P9-CEG-085

NTC's New College FRENCH and ENGLISH Dictionary

NTC's New College FRENCH and ENGLISH Dictionary

NATIONAL TEXTBOOK COMPANY
4255 West Touhy Avenue
Lincolnwood, Illinois 60646-1975 U.S.A.

This edition first published in ©1991 by National Textbook Company,
a division of NTC Publishing Group, 4255 West Touhy Avenue,
Lincolnwood (Chicago), Illinois 60646-1975 U.S.A.

Manufactured in the United States of America.

0 1 2 3 4 5 6 7 8 9 RA 9 8 7 6 5 4 3 2 1

CONTENTS

INTRODUCTION

NTC's New College French and English Dictionary is a comprehensive, authoritative reference designed to aid students, teachers, translators, scholars, business people—virtually anyone working with or studying the French language. This thorough guide to contemporary French offers its users a complete wordlist that includes the full range of formal and informal language encountered in French-speaking countries today, as well as numerous technical, scientific, and business terms. Examples throughout illustrate the proper context in which a word can be used. Colloquial and slang terms are clearly indicated by the symbol *P*, while those that are sometimes considered offensive are accompanied by the symbol ***P****.

Designed especially for English-speakers, this dictionary provides clear pronunciation keys based on the International Phonetic Alphabet (I.P.A.). In this way, users need only consult the French-English section to verify the correct pronunciation of every French word featured in the entries. Proper names are included in the body of the dictionary rather than in separate lists or appendices, thereby making them easier to locate. When American and British usage differ (e.g., *elevator* or *lift* = *ascenseur*), this difference is clearly indicated.

Numerous appendices are also included in this edition, considerably enhancing its value as a reference tool: detailed maps, tables of the principal French and English irregular verbs, a list of false cognates that may cause trouble to English-speakers expressing themselves in French, tables of weights and measures, temperature conversions, monetary units, and commonly used abbreviations. There are also separate sections on letter writing in French, geographical terms in French and English, and an in-depth summary of French grammar for English-speakers. Subjects treated in this summary include the gender of nouns; the position of pronouns; adjective agreement; irregular adjectives; the conjugation of regular verbs in all tenses, voices, and moods; numbers; and question words. This digest of French grammar will be of particular use to students of French, who will find at their fingertips a concise summary of the principal grammar elements of the French language.

For its comprehensiveness, thoroughness, and practicality, *NTC's New College French and English Dictionary* is an invaluable tool for the academic, professional, or general user, working with the French language or with French-speaking people. National Textbook Company is pleased to provide this highly functional reference.

REMARKS

For ease of reference, the reader should note the following:

- As far as is reasonably possible, set or inseparable word groups appear under the first word of the group.
- The swung dash (˜) signifies repetition in the singular of a leading vocabulary word (the word printed in **bold type**). Followed by *s,* (˜s), it signifies the like repetition in the plural.
- The paragraph symbol (¶) also signifies repetition of a leading vocabulary word, but indicates the beginning of the treatment of a new part of speech or a change of gender. This symbol is used to make the point of transition conspicuous.
- An initial letter followed by a period signifies repetition of a translation.
- Separate meanings of each entry are clearly labeled to distinguish the application of each meaning. By careful attention to these labels, the reader should be able to avoid the errors of the French student who wrote his English pen pal "Please send me your new skill [meaning address] as soon as you have removed [meaning moved]."
- Brackets ([ ]) enclose words or parts of words that can be used or omitted at will.
- ʻSee note under H on page 125.
- † Indicates that a regular adverb may be formed by adding *-ment* to the adjective form according to the rules discussed in the grammar note *Adverbs.*

In addition to the explanations of grammar within individual entries, certain points of French grammar have been explained in greater detail in special grammar notes. These notes treat specific instances of French grammar that have proven most troublesome to English speakers (e.g., indirect and direct object pronouns and the subjunctive). For a complete listing of these notes, see page xiv.

In order to assist the reader, reference sections on a variety of topics are included in this dictionary.

The appendices include:

- Abbreviations Most Commonly Used in French
- False Cognates and "Part-Time" Cognates
- Business Correspondence in French
- Monetary Units/Unités monétaires
- Weights and Measures/Poids et mesures
- Numbers/Nombres
- Temperature/Température
- Geographical Names: English-French
- Noms géographiques: français-anglais
- Maps/Cartes

ABBREVIATIONS USED IN THIS DICTIONARY

&	and
&c	et cetera
a	adjective
a.f	adjective, feminine only
a.m	adjective, masculine only
abb	abbreviation
ad	adverb
Adm.	administration
Aero.	aeronautical
Agr.	agriculture; agricultural
Am	America; American
Anat.	anatomy; anatomical
Arch.	architecture; architectural
Arith.	arithmetic
art	article
Artil.	artillery
Astr.	astronomy; astronomical
aux	auxiliary
Bil.	billiards
Biol.	biology; biological
Bkkpg	bookkeeping
Bookb.	bookbinding
Bot.	botanical
Box.	boxing
Build.	building; construction
c	conjunction
Carp.	carpentry; joinery
Cf.	compare
Chem.	chemistry; chemical
Cine	cinema; cinematographic
col	collective, collective noun
Com.	commerce; commercial
compar.	comparative form
comps	compound word
Cook.	cooking
Danc.	dance
dem.	demonstrative
e.g.	for example
Eccl.	ecclesiastical; clerical
Econ.	economy; economics
Elec.	electricity; electrical
Emb.	embroidery
Eng.	England; English
Engin.	engineering
f	feminine
f.pl	feminine plural
f.s	feminine singular
Fenc.	fencing
fig.	figuratively
Fin.	finance; financial
Fish.	fishing
Foot.	football
Fr.	France; French
gen.	generally
Geog.	geography; geographical
Geol.	geology; geological
Geom.	geometry; geometrical
Govt	government; governmental
Gram.	grammar
Gym.	gymnastics
Her.	heraldry
Hist.	history; historical
Hort.	horticulture
Hunt.	hunting; shooting
i	interjection
i.e.	that is
imp	impersonal
Inc. Tax	income tax
Ind.	industry; industrial
inf.	infinitive
Insce	insurance
inv	invariable
ir	irregular, irregular verb
Knit.	knitting
lit.	literally
Liter. or *liter.*	literature; literary
m	masculine*

m, f	masculine and feminine (in nouns)
m.pl	masculine plural
m.s	masculine singular
Mach.	mechanical; machine
Math.	mathematics; mathematical
Meas.	measure; measurement
Mech.	mechanics; mechanical
Med.	medicine; medical
Met.	meteorology; meteorological
Mil.	military
Min.	mining
Mot.	automobile (motoring)
Mus.	music; musical
Myth.	mythology; mythological
N	north
n	noun
Naut.	nautical
Nav.	naval
Need.	needlework
neg.	negative; used negatively
O	obsolete
o.s	oneself
oft.	often
opp.	opposed (to)
Opt.	optics
P	popular; familiar; slang
*P**	indicates familiar and slang words and expressions frequently considered offensive or indecent
p.p	past participle
p.pr	present participle
Path.	pathology; pathological
pej.	pejorative
pers.	person(s)
Phar.	pharmacy; pharmaceutics; pharmacological
Philos.	philosophy; philosophical
Phot.	photography; photographic
Phys.	physics; physical
pl	plural
pn	pronoun
Poet.	poetry; poetical
Pol.	politics; political
pr	preposition or prepositional phrase
pref	prefix
Psych.	psychology; psychological
qch	*quelque chose* (something)
qn	*quelqu'un* (someone)
Rel.	religion
Rly	railroad
s	singular
s.o	someone
Sc	Scotland; Scots
Sch.	school
Sci.	science; scientific
sth	something
Stk Ex.	stock exchange
subj.	subjunctive
Surg.	surgery; surgical
Surv.	surveying
Swim.	swimming
Tech.	technology; technical
Tel.	telecommunications
Ten.	tennis
Theat.	theater; theatrical
Theol.	theology; theological
TV	television
Typ.	typography; printing
Univ.	university
V	see
v.i	intransitive verb
v.i. & t	intransitive and transitive verb
v.pr	pronominal verb
v.t	transitive verb
v.t. & i	transitive and intransitive verb
Vet.	veterinary
Zool.	zoology; zoological

KEY TO PRONUNCIATION IN FRENCH

VOWELS

i	*y*, v*ie*, f*i*ne
e	cr*ée*r, ch*ez*, f*ée*
E	fr*ais*, pr*ès*, bel
a	p*a*p*a*, pl*a*t, f*e*mme
ɑ	b*â*iller, b*a*s, m*â*le
ɔ	b*o*nne, b*o*rne
o	gr*o*s, p*eau*, g*au*che
u	t*ou*t, g*oû*t
Y	v*u*, *u*ne, r*ue*
œ	*oeu*f, p*eu*r, s*eu*l
ǿ	p*eu*, cr*eu*x
ə	d*e*, qu*e*, pr*e*mier
ɛ̃	v*in*, bi*en*, m*ain*
ã	t*emps*, écr*an*, l*en*t
ɔ̃	*on*, m*on*t
œ̃	parf*um*, l*un*di
œ̃	parf*um*, l*un*di

Semi-vowels

j	p*i*ed, fou*ill*e, *y*eux
w	*ou*ate, n*ou*er, *ou*i
y	h*u*ile, c*u*ir, l*u*i

CONSONANTS

p	*p*a*p*ier, ty*p*e
t	*th*éâ*t*re, vi*t*e
k	*qu*i, *k*a*k*i, sa*c*
f	*f*ier, neu*f*
s	*s*i, *c*e*c*i, la*ss*e, *s*ta*t*ion
ʃ	*ch*at, ri*ch*e
b	*b*ain, tom*b*e
d	*d*e*d*ans, ai*d*e
g	*g*ué, ba*gu*e, *g*ant

v	*v*ie, ri*v*e
z	*z*one, mai*s*on, po*s*e
ʒ	*j*e, rou*g*e
l	*l*ong, fo*ll*e
r	*r*ue, *r*i*r*e
m	*m*on, da*m*e
n	*n*ous, *n*o*nn*e
ɲ	bai*gn*er, co*gn*ac
h	*h*olà! (*used in interjections*)
ʻ	*h*ousse (*no liaison or elision*)
ɔ	*used in words borrowed from English:* stand*ing*, camp*ing*

GRAMMAR NOTES

ACCENTS

French uses four accent marks: **acute** *(aigu)*, **grave, circumflex** *(circonflexe)*, and **dieresis** *(tréma)*. In general, the accents function to indicate pronunciation. However, the grave accent is sometimes used to distinguish homonyms, and the circumflex accent is sometimes used for historical reasons.

The Acute Accent

The acute accent *(accent aigu)* is used only on *e*. It indicates the *closed e* pronunciation:

aimé	ému
fée	créer

The Grave Accent

The grave accent *(accent grave)* is used on *a, e,* and *u*. It is used on *e* to indicate the *open e* pronunciation:

près	*compare* chez
gène	*compare* borné

It is also used on *a* and *u* to distinguish homonyms:

la (*fem. art.*)	là *(there)*
ou *(or)*	où *(where)*

The Circumflex Accent

The circumflex accent *(accent circonflexe)* is used on all vowels except *y*. It is used on *e* to indicate open *e* pronunciation and on *o* to indicate *closed o* pronunciation:

bête	*compare* béton
vêtu	*compare* veto
vôtre	*compare* votre

It is used on all vowels to show where Old French had an *s* after the vowel:

bâton	*Old French* baston
bête	*Old French* beste
gît	*Old French* gist
côte	*Old French* coste
coûte	*Old French* couste

Dieresis

The dieresis *(accent tréma)* is used over *e, i,* and *u* to indicate that the vowel is pronounced separately and is not part of a diphthong:

Noël	naïf

On some adjectives ending in *u,* the dieresis is used on the *e* of the feminine although the *e* is silent, as in *aiguë.*

ADJECTIVES

Forms

The adjective in French is a variable part of speech and must agree in gender and number with the noun it modifies. In general, this is a matter of adding *e, s,* or *es* for feminine, masculine plural, or feminine plural respectively: *un bâtiment* **rond,** *une table* **ronde,** *des bâtiments* **ronds,** *des tables* **rondes.**

Some adjectives, however—generally those that end in *e*—have the same ending for both masculine and feminine genders: *un homme* **triste,** *une femme* **triste,** *des hommes* **tristes,** *des femmes* **tristes.**

The pairs below illustrate some generally dependable patterns of changes between masculine and feminine forms not following the above rules:

Masculine	*Feminine*
ancien régime	**ancienne** forteresse
un **gros** chien	une **grosse** lionne
un mur **blanc**	une maison **blanche**
un **faux** sentiment	une **fausse** question
un singe **curieux**	une oie **curieuse**
un vin **doux**	une eau **douce**
un homme **fou**	une femme **folle**
un **beau** garçon	une **belle** fille
un **long** hiver	une **longue** histoire
le monde **entier**	la nuit **entière**
un **bref** discours	une **brève** réponse

Several French adjectives have a special form in the masculine singular. This form is used before a noun beginning with a vowel sound.

Masculine singular: un **vieux** camarade
un **vieil** ami (before noun beginning with a vowel sound)

Feminine singular: une **vieille** camarade   une **vieille** amie

Other adjectives that follow this pattern are:

Masculine singular	*Feminine singular*
beau, bel	belle
fou, fol	folle

mou, mol	molle
nouveau, nouvel	nouvelle

A few adjectives, in general nouns used as adjectives, do not change at all: *un mur* **marron,** *une tasse* **marron,** *des murs* **marron,** *des tasses* **marron.**

Some adjectives are part of set expressions that do not change: **grand**-*chose, à* **grand**-*peine*.

Placement

Most adjectives in French are placed after the noun:

un costume **beige**	un poulet **délicieux**

Several common adjectives are usually placed before the noun:

de **belles** pommes	une **vieille** maison	un **grand** fleuve
un **bon** enfant	de **petits** enfants	un **jeune** homme
une **jolie** robe	un **nouvel** ami	un **mauvais** calcul

Some adjectives may appear before or after the noun, but usually with a difference in meaning. Generally the meaning with the adjective placed after the noun is more concrete or literal:

l'**ancien** regime	the former regime
un peuple **ancien**	an ancient people
pauvre Jean	poor (unfortunate) Jean
une gamine **pauvre**	a poor (moneyless) urchin
une **brave** femme	a good, honest woman
un homme **brave**	a courageous man
un **grand** homme	a great man
un homme **grand**	a tall man

ADVERBS

Formation

The ending *-ment* can be added to many adjectives to form an adverb. This is similar to English *-ly*. In most cases, *-ment* is simply added to the feminine form of the adjective:

Masculine	*Feminine*	*Adverb*
grand	grande	**grandement**
facile	facile	**facilement**
lent	lente	**lentement**
nouveau	nouvelle	**nouvellement**
relatif	relative	**relativement**

When two pronounced consonants immediately precede the ending *-ement,* the first *e* is pronounced (ə), as in *admira*b**l***ement*/admirabləmã/. Otherwise, that *e* is silent.

If the masculine form of the adjective ends in *ai, é, i,* or *u, -ment* is added to the masculine form:

vrai	**vraiment**
carré	**carrément**
hardi	**hardiment**
absolu	**absolument**

Some adverbs end in *-ément* rather than the usual *-ement: aveuglément, communément, conformément, confusément, énormément, expressément, impunément, obscurément, précisément, profondément, uniformément.*

Most adjectives ending in *-ant* and *-ent* follow a special pattern. The ending is *-amment* for adverbs formed from adjectives that end in *-ant,* and *-emment* for adverbs formed from adjectives ending in *-ent.*

élégant	**élégamment**
indépendant	**indépendamment**
négligent	**négligemment**
diligent	**diligemment**

Two exceptions are *lentement* and *véhémentement.*

A few adverbs in *-iment* and *-ument* take a circumflex accent on the *i* or *u*. There is no clear pattern to these:

assidûment **crûment** **gaîment**

For some ordinary English adverbs of manner for which no French form exists (indicated in adjective entries in this dictionary by the omission of the symbol †), the speaker can use *d'une manière* plus the corresponding feminine adjective (*e.g., d'une manière charmante,* charmingly) or by *avec* plus an abstract noun (*e.g., avec entêtement,* stubbornly).

Placement

When the adverb is modifying an adjective or another adverb, it generally precedes the word it modifies: *un livre* **très** *cher,* a very expensive book; *un ciel* **si** *bleu,* a sky so blue.

In general, adverbs follow the entire verb phrase: *je ne la vois pas* **clairement**, I don't see her clearly, *je ne l'ai pas fait* **exprès,** I didn't do it on purpose. However, adverbs may come between an auxiliary verb and a past participle: *il a* **bien** *parlé,* he spoke well.

For adverbs of negation, see the grammar note NEGATION.

ARTICLES

The article in French is a variable part of speech, agreeing with the noun it qualifies in gender and number.

Definite Articles

	Masculine	*Feminine*
Singular	**le** livre (the book)	**la** figure (the face)
Plural	**les** livres (the books)	**les** figures (the faces)

Before a vowel or mute *h, le* and *la* both elide to *l':* **l'***époux,* **l'***épouse.*
With *à* and *de,* definite articles combine to form the following contractions:

	à	*de*
le	**au** bureau	**du** bureau
la	**à la** place	**de la** place
les	**aux** villages	**des** chansons

Uses of the Definite Article

- With abstract nouns or nouns used in a general or abstract sense: **l'***homme est mortel,* man is mortal; **les** *prix montent,* prices are going up.
- With titles: **le** *docteur Marie Dupont,* Doctor Marie Dupont; *monsieur* **le** *Ministre,* Mr. Minister.
- With nouns designating countries, bodies of water, mountains, streets, squares, etc.: **la** *France,* France; **le** *lac Michigan,* Lake Michigan; **la** *rue St-Michel,* St. Michael Street; **la** *place Vendôme,* Vendôme Square.
- With collective nouns: **l'***humanité,* humanity; **les** *gens,* people.
- With nouns denoting sciences, arts, or games: *l'étude* **des** *mathématiques,* the study of mathematics; *jouer* **aux** *échecs,* to play chess.
- With names of illnesses: **l'***asthme,* asthma; **la** *diphtérie,* diphtheria; **la** *poliomyélite,* poliomyelitis.
- With names of meals: *avant* **le** *dîner,* before dinner.
- With the names of holidays: **la** *Toussaint,* All Saints' Day (except: Noël, Pâques).
- In certain set phrases where English omits the article: *à* **la** *maison,* at home; *à* **l'***école,* in school; *à* **l'***église,* to church; *toute* **la** *journée,* all day; *tous* **les** *deux ans,* every two years; **le** *lundi,* on Mondays; **la** *semaine prochaine,* next week.
- In certain phrases where English uses the indefinite article: *dix francs* **le** *kilo,* two francs a kilo.
- With reflexive verbs, where equivalent English phrases use a possessive adjective: *je me lave* **les** *mains,* I wash my hands; *elle se met* **le** *béret,* she's putting on her beret.

The definite article is **not** used:

- In direct address: *bonjour, Docteur,* good morning, Doctor.
- With *de* and *à* desribing composition, purpose, etc.: *chapeau* **de** *paille,* straw hat; *moteur* **à** *vapeur,* steam engine; *verre* **à** *vin,* wine glass.
- In certain descriptive phrases, set phrases, proverbs, and dates and times of day: *avec tristesse,* with sadness; *avoir raison,* to be right; *prendre froid,* to catch cold; *en juin,* in June; *à minuit,* at midnight; *bête comme chou,* stupid as a cabbage.
- After the prepositions *par* and *en: deux fois par jour,* two times per day; *en classe,* in class; *en prison,* in prison, *en été,* in summer.

Indefinite Articles

The indefinite article is used only with singular nouns. The equivalent meaning in plurals is achieved by using *de* plus the definite article.

	Masculine	*Feminine*
Singular	**un** livre (a book)	**une** figure (a face)
Plural	**des** livres (books)	**des** figures (faces)

In negative sentences, *de* (or *d'*) is the *only* form of the definite article.

Je n'ai pas acheté **de** robe hier. Ils n'ont pas **d'**enfants.

The indefinite article is **not** used:

- With nouns expressing profession, trade, nationality, religion, etc., after a linking verb: *sa mère était avocat,* his mother was a lawyer; *il est anglais,* he is an Englishman.
- After *comme* (as, in the capacity of): *il a beaucoup de talent comme poète,* he has a lot of talent as a poet.
- After *sans* and in certain phrases: *sans sou,* without a penny; *une heure et demie,* an hour and a half; *j'ai grand appétit,* I have a big appetite.

Note: The indefinite article precedes *tel,* unlike the English equivalent: **une** *telle chose,* such a thing.

Partitive Articles

Partitive articles are formed by *de* plus the definite article: *de + le = du; de + la = de la; de + les = des.* Partitives are a way of saying "some" or "any," that is, to indicate part of a larger class.

J'ai mangé **des** pommes frites.

Il y a **de la** neige partout.

The definite article is omitted in two cases: after an expression of quantity (such as *peu* or *beaucoup*) and after a negative:

Il y a **beaucoup de** neige.

Il **n'**y a **pas de** neige.

CONJUGATION

Regular Conjugations—Simple Tenses

Most French verbs fall into one of three patterns, or *conjugations.* One model verb for each conjugation can thus serve as the pattern for the formation of many other verbs. Verbs that do not follow any of the three patterns are irregular. Even irregular verbs, however, reflect patterns in their variations. (For the irregular French verbs, see the table at the end of the French-English dictionary, page 257. The listings there give the exceptions to the regular patterns given here.)

The **first conjugation** contains the largest number of verbs, and *new* verbs added to French always follow its pattern. Its model verb is *aimer,* and its infinitive ending is *-er.*

The model verb for the **second conjugation** is *finir.* Its infinitive ending is *-ir.* Verbs in this conjugation contain *-iss-* in certain forms.

The **third conjugation** exhibits a significant number of variant verb forms. The model verb for the conjugation is *rompre,* and its infinitive ending is *-re.*

The following section lists the forms of the three conjugations in the principal *simple tenses,* tenses in which verbs consist of one word only. Subjects are omitted: so, under "Present Indicative," *aim-e* stands for *j'aime, aim-es* for *tu aimes,* and so on.

	Present	*Past Participle*	*Present Participle*
1st	*aim*-**e,-es,-e,-ons,-ez,-ent**	aim-**é**	aim-**ant**
2nd	fin-**is,-is,-it,-issons,-issez,-issent**	fin-**i**	**fin-iss-ant**
3rd	romp-**s,-s,-t,-ons,-ez,-ent**	romp-**u**	romp-**ant**

	Imperfect	*Simple Past*
1st	aim-**ais,-ais,-ait,-ions,-iez,-aient**	aim-**ai,-as,-a,-âmes,-âtes,-èrent**
2nd	finiss-**ais,-ais,-ait,-ions,-iez,-aient**	fin-**is,-is,-it,-îmes,-îtes,-irent**
3rd	romp-**ais,-ais,-ait,-ions,-iez,-aient**	romp-**is,-is,-it,-îmes,-îtes,-irent**
	Future	*Imperative*
1st	aimer-**ai,-as,-a,-ons,-ez,-ont**	aim-**e,-ez**
2nd	finir-**ai,-as,-a,-ons,-ez,-ont**	fin-**is,-issez**
3rd	rompr-**ai,-as,-a,-ons,-ez,-ont**	romp-**s,-ez**
	Present Subjunctive	*Conditional*
1st	aim-**e,-es,-e,-ions,-iez,-ent**	aimer-**ais,-ais,-ait,-ions,-iez,-aient**
2nd	finiss-**e,-es,-e,-ions,-iez,-ent**	finir-**ais,-ais,-ait,-ions,-iez,-aient**
3rd	romp-**e,-es,-e,-ions,-iez,-ent**	rompr-**ais-ais,-ait,-ions,-iez,-aient**

Compound Tenses

There are four commonly used compound tenses, formed by combining the appropriate tense of the auxiliary verbs *avoir* or *être* with the past participle. *Avoir* is used with transitive verbs and intransitive verbs that do not indicate motion. *Être* is used with intransitive verbs of motion and with reflexive verbs. These forms are built up the same way for all verbs, regular and irregular, once the past participle is known:

	Perfect	*Pluperfect*	*Future Perfect*	*Perfect Subjunctive*
Tense of *avoir, être:*	**present**	**imperfect**	**future**	**present subjunctive**
Examples:	j'ai aimé	j'avais aimé	j'aurai aimé	que j'aie aimé
	je suis allé	j'étais allé	je serai allé	que je sois allé
	je me suis trompé	je m'étais trompé	je me serai trompé	que je me sois trompé

For the rules for the agreement of past participles with compound tenses, see pp. xxiv–xxv.

Spelling Changes

Verbs with soft *g* or *c* in the stem preserve it before endings beginning with *a* or *o*—the soft *g* by insertion of an *e* and the soft *c* by use of the cedilla:

ils mang-ent	ils avanc-ent
nous mang**e**-ons	nous avan**ç**-ons
je mang**e**-ais	j'avan**ç**-ais

Mute *e* or *é* in a first-conjugation verb stem changes to *è* when the first syllable of a present-tense ending contains a mute *e:*

p**e**s-er	esp**é**r-er
je p**è**s-e	j'esp**è**r-e
nous p**e**s-ons	nous esp**é**r-ons

The future and conditional have similar changes, but only for verbs with mute *e* in the stem:

p**e**ser	esp**é**rer
je p**è**s-erai	j'esp**é**r-erai
je p**è**s-erais	j'esp**é**r-erais

Single *l* and *t* at the end of the stems after a mute *e (-eler, -eter)* are doubled before endings with mute *e:*

ép**el**-er	cach**et**-er
j'ép**ell**-e	je cach**ett**-e
nous ép**el**-ons	nous cach**et**-ons

A few *-eler* and *-eter* verbs follow the *peser* pattern rather than the *épeler-cacheter* pattern: *acheter, celer, crocheter, démanteler, écarteler, geler, haleter, marteler, modeler, peler.*

ach**e**t-er	c**e**l-er
ach**è**t-e	c**è**l-e
ach**e**t-ons	c**e**l-ons
ach**è**t-erai	c**è**l-erai

In the third conjugation, the third-person singular ending *-t* drops if the stem ends in *d* or *t: il rend, il met.*

In the third conjugation, stems ending in *-m, -t,* and *-v* often drop that consonant in the present singular forms: *je dors, nous dor**m**ons; je pars, nous par**t**ons; je sers, nous ser**v**ons.*

INFINITIVE

The infinitive in French has practically the same uses as the infinitive in English. There are four main differences.

1. An infinitive construction must be used where English uses a gerund. Most often an impersonal construction with an infinitive complement corresponds to an English gerund used as a subject: *il est défendu de fumer,* smoking is forbidden.
2. While the English infinitive is often simply placed next to a verb or adjective, in French an adjective *always* and a verb *often* must be followed by a specific preposition—either *à* or *de*—before the infinitive: *prêt* **à** *partir,* ready to go; *il cherche* **à** *s'échapper,* he's trying to escape; *il a décidé* **de** *partir,* he decided to leave. Some common verbs that take no preposition are *aller, aimer, pouvoir, savoir,* and *vouloir.*
3. An English infinitive can often be used indifferently in an active or a passive sense. In French, this passive sense is always introduced with the preposition *à: il cherche un disque* **à** *écouter,* he is looking for a record to listen to.
4. The infinitive is sometimes used in impersonal commands or instructions:

Ne pas **entrer.**	Do not enter.
Faire cuire à feu doux.	Let it cook over a low fire.

EXPRESSING NEGATION

Negation is expressed by combining *ne* with *pas, personne, rien, jamais, plus, point, que, guère,* or *ni. . . ni:*

Il **ne** vient **pas.**	**Ne** voyez-vous **personne?**
Nous **ne** cherchons **rien.**	Je **n'**ai **que** dix francs.
Tu **ne** comprends **guère.**	L'orphelin **n'**a **ni** père **ni** mère.

Placement of Negatives

Pas, jamais, plus, point, and *guère* usually follow the auxiliary verb:

Il **n'**est **pas** venu.	Je **n'**ai **jamais** dit ça.
Il **n'**a **plus** travaillé.	Elle **n'**a **guère** parlé.

Rien can appear either before or after the past participle in a compound verb. It is more usual, however, to place it after the past participle. *Personne* usually follows the past participle.

Nous **n'**avons **rien** cherché. Je **n'**ai vu **personne.** Nous **n'**avons cherché **rien.**

Personne and *rien* can serve as subjects as well as objects, and *ni. . . ni* can be used with subject nouns:

Personne ne l'a ouvert.	**Rien n'**est arrivé.
Ni Richard **ni** Paule **n'**a téléphoné.	

The two parts of the negation appear together before an infinitive:

Il s'est promis de **ne jamais** revenir à New York.

J'aime mieux **ne pas** sortir ce soir.

Il est allé en taxi pour **ne pas** être en retard.

Omission of Negative Words

Ne is omitted before an infinitive preceded by a preposition with a negative meaning:

Il est parti sans **rien** nous dire.

Personne and *rien* can be used as negatives without *ne* and without a verb:

Qui est-ce qu'ils ont vu? **Personne.**

Qu'est-ce qu'ils ont vu? **Rien.**

Pas sometimes is preceded by *non* when used without a verb:

Prends celui-ci, **(non) pas** celui-là.

Albert va à Moscou, **(non) pas** Marc.

In certain cases, *ne* is used alone, but with no negative meaning. These cases are (1) in subordinate clauses that follow *il y a* or *depuis que,* (2) in subordinate clauses after comparatives, (3) in subordinate clauses that follow conjunctions expressing doubt or fear or that follow main clauses expressing doubt.

Il y a longtemps que nous **ne** vous avons vu. (It's been a long time since we saw you.)

L'enfant est beaucoup plus grand qu'il **ne** l'était il y a un an. (The child is much bigger than he was a year ago.)

J'ai peur que nous **ne** soyons en retard. (I'm afraid we'll be late.)

Vous mangerez bien à ce restaurant à moins que l'on **n'**ait changé de chef. (You'll eat well at that restaurant unless they've changed chefs.)

NUMERALS

Cardinal Numbers

1. Hyphens are used to join most compound numbers under 100 such as 22, 76, 90, 99: *vingt-deux, soixante-seize, quatre-vingt-dix, quatre-vingt-dix-neuf.*

   However, with the numbers 21, 31, 41, 51, 61, 71, *et* is inserted and no hyphens are used: *vingt* **et** *un, soixante* **et** *un, soixante* **et** *onze.*

   With compounds with *cent, mille, million,* etc., neither *et* nor hyphens are commonly used: *cent un, cent vingt-trois, deux cent deux, mille un.* Note that if numbers like 101, 301, 601, 901, 1001, etc. are accompanied by a noun, *et* is added: *mille* **et un** *soucis, un million* **et une** *raisons.*
2. Only *un* agrees with the noun in gender.
3. *Cent* and *mille* are not preceded by *un:* cent hommes, **a** hundred men; mille héroïnes, **a** thousand heroines.
4. *Million, milliard,* etc., when used with no other number following, are followed by *de: un million de francs, dix milliards de personnes,* but *un million et une raisons, deux milliards trois cent mille francs.*
5. Multiples of *vingt* and *cent* are pluralized with an *s: quatre-vingts, trois cents.* However, they lose the *s* when followed by another number: *quatre-vingt-dix, trois cent trois.*

6. Noun forms can be formed from many round numbers by adding *-aine: une dizaine,* about ten; *une douzaine,* about twelve; *une centaine,* about a hundred. **But:** *un millier,* about a thousand. These can be made plural in making estimates: *une vingtaine de personnes est partie pendant l'entracte,* about twenty people left during the intermission; *des milliers d'ouvriers sont actuellement en chômage,* thousands of workers are presently out of work.

Ordinal Numbers

All ordinal numbers except *premier,* first, are formed by adding *-ième* to the corresponding cardinal number:

premier	onzième	vingt et unième	quatre-vingt-unième
deuxième	douzième	vingt-deuxième	quatre-vingt-deuxième
etc.			

PARTICIPLES

Participles are verbal adjectives that agree in gender and number with the nouns they modify. There are some instances, however, when they act more as verbs than as adjectives.

Present Participles

The present participle has three main uses in French: to modify a noun (as an adjective), to attribute an action to a noun or nouns, and to express an action simultaneous with that of another verb in the sentence:

Je connais une histoire **amusante.**	(adjective)
On peut entendre le bruit des enfants **jouant** dans le parc.	(attributing an action to *enfants*)
Elle est tombée en **courant.**	(action simultaneous to *est tombée*)

Only the adjective agrees with the noun in number and gender. The participle is preceded by *en* only when expressing an action *simultaneous* to that of the other verb.

Past Participles

Like the present participle, the past participle agrees with the noun when used as an adjective: *la terre était* **couverte** *de feuilles* **tombées** *des arbres.*

The past participle used in a compound tense agrees with the subject only when it follows the auxiliary verb *être:* elle est **tombée;** but *elle a* **échappé** *au lion.* The past participle also agrees with the subject when used in a passive construction: *La maison a été* **bâtie** *en 1957.*

The past participle used in a compound tense agrees with any *direct* pronoun object that *precedes* it, but not with indirect objects or with any objects that follow it:

D.O.
Les chemises étaient toutes mouillées. Rémi les a **séchées** en rentrant chez lui.

I.O. D.O.
Ils se sont **offert** des cadeaux.

D.O.
Rémi a **séché** les chemises en rentrant chez lui.

Reflexive verbs *(s'ennuyer, s'en aller)* follow the same rule (past participle agreement with the preceeding direct object) but care must be taken to distinguish those in which the pronoun is a direct object from those in which the pronoun is an indirect object. Whether the corresponding nonpronominal verb is transitive can be a general guide.

D.O.
Ils se sont **blessés** en jouant au football.

I.O.
Nous nous sommes **téléphoné** hier soir.

D.O.
Nous nous sommes **rencontrés** au restaurant du coin.

I.O.
Ils se sont **préparé** une bonne soupe.

PASSIVE VOICE

The passive voice *(la tasse était cassée,* the cup was broken) in French is not used as often as a reflexive verb *(la tasse s'est cassée)*. Both will be discussed.

Passive Voice

The passive voice is composed of a form of the verb *être* and the past participle: *casser, être cassé; aimer, être aimé.* The participle agrees with the subject in gender and number:

Le garçon **était accompagné** de sa mère. (The boy was accompanied by his mother.)

La fille **était accompagnée** de sa mère.

Les enfants **étaient accompagnés** de leurs mères.

Les jeunes gens **étaient accompagnées** de leurs mères.

The tense of the passive is the tense of *être* used with the participle. The examples immediately above are imperfect tense, passive voice. Study these examples of other tenses:

L'église **sera construite** par les paroissiens. (*future*)

La maison **a été nettoyée** par la domestique. (*perfect*)

Reflexive Verb for Passive Voice

Many reflexive verbs can have basically the same meaning as the passive voice. Reflexive verbs consist of a verb plus a reflexive pronoun: se promener, to walk; se marier, to get married. Reflexive verbs that are transitive can take on a passive sense:

Ce livre **se lit** beaucoup en ce moment. (This book is read a great deal right now.)

Une voix **s'entend** au loin. (A voice is heard in the distance.)

Ces livres **se sont** bien **vendus.** (These books sold well.)

INTERROGATIVES

French has three ways of changing a statement into a *yes-no* question: by beginning the sentence with *est-ce que,* by a change in intonation, and by inversion.

1. The most general case in written French is to add *est-ce que* to the beginning of a statement to form a question.
   Je t'emmène à la gare en voiture. *(Statement)*
   Est-ce que je t'emmène à la gare en voiture? *(Question)*
2. In speech, it is quite common simply to change the **intonation.** When the sentence is written out, the only difference is that between a period and a question mark:
   Je t'emmène à la gare en voiture. *(Statement)*
   Je t'emmène à la gare en voiture? *(Question)*
   A question that is a polite proposal may begin with *si* and the verb in the imperfect tense. The difference is largely one of politeness or tentativeness:
   Si je t'emmènais à la gare en voiture?
3. **Inversion** is reserved for sentences with pronouns for subjects:
   Il est venu. *(Statement)* **Est-il** venu? *(Question)*
   Elle part. *(Statement)* **Part-elle?** *(Question)*

In the best written French, inversion is used even when the statement form has a noun for a subject. In that case, a pronoun representing the noun is inserted:

Le docteur a dit quelque chose.

Le docteur **a-t-il** dit quelque chose?

Information questions involve the use of question words such as *qui, que, comment, quand, ou,* and *pourquoi.* Such question words always begin a sentence. The use of *est-ce que* or inversion generally occurs with information questions:

Quand **est-ce que** Pierre part?

Quand **part-il?** or Quand Pierre **part-il?**

PERSONAL PRONOUNS

Subject Pronouns

The subject pronouns in French are:

je	**nous**
tu	**vous**
il/elle/on	**ils/elles**

The indefinite pronoun *on* is properly used when the third-person subject is unknown or when the speaker wants to generalize. In spoken French, *on* can replace any pronoun, but most frequently *nous,* which includes the person spoken to:

Si **on** allait au restaurant?	Suppose we go to a restaurant.
Nous, **on** est d'accord.	We agree.

The French tonic pronouns are:

moi	**nous**
toi	**vous**
lui	**eux**
elle	**elles**
soi	**soi**

Tonic pronouns are used in three cases.

1. After a preposition: *on se sent toujours bien chez* **soi,** one always feels good at home.
2. As an emphatic pronoun: **moi,** *je ne suis pas du tout d'accord, I* don't agree at all.
3. In a compound subject: *Jules et* **moi,** *nous allons au cinéma*, Jules and I are going to the movies.

Direct Object Pronouns

The direct object pronouns in French are:

me	**nous**
te	**vous**
le/la/se	**les/se**

These pronouns receive the action of the verb transitively (directly). Except in affirmative commands, they preceed the verbs whose action they receive: *Je* **les** *ai salués de la main. Anne voulait* **te** *frapper.*

Indirect Object Pronouns

The indirect object pronouns in French are:

me	**nous**
te	**vous**
lui	**leur**
se	**se**

Indirect objects express **to whom** or **for whom** an action was done. Like the direct object pronouns, they preceed the verb whose action they receive, except in affirmative commands: *elle* **nous** *chante une belle chanson,* she sings us a beautiful song; *il* **m***'a apporté des nouvelles de ma famille,* he brought me news of my family; *je vais* **leur** *réciter ce poème*, I am going to recite this poem to them.

Se is the reflexive indirect object pronoun: *ils* **se** *parlent très peu ces jours-ci*, they speak very little to each other these days.

En and Y

French has two pronouns that stand for a combination of a preposition and a noun: *en* and *y*. They are used only for things.

à + thing = *y:*	Je vais **y** chercher mes bagages **à la gare.** Je vais **y** chercher mes bagages.
de + thing = *en:*	J'ai pris beaucoup **de photos.** J'**en** ai pris beaucoup.

Order of Object Pronouns

Before the verb (that is, in statements or negative commands), the order of object pronouns is:

me		*le*		*lui*				
te	**before**	*la*	**before**	*leur*	**before**	*y*	**before**	*en*
nous		*les*						
vous								

Tu **me l'**as donné.

Tu **le lui** as donné.

Tu **lui en** as donné.

After the verb (that is, in affirmative commands), the object pronouns occur in the following order:

direct object **before** indirect object **before** *y* + *en*

Donne-**le-moi.**

Donne-**le-lui.**

Donne-**lui-en.**

Note that the object pronouns *me* and *te* (both direct and indirect) become *moi* and *toi* in affirmative commands.

GENDER

All nouns in French have a gender, either masculine or feminine.

Some Observations

1. Nouns denoting living beings often have different forms for the masculine and feminine gender: *travaill***eur,** *travaill***euse,** working man, working woman; *abb***é,** *ab***besse,** abbot, abbess; *act***eur,** *act***rice,** actor, actress; *our***s,** *our***se,** (male) bear, (female) bear.
2. Some nouns have the same form for masculine and feminine. For these nouns the gender is indicated only by the article: **le** *communiste,* **la** *communiste.*

3. To help determine the gender of nouns, there is one general rule *(that has many exceptions):* nouns spelled with a silent *e* at the end tend to be feminine.

Here are some patterns that are also helpful in determining the gender of nouns.

Nouns with the following endings tend to be feminine:

- **-esse:** *la gentillesse, la sagesse, la souplesse*
- **-ion, -tion:** *la compassion, la destruction, la fondation*
- **-té:** *la beauté, la liberté, la simultanéité*
- **-ude:** *la certitude, la multitude, une aptitude*
- **-ure:** *une aventure, la littérature, la sculpture*

Nouns with the following endings tend to be masculine:

- **-age:** *le mariage, le repassage, le témoignage*
- **-isme:** *le mysticisme, le réalisme, le socialisme*
- **-ment:** *le changement, le jugement, le tremblement*

4. For the names of places:

- Countries ending in *-e* tend to be feminine: *la France, l'Italie, la Colombie, la Libye, la Suède.* **But:** *le Mexique, le Cambodge.*
- Countries ending in letters other than *-e* tend to be masculine: *le Portugal, le Danemark, le Gabon, le Sénégal, le Nicaragua.*
- Names of cities tend to be masculine (they are usually used without articles): *New-York est très mouvementé. Jérusalem est ancien.*

FORMATION OF THE PLURAL FOR NOUNS AND ADJECTIVES

Plural in *-s*

Both nouns and adjectives usually form the plural by adding *-s* to the singular.

Singular	*Plural*
un livre vert	des livres verts
la cantatrice chauve	les cantatrices chauves

Certain endings, however, change in different ways to form the plural.

Plural in *-aux*

The ending *-al* in nouns and adjectives changes to *-aux*. (The feminine adjective ending *-ale* simply takes *-s.)*

un cheva**l** origina**l**	des cheva**ux** origina**ux**
une histoire origin**ale**	des histoires origin**ales**

Among adjectives, there are two common exceptions: *idéals* and *finals.* (The noun *idéal,* however, follows the pattern: *des idéaux.)* Among nouns, there are a few common exceptions, as well: *bals, carnavals, chacals, chorals, festivals, récitals,* and *régals.*

un bal idéal	des bals idéals
son récital final	ses récitals finals

There are 7 nouns ending in *-ail* that also change to an *-aux* ending in the plural: *bail, corail, émail, soupirail, vitrail, travail,* and *vantail:*

un b**ail**	des b**aux**
le trav**ail**	les trav**aux**
un vitr**ail**	des vitr**aux**

Plural in *-x*

Nouns and adjectives ending in *-au, -eau,* and *-eu* form the plural by adding *-x:*

un tuyau	deux tuyau**x**
quel beau morceau!	quels beau**x** morceau**x**!
mon neveu	mes neveu**x**

There are 7 nouns ending in *-ou* that also form the plural by adding *-x: bijou, caillou, chou, genou, hibou, joujou,* and *pou:*

le bijou	les bijou**x**
le genou	les genou**x**

There are 2 nouns ending in *-eu* that form their plural in *-s: émeu* and *pneu: émeus, pneus.*

Plural with No Change

Nouns ending in *-s, -x,* and *-z* in the singular do not change in the plural:

la souris	les souris
son nez	leurs nez

Some "adjectives" are really nouns used as adjectives; these do not change for gender *or* number:

le prix **Nobel**	les prix **Nobel**
une carte **marron**	des cartes **marron**

Plurals of Compound Nouns and Loan Words

Elements of compound nouns follow the patterns above. The question is whether *both* elements take a plural ending, or if not, which one. If either element is a noun or an adjective, it takes a plural ending:

une coffre-fort	des coffres-forts	*(n + a)*
un gentilhomme	des gentilshommes	*(a + n)*
l'avant-garde	les avant-gardes	*(ad + n)*

If the compound is a phrase, there is no change in the plural:

un chasse-neige	**des** chasse-neige
un tête-à-tête	**des** tête-à-tête

Loan words do not follow a regular pattern. Latin, Greek, Italian, and often English, tend to follow the source language:

le référendum	les référenda	*(Lat.)*
un credo	des credo	*(Lat.—verb)*
un garden-party	des garden-parties	*(Eng.)*

The Italian loan-words *spaghetti* and *macaroni,* plurals in Italian, are treated as plurals in French: *j'aime les spaghetti,* I like spaghetti.

POSSESSIVE ADJECTIVES AND PRONOUNS

The possessive adjectives and pronouns are:

	Adjectives			*Pronouns*			
	m	**f**	**pl**	**m**	**f**	**m pl**	**f pl**
1s	mon	ma	mes	le mien	la mienne	les miens	les miennes
2s	ton	ta	tes	le tien	la tienne	les tiens	les tiennes
3s	son	sa	ses	le sien	la sienne	les siens	les siennes
1pl	notre	notre	nos	le nôtre	la nôtre	les nôtres	les nôtres
2pl	votre	votre	vos	le vôtre	la vôtre	les vôtres	les vôtres
3pl	leur	leur	leurs	le leur	la leur	les leurs	les leurs

Possessive Adjectives

The possessive adjective is a variable part of speech, agreeing in gender and number with the noun it modifies. The number and gender of the possessive adjective depends on **the noun modified,** not on the possessor. So,

Hélène a oublié **son** portefeuille.

Hélène a oublié **sa** valise.

Hélène a oublié **ses** caoutchoucs.

The possessive adjectives *mon, ton,* and *son* are used before any word beginning with a vowel, whatever the gender. This irregularity is to assure ease of pronunciation:

Anne regardait calmement une affiche.

Anne regardait calmement **son** affiche.

French uses the definite article in places where English uses possessive adjectives (see the grammar note ARTICLES):

Je me lave **les** mains.	I am washing **my** hands.

Possessive Pronouns

The possessive pronoun is used much as in English, but it is a variable part of speech that agrees with the noun it refers to in gender and number:

Hélène a oublié sa valise; j'ai oublié également **la mienne.**

(Helen forgot her suitcase; I also forgot *mine.*)

Hélène a oublié ses gants; Marianne a oublié **également les siens.**

(Helen forgot her gloves; Marianne also forgot *hers.*)

QUANTIFIERS

There are two kinds of quantifiers: **adverbs** and **adjectives.**

Adverbs

Some adverb quantifiers are *beaucoup, peu, trop, assez,* and *bien*. All are followed by *de* plus the noun. The article is omitted after all except *bien de:*

Il y a **beaucoup de** neige.

Il y a **beaucoup de** taxis à la gare.

Il y a **peu de** neige.

Il y a **trop de** neige.

Il y a **assez de** neige.

Bien des taxis à la gare sont rouges.

Adjectives

An adjective quantifier is a variable part of speech that agrees in gender and number with the noun it quantifies. It either replaces the article or, in the case of *tout,* comes before the article:

chaque village	**aucune** ville
tout le village	**toute** la ville
tous les villages	**toutes** les villes

Two adjective quantifiers are always plural and do not change for gender:

quelques villages	**quelques** villes
plusieurs villages	**plusieurs** villes

Numbers are also adjective quantifiers. Only *un* changes for gender:

un enfant	**une** jupe
deux enfants	**vingt** jupes

FRENCH-ENGLISH

A

A, a (a) *m, letter,* A, a.

à (a) (**à le** *is contracted into* **au, à les** *into* **aux**) *pr,* (*destination*) to. *aller ~ Paris, ~ la gare,* go to Paris, to the station. (*position*) *~ Paris,* in Paris; *~ la gare,* at the station. *au 3e étage,* on the 3rd floor. *~ 5 km d'ici,* 5 km away. (*time*) *~ 5 heures,* at 5 o'clock. *au mois de mai,* in May. *au 19e siècle,* in the 19th century. *de 9 ~ 5 heures,* from 9 till 5. *~ demain!* see you (*or* till) tomorrow! (*indirect object*) *parler ~ qn,* speak to s.o. *donner, prêter qch ~ qn,* give, lend sth to s.o. (*ownership*) *ce stylo est ~ moi, ~ Jean,* this pen is mine, John's. *un ami ~ nous,* a friend of ours. (*description*) *la dame aux yeux bleus,* the lady with blue eyes. *chambre ~ 2 lits,* room with 2 beds. *tasse ~ thé,* teacup. *canne ~ pêche,* fishing rod. (*method*) *~ la main,* by hand. *~ pied,* on foot. *~ cheval,* on horseback. *maison ~ vendre, ~ louer,* house for sale, to let. *~ ce qu'il dit,* according to what he says.

abaissement (abɛsmɑ̃) *m,* lowering; pulling down; fall (*value*); humiliation. **abaisser** (se) *v.t,* to lower, let down; humble, humiliate.

abandon (abɑ̃dɔ̃) *m,* abandonment, desertion (*pers., place*); giving up, relinquishment (*rights, studies*); neglected state. *à l'~,* neglected (*garden &c*). lack of constraint. *parler avec ~,* speak freely. **abandonner** (ne) *v.t,* to abandon, leave, desert, forsake; give up, relinquish. **s'~,** *v.pr,* to let o.s go. *s'~ à,* give o.s up to, give way to (*despair &c*).

abaque (abak) *m,* abacus.

abasourdir (abazurdir) *v.t,* to dumbfound, stun.

abâtardir (s') (abɑtardir) *v.pr,* to degenerate.

abat-jour (abaʒur) *m,* lampshade. **abats** (ba) *m.pl,* giblets; (*beef &c*) offal. **abat-son** (abasɔ̃) *m,* louvers. **abattage** (bataʒ) *m,* felling; slaughtering. **abattant** (tɑ̃) *m,* flap (*of table &c*). **abattement** (tmɑ̃) *m,* exhaustion, prostration; dejection, despondency; (*Inc. Tax*) allowance. **abattis** (ti) *m,* giblets; *P* limbs. **abattoir** (twar) *m,* slaughter house, abattoir. **abattre** (tr) *v.t.ir,* to knock down (*wall &c*); cut down, fell (*tree*); bring down (*plane*); shoot down, kill (*bird, pers.*); slaughter (*animal*); depress; exhaust. **s'~,** *v.pr,* to crash down. *s'~ sur,* (*rain*) beat down on; (*troops*) swoop down on. **abattu, e** (ty) *a,* depressed, downcast; exhausted.

abbaye (abɛi) *f,* abbey. **abbé** (be) *m,* abbot; priest. **abbesse** (bɛs) *f,* abbess.

a b c (ɑbese) *m,* A B C, alphabet book; rudiments (*of job*).

abcès (apsɛ) *m,* abscess.

abdication (abdikasjɔ̃) *f,* abdication. **abdiquer** (ke) *v.t. & i,* to abdicate; surrender.

abdomen (abdɔmɛn) *m,* abdomen.

abécédaire (abesedɛr) *m,* spelling primer.

abeille (abɛj) *f,* bee. *~ ouvrière,* worker b.

aberration (abɛrasjɔ̃) *f,* aberration.

abêtir (s') (abɛtir) *v.pr,* to grow dull, stupid.

abhorrer (abɔre) *v.t,* (*liter.*) to abhor, loathe.

abîme (abim) *m,* abyss, gulf, chasm. **abîmer** (bime) *v.t,* to spoil, damage. *s'~,* to get spoiled; (*liter.*) (*ship*) sink; (*pers.*) be sunk in, deep in (*thought &c*).

abject, e (abʒɛkt) *a,* abject, mean, despicable. **abjection** (sjɔ̃) *f,* abjectness, &c.

abjurer (abʒyre) *v.t,* to abjure, renounce.

abnégation (abnegasjɔ̃) *f,* abnegation, self-denial.

aboiement (abwamɑ̃) *m,* bark[ing]. **abois** (bwa) *m.pl, aux ~,* at bay; hard pressed.

abolir (abɔlir) *v.t,* to abolish. **abolition** (lisjɔ̃) *f,* abolition.

abominable† (abɔminabl) *a,* abominable; frightful. **abomination** (sjɔ̃) *f,* abomination. **abominer** (ne) *v.t,* to abominate.

abondance (abɔ̃dɑ̃s) *f,* abundance, plenty; affluence; wealth (*of ideas*). *parler d'~,* to speak extempore. **abondant, e** (dɑ̃, ɑ̃t) *a,* abundant, plentiful, copious. **abondamment** (damɑ̃) *ad,* abundantly, &c. **abonder** (de) *v.i,* to be plentiful, abound (*en,* in). *~ dans le sens de,* be in full agreement with.

abonné, e (abɔne) *n,* subscriber; consumer (*gas, elec.*); season ticket holder. **abonnement** (nmɑ̃) *m,* subscription (*to paper*); (*Rly., Theat.*) season ticket; (*Tel.*) rental. **abonner (s')** (ne) *v.pr, s'~ à,* to subscribe to; take a season ticket for.

abord (abɔr) *m,* approach, access (*to place*); manner (*pers.*). *d'un ~ facile,* easy to reach (*place*); approachable (*pers.*). *~s,* surroundings. *aux ~s de,* around. [*tout*] *d'~,* first of all, at first. *au premier ~, de prime ~,* at first sight, initially. **abordable** (bɔrdabl) *a,* accessible (*place*); approachable (*pers.*); reasonable (*price*). **abordage** (daʒ) *m,* (*Naut.*) boarding; collision. **aborder** (de) *v.t,* to reach (*place*); approach (*pers.*); tackle (*subject*); (*Naut.*) board (*in battle*); collide with. ¶ *v.i,* (*Naut.*) to land.

aborigène (abɔriʒɛn) *a,* aboriginal. ¶ *m,f,* native, aborigine.

aboucher (abuʃe) *v.t,* to join end to end. *s'~ avec qn,* get in touch with s.o.

aboutir (abutir) *v.i,* to succeed. *~ à, ~ dans,*

end up in, result in, lead to. *n'~ à rien*, come to nothing.
aboyer (abwaje) *v.i.* to bark, bay; (*pers.*) yell.
abrasif (abrazif) *a*, abrasive.
abrégé (abreʒe) *m*, summary. *en ~*, in brief, in a nutshell; in miniature. **abréger** (ʒe) *v.t*, to shorten, cut short (*visit*); abridge (*text*); abbreviate (*word*).
abreuver (abrœve) *v.t.* to water (*animal*); soak, drench. (*fig.*) *~ qn de*, shower s.o with. **s'~**, to drink. **abreuvoir** (vwar) *m*, watering place, horse pond; drinking trough.
abréviation (abrevjasjɔ̃) *f*, abbreviation.
abri (abri) *m*, shelter, cover. *~ souterrain*, air-raid shelter. *à l'~ de*, under cover of, sheltered from. *se mettre à l'~*, to [take] shelter (*de*, from).
abricot (abriko) *m*, apricot. **abricotier** (kɔtje) *m*, apricot tree.
abriter (abrite) *v.t*, to shelter, shield, screen.
abrogation (abrɔgasjɔ̃) *f*, abrogation, repeal. **abroger** (ʒe) *v.t*, to abrogate, &c.
abrupt, e (abrypt) *a*, (*pers.*) abrûpt; (*slope*) abrupt, steep, sheer.
abruti, e (abryti) *a*, dazed, stupefied (*with work, drink*). ¶ *m.f*, *P* idiot, moron. **abrutir** (tir) *v.t*, to make stupid; daze, stupefy. **abrutissant, e** (isɑ̃, ɑ̃t) *a*, stupefying; mind-destroying (*work*). **abrutissement** (tismɑ̃) *m*, degradation; stupefied state.
absence (apsɑ̃s) *f*, absence; lack of (*feelings*). *il a des ~s*, his mind wanders. **absent, e** (sɑ̃, ɑ̃t) *a*, absent, away [from home]; lacking, missing. ¶ *m,f*, absentee, missing person. **absentéisme** (eism) *m*, absenteeism. **s'absenter** (sɑ̃te) *v.pr*, to absent o.s, stay *or* go away (*de*, from).
abside (apsid) *f*, apse.
absinthe (apsɛ̃t) *f*, absinth.
absolu, e (apsɔly) *a*, absolute; hard & fast (*rule*); peremptory (*tone*). **~ment** (mɑ̃) *ad*, absolutely. *~ pas!* certainly not!
absolution (apsɔlysjɔ̃) *f*, absolution.
absorbant, e (apsɔrbɑ̃, ɑ̃t) *a*, absorbent; absorbing (*work*). **absorber** (be) *v.t*, to absorb; soak up; take (*food &c*); remove (*stain*); take over (*firm*). **s'~**, to become absorbed, engrossed (*dans*, in). **absorption** (psjɔ̃) *f*, absorption.
absoudre (apsudr) *v.t.ir*, to absolve.
abstenir (s') (apstənir) *v.pr.ir*, to abstain, refrain (*de*, from). **abstention** (stɑ̃sjɔ̃) *f*, abstention. **abstinence** (stinɑ̃s) *f*, abstinence.
abstraction (apstraksjɔ̃) *f*, abstraction. *~ faite de*, apart from, setting aside. **abstraire** (strɛr) *v.t.ir*, to abstract. **abstrait, e** (strɛ, ɛt) *a*, abstract. **l'abstrait**, *m*, the abstract (opp. *concrete*).
abstrus, e (apstry, yz) *a*, abstruse, recondite.
absurde† (apsyrd) *a*, absurd, preposterous. **absurdité** (dite) *f*, absurdity.
abus (aby) *m*, abuse, misuse. **abuser** (ze) *v.t*, to deceive, mislead. *~ de*, to abuse, misuse (*power*); take advantage of (*s.o's age &c*). **s'~**, to be mistaken; delude o.s. **abusif, ive**† (zif, iv) *a*, improper; excessive (*price*).
Abyssinie (l') (abisini) *f*, Abyssinia.
acabit (akabi) *m*, sort, type, stamp.
acacia (akasja) *m*, acacia.
académicien, ne (akademisjɛ̃, ɛn) *n*, academician; member of the Académie française. **académie** (mi) *f*, academy, learned society. *l'A~ française*, the French Academy. (*Univ.*) ≃ regional education authority. **académique** (mik) *a*, academic.
acajou (akaʒu) *m*, mahogany.
acariâtre (akarjɑtr) *a*, peevish, sour, cantankerous.
accablant, e (akablɑ̃, ɑ̃t) *a*, overwhelming; overpowering (*heat*). **accablement** (bləmɑ̃) *m*, despondency, dejection; exhaustion **accabler** (ble) *v.t*, to overwhelm, overcome. *~ qn d'injures*, heap abuse on s.o.
accalmie (akalmi) *f*, lull.
accaparer (akapare) *v.t*, to corner, buy up (*goods*); monopolize (*conversation*); take up one's time & energy. **accapareur, euse** (rœr, øz) *n*, monopolist.
accéder (aksede) *v.i*, *~ à*, to accede to (*request*); comply with (*wishes*); reach (*place*); rise to (*rank*).
accélérateur (akseleratœr) *m*, accelerator. **accélération** (sjɔ̃) *f*, acceleration. **accélérer** (re) *v.t*, to accelerate, speed up, quicken. ¶ *v.i*, (*Mot.*) accelerate.
accent (aksɑ̃) *m*, accent (*all senses*). *~ aigu, grave*, acute, grave a. stress (*word*); tone [*of voice*]; (*fig.*) stress, emphasis. *~s*, accents (*of love, rage*); (*Mus.*) strains. **accentuer** (tɥe) *v.t*, to accent, accentuate, emphasize, stress. *s'~*, to become more pronounced.
acceptable (aksɛptabl) *a*, acceptable. **acceptation** (sjɔ̃) *f*, acceptance. **accepter** (te) *v.t*, to accept; agree (*de faire*, to do). **acception** (psjɔ̃) *f*, meaning (*of word*).
accès (aksɛ) *m*. access, entry; approach. *d'~ facile*, [easily] accessible (*place*); approachable (*pers.*). fit (*rage*); attack (*fever*). **accessible** (sɛsibl) *a*, accessible; approachable.
accession (aksɛsjɔ̃) *f*, accession; rise (*à*, to).
accessit (aksɛsit) *m*, honourable mention.
accessoire† (aksɛswar) *a*, secondary, incidental. ¶ *m*, accessory; (*Theat.*) prop.
accident (aksidɑ̃) *m*, accident; (*car, plane*) crash; setback; (*Med.*) trouble; (*Mus.*) accidental. *par ~*, by chance. *~ de terrain*, undulation. **accidenté, e** (te) *a*, hilly; broken (*ground*); chequered, eventful (*career &c*). **accidentel, le**† (tɛl) *a*, accidental.
acclamation (aklamasjɔ̃) *f*, acclamation. *~s*, cheers. **acclamer** (me) *v.t*, to acclaim, hail,

cheer.

acclimatation (aklimatasjɔ̃) *f,* acclimatization. **acclimater** (te) *v.t,* to acclimatize.

accointances (akwɛ̃tɑ̃s) *f.pl,* dealings, contacts.

accolade (akɔlad) *f,* embrace; (*Typ.*) brace, bracket. **accoler** (le) *v.t,* to bracket together.

accommodant, e (akɔmɔdɑ̃, ɑ̃t) *a,* accommodating. **accommodation** (asjɔ̃) *f,* adaptation. **accommodement** (dmɑ̃) *m,* arrangement, settlement. **accommoder** (de) *v.t,* to suit; make (s.o) comfortable; adapt; prepare (*food*); arrange, settle. **s'~,** *s'~ à,* to adapt [o.s] to. *s'~ de,* put up with. *s'~ avec,* come to an agreement with.

accompagnateur, trice (akɔ̃paɲatœr, tris) *n,* (*Mus.*) accompanist. **accompagnement** (ɲmɑ̃) *m,* (*Mus.*) accompaniment; (*Cook.*) vegetables. **accompagner** (ɲe) *v.t,* to accompany, escort.

accompli, e (akɔ̃pli) *a,* accomplished. **accomplir** (plir) *v.t,* to accomplish, fulfil, perform, carry out; complete. **accomplissement** (plismɑ̃) *m,* accomplishment, &c.

accord (akɔr) *m,* (*gen., Gram.*) agreement; harmony; consent; (*Mus.*) chord; tuning. *en ~ avec,* in keeping with. *d'un commun ~,* of one accord. *être d'~,* to agree. *se mettre d'~,* come to an agreement. *d'~,* agreed, all right; (*Mus.*) in tune. **accordage** (kɔrdaʒ) *m,* tuning. **accordéon** (deɔ̃) *m,* accordion. **accorder** (de) *v.t,* to give, grant, award; concede; match (*colours*); (*Mus.*) tune. (*Gram.*) [*faire*] ~, make (a word) agree. **s'~,** (*gen., Gram.*) agree; (*colours*) match. (*bien, mal*) *s'~ avec qn,* get on (well, badly) with s.o. (*Mus.*) tune [up]. **accordeur** (dœr) *m,* tuner.

accoster (akɔste) *v.t,* to accost; (*Naut.*) come alongside. ¶ *v.i,* to berth.

accotement (akɔtmɑ̃) *m,* (*Mot.*) shoulder, verge. ~ *non stabilisé,* soft verge. **accoter** (te) *v.t,* & **s'~,** *v.pr,* to lean, rest (*à, contre,* against).

accouchement (akuʃmɑ̃) *m,* confinement, delivery. **accoucher** (ʃe) *v.t,* deliver (*qn,* s.o's baby). ¶ *v.i,* to be in labour, have a baby. ~ *de,* give birth to; (*fig.*) bring forth. **accoucheur, euse** (ʃœr, øz), obstetrician; midwife.

accouder (s') (akude) *v.pr,* to lean on one's elbow(s). **accoudoir** (dwar) *m,* armrest.

accoupler (akuple) *v.t,* (*Tech*) to couple, connect; yoke; mate (*animals*). **s'~,** to mate.

accourir (akurir) *v.i.ir,* to run [up], rush.

accoutrement (akutrəmɑ̃) *m,* garb, rig, getup *P.* **accoutrer** (tre) *v.t,* to rig out.

accoutumance (akutymɑ̃s) *f,* habituation; addiction. **accoutumer** (me) *v.t,* to accustom. **s'~,** to get used, accustomed (*à faire,* to doing).

accréditer (akredite) *v.t,* to accredit (*pers.*); substantiate (*rumour*). **s'~,** (*rumour*) to gain ground.

accroc (akro) *m,* rent, tear; snag, hitch.

accroche-cœur (akrɔʃkœr) *m,* kisscurl.

accrocher (akrɔʃe) *v.t,* to hang [up] (*hat, picture*); (*Rly.*) couple, hitch on; catch (*dress: à,* on); bump into (*car*); (*Mil.*) engage. ~ *le regard,* to catch the eye. ¶ *v.i,* to get stuck (*zip, talks*). **s'~ à,** to cling to, hang on to.

accroire (akrwar) *v.t: faire ~ à qn,* to delude s.o into believing.

accroître (akrwatr) *v.t,* & **s'~,** *v.pr,* to increase. **accroissement** (krwasmɑ̃) *m,* increase; (*Econ.*) growth.

accroupir (s') (akrupir) *v.pr,* to squat, crouch [down]. **accroupi, e** (pi) *a,* squatting &c.

accu *P* (aky) *m,* battery.

accueil (akœj) *m,* reception, welcome. *faire bon ~ à,* to welcome. **accueillant, e** (jɑ̃, ɑ̃t) *a,* welcoming. **accueillir** (jir) *v.t.ir,* to receive, welcome, greet; (*hotel*) accommodate.

acculer (akyle) *v.t,* to drive s.o back (*à,* against); [drive into a] corner.

accumulateur (akymylatœr) *m,* accumulator, battery. **accumulation** (sjɔ̃) *f,* accumulation; stockpiling. **accumuler** (le) *v.t,* to accumulate; stockpile; store (*energy*). **s'~,** to accumulate.

accusateur, trice (akyzatœr, tris) *n,* accuser. ¶ *a,* accusing. **accusatif** (tif) *m,* accusative [case]. **accusation** (sjɔ̃) *f,* accusation, charge. **accusé, e** (ze) *n,* accused, defendant. ~ **de réception,** *m,* acknowledgement. ¶ *a,* marked. **accuser** (ze) *v.t,* to accuse, charge (*de,* of, with); blame (*de,* for); show, betray (*age*); bring out, accentuate. ~ *réception de,* to acknowledge receipt of. **s'~ de,** to admit; blame o.s for.

acerbe (asɛrb) *a,* sour; caustic, acid.

acéré, e (asere) *a,* sharp (*point*); cutting, scathing (*remark*).

acétate (asetat) *m,* acetate.

acétique (asetik) *a,* acetic.

acétylène (asetilɛn) *m,* acetylene.

achalandé, e (aʃalɑ̃de) *a: bien ~,* well stocked (*shop*); well patronized.

acharné, e (aʃarne) *a,* fierce, desperate, relentless. ~ *à qch, à faire,* bent on sth, on doing. ~ *contre,* set against. **acharnement** (nəmɑ̃) *m,* fierceness, relentlessness. **acharner (s')** (ne) *v.pr, s'~ sur* or *contre qn,* to be dead against s.o, hound s.o. *s'~ à faire,* try desperately to do.

achat (aʃa) *m,* purchase. *faire des ~s,* to shop.

acheminement (aʃminmɑ̃) *m,* despatch; transporting; routing. **acheminer** (ne) *v.t,* to despatch; transport; route (*train*). **s'~ vers,** to head for.

acheter (aʃte) *v.t,* to buy, purchase (*à qn,* from s.o). **acheteur, euse** (tœr, øz) *n,* buyer, purchaser; shopper.

achevé, e (aʃve) *a,* accomplished; perfect; thorough, out & out. **achèvement** (ʃɛvmɑ̃) *m,* completion. **achever** (ʃve) *v.t,* to finish (*de*

faire, doing); complete; finish off (*pers., animal*). **s'~,** to end.
achopper (aʃɔpe) *v.i,* to stumble (*sur,* over).
acide (asid) *a,* (*lit., fig.*) acid, sour, tart. ¶ *m,* acid. **acidité** (dite) *f,* acidity.
acier (asje) *m,* steel. ~ *rapide,* high-speed steel. *d'*~, steel, of steel; (*fig.*) steely. **aciérie** (ri) *f,* steel works.
acné (akne) *f,* acne.
acolyte (akɔlit) *m,* acolyte.
acompte (akɔ̃t) *m,* instalment; deposit.
aconit (akɔnit) *m,* aconite, monk's-hood.
acoquiner (s') (akɔkine) *v.pr,* to gang up (*avec,* with).
Açores (les) (asɔr) *f.pl,* the Azores.
à-coup (aku) *m,* jerk, jolt. *par* ~*s,* in fits & starts.
acoustique (akustik) *a,* acoustic. ¶ *f,* acoustics.
acquéreur (akerœr) *m,* purchaser, buyer. **acquérir** (rir) *v.t.ir,* to acquire, get, win, obtain; purchase.
acquiescement (akjɛsmɑ̃) *m,* acquiescence. **acquiescer** (se) *v.i,* to acquiesce; agree.
acquis, e (aki, iz) *a,* acquired; established (*fact*). *tenir pour* ~, take for granted. ¶ *m,* experience, knowledge. **acquisition** (kizisjɔ̃) *f,* acquisition; purchase.
acquit (aki) *m,* (*Com.*) receipt. *pour* ~, received [with thanks]. **acquit-à-caution** (kitakosjɔ̃) *m,* bond note. **acquittement** (tmɑ̃) *m,* acquittal; payment, discharge. **acquitter** (te) *v.t,* to acquit; pay, settle; receipt (*bill*). **s'~ de,** to discharge (*debt, duty*); fulfil (*promise*); perform (*task*).
âcre (ɑkr) *a,* acrid, tart, pungent. **âcreté** (ɑkrəte) *f,* acridity, pungency.
acrimonie (akrimɔni) *f,* acrimony. **acrimonieux, euse** (njø, øz) *a,* acrimonious.
acrobate (akrɔbat) *n,* acrobat. **acrobatie** (si) *f,* acrobatics; acrobatic feat. ~ *aérienne,* aerobatics. **acrobatique** (tik) *a,* acrobatic.
acte (akt) *m,* act, action; (*Law*) deed, certificate; (*Theat.*) act. ~*s,* proceedings (*of a society*). ~ *d'accusation,* indictment. ~ *de dernière volonté,* last will & testament. ~ *de naissance, de mariage, de décès,* birth, marriage, death certificate. ~ *sous seing* (sɛ̃) *privé,* private agreement. **acteur, trice** (tœr, tris) *n,* actor, actress.
actif, ive (aktif, iv) *a,* active; regular (*army*). ¶ *m,* active [voice]; (*Fin.*) assets.
action (aksjɔ̃) *f,* (*gen., Law, Mil., Theat.*) action. *passer à l'*~, to take action. *mettre en* ~, put into action. act, deed; effect, action; (*Fin.*) share. ~*s nominatives, au porteur, privilégiées,* registered, bearer, preference shares *or* stock. *société par* ~*s,* joint-stock company. (*Rel.*) ~ *de grâce*[*s*], thanksgiving. **actionnaire** (ɔnɛr) *n,* shareholder.
actionner (aksjɔne) *v.t,* to drive, work, activate; (*Law*) bring an action against, sue.
activement (aktivmɑ̃) *ad,* actively. **activer** (ve) *v.t,* to speed up; stoke (*fire*). **s'~,** to bustle about; get a move on. **activité** (vite) *f,* activity, bustle. *en* ~, in operation; active (*volcano*). *en pleine* ~, in full operation, in full swing.
actuaire (aktɥɛr) *m,* actuary.
actualité (aktɥalite) *f,* topicality; present day event. *d'*~, topical. *l'*~, current events. *les* ~*s,* (*Cine., Radio &c*) the news. **actuel, le** (tɥɛl) *a,* present, current. *à l'heure* ~*le,* at the present time. **actuellement** (lmɑ̃) *ad,* now, at present.
acuité (akɥite) *f,* sharpness; acuteness, keenness (*of sense, pain*); shrillness.
acupuncture (akypɔ̃ktyr) *f,* acupuncture.
adage (adaʒ) *m,* adage.
adaptateur, trice (adaptatœr, tris) *n,* adapter. **adaptation** (sjɔ̃) *f,* adaptation. **adapter** (te) *v.t,* to adapt; (*Tech.*) fit (*plug &c*). *adapté à,* suited to. **s'~ à,** to adapt o.s. to; (*Tech.*) fit.
addition (adisjɔ̃) *f,* addition; bill (*at restaurant*). **additionnel, le** (ɔnɛl) *a,* additional. **additionner** (ne) *v.t,* to add [up], tot up.
adepte (adɛpt) *n,* follower.
adhérence (aderɑ̃s) *f,* adhesion; grip (*tyres: à,* on). **adhérent, e** (rɑ̃, ɑ̃t) *n,* adherent, supporter, member. **adhérer** (re) *v.i,* ~ *à,* to stick to; grip (*road*); be a member of. **adhésif, ive** (zif, iv) *a,* adhesive. **adhésion** (zjɔ̃) *f,* adherence (*à,* to); joining; membership (*à,* of).
adieu (adjø) *i. & m,* good-bye, farewell. *faire ses* ~*x,* to say one's farewells.
adipeux, euse (adipø, øz) *a,* adipose, fatty.
adjacent, e (adʒasɑ̃, ɑ̃t) *a,* adjacent (*à,* to); adjoining.
adjectif, ive (adʒɛktif, iv) *a,* adjectival. ¶ *m,* adjective. **adjectivement** (tivmɑ̃) *ad,* adjectivally, attributively.
adjoindre (adʒwɛ̃dr) *v.t.ir,* to add, attach; appoint as assistant. **adjoint, e** (ʒwɛ̃, ɛ̃t) *a. & n,* assistant, deputy.
adjudant (adʒydɑ̃) *m,* sergeant major. ~ *major,* adjutant.
adjudicataire (adʒydikatɛr) *n,* purchaser; winner of contract. **adjudication** (sjɔ̃) *f,* sale by auction; award of contract. **adjuger** (ʒe) *v.t,* to knock down, auction (*à,* to); award (*contract*).
adjurer (adʒyre) *v.t,* to beseech, implore (*qn de faire*).
admettre (admɛtr) *v.t.ir,* to admit, let in; permit, accept (*conduct*); admit, acknowledge; suppose, assume. *être admis à un examen,* to pass an exam.
administrateur, trice (administratœr, tris) *n,* administrator; director; trustee. **administratif, ive** (tif, iv) *a,* administrative. **administration** (sjɔ̃) *f,* administration, management,

direction; board, governing body; authorities. *l'A~*, the Civil Service. *l'~ locale*, local government. **administré, e** (tre) *n*, citizen. **administrer** (tre) *v.t*, to administer, manage, direct.

admirable† (admirabl) *a*, admirable, wonderful. **admirateur, trice** (tœr, tris) *n*, admirer. **admiratif, ive** (tif, iv) *a*, admiring. **admiration** (sjɔ̃) *f*, admiration. *faire l'~ de qn*, to fill s.o with admiration. **admirer** (re) *v.t*, to admire.

admissible (admisibl) *a*, admissible, acceptable; eligible (*à*, for). **admission** (sjɔ̃) *f*, admission, entry; (*Sch., Univ.*) entrance.

admonester (admɔnɛste) *v.t*, to admonish. **admonestation** (tasjɔ̃) *f*, admonition.

adolescence (adɔlɛsɑ̃s) *f*, adolescence, youth. **adolescent, e** (sɑ̃, ɑ̃t) *a*, adolescent. ¶ *n*, adolescent, teenager.

adonner (s') (adɔne) *v.pr*, *s'~ à*, to devote o.s to; take to (*drink*); go in for (*sport*).

adopter (adɔpte) *v.t*, to adopt; pass (*bill*). **adoptif, ive** (tif, iv) *a*, adopted, foster (*child*); adoptive (*parent &c*). **adoption** (sjɔ̃) *f*, adoption, &c.

adorable (adɔrabl) *a*, adorable, charming, delightful. **adorateur, trice** (tœr, tris) *n*, adorer; worshipper. **adoration** (sjɔ̃) *f*, adoration; worship. **adorer** (re) *v.t*, to adore; worship.

adosser (adose) *v.t*, *~ à qch*, to stand against sth. **s'~ à** *or* **contre**, to lean one's back against.

adoucir (adusir) *v.t*, to sweeten; soften; smooth, soothe, ease (*distress*). **s'~**, to grow sweeter, softer, smoother; (*weather*) grow milder; (*pers.*) mellow.

adresse[1] (adrɛs) *f*, skill, dexterity, deftness; shrewdness. *jeu d'~*, game of skill.

adresse[2] (adrɛs) *f*, address (*letter*); talk, address. *à l'~ de*, for the benefit of. **adresser** (se) *v.t*, to address (*letter, remark*); direct (*look*); send, refer (*pers. to s.o*). *~ la parole à*, speak to, address. **s'~ à**, to address, speak to; apply to, go & see (*pers.*); enquire at (*office*); (*book*) cater for.

adroit, e† (adrwa, at) *a*, skilful, deft, dext[e]rous; shrewd, adroit. *~ de ses mains*, clever with one's hands.

adulateur, trice (adylatœr, tris) *a*, adulatory. ¶ *n*, adulator. **adulation** (sjɔ̃) *f*, adulation. **aduler** (le) *v.t*, to adulate.

adulte (adylt) *a. & n*, adult, grown-up.

adultère (adyltɛr) *n*, adulterer, ess; (*m.*) adultery. ¶ *a*, adulterous.

advenir (advɔnir), *v.i.ir.imp*, to happen, occur. *il m'advint de*, I happened to. *advienne que pourra*, come what may.

adverbe (advɛrb) *m*, adverb. **adverbial, e†** (bjal) *a*, adverbial.

adversaire (advɛrsɛr) *m*, adversary, opponent. **adverse** (vɛrs) *a*, opposing (*forces*); adverse (*lot*). **adversité** (site) *f*, adversity, misfortune.

aération (aerasjɔ̃) *f*, ventilation; airing (*linen*); aeration (*soil, water*). **aérer** (re) *v.t*, to ventilate; air; aerate.

aérien, ne (aerjɛ̃, ɛn) *a*, aerial; air (*raid &c*); overhead (*cable*); light (*step*); ethereal (*music*).

aéro-club (aerɔklœb) *m*, flying club.

aérodrome (aerɔdrom) *m*, airfield.

aerodynamique (aerɔdinamik) *a*, aerodynamic; streamlined. ¶ *f*, aerodynamics.

aérofrein (aerɔfrɛ̃) *m*, air brake.

aérogare (aerɔgar) *f*, air terminal; airport buildings.

aéroglisseur (aerɔglisœr) *m*, hovercraft.

aérogramme (aerɔgram) *m*, air letter.

aéronaute (aerɔnot) *n*, aeronaut. **aéronautique** (notik) *a*, aeronautical, ¶ *f*, aeronautics.

aéronaval, e (aerɔnaval) *a*, air & sea (*forces*). *l'A~e*, the Fleet Air Arm.

aéroport (aerɔpɔr) *m*, airport.

aéroporté, e (aerɔpɔrte) *a*, airborne (*troops*).

aérosol (aerɔsɔl) *m*, aerosol.

affabilité (afabilite) *f*, affability. **affable†** (bl) *a*, affable.

affadir (afadir) *v.t*, to make insipid *or* dull.

affaiblir (afɛblir) *v.t*, to weaken. **s'~**, to grow weaker; (*sound*) fade; (*storm*) die down. **affaiblissement** (ismɑ̃) *m*, weakening.

affaire (afɛr) *f*, affair, matter; business. *ce n'est pas ton ~*, it's none of your business. *ça fait mon ~*, that's just what I want. *c'est toute une ~*, it's quite a business. *tirer qn d'~*, to help s.o out. (*Law, Police*) case. *une ~ de vol*, a case of theft. (*Com.*) business, concern. *une ~ qui marche*, a going concern. transaction, deal, bargain. *une bonne, mauvaise ~*, a good, bad bargain. *avoir ~ à*, to have to deal with, be faced with. *~ de cœur*, love affair. *~s*, (*Com*) business. *homme d'~s*, businessman. (*Pol.*) *~s étrangères*, foreign affairs. *mes ~s*, my things, clothes, belongings. **affairé, e** (fɛre) *a*, busy. **affairement** (mɑ̃), activity, bustling. **affairer (s')** (fɛre) *v.pr*, to bustle about (*à faire*, doing).

affaissement (afɛsmɑ̃) *m*, subsidence; sagging; collapse. **affaisser (s')** (se) *v.pr*, to subside; sag; collapse.

affamé, e (afame) *a*, famished, starving. *être ~ de*, long for, crave. **affamer** (me) *v.t*, to starve.

affectation (afɛktasjɔ̃) *f*, affectation; allocation; appointment; (*Mil.*) posting, attachment. **affecté, e** (te) *a*, affected. **affecter** (te) *v.t*, to affect, feign. *~ de faire*, pretend to do assume, take on (*shape*); allocate, earmark (*funds*); appoint (*pers.*); (*Mil.*) post, attach; move, touch, affect.

affection (afɛksjɔ̃) *f*, affection. *avoir de l'~ pour*, to be fond of. (*Med.*) complaint. **affectionné, e** (ɔne) *a*, affectionate, loving. **affectionner**

(ɔne) *v.t*, to be fond of. **affectueux, euse** (tɥø, øz) *a*, affectionate.
afférent, e (aferɑ̃, ɑ̃t) *a*, ~ *à*, pertaining to.
affermir (afɛrmir) *v.t*, to strengthen; steady (*voice*). **affermissement** (ismɑ̃) *m*, strengthening.
affiche (afiʃ) *f*, poster, [play] bill. *quitter, tenir l'~*, (*play*) come off, keep running. **afficher** (ʃe) *v.t*, to post, stick up; bill. *défense d'~*, stick no bills. display; (*pej*.) flaunt, parade.
affilé, e (afile) *a*, sharp. **d'affilée,** *ad*, at a stretch, on end. **affiler** (le) *v.t*, to sharpen.
affilié, e (afilje) *n*, affiliated member. **affilier** (je) *v.t*, to affiliate.
affinage (afinaʒ) *m*, refining. **affiner** (ne) *v.t*, to refine (*metal*); ripen (*cheese*); (*fig*.) refine, sharpen. **affinement** (mɑ̃) *m*, refinement.
affinité (afinite) *f*, affinity.
affirmatif, ive† (afirmatif, iv) *a*. & *f*, affirmative. **affirmation** (sjɔ̃) *f*, assertion. **affirmer** (me) *v.t*, to affirm, assert.
affleurement (aflœrmɑ̃) *m*, (*Geol*.) outcrop. **affleurer** (re) *v.t*, (*Tech*.) to make flush. ¶ *v.i*, (*reef &c*) to show on the surface; outcrop.
affliction (afliksjɔ̃) *f*, affliction. **affliger** (ʒe) *v.t*, to distress, grieve. *affligé de*, afflicted with. **s'~ de,** to be grieved about. **affligeant, e** (ʒɑ̃, ɑ̃t) *a*, distressing.
affluence (aflyɑ̃s) *f*, crowds. *heure d'~*, rush hour. **affluent** (ɑ̃) *m*, tributary. **affluer** (e) *v.i*, to flow; (*blood*) rush; (*crowd*) flock.
affolant, e (afɔlɑ̃, ɑ̃t) *a*, alarming. **affolé, e** (le) *a*, panic-stricken; driven crazy. **affolement** (mɑ̃) *m*, panic; turmoil. **affoler** (le) *v.t*, to throw into a panic; drive crazy. **s'~,** to panic.
affranchir (afrɑ̃ʃir) *v.t*, to [set] free, emancipate; stamp, frank (*letter*). **affranchissement** (ʃismɑ̃) *m*, emancipation, stamping, franking; postage (*sum*); enfranchisement.
affres (afr) *f.pl*, pangs, throes.
affrètement (afrɛtmɑ̃) *m*, chartering. **affréter** (frete) *v.t*, to charter.
affreux, euse† (afrø, øz) *a*, frightful, hideous; horrible, ghastly.
affrioler (afriɔle) *v.t*, to tempt, entice, excite.
affront (afrɔ̃) *m*, affront; slight.
affronter (afrɔ̃te) *v.t*, to confront, face, brave. **affrontement** (tmɑ̃) *m*, confrontation.
affubler (afyble) *v.t*, ~ *qn de*, to rig s.o out in.
affût (afy) *m*, [gun] carriage; (*Hunt*.) hide. *à l'~*, lying in wait. *à l'~ de qch*, on the lookout for sth.
affûter (afyte) *v.t*, to sharpen, grind.
afin de (afɛ̃) *pr*, in order to, so as to. **afin que,** *c*, (+ *subj*.) in order that, so that.
africain, e (afrikɛ̃, ɛn) *a*. & **A~**, *n*, African. **l'Afrique** (frik) *f*, Africa.
agaçant, e (agasɑ̃, ɑ̃t) *a*, irritating. **agacement** (smɑ̃) *m*, irritation. **agacer** (se) *v.t*, to irritate, get on one's nerves; pester.
agate (agat) *f*, agate.
âge (ɑʒ) *m*, age. *quel ~ a-t-il?* how old is he? *d'~ moyen*, middle-aged. *d'un ~ avancé*, elderly. *prendre de l'~*, to age. *être en ~ de*, to be old enough to. *avoir l'~ légal*, to be of age. *l'~ ingrat*, the awkward age. *l'~ de [la] pierre*, the Stone Age. *l'~ de raison*, the age of reason. **âgé, e** (ɑʒe) *a*, aged, old. ~ *de 8 ans*, 8 years old.
agence (aʒɑ̃s) *f*, agency, bureau; office; branch. ~ *immobilière*, estate agents. ~ *de placement*, employment agency.
agencement (aʒɑ̃smɑ̃) *m*, arrangement; fittings. **agencer** (se) *v.t*, to arrange; fit up, equip.
agenda (aʒɛ̃da) *m*, diary.
agenouiller (s') (aʒnuje) *v.pr*, to kneel [down]. *agenouillé*, kneeling. **agenouilloir** (jwar) *m*, hassock.
agent (aʒɑ̃) *m*, agent; officer; official. ~ [*de police*], policeman. *pardon monsieur l'~*, excuse me officer. (*Sch. &c*) *les ~s*, ancillary staff. ~ *d'assurances*, insurance agent. ~ *de change*, stockbroker. ~ *immobilier*, estate agent. (*Mil*.) ~ *de liaison*, liaison officer. ~ *maritime*, shipping agent. ~ *secret*, secret agent.
agglomération (aglɔmerasjɔ̃) *f*, urban area, built-up a. *l'~ parisienne*, Paris & its suburbs. conglomeration.
aggloméré (re) briquette; chipboard. **agglomérer (s')** (re) *v.pr*, to conglomerate.
agglutiner (aglytine) *v.t*, to agglutinate; bind.
aggraver (agrave) *v.t*, to aggravate; increase.
agile† (aʒil) *a*, agile, nimble. **agilité** (lite) *f*, agility, nimbleness.
agio (aʒjo) *m*, exchange premium. **agioter** (te) *v.i*, to speculate on exchange business. **agioteur** (tœr) *m*, speculator.
agir (aʒir) *v.i*, to act, behave; (*drug &c*) work, take effect. ~ *sur qch*, to act on sth. ~ *auprès de qn*, use one's influence with s.o. **s'~,** *v.imp*, *il s'agit de*, it's a question of, a matter of. *il ne s'agit pas d'argent*, it's not a question of money. *la somme dont il s'agit*, the sum in question. *de quoi s'agit-il?* what's it all about? *il ne s'agit pas de cela*, that's not the point. *il s'agit de trouver*... it's a matter of finding, we have to find... **agissant, e** (ʒisɑ̃, ɑ̃t) *a*, active; effective. **agissements** (smɑ̃) *m.pl*, (*pej*) schemes, goings-on.
agitateur, trice (aʒitatœr, tris) *n*, agitator. **agitation** (sjɔ̃) *f*, agitation; restlessness; bustle; (*Pol*.) unrest. **agité** (te) *a*, agitated (*pers*.); restless (*night*); choppy (*sea*). **agiter** (te) *v.t*, to wave (*arm, flag*); shake (*bottle*); flap (*wings*); wag (*tail*); stir; sway (*trees*); perturb, trouble; debate, discuss.
agneau (aɲo) *m*, lamb; lambskin.
agonie (agɔni) *f*, death agony, d. throes. *à l'~*, at death's door. **agonisant, e** (nizɑ̃, ɑ̃t) *a*,

dying. **agoniser** (ze) *v.i,* to be dying.
agrafe (agraf) *f,* hook, fastener; staple; (*Build*) cramp; (*Med.*) clip. **agrafer** (fe) *v.t,* to do up, fasten (*dress*); staple.
agraire (agrɛr) *a,* agrarian, land (*att.*).
agrandir (agrɑ̃dir) *v.t,* to enlarge. **s'~,** to grow [larger], expand. **aggrandissement** (ismɑ̃) *m,* expansion; (*Build.*) extension; (*Phot.*) enlargement. **aggrandisseur** (disœr) *m,* enlarger.
agréable† (agreabl) *a,* agreeable, pleasant, nice.
agréer (agree) *v.t,* to accept. *veuillez ~ mes sincères salutations,* yours sincerely. *fournisseur agréé,* registered dealer. ¶ *v.i, ~ à,* to please, suit.
agrégation (agregasjɔ̃) *f,* agrégation (*state competitive examination for teachers*). **agrégé, e** (ʒe) *n,* s.o who has passed the above. **agréger** (ʒe) *v.t,* to admit (*as member*). **agrément** (agremɑ̃) *m,* charm, attractiveness. *plein d'~,* very pleasant. *voyage d'~,* pleasure trip. consent, approval; (*Mus.*) ornament. **agrémenter** (te) *v.t,* to adorn, embellish (*de,* with).
agrès (agrɛ) *m.pl.* (*Naut.*) tackle; apparatus (*gym*).
agresseur (agrɛsœr) *m,* attacker; aggressor. **agressif, ive**† (sif, iv) *a,* aggressive. **agression** (sjɔ̃) *f,* attack; aggression.
agricole (agrikɔl) *a,* agricultural; farm (*worker*). **agriculteur** (kyltœr) *m,* farmer. **agriculture** (tyr) *f,* agriculture, farming.
agripper (agripe) *v.t,* to catch hold of, grab. **s'~ à,** to clutch, grip.
agronome (agrɔnɔm) *m,* agronomist. **agronomie** (mi) *f,* agronomy.
aguerrir (agɛrir) *v.t,* to harden (*contre,* against). *aguerri,* seasoned (*troops*).
aguets (agɛ), *m.pl, aux ~,* on the lookout.
aguicher (agiʃe) *v.t,* to entice, tantalize.
ahuri (ayri) *a,* stunned, flabbergasted; stupefied. **ahurir** (ir) *v.t,* to stun, dumbfound. **ahurissant, e** (isɑ̃, ɑ̃t) *a,* staggering, stupefying. **ahurissement** (ismɑ̃) *m,* stupefaction.
aide (ɛd) *f,* aid, help, assistance. *à l'~!* help! *venir en ~ à qn,* to come to s.o's help. *à l'~ de qch,* with the aid *or* help of sth. ¶ *n,* assistant, mate. *~ de camp, m,* aide-de-camp. *~ familiale,* home help. *~-mémoire, m.inv,* memorandum; (*Sch.*) crib. **aider** (ɛde) *v.t,* to aid, help, assist (*qn à faire,* s.o to do). **s'~ de,** to make use of.
aïe (aj) *i,* ow! ouch! (*pain*). *~ ~ ~!* dear oh dear!
aïeul, e (ajœl) *n,* grandfather, -mother. **aïeux** (ajø) *m.pl,* forefathers.
aigle (ɛgl) *n,* eagle. *~ royal,* golden eagle. *ce n'est pas un ~,* he's no genius. **aiglon, ne** (glɔ̃, ɔn) *n,* eaglet.
aigre† (ɛgr) *a,* sour (*taste*); shrill, sharp (*sound*); bitter, keen (*wind*); harsh (*words*). **~-doux, ce** (ɛgrədu, us) *a,* bitter-sweet; sweet & sour. **aigrefin** (fɛ̃) *m,* swindler; haddock. **aigrelet, te** (lɛ, ɛt) *a,* sourish; shrillish.
aigrette (ɛgrɛt) *f,* egret; aigrette, plume.
aigreur (ɛgrœr) *f,* sourness; harshness. **aigrir** (grir) *v.t,* to sour, embitter. **s'~,** (*lit.*) to turn sour; become embittered.
aigu, ë (egy) *a,* acute (*accent, angle, pain*); sharp, pointed; shrill, high (*note*). ¶ *m,* (*Mus.*) *les ~s,* the high notes.
aiguillage (egɥijaʒ) *m,* (*Rly.*) points, shunting. **aiguille** (ij) *f,* needle. *~ à coudre, à tricoter, à repriser,* sewing, knitting, darning needle. hand (*clock*); pointer; spire; (*Rly.*) point. *~ de glace,* icicle. *~ de pin,* pine needle. **aiguiller** (je) *v.t,* to direct, steer; (*Rly.*) shunt, switch. **aiguilleur** (jœr) *m,* pointsman.
aiguillon (egɥijɔ̃) *m,* goad; sting (*insect*); spur, incentive. **aiguillonner** (jɔne) *v.t,* to goad; spur on.
aiguiser (egize) *v.t,* to sharpen, grind; whet (*appetite*).
ail (aj) *m,* garlic.
aile (ɛl) *f,* wing; blade (*propellor*); sail (*windmill*). **ailé, e** (le) *a,* winged. **aileron** (lrɔ̃) *m,* pinion; fin (*shark*); (*Aero.*) aileron.
ailleurs (ajœr) *ad,* elsewhere, somewhere else. *partout ~,* everywhere else. **d'~,** *ad,* besides, moreover. **par ~,** otherwise.
aimable† (ɛmabl) *a,* amiable, kind, nice. **aimant**[1]**, e** (mɑ̃, ɑ̃t) *a,* loving, affectionate.
aimant[2] (ɛmɑ̃) *m,* magnet. **aimanter** (te) *v.t,* to magnetize.
aimer (ɛme) *v.t,* to love; be fond of, like. *~ faire, ~ à faire,* to like doing *or* to do. *j'aimerais mieux, j'aimerais autant sortir,* I would rather, I would just as soon go out. **s'~,** to be in love, love each other. *se faire ~ de qn,* to win s.o's love.
aine (ɛn) *f,* (*Anat.*) groin.
aîné, e (ɛne) *a,* elder; eldest. ¶ *n,* eldest child; senior. *mon ~ de 2 ans,* 2 years my senior.
ainsi (ɛ̃si) *ad,* thus, in this way. *et ~ de suite,* and so on. *pour ~ dire,* so to speak. ¶ *c,* so, and so. *~ tu ne viens pas?* so you're not coming? *~ que,* [just] as.
air (ɛr) *m,* air, breeze. *en plein ~,* in the open air. *sortir prendre l'~,* go out for a breath of fresh air. *regarder en l'~,* look up. *prendre l'~,* (*plane*) to take off. *en l'~,* idle, empty, airy (*words, promises*). *flanquer P* or *ficher P* or *foutre P* en l'~,* to mess up, bugger up **P***; chuck up *P*; chuck away *P.* look, appearance, air. *~ de famille,* family likeness. *d'un ~ perplexe,* with a puzzled look. *avoir l'~,* to look, seem. *elle a l'~ fatiguée,* she looks tired. *il n'a pas l'~ de comprendre,* he doesn't seem to understand. *ça n'a l'~ de rien,* it doesn't look difficult *or* up to much. tune, air; aria.
airain (ɛrɛ̃) (*Poet.*) *m,* bronze, brass.

aire (ɛr) *f*, area; eyrie (*eagle*). ~ *de battage*, threshing floor. ~ *de lancement*, launching site.
airelle (ɛrɛl) *f*, bilberry.
aisance (ɛzɑ̃s) *f*, ease; affluence. *vivre dans l'~*, to be comfortably off. fullness (*in garment*). **aise** (ɛz) *a*, (*liter.*) *bien* ~, very glad. ¶ *f*, ease, comfort. *être à l'~*, to feel at ease, comfortable; to be well off. *en prendre à son* ~, take things easy. (*liter.*) joy, pleasure. **aisé, e** (ɛze) *a*, easy; well off. **aisément** (mɑ̃) *ad*, easily; comfortably; readily.
aisselle (ɛsɛl) *f*, armpit.
ajonc (aʒɔ̃) *m*, gorse.
ajouré, e (aʒure) *a*, openwork (*design*).
ajourner (aʒurne) *v.t*, to adjourn, postpone, put off; (*Law*) summon, subpoena.
ajouter (aʒute) *v.t*, to add. ~ *à*, add to, increase.
ajustage (aʒystaʒ) *m*, (*Mach.*) assembly, fitting. **ajustement** (təmɑ̃) *m*, adjustment. **ajuster** (te) *v.t*, to adjust, regulate; fit (*à*, to, on); settle, put straight; aim at (*with gun*). *ajusté*, (*dress*) close fitting. **s'~**, to tidy oneself up.
alambic (alɑ̃bik) *m*, still.
alanguir (alɑ̃gir) *v.t*, to make languid. **s'~**, to grow 1. **alanguissement** (gismɑ̃) *m*, languor.
alarmant, e (alarmɑ̃, ɑ̃t) *a*, alarming. **alarme** (larm) *f*, alarm. **alarmer** (me) *v.t*, to alarm. **s'~**, to become alarmed (*de, pour*, at, about). **alarmiste** (mist) *a. & n*, alarmist.
albâtre (albɑtr) *m*, alabaster.
albatros (albatros) *m*, albatross.
albinos (albinɔs) *a. inv. & n*, albino.
album (albɔm) *m*, album, book, scrapbook.
albumine (albymin) *f*, albumin.
alcali (alkali) *m*, alkali. **alcalin, e** (lɛ̃, in) *a*, alkaline.
alchimie (alʃimi) *f*, alchemy. **alchimiste** (mist) *m*, alchemist.
alcool (alkɔl) *m*, alcohol, spirit[s]. ~ *à brûler*, methylated spirit. *boire de l'~*, to drink alcohol *or* spirits. **alcoolique** (kɔɔlik) *a. & n*, alcoholic.
alcôve (alkov) *f*, alcove, recess. ~ *de dortoir*, cubicle.
aléa (alea) *m*, risk, hazard. **aléatoire** (twar) *a*, uncertain, chancy, risky.
alène (alɛn) *f*, awl.
alentour (alɑ̃tur) *ad*, around, round about. *d'~*, surrounding. **~s**, *m.pl*, surroundings. *aux ~s de*, in the vicinity of.
alerte (alɛrt) *a*, alert, agile, brisk. ¶ *i*, look out! ¶ *f*, alarm, alert; (*fig.*) warning sign. *donner l'~*, give the alarm *or* alert. ~ *aérienne*, air raid warning.
aléser (aleze) *v.t*, to ream.
alexandrin (alɛksɑ̃drɛ̃) *m*, alexandrine (*verse*).
alézan, e (alezɑ̃, an) *a. & n*, chestnut [horse].
alfa (alfa) *m*, alfa [grass], esparto [grass].
algarade (algarad) *f*, angry outburst; dressing down.
algèbre (alʒɛbr) *m*, algebra. *c'est de l'~*, it's all Greek to me. **algébrique** (ʒebrik) *a*, algebraic.
Alger (alʒe) *m*, Algiers. **l'Algérie** (ʒeri) *f*, Algeria. **algérien, ne** (rjɛ̃, ɛn) *a. &* **A~**, *n*, Algerian.
algue (alg) *f*, seaweed, alga.
alias (aljas) *ad*, alias. **alibi** (alibi) *m*, alibi.
aliénation (aljenasjɔ̃) *f*, alienation. ~ *mentale*, insanity, mental derangement. **aliéné, e** (ne) *n*, mental patient. **aliéner** (ne) *v.t*, to alienate (*à qn*, from s.o); give up, (*Law*) alienate (*rights*). **aliéniste** (nist) *n*, mental specialist.
alignement (aliɲmɑ̃) *m*, lining up; (*Pol.*) alignment; (*Mil.*) dressing; building line. **aligner** (ɲe) *v.t*, to line up, align; (*Mil.*) dress; (*fig.*) reel off. ~ *sur*, bring into line with.
aliment (alimɑ̃) *m*, food. **~s**, food, foodstuffs. **alimentaire** (tɛr) *a*, food (*products*). *denrées ~s*, foodstuffs. **alimentation** (tasjɔ̃) *f*, feeding; supplying; diet; food trade; grocery, groceries (*shop sign*). **alimenter** (te) *v.t*, to feed, supply.
alinéa (alinea) *m*, paragraph.
alité, e (alite) *a*, laid up, bedridden. **aliter** (te) *v.t*, to keep in bed. **s'~**, take to one's bed.
alizé (alize) *a. & m*, [*vent*] ~ , trade wind.
allaiter (alɛte) *v.t*, to suckle, breast-feed. **allaitement** (tmɑ̃) *m*, suckling, feeding.
allant, e (alɑ̃, ɑ̃t) *a*, active, lively. ¶ *m*, go, drive.
allécher (aleʃe) *v.t*, to allure, entice, tempt.
allée (ale) *f*, path; walk, avenue (*in park*); drive (*to house*); aisle (*cinema*). *~s & venues*, comings & goings; running about.
allégation (alegasjɔ̃) *f*, allegation.
allégeance (aleʒɑ̃s) *f*, allegiance.
allégement (alɛʒmɑ̃) *m*, lightening, alleviation. **alléger** (eʒe) to lighten; alleviate (*pain*).
allégorie (alegɔri) *f*, allegory. **allégorique**† (rik) *a*, allegoric(al).
allègre (alɛgr) *a*, lively, cheerful, merry. **allégresse** (alegrɛs) *f*, joy[fulness], elation.
alléguer (alege) *v.t*, to advance, put forward (*pretext, reason*); plead (*ignorance*). ~ *que*, to argue that.
Allemagne (**l'**) (almaɲ) *f*, Germany. ~ *de l'Ouest, de l'Est*, West, East, Germany. **allemand, e** (mɑ̃, ɑ̃d) *a. &* **A~**, *n*, German. **l'allemand,** *m*, German (*language*).
aller (ale) *m*, outward journey; single [ticket]. *~-retour*, ~ *& retour*, journey there & back; return [ticket]. ¶ *v.i.ir*, to go. ~ *à Paris, à l'école, à la chasse*, to go to Paris, to school, hunting. ~ *à pied, à bicyclette, en voiture*, to walk, cycle, drive. (*health &c*) *comment allez-vous?* [*comment*] *ça va?* how are you? how's things? *P. ça va*, I'm fine, all right, O.K. *elle va bien, mal, mieux*, she's well, unwell, better.

les affaires vont mal, business is bad. ~ *à qn,* (*clothes*) to suit, fit; (*food &c*) agree with. ¶ *v.aux,* ~ *faire,* to be going to do. *il va partir,* he's going to leave. to go & do. ~ *voir,* go & see. ~ *chercher,* go & fetch (*s.o, sth*). *cela va sans dire, cela va de soi,* that goes without saying. ¶ *v. imp, il en va de même pour*... the same goes for... *il y va de ma vie,* my life is at stake. *allez! allons!* go on! come on! *allons donc!* (*disbelief*) go on! come off it! *P. allez-y! vas-y!* go on! go ahead! *on y va?* shall we go? **s'en** ~, to go away.
allergie (alɛrʒi) *f,* allergy. **allergique** (ik) allergic.
alliage (aljaʒ) *m,* alloy. **alliance** (jɑ̃s) *f,* alliance; union, marriage. *cousin par* ~, cousin by marriage. wedding ring. **allié, e** (je) *n,* ally; relation [by marriage]. **allier** (je) *v.t,* to ally, unite, combine; match (*à,* with). **s'** ~, to unite; combine; match; ally o.s (*à,* with).
alligator (aligatɔr) *m,* alligator.
allô (alo) (*Tel.*) *i,* hullo!
allocation (allɔkasjɔ̃) *f,* allocation; allowance. ~ *de chômage,* unemployment benefit. ~*s familiales,* family allowance[s].
allocution (allɔkysjɔ̃) *f,* short speech.
allonger (alɔ̃ʒe) *v.t,* to lengthen, prolong; stretch out; deal (*blow*).
allouer (alwe) *v.t,* to allocate, grant; allot, allow (*time*).
allumage (alymaʒ) *m,* lighting; (*Elec.*) switching on; (*Mot.*) ignition. **allume-gaz** (lymgaz) *m.inv,* gas lighter. **allumer** (me) *v.t,* to light, ignite; kindle; (*Elec.*) turn on, switch on. ~ *la cuisine,* switch on the kitchen lights. stir up, arouse. **allumette** (mɛt) *f,* match, ~*s de sûreté,* safety matches. **allumeur** (mœr) *m,* igniter. **allumeuse** (møz) *f* (*pej.*) teaser, flirt.
allure (alyr) *f,* walk, bearing; look, appearance. *avoir fière, piètre* ~, cut a fine, sorry figure. speed, pace. *à toute* ~, at full speed.
allusion (allyzjɔ̃) *f,* allusion, hint, innuendo. *faire* ~ *à,* hint at.
alluvions (allyvjɔ̃) *f.pl,* alluvial deposits.
almanach (almana) *m,* almanac.
aloès (alɔɛs) *m,* aloe.
aloi (alwa) *m, de bon* ~, of sterling worth *or* quality; respectable (*joke*).
alors (alɔr) *ad,* then, at that time; (*consequence*) then, in that case, so; well then. *ça* ~*!* well I never! ~ **que,** when; whereas. ~ **même que,** even though; just when.
alouette (alwɛt) *f,* lark.
alourdir (alurdir) *v.t,* to make heavy, weigh down; to dull (*mind*).
aloyau (alwajo) *m,* sirloin (*beef*).
alpaga (alpaga) *m,* alpaca.
Alpes (les) (alp) *f.pl,* the Alps. **alpestre** (pɛstr) *a,* Alpine.
alphabet (alfabɛ) *m,* alphabet; spelling book. ~ *morse,* Morse code. **alphabétique**† (betik) *a,* alphabetical.
alpin, e (alpɛ̃, in) *a,* alpine. **alpinisme** (pinism) *m,* mountaineering. **alpiniste** (nist) *n,* mountaineer, climber.
Alsace (l') (alzas) *f,* Alsace. **alsacien, ne** (sjɛ̃, ɛn) *a,* & **A**~, *n,* Alsatian.
altérant, e (alterɑ̃, ɑ̃t) *a,* thirst-creating.
altération (alterasjɔ̃) *f,* alteration, change; adulteration; falsification; deterioration.
altercation (altɛrkasjɔ̃) *f,* altercation.
altérer (altere) *v.t,* to alter, change; adulterate, debase; falsify; make thirsty. **s'** ~, (*health*) deteriorate; (*food*) go off.
alternatif, ive† (altɛrnatif, iv) *a,* alternate; (*Elec.*) alternating. ¶ *f,* alternative; option. **alterner** (ne) *v.i. & t,* to alternate.
altesse (altɛs) *f,* highness (*title*).
altier, ère (altje, ɛr) *a,* haughty.
altitude (altityd) *f,* altitude, height.
alto (alto) *m,* viola; alto, contralto (*voice*). ¶ *a,* alto (*saxophone*).
altruisme (altrɥism) *m,* altruism. **altruiste** (ist) *n,* altruist. ¶ *a,* altruistic.
aluminium (alyminjɔm) *m,* aluminium.
alun (alœ̃) *m,* alum.
alunir (alynir) *v.i,* to land on the moon. **alunissage** (nisaʒ) *m,* [moon] landing.
alvéole (alveɔl) *m,* cell; socket (*tooth*).
amabilité (amabilite) *f,* kindness. *ayez l'*~ *de,* be so kind as to.
amadou (amadu) *m,* tinder, touchwood.
amadouer (amadwe) *v.t,* to coax, wheedle, cajole; mollify.
amaigrir (amɛgrir) *v.t,* to [make] thin. **amaigrissant, e** (isɑ̃, ɑ̃t) slimming.
amalgame (amalgam) *m,* amalgam; mixture. **amalgamer** (me) *v.t,* to amalgamate.
amande (amɑ̃d) *f,* almond; kernel. *des yeux en* ~, almond eyes. **amandier** (mɑ̃dje) *m,* almond [tree].
amant (amɑ̃) *m,* lover.
amarrage (amaraʒ) *m,* (*Naut.*) mooring. **amarre** (ar) *f,* [mooring] rope, cable; painter. *les* ~*s,* moorings. **amarrer** (mare) *v.t,* to make fast, moor; belay.
amas (amɑ) *m,* heap, pile, mass, accumulation. **amasser** (se) *v.t,* to amass, pile up, accumulate.
amateur (amatœr) *m,* lover (*of sth*). ~ *de musique,* music lover. *être* [*très*] ~ *de,* to be [very] keen on, fond of. amateur; (*pej.*) dilettante. *équipe* ~, amateur team. *d'*~, amateurish (*work*).
amazone (amazon) *f,* Amazon; horsewoman. [*habit d'*]~, riding habit. **l'A**~, *m,* the Amazon (*river*).
ambages (ɑ̃baʒ) *f.pl, sans* ~, in plain language.
ambassade (ɑ̃basad) *f,* embassy; mission. **am-**

bassadeur, drice (dœr, dris) *n,* ambassador; (*f*) a.'s wife, ambassadress. *l'~ de France,* the French ambassador.
ambiance (ɑ̃bjɑ̃s) *f,* atmosphere; surroundings. **ambiant, e** (ɑ̃, ɑ̃t) *a,* surrounding.
ambigu†, ë (ɑ̃bigy) *a,* ambiguous. **ambiguïté** (gɥite) *f,* ambiguity.
ambitieux, euse† (ɑ̃bisjø, øz) *a,* ambitious. **ambition** (sjɔ̃) *f,* ambition. **ambitionner** (ɔne) *v.t,* to strive for (*sth*); have an ambition (*de faire,* to do).
ambivalent, e (ɑ̃bivalɑ̃, ɑ̃t) *a,* ambivalent.
ambre (ɑ̃br) *m,* amber. *~ gris,* ambergris. **ambré, e** (bre) *a,* amber (*colour*).
ambulance (ɑ̃bylɑ̃s) *f,* ambulance. **ambulancier, ière** (je, jɛr) *n,* a. man, a. woman; a. driver. **ambulant, e** (lɑ̃, ɑ̃t) *a,* travelling, strolling (*player*).
âme (ɑm) *f,* soul; spirit, heart; (*fig.*) moving spirit; (*Mus.*) sound post. *sans ~,* soulless. *grandeur d'~,* noble-mindedness. *~ sœur,* kindred spirit. *musicien dans l'~,* musician to the core. *~ damnée,* henchman. *rendre l'~,* to give up the ghost. *je n'ai vu ~ qui vive,* I didn't see a living soul.
améliorer (ameljɔre) *v.t. & s'~,* to improve.
amen (ɑmɛn) *i. & m,* amen.
aménagement (amenaʒmɑ̃) *m,* fitting up; conversion; development; adjustment. *l'~ du territoire,* regional development. *~s,* fittings. **aménager** (ʒe) *v.t,* to lay out; fit up (*une pièce en bureau,* a room as a study); convert; develop (*region*); adjust.
amende (amɑ̃d) *f,* fine. *faire ~ honorable,* to make amends.
amender (amɑ̃de) *v.t,* to amend; improve.
amène (amɛn) *a,* amiable, affable.
amener (amne) *v.t,* to bring, lead; lead to, cause. *~ qn à faire,* lead, induce s.o to do. to strike (*flag, sail*).
aménité (amenite) *f,* affability.
amenuiser (s') (amənɥize) *v.pr,* to dwindle.
amer, ère† (amɛr) *a,* (*lit., fig.*) bitter.
américain, e (amerikɛ̃, ɛn) *a. &* **A~,** *n,* American. **l'Amérique** (rik) *f,* America.
amerrir (amerir) *v.i,* (*Aero.*) to land on the sea; splash down.
amertume (amɛrtym) *f,* bitterness.
améthyste (ametist) *f,* amethyst.
ameublement (amœbləmɑ̃) *m,* furniture; furnishing. *articles d'~,* furnishings.
ameuter (amøte) *v.t,* to draw, collect (*crowd*); stir up, rouse. **s'~,** to gather.
ami, e (ami) *a,* friendly. ¶ *n,* friend. *petit(e) ami(e),* boyfriend, girlfriend. *se faire un ~ de,* to become friends with. *mes chers ~s,* [ladies &] gentlemen. *mon cher ~,* my dear fellow. **amiable** (amjabl) *a,* (*Law*) *à l'~,* amicable (*agreement*); private (*sale*). *régler à l'~,* settle out of court.
amiante (amjɑ̃t) *m,* asbestos.
amibe (amib) *f,* amoeba.
amical, e† (amikal) *a,* friendly. *peu ~,* unfriendly.
amidon (amidɔ̃) *m,* starch. **amidonner** (dɔne) *v.t,* to starch.
amincir (amɛ̃sir) *v.t,* to thin [down]; slim. **s'~,** to get thinner.
amiral (amiral) *m,* admiral. *vaisseau ~,* flagship. **amirauté** (rote) *f,* admiralty.
amitié (amitje) *f,* friendship. *prendre qn en ~,* to take to s.o. *se lier d'~ avec,* to make friends with. *faites-lui mes ~s,* give him my [kind] regards. (*letter*) [*affectueuses*] *~s, Marie,* love [from] Marie.
ammoniaque (amɔnjak) *f,* ammonia.
amnésie (amnezi) *f,* amnesia.
amnistie (amnisti) *f,* amnesty. **amnistier** (tje) *v.t,* to amnesty.
amocher *P* (amɔʃe) *v.t,* to mess up; bash up *P* (*car*).
amoindrir (amwɛ̃drir) *v.t,* to lessen, weaken; belittle (*s.o*).
amollir (amɔlir) *v.t,* to soften, weaken.
amonceler (amɔsle) *v.t,* to heap up, pile up, accumulate. **amoncellement** (sɛlmɑ̃) *m,* heap; accumulation.
amont (amɔ̃) *m,* upstream waters; uphill slope. *en ~,* upstream, uphill. *en ~ de,* above. *le ski ~,* the uphill ski.
amorce (amɔrs) *f,* bait; percussion cap (*shell*); primer; beginning, start. **amorcer** (se) *v.t,* to bait, entice; prime (*pump, shell*); begin, start (*road, negotiations*).
amorphe (amɔrf) *a,* spiritless, lifeless.
amortir (amɔrtir) *v.t,* to deaden (*sound, pain*); cushion (*blow*); pay off (*debt*); write off, depreciate (*stock*). (*Ten.*) *un amorti,* a drop shot. **amortissement** (tismɑ̃) *m,* deadening &c. **amortisseur** (tisœr) *m,* shock absorber.
amour (amur) *m,* love. *faire l'~,* to make love. love affair; love, sweetheart. *tu seras un ~,* there's a darling. *quel ~ d'enfant!* what a darling child! *pour l'~ de Dieu,* for God's sake. **~-propre** (prɔpr) *m,* self-esteem, pride. **amoureux, euse†** (rø, øz) *a,* in love (*de,* with); amorous (*adventure*); loving (*look*). ¶ *n,* lover, sweetheart.
amovible (amɔvibl) *a,* removable, detachable.
ampère (ɑ̃pɛr) *m,* ampere, amp.
amphibie (ɑ̃fibi) *a,* amphibious. ¶ *m,* amphibian.
amphithéâtre (ɑ̃fiteɑtr) *m,* amphitheatre; lecture theatre; (*Theat.*) gallery.
ample† (ɑ̃pl) *a,* ample, full, roomy (*garment*); spacious; wide-ranging. **ampleur** (ɑ̃plœr) *f,* fullness; scope, range; scale. **amplificateur** (plifikatœr) *m,* amplifier. **amplification** (kasjɔ̃) amplification; expansion. **amplifier** (fje) *v.t,* to amplify; expand, develop.

ampoule (ɑ̃pul) *f,* (*Elec.*) bulb; blister; phial. **ampoulé, e** (le) *a,* bombastic (*style*).
amputer (ɑ̃pyte) *v.t,* to amputate. ~ *qn de la jambe,* a. s.o's leg.
amusant, e (amyzɑ̃, ɑ̃t) *a,* amusing, funny; entertaining. **amusement** (zmɑ̃) *m,* amusement; pastime.
amulette (amylɛt) *f,* amulet.
amuser (amyze) *v.t,* to amuse, entertain; **s'** ~, to amuse o.s; enjoy o.s, have fun (*à faire,* doing). *amuse-toi bien!* have a good time!
amygdale (amigdal) *f,* tonsil. **amygdalite** (lit) *f,* tonsillitis.
an (ɑ̃) *m,* year. *il a 10 ~s,* he is 10 years old. *2 fois par ~,* twice a year. *le jour de l'~,* New Year's Day. *en l'~ 800,* in the year 800.
anachronique (anakrɔnik) *a,* anachronistic. **anachronisme** (nism) *m,* anachronism.
anagramme (anagram) *f,* anagram.
analogie (analɔʒi) *f,* analogy. **analogue** (lɔg) *a,* analogous, similar (*à,* to).
analyse (analiz) *f,* analysis. ~ *grammaticale,* parsing. **analyser** (lize) *v.t,* to analyse; parse. **analyste** (list) *n,* analyst. *~-programmeur,* systems a. **analytique**† (tik) *a,* analytic(al).
ananas (ananɑ) *m,* pineapple.
anarchie (anarʃi) *f,* anarchy. **anarchique**† (ʃik) *a,* anarchic(al). **anarchiste** (ʃist) *n. & a,* anarchist.
anathème (anatɛm) *m,* anathema.
anatomie (anatɔmi) *f,* anatomy. **anatomique**† (mik) *a,* anatomical.
ancestral, e (ɑ̃sɛstral) *a,* ancestral. **ancêtre** (sɛtr) *m,* ancestor.
anche (ɑ̃ʃ) *f,* (*Mus.*) reed.
anchois (ɑ̃ʃwa) *m,* anchovy.
ancien, ne (ɑ̃sjɛ̃, ɛn) *a,* ancient, old. *dans l'~ temps,* in the old days. of long standing (*friendship*); former, old. *mon ~ professeur,* my old teacher. ~ *combattant,* ex-serviceman, veteran. senior. ¶ *m,* elder, old man. (*Hist.*) *les ~s,* the Ancients. **anciennement** (ɛnmɑ̃) *ad,* formerly. **ancienneté** (nte) *f,* age, antiquity; seniority, length of service. *de toute ~,* from time immemorial.
ancrage (ɑ̃kraʒ) *m,* anchorage; mooring. **ancre** (ɑ̃kr) *f,* anchor. *jeter, lever l'~,* to cast, weigh anchor. ~ *à jet,* kedge [a.]. **ancrer** (ɑ̃kre) *v.t,* (*Naut., Build.*) to anchor. **s'** ~, to anchor; (*idea*) take root.
andouille (ɑ̃duj) *f,* (*Cook.*) andouille; (*P*) idiot, clot *P.*
âne (ɑn) *m,* ass, donkey; (*fig.*) ass, fool.
anéantir (aneɑ̃tir) *v.t,* to annihilate, destroy; overwhelm, prostrate. **anéantissement** (aneɑ̃tismɑ̃) *m,* destruction &c (*V anéantir*).
anecdote (anɛgdɔt) *f,* anecdote.
anémie (anemi) *f,* anaemia. **anémique** (mik) *a,* anaemic.
anémone (anemɔn) *f* anemone.
ânerie (ɑnri) *f,* stupidity; stupid remark; blunder. **ânesse** (ɑnɛs) *f,* she-ass.
anesthésie (anɛstezi) *f,* anaesthesia. *faire une ~ à,* give an anaesthetic to. **anesthésier** (zje) *v.t,* to anaesthetize. **anesthésique** (zik) *a. & m,* anaesthetic.
ange (ɑ̃ʒ) *m,* angel. *tu seras un ~,* there's an a. *être aux ~s,* to be in raptures. **angélique**† (ɑ̃ʒelik) *a,* angelic. ¶ *f,* angelica. **angélus** (lys) *m,* angelus.
angine (ɑ̃ʒin) *f,* tonsillitis; sore throat. ~ *de poitrine,* angina [pectoris].
anglais, e (ɑ̃glɛ, ɛz) *a,* English; British (*army &c*). **A~,** *n,* Englishman, -woman, Briton. *l'~, m,* English (*language*).
angle (ɑ̃gl) *m,* angle; corner; point of view. ~ *droit,* right angle.
Angleterre (l') (ɑ̃glətɛr) *f,* England. **anglican** (glikɑ̃) *a,* anglican. **anglicisme,** (glisism) *m,* anglicism. **angliciste** (glisist) *n,* student *or* specialist in English. **les îles Anglo-Normandes,** the Channel Islands. **anglophile** (fil) *a. & n,* anglophile. **anglophobe** (fɔb) *a,* anglophobic. ¶ *n,* anglophobe. **anglo-saxon, ne** (saksɔ̃, ɔn) *a, &* **A ~ -S ~** , *n,* Anglo-Saxon.
angoissant, e (ɑ̃gwasɑ̃, ɑ̃t) *a,* distressing; agonizing. **angoisse** (ɑ̃gwas) *f,* anguish, agony; dread. **angoisser** (se) *v.t,* to distress, cause anguish to.
anguille (ɑ̃gij) *f,* eel. ~ *de mer,* conger [eel]. ~ *sous roche,* something in the wind.
angulaire (ɑ̃gylɛr) *a,* angular; corner (*stone*).
anicroche (anikrɔʃ) *f,* hitch, snag.
ânier, ère (ɑnje, ɛr) *n,* donkey driver.
aniline (anilin) *f,* aniline.
animal, e (animal) *a,* animal. ¶ *m,* animal. *quel ~! P,* what a lout!
animateur, trice (animatœr, tris) *n,* animator, moving spirit; organizer; compère. **animation** (sjɔ̃) *f,* animation, liveliness; bustle, life. **animé, e** (me) *a,* animated, lively; busy (*street*); brisk (*market*); animate. **animer** (me) *v.t,* to enliven, put life into; impel, prompt, actuate; lead, conduct (*group, debate*).
animosité (animozite) *f,* animosity.
anis (ani[s]) *m,* (*Bot.*) anise; (*Cook.*) aniseed.
annales (anal) *f.pl,* annals.
anneau (ano) *m,* ring; coil (*snake*); link (*chain*).
année (ane) *f,* year. *à l'~,* (*pay*) by the year. *de première ~,* first year (*student*). *les ~s trente,* the thirties. ~ *bis-sextile,* leap year. *~-lumière,* light year.
annexe (anɛks) *f,* (*Build.*) annex[e]; annex, appendix (*text*); enclosure (*letter*). **annexer** (kse) *v.t,* (*Pol.*) to annex; attach, append. **annexion** (ksjɔ̃) *f,* annexation.
annihiler (aniile) *v.t,* to annihilate, wipe out; destroy, crush.
anniversaire (anivɛrsɛr) *m,* anniversary; birthday.

annonce (anɔ̃s) *f,* announcement; (*fig.*) indication; call, bid (*Cards*); advertisement. *petites ~s,* classified a-s. **annoncer** (nɔ̃se) *v.t,* to announce; advertise; forecast (*rain*); foreshadow, bode, betoken; announce, show in (*pers.*). **s'~ bien,** to look good, promising. **annonceur** (sœr) *m,* advertiser; announcer. **l'Annonciation** (sjasjɔ̃) *f,* the Annunciation, Lady-day.
annoter (anɔte) *v.t,* to annotate.
annuaire (anɥɛr) *m,* annual, yearbook; (*Tel.*) directory, phone book *P;* (*Army, Navy*) list.
annuel, le† (nɥɛl) *a,* annual, yearly. **annuité** (nɥite) *f,* annual payment.
annulaire (anylɛr) *m,* ring finger, third f.
annuler (anyle) *v.t,* to annul (*marriage*); nullify (*contract*); quash (*sentence*); cancel (*order*).
anoblir (anɔblir) *v.t,* to ennoble.
anode (anɔd) *f,* anode.
anodin, e (anɔdɛ̃, in) *a,* soothing; harmless; insignificant. ¶ *m,* anodyne.
anomalie (anɔmali) *f,* anomaly; (*Biol.*) abnormality.
ânon (ɑnɔ̃) *m,* ass's foal. **ânonner** (nɔne) *v.t,* to drone out, mumble through (*speech*).
anonymat (anɔnima) *m,* anonymity. **anonyme** (nim) *a,* anonymous. *société ~ (SA),* ≃ [public] limited company (PLC).
anormal, e (anɔrmal) *a,* abnormal.
anse (ɑ̃s) *f,* handle (*cup*); (*Geog.*) cove.
antagonisme (ɑ̃tagɔnism) *m,* antagonism. **antagoniste** (nist) *a,* antagonistic. ¶ *n,* antagonist, opponent.
antan (ɑ̃tɑ̃) *m, d'~,* of yesteryear, of long ago.
antarctique (ɑ̃tarktik) *a,* antarctic. ¶ *m, l'A~,* the Antarctic, Antarctica.
antécédent, e (ɑ̃tesedɑ̃, ɑ̃t) *a. & m,* antecedent. *~s,* previous history.
antédiluvien, ne (ɑ̃tedilyvjɛ̃, ɛn) *a,* antediluvian.
antenne (ɑ̃tɛn) *f,* antenna, feeler; (*Radio, T.V.*) aerial. *être, passer à l'~,* to be, go on the air. *gardez l'~,* stay tuned in.
antérieur, e† (ɑ̃terjœr) *a,* previous, former, prior; front. *patte ~e,* forefoot. **antériorité** (rjɔrite) *f,* priority.
anthologie (ɑ̃tɔlɔʒi) *f,* anthology.
anthracite (ɑ̃trasit) *m,* anthracite.
anthrax (ɑ̃traks) *m,* (*Med.*) carbuncle.
anthropologie (ɑ̃trɔpɔlɔʒi) *f,* anthropology. **anthropologiste** (ʒist) *n,* anthropologist.
anthropophage (ɑ̃trɔpɔfaʒ) *a. & m,* cannibal.
anti-aérien, ne (ɑ̃tiaerjɛ̃, ɛn) *a,* anti-aircraft (*gun*); air-raid (*shelter*).
antiatomique (ɑ̃tiatɔmik) *a: abri ~,* fallout shelter.
antibiotique (ɑ̃tibjɔtik) *m,* antibiotic.
antichambre (ɑ̃tiʃɑ̃br) *f,* antechamber, anteroom.
antichar (ɑ̃tiʃar) *a,* anti-tank.
antichoc (ɑ̃tiʃɔk) *a,* shock-proof.
anticipation (ɑ̃tisipasjɔ̃) *f, par ~,* (*payment*) in advance. *roman d'~,* science fiction novel. **anticiper** (pe) *v.i,* to look ahead, anticipate. *~ sur qch,* anticipate sth. *v.t,* anticipate, forestall.
anticyclone (ɑ̃tisiklon) *m,* anticyclone.
antidater (ɑ̃tidate) *v.t,* to antedate.
antidérapant, e (ɑ̃tiderapɑ̃, ɑ̃t) *a,* non-skid.
antidote (ɑ̃tidɔt) *m,* antidote.
antigel (ɑ̃tiʒɛl) *m,* antifreeze.
antillais, e (ɑ̃tijɛ, ɛz) *a. & A~, n,* West Indian. **Antilles (les)** (tij) *f.pl,* the West Indies. *la mer des ~,* the Caribbean sea.
antimoine (ɑ̃timwan) *m,* antimony.
antiparasite (ɑ̃tiparazit) *a, dispositif ~,* suppressor.
antipathie (ɑ̃tipati) *f,* antipathy, aversion. **antipathique** (tik) *a,* unpleasant.
antipodes (ɑ̃tipɔd) *m.pl,* antipodes.
antiquaire (ɑ̃tikɛr) *n,* antique dealer. **antique** (tik) *a,* ancient; antique (*furniture*); (*pej.*) antiquated. **antiquité** (kite) *f,* antiquity; antique. *magasin d'~s,* antique shop.
antisémite (ɑ̃tisemit) *a,* antisemitic.
antiseptique (ɑ̃tisɛptik) *a, & m,* antiseptic.
antithèse (ɑ̃titɛz) *f,* antithesis.
antre (ɑ̃tr) *m,* cave; den, lair.
anus (anys) *m,* anus.
Anvers (ɑ̃vɛr) *m,* Antwerp.
anxiété (ɑ̃ksjete) *f,* anxiety. **anxieux, euse** (ksjø, øz) *a,* anxious, worried.
aorte (aɔrt) *f,* aorta.
août (u, ut) *m,* August.
apache (apaʃ) *m,* Apache; *O* ruffian, tough.
apaisement (apɛzmɑ̃) *m,* calming down; subsiding; relief. **apaiser** (ze) *v.t,* to appease, pacify, calm down (*pers.*); assuage, quench (*hunger, thirst &c*); soothe (*pain*). **s'~,** to calm down; (*storm*) die down.
apanage (apanaʒ) *m,* privilege, exclusive right.
aparté (aparte) *m,* (*Theat.*) aside. *en ~,* in an a.
apathie (apati) *f,* apathy. **apathique** (tik) *a,* apathetic.
apercevoir (apɛrsəvwar) *v.t.ir,* to see, catch sight of; notice; perceive (*danger*). **s'~ de,** to notice, become aware of, realize. **aperçu** (sy) *m,* general idea, outline; insight.
apéritif (aperitif) *m,* aperitif.
apesanteur (apəzɑ̃tœr) *f,* weightlessness.
à-peu-près (apøprɛ) *m,* rough approximation.
aphorisme (afɔrism) *m,* aphorism.
aphrodisiaque (afrɔdizjak) *a. & m,* aphrodisiac.
apiculture (apikyltyr) *f,* bee keeping.
apitoyer (apitwaje) *v.t,* to move to pity. **s'~ sur,** to feel pity for, feel sorry for.
aplanir (aplanir) *v.t,* to level; smooth.
aplatir (aplatir) *v.t,* to flatten. **s'~,** to flatten o.s; fall flat on one's face; grovel.

aplomb (aplɔ̃) *m,* self-possession; verticality, plumb (*wall*); balance (*pers.*). *d'~,* plumb; balanced, steady.
Apocalypse (apɔkalips) *f,* Apocalypse, [book of] Revelation.
apogée (apɔʒe) *m,* (*Astr.*) apogee; (*fig.*) zenith.
apologie (apɔlɔʒi) *f,* defence, vindication.
apoplectique (apɔplɛktik) *a. & m,* apoplectic. **apoplexie** (ksi) *f,* apoplexy.
apostasie (apɔstazi) *f,* apostasy. **apostat** (ta) *a. & n,* apostate, renegade.
apostolat (apɔstɔla) *m,* discipleship; vocation. **apostolique**† (lik) *a,* apostolic.
apostrophe (apɔstrɔf) *f,* apostrophe; rude remark. **apostropher** (fe) *v.t,* to shout at.
apothéose (apɔteoz) *f,* apotheosis.
apôtre (apotr) *m,* apostle.
apparaître (aparɛtr) *v.i.ir,* to appear; seem.
apparat (apara) *m,* pomp. *d'~,* ceremonial.
appareil (aparɛj) *m,* apparatus, appliance, device; camera; (*Radio, T.V.*) set; phone. *qui est à l'~?* who's speaking? aircraft; (*Med.*) splint; (*Pol.*) machinery. *~ [dentaire],* brace. *~ à sous,* slot machine. **~lage** (jaʒ) *m,* fitting up; (*Naut.*) setting sail; equipment. **~ler** (rɛje) *v.t,* to fit up; match up; pair; mate. ¶ *v.i,* (*Naut.*) to set sail, get under way; cast off.
apparemment (aparamɑ̃) *ad,* apparently. **apparence** (rɑ̃s) *f,* appearance, look; *selon toute ~,* in all probability. **apparent, e** (rɑ̃, ɑ̃t) *a,* visible; apparent.
apparenté, e (aparɑ̃te) *a,* related. **apparenter** (te) *v.t,* to ally. **s'~ à,** to marry into; (*Pol.*) ally o.s with.
apparier (aparje) *v.t,* to match, pair.
appariteur (aparitœr) *m,* (*Univ.*) attendant.
apparition (aparisjɔ̃) *f,* appearance, arrival; apparition.
appartement (apartəmɑ̃) *m,* flat, (*Am.*) apartment; suite (*hotel*).
appartenir (apartənir) *v.i.ir, ~ à,* to belong to; concern. *v. imp, il lui appartient de...* it's up to him to... **s'~,** to be one's own master.
appât (apɑ) *m,* bait; lure. *mordre à l'~,* to rise to the bait. **appâter** (te) *v.t,* to lure, entice; bait (*hook*); fatten (*poultry*).
appauvrir (apovrir) *v.t,* to impoverish.
appel (apɛl) *m,* call, appeal; *~ à l'aide,* call for help. *faire ~ à,* appeal to, call on. (*Law*) appeal. *faire ~,* to appeal. (*Mil.*) call-up; roll-call. *faire l'~,* (*Mil., Sch.*) call the roll, register. take-off (*jump*). *~ d'air,* intake of air. *~ de fonds,* call for capital. *~ téléphonique,* phone call. **appelé** (ple) *m,* (*Mil.*) conscript. **appeler** (ple) *v.t,* to call (*pers., dog*); call out (*name*); call, name; call, ring up; summon, call [out] (*doctor*); (*Mil.*) call up; call for, require. **en ~ à,** to appeal to. **en ~ de,** appeal against. **s'~,** to be called. *je m'appelle Adam,* my name is Adam. **appellation** (apɛlasjɔ̃) *f,* designation. *~ d'origine,* mark of the place of origin. *~ contrôlée,* district of origin guaranteed (*wine*).
appendice (apɛ̃dis) *m,* appendage, appendix. **appendicite** (sit) *f,* appendicitis.
appentis (apɑ̃ti) *m,* lean-to, penthouse.
appesantir (apəzɑ̃tir) *v.t,* to make heavy, dull, weigh down. **s'~ sur,** to dwell on.
appétissant, e (apetisɑ̃, ɑ̃t) *a,* appetizing. **appétit** (ti) *m,* appetite. *avoir de l'~,* to have a good a. *bon ~!* enjoy your meal!
applaudir (aplodir) *v.t. & i,* to applaud, clap. *~ à,* to commend, applaud. **s'~,** to congratulate oneself (*de,* for). **applaudissement** (dismɑ̃) *m, ~s,* applause.
application (aplikasjɔ̃) *f,* application. *mettre en ~,* to put into practice. diligence, industry; (*Need.*) appliqué [work]. **applique** (plik) *f,* wall lamp; (*Need.*) appliqué. **appliqué, e** (ke) *a,* industrious; painstaking; applied (*sciences*). **appliquer** (ke) *v.t,* to apply; put (*à, sur,* to, on); give (*kiss, slap*); implement. **s'~ à,** to apply o.s to; (*rule*) apply to.
appoint (apwɛ̃) *m,* exact change; [extra] contribution. **appointements** (tmɑ̃) *m.pl,* salary. **appointer** (te) *v.t,* to pay [a salary to].
appontement (apɔ̃tmɑ̃) *m,* landing stage.
apport (apɔr) *m,* contribution, supply. *~ de capitaux,* capital brought in. **apporter** (pɔrte) *v.t,* to bring, fetch. *~ du soin à faire,* exercise care in doing.
apposer (apoze) *v.t,* to affix, put, append. **apposition** (zisjɔ̃) *f,* (*Gram.*) apposition.
appréciable (apresjabl) *a,* appreciable. **appréciation** (sjɔ̃) *f,* valuation; estimate, assessment. **apprécier** (sje) *v.t,* to value; estimate, assess; appreciate.
appréhender (apreɑ̃de) *v.t,* to arrest; dread. **appréhensif, ive** (sif, iv) *a,* apprehensive (*de,* of). **appréhension** (sjɔ̃) *f,* apprehension.
apprendre (aprɑ̃dr) *v.t.ir,* to learn. *~ à nager,* learn to swim. learn, hear [of] (*news, event, that..*). *~ qch à qn,* tell, teach s.o sth. *ça t'apprendra!* that'll teach you!
apprenti, e (aprɑ̃ti) *n,* apprentice; articled clerk; learner; novice. **apprentissage** (saʒ) *m,* apprenticeship. *mettre en ~,* to apprentice.
apprêt (aprɛ) *m,* dressing (*leather &c*). *~s,* preparations. **apprêté, e** (te) *a,* affected. **apprêter** (te) *v.t,* to prepare; dress. **s'~,** to get ready (*à qch, à faire,* for sth, to do).
apprivoiser (aprivwaze) *v.t,* to tame.
approbateur, trice (aprɔbatœr, tris) *a,* approving. **approbation** (aprɔbasjɔ̃) *f,* approval. approbation.
approchable (aprɔʃabl) *a,* accessible; approachable (*pers.*). **approchant, e** (ʃɑ̃, ɑ̃t) *a,* similar, close (*de,* to). **approche** (prɔʃ) *f,*

approach. **approcher** (ʃe) *v.t*, move near *or* closer (*de*, to); approach (*pers.*). ¶ *v.i*, approach, draw near (*de*, to). **s'~**, to approach, come near. **s' ~ de,** go, come up to, approach.

approfondi, e (aprɔfɔ̃di) *a*, thorough, exhaustive. **approfondir** (dir) *v.t*, to deepen; go deeper into.

approprier (aprɔprie) *v.t*, to adapt, suit. **s' ~**, to appropriate.

approuver (apruve) *v.t*, to approve, pass (*bill*); approve of (*pers., action*).

approvisionner (aprɔvizjɔne) *v.t*, to supply (*en, de*, with). *bien approvisionné en..*, well stocked with... **s' ~**, to stock up (*en*, with). **approvisionnement** (nmɑ̃) *m*, supplying. *~s*, provisions, supplies.

approximatif, ive† (aprɔksimatif, iv) *a*, approximate, rough. **approximation** (sjɔ̃) *f*, approximation, rough estimate.

appui (apɥi) *m*, (*gen., Mil.*) support. *prendre ~ sur*, to lean, rest on. *~ de fenêtre*, window sill. *~-main, m*, maulstick. *~-tête, m*, headrest. **appuyer** (pɥije) *v.t*, to lean, rest (*arms on gate*); support (*pers., theory*). *~ sur*, to press (*bell*); emphasize; (*Mus.*) accentuate. **s'~ sur,** to lean on; rely on.

âpre† (ɑpr) *a*, rough, harsh; bitter (*wind*); fierce (*criticism*). *~ au gain*, grasping.

après (aprɛ) *pr*, after. *~ coup*, after the event, afterwards. *~ J.-C.*, A.D. *courir ~*, to run after. *elle est toujours ~ moi*, she's always on at me *P*. *~ l'avoir vu*, after seeing it. **d'~,** according to. *juger d'~ les apparences*, to judge by appearances. *d'~ Goya*, after Goya. ¶ *ad*, after[wards]. *peu ~*, shortly afterwards. *2 jours ~*, 2 days later. ¶ **~ que,** *c*, after (+ *indic.*). **~-demain,** *ad. & m*, the day after tomorrow. **d' ~-guerre,** *a*, postwar. **~-midi,** *m*, afternoon. *de l'~-midi*, p.m.

âpreté (aprəte) *f*, roughness, &c, *V. âpre*.

à-propos (aprɔpo) *m*, aptness; opportuneness; presence of mind.

apte (apt) *a*, fit[ted], competent qualified; capable (*à qch*, of sth; *à faire*, of doing).

aptitude (aptityd) *f*, aptitude, ability (*à qch, à faire*).

apurer (apyre) *v.t*, to audit.

aquaplane (akwaplan) *m*, aquaplane.

aquarelle (akwarɛl) *f*, water colour.

aquarium (akwarjɔm) *m*, aquarium.

aquatique (akwatik) *a*, aquatic.

aqueduc (akdyk) *m*, aqueduct.

aqueux, euse (akø, øz) *a*, aqueous.

aquilin (akilɛ̃) *a.m*, aquiline.

ara (ara) *m*, macaw.

arabe (arab) *a*, Arab; Arabian; Arabic. ¶ *m*, Arabic (*language*). **A~**, *n*, (*pers.*) Arab.

arabesque (arabesk) *f*, arabesque.

Arabie (arabi) *f*, Arabia. *A~ Séoudite*, Saudi Arabia. **Arabique** (bik) *a*, Arabian (*gulf*).

arable (arabl) *a*, arable.

arachide (araʃid) *f*, groundnut, peanut.

araignée (arɛɲe) *f*, spider.

aratoire (aratwar) *a*, ploughing.

arbitrage (arbitraʒ) *m*, arbitration; refereeing; umpiring. **arbitraire**† (trɛr) *a*, arbitrary; high-handed. **arbitre** (tr) *m*, arbitrator; arbiter; (*Sport*) referee, umpire. **arbitrer** (tre) *v.t*, to arbitrate; referee, umpire.

arborer (arbɔre) *v.t*, to hoist (*flag*); display (*medals*).

arbre (arbr) *m*, tree. *~ fruitier*, fruit t. *~ généalogique*, family t. *~ de Noël*, Christmas t. (*Tech.*) shaft. *~-manivelle*, crankshaft. *~ de transmission*, propeller s. **arbrisseau** (briso) *m*, shrub.

arbuste (arbyst) *m*, small shrub, bush.

arc (ark) *m*, bow (*weapon*); (*Geom., Elec.*) arc; arch. **arcade** (kad) *f*, (*Arch., Anat.*) arch; archway. *~s*, arcade, arches.

arc-boutant (arkbutɑ̃) *m*, flying buttress. **arc-bouter** (te) *v.t*, to buttress. **s'~**, to lean, brace o.s (*contre*, against).

arceau (arso) *m*, arch; (*Croquet*) hoop; (*Med.*) cradle.

arc-en-ciel (arkɑ̃sjɛl) *m*, rainbow.

archaïque (arkaik) *a*, archaic.

archange (arkɑ̃ʒ) *m*, archangel.

arche (arʃ) *f*, arch; ark. *l'~ d'alliance*, the Ark of the Covenant. *l'~ de Noé* (nɔe), Noah's ark.

archéologie (arkeɔlɔʒi) *f*, archaeology. **archéologique** (ʒik) *a*, archaeological. **archéologue** (lɔg) *m*, archaeologist.

archer (arʃe) *m*, archer, bowman. **archet** (ʃɛ) *m*, (*Mus.*) bow. *coup[s] d'~*, bowing.

archevêché (arʃəvɛʃe) *m*, archbishopric; palace. **archevêque** (vɛk) *m*, archbishop.

archi (arʃi) *prefix*, *P* tremendously: *~fou*, raving mad. *~ plein*, chock-a-block *P*. (*title*) arch... *~diacre*, archdeacon, *~duc*, archduke.

archipel (arʃipɛl) *m*, archipelago.

architecte (arʃitɛkt) *m*, architect. **architectural, e** (tyral) *a*, architectural. **architecture** (tyr) *f*, architecture.

archives (arʃiv) *f.pl*, archives, records. **archiviste** (vist) *n*, archivist.

arçon (arsɔ̃) *m*, saddle bow. *vider les ~s*, to take a toss.

arctique (arktik) *a*, arctic.

ardent, e (ardɑ̃, ɑ̃t) *a*, burning, blazing, scorching (*sun, fire &c*); ardent, keen, fervent; spirited; passionate. **ardemment** (damɑ̃) *ad*, ardently, &c. **ardeur** (dœr) *f*, heat (*of sun*); ardour; fervour; keenness; passion.

ardoise (ardwaz) *f*, slate. **ardoisé, e** (dwaze) *a*, slate-grey. **ardoisière** (zjɛr) *f*, slate quarry.

ardu, e (ardy) *a*, steep; arduous, difficult.

are (ar) *m*, are, 100 square metres.
arène (arɛn) *f*, arena. *~s*, amphitheatre.
arête (arɛt) *f*, fishbone; ridge (*mountain, roof*); bridge (*nose*); edge (*cube*); groin (*vault*); beard (*barley*).
argent (arʒɑ̃) *m*, silver. *en ~*, silver. money. *~ de poche*, pocket money. *~ liquide*, ready money. *payer ~ comptant*, to pay cash. *un ~ fou P*, loads of money *P*. *en avoir pour son ~*, to get one's money's worth. **argenter** (te) *v.t*, to silver [-plate]. **argenterie** (tri) *f*, silver, [s.] plate. **argentin, e**[1] (tɛ̃, in) *a*, silvery (*sound*).
argentin, e[2], *a*. & **A~**, *n*, Argentinian. **l'Argentine,** *f*, the Argentine.
argile (arʒil) *f*, clay. *~ réfractaire*, fire clay. **argileux, euse** (lø, øz) *a*, clayey.
argot (argo) *m*, slang. **argotique** (ɔtik) *a*, slangy.
arguer (argɥe) *v.t*, to infer, deduce. **argument** (gymɑ̃) *m*, argument; synopsis. **argumenter** (te) *v.i*, to argue.
aria (arja) *f*, (*Mus.*) aria.
aride (arid) *a*, arid, dry, barren; thankless (*task*); stony (*heart*). **aridité** (dite) *f*, aridity, &c.
aristocrate (aristɔkrat) *n*, aristocrat. **aristocratique**† (tik) *a*, aristocratic. **aristocratie** (si) *f*, aristocracy.
arithmétique† (aritmetik) *a*, arithmetical. ¶ *f*, arithmetic.
arlequin (arləkɛ̃) *m*, harlequin. **arlequinade** (kinad) *f*, harlequinade.
armateur (armatœr) *m*, ship owner.
armature (armatyr) *f*, frame (*tent &c*); (*Build., fig.*) framework; (*Elec.*) armature; (*Mus.*) key signature.
arme (arm) *f*, arm, weapon. *~ à feu*, firearm. (*Mil.*) arm (branch of army). *~s portatives*, small arms. *se battre à l'~ blanche*, fight with cold steel. *appeler sous les ~s*, call up (*reserves*). *en ~s, sous les ~s*, (*men*) under arms; (*people*) up in arms. *prendre, déposer les ~s*, take up, lay down [one's] arms. *faire des ~s*, to fence. *~s*, (*Her.*) coat of arms. *à ~s égales*, on equal terms. *sans ~s*, unarmed.
armée (arme) *f*, army. *~ de l'air*, Air Force. *l'~ du Salut*, the Salvation Army.
armement (arməmɑ̃) *m*, armament; arming; fitting out, commissioning (*ship*); cocking (*gun*); winding on (*camera*). *~s*, arms, armaments.
Arménie (l') (armeni) *f*, Armenia. **arménien, ne** (njɛ̃, ɛn) *a*. & **A~**, *n*, Armenian.
armer (arme) *v.t*, to arm (*de*, with); equip; reinforce (*beam*); fit out, commission (*ship*); cock (*gun*); wind on (*camera*). *armé jusqu'aux dents*, armed to the teeth. *béton armé*, reinforced concrete. **s'~de,** (*lit., fig.*) to arm o.s with.
armistice (armistis) *m*, armistice.
armoire (armwar) *f*, cupboard, wardrobe. *~ à pharmacie*, medicine cabinet.
armoiries (armwari) *f.pl*, [coat of] arms.
armure (armyr) *f*, (*lit., fig.*) armour. (*Phys.*) armature. **armurier** (myrje) *m*, gunsmith; armourer.
arnica (arnika) *f*, arnica.
aromate (arɔmat) *m*, herb; spice. **aromatique** (arɔmatik) *a*, aromatic. **arôme** (rom) *m*, aroma.
arpège (arpɛʒ) *m*, arpeggio.
arpent (arpɑ̃) *m*, (*Hist.*) arpent (*about an acre*). **arpentage** (taʒ) *m*, surveying. **arpenter** (te) *v.t*, to survey; pace up & down. **arpenteur** (tœr) *m*, [land] surveyor.
arquer (arke) *v.t. & i.* & **s'~,** to arch, curve. *jambes arquées*, bandy legs.
arrache-clou (araʃklu) *m*, nail extractor. **d'arrache-pied,** *ad*, relentlessly. **arracher** (ʃe) *v.t*, to pull up (*plant*); dig up, lift (*potatoes*); pull out, extract (*tooth, nail*); tear off (*clothes*). snatch, grab (*à qn*, from s.o). *se faire ~ une dent*, to have a tooth out. *s'~ les cheveux*, to tear one's hair.
arraisonner (arɛzɔne) *v.t*, to inspect (*ship*).
arrangeant, e (arɑ̃ʒɑ̃, ɑ̃t) *a*, obliging. **arrangement** (ʒmɑ̃) *m*, arrangement; settlement. **arranger** (ʒe) *v.t*, to arrange; settle, sort out; mend, fix; suit. *si ça vous arrange*, if that suits you. **s'~,** to come to an agreement; work out. *tout va s'~*, it'll all work out all right. manage. *arrangez-vous pour venir*, see to it that you can come.
arrérages (areraʒ) *m.pl*, arrears.
arrestation (arɛstasjɔ̃) *f*, arrest. *en état d'~*, under arrest. **arrêt** (rɛ) *m*, stopping, stoppage; stop, halt. *10 minutes d'~*, a 10 minute halt. *~ d'autobus*, bus stop. *sans ~*, without stopping. *~ du cœur*, cardiac arrest. *~s, (Mil.) aux ~s*, under arrest. **arrêté, e** (te) *a*, decided, settled. ¶ *m*, order, decree. *~ de compte*, statement *or* settlement of account. **arrêter** (te) *v.t*, to stop, halt, check; arrest (*criminal*); give up (*studies*); fix, decide on (*day*); make up *or* settle (*account*). *~ ses regards sur*, fix one's gaze on. ¶ *v.i*, to stop (*de faire*, doing). **s'~,** to stop, come to a halt. *s'~ net*, stop dead.
arrhes (ar) *f.pl*, deposit.
arrière (arjɛr) *m*, back [part]; rear; (*Naut.*) stern; (*Sport*) [full] back. *à l'~*, at the rear, stern. **en ~,** behind; backwards. (*Mot.*) *faire marche ~*, to reverse. (*Naut.*) *en ~ toute*, full astern. *en ~ de*, behind. ¶ *a. inv*, rear (*wheel &c*); back (*seat*). *pref. inv*, (*the second element only takes the pl. & indicates the gender*): *~-boutique*, back shop. *~-cuisine*, scullery. *~-garde*, rear guard. *~-goût*, aftertaste, *~-grand-mère*, *~-grand-père*, great-

grandmother, -grandfather. ~*-pays*, hinterland. ~*-pensée*, ulterior motive; mental reservation. ~*-petite-fille, -petit-fils, -petits-enfants*, great-granddaughter, -grandson, -grandchildren. ~*-plan*, background. ~*-port*, inner harbour. ~*-saison*, autumn, back end. ~*-train*, hind-quarters. **arriéré, e** (rjere) *a*, (*Com.*) overdue, in arrears; backward (*child*); out of date. ¶ *m*, arrears; backlog (*work*). **arriérer** (re) *v.t*, to defer (*payment*). **s'~**, to get into arrears.

arrimer (arime) *v.t*, to stow (*cargo*). **arrimeur** (mœr) *m*, stevedore.

arrivage (arivaʒ) *m*, arrival. **arrivant, e** (vɑ̃, ɑ̃t) *n*, newcomer, arrival. **arrivée** (ve) *f*, arrival, coming; (*Sport*) finish. *fil d'~*, tape. (*Tech.*) inlet; intake (*air &c*). **arriver** (ve) *v.i*, to arrive, come. *j'arrive!* I'm coming! ~ *à*, reach (*place*). ~ *à faire*, succeed in doing. happen, occur. ¶ *v.imp, il lui est arrivé un accident*, he met with an accident.

arrogance (arɔgɑ̃s) *f*, arrogance. **arrogant, e** (gɑ̃, ɑ̃t) *a*, arrogant. **s'arroger** (ɔʒe) *v.pr*, to assume (*powers, title*).

arrondir (arɔ̃dir) *v.t*, to round [off]; increase (*fortune*). **arrondissement** (dismɑ̃) *m*, rounding; (*Adm.*) district, ward.

arroser (aroze) *v.t*, to water (*plants*); wet, soak; baste (*joint*); drink to (*success*). *ça s'arrose!* that deserves a drink! **arroseur** (zœr) *m*, [lawn] sprinkler. **arroseuse** (zøz) *f*, [street] watering cart. **arrosoir** (zwar) *m*, watering can.

arsenal (arsənal) *m*, arsenal. ~ *maritime*, naval dockyard.

arsenic (arsənik) *m*, arsenic. **arsenical, e** (kal) *a*, arsenical.

art (ar) *m*, art; skill. *l'~ de faire qch*, the art of doing sth. *beaux ~s*, fine arts. *~s d'agrément*, accomplishments. *~s ménagers*, housecraft, home economics. *~s & métiers*, industrial arts & crafts.

artère (artɛr) *f*, artery; main road. **artériel, le** (terjɛl) *a*, arterial. *tension ~le*, blood pressure.

arthrite (artrit) *f*, arthritis. **arthritique** (tik) *a*. & *n*, arthritic. **arthrose** (roz) *f*, osteoarthritis.

artichaut (artiʃo) *m*, [globe] artichoke.

article (artikl) *m*, (*Com., Press, Law, Gram.*) article; entry (*dictionary*). ~ *de fond*, background *or* feature article. *sur cet ~*, on this point. *à l'~ de la mort*, at the point of death. *~s*, accessories, requisites (*office, toilet*); goods. *~s de Paris*, fancy goods.

articulation (artikylasjɔ̃) *f*, (*Anat.*) joint; knuckle; (*Tech., speech*) articulation; [logical] link. **articuler** (le) *v.t. & i, &* **s'~**, to articulate, utter; joint; link.

artifice (artifis) *m*, device contrivance; (*pej.*) artifice, trick. **artificiel, le†** (sjɛl) *a*, artificial.

artificier (sje) *m*, pyrotechnist. **artificieux, euse†** (sjø, øz) *a*, cunning, crafty.

artillerie (artijri) *f*, artillery. ~ *de campagne*, field a. **artilleur** (jœr) *m*, artilleryman, gunner.

artimon (artimɔ̃) *m*, mizzen; m. mast.

artisan, e (artizɑ̃, an) *n*, artisan; craftsman; (*fig.*) author, architect. **artisanal** (anal) *a*, craft (*industry*). **artisanat** (ana) craft industry; artisan class.

artiste (artist) *n*, artist. ~ *peintre*, painter. (*Theat.*) artiste, singer, entertainer; actor, performer. **artiste†** & **artistique†** (tik) *a*, artistic.

aryen, ne (arjɛ̃, ɛn) *a*. & **A~**, *n*, Aryan.

as (ɑs) *m*, ace. ~ *de pique*, ace of spades. *un ~ du ski*, a crack skier. *ficelé comme l'~ de pique P*, dressed like a scarecrow.

asbeste (azbɛst) *m*, asbestos.

ascendance (ɑsɑ̃dɑ̃s) *f*, ancestry. **ascendant, e** (dɑ̃, ɑ̃t) *a*, ascending, upward. ¶ *m*, ascendancy, influence; (*Astr.*) ascendant. *~s*, ancestry. **ascenseur** (sœr) *m*, lift; (*Am.*) elevator. **ascension** (sjɔ̃) *f*, ascent, rising; (*Rel.*) *l'A~*, the Ascension, A. Day. (*mountain*) climb, ascent. *faire l'~ de*, to climb.

ascète (asɛt) *n*. & **ascétique** (setik) *a*, ascetic. **ascétisme** (ism) *m*, asceticism.

asiatique (azjatik) *a*. & **A~**, *n*, Asian. **l'Asie** (zi) *f*, Asia. *l'~ Mineure*, Asia Minor.

asile (azil) *m*, refuge, sanctuary; (*Pol.*) asylum. ~ *[d'aliénés]*, lunatic asylum. ~ *de vieillards*, old people's home.

aspect (aspɛ) *m*, appearance, look; aspect, angle. *vu sous cet ~*, seen from that angle.

asperge (aspɛrʒ) *f*, asparagus.

asperger (aspɛrʒe) *v.t*, to sprinkle with water.

aspérité (asperite) *f*, asperity; roughness.

aspersion (aspɛrsjɔ̃) *f*, sprinkling; (*Rel.*) aspersion. **aspersoir** (swar) *m*, holy-water sprinkler.

asphalte (asfalt) *m*, asphalt.

asphyxie (asfiksi) *f*, asphyxia, suffocation, **asphyxier** (sje) *v.t*, to asphyxiate, &c.

aspic (aspik) *m*, (*Cook.*) dish in aspic; (*Zool.*) asp.

aspirant, e (aspirɑ̃, ɑ̃t) *a*, suction (*pump*). ¶ *n*, candidate. ¶ *m*, (*Mil.*) officer cadet; (*Nav.*) midshipman. **aspirateur** (ratœr) *m*, vacuum cleaner. *passer à l'~*, to vacuum, hoover. **aspiration** (sjɔ̃) *f*, inhaling; aspiration; longing (*à, vers*, for). **aspirer** (re) *v.t*, to inhale; suck up; aspirate. ~ **à**, to aspire to, long for.

aspirine (aspirin) *f*, aspirin.

assaillant (asajɑ̃) *m*, assailant. **assaillir** (jir) *v.t.ir*, to assault, attack; (*lit., fig.*) assail.

assainir (asɛnir) *v.t*, to cleanse; purify (*air*).

assaisonnement (asɛzɔmɑ̃) *m*, seasoning; (*salad*) dressing. **assaisonner** (ne) *v.t*, to season; dress. ~ *qn P*, knock s.o about; to dress s.o down.

assassin, e (asasɛ̃, in) *n,* assassin, murderer. *à l'~!* murder! ¶ *a,* provocative (*glance*). **assassinat** (sina) *m,* assassination, murder. **assassiner** (ne) *v.t,* to assassinate, murder; plague to death.

assaut (aso) *m,* assault, attack, onslaught; (*Sport*) bout. *donner l'~,* to attack. *prendre d'~,* take by storm.

assèchement (asɛʃmɑ̃) *m,* drainage; drying. **assécher** (seʃe) *v.t. & i,* to drain, dry.

assemblage (asɑ̃blaʒ) *m,* assembling, putting together; (*Carp.*) joint; (*Tech.*) assembly; collection. **assemblée** (ble) *f,* meeting, assembly, gathering. *l'A~ Nationale,* (*Fr.*) the National Assembly. **assembler** (ble) *v.t,* (*gen., Mach.*) to assemble; collect; convene. **s'~,** to meet, assemble, gather.

assener (asəne) *v.t,* to strike, deal (*blow*).

assentiment (asɑ̃timɑ̃) *m,* assent, consent.

asseoir (aswar) *v.t.ir,* to seat, sit (s.o) down. *faire ~ qn,* ask s.o to sit down. [*être, rester*] *assis,* [to be, remain] seated *or* sitting. establish (*authority*); base (*theory: sur,* on); *P* stun, amaze. **s'~,** to sit down, take a seat.

assermenter (asɛrmɑ̃te) *v.t,* to swear in.

assertion (asɛrsjɔ̃) *f,* assertion.

asservir (asɛrvir) *v.t,* to enslave; subjugate.

assez (ase) *ad,* enough. *~ de vin,* enough wine. *~ bête pour le croire,* stupid enough to believe it. rather, quite, pretty, fairly. *~ grand,* pretty big. *j'en ai ~!* I'm fed up! (*de,* with).

assidu, e (asidy) *a,* assiduous, painstaking; regular (*at work*). **assiduité** (dɥite) *f,* assiduity; regularity. **assidûment** (dymɑ̃) *ad,* assiduously.

assiégeant (asjeʒɑ̃) *m,* besieger. **assiéger** (ʒe) *v.t,* (*Mil., fig.*) to besiege; beset; hem in.

assiette (asjɛt) *f,* plate. *~ à dessert, creuse, plate* side, soup, dinner plate. (*Arch.*) seating; (*rider's*) seat; (*Naut.*) trim; (*Golf*) lie. *je ne suis pas dans mon ~,* I'm a bit off colour. **assiettée** (te) *f,* plateful.

assignation (asiɲasjɔ̃) *f,* allocation; (*Law*) summons; subpoena. **assigner** (ɲe) *v.t,* to assign, allocate, allot. (*Law*) summons; subpoena.

assimiler (asimile) *v.t,* to assimilate, absorb; liken, compare (*à,* to).

assise (asiz) *f,* bed, foundation; (*Build.*) course. **assises,** *f.pl,* (*Law*) assizes.

assistance (asistɑ̃s) *f,* assistance, help; audience. *~ judiciaire,* legal aid. *l'A~ publique,* ≏ the Social Services. *être à l'A~,* (*child*) to be in care. **assistant, e** (tɑ̃, ɑ̃t) *n,* assistant. *~e sociale,* social worker. *les ~s,* those present. **assister** (te) *v.i, ~* **à,** to attend, be present at. ¶ *v.t,* to assist (*the poor*).

association (asɔsjasjɔ̃) *f,* association; society; (*Com.*) partnership. **associé, e** (sje) *n,* associate; partner. **associer** (sje) *v.t,* to associate, link (*à,* with). *~ qn à,* make s.o a partner in; give s.o a share of. **s'~ à,** to join in, share in (*scheme, grief*).

assoiffé (aswafe) *a, ~ de,* thirsting for.

assolement (asɔlmɑ̃) *m,* rotation (*crops*).

assombrir (asɔ̃brir) *v.t,* to darken; cast a gloom over; cloud (*face*). **s'~,** to darken; grow gloomy.

assommant, e *P* (asɔmɑ̃, ɑ̃t) *a,* deadly dull *P.* **assommer** (me) *v.t,* to batter to death; knock out, stun; overwhelm; *P* bore stiff. **assommoir** *O* (mwar) *m,* club, bludgeon; gin shop.

Assomption (asɔ̃psjɔ̃) *f,* (*Rel.*) Assumption.

assorti, e (asɔrti) *a,* matched; matching; stocked (*shop*); assorted (*sweets*). *bien ~,* well matched; well stocked. **assortiment** (mɑ̃) *m,* assortment; set (*china, tools*); blend (*colours*); match[ing]. **assortir** (tir) *v.t,* to match (*à, avec,* to, with). (*Com.*) supply (*de,* with); stock (*shop*).

assoupir (asupir) *v.t,* to make drowsy, lull; deaden, numb (*senses, pain*). **s'~,** to doze off; grow numb; die down. *assoupi,* dozing. **assoupissement** (pismɑ̃) *m,* doze; drowsiness; numbing.

assouplir (asuplir) *v.t,* to make supple; make tractable; soften; relax (*rule*). **s'~,** to become supple, relax.

assourdir (asurdir) *v.t,* to deafen; muffle (*sound*). **assourdissant, e** (disɑ̃, ɑ̃t) *a,* deafening.

assouvir (asuvir) *v.t,* to satisfy, appease.

assujettir (asyʒɛtir) *v.t,* to subdue, subjugate; subject (*à,* to); secure, make fast.

assumer (asyme) *v.t,* to assume, take on.

assurance (asyrɑ̃s) *f,* assurance, [self-]confidence; assurance, undertaking; (*Fin.*) insurance; insurance company. *~-automobile,* car insurance. *~-incendie,* fire i. *~s sociales* ≏ National Insurance. *~-vie, ~ sur la vie,* life i. **assuré, e** (re) *a,* assured, certain; confident, assured; steady (*voice, step*). *mal ~,* unsteady. *tenir pour ~ que,* to be confident that. ¶ *n,* (*pers.*) insured, policyholder. **assurément** (mɑ̃) *ad,* assuredly, most certainly. **assurer** (re) *v.t, ~ qn de,* to assure s.o of (*support*). *~ à qn que,* assure s.o that. (*Fin.*) insure; ensure (*result*); secure, guarantee; steady, make firm; (*Mountaineering*) belay. **s'~,** to make sure (*de qch, que*). *s'~ sur la vie,* to insure one's life. ensure, secure. **assureur** (rœr) *m,* insurer, underwriter.

astérisque (asterisk) *m,* asterisk.

asthmatique (asmatik) *a. & n,* asthmatic. **asthme** (asm) *m,* asthma.

asticot (astiko) *m,* maggot; (*P*) bloke *P.*

asticoter (astikɔte) *v.t,* to tease, needle.

astigmate (astigmat) *a,* astigmatic.

astiquer (astike) *v.t,* to polish.

astre (astr) *m,* star.
astreindre (astrɛ̃dr) *v.t.ir,* to tie down (*to a task*); compel (*à faire,* to do). **astreinte** (trɛ̃t) *f,* constraint.
astringent, e (astrɛ̃ʒɑ̃, ɑ̃t) *a. & m,* astringent.
astrologie (astrɔlɔʒi) *f,* astrology. **astrologue** (lɔg) *m,* astrologer.
astronaute (astrɔnot) *n,* astronaut. **astronautique** (tik) *f,* astronautics.
astronome (astrɔnɔm) *m,* astronomer. **astronomie** (mi) *f,* astronomy. **astronomique†** (mik) *a,* (*lit., fig.*) astronomic(al).
astuce (astys) *f,* astuteness, shrewdness; trick; *P* pun; wisecrack *P.* **astucieux, euse†** (sjø, øz) *a,* astute, shrewd.
asymétrique (asimetrik) *a,* asymmetrical.
atelier (atəlje) *m,* workshop, workroom, studio; shop (*factory*).
atermoiement (atɛrmwamɑ̃) *m,* procrastination. **atermoyer** (je) *v.i,* to procrastinate.
athée (ate) *m,* atheist. ¶ *a,* atheistic. **athéisme** (teism) *m,* atheism.
Athènes (atɛn) *f,* Athens. **athénien, ne** (tenjɛ̃, ɛn) *a. &* **A ~**, *n,* Athenian.
athlète (atlɛt) *m,* athlete. **athlétique** (letik) *a,* athletic. **athlétisme** (letism) *m,* athletics.
atlantique (atlɑ̃tik) *a,* Atlantic. **l'[océan] A ~**, the A. [ocean].
atlas (atlɑs) *m,* (*book, Anat.*) atlas.
atmosphère (atmɔsfɛr) *f,* atmosphere. **atmosphérique** (ferik) *a,* atmospheric.
atome (atom) *m,* atom. **atomique** (tɔmik) *a,* atomic; (*Mil.*) nuclear. **atomiseur** (izœr) *m,* spray, atomizer. **atomiste** (ist) *n,* atomic scientist.
atone (aton) *a,* lifeless, lacklustre, expressionless; (*Gram.*) unstressed.
atours (atur) *m.pl,* finery.
atout (atu) *m,* trump, trumps. *~ pique,* spades are trumps. (*fig.*) asset, trump card.
âtre (ɑtr) *m,* hearth.
atroce† (atrɔs) *a,* atrocious; heinous (*crime*); excruciating (*pain*); dreadful, terrible. **atrocité** (site) *f,* atrociousness; atrocity.
atrophie (atrɔfi) *f,* atrophy. **atrophier (s')** (fje) *v.pr,* to atrophy.
attabler (s') (atable) *v.pr,* to sit down [to table].
attachant, e (ataʃɑ̃, ɑ̃t) *a,* interesting; engaging. **attache** (taʃ) *f,* clip, fastener; strap, string, tie. *à l'~,* tied up (*animal*). *~s,* (*fig.*) ties. **attaché** (ʃe) *m,* attaché. **attachement** (ʃmɑ̃) *m,* attachment, affection. **attacher** (ʃe) *v.t,* (*lit., fig.*) to attach; tie up, fasten; do up (*lace, button*); rivet (*attention*). *être attaché à,* to be attached to (*s.o*). **s'~,** (*dress*) to fasten, do up; to become attached (*to s.o*).
attaque (atak) *f,* (*Mil., fig.*) attack. *~ aérien,* air raid. *passer à l'~,* move into the a. *d'~ P,* on form. (*Med.*) attack, fit. *~ d'apoplexie,* stroke. *~ cardiaque,* heart a. **attaquer** (ke) *v.t,* to attack (*army, pers., abuse, note*); assault (*s.o*). *~ en justice,* to bring an action against. **s'~ à,** to attack; tackle, grapple with.
attardé, e (atarde) *a,* late, belated; backward (*child*); old-fashioned. **attarder (s')** (de) *v.pr,* to linger, stay late, loiter.
atteindre (atɛ̃dr) *v.t.ir,* to reach; attain; (*bullet*) hit (*à,* in); (*disease*) affect, attack. **atteint, e** (atɛ̃, ɛ̃t) *a, ~ de,* suffering from. *gravement ~,* (*pers.*) seriously ill; (*liver*) badly affected. **atteinte** (tɛ̃t) *f,* (*gen., Med.*) attack (*à,* on; *de,* of). *porter ~ à,* to undermine. *hors d'~,* out of reach *or* range.
attelage (atlaʒ) *m,* harnessing; team. **atteler** (tle) *v.t,* to harness, hitch up; (*Rly.*) couple.
attelle (atɛl) *f,* splint.
attenant, e [à] (atnɑ̃, ɑ̃t) *a,* adjoining.
attendre (atɑ̃dr) *v.t. & i,* to wait for, wait. *attendez qu'il revienne,* wait until he returns. *~ qch avec impatience,* to look forward keenly to sth. *faire ~ qn,* to keep s.o waiting. *se faire ~,* to keep people waiting. *en attendant,* meanwhile. to expect (*pers., baby*). *j'attendais mieux de lui,* I expected better of him. **s'~ à qch, à faire,** to expect sth, to do. *s'~ à ce qu'on fasse,* expect s.o to do.
attendrir (atɑ̃drir) *v.t,* to soften (*heart*); tenderize (*meat*); move (s.o) to pity. **s'~,** to be moved; feel sorry (*sur qn,* for s.o). **attendrissant, e** (isɑ̃, ɑ̃t) *a,* moving, touching. **attendrissement** (mɑ̃) *m,* pity; emotion.
attendu (atɑ̃dy) *pr,* considering. *~* **que,** *c,* seeing that, considering that.
attentat (atɑ̃ta) *m,* attempt on s.o's life. *~ à la bombe,* bomb attack. (*Law*) *~ à la pudeur,* indecent exposure.
attente (atɑ̃t) *f,* wait, waiting; expectation. *dans l'~ de vos nouvelles,* hoping to hear from you.
attenter à (atɑ̃te), to make an attempt on.
attentif, ive† (atɑ̃tif, iv) *a,* attentive, careful; mindful (*à,* of). **attention** (sjɔ̃) *f,* attention; care. *avec ~,* carefully. *~!* look out! careful! *~ à la marche,* mind the step. *fais ~!* be careful! *faire* or *prêter ~ à,* to pay attention to; notice. *~s,* attentions, thoughtfulness.
atténuer (atenɥe) *v.t,* to ease (*pain*); lessen, mitigate. (*Law*) *atténuant,* extenuating (*circumstances*).
atterrer (atɛre) *v.t,* to appal, shatter.
atterrir (atɛrir) *v.i,* to land, touch down. **atterrissage** (isaʒ) *m,* landing. *~ forcé,* forced landing.
attestation (atɛstasjɔ̃) *f,* attestation; certificate. **attester** (te) *v.t,* to testify. *~ [de] qch,* vouch for sth.
attiédir (atjedir) *v.t,* to make lukewarm, cool.
attifer *P* (atife) *v.t,* to get up, doll up *P.*
attirail (atiraj) *m,* gear, paraphernalia.

attirance (atirɑ̃s) *f,* attraction. **attirer** (re) *v.t,* to attract; draw (*attention: sur,* to); lure. **s'~,** to incur, win (*anger, sympathy*). [*s'*]~ *des ennuis,* cause trouble [for o.s].
attiser (atize) *v.t,* to poke (*fire*); (*fig.*) stir up.
attitré, e (atitre) *a,* regular, usual; accredited, registered (*dealer*).
attitude (atityd) *f,* attitude, posture; attitude (*envers qn,* towards s.o); pose.
attraction (atraksjɔ̃) *f,* (*gen., Theat.*) attraction. *~s,* entertainment, cabaret.
attrait (atrɛ) *m,* attraction; appeal.
attrape (atrap) *f,* trick, hoax. **~-nigaud** (nigo) *m,* con *P.* **attraper** (pe) *v.t,* to catch (*ball, train, thief, disease*). *~ froid,* to catch cold. to get (*slap, fine*); take in, trick; tell off *P.*
attrayant, e (atrɛjɑ̃, ɑ̃t) *a,* attractive, engaging. *peu ~,* unattractive.
attribuer (atribɥe) *v.t,* to attribute, ascribe (*à,* to); award, allot, allocate. **s'~,** to claim (*merit*). **attribuable** (abl) *a,* attributable. **attribut** (by) *m,* attribute; (*Gram.*) complement. **attribution** (sjɔ̃) *f,* attribution; awarding, allocation.
attrister (atriste) *v.t,* to sadden.
attrition (atrisjɔ̃) *f,* attrition, abrasion.
attroupement (atrupmɑ̃) *m,* crowd; (*pej.*) mob. **attrouper (s')** (pe) *v.pr,* to gather [together].
aubade (obad) *f,* aubade, dawn serenade.
aubaine (obɛn) *f,* windfall, godsend.
aube (ob) *f,* dawn; (*Eccl.*) alb; blade, vane (*fan, windmill*); paddle. *roue à ~s,* paddle wheel.
aubépine (obepin) *f,* hawthorn, may.
auberge (obɛrʒ) *f,* inn. *~ de jeunesse,* youth hostel. **aubergiste** (ʒist) *n,* innkeeper, landlord, -lady.
aubergine (obɛrʒin) *f,* aubergine, egg plant.
aucun, e (okœ̃, yn) *a,* any; (*neg.*) no, not any. *je n'ai ~e idée,* I've no idea. *sans ~ espoir,* without any hope. ¶ *pn,* any[one]; (*neg.*) none. *~ de mes amis n'est venu,* none of my friends came. **aucunement** (kynmɑ̃) *ad,* in no way, by no means.
audace (odas) *f,* audacity, boldness, daring. **audacieux, euse†** (sjø, øz) *a,* audacious, &c.
au-delà, au-dessous, &c. See *delà, dessous, &c.*
audible (odibl) *a,* audible. **audibilité** (bilite) *f,* audibility. **audience** (odjɑ̃s) *f,* audience (*with s.o*); (*Law*) hearing. **auditeur, trice** (ditœr, tris) *n,* (*gen., Radio*) listener. **audition** (sjɔ̃) *f,* audition; concert, recital; hearing; sound (*in hall*).
auge (oʒ) *f,* trough.
augmentation (ɔgmɑ̃tasjɔ̃) *f,* increase, rise. **augmenter** (te) *v.t,* to increase, raise (*price, salary*); enlarge; supplement. ¶ *v.i,* increase, rise (*de,* by).
augure (ogyr) *m,* augury, omen. *de mauvais ~,* of ill omen. **augurer** (gyre) *v.t,* to augur; forecast.
auguste (ogyst) *a,* august, majestic.
aujourd'hui (oʒurdɥi) *ad,* today; nowadays. *d'~ en huit, en quinze,* to-day week, fortnight.
au[l]ne (on) *m,* alder.
aumône (omon) *f,* alms. *faire l'~,* to give alms. *vivre d'~,* live on charity. **aumônier** (monje) *m,* chaplain.
auparavant (oparavɑ̃) *ad,* before[hand].
auprès (oprɛ) *ad,* nearby. **~ de,** *pr,* close to; next to; with (*pers.*); compared with.
auréole (ɔreɔl) *f,* aureole, halo; ring (*stain*).
auriculaire (ɔrikylɛr) *a,* auricular. ¶ *m,* little finger.
Aurigny (ɔriɲi) *f,* Alderney.
aurore (ɔrɔr) *f,* dawn, daybreak. *~ boréale,* aurora borealis.
auscultation (ɔskyltasjɔ̃) *f,* auscultation. **ausculter** (te) *v.t,* to examine (*patient*).
auspices (ospis) *m.pl,* auspices, omens.
aussi (osi) *ad,* also, too. *j'ai faim–moi aussi,* I'm hungry–so am I. as, so. *~ grand que,* as big as. *un homme ~ riche,* a man so rich, such a r. m. ¶ *c,* therefore, consequently, so. **~ bien que,** *c,* as well as. **aussitôt** (to) *ad,* at once, straight away. *~ dit, ~ fait,* no sooner said than done. **~ que,** *c,* as soon as.
austère† (ostɛr) *a,* austere. **austérité** (terite) *f,* austerity.
austral, e (ɔstral) *a,* southern.
Australie (ɔstrali) *f,* Australia. **australien, ne** (ljɛ̃, ɛn) *a,* & **A~,** *n,* Australian.
autant (otɑ̃) *ad,* as (*or* so) much, as many (*que,* as). *il a ~ de livres que moi,* he has as many books as I do. *pourquoi travaille-t-il ~?* why does he work so much? *deux fois ~ que,* twice as much as. *je ne peux pas en dire ~,* I can't say as much. *d'~ plus urgent,* all the more urgent (*que,* as, since). *~ que je sache,* as far as I know.
autel (otɛl) *m,* altar. *maître ~,* high altar.
auteur (otœr) *m,* author; authoress; writer; composer (*opera*); originator (*plan*); perpetrator (*crime*). *~ d'un accident,* party at fault.
authentique† (ɔtɑ̃tik) *a,* authentic, genuine. **authenticité** (site) *f,* authenticity.
autistique (ɔtistik) *a,* autistic.
auto (ɔtɔ) *f,* [motor] car. ¶ *a. inv,* car. *frais ~,* running costs. ¶ *pref,* auto, self-. *~collant,* self-adhesive. *~portrait,* self-portrait. *~propulsé,* self-propelled. *~suggestion,* autosuggestion.
autobiographie (ɔtɔbiɔgrafi) *f,* autobiography.
autobus (ɔtɔbys) *m,* bus.
autocar (ɔtɔkar) *m,* [motor] coach.
autochenille (ɔtɔʃnij) *f,* half-track.
autochtone (ɔtɔktɔn) *a.* & *n,* native.
autocrate (ɔtɔkrat) *m,* autocrat. **autocratie** (si) *f,* autocracy. **autocratique** (tik) *a,* autocratic.

autodidacte (ɔtɔdidakt) *a*, self-taught.
autodrome (ɔtɔdrom) *m*, motor racing track.
auto-école (ɔtɔekɔl) *f*, driving school.
autographe (ɔtɔgraf) *a. & m*, autograph.
automate (ɔtɔmat) *m*, automation. **automation** (asjɔ̃) *f*, automation. **automatique**† (tik) *a*, automatic. ¶ *m*, (*Tel.*) direct dialing (≃ STD); automatic (*pistol*). **automatisation** (tizasjɔ̃) *f*, automation.
automitrailleuse (ɔtɔmitrɑjøz) *f*, armoured car.
automnal, e (ɔtɔ[m]nal) *a*, autumnal. **automne** (tɔn) *m*, autumn, fall.
automobile (ɔtɔmɔbil) *a*, self-propelled; motor, car (*industry &c*). ¶ *f*, motor car, (*Am.*) automobile. *l'* ~, the car industry, motoring. **automobiliste** (list) *n*, motorist.
autonome (ɔtɔnɔm) *a*, autonomous, self-governing. **autonomie** (mi) *f*, autonomy, self-government. (*Aero., Mot.*) range.
autopsie (ɔtɔpsi) *f*, post mortem, autopsy.
autorail (ɔtɔrɑj) *m*, railcar.
autorisation (ɔtɔrizasjɔ̃) *f*, permission; permit. **autorisé, e** (ze) *a*, authorized; authoritative (*opinion*). **autoriser** (ze) *v.t*, to authorize, give permission to (*qn à faire*). **autoritaire** (tɛr) *a*, authoritarian. **autorité** (te) *f*, authority. (*Adm.*) *les* ~ *s*, the authorities. *d'* ~, straight off, unhesitatingly. *faire* ~ *en matière de*.., to be an authority on...
autoroute (ɔtɔrut) *f*, motorway; (*Am.*) highway.
auto-stop (ɔtɔstɔp) *m*, hitch-hiking. *faire de l'* ~, to hitch[-hike]. *prendre qn en* ~, give s.o a lift. **auto-stoppeur, euse** (pœr, øz) *n*, hitch-hiker.
autour (otur) *ad. &* **autour de,** *pr*, round, around, about.
autre (otr) *a*, other, different. *une* ~ *raison*, another reason. ~ *chose*, something else. *quelqu'un d'* ~, s.o else. ~ *part*, somewhere else. *d'* ~ *part*, on the other hand. *l'* ~ *monde*, the next world. *j'ai d'* ~ *s chats à fouetter*, I've other fish to fry. ¶ *pn*, *un* ~, another [one]. *d'* ~ *s*, others. *l'* ~, the other [one]. *les* ~ *s*, the others. *l'un l'* ~ *&c*, one another (*V un*). *l'un ou l'* ~, either. *ni l'un ni l'* ~, neither. *à d'* ~ *s!* tell that to the marines! **autrefois** (otrəfwa) *ad*, formerly, in the past. **d'** ~, of old, of the past. **autrement** (otrəmɑ̃) *ad*, differently; otherwise, or else. ~ *important*, far more important.
Autriche (l') (otriʃ) *f*, Austria. **autrichien, ne** (ʃjɛ̃, ɛn) *a. &* **A** ~, *n*, Austrian.
autruche (otryʃ) *f*, ostrich.
autrui (otrɥi) *pn*, others, other people.
auvent (ovɑ̃) *m*, canopy; (*Arch.*) penthouse.
auxiliaire (ɔksiljɛr) *a. & m*, auxiliary.
avachi, e (avaʃi) *a*, baggy, out of shape (*garment*); flabby, sloppy (*pers.*); slumped. **avachir (s')** (ʃir) *v.pr*, to become shapeless, limp, sloppy.
aval[1] (aval) *m*, lower waters *or* slope. *le ski* ~, the lower ski. **en** ~, *ad*, down stream, downhill. **en** ~ **de,** *pr*, below.
aval[2], *m*, support, backing; guarantee.
avalanche (avalɑ̃ʃ) *f*, (*lit., fig.*) avalanche.
avaler (avale) *v.t*, to swallow (*food, story, affront*); devour (*book*). ~ *des couleuvres*, swallow an affront.
avaliser (avalize) *v.t*, to guarantee; back.
avance (avɑ̃s) *f*, advance; lead. *avoir de l'* ~, to be ahead (*in work*). *avoir de l'* ~ *sur qn*, have a lead over s.o. *avoir 5 minutes d'* ~, to be 5 minutes early. *en* ~, ahead of time, early; ahead (*in studies*). *en* ~ *sur son temps*, ahead of one's time. **à l'** ~, **d'** ~, beforehand, in advance. ~ [*de fonds*], advance. *faire des* ~ *s*, to make advances. **avancé, e** (se) *a*, advanced (*ideas, post, pupil*). *d'un âge* ~, well on in years. *nous voilà bien avancés!* a lot of good that's done us! **avancement** (smɑ̃) *m*, promotion; advancement; progress. **avancer** (se) *v.t*, move *or* put forward, advance; bring forward (*date*); speed up (*work*); advance (*money*); help. *si cela peut vous* ~, if that helps you. *cela ne t'avancera à rien*, that'll get you nowhere. ¶ *v.i*, to advance, move forward; make progress (*in work*); (*clock*) gain. ~ *de 5 minutes*, to be 5 minutes fast. project, jut out. **s'** ~, advance, move forward.
avanie (avani) *f*, affront, snub.
avant (avɑ̃) *pr*, before. *pas* ~ *6 heures*, not until 6. ~ *peu*, shortly. ~ *tout*, above all. ~ *de partir*, before leaving. ~ *qu'il* [*ne*] *revienne*, before he returns. ¶ *ad*, before [hand]. *3 jours* ~, 3 days before. *la semaine d'* ~, the previous week. *bien* ~ *dans la nuit*, far into the night. *en* ~, forward; ahead (*de*, of). *en* ~, *marche!* quick march. (*Naut.*) *en* ~ *toute!* full steam ahead! ¶ *m*, front; bow (*ship*); (*Sport*) forward; (*Mil.*) front. *aller de l'* ~, to forge ahead. ¶ *a*, *roue* ~, front wheel. *traction* ~, front wheel drive. ¶ *pref. inv*, (*the second element only takes the pl. & indicates the gender*): ~ *-bras*, forearm. ~ *-centre*, centre forward. ~ *-cour*, forecourt. ~ *-coureur*, *a*, premonitory. *signe* ~ *-coureur*, forerunner. ~ *-dernier, ère*, last but one. ~ *-garde* van[guard]; (*Arts*) avant-garde. *d'* ~ *-garde*, avant-garde. ~ *-goût*, foretaste. *d'* ~ *-guerre*, pre-war. ~ *-hier*, the day before yesterday. ~ *-hier soir*, the night before last. ~ *-port*, outer harbour. ~ *-poste*, outpost. ~ *-première*, preview; (*Art*) private view. ~ *-projet*, pilot study. ~ *-propos*, foreword. ~ *-scène*, proscenium; stage box. ~ *-toit*, eaves. *l'* ~ *-veille*, *f*, two days before.
avantage (avɑ̃taʒ) *m*, advantage; benefit. *tirer* ~ *de*, to take advantage of. *j'ai* ~ *à le faire*, it's to my a. to do so. *être à son* ~, to look one's best. (*Ten.*) ~ *service, dehors*, advan-

tage in, out. **avantager** (taʒe) *v.t,* to favour, give an advantage to. **avantageux, euse**† (ʒø, øz) *a,* advantageous; profitable. *occasion ~euse,* good bargain.
avare† (avar) *a,* miserly; sparing (*de,* of). ¶ *n,* miser. **avarice** (varis) *f,* avarice. **avaricieux, euse** (sjø, øz) *a,* miserly.
avarie (avari) *f,* damage. **avarier** (rje) *v.t,* to damage. **s'** ~, to deteriorate, go bad.
avec (avɛk) *pr,* with. **d'** ~, from. ¶ *ad,* with it, with them.
aven (avɛn) *m,* swallow hole, pothole.
avenant, e (avnɑ̃, ɑ̃t) *a,* pleasant. ¶ *m, à l'~ de,* in keeping with. (*Insce*) endorsement.
avènement (avɛnmɑ̃) *m,* accession; advent, coming (*of Christ*).
avenir (avnir) *m,* future; prospect[s]; future generations. **à l'** ~, *ad,* in future. *dans un proche ~,* in the near future.
Avent (l') (avɑ̃) *m,* (*Eccl.*) Advent.
aventure (avɑ̃tyr) *f,* adventure; venture; [love] affair; experience. **à l'**~, *ad,* at random, aimlessly. **d'**~, **par**~, by chance. *dire la bonne ~,* to tell fortunes. **aventuré, e** (re) *a,* risky. **aventurer** (re) *v.t,* to risk (*life*); venture (*remark*). **s'**~, to venture; risk (*à faire,* doing). **aventureux, euse**† (rø, øz) *a,* adventurous; risky. **aventurier, ère** (rje, ɛr) *n,* adventurer, ess.
avenue (avny) *f,* avenue; drive.
avéré, e (avere) *a,* established, recognized. **avérer (s')** (re) *v.pr,* to turn out, prove [to be].
averse (avɛrs) *f,* shower.
aversion (avɛrsjɔ̃) *f,* aversion, dislike.
averti, e (avɛrti) *a,* [well-]informed (*de,* about). **avertir** (ir) *v.t,* to warn; notify (*de qch,* of sth). **avertissement** (tismɑ̃) *m,* warning. ~ *au lecteur,* foreword. **avertisseur** (sœr) *a,* warning. ¶ *m,* (*Mot.*) horn. ~ *d'incendie,* fire alarm.
aveu (avø) *m,* admission, confession; consent.
aveugle (avœgl) *a,* (*lit., fig.*) blind. ~ *de naissance,* born blind. ¶ *n,* blind man, woman. *les ~s, m.pl,* the blind. **aveuglant, e** (glɑ̃, ɑ̃t) *a,* blinding, dazzling. **aveuglement** (gləmɑ̃) *m,* blindness. **aveuglément** (glemɑ̃) *ad,* blindly. **aveugler** (gle) *v.t,* (*lit., fig.*) to blind; dazzle; stop (*leak*). **à l'aveuglette** (glɛt). blindly.
aviateur, trice (avjatœr, tris) *n,* aviator, pilot. **aviation** (sjɔ̃) *f,* aviation, flying; (*Mil.*) air force. ~ *navale,* fleet air arm.
aviculture (avikyltyr) *f,* poultry farming.
avide† (avid) *a,* greedy, grasping; eager, avid (*de qch,* for sth). **avidité** (dite) *f,* greed[iness]; eagerness, avidity.
avilir (avilir) *v.t,* to degrade, debase; depreciate.
aviné e (avine) *a,* intoxicated; drunken (*walk*); (*breath*) smelling of drink.
avion (avjɔ̃) *m,* aeroplane, plane, aircraft. *en ~,* (*go*) by plane. *par ~,* by air[mail]. ~ *de bombardement,* bomber. *~-cargo,* freighter. ~ *de chasse,* fighter [plane]. ~ *de ligne* airliner. ~ *à réaction,* jet plane.
aviron (avirɔ̃) *m,* oar. *l'~,* rowing (*sport*). *faire de l'~,* to row.
avis (avi) *m,* opinion. *à mon ~,* in my opinion. *être de l'~ de qn,* to share s.o's opinion. *changer d'~,* to change one's mind. *je suis d'~ qu'on parte,* I think we should leave. advice. *sur l'~ de qn,* on s.o's advice. notice; (*Fin.*) advice. *jusqu'à nouvel ~,* until further notice. *sauf ~ contraire,* unless otherwise informed. ~ *au lecteur,* foreword. ~ *au public,* notice to the public. **avisé, e** (ze) *a,* wise, sensible. *bien, mal ~,* well-, ill-advised. **aviser** (ze) *v.t,* to notify, inform (*de,* of); catch sight of. ¶ *v.i,* see where one stands, take stock. ~ **à,** to see to. **s'**~ **de faire,** to take it into one's head to do.
aviver (avive) *v.t,* to stir up, arouse; revive; brighten (*colour*).
avocat, e (avɔka, at) *n,* counsel, barrister; (*Sc. & fig.*) advocate. *se faire l'~ de qch,* to advocate sth. *~-conseil,* counsel in chambers. ¶ *m,* avocado [pear].
avoine (avwan) *f,* oats.
avoir (avwar) *m,* possessions; assets; (*Bkkpg.*) credit [side]. *~s,* holdings, assets. ¶ *v.t.ir,* to have; have on (*clothes*); get. give, let out (*cry*); make (*gesture*); take in, trick. *il a 8 ans,* he is 8. *avoir 3 mètres de profondeur,* to be 3 m. deep. ~ *peur, froid, faim &c,* to be afraid, cold, hungry &c. *qu'est-ce qu'il a?* what's the matter with him? *nous en avons pour 2 heures,* it will take us 2 hours. ¶ *v.aux,* (*with p.p*) *il a vu,* he has seen, he saw; *il avait, aurait vu,* he had, would have seen. have to. *j'ai à travailler,* I have to work. *il n'a qu'à demander,* he has only to ask. ¶ *v.imp, il y a,* there is, there are. *combien y en a-t-il?* how many are there? *il y en a deux,* there are two. *il y en a qui disent,* there are some who say. *qu'est-ce qu'il y a?* what's the matter? *il n'y a pas de quoi,* don't mention it. *il y a 3 ans,* 3 years ago. *il y a 20 minutes que j'attends,* I've been waiting 20 minutes.
avoisinant, e (avwazinɑ̃, ɑ̃t) *a,* neighbouring. **avoisiner** (ne) *v.t,* (*lit., fig.*) to border on.
avortement (avɔrtəmɑ̃) *m,* abortion; (*fig.*) failure. **avorter** (te) *v.i,* (*Med.*) to abort; (*fig.*) miscarry, fail. *se faire ~,* to have an abortion. *avorté* abortive (*plan*). **avorton** (tɔ̃) *m,* (*pej: pers.*) little runt.
avoué, e (avwe) *a,* avowed. ¶ *m,* ≃ solicitor. **avouer** (we) *v.t,* to confess, admit; acknowledge. *s'~ coupable,* to admit one's guilt.
avril (avril) *m,* April. *poisson d'~,* April fool.
axe (aks) *m,* axis; axle; trunk road. **axer** (kse) *v.t,* ~ *qch sur,* to centre sth on.
axiome (aksjom) *m,* axiom.

ayant cause (ɛjɑ̃) *m,* assignee. **ayant droit,** *m,* party entitled (*à,* to).
azalée (azale) *f,* azalea.
azote (azɔt) *m,* nitrogen. **azoté, e** (te) *a,* nitrogenous.
aztèque (aztɛk) *a.* & **A ~,** *n,* Aztec.
azur (azyr) *m,* azure. **azuré, e** (zyre) *a,* azure.
azyme (azim) *a,* unleavened.

B

B, b (be) *m, letter,* B, b.
baba (baba) *m, ~ au rhum,* rum baba. ¶ *a, en rester ~ P,* to be flabbergasted.
babeurre (babœr) *m,* butter milk.
babillard, e (babijar, ard) *n,* chatterbox. **babiller** (je) *v.i,* to chatter, prattle; babble.
babines (babin) *f.pl,* chops.
babiole (babjɔl) *f,* trinket; trifle.
bâbord (babɔr) *m,* (*Naut.*) port [side].
babouches (babuʃ) *f.pl,* mules (*slippers*).
babouin (babwɛ̃) *m,* baboon.
bac[1] (bak) *m,* ferry[boat]; tub, vat; sink, tank. *~ à glace,* ice-tray.
bac[2], *abb. of baccalauréat.*
baccalauréat (bakalɔrea) *m, national school examination qualifying for university entrance* ≏ G.C.E. A-levels.
bacchanale (bakanal) *f,* drunken orgy. *~s,* Bacchanalia.
bâche (bɑʃ) *f,* canvas sheet. *~ goudronnée,* tarpaulin.
bachelier, ère (baʃəlje, ɛr) *n, one who has passed the baccalauréat. ~ en droit* ≏ Bachelor of Laws.
bachique (baʃik) *a,* Bacchic; drinking (*song*).
bachot (baʃo) *P m,* = baccalauréat. *boîte à ~,* crammer's. **bachoter** (ʃɔte) *v.i,* to cram. **bachotage** (taʒ) *m,* cramming.
bacille (basil) *m,* bacillus.
bâcler (bɑkle) *v.t,* to scamp, rush through (*work*).
bactérie (bakteri) *f,* bacterium. **bactériologie** (rjɔlɔʒi) *f,* bacteriology. **bactériologiste** (ʒist) *n,* bacteriologist.
badaud, e (bado, od) *n,* curious bystander, rubberneck *P;* stroller.
badge (badʒ) *m,* badge.
badigeon (badiʒɔ̃) *m,* distemper, whitewash. **badigeonner** (ʒɔne) to distemper, whitewash.
badin, e (badɛ̃, in) *a,* light-hearted, playful. **badinage** (inaʒ) *m,* banter.
badine (badin) *f,* switch, cane.
badiner (badine) *v.i,* to jest, banter, joke. *~ avec,* to trifle with.
bafouer (bafwe) *v.t,* to jeer at, ridicule.
bafouiller (bafuje) *v.t.* & *i,* to splutter, stammer [out]. *qu'est-ce qu'il bafouille?* what's he jabbering about?
bâfrer (bɑfre) *v.i.* & *t,* to guzzle, gobble, wolf *P.*
bagage (bagaʒ) *m,* bag, piece of luggage; (*Mil.*) kit. *~s,* luggage, baggage. *faire ses ~s,* to pack.
bagarre (bagar) *f,* fight, brawl, scuffle, set-to. **bagarrer (se)** (re) *v.pr,* to fight, scrap *P.*
bagatelle (bagatɛl) *f,* trifle, bagatelle.
bagne (baɲ) *m,* convict prison; hard labour.
bagnole *P* (baɲɔl) *f,* car, buggy *P.*
bagou (bagu) *m, avoir du ~,* have the gift of the gab.
bague (bag) *f,* ring; collar; (*Mach.*) bush.
baguenauder (se) *P* (bagnode) *v.pr,* to stroll around, mooch about *P.*
baguette (bagɛt) *f,* rod, stick; wand; ramrod; (*conductor's*) baton; stick of bread. *~ de tambour,* drumstick.
bah (bɑ) *i,* pooh!, nonsense!
bahut (bay) *m,* chest; sideboard; *P* school.
bai, e (bɛ) *a,* bay (*horse*).
baie (bɛ) *f,* (*Geog.*) bay; opening (*in wall*); picture window. (*Bot.*) berry.
baignade (bɛɲad) *f,* bathe; dip; bathing place. **baigner** (ɲe) *v.t,* to bathe (*face*); bath (*baby*); wash (*shore*). *baigné de,* bathed in (*tears*); soaked in (*blood*). ¶ *v.i,* (*clothes*) soak (*dans,* in); (*fig.*) be wrapped, shrouded in. **se ~,** to bathe (*swim*); have a bath. **baigneur, euse** (ɲœr, øz) *n,* bather. **baignoire** (ɲwar) *f,* bath (*tub*); (*Theat.*) ground floor box.
bail (baj) *m,* lease. *prendre à ~,* to lease (*house*).
bâiller (bɑje) *v.i,* to yawn, gape; be ajar.
bailleur, eresse (bɑjœr, jrɛs) *n,* lessor. *~ de fonds,* backer, sponsor.
bâillon (bɑjɔ̃) *m,* gag. **bâillonner** (jɔne) *v.t,* to gag.
bain (bɛ̃) *m,* bath; bathe (*sea*); swim (*pool*). *prendre un ~,* to have a bath *or* swim. *faire couler un ~,* run a bath. bath [tub]. *petit, grand ~,* deep, shallow end (*pool*). *être dans le ~,* to be in the picture; to be involved (*crime &c*). *~ de foule,* walkabout. *~-marie, m,* double boiler. *~ de siège,* hipbath. *prendre un ~ de soleil,* to sunbathe. *~s de soleil,* sunbathing. *~ turc,* Turkish bath.
baïonnette (bajɔnɛt) *f,* bayonet.

baisemain (bɛzmɛ̃) *m, faire le ~ à qn,* to kiss s.o's hand.
baiser (bɛze) *m,* kiss. ¶ *v.t,* to kiss (*parts of the body only*); (*P* pers. as object*) to screw *P**, fuck *P**. *se faire ~ P,* to be had, swindled.
baisse (bɛs) *f,* fall, drop. **baisser** (se) *v.t,* to lower, pull down; turn down (*heat*); dip (*headlights*). ¶ *v.i,* to fall, drop; (*sun*) sink; (*tide*) ebb; (*sight*) fail. **se ~,** to stoop, bend down; duck. **baissier** (sje) *m,* (*Stk Ex.*) bear.
bajoues (baʒu) *f.pl,* chops, chaps.
bal (bal) *m,* ball, dance; d. hall. *~ costumé, ~ travesti,* fancy dress ball. *~ masqué,* masked b. *aller au ~,* to go dancing.
balade *P* (balad) *f,* walk, stroll; run (*car*). **balader** *P* (de) *v.t,* to trail round; take for a walk. **se ~,** to go for a walk, stroll *or* run (*car*). **baladeuse** (døz) *f,* inspection lamp. **baladin** (dɛ̃) *m,* street entertainer.
balafre (balafr) *f,* gash, slash; scar. **balafrer** (fre) *v.t,* to gash, &c.
balai (balɛ) *m,* broom; brush. (*Elec.*) brush. *donner un coup de ~,* give the floor a sweep; (*fig.*) make a clean sweep. *~ éponge,* squeezy mop. *~ mécanique,* carpet sweeper.
balance (balɑ̃s) *f,* [pair of] scales; (*Chem &c*) balance. (*Econ., Pol*) *~ des comptes, des forces,* balance of payments, power. **balancé, e** (se) *a, bien ~,* well-turned (*phrase*); well-built (*pers.*). **balancer** (se) *v.t,* to swing (*legs*); rock (*boat*); balance (*account*); (*fig.*) weigh up; *P* chuck *P;* chuck out *P* (*sth, s.o*). ¶ *v.i,* to waver; swing. **se ~,** to swing, sway, rock; seesaw. **balancement** (smɑ̃) *m,* swinging, sway[ing], rocking; (*Mus.*) balance. **balancier** (sje) *m,* pendulum; balancing pole (*tight rope*). **balançoire** (swar) *f,* (*child's*) swing; see-saw.
balayage (balɛjaʒ) *m,* sweeping. **balayer** (je) *v.t,* to sweep [out, up]; (*fig.*) sweep aside; (*radar*) scan. **balayette** (jɛt) *f,* [hand] brush. **balayeur, euse** (jœr, øz) *n,* roadsweeper. ¶ *f,* (*Mach.*) street sweeper. **balayures** (jyr) *f.pl,* sweepings.
balbutiement (balbysimɑ̃) *m,* stammering; mumbling. **balbutier** (sje) *v.t. & i,* to stammer [out]; mumble.
balcon (balkɔ̃) *m,* balcony. [*premier*] *~,* dress circle.
baldaquin (baldakɛ̃) *m,* canopy.
baleine (balɛn) *f,* whale; whalebone; stay (*corset*); rib (*umbrella*). **baleinier, ère** (nje, ɛr) *a,* whaling. ¶ *m,* whaler (*ship*). ¶ *f,* whaleboat.
balise (baliz) *f,* (*Naut., Aero.*) beacon; [marker] buoy; road sign; marker (*ski piste*). **baliser** (lize) *v.t,* to mark with beacons &c.
balivernes (balivɛrn) *f.pl,* nonsense, twaddle.
Balkans (les) (balkɑ̃) *m.pl,* the Balkans. **balkanique** (kanik) *a,* Balkan.
ballade (balad) *f,* ballad (*poem*).
ballant, e (balɑ̃, ɑ̃t) *a,* swinging, dangling.
ballast (balast) *m,* (*Rly*) ballast; (*Naut.*) b. tank.
balle (bal) *f,* (*Sport*) ball. *belle ~,* good shot. (*Ten.*) *faire des ~s,* to knock up. *~ de match,* match point. bullet; bale (*cotton*). *~s P,* francs. *prendre la ~ au bond,* seize the opportunity.
ballerine (balrin) *f,* ballerina, ballet dancer. **ballet** (lɛ) *m,* ballet; b. music.
ballon (balɔ̃) *m,* (*Sport*) ball. *~ de football,* football. (*Aero. & toy*) balloon; (*Chem.*) flask; brandy glass. *~ dirigeable,* airship. *~ d'essai,* trial balloon, feeler. *avoir le ~ P,* to be in the family way. **ballonné, e** (lɔne) *a,* distended; bulging; bloated. **ballonnement** (nmɑ̃) *m,* flatulence.
ballot (balo) *m,* bundle; (*P*) nitwit, clot *P*. **ballottage** (lɔtaʒ) *m,* election result requiring a second ballot. **ballotter** (lɔte) *v.t,* to shake about, jolt; toss. ¶ *v.i,* to roll *or* rattle around; (*boat*) toss.
balnéaire (balneɛr) *a,* bathing. *station ~,* seaside resort.
balourd, e (balur, urd) *n,* dolt, oaf. **~ise** (iz) *f,* oafishness; clumsiness; blunder.
Baltique (la) [mer] (baltik), the Baltic [sea].
balustrade (balystrad) *f,* balustrade; railing.
bambin, e (bɑ̃bɛ̃, in) *n,* small child, little chap.
bambocher *P* (bɑ̃bɔʃe) *v.i,* to live it up *P;* go on the spree.
bambou (bɑ̃bu) *m,* bamboo.
ban (bɑ̃) *m, ~s* [*de mariage*], banns.
banal, e (banal) *a,* banal, commonplace, trite. *peu ~,* unusual. **~iser** (ize) *v.t,* to make trite.
banane (banan) *f,* banana. **bananier** (nje) *m,* banana tree.
banc (bɑ̃) *m,* seat, bench; [work] bench; (*Geol.*) bed, layer; reef. *~ de sable,* sandbank. shoal (*fish*); (*Met.*) bank, patch. *~ des accusés,* dock. *~ d'église,* pew. *~ d'essai,* test bed. *~ des témoins,* witness box.
bancaire (bɑ̃kɛr) *a,* banking; bank (*cheque*).
bancal, e (bɑ̃kal) *a,* bandy[-legged]; rickety.
bandage (bɑ̃daʒ) *m,* bandage; *~ herniaire,* truss.
bande[1] (bɑ̃d) *f,* band, group, gang *P*; flock (*birds*); pack (*wolves &c*). *~ d'imbéciles!* bunch of idiots!
bande[2] (bɑ̃d) *f,* band, strip; bandage; stripe (*pattern*); (*Phot.*) film; (*recording*) tape; (*Bil.*) cushion. *jouer par la ~,* get sth in a roundabout way. (*Naut.*) list. *donner de la ~,* to list. *~ dessinée,* strip cartoon. *~ sonore,* sound track.
bandeau (bɑ̃do) *m,* headband; bandage (*over eyes*). **bander** (de) *v.t,* to bandage, bind; stretch; tense (*muscles*); bend (*bow*). *~ les yeux à qn,* to blindfold s.o.
banderole (bɑ̃drɔl) *f,* banderol[e], streamer.
bandit (bɑ̃di) *m,* bandit; gangster; crook. ~

armé, gunman.
bandoulière (bɑ̃duljɛr) *f*, bandoleer; shoulder strap. *en* ~, slung over the shoulder.
banlieue (bɑ̃liø) *f*, suburbs. *de* ~, suburban. *grande* ~, outer suburbs. **banlieusard, e** (zar, ard) *n*, suburbanite.
banne (ban) *f*, awning; wicker basket.
bannière (banjɛr) *f*, banner.
bannir (banir) *v.t*, to banish; prohibit.
banque (bɑ̃k) *f*, bank; banking. *en* ~, in the bank. ~ *de données*, data b. ~ *du sang*, blood b.
banqueroute (bɑ̃krut) *f*, bankruptcy. *faire* ~, to go bankrupt.
banquet (bɑ̃kɛ) *m*, banquet.
banquette (bɑ̃kɛt) *f*, [bench] seat (*train &c*).
banquier (bɑ̃kje) *m*, banker.
banquise (bɑ̃kiz) *f*, ice field; ice floe.
baptême (batɛm) *m*, baptism, christening. **baptiser** (tize) *v.t*, to baptize, christen; bless (*bell &c*); nickname, dub; water down (*wine*). **baptismal, e** (tismal) *a*, baptismal. **baptistère** (tɛr) *m*, baptistry.
baquet (bakɛ) *m*, tub.
bar (bar) *m*, bar (*drinking*); bass (*fish*).
baragouin (baragwɛ̃) *m*, gibberish. **baragouiner** (gwine) *v.t*, to speak (*a language*) badly; gabble, jabber.
baraque (barak) *f*, hut; stall (*fair*); hovel, dump *P*; (*P home*) place *P*.
baratin *P* (baratɛ̃) *m*, sweet talk; sales talk, patter. ~**er** *P* (tine) *v.t*, to chat up *P*; give the patter to.
baratte (barat) *f*, churn. **baratter** (te) *v.t*, to churn.
Barbade (la) (barbad), Barbados.
barbant, e *P* (barbɑ̃, ɑ̃t) *a*, boring, deadly [dull].
barbare (barbar) *a*, barbarian; barbarous, barbaric. ¶ *m*, barbarian. **barbarie** (bari) *f*, barbarism; barbarity. **barbarisme** (rism) *m*, (*Gram.*) barbarism.
barbe (barb) *f*, beard. *une* ~ *de 5 jours*, 5 days' growth. *à la* ~ *de qn*, under s.o's nose. *rire dans sa* ~, to laugh up one's sleeve. (*P*) *quelle* ~*!* what a drag! *P*. *la* ~*!* damn it! *or* shut up! ~ *à papa*, candy floss. **barbelé, e** (bəle) *a*. & *m*, [*fil de fer*] ~, barbed wire. **barber** *P* (be) *v.t*, to bore stiff. **barbiche** (biʃ) *f*, goatee. **barbier** *O* (bje) *m*, barber.
barbecue (barbəkju) *m*, barbecue.
barboter (barbɔte) *v.i*, to paddle, splash about. ¶ *v.t*, (*P*) pinch *P*, nick *P*. **barbotage** (taʒ) *m*, dabbling, &c; mash (*for cattle*). **barboteuse** (tøz) *f*, (*child's*) rompers.
barbouillage (barbujaʒ) *m*, daub; scrawl. **barbouiller** (buje). *v.t*, to smear (*de*, with); daub, slap paint on; scribble, scrawl.
barbu, e (barby) *a*, bearded. ¶ *f*, brill (*fish*).
Barcelone (barsəlɔn) *f*, Barcelona.
barda *P* (barda) *m*, gear; (*Mil.*) kit.
barde (bard) *m*, bard (*poet*).
barème (barɛm) *m*, table; [price] list; (*salary*) scale.
barguigner (bargiɲe) *v.t*, to shilly-shally.
baril (bari) *m*, barrel, cask. **barillet** (rijɛ) *m*, keg; cylinder (*revolver*).
bariolage (barjɔlaʒ) *m*, medley of colours. **bariolé, e** (le) *a*, motley, multicoloured.
baromètre (barɔmɛtr) *m*, barometer. **barométrique** (metrik) *a*, barometric(al).
baron, ne (barɔ̃, ɔn) *n*, baron, baroness.
baroque (barɔk) *a*, weird (*idea*); (*Art*) baroque.
barque (bark) *f*, small boat.
barrage (baraʒ) *m*, barrier; dam; weir; (*Mil.*) barrage; (*police*) roadblock.
barre (bɑr) *f*, bar, rod (*metal, wood*); (*Danc.*) barre; bar (*of court*); (*Sport*) crossbar; dash, stroke, cross (*on letter t*); (*Naut.*) helm, tiller; (*Geog.*) race, [tidal] bore; [sand] bar. ~ *fixe*, horizontal bar. (*Mus.*) ~ *de mesure*, bar line. [*jeu de*] ~*s*, prisoners' base. **barreau** (baro) *m*, bar, rung; (*Law*) bar. *entrer en* ~, to be called to the bar. **barrer** (re) *v.t*, to bar (*door*); block, close off (*road*); dam; cross (*cheque*); cross out; (*Naut.*) steer, helm *P*. **barrette** (rɛt) *f*, brooch; hair slide; biretta. **barreur** (rœr) *m*, helmsman; cox.
barricade (barikad) *f*, barricade. **barricader** (de) *v.t*, to barricade.
barrière (barjɛr) *f*, fence; gate; barrier.
barrique (barik) *f*, barrel, cask.
barrir (barir) *v.i*, to trumpet (*elephant*).
baryton (baritɔ̃) *m*, baritone.
bas[1]**, se** (bɑ, ɑs) *a*, low (*note, tide*); lower (*branches*). *en* ~ *âge*, very young. *à* ~ *prix*, cheap. lowly (*birth*); mean, base. *à voix* ~*se*, quietly. *être au plus* ~, (*pers.*) to be very low; (*prices*) to be at their lowest. *au* ~ *mot*, at the lowest estimate. ¶ *ad*, (*fly*) low; (*speak*) softly; (*put*) low down. *mettre* ~, (*animals*) give birth; lay down (*arms*). *mettre plus* ~, turn down (*radio*). *à* ~ *les examens!* down with exams. ~ *les mains!* hands off! ¶ *m*, bottom, foot (*hill, page, stairs*); lower part. **en** ~, downstairs, down below. *les gens d'en* ~, the people downstairs. *de haut en* ~, from top to bottom. ¶ *f*, (*Mus.*) bass. (*Typ.*) ~ *de casse*, lower case. ~*-côté*, verge (*road*); side aisle (*church*). ~*se-cour*, farmyard. ~*-fonds*, *m.pl*, (*Naut.*) shallows; dregs (*of society*); slummiest parts (*town*). ~*-relief*, bas relief.
bas[2] (bɑ) *m*, stocking. ~ *bleu*, blue stocking.
basalte (bazalt) *m*, basalt.
basané, e (bazane) *a*, tanned; swarthy.
bascule (baskyl) *f*, seesaw. [*balance à*] ~, weighing machine, scale[s]. *fauteuil à* ~, rocking chair. **basculer** (le) *v.i*, tip over, topple; (*pers.*) overbalance; tip out. *faire* ~, to tip up; tip out.
base (bɑz) *f*, (*lit., Chem., Mil.*) base; basis. ~*s*,

foundation, grounding (*in subject*). *de* ~ basic. **baser** (baze) *v.t*, to base (*sur*, on).
basilic (bazilik) *m*, (*Bot.*) basil; basilisk.
basilique (bazilik) *f*, basilica.
basket[-ball] (baskɛtbol) *m*, basketball.
basque (bask) *f*, skirt; basque.
basse (bɑs) *f*, bass [voice, singer, tuba].
bassement (bɑsmɑ̃) *ad*, meanly, basely. **bassesse** (sɛs) *f*, meanness; servility.
basset (bɑsɛ) *m*, basset hound.
bassin (basɛ̃) *m*, basin, bowl; pan (*scales*); bedpan; pond, pool (*garden*); (*Naut.*) dock; (*Geog.*) basin; pelvis. ~ *de radoub*, dry dock. ~ *houiller*, coal field. **bassine** (sin) *f*, pan, copper. **bassiner** (ne) *v.t*, to warm (*bed*); (*Agr.*) spray, sprinkle; (*P*) bore. **bassinoire** (nwar) *f*, warming pan.
basson (bɑsɔ̃) *m*, bassoon.
bastingage (bastɛ̃gaʒ) *m*, [ship's] rail.
bastion (bastjɔ̃) *m*, bastion.
bât (bɑ) *m*, packsaddle. *voilà où le* ~ *blesse*, that's where the shoe pinches.
bataclan *P* (bataklɑ̃) *m*, junk, clobber. *tout le* ~, the whole bag of tricks.
bataille (bataj) *f*, battle; fight. ~ *rangée*, pitched b. **batailler** (taje) *v.i*, to fight, battle. **batailleur, euse** (jœr, øz) *a*, pugnacious, aggressive. **bataillon** (tajɔ̃) *m*, battalion; (*fig.*) crowd.
bâtard, e (bɑtar, ard) *a. & n*, bastard, illegitimate [child]; mongrel (*dog*). **bâtardise** (tardiz) *f*, bastardy.
bateau (bato) *m*, boat; ship. ~ *à moteur, à rames, à voiles*, motor, rowing, sailing boat. *faire du* ~, to go rowing, sailing. *mener qn en* ~ *P*, take s.o for a ride *P*. ~ *amiral*, flagship. ~*-citerne*, tanker. ~ *de sauvetage*, lifeboat. ~*-feu*, lightship. ~*-mouche*, river boat (*Seine*). ~ *à vapeur*, steamer. **bateleur, euse** *O* (tlœr, øz) *n*, tumbler. **batelier, ère** (təlje, jɛr) *n*, boatman, -woman; ferryman, -woman. **batellerie** (tɛlri) *f*, canal transport.
bâti (bɑti) *m*, (*Need.*) tacking; (*door &c*) frame; (*Mach.*) stand, mounting.
batifoler (batifɔle) *v.i*, to frolic, lark about; dally, flirt.
bâtiment (bɑtimɑ̃) *m*, building; building trade; (*Naut.*) ship. **bâtir** (tir) *v.t*, to build, construct; (*Need.*) tack. *terrain à* ~, building land. **bâtisse** (tis) *f*, building; (*pej.*) hulk, pile. **bâtisseur, euse** (sœr, øz) *n*, builder.
batiste (batist) *f*, cambric, batiste.
bâton (bɑtɔ̃) *m*, stick; cudgel; (*Eccl.*) staff; (*Mil., Mus., Police*) baton. ~ *de rouge* [*à lèvres*], lipstick. (*fig.*) ~ *de vieillesse*, prop of one's old age. *parler à* ~*s rompus*, to talk on casually. *mettre des* ~*s dans les roues*, put a spoke in s.o's wheel.
battage (bataʒ) *m*, beating; threshing; publicity campaign. **battant** (tɑ̃) *m*, clapper (*bell*); door, window. *porte à double* ~, double door. **batte** (bat) *f*, (*Sport*) bat. **battement** (tmɑ̃) *m*, beating, beat (*drum, heart*); banging (*door*); flapping (*sail*). ~*s de mains*, clapping. **batterie** (tri) *f*, (*Mil., Elec.*) battery; (*Mus.*) percussion; drums. ~ *de cuisine*, pots & pans. **batteur** (tœr) *m*, whisk; drummer; thresher (*pers.*); batsman. **batteuse** (tøz) *f*, threshing machine. **battoir** (twar) *m*, beater.
battre (batr) *v.t.ir*, to beat, strike; defeat, beat (*team, record*); scour (*country*); beat (*undergrowth*); thresh; churn (*butter*); (*Cook.*) whisk, beat up; shuffle (*cards*); mint (*money*). (*Mus.*) ~ *la mesure*, beat time. ~ *la retraite*, sound the retreat. ~ *froid à qn*, to cold-shoulder s.o. ~ *pavillon grec*, fly the Greek flag. ~ *son plein*, be in full swing. ¶ *v.i*, (*drum, heart*) to beat; (*door*) bang; (*sail*) flap. ~ *en retraite*, beat a retreat. ~ *des mains*, clap one's hands. ~ *du tambour*, beat the drum. ~ *de l'aile*, flap its wings; (*fig.*) be in a shaky state. **se** ~, to fight (*avec*, with; *contre*, against). **battue** (ty) *f*, (*Hunt.*) beat.
baudet (bodɛ) *m*, donkey.
baudrier (bodrie) *m*, cross belt; baldric.
baume (bom) *m*, (*lit., fig.*) balm.
bavard, e (bavar, ard) *a*, talkative. ¶ *n*, chatterbox; gossip. ~**age** (daʒ) *m*, chatter[ing]; gossip[ing]. **bavarder** (de) *v.i*, to chat, chatter; gossip.
bavarois, e (bavarwa, az) *a. &* **B** ~, *n*, Bavarian.
bave (bav) *f*, dribble; slobber; slime. **baver** (bave) *v.i*, to dribble; slobber. *en* ~, to have a tough time. **baveux, euse** (vø, øz) *a*, dribbling; runny (*omelette*).
Bavière (la) (bavjɛr), Bavaria.
bavoir (bavwar) *m*, bib. **bavure** (vyr) *f*, smudge.
bayer aux corneilles (bɛje), to stand gaping.
bazar (bɑzar) *m*, bazaar; general store. *tout le* ~ *P*, the whole caboodle *P*. ~**der** (de) *P v.t*, to sell off cheap, flog *P*.
béant, e (beɑ̃, ɑ̃t) *a*, gaping, wide open.
béat, e† (bea, at) *a*, blissfully happy; blissful (*smile*); smug. **béatifier** (tifje) *v.t*, to beatify. **béatitude** (tyd) *f*, (*Rel.*) beatitude; bliss.
beau, bel (*before vowel or mute h*), **belle,** *f*, **beaux,** *m.pl*, (bo, bɛl) *a*, beautiful, lovely; handsome, good-looking (*man*); fine (*speech, sentiments*). *il fait* ~ [*temps*], it is fine [weather]. smart, fashionable (*quarter*). *une belle gifle*, a good slap. *une belle peur*, a nasty fright. *à la belle étoile*, (*sleep*) under the stars. *au* ~ *milieu*, right in the middle. *de plus belle*, more than ever. *bel & bien*, well & truly. *se faire* ~, to get dressed up. *l'échapper belle*, have a narrow escape. *il a* ~ *protester*.., it's no good his protesting... ¶ *m*, *être au* ~, to be set fair. *faire le* ~, (*dog*) to beg. ¶ *f*, beauty, belle. *ma belle!* my girl! *B*~ *au bois dormant*, Sleeping Beauty. (*Sport*) deciding

game. (*relations*) *beau-fils, belle-fille, beau-père, belle-mère,* son-, daughter-, father-, mother-in-law; stepson &c. *beau-frère, belle-sœur,* brother-, sister-in-law. *les beaux-arts,* fine arts; Art School. *bel esprit,* wit. *belle-de-jour,* (*Bot.*) morning glory; *P* prostitute. *belles lettres,* great literature. *le ~ monde,* high society. *le ~ sexe,* the fair sex.
beaucoup (boku) *ad,* a lot, a great deal, [very] much. *elle parle ~,* she talks a lot. *merci ~,* thank you very much. *~ de vin,* a lot of wine. *~ de monde,* a lot of people. *~ de choses,* many things, a lot of things. *~ plus court,* much shorter. *de ~,* by far.
beaupré (bopre) *m,* bowsprit.
beauté (bote) *f,* beauty, loveliness; handsomeness (*man*). *de toute ~,* very beautiful. (*woman*) beauty.
bébé (bebe) *m,* baby; dolly.
bec (bɛk) *m,* beak, bill; spout; lip (*jug*); nib; (*Mus.*) mouthpiece; (*Geog.*) bill; *P* mouth. *tomber sur un ~ P,* to hit a snag. *rester le ~ dans l'eau P,* to be left in the lurch. *~ Bunsen,* B. burner. *bec-de-cane,* door handle. *~ fin P,* gourmet. *~ de gaz,* lamp post. *~ de lièvre,* hare lip.
bécane *P* (bekan) *f,* bike.
bécarre (bekar) *m,* (*Mus.*) natural.
bécasse (bekas) *f,* woodcock. **bécasseau** (so) *m,* sandpiper. **bécassine** (sin) *f,* snipe.
bêche (bɛʃ) *f,* spade. **bêcher** (ʃe) *v.t,* to dig.
bécot *P* (beko) *m,* kiss. **~er** *P* (kɔte) *v.t,* to kiss.
becqueter (bɛkte) *v.t,* to peck [at]; *P* eat.
bedaine *P* (bədɛn) *f,* paunch, potbelly.
bedeau (bədo) *m,* beadle; verger.
beffroi (bɛfrwa) *m,* belfry.
bégayer (begɛje) *v.i. & t,* to stutter, stammer [out]. **bégaiement** (gɛmɑ̃) *m,* stuttering, &c.
bégonia (begɔnja) *m,* begonia.
bègue (bɛg) *n,* stutterer, stammerer.
bégueule (begœl) *f,* prude. ¶ *a,* prudish.
béguin (begɛ̃) *m, avoir le ~ pour,* to fancy (s.o).
beige (bɛʒ) *a,* beige.
beignet (bɛɲɛ) *m,* fritter; doughnut.
bêlement (bɛlmɑ̃) *m,* bleat[ing]. **bêler** (le) *v.i,* to bleat.
belette (bəlɛt) *f,* weasel.
belge (bɛlʒ) *a. &* **B ~**, *n,* Belgian. **la Belgique** (ʒik), Belgium.
bélier (belje) *m,* (*Zool., Tech.*) ram; battering ram. (*Astr.*) *le B ~,* Aries.
belladone (bɛladɔn) *f,* belladonna, deadly nightshade.
belle, *V* **beau.**
belligérant, e (bɛliʒerɑ̃, ɑ̃t) *a. & n,* belligerent.
belliqueux, euse (bɛlikø, øz) *a,* warlike, bellicose; quarrelsome (*pers.*)
belvédère (bɛlvedɛr) *m,* belvedere, viewpoint.
bémol (bemɔl) *m,* (*Mus.*) flat.
bénédicité (benedisite) *m,* grace. *dire la ~,* to say grace. **bénédiction** (ksjɔ̃) *f,* blessing; consecration; blessing, godsend.
bénéfice (benefis) *m,* profit. *à ~,* at a profit. *faire du ~,* to make a profit. advantage, benefit; (*Eccl.*) living, benefice. **bénéficiaire** (sjɛr) *a,* profitable. ¶ *n,* beneficiary; payee (*cheque*). **bénéficier de** (sje) *v.i,* to have, enjoy; benefit by.
Bénélux (le) (benelyks) *m,* the Benelux countries.
benêt (bənɛ) *a.m,* silly. ¶ *m,* simpleton.
bénévole† (benevɔl) *a,* voluntary, unpaid.
bénin, igne† (benɛ̃, iɲ) *a,* slight, mild (*illness*); benign (*tumour*). **bénir** (nir) *v.t,* to bless; thank God for. *Dieu vous bénisse!* God bless you! **bénit, e** (ni, ite) *a,* consecrated, holy (*bread, water*). **bénitier** (tje) *m,* stoup.
benjamin, e (bɛ̃jamɛ̃, in) *n,* youngest child.
benne (bɛn) *f,* (*Min.*) skip, tub; bucket, scoop. *~ basculante,* tipper (*lorry*); [cable-]car.
benzine (bɛ̃zin) *f,* benzine.
béquille (bekij) *f,* crutch; stand (*m. cycle*).
berceau (bɛrso) *m,* cradle; crib; arbour. **bercer** (se) *v.t,* to rock; lull, soothe. *~* **de,** to delude with. **berceuse** (søz) *f,* rocking chair; lullaby.
béret (berɛ) *m,* beret.
berge (bɛrʒ) *f,* bank (*river, canal*).
berger (bɛrʒe) *m,* shepherd; sheepdog. *~ allemand,* alsatian. **bergère** (ʒɛr) *f,* shepherdess; wing chair. **bergerie** (ʒəri) *f,* sheep fold. **bergeronette** (rɔnɛt) *f,* wagtail.
berline (bɛrlin) *f,* saloon [car]; berlin (*coach*).
berlingot (bɛrlɛ̃go) *m,* boiled sweet; carton (*milk*).
Bermudes (les) (bɛrmyd) *f.pl,* Bermuda.
bernard-l'ermite (bɛrnarlɛrmit) *m,* hermit crab.
berne (bɛrn) *f, en ~,* at half-mast (*flag*). **berner** (ne) *v.t,* to fool, take in.
bernique (bɛrnik) *f,* limpet. ¶ *i,* not a hope!
besace (bəzas) *f,* beggar's bag; scrip.
besicles (bəzikl) *f.pl,* (*Hist.*) spectacles.
besogne (bəzɔɲ) *f,* [piece of] work, task, job. **besogneux, euse** (ɲø, øz) *a,* needy, poor.
besoin (bəzwɛ̃) *m,* want, need. *être dans le ~,* to be in need. *avoir ~ de qch, de faire, qu'on fasse,* to need sth, to do, s.o to do. *au ~, si ~ est,* if need be, if necessary. *faire ses ~s,* to relieve o.s.
bestial, e† (bɛstjal) *a,* bestial; brutish. **bestiaux** (tjo) *m.pl,* livestock; cattle. **bêta, asse** *P* (bɛta, as) *a. & n,* silly. **bétail** (betaj) *m,* live-stock, cattle.
bête (bɛt) *f,* beast, animal; creature; fool. ¶ *a,* stupid, silly. *~ comme ses pieds,* as thick as two planks. *ce n'est pas si ~,* it's not a bad idea. *~ à bon Dieu,* ladybird. *~ à cornes,* horned animal. *~s fauves,* big cats. *~ noire,* pet aversion. *~ de somme,* beast of burden. **~ment** (mɑ̃) *ad,* stupidly. *tout ~,* quite simply. **bêtise** (betiz) *f,* stupidity; stupid

action; blunder. *dire des ~s,* to talk nonsense. *faire des ~s,* behave stupidly.
béton (betɔ̃) *m,* concrete. *~ armé,* reinforced concrete.
betterave (bɛtrav) *f, ~ [rouge],* beetroot. *~ fourragère,* mangel-wurzel. *~ sucrière,* sugar beet.
beugler (bøgle) *v.i. & t,* to moo; bellow [out].
beurre (bœr) *m,* butter. *~ d'anchois,* anchovy paste. *faire son ~ P,* to make a packet *P.* **beurrer** (re) *v.t,* to butter. **beurrier** (rje) *m,* butter dish.
bévue (bevy) *f,* blunder; bad mistake.
biais (bjɛ) *m,* device, dodge; slant. *en ~,* slantwise. *regarder qn de ~,* give s.o a sideways glance. **biaiser** (ze) *v.i,* to avoid the issue, hedge.
bibelot (biblo) *m,* curio; trinket.
biberon (bibrɔ̃) *m,* baby's bottle.
bible (bibl) *f,* bible. **bibliobus** (ljɔbys) *m,* mobile library. **bibliographie** (grafi) *f,* bibliography. **bibliophile** (fil) *n,* book lover. **bibliothécaire** (tekɛr) *n,* librarian. **bibliothèque** (tɛk) *f* library; bookcase; bookstall. *~ de prêt,* lending library. **biblique** (blik) *a,* biblical.
bicarbonate (bikarbɔnat) *m,* bicarbonate.
bicéphale (bisefal) *a,* two-headed.
biceps (bisɛps) *m,* biceps.
biche (biʃ) *f,* doe. *ma ~,* darling, pet.
bichonner (biʃɔne) *v.t,* to titivate; fuss over.
bicoque (bikɔk) *f,* shanty, shack.
bicorne (bikɔrn) *m,* cocked hat.
bicyclette (bisiklɛt) *f,* bicycle, cycle; cycling. *aller en ~,* to cycle. *faire de la ~,* to go cycling.
bidet (bidɛ) *m,* nag (*horse*); bidet.
bidon (bidɔ̃) *m,* can, tin; (*Mil.*) water bottle; *P* nonsense. ¶ *a. inv,* sham, mock. *~* **ville** (vil) *f,* shantytown.
bidule *P* (bidyl) *m,* thingummy *P,* whats-it *P.*
bief (bjɛf) *m,* race[way] (*mill*); pond (*canal*).
bielle (bjɛl) *f,* (*Mot.*) connecting rod. *couler une ~,* to run a big end.
bien (bjɛ̃) *ad,* well, properly, right[ly]. *il chante ~,* he sings well. *se porter ~,* to be well, in good health. *faire ~ les choses,* to do things properly. *tu as ~ fait,* you did right. *si je me rappelle ~,* if I remember rightly. very, very much. *merci ~,* thank you very much. *~ mieux,* much better. *~ content,* very glad. definitely, really. *c'est ~ ça que tu veux?* is that really what you want? *c'est ~ sa voiture,* that's his car all right. *où peut-il ~ être?* where on earth can he be? *~ en face,* right opposite. *bien sûr,* of course. *tant ~ que mal,* somehow or other. *eh ~!* well! **bien des,** many. *~ des gens,* [a good] many people. *j'ai eu ~ du mal à trouver,* I had a lot of trouble finding. **bien que,** although (+ *subj.*). **si ~ que,** so that, and so. ¶ *a. inv,* good; well, in good health; good-looking. *des gens ~,* decent people. comfortable (*in chair*). *~ avec qn,* on good terms with s.o. *c'est ~ à vous de..* it's good of you to.. *~!* good! fine! ¶ *m,* good. *cela vous fera du ~,* that'll do you good. *dire du ~ de,* speak highly of. possession, property, fortune. *~s mal acquis,* ill-gotten gains. *~***-aimé, e** (bjɛnɛme) *a. & n,* beloved. *~***-être** (bjɛ̃nɛtr) *m,* well-being; welfare, comfort. *~***-fondé** (fɔde) *m,* validity. *~***-pensant, e** (pɑ̃sɑ̃, ɑ̃t) *a,* right-thinking; God-fearing.
bienfaisance (bjɛ̃fəzɑ̃s) *f,* charity. *œuvre de ~,* charitable organization. **bienfaisant, e** (zɑ̃, ɑ̃t) *a,* beneficial; kind, charitable (*pers.*). **bienfait** (fɛ) *m,* kindness, benefit. **bienfaiteur, trice** (tœr, tris) *n,* benefactor, tress.
bienheureux, euse (bjɛ̃nœrø, øz) *a,* (*Rel.*) blessed; happy (*chance*).
biennal, e (bjɛnal) *a,* biennial.
bienséance (bjɛ̃seɑ̃s) *f,* propriety. **bienséant, e** (seɑ̃, ɑ̃t) *a,* proper, becoming.
bientôt (bjɛ̃to) *ad,* soon. *à ~!* see you soon.
bienveillant, e (bjɛ̃vɛjɑ̃, ɑ̃t) *a,* kindly, benevolent. **bienveillance** (ɑ̃s) *f,* kindness, benevolence.
bienvenu, e (bjɛ̃vny) *a. & n,* welcome. *soyez le ~ (la ~e),* you are very welcome. ¶ *f,* welcome. *souhaiter la ~e à qn,* to welcome s.o.
bière[1] (bjɛr) *f,* beer *~ blonde,* lager. *~ brune,* brown ale. *~ pression,* draught beer.
bière[2] (bjɛr) *f,* coffin.
biffer (bife) *v.t,* to cross out, delete.
bifteck (biftɛk) *m,* steak.
bifurcation (bifyrkasjɔ̃) *f,* fork; junction. **bifurquer** (ke) *v.i,* (*road*) to fork, branch off; (*pers.*) turn off. *~ sur la gauche,* bear left.
bigame (bigam) *a,* bigamous, ¶ *n,* bigamist. **bigamie** (mi) *f,* bigamy.
bigarré, e (bigare) *a,* multicoloured, motley. **bigarrure** (ryr) *f,* bright pattern, medley of colours.
bigorneau (bigɔrno) *m,* winkle.
bigot, e (bigo, ɔt) *a,* over-pious, bigoted. ¶ *n,* bigot. **bigoterie** (gɔtri) *f,* bigotry.
bigoudi (bigudi) *m,* hair curler.
bigre (bigr) *i,* gosh! *~***ment** (əmɑ̃) *ad,* darn *P;* (*change*) a hell of a lot *P.*
bijou (biʒu) *m,* jewel; (*fig.*) gem. *mon ~,* my pet. **bijouterie** (tri) *f,* jeweller's shop; jewelery business; j. making. **bijoutier, ère** (tje, ɛr) *n,* jeweller.
bilan (bilɑ̃) *m,* balance sheet; assessment; consequences.
bilboquet (bilbɔkɛ) *m,* cup & ball.
bile (bil) *f,* bile. *se faire de la ~,* to worry. **bileux, euse** (bilø, øz) *a,* easily worried. **bilieux, euse** (ljø, øz) *a,* bilious (*colour*); irritable, morose.
bilingue (bilɛ̃g) *a,* bilingual.
billard (bijar) *m,* billiards; billiard table. *faire un*

~, play a game of billiards. *P* operation table. ~ *japonais,* pin table.
bille (bij) *f,* billiard ball; marble (*game*); (*sawn*) log.
billet (bijɛ) *m,* ticket. ~ *aller-retour,* return t. (*Fin.*) note, (*Am.*) bill. ~ *de banque,* bank note. ~ *doux,* love letter. ~ *de faveur,* complimentary ticket. (*Mil.*) ~ *de logement,* billet.
billevesées (bilvəze) *f.pl,* nonsense.
billion (biljɔ̃) *m,* billion (*million millions*).
billot (bijo) *m,* [chopping] block.
bimbeloterie (bɛ̃blɔtri) *f,* fancy goods.
bimensuel, le (bimɑ̃sɥɛl) *a,* fortnightly.
binaire (binɛr) *a,* binary.
biner (bine) *v.t,* to hoe. **binette** (nɛt) *f,* hoe.
biniou (binju) *m,* Breton bagpipes.
binocle (binɔkl) *m,* pince-nez.
biochimie (bjɔʃimi) *f,* biochemistry.
biographe (biɔgraf) *n,* biographer. **biographie** (fi) *f,* biography.
biologie (biɔlɔʒi) *f,* biology. **biologique** (ʒik) *a,* biological. **biologiste** (ʒist) *n,* biologist.
bipède (bipɛd) *a. & m,* biped.
biplan (biplɑ̃) *m,* biplane.
bique (bik) *f,* nanny-goat. *vieille* ~, old hag.
birman, e (birmɑ̃, an) *a,* & **B**~, *n,* Burmese. **la Birmanie** (mani), Burma.
bis[1], e (bi, iz) *a,* brownish grey; brown (*bread*).
bis[2] (bis) *ad,* (*Theat.*) ~*!* encore! (*Mus.*) repeat. ¶ *m,* encore. ¶ *a, 3* ~, 3a (*house number*).
bisaïeul, e (bizajœl) *n,* great-grandfather, -mother.
bisannuel, le (bizanɥɛl) *a,* biennial.
bisbille *P* (bizbij) *f,* squabble.
biscornu, e (biskɔrny) *a,* misshapen, crooked; queer, cranky (*ideas*).
biscotte (biskɔt) *f,* rusk.
biscuit (biskɥi) *m,* biscuit. ~ [*de Savoie*], sponge cake; biscuit [ware] (*pottery*).
bise (biz) *f,* cold wind; *P* kiss (*on cheek*).
biseau (bizo) *m,* bevel; (*Carp.*) chamfer. **biseauter** (te) *v.t,* to bevel; chamfer.
bismuth (bismyt) *m,* bismuth.
bison (bizɔ̃) *m,* bison.
bisquer *P* (biske) *v.i,* to be riled. *faire* ~, to rile, tease.
bisser (bise) *v.t,* to encore.
bissextile (bisɛkstil) *a, année* ~, leap year.
bistouri (bisturi) *m,* lancet.
bistro[t] *P* (bistro) *m,* bar, café, bistro.
bitte (bit) mooring post; (*P**) cock *P**, prick *P**.
bitume (bitym) *m,* bitumen, asphalt, tarmac. **bitumer** (me) *v.t,* to asphalt, tarmac. **bitumineux, euse** (minø, øz) *a,* bituminous.
bivouac (bivwak) *m,* bivouac. **bivouaquer** (ke) *v.i,* to bivouac.
bizarre† (bizar) *a,* odd, queer, peculiar. **bizarrerie** (zarri) *f,* oddness, &c.
blackbouler *P* (blakbule) *v.t,* to blackball; fail (*in exam*).
blafard, e (blafar, ard) *a,* pale, wan.
blague (blag) *f,* [tobacco] pouch; *P* joke; trick, hoax. *faire une* ~ *à qn,* play a joke *or* trick on s.o. *sans* ~*!* you're kidding! *P.* ~ *à part,* seriously. **blaguer** *P* (ge) *v.i. & t,* to joke, kid, tease. **blagueur, euse** (gœr, øz) *a,* mocking, teasing (*smile*) ¶ *n,* joker.
blaireau (blɛro) *m,* badger; shaving brush.
blâme (blɑm) *m,* blame; reprimand, rebuke. **blâmer** (blɑme) *v.t,* to blame, &c.
blanc, che (blɑ̃, ɑ̃ʃ) *a,* white (*hair, race, wine*); fair, pale (*skin*); blank (*page*); pure, innocent. ~ *comme neige,* pure as the driven snow. *carte blanche,* a free hand. *nuit blanche,* sleepless night. *vers blancs,* blank verse. ¶ *m,* white (*d'œuf,* of egg; *de l'œil,* of the eye). *peindre en* ~, to paint white. white [man]; blank; whites (*laundry*); household linen; white meat, breast (*chicken*). *saigner à* ~, to bleed white. *cartouche à* ~, blank cartridge. *chèque en* ~, blank cheque. ~ *de céruse,* white lead. ~ *de chaux,* whitewash. ~ *d'Espagne,* whiting. ¶ *f,* white woman; (*Mus.*) minim. ~*-bec, P m,* greenhorn *P.* ~**-manger** *m,* blancmange. **Blanche-Neige,** Snow White. ~**-seing** (blɑ̃sɛ̃) *m,* signature on blank document.
blanchâtre (blɑ̃ʃɑtr) *a,* whitish. **blancheur** (blɑ̃ʃœr) *f,* whiteness. **blanchir** (ʃir) *v.t,* to whiten; turn white; bleach; wash, launder. ~ *à la chaux,* to whitewash. (*Cook.*) [*faire*] ~, to blanch. clear, exonerate. ¶ *v.i,* to go white. **blanchisserie** (ʃisri) *f,* laundry. **blanchisseur, euse** (sœr, øz) launderer, laundress.
blaser (blɑze) *v.t,* to make blasé *or* indifferent. *blasé de,* bored with.
blason (blɑzɔ̃) *m,* coat of arms.
blasphémateur, trice (blasfematœr, tris) *n,* blasphemer. **blasphématoire** (twar) *a,* blasphemous. **blasphème** (fɛm) *m,* blasphemy. **blasphémer** (feme) *v.i. & t,* to blaspheme.
blatte (blat) *f,* cockroach, black beetle.
blé (ble) *m,* corn, wheat. ~ *noir,* buckwheat. *manger son* ~ *en herbe,* to spend one's income in advance.
bled *P* (blɛd) *m,* village; dump *P,* hole *P. dans le* ~, up country; in the wilds.
blême (blɛm) *a,* pale, wan. **blêmir** (blemir) *v.i,* to [turn] pale (*de,* with).
blessant, e (blɛsɑ̃, ɑ̃t) *a,* wounding, cutting. **blessé, e** (se) *n,* injured *or* wounded person, casualty. **blesser** (blɛse) *v.t,* to wound (*au bras,* in the arm); injure, hurt. ~ *l'oreille,* grate on the ear. hurt, wound (*feelings*). **blessure** (syr) *f,* wound, injury.
blet, te (blɛ, ɛt) *a,* overripe, soft.
bleu, e (blø) *a,* blue. ¶ *m,* blue. ~ *ciel, marine, roi,* sky, navy, royal blue. bruise; blue cheese; (*P*) novice, (*Mil.*) raw recruit. ~[*s*] [*de*

travail], dungarees. **bleuâtre** (ɑtr) *a,* bluish. **bleuet** (ɛ) *m,* cornflower. **bleuir** (ir) *v.t. & i,* to turn blue. **bleuté, e** (te) *a,* bluish.
blindage (blɛ̃daʒ) *m,* armour-plating. **blindé** (de) *m,* armoured vehicle. *les* ~*s,* the armour. **blinder** (de) *v.t,* to armour; reinforce.
bloc (blɔk) *m,* block, lump; (*Pol.*) bloc, coalition; pad (*paper*); unit; (*P*) clink *P,* jug *P. en* ~, as a whole. *faire* ~ *avec,* to unite with. *visser à* ~, screw up tight. ~*-cuisine,* kitchen unit. ~*-évier,* sink unit. ~*-moteur,* engine block. ~*-notes,* scribbling pad. ~ **age** (aʒ) *m,* (*price, wage*) freeze; (*Build.*) rubble; (*Psych.*) block. ~ **aille** (aj) *f,* rubble.
blockhaus (blɔkos) *m,* blockhouse, pillbox.
blocus (blɔkys) *m,* blockade.
blond, e (blɔ̃, ɔ̃d) *a,* fair, blond (*hair*); fair, fair-haired (*pers.*). ~ *cendré,* ash blonde. ~ *roux,* sandy. ¶ *m,* blond (*colour*); fair- haired man. ¶ *f,* blonde (*woman*); lager (*beer*). ~**inet, te** (dine, ɛt) fair-haired boy, girl. ~ **ir** (dir) *v.i,* to go fairer (*hair*).
bloquer (blɔke) *v.t,* to block [up], obstruct; blockade; hold up (*goods, traffic*); freeze (*wages*); (*Mach.*) jam; chock (*wheels*). ~ *les freins,* jam on the brakes. group *or* lump together. **se** ~, to jam; (*wheel*) lock.
blottir (se) (blɔtir) *v.pr,* to crouch, huddle [up]; curl up; nestle, snuggle up.
blouse (bluz) *f,* overall; smock; (*Med.*) white coat.
blouser *P* (bluze) *v.t,* to take in, trick.
blouson (bluzɔ̃) *m,* windjammer. ~ *noir,* teddy-boy.
blue-jean (bludʒin) *m,* jeans.
bluff (blœf) *m,* bluff. **bluffer** (fe) *v.i. & t,* to bluff.
boa (bɔa) *m,* boa (*wrap, snake*).
bobard *P* (bɔbar) *m,* lie, fib *P;* tall story.
bobine (bɔbin) *f,* reel, bobbin, spool; (*Cine.*) reel; roll (*film*); (*Elec.*) coil; (*P*) face.
bocage (bɔkaʒ) *m,* grove, copse; (*Geog.*) bocage. **bocager, ère** (kaʒe, ɛr) *a,* wooded.
bocal (bɔkal) *m,* jar; goldfish bowl. *mettre en* ~*aux,* to bottle (*fruit*).
bock (bɔk) *m,* glass of beer; beer glass.
bœuf (bœf) *m,* ox, bullock; beef. ¶ *P a. inv,* fantastic (*success*).
bohème (bɔɛm) *n. & a,* bohemian; (*a*) free & easy. *la B*~, Bohemia (*milieu*). **bohémien, ne** (emjɛ̃, ɛn) *n,* gipsy.
boire (bwar) *v.t.ir,* to drink. ~ *un coup,* to have a drink. ~ *comme un trou P,* drink like a fish. drink in (*words*); (*sponge*) absorb. ¶ *m, le* ~ *& le manger,* food & drink.
bois (bwɑ) *m,* wood (*place, timber*). *en* ~, wooden. ~ *blanc,* deal. ~ *à brûler,* firewood. ~ *de charpente,* timber. ~ *de lit,* bedstead. *on va voir de quel* ~ *je me chauffe!* they'll see what I'm made of! antler (*stag*). (*Mus.*) *les* ~, the woodwind. ~**é, e** (ze) *a,* wooded. ~**ement** (zmɑ̃) *m,* afforestation. ~**erie** (zri) *f,* ~[*s*], panelling.
boisseau (bwaso) *m,* bushel.
boisson (bwasɔ̃) *f,* drink. *pris de* ~, drunk.
boîte (bwat) *f,* box; tin, can. *en* ~, tinned, canned (*food*). (*P*) ~ [*de nuit*], night club. school, office, firm; (*pej.*) joint *P.* dump *P.* ~ *d'allumettes,* box of matches. ~ *aux* or *à lettres,* pillar box; letter b. ~ *à musique,* musical b. ~ *à ordures,* dustbin. ~ *à outils,* toolbox. ~ *de vitesses,* gearbox.
boiter (bwate) *v.i,* to limp. **boiteux, euse** (tø, øz) *a,* lame (*pers., excuse*); rickety (*chair*); shaky (*peace, plan*); halting (*verse*).
boitier (bwatje) *m,* (*watch*) case.
boitiller (bwatije) *v.i,* to limp slightly, hobble.
bol (bɔl) *m,* bowl; *P* luck.
bolide (bɔlid) *m,* meteor; racing car.
Bolivie (la) (bɔlivi), Bolivia. **bolivien, ne** (vjɛ̃, ɛn) *a. &* **B** ~, *n,* Bolivian.
bombance (bɔ̃bɑ̃s) *f,* feasting, junketing.
bombardement (bɔ̃bardəmɑ̃) *m,* bombardment, shelling; bombing. **bombarder** (de) *v.t,* to bombard, &c; pitchfork (*à un poste,* into a job). **bombardier** (dje) *m,* bomber (*plane*). **bombe** (bɔ̃b) *f,* bomb; (*fig.*) bombshell; atomizer, spray. *faire la* ~ *P,* go on a binge *P.* ~ *glacée,* ice pudding.
bomber (bɔ̃be) *v.i,* to bulge. ¶ *v.t,* ~ *le torse,* throw out one's chest; (*fig.*) swagger.
bon[1], **ne** (bɔ̃, ɔn) *a,* good, nice (*food, smell*); good, kind (*pers.*); g., competent (*driver*). ~ *en latin,* g. at Latin. right, correct. *le* ~ *train,* the right train. ~ *à,* good for. ~ *à rien,* no good, no use. *puis-je vous être* ~ *à qch?* can I be of any help to you? *à quoi* ~? what's the use? (*Mil.*) ~ *pour le service,* fit for duty. valid (*ticket*). (*considerable*) *un* ~ *moment,* quite some time. *2* ~*nes heures,* 2 full hours. *une* ~*ne râclée,* a g. hiding. ~ *nombre de,* a g. many. [*c'est*] *bon!* all right!, O.K.! *pour de* ~, for good [& all]; in earnest. (*greetings*) ~*ne année!* happy New Year! ~ *appétit!* enjoy your meal! ~ *courage!* g. luck! ~ *voyage!* have a g. journey! *de* ~ *cœur,* (*eat*) heartily; willingly. ~ *débarras!* g. riddance! ~ *enfant,* good-natured. ~*ne femme,* woman; (*pej. wife*) old woman *P. garder pour la* ~*ne bouche,* keep as a tit-bit [for the last]. ~ *gré mal gré,* willy-nilly. *de* ~*ne heure,* early. *à la* ~*ne heure,* that's fine. ~*ne maman,* granny. [*à*] ~ *marché,* cheap. ~ *mot,* witty remark. ~ *papa,* grandad. ~ [*ne*] *à rien, n. & a,* good-for-nothing. ~ *sang!* damn it! ~ *sens,* common sense. ~ *vivant,* jovial fellow. ¶ *ad, sentir* ~, to smell good. *tenir* ~, stand fast. *il fait* ~ *se reposer,* it's good to rest. ¶ *m,* good; g. person; g. part. *f, en voilà une* ~! that's a g. one!
bon[2] (bɔ̃) *m,* coupon, voucher; (*Fin.*) bond.

bonbon (bɔ̃bɔ̃) *m*, sweet. ~ **nière** (bɔnjɛr) *f* sweet box; pretty little flat.
bond (bɔ̃) *m*, leap, bound. *faire un* ~, to start (*surprise*); (*price*) shoot up. *se lever d'un* ~, leap up.
bonde (bɔ̃d) *f*, bung; plug; bunghole; plughole. **bondé, e** (de) *a*, packed, crammed.
bondir (bɔ̃dir) *v.i*, to leap, spring [up]; start; (*ball*) bounce. ~ *de joie*, jump for joy. **bondissement** (dismɑ̃) *m*, leap, bound.
bonheur (bɔnœr) *m*, happiness, bliss; joy, blessing; [good] luck. *j'ai eu le* ~ *de voir*, I had the pleasure of seeing. *par* ~, luckily. *au petit* ~, haphazardly.
bonhomie (bɔnɔmi) *f*, good nature, geniality. **bonhomme** (nɔm) *m*, man, fellow, chap *P*; (*husband*) old man *P*. ~ *de neige*, snowman. *aller son petit* ~ *de chemin*, carry on in one's own sweet way.
bonification (bɔnifikasjɔ̃) *f*, improvement. **bonifier** (fje) *v.t.* & **se** ~, *v.pr*, to improve.
boniment (bɔnimɑ̃) *m*, patter, sales talk.
bonjour (bɔ̃ʒur) *m*, good morning, good afternoon, hullo.
bonne (bɔn) *f*, maid. ~ *à tout faire*, general help, maid of all work. ~ [*d'enfant*], nurse, nanny.
bonnement (bɔnmɑ̃) *ad*, *tout* ~, quite simply.
bonnet (bɔnɛ) *m*, bonnet. ~ *d'âne*, dunce's cap. ~ *de nuit*, (*lit.*) night cap. ~ *de police*, forage cap. *gros* ~, bigwig. *prendre sous son* ~, take on responsibility for. ~**erie** (bɔnɛtri) *f*, hosiery. ~**ier, ère** (bontje, ɛr) *n*, hosier.
bonsoir (bɔ̃swar) *m*, good evening, good night.
bonté (bɔ̃te) *f*, goodness, kindness.
bonze (bɔ̃z) *m*, (*Rel.*) bonze; (*P*) bigwig.
bord (bɔr) *m*, edge; bank (*river*); shore (*lake, sea*); rim (*glass*); hem; (*fig.*) brink, verge (*ruin, tears*). *au* ~ *de la mer*, at the seaside. *à larges* ~*s*, broad-brimmed (*hat*). *remplir à pleins* ~*s*, fill to the brim. (*Naut.*) side (*ship*); tack. *tirer des* ~*s*, to tack. *à* ~ [*d'un navire*], on board [a ship]. *par-dessus* ~, overboard. *les hommes du* ~, the crew.
bordeaux (bɔrdo) *m*, Bordeaux (*wine*); ~ *rouge*, claret.
bordée (bɔrde) *f*, broadside; (*fig.*) volley; (*Naut.*) watch; tack. *tirer des* ~*s*, to tack.
bordel *P* (bɔrdɛl) *m*, brothel; (*fig.*) shambles *P*.
border (bɔrde) *v.t*, to line, run alongside, fringe; (*Need.*) edge, trim; hem; tuck in, t. up (*bed, child*). *bordé de*, bordered *or* lined with.
bordereau (bɔrdəro) *m*, slip, note; statement. ~ *de versement*, paying-in slip.
bordure (bɔrdyr) *f*, edge; (*Hort., Need.*) border; line (*trees*); frame. ~ *de pavés*, kerb. *en* ~ *de*, running along; next to.
borgne (bɔrɲ) *a*, one-eyed; blind in one eye; low, shady (*hotel*).
borne (bɔrn) *f*, post; (*Elec.*) terminal. ~ *kilométrique* (Fr.), mile stone (*Eng.*). ~*s*, bounds, limits. *sans* ~, boundless. *dépasser les* ~*s*, to go too far. **borné, e** (ne) *a*, limited; narrow-minded (*pers.*). **borner** (ne) *v.t*, to bound, mark out; limit, restrict. *se* ~ *à faire*, confine o.s to doing.
bosquet (bɔskɛ) *m*, copse, spinney.
bosse (bɔs) *f*, hump; bump (*head, road*). *avoir la* ~ *de*, to be gifted at. **bosseler** (sle) *v.t*, to dent; emboss. **bosselure** (slyr) *f*, dent. **bossu, e** (sy) *a*, hunchbacked. ¶ *n*, hunchback.
bot (bo) *a*, *pied* ~, club foot.
botanique (bɔtanik) *a*, botanic(al). ¶ *f*, botany. **botaniste** (nist) *n*, botanist.
botte (bɔt) *f*, [high] boot; riding boot. ~ *de caoutchouc*, gumboot, wellington. [~*s*] *cuissardes*, waders. bunch; sheaf; bale. **botter** (te) *v.t*, to put boots on. to kick. ~ *les fesses à qn P*, kick s.o in the pants *P*. **bottier** (tje) *m*, bootmaker. **bottine** (tin) *f*, [ankle] boot.
Bottin (bɔtɛ̃) *m*, directory, phonebook.
bouc (buk) *m*, billy goat. [*barbe de*] ~, goatee. ~ *émissaire*, scapegoat.
boucan *P* (bukɑ̃) *m*, row, racket; fuss (*protest*).
bouche (buʃ) *f*, mouth. *fermer la* ~ *à qn*, to silence s.o. *faire venir l'eau à la* ~, make one's mouth water. ~ *bée*, open-mouthed, gaping. ~ *cousue!* mum's the word! muzzle (*gun*); mouth opening; entrance (*metro*). ~-*à*-~, *m. inv*, kiss of life. ~ *d'égout*, manhole. ~ *d'incendie*, fire hydrant. **bouché, e** (buʃe) *a*, overcast (*weather*); dull-witted, thick *P*. **bouchée** (ʃe) *f*, mouthful. ~ [*au chocolat*], chocolate. *pour une* ~ *de pain*, for a song.
boucher[1] (ʃe) *v.t*, to cork (*bottle*); block [up] (*drain*); fill, stop, plug (*hole, leak*). *se* ~ *le nez*, to hold one's nose. ~**-trou,** (tru) *m*, stopgap.
boucher[2] (buʃe) *m*, butcher. **boucherie** (ʃri) *f*, butcher's shop; butchery (*trade*); slaughter.
bouchon (buʃɔ̃) *m*, stopper, cork; plug, cap, bung; (*Fish.*) float; (*Mot.*) holdup. *sentir le* ~, (*wine*) to be corked.
boucle (bukl) *f*, buckle; loop (*bow, letter, river*); curl, lock (*hair*). ~ *d'oreille*, earring. **bouclé, e** (kle) *a*, curly. **boucler** (kle) *v.t*, to buckle, fasten; lock up, shut up; (*Police*) seal off; settle, clinch (*matter*); balance (*budget*); curl. *la boucle! P.* belt up! *P.* ~ *la boucle*, to loop the loop. **bouclier** (klie) *m*, shield.
bouddhiste (budist) *a.* & *n*, buddhist.
bouder (bude) *v.i*, to sulk. ¶ *v.t*, to shun (*s.o*). **bouderie** (dri) *f*, sulk; sulkiness. **boudeur, euse** (dœr, øz) *a*, sulky.
boudin (budɛ̃) *m*, black pudding.
boue (bu) *f*, mud; sludge.
bouée (bue) *f*, buoy; rubber ring. ~-*culotte*, breeches b. ~ *de sauvetage*, life b.
boueux, euse (buø, øz) *a*, muddy. ¶ *m*, dustman.
bouffant, e (bufɑ̃, ɑ̃t) *a*, puffed out, bouffant. **bouffée** (bufe) *f*, whiff, puff (*smoke*); gust, puff

(*wind*); fit (*anger*). **bouffer**[1] (fe) *v.i*, to puff out, swell out. **bouffi, e** (fi) *a*, puffed up, swollen. **bouffir** (fir) *v.t*, to puff up. ¶ *v.i*, to swell, become bloated.
bouffer[2] *P* (bufe) *v.t. & i*, to eat; gobble [up].
buffon, ne (bufɔ̃, ɔn) *a*, comic(al), farcical. ¶ *m*, buffoon, clown; jester. ~**nerie** (fɔnri) *f*, ~*s*, antics, buffoonery.
bouge (buʒ) *m*, hovel, hole; low dive.
bougeoir (buʒwar) *m*, candlestick.
bougeotte *P* (buʒɔt) *f*, *avoir la* ~, to be fidgety *or* restless. **bouger** (buʒe) *v.i*, to move, stir, budge. ¶ *v.t*, move. ~ *le petit doigt*, move a finger (*to help*).
bougie (buʒi) *f*, candle; (*Mot.*) sparking plug; (*Elec.*) watt.
bougon, ne (bugɔ̃, ɔ̃n) *a*, grumpy. ¶ *n*, grumbler. **bougonner** (bugɔne) *v.i*, to grumble, grouse.
bouillant, e (bujɑ̃, ɑ̃t) *a*, boiling; fiery, hotheaded. **bouille** *P* (buj) *f*, face. **bouillie** (ji) *f*, porridge; baby cereal. *mettre en* ~, reduce to pulp. **bouillir** (jir) *v.i.ir*, to boil; (*fig.*) seethe. *faire* ~, to boil. **bouilloire** (jwar) *f*, kettle. ~ *à sifflet*, singing k. **bouillon** (jɔ̃) *m*, bubble. *couler à gros* ~*s*, to gush out. stock; broth. ~ *cube*, stock cube. **bouillonner** (jɔne) *v.i*, to bubble, boil up, foam; (*lit., fig.*) seethe. **bouillotte** (jɔt) *f*, hot-water bottle.
boulanger, ère (bulɑ̃ʒe, ɛr) *n*, baker. ¶ *f*, baker's wife. ~**ie** (ʒri) *f*, baker's [shop]; bakery [trade].
boule (bul) *f*, (*Bil., Croquet*) ball; (*Bowls*) bowl, wood. *jouer aux* ~*s*, to play bowls *or* boules. *perdre la* ~ *P*, to go crazy. *se mettre en* ~, to get angry. ~ *de neige*, snowball. *faire* ~ *de n.*, (*fig.*) to snowball.
bouleau (bulo) *m*, birch [tree].
bouledogue (buldɔg) *m*, bulldog.
boulet (bulɛ) *m*, cannon ball; ball & chain; (*fig.*) millstone. **boulette** (lɛt) *f*, pellet; meatball; (*P*) clanger *P*.
boulevard (bulvar) *m*, boulevard.
bouleverser (bulvɛrse) *v.t*, to upset, turn upside down; disrupt (*plans*); distress greatly, overwhelm, shatter (*pers.*).
boulier (bulje) *m*, abacus; (*Bil.*) score board.
boulon (bulɔ̃) *m*, bolt. **boulonner** (lɔne) *v.t*, to bolt [down]. ¶ *v.i*, *P* to work, slog *P*.
boulot[1], **te** (bulo, ɔt) *a*, dumpy, tubby.
boulot[2] *P* (bulo) *m*, work; job.
bouquet (bukɛ) *m*, bunch of flowers; bouquet; clump (*trees*); bouquet (*wine*); crowning piece (*fireworks*); prawn. ~**ière** (ktjɛr) *f*, flower girl.
bouquetin (buktɛ̃) *m*, ibex.
bouquin *P* (bukɛ̃) *m*, book. ~**er** *P* (kine) *v.i*, to read. ~**iste** (inist) *m*, secondhand bookseller.
bourbe (burb) *f*, mud. **bourbeux, euse** (bø, øz) *a*, muddy. **bourbier** (bje) *m*, quagmire; scrape, fix; nasty business.
bourde *P* (burd) *f*, blunder, boob *P*; howler.
bourdon (burdɔ̃) *m*, bumble-bee; great bell; (*Mus.*) drone. ~**nement** (dɔnmɑ̃) *m*, buzz; drone (*engine*). ~**ner** (ne) *v.i*, to buzz; drone.
bourg (bur) *m*, market town, village. **bourgade** (burgad) *f*, small town, village.
bourgeois, e (burʒwa, az) *a*, middle-class; (*pej.*) bourgeois. ¶ *n*, middle-class person, bourgeois; (*Hist.*) burgher. **bourgeoisie** (ʒwazi) *f*, middle class[es] (*haute, petite*, upper, lower); bourgeoisie.
bourgeon (burʒɔ̃) *m*, bud. ~**ner** (ʒɔne) *v.i*, to bud.
bourgogne (burgɔɲ) *m*, burgundy (*wine*).
bourrade (burad) *f*, blow, thump.
bourrasque (burask) *f*, squall; gust (*wind*); angry outburst.
bourre (bur) *f*, padding, stuffing; wad.
bourré, e (bure) *a*, crammed (*room*); (*P*) tight *P*.
bourreau (buro) *m*, executioner; hangman; torturer. ~ *d'argent*, spendthrift. ~ *des cœurs*, lady-killer. ~ *d'enfants*, child batterer. **bourreler** (rle) *v.t*, (*fig.*) to torment, rack.
bourrelet (burlɛ) *m*, draught excluder; roll of flesh. **bourrelier** (rəlje) *m*, saddler.
bourrer (bure) *v.t*, to stuff (*de*, with); cram (*bag*); fill (*pipe*); (*Sch.*) cram. ~ *le crâne à qn*, stuff s.o's head with [false] ideas. ~ *de coups*, to beat up.
bourrique (burik) *f*, she-ass; donkey; (*fig.*) ass.
bourru, e (bury) *a*, surly, crusty, gruff.
bourse (burs) *f*, purse. *sans* ~ *délier*, without spending a penny. (*Univ.*) grant, scholarship. *la B*~, the Stock Exchange *or* Market. ~ *du commerce*, commodity market. **boursicoter** (sikɔte) *v.i*, to dabble on the stock exchange. **boursier, ère** (sje, ɛr) *a*, Stock Market (*transaction*). ¶ *n*, grant-holder.
boursouflé, e (bursufle) *a*, bombastic (*style*). **boursoufler** (fle) *v.t*, to puff up, bloat. **se** ~, (*paint*) to blister.
bousculade (buskylad) *f*, crush, scrum *P*; rush. **bousculer** (le) *v.t*, to jostle, hustle; bump into; rush.
bouse (buz) *f*, dung (*cattle*); cow pat.
bousiller *P* (buzije) *v.t*, to botch (*job*); wreck (*car*); bump off *P* (*pers.*).
boussole (busɔl) *f*, compass. *perdre la* ~ *P*, to go off one's head.
bout (bu) *m*, end, tip. *au* ~ *de bras*, at arm's length. *sur le* ~ *des lèvres*, on the tip of one's tongue. *de* ~ *en* ~, from start to finish. ~ *à* ~, end to end. *joindre les deux* ~*s*, to make ends meet. *savoir qch sur le* ~ *du doigt*, to have sth at one's fingertips. piece, bit (*bread, string*). *un bon* ~ *de chemin*, a good way. *être à* ~ [*de forces*], to be exhausted. *à* ~ *de souffle*, out of breath. *pousser qn à bout*, to push s.o to the limit. *au* ~ *de son rouleau*, at the end of one's tether *or* resources. *à* ~

portant, (*fire*) point-blank.
boutade (butad) *f,* witticism; whim.
boute-en-train (butɑ̃trɛ̃) *m, le* ~ *de la soirée,* the life & soul of the party.
bouteille (butɛj) *f,* bottle; cylinder (*gas*). ~ *Thermos,* Thermos flask. *mettre en* ~, to bottle.
boutique (butik) *f,* shop, store; (*P*) dump *P.* **boutiquier, ère** (kje, ɛr) *n,* shopkeeper.
bouton (butɔ̃) *m,* button; stud (*collar*); knob (*door, radio*); (*Med.*) spot, pimple; (*Bot.*) bud. ~ *de manchette,* cuff link. ~*-d'or,* buttercup. ~*-pression,* press stud. ~ *de sonnette,* bell push. **boutonner** (tɔne) *v.t,* to button [up]. **se** ~, to button o.s up; (*garment*) b. up. **boutonnière** (njɛr) *f,* button-hole.
bouture (butyr) *f,* (*Hort.*) cutting.
bouvier (buvje) *m,* herdsman, stockman.
bouvreuil (buvrœj) *m,* bullfinch.
bovin, e (bɔvɛ̃, in) *a,* (*lit., fig.*) bovine.
box (bɔks) *m,* loose box (*horse*); lock-up [garage]; cubicle. ~ *des accusés,* dock.
boxe (bɔks) *f,* boxing. **boxer** (kse) *v.i. & t,* to box, fight; (*v.t, P*) punch, thump *P.* **boxeur** (ksœr) *m,* boxer.
boyau (bwajo) *m,* ~*x,* guts, entrails. ~ [*de chat*], [cat] gut. passageway; racing tyre (*cycle*).
boycottage (bɔjkɔtaʒ) *m,* boycott. **boycotter** (te) *v.t,* to boycott.
bracelet (braslɛ) *m,* bracelet, bangle; [watch] strap. ~**-montre,** *m,* wrist watch.
braconner (brakɔne) *v.i,* to poach. **braconnier** (nje) *m,* poacher.
braguette (bragɛt) *f,* fly, flies (*trousers*).
brahmane (braman) *m,* Brahmin.
brai (brɛ) *m,* pitch, tar.
braillard, e (brajar, ard) *a,* bawling. ¶ *n,* bawler. **brailler** (je) *v.i.* (*& t*), to bawl (out).
braiment (brɛmɑ̃) *m,* bray[ing]. **braire** (brɛr) *v.i.ir,* to bray.
braise (brɛz) *f,* embers. *de* ~, glowing (*eyes*). **braiser** (brɛze) *v.t,* to braise.
brancard (brɑ̃kar) *m,* shaft (*cart*); stretcher. **brancardier** (kardje) *m,* stretcher bearer.
branchage (brɑ̃ʃaʒ) *m,* branches. **branche** (brɑ̃ʃ) *f,* branch (*tree; fig., family, river, science*); leg (*compass*); stick (*celery*); blade (*scissors*); side-piece (*glasses*). ~**ment** (mɑ̃) *m,* (*Rly.*) branch line; (*Elec.*) connection; connecting up; plugging in. **brancher** (ʃe) *v.t,* to connect up (*phone, gas; sur,* with); (*Elec.*) plug in (*radio &c*). ~ *sur,* plug into. *être branché P,* to understand. **branchies** (ʃi) *f.pl,* gills (*fish*).
brandir (brɑ̃dir) *v.t,* to brandish, flourish.
brandon (brɑ̃dɔ̃) *m,* fire brand.
branlant (brɑ̃lɑ̃, ɑ̃t) *a,* shaky; loose (*tooth*). **branle** (brɑ̃l) *m,* swing. *mettre en* ~, set swinging (*bell*); (*fig.*) set in motion. ~**-bas** (brɑ̃lbɑ) *m,* bustle, commotion. (*Nav.*) ~ *de combat,* preparations for action. **branler** (brɑ̃le) *v.i,* to be unsteady; to be loose (*tooth*). ¶ *v.t,* to shake *or* wag (*head*).
braquer (brake) *v.t,* to point (*sur,* at), train (*sur,* on) (*gun, camera &c*). ~ *les yeux sur,* to fix one's eyes on. ¶ *v.i,* ~ *bien,* (*car*) to have a good lock.
bras (brɑ) *m,* arm. *se donner le* ~, to link arms. ~ *dessus,* ~ *dessous,* arm in arm. *les* ~ *croisés,* with folded arms. (*Ind.*) hand, worker; arm (*chair, pick-up*); handle (*pump*); shaft (*oar*); branch (*river*). *en* ~ *de chemise,* in shirt sleeves. *à* ~ *ouverts,* with open arms. *avoir sur les* ~, to have on one's hands. *saisir à* ~ *le corps,* to seize bodily. *les* ~ *m'en tombent,* I'm stunned.
braser (brɑze) *v.t,* to braze.
brasier (brazje) *m,* inferno.
brassage (brasaʒ) *m,* brewing; mixing (*races*).
brassard (brasar) *m,* armlet, armband.
brasse (bras) *f,* breast-stroke. ~ *papillon,* butterfly [stroke]. (*Naut.*) fathom.
brassée (brase) *f,* armful.
brasser (brase) *v.t,* to brew (*beer*); stir up; mix. **brasserie** (sri) *f,* brewery; bar, brasserie. **brasseur** (sœr) *m,* brewer. ~ *d'affaires,* business tycoon.
brassière (brasjɛr) *f,* vest (*baby's*). ~ *de sauvetage,* life jacket.
bravache (bravaʃ) *m,* blusterer, braggart. **bravade** (vad) *f,* act of bravado. **brave** (brav) *a,* brave, gallant; honest, good, decent; nice, fine (*pers.*). *mon* ~, my good man. **bravement** (bravmɑ̃) *ad,* bravely. **braver** (ve) *v.t,* to brave (*danger*); defy (*rule*). **bravo** (vo) *ad,* bravo!, well done!, hear! hear! ¶ *m,* cheer. **bravoure** (vur) *f,* bravery, gallantry.
break (brɛk) *m,* estate car, (*Am.*) station wagon.
brebis (brəbi) *f,* ewe. ~ *égarée,* lost sheep. ~ *galeuse,* black sheep.
brèche (brɛʃ) *f,* breach, gap; nick. *mourir sur la* ~, to die in harness.
bredouille (brəduj) *a,* empty-handed. **bredouiller** (duje) *v.i. & t,* to mumble, stammer.
bref, ève (brɛf, ɛv) *a,* brief, short; curt (*tone*). ¶ *f,* short vowel. ~ **& en** ~, briefly, in short.
breloque (brəlɔk) *f,* charm (*on bracelet*).
brème (brɛm) *f,* bream (*fish*).
Brême (brɛm) *f,* Bremen.
Brésil (le) (brezil), Brazil. **brésilien, ne** (ljɛ̃, ɛn) *a. & B* ~, *n,* Brazilian.
Bretagne (la) (brətaɲ), Brittany.
bretelle (brətɛl) *f,* [shoulder] strap; (*rifle*) sling. ~*s,* braces, (*Am.*) suspenders.
breton, ne (brətɔ̃, ɔn) *a. &* **B** ~, *n,* Breton.
breuvage (brœvaʒ) *m,* beverage, drink.
brevet (brəvɛ) *m,* diploma, certificate; licence (*pilot*); (*Naut.*) ~ *de capitaine,* captain's ticket. ~ [*d'invention*], [letters] patent. **breve-**

ter (vte) *v.t,* to patent.
bréviaire (brevjɛr) *m,* breviary; (*fig.*) bible.
bribes (brib) *f.pl,* scraps; snatches (*conversation*). *par* ~, piecemeal.
bric-à-brac (brikabrak) *m,* bric-à-brac.
brick (brik) *m,* (*Naut.*) brig.
bricolage (brikɔlaʒ) *m,* odd jobs, pottering; do-it-yourself. **bricole** (kɔl) *f,* trifle; small job. **bricoler** (le) *v.i,* to do odd jobs, potter about. **bricoleur, euse** (lœr, øz) *n,* handyman, woman.
bride (brid) *f,* bridle; reins. *à* ~ *abattue,* at full speed. *tenir en* ~, to curb, keep in check. *lâcher la* ~ *à,* to give full rein to. *la* ~ *sur le cou,* without restraint. **brider** (de) *v.t,* to bridle; curb, keep in check. *avoir les yeux bridés,* to have slit eyes.
bridge (bridʒ) *m,* (*cards*) bridge. *faire un* ~, to have a game of b. **bridger** (dʒe) *v.i,* to play bridge. **bridgeur, euse** (dʒœr, øz) *n,* bridge player.
brièvement (briɛvmɑ̃) *ad,* briefly. **brièveté** (vte) *f,* brevity.
brigade (brigad) *f,* (*Mil.*) brigade; (*Police*) squad; gang, team. **brigadier** (dje) *m,* (*Police*) sergeant; (*Mil.*) corporal.
brigand (brigɑ̃) *m,* brigand; crook. ~**age** (daʒ) *m,* brigandage; robbery.
brigue (brig) *f,* (*liter.*) intrigue. **briguer** (ge) *v.t,* to court, covet (*favour, fame*); solicit (*votes*).
brillamment (brijamɑ̃) *ad,* brilliantly, brightly. **brillant, e** (jɑ̃, ɑ̃t) *a,* bright, shining, sparkling; brilliant (*pers., idea*). *ce n'est pas* ~, it's not up to much. ¶ *m,* brightness; shine; brilliance; brilliant (*diamond*). **briller** (je) *v.i,* to shine, glitter, sparkle; (*pers.*) to shine, be outstanding.
brimade (brimad) *f,* vexation; (*Mil., Sch.*) ragging. **brimer** (me) *v.t,* to harass, pick on *P;* (*Mil., Sch.*) rag.
brin (brɛ̃) *m,* blade (*grass*); slip, sprig; strand (*rope*); bit, scrap, touch. *un beau* ~ *de fille,* a fine-looking girl. **brindille** (dij) *f,* twig.
bringue *P* (brɛ̃g) *f, faire la* ~, to go on a binge.
brioche (briɔʃ) *f,* brioche (*bun*); *P* paunch.
brique (brik) *f,* brick; *P* a million old francs. ¶ *a. inv,* brick red.
briquet (brikɛ) *m,* [cigarette] lighter.
briquetage (briktaʒ) *m,* brickwork. **briqueterie** (ktri) *f,* brickyard.
bris (bri) *m,* breaking. (*Law*) ~ *de clôture,* breaking in. **brisant** (zɑ̃) *m,* reef; breaker (*wave*).
brise (briz) *f,* breeze.
brise- (briz) *pref* (*all m. inv.*): ~**-glace,** ice-breaker (*ship*). ~**-lames,** breakwater. ~**-tout,** destructive person. ~**-vent,** windbreak.
brisées (brize) *f.pl, aller sur les* ~ *de qn,* (*fig.*) to poach on s.o's preserves.
brisement (brizmɑ̃) *m,* (*liter.*) ~ *de cœur,* heartbreak.
briser (brize) *v.t,* to break, smash; wreck (*career*); crush (*spirit*); dash (*hopes*). *brisé de fatigue,* exhausted. *brisé de chagrin,* heartbroken. ¶ *v.i,* ~ *avec qn,* to break with s.o. *brisons là!* let's say no more. **se** ~, to break, smash; (*resistance*) break down. **briseur, euse** (zœr, øz) *n,* ~ *de grève,* strike-breaker; blackleg. **brisure** (zyr) *f,* break.
britannique (britanik) *a,* British. *Iles B~s,* British Isles. **B~,** *n,* Briton.
broc (bro) *m,* pitcher, ewer.
brocante (brɔkɑ̃t) *f,* secondhand goods. **brocanteur, euse** (tœr, øz) *n,* secondhand dealer.
broche (brɔʃ) *f,* (*Cook.*) spit; brooch; (*Elec., Med.*) pin. **brocher** (ʃe) *v.t,* (*Bookb.*) to stitch & bind with paper. *livre broché,* paperback. ¶ *v.i, brochant sur le tout,* to cap all. **brochet** (ʃɛ) *m,* pike (*fish*). **brochette** (ʃɛt) *f,* skewer. **brochure** (ʃyr) *f,* brochure, pamphlet; (*Bookb.*) binding with paper.
brocoli (brɔkɔli) *m,* broccoli.
brodequin (brɔdkɛ̃) *m,* laced boot.
broder (brɔde) *v.t,* to embroider. **broderie** (dri) *f,* embroidery. **brodeur, euse** (dœr, øz) *n,* embroiderer, ess.
brome (brom) *m,* bromine. **bromure** (brɔmyr) *m,* bromide.
broncher (brɔ̃ʃe) *v.i,* (*horse*) to stumble; (*pers.*) move, stir. *sans* ~, without flinching *or* faltering.
bronches (brɔ̃ʃ) *f.pl,* bronchial tubes. **bronchite** (brɔ̃ʃit) *f,* bronchitis.
bronze (brɔ̃z) *m,* bronze. **bronzé, e** (ze) *a,* bronzed, [sun]tanned. **bronzer** (ze) *v.t,* to bronze, tan. **se** ~, to get a tan, sunbathe.
brosse (brɔs) *f,* brush. ~ *à cheveux,* hairbrush. ~ *à dents,* tooth b. ~ *à habits,* clothes b. ~ *en chiendent,* scrubbing b. *donner un coup de* ~ *à qch,* to give sth a brush. *les cheveux en* ~, a crew cut. **brosser** (se) *v.t,* to brush; scrub (*floor*). **se** ~, to brush one's clothes. *se* ~ *les cheveux, les dents,* to brush one's hair, teeth. *tu peux te* ~*!* *P* you can whistle for it! *P.*
brou (bru) *m,* husk (*walnut, almond*).
brouette (bruɛt) *f,* wheelbarrow.
brouhaha (bruaa) *m,* hubbub.
brouillage (brujaʒ) *m,* (*Radio*) interference; jamming. **brouillard** (jar) *m,* fog, mist, haze. *il fait du* ~, it's foggy. (*fig.*) *être dans le* ~, to be all at sea. **brouillasser** (jase) *v.imp,* to drizzle. **brouille** (bruj) *f,* quarrel. **brouiller** (bruje) *v.t,* to blur (*vision, signal*); muddle [up] (*ideas, papers*). (*fig.*) ~ *les cartes,* to fog the issue. *œufs brouillés,* scrambled eggs. **se** ~, to become blurred, confused; (*weather*) break up. *se* ~ *avec qn,* to fall out with s.o. **brouillon, ne** (jɔ̃, ɔn) *a,* untidy; muddle-headed. ¶ *n,* muddler. ¶ *m,* [rough] draft; rough copy; rough work. *papier* ~, rough

paper. **broussaille** (brusɑj) *f. oft. pl,* undergrowth, scrub. *en* ~, unkempt, tousled (*hair*). **brousse** (brus) *f,* bush (*scrub*). *en pleine* ~ *P,* at the back of beyond *P.*

brouter (brute) *v.t. & i,* to graze [on], nibble; (*tool*) chatter; (*clutch*) judder.

broutille (brutij) *f,* trifle.

broyer (brwaje) *v.t,* to grind, crush. (*fig.*) ~ *du noir,* to be down in the dumps *P.*

bru (bry) *f,* daughter-in-law.

brugnon (bryɲɔ̃) *m,* nectarine.

bruine (brɥin) *f,* drizzle. **bruiner** (ne) *v.imp,* to drizzle.

bruire (brɥir) *v.i.ir,* to rustle, murmur, hum. **bruissement** (ismɑ̃) *m,* rustle &c.

bruit (brɥi) *m,* noise, sound; din, row; ado, fuss; rumour. *un* ~ *de pas,* footsteps. *le* ~ *court que,* rumour has it that. ~**age** (taʒ) *m,* sound effects. ~**eur** (tœr) *m,* sound effects man.

brûlant, e (brylɑ̃, ɑ̃t) *a,* burning [hot], scorching, boiling; fiery (*glance*). **brûle-gueule** (bryl) *m,* short clay pipe. **à brûle-pourpoint** (purpwɛ̃) *ad,* point-blank. **brûlé** (le) *m,* burning. *odeur de* ~, smell of burning. (*fig.*) *ça sent le* ~, there's trouble brewing. **brûler** (le) *v.t,* to burn; scorch; scald; roast (*coffee*); (*frost*) nip. (*Mot.*) ~ *un feu rouge,* to shoot the lights. (*fig.*) ~ *ses vaisseaux,* to burn one's boats. ¶ *v.i,* to burn, be on fire. *le visage lui brûle,* her face is burning. ~ *d'impatience,* to burn with impatience. *il brûle de parler,* he's burning to speak. **se** ~, to burn o.s. *se* ~ *la main,* to b. one's hand. *se* ~ *la cervelle,* to blow one's brains out. **brûleur** (lœr) *m,* burner. **brûlure** (lyr) *f,* burn; scald. ~*s d'estomac,* heartburn.

brume (brym) *f,* fog, mist, haze. **brumeux, euse** (mø, øz) *a,* foggy, misty; (*fig.*) hazy.

brun, e (brœ̃, yn) *a,* brown; dark; dusky. ¶ *m,* brown; dark-haired man. ¶ *f,* brunette; (*liter.*) dusk. **brunâtre** (brynɑtr) *a,* brownish. **brunette** (nɛt) *f,* brunette. **brunir** (nir) *v.t,* to brown; tan; burnish. ¶ *v.i,* to tan; (*hair*) darken.

brusque† (brysk) *a,* blunt, abrupt, curt, brusque; sudden, abrupt (*movement*). **brusquer** (ke) *v.t,* to rush, hasten (*matters*); treat abruptly, chivvy (*pers.*). *attaque brusquée,* sudden attack. **brusquerie** (kɔri) *f,* bluntness, &c.

brut, e (bryt) *a,* raw (*silk*); crude (*oil*); rough, uncut (*diamond*); extra dry (*champagne*); (*Com.*) gross. *à l'état* ~, (*ideas*) in the rough.

brutal, e† (tal) *a,* brutal; brutish, coarse. *force* ~*e,* brute force. ~**iser** (lize) *v.i,* to ill-treat, abuse, bully. ~**ité** (te) *f,* brutality. **brute** (bryt) *f,* brute; lout.

Bruxelles (brysɛl) *f,* Brussels.

bruyant, e (bryjɑ̃, ɑ̃t) *a,* noisy; boisterous. **bruyamment** (jamɑ̃) *ad,* noisily.

bruyère (bryjɛr) *f,* heather; heath, moor. *pipe en* ~, briar pipe.

buanderie (byɑ̃dri) *f,* washhouse, laundry.

bûche (byʃ) *f,* log. ~ *de Noël,* yule log. *P* fall; *P* blockhead. **bûcher**[1] (byʃe) *m,* woodshed; funeral pyre; stake (*martyr*). **bûcher**[2] *P, v.i.* (*& t*), swot (up) *P.* **bûcheron** (ʃrɔ̃) *m,* woodcutter, lumberjack. **bûcheur, euse** *P* (ʃœr, øz) *n,* swot, slogger *P.*

bucolique (bykɔlik) *a. & f,* bucolic.

budget (bydʒɛ) *m,* budget. ~**aire** (tɛr) *a,* budgetary. *année* ~, financial year.

buée (bɥe) *f,* moisture, condensation; mist (*on windscreen*).

buffet (byfɛ) *m,* sideboard; ~ [*de cuisine*], [kitchen] dresser; buffet (*meal*); refreshment room.

buffle (byfl) *m,* buffalo.

buis (bɥi) *m,* box [tree]; boxwood.

buisson (bɥisɔ̃) *m,* bush. **buissonneux, euse** (sɔnø, øz) *a,* bushy.

bulbe (bylb) *m,* (*Bot., Anat.*) bulb. **bulbeux, euse** (bø, øz) *a,* bulbous.

bulgare (bylgar) *a. &* **B**~, *n,* Bulgarian. **la Bulgarie** (gari), Bulgaria.

bulldozer (buldozɛr) *m,* bulldozer.

bulle (byl) *f,* bubble; blister; (*papal*) bull; balloon (*comic strip*).

bulletin (byltɛ̃) *m,* bulletin; (*Sch.*) report; form; certificate; ballot paper. ~ *météorologique,* weather forecast. ~ *de salaire,* pay-slip.

buraliste (byralist) *n,* tobacconist; (*postal*) clerk. **bureau** (byro) *m,* desk; study; office; department; committee; board. *heures de* ~, office hours. ~ *de location,* box *or* booking office. ~ *de placement,* employment agency. ~ *de poste,* post office. ~ *de tabac,* tobacconist's shop. ~ *de vote,* polling station. **bureaucrate** (krat) *m,* bureaucrat. **bureaucratie** (si) *f,* bureaucracy. **bureaucratique** (tik) *f,* office automation.

burette (byrɛt) *f,* cruet; oil can.

burin (byrɛ̃) *m,* graver, burin; [cold] chisel. **buriner** (rine) *v.t,* to engrave; chisel, chip.

burlesque (byrlɛsk) *a,* burlesque; comical.

bus (bys) *m,* bus.

buse (byz) *f,* buzzard; *P* blockhead.

buste (byst) *m,* bust.

but (by *or* byt) *m,* goal, objective; (*Sport*) goal; target; aim, object, end, purpose. *dans le* ~ *de faire,* with the aim of doing. *de* ~ *en blanc,* (*ask*) point-blank, out of the blue.

butane (bytan) *m,* (*Chem.*) butane; calor gas.

buté, e (byte) *a,* stubborn. **butée,** *f,* (*Arch.*) abutment; (*Mach.*) stop. **buter** (te) *v.i,* ~ *contre,* to bump into, stumble over; come up against (*snag*). (*Foot.*) score a goal. ¶ *v.t,* to antagonize. **se** ~, to dig in one's heels.

butin (bytɛ̃) *m,* booty, spoils, loot. **butiner** (tine)

v.i, (*bees*) to gather nectar.
butoir (bytwar) *m,* (*Mach.*) stop; (*Rly. line*) buffer.
butor (bytɔr) *m,* bittern; lout, boor.
butte (byt) *f,* mound, hillock. ~ *de tir,* (*rifle*) butts. **butter** (te) *v.t,* to ridge (*earth*); earth up (*plant*)
buvable (byvabl) *a,* drinkable. **buvard** (var) *m,* blotter. **buvette** (vɛt) *f,* refreshment bar.
buveur, euse (vœr, øz) *n,* drinker. ~ *de vin,* wine drinker.

C

C, c (se) *m, letter,* C, c.
ça (sa) *pn.* Contraction of *cela.*
çà (sa) *ad:* ~ *& là,* here & there.
cabale (kabal) *f,* cabal. **cabalistique** (listik) *a,* cabalistic.
caban (kabɑ̃) *m,* reefer (*jacket*).
cabane (kaban) *f,* hut, shed; *P* prison, clink *P.* ~ *à lapins,* rabbit hutch. ~ *de rondins,* log cabin. **cabanon** (nɔ̃) *m,* cottage; cabin; shed.
cabaret (kabarɛ) *m,* cabaret, night club; *O* tavern. ~**ier, ère** (bartje, ɛr) *n,* innkeeper.
cabas (kabɑ) *m,* shopping bag.
cabestan (kabɛstɑ̃) *m,* capstan.
cabillaud (kabijo) *m,* cod[fish].
cabine (kabin) *f,* (*Naut., Aero.*) cabin; (*Rly*) cab; lift [cage]; cubicle. ~ *d'aiguillage,* signal box. ~ *de bain,* beach hut. ~ *téléphonique,* phone box.
cabinet (kabinɛ) *m,* small room. ~*s,* toilet, lavatory. office (*lawyer*); (*Med.*) surgery; practice; (*Pol.*) cabinet; minister's advisers. ~ *de débarras,* lumber room. ~ *de toilette,* lavatory, toilet. ~ *de travail,* study.
câble (kɑbl) *m,* (*gen.*) cable. ~ *de frein,* brake c. **câbler** (ble) *v.t,* (*Tel.*) to cable.
caboche *P* (kabɔʃ) *f,* noddle *P,* nut *P,* head. **cabochard, e** *P* (bɔʃar) *a,* pigheaded.
cabosser (kabɔse) *v.t,* to dent.
cabotage (kabɔtaʒ) *m,* coasting; coastal trade. **caboteur** (tœr) *m,* coaster, tramp.
cabotin, e (kabɔtɛ̃, in) *a,* (*pej.*) theatrical. ¶ *n,* ham actor; show-off.
cabrer (kɑbre) *v.t,* to make (*a horse*) rear; antagonize (*pers.*). **se** ~, to rear; (*pers.*) to jib (*contre,* at). **cabri** (kabri) *m,* kid (*goat*). **cabriole** (ɔl) *f,* caper. **cabrioler** (le) *v.i,* to caper. **cabriolet** (lɛ) *m,* (*Hist.*) cabriolet; (*Mot.*) convertible.
caca *P* (kaka) *m, faire* ~, to do jobs *P.*
cacahuète (kakawɛt) *f,* peanut.
cacao (kakao) *m,* cocoa.
cacatoès (kakatɔɛs) *m,* cockatoo.
cachalot (kaʃalo) *m,* sperm whale.
cache (kaʃ) *f,* hiding place; cache. ¶ *m,* (*Phot.*) mask.
cache-, *prefix:* ~**-cache,** *m,* hide-&-seek. ~**-col,** ~**-nez,** *m. inv,* scarf, comforter. ~**-pot,** *m. inv,* flowerpot holder.
cachemire (kaʃmir) *m,* cashmere.
cacher (kaʃe) *v.t,* to hide, conceal. ~ *son jeu,* to hide one's game. *tu me caches le jour,* you're in my light. **se** ~, to hide, be concealed. **cachet** (ʃɛ) *m,* stamp, seal, postmark; style, character; fee; (*Med.*) tablet. **cacheter** (ʃte) *v.t,* to seal. **cachette** (ʃɛt) *f,* hiding place. *en* ~, secretly. **cachot** (ʃo) *m,* dungeon. **cachotterie** (ʃɔtri) *f,* mystery. **cachottier, ère** (tje, ɛr) *a,* secretive.
cacophonie (kakɔfɔni) *f,* cacophony.
cactus (kaktys) *m,* cactus.
cadastre (kadastr) *m,* (*Tax*) cadastre; cadastral survey.
cadavéreux, euse (kadaverø, øz) & **cadavérique** (rik) *a,* cadaverous, corpse-like. **cadavre** (dɑvr) *m,* corpse.
cadeau (kado) *m,* present, gift. *faire* ~ *de,* to give, make a present of.
cadenas (kadnɑ) *m,* padlock. **cadenasser** (dnase) *v.t,* to padlock.
cadence (kadɑ̃s) *f,* rhythm; pace. (*Mus.*) cadence; cadenza. *en* ~, in time; rhythmically. **cadencé, e** (se) *a,* rhythmical.
cadet, te (kadɛ, ɛt) *a. & n,* younger, youngest (child); junior. *mon frère* ~, my younger brother. *mon* ~ *de 3 ans,* 3 years my junior.
cadran (kadrɑ̃) *m,* dial (*clock, phone*); face (*barometer*). ~ *solaire,* sundial.
cadre (kɑdr) *m,* frame (*picture, cycle*); (*fig.*) framework, scope, limits; surroundings, setting; manager, (*Mil.*) officer. *les* ~*s,* managerial staff. **cadrer** (dre) *v.i,* ~ *avec,* to tally with.
caduc, uque (kadyk) *a,* (*Bot.*) deciduous; decrepit; lapsed, obsolete; (*Law*) null & void.
cafard[1] (kafar) *m,* cockroach; (*P*) the blues *P.* *avoir le* ~, to feel blue *P,* depressed.
cafard[2]**, e** (kafar, ard) *n,* (*Sch.*) sneak. ~**er** (de) *v.i.*(*& t*), to sneak (on).
café (kafe) *m,* coffee; café. ~ *au lait,* white coffee. ~ *complet,* continental breakfast.

cafetier, ère (ftje, ɛr) *n,* café owner. ¶ *f,* coffee pot.
cafouillage *P* (kafujaʒ) *m,* muddle, cockup *P.* **cafouiller** *P* (je) *v.i,* to make a cockup *P.*
cage (kaʒ) *f,* cage; case, housing; (*Sport*) goal. ~ *d'ascenseur,* lift shaft. ~ *d'escalier,* stairwell. ~ *à poules,* hen coop.
cagneux, euse (kaɲø, øz) *a,* knock-kneed.
cagnotte (kaɲɔt) *f,* kitty; nest-egg.
cagoule (kagul) *f,* cowl, hood; balaclava.
cahier (kaje) *m,* (*Sch.*) exercise book, notebook. ~ *de brouillon,* rough book. (*Law*) ~ *de charges,* schedule of conditions.
cahin-caha (kaɛ̃kaa) *ad,* so so, middling. *aller* ~, to jog along.
cahot (kao) *m,* jolt, bump; vicissitude. **cahoter** (ɔte) *v.t. & i,* to jolt, bump about.
cahute (kayt) *f,* hovel; shack.
caille (kɑj) *f,* quail.
caillebotis (kajbɔti) *m,* duckboard.
cailler (kɑje) *v.t. &* **se** ~, to curdle; clot (*blood*). ¶ *v.i, P* to be cold; freeze. **caillot** (jo) *m,* clot.
caillou (kaju) *m,* pebble; stone; boulder; *P* head, nut *P. dur comme un* ~, stony (*heart*). ~**teux, euse** (tø, øz) *a,* pebbly, stony. ~**tis** (ti) *m,* gravel; road metal.
Caire (le) (kɛr), Cairo.
caisse (kɛs) *f,* box, crate; tub (*for shrub*); (*Tech.*) casing; body (*vehicle*); (*Mus.*) drum; cashbox, coffer; till; cashdesk; cashier's counter *or* office; office; fund. *de l'argent en* ~, ready cash. (*Ind.*) *passer à la* ~, to get one's cards. *voler la* ~, to raid the till. ~ *à eau,* water tank. ~ *claire,* snare drum, side d. ~ *enregistreuse,* cash register. ~ *d'épargne,* savings bank. ~ *noire,* secret funds. **caissier, ère** (kɛsje, ɛr) *n,* cashier; teller (*bank*).
caisson (kɛsɔ̃) *m,* box, case; (*Mil., Tech.*) caisson. *le mal des* ~*s,* the bends.
cajoler (kaʒɔle) *v.t,* to pet, cuddle, make a fuss of; coax, wheedle. ~**ie** (lri) *f,* cuddle; wheedling.
cake (kɛk) *m,* fruit cake.
calage (kalaʒ) *m,* wedging; chocking.
calamité (kalamite) *f,* calamity. **calamiteux, euse** (tø, øz) *a,* calamitous.
calcaire (kalkɛr) *m,* limestone. ¶ *a,* chalky; hard (*water*); (*Geol.*) limestone.
calciner (kalsine) *v.t,* to burn to ashes; b. to a cinder (*meat*); (*Tech.*) calcine.
calcium (kalsjɔm) *m,* calcium.
calcul (kalkyl) *m,* calculation; sum. *le* ~, arithmetic, calculus; (*Med.*) stone, calculus. ~**ateur, trice** (latœr, trice) *a,* calculating (*sly*). ¶ *m,* computer. ¶ *f,* (*Mach.*) calculator. ¶ *n,* (*pers.*) calculator. ~**er** (le) *v.t. & i,* to calculate, work out.
cale (kal) *f,* hold (*of ship*); wedge, chock. ~ [*de construction*], slipway. ~ *sèche,* ~ *de radoub,* dry dock, graving d.
calé *P* (kale) *a,* clever, bright; tough (*problem*).
calebasse (kalbas) *f,* calabash, gourd.
caleçon (kalsɔ̃) *m,* underpants. ~ *de bain,* bathing trunks.
calembour (kalɑ̃bur) *m,* pun.
calendes (kalɑ̃d) *f.pl,* calends. **calendrier** (lɑ̃drie) *m,* calendar.
calepin (kalpɛ̃) *m,* notebook.
caler (kale) *v.t,* to wedge, chock; prop up (*patient*). **se** ~, to settle o.s (*in chair*). ¶ *v.i,* (*engine*) to stall; (*pers.*) give in. (*Naut.*) ~ *3 mètres,* to draw 3 metres.
calfater (kalfate) *v.t,* to caulk.
calfeutrer (kalføtre) *v.t,* to make draughtproof. **se** ~, to make oneself cosy.
calibre (kalibr) *m,* calibre, bore (*gun &c*); grade, size (*eggs &c*); gauge; (*fig: pers.*) calibre. **calibrer** (bre) *v.t,* to gauge; grade (*eggs &c*).
calice (kalis) *m,* chalice; (*Bot.*) calyx.
calicot (kaliko) *m,* calico.
calife (kalif) *m,* caliph.
Californie (la) (kalifɔrni), California.
califourchon (kalifurʃɔ̃) *ad, à* ~, astride.
câlin, e (kɑlɛ̃, in) *a,* cuddly (*child*); tender (*pers., tone*). ¶ *m,* cuddle. ~**er** (line) *v.t,* to cuddle, fondle. ~**erie** (nri) *f,* caress.
calleux, euse (kalø, øz) *a,* callous, horny.
calligraphie (kaligrafi) *m,* calligraphy.
callosité (kalozite) *f,* callosity.
calmant (kalmɑ̃) *a,* soothing; tranquillizing; pain-killing. ¶ *m,* tranquillizer; painkiller.
calmar (kalmar) *m,* squid.
calme† (kalm) *a,* calm, quiet, still. ¶ *m,* calm, calmness, &c. ~ *plat,* dead calm. *du* ~*!* quiet please! *or* keep calm! **calmer** (me) *v.t,* to calm; quieten [down]; soothe (*pain*); allay (*fears*). **se** ~, to calm down; quieten down; ease; subside.
calomnie (kalɔmni) *f,* calumny, slander; libel. **calomnier** (nje) *v.t,* to slander; libel. **calomnieux, euse** (njø, øz) *a,* slanderous; libellous.
calorie (kalɔri) *f,* calorie. **calorifuge** (kalɔrifyʒ) *a,* [heat-]insulating. ~**age** (aʒ) *m,* insulation, lagging. **calorifuger** (ʒe) *v.t,* to insulate, lag.
calot (kalo) *m,* forage cap. **calotte** (lɔt) *f,* skull cap; *P* slap. ~ *glacière,* icecap.
calque (kalk) *m,* tracing; (*fig.*) exact copy. **calquer** (ke) *v.t,* to trace; copy.
calvaire (kalvɛr) *m,* calvary (*image*); intense suffering. **le C** ~, Calvary (*place*).
calvinisme (kalvinism) *m,* Calvinism.
calvitie (kalvisi) *f,* baldness.
camarade (kamarad) *n,* comrade, companion, mate *P.* ~ *d'atelier, d'école, de jeu,* workmate, schoolmate, playmate.. ~**rie** (dri) *f,* comradeship, companionship, camaraderie.
Cambodge (le) (kɑ̃bɔdʒ) Kampuchea, *O* Cambodia.
cambrer (kɑ̃bre) *v.t. &* **se** ~, to arch, bend,

curve. *cambré*, arched.
cambriolage (kɑ̃briɔlaʒ) *m*, burglary. **cambrioler** (le) *v.t*, to burgle. **cambrioleur** (lœr) *m*, burglar.
cambrure (kɑ̃bryr) *f*, curve; arch; camber (*road*). ~ *du pied*, instep.
cambuse (kɑ̃byz) *f*, (*Naut.*) storeroom; *P* hovel, hole *P*; *P* room.
came (kam) *f*, (*Tech.*) cam; (*P drugs*) junk *P*.
camé, e[1] (kame) *n*, junkie *P*.
camée[2] (kame) *m*, cameo.
caméléon (kameleɔ̃) *m*, chameleon.
camélia (kamelja) *m*, camellia.
camelot (kamlo) *m*, street vendor. **camelote** *P* (lɔt) *f*, rubbish, trash; goods, stuff.
caméra (kamera) *f*, (*Cine, T.V.*) camera; cinecamera.
camion (kamjɔ̃) *m*, lorry, van; (*Am.*) truck. ~-*citerne*, *m*, tanker [lorry]. ~ *de déménagement*, removal van. ~**nage** (ɔnaʒ) *m*, haulage. ~**neur** (nœr) *m*, lorry driver; road haulier.
camisole (kamizɔl) *f*, ~ *de force*, strait jacket.
camomille (kamɔmij) *f*, camomile.
camouflage (kamuflaʒ) *m*, camouflage. **camoufler** (fle) *v.t*, to camouflage; disguise; conceal.
camp (kɑ̃) *m*, camp; party, side. *changer de* ~, to change sides. ~ *volant*, camping trip; temporary stay.
campagnard, e (kɑ̃paɲar, ard) *n*, countryman, -woman. **campagne** (paɲ) *f*, country; countryside. *en pleine* ~, in the depths of the country. (*Mil., Pol*) campaign. *mener une* ~ *pour, contre*, to campaign for, against.
campagnol (kɑ̃paɲɔl) *m*, vole.
campanile (kɑ̃panil) *m*, campanile, bell tower.
campanule (kɑ̃panyl) *f*, campanula.
campement (kɑ̃pmɑ̃) *m*, camp, encampment. **camper** (pe) *v.i*, to camp. ¶ *v.t*, to encamp; put, clap, stick; sketch, portray (*character*). **se** ~, to plant o.s. **campeur, euse** (pœr, øz) *n*, camper. **camping** (piŋ) *m*, campsite; *le* ~, camping. *faire du* ~, to go camping.
camphre (kɑ̃fr) *m*, camphor.
campus (kɑ̃pys) *m*, campus.
camus, e (kamy, yz) *a*, pug-nosed.
Canada (le) (kanada), Canada. **canadien, ne** (djɛ̃, ɛn) *a*. & **C**~, *n*, Canadian.
canaille (kanɑj) *a*, coarse, crude. ¶ *f*, blackguard; bastard *P*; rascal (*child*). *la* ~, the rabble, riff-raff. ~**rie** (jri) *f*, coarseness; dirty trick.
canal (kanal) *m*, canal; channel; (*Anat.*) duct; (*T.V.*) channel. (*Adm.*) *par le* ~ *de qn*, through, via s.o. ~**isation** (lizasjɔ̃) *f*, canalization; piping, pipes (*house*); pipeline, main (*gas, water*). ~**iser** (ze) *v.t*, to channel; canalize.
canapé (kanape) *m*, sofa, settee; (*Cook.*) canapé. ~-*lit*, bed settee.
canard (kanar) *m*, duck, drake; (*Press*) rag *P*; false report; (*Mus.*) wrong note; *P* sugar dipped in drink. *mon petit* ~ *P*, pet *P*. ~ *de Barbarie*, Muscovy duck. ~**er** (narde) *v.t*, to snipe at; pelt (*avec*, with). ~**ière** (djɛr) *f*, duck pond.
canari (kanari) *m*, canary (*bird*). **les [îles] Canaries**, *f.pl*, the Canary Islands.
cancan (kɑ̃kɑ̃) *m*, cancan (*dance*). ~*s*, gossip, tittle-tattle. ~**er** (ane) *v.i*, to gossip.
cancer (kɑ̃sɛr) *m*, cancer. **cancéreux, euse** (serø, øz) *a*, cancerous. ¶ *n*, cancer case. **cancérigène** (riʒɛn) *a*, carcinogenic. **cancérologue** (rɔlɔg) *n*, cancer specialist.
cancre (kɑ̃kr) *m*, dunce.
cancrelat (kɑ̃krəla) *m*, cockroach.
candélabre (kɑ̃delɑbr) *m*, candelabra.
candeur (kɑ̃dœr) *f*, guilelessness, naivety.
candidat, e (kɑ̃dida, at) *n*, candidate; applicant (*à*, for). ~**ure** (tyr) *f*, candidature; application. *poser sa* ~ *à*, to apply for.
candide† (kɑ̃did) *a*, naive, ingenuous.
cane (kan) *f*, duck (*female*). **caner** *P* (ne) *v.i*, to funk it; chicken out. **caneton** (ntɔ̃) *m*, & **canette**[1] (nɛt) *f*, duckling. **canette**[2], *f*, bottle (*beer*).
canevas (kanvɑ) *m*, canvas; tapestry; outline, framework (*book &c*).
caniche (kaniʃ) *m*, poodle.
canicule (kanikyl) *f*, dog days; heatwave.
canif (kanif) *m*, penknife.
canin, e (kanɛ̃, in) *a*, canine, dog (*show*).
caniveau (kanivo) *m*, gutter (*road*).
canne (kan) *f*, walking stick; cane. ~ *à pêche*, fishing rod. ~ *à sucre*, sugar cane.
canneberge (kanbɛrʒ) *f*, cranberry.
cannelé, e (kanle) *a*, fluted (*column*).
cannelle (kanɛl) *f*, cinnamon.
cannelure (kanlyr) *f*, flute. ~*s*, fluting.
canner (kane) *v.t*, to cane (*chairs*).
cannibale (kanibal) *a*. & *n*, cannibal. **cannibalisme** (lism) *m*, cannibalism.
canoë (kanɔe) *m*, canoe. *faire du* ~, to canoe.
canon (kanɔ̃) *m*, (*Artil.*) gun; cannon; barrel; (*Eccl: law & Mus.*) canon. ~ *de campagne*, field gun. ~**ique** (nɔnik) *a*, canonical; venerable (*age*). ~**iser** (nize) *v.t*, to canonize. ~**nade** (nad) *f*, cannonade. ~**ner** (ne) *v.t*, to bombard, shell. ~**nier** (nje) *m*, gunner. ~**nière** (njɛr) *f*, gunboat.
canot (kano) *m*, boat; dinghy. ~ *automobile*, motor boat. ~ *de sauvetage*, lifeboat. ~**age** (nɔtaʒ) *m*, boating, rowing. *faire du* ~, = ~*er*. ~**er** (te) *v.i*, to go boating, rowing. ~**ier** (tje) *m*, boater (*hat*).
cantate (kɑ̃tat) *f*, cantata. **cantatrice** (tris) *f*, singer (*opera, classical*).
cantine (kɑ̃tin) *f*, canteen; tin trunk. **cantinier, ère** (nje, ɛr) *n*, canteen keeper.

cantique (kɑ̃tik) *m,* hymn.
canton (kɑ̃tɔ̃) *m,* canton, district. ~**ade** (tɔnad) *f, à la* ~, for all the world to hear. ~**nement** (nmɑ̃) *m,* (*Mil.*) quarters, billet; billeting. ~**ner** (ne) *v.t,* (*Mil.*) to quarter, billet. *se* ~ *dans,* to withdraw to; confine o.s to. ~**nier** (nje) *m,* roadman.
canular (kanylar) *m,* hoax.
caoutchouc (kautʃu) *m,* rubber; rubber *or* elastic band; raincoat. ~ *mousse,* foam rubber. **caoutchouter** (ʃute) *v.t,* to rubberize.
cap (kap) *m,* cape, headland, point. *doubler un* ~, to round a point; (*fig.*) get over a hump. (*Naut.*) *mettre le* ~ *sur,* to head for. *changer de* ~, to change course. *le* ~ *de Bonne-Espérance,* the Cape of Good Hope.
capable (kapabl) *a,* capable (*de faire,* of doing); able, efficient; qualified. **capacité** (site) *f,* (*gen.*) capacity; ability (*à faire,* to do); efficiency (*pers.*).
cape (kap) *f,* cape; cloak. *rire sous* ~, to laugh up one's sleeve.
capharnaüm (kafarnaɔm) *m,* junk room; mess.
capillaire (kapillɛr) *a,* capillary; hair (*lotion*). ¶ *m,* (*Anat.*) capillary.
capilotade (kapilɔtad) *f,* pulp.
capitaine (kapitɛn) *m,* (*Mil., Naut., Sport*) captain; [military] leader. ~ *au long cours,* master mariner. (*Nav.*) ~ *de corvette,* lieutenant commander. ~ *de frégate,* commander. ~ *de port,* harbour master.
capital, e (kapital) *a,* main, major; capital, essential, cardinal; deadly (*sins*). *peine* ~*e,* capital punishment. ¶ *m,* (*Fin.*) capital; (*fig.*) fund, stock. ~*aux,* funds. *le* ~ *& le travail,* capital & labour. ~ *d'exploitation,* working c. ¶ *f,* capital [city]; capital (*letter*). ~*s d'imprimerie,* block capitals. ~**iser** (lize) *v.t. & i,* to accumulate; save. ~**isme** (lism) *m,* capitalism. ~**iste** (list) *a. & n,* capitalist.
capiteux, euse (kapitø, øz) *a,* heady (*wine*).
capitonner (kapitɔne) *v.t,* to pad; quilt.
capituler (kapityle) *v.i,* to capitulate.
caporal (kapɔral) *m,* corporal.
capot (kapo) *m,* (*Mot.*) bonnet, (*Am.*) hood. **capote** (pɔt) *f,* (*Mot.*) hood, (*Am.*) cover; (*Mil.*) greatcoat. ~ *anglaise P,* French letter *P.* **capoter** (te) *v.i,* to overturn.
câpre (kapr) *f,* (*Cook.*) caper.
caprice (kapris) *m,* caprice, whim, [passing] fancy; vagary; freak (*of fortune*). *faire une* ~, to throw a tantrum. **capricieux, euse**† (sjø, øz) *a,* capricious, whimsical; temperamental, wayward.
capsule (kapsyl) *f,* (*gen.*) capsule; bottle top.
capter (kapte) *v.t,* to win, gain (*confidence, votes*); pick up (*signal*); harness (*river*).
captif, ive (kaptif, iv) *a. & n,* captive. **captiver** (ve) *v.t,* to captivate. **captivité** (vite) *f,* captivity. **capture** (tyr) *f,* capture; catch, prize. **capturer** (tyre) *v.t,* to capture, catch.
capuche (kapyʃ) *f,* hood. **capuchon** (ʃɔ̃) *m,* hood, cowl; hooded coat; cap (*pen*).
capucin, e (kapysɛ̃, in) *n,* Capuchin friar, nun; (*f.*) nasturtium.
caque (kak) *f,* herring barrel.
caquet (kakɛ) *m,* cackle (*hen*); chatter. **caqueter** (kte) *v.i,* to cackle; chatter.
car (kar) *c,* for, because.
carabin *P* (karabɛ̃) *m,* medical student.
carabine (karabin) *f,* carbine, rifle. **carabiné, e** (ne) *a,* stiff (*drink, fine*).
caractère (karaktɛr) *m,* character, nature. *avoir bon, mauvais* ~, to be good-, bad-tempered. characteristic, feature; (*Typ.*) letter, character. ~*s gras,* bold type. ~*s d'imprimerie,* block capitals. **caractériel, le** (terjɛl) *a,* character, emotional (*problems*). ¶ *n,* disturbed *or* problem child. **caractériser** (terize) *v.t,* to characterize. **caractéristique** (ristik) *a,* characteristic. ¶ *f,* characteristic, feature.
carafe (karaf) *f,* carafe; decanter. **carafon** (fɔ̃) *m,* small carafe.
caraïbe (karaib) *a,* Caribbean. *les C*~*s,* the Caribbean.
carambolage (karɑ̃bɔlaʒ) *m,* (*Bil.*) cannon; (*Mot.*) pile-up. **caramboler** (le) *v.i,* (*Bil.*) to cannon. **se** ~, (*Mot.*) to collide, pile up.
caramel (karamɛl) *m,* caramel.
carapace (karapas) *f,* carapace, shell.
carat (kara) *m,* carat.
caravane (karavan) *f,* caravan. **caravanier** (vanje) *m,* caravanner. **caravaning** (niŋ) *m,* caravanning.
carbonate (karbɔnat) *m,* carbonate. **carbone** (bɔn) *m,* carbon. **carbonifère** (nifɛr) *a,* carboniferous. **carbonique** (nik) *a,* carbonic. **carboniser** (ze) *v.t,* to carbonize, char; burn to a cinder (*meat*).
carburant (karbyrɑ̃) *m,* (*Mot.*) fuel. **carburateur** (ratœr) *m,* carburettor. **carbure** (byr) *m,* carbide. **carburer** (re) *v.i,* (*Mot., fig.*) ~ *bien, mal,* to be running well, badly.
carcan (karkɑ̃) *m,* (*Hist.*) iron collar; (*fig.*) yoke.
carcasse (karkas) *f,* carcass; frame[work]; (*Build.*) skeleton, shell.
cardiaque (kardjak) *a,* cardiac. *crise* ~, heart attack. ¶ *n,* heart case (*pers.*).
cardinal, e (kardinal) *a,* cardinal. ¶ *m,* (*Eccl.*) cardinal.
cardiologie (kardjɔlɔʒi) *f,* cardiology. **cardiologue** (lɔg) *n,* heart specialist, cardiologist.
carême (karɛm) *m,* fast. (*Eccl.*) *le C*~, Lent.
carence (karɑ̃s) *f,* shortage, deficiency; incompetence.
carène (karɛn) *f,* hull (*ship*). **caréner** (rene) *v.t,* to careen (*ship*); streamline.
caresse (karɛs) *f,* caress. **caresser** (se) *v.t,* to caress; fondle; stroke (*animal*); toy with (*idea*). ~ *du regard,* look lovingly at.

cargaison (kargɛzɔ̃) *f,* cargo, freight. **cargo** (kargo) *m,* cargo boat, freighter.
caricature (karikatyr) *f,* caricature; cartoon; (*P pers.*) fright *P*. **caricaturer** (tyre) *v.t,* to caricature. **caricaturiste** (rist) *n,* caricaturist, cartoonist.
carie (kari) *f,* caries, (*dental*) decay. **carier** (rje) *v.t.* & **se ~,** to decay.
carillon (karijɔ̃) *m,* peal of bells; chimes; chiming clock. **~ner** (jɔne) *v.i,* to ring, chime. ¶ *v.t,* to chime (*hours*); noise abroad (*news*). **~neur** (nœr) *m,* bell ringer.
carlingue (karlɛ̃g) *f,* (*Aero.*) cabin.
carmin (karmɛ̃) *a.inv.* & *m,* carmine.
carnage (karnaʒ) *m,* carnage, slaughter. **carnassier, ère** (nasje, ɛr) *a,* carnivorous. ¶ *m,* carnivore. ¶ *f,* game-bag.
carnaval, *pl.* **~s** (karnaval) *m,* carnival.
carnet (karnɛ), *m,* notebook; book (*cheques, tickets, stamps*). *~ d'adresses,* address book. *~ d'autobus,* book of bus tickets.
carnivore (karnivɔr) *a,* carnivorous. ¶ *m,* carnivore.
caroncule (karɔ̃kyl) *f,* wattle (*turkey*).
carotide (karɔtid) *a.* & *m,* carotid.
carotte (karɔt) *f,* carrot; (*Min.*) bore core; plug (*tobacco*). ¶ *a. inv,* [*rouge*] *~*, carroty (*hair*). **carotter** *P* (te) *v.t,* to swindle, do *P;* pinch, nick *P.*
carpe (karp) *f,* carp (*fish*).
carpette (karpɛt) *f,* rug.
carquois (karkwɑ) *m,* quiver (*arrows*).
carré, e (kare) *a,* square. *mètre ~*, square metre. forthright (*pers.*); straight (*answer*). ¶ *m,* (*gen.*) square; patch (*land*); (*Naut.*) wardroom. (*Math.*) *5 au ~*, 5 squared. *élever au ~*, to square (*number*). ¶ *P f,* room, pad *P.* **carreau** (ro) *m,* [floor] tile; [tiled] floor; [window] pane; check (*pattern*). *à ~x,* checked. (*Cards*) diamond. **carrefour** (karfur) *m,* crossroads; (*fig.*) forum. **carrelage** (rlaʒ) *m,* tiling; tiled floor. **carreler** (le) *v.t,* to tile. **carrelet** (rlɛ) *m,* plaice. **carrément** (remɑ̃) *ad,* (*tell*) straight [out]; (*go*) straight, direct; definitely. **carrer (se)** (re) *v.pr,* to settle o.s (*dans,* in).
carrière[1] (karjɛr) *f,* career. (*Mil.*) *de ~*, regular. *faire ~ dans,* to make one's career in. *donner ~ à,* to give full play to. **carrière**[2], *f,* quarry, sandpit.
carrosse (karɔs) *m,* [horse-drawn] coach. **~rie** (sri) *f,* (*Mot.*) body, coachwork; coachbuilding. **carrossier** (sje) *m,* coachbuilder.
carrousel (karuzɛl) *m,* carrousel; (*fig.*) merry-go-round.
cartable (kartabl) *m,* satchel; school bag.
carte (kart) *f,* card. *~ [à jouer],* [playing] card; (*Rly*) *~ [d'abonnement],* season ticket. map, chart; menu. *jouer aux ~s,* to play cards. *avoir ~ blanche,* to have a free hand. *tirer les ~s à qn,* to read s.o's cards. *repas à la ~*, à la carte meal. *~ de crédit, d'identité, de visite,* credit, identity, visiting card. *~ d'état-major* ≏ Ordnance Survey map. *~ grise,* logbook (*car*). *~ de lecteur,* library ticket. *~ perforée* punched card. *~ postale,* postcard. *~ routière,* roadmap. *~ des vins,* wine list.
cartel (kartɛl) *m,* (*Econ., Pol.*) cartel; wall clock.
carter (kartɛr) *m,* (*Mach.*) housing; (*Mot.*) crankcase, sump; chain guard (*cycle*).
cartilage (kartilaʒ) *m,* cartilage; gristle.
cartographe (kartɔgraf) *m,* cartographer.
cartomancien, ne (kartɔmɑ̃sjɛ̃, ɛn) *n,* fortune teller (*by cards*).
carton (kartɔ̃) *m,* cardboard; [cardboard] box, carton; sketch; [rifle] target. *~ à chapeaux,* hat box. *~ à dessin,* portfolio. (*Art, Phot.*) *~ de montage,* mount. *~-pâte,* pasteboard. **~nage** (ɔnaʒ) *m,* (*Ind.*) packing; binding in boards (*book*). **~né, e** (tɔne) *a,* hardback (*book*).
cartouche (kartuʃ) *f,* (*gen.*) cartridge; round [of ammunition]. *~ à blanc,* blank c. ¶ *m,* (*Arch.*) cartouche. **~rie** (ʃri) *f,* cartridge factory. **cartouchière** (ʃjɛr) *f,* cartridge pouch; c. belt.
cas (kɑ) *m,* (*gen.*) case; instance; occurrence; situation. *en ce ~*, in that case. *en tout ~*, in any c. *en aucun ~*, on no account. *le ~ échéant,* should the case arise. *en ~ de besoin,* if need be. *en ~ d'urgence,* in an emergency. *faire [grand] ~ de, peu de ~ de,* to set great, little store by. *~ de conscience,* matter of conscience. *~ limite,* borderline case.
casanier, ère (kazanje, ɛr) *a.* & *n,* stay-at-home.
casaque (kazak) *f,* jockey's blouse. *tourner ~*, to change sides, rat *P.*
cascade (kaskad) *f,* cascade, waterfall; (*fig.*) torrent. **cascadeur** (dœr) *m,* (*Cine*) stuntman.
case (kɑz) *f,* compartment; pigeonhole; square (*chessboard*); frame, space (*printed form*); native hut, cabin.
caser (kɑze) *v.t,* to put away; find a husband, wife, job for; put up, house. **se ~,** to settle down. **caserne** (kazɛrn) *f,* barrack. *~ de pompiers,* fire station. **caserner** (ne) *v.t,* to barrack.
casier (kɑzje) *m,* [set of] pigeonholes; cabinet (*drawers*); pigeonhole; locker. *~ à bouteilles,* bottle rack. *~ judiciaire,* police record.
casino (kazino) *m,* casino.
casque (kask) *m,* helmet; crash helmet; headphones, headset; [hair-]drier. **casqué, e** (ke) *a,* wearing a helmet. **casquette** (kɛt) *f,* [peaked] cap.
cassant, e (kɑsɑ̃, ɑ̃t) *a,* brittle; abrupt, curt (*tone*). **cassation** (sasjɔ̃) *f,* (*Law*) cassation; (*Mil.*) reduction to the ranks.
casse (kɑs) *f,* breaking; breakages, damage. ¶ *prefix* (*all inv.*): **~-cou,** *n,* daredevil, reckless

person. ~**-croûte,** *m,* snack. ~**-gueule** *P, a.* (*& m*), dangerous, dicey *P* (business). ~**-noisettes,** ~**-noix,** *m,* nutcrackers. ~**-pieds** *P, n,* crashing bore. ~**-tête,** club; brain teaser.
casser (kɑse) *v.t,* to break, crack, snap; (*Law*) quash, annul; (*Mil.*) cashier; reduce to the ranks. *ça ne casse rien P,* it's no great shakes *P.* ~ *la croûte P,* to have a snack. ~ *la figure* (*la gueule P*) *à qn,* to beat s.o up. ~ *les pieds à qn,* to bore s.o stiff; get on s.o's nerves. ~ *sa pipe P,* to snuff it *P. à tout* ~ *P, a,* stupendous; *ad,* at the most. ¶ *v.i.* & **se** ~, to break. *se* ~ *le bras,* to b. one's arm. *se* ~ *la figure P,* to come a cropper; smash o.s up. *se* ~ *la tête,* to rack one's brains.
casserole (kasrɔl) *f,* saucepan.
cassette (kasɛt) *f,* casket; cassette (*tape*).
casseur (kɑsœr) *m,* breaker. (*P*) tough guy *P.*
cassis (kɑsis) *m,* blackcurrant (*fruit, bush, drink*); (*P head*) nut *P.*
cassonade (kasɔnad) *f,* brown sugar.
cassure (kɑsyr) *f,* break, crack.
castagnettes (kastaɲɛt) *f.pl,* castanets.
caste (kast) *f,* caste.
castor (kastɔr) *m,* beaver.
castration (kastrasjɔ̃) *f,* castration; gelding. **castrer** (re) *v.t,* to castrate; geld (*horse*); neuter (*cat*).
casuistique (kɑzɥistik) *f,* casuistry.
cataclysme (kataklism) *m,* cataclysm.
catacombes (katakɔ̃b) *f.pl,* catacombs.
catafalque (katafalk) *m,* catafalque.
catalogue (katalɔg) *m,* catalogue, list. **cataloguer** (ge) *v.t,* to catalogue, list.
cataplasme (kataplasm) *m,* poultice.
catapulte (katapylt) *f,* catapult. **catapulter** (te) *v.t,* to catapult.
cataracte (katarakt) *f,* (*Med. & falls*) cataract.
catarrhe (katar) *m,* catarrh.
catastrophe (katastrɔf) *f,* catastrophe. **catastropher** *P* (fe) *v.t,* to shatter, stun.
catéchiser (kateʃize) *v.t,* to catechize. **catéchisme** (ʃism) *m,* catechism.
catégorie (kategɔri) *f,* category, class. **catégorique**† (rik) *a,* categorical; flat (*refusal*).
cathédrale (katedral) *f,* cathedral.
cathode (katɔd) *f,* cathode.
catholicisme (katɔlisism) *m,* [Roman] Catholicism. **catholique** (lik) *a. & n,* [Roman] Catholic.
catimini (katimini) *ad, en* ~, on the sly.
Caucase (le) (kokɑz), the Caucasus.
cauchemar (koʃmar) *m,* nightmare.
causant, e (kosɑ̃, ɑ̃t) *a,* chatty, talkative.
cause (koz) *f,* cause, reason; (*Law*) case, action. ~ *célèbre,* famous case. brief. *sans* ~, briefless (*barrister*). *faire* ~ *commune avec,* to make common cause with. *être en* ~, to be involved, at stake, in question. *mettre en* ~, to call into question. **à** ~ **de,** on account of, because of. *en tout état de* ~, in any event. & *pour* ~, & for good reason. **causer**[1] (koze) *v.t,* to cause.
causer[2] (koze) *v.i,* to talk, chat (*de,* about). ~ *politique,* to talk politics. **causerie** (zri) *f,* talk (*lecture*); chat. **causette** (zɛt) *f,* little chat. **causeur, euse** (zœr, øz) *a,* talkative. ¶ *n,* talker.
caustique (kostik) *a,* (*Chem., fig.*) caustic.
cauteleux, euse (kotlø, øz) *a,* wily, crafty.
cautériser (koterize) *v.t,* to cauterize.
caution (kosjɔ̃) *f,* guarantee; (*Pol.*) backing; (*Fin.*) security, guarantee; (*Law*) bail. *se porter* ~, to stand surety. *sujet à* ~, unconfirmed, questionable. ~**nement** (ɔnmɑ̃) *m,* security (*sum*); surety bond; (*Pol*) support, backing. ~**ner** (ne) *v.t,* to guarantee; (*Pol.*) support, back (*pers., policy*).
cavalcade (kavalkad) *f,* rush, stampede; cavalcade.
cavaler *P* (kavale) *v.i,* to run. **se** ~, to clear off.
cavalerie (kavalri) *f,* cavalry. **cavalier, ère**† (lje, ɛr) *a,* offhand, cavalier; riding. *piste* ~*ère,* bridle path. ¶ *n,* rider, horseman, woman; partner (*at dance*). ¶ *m,* (*Mil.*) trooper, cavalryman; (*Chess*) knight.
cave (kav) *f,* cellar, vault. ¶ *a,* hollow, sunken (*cheeks*). **caveau** (kavo) *m,* small cellar; vault, tomb. **caverne** (vɛrn) *f,* cavern, cave. **caverneux, euse** (nø, øz) *a,* cavernous (*voice*).
caviar (kavjar) *m,* caviar.
cavité (kavite) *f,* cavity, hollow.
ce, cet, *m. before vowel or mute h,* **cette,** *f,* **ces,** *pl.* (sə, sɛt, sɛt, se) *dem. a,* this, these; that, those. *cette rue*[*-ci*], [*-là*], this, that street. *ce soir,* this evening. *cette nuit,* tonight; last night. *un de ces jours,* one of these days.
ce (sɛ), **c',** *dem. pn,* it, that. *qui est-ce? c'est un collègue,* who's that? he's *or* that's a colleague. *c'est une actrice,* she's an actress. *c'est moi, lui &c,* it's I, he (me, him *P*) &c. *c'est eux P* or *ce sont eux qui ont tort,* it's they who are wrong. *ce doit être Paul,* it, that must be P. **ce qui, ce que,** what. *je sais ce qui se passe, ce que tu penses,* I know what's happening, what you think. *ce qui est amusant c'est que.* the amusing thing is that . .
ceci (səsi) *dem. pn,* this.
cécité (sesite) *f,* blindness.
céder (sede) *v.t,* to give up, hand over; transfer (*property*). ~ *le pas à,* (*lit., fig.*) to give way to. *le* ~ *à qn,* to be inferior to s.o (*en,* in). ¶ *v.i,* to give in; yield (*à,* to); (*dam, branch*) give way.
cédille (sedij) *f,* cedilla.
cèdre (sɛdr) *m,* cedar.
ceindre (sɛ̃dr) *v.t.ir,* (*liter.*) to surround, encircle (*de,* with); gird on (*sword*).

ceinture (sɛ̃tyr), *f,* belt; sash; waistband; waist; ring, belt (*trees &c*); circle line (*metro*). *se mettre la ~ P,* (*fig.*) to tighten one's belt. ~ *de sauvetage,* life b. ~ *de sécurité,* safety belt (*car*). **ceinturer** (tyre) *v.t,* to seize round the waist; encircle. **ceinturon** (rɔ̃) *m,* (*Mil.*) belt.

cela (səla, sla), **ça** (sa) *dem. pn,* that, it. ~ *est vrai,* that's true. *c'est ça,* that's right. *quand ça? où ça?* when, where was that? *ça alors!* well I never! *rien que ça?* is that all?

célèbre (selɛbr) *a,* famous, celebrated (*par,* for). **célébrer** (lebre) *v.t,* to celebrate (*mass, birthday*); hold (*funeral*); extol. **célébrite** (brite) *f,* celebrity.

céleri (selri) *m,* celery.

célérité (selerite) *f,* speed, promptness.

céleste (selɛst) *a,* celestial, heavenly.

célibat (seliba) *m,* single life; celibacy. **célibataire** (tɛr) *a,* celibate; single, unmarried. ¶ *n,* single man, woman; bachelor, b. girl; (*f*) spinster.

cellier (lje) *m,* storeroom (*food & wine*).

cellophane (sɛlɔfan) *f,* cellophane.

cellulaire (sɛlylɛr) *a,* cellular. *voiture ~,* police van. **cellule** (lyl) *f,* cell. **cellulite** (lit) *f,* cellulitis. **celluloïd** (lɔid) *m,* celluloid. **cellulose** (loz) *f,* (loz) *f,* cellulose.

celte (sɛlt) *a,* celtic. ¶ *n,* **C~,** Celt. **celtique** (tik) *a. & m.* (*language*), Celtic.

celui, *m,* **celle,** *f,* **ceux, celles,** *pl.* (səlɥi, sɛl, sø, sɛl) *dem. pn, celui-ci, celle-ci,* this one; the latter. *celui-là, celle-là,* that one; the former. ~ **qui,** ~ **que &c,** the one that, who, whom &c. ~ *dont tu m'as parlé,* the one you told me about. ~ **de:** *ma voiture & celle de ma fille,* my car & my daughter's.

cénacle (senakl) *f,* [literary] set, coterie.

cendre (sɑ̃dr) *f. oft. pl,* ash[es], cinders; embers. *le jour des C~s,* Ash Wednesday. **cendré, e** (sɑ̃dre) *a,* ashen; grey. *blond ~,* ash blond. ¶ *f,* cinder track. **cendrier** (drie) *m,* ash tray; ash pan (*stove*).

Cendrillon (sɑ̃drijɔ̃) *f,* Cinderella.

Cène (sɛn) *f, la ~,* the Last Supper.

cénotaphe (senɔtaf) *m,* cenotaph.

censé, e (sɑ̃se) *a, être ~ faire qch,* to be supposed to do sth. **censément** (mɑ̃) *ad,* supposedly; virtually. **censeur** (sœr) *m,* censor; (*Sch.*) ≃ deputy head. **censure** (syr) *f,* censorship; [vote of] censure; [board of] censors. **censurer** (syre) *v.t,* to censor; censure.

cent (sɑ̃) *a. & m,* a hundred. *deux ~ dix,* 210. *deux cents francs,* 200 francs. *ordinal inv: la page deux ~,* page 200. *faire les ~ pas,* to pace up & down. **centaine** (tɛn) *f,* hundred [or so], about a hundred.

centaure (sɑ̃tɔr) *m,* centaur.

centenaire (sɑ̃tnɛr), *a,* 100 years old. ¶ *n,* centenarian. ¶ *m,* centenary.

centième (sɑ̃tjɛm) *a. & m,* hundredth.

centigrade (sɑ̃tigrad) *a,* centigrade. **centigramme** (gram) *m,* centigramme. **centilitre** (litr) *m,* centilitre. **centime** (tim) *m,* centime. **centimètre** (mɛtr) *m,* centimetre; tape measure.

central, e (sɑ̃tral) *a,* central; main, head (*office*). ¶ *m,* ~ [*téléphonique*], [telephone] exchange. ¶ *f,* ~*e* [*électrique*], power station. ~*e ouvrière,* group of trade unions. ~**iser** (lize) *v.t,* to centralize.

centre (sɑ̃tr) *m,* (*gen.*) centre. *le C~,* central France. ~*-ville,* town *or* city centre. ~ *commercial,* shopping c. ~ *hospitalier,* hospital complex. ~ *de tri,* [postal] sorting office. **centrer** (tre) *v.t,* (*Sport, Tech.*) to centre. ¶ *v.i,* to centre (*sur,* on). **centrifuge** (trifyʒ) *a,* centrifugal. **centripète** (pɛt) *a,* centripetal.

centuple (sɑ̃typl) *m,* centuple, hundredfold.

cep (sɛp) *m,* vine stock. **cépage** (sepaʒ) *m,* type of vine.

cependant (səpɑ̃dɑ̃) *c,* yet, still, nevertheless. ¶ *ad,* (*liter.*) meanwhile.

céramique (seramik) *f,* ceramics, pottery; ceramic vase, pot.

cerceau (sɛrso) *m,* hoop.

cercle (sɛrkl) *m,* circle, ring; hoop, band; circle (*friends &c*); club; (*fig.*) sphere, range. ~ *d'influence,* sphere of influence. ~ *vicieux,* vicious circle. **cercler** (kle) *v.t,* to ring; hoop (*cask*).

cercueil (sɛrkœj) *m,* coffin.

céréale (sereal) *f,* cereal.

cérébral, e (serebral) *a,* (*Med.*) cerebral; mental, brain (*work*).

cérémonial (seremɔnjal) *m,* ceremonial. **cérémonie** (ni) *f,* ceremony; formality. *sans ~,* simply, informally. **cérémonieux, euse**† (njø, øz) *a,* ceremonious, formal.

cerf (sɛr & sɛrf) *m,* stag.

cerfeuil (sɛrfœj) *m,* chervil.

cerf-volant (sɛrvɔlɑ̃) *m,* kite (*toy*).

cerisaie (sərizɛ) *f,* cherry orchard. **cerise** (riz) *f,* cherry. ¶ *a. inv,* cherry-red, cerise. **cerisier** (rizje) *m,* cherry tree.

cerne (sɛrn) *m,* ring. **cerner** (ne) *v.t,* to surround, encircle; delimit (*subject*); ring (*tree*). *avoir les yeux cernés,* to have rings under the eyes.

certain, e (sɛrtɛ̃, ɛn) *a,* certain; sure. *je le tiens pour ~,* I'm sure of it. (*before n*): *une ~e valeur,* a certain value. *dans ~s cas,* in some *or* certain cases. *d'un ~ âge,* getting on. ~**ement** (tɛnmɑ̃) *ad,* certainly. **certes** (sɛrt) *ad,* most certainly, indeed; of course.

certificat (sɛrtifika) *m,* certificate; diploma; testimonial. ~ *d'aptitude pédagogique,* teaching diploma. **certifier** (fje) *v.t,* to certify; witness (*signature*); guarantee. ~ *qch à qn,* assure s.o of sth.

certitude (sertityd) *f*, certainty. *j'en ai la ~*, I'm sure of it.
cerveau (sɛrvo) *m*, brain; brains, mind. (*fig: pers.*) *le ~ de l'affaire*, the brain behind it all. **cervelle** (vɛl) *f*, brain[s]; head; (*Cook.*) brains. *se creuser la ~*, to rack one's brains. *se brûler la ~*, to blow one's brains out.
Cervin (sɛrvɛ̃), *le ~*, the Matterhorn.
cessation (sɛsasjɔ̃) *f*, cessation; suspension. **cesse** (sɛs), *f*, *sans ~*, continually, incessantly; continuously. **cesser** (se) *v.t*, to stop, end, break off. *~ de faire*, to stop *or* cease doing. ¶ *v.i*, to stop, cease, end. *faire ~*, to put a stop to. **cessez-le-feu,** *m*, ceasefire.
cession (sɛsjɔ̃) *f*, transfer. **cessionnaire** (ɔnɛr) *n*, transferee.
c'est-à-dire (sɛtadir) *ad*, that is [to say]. *~ que*, which means that; actually.
Ceylan (selɑ̃) *m*, Ceylon.
chacal (ʃakal) *m*, jackal.
chacun, e (ʃakœ̃, yn) *pn*, each, each one, every one. *~ d'entre vous*, each of you. *3 francs ~*, 3 francs each. ¶ *m*, everybody, everyone. *~ pour soi*, every man for himself.
chagrin[1], **e** (ʃagrɛ̃, in) *a*, sad, woeful; morose, disgruntled. ¶ *m*, grief, sorrow. *~ d'amour*, disappointment in love. **chagrin**[2], *m*, shagreen. **chagriner** (grine) *v.t*, to grieve, distress; worry, trouble.
chahut (ʃay) *m*, (*Sch.*) uproar, rumpus *P*. **~er** (te) *v.i*, to make a row; fool about, rag. ¶ *v.t*, to rag, play up (*teacher*). **~eux, euse** (tø, øz) *a*, rowdy, unruly.
chaîne (ʃɛn) *f*, chain; range (*hills*); warp (*cloth*); (*Radio, T.V.*) channel; system (*hi-fi*). *~s*, (*fig.*) fetters, bonds. (*Ind.*) *~ de fabrication*, production line. *produire à la ~*, to mass-produce. **chaînette** (nɛt) *f*, [small] chain. **chaînon** (nɔ̃) *m*, (*lit., fig.*) link.
chair (ʃɛr) *f. sometimes pl*, flesh; pulp (*fruit*). *en ~ & en os*, in the flesh. *~ à canon*, cannon-fodder. *~ de poule*, (*fig.*) goose flesh. *ça vous donne la ~ de poule*, it makes your flesh creep.
chaire (ʃɛr) *f*, pulpit; rostrum; (*Univ.*) chair. *la ~ de Saint Pierre*, the Chair of St. Peter.
chaise (ʃɛz) *f*, chair. *~ de bébé*, high chair. *~ de jardin*, garden c. *~ longue*, deck c. *~ à porteurs*, sedan c.
chaland (ʃalɑ̃) *m*, barge; lighter.
châle (ʃɑl) *m*, shawl.
chalet (ʃɑlɛ) *m*, chalet; cottage.
chaleur (ʃalœr) *f*, (*lit, fig.*) heat, warmth; fervour. *les grandes ~s*, the heat of summer. '*craint la ~*', 'keep in a cool place'. **~eux, euse**† (lœrø, øz) *a*, warm (*welcome*).
chaloupe (ʃalup) *f*, launch; (*Hist.*) longboat.
chalumeau (ʃalymo) *m*, (*Tech.*) blowlamp; drinking straw; [shepherd's] pipe.
chalut (ʃaly) *m*, trawl [net]. *pêcher au ~*, to trawl. **chalutier** (tje) *m*, trawler.
chamailler (se) (ʃamaje) *v.pr*, to bicker, squabble. **chamaillerie** (jri) *f*, squabble.
chamarré (ʃamare) *a*, bedecked (*de*, with).
chambard *P* (ʃɑ̃bar) *m*, uproar, rumpus *P*. **~er** *P* (de) *v.t*, to turn upside down; wreck.
chambranle (ʃɑ̃brɑ̃l) *m*, frame (*door, window*); mantlepiece.
chambouler *P* (ʃɑ̃bule) *v.t*, to turn upside down; mess up.
chambre (ʃɑ̃br) *f*, bedroom. *~ à un lit*, single room. *O* room, chamber; (*Pol.*) Chamber, House; (*Law*) court, division; (*Tech.*) chamber. *~ à air*, inner tube. *~ d'amis*, spare room. (*Mot.*) *~ de combustion*, combustion chamber. *~ de commerce*, Chamber of Commerce. *C~ des Communes, des Lords*, House of Commons, of Lords. *C~ des députés*, Chamber of Deputies. *~ forte*, strongroom. *~ froide*, cold store. *~ à gaz*, gas chamber. (*Naut.*) *~ des machines*, engine room. (*Phot.*) *~ noire*, dark room. **chambrée** (ʃɑ̃bre) *f*, [barrack-]room (*occupants*). **chambrer** (bre) *v.t*, to bring to room temperature (*wine*); corner, collar *P* (*pers.*).
chameau (ʃamo) *m*, camel; (*pej: pers.*) beast. **chamelier** (məlje) *m*, camel driver. **chamelle** (mɛl) *f*, she camel.
chamois (ʃamwa) *m*, chamois. [*peau de*] *~*, wash leather, chamois l., shammy.
champ (ʃɑ̃) *m*, field. *les ~s*, the country[side]. *fleurs des ~s*, wild flowers. *à travers ~s*, across the fields. (*fig.*) field (*study &c*); scope, freedom, elbow room; (*Phot. &c*) field of view. *laisser le ~ libre à qn*, to leave s.o a clear field. *~ d'action*, sphere of activity. *~ d'aviation*, airfield. *~ de bataille*, battlefield. *~ de courses*, racecourse. *~ de foire*, fairground. *~ magnétique*, magnetic field. *~ de manœuvre*, parade ground. *~ de tir*, rifle range; field of fire.
champagne (ʃɑ̃paɲ) *m*, champagne. *la C~*, Champagne (*region*). **champenois, e** (pənwa, waz) *a*, of Champagne. *méthode ~e*, c. method.
champêtre (ʃɑ̃pɛtr) *a*, rural, country (*life*).
champignon (ʃɑ̃piɲɔ̃) *m*, mushroom. *~ [vénéneux]*, toadstool; fungus; *P* accelerator.
champion, ne (ʃɑ̃pjɔ̃, ɔn) *a. P*, first-rate. ¶ *n*, champion. **~nat** (ɔna) *m*, championship.
chance (ʃɑ̃s) *f*, [good] luck. *bonne ~!* good luck! *pas de ~!* bad luck! *il a de la ~*, he's lucky. *tenter sa ~*, to try one's luck. *~[s]*, chance. *il a toutes les ~s de gagner*, he has every chance of winning.
chancelant, e (ʃɑ̃slɑ̃, ɑ̃t) *a*, unsteady; faltering; shaky.
chanceler (ʃɑ̃sle) *v.i*, to totter; waver, falter.
chancelier (ʃɑ̃səlje) *m*, chancellor. *C~ de l'Echiquier*, C. of the Exchequer. **chancellerie** (sɛlri)

f, chancellery.
chanceux, euse (ʃɑ̃sø, øz) *a,* lucky.
chancre (ʃɑ̃kr) *m,* (*Med.*) canker; chancre.
chandail (ʃɑ̃daj) *m,* sweater, jersey.
chandelier (ʃɑ̃dəlje) *m,* candlestick. **chandelle** (dɛl) *f,* candle; (*Ten.*) lob. *voir trente-six ~s,* to see stars.
change (ʃɑ̃ʒ) *m,* (*Fin.*) exchange. *perdre, gagner au ~,* to lose, gain on the deal. *donner le ~ à qn,* to put s.o off the scent. **changeant, e** (ʃɑ̃ʒɑ̃, ɑ̃t) *a,* changeable; fickle. **changement** (ʒmɑ̃) *m,* change, alteration. *~ de décor,* change of scenery; (*Theat.*) scene-change. *~ de temps,* c. in the weather. (*Mus.*) *~ de ton,* c. of key. (*Mot.*) *~ de vitesse,* gears; gear lever; g. change. *~ à vue,* transformation scene.
changer (ʃɑ̃ʒe) *v.t,* to change, alter. *~* **de,** to change. *~ d'avis,* to change one's mind. (*Naut.*) *~ de cap,* to c. course. *~ de place avec qn,* to c. places with s.o. *~ de train,* to c. trains. ¶ *v.i,* to change (*en bien, en mal,* for the better, worse). **se ~,** to change [one's clothes]. **changeur** (ʒœr) *m,* money changer.
chanoine (ʃanwan) *m,* (*Eccl.*) canon.
chanson (ʃɑ̃sɔ̃) *f,* song. *c'est toujours la même ~,* it's the same old story. *~ folklorique,* folk song. *~***nette** (ɔnɛt) *f,* ditty; comic song. *~***nier** (nje) *m,* cabaret singer, chansonnier.
chant (ʃɑ̃) *m,* singing; song; chant. *~ du coq,* cockcrow. (*fig.*) *~ du cygne,* swan song. *~ de Noël,* [Christmas] carol. *professeur de ~,* singing teacher. **de ~,** edgeways, on edge.
chantage (ʃɑ̃taʒ) *m,* blackmail.
chantant, e (ʃɑ̃tɑ̃, ɑ̃t) *a,* tuneful (*music*); singing (*voice*).
chanter (ʃɑ̃te) *v.t,* to sing; sing of. *~ victoire,* to crow, exult. *qu'est-ce que tu me chantes là?* what's this you're telling me? ¶ *v.i,* to sing; (*cock*) crow; (*cricket*) chirp; (*stream*) babble. *si ça te chante,* if you feel like it. *faire ~ qn,* to blackmail s.o. **chanteur, euse** (tœr, øz) *n,* singer.
chantier (ʃɑ̃tje) *m,* (*Build.*) yard, depot; building site; roadworks; (*P*) shambles *P. en ~,* on the stocks (*book, work*). *~ naval,* shipyard.
chantonner (ʃɑ̃tɔne) *v.i. & t,* to hum.
chantourner (ʃɑ̃turne) *v.t,* to jig-saw.
chantre (ʃɑ̃tr) *m,* (*Eccl.*) cantor; bard.
chanvre (ʃɑ̃vr) *m,* hemp.
chaos (kao) *m,* chaos. **chaotique** (ɔtik) *a,* chaotic.
chaparder *P* (ʃaparde) *v.t,* to pinch *P,* nick *P.*
chape (ʃap) *f,* (*Eccl.*) cope; tread (*tyre*).
chapeau (ʃapo) *m,* hat; (*Tech.*) cap. *donner un coup de ~ à qn,* (*lit.*) to raise one's hat to s.o. *tirer son ~ à qn,* (*fig.*) to take off one's hat to s.o. *~ haut de forme,* top hat. *~ melon,* bowler [h.] *~ mou,* trilby. (*Mot.*) *~ de roue,* hub cap.
chapelain (ʃaplɛ̃) *m,* chaplain.
chapelet (ʃaplɛ) *m,* rosary; string (*oaths, onions*); stick (*bombs*).
chapelier, ère (ʃapəlje, ɛr) *n,* hatter.
chapelle (ʃapɛl) *f,* chapel; coterie, set. *~ ardente,* chapel of rest.
chapellerie (ʃapɛlri) *f,* hat trade; h. shop.
chapelure (ʃaplyr) *f,* grated bread crumbs.
chaperon (ʃaprɔ̃) *m,* chaperon. *le petit ~ rouge,* Little Red Riding Hood. *~***ner** (prɔne) *v.t,* to chaperon.
chapiteau (ʃapito) *m,* (*Arch.*) capital; big top (*circus*).
chapitre (ʃapitr) *m,* (*Eccl., book*) chapter; heading. *sur ce ~,* on that score. **chapitrer** (tre) *v.t,* to lecture; reprimand.
chapon (ʃapɔ̃) *m,* capon.
chaque (ʃak) *a,* each, every; either.
char (ʃar) *m,* (*Mil.*) tank; cart, waggon; float (*carnival*); chariot.
charabia *P* (ʃarabja) *m,* gibberish.
charade (ʃarad) *f,* charade; riddle.
charançon (ʃarɑ̃sɔ̃) *m,* weevil.
charbon (ʃarbɔ̃) *m,* coal; (*Art*) charcoal; carbon (*arc*); (*Med.*) anthrax. *~ de bois,* charcoal. *être sur des ~s ardents,* to be on tenterhooks. *~***nage** (bɔnaʒ) *m,* coal mining; *~s,* collieries. *~***nier, ère** (nje, ɛr) *a,* coal (*industry*). ¶ *m,* coal merchant; coalman; charcoal burner; collier (*ship*).
charcuter *P* (ʃarkyte) *v.t,* (*Surg.*) to hack about. **charcuterie** (tri) *f,* cooked pork meats; pork butcher's shop *or* trade; delicatessen. **charcutier, ère** (tje, ɛr) *n,* pork butcher; delicatessen dealer.
chardon (ʃardɔ̃) *m,* thistle.
chardonneret (ʃardɔnrɛ) *m,* goldfinch.
charge (ʃarʒ) *f,* (*lit., fig.*) load, burden; freight (*ship*); responsibility; care, custody; duty, office. *~s,* expenses, costs. (*Law, Mil., explosive*) charge; (*Elec.*) charge; charging; caricature. *les ~s de l'Etat,* government expenditure. *~s de famille,* dependants. *à la ~ de qn,* (*pers.*) dependent on s.o; (*costs*) chargeable to s.o. *avoir la ~ de,* to be responsible for. *prendre en ~,* to take responsibility for; (*bus &c*) take on. *à ~ pour lui d'écrire,* on condition that he writes. **chargé, e** (ʒe) *a,* loaded, laden, heavy (*de,* with); full, busy (*day*); overcast (*sky*); furred (*tongue*). *~* **d'affaires,** *m,* chargé d'affaires. **chargement** (ʒəmɑ̃) *m,* loading; load; cargo. **charger** (ʒe) *v.t,* to load (*de,* with). *~ qn de qch,* to put s.o in charge of sth. *~ qn de faire,* to instruct s.o to do. (*Elec.*) charge; (*Law*) charge (*de,* with); (*Mil: attack*) charge [at]; caricature; (*Theat.*) overact, ham (*rôle*). **se ~ de,** to attend to, see to. *se ~ de faire,* undertake to do. **chargeur** (ʒœr) *m,* (*pers.*) loader; shipper; magazine (*gun*); (*Phot.*) cartridge.

chariot (ʃarjo) *m*, waggon; truck; [luggage] trolley; carriage (*typewriter*).
charitable† (ʃaritabl) *a*, charitable; kind. **charité** (te) *f*, (*gen.*) charity; charitable gift; kindness. *faire la ~*, to give to charity.
charivari (ʃarivari) *m*, hubbub.
charlatan (ʃarlatɑ̃) *m*, charlatan, quack. **~erie** (tanri) *f*. & **~isme** (nism) *m*, quackery.
charmant, e (ʃarmɑ̃, ɑ̃t) *a*, charming, delightful. **charme** (ʃarm) *m*, charm, attraction; spell. *sous le ~ de*, spellbound by. **charmer** (me) *v.t*, to charm, delight, enchant. **charmeur, euse** (mœr, øz) *n*, charmer.
charnel, le† (ʃarnɛl) *a*, carnal, sensual. **charnier** (nje) *m*, mass grave.
charnière (ʃarnjɛr) *f*, hinge; (*fig.*) pivot.
charnu, e (ʃarny) *a*, fleshy.
charogne (ʃarɔɲ) *f*, carrion; (*P*) swine *P*.
charpente (ʃarpɑ̃t) *f*, framework; build, frame (*pers.*). **charpenté, e** (pɑ̃te) *a*, *bien ~*, well built (*pers., play*). **charpentier** (tje) *m*, carpenter; shipwright.
charpie (ʃarpi) *f*, shredded linen. *en ~*, in shreds.
charretée (ʃarte) *f*, cartload. **charretier** (tje) *m*, carter. *de ~*, coarse (*language*). **charrette** (rɛt) *f*, cart. *~ anglaise*, trap. *~ à bras*, handcart. **charrier** (rje) *v.t*, to cart, carry, convey; (*river*) carry down. *P ~ qn*, to pull s.o's leg *P*. ¶ *v.i*, to go too far. **charron** (rɔ̃) *m*, wheelwright.
charrue (ʃary) *f*, plough. *mettre la ~ avant les bœufs*, to put the cart before the horse.
charte (ʃart) *f*, charter; deed.
charter (ʃartɛr) *m*, charter flight; chartered plane.
chartreux, euse (ʃartrø, øz) *n*, Carthusian monk, nun. ¶ *f*, C. monastery; chartreuse (*liqueur*).
chas (ʃa) *m*, eye (*needle*).
chasse (ʃas) *f*, hunting; shooting. *~ au renard, au gros gibier*, fox, big game hunting. chase; kill, bag; hunting ground, shoot. *~ gardée*, private shooting. *la ~*, the hunt (*people*). *donner la ~ à*, to give chase to. *prendre en ~*, to pursue. *~ à courre*, hunting. *~ d'eau*, flush (*W.C.*). *~ au furet*, ferreting. *~ à l'homme*, manhunt. **~-mouches** (muʃ) *m. inv*, flyswatter. **~-neige** (nɛʒ) *m. inv*, snowplough.
châsse (ʃɑs) *f*, reliquary, shrine.
chasser (ʃase) *v.t*, to hunt. *~ [au fusil]*, shoot. *~ à l'affût*, hunt from a hide. to drive, chase away *or* off; expel; dismiss (*employee*); dispel (*clouds, doubt*). ¶ *v.i*, to go hunting, shooting; (*car*) skid; (*anchor*) drag. **chasseur, euse** (sœr, øz) *n*, hunter. ¶ *m*, huntsman; commissionaire, page [boy], (*Am.*) bellboy; (*Aero.*) fighter; (*Mil.*) chasseur.
châssis (ʃɑsi) *m*, (*Mot.*) chassis; frame, sash (*window*); (*Hort.*) cold frame; (*Art*) stretcher; (*Typ.*) chase; (*Phot.*) printing frame.
chaste† (ʃast) *a*, chaste. **chasteté** (təte) *f*, chastity.
chasuble (ʃazybl) *f*, chasuble.
chat (ʃa) *m*, **chatte** (ʃat) *f*, cat; (*m*) tomcat. *mon petit ~, ma ~te*, my pet, love. *jouer à ~*, to play tig. *un ~ dans la gorge*, a frog in one's throat. *pas un ~*, no one, not a soul. *le C~ botté*, Puss in Boots. *~ de gouttière*, alley cat. ¶ *a.f*, kittenish (*woman*).
châtaigne (ʃɑtɛɲ) *f*, [sweet] chestnut. **châtaignier** (nje) *m*, chestnut [tree]. **châtain, e** (tɛ̃, ɛn) *a*, chestnut [brown] (*hair*).
château (ʃɑto) *m*, castle; palace; country house, mansion; château (*wine district*). *~ d'eau*, water tower. *~ de cartes*, house of cards. *~ fort*, fortified castle. *C~-la-Pompe*, Adam's ale. *bâtir des ~x en Espagne*, to build castles in the air *or* in Spain. **châtelain, e** (tlɛ̃, lɛn) *n*, owner *or* tenant of a château.
chat-huant (ʃaɥɑ̃) *m*, tawny owl, brown o.
châtier (ʃɑtje) *v.t*, to punish; polish (*style*). **châtiment** (timɑ̃) *m*, punishment.
chatoiement (ʃatwamɑ̃) *m*, shimmer[ing]; sparkle.
chaton (ʃatɔ̃) *m*, kitten; catkin; ball of fluff (*dust*); setting (*jewel*).
chatouille (ʃatuj) *f*, **~ment** (jmɑ̃) *m*, tickle, tickling. **chatouiller** (je) *v.t*, (*lit., fig.*) to tickle. **chatouilleux, euse** (tujø, øz) *a*, ticklish; touchy, sensitive.
chatoyer (ʃatwaje) *v.i*, to shimmer; sparkle.
châtrer (ʃɑtre) *v.t*, to castrate; geld (*horse*); neuter (*cat*); (*fig.*) mutilate (*text*).
chatteries (ʃatri) *f.pl*, playful caresses.
chaud, e† (ʃo, od) *a*, hot; warm; (*fig.*) warm, keen, enthusiastic; fierce (*battle*). *à ~es larmes*, (*weep*) bitterly. ¶ *ad*, *il fait ~*, it is hot, warm. ¶ *m*, heat, warmth. (*Med.*) *~ et froid*, chill. *j'ai ~*, I am hot, warm. *garder qch au ~*, to keep sth warm. *rester au ~*, to stay in the warmth.
chaudière (ʃodjɛr) *f*, boiler. **chaudron** (drɔ̃) *m*, cauldron. **~nerie** (drɔnri) *f*, coppersmith's shop *or* trade; boilermaking; boilerworks. **~nier** (nje) *m*, coppersmith; boilermaker.
chauffage (ʃofaʒ) *m*, heating. *~ central*, central h. **chauffard** (far) *m*, roadhog. **chauffe** (ʃof) *f*, fire chamber; stoking, firing. **~-bain,** *m*, water-heater. **~-eau,** *m*, immersion heater. **~-plats,** *m*, hotplate. **chauffer** (ʃofe) *v.t*, to heat, warm [up]; *~ à blanc*, make white hot; stoke (*boiler*); cram (*for exam*). ¶ *v.i*, to heat [up]; get hot, warm; (*Mot.*) warm up; overheat. *ça va~!* sparks will fly! **se ~**, to warm o.s. *se ~ au gaz*, to have gas heating. **chaufferie** (fri) *f*, boiler room. **chauffeur** (fœr) *m*, (*Mot.*) driver; chauffeur; stoker, boilerman. *~ de camion, de taxi*, lorry, taxi driver.

chaume (ʃom) *m,* stubble; thatch. *couvrir de ~,* to thatch. **chaumière** (ʃomjɛr) *f,* cottage; thatched cottage.
chaussée (ʃose) *f,* road[way]; road surface; causeway. '*~ déformée*', 'uneven surface'.
chausse-pied (ʃospje) *m,* shoehorn. **chausser** (se) *v.t,* to put on (*footwear, skis*). *~ du 40,* to take size 40. supply shoes to; put shoes on (*child*). *~ bien,* to fit well. *chaussé de,* wearing (*footwear*). **chausse-trappe** (trap) *f,* trap. **chaussette** (sɛt) *f,* sock. **chausson** (sɔ̃) *m,* slipper; bootee (*baby*); ballet shoe; (*Cook.*) turnover. **chaussure** (syr) *f,* shoe; boot; shoe trade; s. industry. *~s de ski,* ski boots.
chauve (ʃov) *a,* bald. *~ comme un œuf,* b. as a coot. **~-souris** (ʃovsuri) *f,* bat.
chauvin, e (ʃovɛ̃, in) *a,* chauvinistic. ¶ *n,* chauvinist. **~isme** (vinism) *m,* chauvinism.
chaux (ʃo) *f,* lime. *~ vive,* quicklime. *blanchir à la ~,* to whitewash.
chavirer (ʃavire) *v.i,* to capsize, overturn, upset. ¶ *v.t,* [*faire*] *~,* to capsize &c; (*fig.*) bowl over.
chef (ʃɛf) *m,* head; chief, boss *P;* leader; chief[tain] (*tribe*); *~* [*cuisinier*], chef. *commandant en ~,* commander in chief. *de son propre ~,* on his own initiative. *au premier ~,* exceedingly. ¶ *a,* chief. *~ d'accusation,* charge. *~ d'atelier,* [shop] foreman. *~ de bataillon,* major. *~ de bureau,* chief clerk. *~ d'équipe,* foreman; (*Sport*) captain. *~ d'Etat,* head of state. *~ d'état-major,* chief of staff. *~ de famille,* head of the family. *~ de file,* leader. *~ de gare,* station-master. *~ d'orchestre,* conductor. *~ de train,* guard.
chef-d'œuvre (ʃɛdœvr) *m,* masterpiece.
chef-lieu (ʃɛfljø) *m,* county town, chief town (*department*).
cheftaine (ʃɛftɛn) *f,* [guide] captain; cubmistress.
cheik (ʃɛk) *m,* sheikh.
chelem (ʃlɛm) *m,* (*cards*) slam.
chemin (ʃəmɛ̃) *m,* road, lane, path, track; way. *demander son ~,* to ask one's way. *le ~ de l'église,* the way (*or* the road) to the church. *faire tout le ~ à pied,* to walk all the way. *2 heures de ~,* a 2 hour walk. (*fig.*) *faire du ~,* (*idea*) to gain ground. *~ faisant,* on the way. *~ creux,* sunken lane. *le ~ de* [*la*] *Croix,* the Stations of the Cross. *le ~ des écoliers,* the longest way round. *~ de fer,* railway. *par ~ de f.,* by rail. *~ de halage,* towpath. *~ de table,* runner.
chemineau (ʃəmino) *m,* tramp.
cheminée (ʃəmine) *f,* chimney [stack]; funnel; fireplace; hearth; mantlepiece.
cheminement (ʃəminmɑ̃) *m,* progress; development (*ideas*). **cheminer** (ine) *v.i,* to walk [along], trudge; (*stream*) make its way.
cheminot (ʃəmino) *m,* railwayman.
chemise (ʃəmiz) *f,* shirt (*man*); vest (*woman*); folder. *~ de nuit,* nightdress (*woman*); nightshirt (*man*). *en bras de ~,* in shirtsleeves. **~rie** (sri) *f,* shirt making; shirt department. **chemisier** (zje) *m,* shirtmaker; blouse.
chenal (ʃənal) *m,* (*Naut.*) channel, fairway.
chenapan (ʃnapɑ̃) *m,* rascal; rogue.
chêne (ʃɛn) *m,* oak. **~-liège,** *m,* cork-oak.
chenet (ʃənɛ) *m,* fire-dog, andiron.
chènevis (ʃɛnvi) *m,* hemp seed.
chenil (ʃəni) *m,* kennel.
chenille (ʃənij) *f,* (*Zool., Mot.*) caterpillar. **~tte** (nijɛt) *f,* tracked vehicle.
cheptel (ʃɛptɛl) *m,* livestock.
chèque (ʃɛk) *m,* cheque; voucher. *~-cadeau,* gift token. *~ en blanc,* blank cheque. *~ postal,* c. on a Post Office account. *~ sans provision,* dud c. *~ de voyage,* traveller's c.
cher, ère† (ʃɛr) *a,* dear (*à,* to), beloved. (*letters:*) *C~ Paul,* Dear Paul. *C~ Madame,* Dear Mrs X. *mon ~, ma chère,* my dear. expensive, dear. *pas ~,* cheap. ¶ *ad.* (*cost, pay*) a lot. *vendre ~,* to charge a lot for. (*fig.*) *payer ~ qch,* to pay dearly for sth.
chercher (ʃɛrʃe) *v.t,* to look for, try to find, search for; seek. *~ qn du regard,* to look [around] for s.o. *aller ~,* to go for, go & fetch *or* get. *venez me ~ à la gare,* come & meet me at the station. *envoyer ~ le médecin,* to send for the doctor. *~ à faire,* to try to do. **chercheur, euse** (ʃœr, øz) *n,* seeker; research worker. *~ d'or,* gold digger. ¶ *a,* inquiring (*mind*).
chère (ʃɛr) *f,* food, fare. *faire bonne ~,* to feed well.
chéri, e (ʃeri) *a,* beloved. ¶ *n,* darling. **chérir** (rir) *v.t,* to cherish.
cherté (ʃɛrte) *f,* dearness, high cost.
chérubin (ʃerybɛ̃) *m,* cherub.
chétif, ive† (ʃetif, iv) *a,* puny, sickly (*pers.*); stunted (*plant*); meagre, scanty.
cheval (ʃəval) *m,* horse. (*Mot.*) *~* [*vapeur*], horsepower. *une 4 ~aux* (*une 4 CV*), a 4 h.p. car. *à ~,* on horseback. *à ~ sur,* astride. *à ~ sur le règlement,* very strict on the rules. *~ d'arçons,* vaulting h. *~ à bascule,* rocking h. *~ de bataille,* (*fig.*) hobby h. *~aux de bois,* merry-go-round. *~ de chasse,* hunter. *~ de course,* racehorse. *~ de labour,* cart h.; plough h. *~ de retour,* old lag *P*. *~ de trait,* draught h. **chevaleresque** (lrɛsk) *a,* chivalrous; knightly. **chevalerie** (lri) *f,* knighthood; chivalry. **chevalet** (lɛ) *m,* easel; (*Carp.*) trestle; bridge (*violin &c*). **chevalier** (lje) *m,* knight; chevalier (*légion d'honneur*). *~ errant,* knight-errant. *~ d'industrie,* swindler. **chevalière** (ljɛr) *f,* signet ring. **chevalin, e** (lɛ̃, in) *a,* equine; horsy (*face*); horse meat (*butcher's*). **chevauchée** (voʃe) *f,* ride; cavalcade. **chevauchement** (ʃmɑ̃) *m,*

overlapping. **chevaucher** (ʃe) *v.i,* to ride. ¶ *v.t,* to sit astride; (*bridge*) span; overlap.
chevelu, e (ʃəvly) *a,* long-haired; hairy. **chevelure** (vlyr) *f,* [head of] hair; tail (*comet*).
chevet (ʃəvɛ) *m,* bedhead. *au ~ de qn,* at s.o's bedside.
cheveu (ʃəvø) *m,* (*single*) hair. *~x,* hair. *aux ~x gris,* grey-haired. *ne tenir qu'à un ~,* to hang by a thread. *couper les ~x en quatre,* to split hairs. *tiré par les ~x,* far-fetched. *il y a un ~ P,* there's a snag.
cheville (ʃəvij) *f,* ankle; peg, pin; peg (*violin &c*). *~ ouvrière,* (*lit., fig.*) king pin. **cheviller** (vije) *v.t,* (*Carp.*) to peg.
chèvre (ʃɛvr) *f,* [she-]goat, nanny[-goat]; (*Tech.*) hoist; sawhorse. ¶ *m,* goat['s milk] cheese. **chevreau** (ʃəvro) *m,* kid. **chèvrefeuille** (ʃɛvrəfœj) *m,* honeysuckle. **chevreuil** (ʃəvrœj) *m,* roe deer, roebuck; (*Cook.*) venison. **chevrier, ère** (vrie, ɛr) *n,* goatherd. **chevron** (vrɔ̃) *m,* rafter; chevron; stripe. *~s,* herring bone (*pattern*). *~***né, e** (ɔne) *a,* seasoned, veteran. **chevroter** (vrɔte) *v.i,* (*voice*) to quaver. **chevrotine** (tin) *f,* buckshot.
chez (ʃe) *pr, ~ qn,* at *or* to s.o's house. *~ mon frère,* at *or* to my brother's. *rentrer ~ soi,* to go home. *~ nous,* at home; at our house; in our family *or* country. *allez ~ le boulanger,* go to the baker's. *faites comme ~ vous,* make yourself at home. *un ~-soi,* a home of one's own. care of, c/o (*address*). *~ les Grecs,* among the Greeks.
chiader *P* (ʃjade) *v.i. & t,* to swot [up].
chialer *P* (ʃjale) *v.i,* to cry, blubber.
chiasse *P* (ʃjas) *f, avoir la ~,* to have the runs *P;* be in a funk *P.*
chic (ʃik) *a,* stylish, smart; nice, decent (*avec,* to). ¶ *i, ~* [*alors*]*!* great! ¶ *m,* stylishness, style. *le ~ de, pour,* the knack of. *de ~,* from one's head, off the cuff.
chicane (ʃikan) *f,* quibble; squabble; zigzag [course]. **chicaner** (kane) *v.t,* to quibble *or* squabble with. *~***ie** (nri) *f,* quibbling, wrangling.
chiche† (ʃiʃ) *a,* stingy, mean; scanty (*meal*). *pois ~,* chick pea. *~! P* I bet you! (*que,* that).
chichi *P* (ʃiʃi) *m,* affectation; fuss.
chicorée (ʃikɔre) *f,* endive (*salad*); chicory (*in coffee*).
chicot (ʃiko) *m,* stump.
chien, ne (ʃjɛ̃, ɛn) *m,* dog. *petit ~,* puppy. hammer (*gun*); sex-appeal. ¶ *f,* bitch *de ~,* filthy (*weather*). *une vie de ~,* a dog's life. *entre ~ & loup,* at dusk. *être comme ~ & chat,* to fight like cat & dog. *~ d'arrêt,* pointer. *~ de berger,* sheep d. *~ de chasse,* retriever. *~ couchant,* setter. *faire le ~ couchant,* to toady. *~ courant,* hound. *~ de garde,* watch d. *~-loup,* wolfhound; Alsatian.
chiendent (ʃjɛ̃dɑ̃) *m,* couch grass.
chier *P** (ʃie) *v.i,* to shit *P**. *ça me fait ~,* it's a pain in the arse *P**.
chiffe (ʃif) *f,* (*pej: pers.*) wet *P,* drip *P. ~ molle,* wet rag. **chiffon** (fɔ̃) *m,* rag. *~ de papier,* scrap of paper. *parler ~s P,* to talk clothes. *~***ner** (fɔne) *v.t,* to crumple, crease; *P* annoy, bother. *~***nier** (nje) *m,* rag [& bone] man; chiffonier (*chest*).
chiffre (ʃifr) *m,* figure, numeral; amount, total; cipher, code; monogram. *~ des chômeurs,* unemployment figures. *~ d'affaires,* turnover. **chiffrer** (fre) *v.t,* to encode; assess; number (*pages*). (*Mus.*) figure (*bass*). **se ~ à,** to amount to.
chignon (ʃiɲɔ̃) *m,* chignon, bun.
Chili (le) (ʃili), Chile. **chilien, ne** (ljɛ̃, ɛn) *a. &* **C~,** *n,* Chilean.
chimère (ʃimɛr) *f,* chim[a]era, pipe dream. **chimérique** (merik) *a,* chimerical; fanciful.
chimie (ʃimi) *f,* chemistry. **chimique**† (mik) *a,* chemical. **chimiste** (mist) *n,* chemist (*scientist*).
chimpanzé (ʃɛ̃pɑ̃ze) *m,* chimpanzee.
Chine (la) (ʃin), China. **chinois, e** (nwa, az) *a. &* **C~,** *n,* Chinese. **le ~,** Chinese (*language*). *~***erie** (zri) *f,* Chinese curio. *~s,* complicated formalities, red tape.
chiot (ʃjo) *m,* puppy.
chiottes *P** (ʃjɔt) *f.pl,* bog *P* (*W.C.*).
chiper *P* (ʃipe) *v.t,* to pinch, swipe *P.*
chipie *P* (ʃipi) *f,* ill-natured woman. **chipoter** *P* (pɔte) *v.i,* to pick at one's food; haggle.
chips (ʃips) *m.pl,* [potato] crisps.
chique (ʃik) *f,* quid, chew (*of tobacco*).
chiqué *P* (ʃike) *m,* bluff, sham. *faire du ~,* to put on airs.
chiquenaude (ʃiknod) *f,* flick.
chiquer (ʃike) *v.t. & i,* to chew (*tobacco*).
chiromancie (kirɔmɑ̃si) *f,* palmistry. **chiromancien, ne** (sjɛ̃, ɛn) *n,* palmist.
chiropracteur (kirɔpraktœr) *m,* chiropractor. **chiropraxie** (praksi) *f,* chiropractic.
chirurgical, e (ʃiryrʒikal) *a,* surgical. **chirurgie** (ʒi) *f,* surgery. *~ esthétique* plastic s. **chirurgien** (ʒjɛ̃) *m,* surgeon. *~-dentiste,* dental s.
chiure (ʃjyr) *f,* fly speck.
chlore (klɔr) *m,* chlorine. **chlorer** (re) *v.t,* to chlorinate. **chlorhydrique** (klɔridrik) *a,* hydrochloric. **chloroforme** (rɔfɔrm) *m,* chloroform. **chloroformer** (me) *v.t,* to chloroform. **chlorure** (ryr) *m,* chloride. *~ de chaux,* c. of lime.
choc (ʃɔk) *m,* shock, impact; onslaught, clash; crash, bump, thud; clink (*glasses*); shock (*emotion*). *de ~,* shock (*troops*). *prix ~,* knockdown price. *~ en retour,* (*fig.*) backlash.
chocolat (ʃɔkɔla) *m,* chocolate. *~ à croquer, au lait, en poudre,* plain, milk, drinking c. *~***erie**

(tri) *f,* c. factory. ~**ier, ère** (tje, ɛr) *a,* chocolate. ¶ *n,* c. maker; c.seller.
chœur (kœr) *m,* choir; chorus; chancel. *en* ~, in chorus. *enfant de* ~, altar boy.
choir (ʃwar) *v.i.ir,* (*liter.*) to fall.
choisi, e (ʃwazi) *a,* select, choice. **choisir** (zir) *v.t,* to choose, select. ~ *de faire,* choose to do. **choix** (ʃwa) *m,* choice, selection. *il n'a pas le* ~, he has no choice. *au* ~, according to choice. *de* ~, choice. *de premier* ~, top grade.
choléra (kɔlera) *m,* cholera.
chômage (ʃomaʒ) *m,* unemployment. *être au* ~, to be out of work. *mettre en* ~, to make redundant. *s'inscrire au* ~, to sign on. ~ *partiel,* short time. **chômer** (me) *v.i,* to be idle, out of work; (*factory*) to be shut down. *jour chômé,* public holiday. **chômeur, euse** (mœr, øz) *n,* unemployed person. *les* ~*s,* the unemployed.
chope (ʃɔp) *f,* (*glass*) beer-mug. **choper** *P* (pe) *v.t,* to catch; pinch *P.* **chopine** *P* (pin) *f,* bottle of wine.
choquant, e (ʃɔkɑ̃, ɑ̃t) *a,* shocking; offensive. **choquer** (ke) *v.t,* to shock, offend; shake [up] (*pers.*); (*object*) strike; (*glass*) clink. **se** ~, to be shocked.
choral, e (kɔral) *a,* choral. ¶ *m,* chorale. ¶ *f,* choir, choral society.
chorégraphe (kɔregraf) *n,* choreographer. **chorégraphie** (grafi) *f,* choreography.
choriste (kɔrist) *n,* choir member, chorister; (*Theat.*) chorus singer. **chorus** (rys) *m, faire* ~ *avec qn,* to echo s.o's sentiments.
chose (ʃoz) *f,* thing; matter; property. *peu de* ~, nothing much. *c'est tout autre* ~, that's quite different. *dans l'état actuel des* ~*s,* in the present state of affairs. *dites bien des* ~*s de ma part à..* give my regards to.. ¶ *P m,* thingummy *P;* what's-his-name (*pers.*). ¶ *a, être tout* ~, to feel queer.
chou (ʃu) *m,* cabbage; (*Cook.*) puff; rosette; *P* darling. *faire* ~ *blanc P,* to draw blank. ~ *de Bruxelles,* Brussels sprout. ~*-fleur, m,* cauliflower. ~ *frisé,* kale. **chouchou, te,** *P n,* pet (*child*). ~**ter** *P* (te) to pamper.
choucas (ʃukɑ) *m,* jackdaw.
choucroute (ʃukrut) *f,* sauerkraut.
chouette (ʃwɛt) *f,* owl. ¶ *P a,* great *P,* terrific *P;* nice, sweet (*pers.*). ~ [*alors*]*!* great!
choyer (ʃwaje) *v.t,* to pamper, pet.
chrétien, ne† (kretjɛ̃, ɛn) *a. & n,* Christian. ~**té** (ɛ̃te) *f,* Christendom. **le Christ** (krist), Christ. **christ,** *m,* figure of Christ. **christianiser** (tjanize) *v.t,* to christianize. **christianisme** (nism) *m,* Christianity.
chromatique (krɔmatik) *a,* chromatic.
chrome (krom) *m,* chromium, chrome. **chromer** (me) *v.t,* to chromium-plate.
chronique† (krɔnik) *a,* chronic. ¶ *f,* chronicle; (*Press*) column, page. **chroniqueur** (kœr) *m,* chronicler; columnist.
chrono *P* (krɔno) *m,* stopwatch. *un bon* ~, a good time. ~**logie** (nɔlɔʒi) *f,* chronology. ~**logique** (ʒik) *a,* chronological. ~**métrage** (metraʒ) *m,* (*Sport*) timing. ~**mètre** (mɛtr) *m,* chronometer, stopwatch. ~**métrer** (metre) *v.t,* to time. ~**métreur** (trœr) *m,* timekeeper.
chrysalide (krizalid) *f,* chrysalis.
chrysanthème (krizɑ̃tɛm) *m,* chrysanthemum.
chuchotement (ʃyʃɔtmɑ̃) *m,* whisper[ing]. **chuchoter** (ʃɔte) *v.i. & t,* to whisper.
chuinter (ʃɥɛ̃te) *v.i,* to hiss; (*owl*) hoot.
chut (ʃyt) *i,* sh!
chute (ʃyt) *f,* (*gen.*) fall; drop; loss (*hair*); downfall, collapse; failure (*of a play*); scrap (*cloth*). (*Rel.*) *la* ~, the Fall. ~ *de neige,* snowfall. ~ *d'eau,* waterfall. *la* ~ *des reins,* the small of the back. *la* ~ *du jour,* nightfall.
chuter (ʃyte) *v.i,* to fall; (*play*) flop.
Chypre (ʃipr) *f,* Cyprus. **chypriote** = **cypriote.**
ci (si) *ad, de* ~, *de là, par* ~, *par là,* here & there. *V* **ce, celui, comme.** *comps:* ~*-après,* below. ~*-contre,* opposite. ~*-dessous,* below. ~*-dessus,* above. ~*-devant,* formerly. ~*-gît,* here lies (*grave*). ~*-inclus, e & ci-joint, e,* enclosed.
cible (sibl) *f,* (*lit., fig.*) target.
ciboire (sibwar) *m,* (*Eccl.*) ciborium.
ciboule (sibul) *f,* **ciboulette** (lɛt) *f,* chives.
cicatrice (sikatris) *f,* scar. **cicatrisation** (izasjɔ̃) *f,* healing. **cicatriser** (ze) *v.t. &* **se** ~, to heal [up].
cidre (sidr) *m,* cider.
ciel (sjɛl) *m,* sky. *un* ~ *clair,* a clear sky. (*Rel.*) *le* ~, *les cieux,* heaven. [*juste*] *ciel!* good heavens! *tomber du* ~, to be heaven-sent. canopy (*bed*). *à* ~ *ouvert,* open-air (*life, pool*); opencast (*mine*).
cierge (sjɛrʒ) (*Eccl.*) *m,* candle.
cigale (sigal) *f,* cicada.
cigare (sigar) *m,* cigar. **cigarette** (garɛt) *f,* cigarette. ~ [*à*] *bout filtre,* filter tipped c.
cigogne (sigɔɲ) *f,* stork.
ciguë (sigy) *f,* hemlock.
cil (sil) *m,* eyelash. **ciller** (sije) *v.i,* to blink. *il n'ose pas* ~, he daren't move a muscle.
cime (sim) *f,* (*lit., fig.*) top, summit, peak.
ciment (simɑ̃) *m,* cement. **cimenter** (te) *v.t,* (*lit., fig.*) to cement. ~**ie** (tri) *f,* c. works.
cimeterre (simtɛr) *m,* scimitar.
cimetière (simtjɛr) *m,* cemetery, graveyard, churchyard.
ciné (sine) *m, abb. of* **cinéma. cinéaste** (ast) *n,* film-maker. **ciné-club** (klœb) *m,* film society. **cinéma** (ma) *m,* cinema (*art, place*). *de* ~, film (*star, studio*). *aller au* ~, to go to the c., the pictures, (*Am*) the movies. *c'est du* ~ *P,* it's all an act. ~**thèque** (tɛk) *f,* film library. ~**tographier** (tɔgrafje) *v.t,* to film. ~**togra-**

phique (fik) *a,* film, cinema. **cinéphile** (fil) *n,* film fan.
cinglant, e (sɛ̃glɑ̃, ɑ̃t) *a,* lashing; scathing (*remark*). **cinglé, e** *P* (gle) *a,* crazy, cracked *P.* **cingler** (le) *v.t,* to lash, whip.
cinq (sɛ̃k; *before consonant* sɛ̃) *a.* & *m,* five. *c'était moins* ~ *P,* it was a close shave. *for phrases V* **six** & **sixième. cinquantaine** (sɛ̃kɑ̃tɛn) *f,* about fifty. **cinquante** (kɑ̃t) *a.* & *m,* fifty. **cinquantenaire** (kɑ̃tnɛr) *m,* fiftieth anniversary; golden jubilee. **cinquantième** (tjɛm) *a.* & *n,* fiftieth. **cinquième†** (kjɛm) *a.* & *n,* fifth.
cintre (sɛ̃tr) *m,* (*Arch.*) arch; clothes hanger. (*Theat.*) *les* ~*s,* the flies. **cintré, e** (tre) *a,* arched; waisted (*garment*).
cirage (siraʒ) *m,* [shoe] polish; polishing.
circoncire (sirkɔ̃sir) *v.t.ir,* to circumcise.
circonférence (sirkɔ̃ferɑ̃s) *f,* circumference. **circonflexe** (flɛks) *a,* circumflex. **circonlocution** (lɔkysjɔ̃) *f,* circumlocution. **circonscription** (skripsjɔ̃) *f,* district. ~ *électorale,* constituency. **circonscrire** (skrir) *v.t.ir,* to delimit; limit, confine. **circonspect, e** (spɛ[kt], ɛkt) *a,* circumspect, wary.
circonstance (sirkɔ̃stɑ̃s) *f,* circumstance, occasion. *en pareille* ~, in such a case. *de* ~, appropriate. **circonstancié, e** (stɑ̃sje) *a,* detailed (*account*).
circonvenir (sirkɔ̃vnir) *v.t.ir,* to win over, get round (*pers.*).
circuit (sirkɥi) *m,* (*gen., Elec., Sport*) circuit; [round] trip.
circulaire† (sirkylɛr) *a.* & *f,* circular. **circulation** (lasjɔ̃) *f,* (*gen., Med.*) circulation; traffic; running (*trains*); movement (*goods, people*). **circuler** (le) *v.i,* to circulate; go, move (*car &c*). *circulez!* move along! *faire* ~, to move on (*pers., car*).
cire (sir) *f,* wax; polish. ~ *à cacheter,* sealing wax. **ciré** (sire) *m,* oilskin. **cirer** (re) *v.t,* to polish. **cireur, euse** (rœr, øz) *n,* shoeblack. ¶ *f,* (*Mach.*) floor-polisher.
cirque (sirk) *m,* circus; corrie; *P* bedlam.
cirrhose (siroz) *f,* cirrhosis.
cisaille[s] (sizɑj) *f.* [*pl*], shears; wire-cutters. **cisailler** (zɑje) *v.t,* to clip, cut, shear. **ciseau** (zo) *m,* chisel. ~ *à froid,* cold chisel. [*paire de*] ~*x,* [pair of] scissors; shears. **ciseler** (zle) *v.t,* to chisel; chase, engrave. **ciselet** (zlɛ) *m,* graver. **ciselure** (zlyr) *f,* chasing, engraving.
citadelle (sitadɛl) *f,* (*lit., fig.*) citadel.
citadin, e (sitadɛ̃, in) *a,* urban, town (*life*). ¶ *n,* townsman, city dweller.
citation (sitasjɔ̃) *f,* quotation; summons, subpoena. ~ *à l'ordre de l'armée,* mention in dispatches.
cité (site) *f,* city; town. ~*-jardin, f,* garden c. ~ *ouvrière,* [workers'] housing estate. ~ *universitaire,* halls of residence.
citer (site) *v.t,* to cite, quote; (*Law*) summon, subpœna; (*Mil.*) mention [in dispatches].
citerne (sitɛrn) *f,* tank, cistern.
cithare (sitar) *f,* zither.
citoyen, ne (sitwajɛ̃, ɛn) *n,* citizen. ~**neté** (ɛnte) *f,* citizenship.
citron (trɔ̃) *m,* lemon; (*P*) nut *P.* ~ *pressé,* fresh l. juice. ~ *vert,* lime. ¶ *a. inv,* lemon (*colour*). ~**nade** (ɔnad) *f,* lemon squash. ~**nier** (nje) *m,* lemon tree.
citrouille (sitruj) *f,* pumpkin.
civet de lièvre (sivɛ) *m,* jugged hare.
civière (sivjɛr) *f,* stretcher.
civil, e† (sivil) *a,* civil (*war &c*); civilian; polite, civil. ¶ *m,* civilian. *dans le* ~, in c. life. *en* ~, (*Mil.*) in mufti; in plain clothes. **civilisateur, trice** (lizatœr, tris) *a,* civilizing. **civilisation** (sjɔ̃) *f,* civilization. **civiliser** (ze) *v.t,* to civilize. **civilité** (te) *f,* civility. ~*s,* compliments, civilities.
civique (sivik) *a,* civic. **civisme** (vism) *m,* good citizenship.
clabauder (klabode) *v.i,* to babble (*of hound*); backbite.
clair, e† (klɛr) *a,* bright (*light, room*); fair (*skin*); light (*colour*); clear (*glass, sky, sound, water*); thin (*sauce, hair*); clear, lucid; plain, evident. ¶ *ad,* (*see, speak*) clearly. *il fait* ~, it is [day]light. ¶ *m, tirer au* ~, to clear up, elucidate. (*Tel.*) *en* ~, in clear. *au* ~ *de lune,* in the moonlight.
claire-voie (klɛrvwa) *f,* lattice; (*Arch.*) clerestory. *à* ~, open-work (*fence &c*).
clairière (klɛrjɛr) *f,* clearing; glade.
clairon (klɛrɔ̃) *m,* bugle; bugler. ~**nant, e** (rɔnɑ̃, ɑ̃t) *a,* strident (*voice*). ~**ner** (rɔne) *v.t,* to trumpet.
clairsemé, e (klɛrsəme) *a,* sparse, scattered.
clairvoyance (klɛrvwajɑ̃s) *f,* clear-sightedness, shrewdness. **clairvoyant, e** (jɑ̃, ɑ̃t) *a,* clear-sighted, perceptive, shrewd.
clameur (klamœr) *f,* clamour, outcry.
clan (klɑ̃) *m,* clan, set.
clandestin, e† (klɑ̃dɛstɛ̃, in) *a,* clandestine, secret. *passager* ~, stowaway.
clapet (klapɛ) *m,* (*Tech.*) valve; (*P mouth*) trap *P.*
clapier (klapje) *m,* [rabbit] hutch; (*P*) dump *P;* scree.
clapoter (klapɔte) *v.i,* (*wave*) to lap. **clapotis** (ti) *m,* lapping.
clapper (klape) *v.i,* ~ *de la langue,* to click one's tongue.
claque (klak) *f,* slap, smack; (*Theat.*) claque. ¶ *m,* opera hat.
claquemurer (klakmyre) *v.t,* to coop up.
claquer (klake) *v.i,* (*door*) to bang; (*whip*) crack; (*sail*) flap; (*shot*) ring out. *faire* ~, to bang, crack. *il claque des dents,* his teeth are chattering. (*P die*) snuff it *P;* (*thing*) conk out

P. ¶ *v.t*, to slap (*pers.*); slam (*door*); *P* exhaust; squander, blue *P* (*savings*). *claqué*, dead beat *P*. **claquoir** (kwar) *m*, clapper. **claquettes,** (ket) *f.pl*, tap dancing.

clarifier (klarifje) *v.t*, to clarify.

clarinette (klarinɛt) *f*, clarinet.

clarté (klarte) *f*, light; brightness; clearness (*water*); clarity (*thought*). ~*s*, knowledge (*sur*, about).

classe (klɑs) *f*, (*gen.*) class; category; grade. *les ~s moyennes*. the middle classes. *de première ~*, 1st class; top grade. (*Sch.*) class; year; [*salle de*] ~, classroom. *aller en ~*, to go to school. *faire une ~*, to give a lesson. ~**ment** (smɑ̃) *m*, classification; filing; (*Sch., Sport*) position, placing. **classer** (se) *v.t*, to classify; file (*letters*); grade; close (*case*). *se ~ parmi*, to rank among. **classeur** (sœr) *m*, file; filing cabinet. **classification** (klasifikasjɔ̃) *f*, classification. **classifier** (fje) *v.t*, to classify. **classique†** (sik) *a*, (*Mus. &c*) classical; classic, usual. *études ~s*, classics. ¶ *m*, classic.

clause (kloz) *f*, clause.

claustrophobie (klostrɔfɔbi) *f*, claustrophobia.

clavecin (klavsɛ̃) *m*, harpsichord.

clavette (klavɛt) *f*, (*Tech.*) key, cotter pin.

clavicule (klavikyl) *f*, collarbone.

clavier (klavje) *m*, keyboard; manual; (*Mus.*) compass, range.

clef, *also* **clé** (kle) *f*, (*lit., fig.*) key; spanner; (*Mus.*) clef; peg (*violin*); key (*flute*). *~ de fa, de sol*, bass, treble clef. *~ d'ut*, tenor *or* alto c. *mettre sous ~*, to lock up (*s.o, sth*). ¶ *a.inv*, *position-~ &c*, key position &c. *~ anglaise*, monkey wrench. *~ à molette, à pipe*, adjustable, box spanner. *~ de voûte*, (*lit., fig.*) keystone.

clématite (klematit) *f*, clematis.

clémence (klemɑ̃s) *f*, mildness (*weather*); leniency. **clément, e** (mɑ̃, ɑ̃t) *a*, mild; lenient.

clenche (klɛ̃ʃ) *f*, latch.

cleptomane (klɛptoman) *n*, kleptomaniac. **cleptomanie** (ni) *f*, kleptomania.

clerc. (klɛr) *m*, (*Law*) clerk; (*Rel.*) cleric. **clergé** (klɛrʒe) *m*, clergy. **clérical, e** (klerikal) *a. & m*, (*Rel.*) clerical.

cliché (kliʃe) *m*, cliché; (*Phot.*) negative; (*Typ.*) block, plate.

client, e (kliɑ̃, ɑ̃t) *n*, client, customer; patient; guest, patron (*hotel*). ~**èle** (ɑ̃tɛl) *f*, clientele, customers; (*Pol.*) supporters; (*Law, Med.*) practice; custom, patronage.

clignement (kliɲmɑ̃) *m*, blinking. *~ d'oeil*, wink. **cligner** (ɲe) *v.i*, *~ des* or *les yeux*, to blink, screw up one's eyes. *~ de l'œil*, to wink. **clignotant** (kliɲɔtɑ̃) *m*, (*Mot.*) indicator. **clignoter** (te) *v.i*, to blink; twinkle; flicker; flash (*signal*).

climat (klima) *m*, (*lit., fig.*) climate. ~**ique** (tik) *a*, climatic. ~**isation** (tizasjɔ̃) *f*, air conditioning. ~**iser** (ze) *v.t*, to air-condition.

clin d'œil (klɛ̃dœj) *m*, wink. *en un ~*, in the twinkling of an eye.

clinicien (klinisjɛ̃) *m*, clinician. **clinique** (nik) *a*, clinical. ¶ *f*, clinic; nursing home.

clinquant, e (klɛ̃kɑ̃, ɑ̃t) *a*, flashy. ¶ *m*, tinsel; tawdry jewelry.

clique (klik) *f*, clique, set; (*Mil.*) bugle band. *prendre ses ~s & ses claques*, to pack up & go.

cliquet (klikɛ) *m*, (*Mach.*) pawl, catch. **cliqueter** (kte) *v.i*, to clink; clatter; (*chains*) rattle, jangle; (*swords*) clash. **cliquetis** (kti) *m*, clink; clatter &c.

clivage (klivaʒ) *m*, cleavage, split.

cloaque (klɔak) *m*, cesspool.

clochard, e (klɔʃar, ard) *n*, tramp, down & out.

cloche (klɔʃ) *f*, bell; bell jar; dish cover; cloche. *P* idiot. *~ à fromage*, cheese cover. *~ à plongeur*, diving bell. ~**-pied,** *ad*, *sauter à ~*, to hop.

clocher[1] (klɔʃe) *m*, belfry, church tower, steeple. *de ~*, parochial.

clocher[2] *P* (klɔʃe) *v.i*, *il y a qch qui cloche*, there's sth wrong.

clochette (klɔʃɛt) *f*, small bell; bell flower.

cloison (klwazɔ̃) *f*, partition; (*Naut.*) bulkhead; (*fig.*) barrier. ~**ner** (ne) *v.t*, to partition [off]; compartmentalize.

cloître (klwɑtr) *m*, cloister. **cloîtrer** (wɑtre) *v.t*, to cloister, shut away.

clopin-clopant (klɔpɛ̃klɔpɑ̃) *ad*, hobbling along. **clopiner** (pine) *v.i*, to hobble along.

cloque (klɔk) *f*, blister.

clore (klɔr) *v.t. & i. ir*, to close, shut; enclose; end, conclude. **clos** (klo) *m*, enclosure; vineyard, orchard. **clôture** (klotyr) *f*, fence, railings, hedge, wall; closure, closing. **clôturer** (re) *v.t*, to enclose; close (*debate*).

clou (klu) *m*, nail; stud (*road*). *les ~s*, pedestrian crossing. (*Med.*) boil; star turn, chief attraction (*fête &c*). *vieux ~ P*, old banger *P* (*car*). *mettre au ~ P*, to pawn. *~ de girofle*, clove. **clouer** (klue) *v.t*, to nail [up, down]; (*Mil.*) pin down. *~ le bec à qn P*, to shut s.o up. *cloué sur place*, rooted to the spot. **clouté, e** (klute) *a*, studded; hob-nailed (*boots*). *passage ~*, pedestrian crossing. **clouter** (te) *v.t*, to stud.

clown (klun) *m*, clown. *faire le ~*, to fool about. **clowneries** (nri) *f.pl*, clowning.

club (klœb) *m*, club (*society & golf stick*).

co (kɔ) *pref*, co-, joint. **codétenteur, trice,** joint holder. **codirecteur, trice, cogérant, e,** joint manager. **coéquipier, ère,** team mate.

coaguler (koagyle) *v.t*, to coagulate; (*blood*) clot; (*milk*) curdle.

coaliser (se) (koalize) *v.pr*, to combine, unite. **coalition** (sjɔ̃) *f*, coalition.

coasser (koase) *v.i*, (*frog*) to croak.

cobalt (kɔbalt) *m,* cobalt.
cobaye (kɔbaj) *m,* (*lit., fig.*) guinea pig.
cobra (kɔbra) *m,* cobra.
cocaïne (kɔkain) *f,* cocaine.
cocarde (kɔkard) *f,* cockade, rosette; (*Aero.*) roundel.
cocasse (kɔkas) *a,* droll, comical.
coccinelle (kɔksinɛl) *f,* ladybird.
coche (kɔʃ) *f,* notch. ¶ *m,* stage coach.
cocher[1] (kɔʃe) *m,* coachman; cabman.
cocher[2] (kɔʃe) *v.t,* to tick off; notch.
cochon (kɔʃɔ̃) *m,* pig, hog; pork. ~ *d'Inde,* guinea pig. ~ *de lait,* sucking pig. ¶ ~, **~ne** *P* (ɔn) *a,* filthy, disgusting; smutty. ¶ *P n,* (*pers.*) dirty pig *P;* swine *P.* **~ner** *P* (ɔne) *v.t,* to botch, muck up *P.* **~nerie** (nri) *f,* filth, muck; dirty trick; dirty joke. **~net** (nɛ) *m,* piglet; (*Bowls*) jack.
cocktail (kɔktɛl) *m,* cocktail; c. party; (*fig.*) mixture.
coco (kɔko) *m,* [*noix de*] ~, coconut; liquorice water. *mon* ~ *P,* darling, pet. *drôle de* ~ *P,* odd bloke *P.*
cocon (kɔkɔ̃) *m,* cocoon.
cocorico (kɔkɔriko) *m,* cock-a-doodle-doo.
cocotier (kɔkɔtje) *m,* coconut palm.
cocotte (kɔkɔt) *f,* casserole; *P* hen; (*P pej.*) tart *P. ma* ~, darling. ~ *minute,* pressure cooker.
code (kɔd) *m,* (*gen.*) code. ~ *pénal,* penal code. ~ *de la route,* highway code. *en* ~, in code (*message*); dipped (*headlights*). *se mettre en* ~, to dip one's headlights. **coder** (de) *v.t,* to code.
codicille (kɔdisil) *m,* codicil.
codifier (kɔdifje) *v.t,* to codify.
coefficient (koefisjɑ̃) *m,* coefficient.
coercition (kɔɛrsisjɔ̃) *f,* coercion.
cœur (kœr) *m,* (*Anat., Cards*) heart. *en* ~, heart-shaped. *avoir mal au* ~, to feel sick. (*Hort., fig.*) heart, core; heart (*feelings*). *avoir le* ~ *sensible, léger,* to be tender-, light-hearted. *avoir bon* ~, *le* ~ *gros,* to be kind-, heavy-hearted. *à vous fendre le* ~, heart-rending (*sight*). *au fond de son* ~, in his h. of hearts. *de bon* ~, gladly. *à* ~ *joie,* to one's heart's content. *parler à* ~ *ouvert,* to have a h. to h. talk. *cela me tient à* ~, I've set my h. on it.
coffre (kɔfr) *m,* chest, box; coffer; (*Mot.*) boot. **~-fort** (frəfɔr) *m,* safe. **coffrer** (fre) *v.t,* to lock up (*pers.*). **coffret** (frɛ) *m,* casket. ~ *à bijoux,* jewel box.
cognac (kɔɲak) *m,* cognac, brandy.
cognée (kɔɲe) *f,* felling axe. **cogner** (ɲe) *v.t,* to knock, bump; *P* knock about (*pers.*). ¶ *v.i,* ~ *sur,* to hammer (*nail*); knock on, bang on (*door &c*). (*Box.*) ~ *dur,* to hit hard. *se* ~ *la tête,* to bump one's head (*contre,* on).
cohabiter (koabite) *v.t,* to cohabit.
cohérence (kɔerɑ̃s) *f,* coherence. **cohérent, e** (rɑ̃, ɑ̃t) *a,* coherent. **cohésion** (zjɔ̃) *f,* cohesion.
cohorte (kɔɔrt) *f,* troop; (*Hist.*) cohort.
cohue (kɔy) *f,* crowd; crush.
coi, te (kwa, at) *a,* quiet, silent.
coiffe (kwaf) *f,* head-dress. **coiffer** (fe) *v.t,* ~ *qn,* to do s.o's hair; to put a hat on s.o. *se faire* ~, to get one's hair done. *ça te coiffe bien,* it suits you (*hat*). *coiffé d'un béret,* wearing a b. *coiffé de P,* infatuated with (*s.o, sth*). **se** ~, to do one's hair. **coiffeur, euse** (fœr, øz) *n,* hairdresser. ¶ *f,* dressing table. **coiffure** (fyr) *f,* hairstyle; hairdressing; headgear.
coin (kwɛ̃) *m,* corner, angle. *magasin du* ~, corner shop. *sourire en* ~, half smile. place, spot, district. *petit* ~, lavatory. *l'épicier du* ~, the local grocer. wedge; die, stamp. *au* ~ *du feu,* by the fireside. ~*-repas,* dining area. **coincer** (kwɛ̃se) *v.t,* to wedge; jam (*drawer &c*); pin, corner (*pers.*); catch, nab *P* (*thief*); (*question*) floor, catch out.
coïncidence (kɔɛ̃sidɑ̃s) *f,* coincidence. **coïncider** (de) *v.i,* to coincide.
coing (kwɛ̃) *m,* quince (*fruit*).
coit (kɔit) *m,* coitus.
coke (kɔk) *m,* coke.
col (kɔl) *m,* collar; neck (*bottle*); pass, col. ~ *bleu,* blue collar worker; (*Nav.*) bluejacket. ~ *roulé,* polo neck.
colchique (kɔlʃik) *m,* autumn crocus.
coléoptère (kɔleɔptɛr) *m,* beetle.
colère (kɔlɛr) *f,* anger, rage. [*se mettre*] *en* ~, [to get] angry. *faire une* ~, to get into a temper. ¶ *a,* angry. **coléreux, euse** (lerø, øz), **colérique** (rik) *a,* quick-tempered, irascible.
colibri (kɔlibri) *m,* humming bird.
colifichet (kɔlifiʃɛ) *m,* trinket.
colimaçon (kɔlimasɔ̃) *m,* snail. *en* ~, spiral.
colin (kɔlɛ̃) *m,* hake.
colin-maillard (kɔlɛ̃majar) *m,* blind-man's buff.
colique (kɔlik) *f,* colic, gripes.
colis (kɔli) *m,* parcel. *par* ~ *postal,* by parcel post.
collaborateur, trice (kɔlabɔratœr, tris) *n,* (*gen., Pol.*) collaborator; colleague; (*Press*) contributor. **collaborer** (re) *v.i,* to collaborate. ~ *à,* to contribute to.
collage (kɔlaʒ) *m,* sticking, pasting; gluing; hanging (*paper*); (*Art*) collage. **collant, e** (lɑ̃, ɑ̃t) *a,* sticky; tight-fitting, clinging ¶ *m,* tights; leotard.
collatéral, e (kɔlateral) *a,* collateral.
collation (kɔlasjɔ̃) *f,* light meal, snack. **~ner** (ɔne) *v.t,* to collate.
colle (kɔl) *f,* glue; paste; size; (*Sch. P*) detention; oral test; poser *P* (*question*).
collecte (kɔlɛkt) *f,* collection (*money*); collect. **collecteur** (tœr) *m,* collector; [*égout*] ~, main sewer. **collectif, ive**† (tif, iv) *a,* collective, joint. **collection** (sjɔ̃) *f,* collection; (*Press*) series. **~ner** (ɔne) *v.t,* to collect. **~neur, euse**

(nœr, øz) *n,* collector. **collectivité** (tivite) *f,* group, body; community.
collège (kɔlɛʒ) *m,* college; secondary school. ~ *électoral,* electoral college. **collégial, e** (leʒjal) *a,* collegiate. **collégien, ne** (ʒjɛ̃, ɛn) *n,* schoolboy, -girl.
collègue (kɔlɛg) *m,* colleague.
coller (kɔle) *v.t,* to stick; glue; hang (*paper*); (*P put*) stick, shove *P;* give, hand out (*fine*); stump, catch out (*with question*); (*Sch. P*) put in detention; fail (*in exam*). ¶ *v.i,* to stick, cling; *P* go well. *ça ne colle pas,* that's no good. **se** ~ *P,* to get landed with (*pers., job*).
collet (kɔlɛ) *m,* noose; (*Tech.*) collar, flange. *saisir qn au* ~, to grab s.o by the collar. ~ *monté,* straight-laced. **colleter** (lte) *v.t,* to collar. *se* ~ *avec,* to grapple with.
colleur (kɔlœr) *m,* ~ *d'affiches,* billsticker. ~ *de papiers peints,* wallpaperer.
collier (kɔlje) *m,* necklace; chain (*mayor*); collar (*dog, horse*); (*Tech.*) collar. *donner un coup de* ~, to put one's back into it.
colline (kɔlin) *f,* hill.
collision (kɔlizjɔ̃) *f,* collision; clash. *entrer en* ~ *avec,* to collide with.
colloque (kɔlɔk) *m,* colloquy, conference.
collusion (kɔlysjɔ̃) *f,* collusion.
colmater (kɔlmate) *v.t,* to seal, plug (*leak; fig. gap*).
colombe (kɔlɔ̃b) *f,* dove.
Colombie (la) (kɔlɔ̃bi), Columbia.
colombier (kɔlɔ̃bje) *m,* dovecot[e].
colon (kɔlɔ̃) *m,* colonist, settler.
colonel (kɔlɔnɛl) *m,* colonel; group captain (*Air*).
colonial, e (kɔlɔnjal) *a. & m,* colonial. ~**isme** (ism) *m,* colonialism. **colonie** (ni) *f,* colony, settlement. ~ *de vacances,* holiday camp. **colonisateur, trice** (zatœr, tris) *a,* colonizing. ¶ *n,* colonizer. **coloniser** (nize) *v.t,* to colonize.
colonnade (kɔlɔnad) *f,* colonnade. **colonne** (lɔn) *f,* (*gen.*) column. ~ *vertébrale,* spinal c. ~ *montante,* rising main.
colophane (kɔlɔfan) *f,* resin (*violin*).
colorant, e (kɔlɔrɑ̃, ɑ̃t) *a. & m,* colouring. **coloré, e** (re) *a,* ruddy (*complexion*); colourful (*story*). **colorer** (re) *v.t,* (*lit., fig.*) to colour; dye; stain. **colorier** (rje) *v.t,* to colour. **coloris** (ri) *m,* shade, colour; colouring (*skin*).
colossal, e† (kɔlɔsal) *a,* colossal. **colosse** (lɔs) *m,* colossus; giant.
colporter (kɔlpɔrte) *v.t,* to hawk, peddle. **colporteur, euse** (tœr, øz) *n,* hawker, pedlar. ~ *de rumeurs,* gossipmonger.
coltiner (kɔltine) *v.t,* to carry, hump *P.* **se** ~ *P,* to take on, get landed with.
colza (kɔlza) *m,* rape [seed].
coma (kɔma) *m,* (*Med.*) coma. **comateux, euse** (tø, øz) *a,* comatose.
combat (kɔ̃ba) *m,* (*lit., fig.*) fight; (*Mil.*) battle, action; (*Sport*) match, contest. ~ *de boxe,* boxing match. *tué au* ~, killed in action. ~**if, ive** (tif, iv) *a,* aggressive; (*troops*) ready to fight. ~**ivité** (tivite) *f,* fighting spirit. ~**tant** (tɑ̃) *m,* combatant; fighter. *ancien* ~, ex-serviceman. **combattre** (tr) *v.t, & i. ir,* to fight; (*fig.*) combat, fight against.
combe (kɔ̃b) *f,* coomb, combe.
combien (kɔ̃bjɛ̃) *ad,* how much; how many; how. ~ *ça coûte?* how much is it? ~ *de pain?* how much bread? [*depuis*] ~ *de temps?,* how long? ~ *de fois?* how many times? how often? *tu vois* ~ *elle est triste,* you can see how sad she is. *le* ~ *sommes-nous?* what date is it?
combinaison (kɔ̃binɛzɔ̃) *f,* combination; scheme, device; overalls; flying suit; (*woman's*) slip. **combinard, e** (nar, ard) *n,* schemer. **combine** (in) *f,* scheme; trick. **combiné** (ne) *m,* (*Chem.*) compound; receiver (*phone*). **combiner** (ne) *v.t,* to combine; contrive, devise.
comble (kɔ̃bl) *a,* packed. ¶ *m, le* ~ *de,* the height of. *pour* ~ *de malheur il* ..., to crown his misfortune he ... *c'est le* ~*!* that's the last straw! (*Build.*) roof timbers. **combler** (kɔ̃ble) *v.t,* to fill [in] (*hole, gap*); make good (*loss*); fulfil (*desire*); satisfy (*pers.*). ~ *qn de,* to heap, shower s.o with (*presents &c*).
combustible (kɔ̃bystibl) *a,* combustible. ¶ *m,* fuel. **combustion** (tjɔ̃) *f,* combustion.
comédie (kɔmedi) *f,* comedy; sham; fuss. *jouer la* ~, to put on an act. **comédien, ne** (djɛ̃, ɛn) *n,* actor, actress.
comestible (kɔmɛstibl) *a,* edible. ~**s,** *m.pl,* food, provisions.
comète (kɔmɛt) *f,* comet.
comice agricole (kɔmis) *m,* agricultural show.
comique† (kɔmik) *a,* (*Theat.*) comic; comical, funny. ¶ *m,* comedy; c. writer; comedian; funny side, funny part [of it].
comité (kɔmite) *m,* committee.
commandant (kɔmɑ̃dɑ̃) *m,* commander; commandant; (*Mil.*) major; squadron leader; captain (*plane, ship*). **commande** (mɑ̃d) *f,* (*Com.*) order. *en* ~, on order. *fait sur* ~, made to order. *écrit sur* ~, commissioned (*book &c*). *agir sur* ~, to act on orders. *de* ~, forced, feigned. (*Tech.*) control. ~*s,* controls. *aux* ~*s,* in control. ~**ment** (mɑ̃dmɑ̃) *m,* command, order; (*Rel.*) commandment. *prendre le* ~ *de,* to take command of. **commander** (de) *v.t,* to command (*army*); command, order. *on lui commanda le silence* or *de se taire,* he was ordered to keep quiet. order (*meal, coal*); (*Tech.*) control, operate. ~ *à,* to control (*limbs, anger*). **se** ~, to control o.s.
commanditaire (kɔmɑ̃ditɛr) *m,* sleeping partner. **commanditer** (te) *v.t,* to finance.

commando (kɔmɑ̃do) *m,* commando (*man, unit*).
comme (kɔm) *c,* as (*time*); as, since (*cause*). [*juste*] ~ *je sortais,* just as I was going out. ~ *il neigeait,* since it was snowing. (*similarity*) as, like, such as. ~ *j'ai prévu,* as I foresaw. *blanc* ~ *neige,* white as snow. *un homme* ~ *lui,* a man like him. *boire* ~ *un trou P,* to drink like a fish. ~ *si,* as if. ~ *ça,* like that. ~ *ci,* ~ *ça,* so-so, middling. *maigre* ~ *tout,* as thin as can be. *comme qui dirait P,* as you might say. *c'est tout* ~ *P,* it's the same either way. ¶ *ad,* how. ~ *il fait chaud!* how hot it is! ~ *il est gros!* how fat he is!
commémorer (kɔmemɔre) *v.t,* to commemorate.
commençant, e (kɔmɑ̃sɑ̃, ɑ̃t) *n,* beginner. **commencement** (smɑ̃) *m,* beginning, start. *au* ~, at the start. **commencer** (se) *v.t, & i,* to begin, start, commence. *pour* ~, to start with. ~ *à faire, de f.,* to start to do. ~ *par faire,* start by doing.
comment (kɔmɑ̃) *ad,* how. ~ *allez-vous?* how are you? ~ *s'appelle-t-il?* what's his name? ~*?* what? I beg your pardon? ~*!* what! ~ *donc!* of course!
commentaire (kɔmɑ̃tɛr) *m,* commentary; comment. **commentateur, trice** (tatœr, tris) commentator. **commenter** (te) *v.t,* give a commentary on (*text, match*); to comment on.
commerçant, e (kɔmɛrsɑ̃, ɑ̃t) *a,* commercial; trading; shopping (*street*). *être très* ~, to be a good businessman. ¶ *n,* shopkeeper; tradesman. **commerce** (mɛrs) *m,* commerce, trade, business; shop, business. *le* ~, traders. (*liter.*) [social] intercourse. *d'un* ~ *agréable,* pleasant company. **commercer** (mɛrse) *v.i,* to trade (*avec,* with). **commercial, e**† (sjal) *a,* commercial, business (*prospects*).
commère (kɔmɛr) *f,* gossip.
commettre (kɔmɛtr) *v.t.ir,* to commit (*crime, error*); (*liter.*) entrust (*à,* to). *se* ~ *avec* (*pej.*), to associate with.
commis (kɔmi) *m,* [shop] assistant; clerk. ~ *aux vivres,* ship's steward. ~ *voyageur,* commercial traveller. ~**saire** (sɛr) *m,* superintendent (*police*); steward (*fête &c*); commissioner (*enquiry*). (*Naut.*) ~ *de bord,* purser. ~-*priseur,* auctioneer. ~**sariat** (sarja) *m,* ~ [*de police*], police station.
commission (kɔmisjɔ̃) *f,* committee, commission; message, errand; (*Com.*) commission (*sales*). ~*s,* shopping. *faire les* ~*s,* to go shopping. ~**naire** (ɔnɛr) *m,* (*Com.*) agent; (*hotel*) commissionaire, messenger [boy]; delivery man. ~**ner** (ne) *v.t,* to commission.
commode (kɔmɔd) *f,* chest of drawers. ¶ *a,* convenient, handy; easy; easy to get on with. **commodément** (demɑ̃) *ad,* comfortably. **commodité** (dite) *f,* convenience; comfort.
commotion (kɔmosjɔ̃) *f,* shock; (*fig.*) upheaval. ~ *cérébrale,* concussion. ~**ner** (ɔne) *v.t,* to give a shock to, shake (*pers.*).
commuer (kɔmɥe) *v.t,* to commute (*penalty*).
commun, e (kɔmœ̃, yn) *a,* common, shared, communal; joint (*effort*). *en* ~, in common, shared. *d'un* ~ *accord,* of one accord. common, widespread. *peu* ~, uncommon. (*pej.*) vulgar. ¶ *m,* common run. *hors du* ~, out of the ordinary. ~*s,* outbuildings. ~**al, e** (mynal) *a,* town, district (*offices*); local (*school*). ~**auté** (note) *f,* (*Pol., Rel.*) community; identity (*interests*). *la C~ Economique Européenne,* the European Economic C. ~**autaire** (tɛr) *a,* community. **commune** (myn) *f,* (*Adm.*) commune (*town, parish, district*). *les C~s,* the [House of] Commons. **communément** (nemɑ̃) *ad,* commonly, generally.
communicatif, ive (kɔmynikatif, iv) *a,* communicative; infectious (*laugh*). **communication** (sjɔ̃) *f,* communication (*act, message*); transmission (*documents*). ~*s,* communications. *être en* ~ *avec,* to be in touch with. (*Tel.*) ~ [*téléphonique*], [phone] call. *mettre qn en* ~, to put s.o through. *vous avez la* ~, you are through. ~ *en PCV,* reverse charge call.
communier (kɔmynje) *v.i,* (*Rel.*) to receive communion; (*fig.*) to be at one (*in sth; with s.o*). **communion** (njɔ̃) *f,* (*Rel.*) communion; (*fig.*) agreement, sympathy.
communiqué (kɔmynike) *m,* communiqué; press release. **communiquer** (ke) *v.t,* to communicate; pass (*documents*); transmit (*heat*). ¶ *v.i,* (*pers., room*) to communicate.
communisant, e (kɔmynizɑ̃, ɑ̃t) *n,* communist sympathiser, fellow traveller. **communisme** (nism) *m,* communism. **communiste** (nist) *n,* communist.
commutateur (kɔmytatœr) *m,* (*Elec.*) [light] switch; commutator.
compact, e (kɔmpakt) *a,* dense; compact.
compagne (kɔ̃paɲ) *f,* companion; wife; lady friend. **compagnie** (ɲi) *f,* company. *en* ~ *de,* in the company of. *tenir* ~ *à qn,* to keep s.o c. (*Com., Mil., Theat.*) company; covey (*partridges*). **compagnon** (ɲɔ̃) *m,* companion. ~ *de bord,* shipmate. ~ *de voyage,* fellow traveller.
comparable (kɔ̃parabl) *a,* comparable. **comparaison** (rɛzɔ̃) *f,* comparison. *par* ~ *avec, en* ~ *de,* in comparison with. *sans* ~ *avec,* far superior to. (*Liter.*) simile.
comparaître (kɔ̃parɛtr) *v.i.ir,* (*Law*) to appear.
comparatif, ive† (kɔ̃paratif, iv) *a,* comparative. ¶ *m,* (*Gram.*) comparative. **comparé, e** (re) *a,* comparative (*sciences*). **comparer** (re) *v.t,* to compare (*à, avec,* with); liken (*à,* to).
comparse (kɔ̃pars) *n,* (*Theat.*) [*rôle de*] ~, walk-on [part]; (*fig.*) stooge *P.*

compartiment (kɔ̃partimɑ̃) *m,* compartment.
comparution (kɔ̃parysjɔ̃) *f,* (*Law*) appearance.
compas (kɔ̃pɑ) *m,* [pair of] compasses; (*Naut.*) compass. ~ *à pointes sèches,* dividers.
compassion (kɔ̃pasjɔ̃) *f,* compassion. **compatible** (tibl) *a,* compatible. **compatibilité** (bilite) *f,* compatibility. **compâtir** (tir) *v.i,* to sympathize. ~ *à la douleur de qn,* to feel for s.o in his grief. **compâtissant, e** (tisɑ̃, ɑ̃t) *a,* compassionate, sympathetic.
compatriote (kɔ̃patriɔt) *n,* compatriot, fellow countryman, -woman.
compensateur, trice (kɔ̃pɑ̃satœr, tris) *a,* compensatory. **compensation** (sjɔ̃) *f,* compensation (*de,* for); balancing; (*Fin.*) set-off. **compenser** (se) *v.t,* to compensate for, offset, make up for.
compère (kɔ̃pɛr) *m,* accomplice; *O* comrade.
compétence (kɔ̃petɑ̃s) *f,* (*gen., Law*) competence. **compétent, e** (tɑ̃, ɑ̃t) *a,* competent (*en,* in).
compétitif, ive (kɔ̃petitif, iv) *a,* competitive. **compétition** (sjɔ̃) *f,* competition.
compiler (kɔ̃pile) *v.t,* to compile.
complainte (kɔ̃plɛ̃t) *f,* complaint (*song*).
complaire (kɔ̃plɛr) *v.i.ir,* ~ *à qn,* to [try to] please, humour s.o. **se** ~, to delight (*dans,* in; *à faire,* in doing). **complaisamment** (plɛzamɑ̃) *ad,* complacently; obligingly. **complaisance** (zɑ̃s) *f,* kindness; indulgence; complacency. **complaisant, e** (zɑ̃, ɑ̃t) *a,* obliging, kind; indulgent; complacent.
complément (kɔ̃plemɑ̃) *m,* complement. **~aire** (tɛr) *a,* complementary; additional.
complet, ète† (kɔ̃plɛ, ɛt) *a,* complete, utter, entire; full (*bus, hotel &c*); complete (*musician*). *c'est* ~*!* that's the limit! ¶ *m,* (*man's*) suit. *au* [*grand*] ~, complete, at full strength. **compléter** (plete) *v.t,* to complete.
complexe (kɔ̃plɛks) *a,* complex. ¶ *m,* (*Psych., Ind.*) complex. **complexé, e** *P* (kse) *a, très* ~, full of hang-ups *P.*
complexion (kɔ̃plɛksjɔ̃) *f,* constitution; disposition.
complexité (kɔ̃plɛksite) *f,* complexity.
complication (kɔ̃plikasjɔ̃) *f,* complication; complexity, intricacy.
complice (kɔ̃plis) *a,* knowing (*look*). ~ *de,* a party to. ¶ *n,* accomplice; lover; co-respondent. **complicité** (site) *f,* complicity.
compliment (kɔ̃plimɑ̃) *m,* compliment. ~*s,* congratulations; kind regards. **~er** (te) *v.t,* to compliment, congratulate.
compliqué, e (kɔ̃plike) *a,* complicated; compound (*fracture*). **compliquer** (ke) *v.t,* to complicate. **se** ~, to get complicated.
complot (kɔ̃plo) *m,* plot. **comploter** (plɔte) *v.t,* to plot.
comporter (kɔ̃pɔrte) *v.t,* to consist of, comprise; include, contain; allow, admit of (*exception*); entail. **se** ~, to behave; (*car, team*) perform.
composant, e (kɔ̃pozɑ̃, ɑ̃t) *a. & m,* component. **composé, e** (ze) *a,* compound; studied (*air*). ¶ *m,* (*Chem., Gram.*) compound. **composer** (ze) *v.t,* to form, set up; constitute, make up (*body*); (*Mus., Liter.*) compose; paint (*picture*); dial (*number*); (*Typ.*) set. *se* ~ *de,* to consist of, comprise. **compositeur, trice** (pɔzitœr, tris) *n,* (*Mus.*) composer; (*Typ.*) compositor. **composition** (sjɔ̃) *f,* composition (*gen.*); formation; settlement (*dispute*); [type]setting; (*Sch.*) essay, test.
compost (kɔ̃pɔst) *m,* compost. **composteur** (tœr) *m,* date stamp.
compote (kɔ̃pɔt) *f,* compote, stewed fruit. ~ *de pommes,* stewed apples. *en* ~, (*legs*) like jelly; (*face*) battered. **compotier** (tje) *m,* fruit bowl.
compréhensif, ive (kɔ̃preɑ̃sif, iv) *a,* comprehensive; understanding. **compréhension** (sjɔ̃) *f,* comprehension, understanding. **comprendre** (prɑ̃dr) *v.t.ir,* to understand. *se faire* ~, to make o.s understood. *ça se comprend,* that's understandable. consist of, comprise; include. *y compris,* including. *non compris,* not including, exclusive of.
compresse (kɔ̃prɛs) *f,* (*Med.*) compress. **compresseur** (prɛsœr) *m,* compressor. **compression** (sjɔ̃) *f,* compression; (*spending*) cut, squeeze. **comprimer** (prime) *v.t,* to compress; squeeze; cut down (*spending*); restrain (*tears*).
compromettre (kɔ̃prɔmɛtr) *v.t.ir,* to compromise; jeopardize. **se** ~, to compromise o.s. **compromis** (mi) *m,* compromise.
comptabilité (kɔ̃tabilite) *f,* bookkeeping; accountancy; accounts. **comptable** (bl) *a,* accountable (*de,* for); accounts (*document*); calculating (*machine*). ¶ *n,* accountant. **comptant** (tɑ̃) *a. & m,* [*argent*] ~, cash. *vente au* ~, cash sale. ¶ *ad,* (*pay*) [in] cash.
compte (kɔ̃t) *m,* count, counting; figure, total; account. *faire le* ~ *de,* to count [up]. *tenir les* ~*s,* to keep the accounts. *tenir* ~ *de,* to take into a. *prendre à son* ~, to pay for; take responsibility for. *mettre sur le* ~ *de,* to attribute to. (*Com.*) *s'installer à son* ~, to set up on one's own. (*Ind.*) *donner son* ~ *à qn,* to give s.o his cards *P. à bon* ~, (*buy*) cheap. *s'en tirer à bon* ~, to get off lightly. *se rendre* ~ *de qch, que,* to realize sth, that. *cela fait mon* ~, that suits me; that fits the bill. *son* ~ *est bon,* he's done for. *tout* ~ *fait, en fin de* ~, in the end; when all is said & done. ~ *en banque,* bank account. ~ *cheque postal* ≏ Giro a. ~ *courant, de dépôt,* current, deposit a. ~ *à rebours,* countdown. ~ *rendu,* account, report; review. **~-gouttes** (gut) *m. inv,* dropper. **compter** (kɔ̃te) *v.t,* to count; allow, estimate; charge; pay. ~ *3 heures,* to allow 3 hours. ~ *faire,* to intend, expect, reckon to

do. ¶ *v.i,* to count; matter. ~ *avec qch,* to reckon with sth. ~ *parmi,* to rank among. ~ *sur,* to count on, rely on. **compteur** (tœr) *m,* meter, counter. ~ *à gaz,* gas meter. ~ *Geiger,* G. counter. ~ *[kilométrique],* milometer. ~ *[de vitesse],* speedometer. **comptoir** (twar) *m,* counter; bar; branch, agency.

compulser (kɔ̃pylse) *v.t,* to examine.

comte (kɔ̃t) *m,* count; (*UK*) earl. **comté** (kɔ̃te) *m,* (*Adm.*) county; earldom. **comtesse** (tɛs) *f,* countess.

con, ne *P** (kɔ̃, ɔn) *a,* damn stupid *P.* ¶ *n,* bloody fool *P**. ¶ *m,* cunt *P**.

concasser (kɔ̃kɑse) *v.t,* to crush.

concave (kɔ̃kav) *a,* concave. **concavité** (kavite) *f,* cavity; (*Opt.*) concavity.

concéder (kɔ̃sede) *v.t,* to concede, grant.

concentration (kɔ̃sɑ̃trasjɔ̃) *f,* concentration. *camp de* ~, c. camp. **concentrer** (tre) *v.t,* & **se** ~, *v.pr,* to concentrate. **concentrique** (trik) *a,* concentric.

conception (kɔ̃sɛpsjɔ̃) *f,* conception; idea.

concernant (kɔ̃sɛrnɑ̃) *pr,* concerning. **concerner** (ne) *v.t,* to concern. *en ce qui concerne,* with regard to.

concert (kɔ̃sɛr) *m,* (*Mus.*) concert; agreement; (*fig.*) chorus (*praise*). *de* ~, together; in conjunction. ~**ation** (tasjɔ̃) *f,* consultations. ~**er** (te) *v.t,* to plan, devise. **se** ~, to consult each other. ~**iste** (tist) *n,* concert artiste. **concerto** (sɛrto) *m,* concerto.

concession (kɔ̃sɛsjɔ̃) *f,* concession; (*burial*) plot. ~**naire** (ɔnɛr) *n,* (*Com.*) agent, dealer.

concevable (kɔ̃s[ə]vabl) *a,* conceivable. **concevoir** (səvwar) *v.t. & i.ir,* to conceive; entertain; understand; word, couch; conceive (*child*); conceive, devise; imagine; understand. *ainsi conçu,* couched in these terms.

concile (kɔ̃sil) *m,* (*Eccl.*) council, synod.

conciliant, e (kɔ̃siljɑ̃, ɑ̃t) *a,* conciliatory. **conciliation** (asjɔ̃) *f,* conciliation. **concilier** (kɔ̃silje) *v.t,* to reconcile; win.

concis, e (kɔ̃si, iz) *a,* concise. **concision** (sizjɔ̃) *f,* conciseness, brevity.

concitoyen, ne (kɔ̃sitwajɛ̃, ɛn) *n,* fellow citizen.

concluant, e (kɔ̃klyɑ̃, ɑ̃t) *a,* conclusive. **conclure** (klyr) *v.t. & i.ir,* to conclude; clinch (*deal*). ~ *à l'innocence de qn,* to pronounce s.o innocent. **conclusion** (klyzjɔ̃) *f,* conclusion; (*Law*) submissions; summing up; findings.

concombre (kɔ̃kɔ̃br) *m,* cucumber.

concordance (kɔ̃kɔrdɑ̃s) *f,* agreement, similarity. **concordat** (da) *m,* (*Eccl.*) concordat. **concorde** (kɔrd) *f,* concord, harmony. **concorder** (de) *v.i,* to agree, tally (*avec,* with).

concourir (kɔ̃kurir) *v.i.ir,* to compete; converge. ~ *à,* work towards. **concours** (kur) *m,* competition; contest; [competitive] examination; help, support; combination (*circumstances*). ~ *hippique,* horse show.

concret, ète (kɔ̃krɛ, ɛt) *a,* concrete.

concurrence (kɔ̃kyrɑ̃s) *f,* competition. *jusqu'à* ~ *de,* up to [a limit of]. **concurrent, e** (rɑ̃, ɑ̃t) *n,* competitor; candidate.

concussion (kɔ̃kysjɔ̃) *f,* misappropriation.

condamnation (kɔ̃dɑnasjɔ̃) *f,* condemnation; (*Law*) conviction; sentencing. **condamné, e** (ne) *n,* convict. ~ *à mort,* condemned man, woman. **condamner** (ne) *v.t,* to condemn; convict; sentence; give up hope for (*patient*); block up, bar (*door*); (*Naut.*) batten down.

condensateur (kɔ̃dɑ̃satœr) *m,* (*Elec., Opt.*) condenser. **condensation** (sjɔ̃) *f,* condensation. **condenser** (dɑ̃se) *v.t,* to condense.

condescendance (kɔ̃dɛsɑ̃dɑ̃s) *f,* condescension. **condescendre** (dr) *v.i,* to condescend (*à faire,* to do).

condiment (kɔ̃dimɑ̃) *m,* condiment.

condisciple (kɔ̃disipl) *m,* fellow student; schoolfellow.

condition (kɔ̃disjɔ̃) *f,* condition; state; rank, position. ~*s,* conditions, terms. *à quelles* ~*s?* on what terms? *à* ~, on approval. *sans* ~, unconditional[ly]. *à* ~ *de faire, à* ~ *que tu fasses,* on condition that you do. *se mettre en* ~, to get fit. ~**nel, le**† (ɔnɛl) *a,* conditional. ~**ner** (ne) *v.t,* to condition (*pers.*); package (*goods*).

condoléances (kɔ̃dɔleɑ̃s) *f.pl,* condolences.

conducteur, trice (kɔ̃dyktœr, tris) *a,* (*Elec.*) conductive, conducting. ¶ *n,* (*Mot., Rly*) driver. (*Build.*) ~ *des travaux,* clerk of works. **conduire** (dɥir) *v.t. & i.ir,* to drive (*vehicle*); pilot (*plane*); steer (*boat*); lead, take (*pers.*); run, manage. **se** ~, to behave. **conduit** (dɥi) *m,* pipe, conduit; duct. **conduite** (dɥit) *f,* driving &c; running; behaviour, conduct. ~ *à gauche,* left hand drive.

cône (kon) *m,* cone.

confection (kɔ̃fɛksjɔ̃) *f,* making; preparing; ready-made clothes [business]. ~**ner** (ɔne) *v.t,* to make [up]; prepare (*dish*).

confédération (kɔ̃federasjɔ̃) *f,* confederation, confederacy. **confédéré, e** (re) *a. & n,* confederate.

conférence (kɔ̃ferɑ̃s) *f,* lecture; conference, meeting. **conférencier, ère** (rɑ̃sje, ɛr) *n,* lecturer. **conférer** (re) *v.t,* to give, confer. ¶ *v.i,* to confer (*with s.o*).

confesse (kɔ̃fɛs) *f,* (*Rel.*) confession. **confesser** (se) *v.t,* to confess (*sin*); (*priest*) confess (*s.o*). **se** ~, to make one's confession. **confesseur** (sœr) *m,* confessor. **confession** (sjɔ̃) *f,* confession; denomination. ~**nal** (ɔnal) *m,* confessional (*box*). ~**nel, le** (nɛl) *a,* denominational.

confiance (kɔ̃fjɑ̃s) *f,* confidence, trust; faith (*en,* in). *avoir* ~ *en, faire* ~ *à,* to have confidence in. *de* ~, trustworthy; (*buy*) with confidence. **confiant. e** (ɑ̃, ɑ̃t) *a,* confident; confiding.

confidence (dɑ̃s) *f,* confidence. *faire* ~ *à qn,* to confide in s.o. **confident, e** (dɑ̃, ɑ̃t) *n,* confidant, e. ~**iel, le**† (sjɛl) *a,* confidential. **confier** (fje) *v.t,* to confide (*à,* to); entrust (*qch à qn,* s.o with sth). **se** ~ **à qn,** to confide in s.o.
configuration (kɔ̃figyrasjɔ̃) *f,* configuration, shape; lie [of the land].
confiner (kɔ̃fine) *v.t,* to confine. *confiné,* stuffy (*air*). ¶ *v.i,* ~ **à,** to border. **confins** (fɛ̃) *m.pl,* borders; furthest bounds.
confire (kɔ̃fir) *v.t.ir,* to preserve; pickle.
confirmation (kɔ̃firmasjɔ̃) *f,* confirmation. **confirmer** (me) *v.t,* (*gen., Rel.*) to confirm.
confiscation (kɔ̃fiskasjɔ̃) *f,* confiscation.
confiserie (kɔ̃fizri) *f,* confectionery; confectioner's shop. **confiseur, euse** (zœr, øz) *n,* confectioner.
confisquer (kɔ̃fiske) *v.t,* to confiscate.
confiture (kɔ̃fityr) *f,* jam. ~ *d'oranges,* [orange] marmalade.
conflagration (kɔ̃flagrasjɔ̃) *f,* cataclysm.
conflit (kɔ̃fli) *m,* conflict, clash.
confluent (kɔ̃flyɑ̃) *m,* confluence (*rivers*).
confondre (kɔ̃fɔ̃dr) *v.t,* to confuse, mix up; astound, overwhelm; confound (*critics*). **se** ~, to merge; become confused.
conformation (kɔ̃fɔrmasjɔ̃) *f,* conformation. **conforme** (fɔrm) *a,* ~ *à,* in accordance with, true to. *copie* ~, true copy. **conformé, e** (me) *a, bien, mal* ~, well, badly formed. ~**ment** (mɑ̃) *ad,* ~ *à,* in accordance with. **conformer** (me) *v.t,* ~ *qch à,* to model sth on. **se** ~, to conform. **conformisme** (mism) *m,* conformity. **conformité** (mite) *f,* similarity, agreement. *en* ~ *avec,* in keeping *or* accordance with.
confort (kɔ̃fɔr) *m,* comfort. *tout le* ~ *moderne,* all mod cons. ~**able**† (fɔrtabl) *a,* comfortable (*chair, hotel*).
confrère (frɛr) *m,* colleague, fellow member. **confrérie** (freri) *f,* brotherhood.
confronter (kɔ̃frɔ̃te) *v.t,* to confront; compare.
confus, e (kɔ̃fy, yz) *a,* confused; muddled; ashamed, embarrassed. ~**ément** (fyzemɑ̃) *ad,* confusedly; vaguely. **confusion** (zjɔ̃) *f,* confusion; mistake; embarrassment.
congé (kɔ̃ʒe) *m,* holiday; (*Mil.*) leave. *prendre du* ~, to take time off. *donner* [*son*] ~ *à qn,* to give s.o notice. *prendre* ~ *de qn,* to take leave of s.o. **congédier** (dje) *v.t,* to dismiss.
congélateur (kɔ̃ʒelatœr) *m,* deep-freeze; freezer [compartment]. **congélation** (kɔ̃ʒelasjɔ̃) *f,* freezing. **congeler** (ʒle) *v.t.* & **se** ~, to freeze.
congénital, e (kɔ̃ʒenital) *a,* congenital.
congère (kɔ̃ʒɛr) *f,* snowdrift.
congestion (kɔ̃ʒɛstjɔ̃) *f,* congestion. ~ *cérébrale,* stroke. ~**ner** (ɔne) *v.t,* to congest; flush (*face*).
congratulation (kɔ̃gratylasjɔ̃) *f,* congratulation. **congratuler** (le) *v.t,* to congratulate.
congre (kɔ̃gr) *m,* conger eel.
congrégation (kɔ̃gregasjɔ̃) *f,* (*Eccl.*) congregation.
congrès (kɔ̃grɛ) *m,* congress. **congressiste** (sist) *n,* member of a congress.
conifère (kɔnifɛr) *m,* conifer.
conique (kɔnik) *a,* conical, cone-shaped.
conjecture (kɔ̃ʒɛktyr) *f,* conjecture. **conjecturer** (tyre) *v.t,* to conjecture.
conjoint, e† (kɔ̃ʒwɛ̃, ɛ̃t) *a,* joint. ¶ *n,* spouse. *les* ~*s,* the couple. **conjonction** (ʒɔ̃ksjɔ̃) *f,* conjunction; union. **conjoncture** (ʒɔ̃ktyr) *f,* circumstances.
conjugaison (kɔ̃ʒygɛzɔ̃) *f,* conjugation.
conjugal, e† (kɔ̃ʒygal) *a,* conjugal; married (*life*); marital (*home*).
conjuguer (kɔ̃ʒyge) *v.t,* to conjugate (*verb*); combine (*efforts*).
conjuration (kɔ̃ʒyrasjɔ̃) *f,* conspiracy. **conjuré, e** (re) *n,* conspirator. **conjurer** (re) *v.t,* to avert; ward off; *O* plot. ~ *qn de faire,* beseech s.o to do. **se** ~, to conspire.
connaissance (kɔnɛsɑ̃s) *f,* knowledge; acquaintance (*pers.*); consciousness. *sans* ~, unconscious. ~*s,* learning, knowledge. *à ma* ~, to my knowledge. *en* ~ *de cause,* in full knowledge of the facts. *en pays de* ~, on familiar ground; among familiar faces. **connaisseur, euse** (œr, øz) *a,* expert. ¶ *n,* connoisseur. **connaître** (nɛtr) *v.t.ir,* to know, be acquainted with (*pers., town*); know about (*birds, music*); experience (*success*). *se faire* ~, to make o.s known; make a name for o.s. *s'y* ~ *en qch,* to be well up in sth, know all about sth.
connecter (kɔnɛkte) *v.t,* to connect.
connerie *P** (kɔnri) *f,* bloody stupidity *P**. *dire des* ~*s,* to talk bloody nonsense *P**.
connexion (kɔnɛksjɔ̃) *f,* connection.
connivence (kɔnivɑ̃s) *f,* connivance. *de* ~ *avec,* in connivance with.
conquérant, e (kɔ̃kerɑ̃, ɑ̃t) *a,* conquering. ¶ *n,* conqueror. **conquérir** (rir) *v.t.ir,* to conquer; win; win over. **conquête** (kɛt) *f,* conquest.
consacré, e (kɔ̃sakre) *a,* established, traditional; accepted (*expression*). **consacrer** (kre) *v.t,* (*Rel.*) to consecrate. ~ *à,* to devote (*time &c*) to; dedicate to. *se* ~ *à,* to devote, dedicate o.s to.
conscience (kɔ̃sjɑ̃s) *f,* awareness, consciousness; conscience. *avoir* ~ *que,* to be aware that. *perdre* ~, to lose consciousness. *avoir bonne, mauvaise* ~, to have a clear, guilty c. ~ [*professionnelle*], conscientiousness. **consciencieux, euse**† (ɑ̃sjø, øz) *a,* conscientious. **conscient, e** (sjɑ̃, ɑ̃t) *a,* conscious. ~ *de,* aware of.
conscription (kɔ̃skripsjɔ̃) *f,* conscription. **conscrit** (skri) *m,* conscript.
consécration (kɔ̃sekrasjɔ̃) *f,* consecration; sanc-

tioning (*custom &c*).
consécutif, ive† (kɔ̃sekytif, iv) *a*, consecutive.
conseil (kɔ̃sɛj) *m*, advice. *un petit* ~, a word of a. consultant. *ingénieur-*~, consulting engineer. council, board; meeting. ~ *d'administration*, board [of directors]. ~ *de guerre*, council of war; court martial. *C*~ *des ministres*, the Cabinet. ~ *municipal*, town council. *C*~ *de Sécurité*, Security Council. **conseiller** (sɛje) *v.t*, to advise, recommend (*qch à qn*). ~ *à qn de faire*, to advise s.o to do. ~ *qn*, to advise, counsel s.o. **conseiller, ère** (je, ɛr) *n*, adviser; (*Pol.*) councillor. ~ *matrimonial*, marriage guidance counsellor.
consentement (kɔ̃sɑ̃tmɑ̃) *m*, consent. **consentir** (tir) *v.i.ir*, to consent, agree (*à*, to).
conséquence (kɔ̃sekɑ̃s) *f*, consequence, result; conclusion. *de* ~, *sans* ~, of some, of no importance. *en* ~, consequently. *tirer à* ~, to be important. *tirer les* ~*s*, to draw conclusions. **conséquent, e** (kɑ̃, ɑ̃t) *a*, rational (*mind, act*); important. **par** ~, consequently.
conservateur, trice (kɔ̃sɛrvatœr, tris) *a*, (*Pol.*) conservative. ¶ *n*, curator; librarian; (*Pol.*) conservative. **conservation** (sjɔ̃) *f*, preservation; keeping. **conservatoire** (twar) *m*, school, academy (*music, &c*); conservatoire. **conserve** (sɛrv) *f*, preserve. ~*s*, tinned, canned, bottled food. ~*s au vinaigre*, pickles. (*Naut.*) *de* ~, in convoy. **conserver** (ve) *v.t*, to preserve; keep, maintain, retain; (*Cook.*) preserve, pickle, bottle. **se** ~, (*food*) to keep.
considérable† (kɔ̃siderabl) *a*, considerable; eminent (*pers.*). **consideration** (rasjɔ̃) *f*, consideration; respect, regard. *prendre en* ~, to take into account. *en* ~ *de*, considering; because of. *sans* ~ *de*, regardless of. **considérer** (re) *v.t*, (*gen.*) to consider; respect.
consignataire (kɔ̃siɲatɛr) *m*, (*Com.*) consignee. **consignation** (sjɔ̃) *f*, deposit; consignment. **consigne** (siɲ) *f*, orders; (*Mil.*) confinement to barracks; (*Sch.*) detention; left luggage office; deposit (*bottle*). **consigner** (ɲe) *v.t*, to record (*fact*); deposit (*money, luggage*); (*Mil.*) confine to barracks; (*Sch.*) keep in; put a deposit on. (*non*) *consigné*, (non-) returnable (*bottle*).
consistance (kɔ̃sistɑ̃s) *f*, consistency (*sauce*); (*fig.*) solidity. *sans* ~, unfounded (*rumour*). **consistant, e** (tɑ̃, ɑ̃t) *a*, thick (*liquid*); solid (*food*); well-founded (*rumour*). **consister** (te) *v.i*, to consist (*en*, of; *dans*, in; *à faire*, in doing).
consolateur, trice (kɔ̃sɔlatœr, tris) *a*, consoling. ¶ *n*, comforter. **consolation** (sjɔ̃) *f*, consolation, comfort. **console** (sɔl) *f*, console [table]; (*Mus.*) console. **consoler** (le) *v.t*, to console, comfort; soothe (*grief*). *se* ~ *de*, to get over (*loss*).
consolider (kɔ̃sɔlide) *v.t*, to consolidate, strengthen. **consolidation** (dasjɔ̃) *f*, consolidation, strengthening.
consommateur, trice (kɔ̃sɔmatœr, tris) *n*, consumer; customer (*at café*). **consommation** (sjɔ̃) *f*, consumption; drink; consummation. **consommé, e** (me) *a*, consummate. ¶ *m*, (*Cook.*) clear soup. **consommer** (me) *v.t*, to consume; use; drink (*in café*); consummate (*marriage*); commit (*crime*).
consonne (kɔ̃sɔn) *f*, consonant.
consortium (kɔ̃sɔrsjɔm) *m*, consortium.
conspirateur, trice (kɔ̃spiratœr, tris) *n*, conspirator. **conspiration** (sjɔ̃) *f*, conspiracy, plot. **conspirer** (re) *v.i*, to conspire, plot.
conspuer (kɔ̃spɥe) *v.t*, to boo, barrack.
constamment (kɔ̃stamɑ̃) *ad*, constantly. **constance** (stɑ̃s) *f*, constancy; steadfastness. **constant, e** (stɑ̃, ɑ̃t) *a*, constant; steadfast; continuous. ¶ *f*, (*Math.*) constant.
constater (kɔ̃state) *v.t*, to note, observe; state (*fact*); record (*event*); certify (*death*). **constatation** (tasjɔ̃) *f*, observation; statement (*of fact*); noting; recording.
constellation (kɔ̃stɛllasjɔ̃) *f*, constellation. **constellé, e** (stɛlle) *a*, studded (*de*, with).
consternation (kɔ̃stɛrnasjɔ̃) *f*, consternation, dismay. **consterner** (ne) *v.t*, to dismay.
constipation (kɔ̃stipasjɔ̃) *f*, constipation. **constiper** (pe) *v.t*, to constipate.
constituant, e (kɔ̃stitɥɑ̃, ɑ̃t) *a*, (*gen., Pol.*) constituent. **constituer** (tɥe) *v.t*, to form, set up, build up (*group, collection*); constitute. *bien, mal constitué*, of a healthy, weak constitution. *se* ~ *prisonnier*, to give oneself up. **constitution** (tysjɔ̃) *f*, formation, setting up &c; composition; (*Med., Pol.*) constitution. ~**nel, le**† (ɔnɛl) *a*, constitutional.
constructeur, trice (kɔ̃stryktœr, tris) *n*, maker; builder, constructor. **constructif, ive** (tif, iv) *a*, constructive. **construction** (sjɔ̃) *f*, building, construction (*act*); structure; building (*edifice*). *en* ~, under construction. *la* ~, the building trade. **construire** (strɥir) *v.t.ir*, to construct; build, erect.
consul (kɔ̃syl) *m*, consul. ~**aire** (lɛr) *a*, consular. ~**at** (la) *m*, consulate; consulship.
consultant, e (kɔ̃syltɑ̃, ɑ̃t) *a*, consulting. **consultatif, ive** (tatif, iv) *a*, consultative, advisory. **consultation** (tasjɔ̃) *f*, consultation; (*Med., Law*) opinion, advice. *heures de* ~, surgery hours. **consulter** (te) *v.t*, to consult. ¶ *v.i*, to hold a surgery.
consumer (kɔ̃syme) *v.t*, to consume; (*fig.*) devour; squander. **se** ~, (*pers.*) to waste away.
contact (kɔ̃takt) *m*, (*gen., Elec*) contact; touch. (*Mot.*) *mettre le* ~, to switch on. *prendre* ~ *avec*, to get in touch with.
contagieux, euse (kɔ̃taʒjø, øz) *a*, contagious, infectious. **contagion** (ʒjɔ̃) *f*, contagion.

contamination (kɔ̃taminasjɔ̃) *f*, contamination. **contaminer** (ne) *v.t*, to contaminate.
conte (kɔ̃t) *m*, story; short story. ~ *de fées*, fairy tale.
contemplatif, ive (kɔ̃tɑ̃platif, iv) *a*, contemplative. **contemplation** (sjɔ̃) *f*, contemplation. **contempler** (ple) *v.t*, to contemplate, gaze at.
contemporain, e (kɔ̃tɑ̃pɔrɛ̃, ɛn) *a*, contemporary. ¶ *n*, contemporary.
contenance (kɔ̃tnɑ̃s) *f*, capacity; bearing, attitude. *faire bonne* ~, to put on a bold front. *perdre* ~, to lose one's composure. **contenant** (tnɑ̃) *m*, container. **contenir** (tnir) *v.t.ir*, to contain; hold (*capacity*); contain, restrain (*enemy, mirth*). **se** ~, to contain o.s.
content, e (kɔ̃tɑ̃, ɑ̃t) *a*, pleased, glad, happy (*de*, with, about; *de voir*, to see). ~ *de soi*, pleased with o.s. ¶ *m*, *avoir tout son* ~ *de*, to have one's fill of. **contentement** (tɑ̃tmɑ̃) *m*, contentment; satisfaction. ~ *de soi*, self-satisfaction. **contenter** (te) *v.t*, to satisfy. **se** ~ **de,** to content o.s with, make do with.
contentieux, euse (kɔ̃tɑ̃sjø, øz) *a*, contentious. ¶ *m*, legal department; (*Pol.*) disputes.
contenu (kɔ̃tny) *m*, contents.
conter (kɔ̃te) *v.t*, to tell, recount. *s'en laisser* ~, to be taken in.
contestable (kɔ̃tɛstabl) *a*, questionable, debatable. **contestataire** (tatɛr) *a*, anti-establishment. **contestation** (sjɔ̃) *f*, contesting, disputing; dispute; objection; protest (*against society*). **sans conteste** (tɛst), indisputably. **contester** (te) *v.t*, to challenge, question, dispute.
conteur, euse (kɔ̃tœr, øz) *n*, narrator; storyteller.
contexte (kɔ̃tɛkst) *m*, context.
contigu, ë (kɔ̃tigy) *a*, adjacent (*à*, to); related (*subject*). ~**ïté** (gɥite) *f*, proximity; relatedness.
continence (kɔ̃tinɑ̃s) *f*, continence. **continent**[1], **e** (nɑ̃, ɑ̃t) *a*, continent, chaste.
continent[2] (kɔ̃tinɑ̃) *m*, continent, mainland. **continental, e** (tal) *a*, continental.
contingence (kɔ̃tɛ̃ʒɑ̃s) *f*, contingency. **contingent, e** (ʒɑ̃, ɑ̃t) *a*, contingent. ¶ *m*, (*Mil.*) contingent; call-up class. *le* ~, conscripts. (*Com.*) quota; share. ~**er** (te) *v.t*, (*Com.*) to fix a quota on.
continu, e (kɔ̃tiny) *a*, continuous; unbroken (*line*). ~**ation** (nɥasjɔ̃) *f*, continuation. ~**el, le**† (nɥɛl) *a*, continuous; continual. ~**er** (nɥe) *v.t. & i*, to continue, go on [with]. ~ *de* or *à parler*, to continue, go on talking. ~**ité** (nɥite) *f*, continuation; continuity. **continûment** (nymɑ̃) *ad*, continuously.
contondant, e (kɔ̃tɔ̃dɑ̃, ɑ̃t) *a*, blunt (*instrument*).
contorsion (kɔ̃tɔrsjɔ̃) *f*, contortion. ~**ner (se)** (ɔne) *v.pr*, to contort o.s. ~**niste** (nist) *n*, contortionist.
contour (kɔ̃tur) *m*, contour, outline. ~**ner** (turne) *v.t*, to go round; skirt, bypass (*town*); get round (*difficulty*).
contraception (kɔ̃trasepsjɔ̃) *f*, contraception. **contraceptif, ive** (tif, iv) *a. & m*, contraceptive.
contracter (kɔ̃trakte) *v.t*, to contract, tense (*muscle, face*); contract (*word*); reduce in size; contract (*debt, illness*); take out (*Insce policy*). **se** ~, to shrink, contract; tense; (*pers.*) become tense. **contraction** (sjɔ̃) *f*, contraction. **contractuel, le** (tɥɛl) *a*, contractual. ¶ *n*, ≃ traffic warden.
contradiction (kɔ̃tradiksjɔ̃) *f*, contradiction; discrepancy. **contradictoire** (twar) *a*, conflicting.
contraindre (kɔ̃trɛ̃dr) *v.t.ir*, to constrain, compel, force (*à faire*, to do); restrain. **contrainte** (trɛ̃t) *f*, constraint; restraint. *sous la* ~, under duress. *sans* ~, unrestrainedly.
contraire (kɔ̃trɛr) *a*, opposite, contrary; adverse. ~ *à la santé*, bad for the health. ¶ *m*, opposite. *au* ~, on the contrary. ~**ment** (trɛrmɑ̃) *ad*, ~ *à*, contrary to.
contralto (kɔ̃tralto) *m*, contralto.
contrariant, e (kɔ̃trarjɑ̃, ɑ̃t) *a*, trying, provoking. **contrarier** (rje) *v.t*, to thwart, frustrate (*plans*); annoy. **contrariété** (rjete) *f*, annoyance.
contraste (kɔ̃trast) *m*, contrast. **contraster** (te) *v.i. & t*, to contrast.
contrat (kɔ̃tra) *m*, contract; agreement.
contravention (kɔ̃travɑ̃sjɔ̃) *f*, fine; parking ticket. *dresser* ~ *à qn*, to fine *or* book s.o. (*Law*) contravention (*à*, of).
contre (kɔ̃tr) *pr. & ad*, against; (*Sport*) versus; contrary to. ~ *le mur*, against the wall. ~ *l'ennemi*, a. the enemy. *un remède* ~ *la grippe*, a remedy for 'flu. ~ *l'incendie*, (*insure*) against fire. ~ *toute attente*, against all expectation. *envoi* ~ *remboursement*, cash on delivery. *7 voix* ~ *5*, 7 votes to 5. *parier à cent* ~ *un*, to bet 100 to one. *par* ~, on the other hand. ¶ *m*, *le pour & le* ~, the pros & cons. ¶ *pref. inv*, (*the second element only takes the pl. & indicates the gender*): ~**-allée,** service road; side path (*park*). ~**-attaque, -révolution, -offensive &c**, counterattack, revolution, offensive &c. ~**-amiral,** rear admiral. ~**-braquer,** *v.i*, to steer into the skid. **à** ~**-courant,** against the current. ~**-écrou,** lock nut. ~**-expertise,** second [expert] assessment. **en** ~**-haut [de],** above. ~**-indication,** (*Med.*) contraindication. ~**-interrogatoire,** cross-examination. **à** ~**-jour,** against the light. **prendre le** ~**-pied,** to do the opposite. ~**-plaqué,** *m*, plywood. ~**-torpilleur,** (*Nav.*) destroyer. ~**-ut,** top C. ~**-valeur,** exchange value. ~**-visite,** (*Med.*) second opinion.
contrebalancer (kɔ̃trəbalɑ̃se) *v.t*, to counterbalance; offset.

contrebande (kɔ̃trəbɑ̃d) *f,* smuggling, contraband. *de* ~, smuggled (*goods*). **contrebandier, ère** (bɑ̃dje, ɛr) *n,* smuggler.
contrebas (kɔ̃trəbɑ) *m, en* ~ [*de*], below.
contrebasse (kɔ̃trəbɑs) *f,* double bass.
contrecarrer (kɔ̃trəkɑre) *v.t,* to thwart.
contrecœur (à) (kɔ̃trɔkœr) *ad,* reluctantly.
contrecoup (kɔ̃trəku) *m,* repercussions.
contredire (kɔ̃trədir) *v.i.ir,* to contradict; conflict with (*facts*). **sans contredit** (di), unquestionably.
contrée (kɔ̃tre) *f,* (*liter.*) country, region.
contrefaçon (kɔ̃trəfasɔ̃) *f,* counterfeit[ing]; forgery; imitation; pirated edition. **contrefacteur** (faktœr) *m,* counterfeiter. **contrefaire** (fɛr) *v.t.ir,* to counterfeit, forge; disguise (*voice*); mimic.
contrefort (kɔ̃trəfɔr) *m,* buttress; spur.
contremaître, esse (kɔ̃trəmɛtr, trɛs) *n,* foreman, woman.
contremarque (kɔ̃trəmark) *f,* countermark; (*Theat.*) pass-out ticket.
contrepartie (kɔ̃trəparti) *f,* compensation; opposite view. *en* ~, in return; in compensation.
contrepèterie (kɔ̃trəpɛtri) *f,* Spoonerism.
contrepoids (kɔ̃trəpwa) *m,* counterweight, counterbalance; balancing pole.
contrepoint (kɔ̃trəpwɛ̃) *m,* counterpoint.
contrepoison (kɔ̃trəpwazɔ̃) *m,* antidote.
contresens (kɔ̃trəsɑ̃s) *m,* mistranslation; misinterpretation; absurdity. (*Mot.*) *à* ~, the wrong way.
contresigner (kɔtrəsiɲe) *v.t,* to countersign.
contretemps (kɔ̃trətɑ̃) *m,* mishap, hitch. *à* ~, inopportunely; (*Mus.*) off the beat.
contrevenir à (kɔ̃trəvənir) *v.ir,* to contravene.
contrevent (kɔ̃trəvɑ̃) *m,* outside shutter.
contrevérité (kɔ̃trəverite) *f,* untruth.
contribuable (kɔ̃tribɥabl) *n,* taxpayer; ratepayer. **contribuer** (bɥe) *v.i,* ~ *à,* to contribute to[wards]. **contribution** (bysjɔ̃) *f,* contribution; tax; rate.
contrister (kɔ̃triste) *v.t,* (*liter.*) to grieve.
contrit, e (kɔ̃tri, it) *a,* contrite. **contrition** (sjɔ̃) *f,* contrition.
contrôle (kɔ̃trol) *m,* check[ing]; inspection; supervision; control; (*Theat.*) box office; (*Mil.*) roll, list. ~ *d'identité,* identity check. ~ *de soi-même,* self-control. **contrôler** (trole) *v.t,* to control; check; inspect (*tickets*); supervise. **contrôleur, euse** (lœr, øz) *n,* inspector.
contrordre (kɔ̃trɔrdr) *m,* counter-order.
controverse (kɔ̃trɔvɛrs) *f,* controversy. **controversé, e** (se) *a,* much debated.
contumace (kɔ̃tymas) *f,* (*Law*) *par* ~, in his (her) absence.
contusion (kɔ̃tyzjɔ̃) *f,* bruise, contusion. ~**ner** (ɔne) *v.t,* to bruise.
convaincant, e (kɔ̃vɛ̃kɑ̃, ɑ̃t) *a,* convincing. **convaincre** (vɛ̃kr) *v.t.ir,* to convince (*de qch,* of sth); persuade (*de faire,* to do); convict (*de,* of).
convalescence (kɔ̃valɛsɑ̃s) *f,* convalescence. **convalescent, e** (sɑ̃, ɑ̃t) *a. & n,* convalescent.
convenable† (kɔ̃vnabl) *a,* proper, suitable, fitting; respectable, decent; acceptable, adequate (*pay*). **convenance** (vnɑ̃s) *f,* convenience; suitability (*term*); affinity (*views*). ~*s,* proprieties. ~*s personnelles,* private reasons. *à votre* ~, convenient to you. **convenir** (vnir) *v.i. & t.ir,* to agree (*de qch,* on sth; *de faire,* to do). *comme convenu,* as agreed. ~ **de,** to admit (*mistake*). ~ **à,** to suit, be convenient for. ~ **que** (+ *indic.*), to agree that; admit that. ¶ *v.imp, il convient de faire,* it is advisable *or* polite to do. **convention** (vɑ̃sjɔ̃) *f,* agreement, understanding; (*social &c*) convention. **de** ~ **&** ~**nel, le** (ɔnɛl) *a,* conventional.
converger (kɔ̃vɛrʒe) *v.i,* to converge.
conversation (kɔ̃vɛrsasjɔ̃) *f,* conversation; (*Pol.*) talk. **converser** (se) *v.i,* to converse.
conversion (kɔ̃vɛrsjɔ̃) *f,* conversion; (*Mil.*) wheel; (*Ski*) kickturn. **converti, e** (ti) *n,* convert. **convertible** (tibl) *a,* convertible. ¶ *m,* bed-settee. **convertir** (tir) *v.t,* to convert (*à,* to; *en,* into). **se** ~, (*Rel.*) to be converted.
convertisseur (sœr) *m,* converter.
convexe (kɔ̃vɛks) *a,* convex. **convexité** (ite) *f,* convexity.
conviction (kɔ̃viksjɔ̃) *f,* conviction.
convier (vje) *v.t,* to invite (*à,* to); urge (*à faire,* to do). **convive** (viv) *n,* guest.
convocation (kɔ̃vɔkasjɔ̃) *f,* convening (*meeting*); summons.
convoi (kɔ̃vwa) *m,* convoy; (*Rly*) train; funeral procession.
convoiter (kɔ̃vwate) *v.t,* to covet, lust after. **convoitise** (tiz) *f,* covetousness; lust.
convoler (kɔ̃vɔle) *v.i,* ~ [*en justes noces*], to be wed (*ironic*).
convoquer (kɔ̃vɔke) *v.t,* to call, summon, convene (*pers., meeting*).
convoyer (kɔ̃vwaje) *v.t,* to escort; convoy.
convulser (kɔ̃vylse) *v.t,* to convulse, distort. **convulsif, ive†** (sif, iv) *a,* convulsive. **convulsion** (sjɔ̃) *f,* (*Med., fig.*) convulsion. ~**ner** (ɔne) *v.t,* to convulse.
coopérant (kɔɔperɑ̃) *m,* overseas volunteer. **coopératif, ive** (ratif, iv) *a,* cooperative. ¶ *f,* (*Agr., Com.*) cooperative. **coopération** (sjɔ̃) *f,* cooperation. **coopérer** (re) *v.i,* to cooperate (*à,* in).
coordination (kɔɔrdinasjɔ̃) *f,* coordination. **coordonnées** (dɔne) *f.pl,* (*Math.*) coordinates; *P* address &c. **coordonner** (dɔne) *v.t,* to coordinate.
copain, copine *P* (kɔpɛ̃, in) *n,* pal *P,* mate *P,* chum *P.*

copeau (kɔpo) *m,* [wood] shaving.
Copenhague (kɔpɛnag) *f,* Copenhagen.
copie (kɔpi) *f,* copy. ~ [*certifiée*] *conforme,* certified true c. (*Sch.*) sheet of paper; script. **copier** (pje) *v.t. & i,* (*gen.*) to copy; (*Sch.*) crib (*sur,* from).
copieux, euse† (kɔpjø, øz) *a,* copious; hearty (*meal*); generous (*helping*).
copiste (kɔpist) *n,* copyist.
copropriétaire (koprɔprietɛr) *n,* joint owner.
copulation (kɔpylasjɔ̃) *f,* copulation.
coq[1] (kɔk) *m,* cock. ~ *faisan,* c. pheasant. (*Box.*) *poids* ~, bantam-weight. *comme un* ~ *en pâte,* in clover. ~ *du village,* cock of the walk. **~-à-l'âne,** *m,* jumping from topic to topic.
coq[2] (kɔk) *m,* (*ship's*) cook.
coque (kɔk) *f,* shell (*egg*); hull (*ship*); body (*car*); fuselage (*plane*); cockle (*mollusc*). *œuf à la* ~, boiled egg.
coquelicot (kɔkliko) *m,* poppy.
coqueluche (kɔklyʃ) *f,* whooping cough; idol, darling (*of the public*).
coquet, te† (kɔkɛ, ɛt) *a,* smart, stylish (*pers.*); charming, pretty (*house &c*); (*P*) tidy *P* (*sum*); flirtatious. ¶ *f,* coquette, flirt.
coquetier (kɔktje) *m,* egg cup; egg merchant.
coquetterie (kɔkɛtri) *f,* smartness, stylishness; coquetry.
coquillage (kɔkijaʒ) *m,* shell; shellfish. **coquille** (kij) *f,* (*gen.*) shell; scallop (*dish*); whorl (*butter*); (*Typ.*) misprint. ~ *Saint-Jacques,* scallop.
coquin, e (kɔkɛ̃, in) *a,* mischievous; naughty (*joke*). ¶ *n,* rascal (*child*). ¶ *m,* rogue. ¶ *f,* hussy. **~erie** (kinri) *f,* mischievousness; roguishness; mischievous *or* rascally trick.
cor (kɔr) *m,* (*Mus.*) horn; corn (*foot*); tine (*antler*). ~ *d'harmonie,* French horn. *à* ~ *& à cri,* clamorously.
corail (kɔraj) *m,* coral.
Coran (kɔrɑ̃) *m,* Koran.
corbeau (kɔrbo) *m,* (*gen.*) crow. [*grand*] ~ raven. ~ *freux,* rook.
corbeille (kɔrbɛj) *f,* basket. ~ *à papiers,* waste paper b. ~ *de mariage,* wedding presents. (*Theat.*) [dress] circle.
corbillard (kɔrbijar) *m,* hearse.
cordage (kɔrdaʒ) *m,* rope. ~*s,* rigging. **corde** (kɔrd) *f,* rope; (*fig.*) hanging; (*Mus., Ten., bow*) string. (*Mus.*) *les* ~*s,* the strings. *quatuor à* ~*s,* string quartet. *usé jusqu'à la* ~, threadbare. *toucher la* ~ *sensible,* to touch the right chord (*with s.o*). (*Mot.*) *prendre un virage à la* ~, to hug the bend. ~ *à linge,* clothes line. ~ *raide,* (*lit., fig*) tightrope. ~ *à sauter,* skipping rope. ~*s vocales,* vocal cords. **cordeau** (do) *m,* (*garden*) line; fuse. *tiré à la* ~, dead straight. **cordée** (de) *f,* roped party. **cordelette** (dəlɛt) *f,* cord, string. **corder** (de) *v.t,* to string (*racket*).
cordial, e† (kɔrdjal) *a,* cordial, hearty. ¶ *m,* cordial. **cordialité** (lite) *f,* cordiality.
cordon (kɔrdɔ̃) *m,* cord (*curtain*); string (*apron, purse*); lace (*shoe*). ~ *de sonnette,* bellpull. (*Police*) cordon; [medal] ribbon. ~*-bleu,* cordon-bleu cook. ~ *sanitaire,* (*Med., Pol.*) quarantine line. **~nerie** (ɔnri) *f,* shoe repairer's shop. **~nier, ère** (nje, ɛr) *n,* shoe repairer, cobbler.
Corée (la) (kɔre), Korea. ~ *du Sud,* South K. **coréen, ne** (reɛ̃, ɛn) *a. &* **C~,** *n,* Korean.
coriace (kɔrjas) *a,* tough (*meat, pers.*).
cormoran (kɔrmɔrɑ̃) *m,* cormorant.
corne (kɔrn) *f,* (*gen.*) horn; dog-ear (*page*). *à* ~*s,* horned. ~ *d'abondance,* horn of plenty, cornucopia. ~ *de brume,* foghorn. ~ *à chaussures,* shoe h.
cornée (kɔrne) *f,* cornea.
corneille (kɔrnɛj) *f,* crow (*noire,* carrion; *mantelée,* hooded).
corner[1] (kɔrne) *v.i,* (*Mot.*) to sound one's horn, hoot. ¶ *v.t,* to turn down (*page*); blaze abroad (*news*). **corner**[2] (nɛr) *m,* (*Foot.*) corner [kick].
cornet (nɛ) *m,* cornet (*cone*). ~ *acoustique,* ear trumpet. ~ *à dés,* dice box. (*Mus.*) ~ *à pistons,* cornet.
corniche (kɔrniʃ) *f,* (*Arch.*) cornice; cliff road.
cornichon (kɔrniʃɔ̃) *m,* gherkin; nitwit *P.*
Cornouailles (la) (kɔrnwɑj), Cornwall.
cornu, e (kɔrny) *a,* horned. ¶ *f,* (*Chem.*) retort.
corollaire (kɔrɔlɛr) *m,* corollary.
corolle (kɔrɔl) *f,* (*Bot.*) corolla.
coronaire (kɔrɔnɛr) *a,* coronary.
corporatif, ive (kɔrpɔratif, iv) *a,* corporative. **corporation** (asjɔ̃) *f,* professional body; (*Hist.*) guild. **corporel, le** (rɛl) *a,* corporal (*punishment*); bodily (*pain*). **corps** (kɔr) *m,* (*gen.*) body; corpse. (*Chem.*) ~ *composé,* compound. ~ *simple,* element. ~ *à* ~, *ad.* (*& m*), hand to hand (*fight*). *perdu* ~ *& biens,* lost with all hands. *à* ~ *perdu,* headlong. *donner* ~ *à,* to give substance to (*rumour*). *prendre* ~, to take shape. ~ *d'armée,* army corps. ~ *de bâtiment,* building. ~ *électoral,* electorate. *le* ~ *enseignant,* the teaching profession. ~ *de garde,* guardroom. *le* ~ *médical,* the medical profession. ~ *de métier,* trade association.
corpulence (kɔrpylɑ̃s) *f,* stoutness, corpulence. **corpulent, e** (lɑ̃, ɑ̃t) *a,* corpulent, stout.
corpuscule (kɔrpyskyl) *m,* corpuscle.
correct, e† (kɔrɛkt) *a,* correct. **~eur, trice** (tœr, tris) *n,* marker (*exam*); proof-reader. **~if, ive** (tif, iv) *a. & m,* corrective. ¶ *m,* rider. **~ion** (sjɔ̃) *f,* (*gen.*) correction; marking; proof-reading; correctness; propriety; thrashing. **~ionnel, le** (ɔnɛl) *a,* criminal (*court*).
corrélation (kɔrelasjɔ̃) *f,* correlation.
correspondance (kɔrɛspɔ̃dɑ̃s) *f,* correspond-

ence; relation; (*postal &c*) correspondence; mail; (*Rly &c*) connection. *assurer la ~ avec,* to connect with. **correspondant, e** (dɑ̃, ɑ̃t) *a,* corresponding. ¶ *n,* (*gen., Press*) correspondent. **correspondre** (pɔ̃dr) *v.i,* to correspond (*avec,* with); (*rooms*) communicate; (*Rly &c*) connect (*avec,* with). ~ **à,** to correspond to, fit, tally with.

corrida (kɔrida) *f,* bullfight.

corridor (kɔridɔr) *m,* corridor.

corrigé (kɔriʒe) *m,* fair copy; key (*to exercises*). **corriger** (ʒe) *v.t,* to correct; thrash. ~ *qn de,* to cure s.o of.

corroborer (kɔrɔbɔre) *v.t,* to corroborate.

corroder (kɔrɔde) *v.t,* to corrode.

corrompre (kɔrɔ̃pr) *v.t,* to corrupt; bribe; taint, contaminate.

corrosif, ive (kɔrozif, iv) *a,* corrosive; (*fig.*) caustic. **corrosion** (zjɔ̃) *f,* corrosion.

corruptible (kɔryptibl) *a,* corruptible. **corruption** (sjɔ̃) *f,* corruption, bribery.

corsage (kɔrsaʒ) *m,* blouse; bodice.

corsaire (kɔrsɛr) *m,* (*Hist.*) privateer.

Corse (la) (kɔrs), Corsica. **corse,** *a.* & **C~,** *n,* Corsican.

corsé, e (kɔrse) *a,* full-bodied (*wine*); racy (*story*). **corser** (se) *v.t,* to strengthen; liven up. **se ~,** to become serious, hot up *P.*

corset (kɔrsɛ) *m,* corset.

cortège (kɔrtɛʒ) *m,* procession; retinue.

corvée (kɔrve) *f,* (*Mil.*) fatigue; chore, drudgery; (*Hist.*) statute labour.

corvette (kɔrvɛt) *f,* (*Nav.*) corvette.

cosaque (kɔzak) *m,* Cossack.

cosmétique (kɔsmetik) *a,* cosmetic. ¶ *m,* hair oil.

cosmique (kɔsmik) *a,* cosmic. **cosmonaute** (mɔnot) *n,* cosmonaut. **cosmopolite** (pɔlit) *a,* cosmopolitan. **cosmos** (mos) *m,* cosmos; outer space.

cosse (kɔs) *f,* pod (*peas &c*); (*Naut.*) thimble, eyelet. *avoir la ~ P,* to feel lazy.

cossu, e (kɔsy) *a,* well off; rich.

costaud, e *P* (kɔsto, od) *a,* sturdy, strong.

costume (kɔstym) *m,* costume, dress; suit. ~ *de bain,* bathing suit. **costumer** (me) *v.t,* to dress up (*en,* as).

cotation (kɔtasjɔ̃) *f,* (*Stk Ex.*) quotation; (*Sch.*) marking. **cote** (kɔt) *f,* (*Stk Ex.*) list; quotation, price; value (*car*); odds (*de,* on: *horse*); spot height (*map*); rating, popularity. *avoir la ~ P,* to be rated highly. ~ *d'alerte,* danger mark (*river*). ~ *mal taillée,* rough & ready settlement.

côte (kot) *f,* rib; chop (*pork*); cutlet (*lamb*). *à ~s,* ribbed (*cloth*). ~ *à* ~, side by side. *se tenir les ~s,* to split one's sides (*laughing*). ¶ slope, hill (*road*). *dans la ~,* on the hill. ¶ coast. *la C~ d'Azur,* the Riviera. *la C~ d'Ivoire,* the Ivory Coast.

côté (kote) *m,* side. *de chaque, de l'autre ~,* on either, on the other side (*de,* of). side, aspect. *par certains ~s,* in certain respects. *son ~ faible,* his weak spot. *d'un ~... d'un autre ~...* on the one hand ... on the other h. **du ~ de,** near; towards. *aller, venir du ~ de la rivière,* to go towards, come from the river. *de ce ~,* this way. *de l'autre ~,* the other way. **à ~,** *ad,* nearby. *les gens d'à côté,* the people next door. **à ~ de,** *pr,* beside, next to. **de ~,** *ad,* (*turn, walk*) sideways; (*jump*) aside. *mettre de ~,* to put aside, put by.

coteau (kɔto) *m,* hill, hillside, slope.

côtelette (kotlɛt) *f,* chop, cutlet.

coter (kɔte) *v.t,* to quote the price of (*shares &c*); (*Sch.*) to mark; rate, rank; number, classify. *très coté,* highly thought of.

coterie (kɔtri) *f,* set, clique, circle.

côtier, ère (kotje, ɛr) *a,* coastal (*defence*); inshore (*fishing*).

cotisation (kɔtizasjɔ̃) *f,* subscription (*club*); contributions (*social security &c*). **cotiser** (ze) *v.i,* to pay one's subscription &c. **se ~,** to club together.

coton (kɔtɔ̃) *m,* (*gen.*) cotton. ~ [*hydrophile*], cotton wool. *j'ai les jambes en ~,* my legs feel like c. wool. ¶ *a P,* difficult. **~nade** (tɔnad) *f,* cotton [cloth, goods]. **~neux, euse** (nø, øz) *a,* fluffy; wispy (*fog*). **~nier, ère** (nje, ɛr) *a,* cotton. ¶ *m,* cotton plant.

côtoyer (kotwaje) *v.t,* to run, go along[side], skirt; (*fig.*) border on, verge on; rub shoulders with.

cotre (kɔtr) *m,* (*Naut.*) cutter.

cottage (kɔtaʒ) *m,* (*smart country*) cottage.

cotte (kɔt) *f,* ~ [*de travail*], overalls. (*Hist.*) ~ *de mailles,* coat of mail.

cou (ku) *m,* neck. *sauter au ~ de qn,* to throw one's arms round s.o's neck. *~-de-pied,* instep.

couard, e (kuar, ard) *a,* cowardly. ¶ *n,* coward. **~ise** (diz) *f,* cowardice.

couchage (kuʃaʒ) *m,* sleeping [arrangements]. *sac de ~,* sleeping bag. **couchant** (ʃɑ̃) *m,* west; sunset. **couche** (kuʃ) *f,* layer; coat (*paint*); (*Geol., fig*) stratum; (*liter.*) bed. *~s,* (*Med.*) confinement. *fausse ~,* miscarriage. **coucher** (kuʃe) *m,* going to bed; bedtime; setting (*sun &c*). [*au*] ~ *du soleil,* [at] sunset. ¶ *v.t,* to put to bed. ~ *par écrit,* to commit to (*or* put in) (*or* set down in) writing. put up (*for the night*); lay down; flatten (*crops*); inscribe (*on list*). ~ *qn en joue,* to aim at s.o. ¶ *v.i,* to spend the night, sleep. ~ *avec qn,* to sleep with s.o. **se ~,** to lie down, go to bed; set, go down (*sun, moon*). **couchette** (ʃɛt) *f,* berth, bunk, couchette.

couci-couça *P* (kusikusa) *ad,* so-so *P.*

coucou (kuku) *m,* cuckoo.

coude (kud) *m,* elbow; bend (*pipe, road*). ~ *à* ~, shoulder to shoulder. *se serrer les ~s,* to stick together. *jouer des ~s*, to elbow one's way. **coudée** (de) *f*, *avoir les ~s franches*, to have elbow room, (*fig.*) freedom of action.

cou-de-pied (kudpje) *m*, instep.

couder (kude) *v.t*, to bend (*pipe*). **coudoyer** (dwaje) *v.t*, to rub shoulders with, mix with. **coudre** (kudr) *v.t. & i.ir*, to sew; sew up; sew on; stitch (*book*).

coudrier (kudrie) *m*, hazel tree.

couenne (kwan) *f*, rind (*bacon*); **crackling** (*pork*); (*P skin*) hide *P*.

couilles *P** (kuj) *f.pl*, balls *P** (*testicles*).

couillon *P** (kujɔ̃) *m*, bloody fool *P**. **~nade** *P* (ɔnad) *f*, boob *P*. *~s*, (*nonsense*) cock *P**, crap *P**. **~ner** *P* (ɔne) *v.t*, to swindle.

couiner (kwine) *v.i*, to squeal.

coulant, e (kulɑ̃, ɑ̃t) *a*, runny (*jam*); flowing (*style*). *nœud ~*, slip-knot. **coulé** (le) *m*, (*Mus.*) slur; (*Bil.*) follow [shot]. **coulée** (le) *f*, flow (*lava*); casting (*metal*).

couler (kule) *v.i*, (*liquid*) to flow, run; (*tap*) run, leak; (*words*) flow; (*days*) slip by; (*boat, pers.*) sink. *~ à pic*, sink straight down. *faire ~*, to run (*bath*); shed (*blood*).¶ *v.t*, to pour; cast (*metal*); sink (*boat*); slip (*coin*); steal (*glance*). (*Mot.*) *~ une bielle*, to run a big end. **se ~**, to slip, slide (*dans*, into; *à travers*, through).

couleur (kulœr) *f*, colour; tint, shade; paint; (*Cards*) suit. *de ~*, colourful (*dress*); coloured (*pers.*). *les ~s*, the colours (*flag*); coloureds (*wash*). *photo en ~*, colour photo. *sans ~*, colourless. *sous ~ de*, under the guise of. *en voir de toutes les ~s*, to have every kind of trouble. ¶ *a. inv*, *~ d'azur*, sky blue. *~ paille*, straw-coloured.

couleuvre (kulœvr) *f*, grass snake. *avaler des ~s*, to swallow an affront.

coulisse (kulis) *f*, (*Theat.*) *~s*, wings. *en ~*, *dans la ~*, behind the scenes. unofficial Stock Market; slide (*trombone*); runner (*door*). *porte à ~*, sliding door. *regard en ~*, sidelong look.

couloir (kulwar) *m*, passage, corridor; lane (*air, road, sprint*); gully; (*Ten.*) tramlines. (*Pol.*) *~s*. lobbies.

coup (ku) *m*, blow; stroke; knock. *oft. as object of donner: donner un ~ de pied à*, to kick; *donner un ~ de frein*, to brake. ¶ (*parts of the body*) *~ de corne*, butt. *~ de coude*, nudge. *~ d'œil*, glance; view. *jeter un ~ d'œil à*, to glance at. *~ de main*, (*fig.*) helping hand; raid. *donne-moi un ~ de main*, give me a hand. *avoir le ~ de main*, to have the touch. *~ d'ongle*, scratch. *~ de pouce*, (*fig.*) helping push, boost; final touch. *~ de pied*, kick. *~ de poing*, punch. ¶ (*instrument*) *~ d'archet*, (*Mus.*) bow. *~ de balai*, sweep; (*fig.*) clean sweep. *~ de bâton*, blow with a stick. *~ de chiffon*, wipe, dust. *~ de couteau*, stab. *~ de fer*, press, iron. *~ de fouet*, lash; (*fig.*) fillip, lift. *~ de fusil*, rifle shot; (*fig.*) rip-off *P*. *~ de marteau*, blow with a hammer. *~ de peigne*, comb. *~ de pinceau*, brush stroke. *~ de téléphone*, phone call. ¶ (*sound*) *~ de feu*, shot. *~ de sifflet*, whistle [blast]. *~ de sonnette*, ring. *~ de tonnerre*, clap of thunder; (*fig.*) bombshell. (*Fr. Theat.*) *frapper les trois ~s*, to give the 3 knocks (*before curtain rise*). ¶ (*Sport*) (*Ten., Golf*) stroke; (*Box.*) blow; (*Chess*) move. *~ bas*, blow below the belt. *~ d'envoi*, kick-off. *~ franc*, free kick. *~ roulé*, putt. ¶ (*fig: blow, stroke*) *~ dur*, hard blow. *~ de chance*, stroke of luck. *~ du destin*, stroke of fate. *~ de grâce*, finishing s. *~ de maître*, master s. *~ de massue*, shattering blow. *sale ~ P*, terrible blow; dirty trick. ¶ (*quantity*) *boire un ~*, to have a drink. *~ de rouge*, glass of red wine. *~ de peinture*, coat, lick of paint. *rire un bon ~*, to have a good laugh. ¶ (*time*) *à tous les ~s*, every time. *du premier ~*, first time, f. go. *d'un seul ~*, at one go, time. *à ~ sûr*, for certain. *après ~*, after the event. *~ sur ~*, in quick succession. *être dans le ~*, to be in on it (*job*). *sur le ~*, (*killed*) outright; at the time. *tenir le ~*, to hold out. *tenter le ~ P*, to have a go *P*. *tout à ~*, *tout d'un ~*, suddenly. (*Law*) *~s & blessures*, grievous bodily harm. *~ de chapeau*, raising one's hat. *donner un ~ de collier*, to put one's back into it. *~ d'essai*, first attempt. *~ d'Etat*, coup [d'état]. *~ de filet*, haul. *~ de foudre*, (*fig.*) love at first sight. *~ de froid*, chill. *~ du père François*, stab in the back. *~ de sang*, (*Med.*) stroke. *~[s] de soleil*, sunburn. *~ de vent*, gust of wind. *passer en ~ de vent*, to rush past; pay a flying visit.

coupable (kupabl) *a*, guilty. ¶ *n*, culprit.

coupage (kupaʒ) *m*, blending (*wines*). **coupant, e** (pɑ̃, ɑ̃t) *a*, (*lit., fig.*) sharp.

coupe[1] (kup) *f*, [fruit] dish; goblet; (*Sport*) cup.

coupe[2] (kup) *f*, cutting; cutting out (*garment*); length (*cloth*); felling (*trees*); section (*plan*). *~ de cheveux*, haircut.

coup- (kup) *pref*, (*all m. inv.*) **~-circuit,** (*Elec.*) cut-out. **~-feu,** firebreak. **~-gorge,** death trap. **~-papier,** paper knife. **~-vent,** windbreak.

coupé (kupe) *m*, (*Mot., Danc.*) coupé.

couper (kupe) *v.t*, to cut; cut down (*tree*); c. out (*garment*); c. off (*gas, water &c*); switch off (*current*); take away (*appetite*); (*Cards*) cut; trump; slice (*ball*); blend (*wines*); dilute. *se faire ~ les cheveux*, to get one's hair cut. *~ la tête à qn*, to behead s.o. *~ la gorge à qn*, to cut s.o's throat. (*Mot.*) *~ la route à qn*, to cut in front of s.o. *~ les cheveux en quatre*, to split hairs. *~ l'herbe sous les pieds à qn*, to cut the ground from under s.o's feet. *~ la parole à qn*, to cut s.o short; leave s.o speechless. ~

le souffle à qn, to wind s.o; (*fig.*) take s.o's breath away. ¶*v.i,* to cut. ~ *à travers champs,* to cut across country. **se ~,** to cut o.s. *se ~ au doigt, les ongles,* to cut one's finger, one's nails.
couperet (kuprɛt) *m,* cleaver, chopper.
couperosé, e (kuprɔze) *a,* blotchy (*face*).
couple (kupl) *m,* couple, pair. ~ [*moteur*], torque. **coupler** (ple) *v.t,* to couple, connect. **couplet** (plɛ) *m,* verse (*song*).
coupole (kupɔl) *f,* cupola, dome.
coupon (kupɔ̃) *m,* remnant (*cloth*); coupon. ~-*réponse,* reply coupon. **coupure** (pyr) *f,* (*Gen.*) cut; (*fig.*) break, gap; [press] cutting; (*Fin.*) denomination.
cour (kur) *f,* [court]yard; [barrack] square. ~ *de ferme,* farmyard. ~ *de récréation,* playground. (*Law*) court. ~ *d'appel,* C. of Appeal. ~ *d'assises,* ≏ Crown C. (*Mil.*) ~ *martiale,* c. martial. (*royal*) court. *faire la ~ à,* to court (*woman*).
courage (kuraʒ) *m,* courage, bravery; spirit. *perdre ~,* to lose heart. *je n'ai pas le ~ de,* I haven't the heart to. ¶ *i,* cheer up! *bon ~!* good luck! **courageux, euse†** (raʒø, øz) *a,* courageous, brave.
couramment (kuramɑ̃) *ad,* fluently; commonly. **courant, e** (rɑ̃, ɑ̃t) *a,* running (*water*). *chien ~,* hound. common, everyday; standard (*model*); current (*month*). ¶ *m,* current (*sea, river*); movement, trend; course (*of month*); wave (*feeling*). ~ *d'air,* draught. (*Elec.*) current. ~ *alternatif, continu,* alternating, direct c. *couper le ~,* to cut off the power. *au ~ de,* informed about, up to date with. *mettre qn au ~,* to put s.o in the picture. *tenez-moi au ~,* keep me informed.
courbature (kurbatyr) *f,* stiffness, ache. **courbaturé, e** (re) *a* stiff, aching (*all over*).
courbe (kurb) *a* curved. ¶ *f,* curve. ~ *de niveau,* contour line. **courber** (be) *v.t. & i. &* **se ~,** to bend, bow. **courbette** (bɛt) *f,* low bow. *faire des ~s,* to bow & scrape. **courbure** (byr) *f,* curve.
coureur, euse (kurœr, øz) *n,* runner. ~ *de fond,* long-distance r. ~ *automobile, cycliste,* racing driver, r. cyclist. ¶ *m,* ~ *de bars,* frequenter of bars. ~ [*de filles*], womanizer. ¶ *f,* manhunter.
courge (kurʒ) *f,* gourd; vegetable marrow. **courgette** (ʒɛt) *f,* courgette.
courir (kurir) *v.i.ir,* to run; race; rush; (*water, path &c*) run; (*ship*) sail. *entrer, sortir en courant,* to run in, out. *faire qch en courant,* to do sth in a rush. ~ *à,* to head for (*ruin*). ~ *après qn, qch,* to run after s.o, pursue sth. *le bruit court que,* it is rumoured that. *par le temps qui court,* as things are today. ¶ *v.t,* to run (*race, risk*); face (*danger*); hunt (*stag*); chase (*girls*); to go round (*shops, bars*); roam (*streets, woods*).
courlis (kurli) *m,* curlew.
couronne (kurɔn) *f,* crown, coronet; wreath; crown (*tooth*); (*Astr.*) corona. ~ *d'épines,* crown of thorns. ~ *mortuaire,* funeral wreath. ~**ment** (nmɑ̃) *m,* coronation; crowning; crowning achievement. **couronner** (ne) *v.t,* (*lit., fig.*) to crown; award a prize to.
courrier (kurje) *m,* mail, post, letters; mail (*boat, plane*); *O* courier, messenger; (*Press*) column, page. ~ *du cœur,* agony column.
courroie (kurwa) *f,* strap; (*Tech.*) belt. ~ *de ventilateur,* fan belt.
courroucer (kuruse) *v.t,* (*liter.*) to incense. **courroux** (ru) *m,* (*liter.*) wrath, anger.
cours (kur) *m,* course; flow (*river*). ~ *d'eau,* river, stream, waterway. (*Fin.*) price; currency; rate. ~ *légal,* legal tender. (*Sch.*) lesson; (*Univ.*) lecture; course (*lessons*); course book; school; class, year; avenue, walk (*street name*). ~ *de danse,* school of dancing. ~ *préparatoire,* reception class. *au ~ de,* in the course of, *en ~,* current (*year*); in progress. *en ~ de développement,* in the process of being developed. *avoir ~,* to be legal tender; (*fig.*) to be accepted. *donner libre ~ à,* to give free rein to.
course (kurs) *f,* run; running; race; racing. *de ~,* racing (*car, cycle*); race (*horse*). *faire de la ~,* to go running. flight, course (*arrow, sun*); (*Mach.*) movement; stroke (*piston*); trip, journey; walk, climb; errand, shopping. *faire des ~s,* to go shopping; run errands. *être à bout de ~,* to be worn out. *la ~ aux armements,* the arms race. ~ *de côte,* hill climb. ~ *de fond,* long-distance race *or* running. ~ *de relais,* relay race. ~ *de taureaux,* bull-fight. ~ *de vitesse,* sprint. **coursier** (sje) *m,* messenger; (*liter.*) charger, steed.
court¹, e (kur, urt) *a,* short. *de ~e durée,* short-lived. *à ~ d'argent,* short of money. *prendre au plus ~,* to go the shortest way. *faire la ~e échelle à qn,* to give s.o a leg up. *tirer à la ~e paille,* to draw lots. ¶ *ad,* short. *s'arrêter ~,* to stop short. *couper ~ à,* to cut short. *tourner ~,* to stop suddenly; come to nothing. *tout ~,* simply just (*& no more*).
court² (kur) *m,* (*Ten.*) court.
courtaud, e (kurto, od) *a,* dumpy (*pers.*)
court-circuit (kursirkɥi) *m,* short [circuit].
courtepointe (kurtəpwɛ̃t) *f,* quilt.
courtier, ère (kurtje, ɛr) *n,* broker.
courtisan (kurtizɑ̃) *m,* (*Hist.*) courtier; sycophant. ~**e** (zan) *f,* (*liter.*) courtesan. **courtiser** (ze) *v.t,* to court; woo; fawn on. **courtois, e†** (twa, az) *a,* courteous; courtly (love). **courtoisie** (twazi) *f,* courtesy.
couru, e (kury) *a,* popular (*café, show*).
cousin, e (kuzɛ̃, in) *n,* cousin. ~ *germain,* first

cousin. ¶ *m,* mosquito.
coussin (kusɛ̃) *m,* cushion. **~et** (sinɛ) *m,* [small] cousin; (*Tech.*) bearing.
cousu, e (kuzy) *a,* sewn, stitched. ~ *main,* handsewn. *c'est* ~ *de fil blanc,* it sticks out a mile.
coût (ku) *m,* cost.
couteau (kuto) *m,* knife; knife edge. ~ *à cran d'arrêt,* flick knife. ~ *de cuisine,* kitchen k. ~ *à découper,* carving k. (*fig.*) *à* ~*x tirés,* at daggers drawn. *mettre le* ~ *sous la gorge à qn,* to hold a pistol to s.o's head. **coutelas** (tla) *m,* big kitchen knife. **coutellerie** (tɛlri) *f,* cutlery trade; c. shop *or* works; cutlery (*goods*).
coûter (kute) *v.i,* to cost. ~ *cher,* to cost a lot. *les voitures, ça coûte!* cars are expensive! ~ *les yeux de la tête P,* to cost the earth *P*. *ça lui a coûté sa vie,* it cost him his life. *coûte que coûte,* at all costs. **coûteusement** (tøzmɑ̃) *ad,* expensively. **coûteux, euse** (tø, øz) *a,* costly, expensive.
coutil (kuti) *m,* drill; ticking (*mattress*).
coutume (kutym) *f,* custom. *comme de* ~, as usual. *avoir* ~ *de,* to be in the habit of. **coutumier, ère** (mje, ɛr) *a,* customary. ~ *du fait,* in the habit of doing so.
couture (kutyr) *f,* sewing; needlework; dressmaking; fashion industry; seam; scar. *battre à platte* ~, to beat hollow. **couturier** (rje) *m,* fashion designer, couturier. **couturière** (rjɛr) *f,* dressmaker.
couvée (ve) *f,* clutch (*eggs*); brood.
couvent (kuvɑ̃) *m,* convent; monastery; convent school.
couver (kuve) *v.t,* to sit on (*eggs*); hatch; coddle (*child*); plot; to be sickening for (*illness*). ~ *des yeux,* to gaze longingly *or* lovingly at. ¶ *v.i,* (*hen*) brood, sit; (*fire, anger*) smoulder; (*trouble &c*) brew.
couvercle (kuvɛrkl) *m,* lid; cap, top.
couvert, e (kuvɛr, ɛrt) *a,* covered (*de,* with); wrapped up (*pers.*); overcast (*sky*). *rester* ~, to keep one's hat on. ¶ *m,* place (*at table*); setting. ~*s,* cutlery. *mettre le* ~, to lay the table. shelter. *le vivre & le* ~, board & lodging. *à* ~, under cover, sheltered (*de,* from). (*Mil.*) *se mettre à* ~, to take cover.
couverture (kuvɛrtyr) *f,* blanket; rug (*travelling*); roofing; book jacket; (*Mil., fig.*) cover; (*Fin.*) margin.
couveuse (kuvøz) *f,* broody hen. ~ [*artificielle*], incubator.
couvre-chef (kuvrəʃɛf) *m,* headgear. **couvre-feu** *m,* curfew. **couvre-lit,** *m,* bedspread. **couvre-livre,** *m,* jacket, dust cover (*book*). **couvre-pied,** *m,* quilt. **couvre-théière,** *m,* tea cosy.
couvreur (kuvrœr) *m,* roofer. **couvrir** (kuvrir) *v.t.ir,* to cover (*de,* with); roof; wrap up (*pers.*); conceal; drown (*sound*); cover, shield (*pers.*); (*Mil. & costs*) cover. **se** ~, to wrap up; put on one's hat; cover o.s (*with glory &c*); (*sky, weather*) cloud over.
crabe (krab) *m,* crab.
crac (krak) *i,* crack! bang!
crachat (kraʃa) *m,* spit[tle]. **craché, e** (ʃe) *a, c'est son père tout* ~, he's the spit & image of his father. *c'est lui tout* ~, that's him to a T. **crachement** (ʃmɑ̃) *m,* spitting; (*Radio*) crackle. **cracher** (ʃe) *v.t,* to spit [out]; (*fig.*) belch (*flames &c*); (*P*) cough up *P* (*money*). ¶ *v.i,* to spit; (*pen*) splutter; (*Radio*) crackle. **crachin** (ʃɛ̃) *m,* drizzle. **crachoir** (ʃwar) *m,* spittoon.
crack (krak) *m,* star horse; (*Sport*) ace.
craie (krɛ) *f,* chalk.
craindre (krɛ̃dr) *v.t.ir,* to fear; be afraid of (*de faire,* doing). *je crains la chaleur,* I can't stand the heat. '*craint l'humidité*', keep in a dry place. ~ *pour sa vie,* to fear for one's life. **crainte** (krɛ̃t) *f,* fear. *avoir* ~ *de,* to be afraid of. *de* ~ *de, que,* for fear of, that. **craintif, ive†** (krɛ̃tif, iv) *a,* timid, timorous.
cramoisi, e (kramwazi) *a,* crimson.
crampe (krɑ̃p) *f,* (*Med.*) cramp. **crampon** (krɑ̃pɔ̃) *m,* (*Build.*) cramp; clamp; stud (*boot*). ~ [*à glace*], crampon. (*P pers.*) persistent bore. **~ner** (pɔne) *v.t,* to cramp; clamp; (*fig.*) to cling to, pester (*pers.*). **se** ~ **à,** (*lit., fig.*) to cling to.
cran (krɑ̃) *m,* notch, nick; hole (*belt*). ~ *de sureté,* safety catch (*gun*). *il a du* ~ *P,* he has guts *P*.
crâne (krɑn) *m,* skull; (*fig.*) head. ¶† *a,* plucky, determined. **crâner** (krɑne) *v.i,* to show off, swagger; brazen it out.
crapaud (krapo) *m,* toad.
crapule (krapyl) *f,* scoundrel, scum. **crapuleux, euse†** (lø, øz) *a,* villainous, sordid, debauched.
craqueler (se) (krakle) *v.pr,* to crack. **craquelure** (yr) *f,* crack. **craquer** (ke) *v.i,* (*ice*) to crack; (*branch*) snap; (*coat*) rip; crunch, creak, crackle; (*shoes*) squeak. ¶ *v.t,* to rip; strike (*match*). **craquement** (kmɑ̃) *m,* crack (*sound*); crunch &c. **craqueter** (kte) *v.i,* (*floor*) to creak.
crasse (kras) *a.f,* crass (*ignorance*) ¶ *f,* filth, grime; (*P*) dirty trick. **crasseux, euse** (sø, øz) *a,* filthy, grimy.
cratère (kratɛr) *m,* crater.
cravache (kravaʃ) *f,* riding crop. **cravacher** (ʃe) *v.t,* to whip. ¶ *v.i, P,* to belt along *P*.
cravate (kravat) *f,* [neck]tie.
crayeux, euse (krɛjø, øz) *a,* chalky. **crayon** (jɔ̃) *m,* pencil; p. sketch. ~ *à bille,* ball-point pen. ~ *pour les yeux,* eyeliner. **~ner** (jɔne) *v.t,* to sketch; scribble (*notes*).
créance (kreɑ̃s) *f,* credence, credibility. *donner* ~ *à,* to give credence to; make credible.

(*Fin.*) claim (*on a creditor*). **créancier, ère** (ɑ̃sje, ɛr) *n*, creditor.
créateur, trice (kreatœr, tris) *a*, creative. ¶ *n*, creator. **création** (sjɔ̃) *f*, creation; (*Theat.*) first production; (*Com.*) product. **créature** (tyr) *f*, creature.
crécelle (kresɛl) *f*, rattle (*toy &c*).
crécerelle (kresrɛl) *f*, kestrel.
crèche (krɛʃ) *f*, crib; day nursery, crèche.
crédibilité (kredibilite) *f*, credibility. **crédit** (di) *m*, (*Fin.*) credit. ~*s*, funds. *faire* ~ *à qn*, to give s.o. c. *à* ~, (*buy, sell*) on c. credit, respect; trust. *faire* ~ *à*, to trust in. ~ *hypothécaire*, mortgage. ~*s budgétaires*, budget allocation. **créditer** (te) *v.t*, (*Fin.*) to credit (*de*, with). **créditeur, trice** (tœr, tris) *a*, in credit. *solde* ~, credit balance. ¶ *n*, customer in credit.
credo (kredo) *m*, creed. **crédule** (kredyl) *a*, credulous, gullible. **crédulité** (lite) *f*, credulity, gullibility.
créer (kree) *v.t*, to create; (*Theat.*) create (*rôle*); produce (*new play*).
crémaillère (kremajɛr) *f*, pothook (*with ratchet*); (*Rly*) rack, cog-rail. *pendre la* ~, to give a house-warming.
crémation (kremasjɔ̃) *f*, cremation. **crématoire** (twar) *a*, crematory. ¶ *m*, crematorium.
crème (krɛm) *f*, cream; (*Cook.*) cream, custard. *la* ~, the cream, the best. *café* ~, white coffee. ¶ *a. inv*, cream-coloured. ~ *anglaise*, egg custard. ~ *Chantilly*, ~ *fouettée*, whipped c. ~ *de beauté*, beauty c. ~ *à raser*, shaving c. **crémerie** (mri) *f*, dairy. **crémeux, euse** (kremø, øz) *a*, creamy. **crémier, ère** (mje, ɛr) *n*, dairyman, -woman.
créneau (kreno) *m*, crenel. ~*x*, battlements. (*Mot.*) *faire un* ~, to park between 2 cars. **crénelé, e** (nle) *a*, crenellated.
créole (kreɔl) *a. & n*, Creole.
créosote (kreɔzɔt) *f*, creosote.
crêpe (krɛp) *m*, crape, crêpe; (*f.*) pancake. **crêper** (pe) *v.t*, to back-comb (*hair*).
crépi, e (krepi) *a. & m*, (*Build.*) roughcast.
crépir (krepir) *v.t*, to roughcast.
crépiter (krepite) *v.i*, to crackle; (*gunfire*) rattle; (*fat*) splutter; (*rain*) patter.
crépu, e (krepy) *a*, frizzy, fuzzy (*hair*).
crépuscule (krepyskyl) *m*, (*lit., fig.*) twilight.
crescendo (kreʃɛ̃do) *ad. & m*, crescendo. (*fig.*) *aller* ~, to swell, increase.
cresson (krəsɔ̃) *m*, cress. ~ [*de fontaine*], watercress.
Crète (la) (krɛt), Crete.
crête (krɛt) *f*, crest (*bird, wave*); ridge (*hill, roof*). ~ *de coq*, cockscomb.
crétin, e (kretɛ̃, in) *a*, cretinous *P*. ¶ *n*, (*pej., Med.*) cretin.
creusage (krøzaʒ), **creusement** (zmɑ̃) *m*, digging. **creuser** (ze) *v.t. & i*, to dig (*earth, hole*); sink (*well*); hollow out; (*fig.*) study deeply. *ça creuse*, it makes you hungry. *se* ~ [*la cervelle*], to rack one's brains.
creuset (krøzɛ) *m*, crucible; (*fig.*) melting pot.
creux, euse (krø, øz) *a*, hollow (*box, sound*); sunken (*eyes, road*); empty (*words*); slack (*days &c*). ¶ *m*, hollow (*hand, ground*); trough (*wave*); slack period. *le* ~ *des reins*, the small of the back.
crevaison (krəvɛzɔ̃) *f*, puncture, flat (*tyre*).
crevasse (krəvas) *f*, crack; crevice; crevasse. **crevasser** (se) *v.t*, to crack; chap (*skin*).
crève-cœur (krɛvkœr) *m*, great sorrow, heartbreak. **crevé, e** *P* (krəve) *a*, dead-beat *P;* dead. **crever** (ve) *v.t*, to burst; puncture (*tyre*); break (*heart*); put out (*s.o's eyes*); *P* exhaust, wear out (*pers.*). *ça te crève les yeux*, it's staring you in the face. ¶ *v.i*, to burst, puncture; (*animal*) die; *P* (*pers.*) die, snuff it *P*. ~ *de froid, de soif P*, to die of cold, thirst.
crevette (krəvɛt) *f:* ~ [*grise*], shrimp. ~ [*rose*], prawn.
cri (kri) *m*, cry, shout; scream, shriek; squeal; call (*pers., animal*). ~ *de cœur*, cry from the heart. ~ *de guerre*, war cry. **criailler** (ɑje) *v.i*, (*baby*) to bawl; grouse, nag. **criant, e** (ɑ̃, ɑ̃t) *a*, glaring. **criard, e** (ar, ard) *a*, screaming (*kids*); nagging, scolding; loud (*colours*); pressing (*debts*).
crible (kribl) *m*, sieve, riddle, screen. *passer au* ~, to sift, riddle. **cribler** (ble) *v.t*, to sift, riddle, screen. *criblé de*, riddled with (*holes &c*).
cric (kri) *m*, [lifting] jack.
cricri (krikri) *m*, chirp; cricket (*insect*).
criée (krie) *f*, auction. **crier** (e) *v.i*, to cry, shout; scream, shriek; call out; (*bird*) call; (*floor*) creak; (*brake*) screech. ~ *à tue-tête*, to shout one's head off. ~ *au secours*, to shout for help. ~ *au scandale*, to call it a scandal. ¶ *v.t*, to shout (*orders*); cry (*wares*). ~ *gare*, to shout a warning. **crieur, euse** (œr, øz) *n*, ~ *de journaux*, newsvendor. (*Hist.*) ~ *public*, town crier.
crime (krim) *m*, crime; felony; murder. **criminel, le†** (minɛl) *a*, criminal. ¶ *n*, criminal; murderer.
crin (krɛ̃) *m*, horse hair. *à tous* ~*s*, out & out. **crinière** (krinjɛr) *f*, mane (*animal*); mop of hair.
crique (krik) *f*, creek, inlet (*sea*).
criquet (krikɛ) *m*, locust.
crise (kriz) *f*, (*Med.*) attack, fit; (*fig.*) fit. ~ *de foie*, bilious attack. ~ *de nerfs*, fit of hysterics. *piquer une* ~, to fly off the handle *P*. crisis; shortage. ~ *du logement*, housing problem.
crispation (krispasjɔ̃) *f*, contraction; contortion (*face*); twitching. **crisper** (pe) *v.t*, to tense (*muscles*); contort (*face*); clench (*fist*). **se** ~,

to tense.
cristal (kristal) *m,* crystal; c. object, glass. ~ *taillé,* cut glass. ~*aux de soude,* washing soda. ~**lerie** (lri) *f,* crystal glass making *or* works; crystalware. ~**lin, e** (lɛ̃, in) *a,* crystalline. ¶ *m,* crystalline lens (*eye*). ~**liser** (lize) *v.t. & i. &* **se** ~, to crystallize.
critère (kritɛr) *m,* criterion.
critiquable (kritikabl) *a,* open to criticism. **critique** (tik) *a,* critical; crucial. ¶ *m,* critic; reviewer. ¶ *f,* criticism; critique; review. *la* ~, the critics. *faire la* ~ *de,* to review (*play &c*). **critiquer** (ke) *v.t,* to criticize.
croasser (krɔase) *v.i,* to caw, croak.
croc (kro) *m,* hook; fang. *montrer les* ~*s,* to bare its (*or* one's) teeth. ~**-en-jambe** (krɔkɑ̃ʒɑ̃b) *m, faire un* ~ *à qn,* to trip s.o up; (*fig.*) trick s.o. **croche** (krɔʃ) *f,* (*Mus.*) quaver. *double* ~, semi-quaver. **crochet** (ʃɛ) *m,* (*gen., Box.*) hook; (*Need.*) crochet, c. hook; picklock (*burglar*); fang (*snake*); (*Typ.*) square bracket; (*Mot.*) sudden turn, swerve. *faire un* ~, to swerve; make a detour. *aux* ~*s de qn,* (*live*) at s.o's expense. **crocheter** (ʃte) *v.t,* to pick (*lock*). **crochu, e** (ʃy) *a,* hooked.
crocodile (krɔkɔdil) *m,* crocodile.
crocus (krɔkys) *m,* crocus.
croire (krwar) *v.t.ir,* to believe (*pers., story*); think, consider, believe (*que,* that). *je crois l'avoir vu,* I think I saw him. *on le croit honnête,* he is considered honest. *à l'en* ~, if you listen to him. *je n'en croyais pas mes yeux,* I couldn't believe my eyes. ~ **à,** ~ **en,** to believe in; have confidence in. ~ *en Dieu, aux fantômes,* to believe in God, in ghosts. **se** ~, to be conceited.
croisade (krwazad) *f,* crusade. **croisé, e** (ze) *a,* crossed; double-breasted (*coat*). ¶ *m,* crusader. ¶ *f,* crossing, casement [window]. *à la* ~ *des chemins,* (*lit., fig.*) at the crossroads. **croisement** (zmɑ̃) *m,* (*gen., Biol.*) crossing; cross [breed]; passing (*cars &c*); crossroads. **croiser** (ze) *v.t,* to cross; fold (*arms*); to cut across; to [meet &] pass (*pers., car*); (*Biol.*) cross (*avec,* with). ¶ *v.i,* to overlap; (*Naut.*) cruise. **se** ~, (*gaze*) to meet; (*letters*) cross. **croiseur** (zœr) *m,* (*Nav.*) cruiser. **croisière** (zjɛr) *f,* cruise; cruising. **croisillon** (zijɔ̃) *m,* crossbar; transept.
croissance (krwasɑ̃s) *f,* growth. **croissant** (sɑ̃) *m,* crescent; (*Cook.*) croissant. *en* ~, crescent-shaped. **croître** (krwɑtr) *v.i.ir,* to grow; increase; (*days*) draw out; (*moon*) wax.
croix (krwa) *f,* cross. *la C*~ *Rouge,* the Red Cross. ~ *gammée,* swastika. *mettre en* ~, to crucify. *mise en* ~, crucifixion.
croquant, e (krɔkɑ̃, ɑ̃t) *a,* crisp, crunchy.
croque-mitaine (krɔkmitɛn) *m,* bog[e]y man. **croque-monsieur,** *m,* toasted cheese & ham sandwich. **croque-mort,** *m,* undertaker's man.
croquer (krɔke) *v.t,* to crunch; munch; squander (*money*); sketch. *joli à* ~, pretty as a picture. ¶ *v.i,* (*food*) to be crisp. **croquet** (kɛ) *m,* (*Game*) croquet. **croquette** (kɛt) *f,* (*Cook.*) croquette. **croquis** (ki) *m,* sketch.
crosse (krɔs) *f,* butt (*rifle &c*); (*Eccl.*) crosier, crook; [hockey] stick; [golf] club.
crotte (krɔt) *f,* dung, droppings; mud. ~ *de chocolat,* chocolate. **crotter** (te) *v.t,* to spatter with mud. *crotté,* muddy (*boots*). **crottin** (tɛ̃) *m,* dung (*horse &c*).
croulant *P* (krulɑ̃) *m,* old fogey *P.* **crouler** (le) *v.i,* (*lit., fig.*) to collapse, crumble; totter; stagger (*under weight*).
croup (krup) *m,* croup (*Med.*).
croupe (krup) *f,* rump (*horse; P pers.*); top (*hill*). *monter en* ~, to ride pillion. **croupier** (pje) *m,* croupier (*casino*). **croupion** (pjɔ̃) *m,* rump (*bird*); parson's nose. **croupi,** (pi) *a,* stagnant. **croupir** (pir) *v.t,* (*water*) to stagnate; (*fig: pers.*) wallow (*dans,* in).
croustillant, e (krustijɑ̃, ɑ̃t) *a,* crisp, crusty; (*fig.*) spicey (*story*). **croûte** (krut) *f,* crust; rind (*cheese*); scab; daub (*painting*). **croûton** (tɔ̃) *m,* crusty end (*loaf*); (*Cook.*) crouton; *P* old fogey.
croyable (krwajabl) *a,* credible. **croyance** (jɑ̃s) *f,* belief (*à qch; en Dieu*); creed. **croyant, e** (jɑ̃, ɑ̃t) *n,* (*Rel.*) believer.
cru[1] (kry) *m,* wine district; wine. *du* ~, local. *grand* ~, great wine *or* vintage. *de son propre* ~, of his own invention.
cru[2]**, e**[1] (kry) *a,* raw, uncooked; harsh (*colour*); blunt, coarse (*speech*). *monter à* ~, to ride bareback.
cruauté (kryote) *f,* cruelty.
cruche (kryʃ) *f,* pitcher, jug; (*P*) twit *P.*
crucifiement (krysifimɑ̃) *m,* **crucifixion** (fiksjɔ̃) *f,* crucifixion. **crucifier** (fje) *v.t,* to crucify. **crucifix** (fi) *m,* crucifix.
crudité (krydite) *f,* harshness; bluntness; coarseness (*V* **cru**[2]). (*Cook.*) ~*s,* mixed salad.
crue[2] (kry) *f,* rising (*river level*); flood. *en* ~, in spate.
cruel, le† (kryɛl) *a,* cruel; fierce (*animal*); harsh (*lot*); bitter (*cold*).
crûment (krymɑ̃) *ad,* crudely, bluntly.
crustacé (krystase) *m,* shellfish.
crypte (kript) *f,* crypt.
Cuba (kyba) *f,* Cuba.
cubage (kybaʒ) *m,* cubic content, cubage.
cubain, e (kybɛ̃, ɛn) *a. &* **C**~, *n,* Cuban.
cube (kyb) *m,* cube. ¶ *a,* cubic (*metre*); cube (*root*). **cuber** (be) *v.t,* to cube; measure. **cubique** (bik) *a,* cubic. **cubisme** (bism) *m,* cubism. **cubiste** (bist) *n,* cubist.
cueillette (kœjɛt) *f,* gathering, picking; crop. **cueillir** (jir) *v.t.ir,* to pick, gather (*fruit, flowers*); snatch (*kiss*); pick up (*thief*). ~ *qn à*

froid, to catch s.o off his guard.
cuiller, cuillère (kɥijɛr) *f,* spoon; spoonful; (*Fish.*) spoon [bait]. *petite ~,* teaspoon. *~ à café,* coffee spoon. *~ à soupe,* soupspoon, tablespoon. **cuillerée** (jre) *f,* spoonful. *~ à soupe,* tablespoonful.
cuir (kɥir) *m,* leather; hide. *~ brut,* raw hide. (*Anat.*) *~ chevelu,* scalp. *~ à rasoir,* strop. *~ verni,* patent leather.
cuirasse (kɥiras) *f,* (*Hist.*) cuirass; (*Nav.*) armour [plating]. **cuirassé** (se) *m,* battleship. **cuirasser** (se) *v.t,* (*Nav.*) to armour-plate; (*fig.*) harden (*contre,* against). **cuirassier** (sje) *m,* cuirassier.
cuire (kɥir) *v.t.ir,* (& **faire** ~) to cook; fire (*bricks &c*). *~ au four,* to bake (*cake*), roast (*meat*). *~ à petit feu,* simmer. *~ à la poêle, à l'eau,* fry, boil. *à ~,* cooking (*apples &c*). ¶ *v.i,* to cook. *~ à gros bouillons,* boil hard. (*pers.*) roast (*in sun*); (*body*) burn, smart. **cuisant, e** (kɥizɑ̃, ɑ̃t) *a,* smarting, burning; bitter (*cold*); biting (*words*). **cuisine** (zin) *f,* kitchen; cookery, cooking. *faire la ~,* to do the cooking. shady scheme, fiddle *P*. **cuisiner** (ne) *v.t. & i,* to cook; (*P*) pump *P,* grill *P* (*pers.*). **cuisinier, ère** (nje, ɛr) *n,* cook. ¶ *f,* cooker, kitchen stove.
cuissardes (kɥisard) *f.pl,* (*Fish.*) waders; thigh boots.
cuisse (kɥis) *f,* thigh; leg (*fowl*).
cuisson (kɥisɔ̃) *f,* cooking; firing.
cuissot (kɥiso) *m,* haunch (*venison*).
cuistre (kɥistr) *m,* prig, pedant.
cuit, e (kɥi, it) *a,* cooked. *~ à point,* done to a turn; medium (*steak*). *il est ~ P,* he's had it *P*. ¶ *f, prendre une ~e P,* to get sloshed *P*.
cuivre (kɥivr) *m, ~ [rouge],* copper. *~ jaune,* brass. (*Mus.*) *les ~s,* the brass. **cuivré, e** (kɥivre) *a,* coppery; bronzed (*complexion*); ringing (*voice*); (*Mus.*) brassy (*tone*).
cul (ky) *m,* bottom (*bottle*); (*P**) arse *P**. **culasse** (las) *f,* breech (*gun*); (*Mot.*) cylinder head. **culbute** (kylbyt) *f,* somersault; tumble, fall. **culbuter** (te) *v.i,* to tumble; topple over; (*car*) overturn. ¶ *v.t,* knock over (*table*); overthrow (*government*); (*Mil.*) rout. **cul-de-jatte** (kydʒat) *m,* legless cripple. **cul-de-sac** (kydsak) *m,* blind alley, dead end. **culée** (kyle) *f,* abutment (*bridge*).
culinaire (kylinɛr) *a,* culinary.
culminer (kylmine) *v.i,* to reach its highest point *or* peak. *point culminant,* highest point; climax.
culot (kylo) *m,* cap (*light bulb*); base (*shell*); (*P*) cheek *P*. **culotte** (lɔt) *f,* pair of [knee] breeches; pants, knickers (*underwear*); rump (*beef &c*). *~ courte,* (*boy's*) shorts. *~ de cheval,* riding breeches. *~ de golf,* plus-fours. **culotté, e** *P* (te) *a,* cheeky.
culpabilité (kylpabilite) *f,* culpability, guilt.
culte (kylt) *m,* worship; cult, creed; church service (*protestant*).
cultivateur, trice (kyltivatœr, tris) *n,* farmer. **cultivé, e** (ve) *a,* cultured (*pers.*). **cultiver** (ve) *v.t,* (*lit., fig.*) cultivate; grow (*crop*); work, farm (*land*). **se ~,** to cultivate one's mind. **culture** (tyr) *f,* cultivation; farming. *~ fruitière,* fruit farming. *~ maraichère,* market gardening. *~s,* land under cultivation. *la ~,* culture. *~ générale,* general education. *~ physique,* physical training. (*Biol.*) culture. **culturel, le** (rɛl) *a,* cultural.
cumul (kymyl) *m,* plurality (*of offices*).
cupide† (kypid) *a,* greedy, grasping. **cupidité** (ite) *f,* greed.
curable (kyrable) *a,* curable.
curateur, trice (kyratœr, tris) *n,* guardian, trustee.
curatif, ive (kyratif, iv) *a,* curative. **cure** (kyr) *f,* (*Med.*) course of treatment. *~ de repos,* rest cure. (*Rel.*) living, cure; presbytery. (*liter.*) *n'avoir ~ de,* to care nought for. **curé** (kyre) *m,* parish priest.
cure-dent (kyrdɑ̃) *m,* toothpick.
curée (kyre) *f,* (*Hunt.*) quarry; (*fig.*) scramble.
curer (kyre) *v.t,* to clean out. *se ~ les ongles, les dents,* to clean one's nails, pick one's teeth.
curieux, euse† (kyrjø, øz) *a,* curious (*de savoir,* to know); inquisitive; strange, curious. ¶ *n,* inquisitive person; onlooker; bystander. ¶ *m, le ~,* the curious part *or* thing [about it]. **curiosité** (ozite) *f,* curiosity; inquisitiveness; curio; curious sight.
cutané, e (kytane) *a,* cutaneous, skin. **cuticule** (tikyl) *f,* cuticle.
cuve (kyv) *f,* vat (*wine*); tank (*oil, water*). **cuvée** (kyve) *f,* vatful; vintage. **cuvette** (vɛt) *f,* basin, bowl; washbasin; pan (*W.C*).
cyanure (sjanyr) *m,* cyanide.
cyclable (siklabl) *a, piste ~,* cycle track.
cyclamen (siklamɛn) *m,* cyclamen.
cycle (sikl) *m,* (*gen.*) cycle; bicycle, cycle. **cyclique** (lik) *a,* cyclical. **cyclisme** (klism) *m,* cycling. **cycliste** (klist) *a,* cycle (*race*); cycling (*champion.*) ¶ *n,* cyclist. **cyclomoteur** (lɔmɔtœr) *m,* moped.
cyclone (siklon) *m,* cyclone.
cygne (siɲ) *m,* swan.
cylindre (silɛ̃dr) *m,* (*gen.*) cylinder; roller. **cylindrée** (dre) *f,* (*Mot.*) capacity. **cylindrique** (drik) *a,* cylindrical.
cymbale (sɛ̃bal) *f,* cymbal.
cynique† (sinik) *a,* cynical. ¶ *m,* cynic. **cynisme** (nism) *m,* cynicism.
cyprès (siprɛ) *m,* cypress.
cypriote (siprijɔt) *a. &* **C~,** *n,* Cypriot.
cytise (sitiz) *m,* laburnum.

D

D, d (de) *letter,* D, d.
dactylo (daktilo) *f,* typist. **~graphie** (lɔgrafi) *f,* typewriting, typing. **~graphier** (fje) *v.t,* to type.
dada (dada) *m,* gee-gee; hobby horse; pet subject.
dadais (dadɛ) *m, grand ~,* great booby.
dague (dag) *f,* dagger.
dahlia (dalja) *m,* dahlia.
daigner (dɛɲe) *v.i,* to deign, condescend (*faire,* to do); be so good as to.
daim (dɛ̃) *m,* fallow deer, buck; buckskin, doeskin; suede. **daine** (dɛn) *f,* doe.
dais (dɛ) *m,* canopy.
dallage (dalaʒ) *m,* paving. **dalle** (dal) *f,* flag[stone], paving stone. *~ funéraire,* gravestone (*flat*). *ne faire que ~ P,* to do damn all *P.* **daller** (le) *v.t,* to pave.
daltonien, ne (daltɔnjɛ̃, ɛ̃n) *a,* colour-blind.
Damas (dama[s]) *n,* Damascus.
dame (dam) *f,* lady; wife, lady; (*Cards, Chess*) queen; (*Draughts*) king; (*Tech.*) beetle, rammer. *jeu de ~s,* draughts. ¶ *i, ~ oui, non!* yes, no indeed! *~ d'honneur,* lady-in-waiting. *~ [de nage],* rowlock. *~-jeanne, f,* demijohn. **damer** (me) *v.t,* (*Draughts*) to crown; (*Chess*) queen; tamp, tread down (*earth, ski piste*). **damier** (mje) *m,* draughtboard.
damnation (danasjɔ̃) *f,* damnation. **damné, e** (ne) *a,* cursed, damned. ¶ *n,* (*Rel.*) *les ~s,* the damned. **damner** (ne) *v.t,* to damn.
dancing (dansiŋ) *m,* dance hall.
dandiner (se) (dɑ̃dine) *v.pr,* to waddle.
dandy (dɑ̃di) *m,* dandy.
Danemark (le) (danmark), Denmark.
danger (dɑ̃ʒe) *m,* danger. *en, hors de ~,* in, out of d. *courir un ~,* to run a risk. *sans ~,* safe[ly]. **dangereux, euse**† (ʒrø, øz) *a,* dangerous.
danois, e (danwa, az) *a.* & (*language*) *m,* Danish. **D~** (*pers.*) *n,* Dane.
dans (dɑ̃) *pr,* in; into; within. *entrer ~ le bois,* to enter the wood. *boire ~ un verre,* to drink out of a glass. *prendre qch ~ un tiroir,* to take sth from a drawer. (*time*) *il part ~ 3 jours,* he's leaving in 3 days. *~ l'année,* within the year (*future*). *~ le temps,* at one time (*past*). *coûter ~ les 30 F,* to cost around 30 francs.
dansant, e (dɑ̃sɑ̃, ɑ̃t) *a,* dancing; lively (*music*). *soirée ~e,* dance. **danse** (dɑ̃s) *f,* dance; dancing. *~ classique,* ballet dancing. *de ~,* dancing (*teacher*); dance (*music*). *~ de Saint-Guy,* St. Vitus's dance. **danser** (dɑ̃se) *v.i. & t,* to dance. **danseur, euse** (sœr, øz) *n,* dancer; partner; ballet dancer. *~ de corde,* tightrope walker.
dard (dar) *m,* sting (*insect*); (*Hist.*) dart, spear. **~er** (de) *v.t,* (*liter.*) to shoot (*arrow, glance*).
dare-dare (dardar) *ad,* post-haste.
date (dat) *f,* date. *à quelle ~?* on what date? *en ~ du 3 mai,* (*letter*) dated May the 3rd. *~ limite,* deadline. *de longue, fraîche ~,* long-standing, recent. *faire ~,* (*event*) to be a landmark. **dater** (te) *v.t,* to date. ¶ *v.i, ~ de,* to date from. *à ~ de,* from, on & after.
datif (datif) *m,* dative [case].
datte (dat) *f,* date (*fruit*). **dattier** (tje) *m,* date palm.
daube (dob) *f, bœuf en ~,* casserole of beef.
dauphin (dofɛ̃) *m,* dolphin. **le D~,** the Dauphin.
daurade (dɔrad) *f,* sea bream.
davantage (davɑ̃taʒ) *ad,* more; (*neg.*) any more; [any] longer. *~ que,* more than. *~ de temps,* more time.
de (də) **d'** (d) **(de le** *is contracted into* **du, de les** *into* **des)** *pr,* from, out of (*place*). *venir ~ Lyon,* to come from L. *descendre du train,* to get out of the train. from (*time*). *~ 9 heures à midi,* from 9 till noon. of (*possession*). *la voiture ~ Paul,* P.'s car. (*quantity*) *un verre d'eau,* a glass of water. *un kilo ~ beurre,* a k. of butter. (*definition*) *robe ~ soie,* silk dress. *oiseau ~ nuit,* night bird. *couteau ~ cuisine,* kitchen knife. (*partitive art.*) *boire du lait,* to drink [some] milk. *acheter des œufs,* to buy [some] eggs. *il n'a pas d'argent,* he has no money. to (*with inf.*). *essayer ~ faire,* to try to do. *priez-le ~ venir,* ask him to come. (*manner*) *d'une façon étrange,* in a strange way. *habillé ~ noir,* dressed in black. (*agent, cause*) *suivi d'un chien,* followed by a dog. *couvert ~ neige,* covered with snow. *mourir ~ faim,* to die of hunger. *sauter ~ joie,* to jump for joy.
dé (de) *m, ~ [à coudre],* thimble. (*Game*) die, dice. *~s,* dice. (*Cook.*) *couper en ~s,* to dice.
débâcle (debɑkl) *f,* breaking up (*ice*); (*Mil.*) rout; (*Pol.*) collapse.
déballage (debalaʒ) *m,* unpacking; display (*wares*). **déballer** (le) *v.t,* to unpack.
débandade (debɑ̃dad) *f,* stampede, rout. *à la ~,* helter-skelter, in confusion. **débander** (de) *v.t,* to unbandage. **se ~,** to scatter in confusion.
débaptiser (debatize) *v.t,* to rename.
débarbouiller (se) (debarbuje) *v.pr,* to wash.
débarcadère (debarkadɛr) *m,* landing stage.
débardeur (debardœr) *m,* docker, stevedore.

débarquer (debarke) *v.t,* to land; unload (*cargo*). ¶ *v.i,* to land, disembark. **débarquement** (kəmɑ̃) *m,* landing; unloading.

débarras (debara) *m,* lumber room; box r. *bon ~!* good riddance! **~ser** (rase) *v.t,* to clear (*table*); rid, relieve (*qn de,* s.o of). **se ~ de,** to get rid of; take off (*coat*).

débat (deba) *m,* discussion; debate. *~s,* proceedings. **débattre** (tr) *v.t.ir,* to debate, discuss. **se ~,** (*lit., fig.*) to struggle.

débauchage (deboʃaʒ) *m,* (*Ind.*) laying off. **débauche** (boʃ) *f,* debauchery. *~ de,* profusion of, riot of (*colours*). **débauché, e** (boʃe) *n,* debauchee, rake. **débaucher** (ʃe) *v.t,* to debauch, corrupt; (*Ind.*) incite to strike; lay off.

débile† (debil) *a,* weak, feeble. ¶ *n, ~ mental,* mental defective; (*pej.*) moron. **débilité** (lite) *f,* weakness; mental deficiency. **débiliter** (te) *v.t,* to debilitate, weaken.

débit (debi) *m,* (*Fin.*) debit; (*Com.*) sales, turnover; shop; (*Tech.*) flow, output, discharge; delivery (*speaker*). *~ de tabac,* tobacconist's shop. **~ant, e** (tɑ̃, ɑ̃t) *n,* retailer. *~ de boissons,* licensed grocer. *~ de tabac,* tobacconist. **~er** (te) *v.t,* (*Fin.*) to debit; (*Com.*) retail, sell; (*factory*) produce; (*pipe*) discharge; (*pej.*) spout, pour out (*words*); cut up (*wood*). **~eur, trice** (tœr [illegible] is) *a,* debit (*balance*). ¶ *n,* debtor [illegible]

déblais (deblɛ) *m.pl,* rubble; spoil. **déblayer** (bleje) *v.t,* to clear (*road, site*); clear away.

débloquer (deblɔke) *v.t,* to free, unfreeze (*prices &c*); (*Mach.*) to free, release (*nut, brakes*); clear away.

déboires (debwar) *m.pl,* disappointments; setbacks.

déboiser (debwɑze) *v.t,* to deforest.

déboîtement (debwatmɑ̃) *m,* dislocation (*limb*). **déboîter** (te) *v.t,* to dislocate; disconnect.

débonnaire† (debɔnɛr) *a,* easy-going; good-natured.

débordement (debɔrdəmɑ̃) *m,* overflowing; (*fig.*) outburst. *~s,* excesses. **déborder** (de) *v.i,* to overflow; (*fig.*) *~ de,* to be bursting with (*joy &c*).¶ *v.t,* to go beyond; overlap; outflank; untuck (*bed*). *débordé de travail,* snowed under with work.

débouché (debuʃe) *m,* opening (*career, valley*); end (*street*); (*Com.*) outlet. **déboucher** (ʃe) *v.t,* to uncork (*bottle*); unblock (*pipe*). ¶ *v.i,* to emerge. *~ sur, dans,* (*car, road*) come out on to, into.

déboucler (debukle) *v.t,* to unbuckle; uncurl.

débouler (debule) *v.t. & i,* to tumble down, roll d. (*stairs, slope*); (*rabbit*) bolt.

débours (debur) *m,* out of pocket expense, outlay. **~er** (se) *v.t,* to pay out, lay out.

debout (dəbu) *ad,* (*pers.*) standing; up (*out of bed*). *se mettre ~,* to stand up. *rester ~,* to remain standing; stay up (*late*). *~!* get up! (*object*) upright, on end; standing (*not fallen*). (*fig.*) *mettre qch ~,* to set sth up. *tenir ~,* (*theory &c*) to hold water, stand up.

déboutonner (debutɔne) *v.t,* to unbutton. **se ~** (*fig.*), to open out, speak one's mind.

débraillé, e (debrɑje) *a,* untidy, sloppily dressed, scruffy. ¶ *m,* slovenly dress.

débrayage (debrejaʒ) *m,* (*Mot.*) clutch; (*Ind.*) stoppage. **débrayer** (je) *v.i,* (*Mot.*) to declutch; (*Ind.*) stop work, strike.

débridé, e (debride) *a,* unbridled. **débrider** (de) *v.t,* to unbridle. *sans ~,* non-stop.

débris (debri) *m,* fragment; (*pl*), debris, litter; remains (*army &c*).

débrouiller (debruje) *v.t,* to unravel, disentangle, sort out. **se ~,** to manage, cope, get by *P.* **débrouillard, e** *P* (jar, ard) *a,* resourceful.

débusquer (debyske) *v.t,* to drive out.

début (deby) *m,* beginning, start. *au ~,* at first. *dès le ~,* from the start. *faire ses ~s,* to start; (*Theat.*) make one's début. **~ant, e** (tɑ̃, ɑ̃t) *n,* beginner; novice. **~er** (te) *v.i,* to begin, start; (*Theat.*) make one's début.

deçà (dəsa) *ad,* on this side. *en ~ de,* on this side of; within (*means*). (*liter.*) *~, delà,* here & there, to & fro.

décacheter (dekaʃte) *v.t,* to unseal, open.

décade (dekad) *f,* decade; ten days' period.

décadence (dekadɑ̃s) *f,* decadence, decline. **décadent, e** (dɑ̃, ɑ̃t) *a,* decadent.

décalage (dekalaʒ) (*fig.*) *m,* gap, discrepancy (*between ideas*); interval, time-lag; change of time[table].

décalaminer (dekalamine) *v.t,* (*Mot.*) to decarbonize.

décalcomanie (dekalkɔmani) *f,* transfer (*for china & as toy*).

décaler (dekale) *v.t,* to bring forward *or* put back (*in time*).

décalque (dekalk) *m,* tracing, transfer. **décalquer** (ke) *v.t,* to trace (*design*); transfer.

décamper (dekɑ̃pe) *v.i.* to decamp, clear off.

décanter (dekɑ̃te) *v.t,* to allow (*a liquid*) to settle; (*fig.*) clarify.

décaper (dekape) *v.t,* to strip (*of paint*); scour.

décapiter (dekapite) *v.t,* to behead, decapitate.

décapotable (dekapɔtabl) *a,* (*Mot.*) convertible.

décapsuler (dekapsyle) *v.t,* to take the cap off.

décarcasser (se) *P* (dekarkase) *v.pr,* to go to great trouble; work one's guts out *P.*

décéder (desede) *v.i,* to die.

déceler (desle) *v.t,* to detect; reveal.

décembre (desɑ̃br) *m,* December.

décemment (desamɑ̃) *ad,* decently. **décence** (sɑ̃s) *f,* decency, propriety.

décennal, e (desɛnal) *a,* decennial.

décent, e (desɑ̃, ɑ̃t) *a,* decent; proper.

décentraliser (desɑ̃tralize) *v.t,* to decentralize.

déception (desɛpsjɔ̃) *f,* disappointment.

décerner (desɛrne) *v.t,* to award.
décès (desɛ) *m,* death, decease.
décevant, e (desvɑ̃, ɑ̃t) *a,* disappointing. **décevoir** (s[ə]vwar) *v.t.ir,* to disappoint.
déchaîné, e (deʃene) *a,* wild; furious. **déchaîner** (deʃɛne) *v.t,* to unleash; arouse. **se ~,** to burst out, explode.
déchanter (deʃɑ̃te) *v.i,* to grow disillusioned.
décharge (deʃarʒ) *f,* (*Elec., Law*) discharge; volley (*shots*); (*Com.*) receipt. ~ [*publique*], rubbish dump. **~ment** (ʒmɑ̃) *m,* unloading. **décharger** (ʒe) *v.t,* to unload; (*Law, gun*) discharge; (*fig.*) unburden; vent (*anger*). ~ *qn de,* to relieve s.o of (*duty*). **se ~,** (*battery*) to run down.
décharné, e (deʃarne) *a,* emaciated; gaunt.
déchausser (deʃose) *v.t,* to take s.o's shoes off.
déchéance (deʃeɑ̃s) *f,* decline; degeneration; downfall; lapse (*right*).
déchet (deʃɛ) *m,* scrap; waste. *~s,* waste, refuse.
déchiffrer (deʃifre) *v.t,* to decipher; decode; unravel; (*Mus.*) sight-read.
déchiqueter (deʃikte) *v.t,* to cut *or* tear to pieces. *déchiqueté,* jagged.
déchirant, e (deʃirɑ̃, ɑ̃t) *a,* heart-rending, harrowing. **déchirer** (re) *v.t,* to tear, rip; tear up; t. open; harrow; split (*ears with noise*). **déchirure** (ryr) *f,* tear, rent, rip.
déchoir (deʃwar) *v.i.ir,* to decline; (*pers.*) demean o.s. **déchu, e** (ʃy) *a,* deposed; (*Rel.*) fallen.
décibel (desibɛl) *m,* decibel.
décidé, e (deside) *a,* decided; (*pers.*) determined. **~ment** (mɑ̃) *ad,* undoubtedly. **décider** (de) *v.t,* to decide on; decide (*que,* that; *de faire,* to do). ~ *qn,* to persuade s.o (*à faire,* to do). ~ *de qch,* to decide on sth. **se ~,** to make up one's mind (*à faire,* to do).
décilitre (desilitr) *m,* decilitre.
décimal, e (desimal) *a. & f,* decimal.
décimer (desime) *v.t,* to decimate.
décimètre (desimɛtr) *m,* decimetre.
décisif, ive† (desizif, iv) *a,* decisive; critical. **décision** (zjɔ̃) *f,* decision; decisiveness.
déclamation (deklamasjɔ̃) *f,* declamation; ranting. **déclamer** (me) *v.t. & i,* to declaim; (*pej.*) spout; rant.
déclaration (deklarasjɔ̃) *f,* declaration; statement; admission. ~ *d'impôts,* tax return. ~ *sous serment,* affidavit. **déclarer** (re) *v.t,* to declare, state, announce; (*jury*) find; notify, register (*birth &c*). **se ~,** to declare o.s; d. one's love; (*fire &c*) break out.
déclasser (deklase) *v.t,* to downgrade; relegate; get out of order (*books, cards*).
déclencher (deklɑ̃ʃe) *v.t,* to release (*spring &c*); set off, activate (*alarm*); (*fig.*) trigger off. **déclencheur** (ʃœr) *m,* release mechanism.
déclic (deklik) *m,* trigger, catch; click (*sound*).
déclin (deklɛ̃) *m,* decline, waning. ~ *du jour,* close of day. **~aison** (klinɛzɔ̃) *f,* (*Gram.*) declension. **~er** (ne) *v.t,* (*Gram.*) to decline; state (*name &c*); refuse (*offer*). ¶ *v.i,* to decline, wane; (*day*) draw to a close.
déclivité (deklivite) *f,* slope, incline.
décocher (dekɔʃe) *v.t,* to shoot; let fly.
décoiffer (dekwafe) *v.t,* ~ *qn,* to disarrange s.o's hair. **se ~,** to take off one's hat.
décoller (dekɔle) *v.t,* to unstick; (*P*) shake off (*pers.*). ¶ *v.i,* (*Aero.*) to take off; (*P*) lose weight. **se ~,** to come unstuck.
décolleté, e (dekɔlte) *a,* low-necked (*dress*). ¶ *m,* low neckline.
décolorer (dekɔlɔre) *v.t,* to discolour.
décombres (dekɔ̃br) *m.pl,* rubble, debris.
décommander (dekɔmɑ̃de) *v.t,* to cancel; call off; put off (*guests*). **se ~,** to cancel an engagement.
décomposer (dekɔ̃poze) *v.t,* to break up into its parts; contort (*face*); rot (*meat*).
décompte (dekɔ̃t) *m,* deduction; breakdown (*figures*). **décompter** (kɔ̃te) *v.t,* to deduct.
déconcerter (dekɔ̃sɛrte) *v.t,* to disconcert.
déconfit, e (dekɔ̃fi, it) *a,* downcast. **~ure** (tyr) *f,* failure; defeat; (*Fin.*) ruin.
déconner *P** (dekɔne) *v.i,* to talk drivel; boob *P.*
déconseiller (dekɔ̃sɛje) *v.t,* ~ *qch à qn,* to advise s.o against sth.
déconsidérer (dekɔ̃sidere) *v.t,* to discredit.
décontenancer (dekɔ̃tnɑ̃se) *v.t,* to disconcert.
décontracter (dekɔ̃trakte) *v.t.* & **se ~,** to relax. *en décontracté,* in casual dress.
déconvenue (dekɔ̃vny) *f,* disappointment.
décor (dekɔr) *m,* setting; scenery; (*Theat. Cine*) set; (*& ~s*) scenery, décor. (*Mot.*) *entrer dans le ~,* to run off the road. **~ateur** (ratœr) *m,* [interior] decorator; (*Theat.*) designer. **~atif, ive** (tif, iv) *a,* decorative. **~ation** (sjɔ̃) *f,* decoration; medal. **décorer** (re) *v.t,* (*gen.*) to decorate.
décorum (dekɔrɔm) *m, le ~,* decorum.
découcher (dekuʃe) *v.i,* to sleep out.
découdre (dekudr) *v.t.ir,* to unstitch; unpick.
découler (dekule) *v.i,* to ensue.
découper (dekupe) *v.t,* to carve (*meat*); cut up; cut out. *découpé,* jagged, indented. **se ~,** to stand out (*sur,* against). **découpure** (pyr) *f,* indentation, jagged outline; piece cut out.
découragement (dekuraʒmɑ̃) *m,* discouragement, despondency. **décourager** (ʒe) *v.t,* to discourage, dishearten; deter (*de,* from). **se ~,** to lose heart.
décousu, e (dekuzy) *a,* (*fig.*) disjointed.
découvert, e (dekuvɛr, ɛrt) *a,* bare (*head*); (*& à ~*) exposed (*place*). *agir à ~,* to act openly. ¶ *m,* (*Fin.*) overdraft. *à ~,* overdrawn. ¶ *f,* discovery. *aller à la ~e de,* to go in search of. **découvrir** (vrir) *v.t.ir,* to discover, find out; uncover, bare; disclose; unveil; take the lid off. **se ~,** to take off one's hat *or* clothes;

(*sky*) clear.

décrasser (dekrase) *v.t,* to clean [out]; c. up.

décrépit, e (dekrepi, it) *a,* decrepit. **~ude** (tyd) *f,* decrepitude; decay.

décret (dekrɛ) *m,* decree, order. **décréter** (krete) *v.t,* to order, decree; declare (*curfew &c*).

décrier (dekrie) *v.t,* to disparage.

décrire (dekrir) *v.t.ir,* (*gen.*) to describe.

décrocher (dekrɔʃe) *v.t,* to unhook; take down (*curtains*); (*Tel.*) lift (*receiver*); (*P*) get, land (*prize*). ¶ *v.i,* (*Mil.*) pull out.

décroître (dekrwɑtr) *v.i.ir,* to decrease; dwindle; (*days*) get shorter; (*light*) fade.

décrotter (dekrɔte) *v.t,* to get the mud off. **décrottoir** (twar) *m,* scraper [mat].

décrue (dekry) *f,* fall in level (*river*).

déçu, e (desy) *a,* disappointed.

décupler (dekyple) *v.t. & i,* to increase tenfold.

dédaigner (dedɛɲe) *v.t,* to disdain, scorn. **dédaigneux, euse**† (ɲø, øz) *a,* disdainful, scornful. **dédain** (dɛ̃) *m,* disdain, scorn.

dédale (dedal) *m,* maze, labyrinth.

dedans (dədɑ̃) *ad,* inside, in it. [*au-*]~, indoors. *de* ~, from inside. *en* ~, *au* ~ [*de lui-même*], inwardly, deep down. (*Mot.*) *il m'est rentré* ~, he ran into me. *se ficher* ~ *P,* to make a mistake; boob *P.* ¶ *m,* inside.

dédicace (dedikas) *f,* dedication; inscription. **dédicacer** (se) *v.t,* to autograph, inscribe (*book*). **dédier** (dje) *v.t,* to dedicate.

dédire (se) (dedir) *v.pr,* to go back on one's word. **se ~ de,** to retract. **dédit** (di) *m,* retraction; penalty, forfeit.

dédommagement (dedɔmaʒmɑ̃) *m,* compensation. **dédommager** (ʒe) *v.t,* to compensate.

dédouaner (dedwane) *v.t,* to clear through customs.

dédoubler (deduble) *v.t,* to divide into two. ~ *un train,* to run a relief train.

déductif, ive (dedyktif, iv) *a,* deductive. **déduction** (ksjɔ̃) *f,* (*Com., Log.*) deduction. **déduire** (dɥir) *v.t.ir,* to deduct; deduce, infer.

déesse (deɛs) *f,* goddess.

défaillance (defajɑ̃s) *f,* fainting fit; failing (*pers.*); (*Mach.*) failure; lapse (*memory*). **défaillant, e** (jɑ̃, ɑ̃t) *a,* faint (*pers.*); failing (*strength*); faltering (*step*). **défaillir** (jir) *v.i.ir,* to faint; fail; falter. *sans* ~, without flinching.

défaire (defɛr) *v.t.ir,* to undo; dismantle; unpack; (*liter.*) defeat. **se ~,** to come undone. **se ~ de** to get rid of. **défait, e** (fɛ, ɛt) *a,* worn (*look*). **défaite,** *f,* (*Mil., fig.*) defeat.

défalcation (defalkasjɔ̃) *f,* deduction. **défalquer** (ke) *v.t,* to deduct.

défaut (defo) *m,* defect, fault, flaw; lack, shortage. *faire* ~, to be lacking. **à ~ de,** for lack of. *à* ~, failing that.

défaveur (defavœr) *f,* disfavour. **défavorable**† (vɔrabl) *a,* unfavourable. **défavoriser** (ize) *v.t,* to handicap; [put at a] disadvantage.

défectif, ive (defɛktif, iv) *a,* defective (*verb*). **défection** (sjɔ̃) *f,* defection; absence. **défectueux, euse**† (tɥø, øz) *a,* defective. **défectuosité** (tɥozite) *f,* defect, flaw.

défendable (defɑ̃dabl) *a,* defensible. **défendeur, eresse** (dœr, drɛs) *n,* (*Law*) defendant. **défendre** (fɑ̃dr) *v.t,* to defend; protect; forbid (*qch à qn,* s.o sth; *à qn de faire,* s.o to do). **se ~** [*bien*], to hold one's own; get along [well]. **défense** (fɑ̃s) *f,* (*gen., Law*) defence; protection; prohibition; tusk (*elephant*); (*Naut.*) fender. ~ *d'afficher,* stick no bills. ~ *d'entrer,* no admittance. ~ *de fumer,* no smoking, smoking prohibited. **défenseur** (fɑ̃sœr) *m,* defender; advocate; counsel [for the defence]. **défensif, ive** (sif, iv) *a. & f,* defensive.

déférence (deferɑ̃s) *f,* deference, respect. **déférent, e** (rɑ̃, ɑ̃t) *a,* deferential. **déférer** (re) *v.t,* to refer (*to court*); hand over (*to justice*). ¶ *v.t,* to defer, submit (*à,* to).

déferler (defɛrle) *v.t,* to unfurl. ¶ *v.i,* (*waves*) to break; (*crowd, feeling*) sweep, surge.

défi (defi) *m,* challenge. *mettre qn au* ~, to defy s.o (*de faire,* to do). **~ance** (fjɑ̃s) *f,* mistrust. *sans* ~, unsuspecting[ly]. **défiant, e** (ɑ̃, ɑ̃t) *a,* mistrustful.

déficit (defisi) *m,* deficit. **~aire** (tɛr) *a,* showing a loss; poor (*harvest*).

défier (defje) *v.t,* to challenge; brave; defy. **se ~ de,** to mistrust; beware of.

défigurer (defigyre) *v.t,* to disfigure; distort.

défilé (defile) *m,* procession; march; march past; (*fashion*) parade; (*Geog.*) defile. **défiler** (le) *v.i,* to march *or* file past; pass, go by. **se ~,** to slip away.

défini, e (defini) *a,* definite. **définir** (nir) *v.t,* to define. **définissable** (nisabl) *a,* definable. **définitif, ive**† (tif, iv) *a,* final; decisive (*victory*); definite (*answer*); definitive (*study*). ¶ *f,* **en ~ve,** finally; all things considered. **définition** (sjɔ̃) *f,* definition.

déflagration (deflagrasjɔ̃) *f,* explosion.

déflation (deflasjɔ̃) *f,* (*Econ.*) deflation.

défoncer (defɔ̃se) *v.t,* to stave in; break up (*ground, road*). *défoncé,* potholed (*road*).

déformer (defɔrme) *v.t,* to deform; distort; put out of shape. **déformation** (asjɔ̃) *f,* deformation; distortion; (*fig.*) warping. ~ *professionnelle,* occupational conditioning.

défraîchir (se) (defreʃir) *v.pr,* to fade; become worn.

défrayer (defreje) *v.t,* ~ *qn,* to pay s.o's expenses. ~ *la chronique,* to be the talk of the town.

défricher (defriʃe) *v.t,* to clear (*land for cultivation*).

défroisser (defrwase) *v.t,* to smooth out.

défroque (defrɔk) *f,* cast-off clothing.

défunt, e (defœ̃, œ̃t) *a,* dead; late (*pers.*); defunct. ¶ *n,* deceased.

dégagé, e (degaʒe) *a,* clear (*sky*); open (*view*); free & easy (*manner*). **dégagement** (ʒmɑ̃) *m,* freeing; release; relief &c. *V dégager.* **dégager** (ʒe) *v.t,* to free, release; (*Mil.*) relieve; (*Sport*) clear (*ball*); redeem (*from pawn*); clear (*nose, street*); give off (*smell*); bring out (*meaning*). **se ~,** to free o.s &c; (*sky*) clear; (*idea*) emerge.

dégainer (degene) *v.t,* to draw (*sword &c*).

dégarnir (degarnir) *v.t,* to clear, empty; strip; (*Mil.*) withdraw troops from. **se ~,** (*head*) to go bald; (*tree*) lose its leaves.

dégât (degɑ) *m. oft. pl,* damage.

dégel (deʒɛl) *m,* thaw. **dégeler** (ʒle) *v.t. & i,* to thaw. **se ~,** (*fig: pers.*) to thaw.

dégénéré, e (deʒenere) *a. & n,* degenerate. **dégénérer** *v.i,* to degenerate. **dégénérescence** (resɑ̃s) *f,* degeneration; degeneracy.

dégingandé, e (deʒɛ̃gɑ̃de) *a,* ungainly, gawky.

dégivrer (deʒivre) *v.t,* to defrost; de-ice.

dégonfler (degɔ̃fle) *v.t,* to deflate; reduce (*swelling*). **se ~,** (*tyre*) to go down; (*P*) back out; chicken out *P. dégonflé P,* chicken *P,* yellow *P.*

dégorger (degɔrʒe) *v.t,* to disgorge; clear (*pipe*). ¶ *v.i,* (*drain*) to discharge; (*cloth, meat*) soak.

dégouliner (deguline) *v.i,* to trickle, drip.

dégourdi, e (degurdi) *a,* wide-awake, smart. **dégourdir** (dir) *v.t,* to revive (*numbed fingers &c*); warm up (*water*). **se ~,** *se ~ les jambes,* to stretch one's legs. (*fig.*) to come alive, grow smarter.

dégoût (degu) *m,* disgust, distaste. **~ant, e** (tɑ̃, ɑ̃t) *a,* disgusting. **dégoûter** (te) *v.t,* to disgust. *~ qn de qch,* to put s.o off sth. **se ~ de,** to get sick of. *dégoûté de,* sick of, fed up with *P.*

dégoutter (degute) *v.i,* to drip.

dégradé (degrade) *m,* gradation (*colours*). **dégradation** (sjɔ̃) *f,* degradation; defacement; (*Build.*) dilapidation. **dégrader** (de) *v.t,* to degrade; deface; damage; shade off (*colours*).

dégrafer (degrafe) *v.t,* to unfasten, undo.

dégraisser (degrese) *v.t,* to remove the grease marks *or* fat from (*clothes; meat*); skim (*stock*).

degré (dəgre) *m,* degree (*level*); step (*staircase*); degree (*angle, heat*). *vin de 11 ~s,* 11° wine (*11% alcohol*). (*Sch.*) *enseignement de premier, second ~,* primary, secondary education. *au plus haut ~,* in the extreme. *par ~s,* by degrees.

dégringolade (degrɛ̃gɔlad) *f,* tumble. **dégringoler** (le) *v.i,* to tumble [down]. ¶ *v.t,* to rush down.

dégriser (degrize) *v.t &* **se ~,** to sober up.

dégrossir (degrosir) *v.t,* to rough-hew; sketch out; rub the corners off (*pers.*).

déguenillé, e (degnije) *a,* tattered, ragged.

déguerpir *P* (degɛrpir) *v.i,* to clear off *P.*

déguisement (degizmɑ̃) *m,* disguise; fancy dress. **déguiser** (ze) *v.t,* to disguise; conceal; dress up (*en,* as). **se ~,** to disguise o.s; dress up (*en,* as).

dégustateur (degystatœr) *m,* wine taster. **dégustation** (sjɔ̃) *f,* tasting; sampling. **déguster** (te) *v.t,* to taste (*wine*); sample (*cheese*).

dehors (dəɔr) *ad,* outside; out of doors. *de ~,* from outside. **en ~,** *ad,* outside. **en ~ de,** *pr,* outside; apart from. **au ~,** *ad,* outside; outwardly (*calm*). *flanquer* (*ficher*) *qn ~ P,* to chuck s.o out *P.* ¶ *m,* outside; (*pl.*) appearances.

déifier (deifje) *v.t,* to deify. **déité** (te) *f,* deity.

déjà (deʒa) *ad,* already; before; (*interrogative*) yet. *c'est ~ pas mal,* that's not bad at all, not a bad start.

déjeuner (deʒœne) *v.i,* to [have] lunch; [have] breakfast. ¶ *m,* lunch[eon]. [*petit*] *~,* breakfast; breakfast cup & saucer.

déjouer (deʒwe) *v.t,* to foil, thwart (*plan*).

déjuger (se) (deʒyʒe) *v.pr.* to reverse one's decision.

delà (dəla) *pr,* beyond. **au-~,** beyond; more. **au-~ de,** beyond; more than, over (*sum*). **par-~** beyond. (*liter.*) *par-~ les mers,* over the seas. **l'au-~,** *m,* the beyond (*future life*).

délabré, e (delɑbre) *a,* dilapidated; ramshackle; ruined, broken (*health*). **délabrement** (brəmɑ̃) *m,* dilapidation; poor state (*health, business*). **délabrer** (bre) *v.t,* to ruin. **se ~,** to become dilapidated; (*health*) break down.

délacer (delase) *v.t,* to unlace.

délai (delɛ) *m,* time [limit]; extension [of time]; wait. *dans le ~ de 10 jours,* within 10 days. *dans le plus bref ~,* as soon as possible. *dernier ~,* absolute deadline. *sans ~,* without delay.

délaissement (delɛsmɑ̃) *m,* abandonment, desertion; neglect. **délaisser** (lese) *v.t,* to abandon, desert; neglect.

délassement (delɑsmɑ̃) *m,* relaxation; diversion. **délasser** (se) *v.t,* to refresh, relax; entertain. **se ~,** to relax.

délateur, trice (delatœr, tris) *n,* informer.

délavé, e (delave) *a,* faded; washed out.

délayer (deleje) *v.t,* to add water to, thin; to mix (*flour &c: dans,* with); thin (*sauce*); (*fig.*) spin out, pad out.

delco (dɛlko) *m,* (*Mot.*) distributor.

délecter (se) (delɛkte) *v.pr,* to delight (*de, à,* in).

délégation (delegasjɔ̃) *f,* (*gen.*) delegation. **délégué, e** (ge) *n,* delegate. **déléguer** (ge) *v.t,* to delegate.

délester (delɛste) *v.t,* to unballast; relieve (*de,* of). **délestage** (taʒ) *m,* (*Elec.*) power cut.

délétère (deletɛr) *a,* deleterious.

délibération (deliberasjɔ̃) *f,* deliberation, debate; consideration; decision, resolution.

~*s*, proceedings. **délibéré†, e** (re) *a*, deliberate. **délibérer** (re) *v.i*, to deliberate (*sur*, upon). ~ *de qch*, to deliberate sth. ~ *de faire*, resolve to do.

délicat, e† (delika, at) *a*, (*gen.*) delicate; ticklish, tricky (*question*); tactful; considerate; scrupulous; squeamish. *faire le* ~, to be fussy (*over food*). **délicatesse** (tɛs) *f*, delicacy, &c.

délice (delis) *m*, delight. **~s,** *f.pl*, delights. *faire les* ~*s de qn*, to delight s.o. **délicieux, euse†** (sjø, øz) *a*, delicious; delightful; charming.

délié, e (delje) *a*, thin, slender; lively (*mind*). ¶ *m*, up stroke (*letter*). **délier** (lje) *v.t*, to untie; loosen (*tongue*).

délimiter (delimite) *v.t*, to delimit[ate].

délinquance (delɛ̃kɑ̃s) *f*, delinquency. **délinquant, e** (kɑ̃, ɑ̃t) *a*. & *n*, delinquent.

déliquescence (delikɥɛsɑ̃s) *f*, deliquescence; (*fig.*) decay.

délirant, e (delirɑ̃, ɑ̃t) *a*, delirious; frenzied. **délire** (lir) *m*, delirium; frenzy. **délirer** (lire) *v.i*, to be delirious.

délit (deli) *m*, offence, crime.

délivrance (delivrɑ̃s) *f*, deliverance, release; relief; issue. **délivrer** (vre) *v.t*, to release. ~ *qn de*, to relieve s.o of. issue (*tickets*).

déloger (delɔʒe) *v.t*, to turn out; dislodge. ¶ *v.i*, to move out.

déloyal, e† (delwajal) *a*, disloyal; unfair; dishonest. **déloyauté** (jote) *f*, disloyalty.

delta (dɛlta) *m*, delta.

déluge (delyʒ) *m*, downpour, deluge; (*fig.*) flood (*tears &c*). *le D*~, the Flood.

déluré, e (delyre) *a*, smart; forward, pert.

démagogue (demagɔg) *m*, demagogue.

démailler (demɑje) *v.t*, to undo (*knitting*). **se** ~, to ladder (*stocking, &c*).

demain (dəmɛ̃) *ad.* & *m*, to-morrow. ~ *matin*, to-morrow morning.

demande (dəmɑ̃d) *f*, request (*de*, for); demand, claim; question; application (*job*); proposal (*marriage*); (*Cards*) bid. *sur* ~, on demand. *faire une* ~ *d'emploi*, to apply for a job. **demander** (mɑ̃de) *v.t*, to ask [for], request. ~ *qch à qn*, ask s.o for sth. ~ *à voir*, ask to see. ~ *à qn de faire*, ~ *qu'on fasse*, ask s.o to do. ask (*enquire*) (*à qn*, s.o: *time, way; why, if*); require, need (*time, attention*). **se** ~, to wonder. **demandeur euse** (dœr, øz) *n*, jobhunter; (*Tel.*) caller. **demandeur, eresse** (dœr, drɛs) *n*, plaintiff.

démangeaison (demɑ̃ʒɛzɔ̃) *f*, itch[ing]; (*fig.*) itch, urge (*de faire*, to do). **démanger** (ʒe) *v.i*, to itch. *le bras me démange*, my arm itches. *ça me démange de faire*, I'm itching to do.

démanteler (demɑ̃tle) *v.t*, (*Mil.*) to demolish; break up (*gang*). **démantibuler** *P* (tibyle) *v.t*, to demolish. **se** ~, to fall apart.

démarcation (demarkasjɔ̃) *f*, demarcation.

démarche (demarʃ) *f*, gait, walk; step, measure. *faire une* ~ *auprès de qn*, to approach s.o. ~**(e)ur, euse** (ʃœr, øz) *n*, door-to-door salesman; canvasser.

démarrage (demaraʒ) *m*, (*Mot.*) starting; moving off; (*gen.*) start. **démarrer** (re) *v.i*, to start up; move off; start off, get going; (*Naut.*) cast off. *bien* ~, to get off to a good start. **démarreur** (rœr) *m*, (*Mot.*) starter.

démasquer (demaske) *v.t*, to unmask; reveal.

démêlé (demɛle) *m*, quarrel, dispute. ~*s*, trouble. **démêler** (le) *v.t*, to disentangle; comb out; (*fig.*) unravel, sort out. **se** ~ **de,** to get out of.

démembrer (demɑ̃bre) *v.t*, to divide up.

déménagement (demenaʒmɑ̃) *m*, removal, move. **déménager** (ʒe) *v.t.* & *i*, to remove, move [out] (*house*) ¶ *v.i*, (*P*) to clear off *P;* be off one's head. **déménageur** (ʒœr) *m*, furniture remover.

démence (demɑ̃s) *f*, insanity, madness.

démener (se) (demne) *v.pr*, to throw oneself about; struggle; strive hard.

dément, e (demɑ̃, ɑ̃t) *a* & *n*, insane, mad (person).

démenti (demɑ̃ti) *m*, denial, contradiction; refutation. **démentir** (tir) *v.t.ir*, to contradict; deny, refute; belie. **se** ~, (*jamais*) *se* ~, (never) to fail.

démerdard *P* (demɛrdar) *m*, crafty bugger *P*. **démerder (se)** *P* (de) *v.pr*, to cope; look after o.s; get out of a mess.

démérite (demerit) *m*, (*liter.*) fault, demerit. **démériter** (te) *v.i*, to be at fault.

démesuré†, e (dem[ə]zyre) *a*, inordinate; enormous, huge.

démettre (demɛtr) *v.t.ir*, to dislocate. *se* ~ *le coude*, to d. one's elbow. **se** ~ **de,** to resign [from].

demeurant (au) (dəmœrɑ̃), after all, for all that. **demeure** (mœr) *f*, residence. *à* ~, permanent[ly]. *mettre qn en* ~ *de faire*, to order s.o to do. **demeurer** (mœre) *v.t*, to live. ~ *rue St. Jean*, to live in the rue St. J. stay, remain. *demeurons-en là*, let's leave it at that.

demi (dəmi) *ad*, [*à*] ~ *mort*, half dead. ¶ ~**, e,** *a*, half. *un kilo* & ~, a k. & a half. *une heure* & ~*e*, an hour & a h. ¶ *m*, half[-pint] (*beer*); (*Sport*) half-back. ¶ *f*, half [bottle]; *la* ~*e*, (*strike*) the half hour.

demi (dəmi) *pref. inv.* (*the second element indicates the gender & forms the plural*): ~*-cercle*, semicircle. ~*-dieu*, demigod. ~*-douzaine*, half dozen. ~*-finale*, semi-final. ~*-fond*, middle-distance running. ~*-frère, -soeur*, half-brother, -sister, step-brother, -sister. ~*-jour*, half light. ~*-journée*, half day. *comprendre à* ~*-mot*, [to know how] to take a hint. ~*-pension*, half board (*hotel*). ~*-pensionnaire*, (*Sch.*) half boarder. ~*-tarif*,

half price (*ticket*). ~-*ton*, semitone. ~-*tour*, about turn. *faire* ~-*tour*, to go back.
démission (demisjɔ̃) *f*, resignation. **démissionner** (ɔne) *v.i*, to resign.
démobiliser (demɔbilize) *v.t*, to demobilize.
démocrate (demɔkrat) *a*, democratic. ¶ *n*, democrat. **démocratie** (si) *f*, democracy. **démocratique** (tik) *a*, democratic.
démodé, e (demɔde) *a*, old-fashioned; out of date. **démoder (se)** (de) *v.pr*, to go out of date.
demoiselle (dəmwazɛl) *f*, young lady; single lady, maiden l.; (*Zool.*) dragonfly; (*Tech.*) rammer. ~ *de magasin, du téléphone*, shop, telephone lady. ~ *d'honneur*, bridesmaid.
démolir (demɔlir) *v.t*, to demolish, wreck; (*fig.*) destroy, ruin; shatter (*pers.*). **démolisseur** (lisœr) *m*, demolition worker. **démolition** (sjɔ̃) *f*, demolition.
démon (demɔ̃) *m*, demon, fiend. *mauvais* ~, evil spirit. *le* ~ *de l'alcool*, the demon drink. ~**iaque** (mɔnjak) *a*, demoniacal.
démonstrateur, trice (demɔ̃stratœr, tris) *n*, (*Com.*) demonstrator. **demonstratif, ive** (tif, iv) *a*, demonstrative. **démonstration** (sjɔ̃) *f*, demonstration; proof. ~ *de force*, show of strength.
démonter (te) *v.t*, to dismantle, take to pieces; take down (*curtains*); take off (*tyre*); throw (*rider*); fluster, throw *P* (*pers.*).
démontrer (demɔ̃tre) *v.t*, to demonstrate, prove; show.
démoraliser (demɔralize) *v.t*, to demoralize.
démordre (demɔrdr) *v.i*, *ne pas* ~ *de*, to stick to (*decision &c*).
démunir (demynir) *v.t*, to deprive (*de*, of). **se** ~ **de**, to part with. *démuni de*, lacking in, without.
dénaturé, e (denatyre) *a*, unnatural. **dénaturer** (re) *v.t*, to distort (*facts*); denature (*food*).
dénégation (denegasjɔ̃) *f*, denial; disclaimer.
déniaiser (denjɛze) *v.t*, ~ *qn*, to teach. s.o about the world.
dénicher (deniʃe) *v.t*, to take out of the nest; discover, unearth *P*; track down (*pers.*).
denier (dənje) *m*, (*Hist.*) denier (*coin*: $\frac{1}{12}$ *of a sou*). *les* ~*s publics*, public funds.
dénier (denje) *v.t*, to deny; disclaim. ~ *qch à qn*, to deny s.o sth.
dénigrer (denigre) *v.t*, to denigrate, run down.
dénombrer (denɔ̃bre) *v.t*, to count; enumerate.
dénominateur (denɔminatœr) *m*, denominator. **dénommer** (me) *v.t*, to name. **dénomination** (asjɔ̃) *f*, designation.
dénoncer (denɔ̃se) *v.t*, to denounce; inform against; (*liter.*) proclaim. **dénonciation** (sjasjɔ̃) *f*, denunciation; exposure.
dénoter (denɔte) *v.t*, to denote, betoken.
dénouement (denumɑ̃) *m*, ending, outcome; (*Theat.*) dénouement. **dénouer** (nwe) *v.t*, to untie, undo; unravel, resolve (*situation*).
denrée (dɑ̃re) *f*, food[stuff]. ~*s*, produce.
dense (dɑ̃s) *a*, dense; thick. **densité** (dɑ̃site) *f*, density; thickness.
dent (dɑ̃) *f*, tooth; prong; cog. ~*s de devant, du fond, de lait, de sagesse*, front, back, milk, wisdom teeth. *en* ~ *de scie*, serrated; jagged. *faire ses* ~*s*, to cut one's teeth. *manger du bout des* ~*s*, to pick at one's food. *avoir une* ~ *contre qn*, to have a grudge against s.o. *avoir les* ~*s longues*, to be ambitious. **dentaire** (tɛr) *a*, dental. **denté, e** (te) *a*, (*Tech.*) toothed, cogged; (*Bot.*) dentate. **dentelé, e** (tle) *a*, jagged; indented (*coast*); serrated. **dentelle** (tɛl) *f*, lace. **dentellière** (teljɛr) *f*, lacemaker; lace-making machine. **dentelure** (tlyr) *f*, indentation, serration. **dentier** (tje) *m*, denture, dental plate. **dentifrice** (tifris) *m*, tooth paste; dentifrice. **dentiste** (tist) *n*, dentist. **dentition** (sjɔ̃) *f*, dentition. **denture** (tyr) *f*, set of (*natural*) teeth; (*Tech.*) teeth, cogs.
dénuder (denyde) *v.t*, to bare, strip. **se** ~, (*pers.*) to strip; (*head*) go bald.
dénué, e (denɥe) *a*, ~ *de*, devoid of, lacking in. **dénuement** (nymɑ̃) *m*, destitution.
déodorant (deɔdɔrɑ̃) *m*, [*produit*] ~, deodorant.
dépanner (depane) *v.t*, to repair, fix (*car, T.V.*); help out (*pers.*). **dépannage** (naʒ) *m*, repairing &c. *service de* ~, breakdown service. **dépanneuse** (nøz) *f*, breakdown lorry.
dépareillé, e (deparɛje) *a*, odd (*shoe*); incomplete (*set*).
déparer (depare) *v.t*, to spoil, mar.
départ (depar) *m*, departure; (*Sport, gen.*) start. ~ *lancé, arrêté*, flying, standing start. (*lit., fig.*) *faux* ~, false start. *de* ~, original. *point de* ~, starting point. *au* ~, at the outset. (*liter.*) distinction. (*Com.*) ~ *usines*, ex works.
départager (departaʒe) *v.t*, to decide between. ~ *les voix*, to give the casting vote.
département (departəmɑ̃) *m*, (*gen., Adm.*) department; ministry. ~**al, e** (tal) *a*, departmental; secondary (*road*).
départir (departir) *v.t.ir*, (*liter.*) to assign (*task*). **se** ~ **de**, to abandon.
dépasser (depɑse) *v.t*, to pass (*place*); overtake, pass (*car*); protrude beyond; exceed (*size, sum*); surpass (*en*, in). *cela me depasse!* it's beyond me! *cela dépasse les bornes*, that's going too far.
dépaysé, e (depeize) *a*, lost; out of one's element; disoriented. **dépayser** (ze) *v.t*, to make (s.o) feel strange; disorient.
dépecer (depəse) *v.t*, to cut up (*carcass*).
dépêche (depɛʃ) *f*, dispatch. ~ *télégraphique*, telegram, wire. **dépêcher** (pɛʃe) *v.t*, to dispatch, send. **se** ~, to hurry. *dépêche-toi!* hurry up!
dépeindre (depɛ̃dr) *v.t.ir*, to depict.
dépenaillé, e (depnɑje) *a*, in rags; tattered.

dépendance (depɑ̃dɑ̃s) *f,* dependence; subordination; (*Pol., drug*) dependency; outbuilding. **dépendant, e** (dɑ̃, ɑ̃t) *a,* dependent (*de,* on). **dépendre** (pɑ̃dr) *v.i,* ~ *de,* to depend on; be answerable to; be a dependency of. *ça dépend,* it [all] depends.

dépens (depɑ̃) *m.pl,* (*Law*) costs. *aux* ~ *de,* at the expense of. **dépense** (pɑ̃s) *f,* expense; expenditure; consumption. ~ *de bouche,* living expenses. **dépenser** (pɑ̃se) *v.t,* to spend; expend; use [up]. **dépensier, ère** (sje, ɛr) *a,* extravagant. ¶ *n,* spend-thrift.

déperdition (depɛrdisjɔ̃) *f,* loss (*heat &c*).

dépérir (deperir) *v.t,* to wither, waste away.

dépêtrer (depɛtre) *v.t,* to extricate.

dépeupler (depœple) *v.t,* to depopulate; to empty of (*fish, wild life*).

dépilatoire (depilatwar) *a,* depilatory.

dépister (depiste) *v.t,* to track down, run to earth; throw off the scent.

dépit (depi) *m,* vexation. **en** ~ **de,** in spite of. ~**er** (te) *v.t,* (*liter.*) to vex, frustrate.

déplacé, e (deplase) *a,* out of place, ill-timed; uncalled for. **déplacement** (smɑ̃) *m,* moving, shifting; displacement; journey. **déplacer** (se) *v.t,* to move, shift; transfer (*pers.*); (*Naut.*) displace. **se** ~**,** to move; travel.

déplaire (deplɛr) *v.i.ir,* ~ *à,* to displease. *ça me déplaît,* I don't like it. *n'en déplaise à qn,* with all due respect to s.o. *se* ~ *à Paris,* to dislike it in Paris. **déplaisant, e** (plɛzɑ̃, ɑ̃t) *a,* unpleasant. **déplaisir** (zir) *m,* displeasure.

déplanter (deplɑ̃te) *v.t,* to transplant. **déplantoir** (twar) *m,* (*Hort.*) trowel.

dépliant (depliɑ̃) *m,* folder, leaflet. **déplier** (plie) *v.t,* to unfold.

déploiement (deplwamɑ̃) *m,* spreading out; unfurling; (*Mil.*) deployment; displaying.

déplorable† (deplɔrabl) *a,* deplorable. **déplorer** (re) *v.t,* to deplore; (*liter.*) bewail.

déployer (deplwaje) *v.t,* to spread out; unfurl; (*Mil.*) deploy; display (*strength, zeal*).

déplumer (se) (deplyme) *v.pr,* to moult.

déporter (depɔrte) *v.t,* to deport; carry off course. **déporté, e** (te) *n,* deportee.

déposer (depoze) *v.t,* to put down; deposit; leave; drop (*passenger*); take down (*curtains*); take up (*carpet*); lay down (*arms*); depose (*ruler*); put in, lodge, file (*claim &c*); register (*trade mark*). ¶ *v.i,* (*Law*) to testify. **se** ~**,** (*dregs, dust*) to settle. **dépositaire** (pɔzitɛr) *n,* depositary; trustee; (*Com.*) agent. **déposition** (sjɔ̃) *f,* (*gen.*) deposition.

déposséder (depɔsede) *v.t,* to dispossess.

dépôt (depo) *m,* deposit[ing]; filing; registration; trust. *avoir en* ~, to hold in trust, (*Fin.*) deposit; sediment, scale, fur; warehouse, repository; (*Mil., bus*) depot; jail. ~ *d'ordures,* rubbish tip. **dépotoir** (pɔtwar) *m,* (*lit., fig.*) dumping ground.

dépouille (depuj) *f,* skin, hide (*animal*). ~ [*mortelle*], [mortal] remains. ~*s,* spoils. **dépouiller** (puje) *v.t,* to skin (*animal*); strip (*tree*); go through, examine (*mail, document*); count (*votes*); plunder. **se** ~**,** (*tree*) to shed its leaves. *se* ~ *de,* to shed (*clothes*); cast off, divest o.s of.

dépourvu, e (depurvy) *a,* ~ *de,* lacking in, devoid of. ~ *de tout,* destitute. *prendre qn au* ~, to catch s.o unawares *or* unprepared.

dépravation (depravasjɔ̃) *f,* depravity. **dépraver** (ve) *v.t,* to deprave.

dépréciation (depresjasjɔ̃) *f,* depreciation. **déprécier** (sje) *v.t,* to depreciate; disparage.

déprédations (depredasjɔ̃) *f.pl,* damage.

dépression (deprɛsjɔ̃) *f,* depression. ~ *nerveuse,* nervous breakdown. **déprimer** (prime) *v.t,* to depress.

depuis (dəpɥi) *pr. & ad,* (*time*) since, for. ~ *lundi,* since Monday. ~ *quand est-il là?* how long has he been there? *je la connais* ~ *longtemps,* I've known her for a long time. *il était à Lyon* ~ *3 mois,* he had been in Lyon for 3 months. (*place*) from, since. ~ *Paris jusqu'à Nice,* from P. to N. ~ **que,** *c,* since.

députation (depytasjɔ̃) *f,* deputation; membership (*parliament*). **député** (te) *m,* deputy (*M.P.*); delegate. **députer** (te) *v.t,* to depute, delegate.

déraciner (derasine) *v.t,* to uproot, eradicate.

dérailler (derɑje) *v.i,* to leave the rails; (*P pers.*) rave; (*Mach.*) work badly. **dérailleur** (jœr) *m,* gears (*cycle*).

déraisonnable† (derɛzɔnabl) *a,* unreasonable. **déraisonner** (ne) *v.i,* to talk nonsense; rave.

dérangement (derɑ̃ʒmɑ̃) *m,* trouble; disturbance; journey, trip; disorder. (*Mach.*) *en* ~, out of order. **déranger** (ʒe) *v.t,* to disturb; upset; trouble; (*Mach.*) put out of order; derange (*mind*); upset (*stomach*). **se** ~**,** to move; (*doctor*) come out; put o.s out.

déraper (derape) *v.i,* to skid; slip; (*Naut.*) trip the anchor. **dérapage** (paʒ) *m,* skid.

déréglé, e (deregle) *a,* out of order; upset; dissolute (*life*). **dérèglement** (rɛgləmɑ̃) *m,* disturbance; upset; dissoluteness. **dérégler** (regle) *v.t,* (*Mach.*) to put out of order; upset; disturb.

dérider (deride) *v.t.* & **se** ~**,** to cheer up.

dérision (derizjɔ̃) *f,* derision. *tourner en* ~, to mock. **dérisoire** (zwar) *a,* derisory.

dérivation (derivasjɔ̃) *f,* derivation; diversion (*river*); (*Aero., Naut.*) drift; (*Elec.*) shunt. **dérive** (riv) *f,* drift. *à la* ~, adrift. *aller à la* ~, to drift. (*Aero.*) fin; (*Naut.*) centre-board. **dérivé** (ve) *m,* derivative. **dériver** (ve) *v.t,* to divert (*river*); (*Elec.*) shunt. ¶ *v.i,* to drift. ~ **de,** to derive from.

dernier, ère (dɛrnje, ɛr) *a,* last; latest; final; previous (*owner*); extreme; lowest, poorest (*quality*); top (*floor*). *l'année ~ière, l'an ~*, last year. *au ~ degré*, in the extreme. *en ~ lieu*, lastly. *les ~ières nouvelles*, the latest news. *le ~ cri*, the latest thing. *c'est du ~ ridicule*, it's utterly ridiculous. *mettre la ~ière main à*, to put the finishing touches to. ¶ *n*, last [one]; youngest [child]. *arriver le ~*, to arrive last. *le ~ de mes soucis*, the least of my worries. **dernièrement** (njɛrmɑ̃) *ad*, lately.

dérobé, e (derɔbe) *a*, secret, hidden. *à la ~e*, secretly, surreptitiously. **dérober** (be) *v.t*, to steal (*à*, from); conceal, hide (*à*, from). **se ~**, to hedge, be evasive; (*ground*) give way. **se ~ à**, to shirk (*duty*).

déroger (derɔʒe) *v.i*, *~ à*, to go against (*habit &c*).

dérouler (derule) *v.t*, to unroll; unwind. **se ~**, to unroll; unwind; (*landscape*) unfold; (*event*) take place; (*story*) develop, unfold.

déroute (derut) *f*, rout. *mettre en ~*, to rout. **dérouter** (te) *v.t*, to baffle, nonplus; reroute (*plane &c*); throw off the scent.

derrière (dɛrjɛr) *pr. & ad*, behind; (*Naut.*) aft [of]; astern [of]. *par ~*, (*enter*) by the back; (*attack*) from the rear. ¶ *m*, bottom (*pers.*); hindquarters (*animal*); back (*object, house*). *de ~*, back (*door*); hind (*legs*). back; rear; hinder part; tail (*cart*).

derviche (dɛrviʃ) *m*, dervish.

dès (dɛ) *pr*, from; since. *~ le matin*, from the morning onwards. *~ son enfance*, since his childhood. *~ lors*, from that time on; consequently. *~ Caen*, from C. onwards. *~* **que**, as soon as.

désabuser (dezabyze) *v.t*, to disabuse, undeceive, disillusion.

désaccord (dezakɔr) *m*, quarrel; disagreement; discrepancy. **~er (se)** (kɔrde) *v.pr*, to go out of tune.

désaccoutumer (dezakutyme) *v.t*, *~ qn*, to break s.o of the habit (*de faire*, of doing).

désaffection (dezafɛksjɔ̃) *f*, loss of affection.

désagréable† (dezagreabl) *a*, disagreeable, unpleasant.

désagréger (se) (dezagreʒe) *v.pr*, to disintegrate, break up.

désagrément (dezagremɑ̃) *m*, annoyance; displeasure.

désaltérer (se) (dezaltere) *v.pr*, to quench one's thirst.

désappointement (dezapwɛ̃tmɑ̃) *m*, disappointment. **désappointer** (te) *v.t*, to disappoint.

désapprobation (dezaprɔbasjɔ̃) *f*, disapproval. **désapprouver** (pruve) *v.t*, to disapprove of.

désarçonner (dezarsɔne) *v.t*, (*lit.*) to unseat; (*fig.*) nonplus, throw *P*.

désarmement (dezarməmɑ̃) *m*, disarmament; laying up (*ship*). **désarmer** (me) *v.t*, (*lit., fig.*) to disarm; lay up (*ship*). ¶ *v.i*, to disarm.

désarroi (dezarwa) *m*, disarray, confusion.

désastre (dezastr) *m*, disaster. **désastreux, euse** (trø, øz) *a*, disastrous.

désavantage (dezavɑ̃taʒ) *m*, disadvantage, drawback. **désavantager** (taʒe) *v.t*, to place at a disadvantage, handicap. **désavantageux, euse†** (ʒø, øz) *a*, disadvantageous; unfavourable.

désaveu (dezavø) *m*, disavowal, repudiation; retraction. **désavouer** (vwe) *v.t*, to disclaim; disavow; disown.

desaxé, e (desakse) *a*, unbalanced.

descendance (desɑ̃dɑ̃s) *f*, descent; descendants. **descendant, e** (dɑ̃, ɑ̃t) *a*, descending, downward; down (*train, &c*). ¶ *n*, descendant. **descendre** (sɑ̃dr) *v.i*, to descend, go down; come d., get d. (*de*, from); dismount. *~ de voiture, du train*, get out, off, alight. *~ à l'hôtel, chez des amis*, to put up, stay at a hotel, with friends. (*snow, price*) fall. (*fig.*) *~ à*, stoop to. *~ de*, to be descended from. ¶ *v.t*, to take down, bring d. (*luggage*); go d. (*stairs, river*); shoot d. (*plane*); *P* gun d., shoot (*pers.*). *~ la rue en courant*, to run down the street. **descente** (sɑ̃t) *f*, descent; (*Ski*) run; downhill [race]. *à sa ~ de*, as he alighted from (*car, train*). slope, incline; bringing down; raid (*police*); entrance (*garage*); downspout. *~ de lit*, bedside rug.

description (dɛskripsjɔ̃) *f*, description. **descriptif, ive** (tif, iv) *a*, descriptive.

désemparé, e (dezɑ̃pare) *a*, distraught, bewildered; disabled (*ship*). **désemparer** (re) *v.t*, to disable (*ship*). *sans ~*, without stopping.

désemplir (dezɑ̃plir) *v.i*, *ne pas ~*, to be always full.

désenchanter (dezɑ̃ʃɑ̃te) *v.t*, to disenchant; disillusion.

désenfler (dezɑ̃fle) *v.i*, (*swelling*) to go down.

désennuyer (dezɑ̃nɥije) *v.t*, *~ qn*, to relieve s.o of his boredom.

déséquilibre (dezekilibr) *m*, imbalance; unbalance (*mental*); unsteadiness. **déséquilibré, e** (re) *a*, unbalanced. **déséquilibrer** (re) *v.t*, to throw off balance; unbalance (*mind*).

désert, e (dezɛr, ɛrt) *a*, deserted. ¶ *m*, desert. **déserter** (zɛrte) *v.t. & i*, to desert. **déserteur** (tœr) *m*, deserter. **désertion** (sjɔ̃) *f*, desertion. **désertique** (tik) *a*, desert.

désespérant, e (dezɛsperɑ̃, ɑ̃t) *a*, appalling, maddening. **désespéré†, e** (re) *a*, desperate, hopeless. ¶ *n* desperate person; suicide. **désespérer** (re) *v.i*, to despair (*de*, of). ¶ *v.t*, to drive to despair. **désespoir** (pwar) *m*, despair. *au ~*, in despair.

déshabillé (dɛzabije) *m*, négligée. **déshabiller** (je) *v.t*, to undress. **se ~**, to undress; take off one's coat &c.

déshabituer (dezabitɥe) *v.t*, *~ qn*, to break s.o of the habit (*de faire*, of doing).

désherber (dezɛrbe) *v.t*, to weed.

déshériter (dezerite) *v.t,* to disinherit; deprive. *les déshérités,* the deprived.
déshonneur (dezɔnœr) *m,* dishonour, disgrace. **déshonorant, e** (nɔrɑ̃, ɑ̃t) *a,* dishonourable, discreditable. **déshonorer** (re) *v.t,* to dishonour, disgrace.
déshydrater (dezidrate) *v.t,* to dehydrate.
désigner (deziɲe) *v.t,* to point out; appoint, designate; mark out (*pers.*); (*word*) indicate. **désignation** (ɲasjɔ̃) *f,* designation.
désillusion (dezilyzjɔ̃) *f,* disillusion. ~**ner** (jɔne) *v.t,* to disillusion.
désinence (dezinɑ̃s) *f,* ending (*word*).
désinfectant, e (dezɛ̃fɛktɑ̃, ɑ̃t) *a. & m,* disinfectant. **désinfecter** (te) *v.t,* to disinfect. **désinfection** (sjɔ̃) *f,* disinfection.
désintégration (dezɛ̃tegrasjɔ̃) *f,* disintegration, breakup; (*Phys.*) splitting. **désintégrer** (gre) *v.t,* to break up (*team*); split (*atom*).
désintéressé, e (dezɛ̃terɛse) *a,* disinterested. **désintéressement** (smɑ̃) *m,* disinterestedness; paying off. **désintéresser** (se) *v.t,* to pay off (*creditor*). **se ~ de,** to take no further interest in.
désintoxiquer (dezɛ̃tɔksike) *v.t,* to treat for alcoholism *or* drug addiction.
désinvolte (dezɛ̃vɔlt) *a,* casual, offhand. **désinvolture** (tyr) *f,* casualness.
désir (dezir) *m,* wish; desire (*de,* for; *de faire,* to do). **désirable** (zirabl) *a,* desirable. **désirer** (re) *v.t,* to desire, want (*qch,* sth; *faire,* to do). *laisser à ~,* to leave a lot to be desired. **désireux, euse** (rø, øz) *a,* anxious (*de faire,* to do).
désistement (dezistəmɑ̃) *m,* withdrawal. **désister (se)** (te) *v.pr,* to withdraw.
désobéir (dezɔbeir) *v.i,* to be disobedient. **~ à,** to disobey. **désobéissance** (isɑ̃s) *f,* disobedience. **désobéissant, e** (sɑ̃, ɑ̃t) *a,* disobedient.
désobligeant, e (dezɔbliʒɑ̃, ɑ̃t) *a.* unpleasant, offensive. **désobliger** (ʒe) *v.t,* to offend, hurt.
désœuvré, e (dezøvre) *a,* idle, at a loose end. ¶ *n,* idler. **désœuvrement** (vrəmɑ̃) *m,* idleness.
désolation (dezɔlasjɔ̃) *f,* grief, distress; desolation. **désolé, e** (le) *a,* distressed, very sorry (*de faire,* to do); desolate (*place*). **désoler** (le) *v.t,* to distress, grieve, upset. **se ~,** to get upset.
désopilant, e (dezɔpilɑ̃, ɑ̃t) *a,* hilarious.
désordonné, e (dezɔrdɔne) *a,* untidy; disorderly; disorganized. **désordre** (dr) *m,* (*gen., Med.*) disorder; disorderliness; dissoluteness. *~s,* disturbances.
désorganiser (dezɔrganize) *v.t,* to disorganize.
désorienter (dezɔrjɑ̃te) *v.t,* to disorient.
désormais (dezɔrmɛ) *ad,* henceforth; in future.
désosser (dezɔse) *v.t,* to bone.
despote (dɛspɔt) *m,* despot. **despotique†** (tik) *a,* despotic. **despotisme** (tism) *m,* despotism, tyranny.
dessécher (deseʃe) *v.t,* to dry up (*ground*); parch; wither (*plant*).
dessein (dɛsɛ̃) *m,* (*gen.*) design; plan; intention. *avoir le ~ de faire,* to intend to do. **à ~,** on purpose.
desseller (desɛle) *v.t,* to unsaddle.
desserrer (desɛre) *v.t,* to loosen, slacken. *ne pas ~ les dents,* to keep one's mouth shut.
dessert (desɛr) *m,* dessert.
desserte (desɛrt) *f,* sideboard table; service (*transport*). **desservir** (vir) *v.t.ir,* to clear away (*meal &c*); do a disservice to, harm; (*transport*) serve (*area*); (*priest*) serve, look after (*parish*).
dessin (desɛ̃) *m,* drawing; design, pattern. *~ humoristique,* cartoon. *~ animé,* cartoon film. *~ industriel,* industrial drawing. *cours de ~,* d. lesson. *~ de mode,* fashion design. **~ateur, trice** (sinatœr, tris) *n,* drawer; draughtsman; cartoonist; designer. **dessiner** (sine) *v.t,* to draw, sketch; design; show off; outline. **se ~,** to stand out; show up; take shape.
dessoûler (desule) *v.t. & i,* to sober up.
dessous (dəsu) *ad,* under [it]; underneath, beneath, below. **au-~** (odsu) *ad,* **au-~ de,** *pr,* underneath, beneath, below. **en ~,** *ad,* underneath, below; in an underhand way. *regarder qn en ~,* to give s.o a shifty look. **là-~,** *ad,* under there, underneath. **par-~,** *pr. & ad,* under[neath], beneath. ¶ *m,* underside, bottom; wrong side (*fabric*). *les ~,* undies *P. drap du ~,* bottom sheet. *les gens du ~,* the people downstairs. *avoir le ~,* to get the worst of it. *~ de plat,* table mat. *~ de robe,* petticoat, slip. *~ de verre,* coaster.
dessus (dəsy) *ad,* on [it]; on top [of it]; over, above. *je lui ai tapé ~,* I hit him. **au-~** (odsy) *ad,* over, above; upstairs; on top. **au-~ de,** *pr,* over, above; on top of; beyond (*reproach*). **là-~,** *ad,* on that; thereupon. **par-~,** *pr. & ad,* over. *par-~ bord,* overboard. *par-~ le marché,* into the bargain. *par-~ tout,* above all. *en avoir par-~ la tête,* to be sick of it. ¶ *m,* top, back (*hand*). *drap du ~,* top sheet. *les gens du ~,* the people upstairs. *le ~ du panier,* the pick of the bunch. *prendre le ~,* to get the upper hand. *~ de lit,* bedspread. *~ de table,* table runner.
destin (dɛstɛ̃) *m,* destiny; fate. **~ataire** (tinatɛr) *n,* addressee; consignee (*goods*). **~ation** (sjɔ̃) *f,* destination; purpose. *à ~ de,* bound for. **~ée** (ne) *f,* fate, destiny. **~er** (ne) *v.t,* to intend, mean (*à qn,* for s.o); allot, earmark (*funds*); destine.
destituer (dɛstitɥe) *v.t,* to dismiss; depose. **destitution** (tysjɔ̃) *f,* dismissal.
destructeur, trice (dɛstryktœr, tris) *a,* destructive. ¶ *n,* destroyer. **destructif, ive** (tif, iv) *a,* destructive. **destruction** (sjɔ̃) *f,* destruction.

désuet, te (desɥɛ, ɛt) *a,* obsolete; outdated. **désuétude** (sɥetyd) *f,* disuse.
désunion (dezynjɔ̃) *f,* disunion. **désunir** (nir) *v.t,* to disunite; divide.
détachant (detaʃɑ̃) *m,* stain remover. **détachement** (ʃmɑ̃) *m,* (*gen., Mil.*) detachment. **détacher** (ʃe) *v.t,* to detach, untie, undo, unfasten; take off, t. down (*curtains*); (*Mil., Adm.*) detach, attach, second; (*Mus.*) detach. ~ *le regard de,* to take one's eyes off. to remove stains from. **se ~,** to come loose, c. undone; break off; (*runner*) break away; stand out (*sur,* against).
détail (detaj) *m,* detail, detailed account; breakdown (*figures*); retail. *en ~, dans le ~,* in detail. *vendre au ~,* to retail. **~lant, e** (tajɑ̃, ɑ̃t) *n,* retailer. **~ler** (je) *v.t,* to describe in detail; (*Com.*) sell retail; sell separately.
détaler (detale) *v.i,* to bolt; make off.
détaxer (detakse) *v.t,* to reduce *or* remove tax on.
détecter (detɛkte) *v.t,* to detect. **détecteur** (tœr) *m,* detector (*device*). **détective** (tiv) *m,* detective.
déteindre (detɛ̃dr) *v.t. & i. ir,* to fade. ~ *sur,* (*dye*) to come off on; (*fig.*) influence.
dételer (detle) *v.t,* to unharness. ¶ *v.i, P* stop working. *sans ~,* without a letup.
détendre (detɑ̃dr) *v.t.* & **se ~,** to loosen, slacken, relax; calm [down] (*nerves*).
détenir (detnir) *v.t.ir,* to hold; (*Law*) detain.
détente (detɑ̃t) *f,* relaxation; (*Pol.*) detente; jump, spring; trigger.
détenteur, trice (detɑ̃tœr, tris) *n,* holder; possessor. **détention** (sjɔ̃) *f,* holding; detention, custody. **détenu, e** (tny) *n,* prisoner.
détergent, e, (detɛrʒɑ̃, ɑ̃t) *a. & m,* detergent.
détérioration (deterjɔrasjɔ̃) *f,* deterioration; damage. **détériorer** (re) *v.t,* to damage. **se ~,** to deteriorate.
détermination (detɛrminasjɔ̃) *f,* determining; decision; determination. **déterminé, e** (ne) *a,* definite, specific; determined (*pers.*). **déterminer** (ne) *v.t,* to determine; fix; work out; decide; bring about. **se ~,** make up one's mind.
déterrer (detɛre) *v.t,* to dig up; unearth.
détersif, ive (detɛrsif, iv) *a. & m,* detergent.
détestable† (detɛstabl) *a,* detestable; horrible. **détester** (te) *v.t,* to detest, hate.
détonation (detɔnasjɔ̃) *f,* detonation, report. **détoner** (ne) *v.i,* to detonate.
détonner (detɔne) *v.i,* (*Mus.*) to be out of tune; (*colour*) clash; (*conduct*) be out of place.
détour (detur) *m,* bend, twist (*road*); detour; dodge. *sans ~,* straightforwardly. **~né, e** (turne) *a,* roundabout (*route, method*). **~ner** (ne) *v.t,* to divert; turn away (*head*); put (*s.o*) off, steer (*s.o*) away from (*plan, friend*); hijack (*plane*); misappropriate (*funds*). **~nement** (nəmɑ̃) *m,* diversion; misappropriation; hijacking; abduction (*of minor*).
détraquer (detrake) *v.t,* (*Mach.*) to put out of order; upset (*health*); derange (*mind*).
détrempe (detrɑ̃p) *f,* (*Art*) tempera. **détremper** (trɑ̃pe) *v.t,* to soak. *détrempé,* sodden, waterlogged.
détresse (detrɛs) *f,* distress. *en ~,* in d.
détriment (detrimɑ̃) *m, au ~ de,* to the detriment of.
détritus (detritys) *m,* litter, rubbish.
détroit (detrwa) *m,* strait, straits. *le ~ de Gibraltar,* the Straits of Gibraltar.
détromper (detrɔ̃pe) *v.t,* to disabuse (*de,* of).
détrôner (detrone) *v.t,* to dethrone.
détrousser *O* (detruse) *v.t,* to rob.
détruire (detrɥir) *v.t.ir,* to destroy.
dette (dɛt) *f,* debt. *faire des ~s,* to get into d.
deuil (dœj) *m,* bereavement; mourning. *P faire son ~ de qch,* to say goodbye to sth.
deux (dø; *in liaison* døz) *a,* two. ~ *fois,* twice. *mange-les tous les ~,* eat them both, both of them. *tous les ~ jours,* every other day. second: *venez le ~ mai,* come on the 2nd of May. a couple, a few: *attends ~ minutes,* wait a couple of minutes. *à ~ pas d'ici,* a short walk away. ~ *n, &c,* double n, &c. ¶ *m,* two; (*Cards &c*) two, deuce. *en ~,* (*cut*) in two. ~ *par ~,* (*go*) two by two. (*Naut.*) *~-mats, m,* two-master. *~-pièces, m,* two-piece (*suit, costume*). *~-points, m,* colon. **~ième†** (zjɛm) *a. & n,* second. *for further phrases V* **six & sixième.**
dévaler (devale) *v.i. & t,* to hurtle down.
dévaliser (devalize) *v.t,* to rob; burgle (*house*).
devancer (dəvɑ̃se) *v.t,* to get ahead of; anticipate. **devancier, ère** (sje, ɛr) *n,* predecessor.
devant (d[ə]vɑ̃) *ad,* in front, ahead. ¶ *pr,* in front of; ahead of; before; in the face of (*danger*). *passer ~ qn,* to walk past s.o. *aller au-~ de,* to go to meet (*pers.*); anticipate (*wish*). *par-~, ad. & pr,* in front; in the presence of. ¶ ~ *m,* front. *porte, roue de ~,* front door, wheel. *sur le ~,* (*live*) at the front. *prendre les ~s,* to make the first move. **~ure** (tyr) *f,* [shop] front; [shop] window; display.
dévastation (devastasjɔ̃) *f,* devastation. **dévaster** (te) *v.t,* to devastate.
développement (devlɔpmɑ̃) *m,* development, growth, expansion. **développer** (pe) *v.t,* (*gen., Phot.*) to develop; expand; (*Mil.*) deploy; unwrap; unroll. **se ~,** to develop; expand; deploy.
devenir (dəvnir) *v.i.ir,* to become; grow. *~ riche,* to grow *or* get rich. ~ *fou,* to go mad. *qu'allons-nous ~?* what will become of us?
dévergondé, e (devɛrgɔ̃de) *a,* licentious, shameless. **dévergonder** (de) *v.i,* to run wild.
déverser (devɛrse) *v.t,* to pour out; tip out.
dévêtir (se) (devɛtir) *v.pr.ir,* to undress.

déviation (devjasjɔ̃) *f,* deviation; (*Mot.*) diversion; curvature (*spine*).
dévider (devide) *v.t,* to unwind; (*fig.*) reel off. **dévidoir** (dwar) *m,* reel, spool.
dévier (devje) *v.i,* to deviate; swerve, veer off course. ¶ *v.t,* to divert, deflect.
devin, ineresse (dəvɛ̃, vinrɛs) *n,* sooth-sayer. **deviner** (vine) *v.t,* to guess; foretell (*future*). **devinette** (nɛt) *f,* riddle.
devis (dəvi) *m,* estimate; quotation.
dévisager (devizaʒe) *v.t,* to stare at.
devise (dəviz) *f,* motto; (*Com.*) slogan. *~s étrangères,* foreign currency.
deviser (dəvize) *v.i,* (*liter.*) to converse.
dévisser (devise) *v.t,* to unscrew.
dévoiler (devwale) *v.t,* to unveil; reveal, disclose.
devoir (dəvwar) *m,* duty; (*Sch.*) exercise; ~[*s*], homework. *rendre ses ~s à,* to pay one's respects to. ¶ *v.t.ir,* to owe. ¶ *v.aux,* (*compulsion*) to have to, be due to. *je dois partir demain,* I have to, I must leave tomorrow. *il devait partir dans 3 jours,* he was due to leave in 3 days. *j'ai dû attendre,* I had to wait. *cela devait arriver,* it was bound to happen. (*obligation*) *tu devrais, tu aurais dû le lui dire,* you should (ought to) tell him, should have told him. (*presumably*) *ce doit être mon mari,* that must be my husband. *il a dû savoir,* he must have known. *il n'a pas dû me voir,* he can't have seen me.
dévolu, e (devɔly) *a,* devolved (*à qn,* upon s.o); allotted (*funds*).
dévorant, e (devɔrɑ̃, ɑ̃t) *a,* ravenous (*hunger*); consuming, devouring (*passion*). **dévorer** (re) *v.t,* (*lit., fig.*) to devour, consume.
dévot, e† (devo, ɔt) *a,* devout, pious; (*pej.*) sanctimonious. ¶ *n,* devout person. *faux ~,* hypocrite. **dévotion** (vosjɔ̃) *f,* devotion, devoutness.
dévouement (devumɔ̃) *m,* devotion, self-sacrifice. **dévouer (se)** (vwe) *v.pr,* to devote, dedicate o.s (*à,* to); sacrifice o.s.
dévoyer (devwaje) *v.t,* to lead astray. **se ~**, to go astray.
dextérité (dɛksterite) *f,* dexterity, skill.
diabète (djabɛt) *m,* diabetes.
diable (djɑbl) *m,* devil; [porter's] barrow. ~ [*à ressort*], jack-in-the-box. *petit ~,* little devil (*child*). *pauvre ~,* poor d. *ce ~ de temps,* this horrible weather. *un bruit du ~, de tous les ~s,* the d. of a noise. *il a le ~ au corps,* he's the very d. *envoyer qn au ~,* to tell s.o to go to the d. *tirer le ~ par la queue,* to live from hand to mouth. ¶ *i, ~!* well! (*surprise*). *qui ~, que ~? &c,* who, what the devil? &c. **diabolique**† (bɔlik) *a,* diabolical, devilish.
diacre (djakr) *m,* deacon.
diadème (djadɛm) *m,* diadem.
diagnostic (djagnɔstik) *m,* diagnosis. **diagnostiquer** (ke) *v.t,* to diagnose.
diagonal, e† (djagɔnal) *a. & f,* diagonal. *en ~e,* diagonally. *lire en ~,* to skim through.
diagramme (djagram) *m,* diagram; chart.
dialecte (djalɛkt) *m,* dialect.
dialectique (djalɛktik) *f,* dialectic.
dialogue (djalɔg) *m,* dialogue. **dialoguer** (ge) *v.i,* to converse; have a dialogue.
diamant (djamɑ̃) *m,* diamond.
diamétral, e† (djametral) *a,* diametric. **diamètre** (mɛtr) *m,* diameter.
diantre *O* (djɑ̃tr) *i,* by Jove! *que ~?* what the deuce?
diapason (djapazɔ̃) *m,* (*Mus.*) tuning fork; pitch; compass, range. (*fig.*) *être au ~ de,* to be in tune with.
diaphane (djafan) *a,* diaphanous.
diaphragme (djafragm) *m,* (*gen.*) diaphragm.
diapositive (djapozitiv) *f,* (*Phot.*) slide.
diapré, e (djapre) *a,* many-coloured.
diarrhée (djare) *f,* diarrhoea.
diatribe (djatrib) *f,* diatribe.
dictateur (diktatœr) *m,* dictator. **dictatorial, e** (tɔrjal) *a,* dictatorial. **dictature** (tyr) *f,* dictatorship.
dictée (dikte) *f,* dictation. **dicter** (te) *v.t,* to dictate. **diction** (sjɔ̃) *f,* diction, delivery. **dictionnaire** (ɔnɛr) *m,* dictionary. **dicton** (tɔ̃) *m,* saying, dictum.
didactique (didaktik) *a,* didactic.
dièse (djɛz) *m,* (*Mus.*) sharp. *do ~,* C sharp.
diesel (djezɛl) *m,* diesel.
diète (djɛt) *f,* diet. *~ absolue,* starvation d. (*Hist.*) diet.
dieu (djø) *m,* god. *D~,* God. *le bon D~,* the good Lord. *mon D~!* goodness me! *D~ m'en garde!* God forbid!
diffamation (difamasjɔ̃) *f,* slander; libel. **diffamatoire** (twar) *a,* slanderous; libellous. **diffamer** (me) *v.t,* to slander; libel.
différemment (diferamɑ̃) *ad,* differently. **différence** (rɑ̃s) *f,* difference. **différencier** (rɑ̃sje) *v.t,* to differentiate. **se ~ de,** to differ from. **différend** (rɑ̃) *m,* disagreement; dispute. **différent, e** (rɑ̃, ɑ̃t) *a,* different (*de,* from); various. **différentiel, le** (rɑ̃sjɛl) *a. & m,* differential. **différer** (re) *v.t,* to put off, postpone, defer. ¶ *v.i,* to differ (*de,* from).
difficile (difisil) *a,* difficult, hard; trying; fussy (*pers.*). **~ment** (lmɑ̃) *ad,* with difficulty. **difficulté** (kylte) *f,* difficulty (*à faire,* in doing).
difforme (difɔrm) *a,* deformed, misshapen. **difformité** (mite) *f,* deformity.
diffus, e (dify, yz) *a,* diffused (*heat*); diffuse, wordy. **diffuser** (fyze) *v.t,* to diffuse; spread (*news*); broadcast. **diffusion** (zjɔ̃) *f,* diffusion; spreading; broadcasting.
digérer (diʒere) *v.t,* to digest; (*fig.*) stomach, put up with. **digeste** (ʒɛst) *a,* digestible. **digestif,**

ive (tif, iv) *a,* digestive. ¶ *m,* liqueur. **digestion** (tjɔ̃) *f,* digestion.
digital, e (diʒital) *a,* digital, finger (*print*). ¶ *f,* foxglove; (*Pharm.*) digitalis.
digne (diɲ) *a,* dignified; worthy (*de,* of). **~ment** (ɲmɑ̃) *ad,* with dignity; (*reward*) suitably. **dignitaire** (ɲitɛr) *m,* dignitary. **dignité** (te) *f,* dignity.
digression (digrɛsjɔ̃) *f,* digression.
digue (dig) *f,* dike; sea wall; (*fig.*) barrier.
dilapider (dilapide) *v.t,* to squander; embezzle. **dilapidation** (dasjɔ̃) *f,* squandering &c.
dilater (dilate) *v.t.* & **se ~,** to dilate, expand. **dilatation** (tasjɔ̃) *f,* dilation.
dilemme (dilɛm) *m,* dilemma.
dilettante (dilɛttɑ̃t) *m,* dilettante, amateur.
diligemment (diliʒamɑ̃) *ad,* diligently; promptly. **diligence** (ʒɑ̃s) *f,* (*liter.*) diligence; haste; stage coach. *faire ~,* to make haste. **diligent, e** (ʒɑ̃, ɑ̃t) *a,* (*liter.*) diligent; prompt.
diluer (dilɥe) *v.t,* to dilute; thin (*paint*). **dilution** (lysjɔ̃) *f,* dilution; thinning.
diluvien, ne (dilyvjɛ̃, ɛn) *a,* torrential (*rain*).
dimanche (dimɑ̃ʃ) *m,* Sunday. *le ~ des Rameaux, de Pâques,* Palm, Easter Sunday.
dîme (dim) *f,* (*Hist.*) tithe.
dimension (dimɑ̃sjɔ̃) *f,* size. *à la ~ de,* commensurate with. *~s,* dimensions.
diminuer (diminɥe) *v.t,* to reduce, decrease, diminish; belittle (*pers.*); reduce the salary of. ¶ *v.i,* to decrease, diminish; (*price; milk*) come down; (*storm*) die down; (*days*) grow shorter. **diminutif, ive** (nytif, iv) *a.* & *m,* diminutive. **diminution** (sjɔ̃) *f,* reduction, decrease.
dinde (dɛ̃d) *f,* turkey [hen]; (*P girl*) goose. **dindon** (dɛ̃dɔ̃) *m,* turkey [cock]; (*P man*) sucker. **dindonneau** (dɔno) *m,* turkey poult.
dîner (dine) *m,* dinner; d. party. ¶ *v.i,* to dine. **dînette** (nɛt) *f,* snack; doll's dinner party. **dîneur, euse** (nœr, øz) *n,* diner.
dingue *P* (dɛ̃g) *a,* crazy *P,* daft *P* (*de,* about).
dinosaure (dinozɔr) *m,* dinosaur.
diocèse (djɔsɛz) *m,* diocese.
diphtérie (difteri) *f,* diphtheria.
diphtongue (diftɔ̃g) *f,* diphthong.
diplomate (diplɔmat) *a,* diplomatic. ¶ *n,* diplomat; (*fig.*) diplomatist. **diplomatie** (si) *f,* diplomacy. **diplomatique** (tik) *a,* diplomatic.
diplôme (diplom) *m,* diploma. **diplômé, e** (me) *a,* qualified. ¶ *n,* holder of a diploma.
dire (dir) *m,* saying, assertion; allegation. ¶ *v.t.ir,* to say; tell (*secret*); utter (*word*); state (*name*). *~ à qn que,* to say to s.o, tell s.o that. *~ à qn de faire, ~ qu'on fasse,* to tell s.o to do. *vouloir ~,* to mean. *cette chanson ne me dit rien,* I don't care for this song. *on dirait un renard,* it looks like a fox. *on dirait qu'il va pleuvoir,* it looks like rain. *il n'y a pas à ~,* there's no question about it. *~ que..!* to think that..! *dis donc!* I say!, by the way! *à vrai ~,* to tell you the truth. *pour ainsi ~, autant ~,* so to speak. *cela va sans ~,* it goes without saying. *c'est à ~,* that is to say. *c'est à ~ que..,* well, actually... *comment dirais-je?* how shall I put it? **se ~,** to say to o.s; say to each other. *cela ne se dit pas en français,* you don't say that in French. ¶ *m,* statement. *au ~ de qn,* according to s.o.
direct, e (dirɛkt) *a,* (*gen.*) direct; straightforward; (*Rly*) fast, non-stop (*train*); through (*coach*). ¶ *m,* (*Rly*) fast train. (*Box.*) *~ du gauche,* straight left. (*T.V. &c*) *c'est du ~,* it's live. *en ~ de..,* live from... **~ement** (təmɑ̃) *ad,* (*gen.*) directly; (*go*) straight; (*aaply*) direct; straight away.
directeur, trice (dirɛktœr, tris) *a,* directing; guiding (*principle*). ¶ *n,* manager (*bank, factory*); (*gen., Cine., T.V.*) director. ~ [*d'école*], head, principal. *~ de journal,* newspaper editor. **direction** (sjɔ̃) *f,* direction. *train en ~ de Nice,* train for N. management, directing, running; post of manager &c. *la ~,* the management. manager's &c office; (*Mot.*) steering (*mechanism*). **directive** (tiv) *f,* directive. **Directoire** (twar) *m,* (*Hist.*) Directory, Directoire (*1795-9*). **directorial** (tɔrjal) *a,* managerial. *bureau ~,* manager's &c office. **dirigeable** (riʒabl) *m,* airship. **diriger** (ʒe) *v.t,* to manage, run, direct; (*Mus.*) conduct; steer (*car, boat*); point, aim, train (*gun &c*). **se ~ vers,** to make for, head for, go in the direction of.
discernement (disɛrnəmɑ̃) *m,* discrimination; discernment. **discerner** (ne) *v.t,* to discern; distinguish; discriminate.
disciple (disipl) *m,* disciple, follower. **disciplinaire** (plinɛr) *a,* disciplinary. **discipline** (plin) *f,* (*gen.*) discipline. **discipliner** (ne) *v.t,* to discipline.
discontinu, e (diskɔ̃tiny) *a,* intermittent; dotted (*line*). **~er** (ɥe) *v.t, sans ~,* without a break.
disconvenir (diskɔ̃vnír) *v.i.ir, je n'en disconviens pas,* I don't deny it.
discordance (diskɔrdɑ̃s) *f,* discordance (*sounds*); clash (*colours*); conflict; discrepancy. **discordant, e** (dɑ̃, ɑ̃t) *a,* discordant; clashing; conflicting. **discorde** (kɔrd) *f,* discord, dissension.
discourir (diskurir) *v.i.ir,* to discourse, hold forth; chat. **discours** (kur) *m,* speech, address; talking. *beaux ~,* fine talk.
discourtois, e (diskurtwa, az) *a,* discourteous.
discrédit (diskredi) *m,* discredit, disrepute. **discréditer** (te) *v.t,* to discredit.
discret, ète† (diskrɛ, ɛt) *a,* discreet; unassuming; unobtrusive. **discrétion** (kresjɔ̃) *f,* discretion; unobtrusiveness. *à ~,* ad lib., without limit.
discrimination (diskriminasjɔ̃) *f,* discrimination. **discriminer** (ne) *v.t,* to discriminate.

disculper (diskylpe) *v.t,* to exonerate.

discursif, ive (diskyrsif, iv) *a,* discursive. **discussion** (kysjɔ̃) *f,* discussion, talk; debate; dispute. **discutable** (tabl) *a,* debatable, questionable. **discuter** (te) *v.t,* to discuss, debate; argue about (*price*); question, dispute (*order*). ~ *le coup P,* to have a chat. ¶ *v.i,* to argue; talk. ~ *de,* to discuss.

disette (dizɛt) *f,* scarcity, shortage, dearth.

diseur, euse (dizœr, øz) *n,* ~ *de bonne aventure,* fortune teller.

disgrâce (disgrɑs) *f,* disgrace, disfavour. **disgracier** (grasje) *v.t,* to dismiss from favour, disgrace. **disgracieux, euse** (sjø, øz) *a,* awkward, ungainly.

disjoindre (disʒwɛ̃dr) *v.t.ir,* to separate.

disloquer (dislɔke) *v.t,* to dislocate (*limb*); (*Mach.*) dismantle; break up (*crowd*). **dislocation** (kasjɔ̃) *f,* dislocation, &c.

disparaître (disparɛtr) *v.i.ir,* to disappear, vanish; (*custom*) die out; (*pers.*) die.

disparate (disparat) *a,* disparate, ill-assorted. ¶ *f,* incongruity. **disparité** (rite) *f,* disparity.

disparition (disparisjɔ̃) *f,* disappearance. **disparu, e** (ry) *a,* vanished; dead (*pers.*). *porté* ~, reported missing.

dispendieux, euse (dispɑ̃djø, øz) *a,* expensive, extravagant (*tastes*).

dispensaire (dispɑ̃sɛr) *m,* community clinic. **dispense** (pɑ̃s) *f,* exemption; special permission; (*Rel.*) dispensation. **dispenser** (pɑ̃se) *v.t,* to exempt, excuse (*de,* from); (*liter.*) dispense. **se** ~ **de,** to get out of.

disperser (dispɛrse) *v.t.* & **se** ~, to disperse, scatter. ¶ *v.t,* to dissipate (*efforts*). **dispersion** (sjɔ̃) *f,* dispersal, scattering.

disponibilité (dispɔnibilite) *f,* availability. (*Fin.*) ~*s,* liquid assets. *en* ~, (*Adm.*) on leave of absence; (*Mil.*) unattached. **disponible** (bl) *a,* available; free (*pers.*); receptive (*pupil*).

dispos, e (dispo, oz) *a,* fit, in good form; refreshed. **disposé, e** (poze) *a,* disposed, willing (*à faire,* to do). *bien* ~ *envers qn,* well-disposed towards s.o. **disposer** (ze) *v.t,* to lay, set, place; arrange. ~ *qn à qch, à faire,* to dispose, incline s.o to sth, to do. ¶ *v.i,* (*formal*) to leave. ~ *de,* to have available, at one's disposal. *se* ~ *à faire,* to prepare to do. **dispositif** (zitif) *m,* device, mechanism; plan of action; system; (*Law*) purview. **disposition** (sjɔ̃) *f,* placing, arrangement, layout; disposal: *à votre* ~, at your disposal. frame of mind, mood; (*Law*) provision, clause. ~*s,* aptitude, gift (*pour,* for). *prendre des* ~*s,* to make arrangements.

disproportion (disprɔpɔrsjɔ̃) *f,* disproportion. **disproportionné, e** (ɔne) *a,* disproportionate.

dispute (dispyt) *f,* quarrel, argument. **disputer** (te) *v.t,* to fight over, contest, dispute; fight (*battle*); play (*match*); (*P*) tell off *P*. **se** ~, to quarrel (*avec,* with).

disquaire (diskɛr) *m,* record-dealer.

disqualifier (diskalifje) *v.t,* (*Sport*) to disqualify; (*fig.*) bring discredit on.

disque (disk) *m,* disc; discus; (*Mus.*) record. ~ *souple* & **disquette** (ket) *f,* floppy disc.

dissection (disɛksjɔ̃) *f,* dissection.

dissemblable (disɑ̃blabl) *a,* dissimilar. **dissemblance** (lɑ̃s) *f,* dissimilarity.

disséminer (disemine) *v.t,* to scatter, spread.

dissension (disɑ̃sjɔ̃) *f,* dissension.

dissentiment (disɑ̃timɑ̃) *m,* disagreement.

disséquer (diseke) *v.t,* (*lit, fig.*) to dissect.

dissertation (disɛrtasjɔ̃) *f,* (*Sch.*) essay; (*pej.*) dissertation. **disserter** (te) *v.i,* ~ *sur,* to write, speak [at length] on.

dissidence (disidɑ̃s) *f,* (*Pol.*) dissidence; (*Rel.*) dissent. **dissident, e** (dɑ̃, ɑ̃t) *a,* dissident; dissenting. ¶ *n,* dissident; dissenter.

dissimilitude (disimilityd) *f,* dissimilarity.

dissimulé, e (disimyle) *a,* secretive. **dissimuler** (le) *v.t.,* to conceal, hide; disguise, dissemble.

dissipateur, trice (disipatœr, tris) *n.* & *a,* spendthrift. **dissipation** (sjɔ̃) *f,* unruliness; dissipation; extravagance; dispersal. **dissiper** (pe) *v.t,* to clear, disperse (*smoke*); dispel (*fears*); squander; lead astray (*pers.*). **se** ~, to clear, disperse; (*child*) misbehave; squander one's fortune.

dissocier (disɔsje) *v.t,* to dissociate; separate.

dissolu, e (disɔly) *a,* dissolute. ~**tion** (sjɔ̃) *f,* dissolving; dissolution; rubber solution; dissoluteness. **dissolvant, e** (vɑ̃, ɑ̃t) *a.* & *m,* solvent.

dissonance (disɔnɑ̃s) *f,* dissonance. **dissonant, e** (nɑ̃, ɑ̃t) *a,* discordant; clashing.

dissoudre (disudr) *v.t.ir,* to dissolve.

dissuader (disɥade) *v.t,* to dissuade (*de,* from).

dissymétrique (disimetrik) *a,* unsymmetrical.

distance (distɑ̃s) *f,* distance. *à* ~, at *or* from a distance. *à une grande* ~ *de,* a long way from. (*fig.*) *garder ses* ~*s,* to keep one's distance. **distancer** (tɑ̃se) *v.t,* to outdistance. **distant, e** (tɑ̃, ɑ̃t) *a,* distant. ~ *de 2 km,* 2 km away. aloof, distant.

distendre (distɑ̃dr) *v.t,* to distend; strain. **se** ~, (*ties*) slacken; (*skin*) distend.

distillateur (distilatœr) *m,* distiller. **distillation** (sjɔ̃) *f,* distillation. **distiller** (le) *v.t,* to distil; (*fig.*) exude. **distillerie** (lri) *f,* distillery.

distinct, e† (distɛ̃[kt], ɛ̃kt) *a,* (*gen.*) distinct. ~**if, ive** (tɛ̃ktif, iv) *a,* distinctive. ~**ion** (sjɔ̃) *f,* (*gen.*) distinction. **distingué, e** (tɛ̃ge) *a,* distinguished. *veuillez agréer l'expression de mes sentiments* ~*s,* yours faithfully. **distinguer** (ge) *v.t,* to make out; distinguish (*une chose d'une autre,* one thing from another); set apart; honour. **se** ~, to be distinguished (*de,* from); stand out; distinguish o.s.

distorsion (distɔrsjɔ̃) *f,* distortion.

distraction (distraksjɔ̃) *f,* distraction, amusement; absent-mindedness. **distraire** (trɛr) *v.t.ir,* to distract, (*de,* from); entertain, amuse. **distrait, e†** (trɛ, ɛt) *a,* absent-minded.
distribuer (distribɥe) *v.t,* to distribute, give out; deliver (*mail*); deal (*cards*); allocate (*actors' parts*); arrange; (*Com.*) distribute, supply. **distributeur, trice** (bytœr, tris) *n,* distributor. ¶ *m,* machine; (*Mot.*) distributor. ~ *automatique,* slot machine, vending m. **distribution** (sjɔ̃) *f,* distribution; allotment; delivery; deal; arrangement; supply; (*Theat., Cine*) cast. ~ *des prix,* prize giving. ~ *gratuite,* free gifts.
district (distrikt) *m,* district.
diurne (djyrn) *a,* diurnal.
divagation (divagasjɔ̃) *f,* rambling (*mind*); raving. **divaguer** (ge) *v.i,* to ramble; rave.
divan (divɑ̃) *m,* divan.
divergence (divɛrʒɑ̃s) *f,* divergence. **divergent, e** (ʒɑ̃, ɑ̃t) *a,* divergent. **diverger** (ʒe) *v.i,* to diverge.
divers, e† (divɛr, ɛrs) *a,* different, diverse, varied; various, several; miscellaneous (*expenses*). **diversifier** (vɛrsifje) *v.t,* to diversify, vary. **diversion** (sjɔ̃) *f,* diversion. **diversité** (site) *f,* diversity, variety; difference. **divertir** (tir) *v.t,* to divert; amuse, entertain. *se ~ de qn,* to make fun of s.o. **divertissement** (tismɑ̃) *m,* amusement, entertainment, distraction; (*Mus.*) divertissement.
dividende (dividɑ̃d) *m,* dividend.
divin, e† (divɛ̃, in) *a,* divine; (*P lovely*) heavenly, divine. **~ation** (vinasjɔ̃) *f,* divination. **~iser** (nize) *v.t,* to deify. **~ité** (te) *f,* divinity; god.
diviser (divize) *v.t.* & **se ~,** to divide [up] (*en,* into). **diviseur** (zœr) *m,* divisor. **division** (zjɔ̃) *f,* (*gen.*) division; dissension.
divorce (divɔrs) *m,* divorce. **divorcé, e** (se) *a,* divorced (*de,* from). ¶ *n,* divorcee. **divorcer** (se) *v.i,* to get a divorce. ~ *d'avec qn,* to divorce s.o.
divulguer (divylge) *v.t,* to divulge, disclose.
dix (dis; *in liaison,* diz; *before consonant or 'h,* di) *a.inv.* & *m,* ten. *for phrases V* **six** & **sixième.** **~-huit** (dizɥit; *bef. cons. or 'h,* ɥi) *a.* & *m,* eighteen. **~-huitième** (tjɛm) *a.* & *n,* eighteenth. **dixième†** (dizjɛm) *a.* & *n,* tenth. **dix-neuf** (diznœf; *in liaison,* nœv) *a.* & *m,* nineteen. **dixneuvième** (vjɛm) *a.* & *n,* nineteenth. **dix-sept** (dissɛt) *a.* & *m,* seventeen. **dix-septième** (tjɛm) *a.* & *n,* seventeenth.
dizaine (dizɛn) *f,* ten, about ten.
do (do) (*Mus.*) *m,* C.
docile† (dɔsil) *a,* docile, amenable. **docilité** (lite) *f,* docility.
dock (dɔk) *m,* dock; warehouse. **docker** (kɛr) *m,* docker.
docteur (dɔktœr) *m,* (*Med., Univ.*) doctor (*ès, en,* of). **doctoral, e†** (tɔral) *a,* pompous; pedantic. **doctorat** (ra) *m,* doctorate. **doctoresse** (rɛs) *f,* lady doctor.
doctrinaire (dɔktrinɛr) *a.* & *m,* doctrinaire. **doctrine** (trin) *f,* doctrine.
document (dɔkymɑ̃) *m,* document. **documentaire** (tɛr) *a,* & *m* (*film*), documentary. **documenter** (te) *v.t,* to document.
dodeliner (dɔdline) *v.i,* ~ *de la tête,* to keep nodding one's head [gently].
dodo *P* (dɔdo) *m,* bye-byes *P;* bed. *faire ~,* to sleep.
dodu, e (dɔdy) *a,* plump; chubby (*child*).
dogmatique† (dɔgmatik) *a,* dogmatic. **dogmatiser** (ze) *v.t,* to dogmatize. **dogme** (dɔgm) *m,* dogma; tenet.
dogue (dɔg) *m,* mastiff.
doigt (dwa) *m,* finger; digit; finger's breadth; nip, drop (*wine*). ~ *de pied,* toe. *à deux ~s de réussir* within an ace of succeeding. *au ~ & à l'œil,* (*obey*) slavishly. *se fourrer le ~ dans l'œil P,* to be up the creek *P* (*wrong*). **doigté** (dwate) *m,* (*Mus.*) fingering; tact. **doigtier** (tje) *m,* finger stall.
doléances (dɔleɑ̃s) *f,* complaints, grievances. **dolent, e** (lɑ̃, ɑ̃t) *a,* doleful.
dollar (dɔlar) *m,* dollar.
domaine (dɔmɛn) *m,* domain, estate, property; sphere, domain.
dôme (dom) *m,* dome; canopy (*foliage*).
domesticité (dɔmɛstisite) *f,* domestic staff, household. **domestique** (tik) *a,* domestic, household. ¶ *n,* servant. **domestiquer** (ke) *v.t,* to domesticate (*animal*); harness (*tide*).
domicile (dɔmisil) *m,* residence, home, domicile. **domicilié, e** (lje) *a,* resident, domiciled (*à,* at).
dominant, e (dɔminɑ̃, ɑ̃t) *a,* dominant; prevailing (*wind*); chief, main. ¶ *f,* (*Mus.*) dominant; predominant feature *or* colour. **dominateur, trice** (natœr, tris) *a,* domineering; imperious; ruling (*passion*). **domination** (sjɔ̃) *f,* domination; dominion; rule. **dominer** (ne) *v.t,* (*gen.*) to dominate; outclass; control, master (*feelings*); tower above. ¶ *v.i,* to dominate; predominate, prevail.
dominicain, e (dɔminikɛ̃, ɛn) *n,* Dominican.
dominical, e (dɔminikal) *a,* Sunday (*rest*). *oraison ~e,* Lord's prayer.
domino (dɔmino) *m,* domino.
dommage (dɔmaʒ) *m,* harm, injury. *quel ~!* what a pity! *~s,* damage. *~s corporels,* physical injury. (*Law*) *~s-intérêts,* damages. **~able** (ʒabl) *a,* harmful.
dompter (dɔ̃te) *v.t,* to tame; break in; train (*animal*); subdue (*passions*). **dompteur, euse** (tœr, øz) *n,* trainer; tamer.
don (dɔ̃) *m,* gift, present; donation; gift, talent; knack. *faire ~ de,* to give, donate. **donataire** (dɔnatɛr) *n,* donee. **donateur, trice** (tœr, tris) *n,* donor. **donation** (sjɔ̃) *f,* donation.
donc (dɔ̃k) *c,* therefore, then, so. ¶ (dɔ̃: *empha-*

tic) *dis* ~*!* I say! look here! *allons* ~*!* come on! *comment* ~*?* how do you mean?
donjon (dɔ̃ʒɔ̃) *m,* keep (*castle*).
donnant, e (dɔnɑ̃, ɑ̃t) *a,* generous. *c'est* ~, ~, it's give & take, fifty-fifty. **donne** (dɔn) *f,* (*Cards*) deal. **donné, e** (ne) *a,* given, fixed. *étant* ~ *qch,* given, in view of sth. ¶ *f,* datum, fact. ~*es,* data. **donner** (ne) *v.t,* to give; g. away; g. up (*seat*); deal (*cards*). ~ *à manger à qn,* to give s.o sth to eat. show (*film*); perform (*play*); produce, yield (*crop &c*). *ça m'a donné à penser,* it made me think. ¶ *v.i,* to strike. ~ *de la tête contre,* to knock one's head against. *ne savoir où* ~ *de la tête,* not to know which way to turn. ~ *dans,* to fall into (*trap*). ~ *sur,* (*room &c*) to open onto, look out on. ~ *sur les nerfs,* to get on one's nerves. **se** ~ **à,** to devote o.s to. *se* ~ *de la peine,* to take great trouble. **donneur, euse** (nœr, øz) *n,* giver; (*Cards*) dealer. ~ *de sang,* blood donor.
dont (dɔ̃) *pn,* whose; of whom; of which. *X,* ~ *tu connais le fils,* X, whose son you know. *6 enfants* ~ *2 sont morts,* 6 children, 2 of whom are dead. *la maison* ~ *je parle,* the house I am speaking about.
doré, e (dɔre) *a,* gilt, gilded; golden (*hair*); bronzed (*skin*). ¶ *m,* gilt.
dorénavant (dɔrenavɑ̃) *ad,* from now on.
dorer (dɔre) *v.t,* to gild; bronze; glaze (*pastry*); brown (*meat*). ~ *la pillule,* to sugar the pill. ¶ *v.i,* to brown.
dorique (dɔrik) *a.* & *m,* Doric.
dorloter (dɔrlɔte) *v.t,* to coddle; pamper.
dormant, e (dɔrmɑ̃, ɑ̃t) *a,* still, stagnant (*water*). ¶ *m,* frame (*door*). **dormeur, euse** (mœr, øz) *n,* sleeper. **dormir** (mir) *v.i.ir,* to sleep, be asleep; lie dormant. ~ *comme une souche,* ~ *à poings fermés,* to sleep like a log. *histoire à* ~ *debout,* cock & bull story.
dorsal, e (dɔrsal) *a,* dorsal.
dortoir (dɔrtwar) *m,* dormitory.
dorure (dɔryr) *f,* gilt; gilding; (*Cook.*) glaze.
dos (do) *m,* (*gen.*) back; spine (*book*). *avoir le* ~ *rond,* to be round-shouldered. *en* ~ *d'âne,* humpback (*bridge*). *faire le gros* ~, (*cat*) to arch its back. *se mettre qn à* ~, to make an enemy of s.o. (*fig.*) *avoir qn sur le* ~, to have s.o on one's back.
dose (doz) *f,* dose; quantity. **doser** (doze) *v.t,* to measure out, proportion correctly.
dossier (dosje) *m,* back (*chair*); file, dossier; folder.
dot (dɔt) *f,* dowry. **dotation** (tasjɔ̃) *f,* endowment. **doter** (te) *v.t,* to provide with a dowry; endow (*de,* with).
douairière (dwɛrjɛr) *f,* dowager.
douane (dwan) *f,* customs. *passer à la* ~, to go through customs. **douanier, ère** (nje, ɛr) *a,* customs. ¶ *m,* customs officer.
doublage (dublaʒ) *m,* doubling; lining; dubbing (*film*). **double** (bl) *a,* double; twofold; dual. *à* ~ *commande,* dual control (*car*). (*Mus.*) ~ *croche,* semiquaver. ~ *fond,* false bottom. ¶ *ad,* double. ¶ *m,* double. *le* ~ *de qn,* (*eat, pay*) twice as much as s.o. copy, duplicate; double (*pers.*). *en* ~, (*fold*) in half. *avoir en* ~, to have a copy of. (*Ten.*) doubles. **doublement** (bləmɑ̃) *ad,* doubly. ¶ *m,* doubling; (*Mot.*) overtaking. **doubler** (ble) *v.t,* to double; (*Sch.*) repeat (*class*); understudy; dub (*film*); overtake; round (*cape*); line (*coat*). ¶ *v.i,* to double; overtake. **doublure** (blyr) *f,* lining; understudy; (*Cine.*) stand-in.
douceâtre (dusɑtr) *a,* sickly sweet. **doucement** (smɑ̃) *ad,* gently; softly; slowly; smoothly; carefully; quietly. [*tout*] ~, so-so (*how are you?*). **doucereux, euse** (srø, øz) *a,* sickly sweet; (*fig.*) sugary; unctuous. **douceur** (sœr) *f,* softness; gentleness; sweetness; mildness (*weather*). ~*s,* pleasures; sweets; sweet talk. *en* ~, smoothly, quietly.
douche (duʃ) *f,* shower [bath]; *P* drenching; *P* let-down. **doucher (se)** (ʃe) *v.pr,* to have a shower.
doué, e (dwe) *a,* talented, gifted. *être* ~ *pour,* to have a gift for. ~ *de,* endowed with.
douille (duj) *f,* [cartridge] case; (*Elec.*) bulb socket.
douillet, te† (dujɛ, ɛt) *a,* soft (*pers.*); cosy.
douleur (dulœr) *f,* pain; sorrow, grief, distress. **douloureux, euse**† (lurø, øz) *a,* painful; distressing; pained (*look*).
doute (dut) *m,* doubt, misgiving. *sans* ~, doubtless. **douter** (te) *v.i,* ~ *de,* to doubt, question. *j'en doute,* I doubt it. ~ *que* (+*subj.*), to doubt whether. **se** ~, to suspect (*de qch,* sth; *que,* that). **douteux, euse**† (tø, øz) *a,* doubtful, questionable; (*pej.*) dubious.
douve (duv) *f,* stave (*cask*); moat (*castle*).
Douvres (duvr) *m,* Dover.
doux, ouce (du, us) *a,* soft (*touch, light*); gentle (*breeze, nature, slope*); sweet (*taste, sound*); pleasant (*memories*); quiet (*horse*); fresh (*water*). *cuire à feu* ~, to simmer gently. *en douce P,* on the quiet. *le* ~, sweet things (*opp. bitter*).
douzaine (duzɛn) *f,* dozen. **douze** (duz) *a.* & *m,* twelve. **douzième**† (duzjɛm) *a.* & *n,* twelfth. *for phrases V* **six** & **sixième.**
doyen, ne (dwajɛ̃, ɛn) *n,* (*Rel., Univ.*) dean; senior member, doyen. ~**né** (jɛne) *m,* deanery.
draconien, ne (drakɔnjɛ̃, ɛn) *a,* draconian.
dragée (draʒe) *f,* sugared almond; small shot.
drageon (draʒɔ̃) *m,* (*Bot., Hort.*) sucker.
dragon (dragɔ̃) *m,* dragon; (*Mil.*) dragoon.
drague (drag) *f,* dredge; dredger (*boat*); dragnet. **draguer** (ge) *v.t,* to dredge; drag; fish with a dragnet; sweep (*mines*). **dragueur** (gœr) *m,* dredger (*boat*). ~ *de mines,* minesweeper.

drain (drɛ̃) *m,* (*Agr., Med.*) drain. ~**age** (drɛnaʒ) *m,* drainage. ~**er** (ne) *v.t,* to drain.
dramatique† (dramatik) *a,* (*gen.*) dramatic; tragic. **dramatiser** (ze) *v.t,* to dramatize. **dramaturge** (tyrʒ) *n,* dramatist, playwright. **drame** (dram) *m,* drama; tragedy, drama (*event*).
drap (dra) *m,* woollen cloth; sheet (*bed*). *dans de beaux ~s,* in a pretty pickle. **drapeau** (po) *m,* flag; (*Mil.*) colours. *sous les ~x,* with the colours. **draper** (pe) *v.t,* to drape. **draperie** (pri) *f,* drapery. **drapier** (pje) *m,* draper, cloth manufacturer.
Dresde (drɛzd) *f,* Dresden.
dressage (drɛsaʒ) *m,* erection; pitching; training. **dresser** (se) *v.t,* to erect, raise, set up (*mast, ladder*); pitch (*tent*); draw up, prepare (*list, plan*); lay (*table*); set (*trap*). ~ *qn contre,* to set s.o against. ~ *l'oreille,* to prick up one's ears. train, break in (*animal*). *ça le dressera! P,* that'll teach him! **se** ~, to stand; rise up; (*hair*) stand on end. **dresseur, euse** (sœr, øz) *n,* trainer. **dressoir** (swar) *m,* dresser.
drille (drij) *m, joyeux ~,* cheerful chap.
drisse (dris) *f,* halyard.
drogue (drɔg) *f,* drug. *la ~,* drugs. **drogué, e** (ge) *n,* drug addict. **droguer** (ge) *v.t,* to drug. **se** ~, to be on drugs. **droguerie** (gri) *f,* hardware shop. **droguiste** (gist) *n* hardware merchant.
droit[1]**, e** (drwa, at) *a,* straight. *en ligne ~e,* (*lead*) straight, direct. *le ~ chemin,* the straight & narrow path. upright (*tree*); straight (*not askew*); straight, honest (*pers.*); sound (*judgment*). ¶ *ad,* straight. ~ *devant soi,* s. ahead. *aller tout ~,* to keep s. on. **droit**[2]**, e,** *a,* right (*arm*); right-hand (*tap*). *du côté ~,* on the right-hand side. ¶ *f, la ~e,* (*gen., Pol.*) the right. *à ~e,* (*drive*) on the r.; (*turn*) to the r. **droit**[3]**,** *m,* right. *avoir le ~ de faire,* to have the right to do, be allowed to do. *avoir ~ à,* to be entitled to. (*Law*) *le ~,* law. *faire son ~,* to study law. duty; fee. ~ *d'entrée,* entry fee. ~ *d'aînesse,* birthright. *~s d'adaptation* [*cinématographique*], film rights. *~s d'auteur,* royalties. *~s de douane, de succession,* customs, estate duty. ~**ement** (tmɑ̃) *ad,* uprightly, honestly. ~**ier, ère** (tje, ɛr) *a,* right-handed. ~**ure** (tyr) *f,* uprightness, rectitude.
drôle (drol) *a,* funny, comical; funny, strange, odd. *un ~ de type P,* a strange bloke *P.* ~**ment** (mɑ̃) *ad,* funnily; strangely; *P* awfully, terribly. ~**rie** (drolri) *f,* funniness; funny remark.
dromadaire (drɔmadɛr) *m,* dromedary.
dru, e (dry) *a,* thick; heavy (*rain*). ¶ *ad,* thickly; heavily. *tomber ~,* to fall thick & fast.
druide (drɥid) *m,* druid.
dû, due (dy) *a,* due; owing. ~ *à,* due to. ¶ *m,* due; dues, fees.
duc (dyk) *m,* duke. **ducal, e** (kal) *a,* ducal. **duché** (ʃe) *m,* duchy; dukedom. **duchesse** (ʃɛs) *f,* duchess.
duel (dɥɛl) *m,* duel. *se battre en ~,* to fight a duel. **duelliste** (list) *m,* duellist.
dûment (dymɑ̃) *ad,* duly.
dune (dyn) *f,* dune.
Dunkerque (dœ̃kɛrk) *m,* Dunkirk.
duo (dyo) *m,* duet.
dupe (dyp) *f,* dupe. *être ~ de,* to be fooled by. **duper** (pe) *v.t,* to dupe, take in, fool. **duperie** (pri) *f,* dupery, deception.
duplex (dypleks) *m,* maisonnette; (*Tel.*) link-up.
duplicata (dyplikata) *m,* duplicate. **duplicateur** (tœr) *m,* duplicator.
duplicité (dyplisite) *f,* duplicity.
dur, e (dyr) *a,* hard; stiff; tough; hard-boiled (*egg*); hard, difficult; harsh, severe, tough. ~ *à,* inured to (*pain &c*). *avoir le cœur ~,* to be hard-hearted. ~ *d'oreille,* hard of hearing. ¶ *ad,* (*work*) hard. ¶ *P m,* tough guy *P.* ¶ *f, coucher sur la ~e,* to sleep rough. *en avoir de ~es P,* to have a rough time.
durable (dyrabl) *a,* durable, lasting.
durant (dyrɑ̃) *pr,* during. ~ *des heures,* for hours on end.
durcir (dyrsir) *v.t. & i. &* **se** ~, to harden. **durcissement** (sismɑ̃) *m,* hardening.
durée (dyre) *f,* duration, length; life.
durement (dyrmɑ̃) *ad,* harshly, severely.
durer (dyre) *v.i,* to last. *le temps me dure,* time hangs heavy on me. *faire ~,* to prolong.
dureté (dyrte) *f,* hardness; harshness.
durillon (dyrijɔ̃) *m,* callus.
duvet (dyvɛ) *m,* (*gen.*) down; sleeping bag. ~**eux, euse** (vtø, øz) *a,* downy.
dynamique† (dinamik) *a,* dynamic. ¶ *f,* (*Phys.*) dynamics. **dynamisme** (mism) *m,* dynamism.
dynamite (dinamit) *f,* dynamite.
dynamo (dinamo) *f,* dynamo.
dynastie (dinasti) *f,* dynasty.
dysenterie (disɑ̃tri) *f,* dysentery.
dyslexie (disleksi) *f,* dyslexia.
dyspepsie (dispɛpsi) *f,* dyspepsia.

E

E, e (ə) *m, letter,* E, e.

eau (o) *f,* water; rain. (*ship*) *faire* ~, (*shoes*) *prendre l'*~, to leak. *faire venir l'*~ *à la bouche,* to make one's mouth water. *de la plus belle* ~, of the first water (*gem*); (*fig.*) of the deepest dye. *tomber à l'*~, (*plan*) to fall through. *tourner en* ~ *de boudin P,* to flop. *porter de l'*~ *à la rivière,* to carry coals to Newcastle. ~*x,* waters (*off-shore; spa*); fountains. *aller aux* ~*x,* to take the waters. (*Naut.*) *dans les* ~*x de,* in the wake of. ~*x territoriales,* territorial waters. ~*x usées,* liquid waste. ~ *bénite,* holy water. ~ *de Cologne,* eau de Cologne. ~ *forte,* etching; aqua fortis. ~ *gazeuse,* soda water. ~ *de javel,* bleach. ~ *de vie* (*de prune &c*), (*plum &c*) brandy.

ébahir (ebair) *v.t,* to astound, amaze.

ébattre (s') (ebatr) *v.pr.ir.* ou **prendre ses ébats** (eba), to frolic, gambol about.

ébauche (eboʃ) *f,* [rough] sketch, draft, outline; start. ~ *d'un sourire,* ghost of a smile. **ébaucher** (boʃe) *v.t,* to sketch [out], rough out; outline (*plan*); start (*friendship*). ~ *un sourire,* to give a faint smile. **s'**~, to take shape.

ébène (ebɛn) *f,* ebony. **ébéniste** (nist) *m,* cabinetmaker. **ébénisterie** (tri) *f,* cabinetmaking; cabinetwork.

éblouir (ebluir) *v.t,* (*lit., fig.*) to dazzle. **éblouissement** (ismɑ̃) *m,* dazzle; dazzling sight; (*Med.*) dizzy turn.

ébonite (ebɔnit) *f,* ebonite, vulcanite.

éborgner (ebɔrɲe) *v.t,* to blind in one eye; poke (s.o's) eye out.

éboueur (ebwœr) *m,* dustman.

ébouillanter (ebujɑ̃te) *v.t,* to scald; (*Cook.*) blanch.

éboulement (ebulmɑ̃) *m,* collapse; crumbling; caving in; landslide. **ébouler (s')** (le) *v.pr,* to collapse; crumble; cave in. **éboulis** (li) *m,* fallen earth, rocks &c.

ébouriffer (eburife) *v.t,* to dishevel, ruffle, tousle; (*fig.*) stagger.

ébrancher (ebrɑ̃ʃe) *v.t,* to lop.

ébranlement (ebrɑ̃lmɑ̃) *m,* shaking; weakening; shock. **ébranler** (le) *v.t,* to shake; weaken; undermine (*health, confidence*). *ébranlé,* shaken, shattered (*by news &c*). **s'**~, (*convoy*) to move off.

ébrécher (ebreʃe) *v.t,* to chip (*cup*); nick (*blade*); make a hole in (*fortune*).

ébriété (ebriete) *f,* intoxication.

ébrouer (s') (ebrue) *v.pr,* (*pers., dog*) to shake o.s; (*horse*) snort.

ébruiter (ebrɥite) *v.t,* to spread [around] (*news*).

ébullition (ebylisjɔ̃) *f,* boiling; b. point; turmoil. *en* ~, (*fig.*) in an uproar.

écaille (ekɑj) *f,* scale (*fish*); shell (*oyster*); tortoiseshell; flake (*paint*). **écailler** (kɑje) *v.t,* to scale (*fish*); chip (*paint*). **s'**~, to flake off.

écarlate (ekarlat) *a. & f,* scarlet.

écarquiller (ekarkije) *v.t,* ~ *les yeux,* to stare wide-eyed.

écart (ekar) *m,* gap; interval; difference (*entre,* between). *faire un* ~, (*pers.*) to jump, step aside; (*horse*) shy; (*car*) swerve. *faire le grand* ~, to do the splits. *à l'*~, aside, on one side. *rester, se tenir à l'*~, to stand apart *or* aloof. *à l'*~ *de,* at some distance from. ~ *de conduite,* misdemeanour. **écarté, e** (karte) *a,* remote, secluded, lonely (*house*); outspread (*arms*); apart (*legs*). **écartement** (təmɑ̃) *m,* distance, gap (*de, entre,* between); (*Rly*) gauge. **écarter** (te) *v.t,* to separate, spread, open; turn (*or* push) aside *or* out of the way; avert (*danger*); reject, dismiss (*idea*); distract, divert (*de,* from); (*Cards*) discard. **s'**~, to stand aside; move away; deviate; wander, stray, swerve (*de,* from, off).

ecclésiastique† (eklezjastik) *a,* ecclesiastical, clerical. ¶ *m,* ecclesiastic.

écervelé, e (esɛrvəle) *a,* scatterbrained. ¶ *m,* scatterbrain.

échafaud (eʃafo) *m,* scaffold. ~**age** (daʒ) *m,* scaffolding; heap; (*fig.*) building up. ~**er** (de) *v.t,* to pile up; (*fig.*) build up, construct. ¶ *v.i,* to erect scaffolding.

échalas (eʃalɑ) *m,* pole, stake (*vines &c*).

échalote (eʃalɔt) *f,* shallot.

échancrer (eʃɑ̃kre) *v.t,* to cut away (*neck of garment*); notch, indent. **échancrure** (kryr) *f,* scooped (*or* V) neckline; indentation; serration (*leaf*).

échange (eʃɑ̃ʒ) *m,* (*gen.*) exchange; swap. *en* ~ *de,* in exchange for. **échanger** (ʃɑ̃ʒe) *v.t,* to exchange; swap (*contre,* for). **échangeur** (ʒœr) *m,* (*Mot.*) interchange.

échantillon (eʃɑ̃tijɔ̃) *m,* sample. ~**nage** (ɔnaʒ) *m,* sampling; selection, range. ~**ner** (ne) *v.t,* to sample.

échappatoire (eʃapatwar) *f,* way out, loophole. **échappé, e** (pe) *n,* runaway. ~ *de prison,* escaped prisoner. **échappée** (pe) *f,* (*Sport*) breakaway. ~ [*de vue*], vista, glimpse, (*sea, sun*). **échappement** (pmɑ̃) *m,* (*Mot.*) exhaust; escapement (*clock*). **échapper** (pe) *v.i,* ~ *à,* to escape [from]; evade; elude, slip one's memory. *son nom m'échappe*, his name escapes me. *laisser ~*, to let slip (*word, chance*). *~ des mains*, to slip out of one's hands. *l'~ belle*, to have a narrow escape. **s' ~**, to escape (*de*, from); (*runner*) break away; (*gas*) leak, escape.

écharde (eʃard) *f*, splinter (*wood*).

écharpe (eʃarp) *f*, scarf; sash; sling. *en ~*, in a sling. **écharper** (pe) *v.t*, (*lit., fig.*) to tear in pieces; lynch.

échasse (eʃɑs) *f*, stilt. **échassier** (ʃasje) *m*, wader (*bird*).

échauder (eʃode) *v.t*, to scald. *~ qn*, to teach s.o a lesson.

échauffement (eʃofmɑ̃) *m*, (*Mot.*) overheating; (*Sport*) warm-up. **échauffer** (fe) *v.t*, to make hot (*pers.*); (*Mot.*) overheat; (*fig.*) fire, excite. **s'~**, (*Sport*) to warm up; (*argument*) get heated. **échauffourée** (fure) *f*, clash, skirmish.

échéance (eʃeɑ̃s) *f*, due date; date of payment &c. *à longue, courte ~*, long-, short-term (*plans*). **le cas échéant** (ʃeɑ̃), if the case arises.

échec (eʃɛk) *m*, failure; setback. *tenir qn en ~*, to hold s.o in check. *faire ~ à qn*, to thwart s.o. *les ~s*, chess. *jeu d'~s*, chessmen; chessboard. *~ au roi!* check! *faire ~ & mat*, to checkmate.

échelle (eʃɛl) *f*, ladder; scale (*map, salary*); ladder (*stocking*). *sur une grande ~*, on a large scale. *~ coulissante*, extending ladder. *~ double*, stepladder. *~ mobile*, sliding scale. **échelon** (ʃlɔ̃) *m*, rung; (*Adm.*) grade, level; (*Mil.*) echelon. **échelonner** (ʃlɔne) *v.t*, to spread out, space out (*sur*, over); stagger (*holidays*).

écheveau (eʃvo) *m*, skein, hank; (*fig.*) tangle.

échevelé, e (eʃəvle) *a*, dishevelled, tousled.

échine (eʃin) *f*, spine, backbone; (*Cook.*) loin. *avoir l'~ souple*, to be subservient. **échiner** (s') (ne) *v.pr*, to work o.s. to death.

échiquier (eʃikje) *m*, chessboard.

écho (eko) *m*, echo; reply; report; (*Press*) news *or* gossip item. *faire ~*, (*room*) to echo. *se faire l'~ de*, to echo, repeat.

échoir (eʃwar) *v.i.ir*, to fall due, expire. *~ à qn*, to fall to s.o's lot; f. to s.o (*de faire* to do).

échoppe *O* (eʃɔp) *f*, stall, booth; workshop.

échouer (eʃwe) *v.i*, to fail; fall through; end up; (*Naut.* & **s'~**) run aground. ¶ *v.t*, to ground; beach. *échoué [à sec]*, high & dry.

éclabousser (eklabuse) *v.t*, to splash, [be]spatter (*de*, with). **éclaboussure** (syr) *f*, splash, spatter; (*fig.*) smear (*reputation*).

éclair (eklɛr) *m*, flash of lightning; (*Phot.*) flash; flash (*anger, genius*). *~s de chaleur*, summer lightning. *passer comme l'~* to flash past. (*Cook.*) eclair. ¶ *a*, lightning (*visit, attack*). **~age** (klɛraʒ) *m*, lighting. **~agiste** (aʒist) *m*, electrician; lighting engineer. **~ant, e** (rɑ̃, ɑ̃t) *a*, enlightening.

eclaircie (eklɛrsi) *f*, break (*clouds*); (*Met.*) bright interval. **éclaircir** (sir) *v.t*, to clear up, clarify (*question*); enlighten; lighten (*colour*); thin down (*soup*); thin (*plants, hair*). **s'~**, (*weather*) to clear up. *s'~ la voix*, to clear one's throat.

éclairé, e (eklɛre) *a*, enlightened. **éclairer** (re) *v.t*, to light [up]; throw light upon (*problem*); clear up; enlighten; (*Mil.*) reconnoitre. ¶ *v.i*, *~ bien, mal*, to give a good, bad light. **s'~**, (*face*) to light up; (*problem*) get clearer. **éclaireur** (rœr) *m*, scout; [boy] scout. **éclaireuse** (røz) *f*, [girl] guide.

éclat (ekla) *m*, splinter; fragment (*shell, glass*); burst, roar, shout; clap (*thunder*); brightness, brilliance; lustre, sheen; flash; glare; splendour, glamour; fuss, scandal. **~ant, e** (tɑ̃, ɑ̃t) *a*, bright, brilliant (*light, colour*); loud, shrill (*voice, cry*); radiant (*beauty, health*); resounding (*success*); striking, glaring (*example*). **~ement** (tmɑ̃) *m*, bursting, explosion. **éclater** (te) *v.i*, to burst, explode; (*group*) break up; (*fire, war*) break out; (*cry, shot*) ring out; (*truth, joy*) shine out. *~ de rire*, to burst out laughing. *~ en sanglots*, to b. into tears.

éclectique (eklɛktik) *a*, eclectic.

éclipse (eklips) *f*, eclipse. **éclipser** (se) *v.t*, to eclipse; overshadow. **s'~**, to become eclipsed; (*pers.*) slip away.

éclisse (eklis) *f*, (*Med.*) splint. **éclisser** (se) *v.t*, to splint.

éclopé, e (eklɔpe) *a*, lame, limping.

éclore (eklɔr) *v.i.ir*, to hatch; (*flower*) open; (*fig.*) be born, dawn. **éclosion** (klozjɔ̃) *f*, hatching; opening; birth, dawn.

écluse (eklyz) *f*, lock (*canal*). **éclusier, ère** (zje, ɛr) *n*, lock keeper.

écœurant, e (ekœrɑ̃, ɑ̃t) *a*, sickening, nauseating. **écœurement** (mɑ̃) *m*, (*lit.*) nausea; (*fig.*) disgust. **écœurer** (re) *v.t*, to make (s.o) sick; (*fig.*) sicken, disgust.

école (ekɔl) *f*, school. *aller à l'~*, to attend school. *faire l'~*, to teach. *faire ~*, to gain followers. *faire l'~ buissonnière*, to play truant. *navire-~*, training ship. *~ de l'air*, flying school. *~ maternelle*, nursery s. *~ normale*, teachers training college. **écolier, ère** (lje, ɛr) *n*, schoolboy, -girl; novice.

écologie (ekɔlɔʒi) *f*, ecology. **écologique** (ʒik) *a*, ecological. **écologiste** (ʒist) *n*, ecologist.

éconduire (ekɔ̃dɥir) *v.t.ir*, to get rid of, show out (*visitor*); reject (*suitor*).

économat (ekɔnɔma) *m*, bursarship; bursar's office. **économe** (nɔm) *a*, thrifty; sparing (*de*, of). ¶ *n*, bursar. **économie** (mi) *f*, economy, thrift; saving. *~s*, savings. *faire des ~s*, to save [up]. *~s de bout de chandelle*, cheeseparing economies. (*Econ.*) economy (*system*); economics. (*Univ.*) *~ politique*, economics,

political economy. **économique**† (mik) *a,* economical; economic. **économiser** (ze) *v.t,* to economize [on], save [on]. ~ *sur,* to cut down on. **économiste** (mist) *n,* economist.
écope (ekɔp) *f,* (*Naut.*) baler. **écoper** (pe) *v.t. & i,* to bale [out]; (*P*) to catch it *P* (*suffer*).
écorce (ekɔrs) *f,* bark; peel, skin (*orange*). *l'~ terrestre,* the earth's crust.
écorcher (ekɔrʃe) *v.t,* to flay, skin; graze, scrape; chafe, rub; grate (*on ears*); murder (*language*); fleece (*customer*). **écorchure** (ʃyr) *f,* graze, scrape.
écorner (ekɔrne) *v.t,* to knock the corners off (*furniture*); make a dent in (*fortune*). *écorné,* dog-eared (*book*).
écossais, e (ekɔsɛ, ɛz) *a,* Scottish, Scots; Scotch. **É~, e,** *n,* Scot, Scotsman, -woman. **l'Ecosse** (kɔs) *f,* Scotland.
écosser (ekɔse) *v.t,* to shell, pod (*peas &c*).
écot (eko) *m,* share (*of bill*).
écoulement (ekulmɑ̃) *m,* flow; drainage; (*Med.*) discharge; passing (*time*); (*Com.*) selling. **écouler** (le) *v.t,* (*Com.*) to sell, dispose of. **s'~,** to flow out *or* away; seep out; (*crowd*) disperse; (*time*) pass, elapse; (*Com.*) sell.
écourter (ekurte) *v.t,* to cut short; shorten.
écoute (ekut) *f,* (*Radio, Tel.*) listening; (*Naut.*) sheet. *aux ~s,* listening, on the lookout (*de,* for). **écouter** (te) *v.t,* to listen to; take notice of. *écoutez!* listen!, look here! ~ *qn parler,* to hear s.o speak. ~ *aux portes,* to eavesdrop. **écouteur, euse** (tœr, øz) *n,* listener; eavesdropper. ¶ *m,* (*Tel.*) receiver. *~s,* headphones.
écoutille (ekutij) *f,* (*Naut.*) hatch[way].
écrabouiller (ekrabuje) *v.t,* to crush, squash.
écran (ekrɑ̃) *m,* screen; (*Phot.*) filter. *faire ~ à,* to screen.
écrasant, e (ekrɑzɑ̃, ɑ̃t) *a,* crushing; overwhelming; backbreaking (*work*). **écraser** (ze) *v.t,* to crush; squash; run over; overwhelm. *se faire ~,* to get run over. **s'~,** (*car, plane*) to crash.
écrémer (ekreme) *v.t,* to skim (*milk*).
écrevisse (ekrəvis) *f,* crayfish (*river*).
écrier (s') (ekrie) *v.pr,* to exclaim, cry [out].
écrin (ekrɛ̃) *m,* case, jewelry case.
écrire (ekrir) *v.t. & i.ir,* to write; spell; write down. ~ *à la machine,* to type. *c'était écrit,* it was inevitable. **écrit** (kri) *m,* piece of writing; written exam document. *par ~,* in writing. **écriteau** (to) *m,* notice, sign. **écriture** (tyr) *f,* writing; hand[writing]; style. ~ *moulée,* copperplate handwriting. (*Rel.*) *l'E~ [sainte],* the Scriptures. (*Com.*) *~s,* books, accounts. **écrivailler** (vɑje) *v.i,* (*pej.*) to scribble. **écrivassier, ère** (vasjɛ, ɛr) *n,* scribbler. **écrivain** (vɛ̃) *m,* writer.
écrou (ekru) *m,* (*Tech.*) nut. **écrouer** (krue) *v.t,* to imprison.
écroulement (ekrulmɑ̃) *m,* collapse. **s'écrouler** (le) *v.pr,* to collapse; crumble.
écru, e (ekry) *a,* raw; unbleached (*cloth*).
écu (eky) *m,* shield; (*Hist.*) crown (*coin*). *~s,* money.
écueil (ekœj) *m,* reef; (*fig.*) snag; pitfall.
écuelle (ekɥɛl) *f,* bowl.
éculé, e (ekyle) *a,* down-at-heel (shoe); well-worn, hackneyed (*story*).
écume (ekym) *f,* foam; froth; lather; scum (*jam*). ~ *de mer,* meerschaum. **écumer** (me) *v.t,* to skim (*liquid*); plunder; scour (*town, seas*). ¶ *v.i,* to foam, froth. ~ *de rage,* to foam with rage. **écumeux, euse** (mø, øz) *a,* foamy, frothy. **écumoire** (mwar) *f,* skimmer.
écureuil (ekyrœj) *m,* squirrel.
écurie (ekyri) *f,* stable; (*fig.*) pigsty. ~ *de course,* racing stable.
écusson (ekysɔ̃) *m,* badge; (*Her.*) escutcheon.
écuyer, ère (ekɥije, ɛr) *n,* rider; horseman, -woman; equerry; (*Hist.*) squire.
eczéma (egzema) *m,* eczema.
éden (edɛn) *m,* (*fig.*) Eden. *l'É~,* [the Garden of] Eden.
édenté, e (edɑ̃te) *a,* toothless.
édicter (edikte) *v.t,* to decree.
édification (edifikasjɔ̃) *f,* erection; edification. **édifice** (fis) *m,* edifice, building, structure. **édifier** (fje) *v.t,* to erect, build; build up; edify; enlighten.
Édimbourg (edɛ̃bur) *m,* Edinburgh.
édit (edi) *m,* (*Hist.*) edict.
éditer (edite) *v.t,* to publish; edit (*text*). **éditeur, trice** (tœr, tris) *n,* publisher; editor. **édition** (sjɔ̃) *f,* publishing; editing; edition (*book*); [computer] printout. *l'~,* the publishing business.
éditorial (editɔrjal) *m,* leader; editorial. **~iste** (list) *n,* leader writer.
édredon (edrədɔ̃) *m,* eiderdown.
éducateur, trice (edykatœr, tris) *a,* educational. ¶ *n,* educator. **éducatif, ive** (tif, iv) *a,* educational. **éducation** (sjɔ̃) *f,* education; upbringing; training (*ear &c*). *sans ~,* ill-bred.
édulcorer (edylkɔre) *v.t,* to tone down (*text*).
éduquer (edyke) *v.t,* to educate; bring up; train.
effacé, e (efase) *a,* unobtrusive; retiring; subdued. **effacement** (smɑ̃) *m,* erasing; fading; withdrawal (*candidate*); retiring manner *or* life. **effacer** (se) *v.t,* to efface, obliterate, erase, rub out; wipe off; outshine. **s'~,** to fade; wear off; keep in the background; stand aside.
effarant, e (ɛfarɑ̃, ɑ̃t) *a,* alarming. **effarement** (efarmɑ̃) *m,* alarm. **effarer** (re) *v.t,* to alarm; appal. **effaroucher** (ruʃe) *v.t,* to startle, frighten away. **s' ~,** to take fright (*de,* at); be shocked (*de,* by).
effectif, ive† (efɛktif, iv) *a,* effective; real; actual. ¶ *m,* (*Mil.*) strength; complement; (*Sch.*) size, numbers. **effectuer** (tɥe) *v.t,* to make; carry

out; effect; execute.
efféminé, e (efemine) *a,* effeminate.
effervescence (efɛrvɛsɑ̃s) *f,* effervescence; (*fig.*) ferment, agitation. **effervescent, e** (sɑ̃, ɑ̃t) *a,* effervescent.
effet (efɛ) *m,* effect. *être sans ~,* to have no effect. impression. *faire bon, mauvais ~ sur,* to make a good, bad impression on. (*Theat &c*) *~ comique, de lumière,* comic, lighting effect. *manquer son ~,* (*joke*) to fall flat. (*Sport*) spin (*on ball*). (*Com.*) *~* [*de commerce*], bill [of exchange]. *~s,* clothes, things. *mettre à ~,* to put into effect. *en ~,* you see (*because*); actually; indeed. *sous l'~ de,* under the influence of.
efficace† (efikas) *a,* effective; efficacious; efficient (*pers., tool*). **efficacité** (site) *f,* effectiveness; efficacy; efficiency.
effigie (efiʒi) *f,* effigy.
effilé, e (efile) *a,* slender, tapering. ¶ *m,* fringe. **effiler** (le) *v.t.* & **s'~,** to fray; taper. **effilocher** (s') (lɔʃe) *v.pr,* to fray.
efflanqué, e (eflɑ̃ke) *a,* emaciated; skinny.
effleurer (eflœre) *v.t,* to touch lightly; brush against; graze; (*fig.*) touch upon (*subject*).
effluve (eflyv) *m, ~s,* exhalations.
effondrement (efɔ̃drəmɑ̃) *m,* collapse; breakdown; dejection. **effondrer (s')** (dre) *v.pr,* (*gen.*) to collapse; (*roof*) cave in; (*pers., prices*) slump; (*fig: pers.*) break down.
efforcer (s') (efɔrse) *v.pr,* to try hard, strive, do one's best (*de faire,* to do). **effort** (fɔr) *m,* effort, exertion; (*Mech.*) stress. *faire des ~s,* to make an effort.
effraction (efraksjɔ̃) *f,* breaking in; break-in.
effranger (efrɑ̃ʒe) *v.t,* to fray.
effrayant, e (efrɛjɑ̃, ɑ̃t) *a,* terrifying; frightful, dreadful. **effrayer** (je) *v.t,* to frighten, scare. **s'~,** to be frightened (*de,* by).
effréné, e (efrene) *a,* frantic; unbridled.
effriter (efrite) *v.t,* & **s'~,** to crumble.
effroi (efrwɑ) *m,* terror, dread.
effronté, e (efrɔ̃te) *a,* insolent; shameless, brazen, barefaced. **~ment** (mɑ̃) *ad,* insolently &c. **effronterie** (tri) *f,* effrontery; insolence.
effroyable† (efrwajabl) *a,* appalling, horrifying.
effusion (ɛfyzjɔ̃) *f,* effusion. *avec ~,* effusively. *~ de sang,* bloodshed.
égal, e (egal) *a,* equal (*en,* in; *à,* to); even (*pace*); even, level (*ground*); steady (*wind*); equable (*climate, temperament*). *ça m'est ~,* it's all the same to me. ¶ *n,* equal (*pers.*). *d'~ à ~,* as equals. *à l'~ de,* on a par with; just like. **~ement** (lmɑ̃) *ad,* equally; also, as well. **~er** (le) *v.t,* to equal (*en,* in); match. **~iser** (lize) *v.t,* (*v.i. Sport*) to equalize. **~ité** (te) *f,* equality; evenness, levelness; steadiness; equableness. *~ d'humeur,* evenness of temper. (*Sport*) *être à ~,* to be equal; draw.
égard (egar) *m,* regard, respect. *à cet ~, à tous ~s,* in this, in all respect(s). *à l'~ de,* with regard to, concerning; towards (*pers.*). *~s,* consideration.
égaré, e (egare) *a,* lost; stray (*animal*); remote (*spot*); wild, distraught (*look*). **égarement** (armɑ̃) *m,* distraction; losing. **égarer** (re) *v.t,* (*gen.*) to lead astray; mislead; mislay. **s'~,** to get lost; (*fig.*) to wander off the point.
égayer (egeje) *v.t,* to brighten up (*room*); cheer up, amuse (*pers.*). **s'~,** to amuse o.s.
Égée (la mer) (eʒe), the Aegean sea.
égide (eʒid) *f, sous l'~ de,* under the aegis of.
églantier (eglɑ̃tje) *m,* wild rose (*bush*). **églantine** (tin) *f,* wild (*or* dog) rose.
église (egliz) *f,* church. *l'É~ anglicane* (ɑ̃glikan), the Church of England.
égoïsme (egɔism) *m,* selfishness. **égoïste**† (ist) *a,* selfish, egotistic. ¶ *n,* egotist.
égorger (egɔrʒe) *v.t,* to cut the throat of; massacre; (*fig.*) ruin; (*P*) fleece.
égout (egu) *m,* sewer. **~ier** (tje) *m,* sewerman. **~ter** (te) *v.t,* (*Cook.*) to strain; wring out. ¶ *v.i.* & **s'~,** to drain; (*clothes*) drip. *'laisser ~',* 'drip dry'. **~toir** (twar) *m,* draining board; plate rack.
égratigner (egratiɲe) *v.t,* to scratch. **égratignure** (ɲyr) *f,* scratch.
égrener (egrəne) *v.t,* to pick off; shell; gin (*cotton*); tell (*beads*). **s'~,** to drop off.
égrillard, e (egrijar, ard) *a,* ribald, bawdy.
Égypte (l') (eʒipt) *f,* Egypt. **égyptien, ne** (sjɛ̃, ɛn) *a.* & **É~,** *n,* Egyptian.
eh (e) *i,* [h]eh! *~ bien!* now then!, well!
éhonté, e (eɔ̃te) *a,* shameless, barefaced.
éjaculer (eʒakyle) *v.i,* to ejaculate (*semen*).
éjecter (eʒɛkte) *v.t,* (*Tech.*) to eject; (*P*) kick out.
élaborer (elabɔre) *v.t,* to elaborate; work out.
élagage (elagaʒ) *m,* pruning. **élaguer** (ge) *v.t,* (*lit., fig.*) to prune.
élan[1] (elɑ̃) *m,* elk, moose.
élan[2] (elɑ̃) *m,* bound, spring; dash; run-up (*jump*); momentum; [out]burst, surge (*anger &c*); spirit, fervour. *saut sans ~,* standing jump. **élancé, e** (se) *a,* slender. **élancement** (smɑ̃) *m,* shooting pain. **élancer** (se) *v.i,* (*wound*) to give shooting pains. **s'~,** to rush, dash, dart; (*spire*) soar.
élargir (elarʒir) *v.t,* to widen; broaden; increase, extend; release (*prisoner*).
élasticité (elastisite) *f,* elasticity; spring; flexibility. **élastique** (tik) *a,* elastic, springy (*step*); flexible (*rule*); pliable (*conscience*). ¶ *m,* elastic; elastic *or* rubber band.
Elbe (l'île d') (ɛlb) *f,* the Island of Elba. **l'Elbe,** *m,* the Elbe (*river*).
électeur, trice (elɛktœr, tris) *n,* voter, constituent. **élection** (sjɔ̃) *f,* election. *~ partielle,* by-election. *~s législatives,* general election. **électorat** (tɔra) *m,* electorate

électricien (elɛktrisjɛ̃) *m,* electrician. **électricité** (site) *f,* electricity. **électrification** (fikasjɔ̃) *f,* electrification. **électrifier** (fje) *v.t,* to electrify. **électrique** (trik) *a,* electric(al). **électriser** (ze) *v.t,* (*lit., fig.*) to electrify.

électro (elɛktrɔ) *pref,* electro. ~**-aimant,** *m,* electromagnet. ~ **cardiogramme,** *m,* electrocardiogram. ~**choc(s)** *m(pl),* electric shock treatment.

électrocuter (elɛktrɔkyte) *v.t,* to electrocute. **électrode** (trɔd) *f,* electrode. **électron** (trɔ̃) *m,* electron. **électronique** (ɔnik) *a,* electronic. ¶ *f,* electronics. **électrophone** (fɔn) *m,* record player.

élégamment (elegamɑ̃) *ad,* elegantly; courteously. **élégance** (gɑ̃s) *f,* elegance; courtesy. **élégant, e** (gɑ̃, ɑ̃t) *a,* elegant; courteous. ¶ *n,* man, woman of fashion.

élégie (eleʒi) *f,* elegy.

élément (elemɑ̃) *m,* (*gen., Chem.*) element; (*Mach.*) part; (*Phys.*) cell; (*Mil.*) unit. ~*s,* rudiments; elements (*wind &c*). *dans son* ~, in his element. ~**aire** (tɛr) *a,* elementary.

éléphant (elefɑ̃) *m,* elephant.

élevage (elvaʒ) *m,* breeding, rearing, keeping (*farm animals*); cattle farm. ~ *de poulets,* poultry farm. **élévation** (sjɔ̃) *f,* raising; construction; rise (*level, ground*); (*Arch.*) elevation; loftiness (*style*). (*Rel.*) *l'*~, the Elevation. **élève** (elɛv) *n,* pupil, student. ~ *infirmière,* student nurse. (*Mil., Nav.*) ~ *officier,* [officer] cadet. **élevé, e** (elve) *a,* high; lofty; heavy (*losses*). *bien, mal* ~, well-, ill-mannered. **élever** (ve) *v.t,* (*gen.*) to raise; lift; erect; bring up (*child*); breed, rear, keep (*animals*); grow (*plants*). **s'**~, (*gen.*) to rise; (*house*) rise, stand; (*doubts*) arise. *s'*~ *à,* (*sum*) to amount to. *s'*~ *contre,* to rise up against. **éleveur, euse** (vœr, øz) *n,* breeder.

elfe (ɛlf) *m,* elf.

éligible (eliʒibl) *a,* eligible.

élimer (elime) *v.t,* to wear threadbare.

éliminatoire (eliminatwar) *a,* eliminatory. ¶ *f,* (*Sport*) heat. **éliminer** (ne) *v.t,* to eliminate.

élire (elir) *v.t.ir,* to elect.

élision (elizjɔ̃) *f,* elision.

élite (elit) *f,* élite. *d'*~, first-class (*student*); crack (*troops*).

élixir (eliksir) *m,* elixir.

elle (ɛl) *pn,* (*subject*) she, it. ~*s,* they. (*emphatic*) *c'est* ~ *qui l'a fait,* it's she who did it. *je la connais* ~, I know her all right. *il joue mieux qu'*~, he plays better than her. (*after pr.*) her, it. ~*s,* them. *pour* ~*(s),* for her (them). *un ami à* ~, a friend of hers. ~*-même,* herself, itself. ~*s-mêmes,* themselves.

ellipse (elips) *f,* ellipse; (*Gram.*) ellipsis.

élocution (elɔkysjɔ̃) *f,* diction; delivery.

éloge (elɔʒ) *m,* praise; eulogy. *faire l'*~ *de,* to praise. ~ *funèbre,* funeral oration. **élogieux, euse**† (lɔʒjø, øz) *a,* eulogistic.

éloigné, e (elwaɲe) *a,* distant, far off, remote. **éloignement** (ɲmɑ̃) *m,* removal; postponement; estrangement; distance. *avec l'*~, at a distance (*time, place*). **éloigner** (ɲe) *v.t,* to move away (*de,* from); postpone; estrange; (*fig.*) remove, avert. **s'**~, to go *or* move away (*de,* from); grow away (*from friend*); stray (*from truth*). *éloignez-vous!* stand back!

éloquemment (elɔkamɑ̃) *ad,* eloquently. **éloquence** (kɑ̃s) *f,* eloquence, oratory. **éloquent, e** (kɑ̃, ɑ̃t) *a,* eloquent.

élu, e (ely) *a,* elected; (*Rel.*) chosen. ¶ *n,* elected member. (*Rel.*) *les* ~*s,* the Elect.

élucider (elyside) *v.t,* to elucidate.

éluder (elyde) *v.t,* to elude, evade.

Elysée (elize) *m,* (*Myth.*) Elysium. *le palais de l'*~, the Elysée palace (*Paris*).

émacié, e (emasje) *a,* emaciated.

émail (emaj) *m,* enamel; (*pl.*) pieces of e. ware. ~**lage** (majaʒ) *m,* enamelling. ~**ler** (je) *v.t,* to enamel; (*fig.*) stud; intersperse.

émanciper (emɑ̃sipe) *v.t,* to emancipate. **s'**~, to become liberated.

émaner (emane) *v.i,* ~ *de,* to emanate from, come from.

émarger (emarʒe) *v.t,* to sign [in the margin]; (*Typ.*) trim. ¶ *v.i,* to be paid.

émasculer (emaskyle) *v.t,* to emasculate.

emballage (ɑ̃balaʒ) *m,* packing, wrapping up; package. **emballement** (lmɑ̃) *m,* craze; flare-up (*anger*); bolting (*horse*); racing (*engine*). **emballer** (le) *v.t,* to pack [up], wrap [up]; race (*engine*); (*P*) thrill. **s'**~, to be carried away; flare up; bolt; race.

embarcadère (ɑ̃barkadɛr) *m,* landing stage. **embarcation** (sjɔ̃) *f,* [small] craft, boat.

embardée (ɑ̃barde) *f,* swerve; (*Naut.*) yaw. *faire une* ~, to swerve; yaw.

embargo (ɑ̃bargo) *m,* embargo.

embarquement (ɑ̃barkəmɑ̃) *m,* embarkation; boarding; loading. **embarquer** (ke) *v.t,* to embark; load (*cargo*); (*P*) cart off; nick *P.* ~ *qn dans,* to involve s.o in. ¶ *v.i. &* **s'**~, to embark, [go on] board (*ship, plane, train*); (*v.i.*) to ship water.

embarras (ɑ̃bara) *m,* obstruction, obstacle; embarrassment; predicament. *être dans l'*~, to be in a quandary; to have money troubles. ~ *gastrique,* stomach upset. *faire des* ~, to make a fuss. *avoir l'*~ *du choix,* to have too many choices open. ~**sant, e** (sɑ̃, ɑ̃t) *a,* embarrassing; awkward; cumbersome. ~**sé, e** (se) *a,* embarrassed; cluttered up. **embarrasser** (se) *v.t,* to clutter up (*room*); hamper, get in one's way; to disconcert, embarrass, put in an awkward position. **s'**~, to burden o.s with; bother about.

embaucher (ɑ̃boʃe) *v.t,* to take on, hire (*workers*). **embauche** (boʃ) *f,* hiring.

embaumer (ãbome) *v.t,* to embalm; perfume, scent. ¶ *v.i,* to be fragrant.
embellir (ãbɛlir) *v.t,* to make more beautiful; embellish. ¶ *v.i,* to grow more beautiful.
embêtant, e (ãbɛtã, ãt) *a,* annoying, tiresome. **embêtement** (mã) *m,* annoyance. ~ *s,* bother, trouble. **embêter** (te) *v.t,* to bother; annoy; bore. **s'~,** to be bored.
emblée (d') (ãble) *ad,* right away, straight off, straightaway.
emblème (ãblɛm) *m,* emblem.
embobiner *P* (ãbɔbine) *v.t,* to wheedle.
emboîter (ãbwate) *v.t. &* **s'~,** to fit together. ~ *qch dans,* to fit sth into.
embonpoint (ãbɔ̃pwɛ̃) *m,* stoutness. *prendre de l'~,* to grow stout.
embouché, e (ãbuʃe) *a, mal ~,* coarse, ill-spoken. **embouchure** (ãbuʃyr) *f,* mouth (*river*); (*Mus.*) mouthpiece; embouchure.
embourber (s') (ãburbe) *v.pr,* (*vehicle*) to get stuck in the mud.
embourgeoiser (s') (ãburʒwɑze) *v.pr,* to become middle-class.
embout (ãbu) *m,* tip, ferrule; nozzle (*hose*).
embouteiller (ãbutɛje) *v.t,* to block, jam. **embouteillage** (jaʒ) *m,* traffic jam.
emboutir (ãbutir) *v.t,* to stamp (*metal*); (*P car*) crash into.
embranchement (ãbrãʃmã) *m,* junction; (*Rly*) branch line; side road. **embrancher (s')** (ʃe) *v.pr,* to join up (*sur,* to).
embrasement (ãbrɑzmã) *m,* conflagration; blaze. **embraser** (ze) *v.t,* to set ablaze; illuminate; (*fig.*) fire.
embrassade (ãbrasad) *f,* embrace. **embrasser** (se) *v.t,* to kiss; embrace; embrace (*cause, period*); take up (*career*). ~ *du regard,* to take in at a glance. *'je t'embrasse [affectueusement]',* 'with love' (*letter*).
embrasure (ãbrɑzyr) *f,* embrasure.
embrayer (ãbreje) *v.t,* (*Mach.*) to engage, put into gear. ¶ *v.i,* (*Mot.*) to let in the clutch. **embrayage** (ɛjaʒ) *m,* (*Mot.*) clutch; engaging [the clutch].
embrigader (ãbrigade) *v.t,* to dragoon.
embrocher (ãbrɔʃe) *v.t,* to spit; run through.
embrouiller (ãbruje) *v.t,* to muddle up; tangle. **s'~,** (*pers.*) to get in a muddle; (*ideas*) become confused. **embrouillement** (mã) *m,* muddling, tangling; muddle, tangle.
embroussaillé, e (ãbrusaje) *a,* overgrown (*path*); bushy (*beard*).
embrumer (ãbryme) *v.t,* to mist over. **embruns** (brœ̃) *m.pl,* spray, spindrift.
embryon (ãbriɔ̃) *m,* embryo. **embryonnaire** (ɔnɛr) *a,* embryonic.
embûche (ãbyʃ) *f,* trap. **embuer** (bɥe) *v.t,* to mist over. **embuscade** (byskad) *f,* ambush. *se tenir en ~,* to lie in ambush. **embusquer (s')** (ke) *v.pr,* to lie in ambush.
éméché, e (emeʃe) *a,* merry, tipsy.
émeraude (emrod) *f,* emerald.
émerger (emɛrʒe) *v.i,* to emerge; stand out.
émeri (emri) *m,* emery. *toile ~,* e. paper.
émérite (emerit) *a,* distinguished, eminent.
émerveiller (emɛrvɛje) *v.t,* to fill with wonder. **s'~,** to marvel (*de,* at).
émetteur, trice (emɛtœr, tris) *a,* (*Fin.*) issuing; (*Tel.*) transmitting. ¶ *m,* transmitter. **émettre** (tr) *v.t.ir,* to emit, give out; transmit; (*Fin.*) issue.
émeute (emøt) *f,* riot. **émeutier, ère** (møtje, ɛr) *n,* rioter.
émietter (emjɛte) *v.t. &* **s'~,** to crumble.
émigrant, e (emigrã, ãt) *n,* emigrant. **émigration** (grasjɔ̃) *f,* emigration. **émigré, e** (gre) *n,* (*Hist.*) émigré. **émigrer** (gre) *v.i,* to emigrate.
émincer (emɛ̃se) *v.t,* to slice thinly.
éminemment (eminamã) *ad,* eminently. **éminence** (nãs) *f,* hill, rise; eminence, distinction. *Son E~,* His Eminence (*cardinal*). **éminent, e** (nã, ãt) *a,* eminent; distinguished.
émir (emir) *m,* emir. **~at** (ra) *m,* emirate.
émissaire (emisɛr) *m,* emissary. **émission** (sjɔ̃) *f,* emission; issue; transmission; broadcast.
emmagasiner (ãmagazine) *v.t,* to store; store up, accumulate.
emmailloter (ãmajɔte) *v.t,* to swathe; bandage.
emmêler (ãmɛle) *v.t,* to [en]tangle; muddle.
emménagement (ãmenaʒmã) *m,* moving in (*house*). **emménager** (ʒe) *v.i,* to move in.
emmener (ãmne) *v.t,* to take, t. away *or* off (*pers.*). ~ *qn au bal,* to take s.o to a dance.
emmerdant, e *P** (ãmɛrdã, ãt) *a,* bloody annoying *or* boring *P.* **emmerdement** *P* (dəmã) *m,* bloody nuisance *P.* ~*s,* bloody trouble *P;* hassle *P.* **emmerder** *P* (de) *v.t,* to annoy like hell *P;* bore the pants off *P.* **s'~,** to be bored stiff. **emmerdeur, euse** *P** (dœr, øz) *n,* pain in the neck *P.*
emmitoufler (ãmitufle) *v.t,* to muffle up.
émoi (emwa) *m,* emotion, agitation. *en ~,* (*heart*) in a flutter; (*street*) in a commotion.
émoluments (emɔlymã) *m.pl,* emoluments.
émotif, ive (emɔtif, iv) *a.* (*& n*), emotional (person). **émotion** (emosjɔ̃) *f,* emotion; excitement; fright. **~nel, le** (nɛl) *a,* emotional.
émoulu, e (emuly) *a: frais ~ de,* fresh from (*school, college*).
émousser (emuse) *v.t,* to blunt; (*fig.*) dull.
émoustiller *P* (emustije) *v.t,* to exhilarate.
émouvoir (emuvwar) *v.t.ir,* to move; stir, rouse; disturb, upset.
empailler (ãpɑje) *v.t,* to stuff (*animal*); bottom (*chair*) with straw. **empailleur, euse** (jœr, øz) *n,* taxidermist; chair bottomer.
empaqueter (ãpakte) *v.t,* to pack; wrap up.
emparer (s') (ãpare) *v.pr, ~ de,* to seize; grab; snatch up; take over (*conversation*).
empâter (ãpɑte) *v.t,* to thicken, coarsen (*fea-*

tures); coat (*mouth*). **s'~,** to grow fat.

empêché, e (ɑ̃pɛʃe) *a,* detained, held up; at a loss. **empêchement** (ʃmɑ̃) *m,* obstacle; (*last minute*) difficulty, hitch. **empêcher** (ʃe) *v.t,* to prevent, stop (*qn de faire, que qn fasse,* s.o from doing). *n'empêche que* (+ *indic.*) nevertheless, all the same. *s'~ de faire,* to stop o.s doing. *il n'a pas pu s'~ de voir,* he couldn't help seeing.

empereur (ɑ̃prœr) *m,* emperor.

empesé, e (ɑ̃pəze) *a,* starched; (*fig.*) starchy, stiff. **empeser** (ze) *v.t,* to starch.

empester (ɑ̃pɛste) *v.t,* to make (*place*) stink; reek of (*alcohol*).

empêtrer (s') (ɑ̃pɛtre) *v.pr, s'~ dans,* (*lit.,fig.*) to get tangled up in.

emphase (ɑ̃fɑs) *f,* pomposity. **emphatique†** (fatik) *a,* pompous; (*Gram.*) emphatic.

empiècement (ɑ̃pjɛsmɑ̃) *m,* yoke (*dress*).

empierrer (ɑ̃pjɛre) *v.t,* to metal (*road*).

empiètement (ɑ̃pjɛtmɑ̃) *m,* encroachment. **empiéter sur** (pjete) (*lit., fig.*) to encroach on.

empiffrer *P* **(s')** (ɑ̃pifre) *v.pr,* to stuff o.s (*de,* with).

empiler (ɑ̃pile) *v.t,* to pile [up]; stack.

empire (ɑ̃pir) *m,* empire; authority, sway. *sous l'~ de,* in the grip of; under the influence of. *~ sur soi-même,* self-control.

empirer (ɑ̃pire) *v.t,* to make worse. ¶ *v.i,* to grow worse.

empirique† (ɑ̃pirik) *a,* empirical. **empirisme** (rism) *m,* empiricism.

emplacement (ɑ̃plasmɑ̃) *m,* site, location.

emplâtre (ɑ̃plɑtr) *m,* (*Med.*) plaster (*wound*); (*Mot.*) patch; (*P pers.*) lump, clot *P.*

emplette (ɑ̃plɛt) *f,* purchase. *faire des ~s,* to do some shopping.

emplir (ɑ̃plir) *v.t.* & **s'~,** to fill (*de,* with).

emploi (ɑ̃plwa) *m,* use; usage (*word*); job; employment. *sans ~,* unemployed. *~ du temps,* timetable. **employé, e** (je) *n,* employee. *~ de banque,* bank clerk. *~ de bureau,* office worker. *~ du gaz,* gas man. **employer** (je) *v.t,* to use; employ (*pers., time*). **s'~,** to occupy o.s (*à faire,* doing). **employeur, euse** (jœr, øz) *n,* employer.

empocher (ɑ̃pɔʃe) *v.t,* to pocket.

empoigner (ɑ̃pwaɲe) *v.t,* to grasp; grab [hold of]; (*fig.*) grip. **s'~,** to quarrel; have a scrap.

empoisonnant, e *P* (ɑ̃pwazɔnɑ̃, ɑ̃t) *a,* annoying; deadly [boring]; unbearable (*pers.*). **empoisonnement** (ɔnmɑ̃) *m,* poisoning. (*P*) *~s,* bother, hassle *P.* **empoisonner** (ne) *v.t,* (*lit., fig.*) to poison; (*P*) annoy, drive mad. **empoisonneur, euse** (nœr, øz) *n,* poisoner; (*P*) bore, pain in the neck *P.*

emporté, e (ɑ̃pɔrte) *a,* hasty, quick-tempered. **emportement** (təmɑ̃) *m,* fit of anger.

emporte-pièce (ɑ̃pɔrtəpjɛs) *m,* (*Tech.*) punch. (*fig.*) *à l'~,* incisive.

emporter (ɑ̃pɔrte) *v.t,* to take away; (*wind, wave*) blow, sweep, wash away; (*fig: anger*) carry away. *se laisser ~,* to let o.s be carried away. carry off (*kill*); carry off (*prize*); (*Mil.*) capture (*position*). **l'~ sur,** to get the upper hand of; prevail over; surpass (*en,* in). **s'~,** to lose one's temper (*contre,* with); (*horse*) bolt.

empoté, e, *P* (ɑ̃pɔte) *a,* clumsy. ¶ *n,* clumsy clot *P,* oaf.

empourprer (ɑ̃purpre) *v.t,* to turn crimson.

empreindre (ɑ̃prɛ̃dr) *v.t.ir,* (*liter.*) to imprint. *empreint de,* stamped with, tinged with. **empreinte** (prɛ̃t) *f,* impression, imprint; (*fig.*) stamp; track (*animal*). *~ de pas,* footprint. *~ digitale,* finger print.

empressé, (ɑ̃prɛse) *a,* attentive; assiduous. **empressement** (smɑ̃) *m,* attentiveness; eagerness. **empresser (s')** (se) *v.pr,* to bustle about. *~ auprès de,* to dance attendance on, fuss round. *~ de faire,* to hasten to do.

emprise (ɑ̃priz) *f,* hold, ascendancy.

emprisonnement (ɑ̃prizɔnmɑ̃) *m,* imprisonment. **emprisonner** (ne) *v.t,* to imprison.

emprunt (ɑ̃prœ̃) *m,* borrowing; loan. *faire un ~ à,* to raise a loan from. *d'~,* borrowed; assumed (*name*). **emprunté, e** (te) *a,* awkward, ill-at-ease; sham (*glory*). **emprunter** (te) *v.t,* to borrow (*à,* from); assume (*name*); use, adopt (*style*); take (*route*). **emprunteur, euse** (tœr, øz) *n,* borrower.

empuantir (ɑ̃pɥɑ̃tir) *v.t,* to make (sth) stink.

ému, e (emy) *a,* moved, touched; excited, agitated; emotional (*voice*).

émulation (emylasjɔ̃) *f,* emulation. **émule** (myl) *n,* emulator; equal.

émulsion (emylsjɔ̃) *f,* emulsion.

en¹ (ɑ̃) *pr,* (*place*) in, into, to. *~ France,* in France. *aller ~ Grèce, ~ ville,* to go to Greece, into town. (*time*) in, within. *~ mai, ~ été, ~ 1984,* in May, summer, 1984. *faire le travail ~ 3 jours,* to do the work in 3 days. (*transport*) *aller ~ avion, ~ voiture,* to go by plane, car. (*state, manner*) *~ désordre,* in disorder. *~ noir,* [dressed] in black. *~ colère,* angry. *~ vitesse,* quickly. *parler ~ ami,* to speak as a friend. (*change, translate &c*) into. *couper ~ deux,* to cut into 2. *déguisé ~ marin,* dressed up as a sailor. (*material*) *~ or, ~ bois,* made of gold, wood. (+ *gerund*) *entrer ~ courant,* to run in. *s'instruire ~ lisant,* to educate o.s by reading. *s'assoupir ~ lisant,* to doze off while reading.

en² (ɑ̃) *pn,* (= *de ce lieu*) *j'~ reviens,* I've just got back [from there]. (= *de cela*) *j'~ doute,* I doubt it. *qu'~ penses-tu?* what do you think of it? *il s'~ sert,* he uses it, them. (*quantity*) of it, of them. *il ~ reste un litre,* there's a l. [of it] left. *combien de fils a-t-il? il ~ a trois,* how many sons has he? he has three. *donne-m'~ beaucoup,* give me lots [of it, of them].

encadrer (ãkadre) *v.t,* to frame; surround; train; (*P*) stand, abide (s.o). **encadrement** (mã) *m,* framing; training; frame.
encaisse (ãkɛs) *f,* cash [in hand]. **~ment** (mã) *m,* collection; receipt; cashing (*cheque*). **encaisser** (se) *v.t,* to collect, receive (*money*); cash (*cheque*); take (*blows*); (*P*) stand, stick (*s.o*). *encaissé,* (*road*) hemmed in by hills.
en-cas (ãka) *m,* snack.
encastrer (ãkastre) *v.t,* to embed, sink, fit [flush] (*dans,* into). **s'~,** to fit.
encaustique (ãkostik) *f,* [wax] polish. **encaustiquer** (ke) *v.t,* to polish.
enceindre (ãsɛ̃dr) *v.t.ir,* to enclose, surround. **enceinte**[1] (sɛ̃t) *f,* wall, fence; enclosure; precinct. ~ *acoustique,* loudspeaker system. **enceinte**[2] (sɛ̃t) *a.f,* pregnant (*de 3 mois,* 3 months).
encens (ãsã) *m,* incense. **~er** (se) *v.t,* to incense; flatter. **~oir** (swar) *m,* censer.
encercler (ãsɛrkle) *v.t,* to surround.
enchaînement (ãʃɛnmã) *m,* linking; (*fig.*) series, chain. **enchaîner** (ne) *v.t,* to chain [up]; (*fig.*) enslave; (*secret &c*) bind [together]; link together. ¶ *v.i,* to carry on, continue. **s'~,** to be linked together.
enchantement (ãʃãtmã) *m,* enchantment, spell; delight. **enchanter** (te) *v.t,* to enchant, bewitch; delight, enchant. *enchanté [de vous connaître],* pleased to meet you. **enchanteur, eresse** (tœr, trɛs) *a,* enchanting. ¶ *n,* enchanter, tress; charmer.
enchère (ãʃɛr) *f,* bid. *faire une ~,* to bid. *mettre aux ~s,* to put up for auction. *vente aux ~s,* auction [sale]. **enchérir** (ʃerir) *v.i,* to make a higher bid. ~ *sur,* to outbid; (*fig.*) go one better.
enchevêtrer (ãʃvɛtre) *v.t,* to tangle [up], muddle; confuse. **s'~,** to get in a tangle; become confused.
enclave (ãklav) *f,* enclave. **enclaver** (klave) *v.t,* to enclose, hem in.
enclencher (ãklãʃe) *v.t, &* **s~,** (*Mach.*) to engage.
enclin, e (ãklɛ̃, in) *a,* inclined, prone (*à,* to).
enclore (ãklɔr) *v.t.ir,* to enclose, shut in. **enclos** (klo) *m,* enclosure; paddock; fold.
enclume (ãklym) *f,* anvil.
encoche (ãkɔʃ) *f,* notch, nick.
encoignure (ãkɔɲyr) *f,* corner; corner cupboard.
encoller (ãkɔle) *v.t,* to paste, glue.
encolure (ãkɔlyr) *f,* neck; collar size.
encombrant, e (ãkɔ̃brã, ãt) *a,* bulky, cumbersome; embarrassing (*presence*). **sans encombre** (kɔ̃br), without incident. **encombrement** (kɔ̃brəmã) *m,* congestion; blockage; (*Mot.*) traffic jam; space occupied (*de,* by). **encombrer** (bre) *v.t,* to clutter up; (*Tel.*) block (*lines*); overcrowd (*profession*); burden, encumber. **s'~ de,** to encumber *or* burden o.s with.
encontre (à l'~ de) (ãkɔ̃tr), against. *aller à l'~ de,* to go against, run counter to.
encore (ãkɔr) *ad,* still. *pas ~,* not yet. again; more. ~ *du vin,* some more wine. ~ *une tasse,* another cup. ~ *une fois,* once more. ~ *plus chaud,* hotter still, even hotter. also, as well; even then, still. ~ *ne sait-on pas tout,* we still don't know everything. (*liter.*) ~ *que,* even though.
encourageant, e (ãkuraʒã, ãt) *a,* encouraging. **encourager** (ʒe) *v.t,* to encourage.
encourir (ãkurir) *v.t.ir,* to incur.
encrasser (ãkrase) *v.t,* to foul *or* clog up.
encre (ãkr) *f,* ink. ~ *de Chine,* Indian ink. **encrier** (krie) *m,* inkwell.
encroûter (s') (ãkrute) *v.pr,* to get into a rut.
encyclique (ãsiklik) *a. & f,* encyclical.
encyclopédie (ãsiklɔpedi) *f,* encyclopaedia.
endémique (ãdemik) *a,* endemic.
endetté, e (ãdɛte) *a,* in debt (*fig: envers qn,* to s.o). **endetter** (te) *v.pr,* to get into debt.
endeuiller (ãdœje) *v.t,* to plunge into grief.
endiablé, e (ãdjable) *a,* wild, frenzied.
endiguer (ãdige) *v.t,* to dike; (*fig.*) check.
endimancher (s') (ãdimãʃe) *v.pr,* to put on one's Sunday best.
endive (ãdiv) *f,* chicory.
endoctriner (ãdɔktrine) *v.t,* to indoctrinate.
endolori, e (ãdɔlɔri) *a,* aching, painful.
endommager (ãdɔmaʒe) *v.t,* to damage.
endormant, e (ãdɔrmã, ãt) *a,* deadly dull. **endormi, e** (mi) *a,* asleep; sleeping; drowsy; sluggish; numb. ¶ *n,* sleepyhead. **endormir** (mir) *v.t.ir,* to send to sleep; (*fig.*) lull; deaden. **s'~,** to fall asleep, go to sleep; (*fig.*) slack off.
endos[sement] (ãdo[smã]) *m,* endorsement. **endosser** (se) *v.t,* to put on (*clothes*); shoulder (*responsibility*); (*Fin.*) endorse.
endroit (ãdrwa) *m,* place, spot; point, part (*story &c*). *à l'~ de,* regarding. *à l'~,* right side out (*clothes*).
enduire (ãdɥir) *v.t.ir,* to coat, smear (*de,* with). **enduit** (dɥi) *m,* coating.
endurance (ãdyrãs) *f,* endurance. **endurant, e** (rã, ãt) *a,* hardy; patient.
endurcir (ãdyrsir) *v.t,* to harden; toughen. **s'~,** to grow hard; become tough. **endurcissement** (sismã) *m,* hardening &c; hardness, toughness.
endurer (ãdyre) *v.t,* to endure.
énergie (enɛrʒi) *f,* energy, spirit; (*Phys.*) energy; (*Tech.*) power. **énergique**† (ʒik) *a,* energetic, spirited; vigorous; powerful; strenuous, drastic (*measures*).
énerver (enɛrve) *v.t,* to irritate, annoy. **s'~,** to get worked up.
enfance (ãfãs) *f,* childhood; boyhood; girlhood; (*lit., fig.*) infancy. *l'~,* children.

enfant (ãfã) *n*, child; boy; girl. ~ *de chœur*, altar boy; innocent. ~ *prodige*, infant prodigy. ~ *prodigue*, prodigal son. ~ *trouvé*, foundling. **~ement** (tmã) *m*, (*fig.*) birth. **~er** (te) *v.t*, (*fig.*) to give birth to. **~illage** (tijaʒ) *m*, childishness. **~in, e** (tɛ̃, in) *a*, childlike; childish; simple. *c'est* ~, it's child's play.
enfer (ãfɛr) *m*, (*lit., fig.*) hell. (*Myth.*) *les E~s*, Hades. the underworld. *d'*~, infernal, hellish; raging (*fire*).
enfermer (ãfɛrme) *v.t*, to shut up; lock up; confine; enclose; (*Sport*) box in (*runner*).
enferrer (s') (ãfɛre) *v.pr*, *s'~ dans*, to get involved in, entangled in.
enfiévré, e (ãfjevre) *a*, feverish. **enfiévrer** (re) *v.t*, to fire, rouse, excite.
enfilade (ãfilad) *f*, string; row (*houses*); (*Mil.*) enfilade. **enfiler** (le) *v.t*, to thread (*needle, beads*); slip on (*garment*); go down (*street*). **s'~**, (*P*) to swallow. *s'~ dans*, to turn into (*road*).
enfin (ãfɛ̃) *ad*, at last, finally; lastly. ~ [*bref*], in short. *mais* ~, but; after all; still; come now!
enflammer (ãflame) *v.t*, to set on fire; (*fig.*) fire, inflame. **s'~**, to catch fire; (*fig.*) be fired; flare up.
enfler (ãfle) *v.t*, to [cause to] swell. ¶ *v.i.* & **s'~**, to swell. **enflure** (flyr) *f*, swelling.
enfoncé, e (ãfɔ̃se) *a*, smashed in; sunken, deep set (*eyes*). **enfoncer** (se) *v.t*, to drive, push, thrust in; break down (*door*); (*Mil.*) break through; (*P*) thrash *P* (*opponent*). ¶ *v.i.* & **s'~**, to sink; (*ground*) give way. **enfoncement** (smã) *m*, driving in; breaking down; sinking; giving way; recess.
enfouir (ãfwir) *v.t*, to bury, hide.
enfourcher (ãfurʃe) *v.t*, to mount, get astride.
enfourner (ãfurne) *v.t*, to put in the oven; (*P*) swallow. (*P*) ~ *qch dans*, to stuff sth into *P*.
enfreindre (ãfrɛ̃dr) *v.t.ir*, to infringe.
enfuir (s') (ãfɥir) *v.pr*, to flee, run away; escape; (*time*) fly, vanish.
enfumer (ãfyme) *v.t*, to fill with smoke; smoke out (*hive*).
engagé, e (ãgaʒe) *a*, committed (*writer*). **engageant, e** (ʒã, ãt) *a*, engaging, winning, inviting. **engagement** (ʒmã) *m*, agreement, undertaking; (*Fin., Pol.*) commitment; taking on, engaging (*workers*); (*Mil., Theat.*) engagement; (*Mil.*) enlistment; start (*talks*); (*Sport*) entry; pawing. **engager** (ʒe) *v.t*, to commit, bind; take on, engage; (*Mil.*) enlist; engage (*troops*); involve (*pers: dans*, in); urge (*à faire*, to do); insert (*key*); start, enter into (*discussions*); (*Sport*) enter; pawn. **s'~**, to undertake (*à faire*, to do). **s'~ dans**, to enter into; (*Mach.*) fit into; turn into (*road*); (*Mil.*) enlist in.
engelure (ãʒlyr) *f*, chilblain.
engendrer (ãʒãdre) *v.t*, to beget; engender; breed; generate.
engin (ãʒɛ̃) *m*, instrument; machine; device; [large] vehicle; aircraft; (*Mil.*) missile; (*Fish.* ~*s*) tackle; (*P*) contraption.
englober (ãglɔbe) *v.t*, to include, embody.
engloutir (ãglutir) *v.t*, to gobble up (*food*); engulf (*ship*); swallow up (*fortune*).
engorger (ãgɔrʒe) *v.t*, to choke, block (*pipe*).
engouer (s') (ãgue) *v.pr*, *s'~ pour, de*, to go crazy about (*sth*); become infatuated with (*s.o*).
engouffrer (ãgufre) *v.t*, to engulf, swallow up; gobble up (*food*); shoot (*coal*). **s'~**, to rush.
engourdir (ãgurdir) *v.t*, to numb, dull.
engrais (ãgrɛ) *m*, manure; fertilizer. **~ser** (se) *v.t*, to fatten; manure, fertilize. ¶ *v.i*, (*P*) to put on weight.
engrenage (ãgrənaʒ) *m*, gearing; (*fig.*) chain (*events*). *être pris dans l'*~, to get caught up in the system.
engueulade *P* (ãgœlad) *f*, row, slanging match *P*. **engueuler** *P* (le) *v.t*, to dress down, bawl out *P*. **s'~**, to have a slanging match *P*.
enguirlander (ãgirlãde) *v.t*, to garland; (*P*) to dress down.
enhardir (ãardir) *v.t*, to embolden.
énigmatique† (enigmatik) *a*, enigmatic. **énigme** (nigm) *f*, riddle, enigma.
enivrer (ãnivre) *v.t*, (*lit., fig.*) to intoxicate.
enjambée (ãʒãbe) *f*, stride. **enjamber** (be) *v.t*, to stride (*or* step) over *or* across; straddle; (*bridge*) span.
enjeu (ãʒø) *m*, stake (*wager*).
enjoindre (ãʒwɛ̃dr) *v.t.ir*, to enjoin.
enjôler (ãʒole) *v.t*, to wheedle, get round.
enjoliver (ãʒɔlive) *v.t*, to embellish; set off. **enjoliveur** (vœr) *m*, (*Mot.*) hub cap.
enjoué, e (ãʒwe) *a*, playful. **enjouement** (ʒumã) *m*, playfulness.
enlacer (ãlase) *v.t*, to clasp, hug; entwine. **s'~**, to clasp, hug each other; intertwine.
enlaidir (ãlɛdir) *v.t*, to make ugly; disfigure.
enlèvement (ãlɛvmã) *m*, removal, taking away; abduction; (*Mil.*) capture. **enlever** (lve) *v.t*, to remove; take off (*garment*); take away. ~ *à qn*, to rob, deprive s.o of. abduct, kidnap. *se faire ~ par*, to elope with. win (*victory*); (*Mil.*) capture (*position*); (*Mus.*) play brilliantly.
enliser (s') (ãlize) *v.pr*, to sink [into the sand *or* mud]; (*fig.*) get bogged down (*dans*, in).
enneigé, e (ãneʒe) *a*, snow-covered; snowed up. **enneigement** (nɛʒmã) *m*, depth of snow.
ennemi, e (ɛnmi) *a*, enemy; hostile. ¶ *n*, enemy. ~ *de qch*, opposed to sth.
ennoblir (ãnɔblir) *v.t*, to ennoble, dignify.
ennui (ãnɥi) *m*, boredom; tedium; worry, trouble. *des ~s avec la voiture*, trouble with the car. **ennuyer** (nɥije) *v.t*, to bore; annoy; worry, bother; cause trouble to. **ennuyeux,**

euse† (jø, øz) *a,* boring; annoying, tiresome.
énoncé (enɔ̃se) *m,* statement; (*Sch.*) exposition (*subject*); (*Law*) wording. **énoncer** (se) *v.t,* to state, express.
enorgueillir (ɑ̃nɔrgœjir) *v.t,* to make proud. **s'~,** to pride oneself (*de,* on); boast.
énorme (enɔrm) *a,* enormous, huge, tremendous. **énormément** (memɑ̃) *ad,* enormously, **énormité** (mite) *f,* hugeness; enormity.
enquérir (s') (ɑ̃kerir) *v.pr.ir,* to inquire, ask. **enquête** (kɛt) *f,* inquiry, investigation; inquest. **enquêter** (te) *v.i,* to conduct an investigation (*sur,* into). **enquêteur, euse** (tœr, øz) *n,* [police] officer; pollster.
enquiquiner *P* (ɑ̃kikine) *v.t,* to annoy, bother.
enraciner (ɑ̃rasine) *v.t,* & **s'~,** to root.
enragé, e (ɑ̃raʒe) *a,* furious; rabid; mad keen (*de,* on). ¶ *n,* fanatic. **enrager** (ʒe) *v.i,* to fume. *faire ~,* to infuriate; tease.
enrayer (ɑ̃rɛje) *v.t,* to stop, check; jam (*gun*).
enrégimenter (ɑ̃reʒimɑ̃te) *v.t,* to enroll.
enregistrer (ɑ̃rəʒistre) *v.t,* (*gen.*) to register; record (*fact, Mus.*); tape[-record]; register, check in (*luggage*). **enregistrement** (trəmɑ̃) *m,* registration, check-in; (*Mus. &c*) recording.
enrhumer (ɑ̃ryme) *v.t,* to give a cold to. **s'~,** to catch [a] cold.
enrichir (ɑ̃riʃir) *v.t,* to enrich; make rich. **s'~,** to grow rich.
enrober (ɑ̃rɔbe) *v.t,* to coat (*de,* with).
enrôler (ɑ̃role) *v.t,* to enroll, enlist.
enrouer (ɑ̃rwe) *v.t,* to make hoarse *or* husky.
enrouler (ɑ̃rule) *v.t,* to wind; roll up; coil up.
ensabler (ɑ̃sable) *v.t,* to silt up; run aground (*boat*). **s'~,** to get stuck in the sand.
ensanglanter (ɑ̃sɑ̃glɑ̃te) *v.t,* to stain *or* cover *or* soak with blood.
enseigne (ɑ̃sɛɲ) *f,* shop sign; ensign (*flag*). *~ lumineuse,* neon sign. *à telle ~ que,* so much so that. ¶ *m,* (*Hist.*) ensign. (*Nav.*) *~ de vaisseau,* lieutenant.
enseignement (ɑ̃sɛɲmɑ̃) *m,* teaching; (*Adm.*) education. *être dans l'~,* to be a teacher. **enseigner** (ɲe) *v.t,* to teach (*qch à qn,* sth to s.o; *à qn à faire,* s.o [how] to do).
ensemble (ɑ̃sɑ̃bl) *ad,* together. *être bien, mal ~,* to be on good, bad terms. ¶ *m,* whole; unity; collection; group; (*Mus.*) ensemble. *dans l'~,* on the whole. *vue d'~,* general view.
ensemencer (ɑ̃smɑ̃se) *v.t,* to sow (*land*).
ensevelir (ɑ̃səvlir) *v.t,* to bury; shroud.
ensoleillé, e (ɑ̃sɔlɛje) *a,* sunny. **ensoleiller** (je) *v.t,* to bathe in sunshine; (*fig.*) brighten.
ensommeillé, e (ɑ̃sɔmɛje) *a,* sleepy, drowsy.
ensorceler (ɑ̃sɔrsəle) *v.t,* to bewitch.
ensuite (ɑ̃sɥit) *ad,* then, next; afterwards. **ensuivre (s')** (sɥivr) *v.pr.ir,* to follow, ensue.
entaille (ɑ̃taj) *f,* cut; notch; groove; gash. **entailler** (taje) *v.t,* to cut; notch; gash.
entame (ɑ̃tam) *f,* first slice. **entamer** (me) *v.t,* to cut [into], start on (*loaf &c*); start (*bottle, book, work*): weaken; damage.
entasser (ɑ̃tase) *v.t.* & **s'~,** to heap up, pile up; (*people*) cram into.
entendement (ɑ̃tɑ̃dmɑ̃) *m,* understanding. **entendre** (tɑ̃dr) *v.t,* to hear; listen to; understand; mean; intend. *j'entends être obéi,* I intend to be obeyed. *laisser ~ à qn,* to give s.o to understand. *j'en ai entendu parler,* I've heard about it. **s'~,** to agree; get on (*avec,* with). *s'~ à,* to be good at, know about. [*cela*] *s'entend,* naturally, of course. **entendu, e** (tɑ̃dy) *a,* agreed. *~!* right [you are]! *bien ~!* of course! **entente** (tɑ̃t) *f,* understanding; agreement; harmony. *à double ~,* with a double meaning.
entérite (ɑ̃terit) *f,* enteritis.
enterrement (ɑ̃tɛrmɑ̃) *m,* burial; funeral. **enterrer** (re) *v.t,* to bury; drop (*idea*).
en-tête (ɑ̃tɛt) *m,* heading. *papier à ~,* headed paper.
entêté, e (ɑ̃tete) *a,* obstinate. stubborn. **entêtement** (tmɑ̃) *m,* obstinacy. **entêter (s')** (te) *v.pr,* to persist (*dans,* in; *à faire,* in doing).
enthousiasme (ɑ̃tuzjasm) *m,* enthusiasm. **enthousiasmer** (me) *v.t,* to fill with enthusiasm. **s'~,** to be enthusiastic (*pour,* about). **enthousiaste** (ast) *a,* enthusiastic. ¶ *n,* enthusiast.
enticher (s') (ɑ̃tiʃe) *v.pr,* to become infatuated (*de,* with).
entier, ère (ɑ̃tje, ɛr) *a,* entire, whole; full; intact; complete. *tout ~,* completely, entirely. unbending (*pers.*). ¶ *m,* (*Math.*) whole. *en ~,* entirely; (*read*) right through. **~èrement** (tjɛrmɑ̃) *ad,* entirely, wholly, fully, completely.
entité (ɑ̃tite) *f,* entity.
entomologie (ɑ̃tɔmɔlɔʒi) *f,* entomology.
entonner (ɑ̃tɔne) *v.t,* to strike up (*tune*).
entonnoir (ɑ̃tɔnwar) *m,* funnel (*utensil*); shellhole; crater.
entorse (ɑ̃tɔrs) *f,* sprain. **entortiller** (tije) *v.t,* to twist, wind; wrap up; (*P*) get round (*s.o*).
entour (à l') (ɑ̃tur) *ad,* around. **entourage** (turaʒ) *m,* circle, set; entourage; surround. **entourer** (re) *v.t,* to surround (*de,* with). *~ qn de ses bras,* to put one's arms round s.o. (*fig.*) *~ qn,* to support, comfort s.o.
entracte (ɑ̃trakt) *m,* (*Theat.*) interval; (*fig.*) interlude.
entraide (ɑ̃trɛd) *f,* mutual help. **entraider (s')** (trɛde) *v.pr,* to help one another.
entrailles (ɑ̃traj) *f.pl,* (*liter.*) entrails; womb; (*fig.*) bowels (*earth*); heart.
entrain (ɑ̃trɛ̃) *m,* liveliness, spirit, go, gusto. **entraînant, e** (trɛnɑ̃, ɑ̃t) *a,* stirring, rousing. **entraînement** (nmɑ̃) *m,* (*Mach.*) driving; drive; (*Sport*) training. *manquer d'~,* to be out of training. **entraîner** (ne) *v.t,* to carry *or*

drag along; draw (*s.o*) away; (*Mach.*) drive; entail, involve. (*Sport*) ~ & **s'~**, to train (*à, pour*, for). **entraîneur** (nœr) *m*, trainer; coach.

entrave (ɑ̃trav) *f*, fetter, hobble (*horse*); obstacle, hindrance. (*fig.*) ~*s*, fetters, shackles. **entraver** (trave) *v.t*, to fetter (*animal*); hinder, hamper; hold up (*traffic*).

entre (ɑ̃tr) *pr*, between. ~ *deux âges*, middle-aged. ~ *parenthèses*, in brackets. among[st]. ~ *autres*, among others. *l'un d'~ nous*, one of us. ~ *nous*, between you & me; between ourselves. *tomber ~ les mains de*, to fall into the hands of (*enemy*).

entrebâillé, e (ɑ̃trəbaje) *a*, half-open, ajar.

entrechoquer (ɑ̃trəʃɔke) *v.t.* & **s'~**, to knock together; clash; (*glasses*) clink.

entrecôte (ɑ̃trəkot) *f*, rib steak.

entrecouper (ɑ̃trəkupe) *v.t*, to interrupt, intersperse (*de*, with). **s'~**, to intersect.

entrecroiser (s') (ɑ̃trəkrwaze) *v.pr*, to intersect; criss-cross.

entrée (ɑ̃tre) *f*, entry, entrance (*action*). (*Theat.*) ~ *en scène*, entrance. admission. '~ *interdite*', 'no admittance'. [entrance] ticket; way in, entrance, mouth (*cave*). ~ *des artistes*, stage door. start (*season*); (*Cook.*) entrée, first course. (*Tech.*) ~ *d'air*, air inlet. *avoir ses ~s auprès de qn*, to have easy access to s.o.

entrefaite (ɑ̃trəfɛt) *f*: *sur ces ~s*, in the midst of all this; at that moment.

entrefilet (ɑ̃trəfilɛ) *m*, [short] paragraph (*newspaper*).

entrelacer (ɑ̃trəlase) *v.t.* & **s'~**, to interlace, intertwine.

entremêler (ɑ̃trəmɛle) *v.t*, to intermingle; intersperse. **s'~**, to intermingle.

entremets (ɑ̃trəmɛ) *m*, sweet; dessert.

entremetteur, euse (ɑ̃trəmɛtœr, øz) *n*, go-between. **entremettre (s')** (tr) *v.pr.ir*, to intervene. **entremise** (miz) *f*, intervention; agency. *par l'~ de*, through.

entrepont (ɑ̃trəpɔ̃) *m*, (*Naut.*) steerage.

entreposer (ɑ̃trəpoze) *v.t*, to store, put into storage; warehouse, **entrepôt** (po) *m*, warehouse; bonded warehouse.

entreprenant, e (ɑ̃trəprənɑ̃, ɑ̃t) *a*, enterprising. **entreprendre** (prɑ̃dr) *v.t.ir*, to begin, embark on; tackle, buttonhole (*pers.*). ~ *de faire*, to undertake to do. **entrepreneur, euse** (prənœr, øz) *n*, contractor. ~ *de pompes funèbres*, undertaker. ~ *de transports*, haulage contractor. **entreprise** (priz) *f*, firm, concern; undertaking, venture.

entrer (ɑ̃tre) *v.i*, to enter; come in; go in. ~ *dans*, to enter, go into (*place*); enter into (*details*); join (*club, party, police*); (*Mot.*) run into (*tree*). *on lui est entré dedans*, s.o ran into him. ~ *dans les vues de qn*, to share s.o's views. (*Mil.*) ~ *en action*, to go into action. ~ *en fonction*, to take up one's duties. *laisser ~*, to let in. *faire ~*, to show in (*visitor*). ¶ *v.t*, to put into; bring in. ~ *en fraude*, to smuggle in.

entresol (ɑ̃trəsɔl) *m*, mezzanine.

entre-temps (ɑ̃trətɑ̃) *ad*, meanwhile.

entretenir (ɑ̃trətnir) *v.t.ir*, to maintain; keep in repair; keep up; support (*family*); speak to. **s'~**, to talk, converse (*de*, about); support o.s. **entretien** (tjɛ̃) *m*, maintenance; upkeep; support, keep; conversation; interview.

entretoise (ɑ̃trətwaz) *f*, brace, crosspiece.

entrevoir (ɑ̃trəvwar) *v.t.ir*, to catch a glimpse of; see indistinctly, make out; sense. **entrevue** (vy) *f*, interview; meeting.

entrouvrir (ɑ̃truvrir) *v.t.ir*, to half-open. **entrouvert, e** (vɛr, ɛrt) *a*, half-open, ajar.

énumérer (enymere) *v.t*, to enumerate.

envahir (ɑ̃vair) *v.t*, to invade, overrun; (*water*) flood; (*fig: terror*) take possession of. **envahissement** (ismɑ̃) *m*, invasion. **envahisseur** (sœr) *m*, invader.

envaser (s') (ɑ̃vaze) *v.pr*, to silt up; stick *or* sink in the mud.

enveloppe (ɑ̃vlɔp) *f*, envelope; wrapping (*parcel*); covering; casing; lagging; cover (*tyre*); (*fig.*) exterior. *mettre sous ~*, to put into an envelope. **envelopper** (vlɔpe) *v.t*, to wrap [up]; envelop, shroud, enfold; veil (*thoughts*). *enveloppé de mystère*, shrouded in mystery.

envenimer (ɑ̃vnime) *v.t*, to make septic (*wound*); poison, embitter (*relations*). **s'~**, to go septic; grow bitter, become soured.

envergure (ɑ̃vɛrgyr) *f*, wingspan (*bird, plane*); scale; scope; calibre (*pers.*); range (*mind*). *de grande ~*, large-scale.

envers[1] (ɑ̃vɛr) *pr*, to, towards (*pers.*). *cruel ~ qn*, cruel to s.o. ~ *& contre tous*, despite all opposition.

envers[2] (ɑ̃vɛr) *m*, wrong side, back, reverse. *à l'~*, inside out; back to front; upside down; topsy-turvy.

envi (a' l') (ɑ̃vi), (*liter.*) in emulation, vying.

envie (ɑ̃vi) *f*, desire, longing (*de qch*, for sth; *de faire*, to do). *avoir ~ de*, to want. *je meurs d'~ de voir*, I'm dying to see. envy; birthmark; hangnail. **envier** (vje) *v.t*, to envy, be envious of. **envieux, euse** (vjø, øz) *a*, envious.

environ (ɑ̃virɔ̃) *ad*, about, roughly. **~s**, *m.pl*, surroundings. *aux ~s de*, in the vicinity of (*town*); about, in the region of (*figure*). **~nement** (rɔnmɑ̃) *m*, environment. **~ner** (ne) *v.t*, to surround.

envisager (ɑ̃vizaʒe) *v.t*, to envisage, contemplate (*de faire*, doing).

envoi (ɑ̃vwa) *m*, sending; dispatch; remittance; parcel, package. ~ *contre remboursement*, cash on delivery.

envol (ɑ̃vɔl) *m*, taking flight (*bird*); takeoff (*plane*); (*fig.*) flight. *prendre son ~*, (*bird*) to

take flight. **envoler (s')** (le) *v.pr,* to fly away; (*plane*) take off; (*hat*) blow off; (*fig.*) vanish.
envoûter (ɑ̃vute) *v.t,* to bewitch.
envoyé, e (ɑ̃vwaje) *n,* envoy; messenger. ~ *spécial,* special correspondent. **envoyer** (je) *v.t,* to send; s. off, dispatch; send in, s. out; throw (*stone, punch*); blow (*kiss*). ~ *chercher,* to send for. ~ *promener qn P,* to send s.o packing. **envoyeur, euse** (jœr, øz) *n,* sender.
épagneul, e (epaɲœl) *n,* spaniel.
épais, se (epɛ, ɛs) *a,* thick; thickset (*pers.*); dense (*smoke*); deep (*snow*); dull-witted, dense, thick *P.* ~ *de 2 cm,* 2 cm thick. **épaisseur** (pɛsœr) *f,* thickness; depth; dullness. **épaissir** (sir) *v.t,* to thicken. ¶ *v.i, &* **s'~**, to thicken; get stout.
épanchement (epɑ̃ʃmɑ̃) *m,* effusion (*blood*); outpouring (*feelings*). ~ *de synovie,* water on the knee. **épancher** (ʃe) *v.t,* to pour out. **s'~**, to pour out one's heart.
épanouir (s') (epanwir) *v.pr.* (*flower*) to open out, bloom; (*face*) light up; (*pers.*) blossom.
épargne (eparɲ) *f,* saving, economy; savings. **épargner** (ɲe) *v.t,* to save [up], economize; stint. ~ *qch à qn,* to spare s.o sth.
éparpiller (eparpije) *v.t,* to scatter; fritter away. **épars, e** (par, ars) *a,* scattered.
épatant, e (epatɑ̃, ɑ̃t) *a,* splendid, great *P.* **épaté, e** (epate) *a,* flat (*nose*). **épater** (te) *v.t,* to amaze, stagger; impress; shock.
épaule (epol) *f,* shoulder. **épauler** (le) *v.t,* to back up (*pers.*); bring (*rifle*) to the shoulder. **épaulette** (lɛt) *f,* epaulette; shoulder strap.
épave (epav) *f,* (*lit., fig.*) wreck; piece of wreckage; flotsam [& jetsam].
épée (epe) *f,* sword.
épeler (eple) *v.t,* to spell; spell out.
éperdu†, e (epɛrdy) *a,* distraught, frantic, overwhelmed (*de,* with); passionate (*love*).
éperon (eprɔ̃) *m,* (*gen.*) spur. **~ner** (prɔne) *v.t,* to spur (*horse*); (*fig.*) spur on; (*Naut.*) ram.
épervier (epɛrvje) *m,* sparrow hawk; (*Fish.*) cast net.
éphémère (efemɛr) *a,* ephemeral, fleeting, short-lived. ¶ *m,* mayfly. **éphéméride** (merid) *f,* block calendar.
épi (epi) *m,* ear (*grain*); cob (*corn*); spike (*flower*); tuft (*hair*).
épice (epis) *f,* spice. **épicé, e** (se) *a,* spicy. **épicer** (se) *v.t,* to spice. **épicerie** (sri) *f,* grocer's shop; grocery trade; groceries. **épicier, ère** (sje, ɛr) *n,* grocer.
épicurien, ne (epikyrjɛ̃, ɛn) *a. & n,* epicurean.
épidémie (epidemi) *f,* epidemic. **épidémique** (mik) *a,* epidemic; (*fig.*) contagious.
épiderme (epidɛrm) *m,* epidermis. *avoir l'~ sensible,* to be touchy.
épier (epje) *v.t,* to spy on (*pers.*); watch closely; watch for; listen for.
épigramme (epigram) *f,* epigram.
épigraphe (epigraf) *f,* epigraph.
épilepsie (epilɛpsi) *f,* epilepsy. **épileptique** (tik) *a. & n,* epileptic.
épiler (epile) *v.t,* to remove hairs from; pluck (*eyebrows*).
épilogue (epilɔg) *m,* epilogue; conclusion.
épinard (epinar) *m,* ~[*s*], spinach.
épine (epin) *f,* thorn [bush]; thorn; (*Zool.*) spine, prickle, quill. ~ *dorsale,* backbone. ~ *blanche,* hawthorn. ~ *noire,* blackthorn. **épineux, euse** (nø, øz) *a,* thorny, prickly; (*fig.*) thorny, tricky (*problem*). **épine-vinette** (vinɛt) *f,* (*Bot.*) berberis.
épingle (epɛ̃gl) *f,* pin. [*virage en*] ~ *à cheveux,* hairpin [bend]. ~ *à linge,* clothes peg. ~ *de sûreté,* ~ *de nourrice,* safety pin. *tirer son ~ du jeu,* to get out of a tight spot. **épingler** (pɛ̃gle) *v.t,* to pin.
Épiphanie (epifani) *f,* Epiphany.
épique (epik) *a,* epic.
épiscopal, e (episkɔpal) *a,* episcopal. **épiscopat** (pa) *m,* bishopric; episcopacy.
épisode (epizɔd) *m,* episode. **épisodique** (zɔdik) *a,* occasional; secondary.
épisser (epise) *v.t,* to splice (*rope*).
épistolaire (epistɔlɛr) *a,* epistolary. **épistolier, ère** (lje, ɛr) *n,* letter writer (*pers.*).
épitaphe (epitaf) *f,* epitaph.
épithète (epitɛt) *f,* epithet.
épitomé (epitɔme) *m,* epitome.
épître (epitr) *f,* epistle; letter.
éploré, e (eplɔre) *a,* tearful, in tears.
éplucher (eplyʃe) *v.t,* (*Cook.*) to peel, clean, prepare; (*fig.*) sift (*text*). **épluchures** (ʃyr) *f.pl,* peelings.
épointer (epwɛ̃te) *v.t,* to break the point of; blunt (*needle, pencil*).
éponge (epɔ̃ʒ) *f,* sponge. ~ *métallique,* scourer. *passons l'~!* let's forget about it! **éponger** (pɔ̃ʒe) *v.t,* to sponge; mop up.
épopée (epɔpe) *f,* (*lit., fig.*) epic.
époque (epɔk) *f,* time; (*Hist.*) age, era, period. *à l'~,* at the time.
époumoner (s') (epumɔne) *v.pr,* to make o.s hoarse.
épouse (epuz) *f,* wife, spouse. **épouser** (puze) *v.t,* to marry; take up, espouse (*cause*). ~ [*la forme de*], to fit, take the shape of.
épousseter (epuste) *v.t,* to dust.
époustoufler *P* (epustufle) *v.t,* to flabbergast, stagger.
épouvantable† (epuvɑ̃tabl) *a,* frightful, appalling. **épouvantail** (taj) *m,* scarecrow; bugbear. **épouvante** (vɑ̃t) *f,* terror. *film d'~,* horror film. **épouvanter** (vɑ̃te) *v.t,* to terrify, horrify; appal.
époux (epu) *m,* husband, spouse. *les ~,* husband & wife, [married] couple.
éprendre (s') (eprɑ̃dr) *v.pr.ir, s'~ de,* to fall in

love with.

épreuve (eprœv) *f,* test, trial; ordeal; (*Sch.*) test; (*Typ.*) proof; (*Phot.*) print; (*Sport*) event. ~ *de sélection,* ~ *éliminatoire,* [eliminating] heat. *mettre à l'*~, to put to the test. *à l'*~ *de,* proof against. *à l'*~ *du feu,* fire-proof. *à toute* ~, equal to anything. **éprouver** (pruve) *v.t,* to feel (*pain, joy*); experience, meet with (*difficulties*); test; distress, afflict. **éprouvette** (vɛt) *f,* test-tube.

épuisé, e (epɥize) *a,* exhausted; out of print; (*Com.*) sold out. **épuiser** (ze) *v.t,* (*gen.*) to exhaust; tire out (*pers.*). **s'** ~, to exhaust o.s (*à faire,* doing); (*stocks*) run out; (*strength*) fail. **épuisette** (zɛt) *f,* (*Fish.*) landing net.

épuration (epyrasjɔ̃) *f,* purification; refining; (*Pol.*) purge. **épurer** (pyre) *v.t,* to purify; refine; purge.

équarrir (ekarir) *v.t,* to square off (*stone &c*); quarter, cut up (*carcass*).

équateur (ekwatœr) *m,* equator. *l'É*~, Ecuador.

équation (ekwasjɔ̃) *f,* equation.

équatorial, e (ekwatɔrjal) *a,* equatorial.

équerre (ekɛr) *f,* set square. *d'*~, *en* ~, at right angles.

équestre (ekɛstr) *a,* equestrian.

équilibre (ekilibr) *m,* equilibrium; [mental] stability. *perdre l'*~, to lose one's balance. *en* ~, balanced. **équilibré, e** (bre) *a,* well-balanced, stable (*pers.*). *mal* ~, unbalanced. **équilibrer** (bre) *v.t,* to balance; counterbalance.

équinoxe (ekinɔks) *m,* equinox.

équipage (ekipaʒ) *m,* crew (*ship, plane*); *O* (*royal &c*) train, equipage.

équipe (ekip) *f,* (*gen., Sport*) team; (*Ind.*) shift, gang; crew (*rowing*). *faire* ~ *avec,* to team up with. **équipée** (pe) *f,* escapade; jaunt. **équipier, ère** (pje, ɛr) *n,* team member. **équipement** (pmɑ̃) *m,* equipment, kit; fitting out. **équiper** (pe) *v.t,* to equip, fit out, rig [out] (*de,* with).

équitable† (ekitabl) *a,* equitable, fair.

équitation (ekitasjɔ̃) *f,* riding.

équité (ekite) *f,* equity, fairness.

équivalent, e (ekivalɑ̃, ɑ̃t) *a.* & *m,* equivalent. **équivaloir** (lwar) *v.i.ir,* to be equivalent; be tantamount (*à,* to).

équivoque (ekivɔk) *a,* equivocal, ambiguous; dubious, questionable. ¶ *f,* ambiguity, uncertainty.

érable (erabl) *m,* maple.

érafler (erɑfle) *v.t,* to scratch, graze. **éraflure** (flyr) *f,* scratch, graze.

éraillé, e (erɑje) *a,* hoarse, husky (*voice*).

ère (ɛr) *f,* era, epoch.

érection (erɛksjɔ̃) *f,* erection; setting up.

éreinter (erɛ̃te) *v.t,* to exhaust, wear out; (*fig.*) slate, pull to pieces.

ergot (ɛrgo) *m,* spur (*bird*); (*Tech.*) lug. *monter sur ses* ~*s,* to get one's hackles up. **ergoter** (te) *v.i,* to quibble.

ériger (eriʒe) *v.t,* to erect; (*fig.*) set up. *s'*~ *en juge,* to set o.s up as a judge.

ermitage (ɛrmitaʒ) *m,* hermitage; [country] retreat. **ermite** (mit) *m,* hermit.

éroder (erɔde) *v.t,* to erode. **érosion** (zjɔ̃) *f,* erosion.

érotique (erɔtik) *a,* erotic. **érotisme** (ism) *m,* eroticism.

errant, e (ɛrɑ̃, ɑ̃t) *a,* wandering; roving; stray (*dog*). **erratique** (ratik) *a,* (*Geol., Med.*) erratic.

errements (ɛrmɑ̃) *m.pl,* [erring] ways.

errer (ɛre) *v.t,* to wander, roam; err.

erreur (ɛrœr) *f,* error, mistake; fallacy. ~ *de calcul,* miscalculation. ~ *typographique,* misprint. *par* ~, by mistake. *sauf* ~, if I'm not mistaken. *faire* ~, to be wrong. **erroné, e** (rɔne) *a,* erroneous, wrong, mistaken.

ersatz (ɛrzats) *m,* ersatz; imitation.

éructer (erykte) *v.t,* (*Med.*) to eructate; belch.

érudit, e (erydi, it) *a,* erudite, scholarly. ¶ *n,* scholar. **érudition** (disjɔ̃) *f,* erudition, scholarship.

éruption (erypsjɔ̃) *f,* eruption; rash. *entrer en* ~, to erupt.

ès (ɛs) *pr,* (= *en les*) *licencié* ~ *lettres, sciences* Bachelor of Arts, Science.

escabeau (ɛskabo) *m,* stool; stepladder.

escadre (ɛskadr) *f,* (*Nav.*) squadron; (*Air*) wing. **escadrille** (kadrij) *f,* (*Air*) flight. **escadron** (drɔ̃) *m,* (*Mil.*) squadron.

escalade (ɛskalad) *f,* climbing, scaling. *l'*~, rock climbing; (*Pol.*) escalation. *faire l'*~ *de,* to climb. **escalader** (de) *v.t,* to climb, scale.

escale (ɛskal) *f,* (*Naut.*) port of call; call; (*Aero.*) stop. *faire* ~ *à,* (*ship*) to call at; (*plane*) stop at.

escalier (ɛskalje) *m,* stairs; staircase. *dans l'*~, on the stairs. ~ *d'honneur,* ~ *en colimaçon,* main, spiral staircase. ~ *roulant,* escalator.

escamotable (ɛskamɔtabl) *a,* (*Aero.*) retractable; collapsible (*bed*). **escamoter** (te) *v.t,* to conjure away; filch, pinch *P;* evade, dodge; (*Aero.*) retract (*undercarriage*). **escamoteur, euse** (tœr, øz) *n,* conjurer.

escampette (ɛskɑ̃pɛt) *f: prendre la poudre d'*~, to bolt, skedaddle. **escapade** (kapad) *f, faire une* ~, to skip off, do a bunk *P.*

escargot (ɛskargo) *m,* snail.

escarmouche (ɛskarmuʃ) *f,* (*lit., fig.*) skirmish.

escarpé, e (ɛskarpe) *a,* steep. **escarpement** (pəmɑ̃) *m,* escarpment; steep slope.

escarpin (ɛskarpɛ̃) *m,* flat shoe; pump.

escarpolette *O* (ɛskarpɔlɛt) *f,* swing.

Escaut (l') (ɛsko) *m,* the [river] Scheldt.

escient (ɛsjɑ̃) *m, à bon* ~, advisedly.

esclaffer (s') (ɛsklafe) *v.pr,* to burst out laughing.

esclandre (ɛsklɑ̃dr) *m,* scene; scandal.

esclavage (ɛsklavaʒ) *m,* slavery. **esclave** (klav) *n,* slave.
escompte (ɛskɔ̃t) *m,* discount. **escompter** (kɔ̃te) *v.t,* to discount; count on, bank on.
escorte (ɛskɔrt) *f,* escort. **escorter** (te) *v.t,* to escort.
escouade (ɛskwad) *f,* squad, gang.
escrime (ɛskrim) *f,* fencing. **s'escrimer** (me) *v.pr,* to struggle (*sur,* over; *à faire,* to do).
escroc (ɛskro) *m,* swindler. **escroquer** (krɔke) *v.t,* to swindle (*qch à qn,* s.o out of sth).
espace (ɛspɑs) *m,* space; room. ~ *de temps,* space of time. ~ *parcouru,* distance covered. **espacer** (se) *v.t,* to space [out].
espadon (ɛspadɔ̃) *m,* swordfish.
espadrille (ɛspadrij) *f,* rope-soled canvas shoe.
Espagne (l') (ɛspaɲ) *f,* Spain. **espagnol, e** (ɲɔl) *a.* & (*language*) *m,* Spanish. **E~,** *n,* Spaniard. **espagnolette** (lɛt) *f,* espagnolette (*continental window catch*).
espalier (ɛspalje) *m,* espalier.
espèce (ɛspɛs) *f,* kind, sort; species. ~ *humaine,* human race. *de la plus belle* ~, (*liar*) of the worst sort. ~ *d'idiot!* you idiot! (*Fin.*) [*en*] ~*s,* [in] cash.
espérance (ɛsperɑ̃s) *f,* hope, expectation. ~*s,* promise, prospects. ~ *de vie,* expectation of life. **espérer** (re) *v.t,* to hope for. ~ *faire,* to hope to do. *je l'espère* [*bien*], I hope so. ¶ *v.i,* to have faith, trust (*en,* in).
espiègle (ɛspjɛgl) *a,* mischievous, roguish. ¶ *n,* imp. **espièglerie** (glɔri) *f,* mischievousness, roguishness; prank.
espion, ne (ɛspjɔ̃, ɔn) *n,* spy. **espionnage** (ɔnaʒ) *m,* espionage, spying. **espionner** (ne) *v.t,* to spy on.
esplanade (ɛsplanad) *f,* esplanade.
espoir (ɛspwar) *m,* (*gen.*) hope. *avoir bon* ~ *de faire,* to be confident of doing.
esprit (ɛspri) *m,* mind. *état d'*~, state *or* frame of mind. *avoir l'*~ *large, étroit,* to be broad-, narrow-minded. spirit (*of law, age, group*); spirit (*dead*); wit. *plein d'*~, witty. *mot d'*~, witty remark. ~ *de caste,* class consciousness. ~ *de contradiction,* argumentativeness. ~ *d'équipe, de compétition,* team, competitive spirit. ~ *d'escalier,* slowness in repartee. ~ *fort,* freethinker. *l'E*~ *Saint, le Saint-E*~, the Holy Spirit, the Holy Ghost.
esquimau, aude (ɛskimo, od) *a.* & **E~,** *n,* Eskimo. ¶ *m,* husky (*dog*); choc-ice.
esquinter *P* (ɛskɛ̃te) *v.t,* to spoil, damage; smash up (*car*); (*critic*) tear to shreds; tire (*s.o*) out.
esquisse (ɛskis) *f,* sketch; outline (*plan*); suggestion (*smile*). **esquisser** (se) *v.t,* to sketch; outline; start to make (*gesture*).
esquive (ɛskiv) *f,* dodge; evasion. **esquiver** (kive) *v.t,* to dodge; shirk, evade. **s'~,** to slip *or* sneak away.
essai (esɛ) *m,* testing; test, trial; try, attempt; (*Rugby*) try; essay.
essaim (ɛsɛ̃) *m,* swarm (*bees, &c*). **essaimer** (esɛme) *v.i,* to swarm; (*fig.*) branch out.
essayage (esɛjaʒ) *m,* (*Dress*) fitting. **essayer** (eseje) *v.t,* to test, try out; try on (*clothes*). ~ *de faire,* to try to do. **s'~ à,** to try one's hand at. **essayeur, euse** (jœr, øz) *n,* fitter (*clothes*). **essayiste** (jist) *n,* essayist.
essence (ɛsɑ̃s) *f,* petrol, *Am* gas[oline]; essence, oil (*plants*); species (*trees*); (*Philos.*) essence; gist, essence (*theory*). **essentiel, le**† (sɑ̃sjɛl) *a,* essential (*à, pour,* for). ¶ *m,* essential *or* main thing; essentials. *l'*~ *de,* the main part of. *l'*~ *est de*.. the important thing is to..
essieu (ɛsjø) *m,* axle, axletree.
essor (ɛsɔr) *m,* flight (*bird, imagination*); (*Com.*) expansion, boom. *prendre son* ~, (*bird*) to fly off; (*enterprise*) take off, expand.
essorer (esɔre) *v.t,* to wring out; spin-dry. **essoreuse** (røz) *f,* wringer; spin-drier.
essouffler (esufle) *v.t,* to make breathless. **s'~,** to get out of breath, get puffed *P.*
essuie-glace (esɥi) *m,* windscreen wiper. **essuie-mains,** *m,* [hand] towel. **essuie-verres,** *m,* glass cloth. **essuyer** (sɥije) *v.t,* to wipe [up], dry; mop up; dust; endure, suffer, meet with (*blows, insults*).
est (ɛst) *m,* east. *à l'*~ *de,* e. of. *vent d'*~, e. wind. ¶ *a. inv,* east[ern]; eastward, easterly (*direction*).
estafette (ɛstafɛt) *f,* courier; dispatch rider.
estafilade (ɛstafilad) *f,* gash, slash.
estaminet *O* (ɛstaminɛ) *m,* small café & public house.
estampe (ɛstɑ̃p) *f,* print, engraving; stamp (*metal*). **estamper** (pe) *v.t,* (*Tech.*) to stamp; (*P*) swindle.
estampille (ɛstɑ̃pij) *f,* stamp (*mark*).
esthéticien, ne (ɛstetisjɛ̃, ɛn) *n,* beautician. **esthétique**† (tik) *a,* aesthetic; attractive. ¶ *f,* aesthetics.
estimation (ɛstimasjɔ̃) *f,* valuation; estimate; estimation. **estime** (tim) *f,* esteem, respect; (*Naut.*) dead reckoning. **estimer** (me) *v.t,* to estimate; value (*object*); esteem, respect; consider, reckon, believe.
estival, e (ɛstival) *a,* summer. **estivant, e** (vɑ̃, ɑ̃t) *n,* summer visitor, holiday-maker.
estomac (ɛstɔma) *m,* stomach. (*P*) *avoir de l'*~, to have a nerve; have guts *P.* **estomaquer** *P* (make) *v.t,* to flabbergast.
estomper (ɛstɔ̃pe) *v.t,* (*Art*) to stump, shade off; blur, soften (*outline, memory*). **s'~,** to become blurred.
estourbir *P* (ɛsturbir) *v.t,* to kill, do in *P.*
estrade (ɛstrad) *f,* platform, rostrum, dais.
estragon (ɛstragɔ̃) *m,* tarragon.
estropié, e (ɛstrɔpje) *n,* cripple. **estropier** (pje) *v.t,* to cripple, maim; distort (*words*); murder (*language, music*).

estuaire (ɛstɥɛr) *m*, estuary.
estudiantin, e (ɛstydjɑ̃tɛ̃, in) *a*, student.
et (e) *c*, and. ~ ... ~ .., both ...and .... ~ *ainsi de suite*, and so on. *j'adore cette chanson, ~ toi?* I adore this song, don't you? ~ *alors?* so what? ~ *voilà!* there you are!
étable (etabl) *f*, cowshed.
établi (etabli) *m*, workbench. **établir** (blir) *v.t*, (*gen.*) to establish; set up; lay down (*rules*); draw up (*list, plans*); make out (*cheque*); fix (*price*). **s'~**, to settle; set up (*in trade*); (*custom*) become established; (*friendship*) develop. **établissement** (blismɑ̃) *m*, establishing &c; establishment; institution; settlement (*colony*).
étage (etaʒ) *m*, floor, storey; stage (*rocket*); level; tier; rank. *au premier ~*, on the first floor. **étager** (taʒe) *v.t*, to arrange in tiers. **étagère** (ʒɛr) *f*, shelf; [set of] shelves.
étai (etɛ) *m*, (*gen., Naut.*) stay; prop.
étain (etɛ̃) *m*, tin; pewter.
étalage (etalaʒ) *m*, displaying; display; shop window; show, ostentation. *faire ~ de*, to show off. **étalagiste** (laʒist) *n*, window dresser.
étale (etal) *a.inv*, (*Naut.*) slack (*water*).
étaler (etale) *v.t*, to spread (*butter, payments*); spread out; display (*goods*); flaunt. **s'~**, to spread out; sprawl; flaunt o.s.
étalon (etalɔ̃) *m*, stallion; standard (*measure*). *~-or* gold standard. **~ner** (lɔne) *v.t*, to calibrate; standardize.
étamine (etamin) *f*, muslin; (*Bot.*) stamen.
étanche (etɑ̃ʃ) *a*, (*lit., fig.*) watertight; waterproof. ~ *à l'air*, airtight. **étancher** (tɑ̃ʃe) *v.t*, to staunch, stem (*flow*); quench, slake (*thirst*).
étang (etɑ̃) *m*, pond.
étape (etap) *f*, stage, stopping place. *faire ~ à*, to stop off at. *par petites ~s*, by easy stages.
état (eta) *m*, state; condition. *en bon, mauvais ~*, in good, bad condition. *en ~ de marche*, in working order. *remettre en ~*, to repair. *il n'est pas en ~ de venir*, he's in no state to come. *en ~ de naviguer*, seaworthy. *~ de choses*, situation. *~ d'âme*, mood. *~ d'esprit*, frame of mind. *être dans tous ses ~s*, to be all worked up. *en tout ~ de cause*, in any case. profession; station; (*civil*) status; statement, account; list, inventory. **E~**, *m*, state (*nation, government*). *chef d'E~*, head of state. *homme d'E~*, statesman. *secret d'E~*, state secret. **les E~s-Unis [d'Amérique]**, the United States [of America]. **~iser** (tize) *v.t*, to put under state control. **~isme** (tism) *m*, state control, state socialism. **~-major** (maʒɔr) *m*, (*Mil.*) staff; (*Mil., gen.*) headquarters; headquarters staff.
étau (eto) *m*, (*Tech.*) vice.
étayer (etɛje) *v.t*, to prop up; support.
et cætera (ɛtsetera) *phrase* (*abb.* etc.), et cetera, etc., &c
été (ete) *m*, summer. *en ~*, in summer.
éteignoir (etɛɲwar) *m*, [candle] snuffer; (*fig: pers.*) wet blanket. **éteindre** (tɛ̃dr) *v.t.ir*, to extinguish, put out; turn off, switch off (*gas, light, TV*); switch off the lights in (*room*); calm (*anger*); quench (*thirst*). **s'~**, (*light*) to go out; (*pers.*) die, pass away; die down; die out. **éteint, e** (tɛ̃, ɛ̃t) *a*, extinct; dull, lacklustre (*look*); faded; faint (*voice*).
étendard (etɑ̃dar) *m*, standard, flag.
étendre (etɑ̃dr) *v.t*, to spread [out]; stretch [out]; lay out (*body*); hang out (*washing*); extend, increase; dilute; thin (*sauce*). **s'~**, to extend, stretch; (*pers.*) stretch out, lie down; expatiate, enlarge (*sur*, on); expand, increase; (*disease*) spread. **étendu, e**[1] (dy) *a*, extensive, wide (*view, powers*); stretched out, lying (*pers.*). **étendue**[2], *f*, area, expanse; length, duration (*time*); extent; scope, range; (*Mus.*) compass, range.
éternel, le† (etɛrnɛl) *a*, eternal, everlasting; never-ending. **éterniser** (nize) *v.t*, to draw out, drag out. **s'~**, to drag on; (*pers.*) stay for ever. **éternité** (te) *f*, eternity. *il y a une ~ que* .. [*ne*], it's ages since ...
éternuement (etɛrnymɑ̃) *m*, sneezing; sneeze. **éternuer** (nɥe) *v.i*, to sneeze.
étêter (etɛte) *v.t*, to pollard (*tree*).
éther (etɛr) *m*, ether. **éthéré, e** (tere) *a*, ethereal.
Éthiopie (l') (etjɔpi) *f*, Ethiopia. **éthiopien, ne** (pjɛ̃, ɛn) *a.* & **É~**, *n*, Ethiopian.
éthique (etik) *a*, ethical. ¶ *f*, ethics.
ethnie (ɛtni) *f*, ethnic group. **ethnique** (nik) *a*, ethnic. **ethnologie** (nɔlɔʒi) *f*, ethnology. **ethnologique** (ʒik) *a*, ethnologic(al). **ethnologue** (lɔg) *m*, ethnologist.
étiage (etjaʒ) *m*, low water [mark] (*river*).
étinceler (etɛ̃sle) *v.i*, to sparkle, glitter; (*star*) twinkle. **étincelle** (sɛl) *f*, spark. **étincellement** (mɑ̃) *m*, sparkle, glitter &c; flash.
étioler (s') (etjɔle) *v.pr*, (*plant*) to wilt; (*pers.*) decline.
étique (etik) *a*, emaciated, skinny.
étiqueter (etikte) *v.t*, to label. **étiquette** (kɛt) *f*, label. *l'~*, etiquette.
étirer (etire) *v.t*, to stretch, draw out. *~ ses membres* & **s'~**, (*pers.*) to stretch.
étoffe (etɔf) *f*, stuff, fabric, material. (*fig.*) *il a de l'~*, he is a strong character. *avoir l'~ de*, to have the makings of. **étoffé, e** (fe) *a*, rich, firm (*voice*); meaty (*book*). **étoffer** (fe) *v.t*, to enrich, fill out (*speech*). **s'~**, (*pers.*) to fill out.
étoile (etwal) *f*, star; star (*Cine., ballet*); lucky star. *~ du berger*, evening star. *~ filante*, shooting s. *~ de mer*, starfish. *coucher à la belle ~*, to sleep in the open. *danseuse ~*, prima ballerina. **étoilé, e** (le) *a*, starry, starlit; starred, studded.

étole (etɔl) *f,* stole.
étonnant, e (etɔnɑ̃, ɑ̃t) *a,* astonishing, amazing, surprising. **étonnamment** (namɑ̃) *ad,* astonishingly, &c. **étonnement** (nmɑ̃) *m,* astonishment, &c. **étonner** (ne) *v.t,* to astonish, amaze, surprise. **s'** ~ , to be astonished, wonder, marvel (*de,* at).
étouffant, e (etufɑ̃, ɑ̃t) *a,* stifling. **étouffée** (fe) *f,* (*Cook.*) *cuire à l'* ~, to steam; braise. **étouffer** (fe) *v.t,* to smother, suffocate, choke; muffle, stifle (*cry*); hush up; quell (*revolt*). ¶ *v.i,* to suffocate. **étouffoir** (fwar) *m,* damper (*piano*).
étoupe (etup) *f,* tow; oakum.
étourderie (eturdəri) *f,* thoughtlessness. **étourdi†, e** (di) *a,* thoughtless, heedless. ¶ *n,* scatterbrain. **étourdir** (dir) *v.t,* to stun, daze; deafen; (*wine*) make dizzy. **s'** ~, to drown one's sorrows. **étourdissement** (dismɑ̃) *m,* dizziness; dizzy spell; (*liter.*) intoxication.
étourneau (eturno) *m,* starling (*bird*); young scatterbrain.
étrange† (etrɑ̃ʒ) *a,* strange; odd, queer. **étranger, ère** (trɑ̃ʒe, ɛr) *a,* foreign; strange; unfamiliar; extraneous; irrelevant (*à,* to). ¶ *n,* foreigner, alien; stranger. ¶ *m,* foreign parts. **à l'** ~, *ad,* abroad. *de l'* ~, from abroad. **étrangeté** (ʒte) *f,* strangeness, oddness, queerness.
étranglement (etrɑ̃gləmɑ̃) *m,* strangulation; bottleneck, constriction. **étrangler** (gle) *v.t,* to strangle, throttle, choke; squeeze, constrict; muzzle (*Press*). **s'** ~, to choke.
étrave (etrav) *f,* stem (*ship*).
être (ɛtr) *m,* being. ~ *humain,* human being. heart, soul, being. *de tout son* ~ , with all his heart. ¶ *v.i.ir,* to be. ~ *à,* to belong to. *cette clef est à Jean,* this key is John's. *je n'ai jamais été à Rome,* I have never been to Rome. *en* ~ *: où en est-il dans ..?* how far has he got with ..? *en* ~ *à la page 8,* to have reached page 8. ¶ *v.imp, il est deux heures,* it is 2 o'clock. *il est inutile de crier,* it is useless to shout. *il était une fois,* once [upon a time] there was. *il n'en est rien,* it's nothing of the sort. ¶ *v.aux,* (*compound tenses of aller, venir &c and pr. verbs*) *il est venu,* he came, has come; *elle s'était assise,* she had sat down; (*passive*) *il fut tué,* he was killed.
étreindre (etrɛ̃dr) *v.t.ir,* to embrace, clasp, hug; clutch, grasp; (*emotion*) grip. **étreinte** (trɛ̃t) *f,* grip, grasp; hug, embrace.
étrenner (etrɛne) *v.t,* to use (*or* wear) for the first time, christen. **étrennes** (ɛn) *f.pl,* New Year's gift; ≃ Christmas box (*to postman &c*).
étrier (etrie) *m,* stirrup.
étrille (etrij) *f,* currycomb. **étriller** (trije) *v.t,* to curry; *P* thrash.
étriper (etripe) *v.t,* to gut; draw (*fowl*).
étriqué, e (etrike) *a,* tight, skimpy (*garment*); narrow (*mind*).
étroit, e† (etrwa, at) *a,* narrow; limited, narrow (*pers., mind*); cramped; tight (*garment*); close (*links*); strict (*submission*). *à l'* ~ , in cramped conditions. **étroitesse** (tɛs) *f,* narrowness, &c.
étude (etyd) *f,* (*gen.*) study. *être à l'* ~, to be under consideration. (*Sch., Univ.*) ~*s,* studies. *faire ses* ~*s,* to study. (*Sch.*) preparation; prep room; (*lawyer's*) office, practice. ~*s du marché,* market research. **étudiant, e** (djɑ̃, ɑ̃t) *n,* student. **étudier** (dje) *v.t,* to study; learn (*lesson*); observe closely; (*Mach.*) design.
étui (etɥi) *m,* case. ~ [*de revolver*], holster.
étuve (etyv) *f,* steamroom (*bath*); drying stove, sterilizer; (*fig.*) oven.
étymologie (etimɔlɔʒi) *f,* etymology. **étymologique†** (ʒik) *a,* etymological.
eucalyptus (økaliptys) *m,* eucalyptus.
Eucharistie (l') (økaristi) *f,* the Eucharist.
eugénisme (øʒenism) *m,* eugenics.
euh (ø) *i,* h'm! er!
eunuque (ønyk) *m,* eunuch.
euphémique (øfemik) *a,* euphemistic. **euphémisme** (mism) *m,* euphemism.
euphonie (øfɔni) *f,* euphony.
euphorie (øfɔri) *f,* euphoria. **euphorique** (rik) *a,* euphoric.
Euphrate (l') (øfrat) *m,* the Euphrates.
Europe (l') (ørɔp) *f,* Europe. **européen, ne** (peɛ̃, ɛn) *a.* & **E**~, *n,* European.
euthanasie (øtanazi) *f,* euthanasia.
eux (ø) *pn. m. pl.* See *lui.*
évacué, e (evakɥe) *n,* evacuee. **évacuer** (kɥe) *v.t,* (*gen.*) to evacuate.
évader (s') (evade) *v.pr,* to escape.
évaluation (evalɥasjɔ̃) *f,* valuation; assessment; estimation. **évaluer** (lɥe) *v.t,* to value; assess; estimate.
évanescent, e (evanɛsɑ̃, ɑ̃t) *a,* evanescent.
évangélique† (evɑ̃ʒelik) *a,* evangelic(al). **évangéliste** (list) *m,* evangelist. **évangile & É**~ (ʒil) *m,* (*Rel., fig.*) gospel.
évanouir (s') (evanwir) *v.pr,* to faint; vanish, disappear.
évaporation (evapɔrasjɔ̃) *f,* evaporation. **évaporé, e** (re) *a,* giddy, feather-brained. **évaporer** (re) *v.t.* & **s'**~, to evaporate.
évaser (evase) *v.t.* & **s'**~, to open out; flare.
évasif, ive† (evazif, iv) *a,* evasive. **évasion** (zjɔ̃) *f,* escape, flight.
évêché (evɛʃe) *m,* bishopric, see, diocese; bishop's palace.
éveil (evɛj) *m,* awakening; arousing. *en* ~, on the alert; alerted. *donner l'*~, to raise the alarm. **éveillé, e** (vɛje) *a,* wide-awake; alert. **éveiller** (je) *v.t,* to wake [up]; (*fig.*) arouse. **s'**~, to awaken; be aroused.
événement (evɛnmɑ̃) *m,* event, occurrence. (*Pol.*) ~*s,* incidents.
évent (evɑ̃) *m,* blowhole (*whale*). **éventail** (taj)

m, fan; (*fig.*) range. *en* ~, fanshaped. **éventer** (te) *v.t*, to fan; (*fig.*) get wind of; let out (*secret*). **s'**~, (*beer*) to go flat; go stale.
éventrer (evɑ̃tre) *v.t*, to rip open; disembowel.
éventualité (evɑ̃tɥalite) *f*, possibility, eventuality. **éventuel, le†** (tɥɛl) *a*, possible.
évêque (evɛk) *m*, bishop.
évertuer (s') (evɛrtɥe) *v.pr*, *s'*~ *à faire*, to struggle, strive to do.
éviction (eviksjɔ̃) *f*, eviction.
évidence (evidɑ̃s) *f*, obviousness, evidence. *se rendre à l'*~, to bow to the facts. *en* ~, conspicuous, in evidence. *mettre en* ~, to bring to the fore. *de toute* ~, quite clearly, obviously. **évident, e** (dɑ̃, ɑ̃t) *a*, evident, obvious. **évidemment** (damɑ̃) *ad*, obviously; of course.
évider (evide) *v.t*, to hollow out.
évier (evje) *m*, sink (*kitchen*).
évincer (evɛ̃se) *v.t*, to oust; exclude.
évitable (evitabl) *a*, avoidable. **éviter** (te) *v.t*, to avoid; evade; dodge (*blow*). ~ *de faire*, to avoid doing. ~ *qch à qn*, to spare s.o sth.
évocateur, trice (evɔkatœr, tris) *a*, evocative. **évocation** (kasjɔ̃) *f*, evocation.
évolué, e (evɔlɥe) *a*, advanced (*nation*); enlightened, progressive (*pers.*). **évoluer** (lɥe) *v.i*, to evolve; develop; (*plane*) circle; (*Mil.*) manœuvre. **évolution** (lysjɔ̃) *f*, evolution; development.
évoquer (evɔke) *v.t*, to evoke, conjure up.
ex- (ɛks) *pref*, ex-. *ex-mari*, ex-husband.
exacerber (ɛgzasɛrbe) *v.t*, to exacerbate.
exact, e† (ɛgzakt) *a*, exact, accurate; correct; punctual. **exaction** (ksjɔ̃) *f*, exaction. **exactitude** (tityd) *f*, exactness, exactitude, accuracy; punctuality.
ex æquo (ɛgzeko) *a.inv*. & *ad*, (*Sport. exam*) [placed] equal.
exagération (ɛgzaʒerasjɔ̃) *f*, exaggeration. **exagérer** (re) *v.t*, to exaggerate; overdo. ¶ *v.i*, to go too far.
exaltation (ɛgzaltasjɔ̃) *f*, praising, exalting; excitement, elation. **exalter** (ɛgzalte) *v.t*, to exalt, extol; excite, fire.
examen (ɛgzamɛ̃) *m*, (*gen., Med., Sch.*) examination; scrutiny. **examinateur, trice** (minatœr, tris) *n*, examiner. **examiner** (ne) *v.t*, (*gen.*) to examine; scrutinize; study.
exaspérer (ɛgzaspere) *v.t*, to exasperate; exacerbate (*pain*).
exaucer (ɛgzose) *v.t*, to answer (*prayer*); grant. ~ *qn*, to grant s.o's wish.
excavateur (ɛkskavatœr) *m*, (*Mach.*) excavator. **excavation** (sjɔ̃) *f*, excavation.
excédant, e (ɛksedɑ̃, ɑ̃t) *a*, exasperating. **excédent** (dɑ̃) *m*, surplus, excess. ~ *de bagages*, excess luggage. **excéder** (de) *v.t*, to exceed; exhaust; exasperate.
excellemment (ɛksɛlamɑ̃) *ad*, excellently. **excellence** (lɑ̃s) *f*, excellence. *par* ~, above all else; par excellence. *Son E*~, His Excellency. **excellent, e** (lɑ̃, ɑ̃t) *a*, excellent. **exceller** (le) *v.i*, to excel.
excentricité (ɛksɑ̃trisite) *f*, eccentricity. **excentrique** (trik) *a*, (*gen., Math*) eccentric; outlying. ¶ *n*. (*pers.*) & *m* (*Mach.*), eccentric.
excepté (ɛksɛpte) *pr*, except, apart from. **excepter** (te) *v.t*, to except. **exception** (sjɔ̃) *f*, exception. *d'*~, exceptional. *à l'*~ *de*, except for. *faire* ~, to be an exception. **exceptionnel, le†** (ɔnɛl) *a*, exceptional.
excès (ɛksɛ) *m*, excess; surplus; (*pl.*) excesses; violence; overindulgence. *à l'*~, *avec* ~, to excess, excessively. **excessif, ive†** (sɛsif, iv) *a*, excessive.
excitant, e (ɛksitɑ̃, ɑ̃t) *a*, exciting. ¶ *m*, stimulant. **excitation** (tasjɔ̃) *f*, excitement; stimulation; incitement. **exciter** (te) *v.t*, to excite, arouse, stimulate (*feelings*); thrill, excite; spur on; urge (*à faire*, to do). **s'**~, to get excited; get worked up *P*.
exclamation (ɛksklamasjɔ̃) *f*, exclamation. **exclamer (s')** (me) *v.pr*, to exclaim.
exclure (ɛksklyr) *v.t.ir*, to exclude; turn out, expel (*pers.*). **exclusif, ive†** (klyzif, iv) *a*, exclusive; sole. **exclusion** (zjɔ̃) *f*, exclusion; expulsion. **exclusivité** (zivite) *f*, exclusive rights.
excommunier (ɛkskɔmynje) *v.t*, to excommunicate.
excrément (ɛkskremɑ̃) *m*, excrement.
excroissance (ɛkskrwasɑ̃s) *f*, excrescence.
excursion (ɛkskyrsjɔ̃) *f*, excursion, trip, outing. ~ *à pied*, walk, hike. ~**niste** (ɔnist) *n*, tripper; hiker.
excuse (ɛkskys) *f*, excuse; (*pl.*) apology. *faire des* ~*s*, to apologize. **excuser** (kyze) *v.t*, to excuse; forgive. **s'**~, to apologize (*de*, for).
exécrable† (ɛgzekrabl) *a*, execrable. **exécrer** (kre) *v.t*, to execrate.
exécutable (ɛgzekytabl) *a*, workable, practicable. **exécutant, e** (tɑ̃, ɑ̃t) *n*, (*Mus.*) performer. **exécuter** (te) *v.t*, to execute, carry out, perform, fulfil; (*Mus.*) perform; enforce (*law*); execute, put to death. **s'**~, to pay up; comply. **exécuteur (trice) testamentaire,** executor, trix. **exécutif, ive** (tif, iv) *a*. & *n*, executive. **exécution** (sjɔ̃) *f*, execution, &*c*.
exemplaire (ɛgzɑ̃plɛr) *a*, exemplary. ¶ *m*, copy (*book* &*c*); specimen. **exemple** (zɑ̃pl) *m*, example, instance. *à l'*~ *de son père*, just like his father. *par* ~, for example. [*ça*] *par* ~*!* well I never!
exempt, e (ɛgzɑ̃, ɑ̃t) *a*, exempt, free (*de*, from). ~ *de taxes*, duty free. **exempter** (zɑ̃te) *v.t*, to exempt (*de*, from). **exemption** (zɑ̃psjɔ̃) *f*, exemption.
exercer (ɛgzɛrse) *v.t*, to exercise (*faculty*); train (*à faire*, to do); practise (*profession*); ply

(*trade*); exert (*influence*); exercise (*right*); try (*patience*). **s'~,** (*Mus., Sport*) to practise; train o.s. **exercice** (sis) *m,* (*Mus., Sch., Sport*) exercise. (*Mil.*) *l'~*, drill. *faire de l'~*, to take exercise. practice (*profession*); exercise; exercising; execution (*duty*). *en ~*, in office; (*Med.*) in practice. (*Fin.*) accounting period.
exhalaison (ɛgzalɛzɔ̃) *f,* exhalation (*mist, smell*). **exhaler** (le) *v.t,* to exhale; breathe (*sigh*); express (*joy*). *s'~ de,* to rise from.
exhaustif, ive (ɛgzostif, iv) *a,* exhaustive.
exhiber (ɛgzibe) *v.t,* to show; display. **s'~,** to show off. **exhibition** (bisjɔ̃) *f,* showing; flaunting; showing off. **~niste** (ɔnist) *n,* exhibitionist.
exhorter (ɛgzɔrte) *v.t,* to exhort (*à faire,* to do).
exhumer (ɛgzyme) *v.t,* to exhume; unearth.
exigeant, e (ɛgziʒɑ̃, ɑ̃t) *a,* exacting (*work*); demanding, hard to please (*pers.*). **exigence** (ʒɑ̃s) *f,* requirement, demand; strictness (*pers.*). **exiger** (ʒe) *v.t,* to require, demand (*qch de qn,* sth of s.o); insist on; insist (*qu'il fasse,* on his doing). **exigible** (bl) *a,* [re]payable.
exigu, ë (ɛgzigy) *a,* tiny, cramped (*space*); scanty, meagre. **exiguïté** (gɥite) *f,* smallness, scantiness &c.
exil (ɛgzil) *m,* exile. **exilé, e** (le) *n,* exile. **exiler** (le) *v.t,* to exile.
existence (ɛgzistɑ̃s) *f,* existence; life. **exister** (te) *v.i,* to exist, be. *il existe,* there is, there are.
exode (ɛgzɔd) *m,* exodus, flight. (*Bible*) *l'E~*, Exodus.
exonérer (ɛgzɔnere) *v.t,* (*Fin.*) to exempt (*de,* from).
exorbitant, e (tɑ̃, ɑ̃t) *a,* exorbitant.
exorciser (ɛgzɔrsize) *v.t,* to exorcise.
exotique (ɛgzɔtik) *a,* exotic.
expansif, ive (ɛkspɑ̃sif, iv) *a,* expansive; effusive. **expansion** (sjɔ̃) *f,* expansion; expansiveness. *en ~*, booming (*trade*).
expatrier (ɛkspatrie) *v.t,* to expatriate.
expectative (ɛkspɛktativ) *f, rester dans l'~*, to be waiting (to hear *or* see).
expectorer (ɛkspɛktɔre) *v.t. & i,* to expectorate.
expédient, e (ɛkspedjɑ̃, ɑ̃t) *a. & m,* expedient.
expédier (ɛkspedje) *v.t,* to dispatch, send, forward. *~ par bateau,* ship. dispose of (*business*); polish off (*meal*). **expéditeur, trice** (ditœr, tris) *a,* dispatching. ¶ *n,* sender. **expéditif, ive** (tif, iv) *a,* expeditious. **expédition** (sjɔ̃) *f,* (*Mil., &c*) expedition; (*Com.*) dispatch, forwarding; shipment, consignment (*goods*). **expéditionnaire** (ɔnɛr) *a,* expeditionary. ¶ *m,* dispatch clerk; copying clerk.
expérience (ɛksperjɑ̃s) *f,* experiment; experience. **expérimental, e†** (rimɑ̃tal) *a,* experimental. **expérimentateur, trice** (tatœr, tris) *n,* experimenter. **expérimenté, e** (te) *a,* experienced. **expérimenter** (te) *v.t,* to test [out]; experiment with.
expert, e† (ɛkspɛr, ɛrt) *a,* expert, skilled. ¶ *m,* expert; valuer; surveyor. *~-comptable,* professional accountant. **expertise** (pɛrtiz) *f,* valuation; expert's report. **expertiser** (tize) *v.t,* to value; assess.
expier (ɛkspje) *v.t,* to expiate, atone for.
expiration (ɛkspirasjɔ̃) *f,* expiration; expiry. **expirer** (re) *v.t. & i,* to breathe out. ¶ *v.i,* to expire.
explicatif, ive (ɛksplikatif, iv) *a,* explanatory. **explication** (sjɔ̃) *f,* explanation; discussion; (*Sch.*) commentary (*text*). **explicite†** (sit) *a,* explicit. **expliquer** (ke) *v.t,* to explain; account for; (*Sch.*) comment on (*text*). **s'~,** to make o.s clear; be explained. *tout s'explique,* it's all clear now. *s'~ avec qn,* to have it out with s.o.
exploit (ɛksplwa) *m,* exploit, achievement, feat. **~able** (tabl) *a,* (*gen.*) exploitable. **~ant, e** (tɑ̃, tɑ̃t) *n,* farmer. **~ation** (tasjɔ̃) *f,* working, operating, running; exploitation; undertaking, concern. *~ agricole,* farm. **~er** (te) *v.t,* to work, run, operate; farm; exploit (*idea, pers.*). **~eur, euse** (tœr, øz) *n,* exploiter.
explorateur, trice (ɛksplɔratœr, tris) *n,* explorer. **explorer** (re) *v.t,* to explore.
exploser (ɛksploze) *v.i,* to explode; (*fig.*) burst out. **explosif, ive** (zif, iv) *a. & m,* explosive. **explosion** (zjɔ̃) *f,* explosion; outburst. *faire ~*, to explode.
exportateur, trice (ɛkspɔrtatœr, tris) *a,* exporting. ¶ *n,* exporter. **exportation** (sjɔ̃) *f,* (*gen.*) export. **exporter** (te) *v.t,* to export.
exposant, e (ɛkspozɑ̃, ɑ̃t) *n,* exhibitor. (*m.*) (*Math.*) exponent. **exposé** (ze) *m,* statement; account; talk (*sur,* on). **exposer** (ze) *v.t,* (*gen., Mil., Phot.*) to expose; lay open (*à,* to); endanger (*life*); show, display, exhibit; expound, explain. *exposé à l'est,* facing east. *bien exposé,* well situated. **exposition** (zisjɔ̃) *f,* exposition; exposure; exhibition, show; aspect (*house*).
exprès[1], esse (ɛksprɛs) *a,* formal, express. ¶ *a.inv,* express (*letter, parcel*). *en ~*, (*send*) express. **exprès[2],** (ɛksprɛ) *ad,* on purpose; purposely, specially. ¶ *m,* express, e. messenger. **express** (prɛs) *a.inv. & m,* [*train*] ~, fast train. [*café*] ~, espresso [coffee]. **expressément** (prɛsemɑ̃) *ad,* expressly; specially.
expressif, ive† (ɛksprɛsif, iv) *a,* expressive. **expression** (sjɔ̃) *f,* (*gen.*) expression. **exprimer** (prime) *v.t,* to express; squeeze out (*juice*).
exproprier (ɛksprɔprie) *v.t, ~ qn,* to purchase s.o's land compulsorily.
expulser (ɛkspylse) *v.t,* to expel; deport; evict; eject. **expulsion** (sjɔ̃) *f,* expulsion &c.
expurger (ɛkspyrʒe) *v.t,* to expurgate.
exquis, e (ɛkski, iz) *a,* exquisite.
exsangue (ɛksɑ̃g) *a,* bloodless (*face*).

extase (ɛkstɑz) *f,* ecstasy. **extasier (s')** (zje) *v.pr,* to go into ecstasies (*sur,* over). **extatique** (tatik) *a,* ecstatic, rapturous.
extenseur (ɛkstɑ̃sœr) *a.m,* [*muscle*] ~, extensor. ¶ *m,* chest expander. **extensible** (sibl) *a,* extensible. **extension** (sjɔ̃) *f,* extensor; stretching (*limb*); expansion; spreading. *par* ~ [*de sens*], by extension.
exténuer (ɛkstenɥe) *v.t,* to exhaust, wear out.
extérieur, e† (ɛksterjœr) *a,* outer, outside; external; exterior; outward (*appearance*); foreign (*policy, trade*). ¶ *m,* exterior, outside; foreign countries. *à l'*~, abroad.
exterminer (ɛkstɛrmine) *v.t,* to exterminate.
externat (ɛkstɛrna) *m,* day school. **externe** (tɛrn) *a,* external, exterior. (*Med.*) *à usage* ~, for external use only. ¶ *n,* (*Sch.*) day pupil; (*Med.*) non-resident student.
extincteur (ɛkstɛ̃ktœr) *m,* fire extinguisher. **extinction** (sjɔ̃) *f,* extinguishing; extinction. ~ *de voix,* loss of voice. (*Mil.*) *l'*~ *des feux,* lights out.
extirper (ɛkstirpe) *v.t,* to extirpate, eradicate.
extorquer (ɛkstɔrke) *v.t,* to extort (*à qn,* from s.o). **extorsion** (sjɔ̃) *f,* extortion.
extra (ɛkstra) *a,* top quality; (*P*) terrific *P.* ¶ *m,* extra; special meal; extra help (*home*). ¶ *pref,* extra. ~*-fin,* superfine.
extraction (ɛkstraksjɔ̃) *f,* extraction; mining; quarrying; parentage.
extrader (ɛkstrade) *v.t,* to extradite. **extradition** (disjɔ̃) *f,* extradition.
extraire (ɛkstrɛr) *v.t.ir,* (*gen.*) to extract; mine; excerpt; get, win; quarry. **extrait** (trɛ) *m,* extract; excerpt. ~ *de naissance,* birth certificate.
extraordinaire† (ɛkstraɔrdinɛr) *a,* extraordinary; exceptional; remarkable; (*Pol.*) special. *par* ~, by some strange chance.
extravagance (ɛkstravagɑ̃s) *f,* eccentricity, extravagance (*dress, ideas*). **extravagant, e** (gɑ̃, ɑ̃t) *a,* eccentric (*behaviour*); extravagant, excessive (*price*); wild (*ideas*).
extrême (ɛkstrɛm) *a,* furthest; utmost; drastic (*measures*). ¶ *m,* extreme. *à l'*~, in the e. ~*-onction,* Extreme Unction. *l'E*~*-Orient, m,* the Far East. **extrêmement** (trɛmmɑ̃) *ad,* extremely; exceedingly. **extrémiste** (tremist) *n* extremist. **extrémité** (te) *f,* extremity; end; tip; plight, straights; desperate act. *à la dernière* ~, in desperate straights.
exubérance (ɛgzyberɑ̃s) *f,* exuberance. **exubérant, e** (rɑ̃, ɑ̃t) *a,* exuberant.
exulter (ɛgzylte) *v.i,* to exult.
ex-voto (ɛksvɔto) *m,* votive tablet.

F

F, f (ɛf) *m. & f, letter,* F, f.
fa (fɑ) *m,* (*Mus.*) F.
fable (fɑbl) *f,* fable; story; laughing stock.
fabricant (fabrikɑ̃) *m,* manufacturer, maker. **fabrication** (kasjɔ̃) *f,* manufacture; making; forging; fabricating (*news*). ~ *en série* mass production. *de* ~ *française,* made in France. **fabrique** (brik) *f,* factory, works, mill. **fabriquer** (ke) *v.t,* to manufacture, make; fabricate, invent; forge; (*P*) do. *qu'est-ce que tu fabriques?* what are you up to?
fabuleux, euse† (fabylø, øz) *a,* fabulous.
fac (fak) *f,* (*P Univ.*) *abb. of* **faculté.**
façade (fasad) *f,* (*Arch.*) façade, front; frontage; (*fig.*) façade. *de* ~, sham.
face (fas) *f,* face. *perdre la* ~, to lose f. side (*record*); face, side (*cube*); head side (*coin*). *pile ou* ~*?* heads or tails? **en** ~, opposite; (*look s.o*) in the face. *le magasin d'en* ~, the shop across the road. *voir les choses en* ~, to face facts. ~ **à, en** ~ **de,** opposite, facing. ~ *à* ~, face to f. *de* ~, full-face (*portrait*). *faire* ~ *à,* to face; f. up to; meet (*obligation*). ~ **à** ~, *m,* face to f. encounter. ~**-à-main,** *m,* lorgnette.
facétie (fasesi) *f,* joke; prank. **facétieux, euse** (sjø, øz) *a,* facetious.
facette (fasɛt) *f,* facet.
fâché, e (fɑʃe) *a,* angry; sorry. **fâcher** (ʃe) *v.t,* to make angry, anger; grieve, pain. **se** ~, to get angry (*contre,* with); quarrel (*avec,* with). **fâcherie** (ʃri) *f,* quarrel. **fâcheux, euse**† (ʃø, øz) *a,* unfortunate, tiresome. ¶ *n,* (*liter.*) bore (*pers.*).
facial, e (fasjal) *a,* facial.
facile† (fasil) *a,* easy. ~ *à lire,* e. to read. ~ *d'accès,* e. to reach. facile; fluent; ready. *avoir la parole* ~, to have a ready tongue. ~ *à vivre,* easy to get on with. **facilité** (lite) *f,* easiness, ease; fluency; aptitude, ability; facility, opportunity. **faciliter** (te) *v.t,* to facilitate.
façon (fasɔ̃) *f,* way. *de cette* ~, in this way. *d'une certaine* ~, in a w. *à ma* ~, in my own w. *d'une* ~ *ou d'une autre,* one w. or another. *de toute* ~, in any case. ~ *de parler,* manner of speaking. **de** ~ **à** *faire,* so as to do. **de [telle]** ~ **qu'***il puisse payer,* so that he can pay. ~*s,* manners, behaviour. *faire des* ~*s,* to be affected. *sans* ~, unaffected; unpretentious; without fuss. *merci, sans* ~, no thanks,

honestly. *sans plus de ~s,* without further ado. (*Dress*) making[-up]; cut. *travailler à ~,* to make up customer's material. *~ cuir,* imitation leather (*coat*). **~ner** (sɔne) *v.t,* to make; shape, fashion, form, mould (*pers.*).

fac-similé (faksimile) *m,* facsimile.

facteur (faktœr) *m,* postman; (*gen., Math.*) factor; maker (*pianos*). *~ d'orgues,* organ builder.

factice (faktis) *a,* imitation; artificial; false (*beard*); feigned (*pity*); forced (*smile*).

factieux, euse (faksjø, øz) *a,* seditious.

faction (faksjɔ̃) *f,* faction; guard, sentry duty. *de ~, en ~,* on guard; (*fig.*) on the watch. **~naire** (ɔnɛr) *m,* sentry.

factrice (faktris) *f,* postwoman.

facture (faktyr) *f,* invoice, bill. **facturer** (tyre) *v.t,* to invoice; charge for.

facultatif, ive† (fakyltatif, iv) *a,* optional. *arrêt ~,* request stop. **faculté** (te) *f,* faculty; power. *~ de concentration,* powers of concentration. property (*matter*); (*Univ.*) faculty. *aller à la ~,* to go to university.

fadaise[s] (fadɛz) *f.*[*pl.*], twaddle, nonsense.

fadasse (fadas) *a,* sickly, insipid. **fade** (fad) *a,* insipid, tasteless; flat, dull, insipid (*style &c*). **fadeur** (dœr) *f,* insipidity, *&c.*

fagot (fago) *m,* faggot; bundle of sticks. **fagoter** *P* (gɔte) *v.t,* (*pej: dress*) to rig out *P.*

faible† (fɛbl) *a,* (*gen.*) weak; faint (*light, smell, sound*); low (*sum*); small, slight (*difference*); light (*wind*); feeble (*pulse*). *~ en math,* weak at maths. *~ d'esprit,* feeble-minded. ¶ *m,* weakling. *les ~s,* the weak. weak point; weakness (*for sth*); soft spot (*for s.o*). **faiblesse** (blɛs) *f,* weakness, *&c*; failing, weakness; dizzy spell. **faiblir** (blir) *v.i,* to grow weaker &c; weaken; (*wind*) slacken; (*strength*) flag, fail.

faïence (fajɑ̃s) *f,* [glazed] earthenware; earthenware crockery.

faille[1] (faj) *f,* (*Geol.*) fault; (*fig.*) flaw. **faille**[2] (faj) *V* **falloir. failli, e** (faji) *n,* bankrupt. **faillibilité** (bilite) *f,* fallibility. **faillible** (bl) *a,* fallible. **faillir** (jir) *v.i.ir, j'ai failli mourir,* I nearly *or* all but died. *~* **à,** to fail in (*duty*); fail to keep (*promise*). **faillite** (jit) *f,* bankruptcy.

faim (fɛ̃) *f,* hunger; starvation. *avoir* [*très*] *~,* to be [very] hungry. (*fig.*) *avoir ~ de,* to hunger for. *j'ai une ~ de loup,* I'm ravenous.

fainéant, e (feneɑ̃, ɑ̃t) *a,* idle, lazy. ¶ *n,* idler, loafer. **~er** (ɑ̃te) *v.i,* to idle, loaf about. **~ise** (tiz) *f,* idleness, laziness.

faire (fɛr) *v.t.ir,* (*gen.*) to make; build (*wall*); bake (*cake*); cook (*meal*) &c; do. *ne fais pas ça!* don't do that! make (*speech, mistake*). (*activity*) *~ du piano,* to play the piano; *~ du ski,* ski; *~ des études,* study; *~ le ménage,* do the housework; *~ la vaisselle,* wash up. (*rôle*) *~ l'idiot,* to play the fool; *~ l'innocent,* act the innocent. (*distance, speed*) *~ 50 km,* to cover 50 km; *~ 80 km/h,* do 50 m.p.h. (*total*) *2 & 2 font 4,* 2 & 2 make 4. *ça fait 20F,* that comes to 20F. (*effect*) *ça ne fait rien,* it doesn't matter. *qu'est-ce que ça peut bien lui faire?* what difference does that make to him? *on l'a fait président,* they made him chairman. *qu'as-tu fait de..?* what have you done with..? *elle ne fait que pleurer,* she does nothing but cry. ¶ *v.i,* (*become*) *il veut ~ avocat,* he wants to be a barrister. (*appear*) *~ jeune, vieux, bien,* to look young, old, good. (*do, act*) *~ vite,* to be quick. *vous feriez mieux de..,* you'd do better to... *~ de son mieux,* to do one's best. ¶ *v.imp, il fait froid, du brouillard, une chaleur terrible,* it's cold, foggy, terribly hot. *il fait bon se reposer,* it's good to rest. *ça fait 3 ans que,* it's 3 years since. ¶ *v.aux,* (*causal*) *~ réparer la voiture,* to get the car repaired. *~ opérer son fils,* to have his son operated on. **se ~,** to become. *se ~ vieux,* to grow old. *il se fait tard,* it's getting late. (*cheese, wine*) mature. *se ~ à,* to get used to. *s'en ~,* to worry. *cela se fait souvent,* that's often done. *comment se fait-il que*(+*subj.*)? how is it that? *se ~ écraser,* to get run over. **faire-part** (fɛrpar) *m,* card announcing wedding, birth, death &c. **faisable** (fəzabl) *a,* feasible.

faisan, e (fɛzɑ̃, an) *n,* pheasant. **faisandé, e** (zɑ̃de) *a,* high (*meat*); (*fig.*) rotten, corrupt. **faisandeau** (do) *m,* young pheasant.

faisceau (fɛso) *m,* bundle; (*Opt., Phys.*) beam; stack (*arms*). (*Hist.*) *~x,* fasces.

faiseur, euse (fəzœr, øz) *n,* maker.

fait[1] (fɛ, fɛt) *m,* occurrence, event; fact. *le ~ d'être aveugle,* the fact of being blind. *~ divers,* news item. *~s & gestes,* doings. *~s de guerre,* exploits of war. *au ~* [*de*], informed [about]. *au ~,* by the way. *en ~,* in fact. *de ~,* de facto; in fact. *de ce ~,* for this reason. *dire son ~ à qn,* to speak one's mind to s.o.

fait[2], **e** (fɛ, fɛt) *a, ~ pour,* made for, meant for, designed for. mature (*pers.*); ripe (*cheese*). *idée toute ~e,* ready made idea. *jambe bien ~e,* shapely leg. *c'en est ~ de moi,* it's all up with me.

faîte (fɛt) *m,* top (*roof, tree*); summit (*mountain*); ridgepole.

fait-tout (fɛtu) *m,* stewpan.

fakir (fakir) *m,* fakir.

falaise (falɛz) *f,* cliff.

falbalas (falbala) *m.pl,* frills & furbelows.

fallacieux, euse† (falasjø, øz) *a,* fallacious.

falloir (falwar) *v.imp.ir,* (*need*) *il lui faut du repos,* he needs rest. (*necessity*) *il me faut partir* (or *il faut que je parte*) *demain,* I must leave tomorrow. *s'il le faut,* if necessary. *il m'a fallu attendre,* I had to wait. *il fallait me le dire,* you should have told me. (*probability*) *il*

faut qu'il soit malade, he must be ill. **s'en ~ de:** *il s'en faut de beaucoup qu'elle soit satisfaite,* she is far from being satisfied. *tant s'en faut,* far from it.
falot[1] (falo) *m,* lantern.
falot[2], **e** (falo, ɔt) *a,* colourless (*pers.*).
falsifier (falsifje) *v.t,* to falsify, tamper with; adulterate.
famé, e (fame) *a, mal ~,* disreputable.
famélique (famelik) *a,* half-starved.
fameux, euse† (famø, øz) *a,* first-rate, splendid. *pas ~,* not up to much. *faire une ~se gaffe,* to drop a real *or* proper brick. well known, famous.
familial, e (familjal) *a,* family. ¶ *f,* estate car. **familiariser** (ljarize) *v.t,* to familiarize (*avec,* with). **familiarité** (te) *f,* familiarity. *~s,* familiarities. **familier, ère**† (lje, ɛr) *a,* familiar (*à,* to; *avec,* with); customary; [over]familiar, presumptuous (*pers.*); friendly, informal; colloquial (*expression*). ¶ *m,* regular visitor (*de,* at). **famille** (mij) *f,* family. *air de ~,* family likeness. *en ~,* with the f., as a f.
famine (famin) *f,* famine, starvation.
fan, fana *P* (fan, fana) *n,* fan; enthusiast.
fanal (fanal) *m,* lamp; beacon; (*Rly*) headlight.
fanatique (fanatik) *a,* fanatical ¶ *n,* (*gen., Sport*) fanatic. **fanatisme** (tism) *m,* fanaticism.
fane (fan) *f,* top (*carrot, turnip*).
faner (fane) *v.t,* to ted, toss (*hay*); fade. **se ~,** to fade; wither. **faneuse** (nøz) *f,* (*Agr.*) tedder; swath turner.
fanfare (fɑ̃far) *f,* fanfare; brass band.
fanfaron, ne (fɑ̃farɔ̃, ɔn) *a,* bragging. ¶ *n,* braggart. **~nade** (rɔnad) *f,* bragging. **~ner** (ne) *v.i,* to brag.
fanfreluche (fɑ̃frəlyʃ) *f,* trimming. *~s,* frills.
fange (fɑ̃ʒ) *f,* (*liter.*) mire, mud, filth.
fanion (fanjɔ̃) *m,* pennant.
fantaisie (fɑ̃tezi) *f,* whim; extravagance; fantasy, imagination; (*Mus.*) fantasia. *vivre à sa ~,* to live as one pleases. *bouton ~,* fancy button. **fantaisiste** (zist) *a,* whimsical, fanciful; eccentric; phoney *P* (*pers.*). ¶ *n,* (*Theat.*) entertainer. **fantasque** (task) *a,* whimsical; weird. **fantasme** (asm) *m,* fantasy.
fantassin (fɑ̃tasɛ̃) *m,* infantryman.
fantastique (fɑ̃tastik) *a,* fantastic, weird, uncanny; (*P wonderful*) fantastic *P.*
fantoche (fɑ̃tɔʃ) *m,* puppet (*pers.*).
fantomatique (fɑ̃tomatik) *a,* ghostly. **fantôme** (tom) *m,* phantom, ghost.
faon (fɑ̃) *m,* fawn.
faramineux, euse *P* (faraminø, øz) *a,* staggering.
farce (fars) *f,* practical joke, hoax. *faire une ~ à,* play a joke on. (*Theat.*) farce; (*Cook.*) stuffing. **farceur, euse** (sœr, øz) *n,* joker; practical joker. **farcir** (sir) *v.t,* (*Cook.*) to stuff; cram. **se ~ de,** (*P*) to get landed with (*job, pers.*).
fard (far) *m,* make-up, greasepaint.
fardeau (fardo) *m,* burden, load.
farder (farde) *v.t,* to make up (*face*); (*fig.*) disguise. **se ~,** to make o.s up.
farfelu, e *P* (farfəly) *a,* cranky, crackpot *P.*
farfouiller (farfuje) *v.i,* to rummage [about].
faribole[s] (faribɔl) *f.[pl.],* (*liter.*) twaddle.
farine (farin) *f,* flour. *~ d'avoine, de maïs, de riz,* oatmeal, cornflour, ground rice. **farineux, euse** (nø, øz) *a,* floury, mealy. ¶ *n,* starchy food.
farouche (faruʃ) *a,* shy, timid; unsociable; fierce, grim (*hatred, resistance*); wild, savage.
fart (fart) *m,* [ski] wax. **~er** (te) *v.t,* to wax.
fascicule (fasikyl) *m,* instalment (*book*).
fascination (fasinasjɔ̃) *f,* fascination. **fasciner** (ne) *v.t,* to fascinate; bewitch.
fascisme (fasism) *m,* fascism. **fasciste** (sist) *m,* fascist.
faste[1] (fast) *m,* pomp; splendour.
faste[2] (fast) *a,* (*liter.*) lucky (*day*).
fastidieux, euse† (fastidjø, øz) *a,* tedious.
fastueux, euse† (fastɥø, øz) *a,* luxurious, sumptuous; lavish.
fat (fat) *a.m.* [*& m*], (*liter.*) conceited [person].
fatal, e (fatal) *a,* fatal; fateful (*moment*). *c'était ~,* it was inevitable. **~ement** (mɑ̃) *ad,* inevitably. **~ism** (lism) *m,* fatalism. **~iste** (list) *n,* fatalist. **~ité** (te) *f,* fate; fateful coincidence.
fatidique (fatidik) *a,* fateful (*day, word*).
fatigant, e (fatigɑ̃, ɑ̃t) *a,* tiring; tiresome; tedious. **fatigue** (tig) *f,* fatigue, tiredness; (*Tech.*) fatigue. *~s,* strain. **fatiguer** (ge) *v.t,* to tire; wear out; overwork (*pers.*); exhaust (*land*); strain (*beam*). ¶ *v.i,* to tire; (*ship, engine*) labour. **se ~,** to grow tired (*de,* of).
fatras (fatrɑ) *m,* jumble.
fatuité (fatɥite) *f,* self-conceit.
faubourg (fobur) *m,* suburb. **faubourien, ne** (burjɛ̃, ɛn) *a,* working-class.
fauché, e *P* (foʃe) *a,* broke *P,* skint *P.* **faucher** (ʃe) *v.t,* to mow, reap; mow down; cut off (*limb*); (*P*) pinch *P,* nick *P.* **faucheur, euse** (ʃœr, øz) *n.* (*pers.*) *& f.* (*Mach.*), reaper, mower. **faucille** (sij) *f,* sickle.
faucon (fokɔ̃) *m,* falcon, hawk. *~ pèlerin,* peregrine f. **~nerie** (kɔnri) *f,* falconry.
faufiler (fofile) *v.t,* (*Need.*) to tack. **se ~,** to worm one's way, slip (*in, out, through*).
faune (fon) *m,* (*Myth.*) faun. ¶ *f,* fauna.
faussaire (fosɛr) *n,* forger. **faussement** (smɑ̃) *ad,* falsely; wrongfully. **fausser** (se) *v.t,* to bend; buckle; warp; distort (*facts*); disturb (*mind*). *~ compagnie à qn,* to give s.o the slip. **fausset** (sɛ) *m,* falsetto (*voice*). **fausseté** (ste) *f,* falseness, falsity; falsehood; duplicity.
faute (fot) *f,* mistake, error; fault; sin; (*Law*) offence; (*Foot.*) foul; (*Ten.*) fault. *c'est ma ~,* it's my fault. *~ de,* for want of, through lack

of, failing. *sans* ~, without fail. *prendre qn en* ~, to catch s.o out. ~ *de frappe,* typing error. ~ *d'impression,* misprint. *faire* ~, to be lacking.

fauteuil (fotœj) *m,* armchair, easy chair; chair (*at meeting*); (*Theat.*) seat. ~ *à bascule,* rocking chair. ~ *roulant,* wheelchair.

fautif, ive (fotif, iv) *a,* faulty; at fault.

fauve (fov) *a,* fawn, tawny. ¶ *m,* big cat.

fauvette (fovɛt) *f,* warbler (*bird*).

faux[1] (fo) *f,* scythe.

faux[2], **fausse** (fo, os) *a,* false, wrong, untrue; (*Mus.*) out of tune; false (*nose, teeth*); forged, fake; feigned, sham; blind (*window*). *faire un* ~ *pas,* to stumble, trip; (*fig.*) blunder. *faire fausse route,* to take the wrong road; (*fig.*) to be on the wrong track. ¶ *m,* forgery, fake. *le* ~, the false. ¶ *ad,* (*sing*) out of tune. *sonner* ~, to ring false. *à* ~, (*accuse*) wrongly, unjustly. *fausse clef,* skeleton key. ~ *col,* detachable collar. *fausse couche,* miscarriage. ~ *départ,* (*lit., fig.*) false start. ~ *frais,* incidental expenses. ~*-fuyant, m,* evasion, shift. (*fig.*) *sous un* ~ *jour,* in a false light. ~*-monnayeur, m,* forger. ~*-semblant, m,* pretence, sham. ~ *témoignage,* false evidence; perjury.

faveur (favœr) *f,* favour. *de* ~, complimentary (*ticket*). *régime de* ~, preferential treatment. *en* ~ *de,* in favour of; in aid of (*charity*); on account of. **favorable**† (vɔrabl) *a,* favourable. **favori, ite** (ri, it) *a. & n,* favourite. ¶ ~*s, m.pl,* side whiskers. **favoriser** (ze) *v.t,* to favour; further, promote. **favoritisme** (tism) *m,* favouritism.

fébrile† (febril) *a,* feverish.

fécond, e (fekɔ̃, ɔ̃d) *a,* fruitful, fertile; prolific. ~**er,** (kɔ̃de) *v.t,* to fertilize (*plant, animal*); make pregnant. ~**ité** (dite) *f,* fertility, fruitfulness.

fécule (fekyl) *f,* starch. **féculent, e** (lɑ̃, ɑ̃t) *a,* starchy (*food*).

fédéral, e (federal) *a,* federal. ~**isme** (lism) *m,* federalism. **fédération** (sjɔ̃) *f,* federation. **fédérer** (re) *v.t,* to federate.

fée (fe) *f,* fairy. **féerie** (feri) *f,* enchantment; (*Theat., Cine.*) extravaganza. **féerique** (ferik) *a,* magical.

feindre (fɛ̃dr) *v.t. & i.ir,* to feign; pretend (*de faire,* to do). **feint, e** (fɛ̃, ɛ̃t) *a,* feigned, sham. ¶ *f,* dummy move; (*Sport*) dummy; (*Box.*) feint; ham. **feinter** (te) *v.t,* to dummy; trick. ¶ *v.i,* to feint.

fêler (fɛle) *v.t,* to crack.

félicitations (felisitasjɔ̃) *f.pl,* congratulations. **félicité** (te) *f,* (*liter.*) bliss. **féliciter** (te) *v.t,* to congratulate (*de, sur,* on).

félin, e (felɛ̃, in) *a. & m,* feline.

félon, ne (felɔ̃, ɔn) *a,* disloyal. ¶ *n,* traitor. **félonie** (lɔni) *f,* treachery.

fêlure (fɛlyr) *f,* crack.

femelle (fəmɛl) *f. & a,* female, she; hen; cow (*elephant, &c*). **féminin, e** (feminɛ̃, in) *a,* feminine; female; women's (*team*); womanish (*voice*). ¶ *m,* (*Gram.*) feminine. **féminisme** (nism) *m,* feminism. **féministe** (nist) *a. & n,* feminist.

femme (fam) *f,* woman; wife. ~ *médecin, professeur,* woman doctor, teacher. ~ *au foyer,* housewife (*opp. career woman*). ¶ *a.inv, très* ~, very womanly, feminine. ~ *auteur, f,* authoress. ~ *de chambre,* chambermaid. ~ *de charge,* house-keeper. ~ *d'intérieur* (*att.*), domesticated. ~ *de ménage,* domestic help, cleaner. ~ *du monde,* society woman.

fémur (femyr) *m,* femur, thighbone.

fenaison (fənɛzɔ̃) *f,* haymaking.

fendiller (se) (fɑ̃dije) *v.pr,* (*glaze*) to craze, crack; (*skin*) chap. **fendre** (fɑ̃dr) *v.t,* to split, cleave; crack; slit; break (*heart*). ~ *du bois,* to chop wood. **fendu, e** (fɑ̃dy) *a,* split (*skirt*); with a vent (*jacket*).

fenêtre (f[ə]nɛtr) *f,* window. ~ *à guillotine,* sash w. ~ *à tabatière,* skylight. ~ *en saillie,* bay w. ~ *à battants,* casement w.

fenil (fəni) *m,* hayloft.

fenouil (fənuj) *m,* fennel.

fente (fɑ̃t) *f,* crack, cleft, fissure; slit, split; slot; vent (*coat*).

féodal, e (feɔdal) *a,* feudal. **féodalité** (lite) *f,* feudalism.

fer (fɛr) *m,* iron. *de* ~, iron, of iron (*fig: man, will*). girder; shoe (*horse*); head (*lance &c*); sword. ~*s,* irons, chains; (*Med. O*) obstetrical forceps. ~*-blanc,* tin[plate]. ~ *forgé,* wrought iron. ~ *à friser,* curling tongs. (*fig.*) ~ *de lance,* spearhead. ~ *à repasser,* [flat] iron. ~ *à souder,* soldering iron.

ferblantier (fɛrblɑ̃tje) *m,* tinsmith.

férié, e (ferje) *a, jour* ~, public holiday.

férir (ferir) *v.t: sans coup* ~, without meeting any opposition.

ferler (fɛrle) *v.t,* to furl (*sail*).

ferme[1]† (fɛrm) *a,* firm (*flesh, tone, decision, price*); solid (*ground*); steady (*hand*); tough (*meat*); steadfast (*pers.*). *d'un pas* ~, with a firm step. ¶ *ad,* (*work, hit*) hard; (*discuss*) vigorously.

ferme[2] (fɛrm) *f,* farm; farmhouse; farm lease.

ferment (fɛrmɑ̃) *m,* (*lit., fig.*) ferment. **fermentation** (tasjɔ̃) *f,* fermentation; (*fig.*) ferment. **fermenter** (te) *v.i,* to ferment.

fermer (fɛrme) *v.t. & i,* to shut, s. up, s. down, close, c. up, c. down; do up (*coat*); turn off (*tap, gas*); switch off (*radio*); block, bar (*road, entrance*); enclose. ~ *à clef,* to lock. ~ *les yeux sur,* to close one's eyes to. ~ *la marche,* to bring up the rear. *ferme-la! P,* belt up! *P.* **se**

~, to close, shut; (*dress*) do up.
fermeté (fɛrmǝte) *f,* firmness; steadiness; steadfastness.
fermeture (fɛrmǝtyr) *f,* shutting; closing. (*Com.*) ~ *annuelle,* annual closure. catch; fastening; fastener. ~ *éclair,* zip [fastener].
fermier (fɛrmje) *m,* farmer. **fermière** (ɛr) *f,* farmer's wife; woman farmer.
fermoir (fɛrmwar) *m,* clasp (*necklace*).
féroce† (ferɔs) *a,* ferocious, fierce, savage. **férocité** (site) *f,* ferocity, &c.
ferraille (fɛraj) *f,* scrap iron; (*P*) small change. **ferrailleur** (jœr) *m,* scrap merchant. **ferré, e** (re) *a,* shod (*horse*); hobnailed (*boot*); iron-shod (*wheel*). *voie* ~*e,* (*Rly*) track. (*P*) ~ *sur,* well up in (*subject*). **ferrer** (re) *v.t,* to shoe (*horse*); nail (*boot*); tip *or* bind with metal; strike (*fish*). **ferreux** (rø) *a.m,* ferrous. **ferronnerie** (rɔnri) *f,* ironworks; ironwork. **ferronnier, ère** (nje, ɛr) *n,* craftsman in wrought iron; ironware dealer.
ferroviaire (fɛrɔ̆vjɛr) *a,* railway, rail (*traffic*).
fertile (fɛrtil) *a,* fertile, fruitful. **fertiliser** (lize) *v.t,* to fertilize. **fertilité** (te) *f,* fertility.
féru, e (fery) *a,* ~ *de qch,* passionately fond of sth.
fervent, e (fɛrvɑ̃, ɑ̃t) *a,* fervent, ardent. ¶ *n,* enthusiast, devotee. **ferveur** (vœr) *f,* fervour, ardour.
fesse (fɛs) *f,* buttock. ~*s,* buttocks, bottom. **fessée** (se) *f,* spanking. **fesser** (se) *v.t,* to spank.
festin (fɛstɛ̃) *m,* feast. **festival** (tival) *m,* (*pl,* ~*s*) festival. **festivités** (vite) *f.pl,* festivities.
festoyer (fɛstwaje) *v.i,* to feast.
fête (fɛt) *f,* (*Rel.*) feast; f. day; saint's d.; name d.; birthday; holiday. *les* ~*s,* the holidays (*Christmas, Easter &c*). fair, fête; festival; party, celebration. *air de* ~, festive air. *faire la* ~, to live it up *P. faire* ~ *à qn,* to welcome s.o warmly. *il n'était pas à la* ~, it was no joke for him. *F~-Dieu,* Corpus Christi. ~ *de famille,* family celebration. ~ *foraine,* fun fair. ~ *légale,* public holiday. ~ *de la moisson,* harvest festival. ~ *de village,* village fête. **fêter** (fɛte) *v.t,* to celebrate (*event*); fête, entertain (*pers.*).
fétiche (fetiʃ) *m,* fetish; mascot. **fétichisme** (ʃism) *m,* fetishism.
fétide (fetid) *a,* fetid.
fétu (fety) *m,* [bit of] straw; (*fig.*) straw.
feu[1] (fø) *m,* fire. *prendre* ~, to catch f. *mettre le* ~ *à,* to set f. to. *en* ~, on fire. *au* ~*!* fire! *avez-vous du* ~*?* have you got a light? light (*car, plane, ship*); flash, fire (*diamond*). ~ *arrière,* rear light. *s'arrêter au*[x] *feu*[x], to stop at the [traffic] lights. *les* ~*x de la rampe,* footlights. (*Cook.*) ring; heat. *à* ~ *doux, à petit* ~, over a low heat. (*Mil.*) fire. *faire* ~, to fire. *feu!* fire! ~ *roulant,* running f. (*fig.*) passion, fire. *en* ~, burning (*cheeks*). ~ *d'artifice,* firework. ~ *de cheminée,* chimney fire. ~ *de joie,* bonfire. (*fig.*) ~ *de paille,* flash in the pan. ~ *follet,* will-o'-the-wisp. *faire long* ~, (*plan*) to fall through. (*fig.*) *sous le* ~ *des projecteurs,* in the limelight.
feu[2] (fø) *a,* late, the late (*deceased*). ~ *ma tante,* my late aunt.
feuillage (fœjaʒ) *m,* foliage. **feuille** (fœj) *f,* leaf (*plant*); sheet (*paper, steel*); slip; form; [news]paper. ~ *de chou,* (*pej. newspaper*) rag. ~ *de garde,* end paper. ~ *de paye,* pay slip. ~ *de présence,* time sheet, attendance s. (*Mil.*) ~ *de route,* travel warrant. ~ *de vigne,* vine leaf; (*Art*) fig leaf. ~ *volante,* loose sheet (*paper*). **feuillet** (jɛ) *m,* leaf, page. **feuilleter** (fœjte) *v.t,* to leaf *or* thumb through (*book*). *pâte feuilletée,* puff pastry. **feuilleton** (tɔ̃) *m,* *m,* serial (*magazine, TV*). ~ *à l'eau de rose,* soap-opera. **feuillu, e** (jy) *a,* leafy.
feutre (føtr) *m,* felt; felt hat; felt pen. **feutrer** (føtre) *v.t,* to felt; muffle (*sound*). *à pas feutrés,* with muffled tread.
fève (fɛv) *f,* broad bean.
février (fevrie) *m,* February.
fi (fi) *i,* (*liter.*) bah! (*scorn*). *faire* ~ *de,* to despise, scorn.
fiacre (fjakr) *m,* [horse-drawn] cab.
fiançailles (fjɑ̃sɑj) *f.pl,* engagement. **fiancé, e** (se) *a,* engaged. ¶ *n,* fiancé, e. **fiancer** (se) *v.t,* to betroth. **se** ~, to get engaged (*avec,* to).
fiasco (fjasko) *m,* fiasco. *faire* ~, to be a f.
fibre (fibr) *f,* (*lit., fig.*) fibre; grain (*wood*); (*fig.*) streak. ~ *de verre,* glass fibre; fibre-glass. **fibreux, euse** (brø, øz) *a,* fibrous; stringy (*meat*).
ficelé, e (fisle) *a,* (*pej. dressed*) rigged out *P.* **ficeler** (sle) *v.t,* to tie up [with string]. **ficelle** (sɛl) *f,* string; stick of bread. ~*s du métier,* tricks of the trade.
fiche (fiʃ) *f,* index card; slip; form; (*Elec.*) pin; plug. *mettre en* ~, to index. ~ *de consolation,* consolation [prize].
ficher[1] (fiʃe) *v.t,* to drive in, stick in; file (*papers*).
ficher[2] *P* (fiʃe) *v.t,* to do; give; put, chuck. *fiche-moi la paix,* leave me alone. ~ *par terre,* to knock over, drop. ~ *en l'air,* to chuck up *P;* mess up. ~ *le camp,* to clear off. ~ *à la porte,* to chuck out *P. va te faire fiche! P** get lost! *P**. **se** ~ **de qn,** to make fun of s.o. **se** ~ **de qch,** not to care a damn about sth. *je m'en fiche* [*pas mal*], I couldn't care less. **se** ~ **dedans,** to make a mistake, boob *P.*
fichier (fiʃje) *m,* card index.
fichtre (fiʃtr) *i,* good gracious!, gosh!
fichu[1] (fiʃy) *m,* [head]scarf. **fichu**[2], **e** *P* (fiʃy) *a,* (*before n.*) darned *P;* rotten, lousy *P;* a heck of a *P;* (*after n.*) done for; rigged out *P,* got up *P. mal* ~, out of sorts.
fictif, ive† (fiktif, iv) *a,* fictitious; imaginary.

fiction (sjɔ̃) *f,* fiction; invention.
fidèle† (fidɛl) *a,* (*gen.*) faithful; loyal, true; reliable, accurate (*watch, memory*). ¶ *n,* (*Rel.*) believer. *les ~s,* the faithful; the congregation. **fidélité** (delite) *f,* fidelity; faithfulness; loyalty; reliability.
fief (fjɛf) *m,* (*Hist.*) fief; (*fig.*) preserve; (*Pol.*) stronghold. **fieffé, e** (fe) *a,* arrant, out-&-out.
fiel (fjɛl) *m,* (*lit., fig.*) gall; rancour. **fielleux, euse** (lø, øz) *a,* rancorous.
fiente (fjɑ̃t) *f,* [bird] droppings.
fier[1] **(se)** (fje) *v.pr,* **se ~ à,** to trust (*pers.*); rely on.
fier[2], **ère†** (fjɛr) *a,* proud (*de,* of); proud, haughty; downright, out & out. *faire le ~,* to be aloof, stuck-up *P.* **fierté** (fjɛrte) *f,* pride; haughtiness.
fièvre (fjɛvr) *f,* fever, temperature; (*fig.*) heat, excitement; feverish desire. *~ aphteuse* (aftøz), foot-&-mouth disease. **fiévreux, euse†** (evrø, øz) *a,* feverish. ¶ *n,* fever case (*pers.*).
fifre (fifr) *m,* fife; fife player.
figé, e (fiʒe) *a,* stiff, rigid; set, fixed (*smile*). **figer** (ʒe) *v.t.* & **se ~,** to congeal; coagulate; set; freeze (*pers., smile*).
figue (fig) *f,* fig. *~ de Barbarie,* prickly pear. **figuier** (gje) *m,* fig tree.
figurant, e (figyrɑ̃, ɑ̃t) *n,* (*Theat.*) walk-on; (*Cine.*) extra; cipher; stooge. **figuratif, ive†** (ratif, iv) *a,* (*Art*) representational. **figure** (gyr) *f,* face (*human*); (*Hist., Dance, Math., Skating*) figure; image; diagram. *~s* court cards. *faire ~ de génie,* to be looked on as a genius. *faire bonne ~,* to make a good impression. *faire piètre ~,* to cut a sorry figure. *~ de proue,* figurehead; (*fig.*) key figure. **figuré, e** (gyre) *a,* figurative (*sense*). *au ~,* (*used*) figuratively. **figurer** (re) *v.t,* to represent. ¶ *v.i,* to appear. **se ~,** to imagine, picture to o.s. *figurez-vous* [*que*], just imagine, believe it or not. **figurine** (rin) *f,* figurine.
fil (fil) *m,* thread; yarn; string (*puppet*); (*Elec.*) wire; [cutting] edge; grain (*wood*); linen; thread (*thoughts*); (*Tel.*) line. *avoir qn au bout du ~,* to have s.o on the line. *coup de ~,* phone call. *le ~ de l'eau,* the current. *~ de fer,* wire. *~ à linge,* clothes line. *~ à plomb,* plumb line. *~s de la Vierge,* gossamer. **filament** (lamɑ̃) *m,* filament; thread. **filandreux, euse** (lɑ̃drø, øz) *a,* stringy (*meat*); long-winded (*speech*). **filant, e** (lɑ̃, ɑ̃t) *a,* viscous (*liquid*); shooting (*star*). **filasse** (las) *f,* tow (*flax, hemp*). **filature** (latyr) *f,* spinning; spinning mill; shadowing (*a pers.*).
file (fil) *f,* file, line; (*Mot.*) lane. *~* [*d'attente*], queue. *prendre la ~,* to join the queue. *se ranger en ~,* to line up. *en ~ indienne,* in single file. *à la ~,* one after the other. **filer** (le) *v.t,* to spin; pay out (*cable*); spin out; draw out, hold (*note*); shadow (*pers.*); ladder (*tights*); (*P give*) slip (*money*); land (*blow*). ¶ *v.i,* (*liquid*) to run; (*lamp*) smoke; (*time, train*) fly by; (*pers.*) slip away, make off. *il faut que je file!* I must fly! *~ à l'anglaise,* to take French leave. *~ doux,* to tread carefully (*avec qn,* with s.o).
filet (filɛ) *m,* thread; trickle (*water*); streak (*light*); fillet (*meat, fish*); net; snare. *~* [*à bagages*], luggage rack. *~ de pêche,* fishing net. *~ à provisions,* string bag. **fileter** (lte) *v.t,* to thread (*screw*).
filial, e† (filjal) *a,* filial. ¶ *f,* subsidiary [company].
filière (filjɛr) *f,* (*Adm.*) [usual] channels; path (*career*). *suivre la ~,* to work one's way up.
filigrane (filigran) *m,* filigree [work]; watermark (*paper*).
fille (fij) *f,* daughter. [*jeune*] *~,* girl; (*pej.*) prostitute. *brave ~,* nice girl. *vieille ~,* old maid. *rester ~ O,* to remain unmarried. *~ publique,* prostitute. *~ de ferme,* farm girl. *~ d'honneur,* maid of honour. *~-mère,* unmarried mother. **fillette** (fijɛt) *f,* little girl. **filleul, e** (fijœl) *n,* godchild, godson, god-daughter.
film (film) *m,* film (*material*); film, picture, *Am,* movie. **filmer** (me) *v.t,* to film; shoot (*scene*).
filon (filɔ̃) *m,* vein, seam (*ore &c*); (*fig.*) gold mine; cushy job *P. trouver le ~,* to strike it rich.
filou *P* (filu) *m,* crook; swindler; rascal (*child*). **~ter** *P* (te) *v.t,* to pinch *P;* cheat.
fils (fis) *m,* son. *M. Lucas ~,* Mr Lucas junior. *le ~ L.,* the L. boy. *~ de famille,* young man of means. *~ de ses œuvres,* self-made man. (*pej.*) *~ à papa,* daddy's boy.
filtrage (filtraʒ) *m,* filtration; screening. **filtre** (tr) *m,* (*gen.*) filter; filter tip (*cigarette*). [*café-*]*~,* [filter] coffee. **filtrer** (tre) *v.t,* to filter; screen. ¶ *v.i,* to filter *or* seep through.
fin[1] (fɛ̃) *f,* end. *~ mai,* at the end of May. *à la ~,* eventually, in the end. *en ~ de compte,* in the end. *prendre ~,* to come to an end. *mettre ~ à,* to put an end to. *tirer à sa ~,* to draw to a close. end, death; aim, purpose, object. *parvenir à ses ~s,* to achieve one's ends.
fin[2], **e** (fɛ̃, in) *a,* fine (*thread*); thin (*paper*); slim, slender; sharp (*blade*); pointed; fine, high-class, choice; keen, sharp (*sight*); subtle, smart. *jouer au plus ~,* to try to outwit s.o. (*before n.*) expert: *~ gourmet,* epicure; *~ tireur,* crack shot. extreme: *au ~ fond de,* in the depths of; *le ~ mot de l'affaire,* the truth of the matter. ¶ *f,* liqueur brandy.
final, e† (final) *a,* final. ¶ *m,* (*Mus.*) finale. ¶ *f,* (*Sport*) final. **finalité** (lite) *f,* finality.
finance (finɑ̃s) *f,* finance. *~s,* finances. *les F~s* ≏ the Treasury. **~ment** (smɑ̃) *m,* financing. **financer** (nɑ̃se) *v.i,* to finance. **financier, ère†** (sje, ɛr) *a,* financial. ¶ *m,* financier.

finasser *P* (finase) *v.i*, to use trickery.
finaud, e (fino, od) *a*, wily. ¶ *n*, wily bird.
finement (finmɑ̃) *ad*, finely; shrewdly. **finesse** (nɛs) *f*, fineness &c (*V* **fin**[2]). ~*s*, finer points.
fini, e (fini) *a*, finished; over; out-&-out (*crook*); finite. ¶ *m*, finish. **finir** (nir) *v.t. & i*, to finish, end. ~ *de parler*, to stop talking. ~ *mal*, (*pers.*) to come to a bad end. ~ *par faire*, to end up by doing. *en* ~ *avec*, to have done with, put an end to. *ça n'en finit pas*, there's no end to it.
Finlande (la) (fɛ̃lɑ̃d), Finland. **finnois, e** (finwa, az) & **finlandais, e** (fɛ̃lɑ̃dɛ, ɛz) *a*, Finnish. **F**~, **e**, *n*, Finn. *le finnois*, Finnish (*language*).
fiole (fjɔl) *f*, phial; (*P face*) mug *P*.
fioriture (fjɔrityr) *f*, flourish.
firmament (firmamɑ̃) *m*, firmament.
fisc (fisk) *m*, ≏ Inland Revenue. ~**al, e** (kal) *a*, fiscal, tax (*year*). ~**alité** (lite) *f*, tax system; taxation.
fissure (fisyr) *f*, fissure, crack.
fiston *P* (fistɔ̃) *m*, son, sonny.
fixation (fiksasjɔ̃) *f*, (*Phot.*) fixing; (*Psych. &c*) fixation; fastening; (*Ski*) binding. **fixateur** (tœr) *m*, (*Phot.*) fixer; (*Art*) fixative spray. **fixe**† (fiks) *a*, fixed; steady; intent (*gaze*); fast (*colour*). ¶ *m*, fixed salary. **fixer** (kse) *v.t*, (*gen.*) to fix; fasten, rivet (*gaze*); set, settle (*date*). ~ *qn*, to stare at s.o; brief s.o, fill s.o in *P* (*sur*, on). **se** ~, to settle (*in a place*). **fixité** (ksite) *f*, fixity; steadiness.
flac (flak) *i*, splash!
flacon (flakɔ̃) *m*, [small] bottle; (*Chem.*) flask.
flageller (flaʒɛle) *v.t*, to scourge, flog.
flageoler (flaʒɔle) *v.i*, to tremble, quake. **flageolet** (lɛ) *m*, flageolet (*Mus. & bean*).
flagorner (flagɔrne) *v.t*, to fawn on, toady to.
flagrant, e (flagrɑ̃, ɑ̃t) *a*, flagrant, glaring. *pris en* ~ *délit*, caught red-handed.
flair (flɛr) *m*, sense of smell, nose (*dog*); intuition. **flairer** (flɛre) *v.t*, (*dog*) to sniff [at]; scent (*game*); (*fig.*) scent, sense.
flamand, e (flamɑ̃, ɑ̃d) *a. &* (*language*) *m*, Flemish. **F**~, *n*, Fleming (*pers.*).
flamant (flamɑ̃) *m*, flamingo.
flambant (flɑ̃bɑ̃) *ad*, ~ *neuf*, brand new. **flambeau** (bo) *m*, torch; candlestick. **flambé, e** *P* (be) *a*, done for, ruined. **flambée** (be) *f*, quick blaze; (*fig.*) flare-up. **flamber** (be) *v.i*, to flame, blaze. ¶ *v.t*, to singe; sterilize (*needle*); (*Cook.*) flambé. **flamboyer** (bwaje) *v.i*, to blaze; flame; flash.
flamme (flam) *f*, flame; (*fig.*) fire, ardour, passion; (*liter.*) love; pennant, pennon. **flammèche** (flamɛʃ) *f*, [flying] spark.
flan (flɑ̃) *m*, custard tart.
flanc (flɑ̃) *m*, side, flank. *mettre qn sur le* ~, to exhaust s.o. *tirer au* ~ *P*, to swing the lead *P*.
flancher *P* (flɑ̃ʃe) *v.i*, to give way; pack in *P*.
Flandre (la) (flɑ̃dr) & **les F**~**s**, Flanders.
flanelle (flanɛl) *f*, flannel.
flâner (flɑne) *v.i*, to stroll; saunter; lounge about. **flânerie** (nri) *f*, stroll; strolling; sauntering &c. **flâneur, euse** (nœr, øz) *n*, stroller; idler.
flanquer (flɑ̃ke) *v.t*, to flank; (*P*) to fling, chuck *P*. ~ *qn à la porte*, to chuck s.o out. ~ *une claque à qn*, to clout s.o *P*.
flapi, e (flapi) *a*, dead-beat.
flaque (flak) *f*, pool (*blood &c*). ~ *d'eau*, puddle.
flash (flaʃ) *m*, (*Phot.*) flash; newsflash.
flasque (flask) *a*, flabby; limp (*pers.*).
flatter (flate) *v.t*, to flatter; pander to, humour; delight (*senses*); stroke, pat (*animal*). *se* ~ *de qch, de faire*, to pride o.s on sth, on doing. **flatterie** (tri) *f*, flattery. **flatteur, euse** (tœr, øz) *a*, flattering. ¶ *n*, flatterer.
flatulence (flatylɑ̃s) *f*, flatulence, wind.
fléau (fleo) *m*, flail; scourge, curse; plague, bane; beam (*scale*).
flèche (flɛʃ) *f*, arrow, shaft; spire; jib (*crane*); beam (*plough*); pole (*cart*). ~ *du Parthe*, Parthian shot. *monter en* ~, (*fig.*) to soar, rocket. **flécher** (e) *v.t*, to mark with arrows. **fléchette** (fleʃɛt) *f*, dart.
fléchir (fleʃir) *v.t*, to bend, flex; sway (*pers.*); calm (*anger*). ¶ *v.i*, to bend; sag; yield, give way; (*energy*) flag; (*number, price*) fall, drop. **fléchissement** (ʃismɑ̃) *m*, bending &c.
flegmatique† (flɛgmatik) *a*, phlegmatic. **flegme** (flɛgm) *m*, phlegm, composure.
flemme *P* (flɛm) *f*, laziness. *j'ai la* ~ *de jouer*, I can't be bothered to play. **flemmard, e** *P* (flɛmar, ard) *a*, bone idle. ¶ *n*, lazybones *P*.
flétan (fletɑ̃) *m*, halibut.
flétrir (fletrir) *v.t*, to fade, wither; condemn (*pers., act*).
fleur (flœr) *f*, flower; blossom; bloom. *en* ~[*s*], in flower &c. ~*s des champs*, wild flowers. (*fig.*) *la* ~ *de*, the flower *or* pick of. *la* ~ *de l'âge*, the prime of life. *comme une* ~, easily, without difficulty. *à* ~ *d'eau, de terre*, at water, ground level. **fleurer** (flœrɛ) *v.i*, to smell [of].
fleuret (flœre) *m*, (*Fenc.*) foil.
fleuri, e (flœri) *a*, in bloom; flowery; florid. **fleurir** (rir) *v.i*, to flower, blossom, bloom; flourish. ¶ *v.t*, to decorate with flowers. **fleuriste** (rist) *n*, florist.
fleuve (flœv) *m*, river (*large*).
flexible (flɛksibl) *a*, flexible, pliable; adaptable (*pers.*). **flexion** (ksjɔ̃) *f*, flexion; bending; (*Gram.*) inflection.
flibustier (flibystje) *m*, freebooter.
flic *P* (flik) *m*, cop *P*.
flic flac (flikflak) *i*, splash!; smack! (*slap*).
flirt (flœrt) *m*, flirtation; boyfriend, girlfriend. **flirter** (te) *v.i*, to flirt (*avec*, with).
floc (flɔk) *m*, thud; splash.
flocon (flɔkɔ̃) *m*, flake (*snow*); tuft (*wool*); fleck

(*spray*). ~**neux, euse** (kɔnø, øz) *a,* fluffy, fleecy.
floraison (flɔrɛzɔ̃) *f,* (*lit., fig.*) flowering, blossoming. **floral, e** (ral) *a,* floral; flower (*show*). **floralies** (li) *f.pl,* flower show. **flore** (flɔr) *f,* flora.
Floride (la) (flɔrid), Florida.
florissant, e (flɔrisɑ̃, ɑ̃t) *a,* flourishing, thriving; blooming (*health*).
flot (flo) *m, les ~s,* the waves. *le ~,* the floodtide; (*fig.*) flood, stream. *à ~,* afloat; (*fig.*) on an even keel. *à [grands] ~s,* in torrents. *entrer à ~s,* (*light*) to stream in. **flottage** (flɔtaʒ) *m,* floating (*lumber*), rafting. **flottaison** (tɛzɔ̃) *f: ligne de ~,* waterline. **flottant, e** (tɑ̃, ɑ̃t) *a,* loose, flowing (*dress*); fluctuating; wavering. **flotte** (flɔt) *f,* fleet; float; (*P*) rain; water. **flottement** (tmɑ̃) *m,* swaying; wavering; unevenness (*work*). **flotter** (te) *v.i,* (*gen.*) to float; (*scent*) hang; (*thoughts*) drift; (*smile*) hover; (*clothes*) hang loose; (*pers.*) waver. **flotteur** (tœr) *m,* float; ballcock. **flottille** (tij) *f,* flotilla.
flou, e (flu) *a,* blurred, hazy; woolly, vague; loose (*dress*). ¶ *m,* blurredness, haziness &c.
fluctuation (flyktɥasjɔ̃) *f,* fluctuation.
fluet, te (flyɛ, ɛt) *a,* slender; thin (*voice*).
fluide (flyid) *a,* fluid; free-flowing (*traffic*). ¶ *m,* fluid. **fluidité** (dite) *f,* fluidity.
fluor (flyɔr) *m,* fluorine. **fluorescent, e** (ɔrɛsɑ̃, ɑ̃t) *a,* fluorescent.
flûte (flyt) *f,* flute; flute [glass]; long French loaf. *petite ~,* piccolo. *~ de Pan,* Pan pipes. ¶ *i, ~!* dash it! **flûtiste** (tist) *n,* flautist.
fluvial, e (flyvjal) *a,* river (*police*); fluvial.
flux (fly) *m,* floodtide; (*fig.*) flood; flow (*blood*); (*Phys.*) flux. *le ~ & le reflux,* the ebb & flow. **fluxion** (ksjɔ̃) *f,* swelling (*face*).
foc (fɔk) *m,* jib (*sail*).
focal, e (fɔkal) *a,* focal. ¶ *f,* f. distance.
fœtus (fetys) *m,* foetus.
foi (fwa) *f,* faith, trust; [pledged] word. *digne de ~,* trustworthy. *avoir ~ en qn,* to have faith in s.o. *ajouter ~ à,* to believe (*report*). *ma ~,* well. *ma ~ oui,* yes indeed.
foie (fwa) *m,* (*Anat.*) liver.
foin (fwɛ̃) *m. oft. pl,* hay.
foire (fwar) *f,* fair, market; funfair; (*P*) bedlam. *faire la ~ P,* to go on a binge *P.* **foirer** *P* (re) *v.i,* to fail, go wrong.
fois (fwa) *f,* time. *une ~ pour toutes,* once & for all. *2 ~ par jour,* twice a day. *3 ~ plus de sel,* 3 times as much salt. *à la ~ maigre & fort,* both thin & strong. *des ~ P,* sometimes. *une ~ couché il..,* once in bed he...
foison (fwazɔ̃) *f: à ~,* in abundance. ~**ner** (zɔne) *v.i,* to abound; teem (*de,* with).
folâtre (fɔlɑtr) *a,* playful. **folâtrer** (lɑtre) *v.i,* to play about, romp, frolic.
folichon, ne (fɔliʃɔ̃, ɔn) *a,* entertaining. *pas très ~,* not much fun.
folie (fɔli) *f,* madness; folly; passion; extravagance. *~ furieuse,* (*lit., fig.*) raving madness. *la ~ de la musique,* a passion for music. *la ~ des grandeurs,* delusions of grandeur. *aimer qn à la ~,* to be madly in love with s.o. *faire des ~s,* to act foolishly; be wildly extravagant.
folklore (fɔlklɔr) *m,* folklore. **folklorique** (lɔrik) *a,* folk (*dance*). **folk song** (sɔ̃g) *m,* folk music.
follement (fɔlmɑ̃) *ad,* madly, wildly.
fomenter (fɔmɑ̃te) *v.t,* (*lit., fig.*) to foment, stir up.
foncé, e (fɔ̃se) *a,* dark, deep (*colour*). **foncer** (se) *v.t,* to sink (*well*); make darker (*colour*). ¶ *v.i,* to rush, charge (*sur,* at).
foncier, ère† (fɔ̃sje, ɛr) *a,* fundamental, basic; landed (*property*); land (*tax*).
fonction (fɔ̃ksjɔ̃) *f,* (*Math., gen.*) function. *faire ~ de,* to act as (*s.o, sth*). office, post. *~s,* duties. *entrer en ~s,* to take up one's post. *la ~ publique,* the public service. *en ~ de,* according to. ~**naire** (ɔnɛr) *n,* civil servant; state *or* local authority employee; official. ~**nel, le** (nɛl) *a,* functional. ~**ner** (ne) *v.i,* to work, function, run, operate. ~**nement** (mɑ̃) *m,* working &c. *en bon état de ~,* in good working order.
fond (fɔ̃) *m,* bottom; seat (*chair, trousers*); crown (*hat*); back (*drawer, hall*); far end (*room*). *au ~ de,* at the bottom of &c. (*fig: depths*) *du ~ du cœur,* (*thank*) from the bottom of one's heart. core, heart, substance (*argument*); basis (*thoughts*); (*Liter.*) content; (*Art, fig.*) background. *à ~,* (*study*) thoroughly, in depth; (*screw*) right home. *à ~ de train,* at full speed. *au ~, dans le ~,* in fact, really. *de ~ en comble,* from top to bottom. *de ~,* basic (*work*); (*Sport*) long-distance; cross-country (*skiing*). *article de ~,* background article; feature article. *faire ~ sur,* to rely on. *~ d'artichaut,* artichoke heart. *~ de teint,* foundation (*make-up*).
fondamental, e† (fɔ̃damɑ̃tal) *a,* fundamental, basic.
fondateur, trice (fɔ̃datœr, tris) *n,* founder. **fondation** (sjɔ̃) *f,* (*gen.*) foundation. *~s,* (*Build.*) foundations. **fondé, e** (de) *a,* founded; well-f. *mal ~,* ill-founded. ¶ *m, ~* **de pouvoir,** (*Law*) authorized representative; senior executive (*bank*). **fondement** (fɔ̃dmɑ̃) *m,* foundation. *sans ~,* groundless. **fonder** (de) *v.t,* to found; base. **se ~ sur,** to rely on, go on; (*theory*) be based on.
fonderie (fɔ̃dri) *f,* foundry; smelting works. **fondeur** (dœr) *m,* founder (*metal*).
fondre (fɔ̃dr) *v.t,* to melt; smelt; cast, found; fuse (*en,* into); merge, blend. ¶ *v.i,* to melt, dissolve; (*anger*) melt away. *~ en larmes,* to burst into tears. *~ sur,* to swoop down on.

fondrière (fɔ̃driɛr) *f,* pothole, rut (*road*).
fonds (fɔ̃) *m,* (*lit., fig.*) fund; stock; collection. ~ [*de commerce*], business. ~ *de terre,* land. (*Fin.*) ~, money; funds; capital. ~ *publics,* public funds. *être en* ~, to be in funds. ~ *de roulement,* working capital.
fondu, e (fɔ̃dy) *a,* melted; molten; hazy, blurred. ¶ *f,* (*Cook.*) fondue.
fontaine (fɔ̃tɛn) *f,* spring; fountain.
fonte (fɔ̃t) *f,* melting; smelting; casting, founding. ~ *des neiges,* thaw. cast iron; (*Typ.*) fount.
fonts (fɔ̃) *m.pl:* ~ *baptismaux,* font.
football (futbol) (*P abb:* **foot**) *m,* football, soccer. *jouer au* ~, to play f.
footing (futiŋ) *m: faire du* ~, to go jogging.
for (fɔr) *m:* ~ *intérieur,* heart of hearts.
forage (fɔraʒ) *m,* boring, drilling.
forain, e (fɔrɛ̃, ɛn) *a,* travelling; showground. ¶ *m,* fairground showman. [*marchand*] ~, stallholder; market trader.
forban (fɔrbɑ̃) *m,* (*Hist.*) pirate; (*fig.*) shark.
forçat (fɔrsa) *m,* convict; (*fig.*) slave.
force (fɔrs) *f,* (*&* ~*s*) strength (*physical, moral*); force (*gravity &c*). *la* ~ *brutale,* brute f. *la* ~ *des choses,* f. of circumstances. (*Mil.*) strength; force. ~*s,* forces. *en* ~, in force. *de première* ~ *en,* first-class at. *être de* ~ *à faire,* to be capable of doing. *de* ~, (*enter*) by fórce. *à* ~ *de faire,* by dint of doing, *à toute* ~, at all costs. ~ *lui fut de revenir,* he was forced tc return. (*Naut.*) *faire* ~ *de voiles,* to crowd on sail. ¶ *ad,* many. ~ *d'âme,* fortitude. ~ *de frappe,* strike force. ~ *majeure,* circumstances beyond one's control. *les* ~*s de l'ordre,* the police.
forcé, e (fɔrse) *a,* forced; inevitable. ~**ment** (mɑ̃) *ad,* inevitably. *pas* ~, not necessarily.
forcené, e (fɔrsəne) *a,* deranged; frenzied (*work*). ¶ *m,* maniac.
forceps (fɔrsɛps) *m,* obstetrical forceps.
forcer (fɔrse) *v.t,* to force (*door, pace, plant*); compel (*respect*). ~ *qn,* to force s.o (*à qch,* into sth; *à faire,* to do). run down (*stag*); track down; overcome (*enemy*). ¶ *v.i,* to overdo it, to force it. *se* ~, to force o.s (*à, pour faire,* to do). **forcing** (siŋ) *m,* (*Box.*) pressure.
forer (fɔre) *v.t,* to bore, drill.
forestier, ère (fɔrɛstje, ɛr) *a,* forest (*region*). *exploitation* ~*ère,* forestry. ¶ *m,* forester.
foret (fɔrɛ) *m,* drill.
forêt (fɔrɛ) *f,* forest.
foreuse (fɔrøz) *f,* drill (*well &c*).
forfait (fɔrfɛ) *m,* fixed price; agreed sum. ~-*vacances,* package holiday. (*Sport*) *déclarer* ~, to scratch, withdraw. (*liter.*) crime. ~**aire** (tɛr) *a,* standard, inclusive (*price*).
forfanterie (fɔrfɑ̃tri) *f,* bragging.
forge (fɔrʒ) *f,* forge; smithy. ~*s,* ironworks.
forger (ʒe) *v.t,* to forge (*metal*); mould (*character*); fabricate (*excuse*); coin (*word*). *forgé de toutes pièces,* completely fabricated. **se** ~, to create, form (*ideal*). **forgeron** (ʒərɔ̃) *m,* blacksmith.
formaliser (se) (fɔrmalize) *v.pr,* to take offence (*de,* at). **formaliste** (list) *a,* formal, punctilious. **formalité** (te) *f,* (*gen.*) formality.
format (fɔrma) *m,* format. **formation** (sjɔ̃) *f,* (*gen.*) formation; training; education; (*Mus., Pol.*) group. **forme** (fɔrm) *f,* form, shape. *en* ~ *de poire,* pear-shaped. *prendre* ~, to take shape. form, type; (*Art, Law &c*) form. *de pure* ~, purely formal. last (*shoemaker*). *les* ~*s,* the proprieties. (*health*) *en* ~, fit. *en grande* ~, on peak form. **formel, le**† (mɛl) *a,* positive; categorical; definite. **former** (me) *v.t,* to form (*idea, group, circle*); train (*pers.*) develop (*character, taste*).
formidable† (fɔrmidabl) *a,* enormous; stupendous; (*P*) great *P,* terrific *P,* fantastic *P;* incredible.
formulaire (fɔrmylɛr) *m,* form. **formule** (myl) *f,* formula; form of words; form; method, system. **formuler** (le) *v.t,* to formulate; set out; express.
fornication (fɔrnikasjɔ̃) *f,* fornication.
fort, e (fɔr, ɔrt) *a,* (*gen.*) strong; stout (*pers., legs*); loud (*noise*); heavy (*cold, rain*); big, great (*difference, sum*); steep (*slope*); steadfast, stalwart. ~ *en,* good at, clever at. *elle se fait* ~ *de réussir,* she feels sure of succeeding. *c'est plus* ~ *que moi,* I can't help it. *c'est trop* ~*!* that's too much! ¶ *ad,* (*hit*) hard; (*shout*) loudly; very; very much. ~ *avant dans la nuit,* far into the night. ¶ *m,* (the) strong (*pers.*); market porter; strong point, forte. *avoir* ~ *à faire,* to have difficulty. *au* ~ *de,* in the thick of (*battle*); depths of (*winter*); at the height of (*summer*). (*Mil.*) fort. ~**ement** (təmɑ̃) *ad,* strongly; intensely; (*hit*) hard.
forteresse (fɔrtərɛs) *f,* fortress, stronghold.
fortifiant, e (fɔrtifjɑ̃, ɑ̃t) *a,* invigorating, bracing. ¶ *m,* tonic. **fortification** (fikasjɔ̃) *f,* fortification. **fortifier** (fje) *v.t,* to strengthen, fortify.
fortuit, e (fɔrtɥi, it) *a,* fortuitous, chance. ~**ement** (təmɑ̃) *ad,* fortuitously, by chance.
fortune (fɔrtyn) *f,* luck, chance; fortune (*riches*). *faire* ~, to make one's f. *chercher* ~, to seek one's f. *dîner à la* ~ *du pot,* to take pot luck. **de** ~, makeshift; chance (*companion*). **fortuné, e** (ne) *a,* fortunate, lucky; well-to-do.
forum (fɔrɔm) *m,* forum.
fosse (fos) *f,* pit (*orchestra &c*); grave; deep (*ocean*); (*Sport*) [sand]pit. ~ *d'aisances,* cesspool. (*lit., fig.*) ~ *aux lions,* lions' den. ~ *septique,* septic tank.
fossé (fose) *m,* ditch; (*fig.*) gap, gulf. (*fig.*) *sauter le* ~, to take the plunge. **fossette**

(fosɛt) *f*, dimple.
fossile (fosil) *a. & m*, fossil.
fossoyeur (foswajœr) *m*, grave digger.
fou, fol (*before m. starting with a vowel or 'h*), **folle** (fu, fɔl) *a*, mad, insane; crazy, frantic. ~ *à lier*, raving mad. ~ *d'amour*, madly in love. *avoir le ~ rire*, to have the giggles. (*P*) tremendous, enormous, fantastic *P* (*success &c*). *un monde ~*, an enormous crowd. *un argent ~*, pots of money *P*. *c'est ~ ce qu'il court vite*, he runs incredibly fast. erratic (*compass*); stray (*hair*); runaway (*car, horse*). ¶ *n*, madman, -woman, lunatic. ¶ *m*, fool; (*Hist.*) jester; (*Chess*) bishop; gannet (*bird*).
foudre (fudr) *f*, lightning; (*fig., Myth.*) thunderbolt. (*fig.*) ~*s*, wrath. *frappé par la ~*, struck by lightning. *coup de ~*, love at first sight. **foudroyant, e** (drwajɑ̃, ɑ̃t) *a*, lightning (*attack*); stunning (*success*); devastating (*news*). **foudroyer** (je) *v.t*, (*lightning*) to strike, blast; (*fig.*) strike down. ~ *du regard*, to look daggers at. *foudroyé*, thunderstruck.
fouet (fwɛ) *m*, whip; whisk (*egg*). *le ~*, a whipping. **fouetter** (te) *v.t*, to whip; flog; (*rain*) lash; (*Cook.*) whisk; (*fig.*) whip up, stir.
fougère (fuʒɛr) *f*, fern; bracken.
fougue (fug) *f*, fire, spirit, ardour. **fougueux, euse**† (gø, øz) *a*, fiery, spirited; impetuous; mettlesome (*horse*).
fouille (fuj) *f*, search. ~*s*, excavations. **fouiller** (fuje) *v.t*, to search (*pers., house*); frisk; comb (*area*); dig; excavate; (*animal*) burrow in[to]; (*fig.*) delve into. ¶ *v.i*, ~ *dans*, to rummage in, grope in. **se ~**, to go through one's pockets. **fouillis** (ji) *m*, jumble; muddle, mess. *en ~*, in a mess.
fouine (fwin) *f*, (*Zool.*) stone marten. *à figure de ~*, weaselfaced. **fouiner** (ne) *v.i*, to nose *or* ferret about. **fouineur, euse** (nœr, øz) *a*, prying, nosey *P*. ¶ *n*, nosey parker *P*.
fouir (fwir) *v.t*, to dig.
foulard (fular) *m*, [head]scarf.
foule (ful) *f*, crowd, throng; (*pej.*) mob. *une ~ de*, masses of (*ideas*). *la ~*, the masses.
fouler (fule) *v.t*, to press; tread (*grapes, soil*); full (*cloth*). (*fig.*) ~ *aux pieds*, to trample under foot. *se ~ la cheville*, to sprain one's ankle. **foulure** (fulyr) *f*, sprain.
four (fur) *m*, oven; kiln; furnace. ~ *crématoire*, crematorium furnace. *cuire au ~*, to bake; roast. (*Theat.*) flop, fiasco. *faire un ~*, to flop.
fourbe (furb) *a*, deceitful; treacherous. **fourberie** (bəri) *f*, deceit; treachery.
fourbi *P* (furbi) *m*, gear; clutter.
fourbu, e (furby) *a*, exhausted.
fourche (furʃ) *f*, (*Agr.*) fork; pitchfork. *faire une ~*, (*road*) to fork. **fourcher** (ʃe) *v.i*, to fork. **fourchette** (ʃɛt) *f*, fork (*table*); wishbone; frog (*horse*). *avoir un bon coup de ~*, to have a good appetite. **fourchu, e** (ʃy) *a*, forked. *pied ~*, cloven hoof.
fourgon (furgɔ̃) *m*, waggon; [large] van; (*Rly*) van. ~ *à bagages*, luggage van. ~ *de déménagement*, removal van. ~ *mortuaire*, hearse. ~**ner** (gɔne) *v.i*, to poke about. ~**nette** (nɛt) *f*, small van.
fourmi (furmi) *f*, ant. *avoir des ~s*, to have pins & needles. ~**lière** (ljɛr) *f*, ants' nest; anthill; (*fig.*) hive of activity. **fourmiller** (mije) *v.i*, to swarm; teem (*de*, with).
fournaise (furnɛz) *f*, blaze; (*fig.*) oven, furnace. **fourneau** (no) *m*, stove; furnace; bowl (*pipe*). ~ *à gaz*, gas stove. *haut ~*, blast furnace. **fournée** (ne) *f*, (*lit., fig.*) batch.
fourni, e (furni) *a*, thick (*hair, beard*). *bien ~*, well stocked. **fournil** (ni) *m*, bakehouse.
fourniment (furnimɑ̃) *m*, equipment (*solidier's*). **fournir** (nir) *v.t*, to supply, provide (*qch à qn*, s.o with sth); produce (*passport*); give (*example*); put in (*work*); (*Cards*) follow suit (*à trèfle*, in clubs). ~ *qn en viande*, to supply s.o with meat. ¶ *v.i*, ~ **à**, to provide for. *se ~ chez*, to shop at, get supplied by. **fournisseur** (nisœr) *m*, tradesman; supplier; dealer. ~ *de l'armée*, army contractor. **fourniture** (tyr) *f*, supply. ~*s*, supplies, stationery (*office &c*).
fourrage (furaʒ) *m*, fodder. ~ *vert*, silage. **fourrager** (raʒe) *v.i*, to rummage (*dans*, in).
fourré[1] (fure) *m*, thicket. **fourré**[2], **e** (re) *a*, furlined; filled (*sweets*). *chocolats ~s*, chocolate creams.
fourreau (furo) *m*, scabbard, sheath; case; cover (*umbrella*). *jupe ~*, sheath skirt.
fourrer (fure) *v.t*, to thrust, poke, shove; stuff, cram; line [with fur]; (*P*) stick *P*, shove *P* (*dans*, into). ~ *son nez partout*, to poke one's nose into everything. *se ~ qch dans la tête*, to get sth into one's head. **fourre-tout** (rtu) *m*, junk room; glory-hole; holdall. **fourreur** (rœr) *m*, furrier.
fourrière (furjɛr) *f*, pound (*dogs, cars*).
fourrure (furyr) *f*, coat (*animal*); fur.
fourvoyer (furvwaje) *v.t*, to lead astray; mislead. **se ~**, (*lit., fig.*) to go astray.
foutaise *P* (futɛz) *f*, (*& des ~s*) rot, rubbish.
foutre *P oft. P** (futr) *v.t*, *coarser synonym of* **ficher** *& used in the same phrases* (*V* **ficher**). *qu'est-ce qu'il fout?* what the hell's he up to? *P*. *fous-moi la paix! P**. bugger off! *P**. *va te faire ~! P**, get stuffed! *P**. **foutu, e** *P** (ty) *a*, *coarser synonym of* **fichu**[2] *& used in the same phrases* (*V* **fichu**[2]). (*before n.*) bloody [awful] *P**. (*after n.*) done for, buggered *P**. *être mal ~*, to feel lousy *P* or bloody *P**.
fox[-terrier] (fɔkstɛrje) *m*, fox terrier.
foyer (fwaje) *m*, hearth, fireplace; firebox (*boiler*); home; family; hostel (*students*); home (*old people*); club; (*Theat.*) foyer; seat, source (*fire*); (*Opt.*) focus. ~ *des artistes*,

greenroom. ~ *des jeunes,* youth club.
frac (frak) *m,* tail coat.
fracas (frakɑ) *m,* crash; roar; din. **fracasser** (kase) *v.t,* to smash, shatter.
fraction (fraksjɔ̃) *f, (gen., Math.)* fraction; *(Rel.)* breaking *(bread).* ~**naire** (ɔnɛr) *a,* fractional. ~**ner** (ne) *v.t,* to split up, divide.
fracture (fraktyr) *f, (Med.)* fracture. **fracturer** (tyre) *v.t,* to fracture; break.
fragile (fraʒil) *a,* fragile; brittle; frail; flimsy, shaky *(argument). 'attention ~ ',* 'fragile with care'. **fragilité** (lite) *f,* fragility, &c.
fragment (fragmɑ̃) *m,* fragment, piece; snatch *(song).* ~**aire** (tɛr) *a,* fragmentary. ~**er** (te) *v.t,* to break up; split up.
frai (frɛ) *m,* spawn; spawning; fry.
fraîchement (frɛʃmɑ̃) *ad,* freshly, newly; *(greet)* coolly. **fraîcheur** (ʃœr) *f,* freshness; coolness; chilliness; cool *(evening).* **fraîchir** (ʃir) *v.i,* to get cooler; *(wind)* freshen. **frais**[1], **aîche** (frɛ, ɛʃ) *a,* cool *(wind, reception);* fresh *(colours; news, tracks; air, food; troops);* wet *(paint);* recent *(date). ~ & dispos, ~ comme une rose,* fresh as a daisy. *servir ~,* serve chilled. ¶ *ad, il fait ~,* it's cool. *~ rasé,* freshly shaven. *~ débarqué,* newly arrived. *habillé de ~,* freshly changed. ¶ *m, prendre le ~,* to get some fresh air. *tenir au ~,* to keep in the cool.
frais[2] (frɛ) *m.pl,* expenses; cost; costs; charges, fees. *~ de déplacement,* travelling expenses. *~ divers,* sundry expenses. *~ généraux,* overheads. *~ de justice,* [legal] costs. *~ de scolarité,* school fees. *à peu de ~,* cheaply. *se mettre en ~,* to go to great expense *or* trouble. *en être pour ses ~,* to have wasted one's time *or* effort. *rentrer dans ses ~,* to recover one's expenses. *aux ~ de la princesse P,* at the firm's expense, on the house *P.*
fraise (frɛz) *f,* strawberry. *~ des bois,* wild strawberry. *(Tech.)* countersink [bit]; milling-cutter; drill *(dentist); (Hist.)* ruff. **fraiser** (frɛze) *v.t,* to countersink; mill. **fraisier** (zje) *m,* strawberry plant.
framboise (frɑ̃bwaz) *f,* raspberry. **framboisier** (bwazje) *m,* raspberry bush.
franc[1] (frɑ̃) *m,* franc. *ancien ~,* old f. *(100 old f. = 1 new f.)*
franc[2], **anche** (frɑ̃, ɑ̃ʃ) *a,* frank, candid; open, open-hearted; clear, clear-cut *(difference);* clean *(break);* downright *(idiot);* free *(zone). 3 jours ~s,* 3 clear days. *~ de port (inv.),* carriage free; post free. *corps ~,* irregular force. ¶ *ad, (speak)* frankly. *comps:* ~**-bord,** *m, (Naut.)* freeboard. ~**-maçon,** *m,* freemason. ~**-maçonnerie,** *f,* freemasonry. ~**-parler,** *m,* outspokenness. ~**-tireur,** *m, (Mil.)* irregular; *(fig.)* freelance.
français, e (frɑ̃sɛ, ɛz) *a,* French. **F~, e** *n,* Frenchman, -woman. *les F~,* the French. *le ~,* French *(language).*
France (la) (frɑ̃s), France.
Francfort (frɑ̃kfɔr) *m,* Frankfurt.
franchement (frɑ̃ʃmɑ̃) *ad,* frankly, candidly; openly; *(enter)* boldly; *(ask)* straight out; downright, really *(ugly, good).*
franchir (frɑ̃ʃir) *v.t,* to jump over, clear; cross; pass through; cover *(distance);* surmount; overstep *(bounds).* **franchissement** (ʃismɑ̃) *m,* clearing; crossing &c.
franchise (frɑ̃ʃiz) *f,* frankness; openness, candour; exemption *(customs &c); (Insce)* excess. *~ de bagages,* luggage allowance.
franciscain, e (frɑ̃siskɛ̃, ɛn) *n,* Franciscan.
franciser (frɑ̃size) *v.t,* to Frenchify, gallicize.
franco (frɑ̃ko) *ad,* free. *(Com.) ~ [à] bord,* free on board. *~ de port,* carriage paid; postage p. *y aller ~ P,* to go right ahead; come straight to the point.
francophile (frɑ̃kɔfil) *a. & n,* francophile. **francophobe** (fɔb) *a. & n,* francophobe.
frange (frɑ̃ʒ) *f,* fringe. **franger** (frɑ̃ʒe) *v.t,* to fringe *(de,* with).
frangin, e *P* (frɑ̃ʒɛ̃, in) *m,* brother. ¶ *f,* sister.
franquette (à la bonne) (frɑ̃kɛt), simply, without ceremony.
frappant, e (frapɑ̃, ɑ̃t) *a,* striking. **frappe** (frap) *f,* striking *(medal);* stamp; *(Typ.)* typeface; touch *(typist).* **frapper** (pe) *v.t. & i,* to strike, hit. *~ le regard,* to catch the eye. *~ d'une amende,* to impose a fine on. *frappé de panique,* panic-stricken. *~ du pied,* to stamp [one's foot]. *~ [à une porte],* to knock [on a door]. to strike *(medal, coin);* put on ice *(wine);* ice *(coffee).*
frasque (frask) *f,* escapade.
fraternel, le† (fratɛrnɛl) *a,* fraternal, brotherly. **fraterniser** (nize) *v.i,* to fraternize. **fraternité** (te) *f,* fraternity.
fraude (frod) *f,* fraud; cheating *(exam). en ~,* fraudulently. *la ~ fiscale,* tax evasion. *passer qch en ~,* to smuggle sth in. **frauder** (frode) *v.t,* to defraud, cheat. *~ le fisc,* to evade tax. **fraudeur, euse** (dœr, øz) *n,* defrauder; cheat; smuggler; tax evader. **frauduleux, euse†** (dylø, øz) *a,* fraudulent.
frayer (frɛje) *v.t,* to open up, clear *(way, passage). (fig.) ~ une voie,* to pave the way. *se ~ un chemin dans,* to force one's way through. ¶ *v.i, (fish)* to spawn. *~ avec,* to associate with.
frayeur (frɛjœr) *f,* fright.
fredaine (frədɛn) *f,* prank, escapade.
fredonner (frədɔne) *v.i. & t,* to hum *(tune).*
frégate (fregat) *f,* frigate.
frein (frɛ̃) *m,* brake; bit *(horse); (fig.)* curb, check. *mettre un ~ à,* to check, curb. *ronger son frein, (lit., fig.)* to champ at the bit. *sans ~,* unbridled. *~ à main, à pied,* hand-, footbrake. *~ à disques,* disc brake. **freiner** (frɛne) *v.i. & t,* to brake, pull up; *(fig.)* slow

down, hold up, check.
frelater (frəlate) *v.t,* to adulterate.
frêle (frɛl) *a,* frail.
frelon (frəlɔ̃) *m,* hornet.
freluquet (kɛ) *m,* whipper-snapper.
frémir (fremir) *v.i,* (*pers.*) to shudder, quiver, tremble (*de,* with); (*leaves, lips*) quiver, tremble.
frêne (frɛn) *m,* ash [tree].
frénésie (frenezi) *f,* frenzy. **frénétique**† (tik) *a,* frantic, frenzied.
fréquemment (frekamɑ̃) *ad,* frequently. **fréquence** (kɑ̃s) *f,* (*gen., Radio*) frequency.
fréquent, e (frekɑ̃, ɑ̃t) *a,* frequent. ~**ation** (tasjɔ̃) *f,* frequenting; regular association (*de,* with). ~*s,* company. ~**é, e** (te) *a,* crowded, busy (*place*). ~**er** (te) *v.t,* to frequent (*place*); associate with; see a lot of; go around with (*girl*).
frère (frɛr) *m,* brother. (*fig.*) ~*s d'armes,* brothers in arms. *pays* ~*s,* sister countries. (*Rel.*) brother, friar. *mes* ~*s,* brethren. **frérot** *P* (frero) *m,* kid brother *P.*
fresque (frɛsk) *f,* fresco.
fret (frɛ) *m,* freightage; freight, cargo. *prendre à* ~, to charter. **fréter** (frete) *v.t,* to charter; freight (*ship*). **fréteur** (tœr) *m,* [ship]owner.
frétiller (fretije) *v.i,* to wriggle; fidget. ~ *de la queue,* (*dog*) to wag its tail.
fretin (frətɛ̃) *m,* fry (*fish*). (*lit., fig.*) *menu* ~, small fry.
freux (frø) *m,* rook (*bird*).
friable (friabl) *a,* friable, crumbly.
friand, e (friɑ̃, ɑ̃d) *a,* ~ *de,* fond of. ¶ *m,* meat pasty. ~**ise** (ɑ̃diz) *f,* delicacy, titbit.
fric *P* (frik) *m,* dough *P,* lolly *P.*
fric-frac *P* (frikfrak) *m,* burglary.
friche (friʃ) *f,* fallow land. (*lit., fig.*) *être en* ~, to lie fallow.
fricot *P* (friko) *m,* stew; nosh *P.* **fricoter** *P* (kɔte) *v.i,* to stew, cook; (*fig.*) cook up (*scheme*).
friction (friksjɔ̃) *f,* (*gen.*) friction; rub down (*after bath*); scalp massage. ~**ner** (ɔne) *v.t,* to rub.
frigidaire (friʒidɛr) *m,* refrigerator. **frigide** (ʒid) *a,* frigid. **frigidité** (dite) *f,* frigidity. **frigo** *P* (go) *m,* fridge *P.* **frigorifier** (gɔrifje) *v.t,* to refrigerate; (*P pers.*) *être frigorifié,* to be frozen stiff. **frigorifique** (fik) *a,* refrigerator (*van*). *armoire* ~, cold store.
frileux, euse (frilø, øz) *a,* sensitive to cold, chilly (*pers.*).
frime *P* (frim) *f,* sham, pretence; eyewash. *pour la* ~, just for show.
frimousse *P* (frimus) *f,* little face (*child, girl*).
fringale *P* (frɛ̃gal) *f,* raging hunger; craving (*de,* for).
fringant, e (frɛ̃gɑ̃, ɑ̃t) *a,* frisky (*horse*); dashing, smart (*pers.*). **fringuer** *P* (ge) *v.t,* to dress. **fringues** *P* (ɛ̃g) *f.pl,* clothes, togs *P.*
friper (fripe) *v.t,* to crumple, crease. **friperie** (pri) *f,* secondhand clothes [shop]. **fripier, ère** (pje, ɛr) *n,* secondhand clothes dealer.
fripon, ne (fripɔ̃, ɔn) *a,* mischievous, roguish. ¶ *n,* rascal, rogue (*child*); (*O*) knave. ~**nerie** (nri) *f,* prank, piece of mischief.
frire (frir) *v.t. & i.ir,* (*& faire* ~) to fry.
frise (friz) *f,* frieze.
frisé, e (frize) *a,* curly (*hair*); curly-haired. **friser** (ze) *v.t,* to curl. ~ *qn,* to c. s.o's hair. graze, skim; (*fig.*) be within an ace of. ~ *la soixantaine,* to be close on sixty. ¶ *v.i,* to curl; have curly hair. **frisette** (zɛt) *f,* little curl.
frisquet (friskɛ) *a.m,* chilly.
frisson (frisɔ̃) *m,* shiver, shudder, quiver. *ça me donne le* ~, it gives me the shivers. ~**ner** (sɔne) *v.i,* to shiver &c; tremble (*de,* with).
frit, e (fri, it) *a,* fried. ¶ *f,* chip. ~*es,* chips, French fries. **friteuse** (tøz) *f,* chip pan, deep frier. **friture** (tyr) *f,* frying; deep fat; fried fish; (*Tel.*) crackle.
frivole† (frivɔl) *a,* frivolous; trivial. **frivolité** (lite) *f,* frivolity; triviality.
froc (frɔk) *m,* (*Eccl.*) frock, habit; (*P*) trousers, bags *P.*
froid, e† (frwa, ad) *a,* cold; cool. *garder la tête* ~*e,* to keep a cool head. **à** ~, when cold; (*start*) from cold (*car*). *prendre qn à* ~, to catch s.o off guard. ¶ *m,* cold; c. weather; coolness (*manner*). *il fait* ~, it's cold. *il fait un* ~ *de loup, de canard P,* it's bitterly, freezing c. *j'ai* ~, I'm cold. *j'ai* ~ *aux pieds,* my feet are c. *attraper* ~, *prendre* ~, to catch c. **froideur** (dœr) *f,* coldness; coolness.
froisser (frwase) *v.t,* to crumple, crease; offend, hurt (*pers.*). **se** ~, to take offence (*de,* at); strain (*muscle*).
frôlement (frolmɑ̃) *m,* light touch; rustle. **frôler** (le) *v.t,* to graze, brush against; (*fig.*) come very near to.
fromage (frɔmaʒ) *m,* cheese; (*P*) cushy job *P.* ~ *blanc,* soft white cheese. ~ *de chèvre,* goat's milk c. ~ *à la crème,* cream c. ~ *de tête,* brawn. **fromager, ère** (maʒe, ɛr) *a,* cheese. ¶ *n,* c. maker; cheesemonger. ~**rie** (ʒri) *f,* cheese dairy.
froment (frɔmɑ̃) *m,* wheat.
fronce (frɔ̃s) *f,* (*Need.*) gather. **froncer** (se) *v.t,* (*Need.*) to gather. ~ *les sourcils,* to frown, knit one's brows.
fronde (frɔ̃d) *f,* sling; catapult (*toy*). *esprit de* ~, spirit of revolt. **fronder** (frɔ̃de) *v.t,* to satirize. **frondeur, euse** (dœr, øz) *a,* rebellious, recalcitrant.
front (frɔ̃) *m,* forehead; brow; face; (*gen., Mil., Pol.*) front. ~ *de mer,* sea front. *de* ~, (*crash*) head on; frontal (*attack*). *à cinq de* ~, 5 abreast. *le* ~ *haut,* with one's head held high. *faire* ~ *à,* to face *or* stand up to. *avoir le* ~ *de dire,* to have the face *or* effrontery to say.

frontière (frɔ̃tjɛr) *f.* & *a,* frontier, border. **frontalier, ère** (talje, ɛr) *a,* frontier, border.
fronton (frɔ̃tɔ̃) *m,* pediment.
frottement (frɔtmɑ̃) *m,* rubbing; friction. **frotter** (te) *v.t.* & *i,* to rub; strike (*match*); polish (*floor*); box (*ears*). *se ~ les mains,* to rub one's hands. (*fig.*) **se ~ à,** to cross swords with; rub shoulders with. **frottis** (ti) *m,* (*Med.*) smear.
frou-frou (frufru) *m,* rustling, swish.
frousse *P* (frus) *f,* fright. *avoir la ~,* to be scared stiff. **froussard, e** *P* (sar, ard) *n.* (& *a*), coward(ly).
fructifier (fryktifje) *v.i,* (*lit., fig.*) to bear fruit; yield a profit. **fructueux, euse†** (tɥø, øz) *a,* fruitful, profitable.
frugal, e† (frygal) *a,* frugal. **frugalité** (lite) *f,* frugality.
fruit (frɥi) *m,* fruit; piece of f. *des ~s,* some fruit. (*fig.*) fruit, result, benefit. *sans ~,* fruitlessly. *~s de mer,* seafood. **fruité, e** (te) *a,* fruity. **~erie** (tri) *f,* fruit shop. **~ier, ère** (tje, ɛr) *n,* fruiterer, greengrocer. ¶ *a,* fruit (*tree*).
frusques *P* (frysk) *f.pl,* clothes, togs *P.*
fruste (fryst) *a,* coarse, rough (*pers.*).
frustrer (frystre) *v.t,* to deprive; defraud (*de,* of); frustrate; disappoint.
fuchsia (fyksja) *m,* fuchsia.
fuel[-oil] (fjul-ɔjl) *m,* fuel oil.
fugace (fygas) *a,* fleeting. **fugitif, ive** (ʒitif, iv) *a,* fugitive, runaway (*pers.*); fleeting. ¶ *n,* fugitive.
fugue (fyg) *f, faire une ~,* to run away [from home], abscond. (*Mus.*) fugue.
fuir (fɥir) *v.t.ir,* to flee [from], run away from; shun; evade. ¶ *v.i,* to flee, take to flight; run away, escape; (*time*) fly by; (*liquid, tap*) leak. **fuite** (fɥit) *f,* flight; escape; leak[age].
fulgurant, e (fylgyrɑ̃, ɑ̃t) *a,* flashing, blazing; searing (*pain*); lightning (*speed*).
fulminer (fylmine) *v.i,* to rage, storm; fulminate (*contre,* against).
fume-cigarette, *m,* cigarette holder. **fumée** (me) *f,* smoke, steam. *~s,* fumes. *partir en ~,* (*plans*) to go up in smoke. **fumer** (me) *v.i,* (*pers., fire*) to smoke; steam; fume (*rage*). ¶ *v.t,* to smoke (*pipe*); smoke, cure (*food*); manure. *~ comme un pompier,* to smoke like a chimney. **fumerie** (mri) *f,* opium den. **fumet** (mɛ) *m,* bouquet; aroma. **fumeur, euse** (mœr, øz) *n,* smoker. **fumeux, euse** (mø, øz) *a,* smoky; hazy, woolly (*ideas*). **fumier** (mje) *m,* dung, manure; (*P pers.*) shit *P.*
fumiste (fymist) *m,* heating mechanic; shirker (*work*); humbug, phoney *P.* **~rie** (tri) *f,* fraud; humbug; hoax. **fumoir** (mwar) *m,* smoking room.
fumure (fymyr) *f,* manuring; manure.
funambule (fynɑ̃byl) *n,* tightrope walker.
funèbre (fynɛbr) *a,* funeral; funereal, gloomy; dead (*march*). **funérailles** (nerɑj) *f.pl,* funeral. **funéraire** (rɛr) *a,* funeral. *pierre ~,* tombstone.
funeste (fynɛst) *a,* disastrous, harmful, baneful; fateful (*day*); fatal, deadly.
funiculaire (fynikylɛr) *m,* (*Rly*) funicular.
fur (fyr) *m: au ~ & à mesure,* by degrees; as one goes along. *au ~ & à mesure des besoins,* as [& when] required. *au ~ & à mesure que,* as [soon as], as fast as.
furet (fyrɛ) *m,* ferret. **fureter** (rte) *v.i,* to ferret about, pry. **fureteur, euse** (rtœr, øz) *a,* prying, inquisitive.
fureur (fyrœr) *f,* fury, rage. *~ de qch,* passion, mania for sth. *mettre en ~,* to infuriate. *avec ~,* (*love*) passionately. *faire ~,* to be all the rage. **furibond, e** (ribɔ̃, ɔ̃d) *a,* furious, hopping mad *P.* **furie** (ri) *f,* fury; (*Myth.*) Fury. **furieux, euse†** (rjø, øz) *a,* furious (*contre,* with); tremendous.
furoncle (fyrɔ̃kl) *m,* (*Med.*) boil.
furtif, ive† (fyrtif, iv) *a,* furtive, stealthy.
fusain (fyzɛ̃) *m,* spindle tree; charcoal [pencil]; c. drawing.
fuseau (fyzo) *m,* spindle; bobbin (*lace*); [tapered] ski pants. *en ~,* tapered; slender (*legs*). *~ horaire.* time zone.
fusée (fyze) *f,* rocket; fuse (*shell &c*). *~ éclairante,* flare.
fuselage (fyzlaʒ) *m,* fuselage. **fuselé, e** (zle) *a,* spindle-shaped; tapering; slender.
fusible (fyzibl) *m,* (*Elec.*) fuse.
fusil (fyzi) *m,* rifle, gun; gas lighter; steel (*sharpener*). *un bon ~,* a good shot (*pers.*). *~ de chasse à deux coups,* double barrelled shotgun. *~ mitrailleur,* machine g. *~ sous-marin,* spear-gun. **fusilier** (zilje) *m: ~ marin,* marine. **fusillade** (zijad) *f,* gunfire, shooting. **fusiller** (je) *v.t,* to shoot (*execute*); (*P*) smash up.
fusion (fyzjɔ̃) *f,* fusion; melting; blending (*ideas*); (*Com.*) merger. **fusionner** (ɔne) *v.t.* & *i,* to amalgamate, merge.
fustiger (fystiʒe) *v.t,* (*liter.*) to castigate.
fût (fy) *m,* trunk (*tree*); shaft (*column*); stock (*rifle*); cask, barrel.
futaie (fytɛ) *f,* timber-tree forest.
futé, e (fyte) *a,* crafty; sly; sharp.
futile (fytil) *a,* futile; trivial; frivolous (*pers.*). **futilité** (lite) *f,* futility; frivolousness. *~s,* trivialities.
futur, e (fytyr) *a,* future. ¶ *n,* fiancé(e); husband-, wife-to-be. ¶ *m,* (*gen., Gram.*) future. *~ antérieur,* f. perfect.
fuyant, e (fɥijɑ̃, ɑ̃t) *a,* evasive, shifty (*pers., look*); receding (*chin*); (*Art*) vanishing (*lines*); fleeting. **fuyard, e** (jar, ard) *n,* fugitive, runaway.

G

G, g (ʒe) *m, letter,* G, g.
gabardine (gabardin) *f,* gabardine; raincoat.
gabarit (gabari) *m,* size; (*fig.*) calibre; gauge; template.
gâcher (gɑʃe) *v.t,* to spoil; botch, mess up (*job*); waste; mix (*mortar*). **gâchis** (ʃi) *m,* (*wet*) mortar; slush, sludge; (*fig.*) mess.
gadoue (gadu) *f,* sludge; slush; night soil.
gaffe (gaf) *f,* blunder, boob *P;* gaffe; boathook; (*Fish.*) gaff. **gaffer** (fe) *v.i,* to blunder, boob *P;* drop a brick. ¶ *v.t,* to hook; gaff.
gage (gaʒ) *m,* pledge, security. *mettre qch en ~,* to pawn sth. token, proof; forfeit (*game*). *~s,* wages, pay. *à ~s,* paid, hired. **gager** (gaʒe) *v.t,* to guarantee (*loan*). *~ que,* to bet that. **gageure** (ʒyr) *f,* wager; seemingly impossible feat.
gagnant, e (gɑɲɑ̃, ɑ̃t) *a,* winning. ¶ *n,* winner. **gagne-pain** (ɲpɛ̃) *m,* job; livelihood. **gagner** (ɲe) *v.t,* to earn (*money*). *~ sa vie,* to earn one's living. win; gain; catch (*illness*); win over (*pers.*); reach (*place*); (*sleep*) overcome. ¶ *v.i,* to win; gain, be better off; improve. *~ à être connu,* to improve on acquaintance.
gai, e† (ge) *a,* merry, cheerful, gay (*pers.*); bright, cheerful (*colours &c*); merry, tipsy. (*ironic*) *ça va être ~!* that'll be real fun! *~ luron,* cheery fellow. **gaieté** (te) *f,* gaiety; cheerfulness; liveliness; brightness (*colours*). *de ~ de cœur,* lightheartedly.
gaillard, e† (gajar, ard) *a,* strong, vigorous (*pers.*); lively (*step*); bawdy, ribald. ¶ *m,* [*grand*] *~,* strapping fellow. (*P*) fellow, bloke *P. mon ~,* chum, mate *P.* (*Naut.*) *~ d'arrière,* quarter deck. *~ d'avant,* forecastle, fo'c'sle. ¶ *P f,* strapping lass. *~***ise** (diz) *f,* ribaldry; bawdy remark.
gain (gɛ̃) *m,* gain, profit; earnings; winnings; benefit, advantage; winning (*battle, votes*); saving (*time*). *obtenir ~ de cause,* to win one's case.
gaine (gɛn) *f,* sheath; (*Dress*) girdle.
galamment (galamɑ̃) *ad,* courteously, gallantly. **galant, e** (lɑ̃, ɑ̃t) *a,* courteous, gallant (*to women*); flirtatious (*tone*); amorous, romantic. ¶ *m,* suitor. **galanterie** (lɑ̃tri) *f,* gallantry (*to women*); g. remark; love affair.
galaxie (galaksi) *f,* galaxy.
galbe (galb) *m,* [curved] outline. **galbé, e** (be) *a, bien ~,* shapely (*figure*).
gale (gal) *f,* scabies, itch; mange; scab (*sheep*).
galère (galɛr) *f,* (*Hist.*) galley.
galerie (galri) *f,* gallery; arcade; (*Com: Art*) gallery; room (*museum*); (*Min.*) level, gallery. (*Theat.*) *premières, secondes ~s,* dress, upper circle. audience, gallery; (*Mot.*) roof rack. *~ marchande,* shopping arcade.
galérien (galerjɛ̃) *m,* galley slave.
galet (galɛ) *m,* pebble. *~s,* shingle.
galetas (galta) *m,* garret; hovel.
galette (galɛt) *f,* cake (*round, flat*); pancake; ship's biscuit; (*P*) dough *P. ~ des Rois,* Twelfth Night cake.
galeux, euse (galø, øz) *a,* suffering from scabies; mangy; scabby (*sheep*).
galhauban (galobɑ̃) *m,* (*Naut.*) backstay.
galimatias (galimatjɑ) *m,* gibberish.
galion (galjɔ̃) *m,* (*Hist.*) galleon.
Galles (le pays de) (gal), Wales.
gallicisme (galisism) *m,* gallicism.
gallois, e (galwa, az) *a,* Welsh. **G~, e,** *n,* Welshman, -woman. *le ~,* Welsh (*language*).
gallon (galɔ̃) *m,* gallon.
galoche (galɔʃ) *f,* clog.
galon (galɔ̃) *m,* [piece of] braid; (*Mil.*) stripe. *prendre du ~,* to get promoted. *~***ner** (lɔne) *v.t,* to trim with braid.
galop (galo) *m,* gallop. *petit ~,* canter. *grand ~,* [full] gallop. *se mettre au ~,* to break into a g. *au ~,* (*lit., fig.*) at a gallop. *~***ade** (lɔpad) *f,* stampede. *~***er** (lɔpe) *v.i,* (*lit., fig.*) to gallop; (*imagination*) run wild. **galopin** (pɛ̃) *m,* urchin; rascal.
galvaniser (galvanize) *v.t,* (*Tech., fig.*) to galvanize.
galvauder (galvode) *v.t,* to tarnish, sully (*reputation*); debase (*talent*). ¶ *v.i,* to loaf about.
gambade (gɑ̃bad) *f,* leap, caper, gambol. **gambader** (de) *v.i,* to gambol; caper *or* prance about.
Gambie (la) (gɑ̃bi), [the] Gambia.
gambit (gɑ̃bi) *m,* (*Chess*) gambit.
gamelle (gamɛl) *f,* mess tin; billy-can.
gamin, e (gamɛ̃, in) *a,* mischievous, playful; childish. ¶ *n,* kid *P. ~ des rues,* street urchin. *~***erie** (minri) *f,* childishness, playfulness; foolery.
gamme (gam) *f,* (*Mus.*) scale; (*fig.*) gamut, range. *faire des ~s,* to play scales.
Gand (gɑ̃) *m,* Ghent.
gang (gɑ̃g) *m,* gang (*crooks*).
Gange (le) (gɑ̃ʒ), the Ganges.
ganglion (gɑ̃gliɔ̃) *m,* ganglion.
gangrène (gɑ̃grɛn) *f,* gangrene. **gangrené, e** (grəne) *a,* gangrenous; (*fig.*) corrupt.
gangster (gɑ̃gstɛr) *m,* gangster; crook, shark.
gant (gɑ̃) *m,* glove. *~ de toilette,* face flannel. *jeter, relever le ~,* to throw down, take up the gauntlet. *ça me va comme un ~,* (*dress*) it fits me like a glove; (*plan*) it suits me per-

fectly. **ganter (se)** (te) *v.pr,* to put on one's gloves. **ganterie** (tri) *f,* glove trade; g. shop. **gantier, ère** (tje, ɛr) *n,* glover.

garage (garaʒ) *m,* garage. ~ *d'avions,* hangar. ~ *de bicyclettes,* cycle shed. ~ *de canots,* boathouse. **garagiste** (ʒist) *m,* garage owner; g. mechanic.

garant, e (garɑ̃, ɑ̃t) *n,* guarantor; guarantee. *se porter* ~ *de,* to guarantee, vouch for. **garantie** (ti) *f,* (*Com.*) guarantee; security, surety; safeguard. **garantir** (tir) *v.t,* (*gen.*) to guarantee; assure; protect, shield (*de,* from).

garce (gars) *f,* (*pej.*) bitch *P.*

garçon (garsɔ̃) *m,* boy; young man; fellow, chap; bachelor; waiter; [shop] assistant. ~ *boucher,* butcher's assistant, b.'s boy. ~ [*de café*], waiter. ~ *de courses,* messenger; errand boy. ~ *d'étage,* boots (*hotel*). ~ *de ferme,* farm hand. ~ *d'honneur,* best man. ~ *manqué,* tomboy. **garçonnet** (sɔnɛ) *m,* little boy.

garde[1] (gard) *f,* custody, care, charge. *prendre en* ~, to take into one's care. guard. *sous bonne* ~, under guard. *chien de* ~, watch-dog. guard duty. *de* ~, on duty. (*Mil.*) [*corps de*] ~, guard (*group*). (*Med.*) nurse. ~ *de nuit,* night n. ~ *d'enfants,* childminder. hilt (*sword*). ~*s,* wards (*lock*). *être sur ses* ~*s,* to be on one's guard. *prenez* ~ *de* [*ne pas*] *glisser,* take care you don't slip. *prenez* ~ *aux poutres,* mind the beams. *prends* ~*!* watch out! ~**-à-vous,** *m,* (*Mil.*) position of attention.

garde[2] (gard) *m,* guard (*pers.*); keeper; warden; (*Mil.*) guardsman. ~ *champêtre,* rural policeman. ~ *du corps,* bodyguard. ~ *forestier,* forest warden. ~ *des Sceaux* ≃ Lord Chancellor.

garde- (gard) *pref:* ~*-barrière, n,* level crossing keeper. ~*-boue, m,* mudguard. ~*-chasse, m,* game-keeper. ~*-côte, m,* coastguard ship. ~*-feu, m,* fire guard. ~*-fou, m,* hand rail, railing. ~*-malade, n,* home nurse. ~*-manger, m,* pantry, larder; meat safe. ~*-meuble, m,* furniture store. ~*-robe, f,* wardrobe.

gardénia (gardenja) *m,* gardenia.

garder (garde) *v.t,* to guard, look after, mind; keep, retain; protect (*de,* from). ~ *la chambre, le lit,* to stay in one's room, in bed. ~ *qn à déjeuner,* to have s.o stay to lunch. ~ *rancune à qn,* to bear s.o a grudge. *se* ~ *de faire,* to take care not to do. *chasse gardée,* private shooting *or* hunting. **garderie** (dəri) *f,* day nursery. **gardien, ne** (djɛ̃, ɛn) *n,* keeper; caretaker; warden; warder, [prison] officer; attendant (*museum*); (*fig.*) guardian. ~ *de but,* goal keeper. ~ *de stade,* groundsman. ~ *de nuit,* night watchman. ~ *de la paix,* policeman.

gardon (gardɔ̃) *m,* roach (*fish*).

gare[1] (gar) *f,* (*Rly*) station. *entrer en* ~, (*train*) to come in. ~ *maritime,* harbour station. ~ *routière,* haulage depot; coach station. ~ *de triage,* marshalling yard.

gare[2] (gar) *i,* look out!, take care! ~ *à ta tête!* mind your head! ~ *aux conséquences!* beware of the consequences! ~ *à toi, si..,* woe betide you, if... *sans crier* ~, without warning.

garenne (garɛn) *f,* [rabbit] warren.

garer (gare) *v.t,* to park; garage (*car*); dock (*ship*); switch (*train*). **se** ~, to park; pull to one side; get out of the way, take cover.

gargariser (se) (gargarize) *v.pr,* to gargle. **gargarisme** (rism) *m,* gargle.

gargote (gargɔt) *f,* cheap eating house.

gargouille (garguj) *f,* gargoyle. **gargouiller** (guje) *v.i,* to gurgle; (*stomach*) rumble.

garnement (garnəmɑ̃) *m,* young rascal; tearaway.

garnir (garnir) *v.t,* to furnish; stock; fill (*de,* with); line; cover; trim (*dress*); garnish (*dish*); decorate; (*crowd*) fill (*street*). **se** ~, (*hall*) to fill up. **garni, e** (ni) *a,* (*dish*) served with vegetables; (*larder*) well-stocked. ¶ *m,* furnished rooms. **garnison** (nizɔ̃) *f,* garrison. *en* ~ *à,* stationed at. **garniture** (tyr) *f,* (*Cook.*) garnish; vegetables; trimming; decoration; lining; lagging (*boiler*). ~ *de foyer,* fire irons. ~ *de toilette,* toilet set.

garrot (garo) *m,* withers; tourniquet; garrotte. ~**ter** (rɔte) *v.t,* to tie up.

gars *P* (gɑ) *m,* lad, boy; guy *P. par ici les* ~*!* this way boys!

gaspiller (gaspije) *v.t,* to waste, squander.

gas-oil (gazɔjl) *m,* diesel oil.

gastric (gastrik) *a,* gastric. **gastrite** (trit) *f,* gastritis. **gastronome** (trɔnɔm) *m,* gastronome, gourmet. **gastronomie** (mi) *f,* gastronomy. **gastronomique** (mik) *a,* gastronomic.

gâteau (gɑto) *m,* cake; *P* loot. ~ *de miel,* honeycomb. ~ *de riz,* rice pudding. *c'est du* ~*! P,* it's a piece of cake! *P. papa* ~, indulgent [grand]father.

gâter (gɑte) *v.t,* to spoil, ruin; spoil (*child*). *dents gâtées,* rotten teeth. **se** ~, (*food*) to go bad, rot; deteriorate. **gâterie** (tri) *f,* overindulgence (*to s.o*); little present, treat. **gâteux, euse** (tø, øz) *a,* senile, gaga *P.* ¶ *n,* dodderer.

gauche (goʃ) *a,* left, left-hand; awkward, clumsy; gauche; warped (*plank*). ¶ *m,* (*Box.*) left. ¶ *f, la* ~, (*gen., Pol.*) the left; left-hand side. *à* ~ [*de*], on the left [of]. *à ma* ~, on my left. *de* ~, left-hand (*door*); left-wing (*party*). ~**ment** (ʃmɑ̃) *ad,* awkwardly, clumsily. **gaucher, ère** (ʃe, ɛr) *a,* left-handed. **gaucherie** (ʃri) *f,* awkwardness, clumsiness. **gauchir** (ʃir) *v.t.* & **se** ~, to warp. ¶ *v.t,* to distort (*facts*).

gaudriole *P* (godriɔl) *f,* broad joke.

gaufre (gofr) *f,* waffle. **gaufrer** (gofre) *v.t,* to goffer (*cloth*); emboss (*paper*). **gaufrette** (frɛt) *f,* wafer. **gaufrier** (frije) *m,* goffering iron.
Gaule (la) (gol) (*Hist.*) Gaul.
gaullisme (golism) *m,* Gaullism (*doctrines of de Gaulle*). **gaulliste** (list) *a,* Gaullist.
gaulois, e (golwa, az) *a,* Gallic; bawdy. **G～, e,** *n,* Gaul. **gauloiserie** (lwazri) *f,* bawdiness; bawdy story.
gausser (se) de (gose) *v.pr.* to poke fun at.
gaver (gave) *v.t,* to force-feed (*animal*); stuff (*pers.*); cram (*pupil*).
gavotte (gavɔt) *f,* gavotte.
gaz (gɑz) *m,* gas. *se chauffer au* ～, to have g. heating. (*Mil.*) *les* ～, gas. *avoir des* ～, to have wind. (*Mot.*) *mettre les* ～, to step on the g. *P.* ～ *carbonique,* carbon dioxide. ～ *lacrymogène,* tear gas.
gaze (gɑz) *f,* gauze.
gazelle (gazɛl) *f,* gazelle.
gazer (gɑze) *v.t,* (*Mil.*) to gas. ¶ (*P*) *v.i,* to go well. *ça gaze?* all going well?
gazette (gazɛt) *f,* gazette; (*fig.*) gossip.
gazeux, euse (gɑzø, øz) *a,* gaseous; fizzy (*drink*). **gazier** (zje) *m,* gasman. **gazoduc** (zɔdyk) *m,* gas pipeline. **gazogène** (zɔʒɛn) *m,* gas producer (*plant*). **gazomètre** (mɛtr) *m,* gasometer.
gazon (gɑzɔ̃) *m,* [short] grass, turf; lawn. *une motte de* ～, a turf.
gazouiller (gazuje) *v.i,* to warble, chirp; (*baby, stream*) babble.
geai (ʒe) *m,* jay (*bird*).
géant, e (ʒeɑ̃, ɑ̃t) *a. & n,* giant.
geignard, e (ʒeɲar, ard) *a,* whining, moaning. ¶ *n,* moaner. **geindre** (ʒɛ̃dr) *v.i.ir,* to groan, moan; moan, complain.
gélatine (ʒelatin) *f,* gelatine. **gélatineux, euse** (nø, øz) *a,* gelatinous.
gelé, e (ʒəle) *a,* frozen; frost-bitten; (*fig.*) cold, unenthusiastic. **gelée** (le) *f,* frost; jelly. ～ *blanche,* hoar frost. **geler** (le) *v.t. & i,* to freeze. ¶ *v.imp, il gèle* [*à pierre fendre*], it's freezing [hard]. **se** ～ *P,* (*pers.*) to be freezing.
gelure (ʒəlyr) *f,* frostbite.
gémir (ʒemir) *v.i,* to groan, moan; creak. **gémissement** (mismɑ̃) *m,* groan[ing], &c.
gemme (ʒɛm) *f,* gem; [pine] resin.
gênant, e (ʒɛnɑ̃, ɑ̃t) *a,* awkward; embarrassing. *c'est* ～, it's a nuisance.
gencive (ʒɑ̃siv) *f,* (*Anat.*) gum.
gendarme (ʒɑ̃darm) *m,* gendarme; policeman; battle-axe (*woman*). **gendarmer (se)** (me) *v.pr,* to get up in arms; take a firm line. ～**rie** (məri) *f,* gendarmerie, police force; p. station; p. barracks.
gendre (ʒɑ̃dr) *m,* son-in-law.
gêne (ʒɛn) *f,* discomfort; embarrassment; trouble, bother; financial straits. *sans* ～, offhand, casual, inconsiderate.
généalogie (ʒenealɔʒi) *f,* genealogy. **généalogique** (ʒik) *a,* genealogical.
gêner (ʒɛne) *v.t,* to hinder, hamper, get in one's way; (*smoke, noise*) bother, worry; put out; embarrass; cause financial difficulties to. *ça vous gênerait de faire?* would you mind doing? *être gêné,* to be hard up; feel embarrassed, uncomfortable. **se** ～, to put o.s out; stand on ceremony.
général, e† (ʒeneral) *a,* general. *en* ～, generally. ¶ *m,* (*Mil.*) general. ～ *de brigade,* brigadier; air commodore. ～ *de division,* major general; air vice-marshall. ¶ *f,* general's wife; (*Theat.*) [*répétition*] ～*e,* dress rehearsal. ～**iser** (lize) *v.t. & i,* to generalize. **se** ～, to become general. ～ **isation** (zasjɔ̃) *f,* generalization. ～**ité** (te) *f,* majority. ～*s,* generalities.
générateur, trice (ʒeneratœr, tris) *a,* generating. ¶ *m,* generator. **génération** (sjɔ̃) *f,* generation. **générer** (re) *v.t,* to generate.
généreux, euse† (ʒenerø, øz) *a,* generous.
générique (ʒenerik) *a,* generic. ¶ *m,* (*Cine.*) credits.
générosité (ʒenerozite) *f,* generosity. ～*s,* acts of generosity, kindnesses.
Gênes (ʒɛn) *f,* Genoa.
genèse (ʒənɛz) *f,* genesis. (*Bible*) *la G*～, Genesis.
genêt (ʒənɛ) *m,* (*Bot.*) broom.
génétique (ʒenetik) *a,* genetic. ¶ *f,* genetics.
gêneur, euse (ʒɛnœr, øz) *n,* intruder; nuisance.
Genève (ʒənɛv) *f,* Geneva.
genévrier (ʒənevrie) *m,* juniper.
génial, e (ʒenjal) *a,* of genius; inspired (*idea*). ～**ement** (mɑ̃) *ad,* brilliantly. **génie** (ni) *m,* (*gen.*) genius. *avoir le* ～ *des maths,* to have a g. for maths. spirit. (*Mil.*) *le* ～, the Engineers. ～ *civil,* civil engineering.
genièvre (ʒənjɛvr) *m,* juniper; j. berry; Hollands [gin].
génisse (ʒenis) *f,* heifer.
génital, e (ʒenital) *a,* genital.
génitif (ʒenitif) *m,* genitive [case].
génois, e (ʒenwa, az) *a. &* **G～,** *n,* Genoese.
genou (ʒənu) *m,* knee. ～*x,* lap. *à* ～*x,* on one's knees, kneeling. *se mettre à* ～*x,* to kneel down. *être sur les* ～*x P,* to be on one's knees, exhausted.
genre (ʒɑ̃r) *m,* kind, sort, type. ～ *de vie,* way of life, lifestyle. manner, look. *avoir bon* ～, to be a decent sort. *avoir le* ～ *artiste,* to be the arty type. *ce n'est pas mon* ～, he's (she's) not my type. (*Art, Liter.*) genre; (*Gram.*) gender; genus. *le* ～ *humain,* mankind, the human race.
gens (ʒɑ̃) *m.pl,* (*f.pl. with preceding a.*) people, folk; servants. *de braves* ～, *des* ～ *bien,* good, decent people. *de vieilles* ～, old people. *des jeunes* ～, young men. ～ *d'Église,* clergy. ～ *de lettres,* men of letters. ～ *de mer,* seafarers.

les ~ du pays, the local people. (*Hist.*) *les ~ de robe,* the legal profession.
gentiane (ʒɑ̃sjan) *f,* gentian.
gentil, le (ʒɑ̃ti, ij) *a,* nice, kind (*avec, pour,* to); good (*child*); pretty, sweet; tidy (*sum*). *c'est ~ à vous de..,* it's kind of you to... *tout ça c'est bien ~ mais..,* that's all very well but... ¶ *m,* gentile. **gentilhomme** (tijɔm) *m,* (*Hist.*) nobleman; gentleman. *~ campagnard,* country squire. **gentilhommière** (mjɛr) *f,* country seat.
gentillesse (ʒɑ̃tijɛs) *f,* kindness; sweetness. **gentiment** (mɑ̃) *ad,* kindly; nicely, sweetly.
gentleman (dʒɛntləman) *m,* gentleman.
génuflexion (ʒenyflɛksjɔ̃) *f,* genuflexion.
géographe (ʒeɔgraf) *m,* geographer. **géographie** (fi) *f,* geography. **géographique**† (fik) *a,* geographic(al).
geôle (ʒol) *f,* gaol, jail. **geôlier, ère** (ʒolje, ɛr) *n,* gaoler, jailer.
géologie (ʒeɔlɔʒi) *f,* geology. **géologique** (ʒik) *a,* geological. **géologue** (lɔg) *m,* geologist.
géomètre (ʒeɔmɛtr) *m,* geometrician; surveyor. **géométrie** (metri) *f,* geometry. **géométrique**† (trik) *a,* geometric(al).
Georgie (la) (ʒɔrʒi), Georgia (*USA, USSR*).
gérance (ʒerɑ̃s) *f,* management.
géranium (ʒeranjɔm) *m,* geranium.
gérant, e (ʒerɑ̃, ɑ̃t) *n,* manager, ess.
gerbe (ʒɛrb) *f,* sheaf; shower (*sparks*); spray (*flowers*). *~ d'eau,* spray *or* shower of water. **gerber** (be) *v.t,* to bind; stack.
gerboise (ʒɛrbwas) *f,* jerboa.
gercer (ʒɛrse) *v.t. &* **se ~,** to chap (*lips*); crack (*ground*). **gercure** (syr) *f,* chap; crack.
gérer (ʒere) *v.t,* to manage. *mal ~,* to mismanage.
germain, e (ʒɛrmɛ̃, ɛn) *a: cousin ~,* first cousin.
germe (ʒɛrm) *m,* (*Biol., Med.*) germ; eye (*potato*); (*fig.*) seed (*discord*). **germer** (me) *v.i,* to germinate; shoot, sprout. **germination** (minasjɔ̃) *f,* germination.
gérontologie (ʒerɔ̃tɔlɔʒi) *f,* gerontology.
gérondif (ʒerɔ̃dif) *m,* gerund.
gésier (ʒezje) *m,* gizzard.
gésir (ʒezir) *v.i.ir,* to lie (*sick, dead, &c*).
gestation (ʒɛstasjɔ̃) *f,* gestation.
geste (ʒɛst) *m,* gesture; movement; wave (*hand*); nod, shake (*head*); act, deed. ¶ *f,* epic poem cycle. **gesticuler** (tikyle) *v.i,* to gesticulate.
gestion (ʒɛstjɔ̃) *f,* management, administration. **~naire** (ɔnɛr) *a,* administrative, management. ¶ *n,* administrator.
geyser (ʒezɛr) *m,* geyser (*spring*).
ghetto (gɛto) *m,* ghetto.
gibecière (ʒibsjɛr) *f,* game bag; [leather] shoulder bag; satchel.
gibet (ʒibɛ) *m,* gibbet, gallows.
gibier (ʒibje) *m,* (*Hunt.*) game. *~ à poil,* ground g. *~ à plume,* game birds. *~ d'eau,* waterfowl. *gros ~,* big game. *~ de potence,* gallows bird.
giboulée (ʒibule) *f,* shower; hail storm.
giboyeux, euse (ʒibwajø, øz) *a,* well stocked with game (*land*).
gicler (ʒikle) *v.i,* to spirt, squirt. **giclée** (le) *f,* spurt. **gicleur** (lœr) *m,* (*Mot.*) jet.
gifle (ʒifl) *f,* slap [in the face], smack. **gifler** (fle) *v.t,* to smack, slap in the face.
gigantesque (ʒigɑ̃tɛsk) *a,* gigantic.
gigolo (ʒigɔlo) *m,* gigolo.
gigot (ʒigo) *m,* leg (*of lamb, mutton*). *~ de chevreuil,* haunch of venison. **gigoter** *P* (gɔte) *v.i,* (*baby*) to kick about; wriggle, fidget.
gigue (ʒig) *f,* jig (*dance*); (*Mus.*) gigue.
gilet (ʒilɛ) *m,* waistcoat; cardigan. *~ [de corps],* vest. *~ de sauvetage,* life jacket.
gingembre (ʒɛ̃ʒɑ̃br) *m,* ginger.
girafe (ʒiraf) *f,* giraffe.
giration (ʒirasjɔ̃) *f,* gyration. **giratoire** (twar) *a,* gyratory, girating.
girofle (ʒirɔfl) *m: clou de ~,* clove. **giroflée** (fle) *f,* (*Bot.*) stock. *~ jaune,* wallflower.
giron (ʒirɔ̃) *m,* lap (*of pers.*); (*fig.*) bosom.
girouette (ʒirwɛt) *f,* (*lit., fig.*) weathercock.
gisant (ʒizɑ̃) *m,* recumbent statue (*tomb*). **gisement** (zmɑ̃) *m,* deposit (*coal, ore*); (*Naut.*) bearing.
gitan, e (ʒitɑ̃, an) *a. &* **G~, e,** *n,* gipsy.
gîte (ʒit) *m,* shelter; home; form (*hare*); (*Geol.*) deposit. *le ~ & le couvert,* board & lodging. *~ à la noix,* topside (*beef*).
givre (ʒivr) *m,* hoar frost. **givrer** (re) *v.t. &* **se ~,** to frost over, ice up.
glaçage (glasaʒ) *m,* (*Cook.*) glazing; icing. **glace** (glas) *f,* ice. *~s,* ice fields. *~s flottantes,* ice floes. ice[cream]; mirror; plate glass; window (*train, car*). *à ~,* (*thermometer*) at freezing. *~ à l'eau, à la crème,* water, dairy ice. **glacé, e** (se) *a,* frozen; icy (*room*); iced (*drink*); frosty, stony (*look*); glacé (*fruit*). **glacer** (se) *v.t,* to freeze, chill; ice; glaze (*food, paper*); chill (*blood*). *glacé d'horreur,* frozen with terror. **se ~,** to freeze; (*blood*) run cold. **glaciaire** (sjɛr) *a,* glacial; ice (*age, cap*). **glacial, e** (sjal) *a,* icy, freezing; (*fig.*) frosty. **glacier** (sje) *m,* glacier; ice cream maker *or* seller. **glacière** (sjɛr) *f,* ice box; (*lit., fig.*) ice house. **glacis** (si) *m,* (*Mil.*) glacis; (*Art*) glaze. **glaçon** (sɔ̃) *m,* icicle; block of ice (*river*); ice cube.
gladiateur (gladjatœr) *m,* gladiator.
glaïeul (glajœl) *m,* gladiolus.
glaire (glɛr) *f,* white [of egg]; (*Med.*) phlegm.
glaise (glɛz) *f,* clay. **glaiseux, euse** (zø, øz) *a,* clayey.
glaive (glɛv) *m,* (*Poet.*) sword.
gland (glɑ̃) *m,* acorn; tassel.
glande (glɑ̃d) *f,* gland. *avoir des ~s,* to have swollen glands. **glandulaire** (dylɛr) *a,* glandular.

glaner (glane) *v.t,* (*lit., fig.*) to glean. **glaneur, euse** (nœr, øz) *n,* gleaner. **glanure** (nyr) *f,* gleanings.
glapir (glapir) *v.i,* to yelp, yap.
glas (glɑ) *m,* knell. *sonner le ~,* to toll the knell.
glauque (glok) *a,* grey-green (*eyes, water*).
glissade (glisad) *f,* slide; slip; skid; (*Danc.*) glissade. **glissant, e** (sɑ̃, ɑ̃t) *a,* slippery. **glissement** (smɑ̃) *m,* sliding; gliding; swing (*electoral*). *~ de terrain,* landslide. **glisser** (se) *v.i,* to slide; glide; slip; skid; (*Pol.*) swing. *~ sur,* to skate over (*subject*). ¶ *v.t,* to slip (*qch dans,* sth into). **se ~ dans,** (*pers.*) to slip *or* steal into. **glissière** (sjɛr) *f,* slide. *porte à ~,* sliding door. **glissoire** (swar) *f,* slide (*on ice*).
global, e† (glɔbal) *a,* total, aggregate (*sum*); overall, global (*view*). **globe** (glɔb) *m,* globe; glass cover. *~ oculaire,* eyeball. **globule** (byl) *m,* globule; [blood] corpuscle. **globuleux, euse** (bylø, øz) *a,* globular; protruding (*eyes*).
gloire (glwar) *f,* glory; fame; credit; distinction; (*Rel.*) glory, praise. *~ à Dieu,* glory to God. *se faire ~ de,* to glory in, pride oneself on. **glorieux, euse**† (glɔrjø, øz) *a,* glorious; proud. **glorifier** (rifje) *v.t,* to glorify, praise. *se ~ de,* to glory in, boast of. **gloriole** (rjɔl) *f,* vainglory, vanity.
glossaire (glɔsɛr) *m,* glossary.
glotte (glɔt) *f,* glottis. *coup de ~,* glottal stop.
glouglou (gluglu) *m,* gurgle; gobble (*turkey*). **~ter** (te) *v.i,* to gurgle; gobble.
glousser (gluse) *v.i,* to chuckle; (*hen*) cluck.
glouton, ne† (glutɔ̃, ɔn) *a,* gluttonous. ¶ *n,* glutton. **gloutonnerie** (tɔnri) *f,* gluttony.
glu (gly) *f,* birdlime; glue (*marine*). **gluant, e** (ɑ̃, ɑ̃t) *a,* gluey, sticky.
glucose (glykoz) *f,* glucose.
glycérine (gliserin) *f,* glycerin[e].
glycine (glisin) *f,* wistaria.
gnangnan *P* (ɲɑ̃ɲɑ̃) *n,* wet *P,* drip *P;* moaner *P.*
gnognote *P* (ɲɔɲɔt) *f,* trash (*film &c*).
gnôle *P* (ɲol) *f,* hooch *P.*
gnome (gnom) *m,* gnome.
go (tout de) (go) *ad,* straight off; there & then.
goal (gol) *m,* goalkeeper.
gobelet (gɔblɛ) *m,* mug, tumbler (*metal, plastic*); beaker (*child*). *~ en papier,* paper cup.
gobe-mouches (gɔbmuʃ) *m,* flycatcher (*bird*); sucker. **gober** (be) *v.t,* to swallow [whole] (*food, lie*). **se ~,** to be full of o.s.
goberger (se) (gɔbɛrʒe) *v.pr,* to do oneself well.
godasse *P* (gɔdas) *f,* shoe.
godelureau (gɔdlyro) *m,* young dandy.
godet (gɔdɛ) *m,* pot, jar; (*P drink*) jar *P,* noggin *P.*
godiche (gɔdiʃ) *n,* awkward ass; gawk.
godille (gɔdij) *f,* scull (*stern oar*); (*Ski*) wedel. *à la ~ P,* groggy *P;* ropey *P.* **godiller** (dije) *v.t,* to scull; (*Ski*) wedel.
godillot *P* (gɔdijo) *m,* boot.
goéland (gɔelɑ̃) *m,* seagull, gull.
goélette (gɔelɛt) *f,* schooner.
goémon (gɔemɑ̃) *m,* seaweed, wrack.
gogo *P* (gɔgo) *m,* mug *P,* sucker *P.* **à ~,** galore.
goguenard, e (gɔgnar, ard) *a,* mocking.
goguette *P* (gɔgɛt) *f: être en ~,* to be merry (*with drink*).
goinfre (gwɛ̃fr) *m,* guzzler, pig. **goinfrer** (gwɛ̃fre) *v.i.* **& se ~,** to guzzle, eat like a pig.
goitre (gwatr) *m,* goitre.
golf (gɔlf) *m,* golf; golf course, golf links.
golfe (gɔlf) *m,* gulf, bay. *~ de Gascogne,* Bay of Biscay. *~ du Lion,* Gulf of Lions. *~ Persique,* Persian Gulf.
gommage (gɔmaʒ) *m,* rubbing out. **gomme** (gɔm) *f,* gum; rubber, eraser. *à la ~ P,* useless, pathetic *P.* *~ arabique,* gum arabic. **gommer** (me) *v.t,* to gum; rub out, erase. **gommeux, euse** (mø, øz) *a,* gummy, sticky. **gommier** (mje) *m,* gum tree.
gond (gɔ̃) *m,* hinge. (*fig.*) *sortir de ses ~s,* to fly off the handle.
gondolant, e *P* (gɔ̃dɔlɑ̃, ɑ̃t) *a,* side-splitting.
gondole (gɔ̃dɔl) *f,* gondola.
gondoler (gɔ̃dɔle) *v.i.* **& se ~,** (*wood*) to warp; (*paper*) cockle; (*metal*) buckle. **se ~** *P,* to split one's sides with laughter.
gondolier (gɔ̃dɔlje) *m,* gondolier.
gonfler (gɔ̃fle) *v.t,* to swell (*river, sail*); pump up; inflate (*price, tyre*). ¶ *v.i.* **& se ~,** to swell. *gonflé de joie,* (*heart*) bursting with joy. *il est gonflé! P,* he's got a nerve! *or* he's got some courage! **gonfleur** (lœr) *m,* pump.
gong (gɔ̃g) *m,* gong; (*Box.*) bell.
gorge (gɔrʒ) *f,* throat; bosom, breast; gorge; groove; tumbler (*lock*). *à ~ déployée,* (*sing*) at the top of one's voice; (*laugh*) heartily. (*fig.*) *prendre qn à la ~,* to hold a pistol to s.o's head. *faire des ~s chaudes de qch,* to laugh sth to scorn. **gorgée** (ʒe) *f,* mouthful, gulp. **gorger** (ʒe) *v.t,* to fill, stuff (*pers.*); gorge, saturate (*de,* with).
gorille (gɔrij) *m,* gorilla; (*P*) bodyguard.
gosier (gozje) *m,* throat, gullet.
gosse *P* (gɔs) *n,* kid *P.* *sale ~,* nasty little brat *P.*
gothique (gɔtik) *a,* Gothic.
gouache (gwaʃ) *f,* (*Art*) gouache.
goudron (gudrɔ̃) *m,* tar. **~ner** (rɔne) *v.t,* to tar.
gouffre (gufr) *m,* gulf, abyss, chasm.
gouge (guʒ) *f,* gouge (*tool*).
goujat (guʒa) *m,* boor. **~erie** (tri) *f,* boorishness.
goujon (guʒɔ̃) *m,* gudgeon (*fish*); (*Tech.*) pin, bolt.
goulée (gule) *f,* mouthful, gulp. **goulet** (lɛ) *m,* (*Naut.*) narrows; gully. **goulot** (lo) *m,* neck (*bottle*). *boire au ~,* to drink from the bottle. **goulu, e** (ly) *a,* greedy, gluttonous. **goulûment** (lymɑ̃) *ad,* greedily &c.
goupille (gupij) *f,* (*Tech.*) pin. **goupiller** (je) *v.t,*

to pin; (*P*) arrange, fix. **goupillon** (pijɔ̃) *m,* holy-water sprinkler; bottle brush.
gourbi (gurbi) *m,* hut; hovel; (*P*) slum.
gourd, e (gur, urd) *a,* numb.
gourde (gurd) *f,* gourd; flask; (*P*) clot *P.*
gourdin (gurdɛ̃) *m,* cudgel.
gourmand, e (gurmɑ̃, ɑ̃d) *a,* greedy. ~ *de,* very fond of. ¶ *n,* gourmand. ¶ *m,* (*Agr.*) sucker. ~**er** (mɑ̃de) *v.t,* (*liter.*) to rebuke. ~**ise** (diz) *f,* greediness; titbit.
gourme (gurm) *f,* impetigo (*child*). *jeter sa* ~, to sow one's wild oats.
gourmé, e (gurme) *a,* stiff, formal.
gourmet (gurmɛ) *m,* gourmet.
gourmette (gurmɛt) *f,* curb (*harness*); chain bracelet.
gousse (gus) *f,* pod. ~ *d'ail,* clove of garlic.
gousset (gusɛ) *m,* fob (*pocket*); gusset.
goût (gu) *m,* taste, flavour; (*aesthetic*) taste; liking; style. *sans* ~, tasteless. *de bon, mauvais* ~, in good, bad taste. *à mon* ~, to my liking. *prendre* ~ *à qch,* to get to like sth. **goûter** (te) *m,* tea [party]. ¶ *v.t,* to taste; enjoy. ~ **à,** to try, sample. ~ **de,** to have a taste of.
goutte (gut) *f,* drop; drip; dram, nip *P;* (*Med.*) gout. *tomber* ~ *à* ~, to drip. ~**-à-**~, *m.inv,* (*Med.*) drip. ~**lette,** (tlɛt) *f,* tiny drop; droplet. **goutter** (te) *v.i,* to drip. **goutteux, euse** (tø, øz) *a,* gouty. **gouttière** (tjɛr) *f,* gutter; rainwater pipe; (*Med.*) plaster cast.
gouvernail (guvɛrnaj) *m,* rudder; helm.
gouvernante (guvɛrnɑ̃t) *f,* governess; housekeeper. **gouvernants** (nɑ̃) *m.pl, les* ~, the government. **gouverne** (vɛrn) *f,* guidance; steering. **gouvernement** (nəmɑ̃) *m,* (*gen.*) government. ~**al, e** (tal) *a,* government, governmental. **gouverner** (ne) *v.t,* to govern, rule; control; (*Naut.*) steer. **gouverneur** (nœr) *m,* governor.
grabat (graba) *m,* pallet. **grabataire** (tɛr) *a. & n,* bedridden (person).
grabuge *P* (grabyʒ) *m,* row, rumpus *P.*
grâce (grɑs) *f,* grace, charm; favour; mercy, pardon; thanks. *les* ~*s,* grace (*after meal*). *les trois G*~*s,* the three Graces. *plein de* ~, graceful. *être en* ~, to be in favour. *une semaine de* ~, a week's grace. *de bonne, mauvaise* ~, with [a] good, bad grace. *avoir la bonne* ~ *de,* to have the grace to. *crier* ~, to beg for mercy. *de* ~*!* for goodness' sake! ~ **à,** thanks to. *Sa G*~.., His *or* Her Grace... **gracier** (grasje) *v.t,* to pardon. **gracieuseté** (sjøzte) *f,* graciousness; kindness; free gift. **gracieux, euse**† (sjø, øz) *a,* graceful; kindly, gracious; gratuitous.
gracile (grasil) *a,* slender.
gradation (gradasjɔ̃) *f,* gradation. **grade** (grad) *m,* rank; grade; (*Univ.*) degree. *en prendre son* ~ *P,* to get a dressing-down. **gradé** (de) *m,* non-commissioned officer. **gradin** (dɛ̃) *m,* tier; step (*of terrace*). (*Sport*) *les* ~*s,* the terraces. **gradué, e** (dɥe) *a,* graded; graduated (*scale*). **graduel, le**† (dɥɛl) *a,* gradual. **graduer** (dɥe) *v.t,* to graduate; increase gradually.
grain (grɛ̃) *m,* grain (*corn*); bean (*coffee*); berry (*currant*); speck (*dust*); bead; (*fig.*) grain (*truth*); grain (*texture*); heavy shower; (*Naut.*) squall. (*Rel.*) *le bon* ~, the good seed. ~ *de beauté,* beauty spot; mole. ~ *de plomb,* pellet (*shot*). ~ *de raisin,* grape.
graine (grɛn) *f,* seed. *monter en* ~, (*plant*) to run to seed, bolt. *en prendre de la* ~, to profit by s.o's example. ~ *de lin,* linseed. **grainetier, ère** (tje, ɛr) *n,* seed merchant, seedsman.
graissage (grɛsaʒ) *m,* greasing, lubrication. **graisse** (grɛs) *f,* fat; grease. ~ *de rôti,* dripping. *prendre de la* ~, to put on fat. **graisser** (grɛse) *v.t,* to grease, lubricate; stain with grease. ~ *la patte à qn P,* to grease s.o's palm. **graisseux, euse** (sø, øz) *a,* greasy; fatty; grease-stained.
grammaire (grammɛr) *f,* grammar. **grammairien, ne** (mɛrjɛ̃, ɛn) *n,* grammarian. **grammatical, e**† (matikal) *a,* grammatical.
gramme (gram) *m,* gramme.
grand, e (grɑ̃, ɑ̃d) *a,* big; tall; large (*quantity*); great (*friend, importance*); wide (*margin*); deep (*mourning*); open (*air*); heavy (*drinker*). ~ *âge,* great age, old a. *un* ~ *mois,* a good month. *avoir* ~ *faim,* ~ *peur,* to be very hungry, very frightened. *il a* ~ *envie de partir,* he's very keen to leave. *il est* ~ *temps de commencer,* it's high time to begin. *de* ~ *cœur,* wholeheartedly. *au* ~ *complet,* (*group*) in full strength. *de* ~*e envergure,* large-scale; far-reaching. *au* ~ *jour,* in broad daylight. *de* ~ *matin,* very early in the morning. *à* ~*-peine,* with great difficulty. *en* ~*e tenue,* in full dress. ¶ *ad,* (*open*) wide. *voir* ~, to think big *P.* ¶ *n,* (*Sch.*) *les* ~*(e)s,* the big boys (girls), seniors. *petits &* ~*s,* young & old. *en* ~, on a large scale. *la* ~*e banlieue,* the outer suburbs. *la G*~*e Bretagne,* Great Britain. *ce n'est pas* ~*-chose,* it's not much. (*Univ.*) *les* ~*es écoles, institutes of higher education with national competitive entry. les* ~*es lignes,* (*Rly, fig.*) the main lines. ~ *magasin,* department store. ~*-maman, f,* granny. ~ *mât,* mainmast. ~*-mère, f,* grandmother. ~*-messe, f,* high mass. *le* ~ *monde,* high society. ~*-oncle, m,* great uncle. ~ *ouvert,* wide open. ~*-papa, m,* grandad. ~*-parents, m.pl,* grandparents. ~*-père, m,* grandfather. ~*e personne,* grown-up. *le* ~ *public,* the general public. ~*-route, f,* main road. ~*-rue,* high street. ~*e surface,* hypermarket. ~*-tante, f,* great aunt. *les* ~*es vacances,* the summer holidays. ~*-voile, f,* mainsail.
grandement (grɑ̃dmɑ̃) *ad,* greatly; altogether; amply. *il a* ~ *tort,* he's absolutely wrong.

grandeur (dœr) *f,* size; magnitude; height; greatness; magnanimity; grandeur. ~ *d'âme,* nobility of soul. ~ *nature,* life size.
grandiloquence (grɑ̃dilɔkɑ̃s) *f,* grandiloquence. **grandiloquent, e** (kɑ̃, ɑ̃t) *a,* grandiloquent.
grandiose (grɑ̃djoz) *a,* grandiose, imposing.
grandir (grɑ̃dir) *v.i,* to grow [taller, bigger]; grow up; grow, increase; (*sound*) g. louder. ¶ *v.t,* to magnify; make (*s.o*) look taller.
grange (grɑ̃ʒ) *f,* barn.
granit[e] (granit) *m,* granite.
granule (granyl) *m,* granule. **granuler** (le) *v.t,* to granulate.
graphique† (grafik) *a,* graphic. ¶ *m,* graph.
graphite (grafit) *m,* graphite.
graphologie (grafɔlɔʒi) *f,* graphology.
grappe (grap) *f,* bunch, cluster. ~ *de raisin,* bunch of grapes.
grappin (grapɛ̃) *m,* grapnel. *mettre le* ~ *sur,* to get one's claws on, grab.
gras, se (grɑ, ɑs) *a,* fat (*pers.*); plump (*chicken*); fatty (*food*); greasy; thick (*features*); rich (*food, land*); fat *P* (*reward*); loose (*cough*). *fromage* ~, full fat cheese. *le veau* ~, the fatted calf. *faire la* ~*se matinée,* to have a lie in. ¶ *m,* fat (*on meat*). *le* ~ *de,* the fleshy part of (*arm, leg*). ¶ *ad,* (*Eccl.*) *faire* ~, to eat meat. ~**sement** (grɑsmɑ̃) *ad,* (*pay*) handsomely; (*laugh*) coarsely. *vivre* ~, to live on the fat of the land. **grassouillet, te** (sujɛ, ɛt) *a,* plump; chubby.
gratification (gratifikasjɔ̃) *f,* bonus (*pay*). **gratifier** (fje) *v.t,* to reward (*de,* with).
gratin (grɑtɛ̃) *m,* cheese-topped dish. (*P*) *le* ~, the upper crust.
gratis (gratis) *ad,* free, for nothing.
gratitude (gratityd) *f,* gratitude.
gratte *P* (grat) *f,* pickings, perks. ~**-ciel,** *m,* skyscraper. ~**-papier,** *m,* (*pej.*) pen pusher. **gratter** (te) *v.t,* to scrape; scratch; scratch out; scrape off; make (*s.o*) itch; pick up (*on the side*). ¶ *v.i,* scratch; (*P work*) grind away. **grattoir** (twar) *m,* scraper.
gratuit, e† (gratɥi, it) *a,* free; unjustified (*assertion*); gratuitous (*insult*). **gratuité** (te) *f,* unjustified nature; gratuitousness. *la* ~ *de l'enseignement,* free education.
grave (grav) *a,* grave, solemn; serious, grave, severe (*mistake, wound*); low (*note*); deep (*voice*); grave (*accent*). ¶ *m,* (*Mus.*) lower register. *les* ~*s,* the bass notes. ~**ment** (vmɑ̃) *ad,* solemnly; seriously.
graver (grave) *v.t,* to engrave; cut (*on wood*); carve (*letters*); imprint (*on memory*); cut (*disc*). ~ *à l'eau forte,* to etch. **graveur** (vœr) *m,* engraver.
gravier (gravje) *m,* gravel; bit of gravel. **gravillon** (vijɔ̃) *m,* bit of grit *or* gravel. ~*s,* loose chippings.
gravir (gravir) *v.i* to climb.
gravité (gravite) *f,* gravity, solemnity; seriousness; (*Phys.*) gravity. **graviter** (te) *v.i,* to revolve (*autour de,* round).
gravure (gravyr) *f,* engraving; cutting. ~ *à l'eau forte,* etching. ~ *sur bois,* wood engraving; woodcut. ~ *de mode,* fashion plate.
gré (gre) *m,* will; free will; wish; liking, taste. *à votre* ~, to your liking *or* taste; (*act*) as you wish, like. *de bon* ~, willingly. *de son plein* ~, of one's own free will, own accord. *bon* ~, *mal* ~, willy-nilly. *de* ~ *ou de force,* (*persuade*) by fair means or foul; (*comply*) willy-nilly. *au* ~ *de,* according to; at the mercy of (*wind, current*). *de* ~ *à* ~, by mutual consent. *savoir* ~ *à qn,* to be grateful to s.o.
grèbe (grɛb) *m,* grebe.
grec, ecque (grɛk) *a,* Greek, Grecian. **G~, ecque,** *n,* Greek (*pers.*). *le* ~, Greek (*language*). **la Grèce** (grɛs), Greece.
gredin (grədɛ̃) *m,* scoundrel.
gréement (gremɑ̃) (*Naut.*) *m,* rigging. **gréer** (gree) *v.t,* to rig.
greffe (grɛf) *f,* (*Hort.*) graft; (*Med.*) graft, transplant; grafting. ¶ *m,* (*Law*) Clerk's Office (*court*). **greffer** (fe) *v.t,* to graft; transplant. **greffier** (fje) *m,* clerk (*of court*). **greffon** (fɔ̃) *m,* graft, slip; transplant (*organ*).
grégaire (gregɛr) *a,* gregarious.
grégorien, ne (gregɔrjɛ̃, ɛn) *a,* Gregorian.
grêle[1] (grɛl) *a,* spindly; skinny (*pers.*); shrill (*voice*); small (*intestine*).
grêle[2] (grɛl) *f,* hail; (*fig.*) shower. **grêlé, e** (le) *a,* pock-marked. **grêler** (le) *v.imp, il grêle,* it's hailing. ¶ *v.t,* to damage by hail. **grêlon** (lɔ̃) *m,* hailstone.
grelot (grəlo) *m,* bell, sleigh bell.
grelotter (grəlɔte) *v.i,* to shiver (*de,* with).
grenade (grənad) *f,* pomegranate; grenade. ~ *sous-marine,* depth charge. **G~,** *f,* Granada (*Spain*). **la G~,** Grenada (*W. Indies*). **grenadine** (din) *f,* grenadine (*cordial*).
grenat (grəna) *m,* garnet. ¶ *a. inv,* garnet-red.
grené, e (grəne) *a,* grainy (*leather*); (*Art*) stippled.
grenier (grənje) *m,* loft; garret, attic. ~ *à blé,* granary. ~ *à foin,* hayloft.
grenouille (grənuj) *f,* frog; money box; funds (*club &c*). *manger la* ~ *P,* to make off with the funds.
grès (grɛ) *m,* sandstone; stoneware.
grésil (grezi) *m,* [fine] hail. **grésiller** (je) *v.i,* (*fat*) to sizzle; (*Radio*) crackle. **grésillement** (jmɑ̃) *m,* sizzling; crackling.
grève (grɛv) *f,* (*Ind.*) strike; shore, beach; bank (*river*). *se mettre en* ~, *faire* ~, to [go on] strike. ~ *de la faim,* hunger s. ~ *perlée,* go-slow. ~ *sauvage,* wild-cat s. ~ *de solidarité,* sympathy strike. ~ *sur le tas,* sit-down s.
grever (grəve) *v.t,* to burden, weigh down (*d'impôts,* with taxes); strain (*budget*).

gréviste (grevist) *n,* striker.
gribouillage (gribujaʒ), **gribouillis** (ji) *m,* scribble; doodle. **gribouiller** (je) *v.t,* to scrawl, scribble. ¶ *v.i,* doodle.
grief (griɛf) *m,* grievance. *faire ~ de qch à qn,* to hold sth agaist s.o.
grièvement (griɛvmɑ̃) *ad,* seriously (*injured*).
griffe (grif) *f,* claw, talon. *~s,* (*fig.*) clutches. (*Dress*) maker's label; signature stamp; (*fig.*) stamp (*painter &c*). *coup de ~*, scratch; (*fig.*) dig (*at s.o*); catty remark. **griffer** (fe) *v.t,* to claw, scratch. **griffon** (fɔ̃) *m,* griffon; (*Myth.*) griffin. **griffonner** (fɔne) *v.t,* to scrawl; scribble. ¶ *v.i,* to doodle. **griffure** (fyr) *f,* scratch.
grignoter (griɲɔte) *v.t,* to nibble [at]; (*fig.*) erode.
grigou *P* (grigu) *m,* miser, skinflint.
gril (gri[l]) *m,* grill; g. pan. (*fig.*) *sur le ~*, on tenterhooks. **grillade** (grijad) *f,* grill (*meat*). **grillage** (jaʒ) *m,* wire netting; w. fencing. **grille** (grij) *f,* grating; grille, grid; railings; iron gate; bars (*cell*); grate. **~-pain,** *m,* toaster. **griller** (grije) *v.t,* to grill; toast; roast (*coffee*); (*heat, sun*) scorch; blow (*bulb*); burn out (*engine*); overtake (*runner*). ¶ *v.i,* (*pers.*) to roast. *~ d'envie de faire,* to be itching to do.
grillon (grijɔ̃) *m,* cricket (*insect*).
grimace (grimas) *f,* grimace; [wry] face; grin. **grimacer** (se) *v.i,* to grimace, make a [wry] face; grin; (*cloth*) pucker.
grimer (grime) *v.t,* (*Theat.*) to make up.
grimoire (grimwar) *m,* gibberish; scrawl.
grimper (grɛ̃pe) *v.i,* to climb, clamber up. *~ dans un arbre,* to climb a tree. ¶ *v.t,* to climb.
grincer (grɛ̃se) *v.i,* to grate; creak; (*pen*) scratch. *~ des dents,* to grind one's teeth. *faire ~ des dents,* to set one's teeth on edge.
grincheux, euse (grɛ̃ʃø, øz) *a,* grumpy.
grippe (grip) *f,* influenza, flu. *prendre en ~*, to take a dislike to. **grippé, e** (pe) *a: être ~*, to have flu. **gripper** (pe) *v.i. &* **se ~**, (*Mach.*) to seize up. **grippe-sou,** *m,* skinflint.
gris, e (gri, iz) *a,* grey; dull (*life, weather*); tipsy, fuddled. *faire ~e mine à qn,* to give s.o a cool welcome. ¶ *m,* grey. **grisaille** (grizaj) *f,* greyness; dullness; (*Art*) grisaille. **grisâtre** (zɑtr) *a,* greyish. **griser** (ze) *v.t,* to intoxicate; (*fig.*) go to one's head. *se ~ de,* (*lit., fig.*) to be intoxicated by. **griserie** (zri) *f,* intoxication. **grisonner** (zɔne) *v.i,* to [start to] go grey.
grisou (grizu) *m,* firedamp.
grive (griv) *f,* thrush (*bird*).
grivois, e (grivwa, az) *a,* ribald; spicy. **~erie** (zri) *f,* ribaldry; spicey story.
Groënland (le) (grɔɛnlɑ̃d), Greenland.
grog (grɔg) *m,* grog.
grogner (grɔɲe) *v.i,* to grunt; growl; grumble. **grognon** (ɲɔ̃) *a,* surly; grumpy.
groin (grwɛ̃) *m,* snout (*pig*).
grommeler (grɔmle) *v.i,* to grumble. ¶ *v.t,* to mutter.
gronder (grɔ̃de) *v.t,* to scold. ¶ *v.i,* to growl; (*guns, storm*) rumble, roar; (*crowd*) mutter; (*riot*) be brewing.
groom (grum) *m,* page boy, bellboy.
gros, se (gro, os) *a,* big, large; great; thick; fat; pregnant; coarse (*cloth, features*); heavy (*cold; drinker; industry; shower; sea*); loud (*sound*); rough (*weather*). *avoir le cœur ~*, to have a heavy heart. *faire le ~ dos,* (*cat*) to arch its back. *jouer ~ jeu,* to play for high stakes. ¶ *m, le ~ de,* the bulk of; the worst of (*storm*); the height of (*summer*); the depths of (*winter*). *en ~*, roughly, broadly; (*buy, sell*) wholesale. *mon ~ P,* old man *P.* ¶ *ad,* (*write*) big; (*risk*) a lot. *en avoir ~ sur le cœur,* to be distressed. *~ bonnet P, ~se légume P,* bigwig *P,* big shot *P.* *~se caisse,* bass drum. *~ gibier,* big game. *~ intestin,* large intestine. *~ lot,* jackpot. *~ mot,* coarse word. *~ œuvre,* (*Build.*) main structure. *~ plan,* (*Phot.*) close-up. *~ sel,* cooking salt. *~ titre,* [banner] headline.
gros-bec (grobɛk) *m,* hawfinch.
groseille (grozɛj) *f,* currant (*red, white*). *~ à maquereau,* gooseberry. **groseillier** (zɛje) *m,* currant bush. *~ à maquereau,* gooseberry bush.
grossesse (grosɛs) *f,* pregnancy. **grosseur** (sœr) *f,* size; swelling, lump.
grossier, ère† (grosje, ɛr) *a,* coarse, crude; gross (*error*); crass (*ignorance*); rough (*estimate*); uncouth (*pers.*); rude (*envers,* to). **grossièreté** (ɛrte) *f,* coarseness, &c.
grossir (grosir) *v.i,* to grow [bigger]; (*river, sound*) swell; (*pers.*) put on weight. ¶ *v.t,* to make bigger; enlarge, magnify; swell; exaggerate.
grossiste (grosist) *m,* wholesaler.
grosso-modo (grɔsomɔdo) *ad,* roughly.
grotesque† (grɔtɛsk) *a,* grotesque; ludicrous, absurd.
grotte (grɔt) *f,* cave; grotto.
grouiller (gruje) *v.i,* to swarm, seethe (*de,* with); (*crowd*) mill around.
groupe (grup) *m,* group, knot, party (*people*); clump (*trees*). *~ électrogène,* generating set. *~ de pression,* pressure group. *~ sanguin,* blood group. *~ scolaire,* school complex. **~ment** (pmɑ̃) *m,* grouping; group. **grouper** (pe) *v.t,* to group; pool (*resources*). **se ~**, to gather; cluster; band together.
grouse (gruz) *f,* grouse (*bird*).
gruau (gryo) *m: farine de ~*, fine wheat flour.
grue (gry) *f,* crane (*bird & hoist*).
grume (grym) *f,* bark (*left on felled tree*). *en ~*, in the log.
grumeau (grymo) *m,* lump (*in sauce*).

gruyère (gryjɛr) *m,* gruyère [cheese].
gué (ge) *m,* ford. *passer à* ~, to ford.
guenilles (gənij) *f.pl,* rags, tatters.
guenon (gənɔ̃) *f,* female monkey; fright (*woman*).
guépard (gepar) *m,* cheetah.
guêpe (gɛp) *f,* wasp. **guêpier** (gɛpje) *m,* wasps' nest; (*fig.*) trap.
guère (ne . . .) (nə . . . gɛr) *ad,* hardly, scarcely; not much, not many. *je n'aime* ~, I don't much care for. *il ne tardera* ~, he won't be very long.
guéridon (geridɔ̃) *m,* pedestal table.
guérilla (gerija) *f,* guerrilla warfare. **guérillero** (jero) *m,* guerrilla.
guérir (gerir) *v.t,* to cure; heal. ¶ *v.i,* to recover (*de,* from); be cured (*de,* of); (*wound*) heal. **guérison** (rizɔ̃) *f,* curing; healing; recovery. **guérissable** (sabl) *a,* curable. **guérisseur, euse** (sœr, øz) *n,* healer; quack doctor.
guérite (gerit) *f,* sentry box; (*Build.*) site hut.
Guernesey (gɛrnəzɛ) *f,* Guernsey.
guerre (gɛr) *f,* war; warfare. *en* ~, at war. *faire la* ~, to wage war. *il a fait la* ~, he was in the war. ~ *froide, mondiale,* cold, world war. ~ *de mouvement, de position,* mobile, static warfare. ~ *d'usure,* war of attrition. **guerrier, ère** (gɛrje, ɛr) *a,* warlike; war (*dance*). ¶ *n,* warrior.
guet (gɛ) *m,* watch. *avoir l'œil au* ~, to keep a sharp look-out. **~-apens** (gɛtapɑ̃) *m,* ambush.
guêtre (gɛtr) *f,* gaiter.
guetter (gɛte) *v.t,* to watch; w. out for; lie in wait for. **guetteur** (tœr) *m,* look-out [man].
gueule (gœl) *f,* mouth; muzzle (*animal*); (*P*) mouth; face; look, appearance. [*ferme*] *ta* ~ ! *P**, shut your trap! *P. faire une sale* ~, to pull a face. ~ *de bois P,* hangover. **~-de-loup,** *f,* snapdragon. **gueuler** *P* (le) *v.i. & t,* to bawl; bellyache *P* (*contre,* about). **gueuleton** (ltɔ̃) *m,* blow-out *P,* nosh-up *P.*
gueux, euse (gø, øz) *n,* (*liter.*) beggar, vagabond; rascal, villain.
gui (gi) *m,* mistletoe; (*Naut.*) boom.
guichet (giʃɛ) *m,* (*Rly*) ticket office; (*Theat.*) box office; counter (*bank*); window, hatch; grille (*door*). **guichetier** (ʃtje) *m,* counter clerk.
guide (gid) *m,* guide; guide book. ¶ *f,* [driving] rein. **~-âne,** *m,* simple handbook. **guider** (de) *v.t,* to guide. **guidon** (dɔ̃) *m,* handlebars (*cycle*); foresight (*gun*).
guigne *P* (giɲ) *f,* bad luck.
guigner (giɲe) *v.t,* to eye [covertly]; to have one's eye on.
guignol (giɲɔl) *m,* ≃ Punch & Judy show; (*pej.*) clown. *c'est du* ~, it's a farce.
guillemets (gijmɛ) *m.pl,* quotation marks, inverted commas.
guilleret, te (gijrɛ, ɛt) *a,* lively, perky (*pers.*); spicy (*story*).
guillotine (gijɔtin) *f,* guillotine. **guillotiner** (ne) *v.t,* to guillotine.
guimauve (gimov) *f,* marshmallow.
guimbarde (gɛ̃bard) *f,* Jew's harp; (*P car*) [*vieille*] ~, old rattletrap *P,* old banger *P.*
guimpe (gɛ̃) *f,* wimple; chemisette.
guindé, e (gɛ̃de) *a,* starchy, stiff; stilted.
guinée (gine) *f,* guinea. **la G~,** Guinea.
guingois (de) (gɛ̃gwa) *ad,* askew; lop-sided.
guinguette (gɛ̃gɛt) *f,* open air café with dancing.
guirlande (girlɑ̃d) *f,* garland.
guise (giz) *f, en* ~ *de,* by way of. *n'en faire qu'à sa* ~, to do as one pleases.
guitare (gitar) *f,* guitar. **guitariste** (rist) *n,* guitarist.
guttural, e (gytyral) *a. & f,* guttural.
Guyane (la) (gɥijan), Guiana.
gymnase (ʒimnaz) *m,* gymnasium. **gymnaste** (nast) *m,* gymnast. **gymnastique** (tik) *f,* gymnastics; (*Sch.*) physical education; (*fig.*) ~ *de l'esprit,* mental gymnastics. *quelle* ~ *pour y arriver,* what a hassle to get there *P.*
gynécologie (ʒinekɔlɔʒi) *f,* gynaecology. **gynécologue** (lɔg) *n,* gynaecologist.
gypse (ʒips) *m,* gypsum.
gyroscope (ʒirɔskɔp) *m,* gyroscope.

H

The sign ' denotes that the **h** *is aspirate in the French sense, i.e., no liaison or elision.*
H, h (aʃ) *m. & f, letter,* H, h.
habile† (abil) *a,* skilful, skilled; clever. **habileté** (lte) *f,* skill, skilfulness; cleverness.
habillement (abijmɑ̃) *m,* clothing (*act*); clothes, dress; clothing trade. **habiller** (je) *v.t,* to dress, clothe; cover. *habillé de,* dressed in. **s'~,** to dress, get dressed. *s'~ chez X,* to get one's clothes from X. **habilleuse** (jøz) *f,* (*Theat.*) dresser. **habit** (bi) *m,* costume, dress, outfit; evening dress (*men*), tails; habit (*monk*). *~s,* clothes. *~s du dimanche,* Sunday clothes. ~ *ecclésiastique,* clerical dress. ~ *de gala,* formal dress.
habitable (abitabl) *a,* [in]habitable.

habitacle (abitakl) *m,* (*Naut.*) binnacle; (*Aero.*) cockpit; (*Rel., liter.*) abode.
habitant, e (abitã, ãt) *n,* inhabitant; occupier, occupant. **habitat** (ta) *m,* habitat. **habitation** (sjɔ̃) *f,* house; place of residence. *conditions d'*~, housing conditions. ~ *à loyer modéré* (*HLM*), ≃ council flat; block of c. flats. **habiter** (te) *v.t,* to inhabit (*country*); live in, occupy (*house*). ¶ *v.i,* to live.
habitude (abityd) *f,* habit. *par* ~, out of h. *comme d'*~, as usual. *avoir l'*~ *de faire,* to be used to doing. **habitué, e** (tɥe) *n,* regular [customer], habitué. **habituel, le†** (tɥɛl) *a,* habitual, usual, customary. **habituer** (tɥe) *v.t,* to accustom. **s'**~, to get used *or* accustomed (*à qch,* to sth; *à faire,* to doing).
'hâbleur, euse (ablœr, øz) *n,* braggart.
'hache (aʃ) *f,* axe. ~ *d'armes,* battle-axe. **'haché** (ʃe) *m,* mince. **'hacher** (ʃe) *v.t,* to chop [up]; mince; hack *or* cut to pieces. ~ *menu,* to chop finely. **'hachis** (ʃi) *m,* chopped vegetables; mince. **'hachoir** (ʃwar) *m,* chopper; chopping board; mincer.
'hagard, e (agar, ard) *a,* haggard, wild; distraught.
'haie (ɛ) *f,* hedge; hurdle (*runner*); fence (*horse*); line, row (*people*). ~ *vive,* quickset hedge.
'haillon (ɑjɔ̃) *m,* rag, tatter. *en* ~*s,* in rags.
'haine (ɛn) *f,* hatred, hate (*de, pour,* of). **'haineux, euse** (ɛnø, øz) *a,* full of hatred. **'haïr** (air) *v.t,* to hate, loathe. **'haïssable** (aisabl) *a,* hateful.
Haïti (aiti) *f,* Haiti.
'halage (alaʒ) *m,* towing. *chemin de* ~, towpath.
'hâle (ɑl) *m,* tan, sunburn, **'hâlé, e** (ɑle) *a,* tanned, sunburnt.
haleine (alɛn) *f,* breath; breathing. *hors d'*~, out of breath. *tenir qn en* ~, to keep s.o spellbound *or* on tenterhooks. *de longue* ~, long & exacting (*work*).
'haler (ale) *v.t,* to tow (*boat*); haul in.
'hâler (ɑle) *v.t,* to tan, sunburn.
'haletant, e (altã, ãt) *a,* panting; breathless. **'haleter** (te) *v.i,* to pant, gasp [for breath].
'hall (ɔl) *m,* hall, foyer (*hotel*); (*Rly*) ticket office.
'halle (al) *f,* [covered] market. *les H*~*s* (*Paris*), the central food market.
'hallebarde (albard) *f,* (*Hist.*) halberd.
hallucination (alysinasjɔ̃) *f,* hallucination.
'halo (alo) *m,* halo (*light*).
'halte (alt) *f,* halt, stop (*journey*); break, pause; (*Rly*) halt. ¶ ~**[-là]** *i,* stop!; (*Mil.*) halt!
haltère (altɛr) *m,* dumb-bell. *faire des* ~*s,* to do weight lifting.
'hamac (amak) *m,* hammock.
'Hambourg (ãbur) *m,* Hamburg.
'hameau (amo) *m,* hamlet.
hameçon (amsɔ̃) *m,* fish hook; (*fig.*) bait.
'hampe (ãp) *f,* [flag] pole; shaft (*spear*).
'hanche (ãʃ) *f,* hip; haunch.
'handicap (ãdikap) *m,* (*lit, fig.*) handicap. **handicapé, e** (pe) *a,* handicapped. ¶ *n,* ~ [*mental*], [mentally] handicapped person. **'handicaper** (pe) *v.t,* to handicap.
'hangar (ãgar) *m,* shed; warehouse; (*Aero.*) hangar.
'hanneton (antɔ̃) *m,* cockchafer; maybug.
'hanter (ãte) *v.t,* (*gen.*) to haunt; (*fig.*) obsess. **'hantise** (tiz) *f,* haunting memory; obsession.
'happer (ape) *v.t,* to snap up; snatch; grab.
'harangue (arãg) *f,* harangue. **'haranguer** (ge) *v.t,* to harangue.
'haras (arɑ) *m,* stud farm.
'harassement (arasmã) *m,* exhaustion. **'harasser** (arase) *v.t,* to wear out, exhaust.
'harcèlement (arsɛlmã) *m,* harassment. **'harceler** (səle) *v.t,* to harass; plague, pester.
'harde (ard) *f,* herd (*deer*).
'hardes (ard) *f.pl,* (*pej., liter.*) old clothes.
'hardi†, e (ardi) *a,* bold, daring; brazen. ~*!* come on! (*encouraging*). **'hardiesse** (djɛs) *f,* boldness, daring; effrontery. ~*s,* liberties.
'harem (arɛm) *m,* harem.
'hareng (arã) *m,* herring. ~ *fumé & salé,* kipper. ~ *saur* (sɔr), smoked herring. **'harengère** (ʒɛr) *f,* (*pej.*) fishwife.
'hargne (arɲ) *f,* aggressiveness. **'hargneux, euse†** (arɲø, øz) *a,* aggressive; snappish, fractious.
'haricot (ariko) *m,* bean. ~ *blanc,* haricot bean. ~ *à rames,* ~ *d'Espagne,* runner bean. ~ *vert,* French b. ~ *de mouton,* mutton stew. *des* ~*s!* nothing doing! *c'est la fin des* ~*s! P,* that's the last straw!
harmonica (armɔnika) *m,* harmonica; mouth organ. **harmonie** (ni) *f,* (*gen.*) harmony; wind band. *en* ~ *avec,* in harmony with. **harmonieux, euse†** (njø, øz) *a,* harmonious. **harmonique†** (nik) *a. & m,* harmonic. **harmoniser** (ze) *v.t. &* **s'**~, to harmonize. **harmonium** (njɔm) *m,* harmonium.
'harnachement (arnaʃmã) *m,* harnessing; harness; get-up *P.* **'harnacher** (ʃe) *v.t,* to harness; rig out. **'harnais** (nɛ) *m,* harness.
'harpe (arp) *f,* harp.
'harpie (arpi) *f,* (*Myth., pej.*) harpy.
'harpiste (arpist) *n,* harpist.
'harpon (arpɔ̃) *m,* harpoon. **'harponner** (pɔne) *v.t,* to harpoon; (*P*) waylay.
'hasard (azar) *m,* chance, luck, coincidence; chance (*probability*). ~*s,* risks, hazards. *un heureux* ~, a stroke of luck. *au* ~, at random, haphazardly. *par* ~, by chance; by any c. *à tout* ~, just in case; on the off chance. **'hasarder** (zarde) *v.t,* to risk; venture, hazard (*conjecture*). **se** ~ **dans,** to venture into. **se** ~ **à faire,** to risk doing. **'hasardeux, euse†** (dø, øz) *a,* hazardous, risky; adventurous (*life*).
'hâte (ɑt) *f,* haste, hurry. *à la* ~, hurriedly, hastily. *en toute* ~, with all possible speed. *avoir* ~ *de faire,* to be in a hurry to do. **'hâter**

(ɑte) *v.t,* to hasten; quicken (*pace*). **se ~,** to hurry, hasten (*de faire,* to do). **'hâtif, ive†** (tif, iv) *a,* hasty, hurried; early (*fruit, &c*).

'hauban (obɑ̃) *m,* (*Naut.*) shroud, stay.

'hausse (os) *f,* rise, increase (*pay, price*). *en ~,* rising. **~ment d'épaules** (osmɑ̃) *m,* shrug.

'hausser (se) *v.t,* to raise (*price, voice*); heighten. *~ les épaules,* to shrug one's shoulders.

'haut, e (o, ot) *a,* (*gen.*) high; tall; top (*branches*); high, noble (*birth*); high-ranking (*official*); upper (*classes*); remote (*antiquity*). *~ de 5 mètres,* 5 m. high. *le plus ~ étage,* the top floor. *à ~e voix,* aloud, out loud. *en ~e mer,* on the high seas *or* open sea. *la mer est ~e,* the tide is in. *du plus ~ comique,* highly amusing. *~e bourgeoisie,* upper-middle class. *le H~ Rhin,* the Upper Rhine. (*Mus.*) *~e contre,* counter tenor. *~e fidélité,* high fidelity. *en ~ lieu,* in high places. ¶ *m,* top. *en ~ de,* at the top of (*page, stairs*). *du ~,* top (*shelf*); upstairs (*rooms*). *avoir 2 mètres de ~,* (*wall*) to be 2 m. high. *regarder qn de ~ en bas,* to look s.o up & down. *les ~s & les bas,* the ups & downs (*of life*). ¶ *ad,* (*aim, fly, jump*) high; (*put*) high up; (*speak*) loudly; (*read*) aloud. *'voir plus ~',* 'see above'. *~ les mains!* hands up! **~-de-chausses,** *m,* (*Hist.*) knee breeches. **~-de-forme,** *m,* top hat. **~-fond,** *m,* shoal, shallow. **~-fourneau,** *m,* blast furnace. **~-le-cœur,** *m,* retch, heave. **~-le-corps,** *m,* start, jump. **~-parleur,** *m,* loudspeaker.

'hautain, e (otɛ̃, ɛn) *a,* haughty.

'hautbois (obwɑ) *m,* oboe. **'hautboïste** (bɔist) *n,* oboist.

'hautement (otmɑ̃) *ad,* highly; openly. **'hauteur** (tœr) *f,* height; altitude; level; (*Mus.*) pitch; hill; nobility; haughtiness. *prendre de la ~,* (*plane*) to gain height, climb. *à ~ des yeux,* at eye level. *être à la ~ de,* to be equal to, up to (*job*). *arriver à la ~ de qn,* to draw level with s.o.

'Havane (avan) *m,* Havana (*cigar*). ¶ **la H~,** Havana.

'hâve (ɑv) *a,* gaunt, emaciated; wan.

'havre (ɑvr) *m,* (*liter: lit., fig.*) haven.

'havresac (ɑvrəsak) *m,* haversack.

Hawaï (awai) *m,* Hawaii. **hawaïen, ne** (iɛ̃, ɛn) *a.* & **H~,** *n,* Hawaiian.

'Haye (la) (ɛ), the Hague.

'hé, (e) *i,* hi!, hey! *~! vous, là-bas,* hi! you there!

hebdomadaire (ɛbdɔmadɛr) *a.* & *m,* weekly.

héberger (ebɛrʒe) *v.t,* to put up, take in; accommodate.

hébétement (ebɛtmɑ̃) *m,* stupor. **hébéter** (bete) *v.t,* to stupefy; daze.

hébraïque (ebraik) *a,* Hebraic, Hebrew.

hébreu (ebrø) *a.* & *m* (*language*) Hebrew. *c'est de l'~ P,* it's all Greek to me.

hécatombe (ekatɔ̃b) *f,* hecatomb, slaughter.

hectare (ɛktar) *m,* hectare (=10,000 square metres *or* 2.47 acres).

hecto (ɛktɔ) *pref,* hecto ... *~gramme, ~litre, ~mètre,* hectogramme, -litre, -metre.

hégémonie (eʒemɔni) *f,* hegemony.

'hein ([h]ɛ̃) *i,* eh?; what?; isn't it?

hélas (elɑs) *i,* alas!

'héler ([h]ele) *v.t,* to hail.

hélice (elis) *f,* propeller, screw; (*Geom.*) helix.

hélicoptère (elikɔptɛr) *m,* helicopter. **héligare** (gar) *f,* **héliport** (pɔr) *m,* heliport. **héliporté, e** (pɔrte) *a,* transported by helicopter.

hélium (eljɔm) *m,* helium.

hellénique (ɛlenik) *a,* Hellenic.

helvétique (ɛlvetik) *a,* Swiss.

hématome (ematom) *m,* bruise.

hémicycle (emisikl) *m,* semicircle.

hémisphère (emisfɛr) *m,* hemisphere.

hémoglobine (emɔglɔbin) *f,* haemoglobin. **hémophilie** (fili) *f,* haemophilia. **hémorragie** (raʒi) *f,* haemorrhage. **hémorroïdes** (rɔid) *f.pl* haemorrhoids, piles.

'henné (ɛnne) *m,* henna.

'hennir ([h]ɛnir) *v.i,* to neigh, whinny.

'hep ([h]ɛp) *i,* hey!

hépatite (epatit) *f,* hepatitis.

héraldique (eraldik) *a,* heraldic. ¶ *f,* heraldry. **'héraut** (ro) *m,* (*Hist.*) herald.

herbacé, e (ɛrbase) *a,* herbaceous. **herbage** (baʒ) *m,* pasture. **herbe** (ɛrb) *f,* grass; [species of] g.; blade of g.; herb. *~s potagères, fines ~s,* pot herbs. *mauvaise ~,* weed. *~s folles,* wild grasses. *en ~,* green (*corn*); budding (*artist*). *couper l'~ sous le pied de qn,* to cut the ground from under s.o's feet. **herbeux, euse** (bø, øz) *a,* grassy. **herbier** (bje) *m,* herbarium. **herbicide** (bisid) *a,* herbicidal. ¶ *m,* weed-killer. **herbivore** (bivɔr) *a,* herbivorous. ¶ *m,* herbivore. **herboriser** (bɔrize) *v.i,* to botanize, collect plants. **herboriste** (rist) *n,* herbalist. **herbu, e** (by) *a,* grassy.

hercule (ɛrkyl) *m,* Hercules. **herculéen, ne** (leɛ̃, ɛn) *a,* Herculean.

héréditaire† (ereditɛr) *a,* hereditary. **hérédité** (te) *f,* inheritance (*right*); heredity.

hérésie (erezi) *f,* heresy. **hérétique** (tik) *a,* heretical. ¶ *n,* heretic.

'hérissé, e (erise) *a,* bristly; standing on end (*hair*); bristling (*de,* with). **'hérisser** (se) *v.t,* to make (*sth*) bristle; ruffle (*feathers*); put (*s.o's*) back up. **se ~,** (*hair*) to stand on end, bristle. **hérisson** (sɔ̃) *m,* hedgehog.

héritage (eritaʒ) *m,* inheritance; heritage. **hériter** (te) *v.i.* & *t,* to inherit ([*de*] *qch,* sth; *de qn,* from s.o). **héritier, ère** (tje, ɛr) *n,* heir, heiress.

hermétique† (ɛrmetik) *a,* hermetic; (*fig.*) impenetrable; obscure (*poem*).

hermine (ɛrmin) *f,* ermine, stoat.

herminette (ɛrminɛt) *f,* adze.

'hernie (ɛrni) *f,* hernia, rupture. ~ *discale,* slipped disc.
héroïne (erɔin) *f,* heroine; heroin (*drug*). **héroïque**† (ik) *a,* heroic. **héroïsme** (ism) *m,* heroism.
'héron (erɔ̃) *m,* heron.
'héros (ero) *m,* hero. ~ *de la fête,* guest of honour.
herpès (ɛrpɛs) *m,* herpes.
'herse (ɛrs) *f,* harrow; portcullis. **'herser** (se) *v.t,* to harrow.
hésitant, e (ezitɑ̃, ɑ̃t) *a,* hesitant; faltering. **hésitation** (tasjɔ̃) *f,* hesitation. **hésiter** (te) *v.i,* to hesitate (*à faire,* to do); waver; falter.
hétéroclite (eterɔklit) *a,* assorted, heterogeneous; odd. **hétérodoxe** (dɔks) *a,* heterodox; unorthodox. **hétérogène** (ʒɛn) *a,* heterogeneous. **hétérosexuel, le** (seksɥɛl) *a,* heterosexual.
'hêtre (ɛtr) *m,* beech [tree, wood].
heure (œr) *f,* hour; time; moment. *2 ~s de marche,* a 2 hours' walk. *quelle ~ est-il?* what time is it? *quelle ~ avez-vous?* what t. do you make it? *il est 4 ~s,* it is 4 o'clock; *4 ~s 10,* 10 past 4; *4 ~s moins 10;* 10 to 4; *4 ~s & demie,* half past 4. *l'~ légale,* standard time. *l'~ du dîner,* dinner time. *~s d'affluence,* rush hour. ~ *de pointe,* rush hour; peak time. *~s d'ouverture,* business *or* opening hours. *~s creuses,* slack periods. *~s supplémentaires,* overtime. *à l'~,* on time. *avant l'~,* ahead of t. *de bonne ~,* early. *à la bonne ~!* that's fine! *à l'~ actuelle,* at the present t. *à l'~ qu'il est,* at this moment; by this time. *tout à l'~,* just now (*past*); presently, in a minute. *d'~ en ~,* (*expect*) any time now.
heureusement (œrøzmɑ̃) *ad,* fortunately, luckily. ~ *qu'il est parti,* luckily he has left. **heureux, euse** (rø, øz) *a,* happy; pleased (*de voir,* to see); fortunate, lucky; happy (*chance, choice*).
'heurt (œr) *m,* knock, bump, collision; (*fig.*) clash. *sans ~,* smooth[ly]. **'heurté, e** (œrte) *a,* (*Phot.*) contrasty. **'heurter** (te) *v.t,* to strike, knock, bump [into]; (*fig.*) offend. ¶ *v.i. &* **se** ~, [*se*] ~ *contre,* to bump into, collide with. *se ~ à,* to come up against (*problem*). **'heurtoir** (twar) *m,* [door] knocker; (*Tech.*) stop; (*Rly*) buffer.
hexagone (ɛgzagɔn) *m,* hexagon. ¶ *a,* hexagonal.
hiatus (jatys) *m,* (*Gram., fig.*) hiatus.
hiberner (ibɛrne) *v.i,* to hibernate.
'hibou (ibu) *pl.* ~*x, m,* owl.
'hic (ik) *m: voilà le ~!* there's the snag!
'hideur (idœr) *f,* hideousness. **'hideux, euse**† (dø, øz) *a,* hideous.
hier (iɛr) *ad,* yesterday. ~ [*au*] *soir,* last night.
'hiérarchie (jerarʃi) *f,* hierarchy. **hiérarchique** (ʃik) *a,* hierarchical. *voie ~,* official channels.
hiéroglyphe (jerɔglif) *m,* hieroglyph.
hi-fi (ifi) *a. & f,* hi-fi.
hilare (ilar) *a,* hilarious, laughing. **hilarité** (larite) *f,* hilarity, merriment, laughter.
hindou, e (ɛ̃du) *a. &* **H~,** *n,* Indian; Hindu. **~isme** (ism) *m,* Hinduism.
hippique (ippik) *a,* horse (*show*); equestrian. **hippocampe** (ippɔkɑ̃p) *m,* sea horse. **hippodrome** (drom) *m,* racecourse. **boucherie hippophagique** (faʒik), horsemeat butcher's. **hippopotame** (pɔtam) *m,* hippopotamus.
hirondelle (irɔ̃dɛl) *f,* swallow. ~ *de fenêtre,* house martin. ~ *de rivage,* sand martin.
hirsute (irsyt) *a,* hairy; shaggy; tousled.
'hisser ([h]ise) *v.t,* to hoist; haul up.
histoire (istwar) *f,* history; story, tale; fib; business. *~s,* fuss; trouble. *l'~ de France,* French history. *le plus beau de l'~ c'est que,* the best part of it is that. ~ *drôle,* funny story. *une drôle d'~,* a funny business. *faire des ~s,* to make trouble (*à qn,* for s.o); make a fuss. *pas d'~s!* (*to child*) no nonsense! ~ *de faire P,* just to do. *V dormir.* **historien, ne** (rjɛ̃, ɛn) *n,* historian. **historiette** (rjɛt) *f,* anecdote. **historique**† (rik) *a,* historical; historic. ¶ *m, faire l'~ de,* to give an account *or* review of.
hiver (ivɛr) *m,* winter. *en ~,* in winter. *sports d'~,* w. sports. **hivernal, e** (nal) *a,* winter; wintry. **hiverner** (ne) *v.i. & t,* to winter.
'hochement (ɔʃmɑ̃) *m:* ~ *de tête,* nod; shake of the head. **'hoche-queue** (kø) *m,* wagtail. **'hocher** (ʃe) *v.t:* ~ *la tête,* to nod; shake one's head. **'hochet** (ʃɛ) *m,* rattle.
'hockey (ɔkɛ) *m,* hockey. ~ *sur glace,* ice h.
'holà ([h]ɔla) *i,* hi!, whoa!, hold it! *mettre le ~ à,* to put a stop to.
'hollandais, e (ɔlɑ̃dɛ, ɛz) *a,* Dutch. **'H~,** *n,* Dutchman, -woman. *le ~,* Dutch (*language*). **la Hollande** (lɑ̃d), Holland.
holocauste (ɔlɔkost) *m,* holocaust; sacrifice.
'homard (ɔmar) *m,* lobster.
homélie (ɔmeli) *f,* homily.
homéopathe (ɔmeɔpat) *m,* homoeopath. **homéopathie** (ti) *f,* homoeopathy. **homéopathique** (tik) *a,* homoeopathic.
homérique (ɔmerik) *a,* Homeric.
homicide (ɔmisid) *a,* homicidal. ¶ *n,* murderer. ¶ *m,* murder, homicide. ~ *involontaire,* manslaughter.
hommage (ɔmaʒ) *m,* homage, tribute. *~s,* respects, compliments. *en ~ de,* as a token of. ~ *de l'éditeur,* (*book*) with the publisher's compliments.
hommasse (ɔmas) *a,* mannish (*woman*). **homme** (ɔm) *m,* man. *l'~,* man, mankind. *vêtements d'~,* men's clothes. ~ *d'affaires,* businessman. ~ *de barre,* helmsman. ~ *d'équipage,* member of the crew (*ship*). ~ *d'Etat,* statesman. *~-grenouille,* frogman. ~ *d'intérieur,* domesticated man. *l'~ de la rue,* the man in

the street. ~ *de lettres,* man of letters. ~-*orchestre,* one-man band. ~ *de paille,* puppet, stooge *P.* ~-*sandwich,* sandwich man. ~ *à tout faire,* handyman, odd job man.
homogène (ɔmɔʒɛn) *a,* homogeneous.
homologue (ɔmɔlɔg) *a,* homologous; corresponding (*de,* to). ¶ *m,* (*pers.*) equivalent, counterpart. **homologuer** (ge) *v.t,* to ratify.
homonyme (ɔmɔnim) *m,* homonym; namesake.
homosexuel, le (ɔmɔseksɥɛl) *a.* & *n,* homosexual.
'hongre (ɔ̃gr) *a.m,* gelded. ¶ *m,* gelding.
'Hongrie (la) (ɔ̃gri), Hungary. **'hongrois, e** (grwa, az) *a.* & **'H~,** *n,* Hungarian. *le* ~, Hungarian (*language*).
honnête† (ɔnɛt) *a,* honest, honourable, decent; civil, courteous; fair, reasonable (*price*). ~ *homme,* gentleman. **honnêteté** (nɛtte) *f,* honesty; decency; courtesy; fairness.
honneur (ɔnœr) *m,* honour; credit; reward; pleasure. *mettre son* ~ *à faire,* to make it a point of h. to do. *faire* ~ *à,* to be a credit to (*family*); honour, meet (*obligation*); do justice to (*meal*). *avoir l'*~ *de faire,* to have the h. of doing. (*Adm.*) *j'ai l'*~ *de solliciter,* I am writing to ask. *parole, invité d'*~, word, guest of h. *en l'*~ *de,* (*banquet*) in h. of. ~ *aux dames,* ladies first. *à vous l'*~, after you.
'honnir (ɔnir) *v.t,* to hold in contempt.
honorable† (ɔnɔrabl) *a,* honourable; creditable; respectable. **honoraire** (rɛr) *a,* honorary. **~s,** *m.pl,* fee[s]. **honorer** (re) *v.t,* to honour; respect, esteem; honour, favour (*de,* with); grace; dignify; do credit to; honour (*cheque*). (*Com.*) *votre honorée,* your favour (*letter*). **honorifique** (rifik) *a,* honorary.
'honte (ɔ̃t) *f,* shame, disgrace. *avoir* ~ to be ashamed. *faire* ~ *à qn,* to put s.o to shame. *c'est une* ~*!* it's a disgrace! **'honteux, euse**† (ɔ̃tø, øz) *a,* ashamed (*de,* of); shameful. *c'est* ~, it's disgraceful.
hôpital (ɔpital) *m,* hospital.
'hoquet (ɔkɛ) *m,* hiccup; gulp. *avoir le* ~, to have hiccups. **~er** (kte) *v.i,* to hiccup.
horaire (ɔrɛr) *a,* hourly. ¶ *m,* timetable.
'horde (ɔrd) *f,* horde.
horizon (ɔrizɔ̃) *m,* horizon. *changer d'*~, to have a change of scenery. **~tal, e**† (tal) *a,* horizontal.
horloge (ɔrlɔʒ) *f,* clock. *à l'*~ *de la gare,* (*midday*) by the station clock. ~ *normande,* ~ *de parquet,* grandfather c. ~ *parlante,* speaking c. **horloger** (lɔʒe) *m,* watchmaker, clockmaker. **horlogerie** (ʒri) *f,* watchmaking &c; watchmaker's [shop].
hormis (ɔrmi) *pr,* apart from; except, save.
horoscope (ɔrɔskɔp) *m,* horoscope.
horreur (ɔrrœr) *f,* horror; repugnance, loathing. *quelle* ~*!* how dreadful! *frappé d'*~, horror-struck. *j'ai* ~ *de ça, ça me fait* ~, I detest that. **horrible**† (ɔrribl) *a,* horrible, frightful; hideous; awful, terrible (*bad*). **horripiler** (ɔrripile) *v.t,* to exasperate.
'hors (ɔr) *pr,* apart from, except. ~ **de,** outside, out of. ~ *de la ville,* outside the town. ~ *d'atteinte, de danger, d'haleine,* out of reach, danger, breath. ~ *de soi,* beside o.s (*rage*). ~ *concours,* not competing. *mettre* ~ *de combat,* to put out of the fight. ~ *d'usage,* out of action. [*moteur*] ~-*bord, m,* outboard [motor]. ~-*d'œuvre, m,* (*Cook.*) hors d'œuvre. ~-*jeu, a.* & *m,* (*Sport*) off-side. ~-*la-loi, m,* outlaw. ~ *ligne,* ~ *pair,* outstanding, unequalled. ~-*taxe, a,* duty-free. ~-*texte, m,* plate (*book*). ~ *tout, a,* overall (*length*).
hortensia (ɔrtɑ̃sja) *m,* hydrangea.
horticole (ɔrtikɔl) *a,* horticultural. **horticulteur** (kyltœr) *m,* horticulturist. **horticulture** (tyr) *f,* horticulture.
hospice (ɔspis) *m,* [old people's] home; (*Rel.*) hospice. **hospitalier, ère** (talje, ɛr) *a,* hospitable; hospital. **hospitaliser** (lize) *v.t,* to send to hospital, hospitalize. **hospitalité** (te) *f,* hospitality.
hostie (ɔsti) *f,* (*Rel.*) host.
hostile† (ɔstil) *a,* hostile (*à,* to). **hostilité** (lite) *f,* hostility.
hôte (ot) *m,* host; landlord (*inn*). ¶ *n,* guest.
hôtel (ɔtɛl) *m,* hotel. ~ [*particulier*], mansion; town house. ~-*Dieu,* hospital. ~ *meublé,* lodging house. ~ *de ville,* town hall. ~ *des ventes,* auction rooms. **hôtelier, ère** (tɔlje, ɛr) *a,* hotel. ¶ *n,* hotel keeper, hotelier. **hôtellerie** (tɛlri) *f,* inn; hotel trade.
hôtesse (otɛs) *f,* hostess; landlady. ~ *de l'air,* air hostess.
'hotte (ɔt) *f,* basket (*on back*); hood (*chimney*).
'houblon (ublɔ̃) *m,* hop [plant]; hops.
'houe (u) *f,* hoe. **'houer** (ue) *v.t,* to hoe.
'houille (uj) *f,* coal. ~ *blanche,* water power. **'houiller, ère** (uje, ɛr) *a,* coal (*basin*). ¶ *f,* colliery, coal mine.
'houle (ul) *f,* swell (*sea*). **'houleux, euse** (ulø, øz) *a,* heavy, rough (*sea*); (*fig.*) stormy, turbulent.
'houppe (up) *f,* tuft, tassel. **houppette** (pɛt) *f,* powder puff.
'hourra (hurra) *i.* & *m,* hurrah, hurray.
'houspiller (uspije) *v.t,* to tell off, scold.
'housse (us) *f,* dust cover; loose cover.
'houx (u) *m,* holly.
hovercraft (ɔvɛrkraft) *m,* hovercraft.
'hublot (yblo) *m,* porthole.
'huche (yʃ) *f,* kneading trough; bread bin.
'hue (hy) *i,* gee up! **'huées** (ɥe) *f.pl,* boos. **'huer** (ɥe) *v.t,* to boo. ¶ *v.i,* (*owl*) to hoot.
'huguenot, e (ygno, ɔt) *n,* Huguenot.
huile (ɥil) *f,* oil; oil [painting]; (*P*) bigwig *P.* ~ *de coude,* (*fig.*) elbow grease. ~ *de foie de*

morue, cod liver oil. ~ *de lin,* linseed o. ~ *de paraffine,* (*Med.*) liquid paraffin. ~ *de table,* salad o. *peinture à l'*~, oil paint; o. painting. *mer d'*~, glassy sea. *jeter de l'*~ *sur le feu,* to add fuel to the flames. **huiler** (le) *v.t,* to oil. **huileux, euse** (lø, øz) *a,* oily. **huilier** (lje) *m,* cruet (*oil & vinegar*).
huis clos (à) (ɥi), in camera. **huissier** (sje) *m,* usher; bailiff.
'huit (ɥit; *before a consonant,* ɥi) *a. & m,* eight. ~ *jours,* a week. [*d'*]*aujourd'hui en* ~, a week today. *V* **six** *for phrases.* ~**aine** (tɛn) *f,* about eight. *une* ~ [*de jours*], a week. ~**ante** (tɑ̃t) *a,* (*Swiss*) eighty. **'huitième†** (tjɛm) *a. & n,* eighth.
huître (ɥitr) *f,* oyster.
'hulotte (ylɔt) *f,* tawny owl.
humain, e† (ymɛ̃, ɛn) *a,* human; humane. ¶ *m.pl, les* ~*s,* human beings. **humaniser** (manize) *v.t,* to humanize. **humaniste** (nist) *a. & n,* humanist. **humanitaire** (tɛr) *a. & n,* humanitarian. **humanité** (te) *f,* (*gen.*) humanity. *l'*~, mankind.
humble† (œ̃bl) *a,* humble.
humecter (ymɛkte) *v.t,* to moisten, damp.
'humer (yme) *v.t,* to breathe in; smell.
humérus (ymerys) *m,* humerus.
humeur (ymœr) *f,* humour, mood; temper; ill-humour, bad temper. *de bonne, mauvaise* ~, in a good, bad temper *or* mood. *être d'*~ *à faire,* to be in the mood to do.
humide† (ymid) *a,* damp, moist, humid; wet. **humidifier** (difje) *v.t,* to humidify. **humidité** (te) *f,* damp[ness], humidity. *'craint l'*~*',* 'keep in a dry place'.
humiliation (ymiljasjɔ̃) *f,* humiliation. **humilier** (lje) *v.t,* to humiliate. **humilité** (lite) *f,* humility.
humoriste (ymɔrist) *n,* humorist. **humoristique** (tik) *a,* humorous. **humour** (mur) *m,* humour. *manquer d'*~, to have no sense of h.
humus (ymys) *m,* humus.
'hune (yn) *f,* top (*Naut.*) **'hunier** (nje) *m,* topsail.
'huppe (yp) *f,* hoopoe; crest. **'huppé, e** (pe) *a,* crested (*bird*); (*P*) posh *P.*
'hurler (yrle) *v.i,* to howl; yell; (*siren*) wail; (*colours*) clash.
hurluberlu (yrlybɛrly) *m,* crank.
'hutte (yt) *f,* hut.
hybride (ibrid) *a. & m,* hybrid.
hydrate (idrat) *m,* hydrate. **hydrater** (te) *v.t,* to moisturize (*skin*).
hydraulique (idrolik) *a,* hydraulic. ¶ *f,* hydraulics.
hydravion (idravjɔ̃) *m,* seaplane.
hydrocarbure (idrɔkarbyr) *m,* hydrocarbon. **hydro-électrique** (elɛktrik) *a,* hydroelectric. **hydrofoil** (fɔjl) *m,* hydrofoil. **hydrogène** (ʒɛn) *m,* hydrogen. **hydroglisseur** (glisœr) *m,* hydroplane (*boat*). **hydrolyse** (liz) *f,* hydrolysis. **hydropique** (pik) *a,* dropsical. **hydropisie** (pizi) *f,* dropsy. **hydrophile** (fil) *a,* absorbent (*cotton wool*).
hyène (jɛn) *f,* hyena.
hygiène (iʒjɛn) *f,* hygiene. **hygiénique†** (ʒjenik) *a,* hygienic.
hymen (imɛn) *m,* (*Poet.*) marriage; (*Anat.*) hymen.
hymne (imn) *m,* hymn. ~ *national,* national anthem.
hyper... (ipɛr) *pref,* hyper...
hyperbole (ipɛrbɔl) *f,* hyperbole; hyperbola.
hypermarché (ipɛrmarʃe) *m,* hypermarket. **hypernerveux, euse** (nɛrvø, øz) *a,* over-excitable. **hypertension** (tɑ̃sjɔ̃) *f,* high blood pressure.
hypnose (ipnoz) *f,* hypnosis. **hypnotique** (nɔtik) *a,* hypnotic. **hypnotiser** (tize) *v.t,* to hypnotize. **hypnotiseur** (zœr) *m,* hypnotist. **hypnotisme** (tism) *m,* hypnotism.
hypocrisie (ipɔkrizi) *f,* hypocrisy. **hypocrite†** (krit) *a,* hypocritical. ¶ *n,* hypocrite. **hypodermique** (dɛrmik) *a,* hypodermic. **hypothèque** (tɛk) *f,* mortgage. **hypothéquer** (ke) *v.t,* to mortgage. **hypothèse** (tɛz) *f,* hypothesis. **hypothétique†** (tetik) *a,* hypothetical.
hystérie (isteri) *f,* hysteria. **hystérique** (rik) *a,* hysterical. ¶ *n,* (*Med.*) hysteric.

I

I, i (i) *m, letter,* I, i.
ibérique (iberik) *a,* Iberian.
ibis (ibis) *m,* ibis.
iceberg (isbɛrg) *m,* iceberg.
ici (isi) *ad,* here; now. *par* ~, (*come*) this way. *jusqu'*~, as far as this; up till now. *d'*~ *demain,* by tomorrow. *d'*~ *là,* till then. *d'*~ *peu,* before long. (*Tel.*) ~ *X,* X speaking. ~-**bas,** here below.
icône (ikon) *f,* icon. **iconoclaste** (kɔnɔklast) *m,* iconoclast.
idéal, e† (ideal) *a. & m,* ideal. ~**iser** (lize) *v.t,* to idealize. ~**iste** (list) *a,* idealistic. ¶ *n,* idealist.
idée (ide) *f,* idea, notion; thought; mind. ~*s,*

views. *se faire des ~s,* to imagine things. *on n'a pas ~ de la chaleur,* you can't imagine the heat. *n'en faire qu'à son ~,* to do just as one likes. *se mettre dans l'~ de faire,* to take it into one's head to do. *j'ai dans l'~ que,* I have the notion that. *avoir les ~s larges, étroites,* to be broad-, narrow-minded. *~ fixe,* obsession.

idem (idɛm) *ad,* idem, ditto.

identifier (idɑ̃tifje) *v.t. &* **s'~,** to identify (*à,* with). **identique**† (tik) *a,* identical. **identité** (te) *f,* identity; similarity.

idiomatique (idjɔmatik) *a,* idiomatic. **idiome** (djɔm) *m,* idiom.

idiot, e† (idjo, ɔt) *a,* idiotic, stupid. ¶ *n,* idiot. *faire l'~,* to be stupid; play the fool. **idiotie** (jɔsi) *f,* idiocy. *faire une ~,* to do sth stupid.

idiotisme (idjɔtism) *m,* idiom, locution.

idolâtre (idɔlɑtr) *a,* idolatrous. **idolâtrer** (lɑtre) *v.t,* to idolize. **idolâtrie** (tri) *f,* idolatry. **idole** (dɔl) *f,* (*Rel., fig.*) idol.

idylle (idil) *f,* idyll; romance (*love*).

if (if) *m,* yew [tree].

igname (iɲam) *f,* yam.

ignare (iɲar) *a,* ignorant. ¶ *n,* ignoramus.

ignifuge (ignifyʒ) *a,* fireproof. **ignifuger** (fyʒe) *v.t,* to fireproof.

ignoble† (iɲɔbl) *a,* base, vile; revolting.

ignominie (iɲɔmini) *f,* ignominy. **ignominieux, euse**† (njø, øz) *a,* ignominious.

ignorance (iɲɔrɑ̃s) *f,* ignorance. *dans l'~ de,* in the dark about. **ignorant, e** (rɑ̃, ɑ̃t) *a,* ignorant, unaware (*de,* of). ¶ *n,* ignoramus. **ignoré, e** (re) *a,* unknown (*de tous,* to anyone). **ignorer** (re) *v.t,* to be ignorant (*or* unaware) of, not to know; ignore (*pers.*).

iguane (igwan) *m,* iguana.

il (il) *pn,* he; it; she (*of ship*). *~s,* they. ¶ *pn. imp, ~ fait froid,* it is cold. *~ y a,* there is, are. *~ est vrai que,* it is true that.

île (il) *f,* island, isle. *les ~s Britanniques &c,* see under *britannique &c.*

illégal, e† (illegal) *a,* illegal, unlawful. **~ité** (lite) *f,* illegality. **illégitime**† (ʒitim) *a,* illegitimate; unwarranted. **illégitimité** (mite) *f,* illegitimacy.

illettré, e (illɛtre) *a. & n,* illiterate.

illicite† (illisit) *a,* illicit.

illico (illiko) *ad,* directly, at once.

illimité, e (illimite) *a,* unlimited; boundless; indefinite (*leave*).

illisible† (illizibl) *a,* illegible; unreadable.

illogique† (illɔʒik) *a,* illogical. **illogisme** (ʒism) *m,* illogicality.

illumination (illyminasjɔ̃) *f,* illumination; lighting; floodlighting; inspiration, brainwave. **illuminé, e** (ne) *n,* visionary. **illuminer** (ne) *v.t,* to illuminate; light up; floodlight.

illusion (illyzjɔ̃) *f,* illusion. *~ d'optique,* optical illusion. *se faire des ~s,* to delude o.s. **~niste** (ɔnist) *n,* conjuror. **illusoire** (zwar) *a,* illusory; illusive.

illustration (illystrasjɔ̃) *f,* (*gen.*) illustration. **illustre** (tr) *a,* illustrious. **illustrer** (tre) *v.t,* to illustrate. **s'~,** to become famous.

îlot (ilo) *m,* small island; block (*houses*); (*fig.*) zone, area; pocket (*resistance*).

ilote (ilɔt) *m,* (*Hist.*) Helot; (*fig.*) serf.

image (imaʒ) *f,* image; reflection; picture; likeness; frame (*film*); appearance. *~s,* imagery. **imagé, e** (ʒe) *a,* full of imagery. **imaginaire** (ʒinɛr) *a,* imaginary. **imaginatif, ive** (natif, iv) *a,* imaginative. **imagination** (nasjɔ̃) *f,* imagination. **imaginer** (ne) *v.t,* to imagine; devise, invent. **s'~,** to imagine, think; picture o.s.

imbattable (ɛ̃batabl) *a,* unbeatable.

imbécile† (ɛ̃besil) *a,* idiotic, stupid. ¶ *n,* idiot, imbecile. **imbécilité** (silite) *f,* imbecility, idiocy; idiotic remark *or* act.

imberbe (ɛ̃bɛrb) *a,* beardless.

imbiber (ɛ̃bibe) *v.t,* to soak, impregnate.

imbriquer (s') (ɛ̃brike) *v.pr,* to overlap; (*problems*) be interwoven.

imbroglio (ɛ̃brɔljo) *m,* imbroglio.

imbu, e (ɛ̃by) *a: ~ de,* full of, imbued with.

imbuvable (ɛ̃byvabl) *a,* undrinkable.

imitateur, trice (imitatœr, tris) *n,* imitator, mimic. ¶ *a,* imitative. **imitation** (sjɔ̃) *f,* imitation &c. **imiter** (te) *v.t,* to imitate; mimic; impersonate; forge.

immaculé, e (immakyle) *a,* immaculate.

immangeable (ɛ̃mɑ̃ʒabl) *a,* uneatable.

immanquable† (ɛ̃mɑ̃kabl) *a,* inevitable; impossible to miss.

immatriculer (immatrikyle) *v.t,* to register. **immatriculation** (lasjɔ̃) *f,* registration.

immédiat, e† (immedja, at) *a,* immediate. *dans l'~,* for the time being.

immémorial, e (immemɔrjal) *a,* immemorial.

immense (immɑ̃s) *a,* immense, huge, vast; boundless. **immensément** (mɑ̃semɑ̃) *ad,* immensely. **immensité** (site) *f,* immensity; hugeness, vastness.

immerger (immɛrʒe) *v.t,* to immerse, submerge; dump *or* bury at sea.

immérité, e (immerite) *a,* unmerited, undeserved.

immersion (immɛrsjɔ̃) *f,* immersion; submersion &c.

immeuble (immœbl) *m,* building; block of flats; (*Law*) real estate. *~ de bureaux,* office block.

immigrant, e (imigrɑ̃, ɑ̃t) *a. & n,* immigrant. **immigration** (immigrasjɔ̃) *f,* immigration. **immigrer** (gre) *v.i,* to immigrate.

imminence (imminɑ̃s) *f,* imminence. **imminent, e** (nɑ̃, ɑ̃t) *a,* imminent, impending.

immiscer (s') (immise) *v.pr, s'~ dans,* to interfere in. **immixtion** (mikstjɔ̃) *f,* interference.

immobile (immɔbil) *a,* motionless, still; immobile. **immobilier, ère** (lje, ɛr) *a,* property, real estate (*market*). *société ~ère*, property company. **immobilisation** (lizasjɔ̃) *f*, immobilisation; standstill. **immobiliser** (ze) *v.t*, to immobilize; stop, bring to a halt (*car, Mach.*); (*Fin.*) tie up. **immobilité** (lité) *f*, immobility; stillness.

immodéré†, e (immɔdere) *a*, immoderate; excessive; inordinate.

immolation (immɔlasjɔ̃) *f*, immolation, sacrifice. **immoler** (le) *v.t*, to sacrifice.

immonde (immɔ̃d) *a*, foul, filthy; vile, sordid (*act*). **immondices** (mɔ̃dis) *f.pl*, refuse.

immoral, e (immɔral) *a*, immoral. **immoralité** (lite) *f*, immorality.

immortaliser (immɔrtalize) *v.t*, to immortalize. **immortalité** (te) *f*, immortality. **immortel, le†** (tɛl) *a*, immortal. ¶ *m.pl*, *les I~s*, Academicians. ¶ *f*, everlasting flower.

immuable† (immyabl) *a*, immutable, unchanging.

immuniser (imynize) *v.t*, (*Med.*) to immunize. **immunité** (nite) *f*, (*gen.*) immunity.

impair, e (ɛ̃pɛr) *a*, odd (*number*). ¶ *m*, blunder.

impalpable (ɛ̃palpabl) *a*, impalpable.

impardonnable (ɛ̃pardɔnabl) *a*, unpardonable, unforgivable.

imparfait, e† (ɛ̃parfɛ, ɛt) *a*, imperfect. ¶ *m*, imperfect [tense].

impartial, e† (ɛ̃parsjal) *a*, impartial, unbiassed. **~ité** (lite) *f*, impartiality.

impartir (ɛ̃partir) *v.t*, to impart, bestow.

impasse (ɛ̃pɑs) *f*, blind alley, dead end; (*fig.*) impasse, deadlock.

impassible† (ɛ̃pasibl) *a*, impassive.

impatiemment (ɛ̃pasjamɑ̃) *ad*, impatiently. **impatience** (sjɑ̃s) *f*, impatience. **impatient, e** (ɑ̃, ɑ̃t) *a*, impatient (*de faire*, to do). **impatienter** (te) *v.t*, to put out of patience, irritate. **s'~**, to grow impatient (*contre, de*, with, at).

impayable *P* (ɛ̃pɛjabl) *a*, priceless *P* (*funny*). **impayé, e** (je) *a*, unpaid.

impeccable† (ɛ̃pɛkabl) *a*, impeccable.

impénétrable† (ɛ̃penetrabl) *a*, impenetrable; inscrutable.

impénitent, e (ɛ̃penitɑ̃, ɑ̃t) *a*, unrepentant.

impensable (ɛ̃pɑ̃sabl) *a*, unthinkable; unbelievable.

imper *P* (ɛ̃pɛr) *m*, (*abb. of imperméable*) mac *P*.

impératif, ive† (ɛ̃peratif, iv) *a*, imperative; commanding (*tone*). ¶ *n*, (*Gram.*) imperative; necessity.

impératrice (ɛ̃peratris) *f*, empress.

imperceptible† (ɛ̃pɛrsɛptibl) *a*, imperceptible.

imperfection (ɛ̃pɛrfɛksjɔ̃) *f*, imperfection.

impérial, e (ɛ̃perjal) *a*, imperial. ¶ *f*, imperial (*beard*); top deck (*bus*). **~isme** (lism) *m*, imperialism. **~iste** (list) *a. & m*, imperialist.

impérieux, euse† (ɛ̃perjø, øz) *a*, imperious; pressing (*needs*).

impérissable (ɛ̃perisabl) *a*, imperishable, undying.

imperméabiliser (ɛ̃pɛrmeabilize) *v.t*, to waterproof. **imperméable** (bl) *a*, impermeable; water-proof (*cloth*); (*fig.*) impervious (*à*, to). *~ à l'air*, airtight. ¶ *m*, raincoat, waterproof, mackintosh.

impersonnel, le† (ɛ̃pɛrsɔnɛl) *a*, impersonal.

impertinemment (ɛ̃pɛrtinamɑ̃) *ad*, impertinently. **impertinence** (nɑ̃s) *f*, [piece of] impertinence. **impertinent, e** (nɑ̃, ɑ̃t) *a*, impertinent.

imperturbable† (ɛ̃pɛrtyrbabl) *a*, imperturbable, unruffled.

impétrant, e (ɛ̃petrɑ̃, ɑ̃t) *n*, (*Adm.*) applicant.

impétueux, euse† (ɛ̃petɥø, øz) *a*, impetuous; hot-headed; raging (*wind*). **impétuosité** (tɥozite) *f*, impetuosity.

impie (ɛ̃pi) *a*, impious, ungodly. **impiété** (pjete) *f*, impiety, ungodliness.

impitoyable† (ɛ̃pitwajabl) *a*, pitiless, merciless, ruthless, relentless.

implacable† (ɛ̃plakabl) *a*, implacable.

implanter (ɛ̃plɑ̃te) *v.t*, to establish, set up; settle (*race*); (*fig., Med.*) implant.

implicite† (ɛ̃plisit) *a*, implicit. **impliquer** (ke) *v.t*, to imply; implicate (*dans*, in).

implorer (ɛ̃plɔre) *v.t*, to implore, beseech.

impoli†, e (ɛ̃pɔli) *a*, impolite, rude. **impolitesse** (tɛs) *f*, impoliteness, rudeness.

impondérable (ɛ̃pɔ̃derabl) *a. & m*, imponderable.

impopulaire (ɛ̃pɔpylɛr) *a*, unpopular.

importance (ɛ̃pɔrtɑ̃s) *f*, importance; size, extent. *prendre de l'~*, to increase in importance *or* size. *se donner de l'~*, to put on airs. *d'~*, (*O thrash*) soundly. **important, e** (tɑ̃, ɑ̃t) *a*, important; sizeable (*sum*); extensive (*damage*). *peu ~*, unimportant. ¶ *m*, *l'~*, the main thing. *faire l'~*, to give o.s airs.

importateur, trice (ɛ̃pɔrtatœr, tris) *a*, importing. ¶ *n*, importer. **importation** (sjɔ̃) *f*, import[ation]. **importer**[1] (te) *v.t*, to import.

importer[2] (ɛ̃pɔrte) *v.i*, to matter. *peu importe que*, it doesn't much matter that. *n'importe*, it doesn't matter. *n'importe où, qui, quoi &c*, anywhere, anyone, anything &c.

importun, e (ɛ̃pɔrtœ̃, yn) *a*, importunate, tiresome, troublesome; inopportune. ¶ *n*, intruder; nuisance. **importuner** (tyne) *v.t*, to importune, bother, disturb. **importunité** (nite) *f*, importunity.

imposable (ɛ̃pozabl) *a*, taxable. **imposant, e** (zɑ̃, ɑ̃t) *a*, imposing; impressive. **imposer** (ze) *v.t*, to impose; enforce (*discipline*); (*Rel.*) lay on (*hands*); (*Fin.*) tax. *~ le respect*, to command respect. *~ son nom*, to make a name for o.s. *en ~ à qn*, to impress s.o. **s'~**, to be called for, to be essential. *une visite s'impose*, a visit is a must. *s'~ à qn*, to impose [o.s] on s.o.

imposition (zisjɔ̃) *f,* taxation; (*Rel.*) laying on (*of hands*).

impossibilité (ɛ̃pɔsibilite) *f,* impossibility. *être dans l'~ de faire,* to be unable to do. **impossible** (bl) *a,* impossible. ¶ *m, faire l'~,* to do one's utmost.

imposteur (ɛ̃pɔstœr) *m,* impostor. **imposture** (tyr) *f,* imposture.

impôt (ɛ̃po) *m,* tax; taxation. *~s locaux,* rates. *~ sur le revenu,* income tax.

impotent, e (ɛ̃pɔtɑ̃, ɑ̃t) *a,* disabled, crippled. ¶ *n,* cripple. **impotence** (tɑ̃s) *f,* disability.

impraticable (ɛ̃pratikabl) *a,* impracticable; impassable (*road*); unfit for play (*ground*).

imprécation (ɛ̃prekasjɔ̃) *f,* imprecation, curse.

imprécis, e (ɛ̃presi, iz) *a,* imprecise; vague. **imprécision** (sizjɔ̃) *f,* imprecision &c.

imprégner (ɛ̃preɲe) *v.t,* to impregnate, fill, imbue (*de,* with). **s'~,** (*fig.*) to steep o.s (*de,* in).

imprenable (ɛ̃prənabl) *a,* impregnable.

impresario (ɛ̃prezarjo) *m,* impresario.

impression (ɛ̃prɛsjɔ̃) *f,* (*gen.*) impression; printing; (*Phot.*) exposure; undercoat (*paint*). *j'ai l'~ que,* I have the impression that. *faire bonne, mauvaise ~,* to create a good, bad i. **~nant, e** (ɔnɑ̃, ɑ̃t) *a,* impressive. **~ner** (ne) *v.t,* to impress; affect, upset; expose (*film*). **~niste** (nist) *a. & n,* (*Art*) impressionist.

imprévoyance (ɛ̃prevwajɑ̃s) *f,* improvidence; lack of foresight. **imprévu, e** (vy) *a. & m,* unforeseen; unexpected.

imprimé (ɛ̃prime) *m,* printed book, p. form. *~s,* printed matter. **imprimer** (me) *v.t,* to print; imprint; publish; transmit (*movement*). **imprimerie** (mri) *f,* printing (*art*); p. works. **imprimeur** (mœr) *m,* printer.

improbable (ɛ̃prɔbabl) *a,* improbable.

improductif, ive (ɛ̃prɔdyktif, iv) *a,* unproductive.

impromptu (ɛ̃prɔ̃pty) *ad. & a. inv,* impromptu; extempore. ¶ *m,* (*Mus.*) impromptu.

impropre† (ɛ̃prɔpr) *a,* inappropriate; unsuitable; unfit (*à,* for). **impropriété** (priete) *f,* inaccuracy, error (*language*).

improviser (ɛ̃prɔvize) *v.t. & i,* to improvise. *s'~ médecin,* to act as a doctor. **à l'improviste** (vist) *ad,* unexpectedly. *prendre qn ~,* to take s.o unawares.

imprudemment (ɛ̃prydamɑ̃) *ad,* carelessly; imprudently. **imprudence** (dɑ̃s) *f,* carelessness; imprudence; foolish act. **imprudent, e** (dɑ̃, ɑ̃t) *a,* careless; imprudent; unwise.

impudence (ɛ̃pydɑ̃s) *f,* impudence; shamelessness. **impudent, e** (dɑ̃, ɑ̃t) *a,* impudent; shameless.

impudeur (ɛ̃pydœr) *f,* immodesty. **impudique†** (dik) *a,* immodest; indecent.

impuissance (ɛ̃pɥisɑ̃s) *f,* powerlessness; helplessness; impotence (*sexual*). **impuissant, e** (sɑ̃, ɑ̃t) *a,* powerless; impotent.

impulsif, ive (ɛ̃pylsif, iv) *a,* impulsive. **impulsion** (sjɔ̃) *f,* (*gen.*) impulse; impetus.

impunément (ɛ̃pynemɑ̃) *ad,* with impunity. **impuni, e** (ni) *a,* unpunished, scot-free. **impunité** (te) *f,* impunity.

impur, e† (ɛ̃pyr) *a,* impure. **impureté** (pyrte) *f,* impurity.

imputer (ɛ̃pyte) *v.t,* to impute, ascribe, attribute (*à,* to); (*Fin.*) charge.

inabordable (inabɔrdabl) *a,* inaccessible; unapproachable (*pers.*); prohibitive (*price*).

inacceptable (inaksɛptabl) *a,* unacceptable.

inaccessible (inaksɛsibl) *a,* inaccessible. (*fig.*) *~ à,* impervious to.

inaccoutumé, e (inakutyme) *a,* unusual; unaccustomed (*à,* to).

inachevé, e (inaʃve) *a,* unfinished.

inactif, ive (inaktif, iv) *a,* inactive, idle; ineffectual. **inaction** (sjɔ̃) *f,* inaction, idleness. **inactivité** (tivite) *f,* inactivity.

inadapté, e (inadapte) *a,* maladjusted (*pers.*); not adapted (*à,* to).

inadmissible (inadmisibl) *a,* inadmissible.

inadvertance (inadvɛrtɑ̃s) *f,* inadvertence, oversight. *par ~,* inadvertently.

inaliénable (inaljenabl) *a,* inalienable.

inaltérable (inalterabl) *a,* unchanging, unfailing; fast (*colour*). *~ à,* unaffected by (*heat &c*).

inamical, e (inamikal) *a,* unfriendly.

inamovible (inamɔvibl) *a,* irremovable.

inanimé, e (inanime) *a,* inanimate, lifeless.

inanité (inanite) *f,* inanity, futility.

inanition (inanisjɔ̃) *f: d'~,* (*die*) of hunger.

inaperçu, e (inapɛrsy) *a,* unseen, unnoticed.

inapplicable (inaplikabl) *a,* inapplicable. **inappliqué, e** (ke) *a,* lacking application.

inappréciable (inapresjabl) *a,* inappreciable; inestimable, invaluable.

inapte (inapt) *a, ~ à,* incapable of; unsuited to; (*Mil.*) unfit for (*service*).

inarticulé, e (inartikyle) *a,* inarticulate.

inassouvi, e (inasuvi) *a,* unappeased.

inattaquable (inatakabl) *a,* unassailable.

inattendu, e (inatɑ̃dy) *a,* unexpected.

inattention (inatɑ̃sjɔ̃) *f,* inattention.

inaudible (inodibl) *a,* inaudible.

inaugurer (inogyre) *v.t,* to inaugurate; unveil, open; (*fig.*) usher in.

inavouable (inavuable) *a,* shameful.

incalculable (ɛ̃kalkylabl) *a,* incalculable.

incandescence (ɛ̃kɑ̃dɛsɑ̃s) *f,* incandescence. *en ~,* white hot. **incandescent, e** (sɑ̃, ɑ̃t) *a,* incandescent, white-hot.

incantation (ɛ̃kɑ̃tasjɔ̃) *f,* incantation.

incapable (ɛ̃kapabl) *a,* incapable (*de faire,* of doing); incompetent. **incapacité** (site) *f,* in-

competence. ~ *de faire,* inability to do. (*Med.*) disability, disablement.
incarcérer (ɛ̃karsere) *v.t,* to incarcerate.
incarnation (ɛ̃karnasjɔ̃) *f,* incarnation, embodiment. **incarné, e** (ne) *a,* incarnate; ingrowing (*nail*). **incarner** (ne) *v.t,* to embody.
incartade (ɛ̃kartad) *f,* prank.
incassable (ɛ̃kɑsabl) *a,* unbreakable.
incendiaire (ɛ̃sɑ̃djɛr) *a,* incendiary. ¶ *n,* arsonist. **incendie** (di) *m,* [outbreak of] fire. ~ *criminel,* arson. **incendié, e** (dje) *n,* victim of a fire. **incendier** (dje) *v.t,* to [set on] fire; set f. to.; burn down; (*fig.*) fire.
incertain, e (ɛ̃sɛrtɛ̃, ɛn) *a,* uncertain; indistinct. **incertitude** (tityd) *f,* uncertainty.
incessamment (ɛ̃sɛsamɑ̃) *ad,* very soon. **incessant, e** (sɑ̃, ɑ̃t) *a,* incessant.
inceste (ɛ̃sɛst) *m,* incest. **incestueux, euse**† (tɥø, øz) *a,* incestuous.
incidemment (ɛ̃sidamɑ̃) *ad,* incidentally. **incidence** (dɑ̃s) *f,* effect; incidence. **incident, e** (dɑ̃, ɑ̃t) *a,* incidental; incident (*ray*). ¶ *m,* incident; point of law; setback, hitch.
incinérateur (ɛ̃sineratœr) *m,* incinerator. **incinérer** (re) *v.t,* to incinerate; cremate.
inciser (ɛ̃size) *v.t,* to incise. **incisif, ive** (zif, iv) *a,* incisive. [*dent*] ~*ve,* incisor. **incision** (zjɔ̃) *f,* incision.
incitation (ɛ̃sitasjɔ̃) *f,* incitement. **inciter** (te) *v.t,* to incite, urge (*à faire,* to do).
incivil, e† (ɛ̃sivil) *a,* uncivil. **incivilité** (lite) *f,* incivility, rudeness.
inclinaison (ɛ̃klinɛzɔ̃) *f,* gradient; slope; tilt; pitch (*roof*); list (*ship*). **inclination** (nasjɔ̃) *f,* inclination, leaning; nod (*head*); bow. *avoir de l'~ pour,* to have a taste *or* penchant for. **incliner** (ne) *v.t,* to tilt; bend; bow (*head*). ~ *le buste,* to bow. ¶ *v.i,* ~ *à,* to tend *or* incline towards. **s'~,** to bow; give in. *s'~ devant,* to bow to (*command*).
inclure (ɛ̃klyr) *v.t.ir,* to enclose; include. *inclus,* inclusive (*dates*). **inclusivement** (klyzivmɑ̃) *ad,* inclusively; inclusive (*dates*).
incognito (ɛ̃kɔɲito) *ad.* & *m,* incognito.
incohérence (ɛ̃kɔerɑ̃s) *f,* incoherence. **incohérent, e** (rɑ̃, ɑ̃t) *a,* incoherent.
incolore (ɛ̃kɔlɔr) *a,* colourless.
incomber (ɛ̃kɔ̃be) *v.i,* ~ *à qn,* to be incumbent on s.o; fall to s.o.
incombustible (ɛ̃kɔ̃bystibl) *a,* incombustible.
incommensurable (ɛ̃kɔmɑ̃syrabl) *a,* incommensurable.
incommode (ɛ̃kɔmɔd) *a,* inconvenient, awkward; uncomfortable. **incommodé, e** (de) *a,* unwell, indisposed. **incommodément** (demɑ̃) *ad,* inconveniently &c. **incommoder** (de) *v.t,* (*heat &c*) to bother, trouble. **incommodité** (dite) *f,* inconvenience; awkwardness &c.
incomparable† (ɛ̃kɔ̃parabl) *a,* incomparable.
incompatible (ɛ̃kɔ̃patibl) *a,* incompatible.
incompétent, e (ɛ̃kɔ̃petɑ̃, ɑ̃t) *a,* incompetent.
incomplet, ète† (ɛ̃kɔ̃plɛ, ɛt) *a,* incomplete.
incompréhensible (ɛ̃kɔ̃preɑ̃sibl) *a,* incomprehensible.
incompris, e (ɛ̃kɔ̃pri, iz) *a,* misunderstood.
inconcevable (ɛ̃kɔ̃svabl) *a,* inconceivable.
inconciliable (ɛ̃kɔ̃siljabl) *a,* irreconcilable.
inconditionnel, le† (ɛ̃kɔ̃disjɔnɛl) *a,* unconditional.
inconduite (ɛ̃kɔ̃dɥit) *f,* loose living, wild behaviour.
incongru, e (ɛ̃kɔ̃gry) *a,* improper, unseemly; incongruous. ~**ité** (gryite) *f,* impropriety; incongruity.
inconnu, e (ɛ̃kɔny) *a,* unknown. ¶ *n,* unknown person; stranger. **l'~,** *m,* the unknown. ¶ *f,* (*Math., fig.*) unknown quantity.
inconsciemment (ɛ̃kɔ̃sjamɑ̃) *ad,* unconsciously. **inconscience** (sjɑ̃s) *f,* unconsciousness; recklessness. **inconscient, e** (ɑ̃, ɑ̃t) *a,* unconscious; thoughtless; irresponsible. ¶ *m,* (*Psych.*) *l'~,* the unconscious.
inconséquent, e (ɛ̃kɔ̃sekɑ̃, ɑ̃t) *a,* inconsistent; inconsequent; thoughtless.
inconsidéré†**, e** (ɛ̃kɔ̃sidere) *a,* thoughtless.
inconsistant, e (ɛ̃kɔ̃sistɑ̃, ɑ̃t) *a,* flimsy, weak.
inconsolable† (ɛ̃kɔ̃sɔlabl) *a,* inconsolable.
inconstant, e (ɛ̃kɔ̃stɑ̃, ɑ̃t) *a,* fickle, inconstant; changeable.
inconstitutionnel, le† (ɛ̃kɔ̃stitysjɔnɛl) *a,* unconstitutional.
incontestable† (ɛ̃kɔ̃tɛstabl) *a,* indisputable. **incontesté, e** (te) *a,* undisputed.
incontinent, e (ɛ̃kɔ̃tinɑ̃, ɑ̃t) *a,* incontinent.
incontrôlable (ɛ̃kɔ̃trolabl) *a,* unverifiable; uncontrollable.
inconvenance (ɛ̃kɔ̃vnɑ̃s) *f,* impropriety. **inconvenant, e** (vnɑ̃, ɑ̃t) *a,* improper, unseemly.
inconvénient (ɛ̃kɔ̃venjɑ̃) *m,* inconvenience; drawback, disadvantage.
incorporer (ɛ̃kɔrpɔre) *v.t,* to incorporate; (*Mil.*) enrol; mix, blend.
incorrect, e† (ɛ̃kɔrɛkt) *a,* incorrect; wrong; impolite; improper. **incorrection** (ksjɔ̃) *f,* incorrectness, &c.
incorrigible† (ɛ̃kɔriʒibl) *a,* incorrigible.
incorruptible (ɛ̃kɔryptibl) *a,* incorruptible.
incrédule (ɛ̃kredyl) *a,* incredulous; (*Rel.*) unbelieving. ¶ *n,* (*Rel.*) unbeliever. **incrédulité** (lite) *f,* incredulity; unbelief.
increvable (ɛ̃krəvabl) *a,* puncture-proof (*tyre*); (*P*) indefatigable (*pers.*).
incriminer (ɛ̃krimine) *v.t,* to incriminate, accuse; attack, challenge.
incroyable† (ɛ̃krwajabl) *a,* incredible.
incrustation (ɛ̃krystasjɔ̃) *f,* inlay, inlaid work; fur, scale. **incruster** (te) *v.t,* to inlay; fur up. **s'~,** to become embedded; (*P visitor*) to dig [o.s] in.
incubation (ɛ̃kybasjɔ̃) *f,* incubation.

inculpé, e (ɛ̃kylpe) *n,* accused. **inculper** (pe) *v.t,* to charge (*de,* with).
inculquer (ɛ̃kylke) *v.t,* to inculcate, instil.
inculte (ɛ̃kylt) *a,* uncultivated (*land*); unkempt (*beard*); uncultured (*pers.*).
incurable† (ɛ̃kyrabl) *a. & n,* incurable.
incurie (ɛ̃kyri) *f,* carelessness; negligence.
incursion (ɛ̃kyrsjɔ̃) *f,* incursion, raid, foray.
Inde (l') (ɛ̃d) *f,* India. *les I~s,* the Indies.
indécemment (ɛ̃desamɑ̃) *ad,* indecently. **indécence** (sɑ̃s) *f,* indecency. **indécent, e** (sɑ̃, ɑ̃t) *a,* indecent.
indéchiffrable (ɛ̃deʃifrabl) *a,* indecipherable; unintelligible.
indécis, e (ɛ̃desi, iz) *a,* indecisive; undecided; unsettled (*weather*); vague, indistinct (*form*). **indécision** (sisjɔ̃) *f,* indecision.
indéfendable (ɛ̃defɑ̃dabl) *a,* indefensible.
indéfini†, e (ɛ̃defini) *a,* indefinite; undefined. **indéfinissable** (sabl) *a,* indefinable.
indélébile (ɛ̃delebil) *a,* indelible.
indélicat, e† (ɛ̃delika, at) *a,* indelicate; dishonest. **indélicatesse** (tɛs) *f,* indelicacy; dishonesty.
indémaillable (ɛ̃demajabl) *a,* ladderproof.
indemne (ɛ̃demn) *a,* unscathed, unharmed, unhurt. **indemniser** (nize) *v.t,* to indemnify, compensate (*de,* for). **indemnité** (te) *f,* indemnity, compensation; allowance. *~ de transport,* travel allowance. *~ parlementaire,* M.P's salary.
indéniable† (ɛ̃denjabl) *a,* undeniable.
indépendamment (ɛ̃depɑ̃damɑ̃) *ad,* independently. *~ de,* irrespective of. **indépendance** (dɑ̃s) *f,* independence. **indépendant, e** (dɑ̃, ɑ̃t) *a,* (*gen.*) independent (*de,* of). *chambre ~e,* self-contained bedsitter.
indescriptible (ɛ̃dɛskriptibl) *a,* indescribable.
indésirable (ɛ̃dezirabl) *a. & n,* undesirable.
indestructible (ɛ̃dɛstryktibl) *a,* indestructible.
indéterminé, e (ɛ̃detɛrmine) *a,* indeterminate; unspecified.
index (ɛ̃dɛks) *m,* forefinger; pointer; index. (*Eccl.*) *l'I~,* the Index; (*fig.*) blacklist. **indexer** (se) *v.t,* (*Fin.*) to index.
indicateur, trice (ɛ̃dikatœr, tris) *n,* informer. ¶ *m,* timetable; guide, directory; (*Tech.*) indicator; gauge. *~ de vitesse,* speedometer. **indicatif, ive** (tif, iv) *a,* indicative (*de,* of). ¶ *m,* (*Radio*) signature tune; call sign. (*Gram.*) *l'~,* the indicative. **indication** (sjɔ̃) *f,* indication; clue; [piece of] information; instruction. *sauf ~ contraire,* unless otherwise stated. *~s scéniques,* stage directions. **indice** (dis) *m,* indication, sign; clue; index. *~ du coût de la vie,* cost of living index. **indicible†** (sibl) *a,* inexpressible; unspeakable.
indien, ne (ɛ̃djɛ̃, ɛn) *a. &* **I~,** *n,* Indian.
indifféremment (ɛ̃diferamɑ̃) *ad,* equally [well]; without distinction; indiscriminately. **indifférence** (rɑ̃s) *f,* indifference; unconcern. **indifférent, e** (rɑ̃, ɑ̃t) *a,* indifferent (*à,* to); immaterial.
indigène (ɛ̃diʒɛn) *a,* native; local; indigenous. ¶ *n,* native; local.
indigence (ɛ̃diʒɑ̃s) *f,* poverty, destitution. **indigent, e** (ʒɑ̃, ɑ̃t) *a,* destitute. ¶ *n,* pauper.
indigeste (ɛ̃diʒɛst) *a,* (*lit., fig.*) indigestible. **indigestion** (tjɔ̃) *f,* indigestion.
indignation (ɛ̃diɲasjɔ̃) *f,* indignation. **indigne†** (diɲ) *a,* unworthy (*pers.*); shameful (*act*). *~ de,* unworthy of, not deserving. **indigné, e** (ɲe) *a,* indignant. **indigner** (ɲe) *v.t,* to make (*s.o*) indignant. **s'~,** to get indignant (*de,* about, at). **indignité** (ɲite) *f,* unworthiness; shamefulness; outrage.
indigo (ɛ̃digo) *m,* indigo.
indiquer (ɛ̃dike) *v.t,* to indicate, show, point out; mark; suggest; mention, state. *à l'heure indiquée,* at the stated time.
indirect, e† (ɛ̃dirɛkt) *a,* indirect.
indiscipliné, e (ɛ̃disipline) *a,* unruly.
indiscret, ète† (ɛ̃diskrɛ, ɛt) *a,* indiscreet; prying, inquisitive. **indiscrétion** (kresjɔ̃) *f,* indiscretion; inquisitiveness.
indiscutable† (ɛ̃diskytabl) *a,* indisputable.
indispensable† (ɛ̃dispɑ̃sabl) *a,* indispensable.
indisponible (ɛ̃dispɔnibl) *a,* unavailable.
indisposé, e (ɛ̃dispoze) *a,* indisposed, unwell. **indisposer** (ze) *v.t,* to upset (*make ill*); antagonize. **indisposition** (zisjɔ̃) *f,* indisposition, upset.
indissoluble† (ɛ̃disɔlybl) *a,* indissoluble.
indistinct, e (ɛ̃distɛ̃[kt], ɛ̃kt) *a,* indistinct; confused; blurred. **~ement** (tɛ̃ktəmɑ̃) *ad,* indistinctly; indiscriminately; equally well.
individu (ɛ̃dividy) *m,* individual; (*pej.*) fellow. *son ~,* oneself; one's body. **~aliste** (dɥalist) *n.* (*& a.*), individualist(ic). **~alité** (lite) *f,* individuality. **~el, le†** (dɥɛl) *a,* individual.
indivis (par) (ɛ̃divi) *ad,* (*Law*) jointly. **indivisible†** (zibl) *a,* indivisible.
Indochine (l') (ɛ̃doʃin) *f,* Indo-China.
indocile (ɛ̃dɔsil) *a,* intractable; unruly.
indolemment (ɛ̃dɔlamɑ̃) *ad,* indolently; lazily. **indolence** (lɑ̃s) *f,* indolence; apathy. **indolent, e** (lɑ̃, ɑ̃t) *a,* indolent; apathetic; lethargic.
indolore (ɛ̃dɔlɔr) *a,* painless.
indomptable (ɛ̃dɔ̃tabl) *a,* untamable; indomitable; uncontrollable. **indompté, e** (te) *a,* untamed, wild; undaunted.
Indonésie (l') (ɛ̃dɔnezi) *f,* Indonesia.
indu, e (ɛ̃dy) *a,* undue; ungodly (*hour*).
indubitable† (ɛ̃dybitabl) *a,* indubitable, undoubted.
induction (ɛ̃dyksjɔ̃) *f,* (*gen.*) induction. **induire** (dɥir) *v.t.ir,* to lead; infer; induce. *~ en erreur,* to mislead. **induit** (dɥi) *m,* (*Elec.*) armature.
indulgence (ɛ̃dylʒɑ̃s) *f,* indulgence; leniency.

indulgent, e (ʒɑ̃, ɑ̃t) *a,* indulgent, lenient.
indûment (ɛ̃dymɑ̃) *ad,* unduly; wrongfully.
industrialiser (ɛ̃dystrialize) *v.t,* to industrialize. **industrie** (tri) *f,* industry; business, trade; ingenuity. ~ *légère, lourde,* light, heavy industry. ~ *du bâtiment,* building trade. ~ *du spectacle,* show business. **industriel, le**† (ɛl) *a,* industrial. ¶ *m,* manufacturer; industrialist. **industrieux, euse**† (ø, øz) *a,* industrious.
inébranlable† (inebrɑ̃labl) *a,* unshakable; unwavering; steadfast.
inédit, e (inedi, it) *a,* unpublished (*book*); novel, original.
ineffable (inefabl) *a,* ineffable.
ineffaçable (inefasabl) *a,* indelible.
inefficace† (inefikas) *a,* ineffectual, ineffective; inefficient (*pers.*).
inégal, e† (inegal) *a,* unequal; uneven. **inégalable** (labl) *a,* incomparable. **inégalité** (lite) *f,* inequality; unevenness.
inélégant, e (inelegɑ̃, ɑ̃t) *a,* inelegant; discourteous.
inéligible (ineliʒibl) *a,* ineligible.
inéluctable (inelyktabl) *a,* inescapable.
inénarrable (inenarabl) *a,* indescribable; priceless *P.*
inepte† (inɛpt) *a,* inept; stupid, silly. **ineptie** (si) *f,* ineptitude; [piece of] stupidity.
inépuisable† (inepɥizabl) *a,* inexhaustible.
inerte (inɛrt) *a,* inert; lifeless; apathetic. **inertie** (si) *f,* inertia; apathy.
inespéré, e (inɛspere) *a,* unhoped for, unexpected.
inestimable (inɛstimabl) *a,* inestimable; incalculable.
inévitable† (inevitabl) *a,* inevitable; unavoidable.
inexact, e† (inɛgzakt) *a,* inexact, inaccurate; unpunctual. ~**itude** (tityd) *f,* inaccuracy; unpunctuality.
inexcusable (inɛkskyzabl) *a,* inexcusable.
inexécutable (inɛgzekytabl) *a,* unworkable; impracticable.
inexistant, e (inɛgzistɑ̃, ɑ̃t) *a,* non-existent.
inexorable† (inɛgzɔrabl) *a,* inexorable.
inexpérience (inɛksperjɑ̃s) *f,* inexperience. **inexpérimenté, e** (rimɑ̃te) *a,* inexperienced, unskilled.
inexplicable (inɛksplikabl) *a,* inexplicable. **inexpliqué, e** (ke) *a,* unexplained.
inexploité, e (inɛksplwate) *a,* unexploited.
inexpressif, ive (inɛkspresif, iv) *a,* expressionless. **inexprimable** (primabl) *a,* inexpressible.
in extenso (inɛkstɛ̃so) *ad,* in extenso, in full.
inextinguible (inɛkstɛ̃gɥibl) *a,* inextinguishable; unquenchable; uncontrollable (*laugh*).
in extremis (inɛkstremis) *ad,* at the last minute.
inextricable† (inɛkstrikabl) *a,* inextricable.
infaillible† (ɛ̃fajibl) *a,* infallible; unerring.
infamant, e (ɛ̃famɑ̃, ɑ̃t) *a,* infamous; defamatory. **infâme** (fɑm) *a,* infamous, foul; vile; revolting (*slum*). **infamie** (fami) *f,* infamy; vile act *or* words.
infanterie (ɛ̃fɑ̃tri) *f,* infantry.
infanticide (ɛ̃fɑ̃tisid) (*act*) *m.* & (*pers.*) *n,* infanticide. **infantile** (til) *a,* infantile, childish; child (*care*).
infarctus (ɛ̃farktys) *m,* ~ [*du myocarde*], coronary thrombosis.
infatigable† (ɛ̃fatigabl) *a,* indefatigable, tireless.
infatuation (ɛ̃fatɥasjɔ̃) *f,* self-conceit. **infatué, e** (tɥe) *a,* conceited. ~ *de soi-même,* full of o.s. **s'infatuer de** (tɥe) *v.pr,* to become infatuated with.
infécond, e (ɛ̃fekɔ̃, ɔ̃d) *a,* barren; infertile.
infect, e (ɛ̃fɛkt) *a,* foul, disgusting; rotten *P* (*film*). ~**er** (te) *v.t,* to infect, contaminate. ~**ieux, euse** (sjø, øz) *a,* (*Med.*) infectious. ~**ion** (sjɔ̃) *f,* infection; stench.
inférence (ɛ̃ferɑ̃s) *f,* inference. **inférer** (re) *v.t,* to infer.
inférieur, e (ɛ̃ferjœr) *a,* lower (*jaw, class*); inferior; smaller (*quantity*). ¶ *n,* inferior (*pers.*). **infériorité** (rjɔrite) *f,* inferiority.
infernal, e (ɛ̃fɛrnal) *a,* infernal, hellish.
infertile (ɛ̃fɛrtil) *a,* (*lit., fig.*) infertile, barren.
infester (ɛ̃fɛste) *v.t,* to infest, overrun.
infidèle† (ɛ̃fidɛl) *a,* unfaithful; untrustworthy (*memory*); (*Rel.*) infidel. ¶ *n,* (*Rel.*) infidel. **infidélité** (delite) *f,* infidelity; unfaithfulness &c.
infiltrer (s') (ɛ̃filtre) *v.pr,* to infiltrate, percolate; (*light*) filter through.
infime (ɛ̃fim) *a,* tiny, minute.
infini, e (ɛ̃fini) *a,* infinite; endless (*talk*). ¶ *m, l'*~, the infinite. (*Math., Phot.*) infinity. *à l'*~, ad infinitum; endlessly. ~**ment** (mɑ̃) *ad,* infinitely. *regretter* ~, to be terribly sorry. ~**té** (te) *f,* infinity. *une* ~ *de,* no end of. ~**tésimal, e** (tezimal) *a,* infinitesimal. ~**tif, ive** (tif, iv) *a.* & *m,* infinitive.
infirme (ɛ̃firm) *a,* disabled, crippled; infirm (*old age*). ¶ *n,* disabled person, cripple. **infirmer** (me) *v.t,* to invalidate; (*Law*) quash. **infirmerie** (məri) *f,* infirmary, sick bay (*Sch., ship*). **infirmier, ère** (mje, ɛr) *m,* [male] nurse. ¶ *f,* nurse. ~*ère chef,* sister. ~*ère en chef,* matron; chief nursing officer. **infirmité** (mite) *f,* disability; infirmity (*old age*).
inflammable (ɛ̃flamabl) *a,* [in]flammable. **inflammation** (sjɔ̃) *f,* inflammation.
inflation (ɛ̃flasjɔ̃) *f,* (*Econ.*) inflation. ~**niste** (ɔnist) *a,* inflationary.
infléchir (ɛ̃fleʃir) *v.t,* to bend; inflect. **inflexible**† (flɛksibl) *a,* inflexible. **inflexion** (ksjɔ̃) *f,* bend; inflexion (*voice*); shift (*policy*). ~ *du corps,* bow.
infliger (ɛ̃fliʒe) *v.t,* to inflict.

influence (ɛ̃flyɑ̃s) *f,* influence (*sur,* on). **influencer** (ɑ̃se) *v.t,* to influence. **influent, e** (ɑ̃, ɑ̃t) *a,* influential. **influer** (e) *v.i:* ~ *sur,* to influence.
influx (ɛ̃fly) *m:* ~ *nerveux,* [nerve] impulse.
in-folio (ɛ̃fɔljo) *a.m. & m,* folio (*book*).
informateur, trice (ɛ̃fɔrmatœr, tris) *n,* informant. **informaticien, ne** (tisjɛ̃, ɛn) *n,* computer scientist. **information** (sjɔ̃) *f,* (*gen.*) information; piece of i.; piece of news. (*Radio, TV*) *les* ~*s,* the news. ~ *officielle,* [judicial] inquiry. **informatique** (tik) *f,* data processing; computer science. **informatiser** (tize) *v.t,* to computerize.
informe (ɛ̃fɔrm) *a,* shapeless; misshapen.
informer (ɛ̃fɔrme) *v.t,* to inform. **s'**~, to inquire, find out (*de,* about).
infortune (ɛ̃fɔrtyn) *f,* misfortune. **infortuné, e** (ne) *a,* wretched, hapless. ¶ *n,* [poor] wretch.
infraction (ɛ̃fraksjɔ̃) *f,* infringement, breach (*à,* of); offence.
infranchissable (ɛ̃frɑ̃ʃisabl) *a,* impassable; (*fig.*) insuperable.
infrarouge (ɛ̃fraruʒ) *a. & m,* infrared. **infrastructure** (stryktyr) *f,* infrastructure; substructure (*Rly, road*).
infroissable (ɛ̃frwasabl) *a,* uncrushable, crease-resistant.
infructueux, euse† (ɛ̃fryktɥø, øz) *a,* fruitless.
infuse (ɛ̃fyz) *a.f: science* ~, innate knowledge. **infuser** (ze) *v.t,* (*& faire* ~) to infuse; instil (*à,* into). **infusion** (zjɔ̃) *f,* infusion; herb tea.
ingambe (ɛ̃gɑ̃b) *a,* nimble.
ingénier (s') (ɛ̃ʒenje) *v.pr,* to try hard (*à,* to). **ingénieur** (jœr) *m,* engineer. ~ *chimiste, électricien, en génie civil, mécanicien,* chemical, electrical, civil, mechanical e. **ingénieux, euse**† (jø, øz) *a,* ingenious. **ingéniosité** (jozite) *f,* ingenuity.
ingénu†, **e** (ɛ̃ʒeny) *a,* ingenuous, artless. ¶ *f,* (*Theat.*) ingénue. ~**ité** (nɥite) *f,* artlessness, naïvety.
ingérer (s') (ɛ̃ʒere) *v.pr,* to interfere (*dans,* in).
ingouvernable (ɛ̃guvɛrnabl) *a,* ungovernable.
ingrat, e (ɛ̃gra, at) *a,* ungrateful; thankless (*task*); unattractive (*face*). **ingratitude** (tityd) *f,* ingratitude.
ingrédient (ɛ̃gredjɑ̃) *m,* ingredient.
inguérissable (ɛ̃gerisabl) *a,* incurable; inconsolable (*grief*).
ingurgiter (ɛ̃gyrʒite) *v.t,* to swallow; swill (*drink*).
inhabile† (inabil) *a,* unskilful; inept.
inhabitable (inabitabl) *a,* uninhabitable. **inhabité, e** (te) *a,* uninhabited.
inhaler (inale) *v.t,* to inhale.
inhérent, e (inerɑ̃, ɑ̃t) *a,* inherent (*à,* in).
inhospitalier, ère (inɔspitalje, ɛr) *a,* inhospitable.
inhumain, e† (inymɛ̃, ɛn) *a,* inhuman. **inhumanité** (manite) *f,* inhumanity.
inhumer (inyme) *v.t,* to inter, bury.
inimaginable (inimaʒinabl) *a,* unimaginable.
inimitable (inimitabl) *a,* inimitable.
inimitié (inimitje) *f,* enmity.
ininflammable (inɛ̃flamabl) *a,* non-flammable.
inintelligent, e (inɛ̃tɛliʒɑ̃, ɑ̃t) *a,* unintelligent. **inintelligible**† (ʒibl) *a,* unintelligible.
ininterrompu, e (inɛ̃tɛrɔ̃py) *a,* uninterrupted; unbroken (*line*).
inique† (inik) *a,* iniquitous. **iniquité** (kite) *f,* iniquity.
initial, e† (inisjal) *a. & f,* initial. **initiation** (sjɔ̃) *f,* initiation. **initiative** (tiv) *f,* initiative. **initié, e** (sje) *n,* initiate. **initier** (sje) *v.t,* to initiate (*à,* into).
injecter (ɛ̃ʒɛkte) *v.t,* to inject. *injecté de sang,* bloodshot (*eye*). **injecteur** (tœr) *m,* injector. **injection** (ksjɔ̃) *f,* injection.
injonction (ɛ̃ʒɔ̃ksjɔ̃) *f,* injunction, order.
injure (ɛ̃ʒyr) *f,* insult; affront; (*liter.*) ravages (*of time*). ~*s,* abuse. **injurier** (ʒyrje) *v.t,* to abuse, insult. **injurieux, euse**† (rjø, øz) *a,* abusive, insulting.
injuste† (ɛ̃ʒyst) *a,* unjust; unfair. **injustice** (tis) *f,* injustice; unfairness. **injustifiable** (tifjabl) *a,* unjustifiable.
inlassable† (ɛ̃lasabl) *a,* tireless, unflagging.
inné, e (ine) *a,* innate, inborn.
innocemment (inɔsamɑ̃) *ad,* innocently. **innocent, e** (sɑ̃, ɑ̃t) *a,* innocent (*de,* of); harmless. ¶ *n,* innocent; simpleton. **innocence** (sɑ̃s) *f,* innocence; harmlessness. **innocenter** (sɑ̃te) *v.t,* to find not guilty, clear.
innocuité (inɔkɥite) *f,* harmlessness.
innombrable (inɔ̃brabl) *a,* innumerable, countless; vast (*crowd*).
innommable (inɔmabl) *a,* unspeakable.
innovateur, trice (inɔvatœr, tris) *a,* innovative. ¶ *n,* innovator. **innovation** (vasjɔ̃) *f,* innovation. **innover** (ve) *v.i,* to innovate.
inoccupé, e (inɔkype) *a,* unoccupied; idle.
inoculation (inɔkylasjɔ̃) *f,* inoculation. **inoculer** (le) *v.t,* to inoculate; infect (*qch à qn,* s.o with sth).
inodore (inɔdɔr) *a,* odourless; scentless.
inoffensif, ive (inɔfɑ̃sif, iv) *a,* innocuous; inoffensive; harmless.
inondation (inɔ̃dasjɔ̃) *f,* flood; flooding, inundation. **inonder** (de) *v.t,* (*lit., fig.*) to flood, inundate, swamp.
inopérant, e (inɔperɑ̃, ɑ̃t) *a,* ineffective.
inopiné†, **e** (inɔpine) *a,* unexpected, sudden.
inopportun, e (inɔpɔrtœ̃, yn) *a,* inopportune; ill-timed. ~**ément** (tynemɑ̃) *ad,* inopportunely.
inorganique (inɔrganik) *a,* inorganic.
inoubliable (inubliabl) *a,* unforgettable.
inouï, e (inwi) *a,* unheard of; incredible.
inoxydable (inɔksidabl) *a,* stainless (*steel*).
inquiet, ète (ɛ̃kjɛ, ɛt) *a,* uneasy; worried, anxious. ¶ *n,* worrier. **inquiéter** (jete) *v.t,* to worry;

disturb; trouble. **s'~**, to worry. *s'~ de*, to worry *or* bother about; inquire about. **inquiétude** (tyd) *f*, anxiety.
inquisiteur, trice (ɛ̃kizitœr, tris) *a*, inquisitive. ¶ *m*, inquisitor. **inquisition** (sjɔ̃) *f*, inquisition.
insaisissable (ɛ̃sɛzisabl) *a*, elusive; imperceptible.
insalubre (ɛ̃salybr) *a*, unhealthy; insanitary.
insanité (ɛ̃sanite) *f*, insanity; insane act.
insatiable† (ɛ̃sasjabl) *a*, insatiable.
inscription (ɛ̃skripsjɔ̃) *f*, writing, entering, recording; registration, enrolment; (*Univ.*) matriculation; inscription (*tomb*). **inscrire** (skrir) *v.t.ir*, to write down, enter, record; register, enrol. **s'~**, to put one's name down; register, enrol. *s'~ à*, to join (*club*). *s'~ en faux contre*, to deny the truth of.
insecte (ɛ̃sɛkt) *m*, insect. **insecticide** (tisid) *a.* & *m*, insecticide.
insécurité (ɛ̃sekyrite) *f*, insecurity.
insensé, e (ɛ̃sɑ̃se) *a*, mad; senseless. **insensible** (sibl) *a*, insensible, insensitive (*à*, to); imperceptible. **~ment** (mɑ̃) *ad*, imperceptibly.
inséparable† (ɛ̃separabl) *a*, inseparable.
insérer (ɛ̃sere) *v.t*, to insert. **s'~**, to fit into. **insertion** (sɛrsjɔ̃) *f*, insertion.
insidieux, euse† (ɛ̃sidjø, øz) *a*, insidious.
insigne (ɛ̃siɲ) *a*, distinguished; signal, conspicuous; remarkable. ¶ *m*, badge. *~s*, insignia.
insignifiant, e (ɛ̃siɲifjɑ̃, ɑ̃t) *a*, insignificant; trifling. **insignifiance** (ɑ̃s) *f*, insignificance.
insinuation (ɛ̃sinɥasjɔ̃) *f*, insinuation; innuendo. **insinuer** (nɥe) *v.t*, to insinuate. **s'~**, to worm one's way; (*water*) seep (*dans*, into).
insipide (ɛ̃sipid) *a*, insipid; tasteless.
insistance (ɛ̃sistɑ̃s) *f*, insistence. **insister** (te) *v.i*, to insist. *~ sur*, to stress.
insociable (ɛ̃sɔsjabl) *a*, unsociable.
insolation (ɛ̃sɔlasjɔ̃) *f*, sunstroke. *une ~*, a touch of s. exposure (*to sun*); [hours of] sunshine.
insolemment (ɛ̃sɔlamɑ̃) *ad*, insolently; unashamedly. **insolence** (lɑ̃s) *f*, insolence. **insolent, e** (lɑ̃, ɑ̃t) *a*, insolent; unashamed; extraordinary (*health*).
insolite (ɛ̃sɔlit) *a*, unusual; strange.
insoluble (ɛ̃sɔlybl) *a*, insoluble.
insolvabilité (ɛ̃sɔlvabilite) *f*, insolvency. **insolvable** (bl) *a*, insolvent.
insomnie (ɛ̃sɔmni) *f*. *oft. pl*, insomnia.
insondable (ɛ̃sɔ̃dabl) *a*, unfathomable.
insonore (ɛ̃sɔnɔr) *a*, soundproof. **insonoriser** (rize) *v.t*, to soundproof.
insouciant, e (ɛ̃susjɑ̃, ɑ̃t) *a*, carefree, happy-go-lucky. *~ de*, unconcerned by. **insoucieux, euse** (sjø, øz) *a*, carefree.
insoumis, e (ɛ̃sumi, iz) *a*, unsubdued; rebellious (*child*). ¶ *m*, (*Mil.*) absentee.
insoutenable (ɛ̃sutnabl) *a*, untenable; unbearable (*heat*).
inspecter (ɛ̃spɛkte) *v.t*, to inspect. **inspecteur, trice** (tœr, tris) *n*, inspector. *~ d'Académie* ≃ Chief Education Officer. *~ général*, Inspector of Schools. **inspection** (ksjɔ̃) *f*, inspection; inspectorate.
inspiration (ɛ̃spirasjɔ̃) *f*, inspiration. **inspirer** (re) *v.t*, (*gen.*) to inspire. ¶ *v.i*, breathe in.
instabilité (ɛ̃stabilite) *f*, instability. **instable** (bl) *a*, unstable, unsteady.
installation (ɛ̃stalasjɔ̃) *f*, installation; fitting out; settling in. *~s*, fittings. **installer** (le) *v.t*, to install; put in; set up; fit out (*flat*); settle (*pers.*). **s'~**, to set up house; settle [in]; settle down (*in chair &c*); (*Com. &c*) set up (*comme*, as).
instamment (ɛ̃stamɑ̃) *ad*, earnestly; insistently. **instance** (stɑ̃s) *f*, *~s*, entreaties. *avec ~*, earnestly. (*Law*) proceedings. *tribunal d'~*, *de grande ~* ≃ magistrates' court, High C. *en ~*, pending. *en ~ de*, on the point of. **instant,**[1] **e** (stɑ̃, ɑ̃t) *a*, earnest, insistent.
instant[2] (ɛ̃stɑ̃) *m*, moment, instant. *à l'~*, at once; a moment ago. *par ~s*, at times. *à chaque ~*, *à tout ~*, all the time; at any moment. *de tous les ~s*, constant. **~ané**†, **e** (tane) *a*, instantaneous; instant (*coffee*). ¶ *m*, snap[shot].
instar de (à l') (ɛ̃star) *pr*, (*liter.*) after the fashion of, like.
instaurer (ɛ̃stɔre) *v.t*, to institute.
instigation (ɛ̃stigasjɔ̃) *f*, instigation.
instinct (ɛ̃stɛ̃) *m*, instinct. **instinctif, ive**† (stɛ̃ktif, iv) *a*, instinctive.
instituer (ɛ̃stitɥe) *v.t*, to institute; appoint.
institut (ɛ̃stity) *m*, institute. *l'I~*, the Institute (*the 5 Fr. Academies*). *~ de beauté*, beauty parlour. *~ médicolégal*, mortuary. **~eur, trice** (tœr, tris) *n*, [primary school] teacher. **~ion** (sjɔ̃) *f*, institution; private school.
instructeur (ɛ̃stryktœr) *m*, instructor. **instructif, ive** (tif, iv) *a*, instructive. **instruction** (sjɔ̃) *f*, education; (*Mil.*) training. *sans ~*, uneducated. (*Law*) investigation (*by juge d'~*); directive. *~s*, instructions. **instruire** (strɥir) *v.t.ir*, to teach; educate; train; inform (*de*, of); (*Law*) investigate.
instrument (ɛ̃strymɑ̃) *m*, instrument; implement; tool. *~ de musique*, musical i. **~al, e** (tal) *a*, instrumental. **~er** (te) *v.t*, to orchestrate. **~iste** (tist) *n*, instrumentalist.
insu de (à l') (ɛ̃sy) *pr*, unknown to. *à mon ~*, without my knowledge *or* knowing.
insubmersible (ɛ̃sybmɛrsibl) *a*, unsinkable.
insubordonné, e (ɛ̃sybɔrdɔne) *a*, insubordinate.
insuccès (ɛ̃syksɛ) *m*, failure.
insuffisamment (ɛ̃syfizamɑ̃) *ad*, insufficiently. **insuffisance** (zɑ̃s) *f*, insufficiency, shortage; inadequacy. **insuffisant, e** (zɑ̃, ɑ̃t) *a*, insufficient, inadequate; incompetent.
insulaire (ɛ̃sylɛr) *a*, insular. ¶ *n*, islander.

insuline (ɛ̃sylin) *f,* insulin.
insulte (ɛ̃sylt) *f,* insult. **insulter** (te) *v.t,* to insult. ~ *à,* to be an insult to.
insupportable† (ɛ̃sypɔrtabl) *a,* unbearable; insufferable.
insurgé, e (ɛ̃syrʒe) *a. & n,* insurgent, rebel. **insurger (s')** (ʒe) *v.pr,* to revolt, rebel.
insurmontable (ɛ̃syrmɔ̃tabl) *a,* insurmountable, insuperable.
insurrection (ɛ̃syrɛksjɔ̃) *f,* insurrection.
intact, e (ɛ̃takt) *a,* intact.
intangible (ɛ̃tɑ̃ʒibl) *a,* intangible; inviolable.
intarissable† (ɛ̃tarisabl) *a,* inexhaustible.
intégral, e† (ɛ̃tegral) *a,* complete; full, unabridged (*text*). ¶ *f,* (*Math.*) integral. **l'intégralité** (lite) *f,* the whole. **intègre** (tɛgr) *a,* upright; honest. **intégrer** (tegre) *v.t,* to integrate (*à, dans,* into). **intégrité** (tegrite) *f,* (*gen.*) integrity.
intellect (ɛ̃tɛlɛkt) *m,* intellect. ~ **uel, le**† (tɥɛl) *a. & n,* intellectual; highbrow. ¶ *a,* mental (*powers*).
intelligemment (ɛ̃tɛliʒamɑ̃) *ad,* intelligently. **intelligence** (ʒɑ̃s) *f,* intelligence; understanding (*de,* of); complicity. *d'*~, in [secret] agreement. *vivre en bonne* ~ *avec,* to be on good terms with. ~*s,* secret dealings. **intelligent, e** (ʒɑ̃, ɑ̃t) *a,* intelligent. **intelligible**† (ʒibl) *a,* intelligible; clear.
intempérance (ɛ̃tɑ̃perɑ̃s) *f,* intemperance; excess. **intempérant, e** (rɑ̃, ɑ̃t) *a,* intemperate. **intempéries** (ri) *f.pl,* bad weather.
intempestif, ive† (ɛ̃tɑ̃pɛstif, iv) *a,* untimely.
intenable (ɛ̃tnabl) *a,* intolerable; untenable.
intendance (ɛ̃tɑ̃dɑ̃s) *f,* (*Sch.*) bursar's department; (*Mil.*) Service Corps. **intendant, e** (dɑ̃, ɑ̃t) *n,* steward; bursar; (*Mil.*) quartermaster.
intense (ɛ̃tɑ̃s) *a,* intense; dense (*traffic*). **intensément** (semɑ̃) *ad,* intensely. **intensif, ive**† (tɑ̃sif, iv) *a,* intensive. **intensifier** (fje) *v.t,* to intensify. **intensité** (te) *f,* intensity; density.
intenter (ɛ̃tɑ̃te) *v.t,* (*Law*) to bring (*action*); institute (*proceedings*).
intention (ɛ̃tɑ̃sjɔ̃) *f,* intention. *avoir l'*~ *de faire,* to intend to do. ~**né, e** (ɔne) *a, bien, mal* ~, well-, ill-intentioned. ~**nel, le**† (nɛl) *a,* intentional.
inter (ɛ̃tɛr) *m,* (*Tel.*) *abb. of* **interurbain.** (*Sport*) inside (*right, left*). ¶ *pref,* inter... ~*continental,* intercontinental. ~*scolaire,* inter-school.
interaction (ɛ̃teraksjɔ̃) *f,* interaction.
intercaler (ɛ̃tɛrkale) *v.t,* to insert.
intercéder (ɛ̃tɛrsede) *v.t,* to intercede.
intercepter (ɛ̃tɛrsɛpte) *v.t,* to intercept.
interchangeable (ɛ̃tɛrʃɑ̃ʒabl) *a,* interchangeable.
interdiction (ɛ̃tɛrdiksjɔ̃) *f,* prohibition; ban. **interdire** (dir) *v.t.ir,* to prohibit; forbid; ban; preclude; ban from office. *s'*~ *qch,* to abstain from sth. **interdit** (di) *a,* forbidden; banned; dumbfounded. ¶ *m,* (*Eccl.*) interdict.
intéressant, e (ɛ̃terɛsɑ̃, ɑ̃t) *a,* interesting; attractive (*price*). **intéressé, e** (ɛ̃terɛse) *a,* concerned; self-interested. *les* ~*s,* the interested parties. **intéresser** (se) *v.t,* to interest; concern. **s'**~ **à,** to be interested in; take an interest in. **intérêt** (rɛ) *m,* (*gen., Fin.*) interest; stake. *l'*~ *général,* the general i. *5% d'*~, 5% interest.
intérieur, e† (ɛ̃terjœr) *a,* interior; inner; inward; inside; inland; internal, home, domestic (*market, policy*). ¶ *m,* (*gen., Foot.*) inside; interior. *rester à l'*~, to stay indoors. *d'*~, indoor (*clothes*); domesticated (*man, woman*). *à l'*~ *de,* inside. *à l'*~ *de lui-même,* inwardly. ~**ement** (mɑ̃) *ad,* inwardly.
intérim (ɛ̃terim) *m,* interim. *faire l'*~, to deputize. *par* ~, acting. **intérimaire** (mɛr) *a,* interim; acting; temporary.
interjection (ɛ̃tɛrʒɛksjɔ̃) *f,* interjection.
interligne (ɛ̃tɛrliɲ) *m,* space between lines.
interlocuteur, trice (ɛ̃tɛrlɔkytœr, tris) *n, son* ~, the person he was speaking to.
interlope (ɛ̃tɛrlɔp) *a,* suspect, shady.
interloquer (ɛ̃tɛrlɔke) *v.t,* to take aback.
interlude (ɛ̃tɛrlyd) *m,* (*Mus., TV*) interlude.
intermède (ɛ̃tɛrmɛd) *m,* (*Theat., fig.*) interlude. **intermédiaire** (medjɛr) *a,* intermediate. ~ *entre,* halfway between. ¶ *n,* intermediary, go-between. ¶ *m, par l'*~ *de qn,* through s.o. *sans* ~, (*sell*) directly.
interminable† (ɛ̃tɛrminabl) *a,* interminable.
intermittent, e (ɛ̃tɛrmitɑ̃, ɑ̃t) *a,* intermittent.
internat (ɛ̃tɛrna) *m,* boarding school; boarding; boarders; (*Med.*) house job.
international, e (ɛ̃tɛrnasjɔnal) *a,* international. ¶ *n,* (*Sport*) international [player].
interne (ɛ̃tɛrn) *a,* internal; inner (*ear*). ¶ *n,* (*Sch.*) boarder; (*Med.*) houseman, (*Am.*) intern. **interné, e** (ne) *n,* internee; [mental] patient. **interner** (ne) *v.t,* (*Pol.*) to intern; commit to a mental hospital.
interpeller (ɛ̃tɛrpɛlle) *v.t,* to shout to, s. at; (*Pol., police*) question.
interphone (ɛ̃tɛrfɔn) *m,* intercom.
interpoler (ɛ̃tɛrpɔle) *v.t,* to interpolate.
interposer (ɛ̃tɛrpoze) *v.t,* to interpose. **s'**~, to intervene.
interprétation (ɛ̃tɛrpretasjɔ̃) *f,* interpretation. **interprète** (prɛt) *n,* (*gen. Mus. &c*) interpreter; performer. **interpréter** (prete) *v.t,* (*gen.*) to interpret; perform; (*Mus.*) play, sing.
interrogateur, trice (ɛ̃tɛrɔgatœr, tris) *a,* questioning. ¶ *m,* [oral] examiner. **interrogatif, ive**† (tif, iv) *a,* interrogative. **interrogation** (sjɔ̃) *f,* interrogation; examination; test; question. **interrogatoire** (twar) *m,* (*Law*) questioning; cross-examination. **interroger** (ʒe) *v.t,* to interrogate; question; examine; (*Sch.*) test (*orally*).

interrompre (ɛ̃tɛrɔ̃pr) *v.t*, to interrupt, break off. **interrupteur** (ryptœr) *m*, (*Elec.*) switch. **interruption** (sjɔ̃) *f*, interruption, break.
intersection (ɛ̃tɛrsɛksjɔ̃) *f*, intersection.
interstice (ɛ̃tɛrstis) *m*, interstice, crack.
interurbain, e (ɛ̃tɛryrbɛ̃, ɛn) *a. & m*, (*Tel.*) long distance (phone service).
intervalle (ɛ̃tɛrval) *m*, space; interval (*time, Mus.*). *dans l'~*, meanwhile. *par ~s*, at intervals.
intervenir (ɛ̃tɛrvənir) *v.i.ir*, to intervene, interfere; (*Med.*) operate; happen, occur, arise. **intervention** (vɑ̃sjɔ̃) *f*, intervention; (*Med.*) operation.
intervertir (ɛ̃tɛrvɛrtir) *v.t*, to reverse [the order of].
interview (ɛ̃tɛrvju) *f*, (*Press &c*) interview. **interviewer**[1] (vjuve) *v.t*, to interview. **interviewer**[2] (vœr) *m*, interviewer.
intestin, e (ɛ̃tɛstɛ̃, in) *a*, (*fig.*) internal (*feud*). ¶ *m*, intestine. *~s*, bowels, intestines. **intestinal, e** (tinal) *a*, intestinal.
intime† (ɛ̃tim) *a*, intimate; private; close (*friend*). ¶ *n*, close friend. **intimer** (me) *v.t*, *~ l'ordre à qn*, to order s.o.
intimider (ɛ̃timide) *v.t*, to intimidate.
intimité (ɛ̃timite) *f*, intimacy; privacy. *dans l'~*, privately, quietly.
intitulé (ɛ̃tityle) *m*, title. **intituler** (le) *v.t*, to entitle, call, name.
intolérable† (ɛ̃tɔlerabl) *a*, intolerable. **intolérance** (rɑ̃s) *f*, intolerance. **intolérant, e** (rɑ̃, ɑ̃t) *a*, intolerant.
intonation (ɛ̃tɔnasjɔ̃) *f*, intonation.
intoxication (ɛ̃tɔksikasjɔ̃) *f*, poisoning. **intoxiqué, e** (ke) *n*, drug addict; alcoholic. **intoxiquer** (ke) *v.t*, to poison; brainwash.
intraduisible (ɛ̃tradɥizibl) *a*, untranslatable.
intraitable (ɛ̃trɛtabl) *a*, intractable, uncompromising.
intransigeant, e (ɛ̃trɑ̃ziʒɑ̃, ɑ̃t) *a*, intransigent, uncompromising.
intransitif, ive† (ɛ̃trɑ̃zitif, iv) *a*, intransitive.
intraveineux, euse (ɛ̃travɛnø, øz) *a*, intravenous. ¶ *f*, i. injection.
intrépide† (ɛ̃trepid) *a*, intrepid, dauntless. **intrépidité** (dite) *f*, intrepidity, &c.
intrigant, e (ɛ̃trigɑ̃, ɑ̃t) *a*, scheming. ¶ *n*, intriguer, schemer. **intrigue** (trig) *f*, intrigue; love affair; (*Theat.*) plot. **intriguer** (ge) *v.t*, to intrigue, puzzle. ¶ *v.i*, to intrigue, scheme.
intrinsèque† (ɛ̃trɛ̃sɛk) *a*, intrinsic.
introducteur, trice (ɛ̃trɔdyktœr, tris) *n*, introducer. **introduction** (ksjɔ̃) *f*, (*gen.*) introduction. **introduire** (dɥir) *v.t.ir*, to introduce; show in, usher in; insert. **s'~**, to get in, gain admittance.
introuvable (ɛ̃truvabl) *a*, not to be found.
intrus, e (ɛ̃try, yz) *n*, intruder; trespasser. **intrusion** (tryzjɔ̃) *f*, intrusion.
intuitif, ive† (ɛ̃tɥitif, iv) *a*, intuitive. **intuition** (sjɔ̃) *f*, intuition.
inusable (inyzabl) *a*, hard-wearing.
inusité, e (inyzite) *a*, uncommon (*word*).
inutile† (inytil) *a*, useless; unnecessary, needless. **inutilisable** (lizabl) *a*, unusable. **inutilisé, e** (ze) *a*, unused. **inutilité** (te) *f*, uselessness; needlessness.
invalide (ɛ̃valid) *a*, (*Med.*) disabled. ¶ *n*, disabled person. *~ de guerre*, d. ex-serviceman. **invalider** (de) *v.t*, to invalidate; unseat (*député*). **invalidité** (dite) *f*, disablement, disability.
invariable† (ɛ̃varjabl) *a*, invariable.
invasion (ɛ̃vɑzjɔ̃) *f*, invasion.
invective (ɛ̃vɛktiv) *f*, invective. *~s*, abuse. **invectiver** (ve) *v.i*, to rail. ¶ *v.t*, to abuse.
invendable (ɛ̃vɑ̃dabl) *a*, unsaleable. **invendu, e** (dy) *a*, unsold.
inventaire (ɛ̃vɑ̃tɛr) *m*, inventory; stocklist; stocktaking. (*fig.*) *faire l'~ de*, to take stock of.
inventer (ɛ̃vɑ̃te) *v.t*, to invent; devise. **inventeur, trice** (tœr, tris) *n*, inventor. **inventif, ive** (tif, iv) *a*, inventive. **invention** (sjɔ̃) *f*, invention; inventiveness.
inverse† (ɛ̃vɛrs) *a*, opposite (*direction*); inverse, reverse (*order*). ¶ *m*, opposite, reverse. **inverser** (se) *v.t*, to reverse, invert. **inversion** (sjɔ̃) *f*, inversion; reversal.
invertébré, e (ɛ̃vɛrtebre) *a. & m*, invertebrate.
inverti, e (ɛ̃vɛrti) *n*, homosexual.
investigation (ɛ̃vɛstigasjɔ̃) *f*, investigation.
investir (ɛ̃vɛstir) *v.t*, (*Fin., Mil.*) invest; [in]vest (*de*, with); induct (*pers.*). **investissement** (tismɑ̃) *m*, (*Fin.*) investment; siege. **investiture** (tyr) *f*, appointment; investiture.
invétéré, e (ɛ̃vetere) *a*, inveterate.
invincible† (ɛ̃vɛ̃sibl) *a*, invincible; insurmountable.
inviolable† (ɛ̃vjɔlabl) *a*, inviolable, immune.
invisible† (ɛ̃vizibl) *a*, invisible; unseen (*danger*); not available (*pers.*).
invitation (ɛ̃vitasjɔ̃) *f*, invitation. **invité, e** (te) *n*, guest. **inviter** (te) *v.t*, to invite (*à dîner*, to dinner; *à faire*, to do).
invivable (ɛ̃vivabl) *a*, unbearable.
invocation (ɛ̃vɔkasjɔ̃) *f*, invocation.
involontaire† (ɛ̃vɔlɔ̃tɛr) *a*, involuntary; unintentional.
invoquer (ɛ̃vɔke) *v.t*, to invoke, call upon.
invraisemblable† (ɛ̃vrɛsɑ̃blabl) *a*, unlikely; improbable; implausible (*thesis*); incredible. **invraisemblance** (blɑ̃s) *f*, unlikelihood, improbability; implausibility.
invulnérable (ɛ̃vylnerabl) *a*, invulnerable.
iode (jɔd) *m*, iodine.
ion (iɔ̃) *m*, ion.
Irak (l') (irak) *m*, Iraq. **irakien, ne** (kjɛ̃, ɛn) *a. &* **I~**, *n*, Iraqi.

Iran (l') (irɑ̃) *m*, Iran. **iranien, ne** (ranjɛ̃, ɛn) *a. &* **I ~,** *n*, Iranian.
irascible (irasibl) *a*, irascible.
iris (iris) *m*, (*Anat., Bot., Phot.*) iris. **~ ation** (zasjɔ̃) *f*, iridescence. **irisé, e** (ze) *a*, iridescent.
irlandais, e (irlɑ̃dɛ, ɛz) *a*, Irish. **I ~,** *n*, Irishman, -woman. **l' ~,** *m*, Irish (*language*). **Irlande (l')** (lɑ̃d) *f*, Ireland. *l'~ du Nord*, Northern Ireland. *la mer d'~*, the Irish sea.
ironie (irɔni) *f*, irony. **ironique†** (nik) *a*, ironic(al). **ironiser** (nize) *v.i*, to be ironical.
irradier (iradje) *v.t*, to irradiate. ¶ *v.i. &* **s' ~,** to radiate.
irraisonné, e (irɛzɔne) *a*, irrational.
irrationnel, le (irasjɔnɛl) *a*, irrational.
irréalisable (irealizabl) *a*, unrealizable.
irréconciliable (irekɔ̃siljabl) *a*, irreconcilable.
irrécouvrable (irekuvrabl) *a*, irrecoverable.
irrécupérable (irekyperabl) *a*, irretrievable.
irrécusable (irekyzabl) *a*, unimpeachable.
irréductible (iredyktibl) *a*, irreducible; indomitable (*will*); insurmountable.
irréel, le (ireɛl) *a*, unreal.
irréfléchi, e (irefleʃi) *a*, unconsidered. **irréflexion** (flɛksjɔ̃) *f*, thoughtlessness.
irréfutable† (irefytabl) *a*, irrefutable.
irrégularité (iregylarite) *f*, irregularity. **irrégulier, ère†** (lje, ɛr) *a*, irregular; erratic.
irréligieux, euse† (irelizjø, øz) *a*, irreligious.
irrémédiable† (iremedjabl) *a*, irremediable.
irremplaçable (irɑ̃plasabl) *a*, irreplaceable.
irréparable† (ireparabl) *a*, irreparable.
irréprochable† (ireprɔʃabl) *a*, irreproachable.
irrésistible† (irezistibl) *a*, irresistible.
irrésolu, e (irezɔly) *a*, irresolute.
irrespectueux, euse† (irɛspɛktɥø, øz) *a*, disrespectful.
irresponsable (irɛspɔ̃sabl) *a*, not responsible (*de*, for).
irrétrécissable (iretresisabl) *a*, unshrinkable.
irrévérencieux, euse (ireverɑ̃sjø, øz) *a*, irreverent.
irréversible (ireversibl) *a*, irreversible.
irrévocable† (irevɔkabl) *a*, irrevocable.
irrigation (irigasjɔ̃) *f*, irrigation. **irriguer** (ge) *v.t*, to irrigate.
irritable (iritabl) *a*, irritable. **irritation** (sjɔ̃) *f*, irritation. **irriter** (te) *v.t*, (*gen.*) to irritate; annoy. **s' ~,** to be *or* get annoyed (*de*, about, by).
irruption (irypsjɔ̃) *f*, irruption. *faire ~*, to burst in.
Islam (islam) *m*, Islam.
islandais, e (islɑ̃dɛ, ɛz) *a. &* (*language*) *m*, Icelandic. **I ~,** *n*, Icelander. **Islande (l')** (lɑ̃d) *f*, Iceland.
isolant, e (izɔlɑ̃, ɑ̃t) *a*, insulating. ¶ *m*, insulator. **isolé, e** (le) *a*, isolated; remote; lone. **isolement** (lmɑ̃) *m*, isolation; loneliness; insulation. **isolément** (lemɑ̃) *ad*, separately; in isolation. **isoler** (le) *v.t*, to isolate; insulate. **isoloir** (lwar) *m*, polling booth.
isorel (izɔrɛl) *m*, hardboard.
Israël (l') (israɛl) *m*, Israel. **israélien, ne** (eljɛ̃, ɛn) *a. &* **I ~,** *n*, Israeli. **israélite** (elit) *a*, Jewish. ¶ *n*, Jew, Jewess; (*Hist.*) Israelite.
issu, e (isy) *a*, *~ de*, descended from; stemming from. **issue** (sy) *f*, exit, way out; solution, way out; outcome. **à l' ~ de,** *ad*, at the end of. *voie sans ~*, (*lit., fig.*) dead end.
isthme (ism) *m*, isthmus.
Italie (l') (itali) *f*, Italy. **italien, ne** (ljɛ̃, ɛn) *a. &* **I ~,** *n*, Italian. *l'~*, Italian (*language*).
italique (italik) *a*, italic. ¶ *m*, italics.
item (itɛm) *ad*, (*Com.*) item, likewise; ditto.
itinéraire (itinerɛr) *m*, itinerary, route.
ivoire (ivwar) *m*, ivory.
ivraie (ivrɛ) *f*, rye grass; (*fig.*) tares.
ivre (ivr) *a*, drunk. *~ mort*, dead drunk. *~ de joie*, wild with joy. **ivresse** (ivrɛs) *f*, drunkenness, intoxication; (*fig.*) exhilaration, ecstasy, rapture. **ivrogne** (vrɔɲ) *n*, drunkard. **ivrognerie** (ɲri) *f*, drunkenness.

J

J, j (ʒi) *m*, *letter*, J, j.
jabot (ʒabo) *m*, crop (*bird*); (*Dress*) jabot.
jacasser (ʒakase) *v.i*, to jabber, chatter.
jachère (ʒaʃɛr) *f*, fallow [land]. *rester en ~*, to lie fallow.
jacinthe (ʒasɛ̃t) *f*, hyacinth. *~ des bois*, bluebell.
jactance (ʒaktɑ̃s) *f*, conceit; bragging.
jade (ʒad) *m*, jade; j. object.
jadis (ʒɑdis) *ad*, formerly, long ago. *au temps ~*, in olden times.
jaguar (ʒagwar) *m*, jaguar.
jaillir (ʒajir) *v.i*, to gush, spirt; flash; (*flame*) shoot up; (*tears*) well up; (*cry*) burst out.
jais (ʒɛ) *m*, jet; jet black.
jalon (ʒalɔ̃) *m*, peg, stake; range pole. (*fig.*) *planter des ~s*, to prepare the ground. **~ner** (lɔne) *v.t*, to stake out, mark out.
jalouser (ʒaluze) *v.t*, to be jealous of; envy. **jalousie** (zi) *f*, jealousy; Venetian blind. **jaloux, ouse†** (lu, uz) *a*, jealous.

Jamaïque (la) (ʒamaik), Jamaica.
jamais (ʒamɛ) *ad,* never, ever. *ne . . .* ~, never. *on ne sait* ~, you never know. ~ *de la vie!* never! *à [tout]* ~, for ever [& ever]. ~ *plus!* never again! *si* ~ *vous . .*, if you ever . . .
jambe (ʒɑ̃b) *f,* leg. ~ *de force,* strut. *à toutes* ~*s,* at full speed. *prendre ses* ~*s à son cou,* to take to one's heels.
jambon (ʒɑ̃bɔ̃) *m,* ham.
jante (ʒɑ̃t) *f,* rim (*wheel*); felly.
janvier (ʒɑ̃vje) *m,* January.
Japon (le) (ʒapɔ̃) *m,* Japan. **japonais, e** (pɔnɛ, ɛz) *a. & J*~, *n,* Japanese. *le* ~, Japanese (*language*). **japonerie** (nri) *f,* Japanese curio.
japper (ʒape) *v.i,* to yap, yelp.
jaquette (ʒakɛt) *f,* morning coat (*man*); jacket (*woman*); [book] jacket.
jardin (ʒardɛ̃) *m,* garden. ~ *anglais,* landscape g. ~ *botanique,* ~ *des plantes,* botanical gardens. ~ *d'enfants,* kindergarten, nursery school. ~ *potager,* kitchen garden. ~ *public,* park. **jardinage** (dinaʒ) *m,* gardening. **jardiner** (ne) *v.i,* to garden. **jardinet** (nɛ) *m,* small garden. **jardinier, ère** (nje, ɛr) *a,* garden. ¶ *n,* gardener. ¶ *f,* window box; jardinière. (*Cook.*) ~*ere de légumes,* mixed vegetables.
jargon (ʒargɔ̃) *m,* jargon, lingo; gibberish. ~**ner** (gɔne) *v.i,* to jabber; talk jargon.
jarre (ʒar) *f,* [earthenware] jar.
jarret (ʒarɛ) *m,* back of the knee (*man*); hock (*horse*); knuckle (*veal*); shin (*beef*). ~**elle** (rtɛl) *f,* suspender. ~**ière** (rtjɛr) *f,* garter.
jars (ʒar) *m,* gander.
jaser (ʒɑze) *v.i,* to chatter; babble; blab.
jasmin (ʒasmɛ̃) *m,* jasmine.
jaspe (ʒasp) *m,* jasper. ~ *sanguin,* bloodstone. **jasper** (pe) *v.t,* to marble.
jatte (ʒat) *f,* bowl.
jauge (ʒoʒ) *f,* gauge; dipstick; tonnage (*ship*). **jauger** (ʒoʒe) *v.t,* to measure the capacity *or* tonnage of; size up (*pers.*). ¶ *v.i,* to have a capacity of.
jaunâtre (ʒonɑtr) *a,* yellowish. **jaune** (ʒon) *a,* yellow; sallow. ¶ *m,* yellow; yolk (*egg*); (*Ind.*) blackleg. *les J*~*s,* the yellow races. **jaunir** (ʒonir) *v.i,* to turn yellow. **jaunisse** (nis) *f,* jaundice.
Java (ʒava) *f,* Java. **javanais, e** (nɛ, ɛz) *a. &* **J**~, *n,* Javan[ese].
javelle (ʒavɛl) *f,* swath (*corn*).
javelliser (ʒavɛlize) *v.t,* to chlorinate.
javelot (ʒavlo) *m,* javelin.
je, j' (ʒə, ʒ) *pn,* I.
jean (dʒin) *m,* [pair of] jeans.
jeep (ʒip) *f,* jeep.
jérémiades (ʒeremjad) *f.pl,* moaning, whining.
jersey (ʒɛrzɛ) *m,* jersey (*cloth*). **J**~, *f,* Jersey. **jersiais, e** (zjɛ, ɛz) *a,* Jersey (*cattle*).
Jérusalem (ʒeryzalɛm) *f,* Jerusalem.
jésuite (ʒezɥit) *m,* Jesuit.
Jésus (ʒezy) *m,* Jesus. **Jésus-Christ** (kri) *m,* Jesus Christ. *avant, après* ~, B.C., A.D.
jet[1] (ʒɛ) *m,* throw (*discus &c*); jet, spurt (*liquid*); ray, beam (*light*). *premier* ~, first sketch (*book*). *du premier* ~, straight off, first go. (*Bot.*) shoot; (*Tech.*) pouring (*metal*). ~ *d'eau,* fountain; spray; nozzle (*pipe*). ~ *à la mer,* jettison. **jet**[2] (dʒɛt) *m,* (*Aero.*) jet. **jetée** (te) *f,* jetty; pier. **jeter** (te) *v.t,* to throw; fling; hurl; throw away; lay (*foundations*); shed, cast (*light*); utter, let out (*cry*). ~ *l'effroi parmi,* to spread alarm among. ~ *un coup d'œil sur,* to glance at. ~ *un sort à qn,* to cast a spell on s.o. **se** ~, to throw o.s, rush. (*fig.*) *se* ~ *à l'eau,* to take the plunge. *s'en* ~ *un derrière la cravate P,* to have a quick one *P.*
jeton (tɔ̃) *m,* counter; token; chip (*casino*). ~*s de présence,* directors' fees; fees.
jeu (ʒø) *m,* game. ~ *d'adresse,* g. of skill. (*Sport*) *3* ~*x à 2,* (*lead*) 3 games to 2. (*space*) ~ *de boules,* bowling ground *or* green. *hors* ~, (*Ten.*) out; (*Foot.*) off-side. set (*keys; chess &c*); pack (*cards*); stop (*organ*); (*Cards*) hand. (*fig.*) *cacher son* ~, to conceal one's hand. play (*opp. work*); gambling; stake; (*Theat.*) acting; (*Mus.*) playing; action, working; play (*sun, light*); (*Mech.*) play. *être en* ~, to be at stake. *entrer en* ~, to come into play. *les forces en* ~, the forces at work. *ce n'est pas de* ~, it's not fair. *faire le* ~ *de qn,* to play into s.o's hands. *jouer gros* ~, to play for high stakes. *avoir beau* ~ *de,* to be well placed to. ~ *de barres,* prisoners' base. ~ *de construction,* building set. ~ *d'enfant,* child's play. ~ *d'esprit,* witticism. ~ *de massacre,* Aunt Sally; wholesale slaughter. ~ *de mots,* pun. *J*~*x Olympiques,* Olympic games. ~ *de quilles,* skittle alley. ~ *de scène,* stage business. ~ *de société,* parlour game.
jeudi (ʒødi) *m,* Thursday.
jeun (à) (ʒœ̃) *ad,* fasting; on an empty stomach.
jeune (ʒœn) *a,* young; youthful; younger (*brother, generation*); inexperienced. *Durand*~, D. junior. ¶ *n,* youth, girl. *les* ~*s,* young people. ~ *fille,* girl. ~*s gens,* young people. ~*s mariés,* newly-weds. (*Theat.*) ~ *premier, ère,* leading man, lady.
jeûne (ʒøn) *m,* fast[ing]. **jeûner** (ne) *v.i,* to fast; go without food.
jeunesse (ʒœnɛs) *f,* youth; youthfulness. *la* ~, young people.
joaillerie (ʒwɑjri) *f,* jewel[le]ry; jeweller's shop. **joaillier, ère** (je, ɛr) *n,* jeweller.
jobard, e *P* (ʒɔbar, ard) *n,* mug *P,* sucker *P.*
jockey (ʒɔkɛ) *m,* jockey.
joie (ʒwa) *f,* joy, delight; pleasure. *faire la* ~ *de qn,* to delight s.o. *se faire une* ~ *de faire,* to be delighted to do; look forward to doing.
joindre (ʒwɛ̃dr) *v.t,* to join; link; fold (*hands*); unite; combine; attach, enclose (*cheque*);

contact (*pers.*). ~ *les deux bouts P*, to make ends meet. ¶ *v.i*, to join, meet; (*door &c*) shut. **se ~ à,** to join (*group*). **joint** (ʒwɛ̃) *m*, joint; join; pointing (*wall*); washer; gasket; (*P Drugs*) joint *P*. **jointoyer** (twaje) *v.t*, to point (*masonry*). **jointure** (tyr) *f*, joint; join.

joli, e (ʒɔli) *a*, pretty; attractive; nice, fine. *une ~e somme*, a tidy sum. (*ironic*) *un ~ gâchis*, a fine mess. **~ment** (mɑ̃) *ad*, prettily &c. ~ *bête*, jolly stupid, really s.

jonc (ʒɔ̃) *m*, rush, bulrush; cane. **joncher** (ʃe) *v.t*, ~ *qch de*, to strew sth with.

jonction (ʒɔ̃ksjɔ̃) *f*, junction; meeting.

jongler (ʒɔ̃gle) *v.i*, to juggle. **jonglerie** (glǝri) *f*, juggling. **jongleur, euse** (glœr, øz) *n*, juggler. ¶ *m*, (*Hist.*) minstrel.

jonque (ʒɔ̃k) *f*, (*Naut.*) junk.

jonquille (ʒɔ̃kij) *f*, daffodil; jonquil.

Jordanie (la) (ʒɔrdani) Jordan. **jordanien, ne** (njɛ̃, ɛn) *a. &* **J~,** *n*, Jordanian.

joue (ʒu) *f*, cheek. *mettre* (ou *coucher*) *en ~*, to aim at. (*Mil.*) *en ~!* take aim!

jouer (ʒwe) *v.i*, to play. ~ *au football, aux soldats*, to play football, soldiers. ~ *du violon*, to play the violin. gamble. ~ *avec sa vie*, to gamble with one's life. (*Theat. &c*) act; (*Mech.*) be loose; (*wood*) warp; work. *faire ~*, to operate (*spring*). ~ *sur les mots*, to play on words. ~ *au plus fin*, to try to outwit s.o. ~ **de,** to make use of. ~ *des coudes*, to elbow one's way. ¶ *v.t*, to play, act (*part, play*); (*Mus., Sport*) play (*note, set, card*); (*Chess*) move (*piece*); bet, stake, wager; back (*horse*). ~ *un tour à*, to play a trick on. **se ~ de,** to deceive (*s.o*); make light of. **jouet** (ʒwɛ) *m*, toy; plaything. **joueur, euse** (ʒwœr, øz) *n*, player; gambler. *bon, mauvais ~*, good, bad loser.

joufflu, e (ʒufly) *a*, chubby.

joug (ʒu) *m*, yoke.

jouir (ʒwir) *v.i*, ~ *de*, to enjoy; be in possession of (*faculties*); possess, have. ~ *P*, to have fun; come *P* (*sex*). **jouissance** (ʒwisɑ̃s) *f*, enjoyment, pleasure; (*Law*) use, possession; (*P*) orgasm.

joujou (ʒuʒu) *m*, (*pl.* ~*x*) toy.

jour (ʒur) *m*, [day]light; day[time]; day. *il fait ~*, it is [day]light. *à la pointe du ~, au petit ~*, at dawn, daybreak. *au grand ~, en plein ~*, in broad daylight. *voyager de ~*, to travel by day. *dans 2 ~s, huit ~s*, in 2 days, a week. *le ~ d'avant, d'après*, the d. before, the next d. *tous les ~s*, every d. *un de ces ~s*, one of these days. *au ~ le ~*, (*live*) from d. to d. *du ~ au lendemain*, overnight. *de nos ~s*, nowadays. *le goût du ~*, the style of the day. ¶ light. *il a le ~ dans les yeux*, he has the light in his eyes. *mettre au ~*, to bring to l. (*fig.*) *voir sous un ~ favorable*, to view in a favourable l. gap (*hedge &c*). (*Need.*) ~*s*, hemstitching. *à ~*, openwork. *mettre fin à ses ~s*, to put an end to one's life. *donner le ~ à*, to give birth to. *être, mettre à ~*, to be, bring up to date. *le ~ de l'An*, New Year's day. ~ *férié*, public holiday. ~ *de fête*, feast day, holiday. *le ~ J*, D-day. ~ *maigre*, fast day. *le ~ de Pâques*, Easter Day. *le ~ des Morts*, All Souls' day. *le ~ des Rois*, Epiphany, Twelfth Night.

Jourdain (le) (ʒurdɛ̃), the Jordan.

journal (ʒurnal) *m*, [news]paper; magazine; journal; diary, journal. ~ *parlé, télévisé*, radio, TV news. ~ *de bord*, (*ship's*) log [book]. **~ier, ère** (lje, ɛr) *a*, daily; everyday, humdrum. ¶ *m*, (*Agr.*) day labourer. **~isme** (lism) *m*, journalism. **~iste** (list) *n*, journalist.

journée (ʒurne) *f*, day; day's work; day's pay. *toute la ~*, all day long. *à la ~*, (*pay*) by the day. *à petites ~s*, (*travel*) by easy stages. **journellement** (nɛlmɑ̃) *ad*, daily.

joute (ʒut) *f*, joust; contest. ~ *s nautiques*, water tournament. **jouter** (te) *v.i*, (*Hist., fig.*) to joust.

jouvenceau, elle (ʒuvɑ̃so, ɛl) *n*, youth, damsel.

jovial, e† (ʒɔvjal) *a*, jovial, merry, jolly.

joyau (ʒwajo) *m*, jewel.

joyeux, euse† (ʒwajø, øz) *a*, joyful; jolly, merry, cheerful. *J~ Noel!* Merry Christmas!

jubilation (ʒybilasjɔ̃) *f*, jubilation. **jubilé** (le) *m*, jubilee. **jubiler** (le) *v.i*, to be jubilant.

jucher (ʒyʃe) *v.t. &* **se ~,** to perch.

judaïque (ʒydaik) *a*, Judaic, Jewish.

judas (ʒydɑ) *m*, peephole, judas-hole.

judiciaire† (ʒydisjɛr) *a*, judicial; legal.

judicieux, euse† (ʒydisjø, øz) *a*, judicious.

juge (ʒyʒ) *m*, (*gen.*) judge. ~ *d'instruction*, examining magistrate. ~ *de paix*, justice of the peace, magistrate. ~ *de touche*, touch judge, linesman. **jugé** (ʒe) *m*, *au ~*, by guesswork; (*fire*) blind. **jugement** (ʒyʒmɑ̃) *m*, (*gen.*) judg[e]ment. *porter ~ sur*, to pass j. on. (*Law*) sentence; award. *passer en ~*, to stand trial. **jugeote** *P* (ʒɔt) *f*, common sense, nous. **juger** (ʒe) *v.t*, (*gen.*) to judge; try (*case*); decide; consider. ~ *bon de faire*, to think fit to do. *jugez de ma surprise!* imagine my surprise! *à en ~ par*, judging by.

jugulaire (ʒygylɛr) *f*, chin strap. **[veine] ~,** *f*, jugular [vein]. **juguler** (le) *v.t*, to arrest (*disease*); quell, suppress.

juif, ive (ʒɥif, iv) *a*, Jewish. ¶ **J~,** *n*, Jew, Jewess.

juillet (ʒɥijɛ) *m*, July.

juin (ʒɥɛ̃) *m*, June.

jules *P* (ʒyl) *m*, bloke *P*, boyfriend.

jumeau, elle (ʒymo, ɛl) *a*, twin; semidetached. ¶ *n*, twin; double. ¶ *f*.[*pl*], binoculars. ~[*s*] *de théâtre*, opera glasses. **jumelage** (laʒ) *m*, twinning. **jumeler** (mle) *v.t*, to twin (*towns*);

double up.
jument (ʒymɑ̃) *f,* mare.
jungle (ʒɔ̃gl) *f,* jungle.
junior (ʒynjɔr) *a. & n,* junior.
jupe (ʒyp) *f,* skirt. *~-culotte,* divided s. **jupon** (pɔ̃) *m,* waist petticoat.
juré, e (ʒyre) *a,* sworn. ¶ *n,* juror; juryman, -woman. **jurer** (re) *v.t,* to swear; vow. *~ de,* to swear to. ¶ *v.i,* to swear, curse; (*colours*) clash.
juridiction (ʒyridiksjɔ̃) *f,* jurisdiction; courts. **juridique**† (dik) *a,* legal. **juriste** (rist) *m,* lawyer; jurist.
juron (ʒyrɔ̃) *m,* oath, swearword.
jury (ʒyri) *m,* jury; (*Sport &c*) judges; (*Sch.*) board of examiners.
jus (ʒy) *m,* juice; gravy; (*P*) coffee; water. *~ de réglisse,* liquorice.
jusant (ʒyzɑ̃) *m,* ebb tide.
jusque (ʒysk) *pr,* (*space*) to; as far as; up to; (*time*) till, until, up to. *jusqu'à présent,* up to now. *jusqu'au moment où,* until. even. *des souris ~ dans les tiroirs,* mice even in the drawers. *aller jusqu'à faire,* to go so far as to do. ¶ *c, jusqu'à ce que* (+ *subj.*) until.
juste (ʒyst) *a,* just, fair; legitimate (*claim*); right, correct (*time, answer*); true (*value*); (*Mus.*) in tune; true (*voice*); right (*note*); tight, skimpy (*garment*). *3 jours pour ce travail -c'est un peu ~,* 3 days for this work - it's running it a bit fine. *très ~!* very true! *à 6 heures ~s,* at 6 o'clock sharp. *~ milieu,* happy medium, golden mean. *à ~ titre,* with [good] reason; rightly [so]. ¶ *ad,* rightly; correctly; (*sing*) in tune; just; exactly. *au ~,* exactly. *comme de ~,* naturally, as usual. *tout ~,* only just; barely. **justement** (təmɑ̃) *ad,* justly; exactly, just. **justesse** (tɛs) *f,* accuracy; correctness; (*Mus.*) correct intonation. *de ~,* (*win*) narrowly. **justice** (tis) *f,* justice; fairness; court of law. *la ~,* the law (*authorities*). *en toute ~,* in all fairness. *passer en ~,* to stand trial. **justiciable** (sjabl) *a, ~ de,* subject to (*court*). **justifiable** (fjabl) *a,* justifiable. **justificatif, ive** (fikatif, iv) *a,* supporting. *pièce ~ ive,* written proof. **justifier** (fje) *v.t,* to justify. *~* **de,** to prove. **se ~,** to justify o.s; clear o.s (*de,* of).
jute (ʒyt) *m,* jute.
juteux, euse (ʒytø, øz) *a,* juicy.
juvénile (ʒyvenil) *a,* youthful.
juxtaposer (ʒykstapoze) *v.t,* to juxtapose.

K

K, k (ka) *m, letter,* K, k.
kaki (kaki) *a. & m,* khaki.
kaléidoscope (kaleidɔskɔp) *m,* kaleidoscope.
kangourou (kɑ̃guru) *m,* kangaroo.
kaolin (kaɔlɛ̃) *m,* kaolin, china clay.
kascher (kaʃɛr) *a. inv,* kosher.
kayak (kajak) *m,* kayak; canoe.
Kenya (le) (kenja) Kenya.
képi (kepi) *m,* kepi (*peaked cap*).
kermesse (kɛrmɛs) *f,* fair; fête, bazaar.
kérosène (kerozɛn) *m,* kerosene, aviation fuel.
kidnapper (kidnape) *v.t,* to kidnap.
kilo (kilo) *m,* kilo. ¶ *pref,* kilo . . . **kilogramme** (lɔgram) *m,* kilogramme. **kilométrage** (metraʒ) *m,* mileage (*car*). **kilomètre** (mɛtr) *m,* kilometre. **kilowatt** (wat) *m,* kilowatt.
kimono (kimɔno) *m,* kimono.
kinésithérapeute (kineziterapøt) *n,* physiotherapist. **kinésithérapie** (rapi) *f,* physiotherapy.
kiosque (kjɔsk) *m,* kiosk; stall; bookstall; conning tower (*submarine*). *~ à musique,* bandstand. *~ de jardin,* summer house.
knock-out (nɔkawt) *a,* (*Box.*) knocked out. ¶ *m,* knock-out.
krach (krak) *m,* (*Fin.*) crash.
kyrielle (kirjɛl) *f,* string, stream; crowd.
kyste (kist) *m,* cyst.

L

L, l (ɛl) *m. & f, letter,* L, l.
la[1] (la) *m,* (*Mus.*) A. *donner le ~,* to set the fashion.
la[2] (la) *art. & pn, V* **le**[1] **& le**[2]**.**
là (la) *ad,* there; then; that. *ma clef n'est pas ~,* my key is not there. *c'est ~ que je compris,* it

was then that I understood. *à cette epoque-* ~, at that time. *~-bas,* over there. *~-dedans,* in there; within. *~-dessous,* under there, underneath. *~-dessus,* on that, thereupon. *~-haut,* up there. *de* ~, away, off; out of there; from then. *par* ~, that way; through there; thereby. ¶ *i, oh* ~ *~!* O dear me!
labeur (labœr) *m,* labour.
labial, e (labjal) *a. & f,* labial.
laborantin, e (labɔrɑ̃tɛ̃, in) *n,* lab assistant. **laboratoire** (ratwar) *m,* laboratory.
laborieux, euse† (labɔrjø, øz) *a,* laborious, arduous (*task*); laboured (*account*); hard-working; working (*class*).
labour (labur) *m,* ploughing; digging; ploughed field. **~age** (raʒ) *m,* ploughing; digging. **~er** (re) *v.t,* to plough [up]; dig; (*fig.*) furrow. **~eur** (rœr) *m,* ploughman.
labyrinthe (labirɛ̃t) *m,* labyrinth, maze.
lac (lak) *m,* lake.
lacer (lase) *v.t,* to lace [up], tie [up] (*shoes*).
lacérer (lasere) *v.t,* to lacerate; tear [up].
lacet (lasɛ) *m,* lace (*boot &c*); bend (*road*). *en ~s,* winding. snare, noose.
lâche† (lɑʃ) *a,* loose; lax; cowardly. **lâcher** (lɑʃe) *v.t,* to loosen, slacken; let go, release; let out (*oath*); drop (*friend, studies*). ~ *pied,* to give way. ~ *prise,* to let go. **lâcheté** (ʃte) *f,* cowardice; cowardly act.
laconique† (lakɔnik) *a,* laconic.
lacrymal, e (lakrimal) *a,* lachrymal, tear (*duct*).
lacrymogène (lakrimɔʒɛn) *a, gaz* ~, tear gas.
lacté, e (lakte) *a,* milky; milk (*diet*).
lacune (lakyn) *f,* lacuna; gap.
ladre (lɑdr) *n.* (*& a.*) (*liter.*) miser(ly).
lagune (lagyn) *f,* lagoon.
lai (lɛ) *a.m,* lay (*brother*). ¶ *m,* lay (*poem*).
laiciser (laisize) *v.t,* to laicize, secularize.
laid, e (lɛ, ɛd) *a,* ugly, plain; horrible; mean (*act*). **laideron** (drɔ̃) *m,* plain girl. **laideur** (dœr) *f,* ugliness &c.
lainage (lɛnaʒ) *m,* woollen goods, woollens. **laine** (lɛn) *f,* wool. ~ *peignée,* worsted. **laineux, euse** (nø, øz) *a,* woolly. **lainier, ère** (nje, ɛr) *a,* wool[len] (*trade &c*).
laïque (laik) *a,* lay; secular; non-religious. ¶ *n,* layman, -woman. *les ~s,* the laity.
laisse (lɛs) *f,* leash, lead.
laissé pour compte (lɛse) *m,* article left unsold; reject.
laisser (lɛse) *v.t,* to leave; bequeath. *laisse les chaises au jardin,* leave the chairs in the garden. *laisse-le tranquille,* leave him in peace. let, allow. *laissez-moi sortir,* let me go out. ~ *aller &* ~ *échapper,* to let go. ~ *tomber,* to drop; let fall. **se ~,** *se* ~ *aller,* to let o.s go. *se* ~ *arrêter,* to let o.s be arrested. **laisser-aller,** *m,* carelessness. **laisser-faire,** *m,* non-interference, laissez-faire. **laissez-passer,** *m,* pass.
lait (lɛ) *m,* milk. ~ *condensé,* condensed m. ~ *de chaux,* whitewash. **~age** (taʒ) *m,* milk product. **~ance** (tɑ̃s) *f,* soft roe. **~erie** (tri) *f,* dairy. **~eux, euse** (tø, øz) *a,* milky.
laitier, ère (lɛtje, ɛr) *n,* milkman, -woman, dairyman. ¶ *f,* milker (*cow*). ¶ *a,* dairy.
laiton (lɛtɔ̃) *m,* brass.
laitue (lɛty) *f,* lettuce. ~ *romaine,* cos lettuce.
lama (lama) *m,* (*Rel.*) lama; (*Zool.*) llama.
lambeau (lɑ̃bo) *m,* rag, tatter; shred.
lambin, e (lɑ̃bɛ̃, in) *a,* dawdling, leisurely. ¶ *n,* dawdler, slowcoach. **lambiner** (bine) *v.i,* to dawdle, lag.
lambris (lɑ̃bri) *m,* panelling; wainscot.
lame (lam) *f,* [thin] sheet (*metal, glass*); lamina; [microscope] slide; [knife] blade; swordsman; wave (*sea*). **lamé, e** (lame) *a. & m,* lamé. **lamelle** (mɛl) *f,* small strip; slat (*blind*).
lamentable† (lamɑ̃tabl) *a,* lamentable; appalling; pitiful (*sight*). **lamentation** (sjɔ̃) *f,* lament[ation]. **lamenter (se)** (te) *v.pr,* to lament. *se* ~ *sur,* to bewail, deplore.
laminer (lamine) *v.t,* to laminate. **laminoir** (nwar) *m,* rolling mill.
lampadaire (lɑ̃padɛr) *m,* standard lamp; street lamp.
lampe (lɑ̃p) *f,* lamp; bulb; (*Radio*) valve. ~ *de poche,* electric torch. ~ *de travail,* reading lamp.
lampée *P* (lɑ̃pe) *f,* gulp, swig *P.*
lampion (lɑ̃pjɔ̃) *m,* paper lantern.
lance (lɑ̃s) *f,* spear; lance; hose. **~-flamme,** *m,* flame thrower. **lancement** (lɑ̃smɑ̃) *m,* throwing; launch[ing] (*ship*); floating (*loan*). ~ *du javelot,* throwing the javelin. ~ *du poids,* putting the shot. **lancer** (se) *m,* throw. ¶ *v.t,* to throw; put (*the shot*); fling; drop (*bombs*); dart (*glance*); launch (*ship, product*); send out (*message*); float (loan). **se ~,** to leap; dash, rush. *se* ~ *dans,* to launch into (*discussion*). **lancette** (sɛt) *f,* lancet. **lancinant, e** (sinɑ̃, ɑ̃t) *a,* shooting (*pain*); haunting (*memory*). **lanciner** (ne) *v.i,* to throb. ¶ *v.t,* to haunt.
landau (lɑ̃do) *m,* landau. ~ [*pour enfant*], pram. ~ *pliant,* folding pram.
lande (lɑ̃d) *f,* heath, moor[land].
langage (lɑ̃gaʒ) *m,* language, speech. ~ *argotique,* slang [speech].
lange (lɑ̃ʒ) *m,* baby's blanket. *~s,* (*Hist.*) swaddling clothes.
langoureux, euse† (lɑ̃gurø, øz) *a,* languorous.
langouste (lɑ̃gust) *f,* spiny lobster, (*sea*) crayfish. **langoustine** (tin) *f,* Dublin bay prawn. *~s,* scampi.
langue (lɑ̃g) *f,* tongue; language, speech. *tirer la ~,* to stick out one's tongue. *avoir la* ~ *bien pendue,* to have a ready tongue in one's head. **languette** (lɑ̃gɛt) *f,* tongue (*wood, leather*).
langueur (lɑ̃gœr) *f,* languor; listlessness. **languir**

(gir) *v.i,* to languish; pine [away]; (*conversation*) flag. **languissant, e** (gisɑ̃, ɑ̃t) *a,* languishing; languid; dull; slack (*business*).
lanière (lanjɛr) *f,* strap; strip; lash.
lanterne (lɑ̃tɛrn) *f,* lantern; lamp; (*pl.*) side lights (*car*). ~ *de projection,* slide projector. ~-*tempête,* hurricane lamp. ~ *vénitienne,* paper lantern. **lanterner** (ne) *v.i,* to dawdle. ¶ *v.t,* to fool, mislead.
lapalissade (lapalisad) *f,* truism.
laper (lape) *v.i. & t,* to lap [up], lick up.
lapereau (lapro) *m,* young rabbit.
lapider (lapide) *v.t,* to stone [to death]; throw stones at.
lapin, e (lapɛ̃, in) *n,* [buck, doe] rabbit. ~ *domestique,* ~ *de choux,* tame r. ~ *de garenne,* wild r.
Laponie (la) (lapɔni) Lapland.
laps de temps (laps) *m,* lapse of time. **lapsus** (sys) *m,* lapse, slip.
laquais (lakɛ) *m,* footman; (*Hist. & pej.*) lackey.
laque (lak) *f,* lac, shellac; lacquer; hair lacquer. ¶ *m,* lacquer [work]. **laquer** (ke) *v.t,* to lacquer.
larbin (larbɛ̃) *P m,* (*pej.*) flunkey.
larcin (larsɛ̃) *m,* theft, larceny; booty.
lard (lar) *m,* bacon; fat. *un gros* ~ *P,* a fat lump *P.* **larder** (larde) *v.t,* (*Cook.*) to lard. **lardon** (dɔ̃) *m,* lardon.
large (larʒ) *a,* broad, wide; large; extensive (*powers*); liberal (*pers., ideas*). ~ *d'esprit,* broadminded. ¶ *m,* width. *2 mètres de* ~, 2m. wide. *le* ~, the open sea. *au* ~, out at sea. *au* ~ *de Brest,* off Brest. ~**ment** (mɑ̃) *ad,* (*space*) widely; (*exceed*) far, greatly. ~ *suffisant,* easily enough, plenty. **largesse** (ʒɛs) *f,* generosity, largess[e]. **largeur** (ʒœr) *f,* breadth; width.
larguer (large) *v.t,* to cast off (*moorings*); drop (*bombs*); (*P*) chuck *P* (*job*).
larme (larm) *f,* tear; drop (*liquid*). **larmoiement** (mwamɑ̃) *m,* watering of the eyes; snivelling. **larmoyant, e** (jɑ̃, ɑ̃t) *a,* weeping; tearful; maudlin. **larmoyer** (je) *v.i,* (*eyes*) to water; snivel.
larron (larɔ̃) *m,* (*Hist.*) thief.
larve (larv) *f,* larva, grub.
laryngite (larɛ̃ʒit) *f,* laryngitis. **larynx** (rɛ̃ks) *m,* larynx.
las, asse (lɑ, ɑs) *a,* tired, weary.
lascar *P* (laskar) *m,* rogue.
lascif, ive† (lasif, iv) *a,* lascivious, lustful.
laser (lazɛr) *m,* laser.
lasser (lɑse) *v.t,* to tire; weary. **se** ~, to grow weary (*de,* of). **lassitude** (ityd) *f,* weariness, lassitude.
lasso (laso) *m,* lasso.
latence (latɑ̃s) *f,* latency. **latent, e** (tɑ̃, ɑ̃t) *a,* latent, hidden.
latéral, e† (lateral) *a,* lateral, side.
latex (latɛks) *m,* latex.
latin, e (latɛ̃, in) *a. & m,* Latin. ~ *de cuisine,* dog Latin.
latitude (latityd) *f,* latitude; scope.
latte (lat) *f,* lath. **lattis** (ti) *m,* lathing.
laudatif, ive (lodatif, iv) *a,* laudatory.
lauréat, e (lɔrea, at) *a,* prizewinning. ¶ *n,* prize winner. **laurier** (rje) *m,* laurel; (*Cook.*) bay. ~-*rose, m,* oleander.
lavable (lavabl) *a,* washable. **lavabo** (bo) *m,* washbasin. *les* ~*s,* toilets. **lavage** (vaʒ) *m,* washing, wash.
lavande (lavɑ̃d) *f,* lavender.
lave (lav) *f,* lava.
laver (lave) *v.t,* to wash; w. out (*stain*); w. away (*shame*); bathe (*wound*). ~ *la vaisselle,* to w. up, do the dishes. **se** ~, to have a wash; to clear o.s (*of an accusation*). *se* ~ *la figure,* to wash one's face. *se* ~ *les dents,* to clean one's teeth. *je m'en lave les mains,* I wash my hands of the matter. **lave-glace,** *m,* windscreen washer. **lave-vaisselle,** *m,* dishwasher. **lavement** (vmɑ̃) *m,* enema. **laverie** (vri) *f,* launderette. **lavette** (vɛt) *m,* dish cloth. **laveur, euse** (vœr, øz) *n,* washer. ~ *de carreaux,* window cleaner. ~*euse de linge,* washerwoman. **lavis** (vi) *m,* (*Art*) wash [drawing].
laxatif, ive (laksatif, iv) *a. & m,* laxative.
laxisme (laksism) *m,* laxity.
layette (lɛjɛt) *f,* baby clothes, layette.
le[1]**; la; l'; les** (lə; la; l; le) *definite art* (**le, les** *with à,* **au, aux;** *with de,* **du, des**), the. *voici la clef,* here is the key. *le lundi,* on Mondays. *le 3 mai,* on the 3rd of May. *le soir,* in the evening. *la nuit,* at night. *la France,* France. *l'histoire,* history. *2F le kilo, la pièce,* 2 francs a kilo, each. *80 km à l'heure,* 80 km an hour. *j'aime le vin,* I like wine. *le père de cette fille,* this girl's father. *il ferma les yeux,* he closed his eyes. *oh la belle robe!* what a beautiful dress!
le[2]**; la; l'; les** (lə; la; l; le) *pn,* him, her, it, them. *il le donna à Marie,* he gave it to Marie. *je le crois bien,* I believe, think so.
leader (lidœr) *m,* (*Pol., Sport*) leader.
lécher (leʃe) *v.t,* to lick; polish up (*text*). *se* ~ *les doigts,* to lick one's fingers. (*fig*) *s'en* ~ *les doigts,* to lick one's lips over sth. ~ *les bottes de qn P,* to suck up to s.o *P.* **lèche-vitrines** *P* (lɛʃ-) *m, faire du* ~, to go window-shopping.
leçon (ləsɔ̃) *f,* lesson. *cela lui donnera une bonne* ~, that will teach him a lesson.
lecteur, trice (lɛktœr, tris) *n,* reader; (*Univ.*) [foreign language] assistant. **lecture** (tyr) *f,* reading; sth to read.
ledit, ladite, lesdits, lesdites (lədi, ladit, ledi, ledit) *a,* (*Law*) the [afore]said.
légal, e† (legal) *a,* legal; statutory; lawful. **légaliser** (lize) *v.t,* to legalize. **légalité** (lite) *f,* legality.
légat (lega) *m,* legate. ~**aire** (tɛr) *n,* legatee. ~

universel, sole l. ~**ion** (sjɔ̃) *f,* legation.
légendaire (leʒɑ̃dɛr) *a,* legendary. **légende** (ʒɑ̃d) *f,* legend; key (*map*); caption (*illustration*).
léger, ère† (leʒe, ɛr) *a,* light; lightweight, flimsy (*construction, argument*); slight, mild (*illness*); weak (*tea*); light (*wine*); springy, nimble (*step*); faint (*noise*). *à la ~ère,* thoughtlessly, without due consideration. **légèreté** (ʒɛrte) *f,* lightness &c.
légion (leʒjɔ̃) *f,* legion. *ils sont ~,* they are legion. **legionnaire** (ʒɔnɛr) *m,* legionary.
législateur, trice (leʒislatœr, tris) *n,* legislator. **législatif, ive** (tif, iv) *a,* legislative; parliamentary (*election*). **législation** (sjɔ̃) *f,* legislation. **législature** (tyr) *f,* legislature; term (*of office*). **légiste** (ʒist) *m,* jurist. **légitime†** (ʒitim) *a,* legitimate; lawful; rightful. *~ défense,* self-defence. **légitimer** (me) *v.t,* to legitimatize; legitimate. **légitimité** (mite) *f,* legitimacy, lawfulness.
legs (lɛg *ou* lɛ) *m,* legacy, bequest. **léguer** (lege) *v.t,* to bequeath, leave, hand down.
légume (legym) *m,* vegetable. ¶ *f, une grosse ~ P,* a bigwig *P.* **légumier** (mje) *m,* vegetable dish. **légumineux, euse** (minø, øz) *a,* leguminous. ¶ *f,* legume, pulse.
leitmotiv (laitmɔtif) *m,* leitmotiv, -if.
Léman (le lac) (lemɑ̃), the Lake of Geneva.
lendemain (lɑ̃dmɛ̃) *m, le ~,* the next day, day after; the future. *les ~s,* consequences. *sans ~,* short-lived.
lent, e† (lɑ̃, ɑ̃t) *a,* slow; lingering; low (*fever, speed*). **lenteur** (lɑ̃tœr) *f,* slowness.
lentille (lɑ̃tij) *f,* (*Bot., Cook.*) lentil; (*Opt.*) lens. *~s cornéennes,* contact lenses.
léopard (leɔpar) *m,* leopard.
lèpre (lɛpr) *f,* leprosy. **lépreux, euse** (leprø, øz) *a,* leprous; peeling (*wall*). ¶ *n,* leper. **léproserie** (prozri) *f,* leper hospital.
lequel, laquelle, lesquels, lesquelles (ləkɛl, lakɛl, lekɛl) *pn,* (*with à, de, auquel, auxquels, auxquelles, duquel, desquels, desquelles*) who, whom; which. (*relative*) *la route par laquelle il est passé,* the road by which he came. *auquel cas,* in which case. (*interrogative*) *lequel des garçons est le plus jeune?* which of the boys is the youngest?
lesbienne (lɛsbjɛn) *f,* lesbian.
lèse-majesté (lɛzmaʒɛste) *f,* treason; lese-majesty. **léser** (leze) *v.t,* to injure; wrong; infringe on (*rights*); damage (*interests*).
lésiner (lezine) *v.i,* to skimp (*sur qch,* on sth). **lésinerie** (nri) *f,* stinginess.
lésion (lezjɔ̃) *f,* lesion.
lessive (lɛsiv) *f,* washing powder; washing; wash. *faire la ~,* to do the washing. **lessivé, e** *P* (ve) *a,* washed out *P,* dead beat *P.* **lessiver** (sive) *v.t,* to wash; (*P: gambling*) to clean out *P.* **lessiveuse** (vøz) *f,* [laundry] boiler.
lest (lɛst) *m,* ballast.
leste† (lɛst) *a,* nimble, sprightly (*step*); risqué, rude (*joke*).
lester (lɛste) *v.t,* to ballast. *se ~ l'estomac,* to line one's stomach.
léthargie (letarʒi) *f,* lethargy. **léthargique** (ʒik) *a,* lethargic.
lettre (lɛtr) *f,* letter. *en toutes ~s,* written [out] in full, spelled out. *mettre une ~ à la poste,* to post a l. *les [belles] ~s,* literature. *professeur de ~s,* teacher of French (*in Fr.*). *~ morte,* dead letter. *~ de change,* bill of exchange. *~ de crédit,* letter of credit. *~s de créance,* credentials. *~ recommandée,* registered l., recorded delivery l. **lettré, e** (tre) *a,* well-read.
leucémie (løsemi) *f,* leukemia.
leur (lœr) *a,* their. *~ fils est malade,* their son is ill. ¶ **le ~, la ~, les ~s,** *pn,* theirs. *ce sac est le ~,* this bag is theirs. *les ~s,* their family. ¶ *personal pn, V* **lui.**
leurre (lœr) *m,* (*Hunt.*) lure; (*lit., fig.*) snare, trap; deception. **leurrer** (re) *v.t,* to delude.
levain (ləvɛ̃) *m,* leaven. *sans ~,* unleavened.
levant (ləvɑ̃) *a.m,* rising (*sun*). ¶ *m,* east. *le L~,* the Levant.
levé (ləve) *m,* (*Surv.*) survey. **levée** (ve) *f,* raising (*siege*); lifting (*ban*); levying (*tax*); closing (*sitting*); collection (*letters*); (*Cards*) trick; embankment. **lever** (ve) *m,* rising, getting up (*from bed*). *~ du jour,* daybreak. *~ du soleil,* sunrise. *~ de rideau,* (*Theat.*) curtain; curtain raiser. ¶ *v.t,* to lift; raise (*object*); lift up (*head*); remove (*difficulty*); levy (*tax*); clear (*letter box*); close (*sitting*); break (*camp*); weigh (*anchor*); draw up (*plan*). ¶ *v.i,* (*plant*) to come up; (*Cook.*) rise. *faire ~ la pâte,* make the dough rise. **se ~,** (*pers.*) to get up; stand up; (*curtain*) go up; (*sun*) rise; (*wind*) get up; (*mist*) clear.
levier (ləvje) *m,* lever.
lévite (levit) *m,* Levite.
lèvre (lɛvr) *f,* lip.
lévrier (levrie) *m,* greyhound.
levure (ləvyr) *f,* yeast.
lexicographe (lɛksikɔgraf) *m,* lexicographer. **lexique** (sik) *m,* vocabulary; lexicon.
lézard (lezar) *m,* lizard.
lézarde (lezard) *f,* crack. **lézarder** (de) *v.i,* to sun oneself. **se ~,** to crack.
liaison (ljɛzɔ̃) *f,* [love] affair; [business] relationship, contact; [transport] link. *entrer en ~ avec qn,* to get in contact with s.o.
liane (ljan) *f,* liana, creeper.
liant, e (ljɑ̃, ɑ̃t) *a,* sociable.
liard (ljar) *m,* (*Hist.*) farthing.
liasse (ljas) *f,* bundle (*papers*); wad (*banknotes*).
Liban (le) (libɑ̃), [the] Lebanon. **libanais, e** (banɛ, ɛz) *a.* & **L~,** *n,* Lebanese.
libelle (libɛl) *m,* libel; lampoon.
libellé (libɛlle) *m,* wording. **libeller** (le) *v.t,* to draw up (*document*); make out (*cheque*);

word (*letter*).
libellule (libɛlyl) *f*, dragonfly.
libéral, e† (liberal) *a*, liberal; learned (*profession*). ¶ *m*, liberal. ~**isation** (lizasjɔ̃) *f*, liberalisation. ~**iser** (lize) *v.t*, to liberalize. ~**isme** (lism) *m*, liberalism. ~**ité** (te) *f*, liberality.
libérateur, trice (liberatœr, tris) *n*, liberator. ¶ *a*, liberating; (*war*) of liberation. **libération** (sjɔ̃) *f*, liberation; discharge; release. **libérer** (re) *v.t*, to release (*prisoner*); discharge (*soldier*); free (*from debts &c*); deliver (*country*). **se** ~, to make o.s free. **liberté** (bɛrte) *f*, liberty, freedom; free time.
libertin, e (libɛrtɛ̃, in) *a*. & *n*, libertine. ~**age,** (tinaʒ) *m*, licentiousness, debauchery.
libraire (librɛr) *m*, bookseller. ~*-editeur*, b. & publisher. **librairie** (brɛri) *f*, bookshop; book trade.
libre† (libr) *a*, free; vacant (*seat*); spare (*time*); open (*sale*); clear (*way*); independent, private (*education*); blunt (*manners*). ~ *arbitre, m*, free will. ~*-échange, m*, f. trade. ~ *penseur*, freethinker. ~*-service, m*, self-service restaurant, shop.
librettiste (librɛtist) *m*, librettist.
Libye (la) (libi), Libya. **libyen, ne** (bjɛ̃, ɛn) *a*. & **L**~, *n*, Libyan.
licence (lisɑ̃s) *f*, (*Univ.*) degree. ~ *ès lettres*, Arts degree, ≃ B.A. licence, permit; licentiousness. **licencié, e** (sɑ̃sje) *n*, graduate, bachelor (*law, arts &c*). **licencier** (sje) *v.t*, to make redundant; dismiss. **licenciement** (simɑ̃) *m*, redundancy; dismissal. **licencieux, euse†** (sjø, øz) *a*, licentious.
lichen (likɛn) *m*, lichen.
licite† (lisit) *a*, licit, lawful.
licorne (likɔrn) *f*, unicorn.
lie (li) *f*, sediment, dregs. ~ *de vin, a*, wine[-coloured].
lié, e (lje) *a*, bound, tied; (*pl*) close [friends].
liège (ljɛʒ) *m*, cork.
lien (ljɛ̃) *m*, bond; tie; link. **lier** (lje) *v.t*, to bind; tie [up]; link; connect; (*Mus.*) slur, tie; thicken (*sauce*). **se lier,** to bind o.s; make friends (*avec*, with).
lierre (ljɛr) *m*, ivy.
lieu (ljø) *m*, place. *les* ~*x*, the premises. *sur les* ~*x*, on the spot, at the scene. ~ *de naissance, travail*, place of birth, work. ~ *d'aisances O*, lavatory. ~ *commun*, commonplace. *en haut* ~, in high places. *en premier* ~, in the first place. *ce n'est pas le* ~ *de*, this is not the [right] place to. *au* ~ *de qch, de faire*, instead of sth, doing. *avoir* ~, to take place. *il y a* ~ *de*, there are [good] grounds for. *s'il y a* ~, if necessary.
lieue (ljø) *f*, league (≃ 4 km).
lieuse (ljøz) *f*, (*Agr.*) binder.
lieutenant (ljøtnɑ̃) *m*, lieutenant; mate (*ship*). ~*-colonel*, lieutenant colonel. ~ *de vaisseau*, [naval] lieutenant.
lièvre (ljɛvr) *m*, hare.
ligament (ligamɑ̃) *m*, ligament. **ligature** (tyr) *f*, ligature.
ligne (liɲ) *f*, (*gen., Rly, Fish.*) line; row; figure (*woman*). ~ *d'autobus*, bus company; bus route. ~ *de but*, goal l. ~ *de départ*, starting l. ~ *de flottaison* (flɔtɛzɔ̃), water l. ~ *d'horizon*, skyline. (*Sport*) ~ *médiane*, halfway l. ~ *de touche*, touchline.
lignée (liɲe) *f*, decendants, line.
ligneux, euse (liɲø, øz) *a*, ligneous, woody. **lignite** (ɲit) *m*, lignite.
ligoter (ligɔte) *v.t*, to bind, lash.
ligue (lig) *f*, league. **liguer** (ge) *v.t*, to unite (*contre*, against). **se liguer,** to form a league, be in league.
lilas (lilɑ) *m*. & *a. inv*, lilac.
limace (limas) *f*, (*Zool.*) slug; (*P*) shirt. *quelle* ~*!* what a slowcoach! **limaçon** (sɔ̃) *m*, snail.
limande (limɑ̃d) *f*, dab (*fish*). ~*-sole*, lemon sole.
limbe (lɛ̃b) *m*, *les* ~*s*, limbo.
lime (lim) *f*, file (*tool*). **limer** (me) *v.t*, to file.
limier (limje) *m*, bloodhound; (*fig.*) sleuth.
limitation (limitasjɔ̃) *f*, limitation. ~ *des naissances*, birth control. **limite** (mit) *f*, limit; boundary. *sans* ~, boundless. *à la* ~, almost, at a pinch. *dans une certaine* ~, to a certain extent. ¶ *a*, *cas* ~, borderline case. *vitesse* ~, maximum speed. **limiter** (te) *v.t*, to limit; restrict; (*frontier*) border. **se limiter,** to restrict o.s; be limited (*à*, to). **limitrophe** (trɔf) *a*, bordering.
limoger (limɔʒe) *v.t*, to dismiss, fire.
limon (limɔ̃) *m*, silt; shaft (*cart*). **limonade** (mɔnad) *f*, lemonade. **limoneux, euse** (nø, øz) *a*, muddy, silt-laden.
limpide (lɛ̃pid) *a*, limpid; lucid (*account*).
lin (lɛ̃) *m*, flax. [*toile de*]~, linen.
linceul (lɛ̃sœl) *m*, shroud.
linéaire (lineɛr) *a*, linear.
linge (lɛ̃ʒ) *m*, *le* ~, *du* ~, [household] linen; underwear. *laver le* ~, to do the washing. *un* ~, a cloth. *blanc comme un* ~, as white as a sheet. **lingerie** (ʒri) *f*, underwear, lingerie; linen room.
lingot (lɛ̃go) *m*, ingot.
linguiste (lɛ̃gɥist) *n*, linguist. **linguistique** (tik) *f*, linguistics. ¶ *a*, linguistic.
liniment (linimɑ̃) *m*, liniment.
linoléum (linɔleɔm) *m*, linoleum, lino.
linotte (linɔt) *f*, linnet.
linteau (lɛ̃to) *m*, lintel.
lion (ljɔ̃) *m*, lion. **lionceau** (so) *m*, lion cub. **lionne** (ɔn) *f*, lioness.
lippe (lip) *f*, thick underlip. *faire la* ~, to pout. **lippu, e** (py) *a*, thick-lipped.
liquéfaction (likefaksjɔ̃) *f*, liquefaction. **liquéfier**

(fje) *v.t*, to liquefy. **liqueur** (kœr) *f*, liqueur; (*Chem.*) solution.
liquidateur (likidatœr) *m*, liquidator. **liquidation** (sjɔ̃) *f*, liquidation, winding up; settlement; payment; sale.
liquide (likid) *a*, liquid; runny, thin. ¶ *m*, liquid. *du* ~, ready money.
liquider (likide) *v.t*, to liquidate, wind up (*company*); close, settle (*account*); sell off (*stock*); pay off (*debt*); (*P*) eliminate, get rid of (*rival*). **liquidité** (dite) *f*, (*Law, Chem.*) liquidity. ~ *s*, liquid assets.
liquoreux, euse (likɔrø, øz) *a*, syrupy (*wine*).
lire[1] (lir) *v.t.ir*, to read; r. out (*speech*). *nous esperons vous* ~ *bientôt*, we hope to hear from you soon.
lire[2] (lir) *f*, lira.
lis (lis) *m*, lily.
Lisbonne (lizbɔn) *f*, Lisbon.
liseron (lizrɔ̃) *m*, bindweed.
liseur, euse (lizœr, øz) *n*, reader. ¶ *f*, bed jacket. **lisible†** (zibl) *a*, legible; readable.
lisière (lizjɛr) *f*, selvedge (*cloth*); edge (*place*).
lisse (lis) *a*, smooth; sleek (*hair*). **lisser** (se) *v.t*, to smooth; preen (*feathers*).
liste (list) *f*, list. ~ *électorale*, electoral roll. ~ *noire*, blacklist.
listing (listiŋ) *m*, [computer] printout.
lit (li) *m*, bed; bed (*river*); layer (*soil &c*). ~ *d'une personne/de deux personnes*, single/double bed. ~ *de fer*, iron bedstead. ~ *de repos*, couch. ~ *de douleur*, sick b. *se mettre au* ~, to go to b. *faire le* ~, to make the b. *de premier* ~, (*child*) of the first marriage.
litanie (litani) *f*, (*Rel., pej.*) litany.
literie (litri) *f*, bedding.
lithographie (litɔgrafi) *f*, lithography (*technique*); lithograph (*print*).
litière (litjɛr) *f*, litter (*animal bedding*).
litige (litiʒ) *m*, litigation; dispute. **litigieux, euse** (tiʒjø, øz) *a*, litigious; contentious.
litre, (litr) *m*, litre; litre bottle.
littéraire† (literɛr) *a*, literary.
littéral, e† (literal) *a*, literal.
littérature (literatyr) *f*, literature; writing (*profession*).
littoral, e (litɔral) *a*, coastal. ¶ *m*, coast.
liturgie (lityrʒi) *f*, liturgy. **liturgique** (ʒik) *a*, liturgical.
livide (livid) *a*, livid, pallid.
Livourne (livurn) *f*, Leghorn.
livraison (livrɛzɔ̃) *f*, delivery.
livre[1] (livr) *f*, pound = $\frac{1}{2}$ kilogram. ~ [*sterling*], pound [sterling].
livre[2] (livr) *m*, book. ~ *à succès*, bestseller. ~ *d'images*, picture b. ~ *de bord*, log[book]. ~ *de caisse*, cashbook. ~ *de classe*, schoolbook. ~ *de chevet*, bedside b. ~ *d'or*, visitors' b. ~ *de poche*, paperback. *à* ~ *ouvert*, (*translate*) at sight.
livrée (livre) *f*, livery.
livrer (livre) *v.t*, (*Com.*) to deliver; hand over (*pers.*); give away (*secret*). ~ *bataille*, to join battle. ~ *passage à qn*, let s.o pass. **se** ~ **à**, to confide in; give o.s up to; abandon o.s. to (*fate*); give o.s over to (*grief*); indulge in (*drink*); devote o.s to (*research*).
livret (livrɛ) *m*, (*Mus.*) libretto. ~ *de caisse d'épargne*, savings bank book. ~ *scolaire*, school report book. ~ *de famille*, family record book.
livreur, euse (livrœr, øz) *n*, delivery man *or* boy *or* girl.
lobe (lɔb) *m*, lobe.
local, e† (lɔkal) *a*, local. ¶ *m. oft. pl*, premises; offices. **localiser** (lize) *v.t*, to localize; confine (*fire &c*). **localité** (te) *f*, locality. **locataire** (tɛr) *n*, tenant (*house*); lodger (*room*). **location** (sjɔ̃) *f*, (*by owner*) letting; (*by tenant*) renting (*house*); hiring (*car*); reservation (*seat*). *contrat de* ~, lease. ~*-vente*, hire purchase.
lock-out (lɔkaut) *m*, lockout.
locomotion (lɔkɔmɔsjɔ̃) *f*, locomotion. **locomotive** (tiv) *f*, locomotive, [railway] engine.
locution (lɔkysjɔ̃) *f*, phrase.
lofer (lɔfe) *v.i*, (*Naut.*) to luff.
logarithme (lɔgaritm) *m*, logarithm.
loge (lɔʒ) *f*, lodge (*porter, freemason*); (*Theat.*) box; dressing room (*actor*). ~ **able** (ʒabl) *a*, habitable, roomy. ~ **ment** (ʒmɑ̃) *m*, housing. *la crise du* ~, the housing crisis. accommodation, lodgings; (*Mil.*) quarters; billeting. **loger** (ʒe) *v.t*, to house; accommodate; put up. ¶ *v.i*, to live (*dans* in, *chez* with, at). *se* ~, to find somewhere to live, stay. **logeur, euse** (ʒœr, øz) *n*, landlord, -lady.
logiciel (lɔʒisjɛl) *m*, software (*computer*).
logique† (lɔʒik) *a*, logical. ¶ *f*, logic.
logis (lɔʒi) *m*, (*liter.*) dwelling, home.
loi (lwa) *f*, law. *appliquer la* ~, to carry out the law. *c'est lui qui fait la* ~, his word is law. *se faire une* ~ *de faire*, to make a rule of doing. ~ *martiale*, martial law.
loin (lwɛ̃) *ad*, far; f. off, f. away (*place, time*). *au* ~, in the distance. *de* ~, from a long way off. *l'été n'est pas* ~, summer's not far off. *de* ~ *en* ~, here & there; every now & then. ~ *de là*, far from it. **lointain, e** (tɛ̃, ɛn) *a*, remote, distant. ¶ *m*, *dans le* ~, in the distance.
loir (lwar) *m*, dormouse.
loisible (lwazibl) *a*, *il lui est* ~ *de*, he is free, permitted to. **loisir** (zir) *m. oft. pl*, leisure; spare time; leisure activities. *à* ~, at leisure.
lombaire (lɔ̃bɛr) *a*, lumbar.
Lombardie (la) (lɔ̃bardi), Lombardy.
londonien, ne (lɔ̃dɔnjɛ̃, ɛn) *a*, London. **L** ~, *n*, Londoner. **Londres** (lɔ̃dr) *m*, London.
long, ongue (lɔ̃, ɔ̃g) *a*, long; lengthy; long-standing (*friendship*). *une corde* ~*ue de 2*

mètres, a rope 2 m. long. *il était ~ à venir,* he was a l. time coming. ¶ *ad, en savoir ~,* to know a lot (*sur,* about). ¶ *m,* length. *en ~,* lengthways. *un jardin de 20 mètres de ~,* a garden 20 m. long. *le ~ du canal,* along the canal. *tout au ~ de,* all through, throughout. *étendu de tout son ~,* lying full length. ¶ *f, à la ~ue,* in the long run.

longanimité (lɔ̃ganimite) *f,* (*liter.*) long-suffering, forbearance.

long-courrier (lɔ̃kurje) *m,* ocean liner; long-haul aircraft.

longe (lɔ̃ʒ) *f,* lead; tether; loin (*veal*).

longer (lɔ̃ʒe) *v.t,* (*road, wall*) to border, skirt; (*pers.*) go along.

longévité (lɔ̃ʒevite) *f,* longevity.

longitude (lɔ̃ʒityd) *f,* longitude. **longitudinal, e†** (dinal) *a,* longitudinal.

longtemps (lɔ̃tɑ̃) *ad,* [for] long; [for] a long while. *je n'en ai pas pour ~,* it won't take me long. *il y a ~ que j'attends,* I've been waiting a long time. **longuement** (lɔ̃gmɑ̃) *ad,* [for] a long time; at length. **longuet, te** (gɛ, ɛt) *a,* longish. **longueur** (gœr) *f,* length. *en ~,* lengtnways. *~ d'onde,* wavelength. *traîner en ~,* to drag out. *gagner de 3 ~s,* to win by three lengths. *~s,* tedious moments (*film, novel*). **longue-vue** (lɔ̃gvy) *f,* telescope.

lopin (lɔpɛ̃) *m,* patch, plot (*of ground*).

loquace (lɔkwas) *a,* loquacious, talkative.

loque (lɔk) *f, en ~s,* in rags, tatters. (*fig., pej.*) *c'est une ~,* he, she is a wreck.

loquet (lɔkɛ) *m,* latch (*door*).

lorgner (lɔrɲe) *v.t,* to eye (*object*); ogle (*woman*); have one's eye on (*inheritance*). **lorgnette** (ɲɛt) *f,* spyglass. **lorgnon** (ɲɔ̃) *m,* pince-nez.

loriot (lɔrjo) *m,* [golden] oriole.

lors (lɔr) *ad,* then. *dès ~,* from then on. *~ de,* at the time of. *~ même que,* even though. **lorsque** (lɔrskə) *c,* when.

losange (lɔzɑ̃ʒ) (*Geom.*) *m,* lozenge, diamond.

lot (lo) *m,* lot (*auction & fig.*); portion; prize (*lottery*). **loterie** (lɔtri) *f,* lottery.

lotion (losjɔ̃) *f,* lotion.

lotir (lɔtir) *v.t,* to divide up; provide (*qn de,* s.o with). *bien loti,* well-off. **lotissement** (ismɑ̃) *m,* housing estate.

loto (lɔto) *m,* lotto (*game*).

lotus (lɔtys) *m,* lotus.

louable (lwabl) *a,* laudable, praiseworthy.

louange (lwɑ̃ʒ) *f,* praise. **louangeur, euse** (ʒœr, øz) *a,* laudatory.

louche (luʃ) *a,* shady, suspicious. ¶ *f,* soup ladle. **loucher** (ʃe) *v.i,* to squint.

louer[1] (lwe) *v.t,* to praise. *~ qn de qch,* to praise s.o for sth. **se ~ de,** to be pleased with.

louer[2] (lwe) *v.t,* (*owner*) to let [out]; (*tenant*) rent (*house*); hire (*car*); reserve, book (*seat*). *à ~,* to let; for hire. **loueur, euse** (wœr, øz) *n,* hirer.

loufoque *P* (lufɔk) *a,* crazy, barmy *P.* ¶ *n,* crackpot.

Louisiane (lwizjan) *f,* Louisiana.

loulou (lulu) *m,* Pomeranian [dog], pom.

loup (lu) *m,* wolf; bass (*fish*). *~ de mer P,* old salt *P* (*sailor*).

loupe (lup) *f,* magnifying glass. **louper** *P* (pe) *v.t,* to miss (*train*); mess up *P,* bungle *P* (*job*).

loup-garou (lugaru) *m,* werewolf.

lourd, e† (lur, urd) *a,* (*lit., fig.*) heavy; weighty; close, sultry (*weather*); serious (*mistake*). *yeux ~s,* eyes heavy with sleep. *avoir la tête ~e,* to be headachy. *avoir l'esprit ~,* to be slow-witted. **lourdaud, e** (lurdo, od) *a,* oafish. ¶ *n,* oaf. **lourdeur** (dœr) *f,* heaviness, &c.

loustic *P* (lustik) *m,* funny guy, [practical] joker.

loutre (lutr) *f,* otter.

louve (luv) *f,* [she-]wolf. **louveteau** (luvto) *m,* wolf cub; cub scout.

louvoyer (luvwaje) *v.i,* (*Naut.*) to tack; (*fig.*) evade the issue.

loyal, e† (lwajal) *a,* honest, fair; true, loyal, trusty. **loyauté** (jote) *f,* honesty, fairness; loyalty.

loyer (lwaje) *m,* rent.

lubie (lybi) *f,* whim, fad, craze.

lubrifiant, e (lybrifjɑ̃, ɑ̃t) *a,* lubricating. ¶ *m,* lubricant. **lubrifier** (fje) *v.t,* to lubricate. **lubrique** (brik) *a,* lewd.

lucarne (lykarn) *f,* dormer window; skylight.

lucide† (lysid) *a,* lucid, clear; conscious; clear-headed. **lucidité** (dite) *f,* lucidity; consciousness; clear-headedness.

luciole (lysjɔl) *f,* firefly.

lucratif, ive† (lykratif, iv) *a,* lucrative. **lucre** (lykr) *m,* lucre, gain.

luette (lɥɛt) *f,* uvula.

lueur (lɥœr) *f,* glimmer (*candle, hope*); gleam (*anger*); glow (*embers*).

luge (lyʒ) *f,* sledge, toboggan.

lugubre† (lygybr) *a,* lugubrious, gloomy.

lui[1], (*pl.*) **leur** (lɥi, lœr) *pn,* (*indirect object*) [to] him, her, it, (*pl.*) them. *je le ~ ai dit,* I told him (her). *montrez-le-leur,* show it to them. *il ~ est facile de venir,* it's easy for him (her) to come.

lui[2], (*pl.*) **eux** (lɥi, ø) *pn.m,* (*emphatic*) he, him, it, (*pl.*) they, them. *c'est ~ qui l'a fait,* it's he who did it. *je le connais ~,* I know him all right. *j'ai bu plus que ~,* I drank more than he did. (*after pr.*) him, it, them. *pour ~,* for him. *avec eux,* with them. *cette clef est à ~,* this key is his. *lui-même, eux-mêmes,* himself, itself, themselves.

luire (lɥir) *v.i.ir,* to shine, gleam. **luisant, e** (lɥizɑ̃, ɑ̃t) *a,* shining, gleaming; bright; glossy. ¶ *m,* shine, gloss.

lumbago (lɔ̃bago) *m,* lumbago.

lumière (lymjɛr) *f,* light. *la ~ du jour,* daylight.

(*fig.*) *avoir quelque* ~ *sur,* to have some knowledge of. *jeter une nouvelle* ~ *sur,* to throw new light on. **luminaire** (nɛr) *m,* light, lamp. **lumineux, euse†** (nø, øz) *a,* luminous; bright.
lunaire (lynɛr) *a,* lunar.
lunatique (lynatik) *a,* whimsical, quirky.
lunch (lœntʃ) *m,* buffet lunch.
lundi (lœ̃di) *m,* Monday.
lune (lyn) *f,* moon. *pleine, nouvelle* ~, full, new moon. ~ *de miel,* honeymoon.
luné, e *P* (lyne) *a, bien* ~, in a good mood.
lunette (lynɛt) *f,* ~*s,* glasses; goggles (*protective*). ~ *d'approche,* telescope. (*Mot.*) ~ *arrière,* rear window. ~*s de soleil,* sunglasses.
lurette (lyrɛt) *f: il y a belle* ~ *que,* it is ages since.
luron *P* (lyrɔ̃) *m,* lad *P. joyeux* ~, gay dog.
lustre (lystr) *m,* lustre; gloss; (*fig.*) lustre; chandelier. **lustrer** (tre) *v.t,* to lustre; shine, make shiny.
luth (lyt) *m,* lute.
luthérien, ne (lyterjɛ̃, ɛn) *a. & n,* Lutheran.
luthier (lytje) *m,* musical instrument maker.
lutin, e (lytɛ̃, in) *a,* impish. ¶ *m,* imp.
lutrin (lytrɛ̃) *m,* lectern.
lutte (lyt) *f,* struggle; fight; (*Sport*) wrestling. *la* ~ *des classes,* the class struggle, war. *la* ~ *contre le cancer,* the fight against cancer. (*Sport*) ~ *libre,* all-in wrestling. **lutter** (te) *v.i,* to struggle, fight (*contre,* against); (*Sport*) wrestle. **lutteur** (tœr) *m,* wrestler; (*fig.*) fighter.
luxation (lyksasjɔ̃) *f,* dislocation.
luxe (lyks) *m,* luxury; luxuriousness. (*Com.*) *de* ~, de luxe. *voiture de* ~, luxury car.
Luxembourg (lyksɑ̃bur) *m,* Luxemburg.
luxer (lykse) *v.t,* to dislocate.
luxueux, euse (lyksɥø, øz) *a,* luxurious. **luxure** (ksyr) *f,* lust. **luxuriant, e** (ksyrjɑ̃, ɑ̃t) *a,* luxuriant, lush, rank. **luxurieux, euse** (rjø, øz) *a,* lustful, lewd.
luzerne (lyzɛrn) *f,* lucerne, alfalfa.
lycée (lise) *m,* secondary school. ~ *technique,* technical school. **lycéen, ne** (seɛ̃, ɛn) *n,* secondary school pupil.
lymphe (lɛ̃f) *f,* lymph. **lymphatique** (fatik) *a,* lymphatic; (*fig.*) sluggish.
lyncher (lɛ̃ʃe) *v.t,* to lynch.
lynx (lɛ̃ks) *m,* lynx.
Lyon (ljɔ̃) *m,* Lyons.
lyre (lir) *f,* lyre. **lyrique** (lirik) *a,* lyric; lyrical. *artiste* ~, opera singer. ¶ *m,* lyric poet. **lyrisme** (rism) *m,* lyricism.
lys (lis) *m, V* **lis.**

M

M, m (ɛm) *m. & f, letter,* M, m.
ma (ma) *a, V* **mon.**
maboul *P* (mabul) *a. & n,* loony *P.*
macabre (makɑbr) *a,* macabre; gruesome.
macadam (makadam) *m,* macadam; tarmac. ~**iser** (mize) *v.t,* to macadamize; tarmac.
macareux (makarø) *m,* puffin.
macaron (makarɔ̃) *m,* (*Cook.*) macaroon; round badge; round sticker.
macaroni (makarɔni) *m,* piece of macaroni. *des* ~*s,* macaroni.
macchabée *P* (makabe) *m,* corpse, stiff *P.*
macédoine (masedwan) *f:* ~ *de fruits,* fruit salad. ~ *de legumes,* mixed vegetables, macedoine.
macérer (masere) *v.t,* to macerate.
mâchefer (mɑʃfɛr) *m,* clinker, cinders.
mâcher (mɑʃe) *v.t,* to chew; munch; (*animal*) champ. *il ne mâche pas ses mots,* he doesn't mince his words.
machiavélique (makjavelik) *a,* Machiavellian.
machin, e *P* (maʃɛ̃, in) *n,* thingumajig *P,* what-d'you-call-it *P. M*~, *e* (*pers.*) what's-his-(her)-name *P.*
machinal, e† (maʃinal) *a,* (*fig.*) mechanical. **machination** (sjɔ̃) *f,* machination. **machine** (ʃin) *f,* machine; (*Rly.*) engine, locomotive; (*Naut.*) engine; vehicle; motorcycle. ~ *à affranchir,* franking m. ~ *à calculer,* calculator. ~ *à coudre,* sewing machine. ~ *à écrire,* typewriter. ~ *à laver,* washing m. ~ *à laver la vaisselle,* dishwasher. ~ *à sous,* fruit m., one-armed bandit; slot m. ~ *à traitement de texte,* word processor. ~ *à vapeur,* steam engine. ~*-outil, f,* machine tool. **machiner** (ne) *v.t,* to scheme, plot. **machinerie,** (nri) *f,* machinery; engine room. **machinisme** (nism) *m,* mechanization. **machiniste** (nist) *m,* stage-hand; driver.
mâchoire (mɑʃwar) *f,* jaw.
mâchonner (mɑʃɔne) *v.t,* to chew; mumble.
maçon (masɔ̃) *m,* builder; [stone]mason; bricklayer. **maçonnerie** (nri) *f,* masonry; stonework; brickwork.
maculer (makyle) *v.t,* to stain (*de,* with).
Madame (madam), *pl,* **Mesdames** (medam) *f,*

Mrs, Madam. ~ *X*, Mrs X. *bonjour* ~, good morning; good morning Mrs X. ~, dear Madam (*letter*). *chère* ~, dear Mrs X. ~ *désire?* what would you like, Madam? ~ *la Présidente*, Madam chairman; the chairman. *Mesdames, Messieurs*, ladies and gentlemen.

Mademoiselle (madmwazɛl), *pl*, **Mesdemoiselles** (medmwazɛl) *f*, Miss. ~ *X*, Miss X. *bonjour* ~, good morning; good morning Miss X. *bonjour Mesdemoiselles*, good morning ladies *or* girls. ~, dear Madam (*letter*). *cher* ~, dear Miss X (*letter*).

Madère (madɛr) *f*, Madeira.

madone (madɔn) *f*, madonna.

madré, e (madre) *a*, crafty, deep.

madrier (madrie) *m*, beam.

magasin (magazɛ̃) *m*, shop, store; warehouse; magazine (*gun, camera*). ~ *à grande surface*, hypermarket. ~ *à succursales multiples*, chain store. *en* ~, in stock. **magasinier** (nje) *m*, storekeeper, warehouseman. **magazine** (zin) *m*, magazine (*periodical*).

mage (maʒ) *m*, magus. ¶ *a*, *les Rois* ~*s*, the Magi.

magicien, ne (maʒisjɛ̃, ɛn) *n*, magician. **magie** (ʒi) *f*, magic. **magique**† (ʒik) *a*, (*lit.*) magic; (*fig.*) magical.

magistral, e† (maʒistral) *a*, masterly (*work, address*); brilliant (*success*); masterful (*tone*). *cours* ~, (*Univ.*) lecture. **magistrat** (tra) *m*, magistrate. **magistrature** (tyr) *f*, (*Law*) magistracy; (*Adm., Pol.*) public office. *la* ~ *suprême*, the highest office.

magma (magma) *m*, (*Sci.*) magma; (*fig.*) muddle.

magnanime† (maɲanim) *a*, magnanimous. **magnanimité** (mite) *f*, magnanimity.

magnat (magna) *m*, magnate, tycoon.

magner (se) *P* (maɲe) *v.pr*, to hurry up, get cracking *P*.

magnésium (maɲezjɔm) *m*, magnesium.

magnétique (maɲetik) *a*, magnetic. **magnétisation** (zasjɔ̃) *f*, magnetization; hypnotisation. **magnétiser** (ze) *v.t*, to magnetize; hypnotize. **magnétiseur** (zœr) *n*, hypnotizer. **magnétisme** (tism) *m*, (*Phys., fig.*) magnetism; hypnotism.

magnéto (maɲeto) *f*, (*Elec.*) magneto. ¶ (*P*) *m*, tape recorder. ~**phone** (tɔfɔn) *m*, tape recorder. ~ *à cassettes*, cassette recorder. ~**scope** (skɔp) *m*, video-recorder; videotape.

magnificence (maɲifisɑ̃s) *f*, magnificence. **magnifique**† (fik) *a*, magnificent; gorgeous, superb. (*P*) ~*!*, great!, fantastic! *P*.

magot (mago) *m*, (*Zool.*) Barbary ape; (*P*) hoard, stash *P*; nest egg.

mai (mɛ) *m*, May (*month*).

maigre (mɛgr) *a*, (*pers.*) thin, skinny; thin, lean (*face*); meagre, scanty (*ration*); poor (*harvest, profit*); straggling, sparse (*beard, grass*); lean (*meat*); low-fat (*cheese*); clear (*bouillon*). *jour* ~, day of abstinence. ¶ *n*, thin person. ¶ *m*, lean [meat]. ~**ment** (grəmɑ̃) *ad*, meagrely, scantily. **maigreur** (grœr) *f*, thinness. **maigrir** (grir) *v.i*, to get thinner, lose weight. ¶ *v.t*, (*illness*) to make s.o lose weight; (*dress*) to make s.o look slim.

maille (maj) *f*, (*Knit.*) stitch; mesh (*net*); link (*armour*). ~*s*, mail (*armour*). ~ *filée*, ladder (*stocking*). ~ *échappée*, (*Knit.*) dropped stitch. *une* ~ *à l'endroit, une* ~ *à l'envers*, knit one, purl one.

maillet (majɛ) *m*, mallet.

maillon (majɔ̃) *m*, link (*chain*).

maillot (majo) *m*, (*gen.*) vest; (*Sport*) vest, jersey; leotard; baby's wrap. ~ *de bain*, swimming trunks (*man*); swimsuit, swimming costume (*woman*).

main (mɛ̃) *f*, hand. *la* ~ *dans la* ~, hand in hand (*lovers*), h. in glove (*criminals*). *donne-moi la* ~, hold my h. *trouver une* ~ *secourable*, to find a helping h. *donne-moi un coup de* ~, give me a h. *demander la* ~ *d'une femme*, to ask for a woman's h. [in marriage]. *à* ~ *droite, gauche*, on the right-, left-h. side. *fait* [*à la*] ~, handmade. (*fig.*) *avoir les* ~*s libres, liées*, to have a free h., have one's hands tied. *j'ai une belle* ~, I have a good h. (*cards*). *en venir aux* ~*s*, to come to blows. ~ *courante*, handrail. ~ *d'œuvre*, manpower, labour.

mainmise (mɛ̃miz) *f*, (*Law, Pol.*) seizure (*sur*, of).

maint, e (mɛ̃, ɛ̃t) *a*, (*liter.*) many, many a. ~*es fois*, many a time.

maintenant (mɛ̃tnɑ̃) *ad*, now. **maintenir** (tnir) *v.t.ir*, to maintain, keep; uphold (*tradition*); stand by (*decision*). **se** ~, to hold one's own; (*price, health*) stay the same. **maintien** (tjɛ̃) *m*, maintenance, upholding; deportment, bearing.

maire (mɛr) *m*, mayor. **mairie** (meri) *f*, town hall; town council.

mais (mɛ) *c*, but. ~ *non!* not at all! ~ *oui!* certainly!, of course! ¶ *m*, but, objection.

maïs (mais) *m*, maize, Indian corn.

maison (mɛzɔ̃) *f*, house; block of flats. ~ *individuelle*, detached house. home. *venez à la* ~, come home with me. *rester à la* ~, to stay at home. *fait à la* ~, home-made. firm, company; store, shop; household. *employés de* ~, domestic staff. ~ *d'arrêt*, prison. ~ *close*, brothel. ~ *de jeu*, gaming house. ~ *de retraite*, old people's home. ~ *de santé*, nursing home. ~ *des étudiants*, hostel. ~ *des jeunes et de la culture*, youth club and arts centre. ~**née** (zɔne) *f*, household, family. ~**nette** (nɛt) *f*, small house.

maître, esse (mɛtr, trɛs) *a*, main, chief, major. *idée* ~*esse*, principal, main idea. *poutre* ~*esse*, main beam. *une* ~*esse femme*, a masterful woman. ¶ *m,* master; (*Pol.*) ruler. *parler en* ~, to speak with authority, authoritatively. *rester* ~ *de soi,* to be in control of o.s. ~ *de maison,* host. ~ [*d'école*], teacher, schoolmaster. *M*~, Sir. *M*~ *X,* (*Law*) Mr. X. ~ *chanteur,* blackmailer. ~ *d'armes,* fencing master. ~ *d'équipage,* boatswain. ~ *d'hôtel,* head waiter. ~ *de cérémonie,* master of ceremonies. ~ *de conférences,* lecturer. ¶ *f,* mistress; (*Sch.*) teacher, schoolmistress. **maîtrise** (triz) *f,* control, mastery. ~ [*de soi*], self-control. skill, expertise; (*Rel.*) choir; (*Univ.*) ≏ master's degree. **maîtriser** (trize) *v.t,* to control; overpower (*pers.*); subdue, suppress (*revolt*); master (*language*). **se** ~, to control o.s.

majesté (maʒɛste) *f,* majesty. *Sa M*~, His (Her) Majesty. **majestueux, euse**† (tɥø, øz) *a,* majestic; imposing.

majeur, e (maʒœr) *a,* (*gen., Mus.*) major. *en* ~*e partie,* for the most part. (*Law*) *être* ~, to be of age. ¶ *n,* (*Law*) major. ¶ *m,* middle finger.

major (maʒɔr) *m,* (*Mil.*) medical officer. (*Univ.*) *être* ~ *de promotion,* to be first in one's year. **majoration** (ʒɔrasjɔ̃) *f,* increase (*price*); surcharge. **majordome** (dɔm), major-domo. **majorer** (re) *v.t,* to increase (*de,* by). **majorité** (rite) *f,* (*gen., Law*) majority; government, party in power. *être en* ~, to be in the majority. **majoritaire** (tɛr) *a,* majority.

Majorque (maʒɔrk) *f,* Majorca.

majuscule (maʒyskyl) *a.* & *f,* capital (letter).

mal (mal) *m,* evil, ill. *le* ~, evil. *dire du* ~ *de qn,* to speak ill of s.o. harm. *faire du* ~, to harm, hurt. pain; sorrow; illness. *se faire du* ~, to hurt o.s. *ça fait* ~, it hurts. *j'ai* ~ *à la tête,* I have a headache. ~ *de mer,* seasickness. ~ *du pays,* homesickness. trouble, difficulty. *se donner du* ~ *à faire qch,* to take pains over sth. ¶ *ad,* badly, not properly. *la porte ferme* ~, the door doesn't close properly. ~ *choisi,* ill-chosen. ~ *famé,* disreputable. ~ *comprendre,* to misunderstand. *se sentir* ~, to feel ill. *se trouver* ~, to be taken ill. (*P*) *pas* ~ [*de*], a good deal [of], a lot [of]. ¶ *a. inv,* wrong, bad. *il est, c'est* ~ *de faire ça,* it's wrong to do that. *il est* ~ *dans sa peau,* he is at odds with himself. *être* ~ *avec qn,* to be on bad terms with s.o. (*P*) *pas* ~, not bad *P,* quite good.

malade (malad) *a,* ill, sick, unwell (*pers.*); diseased (*plant*); bad (*tooth*); ailing (*business*). ¶ *n,* sick person; invalid; patient. ~ *mental,* mentally ill person. **maladie** (di) *f,* illness; disease. ~ *de cœur,* heart complaint, disease. mania. *avoir la* ~ *de la vitesse,* to be a speed maniac. **maladif, ive** (dif, iv) *a,* sickly; morbid.

maladresse (maladrɛs) *f,* awkwardness, clumsiness. **maladroit, e**† (drwa, at) *a.* & *n,* awkward, clumsy (person).

malaise (malɛz) *m,* dizzy turn; (*fig.*) uneasiness; (*Pol.*) unrest. **malaisé, e** (lɛze) *a,* difficult. **malaisément** (mɑ̃) *ad,* with difficulty.

Malaisie (la) (malɛzi), Malaya.

malappris, e (malapri, iz) *a,* boorish. ¶ *n,* lout.

malaria (malarja) *f,* malaria.

malavisé, e (malavize) *a,* ill-advised; unwise.

malaxer (malakse) *v.t,* to mix; knead.

malchance (malʃɑ̃s) *f,* bad luck, misfortune. *par* ~, unfortunately. **malchanceux, euse** (ʃɑ̃sø, øz) *a,* unlucky.

malcommode (malkɔmɔd) *a,* inconvenient.

mâle (mɑl) *a,* (*Biol.* &*c*) male; manly; bull (*elephant*); buck (*rabbit*); cock (*bird*). ¶ *m,* male &c.

malédiction (malediksjɔ̃) *f,* curse.

maléfice (malefis) *m,* [evil] spell. **maléfique** (fik) *a,* evil.

malencontreux, euse† (malɑ̃kɔ̃trø, øz) *a,* unfortunate; inadvertent.

malentendu (malɑ̃tɑ̃dy) *m,* misunderstanding.

malfaçon (malfasɔ̃) *f,* fault, defect.

malfaisant, e (malfəzɑ̃, ɑ̃t) *a,* malicious; harmful. **malfaiteur** (fɛtœr) *m,* law-breaker; burglar, thief.

malformation (malfɔrmasjɔ̃) *f,* malformation.

malgré (malgre) *pr,* in spite of. ~ *moi,* (*consent*) against my better judgement. ~ *tout,* in spite of everything; all the same.

malhabile† (malabil) *a,* clumsy, unskilful.

malheur (malœr) *m,* misfortune; accident. *le* ~, adversity, bad luck. *par* ~, unfortunately. **malheureux, euse**† (lœrø, øz) *a,* unfortunate (*remark*); unhappy, miserable (*life*); unsuccessful (*candidate*). ¶ *n,* wretch.

malhonnête† (malɔnɛt) *a,* dishonest; rude. ~**té** (nɛtte) *f,* dishonesty; rudeness.

malice (malis) *f,* malice, spite; mischief, mischievousness. **malicieux, euse**† (sjø, øz) *a,* mischievous.

malin, igne† (malɛ̃, iɲ) *a,* clever, bright, smart; (*P*) difficult; malicious; (*Med.*) malignant. *le M*~, the Devil.

malingre (malɛ̃gr) *a,* sickly, puny.

malintentionné, e (malɛ̃tɑ̃sjɔne) *a,* ill-intentioned (*envers,* towards).

malle (mal) *f,* trunk; (*Mot.*) boot. (*P*) *faire la* ~, to scarper *P.* ~**tte** (lɛt) *f,* small suitcase.

malléable (malleabl) *a,* malleable.

malmener (malməne) *v.t,* to abuse; handle roughly.

malnutrition (malnytrisjɔ̃) *f,* malnutrition.

malodorant, e (malɔdɔrɑ̃, ɑ̃t) *a,* foul-smelling.

malotru, e (malɔtry) *n,* lout.

malpropre† (malprɔpr) *a,* dirty; smutty (*joke*); dishonest (*conduct*); shoddy (*work*). **malpropreté** (prəte) *f,* dirtiness.

malsain, e (malsɛ̃, ɛn) *a,* unhealthy.

malséant, e (malseɑ̃, ɑ̃t) *a,* unseemly.

malt (malt) *m,* malt.
maltais, e (maltɛ, ɛz) *a. & M~, n,* Maltese. **Malte** (malt) *f,* Malta.
maltraiter (maltrɛte) *v.t,* to illtreat (*pers.*); misuse (*grammar*).
malveillance (malvɛjɑ̃s) *f,* malevolence. **malveillant, e** (jɑ̃, ɑ̃t) *a,* malevolent.
malversation (malvɛrsasjɔ̃) *f,* embezzlement.
maman (mamɑ̃) *f,* mummy, mum *P.*
mamelle (mamɛl) *f,* breast (*woman*); udder (*cow*); (*Zool.*) teat. **mamelon** (mlɔ̃) *m,* nipple; (*Geog.*) hillock.
mamie (mami) *f,* granny *P.*
mammifère (mamifɛr) *m,* mammal.
mammouth (mamut) *m,* mammoth.
mamours (mamur) *m.pl: faire des ~ à,* to fondle, caress.
manager (manadʒɛr) *m,* (*Sport &c*) manager.
manche (mɑ̃ʃ) *m,* handle; shaft; neck (*violin*). *~ à balai,* broomstick. (*P*) clumsy oaf. ¶ *f,* sleeve. *à ~s courtes,* short-sleeved. *sans ~s,* sleeveless. *avoir qn dans sa ~,* to have s.o in one's pocket. (*Cards*) game; (*Sport, Pol.*) round. *~ à air,* ventilator (*ship*); (*Aero.*) wind-sock. **la M~,** the [English] Channel. **manchette** (mɑ̃ʃɛt) *f,* cuff; over-sleeve; (*Press*) headline. **manchon** (ʃɔ̃) *m,* muff.
manchot, e (mɑ̃ʃo, ɔt) *a. & n,* one-handed, one-armed (person); (person) with no hands, arms. (*m.*) (*Zool.*) penguin.
mandarin (mɑ̃darɛ̃) *m,* (*Hist., pej.*) mandarin. **mandarine** (rin) *f,* mandarin [orange], tangerine.
mandat (mɑ̃da) *m,* (*gen., Pol.*) mandate. *~ [-poste],* postal order. (*Law*) power of attorney, proxy; (*Police*) warrant. *~ d'amener,* summons. *~ d'arrêt,* warrant for arrest. *~ de dépôt,* committal order. *~ de perquisition,* search warrant. **~aire** (tɛr) *m,* attorney; proxy; representative. **~er** (te) *v.t,* to authorize [the payment of]; commission (*pers.*).
mandibule (mɑ̃dibyl) *f,* mandible; jaw.
mandoline (mɑ̃dɔlin) *f,* mandolin[e].
manège (manɛʒ) *m,* riding school; (*fig.*) trick, ploy. *~ [de chevaux de bois],* merry-go-round.
manette (manɛt) *f,* handle, lever; tap.
manganèse (mɑ̃ganɛz) *m,* manganese.
mangeable (mɑ̃ʒabl) *a,* eatable. **mangeaille** (ʒɑj) *f,* (*pej.*) food. **mangeoire** (ʒwar) *f,* manger. **manger** (ʒe) *v.t,* to eat; (*rust &c*) eat away; (*sun*) fade; take up (*time*); go through (*money &c*); swallow (*words*). *donner à ~ à,* to feed. *on mange bien ici,* the food's good here. *~ sur le pouce,* to have a quick snack. *~ comme quatre,* to eat like a horse. *~ du bout des doigts,* to pick at one's food. *~ qn des yeux,* to devour s.o with one's eyes. *~ le morceau P,* to spill the beans *P.* ¶ *m,* food. **mangeur, euse** (ʒœr, øz) *n,* eater.
mangue (mɑ̃g) *f,* mango.
maniable (manjabl) *a,* manageable; handy.
maniaque (manjak) *a,* fussy; fanatical. ¶ *n,* crank; fanatic; lunatic, maniac. **manie** (ni) *f,* funny habit; mania.
maniement (manimɑ̃) *m,* handling. *~ d'armes,* arms drill. **manier** (nje) *v.t,* to handle.
manière (manjɛr) *f,* way; (*Art*) style. *~ de penser,* way of thinking. *~ de vivre,* way of life. *une ~ de,* a sort of. *de toute[s] ~[s],* in any case. *de ~ à faire,* so as to do. *~s,* manners. *faire des ~s,* to put on airs; make a fuss. **maniéré, e** (jere) *a,* affected; mannered (*style*). **maniérisme** (rism) *m,* mannerism.
manifestant, e (manifɛstɑ̃, ɑ̃t) *n;* demonstrator. **manifestation** (tasjɔ̃) *f,* (*gen.*) expression; appearance; (*Pol.*) demonstration. **manifeste**† (fɛst) *a,* manifest, obvious, evident. ¶ *m,* manifesto. **manifester** (te) *v.t,* to show, express (*emotion*); demonstrate (*virtue*). (*v.i,*) (*Pol. &c*) to demonstrate. **se ~,** to be shown, appear.
manigance (manigɑ̃s) *f,* scheme. **manigancer** (gɑ̃se) *v.t,* to plot, scheme.
manipulateur, trice (manipylatœr, tris) *n,* technician. **manipulation** (lasjɔ̃) *f,* handling; (*Sch., Chem. &c*) experiment. *~s,* (*Med., pej.*) manipulation. **manipuler** (le) *v.t,* to handle; manipulate; fiddle *P* (*accounts*).
manitou (manitu) *m, grand ~ P,* big shot *P.*
manivelle (manivɛl) *f,* crank; starting handle.
manne (man) *f,* manna; (*fig.*) godsend.
mannequin (mankɛ̃) *m,* [dressmaker's] dummy; model (*pers.*).
manœuvre (manœvr) *f,* manœuvre; (*Rly*) shunting. *~s électorales,* electioneering. *~s frauduleuses,* swindling. ¶ *m,* labourer; unskilled worker. **manœuvrer** (nœvre) *v.t. & i,* to manœuvre; operate (*lever*).
manoir (manwar) *m,* manor [house].
manomètre (manɔmɛtr) *m,* gauge, manometer.
manquant, e (mɑ̃kɑ̃, ɑ̃t) *a,* missing. **manque** (mɑ̃k) *m,* want, lack, shortage (*de,* of). *~s,* faults, shortcomings; gaps (*knowledge*). *à la ~ P,* grotty *P.* **manqué, e** (mɑ̃ke) *a,* failed (*attempt*); missed (*chance*); spoilt (*photo*). *c'est un artiste ~,* he's a failed artist; he should have been an artist. **manquement** (kmɑ̃) *m,* breach (*law*); lapse. **manquer** (ke) *v.t,* to miss (*train, pers.*); spoil, mess up *P* (*life, photo*). (*v.i.*) to be lacking; be absent, missing; fail. *le temps me manque pour écrire,* I have no time for writing. *~ à son honneur,* to fail in one's honour. *tu nous manques,* we miss you. *~* **de,** to lack, be short of. *il a manqué de tomber,* he nearly fell. *il me manque 3 francs,* I am 3 francs short.
mansarde (mɑ̃sard) *f,* attic.
mansuétude (mɑ̃sɥetyd) *f,* leniency.
manteau (mɑ̃to) *m,* coat. *~ de cheminée,* man-

telpiece. *sous le ~*, secretly; (*sold*) under the counter. **mantille** (tij) *f*, mantilla.
manucure (manykyr) *n*, manicurist.
manuel, le† (manɥɛl) *a*, manual. ¶ *m*, manual, handbook.
manufacture (manyfaktyr) *f*, factory; manufacture. **manufacturer** (re) *v.t*, to manufacture.
manuscrit, e (manyskri, it) *a*, handwritten. ¶ *m*, manuscript.
manutention (manytɑ̃sjɔ̃) *f*, handling; storehouse. **~naire** (ɔnɛr) *n*, packer.
mappemonde (mapmɔ̃d) *f*, map of the world; globe.
maquereau (makro) *m*, mackerel; (*P*) pimp.
maquette (makɛt) *f*, [scale] model.
maquillage (makijaʒ) *m*, makeup. **maquiller** (je) *v.t*, to make up (*face*); doctor (*facts*); fiddle, massage *P* (*figures*).
maquis (maki) *m*, scrub[land]; (*fig.*) maze; maquis (*resistance movement 1940–1944*). **~ard, e** (zar, ard) *n*, member of the maquis.
maraîcher, ère (marɛʃe, ʃɛr) *a*, market garden (*produce*). ¶ *n*, market gardener. **marais** (rɛ) *m*, marsh, swamp. *~ salant*, salt marsh.
marasme (marasm) *m*, stagnation; slump.
marathon (maratɔ̃) *m*, marathon.
marâtre (marɑtr) *f*, cruel mother.
maraude (marod) *f*, marauding, pilfering. *en ~*, cruising (*taxi*). **marauder** (rode) *v.i*, to maraud, thieve, pilfer. **maraudeur, euse** (dœr, øz) *n*, marauder, thief.
marbre (marbr) *m*, marble; [marble] slab *or* top; (*Typ.*) stone, bed. **marbrer** (bre) *v.t*, to marble; mottle. **marbrier** (brie) *m*, monumental mason. **marbrure** (bryr) *f*, marbling.
marc (mar) *m*, marc; grounds (*coffee*); brandy.
marcassin (markasɛ̃) *m*, young wild boar.
marchand, e (marʃɑ̃, ɑ̃d) *a*, market (*value*); merchant (*ship*). ¶ *n*, shopkeeper; merchant; dealer; stallholder. *~ au détail*, retailer. *~ en gros*, wholesaler. *~ de biens*, ≃ estate agent. *~ de couleurs*, ironmonger. *~ de journaux*, newsagent. *~ de légumes*, greengrocer. *~ des quatre saisons*, costermonger. **~age** (ʃɑ̃daʒ) *m*, bargaining, haggling. **~er** (de) *v.t*, to bargain [over], haggle [over]; be grudging *or* sparing with. **~ise** (diz) *f*, commodity. *~s*, goods, merchandise.
marche[1] (marʃ) *f*, step. *les ~s*, the stairs, steps.
marche[2] (marʃ) *f*, walking (*action*); step, gait; pace; walk. *une heure de ~*, an hour's walk. (*Mil. &c*) march. *faire ~ sur*, to march on. *fermer la ~*, to bring up the rear. running (*car*); working (*machine*); course (*events*); progress (*illness*); march (*time*). *faire ~ arrière*, (*car*) to reverse; (*fig.*) to back-pedal. *~ à suivre*, procedure. *en ~*, (*machine*) running; (*pers.*) on the move. *mettre en ~*, to start up (*engine*). *se mettre en ~*, (*machine*) to start; (*pers.*) get moving.
marché (marʃe) *m*, (*gen., Econ., Fin.*) market; trading centre; bargain; deal. *faire son ~*, to go shopping. *conclure un ~*, to make a deal. *le M~ Commun*, the Common Market. *le ~ noir*, the black market. *~ aux puces*, flea market. *le ~ des valeurs*, the stockmarket.
marchepied (marʃəpje) *m*, (*Rly*) step; (*fig.*) stepping stone.
marcher (marʃe) *v.i*, to walk; step; march. *~ à grands pas*, to stride. *~ sur les pieds de qn*, to tread on s.o's toes. *~ sur mes plates-bandes, sur mes brisées*, to trespass on my preserves. (*vehicle*) travel, go (*fast, slow*); (*Mach. &c*) run, work. *ma montre marche bien*, my watch is going well. *le chauffage marche*, the heating is working. *comment ça marche?* how are things going? *les affaires marchent*, business is good. (*P*) to agree; be taken in. *faire ~ qn*, to take s.o in. **marcheur, euse** (ʃœr, øz) *n*, walker; (*Pol.*) marcher.
mardi (mardi) *m*, Tuesday. *M~ gras*, Shrove Tuesday.
mare (mar) *f*, pond, pool. **marécage** (marekaʒ) *m*, marsh, swamp, bog. **marécageux, euse** (kaʒø, øz) *a*, marshy, swampy, boggy.
maréchal (mareʃal) *m*, (*Mil.*) marshal (*Fr.*); field marshal (*UK*). *~ des logis*, sergeant. **~-ferrant** (fɛrɑ̃) *m*, blacksmith.
marée (mare) *f*, tide. *~ haute, basse*, high, low tide. (*fig.*) surge; fresh [sea] fish.
marelle (marɛl) *f*, hopscotch.
margarine (margarin) *f*, margarine.
marge (marʒ) *f*, margin. *~ bénéficiaire*, profit m. *~ d'erreur*, m. of error. *en ~ de la société*, on the fringes of society. *tu as de la ~*, you've got time. **marginal, e** (ʒinal) *a*, marginal. *les marginaux*, dropouts; second-class citizens.
marguerite (margərit) *f*, marguerite, ox-eye daisy.
mari (mari) *m*, husband. **mariage** (rjaʒ) *m*, marriage; wedding; blend (*colours*). *~ d'amour*, love match. *faire un ~ d'argent*, to marry for money. **marié, e** (rje) *n*, bridegroom, bride. *les ~s*, the bride and groom; the newly-weds. **marier** (rje) *v.t*, to marry (*couple*); blend, match (*colours*). **se ~ à qn, avec qn,** to get married to s.o, marry s.o.
marijuana (mariʒɥana) *f*, marijuana, pot *P*.
marin, e (marɛ̃, in) *a*, marine; sea (*breeze*); sailor (*suit*). ¶ *m*, sailor; seaman. *~ d'eau douce*, landlubber. **marine** (rin) *f*, navy; (*Art*) seascape. *~ de guerre*, navy. *~ marchande*, merchant n. ¶ *m*, (*Mil.*) marine. **mariner** (ne) *v.t*, to marinade; souse (*herrings*).
marionette (marjɔnɛt) *f*, (*lit., fig.*) puppet. *~ à fils*, marionette. *~ à gaine*, glove puppet.
marital, e† (marital) *a*, marital. *vivre ~ement*, to live as husband and wife.
maritime (maritim) *a*, maritime; shipping (*company*); coastal (*town*).

marjolaine (marʒɔlɛn) *f,* [sweet] marjoram.
marmaille *P* (marmɑj) *f,* gang of kids *P.*
marmelade (marməlad) *f,* stewed fruit. *en* ~, (*reduce*) to a pulp.
marmite (marmit) *f,* [cooking-]pot; (*Geol.*) pothole; (*Artil.*) heavy shell.
marmonner (marmɔne) *v.t. & i,* to grumble, mutter.
marmot *P* (marmo) *m,* kid *P.* ~**te** (mɔt) *f,* (*Zool.*) marmot; (*fig.*) sleepyhead. ~**ter** (mɔte) *v.t. & i,* to mumble, mutter.
Maroc (le) (marɔk), Morocco. **marocain, e** (kɛ̃, ɛn) *a. &* **M**~, *n,* Moroccan.
maronner *P* (marɔne) *v.i,* to grumble, grouse *P.*
maroquin (marɔkɛ̃) *m,* morocco [leather]; (*fig.*) [minister's] portfolio. **maroquinerie** (kinri) *f,* shop selling fancy leather goods. [*articles de*] ~, fancy leather goods.
marotte (marɔt) *f,* craze, hobby.
marquant, e (markɑ̃, ɑ̃t) *a,* outstanding, striking. **marque** (mark) *f,* mark; sign; (*fig.*) token; (*Com.*) brand, make; (*Sport*) score. ~*s de pas,* footprints. ~ *de fabrique,* trademark. ~ *déposée,* registered t. *de* ~, high-class (*products*). **marqué, e** (ke) *a,* marked, pronounced. **marquer** (ke) *v.t,* to mark; label, stamp (*goods*); brand (*animal*); show; (*scales*) register; (*clock*) say, point to; note down; (*Sport*) mark (*player*); score (*goal*). ~ *le pas,* (*lit., fig.*) to mark time. ¶ *v.i,* to stand out; leave a mark. **marqueur** (kœr) *m,* (*Sport*) scorer; felt[-tip] pen.
marquis (marki) *m,* marquess. **marquise** (kis) *f,* marchioness; glass canopy.
marraine (marɛn) *f,* godmother; christener (*ship*).
marrant, e *P* (marɑ̃, ɑ̃t) *a,* funny, killing *P.*
marre *P* (mar) *ad, en avoir* ~, to be fed up *P* (*de,* with).
marrer (se) *P* (mare) *v.pr,* to laugh, kill o.s laughing *P.*
marron (marɔ̃) *m,* chestnut; (*P*) thump. ~ *d'Inde,* horse chestnut. ¶ *a. inv,* brown. *être* ~ *P,* to be had *P.* ~**nier** (ɔnje) *m,* chestnut tree.
mars (mars) *m,* March. **M**~, Mars.
marseillais, e (marsɛjɛ, ɛz) *a. &* **M**~, *n,* [person] from Marseilles. *la M*~*e,* the Marseillaise (*Fr. national anthem*).
marsouin (marswɛ̃) *m,* porpoise.
marteau (marto) *m,* hammer; [door] knocker. *être* ~ *P,* to be mad, nutty *P.* ~**-pilon** (pilɔ̃) *m,* power hammer. ~**-piqueur** (pikœr) *m,* pneumatic drill. **martèlement** (tɛlmɑ̃) *m,* hammering, pounding. **marteler** (təle) *v.t,* to hammer, pound.
martial, e (marsjal) *a,* martial, warlike.
martien, ne (marsjɛ̃, jɛn) *a. & n,* Martian.
martinet (martinɛ) *m,* swift (*bird*); small whip.
martin-pêcheur (martɛ̃pɛʃœr) *m,* kingfisher.
martre (martr) *f,* marten. ~ *zibeline,* sable.
martyr, e (martir) *a,* martyred; battered (*child*). ¶ *n,* martyr. **martyre,** *m,* martyrdom; torment. **martyriser** (tirize) *v.t,* (*Rel.*) to martyr; torture; bully (*schoolchild*); batter (*baby*).
marxisme (marksism) *m,* Marxism. **marxiste** (ist) *a. & n,* Marxist.
mascarade (maskarad) *f,* masquerade.
mascotte (maskɔt) *f,* mascot.
masculin, e (maskylɛ̃, in) *a,* male; manly; (*pej.*) mannish (*woman*); (*Gram.*) masculine. ¶ *m,* (*Gram.*) masculine.
masochisme (mazɔʃism) *m,* masochism. **masochiste** (ist) *a,* masochistic. ¶ *n,* masochist.
masque (mask) *m,* (*gen., fig.*) mask. ~ *antirides,* face pack. ~ *à gaz,* gas mask. **masqué, e** (ke) *a,* masked; concealed (*exit*). **masquer** (ke) *v.t,* to mask, conceal (*à qn,* from s.o); screen; obscure.
massacre (masakr) *m,* massacre, slaughter. *quel* ~! *P,* what a mess! **massacrer** (kre) *v.t,* to massacre; slaughter; (*P*) murder (*play*), make a mess of (*task*). **massacreur, euse** (krœr, øz) *n,* slaughterer; (*P*) botcher.
massage (masaʒ) *m,* massage.
masse (mas) *f,* mass; massive shape. ~ *monétaire,* amount of money in circulation. *tailler dans la* ~, to carve from the block. *la* ~, *les* ~*s,* the masses. *la* ~ *des électeurs,* the majority of voters. *une* ~ *de P,* masses of. *de* ~, mass (*protest*). *en* ~, mass (*killings*), en masse. sledgehammer. ~ [*d'armes*], mace.
massepain (maspɛ̃) *m,* marzipan.
masser (mase) *v.t,* to massage; mass (*troops*). **se** ~, (*crowd*) to mass.
masseur, euse (masœr, øz) *n,* masseur, euse. ~ *kinésithérapeute,* physiotherapist.
massif, ive† (masif, iv) *a,* massive; sturdy, hefty (*pers.*); heavy (*face*); solid (*gold*); mass (*exodus*). ¶ *m,* (*Geog.*) massif; clump (*trees*); bank (*flowers*).
massue (masy) *f,* club, bludgeon.
mastic (mastik) *m,* mastic; putty. ¶ *a,* off-white.
mastiquer (mastike) *v.t,* to chew, masticate; putty (*window*); fill (*crack*).
mastodonte (mastɔdɔ̃t) *m,* (*Zool.*) mastodon; (*fig.*) great hulk (*pers.*).
masturber (se) (mastyrbe) *v.pr,* to masturbate.
masure (mazyr) *f,* hovel, ruin.
mat[1], e (mat) *a,* mat (*colour &c*); dull. *bruit* ~, thud.
mat[2] (mat) *a. inv. & m,* (*Chess*) checkmate. *faire* ~, to [check]mate.
mât (mɑ) *m,* mast; pole (*flag, tent*). ~ *de charge,* derrick. ~ *de cocagne* (kɔkaɲ), greasy pole. ~ *de misaine,* foremast.
matamore (matamɔr) *m,* swaggerer.
match (matʃ) *m,* (*Sport*) match. ~ *aller, retour,* first, second leg. ~ *nul,* draw.
matelas (matla) *m,* mattress. ~ *pneumatique,*

air bed, Lilo. ~**ser** (lase) *v.t*, to pad, quilt. ~**sier, ère** (sje, ɛr) *n*, mattress maker.
matelot (matlo) *m*, sailor, seaman.
mater (mate) *v.t*, (*Chess*) to [check]mate; subdue; quell; control, check (*fire*).
matérialiser (materjalize) *v.t*, & **se** ~, to materialize. **matérialisme** (lism) *m*, materialism. **matérialiste** (list) *n*, materialist. ¶ *a*, materialistic. **matériau** (rjo) *m*, (*Build.*) material. ~**x**, *m.pl*, (*Build.*) materials; material (*book*). **matériel, le**† (rjɛl) *a*, material; physical; financial. *il est dans l'impossibilité ~le de le faire*, he simply cannot do it. ¶ *m*, materials, equipment; hardware (*computer*). ~ *d'exploitation*, plant. ~ *roulant*, rolling stock.
maternel, le† (matɛrnɛl) *a*, maternal, motherly; mother's (*side*); mother (*tongue*); nursery (*school*). **maternité** (nite) *f*, maternity, motherhood; maternity hospital.
mathématicien, ne (matematisjɛ̃, ɛn) *n*, mathematician. **mathématique**† (tik) *a*, mathematical. ¶ *f*. & ~*s*, mathematics. **matheux, euse** *P* (tø, øz) *n*, maths student; m. expert. **maths** *P* (mat) *f.pl*, maths *P*.
matière (matjɛr) *f*, matter; material; substance; (*Sch.*) subject; [subject] matter, contents (*book*). *donner ~ à plaisanter*, to give cause for laughter. ~[*s*] grasse[*s*], fat [content]. ~ *première*, raw material.
matin (matɛ̃) *m*, morning. *le* ~, in the m. *3 heures du* ~, 3 in the m. *de grand, bon* ~, very early. ~**al, e** (tinal) *a*, morning (*routine*); early (*hour*). *être* ~, to be an early riser, be up early. ~**ée** (tine) *f*, morning; (*Theat.* &c) matinee, afternoon performance.
matois, e (matwa, az) *a*, sly, wily.
matou (matu) *m*, tom [cat].
matraquage (matrakaʒ) *m*, beating up; plugging (*slogan*); bombardment (*public*). **matraque** (ak) *f*, truncheon; cosh. **matraquer** (ke) *v.t*, to beat up; (*P*) overcharge; plug (*slogan*); bombard (*public*).
matrice (matris) *f*, womb; (*Tech.*) mould; (*Math.* &c) matrix. **matricule** (kyl) *m*, reference number; (*Mil.*) regimental n.
matrimonial, e (matrimɔnjal) *a*, matrimonial.
matrone (trɔn) *f*, matronly woman.
mâture (mɑtyr) *f*, masts (*col.*).
maturité (matyrite) *f*, maturity.
maudire (modir) *v.t.ir*, to curse. **maudit, e** (di, it) *a*, damned (*soul*); cursed; (*P*) blasted *P*, damned *P*. *les ~s*, the damned. *le M~*, the Devil.
maugréer (mogree) *v.i*, to grumble (*contre*, at, about).
Maurice (l'île) (mɔris) *f*, Mauritius.
mausolée (mozɔle) *m*, mausoleum.
maussade (mosad) *a*, sullen, gloomy.
mauvais, e (movɛ, ɛz) *a*, (*gen.*) bad; faulty (*goods*); wrong (*number*); poor (*health, excuse*); unpleasant (*taste*). *il fait* ~, the weather's bad. *la mer est ~e*, the sea is rough. *passer un ~ quart d'heure*, to have a bad time of it. ~ *coucheur*, awkward customer. ~ *coup*, nasty blow; crime. ~*e herbe*, weed. ~*e langue*, scandalmonger. ~ *lieu*, place of ill repute. ~ *pas*, tight corner. ~*e passe*, difficult situation. ~ *plaisant*, hoaxer. *faire la ~e tête*, to sulk. ¶ *m*, bad; evil; bad bit (*food*).
mauve (mov) *f*, (*Bot.*) mallow. ¶ *a*. & *m*, mauve.
mauviette *P* (movjɛt) *f*, weakling.
maxillaire (maksillɛr) *a*, maxillary. ¶ *m*, jawbone.
maxime (maksim) *f*, maxim.
maximum (maksimɔm) *a*. & *m*, maximum. *au grand* ~, at the very most. **maximal** (mal) *a*, maximal.
mayonnaise (majɔnɛz) *f*, mayonnaise.
mazette (mɑzɛt) *i*, my goodness!
mazout (mazut) *m*, [fuel] oil.
me, m' (mə, m) *personal pn*, me; [to] me; myself. ~ *voici*, here I am.
méandre (meɑ̃dr) *m*, meander, winding.
mec *P* (mɛk) *m*, guy *P*, bloke *P*.
mécanicien, ne (mekanisjɛ̃, jɛn) *n*, (*Mot.*) [garage, motor] mechanic; (*Rly*) engine driver; (*Naut.*) engineer. ~*ne*, [sewing] machinist. **mécanique**† (nik) *a*, mechanical; clockwork (*toy*). ¶ *f*, mechanics; mechanism; mechanical engineering. **mécaniser** (ze) *v.t*, to mechanize. **mécanisme** (nism) *m*, mechanism. **mécanographie** (ɔgrafi) *f*, punched card system.
mécène (mesɛn) *m*, patron (*of the arts*).
méchant, e (meʃɑ̃, ɑ̃t) *a*, wicked; nasty; naughty (*child*); miserable (*scrap*); wretched; (*P*) fantastic *P*. *ce n'est pas bien ~ P*, it's not too bad. ¶ *n*, wicked person; naughty child. *les ~s P*, the baddies *P*. **méchamment** (ʃamɑ̃) *ad*, wickedly; badly; (*P*) fantastically *P*. **méchanceté** (ʃɑ̃ste) *f*, wickedness; spite. *par* ~, out of spite. wicked action; spiteful remark.
mèche (mɛʃ) *f*, wick (*lamp*); fuse (*bomb*); lock (*hair*); bit (*drill*). (*P*) *être de ~ avec qn*, to be in league with s.o. *vendre la ~ P*, to blow the gaff *P*.
mécompte (mekɔ̃t) *m*, disappointment.
méconnaissable (mekɔnɛsabl) *a*, unrecognizable. **méconnaissance** (ɑ̃s) *f*, lack of knowledge; ignorance. **méconnaître** (nɛtr) *v.t.ir*, to fail to recognize, not to know; misjudge; underestimate; ignore. **méconnu, e** (ny) *a*, unrecognised; misunderstood.
mécontent, e (mekɔ̃tɑ̃, ɑ̃t) *a*, dissatisfied; annoyed (*de*, with). ¶ *n*, malcontent; grumbler. ~**ement** (tɑ̃tmɑ̃) *m*, discontent; dissatisfaction; annoyance. ~**er** (te) *v.t*, to dissatisfy, displease; annoy.

Mecque (la) (mɛk), Mecca.
médaille (medaj) *f,* medal; badge. **médaillé, e** (daje) *n,* medal-holder, medallist. **médailler** (je) *v.t,* to award a medal to. **médaillon** (jɔ̃) *m,* medallion; locket.
médecin (medsɛ̃) *m,* doctor; physician. ~ *généraliste,* general practitioner. ~ *d'hôpital,* consultant; hospital doctor. ~ *légiste,* forensic surgeon. **médecine** (sin) *f,* medicine. ~ *légale,* forensic m. ~ *du travail,* occupational m.
media or **média** (medja) *m.pl,* media.
médiateur, trice (medjatœr, tris) *n,* mediator; (*Ind.*) arbitrator. **médiation** (sjɔ̃) *f,* mediation; (*Ind.*) arbitration.
médical, e† (medikal) *a,* medical. **médicament** (mɑ̃) *m,* medicine; drug. **médicinal, e** (sinal) *a,* medicinal.
médiéval, e (medjeval) *a,* medi[a]eval.
médiocre (medjɔkr) *a,* mediocre; poor (*quality*); second-rate (*pers.*). ¶ *n,* mediocrity. ~**ment** (rəmɑ̃) *ad,* (*work*) indifferently; barely (*satisfied*). **médiocrité** (krite) *f,* mediocrity; poorness.
médire (medir) *v.i.ir,* ~ *de,* to speak ill of, slander. **médisance** (dizɑ̃s) *f,* [piece of] scandal; scandalmongering. **médisant, e** (zɑ̃, ɑ̃t) *a,* slanderous. ¶ *n,* slanderer, scandalmonger.
méditatif, ive (meditatif, iv) *a,* meditative. **méditation** (sjɔ̃) *f,* meditation. **méditer** (te) *v.t,* to meditate [up]on, ponder [over]; meditate, plan. ¶ *v.i,* to meditate.
Méditerranée (meditɛrane) *f, la* [*mer*] ~, the Mediterranean [Sea]. **méditerranéen, ne** (neɛ̃, ɛn) *a,* Mediterranean.
méduse (medyz) *f,* jelly fish. (*Myth.*) *M*~, Medusa. **méduser** (dyze) *v.t,* to dumbfound.
meeting (mitiŋ) *m,* (*Pol., Sport*) meeting.
méfait (mefɛ) *m,* misdemeanour, misdeed. ~*s,* ill-effects (*of drug, weather*).
méfiance (mefjɑ̃s) *f,* mistrust, distrust; suspicion. **méfiant, e** (jɑ̃, ɑ̃t) *a,* mis-, distrustful; suspicious. **se méfier de** (fje), *v.pr,* to mistrust, distrust; beware of. *méfie-toi!* be careful!
méga (mega) *pref.,* mega. ¶ *P a.inv,* enormous.
mégalomane (megalɔman) *a. & n,* megalomaniac. **mégalomanie** (ni) *f,* megalomania.
mégarde (par) (megard) *ad,* inadvertently; accidentally.
mégère (meʒɛr) *f,* (*pej.*) shrew.
mégot *P* (mego) *m,* cigarette end.
meilleur, e (mɛjœr) *a,* better (*que,* than). ~ *marché,* cheaper. *le* ~ *marché,* the cheapest. ~*s vœux,* best wishes. ¶ *ad,* (*smell*) better. ¶ *n, le* ~, *la* ~*e,* the best one. *les* ~*s,* the best ones. ¶ *m, le* ~, the best. *pour le* ~ *et pour le pire,* for better or for worse. *le* ~ *de sa vie,* the best part of his life.
mélancolie (melɑ̃kɔli) *f,* melancholy. **mélancolique**† (lik) *a,* melancholy.
mélange (melɑ̃ʒ) *m,* mixture; blend; mixing, blending. ~*s,* (*Liter.*) miscellany. **mélanger** (lɑ̃ʒe) *v.t,* to mix, blend; mix up, muddle up. **se** ~, to mix, blend.
mélasse (melas) *f,* (*Cook.*) treacle; muck. *être dans la* ~ *P,* to be in the soup *P.*
mêlé, e (mele) *a,* mixed, mingled. ¶ *f,* mêlée; (*Rugby*) scrum. **mêler** (le) *v.t,* to mix; mingle; blend; combine; muddle up (*dates*); shuffle (*cards*). ~ *qn à,* to involve s.o in (*deal*). **se** ~, to mix, mingle; combine. *se* ~ *à,* to get involved in, join in. *se* ~ *de,* to meddle with. *se* ~ *de faire,* to take it upon o.s to do.
mélèze (melɛz) *m,* larch [tree].
méli-mélo *P* (melimelo) *m,* jumble; muddle.
mélodie (melɔdi) *f,* tune, melody. **mélodieux, euse**† (djø, øz) *a,* melodious, tuneful. **mélodique** (dik) *a,* melodic.
mélodramatique (melɔdramatik) *a,* melodramatic. **mélodrame** (dram) *m,* melodrama.
mélomane (melɔman) *a. & n, être* ~, to be a music lover.
melon (məlɔ̃) *m,* melon. **[chapeau]** ~, bowler [hat].
membrane (mɑ̃bran) *f,* membrane.
membre (mɑ̃br) *m,* (*gen., Math., Gram.*) member; (*Anat.*) limb. *état* ~, member state.
même (mɛm) *a,* same. *la* ~ *jupe qu'hier,* the same skirt as yesterday. *ils sont du* ~ *avis,* they are of the same opinion. *ses propos* ~*s,* his very remarks. *moi-*~, myself, *lui-*~, himself &c. ¶ *n, le* ~, *la* ~, the same, the s. thing, s. one. ¶ *ad,* even. ~ *lui comprend,* even he understands. *aujourd'hui* ~, this very day. *quand* ~, *tout de* ~, all the same. *à* ~ *la bouteille,* straight from the bottle. *à* ~ *la peau,* next to the skin. *être à* ~ *de,* to be in a position to, able to.
mémé *P* (meme) *f,* granny *P;* old dear *P.*
mémento (memɛ̃to), *m,* engagement diary.
mémoire (memwar) *f,* memory. *avoir une bonne* ~, *la* ~ *courte,* to have a good, a short m. *à la* ~ *de,* in m. of. *de* ~, from memory, by heart. ¶ *m,* memorandum; (*learned*) paper; bill; report. ~*s,* memoirs. **mémorable** (mɔrabl) *a,* memorable. **mémorandum** (rɑ̃dɔm) *m,* memorandum. **mémorial** (rjal) *m,* (*Arch.*) memorial.
menaçant, e (mənasɑ̃, ɑ̃t) *a,* menacing, threatening. **menace** (as) *f,* threat. *sous la* ~ *de,* under threat of. **menacer** (se) *v.t,* to threaten (*de,* with). *la pluie menace,* it looks like rain.
ménage (menaʒ) *m,* couple. *se mettre en* ~, to set up house. *querelle de* ~, domestic quarrel. *faire bon* ~ *avec,* to get on well with. housework. *faire le* ~, to do the housework. *faire des* ~*s,* to go out cleaning. **ménagement** (naʒmɑ̃) *m,* care. ~*s,* consideration. **ménager**

(ʒe) *v.t,* to economize, conserve, use sparingly (*money, strength*); spare (*feelings*); handle carefully (*pers.*); take care of (*health*); moderate (*remarks*); arrange, organize; put in (*window*); cut (*path*). **ménager, ère** (ʒe, ɛr) *a,* economical, sparing (*de,* of); household (*items*). *travaux ~s,* housework. ¶ *f,* housewife; canteen of cutlery. **ménagerie** (ʒri) *f,* menagerie.

mendiant, e (mɑ̃djɑ̃, ɑ̃t) *n,* beggar. **mendicité** (disite) *f,* begging. **mendier** (dje) *v.i. & t,* to beg (*qch à qn,* s.o for sth).

menée (məne) *f, ~s,* intrigues. **mener** (ne) *v.t,* to lead, take (*to a place*); drive; run, manage (*business*); conduct (*enquiry*); (*Sport & v.i.*) lead, be in the lead. *~ une vie de chien,* to lead a dog's life.

ménestrel (menɛstrɛl) *m,* minstrel.

meneur, euse (mənœr, øz) *n,* ringleader; agitator. *~ de jeu,* compère; quiz-master.

menhir (mɛnir) *m,* menhir.

méningite (menɛ̃ʒit) *f,* meningitis.

ménopause (menɔpoz) *f,* menopause.

menotte (mənɔt) *f, ~s,* handcuffs. (*P*) hand, handy *P*.

mensonge (mɑ̃sɔ̃ʒ) *m,* lie, untruth; fib *P*. *le ~,* untruthfulness, lying. **mensonger, ère†** (sɔ̃ʒe, ɛr) *a,* untrue, false, deceitful.

menstruation (mɑ̃stryɑsjɔ̃) *f,* menstruation.

mensualité (mɑ̃sɥalite) *f,* monthly payment, salary. **mensuel, le†** (sɥɛl) *a,* monthly (*a. & ad.*). ¶ *n,* monthly paid employee. ¶ *m,* monthly magazine.

mensuration (mɑ̃syrasjɔ̃) *f,* mensuration. *~s,* measurements.

mental, e† (mɑ̃tal) *a,* mental. **mentalité** (lite) *f,* mentality.

menteur, euse (mɑ̃tœr, øz) *n,* liar, fibber *P*. ¶ *a,* lying, deceptive, false.

menthe (mɑ̃t) *f,* mint; peppermint cordial. *~ poivrée,* peppermint. *~ verte,* spearmint. *de ~, à la ~,* mint.

mention (mɑ̃sjɔ̃) *f,* mention; note; reference; (*Sch.*) [examination] grade; (*Univ.*) class. *~ très bien,* grade A pass, first class honours. *faire ~ de,* to mention. *rayer la ~ inutile,* delete as appropriate. **mentionner** (ɔne) *v.t,* to mention.

mentir (mɑ̃tir) *v.i.ir,* to lie. *sans ~,* to be quite honest.

menton (mɑ̃tɔ̃) *m,* chin.

menu[1] (məny) *m,* menu; meal. *~ à prix fixe,* set menu. *~ touristique,* standard m. *~ gastronomique,* gourmet's m.

menu[2], e (məny) *a,* slender, slim; slight; small; petty, trifling; minute (*detail*). ¶ *ad,* (*chop*) fine.

menuet (mənɥɛ) *m,* minuet.

menuiserie (mənɥizri) *f,* joinery; carpentry; joiner's workshop; piece of woodwork. **menuisier** (zje) *m,* joiner; carpenter; cabinet maker.

méprendre (se) (meprɑ̃dr) *v.pr.ir,* to be mistaken (*sur,* about).

mépris (mepri) *m,* contempt, scorn. **méprisable** (zabl) *a,* contemptible, despicable. **méprisant, e** (zɑ̃, ɑ̃t) *a,* contemptuous, scornful. **méprise** (prize) *f,* mistake; misunderstanding. **mépriser** (prize) *v.t,* to despise, scorn; disregard.

mer (mɛr) *f,* sea. *~ fermée,* inland s. *~ d'huile,* glassy s. *en haute, pleine ~,* on the open s. tide. *la ~ est haute,* the tide is high. *~ du Nord,* North Sea.

mercenaire (mɛrsənɛr) *a. & m,* mercenary.

mercerie (mɛrsri) *f,* haberdashery.

merci (mɛrsi) *i,* thank you (*de, pour,* for); no, thank you. *~ beaucoup, ~ bien,* thank you very much. ¶ *m,* thank-you. *dis-lui un grand ~,* tell him thank you very much. ¶ *f,* mercy. *à la ~ de,* at the mercy of. *sans ~,* merciless. *crier ~,* to cry for m.

mercier, ère (mɛrsje, ɛr) *n,* haberdasher.

mercredi (mɛrkrədi) *m,* Wednesday. *le ~ des Cendres,* Ash Wednesday.

mercure (mɛrkyr) *m,* mercury.

merde *P** (mɛrd) *f,* shit *P**; (*fig.*) bloody muddle *P**. ¶ *i,* hell *P,* shit *P**.

mère (mɛr) *f,* mother. *~ de famille,* mother, housewife. *~ porteuse,* surrogate mother. (*pej.*) *la ~ N,* old Mrs. N. *maison ~,* parent company.

méridien, ne (meridjɛ̃, ɛn) *a. & m,* meridian. **méridional, e** (djɔnal) *a,* southern, south. ¶ *n,* southerner.

meringue (mərɛ̃g) *f,* meringue.

merise (məriz) *f,* wild cherry. **merisier** (rizje) *m,* wild cherry [tree].

méritant, e (meritɑ̃, ɑ̃t) *a,* deserving. **mérite** (rit) *m,* merit. *de grand ~,* of great worth. **mériter** (te) *v.t,* to merit, deserve. *ça mérite d'être vu,* that's worth seeing. *son courage lui a mérité le respect,* his courage earned him respect. *ceci mérite réflexion,* this requires some thought. **méritoire** (twar) *a,* meritorious.

merlan (mɛrlɑ̃) *m,* whiting.

merle (mɛrl) *m,* blackbird.

merluche (mɛrlyʃ) *f,* dried cod.

merveille (mɛrvɛj) *f,* marvel, wonder. *à ~,* excellently; (*function*) perfectly; (*work out*) just right. *faire ~,* to work wonders. **merveilleux, euse†** (vɛjø, øz) *a,* marvellous, wonderful. **le ~,** the supernatural.

mes (me) *possessive a, V* **mon.**

mésalliance (mezaljɑ̃s) *f,* misalliance.

mésange (mezɑ̃ʒ) *f,* tit[mouse]. *~ charbonnière,* great tit, tomtit.

mésaventure (mezavɑ̃tyr) *f,* misadventure, mishap.

Mesdames (medam) *f.pl, V* **Madame.**

Mesdemoiselles (medmwazɛl) *f.pl, V* **Mademoiselle.**
mésentente (mezɑ̃tɑ̃t) *f,* disagreement.
mésestimer (mezɛstime) *v.t,* to undervalue, underestimate, underrate.
mésintelligence (mezɛ̃tɛliʒɑ̃s) *f,* discord; disagreement.
mesquin, e† (mɛskɛ̃, in) *a,* mean; shabby; stingy. **mesquinerie** (kinri) *f,* meanness, &c.
mess (mɛs) *m, (Mil.)* mess.
message (mɛsaʒ) *m,* message. **messager, ère** (saʒe, ɛr) *n,* messenger. **messageries** (ʒri) *f.pl,* freight service.
messe (mɛs) *f, (Eccl.)* mass. ~ *basse,* low m. ~ *chantée,* high m.
messie (mɛsi) *m,* messiah. *le M* ~, the M.
messieurs (mesjø) *m.pl, V* **monsieur.**
mesure (məzur) *f,* measurement; measure; *(Mus.)* tempo; *(Mus.)* bar; *(Poet.)* metre. *en* ~, *(play)* in time. *sur* ~, *(made)* to measure. *faire bonne* ~, to give good measure. moderation. *avec* ~, in moderation. *passer toute* ~, to go too far. step. *prendre des* ~*s,* to take measures, steps. *être en* ~ *de faire,* to be able to do. [*au fur et*] *à* ~ *que,* as. [*au fur et*] *à* ~, gradually, bit by bit. *à la* ~ *de l'homme,* on a human scale. *à sa* ~, within his capabilities. *dans une certaine* ~, to some extent. **mesuré, e** (zyre) *a,* guarded *(language)*; measured *(pace)*; moderate *(pers.)*. **mesurer** (re) *v.t,* to measure; m. out; calculate; *(fig.)* weigh; evaluate; limit *(money &c)*. **se** ~ **avec,** to pit o.s against.
métal (metal) *m,* metal. **métallique** (tallik) *a,* metallic; metal. **métallurgie** (tallyrʒi) *f,* metallurgy; metallurgical industry. **métallurgique** (ʒik) *a,* metallurgic. **métallurgiste** (ʒist) *m,* metallurgist; steel-, metal-worker.
métamorphose (metamɔrfoz) *f,* metamorphosis. **métamorphoser** (foze) *v.t,* to metamorphose; transform *(en,* into).
métaphore (metafɔr) *f,* metaphor. **métaphorique†** (fɔrik) *a,* metaphorical.
métaphysicien (metafizisjɛ̃) *m,* metaphysician. **métaphysique** (zik) *f,* metaphysics. ¶ *a,* metaphysical.
météore (meteɔr) *m,* meteor. **météorique** (ɔrik) *a,* meteoric. **météorite** (rit) *f,* meteorite. **météorologie** (rɔlɔʒi) *f,* meteorology; Meteorological Office. **météorologique** (ʒik) *a,* meteorological; weather *(forecast)*. **météorologiste** (ʒist) *n,* **météorologue** (lɔg) *n,* meteorologist.
métèque (metɛk) *n, (pej.)* wog *P**.
méthane (metan) *m,* methane.
méthode (metɔd) *f,* method, way, system; manual, tutor. *avec* ~, methodically. **méthodique†** (dik) *a,* methodical.
méticuleux, euse† (metikylø, øz) *a,* meticulous, punctilious.
métier (metje) *m, (gen.)* job; occupation; trade; craft; profession. *connaître son* ~, to know one's job. skill; technique; experience. *avoir du* ~, to have practical experience. ~ *à tisser,* [weaving] loom.
métis, se (metis) *a. & n,* half-caste *(pers.)*; crossbreed; mongrel; hybrid *(plant)*. **métisser** (se) *v.t,* to cross[breed].
métonymie (metɔnimi) *f,* metonymy.
métrage (metraʒ) *m,* measurement; *(Dress)* length, yardage. **mètre** (mɛtr) *m, (Meas., Poet.)* metre; [metre] rule, ruler. ~ *à ruban,* tape measure. ~ *carré,* square m. ~ *cube,* cubic m. **métrer** (metre) *v.t,* to measure, survey. **métreur, euse** (trœr, øz) *n,* quantity surveyor. **métrique** (trik) *a,* metrical; metric. ¶ *f,* metrics, prosody.
métro (metro) *m,* underground; tube *P*.
métronome (metrɔnɔm) *m,* metronome.
métropole (metrɔpɔl) *f,* metropolis; home country. **métropolitain, e** (litɛ̃, ɛn) *a,* metropolitan.
mets (mɛ) *m, (Cook.)* dish.
mettable (mɛtabl) *a,* wearable. **metteur** (tœr) *m,* ~ *en scène (Theat.)* producer, *(Cine.)* director. **mettre** (tr) *v.t.ir,* to put; place. ~ *à plat,* to lay flat. ~ *droit,* to put straight. ~ *un enfant à l'école,* to send a child to school. take *(to a place)*. ~ *qn à la gare,* to drop s.o at the station. put on *(clothes)*; take, spend *(time)*; switch on, turn on *(radio)*; put in, install *(fittings)*; suppose. *mettons que j'aie tort,* let's say I'm wrong. ~ *les bouts P, les* ~ *P,* to clear off *P*. **se** ~, *(pers.)* to put o.s; *(object)* to go. *mets-toi là,* go and sit, stand there. *se* ~ *au lit,* to go to bed. *(fig.) je ne savais pas où me* ~, I didn't know where to put myself. *(weather)* turn *(cold &c)*; put on *(clothes)*. *se* ~ *en habit,* to put on a suit. *elle n'a rien à se* ~, she hasn't a thing to wear. *se* ~ *en colère,* to get angry. **se** ~ **à:** *se* ~ *à pleurer,* to start crying; *se* ~ *au travail,* to set to work. *se* ~ *avec qn,* to team up with s.o.
meuble (mœbl) *a,* movable *(property)*; loose *(earth)*; soft *(stone)*. ¶ *m,* piece of furniture. *le*[*s*] *meuble*[*s*], the furniture. ~ *de rangement,* storage unit. **meublé, e** (ble) *a,* furnished. ¶ *m,* furnished flat. **meubler** (ble) *v.t,* to furnish; fill *(memory)*. **se** ~, to buy furniture.
meugler (møgle) *v.i, (cow)* to moo.
meule (møl) *f,* millstone; buff wheel; [hay] stack; round *(of gruyere)*. ~ *à aiguiser,* grindstone.
meunier, ère (mønje, ɛr) *a,* milling. *sole* ~*ière,* sole meunière. ¶ *n,* miller. ¶ *f,* miller's wife.
meurtre (mœrtr) *m,* murder. **meurtrier, ère** (trie, ɛr) *a,* murderous *(intent)*; deadly *(weapon)*. ¶ *n,* murderer, ess; *(f.) (Arch.)* loophole.
meurtrir (mœrtrir) *v.t,* to bruise. **meurtrissure** (trisyr) *f,* bruise.
meute (møt) *f, (Hunt., fig.)* pack.
mévente (mevɑ̃t) *f,* slump [in trade].

mexicain, e (mɛksikɛ̃, ɛn) *a.* & **M ~**, *n,* Mexican. **Mexico** (ko) *m,* Mexico City. **le Mexique** (sik), Mexico.
mi (mi) *m,* (*Mus.*) E; mi. ¶ ~ - *pref,* half, mid-. *la mi-carême,* mid-lent. *à mi-chemin,* midway, half way. *mi-clos,* half-closed (*eye*). *à mi-corps,* to the waist, waisthigh *or* deep. *à mi-côte,* half way up [the hill]. *la mi-juin &c,* mid June &c. *à mi-vitesse,* at half speed. *à mi-voix,* in a low voice. *V* **mi-temps.**
miaou (mjau) *m,* miaow.
miauler (mjole) *v.i,* to miaow, mew. **miaulement** (lmɑ̃) *m,* mewing, caterwauling.
mica (mika) *m,* mica.
miche (miʃ) *f,* round loaf (*bread*).
micmac *P* (mikmak) *m,* funny business *P;* fuss *P.*
micro (mikro) *m,* microphone, mike *P.*
microbe (mikrɔb) *m,* microbe. **microbien, ne** (bjɛ̃, jɛn) *a,* bacterial (*disease*).
microfilm (mikrofilm) *m,* microfilm.
microphone (mikrɔfɔn) *m,* microphone.
microplaquette (mikrɔplakɛt) *f,* (*Electronics*) [micro]chip.
miscroscope (mikrɔskɔp) *m,* microscope. *au* ~, under a m. **microscopique** (pik) *a,* microscopic.
microsillon (mikrɔsijɔ̃) *m,* [*disque*] ~, long-playing record, L.P.
midi (midi) *m,* noon, midday, twelve o'clock; lunchtime; (*Geog.*) south. *le M* ~, the South [of France], the Midi.
mie (mi) *f,* crumb (*bread,* opp. *crust*).
miel (mjɛl) *m,* honey. **mielleux, euse**† (lø, øz) *a,* honeyed; sickly-sweet; unctuous (*pers.*).
mien, ne (mjɛ̃, ɛn) *pn, le* ~, *la* ~*ne, les* ~*s, les* ~*nes,* mine, my own. ¶ *n, les* ~*s,* my family. ¶ *a, un* ~ *ami O,* a friend of mine.
miette (mjɛt) *f,* crumb (*bread*); scrap; snippet (*talk*). *en* ~*s,* in bits; (*break*) to bits.
mieux (mjø) *ad,* better. *aller* ~, to be better. *tu chantes* ~ *que lui,* you sing better than he does. *le* ~, *la* ~, *les* ~, [the] best; [the] better (*of 2*). *ce projet me convient le* ~, this plan suits me [the] best. *de* ~ *en* ~, better and better. ~ *que jamais,* better than ever. ¶ *a.inv,* better; better-looking. *être le* ~ *du monde,* to be in the best of health. *au* ~, at best. *qui* ~ *est,* better still. ¶ *m, faire de son* ~, to do one's best.
mièvre (mjɛvr) *a,* precious; vapid; mawkish.
mignard, e (miɲar, ard) *a,* (*liter.*) mannered. **mignon, ne** (ɲɔ̃, ɔn) *a,* sweet; pretty; nice. ¶ *n,* pet, darling.
migraine (migrɛn) *f,* (*Med.*) migraine, headache.
migrateur, trice (migratœr, tris) *a,* migratory; migrant. ¶ *n,* migrant; migratory bird. **migration** (sjɔ̃) *f,* migration.
mijaurée (miʒɔre) *f,* affected woman.
mijoter (miʒɔte) *v.t,* (*Cook.*) *faire* ~, to simmer. (*P*) cook up *P,* hatch (*scheme*). ¶ *v.i,* to simmer.
mil (mil) *m,* one thousand (*in dates*).
milice (milis) *f,* militia. **milicien, ne** (sjɛ̃, ɛn) *n,* militiaman, -woman.
milieu (miljø) *m,* middle. *au* ~ *de,* in the middle of, midst of, among. middle course. *le juste* ~, the happy medium. (*gen., Bio., Geog.*) environment; (*Phys.,*) medium; milieu, circle. *le* ~ *familial,* the family circle, background.
militaire† (militɛr) *a,* military. ¶ *m,* soldier, serviceman. ~ *de carrière,* regular [soldier]. **militant, e** (tɑ̃, ɑ̃t) *a.* & *n,* militant. **militantisme** (ɑ̃tism) *m,* militancy. **militarisation** (tarizasjɔ̃) *f,* militarisation. **militariser** (ze) *v.t,* to militarize. **militer** (te) *v.i,* (*pers.*) to be a militant; (*reason*) militate.
mille (mil) *a.inv,* a (one) thousand. *trois* ~ *deux cents,* three thousand two hundred. ~ *regrets,* I'm extremely sorry. ~ *fois trop cher,* far too expensive. ¶ *m,* (*Com., Math.*) a (one) thousand; nautical mile; bull's eye. **millénaire** (millenɛr) *m,* millennium. ¶ *a,* millennial; (*fig.*) ancient. **mille-pattes** (pat) *m.inv,* centipede.
millésime (millezim) *m,* date, year; vintage
millet (mijɛ) *m,* (*Agr.*) millet.
milliard (miljar) *m,* milliard, thousand million. **milliardaire** (jardɛr) *n.* & *a,* multi-millionaire.
millième (miljɛm) *a.* & *m,* thousandth. **millier** (je) *m,* thousand [or so]. **milligramme** (milligram) *m,* milligram[me]. **millimètre** (millimɛtr) *m,* millimetre.
million (miljɔ̃) *m,* million. *4* ~*s de francs,* 4 million francs. **millionième** (jɔnjɛm) *a.* & *n,* millionth. **millionnaire** (nɛr) *n,* millionaire.
mime (mim) *m,* mime; mimic. **mimer** (me) *v.t,* (*Theat.*) to mime; mimic; take off *P.* **mimétisme** (metism) *m,* (*Zool.*) m, mimicry. **mimique** (mik) *f,* dumb show, mime.
mimosa (mimoza) *m,* mimosa.
minable (minabl) *a,* wretched; shabby; hopeless *P,* pathetic *P.*
minauder (minode) *v.i,* to mince. **minauderie** (dri) *f,* ~*s,* mincing ways.
mince (mɛ̃s) *a,* thin, slender; slight (*knowledge*); meagre (*wage*). ¶ *ad,* (*cut*) thinly. ¶ *i, P,* ~ [*alors*]*!* blast [it]! *P.* **minceur** (mɛ̃sœr) *f,* thinness.
mine[1] (min) *f,* appearance, face; look, expression. *faire la* ~, to pull a face. *avoir bonne* ~, to look well. *faire* ~ *de faire,* to pretend to do.
mine[2] (min) *f,* (*gen., fig., Mil.*) mine. ~ *de charbon,* coalmine; pit; colliery. ~ [*de crayon*], [pencil] lead. **miner** (ne) *v.t,* (*Mil.*) to mine; undermine (*cliff*); wear down, away. **minerai** (nrɛ) *m,* ore. **minéral, e** (neral) *a,*

mineral; (*Chem.*) inorganic. ¶ *m,* mineral. **minéralogie** (lɔʒi) *f,* mineralogy. **minéralogique** (ʒik) *a,* mineralogical. *plaque ~,* (*Mot.*) number plate. **minéralogiste** (ʒist) *m,* mineralogist.

minet, te *P* (minɛ, ɛt) *n,* puss[y-cat] *P;* pet *P.*

mineur, e (minœr) *a,* (*gen., Law, Mus.*) minor. ¶ *n,* (*Law*) minor. ¶ *m,* (*Mus.*) minor; (*Ind.*) miner. *~ de fond,* pitface worker.

mini (mini) *pref,* mini. *~bus m,* minibus. *~-cassette f,* cassette recorder. *~jupe f,* miniskirt.

miniature (minjatyr) *f,* miniature. *en ~,* in miniature. **miniaturiser** (rize) *v.t,* to miniaturize.

minier, ère (minje, ɛr) *a,* mining.

minimal, e (minimal) *a,* minimum. **minime** (minim) *a,* minor; trivial. **minimiser** (ize) *v.t,* to minimize. **minimum, ma** (minimɔm, ma) *a,* minimum. ¶ *m,* minimum; (*Law*) m. sentence. *au ~,* at least.

ministère (ministɛr) *m,* ministry; department; government; (*Rel.*) ministry. *M~ de l'Intérieur* (*Fr.*), Home Office (*UK*). *M~ des Finances,* Treasury. *~ public,* public prosecutor. **ministériel, le** (terjɛl) *a,* ministerial; cabinet (*reshuffle*). **ministre** (tr) *m,* minister; secretary [of state]; (*Diplomacy*) envoy. *~ des Finances,* Chancellor of the Exchequer. *~ [du culte],* minister [of religion].

minium (minjɔm) *m,* red lead paint.

minois (minwa) *m,* [pretty] little face.

minoritaire (minɔritɛr) *a,* minority. *être ~,* to be in the minority. **minorité** (te) *f,* (*gen., Law, group*) minority. *être en ~,* to be in the m.

Minorque (minɔrk) *f,* Minorca.

minoterie (minɔtri) *f,* [flour] milling; flour mill. **minotier** (tje) *m,* miller.

minou *P* (minu) *m,* puss[y-cat] *P.*

minuit (minɥi) *m,* midnight, twelve o'clock [at night].

minuscule (minyskyl) *a,* minute, tiny. ¶ *f,* small letter.

minutage (minytaʒ) *m,* timing. **minute** (yt) *f,* minute; moment; (*Law*) minute, draft. *la ~ de verité,* the moment of truth. *à la ~,* (*arrive*) on time; at that moment; (*act*) there and then. **minuter** (te) *v.t,* to time. **minuterie** (tri) *f,* time-switch.

minutie (minysi) *f,* meticulousness; precision; detail. *~s* (*pej.*) minutiae, trifling details. **minutieux, euse†** (sjø, øz) *a,* meticulous; minute.

mioche *P* (miɔʃ) *n,* kid *P;* brat *P.*

mirabelle (mirabɛl) *f,* cherry plum.

miracle (mirɑkl) *m,* miracle. *par ~,* miraculously. **miraculé, e** (kyle) *a. & n,* s.o who has been cured, saved miraculously. **miraculeux, euse†** (rakylø, øz) *a,* miraculous.

mirador (miradɔr) *m,* (*Mil.*) watchtower.

mirage (miraʒ) *m,* mirage. **mire** (mir) *f,* (*TV*) test card. **mirer (se)** (re) *v.pr,* to gaze at o.s; (*object*) to be reflected.

mirifique *P* (mirifik) *a,* marvellous, fabulous *P.*

mirobolant, e *P* (mirɔbɔlɑ̃, ɑ̃t) *a,* wonderful.

miroir (mirwar) *m,* (*lit., fig.*) mirror. **miroiter** (rwate) *v.i,* to gleam, glisten, sparkle. (*fig.*) *faire ~ qch,* to paint sth in glowing colours. **miroiterie** (tri) *f,* mirror trade; m. industry. **miroitier, ère** (tje, jɛr) *n,* mirror manufacturer *or* dealer.

mis, e (mi, iz) *a: bien ~,* well-dressed.

misanthrope (mizɑ̃trɔp) *n,* misanthropist. ¶ *a,* misanthropic.

mise (miz) *f,* putting, setting; stake (*gaming*); clothing. *~ à jour,* updating. *~ à mort,* kill. *~ à prix,* reserve [price]. *~ au point,* (*Phot.*) focussing; (*Tech.*) adjustment; (*Mot.*) tuning; clarification. *~ de fonds,* capital outlay. *~ en accusation,* indictment. *~ en garde,* warning. *~ en marche,* starting. *~ en pages,* (*Typ.*) making up. *~ en plis,* set (*hair*). *~ en scène,* staging; production. *~ en valeur,* development, improvement (*property*). *être de ~,* (*remark*) to be in place. **miser** (mize) *v.t. & i,* to stake, bet. (*P*) *~ sur,* to count on.

misérable† (mizerabl) *a,* destitute, poverty-stricken; miserable (*condition*); wretched, pitiful; paltry (*sum*). ¶ *n,* [poor] wretch; scoundrel. **misère** (zɛr) *f,* destitution, poverty. *~s,* miseries, woes; (*P*) troubles. *avoir qch pour une ~,* to get sth for a song. **miséreux, euse** (zerø, øz) *a,* poverty-stricken. ¶ *n,* down-and-out.

miséricorde (mizerikɔrd) *f,* mercy. **miséricordieux, euse†** (djø, øz) *a,* merciful.

misogyne (mizɔʒin) *a,* misogynous. ¶ *n,* misogynist. **misogynie** (ni) *f,* misogyny.

missel (misɛl) *m,* missal.

missile (misil) *m,* missile.

mission (misjɔ̃) *f,* mission; assignment. **missionnaire** (ɔnɛr) *n,* missionary. **missive** (siv) *f,* missive.

mistral (mistral) *m,* mistral (*wind*).

mitaine (mitɛn) *f,* mitten.

mite (mit) *f,* [clothes] moth. **mité, e** (te) *a,* moth-eaten. **miteux, euse** (tø, øz) *a,* shabby.

mi-temps (mitɑ̃) *f.inv,* (*Sport*) half; half-time. *à ~,* (*work*) part-time.

mitigé (mitiʒe) *a,* mitigated; half-hearted; (*P*) mixed (*feelings*).

mitonner (mitɔne) *v.t. & i,* to simmer.

mitoyen, ne (mitwajɛ̃, ɛn) *a,* party (*wall, structure*).

mitraille (mitrɑj) *f,* grape shot; hail of bullets. **mitrailler** (je) *v.t,* to machine-gun; (*fig.*) bombard (*with questions*). *~***tte** (jɛt) *f,* sub-machine gun. **mitrailleur** (jœr) *n,* machine gunner. **mitrailleuse** (jøz) *f,* machine gun.

mitre (mitr) *f,* (*Eccl.*) mitre. **mitron** (trɔ̃) *m,*

baker's boy.
mixage (miksaʒ) *m,* (*Cine. &c*) sound mixing.
mixer (miksœr) *m,* [food] mixer.
mixité (miksite) *f,* coeducation. **mixte** (st) *a,* (*gen.*) mixed; coeducational (*school*); joint (*commission*); combined (*team*). **mixture** (tyr) *f,* mixture; (*fig., pej.*) [vile] concoction.
mobile (mɔbil) *a,* movable (*shelf*); moving (*parts*); mobile; changeable; loose (*pages*). ¶ *m,* (*Mech.*) moving body; motive (*de,* for); (*Art*) mobile. **mobilier, ère** (lje, ɛr) *a,* personal (*belongings*); transferable (*securities*). ¶ *m,* furniture; (*Law*) movable property. **mobilisation** (lizasjɔ̃) *f,* mobilization. **mobiliser** (ze) *v.t,* to mobilize. **mobilité** (te) *f,* mobility.
mobylette (mɔbilɛt) *f,* moped.
mocassin (mɔkasɛ̃) *m,* mocassin.
moche *P* (mɔʃ) *a,* ugly, ghastly *P;* rotten *P.* **~té** *P* (te) *f,* ugliness; eyesore.
modal, e (mɔdal) *a,* modal (*verb*). **modalité** (lite) *f,* method, mode. **mode** (mɔd) *f,* fashion; (*pej.*) craze. *à la ~,* in fashion, fashionable, trendy *P. ad,* fashionably. *suivre la ~,* to keep in fashion. *dans la ~,* (*work*) in the fashion business. *à la ~ de,* in the style of. ¶ *m,* method, way; (*Gram.*) mood; (*Mus., Philos.*) mode. *~ d'emploi,* instructions for use. *~ de vie,* way of life.
modelage (mɔdlaʒ) *m,* modelling. **modèle** (dɛl) *m,* (*gen., Econ.*) model; (*Tech.*) pattern; specimen. *~ déposé,* registered design. *~ réduit,* small scale model. ¶ *a,* model. **modelé** (dle) *m,* (*Geog., Art*) relief; contours. **modeler** (dle) *v.t,* to model; mould, shape. **se ~,** to model o.s (*sur qch,* on sth).
modération (mɔderasjɔ̃) *f,* moderation; restraint; reduction. **modéré, e** (re) *a,* moderate. **~ment** (mɑ̃) *ad,* moderately; in moderation. **modérer** (re) *v.t,* to moderate; curb; reduce (*speed*). **se ~,** to calm down; restrain o.s.
moderne (mɔdɛrn) *a,* modern; up to date. ¶ *m,* modern style; modern [writer &c]. **moderniser** (nize) *v.t,* to modernize.
modeste† (mɔdɛst) *a,* modest, unpretentious. **modestie** (ti) *f,* modesty.
modicité (mɔdisite) *f,* lowness (*price &c*).
modification (mɔdifikasjɔ̃) *f,* modification, alteration. **modifier** (fje) *v.t,* to modify, alter.
modique† (mɔdik) *a,* low, small (*sum &c*).
modiste (mɔdist) *f,* milliner.
modulation (mɔdylasjɔ̃) *f,* modulation. **module** (dyl) *m,* (*Space*) module; (*Math. &c*) modulus. **moduler** (le) *v.i. & t,* to modulate.
moelle (mwal) *f,* (*Anat.*) marrow; (*Bot.*) pith. *~ épinière,* spinal cord. **moelleux, euse**† (lø, øz) *a,* mellow; soft; creamy (*food*). ¶ *m,* mellowness &c.
moellon (mwalɔ̃) *m,* rubble [stone].
mœurs (mœrs) *f.pl,* manners, habits; morals, morality. *bonnes ~,* accepted moral standards. *affaire de ~,* (*Law*) sex case.
moi (mwa) *pn,* me, to me, I. (*object*) *regardez-~!* look at me! *donne-le-~!* give it to me! (*emphatic*) *c'est ~ qui l'ai vu,* it's I who saw it. *ils nous ont suivis, mon fils & ~,* they followed me & my son. *~, je le ferai,* I'll do it. *il parle plus que ~,* he talks more than I do. (*after pr.*) *pour ~,* for me. *c'est à ~,* it's mine. ¶ *m,* self; ego. **~-même,** *pn,* myself.
moignon (mwaɲɔ̃) *m,* stump (*limb, tree*).
moindre (mwɛ̃dr) *a,* less; lesser, lower. **le, la, ~,** the least; the slightest. **~ment** (drəmɑ̃) *ad,* [*ne . . .*] *pas le ~,* not in the least.
moine (mwan) *m,* monk, friar.
moineau (mwano) *m,* sparrow.
moins (mwɛ̃) *ad,* less. *~ cher,* less expensive. *il a ~ d'argent, ~ de livres que vous,* he has less money, fewer books than you. *le ~, la ~ &c,* [the] least. *le ~ poli de ses fils,* the least polite of her sons. *le ~ souvent,* [the] least often. *pas le ~ du monde,* not in the very least. **~ de,** less than (*number, age*); not yet (*time*). *en ~ de rien,* in less than no time. *au ~,* at least (*not less than*). *du ~,* at least, at all events. *pour le ~,* to say the least. *de ~ en ~,* less & less. **à ~ que:** *à ~ qu'il ne soit mort,* unless he's dead. ¶ *pr,* minus. *9 ~ 3 font 6,* 9 minus 3 equals 6. *il fait ~ 7°,* it's minus 7°. *il est 9 heures ~ 20,* it is 20 to 9. ¶ *m,* minus sign. **~-value** (valy) *f,* (*Com.*) depreciation.
moiré (mware) *a,* watered, moiré (*silk*). ¶ *m,* moiré.
mois (mwa) *m,* month; monthly pay *or* salary. *au ~,* (*paid*) monthly, by the month.
moïse (mɔiz) *m,* wicker cradle; Moses basket.
moisi, e (mwazi) *a,* mouldy, mildewy. ¶ *m,* mould, mildew. **moisir** (zir) *v.t,* to make mouldy. ¶ *v.i,* to go mouldy; (*P*) (*pers.*) to hang around *P.* **moisissure** (zisyr) *f,* mildew, mould, mouldiness.
moisson (mwasɔ̃) *f,* harvest. **moissonner** (sɔne) *v.t,* to reap, harvest; (*fig.*) gather, collect. **moissonneur, euse** (nœr, øz) *n,* harvester (*pers.*). ¶ *f,* harvester (*machine*). *~euse-batteuse f,* combine harvester.
moite (mwat) *a,* moist, clammy, sweaty; muggy (*weather*). **moiteur** (tœr) *f,* moistness &c.
moitié (mwatje) *f,* half; half-way mark; (*P*) better half *P* (*wife*). *partager en deux ~s,* to divide in h. ¶ *ad,* half. *à ~,* half, by halves. *à ~ chemin,* half-way. *à ~ prix,* [at] half-price. *à ~ vide,* half-empty. *par ~,* (*divide*) in half. *~ filles, ~ garçons,* (*group*) half girls and half boys. *~-~,* half-and-half; (*P*) so-so *P.*
moka (mɔka) *m,* mocha coffee; coffee cream cake.
molaire (mɔlɛr) *f,* molar.
môle (mol) *m,* breakwater, jetty.
moléculaire (mɔlekylɛr) *a,* molecular. **molécule** (kyl) *f,* molecule.

moleskine (mɔlɛskin) *f,* imitation leather.
molester (mɔlɛste) *v.t,* to molest, manhandle.
molette (mɔlɛt) *f,* toothed *or* milled wheel.
mollasse (mɔlas) *a,* flabby; flimsy; spineless. **mollement** (lmɑ̃) *ad,* (*fall*) softly; (*run*) gently; (*object*) feebly; half-heartedly; (*relax*) lazily. **mollesse** (lɛs) *f,* softness; mildness; feebleness; flabbiness; laxness. **mollet, te** (lɛ, ɛt) *a,* soft, soft-boiled (*eggs*). ¶ *m,* (*Anat.*) calf. **molleton** (ltɔ̃) *m,* flannelette. **molletonné, e** (ɔne) *a,* fleece-lined (*gloves*). **mollir** (lir) *v.i,* to soften; slacken; weaken.
mollusque (mɔlysk) *m,* mollusc; (*P*) lazy slob *P.*
molosse (mɔlɔs) *m,* big [fierce] dog.
môme *P* (mom) kid *P;* brat *P;* bird *P.*
moment (mɔmɑ̃) *m,* moment, while; (*Tech.*) moment; (*Phys.*) momentum. *un bon* ~, quite a while. *un* ~*!* just a minute! time. *à tout* ~, all the time; at any time. *au* ~ *où il arrivait,* just as he was arriving. *en ce* ~, at present. *par* ~*s,* now and then. *pour le* ~, for the time being. *sur le* ~, at the time. **momentané, e** (tane) *a,* momentary. ~**ment** *ad,* at the moment; momentarily.
momie (momi) *f,* mummy. **momifier** (fje) *v.t,* to mummify.
mon, ma, mes (mɔ̃, ma, me) *a,* my. *oui* ~ *mon colonel &c,* yes, sir. (*Eccl.*) *oui* ~ *Père,* yes Father. ~ *vieux P,* old chap *P.* ~ *Dieu!* good heavens!
monarchie (mɔnarʃi) *f,* monarchy. **monarchique** (ʃik) *a,* monarchic(al). **monarchiste** (ʃist) *a. & n,* monarchist. **monarque** (nark) *m,* monarch.
monastère (mɔnastɛr) *m,* monastery; convent. **monastique** (tik) *a,* monastic.
monceau (mɔ̃so) *m,* heap, pile.
mondain, e (mɔ̃dɛ̃, ɛn) *a,* (*Rel.*) worldly; (*Philos.*) mundane; society, social; fashionable; refined (*manners*). *la police* ~*e,* ≏ the vice squad. ¶ *n,* society man, woman; socialite. **mondanité** (danite) *f,* society life; small talk. **monde** (mɔ̃d) *m,* world. *dans le* ~ *entier,* throughout the world. *le meilleur du* ~, the best in the world. *pour rien au* ~, not for all the world. people. *il y a beacoup de* ~, there's a crowd. *nous avons du* ~, we have visitors. set, circle. *le* [*grand*] ~, high society. **mondial, e**† (jal) *a,* world (*war*); world-wide. **mondiovision** (jɔvizjɔ̃) *f,* television broadcast by satellite.
monétaire (mɔnetɛr) *a,* monetary.
mongolien, ne (mɔ̃gɔljɛ̃, ɛn) *a. & n,* (*Med.*) mongol. **mongolisme** (lism) *m,* mongolism.
moniteur, trice (mɔnitœr, tris) *n,* instructor, tress; supervisor (*camp*).
monnaie (mɔnɛ) *f,* currency; coin; coinage. [*petite*] ~, [small] change. *faire la* ~ *de 50 F,* to get change for 50 francs. *la* ~ *courante,* common practice, a common occurrence. **monnayer** (nɛje) *v.t,* to convert into cash; capitalize on (*talent*).
mono... (mɔnɔ) *pref,* mono... ~**chrome** (krom) *a,* monochrome, monochromatic. ~**cle** (kl) *m,* monocle, eyeglass. ~**corde** (kɔrd) *a,* monotonous (*voice*). ~**gamie** (gami) *f,* monogamy. ~**gramme** (gram) *m,* monogram. ~**graphie** (grafi) *f,* monograph. ~**kini** (kini) *m,* topless swimsuit. ~**lingue** (lɛ̃g) *a,* monolingual. ~**lithique** (litik) *a,* (*lit., fig.*) monolithic. ~**logue** (lɔg) *m,* monologue. ~**loguer** (ge) *v.i,* to soliloquize. ~**pole** (pɔl) *m,* monopoly. ~**poliser** (ize) *v.t,* to monopolize. ~**syllabe** (silab) *m,* monosyllable. ¶ *a,* & ~**syllabique** (bik) *a,* monosyllabic. ~**théisme** (teism) *m,* monotheism. ~**tone** (tɔn) *a,* monotonous; dull; humdrum. ~**tonie** (ni) *f,* monotony; dullness.
monôme (monom) *m,* students' procession.
monseigneur (mɔ̃sɛɲœr) *m,* His, Your Royal Highness (*prince*); My Lord, His, Your Grace (*bishop*); His, Your Eminence (*cardinal*). **monsieur** (məsjø) *m,* gentleman. **M**~, **Messieurs** (mesjø) *pl,* Mr., sir. ~ *X,* Mr. X. *bonjour* ~, good morning; good morning Mr. X. (*pl.*) good morning gentlemen. ~, dear sir (*letter*). *cher* ~, dear Mr. X (*letter*). ~ *le Président,* Mr. President, the President, dear Mr. President (*letter*). ~ *le Ministre,* Minister, the Minister. ~ *le Juge,* His, Your Honour.
monstre (mɔ̃str) *m,* (*lit., fig*) monster. (*Cine. &c*) ~ *sacré,* superstar. ¶ *a,* (*P*) colossal. **monstrueux, euse**† (mɔ̃stryø, øz) *a,* monstrous. **monstruosité** (ozite) *f,* monstrosity; deformity.
mont (mɔ̃) *m,* mountain. *le* ~ *Blanc &c,* Mont Blanc &c. *être par* ~*s et par vaux,* to be on the move. ~**-de-piété** (dəpjete) *m,* pawn shop.
montage (mɔ̃taʒ) *m,* (*Ind.*) assembly (*car &c*); setting (*gem*); pitching (*tent*); (*Cine.*) editing.
montagnard, e (mɔ̃taɲar, ard) *a,* highland, mountain. ¶ *n,* mountain dweller. **montagne** (taɲ) *f,* mountain. *la* ~, the mountains. *une* ~ *de,* masses of. *se faire une* ~ *de qch,* to make too much of sth. ~*s russes,* big dipper. **montagneux, euse** (ɲø, øz) *a,* mountainous; hilly.
montant, e (mɔ̃tɑ̃, ɑ̃t) *a,* rising, incoming (*tide*); upward; up-hill; up (*train*); high-necked (*dress*). ¶ *m,* upright (*ladder*); post (*bed*); total (*amount*). **monte-charge** (mɔ̃tʃarʒ) *m,* service lift. **montée** (mɔ̃te) *f,* ascent; climb, climbing; rise (*price*); hill.
monter (mɔ̃te) *v.i,* to go up (*à,* to; *dans,* into). ~ *à pied,* to walk up. ~ *sur,* to climb up on (*chair*). ~ *dans un train,* to board a train. ~ *à cheval,* to mount; ride. (*sun, price*) to rise; (*sea*) come in. ~ [*en graine*], run to seed. ~ *en grade,* be promoted. ~ *sur ses grands*

chevaux, to get on one's high horse. ¶ *v.t,* to climb (*stairs*); take, carry up (*baggage*); ride (*horse*); assemble (*machine*); pitch (*tent*); edit (*film*); put on, produce (*play*); hatch (*plot*); equip. *se ~ à,* (*price*) to come to, add up to. **monteur, euse** (tœr, øz) *n,* (*Tech.*) fitter; (*Cine.*) editor.

monticule (mɔ̃tikyl) *m,* hillock, mound.

montre (mɔ̃tr) *f,* watch. *~-bracelet,* wrist watch. *à ma ~,* by my watch. *~ en main,* exactly, precisely. *faire ~ de,* to show. **montrer** (mɔ̃tre) *v.t,* to show; point out; display. **se ~,** to appear, show o.s; prove; prove o.s.

monture (mɔ̃tyr) *f,* mount (*animal*); setting (*gem*); (*Tech.*) mounting; frame (*glasses*).

monument (mɔnymɑ̃) *m,* (*gen., fig.*) monument, memorial. *~ aux morts,* war memorial. *~ funéraire,* monument. *~ historique,* ancient monument. **monumental, e** (tal) *a,* monumental.

moquer (se) (mɔke) *v.pr, se ~ de,* to make fun of, laugh at. *je m'en moque pas mal P,* I couldn't care less. **moquerie** (kri) *f, ~[s],* mockery. **moquette** (kɛt) *f,* fitted carpet. **moqueur, euse†** (kœr, øz) *a,* mocking.

moral, e (mɔral) *a,* moral; mental. ¶ *m,* morale. *avoir bon ~,* to be in good spirits. *au ~,* mentally; morally. **morale** (ral) *f,* morals; moral code, standard; moral (*of story*). **moralement** (lmɑ̃) *ad,* morally. **moraliser** (lize) *v.i,* to moralize. ¶ *v.t,* to lecture. **moraliste** (list) *a,* moralistic. ¶ *n,* moralist. **moralité** (te) *f,* morality; morals, moral standards; moral (*of fable*).

morbide (mɔrbid) *a,* morbid; unhealthy. **morbidité** (ite) *f,* morbidity.

morceau (mɔrso) *m,* (*gen., Mus.*) piece; bit; (*Liter., Mus.*) passage; lump (*sugar*); patch, plot (*land*); cut (*meat*). *manger un ~,* to have a bite to eat. *~x choisis,* selected extracts. **morceler** (səle) *v.t,* to divide, split up. **morcellement** (sɛlmɑ̃) *m,* division.

mordant, e (mɔrdɑ̃, ɑ̃t) *a,* biting (*cold*); cutting, scathing (*tone*). ¶ *m,* spirit, drive (*pers.*); bite (*style, saw*). **mordicus** (dikys) *ad,* doggedly. **mordiller** (dije) *v.t,* to nibble [at].

mordoré, e (mɔrdɔre) *a,* lustrous bronze.

mordre (mɔrdr) *v.t,* to bite; (*saw*) bite into. *la balle a mordu la ligne,* the ball just touched the line. *~* **sur,** to overlap, go over [into]. ¶ *v.i, ~ dans une poire,* to bite into a pear. (*Fish., fig.*) to bite. *~ à qch P,* to take to sth. **se ~,** *se ~ la langue,* (*lit., fig.*) to bite one's tongue. *je m'en mords les doigts,* I could kick myself. **mordu, e** *P* (dy) *a, être ~ de,* to be crazy about *P.*

morfondre (se) (mɔrfɔ̃dr) *v.pr,* to mope, fret. **morfondu, e** (fɔ̃dy) *a,* dejected.

morgue (mɔrg) *f,* haughtiness; pride; mortuary; morgue.

moribond, e (mɔribɔ̃, ɔ̃d) *a.* (*& n*), dying, moribund (man, woman).

morigéner (mɔriʒene) *v.t,* to take to task.

morne (mɔrn) *a,* gloomy, dismal, dreary; bleak (*country*); glum (*face*).

morose (mɔroz) *a,* morose, sullen, moody. **morosité** (rozite) *f,* moroseness, &c.

morphine (mɔrfin) *f,* morphine.

morphologie (mɔrfɔlɔʒi) *f,* morphology.

mors (mɔr) *m,* bit (*bridle*); jaw (*vice*).

morse (mɔrs) *m,* (*Zool.*) walrus; morse (*code*).

morsure (mɔrsyr) *f,* bite.

mort (mɔr) *f,* death. *à la ~ de son père,* on the death of his father. *donner la ~ à qn,* to kill s.o. *de ~,* deadly (*weapon*); deathly (*hush*); death (*penalty*). *à ~,* mortally (*wounded*); fatally (*injured*); (*fight*) to the death; death (*sentence*). *mettre qn à ~,* to put s.o to death. *souffrir mille ~s,* to suffer agonies. **mort, e** (mɔr, ɔrt) *a,* dead. *il est ~ depuis une semaine,* he has been dead a week. *~ [de fatigue],* dead tired. ¶ *n,* dead man, woman. *les ~s,* the dead. ¶ *m,* (*Cards*) dummy.

mortadelle (mɔrtadɛl) *f,* mortadella.

mortaise (mɔrtɛz) *f,* mortise.

mortalité (mɔrtalite) *f,* mortality; death rate. **mort-aux-rats** (mɔrora) *f,* rat poison. **mortel, le†** (tɛl) *a,* mortal, deadly, lethal; fatal (*accident*); deathly (*silence*); deadly boring (*film; P pers.*). ¶ *n,* mortal. **morte-saison** (təsɛzɔ̃) *f,* off season.

mortier (mɔrtje) *m,* (*gen.*) mortar.

mortifier (mɔrtifje) *v.t,* to mortify. **mort-né, e** (mɔrne) *a,* still-born. **mortuaire** (mɔrtɥɛr) *a,* mortuary, funeral (*rites*); [of] death; (*house*) of the deceased.

morue (mɔry) *f,* (*Zool.*) cod.

morve (mɔrv) *f,* mucus of the nose; snot *P.*

mosaïque (mɔzaik) *f,* mosaic.

Moscou (mɔsku) *m,* Moscow.

mosquée (mɔske) *f,* mosque.

mot (mo) *m,* word; note (*letter*). *à, sur ces ~s,* with, at these words. *en un ~,* in a word. *~ d'excuse,* [excuse] note. *dire deux ~s à qn,* to have a word with s.o; give s.o a piece of one's mind. *avoir le ~ de la fin,* to have the last word. *prendre qn au ~,* to take s.o at his word. *le ~ de l'enigme,* the key to the mystery. *~-clé m,* key word. *~ de passe,* password. *~ à ~* (motamo), *~ pour ~,* word for word, verbatim. *~s croisés* crossword [puzzle]. *~ d'ordre,* watchword.

moteur[1] (mɔtœr) *m,* engine, motor; (*fig.*) mover, driving force. *~ électrique,* electric motor. *~ à 2 temps,* 2-stroke engine. *à ~* power-driven.

moteur[2], **trice** (tœr, tris) *a,* motor (*muscles*); driving (*force*). **motif** (tif) *m,* motive; reason; grounds (*de,* for); pattern (*fabric*); (*Mus. &c*)

motif. **motion** (mosjɔ̃) *f,* (*Pol.*) motion. **motivation** (mɔtivɑsjɔ̃) *f,* motivation. **motivé, e** (ve) *a,* justified, well-founded (*belief*); motivated (*pers.*). **motiver** (mɔtive) *v.t,* to state the reason for; justify.

moto-cross (mɔtɔkrɔs) *m.inv,* motocross. **motoculteur** (kyltœr) *m,* [motor] cultivator. **motocyclette** (siklɛt), *abb.* **moto** (mɔto) *f,* motorcycle, [motor] bike *P.* **motocycliste** (klist) *n,* motorcyclist. **motopompe** (pɔ̃p) *f,* motor-pump. **motoriser** (ze) *v.t,* (*Tech. &c*) to motorize. *être motorisé P,* to have transport, a car.

motrice (mɔtris) *f,* motor unit. *V* **moteur²**.

motte (mɔt) *f,* clod (*earth*). ~ *de gazon,* turf. ~ *de beurre,* block of butter.

motus *P* (mɔtys) *i,* not a word!

mou, mol, molle (mu, mɔl) *a,* (*gen.*) soft; limp (*leaf*); flabby (*face*); weak (*protest, features*); dull (*style*); lax, indolent (*pers.*); muffled (*sound*). **mou,** *m,* lights (*animal lungs*). *avoir du* ~, to be slack.

mouchard (muʃar) *m,* (*P*) grass *P;* (*Sch.*) sneak *P;* (*Mil.*) spy plane. ~**er** *P* (rde) *v.t,* to grass on *P;* (*Sch.*) sneak on *P.*

mouche (muʃ) *f,* fly; patch, beauty spot (*on face*). ~ *bleue,* bluebottle. ~ *à vers,* blowfly. *prendre la* ~, to get in a huff *P. faire* ~, (*lit., fig.*) to score a bull's-eye.

moucher (muʃe) *v.t,* ~ *qn,* to blow, wipe s.o's nose [for them]; (*fig.*) snub s.o. **se** ~, to blow one's nose.

moucheté, e (muʃte) *a,* spotted, speckled.

mouchoir (muʃwar) *m,* handkerchief; headscarf. ~ *en papier,* tissue, paper hanky.

moudre (mudr) *v.t.ir,* to grind.

moue (mu) *f,* pout. *faire la* ~, to pout; pull a face.

mouette (mwɛt) *f,* [sea] gull.

mouffette (mufɛt) *f,* (*Zool.*) skunk.

moufle (mufl) *f,* mitten.

mouillage (mujaʒ) *m,* (*Naut.*) mooring; anchorage. **mouillé, e** (je) *a,* wet. **mouiller** (je) *v.t,* to wet; water down (*wine &c*); (*Naut.*) lay (mines). ~ *l'ancre,* to cast anchor. ¶ *v.i,* (*Naut.*) to anchor. **se** ~, to get [o.s] wet; (*eyes*) to fill with tears.

moulage (mulaʒ) *m,* moulding (*act*); casting; (*plaster*) cast. **moule** (mul) *m,* (*lit., fig.*) mould; (*Typ.*) matrix. ~ *à gâteaux,* cake tin. ¶ *f,* (*Zool.*) mussel; (*P*) idiot. **mouler** (le) *v.t,* to mould; cast (*statue*); (*dress*) hug, fit tightly. ~ *sa pensée sur,* to model one's ideas on.

moulin (mulɛ̃) *m,* mill. ~ *à eau,* water mill. ~ *à paroles P,* chatterbox. ~ *à vent,* windmill. ~**et** (nɛ) *m,* (*Fish.*) reel. *faire le* ~ *avec,* to whirl, twirl. **moulu, e** (ly) *a,* (*beaten*) black and blue. ~ *de fatigue P,* dead beat *P.*

moulure (mulyr) *f,* (*Arch. &c*) moulding.

mourant, e (murɑ̃, ɑ̃t) *a,* dying (*pers., fire*); languishing (*eyes*); faint (*voice*). *un* ~, a dying man. *les* ~*s,* the dying. **mourir** (rir) *v.i.ir,* to die. ~ *assassiné,* to be murdered. *faire* ~, to kill. die away (*noise*); die out (*fire*); d. down (*flame*). ~ *de faim,* (*lit.*) to starve to death; (*fig.*) to be starving. **se** ~, to be dying.

mouron (murɔ̃) *m,* pimpernel.

mousquetaire (muskətɛr) *m,* musketeer.

mousse (mus) *m,* ship's boy. ¶ *f,* (*Bot.*) moss; froth, foam (*water*); lather (*soap*); head (*beer*); (*Cook.*) mousse. ~ *au chocolat,* chocolate mousse. *balle* ~, rubber ball. *caoutchouc* ~, foam rubber.

mousseline (muslin) *f,* muslin; chiffon.

mousser (muse) *v.i,* (*water*) to froth, foam; (*soap*) lather; (*champagne*) sparkle. *se faire* ~ *P,* to give o.s a boost *P.* **mousseux, euse** (sø, øz) *a,* frothy; sparkling. ¶ *m,* sparkling wine.

mousson (musɔ̃) *f,* monsoon.

moustache (mustaʃ) *f,* moustache; whiskers (*animal*).

moustiquaire (mustikɛr) *f,* mosquito net. **moustique** (tik) *m,* mosquito.

moutarde (mutard) *f,* mustard. ~ *forte,* English m. ~ *à l'estragon,* French m. *la* ~ *lui monta au nez,* he lost his temper.

mouton (mutɔ̃) *m,* (*Zool., fig.*) sheep; (*Cook.*) mutton; sheepskin. ~*s,* white horses (*waves*); bits of fluff; fleecy clouds. *ce sont de vrais* ~*s de Panurge,* they're like a flock of sheep. ~**neux, euse** (ɔnø, øz) *a,* (*sky*) dotted with fleecy clouds; (*sea*) dotted with white horses. ~**nier, ère** (nje, ɛr) *a,* sheep-like (*pers.*).

mouvant, e (muvɑ̃, ɑ̃t) *a,* moving, shifting, unstable (*situation*). **mouvement** (vmɑ̃) *m,* (*gen., Pol., Mus., Tech.*) movement. ~*s de gymnastique,* [physical] exercises. ~ *de tête,* nod. *avoir un* ~ *de recul,* to start back. impulse; reaction. ~ *de colère,* upsurge of anger. *de son propre* ~, of one's own accord. action; bustle, stir. *place pleine de* ~, busy, bustling square. action (*of play*); rhythm (*of phrase*); drape (*of curtain*); (*Mil.*) move. *être sans cesse en* ~, to be continually on the move, go *P. suivre le* ~, to follow the trend. *être dans le* ~, to keep up to date. *par un* ~ *d'horlogerie,* by clockwork. **mouvementé, e** (te) *a,* eventful; turbulant, stormy; broken (*ground*). **mouvoir** (vwar) *v.t.ir,* (*Mach.*) to drive; move (*leg*); (*emotion*) prompt, drive. **se** ~, to move.

moyen, ne (mwajɛ̃, ɛn) *a,* average; mediocre (*result*); medium (*height*); medium-sized; mixed (*weather*); (*Sch.*) intermediate (*classes*). *le* ~ *âge,* the middle ages. *du* ~ *âge,* medi[a]eval. ¶ *m,* means, way. *au* ~ *de,* by means of. ~*s,* (*financial*) means; abilities. *c'est au-dessus de mes* ~*s,* I can't afford it, I can't manage it. *est-ce qu'il y a* ~ *de leur parler?* is it possible to speak to them? ~ **âgeux, euse** (ʒɛnaʒø, øz) *a*, medi[a]eval. ~**-courrier** (kurje) *m*, medium-haul aeroplane. ~**nant** (nɑ̃) *pr*, for (*sum*); in return for (*service*); with (*effort*). ~**ne** (ʒɛn) *f*, average. *la* ~ *d'âge*, the average age. *la* ~ *des gens*, most people. (*Sch.*) *avoir la* ~, to get half marks. *être dans la bonne* ~, to be above average. *faire du 80 de* ~, to average 80 km/h. ~**nement** (nmɑ̃) *ad*, moderately, fairly; moderately well. **M~-Orient** (ɔrjɑ̃) *m*, *le* ~, the Middle East.

moyeu (mwajø) *m*, hub (*wheel*).

mucosité (mykozite) *f*, (*Med.*) mucus.

mue (my) *f*, moult[ing]; slough[ing]; breaking (*voice*). **muer** (mɥe) *v.i*, to moult; (*snake*) slough; (*voice*) break. **se** ~, to change (*en*, into).

muet, te (mɥɛ, ɛt) *a*, dumb; silent; (*Linguistics*) mute, silent. *rester* ~, to stand speechless. ¶ *n*, dumb man, woman. ¶ *m*, *le* ~, the silent cinema.

mufle (myfl) *m*, (*Zool.*) muzzle; (*P*) boor, lout. ~**rie** (ləri) *f*, boorishness. **muflier** (flie) *m*, antirrhinum, snapdragon.

mugir (myʒir) *v.i*, (*cow*) to moo; (*bull*) bellow; (*wind*) howl. **mugissement** (ʒismɑ̃) *m*, mooing &c.

muguet (mygɛ) *m*, lily of the valley.

mulâtre, esse (mylɑtr, ɛs) *a. & n*, mulatto. **mule** (myl) *f*, [she] mule; mule (*slipper*). **mulet** (lɛ) *m*, [he] mule; mullet (*fish*). **muletier, ère** (ltje, ɛr) *a*, mule (*track*). ¶ *n*, muleteer.

mulot (mylo) *m*, field mouse.

multi... (mylti) *pref*, multi... ~**colore** (kɔlɔr) *a*, multicoloured. ~**forme** (fɔrm) *a*, multiform, many-sided. ~**millionnaire** (miljɔnɛr) *n*, multimillionaire. ~**national, e** (nasjɔnal) *a*, multinational. **multiple** (tipl) *a*, multiple (*fracture*); manifold (*aspects*); numerous. *à usages* ~*s*, multi-purpose. ¶ *m*, multiple. ~**plication** (plikɑsjɔ̃) *f*, (*Math., Bot.*) multiplication; increase in number. ~**plicité** (site) *f*, multiplicity. ~**plier** (plie) *v.t*, & **se** ~, to multiply. ~**tude** (tyd) *f*, multitude; vast number, amount.

municipal, e (munisipal) *a*, municipal, town (*council*); local (*by-law*); public (*swimming bath*). ~**ité** (lite) *f*, town; town council.

munir (mynir) *v.t*, to supply, provide; equip (*de*, with). **se** ~, provide, arm o.s (*de*, with). **munitions** (nisjɔ̃) *f.pl*, ammunition.

muqueuse (mykøz) *f*, mucous membrane.

mur (myr) *m*, wall. *le* ~ *du son*, the sound barrier.

mûr, e (myr) *a*, ripe (*fruit*); mature (*pers.*); worn (*fabric*). *pas* ~, unripe. *trop* ~, overripe.

muraille (myrɑj) *f*, [high] wall. **mural, e** (ral) *a*, wall; (*Art*) mural.

mûre (myr) *f*, blackberry; mulberry.

mûrement (myrmɑ̃) *ad*: *ayant* ~ *réfléchi*, after careful thought.

murer (myre) *v.t*, to wall, brick up (*window &c*). **se** ~, to shut o.s up (*at home*); isolate o.s.

mûrier (myrje) *m*, mulberry tree.

mûrir (myrir) *v.i. & t*, to ripen, mature; mellow.

murmure (myrmyr) *m*, murmur ~*s*, grumblings; objections. **murmurer** (myre) *v.t*, to murmur. ¶ *v.i*, to murmur, grumble.

musaraigne (myzarɛɲ) *f*, (*Zool.*) shrew.

musarder (myzarde) *v.i*, to dawdle.

musc (mysk) *m*, musk. ~**ade** (kad) *f*, nutmeg. ~**at** (ka) *m*, muscat grape; muscatel (*wine*).

muscle (myskl) *m*, muscle. **musclé, e** (kle) *a*, muscular. **musculaire** (kylɛr) *a*, muscular (*force*); muscle (*fibre*).

Muse (myz) *f*, Muse.

museau (myzo) *m*, muzzle, snout.

musée (myze) *m*, museum; art gallery.

museler (myzle) *v.t*, to muzzle. **muselière** (zəljɛr) *f*, muzzle (*dog*).

musette (myzɛt) *f*, haversack; bag; nosebag; (*Mus.*) musette (*bagpipes*).

muséum (myzeɔm) *m*, natural history museum.

musical, e† (myzikal) *a*, musical. **music-hall** (myzik hɔl) *m*, music hall; variety theatre. **musicien, ne** (sjɛ̃, ɛn) *n*, musician. ¶ *a*, musical. **musique** (zik) *f*, music; band. *il fait de la* ~, he plays an instrument.

musulman, e (myzylmɑ̃, an) *a. & n*, Muslim, Moslem.

mutation (mytɑsjɔ̃) *f*, (*Adm.*) transfer; (*Biol.*) mutation. **muter** (te) *v.t*, to transfer.

mutilation (mytilasjɔ̃) *f*, mutilation, maiming (*pers.*); defacement. **mutilé, e** (le) *a. & n*, disabled (person). ~ *de guerre*, disabled ex-serviceman. **mutiler** (le) *v.t*, to mutilate, maim; deface.

mutin, e (mytɛ̃, in) *a*, mischievous (*child*). ¶ *m*, mutineer. **mutiné, e** (tine) *a*, mutinous. ¶ *m*, mutineer. **mutiner (se)** (ne) *v.pr*, (*Mil., Naut.*) to mutiny; rebel. ~**erie** (nri) *f*, mutiny; revolt.

mutisme (mytism) *m*, silence; dumbness.

mutuel, le (mytɥɛl) *a*, mutual. ¶ *f*, mutual benefit society. ~**lement** (ɛlmɑ̃) *ad*, (*help*) each other, one another; mutually (*felt*).

myope (mjɔp) *a. & n*, short-sighted (person). **myopie** (pi) *f*, myopia; short-sightedness.

myosotis (mjɔzɔtis) *m*, forget-me-not.

myriade (mirjad) *f*, myriad.

myrrhe (mir) *f*, myrrh.

myrte (mirt) *m*, myrtle. **myrtille** (til) *f*, whortleberry, bilberry.

mystère (mistɛr) *m*, mystery. **mystérieux, euse†** (terjø, øz) *a*, mysterious. **mysticisme** (tisism) *m*, mysticism. **mystificateur, trice** (fikatœr, tris) *n*, hoaxer. **mystifier** (fje) *v.t*, to mystify; fool. **mystique†** (tik) *a*, mystical. ¶ *n*, mystic

(*pers.*). ¶ *f,* mysticism; mystique; blind belief in.
mythe (mit) *m,* myth. **mythique** (tik) *a,* mythical. **mythologie** (tɔlɔʒi) *f,* mythology. **mythologique** (ʒik) *a,* mythological. **mythomane** (man) *f,* mythomaniac.
myxomatose (miksɔmatoz) *f,* myxomatosis.

N

N, n (ɛn) *m, letter,* N, n.
nabot, e (nabo, ɔt) *n,* (*pej.*) midget (*pers.*).
nacre (nakr) *f,* mother of pearl. **nacré, e** (kre) *a,* pearly.
nage (naʒ) *f,* swimming; stroke; style of swimming. ~ *libre,* freestyle. ~ *sur le dos,* backstroke. *traverser la Manche à la* ~, to swim the Channel. *en* ~, bathed in sweat. ~**oire** (war) *f,* fin (*fish*); flipper (*seal*). **nager** (ʒe) *v.i,* to swim; (*object*) float; (*P fig.*) to be at sea *P.* ~ *dans la graisse,* (*food*) to be swimming in fat. **nageur, euse** (ʒœr, øz) *n,* swimmer.
naguère (nagɛr) *ad,* not long ago; formerly.
naïf, ïve (naif, iv) *a,* naive. ¶ *n,* gullible fool.
nain, e (nɛ̃, ɛn) *n,* dwarf. ¶ *a,* dwarfish; dwarf (*tree*).
naissance (nɛsɑ̃s) *f,* birth; source (*river*); root (*hair*). *de* ~, (*blind*) from birth; (*English*) by birth. ~ *du jour,* dawn. *donner* ~, to give birth (*à,* to); give rise (*to rumours*). **naître** (nɛtr) *v.i.ir,* (*pers., idea*) to be born; (*problem*) arise; (*town*) spring up; (*plant*) bud. *elle est née le 7 juin,* she was born on June 7. *il est né musicien,* he's a born musician. *faire* ~, to create (*industry*); arouse (*hate*).
naïvement (naivmɑ̃) *ad,* naively. **naïveté** (vte) *f,* naivety.
nana *P* (nana) *f,* bird *P,* chick *P.*
nanti, e (nɑ̃ti) *a,* affluent, well-off. **nantir** (ir) *v.t,* to provide (*de,* with).
napalm (napalm) *m,* napalm.
naphtaline (naftalin) *f,* mothballs.
napolitain, e (napɔlitɛ̃, ɛn) *a.* & **N**~, *n,* Neapolitan.
nappe (nap) *f,* tablecloth; sheet (*water, flame*); layer (*oil*). ~**ron** (prɔ̃) *m,* [tray] cloth; doily.
narcisse (narsis) *m,* narcissus.
narcotique (narkɔtik) *a.* & *m,* narcotic.
narguer (narge) *v.t,* to flout; scoff at.
narine (narin) *f,* nostril.
narquois, e† (narkwa, az) *a,* mocking.
narrateur, trice (narratœr, tris) *n,* narrator. **narratif, ive** (tif, iv) *a,* narrative. **narration** (sjɔ̃) *f,* narrative, story; narration; (*Sch.*) essay. **narrer** (re) *v.t,* to narrate.
nasal, e (nazal) *a,* nasal. **naseau** (zo) *m,* nostril (*horse*). **nasillard, e** (ijar, ard) *a,* nasal, whining. **nasillement** (jmɑ̃) *m,* twang; whine. **nasiller** (je) *v.i,* to speak with a nasal twang; (*microphone*) to whine.
nasse (nas) *f,* (*Fish.*) hoop net.
natal, e (natal) *a,* native. **natalité** (lite) *f,* birth rate.
natation (natasjɔ̃) *f,* swimming.
natif, ive (natif, iv) *a,* native.
nation (nasjɔ̃) *f,* nation. ~**al, e** (ɔnal) *a,* national; state (*funeral*). *route* ~*e,* ≃ 'A' road. ~**alisation** (izɑsjɔ̃) *f,* nationalization. ~**aliser** (ize) *v.t,* to nationalize. ~**alisme** (lism) *m,* nationalism. ~**aliste** (list) *a.* & *n,* nationalist. ~**alité** (te) *f,* nationality.
nativité (nativite) *f,* nativity.
natte (nat) *f,* plait, pigtail (*hair*); mat.
naturalisation (natyralizasjɔ̃) *f,* naturalization. **naturaliser** (ze) *v.t,* to naturalize. *se faire* ~ *français,* to become a naturalised Frenchman. **nature** (tyr) *f,* nature; kind. *la* ~ *humaine,* human nature. *de toute*[*s*] ~[*s*], of all kinds. ~ *morte,* still life. *en* ~, (*pay*) in kind. ¶ *a. inv,* plain (*food*); black (*coffee*); straight (*whisky*). **naturel, le**† (tyrɛl) *a,* natural; normal. ¶ *m,* naturalness; nature, disposition; native (*pers*). *au* ~, (*Cook.*) served plain.
naufrage (nofraʒ) *m,* wreck, shipwreck. *faire* ~, to be [ship]wrecked. **naufragé, e** (fraʒe) *n,* shipwrecked person, castaway.
nauséabond, e (nozeabɔ̃, ɔ̃d) *a,* nauseating, sickening. **nausée** (ze) *f,* nausea; sickness. *avoir la* ~, to feel sick. (*lit., fig.*) *donner la* ~ *à qn,* to make s.o feel sick.
nautique (notik) *a,* nautical; water (*sport*).
naval, e (naval) *a,* naval, ship-building (*industry*).
navet (navɛ) *m,* turnip; (*P*) third-rate film, painting &c.
navette (navɛt) *f,* shuttle (*loom*); s. service. *faire la* ~ to commute; shuttle to & fro.
navigabilité (navigabilite) *f,* navigability (*river*); seaworthiness (*boat*). **navigable** (abl) *a,* navigable. **navigateur** (tœr) *m,* navigator. **navigation** (sjɔ̃) *f,* navigation; sailing; shipping. **naviguer** (ge) *v.i,* to navigate, sail; (*pilot*) to fly. (*fig.*) *il sait* ~ *P,* he knows the ropes.
navire (navir) *m,* ship; vessel. ~ *amiral,* flagship.

navrant, e (navrɑ̃, ɑ̃t) *a,* distressing, upsetting; annoying. **navrer** (vre) *v.t,* to distress, upset; annoy.
nazi, e (nazi) *a. & n,* Nazi. **~sme** (ism) *m,* Nazism.
ne, n' (nə, n) *neg. particle, je ~ sais pas,* I don't know. *il n'a pas d'amis,* he has no friends. *elle ~ l'aime point,* she doesn't like it at all. *aucune lettre n'est arrivée,* no letter has arrived. *~... que,* only. *avant qu'elle ~ vienne,* before she comes. *il est plus fort que tu ~ penses,* he is stronger than you think.
néanmoins (neɑ̃mwɛ̃) *ad,* nevertheless, yet.
néant (neɑ̃) *m,* nothing[ness]; nil, none.
nébuleux, euse (nebylø, øz) *a,* nebulous, cloudy; clouded. ¶ *f,* (*Astr.*) nebula.
nécessaire† (nesesɛr) *a,* necessary, needful; indispensable (*pers.*). ¶ *m, le ~,* what is needed, necessary. *le strict ~,* the bare necessities. *peux-tu faire le ~?* can you see to it? *~ à couture,* sewing box. *~ de voyage,* grip. **nécessité** (site) *f,* necessity; destitution. *être dans la ~ de faire,* to be compelled to do. **nécessiter** (te) *v.t,* to necessitate; require. **nécessiteux, euse** (tø, øz) *a,* needy.
nécrologie (nekrɔlɔʒi) *f,* obituary; o. column.
nécropole (pol) *f,* necropolis.
nectar (nektar) *m,* (*Bot., Myth., fig.*) nectar.
néerlandais, e (neɛrlɑ̃dɛ, ɛz) *a,* Dutch. **N~,** *n,* Dutchman, -woman. ¶ *m,* Dutch (*language*).
nef (nɛf) *f,* nave (*church*).
néfaste (nefast) *a,* ill-fated, disastrous; harmful.
négatif, ive† (negatif, iv) *a,* negative. ¶ *m,* (*Phot.*) negative. ¶ *f, par la ~ ive* (*answer*) in the negative. **négation** (sjɔ̃) *f,* negation.
négligé, e (negliʒe) *a,* neglected; slovenly (*appearance*); slipshod (*work*). ¶ *m,* slovenliness; negligée (*garment*). **négligeable** (ʒabl) *a,* negligible; trivial. *non ~,* not inconsiderable. **négligemment** (ʒamɑ̃) *ad,* negligently, carelessly; casually. **négligence** (ʒɑ̃s) *f,* negligence; carelessness; slovenliness; omission. **négligent, e** (ʒɑ̃, ɑ̃t) *a,* negligent; careless; casual. **négliger** (ʒe) *v.t,* to neglect, disregard (*advice*); miss (*chance*); be careless about (*dress*). **se ~,** to neglect o.s; be careless about one's dress.
négoce (negɔs) *m,* (*O*) business. **négociable** (sjabl) *a,* negotiable. **négociant, e** (sjɑ̃, ɑ̃t) *n,* trader, merchant. *~ en gros,* wholesaler. **négociateur, trice** (atœr, tris) *n,* negotiator. **négociation** (sjɔ̃) *f,* negotiation. **négocier** (sje) *v.t,* to negotiate.
nègre (nɛgr) *a,* (*pej.*) Negro. ¶ *m,* (*pej.*) Negro; ghost writer. **négresse** (negrɛs) *f,* (*pej.*) Negress. **négrier** (grie) *m,* slave trader; s. driver (*employer*).
neige (nɛʒ) *f, oft. pl,* snow. *~ carbonique,* dry ice. *~ fondue,* sleet. *sports de ~,* winter sports. **neiger** (nɛʒe) *v.imp,* to snow. **neigeux, euse** (ʒø, øz) *a,* snowy, snow-clad (*peak*).
nénuphar (nenyfar) *m,* water lily.
néologisme (neɔlɔʒism) *m,* neologism.
néon (neɔ̃) *m,* neon; neon lighting.
néophyte (neɔfit) *n,* (*Rel.*) neophyte; beginner.
néo-zélandais, e (neɔzelɑ̃dɛ, ɛz) *a,* New Zealand. **N~,** *n,* New Zealander.
népotisme (nepɔtism) *m,* nepotism.
nerf (nɛr & nɛrf) *m,* nerve. *avoir les ~s malades,* to suffer from nerves. *avoir les ~s tendues,* to be on edge. *ça me porte* (*P tape*) *sur les ~s,* that's getting on my nerves. *allons, du ~!* come on, buck up!
nerveux, euse† (nɛrvø, øz) *a,* (*Anat., gen.*) nervous; nerve (*cell*); tense; fidgety; highly-strung; vigorous, energetic. **nervosité** (vozite) *f,* irritability; nervousness. **nervure** (vyr) *f,* (*Arch.*) rib; (*Bot.*) nervure, vein.
net, te (nɛt) *a,* clean (*cloth &c*); neat (*room, work*); clear (*conscience, voice, memory*); (*Phot.*) sharp (*image*); net (*profit, weight*); outright (*refusal*). *~ de,* free of. *mettre au ~,* to make a clean copy of. **net** *ad,* (*speak*) plainly, bluntly; (*refuse*) flatly; (*killed*) outright; (*stop*) dead; (*Com.*) net. **nettement** (tmɑ̃) *ad,* (*gen.*) clearly; (*speak*) frankly, plainly; (*refuse*) flatly; (*appear*) distinctly. **netteté** (nɛtte) *f,* cleanness; clearness; sharpness. **nettoiement** (nɛtwamɑ̃) *m,* cleaning, cleansing. **nettoyage** (jaʒ) *m,* cleaning; (*Mil.*) cleaning up. *~ à sec,* dry cleaning. **nettoyer** (je) *v.t,* to clean; clear (*garden*); (*P*) to bump off *P;* clean out (*ruin*); (*Mil., Police*) clean up. *~ à sec,* to dry-clean.
neuf[1] (nœf) *a. & m,* nine; ninth. *~ fois sur dix,* 9 times out of 10. *for phrases V* **six** *&* **sixième.**
neuf[2], **euve** (nœf, œv) *a,* new; young (*country*); fresh (*idea*). *à l'etat ~,* as good as new. ¶ *m, du ~,* new ideas, developments. *habillé de ~,* dressed in new clothes. *remettre à ~,* to do up like new.
neurasthénie (nørasteni) *f,* depression. **neurasthénique** (nik) *a,* depressed. **neurologiste** (rɔlɔʒist) *n,* neurologist.
neutraliser (nøtralize) *v.t,* to neutralize. **neutralité** (te) *f,* neutrality. **neutre** (nøtr) *a,* neutral; (*Gram., Zool.*) neuter. ¶ *m,* (*Gram.*) neuter; (*Elec.*) neutral; (*Pol.*) neutral country. **neutron** (trɔ̃) *m,* neutron.
neuvième† (nœvjɛm) *a. & n,* ninth.
neveu (nəvø) *m,* nephew.
névralgie (nevralʒi) *f,* neuralgia. **névralgique** (ʒik) *a,* neuralgic. *point ~,* nerve centre. **névrose** (vroz) *f,* neurosis. **névrosé, e** (vroze) *a,* neurotic.
nez (ne) *m,* nose. *baisser le ~,* to look down. *rire au ~ de qn,* to laugh in s.o's face. *parler du ~,* to speak through one's nose. *ça sent le gaz à plein ~,* there's a strong smell of gas. *avoir du ~,* to have flair.

ni (ni) *c*, nor; or. ~ . . . ~ . . . neither . . . nor . . . *~ plus ~ moins*, no more nor less. *~ l'un ~ l'autre*, neither one nor the other.
niais, e† (njɛ, ɛz) *a*, silly; inane (*laugh*). ¶ *n*, simpleton. **niaiserie** (zri) *f*, silliness. *~s*, foolish remarks.
niche (niʃ) *f*, niche; [dog] kennel; trick, prank. **nichée** (ʃe) *f*, brood (*chicks*); litter (*puppies*). **nicher** (ʃe) *v.i*, to nest; (*P*) (*pers.*) to hang out *P*. **se ~**, (*bird*) to nest; (*cottage*) nestle; (*object*) lodge itself, get stuck.
nickel (nikɛl) *m*, nickel. ¶ *a*, (*P*) spick and span. **nickeler** (kle) *v.t*, to nickle-plate.
nicotine (nikɔtin) *f*, nicotine.
nid (ni) *m*, nest; den (*thieves*). (*Naut.*) *~ de pie*, crow's nest. *~ de poule*, pothole.
nièce (njɛs) *f*, niece.
nier (nje) *v.t*, to deny (*avoir fait*, having done); (*Law*) deny the charges.
nigaud, e (nigo, od) *a*, silly. ¶ *n*, *gros ~!* big silly!
nipper *P* (nipe) *v.t*, to tog out *P*. **se ~**, to get all dressed up. **nippes** *P* (nip) *fpl*, old clothes.
nippon, e (nipɔ̃, ɔn) *a*, & **N~**, *n*, Japanese.
nitrate (nitrat) *m*, nitrate. **nitrique** (trik) *a*, nitric. **nitroglycérine** (trɔgliserin) *f*, nitroglycerin[e].
niveau (nivo) *m*, level; (*Sch.*) standard. *de ~ avec, au même ~ que*, level with. *être de, à ~*, to be level. *~ à bulle*, spirit level. *~ de vie*, standard of living. **niveler** (vle) *v.t*, to level; wear away. **nivellement** (vɛlmɑ̃) *m*, levelling.
noble† (nɔbl) *a*, noble. ¶ *n*, noble[man], noblewoman. **noblesse** (blɛs) *f*, nobility.
noce (nɔs) *f*, wedding; w. party. *~s*, wedding. *être de ~*, to be invited to a wedding. *~s d'or*, golden wedding. *faire la ~ P*, to have a wild time. **noceur, euse** (sœr, øz) *n*, reveller.
nocif, ive (nɔsif, iv) *a*, noxious.
noctambule (nɔktɑ̃byl) *n*, night-bird (*pers.*). **nocturne** (tyrn) *a*, nocturnal, night. ¶ *m*, (*Mus.*) nocturne.
Noël (nɔɛl) *m*, Christmas; [Christmas] carol; Christmas present. *à la [fête de] ~, à ~*, at Christmas.
nœud (nø) *m*, knot; bow; (*Phys.*) node; crux (*of problem*). *~s O*, ties (*of friendship*). *~ coulant*, slip knot. *~ papillon*, bow tie.
noir, e (nwar) *a*, black; dark (*hair, eyes*); sunburnt (*skin*); brown (*bread*); black & blue (*bruised*). *~ sur blanc*, (*see sth written*) in black and white. black, coloured (*race, pers.*). *l'Afrique ~e*, black Africa. *il fait nuit ~e*, it's pitch-dark. gloomy; macabre; (*P*) drunk. *marché ~*, black market. *travail ~*, moonlighting. ¶ *m*, black (*colour*); mascara (*make-up*); black mark. *N~*, Black (*pers.*). *en ~*, (*dressed*) in black, in mourning. ¶ *f*, (*Mus.*) crotchet. *N~e*, Black [woman]. **~âtre** (rɑtr) *a*, blackish. **~aud, e** (ro, od) *a*. & *n*, swarthy (man &c). **~ceur** (sœr) *f*, blackness; darkness; black deed. **~cir** (sir) *v.t*, (*gen., fig.*) to blacken; dirty; darken; cover (*paper*) with writing. ¶ *v.i*, (*skin*) to tan; (*colour*) darken. **se ~**, to darken; (*weather*) turn stormy. **~cissement** (sismɑ̃) *m*, blackening; dirtying; darkening. **~cissure** (yr) *f*, smudge.
noise (nwaz) *f*: *chercher ~ à qn*, to pick a quarrel with s.o.
noisetier (nwaztje) *m*, hazel [tree]. **noisette** (zɛt) *f*, hazel nut. ¶ *a.inv*, hazel.
noix (nwɑ) *f*, walnut; nut. *~ de coco*, coconut. *~ de beurre*, knob of butter. *à la ~ P*, rubbishy.
nom (nɔ̃) *m*, name; (*Gram.*) noun. *au ~ de qn*, (*speak*) on s.o's behalf. *au ~ de la loi*, in the name of the law. *petit ~*, first name. *~ de baptême*, Christian name. *~ commun*, common noun. *~ déposé*, [registered] trademark. *~ d'emprunt*, assumed name, alias. *~ de famille*, surname. *~ de guerre*, nom de guerre, assumed name. *~ de jeune fille*, maiden name. *~ propre*, proper noun. *~ de plume*, nom de plume, pen name. *~ de théâtre*, stage n. *~ & prénoms*, full name.
nomade (nɔmad) *a*, nomadic. ¶ *m*, nomad.
nombre (nɔ̃br) *m*, number. *depuis ~ d'années*, for a number of years. *sans ~*, innumerable. *être en ~*, to be in large numbers. *il me compte au ~ de ses amis*, he numbers me among his friends. **nombrer** (nɔ̃bre) *v.t*, to number, count. **nombreux, euse** (brø, øz) *a*, numerous; many; large (*crowd*). *peu ~*, few.
nombril (nɔ̃bri) *m*, navel; belly button *P*.
nomenclature (nɔmɑ̃klatyr) *f*, nomenclature; list. **nominal, e†** (minal) *a*, nominal; (*Gram.*) noun. *liste ~e*, list of names. **nominatif, ive** (tif, iv) *a*, (*Fin.*) registered (*securities*); (*list*) of names. ¶ *m*, (*Gram.*) nominative [case]. **nomination** (sjɔ̃) *f*, nomination; appointment (*à*, to). **nominativement** (tivmɑ̃) *ad*, by name. **nommément** (memɑ̃) *ad*, by name; particularly. **nommer** (me) *v.t*, to name; call; nominate; appoint. **se ~**, to give one's name; be called.
non (nɔ̃) *neg. particle*, no. *certes ~!* certainly not! not. *je crains que ~*, I'm afraid not. *~ [pas] que . . .* not that . . . *c'est vrai ~?* it's true isn't it? *ni moi ~ plus*, nor I either. *~ seulement*, not only. *~ moins connu*, no less famous. ¶ *m*, no; nay; vote against. ¶ *pref* non-, un-. **~-assistance** (nɔ̃asistɑ̃s) *f*, failure to render assistance (*to pers. in danger*). **~-lieu** (ljø) *m*, (*Law*) no case to answer. **~-sens** (sɑ̃s) *m*, nonsense; meaningless word.
nonante (nɔ̃nɑ̃t) *a*, (*Belgian, Swiss*) ninety.
nonce apostolique (nɔ̃s) *m*, papal nuncio.
nonchalamment (nɔ̃ʃalamɑ̃) *ad*, nonchalantly. **nonchalance** (lɑ̃s) *f*, nonchalance. **nonchalant, e** (lɑ̃, ɑ̃t) *a*, nonchalant.

nonobstant (nɔnɔpstɑ̃) *pr,* notwithstanding.
nord (nɔr) *m,* north. *au ~,* (*place*) in the n.; (*travel*) northwards. *au ~ de,* [to the] n. of. *vent du ~,* n. wind. ¶ *a.inv,* north, northern; northward (*direction*). **~-americain, e** &c (amerikɛ̃, ɛn) *a. & n,* North Americain &c. **~-est** (nɔr[d]ɛst) *m. & a.inv,* north-east. **~ique** (dik) *a,* Nordic. ¶ **N~,** *n,* Scandinavian (*pers.*). **~-ouest** (nɔr[d]wɛst) *m. & a.inv,* north-west.
normal, e† (nɔrmal) *a,* normal; standard; usual. *de dimension ~e,* standard-sized. ¶ *f, la ~e,* (*get back to*) normal, normality; (*deviate from*) the norm; (*above*) average. **~isation** (izɑsjɔ̃) *f,* normalization; standardization. **~iser** (ze) *v.t,* to normalize; standardize.
normand, e (nɔrmɑ̃, ɑ̃d) *a,* Norman, *les îles N~es,* the Channel Islands. N~, *n,* Norman. **la Normandie** (mɑ̃di), Normandy.
norme (nɔrm) *f,* norm; (*Tech.*) standard. *dans la ~,* (*stay*) within limits.
Norvège (la) (nɔrvɛʒ), Norway. **norvégien, ne** (veʒjɛ̃, ɛn) *a. &* **N~,** *n,* Norwegian.
nos (no) *possessive a, V* **notre.**
nostalgie (nɔstalʒi) *f,* nostalgia. **nostalgique** (ʒik) *a,* nostalgic.
notabilité (nɔtabilite) *f,* notability. **notable†** (bl) *a. & m,* notable.
notaire (nɔtɛr) *m,* ≏ solicitor; notary.
notamment (nɔtamɑ̃) *ad,* especially, notably.
notation (nɔtasjɔ̃) *f,* notation; (*Sch.*) marking.
note (nɔt) *f,* (*gen., Mus.*) note; (*Sch.*) mark; bill (*restaurant*). *prendre qch en ~,* to make a note of sth. *~ en bas de page,* footnote. *~ de service,* memorandum. (*fig.*) *être dans la ~,* to strike the right note. **noter** (te) *v.t,* to note; n. down; write down; mark (*pupil, with a cross &c*); notice. **notice** (tis) *f,* note; directions (*for use*). **notification** (tifikɑsjɔ̃) *f,* notification. **notifier** (je) *v.t,* to notify.
notion (nosjɔ̃) *f,* notion. *quelques ~s de,* some notion of (*subject*).
notoire† (nɔtwar) *a,* notorious, well known. *il est ~ que,* it is common knowledge that. **notoriété** (tɔrjete) *f,* notoriety. *~ publique,* common knowledge.
notre (nɔtr) *pl.* **nos** (no) *possessive a,* our; our own. *N~ Dame,* Our Lady. *N~ Seigneur,* our Lord. **le nôtre, la ~, les ~s** (notr) *pn,* ours; our own. ¶ *m, nous y avons mis du ~,* we did our bit. *il est des ~s,* he is one of us, our family.
nouer (nwe) *v.t,* to tie; knot; tie up (*parcel*); form (*alliance*); strike up (*conversation*). **se ~,** (*hands*) to join together; (*alliance*) be formed. **noueux, euse** (nuø, øz) *a,* gnarled.
nougat (nugɑ) *m,* nougat. *~s P,* feet. *c'est du ~ P,* it's a cinch *P.*
nouille (nuj) *f, ~s,* noodles, pasta. (*P*) noodle *P,* idiot; drip *P.*
nounou *P* (nunu) *f,* nanny.
nourri, e (nuri) *a,* fed. *bien ~,* well-fed. *mal ~,* under-fed, under-nourished. (*Mil.*) heavy (*fire*); lively (*conversation*). **~ce** (ris) *f,* [wet] nurse; child-minder; jerrycan. **nourrir** (rir) *v.t,* to feed; nurse (*project*); cherish, nourish (*hopes*); (*industry*) provide a living *or* work for. *~ au sein,* to breast-feed. ¶ *v.i,* to be nourishing. **se ~,** to eat. *se ~ de* to eat (*food*); feed on (*illusions*). **~ssant, e** (sɑ̃, ɑ̃t) *a,* nourishing, nutritious. **~sson** (sɔ̃) *m,* infant. **~ture** (tyr) *f,* food; diet.
nous (nu) *pn,* we; us; to us; ourselves; each other. *il ~ appelle,* he's calling us. *il ~ parle,* he's talking to us. *cette voiture est à ~,* this car is ours. *~ ~ sommes amusés,* we enjoyed ourselves. *~ ~ sommes aidés,* we helped each other. *~-mêmes,* ourselves.
nouveau, elle (el, *m, before vowel or mute h*) (nuvo, ɛl) *a,* (*gen.*) new; novel (*idea*); up-to-date (*method*); fresh (*evidence*); recent, latest (*book*); further (*development*). ¶ *ad,* newly (*wed*). ¶ *n,* new man, woman; (*Sch.*) new boy, girl. ¶ *m, du ~,* fresh, new development, idea. *faire qch de ~, à ~,* to do sth again. *Nouvel An,* New Year. *N~ Monde,* New World. *~-né, e, a. & n,* new-born (*child*). *~ venu, nouvelle venue,* new-comer. **Nouvelle-Zélande (la)** (zelɑ̃d), New Zealand. **~té** (te) *f,* novelty; new thing, book, play &c; innovation; (*pl.*) new styles, latest fashions.
nouvelle (nuvɛl) *f,* [piece of] news; short story. *avez-vous de ses ~s?* have you heard from him? (*Press*) *voici les ~s,* here is the news.
nouvellement (nuvɛlmɑ̃) *ad,* newly, recently.
novateur, trice (nɔvatœr, tris) *n,* innovator.
novembre (nɔvɑ̃br) *m,* November.
novice (nɔvis) *n,* (*Rel., gen.*) novice; beginner. ¶ *a,* inexperienced (*dans,* in); green.
noyade (nwajad) *f,* drowning (*fatality*).
noyau (nwajo) *m,* stone (*fruit*); (*Sci.*) nucleus; [close-knit] group, circle. *~ de résistance,* centre of resistance.
noyé, e (nwaje) *a,* drowned; shrouded (*in darkness*); lost (*in a crowd*); (*fig.*) out of one's depth; bogged down (*with paperwork*). ¶ *n,* drowned man, woman. **noyer** (je) *v.t,* to drown; flood (*engine, land*); swamp. **se ~,** to drown; drown o.s; (*fig.*) become bogged down.
noyer (nwaje) *m,* walnut [tree, wood].
nu, e (ny) *a,* naked, nude; bare (*room*); plain (*truth*). *se mettre ~,* to strip [off]. *mettre à ~,* to lay bare (*soul*); (*Elec.*) strip (*cable*). *à l'œil ~,* with the naked eye. *~ comme un ver,* stark naked. *~-pieds, inv.* ou *pieds ~s,* barefoot[ed]. *~-tête, inv.* ou *tête ~e,* bareheaded. ¶ *m,* nude. **~-pieds** (pje) *m.pl,* flip-flops.
nuage (nyaʒ) *m,* cloud; drop (*milk*). *sans ~s,*

cloudless (*sky*); unmarred (*happiness*). **nuageux, euse** (ʒø, øz) *a*, cloudy, overcast.
nuance (nyɑ̃s) *f*, shade (*colour*); nuance (*meaning*); slight difference. *tout en ~s*, subtle. *sans ~*, unsubtle. **nuancer** (ɑ̃se) *v.t*, to qualify (*opinion*).
nucléaire (nykleɛr) *a*, nuclear.
nudisme (nydism) *m*, nudism. **nudiste** (st) *a. & n*, nudist. **nudité** (ite) *f*, nudity, nakedness (*pers.*); bareness (*room*).
nuée (nye) *f*, (*liter.*) cloud; (*fig.*) host; swarm. **nues** (ny) *f.pl*, *porter qn aux ~*, to praise s.o to the skies. *tomber des ~*, to be taken aback.
nuire (nɥir) *v.i.ir*, *~ à*, to harm, injure; prejudice (*outcome*). **se ~**, to do o.s harm; harm each other. **nuisible** (nɥizibl) *a*, harmful, hurtful, injurious. *animaux ~s*, pests.
nuit (nɥi) *f*, night; darkness. *la ~*, (*open*) at night. *de ~*, night (*service*); (*drive*) at night. *cette ~*, tonight; last night. *dans la ~ de mardi*, during Tuesday n. *~ blanche*, sleepless n. *à la ~ tombante*, at nightfall. *il fait ~ noire*, it's pitch dark.
nul, le (nyl) *a*, no; not any. *je n'ai ~ besoin de*, I have no need to (*do*), of (*help*). *~ autre*, no one else. *~ le part*, nowhere. nil; null and void; non-existent (*crop*); (*Sport*) draw; nil draw. *~ et non avenu*, null and void. worthless; useless. *~ en chimie*, useless at chemistry. **nul,** *pn*, no one, none. **nullement** (lmɑ̃) *ad*, not at all. **nullité** (lite) *f*, nullity; uselessness; nonentity (*pers.*).
nûment (nymɑ̃) *ad*, openly, frankly.
numéraire (nymerɛr) *m*, cash. **numéral, e** (ral) *a*, numeral. **numérique†** (rik) *a*, numerical. **numéro** (ro) *m*, number; (*Press*) issue; (*Theat.*) number; act. *composer un ~*, to dial a number. *~ minéralogique*, registration n. (*car*). *c'est un drôle de ~! P* he's a real character! *P*. **numérotage** (rɔtaʒ) *m*, numbering. **numéroter** (te) *v.t*, to number.
nuptial, e (nypsjal) *a*, nuptial, wedding.
nuque (nyk) *f*, nape [of the neck].
nutritif, ive (nytritif, iv) *a*, nutritive; nutritious; food (*value*). **nutrition** (sjɔ̃) *f*, nutrition.
nylon (nilɔ̃) *m*, nylon.
nymphe (nɛ̃f) *f*, nymph.

O

O, o (o) *m*, *letter*, O, o.
oasis (oazis) *f*, (*lit., fig.*) oasis.
obéir (ɔbeir) *v.i*, *~ à*, to obey; comply with; (*boat &c*) respond to. **obéissance** (isɑ̃s) *f*, obedience. **obéissant, e** (sɑ̃, ɑ̃t) *a*, obedient.
obélisque (ɔbelisk) *m*, obelisk.
obèse (ɔbɛz) *a*, obese. **obésité** (bezite) *f*, obesity.
objecter (ɔbʒɛkte) *v.t*, to object (*que*, that); o. to; plead (*tiredness &c*). **objecteur [de conscience]**, *m*, conscientious objector. **objectif, ive†** (tif, iv) *a. & m*, objective (*Philos.*). ¶ *m*, objective, aim; objective, lens (*camera*). **objection** (ksjɔ̃) *f*, objection. **objet** (ʒɛ) *m*, object; subject (*discussion, enquiry*). *~ d'art*, objet d'art.
obligation (ɔbligasjɔ̃) *f*, obligation; bond; debenture. *avoir l'~ de*, to be under the obligation to. **obligatoire** (twar) *a*, obligatory, compulsory; (*P*) inevitable. **obligé, e** (ʒe) *a*, obliged; indebted; (*P*) inevitable; (*Mus.*) obbligato. ¶ *n*, debtor. **obligeamment** (ʒamɑ̃) *ad*, obligingly. **obligeant, e** (ʒɑ̃, ɑ̃t) *a*, obliging, kind. **obliger** (ʒe) *v.t*, to oblige, require, compel (*qn à faire*, s.o to do). *être obligé*, to be obliged (*de faire*, to do).
oblique† (ɔblik) *a*, oblique; side[long] (*glance*). ¶ *f*, (*Math.*) oblique line. **obliquer** (ke) *v.i*, to turn off (*road &c*).
oblitérer (ɔblitere) *v.t*, to obliterate; cancel.
oblong, ongue (ɔblɔ̃, ɔ̃g) *a*, oblong.
obnubiler (ɔbnybile) *v.t*, to obsess.
obole (ɔbɔl) *f*, offering, mite.
obscène (ɔpsɛn) *a*, obscene. **obscénité** (senite) *f*, obscenity.
obscur, e (ɔpskyr) *a*, dark; dim, murky; obscure. **obscurcir** (skyrsir) *v.t*, to darken, obscure. **s'~**, to grow dark &c; become obscure; (*mystery*) deepen. **obscurément** (remɑ̃) *ad*, obscurely. **obscurité** (rite) *f*, dark[ness], obscurity.
obsédant, e (ɔpsedɑ̃, ɑ̃t) *a*, obsessive; haunting. **obsédé, e** (sede) *n*, fanatic. *~ [sexuel]*, sex maniac. **obséder** (sede) *v.t*, obsess, haunt.
obsèques (ɔpsɛk) *f.pl*, obsequies. **obséquieux, euse†** (sekjø, øz) *a*, obsequious. **obséquiosité** (kjozite) *f*, obsequiousness.
observance (ɔpsɛrvɑ̃s) *f*, observance. **observateur, trice** (vatœr, tris) *n*, observer. ¶ *a*, observant. **observation** (sjɔ̃) *f*, observance; observation; remark; objection; reproof. **observatoire** (twar) *m*, observatory; (*Mil.*) observation post. **observer** (ve) *v.t*, to observe; watch; spot; examine (*microscope*); keep (*rule, feast*). **s'~**, keep a check on o.s.
obsession (ɔpsɛsjɔ̃) *f*, obsession.
obstacle (ɔpstakl) *m*, obstacle; fence, jump

(*horse*). *faire* ~ *à,* to stand in the way of; block, hinder.
obstétrique (ɔpstetrik) *f,* obstetrics.
obstination (ɔpstinasjɔ̃) *f,* obstinacy, stubbornness. **obstiné†, e** (ne) *a,* obstinate; persistent. **obstiner (s')** (ne) *v.pr,* to persist (*à faire,* in doing); insist, dig one's heels in.
obstruction (ɔpstryksjɔ̃) *f,* obstruction; stoppage. **obstruer** (strye) *v.t,* to obstruct; block.
obtempérer à (ɔptɑ̃pere), to obey.
obtenir (ɔptənir) *v.t.ir,* to obtain, secure, get; reach, arrive at (*total*); achieve (*result*). *j'ai obtenu de la voir,* I managed to see her.
obturateur (ɔptyratœr) *m,* obturator; (*Phot.*) shutter. **obturer** (re) *v.t,* to seal; fill (*tooth*).
obtus, e (ɔpty, yz) *a,* obtuse.
obus (obys) *m,* (*Artil*) shell.
obvier à (ɔbvje), to obviate, prevent.
occasion (ɔkazjɔ̃) *f,* chance; opportunity, opening; occasion; bargain. *d'*~, second-hand, used. **occasionnel, le** (ɔnɛl) *a,* occasional; chance; casual (*customer*). **occasionnellement** (lmɑ̃) *ad,* occasionally. **occasionner** (ne) *v.t,* to bring about, cause.
occident (ɔksidɑ̃) *m,* west. **occidental, e** (tal) *a,* west[ern].
occulte (ɔkylt) *a,* occult.
occupant, e (ɔkypɑ̃, ɑ̃t) *a,* (*Mil.*) occupying. ¶ *n,* occupant, occupier. **occupation** (pasjɔ̃) *f,* (*gen.*) occupation; occupancy (*dwelling*); job. **occupé, e** (pe) *a,* busy; (*toilets, telephone*) engaged; (*places &c*) taken, occupied. **occuper** (pe) *v.t,* to occupy; live in (*dwelling*); hold (*job*); employ (*work-force*). **s'~ à,** to busy o.s with. **s'~ de,** to attend to, see to; look after (*children*); deal with; take an interest in. *occupe-toi de tes affaires P,* mind your own business.
occurrence (ɔkyrɑ̃s) *f,* occurrence; instance, case.
océan (ɔseɑ̃) *m,* ocean; (*fig.*) sea. **l'Océanie** (ani) *f,* Oceania. **océanique** (anik) *a,* oceanic.
ocre (ɔkr) *f,* ochre.
octane (ɔktan) *m,* octane.
octante (ɔktɑ̃t) *a.inv,* (*Dialect*) eighty. **octave** (ɔktav) *f,* octave. **octobre** (tɔbr) *m,* October. **octogénaire** (ʒenɛr) *a. & n,* octogenarian. **octogone** (gɔn) *a,* octagonal. ¶ *m,* octagon.
octroi (ɔktrwa) *m,* octroi (*duty on goods entering town*). **octroyer** (trwaje) *v.t,* to grant.
oculaire (ɔkylɛr) *a,* ocular. **oculiste** (list) *m,* oculist, eye specialist.
ode (ɔd) *f,* ode.
odeur (odœr) *f,* odour, smell, scent. *en ~ de sainteté,* in favour (*auprès de,* with).
odieux, euse† (ɔdjø, øz) *a,* odious, heinous; obnoxious; unbearable.
odorant, e (ɔdɔrɑ̃, ɑ̃t) & **odoriférant, e** (riferɑ̃, ɑ̃t) *a,* fragrant, [sweet-]scented. **odorat** (ra) *m,* [sense of] smell.
odyssée (ɔdise) *f,* Odyssey.
œil (œj) *m,* (*Anat. & gen.*) eye; look; (*Bot.*) bud; (*Typ.*) face. *avoir l'*~, to have sharp eyes. *à l'~ P,* for nothing. *risquer un* ~, take a peep, quick look. **œillade** (jad) *f,* wink. *faire des ~s à,* make eyes at. **œillères** (jɛr) *f.pl,* blinkers. **œillet** (jɛ) *m,* eyelet; (*Bot.*) carnation. ~ *d'Inde,* marigold. ~[*mignardise*], pink.
œsophage (ezɔfaʒ) *m,* oesophagus.
œuf (œf) *m,* egg. ~ *à la coque,* boiled egg. ~ *de Pâques,* Easter egg.
œuvre (œvr) *f,* work; (*col.*) works; undertaking, task; deed; (*pl.*) charitable works. ~ [*de bienfaisance*], charity, charitable organisation. *mettre en* ~, to implement. ¶ *m,* works (*of an artist*).
offensant, e (ɔfɑ̃sɑ̃, ɑ̃t) *a,* offensive, insulting. **offense** (fɑ̃s) *f,* offence; insult; (*Rel.*) trespass. **offensé, e** (fɑ̃se) *n,* injured party. **offenser** (se) *v.t,* to offend [against]. **s'~,** to take offence. **offenseur** (sœr) *m,* offender. **offensif, ive†** (sif, iv) *a. & f,* (*Mil., Pol.*). offensive.
office (ɔfis) *m,* (*Adm.*) office; function; duties; agency, bureau; [church] service; worship. *d'*~, official[ly]; as a matter of course. ¶ *f,* pantry. **officiel, le†** (sjɛl) *a,* official. ¶ *m,* (*Sport &c*) official. **officier** (sje) *v.i,* (*Eccl.*) to officiate. ¶ *m,* officer. ~ *de l'état civil,* registrar (*births &c.*). ~ *de marine,* naval officer. ~ *ministériel,* member of the legal profession. **officieux, euse†** (sjø, øz) *a,* unofficial.
offrande (ɔfrɑ̃d) *f,* offering. **le plus offrant** (frɑ̃), the highest bidder. **offre** (fr) *f,* offer; tender; bid. ~ *d'emploi,* situation vacant. *l'~ & la demande,* supply & demand. **offrir** (frir) *v.t.ir,* give, buy (*gift*); offer, tender; offer up; present; provide (*example, explanation*). *c'est pour ~?* is it for a present?
offusquer (ɔfyske) *v.t,* to offend. **s'~,** to take offence.
ogive (ɔʒiv) *f,* (*Arch.*) rib; nose cone (*rocket*). ~ *nucléaire,* nuclear warhead.
ogre, ogresse (ɔgr, grɛs) *n,* ogre, ogress.
oie (wɑ) *f,* goose.
oignon (ɔɲɔ̃) *m,* onion; (*Bot.*) bulb; bunion. *occupe-toi de tes ~s P,* mind your own business.
oindre (wɛ̃dr) *v.t.ir,* to anoint.
oiseau (wazo) *m,* bird. *drôle d'~ P,* queer fish *P. trouver l'~ rare,* to find the man (*or* woman) in a million. ~ *de mauvais augure,* bird of ill omen. ~*-mouche, m,* humming bird. **oiseleur** (zlœr) *m,* bird catcher. **oiselier, ère** (zəlje, ɛr) *n,* bird-seller. **oisellerie** (zɛlri) *f,* birdshop, b. selling.
oiseux, euse (wazø, øz) *a,* pointless, trifling (*words &c*). **oisif, ive†** (zif, iv) *a,* idle (*pers., money*).
oisillon (wazijɔ̃) *m,* fledgeling.

oisiveté (wazivte) *f,* idleness.
oison (wazɔ̃) *m,* gosling.
oléagineux, euse (ɔleaʒinø, øz) *a,* oleaginous. ¶ *m,* oleaginous plant.
oléoduc (ɔleɔdyk) *m,* oil pipeline.
oligarchie (ɔligarʃi) *f,* oligarchy.
olivâtre (ɔlivatr) *a,* olive-greenish; sallow (*complexion*). **olive** (liv) *f,* olive. ¶ *a,* olive[-green]. **oliveraie** (livrɛ) *f,* o. grove. **olivier** (livje) *m,* o. [tree]; o. [wood].
olympique (ɔlɛ̃pik) *a,* Olympic.
ombilic (ɔ̃bilik) *m,* umbilicus; navel.
ombrage (ɔ̃braʒ) *m,* [spread of] foliage; shade; umbrage. **ombragé, e** (braʒe) *a,* shady. **ombrager** (ʒe) *v.t,* to shade. **ombrageux, euse** (ʒø, øz) *a,* touchy; skittish (*beast*). **ombre** (ɔ̃br) *f,* shade; shadow; ghost; darkness; (*fig.*) obscurity, dark. *une ~ au tableau,* a fly in the ointment. *~s chinoises,* shadowgraph, s. show. *~ portée,* shadow. ¶ *m,* (*fish*), grayling. **ombrelle** (ɔbrɛl) *f,* sunshade, parasol. **ombrer** (bre) *v.t,* (*Art*) to shade. **ombreux, euse** (brø, øz) *a,* (*Poet.*) shady.
omelette (ɔmlɛt) *f,* omelet[te].
omettre (ɔmɛtr) *v.t.ir,* to omit, leave out. **omission** (misjɔ̃) *f,* omission.
omnibus (ɔmnibys) *m,* slow train; (*O*) omnibus.
omnipotence (ɔmnipɔtɑ̃s) *f,* omnipotence. **omnipotent, e** (tɑ̃, ɑ̃t) *a,* omnipotent.
omniscience (ɔmnisjɑ̃s) *f,* omniscience. **omniscient, e** (jɑ̃, ɑ̃t) *a,* omniscient.
omnivore (ɔmnivɔr) *a,* omnivorous.
omoplate (ɔmɔplat) *f,* shoulder blade.
on (ɔ̃) *pn,* one, you, we; they, people; someone; (*P*) we. *Also used for passive & indeterminate phrases. ~ demande*... wanted... (*advertisement*). *~ dit, ~ prétend,* it is said, they say. *~ y va?* let's go. **~-dit,** (ɔ̃di) *m,* rumour.
once (ɔ̃s) *f,* ounce.
oncle (ɔ̃kl) *m,* uncle.
onctueux, euse† (ɔ̃ktyø, øz) *a,* creamy; (*fig.*) unctuous, smooth. **onctuosité** (tyozite) *f,* smoothness, unctuousness; creaminess.
onde (ɔ̃d) *f,* wave; (*Poet.*) sea, main. **ondée** (de) *f,* heavy shower. **ondulation** (dylasjɔ̃) *f,* undulation; (*pl: hair*) waves. **ondulé, e** (le) *a,* undulating, wavy. **onduler** (le) *v.i,* to undulate; wave; (*hair*) be wavy. **onduleux, euse** (lø, løz) *a,* undulating; wavy; swaying (*walk*).
onéreux, euse (ɔnerø, øz) *a,* costly.
ongle (ɔ̃gl) *m,* [finger] nail; claw (*animal*). *~ de pied,* toenail.
onomatopée (ɔnɔmatɔpe) *f,* onomatopoeia.
onyx (ɔniks) *m,* onyx.
onze (ɔ̃z) *a. & m,* eleven; eleventh. *for phrases V* **six** *&* **sixième. onzième**† (ɔ̃zjɛm) *a. & n,* eleventh. (*Note.—Say* le onze, le onzième, *not* l'onze, l'onzième.).
opacité (ɔpasite) *f,* opacity; impenetrability.
opale (ɔpal) *f,* opal.
opaque (ɔpak) *a,* opaque; (*darkness &c*) impenetrable.
opéra (ɔpera) *m,* opera; o. [house]. *~ bouffe,* comic opera. *~-comique,* light opera, opéra comique.
opérateur, trice (ɔperatœr, tris) *n,* operator; camera man (*film*). **opération** (sjɔ̃) *f,* (*gen., Med., Math., Mil.*) operation; (*Com.*) deal; (*pl.*) dealings; (*Tech.*) process, operation. **opéré, e** (re) *n,* (*Med.*) patient. **opérer** (re) *v.t,* (*Surg.*) to operate on (*de,* for); remove (*tumour &c*); carry out, implement (*reform &c*); make (*choice*); work (*wonder &c*); bring about (*change*). ¶ *v.i,* to work, take effect; proceed.
opérette (ɔperɛt) *f,* operetta, light opera.
ophtalmique (ɔftalmik) *a,* ophthalmic. **ophtalmologie** (ɔlɔʒi) *f,* ophthalmology. **ophtalmologiste** (ɔlɔʒist) *n,* ophthalmologist.
opiner (ɔpine) *v.i,* to opine; vote. *~ de la tête,* nod assent. *~ du bonnet,* to be in agreement with everything said. **opiniâtre**† (njɑtr) *a. & n,* self-willed; obstinate, stubborn (person); (*hate &c*) unrelenting. **opiniâtrer (s')** (ɑtre) *v.pr,* to persist. **opiniâtreté** (trəte) *f,* obstinacy, &c. **opinion** (njɔ̃) *f,* opinion; view.
opium (ɔpjɔm) *m,* opium.
opportun, e (ɔpɔrtœ̃, yn) *a,* opportune, timely, well-timed. **opportunément** (tynemɑ̃) *ad,* opportunely. **opportunisme** (nism) *m,* opportunism. **opportuniste** (nist) *n,* opportunist. **opportunité** (te) *f,* opportuneness.
opposant, e (ɔpozɑ̃, ɑ̃t) *n,* opponent. ¶ *a,* opposing. **opposé, e** (ze) *a,* opposite; opposing (*team*); contrasting; conflicting. ¶ *m,* opposite, reverse, contrary. *à l'~,* the other way, on the other side. **opposer** (ze) *v.t,* to bring together (*teams &c*); bring into conflict (*rivals &c*); contrast (*à,* with); put forward (*argument*); put up (*resistance*). **s'~,** to confront each other; conflict; clash; contrast. *s'~ à,* rebel against; oppose. **opposition** (sjɔ̃) *f,* opposition; contrast; conflict. *mettre ~ à,* to oppose (*decision*); stop (*cheque*). *mettre en ~,* to contrast, oppose. *par ~ à,* as opposed to; in contrast with.
oppresser (ɔprɛse) *v.t,* to oppress; (*clothes*) suffocate. **oppressant, e** (sɑ̃, ɑ̃t) *a,* oppressive. **oppresseur** (sœr) *m,* oppressor. **oppressif, ive** (sif, iv) *a,* oppressive. **oppression** (sjɔ̃) *f,* oppression. **opprimer** (prime) *v.t,* to oppress; suppress; stifle; suffocate.
opprobre (ɔprɔbr) *m,* disgrace, opprobrium.
opter (ɔpte) *v.i,* to choose. *~ pour,* opt for.
opticien, ne (ɔptisjɛ̃) *n,* optician.
optimisme (ɔptimism) *m,* optimism. **optimiste** (mist) *a,* optimistic. ¶ *n,* optimist.
optimum (ɔptimɔm) *a,* optimum, optimal. ¶ *n,* optimum.

option (ɔpsjɔ̃) *f,* option.
optique (ɔptik) *a,* optic; optical. ¶ *f,* optics; perspective, viewpoint.
opulence (ɔpylɑ̃s) *f,* opulence, affluence, wealth. **opulent, e** (lɑ̃, ɑ̃t) *a,* opulent, &c.
opuscule (ɔpyskyl) *m,* opuscule.
or[1] (ɔr) *c,* now. ~ *ça,* now then.
or[2] (ɔr) *m,* gold. *ni pour ~ ni pour argent,* for love or money. *d'~, en ~,* gold; golden.
oracle (ɔrakl) *m,* oracle.
orage (ɔraʒ) *m,* thunderstorm; storm. **orageux, euse†** (raʒø, øz) *a,* stormy; thundery.
oraison (ɔrɛzɔ̃) *f,* prayer. ~ *dominicale,* Lord's prayer. ~ *funèbre,* funeral oration.
oral, e† (ɔral) *a. & m,* oral, viva [voce].
orange (ɔrɑ̃ʒ) *f,* orange. ~ *amère,* Seville o. ~ *sanguine,* blood o. **orange,** *m. & a. &* **orangé, e** (rɑ̃ʒe) *a. & m,* orange (*colour*). **orangeade** (ʒad) *f,* orangeade. **oranger** (ʒe) *m,* orange [tree]. **orangerie** (ʒri) *f,* orangery.
orang-outang (ɔrɑ̃utɑ̃) *m,* orang-outang.
orateur (ɔratœr) *m,* orator, speaker. **oratoire** (twar) *a,* oratorical. *l'art ~,* oratory. ¶ *m,* oratory (*chapel*). **oratorio** (tɔrjo) *m,* oratorio.
orbite (ɔrbit) *f,* orbit; socket (*eye*); sphere of influence. *mettre sur ~,* to launch, put into orbit.
Orcades (les) (ɔrkad) *f.pl,* the Orkneys.
orchestral, e (ɔrkɛstral) *a,* orchestral. **orchestre** (tr) *m,* orchestra, band; (*Theat.*) stalls. **orchestration** (trasjɔ̃) *f,* orchestration; organization. **orchestrer** (tre) *v.t,* to orchestrate, score; organize.
orchidée (ɔrkide) *f,* orchid.
ordinaire† (ɔrdinɛr) *a,* ordinary; common; customary; usual, everyday. ¶ *m,* ordinary; (*food*) everyday fare.
ordinal (ɔrdinal) *a. & m,* ordinal [number].
ordinateur (ɔrdinatœr) *m,* computer. *mettre sur ~,* to computerize.
ordonnance (ɔrdɔnɑ̃s) *f,* (*Med.*) prescription; (*Law*) order; ruling; organization, layout, plan. ¶ *f. or m,* orderly, batman. **ordonné, e** (ne) *a,* (*pers., place*) tidy, orderly; methodical; (*life*) well-ordered. ¶ *f,* ordinate. **ordonner** (ne) *v.t,* to order (*à qn de faire,* s.o to do). ~ *le silence à qn,* order s.o to be quiet. organize; prescribe; ordain. **ordre** (dr) *m,* (*gen.*) order; command. *à l'~ de,* payable to. *à vos ~s!* yes sir! *dans le même ~ d'idées,* similarly. *de dernier ~,* third-rate. *de premier ~,* first-rate. *en ~,* tidy, in order. *l'~ du jour,* (*Mil.*) the order of the day; (*gen.*) the agenda. *cité à l'~ du jour,* mentioned in dispatches. *l'~ public,* law & order. *sans ~,* untidy, disorderly.
ordure (ɔrdyr) *f,* filth, dirt, muck; rubbish; (*fig.*) smut, filth; (*pej: pers.*) swine *P;* (*pl.*) refuse, rubbish; dirt; obscenities, filth. **ordurier, ère** (dyrje, ɛr) *a,* filthy; smutty.
orée (ɔre) *f,* edge (*of a wood*).
oreille (ɔrɛj) *f,* ear; hearing; wing (*nut, chair*); handle (*tureen*). *avoir de l'~,* to have a good ear (*for music*). *avoir l'~ dure,* be hard of hearing. *avoir les ~s rebattus de qch,* be sick of hearing sth. *l'~ basse,* crestfallen. *tirer les ~s à qn,* (*lit.*) tweak s.o's ears; (*fig.*) tell s.o off. **oreiller** (rɛje) *m,* pillow. **oreillette** (jɛt) *f,* auricle (*heart*); ear-flap. **oreillons** (jɔ̃) *m.pl,* mumps.
ores (ɔr) *ad: d'~ & déjà,* already.
orfèvre (ɔrfɛvr) *m,* goldsmith &/*or* silversmith. **orfèvrerie** (fɛvrəri) *f,* gold[smith's] &/*or* silver[smith's] work *or* shop.
organe (ɔrgan) *m,* organ; spokesman; (*pl, Mach.*) parts, gear. **organigramme** (igram) *m,* organization chart; flow chart. **organique** (nik) *a,* organic. **organisateur, trice** (zatœr, tris) *n,* organizer. ¶ *a,* organizing. **organisation** (zasjɔ̃) *f,* organization. **organiser** (ze) *v.t,* to organize, arrange. **organisme** (nism) *m,* organism. **organiste** (nist) *n,* (*Mus.*) organist.
orge (ɔrʒ) *f,* barley. **orgelet** (ʒəlɛ) *m,* sty[e] (*eye*).
orgie (ɔrʒi) *f,* orgy; (*fig.*) riot.
orgue (ɔrg) *m, the pl. is f,* organ; o. loft. ~ *de Barbarie,* barrel organ.
orgueil (ɔrgœj) *m,* pride. **orgueilleux, euse†** (gœjø, øz) *a,* proud.
orient (ɔrjɑ̃) *m,* orient, east. **l'O~** (*Geog.*), the Orient, the East. **orientable** (tabl) *a,* adjustable. **oriental, e** (tal) *a,* oriental, eastern. **O~,** *n,* Oriental. **orientation** (tasjɔ̃) *f,* positioning, adjustment; orientation, directing; aspect; direction; trends; leanings, tendencies. *l'~ professionnelle,* careers advising. **orienter** (te) *v.t,* to orient[ate]; direct, point; adjust, position. **s'~,** to find one's bearings. ~ *vers,* turn *or* move towards.
orifice (ɔrifis) *m,* opening; orifice; mouth (*pipe &c*).
originaire† (ɔriʒinɛr) *a,* original. *être ~ de,* to come from, be a native of. **original, e†** (nal) *a,* original; odd, eccentric. ¶ *n,* eccentric. ¶ *m,* original; top copy (*typing*). **originalité** (lite) *f,* originality; eccentricity, oddness. **origine** (ʒin) *f,* origin; beginning, outset. **d'~,** (*tyres*) original; (*country*) of origin. **originel, le†** (nɛl) *a,* original.
oripeaux (ɔripo) *m.pl,* rags.
orme (ɔrm) *m,* elm [tree].
orné, e (ɔrne) *a,* ornate. **ornement** (mɑ̃) *m,* ornament; embellishment, adornment. *sans ~s,* unadorned. **ornemental, e** (tal) *a,* ornamental. **ornementation** (tasjɔ̃) *f,* ornamentation. **orner** (ne) *v.t,* to decorate, adorn, embellish.
ornière (ɔrnjɛr) *f,* rut. *être sorti de l'~,* to be out of the wood.
ornithologie (ɔrnitɔlɔʒi) *f,* ornithology. **ornithologique** (ʒik) *a,* ornithological. **ornithologiste**

(ʒist) *ou* **ornithologue** (lɔg) *n*, ornithologist.
orphelin, e (ɔrfəlɛ̃, in) *n. & a*, orphan. ~ *de père*, fatherless. **orphelinat** (lina) *m*, orphanage; children of an o.
orteil (ɔrtɛj) *m*, toe.
orthodoxe (ɔrtɔdɔks) *a. & n*, orthodox. **orthodoxie** (ksi) *f*, orthodoxy. **orthographe** (graf) *f*, orthography, spelling. **orthographier** (fje) *v.t*, to spell. *mal* ~, to misspell. **orthographique** (fik) *a*, orthographic(al); spelling. **orthopédie** (pedi) *f*, orthopaedics. **orthopédique** (dik) *a*, orthopaedic.
ortie (ɔrti) *f*, [stinging] nettle. ~ *blanche*, white dead-nettle.
orvet (ɔrvɛ) *m*, slow-worm.
os (ɔs, *pl.* o) *m*, bone. ~ *à moelle*, marrow b. *tomber sur un* ~, to hit a snag *P*.
osciller (ɔsile) *v.i*, to oscillate, swing, sway about; fluctuate; waver. **oscillation** (lasjɔ̃) *f*, oscillation, &c.
osé, e (oze) *a*, daring, bold.
oseille (ozɛj) *f*, sorrel; (*P: money*) dough *P*.
oser (oze) *v.t*, to dare (*faire*, to do).
osier (ozje) *m*, (*Bot.*) willow; wicker.
ossature (ɔsatyr) *f*, frame[work]. **osselet** (slɛ) *m*, ossicle; (*pl.*) knuckle bones. **ossements** (smɑ̃) *m.pl*, bones (*dead*). **osseux, euse** (sø, øz) *a*, bony, osseous.
ostensible† (ɔstɑ̃sibl) *a*, conspicuous. **ostentatoire** (twar) *a*, ostentatious. **ostentation** (sjɔ̃) *f*, ostentation.
ostraciser (ɔstrasize) *v.t*, to ostracize. **ostracisme** (sism) *m*, ostracism.
otage (ɔtaʒ) *m*, hostage.
otarie (ɔtari) *f*, sea lion.
ôter (ote) *v.t*, to remove, take away (*à qn*, from s.o); t. off; pull off (*clothes*). **s'**~, to get out (*of way &c*).
otite (ɔtit) *f*, ear infection.
oto-rhino-laryngologiste (ɔtɔrinɔlarɛ̃gɔlɔʒist) *n*, ear, nose & throat specialist.
ou (u) *c*, or, either. ~ *bien*, or [else].
où (u) *ad. & pn*, where; when; in, on, from &c which. *par* ~, which way; through which. ~ *voulez-vous en venir?* what are you getting at?
ouailles (wɑj) *f.pl*, (*liter.*) flock (*Christians*).
ouate (wat) *f*, cotton wool; padding. **ouaté** (te) *a*, quilted; padded; muffled (*sound*).
oubli (ubli) *m*, forgetfulness; oblivion; oversight, omission; lapse of memory. **oublier** (blie) *v.t. & i*, to forget (*de faire* to do); f. about; miss, leave out, omit.
ouest (wɛst) *m*, west. *à l'* ~, in the w.; to the w., westwards. ¶ *a*, west, western; westerly, westward. ~*-allemand*, West German. *l'O* ~ (*Pol.*), the West.
ouf (uf) *i*, oh!, what a relief!
oui (wi) (*particle*), yes. *je pense que* ~, I think so. ¶ *m*, (*le* ~, *un* ~) yes, aye. *pour un* ~ *ou pour un non*, at the drop of a hat.
ouï-dire (widir) *m*, hearsay. **ouïe** (wi) *f*, hearing; (*pl: Mus.*) sound holes; gills (*fish*). **ouïr** (wir) *v.t.ir*, (*liter., Law*) to hear.
ouragan (uragɑ̃) *m*, hurricane.
ourler (urle) *v.t*, to hem. **ourlet** (lɛ) *m*, hem; rim.
ours (urs) *m*, bear. ~ *blanc*, polar b. ~ [*en peluche*], teddy b. ~ *mal léché*, lout. **ourse** (urs) *f*, [she-] bear; (*Astr.*) Bear. **oursin** (sɛ̃) *m*, sea urchin. **ourson** (sɔ̃) *m*, bear cub.
outil (uti) *m*, tool; (*Agr.*) implement. **outillage** (tijaʒ) *m*, [set of] tools; machinery; equipment. **outiller** (je) *v.t*, to equip, fit out.
outrage (utraʒ) *m*, insult. *faire* ~ *à*, to insult, offend; outrage. ~ *à magistrat*, contempt of court. ~ *à la pudeur*, indecent behaviour. **outragé, e** (ʒe) *a*, gravely offended. **outrageant, e** (traʒɑ̃, ɑ̃t) *a*, offensive. **outrager** (ʒe) *v.t*, to insult; outrage. **outrageux, euse**† (ʒø, øz) *a*, outrageous, excessive.
outrance (utrɑ̃s) *f*, excess; excessiveness. *à* ~, in the extreme, to excess. **outrancier, ère** (trɑ̃sje, ɛr) *a*, extreme, extremist.
outre (utr) *pr. & ad*, beyond; further. ~*-Manche*, across the Channel. *en* ~, moreover, besides. *en* ~ *de*, on top of. ~ *mesure*, to excess. **~-mer,** *ad.* & **d'~-mer,** *a*, oversea[s].
outré, e (utre) *a*, excessive; extravagant; exaggerated; outraged.
outrepasser (utrəpɑse) *v.t*, to go beyond, overstep.
outrer (utre) *v.t*, to overdo; exaggerate; outrage.
ouvert, e† (uvɛr, ɛrt) *a*, open; o.-ended; wide (*angle*); (*tap*) on, running. **overture** (vɛrtyr) *f*, opening; o.-out; o. up, unlocking; (*Phot.*) aperture; overture.
ouvrable (uvrabl) *a*, *jour* ~, working day, weekday. **ouvrage** (vraʒ) *m*, work; piece of w. ~ *d'art*, structure (*bridge &c*). **ouvragé, e** (vraʒe) *a*, finely worked, carved, embroidered &c.
ouvre-boîte (uvrə) *m*, tin opener. **ouvre-bouteille[s]**, *m*, bottle-opener.
ouvreuse (uvrøz) *f*, usherette.
ouvrier, ère (uvrie, ɛr) *a*, working; w. class (*district*); industrial, labour (*relations &c*). ¶ *m*, worker, workman, labourer. ¶ *f*, female worker.
ouvrir (uvrir) *v.t.ir*, to open; unlock; spread (*wings*); undo, unfasten (*coat*); open up; cut open; build (*motorway*); head (*list*); turn on, switch on; draw back (*curtains*); sharpen (*appetite*). ¶ *v.i.ir*. to open. **s'**~, to open, o. out. ~ *à*, become aware of; open one's heart to.
ovaire (ɔvɛr) *m*, ovary.
ovale (ɔval) *a. & m*, oval.
ovation (ɔvasjɔ̃) *f*, ovation.
ovin, e (ɔvɛ̃, in) *a*, ovine. ¶ *m.pl*, ovine race.
ovule (ɔvyl) *m*, ovum. **ovulation** (ylasjɔ̃) *f*,

ovulation.
oxydant, e (ɔksidɔ̃, ɔ̃t) *a,* oxidizing. ¶ *m,* oxidizer. **oxydation** (sidasjɔ̃) *f,* oxidization, oxidation. **oxyde** (sid) *m,* oxide. ~ *de carbone,* carbon monoxide. **oxyder** (de) *v.t,* to oxidize. **oxygénation** (ʒenasjɔ̃) *f,* oxygenation. **oxygène** (ʒɛn) *m,* oxygen. **oxygéner** (ʒene) *v.t,* to oxygenate. **s'~** *P,* get some fresh air.
ozone (ɔzɔn) *m,* ozone.

P

P, p (pe) *m, letter,* P, p.
pacage (pakaʒ) *m,* pasture [land].
pacha (paʃa) *m,* pasha.
pachyderme (paʃidɛrm) *m,* elephant.
pacificateur, trice (pasifikatœr, tris) *n,* peacemaker; pacifier. ¶ *a,* pacifying. **pacifier** (fje) *v.t,* to pacify; appease. **pacifique**† (fik) *a,* pacific, peaceable; peaceful. **le P~,** the Pacific. **pacifisme** (fism) *m,* pacifism. **pacifiste** (fist) *n. & a,* pacifist.
pacotille (pakɔtij) *f,* cheap & nasty goods, trash; showy stuff.
pacte (pakt) *m,* pact. **pactiser avec** (tize), come to terms with; take sides with; compound (*felony*).
pactole (paktɔl) *m,* gold mine.
pagaie (pagɛ) *f,* paddle (*canoe*).
pagaïe *ou* **pagaille** (pagaj) *f,* mess, shambles. *en ~,* in vast quantities.
paganisme (paganism) *m,* paganism, heathenism.
pagayer (pagɛje) *v.t,* to paddle (*canoe*). **pagayeur, euse** (jœr, øz) *n,* paddler.
page[1] (paʒ) *f,* page (*book*); chapter (*of one's life*). *être à la ~,* to be up to date, with it *P;* keep in touch *or* up to date.
page[2] (paʒ) *m,* (*Hist.*) page [boy].
pagne (paɲ) *m,* loincloth.
pagode (pagɔd) *f,* pagoda.
paie (pɛ) *f,* pay, wages. **paiement** (mɑ̃) *m,* payment.
païen, ne (pajɛ̃, ɛn) *a. & n,* pagan, heathen.
paillasse (pajas) *f,* straw mattress. **paillasson** (sɔ̃) *m,* doormat. **paille** (paj) *f,* straw; (*Tech.*) flaw. ~ *de fer,* wire wool. *être sur la ~,* to be penniless. **paillé, e** (je) *a,* straw-bottomed. **pailleté, e** (jte) *a,* sequined, spangled. **paillette** (jɛt) *f,* sequin, spangle; speck (*gold*); flake.
pain (pɛ̃) *m,* bread; loaf (*bread, sugar*); biscuit (*dog*); cake (*soap, fish, &c*); tablet; pat (*butter*). ~ *à cacheter,* sealing wax. ~ *de campagne,* farmhouse loaf. ~ *complet,* wholemeal bread. ~ *d'épice,* gingerbread. ~ *de mie,* sandwich loaf. ~ *grillé,* toast.
pair[1] (pɛr) *m,* (*pers.*) peer; (*Fin.*) par. *au ~,* au pair (*girl*). *de ~ avec,* hand in hand with.
pair[2], **e** (pɛr) *a,* even (*number*).
paire (pɛr) *f,* pair; brace; yoke (*oxen, &c*).
pairesse (pɛrɛs) *f,* peeress. **pairie** (ri) *f,* peerage.
paisible† (pɛzibl) *a,* peaceable, peaceful.
paître (pɛtr) *v.t. & i. ir,* to graze. *envoyer ~ qn P,* to send s.o packing.
paix (pɛ) *f,* peace; quiet; stillness, peacefulness. *fiche-moi la ~ P,* leave me alone. ¶ *i,* shut up!
Pakistan (pakistɑ̃) *m,* Pakistan. **pakistanais, e** (anɛ, ɛz) *a. &* **P~,** *n,* Pakistani.
palace (palas) *m,* luxury hotel.
palais (palɛ) *m,* palace; [law] courts; court; palate. ~ *dur,* hard palate. ~ *mou,* soft p.
palan (palɑ̃) *m,* pulley block; tackle.
palatal, e (palatal) *a,* palatal.
pale (pal) *f,* blade (*oar, air propeller*); paddle.
pâle (pɑl) *a,* pale, pallid, wan; weak; poor (*imitation*).
palefrenier (palfrɔnje) *m,* groom, ostler.
paléographie (paleɔgrafi) *f,* pal[a]eography. **paléontologie** (ɔ̃tɔlɔʒi) *f,* pal[a]eontology.
Palestine (la) (palɛstin), Palestine. **palestinien, ne** (stinjɛ̃, jɛn) *a. &* **P~,** *n,* Palestinian.
palet (palɛ) *m,* quoit; quoits; puck (*Ice hockey*).
paletot (palto) *m,* knitted jacket.
palette (palɛt) *f,* palette; (*meat*) shoulder; paddle.
pâleur (pɑlœr) *f,* pallor, paleness.
palier (palje) *m,* landing (*stairs*); floor; (*Tech.*) bearings; level; (*fig.*) stage.
pâlir (pɑlir) *v.i. & t,* to [turn] pale; blanch; (*stars*) grow dim; wane; fade.
palissade (palisad) *f,* fence; boarding.
palliatif, ive (palljatif, iv) *a. & m,* palliative; makeshift, stopgap. **pallier** (pallje) *v.t,* to get round (*difficulty*); offset, compensate for, make up for (*loss*).
palmarès (palmarɛs) *m,* prize list, honours list.
palme (palm) *f,* palm [leaf]; (*Swim.*) flipper. **palmé, e** (me) *a,* webbed; webfooted (*bird*). **palmeraie** (mɔrɛ) *f,* palm grove. **palmier** (mje) *m,* palm [tree].
palombe (palɔ̃b) *f,* ring dove, wood pigeon.
pâlot, te (pɑlo, ɔt) *a,* pale, wan, peaky *P.*
palourde (palurd) *f,* clam.
palpable (palpabl) *a,* palpable. **palper** (pe) *v.t,* to feel, finger; (*Med.*) palpate; (*P*) make (*money*). **palpitant, e** (pitɑ̃, ɑ̃t) *a,* thrilling,

exciting. **palpitation** (pitasjɔ̃) *f,* palpitation, throbbing, fluttering. **palpiter** (te) *v.i,* to palpitate; throb; beat; pound; (*flame, nostril*) quiver.
paludéen, ne (palydeɛ̃, ɛn) *a,* marshy; malarial. **paludisme** (dism) *m,* malaria.
pâmer (se) (pɑme) *v.pr,* to swoon.
pampas (pɑ̃pɑs) *f.pl,* pampas.
pamphlet (pɑ̃flɛ) *m,* lampoon.
pamplemousse (pɑ̃pləmus) *f,* grapefruit.
pan[1] (pɑ̃) *m,* piece, section; side, face; tail (*coat, shirt*); skirt. ~ *de mur,* [section of] wall.
pan[2] (pɑ̃) *i,* bang!, whack!
panacée (panase) *f,* panacea.
panache (panaʃ) *m,* plume; panache; gallantry. **panaché, e** (naʃe) *a,* multi-coloured; mixed; motley. ¶ *m,* shandy.
panais (panɛ) *m,* parsnip.
panaris (panari) *m,* whitlow.
pancarte (pɑ̃kart) *f,* sign, notice; road sign; placard.
pancréas (pɑ̃kreɑs) *m,* pancreas.
pandit (pɑ̃di) *m,* pundit.
paner (pane) *v.t,* (*Cook.*) to coat with breadcrumbs.
panier (panje) *m,* (*gen., Sport*) basket; basket[ful]. ~ *à ouvrage,* workbasket. ~ *à papiers,* wastepaper b. ~ *à provisions,* shopping b. ~ *percé,* spendthrift. ~*-repas,* packed lunch. ~ *à salade,* salad shaker; (*P*) police van, Black Maria.
panique (panik) *a. & f,* panic. **paniquer** (ke) *v.i,* to panic.
panne (pan) *f,* breakdown, failure. *avoir une* ~ *d'essence* ou *une* ~ *sèche,* to run out of petrol. *laisser en* ~, to leave in the lurch. *mettre en* ~ (*Naut.*), to heave to. *tomber en* ~, to break down.
panneau (pano) *m,* panel; sign, notice. ~ *d'affichage,* notice board; hoarding. ~ *indicateur,* signpost. ~ *de signalisation,* road sign. ~ *vitré,* glass panel.
panonceau (panɔ̃so) *m,* plaque; sign.
panoplie (panɔpli) *f,* panoply, range; (*toy*) outfit. ~ *d'armes,* display of weapons; armoury.
panorama (panɔrama) *m,* panorama. **panoramique** (ik) *a,* panoramic.
panse (pɑ̃s) *f,* belly, paunch.
pansement (pɑ̃smɑ̃) *m,* dressing (*wound*); bandage. ~ [*adhésif*], [sticking] plaster (*with dressing*). **panser** (se) *v.t,* to dress; groom (*horse*).
pantalon (pɑ̃talɔ̃) *m,* [pair of] trousers.
pantelant, e (pɑ̃tlɑ̃, ɑ̃t) *a,* panting; heaving (*flesh*).
panthéon (pɑ̃teɔ̃) *m,* pantheon.
panthère (pɑ̃tɛr) *f,* panther.
pantin (pɑ̃tɛ̃) *m,* (*toy*) jumping jack; (*pers.*) puppet.
pantomime (pɑ̃tɔmim) *n,* mime; m. show; (*fig.*) fuss, scene.
pantoufle (pɑ̃tufl) *f,* slipper. **pantouflard, e** *P* (lar, ard) *a. & n,* stay-at-home; quiet (*life*).
paon (pɑ̃) *m,* peacock; p. butterfly. **paonne** (pan) *f,* peahen.
papa (papa) *m,* dad[dy].
papal, e (papal) *a,* papal. **papauté** (pote) *f,* papacy. **pape** (pap) *m,* pope.
papelard *P* (paplar) *m,* paper.
paperasse (papras) *f,* (*pej.*) papers; forms. **paperasserie** (sri) *f,* bumf; red tape; forms. **papeterie** (pap[ɛ]tri) *f,* paper mill; p. making; p. trade; stationer's shop; stationery. **papetier, ère** (paptje, ɛr) *n,* paper maker; stationer. **papier** (pje) *m,* paper; piece of p; article (*newspaper*). *mettre qch à* ~, to write sth down; put sth in writing. ~ *à signer,* form to sign. ~ *aluminium,* ~ *alu P,* tinfoil, aluminium foil. ~ *d'argent,* silver foil, s. paper. ~ *brouillon,* scrap paper. ~ *buvard,* blotting p. ~ *calque,* tracing p. ~ *carbone,* carbon p. ~ *à cigarettes,* cigarette p. ~ *collant,* sticky p. ~ *cul P**, bog roll *P**. ~ *à dessin,* drawing p. ~ *d'emballage,* wrapping p. ~ *filtre,* filter p. ~ *hygiénique,* toilet p. ~ *journal,* newspaper. ~ *à lettres,* notepaper, writing p. ~ *mâché,* papier-mâché. ~ *machine,* typing p. ~ *monnaie,* paper money. ~ *peint,* wallpaper. ~ *de soie,* tissue p. ~ *sulfurisé,* greaseproof p. ~ *timbré,* stamped p. ~ *de tournesol,* litmus p. ~ *de verre,* glasspaper, sandpaper.
papillon (papijɔ̃) *m,* butterfly; wing nut; bow tie; parking ticket; sticker. ~ *de nuit,* moth.
papillote (papijɔt) *f,* curlpaper; [sweet] wrapper; frill (*for leg of lamb*); (*Cook.*) buttered paper. **papilloter** (te) *v.i,* to flicker; blink; twinkle.
papoter (papɔte) *v.i,* to gossip; chatter.
pâque (pɑk) *f,* passover. **Pâques** (pɑk) *m.s,* Easter.
paquebot (pakbo) *m,* liner, [steam] ship.
pâquerette (pɑkrɛt) *f,* daisy.
paquet (pakɛ) *m,* packet (*cigarettes &c*); bag (*sugar &c*); pack (*cards*); bundle (*linen*); parcel; (*fig.*) pile, mass, lump. *faire un* ~ *cadeau,* to gift-wrap. *un* ~ *de mer,* a heavy sea; big wave. **paquetage** (ktaʒ) *m,* pack (*soldier's*).
par (par) *pr,* by (*s.o, sth*). *cassé* ~ *mon frère,* ~ *le vent,* broken by my brother, by the wind. ~ *chèque,* (*pay*) by cheque. ~ *erreur,* by mistake. by way of, through, via, across. ~ *la fenêtre,* (*enter*) through *or* by the window; (*throw*) out of the w. ~ *les rues,* (*walk*) through the streets. *3 fois* ~ *jour,* 3 times a day. ~ *an.* per annum. ~*-ci,* ~*-là, ad,* here & there, hither & thither; at odd times. ~*-dessous,* ~*-dessus, V dessous, dessus.* ~ *ici,* this way, through here. ~ *là,* that way, through there; by that. *de* ~ *le monde,* all over the world. ~ *où?* which way? ~ *trop,* far

too, too much, unduly.
parabole (parabɔl) *f,* parable; parabola. **parabolique**† (lik) *a, (Geom),* parabolic. ¶ *m,* electric fire.
parachever (paraʃve) *v.t,* to finish [off], perfect.
parachute (paraʃyt) *m,* parachute. **parachuter** (te) *v.t,* to parachute. **parachutisme** (tism) *&* **parachutage** (taʒ) *m,* parachuting. **parachutiste** (tist) *n,* parachutist; *(Mil.)* paratrooper.
parade (parad) *f,* parade; show; *(Box., Fenc.)* parry; *(fig.)* answer, reply. *de* ~, ceremonial *(uniform). faire* ~ *de,* to show off. **parader** (de) *v.i,* to parade; show off.
paradis (paradi) *m,* paradise, heaven; *(Theat.)* the gods. *le P~ terrestre,* the Garden of Eden; *(fig.)* heaven on earth.
paradoxal, e† (paradɔksal) *a,* paradoxical. **paradoxe** (dɔks) *m,* paradox.
paraffine (parafin) *f,* paraffin wax.
parages (paraʒ) *m.pl,* region; waters. *dans les* ~, in the area, in the vicinity. *dans les* ~ *de,* round about, near.
paragraphe (paragraf) *m,* paragraph.
paraître (parɛtr) *v.i.ir,* to appear; show; be published, come out; seem, look. *'vient de* ~*'* 'just out' *(publication).*
parallèle† (paralɛl) *a, (Math.)* parallel; similar; separate; unofficial. ¶ *f, (Math.)* parallel line. ¶ *m, (Geog., fig.)* parallel. **parallélisme** (lelism) *m,* parallelism; *(Mot.)* wheel alignment. **parallélogramme** (lɔgram) *m,* parallelogram.
paralyser (paralize) *v.t,* to paralyse. **paralysie** (zi) *f,* paralysis. **paralytique** (tik) *a. & n,* paralytic.
paramètre (paramɛtr) *m,* parameter.
paranoïaque (paranojak) *a. & m,* paranoiac.
parapet (parapɛ) *m,* parapet.
paraphe (paraf) *m,* initials; flourish; signature. **parapher** (fe) *v.t,* to initial; sign.
paraphrase (parafrɑz) *f,* paraphrase. **paraphraser** (frɑze) *v.t,* to paraphrase.
parapluie (paraplɥi) *m,* umbrella.
parasite (parasit) *m,* parasite; sponger; *(pl: Radio, TV)* interference, atmospherics. ¶ *a,* parasitical.
parasol (parasɔl) *m,* parasol, sunshade; beach umbrella.
paratonnerre (paratɔnɛr) *m,* lightning conductor.
paravent (paravɑ̃) *m,* screen *(folding & fig.).*
parbleu *O* (parblø) *i,* why, of course!
parc (park) *m,* park; grounds *(big house)*; *(Mil.)* depot; *(Econ.)* stock. ~ *à bébé,* playpen. ~ *à huîtres,* oyster bed. ~ *à moutons,* sheep pen. ~ *automobile,* car fleet. ~ *d'attractions,* amusement part. ~ *naturel,* nature reserve. **parcage** (kaʒ) *m,* parking; penning.
parcelle (parsɛl) *f,* scrap, fragment; grain *(truth)*; bit; parcel *(of land)*; plot.
parce que (pars[ə]kə) *c,* because.
parchemin (parʃəmɛ̃) *m,* parchment; *(fig.)* title; diploma.
parcimonie (parsimɔni) *f,* parsimony. **parcimonieux, euse**† (njø, øz) *a,* parsimonious.
parcmètre (parkmɛtr) *m,* parking meter.
parcourir (parkurir) *v.t.ir,* to cover, travel *(distance)*; go all over *(place)*; run through; skim *or* glance through *(book).* **parcours** (kur) *m,* distance; journey; route; stretch; course *(river &c)*; round *(Golf).*
par-dessous, *V* **dessous. par-dessus,** *V* **dessus.**
pardessus (pardəsy) *m,* overcoat.
pardi (pardi) *i,* of course!
pardon (pardɔ̃) *m,* pardon, forgiveness. *[je vous demande]* ~, I'm sorry, excuse me, I beg your pardon. **pardonnable** (dɔnabl) *a,* pardonable. **pardonner** (ne) *v.t,* to pardon, forgive *(qch à qn,* s.o for sth); excuse.
pare- (par) *pref:* ~*-balles, m,* bullet shield; *a,* b. proof. ~*-boue, m,* mudguard. ~*-brise, m,* windscreen. ~*-chocs, m,* bumper. ~*-étincelles, m,* fireguard. ~*-soleil, m,* sun visor.
pareil, le (parɛj) *a,* similar, like, alike, same; such. ~ *à,* ~ *que,* the same as, similar to, just like. *c'est toujours* ~, it's always the same. ¶ *n,* equal, peer; *(pl.)* fellow men. *sans* ~, unequalled. **pareillement** (rɛjmɑ̃) *ad,* also, likewise.
parent, e (parɑ̃, ɑ̃t) *a,* related *(de,* to). ¶ *n,* relation, relative; *(Biol.)* parent; *(m.pl.)* parents; ancestors, forefathers. **parenté** (rɑ̃te) *f,* relationship, kinship; relations.
parenthèse (parɑ̃tɛz) *f,* parenthesis; bracket. *entre* ~*s,* in brackets, incidentally.
parer[1] (pare) *v.t,* to adorn, deck; dress.
parer[2] (pare) *v.t,* to ward off, fend off, stave off; *(Box., Fenc., fig.)* parry. ~ *à,* to prepare for; deal with; ward off; remedy. *(Naut.) parez à virer!* ready about!
paresse (parɛs) *f,* laziness, idleness, sloth; sluggishness. **paresser** (se) *v.i,* to laze around, lounge about. **paresseux, euse**† (sø, øz) *a. & n,* idle, &c (person). ¶ *(Zool.) m,* sloth.
parfaire (parfɛr) *v.t.ir,* to perfect. **parfait, e** (fɛ, ɛt) *a,* perfect; faultless, flawless; complete, total, utter. ¶ *m,* perfect [tense]. **parfaitement** (tmɑ̃) *ad,* perfectly, totally, utterly; quite so, exactly.
parfois (parfwa) *ad,* sometimes, at times, now & again.
parfum (parfœ̃) *m,* perfume, fragrance; scent; flavour *(ice-cream)*; aroma *(coffee).* **parfumé, e,** (fyme) *a,* fragrant, scented; flavoured. **parfumer** (fyme) *v.t,* to scent, perfume; *(Cook.)* flavour. **parfumerie** (mri) *f,* perfumery. **parfumeur, euse** (mœr, øz) *n,* perfumer.
pari (pari) *m,* bet, wager. **parier** (rje) *v.t,* to bet, wager, lay, punt. ~ *sur,* to back *(horse). il y a*

à ~ que..., the odds are that... **parieur, euse** (jœr, øz) *n,* punter.
parisien, ne (parizjɛ̃, ɛn) *a.* & **P~,** *n,* Parisian.
parité (parite) *f,* parity, equality.
parjure (parʒyr) *m,* perjury; betrayal. ¶ *n,* perjurer; traitor. ¶ *a,* faithless (*pers.*); false (*oath*). **parjurer (se)** (ʒyre) *v.pr,* to perjure o.s; fail to honour one's promise.
parking (parkiŋ) *m,* car park, (*Am.*) parking lot; parking.
parlant, e (parlɑ̃, ɑ̃t) *a,* speaking, talking; lifelike (*portrait*); eloquent (*look*); graphic (*description &c*). **parlé, e** (le) *a,* spoken.
parlement (parləmɑ̃) *m,* parliament. **parlementaire** (tɛr) *a,* parliamentary. ¶ *m,* member of parliament. **parlementer** (te) *v.i,* to parley.
parler (parle) *v.i,* to speak, talk (*de,* about). *quand on parle du loup [on en voit la queue],* talk of the devil [& he's sure to appear]. *sans ~ de,* not to mention. *tu parles!* you're telling me!; you must be joking! *vous n'avez qu'à ~,* just say the word. ¶ *v.t, ~ politique,* to talk politics. ¶ *m,* dialect. **parleur, euse** (lœr, øz) *n,* talker. **parloir** (lwar) *m,* parlour (*convent*); visiting room (*prison*).
parmi (parmi) *pr,* among[st], amid[st].
parodie (parɔdi) *f,* parody. **parodier** (dje) *v.t,* to parody.
paroi (parwa) *f,* (*gen., Anat.*) wall; partition; side (*vehicle*). *~ rocheuse,* rock face.
paroisse (parwas) *f,* parish. **paroissial, e** (sjal) *a,* parish. **paroissien, ne** (sjɛ̃, ɛn) *n,* parishioner.
parole (parɔl) *f,* word; remark; speech; parole; (*pl.*) words, lyrics (*song*). *~ d'évangile,* gospel [truth]. *droit de ~,* right to speak. *tenir ~,* to keep one's word.
paroxysme (parɔksism) *m,* paroxysm; height (*emotion*); crisis [point] (*illness*).
parpaing (parpɛ̃) *m,* breeze-block.
parquer (parke) *v.t,* to pen; park.
parquet (parkɛ) *m,* [wooden *or* parquet] floor; (*Law*) public prosecutor's department. **parqueter** (kəte) *v.t,* to floor, parquet.
parrain (parɛ̃) *m,* godfather; sponsor; (*pl.*) godparents. **parrainage** (rɛnaʒ) *m,* sponsorship. **parrainer** (ne) *v.t,* to sponsor.
parricide (parisid) (*pers.*) *n.* & (*act*) *m,* parricide. ¶ *a,* parricidal.
parsemer (parsəme) *v.t,* to strew, sprinkle, scatter.
part (par) *f,* share; part; portion. *~ du lion,* lion's share. *à ~,* apart; aside; except. *autre ~,* elsewhere, somewhere else. *d'autre ~,* on the other hand. *de ~ & d'autre,* on either side. *de la ~ de,* on behalf of, from. *c'est de la ~ de qui?* (*Tel.*) who's speaking *or* calling? *de ~ en ~,* right through. *faire ~,* to acquaint, inform (*de qch à qn,* s.o of sth).
partage (partaʒ) *m,* division, sharing; share; cutting (*cake*); (*fig.*) portion, lot. *recevoir qch en ~,* to receive sth in a will. **partagé, e** (taʒe) *a,* divided; endowed; mutual (*love*). **partageable** (ʒabl) *a,* divisible. **partager** (ʒe) *v.t,* to divide [up]; share [out]; agree with (*idea*).
partance (partɑ̃s) *f, en ~,* due to leave; outbound, sailing. **partant** (tɑ̃) *m,* starter (*runner*); runner (*horse*); person leaving.
partenaire (partənɛr) *n,* partner.
parterre (partɛr) *m,* [flower] bed, border; (*Theat.*) stalls; audience.
parti (parti) *m,* party, side; option; decision; match (*marriage*). *~ pris,* prejudice, bias. *faire un mauvais ~ à,* to ill-treat. *prendre ~,* to take sides, to side. *tirer ~ de,* to make use of, turn to account.
partial, e† (parsjal) *a,* partial, bias[s]ed, unfair. **partialité** (lite) *f,* partiality, &c.
participant, e (partisipɑ̃, ɑ̃t) *a,* participant, participating. ¶ *n,* participant; entrant (*competition &c*); member. **participation** (ipasjɔ̃) *f,* participation; appearance; involvement; (*Fin.*) interest. *~ aux bénéfices,* profit-sharing. **participe** (sip) *m,* (*Gram.*) participle. **participer** (pe) *v.i,* to participate, share; partake. *~ à,* to take part in; enter; participate in; be involved in.
particulariser (partikylarize) *v.t,* to particularize. **se ~ par,** be distinguished by. **particularité** (te) *f,* particularity; peculiarity; distinctive feature. **particule** (kyl) *f,* particle. **particulier, ère†** (lje, ɛr) *a,* particular; distinctive; peculiar, odd; private (*lessons &c*). *en ~,* in private; separately, in particular. ¶ *n,* [private] individual.
partie (parti) *f,* (*gen., Mus.*) part; field, subject; (*Sport, Cards*) game; (*Mil.*) opponent; (*Law*) party; litigant; outing, party. *faire ~ de,* to take part in; belong to; be among. *faire ~ intégrale,* be part & parcel. *prendre ~ à,* to take to task. *se mettre de la ~,* to join in. *~s sexuelles,* private parts.
partiel, le (parsjɛl) *a,* partial (*not entire*). **partiellement** (lmɑ̃) *ad,* partially, partly.
partir (partir) *v.i.ir,* to go away *or* off; leave; depart, set off; set out (*pour,* for); (*engine*) start; (*plane*) take off; (*plant*) take; come from, emanate; (*stain*) come out; (*button*) come off; (*smell*) clear. *à ~ de,* from, on & after. *~ de,* (*contract*) to begin on; (*bus*) start *or* run from. *faire ~,* to remove (*stain*); get rid of; launch (*rocket*); set off.
partisan, e (partizɑ̃, an) *m,* partisan, supporter. ¶ *a,* partisan.
partitif, ive (partitif, iv) *a,* (*Gram.*) partitive. **partition** (sjɔ̃) *f,* (*Mus.*) score; partition.
partout (partu) *ad,* everywhere. (*Ten.*) *3 ~,* 3 all. *~ où,* wherever.
parure (paryr) *f,* finery; ornament; [set of] jewels; [set of] underwear.
parvenir (parvənir) *v.i.ir,* to arrive; succeed. ~

à, to arrive at, reach; attain [to]. ~ *à faire,* to succeed in doing, manage to do. **parvenu, e** (ny) *n,* upstart, parvenu.

parvis (parvi) *m,* square (*in front of a church*).

pas[1] (pɑ) *m,* step, footstep; footprint; pace; (*horse*) walk; (*Geog.*) pass; straits; thread (*screw*). *P~ de Calais,* Straits of Dover. ~ *de la porte,* doorstep. ~ *de porte,* key money. *au ~,* slowly, dead slow (*roadsign*). *au ~ cadencé,* in quick time. *au ~ de course,* at a run. *au ~ de gymnastique,* at a jog trot. *avoir le ~ sur,* take precedence over. *prendre le ~ sur,* to supplant; override; steal a march on. *sauter le ~,* to take the plunge.

pas[2] (pɑ) *neg. particle usually coupled with* **ne,** not; no. ~ *de,* no. ~ *du tout,* not at all. ~ *encore,* not yet. ~ *mal de,* quite a few, quite a lot of. ~ *possible!* you don't say! ~ *vrai?* isn't that so? &c. *ce n'est ~ trop tôt,* not before time.

passable† (pɑsabl) *a,* passable, tolerable, fair, pretty good. **passade** (sad) *f,* passing fancy. **passage** (saʒ) *m,* passage; way; route; passageway; alley way; crossing. *attendre le ~ de l'autobus,* to wait for the bus to come. *barrer le ~ à qn,* to block s.o's way. *laisser le ~ à,* to make way for. ~ *à niveau,* level crossing. ~ *clouté,* pedestrian crossing. ~ *interdit* [*au public*], no thoroughfare. ~ *souterrain,* subway.

passager, ère (pɑsaʒe, ɛr) *a,* passing; temporary; transient; short-lived; busy (*street*). *pluies ~ères,* intermittant *or* occasional showers. ¶ *n,* passenger. ~ *clandestin,* stowaway. **passagèrement** (ʒɛrmɑ̃) *ad,* in passing, temporarily. **passant, e** (pɑsɑ̃, ɑ̃t) *n,* passer-by. ¶ *m,* loop (*belt*).

passation (pasasjɔ̃) *f,* signing (*contract*). ~ *de pouvoir,* transfer of power.

passe (pɑs) *f,* pass; channel. ~ *d'armes,* heated exchange. *en ~ de,* on the way to. *mauvaise ~,* bad patch.

passé, e (pɑse) *a,* last (*month &c*); past, former; bygone; faded. ~ *de la mode,* out of fashion. *3 heures ~es,* past 3 o'clock. ¶ *m,* past; p. [tense]. ~ *antérieur,* past anterior. ~ *composé,* perfect. ~ *simple,* past historic. **passé,** *pr,* after.

passe-droit (pɑsdrwa) *m,* undeserved privilege.

passement (pɑsmɑ̃) *m,* braid. **passementerie** (tri) *f,* braid, trimming.

passe-montagne (pɑsmɔ̃taɲ) *m,* balaclava.

passe-partout (pɑspartu) *m,* master key, skeleton key.

passe-plats (pɑspla) *m,* service hatch.

passeport (pɑspɔr) *m,* passport.

passer (pɑse) *v.i,* to pass; call; go past; go (*from one place or state to another*); go by; go through; (*film &c*) be on *or* showing; appear; (*ears &c*) stick out; (*colour*) fade. ~ *devant la jurisdiction,* to come up before a court. ~ *en seconde* (*Mot.*), to change into second. ~ *pour un idiot,* to be taken for a fool. *faire ~ qn pour,* to make s.o out to be. ¶ *v.t,* to cross; go through &c; spend (*time*); take, sit (*exam*); clear (*customs*); pass, p. on, give, hand; strain (*liquid*); put on (*record*); show (*film*). **se ~ de,** to do without, manage without.

passerelle (pɑsrɛl) *f,* footbridge; bridge (*ship*); gangway.

passe-temps (pɑstɑ̃) *m,* pastime.

passeur (pɑsœr) *m,* ferryman; smuggler.

passible (pasibl) *a,* liable. ~ *de droits,* dutiable. ~ *d'un impôt,* liable for tax.

passif, ive (pasif, iv) *a,* passive. ¶ *m,* passive [voice]; liabilities.

passiflore (pasiflɔr) *f,* passion flower.

passion (pɑsjɔ̃) *f,* passion. *la P~* (*Rel.*) the Passion. *sans ~,* dispassionately. **passionnant, e** (ɔnɑ̃, ɑ̃t) *a,* thrilling; fascinating. **passionné**†, **e** (ne) *a,* passionate; impassioned. *il est ~ pour,* he is passionately fond of; he has a passion for. ¶ *n, un ~ de jazz,* a jazz fanatic. **passionner** (ne) *v.t,* enthral[l], fascinate. **se ~ pour,** to have a passion for; be fascinated by.

passivement (pasivmɑ̃) *ad,* passively. **passivité** (vite) *f,* passivity.

passoire (pɑswar) *f,* colander; strainer, sieve.

pastel (pastɛl) *m,* pastel; woad.

pastèque (pastɛk) *f,* water melon.

pasteur (pastœr) *m,* shepherd; pastor, minister.

pasteuriser (pastœrize) *v.t,* to pasteurize.

pastiche (pastiʃ) *m,* pastiche. **pasticher** (ʃe) *v.t,* to write a pastiche of.

pastille (pastij) *f,* pastille, lozenge; block (*colour*); disc (*paper*).

pastoral, e (pastɔral) *a,* pastoral. ¶ *f,* pastoral; pastorale.

pat (pat) *m,* (*Chess*) stalemate.

patate (patat) *f,* (*P*) spud *P*; fathead *P*. ~ [*douce*], sweet potato.

patati *P* (patati) *i, & ~ & patata,* & so on & so forth.

patatras (patatrɑ) *i,* crash!

pataud, e (pato, od) *a. & n,* clumsy (person).

patauger (patoʒe) *v.i,* to wade, splash about; flounder.

pâte (pɑt) *f,* pastry; dough; mixture (*cake*); batter (*frying*); (*substance*) paste, cream. *~s* [*alimentaires*], pasta. ~ *à choux,* choux pastry. ~ *à papier,* paper pulp. ~ *brisée,* shortcrust pastry. ~ *d'amandes,* almond paste. ~ *dentifrice,* toothpaste. ~ *de fruits,* fruit jelly. ~ *feuilletée,* flaky *or* puff pastry. **pâté** (pɑte) *m,* pâté; [ink] blot; block (*houses*). ~ *en croûte,* meat pie. ~ [*de sable*], sandpie, sandcastle. **pâtée** (te) *f,* mash (*poultry*); swill (*pigs*).

patelin (patlɛ̃) *m,* village.

patelle (patɛl) *f,* limpet.
patent, e[1] (patɑ̃, ɑ̃t) *a,* patent, obvious.
patente[2] (patɑ̃t) *f,* licence. **patenté, e** (te) *a,* licensed.
patère (patɛr) *f,* hat *or* coat peg.
paterne (patɛrn) *a,* patronizing. **paternel, le†** (nɛl) *a,* paternal, fatherly; father's (*side*). ¶ *m,* (*P*) old man *P*. **paternité** (nite) *f,* paternity.
pâteux, euse (pɑtø, øz) *a,* pasty; furred (*tongue*); thick, husky (*voice*).
pathétique† (patetik) *a,* pathetic. ¶ *m,* pathos.
pathologie (patɔlɔʒi) *f,* pathology. **pathologique†** (ʒik) *a,* pathological. **pathologiste** (ʒist) *n,* pathologist.
pathos (patɔs) *m,* pathos, emotionalism.
patibulaire (patibylɛr) *a,* sinister.
patiemment (pasjamɑ̃) *ad,* patiently. **patience** (sjɑ̃s) *f,* patience; (*Cards*) patience; (*Bot.*) dock. **patient, e** (sjɑ̃, ɑ̃t) *a,* patient; laborious. ¶ *n,* patient. **patienter** (ɑ̃te) *v.i,* to have patience; wait, hang on *P*.
patin (patɛ̃) *m,* skate, runner (*sledge*). *~s à glace,* ice skates. *~s à roulettes,* roller skates. *~ [de frein],* brake block. **patinage** (tinaʒ) *m,* skating; spinning (*wheel*); slipping (*clutch*). *~ artistique,* figure skating. **patine** (tin) *f,* patina. **patiner** (ne) *v.i,* to skate; spin; slip. **patinette** (nɛt) *f,* scooter. **patineur, euse** (nœr, øz) *n,* skater. **patinoire** (nwar) *f,* skating rink, ice rink.
patio (patjo) *m,* patio.
pâtir (pɑtir) *v.i,* to suffer.
pâtisserie (patisri) *f,* cake, pastry; cake shop; confectioner's; cake- *or* pastry-making, baking; confectionery. **pâtissier, ère** (sje, ɛr) *n,* pastry-cook, confectioner.
patois (patwa) *m,* patois.
patraque (patrak) *a,* out of sorts, peaky *P*.
pâtre (pɑtr) *m,* (*liter.*) shepherd.
patriarcal, e (patriarkal) *a,* patriarchal. **patriarche** (arʃ) *m,* patriarch.
patricien, ne (patrisjɛ̃, ɛn) *a. & n,* patrician. **patrie** (tri) *f,* native land, country, fatherland; home. **patrimoine** (trimwan) *m,* patrimony; inheritance, heritage. **patriote** (ɔt) *n,* patriot. ¶ *~* & **patriotique** (tik) *a,* patriotic. **patriotisme** (tism) *m,* patriotism. **patron**[1], **ne** (trɔ̃, ɔn) *n,* owner, boss *P;* employer; governor *P;* proprietor, tress (*restaurant*); manager, ess (*hotel*); landlord, lady (*bar*); (*Hist., Rel.*) patron, ess. *~ [pêcheur],* skipper.
patron[2] (patrɔ̃) *m,* pattern (*dress &c*); stencil.
patronage (patrɔnaʒ) *m,* patronage; youth club; (*Rel.*) y. fellowship. **patronal, e** (nal) *a,* patronal; employer's, -ers'. **patronat** (na) *m,* employers (*col.*). **patronner** (ne) *v.t,* to support, sponsor.
patrouille (patruj) *f,* patrol. **patrouiller** (truje) *v.i,* to patrol.
patte (pat) *f,* paw; foot; leg; claw; (*P*) hand, paw *P;* fluke (*anchor*); tongue; strap; epaulette. *à ~s d'éléphant,* bell-bottom (*trousers*). *à quatre ~s,* on all fours. *~ [de lapin],* side burns. *~s de mouche,* spidery scrawl. *~-***d'oie,** *f,* multiple fork (*of roads*); crow's-foot (*wrinkle*).
pâturage (pɑtyraʒ) *m,* pasture, grazing. **pâture** (tyr) *f,* pasture; (*fig.*) food. **pâturer** (tyre) *v.i,* to pasture, graze.
paume (pom) *f,* palm (*hand*); (*Sport*) real tennis (*ancient game*).
paumé, e *P* (pome) *a,* lost; godforsaken *P*. ¶ *n,* drop-out. **paumer** (me) *v.t,* to lose.
paupière (popjɛr) *f,* eyelid.
paupiette (popjɛt) *f, ~ de bœuf,* beef olive.
pause (poz) *f,* pause; break; (*Sport*) half-time.
pauvre† (povr) *a,* (*gen.*) poor; shabby (*clothes*). *~ en,* lacking, short of. ¶ *n,* poor man, woman; (*pl.*) p. people, poor. *le ~!* poor thing! *mon ~ ami,* my dear fellow. **pauvreté** (vrɔte) *f,* poverty; shabbiness.
pavage (pavaʒ) *m,* paving; cobbles.
pavaner (se) (pavane) *v.pr,* to strut [about].
pavé (pave) *m,* paving stone; cobblestones; (*fig.*) streets; thick steak; heavy book. *jeter un ~ dans la mare,* to put the cat among the pigeons. **paver** (ve) *v.t,* to pave; cobble.
pavillon (pavijɔ̃) *m,* house; lodge; ward, pavilion (*hospital*); (*Naut.*) flag; (*Mus.*) bell; pinna (*ear*).
pavoiser (pavwaze) *v.t,* to dress (*ship*); deck with flags. ¶ *v.i,* to put out the flags; (*fig.*) exult.
pavot (pavo) *m,* poppy.
payable (pɛjabl) *a,* payable. **payant, e** (jɑ̃, ɑ̃t) *a,* paying. ¶ *n,* payer. **paye** (pɛj) *V* **paie. payement** (pɛ[j]mɑ̃) *V* **paiement. payer** (je) *v.t,* to pay; settle; pay for; reward; stand (*drink &c*). *~ les pots cassés,* (*lit.*) to pay for the damage; (*fig.*) pick up the pieces; carry the can. ¶ *v.i,* (*effort*) pay off; (*job*) be well paid. *~ pour qn,* pay for s.o; (*fig.*) carry the can for s.o. **se** *~ P,* to treat o.s (*qch,* to sth); get (*illness*). *se ~ la tête de qn,* to make fun of s.o. **payeur, euse** (jœr, øz) *n,* payer; paymaster.
pays (pei) *m,* country, land; region; village. *~ de cocagne* (kɔkaɲ), land of plenty. *les P~-Bas,* the Netherlands. *le P~ de Galles,* Wales. **paysage** (zaʒ) *m,* landscape; scenery. **paysagiste** (zaʒist) *m,* landscape painter. [*jardinier*] *~,* landscape (gardener).
paysan, ne (peizɑ̃, an) *a,* farming; farmers'; country (*customs*); (*pej.*) peasant. ¶ *m,* countryman, farmer; peasant. ¶ *f,* countrywoman, peasant woman. **paysannerie** (zanri) *f,* peasantry, farmers.
péage (peaʒ) *m,* toll; tollgate. *autoroute à ~,* toll motorway.
peau (po) *f,* skin, pelt; scruff (*neck*); leather; rind, peel; hide. *être bien dans sa ~,* to feel great; feel at ease. *risquer sa ~,* to risk one's

neck. ~ *de chamois*, chamois leather, shammy. *P*~ *Rouge*, *m*, redskin, red Indian. ~ *de vache P*, bastard *P*; bitch *P*.
pébroque *P* (pebrɔk) *m*, brolly *P*.
peccadille (pɛkadij) *f*, peccadillo; trifle.
pêche[1] (pɛʃ) *f*, peach; (*P*) slap.
pêche[2] (pɛʃ) *f*, fishing; f. season; catch. ~ *à la ligne*, line fishing (*sea*); angling (*river*).
péché (peʃe) *m*, sin. ~ *de jeunesse*, youthful indiscretion. ~ *mignon*, pet vice, weakness. **pécher** (ʃe) *v.i*, to sin; err; offend.
pêcher[1] (pɛʃe) *m*, peach [tree].
pêcher[2] (pɛʃe) *v.t*, to fish for; catch, land; gather (*shellfish*). ~ *la crevette*, to go shrimping. ¶ *v.i*, to go fishing, go angling. ~ *à l'asticot*, to fish with maggots. **pêcheur, euse** (ʃœr, øz) *n*, fisherman, angler; fisher (*pearl*).
pécheur, eresse (peʃœr, ʃrɛs) *n*, sinner.
pécule (pekyl) *m*, savings, nest-egg; earnings, wages (*prisoner, soldier*.).
pécuniaire† (pekynjɛr) *a*, financial.
pédagogie (pedagɔʒi) *f*, educational method. **pédagogique** (gɔʒik) *a*, educational, pedagogical; clear (*exposition*). **pédagogue** (gɔg) *m*, teacher.
pédale (pedal) *f*, pedal; treadle; (*P**) queer *P**. **pédaler** (le) *v.i*, to pedal; cycle. **pédalier** (lje) *m*, pedal [key]board; crank gear (*cycle*). **pédalo** (lo) *m*, pedal-boat.
pédant, e (pedɑ̃, ɑ̃t) *a*, pedantic. ¶ *n*, pedant. **pédantisme** (tism) *m*, pedantry.
pédé *P** (pede) *m*, queer *P**, gay *P*. **pédéraste** (rast) *m*, homosexual.
pédiatre (pedjatr) *n*, paediatrician. **pédiatrie** (tri) *f*, paediatrics.
pédicure (pedikyr) *n*, chiropodist.
pedigree (pedigri) *m*, pedigree (*beast*).
pègre (pɛgr) *f*, *la* ~, the underworld.
peignage (pɛɲaʒ) *m*, combing, carding (*textiles*). **peigne** (pɛɲ) *m*, comb; card. ~ *fin*, fine tooth comb. **peignée** (ɲe) *f*, thrashing. **peigner** (ɲe) *v.t*, to comb; card. **se** ~, to comb one's hair. **peignoir** (ɲwar) *m*, dressing gown. ~ *de bain*, bath robe.
peinard, e *P* (pɛnar, ard) *a*, cushy *P*.
peindre (pɛ̃dr) *v.t.ir*, to paint; depict, portray.
peine (pɛn) *f*, sorrow, sadness; trouble, effort; difficulty; penalty, punishment; sentence. *à* ~, hardly, scarcely, barely. *avoir de la* ~, to be sad *or* upset. [*ce n'est* ou *il ne vaut*] *pas la* ~ *de*, it's not worth, there's no point in. *sans* ~, easily. **peiner** (ne) *v.t*, to sadden, grieve, distress. ¶ *v.i*, to work hard, labour.
peintre (pɛ̃tr) *m*, painter; portrayer. ~ *en bâtiment*, house painter. ~*-décorateur*, painter & decorator. **peinture** (pɛ̃tyr) *f*, painting; picture; paintwork; paint; (*fig*.) portrayal. ~ *à l'eau*, watercolour. **peinturlurer** (tyrlyrer) *v.t*, to daub.
péjoratif, ive (peʒɔratif, iv) *a*, pejorative, derogatory.
Pékin (pekɛ̃) *m*, (*Geog*.) Peking. **pékinois, e** (kinwa, az) *a*. & *m*. & **P**~, *n*, Pekinese.
pelage (pəlaʒ) *m*, coat, fur.
pêle-mêle (pɛlmɛl) *ad*, higgeldy-piggeldy.
pelé, e (pəle) *a*, bare; bald; hairless, threadbare. **peler** (le) *v.t*. & *i*, to peel.
pèlerin, e (pɛlrɛ̃, in) *n*, pilgrim. **pèlerinage** (lrinaʒ) *m*, pilgrimage. **pèlerine** (rin) *f*, cape.
pélican (pelikɑ̃) *m*, pelican.
pelisse (pəlis) *f*, pelisse.
pelle (pɛl) *f*, shovel; spade (*child*). ~ *à ordures*, dustpan. ~ *à tarte*, cake server. **pelletée** (lte) *f*, shovelful, spadeful. **pelleteuse** (tøz) *f*, mechanical shovel *or* digger.
pellicule (pɛllikyl) *f*, film; (*pl*.) dandruff.
pelote (plɔt) *f*, ball (*wood, string*); pincushion; pile (*money*). ~ [*basque*], pelota. **peloter** *P* (te) *v.t*, to paw *P*, pet *P*. **peloton** (tɔ̃) *m*, (*Mil*.) platoon; (*Sport*) pack. ~ *d'exécution*, firing squad.
pelouse (pluz) *f*, lawn; (*Foot*. &c) ground, field.
peluche (plyʃ) *f*, plush; bit of fluff. **pelucher** (ʃe) *v.i*, to fluff up. **pelucheux, euse** (ʃø, øz) *a*, fluffy.
pelure (plyr) *f*, peel, skin, rind; (*P*) [over]coat.
pénal, e (penal) *a*, penal. **pénaliser** (lize) *v.t*, to penalise. **pénalité** (lite) *f*, penalty. **penalty** (lti) *m*, (*Foot*.) penalty [kick].
pénates (penat) *m.pl*, home. *dieux* ~, Penates, household gods.
penaud, e (pəno, od) *a*, sheepish.
penchant (pɑ̃ʃɑ̃) *m*, tendency, propensity; fondness, liking. *avoir un* ~ *pour*, to be partial to. **penché, e** (ʃe) *a*, sloping; slanting; tipping, tilting. **pencher** (ʃe) *v.t*, to tip, tilt; lean. ¶ *v.i*, to lean over; tilt, be slanting. *faire* ~ *la balance*, to tip the scales. **se** ~, to lean over, bend down.
pendable (pɑ̃dabl) *a*, [deserving of] hanging. **pendaison** (dɛzɔ̃) *f*, hanging. **pendant**[1], **e** (dɑ̃, ɑ̃t) *a*, hanging [down]; dangling; drooping; pending; outstanding (*question* &c). ¶ *m*, matching piece; counterpart. ~ [*d'oreille*], drop earring. *faire* ~ *à*, *se faire* ~, to match.
pendant[2] (pɑ̃dɑ̃) *pr*, during, for. ~ *que*, while, whilst.
pendentif (pɑ̃dɑ̃tif) *m*, pendant. **penderie** (dri) *f*, wardrobe; walk-in cupboard. **pendre** (dr) *v.t*. & *i*, to hang; h. up, h. out; (*arms, legs*) dangle; (*cheek*) sag. ~ *la crémaillère*, to have a house-warming party. **se** ~, to hang o.s. ~ *à*, to hang from. ~ *au cou de qn*, to throw one's arms round s.o's neck. **pendule** (dyl) *f*, clock. ¶ *m*, pendulum. **pendulette** (lɛt) *f*, small clock.
pénétrable (penetrabl) *a*, penetrable. **pénétrant, e** (trɑ̃, ɑ̃t) *a*, penetrating, piercing, searching; shrewd (*pers*.); drenching, which soaks right through; bitter (*cold*). **pénétration** (trasjɔ̃) *f*,

penetration; insight. **pénétré, e** (tre) *a,* earnest. *être ~ de,* to be highly conscious of; be full of. **pénétrer** (tre) *v.t,* to penetrate; fill, permeate; fathom (*meaning*). ¶ *v.i, ~ dans,* to enter; penetrate; (*burglar*) break into, get into.

pénible† (penibl) *a,* painful; difficult; hard; tiresome, tedious.

péniche (peniʃ) *f,* barge.

pénicilline (penisilin) *f,* penicillin.

péninsulaire (penɛ̃sylɛr) *a,* peninsular. **péninsule** (syl) *f,* peninsula.

pénis (penis) *m,* penis.

pénitence (penitɑ̃s) *f,* penitence; penance; punishment; penalty, forfeit (*at play*). *faire ~,* to repent. *mettre qn en ~,* to make s.o stand in the corner. **pénitencier** (tɑ̃sje) *m,* penitentiary. **pénitent, e** (tɑ̃, ɑ̃t) *a. & n,* penitent. **pénitentiaire** (tɑ̃sjɛr) *a,* prison.

pénombre (penɔ̃br) *f,* half-light; darkness.

pensant, e (pɑ̃sɑ̃, ɑ̃t) *a,* thinking; -minded (*bien,* right), -disposed (*mal,* ill). **pensée**[1] (pɑ̃se) *f,* (*Bot.*) pansy. **pensée**[2] (pɑ̃se) *f,* thought, thinking, mind. **penser** (se) *v.i. & t,* to think; t. out. *~ bien, mal de,* to have a high, low opinion of. *faire ~ à,* to remind, make (*s.o*) think of. *~ faire,* to consider doing, intend to do. **penseur** (sœr) *m,* thinker. **pensif, ive†** (sif, iv) *a,* pensive, thoughtful.

pension (pɑ̃sjɔ̃) *f,* board & lodging; boarding house; b. school; pension. *~ alimentaire,* alimony; living allowance (*student*). *demi-~,* half-board. *~ de retraite,* old-age (*or* retirement) pension. **pensionnaire** (ɔnɛr) *n,* (*Sch.*) boarder; resident (*hotel*); lodger. **pensionnat** (na) *m,* boarding school. **pensionné, e** (ne) *n,* pensioner. **pensionner** (ne) *v.t,* to pension, to give a pension to.

pentagone (pɑ̃tagɔn) *m,* pentagon.

pente (pɑ̃t) *f,* slope; (*fig.*) bent, tendency. *en ~,* sloping, on a slope. *~ glissante,* (*fig.*) slippery slope. *sur une mauvaise ~,* (*fig.*) going downhill.

Pentecôte (la) (pɑ̃tkot), Whit Sunday; Whitsun[tide]; Pentecost.

pénultième (penyltjɛm) *a,* penultimate.

pénurie (penyri) *f,* shortage.

pépé *P* (pepe) *m,* grandpa, grandad.

pépée *P* (pepe) *f,* (*girl*) bird *P.*

pépère *P* (pepɛr) *m,* grandpa; [old] man, old boy. ¶ *a,* quiet (*life &c*); cushy (*job*).

pépie (pepi) *f,* thirst. *avoir la ~,* to be parched.

pépier (pepje) *v.i,* to chirp, cheep, chirrup.

pépin (pepɛ̃) *m,* pip (*fruit*); (*P fig.*) snag, hitch. **pépinière** (pinjɛr) *f,* (*Hort.*) nursery; (*fig.*) nest. **pépiniériste** (njerist) *m,* nurseryman.

pépite (pepit) *f,* nugget.

perçant, e (pɛrsɑ̃, ɑ̃t) *a,* piercing; keen, sharp; shrill. **mettre en perce** (pɛrs), to broach, tap (*cask*). **percée** (se) *f,* opening; breach, gap; breakthrough; (*Rugby*) break. **percement** (səmɑ̃) *m,* drilling, boring (*hole*); building, driving (*road*); making (*window*). **perce-neige,** *f,* snowdrop. **perce-oreille,** *m,* earwig.

percepteur (pɛrsɛptœr) *m,* collector (*tax*). **perceptible** (tibl) *a,* collectable; perceptible, discernible. *~ à l'ouïe,* audible. **perception** (sjɔ̃) *f,* collection; collector's office; perception.

percer (pɛrse) *v.t,* to pierce; drill, bore, d. *or* b. through; lance; burst; break through; b. open (*safe &c*); wear a hole in (*shoes*); penetrate (*mystery*). *~ une dent,* to cut a tooth. ¶ *v.i,* (*abscess*) to burst; (*plant*) come up; (*sun &c*) break through; (*emotion*) show; (*actor &c*) become famous. **perceur** (sœr) *m,* driller (*pers.*). *~ de coffre-fort,* safebreaker. **perceuse** (søz) *f,* drill.

percevable (pɛrsəvabl) *a,* collectable, payable (*tax*). **percevoir** (səvwar) *v.t,* to collect (*tax*); receive, get (*indemnity*); perceive, detect.

perche (pɛrʃ) *f,* pole; perch (*fish*). **percher** (ʃe) *v.i,* to perch, roost. **perchoir** (ʃwar) *m,* perch.

perclus, e (pɛrkly, yz) *a,* crippled, paralyzed.

percolateur (pɛrkɔlatœr) *m,* [commercial] percolator.

percussion (pɛrkysjɔ̃) *f,* percussion. **percutant, e** (tɑ̃, ɑ̃t) *a,* forceful. **percuter** (te) *v.t,* to strike. ¶ *v.i,* (*car &c*) to crash into. **percuteur** (tœr) *m,* firing pin.

perdant, e (pɛrdɑ̃, ɑ̃t) *n,* loser. ¶ *a,* losing. **perdition** (disjɔ̃) *f,* perdition. *en ~,* (*ship*) in distress. **perdre** (dr) *v.t,* to lose; waste (*time, money*); forget (*name &c*); cause ruin to. ¶ *v.i,* to lose; leak (*tank*). **se ~,** to get lost, lose one's way; disappear, vanish; (*custom*) die out; (*ship*) sink; be wasted; go to the bad.

perdreau (pɛrdro) *m,* young partridge. **perdrix** (dri) *f,* partridge.

père (pɛr) *m,* father, parent; (*beast*) sire; senior; (*pl.*) ancestors, forefathers. *le ~ Noël,* Father Christmas, Santa Claus.

pérégrination (peregrinasjɔ̃) *f,* peregrination.

péremptoire† (perɑ̃ptwar) *a,* peremptory.

perfection (pɛrfɛksjɔ̃) *f,* perfection. **perfectionné, e** (ɔne) *a,* sophisticated. **perfectionnement** (ɔnmɑ̃) *m,* improvement, perfection. **perfectionner** (ɔne) *v.t,* to perfect; improve.

perfide† (pɛrfid) *a. & n,* treacherous, perfidious (person). **perfidie** (di) *f,* treachery, perfidy.

perforateur, trice (pɛrfɔratœr, tris) *n,* punch card operator. ¶ *f,* (*computers*) card punch. **perforation** (asjɔ̃) *f.* (*Med.*) perforation; (*computers*) punch. **perforer** (re) *v.t,* to perforate; drill; punch.

performance (pɛrfɔrmɑ̃s) *f,* performance.

perfusion (pɛrfyzjɔ̃) *f,* perfusion.

péricliter (periklite) *v.i,* to collapse.

péril (peril) *m,* peril. **périlleux, euse†** (rijø, øz) *a,* perilous.

périmé, e (perime) *a,* out of date (*ticket &c*); exploded (*theory*). **périmer** (me) *v.i,* to lapse, expire.

périmètre (perimɛtr) *m,* perimeter; limit.

période (perjɔd) *f,* period, spell. **périodicité** (disite) *f,* periodicity. **périodique†** (dik) *a,* periodic. ¶ *m,* periodical.

péripétie (peripesi) *f,* vicissitude; event.

périphérie (periferi) *f,* periphery; outskirts (*town*). **périphérique** (rik) *a,* peripheral; outlying. ¶ *m,* [*boulevard*] ~, ring road. [*terminal*] ~, computer terminal.

périphrase (perifrɑz) *f,* periphrasis.

périr (perir) *v.i,* to perish, be lost; die; lapse.

périscope (periskɔp) *m,* periscope.

périssable (perisabl) *a,* perishable.

péritonite (peritɔnit) *f,* peritonitis.

perle (pɛrl) *f,* pearl; bead; (*fig.*) gem. ~ *de culture,* cultured pearl.

permanence (pɛrmanɑ̃s) *f,* permanence; committee room; [duty] office; study room. *de* ~, on duty. *en* ~, permanently; continuously. **permanent, e** (nɑ̃, ɑ̃t) *a,* permanent, standing; continuous. ¶ *m,* (*Pol.*) official. ¶ *f,* perm.

permanganate (pɛrmɑ̃ganat) *m,* permanganate.

perméable (pɛrmeabl) *a,* permeable.

permettre (pɛrmɛtr) *v.t.ir,* to permit, allow (*à qn de faire,* s.o to do). **se** ~, to allow o.s, indulge in. *se* ~ *de,* to venture to. **permis** (mi) *m,* permit, licence. ~ *de conduire,* driving licence. **permission** (sjɔ̃) *f,* permission; (*Mil.*) leave, pass. **permissionnaire** (ɔnɛr) *m. & a,* (soldier) on leave.

permutation (pɛrmytasjɔ̃) *f,* permutation. **permuter** (te) *v.t,* to permutate, change round. ¶ *v.i,* to change, swap (*jobs &c*).

pernicieux, euse† (pɛrnisjø, øz) *a,* pernicious.

péroraison (perɔrɛzɔ̃) *f,* peroration. **pérorer** (re) *v.i,* to hold forth, speechify.

Pérou (le) (peru), Peru.

peroxyde (perɔksid) *m,* peroxide.

perpendiculaire† (pɛrpɑ̃dikylɛr) *a. & f,* perpendicular.

perpétrer (pɛrpetre) *v.t,* to perpetrate.

perpétuation (pɛrpetɥasjɔ̃) *f,* perpetuation. **perpétuel, le†** (tɥɛl) *a,* perpetual, permanent; for life. **perpétuer** (tɥe) *v.t,* to perpetuate. **perpétuité** (tɥite) *f,* perpetuity. *à* ~, in perpetuity; for life.

perplexe (pɛrplɛks) *a,* perplexed, puzzled; perplexing. **perplexité** (ksite) *f,* perplexity.

perquisition (pɛrkizisjɔ̃). *f,* (*Law*) search. **perquisitionner** (ɔne) *v.i,* to carry out a search.

perron (pɛrɔ̃) *m,* steps (*at entrance*).

perroquet (pɛrɔkɛ) *m,* parrot. **perruche** (ryʃ) *f,* budgerigar, budgie; chatterbox.

perruque (pɛryk) *f,* wig.

pers, e (pɛr, ɛrs) *a,* greenish-blue.

persan, e (pɛrsɑ̃, an) *a. &* **P**~, *n,* Persian (*modern*). *le* ~, Persian (*language*). **la Perse** (pɛrs), Persia. **perse,** *a. &* **P**~, *n,* Persian (*ancient*).

persécuter (pɛrsekyte) *v.t,* to persecute. **persécuteur, trice** (tœr, tris) *n,* persecutor. **persécution** (sjɔ̃) *f,* persecution.

persévérance (pɛrseverɑ̃s) *f,* perseverance. **persévérer** (re) *v.i,* to persevere.

persienne (pɛrsjɛn) *f,* sun shutter.

persiflage (pɛrsiflaʒ) *m,* mockery. **persifler** (fle) *v.t,* to mock, make fun of.

persil (pɛrsi) *m,* parsley. **persillé, e** (sije) *a,* sprinkled with parsley; blue-veined (*cheese*); marbled (*meat*).

persistance (pɛrsistɑ̃s) *f,* persistence. *avec* ~, persistently, stubbornly. **persistant, e** (tɑ̃, ɑ̃t) *a,* persistent. **persister** (te) *v.i,* to persist.

personnage (pɛrsɔnaʒ) *m,* personage; character. *être un* ~, to be somebody. **personnalité** (nalite) *f,* personality; (*pl.*) [well known] people. **personne** (sɔn) *f,* person; self; (*pl.*) people. ~ *âgée,* elderly person. ~ *à charge,* dependent. *la* ~ *humaine,* the individual. ~ *morale* ou *civile,* (*Law*) artificial person. ~ *physique,* (*Law*) individual. ¶ *pn.m,* anybody, anyone; nobody, no one, none. *je ne vois* ~, I can't see anyone. **personnel, le†** (nɛl) *a,* personal; private; selfish. ¶ *m,* staff, personnel. **personnifier** (nifje) *v.t,* to personify; embody.

perspective (pɛrspɛktiv) *f,* perspective; outlook, view, prospect; viewpoint, angle.

perspicace (pɛrspikas) *a,* perspicacious. **perspicacité** (site) *f,* perspicacity.

persuader (pɛrsɥade) *v.t,* to persuade; convince (*qn de qch, de faire,* s.o of sth, to do). *j'en suis persuadé,* I'm convinced of it. ¶ *v.i,* ~ *à qn,* to persuade s.o (*de faire,* to do). **persuasif, ive** (zif, iv) *a,* persuasive; convincing. **persuasion** (zjɔ̃) *f,* persuasion; belief.

perte (pɛrt) *f,* loss; leak[age]; waste; (*Mil.*) casualty; ruin. ~ *sèche,* dead loss. *à* ~, at a loss. *à* ~ *de vue,* as far as the eye can see. *en pure* ~, to no purpose.

pertinent, e (pɛrtinɑ̃, ɑ̃t) *a,* pertinent, apposite, relevant; discerning; (*Linguistics*) significant. **pertinemment** (namɑ̃) *ad,* pertinently &c. **pertinence** (nɑ̃s) *f,* relevance, pertinence.

perturbateur, trice (pɛrtyrbatœr, tris) *a,* disruptive. ¶ *n,* troublemaker. **perturbation** (sjɔ̃) *f,* disturbance, perturbation; disruption. **perturber** (be) *v.t,* to disrupt; disturb; perturb.

péruvien, ne (peryvjɛ, ɛn) *a. &* **P**~, *n,* Peruvian.

pervenche (pɛrvɑ̃ʃ) *f,* (*Bot.*) periwinkle.

pervers, e (pɛrvɛr, ɛrs) *a,* perverse; perverted. ¶ *m,* pervert. **perversion** (vɛrsjɔ̃) *f,* perversion. **perversité** (site) *f,* perversity. **pervertir** (tir) *v.t,* to pervert.

pesage (pəzaʒ) *m,* weighing; (*Turf*) w. in. **pesamment** (zamɑ̃) *ad,* heavily. **pesant, e** (zɑ̃, ɑ̃t) *a,* heavy, weighty; ponderous; massive;

deep (*sleep*). *son* ~ *d'or*, his, its, weight in gold. **pesanteur** (zɑ̃tœr) *f*, heaviness, weight; (*Phys.*) gravity. **pesée** (ze) *f*, weighing; thrust, push. **pèse-lettre** (pɛzlɛtr) *m*, letter scales. **pèse-personne** (pəzpɛrsɔn) *m*, scales. **peser** (pəze) *v.t*, to weigh; ponder; weigh up. ¶ *v.i*, to weigh; lie heavy; bear, press; carry weight; be heavy.

pessimisme (pɛsimism) *m*, pessimism. **pessimiste** (mist) *m*, pessimist. ¶ *a*, pessimistic.

peste (pɛst) *f*, plague; (*fig: pers.*) pest, nuisance. **pester** (te) *v.i*, to curse. **pestilence** (tilɑ̃s) *f*, stench. **pestilentiel, le** (lɑ̃sjɛl) *a*, stinking.

pet (pɛ) *m*, fart *P**. *faire le* ~ *P*, to be on the look-out.

pétale (petal) *m*, petal.

pétarade (petarad) *f*, backfire. **pétarader** (de) *v.i*, to backfire. **pétard** (tar) *m*, banger, firecracker; (*Rly*) detonator; (*P*) row, racket; gun.

péter (pete) *v.i*, (*P**) to fart *P**; (*P*) go off; burst; bust, snap. ¶ *v.t*, (*P*) to bust, snap.

pétiller (petije) *v.i*, to crackle; sparkle; fizz[le], bubble [over].

petit, e (pəti, it) *a*, small, little; short; slim, thin, slender (*waist &c*); young; (*pej.*) mean, petty; slight (*cold &c*); minor; light (*tap*). ¶ *ad*, ~ *à* ~, little by l. **petit,** *comps:* ~ *ami*, boyfriend. *P*~ *Chaperon Rouge*, Little Red Riding Hood. ~ *chat*, kitten. ~ *chien*, puppy. ~ *cousin*, young cousin; distant c. ~ *déjeuner*, breakfast. *le* ~ *doigt*, the little finger. *le* ~ *écran*, television, the small screen. ~*-enfant*, grandchild. ~*s-enfants*, grandchildren. ~*-fils*, grandson. ~*s fours*, petits fours. ~*-gris*, garden snail. ~*-lait*, whey. ~*-nègre*, pidgin [French]. ~*-neveu*, great-nephew. ~ *nom*, first name. ~*-pois*, [garden] peas. *le P*~ *Poucet*, Tom Thumb. ~ *salé*, streaky bacon. ~*-suisse*, petit suisse. **petite,** *comps:* ~ *amie*, girlfriend. ~ *classe*, junior form. ~ *cousine*, young cousin; distant c. ~*-fille*, granddaughter. ~*-nièce*, great niece. ~ *noblesse*, gentry. ~ *vérole*, smallpox. **petit, e,** *n*, little boy, l. girl, l. one. **un petit,** a young one, cub, pup, whelp. **les petits,** little ones, children; the young. *les tout* ~, the very young, the tiny tots; (*Sch.*) the infants. **petitement** (titmɑ̃) *ad*, poorly; meanly, pettily. **petitesse** (tɛs) *f*, smallness, small size; pettiness, meanness.

pétition (petisjɔ̃) *f*, petition. ~ *de principe*, begging the question. *faire une* ~ *auprès de qn*, to petition s.o. **pétitionnaire** (sjɔnɛr) *n*, petitioner.

pétrel (petrɛl) *m*, petrel.

pétrification (petrifikasjɔ̃) *f*, petrifaction. **pétrifier** (fje) *v.t*, to petrify.

pétrin (petrɛ̃) *m*, kneading trough; fix, mess. *être dans le* ~, to be in a fix. **pétrir** (trir) *v.t*, to knead.

pétrole (petrɔl) *m*, petroleum, oil. ~ [*lampant*] (lɑ̃pɑ̃), paraffin [oil]. **pétrochimie** (trɔʃimi) *f*, petrochemistry. **pétrolier, ère** (lje, ɛr) *a*, petroleum, oil; oil-producing (*country*). ¶ *m*, [oil] tanker; oil magnate. **pétrolifère** (lifɛr) *a*, oil-bearing.

pétulant, e (petylɑ̃, ɑ̃t) *a*, lively, impetuous.

pétunia (petynja) *m*, petunia.

peu (pø) *ad*, little, not much; few, not many; not very. ~ *de temps*, little time. ~ *de verres*, few glasses. *il mange très* ~, he eats very little. ¶ *m*, little. *un* ~ *de vin*, a l. wine. *un tout petit* ~, a tiny bit. *le* ~ *d'amis qu'il a*, the few friends he has. *un* ~ *partout*, all over the place. *à* ~ [*de chose*] *près*, about, nearly.

peuplade (pœplad) *f*, tribe. **peuple** (pl) *m*, people, nation; crowd [of people]. *les gens du* ~, the common *or* ordinary people. **peuplé, e,** (ple) *a*, populated. **peupler** (ple) *v.t*, to populate; stock; plant out; fill; inhabit. **peuplement** (pləmɑ̃) *m*, stocking; populating; planting (*trees*); population.

peuplier (pœplie) *m*, poplar.

peur (pœr) *f*, fear, fright. *avoir* ~, to be afraid. **peureux, euse**† (pœrø, øz) *a*, timid, nervous.

peut-être (pœtɛtr) *ad*, perhaps, maybe.

phalange (falɑ̃ʒ) *f*, phalanx.

pharaon (faraɔ̃) *m*, Pharaoh.

phare (far) *m*, lighthouse; light; beacon; headlight, headlamp. ~ *antibrouillard*, foglamp. ~*s code*, dipped headlights. ~ *de recul*, reversing light. *pleins* ~*s*, full beam.

pharisien, ne [zjɛ̃, ɛn] *n*, Pharisee.

pharmaceutique (farmasøtik) *a*, pharmaceutical. **pharmacie** (si) *f*, pharmacy; dispensary; chemist's shop; medicine chest; pharmacology; medicines, pharmaceuticals. ~ *portative*, first-aid kit. **pharmacien, ne** (sjɛ̃, ɛn) *n*, chemist, druggist, pharmacist.

pharyngite (farɛ̃ʒit) *f*, pharyngitis. **pharynx** (rɛ̃ks) *m*, pharynx.

phase (fɑz) *f*, phase; stage.

phénix (feniks) *m*, phoenix; paragon.

phénol (fenɔl) *m*, phenol.

phénoménal, e† (fenɔmenal) *a*, phenomenal. **phénomène** (mɛn) *m*, phenomenon; freak.

philanthrope (filɑ̃trɔp) *n*, philanthropist. **philanthropie** (pi) *f*, philanthropy. **philanthropique** (pik) *a*, philanthropic.

philatélisme (filatelism) *m*, philately. **philatéliste** (list) *n*, philatelist.

philharmonique (filarmɔnik) *a*, philharmonic.

philistin (filistɛ̃) *m*, Philistine.

philosophe (filɔzɔf) *n*, philosopher. ¶ *a*, philosophic(al) (*calm*). **philosopher** (fe) *v.i*, to philosophize. **philosophie** (fi) *f*, philosophy. **philosophique**† (fik) *a*, philosophic(al).

phlébite (flebit) *f*, phlebitis.

phlox (flɔks) *m*, phlox.

phobie (fɔbi) *f,* phobia.
phonétique (fɔnetik) *a,* phonetic. ¶ *f,* phonetics. **phonographe** (nɔgraf) *m,* gramophone, phonograph. **phonologie** (nɔlɔʒi) *f,* phonology.
phoque (fɔk) *m,* (*Zool.*) seal.
phosphate (fɔsfat) *m,* phosphate. **phosphore** (fɔr) *m,* phosphorus. **phosphorescence** (fɔrɛsɑ̃s) *f,* phosphorescence. **phosphorescent, e** (sɑ̃, ɑ̃t) *a,* phosphorescent.
photo (fɔtɔ) *f,* photo, snapshot. ~**copie** (kɔpi) *f,* photocopy[ing], photostat[ting]. ~**copier** (pje) *v.t,* to photocopy, photostat. ~**copieur** (pjœr) *m,* photocopier. ~**-électrique** (elɛktrik) *a,* photo-electric. **photographe** (fɔtɔgraf) *n,* photographer; camera dealer. **photographie** (fi) *f,* photography; photograph. **photographier** (fje) *v.t,* to photograph. **photographique** (fik) *a,* photographic. **photogravure** (vyr) *f,* photoengraving.
phrase (frɑs) *f,* sentence; (*Mus., fig.*) phrase. ~ *toute faite,* stock phrase. *faire des ~s,* to use flowing language.
phtisie (ftizi) *f,* consumption.
physicien, ne (fizisjɛ̃, ɛn) *n,* physicist.
physiologie (fizjɔlɔʒi) *f,* physiology.
physionomie (fizjɔnɔmi) *f,* face.
physique† (fizik) *a,* physical. ¶ *f,* physics. ¶ *m,* physique.
piaffer (pjafe) *v.i,* to paw the ground; prance.
piailler (pjɑje) *v.i,* to squawk.
pianiste (pjanist) *n,* pianist. **piano** (no) *m,* piano. ~ *à queue,* grand piano. ~ *droit,* upright piano. ¶ *ad,* piano; (*fig.*) gently.
piauler (pjole) *v.i,* to cheep; whimper.
pic (pik) *m,* pick; peak; woodpecker. *à ~,* sheer, precipitous.
piccolo (pikɔlo) *m,* piccolo.
pichet (piʃɛ) *m,* pitcher, jug.
picoler *P* (pikɔle) *v.i,* to booze *P,* tipple *P.*
picorer (pikɔre) *v.i,* to peck.
picotement (pikɔtmɑ̃) *m,* pricking; tickling; stinging; smarting. **picoter** (te) *v.t,* to prick; peck; sting, make smart. ¶ *v.i,* to tickle, prick, smart, sting, prickle.
picrate *P* (pikrat) *m,* plonk *P;* [cheap] wine.
pie (pi) *f,* magpie; chatterbox. ¶ *a,* piebald, black & white.
pièce (pjɛs) *f,* (*gen., Mus., Liter., chess &c*) piece; bit, fragment; (*Mil.*) gun; (*Fish. &c*) specimen; document, paper; (*Need.*) patch; room; head (*cattle &c*); (*P*) tip (*gratuity*); cask (*wine*). [*la*] ~, each, apiece. ~ *à conviction* (*Law*), exhibit. ~ *de blé,* wheat field. ~ [*détachée*] (*Tech.*), part, component. ~ *d'eau,* ornamental lake. ~ *d'identité,* identity paper. ~ [*de monnaie*], coin. ~ *de rechange,* spare part. ~ [*de théâtre*], [stage] play. ~ *montée,* tiered cake; wedding c.
pied (pje) *m,* foot; trotter; base, bottom; leg (*chair, &c*); stalk; footing; foothold; stand; standard; stem (*glass*); plant (*lettuce &c*); head (*celery*); (*P*) idiot. ~ *à* ~, every inch of the way. ~*-à-terre,* pied-à-terre. ~*-de-poule,* hound's tooth (*cloth*). ~*-d'alouette,* delphinium. ~ *de vigne,* vine. ~ *noir,* pied-noir (*Algerian born Frenchman*). *à ~ sec,* without getting one's feet wet. *au ~ de la lettre,* literally. *au ~ levé,* at a moment's notice. *avoir bon ~ bon œil,* to be fit as a fiddle. *avoir le ~ marin,* to be a good sailor. *de ~ ferme,* resolutely. *faire le ~ de grue P,* to kick one's heels. *faire un ~ de nez à qn,* to thumb one's nose at s.o. *mettre qn à ~,* to dismiss s.o. *mettre qn au ~ de mur,* to put s.o. to the test. *sur ~,* on foot; standing (*crops*). *vivre sur un grand ~,* to live in a grand style. **piédestal** (pjedɛstal) *m,* pedestal.
piège (pjɛʒ) *m,* trap, snare, pitfall; pit. ~ *à loups,* mantrap. **piéger** (pjeʒe) *v.t,* to trap; set a trap in; booby-trap. *engin piégé,* booby trap.
pierraille (pjɛrɑj) *f,* loose stones, chippings. **pierre** (pjɛr) *f,* stone. ~ *à aiguiser,* whetstone, hone. ~ *à briquet* & ~ *à fusil,* flint. ~ *à chaux,* limestone. ~ *d'achoppement* (aʃɔpmɑ̃) stumbling block. ~ *d'aimant,* lodestone. ~ *de touche,* touchstone. ~ *ponce,* pummice [stone]. ~ *précieuse,* precious stone, gem. ~ *tombale* (tɔ̃bal), tombstone. **pierreries** (pjɛr[ə]ri) *f.pl,* precious stones, gems, jewels. **pierreux, euse** (rø, øz) *a,* stony; gritty.
pierrot (pjɛro) *m,* pierrot; sparrow.
piété (pjete) *f,* piety, godliness; devotion.
piétiner (pjetine) *v.t,* to trample on; t. underfoot; tread on. ¶ *v.i,* to stamp [one's foot *or* feet]; stand about; be at a standstill. **piétinement** (tinmɑ̃) *m,* stamping; standing about. **piéton** (tɔ̃) *m,* pedestrian. **piéton, ne** (tɔ̃, ɔn) & **piétonnier, ère** (tɔnje, ɛr) *a,* pedestrian.
piètre† (pjɛtr) *a,* poor, mediocre; wretched.
pieu (pjø) *m,* stake, post; pile; (*P*) bed.
pieuvre (pjœvr) *f,* octopus.
pieux, euse† (pjø, øz) *a,* pious, devout. ~ *mensonge,* white lie.
pigeon, ne (piʒɔ̃, ɔn) *n,* pigeon. (*P*) mug *P.* ~ *ramier,* wood pigeon. ~ *voyageur,* carrier pigeon. **pigeonneau** (ʒɔno) *m,* young pigeon, squab. **pigeonnier** (nje) *m,* dovecot[e].
pigment (pigmɑ̃) *m,* pigment.
pignocher (piɲɔʃe) *v.i,* to pick at one's food.
pignon (piɲɔ̃) *m,* gable; pinion; gearwheel; (*Bot.*) pine kernel.
pilastre (pilastr) *m,* pilaster; newel.
pile (pil) *f,* pile, heap; stack (*of wood*); pier (*bridge*); (*Elec.*) battery, cell; reverse (*coin*). ~ *atomique,* atomic reactor. ~ *ou face?* heads or tails? ¶ *ad,* (*P stop*) dead *P. tomber ~,* to be just right.

piler (pile) *v.t,* to pound, crush.
pilier (pilje) *m,* pillar.
pillage (pijaʒ) *m,* pillage, looting; ransacking; fleecing; plagiarizing. **piller** (je) *v.t,* to pillage, plunder, loot, ransack; (*pers.*) fleece; (*fig.*) plagiarize.
pilon (pilɔ̃) *m,* pestle; drumstick (*fowl*); wooden leg. **pilonner** (lɔne) *v.t,* to pound; shell, bombard. **pilonnage** (lɔnaʒ) *m,* pounding &c.
pilori (pilɔri) *m,* pillory. *mettre au* ~, to pillory.
pilotage (pilɔtaʒ) *m,* piloting; flying. **pilote** (lɔt) *m,* pilot; driver; (*fig.*) guide. ¶ *a,* experimental; cut-price (*shop*). **piloter** (te) *v.t,* to pilot; fly; drive. ~ *dans,* to show (*pers.*) round (*town*). **pilotis** (ti) *m,* pile (*stake*).
pilou (pilu) *m,* flannelette.
pilule (pilyl) *f,* pill.
piment (pimɑ̃) *m,* chilli; (*fig.*) spice. ~ *doux,* pepper, capsicum.
pimpant, e (pɛ̃pɑ̃, ɑ̃t) *a,* smart, spruce, spick & span.
pin (pɛ̃) *m,* pine [tree].
pinacle (pinakl) *m,* pinnacle.
pince (pɛ̃s) *f,* (*oft. pl.*) pliers, nippers; forceps; tweezers; tongs; (*s.*) clip; clamp; crowbar; claw, pincer (*crab &c*); pleat; (*Need,*) dart; (*P*) hand, mitt *P*; leg. ~*s à épiler,* eyebrow tweezers. ~ *à linge,* clothes peg. ~-*monseigneur, f,* jemmy (*burglar's*). ~-*sans-rire, m,* man of dry humour. **pincé, e** (pɛ̃se) *a,* prim; stiff.
pinceau (pɛ̃so) *m,* paint brush. ~ *lumineux,* pencil of light.
pincée (pɛ̃se) *f,* pinch (*snuff &c*). **pincer** (se) *v.t,* to pinch, nip, squeeze; purse (*lips*); pluck (*strings*); play (*harp &c*), twang; grip; catch; (*Need.*) put darts in. **pincement au cœur** (smɑ̃) lump in one's throat. **pincettes** (sɛt) *f.pl,* tweezers; tongs (*fire*). **pinçon** (sɔ̃) *m,*pinch-mark.
pinède (pinɛd) *f,* pinewood, pine forest.
pingouin (pɛ̃gwɛ̃) *m,* auk; penguin.
ping-pong (piŋpɔ̃g) *m,* ping-pong, table tennis.
pingre (pɛ̃gr) *a,* stingy. ¶ *m,* skinflint.
pinson (pɛ̃sɔ̃) *m,* chaffinch.
pintade (pɛ̃tad) *f,* guinea fowl.
pioche (pjɔʃ) *f,* pick; pickaxe; mattock. **piocher** (ʃe) *v.t. & i,* to pick up; work hard, grind.
piolet (pjɔlɛ) *m,* ice axe.
pion (pjɔ̃) *m,* (*Chess.*) pawn; piece; (*Sch.*) supervisor.
pionnier (pjɔnje) *m,* pioneer.
pipe (pip) *f,* pipe. **pipeau** (po) *m,* [reed] pipe.
pipe-line (pajplajn, piplin) *m,* pipeline.
pipi *P* (pipi) *m,* wee[wee] *P.*
piquant, e (pikɑ̃, ɑ̃t) *a,* prickly; thorny; biting (*cold*); cutting (*remark*); spicy, titillating; sour, tart; piquant; hot (*mustard*). ¶ *m,* prickle; thorn; spine; barb; piquancy; spice. **pique** (pik) *f,* pike (*weapon*); cutting remark. ¶ *m,* (*Cards*) spade[s]. ~ *-assiette, m,* sponger. ~*-nique* (nik) *m,* picnic. ~*-niquer,* to picnic. **piqué, e** (ke) *a,* quilted; [machine] stitched; (*P*) crazy; mildewed; worm-eaten; sour (*wine*). ¶ *m,* piqué; (*Aero.*) dive. **piquer** (ke) *v.t,* to prick; sting; bite; arouse, excite; nettle, pique; (*P*) to pick up (*illness &c*); pinch *P,* nick *P;* (*Need.*) stitch. ~ *une crise,* to have a fit (*of tears, giggles*). ~ *une tête,* to dive [head first]. ¶ *v.i,* to be hot, be sour, be pungent. ~ *du nez* (*Aero.*), to nose dive; (*Naut.*) dip her head; (*flowers*) droop; (*pers.*) fall head first. **se** ~, to pride o.s (*de qch, de faire,* on sth, on doing). **piquet** (kɛ) *m,* peg, stake; picket; (*Cards*) piquet. **piquette** (kɛt) *f,* [cheap] wine; thrashing *P;* hammering *P.* **piqûre** (kyr) *f,* prick; sting; bite; hole; (*Med.*) injection, shot; stitch[ing].
pirate (pirat) *m,* pirate; swindler. ~ *de l'air,* hijacker. ¶ *a,* pirate. **pirater** (te) *v.i,* to pirate. **piraterie** (tri) *f,* piracy. ~ *aérienne,* hijacking.
pire (pir) *a,* worse. *le* ~, the worst.
pirogue (pirɔg) *f,* [dug-out] canoe.
pirouette (pirwɛt) *f,* pirouette; about-turn; evasive reply.
pis[1] (pi) *m,* udder.
pis[2] (pi) *ad,* worse. *le* ~, the worst. ~ *aller, m,* last resource; makeshift. *au* ~ *aller,* at the worst.
pisciculture (pisikyltyr) *f,* fish breeding. **piscine** (sin) *f,* swimming pool.
pissenlit (pisɑ̃li) *m,* dandelion.
pisser *P** (pise) *v.i,* to pee *P;* gush out.
pistache (pistaʃ) *f,* pistachio [nut].
piste (pist) *f,* track (*running, racing*); run (*ski &c*); (*Aero.*) runway; ring (*circus*); [dance] floor; rink (*skating*); racecourse; track, trail; (*police*) lead, clue. ~ *cavalière,* bridle path. ~ *cyclable,* cycle track. ~ *sonore,* sound track. **pister** (te) *v.t,* to track, trail.
pistil (pistil) *m,* pistil.
pistolet (pistɔlɛ) *m,* pistol; spray gun.
piston (pistɔ̃) *m,* piston; (*Mus.*) valve; (*P*) string-pulling. **pistonner** *P* (tɔne) *v.t,* to pull strings for.
pitchpin (pitʃpɛ̃) *m,* pitchpine.
piteux, euse† (pitø, øz) *a,* pathetic; pitiful; shamefaced. **pitié** (tje) *f,* pity, mercy.
piton (pitɔ̃) *m,* (*climbing*) peg, piton; (*Geog.*) peak.
pitoyable† (pitwajabl) *a,* pitiable, pitiful.
pitre (pitr) *m,* clown; buffoon.
pittoresque† (pitɔrɛsk) *a,* picturesque; quaint; graphic. ¶ *m,* picturesqueness.
pivert (pivɛr) *m,* green woodpecker.
pivoine (pivwan) *f,* peony.
pivot (pivo) *m,* pivot; tap root. **pivoter** (vɔte) *v.i,* to pivot, turn, revolve, swivel.
placage (plakaʒ) *m,* veneer; facing.
placard (plakar) *m,* cupboard; poster, notice;

(*P*) thick layer. **placarder** (karde) *v.t*, to stick up (*bills*); placard.
place (plas) *f*, place; square (*in town*); seat; room, space; fare (*transport*); (*Sport*) place, placing; job, position, situation; (*Com., Fin.*) market. ~ *d'armes*, parade ground. ~ *forte*, fortified town. *à la* ~ *de*, instead of, in place of. *de* ~ *en* ~, here, there & everywhere. *être en* ~, to be ready. *faire* ~ *à qn*, to let s.o pass; give way to s.o. *faire* ~ *nette*, to make a clean sweep. *faire de la* ~, to make room. *les gens en* ~, influential people. *payer* ~ *entière*, to pay a full fare (*or* price). *prenez* ~, take your place (*or* seat). **placement** (smɑ̃) *m*, investment. **placer** (se) *v.t*, to place, put, set; post; station; land (*punch*); put (*or* get) in (*word*); fit, put in; (*Com.*) place, sell; invest (*money*); deposit, pay in. **se** ~, to take up position; stand; sit down; take place, happen, occur; find a job.
placide† (plasid) *a*, placid. **placidité** (dite) *f*, placidity.
placier (plasje) *m*, canvasser, traveller.
plafond (plafɔ̃) *m*, ceiling; roof (*car*); maximum. **plafonner** (fɔne) *v.i*, to reach a ceiling (*or* maximum). **plafonnier** (nje) *m*, interior light (*car*); ceiling light.
plage (plaʒ) *f*, beach; seaside resort; track (*record*); (*fig.*) zone. ~ *arrière*, (*Naut.*) quarter deck; (*Mot.*) back shelf. ~ *de prix*, price range (*or* bracket).
plagiaire (plaʒjɛr) *m*, plagiarist. **plagiat** (ʒja) *m*, plagiarism. **plagier** (ʒje) *v.t*, to plagiarize.
plaider (plɛde) *v.i. & t*, to plead. ~ *pour qn*, to be a point in s.o's favour; speak for s.o. **plaideur, euse** (dœr, øz) *n*, litigant. **plaidoirie** (dwari) *f*, pleading; counsel's speech. **plaidoyer** (dwaje) *m*, speech for the defence.
plaie (plɛ) *f*, wound; cut; (*fig.*) scourge.
plaignant, e (plɛɲɑ̃, ɑ̃t) *a*, litigant. ¶ *n*, plaintiff.
plaindre (plɛ̃dr) *v.t.ir*, to pity, be sorry for; begrudge. **se** ~, to complain; moan, groan, make a complaint (*de*, about).
plaine (plɛn) *f*, (*Phys., Geog.*) plain.
plain-pied (plɛ̃pje) *ad*, *de* ~, on the same level (*avec*, as); (*house*) at street level. *entrer de* ~ *dans le sujet*, to come straight to the point.
plainte (plɛ̃t) *f*, moan, groan, complaint; (*Law*) action. **plaintif, ive**† (plɛ̃tif, iv) *a*, plaintive, doleful.
plaire (plɛr) *v.i.ir*, ~ *à qn*, to please s.o, be liked by s.o. *ça lui plaît*, he likes *or* enjoys it. *ça te plairait de venir?* would you like to come? *plaît-il?* I beg your pardon? *s'il te plaît, s'il vous plaît*, [if you] please. *plût au ciel que ...*, would to heaven that ... **se** ~, *elle se plaît à Paris*, she likes being in P. *se* ~ *à faire*, to enjoy doing. **plaisamment** (plɛzamɑ̃) *ad*, laughably; amusingly; pleasantly, agreeably. **de plaisance** (zɑ̃s), pleasure (*boat*); week-end (*cottage*). **plaisant, e** (zɑ̃, ɑ̃t) *a*, funny, amusing; pleasant, agreeable; laughable, ridiculous. **plaisanter** (zɑ̃te) *v.i*, to joke. ¶ *v.t*, to tease. **plaisanterie** (tri) *f*, joke; practical j.; prank. **plaisir** (zir) *m*, pleasure; will, wish; hobby. *au* ~ [*de vous revoir*], [I'll] see you again sometime. *faire* ~ *à qn*, to please s.o, make s.o happy.
plan, e (plɑ̃, an) *a*, (*Math.*) plane; flat. ¶ *m*, plan; map (*town*); (*Math. &c*) plane; (*Cine.*) shot. ~ *d'eau*, stretch of water. ~ *de travail*, worktop (*kitchen*). *au deuxième* ~, in the middle distance. *dernier* ~, background. *premier* ~, foreground. *laisser en* ~, to leave in the lurch; abandon.
planche (plɑ̃ʃ) *f*, plank; board; shelf; gangplank; diving board; (*Hort.*) bed; (*Typ.*) plate. ~ *à repasser*, ironing board. ~ *à voile*, sailboard; windsurfing. ~ *de salut*, last hope. *cabine en* ~*s*, wooden hut. *faire la* ~ (*Swim.*) to float. **plancher** (ʃe) *m*, floor.
plancton (plɑ̃ktɔ̃) *m*, plankton.
planer (plane) *v.i*, to glide; soar; hover; look down (*sur*, on, over).
planétaire (planetɛr) *a*, planetary. **planète** (nɛt) *f*, planet.
planeur (planœr) *m*, (*Aero.*) glider.
planification (planifikasjɔ̃) *f*, [economic] planning. **planifier** (nifje) *v.t*, to plan. **planning** (planiŋ) *m*, programme, schedule. ~ *familial*, family planning.
planque *P* (plɑ̃k) *f*, hideout; cushy job *P*. **planquer** *P* (ke) *v.t*, to hide away. **se** ~, to take cover.
plant (plɑ̃) *m*, sapling, seedling, young plant; plantation (*trees*); bed (*plants*). **plantain** (tɛ̃) *m*, plantain. **plantation** (tasjɔ̃) *f*, planting; plantation; bed; plant. **plante** (plɑ̃t) *f*, sole (*foot*); (*Bot.*) plant. ~ *vivace*, perennial. **planter** (te) *v.t*, to plant, set; plant (*garden*); plant out; pitch (*tent*); hammer in (*nail*); drive in (*post*); stick in (*needle*); put, stick *P*. ~ *là*, to dump; ditch, walk out on (*pers.*). **planteur** (tœr) *n*, planter, grower. **plantoir** (twar) *m*, dibble.
planton (plɑ̃tɔ̃) (*Mil.*) *m*, orderly; o. duty. *faire le* ~ *P*, to hang about *P*.
plantureux, euse† (plɑ̃tyrø, øz) *a*, copious, fertile; bumper (*crop*).
plaquage (plakaʒ) *m*, (*Rugby*) tackle. **plaque** (plak) *f*, plate; sheet; slab; plaque; tablet; badge. ~ *d'identité*, identity disc. ~ *minéralogique*, (*Mot.*) number plate. ~ *tournante*, (*Rly.*) turntable. **plaqué, e** (ke) *a*, plated (*gold &c*). ¶ *m*, [electro]plate. **plaquer** (ke) *v.t*, to plate; veneer; (*Rugby*) tackle; plaster down (*hair*); (*P*) pack in *P*; ditch *P*, jilt (*pers.*).
plasma (plasma) *m*, plasma.
plastic (plastik) *m*, gelignite. **plastifier** (tifje) *v.t*, to coat with plastic. **plastique** (tik) *a. & m*,

plastic. ¶ *f,* plastic art. **plastiquer** (tike) *v.t,* to plant a plastic bomb in.
plastron (plastrɔ̃) *m,* breastplate; shirt front.
plat[1] (pla) *m,* dish; course (*meal*). ~ *du jour,* today's special. ~ *de résistance,* main course; (*fig.*) pièce de résistance.
plat[2], **e** (pla, at) *a,* flat; straight (*hair, angle*); dull; smooth; dead (*calm*). *à* ~, flat. *à* ~ *ventre,* flat on one's face. *mettre qn à* ~, to lay s.o low. ¶ *m,* flat part. ~*s de côtes,* best rib (*beef*). *faire du* ~ *à P,* to crawl to; sweet-talk *P* (*woman*).
platane (platan) *m,* plane [tree].
plat-bord (plabɔr) *m,* gunwale.
plateau (plato) *m,* tray; pan (*scale*); turntable, deck (*record player*); top (*table*); (*Geog.*) plateau; (*Theat.*) stage; (*Cine.*) set; (*Rly.*) flat wagon; trailer.
plate-bande (platbɑ̃d) (*Hort.*) *f,* border; bed.
plate-forme (platfɔrm) *f,* platform, stage; flat roof.
platement (platmɑ̃) *ad,* flatly; dully.
platine (platin) *f,* turntable, deck (*record player*). ¶ *m,* platinum.
platitude (platityd) *f,* dullness; platitude.
plâtras (platra) *m,* rubble. **plâtre** (tr) *m,* plaster; p. cast. **plâtrer** (plɑtre) *v.t,* to plaster; set in plaster. **plâtrier** (trie) *m,* plasterer. **plâtrière** (ɛr) *f,* gypsum quarry.
plausible† (plozibl) *a,* plausible.
plébiscite (plebisit) *m,* plebiscite. **plébisiter** (site) *v.t,* to elect by plebiscite.
plein, e† (plɛ̃, ɛn) *a,* full; complete, total; solid; continuous, unbroken (*line*); rich (*voice*); pregnant (*animal*); open (*air*). ~ *de,* full of; covered with; bursting with. *en* ~ *jour,* in broad daylight. ¶ *ad,* all over, completely. ~ *de,* lots of. *à* ~, to full capacity, to the full. *en avoir* ~ [*le dos*] *de qch P,* to be fed up with sth. ¶ *m,* height. *faire le* ~, (*Mot.*) to fill up; (*Theat.*) have a full house. **plénipotentiaire** (nipɔtɑ̃sjɛr) *m.* & *a,* plenipotentiary. **plénitude** (tyd) *f,* plenitude, fullness; completeness.
pléonasme (pleɔnasm) *m,* pleonasm.
pléthore (pletɔr) *f,* plethora, glut. **pléthorique** (rik) *a,* excessive; overabundant.
pleur (plœr) *m. usually pl,* tear. **pleurard, e** (plœrar, ard) *n,* crybaby, grizzler. ¶ *a,* whining, whimpering, grizzling. **pleurer** (re) *v.i.* to weep; cry; (*eyes*) water, run; (*violin &c*) wail; (*pej.*) moan. ¶ *v.t,* to moan [for]; bewail; weep, shed (*tears*); shout for; begrudge. *à* ~, dreadfully, terribly.
pleurésie (plœrezi) *f,* pleurisy.
pleurnicher (plœrniʃe) *v.i,* to whimper, whine, snivel. **pleurnicherie** (ʃri) *f,* whining, snivelling. **pleurnicheur, euse** (ʃœr, øz) *n,* crybaby. ¶ *a,* snivelling, whining.
pleuviner (pløvine) *v.i,* to drizzle. **pleuvoir** (war) *v.i.ir,* to rain; (*blows*) shower. *il pleut à verse, à torrents, il pleut des cordes,* it's pouring, teeming down.
pli (pli) *m,* fold; pleat; wrinkle, pucker, crease; bend; line (*brow*); habit; envelope, letter; (*Cards*) trick. *prendre le* ~ *de,* to get into the habit of. *prendre un mauvais* ~, (*garment*) to get out of shape. **pliable** (abl) *a,* pliable. **pliant, e** (ɑ̃, ɑ̃t) *a,* pliant; folding; collapsible. ¶ *m,* camp stool.
plie (pli) *f,* plaice.
plier (plie) *v.t.* & *i,* to fold; f. up; f. back; bend; sag; (*pers.*) yield, give in; g. way. **se** ~ **à,** to submit to; yield to; bow to; give in to.
plinthe (plɛ̃t) *f,* plinth; skirting [board].
plisser (plise) *v.t.* & *i,* to pleat, fold; crease, wrinkle, pucker; screw up (*eyes*). **plissure** (syr) *f,* pleats.
pliure (plijyr) *f,* fold; bend.
plomb (plɔ̃) *m,* lead; [1.] shot; (*Fish.*) sinker; (*Typ.*) type; (*Elec.*) fuse. *à* ~, straight down. *de* ~, leaden; deep (*sleep*); blazing (*sun*). **plombage** (baʒ) *m,* filling (*teeth*). **plomber** (be) *v.t,* to weight [with lead]; fill (*tooth*); seal; plumb (*wall*). **plomberie** (bri) *m,* plumbing; plumber's workshop. **plombier** (bje) *m,* plumber.
plongeoir (plɔ̃ʒwar) *m,* diving board. **plongeon** (ʒɔ̃) *m,* dive. **plongée** (ʒe) *f,* diving; dive, submersion. **plonger** (ʒe) *v.i.* & *t,* to plunge; dive; submerge; dip; duck; immerse; thrust. **plongeur, euse** (ʒœr, øz) *n,* diver; skin d.; dishwasher (*restaurant*).
ployer (plwaje) *v.t.* & *i,* to bend, sag; give way, yield.
pluie (plɥi) *f,* rain; shower; wet. ~ *fine,* drizzle. (*fig.*) *faire la* ~ *& le beau temps,* carry a lot of weight.
plumage (plymaʒ) *m,* plumage, feathers. **plume** (plym) *f,* (*bird & Box.*) feather; pen; vaccine point. **plumeau** (mo) *m,* feather duster. **plumer** (me) *v.t,* to pluck; (*fig.*) fleece. **plumet** (mɛ) *m,* plume. **plumier** (mje) *m,* pencil box.
plupart (la) (plypar), most, the majority.
pluriel, le (plyrjɛl) *a.* & *m,* (*Gram.*) plural.
plus (ply) *ad,* more, -er (*suffix*); (*with* ne..) longer, any l., no l., any more, no more. *de* ~ *en* ~, more & more. **le** ~, the most, -est (*suffix*). *au* ~, at the most, at the outside. *tout au* ~, at the very most. ¶ *c.* (plys) plus, and. **[signe]** ~ (plys) *m,* plus [sign]. **plusieurs** (zjœr) *a.* & *pn,* several. **plus-que-parfait** (plykəparfɛ) *m,* pluperfect. **plus-value** (plyvaly) *f,* appreciation; profit, surplus.
plutôt (plyto) *ad,* rather, sooner, instead.
pluvier (plyvje) *m,* plover.
pluvieux, euse (plyvjø, øz) *a,* rainy; wet.
pneumatique (pnømatik) (*abb.* **pneu**) *m,* tyre; letter sent by pneumatic despatch.
pneumonie (pnømɔni) *f,* pneumonia.

poche (pɔʃ) *f,* pocket; bag; pouch (*kangaroo*). ~ *revolver,* hip pocket. *avoir des ~s sous les yeux,* to have bags under one's eyes. *de ~,* pocket; paperback (*book*). *faire des ~s,* (*clothes*) to go out of shape, bag. **pocher** (ʃe) *v.t,* to poach (*eggs*); black (*eye*). **pochette** (ʃɛt) *f,* breast pocket; pocket handkerchief; case (*needles &c*); envelope; book (*matches*).
poêle[1] (pwal) *f,* frying pan.
poele[2] (pwal) *m,* stove.
poème (pɔɛm) *m,* poem. **poésie** (ezi) *f,* poetry; poem, piece of poetry. **poète** (ɛt) *m,* poet. **poétesse** (tɛs) *f,* poetess. **poétique**† (tik) *a,* poetic; poetical.
pognon *P* (pɔɲɔ̃) *m,* dough *P,* lolly *P,* bread *P.*
poids (pwɑ) *m,* weight; (*Sport*) shot. ~ *lourd,* lorry; (*Sport & fig.*) heavyweight. ~ *mort,* dead load. ~ *plume,* (*Sport & fig.*) featherweight. ~ *spécifique,* specific gravity.
poignant, e (pwaɲɑ̃, ɑ̃t) *a,* poignant.
poignard (pwaɲar) *m,* dagger. **poignarder** (ɲarde) *v.t,* to stab, knife. **poigne** (pwaɲ) *f,* grip; energy. **poignée** (ɲe) *f,* handful; handle; grip. ~ *de main,* handshake. **poignet** (ɲɛ) *m,* wrist; cuff.
poil (pwal) *m,* hair (*on animal & body pers.*); fur, coat; pile, nap; bristle. *à ~ P,* naked, starkers *P*. au ~ P,* fantastic, great *P.* ~ *de carotte,* red [haired]. **poilu, e** (ly) *a,* hairy. ¶ *m,* French soldier (*1st World War*).
poinçon (pwɛ̃sɔ̃) *m,* awl; style; die, stamp; hallmark. **poinçonner** (sɔne) *v.t,* to punch; clip (*ticket*); stamp; hall-mark. **poinçonneur, euse** (sɔnœr, øz) *n,* ticket-puncher. ¶ *f,* punching machine.
poindre (pwɛ̃dr) *v.i.ir,* to dawn, break; come up.
poing (pwɛ̃) *m,* fist, hand.
point[1] (pwɛ̃) *m,* (*gen.*) point; (*Naut., Aero.*) position; dot, spot, speck; pip (*dice*); full stop, period; (*score*) point, mark, unit; (*Need.*) stitch. ~ *d'appui,* fulcrum. ~ *chaud* (*Mil.*), trouble spot; (*gen.*) major issue. ~ *de côté,* stitch (*pain*). ~ *d'exclamation,* exclamation mark. ~ *d'interrogation,* question mark. ~ *de mire,* target; (*fig.*) focal point. ~ *de repère,* landmark; point of reference. ~ *de vue,* view point; point of view. ~ *mort,* (*Mot.*) neutral. *au ~ mort,* at a standstill. ~ *névralgique,* (*Med.*) nerve centre; (*fig.*) sensitive spot. ~ *noir,* blackhead. ~ *virgule,* semicolon. *à ~,* medium (*steak*). *au ~,* in focus; perfected, up to scratch.
point[2] (pwɛ̃) (*liter.*) *same as* **pas**[2].
pointage (pwɛ̃taʒ) *m,* ticking off; checking off; c. in; c. out; aiming (*gun*); check.
pointe (pwɛ̃t) *f,* point (*sharp end*); tip; head; top; peak; toe (*shoe, sock*); tack; spike; hint, touch; triangular scarf. ~ *d'asperge,* asparagus tip. ~ *de terre,* spit of land. ~ *du jour* (*liter.*), daybreak. *à la ~ de,* in the forefront of. *de ~,* leading; maximum (*speed*); latest (*idea*). *heure de ~,* rush hour. *en ~,* pointed. *faire des ~s,* to dance on points. *sur la ~ des pieds,* on tiptoe.
pointer (pwɛ̃te) *v.t,* to tick off; mark off, check; c. in; c. out; (*Naut.*) plot (*position*); aim (*gun*); point (*finger*); train, direct; prick up (*ears*). ¶ *v.i,* to clock in; c. out, appear; peep out, pierce through; (*day*) break, dawn; soar up. **se ~,** to turn up *P.* **pointillé, e** (tije) *a,* dotted. ¶ *m,* dotted line. **pointilleux, euse** (jø, øz) *a,* particular, pernickety.
pointu, e (pwɛ̃ty) *a,* pointed; sharp; shrill.
pointure (pwɛ̃tyr) *f,* size (*shoes, gloves &c*).
poire (pwar) *f,* pear; (*P*) mug *P.* ~ *électrique,* switch. **poiré** (pware) *m,* perry.
poireau (pwaro) *m,* leek. *faire le ~,* & **poireauter** *P* (rote) *v.i,* to hang about *P.*
poirier (pwarje) *m,* pear tree. *faire le ~,* to do a headstand.
pois (pwɑ) *m,* pea; dot, spot. ~ *cassés,* split peas. ~ *chiche,* chickpea. ~ *de senteur,* sweet pea. *petits ~,* [garden] peas.
poison (pwazɔ̃) *m,* poison.
poisse *P* (pwas) *f,* rotten luck *P.* **poisser** (se) *v.t,* to make sticky; (*P*) nab *P.* **poisseux, euse** (sø, øz) *a,* sticky.
poisson (pwasɔ̃) *m,* fish. *faire un ~ d'avril à,* to make an April fool of. ~ *rouge,* goldfish. **poissonnerie** (nri) *f,* fish market; f. shop. **poissonneux, euse** (nø, øz) *a,* full of fish. **poissonnier, ère** (nje, ɛr) *n,* fishmonger.
poitrail (pwatrɑj) *m,* breast (*horse*). **poitrine** (trin) *f,* chest, breast; bust, bosom; breast (*veal, lamb*); belly (*pork*). ~ *salée* ou *fumée,* streaky bacon.
poivre (pwavr) *m,* pepper. ~ *de Cayenne* (kajɛn), ~ *rouge,* Cayenne p., red p. ~ *en grains,* peppercorns. **poivré, e** (pwavre) *a,* peppery; spicy (*tale*). **poivrer** (vre) *v.t,* to pepper. **poivrier** (vrie) *m,* pepper plant; p. pot. **poivron** (vrɔ̃), *m,* ~ [*vert*], ~ *rouge,* green, red pepper, capsicum.
poivrot, e *P* (pwavro, ɔt) *n,* drunkard.
poker (pɔkɛr) *m,* poker; game of p.
poix (pwɑ) *f,* pitch.
polaire (pɔlɛr) *a,* polar; pole (*star*). **polariser** (larise) *v.t,* to polarize; (*fig.*) focus, attract. **pôle** (pol) *m,* (*Astr., Phys. &c*) pole. ~ *d'attraction,* (*fig.*) focus of attention.
polémique (pɔlemik) *a,* polemic(al); controversial. ¶ *f,* polemic; controversy.
poli, e (pɔli) *a,* polished; smooth; polite. ¶ *m,* polish, shine.
police (pɔlis) *f,* police [force]; policing; police regulations; (*Insce*) policy.
polichinelle (pɔliʃinɛl) *m,* Punch; buffoon.
policier, ère (pɔlisje, ɛr) *a,* (*gen.*) police; detective (*novel*). ¶ *m,* policeman.
poliment (pɔlimɑ̃) *ad,* politely.

polio[myélite] (pɔljɔ[mjelit]) *f,* polio[myelitis].
polir (pɔlir) *v.t,* to polish; refine.
polisson, ne (pɔlisɔ̃, ɔn) *a,* naughty; saucy. ¶ *n,* [little] monkey *P.* **polissonnerie** (nri) *f,* naughty trick.
politesse (pɔlitɛs) *f,* politeness; compliment.
politicien, ne (pɔlitisjɛ̃, ɛn) *a,* politicking. ¶ *n,* political schemer, politician. **politique†** (tik) *a,* political; politic. *homme ~,* politician. ¶ *m,* politician. ¶ *f,* policy; politics. **politiser** (tise) *v.t,* to politicize, bring politics into.
polka (pɔlka) *m,* polka.
pollen (pɔllɛn) *m,* pollen.
polluer (pɔllɥe) *v.t,* to pollute. **pollution** (pɔllysjɔ̃) *f,* pollution.
polo (pɔlo) *m,* polo; sweat shirt.
Pologne (la) (pɔlɔɲ), Poland. **polonais, e** (nɛ, ɛz) *a,* Polish. **P~,** *n,* Pole. **le ~,** Polish (*language*). **polonaise,** *f,* polonaise.
poltron, ne (pɔltrɔ̃, ɔn) *a,* cowardly. ¶ *n,* coward. **poltronnerie** (trɔnri) *f,* cowardice.
polychrome (pɔlikrom) *a,* polychrome, polychromatic. **polyclinique** (klinik) *f,* polyclinic. **polycopier** (kɔpje) *v.t,* to duplicate, stencil. **polyculture** (kyltyr) *f,* mixed farming. **polyester** (ɛstɛr) *m,* polyester. **polygame** (gam) *n,* polygamist. ¶ *a,* polygamous. **polygamie** (mi) *f,* polygamy. **polyglotte** (glɔt) *a. & n,* polyglot. **polygone** (gɔn) *m,* polygon; (*fig.*) area, space. **la Polynésie** (nezi), Polynesia. **polype** (lip) *m,* polyp; polypus. **polysémie** (semi) *f,* polysemy. **polysyllabe** (silab) *a,* polysyllabic. ¶ *m,* polysyllable. **polyvalent, e** (valɑ̃, ɑ̃t) *a,* polyvalent; varied; various, many; versatile; (*Sch.*) general.
pommade (pɔmad) *f,* cream, pomade; ointment.
pomme (pɔm) *f,* apple; cone (*fir, pine*); knob; head (*stick, cabbage*); rose (*can*). *~ d'Adam* (adɑ̃), Adam's apple. *~ de terre,* potato. *~s frites,* chips. *~ sauvage,* crab [apple]. **pommeau** (mo) *m,* pommel. **pommelé, e** (mle) *a,* dapple[d]; mackerel (*sky*). **pommette** (mɛt) *f,* cheek bone. **pommier** (mje) *m,* apple tree.
pompe (pɔ̃p) *f,* pomp; pump; (*P*) shoe. *~ à air,* air pump. *~ à incendie,* fire engine. *~ aspirante,* suction pump. *~s funèbres,* funeral director's, undertaker's. **pomper** (pɔ̃pe) *v.t. & i,* to pump [out]; (*P Sch.*) crib; (*P*) wear out, tire out; (*P**) knock back *P**, drink. **pompeux, euse†** (pɑ̃pø, øz) *a,* pompous; solemn. **pompier** (pɑ̃pje) *m,* fireman; (*pl.*) fire brigade. ¶ *a,* (*P*) pompous. **pompiste** (pist) *n,* petrol pump attendant.
pompon (pɔ̃pɔ̃) *m,* pompon.
ponce (pɔ̃s) *f,* pumice. **poncer** (pɔ̃se) *v.t,* to sand, rub down. **ponceuse** (søz) *f,* sander.
ponction (pɔ̃ksjɔ̃) *f,* (*Surg.*) puncture, tapping; withdrawal (*money*).
ponctualité (pɔ̃ktɥalite) *f,* punctuality.
ponctuation (pɔ̃ktɥasjɔ̃) *f,* punctuation.
ponctuel, le† (pɔ̃ktɥɛl) *a,* punctual.
ponctuer (pɔ̃ktɥe) *v.t,* to punctuate.
pondération (pɔ̃derasjɔ̃) *f,* level-headedness; balancing, weighing. **pondéré, e** (re) *a,* level-headed. **pondérer** (re) *v.t,* to balance; weight.
pondre (pɔ̃dr) *v.t,* to lay (*eggs*); (*P fig.*) produce (*child &c*).
poney (pɔnɛ) *m,* pony.
pont (pɔ̃) *m,* bridge; deck (*ship*); (*fig.*) link, bridge; (*Mot.*) axle. *faire le ~,* to make a long weekend (*between weekend & bank holiday*). *faire un ~ d'or à qn,* to offer s.o a fortune to take on a job. *~ aérien,* airlift. *~ basculant,* bascule bridge. *~ de graissage,* ramp (*garage*). *~ suspendu,* suspension bridge. *~ tournant,* swing bridge.
ponte[1] (pɔ̃t) *f,* laying (*eggs*).
ponte[2] *P* (pɔ̃t) *m,* big shot *P.*
ponter (pɔ̃te) *v.i,* (*Cards &c*) to punt.
pontife (pɔ̃tif) *m,* pontiff. **pontifical, e** (fikal) *a,* pontifical; papal. **pontificat** (ka) *m,* pontificate. **pontifier** (fje) *v.i,* to pontificate.
pont-levis (pɔ̃ləvi) *m,* drawbridge (*castle*).
ponton (pɔ̃tɔ̃) *m,* pontoon; landing stage.
pop (pɔp) *a.inv,* pop.
pope (pɔp) *m,* [Orthodox] priest.
popeline (pɔplin) *f,* poplin.
populace (pɔpylas) *f,* rabble. **populaire†** (lɛr) *a,* popular; working-class (*area*); vernacular (*speech*). **populariser** (larize) *v.t,* to popularize. **popularité** (larite) *f,* popularity. **population** (sjɔ̃) *f,* population. **populeux, euse** (lø, øz) *a,* densly populated.
porc (pɔr) *m,* pig; pork; pigskin.
porcelaine (pɔrsəlɛn) *f,* porcelain, china; piece of porcelain.
porcelet (pɔrsəlɛ) *m,* piglet.
porc-épic (pɔrkepik) *m,* porcupine.
porche (pɔrʃ) *m,* porch.
porcherie (pɔrʃəri) *f,* pigsty.
pore (pɔr) *m,* pore. **poreux, euse** (pɔrø, øz) *a,* porous.
pornographie (pɔrnɔgrafi) *f,* pornography. **pornographique** (fik) *a,* pornographic.
port[1] (pɔr) *m,* harbour, port. *~ d'attache,* port of registry; (*fig.*) home base. *à bon ~,* safe[ly].
port[2] (pɔr) *m,* postage; carriage; bearing; wearing. **portable** (pɔrtabl) *a,* wearable; portable. **portatif, ive** (tatif, iv) *a,* portable.
portail (pɔrtaj) *m,* portal.
portant, e (pɔrtɑ̃, ɑ̃t) *a,* bearing. *bien ~,* in good health. *mal ~,* in bad h.
porte (pɔrt) *f,* door, doorway; doorstep; gate, gateway; arch. *~ cochère* (kɔʃɛr), carriage entrance. *~ d'embarquement,* departure gate. *~ d'entrée,* front door. *~ de service,* back door, tradesmen's entrance. *~-fenêtre,* French window.
porte- (pɔrt; *sometimes* pɔrtə *as noted*) *comps,*

all m: ~ *à faux,* overhang. ~*-avions,* aircraft carrier. ~*-bagages,* luggage rack. ~*-bonheur,* mascot, lucky charm. ~*-cigarettes,* cigarette case. ~*-clefs* (təkle), key ring. ~*-couteau,* knife rest. ~*-documents* (tədɔkymɑ̃), attaché case. ~*-drapeau* (tədrapo), standard bearer. ~*-mine* (təmin), propelling pencil. ~*-monnaie,* purse. ~*-parapluies,* umbrella stand. ~*-parole,* spokesman, mouthpiece. ~*-plume* (təplym), penholder. ~*-revues,* magazine rack. ~*-savon,* soapdish. ~*-serviettes,* towel rail. ~*-voix* (təvwa), megaphone.

porté, e (pɔrte) *a,* inclined, disposed, prone, apt (*à faire,* to do). ~ *sur,* fond of.

portée (pɔrte) *f,* reach, range; scope, capacity; significance; impact, import; (*Mus.*) stave, staff; (*Arch.*) span, loading; litter (*pups*). *à ~ de voix,* within earshot.

portefeuille (pɔrtəfœj) *m,* portfolio; wallet.

portemanteau (pɔrtmɑ̃to) *m,* coat hanger; c. rack; hat stand.

porter (pɔrte) *v.t,* to bear, carry; take; bring; lift; put; wear, have [on]; write down; (*Com.*) enter; report; feel (*sentiment*); yield (*harvest*); turn (*discussion*). ¶ *v.i,* to carry; be effective; (*shot, word*) tell; (*animal*) carry its young. ~ *sur,* to be supported by; focus on; (*discussion*) turn on; (*stress*) fall on. **se ~,** to stand as (*candidate*). ~ *bien,* to be well. ~ *mal,* to be unwell. **porteur, euse** (tœr, øz) *n,* porter; carrier; (*m.*) bearer; holder. ¶ *a,* carrier; booster (*rocket*).

portier, ère (pɔrtje, ɛr) *n,* porter, commissionaire. ¶ *f,* door (*carriage, car*).

portion (pɔrsjɔ̃) *f,* portion, share, part; helping (*food*).

portique (pɔrtik) *m,* portico; (*Sport*) crossbar.

Porto (pɔrto) *m,* Oporto. **porto** *ou* **vin de Porto,** *m,* port [wine].

portrait (pɔrtrɛ) *m,* portrait, likeness; image; description; photograph. ~*-robot,* identikit (*or* photo-fit) picture.

portugais, e (pɔrtygɛ, ɛz) *a.* & **P~,** *n,* Portuguese. *le ~,* Portuguese (*language*). **le Portugal** (gal), Portugal.

pose (poz) *f,* pose; posing; (*Phot.*) exposure, time e; installation. **posé, e** (ze) *a,* calm, steady, sober, level-headed. **poser** (ze) *v.i,* to rest; pose, sit (*portrait*); show off. ¶ *v.t,* to place, put [down], lay [down], set down; stand; write [down]; install (*gas*); hang (*curtains &c*); fit; put in, p. up; set out, state. ~ *un lapin à qn P,* to stand s.o up *P.* ~ *une question,* to ask a question. **se ~,** to settle, alight; land, touch down; (*question*) arise, crop up. ~ *comme,* to pretend (*or* claim) to be. **poseur, euse** (zœr, øz) *a,* affected. ¶ *n,* layer (*pipes &c*); show-off, poseur.

positif, ive† (pozitif, iv) *a.* & *n,* positive.

position (pozisjɔ̃) *f,* position; stand; stance; balance (*bank account*).

possédant, e (pɔsedɑ̃, ɑ̃t) *a,* propertied. ¶ *n.pl, les ~s,* the wealthy. **possédé, e** (de) *a,* possessed (*mad*). ¶ *n,* one possessed. **posséder** (de) *v.t,* to possess, own, have, hold; (*P*) take in, dupe (*pers.*). **se ~,** to control o.s. **possesseur** (sɛsœr) *m,* possessor, owner, holder. **possessif, ive** (sif, iv) *a,* possessive. **possession** (sjɔ̃) *f,* possession; ownership.

possibilité (pɔsibilite) *f,* possibility. **possible** (bl) *a,* possible; feasible. *aussitôt que ~,* as soon as possible. *pas ~!* well I never! ¶ *m,* possibility. *faire son ~,* to do one's utmost.

postal, e (pɔstal) *a,* postal, post, mail.

postdater (pɔstdate) *v.t,* to postdate.

poste[1] (pɔst) *f,* post, mail; post office. ~ *aérienne,* airmail. ~ *restante,* poste restante.

poste[2] (pɔst) *m,* post, station; job, position; appointment; (*Radio, TV*) set; (*Tel.*) extension; (*Ind.*) shift; item (*budget*). ~ *d'aiguillage,* signal box. ~ *de contrôle,* checkpoint. ~ *d'équipage,* crew's quarters. ~ *d'essence,* petrol station. ~ *d'incendie,* fire point. ~ *de pilotage,* cockpit. ~ *de police,* police station. **poster** (te) *v.t,* to post, station.

poster (pɔstɛr) *m,* poster.

postérieur, e† (pɔsterjœr) *a,* later; back. ¶ *m,* posterior.

postérité (pɔsterite) *f,* posterity, issue.

posthume (pɔstym) *a,* posthumous.

postiche (pɔstiʃ) *a,* false. ¶ *m,* hair-piece, postiche.

postier, ère (pɔstje, ɛr) *n,* post office worker.

postillon (pɔstijɔ̃) *m,* postillion.

postopératoire (pɔstɔperatwar) *a,* post-operative.

post-scriptum (pɔstskriptɔm) (*abb.* P.-S.) *m,* postscript, P.S.

postsynchroniser (pɔstsɛ̃krɔnize) *v.t,* to dub (*film.*).

postulant, e (pɔstylɑ̃, ɑ̃t) *n,* applicant. **postulat** (la) *m,* postulate. **postuler** (le) *v.t,* to apply for (*job*); postulate.

posture (pɔstyr) *f,* posture; position.

pot (po; *before à, au,* pɔt) *m,* pot, jar; jug; potty (*child's*); (*P*) luck; (*Cards*) kitty; pile. ~*-au-feu,* stock pot; stew, stewing beef. ~ *d'échappement,* exhaust pipe. ~*-de-vin,* bribe. ~*-pourri,* potpourri, medley.

potable (pɔtable) *a,* drinkable, drinking (*water*).

potage (pɔtaʒ) *m,* soup. **potager, ère** (taʒe, ɛr) *a,* vegetable. ¶ *m,* vegetable *or* kitchen garden.

potasse (pɔtas) *f,* potash.

potasser *P* (pɔtase) *v.t.* & *i,* to swot [up] *P.*

potassium (pɔtasjɔm) *m,* potassium.

pote *P* (pɔt) *m,* mate *P,* pal *P.*

poteau (pɔto) *m,* post, pole; execution post. ~ [*d'arrivée*], [winning] post. ~ *de départ,* starting p. ~ *indicateur,* sign post. *au ~! P* down with him! *P*.

potelé, e (pɔtle) *a*, plump; chubby.

potence (pɔtɑ̃s) *f*, gallows, gibbet; bracket.

potentat (pɔtɑ̃ta) *m*, potentate.

potentiel, le† (pɔtɑ̃sjɛl) *a. & m*, potential.

poterie (pɔtri) *f*, pottery; piece of p. **potiche** (pɔtiʃ) *f*, vase (*Chinese &c*). **potier** (pɔtje) *m*, potter.

potin (pɔtɛ̃) *m*, gossip; row, fuss.

potion (posjɔ̃) *f*, potion.

potiron (pɔtirɔ̃) *m*, pumpkin.

pou (pu) *m*, louse.

pouah (pwa) *i*, ugh!

poubelle (pubɛl) *f*, dustbin.

pouce (pus) *m*, thumb; big toe; (*Meas.*) inch.

pouding (pudiŋ) *m*, pudding.

poudre (pudr) *f*, powder; dust. *en* ~, powdered, dried (*milk*); drinking (*chocolate*); granulated (*sugar*). **poudrer** (pudre) *v.t*, to powder. **poudreux, euse** (drø, øz) *a*, dusty. **poudrier** (drie) *m*, powder compact. **poudrière** (ɛr) *f*, powder magazine; p. keg.

pouf (puf) *m*, pouffe. ¶ *i*, thud.

pouffer [de rire] (pufe), to snigger.

pouilleux, euse (pujø, øz) *a*, lousy, verminous; squalid, seedy (*area*); filthy (*pers.*). ¶ *n*, down-and-out.

poulailler (pulaje) *m*, hen house; (*Theat.*) gods.

poulain (pulɛ̃) *m*, foal; (*fig.*) promising young athlete; protégé.

poularde (pulard) *f*, fattened chicken. **poule**[1] (pul) *f*, hen; boiling fowl; (*P*) mistress, whore. ~ *au pot*, boiled chicken. ~ *d'eau*, moorhen. ~ *faisane*, hen pheasant. ~ *mouillée*, coward, softy. **poule**[2] (pul) (*Sport*) *f*, pool; kitty; tournament; (*Rugby*) group.

poulet (lɛ) *m*, chicken; (*P*) cop *P*.

pouliche (puliʃ) *f*, filly, foal.

poulie (puli) *f*, pulley, block.

poulpe (pulp) *m*, octopus.

pouls (pu) *m*, (*Anat.*) pulse.

poumon (pumɔ̃) *m*, lung. ~ *d'acier*, iron lung.

poupe (pup) *f*, stern, poop.

poupée (pupe) *f*, doll; (*P*) bird *P* (*girl*); finger bandage. **poupon, ne** (pɔ̃, ɔn) *n*, baby. **pouponner** (pɔne) *v.t*, to fondle, dandle, cuddle. **pouponnière** (njɛr) *f*, day nursery, crèche.

pour (pur) *pr*, for; on account of; in favour of. *partir* ~ *Paris*, to leave for P. ~ *toujours*, for ever. ~ *moi*, in my view. ~ *20F de*, 20 francs' worth of. ~ *ainsi dire*, so to speak. ~ *cent*, per cent. ~ *que*, in order that. *le* ~ *& le contre*, the pros & cons.

pourboire (purbwar) *m*, tip.

pourcentage (pursɑ̃taʒ) *m*, percentage.

pourchasser (purʃase) *v.t*, to pursue; hunt down; hound.

pourparlers (purparle) *m.pl*, negotiations, talks, discussions.

pourpre (purpr) *a. & m*, crimson. ¶ *f*, purple.

pourquoi (purkwa) *ad. & c*, why, what for. ¶ *m*, reason; question.

pourri, e (puri) *a*, rotten, bad, rotting; spoilt (*child*). ¶ *m*, rotten part; foul smell; (*P* pers.*) bastard *P**. **pourrir** (rir) *v.i*, to go rotten (*or* bad); rot [away]. ¶ *v.t*, to make rotten, rot. **pourriture** (rityr) *f*, rotting; rot; rottenness.

poursuite (pursɥit) *f*, pursuit, chase; (*oft. pl.*) lawsuit, proceedings; prosecution; continuation. [*course*] ~, track race. **poursuivant, e** (vɑ̃, ɑ̃t) *n*, pursuer. **poursuivre** (vr) *v.t.ir*, to pursue, chase; hunt; seek; strive towards; continue; carry on with; follow up; prosecute, sue. ¶ *v.i*, to carry on, continue; keep it up. **se** ~, to go on.

pourtant (purtɑ̃) *ad*, yet, nevertheless.

pourtour (purtur) *m*, circumference; surround; perimeter.

pourvoir (purvwar) *v.t*, to provide, equip, supply. ~ *qn de qch*, to provide s.o with sth. ~ **à**, to provide for, cater for; deal with; fill (*job*). **pourvoyeur, euse** (jœr, øz) *n*, supplier. **pourvu que** (vy) *c*, provided [that], so long as; let's hope.

pousse (pus) *f*, growth; shoot, sprout. **poussé, e** (se) *a*, advanced (*studies*); exhaustive (*enquiries*). **poussée** (se) *f*, push, shove; thrust; pressure; outburst; rise, upsurge; attack (*acne*). **pousser** (se) *v.t*, to push, shove, nudge; move, shift; drive, urge on; press; utter, let out (*cry*); continue, carry on [with] (*studies &c*); pursue, follow up. ¶ *v.i*, to grow; (*tooth*) come through; shoot, spring up. **poussette** (sɛt) *f*, push chair.

poussière (pusjɛr) *f*, dust. **poussiéreux, euse** (sjerø, øz) *a*, dusty; (*fig.*) fusty.

poussif, ive (pusif, iv) *a*, short-winded; wheezing.

poussin (pusɛ̃) *m*, chick; spring chicken.

poussoir (puswar) *m*, [push] button.

poutre (putr) *f*, beam; girder. **poutrelle** (trɛl) *f*, girder.

pouvoir (puvwar) *m*, power; authority; capacity, ability; (*Pol.*) power, government; (*Law*) proxy. ¶ *v. aux. ir*, to be able; can; may; be allowed. (*permission*) *puis-je entrer?* may I come in? (*ability*) *je peux le voir*, I can see him. *elle n'a pas pu venir*, she wasn't able to come. *pourriez-vous m'écrire?* could you write to me? *tu aurais pu m'écrire*, you could have written to me. (*possibility*) *il peut être fatigué*, he may be tired. **se** ~, *ça se peut*, that's possible, *cela se pourrait bien*, that could well be.

prairie (prɛri) *f*, meadow.

praline (pralin) *f*, sugared almond, praline. **praliné, e** (ne) *a*, praline flavoured.

praticable (pratikabl) *a*, practicable, feasible; passable (*road*). **praticien, ne** (sjɛ̃, ɛn) *n*, practitioner. **pratique** (tik) *a*, practical;

convenient, handy. ¶ *f,* practice; practical experience; observance (*rule &c*); practising; exercise. **pratiquement** (kmɑ̃) *ad,* practically; in practice. **pratiquer** (ke) *v.t,* to practise; observe; exercise; play (*sport*); make, pierce, bore (*hole*); build (*road*); carry out (*operation*). ¶ *v.i,* to go to church; (*Med.*) practise.

pré (pre) *m,* meadow.

préalable† (prealabl) *a,* previous; preliminary; prior. ¶ *m,* precondition, prerequisite.

préambule (preɑ̃byl) *m,* preamble; prelude.

préau (preo) *m,* courtyard, quadrangle; playground (*covered*).

préavis (preavi) *m,* [previous] notice, warning.

précaire† (prekɛr) *a,* precarious.

précaution (prekosjɔ̃) *f,* precaution; caution, care. **précautionneux, euse** (sjɔnø, øz) *a,* cautious, careful.

précédemment (presedamɑ̃) *ad,* previously. **précédent, e** (dɑ̃, ɑ̃t) *a,* preceding, previous, before. ¶ *m,* precedent. **précéder** (de) *v.t,* to precede.

précepte (presɛpt) *m,* precept. **précepteur** (tœr) *m,* tutor.

prêche (prɛʃ) *m,* sermon. **prêcher** (ʃe) *v.t. & i,* to preach, p. to.

precieux, euse† (presjø, øz) *a,* precious; invaluable (*help &c*); valued; valuable; affected.

précipice (presipis) *m,* precipice; chasm; (*fig.*) abyss.

précipitamment (presipitamɑ̃) *a,* precipitately, hastily. **précipitation** (sjɔ̃) *f,* haste; (*pl Met.*) precipitation. **précipité, e** (te) *a,* precipitate, hasty, hurried, headlong. ¶ *m,* precipitate. **précipiter** (te) *v.t,* to precipitate; hasten; plunge; throw, hurl down. **se ~,** to rush; hurry; speed up; (*pulse*) quicken; throw (*or* hurl) o.s.

précis, e (presi, iz) *a,* precise, exact; definite. *à 8 heures ~es,* at 8 o'clock sharp. ¶ *m,* abstract, summary, précis. **précisément** (sizemɑ̃) *ad,* precisely, exactly. **préciser** (ze) *v.t,* to state precisely, specify; clarify, make clear; be more specific about; point out, explain. **précision** (zjɔ̃) *f,* precision, accuracy; distinctness; point, piece of information; explanation.

précité, e (presite) *a,* aforesaid, above.

précoce (prekɔs) *a,* precocious; early, forward; premature (*senility &c*). **précocité** (site) *f,* precociousness &c.

préconçu, e (prekɔ̃sy) *a,* preconceived.

préconiser (prekɔnize) *v.t,* to recommend, advocate.

précurseur (prekyrsœr) *m,* precursor, forerunner. ¶ *a,* precursory.

prédécesseur (predesɛsœr) *m,* predecessor.

prédestination (predɛstinasjɔ̃) *f,* predestination. **prédestiner** (ne) *v.t,* to predestine.

prédicat (predika) *m,* predicate.

prédicateur (predikatœr) *m,* preacher.

prédiction (prediksjɔ̃) *f,* prediction; forecast.

prédilection (predilɛksjɔ̃) *f,* predilection, partiality. *de ~,* favourite.

prédire (predir) *v.t.ir,* to predict, foretell.

prédisposer (predispoze) *v.t,* to predispose.

prédominer (predɔmine) *v.i,* to predominate, prevail.

prééminent, e (preeminɑ̃, ɑ̃t) *a,* pre-eminent.

préfabriqué, e (prefabrike) *a,* prefabricated. ¶ *m,* prefabricated house.

préface (prefas) *f,* preface.

préfecture (prefɛktyr) *f,* prefecture; headquarters (*of police*).

préférable (preferabl) *a,* preferable, better. **préférence** (rɑ̃s) *f,* preference. **préférentiel, le** (rɑ̃sjɛl) *a,* preferential. **préférer** (re) *v.t,* to prefer.

préfet (prefɛ) *m,* prefect.

préfigurer (prefigyre) *v.t,* to foreshadow.

préfixe (prefiks) *m,* prefix.

préhistorique (preistɔrik) *a,* prehistoric.

préjudice (preʒydis) *m,* detriment; injury; harm; loss. **préjudiciable** (sjabl) *a,* prejudicial, detrimental; harmful. **préjugé** (ʒe) *m,* prejudice. **préjuger de** (ʒe) *v.t,* to prejudge.

prélasser (se) (prelɑse) *v.pr,* to loll. **prélat** (la) *m,* prelate.

prélèvement (prelɛvmɑ̃) *m,* deduction, levy; withdrawal. *~ de sang,* blood test. **prélever** (lve) *v.t,* to deduct, levy; withdraw (*from bank*).

préliminaire (preliminɛr) *a. & m,* preliminary.

prélude (prelyd) *m,* prelude. **préluder à** (de) *v.t,* to be a prelude to, lead up to.

prématuré†, **e** (prematyre) *a,* premature, untimely. ¶ *n,* premature baby.

préméditation (premeditasjɔ̃) *f,* premeditation. **préméditer** (te) *v.t,* to premeditate.

premier, ère (prəmje, ɛr) *a,* first, initial; early (*childhood*); earliest; front (*row*); leading, foremost; prime; primary; lowest, bottom (*price &c*); (*after n.*) basic. *au ~ abord,* at first sight. *en ~ lieu,* in the first place. *le ~ âge,* the first 3 months of life. *~ choix,* best quality, finest q. *~ ministre,* prime minister, premier. *~-né, m,* firstborn. *de ~ ordre,* first-class, first-rate. *~ plan,* foreground. *~s secours,* first aid. *le ~ venu,* the first to come; (*fig.*) anybody. ¶ *m,* first; first floor; first child. *le ~ de l'an,* New Year's Day. ¶ *f,* first; (*Rly.*) f. class; (*Theat.*) f. night; première; (*Mot.*) first gear. **premièrement** (mjɛrmɑ̃) *ad,* first[ly]; for a start, to start with, in the first place.

prémonition (premɔnisjɔ̃) *f,* premonition. **prémonitoire** (nitwar) *a,* premonitory.

prémunir (premynir) *v.t,* to protect.

prenant, e (prənɑ̃, ɑ̃t) *a,* absorbing, engrossing, captivating. **prendre** (prɑ̃dr) *v.t.ir,* to take; t. up; t. in; t. down; t. off (*or* away); t. on; catch (*fish, cold*); capture; (*pain*) strike; seize; get, pick up (*illness &c*); make a note of; gain, put on (*weight*); handle, deal with.¶ *v.i,* to set; (*plant &c*) take, strike; catch on, be a success; go; turn, bear (*left &c*); start, light, catch fire. *à tout* ~, on the whole, all in all. **se** ~, to take o.s; set hard, freeze over. **s'en** ~ **à,** to blame; set about; take it out on; challenge; take on. **s'y** ~, to set about it. **preneur, euse** (prənœr, øz) *n,* taker; buyer; lessee.

prénom (prenɔ̃) *m,* first name, Christian n. **prénommer** (nɔme) *v.t,* to call, name (*pers.*).

préoccupation (preɔkypasjɔ̃) *f,* preoccupation; worry, anxiety. **préoccuper** (pe) *v.t,* to preoccupy; worry. **se** ~, to be concerned, worry.

préparateur, trice (preparatœr, tris) *n,* assistant. **préparatifs** (tif) *m.pl,* preparations. **préparation** (sjɔ̃) *f,* preparation. **préparatoire** (twar) *a,* preparatory. **préparer** (re) *v.t,* to prepare, get ready; lay (*table &c*); study for (*exam*). **se** ~, to prepare, get ready; (*storm*) brew.

prépondérance (prepɔ̃derɑ̃s) *f,* preponderance; supremacy, domination. **prépondérant, e** (rɑ̃, ɑ̃t) *a,* dominating.

préposé, e (prepoze) *n,* employee; attendant (*cloakroom*); postman, woman. **préposer** (ze) *v.t,* to appoint.

préposition (prepɔzisjɔ̃) *f,* preposition.

prérogative (prerɔgativ) *f,* prerogative.

près (prɛ) *ad,* near [by]; close [by]. ~ *de,* close to, near [to]; almost, nearly. *à* ... ~, apart from, except for; to within. *à un franc* ~, (*price*) to within about a franc. *à peu* ~, nearly, about, pretty much. *à peu de chose* ~, more or less. *de* ~, closely, carefully.

présage (prezaʒ) *m,* omen, sign. **présager** (zaʒe) *v.t,* to be an omen (*or* a sign) of; predict, foresee.

presbyte (prɛzbit) *n. & a,* long-sighted (person).

presbytère (prɛzbitɛr) *m,* presbytery.

prescience (presjɑ̃s) *f,* prescience, foreknowledge.

prescription (prɛskripsjɔ̃) *f,* prescription; order; stipulation. **prescrire** (skrir) *v.t.ir,* to prescribe; stipulate; command, order.

préséance (preseɑ̃s) *f,* precedence (*in rank*).

préselection (preselɛksjɔ̃) *f,* preselection; short-listing (*candidates*). **préselectionner** (sjɔne) *v.t,* to short-list; (*Radio*) preset.

présence (prezɑ̃s) *f,* presence; attendance. *en* ~, face to face; opposing (*armies*). **présent, e** (zɑ̃, ɑ̃t) *a,* present. ¶ *m,* present tense; gift, present. *à* ~, at present, now; nowadays. *le* ~, the present (*time*). *les* ~*s,* the people present. **présentable** (zɑ̃tabl) *a,* presentable. **présentateur, trice** (tatœr, tris) *n,* (*Radio, TV*) presenter, introducer. **présentation** (sjɔ̃) *f,* presentation; introduction; appearance. **présentement** (zɑ̃tmɑ̃) *ad,* at present, now. **présenter** (te) *v.t,* to present; introduce; display, set out (*goods*); show; (*TV*) compere; offer; pay (*respects*); (*Tech.*) line up, position. ¶ *v.i,* ~ *bien, mal,* to have a good, bad appearance. **se** ~, to go; come; appear; arise, crop up; come forward; introduce o.s; present itself. ~ *à,* to stand for, sit for, enter for.

préservatif, ive (prezɛrvatif, iv) *a,* preventive, protective. ¶ *m,* sheath, condom. **préservation** (sjɔ̃) *f,* preservation, protection. **préserver** (ve) *v.t,* to protect.

présidence (prezidɑ̃s) *f,* presidency; chairmanship; vice-chancellorship; presidential residence. **président, e** (dɑ̃, ɑ̃t) *n,* president; chairman; presiding judge; (*Univ.*) vice-chancellor. ~ *du conseil,* prime minister. ~ *du jury,* (*Law*), foreman of the jury; (*Sch.*) chief examiner. **présidentiel, le** (dɑ̃sjɛl) *a,* presidential. **présider [à]** (de) *v.t. & i,* to preside at, over; chair; govern.

présomptif, ive (prezɔ̃ptif, iv) *a,* (*heir*) apparent. **présomption** (sjɔ̃) *f,* presumption. **présomptueux, euse†** (tɥø, øz) *a,* presumptuous.

presque (prɛsk) *ad,* almost, nearly, all but. ~ *jamais,* hardly ever. **presqu'île** (kil) *f,* peninsula.

pressant, e (prɛsɑ̃, ɑ̃t) *a,* pressing, urgent. **presse** (prɛs) *f,* press; [news]papers; [printing] press; (*liter.*) throng, crowd, hurry. **presse-citrons,** *m,* lemon squeezer.

pressentiment (presɑ̃timɑ̃) *m,* presentiment, foreboding, premonition; feeling. **pressentir** (tir) *v.t.ir,* to have a presentiment of; sound (*pers.*).

presse-papiers (prɛspapje) *m,* paperweight. **presse-purée** (pyre) *m,* potato-masher. **presser** (se) *v.t,* to press; squeeze; hasten, speed up, hurry, push, urge. ¶ *v.i,* to be urgent; press. *cela ne presse pas,* there's no hurry. **se** ~, to press, crowd, throng; hurry. **pressing** (siŋ) *m,* steam-pressing; dry cleaner's; (*Sport*) pressure. **pression** (sjɔ̃) *f,* pressure; press stud. *à la* ~, draught (*beer*). **pressoir** (swar) *m,* press (*wine, &c*).

pressurisation (prɛsyrizasjɔ̃) *f,* pressurization. **pressuriser** (rize) *v.t,* to pressurize.

prestance (prɛstɑ̃s) *f,* presence, bearing.

prestation (prɛstasjɔ̃) *f,* benefit, allowance (*social security &c*); performance; service (*hotel &c*).

preste† (prɛst) *a,* quick, nimble.

prestidigitateur (prɛstidiʒitatœr) *m,* conjurer. **prestidigitation** (sjɔ̃) *f,* conjuring.

prestige (prɛstiʒ) *m,* prestige. **prestigieux, euse** (tiʒjø, øz) *a,* prestigious.

présumer (prezyme) *v.t,* to presume, assume. *trop* ~ *de,* to overestimate, overrate.

présupposer (presypoze) *v.t,* to presuppose.

présure (prezyr) *f,* rennet.

prêt (prɛ) *m,* loan; advance.

prêt, e (prɛ, ɛt) *a,* ready; prepared, willing *être*

~ *à tout*, to stop at nothing. **prêt-à-porter,** ready to wear *or* off-the-peg [clothes].

prétendant, e (pretɑ̃dɑ̃, ɑ̃t) *n*, candidate. ¶ *m*, pretender (*to throne*); suitor. **prétendre** (tɑ̃dr) *v.t. & i*, to claim, pretend; assert; contend; (*liter.*) want; mean, intend. ~ **à,** aspire to; lay claim to. **prétendu, e** (tɑ̃dy) *a*, alleged; would-be; so-called.

prête-nom (prɛtnɔ̃) *m*, figurehead.

prétentieux, euse (pretɑ̃sjø, øz) *a*, pretentious. **prétention** (sjɔ̃) *f*, claim; pretension.

prêter (prɛte) *v.t*, to lend; give; take (*oath*); attribute. ~ *attention*, to pay attention. *un prêté [pour un] rendu*, tit for tat. ~ **à,** to be open to, give rise to. ~ *à rire*, to be ridiculous. **se** ~, to give, stretch (*shoes &c*).

prétérit (preterit) *m*, preterite.

prêteur, euse (prɛtœr, øz) *a*, unselfish. ¶ *n*, lender. ~ *sur gages*, pawnbroker.

prétexte (pretɛkst) *m*, pretext, pretence, excuse. **prétexter** (te) *v.t*, to give as a pretext *or* excuse.

prêtre (prɛtr) *m*, priest. **prêtresse** (prɛtrɛs) *f*, priestess. **prêtrise** (triz) *f*, priesthood.

preuve (prœv) *f*, proof; evidence; token. ~ *par l'absurde*, reductio ad absurdum.

prévaloir (prevalwar) *v.i.ir*, to prevail. **se** ~ **de,** to take advantage of; pride o.s on.

prévenance (prevnɑ̃s) *f*, [kind] attention. **prévenant, e** (vnɑ̃, ɑ̃t) *a*, attentive, kind, considerate, thoughtful. **prévenir** (vnir) *v.t.ir*, to warn (*de* about); inform, tell; prevent, avoid; forestall; anticipate; prejudice. **préventif, ive** (vɑ̃tif, iv) *a*, preventive. **prévention** (vɑ̃sjɔ̃) *f*, custody, detention; prevention. **prévenu, e** (vny) *n*, accused.

prévisible (previzibl) *a*, foreseeable. **prévision** (zjɔ̃) *f*, prediction; expectation; forecast. **prévoir** (vwar) *v.t.ir*, to foresee, forecast; provide for; plan; provide, allow.

prévôt (prevo) *m*, provost.

prévoyance (prevwajɑ̃s) *f*, foresight, forethought. **prévoyant, e** (jɑ̃, ɑ̃t) *a*, provident.

prier (prije) *v.t*, to pray to (*God*); beg, ask, request (*qn de faire*, s.o to do). *je vous en prie*, please do, of course; don't mention it, not at all; after you. ¶ *v.i*, to pray. **prière** (ɛr) *f*, prayer; request, entreaty. ~ *de* ..., please ... **prieur, e** (œr) *n*, prior, ess. **prieuré** (œre) *m*, priory.

primaire (primɛr) *a*, primary; simplistic; simple-minded (*pers.*). ¶ *m*, primary; p. school.

primat (prima) *m*, primate.

primate (primat) *m*, (*Zool.*) primate.

primauté (primote) *f*, primacy.

prime[1] (prim) *a*, first; earliest; (*Math.*) prime.

prime[2] (prim) *f*, free gift; bonus; premium; subsidy; allowance. **primer** (me) *v.t*, to prevail over, take precedence over; award a prize to. ¶ *v.i*, to be of prime importance.

primeur (primœr) *f*, early vegetable, early fruit. *avoir la ~ sur une nouvelle*, to be the first to hear the news. *marchand de ~s*, greengrocer.

primevère (primvɛr) *f*, primrose.

primitif, ive† (primitif, iv) *a*, primitive, original; crude.

primo (primo) *ad*, first[ly].

primordial, e† (primɔrdjal) *a*, primordial, essential.

prince (prɛ̃s) *m*, prince. *être bon* ~, to be generous. **princesse** (sɛs) *f*, princess. **princier, ère** (sje, ɛr) *a*, princely.

principal, e† (prɛ̃sipal) *a*, principal, chief, head, main; staple (*product*). ¶ *m*, principal; chief; headmaster; main thing. ¶ *f*, (*Gram.*) main clause.

principauté (prɛ̃sipote) *f*, principality.

principe (prɛ̃sip) *m*, principle. *de* ~, mechanical, automatic (*opposition &c*). *faire qch de* ~, to do sth on principle. *en* ~, as a rule; in principle. *par* ~, on principle. *partir du ~ que*, to work on the assumption that.

printanier, ère (prɛ̃tanje, ɛr) *a*, spring; s.-like. **printemps** (tɑ̃) *m*, spring[-time].

priorité (priɔrite) *f*, priority; (*Mot.*) right of way.

pris, e (pri, iz) *a*, taken; sold out; busy (*pers.*); stuffed up (*hose*); hoarse (*throat*); set (*cream*); frozen (*water*); stricken.

prise (priz) *f*, taking; catch; hold, purchase, grip; setting (*cement*); (*Naut.*) prize; pinch (*snuff &c*); dose. ~ *d'air*, air inlet *or* intake. ~ *d'eau*, hydrant, water supply point; tap. ~ *de bec*, altercation, set-to. ~ *de conscience*, realization. ~ *de contact*, initial contact. ~ *de courant*, plug; socket. ~ *de position*, stand. ~ *de sang*, blood test. ~ *de son*, sound recording. ~ *de terre*, (*Elec.*) earth. ~ *de vue*, filming, shooting; shot. *donner ~ à*, to give rise to. *en* ~, (*Mot.*) in gear.

priser (prise) *v.t*, to take (*snuff &c*); (*fig.*) prize, value. ¶ *v.i*, to take snuff.

prisme (prism) *m*, prism.

prison (prizɔ̃) *f*, prison, gaol, jail; imprisonment (*term*). **prisonnier, ère** (zɔnje, ɛr) *n*, prisoner.

privation (privasjɔ̃) *f*, deprivation, loss; privation, hardship.

privauté (privote) *f*, liberty.

privé†, **e** (prive) *a*, private. ¶ *m*, privy; private life; (*Ind.*) private sector.

priver (prive) *v.t*, to deprive. *privé de conscience*, unconscious. *privé de voix*, speechless, unable to speak. **se** ~ **de,** to go *or* do without.

privilège (privilɛʒ) *m*, privilege. **privilégié, e** (leʒje) *a*, privileged; favoured. **privilégier** (ʒje) *v.t*, to favour.

prix (pri) *m*, price, cost; prize; prizewinner; prizewinning book; race. *à aucun* ~, on no account. *à tout* ~, at all costs. *donner du ~ à qch*, to make sth more precious.

probabilité (prɔbabilite) *f,* probability, likelihood. **probable†** (bl) *a,* probable, likely.

probant, e (prɔbɑ̃, ɑ̃t) *a,* convincing, cogent. **probité** (bite) *f,* probity, honesty, integrity.

problématique (prɔblematik) *a,* problematic(al). **problème** (blɛm) *m,* problem.

procédé (prɔsede) *m,* behaviour; process. **procéder** (de) *v.i,* to proceed; behave. ~ **à,** to conduct, carry out. ~ **de,** to come from, proceed from. **procédure** (dyr) *f,* procedure; proceedings. **procès** (sɛ) *m,* (*Law*) proceedings, action, case. ~ [*civil*], [law]suit. ~ [*criminel*], [criminal] trial. **procession** (sjɔ̃) *f,* procession. **processus** (sys) *m,* process, course. **procès-verbal,** *m,* report; minute(s); statement. *dresser un ~ contre qn,* to book s.o.

prochain, e (prɔʃɛ̃, ɛn) *a,* next; near, immediate; forthcoming; imminent. *au revoir, à la ~e* [*fois*]*!* goodbye, see you [again]! *un jour ~,* soon, in the near future. **prochainement** (ʃɛnmɑ̃) *ad,* shortly, soon. **proche** (prɔʃ) *a,* close, near; nearby, neighbouring; at hand; imminent. ~ *de,* near, close to. *de ~ en ~,* gradually. *P~ Orient,* Near-East. ¶ *m.pl,* next of kin, close relations.

proclamation (prɔklamasjɔ̃) *f,* proclamation; declaration, announcement. **proclamer** (me) *v.t,* to proclaim, publish; declare; announce (*exam results*).

procréer (prɔkree) *v.t,* to procreate.

procuration (prɔkyrasjɔ̃) *f,* proxy, power of attorney. **procurer** (re) *v.t,* to procure, obtain; bring, give (*joy &c*). **se ~,** to get, obtain [for o.s]; buy [for o.s]. **procureur** (rœr) *m,* ~ [*de la République*], state *or* public prosecutor.

prodigalité (prɔdigalite) *f,* prodigality, extravagance; profusion; (*pl.*) extravagance.

prodige (prɔdiʒ) *m,* prodigy, wonder. **prodigieux, euse†** (diʒjø, øz) *a,* prodigious; incredible, fantastic.

prodigue (prɔdig) *a,* prodigal, lavish, unsparing, profuse; wasteful. ¶ *n,* prodigal, spendthrift. **prodiguer** (ge) *v.t,* to lavish; be unsparing with; be lavish with; give.

producteur, trice (prɔdyktœr, tris) *n,* producer. ¶ ~ *&* **productif, ive** (tif, iv) *a,* producing, productive, bearing. **production** (sjɔ̃) *f,* production, output, yield; product; (*pl.*) produce, goods. **productivité** (tivite) *f,* productivity. **produire** (dɥir) *v.t.ir,* to produce, make; grow; yield, return; show. **se ~,** to occur, happen; (*actor*) appear. **produit** (dɥi) *m,* product, produce, proceeds, yield; takings, receipts; profits; income. ~ [*chimique*], chemical. ~ *national brut,* gross national product.

proéminent, e (prɔeminɑ̃, ɑ̃t) *a,* prominent.

profanateur, trice (prɔfanatœr, tris) *a,* profaning. ¶ *n,* profaner. **profanation** (sjɔ̃) *f,* profanation, desecration, defilement. **profane** (fan) *a,* profane; secular. ¶ *n,* layman; lay person; (*Rel.*) non-believer. *le ~,* the secular. **profaner** (ne) *v.t,* to profane, desecrate; defile.

proférer (prɔfere) *v.t,* to utter.

professer (prɔfɛse) *v.t,* to profess; teach. **professeur** (sœr) *m,* professor; teacher; master, mistress; lecturer; instructor. **profession** (sjɔ̃) *f,* profession; occupation; trade. **professionnel, le** (ɔnɛl) *a,* professional; occupational; vocational. ¶ *n,* professional. **le professorat** (sɔra) [the] teaching [profession].

profil (prɔfil) *m,* profile; outline; line (*car*). **profiler** (le) *v.t,* to profile; shape. **se ~,** to stand out, be outlined, emerge.

profit (prɔfi) *m,* profit, benefit, advantage. **profitable** (tabl) *a,* profitable; beneficial. **profiter** (te) *v.i,* to benefit, profit; (*de,* from); take advantage, make the most (*de,* of); thrive. **profiteur, euse** (tœr, øz) *n,* profiteer.

profond, e (prɔfɔ̃, ɔ̃d) *a,* deep, profound; low (*bow*); sound (*sleep*); underlying (*reason &c*). *peu ~,* shallow. *au plus ~ de,* in the depths of. **profondément** (demɑ̃) *ad,* deeply &c. **profondeur** (dœr) *f,* depth; profundity. *en ~,* in depth, radical.

profusion (prɔfyzjɔ̃) *f,* profusion, wealth.

progéniture (prɔʒenityr) *f,* progeny, offspring.

programmation (prɔgramasjɔ̃) *f,* (*gen.*) programming; softwear (*computer*). **programme** (gram) *m,* programme; syllabus; curriculum. **programmer** (me) *v.t,* to programme (*computer*); (*Radio &c*) bill; (*P*) plan. **programmeur, euse** (mœr, øz) *n,* [computer] programmer.

progrès (prɔgrɛ) *m. oft. pl,* progress. **progresser** (grɛse) *v.i,* to progress, make headway. **progressif, ive†** (sif, iv) *a,* progressive. **progression** (sjɔ̃) *f,* progression; progress, advance. **progressiste** (sist) *n,* progressive.

prohiber (prɔibe) *v.t,* to prohibit, forbid. **prohibitif, ive** (bitif, iv) *a,* prohibitive. **prohibition** (sjɔ̃) *f,* prohibition.

proie (prwa) *f,* prey.

projecteur (prɔʒɛktœr) *m,* projector; search light; spotlight; floodlight. **projectile** (til) *m,* projectile, missile. **projection** (sjɔ̃) *f,* projection; showing; throwing; discharge. **projet** (ʒɛ) *m,* project, scheme, plan; draft. ~ *de loi,* bill, measure. **projeter** (ʒte) *v.t,* to project, throw, cast; plan, contemplate (*de faire,* to do, doing).

prolétaire (prɔletɛr) *m,* proletarian. **prolétariat** (tarja) *m,* proletariat. **prolétarien, ne** (rjɛ̃, ɛn) *a,* proletarian.

prolifération (prɔliferasjɔ̃) *f,* proliferation. **proliférer** (fere) *v.i,* to proliferate. **prolifique** (fik) *a,* prolific.

prologue (prɔlɔg) *m,* prologue.
prolongation (prɔlɔ̃gasjɔ̃) *f,* prolongation; extension. **prolongement** (lɔ̃ʒmɑ̃) *m,* continuation, extension; (*pl.*) repercussions, effects. **prolonger** (lɔ̃ʒe) *v.t,* to prolong, protract, extend, lengthen. **se ~,** to continue; last, persist.
promenade (prɔmnad) *f,* walk, stroll; ride; drive; trip, outing, ramble; promenade. *~ en bateau,* row; sail. **promener** (mne) *v.t,* to take for a walk; pass, run, cast. *~ par, ~ dans,* to show round. **se ~,** to [go for a] walk, stroll. *allez vous ~!* be off with you! **promeneur, euse** (mnœr, øz) *n,* walker; tripper.
promesse (prɔmɛs) *f,* promise. **prometteur, euse** (tœr, øz) *a,* promising. **promettre** (mɛtr) *v.t.ir,* to promise (*de faire,* to do).
promiscuité (prɔmiskɥite) *f,* lack of privacy.
promontoire (prɔmɔ̃twar) *m,* promontory.
promoteur, trice (prɔmɔtœr, tris) *n,* promoter; property developer. **promotion** (sjɔ̃) *f,* promotion; (*Sch.*) year. [*en*] *~*, [on] special offer. **promouvoir** (muvwar) *v.t.ir,* to promote.
prompt, e† (prɔ̃, ɔ̃t) *a,* prompt, quick; sudden. **promptitude** (prɔ̃tityd) *f,* promptness &c.
promulguer (prɔmylge) *v.t,* to promulgate.
prôner (prone) *v.t,* to extoll; advocate.
pronom (prɔnɔ̃) *m,* pronoun. **pronominal, e** (nɔminal) *a,* pronominal.
prononcer (prɔnɔ̃se) *v.t,* to pronounce; utter; speak; mention; deliver (*speech*); pass (*sentence*). **se ~,** to declare oneself; be pronounced (*letter, syllable*); reach a decision; give a verdict. **prononciation** (sjasjɔ̃) *f,* pronunciation.
pronostic (prɔnɔstik) *m,* forecast. **pronostiquer** (ke) *v.t,* to prognosticate, forecast. **pronostiqueur, euse** (kœr, øz) *n,* forecaster; tipster.
propagande (prɔpagɑ̃d) *f,* propaganda.
propager (prɔpaʒe) *v.t,* to propagate, spread.
propension (prɔpɑ̃sjɔ̃) *f,* propensity.
prophète, étesse (prɔfɛt, etɛs) *n,* prophet, ess, seer. **prophétie** (fesi) *f,* prophecy. **prophétique**† (tik) *a,* prophetic. **prophétiser** (ze) *v.t,* to prophesy.
propice (prɔpis) *a,* propitious, auspicious, lucky.
proportion (prɔpɔrsjɔ̃) *f,* proportion, ratio. *toutes ~s gardées,* relatively speaking. **proportionnel, le**† (ɔnɛl) *a,* proportional; proportionate. **proportionner** (ɔne) *v.t,* to proportion.
propos (prɔpo) *m,* purpose; subject, matter; remark, (*pl.*) talk. **à ~,** *a. & ad,* to the point; by the way. **à ~ de,** *pr,* with regard to, about. *à tout ~*, at every turn. *de ~ délibéré,* deliberately, purposely. **proposer** (ze) *v.i,* to propose, suggest; offer; put forward; recommend. **se ~,** to offer oneself; propose, mean (*de faire,* to do). **proposition** (zisjɔ̃) *f,* proposal, proposition; motion; (*Gram.*) clause.
propre[1] (prɔpr) *a,* own; suitable, appropriate; literal (*meaning*); proper (*noun*). *~ à,* peculiar to, characteristic of. *un ~-à-rien,* a good-for-nothing. *par ses ~s moyens,* in one's own way; under one's own steam. ¶ *m,* peculiarity, [distinctive] feature; literal sense (*word*).
propre[2] (prɔpr) *a,* clean, neat, tidy; decent, honest; toilet trained (*child*); house-trained (*dog*). *c'est du ~! P* what a mess!, it's a disgrace!
proprement (prɔprmɑ̃) *ad,* cleanly, neatly, tidily; properly; decently; exactly, strictly, specifically, literally. *à ~ parler,* strictly speaking. *les Parisiens ~ dits,* the Parisians themselves.
propret, te (prɔprɛ, ɛt) *a,* neat, tidy. **propreté** (prəte) *f,* cleanliness; neatness, tidiness; hygiene.
propriétaire (prɔprietɛr) *n,* proprietor, tress, owner; landlord, -lady. **propriété** (te) *f,* ownership; property; land; suitability, appropriateness (*word*). *~ artistique,* artistic copyright.
propulser (prɔpylse) *v.t,* to propel, drive; fling, hurl. **propulseur** (sœr) *a,* propulsive, driving. ¶ *m,* propeller. **propulsion** (sjɔ̃) *f,* propulsion.
prorata (prɔrata) *au ~ de, pr,* in proportion to.
prorogation (prɔrɔgasjɔ̃) *f,* prorogation; extension; deferment, adjournment. **proroger** (rɔʒe) *v.t,* to prorogue; extend; defer, adjourn.
prosaïque† (prɔzaik) *a,* prosaic.
proscrire (prɔskrir) *v.t.ir,* to proscribe, outlaw, banish; ban, prohibit; exile. **proscrit, e** (skri, it) *n,* outlaw; exile.
prose (proz) *f,* prose.
prospecter (prɔspɛkte) *v.t,* (*Min.*) to prospect; (*Com.*) canvas. **prospecteur, trice** (tœr, tris) *n,* prospector. **prospection** (sjɔ̃) *f,* prospecting; canvassing.
prospectus (prɔspɛktys) *m,* leaflet, brochure, handout.
prospère (prɔspɛr) *a,* prosperous, thriving, flourishing. **prospérer** (pere) *v.i,* to prosper, thrive. **prospérité** (rite) *f,* prosperity.
prostate (prɔstat) *f,* prostate [gland].
prosterné, e (prɔstɛrne) *a,* prostrate. **prosterner** (ne) *v.t,* to bow low. **se ~,** to prostrate o.s, bow down; (*fig.*) grovel.
prostituée (prɔstitɥe) *f,* prostitute. **prostituer** (tɥe) *v.t,* to prostitute. **prostitution** (tɥsjɔ̃) *f,* prostitution.
prostration (prɔstrasjɔ̃) *f,* prostration. **prostré, e** (tre) *a,* prostrate[d].
protagoniste (prɔtagɔnist) *m,* protagonist.
protecteur, trice (prɔtɛktœr, tris) *n,* protector; guardian; patron. ¶ *m,* pimp. ¶ *a,* protective;

patronizing. **protection** (sjɔ̃) *f,* protection; patronage; armour-plating. **protectionnisme** (ɔnism) *m,* protectionism. **protectionniste** (ɔnist) *m. & a,* protectionist. **protectorat** (tɔra) *m,* protectorate. **protégé, e** (teʒe) *n,* protégé, e. **protéger** (ʒe) *v.t,* to protect, shield, guard; patronize.

protestant, e (prɔtɛstɑ̃, ɑ̃t) *n. & a,* protestant. **protestantisme** (tɑ̃tism) *m,* protestantism. **protestataire** (tatɛr) *n,* protester. ¶ *a,* protesting (*pers.*); protest (*march*). **protestation** (tasjɔ̃) *f,* protest[ation]. **protester** (te) *v.t. & i,* to protest.

protocolaire (prɔtɔkɔlɛr) *a,* formal. **protocole** (kɔl) *m,* protocol; etiquette. ~ *d'accord,* draft treaty.

prototype (prɔtɔtip) *m,* prototype.

protubérance (prɔtyberɑ̃s) *f,* protuberance. **protubérant, e** (rɑ̃, ɑ̃t) *a,* bulging, protuberant, protruding.

proue (pru) *f,* prow.

prouesse (pruɛs) *f,* prowess, valour; feat.

prouver (pruve) *v.t,* to prove; show.

provenance (prɔvnɑ̃s) *f,* origin, source. *en ~ de,* from. **provenir de** (vnir) *v.i.ir,* to come from; be due to, be the result of.

proverbe (prɔvɛrb) *m,* proverb. **proverbial, e†** (bjal) *a,* proverbial.

providence (prɔvidɑ̃s) *f,* providence; godsend; good angel. **providentiel, le†** (dɑ̃sjɛl) *a,* providential.

province (prɔvɛ̃s) *f,* province; provinces, country. *en ~,* in the provinces. *de ~,* provincial (*town*). **provincial, e** (vɛ̃sjal) *a,* provincial.

proviseur (prɔvizœr) *m,* headmaster. **provision** (zjɔ̃) *f,* stock, supply; deposit (*bank*), funds; (*pl.*) provisions, food, groceries. **provisoire†** (zwar) *a,* provisional, temporary.

provocateur, trice (prɔvɔkatœr, tris) *n,* agitator. ¶ *a,* provocative. **provocation** (kasjɔ̃) *f,* provocation. **provoquer** (ke) *v.t,* to provoke, incite; challenge; induce, cause; arouse.

proximité (prɔksimite) *f,* proximity. *à ~,* close by, near at hand.

prude (pryd) *a,* prudish. ¶ *f,* prude.

prudemment (prydamɑ̃) *ad,* prudently. **prudence** (dɑ̃s) *f,* prudence, discretion; wisdom. **prudent, e** (dɑ̃, ɑ̃t) *a,* prudent.

prune (pryn) *f,* plum. **pruneau** (no) *m,* prune. **prunelle** (nɛl) *f,* sloe; pupil (*eye*); apple (*eye*). [*liqueur de*] ~, sloe gin. **prunellier** (lje) *m,* blackthorn. **prunier** (nje) *m,* plum [tree].

psalmodier (psalmɔdje) *v.i. & t,* to chant. **psaume** (psom) *m,* psalm. **psautier** (psotje) *m,* psalter.

pseudonyme (psødɔnim) *m,* pseudonym; pen name; stage name.

psychanalyse (psikanaliz) *f,* psychoanalysis. **psychanalyser** (se) *v.t,* to psychoanalyze. **psychanaliste** (list) *n,* psychoanalyst. **psychiatre** (kjatr) *n,* psychiatrist. **psychiatrie** (tri) *f,* psychiatry. **psychiatrique** (trik) *a,* psychiatric, mental (*hospital*). **psychique** (ʃik) *a,* psychic(al); psychological. **psychisme** (ʃism) *m,* psyche. **psychologie** (kɔlɔʒi) *f,* psychology. **psychologique** (ʒik) *a,* psychological. **psychologue** (lɔg) *n,* psychologist. **psychose** (koz) *f,* psychosis; (*fig.*) obsessive fear.

puant, e (pyɑ̃, ɑ̃t) *a,* stinking; foul. **puanteur** (ɑ̃tœr) *f,* stink, stench.

puberté (pybɛrte) *f,* puberty.

public, ique (pyblik) *a,* public. ¶ *m,* public; audience. **publication** (kasjɔ̃) *f,* publication. **publicitaire** (sitɛr) *a,* advertising, publicity, promotional. **publicité** (te) *f,* publicity, advertising; advertisement. **publier** (e) *v.t,* to publish.

puce (pys) *f,* flea; (*P Electronics*) [micro]chip. *mettre une ~ à l'oreille de qn,* to arouse s.o's suspicions. **puceron** (srɔ̃) *m,* green fly.

pudeur (pydœr) *f,* modesty, decency, shame. **pudibond, e** (dibɔ̃, ɔ̃d) *a,* prudish. **pudibonderie** (dri) *f,* prudishness. **pudique†** (dik) *a,* chaste, modest.

puer (pɥe) *v.i,* to stink, smell. ¶ *v.t,* to stink of, smell of.

puéricultrice (pɥerikyltris) *f,* paediatric nurse. **puériculture** (tyr) *f,* paediatric nursing. **puéril, e†** (ril) *a,* puerile, childish. **puérilité** (lite) *f,* puerility, childishness.

pugilat (pyʒila) *m,* [fist] fight.

puîné, e (pɥine) *a. & n,* younger (brother, sister).

puis (pɥi) *ad,* then, afterwards, next; besides.

puisard (pɥizar) *m,* cesspool. **puiser** (ze) *v.t. & i,* (*lit. fig.*) to draw (*dans,* from).

puisque, puisqu' (pɥisk[ə]) *c,* since, as, seeing that.

puissamment (pɥisamɑ̃) *ad,* powerfully, mightily. **puissance** (sɑ̃s) *f,* power; might; strength, force; authority. ~ *fiscale,* (*Mot.*) engine rating. **puissant, e** (sɑ̃, ɑ̃t) *a,* powerful; mighty.

puits (pɥi) *m,* well; (*Min.*) shaft.

pull *P* (pul), **pull-over** (pulɔvœr) *m,* sweater, pullover, jumper.

pulluler (pyllyle) *v.i,* to multiply, proliferate; swarm, abound.

pulmonaire (pylmɔnɛr) *a,* pulmonary.

pulpe (pylp) *f,* pulp.

pulsation (pylsasjɔ̃) *f,* pulsation; beating.

pulsion (pylsjɔ̃) *f,* drive, urge.

pulvérisateur (pylverizatœr) *m,* spray, atomizer. **pulvérisation** (zasjɔ̃) *f,* pulverization; spraying. **pulvériser** (ze) *v.t,* to pulverize, powder; spray.

puma (pyma) *m,* puma.

punaise (pynɛz) *f,* bug; drawing pin.

punch (pɔ̃ʃ) *m,* punch (*drink*).

punir (pynir) *v.t,* to punish; avenge. **punissable** (nisabl) *a,* punishable. **punitif, ive** (nitif, iv) *a,*

punitive. **punition** (sjɔ̃) *f,* punishment.
pupille[1] (pypil) *n,* ward.
pupille[2] (pypil) *f,* pupil (*eye*).
pupitre (pypitr) *m,* desk; music stand, lectern; rostrum.
pur, e† (pyr) *a,* pure; clear; undiluted; straight, neat (*gin &c*); plain, mere, sheer. *~-sang,* thoroughbred, purebred.
purée (pyre) *f,* purée. *~ [de pommes de terre],* mashed potatoes. *être dans la ~ P,* to be in the soup *P.*
pureté (pyrte) *f,* purity; clearness (*sky*).
purgatif, ive (pyrgatif, iv) *a. & m,* purgative. **purgatoire** (twar) *m,* purgatory. **purge** (pyrʒ) *f,* purge. **purger** (ʒe) *v.t,* to purge, drain; bleed (*brakes*); serve (*sentence*). **se ~**, to take a purgative.
purification (pyrifikasjɔ̃) *f,* purification, cleansing; refinement. **purifier** (fje) *v.t,* to purify, cleanse; refine.
purin (pyrɛ̃) *m,* liquid manure.
puritain, e (pyritɛ̃, ɛn) *n,* Puritan. ¶ *a,* Puritan; puritanic(al).
pus (py) *m,* pus, matter.
pustule (pystyl) *f,* pustule, pimple.
putain *P** (pytɛ̃) *f,* whore. ¶ *i, ~!* hell!
putatif, ive (pytatif, iv) *a,* putative, reputed.
putois (pytwa) *m,* polecat.
putréfaction (pytrefaksjɔ̃) *f,* putrefaction. **putréfier** (fje) *v.t,* to putrefy. **putride** (trid) *a,* putrid.
puy (pɥi) *m,* mountain, peak.
puzzle (pœzl) *m,* jigsaw [puzzle].
pyjama (piʒama) *m,* pyjamas.
pylône (pilon) *m,* pylon.
pyramide (piramid) *f,* pyramid.
pyromane (pirɔman) *n,* arsonist; pyromaniac.
python (pitɔ̃) *m,* python.

Q

Q, q (ky) *m, letter,* Q, q.
quadragénaire (kwadraʒenɛr) *a,* forty years old.
quadrangulaire (kwadrɑ̃gylɛr) *a,* quadrangular.
quadri- (kadri) *pref:* four- *~moteur,* four-engined. *~-réacteur,* four-engined jet.
quadrilatère (kadrilatɛr) *m,* quadrilateral.
quadrillage (kadrijaʒ) *m,* (*Police &c*) covering, control; grid pattern (*paper*). **quadrillé, e** (je) *a,* squared (*paper*). **quadriller** (je) *v.t,* to cover, control.
quadrupède (k[w]adrypɛd) *a. & m,* quadruped.
quadruple (k[w]adrypl) *a. & m,* quadruple, fourfold. **quadrupler** (ple) *v.t,* to quadruple. **quadruplés, ées** (ple) *n.pl,* quadruplets, quads.
quai (ke) *m,* quay, wharf; embankment (*river*); (*Rly.*) platform.
qualificatif, ive (kalifikatif, iv) *a,* qualifying. ¶ *m,* (*Gram.*) qualifier; (*fig.*) term. **qualification** (kasjɔ̃) *f,* qualification; label, description. **qualifié, e** (fje) *a,* qualified; skilled (*worker*); aggravated (*robbery*). **qualifier** (kalifje) *v.t,* to qualify; call, style; describe. **qualité** (te) *f,* quality; capacity; skill; position, occupation.
quand (kɑ̃) *c,* when. *~ bien même,* even if, though. *~ même,* all the same, nevertheless. ¶ *ad,* when?
quant à (kɑ̃ta) *pr,* as for, as to, as regards.
quantifier (kɑ̃tifje) *v.t,* to quantify. **quantitatif, ive** (titatif, iv) *a,* quantitive. **quantité** (tite) *f,* quantity; amount; lots, a lot.
quarantaine (karɑ̃tɛn) *f,* [about] forty; quarantine. *mettre en ~,* to quarantine (*ship*); send (*pers.*) to Coventry. **quarante** (rɑ̃t) *a,* forty. ¶ *m,* forty; 40th. **quarantième** (rɑ̃tjɛm) *a. & n,* fortieth.
quart (ka) *m,* quarter; ¼ litre; (*Naut.*) watch. *~ d'heure,* quarter of an hour. *une heure et ~,* a quarter past one. *de ~,* on watch. *partir au ~ de bouton,* (*Mot.*) to start first time. *passer un mauvais ~ d'heure,* to have a bad time of it. **quartette** (kwartɛt) *m,* jazz quartet[te].
quartier (kartje) *m,* district, area; quarter; chunk (*meat*); segment, piece (*fruit*); (*pl.*) quarters. *~ général,* headquarters. *de ~,* local. *mettre en ~s,* to tear to pieces.
quartz (kwarts) *m,* quartz.
quasi (kɑzi) *ad,* almost, nearly. ¶ *pref:* near. **quasiment** (zimɑ̃) *ad,* almost, nearly.
quatorze (katɔrz) *a. & m,* fourteen; 14th (*date*). *la guerre de ~,* the First World War. **quatorzième** (zjɛm) *a. & n,* fourteenth.
quatrain (katrɛ) *m,* quatrain.
quatre (katr) *a. & m,* four; 4th (*date*). *dire à qn ses ~ vérités,* to tell s.o a few home truths. *faire les ~ cent coups,* to be a real troublemaker. *faire ses ~ volontés,* to do exactly as one pleases. *se mettre en ~ pour qn,* to go out of one's way for s.o. *tiré à ~ épingles,* dressed up to the nines. *à ~ pattes,* on all fours. *for other phrases V* **six & sixième.** *~-vingt-dix* (trəvɛ̃di[s]) *a. & m,* ninety. *~-vingt-onze* (vɛ̃ɔ̃z), 91. *~-vingt-dixième* (zjɛm) *a. & n,* ninetieth. *~-vingtième* (tjɛm) *a. & n,* eight-

ieth. ~*-vingts, a. & m,* eighty. ~*-vingt-un* (vɛ̃œ̃), 81. **quatrième**† (triɛm) *a. & n,* fourth.
quatuor (kwatɥɔr) *m,* quartet[te].
que, qu' (kə, k) *c,* that; *il dit* ~, he says that. (*comparisons*) than, as. *qu'il le veuille ou non,* whether he wants it or not. *si elle revient et qu'il fasse beau,* if she returns & it is fine. *qu'il vienne,* let him come. ~ *m'importe!* what do I care? ¶ *ad,* [*ce*] ~ *tu es bête!* how stupid you are! ¶ *pr,* (*relative; object*) whom, which, that. *un jour* ~, one day when. (*interrogative*) ~*?* & *qu'est-ce que?* (kɛskə) what? (*object*). *qu'est-ce qui?* (ki) what? (*subject*).
quel, le (kɛl) *a,* (*interrogative*) which?, what?, who? (*exclamatory*) ~*le idée!* what an idea! ~*le chance,* what luck! ~ *que,* whatever; whoever.
quelconque (kɛlkɔ̃k) *a,* any; some. *pour une raison* ~, for some reason or other. ordinary; plain-looking; poor, indifferent.
quelque (kɛlk[ə]) *a,* some, any; a few. ~ *chose, m,* something; anything. ~*fois, ad,* sometimes. ~ *part, ad,* somewhere.
quelqu'un, quelqu'une (kɛlkœ̃, kyn) *pn,* somebody, someone, anybody, anyone. *quelques-uns, unes* (kəzœ̃, yn) *pl,* some [people], a few.
quémander (kemɑ̃de) *v.t,* to beg for.
qu'en-dira-t-on (le) (kɑ̃diratɔ̃) *m,* what people may say.
quenelle (kənɛl) *f,* quenelle.
quenotte *P* (kənɔt) *f,* toothy-peg *P;* tooth.
querelle (kərɛl) *f,* quarrel, row. **quereller** (le) *v.t,* to scold, nag. **se** ~, to quarrel, wrangle. **querelleur, euse** (lœr, øz) *a,* quarrelsome.
question (kɛstjɔ̃) *f,* question; query; point, matter, issue. *hors de* ~, out of the question. *poser la* ~ *de confiance,* to ask for a vote of confidence. *remettre en* ~, to challenge, [call in] question. **questionnaire** (ɔnɛr) *m,* questionnaire. **questionner** (ne) *v.t,* to question.
quête (kɛt) *f,* quest, search; collection. **quêter** (kɛte) *v.t,* to seek for; collect (*alms*). ¶ *v.i,* to take the collection, collect money. **quêteur, euse** (tœr, øz) *n,* collector.
queue (kø) *f,* tail; handle (*pan*); stem; stalk; rear (*train*); bottom (*class*); queue, file; (*Bil.*) cue. ~ *de cheval,* ponytail. ~*-de-pie,* tails. *à la* ~ *leu leu,* in single file, one after the other. *faire une* ~ *de poisson,* (*Mot.*) to cut in front of s.o.
qui (ki) *pn,* (*interrogative*) ~ & ~ *est-ce* ~*?* who? (*subject*). ~ & ~ *est-ce que?* who[m]? (*object*). *à* ~ *penses-tu?* who are you thinking of? (*relative: subject*) who. ~ *que,* whoever, anyone that. ~*-vive?* who goes there? *sur le* ~*-vive,* on the alert. *à* ~ *mieux, mieux,* each one more than the other.
quiconque (kikɔ̃k) *pn,* who[so]ever; anyone that.
quiétude (kɥietyd) *f,* quiet; peace [of mind].
quignon (kiɲɔ̃) *m,* [c]hunk.
quille (kij) *f,* skittle, ninepin; keel.
quincaillerie (kɛ̃kajri) *f,* hardware, ironmongery. **quincaillier** (je) *m,* ironmonger.
quinconce (kɛ̃kɔ̃s) *m, en* ~, in staggered rows.
quinine (kinin) *f,* quinine.
quinquennal, e (kɥɛ̃kɛnnal) *a,* quinquennial; five-year (*plan*).
quintal (kɛ̃tal) *m,* quintal = 100 kilos.
quinte (kɛ̃t) *f,* (*Cards*) quint; (*Mus.*) fifth. ~ [*de toux*], fit of coughing.
quintessence (kɛ̃tɛsɑ̃s) *f,* quintessence.
quintette (kɛ̃tɛt) *f,* quintet[te].
quintuple (kɛ̃typl) *a. & m,* quintuple. **quintupler** (ple) *v.t. & i,* to quintuple, increase fivefold. **quintuplés, ées** (ple) *n.pl,* quintuplets, quins.
quinzaine (kɛ̃zɛn) *f,* [about] fifteen; fortnight. **quinze** (kɛ̃z) *a. & m,* fifteen; 15th (*date*). ~ *jours,* fortnight. *le* ~ *août,* Assumption. **quinzième**† (kɛ̃zjɛm) *a. & n,* fifteenth.
quiproquo (kiprɔko) *m,* mistake (*of one pers. for another*); misunderstanding.
quittance (kitɑ̃s) *f,* receipt; bill. **quitte** (kit) *a,* quit, rid, free. ~ *à perdre,* although it may mean losing. ~ *envers qn,* quits with s.o. ~ *ou double,* double or quits. **quitter** (te) *v.t. & i,* to leave, quit, vacate; give up; swerve from. *ne quittez pas!* (*Tel.*) hold on!, hold the line!
quoi (kwa) *pn,* (*interrogative*) what? ~ *de neuf?* what's the news? *à* ~ *bon?* what's the use? (*relative*) *après* ~, *sur* ~, whereupon. *de* ~ *écrire,* writing materials. *il n'y a pas de* ~, (*after thanks*) not at all, don't mention it. ~ *que,* whatever. ~ *que ce soit,* anything at all. ~ *qu'il en soit,* be that as it may.
quoique, quoiqu' (kwak[ə]) *c,* [al]though (+ *subj.*).
quolibet (kɔlibɛ) *m,* gibe.
quorum (kɔrɔm) *m,* quorum.
quote-part (kɔtpar) *f,* share, quota.
quotidien, ne (kɔtidjɛ̃, ɛn) *a,* daily; everyday. **[journal]** ~ *m,* daily [paper]. **quotidiennement** (ɛnmɑ̃) *ad,* daily.
quotient (kɔsjɑ̃) *m,* quotient.

R

R, r (ɛr) *m, letter,* R, r.
rabâchage (rabɑʃaʒ) *m,* endless repetition. **rabâcher** (ʃe) *v.t.* (*& i*), to harp on; keep on repeating (*o.s*). **rabâcheur, euse** (ʃœr, ʃøz) *n,* repetitive bore.
rabais (rabɛ) *m,* reduction, discount. *au* ~, at a reduced price; (*pej.*) third rate. **rabaisser** (se) *v.t,* to lower; disparage, belittle.
rabat (raba) *m,* flap (*table &c*). ~**-joie,** *m,* killjoy. **rabatteur, euse** (tœr, øz) *n,* tout; beater. **rabattre** (tr) *v.t.ir,* to close; turn down; pull d.; push back (*covers*); reduce, lower; deduct, take off; drive (*game*); beat. **se** ~, (*car &c*) to cut in; fall short. ~ *sur,* fall back on, make do with.
rabbin (rabɛ̃) *m,* rabbi.
rabibocher *P* (rabibɔʃe) *v.t,* to reconcile.
rabiot *P* (rabjo) *m,* extra [food]; e. time. **rabioter** *P* (jɔte) *v.t,* to scrounge; fiddle *P.*
râble (rɑbl) *m,* back (*hare &c*); (*Cook.*) saddle. **râblé, e** (ble) *a,* stocky.
rabot (rabo) *m,* plane (*tool*). **raboter** (bɔte) *v.t,* to plane; (*fig.*) polish. **raboteux, euse** (tø, øz) *a,* rough, rugged; knotty.
rabougrir (rabugrir) *v.t,* to stunt (*growth*).
rabouter (rabute) *v.t,* to join [up].
rabrouer (rabrue) *v.t,* to rebuff, snub; rebuke.
racaille (rakɑj) *f,* rabble, riff-raff.
raccommodage (rakɔmɔdaʒ) *m,* mending, repairing. **raccommodement** (dmɑ̃) *m,* reconciliation. **raccommoder** (de) *v.t,* to mend, repair; reconcile. **se** ~, to make it up.
raccord (rakɔr) *m,* join; joint; link; (*Cine.*) l. scene. ~ [*de maçonnerie*], pointing. ~ [*de peinture*], touch up. **raccorder** (kɔrde) *v.t,* to join, connect, couple, link up.
raccourci (rakursi) *m,* short cut; summary. *en* ~, in miniature; in a nutshell. **raccourcir** (sir) *v.t,* to shorten; abridge, curtail. **[se]** ~, to draw in (*days*); shrink.
raccroc (rakro) *m,* fluke, lucky stroke. **raccrocher** (krɔʃe) *v.t,* to hang up again; replace (*receiver*); grab hold of; connect, link. ¶ *v.i,* (*Tel.*) to hang up, ring off. **se** ~ **à,** to clutch, catch; cling to.
race (ras) *f,* race; strain, breed, stock. *de* ~, purebred, pedigree, thoroughbred. **racé, e** (se) *a,* thoroughbred, purebred, pedigree.
rachat (raʃa) *m,* repurchase; redemption; ransom; (*Insce*) surrender; (*Fin.*) take-over. **racheter** (ʃte) *v.t,* to repurchase, buy back; redeem; surrender; ransom; atone for; take over.
rachitique (raʃitik) *a,* (*Med.*) rickety; (*pej.*) scrawny. **rachitisme** (tism) *m,* rickets.
racine (rasin) *f,* root.
racisme (rasism) *m,* racialism, racism. **raciste** (sist) *a. & n,* racialist, racist.
raclée (rɑkle) *f,* thrashing, hiding. **racler** (kle) *v.t,* to scrape; s. off; s. away. *se* ~ *la gorge,* to clear one's throat.
racoler (rakɔle) *v.t,* to tout for; solicit.
racontar (rakɔ̃tar) *m,* story, lie. **raconter** (te) *v.t,* to tell, relate; recount. ~ *des histoires,* to tell stories. *qu'est-ce que tu racontes?* what are you talking about *or* saying?
racornir (rakɔrnir) *v.t,* to harden; shrivel.
radar (radar) *m,* radar.
rade (rad) *f,* (*Naut.*) roads; [natural] harbour. *laisser en* ~ *P,* to leave in the lurch; shelve (*project*); leave behind.
radeau (rado) *m,* raft.
radial, e (radjal) *a,* radial. **radiateur** (tœr) *m,* radiator; (*gas, elec.*) heater. **radiation** (sjɔ̃) *f,* striking out; s. off; radiation.
radical, e† (radikal) *a. & m,* radical; root. **radicaliser (se)** (lize) *v.pr,* to toughen, harden.
radier (radje) *v.t,* to strike out; s. off.
radieux, euse (radjø, øz) *a,* radiant, beaming.
radio (radjo) *f,* radio; r. [set]; X-ray photograph. ¶ *m,* radio operator; radio[tele]gram. **radioactif, ive** (aktif, iv) *a,* radioactive. **radioactivité** (vite) *f,* radioactivity. **radiodiffuser** (ɔdifyze) *v.t,* to broadcast. **radiodiffusion** (zjɔ̃) *f.* broadcasting. **radiographie** (fi) *f,* radiography; X-ray photograph. **radiographier** (fje) *v.t,* to X-ray. **radiographique** (fik) *a,* X-ray. **radioguidage** (gidaʒ) *m,* radio control. **radiologie** (lɔʒi) *f,* radiology. **radiologue** (lɔg) *n,* radiologist. **radiophonie** (fɔni) *f,* radiotelephony. **radiophonique** (fɔnik) *a,* radio. **radioreportage** (r[e]pɔrtaʒ) *m,* radio report. **radioreporter** (rəpɔrtɛr) *m,* radio reporter. **radioscopie** (skɔpi) *f,* radioscopy. **radiotélégraphie** (telegrafi) *f,* radiotelegraphy. **radiotélévisé, e** (televize) *a,* broadcast & televised.
radis (radi) *m,* radish; (*P*) penny, bean *P.*
radium (radjɔm) *m,* radium.
radius (radjys) *m,* (*Anat.*) radius.
radoter (radɔte) *v.i,* to drivel, ramble. **radoteur, euse** (tœr, øz) *n,* dotard.
radoucir (radusir) *v.t,* to soften. **se** ~, to become milder; calm down; (*voice*) soften. **radoucissement** (sismɑ̃) *m,* milder weather.
rafale (rafal) *f,* squall, gust; hail (*bullets*); burst (*fire*).
raffermir (rafɛrmir) *v.t,* to strengthen; steady (*voice*).
raffinage (rafinaʒ) *m,* refining. **raffiné, e** (ne) *a,*

refined; sophisticated. **raffinement** (nmɑ̃) *m,* refinement, sophistication. **raffiner** (ne) *v.t,* to refine; polish. ¶ *v.i,* to be meticulous. **raffinerie** (nri) *f,* refinery. **raffineur, euse** (nœr, øz) *n,* refiner.
raffoler de (rafɔle), to be very fond of, dote on.
rafistoler (rafistɔle) *v.t,* to patch up.
rafle (rɑfl) *f,* [police] roundup *or* raid. **rafler** *P* (rafle) *v.t,* to swipe *P.*
rafraîchir (rafrɛʃir) *v.t. & i,* to cool, refresh, freshen; revive; trim (*hair, grass*). **rafraîchissant, e** (ʃisɑ̃, ɑ̃t) *a,* refreshing. **rafraîchissement** (ʃismɑ̃) *m,* cooling; cold drink; (*pl.*) refreshments.
ragaillardir (ragajardir) *v.t,* to cheer up.
rage (raʒ) *f,* rage; rabies, madness; mania. ~ *de dents,* raging toothache. **rager** (raʒe) *v.i,* to fume. **rageur, euse†** (ʒœr, øz) *a,* furious; bad tempered.
ragot (rago) *m,* gossip, scandal.
ragoût (ragu) *m,* stew. **ragoûtant, e** (tɑ̃, ɑ̃t) *a,* tempting.
raid (rɛd) *m,* raid; endurance test.
raide (rɛd) *a,* stiff; straight (*hair*); tight, taut; steep; rigid; rough (*alcohol*); (*fig.*) far-fetched. ¶ *ad,* ~ *mort,* stone dead. **raideur** (dœr) *f,* stiffness, &c. **raidillon** (dijɔ̃) *m,* [steep] incline. **raidir** (dir) *v.t,* to stiffen; tighten; harden, toughen. **raidissement** (dismɑ̃) *m,* stiffening; hard line.
raie (rɛ) *f,* line; scratch, mark; stripe; parting (*hair*); ray, skate (*fish*).
raifort (rɛfɔr) *m,* horseradish.
rail (rɑj) *m,* rail. ~ *conducteur,* live rail.
railler (rɑje) *v.t,* to jeer at, scoff at. **raillerie** (jri) *f,* mockery. **railleur, euse** (jœr, øz) *a,* mocking.
rainure (rɛnyr) *f,* groove, slot. **rainurer** (re) *v.t,* to groove.
raisin (rɛzɛ̃) *m,* grapes. *grappe de* ~, bunch of grapes. ~*s de Corinthe,* currants (*dried*). ~*s de Smyrne,* sultanas. ~*s secs,* raisins.
raison (rɛzɔ̃) *f,* (*gen.*) reason; (*Math.*) ratio, ~ *de plus,* all the more reason. ~ *d'État,* reason of State. ~ *d'être,* raïson d'être. ~ *sociale,* (*Com.*) corporate name. *avec* [*juste*] ~, with good reason. *avoir* ~, to be right. *donner* ~ *à qn,* to prove s.o. right. ~**nable†** (zɔnabl) *a,* reasonable; rational; fair; sound, sane. ~**nement** (nmɑ̃) *m,* reasoning; argument. ~**ner** (ne) *v.i,* to reason; argue. ¶ *v.t,* to reason with. ~**neur, euse** (nœr, øz) *n,* arguer. ¶ *a,* argumentative.
rajeunir (raʒœnir) *v.t,* to rejuvenate; make look younger; renovate; update; modernize; brighten up. **rajeunissement** (nismɑ̃) *m,* rejuvenation &c.
rajuster (raʒyste) *v.t,* to readjust; put straight.
râle (rɑl) *m,* rail (*bird*); [death] rattle.
ralenti, e (ralɑ̃ti) *a,* slow. ¶ *m,* slow-motion; (*Mot.*) tick-over. **ralentir** (ralɑ̃tir) *v.t. & i,* to slacken, slow down; reduce speed; flag. **ralentissement** (tismɑ̃) *m,* slowing down; slackening off; flagging.
rallier (ralje) *v.t,* to rally; rejoin; unite; win [over]. **se** ~ **à,** to join; go over to (*enemy*); rally round; come round to.
rallonge (ralɔ̃ʒ) *f,* leaf (*table*); extension piece (*flex &c*). **rallonger** (lɔ̃ʒe) *v.t,* to lengthen, extend.
rallumer (ralyme) *v.t,* to relight, rekindle.
rallye (rali) *m,* rally.
ramage (ramaʒ) *m,* floral design; song (*of birds*).
ramassage (ramasaʒ) *m,* collection, gathering; picking up. ~*scolaire,* school bus service. **ramassé, e** (se) *a,* stocky; condensed, compact. **ramasser** (se) *v.t,* to gather, collect; pick up. **se** ~, to curl up; crouch; (*P*) come a cropper *P.* **ramasseur, euse** (sœr, øz) *n,* collector, gatherer. **ramassis** (si) *m,* pack, bunch; jumble.
rame (ram) *f,* (*Hort.*) stick; oar; ream; (*Rly*) train.
rameau (ramo) *m,* branch; (*Eccl.*) palm.
ramener (ramne) *v.t,* to bring back; restore. ~ *en arrière,* draw back; brush back (*hair*). **se** ~ **à,** to boil down to.
ramer (rame) *v.i,* to row. ~ *en couple,* to scull. **rameur, euse** (mœr, øz) *n,* rower, oarsman, -woman.
ramier (ramje) *m,* [*pigeon*] ~, wood pigeon.
ramification (ramifikasjɔ̃) *f,* ramification. **ramifier (se)** (fje) *v.pr,* to ramify; branch out.
ramolli, e (ramɔli) *a,* soft. **ramollir** (lir) *v.t,* to soften. **ramollissement** (lismɑ̃) *m,* softening.
ramoner (ramɔne) *v.t,* to sweep (*chimney*). **ramoneur** (nœr) *m,* chimney sweep.
rampant, e (rɑ̃pɑ̃, ɑ̃t) *a,* rampant; creeping; crawling; grovelling. **rampe** (rɑ̃p) *f,* slope; ramp; banisters, hand rail; footlights. **ramper** (rɑ̃pe) *v.i,* to creep, crawl; cringe, grovel.
ramure (ramyr) *f,* branches; antlers.
rancard *P* (rɑ̃kar) *m,* tip; date.
rancart (mettre au) *P* (rɑ̃kar) to chuck out, scrap.
rance (rɑ̃s) *a,* rancid, rank. **rancir** (rɑ̃sir) *v.i,* to become rancid.
rancœur (rɑ̃kœr) *f,* rancour, bitterness.
rançon (rɑ̃sɔ̃) *f,* ransom. **rançonner** (sɔne) *v.t,* to ransom; fleece.
rancune (rɑ̃kyn) *f,* rancour, spite; grudge. **rancunier, ère** (nje, ɛr) *a,* spiteful. *être* ~, to bear a grudge.
randonnée (rɑ̃dɔne) *f,* circuit; trip, run.
rang (rɑ̃) *m,* row, line; tier; rank, station, place. **rangé, e** (ʒe) *a,* tidy; [well-]ordered; orderly; settled. **rangée** (ʒe) *f,* row, line. **rangement** (ʒmɑ̃) *m,* putting away; arrangement; storage space. **ranger** (ʒe) *v.t,* to arrange, tidy, put away; park (*car*); line up; place (*guests*). **se**

~, to line up; pull in; park; stand aside; (*P*) settle down. ~ *à*, to fall in with. ~ *du côté de qn*, to side with s.o.
ranimer (ranime) *v.t*, to revive; restore; rekindle.
rapace (rapas) *a*, rapacious; predatory. ¶ *m*, bird of prey.
rapatrier (rapatrie) *v.t*, to repatriate, send home.
râpe (rɑp) *f*, rasp; grater (*nutmeg, &c*). **râpé, e** (rɑpe) *a*, grated; threadbare, shabby. **râper** (pe) *v.t*, to rasp; grate.
rapetisser (raptise) *v.t. & i*, to shorten; dwarf; belittle.
rapeux, euse (rapø, øz) *a*, rough.
raphia (rafja) *m*, raffia.
rapiat, e (rapja, at) *a*, tight-fisted. ¶ *n*, skinflint.
rapide† (rapid) *a*, rapid, fast, swift; speedy; cursory; steep. ¶ *m*, rapid (*river*); fast train, express. **rapidité** (dite) *f*, speed, rapidity, swiftness &c.
rapiécer (rapjese) *v.t*, to piece, patch.
rappel (rapɛl) *m*, recall; call[ing]; reminder; (*Com.*) quote; back pay; booster (*vaccination*). *faire un* ~, (*climbing*) to rope down, abseil. **rappeler** (ple) *v.t*, to recall; call (*to order &c*); remind; r. of; remember; be reminiscent of; quote (*reference*); mention; (*Tel.*) ring back. ~ *qn à la vie*, to revive s.o. **se** ~, to recollect, remember.
rappliquer *P* (raplike) *v.i*, to come back, turn up.
rapport (rapɔr) *m*, connection, relationship, link; report; conference; yield, return; (*pl.*) relations; (*Math.*) ratio. ~*s* [*sexuels*], sexual relations. *être en* ~ *avec*, to be in keeping with. *par* ~ *à*, in relation to; compared with. *les* ~ *des forces*, the balance of power. *sous tous les* ~*s*, in every respect. **rapporter** (pɔrte) *v.t*, to bring *or* take back; bring in, yield; report; quote; mention; add [on]; relate; revoke. ¶ *v.i*, (*dog*) to retrieve; give a good yield. **se** ~, to refer, relate. **rapporteur, euse** (tœr, øz) *n*, (*Sch.*) sneak. ¶ *m*, reporter; (*Geom.*) protractor.
rapprochement (raprɔʃmɑ̃) *m*, reconciliation; comparison; bringing together; connection. **rapprocher** (ʃe) *v.t*, to bring nearer; b. together; reconcile; compare. **se** ~, to come *or* move *or* get nearer (*de*, to); c. together; become more frequent.
rapt (rapt) *m*, abduction; kidnapping.
raquette (rakɛt) *f*, racket, -quet; (*table tennis*) bat; snow shoe.
rare (rɑr) *a*, rare; scarce; uncommon; unusual; sparse, thin; few. **raréfier (se)** (rarefje) *v.pr*, to become scarce; rarefy, get thin. **rarement** (rarmɑ̃) *ad*, rarely, seldom. **rareté** (te) *f*, rarity; scarcity; curiosity. **rarissime** (risim) *a*, extremely rare.
ras, e (rɑ, ɑz) *a*, short (*grass*); close-cropped; full (*measure &c*). ~ *du cou*, crew-neck jumper. *à* ~ *bords*, to the brim. *à* ~ *de terre*, level with the ground. *en avoir* ~ *le bol P*, to be fed up to the back teeth *P*. **rasade** (rasad) *f*, glassful.
rasage (rɑzaʒ) *m*, shaving. **rasant, e** (zɑ̃, ɑ̃t) *a*, (*P*) boring; low-angled (*light*). **raser** (ze) *v.t*, to shave; raze; graze, brush, skim; (*P*) bore. **raseur, euse** *P* (zœr, øz) *n*, bore. **rasoir** (zwar) *m*, razor; (*P*) bore.
rassasier (rasazje) *v,t*, to satisfy; satiate.
rassembler (rasɑ̃ble) *v.t*, to gather; g. together, assemble; collect, bring together; reassemble; summon up (*courage*).
rasseoir (raswar) *v.t.ir*, to sit up again (*baby*); put back straight (*object*). **se** ~, to sit down again.
rasséréner (se) (raserene) *v.pr*, to become serene again.
rassis, e (rasi, iz) *a*, stale (*bread*).
rassurer (rasyre) *v.t*, to reassure, cheer.
rat, e (ra, at) *n*, rat. ~ *de bibliothèque*, bookworm (*pers.*). ~ *des champs*, field mouse. ~ *musqué*, musk rat, musquash.
ratatiné, e (ratatine) *a*, shrivelled, shrunken; wizened, wrinkled.
rate (rat) *f*, (*Anat.*) spleen.
râteau (rɑto) *m*, rake. **râteler** (tle) *v.t*, to rake up. **râtelier** (təlje) *m*, rack; denture.
rater (rate) *v.i*, to misfire; fail, go wrong, backfire. ¶ *v.t*, to miss (*shot, train*); spoil, mess up (*job*); fail.
ratifier (ratifje) *v.t*, to ratify, confirm.
ration (rasjɔ̃) *f*, ration, allowance.
rationaliser (rasjɔnalize) *v.t*, to rationalize. **rationalisme** (ism) *m*, rationalism. **rationnel, le†** (nɛl) *a*, rational.
rationner (rasjɔne) *v.t*, to ration.
ratisser (ratise) *v.t*, to rake; r. up; (*police &c*) comb; (*P*) clean up.
raton (ratɔ̃) *m*, young rat. ~ *laveur*, racoon.
rattacher (rataʃe) *v.t*, to refasten; bind; connect; tie up; join, unite; relate (*fact*).
rattraper (ratrape) *v.t*, to recapture; overtake, catch up; recover; salvage; make up for. ~ *qn*, (*Sch.*) to allow s.o to pass (*exam.*). **se** ~, to stop o.s falling; make up for it. *rattrapage scolaire*, remedial teaching.
rature (ratyr) *f*, erasure; deletion; alteration. **raturer** (tyre) *v.t*, to erase, scratch out; alter.
rauque (rok) *a*, hoarse, raucous, harsh.
ravage (ravaʒ) *m. oft. pl*, ravage, havoc, devastation. **ravager** (vaʒe) *v.t*, to ravage, devastate, lay waste. **ravageur, euse** (œr, øz) *a*, devastating.
ravaler (ravale) *v.t*, to swallow, choke back; (*pers: dignity*) lower; clean, restore, give a face lift to.
ravauder (ravode) *v.t*, to mend; darn.

rave (rav) *f,* [cole] rape.
ravi, e (ravi) *a,* delighted.
ravigoter *P* (ravigɔte) *v.t,* to revive, buck up *P.*
ravin (ravɛ̃) *m,* ravine, gully. **raviner** (vine) *v.t,* to gully; furrow.
ravir (ravir) *v.t,* to ravish, carry off; delight, enrapture.
raviser (se) (ravize) *v.pr,* to change one's mind.
ravissant, e (ravisɑ̃, ɑ̃t) *a,* ravishing, delightful. **ravissement** (vismɑ̃) *m,* rapture. **ravisseur, euse** (sœr, øz) *n,* kidnapper, abductor.
ravitailler (ravitaje) *v.t,* to refuel; provide with fresh supplies.
raviver (ravive) *v.t,* to revive; rekindle; brighten up.
ravoir (ravwar) *v.t,* to get (*something*) back; (*P*) get clean.
rayer (rɛje) *v.t,* to scratch, score; rule; stripe, streak; delete, cross out.
rayon (rɛjɔ̃) *m,* ray, beam; gleam; radius; spoke; comb (*honey*); drill, furrow, row; shelf; department; counter. ~ *d'action,* range. (*Mot.*) ~ *de braquage,* lock, **rayonnage** (jɔnaʒ) *m. oft. pl,* shelving, set of shelves. **rayonnant, e** (jɔnɑ̃, ɑ̃t) *a,* radiant.
rayonne (rɛjɔn) *f,* rayon.
rayonnement (rɛjɔnmɑ̃) *m,* radiation; radiance; influence; extension. **rayonner** (ne) *v.i,* to radiate, beam, shine; extend; be radiant. ~ *dans une région,* to tour around a region; (*buses*) service a region.
rayure (rɛjyr) *f,* scratch, &c, as *rayer.*
raz-de-maree (rɑ) *m,* tidal wave.
razzia (razja) *f,* raid, foray.
ré (re) *m,* (*Mus.*) D.
réacteur (reaktœr) *m,* (*Aero.*) jet engine; (*Phys.*) reactor. **réaction** (sjɔ̃) *f,* reaction. **réactionnaire** (ɔnɛr) *a.* & *n,* reactionary.
réadapter (readapte) *v.t,* to readjust; rehabilitate; re-educate.
réagir (reaʒir) *v.t,* to react.
réalisateur, trice (realizatœr, tris) *n,* (*Cine.*) director. **réalisation** (zasjɔ̃) *f,* production; achievement; creation; fulfilment, realization. **réaliser** *v.t,* (lize) to achieve; make; carry out; realize; (*Cine.*) produce. **réalisme** (lism) *m,* realism. **réaliste** (list) *a,* realistic. ¶ *n,* realist. **réalité** (te) *f,* reality.
réanimer (reanime) *v.t,* to resuscitate, revive.
réapparition (reaparisjɔ̃) *f,* reappearance.
réassortir (reasɔrtir) *v.t,* to stock; replenish; match [up].
rébarbatif, ive (rebarbatif, iv) *a,* forbidding.
rebâtir (rəbɑtir) *v.t,* to rebuild; reconstruct.
rebattre (rəbatr) *v.t.ir,* to repeat. **rebattu, e** (ty) *a,* hackneyed.
rebelle (rəbɛl) *a,* rebellious; rebel; stubborn; unruly. ¶ *n,* rebel. **rebeller (se)** (le) *v.pr,* to rebel. **rébellion** (rebɛljɔ̃) *f,* rebellion.
rebiffer (se) (rəbife) *v.pr,* to show temper.
rebond (rəbɔ̃) *m,* bounce, rebound. **rebondi, e** (ɔ̃di) *a,* rounded, plump; pot-bellied. **rebondir** (dir) *v.i,* to rebound, bounce; crop up again.
rebord (rəbɔr) *m,* edge, rim; hem; ledge.
rebours (rəbur) *m,* wrong way; contrary, reverse. *à* ~, the wrong way; backwards. *comprendre à* ~, to misconstrue.
rebouteux, euse (rəbutø, øz) *n,* bonesetter.
rebrousse-poil (à) (rəbruspwal) *ad,* against the nap, the wrong way. **rebrousser** (se) *v.t,* to rub the wrong way. ~ *chemin,* to retrace one's steps.
rebuffade (rəbyfad) *f,* rebuff.
rébus (rebys) *m,* rebus.
rebut (rəby) *m,* scrap, waste; (*fig.*) scum; (*pl. Post*) dead letters. **rebutant, e** (tɑ̃, ɑ̃t) *a,* disheartening; repellent. **rebuter** (te) *v.t,* to repulse; dishearten, discourage; repel.
récalcitrant, e (rekalsitrɑ̃, ɑ̃t) *a.* & *n,* recalcitrant.
récapituler (rekapityle) *v.t,* to recapitulate.
receler (rəsle) *v.t,* to conceal; harbour (*criminal*); receive (*stolen goods.*) **receleur, euse** (slœr, øz) *n,* receiver, fence.
récemment (resɑmɑ̃) *ad,* recently, lately.
recensement (rəsɑ̃smɑ̃) *m,* census; inventory; registration. **recenser** (se) *v.t,* to take the census of; count.
récent, e (resɑ̃, ɑ̃t) *a,* recent, late; fresh.
récépissé (resepise) *m,* receipt. **réceptacle** (sɛptakl) *m,* receptacle; meeting point. **récepteur, trice** (tœr, tris) *a,* receiving. ¶ *m,* (*Tel.* &*c*). receiver. **réception** (sjɔ̃) *f,* reception; welcome; reception room; r. desk; lobby; receipt (*letter &c*); (*Sport*) catching; landing.
récessif, ive (resɛsif, iv) *a,* recessive. **récession** (sjɔ̃) *f,* recession.
recette (rəsɛt) *f,* recipe; formula; takings; collection; (*pl.*) receipts. ~*-perception,* tax office. *faire* ~, to be a big success.**recevabilité** (rəsvabilite) *f,* admissability. **recevable** (səvabl) *a,* admissible. **receveur, euse** (vœr, øz) *n,* (*Med.*) recipient; collector (*taxes &c*); conductor (*bus*). ¶ *f.* attendant (*Theat.*). ~ *des postes,* postmaster, -mistress. **recevoir** (vwar) *v.t,* to receive; admit; get; meet with; accept; welcome; take in (*boarders*); entertain; (*hotel*) hold, accommodate. *être reçu à,* to pass (*exam*). **se** ~, to land (*jump*).
rechange (rəʃɑ̃ʒ) *m,* change (*clothes*). *de* ~, spare.
réchapper (reʃape) *v.i,* to escape; recover.
recharge (rəʃarʒ) *f,* reload; refill. **recharger** (ʒe) *v.t,* to recharge; reload; refill.
réchaud (reʃo) *m,* stove. **réchauffer** (ʃofe) *v.t,* to reheat, warm up; revive.
rêche (rɛʃ) *a,* rough, harsh.
recherche (rəʃɛrʃ) *f,* search, quest, pursuit; research, inquiry; prospecting; studied

elegance. **recherché, e** (ʃe) *a,* sought after, much in demand; choice, exquisite; studied; meticulous. **rechercher** (ʃe) *v.t,* to search for, seek, look for, pursue.
rechigner (rəʃiɲe) *v.i,* to jib, balk. **en rechignant** (ɲɑ̃), with a bad grace.
rechute (rəʃyt) *f,* relapse; backsliding.
récidive (residiv) *f,* (*Law*) second *or* subsequent offence; (*Med.*) recurrence; (*fig.*) repetition. **récidiver** (ve) *v.i,* to commit a further offence; recur; do it again. **récidiviste** (vist) *n,* old offender; recidivist.
récif (resif) *m,* reef (*of rocks*).
récipient (resipjɑ̃) *m,* receptacle, container.
réciproque (resiprɔk) *a,* reciprocal. ¶ *f,* reverse, opposite; same. **réciproquement** (kmɑ̃) *ad,* each other, one another; vice versa.
récit (resi) *m,* account, narrative; (*Theat.*) monologue. **récital** (tal) *m,* recital. **récitation** (sjɔ̃) *f,* recitation. **réciter** (te) *v.t,* to recite.
réclamation (reklamasjɔ̃) *f,* complaint. **réclame** (klam) *f,* advertisement, puff. *article en ~,* special offer. **réclamer** (me) *v.i,* to complain, protest. ¶ *v.t,* to claim; crave; call for; ask for.
reclasser (rəklɑse) *v.t,* to redeploy; rehabilitate.
reclus, e (rəkly, yz) *n,* recluse. ¶ *a,* cloistered. **réclusion** (reklyzjɔ̃) *f,* reclusion; imprisonment.
recoin (rəkwɛ̃) *m,* nook, recess.
récolte (rekɔlt) *f,* harvest[ing]; crop. **récolter** (te) *v.t,* to harvest; collect.
recommandable (rəkɔmɑ̃dabl) *a,* commendable. **recommandation** (dasjɔ̃) *f,* commendation. **recommander** (rəkɔmɑ̃de) *v.t,* to [re]commend; (*Post*) register, record. **se ~ de qn,** to give s.o's name as a reference.
recommencer (rəkɔmɑ̃se) *v.t. & i,* to begin *or* start again; repeat (*error*); renew.
récompense (rekɔ̃pɑ̃s) *f,* reward; award. *en ~ de,* in return for. **récompenser** (pɑ̃se) *v.t,* to reward.
réconcilier (rekɔ̃silje) *v.t,* to reconcile.
reconduire (rəkɔ̃dɥir) *v.t.ir,* to escort; see home; show out; renew (*policy*).
réconfort (rekɔ̃fɔr) *m,* comfort. **réconforter** (fɔrte) *v.t,* to comfort; strengthen.
reconnaissable (rəkɔnɛsabl) *a,* recognizable. **reconnaissance** (sɑ̃s) *f,* recognition; acknowledgement; gratitude, thankfulness; reconnaissance, exploration. **reconnaissant, e** (sɑ̃, ɑ̃t) *a,* grateful, **reconnaître** (nɛtr) *v.t.ir,* to recognize; admit, acknowledge; reconnoitre.
reconquérir (rəkɔ̃kerir) *v.t.ir,* to reconquer; regain.
reconstituant, e (rəkɔ̃stitɥɑ̃, ɑ̃t) *a,* energizing. ¶ *m,* tonic. **reconstituer** (tɥe) *v.t,* to reconstitute; reconstruct; piece together; (*Biol.*) regenerate. **reconstitution** (tysjɔ̃) *f,* reconstitution &c.
reconstruction (rəkɔ̃stryksjɔ̃) *f,* rebuilding. **reconstruire** (strɥir) *v.t.ir,* to rebuild.
record (rəkɔr) *m,* (*Sport &c*) record. **recordman** (kɔrdman) *m,* record holder.
recoupement (rəkupmɑ̃) *m,* cross-check. **recouper** (pe) *v.t,* to cut again, c. more; intersect; match up with.
recourbé, e (rəkurbe) *a,* curved; hooked (*nose*).
recourir (rəkurir) *v.t.ir,* to have recourse, resort (*à,* to); turn, appeal. **recours** (kur) *m,* recourse, resort; (*Law*) appeal.
recouvrement (rəkuvrəmɑ̃) *m,* recovery; collection. **recouvrer** (vre) *v.t,* to recover; collect.
recouvrir (rəkuvrir) *v.t.ir,* to re-cover; cover. **se ~,** to overlap.
récréation (rekreasjɔ̃) *f,* recreation; playtime, break.
recréer (rəkree) *v.t,* to re-create.
récrier (se) (rekrie) *v.pr,* to cry out, exclaim.
récrimination (rekriminasjɔ̃) *f,* recrimination.
récrire (rekrir) *v.t.ir,* to rewrite; write again.
recroqueviller (se) (rəkrɔkvije) *v.pr,* to shrivel up, curl up.
recrudescence (rəkrydɛsɑ̃s) *f,* upsurge.
recrue (rəcry) *f,* recruit. **recruter** (te) *v.t,* to recruit.
rectangle (rɛktɑ̃gl) *a,* right-angled. ¶ *m,* rectangle. **rectangulaire** (tɑ̃gylɛr) *a,* rectangular.
rectificatif (rɛktifikatif) *m,* & **rectification** (kasjɔ̃) *f,* correction. **rectifier** (fje) *v.t,* to rectify; correct; adjust, straighten.
rectiligne (rɛktiliɲ) *a,* rectilinear; straight.
rectitude (rɛktityd) *f,* straightness; rectitude.
recto (rɛkto) *m,* recto, front, face.
rectum (rɛktɔm) *m,* rectum.
reçu (rəsy) *m,* receipt. ¶ *a,* accepted; successful (*candidate*).
recueil (rəkœj) *m,* collection; book. **recueillement** (kœjmɑ̃) *m,* meditation, contemplation. **recueillir** (jir) *v.t.ir,* to collect, gather; take in; t. note of, record. **se ~,** to meditate, gather one's thoughts.
recul (rəkyl) *m,* retreat; recession; decline; recoil, kick; deferment; backward movement. **reculade** (lad) *f,* retreat. **reculé, e** (le) *a,* distant, remote. **reculer** (le) *v.i. & t,* to draw back; move back; recede; retreat; back; recoil, kick; postpone; reverse. **à reculons** (lɔ̃) *ad,* backward[s].
récupérer (rekypere) *v.t,* to recover, recoup; salvage; repossess; retrieve, rescue. ¶ *v.i,* to recover, recuperate.
récurer (rekyre) *v.t,* to scour, clean.
récuser (rekyze) *v.t,* to challenge, object to.
rédacteur, trice (redaktœr, tris) *n,* writer; drafter; editor; compiler. *~ en chef.* chief editor. **rédaction** (sjɔ̃) *f,* drafting; editing; editorial staff; (*Sch.*) essay, composition.
reddition (rɛddisjɔ̃) *f,* surrender.
redemander (rədmɑ̃de) *v.t,* to ask for again; ask

for more; ask for back.
rédempteur, trice (redɑ̃ptœr, tris) *a*, redeeming. ¶ *n*, redeemer. **rédemption** (psjɔ̃) *f*, redemption.
redescendre (rədɛsɑ̃dr) *v.i*, to come down again; fall again (*barometer*).
redevable (rədəvabl) *a*, indebted, beholden; liable. **redevance** (vɑ̃s) *f*, tax; fees, dues; licence fee; rental charge. **redevoir** (vwar) *v.t*, to still owe.
rédiger (rediʒe) *v.t*, to draw up, draft; write.
redire (rədir) *v.t.ir*, to say again; repeat. *trouver à ~ à*, to find fault with. **redite** (dit) *f*, repetition.
rédondance (rədɔ̃dɑ̃s) *f*, superfluity. **redondant, e** (dɑ̃, ɑ̃t) *a*, redundant; superfluous.
redonner (rədɔne) *v.t*, to give again; restore; give back; give more.
redoublement (rədubləmɑ̃) *m*, increase, intensification; reduplication; (*Sch.*) repeating a year. **redoubler** (ble) *v.t. & i*, to increase, intensify; redouble, step up; repeat a year.
redoutable (rədutabl) *a*, redoubtable, formidable. **redouter** (te) *v.t*, to dread, fear.
redressement (rədrɛsmɑ̃) *m*, setting upright, straightening, putting right, righting, correcting. **redresser** (se) *v.t*, to straighten; redress; right; put right.
réduction (redyksjɔ̃) *f*, reduction; reducing; cut; (*Mil.*) capture; quelling (*riot*). **réduire** (dɥir) *v.t.ir*, to reduce; boil down; shorten, lessen, cut; capture; quell. **réduit, e** (dɥi, it) *a*, scaled down; miniature; reduced; limited. ¶ *m*, small room, cubbyhole, recess; hideout.
rééditer (reedite) *v.t*, to republish, re-issue.
réel, le† (reɛl) *a*, real; actual. ¶ *m*, real[ity].
réélection (reelɛksjɔ̃) *f*, re-election. **rééligible** (liʒibl) *a*, re-eligible. **réélire** (lir) *v.t.ir*, to re-elect.
refaire (rəfɛr) *v.t.ir*, to remake, do [over] again; do up, repair; recover. **réfection** (refɛksjɔ̃) *f*, restoration. **réfectoire** (twar) *m*, refectory.
référence (referɑ̃s) *f*, reference; testimonial; footnote. **référendum** (referɛ̃dɔm) *m*, referendum. **référer** (fere) *v.t. & i*, **& se ~**, to refer. [*s*']*en ~ à qn*, to submit a matter to s.o.
refiler *P* (rəfile) *v.t*, to give; pass on; palm off *P*.
réfléchi, e (refleʃi) *a*, reflective; thoughtful; considered, deliberate; (*Gram.*) reflexive. **réfléchir** (ʃir) *v.t. & i*, to reflect; think over, ponder, consider. **réflecteur** (flɛktœr) *m*, reflector. **reflet** (rəflɛ) *m*, reflection; reflex; shimmer, glint; light, highlight (*hair*). **refléter** (flete) *v.t*, to reflect. **réflexe** (reflɛks) *a. & m*, reflex. **réflexif, ive** (ksif, iv) *a*, reflexive; introspective. **réflexion** (ksjɔ̃) *f*, reflection; thought; remark, comment.
refluer (rəflye) *v.i*, to flow back, ebb; surge. **reflux** (fly) *m*, reflux, ebb.
refondre (rəfɔ̃dr) *v.t*, to recast, remodel.
réformateur, trice (refɔrmatœr, tris) *n*, reformer. **réformation** (sjɔ̃) *f*, reformation. **réforme** (fɔrm) *f*, reform[ation]; (*Mil., Nav.*) discharge, invaliding.
reformer (rəfɔrme) *v.t*, to re-form.
réformer (refɔrme) *v.t*, to reform, amend; discharge, retire, invalid; (*Law*) reverse. **réformisme** (mism) *m*, reformism. **réformiste** (mist) *a. & n*, reformist.
refoulé, e (rəfule) *a*, inhibited, frustrated. **refouler** (rəfule) *v.t*, to drive back; stem; repress; force back (*tears*).
réfractaire (refraktɛr) *a*, refractory; fire[-proof]; ovenproof. *~ à*, impervious to; resistant to. ¶ (*Mil.*) *m*, defaulter.
réfracter (refrakte) *v.t*, to refract.
refrain (rəfrɛ̃) *m*, refrain, chorus.
refréner (rəfrene) *v.t*, to curb, bridle.
réfrigérateur (refriʒeratœr) *m*, refrigerator, fridge. **réfrigération** (rasjɔ̃) *f*, refrigeration; cooling. **réfrigérer** (ʒere) *v.t*, to refrigerate; cool.
refroidir (rəfrwadir) *v.t. & i*, **& se ~**, to cool, chill; (*fig.*) damp; get cold. **refroidissement** (dismɑ̃) *m*, cooling; (*Med.*) chill.
refuge (rɛfyʒ) *m*, refuge, shelter; traffic island; [mountain] hut. **réfugié, e** (refyʒje) *n*, refugee. **réfugier (se)** (ʒje) *v.pr*, to take refuge.
refus (rəfy) *m*, refusal. **refuser** (ze) *v.t*, to refuse, decline; deny; reject, turn down; fail (*exam*). **se ~**, to object, refuse, decline.
réfuter (refyte) *v.t*, to refute.
regagner (rəgaɲe) *v.t*, to regain, win back, recover; make up for; get back to.
regain (rəgɛ̃) *m*, (*Agric.*) second crop of hay; renewal; new lease (*of life*).
régal (regal) *m*, feast; treat. **régaler** (le) *v.t*, to entertain, feast; treat; regale. **se ~ de**, to have a feast on.
regard (rəgar) *m*, look, gaze, glance, eye(s); attention, notice; peep hole; manhole. *~ appuyé*, stare. *en ~*, opposite, facing. *en ~ de*, compared with. **regardant, e** (gardɑ̃, ɑ̃t) *a*, close-fisted, mean. **regarder** (de) *v.t*, to look (*at, on*), watch; see, eye; consider, regard, mind, be one's business; face, front. *~ fixement*, to stare at.
régate (regat) *f*, regatta.
régence (reʒɑ̃s) *f*, regency.
régénérer (reʒenere) *v.t*, to regenerate; revive, restore.
régent, e (reʒɑ̃, ɑ̃t) *n. & a*, regent. **régenter** (ʒɑ̃te) *v.t*, to dictate to; dominate; domineer.
régie (reʒi) *f*, (*Cine., Theat. &c*) production department; administration. *~ d'État*, State-owned company.
regimber (rəʒɛ̃be) *v.i*, to kick, jib.
régime (reʒim) *m*, system; [s. of] government; régime; regulations; diet; [engine] speed; (*Gram.*) object; bunch (*bananas &c*). ~

[*matrimonial*], marriage settlement. *à ce* ~, at this rate.
régiment (reʒimɑ̃) *m*, regiment. **régimentaire** (tɛr) *a*, regimental.
région (reʒjɔ̃) *f*, region, district. **régional, e** (ɔnal) *a*, regional.
régir (reʒir) *v.t*, to govern, rule, manage. **régisseur** (ʒisœr) *m*, manager, steward; stage manager; (*Cine. &c*) assistant director.
registre (rəʒistr) *m*, register. ~ *d'état civil*, register of births, marriages & deaths.
règle (rɛgl) *f*, rule; ruler; order. ~ *à calculer*, slide rule. **réglé, e** (regle) *a*, regular, steady; set, stated; ruled (*paper*). **règlement** (rɛgləmɑ̃) *m*, settlement, adjustment; regulation, rule. ~**aire** (tɛr) *a*, regulation; statutory. ~**er** (te) *v.t*, to regulate, control. **régler** (regle) *v.t*, to settle; s. up [with], pay; regulate, adjust; time; set, fix, decide on; determine; model (*sur*, on); rule [lines on].
réglisse (reglis) *f*, liquorice.
règne (rɛɲ) *m*, reign; sway; (*Nat. Hist.*) kingdom. **régner** (ɲe) *v.i*, to reign, rule; obtain; prevail.
regorger (rəgɔrʒe) *v.i. & t*, to overflow, brim, abound, teem; burst.
régresser (regrese) *v.i*, to regress; diminish; recede. **régressif, ive** (sif, iv) *a*, regressive. **régression** (sjɔ̃) *f*, regression; decline.
regret (rəgrɛ) *m*, regret. *à* ~, reluctantly. **regrettable** (tabl) *a*, regrettable, unfortunate. **le (la) regretté, e...** (te) the late lamented... **regretter** (te) *v.t*, to regret, be sorry (for); miss.
regrouper (rəgrupe) *v.t*, to group together; reassemble, regroup; round up (*cattle*).
régulariser (regylarize) *v.t*, to regularize, sort out; put in order, regulate. **régularité** (te) *f*, regularity, evenness; steadiness. **régulateur, trice** (tœr, tris) *a*, regulating. ¶ *m*, regulator. **régulation** (sjɔ̃) *f*, regulation; control. **régulier, ère†** (lje, ɛr) *a*, regular; steady, even; legitimate, in order; legal, official; aboveboard (*business*). ¶ (*Mil. &c*) *m*, regular.
réhabiliter (reabilite) *v.t*, to rehabilitate, reinstate; discharge (*bankrupt*).
rehausser (rəose) *v.t*, to raise; enhance; heighten; brighten up; emphasize (*detail &c*).
réimpression (reɛ̃prɛsjɔ̃) *f*, reprint[ing]. **réimprimer** (prime) *v.t*, to reprint.
rein (rɛ̃) *m*, kidney; (*pl.*) back. *avoir mal aux* ~*s*, to have backache.
reine (rɛn) *f*, queen (*pers. & Chess*). ~*-claude* (klod), greengage. ~*-des-prés*, meadowsweet. ~*-marguerite*, [China] aster.
reinette (rɛnɛt) *f*, pippin, rennet. ~ *grise*, russet (*apple*).
réintégrer (reɛ̃tegre) *v.t*, to reinstate; return to (*place*).
réitérer (reitere) *v.t*, to reiterate, repeat.
rejaillir (rəʒajir) *v.i*, to gush out; reflect, redound.
rejet (rəʒɛ) *m*, throwing out; rejection; (*Hort.*) shoot. **rejeter** (ʒ[ə]te) *v.t*, to throw back; t. out; t. up; reject, set aside, negative; dismiss; disallow. **rejeton** (ʒtɔ̃) *m*, shoot; offspring.
rejoindre (rəʒwɛ̃dr) *v.t.ir*, to rejoin, meet again; join; catch up.
rejouer (rəʒwe) *v.t. & i*, to replay; play again.
réjoui, e (reʒwi) *a*, joyous, joyful. **réjouir** (ʒwir) *v.t*, to delight. **se** ~, to be delighted (*or* thrilled) (*de*, about); rejoice. **réjouissance** (ʒwisɑ̃s) *f*, rejoicing; festivities. **réjouissant, e** (sɑ̃, ɑ̃t) *a*, amusing, entertaining; cheering; delightful.
relâche (rəlɑʃ) *m*, respite; (*Theat.*) closure. ¶ *f*, (*Naut.*) port of call. **relâcher** (lɑʃe) *v.t. & i*, to loosen, slacken; relax; release; (*Naut.*) put in.
relais (rəlɛ) *m*, (*gen.*) relay; shift; restaurant; coaching inn.
relancer (rəlɑ̃se) *v.t*, to throw back; revive, relaunch; badger, pester; (*Ind.*) boost.
relater (rəlate) *v.t*, to relate, state. **relatif, ive†** (tif, iv) *a*, relative, comparative; relating. ¶ (*Gram.*) *m*, relative pronoun. ¶ (*Gram.*) *f*, relative clause. **relation** (sjɔ̃) *f*, relationship; connection; (*pers.*) acquaintance; account, report. *en* ~ *avec*, in touch (*or* contact) with.
relativité (rəlativite) *f*, relativity.
relaxer (rəlakse) *v.t*, to relax; release; acquit.
relayer (rəleje) *v.t*, to relieve, take over from; (*Tel.*) relay. **relayeur, euse** (jœr, øz) *n*, relay runner.
reléguer (rəlege) *v.t*, to relegate.
relent (rəlɑ̃) *m*, bad odour.
relève (rəlɛv) *f*, relief (*from turn of duty*). **relevé, e** (lve) *a*, high, exalted, lofty; strong (*flavour*). ¶ *m*, statement, list; reading (*meter*); bill. ~ *de compte*, bank statement. **relèvement** (lɛvmɑ̃) *m*, raising, increasing; rise, increase; recovery (*economy &c*); (*Naut.*) plotting. **relever** (lve) *v.t*, to raise, lift [up]; pick up; turn up (*collar*); take up; restore; make out (*account*); read (*meter*); point out, note; set off, enhance; (*Cook*) season; relieve; release; (*Naut.*) plot. ¶ *v.i*, ~ *de*, to recover from (*illness*); to be a matter for *or* the concern of. **se** ~, to stand up [again]; turn up; lift up; recover. **releveur** (vœr)*m*, meter reader.
relief (rəljɛf) *m*, relief. *en* ~, in relief; raised, embossed. *mettre en* ~, to bring out, set off, enhance; emphasize, stress.
relier (rəlje) *v.t*, to link, join up; connect; bind (*book*). **relieur, euse** (jœr, øz) *n*, [book]binder.
religieux, euse† (rəliʒjø, øz) *a*, religious; sacred (*song &c*); church (*school &c*). ¶ *m*, monk. ¶ *f*, nun. **religion** (ʒjɔ̃) *f*, religion; vows; [religious] faith; monastic life.
reliquaire (rəlikɛr) *m*, reliquary.
reliquat (rəlika) *m*, balance, residue.

relique (rəlik) *f,* relic.
reliure (rəljyr) *f,* [book]binding.
relogement (rəlɔʒmɑ̃) *m,* rehousing. **reloger** (ʒe) *v.t,* to rehouse.
reluire (rəlɥir) *v.i.ir,* to shine, glitter. **reluisant, e** (lɥizɑ̃, ɑ̃t) *a,* shining; creditable; brilliant.
reluquer *P* (rəlyke) *v.t,* to ogle.
remâcher (rəmɑʃe) *v.t,* to chew again; ruminate on, brood over.
remanier (rəmanje) *v.t,* to revise; reshape; recast; reshuffle.
remarquable† (rəmarkabl) *a,* remarkable; noteworthy; conspicuous. **remarque** (mark) *f,* remark, note. **remarquer** (ke) *v.t,* to notice; remark, observe. *faire ~,* to point out.
remballer (rɑ̃bale) *v.t,* to repack.
rembarquer (rɑ̃barke) *v.t. & i,* to reembark.
rembarrer (rɑ̃bare) *v.t,* to rebuff.
remblai (rɑ̃blɛ) *m,* embankment. [*terre de*] *~,* ballast, hard core; (*Build.*) backfill. *~s récents,* soft verges. **remblayer** (je) *v.t,* to fill in; bank up.
remboîter (rɑ̃bwate) *v.t,* to put back in place; fit together again.
rembourrer (rɑ̃bure) *v.t,* to stuff, pad.
rembourser (rɑ̃burse) *v.t,* to repay; refund; reimburse.
rembrunir (rɑ̃brynir) *v.t.* & **se ~,** to darken.
remède (rəmɛd) *m,* remedy, cure; medicine. *~ de bonne femme,* folk remedy. **remédier à** (medje), to remedy, cure; solve.
remémorer (se) (rəmemɔre) *v.pr,* to remember.
remerciement (rəmɛrsimɑ̃) *m. oft. pl,* thanks. **remercier** (sje) *v.t,* to thank; dismiss.
remettre (rəmɛtr) *v.t.ir,* to put back [again]; put on again; restore; remit, send [in]; hand [over], deliver; commend; put off, postpone; remember; add. *~ ça P,* to go through it all again. *~ en question,* to challenge; cast doubt on. **se ~,** to recover, get better; start again. *~ avec qn,* to make it up with s.o.
réminiscence (reminisɑ̃s) *f,* reminiscence.
remise (rəmiz) *f,* putting back; restoration; remittance; remission; delivery; postponement; allowance, discount; reduction; shed. *~ à jour,* updating. *~ en cause,* calling into question. *~ en jeu,* throw-in. **remiser** (mize) *v.t,* to put away.
remontant, e (rəmɔ̃tɑ̃, ɑ̃t) *a,* invigorating. ¶ *m,* stimulant, tonic, pick-me-up. **remontée** (te) *f,* ascent, rise; recovery. **remonte-pente** (mɔ̃tpɑ̃t) *m,* (*Ski*) draglift. **remonter** (mɔ̃te) *v.i,* to go, come, climb back up; get back (*en voiture,* into a car). *~ à cheval,* to remount. (*skirt*) ride up; (*memories*) go back. ¶ *v.t,* to climb back up (*stairs*); take back up; raise (*wall*); wind up (*spring*); restock, replenish; set up again; cheer up. **se ~,** to stock up (*en* in); cheer o.s up. **remontoir** (twar) *m,* winder.
remontrance (rəmɔ̃trɑ̃s) *f,* remonstrance; reproof, reprimand. **remontrer** (tre) *v.t,* to show again.
remords (rəmɔr) *m,* remorse.
remorque (rəmɔrk) *f,* tow[ing]; trailer; tow-line. **remorquer** (ke) *v.t,* to tow, haul. **remorqueur** (kœr) *m,* tug [boat].
remous (rəmu) *m,* eddy, [back]wash, swirl.
rempart (rɑ̃par) *m,* rampart; (*fig.*) bulwark.
remplaçant, e (rɑ̃plasɑ̃, ɑ̃t) *n,* replacement, substitute; stand-in; supply teacher; locum; (*Sport*) reserve. **remplacement** (smɑ̃) *m,* replacement. **remplacer** (se) *v.t,* to replace; take the place of; substitute for, stand in for.
remplir (rɑ̃plir) *v.t,* to fill up, refill, replenish; fill; fulfil, comply with; perform. **remplissage** (plisaʒ) *m,* filling [up]; padding.
remplumer (se) *P* (rɑ̃plyme) *v.pr,* to put on flesh again; get back on one's feet.
remporter (rɑ̃pɔrte) *v.t,* to take away; carry off, win, gain.
remuant, e (rəmɥɑ̃, ɑ̃t) *a,* restless. **remue-ménage** (mymenaʒ) *m,* bustle, stir, upset. **remuement** (mɑ̃) *m,* moving. **remuer** (mɥe) *v.t. & i,* to move; stir (*tea*); poke, rake up; shake; wag, flick (*tail*); remove, shift; toss (*salad*).
rémunérateur, trice (remyneratœr, trice) *a,* remunerative, paying. **rémunération** (sjɔ̃) *f,* remuneration, payment. **rémunérer** (re) *v.t,* to remunerate, pay for, reward.
renâcler (rənɑkle) *v.i,* to snort; hang back.
renaissance (rənɛsɑ̃s) *f,* rebirth; revival; renaissance. **renaître** (nɛtr) *v.i.ir,* to be revived; spring up again; recur; (*day*) dawn; come back to life.
renard (rənar) *m,* fox. **renarde** (nard) *f,* vixen. **renardeau** (do) *m,* fox cub.
renchérir (rɑ̃ʃerir) *v.i,* to get dearer, go up; (*pers.*) go further. *~ sur,* to go further than, improve on. **renchérissement** (rismɑ̃) *m,* rise in the price.
rencontre (rɑ̃kɔ̃tr) *f,* meeting, encounter; collision. *aller à la ~ de,* to go to meet. **rencontrer** (kɔ̃tre) *v.t,* to meet, m. with, encounter, come across, strike; run into, collide with.
rendement (rɑ̃dmɑ̃) *m,* yield, return; output, capacity; efficiency. **rendez-vous** (devu) *m,* appointment; place of meeting; date. *~ de chasse,* meet. *~ spatial,* docking [in space].
rendormir (rɑ̃dɔrmir) *v.t.ir,* to send to sleep again. **se ~,** to go to sleep again.
rendre (rɑ̃dr) *v.t,* to give back, return; restore; give up; render; give; pay; dispense; repay; yield; deliver; surrender; bring up (*food*); make; drive (*one mad*). *~ du poids,* (*Turf*), to have a weight handicap. *~ hommage,* to pay tribute. *~ la pareille à qn,* to do the same for s.o. *~ visite à,* to visit (*pers.*) ¶ *v.i,* to yield, be productive; be sick, vomit. **se ~,** to make oneself; go; surrender, yield. *~ compte*

de, to realize, be aware of. **rendu, e** (rɑ̃dy) *a,* exhausted, worn out. ¶ *m,* (*Com.*) return.
rêne (rɛn) *f,* rein.
renégat, e (rənega, at) *n,* renegade.
renfermé (rɑ̃fɛrme) *m,* musty smell. **renfermer** (me) *v.t,* to contain. **se ~,** to withdraw.
renflement (rɑ̃fləmɑ̃) *m,* bulge. **renfler** (fle) *v.i,* to swell.
renflouer (rɑ̃flue) *v.t,* to refloat (*ship*).
renfoncement (rɑ̃fɔ̃smɑ̃) *m,* recess. **renfoncer** (se) *v.t,* to drive in; knock in; indent.
renforcer (rɑ̃forse) *v.t,* to reinforce; strengthen, brace; intensify. **renfort** (fɔr) *m,* (*Mil.*) reinforcement. *de ~,* strengthening, supporting; extra. *à grand ~ de,* with plenty of.
renfrogner (se) (rɑ̃frɔɲe) *v.pr,* to frown, scowl, look sullen.
rengager (rɑ̃gaʒe) *v.t,* to re-engage; start up again; reinvest. **se ~,** to re-enlist.
rengaine (rɑ̃gɛn) *f,* hackneyed expression; old song.
rengainer (rɑ̃gɛne) *v.t,* to sheathe; suppress.
rengorger (se) (rɑ̃gɔrʒe) *v.pr,* to strut, swagger.
renier (rənje) *v.t,* to disown, deny.
renifler (rənifle) *v.i. & t,* to sniff; snuffle; snort.
renne (rɛn) *m,* reindeer.
renom (rənɔ̃) *m,* renown, fame; repute. **renommé, e** (nɔme) *a,* renowned, famed, noted. ¶ *f,* fame, renown, name. **renommer** (me) *v.t,* to reappoint.
renoncement (rənɔ̃smɑ̃) *m,* renunciation, self-denial. **renoncer** (se) *v.i. & t. & ~* **à,** to renounce, give up, forgo. **renonciation** (sjasjɔ̃) *f,* renunciation, giving up.
renoncule (rənɔ̃kyl) *f,* ranunculus, buttercup.
renouer (rənwe) *v.t,* to retie; renew, resume.
renouveau (rənuvo) *m,* revival, renewal. **renouvelable** (vlabl) *a,* renewable. **renouveler** (vle) *v.t,* to renew; revive; replenish; repeat; re-elect. **se ~,** to recur, be renewed. **renouvellement** (vɛlmɑ̃) *m,* renewal, revival; repetition; replenishment. **rénover** (renɔve) *v.t,* to renovate, restore; reform; renew.
renseignement (rɑ̃sɛɲmɑ̃) *m. oft. pl,* information, intelligence, particular; inquiry. **renseigner** (ɲe) *v.t,* to inform. **se ~,** to inquire.
rentable (rɑ̃tabl) *a,* profitable. **rentabilité** (bilite) *f,* profitability.
rente (rɑ̃t) *f,* annuity; pension; interest; stock; private income; allowance. **rentier, ère** (tje, ɛr) *n,* person of independent means.
rentrant, e (rɑ̃trɑ̃, ɑ̃t) *a,* retractable; (*Math.*) reflex (*angle*). **rentrée** (tre) *f,* start of a new school (*or* academic) year (*or* term); return; re-entry; reopening; reassembly; (*Theat. &c*) comeback; (*Com. pl*) income. **rentrer** (tre) *v.i,* to re-enter; return; reappear; reopen; come (*or* go) back in; start [school] again. *~ dans l'ordre,* to return to normal. *se ~ dans ses frais,* to recover one's expenses. ¶ *v.t,* to bring in, put away (*car*); draw in (*claws*).
renverse (à la) (rɑ̃vɛrs) *ad,* (*fall*) backwards, on one's back. **renversement** (smɑ̃) *m,* reversal, inversion; overthrow (*government &c*); defeat. **renverser** (se) *v.t,* to overturn, upset; overthrow; invert, reverse; astound. *se ~ sur sa chaise,* to lean (*or* lie) back (*or* recline) in one's chair.
renvoi (rɑ̃vwa) *m,* return; dismissal; postponement; reference; footnote. **renvoyer** (je) *v.t,* to send back, return; dismiss; suspend; expel; put off, adjourn; refer; echo; reflect. *~ à une autre audience,* to remand.
réorganiser (reɔrganize) *v.t,* to reorganize.
réouverture (reuvɛrtyr) *f,* reopening.
repaire (rəpɛr) *m,* den, lair; nest; haunt.
repaître (se) (rəpɛtr) *v.pr, ~ de,* to gorge o.s on; revel in.
répandre (repɑ̃dr) *v.t,* to pour out, spill, shed; spread, diffuse; waft; scatter, sprinkle. **répandu, e** (pɑ̃dy) *a,* widespread; well known.
réparable (reparabl) *a,* repairable.
reparaître (rəparɛtr) *v.i.ir,* to reappear.
réparateur, trice (reparatœr, tris) *n,* repairer, mender. ¶ *a,* refreshing (*sleep*). **réparation** (sjɔ̃) *f,* repair, mending, fixing; compensation, damages, reparation; amends, atonement, redress. **réparer** (re) *v.t,* to repair, mend; retrieve; make amends for; make up for; redress; rectify.
repartie (rəparti) *f,* repartee, retort, rejoinder. **repartir** (tir) *v.i.ir,* to set out again.
répartir (repartir) *v.t,* to distribute, apportion, allot; assess; spread. **répartition** (tisjɔ̃) *f,* distribution, &c.
repas (rəpɑ) *m,* meal. *~ de noce,* wedding breakfast.
repassage (rəpasaʒ) *m,* ironing; sharpening. **repasser** (se) *v.t,* to cross again; resit (*exam*); show again (*film*); put back; iron (*linen &c*); sharpen (*blade*); go over, think over; hand over (*or* back); go past again. ¶ *v.i,* to come (*or* go) back.
repêcher (rəpɛʃe) *v.t,* to fish up, f. out; give a second chance to (*athlete*); (*Sch.*) let through (*candidate*).
repentir (rəpɑ̃tir) *m,* repentance. **se ~,** *v.pr.ir,* to repent. **se ~ de,** to repent, be sorry for.
répercussion (repɛrkysjɔ̃) *f,* repercussion. **répercuter** (te) *v.t,* to reverberate.
repère (rəpɛr) *m,* reference mark, landmark; marker, indicator. **repérer** (pere) *v.t,* to mark; locate, spot. **se ~,** to find one's way about, get one's bearings.
répertoire (repɛrtwar) *m,* index, list; catalogue; repertory; repertoire. **répertorier** (tɔrje) *v.t,* to list, itemize.
répéter (repete) *v.t,* to repeat; rehearse; learn, practice. **répétition** (sjɔ̃) *f,* repetition; rehearsal. *~ générale,* dress rehearsal.

repeupler (rəpœple) *v.t*, to repopulate; restock; replant.
repiquer (rəpike) *v.t*, to prick again; restitch; plant out; (*mosquito*) bite again; record, tape.
répit (repi) *m*, respite.
replacer (rəplase) *v.t*, to replace; reinvest.
replanter (rəplɑ̃te) *v.t*, to replant.
replâtrer (rəplɑtre) *v.t*, to replaster; patch up.
replet, ète (rəplɛ, ɛt) *a*, stout, podgy (*pers.*).
repli (rəpli) *m*, fold, crease; recess (*heart*); (*Mil.*) falling back. **replier** (plie) *v.t*, to fold up, f. over; withdraw (*troops*). **se ~**, to fall back, withdraw.
réplique (replik) *f*, retort, rejoinder, answer; (*Theat.*) cue; replica. **répliquer** (ke) *v.t*, to retort, rejoin, answer [back].
répondant, e (repɔ̃dɑ̃, ɑ̃t) *n*, surety, guarantor. *avoir du ~*, to have money behind one. **répondeur** (dœr) *m*, telephone answering machine. **répondre** (pɔ̃dr) *v.t. & i*, to answer, reply; (*controls*) respond; *~ à*, to answer (*description*); come up to (*expectation*). *~ de*, to answer for, vouch for. **réponse** (pɔ̃s) *f*, answer, reply; response. *~ de Normand*, evasive answer.
report (rəpɔr) *m*, carry forward; c. over; continuation; postponement. **reportage** (pɔrtaʒ) *m*, reporting; report (*news*). **reporter** (te) *v.t*, to carry forward; c. over; bring forward; take back; put off, postpone; defer; transfer (*vote &c*). **se ~ à**, to refer to; think back to. **reporter** (tɛr) *m*, reporter (*news*).
repos (rəpo) *m*, rest, repose; peace & quiet; pause (*in speech*); (*Mus.*) cadence. *jour de ~*, day off. **reposant, e** (zɑ̃, ɑ̃t) *a*, restful. **reposer** (ze) *v.t*, to replace, put back [down]; rest; order (*arms*); repeat (*question*); bring up again (*problem*). ¶ *v.i*, to rest, lie; (*liquid*) settle. **se ~**, to rest, lie down. *~ sur qn*, to rely on s.o.
repoussant, e (rəpusɑ̃, ɑ̃t) *a*, repulsive. **repoussé, e** (se) *a*, repoussé; embossed. **repousser** (se) *v.t*, to push back; repel, repulse; reject; put off, postpone. ¶ *v.i*, to grow again.
répréhensible (repreɑ̃sibl) *a*, reprehensible.
reprendre (rəprɑ̃dr) *v.t.ir*, to recapture; take up [again]; take back; resume; take more; regain, recover; (*Com.*) take in part exchange; take over (*factory*); reopen (*hostilities*); catch [again]; (*Need.*) alter; take in (*or* up), let out (*or* down); touch up (*picture*); go over again; reprimand, tell off *P*; correct. ¶ *v.i.ir*, to take root again; pick up; start again. **se ~**, to correct o.s; stop o.s, pull o.s together.
représaille (rəprezɑj) *f. oft. pl*, reprisal, retaliation.
représentant, e (rəprezɑ̃tɑ̃, ɑ̃t) *n*, representative; agent. **représentatif, ive** (tatif, iv) *a*, representative. **représentation** (sjɔ̃) *f*, representation; description, portrayal; (*Theat. &c*) performance; commercial travelling. **représenter** (te) *v.t*, to represent; depict, portray, show; perform, play; put on, stage. ¶ *v.i*, *~ bien*, to have a fine presence. **se ~**, to imagine; occur again, arise again. *~ à*, to resit (*exam*); stand again (*election*).
répression (reprɛsjɔ̃) *f*, repression.
réprimande (reprimɑ̃d) *f*, reprimand, reproof, rebuke. **réprimander** (mɑ̃de) *v.t*, to reprimand, reprove, rebuke.
réprimer (reprime) *v.t*, to suppress; quell, put down; hold back (*tears &c*).
repris de justice (rəpri) *m*, ex-convict. **reprise** (priz) *f*, resumption; renewal, re-opening; return; revival, recovery; rerun (*film*); (*TV &c*) repeat; (*Box.*) round; (*Mot. pl.*) acceleration; (*Com.*) taking back, part exchange; darn[ing]; repair. *à plusieurs ~s*, several times, on several occasions. *~ perdue*, invisible mending. **repriser** (prize) *v.t*, to darn, mend.
réprobation (reprɔbasjɔ̃) *f*, reprobation.
reproche (rəprɔʃ) *m*, reproach, blame. **reprocher** (ʃe) *v.t*, to reproach, blame. *~ à*, to find fault with, hold against.
reproduction (rəprɔdyksjɔ̃) *f*, reproduction; repeat, copy. **reproduire** (dɥir) *v.t.ir*, to reproduce, repeat, copy. **se ~**, to recur; reproduce, breed.
réprouvé, e (repruve) *n*, reprobate. **réprouver** (ve) *v.t*, to reprove; disapprove of; condemn; damn.
reptile (rɛptil) *m*, reptile; snake; (*pej: pers.*) creep.
républicain, e (repyblikɛ̃, ɛn) *a. & n*, republican. **république** (lik) *f*, republic.
répudier (repydje) *v.t*, to repudiate; renounce.
répugnance (repyɲɑ̃s) *f*, repugnance; reluctance. **répugnant, e** (ɲɑ̃, ɑ̃t) *a*, repugnant, revolting, disgusting. **répugner** (ɲe) *v.i*, to be repugant (*à*, to); be loath, reluctant (*à faire*, to do).
répulsif, ive (repylsif, iv) *a*, repulsive. **répulsion** (sjɔ̃) *f*, repulsion.
réputation (repytasjɔ̃) *f*, reputation, repute; name. **réputé, e** (te) *a*, well known; of repute, reputable, renowned.
requérir (rəkerir) *v.t.ir*, to require, call for; request, demand. **requête** (kɛt) *f*, request, petition.
requiem (rekɥiɛm) *m*, requiem.
requin (rəkɛ̃) *m*, shark (*also fig.*).
requinquer (se) *P* (rəkɛ̃ke) *v.pr*, to perk up.
requis, e (rəki, iz) *a*, requisite, required. ¶ *m*, labour conscript (*in war &c*).
réquisition (rekizisjɔ̃) *f*, requisition; conscription. **réquisitionner** (ɔne) *v.t*, to requisition, commandeer; conscript. **réquisitoire** (twar) *m*, indictment; closing speech for the prosecution.

rescapé, e (rɛskape) *n,* survivor.
rescousse (à la) (rɛskus), to the rescue.
réseau (rezo) *m,* network; system. ~ *express régional* (*RER*), fast commuter service (*Paris region*).
réséda (rezeda) *m,* reseda, mignonette.
réservation (rezɛrvasjɔ̃) *f,* reservation. **réserve** (zɛrv) *f,* (*gen., Mil.*) reserve; reservation; stock; (*Hunt.*) preserve; sanctuary (*animals*). *sous ~ de,* subject to. *sous ~ que,* on condition that. **réservé, e** (ve) *a,* reserved; cautious, guarded. **réserver** (ve) *v.t,* to reserve, keep, save; book; have in store. **réserviste** (vist) *m,* reservist. **réservoir** (vwar) *m,* reservoir; tank, cistern; gasometer; fishpond.
résidence (rezidɑ̃s) *f,* residence, dwelling. **résident, e** (dɑ̃, ɑ̃t) *n. & a,* resident. **résider** (de) *v.i,* to reside, dwell, live; lie, rest. **résidu** (dy) *m,* residue; (*Math.*) remainder; (*pl.*) remnants, residue; waste. **résiduel, le** (dyɛl) *a,* residual.
résignation (reziɲasjɔ̃) *f,* resignation. **résigner (se)** (ɲe) *v.pr,* to resign o.s.
résilier (rezilje) *v.t,* to terminate (*contract*).
résine (rezin) *f,* resin, rosin. **résineux, euse** (nø, øz) *a,* resinous.
résistance (rezistɑ̃s) *f,* resistance; opposition; endurance, stamina; element (*heater &c*). **résistant, e** (tɑ̃, ɑ̃t) *a,* resistant, strong, tough. ¶ *n,* Resistance fighter. **résister à** (te), to resist, withstand; stand [up to]; hold out against.
résolu†, e (rezɔly) *a,* resolute, determined. **résolution** (sjɔ̃) *f,* resolution; solution; resolve.
résonance (rezɔnɑ̃s) *f,* resonance. **résonateur** (natœr) *m,* resonator. **résonnant, e** (nɑ̃, ɑ̃t) *a,* resonant. **resonner** (ne) *v.i,* to resound; reverberate, resonate; echo, ring.
résorber (rezɔrbe) *v.t,* to resorb, absorb; reduce gradually. **résorption** (ɔrpsjɔ̃) *f,* resorption &c.
résoudre (rezudr) *v.t.ir,* to resolve, solve; decide on. ~ *de faire & se ~ à faire,* to decide to do.
respect (rɛspɛ) *m,* respect, regard, deference. **respectable** (pɛktabl) *a,* respectable. **respecter** (te) *v.t,* to respect; have respect for. **respectif, ive†** (tif, iv) *a,* respective. **respectueux, euse†** (tɥø, øz) *a,* respectful. ~ *des lois,* law-abiding.
respiration (rɛspirasjɔ̃) *f,* respiration, breathing, breath. **respiratoire** (ratwar) *a,* respiratory, breathing. **respirer** (re) *v.i. & t,* to breathe; get one's breath; inhale; exude, radiate.
resplendir (rɛsplɑ̃dir) *v.i,* to shine, glitter. **resplendissant, e** (disɑ̃, ɑ̃t) *a,* resplendent; aglow; glorious.
responsabilité (rɛspɔ̃sabilite) *f,* responsibility; liability. **responsable** (bl) *a,* responsible, answerable, liable. ¶ *n,* person in charge, official; person responsible (*or* to blame), culprit.
resquiller (rɛskije) *v.i,* to fiddle a free seat (*bus*); get in without paying; jump the queue. **resquilleur, euse** (kijœr, øz) *n,* queue-jumper; faredodger.
ressac (rəsak) *m,* undertow; surf.
ressaisir (rəsɛzir) *v.t,* to recover; recapture; take (*or* catch) hold of again. **se ~,** to regain one's self-control; rally, pull o.s together. ~ *de,* to seize again.
ressasser (rəsase) *v.t,* to repeat again & again; turn over (*in one's mind*).
ressemblance (rəsɑ̃blɑ̃s) *f,* resemblance, likeness. **ressemblant, e** (blɑ̃, ɑ̃t) *a,* [a]like; lifelike, true to life (*portrait*). **ressembler à** (ble), to resemble, be like, look like.
ressemeler (rəsəmle) *v.t,* to resole.
ressentiment (rəsɑ̃timɑ̃) *m,* resentment. **ressentir** (tir) *v.t.ir,* to feel; experience. **se ~ de,** to feel the effects of.
resserre (rəsɛr) *f,* store [room]. **resserrer** (sɛre) *v.t,* to tighten; strengthen; squeeze (*credit*). **se ~,** to tighten; grow stronger; draw in; narrow; close.
ressort (rəsɔr) *m,* spring; spirit; (*Law*) jurisdiction; responsibility. ~ *à boudin,* spiral spring. *à ~,* spring-loaded. *être du ~ de,* to fall within the competence of. **ressortir** (sɔrtir) *v.i,* to be under the jurisdiction of. ¶ *v.i.ir,* to go out again; stand out (*in relief*); result, appear. ¶ *v.t.ir,* to bring (*or* take) out again. **ressortissant, e** (tisɑ̃, ɑ̃t) *n,* national.
ressource (rəsurs) *f,* resource; possibility; means; resort.
ressouvenir (se) (rəsuvnir) *v.pr.ir,* to remember.
ressusciter (resysite) *v.t,* to resuscitate, revive; raise (*the dead*). ¶ *v.i,* to revive; come back to life; rise [from the dead].
restant, e (rɛstɑ̃, ɑ̃t) *a,* remaining, left. ¶ *m,* remainder, rest.
restaurant (rɛstɔrɑ̃) *m,* restaurant. **restaurateur, trice** (ratœr, tris) *n,* restorer; restaurant keeper, caterer. **restauration** (sjɔ̃) *f,* restoration. **restaurer** (re) *v.t,* to restore, refresh. **se ~,** to have sth to eat.
reste (rɛst) *m,* rest, remainder, remains; leavings, remnant; (*pl.*) left-overs; [mortal] remains. *du ~,* besides, moreover. **rester** (te) *v.i,* to remain, be left; stay, stop; stand, sit; stick; last; live. *reste à savoir si,* it remains to be seen whether. *y ~ P,* to meet one's end.
restituer (rɛstitɥe) *v.t,* to restore, return; release (*energy &c*); reproduce (*sound*). **restitution** (tysjɔ̃) *f,* restitution; restoration, return; release.
restreindre (rɛstrɛ̃dr) *v.t.ir,* to restrict, limit; cut down; decrease; narrow. **restriction** (triksjɔ̃) *f,* restriction; reservation; qualification.
résultante (rezultɑ̃t) *f,* resultant; outcome, result, consequence. **résultat** (ta) *m,* result, outcome. **résulter** (te) *v.i,* to result, follow,

ensue.
résumé (rezyme) *m,* summary, abstract. *en* ~, in short; to sum up; in miniature. **résumer** (me) *v.t,* to summarize; sum up; typify. **se** ~ **à,** to amount to.
résurrection (rezyrɛksjɔ̃) *f,* resurrection.
rétablir (retablir) *v.t,* to re-establish, restore; retrieve; reinstate. **se** ~, to recover; return, be restored; pull o.s up. **rétablissement** (blismɑ̃) *m,* re-establishment &c.
retaper (rətape) *v.t,* to do up; fix up; straighten (*bed*); retype. **se** ~ *P,* to get back on one's feet.
retard (rətar) *m,* delay; lateness; (*country &c*) backwardness. *en* ~, late, behind[-hand]; overdue; in arrears; slow (*clock*). **retardataire** (tardatɛr) *a,* late; obsolete. ¶ *n,* late-comer. **à retardement** (dmɑ̃) delayed action; time[d]; self-timing. **retarder** (de) *v.t,* to retard, delay; hinder; put off; put back (*clock*). ¶ *v.i,* be slow; lose.
retenir (rətnir) *v.t.ir,* to keep back, retain, withhold, stop; keep; engage; reserve, book; detain; hold; h. back, check, restrain; remember; (*Arith.*) carry; accept (*plan &c*). **se** ~, to restrain o.s. ~ *à,* to hold on to. **rétention** (retɑ̃sjɔ̃) *f,* retention.
retentir (rətɑ̃tir) *v.i,* to [re]sound, ring. ~ *sur,* to affect. **retentissement** (tismɑ̃) *m,* effect, stir; (*pl.*) repercussions.
retenue (rətny) *f,* self-control, restraint; reserve; discretion; stoppage (*pay &c*); (*Arith.*) carry; (*Sch.*) detention.
réticence (retisɑ̃s) *f,* reticence; reluctance; (*pl.*) hesitations, reservations. **réticent, e** (sɑ̃, ɑ̃t) *a,* reticent &c.
rétif, ive (retif, iv) *a,* restive.
rétine (retin) *f,* retina.
retiré, e (rətire) *a,* solitary, secluded, remote. **retirer** (re) *v.t,* to redraw; draw back; withdraw; take out; remove; extract; draw, get, derive; recall. **se** ~, to retire, withdraw; stand down; recede; shrink.
retombée (rətɔ̃be) *f,* spring[ing] (*arch*); spin off; (*pl.*) fall-out. **retomber** (be) *v.i,* to fall [again], land; come down; fall [back] down; (*interest &c*) fall away. ~ *dans,* to lapse into; sink into. ~ *sur ses pieds,* to land on one's feet.
rétorquer (retɔrke) *v.t,* to retort.
retouche (rətuʃ) *f,* retouch[ing], alteration. **retoucher** (ʃe) *v.t.* & ~ **à,** to retouch, touch up; alter (*garment*); hit again.
retour (rətur) *m,* return; r. ticket; r. journey. ~ *d'âge,* change of life. ~ *de flamme,* backfire; blowback. ~ *de manivelle,* kick; backlash. ~ *en arrière,* flashback; look back; retreat. *en* ~, in return. *être de* ~, to be back [home]. *sans* ~, (*go*) for ever; final (*journey*). **retourner** (ne) *v.t,* to turn; t. up; t. upside down; t. over; t. round; t. back; return; toss (*salad*); (*P*) shake (*pers.*). ¶ *v.i,* to return, go back. ~ *sur ses pas,* to retrace one's steps. **se** ~, to turn over; t. [round]; look back; wrench, twist. *s'en* ~, to go back. ~ *contre,* to turn against, rebound on.
retracer (rətrase) *v.t,* to recount; redraw.
rétracter (retrakte) *v.t,* to retract; withdraw.
retrait (rətrɛ) *m,* ebb; retreat; withdrawal; collection; redemption. **retraite** (trɛt) *f,* retreat; retirement; r. pension; hideout, lair. **retraité, e** (te) *a,* retired. ¶ *n,* [old age] pensioner.
retranchement (rətrɑ̃ʃmɑ̃) *m,* (*Mil.*) entrenchment, retrenchment. **retrancher** (ʃe) *v.t,* to take away, subtract, deduct; cut off; remove; take out. **se** ~, to entrench o.s; take refuge.
rétrécir (retresir) *v.t,* to shrink; take in; contract; narrow; tighten. ¶ *v.i.* & **se** ~, to shrink; contract; [grow] narrow; get smaller.
rétribuer (retribɥe) *v.t,* to pay. **rétribution** (bysjɔ̃) *f,* payment, reward.
rétroactif, ive† (retroaktif, iv) *a,* retroactive, retrospective (*law*).
rétrograde (retrɔgrad) *a,* retrograde, backward. **rétrograder** (de) *v.t,* to fall back; move back; regress; (*Mot.*) change down. ¶ *v.t,* to demote.
rétrospectif, ive† (retrɔspɛktif, iv) *a,* retrospective.
retroussé, e (rətruse) *a,* turned-up (*nose*); curled up (*moustache*). **retrousser** (se) *v.t,* to tuck up; hitch up; roll up; curl up (*lip*). **se** ~, (*edges*) to turn outwards.
retrouvailles (rətruvaj) *f.pl,* reunion.
retrouver (rətruve) *v.t,* to find [again], rediscover; regain; meet (*or* see) again. *s'y* ~, to find one's way; (*P*) break even; make a profit.
rétroviseur (retrɔvizœr) *m,* rear-view mirror. ~ [*d'aile*], wing mirror.
réunion (reynjɔ̃) *f,* reunion; assembly, gathering, function, meeting. ~ *hippique,* horse-show, gymkhana. **réunir** (nir) *v.t,* to collect, gather; combine; join, unite; raise (*funds*); call a meeting of; entertain (*friends &c*); reunite. **se** ~, to meet, get together; combine, unite; (*rivers*) merge.
réussi, e (reysi) *a,* successful. **réussir** (sir) *v.i,* to succeed; prosper; do well; pass (*à un examen,* an exam). ~ *à faire,* to succeed in doing, manage to do. ~ *à qn* (*climate &c*) to agree with s.o.¶ *v.t,* to make a success of; bring off. **réussite** (sit) *f,* success; (*Cards*) patience.
revaloir (rəvalwar) *v.t.ir,* to pay (*s.o*) back; get even with (*s.o*).
revanche (rəvɑ̃ʃ) *f,* revenge; return match. *en* ~, on the other hand.
rêvasser (rɛvase) *v.i,* to daydream. **rêve** (rɛv) *m,* dream; day dream.
revêche (rəvɛʃ) *a,* cantankerous.
réveil (revɛj) *m,* waking, awakening; (*Rel.*) revival; reveille; alarm clock. **réveille-matin**

(vɛj) *m,* alarm clock. **réveiller** (vɛje) *v.t,* to awake[n], wake[n], call, [a]rouse; revive. **se ~**, to wake [up]; revive; start up again; regain consciousness; be roused. **réveillon** (jɔ̃) *m,* Christmas Eve *or* New Year's Eve dinner. **réveillonner** (jɔne) *v.i,* to celebrate Christmas *or* New Year's Eve.

révélateur, trice (revelatœr, tris) *a,* revealing. ¶ *m,* (*Phot.*) developer; (*liter.*) revelation. **révélation** (sjɔ̃) *f,* revelation; disclosure; eye-opener. **révéler** (le) *v.t,* to reveal, disclose, make known; discover, bring to fame (*actor &c*).

revenant (rəvnɑ̃) *m,* ghost.

revendeur, euse (rəvɑ̃dœr, øz) *n,* secondhand dealer; retailer.

revendiquer (rəvɑ̃dike) *v.t,* to claim, demand.

revendre (rəvɑ̃dr) *v.t,* to resell. *avoir à ~*, to have enough & to spare.

revenir (rəvnir) *v.i.ir,* to come [back], return; come again, recur; revert. *~ à,* to amount to, cost. *~ de,* to recover from. *~ sur,* to retrace; go back on; reconsider; rake up (*past*). *faire ~*, (*Cook.*) to brown. **s'en ~**, to come back.

revente (rəvɑ̃t) *f,* resale.

revenu (rəvny) *m,* revenue, income.

rêver (rɛve) *v.i. & t,* to dream; d. of; muse; ponder.

réverbère (revɛrbɛr) *m,* street lamp. **réverbérer** (bere) *v.t,* to reverberate; reflect (*light*).

révérence (reverɑ̃s) *f,* reverence; bow, curts[e]y. **révérencieux, euse**† (sjø, øz) *a,* obsequious; reverential. **révérend, e** (rɑ̃, ɑ̃d) *a,* reverend. **révérer** (re) *v.t,* to revere, reverence.

rêverie (rɛvri) *f,* reverie, musing; idle fancy.

revers (rəvɛr) *m,* reverse; back; backhand [stroke, blow]; lapel; turn-up (*trousers*); cuff; top (*boots*).

reverser (rəvɛrse) *v.t,* to pour out more; put back, pay back.

réversible (revɛrsibl) *a,* reversible; revertible. **réversion** (sjɔ̃) *f,* reversion.

revêtement (rəvɛtmɑ̃) *m,* facing (*wall &c*); coating; covering; surface (*road*); flooring. **revêtir** (tir) *v.t.ir,* to clothe, dress; don, put on; assume; face, cover, surface; coat.

rêveur, euse† (rɛvœr, øz) *a,* dreamy. ¶ *n,* dreamer.

revigorer (rəvigɔre) *v.t,* to reinvigorate.

revirement (rəvirmɑ̃) *m,* change, reversal.

reviser (rəvize) *v.t,* to revise; review, reconsider; (*Mot.*) service; overhaul; audit. **revision** (zjɔ̃) *or* **révision** (revizjɔ̃) *f,* revision; review[ing] &c.

revivifier (rəvivifje) *v.t,* to revive. **revivre** (vivr) *v.i.ir,* to live again, come to life again; revive. ¶ *v.t,* to relive.

révocation (revɔkasjɔ̃) *f,* revocation; repeal; dismissal, removal.

revoici (rəvwasi) *pr,* here . . . again. *le ~*, here he is again. **revoilà** (la) *pr,* there . . . again.

revoir (rəvwar) *v.t.ir,* to see again, meet again; revise; review. *au ~!* good-bye!

revoler (rəvɔle) *v.i,* to fly again; fly back.

révoltant, e (revɔltɑ̃, ɑ̃t) *a,* revolting. **révolte** (vɔlt) *f,* revolt. **révolté, e** (te) *n,* rebel. **révolter** (te) *v.t,* to revolt, outrage, appal. **se ~**, to revolt, rebel.

révolu, e (revɔly) *a,* past. *des jours ~s,* days gone by. *il a 10 ans ~s,* he is over 10. **révolution** (sjɔ̃) *f,* revolution; uproar. **~naire** (ɔnɛr) *a. & n,* revolutionary. **~ner** (ne) *v.t,* to revolutionize; upset. **revolver** (revɔlvɛr) *m,* revolver (*gun*).

révoquer (revɔke) *v.t,* to revoke, repeal; dismiss; recall.

revue (rəvy) *f,* review, inspection; magazine; revue.

révulser (se) (revylse) *v.pr,* to contort; roll upwards (*eyes*).

rez-de-chaussée (redʃose) *m,* ground floor.

rhabiller (rabije) *v.t,* to dress again, reclothe.

rhapsodie (rapsɔdi) *f,* rhapsody.

rhénan, e (renɑ̃, an) *a,* Rhine.

rhésus (rezys) *m,* Rhesus.

rhétorique (retɔrik) *f,* rhetoric. ¶ *a,* rhetorical.

Rhin (le) (rɛ̃), the Rhine.

rhinocéros (rinɔserɔs) *m,* rhinoceros.

rhinopharyngite (rinɔfarɛ̃ʒit) *f,* sore throat; throat infection.

rhododendron (rɔdɔdɛ̃drɔ̃) *m,* rhododendron.

rhubarbe (rybarb) *f,* rhubarb.

rhum (rɔm) *m,* rum.

rhumatismal, e (rymatismal) *a,* rheumatic. **rhumatisme** (tism) *m. oft. pl,* rheumatism. **rhumatologie** (tɔlɔʒi) *f,* rheumatology. **rhume** (rym) *m,* cold (*de cerveau, de poitrine.* in the head, on the chest). *~ des foins,* hay fever.

riant, e (riɑ̃, ɑ̃t) *a,* smiling; cheerful.

ribambelle (ribɑ̃bɛl) *f,* string; swarm.

ribouldingue *P* (ribuldɛ̃g) *f,* spree.

ricaner (rikane) *v.i,* to snigger, giggle.

richard, e *P* (riʃar) *n,* moneybags *P.* **riche**† (riʃ) *a,* rich, wealthy; copious; valuable; handsome. *~ de,* full of. *~ en,* rich in, well-off for. ¶ *n,* rich (*or* wealthy) person. **richesse** (ʃɛs) *f,* wealth, riches; richness. **richissime** (ʃisim) *a,* rolling in wealth.

ricin (risɛ̃) *m,* castor oil plant.

ricocher (rikɔʃe) *v.i,* to ricochet. **ricochet** (ʃɛ) *m,* ricochet; (*pl.*) ducks & drakes.

rictus (riktys) *m,* grin.

ride (rid) *f,* wrinkle, line; ripple; ridge. **rideau** (do) *m,* curtain; shutter. *~ de fer,* (*Theat.*) safety curtain; (*shop*) [metal] shutters. *le ~ de fer,* the Iron Curtain. **rider** (de) *v.t,* to wrinkle, line; ripple, ruffle.

ridicule† (ridikyl) *a,* ridiculous. ¶ *m,* ridiculousness; ridicule. **ridiculiser** (lize) *v.t,* to ridicule.

rien (ryɛ̃) *pn,* (*with ne*) nothing; anything;

(*Sport*) nil, nothing; (*Ten.*) love. *~d'autre*, nothing else. ~ *que*, merely, just. ~ *de* ~, absolutely nothing. *de* ~ (*after thanks*), not at all. ¶ *m*, nothingness; mere nothing; trifle, hint. *des* ~*s*, trivia.

rieur, euse (rjœr, øz) *n*, person laughing. ¶ *a*, laughing, cheerful.

rigide† (riʒid) *a*, rigid; stiff; strict. **rigidité** (dite) *f*, rigidity; stiffness; strictness. ~ *cadavérique* (kadaverik), rigor mortis.

rigole (rigɔl) *f*, channel, ditch, trench.

rigoler *P* (rigɔle) *v.i*, to laugh; have fun; joke. *tu rigoles!* you're joking! **rigolo, te** *P* (lo, ɔt) *a*, funny, killing *P*. ¶ *n*, comic; fraud.

rigoureux, euse† (rigurø, øz) *a*, rigorous, severe; strict. **rigueur** (gœr), *f*, rigour, severity; hardship; strictness. *à la* ~, at a pinch, if need be; possibly. *de* ~, the done thing.

rime (rim) *f*, rhyme. **rimer** (me) *v.t*, to put into verse. ¶ *v.i*, to rhyme; write verse. *cela ne rime à rien*, it does not make sense.

rincer (rɛ̃se) *v.t*, to rinse; r. out.

riper (ripe) *v.i*, to slip, slide.

riposte (ripɔst) *f*, riposte, retort; counter-attack, reprisal. **riposter** (te) *v.t*, to answer back, retaliate; counterattack.

rire (rir) *m*, laughter; laugh. ¶ *v.i.ir*, to laugh, have fun; joke. ~ *aux éclats*, to roar with laughter. ~ *de*, to laugh (*or* scoff) at. **se** ~ **de**, to make light of; laugh at.

ris (ri) *m*, ~ *de veau*, sweetbread.

risée (rize) *f*, laughing stock. **risible**† (zibl) *a*, ludicrous, laughable.

risque (risk) *m*, risk, hazard. **risqué, e** (ke) *a*, risky; risqué, daring. **risquer** (ke) *v.t*, to risk, chance; venture, hazard. ~ *le coup P*, to chance it. **se** ~, to venture into (*or* on); have a try. **risque-tout**, daredevil.

rissole (risɔl) *f*, rissole. **rissoler** (le) *v.t*, (*Cook.*) to brown.

ristourne (risturn) *f*, rebate, discount.

rite (rit) *m*, rite; (*fig.*) ritual. **rituel, le**† (tɥɛl) *a.* & *m*, ritual.

rivage (rivaʒ) *m*, shore.

rival, e (rival) *n.* & *a*, rival. **rivaliser avec** (lize), to rival, vie with. **rivalité** (te) *f*, rivalry.

rive (riv) *f*, bank, side, shore.

river (rive) *v.t*, to rivet, clinch.

riverain, e (rivrɛ̃, ɛn) *a*, waterside. ¶ *m*, waterside resident; (*pl.*) residents of a street.

rivet (rivɛ) *m*, rivet.

rivière (rivjɛr) *f*, river; rivière (*gems*); water-jump.

rixe (riks) *f*, scuffle, brawl, affray.

riz (ri) *m*, rice. **rizière** (zjɛr) *f*, rice field.

robe (rɔb) *f*, dress, gown, frock; robe; robe (*legal dress*); cloth (*clerical dress*); coat (*animal's*); colour (*wine*). ~ *de chambre*, dressing gown. ~ *de mariée*, wedding dress.

robinet (rɔbinɛ) *m*, tap.

robot (rɔbo) *m*, robot. ~ *ménager*, food processor. ~**ique** (bɔtik) *a*, robot. ¶ *f*, robotics.

robuste (rɔbyst) *a*, robust, sturdy, sound, firm, strong; hardy (*plant*). **robustesse** (tɛs) *f*, robustness, strength.

roc (rɔk) *m*, rock.

rocade (rɔkad) *f*, bypass.

rocaille (rɔkaj) *f*, loose stones; stony ground; rockery, rock garden. **rocailleux, euse** (kajø, øz) *a*, rocky, stony; rugged.

rocambolesque (rɔkɑ̃bɔlɛsk) *a*, incredible, fantastic.

roche (rɔʃ) *f*, rock. **rocher** (ʃe) *m*, rock. **rocheux, euse** (rɔʃø, øz) *a*, rocky.

rock [and roll] (rɔk[ɛnrɔl]) *m*, rock-'n'-roll, jive.

rococo (rɔkɔko) *m.* & *a*, rococo.

rodage (rɔdaʒ) *m*, (*Mot.*) running-in; grinding. **roder** (rɔde) *v.t*, to grind (*valves*); run in.

rôder (rɔde) *v.i*, to prowl, hang about. **rôdeur** (dœr) *m*, prowler.

rogne (rɔɲ) *f*, [bad] temper.

rogner (rɔɲe) *v.t*, to clip, trim, pare; cut down.

rognon (rɔɲɔ̃) *m*, kidney (*animal*).

rognure (rɔɲyr) *f*, clipping, paring (*bit*).

roi (rwa) *m*, king; champion. *les R~s Mages*, the 3 Wise Men. *le jour des R~s*, Twelfth Night.

roide (rɛd & rwad) *a*, **roideur** (dœr) *f*, **roidir** (dir) *v.t.* Same as *raide*, *&c*.

roitelet (rwatlɛ) *m*, kinglet; wren.

rôle (rol) *m*, (*Theat.* & *fig.*) role, part; roll, list. *à tour de* ~, in turn.

romain, e (rɔmɛ̃, ɛn) *a.* & **R** ~ (*pers.*) *n*, Roman. **romaine**, *f*, cos lettuce; steelyard.

roman[1], **e** (rɔmɑ̃, an) *a.* & *m*, Romance (*language*); Romanesque (*Arch.*).

roman[2] (rɔmɑ̃) *m*, novel; romance; story. ~ *d'amour*, love story. ~ *de cape & d'épée*, historical romance. ~*-feuilleton*, serial[ized novel]. ~ *policier*, detective novel. ~ *série noire*, thriller. **romance** (mɑ̃s) *f*, lovesong, sentimental ballad. **romancier, ère** (mɑ̃sje, ɛr) *n*, novelist. **romanesque** (manɛsk) *a*, fantastic, fabulous, romantic. ¶ *m*, romantic side; fancy.

romanichel, le (rɔmaniʃɛl) *n*, gypsy.

romantique (rɔmɑ̃tik) *a.* & *n*, romantic.

romarin (rɔmarɛ̃) *m*, rosemary.

rompre (rɔ̃pr) *v.t.* & *i*, to break; b. up; b. in; b. off; snap; rupture; disrupt; burst; interrupt, cut off; upset (*balance*); cancel. (*Mil.*) ~ [*les rangs*], to fall out, dismiss. **rompu, e** (rɔ̃py) *a*, worn-out, exhausted; experienced, inured.

romsteck (rɔmstɛk) *m*, rump steak.

ronce (rɔ̃s) *f*, bramble; blackberry bush.

rond, e (rɔ̃, ɔ̃d) *a*, round; rounded; plump; (*P*) drunk, tight *P*; straight, on the level (*in business*). ¶ *m*, circle, ring; slice (*onion &c*); (*P pl.*) cash. ~ *de serviette*, napkin ring. *en* ~, in a ring. ¶ *f*, rounds, beat, patrol; round [dance], dance in a ring; circle, ring; roundhand (*writing*); (*Mus.*) semibreve. *à la ~e,* around. **rondelet, te** (rɔ̃dlɛ, ɛt) *a,* plumpish; tidy (*sum*). **rondelle** (dɛl) *f,* washer; disc; slice. **rondement** (dmɑ̃) *ad,* roundly, briskly; bluntly. **rondeur** (dœr) *f,* roundness, plumpness; friendly directness. **rondin** (dɛ̃) *m,* log. **rond-point** (rɔ̃pwɛ̃) *m,* roundabout.

ronéoter (rɔneɔte) *v.t,* to roneo, duplicate.

ronflant, e (rɔ̃flɑ̃, ɑ̃t) (*fig.*) *a,* high-flown; pompous. **ronflement** (flamɑ̃) *m,* snore[s]; hum; purr; roar. **ronfler** (fle) *v.i,* to snore; boom, roar, (*engine*) hum, purr, throb.

ronger (rɔ̃ʒe) *v.t,* to gnaw; eat [away, into]; fret. *~ son frein,* to champ at the bit. *se ~ les ongles,* to bite one's nails. *se ~ les sangs,* to eat one's heart out. **rongeur, euse** (ʒœr, øz) *a. & m,* rodent.

ronronnement (rɔ̃rɔnmɑ̃) *m,* purr; hum. **ronronner** (ne) *v.i,* to purr, hum.

roquet (rɔkɛ) *m,* [nasty little] dog.

roquette (rɔkɛt) *f,* rocket.

rosace (rozas) *f,* rosette; rose; rose window. **rosaire** (zɛr) *m,* rosary (*beads*).

rosbif (rɔzbif) *m,* roast beef; roast sirloin.

rose (roz) *f,* rose; rose window; rose diamond. *~ moussue,* moss rose. *~ muscade,* musk r. *~ thé,* tea r. *~ trémière* (tremjɛr), hollyhock. ¶ *m. & a,* pink. **rosé, e** (roze) *a,* pinkish; rosé (*wine*).

roseau (rozo) *m,* reed.

rosée (roze) *f,* dew.

roseraie (rozrɛ) *f,* rose garden. **rosette** (zɛt) *f,* rosette; bow (*ribbon*). **rosier** (zje) *m,* rose tree. *~ grimpant,* rambler *or* climbing rose.

rosse (rɔs) *f,* (*horse*) nag; (*pers.*) beast. ¶ *a,* nasty. **rosser** (se) *v.t,* to thrash, beat.

rossignol (rɔsiɲɔl) *m,* nightingale; picklock; unsaleable article.

rot (ro) *m,* belch, burp.

rotation (rɔtasjɔ̃) *f,* rotation; turnover; frequency (*buses &c*). **rotatoire** (twar) *a,* rotary.

roter (rɔte) *v.i,* to belch, burp.

rôti (roti) *m,* roast [meat]; roasting meat. *~ de porc,* r. pork.

rotin (rɔtɛ̃) *m,* rat[t]an; r. cane.

rôtir (rotir) *v.t. & i,* to roast. **rôtisserie** (tisri) *f,* steakhouse; shop selling roast meat. **rôtissoire** (tiswar) *f,* rotisserie, spit.

rotonde (rɔtɔ̃d) *f,* rotunda. **rotondité** (tɔ̃dite) *f,* rotundity.

rotor (rɔtɔr) *m,* rotor.

rotule (rɔtyl) *f,* knee cap. *être sur les ~s P,* to be all in.

rouage (rwaʒ) *m,* cog [wheel]; gearwheel; part (*watch*); (*pl.*) workings, works, parts.

rouan, ne (rwɑ̃, an) *a. & n,* roan (*animal*).

roublard, e *P* (rublar, ard) *a. & n,* crafty (person).

roucouler (rukule) *v.i,* to coo; bill & coo. ¶ *v.t,* (*pej., pers.*) to warble.

roue (ru) *f,* wheel. *~ libre,* free w. *faire la ~,* to spread its tail (*peacock*); do a cartwheel. **roué, e** (rwe) *a,* artful, wily. **rouelle** (rwɛl) *f,* round [slice]; fillet (*veal*).

rouer (rwe) *v.t,* to coil (*rope*); break upon the wheel. *~ de coups,* to thrash. **rouerie** (ruri) *f,* trickery. **rouet** (rwɛ) *m,* spinning wheel.

rouflaquette (ruflakɛt) *f,* sideburn.

rouge (ruʒ) *m,* (*colour*) red; r. wine; rouge. *voter ~,* to vote Communist. ¶ *n,* (*Pol.*), Red *P.* ¶ *a,* red; red-hot; flushed, blushing. *~-gorge, m,* robin [redbreast]. **rougeâtre** (ruʒɑtr) *a,* reddish. **rougeaud, e** (ʒo, od) *a,* red-faced, ruddy. **rougeole** (ʒɔl) *f,* measles. **rouget** (ʒɛ) *m,* red mullet. **rougeur** (ʒœr) *f,* redness; blush, flush; red spot (*skin*). **rougir** (ʒir) *v.t. & i,* to redden; blush, flush; to go (*or* turn) red; get (*or* make) red-hot. *~ de,* to be ashamed of.

rouille (ruj) *f,* rust. **rouillé, e** (ruje) *a,* rusty, rusted; stiff (*muscle*). **rouiller** (je) *v.i,* to rust, get (*or* go) rusty. ¶ *v.t,* rust, make rusty.

roulade (rulad) *f,* roll (*downhill*); (*Mus.*) roulade, run; rolled meat. **roulant, e** (lɑ̃, ɑ̃t) *a,* on wheels; (*P*) killing *P* (*funny*). **rouleau** (lo) *m,* roller; roll; curler. *~ compresseur,* steamroller *~ à pâtisserie,* rolling pin. **roulement** (lmɑ̃) *m,* rotation; roll[ing]; rumble, rattle; movement (*traffic*); circulation (*capital*). *~ [à billes],* ball bearings. **rouler** (le) *v.t,* to roll, r. along; wheel along; wind up, wrap up; roll up; r. out (*pastry*); wiggle (*hips*); sway (*shoulders*); (*P*) con *P,* diddle *P.* *~ sa bosse,* to travel widely, knock about. ¶ *v.i,* (*cars &c*) to run, go; drive; drift around. *~ sur,* (*conversation*) to be centred on, turn on. *~ sur l'or,* to be rolling [in money] *P.* **roulette** (lɛt) *f,* castor; roulette; r. wheel. *~ de dentiste,* dentist's drill. **roulis** (li) *m,* rolling (*ship*). **roulotte** (lɔt) *f,* caravan.

roumain, e (rumɛ̃, ɛn) *a. &* **R~,** *n. &* **le roumain** (*language*), R[o]umanian. **la Roumanie** (mani), R[o]umania.

roupie (rupi) *f,* rupee.

roupiller *P* (rupije) *v.i,* to snooze. **roupillon** (pijɔ̃) *m,* snooze, kip *P.*

rouquin, e (rukɛ̃, in) *a,* red-haired (*pers.*); red. ¶ *n,* redhead.

rouspéter (ruspete) *v.i,* to grouse.

rousseur (rusœr) *f,* redness; russet colour; (*pl.*) brown marks (*on skin*). **roussi** (si) *m,* [smell of] burning. **roussir** (sir) *v.t,* to scorch, singe. ¶ *v.i,* to turn brown. *faire ~,* (*Cook.*) to brown.

route (rut) *f,* road, path, track; route, course, way; transit; journey. *~ nationale, départementale,* main, secondary road. *en ~,* on the way. *faire ~ avec qn,* to travel with s.o. *faire ~ vers,* head towards. **routier, ère** (tje, ɛr) *a,*

road. ¶ *m*, long distance lorry driver. **routine** (tin) *f*, routine. **routinier, ère** (nje, ɛr) *a*, humdrum, routine.
rouvrir (ruvrir) *v.t.ir*, to reopen.
roux, rousse (ru, rus) *a*, red-haired; russet; red, auburn, ginger (*hair*) ¶ *n*, redhead. ¶ *m*, red &c (*colour*); (*Cook.*) roux.
royal, e† (rwajal) *a*, royal, regal, kingly; princely (*sum*). **royaliste** (list) *a. & n*, royalist. **royaume** (jom) *m*, kingdom, realm. *le R ~ Uni*, the United Kingdom. **royauté** (ote) *f*, kingship; monarchy.
ruade (rɥad) *f*, lashing out; kick (*horse*).
ruban (rybɑ̃) *m*, ribbon; band; tape.
rubéole (rybeɔl) *f*, German measles.
rubicond, e (rybikɔ̃, ɔ̃d) *a*, rubicund, florid.
rubis (rybi) *m*, ruby; jewel (*watch*).
rubrique (rybrik) *f*, rubric; heading; column (*special subject news*).
ruche (ryʃ) *f*, [bee]hive.
rude (ryd) *a*, rough; rugged; harsh; hard; severe; rude; crude, unpolished; tough; hearty (*appetite*). **~ment** (dmɑ̃) *ad*, roughly &c; (*P*) awfully *P*, terribly *P*. **rudesse** (dɛs) *f*, roughness &c.
rudiment (rydimɑ̃) *m*, rudiment. **rudimentaire** (tɛr) *a*, rudimentary.
rudoyer (rydwaje) *v.t*, to use roughly, browbeat.
rue (ry) *f*, street; (*Bot.*) rue. *~ à sens unique*, one way street.
ruée (rɥe) *f*, rush, onrush, onslaught.
ruelle (rɥɛl) *f*, lane, alley.
ruer (rɥe) *v.t*, to lash out, kick (*horse*). *se ~ sur*, to hurl oneself at, rush at.
rugir (ryʒir) *v.i*, to roar. **rugissement** (ʒismɑ̃) *m*, roar, howl.
rugueux, euse (rygø, øz) *a*, rough, rugged.
ruine (rɥin) *f*, ruin, [down]fall. *~ [humaine]*, (*pej.*) [human] wreck. **ruiner** (ne) *v.t*, to ruin. **ruineux, euse** (nø, øz) *a*, ruinous.
ruisseau (rɥiso) *m*, stream, brook; gutter (*street & fig.*). **ruisseler** (sle) *v.i*, to stream, run down, flow.
rumeur (rymœr) *f*, rumour; hum (*voices &c*); murmer[ing]; hubbub; rumblings.
ruminant, e (ryminɑ̃, ɑ̃t) *a. & m*, ruminant. **ruminer** (ne) *v.t. & i*, to ruminate; ponder, meditate; brood over.
rupture (ryptyr) *f*, breaking; rupture; fracture; breaking off, breach; breakdown; split.
rural, e (ryral) *a*, rural, country.
ruse (ryz) *f*, ruse, trick[ery], dodge; stratagem; cunning, slyness; guile. **rusé, e** (ryze) *a*, artful, crafty, wily. **ruser** (ze) *v.i*, to use cunning.
russe (rys) *a. &* **R ~**, *n. &* **le russe** (*language*), Russian. **la Russie** (si), Russia.
rustaud, e (rysto, od) *a*, coarse. ¶ *n*, country bumpkin.
rustine (rystin) *f*, rubber patch (*for repair*).
rustique (tik) *a*, rustic; country; hardy (*plant*). **rustre** (str) *m*, boor, lout. ¶ *a*, boorish.
rut (ryt) *m*, rut, heat (*animals*). *en ~*, on heat.
rutabaga (rytabaga) *m*, swede.
rutiler (rytile) *v.i*, to shine brightly, gleam.
rythme (ritm) *m*, rhythm; pace, tempo, rate. **rythmer** (me) *v.t*, to give rhythm to; punctuate. **rythmique** (mik) *a*, rhythmic(al). ¶ *f*, rhythmics.

S

S, s (ɛs) *m*, *letter*, S, s.
sabbat (saba) *m*, sabbath; (*P*) row, racket.
sablage (sablaʒ) *m*, sanding, sandblasting. **sable** (sɑbl) *m*, sand. *~s mouvants*, quicksands. ¶ *a*, sand-coloured; sandy. **sablé** (ble) *m*, shortbread biscuit. **sabler** (sɑble) *v.t*, to sand (*road*); sandblast; drink (*champagne*). **sablier** (blie) *m*, hour glass, sand g. **sablière** (ɛr) *f*, sand pit, gravel pit. **sablonneux, euse** (blɔnø, øz) *a*, sandy.
sabord (sabɔr) *m*, scuttle. **saborder** (bɔrde) *v.t*, to scuttle (*ship*); wind up, shut down (*business*).
sabot (sabo) *m*, clog; hoof (*animal*). *~ de frein*, break shoe.
sabotage (sabɔtaʒ) *m*, sabotage, act of s.; botching. **saboter** (te) *v.t*, to sabotage; botch; damage wilfully, wreck. **saboteur, euse** (tœr, øz) *n*, saboteur; botcher.
sabre (sɑbr) *m*, sabre, cutlass. **sabrer** (sɑbre) *v.t*, to sabre; cut down; slash (*text*).
sac[1] (sak) *m*, bag; sack; bagful; sackful; (*P*) 10 francs. *~ à dos*, rucksack. *~ à main*, handbag. *~ à provisions*, shopping bag. *~ de couchage*, sleeping bag. *~ de voyage*, overnight bag.
sac[2] (sak) *m*, sacking (*town*). *mettre à ~*, to sack.
saccade (sakad) *f*, jerk, start. **saccadé, e** (de) *a*, jerky; irregular; staccato (*voice*).
saccager (sakaʒe) *v.t*, to sack; ransack; upset; wreck, turn upside down.
saccharine (sakarin) *f*, saccharin[e].
sacerdoce (sasɛrdɔs) *m*, priesthood; ministry. **sacerdotal, e** (tal) *a*, sacerdotal, priestly.
sachet (saʃɛ) *m*, sachet; bag. *~ à thé*, tea bag.

sacoche (kɔʃ) *f,* bag; satchel; saddlebag; toolbag; panier.
sacquer *P* (sake) *v.t,* to give the sack to *P;* give a rotten mark to *P,* fail (*student*).
sacraliser (sakralise) *v.t,* to regard as sacred.
sacre (kr) *m,* anointing, coronation; consecration (*bishop*). **sacré, e** (kre) *a,* holy, sacred; (*P*) damned *P,* blasted *P.* **sacrement** (krəmɑ̃) *m,* sacrament. **sacrer** (kre) *v.t,* to anoint, crown; consecrate. ¶ *v.i,* (*O*) curse, swear. **sacrifice** (krifis) *m,* sacrifice. **sacrifier** (fje) *v.t,* to sacrifice; (*Com.*) give away (*for next to nothing*). ~ *à,* to conform to. **sacrilège** (lɛʒ) *m,* sacrilege. ¶ *a,* sacrilegious.
sacripant (sakripɑ̃) *m,* rascal, bully.
sacristain (sakristɛ̃) *m,* sacristan. **sacristie** (ti) *f,* vestry, sacristy. **sacro-saint, e** (krɔsɛ̃, ɛ̃t) *a,* sacrosanct.
sadique† (sadik) *a,* sadistic. ¶ *n,* sadist. **sadisme** (ism) *m,* sadism.
safari (safari) *m,* safari.
safran (safrɑ̃) *m,* saffron.
sagace (sagas) *a,* sagacious, shrewd. **sagacité** (site) *f,* sagacity, shrewdness.
sage† (saʒ) *a,* wise, sage; judicious, prudent, sensible; well-behaved, good (*child*); chaste. ¶ *m,* sage, wise man. ~*-femme, f,* midwife. **sagesse** (ʒɛs) *f,* wisdom &c; good conduct.
sagouin *P* (sagwɛ̃) *m,* filthy pig; slob *P**; bastard *P**.
saignant, e (sɛɲɑ̃, ɑ̃t) *a,* bleeding; raw; rare, underdone (*meat*). **saignée** (ɲe) *f,* (*Med.*) bleeding; savage cut; (*pl.*) heavy losses (*war*); trench, ditch; groove. ~ *du bras,* bend in the arm. **saigner** (ɲe) *v.i. & t,* to bleed; stick (*pig*). ~ *du nez,* to have a nosebleed. *se ~ aux 4 veines,* to bleed o.s white.
saillant, e (sajɑ̃, ɑ̃t) *a,* salient, projecting prominent; striking, outstanding. **saillie** (ji) *f,* projection; witticism; covering. **saillir** (jir) *v.i.ir,* to project; protrude; stick out; bulge. ¶ *v.t.ir,* (*animals*) to cover.
sain, e† (sɛ̃, ɛn) *a,* healthy, sound; wholesome; sane. ~ *& sauf,* safe & sound.
saindoux (sɛ̃du) *m,* lard.
saint, e (sɛ̃, ɛ̃t) *n,* saint; statue of a saint. ¶ *a,* holy; saintly, godly. ~*-frusquin,* gear *P,* clobber *P. à la ~-glinglin,* never in a month of Sundays. ~ *patron,* patron saint. *S~-Siège,* Holy See. *la S~e Vierge,* the Blessed Virgin. **Saint,** *comps;* ~*-bernard,* St. Bernard (*dog*); good Samaritan. *le ~-Esprit* (sɛ̃tɛspri), the Holy Ghost, the Holy Spirit. *la ~-Jean* (sɛ̃ʒɑ̃), Midsummer day. *la ~-Michel* (miʃɛl), Michaelmas. *la ~-Sylvestre* (silvɛstr), new-year's eve. **saintement** (tmɑ̃) *ad,* like a saint. **sainteté** (təte) *f,* holiness, saintliness; sanctity.
saisie (sɛzi) *f,* seizure. ~*-arrêt,* distraint. **saisir** (zir) *v.t,* to seize, grab; catch hold of; catch; grasp, understand; grip; (*Law*) submit to; (*Cook.*) fry quickly. **saisissant, e** (zisɑ̃, ɑ̃t) *a,* piercing (*cold*); startling, striking; thrilling. **saisissement** (smɑ̃) *m,* shock; thrill.
saison (sɛzɔ̃) *f,* season, time (*of year*); cure.
salade (salad) *f,* salad; lettuce; green salad; muddle, jumble; (*P pl.*) lies, stories. **saladier** (dje) *m,* salad bowl.
salage (salaʒ) *m,* salting, curing.
salaire (salɛr) *m,* wage[s], pay; salary; reward. ~ *de famine,* starvation wage.
salaison (salɛzɔ̃) *f,* salting, curing; (*pl.*) salt provisions.
salamandre (salamɑ̃dr) *f,* salamander; slow-combustion stove.
salami (salami) *m,* salami.
salarié, e (salarje) *a,* salaried, wage-earning, paid (*work*). ¶ *n,* wage-earner; salaried employee.
salaud *P** (salo) *m,* bastard *P**, swine.
sale† (sal) *a,* dirty, filthy; foul; nasty.
salé, e (sale) *a,* salted, salty, salt; stiff (*punishment*); steep (*price*); (*P*) spicy, fruity. ¶ *m,* salty food; salt pork. **saler** (le) *v.t,* to salt; be tough on; fleece; bump up (*price*).
saleté (salte) *f,* dirtiness; dirt, filth; mess; rubbish, trash, junk; dirty remark; d. trick; nasty character.
salière (saljɛr) *f,* saltcellar. **salin, e** (lɛ̃, in) *a,* saline.
salir (salir) *v.t,* to dirty, soil.
salive (saliv) *f,* saliva, spittle. **saliver** (live) *v.i,* to salivate.
salle (sal) *f,* hall; room; ward (*hospital*); (*Theat. &c*) auditorium, theatre; audience; cinema. ~ *à manger,* dining room; d. r. suite. ~ *d'attente,* waiting room. ~ *de bain*[*s*], bathroom. ~ *de classe,* classroom. ~ *d'eau,* shower room. ~ *des fêtes,* village hall. ~ *d'opération,* operating theatre. ~ *des ventes,* saleroom, auction room.
salmigondis (salmigɔ̃di) *m,* hotchpotch.
salon (salɔ̃) *m,* lounge, sitting room; lounge suite; saloon; (*hairdressing*) salon; exhibition, show. *S~ de l'Auto,* Motor Show. ~ *de thé,* tearoom.
salope *P** (salɔp) *f,* bitch *P**; slut; tart *P**. **saloperie** *P** (pri) *f,* muck, trash, junk, rubbish; filth; filthy remark; dirty trick.
salopette (salɔpɛt) *f,* dungarees; overall[s].
salpêtre (salpɛtr) *m,* saltpetre.
salsifis (salsifi) *m,* salsify.
saltimbanque (saltɛ̃bɑ̃k) *n,* [travelling] acrobat.
salubre (salybr) *a,* salubrious, healthy; wholesome. **salubrité** (brite) *f,* salubrity &c; (*public*) health.
saluer (salɥe) *v.t,* to salute, bow to; greet; hail.
salut (saly) *m,* wave; nod; bow; (*Mil. &c*) salute; safety; (*Rel.*) salvation. ¶ *i,* hello!, hi! *P;* bye! *P,* see you! *P;* (*liter.*) [all] hail. **salutaire** (tɛr)

a, salutary, wholesome, beneficial. **salutation** (tasjɔ̃) *f*, salutation, greeting.
salve (salv) *f*, salvo.
samedi (samdi) *m*, Saturday.
sanatorium (sanatɔrjɔm) *m*, sanatorium.
sanctifier (sɑ̃ktifje) *v.t*, to sanctify, hallow. **sanction** (sjɔ̃) *f*, sanction, assent; penalty, punishment. **sanctionner** (ɔne) *v.t*, to sanction, approve; punish. **sanctuaire** (tɥɛr) *m*, sanctuary.
sandale (sɑ̃dal) *f*, sandal.
sandwich (sɑ̃dwitʃ) *m*, sandwich.
sang (sɑ̃) *m*, blood. *être en ~*, to be bleeding. *se ronger les ~s, se faire du mauvais ~*, to worry, get in a state. **sang-froid** (sɑ̃frwa) *m*, self-control, sangfroid; coolness. **sanglant, e** (glɑ̃, ɑ̃t) *a*, bloody; scathing, savage.
sangle (sɑ̃gl) *f*, strap, band, girth, webbing. **sangler** (sɑ̃gle) *v.t*, to strap; girth; lash. **se ~**, to strap up.
sanglier (sɑ̃glje) *m*, wild boar.
sanglot (sɑ̃glo) *m*, sob. **sangloter** (glɔte) *v.i*, to sob.
sangsue (sɑ̃sy) *f*, leech. **sanguin, e** (gɛ̃, in) *a*, passionate; ruddy; blood. ¶ *f*, blood orange; red pencil drawing. **sanguinaire** (ginɛr) *a*, bloody; bloodthirsty. **sanguinolant, e** (nɔlɑ̃, ɑ̃t) *a*, streaked with blood; slightly bleeding (*wound*).
sanitaire (sanitɛr) *a*, sanitary, health. ¶ *m.pl*, bathroom; b. suite; b. plumbing.
sans (sɑ̃) *pr*, without; but for; -less; non-. *~ manger*, without eating. *~ arrêt*, non-stop. *~ cela, ~ quoi*, otherwise. *~ que*, without. *~-le-sou*, penniless. *il va ~ dire que*, it goes without saying that.
sans-abri (sɑ̃zabri) *n*, homeless person.
sans-cœur (sɑ̃kœr) *n*, heartless person.
sans-gêne (sɑ̃ʒɛn) *m*, lack of consideration. ¶ *n*, inconsiderate *or* offhand person.
sansonnet (sɑ̃sɔnɛ) *m*, starling (*bird*).
sans-souci (sɑ̃susi) *a*, carefree.
sans-travail (les) (sɑ̃travaj) *m.pl*, the unemployed.
santé (sɑ̃te) *f*, health. *à votre ~!* cheers!
sape (sap) *f*, undermining, sapping; approach trench; (*pl. P*) gear *P*. **saper** (pe) *v.t*, to undermine, sap. (*P*) *bien sapé*, well dressed. **sapeur** (pœr) *m*, sapper. *~-pompier*, fireman.
saphir (safir) *m*, sapphire.
sapin (sapɛ̃) *m*, fir [tree]. *~ de Noël*, Christmas tree. **sapinière** (pinjɛr) *f*, fir plantation.
sarabande (sarabɑ̃d) *f*, saraband (*dance*); (*P*) racket *P*, din.
sarbacane (sarbakan) *f*, pea shooter; blow gun, blowpipe, blow tube (*dart tube*).
sarcasme (sarkasm) *m*, sarcasm, sarcastic remark. **sarcastique** (tik) *a*, sarcastic.
sarcler (sarkle) *v.t*, to weed. **sarcloir** (klwar) *m*, weeding hoe, weeder.
sarcophage (sarkɔfaʒ) *m*, sarcophagus.
Sardaigne (la) (sardɛɲ), Sardinia. **sarde** (sard) *a*. & **S~**, *n*, Sardinian.
sardine (sardin) *f*, sardine.
sardonique† (sardɔnik) *a*, sardonic.
sarigue (sarig) *m*. & *f*, opossum.
sarment (sarmɑ̃) *m*, vine shoot.
sarrasin (sarazɛ̃) *m*, buckwheat.
sarriette (sarjɛt) *f*, (*Bot.*) savory.
sas (sɑ) *m*, sieve; (*Naut.*) airlock; lock (*canal*).
Satan (satɑ̃) *m*, Satan. **satané, e** *P* (tane) *a*, blasted, confounded *P*. **satanique** (nik) *a*, satanic.
satelliser (satɛlize) *v.t*, to put into orbit; make into a satellite (*country*). **satellite** (lit) *m*, satellite.
satiété (sasjete) *f*, satiety, satiation. *à ~*, to satiety &c; ad nauseum.
satin (satɛ̃) *m*, satin. **satiné, e** (tine) *a*, satiny, satin-like; with a silk finish. **satiner** (ne) *v.t*, to put a satin (*or* silk) finish on.
satire (satir) *f*, satire. **satirique†** (tirik) *a*, satiric, satirical. **satiriser** (ze) *v.t*, to satirize.
satisfaction (satisfaksjɔ̃) *f*, satisfaction, gratification. **satisfaire** (fɛr) *v.t.ir*, to satisfy, please, gratify, answer. **~ à**, to satisfy; answer, meet; fulfil. **satisfaisant, e** (fəzɑ̃, ɑ̃t) *a*, satisfactory.
saturer (satyre) *v.t*, to saturate.
satyre (satir) *m*, satyr; (*P*) sex-maniac *P*.
sauce (sos) *f*, sauce, dressing; gravy. *mettre qn à toutes les ~s*, to make s.o do any job going. *recevoir la ~ P*, to get soaked. **saucer** (sose) *v.t*, to dip in (*or* mop up) the sauce; drench, soak. **saucière** (sjɛr) *f*, sauce boat, gravy b.
saucisse (sosis) *f*, sausage. **saucisson** (sɔ̃) *m*, slicing sausage (*large*).
sauf[1], sauve (sof, sov) *a*, safe, unhurt, unscathed; saved. **sauf[2]**, *pr*, except, save, but; unless. *~ avis contraire*, unless you hear otherwise. **~-conduit**, *m*, safe conduct.
sauge (soʒ) *f*, sage; salvia.
saugrenu, e (sogrəny) *a*, absurd, preposterous.
saule (sol) *m*, willow [tree].
saumâtre (somɑtr) *a*, brackish, briny.
saumon (somɔ̃) *m*, salmon.
saumure (somyr) *f*, brine.
sauna (sona) *m*, sauna.
saupoudrer (sopudre) *v.t*, to sprinkle, dredge, dust, powder.
saut (so) *m*, leap, jump, vault; hop; skip; fall[s] (*water*). *~ à la perche*, pole vault. *~ en hauteur*, high jump. *~ en longueur*, long j. *le ~ périlleux*, a somersault. *faire qch au ~ de lit*, to do sth as soon as one gets out of bed. **saute** (sot) *f*, shift, change. **~-mouton** (sotmutɔ̃) *m*, leap-frog. **sauter** (sote) *v.i*, to leap, jump; hop; vault; fly (*at s.o*); blow up, explode; fuse, blow; toss (*pancake*); break open (*lock*); *P* cancel; (*P*) get the sack;

(*lesson*) be cancelled; (*Cook.*) sauté. ~ *à cloche-pied,* to hop. ~ *à la corde,* to skip. *faire* ~, to blow up. *se faire* ~ *la cervelle P,* to blow one's brains out. ¶ *v.t,* to jump [over]; skip (*class*). **sauterelle** (trɛl) *f,* grasshopper. [*grande*] ~ *P,* beanpole. **sauteur, euse** (tœr, øz) *n,* jumper. (*f.*) sauté pan. **sautiller** (tije) *v.i,* to hop, skip.
sautoir (twar) *m,* chain (*jewellery*).
sauvage† (sovaʒ) *a,* wild; savage; (*fig.*) unsociable; unauthorized (*camping &c*); unfair (*competition*); unofficial (*strike &c*). ¶ *n,* recluse, unsociable type; savage; brute. **sauvagerie** (ʒri) *f,* savagery.
sauvegarde (sovgard) *f,* safeguard, protection. **sauve-qui-peut** (kipø) *m,* stampede, headlong flight. **sauver** (ve) *v.t,* to save, rescue; salvage. **se** ~, to escape; run away, be off. **sauvetage** (vtaʒ) *m,* life saving, rescue; salvage; salvation. **sauveteur** (vtœr) *m,* rescuer. **sauveur** (vœr) *m,* saviour. **à la sauvette** (vɛt) *ad,* hastily, hurriedly.
savamment (savamɑ̃) *ad,* learnedly; knowingly, skilfully, cleverly.
savane (savan) *f,* savannah.
savant, e (vɑ̃, ɑ̃t) *a,* learned, scholarly; skilful; performing (*dog*). ¶ *n,* scientist, scholar.
savate (savat) *f,* old shoe.
saveur (savœr) *f,* savour, flavour.
savoir (savwar) *v.t.ir,* to know; be aware of; know how to; be able to; hear [of], learn of (*news*). *faire* ~ *à qn,* to let s.o know, tell s.o. *sais-tu nager?* can you swim? *à* ~, namely, that is. *sachez que,* let me tell you. *autant que je sache,* as far as I know. ¶ *m,* knowledge, learning. ~**-faire** (vwarfɛr) *m,* savoir faire; know-how *P.* ~**-vivre,** *m,* good manners.
savon (savɔ̃) *m,* soap; bar of s. ~ *à barbe,* shaving s. ~ *en poudre,* soap powder. *passer un* ~ *à qn P,* to give s.o a ticking-off *P.* **savonner** (vɔne) *v.t,* to soap. **savonnette** (nɛt) *f,* bar of [toilet] soap. **savonneux, euse** (nø, øz) *a,* soapy.
savourer (savure) *v.t,* to savour. **savoureux, euse** (rø, øz) *a,* tasty; juicy (*story*).
saxifrage (saksifraʒ) *f,* saxifrage.
saxophone (saksɔfɔn) *m,* saxophone.
sbire (zbir) *m,* (*pej.*) henchman.
scabreux, euse (skabrø, øz) *a,* improper, shocking; risky.
scalpel (skalpɛl) *m,* scalpel.
scalper (skalpe) *v.t,* to scalp.
scandale (skɑ̃dal) *m,* scandal; fuss, scene. *à* ~, (*book &c*) controversial. **scandaleux, euse**† (lø, øz) *a,* scandalous, shocking. **scandaliser** (lize) *v.t,* to scandalize, shock.
scander (skɑ̃de) *v.t,* to scan (*verse*); (*Mus.*) stress, syllabize (*articulate by syllables*).
scandinave (skɑ̃dinav) *a.* & **S**~, *n,* Scandinavian. **la Scandinavie** (navi), Scandinavia.
scansion (skɑ̃sjɔ̃) *f,* scansion, scanning.
scaphandre (skafɑ̃dr) *m,* diving suit; space suit. **scaphandrier** (fɑ̃drie) *m,* diver (*underwater*).
scarabée (skarabe) *m,* beetle; scarab.
scarifier (skarifje) *v.t,* to scarify.
scarlatine (skarlatin) *f,* scarlatina, scarlet fever.
scarole (skarɔl) *f,* endive.
sceau (so) *m,* seal; (*fig.*) stamp.
scélérat, e (selera, at) *a,* villainous, wicked. ¶ *n,* villain, scoundrel, miscreant.
scellé (sɛle) *m,* seal (*official*). **sceller** (le) *v.t,* to seal; s. up; (*Build.*) embed.
scénario (senarjo) *m,* scenario, screenplay; (*fig.*) pattern. **scénariste** (rist) *n,* scriptwriter. **scène** (sɛn) *f,* stage; scene. *mettre en* ~, to present; stage; direct. **scénique** (senik) *a,* scenic, theatrical, stage.
scepticisme (sɛptisism) *m,* scepticism. **sceptique** (tik) *a,* sceptical. ¶ *n,* sceptic.
sceptre (sɛptr) *m,* sceptre.
schéma (ʃema) *m,* diagram, plan. **schématique**† (matik) *a,* schematic; diagrammatic; oversimplified. **schématiser** (tise) *v.t,* to schematize; oversimplify.
schisme (ʃism) *m,* schism.
schiste (ʃist) *m,* schist.
schizophrène (skizɔfrɛn) *a.* & *n,* schizophrenic. **schizophrénie** (ni) *f,* schizophrenia.
sciage (sjaʒ) *m,* sawing.
sciatique (sjatik) *a,* sciatic. ¶ *f,* sciatica.
scie (si) *f,* saw; (*pej.*) bore; catch-tune. ~ *à découper,* fretsaw, jigsaw. ~ *à métaux,* hacksaw. ~ *à ruban,* bandsaw.
sciemment (sjamɑ̃) *ad,* knowingly, wittingly. **science** (sjɑ̃s) *f,* science; art, skill; knowledge. ~*-fiction,* science fiction. ~*s humaines,* social sciences. ~*s naturelles,* biology. **scientifique**† (ɑ̃tifik) *a,* scientific. ¶ *n,* scientist.
scier (sje) *v.t,* to saw; saw off; (*P*) bowl over, stagger. **scierie** (siri) *f,* saw mill. **scieur** (sjœr) *m,* sawyer.
scinder (sɛ̃de) *v.t,* (*fig.*) to divide, split.
scintiller (sɛ̃tije) *v.i,* to scintillate; twinkle, glitter, sparkle, glisten.
scission (sisjɔ̃) *f,* scission, split, cleavage; secession.
sciure (sjyr) *f,* sawdust.
sclérose (skleroz) *f,* sclerosis; ossification. ~ *en plaques,* multiple sclerosis.
scolaire (skɔlɛr) *a,* school; academic (*year*). **scolarisation** (arizasjɔ̃) *f,* schooling. **scolariser** (ze) *v.t,* to provide schooling for. **scolarité** (rite) *f,* schooling; school-leaving age.
scolopendre (skɔlɔpɑ̃dr) *f,* centipede.
sconse (skɔ̃s) *m,* skunk (*fur*).
scooter (skutœr) *m,* [motor] scooter.
scorbut (skɔrby) *m,* scurvy.
scorie (skɔri) *f. oft. pl,* slag, scoria.
scorpion (skɔrpjɔ̃) *m,* scorpion.
scotch (skɔtʃ) *m,* scotch [whisky]; sellotape.

scout (skut) *m,* [boy] scout.
scribe (skrib) *m,* scribe. **scribouillard, e** (bujar, ard) *n,* penpusher.
script (skript) *m,* printing (*hand*). *écrire en ~,* to print. *~-girl,* continuity girl.
scrupule (skrypyl) *m,* scruple, qualm. **scrupuleux, euse**† (lø, øz) *a,* scrupulous.
scrutateur, trice (skrytatœr, tris) *a,* searching. ¶ *m,* (*Pol.*) scrutineer. **scruter** (te) *v.t,* to scrutinize, scan; peer into; search. **scrutin** (tɛ̃) *m,* poll, ballot, voting, vote.
sculpter (skylte) *v.t,* to sculpture; carve; sculpt. **sculpteur** (tœr) *m,* sculptor; carver. **sculpture** (tyr) *f,* sculpture. *~ sur bois,* wood carving.
se, s' (sə, s) *pn,* oneself; himself, herself, itself; themselves; each other, one another. *Note:* An English intransitive is often expressed in French by the pronominal form (*se, s'*); thus, to depreciate, *v.t, déprécier, avilir;* to depreciate, *v.i, se déprécier, s'avilir.* The pronominal form also serves to give to a transitive verb a passive meaning; as, *lettre qui se prononce,* letter which is pronounced.
séance (seɑ̃s) *f,* seat (*at a council*); sitting, session, meeting; performance. *~ de spiritisme,* seance. *~ tenante,* forthwith. **séant**[1], **e** (seɑ̃, ɑ̃t) *a,* becoming, seemly, proper. **séant**[2] *m, se mettre sur son ~,* to sit up.
seau (so) *m,* pail, bucket; pailful. *~ hygiénique,* slop pail.
sébile (sebil) *f,* wooden bowl.
sec, sèche (sɛk, sɛʃ) *a,* dry; dried; thin; hard (*heart*); curt; neat (*alcohol*). *bruit ~,* sharp snap. **sec,** *ad,* hard (*hit, drink*); with a jolt. **à sec,** *ad,* dry; dried up; broke *P;* empty. **sec,** *m,* dry; dry place; dry land.
sécateur (sekatœr) *m,* pruning shears, secateurs.
sécession (sesɛsjɔ̃) *f,* secession.
sèchement (sɛʃmɑ̃) *ad,* drily, curtly. **sécher** (seʃe) *v.t. & i,* to dry; d. up; d. out; (*Sch. P*) be stumped *P;* skip (*classes*). **sécheresse** (ʃrɛs) *f,* dryness; drought; hardness &c, as *sec.* **séchoir** (ʃwar) *m,* drying room; drier; airer; clothes horse.
second, e† (səgɔ̃, ɔ̃d) *a,* second; secondary. *de ~ choix,* low-grade; class two (*fruit &c*). ¶ *n,* second. ¶ *m,* second floor; second in command; (*Naut.*) first mate. ¶ *f,* second; second class; second-class ticket; second gear; (*Sch.*) fifth form. **secondaire** (gɔ̃dɛr) *a,* secondary; minor; side. **seconder** (gɔ̃de) *v.t,* to help, assist.
secouer (səkwe) *v.t,* to shake; s. up; s. down; s. off. *~ la tête,* to nod; shake one's head.
secourable (səkurabl) *a,* helpful. **secourir** (rir) *v.t.ir,* to help, assist, aid. **secourisme** (rism) *m,* first aid. **secours** (kur) *m,* help, aid, assistance; rescue. (*Mil.*) relief. *au ~ !* help! *de ~,* emergency (*exit*); spare (*wheel*). *équipe de ~,* rescue party.
secousse (səkus) *f,* shake, jerk, jolt, shock. *~ politique,* political upheaval. *~ sismique,* earth tremor.
secret, ète (səkrɛ, ɛt) *a,* secret; (*pers.*) reserved. ¶ *m,* secret; secrecy, privacy; solitary confinement. *~ de Polichinelle,* open secret. *en ~,* secretly. **secrétaire** (kretɛr) *m,* secretary; writing desk, secretaire. *~ de direction,* executive secretary. *~ d'État,* junior minister. **secrétariat** (tarja) *m,* secretaryship; secretariat; secretarial work; s. offices; s. staff; (*Sch.*) [secretary's] office.
sécréter (sekrete) *v.t,* to secrete. **sécrétion** (sjɔ̃) *f,* secretion.
sectaire (sɛktɛr) *m. & a,* sectarian. **sectarisme** (tarism) *m,* sectarianism. **secte** (sɛkt) *f,* sect.
secteur (sɛktœr) *m,* sector; district; area; (*Elec.*) local supply area. *le ~,* the mains [supply]. **section** (sjɔ̃) *f,* section; department; fare stage (*bus &c*); (*Mil.*) platoon. **sectionnement** (sjɔnmɑ̃) *m,* severance. **sectionner** (ne) *v.t,* to sever.
séculaire (sekylɛr) *a,* age-old. **séculier, ère** (lje, ɛr) *a. & n,* secular.
sécuriser (sekyrize) *v.t,* to give [a feeling of] security to. **sécurité** (rite) *f,* safety, security. *la ~ routière,* road safety. *la S~ Sociale,* Social Security.
sédatif, ive (sedatif, iv) *a. & m,* sedative.
sédentaire (sedɑ̃tɛr) *a,* sedentary. **sédantariser** (tarize) *v.t,* to settle.
sédiment (sedimɑ̃) *m,* sediment, deposit.
séditieux, euse† (sedisjø, øz) *a,* seditious; insurrectionary. **sédition** (sjɔ̃) *f,* sedition; insurrection.
séducteur, trice (sedyktœr, tris) *a,* seductive. ¶ *m,* seducer; womanizer. ¶ *f,* seductress. **séduction** (ksjɔ̃) *f,* seduction, seducing; charming, captivation; charm, appeal. **séduire** (dɥir) *v.t.ir,* to seduce; charm, captivate; appeal to. **séduisant, e** (dɥizɑ̃, ɑ̃t) *a,* seductive, tempting; charming, appealing; attractive.
segment (sɛgmɑ̃) *m,* segment.
ségrégation (segregasjɔ̃) *f,* segregation.
seiche (sɛʃ) *f,* cuttle fish.
seigle (sɛgl) *m,* rye.
seigneur (sɛɲœr) *m,* lord. **seigneurie** (ɲœri) *f,* lordship; manor.
sein (sɛ̃) *m,* breast; bosom; womb. *au ~ de,* in the midst of; within. *donner le ~ à,* to breastfeed.
séisme (seism) *m,* earthquake.
seize (sɛz) *a. & m,* sixteen; 16th (date). **seizième**† (sɛzjɛm) *a. & n,* sixteenth.
séjour (seʒur) *m,* stay; abode, dwelling place; living room. **séjourner** (ʒurne) *v.i,* to stay; (*snow &c*) lie.

sel (sɛl) *m,* salt; piquancy, wit. ~ *fin,* table salt. ~ *gemme,* rock salt. ~*s pour bains,* bath salts.
sélection (selɛksjɔ̃) *f,* selection, choice. **sélectionner** (ɔne) *v.t,* to select.
selle (sɛl) *f,* saddle; seat; (*Med.*) stool, motion. **seller** (le) *v.t,* to saddle. **sellerie** (lri) *f,* saddlery. **sellette** (lɛt) *f,* stool; pedestal (*vase*). *tenir quelqu'un sur la* ~, to interrogate s.o, grill s.o *P.* **sellier** (lje) *m,* saddler.
selon (səlɔ̃) *pr,* [according] to; in accordance with. ~ *moi,* in my opinion. *c'est* ~, it all depends.
semailles (səmɑj) *f.pl,* seed time; sowing.
semaine (səmɛn) *f,* week; week's work, pay &c. *la* ~ *seulement,* week days only.
sémantique (semɑ̃tik) *a,* semantic. ¶ *f,* semantics.
sémaphore (semafɔr) *m,* semaphore.
semblable† (sɑ̃blabl) *a,* [a]like, similar; such. ¶ *m,* fellow [man], like. **semblant** (blɑ̃) *m,* semblance, appearance, show. [*faux*] ~, pretence, sham. *un* ~ *de sourire,* a shadow of a smile. *faire* ~ *de,* to pretend. **sembler** (ble) *v.i,* to seem, appear, look, strike.
semelle (səmɛl) *f,* sole.
semence (səmɑ̃s) *f,* seed; tack (*nail*). ~ *de perles,* seed pearls. **semer** (me) *v.t,* to sow; scatter, strew, spread; shake off (*pursuer*); shed, lose.
semestre (səmɛstr) *m,* half-year; semester. **semestriel, le** (triɛl) *a,* half-yearly.
semi- (səmi) *pref,* semi-, half-. ~*-remorque, f,* articulated lorry; trailer.
sémillant, e (semijɑ̃, ɑ̃t) *a,* vivacious; dashing.
séminaire (seminɛr) *m,* seminary; seminar.
semis (səmi) *m,* seedling; sowing; seedbed.
sémitique (semitik) *a,* Semitic.
semonce (səmɔ̃s) *f,* reprimand. *coup de* ~ (*Naut.*), warning shot.
semoule (səmul) *f,* semolina.
sempiternel, le (sɑ̃pitɛrnɛl) *a,* eternal, never-ending.
sénat (sena) *m,* senate. **sénateur** (tœr) *m,* senator.
Sénégal (le) (senegal), Senegal. **senegalais, e** (lɛ, ɛz) *a.* & **S** ~, *n,* Senegalese.
sénile (senil) *a,* senile. **sénilité** (lite) *f,* senility.
sens (sɑ̃s) *m,* sense; meaning; direction, way. ~ *commun,* [common] sense. *au* ~ *propre, figuré,* in the literal, figurative sense. ~ *dessus dessous,* upside down. ~ *giratoire,* roundabout (*traffic*). ~ *interdit,* no entry, one way street. ~ *unique,* one way street. *reprendre ses* ~, to regain consciousness. **sensation** (sɑ̃sasjɔ̃) *f,* sensation; feel[ing], sense. *à* ~ & **sensationnel, le** (sjɔnɛl) *a,* sensational, fantastic *P.* **sensé**†, **e** (se) *a,* sensible. **sensibiliser** (sibilize) *v.t,* to make sensitive (*or* alive) (*à,* to). **sensibilité** (sibilite) *f,* sensitivity. **sensible** (sibl) *a,* sensitive. *endroit* ~, *côté* ~, tender, sore spot. appreciable, palpable, perceptible. **sensiblement** (bləmɑ̃) *a,* appreciably; noticeably; approximately, more or less. **sensiblerie** (ri) *f,* sentimentality; squeamishness. **sensitif, ive** (tif, iv) *a,* sensory, ¶ *f,* sensitive plant.
sensoriel, le (sɑ̃sɔrjɛl) *a,* sensory.
sensualité (sɑ̃sɥalite) *f,* sensuality, sensuousness. **sensuel, le**† (sɥɛl) *a,* sensual; sensuous.
sentence (sɑ̃tɑ̃s) *f,* maxim; (*Law*) sentence. **sentencieux, euse**† (tɑ̃sjø, øz) *a,* sententious.
senteur (sɑ̃tœr) *f,* scent, odour, perfume.
senti, e (sɑ̃ti) *a,* well expressed, strong. *bien* ~, heartfelt (*words*); home (*truths*).
sentier (sɑ̃tje) *m,* footpath, path, track. *sur le* ~ *de la guerre,* (*fig.*) on the warpath.
sentiment (sɑ̃timɑ̃) *m,* feeling, emotion; sentiment. **sentimental, e** (tal) *a,* sentimental. ¶ *n,* sentimentalist. **sentimentalité** (lite) *f,* sentimentality.
sentinelle (sɑ̃tinɛl) *f,* sentry; guard.
sentir (sɑ̃tir) *v.t.ir,* to smell; taste; feel; smell of; taste of; smack of; be aware (*or* conscious) of; sense; appreciate. *je ne peut pas le* ~, I can't stand [the sight of] him. **se** ~, to feel; be felt, show. *se* ~ *fatigué,* to feel tired.
seoir (swar) *v.i.ir,* to suit, become (*à qn,* s.o).
séparation (separasjɔ̃) *f,* separation, parting, severance; dispersal. *mur de* ~, partition wall. **séparatisme** (ratism) *m,* separatism. **séparatiste** (tist) *a.* & *n,* separatist. **séparé**†, **e** (re) *a,* separate, distinct; apart; separated. **séparer** (re) *v.t,* to separate; part; distinguish between; split, divide. **se** ~, to part (*de,* with); divide; split off; break apart, separate; disperse; (*couple*) split up.
sept (sɛt) *a.* & *m,* seven; 7th (*date*). *for phrases V* **six.**
septembre (sɛptɑ̃br) *m,* September.
septennat (sɛptena) *m,* seven-year term [of office].
septentrional, e (sɛptɑ̃triɔnɛl) *a,* northern.
septicémie (sɛptisemi) *f,* septicaemia; blood poisoning.
septième† (sɛtjɛm) *a.* & *n,* seventh. *le* ~ *art,* the cinema. *for other phrases V* **sixième.**
septique (sɛptik) *a,* septic.
septuagénaire (sɛptɥaʒenɛr) *a.* & *n,* septuagenarian.
sépulcral, e (sepylkral) *a,* sepulchral. **sépulcre** (kr) *m,* sepulchre. **sépulture** (tyr) *f,* burial; burial place.
séquelles (sekɛl) *f.pl,* after-effects; aftermath.
séquence (sekɑ̃s) *f,* sequence.
séquestration (sekɛstrasjɔ̃) *f,* illegal confinement. **séquestre** (str) *m,* sequestration. **séquestrer** (stre) *v.t,* to confine illegally.
sérail (seraj) *m,* seraglio.

séraphin (serafɛ̃) *m*, seraph.
serein, e† (sərɛ̃, ɛn) *a*, serene, calm; dispassionate; clear (*sky*).
sérénade (serenad) *f*, serenade; (*P*) din, racket *P*.
sérénité (serenite) *f*, serenity; calmness &c *as* **serein.**
serf, serve (sɛrf, sɛrv) *n*, serf.
serge (sɛrʒ) *f*, serge.
sergent (sɛrʒɑ̃) *m*, sergeant. ~ *de ville*, policeman. ~ *instructeur*, drill sergeant.
sériciculture (serisikyltyr) *f*, silkworm breeding.
série (seri) *f*, series; range; set; chapter (*accidents*); (*Naut.*) class; (*Sport*) rank; qualifying round (*or* heat). *article de* ~, standard article. *en* ~ mass (*production*).
sérieux, euse† (serjø, øz) *a*, serious; earnest; reliable, dependable; serious-minded; genuine; strong, good (*reasons &c*); considerable (*difference*). ¶ *m*, seriousness; earnestness; serious-mindedness; dependability.
serin, e (s[ə]rɛ̃, in) *n*, canary. **seriner** (rine) *v.t*, ~ *qch à qn*, to din *or* drum sth into s.o.
seringue (s[ə]rɛ̃g) *f*, syringe.
serment (sɛrmɑ̃) *m*, oath, pledge.
sermon (sɛrmɔ̃) *m*, sermon. **sermonner** (mɔne) *v.t*, to lecture.
serpe (sɛrp) *f*, bill hook.
serpent (sɛrpɑ̃) *m*, serpent, snake. ~ *à sonnettes*, rattlesnake. **serpenter** (te) *v.i*, to wind, meander. **serpentin** (tɛ̃) *m*, coil; [paper] streamer.
serpillière (sɛrpijɛr) *f*, floorcloth.
serpolet (sɛrpɔlɛ) *m*, wild thyme.
serrage (sɛraʒ) *m*, tightening, clamping.
serre (sɛr) *f*, greenhouse, glasshouse, conservatory; claw, talon. ~ *chaude*, hothouse.
serré, e (sɛre) *a*, tight, close, serried; clenched (*fist*); tightly packed; closely woven; dense. **serrement** (rmɑ̃) *m*, pressure; squeeze, shake (*hand*). ~ *de cœur*, pang. **serrer** (re) *v.t*, to press, squeeze; clasp, hug, wring, grip; clench; shake (*hand*); tighten; put on (*brake*); keep close to; close up; (*O*) put away. ~ *à droite*, (*Mot.*) to move in to the right. **se** ~, to squeeze up; huddle, cuddle up (*contre*, to, against). **serrure** (ryr) *f*, lock. **serrurerie** (ryrri) *f*, locksmith's trade. **serrurier** (rje) *m*, locksmith.
sertir (sɛrtir) *v.t*, to set (*gem*).
sérum (serɔm) *m*, serum.
servant (sɛrvɑ̃) *m*, server. **servante** (vɑ̃t) *f*, [maid]servant. **serviable** (vjabl) *a*, obliging. **service** (vis) *m*, duty; service (*all senses*); department, section; set (*plates &c*). *rendre* ~, to be helpful. *rendre un* ~ *à qn*, to do s.o a good turn. ~ *après-vente*, after sales service. ~ *compris*, service included. ~ *des urgences*, casualty department. ~ *d'ordre*, police patrol; team of stewards (*crowd control &c*). ~*s secrets*, secret service. **serviette** (vjɛt) *f*, briefcase. ~ [*de table*], [table] napkin, serviette. ~ [*de toilette*], towel. ~*-éponge*, towel. ~ *périodique*, sanitary towel.
servile† (sɛrvil) *a*, servile, menial; slavish. **servilité** (lite) *f*, servility; slavishness.
servir (sɛrvir) *v.t.ir*, to serve; be of use; wait (on); attend to; serve up; (*Cards*) deal. ~ **à,** (*pers.*) to be of use to, be useful to. ~ **à faire,** to be used for doing. ~ **de qch,** to be used as, serve as sth. ~ *de leçon à qn*, to be a lesson to s.o. ~ *des intérêts à qn*, to pay s.o interest. *à quoi ça sert?* what's that [used] for? *ça ne sert à rien*, it's no use. **se** ~ **chez,** to shop at. **se** ~ **de,** to use. **serviteur** (vitœr) *m*, servant. **servitude** (tyd) *f*, servitude, slavery; constraint.
session (sɛsjɔ̃) *f*, session.
seuil (sœj) *m*, threshold, sill; doorstep, doorway.
seul, e (sœl) *a*, alone, by oneself, on one's own; lonely; sole, only; one, single; mere, very. ~ *& unique*, one & only. *d'un* ~ *coup*, suddenly. ¶ *ad*, on one's own; (*speak*) to o.s. ¶ *n*, *un* ~, only one. **seulement** (lmɑ̃) *ad*, only; solely, merely.
sève (sɛv) *f*, sap (*plant*).
sévère† (sevɛr) *a*, severe, stern; hard; strict. **sévérité** (verite) *f*, severity &c.
sévices (sevis) *m.pl*, maltreatment, cruelty (*in law*).
sévir (sevir) *v.i*, to deal severely (*contre*, with); rage, be rife, be rampant.
sevrage (səvraʒ) *m*, weaning. **sevrer** (vre) *v.t*, to wean; deprive.
sexe (sɛks) *m*, sex; sex organs.
sextant (sɛkstɑ̃) *m*, sextant.
sextuor (sɛkstɥɔr) *m*, sextet[te].
sexué, e (sɛksɥe) *a*, sexual. **sexuel, le**† (sɥɛl) *a*, sexual, sex (*education &c*).
shampooing (ʃɑ̃pwɛ̃) *m*, shampoo.
shoot (ʃut) *m*, (*Foot.*) shot. **shooter** (te) *v.i*, to shoot.
short (ʃɔrt) *m*, [pair of] shorts.
seyant, e (sɛjɑ̃, ɑ̃t) *a*, becoming.
si¹ (si) *c*, if; whether; what if; while. ~ *ce n'est que*, unless. ~ *tant est que*, that is if. ¶ *m*, if.
si² (si) *ad*, yes (*contradicting negative*). ¶ so, as; however. *un* ~ *bon vin*, such a good wine. *il marche* ~ *vite que...* , he walks so fast that... *il n'est pas* ~ *riche que son fils*, he's not as rich as his son. ~ *malade qu'il soit*, however ill he is. ~ *bien que*, so that.
si³ (si) *m*, (*Mus.*) **B**; ti.
siamois, e (sjamwa, az) *a*, Siamese. ¶ *n.pl*, Siamese twins. ¶ *m*, Siamese [cat].
Sicile (la) (sisil), Sicily. **sicilien, ne** (ljɛ̃, ɛn) *a*. & **S**~, *n*, Sicilian.
SIDA, Sida (sida) *m*, (*Med.*: *syndrome immunodéficitaire acquis*) AIDS, Aids.
sidérer *P* (sidere) *v.t*, to stagger, shatter *P*.

sidéral, e (sideral) *a,* sidereal.
sidérurgie (sideryrʒi) *f,* iron & steel metallurgy *or* industry.
siècle (sjɛkl) *m,* century; age. *de ~ en ~,* through the ages. *le S~ des lumières,* the Enlightenment.
siège (sjɛʒ) *m,* seat; bench; headquarters; head office; (*Eccl.*) see; centre (*nerves &c*); siege. *~ éjectorable,* ejector seat. *~ social,* registered office. **siéger** (eʒe) *v.i,* to have its headquarters; sit; be seated.
sien, ne (*with* **le, la, les**) (sjɛ̃, ɛn) *pn.* his, hers; one's own, his own, her own. ¶ *m, y mettre du ~,* to pull one's weight. *les ~ s,* one's family.
sieste (sjɛst) *f,* siesta, nap.
siffler (sifle) *v.i,* to whistle; blow one's (*or* a) whistle; hiss; wheeze. ¶ *v.t,* to whistle for; blow one's w. at; hiss, boo (*play &c*); (*P**) guzzle *P.* **sifflet** (flɛ) *m,* whistle; hiss, catcall. **siffleur, euse** (flœr, øz) *n,* whistler; hisser, booer.
sigle (sigl) *m,* abbreviation, acronym.
signal (siɲal) *m,* signal. *signaux [lumineux],* traffic lights. **signalé, e** (le) *a,* signal; conspicuous. **signalement** (lmɑ̃) *m,* description. **signaler** (le) *v.t,* to indicate; point out; signal; report (*fact &c*). **se ~,** to distinguish o.s, stand out. **signalisation** (lizasjɔ̃) *f,* signals; erection of [road] signs (*or* signals). *~ routière,* roadsigns.
signataire (siɲatɛr) *n,* signatory. **signature** (tyr) *f,* signing, signature. **signe** (siɲ) *m,* sign, token, mark; motion, wave (*hand*). *~ de ponctuation,* punctuation mark. *~ de ralliement,* rallying symbol. *~ de tête affirmatif* (*négatif*), nod (shake) of the head. **signer** (ɲe) *v.t,* to sign. **se ~,** to cross o.s. **signet** (ɲɛ) *m,* bookmark.
significatif, ive (siɲifikatif, iv) *a,* significant. **signification** (sjɔ̃) *f,* signification, meaning. **signifier** (fje) *v.t,* to signify, mean; notify, intimate; (*Law*) serve (*a notice*).
silence (silɑ̃s) *m,* silence, stillness, hush; pause; (*Mus.*) rest. **silencieux, euse**† (lɑ̃sjø, øz) *a,* silent, noiseless, still. ¶ *m,* silencer.
silex (silɛks) *m,* silex, flint.
silhouette (silwɛt) *f,* silhouette, outline; figure.
silicate (silikat) *m,* silicate. **silice** (lis) *f,* silica.
silicium (silisjɔm) *m,* silicon.
silicone (silikɔn) *f,* silicone.
sillage (sijaʒ) *m,* wake, trail; [vapour] t. **sillon** (jɔ̃) *m,* furrow; (*pl., Poet.*) fields; groove. **sillonner** (ɔne) *v.t,* to furrow; (*roads &c*) cut across.
silo (silo) *m,* silo.
simagrée (simagre) *f. oft. pl,* fuss.
simiesque (simjɛsk) *a,* ape-like, apish.
similaire (similɛr) *a,* similar, like. **simili-** (li) *pref,* imitation. **similitude** (tyd) *f,* similarity.
simple† (sɛ̃pl) *a,* simple; single; ordinary; straightforward; private (*soldier*); plain; mere. *~ comme bonjour,* as easy as pie. *~ d'esprit, a,* simple-minded; *n,* simpleton. ¶ *m,* (*Ten.*) singles; (*O Bot*) simple *O.* *~ dames,* ladies' singles. *passer du ~ au double,* to double. **simplet, te** (plɛ, ɛt) *a,* simple; simplistic. **simplicité** (sɛ̃plisite) *f,* simplicity &c. **simplifier** (fje) *v.t,* to simplify.
simulacre (simylakr) *m,* enactment; (*pej.*) pretence. *~ de combat,* sham fight, mock f. **simulateur, trice** (latœr, tris) *n,* shammer, pretender; malingerer. **simulation** (lasjɔ̃) *f,* simulation, feigning. **simulé, e** (le) *a,* feigned, sham. **simuler** (le) *v.t,* to simulate, feign, sham. *~ la maladie,* to malinger.
simultané†, e (simyltane) *a,* simultaneous.
sinapisme (sinapism) *m,* mustard plaster.
sincère† (sɛ̃sɛr) *a,* sincere, unfeigned, genuine. **sincérité** (serite) *f,* sincerity &c.
sinécure (sinekyr) *f,* sinecure.
Singapour (sɛ̃gapur) *m,* Singapore.
singe (sɛ̃ʒ) *m,* monkey, ape; copy cat. **singer** (sɛ̃ʒe) *v.t,* to ape, take off *P;* feign. **singerie** (ʒri) *f,* monkey house; grimace, monkey trick; grotesque imitation; (*pl.*) airs & graces.
singulariser (sɛ̃gylarize) *v.t,* to make conspicuous. **singulier, ère**† (lje, ɛr) *a,* singular; peculiar; odd, strange; remarkable. ¶ *m,* (*Gram.*) singular. **singularité** (larite) *f,* singularity &c.
sinistre† (sinistr) *a,* sinister, ominous. ¶ *m,* disaster; blaze; (*Insce.*) accident. **sinistré, e** (tre) *n,* disaster victim.
sinon (sinɔ̃) *c,* otherwise, else; except, other than; if not; or else.
sinueux, euse (sinɥø, øz) *a,* sinuous, winding. **sinuosité** (nɥozite) *f,* sinuosity, bend.
sinus (sinys) *m,* sinus; sine. **sinusite** (sit) *f,* sinusitis.
siphon (sifɔ̃) *m,* siphon; U-bend. **siphonner** (fɔne) *v.t,* to siphon.
sire (sir) *m,* sire (*to king*); lord.
sirène (sirɛn) *f,* siren, mermaid; hooter.
sirop (siro) *m,* syrup. **siroter** (rɔte) *v.t,* to sip. **sirupeux, euse** (rypø, øz) *a,* syrupy.
sis, e (si, iz) *a,* (*Adm., Law*) located.
sismique (sismik) *a,* seismic. **sismographe** (mɔgraf) *m,* seismograph.
site (sit) *m,* site. *~ pittoresque,* beauty spot.
sitôt (sito) *ad,* as soon, so soon.
situation (sitɥasjɔ̃) *f,* situation, position; job; location; (*Fin.*) statement of finances. **situé, e** (tɥe) *a,* situated. **situer** (tɥe) *v.t,* to site, situate; locate; set, place.
six (si; *in liaison,* siz; *at end of phrase,* sis) *a. & m,* six; 6th (*date*). *~-huit* (*Mus.*) *m,* six-eight [time]. *~-mâts* (*Naut.*) *m,* six-master. *~ mille,* six thousand. *~ par ~,* 6 at a time. *à ~ contre un,* 6 against one. *à ~ faces,* six-

sided. *Henri* ~, Henry the Sixth. *il a* ~ *ans,* he is 6 years old. *il est* ~ *heures,* it is 6 o'clock. *il habite au [numéro]* ~, he lives at number 6. *le* ~ *mai,* [on the] sixth of May. *tous les* ~, all 6 of them (us, you). **sixième†** (sizjɛm) *a. & n,* sixth. *dans le* ~ *[arrondissement],* in the sixth arrondissement (*of Paris*). *elle est arrivée la* ~, she was the sixth to arrive. *il habite au* ~, he lives on the sixth floor. ¶ *m,* sixth (*portion*). ¶ *f,* first year (*or* form). *entrer en* ~, to go into the first year; start at secondary school.

skaï (skɑj) *m,* leatherette.

sketch (skɛtʃ) *m,* [variety] sketch.

ski (ski) *m,* ski; skiing. *faire du* ~, to ski, go skiing. ~ *de fond,* langlauf, cross-country skiing. ~ *nautique,* water-skiing. **skier** (skje) *v.i,* to ski.

slave (slav) *a,* Slavic; Slavonic. **S~,** *n,* Slav.

slip (slip) *m,* pants, briefs. ~ *de bain,* trunks; bikini briefs.

slogan (slɔgɑ̃) *m,* slogan.

slow (slo) *m,* slow number.

smicard, e *P* (smikar, ard) *n,* minimum wage earner.

smoking (smɔkiŋ) *m,* dinner jacket.

snob (snɔb) *a,* posh *P;* snobby. ¶ *n,* snob. **snobisme** (bism) *m,* snobbery.

sobre† (sɔbr) *a,* sober, temperate, abstemious; sparing. **sobriété** (briete) *f,* sobriety &c.

sobriquet (sɔbrikɛ) *m,* nickname.

soc (sɔk) *m,* ploughshare.

sociable (sɔsjabl) *a,* sociable; hospitable. **social, e†** (sjal) *a,* social. **socialiser** (lize) *v.t,* to socialize. **socialisme** (lism) *m,* socialism. **socialiste** (list) *n. & a,* socialist. **sociétaire** (sjetɛr) *n,* member (*of a society*). **société** (te) *f,* society; club; company; firm; gathering. ~ *à responsabilité limitée,* limited liability company. ~ *anonyme,* [public] limited company. ~ *par actions,* joint stock company. **sociologie** (sjɔlɔʒi) *f,* sociology. **sociologique†** (ʒik) *a,* sociological. **sociologue** (lɔg) *n,* sociologist.

socle (sɔkl) *m,* pedestal, stand.

soquette (sɔkɛt) *f,* ankle sock.

soda (sɔda) *m,* fizzy drink.

sodium (sɔdjɔm) *m,* sodium.

sœur (sœr) *f,* sister. *& ta* ~*! P** get lost! *P**

sofa (sɔfa) *m,* sofa.

soi (swa) *m,* self; id. ¶ *pn. &* ~**-même,** oneself; himself, herself, itself. *cela va de* ~, that goes without saying, stands to reason. ~**-disant** (dizɑ̃) *a.inv,* self-styled, would-be; so-called. ¶ *ad,* supposedly.

soie (swa) *f,* silk; bristle (*hog*). **soierie** (ri) *f,* silk goods, silks; silk trade.

soif (swaf) *f,* thirst; craving, hankering. *avoir* ~, to be thirsty, to thirst.

soigné, e (swaɲe) *a,* tidy, neat, well-groomed; well-kept; careful; well-cared-for; carefully-prepared (*meal*); (*P*) massive *P.* **soigner** (ɲe) *v.t,* to take care of, look after, attend to; tend; nurse; treat. **soigneur** (ɲœr) *m,* (*Box.*) second; trainer. **soigneux, euse†** (ɲø, øz) *a,* careful; tidy, neat. **soin** (swɛ̃) *m,* care; neatness, tidiness; (*pl.*) care; attention, treatment. *aux bons* ~*s de,* care of, c/o. *avoir, prendre* ~ *de faire,* to take care to do.

soir (swar) *m,* evening, night; afternoon. **soirée** (sware) *f,* evening; [evening] party. *de* ~, evening (*dress &c*).

soit (swa) *c,* that is to say. ~ ... ~, [either] ... or, ~ *que* ... ~ *que* (+*subj.*), whether ... or ... ¶ *ad,* very well, well & good.

soixantaine (swasɑ̃tɛn) *f,* sixty [or so], around sixty, sixty odd. *il a la* ~, he is in his sixties (*or* sixtyish). **soixante** (sɑ̃t) *a. & m,* sixty. ~ *& un,* sixty-one. *les années* ~, the sixties. ~**-dix** (sɑ̃tdis) *a. & m,* seventy. ~ *& onze,* ~*-douze,* 71, 72. ~**-dixième** (zjɛm) *a. & n,* seventieth. **soixantième** (tjɛm) *a. & n,* sixtieth.

soja (sɔja) *m,* soya.

sol[1] (sɔl) *m,* ground, soil; floor. ~*-air,* ground-to-air.

sol[2] (sɔl) (*Mus.*) *m.inv,* G.

solaire (sɔlɛr) *a,* solar, sun.

soldat (sɔlda) *m,* soldier. ~ *de plomb,* tin soldier. *le S~ inconnu,* the Unknown Warrior *or* Soldier.

solde (sɔld) *f,* pay. ¶ *m,* balance; b. outstanding; settlement; [clearance] sale. *en* ~, sale price; sale (*item*). *les* ~*s,* the sales. **solder** (de) *v.t,* to balance (*a/c*); pay off, settle; sell off, clear.

sole (sɔl) *f,* sole. ~ *limande,* lemon sole.

solécisme (sɔlesism) *m,* solecism.

soleil (sɔlɛj) *m,* sun; sunshine; sunflower; catherine wheel (*firework*); grand circle (*acrobatics*); (*fig.*) somersault. ~ *couchant,* setting sun, sunset. *il fait du* ~, it's sunny.

solennel, le† (sɔlanɛl) *a,* solemn; formal; ceremonial. **solennité** (nite) *f,* solemnity; celebration.

solfège (sɔlfɛʒ) *m,* musical theory.

solidaire† (sɔlidɛr) *a,* interdependent; (*Law*) binding all parties; jointly liable. *être* ~*s,* to show solidarity, stick together. *être* ~ *de,* to be dependent on. **solidarité** (darite) *f,* solidarity; interdependence; joint liability. **solide†** (lid) *a,* solid; strong; sturdy; sound; reliable; hefty, substantial. ¶ *m,* solid. **solidifier** (difje) *v.t,* to solidify. **solidité** (te) *f,* solidity; strength; soundness.

soliloque (sɔlilɔk) *m,* soliloquy.

soliste (sɔlist) *n,* soloist.

solitaire† (sɔlitɛr) *a,* solitary, lonely. ¶ *n,* recluse; loner, lone wolf. ¶ *m,* old boar; solitaire (*gem & game*). **solitude** (tyd) *f,* solitude, loneliness.

solive (sɔliv) *f,* joist.

solliciter (sɔllisite) *v.t,* to solicit, ask for, apply

for; seek; appeal to; attract (*attention*). **sollicitation** (tasjɔ̃) *f*, entreaty, appeal; solicitation. **solliciteur, euse** (tœr, øz) *n*, supplicant. **sollicitude** (tyd) *f*, solicitude; anxiety.
solo (sɔlo) *m*, (*Mus.*) solo.
solstice (sɔlstis) *m*, solstice.
soluble (sɔlybl) *a*, soluble; solvable. **solution** (sjɔ̃) *f*, solution.
solvabilité (sɔlvabilite) *f*, (*Fin.*) solvency. **solvable** (bl) *a*, solvent.
sombre† (sɔ̃br) *a*, dark, sombre, gloomy; dim.
sombrer (sɔ̃bre) *v.i*, to founder, sink, go down.
sommaire† (sɔmɛr) *a*, summary, brief; basic; scanty, cursory. ¶ *m*, summary, synopsis.
sommation (sɔmasjɔ̃) *f*, summons; demand; (*Mil.*) warning.
somme[1] (sɔm) *f*, sum, amount. ~ *toute, en* ~, all in all, when all is said & done. *faire la* ~ *de*, to add up.
somme[2] (sɔm) *m*, nap, snooze. **sommeil** (mɛj) *m*, sleep, slumber; sleepiness. *avoir* ~, to feel sleepy. *laisser en* ~, to leave in abeyance. **sommeiller** (mɛje) *v.i*, to doze; lie dormant.
sommelier (sɔməlje) *m*, wine waiter.
sommer (sɔme) *v.t*, to summon, call on.
sommet (sɔmɛ) *m*, summit, top; vertex; crown (*head*); crest (*wave*).
sommier (sɔmje) *m*, bedsprings; divan base.
sommité (sɔmmite) *f*, leading light.
somnambule (sɔmnɑ̃byl) *n*, somnambulist, sleep walker. **somnambulisme** (lism) *m*, somnambulism.
somnifère (sɔmnifɛr) *m*, soporific, sleeping drug; s. pill. ¶ *a*, soporific.
somnolent, e (sɔmnɔlɑ̃, ɑ̃t) *a*, somnolent, sleepy, drowsy. **somnoler** (le) *v.i*, to doze; lie dormant.
somptueux, euse† (sɔ̃ptɥø, øz) *a*, sumptuous, magnificent; lavish. **somptuosité** (tɥozite) *f*, sumptuousness &c.
son, sa, ses (sɔ̃, sa, se) *a*, his, her, its, one's.
son[1] (sɔ̃) *m*, sound; ringing. **son**[2] (sɔ̃) *m*, bran.
sonate (sɔnat) *f*, sonata.
sondage (sɔ̃daʒ) *m*, probing, sounding; boring, drilling; catheterization. ~ [*d'opinion*], [opinion] poll. **sonde** (sɔ̃d) *f*, probe; sonde; (*Naut.*) sounding line; borer, drill; feeding tube; catheter. **sonder** (sɔ̃de) *v.t*, to sound; probe &c.
songe (sɔ̃ʒ) *m*, dream. **songer** (sɔ̃ʒe) *v.i*, to dream; reflect, consider; imagine. ~ *à*, to think over, reflect on; think of, contemplate. **songerie** (ʒri) *f*, reverie. **songeur, euse** (ʒœr, øz) *a*, dreamy; pensive. ¶ *n*, dreamer.
sonnant, e (sɔnɑ̃, ɑ̃t) *a*, *à 6 heures* ~*es*, on the stroke of 6. **sonné, e** (ne) *a*, past, struck (*hour*); turned (*a certain age*); (*P*) groggy; (*P*) cracked *P*. **sonner** (ne) *v.i. & t*, to sound; ring; r. for; toll; strike; (*P*) take aback; knock out. ~ *à toute volée*, to peal out. ~ *de*, to sound (*horn &c*). **sonnerie** (nri) *f*, ringing; sound; chimes; bell; call (*trumpet, bugle*). **sonnet** (nɛ) *m*, sonnet. **sonnette** (nɛt) *f*, bell. ~ *d'alarme*, alarm bell. ~ *de nuit*, night-bell. **sonneur** (nœr) *m*, bell ringer. **sonore** (nɔr) *a*, sonorous; resonant, ringing; echoing; voiced (*consonant*); sound (*vibrations*). **sonorisation** (rizasjɔ̃) *f*, public address system. **sonorité** (rite) *f*, (*Mus.*) tone; acoustics; resonance.
sophistiqué, e (sɔfistike) *a*, sophisticated.
soporifique (sɔpɔrifik) *a. & m*, soporific.
soprano (sɔprano) *m*, soprano.
sorbet (sɔrbɛ) *m*, water ice, sorbet. **sorbetière** (btjɛr) *f*, ice cream maker (*churn*).
sorcellerie (sɔrsɛlri) *f*, sorcery, witchcraft. **sorcier, ère** (sje, ɛr) *n*, sorcerer, ess, wizard, witch; hag.
sordide† (sɔrdid) *a*, sordid; squalid.
Sorlingues (îles) (sɔrlɛ̃g) *f.pl*, Scilly Isles.
sornettes *O* (sɔrnɛt) *f.pl*, nonsense, balderdash.
sort (sɔr) *m*, lot, fate; spell. *le* ~ *est tombé sur lui*, it fell to his lot. *tirer au* ~, to draw lots. **sortable** *P* (tabl) *a*, presentable (*pers.*).
sorte (sɔrt) *f*, sort, kind. *de la* ~, in that way. *de* ~ *à*, so as to, in order to. *de* ~ *que*, in such a way that, so that. *en quelque* ~, in a way, as it were.
sortie (sɔrti) *f*, leaving; exit; way out; (*Mil.*) sortie; outing; evening out; outburst; sally; odd remark; (*Com: car &c*) launching; (*record*) release; (*book*) appearance; export; (*Fin.*) outlay; (*pl.*) outgoings. ~ *de bain*, bathrobe.
sortilège (sɔrtilɛʒ) *m*, witchcraft, spell.
sortir (sɔrtir) *v.i.ir*, to go out; come out; leave; emerge, issue, spring; stand out; stick out. ~ *de* to overstep (*limits &c*); come from (*place &c*). ¶ *v.t.ir*, to take out; bring out, pull out; release (*film*); lower (*undercarriage*).
sosie (sɔzi) *m*, double (*pers.*).
sot, te† (so, ɔt) *a*, silly, foolish, stupid. ¶ *n*, fool. **sottise** (sɔtiz) *f*, silliness, foolishness, stupidity; silly remark (*or* action).
sou (su) *m*, sou; (*fig.*) penny.
soubassement (subɑsmɑ̃) *m*, base.
soubresaut (subrəso) *m*, start (*nervous*); jolt.
souche (suʃ) *f*, stump, stock, stub; founder (*family*); counterfoil; (*Linguistics*) root; colony, clone (*microbes*).
souci (susi) *m*, worry, care; concern; marigold. *se faire du* ~, to worry. ~ *d'eau*, marsh marigold. **se soucier de** (sje), to care about, be concerned for. **soucieux, euse** (sjø, øz) *a*, anxious, concerned, worried.
soucoupe (sukup) *f*, saucer.
soudain, e† (sudɛ̃, ɛn) *a*, sudden. **soudain,** *ad*, suddenly. **soudaineté** (dɛnte) *f*, suddenness.
soude (sud) *f*, soda.
souder (sude) *v.t*, to solder; weld; bind together; fuse.

soudoyer (sudwaje) *v.t,* to bribe.
soudure (sudyr) *f,* soldering; solder; welding; joint; weld.
souffle (sufl) *m,* breath; puff, blow; breathing; blast; inspiration. ~ *au cœur,* heart murmur. *à bout de* ~, out of breath. **souffler** (fle) *v.i,* to blow; puff; get one's breath back. ¶ *v.t,* to blow out; (*bomb &c*) blast, shatter; whisper; (*Theat.*) prompt; breathe; (*P*) flabbergast *P;* (*P*) pinch *P.* **soufflé** (fle) *m,* soufflé. **soufflerie** (fləri) *f,* bellows (*organ &c*); wind tunnel; ventilating fan; blowing engine. **soufflet** (flɛ) *m,* bellows; (*Rly.*) vestibule; gusset; (*O*) slap. **souffleur, euse** (flœr, øz) *n,* blower; prompter.
souffrance (sufrɑ̃s) *f,* suffering. *en* ~, awaiting delivery, held up; pending. **souffrant, e** (frɑ̃, ɑ̃t) *a,* suffering; ailing, unwell. **souffre-douleur** (frədulœr) *m,* scapegoat, whipping boy. **souffreteux, euse** (tø, øz) *a,* sickly. **souffrir** (frir) *v.t. & i.ir,* to suffer; bear; endure, stand; undergo; (*liter.*) allow.
soufre (sufr) *m,* sulphur, brimstone.
souhait (swɛ) *m,* wish. ~*s de bonne année,* new-year's wishes. *à tes* ~*s!* bless you! (*after sneeze*). *à* ~, to perfection. **souhaitable** (tabl) *a,* desirable. **souhaiter** (te) *v.t,* to wish; w. for; hope. ~ *la bonne année à qn,* to wish s.o a happy New Year.
souiller (suje) *v.t,* to soil, dirty; stain, sully. **souillon** (jɔ̃) *f,* slut, slattern. **souillure** (jyr) *f,* spot, stain.
soûl, e (su, ul) *a,* drunk. ¶ *m, manger tout son* ~, to eat one's fill.
soulagement (sulaʒmɑ̃) *m,* relief. **soulager** (ʒe) *v.t,* to relieve, ease, alleviate; comfort.
soûlard, e *P* (sular, ard) *n,* drunkard. **soûler** (le) *v.t,* to make drunk, intoxicate. **se** ~, to get drunk. **soûlerie** (lri) *f,* drunken bout.
soulèvement (sulɛvmɑ̃) *m,* rising; heaving; (*Geol.*) upheaval; revolt. **soulever** (lve) *v.t,* to raise, lift; make heave; rouse. **se** ~, to rise, heave; revolt.
soulier (sulje) *m,* shoe. *être dans les petits* ~*s,* to feel awkward.
souligner (suliɲe) *v.t,* to underline; emphasize.
soumettre (sumɛtr) *v.t.ir,* to subdue; submit; subject. **se** ~, to submit. **soumis, e** (mi, iz) *a,* submissive. **soumission** (misjɔ̃) *f,* submission; tender. **soumissionner** (ɔne) *v.t,* to tender for.
soupape (supap) *f,* valve.
soupçon (supsɔ̃) *m,* suspicion; dash; touch. **soupçonner** (sɔne) *v.t,* to suspect, **soupçonneux, euse** (nø, øz) *a,* suspicious.
soupe (sup) *f,* soup. ~ *au lait,* quick tempered. ~ *populaire,* soup kitchen.
soupente (supɑ̃t) *f,* cupboard under the stairs.
souper (supe) *m,* supper. ¶ *v.i,* to have supper.
soupeser (supəze) *v.t,* to feel the weight of.
soupière (supjɛr) *f,* soup tureen.
soupir (supir) *m,* sigh; (*Mus.*) crotchet rest. **soupirail** (piraj) *m,* [small] basement window. **soupirant** (rɑ̃) *m,* suitor. **soupirer** (re) *v.i,* to sigh; yearn (*après, pour,* for).
souple (supl) *a,* supple, pliable; flexible; lithe; floppy (*disc*). **souplesse** (plɛs) *f,* suppleness &c.
source (surs) *f,* source, spring. **sourcier, ère** (sje, ɛr) *n,* water diviner, dowser.
sourcil (sursi) *m,* eyebrow. **sourciller** (je) *v.i,* to flinch; bat an eyelid *P.* **sourcilleux, euse** (jø, øz) *a,* finicky.
sourd, e (sur, urd) *a,* deaf; dull (*pain*); muted, muffled (*sound*); subdued (*anger*); hidden, secret (*intrigue*); voiceless (*consonant*). ¶ *n,* deaf person. **sourdement** (surdəmɑ̃) *ad,* dully; secretly. **sourdine** (din) *f,* (*Mus.*) mute, damper. *en* ~, quietly. **sourd-muet, sourde-muette** (surmɥɛ, dmɥɛt) *a,* deaf & dumb. ¶ *n,* deaf-mute.
sourdre (surdr) *v.i,* to spring, well up.
souriant, e (surjɑ̃, ɑ̃t) *a,* smiling; agreeable; cheerful.
souricière (surisiɛr) *f,* mouse trap; trap (*police, &c*).
sourire (surir) *m,* smile. ¶ *v.i.ir,* to smile. ~ *à,* (*idea*) to be attractive to, please.
souris (suri) *f,* mouse; (*P woman*) bird *P.*
sournois, e† (surnwa, az) *a,* sly, underhand.
sous (su; *in liaison,* suz) *pr,* under[neath], beneath, below. ~ *huitaine,* within a (*or* the) week. ~ *peu,* shortly. ~ *terre,* underground. ~ *vide,* vacuum-packed. **sous,** *comps:* ~-*agence, f,* sub-branch. ~-*alimenté, e, a,* undernourished, underfed. ~-*art,* pseudo-art. ~-*bois, m,* undergrowth. ~-*cutané, e, a,* subcutaneous. ~-*développement, m,* underdevelopment. ~-*entendre, v.t,* to imply. ~-*entendu, e, a,* implied, understood; *m,* innuendo, insinuation. *sous-estimer, v.t,* to under-estimate, undervalue, underrate. ~-*fifre, m, P,* underling. ~-*gouverneur, m,* deputy governor. ~-*jacent, e* (suʒasɑ̃, ɑ̃t) *a,* underlying. ~-*lieutenant, m,* sublieutenant, second l. ~-*louer, v.t,* to sublet. ~-*main, m,* blotting pad. *en* ~-*main,* secretly. ~-*marin, e, a. & m,* submarine. ~-*officier, m,* non-commissioned officer. ~-*secrétaire, m,* under secretary. ~-*sol, m,* subsoil; basement. ~-*tendre, v.t,* to subtend; underlie. ~-*titre, m,* subtitle, caption. ~-*vêtement, m,* undergarment; (*pl.*) underwear.
souscripteur, trice (suskriptœr, tris) *n,* subscriber. **souscription** (sjɔ̃) *f,* subscription. **souscrire** (skrir) *v.t,* to sign. ~ *à,* to subscribe to.
soussigné, e (susiɲe) *a. & n,* undersigned.
soustraction (sustraksjɔ̃) *f,* abstraction; subtraction. **soustraire** (strɛr) *v.t.ir,* to remove, abstract; (*Arith.*) subtract; shield, conceal. **se** ~ **à,** to elude, avoid. *se* ~ *à la justice,* to

abscond.
soutane (sutan) *f,* cassock; cloth (*clergy*).
soute (sut) *f,* hold (*ship*); tank; bunker.
soutenable (sutnabl) *a,* tenable, defensible. **soutenir** (tnir) *v.t.ir,* to sustain, support, hold up; uphold; keep, maintain; back [up]; stand, bear; afford. **soutenu, e** (tny) *a,* sustained; unremitting; lofty (*style*).
souterrain, e (sutɛrɛ̃, ɛn) *a,* underground, subterranean. ¶ *m,* tunnel; cavern.
soutien (sutjɛ̃) *m,* support. *~-gorge, m,* bra.
soutirer (sutire) *v.t,* to extract, squeeze out; decant (*wine*).
souvenir (suvnir) *m,* memory; remembrance, recollection; keepsake, memento; souvenir. **se ~,** *v.pr.ir,* to remember, recollect (*de qn, de qch,* s.o, sth; *que,* that).
souvent (suvɑ̃) *ad,* often.
souverain, e† (suvrɛ̃, ɛn) *a,* sovereign; supreme, superlative. ¶ *n,* sovereign. **souveraineté** (vrɛnte) *f,* sovereignty.
soviet (sɔvjɛt) *m,* soviet. **soviétique** (etik) *a,* Soviet. **S~,** *n,* Soviet citizen.
soyeux, euse (swajø, øz) *a,* silky.
spacieux, euse† (spasjø, øz) *a,* spacious, roomy, capacious.
sparadrap (sparadra) *m,* sticking plaster.
spartiate (sparsjat) *a. & n,* Spartan.
spasme (spasm) *m,* spasm. **spasmodique** (mɔdik) *a,* (*Med.*) spasmodic.
spatial, e (spasjal) *a,* spatial; space.
spatule (spatyl) *f,* spatula.
speaker (spikœr) *m,* (*Radio*) announcer. **speakerine** (krin) *f,* [female] announcer.
spécial, e† (spesjal) *a,* special; peculiar. **se spécialiser dans** (lize), to specialize in. **spécialiste** (list) *n,* specialist. **spécialité** (te) *f,* speciality; (*Univ.*) special field.
spécieux, euse† (spesjø, øz) *a,* specious.
spécification (spesifikasjɔ̃) *f,* specification. **spécifier** (fje) *v.t,* to specify. **spécifique†** (fik) *a, & m,* specific.
spécimen (spesimɛn) *m,* specimen; sample copy (*book*).
spectacle (spɛktakl) *m,* spectacle, sight; entertainment, show. *le ~,* show business. **spectaculaire** (kylɛr) *a,* spectacular, dramatic. **spectateur, trice** (tœr, tris) *n,* spectator, onlooker; (*m.pl.*) audience.
spectral, e (spɛktral) *a,* spectral. **spectre** (tr) *m,* spectre; spectrum.
spéculateur, trice (spekylatœr, tris) *n,* speculator. **spéculatif, ive** (tif, iv) *a,* speculative. **spéculation** (sjɔ̃) *f,* speculation. **spéculer** (le) *v.i,* to speculate. *~ sur,* (*fig.*) to bank on, rely on.
spéléologie (speleɔlɔʒi) *f,* speleology, potholing.
sperme (spɛrm) *m,* sperm, semen.
sphère (sfɛr) *f,* sphere, orb, globe. **sphérique** (sferik) *a,* spherical.
sphincter (sfɛ̃ktɛr) *m,* sphincter.
sphinx (sfɛ̃ks) *m,* sphinx.
spiral, e (spiral) *a,* spiral. ¶ *m,* hair spring. ¶ *f.* spiral.
spirite (spirit) *n,* (*Psychics*) spiritualist. **spiritisme** (tism) *m,* spiritualism. **spiritualisme** (tɥalism) *m,* (*Philos.*) spiritualism. **spiritualiste** (list) *n,* spiritualist. **spirituel, le†** (tɥɛl) *a,* spiritual; sacred (*concert*); witty. **spiritueux** (tɥø) *m.pl,* spirits.
splendeur (splɑ̃dœr) *f,* splendour. **splendide†** (did) *a,* splendid, gorgeous.
spolier (spɔlje) *v.t,* to despoil.
spongieux, euse (spɔ̃ʒjø, øz) *a,* spongy.
spontané†, e (spɔ̃tane) *a,* spontaneous. **spontanéité** (neite) *f,* spontaneity.
sporadique† (spɔradik) *a,* sporadic.
sport (spɔr) *m,* sport, sports. ¶ *a. inv,* casual (*clothes*). **sportif, ive** (spɔrtif, iv) *a,* fond of sport[s]; sporting; sports; athletic (*meeting*); competitive (*fishing*). *un ~,* a sportsman.
spot (spɔt) *m,* spotlight; (*Phys.*) lightspot.
square (skwar) *m,* public garden.
squelette (skəlɛt) *m,* skeleton.
stabilisateur, trice (stabilizatœr, tris) *a,* stabilizing. ¶ *m,* stabilizer. **stabiliser** (ze) *v.t,* to stabilize. **stabilité** (lite) *f,* stability. **stable** (bl) *a,* stable; steady.
stade (stad) *m,* stadium; (*Med.*) stage.
stage (staʒ) *m,* training period; t. course. **stagiaire** (staʒjɛr) *n,* trainee.
stagnant, e (stagnɑ̃, ɑ̃t) *a,* stagnant. **stagnation** (nasjɔ̃) *f,* stagnation. **stagner** (ne) *v.i,* to stagnate.
stalactite (stalaktit) *f,* stalactite.
stalagmite (stalagmit) *f,* stalagmite.
stalle (stal) *f,* stall; box (*horse*).
stand (stɑ̃d) *m,* stand (*exhibition*); stall (*fair*); shooting gallery, rifle range.
standard (stɑ̃dar) *m,* switchboard. *~ de vie,* standard of living. ¶ *a,* standard. **standardisation** (disasjɔ̃) *f,* standardization. **standardiser** (dize) *v.t,* to standardize. **standardiste** (dist) *n,* switchboard operator.
standing (stɑ̃diŋ) *m,* standing. *grand ~,* luxury.
starter (startɛr) *m,* (*Mot.*) choke.
station (stasjɔ̃) *f,* station; halt; stop (*bus*); rank (*cab*); resort; posture, stance. *~ balnéaire,* seaside resort. *~ de taxis,* taxi rank. *~-service,* petrol station. *~ thermale,* thermal spa. **stationnaire** (ɔnɛr) *a,* stationary. **stationnement** (nmɑ̃) *m,* parking. *~ interdit,* no parking. **stationner** (ne) *v.i,* to park.
statique (statik) *a,* static.
statisticien, ne (statistisjɛ̃, ɛn) *n,* statistician. **statistique†** (tik) *a,* statistical. ¶ *f,* statistics.
statue (staty) *f,* statue.
statuer (statɥe) *v.t,* to ordain. *~ sur,* to decide, resolve on.
statuette (statɥɛt) *f,* statuette.

statu quo (statykwo) *m*, status quo.
stature (statyr) *f*, stature.
statut (staty) *m*, statute; status. **statutaire** (tɛr) *a*, statutory.
stencil (stɛnsil) *m*, stencil.
sténodactylo (stenɔdaktilɔ) *n*, shorthand-typist. **sténographie** (fi) *f*, shorthand, stenography. **sténographier** (fje) *v.t*, to take down [in shorthand].
stéréo (stereo) *a*. & *f*, stereo. ~**phonie** (fɔni) *f*, stereophony. ~**phonique** (nik) *a*, stereophonic.
stéréotype (stereɔtip) *m*, stereotype. **stéréotyper** (pe) *v.t*, to stereotype.
stérile (steril) *a*, sterile, barren; fruitless. **stérilet** (lɛ) *m*, (*Med.*) coil, loop. **stérilisateur** (lizatœr) *m*, sterilizer. **stérilisation** (zasjɔ̃) *f*, sterilization. **stériliser** (lize) *v.t*, to sterilize. **stérilité** (te) *f*, sterility &c.
sternum (stɛrnɔm) *m*, sternum, breast bone.
stéthoscope (stetɔskɔp) *m*, stethoscope.
stigmate (stigmat) *m*, stigma, brand; (*Rel. pl.*) stigmata. **stigmatiser** (tize) *v.t*, to stigmatize, condemn.
stimulant, e (stimylɑ̃, ɑ̃t) *a*, stimulating. ¶ *m*, stimulant; stimulus, incentive, spur. **stimuler** (le) *v.t*, to stimulate.
stipuler (stipyle) *v.t*, to stipulate.
stock (stɔk) *m*, stock. **stockage** (kaʒ) *m*, stocking. **stocker** (ke) *v.t*, to stock, stockpile.
stoïque† (stɔik) *a*, stoical.
stomacal, e (stɔmakal) *a*, stomach; gastric.
stop (stɔp) *i*, stop. ¶ *m*, stop sign; brake light. *faire du* ~ *P*, to hitch-hike. **stoppage** (stɔpaʒ) *m*, invisible mending. **stopper** (pe) *v.t*. & *i*, to stop; stop from running (*stocking &c*). *faire* ~, to get [invisibly] mended.
store (stɔr) *m*, blind, shade; awning; net curtain. ~ *vénitien*, Venetian blind.
strabisme (strabism) *m*, squint.
strangulation (strɑ̃gylasjɔ̃) *f*, strangulation.
strapontin (strapɔ̃tɛ̃) *m*, tip-up seat.
stratagème (strataʒɛm) *m*, stratagem.
strate (strat) *f*, stratum.
stratège (tɛʒ) *m*, strategist. **stratégie** (teʒi) *f*, strategy. **stratégique** (ʒik) *a*, strategic(al).
stratification (stratifikasjɔ̃) *f*, stratification. **stratifier** (fje) *v.t*, to stratify.
strict, e† (strikt) *a*, strict; plain; literal; basic.
strident, e (stridɑ̃, ɑ̃t) *a*, strident, shrill.
strie (stri) *f*, stria; ridge; streak. **strier** (je) *v.t*, to striate; ridge; streak.
strophe (strɔf) *f*, stanza, verse.
structure (stryktyr) *f*, structure. **structural, e**† (tyral) & **structurel, le** (rɛl) *a*, structural.
stuc (styk) *m*, stucco.
studieux, euse† (stydjø, øz) *a*, studious.
stupéfaction (stypefaksjɔ̃) *f*, stupefaction, amazement. **stupéfaire** (fɛr) *v.t*, to astound, stun. **stupéfiant** (stypefjɑ̃) *m*, narcotic, drug. **stupéfier** (fje) *v.t*, to stupefy; amaze. **stupeur** (pœr) *f*, stupor; amazement. **stupide**† (pid) *a*, stupid; stunned. **stupidité** (dite) *f*, stupidity; stupid remark (*or* action).
style (stil) *m*, style; stylus. **styler** (le) *v.t*, to train. **styliser** (lize) *v.t*, to stylize.
stylo (stilo) *m*, pen. ~ [-*bille*], ball-point [pen]. ~ [*à encre*], fountain pen.
su (sy) *m*: *au* ~ *de*, to the knowledge of.
suaire (sɥɛr) *m*, shroud, winding sheet.
suant, e (sɥɑ̃, ɑ̃t) *a*, sweating; sweaty; (*P*) deadly [dull] *P*.
suave† (sɥav) *a*, suave, smooth; sweet (*music &c*). **suavité** (avite) *f*, suavity &c.
subalterne (sybaltɛrn) *a*, subordinate, subsidiary; junior. ¶ *n*, subordinate, inferior.
subconscient, e (sybkɔ̃sjɑ̃, ɑ̃t) *a*. & *m*, subconscious.
subdiviser (sybdivize) *v.t*, to subdivide.
subir (sybir) *v.t*, to undergo, submit to, suffer; endure; be subjected to.
subit, e† (sybi, it) *a*, sudden. **subito** (to) *ad*, all of a sudden.
subjectif, ive† (sybʒɛktif, iv) *a*, subjective.
subjonctif (sybʒɔ̃ktif) *m*, subjunctive [mood].
subjuguer (sybʒyge) *v.t*, to subjugate, subdue; enthrall, captivate.
sublime† (syblim) *a*, sublime. **sublimer** (me) *v.t*, to sublimate.
submerger (sybmɛrʒe) *v.t*, to submerge, flood; overwhelm, engulf. **submersion** (sjɔ̃) *f*, submersion; flooding.
subordonné, e (sybɔrdɔne) *a*. & *n*, subordinate. **subordonner** (ne) *v.t*, to subordinate.
suborner (sybɔrne) *v.t*, to bribe; seduce.
subreptice† (sybrɛptis) *a*, surreptitious.
subside (sypsid) *m*, grant; (*pl.*) allowance.
subsidiaire† (sypsidjɛr) *a*, subsidiary.
subsistance (sypsistɑ̃s) *f*, subsistence. **subsister** (te) *v.i*, to subsist.
substance (sybstɑ̃s) *f*, substance. ~ *alimentaire*, food. **substantiel, le**† (stɑ̃sjɛl) *a*, substantial. **substantif** (tif) *m*, substantive, noun.
substituer (sybstitɥe) *v.t*, to substitute. **substitut** (ty) *m*, substitute; deputy public prosecutor.
subterfuge (syptɛrfyʒ) *m*, subterfuge.
subtil, e† (syptil) *a*, subtle; fine. **subtiliser** (lize) *v.t*, to spirit away. **subtilité** (te) *f*, subtlety.
subvenir à (sybvənir) *v.ir*, to provide for, meet, cover (*expenses*). **subvention** (vɑ̃sjɔ̃) *f*, subsidy, grant. ~**ner** (ɔne) *v.t*, to subsidize; grant funds to.
subversif, ive (sybvɛrsif, iv) *a*, subversive. **subversion** (sjɔ̃) *f*, subversion.
suc (syk) *m*, juice.
succédané (syksedane) *m*, substitute (*product*). **succéder à** (de), to succeed; s. to; follow; inherit. **succès** (sɛ) *m*, success; hit; bestseller. *à* ~, successful. **successeur** (sɛsœr) *m*, successor. **successif, ive**† (sif, iv) *a*, successive.

succession (sjɔ̃) *f,* succession; inheritance, estate.
succinct, e† (syksɛ̃, ɛ̃kt) *a,* succinct; meagre.
succion (syksjɔ̃) *f,* suction. *de ~,* sucking (*noise*).
succomber (sykɔ̃be) *v.i,* to succumb; die.
succulent, e (sykylɑ̃, ɑ̃t) *a,* succulent, juicy.
succursale (sykyrsal) *f,* branch.
sucer (syse) *v.t,* to suck. **sucette** (sɛt) *f,* lollypop; dummy.
sucre (sykr) *m,* sugar; lump of s. *~ cristalisé,* preserving s. *~ de canne,* cane s. *~ d'orge,* barley s. *~ en morceaux,* lump s. *~ en poudre,* castor s. *~ semoule,* granulated s. **sucré, e** (kre) *a,* sweet, sweetened; sugary. **sucrer** (kre) *v.t,* to sugar, sweeten; (*P*) stop. **se ~,** to help o.s to sugar; (*P*) line one's pockets. **sucrerie** (krəri) *f,* sugar refinery; (*pl.*) sweets, sweet things. *aimer les ~s,* to have a sweet tooth. **sucrier, ère** (krie, ɛr) *a,* sugar; s. producing. ¶ *m,* sugar basin; sugar producer. *~* [*verseur*], sugar shaker.
sud (syd) *a. inv,* south[ern]; southerly; southward. ¶ *m,* south. *au ~ de,* to the south of. *~-africain, e,* South African. *~-américain, e,* South American. **~-est** (sydɛst) *m,* south east. **~-ouest** (sydwɛst) *m,* south west.
Suède (la) (sɥɛd), Sweden. **s~,** *m,* suede. **suédine** (sɥedin) *f,* suedette. **suédois, e** (edwa, az) *a. &* (*language*) *m,* Swedish. **S~,** *n,* Swede (*pers.*).
suée (sɥe) *f,* sweat (*state*). **suer** (e) *v.i. & t,* to sweat, perspire; ooze, exude. *~ à grosses gouttes,* to sweat profusely. **sueur** (œr) *f,* sweat, perspiration.
suffire (syfir) *v.i.ir,* to suffice, be enough, do. *~ à,* to be equal to, satisfy, cope with. *suffit que,* suffice it to say that. **suffisamment** (fizamɑ̃) *ad,* sufficiently, enough, adequately. **suffisance** (zɑ̃s) *f,* (*liter.*) sufficiency; self-importance, bumptiousness. **suffisant, e** (zɑ̃, ɑ̃t) *a,* sufficient &c.
suffixe (syfiks) *m,* suffix. ¶ *a,* suffixed.
suffocation (syfɔkasjɔ̃) *f,* suffocating feeling. **suffoquer** (ke) *v.t. & i,* to suffocate, stifle, choke; stagger (*amaze*).
suffrage (syfraʒ) *m,* suffrage, vote; approval.
suggérer (sygʒere) *v.t,* to suggest. **suggestion** (sygʒɛstjɔ̃) *f,* suggestion. **suggestif, ive** (tif, iv) *a,* suggestive.
suicidaire (sɥisidɛr) *a,* suicidal. **suicide** (sɥisid) *m. &* **suicidé, e** (de) (*pers.*) *n,* suicide. **suicider (se)** (de) *v.pr,* to commit suicide.
suie (sɥi) *f,* soot.
suif (sɥif) *m,* tallow.
suinter (sɥɛ̃te) *v.i,* to ooze. **suintement[s]** (tmɑ̃) *m.* (*pl*), oozing.
suisse (sɥis) *a,* Swiss. ¶ *m,* Swiss (*man*); Swiss guard, beadle. **la S~,** Switzerland. **Suissesse** (sɛs) *f,* Swiss (*woman*).
suite (sɥit) *f,* continuation; following episode; follow-up, sequel; rest, remainder; retinue; suite; result; series; succession, train; coherence; (*pl.*) consequences, after-effects, repercussions. *~ & fin,* final episode. *à la ~ de,* behind; following. *de ~,* at once; running, in a row. *par ~,* consequently, therefore. *par ~ de,* as a result of. *par la ~,* afterwards. **suivant, e** (vɑ̃, ɑ̃t) *a,* next, following. ¶ *n,* next [one], following [one]. *au ~!* next please! **suivant,** *pr,* along; according to. *~ que,* according to whether. **suivi, e** (vi) *a,* consistent; steady; well-attended; (*Com.*) in general production. **suivre** (sɥivr) *v.t.ir,* to follow; attend (*class*); attend to; (*Com.*) stock. *à ~,* to be continued (*serial*). *faire ~,* to forward, readdress.
sujet, te (syʒɛ, ɛt) *a,* subject, liable, prone (*à,* to). *~ à caution,* unconfirmed; questionable. ¶ *n,* subject (*of a State*). ¶ *m,* subject, topic, matter, theme; cause, grounds. *au ~ de,* about, concerning. *brillant ~,* brilliant pupil. *mauvais ~,* bad lot; bad boy. **sujétion** (ʒesjɔ̃) *f,* subjection, constraint.
sulfate (sylfat) *m,* sulphate. **sulfite** (fit) *m,* sulphite. **sulfure** (fyr) *m,* sulphide. **sulfureux, euse** (rø, øz) *a,* sulphur[ous]. **sulfurique** (rik) *a,* sulphuric. **sulfurisé** (rize) *a,* greaseproof (*paper*).
sultan (syltɑ̃) *m,* sultan. **sultane** (tan) *f,* sultana (*pers.*).
summum (sɔmɔm) *m,* height.
super (sypɛr) *a.inv,* (*P*) great *P,* fantastic *P.* ¶ *m, ~* [*carburant*], super, four-star [petrol]. ¶ *pref:* super-. *les ~-grands,* the super-powers.
superbe† (sypɛrb) *a,* superb, magnificent.
supercherie (sypɛrʃəri) *f,* fraud, trickery.
superficie (sypɛrfisi) *f,* area. **superficiel, le**† (sjɛl) *a,* superficial, shallow, skin-deep.
superflu, e (sypɛrfly) *a,* superfluous. **superflu,** *m.* **& superfluité** (ite) *f,* superfluity, surplus.
supérieur, e (syperjœr) *a,* superior; upper; higher. *~ à,* above; greater (*or* higher) than; superior to. ¶ *n,* superior. **supérieurement** (œrmɑ̃) *ad,* superlatively, exceptionally well. **supériorité** (rjɔrite) *f,* superiority.
superlatif, ive (sypɛrlatif, iv) *a. & m,* superlative.
supermarché (sypɛrmarʃe) *m,* supermarket.
superposer (sypɛrpoze) *v.t,* to super[im]pose.
superproduction (sypɛrprɔdyksjɔ̃) *f,* spectacular.
superstitieux, euse† (sypɛrstisjø, øz) *a,* superstitious. **superstition** (sjɔ̃) *f,* superstition.
supplanter (syplɑ̃te) *v.t,* to supplant.
suppléance (sypleɑ̃s) *f,* supply post; temporary replacement. **suppléant, e** (ɑ̃, ɑ̃t) *n. & a,* supply [teacher]; deputy; locum. **suppléer** (ee) *v.t,* to supply, make up for; deputize for; stand in for; replace. *~ à,* to make up for; fill (*vacancy*). **supplément** (mɑ̃) *m,* supplement,

addition; excess, extra [charge, fare]. **supplémentaire** (tɛr) *a,* supplementary, additional, extra, further, relief (*train*).

suppliant, e (sypliɑ̃, ɑ̃t) *a,* beseeching, imploring. ¶ *n,* suppliant, supplicant. **supplication** (kasjɔ̃) *f,* supplication, entreaty. **supplice** (plis) *m,* punishment, torture, torment; execution. **supplier** (plie) *v.t,* to beseech, entreat, implore. **supplique** (plik) *f,* petition.

support (sypɔr) *m,* support, rest, stand, prop. ~ *audio-visuel,* audio-visual aid. ~ *publicitaire,* advertising medium. **~able** (pɔrtabl) *a,* bearable, endurable, tolerable. **~er** (te) *v.t,* to support; endure, bear, suffer; stand, take (*alcohol, food &c*). **~er** (tɛr) *m,* (*Sport*) supporter.

supposé, e (sypoze) *a,* supposed; estimated. **suppose que,** supposing [that]. **supposer** (ze) *v.t,* to suppose; assume, infer, take; imply. **supposition** (zisjɔ̃) *f,* supposition.

suppositoire (sypɔzitwar) *m,* suppository.

suppression (syprɛsjɔ̃) *f,* suppression; abolition; elimination, removal; cancellation; deletion; withdrawal. **supprimer** (prime) *v.t,* to suppress, do away with, cut out; abolish, eliminate, remove; cancel; delete. ~ *qch à qn,* to deprive s.o of sth. **se ~,** to take one's own life.

suppurer (sypyre) *v.i,* to suppurate.

supputer (sypyte) *v.t,* to calculate.

suprématie (sypremasi) *f,* supremacy. **suprême†** (prɛm) *a. & m,* supreme.

sur[1] (syr) *pr,* on, upon; onto; on top of; over. ~ *ce,* thereupon, whereupon. *4 ~ 5,* 4 out of 5. *une personne ~ 10,* one person in 10. *tourner ~ la droite,* to turn [to the] right. ~ *les 4 heures,* around 4 o'clock. *une chambre ~ le lac,* a room looking onto the lake. ¶ *pref:* over-.

sur[2]**, e** (syr) *a,* sour, tart.

sûr, e (syr) *a,* sure, safe, secure; reliable; settled (*weather*); trustworthy; sound (*reasoning &c*); steady. ~ *de soi,* self-assured. ~ *& certain,* absolutely certain, positive.

surabondant, e (syrabɔ̃dɑ̃, ɑ̃t) *a,* superabundant; overabundant. **surabonder** (de) *v.i,* to be superabundant &c.

suranné, e (syrane) *a,* outdated, outmoded.

surcharge (syrʃarʒ) *f,* overloading; excess (*or* extra) [load]; alteration (*M.S.*). **surcharger** (ʒe) *v.t,* to overload; correct, alter (*write over*).

surchauffer (syrʃofe) *v.t,* to overheat; superheat.

surchoix (syrʃwa) *a. inv,* top-quality.

surclasser (syrklase) *v.t,* to outclass.

surcroît (syrkrwa) *m,* increase. *par ~,* in addition, to boot.

surdité (syrdite) *f,* deafness.

sureau (syro) *m,* elder [tree].

surélever (syrelve) *v.t,* to heighten; raise.

sûrement (syrmɑ̃) *ad,* surely &c, as *sûr.*

surenchère (syrɑ̃ʃɛr) *f,* higher bid. **surenchérir sur** (ʃerir), to bid higher than, outbid.

surestimer (syrɛstime) *v.t,* to overestimate, overvalue, overrate.

sûreté (syrte) *f,* safety, security; precaution; sureness, reliability, soundness; safe place; safety device; assurance, guarantee. *la S~* [*nationale*] ≃ the C.I.D.

surexciter (syrɛksite) *v.t,* to overexcite.

surface (syrfas) *f,* surface; area. (*Foot.*) ~ *de but,* goal area. ~ *de réparation,* penalty a. ~ *des étages,* floor space (*building*).

surfaire (syrfɛr) *v.t.ir,* to overrate, overvalue.

surfin, e (syrfɛ̃, in) *a,* superfine.

surgelé, e (syrʒəle) *a,* deep-frozen.

surgir (syrʒir) *v.i,* to arise; appear suddenly. ~ *de terre,* to shoot up.

surhomme (syrɔm) *m,* superman.

surhumain, e (syrymɛ̃, ɛn) *a,* superhuman.

surimpression (syrɛ̃prɛsjɔ̃) *f,* double exposure.

surir (syrir) *v.i,* to turn sour.

sur-le-champ (syrləʃɑ̃) *ad,* at once; there & then.

surlendemain (syrlɑ̃dmɛ̃) *m, le ~,* 2 days later. *le ~ de,* 2 days after.

surmenage (syrmənaʒ) *m,* overwork. **surmener** (məne) *v.t,* to overwork.

surmonter (syrmɔ̃te) *v.t,* to surmount, overcome.

surnager (syrnaʒe) *v.i,* to float [on the surface]; survive.

surnaturel, le† (syrnatyrɛl) *a. & m,* supernatural.

surnom (syrnɔ) *m,* nickname. **surnommer** (nɔme) *v.t,* to [nick]name, call.

suroît (syrwa) *m,* sou'wester (*wind, hat*).

surpasser (syrpɑse) *v.t,* to surpass, outdo.

surpeuplement (syrpœpləmɑ̃) *m,* overpopulation.

surplis (syrpli) *m,* surplice.

surplomb (syrplɔ̃) *m,* overhang. **surplomber** (be) *v.i. & t,* to overhang.

surplus (syrply) *m,* surplus, excess; rest. *au ~,* moreover.

surprenant, e (syrprənɑ̃, ɑ̃t) *a,* surprising. **surprendre** (prɑ̃dr) *v.t.ir,* to surprise; catch [unawares]; intercept; detect, discover; overhear; catch out. **surprise** (priz) *f,* surprise. *prendre qn par ~,* to catch s.o off guard. **~-partie,** (parti) *f,* party.

surproduction (syrprɔdyksjɔ̃) *f,* overproduction.

sursaut (syrso) *m,* start, jump; burst (*energy*).

surseoir à (syrswar) (*Law*) *v.ir,* to suspend, delay, stay. ~ *l'exécution de,* to reprieve. **sursis** (si) *m,* reprieve. ~ [*d'incorporation*], (*Mil.*) deferment. *peine avec ~,* suspended sentence. **sursitaire** (sitɛr) *a,* (*Mil.*) deferred.

surtaxe (syrtaks) *f,* surcharge. **surtaxer** (kse) *v.t,* to surcharge.

surtout (syrtu) *ad,* above all, especially.

surveillance (syrvɛjɑ̃s) *f,* supervision; watch; invigilation; surveillance. **surveillant, e** (jɑ̃, ɑ̃t) *n,* supervisor, overseer; invigilator; warder (*prison*); floor-walker (*shop*). **surveiller** (je) *v.t,* to supervise, superintend, watch [over], look after; invigilate.
survenir (syrvənir) *v.i.ir,* to occur, arise; take place.
survêtement (survɛtmɑ̃) *m,* tracksuit.
survie (syrvi) *f,* survival. *la* ~, the afterlife. **survivance** (vɑ̃s) *f,* survival. **survivant, e** (vɑ̃, ɑ̃t) *n,* survivor. **survivre à** (vivr) *v.ir,* to survive, outlive. **se survivre,** to live on (*dans,* in).
survoler (syrvɔle) *v.t,* to fly over; skim through; s. over.
survolté, e (syrvɔlte) *a,* worked up; (*Elec.*) boosted.
sus (sy[s]) *ad, en* ~, in addition.
susceptibilité (sysɛptibilite) *f,* susceptibility; touchiness. **susceptible** (bl) *a,* touchy, sensitive; susceptible. ~ *de faire,* able *or* likely to do.
susciter (sysite) *v.t,* to arouse; give rise to; stir up; create.
suspect, e (syspɛkt) *a,* suspicious, suspect. **suspecter** (te) *v.t,* to suspect, question.
suspendre (syspɑ̃dr) *v.t,* to suspend, hang up; sling; adjourn, defer, postpone. **en suspens** (pɑ̃), in suspense; in abeyance; in suspension. **suspense** (pɑ̃s) *m,* suspense. **suspension** (sjɔ̃) *f,* suspension, hanging; adjournment, deferment, postponement; breaking off.
suspicion (syspisjɔ̃) *f,* suspicion.
susurrer (sysyre) *v.i. & t,* to murmur, whisper.
suture (sytyr) *f,* suture.
suzerain, e (syzrɛ̃, ɛn) *a,* paramount. ¶ *n,* suzerain. **suzeraineté** (rɛnte) *f,* suzerainty.
svelte (svɛlt) *a,* slender, slim.
sycomore (sikɔmɔr) *m,* sycamore.
syllabe (silab) *f,* syllable. **syllabique** (bik) *a,* syllabic.
syllogisme (silɔʒism) *m,* syllogism.
sylphe (silf) *m,* **sylphide** (fid) *f,* sylph.
sylviculture (silvikyltyr) *f,* forestry.
symbole (sɛ̃bɔl) *m,* symbol. **symbolique**† (lik) *a,* symbolic(al); token. **symboliser** (ze) *v.t,* to symbolize.
symétrie (simetri) *f,* symmetry. **symétrique**† (trik) *a,* symmetric(al).
sympa *P* (sɛ̃pa) *a.inv,* nice, friendly. **sympathie** (pati) *f,* sympathy, fellow feeling; liking. **sympathique** (tik) *a,* nice, friendly; likeable, pleasant; sympathetic; invisible (*ink*). **sympathisant, e** (tizɑ̃, ɑ̃t) *n,* (*Pol.*) sympathizer. **sympathiser** (tize) *v.i,* to get on [well]; make friends.
symphonie (sɛ̃fɔni) *f,* symphony.
symptôme (sɛ̃ptom) *m,* symptom.
synagogue (sinagɔg) *f,* synagogue.
synchronie (sɛ̃krɔni) *f,* synchrony. **synchronique** (nik) *a,* synchronic. **synchroniser** (nize) *v.t,* to synchronize.
syncope (sɛ̃kɔp) *f,* syncope; syncopation; fainting fit, blackout. **syncopé, e** (pe) *a,* syncopated.
syndic (sɛ̃dik) *m,* agent; (*Law*) receiver. **syndical, e** (kal) *a,* trade union. **syndicaliste** (kalist) *m,* trade unionist. **syndicat** (ka) *m,* [trade] union; union, syndicate; association. ~ *d'initiative,* tourist information office. **syndiquer** (ke) *v.i,* to unionize. **se** ~, to form a trade union; join a t.u.
syndrome (sɛ̃drom) *m,* syndrome.
synode (sinɔd) *m,* synod.
synonyme (sinɔnim) *a,* synonymous. ¶ *m,* synonym.
syntaxe (sɛ̃taks) *f,* syntax.
synthèse (sɛ̃tɛz) *f,* synthesis. **synthétique**† (tetik) *a,* synthetic. **synthétiser** (tize) *v.t,* to synthesize.
Syrie (la) (siri), Syria. **syrien, ne** (rjɛ̃, ɛn) *a. &* **S**~, *n,* Syrian.
systématique† (sistematik) *a,* systematic; (*fig.*) hidebound. **systématiser** (tize) *v.t,* to systematize. **se** ~, to become the rule. **système** (tɛm) *m,* system.

T

T, t (te) *m, letter,* T, t.
tabac (taba) *m,* tobacco; tobacconist's [shop]. ~ *à priser,* snuff. *c'est toujours le même* ~, it's always the same old thing. *passer à* ~ *P,* to beat up. ¶ *a.inv,* buff.
tabasser *P* (tabase) *v.t,* to beat up. **se** ~, to have a punch-up *P.*
tabatière (tabatjɛr) *f,* snuff box; skylight.
tabernacle (tabɛrnakl) *m,* tabernacle.
table (tabl) *f,* table (*all senses*); tableland, plateau. ~ *à dessin,* drawing board. ~ *à repasser,* ironing board. ~ *alphabétique,* alphabetical table. ~ *de conférence,* conference table. ~ *des matières,* [list of] contents

(*book*). ~ *de nuit*, bedside table. ~ *d'orientation*, viewpoint indicator. ~ *de travail*, work desk. ~ *roulante*, trolley. *à* ~*!* come & eat! **tableau** (blo) *m*, picture, painting; board; box (*fuses*); rack (*keys*); table, chart; list, register, roll; (*Theat.*) scene. ~ *d'affichage*, notice board. ~ *de bord*, dashboard, instrument panel. ~ *de chasse*, bag. ~ *des horaires*, timetable. ~ *de maître*, masterpiece. ~ *de service*, duty roster. ~ [*noir*], blackboard. **tablée** (ble) *f*, table (*of people*). **tabler sur** (ble), to count on. **tablette** (blɛt) *f*, bar (*chocolate*); slab; stick (*chewing gum*); block; shelf; flap (*desk*); tablet (*writing*). **tablier** (blie) *m*, apron, pinafore; overall, smock (*child's*); roadway (*bridge*); shutter.

tabou (tabu) *m*, taboo.

tabouret (taburɛ) *m*, stool; footstool. ~ *de piano*, music stool.

tache (taʃ) *f*, mark, spot, blotch; stain; blob, blot; blemish. ~ *d'encre*, ink stain, i. blot. ~ *de rousseur*, freckle. ~ *de sang*, bloodstain. *faire* ~ *d'huile*, to spread.

tâche (tɑʃ) *f*, task; job. *à la* ~, piece (*work*).

tacher (taʃe) *v.t*, to mark, spot &c *as* **tache.**

tâcher (tɑʃe) *v.i*, to try, endeavour (*de faire*, to do).

tacheter (taʃte) *v.t*, to spot, speckle.

tacite† (tasit) *a*, tacit.

taciturne (tasityrn) *a*, taciturn, silent.

tact (takt) *m*, tact.

tactile (taktil) *a*, tactile.

tactique (taktik) *a*, tactical. ¶ *f*, tactics.

taffetas (taftɑ) *m*, taffeta.

taie (tɛ) *f*, case, slip (*pillow*); cover (*cushion*).

taillade (tajad) *f*, cut, slash, gash. **taillader** (de) *v.t*, to slash, slit, gash.

taille[1] (taj) *f*, height, size; waist. *avoir la* ~ *fine*, to have a slim waist. *de* ~, considerable, sizeable. *la* ~ *38*, size 38.

taille[2] (taj) *f*, cutting; carving; trimming, pruning; cut. ~*-crayon*, pencil sharpener. **tailler** (tɑje) *v.t*, to cut; cut out; prune; trim; clip; carve; sharpen; make (*clothes*). **se** ~ *P*, to clear off *P*. **tailleur** (tajœr) *m*, tailor; [woman's] suit. **taillis** (ji) *m*, copse, coppice.

tain (tɛ̃) *m*, silvering (*for mirror*).

taire (tɛr) *v.t.ir*, to say nothing about; hush up; conceal. *faire* ~, to silence, hush. **se** ~, to be silent, keep quiet.

talc (talk) *m*, talc; talcum powder.

talent (talɑ̃) *m*, talent; gift.

talisman (talismɑ̃) *m*, talisman.

taloche (talɔʃ) *f*, cuff, clout.

talon (talɔ̃) *m*, heel; stub, counterfoil (*cheque*); (*Cards*) talon. **talonner** (lɔne) *v.t*, to follow on the heels of; hound; (*horse*) kick; (*hunger*) gnaw at; (*Rugby*) heel. **talonneur** (nœr) *m*, (*Rugby*) hooker.

talquer (talke) *v.t*, to put talc on.

talus (taly) *m*, bank, embankment.

tambour (tɑ̃bur) *m*, drum; drummer; embroidery hoop; tambour, revolving door; spool. ~ *de basque*, tambourine. ~ *de frein*, brake drum. ~*-major*, drum major. **tambourin** (rɛ̃) *m*, tambourine. **tambouriner** (burine) *v.i*, to drum. ¶ *v.t*, to drum out; (*fig.*) broadcast.

tamis (tami) *m*, sieve; sifter.

Tamise (la) (tamiz), the Thames.

tamiser (tamize) *v.t*, to sift; sieve; filter, subdue (*light*).

tampon (tɑ̃pɔ̃) *m*, stopper; plug, bung; wad; pad; tampon; stamp; (*Rly*) buffer. ~ *à récurer*, scouring pad. ~ *de la poste*, postmark. ~ *encreur*, inking pad. **tamponner** (pɔne) *v.t*, to mop up; dab; ram, crash into; stamp.

tam-tam (tamtam) *m*, tomtom.

tancer (tɑ̃se) *v.t*, (*liter.*) to rate, scold.

tandem (tɑ̃dɛm) *m*, tandem (*cycle*); (*fig.*) pair.

tandis que (tɑ̃di[s]) *c*, while, whilst; whereas.

tangage (tɑ̃gaʒ) *m*, pitching (*ship*).

tangent, e (tɑ̃ʒɑ̃, ɑ̃t) *a*, tangent[ial]. ¶ *f*, tangent.

tangible (tɑ̃ʒibl) *a*, tangible.

tanguer (tɑ̃ge) *v.i*, to pitch (*ship*); (*fig.*) reel.

tanière (tanjɛr) *f*, den, lair; hole, earth.

tank (tɑ̃k) *m*, (*Mil.*) tank. **tanker** (kɛr) *m*, tanker.

tan[n]in (tanɛ̃) *m*, tannin. **tannage** (naʒ) *m*, tanning. **tannant, e** *P* (nɑ̃, ɑ̃t) *a*, maddening. **tanner** (ne) *v.t*, to tan; weather; (*P*) pester. ~ *le cuir à qn*, to tan s.o's hide. **tannerie** (nri) *f*, tannery; tanning. **tanneur** (nœr) *m*, tanner.

tant (tɑ̃) *ad*, so much; so many; such; so; as much. ~ *bien que mal*, so-so; after a fashion. ~ *de fois*, so many times. ~ *que ça?* as much as that? ~ *& plus*, ever so much (*or* many). ~ *mieux*, so much the better; that's fine. ~ *pis*, too bad; never mind. ~ *que*, as long as, while. ~ *s'en faut*, far from it. ~ *soit peu*, ever so little, somewhat.

tante (tɑ̃t) *f*, aunt; (*P**) poof *P**.

tantième (tɑ̃tjɛm) *m*, percentage.

tantinet (tɑ̃tinɛ) *m*, tiny bit, little bit.

tantôt (tɑ̃to) *ad*, this afternoon; sometimes.

taon (tɑ̃) *m*, gad-fly, horse fly.

tapage (tapaʒ) *m*; noise, uproar, disturbance, row; fuss. **tapageur, euse** (paʒœr, øz) *a*, noisy, rowdy, uproarious; loud, flash[y], showy, garish.

tape (tap) *f*, slap. **tapé, e** (pe) *a*, pat (*answer*); mad, cracked (*pers.*). **tape-à-l'œil** (palœj) *a.inv*, flashy, showy. ¶ *n*, show. **tapecul** (pky) *m*, rattletrap (*car*). **tapée** (pe) *f*, heaps, swarm. **taper** (pe) *v.t. & i*, to beat; slap; bang; stamp (*foot*). ~ [*à la machine*], to type [out]. ~ *dans*, to dig into (*food*). (*sun*) beat down. ~ *dans l'œil de qn P*, to take s.o's fancy. ~ *qn*, to cadge off s.o, touch s.o *P*. ~ *sur*, to hit; bang on; thump. **se** ~, to get landed with

(*task &c*). **tapette** (pɛt) *f*, carpet beater; flyswatter; mousetrap; (*P*) chatterbox; (*P**) queer *P**, poof *P**. **tapeur, euse** *P* (pœr, øz) *n*, cadger *P*.
tapinois (en) (tapinwa) *ad*, furtively.
tapioca (tapjɔka) *m*, tapioca.
tapir (tapir) *m*, tapir.
tapir (se) (tapir) *v.pr*, to crouch; lurk; hide away.
tapis (tapi) *m*, carpet; rug, mat; cloth, cover. ~-*brosse*, doormat. ~ *roulant*, conveyor belt; moving walkway. ~ *vert*, green baize; gambling table. *aller au* ~, to go down for the count. **tapisser** (se) *v.t*, to paper (*wall*); hang; cover, plaster (*posters &c*); line; (*moss &c*) carpet. **tapisserie** (sri) *f*, wallpaper; tapestry; tapestrymaking. *faire* ~, to be a wallflower (*dance*). **tapissier, ère** (sje, ɛr) *n*, tapestry maker; upholsterer; interior decorator.
tapoter (tapɔte) *v.t*, to tap; pat (*cheek*); strum.
taquin, e (takɛ̃, in) *a*, teasing. ¶ *n*, tease. **taquiner** (kine) *v.t. & i*, to tease, torment; worry.
tarabiscoté, e (tarabiskɔte) *a*, over-ornate.
tarabuster (tarabyste) *v.t*, to badger; bother.
taratata (taratata) *i*, rubbish!
tard (tar) *ad*, late. *plus* ~, later. *sur le* ~, late in life. **tarder** (tarde) *v.i*, to delay, be long (*à venir*, [in] coming); loiter. ¶ *v.imp*, *il me tarde de voir*, I'm longing to see. **tardif, ive**† (dif, iv) *a*, tardy, belated; late.
tare (tar) *f*, defect; taint; (*Com.*) tare.
taré, e (tare) *a*, tainted, corrupt; with a defect (*child*). ¶ *n*, degenerate; cretin.
tarentelle (tarɑ̃tɛl) *f*, tarantella. **tarentule** (tyl) *f*, tarantula.
targette (tarʒɛt) *f*, bolt (*door*).
targuer (se) de (targe), to pride oneself on.
tarif (tarif) *m*, tariff, rate, rates, scale; price list; fare. **tarifer** (fe) *v.t*, to fix a price (*or* rate) for.
tarir (tarir) *v.t. & i*, to dry up; stop talking.
tarte (tart) *f*, (*Cook.*) tart; (*P*) clout. ¶ *a. inv*, (*P*) daft; ugly. **tartelette** (tlɛt) *f*, tart[let]. **tartine** (tin) *f*, slice of bread & butter; screed. **tartiner** (ne) *v.t*, to spread. *pâte à* ~, spread.
tartre (tartr) *m*, tartar; scale, fur. **tartrique** (trik) *a*, tartaric.
tartufe (tartyf) *m*, sanctimonious hypocrite.
tas (tɑ) *m*, heap, pile; pack (*lies*). ~ *de compost*, compost heap. *un* ou *des* ~ *de*, lots of, loads of, heaps of.
tasse (tɑs) *f*, cup; mug.
tassé, e (tɑse) *a*, strong (*coffee*); well-filled. **tassement** (tɑsmɑ̃) *m*, settling (*wall*); packing (*snow*); compression. **tasser** (se) *v.t*, to press down; pack [down]; cram. **se** ~, to settle, sink; settle down; (*old pers.*) shrink; squeeze up.
tâter (tɑte) *v.t*, to feel; (*fig.*) sound out. ~ *le terrain*, to see how the land lies. ¶ *v.i*, ~ *de*, to try, taste.
tatillon, ne (tatijɔ̃, ɔn) *a*, fussy, pernickety.
tâtonnement (tɑtɔnmɑ̃) *m*, groping; tentative effort; (*pl.*) trial & error. **tâtonner** (ne) *v.i*, to grope; fumble. **à tâtons** (tɔ̃) *ad*, gropingly; warily. *avancer* ~, to grope one's way.
tatou (tatu) *m*, armadillo.
tatouage (tatwaʒ) *m*, tattooing; tattoo (*on skin*). **tatouer** (twe) *v.t*, to tattoo.
taudis (todi) *m*, hovel; slum.
taule *P* (tol) *f*, clink *P* (*prison*).
taupe (top) *f*, (*Zool.*) mole; moleskin. **taupinière** (pinjɛr) *f*, molehill.
taureau (tɔro) *m*, bull.
tautologie (totɔlɔʒi) *f*, tautology.
taux (to) *m*, rate; level, degree. ~ *de change*, exchange rate.
taverne (tavɛrn) *f*, tavern, inn.
taxation (taksasjɔ̃) *f*, taxation, taxing, fixing the price. **taxe** (taks) *f*, tax; duty. ~ *à la valeur ajoutée* (*T.V.A.*), value added tax (V.A.T.). **taxer** (kse) *v.t*, to tax; fix the price of.
taxi (taksi) *m*, taxi [cab]. ~**phone** (fɔn) *m*, pay phone.
tchécoslovaque (tʃekɔslɔvak) *a.* & **T**~, *n*, Czechoslovak. **Tchécoslovaquie** (ki) *f*, Czechoslovakia. **tchèque** (tʃɛk) *a.* & (*language*) *m.* & **T**~ (*pers.*) *n*, Czech.
te, t' (tə, t) *pn*, (*object*) you, yourself.
technique† (tɛknik) *a*, technical. ¶ *f*, technique. **technologie** (nɔlɔʒi) *f*, technology.
teck (tɛk) *m*, teak.
teckel (tekɛl) *m*, dachshund.
teigne (tɛɲ) *f*, ringworm; (*pers.*) pest.
teindre (tɛ̃dr) *v.t.ir*, to dye. **teint** (tɛ̃) *m*, colour; complexion. **teinte** (tɛ̃t) *f*, tint, shade, hue; tinge. **teinter** (tɛ̃te) *v.t*, to tint; stain (*wood*); tinge. **teinture** (tyr) *f*, dyeing; dye; tinge; smattering; tincture. **teinturerie** (tyrri) *f*, dyeing; [dry] cleaners. **teinturier, ère** (tyrje, ɛr) *n*, dyer; dry cleaner.
tel, telle (tɛl) *a*, such; like *un* ~ *bruit*, such a noise. ~ *que*, like, such as. *comme* ~, *en tant que* ~, as such. *de* ~ *le façon que*, in such a way that. *de* ~ *le sorte que*, so that. ¶ *pn*, such a one, some. *un* ~, *une* ~ *le*, so-&-so.
télé *P* (tele) *f*, telly *P*, T.V. *P*.
télécommande (telekɔmɑ̃d) *f*, remote control.
télécommunications (telekɔmynikasjɔ̃) *f.pl*, telecommunications.
téléférique (teleferik) *m*, [aerial] cable-car.
télégramme (telegram) *m*, telegram, wire. **télégraphe** (graf) *m*, telegraph. **télégraphie** (fi) *f*, telegraphy. **télégraphier** (fje) *v.t*, to telegraph, wire, cable. **télégraphique**† (fik) *a*, telegraphic, telegraph; Morse (*alphabet*). **télégraphiste** (fist) *n*, telegraph messenger.
téléguidage (telegidaʒ) *m*, radio control.
télématique (telematik) *f*, information technology.
téléobjectif (teleɔbʒɛktif) *m*, telephoto lens.

télépathie (telepati) *f*, telepathy.
téléphone (telefɔn) *m*, telephone. ~ *arabe*, bush telegraph. ~ *rouge*, (*Pol.*) hot line. **téléphoner** (ne) *v.t. & i*, to [tele]phone; be on the phone. **téléphonique** (nik) *a*, telephone. **téléphoniste** (nist) *n*, telephonist.
télescope (telɛskɔp) *m*, telescope. **télescoper (se)** (pe) *v.pr*, (*trains*) to telescope. **télescopique** (pik) *a*, telescopic.
téléscripteur (teleskriptœr) *m*, teleprinter.
téléspectateur, trice (telespɛktatœr, tris) *n*, [television] viewer.
téléviser (televize) *v.t*, to televise. **téléviseur** (zœr) *m*, television [set]. **télévision** (zjɔ̃) *f*, television.
tellement (tɛlmɑ̃) *ad*, so, so much, so many. *pas* ~, not all that much, not very much.
téméraire† (temerɛr) *a*, rash, reckless, foolhardy. **témérité** (rite) *f*, temerity, rashness &c.
témoignage (temwaɲaʒ) *m*, testimony, evidence; mark, token. **témoigner** (ɲe) *v.i. & t*, to testify, bear witness, give evidence; show. ~ *de*, to attest, show. **témoin** (mwɛ̃) *m*, witness; second (*duel*); testimony, evidence; baton (*relay race*). ~ *à charge*, witness for the prosecution. ~ *à décharge*, w. for the defence. ¶ *a*, control; warning (*light*); pilot (*scheme*); show (*house*).
tempe (tɑ̃p) *f*, (*Anat.*) temple.
tempérament (tɑ̃peramɑ̃) *m*, temperament, constitution. *à* ~, (*buy*) on hire purchase.
tempérance (tɑ̃perɑ̃s) *f*, temperance. **tempérant, e** (rɑ̃, ɑ̃t) *a*, temperate.
température (tɑ̃peratyr) *f*, temperature. **tempéré** (re) *a*, temperate. **tempérer** (re) *v.t*, to temper, moderate; soothe.
tempête (tɑ̃pɛt) *f*, storm, tempest. **tempêter** (pɛte) *v.i*, to storm, rage. **tempétueux, euse** (petɥø, øz) *a*, tempestuous, stormy.
temple (tɑ̃pl) *m*, temple; church (*Protestant*).
temporaire† (tɑ̃pɔrɛr) *a*, temporary. **temporel, le**† (rɛl) *a*, temporal. **temporiser** (rize) *v.i*, to temporize; stall. **temps**[1] (tɑ̃) *m*, time; times, days; (*Gram.*) tense; (*Mus.*) beat; (*Tech.*) stroke (*engine &c*). ~ *d'arrêt*, pause, halt. ~ *mort*, slack period, lull. *à* ~, in time. *à* ~ *perdu*, in one's spare time. *ces derniers* ~, of late, lately. *dans le* ~, at one time. *dans le bon vieux* ~, in the good old days. *de* ~ *en* ~, from time to time. *il était* ~*!* not before time!
temps[2] (tɑ̃) *m*, weather. *il fait beau, mauvais* ~, the weather's fine, bad. *prendre le* ~ *comme il vient*, to take things as they come.
tenable (tənabl) *a*, tenable; bearable.
tenace† (tənas) *a*, stubborn, persistent; tenacious; strong (*glue*). **ténacité** (tenasite) *f*, stubbornness &c.
tenaille (tənɑj) *f*, *oft. pl.* tongs; pincers. **tenailler** (je) *v.t*, to torture, torment.
tenancier, ère (tənɑ̃sje, ɛr) *n*, manager, ess (*bar*).
tenant (nɑ̃) *m*, champion, supporter, upholder; (*Sport*) holder (*title*). *d'un* [*seul*] ~, all in one piece.
tendance (tɑ̃dɑ̃s) *f*, tendency, trend. **tendancieux, euse** (dɑ̃sjø, øz) *a*, tendentious; leading (*question*).
tender (tɑ̃dɛr) *m*, tender (*locomotive*).
tendon (tɑ̃dɔ̃) *m*, tendon, sinew.
tendre (tɑ̃dr) *v.t*, to stretch, tighten, strain; tense (*muscles*); stretch [out]; crane (*neck*); hold out (*hand &c*); set (*trap &c*). ~ *l'oreille*, to prick up one's ears. ¶ *v.i*, to tend; aim.
tendre† (tɑ̃dr) *a*, tender, soft; sensitive; early (*youth*); fond. **tendresse** (tɑ̃drɛs) *f*, tenderness, fondness, love; (*pl.*) caresses. **tendreté** (drəte) *f*, tenderness (*meat &c*). **tendron** (drɔ̃) *m*, tender shoot; gristle (*veal*); (*O or P*) young girl.
tendu, e (tɑ̃dy) *a*, tense, taut, tight; strained, tensed; outstretched (*arms*).
ténèbres (tenɛbr) *f.pl*, dark[ness], gloom. **ténébreux, euse**† (nebrø, øz) *a*, dark, murky; gloomy; obscure.
teneur (tənœr) *f*, content; terms.
ténia (tenja) *m*, taenia, tapeworm.
tenir (tənir) *v.t.ir*, to hold; h. on; keep; have; contain; take; t. up (*space*); consider; have control over (*class &c*); take on; honour (*bet*). ~ *de qn*, to have [got] from s.o. ¶ *v.i.ir*, to hold; stay up; stand firm; (*colour*) be fast; last. ~ **à**, to value, care about; be fond of; be anxious to; be due to, stem from. ~ *dans*, to fit in to. ~ **de**, to take after. ¶ *v.imp.ir*, to depend. *il ne tient qu'à lui de décider*, it's up to him to decide. **se** ~, to keep, hold; stand; sit; behave; be held; hang together; consider. **s'en** ~ **à**, to confine o.s to; content o.s with.
tennis (tɛnis) *m*, tennis; t. court. ~ *de table*, table tennis. ¶ *f.pl*, gym shoes, tennis shoes. **tennisman** (man) *m*, tennis player.
tenon (tənɔ̃) *m*, tenon.
ténor (tenɔr) *m*, tenor (*voice, singer*).
tension (tɑ̃sjɔ̃) *f*, tension; strain; pressure; voltage. ~ *artérielle*, blood pressure.
tentaculaire (tɑ̃takylɛr) *a*, tentacular; (*fig.*) sprawling. **tentacule** (kyl) *m*, tentacle.
tentateur, trice (tɑ̃tatœr, tris) *n*, tempter, temptress. **tentation** (sjɔ̃) *f*, temptation.
tentative (tɑ̃tativ) *f*, attempt, endeavour. ~ *de meurtre*, attempted murder.
tente (tɑ̃t) *f*, tent.
tenter (tɑ̃te) *v.t*, to attempt, try (*de faire*, to do); tempt. ~ *le coup P*, to have a go, give it a try *P*.
tenture (tɑ̃tyr) *f*, hangings; curtain.
tenu, e (təny) *a*, (*well, ill*) kept; looked after; turned out (*child*); (*to be*) bound (*à*, by); obliged (*de faire*, to do). ¶ *f*, upkeep, running (*house &c*); control, handling; good manners, g. behaviour; standard, quality; posture;

appearance; dress; uniform. ~ *de route,* road holding. ~ *de soirée,* evening dress.
ténu, e (teny) *a,* thin, fine; tenuous. **ténuité** (nɥite) *f,* thinness &c.
tercet (tɛrsɛ) *m,* (*Poetry*) tercet, triplet.
térébenthine (terebɑ̃tin) *f,* turpentine.
tergal (tɛrgal) *m,* Terylene.
tergiverser (tɛrʒivɛrse) *v.i,* to procrastinate.
terme (tɛrm) *m,* term; end; time limit, deadline; quarter (*year*); quarterly rent; (*pl.*) terms: *en bons ~s avec,* on good terms with. *à ~,* (*Med.*) full-term; at t.; (*Stk.Ex.*) forward. *arriver à ~,* to expire; fall due. *avant ~,* (*Med.*) premature[ly]. **terminaison** (minɛzɔ̃) *f,* termination, ending. **terminal, e** (nal) *a,* final, terminal. (*Sch.*) [*classe*] *~e,* Upper 6th. ¶ *m,* terminal (*computer, oil*). **terminer** (ne) *v.t,* to terminate, end, wind up, finish, complete. **terminologie** (nɔlɔʒi) *f,* terminology. **terminus** (nys) *m,* terminus.
termite (tɛrmit) *m,* termite, white ant.
terne (tɛrn) *a,* dull, lustreless, drab. **ternir** (nir) *v.t,* to tarnish, dull.
terrain (tɛrɛ̃) *m,* ground, soil; (*Geol.*) formation; plot [of land], site; (*Golf &c*) course; (*Foot.*) pitch, field; basketball court; (*Mil.*) terrain; breeding ground (*epidemic*). ~ *d'aviation,* airfield. ~ *de camping,* campsite. ~ *vague,* waste ground. *sur le ~,* in the field (*research &c*).
terrasse (tɛras) *f,* terrace; flat roof; [pavement] outside (*café*). **terrassement** (smɑ̃) *m,* earthwork; embankment; excavation. **terrasser** (se) *v.t,* to floor, bring down; overcome, overwhelm; excavate, dig out. **terrassier** (sje) *m,* navvy.
terre (tɛr) *f,* earth, world; ground, soil; clay; (*Naut.*) shore; land, country; estate. ~ *à foulon,* fuller's earth. ~ *battue,* hard-packed surface; (*Ten.*) hard court. ~ *brûlée,* scorched earth (*policy*). ~ *cuite,* terracotta; baked clay. *la ~ ferme,* dry land, terra firma. ~ *glaise,* clay. *T~ Sainte,* Holy Land. *dans les ~s,* inland. **terreau** (tɛro) *m,* compost. ~ *de feuilles,* leaf mould. **Terre-Neuve,** *f,* Newfoundland. **terre-neuve,** *m,* N. [dog]. **terre-plein,** *m,* terreplein; (*Build.*) platform. **terrer (se)** (tɛre) *v.pr,* to crouch down; go to ground; hide away. **terrestre** (rɛstr) *a,* terrestrial; land; earthly.
terreur (tɛrœr) *f,* terror, dread.
terreux, euse (tɛrø, øz) *a,* earthy; muddy, dirty; sallow (*complexion*).
terrible† (tɛribl) *a,* terrible, dreadful; (*P excellent*) terrific.
terrien, ne (tɛrjɛ̃, ɛn) *a,* landed (*proprietor*); country. ¶ *n,* countryman, woman; landsman, woman; Earthman, woman. **terrier** (rje) *m,* burrow, hole; earth (*fox*); terrier (*dog*).
terrifier (tɛrifje) *v.t,* to terrify.
terrine (tɛrin) *f,* terrine; pâté.
territoire (tɛritwar) *m,* territory; area; jurisdiction. **territorial, e** (tɔrjal) *a,* territorial. ¶ *f,* Territorial Army. **terroir** (rwar) *m,* soil.
terroriser (tɛrɔrize) *v.t,* to terrorize. **terrorisme** (rism) *m,* terrorism. **terroriste** (rist) *a. & n,* terrorist.
tertiaire (tɛrsjɛr) *a,* tertiary. [*secteur*] ~, (*Econ.*) service industries. **tertio** (sjo) *ad,* third[ly].
tertre (tɛrtr) *m,* hillock, mound.
tesson (tɛsɔ̃) *m,* piece of broken glass.
test (tɛst) *m,* test.
testament (tɛstamɑ̃) *m,* will, testament. **testamentaire** (tɛr) *a,* of a will. **testateur, trice** (tœr, tris) *n,* testator, trix. **tester**[1] (te) *v.i,* to make one's will. **tester**[2] (tɛste) *v.t,* to test.
testicule (tɛstikyl) *m,* testicle.
tétanos (tetanɔs) *m,* tetanus, lockjaw.
têtard (tɛtar) *m,* tadpole.
tête (tɛt) *f,* head; top; front, lead; face (*expression*); brains, wits; (*fig.*) neck; (*Foot.*) header. *avoir toute sa ~,* to have one's wits about one. *avoir une ~ de plus,* to be a head taller. *avoir une petite ~,* to be dim-witted. *faire la ~,* to sulk. *en mettre sa ~ à couper,* to stake one's life on it. *risquer sa ~,* to risk one's neck. *se laver la ~ P,* to wash one's hair. *~-à-~,* tête-à-tête, private conversation. *en ~-à-~,* alone together. *~-à-queue,* (*Mot.*) spin (*right round*). *~-bêche,* head to tail. ~ *brûlée,* wild adventurer. ~ *chaude,* hothead. ~ *chercheuse,* homing device. ~ *d'affiche,* top of the bill. ~ *de bielle,* (*Mot.*) big end. ~ *de lecture,* pickup head (*record player*). ~ *de ligne* (*Rly*), terminus, end of line. ~ *de linotte,* scatterbrain. ~ *de mort,* death's head; skull & crossbones; (*Cook.*) Gouda cheese. *~-de-nègre,* nigger brown. ~ *de pont,* bridgehead, beachhead. ~ *de série,* (*Ten.*) seeded player. ~ *de Turc,* whipping boy. ~ *nucléaire,* nuclear warhead.
tétée (tete) *f,* (*baby*) sucking; feeding; f. time. **téter** (te) *v.t,* to suck; s. at (*bottle, pipe*). ~ *sa mère,* to suck at one's mother's breast. **tétine** (tin) *f,* teat (*bottle, cow*); dummy. **téton** *P* (tɔ̃) *m,* breast, tit *P.*
têtu, e (tety) *a,* stubborn, mulish.
texte (tɛkst) *m,* text; passage, piece; topic, subject; (*Theat.*) lines.
textile (tɛkstil) *a. & m,* textile. *~s synthétiques,* manmade fibres.
textuel, le† (tɛkstɥɛl) *a,* literal, word for word; verbatim, exact.
texture (tɛkstyr) *f,* texture.
thé (te) *m,* tea; t. plant; t. party.
théâtral, e† (teɑtral) *a,* theatrical; dramatic; theatre (*season &c*). **théâtre** (ɑtr) *m,* theatre, stage; drama, dramatic works, plays; scene (*crime*); (*fig.*) histrionics, theatricals;

playacting.
théière (tejɛr) *f,* teapot.
thème (tɛm) *m,* theme; (*Sch.*) prose, translation (*into foreign language*); (*Gram*) stem.
théodolite (teɔdɔlit) *m,* theodolite.
théologie (teɔlɔʒi) *f,* theology. **théologien, ne** (ʒjɛ̃, ɛn) *n,* theologian. **théologique†** (ʒik) *a,* theological.
théorème (teɔrɛm) *m,* theorem. **théoricien, ne** (risjɛ̃, ɛn) *n,* theorist. **théorie** (ri) *f,* theory. **théorique†** (rik) *a,* theoretic(al).
thérapeutique (terapøtik) *a,* therapeutic. ¶ *f,* therapeutics; therapy.
thermal, e (tɛrmal) *a,* thermal, hot. *cure ~e,* water cure. *station ~e,* spa. **thermique** (mik) *a,* thermal (*unit*); thermic (*energy*). **thermoélectrique** (mɔelɛktrik) *a,* thermoelectric(al).
thermomètre (tɛrmɔmɛtr) *m,* thermometer. ~ *médical,* clinical thermometer.
thermonucléaire (tɛrmɔnykleɛr) *a,* thermonuclear.
thermos (tɛrmɔs) *m. or f,* Thermos *or* vacuum flask.
thésauriser (tezɔrize) *v.i. & t,* to hoard.
thèse (tɛz) *f,* thesis.
thon (tɔ̃) *m,* tunny (*fish*), tuna.
thorax (tɔraks) *m,* thorax.
thrombose (trɔ̃boz) *f,* thrombosis.
thym (tɛ̃) *m,* thyme.
thyroïde (tirɔid) *a,* thyroid.
tiare (tjar) *f,* tiara.
tibia (tibja) *m,* tibia, shin bone; shin.
tic (tik) *m,* tic; twitching; mannerism.
ticket (tikɛ) *m,* ticket. ~ *de quai,* platform ticket.
tic-tac (tiktak) *m,* tick-tock, ticking.
tiède† (tjɛd) *a,* tepid, lukewarm; (*fig.*) half-hearted; mild (*weather*). **tiédeur** (tjedœr) *f,* tepidness &c. **tiédir** (dir) *v.i,* to become tepid; cool down (*or* off); warm up.
tien, ne (*with,* **le, la, les**) (tjɛ̃, ɛn) *pn. & m,* yours, your own. *à la ~ne,* cheers *P. les ~s,* your family; your group.
tiens (tjɛ̃) *v. imperative,* here [you are], take this; look!, ah! ~ *~! P,* well, well!, fancy that!.
tiers, tierce (tjɛr, ɛrs) *a,* third. *le T~ Monde,* the Third World. ¶ *m,* third [part]; third person, third party. ¶ *f,* (*Mus.*) third; (*Cards &c*) tierce. **tiercé** (se) *m,* tiercé (*Fr. betting system*).
tige (tiʒ) *f,* stem, stalk; shaft; leg (*boot, stocking*).
tignasse (tiɲas) *f,* shock, mop (*hair*).
tigre, tigresse (tigr, grɛs) *n,* tiger, tigress. **tigré, e** (gre) *a,* striped, tabby; streaked; spotted.
tilleul (tijœl) *m,* lime [tree]; limeflower tea.
timbale (tɛ̃bal) *f,* kettledrum; (*pl.*) timpani; cup (*metal*); (*Cook.*) timbale. **timbalier** (lje) *m,* timpanist.
timbrage (tɛ̃braʒ) *m,* stamping, postmarking. **timbre** (tɛ̃br) *m,* stamp; postmark; tone, timbre; bell. ~ [*-poste*], [postage] stamp. ~ *fiscal,* excise s. **timbré, e** (tɛ̃bre) *a,* stamped; (*P*) cracked, daft. **timbrer** (bre) *v.t,* to stamp; postmark.
timide† (timid) *a,* timid; nervous; shy, bashful, diffident. **timidité** (dite) *f,* timidity &c.
timon (timɔ̃) *m,* shaft; beam; tiller. **timonier** (mɔnje) *m,* (*Naut.*) helmsman, steersman.
timoré, e (timɔre) *a,* timorous.
tintamarre (tɛ̃tamar) *m,* din, racket, noise.
tinter (tɛ̃te) *v.i. & t,* to ring, toll; tinkle; jingle; clink; chink; tingle, buzz. **tintement** (tmɑ̃) *m,* ringing &c; singing (*ears*).
tintin *P* (tɛ̃tɛ̃) *i,* no chance!, nothing doing! *faire ~,* to go without.
tintouin *P* (tɛ̃twɛ̃) *m,* trouble, worry.
tipule (tipyl) *f,* daddy-longlegs, crane fly.
tique (tik) *f,* tick (*insect*). **tiquer** (ke) *v.i,* to pull a face.
tiqueté (tikte) *a,* speckled, variegated.
tir (tir) *m,* shooting; fire, firing; rifle range; shooting gallery. ~ *à l'arc,* archery. *à ~ rapide,* quickfiring.
tirade (tirad) *f,* tirade; soliloquy.
tirage (tiraʒ) *m,* (*Phot.*) printing; print; (*Press*) circulation; edition (*book*); draw (*lottery*); draught (*fire*); (*P*) friction. ~ *au sort,* drawing of lots.
tiraillement (tirɑjmɑ̃) *m,* tugging; gnawing (*stomach*); wrangling; doubt. **tirailler** (je) *v.t,* to pull at, tug at; gnaw at; plague, pester. ¶ *v.i,* (*Mil.*) to fire. **tirailleur** (jœr) *m,* skirmisher.
tirant (tirɑ̃) *m,* draw string; strap; facing (*shoe*). ~ *d'eau,* draught (*boat*).
tire (tir) *comps, all m: ~-au-flanc P,* skiver *P. ~-bouchon,* corkscrew. *à ~ d'aile,* (*fly*) swiftly. *~-fesses P,* ski tow. *~-lait,* breast pump. *à ~-larigot P,* to one's heart's content. *~-ligne,* drawing pen. ¶ *voleur à la ~, m,* pickpocket.
tiré, e (tire) *a,* drawn, pinched, haggard. ~ *à quatre épingles,* dressed up to the nines. ~ *par les cheveux,* far-fetched. ¶ *m,* drawee. ¶ *f,* long haul *P. une ~ de,* heaps of *P,* a load of *P.*
tirelire (tirlir) *f,* moneybox, piggy bank; (*P*) nut *P* (*head*); face.
tirer (tire) *v.t,* to draw; d. up; pull; p. up; p. down; p. out; put out (*tongue*); tug, tow (*boat, car &c*); slide, shoot (*bolt*); take, extract, derive; (*Phot., Typ.*) print; fire (*weapon*); shoot (*game*); set off (*fireworks*). ~ *les ficelles,* (*fig.*) to pull the strings. ~ *l'œil,* to get noticed. ~ *les oreilles à qn,* to tell s.o off. ~ *qn de,* to rescue s.o from; get s.o out of (*prison &c*). ~ *qn de l'erreur,* to disabuse s.o. ~ *qn du doute,* to dispel s.o's doubts. ~

qn du sommeil, to arouse s.o from sleep. ¶ *v.i,* to fire, shoot; throw; draw, pull. ~ *à,* (*Press*) to have a circulation of. ~ *à conséquence,* to matter. ~ *à sa fin,* to draw to a close. ~ *au flanc P,* to skive. ~ *sur,* to verge on (*colour*); be getting on for (*age*); pull at, tug at; draw on; shoot at, fire on. ~ *sur la ficelle P,* to push one's luck. **se ~,** to extricate o.s; (*P*) clear off *P;* (*features*) become drawn. ~ *de,* to get out of; manage, cope, get through. *s'en ~ P,* to get away with it; pull through, manage, get by.

tiret (tirɛ) *m,* dash (*line*); hyphen.

tireur, euse (tirœr, øz) *n,* drawer; marksman, shot. ~ *d'armes,* fencer. ~ *de cartes,* fortune teller. ~ *isolé,* sniper.

tiroir (tirwar) *m,* drawer. ~*-caisse,* till.

tisane (tizan) *f,* infusion, herb tea.

tison (tizɔ̃) *m,* brand. **tisonner** (zɔne) *v.i,* to poke. **tisonnier** (nje) *m,* poker.

tissage (tisaʒ) *m,* weaving. **tisser** (se) *v.t,* to weave, spin (*web*). **tisserand, e** (srɑ̃, ɑ̃d) & **tisseur, euse** (sœr, øz) *n,* weaver. **tissu** (sy) *m,* cloth, fabric, material; (*Anat. & fig.*) tissue. ~*-éponge,* [terry] towelling.

titiller (titille) *v.t,* to titillate.

titre (titr) *m,* title; heading; name; (*Stk. Ex.*) security; (*pl.*) stocks, securities; fineness (*gold &c*); titre (*solution*); qualification; claim. ~ *au porteur,* bearer bond. ~ *d'alcool,* alcohol content. ~ *de transport,* ticket. *à aucun ~,* on no account. *à ce ~,* as such; therefore. *au même ~,* in the same way. *à ~ de,* by virtue of, by way of, as. *en ~,* titular. **titré, e** (tre) *a,* titled. **titrer** (tre) *v.t,* to confer a title on; run as a headline; titrate.

tituber (titybe) *v.i,* to stagger, lurch.

titulaire (titylɛr) *a,* titular. ¶ *n,* holder; occupant; incumbent. **titulariser** (larize) *v.t,* to give tenure to.

toast (tɔst) *m,* toast (*health*); slice of toast.

toboggan (tɔbɔgɑ̃) *m,* toboggan; slide; (*Mot.*) flyover.

toc (tɔk) *m,* (*P*) *du ~,* fake, rubbish. *en ~,* imitation. ¶ *i, ~ ~!* knock knock!

tocsin (tɔksɛ̃) *m,* alarm bell; tocsin.

toge (tɔʒ) *f,* toga; gown, robe.

Togo (le) (tɔgo) Togo.

tohu-bohu (tɔybɔy) *m,* chaos; hubbub.

toi (twa) *pn,* (*after pr. & emphatic*) you. ~*-même,* yourself, *à ~,* yours, your own.

toile (twal) *f,* cloth; piece of c.; canvas; linen, cotton; (*Naut.*) sails. ~ *à bâche,* tarpaulin. ~ *à matelas,* ticking. ~ *à sac,* sacking. ~ *à voile,* sailcloth. ~ *cirée,* oilcloth. ~ *d'araignée,* spider's web, cobweb. ~ *de fond,* (*Theat.*) backcloth. ~ *de jute,* hessian. ~ *de tente,* tent canvas.

toilette (twalɛt) *f,* washing; cleaning; (*dog*) grooming; washstand; clothes; (*pl.*) toilet, lavatory. ~ *de mariée,* wedding dress. *faire sa ~,* to have a wash; (*cat*) wash itself. *faire la ~ de,* to clean (*car*); groom (*dog*). *nécessaire de ~,* toilet bag.

toiser (twaze) *v.t,* to measure; look (*one*) up & down.

toison (twazɔ̃) *f,* fleece; mop, mane (*hair*).

toit (twa) roof; (*fig.*) home. **toiture** (tyr) *f,* roof[ing].

tôle (tol) *f,* sheet metal; iron *or* steel sheet. ~ *ondulée,* corrugated iron.

tolérable (tɔlerabl) *a,* tolerable. **tolérance** (rɑ̃s) *f,* (*gen., Med., Tech.*) tolerance; toleration; margin, limit. **tolérant, e** (rɑ̃, ɑ̃t) *a,* tolerant. **tolérer** (re) *v.t,* to tolerate, bear, stand; allow.

tôlerie (tolri) *f,* sheet metal trade *or* workshop; steel-work, plates. **tôlier** (lje) *m,* sheet metal worker. ~ *en voitures,* panel beater.

tollé (tɔlle) *m,* outcry.

tomate (tɔmat) *f,* tomato.

tombe (tɔ̃b) *f,* tomb, grave; tombstone, gravestone. **tombeau** (tɔ̃bo) *m,* tomb, vault; (*fig.*) grave. *à ~ ouvert,* at breakneck speed.

tombée (tɔ̃be) *f,* fall. *la ~ de la nuit,* nightfall. **tomber** (be) *v.i,* to fall, f. over, f. down; (*fog &c*) come down; (*lightning*) strike; die down; hang [down]; fall away; (*moustache*) droop. ~ *à l'eau,* (*plans*) to fall through. ~ *à plat,* to fall flat. ~ *de Charybde en Scylla,* to jump out of the frying pan into the fire. ~ *de haut,* to be bitterly disappointed. ~ *juste,* to be right, come out right. ~ *sous le sens,* to stand to reason. *laisser ~,* to drop. ¶ *v.t,* (*Sport*) to throw. ~ *la veste P,* to slip off one's jacket. ~ **sur,** to run into; come across; (*conversation*) come round to; (*eyes*) light upon; (*P*) go for (*attack*). ~ *sur un bec, P* to hit a snag. **tombereau** (bro) *m,* [tip] cart; cartload. **tombola** (bɔla) *f,* tombola.

tome (tom) *m,* volume; part, book.

ton, ta, tes (tɔ̃, ta, te) *a,* your.

ton (tɔ̃) *m,* tone; pitch (*voice*); (*Mus.*) key; tone (*interval*); shade (*colour*). *de bon ~* in good taste. *être dans le ~,* (*Mus.*) to be in tune; (*gen.*) fit in, match, tone in. **tonal, e** (tɔnal) *a,* tonal. **tonalité** (lite) *f,* tone; (*Mus.*) tonality, key; (*Tel.*) dialling tone.

tondeuse (tɔ̃døz) *f,* clippers; shears. ~ [*à gazon*], [lawn] mower. **tondre** (tɔ̃dr) *v.t,* to shear, clip, crop; mow; fleece (*pers.*).

tonifier (tɔnifje) *v.t,* to tone up; stimulate, invigorate. **tonique** (nik) *a,* tonic; toning; stimulating, invigorating; bracing. ¶ *m,* (*Med., fig.*) tonic; toning lotion.

tonnage (tɔnaʒ) *m,* tonnage. **tonne** (tɔn) *f,* [metric] ton, tonne. **tonneau** (no) *m,* cask, barrel; (*Naut.*) ton; (*Aero.*) flick roll; (*Mot.*) somersault. **tonnelet** (nlɛ) *m,* keg. **tonnelier** (nəlje) *m,* cooper. **tonnelle** (nɛl) *f,* arbour, bower. **tonnellerie** (lri) *f,* cooperage.

tonner (tɔne) *v.i. & imp,* to thunder; boom; roar; rage. **tonnerre** (nɛr) *m,* thunder. (*P*) *du* ~, fantastic *P.*
tonsure (tɔ̃syr) *f,* tonsure; (*P*) bald patch.
tonte (tɔ̃t) *f,* shearing; clipping; mowing.
top (tɔp) *m,* (*Radio*) pip. ~ *secret,* top secret.
topaze (tɔpɑz) *f,* topaz.
toper (tɔpe) *v.t,* to agree. *topez-là,* it's a deal!
topinambour (tɔpinɑ̃bur) *m,* Jerusalem artichoke.
topo *P* (tɔpo) *m,* rundown *P,* spiel *P.*
topographie (tɔpɔgrafi) *f,* topography.
toquade (tɔkad) *f,* craze, fancy.
toque (tɔk) *f,* cap; fur hat.
toqué, e *P* (tɔke) *a,* crazy, cracked. ¶ *n,* nutcase *P.*
torche (tɔrʃ) *f,* torch. **torcher** (ʃe) *v.t,* to wipe. **torchère** (ʃɛr) *f,* flare. **torchis** (ʃi) *m,* (*Build.*) cob. **torchon** (ʃɔ̃) *m,* cloth; teacloth, tea towel; duster; (*pej.*) mess; rag (*newspaper*).
tordant, e *P* (tɔrdɑ̃, ɑ̃t) *a,* screamingly funny, killing *P.* **tordre** (tɔrdr) *v.t,* to wring; w. out; twist, contort. **se** ~, to be doubled up (*laughter*); bend; buckle, twist; sprain (*limb*). **tordu, e** (dy) *a,* crooked, twisted, bent, buckled; warped (*mind*).
toréador (tɔreadɔr) *m,* toreador.
tornade (tɔrnad) *f,* tornado.
torpeur (tɔrpœr) *f,* torpor. **torpide** (pid) *a,* torpid.
torpille (tɔrpij) *f,* torpedo. **torpiller** (pije) *v.t,* to torpedo. **torpilleur** (jœr) *m,* torpedo boat.
torréfier (tɔrrefje) *v.t,* to roast.
torrent (tɔrɑ̃) *m,* torrent. **torrentiel, le** (rɑ̃sjɛl) *a,* torrential.
torride (tɔrid) *a,* torrid; scorching (*heat*).
torsade (tɔrsad) *f,* twist. **torsader** (de) *v.t,* to twist. **torse** (tɔrs) *m,* torso, chest. **torsion** (sjɔ̃) *f,* torsion; twisting.
tort (tɔr) *m,* wrong; fault; mistake; injury, harm. *à* ~, wrongly. *à* ~ *& à travers,* at random, wildly. *avoir* ~, to be wrong. *avoir des* ~*s envers qn,* to have wronged s.o. *donner* ~ *à,* to blame; prove wrong.
torticolis (tɔrtikɔli) *m,* stiff neck.
tortiller (tɔrtije) *v.t,* to twist; twirl. ~ *des hanches,* to wiggle one's hips. **se** ~, to wriggle; writhe; wiggle. **tortillon** *P* (jɔ̃) *m,* twist.
tortionnaire (tɔrsjɔnɛr) *m,* torturer.
tortue (tɔrty) *f,* tortoise. ~ *de mer,* turtle.
tortueux, euse† (tɔrtɥø, øz) *a,* tortuous; winding; devious.
torture (tɔrtyr) *f,* torture. **torturer** (tyre) *v.t,* to torture. *se* ~ *l'esprit,* to rack, cudgel, one's brains.
tôt (to) *ad,* soon; early. ~ *ou tard,* sooner or later. *le plus* ~ *possible,* as soon as possible.
total, e† (tɔtal) *a. & m,* total, comptete, utter. **totalis[at]eur** (liz[at]œr) *m,* totalizator. **totaliser** (ze) *v.t,* to total. **totalitaire** (litɛr) *a,* (*Pol.*) totalitarian. **totalité** (te) *f,* whole, totality. *la* ~ *de,* all of.
toubib *P* (tubib) *m,* doctor.
toucan (tukɑ̃) *m,* toucan.
touchant, e (tuʃɑ̃, ɑ̃t) *a,* touching, moving. **touchant,** *pr,* concerning, about. **touche** (tuʃ) *f,* touch, stroke; (*piano &c*) key; (*Foot., Rugby*) touchline; touch; line-out; throw-in; (*Fish.*) bite; (*Fenc. & fig.*) hit. *quelle drôle de* ~*!* what a sight! *P.* **touche-à-tout,** *m,* meddler; dabbler. **toucher** (ʃe) *m,* touch; feel. ¶ *v.t,* to touch, feel; adjoin; (*fig.*) concern; hit; contact, get in touch with; draw, get, receive (*salary &c*); cash (*cheque*); win (*prize*); affect, move. ~ *le fond,* to touch the bottom. ~ *terre,* to land. ~ **à,** to touch, break into (*savings*); meddle in, dabble in; tamper with, meddle with; question; near, approach (*end, goal*); border on, adjoin; affect, have to do with.
touffe (tuf) *f,* tuft; clump.
touffu, e (tufy) *a,* bushy, thick; complex (*story &c*).
toujours (tuʒur) *ad,* always, ever; still; anyhow, anyway. ~ *est-il que,* the fact remains that. *comme* ~, as ever, as always. *il pleut* ~, it's still raining.
toupet (tupɛ) *m,* quiff (*hair*); cheek, sauce *P.*
toupie (tupi) *f,* [spinning] top.
tour[1] (tur) *f,* tower; tower block; (*Chess*) castle, rook. ~ *de contrôle,* control tower.
tour[2] (tur) *m,* turn; revolution; trip, outing, walk; drive, ride; tour; feat, stunt, trick; circumference, measurement (*waist &c*); (*Tech.*) lathe. ~ *à* ~, *à* ~ *de rôle,* in turn. ~ *de force,* (*lit.*) feat of strength; (*fig.*) amazing feat. ~ *d'honneur,* lap of honour. ~ *d'horizon,* general survey. ~ *de main,* knack, dexterity. *en un* ~ *de main,* in a jiffy; quick as a flash. ~ *de passe-passe,* sleight of hand, trick. ~ [*de phrase*], turn of phrase. ~ [*de piste*], (*Sport*) lap, circuit. ~ *de potier,* potter's wheel. ~ *de reins,* strained back. ~ [*de scrutin*], ballot. ~ *de taille,* waist measurement. *à* ~ *de bras,* with all one's might; (*fig.*) prolifically. *faire le* ~ *de,* to go round; consider from all angles. *faire le* ~ *de cadran,* to sleep round the clock.
tourbe (turb) *f,* peat. **tourbeux, euse** (bø, øz) *a,* peaty. **tourbière** (bjɛr) *f,* peat bog.
tourbillon (turbijɔ̃) *m,* whirlwind; whirl, swirl; whirlpool; vortex; bustle. **tourbillonner** (jɔne) *v.i,* to whirl, swirl, eddy.
tourelle (turɛl) *f,* turret; (*Naut.*) conning-tower.
tourisme (turism) *m,* tourism; touring, sightseeing. **touriste** (rist) *n,* tourist; tripper.
tourment (turmɑ̃) *m,* torment, torture; agony. **tourmente** (mɑ̃t) *f,* storm, turmoil; upheaval. **tourmenté, e** (mɑ̃te) *a,* tormented, tortured,

anguished. **tourmenter** (te) *v.t,* to torment, torture, rack; worry; plague. **se ~,** to fret.

tournage (turnaʒ) *m,* (*Cine.*) shooting; turning. **tournant, e** (nɑ̃, ɑ̃t) *a,* revolving; swivel (*chair*); encircling (*movement*); spiral (*stairs*). ¶ *m,* bend. ~ *décisif,* watershed. *avoir qn au ~ P,* to get one's own back. **tourné, e** (ne) *a,* (*Carp.*) turned; sour (*milk*). *bien ~,* shapely (*figure &c*); trim, neat; well-turned. *mal ~,* badly expressed; unfortunate (*expression*). **tourneboüler** *P* (nəbule) *v.t,* to put in a whirl. **tournebroche** (nəbrɔʃ) *m,* roasting jack. **tourne-disque** (nədisk) *m,* record player. **tournée** (ne) *f,* round, tour; circuit. **tourner** (ne) *v.t,* to turn; t. over; stir (*sauce*); round, get round; throw (*pot*); shoot, film; turn (*phrase*); phrase, express (*wording*). ~ *& retourner,* to turn over & over. ~ *en ridicule,* to ridicule. *se ~ les pouces,* to twiddle one's thumbs. ¶ *v.i,* to turn [round]; t. out (*well, badly*); revolve; (*top*) spin; (*engine &c*) turn over; (*milk*) turn [sour]. ~ *autour du pot P,* to beat about the bush. ~ *au vinaigre,* (*wine*) to turn vinegary; (*fig.*) turn sour. ~ *court,* to come to an abrupt end. ~ *de l'œil P,* to faint, pass out. ~ *rond,* to run smoothly. **se ~,** to turn. **tournesol** (nəsɔl) *m,* sunflower; litmus. **tourneur** (nœr) *m,* turner. **tournevis** (nəvis) *m,* screwdriver. **tourniquet** (nikɛ) *m,* turnstile; revolving door; sprinkler hose; revolving stand; (*Med.*) tourniquet. **donner le tournis à qn** *P,* to make s.o. feel giddy.

tournoi (turnwa) *m,* tournament. **tournoyer** (nwaje) *v.i,* to spin, whirl; wheel; swirl.

tournure (turnyr) *f,* turn, course; cast; shape; turn of phrase; form. *prendre ~,* to take shape.

tourte (turt) *f,* pie, tart. **tourteau** (to) *m,* oil cake; [sort of] crab.

tourterelle (turtərɛl) *f,* turtle dove.

Toussaint (la) (tusɛ̃), All Saints' day.

tousser (tuse) *v.i,* to cough.

tout (tu) *pn,* all, everything. ~ *compris,* all-in, inclusive. *à ~ prendre,* all things considered. *en ~,* in all. **le ~,** the whole, the lot. **tout, e** (tu, tut) *a.s,* **tous** (tu & tus) *a.m.pl,* all, the whole [of], every; any. *tout le monde,* everybody, every one. *tout le temps,* all the time. *à tout instant,* constantly. *de toute façon,* in any case, anyway. ¶ *ad,* quite; very; thoroughly; all; right; ready (*made, cooked*); stark (*naked*); bolt (*upright*); just. ~ *... que,* however, [al]though. **tout,** *comps:* ~ *à coup,* ~ *d'un coup,* suddenly, all of a sudden. ~ *à fait,* quite; altogether; perfectly. ~ *à l'heure,* presently, by & by; just now. ~ *de suite,* at once, directly. ~ *en parlant,* while speaking. **tout-à-l'égout,** *m,* main drainage. **toute-épice,** *f,* allspice. **toutefois,** *ad,* yet, however, nevertheless, still. **tout-petit,** *m,* little one. **toute-puissance,** *f,* omnipotence. **tout-puissant, toute-puissante,** *a,* almighty, omnipotent; all-powerful. *le Tout-Puissant,* the Almighty.

toutou (tutu) *m,* bow-wow, doggie.

toux (tu) *f,* cough[ing].

toxine (tɔksin) *f,* toxin. **toxique** (ksik) *a,* toxic, poisonous, poison (*gas*). ¶ *m,* poison.

trac (trak) *m,* stage fright; nerves.

tracas (trakɑ) *m,* worry, bother. **tracasser** (kase) *v.t,* to worry.

trace (tras) *f,* mark; trace; track[s]; sign; [foot]step. ~*s de doigt,* finger marks. ~*s de pas,* footprints. **tracé** (se) *m,* layout, plan; line, course; route (*road*). **tracer** (se) *v.t,* to trace; lay out; mark out; map out; draw, sketch, outline; open up (*road*).

trachée-artère (traʃeartɛr) *f,* trachea, windpipe.

tract (trakt) *m,* leaflet. **tractations** (tasjɔ̃) *f.pl,* dealings, negotiations.

tracteur (traktœr) *m,* tractor. **traction** (ksjɔ̃) *f,* traction.

tradition (tradisjɔ̃) *f,* tradition. **traditionnel, le†** (sjɔnɛl) *a,* traditional; (*P*) good old *P,* usual.

traducteur, trice (tradyktœr, tris) *n,* translator. **traduction** (ksjɔ̃) *f,* translation; rendering, expression. **traduire** (dɥir) *v.t.ir,* to translate; express, convey, render. ~ *qn en justice,* to bring s.o before the courts. **se ~,** to be translated; show. **traduisible** (dɥizible) *a,* translatable.

trafic (trafik) *m,* (*Mot., Rly, Aero., pej.*) traffic; (*O*) trade; trafficking; dealings; (*P*) funny business *P.* ~ *d'armes,* gunrunning. **trafiquant** (kɑ̃) *m,* trafficker. **trafiquer** (ke) *v.i,* to traffic, trade (*illegally*). ¶ *v.t,* (*P*) to doctor *P* (*drink &c*).

tragédie (traʒedi) *f,* tragedy. **tragédien, ne** (djɛ̃, ɛn) *n,* tragic actor, tress. **tragique†** (ʒik) *a,* tragic(al). ¶ *m,* tragedy; tragic author.

trahir (trair) *v.t,* to betray; reveal. **trahison** (izɔ̃) *f,* treachery; treason; betrayal.

train (trɛ̃) *m,* train; pace, rate; line; raft (*timber*); batch, set (*tyres &c*). ~ *avant* (*arrière*), front (rear) wheel-axle unit. ~ *d'atterrissage,* undercarriage. ~ *de derrière,* hindquarters. ~ *de devant,* forequarters. ~ *de vie,* life style. ~ *direct,* fast train. ~ *omnibus,* slow t. *à un ~ d'enfer,* hell for leather. *aller bon ~,* to make good progress; be rife. *aller son petit ~,* to go along at one's own pace. *en ~ de faire,* in the course of doing. *être en ~,* to be in good form; be in good spirits. *mise en ~,* starting up, start; (*Gym.*) warm-up. *prendre le ~ en marche,* (*lit.*) to jump onto a moving train; (*fig.*) jump on the bandwagon.

traînant, e (trɛnɑ̃, ɑ̃t) *a,* drawling (*voice*). **traînard** (nar) *m,* straggler; slowcoach. **traîne** (trɛn) *f,* train (*of dress*). *à la ~,* in tow. **traîneau** (trɛno) *m,* sledge, sleigh; dragnet. **traînée** (ne) *f,* trail; tracks; streak (*mark*).

traîner (ne) *v.t,* to drag along; trail. ~ *la jambe,* to limp, hobble. ~ *les pieds,* to shuffle along. ~ *un boulet,* to have a millstone round one's neck. ¶ *v.i,* to trail; lag behind; hang about, linger, loiter. ~ *[en longueur],* to drag on. **se ~,** to drag on; drag o.s about. ~ *aux pieds de qn,* to grovel at s.o's feet.
train-train (trɛ̃trɛ̃) *m,* humdrum, routine.
traire (trɛr) *v.t.ir,* to milk; draw.
trait (trɛ) *m,* line, stroke (*pen*); feature, trait; act; (*pl.*) features; (*O*) dart, arrow; (*liter.*) taunt; trace (*harness*). *de* ~, draught (*animal*). ~ *d'union,* hyphen; (*fig.*) link. *à grands ~s,* roughly. *avoir ~ à,* to relate to, have to do with. *d'un ~,* (*drink*) in one gulp; (*sleep*) uninterruptedly. **traîtable** (tabl) *a,* tractable, manageable. **traite** (trɛt) *f,* stretch; stage (*journey*); trade; draft, bill; milking. *la ~ des noirs,* the slave trade. **traité** (te) *m,* treatise; treaty. **traitement** (tmɑ̃) *m,* treatment; course of t.; salary; processing, treating (*raw materials*). **traiter** (te) *v.t,* to treat; (*O*) entertain; deal with; handle; call. ~ *de,* to deal with, treat of. ~ *qn de menteur,* to call s.o a liar. ¶ *v.i,* to have dealings, deal. **traiteur** (tœr) *m,* caterer.
traître, traîtresse (trɛtr, trɛtrɛs) *n,* traitor, traitress; (*Theat.*) villain. ¶ *a,* treacherous, traitorous. **traîtreusement** (trøzmɑ̃) *ad,* treacherously. **traîtrise** (triz) *f,* treachery.
trajectoire (traʒɛktwar) *f,* trajectory; path (*storm &c*). **trajet** (ʒɛ) *m,* journey, voyage; route; distance; course.
trame (tram) *f,* woof, weft; web, thread (*of life*); plot. **tramer** (me) *v.t,* to weave; hatch (*plot*).
tramway (tramwɛ) *m,* tram[car].
tranchant, e (trɑ̃ʃɑ̃, ɑ̃t) *a,* cutting, sharp, keen. ¶ *m,* [cutting] edge. **tranche** (trɑ̃ʃ) *f,* slice; rasher; edge (*book, coin*); bracket (*age, salary*). **tranché, e** (trɑ̃ʃe) *a,* well-marked; distinct. **tranchée** (ʃe) *f,* trench. **trancher** (ʃe) *v.t,* to slice; cut; chop off; cut short; settle, decide; conclude. ¶ *v.i,* to contrast strongly; stand out.
tranquille† (trɑ̃kil) *a,* tranquil, quiet, calm, peaceful. *laisse-moi* ~, leave me alone *or* in peace. **tranquillisant, e** (lizɑ̃, ɑ̃t) *a,* soothing; tranquillizing; reassuring. ¶ *m,* tranquillizer. **tranquilliser** (lize) *v.t,* to calm, soothe; reassure. **tranquillité** (te) *f,* tranquillity, peace &c.
transaction (trɑ̃zaksjɔ̃) *f,* transaction.
transatlantique (trɑ̃zatlɑ̃tik) *a,* transatlantic. ¶ *m,* transatlantic liner; deckchair.
transbahuter *P* (trɑ̃zbayte) *v.t,* to shift, lug along *P.*
transborder (trɑ̃sbɔrde) *v.t,* to tran[s]ship; (*Rly*) transfer. **transbordeur** (dœr) *m,* transporter bridge.
transcendant, e (trɑ̃sɑ̃dɑ̃, ɑ̃t) *a,* transcendent. ~ & **transcendental, e** (dɑ̃tal) *a,* transcendental.
transcender (de) *v.t,* to transcend.
transcription (trɑ̃skripsjɔ̃) *f,* transcript[ion]; copy. **transcrire** (skrir) *v.t.ir,* to transcribe; copy out.
transe (trɑ̃s) *f,* trance; (*pl.*) agony.
transept (trɑ̃sɛpt) *m,* transept.
transférer (trɑ̃sfere) *v.t,* to transfer; translate (*bishop*). **transfert** (fɛr) *m,* transfer; transference.
transfiguration (trɑ̃sfigyrasjɔ̃) *f,* transfiguration. **transfigurer** (re) *v.t,* to transfigure; transform.
transformateur (trɑ̃sfɔrmatœr) *m,* transformer. **transformation** (masjɔ̃) *f,* transformation, change; conversion; processing. **transformer** (me) *v.t,* to transform, change, convert; process. ~ *qch en,* to turn sth into.
transfuge (trɑ̃sfyʒ) *m,* (*Mil., Pol.*) renegade.
transfuser (trɑ̃sfyze) *v.t,* to transfuse. **transfusion** (fyzjɔ̃) *f,* transfusion.
transgresser (trɑ̃sgrɛse) *v.t,* to contravene, infringe; disobey. **transgression** (sjɔ̃) *f,* contravention &c.
transiger (trɑ̃zige) *v.i,* to compound, compromise.
transir (trɑ̃sir) *v.t,* to chill, numb; (*fig.*) paralyse.
transistor (trɑ̃zistɔr) *m,* transistor. **transistorisé** (rize) *a,* transistorized.
transit (trɑ̃zit) *m,* transit. **transiter** (te) *v.t. & i,* to pass in transit.
transitif, ive† (trɑ̃zitif, iv) *a,* transitive.
transition (trɑ̃zisjɔ̃) *f,* transition. **transitoire** (twar) *a,* transitory, transient; transitional.
translucide (trɑ̃slysid) *a,* translucent.
transmetteur (trɑ̃smɛtœr) *m,* transmitter. **transmettre** (tr) *v.t.ir,* to transmit; pass on; hand down; transfer, convey; forward, send on (*letter*); (*Radio, TV*) broadcast; (*Sport*) pass; pass on, hand over. **transmission** (misjɔ̃) *f,* (*gen., Mot.*) transmission; passing on &c.
transparaître (trɑ̃sparɛtr) *v.i,* to show [through]. **transparence** (rɑ̃s) *f,* transparency; transparence; limpidity, clearness. **transparent, e** (rɑ̃, ɑ̃t) *a,* transparent; limpid, clear.
transpercer (trɑ̃spɛrse) *v.t,* to transfix, pierce.
transpiration (trɑ̃spirasjɔ̃) *f,* perspiration. **transpirer** (re) *v.i,* to perspire; (*secret*) leak out, come to light. ~ *sur qch P,* to sweat over sth *P.*
transplantation (trɑ̃splɑ̃tasjɔ̃) *f,* transplantation; (*Med.*) transplant. **transplanter** (te) *v.t,* to transplant.
transport (trɑ̃spɔr) *m,* transport[ation], carrying; conveyance; transport (*delight &c*). ~ *au cerveau,* seizure, stroke. *~s en commun, ~s publics,* public transport. ~[*s*] *routier*[*s*], road haulage. **transporter** (te) *v.t,* to transport &c; carry away, send into raptures. **se ~,** to betake o.s, repair.

transposer (trɑ̃spoze) *v.t,* to transpose.
transvaser (trɑ̃svɑze) *v.t,* to decant.
transversal, e† (trɑ̃svɛrsal) *a,* transverse, cross.
trapèze (trapɛz) *m,* trapeze; (*Geom.*) trapezium.
trappe (trap) *f,* trap, pitfall; trap door; hatch; exit door (*parachute*). **trappeur** (pœr) *m,* trapper.
trapu, e (trapy) *a,* thick-set, dumpy, squat, stocky; (*P Sch.*) brainy *P* (*pers.*); tough (*problem*).
traquenard (traknar) *m,* trap. **traquer** (ke) *v.t,* to track down; hunt down; hound, pursue.
travail (travaj) *m,* (*gen.*) work; piece of w., occupation; working[s]; operation; (*opp. capital, Med.*) labour; warp[ing] (*wood*); (*pl.*) work[s]. ~ *à la chaîne,* production line work. ~ *à la pièce,* piecework. ~ *au noir P,* moonlighting *P. travaux forcés,* hard labour. *travaux manuels,* (*Sch.*) handicrafts. *travaux ménagers,* housework. **travaillé, e** (vaje) *a,* worked, wrought; polished; elaborate, finely-worked. ~ *par,* tormented by. **travailler** (je) *v.i,* to work, train, practise. ¶ *v.t,* to work, w. on; practise; distract, worry; torment. ~ *à,* to work on, work for, work towards. **travailleur, euse** (jœr, øz) *n,* worker; workman; labourer. ~ *indépendant,* self-employed person. ¶ *a,* hard-working. **travailliste** (jist) *a,* Labour. ¶ *n,* Labour party member. *les* ~*s,* Labour.
travée (trave) *f,* (*Arch.*) bay; span (*bridge, roof*); row [of seats].
travers[1] (travɛr) *m,* fault, failing, shortcoming.
travers[2] (travɛr) *m,* breadth; beam (*ship*). *par le* ~, *en* ~, on the beam, abeam. **à** ~, through, across. **de** ~, crooked; awry, amiss, wrong. *regarder qn de* ~, to look askance at s.o. **en** ~, *ad,* across, crosswise. **en** ~ **de,** *pr,* across. **traverse** (vɛrs) *f,* crosspiece, strut; sleeper (*rail track*). **traversée** (se) *f,* crossing, passage. **traverser** (se) *v.t,* to cross, go through; run across. **traversin** (sɛ̃) *m,* bolster (*bed*).
travesti (travɛsti) *m,* transvestite; drag artist; fancy dress. **travestir** (travɛstir) *v.t,* to dress up; travesty; misrepresent.
trébucher (trebyʃe) *v.i,* to stumble, trip.
trèfle (trɛfl) *m,* trefoil; clover; (*Cards*) clubs.
tréfonds (trefɔ̃) *m,* inmost depths; core. *dans le* ~ *de mon cœur,* deep down in my heart.
treillage (trɛjaʒ) *m,* lattice work; trellis; trellis fence. **treille** (trɛj) *f,* vine arbour; climbing vine. **treillis** (ji) *m,* trellis; wire-mesh; lattice work; canvas; (*Mil.*) combat uniform.
treize (trɛz) *a.* & *m,* thirteen. **treizième†** (trɛzjɛm) *a.* & *n,* thirteenth.
tréma (tremɑ) *m,* dieresis.
tremble (trɑ̃bl) *m,* aspen.
tremblement (trɑ̃bləmɑ̃) *m,* shiver; trembling, quavering, shaking. ~ *de terre,* earthquake. **trembler** (ble) & **trembloter** (blɔte) *v.i,* to tremble, shake, vibrate, quake, quiver, quaver, quail, shiver, flutter, flicker.
tremolo (tremɔlo) *m,* (*Mus.*) tremolo.
trémousser (se) (tremuse) *v.pr,* to fidget; wriggle; wiggle (*walking*).
trempe (trɑ̃p) *f,* temper, quenching (*steel*); (*pers.*) calibre; (*P*) slap, beating. **tremper** (trɑ̃pe) *v.t,* to soak, drench; steep; damp, wet, stand in water; dip; (*Tech.*) quench; (*liter.*) steel, strengthen. ¶ *v.i,* to stand in water, soak. ~ *dans,* to be involved in (*crime*). **se** ~, to get soaked *or* drenched; have a quick dip. **trempette** *P* (pɛt) *f,* quick dip.
tremplin (trɑ̃plɛ̃) *m,* spring board, diving b.; ski jump.
trentaine (trɑ̃tɛn) *f,* thirty [or so]; about 30. **trente** (trɑ̃t) *a,* thirty. ¶ *m,* thirty; 30th (*date*). ~*-six* (*fig.*), umpteen *P,* any number of. *voir* ~*-six chandelles P,* to see stars. *se mettre sur son* ~ *& un,* to put on one's Sunday best. *les années* ~, the thirties. **trentième** (trɑ̃tjɛm) *a.* & *n,* thirtieth. *for phrases V* **six & sixième.**
trépan (trepɑ̃) *m,* trepan. **trépaner** (pane) *v.t,* to trepan.
trépas (trepɑ) *m,* (*liter*) death, decease. **trépasser** (se) *v.i,* (*liter.*) to die, pass away. **les trépassés** (se), the dead, the departed.
trépidant, e (trepidɑ̃, ɑ̃t) *a,* vibrating; pulsating; hectic, busy (*life*). **trépidation** (trepidasjɔ̃) *f,* vibration, reverberation. **trépider** (de) *v.i,* to vibrate, reverberate.
trépied (trepje) *m,* tripod.
trépigner (trepiɲe) *v.i,* to stamp (*rage &c*).
très (trɛ) *ad,* very, most, [very] much. ~ *bien,* very well, all right. *être* ~ *amis,* to be great friends.
trésor (trezɔr) *m,* treasure; t. trove; treasury; treasure-house; (*Fin.*) exchequer, finances. *T*~ *public,* public revenue department. *des* ~*s de,* a wealth of. **trésorerie** (zɔrri) *f,* finances, funds; accounts; public revenue office; accounts department. **trésorier, ère** (zɔrje, ɛr) *n,* treasurer; paymaster.
tressaillir (trɛsajir) *v.i.ir,* to start; thrill; wince; shudder.
tressauter (trɛsote) *v.i,* to start, jump; be jolted; shake about.
tresse (trɛs) *f,* plait, tress; braid. **tresser** (se) *v.t,* to plait; braid; weave (*wicker &c*).
tréteau (treto) *m,* trestle; (*pl.*) boards, stage.
treuil (trœj) *m,* winch, windlass, hoist.
trêve (trɛv) *f,* truce; respite.
tri (tri) *m,* sorting [out]; selection. *le* [*bureau de*] ~, the sorting office. **triage** (aʒ) *m,* sorting [out]; marshalling yard; shunting.
triangle (triɑ̃gl) *m,* (*Geom.* & *Mus.*) triangle. **triangulaire** (ɑ̃gylɛr) *a,* triangular; three-cornered (*fight &c*).
tribal, e (tribal) *a,* tribal.
tribord (tribɔr) *m,* starboard.

tribu (triby) *f,* tribe.
tribulation (tribylasjɔ̃) *f,* tribulation, trial.
tribun (tribœ̃) (*pers.*) *m,* tribune. **tribunal** (bynal) *m,* tribunal; bench; court. **tribune** (byn) *f,* tribune; rostrum; platform; gallery; loft (*organ*); [grand]stand; (*fig.*) forum. ~ *libre d'un journal,* opinion column of a newspaper.
tribut (triby) *m,* tribute. **tributaire** (tɛr) *a. & m,* tributary (*pers., river*); dependent.
tricentaire (trisɑ̃tɛr) *a,* 300-year-old. ¶ *m,* tercentenary, tricentennial.
triceps (trisɛps) *a. & m,* triceps.
triche *P* (triʃ) *f,* cheating. **tricher** (ʃe) *v.i,* to cheat, trick. ~ *sur,* to lie about, cheat over. **tricherie** (ʃri) *f,* cheating; trickery. **tricheur, euse** (ʃœr, øz) *n,* cheat.
tricolore (trikɔlɔr) *a,* three-coloured. *le [drapeau]* ~, the tricolour, the French flag.
tricot (triko) *m,* knitting (*art*); knitted fabric; sweater, jumper. ~ *de corps,* vest. **tricoter** (te) *v.t. & i,* to knit. **tricoteuse** (tøz) *f,* knitter (*pers.*); knitting machine.
trictrac (triktrak) *m,* backgammon; b. board.
tricycle (trisikl) *m,* tricycle.
trident (tridɑ̃) *m,* trident.
triennal, e (triɛnnal) *a,* triennial, 3-yearly; 3-year.
trier (trie) *v.t,* to sort; pick, select; grade; sift. *trié sur le volet,* (*fig.*) handpicked. **trieur, euse** (œr, øz) *n,* sorter; grader.
trille (trij) *m,* trill.
trilogie (trilɔʒi) *f,* trilogy.
trimbaler (trɛ̃bale) *v.t,* to drag about; cart around *P;* trail along (*pers.*).
trimer *P* (trime) *v.i,* to slave away.
trimestre (trimɛstr) *m,* quarter, 3 months; (*Sch.*) term; quarter's rent, salary &c. **trimestriel, le** (triɛl) *a,* quarterly, 3-monthly; (*Sch.*) termly.
tringle (trɛ̃gl) *f,* rod (*stair, curtain*).
Trinité (la) (trinite), the Trinity; Trinidad. *à la* ~, on Trinity Sunday.
trinquer (trɛ̃ke) *v.i,* to clink glasses; (*P*) cop it *P.* ~ *à qch,* to drink to sth.
trio (trio) *m,* trio.
triomphal, e† (triɔ̃fal) *a,* triumphal; triumphant. **triomphant, e** (fɑ̃, ɑ̃t) *a,* triumphant. **triomphateur, trice** (fatœr, tris) *n,* triumphant victor. **triomphe** (ɔ̃f) *m,* triumph; victory. **triompher** (ɔ̃fe) *v.i,* to triumph; prevail, be triumphant; (*illness*) have its victory. ~ **de**,. to triumph over.
triperie (tripri) *f,* tripe shop. **tripes** (trip) *f.pl,* tripe; (*P*) guts *P.* **tripier, ère** (pje, ɛr) *n,* tripe butcher.
triple† (tripl) *a. & m,* treble, triple, threefold, 3 times; triplicate. ~ *croche, f,* demisemiquaver. ~ *menton,* row of chins. ~ *saut,* triple jump. **tripler** (ple) *v.t. & i,* to treble, triple. **triplés, ées** (ple) *n.pl,* triplets.
triporteur (tripɔrtœr) *m,* delivery bicycle.
tripot *P* (tripo) *m,* dive *P,* joint *P.* **tripotage** *P,* (pɔtaʒ) *m,* fiddling, jiggery-pokery *P.* **tripotée** *P** (te) *f,* hiding *P,* beating. *une* ~ *de,* loads of *P.* **tripoter** *P* (te) *v.t,* to fiddle with; speculate with (*funds*); paw *P* (*woman*). ¶ *v.i,* to mess about.
trique (trik) *f,* cudgel.
triste† (trist) *a,* sad, sorrowful, woeful; dreary, gloomy, dismal; bleak, depressing; sorry, wretched. **tristesse** (tɛs) *f,* sadness &c.
triturer (trityre) *v.t,* to knead (*dough*); manipulate. *se* ~ *la cervelle P,* to rack one's brains.
trivial, e† (trivjal) *a,* vulgar, coarse, crude; commonplace, mundane. **trivialité** (lite) *f,* vulgarity &c.
troc (trɔk) *m,* exchange, barter.
troène (trɔɛn) *m,* (*Bot.*) privet.
troglodyte (trɔglɔdit) *m,* troglodyte, cave dweller.
trognon (trɔɲɔ̃) *m,* core (*apple*); stump (*cabbage*).
trois (trwɑ) *a. & m,* three; third (*date*). ~ *étoiles,* three-star hotel (*or* restaurant). ~ *fois,* three times, thrice. ~ *fois rien,* next to nothing. ~-*mâts, m,* three-master. ~-*pièces,* three-room flat; three-piece suit. ~-*quarts,* three-quarters; (*Rugby*) three-quarter. *for other phrases V* **six & sixième. troisième†** (zjɛm) *a,* third. *le* ~ *âge,* senior citizens; the years of retirement. ¶ *m,* third (*number, pers., floor*). ¶ *f,* third (*class*).
trolleybus (trɔlɛbys) *m,* trolley bus.
trombe (trɔ̃b) *f,* waterspout. ~ *d'eau,* cloudburst. *entrer en* ~, to burst in.
trombone (trɔ̃bɔn) *m,* trombone; trombonist; paper clip.
trompe (trɔ̃p) *f,* horn; proboscis; trunk. ~ *d'Eustache* (østaʃ), Eustachian tube.
trompe-l'œil (trɔ̃plœj) *m,* (*Art*) trompe-l'œil; (*fig.*) eyewash *P,* bluff. **tromper** (pe) *v.t,* to deceive, delude; cheat; mislead; elude (*pursuer*); stave off (*hunger &c*); disappoint, outwit; while away. **se** ~, to be mistaken. *se* ~ *de chemin,* to take the wrong road. **tromperie** (pri) *f,* deceit, deception.
trompette (trɔ̃pɛt) *f,* trumpet. ¶ *m,* trumpeter.
trompeur, euse† (trɔ̃pœr, øz) *n,* deceiver, cheat. ¶ *a,* deceitful; deceptive.
tronc (trɔ̃) *m,* trunk; collection box. ~ *commun,* (*Sch.*) common-core syllabus. **tronçon** (sɔ̃) *m,* section. **tronçonner** (sɔne) *v.t,* to cut up. **tronçonneuse** (øz) *f,* chain saw.
trône (tron) *m,* throne. **trôner** (trone) *v.i,* to sit enthroned, sit in state.
tronquer (trɔ̃ke) *v.t,* to truncate.
trop (tro) *ad,* (*with a, ad*) too, over-; (*with v.*) too much; (*time*) [for] too long; (*superlative*) too, so [very]. ~ *de,* too much, too many; excessive. *de* ~, *en* ~, too many, too much,

[left] over. *être de* ~, (*pers.*) to be in the way, be unwelcome; (*remark*) be uncalled for. ¶ *m*, excess, extra.
trophée (trɔfe) *m*, trophy.
tropical, e (trɔpikal) *a*, tropical. **tropique** (pik) *m*, tropic. ~ *du Cancer* (kɑ̃sɛr), t. of Cancer. ~ *du Capricorne* (kaprikɔrn), t. of Capricorn.
trop-plein (trɔplɛ̃) *m*, overflow; excess.
troquer (trɔke) *v.t*, to barter, exchange.
trot (tro) *m*, trot. **trotte** *P* (trɔt) *f*, fair distance. **trotter** (te) *v.i. & t*, to trot; t. along; run around, scamper [about]; run (*in one's head*). **trotteur, euse** (tœr, øz) *n*, trotter (*horse*). ¶ *f*, second hand (*watch*). **trottiner** (tine) *v.i*, to trot; toddle. **trottinette** (nɛt) *f*, scooter. **trottoir** (twar) *m*, pavement, (*Am.*) sidewalk; walkway. *faire le* ~ *P*, to be on the game *P*.
trou (tru) *m*, hole; gap; deficit; lapse (*memory*); (*pej: place*) hole *P*, dump *P*. ~ *d'aération*, air vent. ~ *d'air*, air pocket. ~ *d'homme*, manhole.
troubadour (trubadur) *m*, troubadour.
trouble (trubl) *a*, cloudy; dim, blurred, misty; murky, shady. ¶ *m*, disorder; disturbance; trouble, discord; turmoil, tumult; agitation, distress; confusion, embarrassment. ~**-fête** (bləfɛt) *m*, spoilsport, kill joy. **troubler** (ble) *v.t*, to disturb, disrupt; trouble, bother; blur, make cloudy. **se** ~, to get flustered; (*water*) cloud.
troufion *P* (trufjɔ̃) *m*, private [soldier].
trouée (true) *f*, gap; (*Mil.*) breach. **trouer** (e) *v.t*, to make a hole in; pierce. *tout troué*, full of holes.
troupe (trup) *f*, troop, band; troupe; group. *la* ~, (*Mil.*) the army; the troups. **troupeau** (po) *m*, herd, drove; flock.
trousse (trus) *f*, case, kit; instrument case (*doctor*); pencil case. ~ *à outils*, toolkit. ~ *de maquillage*, makeup purse. ~ *de toilette*, sponge bag; travelling bag. *aux* ~*s de*, hot on the heels of. **trousseau** (so) *m*, bunch (*keys &c*); outfit, kit; trousseau. **trousser** (se) *v.t*, to truss; tuck up (*skirt*).
trouvaille (truvaj) *f*, [lucky] find; stroke of inspiration. **trouver** (ve) *v.t*, to find; discover; come across; meet with (*difficulties*); meet (*death &c*); get; think. ~ *à qui parler*, to meet one's match. ~ *le moyen*, to manage, contrive. ~ *son compte à faire*, to be better [off] doing. *aller* ~ *qn*, to go & see s.o. **se** ~, to be; feel; happen. ~ *mal*, to pass out, faint. *il se trouve que*, it turns out, it happens that.
truand *P* (tryɑ̃) *m*, cook. **truander** *P* (de) *v.t*, to swindle.
trublion (tryblijɔ̃) *m*, troublemaker, agitator.
truc *P* (tryk) *m*, knack, trick, way; thingummy *P*, whatsit *P*, thing.
truchement (tryʃmɑ̃) *m*, *par le* ~ *de*, through [the intervention of]; by means of.
truculent, e (trykylɑ̃, ɑ̃t) *a*, colourful.
truelle (tryɛl) *f*, trowel. ~ *à poisson*, fish slice.
truffe (tryf) *f*, truffle; nose (*dog*). **truffer** (fe) *v.t*, to garnish with truffles; (*fig.*) lard, pepper (*de*, with).
truie (trɥi) *f*, sow.
truite (trɥit) *f*, trout. **truité, e** (te) *a*, speckled, mottled.
truquage (trykaʒ) *m*, faking; fixing *P*, rigging *P*; fiddling *P*; (*Cine.*) effect, trick. **truquer** (ke) *v.t*, to fake; fix *P*, rig *P*; fiddle *P*.
trust (trœst) *m*, trust; corporation. **truster** (te) *v.t*, to monopolize.
tsar (tzar) *m*, tsar.
tsé-tsé (tsetse) *f*, [*mouche*] ~, tsetse fly.
tu (ty) *pn. subject*, you (*familiar form, also used to child*); (*Rel.*, *O*) thou.
tuant, e (tɥɑ̃, ɑ̃t) *a*, boring; killing; exasperating.
tuba (tyba) *m*, tuba; snorkel.
tube (tyb) *m*, tube; pipe; (*P*) hit song. ~ *digestif*, digestive tract.
tubercule (tybɛrkyl) *m*, tuber; tubercle. **tuberculeux, euse** (lø, øz) *a*, tuberculous; tubercular. ¶ *n*, tuberculosis patient. **tuberculose** (loz) *f*, tuberculosis.
tubulaire (tybylɛr) *a*, tubular.
tuer (tɥe) *v.t*, to kill; shoot; (*fig.*) exhaust, wear out. ~ *la poule aux œufs d'or*, to kill the goose that lays the golden egg. *un tué, une tuée*, a person killed. *les tués*, the dead. **se** ~, to be killed; kill o.s; wear o.s out. **tuerie** (tyri) *f*, slaughter, butchery, carnage. *à tue-tête*, at the top of one's voice. **tueur, euse** (tɥœr, øz) *n*, killer. ~ [*à gages*], hired killer. ¶ *m*, slaughterman, slaughterer.
tuile (tɥil) *f*, tile; wafer; (*P*) blow.
tulipe (tylip) *f*, tulip. **tulipier** (pje) *m*, tulip tree.
tulle (tyl) *m*, tulle, net.
tumeur (tymœr) *f*, tumour.
tumulte (tymylt) *m*, tumult, uproar, turmoil; riot; commotion, hubbub. **tumultueux, euse**† (tɥø, øz) *a*, tumultuous, riotous, turbulent, stormy.
tunique (tynik) *f*, tunic.
Tunisie (la) (tynizi) Tunisia. **tunisien, ne** (zjɛ̃, ɛn) *a. &* **T**~, *n*, Tunisian.
tunnel (tynɛl) *m*, tunnel.
turban (tyrbɑ̃) *m*, turban.
turbine (tyrbin) *f*, turbine.
turboréacteur (tyrbɔreaktœr) *m*, turbojet.
turbot (tyrbo) *m*, turbot.
turbulence (tyrbylɑ̃s) *f*, turbulence. **turbulent, e** (lɑ̃, ɑ̃t) *a*, turbulent, unruly, restless; boisterous.
turc, turque (tyrk) *a*, Turkish. **T**~, *n*, Turk. **le** ~, Turkish (*language*).
turf (tyrf) *m*, racecourse. *le* ~, the turf. **turfiste** (fist) *n*, racegoer.

turlupiner *P* (tyrlypine) *v.t,* to bother, worry.
turne (tyrn) (*P Sch.*) *f,* room.
Turquie (tyrki) *f,* Turkey.
turquoise (tyrkwaz) *f.* & *a,* turquoise.
tutelle (tytɛl) *f,* tutelage, guardianship; trusteeship; supervision. **tuteur, trice** (tœr, tris) *n,* guardian. ¶ *m,* (*Hort.*) prop, stake.
tutoiement (tytwamɑ̃) *m,* use of 'tu'. **tutoyer** (je) *v.t,* to address as 'tu'; be on first name terms with.
tutu (tyty) *m,* ballet skirt, tutu.
tuyau (tɥijo) *m,* pipe; tubing; (*P*) tip. ~ *d'arrosage,* hosepipe, garden hose. ~ *de cheminée,* chimney pipe. ~ *d'échappement,* exhaust [pipe]. **tuyauter** (te) *v.t,* to give a tip to; put in the know *P.* **tuyauterie[s]** (tri) *f.* [*pl*], piping; pipes (*organ*).
tympan (tɛ̃pɑ̃) *m,* tympanum, eardrum.
type (tip) *m,* type; (*P*) bloke *P.* ¶ *a.inv,* standard; typical, classic.
typhoïde (tifɔid) *a,* typhoid.
typhon (tifɔ̃) *m,* typhoon.
typhus (tifys) *m,* typhus.
typique† (tipik) *a,* typical.
typographe (tipɔgraf) *n,* typographer. **typographie** (fi) *f,* typography. **typographique** (fik) *a,* typographic(al).
typologie (tipɔlɔʒi) *f,* typology.
tyran (tirɑ̃) *m,* tyrant. **tyrannie** (rani) *f,* tyranny. **tyrannique**† (nik) *a,* tyrannic(al); high-handed. **tyranniser** (nize) *v.t,* to tyrannize [over].
tzigane (tsigan) *n.* & *a,* gipsy, Tzigane.

U

U, u (y) *m, letter,* U, u.
ubiquité (ybikɥite) *f,* ubiquity.
ulcération (ylserasjɔ̃) *f,* ulceration. **ulcère** (sɛr) *m,* ulcer. **ulcérer** (sere) *v.t,* to ulcerate; appal.
ultérieur, e (ylterjœr) *a,* ulterior, later, subsequent. **ultérieurement** (œrmɑ̃) *ad,* later [on].
ultime (yltim) *a,* ultimate, final.
ultra (yltra) *pref:* ultra. **~-son,** ultrasonic sound. **~-violet,** *a,* ultraviolet. ¶ *m,* ultraviolet ray.
un (œ̃) *m,* one. **un, une** (œ̃, yn) *a,* one; a, an; some. ¶ *pn,* one. ~ *à* ~, one by one; one after another. *l'*~, each (*price of articles*); one. *la une,* (*Press*) the front page. *l'*~ *l'autre, les uns* (*les unes*) *les autres,* one another, each other. *l'*~ *& l'autre,* both. *l'*~ *ou l'autre,* either. *les* ~*s,* some. *ni l'*~ *ni l'autre,* neither. ~ *seul,* one only, just one. *une fois,* once. *une fois pour toutes,* once and for all. *il y avait une fois,* once upon a time there was.
unanime† (ynanim) *a,* unanimous. **unanimité** (mite) *f,* unanimity. *à l'*~, unanimously.
uni, e (yni) *a,* united; close (*friend &c*); even, smooth; plain (*colour, paper*).
unième† (ynjɛm) *a,* first (*only after* 20, 30 *&c,* e.g, *vingt &* ~, 21st; *cent* ~, 101st).
unificateur, trice (unifikatœr, tris) *a,* unifying. **unification** (kasjɔ̃) *f,* unification. **unifier** (ynifje) *v.t,* to unify. **uniforme** (fɔrm) *a,* uniform, even. ¶ *m,* uniform. **uniformément** (memɑ̃) *ad,* uniformly, evenly. **uniformisation** (mizasjɔ̃) *f,* standardization. **uniformiser** (ze) *v.t,* to standardize. **uniformité** (mite) *f,* uniformity.
unijambiste (yniʒɑ̃bist) *a.* & *n,* one-legged (person).
unilatéral, e† (ynilateral) *a,* unilateral; one-sided.
union (ynjɔ̃) *f,* union; unity; combination; association. *l'U*~ *Soviétique,* the Soviet Union.
unique (ynik) *a,* only; sole; single; one; unique. *fils* ~, only son. ~ *au monde,* absolutely unique. *à voie* ~, single-lane (*road*). **uniquement** (kmɑ̃) *ad,* solely, uniquely; only, merely, just.
unir (ynir) *v.t,* to unite, join; j. up, link; combine. **s'**~, to unite; be joined in marriage; combine. **unisexe** (nisɛks) *a.inv,* unisex. **unisson** (nisɔ̃) *m,* unison. **unitaire** (tɛr) *a,* unitary; (*Pol.*) unitarian. **unité** (te) *f,* unity; (*Com., Math., Mil.*) unit; (*Naut.*) warship; (*P*) ten thousand francs.
univers (ynivɛr) *m,* universe. **universalité** (vɛrsalite) *f,* universality. **universel, le**† (sɛl) *a,* universal; world[-wide]. **universitaire** (sitɛr) *a,* university; academic. ¶ *n,* academic. **université** (te) *f,* university.
uranium (yranjɔm) *m,* uranium.
urbain, e (yrbɛ̃, ɛn) *a,* urban, city; (*liter.*) urbane. **urbanisme** (banism) *m,* town planning. **urbaniste** (ist) *n,* town planner. **urbanité** (te) *f,* urbanity.
urée (yre) *f,* urea.
urgence (yrʒɑ̃s) *f,* urgency; (*Med.*) emergency case. *d'*~, urgently, immediately; emergency (*measure &c*). **urgent, e** (ʒɑ̃, ɑ̃t) *a,* urgent. *l'*~, the most urgent thing. **urger** *P* (ʒe) *v.i,* to be urgent.

urine (yrin) *f,* urine. **uriner** (ne) *v.i,* to urinate. **urinoir** (nwar) *m,* urinal (*place*).
urne (yrn) *f,* urn. ~ *électorale,* ballot box.
urticaire (yrtikɛr) *f,* nettle rash.
us & coutumes (ys) *m.pl,* [habits &] customs. **usage** (zaʒ) *m,* use; purpose; wear; usage, custom, practice. (*Med.*) *à* ~ *externe,* for external use. *à l'*~, with use. *à l'*~ *de,* for. *d'*~, usual, customary, set (*formula*). *en* ~, in use. *faire de l'*~, (*shoes &c*) to wear *or* last well. **usagé, e** (zaʒe) *a,* used, worn. **usager, ère** (ʒe, ɛr) *n,* user. **usé, e** (ze) *a,* worn [out]; shabby. ~ [*jusqu'à la corde*], threadbare, hackneyed, stale. **user** (ze) *v.t,* to use; wear [out, away]. ~ *de,* to use, exercise. *en* ~ *bien, mal avec qn,* to treat s.o well, badly. **s'**~, to wear [away].
usine (yzin) *f,* works; factory; mill; plant. **usiner** (ne) *v.t,* to manufacture; machine.
usité, e (yzite) *a,* used, in use; common (*word*).
ustensile (ystɑ̃sil) *m,* utensil; implement, tool.
usuel, le† (yzɥɛl) *a,* ordinary, everyday; common. ¶ *m,* book on the open shelf (*library*).
usufruit (yzyfrɥi) *m,* usufruct.
usuraire (yzyrɛr) *a,* usurious. **usure** (zyr) *f,* usury; wear [& tear], wearing; worn state. **usurier, ère** (zyrje, ɛr) *n,* usurer.
usurpateur, trice (yzyrpatœr, tris) *n,* usurper. **usurpation** (sjɔ̃) *f,* usurpation. **usurper** (pe) *v.t,* to usurp.
ut (yt) *m,* (*Mus.*) C.
utérin, e (yterɛ̃, in) *a,* uterine. **utérus** (rys) *m,* uterus, womb.
utile† (ytil) *a,* useful, helpful. **utilisateur, trice** (lizatœr, tris) *n,* user. **utilisation** (zasjɔ̃) *f,* use. **utiliser** (lize) *v.t,* to make use of, use. **utilitaire** (tɛr) *a. & n,* utilitarian. **utilité** (te) *f,* use[fulness].
utopie (ytɔpi) *f,* utopia. **utopique** (pik) *a. &* **utopiste** (pist) *n,* utopian.

V

V, v (ve) *m, letter,* V, v.
vacance (vakɑ̃s) *f,* vacancy; (*pl.*) holiday[s]; vacation, recess; (*Law*) abeyance. **vacancier, ère** (sje, ɛr) *n,* holiday-maker. **vacant, e** (kɑ̃, ɑ̃t) *a,* vacant, unoccupied.
vacarme (vakarm) *m,* uproar, din, row.
vacation (vakasjɔ̃) *f,* (*Law*) sitting, session (*experts*); (*Law*) (*pl.*) fees; vacation.
vaccin (vaksɛ̃) *m,* vaccine. **vaccination** (sinasjɔ̃) *f,* vaccination. **vacciner** (ne) *v.t,* to vaccinate.
vache (vaʃ) *f,* cow; cow hide; (*P**) bitch *P**; swine *P**. ~ *laitière,* dairy cow. *la* ~*! P* hell! *P manger la* ~ *enragée,* to go through hard times. *parler français comme une* ~ *espagnole,* to speak appallingly bad French. ¶ *a,* rotten *P,* mean. **vachement** *P* (ʃmɑ̃) *ad,* bloody *P**, damned *P;* like hell *P;* in a rotten way. **vacher** (ʃe) *n,* cowherd. **vacherie** (ʃri) *f,* cowshed; (*P*) rottenness *P;* dirty trick *P;* bitchy remark *P. quelle* ~ *de temps!* what bloody awful weather! *P**.
vaciller (vasile) *v.i,* to be unsteady, wobble; vacillate, waver; flicker.
va-comme-je-te-pousse (à la) *P* (vakɔmʒətəpus) any old how *P.*
vadrouille *P* (vadruj) *f,* ramble. **vadrouiller** *P* (je) *v.i,* to rove around.
va-et-vient (vaevjɛ̃) *m,* comings & goings, to-ings & fro-ings; backwards & forwards motion; (*Elec.*) two-way switch.
vagabond, e (vagabɔ̃, ɔ̃d) *a,* wandering; restless (*mind*). ¶ *n,* vagabond, vagrant, tramp. **vagabondage** (bɔ̃daʒ) *m,* vagrancy; wandering. **vagabonder** (de) *v.i,* to rove, wander.
vagin (vaʒɛ̃) *m,* vagina.
vagir (vaʒir) *v.i,* to wail, cry (*of baby*). **vagissement** (ʒismɑ̃) *m,* wailing, cry.
vague[1] (vag) *f,* wave; surge. ~[*s*] *de fond,* ground swell.
vague†[2] (vag) *a,* vague; hazy; waste (*land*); loose-fitting (*garment*). ¶ *m,* vagueness; void. ~ *à l'âme,* vague melancholy. **vaguer** (vage) *v.i,* to wander [about].
vaillamment (vajamɑ̃) *ad,* valiantly, gallantly; bravely, courageously. **vaillance** (jɑ̃s) *f,* gallantry, valour; bravery, courage. **vaillant, e** (jɑ̃, ɑ̃t) *a,* valiant, gallant &c; robust, vigorous.
vain, e† (vɛ̃, ɛn) *a,* vain; empty, useless, futile. *en* ~, in vain, fruitless.
vaincre (vɛ̃kr) *v.t.ir,* to vanquish, conquer; beat; overcome. **les vaincus** (vɛ̃ky) *m.pl,* the vanquished. **vainqueur** (kœr) *m,* conqueror, victor; (*Sport*) winner.
vaisseau (vɛso) *m,* vessel; ship; (*Arch.*) nave. ~ *amiral,* flagship. ~ *sanguin,* blood vessel. ~ *spatial,* spaceship. **vaisselier** (səlje) *m,* dresser. **vaisselle** (sɛl) *f,* crockery, dishes; washing up. *faire la* ~, to wash up.
val (val) *m,* valley.
valable† (valabl) *a,* valid, good; worthwhile, decent.
valet (valɛ) *m,* [man] servant; (*Cards*) knave, jack. ~ *de chambre,* valet. ~ *de ferme,* farm

hand. ~ *de pied,* footman.
valeur (valœr) *f,* (*gen.*) value; worth, merit; price; (*Fin.*) security; (*pl.*) stocks & shares. ~ *marchande,* market value. ~*s mobilières,* transferable securities. ~*s morales,* moral values. ~ *vénale,* monetary value. *mettre en* ~, to exploit (*land*); highlight, set off; show to advantage. *objets de* ~, valuables. **valeureux, euse**† (lœrø, øz) *a,* valorous.
valide† (valid) *a,* valid; available; able-bodied, fit for service (*pers.*). **valider** (de) *v.t,* to validate; authenticate (*document*). **validité** (dite) *f,* validity.
valise (valiz) *f,* [suit]case. ~ [*diplomatique*], diplomatic bag.
vallée (vale) *f,* valley. **vallon** (lɔ̃) *m,* vale. **vallonné, e** (lɔne) *a,* undulating.
valoir (valwar) *v.t,* to be worth; be as good as; be equivalent to; apply, be valid. *cela vaut la peine* ou *le coup P,* it is worth while. *ça ne vaut rien,* it's no good. *il vaut mieux partir,* it is better to leave. *à* ~ *sur,* on account of. *faire* ~, to highlight; emphasize; show off to advantage; assert (*right*); exploit, develop (*land*). ¶ *v.t,* to earn, gain.
valoriser (valɔrize) *v.t,* to enhance the value of.
valse (vals) *f,* waltz; (*fig.*) musical chairs. ~ *hésitation,* pussyfooting *P.* **valser** (se) *v.i,* to waltz. *envoyer* ~, to send flying. *faire* ~, to throw around. **valseur, euse** (sœr, øz) *n,* waltzer.
valve (valv) *f,* valve.
vampire (vɑ̃pir) *m,* vampire; v. bat.
vandale (vɑ̃dal) *m,* vandal. **vandalisme** (lism) *m,* vandalism, wanton destruction.
vanille (vanij) *f,* vanilla.
vanité (vanite) *f,* vanity, conceit; uselessness, futility. **vaniteux, euse** (tø, øz) *a,* vain, conceited.
vanne (van) *f,* sluice gate, flood gate; gate. **vanneau** (no) *m,* lapwing, pe[e]wit. **vanner** (ne) *v.t,* to winnow; (*P*) exhaust. **vannerie** (nri) *f,* basketwork. **vannier** (nje) *m,* basket maker.
vantail (vɑ̃taj) *m,* leaf (*door, shutter*).
vantard, e (vɑ̃tar, ard) *a,* boastful. ¶ *n,* boaster, braggart. **vantardise** (tardiz) *f,* boast[ing], brag[ging]. **vanter** (te) *v.t,* to praise, extol, vaunt. **se** ~, to boast, vaunt, brag.
va-nu-pieds (vanypje) *n,* beggar, tramp.
vapeur (vapœr) *f,* vapour; haze; steam. *à* ~, steam (*engine, boat*). *à toute* ~, full steam ahead. [*cuit à la*] ~, (*Cook.*) steamed. **vaporeux, euse** (pɔrø, øz) *a,* vaporous; misty; hazy; filmy, gauzy. **vaporisateur** (rizatœr) *m,* spray, atomizer. **vaporiser** (ze) *v.t,* to vaporize; spray.
vaquer (vake) *v.i,* to be on vacation. ~ *à,* to attend to.
varappe (varap) *f,* rock climbing.
varech (varɛk) *m,* seaweed, wrack.
vareuse (varøz) *f,* (*Mil.*) tunic; pea jacket (*sailor*).
variable (varjabl) *a,* variable, changeable, unsettled. *au* ~, at change (*barometer*). ¶ *f,* variable. **variante** (rjɑ̃t) *f,* variant. **variation** (rjasjɔ̃) *f,* variation, change.
varice (varis) *f,* varicose vein.
varicelle (varisɛl) *f,* chicken pox.
varié, e (varje) *a,* varied; various, divers. **varier** (je) *v.t. & i,* to vary. **variété** (rjete) *f,* variety; (*pl.*) variety show.
variole (varjɔl) *f,* smallpox.
Varsovie (varsɔvi) *f,* Warsaw.
vase[1] (vɑz) *f,* mud, silt, slime.
vase[2] (vɑz) *m,* vase, vessel. ~ *de nuit,* chamber pot. (*fig.*) *en* ~ *clos,* in seclusion.
vaseline (vazlin) *f,* vaseline.
vaseux, euse (vɑzø, øz) *a,* muddy, slimy; (*P*) hazy; washed out *P* (*pers.*).
vasistas (vazistɑs) *m,* fanlight.
vassal, e (vasal) *n,* (*Hist.*) vassal.
vaste (vast) *a,* vast, immense, huge.
va-tout (vatu) *m, jouer son* ~, to stake one's all.
vaudeville (vodvil) *m,* vaudeville.
vau-l'eau (à) (volo) *ad,* to rack & ruin.
vaurien, ne (vorjɛ̃, ɛn) *n,* good-for-nothing.
vautour (votur) *m,* vulture.
vautre (votr) *m,* boar hound.
vautrer (se) (votre) *v.pr,* to wallow; sprawl.
veau (vo) *m,* calf; veal; calf[skin]. (*P pej.*) lump *P.* ~ *d'or,* golden calf. ~ *gras,* fatted c.
vecteur (vɛktœr) *m,* vector.
vécu, e (veky) *a,* real-life (*story*).
vedette (vədɛt) *f,* (*Theat., Cine.*) star; leading light; launch (*boat*); (*Mil.*) patrol boat. *avoir la* ~, to top the bill; make the headlines; be in the limelight. *en* ~, in the limelight; with star billing.
végétal, e (veʒetal) *a,* plant (*life*); vegetable. ¶ *m,* plant. **végétarien, ne** (tarjɛ̃, ɛn) *a. & n,* vegetarian. **végétarisme** (rism) *m,* vegetarianism. **végétation** (sjɔ̃) *f,* vegetation; growth. ~*s* [*adénoïdes*], adenoids. **végéter** (te) *v.i,* to vegetate.
véhémence (veemɑ̃s) *f,* vehemence. **véhément, e**† (mɑ̃, ɑ̃t) *a,* vehement.
véhicule (veikyl) *m,* vehicle; medium. **véhiculer** (le) *v.t,* to convey.
veille (vɛj) *f,* wakefulness, staying up; [night] watch; day before, eve; brink, point. *la* ~ *au soir,* the previous evening, the e. before. **veillée** (je) *f,* evening gathering. ~ [*funèbre*], wake, watch. **veiller** (je) *v.i,* to stay up, sit up, lie awake; be watchful; spend the evening in company. ¶ *v.t,* to watch over, sit up with. ~ *à,* to see to, attend to, look after. ~ *au grain,* to keep an eye open for trouble. ~ *sur,* to watch over. **veilleuse** (jøz) *f,* nightlight; (*Mot.*) sidelight.

veine (vɛn) *f,* vein; seam (*coal*); (*fig.*) inspiration; (*P*) luck. *de la même ~*, in the same vein. *être en ~*, to be inspired. *pas de ~!* bad luck! **veiner** (ne) *v.t,* to vein, grain.
vêler (vɛle) *v.i,* to calve.
vélin (velɛ̃) *m,* vellum.
véliplanchiste (veliplɑ̃ʃist) *n,* windsurfer (*pers.*).
velléitaire (vɛleitɛr) *a,* irresolute. ¶ *n,* waverer. **velléité** (eite) *f,* irresolute *or* vague intention.
vélo (velo) *m,* bike. **vélocité** (te) *f,* swiftness. **vélodrome** (drom) *m,* cycle track. **vélomoteur** (mɔtœr) *m,* moped.
velours (vəlur) *m,* velvet; bloom (*peach*). *~ côtelé,* corduroy. **velouté, e** (lute) *a,* velvet[y]; smooth; mellow (*voice &c*). ¶ *m,* velvetiness, smoothness; (*Cook.*) velouté sauce; velouté, cream soup.
velu, e (vəly) *a,* hairy (*skin, caterpillar, leaf*).
venaison (vənɛzɔ̃) *f,* venison.
vénal, e† (venal) *a,* venal. **vénalité** (lite) *f,* venality.
venant (vənɑ̃) *m,* comer.
vendable (vɑ̃dabl) *a,* saleable, marketable.
vendange (vɑ̃dɑ̃ʒ) *f.oft.pl,* grape harvest; vintage. **vendanger** (ʒe) *v.t,* (*& i*), to pick (grapes). **vendangeur, euse** (ʒœr, øz) *n,* grape-picker.
vendetta (vɑ̃dɛtta) *f,* vendetta, feud.
vendeur, euse (vɑ̃dœr, øz) *n,* seller, vendor; salesman, -woman. **vendre** (dr) *v.t,* to sell, sell at; sell for; sell up. *~ la mèche P,* to give the game away. *~ la peau de l'ours avant de l'avoir tué,* to count one's chickens before they are hatched. **se ~**, to sell, be sold; sell o.s, give o.s away.
vendredi (vɑ̃drədi) *m,* Friday. *le ~ saint,* Good Friday.
vénéneux, euse (venenø, øz) *a,* poisonous.
vénérable (venerabl) *a,* venerable. **vénération** (sjɔ̃) *f,* veneration. **vénérer** (re) *v.t,* to venerate.
vénérien, ne (venerjɛ̃, ɛn) *a,* venereal (*disease*). ¶ *n,* V.D. patient.
vengeance (vɑ̃ʒɑ̃s) *f,* vengeance; revenge. **venger** (ʒe) *v.t,* to avenge, revenge. **se ~**, to have one's revenge (*de qn,* on o.s; *de qch,* for sth). **vengeur, eresse** (ʒœr, ʒrɛs) *n,* avenger. ¶ *a,* avenging, vengeful.
véniel, le† (venjɛl) *a,* venial.
venimeux, euse (vənimø, øz) *a,* venomous. **venin** (nɛ̃) *m,* venom.
venir (vənir) *v.i.ir,* to come; (*idea*) strike; occur, happen. *les années à ~*, the years to come. *~ au monde,* to come into the world, be born. *~ de,* to come from. *~ [jusqu']à,* to reach, come up to, down to. *en ~ à,* to reach, get to, come to. *où voulez-vous en ~?* what are you getting at? *en ~ aux mains,* to come to blows. *faire ~*, to call, send for. *je viens de voir,* I have just seen. *s'il vient à neiger,* if it should [happen to] snow. *s'en ~*, to come.
vent (vɑ̃) *m,* wind. *~ coulis,* draught. *avoir ~ de,* to get wind of. *au ~*, to windward. *sous le ~*, to leeward. *dans le ~ P,* trendy *P.*
vente (vɑ̃t) *f,* sale. *~ [aux enchères],* auction, [a.] sale. *~ de charité,* charity bazaar, jumble sale. *en ~*, on sale, for sale.
venter (vɑ̃te) *v.imp,* to be windy, blow. **venteux, euse** (tø, øz) *a,* windy; breezy. **ventilateur** (tilatœr) *m,* fan, ventilator. **ventilation** (sjɔ̃) *f,* ventilation, airing; breakdown, analysis. **ventiler** (le) *v.t,* to ventilate &c.
ventouse (vɑ̃tuz) *f,* cupping glass; sucker (*of leech*); suction pad.
ventre (vɑ̃tr) *m,* abdomen; stomach, tummy *P;* womb; belly; bulb. *avoir le ~ creux,* to have an empty stomach. *mal au ~*, stomach ache. *il n'a rien dans le ~ P,* he's got no guts *P.*
ventricule (vɑ̃trikyl) *m,* ventricle.
ventriloque (vɑ̃trilɔk) *n,* ventriloquist. **ventriloquie** (ki) *f,* ventriloquism, ventriloquy.
ventripotent, e (vɑ̃tripɔtɑ̃, ɑ̃t) *&* **ventru, e** (ry) *a,* potbellied; bulbous.
venu, e (vəny) *n,* comer; (*f.*) coming. ¶ *a, bien ~*, timely, apposite; (*child &c*) sturdy; well-developed. *mal ~*, untimely; stunted.
vêpres (vɛpr) *f. pl,* vespers.
ver (vɛr) *m,* worm; grub; maggot. *~ à soie,* silkworm. *~ luisant,* glow-worm. *~ solitaire,* tapeworm. *tirer les ~s du nez à qn P,* to get information out of s.o.
véracité (verasite) *f,* veracity, truthfulness.
véranda (verɑ̃da) *f,* veranda[h].
verbal, e† (vɛrbal) *a,* verbal. **verbaliser** (lize) *v.i,* to take particulars; draw up a report. **verbe** (vɛrb) *m,* verb; [tone of] voice. *le V~* (*Theol.*) the Word. **verbeux, euse** (bø, øz) *a,* verbose, wordy. **verbiage** (bjaʒ) *m,* verbiage. **verbosité** (bozite) *f,* verbosity, wordiness.
verdâtre (vɛrdɑtr) *a,* greenish. **verdeur** (dœr) *f,* tartness, sharpness; acidity; forthrightness; vigour, vitality.
verdict (vɛrdikt) *m,* verdict.
verdier (vɛrdje) *m,* greenfinch. **verdir** (dir) *v.t. & i,* to turn green. **verdoyant, e** (dwajɑ̃, ɑ̃t) *a,* verdant. **verdure** (dyr) *f,* verdure, greenery; greenness; greensward; green stuff, greens.
véreux, euse (verø, øz) *a,* wormy, maggoty; shady, bogus, fishy.
verge (vɛrʒ) *f,* rod; (*Anat.*) penis.
verger (vɛrʒe) *m,* orchard.
verglas (vɛrgla) *m,* [black] ice (*road*).
vergogne (sans) (vɛrgɔɲ), shameless.
vergue (vɛrg) *f,* (*Naut.*) yard.
véridique† (veridik) *a,* truthful, veracious; authentic, genuine, **vérifiable** (rifjabl) *a,* verifiable. **vérificateur, trice** (fikatœr, tris) *n,* controller, checker; inspector. *~ des comptes,* auditor. **vérification** (sjɔ̃) *f,* verification, checking, ascertaining; auditing; confirmation;

proof. ~ *d'identité*, identity check. ~ *faite*, on checking. **vérifier** (fje) *v.t*, to verify &c.
vérin (verɛ̃) *m*, (*Mot.*) jack.
véritable† (veritabl) *a*, true; real, genuine; veritable. **vérité** (te) *f*, truth; truthfulness, sincerity; lifelikeness, trueness to life (*portrait &c*).
vermeil, le (vɛrmɛj) *a*, vermilion; ruby, rosy. ¶ *m*, vermeil.
vermicelle (vɛrmisɛl) *m*, vermicelli; v. soup.
vermillon (vɛrmijɔ̃) *m*, vermilion.
vermine (vɛrmin) *f*, vermin. **vermoulu, e** (muly) *a*, worm-eaten. **vermoulure** (lyr) *f*, worm hole.
vermouth (vɛrmut) *m*, verm[o]uth.
verni, e (vɛrni) *a*, shiny, glossy; (*P*) lucky; patent (*leather*), patent leather (*shoes*). **vernir** (nir) *v.t*, to varnish; glaze. **vernis** (ni) *m*, varnish; glaze; shine, gloss; (*fig.*) veneer. ~ [*à ongles*], nail varnish. **vernissage** (nisaʒ) *m*, varnishing; glazing; preview (*art gallery*).
vérole *P** (verɔl) *f*, pox *P**.
véronique (verɔnik) *f*, speedwell, veronica.
verrat (vɛra) *m*, boar.
verre (vɛr) *m*, glass; (*Opt.*) lens; drink. ~ *à dents*, tooth mug. ~ *blanc*, plain glass. ~*s de contact*, contact lenses. ~ *dépoli*, frosted glass. ~*s fumés*, tinted lenses. *prendre un* ~, to have a drink. **verrerie** (vɛrri) *f*, glass making; g. works; glass[ware]. **verrier** (rje) *m*, glass maker; g. artist. **verrière** (rjɛr) *f*, window; glass roof; g. wall. **verroterie** (rɔtri) *f*, [glass] beads.
verrou (vɛru) *m*, bolt. *sous les* ~*s*, under lock & key, locked up. **verrouiller** (ruje) *v.t*, to bolt; lock up (*prisoner*).
verrue (vɛry) *f*, wart. ~ *plantaire*, verruca.
vers¹ (vɛr) *m*, line (*poetry*); (*pl.*) verse. ~ *blancs*, blank verse.
vers² (vɛr) *pr*, toward[s], to; about, around. ~ *9 heures*, about 9 o'clock. ~ *la fin du siècle*, towards the end of the century.
versant (vɛrsɑ̃) *m*, side, slope (*hill &c*).
versatile (vɛrsatil) *a*, fickle; changeable. **versatilité** (lite) *f*, fickleness &c.
verse (à) (vɛrs) (*rain*) in torrents, **versé(e) dans** (se), versed in, conversant with. **versement** (səmɑ̃) *m*, payment, paying in; instalment. **verser** (se) *v.t*, to pour [out], tip; shed (*tears*); pay; assign (*dans*, to). ~ *des arrhes*, to pay a deposit. ¶ *v.i*, to overturn. ~ *dans*, to lapse into. **verset** (sɛ) *m*, verse (*Bible*). **verseuse** (søz) *f*, pourer.
version (vɛrsjɔ̃) *f*, version; translation (*into one's own language*); unseen [translation]. *en* ~ *originale*, (*film*) in the original language *or* version. *en* ~ *anglaise*, dubbed in English.
verso (vɛrso) *m*, back. *au* ~, overleaf.
vert, e (vɛr, ɛrt) *a*, green; unripe; young (*wine*); sprightly (*pers.*); sharp, stiff (*reprimand*); saucy, spicy (*remark*). ¶ *m*, green; grass. **vert-de-gris** (vɛrdəgri) *m*, verdigris. ¶ *a*, grey[ish]-green.
vertébral, e (vɛrtebral) *a*, vertebral; spinal (*column*). **vertèbre** (tɛbr) *f*, vertebra. **vertébré, e** (tebre) *a*. & *m*, vertebrate.
vertement (vertəmɑ̃) *ad*, (*scold*) sharply, soundly.
vertical, e (vɛrtikal) *a*, vertical, upright. ¶ *f*, vertical. **verticalement** (lmɑ̃) *ad*, vertically; down (*crossword clues*).
vertige (vɛrtiʒ) *m*, dizziness; giddiness; vertigo; (*fig.*) fever. **vertigineux, euse†** (tiʒinø, øz) *a*, dizzy, giddy; breathtaking; breathtakingly high.
vertu (vɛrty) *f*, virtue. *en* ~ *de*, in (*or* by) v. of; in accordance with. **vertueux, euse†** (tɥø, øz) *a*, virtuous.
verve (vɛrv) *f*, verve.
verveine (vɛrvɛn) *f*, verbena.
vésicule (vezikyl) *f*, vesicle. ~ [*biliaire*], gall-bladder.
vespasienne (vɛspazjɛn) *f*, urinal (*street*).
vessie (vɛsi) *f*, bladder.
veste (vɛst) *f*, jacket. **vestiaire** (tjɛr) *m*, cloakroom; changing room.
vestibule (vɛstibyl) *m*, vestibule, [entrance] hall, lobby.
vestige (vɛstiʒ) *m*, vestige, relic, remnant, trace; (*pl.*) vestiges, remains, relics.
vestimentaire (vɛstimɑ̃tɛr) *a*, sartorial, of dress.
veston (vɛstɔ̃) *m*, jacket.
vêtement (vɛtmɑ̃) *m*, garment; item of clothing; (*pl.*) clothes; clothing industry. ~*s de dessous*, underclothes.
vétéran (veterɑ̃) *m*, veteran.
vétérinaire (veterinɛr) *a*, veterinary. ¶ *m*, veterinary surgeon, vet.
vétille (vetij) *f*, trifle.
vêtir (vɛtir) *v.t.ir*, to clothe, dress.
veto (veto) *m*, veto.
vétuste (vetyst) *a*, ancient, dilapidated. **vétusté** (te) *f*, great age, dilapidation.
veuf, veuve (vœf, vœv) *a*, widowed. ¶ *m*, widower. ¶ *f*, widow.
veule (vœl) *a*, spineless.
veuvage (vœvaʒ) *m*, widowhood.
vexant, e (vɛksɑ̃, ɑ̃t) *a*, annoying, vexing; hurtful. **vexation** (asjɔ̃) *f*, humiliation. **vexatoire** (atwar) *a*, *mesures* ~*s*, harassment. **vexer** (kse) *v.t*, to vex, hurt, upset.
viabilité (vjabilite) *f*, good condition (*of roads*); viability. *avec* ~, with services [laid on]. **viable** (bl) *a*, viable.
viaduc (vjadyk) *m*, viaduct.
viager, ère (vjaʒe, ɛr) *a*, life, for life. ¶ *m*, life annuity.
viande (vjɑ̃d) *f*, meat. ~ *de boucherie*, butcher's meat.
viatique (vjatik) *m*, provision for journey.
vibrant, e (vibrɑ̃, ɑ̃t) *a*, vibrating; vibrant,

resonant; emotive. **vibratoire** (bratwar) *a,* vibratory. **vibration** (brasjɔ̃) *f,* vibration. **vibrer** (bre) *v.i,* (*Phys. & fig.*) to vibrate; thrill; (*voice*) quiver; be vibrant.

vicaire (vikɛr) *m,* curate. ~ *général,* vicar-general.

vice (vis) *m,* vice; defect, fault, flaw. ~ *de conformation,* malformation. ~ *de construction,* constructional defect. ~ *de forme,* legal flaw *or* irregularity. ~ *de prononciation,* mispronunciation.

vice- (vis) *pref,* vice: ~*-président, e, n,* vice- (*or* deputy) chairman *or* president. ~*-roi, m,* viceroy.

vice versa (viseversa) *ad,* vice versa.

vicier (visje) *v.t,* to taint; pollute; contaminate. **vicieux, euse†** (sjø, øz) *a,* perverted, depraved (*pers.*); restive (*horse*); incorrect (*pronunciation*). ¶ *n,* pervert.

vicinal, e (visinal) *a,* local (*road*).

vicissitude (visisityd) *f,* vicissitude.

victime (viktim) *f,* victim; casualty.

victoire (viktwar) *f,* victory; win. ~ *aux points,* win on points. **victorieux, euse†** (rjø, øz) *a,* victorious, triumphant.

victuailles (viktɥaj) *f.pl,* provisions.

vidange (vidɑ̃ʒ) *f,* emptying; (*Mot.*) oil change; waste outlet (*sink*). **vidanger** (dɑ̃ʒe) *v.t,* to empty. **vide** (vid) *a,* empty, vacant. ~ *de,* devoid of; empty of. ~ *de sens,* meaningless. ¶ *m,* void, emptiness; vacuum; gap, space, blank. *à* ~, empty. *sous* ~, under vacuum. *emballée sous* ~, vacuum-packed. ~*-ordures, m.inv,* rubbish chute. ~*-poches,* tidy; (*Mot.*) glove compartment. ~ *sanitaire,* underfloor space.

vidéocassette (videokasɛt) *f,* video-cassette.

vider (vide) *v.t,* to empty; e. out; drain (*glass &c*); draw (*fowl*); gut (*fish*); core (*apple*); throw (*rider*); settle (*dispute*); vacate (*les lieux,* the premises); (*P*) throw out *P;* (*P*) wear out. ~ *l'abcès,* to root out the evil. ~ *son sac P,* to come out with it *P.*

vie (vi) *f,* life; lifetime; living; life[story]. *à* ~, *pour la* ~, for life. *c'est la* ~*!* that's life! *faire la* ~, to lead a life of pleasure; (*P*) kick up a fuss *P. jamais de la* ~*!* not on your life!, never! *la* ~ *chère,* the high cost of living. [*mode de*] ~, lifestyle.

vieillard (vjɛjar) *m,* old man. *les* ~*s,* the aged (*either sex*). **vieillesse** (jɛs) *f,* [old] age. **vieillir** (jir) *v.i,* to grow old, age; become obsolete. ¶ *v.t,* to age, make [look] old[er]. **vieillissant, e** (jisɑ̃, ɑ̃t) *a,* ageing. **vieillot, te** (jo, ɔt) *a,* quaint, antiquated.

vierge (vjɛrʒ) *f,* virgin. ¶ *a,* virgin; blank (*page*); free; unexposed (*film*); clean (*record*).

vieux, vieil, vieille (vjø, vjɛj) *a,* old; ancient; long-standing (*friendship*); former, previous. ~ *comme le monde,* as old as the hills. ~ *bique P*,* old bag P*. *vieille fille,* spinster, old maid. ~ *garçon,* bachelor. ~ *jeu, inv,* old-fashioned, old hat. **vieux, vieille,** *n,* old man, old woman. *le* ~, the old (*opp.* the new). *les* ~, the old (*either sex*). *mon* ~, old man, old boy. *un* ~ *de la vieille,* one of the old brigade.

vif, vive (vif, iv) *a,* lively, vivacious; sharp, quick, keen; brusque; intense; strong, deep, great (*satisfaction &c*); bright, brilliant (*light*); biting, bitter (*cold*); (*burn*) alive. *de vive voix,* by word of mouth, in person. ¶ *m,* (*Law*), living person. **le vif,** the quick (*flesh &c*); the heart (*of a matter*). (*Art*) *sur le* ~, from life.

vigie (viʒi) *f,* look-out, watch; look-out post.

vigilance (viʒilɑ̃s) *f,* vigilance, watchfulness. **vigilant, e** (lɑ̃, ɑ̃t) *a,* vigilant, watchful. **vigile** (ʒil) *f,* watch; watchman.

vigne (viɲ) *f,* vine; vineyard. ~ *vierge,* Virginia creeper. **vigneron, ne** (ɲərɔ̃, ɔn) *n,* wine grower. **vignette** (ɲɛt) *f,* vignette; illustration; label; (*Mot.*) tax disc. **vignoble** (ɲɔbl) *m,* vineyard.

vigoureux, euse† (vigurø, øz) *a,* vigorous, strong, sturdy, robust. **vigueur** (gœr) *f,* vigour, strength &c. *en* ~, in force; current, in use.

vil, e† (vil) *a,* vile, base, mean. *à* ~ *prix,* dirt-cheap. **vilain, e†** (lɛ̃, ɛn) *a,* ugly; wretched; nasty; naughty; wicked. ¶ *n,* villain; (*Hist.*) villein.

vilebrequin (vilbrəkɛ̃) *m,* brace; crankshaft.

villa (villa) *f,* detached house. **village** (vilaʒ) *m,* village. **villageois, e** (laʒwa, az) *n,* villager. ¶ *a,* village. **ville** (vil) *f,* town, city. ~ *d'eaux,* spa. **villégiature** (leʒjatyr) *f,* stay in the country; holiday.

vin (vɛ̃) *m,* wine. ~ *chaud,* mulled wine. ~ *d'honneur,* reception (*with wine*). *entre deux* ~*s,* tipsy. **vinaigre** (nɛgr) *m,* vinegar. (*fig.*) *tourner au* ~, to turn sour. **vinaigrer** (nɛgre) *v.t,* to vinegar. **vinaigrette** (grɛt) *f,* French dressing.

vindicatif, ive (vɛ̃dikatif, iv) *a,* vindictive.

vingt (vɛ̃) *a,* twenty. ¶ *m,* twenty; 20th (*date*). *for phrases V* **six** *&* **sixième.** ~*-deux!* look out! **vingtaine** (tɛn) *f,* score, twenty [or so]. **vingtième** (tjɛm) *a. & n,* twentieth.

vinicole (vinikɔl) *a,* wine-growing; wine-producing; wine-making; wine (*industry &c*).

vinyle (vinil) *m,* vinyl.

viol (vjɔl) *m,* rape; violation.

violacé, e (vjɔlase) *a,* mauvish, purplish.

violateur, trice (vjɔlatœr, tris) *a,* violator; transgressor. **violation** (sjɔ̃) *f,* violation, transgression, breach; desecration.

violâtre (vjɔlɑtr) *a,* purplish.

violemment (vjɔlamɑ̃) *ad,* violently. **violence** (lɑ̃s) *f,* violence. *se faire* ~, to force o.s. **violent, e** (lɑ̃, ɑ̃t) *a,* violent; strenuous; urgent.

intense (*need &c*). **violenter** (lɑ̃te) *v.t*, to assault [sexually]; do violence to. **violer** (le) *v.t*, to violate, transgress, break; rape; desecrate.

violet, te (vjɔlɛ, ɛt) *a*, violet, purple. **violet,** *m*, violet, purple (*colour*). **violette,** *f*, (*Bot.*) violet. ~ *de Parme*, Parma v. ~ *odorante*, sweet v.

violon (vjɔlɔ̃) *m*, violin, fiddle; lock-up, clink *P*. **violoncelle** (sɛl) *m*, cello. **violoncelliste** (list) *n*, cellist. **violoniste** (lɔnist) *n*, violinist.

vipère (vipɛr) *f*, viper, adder.

virage (viraʒ) *m*, (*Mot.*) bend; turn; (*fig.*) change in direction *or* policy; (*Phot.*) toning.

virago (virago) *f*, virago.

virée *P* (vire) *f*, drive, run; walk; tour, trip. **virement** (rmɑ̃) *m*, & ~ *bancaire*, credit transfer. (*Naut.*) ~ *de bord*, tacking. **virer** (re) *v.i*, to turn; change; (*Naut.*) go about; (*Phot.*) tone; (*Med: skin test*) come up positive. ~ *à l'aigre*, to turn sour. ~ *de bord*, to tack. ~ *sur l'aile*, (*Aero.*) to bank. ¶ *v.t*, to transfer; (*P*) kick out *P*.

vireux, euse (virø, øz) *a*, noxious.

virevolte (virvɔlt) *f*, (*Danc.*) twirl; (*fig.*) volte-face.

virginal, e (virʒinal) *a*, virginal, maiden[ly]. **virginité** (te) *f*, virginity, maidenhood; purity.

virgule (virgyl) *f*, comma. ~ [*décimale*], [decimal] point. *Note:*—The decimal point is indicated in French by a comma.

viril, e (viril) *a*, virile, manly; masculine, male. **virilité** (lite) *f*, virility, manliness; masculinity.

virtuel, le† (virtɥɛl) *a*, potential; virtual.

virtuose (virtɥoz) *n*, virtuoso. **virtuosité** (ozite) *f*, virtuosity.

virulence (virylɑ̃s) *f*, virulence. **virulent, e** (lɑ̃, ɑ̃t) *a*, virulent. **virus** (rys) *m*, virus.

vis (vis) *f*, screw. ~ *platinées*, (*Mot.*) [contact] points. ~ *sans fin*, worm.

visa (viza) *m*, stamp; initials, signature; visa (*passport*).

visage (vizaʒ) *m*, face. *à* ~ *découvert*, openly. *V*~ *pâle*, paleface.

vis-à-vis (vizavi) & ~ **de**, *pr. & ad*, opposite, o. to; face to face; facing; vis-à-vis; towards; in front of. ¶ *m*, person opposite; opposite number; house opposite; meeting.

viscéral, e (viseral) *a*, (*Anat.*) visceral; (*fig.*) deep-seated. **viscères** (sɛr) *m.pl*, intestines.

viscosité (viskɔzite) *f*, viscosity, stickiness.

visée (vize) *f*, aiming; aim; (*pl.*) designs, aims. **viser** (ze) *v.t*, to aim at; (*remarks*) be directed at; (*P*) take a look at; visa, stamp. ¶ *v.i*, to [take] aim; (*fig.*) set one's sights. ~ *à*, to aim at; be aimed at. **viseur** (zœr) *m*, (*Phot.*) view finder; sights; telescopic sight. **visibilité** (zibilite) *f*, visibility. **visible**† (bl) *a*, visible; obvious; at home. **visière** (zjɛr) *f*, peak (*cap*); eyeshade; (*Hist.*) visor. **vision** (zjɔ̃) *f*, vision, sight; seeing. **visionnaire** (zjɔnɛr) *a. & n*, visionary. **visionner** (ne) *v.t*, to view. **visionneuse** (nøz) *f*, (*Phot.*) viewer.

visite (vizit) *f*, visit, call; attendance; inspection, examination; visiting; visitor. *rendre* ~ *à qn*, to visit s.o, call on s.o. ~ [*à domicile*], housecall. ~ *de contrôle*, follow-up visit. ~ *médicale*, medical examination. *la* ~, [medical] consultations; (*Mil.*) sick parade. **visiter** (te) *v.t*, to visit (*place*); go round (*castle*); view (*house*); inspect (*ship*); examine (*luggage*). **visiteur, euse** (tœr, øz) *n*, visitor, caller.

vison (vizɔ̃) *m*, mink (*Zool. & fur*).

visqueux, euse (viskø, øz) *a*, viscous, sticky, tacky; (*fig.*) smarmy.

visser (vise) *v.t*, to screw [on, down, up]; (*P*) keep a tight rein on.

visuel, le† (vizɥɛl) *a*, visual.

vital, e (vital) *a*, vital. **vitalité** (lite) *f*, vitality. **vitamine** (min) *f*, vitamin.

vite (vit) *a*, fast, swift, quick. ¶ *ad*, quick[ly], fast; in a hurry; soon, in no time. *c'est* ~ *fait*, it doesn't take long. *fais* ~*!* hurry! **vitesse** (tɛs) *f*, speed, quickness; (*Mot.*) gear. ~ *acquise*, momentum. ~ *de croisière*, cruising speed. *à toute* ~, at full speed. *en* ~, in a hurry, quickly.

viticole (vitikɔl) *a*, wine; wine-growing, -producing, -making. **viticulteur** (kyltœr) *m*, wine grower. **viticulture** (tyr) *f*, wine-growing.

vitrage (vitraʒ) *m*, glazing; windows; glass partition. **vitrail** (traj) *m*, stained-glass window. **vitre** (tr) *f*, [window] pane. **vitrer** (tre) *v.t*, to glaze (*window*). **vitrerie** (trəri) *f*, glaziery, glazing; glass (*goods*). **vitreux, euse** (trø, øz) *a*, vitreous, glassy; lack-lustre. **vitrier** (trie) *m*, glazier. **vitrifier** (fje) *v.t*, to vitrify; glaze. **vitrine** (trin) *f*, shop window; display cabinet.

vitriol (vitriɔl) *m*, vitriol.

vitupérer (vitypere) *v.i*, to vituperate; rant & rave.

vivable (vivabl) *a*, fit to live in; (*pers.*) livable-with.

vivace (vivas) *a*, inveterate; (*Bot.*) hardy, h. perennial. **vivacité** (site) *f*, vivacity, liveliness; quickness; keenness, sharpness; brightness, intensity; vividness. ~ *d'esprit*, quick-wittedness. ~ *d'humeur*, quickness of temper.

vivant, e (vivɑ̃, ɑ̃t) *a*, alive, living; lifelike; live; modern (*language*); lively; vivid. ¶ *m*, living being; lifetime, life. *de son* ~, in his lifetime. **vivat** (vat) *m*, cheer. **vive** (viv) *i*, long live, 3 cheers for . . **vivement** (vmɑ̃) *ad*, briskly; sharply; keenly; warmly; (*feel*) deeply; brightly, vividly. **viveur** (vœr) *m*, high liver, pleasure-seeker. **vivier** (vje) *m*, fishpond; fish-tank. **vivifier** (vifje) *v.t*, to invigorate. **vivisection** (sɛksjɔ̃) *f*, vivisection. **vivoter** (vɔte) *v.i*, to get along, manage. **vivre** (vivr) *v.i.ir,* to live; be alive; subsist; (*portrait*) be lifelike. ~ *de qch,* to live on sth. *facile à* ~, easy to get on with. ¶ *v.t,* to live through. ¶ *m.(pl.)* provisions, supplies. *le* ~ *& le couvert,* board & lodging.

vocabulaire (vɔkabylɛr) *m,* vocabulary. *quel* ~*!* what language! **vocal, e†** (kal) *a,* vocal. **vocalique** (lik) *a,* vocalic, vowel. **vocaliser** (lize) *v.t,* to vocalize. **vocatif** (katif) *m,* vocative [case]. **vocation** (sjɔ̃) *f,* vocation, calling; call (*divine*).

vociférer (vɔsifere) *v.i,* to shout angrily, yell.

vœu (vø) *m,* vow; wish.

vogue (vɔg) *f,* fashion, vogue.

voguer (vɔge) *v.i,* to sail; wander, drift.

voici (vwasi) *pr,* here is, here are; here; this is. ~ *2 ans qu'on ne s'est pas vu,* it's 2 years since we saw each other. *il est parti* ~ *10 minutes,* he left 10 minutes ago. *me* ~*!* here I am.

voie (vwa) *f,* way; road; route; lane (*of road*); (*Rly*) track, line; gauge. ~ *d'accès,* access. ~ *d'eau,* leak. ~*s de fait,* assault [& battery]. ~ *de garage,* (*Rly*) siding. ~*s digestives,* digestive tract. ~ *ferrée,* railway. *par la* ~ *hiérarchique,* through official channels. ~ *lactée,* Milky Way. ~ *navigable,* waterway. ~ *publique,* public thoroughfare, highway. *en* ~ *de,* in the process of; on the way to. *par* ~ *de conséquence,* as a result, in consequence.

voilà (vwala) *pr,* there is, there are; that is, those are. ~ *2 ans qu'on ne s'est pas vu,* we haven't seen each other for 2 years. *la* ~, there she is. *l'homme que* ~, that man there. ¶ *i,* there!, there you are!, right then!, that's it!, that's done!

voilage (vwalaʒ) *n,* net [curtain].

voile¹ (vwal) *f,* sail; sailing. *faire* ~, to sail (*vers,* towards). *faire de la* ~, to sail, go sailing. *toutes* ~*s dehors,* under full sail. *mettre les* ~*s P,* to clear off *P.*

voile² (vwal) *m,* veil; net (*fabric*); (*Med.*) shadow (*on lung*); film. ~ *de palais,* soft palate. **voilé, e** (le) *a,* veiled; hazy, misty; dimmed; husky (*voice*). **voiler** (le) *v.t,* to veil; buckle; warp. **se** ~, to mist over, become hazy; buckle, warp. ~ *la face,* to hide one's face. ~ *le visage,* to wear a veil.

voilier (vwalje) *m,* sailing ship, s. boat. **voilure** (lyr) *f,* sails (*col.*).

voir (vwar) *v.t. & i.ir,* to see; look at; look into; go over, read; find [out]. ~ *loin,* to see ahead. ~ *venir,* to wait & see. *c'est à* ~, it remains to be seen. *faire* ~, to show. *fais* ~*!* let me look or see! *voyons!* let's see now!, come on now! ~ *trente-six chandelles,* to see stars. *cela n'a rien à* ~ *avec...* that has nothing to do with... ~ **à,** to make sure that; see to it that. **se** ~, to show, be obvious; find o.s; be seen. *ça se voit,* that's obvious, that can be seen.

voire (vwar) *ad,* even. ~ *même,* & even, indeed.

voirie (vwari) *f,* highway maintenance; refuse collection.

voisin, e (vwazɛ̃, in) *a,* neighbouring; next; akin; connected. ¶ *n,* neighbour. ~ *d'à-côté,* next-door neighbour. **voisinage** (zinaʒ) *m,* neighbourhood; vicinity; proximity, closeness. **voisiner** (ne) *v.i,* to be side by side.

voiture (vwatyr) *f,* [motor] car; carriage, coach; cart. ~ *à bras,* handcart. ~ *d'enfant,* pram, perambulator. ~ *de sport,* sports car. ~ *de tourisme,* saloon.

voix (vwa) *f,* voice; vote; opinion. *à* ~ *basse, haute,* in a low, loud voice. *d'une* ~ *juste,* (*sing*) in tune. *en* ~, in good voice.

vol¹ (vɔl) *m,* flying, flight; wing; flock (*birds*). ~ *à voile,* (*Aero.*) gliding. ~ *libre,* hang-gliding. *à* ~ *d'oiseau,* as the crow flies.

vol² (vɔl) *m,* theft, stealing, robbery. ~ *à l'étalage,* shoplifting. ~ *à la tire,* pickpocketing. ~ *à main armée,* armed robbery.

volage (vɔlaʒ) *a,* fickle, inconstant.

volaille (vɔlaj) *f,* poultry; fowl. **volailler** (je) *m,* poulterer.

volant, e (vɔlɑ̃, ɑ̃t) *a,* flying.

volant (vɔlɑ̃) *m,* steering wheel; (*Tech.*) flywheel; [hand]wheel; flounce (*skirt &c*); shuttlecock.

volatil, e (vɔlatil) *a,* volatile. **volatile** (til) *m,* winged creature. **volatiliser** (lize) *v.t,* to volatilize. **se** ~, to volatilize; vanish.

vol-au-vent (vɔlovɑ̃) *m.inv,* vol-au-vent.

volcan (vɔlkɑ̃) *m,* volcano; (*fig.*) powder keg; spitfire (*pers.*). **volcanique** (kanik) *a,* volcanic.

volée (vɔle) *f,* flight; flock; volley; peal (*bells*). ~ *de coups,* volley of shots. ~ *d'escalier,* flight of stairs. *à la* ~, in the air; on the wing; broadcast; at random. *à toute* ~, vigorously, with full force. **voler¹** (le) *v.i,* to fly. (*fig.*) ~ *de ses propres ailes,* to fend for o.s.

voler² (vɔle) *v.t,* to steal (*qch à qn,* sth from s.o); rob (s.o); cheat.

volet (vɔlɛ) *m,* shutter; (*Mot.*) bonnet flap; panel (*triptych*); section.

voleter (vɔlte) *v.i,* to flutter; flit; skip.

voleur, euse (vɔlœr, øz) *n,* thief; swindler. *au* ~*!* stop thief! ~ *de grand chemin,* highwayman.

volière (vɔljɛr) *f,* aviary.

volley-ball (vɔlɛbol) *m,* volleyball. **volleyeur, euse** (ɛjœr, øz) *n,* volleyball player; (*Ten.*) volleyer.

volition (vɔlisjɔ̃) *f,* volition.

volontaire† (vɔlɔ̃tɛr) *a,* voluntary; intentional; self-willed, wilful; determined. ¶ *n,* volunteer. **volonté** (te) *f,* will; intention; willpower, determination. *à* ~, at will; to taste; as you like. *bonne* ~, goodwill, willingness. *mauvaise* ~, unwillingness, bad grace. **volontiers** (tje) *ad,* willingly, gladly, with pleasure; readily.

volt (vɔlt) *m,* volt. **voltage** (taʒ) *m,* voltage.
volte-face (vɔltəfas) *f,* about-turn, volte-face.
voltige (vɔltiʒ) *f,* trick riding; aerobatics. **voltiger** (tiʒe) *v.i,* to fly about, flutter.
volubile (vɔlybil) *a,* voluble. **volubilis** (lis) *m,* convolvulus. **volubilité** (lite) *f,* volubility.
volume (vɔlym) *m,* volume; bulk. *faire du* ~, to be bulky. **volumineux, euse** (minø, øz) *a,* voluminous, bulky.
volupté (vɔlypte) *f,* sensual *or* voluptuous pleasure. **voluptueux, euse†** (tɥø, øz) *a,* voluptuous.
volute (vɔlyt) *f,* volute, scroll; curl (*smoke*).
vomi (vɔmi) *m,* vomit. **vomir** (mir) *v.t,* to vomit, bring up; spew out (*hate, flames &c*); (*fig.*) loathe, detest. *c'est à* ~, it makes you sick. **vomissement** (mismɑ̃) *m. oft.pl,* vomiting.
vorace† (vɔras) *a,* voracious. **voracité** (site) *f,* voracity, voraciousness.
votant, e (vɔtɑ̃, ɑ̃t) *n,* voter. **vote** (vɔt) *m,* vote; voting; passing (*law*). ~ *par procuration,* proxy vote. **voter** (te) *v.i. & t,* to vote; v. for; pass, carry. ~ *à main levée,* to vote by a show of hands. **votif, ive** (tif, iv) *a,* votive.
votre, *pl.* **vos** (vɔtr, vo) *a,* your. **vôtre** (votr) *a,* yours. *le* ~, *la* ~, *les* ~*s,* yours, your own. *à la* ~*!* cheers! **les vôtres,** your family; your kind.
vouer (vwe) *v.t,* to vow; dedicate; devote.
vouloir (vulwar) *m,* will. ¶ *v.t.ir,* to want, wish; like, be pleased to; be willing; require; intend, mean, expect. ~ *absolument,* to be set on, determined. ~ *dire,* to mean. *qu'est-ce que ça vent dire?* what does that mean? *en* ~ *à qch,* to be after sth. *en* ~ *à qn,* to have sth against s.o; bear a grudge against s.o. *s'en* ~ *de,* to be angry with o.s for. *sans le* ~, unintentionally, inadvertently. *vous l'avez voulu,* you asked for it. *voulez-vous. . ., veux-tu . . ?* will you . .? **voulu, e** (ly) *a,* required, requisite; deliberate, intentional.
vous (vu) *pn,* you (*subject, object & after pr.*), to you; yourself, yourselves; each other. *c'est à* ~, it's yours. *for examples V* **nous.** ~*-même,* ~*-mêmes,* yourself, yourselves.
voûte (vut) *f,* vault, arch; dome; canopy. ~ *palatine,* ~ *du palais,* roof of the mouth. **voûté, e** (te) *a,* vaulted; arched; stooping, bent, round-shouldered. **voûter** (te) *v.t,* to vault, arch; bow.
vouvoyer (vuvwaje) *v.t,* to address as 'vous'.
voyage (vwajaʒ) *m,* journey, trip, tour; travel; voyage; travelling. ~ *de noces,* honeymoon. **voyager** (jaʒe) *v.i,* to travel. **voyageur, euse** (ʒœr, øz) *n,* traveller. ¶ *a,* wayfaring.
voyant, e (vwajɑ̃, ɑ̃t) *a,* gaudy, garish; showy. ¶ *m,* [signal] light.
voyelle (vwajɛl) *f,* vowel.
voyeur, euse (vwajœr, øz) *n,* peeping Tom, voyeur.
voyou (vwaju) *m,* hooligan, lout; rascal (*child*).
vrac (en) (vrak), in bulk; loose; (*fig.*) in a jumble.
vrai, e (vrɛ) *a,* true; real, genuine; right; downright. **vrai & vraiment** (mɑ̃) *ad,* truly, really; indeed. **vrai,** *m,* truth. *être dans le* ~, to be in the right. **vraisemblable†** (sɑ̃blabl) *a,* probable, likely; plausible, convincing. **vraisemblance** (blɑ̃s) *f,* probability, likelihood; plausibility.
vrille (vrij) *f,* tendril; gimlet, spiral. **vriller** (vrije) *v.t,* to bore. ¶ *v.i,* to spiral, spin; become twisted.
vrombir (vrɔ̃bir) *v.i,* to hum. **vrombissement** (bismɑ̃) *m,* humming.
vu, e (vy) *a,* thought of. *bien* ~, well thought of; good form. *mal* ~, poorly thought of; bad form. *c'est* ~*?* all right? *au* ~ *& au su de tous,* openly & publicly. **vu,** *pr,* in view of. ~ *que,* seeing that, in view of the fact that.
vue, (vy) *f,* [eye] sight; view; sight; photo[graph]; (*pl.*) views; plans; designs (on sth). *à* ~, at sight, visually; visual. *à* ~ *de nez P,* at a rough guess. *à* ~ *d'œil,* before one's very eyes. *de* ~, (*know*) by sight. *en* ~, in sight; conspicuous. *en* ~ *de,* with a view to, with the idea of.
vulcain (vylkɛ̃) *m,* red admiral (*butterfly*).
vulcaniser (vylkanize) *v.t,* to vulcanize.
vulgaire† (vylgɛr) *a,* vulgar, coarse; common. **vulgarisation** (garizasjɔ̃) *f,* popularization. **vulgariser** (ze) *v.t,* to popularize. **vulgarité** (te) *f,* vulgarity.
vulnérable (vylnerabl) *a,* vulnerable.
vulve (vylv) *f,* vulva.

W

W, w (dubləve) *m, letter,* W, w.
wagon (vagɔ̃) *m,* (*Rly*) carriage, coach, car; wagon, truck; truckload, wagonload. *~-citerne,* tanker, tank wagon. *~-lit,* sleeping car. *~-poste,* mail van. *~-restaurant,* restaurant car, dining car. **wagonnet** (gɔnɛ) *m,* small truck.
waters (watɛr) *m.pl,* toilet, lavatory.
watt (wat) *m,* watt.
week-end (wikɛnd) *m,* weekend.
western (wɛstɛrn) *m,* western.
whisky (wiski) *m,* whisky.
whist (wist) *m,* whist.

X Y

X, x (iks) *m, letter,* X, x.
xénophobe (ksenɔfɔb) *a,* xenophobic. ¶ *n,* xenophobe. **xénophobie** (bi) *f,* xenophobia.
xérès (kserɛs) *m,* sherry.
xylophone (ksilɔfɔn) *m,* xylophone.

Y, y (igrɛk) *m, letter,* Y, y.
y (i) *ad,* there; here. ¶ *pn,* (= *à qch*) to it (*or* them), at it, about it &c. *je m'y attendais,* I expected it. *réfléchissez-y,* think about it. *~ compris,* including.
yacht (jɔt) *m,* yacht.
yaourt (jaur[t]) & **yoghourt** (jɔgur[t]) *m,* yog[h]urt.
yoga (jɔga) *m,* yoga.
yole (jɔl) *f,* skiff.
yougoslave (jugɔslav) *a.* & Y~, *n,* Yugoslav[ian]. **la Yougoslavie** (slavi), Yugoslavia.
youyou (juju) *m,* dinghy.
ypérite (iperit) *f,* mustard gas.

Z

Z, z (zɛd) *m, letter,* Z, z.
zèbre (zɛbr) *m,* zebra; (*P*) bloke *P.* **zébré, e** (zebre) *a,* striped.
zébu (zeby) *m,* zebu.
zélateur, trice (zelatœr, tris) *n,* zealot. **zèle** (zɛl) *m,* zeal. **zélé, e** (zele) *a,* zealous.
zénith (zenit) *m,* zenith.
zéro (zero) *m,* zero, nought, 0; (*Ten.*) love; (*Foot.*) nil; (*P pers.*) nonentity. *~ heure,* zero hour. *recommencer à ~,* to go back to square one.
zeste (zɛst) *m,* peel, zest (*orange, lemon*).
zézayer (zezɛje) *v.i,* to lisp.
zibeline (ziblin) *f,* sable.
zigouiller *P* (ziguje) *v.t,* to do in *P.*
zigzag (zigzag) *m,* zigzag. **zigzaguer** (ge) *v.i,* to zigzag [along].
zinc (zɛ̃g) *m,* zinc; (*P*) bar, counter; (*P*) plane.
zinzin *P* (zɛ̃zɛ̃) *a,* barmy *P.* ¶ *m,* what's it *P.*
zizanie (zizani) *f,* discord, ill-feeling.
zodiaque (zɔdjak) *m,* zodiac.
zona (zona) *m,* shingles.

zone (zon) *f,* zone; belt; area. ~ *bleue,* restricted parking area. ~ *franche,* free zone. *la* ~ , the slum belt.

zoo (zoo) *m,* zoo. **zoologie** (zɔɔlɔʒi) *f,* zoology. **zoologique** (ʒik) *a,* zoological. **zoologiste** (ʒist) *n,* zoologist.

zoom (zum) *m,* zoom; z. lens.

zouave (zwav) *m,* Zouave, zouave. *faire le* ~ *P,* to fool around.

zozoter (zɔzɔte) *v.i,* to lisp.

zut *P* (zyt) *i,* drat [it]! *P;* shut up! *P.*

French Irregular Verbs

Numbering of tenses & parts:-

(1) **Present Indicative**
(2) **Present Participle**
(3) **Past Participle**
(4) **Past Historic**
(5) **Future**
(6) **Imperative**
(7) **Present Subjunctive**
(8) **Imperfect Indicative.**

These tenses can normally be formed from another part of the verb as follows:-

(5) **Future:** add Future endings to the Infinitive (or Infinitive less the final *e,* if it ends in *-re*).
(6) **Imperative:** the same as the *tu, nous & vous* forms of the Present Indicative (but with regular *-er* verbs omit the final *s* of the *tu* form).
(7) **Present Subjunctive** & (8) **Imperfect Indicative:** add the appropriate tense endings to the Present Participle less the final *-ant.* e.g, battre, *p.pr* battant: (7) je batte. (8) je battais.

Tenses (5)–(8) are given only when not formed as above.

Prefixed verbs not included in the list, such as **abattre, sourire, désapprendre, satisfaire,** follow the second or last element (**battre, rire, prendre, faire**).

absoudre—(1) j'absous, tu absous, il absout, nous absolvons, vous absolvez, ils absolvent. (2) absolvant. (3) absous, oute.

abstraire—*like* **traire,** *but only used in* (1) (8) *and compound tenses.*

accroître—*like* **croître,** *but* (3) accru, *no circumflex accent.*

acquérir—(1) j'acquiers, tu acquiers, il acquiert, nous acquérons, vous acquérez, ils acquièrent. (2) acquérant. (3) acquis, e. (4) j'acquis. (5) j'acquerrai. (7) j'acquière.

aller—(1) je vais, tu vas, il va, nous allons, vous allez, ils vont. (2) allant. (3) allé, e. (4) j'allai. (5) j'irai. (6) va (*but* vas-y), allons, allez. (7) j'aille.

s'en aller—*like* **aller.** (6) va-t-en, allons-nous-en, allez-vous-en. *Perfect:* je m'en suis allé.

apercevoir—*like* **recevoir.**

apparaître—*like* **connaître.**

assaillir—(1) j'assaille, tu assailles, il assaille, nous assaillons, vous assaillez, ils assaillent. (2) assaillant. (3) assailli, e. (4) j'assaillis.

asseoir—(1) j'assieds, tu assieds, il assied, nous asseyons, vous asseyez, ils asseyent. (2) asseyant. (3) assis, e. (4) j'assis. (5) j'assiérai *ou* j'asseyerai.
Sometimes conjugated keeping the oi *of the radical, thus:* (1) j'assois, nous assoyons. (5) j'assoirai. (8) j'assoyais.

astreindre—*like* **atteindre.**

atteindre—(1) j'atteins, tu atteins, il atteint, nous atteignons, vous atteignez, ils atteignent. (2) atteignant. (3) atteint, e. (4) j'atteignis.

avoir—(1) j'ai, tu as, il a, nous avons, vous avez, ils ont. (2) ayant. (3) eu, e. (4) j'eus. (5) j'aurai. (6) aie, ayons, ayez. (7) j'aie. (8) j'avais.

battre—(1) je bats, tu bats, il bat, nous battons, vous battez, ils battent. (2) battant. (3) battu, e. (4) je battis.

boire—(1) je bois, tu bois, il boit, nous buvons, vous buvez, ils boivent. (2) buvant. (3) bu, e. (4) je bus.

bouillir—(1) je bous, tu bous, il bout, nous bouillons, vous bouillez, ils bouillent. (2) bouillant. (3) bouilli, e. (4) je bouillis.

braire—*like* **traire;** *but seldom used except in infinitive & in 3rd persons of* (1) & (5).

bruire—*Seldom used except in infinitive,* (1) il bruit, and (8) il bruissait, ils bruissaient.

ceindre—*like* **atteindre.**

choir—(3) chu, e. *Others not used.*

circoncire—*like* **confire,** *but* (3) circoncis, e.

circonscrire—*like* **écrire.**

clore—(1) je clos, tu clos, il clôt. (3) clos, e. *Other forms not used.* (5) je clorai. (6) clos. (7) je close.

comparaître—*like* **connaître,** *but* (3) comparu (*inv.*).

concevoir—*like* **recevoir.**

conclure—(1) je conclus, tu conclus, il conclut, nous concluons, vous concluez, ils concluent. (2) concluant. (3) conclu, e. (4) je conclus.

conduire—(1) je conduis, tu conduis, il conduit, nous conduisons, vous conduisez, ils conduisent. (2) conduisant. (3) conduit, e. (4) je conduisis.

confire—(1) je confis, tu confis, il confit, nous confisons, vous confisez, ils confisent. (2) confisant. (3) confit, e. (4) je confis.

connaître—(1) je connais, tu connais, il connaît, nous connaissons, vous connaissez, ils connaissent. (2) connaissant. (3) connu, e. (4) je connus.

conquérir—*like* **acquérir.**

construire—*like* **conduire.**

contraindre—*like* **craindre.**

contredire—*like* **dire,** *except* (1) vous contredisez. (6) contredisez.
coudre—(1) je couds, tu couds, il coud, nous cousons, vous cousez, ils cousent. (2) cousant. (3) cousu, e. (4) je cousis.
courir—(1) je cours, tu cours, il court, nous courons, vous courez, ils courent. (2) courant. (3) couru, e. (4) je courus. (5) je courrai.
couvrir—*like* **ouvrir.**
craindre—(1) je crains, tu crains, il craint, nous craignons, vous craignez, ils craignent. (2) craignant. (3) craint, e. (4) je craignis.
croire—(1) je crois, tu crois, il croit, nous croyons, vous croyez, ils croient. (2) croyant. (3) cru, e. (4) je crus. (7) je croie.
croître—(1) je croîs, tu croîs, il croît, nous croissons, vous croissez, ils croissent. (2) croissant. (3) crû, crue (*pl.* crus, crues). (4) je crûs.
cueillir—(1) je cueille, tu cueilles, il cueille, nous cueillons, vous cueillez, ils cueillent. (2) cueillant. (3) cueilli, e. (4) je cueillis. (5) je cueillerai. (6) cueille, cueillons, cueillez.
cuire—*like* **conduire.**
décevoir—*like* **recevoir.**
déchoir—(1) je déchois, tu déchois, il déchoit. (3) déchu, e. (4) je déchus. (5) je décherrai. (7) je déchoie.
découvrir—*like* **ouvrir.**
décrire—*like* **écrire.**
décroître—*like* **croître,** *except* (3) décru, e.
dédire—*like* **dire,** *except* (1) vous dédisez. (6) dédisez.
déduire—*like* **conduire.**
défaillir—(1) nous défaillons, vous défaillez, ils défaillent. (2) défaillant. (4) je défaillis. (8) je défaillais. *Other forms seldom used.*
démentir—*like* **sentir.**
dépeindre—*like* **atteindre.**
dépourvoir—(3) dépourvu, e.
déteindre—*like* **atteindre.**
détruire—*like* **conduire.**
devoir—(1) je dois, tu dois, il doit, nous devons, vous devez, ils doivent. (2) devant. (3) dû, due (*pl.* dus, dues). (4) je dus. (5) je devrai. (7) je doive.
dire—(1) je dis, tu dis, il dit, nous disons, vous dites, ils disent. (2) disant. (3) dit, e. (4) je dis.
disparaître—*like* **connaître.**
dissoudre—*like* **absoudre.**
dormir—(1) je dors, tu dors, il dort, nous dormons, vous dormez, ils dorment. (2) dormant. (3) dormi. (4) je dormis.
échoir—(1) il échoit *ou* il échet. (2) échéant. (3) échu, e. (5) il écherra. *Other forms hardly ever used.*
éclore—(1) il éclôt, ils éclosent. (3) éclos, e. (5) il éclora. (7) il éclose.
écrire—(1) j'écris, tu écris, il écrit, nous écrivons, vous écrivez, ils écrivent. (2) écrivant. (3) écrit, e. (4) j'écrivis.
élire—*like* **lire.**
empreindre—*like* **atteindre.**
enceindre—*like* **atteindre.**
enduire—*like* **conduire.**
enfreindre—*like* **atteindre.**
enquérir—*like* **acquérir.**
éteindre—*like* **atteindre.**
être—(1) je suis, tu es, il est, nous sommes, vous êtes, ils sont. (2) étant. (3) été (*inv.*). (4) je fus. (5) je serai. (6) sois, soyons, soyez. (7) je sois.
étreindre—*like* **atteindre.**
exclure—*like* **conclure.**
faillir—(1) il faut (*in* s'en faut). (3) failli, e. (4) je faillis &c. *Seldom used in other forms.*
faire—(1) je fais, tu fais, il fait, nous faisons, vous faites, ils font. (2) faisant. (3) fait, e. (4) je fis. (5) je ferai. (7) je fasse.
falloir—(1) il faut. (3) fallu (*inv.*). (4) il fallut. (5) il faudra. (7) il faille. (8) il fallait.
feindre—*like* **atteindre.**
frire—(1) je fris, tu fris, il frit, nous faisons frire, vous faites frire, ils font frire. (3) frit, e. (6) fris. (8) je faisais frire.
fuir—(1) je fuis, tu fuis, il fuit, nous fuyons, vous fuyez, ils fuient. (2) fuyant. (3) fui, e. (4) je fuis. (7) je fuie.
geindre—*like* **atteindre.**
gésir—(1) je gis, tu gis, il gît, nous gisons, vous gisez, ils gisent. (2) gisant. (8) je gisais &c. *Other forms not used.*
inclure—*like* **conclure.**
induire—*like* **conduire.**
inscrire—*like* **écrire.**
instruire—*like* **conduire.**
interdire—*like* **dire,** *except* (1) vous interdisez. (6) interdisez.
introduire—*like* **conduire.**
joindre—(1) je joins, tu joins, il joint, nous joignons, vous joignez, ils joignent. (2) joignant. (3) joint, e. (4) je joignis.
lire—(1) je lis, tu lis, il lit, nous lisons, vous lisez, ils lisent. (2) lisant. (3) lu, e. (4) je lus.
luire—*like* **conduire,** *except* (3) lui (*inv.*) *& no* (4).
maudire—(1) je maudis, tu maudis, il maudit, nous maudissons, vous maudissez, ils maudissent. (2) maudissant. (3) maudit, e. (4) je maudis.
méconnaître—*like* **paraître.**
médire—*like* **dire,** *except* (1) vous médisez. (6) médisez.
mentir—*like* **sentir.**
mettre—(1) je mets, tu mets, il met, nous mettons, vous mettez, ils mettent. (2) mettant. (3) mis, e. (4) je mis.
moudre—(1) je mouds, tu mouds, il moud, nous moulons, vous moulez, ils moulent. (2) moulant. (3) moulu, e. (4) je moulus.
mourir—(1) je meurs, tu meurs, il meurt, nous

mourons, vous mourez, ils meurent. (2) mourant. (3) mort, e. (4) je mourus. (5) je mourrai. (7) je meure.
mouvoir—(1) je meus, tu meus, il meut, nous mouvons, vous mouvez, ils meuvent. (2) mouvant. (3) mû, mue (*pl.* mus, mues). (4) je mus. (5) je mouvrai. (7) je meuve.
naître—(1) je nais, tu nais, il naît, nous naissons, vous naissez, ils naissent. (2) naissant. (3) né, e. (4) je naquis.
nuire—*like* **conduire.**
offrir—*like* **ouvrir.**
oindre—*like* **joindre.**
ouïr—(3) ouï, ïe.
ouvrir—(1) j'ouvre, tu ouvres, il ouvre, nous ouvrons, vous ouvrez, ils ouvrent. (2) ouvrant. (3) ouvert, e. (4) j'ouvris. (6) ouvre, ouvrons, ouvrez.
paître—*like* **connaître.**
paraître—*like* **connaître,** *but* (3) paru (*inv.*).
partir—(1) je pars, tu pars, il part, nous partons, vous partez, ils partent. (2) partant. (3) parti, e. (4) je partis.
peindre—*like* **atteindre.**
plaindre—*like* **craindre.**
plaire—(1) je plais, tu plais, il plaît, nous plaisons, vous plaisez, ils plaisent. (2) plaisant. (3) plu (*inv.*). (4) je plus.
pleuvoir—(1) il pleut. (2) pleuvant. (3) plu (*inv.*). (4) il plut. (5) il pleuvra.
poindre—*like* **joindre,** *but seldom used except in infinitive &* (5).
pourvoir—(1) je pourvois, tu pourvois, il pourvoit, nous pourvoyons, vous pourvoyez, ils pourvoient. (2) pourvoyant. (3) pourvu, e. (4) je pourvus. (7) je pourvoie.
pouvoir—(1) je peux *ou* je puis, tu peux, il peut, nous pouvons, vous pouvez, ils peuvent. (2) pouvant. (3) pu (*inv.*). (4) je pus. (5) je pourrai. (7) je puisse.
prédire—*like* **dire,** *except* (1) vous prédisez. (6) prédisez.
prendre—(1) je prends, tu prends, il prend, nous prenons, vous prenez, ils prennent. (2) prenant. (3) pris, e. (4) je pris. (7) je prenne.
prescrire—*like* **écrire.**
prévaloir—*like* **valoir,** *but* (7) je prévale.
prévoir—*like* **voir,** *except* (5) je prévoirai.
produire—*like* **conduire.**
promouvoir—*like* **mouvoir,** *but seldom used except in infinitive &* (3) promu, e.
proscrire—*like* **écrire.**
recevoir—(1) je reçois, tu reçois, il reçoit, nous recevons, vous recevez, ils reçoivent. (2) recevant. (3) reçu, e. (4) je reçus. (5) je recevrai. (7) je reçoive.
réduire—*like* **conduire.**
reluire—*like* **luire.**
renaître—*like* **naître,** *but no* (3) *or compound tenses.*
repentir (se)—*like* **sentir.**
requérir—*like* **acquérir.**
résoudre—(1) je résous, tu résous, il résout, nous résolvons, vous résolvez, ils résolvent. (2) résolvant. (3) résolu, e. (4) je résolus.
restreindre—*like* **atteindre.**
rire—(1) je ris, tu ris, il rit, nous rions, vous riez, ils rient. (2) riant. (3) ri (*inv.*). (4) je ris.
saillir—*like* **assaillir.**
savoir—(1) je sais, tu sais, il sait, nous savons, vous savez, ils savent. (2) sachant. (3) su, e. (4) je sus. (5) je saurai. (6) sache, sachons, sachez. (7) je sache. (8) je savais.
séduire—*like* **conduire.**
sentir—(1) je sens, tu sens, il sent, nous sentons, vous sentez, ils sentent. (2) sentant. (3) senti, e. (4) je sentis.
seoir—*In sense to suit,* (1) il sied, ils siéent. (2) séant *ou* seyant. (5) il siéra, ils siéront. (7) il siée, ils siéent. (8) il seyait, ils seyaient. *No other forms.*
servir—(1) je sers, tu sers, il sert, nous servons, vous servez, ils servent. (2) servant. (3) servi, e. (4) je servis.
sortir—(1) je sors, tu sors, il sort, nous sortons, vous sortez, ils sortent. (2) sortant. (3) sorti, e. (4) je sortis.
souffrir—*like* **ouvrir.**
souscrire—*like* **écrire.**
suffire—*like* **confire,** *but* (3) suffi (*inv.*).
suivre—(1) je suis, tu suis, il suit, nous suivons, vous suivez, ils suivent. (2) suivant. (3) suivi, e. (4) je suivis.
surseoir—(1) je sursois, tu sursois, il sursoit, nous sursoyons, vous sursoyez, ils sursoient. (2) sursoyant. (3) sursis, e. (4) je sursis. (7) je sursoie.
taire—*like* **plaire,** *except* (1) il tait (*no circumflex*) & (3) tu, e.
teindre—*like* **atteindre.**
tenir—(1) je tiens, tu tiens, il tient, nous tenons, vous tenez, ils tiennent. (2) tenant. (3) tenu, e. (4) je tins. (5) je tiendrai. (7) je tienne.
traduire—*like* **conduire.**
traire—(1) je trais, tu trais, il trait, nous trayons, vous trayez, ils traient. (2) trayant. (3) trait, e. (7) je traie.
transcrire—*like* **écrire.**
tressaillir—*like* **assaillir.**
vaincre—(1) je vaincs, tu vaincs, il vainc, nous vainquons, vous vainquez, ils vainquent. (2) vainquant. (3) vaincu, e. (4) je vainquis.
valoir—(1) je vaux, tu vaux, il vaut, nous valons, vous valez, ils valent. (2) valant. (3) valu, e. (4) je valus. (5) je vaudrai. (7) je vaille.
venir—(1) je viens, tu viens, il vient, nous venons, vous venez, ils viennent. (2) venant. (3) venu, e. (4) je vins. (5) je viendrai. (7) je vienne.
vêtir—(1) je vêts, tu vêts, il vêt, nous vêtons,

vous vêtez, ils vêtent. (2) vêtant. (3) vêtu, e. (4) je vêtis.

vivre—(1) je vis, tu vis, il vit, nous vivons, vous vivez, ils vivent. (2) vivant. (3) vécu (*inv.*). (4) je vécus.

voir—(1) je vois, tu vois, il voit, nous voyons, vous voyez, ils voient. (2) voyant. (3) vu, e. (4) je vis. (5) je verrai. (7) je voie.

vouloir—(1) je veux, tu veux, il veut, nous voulons, vous voulez, ils veulent. (2) voulant. (3) voulu, e. (4) je voulus. (5) je voudrai. (6) veuille & veux, veuillons & voulons, veuillez & voulez. (7) je veuille.

ENGLISH-FRENCH

A

A, a, *n,* A, a, *m;* (*Mus.*) la, *m;* (*house number*) bis. **A1,** *a,* de première qualité, champion *P.* **A-levels,** *n.pl,* ≃ baccalauréat, *m.*

a, an, *indefinite art,* un, une. *3 times ~ day,* 3 fois par jour. *50 francs ~ head,* 50 F par personne. *4 francs ~ kilo,* 4 F le kilo. (*not a*) *I haven't ~ pen,* je n'ai pas de stylo. *don't make ~ noise,* ne fais pas de bruit. *not ~ single word,* pas un [seul] mot. *as ~ friend,* en ami. *act like ~ friend,* agir en ami. *what ~ surprise!* quelle surprise! *a man with ~ white beard,* un homme à la barbe blanche. *to have ~ good ear,* avoir de l'oreille.

aback, *ad, taken ~,* interloqué, déconcerté.

abacus, *n,* abaque, *m.*

abandon, *v.t,* abandonner, délaisser. ¶ *n,* abandon, *m,* désinvolture, *f.*

abase, *v.t,* abaisser, humilier.

abash, *v.t,* décontenancer. *~ed,* confus.

abate, *v.i,* diminuer; (*anger, pain, storm*) s'apaiser, se calmer; (*wind*) se modérer. **~ment,** *n,* diminution; (*noise*) suppression, *f.*

abattoir, *n,* abattoir, *m.*

abbess, *n,* abbesse, *f.* **abbey,** *n,* abbaye, *f.* **abbot,** *n,* abbé, *m.*

abbreviate, *v.t,* abréger. **abbreviation,** *n,* abréviation, *f.*

A B C, *n,* A b c, alphabet, *m. as easy as ~,* simple comme bonjour.

abdicate, *v.t. & i,* abdiquer. **abdication,** *n,* abdication, *f.*

abdomen, *n,* abdomen, *m.* **abdominal,** *a,* abdominal.

abduct, *v.t,* enlever, kidnapper.

abeam, *ad,* par le travers.

abed, *ad,* au lit, couché.

aberration, *n,* aberration, *f,* égarement, *m.*

abet, *v.t,* soutenir, encourager.

abeyance, *n, in ~,* en suspens.

abhor, *v.t,* abhorrer, avoir en horreur. **~rence,** *n,* horreur, *f.* **~rent,** *a,* répugnant.

abide, *v.t.ir,* souffrir, supporter. ¶ *v.i, ~ by,* s'en tenir à. **abiding,** *a,* constant.

ability, *n,* compétence (en qch; pour faire); aptitude, *f* (à faire); (*skill*) talent, *m,* habileté, *f.*

abject, *a,* abject. **~ion,** *n,* abjection, *f.*

abjure, *v.t,* renoncer à; (*Rel.*) abjurer.

ablaze, *ad,* en feu, en flammes. *~ with anger,* bouillant de colère.

able, *a,* (*clever*) capable, compétent. *an ~ man,* un homme de talent. *~-bodied,* robuste. ~[-*bodied*] *seaman,* matelot de deuxième classe, *m. to be ~ to,* pouvoir, être capable de; (*know how to*) savoir; (*be in a position to*) être en mesure (*ou* à même) de. **ably,** *ad,* habilement.

abnormal†, *a,* anormal. **~ity,** *n,* caractère anormal *m;* (*Biol.*) anomalie, *f.*

aboard, *ad,* à bord. ¶ *pr,* à bord de.

abode, *n,* domicile, *m,* demeure, *f.*

abolish, *v.t,* abolir, supprimer. **abolition,** *n,* abolition, suppression, *f.*

abominable†, *a,* abominable. **abominate,** *v.t,* abominer, exécrer. **abomination,** *n,* abomination, *f.*

aboriginal, *a. & n,* aborigène, *m,f.* **aborigine,** *n,* aborigène, *m,f.*

abort, *v.i,* (*Med., fig.*) avorter. **~ion,** *n,* avortement, *m. to have an ~,* se faire avorter. **~ionist,** *n,* avorteur, euse. **~ive,** *a,* (*fig.*) manqué, raté.

abound, *v.i,* abonder (*in,* en).

about, *pr,* (*concerning*) au sujet de, à propos de, concernant. *what's it all ~?* de quoi s'agit-il?, qu'est-ce qu'il y a? *find out ~,* se renseigner sur. (*around*) *wander ~ the town, the streets,* flâner dans la ville, par les rues. ¶ *ad,* (*approx.*) vers, à peu près, environ. *~ 9 o'clock,* vers neuf heures. *~ 8 km from here,* à 8 km environ d'ici. *~ 20 friends,* une vingtaine d'amis. (*here & there*) ça & là. *round ~,* tout autour. *lie ~,* (*clothes, books*) traîner. (*Naut.*) *go ~,* virer [vent devant]. *ready ~!* parez à virer! *to be ~ to do,* être sur le point de faire, aller f. *~-turn, n,* (*Mil.*) demi-tour, *m.*

above, *pr,* au-dessus de; (*more than*) plus de; (*upstream of*) en amont de. (*fig.*) *~ suspicion,* au-dessus de tout soupçon. *~ all,* surtout. ¶ *ad,* au-dessus, en haut; (*in text*) ci-dessus. *from ~,* d'en haut. *~-board,* (*pers.*) franc; (*deal*) régulier; (*ad.*) cartes sur table. *~-mentioned,* susmentionné, ci-dessus. *~-named,* susnommé.

abrasion, *n,* frottement, *m;* (*Med.*) écorchure, *f.* **abrasive,** *a,* abrasif; (*tone*) caustique.

abreast, *ad,* de front; (*Naut.*) par le travers. *~ of,* à la hauteur de; (*news*) au courant de.

abridge, *v.t,* abréger, raccourcir. **abridg[e]ment,** *n,* abrégé, *m.*

abroad, *ad,* à l'étranger. *from ~,* de l'étranger. *there is a rumour ~ that...,* le bruit court que...

abrogate, *v.t,* abroger. **abrogation,** *n,* abrogation, *f.*

abrupt†, *a,* (*pers., tone, turn*) brusque; (*slope*) abrupte. **~ness,** *n,* brusquerie, *f.*

abscess, *n,* abcès, *m.*

abscond, *v.i,* s'enfuir, se soustraire à la justice.

abseil, *n,* rappel, *m.* ¶ *v.i,* descendre en r.

absence, *n,* absence, *f.* (*Law*) *in his, her* ~, par contumace. ~ *of mind,* distraction, *f.* **absent,** *a,* absent. ¶ *v.t,* ~ *o.s,* s'absenter. ~**ee,** *n,* absent, e; (*Mil.*) insoumis, *m.* ~**-minded,** *a,* distrait. ~**-mindedly,** *ad,* distraitement.
absinth, *n,* absinthe, *f.*
absolute, *a,* absolu; (*disaster*) véritable; (*idiot*) parfait. ~**ly,** *ad,* absolument.
absolution, *n,* absolution, *f.* **absolve,** *v.t,* absoudre.
absorb, *v.t,* (*lit., fig.*) absorber; (*shock*) amortir. ~**ent,** *a,* absorbant. ~**ing,** *a,* (*book, film*) passionnant. **absorption,** *n,* absorption, *f.*
abstain, *v.i,* s'abstenir (*from,* de). **abstemious,** *a,* sobre, frugal. **abstention,** *n,* abstention, *f.* **abstinence,** *n,* abstinence, *f.*
abstract, *a,* abstrait. ¶ *n,* résumé, *m.* (*Philos.*) *the* ~, l'abstrait, *m.* (*Art*) œuvre abstraite. ¶ *v.t,* (*steal*) soustraire; (*summarize*) résumer. ~**ion,** *n,* (*idea*) abstraction; (*theft*) soustraction, *f.*
abstruse, *a,* abstrus.
absurd†, *a. & n,* absurde, *m.* ~**ity,** *n,* absurdité, *f.*
abundance, *n,* abondance, *f.* **abundant,** *a,* abondant. ~**ly,** *ad,* abondamment.
abuse, *n,* (*misuse*) abus, *m;* (*insults*) injures, insultes, *f.pl.* ¶ *v.t,* abuser de; injurier; (*child*) maltraiter. **abusive**†, *a,* injurieux; (*use*) abusif.
abut, *v.i,* ~ *on,* être contigu à, confiner à.
abysmal, *a,* (*ignorance*) sans bornes.
abyss, *n,* abîme, gouffre, *m.*
Abyssinia, *n,* l'Abyssinie, *f.* **Abyssinian,** *a,* abyssinien. ¶ *n,* Abyssinien, ne.
acacia, *n,* acacia, *m.*
academic, *a,* universitaire; (*question*) théorique; (*art*) académique; (*year*) scolaire. ¶ *n,* (*pers.*) universitaire, *m,f.* ~**ian,** *n,* académicien, ne. **academy,** *n,* académie; école, *f,* collège, *m.*
accede, *v.i,* ~ *to,* (*request*) agréer; (*throne*) monter sur.
accelerate, *v.t,* accélérer. **accelerator,** *n,* accélérateur, *m.*
accent, *n,* accent, *m.* **accent & accentuate,** *v.t,* accentuer.
accept, *v.t,* accepter; (*facts*) admettre. ~**able,** *a,* acceptable; (*manners*) convenable; (*gift*) le bienvenu. ~**ance,** *n,* acceptation, *f.* ~**ed,** *a,* (*fact*) reconnu; (*behaviour*) admis; (*expression*) consacré.
access, *n,* accès, abord, *m.* ~ *road,* route d'accès, *f.* ~**ible,** *a,* accessible. ~**ion,** *n,* (*to throne*) avènement, *m.*
accessory†, *a,* accessoire. ¶ *n,* accessoire, *m;* (*Law*) complice, *m,f.*
accident, *n,* accident, *m. by* ~, accidentellement; (*by chance*) par hasard. ~ *insurance,* assurance contre les accidents, *f.* **accidental**†, *a,* accidentel; fortuit. ¶ (*Mus.*) *n,* accident, *m.*
acclaim, *v.t,* acclamer. **acclamation,** *n,* acclamation, *f.*
acclimatization, *n,* acclimatation, *f.* **acclimatize,** *v.t,* acclimater; (*fig.*) acclimater (*to,* à).
accommodate, *v.t,* (*lodge*) loger; (*hold*) contenir; (*supply*) fournir (*s.o with sth,* qch à qn). ~ *o.s to,* s'accommoder à. **accommodating,** *a,* accommodant, complaisant. **accommodation,** *n,* logement, *m.* ~ *bill* (*Com.*), billet de complaisance, *m.*
accompaniment, *n,* accompagnement, *m.* **accompanist,** *n,* accompagnateur, trice. **accompany,** *v.t,* accompagner.
accomplice, *n,* complice, *m,f.*
accomplish, *v.t,* accomplir, réaliser. ~ *one's aim,* atteindre son but. ~**ed,** *a,* accompli. ~**ment,** *n,* accomplissement, *m;* (*achievement*) réussite, *f;* (*skill*) talent, *m.*
accord, *n,* accord, consentement, *m. of one's own* ~, de son plein gré. *with one* ~, d'un commun accord. ¶ *v.t.* (*& i*), (s')accorder. ~**ance,** *n,* accord, *m. in* ~ *with,* conformément à. ~**ing as,** *c,* dans la mesure où. ~**ing to,** *pr,* selon, d'après; suivant. ~*ing to him,* selon *ou* d'après lui. ~**ingly,** *ad,* en conséquence.
accordion, *n,* accordéon, *m.*
accost, *v.t,* accoster, aborder.
account, *n,* (*Com.*) compte, *m,* note, *f. keep the* ~*s,* tenir les comptes *ou* la comptabilité. *bank* ~, compte en banque. *current* ~, compte courant. *put it on my* ~, vous le mettrez sur mon c. *pay £20 on* ~, verser un acompte de £20. (*report*) récit, compte rendu, *m;* (*importance*) importance, valeur, *f. of no* ~, sans importance. *take into* ~, tenir compte de. *turn sth to* ~, tirer parti de qch, profiter de qch. *on* ~ *of,* à cause de. *on no* ~, en aucun cas, sous aucun prétexte. ¶ *v.t,* ~ *for,* rendre compte de, expliquer. ~**able,** *a,* responsable (*for,* de). ~**ancy,** *n,* comptabilité, *f.* ~**ant,** *n,* comptable, *m,f. chartered* ~, expert-comptable, *m.* ~**ing,** *n,* comptabilité, *f.* ~ *machine,* machine comptable, *f.*
accredit, *v.t,* accréditer (*to,* auprès de).
accrue, *v.i,* dériver (*from,* de); revenir (*to,* à); (*interest*) courir. ~*d interest,* intérêt couru, *m.*
accumulate, *v.t.* (*& i*), (s')accumuler, (s')amasser. **accumulation,** *n,* accumulation, *f;* (*heap*) tas, amas, *m.* **accumulator,** *n,* accumulateur, *m.*
accuracy, *n,* exactitude, justesse, *f.* **accurate**†, *a,* exact, juste, précis.
accursed, *a,* maudit.
accusation, *n,* accusation, *f.* **accusative [case],** accusatif, *m.* **accuse,** *v.t,* accuser (de qch; de faire). *the* ~*d,* l'accusé, e. **accuser,** *n,* accusateur, trice. **accusing,** *a,* accusateur.
accustom, *v.t,* accoutumer, habituer (*to,* à; *to*

doing, à faire). **~ed,** *a,* (*pers.*) accoutumé; (*usual*) coutumier, habituel. *grow ~ed to,* s'habituer à, s'accoutumer à.
ace, *n,* as, *m. within an ~ of,* à deux doigts de.
acerbity, *n,* âpreté, aigreur, *f.*
acetate, *n,* acétate, *m.* **acetic,** *a,* acétique.
acetylene, *n,* acétylène, *m. ~ lamp,* lampe à acétylène, *f.*
ache, *n,* mal, *m,* douleur, *f. head ~,* mal de tête. ¶ *v.i,* faire mal. *my head aches,* j'ai mal à la tête.
achieve, *v.t,* accomplir, exécuter; (*aim*) atteindre. **~ment,** *n,* accomplissement; (*feat*) exploit, *m,* réussite, *f.*
aching, *a,* douloureux; (*tooth*) malade. *I'm ~ all over,* j'ai mal partout.
acid, *a.* (*lit., fig.*) & *n,* acide, *m. ~ rain,* pluies acides *f.pl. ~ test,* épreuve décisive. **~ity,** *n,* acidité, *f.*
acknowledge, *v.t,* (*son, debt*) reconnaître; avouer, admettre (*that,* que); (*greeting*) répondre à. *~ receipt of,* accuser réception de. **~ment,** *n,* (*letter*) accusé de réception; (*money*) reçu, *m;* (*help*) reconnaissance, *f.*
acme, *n,* apogée, comble, sommet, *m.*
acne, *n,* acné, *f.*
acorn, *n,* gland, *m.*
acoustic, *a,* acoustique. **~s,** *n.pl,* acoustique, *f.*
acquaint, *v.t, ~ with,* informer de, renseigner sur; (*situation*) mettre au courant de. **~ance,** *n,* connaissance, relation, *f. make s.o's ~,* faire la connaissance de qn.
acquiesce, *v.i,* acquiescer, consentir (*in,* à). **acquiescence,** *n,* consentement, *m.*
acquire, *v.t,* acquérir; (*habit*) prendre. *~ a taste for,* prendre goût à. **acquisition,** *n,* acquisition, *f.* **acquisitive,** *a,* âpre au gain.
acquit, *v.t,* acquitter (*of,* de). *~ o.s well,* bien s'en tirer. **~tal,** *n,* acquittement, *m.*
acre, *n,* ≏ arpent, demi-hectare, *m.*
acrid, *a,* âcre; (*fig.*) acerbe.
acrimonious, *a,* acrimonieux. **acrimony,** *n,* acrimonie, *f.*
acrobat, *n,* acrobate, *m,f.* **acrobatic,** *a,* acrobatique. **~s,** *n.pl,* acrobatie, *f.*
across, *ad,* en travers. (*river*) *2 km ~,* large de 2 km. ¶ *pr,* (*sited*) (*hills*) *~ the river,* de l'autre côté de la rivière; (*bridge*) *~ the Seine,* sur la S.; (*tree*) *~ the road,* en travers de la route; (*shop*) *~ the road,* d'en face; (*allies*) *~ the Channel,* d'outre-Manche. (*moving*) d'un côté à l'autre de, à travers. *go, walk ~,* traverser. *run, swim ~,* traverser en courant, à la nage. *~ the fields,* à travers champs. *get sth ~ to s.o,* faire comprendre qch à qn.
acrylic, *a,* acrylique.
act, *n,* (*deed*) action, *f,* acte, *m. in the ~ of doing,* en train de faire. *caught in the ~,* pris en flagrant délit. (*~ of Parliament*) loi, *f;* (*Theat.*) acte. *put on an ~,* jouer la comédie. ¶ *v.t, ~ a part,* jouer, tenir un rôle. *~ the fool,* faire l'idiot. ¶ *v.i,* agir, se comporter. *~ like a friend,* agir en ami. *~ as manager,* faire fonction de directeur. **~ing,** *n,* jeu, *m.* ¶ *a,* suppléant, intérimaire.
action, *n,* action, *f. take ~,* agir. *put into ~,* (*plan*) mettre à l'exécution. *out of ~,* (*pers.*) hors de combat; (*Mach.*) hors d'usage. (*Law*) procès, *m. bring an ~ against,* intenter une action contre. (*Mil.*) combat, *m. go into ~,* engager le c.
activate, *v.t,* activer; (*mechanism*) actionner.
active, *a,* (*pers., life*) actif; (*volcano*) en activité. *take an ~ part in,* prendre une part active à. (*Mil.*) *on ~ service,* en campagne. (*Gram.*) *in the ~,* à l'actif. **activity,** *n,* activité, *f.*
actor, tress, *n,* acteur, trice, comédien, ne.
actual, *a,* réel, effectif, véritable. **~ity,** *n,* réalité, *f.* **~ly,** *ad,* effectivement, réellement, véritablement, en fait.
actuary, *n,* actuaire, *m,f.*
actuate, *v.t,* (*pers.*) animer, pousser; (*mechanism*) actionner.
acumen, *n,* flair, *m,* finesse, *f.*
acupuncture, *n,* acuponcture, *f.*
acute, *a,* (*Med., pain, accent, angle*) aigu; (*shortage*) grave; (*mind*) perspicace. **~ly,** *ad,* vivement. **~ness,** *n,* (*pain*) intensité; (*pers.*) perspicacité, *f.*
A.D. (*Anno Domini*), après Jésus-Christ.
adage, *n,* adage, *m.*
adamant (to be), être inflexible.
Adam, *n,* Adam, *m. ~'s apple,* pomme d'Adam, *f. ~'s ale,* Château-la-Pompe, *m.*
adapt, *v.t,* adapter, approprier. **~ation,** *n,* adaptation, *f.* **~er,** *n,* (*pers.*) adapteur, trice; (*Tech.*) adapteur, *m;* (*Elec.*) prise multiple, *f,* adaptateur, *m.*
add, *v.t,* ajouter; (*figures & ~ up*) additionner, totaliser. *his story doesn't ~ up,* son histoire ne tient pas debout. *~ up to,* s'élever à. *~ing machine,* machine à calculer, *f.*
adder, *n,* vipère, *f.*
addict, *n,* (*Med.*) intoxiqué, e; (*fig.*) fanatique, *m,f. drug ~,* toxicomane, *m,f.* **~ed,** *a,* adonné (*to,* à). *become ~ed to,* s'adonner à. **~ion,** *n,* (*Med.*) dépendance, *f.*
addition, *n,* addition; (*of staff &c*) adjonction, *f. in ~,* de plus. *in ~ to,* en plus de. **~al,** *a,* additionnel, supplémentaire, de plus.
addled, *a,* (*egg*) pourri.
address, *n,* (*letter*) adresse, *f;* (*talk*) discours, *m,* allocution, *f.* ¶ *v.t,* (*letter*) adresser; (*pers.*) s'adresser à; (*Golf*) viser. **~ee,** *n,* destinataire, *m,f.*
adduce, *v.t,* alléguer, fournir.
adenoids, *n.pl,* végétations [adénoïdes], *f.pl.*
adept, *a,* habile (à), expert (à, en). ¶ *n,* expert, *m* (*in, at,* en).
adequate, *a,* suffisant; satisfaisant. **~ly,** *ad,*

suffisamment.
adhere, *v.i,* adhérer (*to,* à). **adherence,** *n,* adhésion, *f* (*to,* à). **adhesion,** *n,* (*Tech.*) adhérence, *f.* **adhesive,** *a,* adhésif. ~ *plaster,* (*Med.*) sparadrap, *m.* ~ *tape,* ruban adhésif, Scotch, *m.*
adieu, *i. & n,* adieu, *m.*
ad infinitum, *ad,* à l'infini.
adjacent, *a,* (*Math.*) adjacent; (*gen.*) voisin (*to,* de).
adjectival, *a.* & **adjective,** *n,* adjectif, *m.*
adjoin, *v.i,* être contigu à. ~**ing,** *a,* attenant, voisin.
adjourn, *v.t,* ajourner, renvoyer, remettre. ~ *a meeting,* (*break off*) suspendre la séance, (*close*) lever la s. ~**ment,** *n,* ajournement, renvoi, *m,* remise, suspension, *f.*
adjudicate, *v.t,* juger. **adjudicator,** *n,* juge, *m.*
adjunct, *n,* accessoire, *m.*
adjust, *v.t,* ajuster, régler, mettre au point. ¶ *v.i,* s'adapter (*to,* à). ~*able spanner,* clef à molette, *f.* ~**ment,** *n,* (*Tech.*) réglage, *m,* mise au point, *f;* (*pers.*) adaptation, *f.*
adjutant, *n,* adjudant major, *m.*
ad lib, *ad,* à volonté, à discrétion. ¶ *v.i. & t,* improviser.
administer, *v.t,* administrer, gérer. **administration,** *n,* administration, direction, *f.* **administrative,** *a,* administratif. **administrator,** *n,* administrateur, trice.
admirable†, *a,* admirable.
admiral, *n,* amiral, *m.* ~ *of the fleet,* a. à cinq étoiles. **Admiralty [Board],** *n,* ≏ ministère de la Marine, *m.*
admiration, *n,* admiration, *f.* **admire,** *v.t,* admirer. **admirer,** *n,* admirateur, trice. **admiring,** *a,* admiratif. ~**ly,** *ad,* avec admiration.
admissible, *a,* admissible, acceptable.
admission, *n,* admission, entrée, *f;* (*of fact*) aveu, *m.* **admit,** *v.t,* (*pers.*) admettre, laisser entrer; (*fact*) admettre, reconnaître, avouer. ~ *of,* permettre. ~**tance,** *n,* admission, entrée, *f.*
admonish, *v.t,* réprimander; (*urge*) exhorter (à faire). **admonition,** *n,* réprimande, remontrance, *f.*
ado, *n, without further* ~, sans plus de cérémonies.
adolescence, *n,* adolescence, *f.* **adolescent,** *a. & n,* adolescent, e.
adopt, *v.t,* adopter. ~**ed,** ~**ive,** *a,* (*pers.*) adoptif. ~**ion,** *n,* adoption, *f;* choix, *m.*
adorable, *a,* adorable. **adoration,** *n,* adoration, *f.* **adore,** *v.t,* adorer. **adoringly,** *ad,* avec adoration.
adorn, *v.t,* parer, orner. ~**ment,** *n,* parure, *f,* ornement, *m.*
adrenalin, *n,* adrénaline, *f.*
Adriatic, *a. & n,* Adriatique, *f.*
adrift, *a. & ad,* (*Naut.*) à la dérive. *come* ~, (*rope &c*) se détacher; (*plans*) tomber à l'eau.
adroit†, *a,* adroit. ~**ness,** *n,* dextérité, *f.*
adulate, *v.t,* aduler. **adulation,** *n,* adulation, *f.* **adulatory,** *a,* adulateur.
adult, *a. & n,* adulte, *m,f.*
adulterate, *v.t,* frelater. **adulteration,** *n,* frelatage, *m.*
adulterer, ess, *n,* adultère, *m,f.* **adulterous,** *a,* adultère. **adultery,** *n,* adultère, *m.*
advance, *n,* (*gen., Mil.*) avance, *f. make* ~*s,* (*in science &c*) faire des progrès; (*to s.o*) faire des avances. *in* ~, à l'avance, d'a., par a. *in* ~ *of his time,* en avance sur son temps. (*payment*) avance. (*Mil.*) ~ *guard,* avant-garde, *m.* ~ *notice,* préavis, *m.* ¶ *v.t,* avancer. ¶ *v.i,* [s']avancer; (*work, studies*) progresser, faire des progrès. ~**ment,** *n,* avancement, *m.*
advantage, *n,* avantage, *m. to have an* ~ *over s.o,* avoir un a. sur qn. *take* ~ *of,* (*opportunity*) profiter de; (*age, kindness*) abuser de, exploiter. (*Ten.*) ~ *in, out,* avantage service, dehors. ~**ous†,** *a,* avantageux.
advent, *n,* venue, *f,* avènement, *m;* (*of Christ*) avènement. (*Eccl.*) *A*~, l'Avent, *m.*
adventure, *n,* aventure, *f.* ¶ *a,* (*story &c*) d'aventures. **adventurer,** *n,* aventurier, *m.* **adventuress,** *n,* aventurière, *f.* **adventurous,** *a,* aventureux.
adverb, *n,* adverbe, *m.* ~**ial†,** *a,* adverbial.
adversary, *n,* adversaire, *m.* **adverse,** *a,* défavorable; (*wind*) contraire. **adversity,** *n,* adversité, infortune, *f.*
advert, *n, abb. of* **advertisement.**
advertise, *v.t,* (*Com.*) faire de la publicité *ou* de la réclame pour; (*sth for sale*) mettre une annonce (pour vendre qch); (*ignorance*) afficher. ¶ *v.i,* faire de la publicité &c. ~ *for,* demander par voie d'annonces. ~**ment,** *n,* publicité, réclame; (*personal*) annonce, *f.* ~ *column,* petites annonces. ~ *hoarding,* panneau-réclame, *m.* **advertiser,** *n,* annonceur, *m.* **advertising,** *n,* publicité, réclame, *f.* ¶ *a,* publicitaire; (*agency*) de publicité.
advice, *n,* avis, *m,* conseils, *m.pl. piece of* ~, un conseil. **advisable,** *a,* à conseiller, recommandable. **advise,** *v.t,* conseiller (qch à qn; à qn de faire); recommander (qch); (*counsel*) conseiller (qn sur qch); (*Com: notify*) aviser (qn de qch). ~ *against,* déconseiller (qch à qn). **advisedly,** *ad,* en toute connaissance de cause. **adviser,** *n,* conseiller, ère. **advisory,** *a,* consultatif.
advocate, *n,* avocat, défenseur; partisan, *m.* ¶ *v.t,* préconiser, recommander.
adze, *n,* herminette, *f.*
Aegean Sea (the), la mer Égée.
aegis, *n,* égide, *f.*
aerate, *v.t,* (*soil*) aérer; (*drink*) gazéfier. ~*d water,* eau gazeuse, *f.*
aerial, *a,* aérien. ~ *cable car,* téléférique, *m.* ¶

(*Radio*) *n*, antenne, *f*.
aerobatics, *n*, acrobatie aérienne, *f*. **aerodrome,** *n*, aérodrome, *m*. **aerodynamic,** *a*. & **~s,** *n*, aérodynamique, *f*.
aeronaut, *n*, aéronaute, *m,f*. **~ic(al),** *a*, aéronautique. **~ics,** *n*, aéronautique, *f*.
aeroplane, *n*, avion, *m*.
aerosol, *n*, aérosol, *m*; (*spray*) bombe, *f*.
aesthetic(al), *a*, esthétique.
afar, *ad*, loin, au loin. *from* ~, de loin.
affability, *n*, affabilité, *f*. **affable,** *a*, affable, aimable. **affably,** *ad*, avec affabilité.
affair, *n*, affaire; (*love* ~) liaison, affaire de cœur, *f*. *state of* ~*s*, état des choses, *m*, situation, *f*.
affect, *v.t*, avoir un effet sur; influer sur; (*emotionally*) émouvoir, affecter; (*feign*) affecter. **~ation,** *n*, affectation, *f*. **~ed,** *a*, affecté. **~edly,** *ad*, avec affectation. **~ing,** *a*, touchant. **affection,** *n*, affection, *f*. **~ate†,** *a*, affectueux; (*letter ending*) affectionné.
affidavit, *n*, déclaration sous serment, *f*.
affiliate, *v.t*, affilier.
affinity, *n*, affinité, *f*.
affirm, *v.t*, affirmer. **~ation,** *n*, affirmation, *f*. **~ative†,** *a*, affirmatif. ¶ *n*, affirmative, *f*. *in the* ~, (*reply*) affirmativement.
affix, *n*, affixe, *m*. ¶ *v.t*, apposer.
afflict, *v.t*, affliger. ~*ed with*, affligé de. **~ion,** *n*, affliction, *f*.
affluence, *n*, richesse, abondance, *f*. **affluent,** *a*, riche; (*society*) d'abondance. ¶ (*Geog.*) *n*, affluent, *m*.
afford, *v.t*, (*provide*) donner, fournir; (*holiday &c*) s'offrir, se payer *P*. ~ *to*, avoir les moyens de; (*be late*) se permettre de.
afforestation, *n*, [re]boisement, *m*.
affray, *n*, échauffourée, rixe, *f*.
affront, *n*, affront, *m*, insulte, *f*. ¶ *v.t*, offenser, insulter.
Afghan, *a*, afghan. ¶ *n*, Afghan, e.
afield, *ad*: *far* ~, très loin.
afloat, *ad*. & *a*, à flot, sur l'eau; (*fig.*) en circulation.
aforesaid, *a*, susdit, précité. ¶ *n*, susdit, e.
afraid, *a*, effrayé. *to be* ~ *of*, avoir peur de, craindre.
afresh, *ad*, de nouveau, à nouveau.
Africa, *n*, l'Afrique, *f*. **African,** *a*, africain. ¶ *n*, Africain, e.
aft, *ad*, (*Naut.*) vers *ou* sur *ou* à l'arrière.
after, *pr*, après. ~ *dinner*, après le dîner. *it is* ~ *6 o'clock*, il est 6 heures passées. ~ *finishing*, après avoir fini. *day* ~ *day*, jour après j. ~ *all*, après tout. ~ *the event*, après coup. *run* ~ *s.o*, courir après qn. ~ *you*, après vous. (*style, manner*) d'après, suivant. ¶ *ad*, = ~*wards*. ¶ *c*, après que (+ *indic.*). *come* ~ *he has left*, viens après qu'il sera parti. ~*birth*, délivre; placenta, *m*. ~*deck*, arrière-pont, *m*. ~*-effect*, suite, répercussion, *f*. ~*life*, vie future. ~*math*, suites, conséquences, *f.pl*. ~*noon*, après-midi, *m*. *good* ~*noon*, bonjour. ~*-taste*, arrière-goût, *m*. ~*thought*, réflexion après coup, *f*. ~*wards*, après, plus tard, par la suite.
again, *ad*, encore [une fois], de nouveau. ~ & ~, maintes & maintes fois. *now* & ~, de temps en temps. *never* ~, plus jamais. *as much* ~, deux fois autant. **again** *after a verb is often expressed by the prefix* re- *as, to begin* ~, recommencer.
against, *pr*, contre. ~ *my will*, à contre-cœur, malgré moi. *I've nothing* ~ *it*, je n'ai rien contre cela. *to be dead* ~ *sth*, s'opposer absolument à qch. ~ *the law*, contraire à la loi. ~ *the wall*, contre le mur. ~ *the light*, à contrejour. *as* ~, en comparaison de.
agate, *n*, agate, *f*.
age, *n*, âge, *m*. *what's his* ~? quel âge a-t-il? *9 years of* ~, âgé de 9 ans. *come of* ~, atteindre sa majorité. *she's under* ~, elle n'a pas encore l'âge légal. *she doesn't look her* ~, elle ne fait pas son âge. (*old* ~) vieillesse, *f*. (*period*) âge, époque, *f*. *it is* ~*s since I saw him*, il y a une éternité que je ne l'ai vu. ¶ *v.i*, vieillir.
aged, *a*, âgé, vieux. ~ *9*, âgé de 9 ans. ¶ *n.pl*, *the* ~, les personnes âgées.
agency, *n*, agence, *f*, bureau, *m*. *through the* ~ *of s.o*, par l'intermédiaire de qn.
agenda, *n*, ordre du jour, *m*.
agent, *n*, agent, *m*; représentant, e; (*dealer*) concessionnaire, *m,f*.
agglomeration, *n*, agglomération, *f*.
aggravate, *v.t*, aggraver; (*annoy*) exaspérer, agacer.
aggregate, *a*, global, total. ¶ *n*, total, ensemble, *m*.
aggression, *n*, agression, *f*. **aggressive,** *a*, agressif. **aggressor,** *n*, agresseur, *m*.
aggrieved, *a*, chagriné.
aghast, *a*, stupéfait, atterré (*at*, de).
agile†, *a*, agile. **agility,** *n*, agilité, *f*.
agitate, *v.t*, agiter. ¶ *v.i*, (*Pol.*) faire de l'agitation (contre; en faveur de). **agitation,** *n*, agitation, *f*. **agitator,** *n*, agitateur, trice.
agnostic, *a*, agnostique.
ago, *ad*, *a year* ~, il y a un an.
agog, *a*, en émoi, impatient.
agonizing, *a*, déchirant, angoissant. **agony,** *n*, douleur déchirante; (*mental*) angoisse, *f*. *death* ~, agonie, *f*. *suffer agonies*, être au supplice. ~ *column*, annonces personnelles, *f.pl*.
agrarian, *a*, agraire.
agree, *v.t*, (*to do*) consentir (à faire), accepter (de f.); (*admit*) avouer, admettre, reconnaître (*that*, que); (*price*) se mettre d'accord sur. ¶ *v.i*, ~ *with s.o*, être *ou* tomber *ou* se mettre

d'accord avec qn (*about, on*, sur). (*Gram.*) s'accorder (*with*, avec). *garlic doesn't ~ with me*, l'ail ne me réussit pas. *~d price*, prix convenu. *~d!* d'accord!, entendu! **~able,** *a*, agréable, aimable; consentant (*to*, à). **~ment,** *n*, accord, *m*, convention *f;* contrat; pacte, *m*.

agricultural, *a*, agricole; (*engineer*) agronome. *~ show*, exposition agricole, *f*. **agricultur[al]ist,** *n*, (*scientist*) agronome, *m,f;* (*farmer*) agriculteur, *m*. **agriculture,** *n*, agriculture, *f*.

aground, *a*, échoué. **to run ~,** *v.i*, s'échouer.

ahead, *ad*, en avant, devant. *go on ~*, aller en avant. (*Naut.*) *full steam ~!* en avant toute! *get ~*, (*lit., fig.*) prendre de l'avance. *to be ~ of s.o*, être en avance *ou* avoir de l'avance sur qn. (*book*) *a month ~*, un mois à l'avance.

ahoy, *i*, ohé! *ship ~!* ohé du navire!

aid, *n*, aide, *f*. *with the ~ of*, (*s.o*) avec l'aide de; (*sth*) à l'aide de. (*pers.*) aide, *m,f*. assistant, e. *audio-visual ~s*, support audio-visuel. ¶ *v.t*, aider (à faire).

aide, *n*, aide, *m,f*. *~-de-camp*, aide de c., *m*.

Aids, AIDS (*Med: acquired immune deficiency syndrome*) *n*, Sida, SIDA (syndrome immuno-déficitaire acquis), *m*.

ail, *v.t*, *what ~s him?* qu'est-ce qu'il a? **~ing,** *a*, maladif, souffrant. **~ment,** *n*, mal, ennui de santé, *m*.

aim, *n*, *to take ~*, viser. (*Mil.*) *take ~!* en joue! (*purpose*) but, objet, *m*. *with the ~ of doing*, dans le but de faire. ¶ *v.t*, (*gun*) braquer (*at*, sur); (*remark*) diriger (*at*, contre). ¶ *v.i*, viser. *~ at*, (*sth*) viser; (*s.o*) coucher en joue. *~ to do*, viser à faire, avoir l'intention de f. **~less,** *a*, **~lessly,** *ad*, sans but.

air, *n*, air, *m*. *in the open ~*, en plein air. *go out for some fresh ~*, sortir prendre l'air. *throw up in the ~*, jeter en l'air. (*Radio*) *on the ~*, à la radio, à l'antenne. (*Mus.*) air, *m;* (*look*) air, mine, *f*. *give o.s ~s*, se donner des airs. *~ base*, base aérienne. *~borne*, (*plane*) en vol, (*troops*) aéroporté. *~craft*, avion, appareil, *m*. *~craft carrier*, porte-avions, *m*. *~-conditioned*, climatisé. *~crew*, *n*, équipage, *m*. *~field*, terrain d'aviation, aérodrome, *m*. *~ force*, armée de l'air, *f*. *~gun*, fusil à air comprimé, *m*. *~ hostess*, hôtesse de l'air, *f*. *~lift*, pont aérien, *m*. *~line*, ligne aérienne. *~lock*, bouchon, *m*, bulle d'air, *f*. *by ~mail*, par avion. *~man*, aviateur, *m*. *~port*, aéroport, *m*. *~ raid*, raid aérien, *m*. *~ ship*, dirigeable, *m*. *to be ~sick*, avoir le mal de l'air. *~ terminal*, aérogare, *f*. *~tight*, étanche. *~worthy*, en état de navigation. ¶ *v.t*, (*clothes, room*) aérer; (*views*) faire parade de. **~ing,** *n*, aérage, *m*, aération, ventilation, *f*. **~less,** *a*, sans air, privé d'air. **~y,** *a*, (*room*) clair; (*casual*) dégagé. désinvolte; (*promises*) en l'air.

aisle, *n*, (*church*) allée centrale; (*side*) bas-côté, *m*, nef latérale; (*Theat.*) allée, *f;* (*bus*) couloir, *m*.

ajar, *a*, entrouvert.

akimbo, *ad*: *with arms ~*, les mains sur les hanches.

akin to, *a*, qui ressemble à, qui tient de.

alabaster, *n*, albâtre, *m*.

alacrity, *n*, empressement, *m*.

alarm, *n*, alarme, alerte, *f*. *raise the ~*, donner l'alarme. *~ clock*, réveille-matin, réveil, *m*. ¶ *v.t*, alarmer. **~ing,** *a*, alarmant. **~ist,** *a. & n*, alarmiste, *m,f*.

alas *i*, hélas!

alb, *n*, aube, *f*.

Albania, *n*, l'Albanie, *f*. **Albanian,** *a*, albanais. ¶ *n*, Albanais, e.

albatross, *n*, albatros, *m*.

albino, *n*, albinos, *m,f*.

album, *n*, album, *m*.

albumen, *n*, albumen, *m*. **albumin,** *n*, albumine, *f*.

alchemist, *n*, alchimiste, *m*. **alchemy,** *n*, alchimie, *f*.

alcohol, *n*, alcool, *m*. **~ic,** *a*, alcoolique; (*drink*) alcoolisé. ¶ *n*, alcoolique, *m,f*. **~ism,** *n*, alcoolisme, *m*.

alcove, *n*, alcôve, *f*.

alder, *n*, aune, *m*.

alderman, *n*, ≃ conseiller (ère) municipal(e).

ale, *n*, bière, *f*. *brown ~*, bière brune.

alert, *a*, vigilant, éveillé. ¶ *n*, alerte, *f*. *on the ~*, (*pers.*) sur le qui-vive; (*troops*) en état d'alerte. ¶ *v.t*, alerter (*to*, sur).

Alexandria, *n*, Alexandrie, *f*.

alfresco, *a. & ad*, en plein air.

algebra, *n*, algèbre, *m*.

Algeria, *n*, l'Algérie, *f*. **Algerian,** *a*, algérien. ¶ *n*, Algérien, ne. **Algiers,** *n*, Alger, *m*.

alias, *ad*, alias. ¶ *n*, faux nom, *m*.

alibi, *n*, alibi, *m*.

alien, *a*, & *n*, étranger, ère; (*from space*) extraterrestre, *m,f*. **alienate,** *v.t*, aliéner.

alight[1], *a*, allumé. *set ~*, mettre le feu à.

alight[2], *v.i*, (*pers.*) descendre; (*bird*) se poser.

align, *v.t*, aligner. **~ment,** *n*, alignement, *m*.

alike, *a*, semblable, pareil. *to be ~*, se ressembler. ¶ *ad*, également; à la fois; (*dress*) de la même façon.

alimentary, *a*, alimentaire.

alimony, *n*, pension alimentaire, *f*.

alive, *a*, en vie, vivant. *burn ~*, brûler vif. *keep ~*, maintenir en vie. (*alert*) éveillé, dégourdi. *~ to*, sensible à. *to be ~ with vermin*, grouiller de vermine.

alkali, *n*, alcali, *m*. **alkaline,** *a*, alcalin.

all, *a*, tout. *~ the year* [*round*], [pendant] toute l'année. *~* [*those*] *who*, tous ceux qui, toutes celles qui. *at ~ hours*, à toute heure. *on ~*

occasions, en toute occasion. ~ *three,* tous les trois. ¶ *ad,* tout, entièrement. ~ *at once,* tout à coup. ~ *but,* presque, à peu de choses près. *he* ~ *but died,* il a failli mourir. ~ *told,* en tout. ~ *right!* très bien!, bon!, ça va! ~ *the better,* tant mieux. ~ *the same,* tout de même, quand même. *it's* ~ *the same to me,* ça m'est égal. *not at* ~, pas du tout. *nothing at* ~, rien du tout. *Thank you!* — *not at* ~, Merci! — je vous en prie, [il n'y a] pas de quoi. ¶ *pr,* tout, tous, *m,pl.* ~ *of us,* nous tous. *that is* ~, c'est tout, voilà tout. *after* ~, après tout. ~ *that you say,* tout ce que vous dites. *for* ~ *I know,* autant que je sache. *for* ~ *I care,* pour ce que cela me fait. *when* ~ *is said and done,* en fin de compte, tout compte fait. (*Games*) *two* ~, deux à deux; (*Ten.*) deux partout; *fifteen* ~, quinze à. ~ *change!* tout le monde descend! ~ *clear,* fin d'alerte, *f.* ~*-in,* (*pers.*) éreinté; (*price*) tout compris; (*policy*) tous risques. *A*~ *Hallows, A*~ *Saints' Day,* la Toussaint. ~*-out,* (*effort*) maximum. ~*-powerful,* tout-puissant. ~*-round,* (*athlete*) complet; (*improvement*) général.

Allah, *n,* Allah, *m.*

allay, *v.t,* calmer, apaiser.

allegation, *n,* allégation, *f.* **allege,** *v.t,* alléguer, prétendre.

allegiance, *n,* allégeance, *f.*

allegoric(al†) *a,* allégorique. **allegory,** *n,* allégorie, *f.*

allergic, *a,* allergique (*to,* à). **allergy,** *n,* allergie, *f.*

alleviate, *v.t,* alléger, soulager, adoucir. **alleviation,** *n,* allégement, soulagement, adoucissement, *m.*

alley, *n,* ruelle; (*in garden*) allée, *f.*

alliance, *n,* alliance, *f.*

allied, *a,* allié (*to,* à; *with,* avec).

alligator, *n,* alligator, *m.*

allocate, *v.t,* allouer; (*money*) affecter. **allocation,** *n,* allocation, *f.*

allot, *v.t,* attribuer, assigner. ~**ment,** *n,* distribution, *f;* (*Agric.*) lopin de terre, *m.*

allow, *v.t,* permettre (qch à qn; à qn de faire); autoriser (qn à faire); souffrir, tolérer; (*money*) allouer, accorder. (*time*) ~ *2 hours,* compter 2 heures. (*admit*) admettre. ~**ance,** *n,* (*personal*) pension, rente; (*travel, lodging &c*) indemnité, allocation, *f;* (*discount*) rabais, *m,* réduction, *f.* *make* ~[*s*] *for,* se montrer indulgent envers qn; tenir compte de qch.

alloy, *n,* alliage, *m.*

allude, *v.i,* faire allusion (*to,* à).

allure, *n,* charme, attrait, *m.* ¶ *v.t,* attirer, séduire. **alluring,** *a,* séduisant.

allusion, *n,* allusion, *f.*

alluvial, *a,* alluvial.

ally, *n,* allié, e. ¶ *v.t,* ~ *o.s with,* s'allier avec.

almanac, *n,* almanach, *m.*

almighty, *a,* tout-puissant; (*din*) du diable. ¶ *n, the A*~, le Tout-Puissant.

almond, *n,* amande, *f.* ~ *eyes,* des yeux en amande, *m.pl.* ~ [*tree*], amandier, *m.*

almost, *ad,* presque.

alms, *n,* aumône, *f.* *give* ~, faire l'aumône. ~*house,* hospice, *m.*

aloft, *ad,* en haut; (*Naut.*) dans la mâture.

alone, *a,* seul. *all* ~, tout(e) seul(e). ~ *in doing,* seul à faire. *let, leave* ~, (*pers.*) laisser tranquille; (*object*) ne pas toucher à.

along, *pr,* le long de. *run* ~ *the beach,* courir le l. de la plage. (*trees*) ~ *the road,* au bord de la route. *the path runs* ~[*side*] *the wood,* le sentier longe le bois. *somewhere* ~ *the road,* quelque part en chemin. ¶ *ad, come* ~, *be* ~, venir. *come* ~*!* venez donc! ~ *with,* avec. ~**side,** *pr. & ad,* (*beside*) à côté de; (*along*) le long de. (*Naut: ships*) bord à bord. *to be* ~ *the quay,* être à quai. *come* ~ *the quay,* accoster le quai.

aloof, *ad,* à l'écart. ¶ *a,* distant.

aloud, *ad,* à haute voix, tout haut.

alpaca, *n,* alpaga, *m.*

alpha, *n,* alpha, *m.* **alphabet,** *n,* alphabet, *m.* ~**ical†,** *a,* alphabétique.

Alpine, *a,* alpin; alpestre. **the Alps,** les Alpes, *f.pl.*

already, *ad,* déjà.

Alsace, *n,* l'Alsace, *f.* **Alsatian,** *a,* alsacien. ¶ *n,* (*pers.*) Alsacien, ne; (*dog*) chien-loup, *m.*

also, *ad,* aussi, également.

altar, *n,* autel, *m.* ~ *boy,* enfant de chœur, *m.* ~ *piece,* retable, *m.*

alter, *v.t,* changer, modifier; (*speech &c*) remanier. ¶ *v.i,* changer. ~**ation,** *n,* changement, *m,* modification, *f;* remaniement, *m.*

altercation, *n,* altercation, prise de bec, *f.*

alternate†, *a,* alternatif, alterné. *on* ~ *days,* tous les deux jours. ¶ *v.i.* (*& t*), (faire) alterner. ~**ly,** *ad,* alternativement, tour à tour. **alternating,** *a,* alternant; (*current*) alternatif. **alternative,** *a,* autre. ¶ *n,* alternative, *f.* *he has no* ~, il n'a pas le choix.

although, *c,* quoique, bien que (+*subj*).

altimeter, *n,* altimètre, *m.*

altitude, *n,* altitude, *f.*

alto, *n,* (*female*) contralto, *m;* (*male*) haute-contre, *f.* ¶ *a,* (*part*) de contralto &c; (*saxophone*) alto; (*clef*) d'ut.

altogether, *ad,* tout à fait, entièrement, complètement; (*in total*) en tout.

altruist, *n.* & ~**ic,** *a,* altruiste, *m,f.*

aluminium, *n,* aluminium, *m.*

always, *ad,* toujours.

amalgam, *n,* amalgame, *m.* ~**ate,** *v.t,* amalgamer, fusionner.

amass, *v.t,* amasser.

amateur, *n,* amateur, *m.* ¶ *a,* (*player &c*) amateur; (*work*) d'a. ~ *status,* statut d'a., *m.*
amaze, *v.t,* étonner, stupéfier. ~**ment,** *n,* étonnement, *m,* stupéfaction, *f.*
Amazon (*woman*) *n,* amazone, *f.* **the** ~ (*river*), l'Amazone, *m.*
ambassador, dress, *n,* ambassadeur, drice. *French* ~, ambassadeur de France.
amber, *n,* ambre, *m.* ~ *light,* feu orange. ~**gris,** *n,* ambre gris, *m.*
ambidextrous *a,* ambidextre.
ambiguity, *n,* ambiguïté, équivoque, *f.* **ambiguous**†, *a,* ambigu, équivoque.
ambition, *n,* ambition, *f. it's my* ~ *to do,* j'ambitionne de faire. **ambitious**†, *a,* ambitieux.
amble, *v.i,* ~ [*along*], aller d'un pas tranquille.
ambulance, *n,* ambulance, *f.*
ambush, *n,* embuscade, *f,* guetapens, *m. in* ~, (*troops*) embusqué. ¶ *v.t, to* ~ *s.o,* tendre une embuscade à qn.
ameliorate, *v.t.* (& *i*), (s')améliorer. **amelioration,** *n,* amélioration, *f.*
amen, *i.* & *n,* amen, *m.*
amenable, *a,* maniable. ~ *to kindness,* sensible à la douceur. ~ *to reason,* raisonnable.
amend, *v.t,* (*law*) amender; (*habits*) réformer; (*text*) modifier. ~**ment,** *n,* amendement, *m.* ~**s,** *n.pl,* réparation, *f. make* ~, faire amende honorable; se racheter.
amenity, *n,* agrément, *m.* (*pl*) commodités, *f.pl.*
America, *n,* l'Amérique. *f.* **American,** *a,* américain. ~ *cloth,* toile cirée. ¶ *n,* Américain, e.
amethyst, *n,* améthyste, *f.*
amiability, *n,* amabilité, *f.* **amiable,** *a,* aimable. **amiably,** *ad,* avec amabilité.
amicable†, *a,* amical. ~ *settlement,* arrangement à l'amiable, *m.*
amid, amidst, *pr,* au milieu de, parmi. **amidships,** *ad,* au milieu du navire.
amiss, *ad.* & *a, take sth* ~, prendre qch de travers *ou* en mauvaise part. *it wouldn't come* ~, cela ne ferait pas de mal. *there's sth* ~, il y a qch qui ne va pas; il y a un os *P.*
ammonia, *n,* ammoniaque, *f.*
ammunition, *n,* munitions, *f.pl.* ~ *dump,* parc de munitions, *m.*
amnesia, *n,* amnésie, *f.*
amnesty, *n,* amnistie, *f.*
among[st], *pr,* parmi, entre, au milieu de. ~ *friends,* entre amis. (*count s.o*) ~ *one's friends,* au nombre de ses amis.
amorous†, *a,* amoureux.
amorphous, *a,* amorphe.
amount, *n,* quantité; (*sum*) somme, *f,* montant, total, *m. any* ~ *of,* des quantités de, énormément de. ¶ *v.i,* ~ *to,* se monter à, s'élever à. (*fig.*) *it* ~*s to the same thing,* cela revient au même.
ampere, *n,* ampère, *m.*
amphibian, *n,* amphibie, *m.* **amphibious,** *a,* amphibie.
amphitheatre, *n,* amphithéâtre, *m.*
ample†, *a,* abondant, copieux; largement suffisant; (*garment*) ample.
amplification, *n,* amplification, *f.* **amplifier,** *n,* amplificateur, *m.* **amplify,** *v.t,* (*sound*) amplifier; (*idea*) développer.
amputate, *v.t,* amputer. ~ *s.o's leg,* amputer qn de la jambe.
amulet, *n,* amulette, *f.*
amuse, *v.t,* amuser, divertir, faire rire. *to be* ~*d at,* s'amuser de. (*entertain*) amuser, distraire. ~ *o.s by doing,* s'amuser à faire. ~**ment,** *n,* amusement, *m;* distraction, *f. much to my* ~, à mon grand amusement. **amusing,** *a,* amusant, drôle.
an, *indefinite art. V* **a.**
anachronism, *n,* anachronisme, *m.* **anachronistic,** *a,* anachronique.
anaemia, *n,* anémie, *f.* **anaemic,** *a,* anémique.
anaesthesia, *n,* anesthésie, *f.* **anaesthetic,** *a.* & *n,* anesthésique, *m.* **anaesthetize,** *v.t,* anesthésier.
anagram, *n,* anagramme, *f.*
analgesic, *a,* analgésique.
analogue, *n,* analogue, *m.* ~ *computer,* calculateur analogique, *m.*
analogous, *a,* analogue (*to, with,* à). **analogy,** *n,* analogie, *f.*
analyse, *v.t,* analyser, faire l'analyse de; (*Bkkpg*) ventiler. **analysis,** *n,* analyse; ventilation, *f.* **analyst,** *n,* analyste; (*Psych.*) psychanalyste, *m,f.* **analytic(al**†**),** *a,* analytique.
anarchic(al), *a,* anarchique. **anarchist,** *n,* anarchiste, *m,f.* **anarchy,** *n,* anarchie, *f.*
anatomical†, *a,* anatomique. **anatomy,** *n,* anatomie, *f.*
ancestor, *n,* ancêtre, *m.* **ancestral,** *a,* ancestral. **ancestry,** *n,* ascendance, *f.*
anchor, *n,* ancre, *f. lie at* ~, être à l'a., mouiller. ¶ *v.i,* jeter l'ancre, s'ancrer. ¶ *v.t,* (*Naut.*) mettre à l'a.; (*Build., fig.*) ancrer. ~**age,** *n,* mouillage, *m.*
anchovy, *n,* anchois, *m.*
ancient†, *a,* ancien; (*world, Rome*) antique; (*monument*) historique; (*pers., clothes*) très vieux. ¶ *n, the* ~*s,* les anciens, *m.pl.*
and, *c,* et. *a table* ~ *chair,* une table et une chaise. (*numbers*) *a hundred* ~ *two,* cent deux; *2* ~ *a half,* deux et demi; *2* ~ *three quarters,* deux trois quarts; *an hour* ~ *ten minutes,* une heure dix minutes. ~ *so on,* ~ *so forth,* et ainsi de suite. ~ *so on & so forth,* et patati et patata. *go* ~ *see,* allez voir. *try* ~ *find,* essayez de trouver. *faster* ~ *faster,* de plus en plus vite. *strawberries* ~ *cream,* fraises à la crème.
anecdote, *n,* anecdote, *f.*

anemone, *n,* anémone, *f.*
aneroid [barometer], baromètre anéroïde, *m.*
aneurism, *n,* anévrisme, *m.*
anew, *ad,* de nouveau; à nouveau.
angel, *n,* ange, *m.* ~**ic**†, *a,* angélique. **angelica** (*Bot.*) *n,* angélique, *f.* **Angelus,** *n,* (*prayer, bell*) Angélus, *m.*
anger, *n,* colère, *f.* ¶ *v.t,* mettre en colère, fâcher.
angina, *n,* angine, *f.* ~ *pectoris,* angine de poitrine.
angle[1], *n,* angle, *m. at en* ~, en biais. *seen from that* ~, vu sous cet angle. (*fig.*) point de vue, *m.* ~ *iron,* cornière, *f.*
angle[2], *v.i,* pêcher à la ligne. ~ *for* (*compliments*) chercher. **angler,** *n,* pêcheur à la ligne, *m.* **angling,** *n,* pêche à la ligne, *f.*
Anglican, *a.* & *n,* (*Eccl.*) anglican, e.
anglicism, *n,* anglicisme, *m.* **anglicize,** *v.t,* angliciser.
Anglo-French, *a,* franco-britannique.
anglophile, *a.* & *n,* anglophile, *m,f.* **anglophobe,** *n,* anglophobe, *m,f.*
Anglo-Saxon, *a,* anglo-saxon.
angora, *a.* & *n,* angora, *inv.* & *m.*
angrily, *ad,* avec colère, en colère. **angry,** *a,* en colère, fâché, irrité (*with s.o,* contre qn). *to get* ~, se fâcher, se mettre en colère.
anguish, *n,* angoisse, *f.*
angular, *a,* anguleux.
animal, *a,* animal. ¶ *n,* animal, *m.*
animate, *a,* vivant, animé. ¶ *v.t,* animer. ~**d,** *a,* animé. ~ *cartoon,* dessin animé. **animation,** *n,* animation, *f;* entrain, *m.*
animosity, animus, *n,* animosité, *f.*
aniseed, *n,* anis, *m,* graine d'anis, *f.*
ankle, *n,* cheville. ~ *socks,* socquettes, *f.pl.*
annals, *n.pl,* annales, *f.pl.*
annex, *v.t,* annexer. ¶ (& ~**e**) *n,* annexe, *f.* ~**ation,** *n,* annexion, *f.*
annihilate, *v.t,* anéantir, annihiler. **annihilation,** *n,* anéantissement, *m.*
anniversary, *a.* & *n,* anniversaire, *m.*
annotate, *v.t,* annoter. **annotation,** *n,* annotation, *f.*
announce, *v.t,* annoncer; (*birth, marriage &c*) faire part de. ~**ment,** *n,* annonce, *f,* avis; faire-part, *m.* **announcer** (*Radio*) *n,* speaker(ine), *m*(*f*).
annoy, *v.t,* agacer, contrarier, irriter, énerver, embêter *P. to get* ~*ed with s.o,* se mettre en colère contre qn. ~**ance** *n,* contrariété *f,* mécontentement, *m.* ~**ing,** *a,* agaçant, énervant, embêtant *P;* (*tiresome*) ennuyeux.
annual†, *a,* annuel. ¶ *n,* plante annuelle, *f;* (*book*) annuaire, *m.* **annuitant,** *n,* rentier, ère.
annuity, *n,* rente [viagère] *f.*
annul, *v.t,* annuler; (*law*) abroger; (*judgment*) casser.
annum, *n: per* ~, par an.
Annunciation (the), l'Annonciation, *f.*
anode, *n,* anode, *f.*
anoint, *a,* oindre, sacrer.
anomalous, *a,* anormal. **anomaly,** *n,* anomalie, *f.*
anon, *ad,* tantôt, tout à l'heure.
anonymity, *n,* anonymat, *m.* **anonymous,** *a,* anonyme.
anorak, *n,* anorak, *m.*
another, *a.* & *pn,* (*one more*) encore un(e), un(e) de plus. *in* ~ *2 years,* dans 2 ans d'ici. (*different*) un(e) autre; (*similar*) un(e) autre, un(e) second(e).
answer, *n,* réponse, *f. in* ~ *to your letter,* en r. à votre lettre. *he always has a ready* ~, il a la réplique facile. (*to problem*) solution, *f;* (*to riddle*) mot de l'énigme, *m.* ~*-phone,* répondeur automatique, *m.* ¶ *v.t,* répondre à. ~ *back,* répliquer [avec impertinence]. ~ *for,* répondre de. ~**able,** *a,* responsable (*for,* de).
ant, *n,* fourmi, *f.* ~*-eater,* fourmilier, *m.* ~*hill,* fourmilière, *f.*
antagonism, *n,* antagonisme, *m.* **antagonist,** *n,* antagoniste, *m.* **antagonize,** *v.t,* provoquer l'hostilité de.
antarctic, *a,* antarctique. *the A*~ *Ocean,* l'océan antarctique, *m.*
antecedent, *a.* & *n,* antécédent, *m.*
antechamber, *n,* antichambre, *f.*
antedate, *v.t,* antidater.
antediluvian, *a,* antédiluvien.
antelope, *n,* antilope, *f.*
ante meridiem (*abb.* a.m.), avant midi; du matin.
antenatal, *a,* prénatal. ~ *clinic,* visite prénatale, *f.*
antenna, *n,* antenne, *f.*
anterior†, *a,* antérieur.
anteroom, *n,* antichambre, *f.*
anthem, *n,* motet, *m;* (*national*) hymne, *m.*
anthology, *n,* anthologie, *f.*
anthracite, *n,* anthracite, *m.*
anthropology, *n,* anthropologie, *f.*
anti-aircraft, *a,* (*gun*) antiaérien. ~ *defence,* défense contre avions, D.C.A., *f.*
antibiotic, *a.* & *n,* antibiotique, *m.*
antibody, *n,* anticorps, *m.*
antic, *n,* ~*s,* bouffonnerie; gambades, *f*(*pl*).
anticipate, *v.t,* prévoir, s'attendre à; (*event, profits*) anticiper sur. **anticipation,** *n,* anticipation, prévision, *f.* (*Com.*) *thanking you in* ~, en vous remerciant d'avance.
anticyclone, *n,* anticyclone, *m.*
antidote, *n,* antidote, *m.*
antifreeze, *n,* antigel, *m.*
antipathetic, *a,* antipathique. **antipathy,** *n,* antipathie, aversion, *f.*
antipodes, *n.pl,* antipodes, *m.pl.*
antiquary, antiquarian, *n,* archéologue, amateur d'antiquités, *m.* **antiquated,** *a,* suranné, vieilli. **antique,** *a,* ancien, antique. ~ *furni-*

ture, meubles anciens, *m,pl.* ¶ *n,* objet d'art ancien. ~ *dealer,* antiquaire, *m.* ~ *shop,* magasin d'antiquités, *m.* **antiquity,** *n,* antiquité, *f.*
antirrhinum, *n,* muflier, *m,* gueule-de-loup, *f.*
anti-semitic, *a,* antisémite, antisémitique.
antiseptic, *a. & n,* antiseptique, *m.*
antisocial, *a,* antisocial.
anti-tank, *a,* antichar.
antithesis, *n,* antithèse, *f.*
antler, *n,* merrain, *m.* ~*s,* bois, *m.pl.*
Antwerp, *n,* Anvers, *m.*
anus, *n,* anus, *m.*
anvil, *n,* enclume, *f.*
anxiety, *n,* anxiété, inquiétude, *f;* soucis, *m.pl.* **anxious,** *a,* anxieux; inquiet, soucieux (*about,* de). *to be* ~ *to do,* être désireux *ou* impatient de faire; tenir beaucoup à f. ~**ly,** *ad,* avec anxiété.
any, *a, ad, & pn,* (*interrog.*) du, de la, des. *Who has* ~ *money?* Qui a de l'argent? (*neg.*) de. *I haven't* ~ *money,* je n'ai pas d'a. ne... aucun. *I haven't* ~ *idea,* je n'ai aucune idée. (*no matter which*) n'importe quel, quelconque, tout. *buy* ~ *paper* [*you like*], achetez n'importe quel journal. *at* ~ *hour of the day,* à toute heure du jour. *in* ~ *case,* en tout cas. *has he* ~? en a-t-il? (*go*) ~ *further,* plus loin. ~ *more,* encore (du, de la, des), (*neg.*) ne... plus (de). (*we expect him*) ~ *day,* d'un jour à l'autre.
anybody, anyone, *n. & pn,* (*interrog.*) quelqu'un; (*neg.*) ne... personne; (*no matter who*) n'importe qui, le premier venu, tout le monde. ~ *would think,* on croirait. ~ *who,* quiconque.
anyhow, *ad,* de toute façon; en tout cas, toujours; n'importe comment; tant bien que mal.
anything, *pn,* (*V anybody*) quelque chose; (*neg.*) ne... rien; n'importe quoi, quoi que ce soit.
anywhere, *ad,* (*V anybody*) quelque part; (*neg.*) ne... nulle part; n'importe où.
aorta, *n,* aorte, *f.*
apace, *ad,* à grands pas, rapidement.
apart, *ad, 5 km* ~, à 5 km l'un de l'autre. *with one's feet* ~, les jambes écartées. (*aside*) à part, à l'écart; (*separately*) séparément. ~ *from,* à part, en dehors de.
apartment, *n,* (*room*) pièce, chambre, *f;* (*Am: flat*) appartement, logement, *m.*
apathetic, *a,* apathique, indolent. **apathy,** *n,* apathie, indolence, *f.*
ape, *n,* [grand] singe, *m.* ¶ *v.t,* singer.
aperient, *a. & n,* laxatif, *m.*
aperture, *n,* ouverture, *f.*
apex, *n,* sommet, *m.*
aphorism, *n,* aphorisme, *m.*
apiary, *n,* rucher, *m.*
apiece, *ad,* [la] pièce, chacun(e).
apogee, *n,* apogée, *m.*
apologetic, *a,* (*tone &c*) d'excuse. *to be* ~, s'excuser. **apologize,** *v.i,* s'excuser (de qch auprès de qn); faire ses excuses (à qn pour qch). **apology,** *n,* excuses, *f.pl.*
apoplectic, *a. & n,* apoplectique, *m,f.* ~ *fit,* attaque d'apoplexie, *f.* **apoplexy,** *n,* apoplexie, *f.*
apostle, *n,* apôtre, *m. the* [*A* ~*s*] *Creed,* le symbole [des apôtres]. **apostleship,** *n,* apostolat, *m.* **apostolic,** *a,* apostolique.
apostrophe, *n,* apostrophe, *f.*
appal, *v.t,* consterner, épouvanter. **appalling,** *a,* épouvantable.
apparatus, *n,* appareil, dispositif, *m.*
apparel, *n,* habillement, *m,* vêtements, *m.pl.*
apparent, *a,* apparent; (*heir*) présomptif. ~**ly,** *ad,* apparemment.
apparition, *n,* apparition, *f.*
appeal, *n,* appel, *m.* (*Law*) *A*~ *Court,* cour d'appel, *f.* (*attraction*) attrait, charme, *m.* ¶ *v.i,* faire appel (*to,* à); (*charity*) lancer un appel; (*Law*) se pourvoir en appel. ~ *to,* (*good sense*) en appeler à; (*attract*) plaire à, attirer. *that doesn't* ~ *to me,* cela ne me dit rien *P.*
appear, *v.i,* apparaître, se montrer; (*before a court*) comparaître; (*on TV*) passer à la télévision; (*seem*) paraître, sembler. ~**ance,** *n,* apparition; (*book*) parution; (*before a court*) comparution; (*look*) apparence, mine, *f,* aspect, *m. to all* ~*s,* selon toute apparence.
appease, *v.t,* apaiser, calmer. ~**ment,** *n,* apaisement, *m.*
append, *v.t,* joindre, attacher; (*signature*) apposer. ~**age, appendix,** *n,* appendice, *m.* **appendicitis,** *n,* appendicite, *f.*
appertain, *v.i,* appartenir.
appetite, *n,* appétit, *m.* **appetizer,** *n,* apéritif, *m.* **appetizing,** *a,* appétissant.
applaud, *v.t,* applaudir. **applause,** *n,* applaudissements, *m.pl.*
apple, *n,* pomme, *f.* ~ *core,* trognon de p., *m.* ~ *pie,* tourte aux pommes, *f.* ~ *sauce,* compote de pommes, *f.* ~ *tree,* pommier, *m.*
appliance, *n,* appareil; dispositif, *m.*
applicant, *n,* (*job*) candidat, e (*for,* à); (*Adm.*) demandeur, euse. **application,** *n,* (*paint, rule*) application; (*for job*) demande d'emploi; (*to studies*) application, attention, *f.*
apply, *v.t,* (*paint, bandage*) appliquer, mettre; (*pressure*) exercer; (*brakes*) actionner. ~ *for,* demander, faire une demande de. ~ *to,* s'adresser à.
appoint, *v.t,* (*to a post*) nommer, désigner; (*date, place*) fixer, désigner. *well* ~*ed house,* maison bien installée. ~**ment,** *n,* rendez-vous, *m. make an* ~ *with s.o.* donner r-v. à qn. (*post*) poste, emploi, *m;* (*selection*) nomination, désignation, *f.* ~*s,* aménagement, *m,* instal-

lation, *f.*
apportion, *v.t,* répartir, partager.
apposite, *a,* à propos, pertinent.
apposition, *n,* apposition, *f.*
appraisal, *n,* estimation, évaluation, *f.*
appraise, *v.t,* évaluer, estimer.
appreciable, *a,* appréciable, sensible. **appreciably,** *ad,* sensiblement. **appreciate,** *v.t,* (*art, wine*) apprécier; (*help, kindness*) être reconnaissant de; (*realize*) se rendre compte (*sth,* de qch; *that,* que). ¶ *v.i,* (*Fin.*) monter, augmenter de valeur. **appreciation,** *n,* appréciation, estimation; reconnaissance; (*Fin.*) hausse, *f.*
appreciative, *a,* reconnaissant; (*comment*) élogieux.
apprehend, *v.t,* arrêter, appréhender; (*fear*) craindre, redouter. **apprehension,** *n,* arrestation; crainte, appréhension, *f.* **apprehensive,** *a,* inquiet, appréhensif.
apprentice, *n,* apprenti, e. ¶ *v.t,* mettre en apprentissage. **~ship,** *n,* apprentissage, *m.*
apprise *v.t,* informer (*s.o of sth,* qn de qch).
approach, *n,* approche, *f;* (*to job, problem*) façon de s'y prendre, *f.* *~s* (*to town*) abords, *m.pl,* approches, *f.pl.* ¶ *v.t,* [s']approcher de; (*pers., question*) aborder. *~ s.o* (*to obtain sth*) faire des démarches auprès de qn. ¶ *v.i,* [s']approcher. ~ **able,** *a,* approchable.
approbation, *n,* approbation, *f.*
appropriate†, *a,* propre, approprié (*for, to,* à). *at the ~ time,* en temps opportun. ¶ *v.t,* s'approprier.
approval, *n,* approbation, *f,* assentiment, *m.* *on ~,* à condition. **approve,** *v.t.,* approuver, sanctionner. **approving,** *a,* approbateur.
approximate†, *a,* approximatif. **approximation,** *n,* approximation, *f.*
apricot, *n,* abricot, *m.* *~ tree,* abricotier, *m.*
April, *n,* avril, *m.* *to make an ~ fool of,* faire un poisson d'avril à.
apron, *n,* tablier, *m.*
apropos, *ad,* à propos.
apse, *n,* abside, *f.*
apt, *a,* *~ to do,* (*pers.*) enclin, disposé, porté à faire; (*thing*) susceptible de faire. (*remark*) à propos, juste, pertinent; (*pupil*) doué. **~ly,** *ad,* à propos. **aptitude,** *n,* aptitude, *f* (*for,* à), dispositions, *f.pl* (*for,* pour).
aqualung, *n,* scaphandre autonome, *m.*
aquarium, *n,* aquarium, *m.*
aquatic, *a,* (*plant*) aquatique; (*sport*) nautique.
aqueduct, *n,* aqueduc, *m.*
aquiline, *a,* aquilin.
Arab, *a,* arabe. ¶ *n,* Arabe, *m,f.* **arabesque,** *n,* arabesque, *f.* **Arabia,** *n,* l'Arabie, *f.* **Arabian,** *a,* arabe. *~ gulf,* golfe Arabique, *m.* *the ~ nights,* les Mille & une Nuits. ¶ *n,* Arabe, *m,f.* **Arabic** (*language*) *n,* l'arabe, *m.* ~ **numerals,** chiffres arabes, *m.pl.*
arable, *a,* arable.
arbitrary†, *a,* arbitraire. **arbitrate,** *v.t,* arbitrer. **arbitration,** *n,* arbitrage, *m.* **arbitrator,** *n,* arbitre, *m.*
arbour, *n,* tonnelle, charmille, *f.*
arc, *n,* arc, *m.* *~ lamp,* lampe à arc, *f.*
arcade, *n,* arcades, *f.pl.* *shopping ~,* galerie marchande, *f.*
arch[1]**,** *n,* (*Arch., eyebrow*) arc, *m,* arcade, *f;* (*foot*) voûte plantaire, *f.* *~way,* passage voûté. ¶ *v.t,* arquer. *~ed,* (*back*) cambré; (*door*) cintré.
arch[2]**,** *a,* (*roguish*) espiègle, coquin.
arch[3]**,** *a,* (*supreme*) grand, achevé. ¶ *pref,* arch[i]... *~angel,* archange, *m.* *~bishop,* archevêque, *m.* *~bishopric,* archevêché, *m.* *~deacon,* archidiacre, *m.*
archaeologic(al), *a,* archéologique. **archaeologist,** *n,* archéologue, *m.* **archaeology,** *n,* archéologie, *f.*
archaic, *a,* archaïque.
archer, *n,* archer, *m.* **~y,** *n,* tir à l'arc, *m.*
archetype, *n.* & **archetypal,** *a,* archétype.
Archimedes' screw, vis d'Archimède, *f.*
archipelago, *n,* archipel, *m.*
architect, *n,* architecte; (*fig.*) artisan, *m.* **architectural,** *a,* architectural. **architecture,** *n,* architecture, *f.*
archives, *n.pl,* archives, *f.pl.*
arctic, *a,* arctique. *the A~ Ocean,* l'océan arctique, *m.* ¶ *n, the A~,* l'Arctique, *m.*
ardent, *a,* ardent, fervent. **~ly,** *ad,* ardemment. **ardour,** *n,* ardeur, ferveur, *f.*
arduous, *a,* ardu, pénible, laborieux.
are, *V be.*
area, *n,* aire, superficie; (*region*) zone, région, *f.* (*fig.*) *~ of agreement,* terrain d'entente, *m.*
arena, *n,* arène, *f.*
Argentina & the Argentine, l'Argentine, *f.* **Argentinian,** *a,* argentin. ¶ *n,* Argentin, e.
arguable, *a,* discutable. *it is ~ that..,* on peut soutenir que.. **argue,** *v.i,* argumenter, raisonner; (*quarrel*) se disputer. ¶ *v.t,* (*case*) discuter, débattre. *~ the toss P,* discuter le coup *P.* **argument,** *n,* argument, raisonnement, *m;* (*quarrel*) dispute, discussion, *f.* **~ative,** *a,* raisonneur.
aria (*Mus.*) *n,* aria, *f.*
arid, *a,* aride. **~ity,** *n,* aridité, *f.*
aright, *ad,* bien, correctement.
arise, *v.i.ir,* (*problem &c*) surgir, survenir; (*opportunity*) se présenter; (*cry, doubts*) s'élever. *should the case ~,* le cas échéant.
aristocracy, *n,* aristocratie, *f.* **aristocrat,** *n,* aristocrate, *m,f.* **aristocratic†,** *a,* aristocratique.
arithmetic, *n.* & **~al†,** *a,* arithmétique, *f.*
ark, *n,* arche, *f.* *the A~ of the Covenant,* l'arche d'alliance. *Noah's ~,* l'a. de Noé.
arm[1]**,** *n,* (*limb*) bras, *m.* *~ in ~,* bras dessus

bras dessous. *with open* ~*s*, à bras ouverts. *at* ~*'s length,* à bout de b. *keep s.o at* ~*'s length,* tenir qn à distance. ~[*rest*], bras, accoudoir, *m.* ~*band &* ~*let,* brassard, *m.* ~*chair,* fauteuil, *m.* ~*ful,* brassée, *f.* ~*hole,* emmanchure, *f.* ~*pit,* aisselle, *f.*

arm[2], *n,* (*weapon*) arme, *f. take up* ~*s,* prendre les armes. *to be up in* ~*s,* être en révolte (*against,* contre). ~*s race,* course aux armements, *f.* ~*s,* (*Her.*) armes, *f.pl.* ¶ *v.t.* (*& i*) (s')armer. ~**ed,** *a,* armé (*with,* de). ~ *to the teeth,* armé jusqu'aux dents. ~ *robbery,* vol à main armée, *m.*

armadillo, *n,* tatou, *m.*

armament & ~**s,** *n*(*pl*), armement, *m.*

armature, *n,* armature, *f.*

Armenia, *n,* l'Arménie, *f.* **Armenian,** *a,* arménien. ¶ *n,* Arménien, ne.

armistice, *n,* armistice, *m.*

armour, *n,* armure, *f;* (*Mil: vehicles*) blindés, *m.pl.* ~ *plating,* blindage, *m;* (*Naut.*) cuirasse, *f.* ~**ed,** *a,* (*car, division*) blindé; (*Naut.*) cuirassé. ~**er,** *n,* armurier, *m.* ~**y,** *n,* dépot d'armes, *m.*

army, *n,* armée [de terre]; (*fig.*) foule, *f. join the* ~, s'engager [dans l'a.]. ¶ *a,* (*life, uniform*) militaire. ~ *corps,* corps d'armée, *m.*

aroma, *n,* arôme, *m.* ~**tic,** *a,* aromatique.

around, *ad,* autour. *all* ~, tout autour. (*nearby*) alentour, près d'ici. *somewhere* ~, quelque part. *he's not* ~, il n'est pas là. ¶ *pr,* autour de. *wander* ~ *the town,* errer dans la ville. (*approx.*) environ, à peu près. ~ *3 o'clock,* vers 3 heures.

arouse, *v.t,* (*feelings*) éveiller, provoquer, susciter; (*O wake*) réveiller.

arpeggio, *n,* arpège, *m.*

arrange, *v.t,* (*gen., flowers, Mus.*) arranger; (*books &c*) ranger, mettre en ordre; (*furniture*) disposer; (*date*) fixer. ¶ *v.i,* ~ *to do,* s'arranger pour faire. ~**ment,** *n,* arrangement, *m,* disposition, *f. make* ~*s for,* faire des préparatifs pour. *make* ~ *for sth to be done,* prendre des mesures pour faire faire qch.

array, *n,* (*Mil.*) *battle* ~, ordre de bataille, *m.* (*objects*) étalage, *m;* (*people*) assemblée, *f.*

arrears, *n.pl,* arriéré, *m. in* ~, (*rent*) arriéré. *fall into* ~, s'arriérer.

arrest, *n,* arrestation, *f. under* ~, (*Civil*) en état d'arrestation; (*Mil.*) aux arrêts. ¶ *v.t,* (*pers., growth*) arrêter; (*disease*) enrayer.

arrival, *n,* arrivée, *f.* **arrive,** *v.i,* arriver. ~ *at,* arriver à, parvenir à, atteindre; (*solution*) aboutir à. ~ *unexpectedly,* (*pers.*) survenir.

arrogance, *n,* arrogance, *f.* **arrogant,** *a,* arrogant, rogue. ~**ly,** *ad,* arrogamment.

arrow, *n,* flèche, *f.* ~*head,* pointe de f., *f.*

arse *P**, *n,* cul *P**, *m.*

arsenal, *n,* arsenal, *m.*

arsenic, *n,* arsenic, *m.*

arson, *n,* incendie volontaire, *m.* ~**ist,** *n,* incendiaire, *m,f.*

art, *n,* art, *m;* (*skill*) habileté, *f;* (*cunning*) artifice, *m. study* ~, faire les beaux arts. ~ *gallery,* musée d'art, *m;* (*dealer's*) galerie, *f.* ~ *school,* école des beaux arts, *f. A*~*s Faculty,* faculté des Lettres, *f. A*~*s degree,* licence ès lettres, *f.*

artery, *n,* artère, *f.*

artesian, *a,* ~ *well,* puits artésien, *m.*

artful†, *a,* astucieux, rusé, malin. ~**ness,** *n,* astuce, ruse, *f.*

arthritis, *n,* arthrite, *f.* **arthritic,** *a,* arthritique.

artichoke, *n,* (*globe*) artichaut; (*Jerusalem*) topinambour, *m.*

article, *n,* (*Com., Gram., Law, Press*) article; objet, *m.* ~*s,* (*craft*) [contrat d']apprentissage; (*profession*) stage, *m.* ¶ *v.t,* mettre en apprentissage; m. en stage (*to,* chez). ~*d clerk,* stagiaire, *m,f.*

articulate, *a,* (*pers.*) qui s'exprime bien. ¶ *v.t. & i,* articuler. ~*d lorry,* semi-remorque, *m.* **articulation,** *n,* articulation, *f.*

artifice, *n,* artifice, *m,* ruse, *f.*

artificial†, *a,* artificiel; (*imitation*) factice, simili.

artillery, *n,* artillerie, *f.* ~**man,** *n,* artilleur, *m.*

artisan, *n,* artisan, e.

artist & artiste, *n,* artiste, *m,f.* **artistic,** *a,* artistique; (*pers., temperament*) artiste. ~**ally,** *ad,* artistiquement.

artless†, *a,* naturel; ingénu.

Aryan, *a,* aryen.

as, *ad & c,* (*degree*) ~ *big* ~, aussi grand que; (*neg.*) pas si (*ou* aussi) grand que. ~ *often* ~, aussi souvent que. ~ *much* ~ *possible,* autant que possible. (*while*) comme, pendant que; (*since*) puisque, comme; (*manner*) comme. *do* ~ *you like,* faites comme vous voudrez. *just* ~, ainsi que. ~ [*& when*], au fur & à mesure que. ~ [*& when*] *required,* au fur & à mesure des besoins. (*concessive*) *be that* ~ *it may,* quoi qu'il en soit. *try* ~ *he might, he couldn't* . . . il a eu beau essayer, il n'a pas pu . . . (*capacity*) comme, en tant que, en. *act* ~ *a father,* agir en père. *treat s.o as a friend,* traiter qn en ami. ~ *for,* ~ *to,* ~ *regards,* quant à. ~ *it were,* pour ainsi dire; en quelque sorte. ~ *yet,* jusqu'à présent.

asbestos, *n,* amiante, *f.*

ascend, *v.t. & i,* [re]monter, faire l'ascension de. ~ *the throne,* monter sur le trône. ~**ancy** & ~**ant,** *n,* ascendant, *m.* **ascension,** *n,* ascension, *f. A*~ *day,* l'Ascension. **ascent,** *n,* ascension; montée, *f.*

ascertain, *v.t,* découvrir, s'informer de; établir.

ascetic, *a,* ascétique. ¶ *n,* ascète, *m,f.*

ascribe, *v.t,* attribuer, imputer.

ash[1], *n, oft. pl,* cendre, *f. oft. pl.* ~ *blonde,* blond cendré, *m.* ~ *pan,* ~ *tray,* cendrier, *m.*

A~ Wednesday, le mercredi des Cendres.
ash², *n,* ~ [*tree*], frêne, *m.*
ashamed, *a,* honteux, confus. *to be* ~, avoir honte (*of s.o, sth,* de qn, qch.).
ashen, *a,* (*face*) cendreux, blême.
ashore, *ad,* à terre. *go* ~, débarquer. *put s.o* ~, débarquer qn.
Asia, *n,* l'Asie, *f.* ~ *Minor,* l'Asie Mineure. **Asiatic,** *a,* asiatique. ¶ *n,* Asiatique, *m,f.*
aside, *ad,* de côté; à part; à l'écart. *put* ~, mettre de côté. *take s.o* ~, prendre qn à part. ¶ *n,* (*Theat.*) aparté, *m. in an* ~, en aparté.
ask, *v.t,* (*inquire*) demander (qch à qn); interroger (qn), poser une question à (qn) (*about,* au sujet de); (*request*) demander (à qn de faire), prier (qn de faire). ~ *s.o for sth,* demander qch à qn. ~ *a favour from s.o,* demander une faveur à qn; (*formal*) solliciter une f. de qn. (*invite*) inviter (qn à déjeuner, à faire). ~ *about,* se renseigner sur, s'informer de. ~ *after,* demander des nouvelles de. ~ *for,* demander.
askance, *ad, look* ~ *at,* regarder de travers, r. avec méfiance.
askew, *ad,* de travers, de guingois.
aslant, *ad,* en biais, obliquement.
asleep, *a,* endormi. *to fall* ~, s'endormir. *to be sound* ~, dormir profondément *ou* à poings fermés.
asparagus, *n,* asperge, *f;* asperges, *f.pl.*
aspect, *n,* (*pers.*) aspect, *m,* mine, *f;* (*question*) aspect, *m,* face, *f;* (*house*) exposition, *f.*
aspen, *n,* tremble, *m.*
asperity, *n,* aspérité; (*pers.*) rudesse, *f.*
aspersion, *n,* calomnie, *f. cast* ~*s on,* dénigrer.
asphalt, *n,* asphalte, *m.* ¶ *v.t,* asphalter.
asphyxia, *n,* asphyxie, *f.* **asphyxiate,** *v.t.* (*& i*), (s')asphyxier.
aspirate, *v.t,* aspirer. **aspiration,** *n,* aspiration, *f.* **aspire,** ~ *to,* aspirer à (qch, faire); ambitionner (qch, de faire); (*post &c*) briguer.
aspirin, *n,* aspirine, *f.*
ass, *n,* âne, *m,* (*she*) ânesse, *f.* ~*'s foal,* ânon, *m.* (*P*) imbécile, *m,f;* idiot, e. *don't be an* ~, ne fais pas l'idiot.
assail, *v.t,* assaillir. ~**ant,** *n,* agresseur, *m.*
assassin, *n,* assassin, e. ~**ate,** *v.t,* assassiner. ~**ation,** *n,* assassinat, *m.*
assault, *n,* (*Mil.*) assaut, *m* (*on,* de); (*Law*) agression, *f.* ~ *& battery,* coups & blessures, *m.pl.* ¶ *v.t,* (*Mil.*) donner l'assaut à; (*sexually*) violenter.
assay, *n,* (*metal*) essai, *m.* ¶ *v.t,* essayer.
assemble, *v.t,* (*objects*) assembler; (*people*) rassembler, réunir; (*Mach.*) monter. ¶ *v.i,* se rassembler, se réunir. **assembly,** *n,* (*people*) assemblée, réunion, *f;* (*Mach.*) montage, *m. engine* ~, bloc moteur, *m.* ~ *line,* chaîne de montage, *f.*
assent, *n,* assentiment, *m.* ¶ *v.i,* ~ *to,* donner son assentiment à.
assert, *v.t,* soutenir; affirmer (*that,* que); (*authority*) affirmer; (*rights*) faire valoir. ~**ion,** *n,* assertion, affirmation, *f.* ~**ive,** *a,* autoritaire.
assess, *v.t,* estimer, évaluer; (*tax &c*) déterminer le montant de. ~**ment,** *n,* estimation, évaluation, *f.*
asset, *n,* avantage, *m.* ~*s,* biens, *m.pl;* (*Fin.*) avoir, actif, *m.*
assiduity, *n,* assiduité, *f.* **assiduous,** *a,* assidu. ~**ly,** *ad,* assidûment.
assign, *v.t,* assigner, attribuer; (*pers. to duties*) affecter. ~**ation,** *n,* (*meeting*) rendez-vous, *m.* ~**ment,** *n,* attribution; affectation; (*task*) mission, *f.*
assimilate, *v.t,* assimiler.
assist, *v.t,* aider, assister (qn à faire); prêter secours à. ~**ance,** *n,* aide, assistance, *f. come to s.o's* ~, venir à l'aide de qn, prêter main-forte à qn. ~**ant,** *n,* aide, auxiliaire, *m,f;* (*Sch.*) assistant, e. ¶ *a,* adjoint. sous-. ~*commissioner,* commissaire adjoint. ~ *director,* sous-directeur, *m.*
assizes, *n.pl,* assises, *f.pl.*
associate, *n,* associé, e, collègue, *m,f,* ¶ *v.t,* associer. *to be* ~*d with s.o.,* s'associer avec qn. ¶ *v.i,* ~ *with s.o.,* fréquenter qn. **association,** *n,* association; société; fréquentation, *f.* ~ *football,* football [association], *m.*
assorted, *a,* assorti. **assortment,** *n,* assortiment, *m.*
assuage, *v.t,* apaiser.
assume, *v.t,* (*take on*) prendre, assumer; (*an air*) affecter; (*rights*) s'arroger; (*suppose*) supposer, admettre. *let's* ~ *that,* supposons que (+ *subj.*). ~*d name,* nom d'emprunt, *m.* **assumption,** *n,* supposition. (*Rel.*) *the A*~, l'Assomption, *f.*
assurance, *n,* assurance, *f.* **assure,** *v.t,* assurer (*s.o of sth,* qn de qch). **assured,** *a,* (*all senses*) assuré. ~**ly,** *ad,* assurément, à coup sur.
aster, *n,* aster, *m.*
asterisk, *n,* astérisque, *m.*
astern, *ad,* à (*ou* sur) l'arrière. *go* ~, battre en arrière.
asteroid, *n,* astéroïde, *m.*
asthma, *n,* asthme, *m.* **asthmatic,** *a,* asthmatique.
astigmatic, *a,* astigmate.
astonish, *v.t,* étonner, surprendre. ~**ing,** *a,* étonnant. ~**ingly,** *ad,* étonnamment. ~**ment,** *n,* étonnement, *m,* surprise, *f.*
astound, *v.t,* ahurir, ébahir, stupéfier. ~**ing,** *a,* ahurissant, stupéfiant.
astray, *ad, go* ~, s'égarer. (*fig.*) *lead* ~, détourner du droit chemin.
astride, *ad.* (*& pr*), à califourchon, à cheval (sur).
astringent, *a. & n,* astringent, *m.*

astrologer, *n,* astrologue, *m.* **astrology,** *n,* astrologie, *f.*
astronaut, *n,* astronaute, *m,f.*
astronomer, *n,* astronome, *m.* **astronomic(al†),** *a,* astronomique. **astronomy,** *n,* astronomie, *f.*
astute, *a,* fin, rusé; astucieux.
asylum, *n,* asile, *m.*
at, *pr,* (*place*) à, chez. ~ *table,* à table. ~ *school,* à l'école. ~ *home,* à la maison, chez soi. ~ *my mother's,* chez ma mère. ~ *sea,* en mer. *go in* ~ *the door,* entrez par la porte. ~ *hand,* à portée de main, sous la main. (*towards*) *rush, charge* ~, se précipiter vers, contre; foncer sur. (*time*) ~ *ten o'clock,* à dix heures. ~ *night,* la nuit. ~ *once,* tout de suite. ~ *last,* enfin. ~ *the same time,* en même temps. ~ *war,* en guerre. *good* ~ *history,* fort en histoire.
atheism, *n,* athéisme, *m.* **atheist,** *n,* athée, *m.* **atheistic,** *a,* athée.
Athenian, *a,* athénien. ¶ *n,* Athénien, ne. **Athens,** *n,* Athènes, *f.*
athirst, *a,* assoiffé (*for,* de).
athlete, *n,* athlète, *m.* **athletic,** *a,* athlétique. **athletics,** *n.pl,* athlétisme, *m.* ~ *meeting,* meeting d'athlétisme, *m.*
athwart, *ad,* en travers. ¶ *pr,* en travers de.
Atlantic, *a,* atlantique. ~ *liner,* transatlantique, *m. the A~ [Ocean],* l'[océan] Atlantique, *m.*
atlas, *n,* atlas, *m.*
atmosphere, *n,* atmosphère, *f.* **atmospheric(al),** *a,* atmosphérique. **atmospherics** (*Radio*), *n.pl,* parasites, *m.pl.*
atom, *n,* atome, *m;* (*fig.*) brin, grain, *m,* miette, *f.* ~ *bomb,* bombe atomique, *f.* **~ic,** *a,* atomique. ~ *warfare,* guerre nucléaire, *f.* **~izer,** *n,* atomiseur, *m.*
atone for (to), expier, racheter. **atonement,** *n,* expiation, réparation, *f.*
atrocious†, *a,* atroce. **atrocity,** *n,* atrocité, *f.*
atrophy, *n,* atrophie, *f.* ¶ *v.i,* s'atrophier.
attach, *v.t,* attacher, lier; (*document*) joindre, annexer. *the ~ed letter,* la lettre ci-jointe. (*Law: goods*) saisir. ~ *credence to,* ajouter foi à. ~ *o.s. to,* s'attacher à. **attaché,** *n,* attaché, *m.* ~ *case,* mallette, *f.* **attachment,** *n,* fixation, *f;* (*Mach.*) accessoire; (*affection*) attachement, *m* (*to,* à); (*Law*) saisie, *f.*
attack, *n,* attaque, *f;* (*on s.o's life*) attentat, *m;* (*Med.*) crise, *f;* (*fever*) accès, *m.* ¶ *v.t,* attaquer; (*task*) s'attaquer à. **~er,** *n,* attaquant, agresseur, *m.*
attain, *v.t,* atteindre, parvenir à. **~ment,** *n,* (*of ends*) réalisation, *f.* *~s,* compétences, *f.pl.*
attempt, *n,* tentative, *f,* essai, effort; (*on s.o's life*) attentat, *m. first* ~, coup d'essai, *m.* ¶ *v.t,* essayer, tenter (de faire). *~ed murder,* tentative de meurtre, *f.*
attend, *v.t,* (*event*) assister à; (*school, church*) aller à; (*classes*) suivre; (*pers.*) accompagner; (*the sick*) soigner. ¶ *v.i,* faire attention. *~ to,* s'occuper de (qn, qch). **~ance,** *n,* présence, *f, regular* ~ *at,* assiduité à. (*those present*) assistance, *f;* (*Med: on a patient*) visites, *f.pl.* **~ant,** *n,* (*personal*) domestique, *m,f;* (*museum*) gardien, ne; (*Theat.*) ouvreuse, *f.*
attention, *n,* attention, *f. pay* ~, faire attention. *pay* ~ *to,* prêter attention à. (*shop, hotel*) service, *m.* *~s,* soins, *m.pl,* prévenances, *f.pl.* (*Mil.*) ~ *!* garde-à-vous! **attentive,** *a,* attentif; (*to s.o*) prévenant (envers), empressé (auprès de); (*to sth*) soucieux (de).
attenuate, *v.t,* atténuer.
attest, *v.t,* attester. **~ation,** *n,* attestation, *f.*
attic, *n,* mansarde, *f,* grenier, *m.*
attire, *n,* vêtements, habits, *m.pl.* ¶ *v.t,* vêtir.
attitude, *n,* attitude, pose; (*of mind*) attitude, disposition, *f,* état d'esprit, *m.*
attorney, *n,* mandataire, *m,f. A~ General* (*UK*), ≏ Procureur Général, *m.*
attract, *v.t,* attirer. **~ion,** *n,* attraction, *f;* (*pers., place*) attraits, charmes, *m.pl.* **~ive,** *a,* attrayant, attirant; (*price, scheme*) intéressant; (*Phys.*) attractif.
attributable, *a,* attribuable. **attribute,** *n,* attribut, *m;* (*Gram.*) épithète, *f.* ¶ *v.t,* attribuer.
attrition, *n,* usure, *f.*
attuned, *a,* ~ *to,* en accord avec.
aubergine, *n,* aubergine, *f.*
auburn, *a,* auburn, châtain roux, *inv.*
auction, *n,* [vente (*f*) aux] enchères, *f.pl.* ~ *bridge,* bridge aux enchères, *m.* ~ *mart,* ~ *rooms,* salle des ventes, *f.* ¶ *v.t,* vendre aux enchères. **~eer,** *n,* commissaire priseur, *m.*
audacious†, *a,* audacieux. **audacity,** *n,* audace, *f.*
audible, *a,* perceptible, audible.
audience, *n,* (*hearing*) audience; (*pers.*) assistance, *f;* spectateurs, *m.pl;* (*Mus., Radio*) auditeurs; (*TV*) téléspectateurs, *m.pl.*
audio-visual, *a,* audio-visuel.
audit, *v.t,* vérifier. **~[ing],** *n,* vérification des comptes, *f.* **audition,** *n,* (*Mus., Theat.*) audition; (*Cine., TV*) séance d'essai, *f.* ¶ *v.t,* auditionner. **auditor,** *n,* vérificateur des comptes, *m.* **auditorium,** *n,* salle, *f.*
auger, *n,* tarière, vrille, *f.*
aught, *n, for* ~ *I know,* autant que je sache.
augment, *v.t,* augmenter.
augur, *n,* augure, *m.* ¶ *v.t,* augurer, présager. ¶ *v.i,* augurer (bien, mal). **~y,** *n,* augure, présage, *m.*
august, *a,* auguste. **A~,** *n,* août, *m.*
auk, *n,* pingouin, *m.*
aunt, *n,* tante, *f. A~ Sally,* jeu de massacre, *m;* (*pers.*) tête de Turc, *f.*
au pair, *a,* ~ *girl,* jeune fille au pair.
aureole, *n,* auréole, *f.*
aurora, *n,* aurore, *f.* ~ *borealis,* a. boréale.

auspice, *n,* auspice, *m.* **auspicious,** *a,* propice, favorable, de bon augure.
austere†, *a,* austère, sévere. **austerity,** *n,* austérité, *f.*
Australasia, *n,* l'Australasie, *f.* **Australia,** *n,* l'Australie, *f.* **Australian,** *a,* australien. ¶ *n,* Australien, ne.
Austria, *n,* l'Autriche, *f.* **Austrian,** *a,* autrichien. ¶ *n,* Autrichien, ne.
authentic†, *a,* authentique. **~ity,** *n.* authenticité, *f.*
author, *n,* auteur; (*fig.*) auteur, créateur, *m.* **~ess,** *n,* femme auteur, *f.*
authoritative, *a,* (*statement*) autorisé; (*pers.*) autoritaire; (*document*) qui fait autorité. **authority,** *n,* autorité, *f,* pouvoir, *m;* (*to act*) autorisation, *f. on his own ~,* de son propre chef. (*pers.*) autorité, *f,* expert, *m. to be an ~,* faire autorité (en matière de). *on good ~,* de source sûre. *the authorities,* les autorités, l'administration, *f.*
authorization, *n,* autorisation, *f.* **authorize,** *v.t,* autoriser (qch; qn à faire).
authorship, *n,* (*book &c*) paternité, *f.*
autistic, *a,* autistique.
autobiography, *n,* autobiographie, *f.*
autocracy, *n,* autocratie, *f.* **autocrat,** *n,* autocrate, *m.* **~ic,** *a,* autocratique.
autograph, *n,* autographe, *m.* ¶ *v.t,* (*a book*) signer, dédicacer.
automatic, *a,* automatique. ¶ *n,* (*pistol*) automatique, *m;* (*car*) voiture [à transmission] automatique, *f.* **automation,** *n,* automatisation, *f.* **automaton,** *n,* automate, *m.*
automobile, *n,* automobile, auto, *f.*
autonomous, *a,* autonome. **autonomy,** *n,* autonomie, *f.*
autopsy, *n.* autopsie, *f.*
autumn, *n,* automne, *m.* **~al,** *a,* d'automne.
auxiliary, *a.* & *n,* auxiliaire, *m,f.*
avail, *n, of no ~,* sans résultat, inutile. ¶ *v.t, ~ o.s. of,* profiter de; (*service*) utiliser. **~able,** *a,* disponible; libre; (*ticket*) valable, valide.
avalanche, *n,* avalanche, *f.*
avarice, *n,* avarice, *f.* **avaricious,** *a,* avare.
avenge, *v.t,* venger. *to ~ o.s,* se venger (de qn, qch); prendre sa revanche (sur qn). **avenger,** *n,* vengeur, eresse. **avenging,** *a,* vengeur.
avenue, *n,* avenue, *f,* boulevard, *m.*
aver, *v.t,* soutenir, affirmer.
average, *a,* moyen. *the ~ Frenchman,* le Français moyen. ¶ *n,* moyenne, *f. on ~,* en moyenne. ¶ *v.t,* (*figures*) établir la moyenne de. (*Mot.*) *to ~ 50* [*mph*], faire une moyenne de 80 km/h, faire du 80 de moyenne *P.*
averse to, *a,* opposé à, ennemi de. *to be ~ to doing,* répugner à faire. **aversion,** *n,* aversion, répugnance, *f,* dégoût, *m.*
avert, *v.t,* (*blow, eyes*) détourner; (*suspicion*) écarter; (*accident*) prévenir.
aviary, *n,* volière, *f.*
aviation, *n,* aviation, *f.* **aviator,** *n,* aviateur, trice.
avid†, *a,* avide (*for,* de). **~ity,** *n,* avidité, *f.*
avocado, *n, ~* [*pear*], avocat, *m.*
avoid, *v.t,* éviter (*doing,* de faire); (*duties, tax*) se soustraire à; (*blow*) esquiver. **~able,** *a,* évitable.
avow, *v.t,* avouer, admettre. *~ed enemy,* ennemi déclaré. **~al,** *n,* aveu, *m.*
await, *v.t,* attendre.
awake, *a,* [r]éveillé; (*alert*) vigilant. (*fig.*) *~ to,* conscient de. ¶ *v.t,* réveiller. ¶ *v.i,* se réveiller, s'éveiller. **awaken,** *v.t. & i,* = **awake. ~ing,** *n,* réveil, *m.*
award, *n,* prix, *m;* (*Univ.*) bourse; (*Court*) décision, *f.* ¶ *v.t,* (*prize*) décerner; (*honour*) conférer; (*contract*) adjuger; (*damages*) accorder.
aware, *a, ~ of,* conscient de. *be ~ of,* être au courant de, ne pas ignorer. *become ~ of,* prendre conscience de, se rendre compte de.
away, *ad, far ~,* au loin. *5 km ~,* à 5 km d'ici, de là; à une distance de 5 km. *~ from home,* absent. *~ on holiday,* parti en vacances. *go ~,* s'en aller. *~ match,* match à l'extérieur.
awe, *n,* crainte, *f,* respect mêlé de crainte, *m. hold in ~,* craindre, redouter. **~-inspiring,** *a,* impressionnant, imposant. **awful,** *a,* affreux, terrible, effroyable. **~ly,** *ad,* très, terriblement, rudement *P. thanks ~,* merci infiniment.
awhile, *ad,* un instant, un peu.
awkward, *a,* (*pers.*) gauche, maladroit; (*inconvenient*) peu commode, gênant, difficile; (*problem, question*) délicat, embarrassant. *the ~ age,* l'âge ingrat. *feel ~,* se sentir mal à l'aise, gêné.
awl, *n,* alène, *f,* poinçon, *m.*
awning, *n,* tente; (*shop*) banne; (*cart*) bâche; (*hotel*) marquise, *f.*
awry, *ad. & a,* de travers, de guingois.
axe, *n,* hache, *f.*
axiom, *n,* axiome, *m.*
axis, *n,* axe, *m.*
axle, *n,* axe, *m;* (*Mot.*) essieu, *m.*
ay, *i. & n,* oui, *m. the ~s have it,* les oui l'emportent.
azalea, *n,* azalée, *f.*
Azores (the), les Açores, *f.pl.*
azure, *a,* azuré. ¶ *n,* azur, *m.*

B

B (*Mus.*) *letter,* si, *m.*
baa, *v.i,* bêler. **baa[ing],** *n,* bêlement, *m.*
babble, *n,* (*baby, stream*) gazouillement, *m;* (*voices*) rumeur, *f.* ¶ *v.i,* babiller; gazouiller; (*chatter*) bavarder; (*stupidly*) bafouiller.
babel (*fig.*) *n,* tour de Babel, *f;* brouhaha, *m.*
baboon, *n,* babouin, *m.*
baby, *n,* bébé, *m.* ~ *of the family,* benjamin, e. ~ *carriage,* voiture d'enfant, *f.* ~ *face,* visage poupin, *m.* ~ *grand,* piano à demi-queue, *m.* ~ *linen,* layette, *f.* ~*-sit,* garder les enfants. ~*-sitter,* baby-sitter, *m,f.* ~**hood,** *n,* première enfance, *f.* ~**ish,** *a,* enfantin.
bachelor, *n,* célibataire, *m.* (*Univ.*) *B~ of Arts, of Science,* licencié ès lettres, ès sciences. ~ *flat,* garçonnière, *f.* ~ *girl,* célibataire, *f.*
back, *a,* arrière *inv;* (*door, garden, seat*) de derrière. ~ *room,* chambre sur le derrière, *f.* ¶ *ad,* en arrière, vers l'arrière. *Note: after a verb* **back** *is sometimes expressed by* **re-** *as, to come back,* revenir. *to be* ~, être de retour. ¶ *n,* dos, *m,* reins, *m.pl;* (*hand*) revers; (*house*) derrière; (*chair*) dossier; (*book*) dos; (*page, cheque*) verso; (*cupboard, hall*) fond; (*Foot.*) arrière, *m.* ~ *to front,* [sens] devant derrière. *with one's* ~ *to the light,* à contre-jour. ¶ *v.t,* (*support*) appuyer, soutenir; (*candidate*) pistonner *P;* (*car*) faire reculer; (*bet on*) parier sur, miser sur. ¶ *v.i,* (*pers.*) reculer; (*car*) faire marche arrière; (*wind: opp. veer*) tourner [du nord vers l'ouest &c]. ~ *down,* se dégonfler *P.* ~ *out of,* se soustraire à.
backbite, *v.i,* médire de. **backbiting,** *n,* médisance, *f.*
backbone, *n,* échine, colonne vertébrale; (*fig.*) énergie, *f.*
backdate, *v.t,* antidater.
back-end, *n,* (*of year*) arrière-saison, *f.*
backer, *n,* partisan; (*Betting*) parieur, *m.*
backfire, *n,* pétarade, *f.* ¶ *v.i,* pétarader.
backgammon, *n.* & ~ *board,* trictrac, *m.*
background, *n,* arrière-plan, fond, *m.* (*fig.*) *in the* ~, dans la pénombre.
backhand, *n,* (*Ten.*) revers, *m.*
backing, *n,* soutien; (*Mus.*) accompagnement; (*vehicle*) recul, *m,* marche arrière, *f.*
backlog, *n,* arriéré, *m.*
back number *n,* (*news*), vieux numéro, *m.*
backside, *P, n,* (*buttocks*) derrière, *m.*
backstage, *ad,* dans les coulisses, *f.pl.*
backstay (*Naut.*) *n,* galhauban, *m.*
backstitch, *n,* point arrière, *m.*
back tooth, *n,* dent du fond, *f.*
backward, *a,* (*step*) en arrière, rétrograde; (*nation*) peu avancé; (*child*) arriéré. ¶ ~**[s],** *ad,* en arrière; (*go, walk*) à reculons. *fall* ~, tomber à la renverse. ~ *& forwards,* de long en large.
backwash, *n,* remous, *m.*
back water (to), scier, ramer à rebours.
backwater, *n,* (*river*) bras mort; (*fig.*) trou perdu, coin tranquille, *m.*
bacon, *n,* lard, *m;* (*in rashers*) bacon, *m.* ~ & *eggs,* oeufs au jambon, *m.pl.*
bacteria, *n.pl,* bactéries, *f.pl.*
bacteriology, *n,* bactériologie, *f.*
bad, *a,* (*wicked*) (*action*) mauvais, (*pers.*) méchant. ~ *language,* gros mots, *m.pl.* ~ *lot,* mauvais sujet, sale type, *m.* ~ *dog!* vilain chien! (*inferior*) mauvais, de mauvaise qualité; (*food*) gâté, pourri; (*tooth*) carié. *to go* ~, se gâter, pourrir. (*ill*) malade. *to feel* ~, se sentir mal. *be in a* ~ *way,* être très mal. (*accident, illness*) grave; (*cold*) gros. *it's too* ~, c'est un peu fort! *have a* ~ *time* [*of it*], passer un mauvais quart d'heure, en baver *P.* *in a* ~ *temper,* de mauvaise humeur. *to be* ~ *tempered,* avoir mauvais caractère. ¶ *n,* mauvais, *m.* *from* ~ *to worse,* de mal en pis.
badge, *n,* insigne, *m,* plaque, *f;* (*sew-on*) badge, *m;* (*fig.*) symbole, *m.*
badger, *n,* blaireau, *m.* ¶ *v.t,* harceler, importuner.
badly, *ad,* mal; gravement. grièvement. *I* ~ *want,* j'ai grande envie de. *I* ~ *need,* il me faut absolument.
badminton, *n,* badminton, *m.*
badness, *n,* mauvais état, *m,* mauvaise qualité; méchanceté, *f.*
baffle, *v.t,* (*pers.*) confondre, dérouter; (*plot*) déjouer; (*description*) échapper à, défier. ~ **[plate],** *n,* chicane, *f,* déflecteur, *m.*
bag, *n,* sac, *m;* (*tools, post*) sacoche, *f;* (*tea*) sachet, *m;* (*luggage*) valise, *f.* (*game*) *a good* ~, un beau tableau. ¶ *v.t,* mettre en sac, ensacher; (*steal*) chiper *P,* faucher *P.* ¶ *v.i,* (se) gonfler, (*trousers*) goder.
bagatelle (*trifle*) *n,* bagatelle, *f.* **bagatelle** (*game*) *n.* & ~ *board,* billard anglais, *m.*
baggage, *n,* bagages, *m.pl;* (*Mil.*) équipement, *m.*
baggy, *a,* (*garment*) flottant, avachi.
bagpipe[s], *n,* cornemuse, *f.*
bail, *n,* caution; (*pers.*) caution, *f,* répondant, e. *release on* ~, mettre en liberté provisoire sous caution. *stand* ~ *for,* se porter garant de. ¶ *v.t,* ~ **out** (*boat*), écoper, vider. ¶ *v.i,* (*Aero.*) sauter en parachute. ~**er,** *n,* écope, *f.*
bailiff, *n,* huissier; intendant, régisseur, *m.*
bairn, *n, Sc & N,* enfant, *m, f.*

bait, *n,* amorce, *f,* appât. *m. rise to the* ~, mordre à l'hameçon. ¶ *v.t,* amorcer, appâter; tourmenter, harceler.
baize, *n,* serge, *f,* reps, *m.* ~ *door,* porte matelassée, *f.*
bake, *v.t,* [faire] cuire au four. ¶ *v.i,* cuire [au four]. **baker,** *n,* boulanger, ère. ~**y,** *n,* boulangerie, *f.* **baking,** *n,* cuisson; boulangerie, *f.* ~ *powder,* levure chimique, *f.* ~ *tin,* tourtière, *f.*
balance, *n,* (*scales*) balance, *f;* (*poise*) équilibre, aplomb, *m. lose one's* ~, perdre l'équilibre. (*Com.*) *credit, debit* ~, solde créditeur, débiteur, *m.* ~ *sheet,* bilan, *m.* ~ *of payments,* balance des paiements. ~ *of power,* balance politique, équilibre des forces. ~ *weight,* contrepoids, *m.* ~ *wheel* (*watch*) balancier, *m.* ¶ *v.t,* équilibrer, tenir en équilibre; (*weigh up*) balancer; (*Com.*) solder. **balancing,** *n,* balancement, *m.* ~ *pole* (*tight rope*), balancier, *m.*
balcony, *n,* balcon, *m.*
bald, *a,* chauve; (*style*) plat, sec; (*tyre*) lisse.
balderdash, *n,* bêtises, balivernes, *f.pl.*
baldness, *n,* calvitie; nudité, *f.*
bale, *n,* balle, *f,* ballot, *m.* ¶ *v.t,* emballer. ~ **[out]** (*boat*), *v.t,* écoper, vider.
baleful, *a,* sinistre, funeste.
balk, *n,* obstacle, *m;* (*Build.*) solive; (*timber*) bille, *f.* ¶ *v.t,* frustrer, déjouer. ¶ *v.i,* reculer, hésiter (*at,* devant).
Balkan, *a,* balkanique. *the* ~ *States,* les États des Balkans, *m.pl.* **the** ~**s,** les Balkans, *m.pl.*
ball[1], *n,* (*Golf, Ten.*) balle, *f;* (*Foot.*) ballon, *m;* (*Bil.*) bille, boule, *f;* (*eye, lightning*) globe, *f;* (*string, wool*) pelote, *f,* peloton, *m.* ~ *bearings,* roulement à billes, *m.* ~ *cock,* robinet à flotteur, *m.* ~ *point pen,* stylo à bille, *m.* ~*s P**, (*Anat.*) couilles *P**; (*rubbish*) conneries *P**, *f.pl. a* ~*s-up P,* un vrai bordel *P.* ¶ *v.t,* · (*wool*) pelotonner.
ball[2], *n,* (*Danc.*) bal, *m.* ~ *room,* salle de bal, *f.*
ballad, *n,* (*poem*) ballade; (*song*) romance, *f.*
ballast, *n,* (*road, Rly*) ballast, *m;* (*Build.*) blocaille, *f;* (*Naut., Aero.*) lest; (*fig.*) plomb, *m.* ¶ *v.t,* lester.
ballerina, *n,* ballerine, *f.* **ballet,** *n,* ballet, *m.* ~ *dancer,* danseur, euse de b.
ballistic, *a,* balistique. ~ *missile,* engin balistique, *m.*
balloon, *n,* ballon; aérostat, *m.* ~ *fabric,* toile d'avion, *f.* ~**ed** (*dress*) *a,* ballonné. **go** ~**ing,** monter en ballon. ~**ist,** *n,* aéronaute, *m,f.*
ballot, *n,* [tour de] scrutin, *m.* ~ *box,* urne électorale, *f.* ~ *paper,* bulletin de vote, *m.* ¶ *v.i,* voter au scrutin. ~ *for,* (*place*) tirer au sort.
ballyhoo, *P, n,* battage *P, m.*
balm, *n,* baume, *m.* ~**y,** *a,* embaumé; (*P crazy*) toqué *P,* timbré *P.*
baloney, *P, n,* balivernes *P, f.pl.*
balsam, *n,* baume, *m;* (*Bot.*) balsamine, *f.*
Baltic [Sea] (the), la [mer] Baltique.
baluster, *n,* balustre, *m.* **balustrade,** *n,* balustrade, *f.*
bamboo, *n,* bambou, *m.*
bamboozle, *v.t,* mettre dedans, embobiner.
ban, *n,* interdiction, *f.* ¶ *v.t,* interdire.
banana, *n,* banane, *f.* ~ [*tree*], bananier, *m.*
band[1], *n,* bande, *f;* (*iron*) lien; (*barrel*) cercle; (*hat*) ruban, *m;* (*Radio*) bande; (*gram. record*) plage, *f. elastic* ~, elastique, *m.* ~ *saw,* scie à ruban, *f.*
band[2], *n,* bande, troupe, *f;* (*Mus.*) orchestre, *m,* musique; (*brass*) fanfare; (*wind*) harmonie, *f.* ~ *master,* chef d'orchestre, de musique *etc.* ~ *stand,* kiosque à musique, *m.* ¶ *v.i,* ~ *together,* se liguer, former une bande.
bandage, *n,* bande, *f,* bandage, pansement, *m.* ¶ *v.t,* bander, mettre un pansement sur.
bandit, *n,* bandit, *m.*
bandoleer, *n,* bandoulière, *f.*
bandsman, *n,* musicien, *m.*
bandy, *v.t,* se renvoyer. ~ *words with,* avoir des mots avec. ~ **[-legged],** *a,* bancal.
bane, *n,* fléau, *m.* ~ **ful,** *a,* funeste.
bang, *n,* détonation, *f,* fracas; (*door*) claquement, *m.* ¶ *i,* pan! vlan! ¶ *ad,* ~ *in the middle,* au beau milieu. ¶ *v.t,* frapper [violemment]; (*door*) faire claquer. ~ *one's head against,* se cogner la tête contre. ¶ *v.i,* (*door*) claquer. *go off* ~, éclater, détoner.
bangle, *n,* bracelet, *m.*
banish, *v.t,* bannir.
banister, *n,* balustre, *m.* ~*s,* rampe, *f.*
bank[1], *n,* (*river, lake*) bord, *m,* rive, berge, *f;* (*earth*) talus; (*sand*) banc; (*Aero.*) virage incliné, *m.* ¶ *v.t,* ~ *up,* (*road*) remblayer; (*earth*) amonceler. ¶ *v.i,* (*clouds &c*) s'entasser, s'amonceler; (*Aero.*) virer sur l'aile.
bank[2], *n,* (*Fin.*) banque, *f.* ~ *account,* compte en b. ~ *book,* carnet de b., *m.* ~ *card,* carte d'identité bancaire, *f.* ~ *clerk,* employé de b. ~ *holiday,* jour férié. ~ *note,* billet de b. ~ *rate,* taux d'escompte, *m.* ¶ *v.t,* (*money*) déposer en banque. ¶ *v.i,* ~ *on,* compter sur. ~**er,** banquier, *m.*
bankrupt, *n,* failli, *m. to go* ~, faire faillite. ~**cy,** *n,* faillite; (*fraudulent*) banqueroute, *f.*
banner, *n,* bannière, *f;* étendard, *m.* ~ *headline,* gros titre.
banns, *n.pl,* bans de mariage, *m.pl.*
banquet, *n,* banquet, festin, *m.* ~ *ing hall,* salle des festins, *f.*
bantam weight *n,* (*Box.*) poids coq, *m.*
banter, *n,* badinage, *m.* ¶ *v.t,* badiner.
baptism, *n,* baptême, *m.* ~**al,** *a,* baptismal. **baptist,** *a. & n,* (*Rel.*) *B*~, baptiste, *m,f.* ~**[e]ry,** *n,* baptistère, *m.* **baptize,** *v.t,* baptiser.

bar, *n,* (*metal, harbour*) barre; (*chocolate*) tablette. ~ *of soap,* savonnette. (*Mus.*) mesure. ~ *line,* barre, *f.* (*Law*) barreau, *m. call to the* ~, inscrire au barreau. *put behind* ~*s,* mettre sous les verrous, écrouer. (*pub*) bar, bistro(t); (*counter*) comptoir, *m.* ¶ *v.t,* barrer.
barb, *n,* (*fish hook*) barbillon, *m;* (*arrow*) barbelure, *f.* ~[*ed*] *wire,* fil de fer barbelé, *m.*
Barbados, *n,* la Barbade.
barbarian, *a.* & *n,* barbare, *m,f.* **barbaric, barbarous,** *a,* barbare. **barbarism,** *n,* barbarie, *f;* (*Gram.*) barbarisme, *m.* **barbarity,** *n,* barbarie, *f.*
barber, *n,* coiffeur, *m.*
barbiturate, *n,* barbiturique, *m.*
Barcelona, *n,* Barcelone, *f.*
bard, *n,* (*poet*) barde; chantre, *m.*
bare, *a,* nu; (*landscape*) dénudé, pelé; (*garden, style*) dépouillé; (*cupboard*) vide, dégarni; (*majority*) faible. ~*back* (*Riding*), à nu, à cru. ~*faced,* éhonté, effronté. ~*foot*[*ed*], nu-pieds, pieds nus. ~*headed,* nu-tête, tête nue. ¶ *v.t,* mettre à nu; (*head*) découvrir; (*Elec: wire*) dénuder. ~**ly,** *ad,* à peine, tout juste, ne... guère. ~**ness,** *n,* nudité, *f.*
bargain, *n,* marché, *m,* affaire; occasion. *a good, bad* ~, une bonne, mauvaise affaire. *a real* ~, une véritable occasion. *into the* ~, pardessus le marché. *it's a* ~! entendu! ¶ *v.i,* marchander. ~ *for,* s'attendre à. ~**ing,** *n,* marchandage, *m.*
barge, *n,* chaland, *m,* péniche, *f.* **bargee, bargeman,** *n,* batelier, marinier, *m.*
baritone, *n,* baryton, *m.*
barium, *n,* ~ *meal,* sulfate de baryum, *m.*
bark[1], *n,* (*tree*) écorce, *f.* ¶ *v.t,* écorcer. ~ *one's shins,* s'écorcher les jambes.
bark[2], *n,* (*dog*) aboiement; (*fox*) glapissement, *m.* ¶ *v.i.* aboyer, glapir. ~ *up the wrong tree,* se tromper d'adresse.
bark[3], *n,* (*boat*) barque, *f.*
barley, *n,* orge, *f.* ~ *sugar,* sucre d'orge, *m.* ~ *water,* boisson d'orge, *f.*
barm, *n,* levure, *f.* ~**y,** *a,* (*P daft*) toqué *P,* timbré *P.*
barn, *n,* grange, *f.* ~ *owl,* effraie, *f.* ~*yard,* basse-cour, *f.*
barnacle & ~ **goose,** *n,* bernacle, bernache, *f.*
barometer, *n,* baromètre, *m.* **barometric(al),** *a,* barométrique.
baron, ess, *n,* baron, ne.
barque, *n,* barque, *f.*
barrack, *n. oft. pl,* caserne, *f.* ~ *room,* chambrée [militaire], *f.* ¶ *v.t,* caserner; (*jeer*) huer, conspuer.
barrage, *n,* barrage, *m.*
barrel, *n,* (*wine*) tonneau, fût, *m,* barrique, *f;* (*oil*) baril, *m;* (*herrings*) caque, *f;* (*rifle &c*) canon, *m.* ~ *organ,* orgue de Barbarie, *m.* ¶ *v.t,* mettre en tonneau &c.
barren, *a,* stérile, aride. ~**ness,** *n,* stérilité, aridité, *f.*
barricade, *n,* barricade, *f.* ¶ *v.t,* barricader.
barrier, *n,* barrière, *f;* (*Rly*) portillon, *m;* (*fig.*) obstacle, *m.*
barring, *pr,* sauf, à part, excepté, à moins de.
barrister [at law], *n,* avocat, *m.*
barrow[1], *n,* (*wheel* ~) brouette; (*handcart*) charrette, *f.* ~ *boy,* marchand des quatre saisons, *m.*
barrow[2], *n,* (*mound*) tumulus, *m.*
barter, *n,* échange, troc, *m.* ¶ *v.t,* échanger, troquer.
basalt, *n,* basalte, *m.*
base[1], *n,* base, *f;* (*Build.*) soubassement; (*Elec: bulb*) culot, *m.* ~*ball,* base-ball, *m.* ~ *line* (*Ten.*), ligne de fond, *f.* ¶ *v.t,* baser, fonder (*on,* sur). ~**less,** *a,* sans fondement. ~**ment,** *n,* sous-sol, *m.*
base[2], *a,* bas, ignoble, indigne; (*metal*) vil. ~ *coin,* fausse monnaie, *f.* ~**ly,** *ad,* bassement, lâchement. ~**ness,** *n,* bassesse, *f.*
bash, *P, n,* coup, coup de poing, *m.* ¶ *v.t,* frapper, cogner. ~ *in,* défoncer. ~ *up,* (*car*) bousiller *P;* (*pers.*) tabasser *P.*
bashful, *a,* timide, pudique. ~**ness,** *n,* timidité, modestie, *f.*
basic, *a,* fondamental; (*Chem. &c*) basique.
basil, *n,* (*Bot.*) basilic, *m.*
basilica, *n,* basilique, *f.*
basilisk, *n,* basilic, *m.*
basin, *n,* (*Geog.*) bassin; (*Cook.*) bol, *m;* (*wash*~) cuvette, *f,* lavabo, *m.*
basis, *n,* base, fondement, *m.*
bask, *v.i,* se chauffer.
basket, *n,* (*shopping*) panier, *m;* (*laundry, waste-paper*) corbeille; (*on back*) hotte, *f.* ~*ball,* basket[-ball], *m.* ~ *maker,* vannier, *m.* ~*work,* vannerie, *f.*
bas-relief, *n,* bas-relief, *m.*
bass[1], *n,* (*fish*) perche, *f;* (*sea*) bar, *m.*
bass[2], *n,* (*Mus.*) (*singer, voice, tuba*) basse, *f.* ~ *clef,* clef de fa, *f.* ~ *drum,* grosse caisse, *f.*
bassoon, *n,* basson, *m.*
bastard, *a,* bâtard. ¶ *n,* bâtard, e; (*pej. P**) salaud *P**, *m.* ~**y,** *n,* bâtardise, *f.*
baste, *v.t,* (*Need.*) bâtir; (*meat*) arroser.
bat[1], *n,* (*Zool.*) chauve-souris, *f.*
bat[2], *n,* (*cricket, baseball*) batte, *f;* (*table-ten.*) raquette, *f.* ¶ *v.i,* manier la batte. *he didn't* ~ *an eyelid,* il n'a pas bronché.
batch, *n,* fournée, *f;* groupe, *m.*
bath, *n,* bain, *m;* (~*tub*) baignoire, *f. to have a*~, prendre un bain. *b*~ *chair,* fauteuil roulant, *m.* ~*mat,* tapis de bain. ~*robe,* peignoir de b., *m.* ~*room,* salle de bains, *f.* ~ *salts,* sels de b., *m.pl.* ¶ *v.t,* baigner, donner un b. à. ¶ *v.i,* prendre un b.
bathe, *n,* bain, *m,* baignade, *f.* ¶ *v.t,* baigner. ¶ *v.i,* se baigner. **bather,** *n,* baigneur, euse.

bathing, *n,* bains, *m.pl;* bain, *m.* ~ *costume,* ~ *trunks,* maillot de bain, *m.* ~ *hut,* cabine [de bains] *f.*
batman, *n,* (*Mil.*) ordonnance, *f.*
bâton, *n,* (*Mil., Mus.*) bâton, *m,* baguette, *f.* ~ *charge,* (*police*) charge à la matraque. *f.*
battalion, *n,* bataillon, *m.*
batten, *n,* latte; volige, *f.* ¶ *v.t,* (*Naut.*) ~ **down** condamner. ¶ *v.i,* ~ **on,** s'engraisser de.
batter, *n,* (*Cook.*) pâte [à frire], *f.* ¶ *v.t,* battre, frapper. ~ *in,* défoncer. ~**ed,** *a,* (*hat, car &c*) bosselé, cabossé; (*baby*) maltraité.
battery, *n,* (*Mil., car*) batterie, *f;* (*Elec.*) accumulateur, *m;* (*dry*) pile, *f.*
battle, *n,* bataille, *f,* combat, *m.* ~*-axe,* hache d'armes, *f.* ~*field,* champ de bataille, *m.* ~*ship,* cuirassé, *m.* ¶ *v.i,* se battre, lutter, batailler.
battledore, *n,* raquette, *f.* ~ *& shuttlecock,* [jeu de] volant, *m.*
battlement, *n,* créneau, *m.* ~**ed,** *a,* crénelé.
bauble, *n,* babiole, *f.*
baulk, *n. & v.t.* = **balk**.
Bavaria, *n,* la Bavière. **Bavarian,** *a,* bavarois. ¶ *n,* Bavarois, e.
bawdy, *a,* paillard. ~ *house,* bordel *P, m.*
bawl, *v.i,* brailler, beugler. gueuler *P.* ~ *s.o. out,* engueuler qn *P.*
bay, *n,* (*Geog.*) baie, anse, *f. B~ of Biscay,* Golfe de Gascogne, *m.* (*Arch.*) travée, *f.* ~ *window,* fenêtre en saillie, *f.*
bay[2], *n,* (*tree*) laurier, *m.* ~ *rum,* lotion capillaire, *f.*
bay[3], *a,* (*horse*) bai. ¶ *n,* cheval bai, *m.*
bay[4], *n,* (*dog*) aboiement, aboi, *m. at* ~, aux abois. *bring to* ~, acculer. ¶ *v.i,* aboyer.
bayonet, *n,* baïonnette, *f.*
bazaar, *n,* bazar, *m;* vente de charité, *f.*
B.C. (*before Christ*), avant Jésus-Christ.
be, *v.i.ir,* être, exister. *there is, there are,* il y a. (*place, situation*) se trouver; (*health*) aller, se porter. *how are you?* comment allez-vous? (*feel*) *to* ~ *cold, hungry, afraid &c,* avoir froid, faim, peur &c. *to* ~ *right, wrong,* avoir raison, tort. (*age*) *he is 40,* il a 40 ans. (*Math.*) *twice 4 is 8,* 2 fois 4 font 8. (*weather*) *it is fine, warm &c,* il fait beau, chaud &c. (*time*) *it is 6 o'clock,* il est 6 heures. *he is* [*engaged in*] *writing a letter,* il est en train d'écrire une lettre. (*go*) *I have been to Rome,* j'ai été à Rome. *I have just been writing,* je viens d'écrire. *I have been waiting for 10 minutes,* j'attends depuis 10 minutes. *you are to stay here,* vous devez rester ici. *When used to express the passive voice, often translated by on + active verb: he was* (*has been*) *arrested,* on l'a arrêté.
beach, *n,* plage, grève, *f;* (*lake*) rivage, *m.* ~*comber,* rôdeur de grève, (*fig.*) propre à rien. ~*head,* tête de pont, *f.* ~ *umbrella,* parasol, *m.* ~ *wear,* tenue de plage, *f.* ¶ *v.t,* (*boat*) échouer.
beacon, *n,* balise, *f;* phare, *m. to mark with* ~*s,* baliser.
bead, *n,* perle, *f,* grain, *m;* (*sweat*) goutte, *f.* [*string of*] ~*s,* collier, *m. tell one's* ~*s* (*rosary*), dire son chapelet, *m.*
beadle, *n,* bedeau; (*Univ.*) appariteur, *m.*
beak, *n,* bec, *m.* ~**ed,** *a,* (*nose*) crochu.
beaker, *n,* gobelet; (*Chem.*) vase à bec, *m.*
beam, *n,* (*Arch.*) poutre, solive, *f;* (*Mach.*) balancier; (*scale*) fléau, *m;* (*light*) rayon; (*headlight &c*) faisceau, *m;* (*Naut.*) (*breadth*) largeur, *f. on the* ~, par le travers. *on the port, starboard* ~, à babord, tribord. (*fig.*) *on one's* ~ *ends,* dans la gêne. ¶ *v.i,* rayonner. ~**ing,** *a,* (*face, smile*) radieux, épanoui.
bean, *n,* haricot, *m. broad* ~, fève, *f. French* ~, haricot vert. *haricot* ~, h. blanc. *runner* ~, h. à rames, h. d'Espagne. (*coffee*) grain, *m. I haven't a* ~ *P,* je n'ai pas un radis *P. full of* ~*s,* plein d'entrain.
bear[1], *n,* ours(e), *m,f.* (*Astr.*) *the Great B*~, la Grande Ourse. (*pers.*) ours, homme maussade, *m;* (*Stk Ex.*) baissier, *m.* ~ *cub,* ourson, *m.* ~ *garden,* (*fig.*) pétaudière, *f.*
bear[2], *v.t.ir,* porter; (*endure*) supporter, tolérer, souffrir; (*give birth to*) donner naissance à, mettre au monde; (*yield*) donner, produire; (*Fin.*) rapporter. ~ *down,* vaincre, abattre. ~ *on* (*press*) appuyer, peser sur. ~ *out,* confirmer. ~ *upon,* (*subject*) se rapporter à. ~ *with,* supporter [avec patience]. ¶ *v.i,* ~ *left, right,* prendre sur la gauche, la droite. ~ *up,* tenir le coup *P.* ~**able,** *a,* supportable, tenable.
beard, *n,* barbe; (*Bot.*) barbe, arête, *f.* ~**ed,** *a,* barbu, à barbe. ¶ *v.t,* défier, braver. ~**less,** *a,* imberbe.
bearer, *n,* porteur, euse; (*passport*) titulaire, *m,f;* (*Fin.*) porteur, *m.* ~ *cheque, shares,* chèque, actions, au porteur.
bearing, *n,* (*pers.*) allure, *f,* maintien, port, *m. compass* ~, relèvement au compas. (*Naut.*) *take a ship's* ~, faire le point. *take one's* ~*s,* s'orienter, se repérer. *lose one's* ~*s,* être désorienté, perdre le nord *P.* (*Mech.*) coussinet, palier, *m. have no* ~ *on,* n'avoir aucun rapport avec.
beast, *n,* bête, *f;* animal, *m;* (*pers.*) brute, vache *P, f,* ~ *of burden,* bête de somme. ~**ly,** *a,* bestial; dégoûtant, infect *P,* dégueulasse *P**.
beat, *n,* (*heart, drum*) battement, *m;* (*Mus.*) mesure, *f. strong, weak* ~, temps fort, faible, *m.* (*Hunt.*) battue, *f;* (*police*) ronde, *f. that's off my* ~, cela n'est pas de mon rayon. ¶ *v.t.ir,* battre, frapper. ~ *black & blue,* rouer de coups. (*Mus.*) ~ *time,* battre la mesure. (*Hunt.*) battre. ~ *a retreat,* battre en retraite. ~ *a way through,* se frayer un chemin. ~

back, ~ **off,** repousser. ~ **in,** (*door, skull*) défoncer. ~ **up,** (*eggs &c*) fouetter, (*pers.*) passer à tabac *P.* (*defeat*) vaincre, battre, l'emporter sur. ¶ *v.i,* (*Naut.*) ~ *to windward,* louvoyer au plus près. ~ *about the bush,* tourner autour du pot. ~**er,** *n,* (*eggs*) batteur, fouet, *m;* (*Hunt.*) rabatteur, traqueur, *m.* ~**ing,** *n,* (*thrashing*) correction, raclée, rossée *P,f;* (*drums*) battement, roulement, *m;* (*defeat*) défaite, *f;* (*Hunt.*) rabattage, *m.*

beatitude, *n,* béatitude, *f. the B~s,* les béatitudes.

beau, *n,* beau, élégant, dandy, *m.*

beautiful, *a,* beau; magnifique. ~**ly,** *ad,* (*suit, work*) parfaitement, à merveille. **beautify,** *v.t,* embellir. **beauty,** *n,* beauté; (*woman*) belle, *f. B~ & the Beast,* la Belle & la Bête. ~ *parlour,* institut de beauté, *m.* ~ *spot,* site pittoresque, *m;* (*patch on face*) mouche, *f;* (*mole*) grain de beauté, *m.*

beaver, *n,* castor, *m.*

becalmed, *a,* encalminé, pris par le calme.

because, *c,* parce que. ~ *of,* à cause de.

beck[1], *n, N,* ruisseau, *m.*

beck[2], *n,* signe, *m. be at s.o's ~ & call,* obéir à qn au doigt et à l'œil. **beckon,** *v.i,* faire signe.

become, *v.i.ir,* devenir, se faire. *to ~ a priest,* se faire prêtre. ~ *old, thin,* vieillir, maigrir. ~ *accustomed to,* s'habituer à, s'accoutumer à. ~ *known,* se faire connaître. *what has become of him?* qu'est-il devenu? ¶ *v.t,* (*befit*) convenir à; (*suit*) aller [bien] à. **becoming,** *a,* convenable; [bien]séant; (*dress*) seyant; qui va bien.

bed, *n,* lit, *m;* (*Liter.*) couche, *f;* (*sea*) fond, (*river*) lit; (*flowers*) parterre, *m,* plate-bande, *f,* (*vegetables*) planche; (*Geol.*) couche, *f,* gisement, *m;* (*Arch.*) assise, *f;* (*machine*) berceau; (*lathe, oysters*) banc, *m. go to ~,* se coucher. *put to ~,* coucher, mettre au lit. *go to ~ with P,* coucher avec *P. get out of ~,* se lever. ~ *clothes,* draps & couvertures. ~*head,* chevet, *m.* ~ *pan,* bassin de lit, *m.* ~*ridden,* alité, grabataire. ~*room,* chambre [à coucher], *f.* ~*side,* chevet, *m.* ~*side carpet,* descente de lit, *f.* ~*side table,* table de chevet, *f.* ~*spread,* couvrelit, dessus de lit, *m.* ~*stead,* bois de lit; lit, *m.* ~*time,* l'heure du coucher, *f.* ¶ *v.t,* (*foundations*) asseoir. ~ *out,* (*plants*) repiquer. **bedding,** *n,* literie, *f.*

bedeck, *v.t,* parer, orner, attifer.

bedlam, *n,* maison de fous; (*fig.*) pétaudière, *f;* chambard *P, m.*

bedraggled, *a,* débraillé.

bee, *n,* abeille, *f.* ~ *eater,* guêpier, *m.* ~*hive,* ruche, *f.* ~ *keeping,* apiculture, *f. a ~ in one's bonnet,* marotte, idée fixe, *f.*

beech [tree], *n,* hêtre, *m.* ~ *copse,* hêtraie, *f.* ~*mast,* faînes, *f.pl.* ~*nut,* faîne, *f.*

beef, *n,* bœuf, *m.* ~ *steak,* bifteck, *m. roast ~,* rôti de b., rosbif, *m.* ~ *tea,* bouillon de b.

beer, *n,* bière, *f.* ~ *bottle,* canette, *f.* ~ *glass,* bock, *m,* chope, *f.*

beet, *n,* bette; betterave, *f.* ~ *sugar,* sucre de betterave, *m.* **beetroot,** *n,* betterave, *f.*

beetle, *n,* coléoptère, scarabée; (*black*) cafard, *m,* blatte, *f;* (*tool*) mailloche, *f.* **beetling brows,** sourcils touffus, *m.pl.* **beetling crag,** rocher qui surplombe, *m.*

befall, *v.i.ir,* arriver, advenir, survenir.

befit, *v.t,* convenir à. **befitting,** *a,* convenable.

before, *ad,* (*time*) avant, auparavant. *never ~,* (ne) jamais ... jusqu'ici. (*place*) devant; en avant. ¶ *c,* avant de + *infin;* avant que + [ne] + *subj.* ¶ *pr,* (*time*) avant. ~ *long,* sous peu. ~ *doing,* avant de faire. (*place*) devant. ~**hand,** *ad,* à l'avance, d'a., par a., au préalable.

befriend, *v.t,* venir en aide à; traiter en ami.

beg, *v.t. & i,* (*for alms, food*) mendier; (*favour*) quémander, solliciter; (*Com. to inform*) avoir l'honneur de; (*beseech*) prier, supplier (qn de faire); (*dog*) faire le beau. *I ~ your pardon,* je vous demande pardon.

beget, *v.t.ir,* engendrer; (*fig.*) causer, créer.

beggar, *n,* mendiant, e. *poor ~!* pauvre diable! *m. lucky ~,* veinard *P, m.* ¶ *v.t,* ruiner. ~**ly,** *a,* piètre, misérable, dérisoire. ~**y,** *n,* mendicité, misère, *f.*

begin, *v.t.ir,* (*work &c*) commencer, se mettre à; (*conversation &c*) entamer, amorcer. ~ *to do,* commencer à *ou* de faire, se mettre à f. ¶ *v.i,* commencer (*with* par; *by doing,* par faire); débuter (*with,* par). ~ *again, v.t. & i,* recommencer; reprendre. ~**ner,** *n,* débutant, e. ~**ning,** *n,* commencement, début *m.*

begonia, *n,* bégonia, *m.*

begrudge, *v.t,* envier (qch à qn).

beguile, *v.t,* tromper; (*charm*) distraire, amuser. ~**ing,** *a,* séduisant.

behalf of (on), de la part de; pour le compte de; (*plead*) en faveur de.

behave, *v.i. & reflexive,* se comporter, se conduire. ~ [*properly*]! (*to child*), tiens-toi bien! **behaviour,** *n,* conduite, *f,* comportement, *m,* (*towards s.o,* envers qn).

behead, *v.t,* décapiter.

behest, *n,* commandement, ordre, *m.*

behind, *ad,* derrière, en arrière. ¶ *pr,* derrière, en arrière de; (*other pupils*) en retard sur. ¶ *n,* (*buttocks*) derrière, *m.* ~**hand,** *ad,* en retard.

behold, *v.t. & i.ir,* voir. ¶ *i,* voyez! ~*en to,* redevable à. ~**er,** *n,* spectateur, trice.

being, *n,* être, *m;* existence, *f. human ~s,* êtres humains. *come into ~,* prendre naissance.

belabour, *v.t,* rouer de coups.

belated, *a,* tardif.

belay, *v.t,* amarrer.

belch, *n,* renvoi, rot *P, m.* ¶ *v.i,* faire un renvoi, roter *P;* (*fig: flames &c*) vomir; cracher.

beleaguer, *v.t,* assiéger.
belfry, *n,* beffroi, clocher, *m.*
Belgian, *a,* belge. ¶ *n,* Belge, *m,f.* **Belgium,** *n,* la Belgique.
belie, *v.t,* démentir.
belief, *n,* croyance, foi; conviction, *f. beyond ~,* incroyable. *to the best of my ~,* autant que je sache. **believable,** *a,* croyable. **believe,** *v.t. & i,* croire (*in sth,* à qch; *in God,* en Dieu); (*story &c*) ajouter foi à. **believer,** *n,* partisan (*in,* de) *m;* (*Rel.*) croyant, e.
belittle, *v.t,* décrier, rabaisser.
bell, *n,* cloche; (*hand*) clochette; (*door*) sonnette; (*phone*) sonnerie, *f;* (*cycle*) timbre; (*globular*) grelot, *m.* *~boy,* groom, chasseur, *m.* *~ push,* bouton de sonnette, *m.* *~ ringer,* sonneur, carillonneur, *m.* *~ tent,* tente conique, *f.* *~ tower,* clocher, *m.*
belladonna, *n,* belladone, *f.*
belle, *n,* beauté, reine, *f.*
bellicose, *a,* belliqueux. **belligerent,** *a. & n,* belligérant, e.
bellow, *v.i,* beugler, mugir.
bellows, *n.pl,* soufflet, *m;* soufflerie, *f.*
belly, *n,* ventre, *m,* panse *P,* bedaine *P, f.* *~ band,* sous-ventrière, *f.* *~ landing,* atterrissage sur le ventre. ¶ *v.i,* s'enfler, bomber.
belong to, *v.i,* appartenir à, être à; (*club &c*) faire partie de. *~***ings,** *n.pl,* affaires, possessions, *f.pl.*
beloved, *a. & n,* [bien] aimé, e, chéri, e.
below, *ad,* en bas; en dessous, plus bas; (*documents*) ci-dessous. ¶ *pr,* sous; au-dessous de; (*river*) en aval de.
belt, *n,* ceinture, *f;* (*Mil.*) ceinturon, *m;* (*Tech.*) courroie, *f;* (*Geog.*) bande, zone, *f.* ¶ *v.t,* (*thrash*) donner une raclée à. *~ up! P*,* ferme-la! *P*.*
bemoan, *v.t,* déplorer; pleurer.
bench, *n,* banc, *m;* banquette, *f;* (*workshop*) établi, *m;* (*Law*) siège, tribunal, *m,* les magistrats, *m.pl.* *~ mark,* repère de niveau, *m.*
bend, *n,* courbe, *f;* (*road*) tournant, virage, *m;* (*river, pipe*) coude, *f;* (*limb*) pli; (*knot*) nœud, *m.* ¶ *v.t,* courber, plier, fléchir; (*buckle*) fausser. ¶ *v.i,* se courber, plier; (*branch*) ployer; se fausser. *~ forward,* se pencher en avant. *on ~ed knees,* à genoux.
beneath, *ad,* dessous; au-dessous; en bas. ¶ *pr,* au-dessous de, sous.
benediction, *n,* bénédiction, *f.*
benefaction, *n,* bienfait, *m.* **benefactor, tress,** *n,* bienfaiteur, trice.
benefice, *n,* bénéfice, *m.*
beneficence, *n,* bienfaisance, *f.* **beneficent,** *a,* bienfaisant.
beneficial, *a,* avantageux, profitable, salutaire. **beneficiary,** *n,* bénéficiaire, *m,f.* **benefit,** *n,* avantage, profit, *m. to his ~,* dans son intérêt. *unemployment ~,* allocations de chômage, *f.pl.* *~ match,* match au profit de qn. *~ society,* société de secours mutuels, *f.* ¶ *v.t,* faire du bien à, profiter à. ¶ *v.i,* gagner (*by doing,* à faire).
benevolence, *n,* bienveillance, bonté; bienfaisance, *f.* **benevolent,** *a,* (*kind*) bienveillant; (*charitable*) bienfaisant.
Bengal, *n,* le Bengale. *~ light,* feu de bengale, *m.* **Bengali,** *a,* bengali, *inv.* ¶ *n,* (*pers.*) Bengali, *m,f.*
benighted, *a,* surpris par la nuit; (*fig.*) plongé dans les ténèbres.
benign, benignant, *a,* (*kindly*) bienveillant; (*Med.*) bénin (*f.* -igne). *~***ly,** *ad,* avec bienveillance.
bent[1], *p.p of* **bend,** *~ on,* résolu, décidé (à faire).
bent[2], *n,* aptitude, disposition, *f;* penchant, goût, *m.*
benumb, *v.t,* engourdir. *~ed with cold, fear,* transi de froid, peur.
benzine, *n,* benzine, *f.* **benzoin,** *n,* benjoin, *m.*
benzol[e], *n,* benzol, *m.*
bequeath, *v.t,* léguer. **bequest,** *n,* legs, *m.*
berberis, *n,* (*Bot.*) épine-vinette, *f.*
bereave, *v.t.ir,* priver, déposséder (qn de qch); (*by death*) ravir (qn à qn). *the ~d,* la famille du défunt. *~***ment,** *n,* deuil, *m;* perte, *f.*
beret, *n,* béret [basque], *m.*
Bermuda, les Bermudes, *f.pl.*
berry, *n,* baie, *f;* (*coffee*) grain, *m.*
berth, *n,* couchette, *f;* (*Naut.*) mouillage, poste d'amarrage, *m.*
beryl, *n,* béryl, *m.*
beseech, *v.t.ir,* supplier, implorer.
beset, *v.t.ir,* entourer, assaillir. *~ting sin,* péché d'habitude, *m.*
beside, *pr,* à côté de; auprès de; (*compared to*) en comparaison de. *~ o.s,* (*anger*) hors de soi, (*joy*) transporté de joie. **besides,** *ad,* d'ailleurs, du reste, en outre. ¶ *pr,* excepté, hormis, à part, en dehors de. *nothing ~,* rien d'autre, rien de plus.
besiege, *v.t,* assiéger. **besieger,** *n,* assiégeant, *m.*
besmear, *v.t,* barbouiller.
besmirch, *v.t,* souiller.
besom, *n,* balai [de bouleau], *m.*
besotted, *a,* abruti; (*infatuated*) entiché (*with,* de).
bespatter, *v.t,* eclabousser (*with,* de).
bespeak, *v.t.ir,* retenir; commander. **bespoke,** *a,* (*suit &c*) sur commande, sur mesure; (*tailor*) à façon.
besprinkle, *v.t,* arroser.
best, *a,* le meilleur, le plus beau. *~ man,* (*wedding*) garçon d'honneur, *m.* *~ quality,* de premier choix. *~ seller,* livre à succès, *m.* ¶ *ad,* le mieux. ¶ *n, the ~,* le mieux. *the ~ of it is that..,* le plus beau de l'affaire c'est que.. *the ~ plan would be to wait,* le mieux serait d'attendre. *in one's [Sunday] ~,* en-

dimanché. *to do one's* ~, faire de son mieux.
bestial†, *a*, bestial.
bestir oneself (to), se remuer, s'empresser.
bestow, *v.t*, accorder, conférer (*on*, à).
bestride, *v.t.ir*, enjamber, enfourcher.
bet, *n*, pari, *m*. ¶ *v.t*, parier; gager.
betake o.s. (to), *v. reflexive ir*, se rendre (*to*, à).
bethink o.s. (to), *v. reflexive ir*, s'aviser (de qch, de faire).
betide, *v.t*, arriver à. *whate'er* ~, quoiqu'il arrive (*ou* advienne).
betimes, *ad*, de bonne heure, tôt.
betoken, *v.t*, présager; dénoter; annoncer; être signe de.
betray, *v.t*, trahir; tromper; (*secret*) livrer; (*disclose*) révéler. ~**al,** *n*, trahison, *f*. ~**er,** *n*, traître, traîtresse.
betroth, *v.t*, fiancer. ~**al,** *n*, fiançailles, *f.pl*. ~**ed,** *n*. & *a*, fiancé, e.
better[1], *a*, meilleur. ~*-looking*, mieux. *to be* ~, (*health*) se porter (*ou* aller) mieux. *to get* ~, (*illness*) se remettre d'une maladie; (*weather*) s'améliorer, se remettre au beau. *it is* ~ *to*, il vaut mieux. ¶ *ad*, mieux. *so much the* ~, tant mieux. ¶ (*pers*.) *n*, supérieur, e. ¶ *v.t*, améliorer. ~**ment,** *n*, amélioration, *f*.
better[2] *or* **bettor,** *n*, parieur, euse; turfiste, *m,f*. **betting,** *n*, pari, *m*; (*odds*) cote, *f*. ~ *on the tote*, pari mutuel. ~ *shop*, bureau de paris, *m*.
between, *pr*, entre. ~ *now & then*, d'ici là. ~ *here & Paris*, d'ici à Paris. ¶ *ad*, au milieu. ~ *times*, dans l'intervalle. ~**-decks,** *n*, entrepont, *m*.
bevel, *n*, biseau, *m*. ~ [*square*], fausse équerre, *f*. ~ *gear*, engrenage conique, *m*. ¶ *v.t*, biseauter.
beverage, *n*, boisson, *f*.
bevy, *n*, bande, troupe, *f*.
bewail, *v.t*, pleurer, déplorer, se lamenter sur.
beware, *v.i*, se mefier. *to* ~ *of*, prendre garde à (qn, qch); se méfier de (qch); se garder de (*doing*, faire) '~ *of thieves!*', 'attention aux voleurs!' '~ *of the dog!*', '[attention] chien méchant!'
bewilder, *v.t*, désorienter, dérouter, ahurir. ~**ment,** *n*, perplexité, désorientation, *f*, ahurissement, *m*.
bewitch, *v.t*, ensorceler, enchanter. ~**ing,** *a*, ensorcelant, enchanteur, séduisant. ~**ingly,** *ad*, ~ *beautiful*, belle à ravir.
beyond, *ad*, au-delà, plus loin. ¶ *pr*, au-delà de, par-delà, de l'autre côte de; (*strength, means*) au-dessus de; excepté, sauf, en dehors de. *go* ~, dépasser. *that's* ~ *me*, ça me dépasse.
bias, *n*, biais; (*fig*.) penchant, parti pris, préjugé, *m*; partialité, *f*. ¶ *v.t*, prévenir (*against*, contre; *towards*, en faveur de). **bias(s)ed,** *a*, partial.
bib, *n*, bavoir, *m*, bavette, *f*.
Bible, *n*, Bible, *f*. **biblical,** *a*, biblique.
bibliography, *n*, bibliographie, *f*. **bibliophil[e]**, *n*, bibliophile, *m*.
bibulous, *a*, adonné à la boisson.
biceps, *n*, biceps, *m*.
bicker, *v.i*, se chamailler.
bicycle, *n*, bicyclette, *f*, vélo, *m*. ¶ *v.i*, aller à bicyclette, aller en vélo. *go* ~*ing*, faire de la b., faire du v.
bid, *n*, offre; (*auction*) enchère; (*cards*) demande, *f*. *higher* ~, surenchère, *f*. ¶ *v.t. & i.ir*, commander, ordonner (à qn de faire); (*adieu &c*) dire; (*auction*) faire une enchère. ~ *higher than*, [sur]enchérir sur. **bidder,** *n*, enchérisseur, *m*.
bide one's time (to), attendre son heure, se réserver.
biennial, *a*, biennal, bisannuel.
bier, *n*, civière, *f*, brancards, *m.pl*.
bifurcation, *n*, bifurcation, *f*.
big, *a*, grand, gros; (*sum, impression*) fort; (*with child*) enceinte; (*pers*.) important, remarquable. *to earn* ~ *money*, gagner gros. ~ *dipper*, montagnes russes, *f.pl*. ~ *game*, gros gibier, *m*. ~ *end*, (*Mot*.) tête de bielle, *f*. ~*head P*, crâneur *P*, *m*. *to be* ~*-hearted*, avoir bon coeur. ~ *shot*, ~*wig*, gros bonnet, *m*, grosse légume *P*.
bigamist, *n*, bigame, *m,f*. **bigamous,** *a*, bigame. **bigamy,** *n*, bigamie, *f*.
bight, *n*, baie, *f*, golfe, *m*; (*rope*) boucle, *f*.
bigness, *n*, grosseur; grandeur, *f*.
bigot, *n*. & ~**ed,** *a*, (*Rel*.) bigot, e; (*Pol*.) fanatique, sectaire. ~**ry,** *n*, bigoterie, *f*; fanatisme, *m*.
bike *P*, *n*, vélo, *m*, bécane *P*, *f*.
bilberry, *n*, airelle, myrtille, *f*.
bile, *n*, bile, *f*; (*fig*.) mauvaise humeur, *f*.
bilge, *n*, (*ship*) fond de cale; (*P nonsense*) idioties, foutaises *P*, *f.pl*. ~ *water*, eau de cale, *f*.
bilious, *a*, bilieux.
bilk, *v.t*, frustrer; flouer.
bill[1], *n*, (*account*) note, facture; (*restaurant*) addition, *f*; (*Com*.) effet, *m*, traite, *f*; (*Pol*.) projet de loi, *m*; (*poster*) affiche, *f*, écriteau, *m*. ~ *of exchange*, lettre de change, *f*. ~ *of sale*, acte de vente, *m*. ~ *of fare*, menu, *m*, carte du jour, *f*. (*Naut*.) ~ *of health*, patente de santé, *f*. ~ *of lading*, connaissement, *m*. ~*board*, panneau d'affichage, *m*. ~*sticker*, afficheur, *m*. *to top the* ~, être en tête d'affiche. *stick no* ~*s!* défense d'afficher! ¶ *v.t*, (*goods*) facturer; (*play*) annoncer, mettre à l'affiche.
bill[2], *n*, (*bird*) bec; (*Geog*.) cap, promontoire, bec, *m*. ¶ *v.i*, (*birds*) se becqueter. ~ *& coo*, roucouler.
billet[1], *n*, (*Mil*.) billet de logement; (*pl*.) cantonnement, *m*. ¶ *v.t*, cantonner; loger. ~*ing officer*, chef de cantonnement, *m*.

billet[2], *n,* (*wood*) bûche, billette, *f.*
billhook, *n,* serpe, *f.*
billiard, *n,* ~*s,* [jeu de] billard, *m.* ~ *ball, cue, room,* boule, queue, salle de billard, *f.* ~ *table,* table de b., *f,* billard, *m. play* ~*s,* jouer au b., faire une partie de b.
billion, *n,* (*thousand million*) milliard, (*million million*) billion, *m.*
billow, *n,* vague, lame, *f,* flot, *m;* (*smoke*) tourbillon, *m.* ¶ *v.i, fig.* (*sail*) se gonfler; (*smoke*) sortir en tourbillons. ~**y,** *a,* houleux.
billy goat, *n,* bouc, *m.*
bimonthly, *a,* (*every 2 months*) bimestriel; (*twice a month*) bimensuel.
bin, *n,* coffre, *m;* (*bread*) boîte, huche, *f;* (*wine*) casier à bouteilles, *m. dust*~, *waste*~, poubelle, boîte à ordures, *f.*
binary, *a,* binaire. ~ *notation,* numération b., *f.*
bind, *v.t.ir,* lier, attacher; (*prisoner*) ligoter; (*wound*) bander; (*book*) relier; (*commit*) obliger, engager (qn à faire); (*bowels*) resserrer. *I'll be bound,* j'en réponds. ¶ *v.i,* (*P complain*) rouspéter *P.* ¶ *n,* (*P bore*) (*pers.*) casse-pieds *P, m.f,* (*thing*) barbe *P, f.* ~**er,** *n,* (*sheaf: pers.*) lieur, *m;* (*Mach.*) lieuse, *f;* (*book*) relieur, euse; (*papers*) classeur, *m.* ~**ing,** *a,* obligatoire. ¶ *n,* (*book*) reliure, *f;* (*Need.*) ruban, *m;* (*skis*) fixation, *f.*
bindweed, *n,* liseron, *m.*
bine, *n,* sarment, *m.*
binge *P, n,* bombe *P, f. have a* ~, faire la bombe *ou* la bringue *P.*
bingo, *n,* [jeu de] loto, *m.*
binnacle, *n,* habitacle, *m.*
binoculars, *n.pl,* jumelle(s), *f* (*pl*).
biochemistry, *n,* biochimie, *f.*
biographer, *n,* biographe, *m.f.* **biography,** *n,* biographie, *f.*
biologist, *n,* biologiste, *m.f.* **biology,** *n,* biologie, *f.*
biped, *n,* bipède, *m.*
biplane, *n,* biplan, *m.*
birch, *n,* (*tree*) bouleau, *m;* (*rod*) verge, *f,* fouet, *m.* ¶ *v.t,* fouetter.
bird, *n,* oiseau; (*young*) oisillon, *m;* (*Cook.*) volaille, *f.* ~ *of prey,* oiseau de proie. ~ *of ill omen,* oiseau de mauvais augure. (*P girl*) nana *P, f. give s.o the* ~ *P,* envoyer promener, envoyer paître qn *P.* (*Theat.*) *get the* ~, se faire huer *ou* siffler. ~ *'s-eye view,* vue à vol d'oiseau. ~*-seller,* oiselier. ~*-catcher,* oiseleur, *m.* ~ *sanctuary,* réserve d'oiseaux, *f.* ~ *watcher,* ornithologue amateur *m.f.*
birth, *n,* naissance, *f;* (*child* ~) accouchement, *m,* couches, *f.pl;* (*animal*) mise au monde, *f;* (*parentage*) extraction, *f.* ~ *certificate,* extrait de naissance, *m.* ~ *control,* limitation des naissances, *f.* ~*day,* anniversaire *m.* ~*mark,* envie, tache de vin, *f.* ~*place,* lieu de naissance, *m.* ~ *rate,* natalité, *f.*
biscuit, *n,* biscuit, *m.* ~ *barrel,* seau à biscuits, *m.* ~[*ware*], biscuit, *m.*
bisect, *v.t,* diviser en deux parties égales. **bisection,** *n,* bissection, *f.*
bishop, *n,* évêque, *m;* (*Chess*) fou, *m.* ~**'s house** & **bishopric,** *n,* évêché, *m.*
bismuth, *n,* bismuth, *m.*
bison, *n,* bison, *m.*
bit[1], *n,* morceau; (*paper, string*) bout, *m;* un peu; (*tiny*) brin, *m,* un tout petit peu. ~ *of advice,* un conseil. ~ *of luck,* une chance. ~ *of news,* une nouvelle. *a good* ~ *bigger,* bien plus grand. *come to* ~*s,* tomber en morceaux.
bit[2], *n,* (*horse*) mors, *m. take the* ~ *between one's teeth,* prendre le mors aux dents. (*tool*) mèche, *f.*
bit[3], *past of* **bite.**
bitch, *n,* chienne, *f.* ~ *fox,* renarde, *f.* ~ *wolf,* louve, *f.* (*P pej. woman*) garce *P, f.* ¶ *v.i,* (*complain*) rouspéter *P.* ~**y,** *a,* (*P spiteful*) vache *P.*
bite, *n,* morsure; (*insect*) piqûre; (*mouthful*) bouchée, *f;* (*to eat*) morceau, *m;* (*Fish.*) touche, *f. I've got a* ~, ça mord. *speech full of* ~, discours plein de mordant. ¶ *v.t. & i.ir,* mordre, piquer. ~**ing,** *a,* (*cold*) mordant, cuisant; (*wind*) cinglant; (*wit, sarcasm*) mordant.
bitten, *p.p. of* **bite.**
bitter, *a,* amer, âpre; (*cold, wind*) glacial, cinglant; (*enemy, hatred*) acharné; (*suffering*) cruel. ~ *sweet, a,* aigre-doux; (*n. Bot.*) douce-amère, *f.* ¶ *n,* (*beer*) bière anglaise, *f.* ~*s,* amer, bitter, *m.* ~**ly,** *ad,* amèrement, avec amertume; cruellement, profondément. *it's* ~ *cold,* il fait un froid de loup. *cry* ~, pleurer à chaudes larmes. ~**ness,** *n,* amertume, *f.*
bittern, *n,* butor, *m.*
bitumen, *n,* bitume, *m.* **bituminous,** *a,* bitumineux.
bivalve, *a. & n,* bivalve, *m.*
bivouac, *n,* bivouac, *m.* ¶ *v.i,* bivouaquer.
blab, *v.i,* (*chatter*) jaser; (*secret*) manger le morceau *P.*
black, *a,* noir; (*Negro*) noir, nègre; (*dark*) obscur, noir. *it is pitch* ~, il fait nuit noire. ~ *& blue,* couvert de bleus. *beat* ~ *& blue,* battre comme plâtre. ~ *eye,* œil poché, *m. give s.o. a* ~ *eye,* pocher l'œil à qn. ~ *look,* regard noir, *m.* ¶ *n,* noir, *m;* (*Negro*) Noir, e. *dressed in* ~, habillé de noir. [*down*] *in* ~ *& white,* (écrit) noir sur blanc. ~*ball,* (*v.i.*) blackbouler. ~ *beetle,* cafard, *m.* ~*berry,* mûre, *f.* ~*berry bush,* ronce, *f,* mûrier, *m.* ~*bird,* merle, *m.* ~*board,* tableau [noir], *m.* ~*cap,* fauvette à tête noire, *f.* ~*-cock,* coq de bruyère, *m.* ~ *currant* (*fruit, bush, drink*)

cassis, *m.* ~*guard,* canaille, *f,* ~*head,* point noir, *m,* ~*lead,* mine de plomb, *f,* graphite, *m.* ~*leg,* jaune, briseur de grève, *m.* ~*list,* liste noire; (*v.t.*) mettre sur la liste n., (*book*) mettre à l'index. ~ *magic,* magie noire, *f.* ~*mail, n,* chantage, *m;* (*v.t.*) faire chanter. ~*mailer,* maître chanteur, *m. B*~ *Maria P,* panier à salade *P, m.* ~ *market,* marché noir, *m.* ~ *marketeer,* trafiquant du marché n., *m.* ~*out,* (*faint*) syncope, *f; v.i,* s'évanouir; (*wartime*) black-out, *m.* ~ *pudding,* boudin, *m. B*~ *Sea,* mer Noire, *f.* ~ *sheep* (*fig.*), brebis galeuse, *f.* ~*smith,* forgeron, *m;* (*horses*) maréchal ferrant, *m.* (*accident*) ~ *spot,* point noir, *m.* ~*thorn,* épine noire, *f,* prunellier, *m.* ¶ *v.t,* noircir; (*boots*) cirer; (*cargo &c*) boycotter.

blackamoor, *n,* moricaud, e.

blacken, *v.t. & i,* noircir. **blacking,** *n,* (*boots*) cirage [noir], *m.* **blackish,** *a,* noirâtre. **blackness,** *n,* noirceur, *f.*

bladder, *n,* vessie; (*Bot.*) vésicule, *f.*

blade, *n,* (*knife &c*) lame; (*propeller, fan*) aile; (*oar*) pale, *f,* plat, *m;* (*grass*) brin; (*windscreen wiper*) caoutchouc, *m.*

blame, *n,* blâme, *m,* reproches, *m.pl,* faute, *f.* ¶ *v.t,* blâmer, reprocher (qch à qn; à qn de faire), s'en prendre à. *he is to* ~, c'est sa faute. ~**less,** *a,* innocent, irréprochable. ~**worthy,** *a,* blâmable.

blanch, *v.t,* blanchir. ¶ *v.i,* (*hair*) blanchir; (*pers.*) pâlir, blémir.

bland, *a,* doux, suave, doucereux, mielleux. ~**ishment,** *n,* flatterie, *f.*

blank, *a,* blanc, vierge; (*cheque*) en blanc. ~ *cartridge,* cartouche à blanc, *f.* ~ *verse,* vers blancs, *m.pl.* ¶ *n,* blanc, *m;* lacune, *f,* trou, *m;* vide, *m. draw* ~, échouer, faire chou blanc.

blanket, *n,* couverture; (*snow, fog, smoke*) couche, *f,* manteau, nuage, *m.* ~ *stitch,* (*Emb.*) point de feston, *m.*

blare, *n,* (*trumpet*) sonnerie, *f;* (*radio*) beuglement; vacarme, *m.* ¶ *v.i,* retentir.

blarney, *n,* boniments, *m.pl,* baratin *P, m.*

blaspheme, *v.i. & t,* blasphémer. **blasphemer,** *n,* blasphémateur, trice. **blasphemous,** *a,* blasphématoire. **blasphemy,** *n,* blasphème, *m.*

blast, *n,* explosion, *f,* coup de mine, *m;* (*trumpet*) sonnerie, *f;* (*bomb*) souffle; (*siren*) coup; (*wind*) coup de vent, *m,* rafale, *f.* ~ *furnace,* haut fourneau. ~*-off,* (*rocket*) lancement, *m,* mise à feu, *f. at full* ~, à plein. ¶ *v.t,* (*blow up*) faire sauter; (*lightning*) foudroyer. ~**ing,** *n,* minage, *m.*

blatant, *a,* (*lie &c*) flagrant, criant; (*liar*) éhonté; (*colour*) criard.

blaze[1], *n,* flambée, flamme(s), *f,* incendie, *m;* (*fig.*) éclat, *m. how the* ~*s?* comment diable? *work like* ~*s,* travailler comme un dingue *P.* ¶ *v.i,* flamber; flamboyer. ~ *abroad,* claironner. ~ *away,* tirailler. **blazing,** *a,* en feu, en flammes; (*eyes, colour*) flamboyant; (*sun*) ardent.

blaze[2], *n,* (*horse*) étoile; (*tree*) marque, encoche, *f.* ¶ *v.t,* marquer. ~ *a trail,* frayer un chemin.

blazon, *n,* (*Her.*) blason, *m.* ¶ *v.t,* ~ *forth,* proclamer, claironner.

bleach, *n,* décolorant, *m,* eau oxygénée; (*domestic*) eau de Javel, *f.* ¶ *v.t,* blanchir. ~**ers,** (*Am.*) *n.pl,* gradins, *m.pl.*

bleak, *a,* morne, triste, désolé.

bleary, *a,* (*eyes*) trouble, chassieux, larmoyant.

bleat, *v.i,* bêler; (*goat & fig.*) chevroter. **bleat[ing],** *n,* bêlement, *m.*

bleed, *v.t. & i.ir,* saigner. *have a nose-*~, saigner du nez. ~**ing,** *m,* saignement, *m,* hémorragie, *f;* (*blood letting*) saignée, *f.*

bleep, bleeper, *n,* (*hospital &c*) bip, *m.* ¶ *v.t,* biper.

blemish, *n,* défaut, *m,* tare; (*fruit*) tache; (*reputation*) souillure, *f.* ¶ *v.t,* gâter, abîmer; (*fig.*) ternir.

blend, *n,* (*tea &c*) mélange; (*colours*) mariage, *m.* ¶ *v.t,* mêler, mélanger; (*wines*) couper; (*colours*) marier. ¶ *v.i,* se mêler, se mélanger; se marier, s'allier.

bless, *v.t,* bénir; (*bell &c*) baptiser. ~ *you!* vous êtes un ange!; (*sneezing*) à vos souhaits! **blessed, blest,** *a,* béni; heureux; bienheureux; (*P cursed*) sacré *P,* fichu *P* (*both before n.*) *the Blessed Virgin* [*Mary*], la Sainte Vierge. *to be* ~ *with,* avoir le bonheur d'avoir, de posséder. **blessedness,** *n,* béatitude; félicité, *f.* **blessing,** *n,* bénédiction, *f;* bonheur; (*at meal*) bénédicité, *m.*

blew, *past of* **blow.**

blight, *n,* (*crops*) rouille, nielle, *f,* mildiou, *m;* (*fruit trees*) cloque, *f;* (*fig.*) fléau, *m.* ¶ *v.t,* rouiller, nieller; (*fig.*) gâcher.

blind, *a,* aveugle; (*in one eye*) borgne; (*corner, flying*) sans visibilité. ~ *man, woman,* un, une aveugle. *the* ~, les aveugles. ~ *alley,* impasse, *f,* cul-de-sac, *m.* ~ *man's buff,* colin-maillard, *m. turn a* ~ *eye to,* fermer les yeux sur. ¶ *n,* store, *m;* jalousie, *f;* (*fig.*) masque, *m,* feinte, *f.* ¶ *v.t,* aveugler; (*dazzle*) éblouir. ~**fold,** *v.t,* bander les yeux à, de. ~**ly,** *ad,* aveuglément. ~**ness,** *n,* cécité, *f;* (*fig.*) aveuglement, *m.*

blink, *n,* clignotement, *m.* ¶ *v.i,* cligner des yeux; (*light*) clignoter. ~**ing** *P, a,* sacré *P,* fichu *P* (*both before n.*) ~**er,** *n,* œillère, *f.*

bliss, *n,* béatitude, félicité, *f.* ~**ful**†, *a,* bienheureux; merveilleux.

blister, *n,* ampoule, cloque, *f;* (*paint*) boursouflure, *f.* ¶ *v.i,* se couvrir d'ampoules; (*paint*) se boursoufler, cloquer.

blithe, *a,* gai, joyeux.

blitz, *n,* bombardement [aérien], *m;* attaque éclair, *f. the B*~, le Blitz. ~*krieg,* guerre éclair, *f.* ¶ *v.t,* bombarder.

blizzard, *n,* tempête de neige, *f.*

bloated, *a,* gonflé, bouffi, boursouflé.

bloater, *n,* hareng saur, *m.*

block, *n,* bloc, *m;* (*wood*) bille, *f;* (*chopping*) billot, *m;* (*of flats*) immeuble, *m;* (*houses*) pâté; (*mental*) blocage, *m;* (*pulley*) moufle, poulie, *f;* (*traffic*) embouteillage, encombrement, *m;* (*Typ.*) cliché, *m;* (*shares*) tranche, *f.* ~ *capitals,* majuscules d'imprimerie, *f.pl.* ~*head P,* imbécile, *m.f,* crétin, e *P.* ~*house,* blockhaus, *m.* ¶ *v.t,* bloquer, barrer; (*pipe &c*) boucher, obstruer.

blockade, *n,* blocus, *m.* ¶ *v.t,* bloquer.

bloke *P, n,* type *P,* mec *P, m.*

blond, *a. & n,* (*pers.*) blond, e.

blood, *n,* sang, *m;* race, *f;* (*dandy*) petit-maître, *m.* ~ *bank,* banque du sang, *f.* ~ *bath,* bain de s., massacre, *m.* ~ *cell,* globule sanguin, *m.* ~*curdling,* à vous figer le sang. ~ *donor,* donneur, -euse de s. ~ *group,* groupe sanguin, *m.* ~ *heat,* température du s., *f.* ~*hound,* limier, *m.* ~ *letting,* saignée, *f.* ~ *orange,* orange sanguine, *f.* ~ *poisoning,* empoisonnement du.s., *m.* ~ *pressure,* tension artérielle, *f.* ~ *red,* rouge sang, *m.* ~ *relation,* parent(e) par le sang. ~*shed,* effusion de s., *f;* carnage, *m.* ~*shot,* injecté de sang. ~ *test,* analyse de s. ~*thirsty,* altéré de s., sanguinaire. ~ *transfusion,* transfusion de s. ~ *vessel,* vaisseau sanguin, *m.* ~**less,** a, exsangue; (*victory*) sans effusion de s. ~**y,** *a,* ensanglanté, sanglant, en sang; sanguinaire; (*P**) sacré *P,* foutu *P** (*both before n.*) ¶ *ad P,* vachement *P.* ~ *annoying,* emmerdant *P*.* ~ *fool,* pauvre con *P*, m.*

bloom, *n,* fleur; floraison, *f;* (*cheek, peach*) velouté, *m. in full* ~, en pleine floraison, épanoui. ¶ *v.i,* fleurir, s'épanouir. ~**ing,** *a,* en fleur, fleuri[ssant]; (*fig.*) florissant. *P* = **blinking** *P.*

bloomer *P, n,* bévue, gaffe, *f.*

blossom, *n,* fleur, *f.* ¶ *v.i,* fleurir. ~**ing,** *n,* floraison, *f.*

blot, *n,* pâté, *m,* tache, *f.* ¶ *v.t,* faire un pâté sur, tacher; (*with blotting paper*) sécher. ~ *out,* effacer. *blotting paper,* [papier] buvard, *m.*

blotch, *n,* tache, marbrure, *f.* ~**y,** *a,* (*skin*) marbré.

blotter, *n,* buvard, sous-main, *m.*

blouse, *n,* (*woman*) chemisier, *m;* (*artist*) blouse, *f.*

blow[1], *n,* coup, *m;* (*fist*) coup de poing; (*stick*) c. de bâton; (*misfortune*) coup, malheur, *m. come to* ~*s,* en venir aux mains.

blow[2], *n,* (*wind*) coup de vent, *m. go out for a* ~, sortir prendre l'air. ~*fly,* mouche à viande, *f.* ~*hole,* (*whale*) évent, *m.* ~*lamp,* lampe à souder, *f.* ~*-out,* (*tyre*) éclatement; (*P meal*) gueuleton *P, m.* ¶ *v.t.ir,* (*wind instrument*) souffler dans; (*ship*) pousser; (*leaves*) chasser. ~ *one's horn,* (*car*) corner, klaxonner. ~ *one's nose,* se moucher. ~ *a kiss,* envoyer un baiser. ~ *the gaff,* vendre la mèche. ~ *one's own trumpet,* se faire mousser *P.* ~ **away,** ~ **off,** emporter. ~ **down,** (*tree*) abattre. ~ **out,** (*candle*) souffler; (*one's brains*) se brûler la cervelle. ~ **up,** (*bridge*) faire sauter; (*tyre*) gonfler. *v.i.ir,* (*wind*) souffler. ~ *hard,* souffler en tempête. ~**over** (*storm*) se calmer. ~**up,** (*storm*) se préparer; (*mine*) sauter, exploser, faire explosion; (*P in anger*) sauter au plafond *P.* ~**er,** *n,* ventilateur; *P* hautparleur, (*phone*) bigophone *P, m.*

blubber, *n,* blanc de baleine, *m.* ¶ *v.i,* sangloter.

blue, *a,* bleu; (*sad*) triste; (*bawdy: joke*) grivois, (*film*) porno *P. to feel* ~, broyer du noir, avoir le cafard *P. be in a* ~ *funk,* avoir la frousse *P.* ¶ *n,* azur, *m. out of the* ~, tombé du ciel. *the* ~*s,* (*gloom*) le cafard *P;* (*Mus.*) le blues. *Bluebeard,* Barbe-Bleue, *m.* ~*bell,* jacinthe des bois, *f.* ~*bottle,* mouche à viande, *f.* ~ *collar worker,* col bleu, *m.* ~*-eyed,* aux yeux bleus. *B*~ *Peter,* pavillon de partance, *m.* ~*print,* bleu, *m.* ~*stocking,* bas-bleu, *m.* ~ *tit,* mésange bleue, *f.* ¶ *v.t,* (*P squander*) manger, gaspiller.

bluff[1], *a,* (*pers.*) franc, carré; (*cliff*) escarpé, à pic. ¶ *n,* cap à pic, *m,* falaise, *f.*

bluff[2], *n,* bluff, *m.* ¶ *v.t. & i,* bluffer.

bluish, *a,* bleuâtre.

blunder, *n,* bévue, gaffe, *f,* impair, *m.* ¶ *v.i,* faire une bévue &c; gaffer. ~**ing,** *a,* maladroit.

blunt, *a,* émoussé; (*instrument*) contondant; (*pers.*) brusque, carré. ¶ *v.t,* (*blade*) émousser; (*pencil*) épointer. ~**ly,** *ad,* brusquement, carrément, roundement. ~**ness,** *n,* état émoussé, *m;* brusquerie, *f.*

blur, *n,* tache, forme confuse, *f.* ¶ *v.t,* estomper; (*sight*) brouiller, troubler. ~**red,** (*image*) flou; (*sight*) trouble. *become* ~*red,* s'estomper.

blurb, *n,* baratin publicitaire *P, m.*

blurt out, *v.t,* lâcher, laisser échapper.

blush, *n,* rougeur, *f. without a* ~, sans rougir. ¶ *v.i,* rougir.

bluster, *n,* fracas, *m;* (*pers.*) air bravache, *m,* fanfaronnade, rodomontade, *f.* ¶ *v.i,* (*wind*) faire rage; (*pers.*) tempêter; faire le bravache. ~**er,** *n,* bravache, *m.*

boar, *n,* verrat; (*wild*) sanglier, *m.*

board, *n,* planche, *f;* (*games*) tableau; (*notice*) écriteau; (*Naut.*) bord, *m. on* ~ *a ship,* à bord d'un navire. *go on* ~, s'embarquer. (*officials*) comité, commission, *f.* ~ *of directors,* conseil d'administration, *m.* ~ *of examiners,* jury d'examen, *m. B*~ *of Trade,* Ministère du Commerce, *m.* (*meals*) pension, *f.* ~ *& lodging,* chambre avec pension. *full* ~, pension complète. ¶ *v.t,* (*train, bus*) monter dans;

(*ship, plane*) monter à bord de; (*pers.*) prendre en pension. ~ *out*, mettre en pension. ¶ *v.i*, être en pension, loger. ~**er,** *n*, pensionnaire, *m,f;* (*Sch.*) interne, pensionnaire, *m,f.* ~**ing,** *n*, (*floor*) planchéiage; (*ship: attack*) abordage, *m.* ~ *card, pass*, carte d'embarquement, *f.* ~ *house*, pension, *f;* (*Sch.*) internat, *m.* ~ *school*, pensionnat, internat, *m*, pension, *f.*

boast, *n*, fanfaronnade, *f.* ¶ *v.i*, se vanter (de qch, de faire). ¶ *v.t*, [être fier de] posséder. ~**er,** ~**ful,** *n. & a*, vantard, e, fanfaron, ne. ~**ing,** *n*, vantardise, *f.*

boat, *n*, bateau; (*ship*) navire, bâtiment, vaisseau, *m;* (*small*) embarcation, barque, *f*, canot, *m.* ~*builder*, constructeur naval *ou* de bâteaux, *m.* ~ *deck*, pont des embarcations, *m.* ~ *hook*, gaffe, *f.* ~*house*, hangar à bâteaux, *m.* ~*man*, ~*woman*, batelier, ère, (*ferry*) passeur, *m.* ~ *race*, course d'aviron, *f.* ~*yard*, chantier de bâteaux, *m.* ¶ *v.i*, *to go* ~*ing*, se promener en bateau; faire du canotage. ~**er,** *n*, (*hat*) canotier. ~**ing,** *n*, canotage, *m.* **boatswain,** *n*, maître d'équipage, *m.*

bob[1], *n*, (*curtsy*) petite révérence; (*haircut*) coiffure à la Jeanne d'Arc, *f;* (*weight*) plomb; (*float*) bouchon, *m.* ¶ *v.i*, ~ *about*, s'agiter. ~ *up & down*, ballotter; (*on water*) danser sur l'eau.

bob[2] *P, n*, shilling, *m.*

bobbin, *n*, bobine, *f;* (*lace*) fuseau, *m.*

bobby *P, n*, (*policeman*) flic *P, m.*

bobsleigh, *n*, bobsleigh, *m.*

bobtail, *n*, queue écourtée, *f.*

bode, *v.t*, présager. ~ *well, ill*, être de bon, mauvais augure.

bodice, *n*, corsage, *m.* **bodily,** *a*, corporel; physique; matériel; (*fear*) pour sa personne. ¶ *ad*, corporellement; en masse.

bodkin, *n*, passe-lacet, *m.*

body, *n*, corps; (*dead*) cadavre, *m;* (*people*) masse, foule, *f*, groupe, ensemble, *m. in a* ~, en masse. (*pers.*) bonhomme, type, *m*, bonne femme, *f.* (*car* ~ *&* ~*work*) carosserie, *f.* ~*guard*, garde du corps, *m.*

bog, *n*, marais, marécage, *m.* ¶ *v.t*, embourber. *get* ~*ged down*, s'embourber.

bog[e]y[1], *n*, épouvantail, *m;* bête noire, *f.* ~*man*, croque-mitaine, *m.*

bogey[2], **bogie,** (*Rly*) *n*, bogie, *f;* (*trolley*) diable, *m.*

bogey[3], (*Golf*) *n*, bogey, *m.*

boggle, *v.i*, reculer, hésiter; être ahuri.

boggy, *a*, marécageux, tourbeux.

bogus, *a*, faux, simulé.

Bohemia (*fig.*) *n*, la bohème. **Bohemian** (*fig.*) *n. & a*, bohème, *m,f.*

boil[1] (*Path.*) *n*, furoncle, clou, *m.*

boil[2], *v.t*, faire bouillir; [faire] cuire à l'eau. ¶ *v.i*, bouillir; (*sea*) bouillonner. ~ *down*, se réduire. ~ *over*, déborder. ~**ed,** *a:* ~ *beef*, bœuf bouilli, *m.* ~ *egg*, œuf à la coque, *m.* ~ *potatoes*, pommes vapeur, *f.pl.* ~**er,** *n*, (*hot water, steam*) chaudière; (*laundry*) lessiveuse, *f;* (*Cook. double*) bain-marie, *m.* ~*maker*, chaudronnier, *m.* ~ *room*, chambre de chauffe, chaufferie, *f.* ~**ing,** *n*, ébullition, *f;* bouillonnement, *m.* ~ *point*, point d'ébullition, *m.* ¶ *a*, bouillant.

boisterous†, *a*, bruyant, turbulent.

bold, *a*, hardi, osé, audacieux, courageux. ~ *type*, caractères gras, *m.pl. in* ~ [*type*], en grasse. ~**ly,** *ad*, hardiment, audacieusement. ~**ness,** *n*, hardiesse, audace, *f.*

Bolivia, *n*, la Bolivie. **Bolivian,** *a*, bolivien. ¶ *n*, Bolivien, ne.

bollard, *n*, bollard, *m.*

bollocks *P** = **balls** *P**.

Bologna, *n*, Bologne, *f.*

Bolshevik, *a*, bolchevique. ¶ *n*, Bolchevik, *m,f.* **Bolshevism,** *n*, bolchevisme, *m.* **bolshy** *P, n*, (*Pol.*) rouge, *m,f.* ¶ *a*, récalcitrant, mauvais coucheur *P.*

bolster, *n*, traversin, *m.* ~ **up,** *v.t*, étayer; soutenir.

bolt, *n*, (*Tech.*) boulon; (*door*) verrou, *m;* (*lock*) pêne, *m;* (*flight*) fuite soudaine, *f;* (*cloth*) rouleau, *m. make a* ~ *for it*, se sauver à toutes jambes. ¶ *v.t*, boulonner; verrouiller; (*food*) engouffrer. ¶ *v.i*, (*pers.*) se sauver à toutes jambes; (*horse*) s'emballer. ¶ *ad*, ~ *upright*, tout droit; droit comme un i.

bomb, *n*, bombe, *f. cost a* ~ *P*, coûter les yeux de la tête. ~ *aimer*, bombardier. ~ *crater*, entonnoir. ~ *disposal*, désamorçage, *m. come like a* ~*shell*, tomber, éclater comme une bombe. ~ *shelter*, abri [antiaérien], *m.* ¶ *v.t*, bombarder. ~*ed out*, (*family*) sinistré.

bombard, *v.t*, bombarder. ~**ier,** *n*, (*Mil.*) caporal d'artillerie, *m.* ~**ment,** *n*, bombardement, *m.*

bombast, *n*, emphase, boursouflure, *f.* ~**ic,** *a*, grandiloquent; (*style*) ampoulé, boursouflé.

bomber, *n*, (*plane*) bombardier; (*terrorist*) plastiqueur, *m.*

bona fide, *a. & ad*, de bonne foi; sérieux.

bond, *n*, lien, *m*, attache, *f;* (*Fin.*) bon, *m;* obligation, *f;* titre, *m.* ~*holder*, porteur d'obligations, *m.* (*Law*) contrat; engagement, *m. enter into a* ~, s'engager [à faire]. ~*s*, (*chains*) fers, *m.pl*, chaines, *f.pl.* ~*ed warehouse*, entrepôt des douanes, *m. in* ~, à l'entrepôt. ¶ *v.t*, (*Build.*) liaisonner; (*put into* ~) entreposer en douane. ~**age,** *n*, esclavage, *m.* ~**ing,** *n*, (*Build.*) liaison, *f.*

bone, *n*, os, *m;* (*fish*) arête, *f;* (*pl, dead*) ossements, *m.pl.* ~ *of contention*, pomme de discorde, *f.* ~*head*[*ed*] *P*, crétin, e *P*, imbécile. ~*setter*, rebouteur, *m.* ¶ *v.t*, désosser;

ôter les arêtes de; (*P steal*) chiper *P*, piquer *P*.
bonfire, *n*, feu de joie, *m*.
bonkers *P*, *a*, cinglé *P*, dingue *P*.
bonnet, *n*, (*woman*) capote, *f*, bonnet, chapeau à brides, *m*; (*Sc: man*) bonnet, béret [écossais], *m*; (*car*) capot, *m*.
bonny (*Sc.*) *a*, joli, beau.
bonus, *n*, gratification, prime, *f*. ~ *shares*, actions gratuites, *f.pl*.
bony, *a*, (*Anat.*) osseux; (*limbs*) maigre, décharné.
boo, *v.t*, huer, conspuer. ¶ *n*, huée, *f*.
booby, *n*, nigaud, e, *f*. ~ *prize*, prix de consolation, *m*. ~ *trap*, piège, traquenard, *m*; (*Mil.*) objet piégé, *m*.
book, *n*, livre, bouquin *P*; (*exercise*) cahier; (*note*) carnet; (*tickets, cheques &c*) carnet, *m*. ~*binder*, relieur, euse. ~*binding*, reliure, *f*. ~*case*, bibliothèque, *f*. ~*-ends*, serre-livres, *m*. ~*keeper*, comptable, *m,f*. ~*keeping*, comptabilité, *f*. ~ *lover*, bibliophile, *m*. ~*maker*, bookmaker, *m*. ~*mark*, signet, *m*, marque, *f*. ~ *plate*, ex-libris, *m*. ~*seller*, libraire, (*secondhand*) bouquiniste, *m*. ~*shop*, librairie, *f*. ~*shelf*, rayon, *m*. ~*stall*, kiosque à journaux, étalage de bouquiniste, *m*. ~ *token*, chèque-livre, *m*. ~*worm* (*pers.*), rat de bibliothèque, *m*. *to make a* ~ (*Betting*), inscrire des paris. ¶ *v.t*, (*room*) retenir, réserver; (*seat*) louer; (*performer*) engager; (*Com: order*) inscrire, enregistrer; (*Police: driver*) donner un procès-verbal à; (*Foot.*) prendre le nom de. ~*ed up* (*hotel*) complet. ¶ *v.i*, prendre un billet. ~**ing,** *n*, (*Theat.*) location; (*Rly*) réservation, *f*. ~ *office*, (*Theat., Rly*) guichet, *m*. **booklet,** *n*, brochure, *f*.
boom[1], *n*, (*harbour*) barrage; (*Naut.*) gui, *m*; (*crane*) flèche; (*microphone*) perche, *f*.
boom[2], *n*, grondement, mugissement, *m*. ¶ *v.i*, gronder, tonner.
boom[3], *n*, (*Com.*) forte hausse, *f*, boom, *m*. ¶ *v.i*, être en hausse, marcher très bien.
boon, *n*, bénédiction, aubaine; faveur, *f*. ~ *companion*, bon camarade, *m*.
boor, *n*, rustre, goujat, mufle *P*, *m*. ~**ish,** *a*, grossier, rustre. ~**ishness,** *n*, goujaterie, muflerie, *f*.
boot, *n*, botte, chaussure [montante], *f*; (*Mil.*) brodequin, *m*. *gum* ~, botte en caoutchouc. *riding* ~, botte à l'écuyère. (*lady's button*) bottine, *f*; (*car*) coffre, *m*, malle, *f*. *to get the* ~ *P*, être flanqué à la porte *P*. ~*s*, garçon d'hôtel, *m*. ~*lace*, lacet de chaussure, *m*. ~*maker*, bottier, *m*. ~*polish*, cirage, *m*. ~ *scraper*, décrottoir, *m*. ¶ *v.t*, (*kick*) botter, donner un coup de pied à. ~**ee,** *n*, [petit] chausson, *m*.
booth, *n*, (*fair*) baraque; (*phone &c*) cabine, *f*.
booty, *n*, butin, *m*.
booze *P*, *n*, alcool, *m*. ¶ *v.i*, picoler *P*, biberonner *P*.
boracic, *a*, borique. **borax,** *n*, borax, *m*.
border, *n*, (*edge*) bord, *m*, bordure; (*woods*) lisière; (*boundary*) frontière, limite; (*garden*) plate-bande, *f*. ~*line*, ligne de démarcation, *f*. ~*line case*, cas limite, *m*. ¶ *v.t*, border. ~*ing country*, pays limitrophe, *m*. ~ [*up*]*on*, avoisiner; (*fig.*) côtoyer, toucher à, friser.
bore[1], *n*, (*gun*) calibre, *m*; (*tidal*) barre d'eau, *f*. ~*hole*, trou de sonde, *m*. ¶ *v.t*, percer, forer; (*well, tunnel*) creuser; (*cylinder*) aléser. ¶ *v.i*, forer, sonder.
bore[2], *n*, (*event*) ennui, *m*, scie *P*, *f*. *what a* ~! quelle barbe! (*pers.*) raseur, euse *P*, casse-pieds *P*, *m,f*, *inv*. ¶ *v.t*, ennuyer, assommer, raser *P*, casser les pieds à. *to be* ~*d to death*, s'ennuyer à mourir.
boric, *a*, borique.
born, *p.p.* & *a*, né; de naissance. ~ *blind*, aveugle de naissance. *to be* ~, naître.
borne, *p.p. of* **bear.**
borrow, *v.t*, emprunter (*from*, à). ~**er,** *n*, emprunteur, euse. ~**ing,** *n*, emprunt, *m*.
borzoi, *n*, lévrier russe; borzoï, *m*.
bosom, *n*, poitrine, *f*, seins *m.pl*; (*fig.*) sein. *in the* ~ *of the family*, au sein de la famille. ~ *friend*, ami de cœur, *m*.
Bosphorus (the), le Bosphore.
boss *P*, *n*, patron, ne, chef, *m*. ¶ *v.t*, mener, régenter; diriger. ~**y,** *a*, autoritaire.
botanic(al), *a*, botanique. ~ *gardens*, jardin des plantes, j. botanique, *m*. **botanist,** *n*, botaniste, *m*. **botanize,** *v.i*, herboriser. **botany,** *n*, botanique, *f*.
botch, *v.t*, (& *make a* ~ *of*) bousiller *P*.
both, *a*. & *ad*, tous [les] deux; l'un(e) & l'autre. ~ *...and...*, et...et... *on* ~ *sides*, des deux côtés. *in* ~ *hands*, à deux mains. ~ *tall & strong*, à la fois grand & fort.
bother, *n*, ennui[s], embêtement, *m*. ¶ *i*, zut!; *P* flûte!; *P* la barbe! *P* ¶ *v.t*, ennuyer, gêner, embêter *P*; (*worry*) tracasser, inquiéter. *I'm sorry to* ~ *you*, je m'excuse de vous déranger. ¶ *v.i*, se donner la peine (de faire). ~ *about*, s'inquiéter de.
bottle, *n*, bouteille, *f*; (*small*) flacon; (*fruit*) bocal; (*baby's*) biberon, *m*; (*beer*) canette, *f*. ~ *rack*, porte-bouteilles, *m*. ~*neck*, goulot; (*traffic*) embouteillage, *m*. ¶ *v.t*, mettre en bouteille(s); (*fruit*) m. en bocal. ~ *up*, (*feelings*) ravaler, refouler.
bottom, *n*, fond; (*stairs, page*) bas; (*hill*) pied; (*buttocks*) derrière, *m*. *at* ~, au fond. *from the* ~ *of my heart*, du fond de mon coeur. ¶ *a*, inférieur. ~ *floor*, rez-de-chaussée, *m*. ~ *gear*, première vitesse. ~ *step*, première marche, *f*.
bough, *n*, branche, *f*; rameau, *m*.
bought, *p.p. of* **buy.**

boulder, *n,* rocher, *m,* grosse pierre, *f.*

bounce, *n,* bond, rebond, *m. full of* ~, (*pers.*) dynamique, plein d'entrain. ¶ *v.i,* rebondir; (*pers.*) bondir. ~ *into,* entrer d'un bond. ¶ *v.t,* (*P eject*) vider *P.* ~**r** *P, n,* videur *P.*

bound[1], *n,* bond, saut, *m. at a* ~, d'un bond. ¶ *v.i,* bondir, sauter.

bound[2], *n,* ~*s,* bornes, limite(s), *f* (*pl*). *to exceed all* ~*s,* dépasser la mesure. *within the* ~*s of possibility,* dans la limite du possible. ~**ed by,** borné, limité par. ~**less,** *a,* illimité, sans bornes.

bound[3], *p.p. of* **bind.** ¶ *a,* sûr, certain (*to do,* de faire); (*obliged*) obligé, tenu (de faire). ~*en duty,* devoir impérieux. ~ *for,* à destination de, en route pour; (*train*) en direction de.

bounteous†, bountiful†, *a,* (*pers.*) généreux, libéral; (*crop*) abondant, fécond. **bounty,** *n,* générosité, *f.*

bouquet, *n,* bouquet; (*wine*) bouquet, fumet, *m.*

bout, *n,* (*fever &c*) accès, *m,* attaque, *f;* (*Box.*) combat; (*Fenc.*) assaut, *m. drinking* ~, beuverie, *f.*

bovine, *a,* bovin.

bow[1] (bou) *n,* (*weapon, curve*) arc; (*knot*) noeud; (*Mus.*) archet; (*saddle*) arçon, *m.* ~*-legged,* aux jambes arquées. ~*man,* archer, *m.* ~ *tie,* noeud papillon, *m.* ~ *window,* fenêtre en saillie, *f,* bow-window, *m.*

bow[2] (bau) *n,* (*head*) salut, *m;* (*body*) révérence, *f.* ¶ *v.i,* saluer, incliner la tête. *to* ~ *to s.o,* saluer qn. ~ *& scrape,* faire des courbettes. (*bend*) se courber, fléchir. ~ *before,* (*fig.*) s'incliner devant, se soumettre à.

bow[3] (bau) *n,* (*ship*) avant, *m,* proue, *f;* (*oarsman*) nageur de l'avant, *m.* ~**sprit,** beaupré, *m.*

bowdlerize, *v.t,* expurger.

bowels, *n.pl,* intestins, *m.pl;* entrailles, *f.pl.*

bower, *n,* tonnelle, *f,* berceau de verdure, *m.*

bowing, *n,* (*Mus.*) coup d'archet, *m.*

bowl[1], *n,* bol, *m;* (*water*) cuvette; (*crystal*) coupe; (*dog*) écuelle; (*beggar*) sébile, *f;* (*pipe*) fourneau, *m.*

bowl[2], *n,* (*Sport*) boule, *f.* [*game of*] ~*s,* [jeu de] boules; pétanque, *f.* ¶ *v.t,* ~ *over,* renverser; (*fig.*) stupéfier.

bowler [hat], *n,* [chapeau] melon, *m.*

bowling: ~ *alley,* bowling, *m.* ~ *green,* terrain de boules [sur gazon], *m.*

bow-wow, *n,* toutou, *m.*

box[1], *n,* boîte; (*large*) caisse, *f;* (*cardboard*) carton; (*casket*) coffret; (*coach*) siège, *m;* (*Theat.*) loge; (*witness*) barre, *f;* (*jury*) banc, *m.* (*P TV*) *on the* ~, à la télé *P.* ~ *office,* bureau de location, guichet, *m.* ~ *pleat,* pli creux, *m.* ~ *room,* débarras, *m.* ~ *spanner,* clef à pipe, *f.* ¶ *v.t,* mettre en boîte, m. en caisse. ~ *in,* (*pipes*) encastrer.

box[2], *n,* ~ *on the ear,* claque, gifle, *f.* ¶ *v.i. & t,* faire de la boxe, boxer (avec qn). ~ *s.o's ears,* claquer, gifler qn. ~**er,** *n,* boxeur, *m.* ~**ing,** *n,* boxe, *f.* ~ *match,* match de b., *m.* ~ *ring,* ring, *m.*

box[3], *n,* (*tree & wood*) buis, *m.*

boy, *n,* garçon, enfant; (*small*) petit garçon, garçonnet; jeune [homme]. *French* ~, jeune Français, *m. old* ~, mon vieux. *come on* ~*s* (*fellows*)! allez les gars! ~*friend,* petit ami. ~ *scout,* scout, éclaireur, *m.* ~**hood,** *n,* enfance, jeunesse, *f.* ~**ish,** *a,* de garçon, enfantin.

brace, *n,* (*strut, stay*) entretoise, *f,* étrésillon; (*tool*) vilebrequin, *m;* (*pair*) paire; (*Typ.* } *or* {) accolade, *f;* (*dental*) appareil dentaire, *m.* ~*s,* (*Dress*), bretelles, *f.pl.* ¶ *v.t,* renforcer, étayer, soutenir. ~ *o.s,* fortifier son âme (pour faire). ~**ing,** *a,* (*climate*) fortifiant, tonifiant.

bracelet, *n,* bracelet, *m.*

bracken, *n,* fougère, *f.*

bracket, *n,* (*angle*) support, *m,* potence, *f.* (*Typ.*) [ ] crochet, *m;* ( ) parenthèse; { } accolade, *f.* ¶ *v.t,* mettre entre parenthèses.

brackish, *a,* saumâtre.

bradawl, *n,* poinçon, *m.*

brag, *n,* vanterie, fanfaronnade, *f.* ¶ *v.i,* se vanter. **braggart,** *n,* vantard, e, fanfaron, ne.

brahmin, *n,* brahmane, *m.*

braid, *n,* soutache, *f,* galon, *m;* (*hair*) tresse, natte, *f.* ¶ *v.t,* (*trim with* ~) soutacher, galonner; (*plait*) tresser, natter.

brain, *n.* & ~**s,** *pl,* cerveau, *m,* cervelle, *f;* (*pl. Cook.*) cervelle. *to blow out one's* ~*s,* se brûler la cervelle. ~ *fever,* fièvre cérébrale, *f.* ~ *washing,* lavage de cerveau, *m.* ~ *wave,* idée géniale, *f.* ~**less,** *a,* sans cervelle.

braise, *v.t,* braiser.

brake[1], *n,* (*thicket*) fourré, *m;* (*bracken*) fougère, *f.*

brake[2], *n,* (*vehicle*) break, *m.*

brake[3], *n,* (*wheel*) frein, *m.* ~ *block,* sabot de f., *m.* ~ *drum,* tambour de f., *m.* ~ *shoe,* mâchoire de f., *f.* ~ *van* (*Rly*) fourgon à f., *m.* ¶ *v.i,* freiner.

bramble, *n,* ronce, *f.*

bran, *n,* son, *m.*

branch, *n,* (*tree, family, river*) branche, *f;* (*Rly, road, pipe*) embranchement; (*river*) bras, *m;* (*store, bank*) succursale, *f.* ¶ *v.i,* (*road*) bifurquer; (*tree, river*) se ramifier. ~ *out,* étendre ses activités.

brand, *n,* (*cattle, Com.*) marque; (*prisoner*) flétrissure, *f;* (*wood*) tison, brandon; (*fig.*) stigmate, *m.* ~*-new,* tout neuf. ¶ *v.t,* marquer au fer rouge; (*fig.*) stigmatiser, flétrir.

brandy, *n,* cognac, *m,* fine [champagne]; eau de vie, *f.* ~ *& soda,* fine à l'eau, *f.*

brash, *a,* effronté; suffisant.

brass, *n,* cuivre [jaune]; laiton, *m.* (*Mus.*) *the* ~, les cuivres. (*P cheek*) toupet, culot *P, m;* (*P*

money) fric *P*, pognon *P*, *m*. ~ *band*, fanfare, *f*. (*Mil*.) ~ *hat P*, huile *P*, *f*. ~**y**, *a*, cuivré.
brassière, *n*, soutien-gorge, *m*.
brat, *n*, gamin, e, marmot, *m*, gosse, *m*,*f*; (*pl*, *col*.) marmaille, *f*.
bravado, *n*, bravade, *f*.
brave†, *a*, courageux, brave. ~ *man*, [homme] brave, *m*. *be* ~! du courage! ¶ *v.t*, braver, affronter. ~**ry**, *n*, courage, *m*, bravoure, *f*.
bravo, *i*, bravo! **bravura**, *n*, bravoure, *f*.
brawl, *n*, bagarre, rixe, *f*. ¶ *v.i*, se bagarrer *P*. ~**er**, *n*, bagarreur *P*, *m*.
brawn, *n*, (*Cook*.) fromage de tête, *m*; (*fig*.) du muscle. ~**y**, *a*, (*arm*) musculeux; (*pers*.) musclé.
bray, *v.i*, braire; (*trumpet*) résonner, éclater. ~[**ing**], *n*, braiment, *m*.
braze, *v.t*, souder au laiton, braser. **braze** (*joint*) & **brazing**, *n*, brasure, *f*.
brazen, *a*, de cuivre. ~[-*faced*], effronté. *to* ~ *it out*, crâner, payer d'effronterie.
brazier, *n*, (*pers*.) chaudronnier; (*fire*) brasero, *m*.
Brazil, *n*, le Brésil. **Brazilian**, *a*, brésilien. ¶ *n*, Brésilien, ne.
breach, *n*, (*gap*) brèche; (*Law*) infraction, violation, *f*; (*manners &c*) manquement (*of*, à), *m*. ~ *of contract*, rupture de contrat, *f*. ~ *of faith*, manque de parole, *m*. ~ *of promise*, violation de promesse de mariage, *f*. ~ *of trust*, abus de confiance, *m*.
bread, *n*, pain, *m*. *loaf of* ~, pain, miche, *f*. ~ *& butter*, tartine, *f*; (*fig*.) gagne-pain, *m*. *inv*. ~*crumb*, miette de pain. ~*crumbs* (*Cook*.), chapelure, *f*. ~*knife*, couteau à pain, *m*. ~*winner*, soutien de famille, *m*.
breadth, *n*, largeur; (*wing*) envergure; (*style*) ampleur, *f*.
break, *n*, rupture, cassure, *f*; (*interval*) interruption, pause, *f*; (*gap*) trouée, brèche, *f*; (*journey*) arrêt, *m*; (*Sch*.) récréation; (*boy's voice*) mue, *f*; (*weather*) changement, *m*; (*clouds*) éclaircie; (*Bil*.) série, *f*. *at* ~ *of day*, au point du jour. *lucky* ~, chance, veine *P*, *f*. *make a* ~ *for it*, s'évader. ¶ *v.t.ir*, casser, briser; rompre; (*bone*) casser, fracturer. ~ *one's leg*, se casser la jambe. (*Elec. circuit*) couper; (*heart*) briser; (*law, treaty*) violer; (*news*) annoncer; (*oath*) rompre; (*record*) battre; (*sound barrier*) franchir; (*gaming; bank*) faire sauter. ~ *one's word*, manquer de parole. (See also *broken*). ¶ *v.i.ir*, [se] casser, se briser &c; (*dawn*) poindre; (*waves*) déferler; (*clouds*) se dissiper; (*news*) éclater; (*voice*) s'altérer, s'étrangler; (*boy's voice*) muer. ~ **down**, (*Mach*.) tomber en panne; (*project*) échouer; (*pers*.) fondre en larmes. ~ **in**, (*door*) enfoncer. ~ **into**, (*house*) entrer par effraction; (*savings*) entamer. ~ **off**, rompre; détacher. ~ **out**, (*fire, war*) éclater, se déclarer. ~ **through**, percer. ~ **up**, (*weather*) se gâter; (*marriage*) se briser; (*Sch*.) entrer en vacances. **breakable**, *a*, fragile. **breakage**, *n*, rupture; (*crockery*) casse, *f*, bris, *m*. **breakaway**, *a*, (*group*) dissident, séparatiste. **breakdown**, *n*, (*Mach*.) panne, *f*; (*mental*) dépression nerveuse. ~ *gang*, équipe de dépannage. ~*truck*, dépanneuse, *f*. **breaker**, *n*, (*pers*.) casseur; briseur; (*wave*) brisant, *m*. **breakfast**, *n*, petit déjeuner, *m*. ¶ *v.i*, déjeuner, prendre le petit d. **breaking**, *n*, fracture, rupture; (*law*) violation; (*word*) manquement, *m*; (*voice*) mue, *f*. **at breakneck speed**, à une vitesse folle. **breakout**, *n*, (*jail*) évasion, *f*. **breakwater**, *n*, brise-lames, *m*.
bream, *n*, brème, *f*.
breast, *n*, (*chest*) poitrine, *f*; (*woman*) sein, *m*, mamelle, *f*. *at the* ~, au sein. (*horse*) poitrail; (*fowl*) blanc, *m*. ~*bone*, sternum, *m*. ~*-feed*, allaiter, donner le sein à. ~*plate*, plastron, *m*. ~*-pocket*, poche de poitrine, *f*. ~*-stroke*, brasse, *f*. ¶ *v.t*, (*waves &c*) affronter.
breath, *n*, haleine, *f*; souffle, *m*. ~ *of wind*, souffle d'air. *out of* ~, hors d'haleine, à bout de souffle. *get one's* ~ *back*, reprendre haleine. *take a deep* ~, respirer à fond. ~*taking*, à vous couper le souffle. **breathe**, *v.i*, respirer; souffler. ~ *hard*, haleter. ¶ *v.t*, (*sigh*) pousser; (*words*) murmurer. **breathing**, *n*, respiration, *f*. ~ *space*, le temps de respirer, *m*. **breathless**, *a*, haletant, essoufflé.
breech, *n*, (*gun*) culasse, *f*. (*Med*.) ~ [*delivery*], [accouchement par le] siège, *m*. **breeches**, *n.pl*, culotte, *f*. ~ *buoy*, bouée culotte, *f*.
breed, *n*, race, espèce, *f*. ¶ *v.t.ir*, élever; (*fig*.) engendrer, faire naître. ¶ *v.i.ir*, se reproduire, se multiplier. ~**er** (*stock*) *n*, éleveur, *m*. (*Phys*.) ~ *reactor*, réacteur nucléaire. ~**ing**, *n*, reproduction, *f*; élevage, *m*; (*pers*.) bonnes manières, *f.pl*, savoir-vivre, *m*.
breeze[1], *n*, cendres, *f.pl*. ~ *block*, parpaing, *m*.
breeze[2], *n*, brise, *f*. **breezily**, *ad*, d'un air dégagé. **breezy**, *a*, (*weather*) frais; (*pers*.) désinvolte.
Bremen, *n*, Brême, *f*.
brethren, *n.pl*, frères, *m.pl*.
breviary, *n*, bréviaire, *m*.
brevity, *n*, concision; brièveté, *f*.
brew, *v.t*, brasser; (*tea*) faire infuser. ¶ *v.i*, faire de la bière; (*storm*) couver, se préparer; (*fig*.) couver, se tramer, se mijoter. ~**er**, *n*, brasseur, *m*. ~**ery**, *n*, brasserie, *f*. ~**ing**, *n*, brassage, *m*.
briar, *n*, églantier, *m*; (*pipe, wood*) bruyère, *f*.
bribe, *n*, pot-de-vin, *m*. ¶ *v.t*, corrompre, soudoyer, suborner. ~**ry**, *n*, corruption, *f*.
brick, *n*, brique, *f*; (*pl*.—*child's game*) jeu de construction, *m*. ~ *kiln*, four à briques, *m*. ~*layer*, maçon, *m*. ~*maker*, briquetier, *m*. ~*work*, briquetage, *m*. ~*works*, briqueterie, *f*.

bridal, *a,* nuptial; de mariée. **bride,** *n,* [jeune] mariée. ~ *to be,* future mariée. ~ & ~*groom,* jeunes mariés. *m.pl.* ~*groom,* [jeune] marié. ~*groom to be,* futur m. *bridesmaid,* demoiselle d'honneur, *f.*

bridge[1], *n,* pont, *m;* (*foot & ship's*) passerelle, *f;* (*violin*) chevalet; (*nose*) dos, *m;* (*spectacles*) arcade, *f.* (*Mil.*) ~*head,* tête de pont, *f.* ¶ *v.t,* jeter un pont sur; franchir.

bridge[2], *n,* (*Cards*) bridge, *m. play* ~, jouer au bridge, faire un bridge. ~ *party,* soirée de b. ~ *player,* bridgeur, euse.

bridle, *n,* bride, *f.* ~ *path,* sentier *m,* piste cavalière, *f.* ¶ *v.t,* (*horse*) brider; (*feelings*) refréner. ¶ *v.i,* se rebiffer, regimber.

brief, *a,* bref, concis; de courte durée. ¶ *n,* cause, *f,* dossier, *m;* instructions, *f.pl.* ~*s* (*Dress*), slip, *m.* ~*case,* serviette, *f.* ¶ *v.t,* confier une cause à; (*Mil. &c*) donner des instructions à; mettre au fait (*on sth,* de qch). ~**ing,** *n,* briefing, *m.* ~**ly,** *ad,* brièvement, bref, en deux mots.

brier, *n,* églantier, *m;* (*pipe, wood*) bruyère, *f.*

brig, *n,* brick, *m.*

brigade, *n,* brigade, *f.*

brigadier, *n,* (*Mil.*) général de brigade, *m.*

brigand, *n,* brigand, *m.* ~**age,** *n,* brigandage, *m.*

bright, *a,* brillant, vif; (*weather, room*) clair; (*sunshine*) éclatant; (*colour*) vif, lumineux; (*metal*) luisant; (*pers.*) gai, animé; intelligent; (*smile*) radieux. ~ *interval* (*Met.*), éclaircie, *f.* ~**en,** *v.t,* faire briller; polir; (*pers.*) animer, égayer. ¶ *v.i,* (*weather*) s'éclaircir, se dégager. ~**ly,** *ad,* brillamment, avec éclat. ~**ness,** *n,* brillant, éclat, *m;* (*light*) intensité, *f.*

brill, *n,* barbue, *f.*

brilliance, brilliancy, *n,* éclat, brillant, *m.* **brilliant,** *a,* brillant, éclatant. ¶ *n,* brillant, *m.* ~**ly,** *ad,* brillamment; avec éclat.

brim, *n,* bord, *m.* ~ *over,* déborder. ~**-full** *or* ~**ful,** *a,* plein jusqu'aux bords, à pleins bords.

brimstone, *n,* soufre, *m.*

brindled, *a,* tacheté, moucheté.

brine, *n,* eau salée; saumure, *f.*

bring, *v.t.ir,* (*thing*) apporter; (*pers., animal*) amener; (*good & bad luck*) porter. ~ *up, down,* monter, descendre. ~ *an action against,* intenter un procès à. ~ *about,* causer, provoquer. ~ *back,* rapporter; ramener. ~ *down,* (*plane*) faire atterrir; (*enemy*) abattre. ~ *to an end,* mettre fin à. ~ *forward,* avancer. ~ *in,* (*money*) rapporter. ~ *to s.o's knowledge,* signaler à qn. ~ *off,* réaliser, mener à bien, réussir. ~ *up,* (*child*) élever; (*food*) rendre, vomir; (*the rear*) fermer la marche.

brink, *n,* bord, *m. on the* ~ *of,* à deux doigts de.

briny, *a,* saumâtre, salé.

briquet[te], *n,* briquette, *f.*

brisk†, *a,* vif, animé; (*trade*) actif. *walk* ~*ly,* marcher d'un bon pas, d'un pas allègre. ~**ness,** *n,* vivacité, animation; (*trade*) activité, *f.*

brisket, *n,* poitrine [de boeuf], *f.*

bristle, *n,* (*beard, brush*) poil, *m;* (*boar*) soie, *f.* ¶ *v.i,* se hérisser. **bristling,** & **bristly,** *a,* hérissé (*with,* de).

Britain, *n,* la Grande-Bretagne. **British,** *a,* britannique; anglais. ~ *ambassador,* ambassadeur de Grande-Bretagne, *m.* ~ *consul,* consul britannique, *m.* ~ *Isles,* îles Britanniques, *f.pl.* ¶ *n, the* ~, les Britanniques, les Anglais, *m.pl.*

Brittany, *n,* la Bretagne.

brittle, *a,* cassant, fragile. ~**ness,** *n,* fragilité, *f.*

broach, *n,* (*spit*) broche, *f;* (*tool*) perçoir, *m.* ¶ *v.t,* (*cask*) percer; (*fig.*) entamer, aborder.

broad, *a,* large; (*plain, ocean*) vaste, immense; (*accent*) prononcé; (*ribald*) grivois. ~ *bean,* fève, *f.* ~*-brimmed hat,* chapeau à grands bords, *m. in* ~ *daylight,* au grand jour, en plein jour. ~ *hint,* allusion à peine voilée. ~ *outlines,* les grandes lignes. ~*- minded,* à l'esprit large. ~*-shouldered,* large d'épaules. ~**en,** ~**en out,** (*lit. & fig.*) *v.t,* élargir. ¶ *v.i,* s'élargir.

broadcast, *n,* émission, *f.* ¶ *a,* [radio]diffusé; télévisé. ¶ *v.t,* [radio]diffuser, émettre; téléviser; (*seed*) semer à la volée. ~**ing,** *n,* radiodiffusion; télévision, *f.* ~*ing station,* station radiophonique, *f.*

broadly, *ad,* généralement, en gros. **broadness,** *n,* largeur; grossièreté, *f;* (*accent*) caractère prononcé.

broadside, *n,* (*Naut.*) (*ship*) flanc, *m.* ~ *on,* par le travers; (*gunfire & fig.*) bordée, *f.*

brocade, *n,* brocart, *m.*

broil, *v.t. & i,* (*Cook.*) griller. ~**ing,** *a,* (*sun*) brûlant. ~**er,** *n,* (*fowl*) poulet [à rôtir].

broke, *past of* **break.** ¶ *a,* (*P hard up*) fauché *P,* à sec *P.*

broken, *p.p. of* **break.** ¶ *a,* (*country*) accidenté; (*health*) délabré, (*sleep*) interrompu; (*speech*) entrecoupé; (*English, French, &c*) mauvais. ~*-down* (*car*), en panne. ~*-hearted,* au coeur brisé. ~*-winded,* poussif.

broker, *n,* courtier, agent, *m.* ~**age,** *n,* courtage, *m.*

bromide, *n,* bromure, *m.*

bronchial, *a,* des bronches, bronchique. ~ *tubes,* bronches, *f.pl.* **bronchitis,** *n,* bronchite, *f.*

bronze, *n,* bronze, *m.* ¶ *v.t,* (*metal & skin*) bronzer. ¶ *v.i,* (*get a tan*) se bronzer.

brooch, *n,* broche, *f.*

brood, *n,* couvée; nichée; (*children*) progéniture, *f.* ~ *hen,* couveuse, *f.* ~ *mare,* [jument] poulinière, *f.* ¶ *v.i,* couver; (*pers.*) broyer du noir. ~ *on sth,* ruminer qch.

brook¹, *n*, ruisseau, *m*. ~**let**, *n*, ruisselet, *m*.
brook², *v.t*, souffrir, tolérer, admettre.
broom, *n*, balai; (*Bot.*) genêt, *m*. ~*stick*, manche à balai, *m*.
broth, *n*, bouillon, *m*.
brother, *n*, frère, *m*. ~*-in-law*, beau-frère. ~*hood*, *n*, fraternité, confrérie; confraternité, *f*. ~**ly**, *a*, fraternel.
brow, *n*, (*forehead*) front; (*eye* ~) sourcil; (*hill*) sommet; (*cliff*) bord, *m*. ~**beat**, *v.t*, rudoyer; intimider.
brown, *a*, brun; marron *inv;* (*hair*) châtain; (*shoes*) marron. ~ *ale*, bière brune. ~ *bread*, pain bis, *m*. ~ *owl*, chat-huant, *m*. ~ *paper*, papier d'emballage, *m*. ~ *study*, rêverie, *f*. ~ *sugar*, cassonade, *f*. *to go* ~, (*pers.*) brunir; (*leaves*) roussir. ¶ *n*, brun, marron, *m*. ¶ *v.t*, (*Cook.*) (*meat*) faire dorer, (*sauce*) faire roussir. *I'm* ~*ed off P*, j'en ai marre *P*. ~**ish**, *a*, brunâtre.
brownie, *n*, elfe, *m*, lutin, *m*. *B*~ (*Guide*) jeannette, *f*.
browse, *v.i*. & *t*, brouter, paître. ~ *through*, (*book*) feuilleter.
bruise, *n*, bleu, *m*, contusion, meurtrissure; (*fruit*) talure, *f*. ¶ *v.t*, contusionner, meurtrir, faire un bleu à; taler; (*fig.*) meurtrir.
brunt, *n*, *bear the* ~ *of*, porter le poids de; (*attack*) soutenir le plus fort de.
brush, *n*, brosse, *f;* (*paint*) pinceau; (*broom*) balai; (*hearth &c*) balayette, *f*. *hair, tooth* ~, brosse à cheveux, à dents. *give sth a* ~, donner un coup de brosse à qch. (*clash*) échauffourée, *f*, accrochage; (*Elec.*) balai, *m;* (*fox*) queue, *f*. *give s.o. the* ~*off P*, envoyer promener *ou* balader *P* qn. ~*wood*, broussailles, *f.pl*, taillis, *m*. ¶ *v.t*, brosser, balayer; (*mud off*) décrotter; (*graze*) effleurer, frôler, raser. ~ *one's hair* &c, se brosser les cheveux &c. ~ *up one's French*, se remettre au français.
brusque, *a*, brusque. ~**ly**, *ad*, avec brusquerie.
Brussels, *n*, Bruxelles, *f*. ~ *sprouts*, choux de Bruxelles, *m.pl*.
brutal†, *a*, brutal. ~**ity**, *n*, brutalité, *f*. **brute**, *n*, (*animal*) brute, bête, *f;* (*pers.*) brute, *f*, brutal, *m*. ~ *beast*, bête brute, *f*. ~ *force*, force brutale, *f*. **brutish**†, *a*, brutal, bestial.
bubble, *n*, bulle, *f;* (*in liquid*) bouillon, *m;* (*in metal, glass*) soufflure, *f;* (*fig.*) chimère, *f*. ¶ *v.i*, bouillonner; pétiller.
buccaneer, *n*, boucanier, pirate, *m*.
buck, *n*, (*deer*) daim; (*rabbit, hare &c*) mâle; (*pers.*) dandy, élégant, *m;* (*Am. P*) dollar, *m*. *pass the* ~ *P*, se soustraire à la responsabilité. ~*skin*, peau de daim, *f*, daim, *m*. ~*wheat*, sarrasin, blé noir, *m*. ¶ *v.i*, (*horse*) lancer une ruade. ~ *up*, (*hurry*) se remuer, se grouiller *P*. ¶ *v.t*, (*cheer*) ravigoter *P*.
bucket, *n*, seau; (*dredger &c*) godet, *m*. ¶ *v.i*, (*rain*) *it's* ~*ing down*, il pleut à seaux. ~ *seat*, siège-baquet, *m*.
buckle, *n*, boucle, *f*. ¶ *v.t*, boucler; (*metal*) fausser, gauchir; (*wheel*) voiler. ¶ *v.i*, gauchir; se voiler.
buckram, *n*, bougran, *m*.
bucolic, *a*, bucolique.
bud, *n*, bourgeon, bouton, *m;* (*Hort. graft*) écusson, *m*. ¶ *v.t*, (*Hort.*) greffer, écussonner. ¶ *v.i*, bourgeonner. ~**ding**, *a*, (*artist &c*) en herbe; naissant.
Buddhist, *a*, bouddhique. ¶ *n*, Bouddhiste, *m,f*.
buddy *P*, *n*, copain, *m*.
budge, *v.i*, bouger.
budget, *n*, budget, *m*. ¶ *v.i*, ~ **for**, porter au b.
buff, (*colour*) *a*. & *n*, chamois, *m*. ~ [*leather*], buffle, *m*, peau de buffle, *f*. *in the* ~ *P*, à poil *P*. ¶ *v.t*, polir. **buffalo**, *n*, buffle, *m*.
buffer, *n*, tampon; (*in station*) butoir, *m*. ~ *state*, état tampon, *m*.
buffet¹, *n*, (*slap*) gifle, *f*, soufflet; (*fist*) coup de poing, *m*. ¶ *v.t*, frapper; (*wind*) secouer.
buffet², *n*, (*sideboard*) buffet, *m*. ~ *car*, voiture-buffet, *f*, buffet. ~ *supper*, souper-buffet, *m*.
buffoon, *n*, bouffon, pitre, *m*, ~**ery**, *n*, bouffonnerie, *f*.
bug, *n*, punaise, *f;* (*P*) insecte, *m*, bestiole *P*, *f*. ~*-ridden*, infesté de punaises. ¶ *v.t*, (*room*) installer des micros dans. ~**bear**, *n*, epouvantail, cauchemar, *m*.
bugger, *n*, (*Law*) pédéraste, *m*. (*P* blighter*) *silly* ~, pauvre con *P**. ~ [*it*]! *P**, merde! *P**. ~ *off! P**, fous-moi le camp! *P**.
bugle, *n*, clairon, *m*. ~ *call*, sonnerie de clairon, *f*. **bugler**, *n*, clairon, *m*.
build, *n*, carrure, charpente, *f*. *of sturdy* ~, (*man*) bien bâti, solidement charpenté, costaud. ¶ *v.t.ir*, bâtir, construire. ~ *up*, édifier; (*theory*) échafauder; accumuler, augmenter; (*strength*) prendre des forces. ~**er**, *n*, constructeur, entrepreneur [en bâtiment], *m*. ~**ing**, *n*, construction, *f*, bâtiment, édifice; immeuble, *m*. ~ *materials*, matériaux de construction, *m.pl*. ~ *plot*, terrain à bâtir, *m*. ~ *site*, chantier [de construction], *m*. ~ *society*, société de crédit immobilier, *f*.
built, *past & p.p. of* **build**. ¶ *a*, ~*-in*, (*cupboard &c*) encastré. ~*-up area*, agglomération, *f*.
bulb, *n*, (*Bot.*) bulbe, *f*, oignon, *m;* (*garlic*) tête; (*Elec.*) ampoule, *f;* (*Chem.*) ballon, *m*. ~**ous**, *a*, bulbeux.
Bulgaria, *n*, la Bulgarie. **Bulgarian**, *a*, bulgare. ¶ *n*, Bulgare, *m,f*.
bulge, *n*, bombement, renflement, ventre, *m;* (*birth rate*) poussée, *f*. ¶ *v.i*, bomber, se renfler, faire saillie. **bulging**, *a*, (*forehead*) bombé; (*eyes*) protubérant; (*bag &c*) bourré.
bulk, *n*, volume; masse; grosseur, *f;* le [plus] gros, la plus grande partie. *in* ~, en gros; (*unpacked*) en vrac. ~*head*, cloison, *f*. ~**y**, *a*,

volumineux; encombrant.
bull, *n,* taureau, *m.* ~ *calf,* taurillon. (*elephant &c*) mâle, *m;* (*Stk Ex.*) haussier, *m.* *P* (& ~ *shit P**) (*spit & polish*) fourbissage, *m;* (*nonsense*) conneries *P, f.pl.* ~ *dog,* bouledogue, *m.* ~ *fight,* course de taureaux, *f.* **bull's-eye,** (*target*) noir, *m. score a* ~, (*& fig.*) faire mouche.
bulldoze, *v.t,* passer au bulldozer. **bulldozer,** *n,* bulldozer, *m.*
bullet, *n,* balle, *f.* ~ *proof,* (*vest*) pare-balles, *inv;* (*car*) blindé.
bulletin, *n,* bulletin, communiqué, *m.*
bullfinch, *n,* bouvreuil, *m.*
bullion, *n,* or en barre; or (*ou* argent) en lingots, *m.*
bullock, *n,* bœuf, *m.*
bully, *n,* tyran, brutal, *m;* (*Sch.*) [petite] brute, *f.* ¶ *v.t,* malmener, brutaliser, persécuter.
bulrush, *n,* jonc, *m.*
bulwark, *n,* rempart; (*Naut.*) pavois, *m.*
bum[1] *Am P, n,* clochard, fainéant, *m.* ¶ *a,* moche *P,* minable *P.*
bum[2] *P, n,* derrière, *m.*
bumble-bee, *n,* bourdon, *m.*
bumf *P, n,* paperasses, *f.pl.*
bump, *n,* (*ground*) bosse, *f;* (*shock*) choc, heurt; (*jolt*) cahot, *m.* ¶ *v.t,* (*car*) heurter. *to* ~ *one's head,* se cogner la tête. ¶ *v.i,* ~ *along,* cahoter. ¶ *v.t,* ~ *off P,* liquider *P.*
bumper, *n,* (*brim-full glass*) rasade, *f;* (*Mot.*) pare-chocs, *m inv.* ¶ *a,* (*crop*) exceptionnel.
bumpkin, *n,* rustre, lourdaud, *m.*
bumptious, *a,* suffisant. ~**ness,** *n,* suffisance, *f.*
bun, *n,* petit pain au lait; (*hair*) chignon, *m.*
bunch, *n,* (*flowers*) bouquet, *m;* (*asparagus*) botte; (*grapes*) grappe, *f;* (*bananas*) régime; (*keys*) trousseau; (*people*) groupe, *m,* bande, *f.* ¶ *v.i,* ~ *together,* se grouper, se serrer.
bundle, *n,* paquet, ballot; (*wood*) fagot, *m;* (*bank notes, letters*) liasse, *f.* ¶ *v.t,* (& ~ *up*) empaqueter, mettre en paquet, liasse &c.
bung & ~ **hole,** *n,* bonde, *f.* ¶ *v.t,* (& ~ *up*) boucher; (*P throw*) flanquer *P.*
bungalow, *n,* bungalow, *m.*
bungle, *n,* bousillage, gâchis, *m.* ¶ *v.t,* bousiller, gâcher. **bungler,** *n,* bousilleur, euse, maladroit, e.
bunion, *n,* oignon, *m.*
bunk, *n,* couchette, *f. do a* ~ *P,* mettre les bouts *P.*
bunker, *n,* (*ship*) soute, *f;* (*Golf*) bunker, *m.*
bunkum *P, n,* blague, *f,* foutaises *P, f.pl.*
bunting[1], *n,* drapeaux, *m.pl.,* pavoisement, *m.*
bunting[2], *n,* (*bird*) bruant, *m.*
buoy, *n,* bouée, *f.* ¶ *v.t,* (*channel*) baliser. ~ *up,* soutenir. ~**ancy,** *n,* (*ship*) flottabilité; (*liquid*) poussée, *f.* ~**ant,** *a,* flottable; (*pers.*) animé, plein d'entrain.
bur[r] & burdock, *n,* (*Bot.*) bardane, *f.*
burden, *n,* fardeau, *m,* charge, *f,* faix; (*years*) poids, *m;* (*ship*) port, tonnage; (*song*) refrain, *m.* ¶ *v.t,* charger; accabler. ~**some,** *a,* lourd, écrasant.
bureaucracy, *n,* bureaucratie, *f.* **bureaucrat,** *n,* bureaucrate, *m,f.*
burglar, *n,* cambrioleur, euse. ~ *alarm,* sonnerie antivol, *f.* ~**y,** *n,* cambriolage, *m.* **burgle,** *v.t,* cambrioler.
Burgundian, *a,* bourguignon. ¶ *n,* Bourguignon, ne.
Burgundy, *n,* la Bourgogne; (*wine*) bourgogne, vin de B., *m.*
burial, *n,* enterrement, *m,* sépulture, *f.* ~ *ground,* cimetière, *m.* ~ *place,* lieu de sépulture, *m.* ~ *service,* office des morts, *m.*
burlesque, *n,* caricature, *f,* burlesque, *m.* ¶ *v.t,* tourner en ridicule.
burly, *a,* solidement bâti; costaud *P.*
Burma, *n,* la Birmanie. **Burmese,** *a,* birman. ¶ *n,* Birman, e.
burn, *n,* brûlure, *f.* ¶ *v.t.ir,* brûler; (*house, town*) incendier, mettre le feu à; (*to a cinder*) calciner; (*acid*) ronger. ~ *one's hand,* se brûler la main. ~ *one's fingers,* (*fig.*) se faire échauder. ~ *one's boats,* brûler ses vaisseaux. ¶ *v.i,* brûler. ~**er,** *n,* (*stove*) brûleur; (*gas lamp*) bec, *m.* ~**ing,** *a,* en flammes, incendié; (*fig.*) brûlant, ardent. ¶ *n,* (*of town* &c) incendie, *m. there's a smell of* ~, ça sent le brûlé.
burnish, *v.t,* (*metal*) brunir, polir.
burnt, *a:* ~ *almond,* praline, *f.* ~ *offering,* holocauste, *m.* ~ *Sienna,* terre de Sienne brûlée, *f.*
burr, *n,* (*Tech.*) bavure, barbe, *f. to speak with a* ~, grasseyer.
burrow, *n,* terrier, *m.* ¶ *v.i,* creuser [la terre]; (*fig.*) fouiller.
bursar, *n,* (*Sch.*) économe, *m,f;* (*student*) boursier, ère. ~**y,** *n,* bourse, *f.*
burst, *n,* (*shell*) explosion, *f,* éclatement; (*laughter, anger*) éclat; (*passion &c*) transport, élan, *m.* ¶ *v.t.ir,* faire éclater, [faire] crever; rompre. ¶ *v.i,* éclater, faire explosion; (*tyre*) crever; (*rush*) se précipiter. ~ *in,* faire irruption. ~ *into tears,* fondre en larmes. ~ *out,* s'exclamer; (*laughing*) éclater de rire.
bury, *v.t,* enterrer, ensevelir.
bus, *n,* autobus, bus *P;* (*coach*) [auto]car, *m;* (*P car*) bagnole, *P, f.* ~ *conductor,* receveur d'autobus. ~ *driver,* conducteur d'a. ~ *stop,* arrêt d'a.
bush[1], *n,* buisson, arbuste, *m;* (*scrub*) (*Africa*) brousse, *f,* (*Corsica*) maquis, *m.*
bush[2], *n,* (*Mach.*) bague, *f.*
bushel, *n,* boisseau, *m.* (= 8 gallons).
bushy, *a,* (*beard*) touffu; (*ground*) broussailleux.
busily, *a,* activement.
business, *n,* affaires, *f.pl. a small* ~, un petit

commerce. ~ *of the day*, ordre du jour, *m. to know one's* ~, connaître son affaire, s'y connaître. *quite a* ~, toute une affaire. *a bad* ~, une sale histoire. *a strange* ~, une drôle d'histoire. *that's none of my* ~, cela ne me regarde pas. *mind your own* ~, mêlez-vous de vos affaires. ~ *hours*, heures d'ouverture, *f.pl.* ~*man*, homme d'affaires. ~ *trip*, voyage d'affaires. *the* ~ *world*, le monde des affaires. ~**like**, *a*, pratique, méthodique; sérieux.

bust[1], *n*, buste, *m;* poitrine, *f.* ~ *measurement*, tour de poitrine, *m.*

bust[2] *P*, *a*, cassé, fichu *P; (penniless)* fauché *P. go* ~ *P*, faire faillite. ¶ *n*, *(spree)* bringue *P, f.* ¶ *v.i*, ~ *up P*, *(with friends)* se brouiller.

bustard, *n*, outarde, *f.*

bustle, *n*, affairement, remue-ménage, *m.* ¶ *v.i*, s'affairer.

busy, *a*, occupé *(doing*, à faire); affairé, actif. ¶ *v.t*, ~ *o.s*, s'occuper (à faire, à qch). ~**body**, *to be a* ~, fourrer son nez partout.

but, *c*, mais; sans: *(I never hear that song)* ~ *I think of you*, sans penser à vous. que... (ne): *(never a week passes)* ~ *she writes*,... qu'elle n'écrive. ¶ *ad*, *(only)* seulement, ne... que. *(liter.) he is* ~ *a child*, ce n'est qu'un enfant. ¶ *pr*, *(except)* sauf, excepté, à part; sinon. ~ *for*, sans. *no one* ~ *you*, personne sauf vous. ¶ *n*, mais, *m.*

butcher, *n*, boucher, *m.* ~*'s boy*, garçon boucher, *m.* ~*'s meat*, viande de boucherie, *f.* ~*'s shop*, boucherie, *f.* ~*'s wife*, bouchère, *f.* ¶ *v.t*, *(animal)* abattre; *(pers.)* égorger, massacrer. ~**y**, *n*, boucherie, *f.*

butler, *n*, sommelier; maître d'hôtel, *m.*

butt[1], *n*, *(cask)* tonneau; *(end)* [gros] bout, *m; (rifle)* crosse, *f; (cigarette)* mégot, *m.*

butt[2], *n*, *(target)* cible, *f.* ~*s*, champ de tir, *m.* *(of s.o's wit)* objet de risée, *m; (ram &c)* coup de corne, coup de tête, *m.* ¶ *v.t*, donner un coup de corne *ou* de tête à. ~ *in*, intervenir.

butter, *n*, beurre, *m.* ~ *dish*, beurrier, *m.* ~ *milk*, babeurre, *m.* ¶ *v.t*, beurrer.

buttercup, *n*, bouton d'or, *m.*

butterfly, *n*, papillon, *m.* ~*-stroke*, brasse papillon, *f.*

buttocks, *n.pl*, *(pers.)* fesses, *f.pl; (animal)* croupe, *f.*

button, *n*, bouton, *m.* ~*s*, *(boy)* groom, chasseur; *m.* ~*hole*, boutonnière, *f.* ~*hole stitch*, point de boutonnière, *m.* *(v.t) to* ~*hole*, *(pers.)* accrocher. ~*hook*, tire-bouton, *m.* ~ *mushroom*, champignon de Paris, *m.* ¶ *v.t*, boutonner.

buttress, *n*, contrefort, éperon; *(flying)* arc-boutant, *m.* ¶ *v.t*, arc-bouter; soutenir.

buxom, *a*, rondelet, opulent, bien en chair.

buy, *v.t.ir*, acheter, acquérir; *(bribe)* acheter, corrompre. ~ *back*, racheter. ~ *out*, *(Fin.)* désintéresser. ~ *up*, acheter en bloc, rafler *P.* ~**er**, *n*, acheteur, euse, acquéreur, *m.* ~*'s market*, marché acheteur. ~**ing**, *n*, achat, *m*, acquisition, *f.*

buzz, *n*, bourdonnement, vrombissement, *m; (P phone call)* coup de fil, *m.* ¶ *v.i*, bourdonner, vrombir; *(ears)* tinter. ~ *off P*, ficher le camp *P.*

by, *pr*, *(agent)* par: *helped* ~ *his brother*, aidé par son frère; *(method)* par, en, à. ~ *bicycle*, à bicyclette, en vélo. ~ *car*, en voiture. ~ *train*, par le train, en train. *(near)* près de, à côté de. *(via)* ~ *Calais*, par Calais. *pay* ~ *the hour*, payer à l'heure. ~ *Thursday*, avant jeudi. ~ *day*, *night*, le jour, la nuit. *(sell)* ~ *the metre*, au mètre. ¶ *ad*, *(near)* près. *close* ~, tout près. ~ *&* ~, bientôt, tout à l'heure. ~ *the* ~[*e*], ~ *the way*, à propos. *to get* ~, *(cope)* se débrouiller. *to put* ~, mettre de côté.

by-,... ~*-election*, élection partielle. ~[*e*]*-law*, arrêté municipal, *m.* ~*gone*, passé, d'autrefois. ~*path*, sentier écarté, *m.* ~*-product*, sous-produit, *m.* ~*-road*, chemin détourné, *m.* ~*stander*, spectateur, trice assistant, e. ~*word for*, synonyme de.

bye-bye *P*, *i*, au revoir, salut *P. go to* ~*s*, *(baby)* faire dodo.

bypass, *n*, route de détournement, *f.* ¶ *v.t*, *(town)* contourner, éviter.

Byzantine, *a*, byzantin. **Byzantium**, *n*, Byzance, *f.*

C

C *(Mus.) letter*, ut, do, *m.* ~ *clef*, clef d'ut, *f.*

cab, *n*, fiacre, taxi, *m. by* ~ en f., en t. *(truck, Rly)* cabine, *f.* ~ *driver*, cocher [de fiacre], chauffeur de taxi, *m.* ~ *rank*, station de fiacres, de taxis, *f.*

cabal, *n*, cabale, *f.*

cabaret, *n*, cabaret, *m.* ~ *show*, spectacle de c., *m.*

cabbage, *n*, chou, *m.* ~ *lettuce*, laitue pommée, *f.* ~ *white (butterfly)*, piéride du chou, *f.*

cabin, *n,* (*hut*) cabane, hutte, case, *f;* (*ship*) cabine, *f.* ~ *boy,* mousse, *m.* ~ *cruiser,* yacht de croisière, *m.* ~ *trunk,* malle de cabine, *f.*
cabinet, *n,* meuble, *m;* (*glass-fronted*) vitrine, *f;* (*filing*) classeur, *m;* (*Pol.*) Conseil des ministres, cabinet, *m.* ~ *maker,* ébéniste, *m.* ~ *minister,* membre du cabinet, *m.*
cable, *n,* câble, *m.* ~*car,* téléférique, *m.* ~ *railway,* funiculaire, *m.* ¶ (*Tel.*) *v.t,* câbler, télégraphier.
caboodle *P, n, the whole* ~, tout le saint-frusquin *P.*
cacao, *n,* cacao. ~ [*tree*], cacaoyer, *m.*
cache, *n,* (*place*) cachette, *f.* **cachet,** *n,* cachet, *m.*
cackle, *n,* caquet, *m.* ¶ *v.i,* caqueter.
cactus, *n,* cactus, *m.*
cad, *n,* goujat, mufle, *m.*
caddie, *n,* (*Golf*) caddie, *m.*
caddy, *n,* boîte à thé, *f.*
cadence & cadenza, *n,* cadence, *f.*
cadet, *n,* cadet; élève officier, *m.*
cadge, *v.t,* taper *P* (*5F from s.o,* qn de 5F); écornifler *O.* **cadger,** *n,* parasite, *m;* (*meals*) pique-assiette, *m,f;* tapeur, euse *P.*
Cadiz, *n,* Cadix, *m.*
Caesarean [section], *n,* (*Med.*) césarienne, *f.*
cage, *n,* cage; (*lift*) cabine, *f.* ~ *bird,* oiseau de volière, *n.* ¶ *v.t,* encager, mettre en cage.
cagey *P, a,* dissimulé, cachottier; prudent.
cairn, *n,* cairn, *m.*
Cairo, *n,* le Caire.
caisson, *n,* caisson, *m.*
cajole, *v.t,* cajoler, amadouer. ~**ry,** *n,* cajolerie, *f.*
cake, *n,* gâteau, *m;* (*small*) pâtisserie, *f.* ~ *of soap,* savonnette, *f,* pain de savon, *m. cattle* ~, tourteau, *m.* ¶ *v.t,* ~*ed,* (*mud*) séché; (*blood*) coagulé.
calabash, *n,* calebasse, *f.*
calamitous, *a,* calamiteux, catastrophique. **calamity,** *n,* calamité, *f.*
calcareous, *a,* calcaire.
calcine, *v.t,* calciner.
calcium, *n,* calcium, *m.*
calculate *v.t,* calculer; évaluer. ¶ *v.i,* faire des calculs. ~**d,** *a,* délibéré. ~*d to,* propre à, de nature à. **calculating,** *a,* (*pers.*) calculateur. ~ *machine,* machine à calculer, *f.* **calculation & calculus,** *n,* calcul, *m.*
calendar, *n,* calendrier, *m.* ~ *year,* année civile, *f.*
calf[1], *n,* veau, *m.* ~[*skin*], [cuir de] veau, *m.*
calf[2], (*leg*) mollet, *m.*
calibrate, *v.t,* calibrer. **calibre,** *n,* calibre, *m.*
calico, *n,* calicot, *m.*
California, *n,* la Californie. **Californian,** *a,* californien. ¶ *n,* Californien, ne.
calipers, *n.pl,* compas d'épaisseur; (*Med.*) appareil orthopédique, *m.*
caliph, *n,* calife, *m.*
call, *n,* cri, appel, *m;* (*phone*) coup de téléphone, coup de fil, *m;* (*bugle*) sonnerie; (*on s.o*) visite; (*Rel.*) vocation; (*Bridge*) annonce, *f. port of* ~, escale, *f.* ~*box,* cabine téléphonique, *f.* ~*boy* (*Theat.*) avertisseur. ~ *girl,* prostituée, call-girl. ~*-up,* (*Mil.*) convocation, mobilisation, *f.* ¶ *v.t,* appeler, nommer. *be* ~*ed,* s'appeler. ~ *s.o. a fool,* traiter qn d'idiot. (*summon*) (*meeting*) convoquer, (*doctor, taxi*) faire venir, appeler; (*waken*) réveiller; (*phone*) téléphoner à qn. ~ *into play,* mettre en jeu. ~ *in question,* mettre en doute. ~ *a halt to,* mettre fin à. ~ **at,** (*butcher's*) passer chez (le boucher); (*ship*) faire escale à. ~ **back,** rappeler. ~ **in,** faire venir. ~ **for,** demander; (*fig.*) exiger. ~ **on,** rendre visite à. ~ **off,** annuler, rompre. ~ **out,** (*workers on strike*) donner la consigne de grève. ~ **up,** (*Mil.*) mobiliser. ~**ing,** *n,* métier, *m,* vocation, *f.*
callous, *a,* endurci, sans pitié. ~ *to,* insensible à. (*skin*) calleux. **callus,** *n,* durillon, *m.*
callow, *a,* inexpérimenté. *a* ~ *youth,* un blanc-bec, *m.* ~ *youth,* la verte jeunesse.
calm, *a,* calme, tranquille. ¶ *v.t,* calmer. ¶ *v.i,* ~ *down,* se calmer. *keep* ~*!* du calme! ~**ly,** *ad,* tranquillement. ~**[ness],** *n,* calme, *m,* tranquillité, *f.*
calorie, *n,* calorie, *f.*
calumniate, *v.t,* calomnier. **calumny,** *n,* calomnie, *f.*
Calvary (*place*) *n,* Calvaire, *m.* **calvary** (*representation*) *n,* calvaire, *m.*
calve, *v.i,* vêler, mettre bas.
calyx, *n,* calice, *m.*
cam, *n,* came, *f.* ~*shaft,* arbre à cames, *m.*
camber, *n,* bombement, *m,* cambrure, *f.*
cambric, *n,* batiste, *f.*
came, *past of* **come.**
camel, *n,* chameau, *m.* ~ *driver,* chamelier, *m.* ~ *hair,* poil de chameau, *m.*
camellia, *n,* camélia, *m.*
cameo, *n,* camée, *m.*
camera, *n,* appareil [photographique], *m;* (*movie*) caméra, *f.* (*Law*) *in* ~, à huis clos. ~*man,* caméraman, *m.* ~ *obscura,* chambre noire, *f.* ~*work,* prise de vues, *f.*
camomile, *n,* camomille, *f.*
camouflage, *n,* camouflage, *m.* ¶ *v.t,* camoufler.
camp[1], *n,* camp, *m.* ~ *bed,* lit de camp, *m.* ~ *site,* [terrain de] camping, *m.* ~ *stool,* pliant, *m.* ¶ *v.i,* camper. *go* ~*ing,* faire du camping. ~**ing,** *n,* camping, *m.*
camp[2] *P, a,* affecté; cabotin. ¶ *v.t, to* ~ *it up,* cabotiner *P.*
campaign, *n,* campagne, *f.* ¶ *v.i,* ~ *for, against,* mener une campagne pour, contre. ~**er,** *n,* (*old*) vétéran; (*for a cause*) militant, e.
campanula, *n,* campanule, *f.*
camphor, *n,* camphre, *m.* ~**ate,** *v.t,* camphrer.

can[1], *n,* bidon, *m;* (*food, drink*) boîte; (*garbage*) poubelle, boîte à ordures, *f.* ¶ *v.t,* mettre en boîte(s), m. en conserve.
can[2], *v. modal ir,* pouvoir; (*omit with verbs of perception*) ~ *you see him?* vous le voyez? *he could be heard shouting,* on l'entendait crier. (*know how to*) savoir: *she* ~ *read,* elle sait lire; ~ *you swim?* savez-vous nager? (*permission*) *you* ~ (*may*) *go,* vous pouvez partir; *could I speak to...?* est-ce que je pourrais parler à...? *he could be dead,* il se peut qu'il soit mort. *you could* (*might*) *have warned me,* vous auriez pu m'avertir. (*neg. of must*) *he can't be very strong,* il ne doit pas être très fort. *he can't have found it,* il n'a pas dû le trouver. *Cf: he couldn't find it,* il n'a pas pu le trouver. *he could have come yesterday,* il aurait pu venir hier.
Canada, *n,* le Canada. **Canadian,** *a,* canadien. ¶ *n,* Canadien, ne.
canal, *n,* canal, *m.* ~**ize,** *v.t,* canaliser.
canary, *n,* serin, e, canari, *m.* ~ *seed,* millet, *m. the C~ Islands, the Canaries,* les [îles] Canaries, *f.pl.*
cancel, *v.t,* (*delete*) biffer, rayer; (*stamp*) oblitérer; (*event*) annuler, décommander; (*train*) supprimer; (*contract*) résilier.
cancer (*Med.*) *n,* cancer, *m.* ~**ous,** *a,* cancéreux.
candelabra, *n,* candélabre, *m.*
candid†, *a,* sincère, franc.
candidate, *n,* candidat, e.
candied, *a,* (*fruit*) glacé, confit. ~ *peel,* écorce confite, *f.*
candle, *n,* bougie, chandelle; (*church*) cierge, *f.* ~ *grease,* suif, *m. a 60 c.p. lamp,* une lampe de 60 bougies. ~*stick,* bougeoir; chandelier, *m.*
candour, *n,* sincérité, franchise, *f.*
candy, *n,* (*Am.*) bonbon *m.* [*sugar*] ~, sucre candi, *m.*
cane, *n,* (*walking stick*) canne; badine, *f,* jonc, *m;* (*basketry*) rotin; (*Sch.*) fouet, *m.* ~ *sugar,* sucre de canne, *m.* ¶ *v.t,* (*Sch.*) fouetter; (*chair*) canner.
canine, *a,* canin.
canister, *n,* boîte [métallique], *f.*
canker, *n,* (*Med.*) ulcère; (*lit., fig.*) chancre, *m.*
cannibal, *n. & a,* cannibale, anthropophage, *m,f.*
cannon, *n,* canon; (*Bil.*) carambolage, *m.* ~*ball,* boulet, *m.* ~ *shot,* coup de canon, *m.* ¶ *v.i,* (*Bil.*) caramboler. ~**ade,** *n,* canonnade, *f.*
canny, *a,* prudent; malin, rusé.
canoe, *n,* canoë, *m;* (*dugout*) pirogue, *f;* (*sport*) kayak. ¶ *v.i,* faire du canoë, du kayak.
canon, *n,* (*Eccl., Mus.*) canon; (*rule*) canon, critère, *m,* règle, *f;* (*pers.*) chanoine, *m.* ~ *law,* droit canon, *m.* ~**ize,** *v.t,* canoniser.
canopy, *n,* (*throne*) dais; (*Arch., bed*) baldaquin, *m;* (*fig.*) voûte, *f.*
cant[1], *n,* langage hypocrite, *m,* tartuferie, *f.*
cant[2], *n,* pente, inclinaison, *f.* ¶ *v.t,* incliner, pencher.
cantankerous, *a,* revêche, hargneux.
cantata, *n,* cantate, *f.*
canteen, *n,* cantine, *f;* (*flask*) bidon, *m;* (*mess tin*) gamelle; (*cutlery*) ménagère, *f.*
canter, *n,* petit galop, *m.* ¶ *v.i,* aller au petit galop.
Canterbury, *n,* Cantorbéry. ~ *bell,* campanule, *f.*
canticle, *n,* cantique, *m.*
cantilever, *n,* (*Engin.*) cantilever; (*Arch.*) corbeau, *m.*
canto, *n,* chant, *m.* **cantor,** *n,* chantre, *m.*
canvas, *n,* (*Naut., Art*) toile, *f;* (*Emb.*) canevas, *m. under* ~, sous la tente.
canvass, *v.i,* (*Pol.*) solliciter des suffrages *ou* des voix. ~**er,** démarcheur, *m.* ~**ing,** démarchage électoral, *m.*
canyon, cañon, *n,* cañon, *m,* gorge, *f.*
cap, *n,* (*peaked*) casquette, *f;* (*sailor*) bonnet; (*officer*) képi; (*soldier*) calot, *m;* (*lace*) coiffe; (*judge*) toque; (*skull*) calotte; (*bottle*) capsule, *f;* (*radiator*) bouchon, *m.* ¶ *v.t,* (*pers.*) coiffer; (*bottle*) capsuler; (*outdo*) surpasser.
capability, *n,* capacité, aptitude, *f.* **capable,** *a,* (*pers.*) capable (de), apte (à); compétent; (*event*) susceptible (de).
capacious, *a,* spacieux, vaste. **capacity,** *n,* capacité; (*ability*) aptitude, capacité[s], *f.*[*pl*]; (*status*) titre, *m,* qualité, *f. in his* ~ *as mayor,* en sa qualité de maire. *filled to* ~, (*hall &c*) comble *inv,* bondé.
cape[1], *n,* pèlerine, cape, *f.*
cape[2], *n,* (*Geog.*) cap, *m,* promontoire, *f. the C~ of Good Hope,* le cap de Bonne-Espérance. *C~ Town,* le Cap.
caper[1], *n,* cabriole, gambade, *f.* ¶ *v.i,* gambader.
caper[2], *n,* (*Cook.*) câpre, *f.*
capillary, *a,* capillaire.
capital†, *a,* capital; *P* fameux; (*letter &* ~ *letter, n*) majuscule, capitale, *f.* ¶ *n,* (*country*) [ville] capitale, *f;* (*department*) chef-lieu, *m;* (*Arch.*) chapiteau, *m;* (*Fin.*) capital, *m,* capitaux, fonds, *m.pl.* ~ *& labour,* le capital & la main d'oeuvre. ~ *gains,* plus-values [en capital] *f.pl.* ~ *transfer tax,* ≏ droits de succession, *m.pl.* ~**ist,** *n,* capitaliste, *m,f.* ~**ize,** *v.t,* capitaliser. ~ *on* (*fig.*) tirer parti de.
capitulate, *v.i,* capituler.
capon, *n,* chapon, *m.*
caprice, *n,* caprice, *m.* **capricious,** *a,* capricieux.
capsicum, *n,* piment, *m.*
capsize, *v.t,* renverser; (*boat*) faire chavirer. ¶ *v.i,* se renverser; chavirer.
capstan, *n,* cabestan, *m.* ~ *lathe,* tour revolver, *m.*
capsule, *n,* capsule, *f.*
captain, *n,* (*Mil., Naut., Sport*) capitaine; (*Nav.*)

capitaine de vaisseau, *m*.
caption, *n,* sous-titre, *m*.
captious, *a,* chicaneur, vétilleux.
captivate, *v.t,* captiver. **captive,** *a,* captif. ¶ *n,* captif, ive. **captivity,** *n,* captivité, *f*. **capture,** *n,* capture, prise, *f*. ¶ *v.t,* capturer, prendre, faire prisonnier.
Capuchin friar, nun, capucin, e.
car, *n,* (*Mot.*) voiture, automobile, auto, *f;* (*tram*~) [voiture de] tramway, tram, *m;* (*Rly*) wagon. *dining* ~, wagon-restaurant. *sleeping* ~, wagon-lit, *m*. ~ *park,* parking, *m*.
caramel, *n,* caramel, *m*.
carapace, *n,* carapace, *f*.
carat, *n,* carat, *m*. *18* ~ *gold,* or à 18 carats, *m*.
caravan, *n,* caravane; (*gipsy*) roulotte, *f*. ~ *site,* camping pour caravanes, *m*.
caraway, *n,* carvi, *m*. ~ *seed,* graine de c., *f*.
carbide, *n,* carbure, *m*.
carbine, *n,* carabine, *f,* mousqueton, *m*.
carbohydrates, *n.pl,* farineux, féculents, *m.pl*.
carbolic acid, *n,* phénol, *m*.
carbon, *n,* (*Chem.*) carbone; (*Elec.*) charbon, *m*. ~ [*copy*], carbone, *f*. ~ *monoxide,* oxyde de carbone, *m*. ~ [*paper*], papier carbone, *m*. **carbonate,** *n,* carbonate, *m*. **carbonic,** *a,* carbonique. **carboniferous,** *a,* carbonifère. **carbonize,** *v.t,* carboniser.
carboy, *n,* bonbonne [clissée], *f*.
carbuncle, *n,* (*Med.*) anthrax, furoncle, *m*.
carburettor, *n,* carburateur, *m*.
carcass, *n,* carcasse, *f,* cadavre, *m;* (*ship*) carcasse.
card[1], *n,* carte; (*index* ~) fiche, *f*. *game of* ~*s,* partie de cartes, *f*. *play* ~*s,* jouer aux cartes. *to get one's* ~*s,* être mis à la porte. ~*board,* carton, *m*. ~ *index,* fichier, *m*. ~ *sharper,* tricheur, euse. ~ *table,* table de jeu, *f*. ~ *trick,* tour de cartes, *m*.
card[2], *n,* (*wool*) carde, *f*. ¶ *v.t,* carder.
cardigan, *n,* cardigan, gilet, *m*.
cardinal, *a,* cardinal. ¶ *n,* cardinal, *m*.
care, *n,* (*heed*) soin, *m,* attention, *f;* (*charge*) soins, *m.pl,* charge, garde, *f;* (*anxiety*) souci, *m*. *take* ~*!* [faites] attention! ~ *of,* c/o, chez, aux bons soins de, c/o. *driving without due* ~ *& attention,* conduite négligente, *f*. *take* ~ *of* (*look after*) s'occuper de, se charger de. ~*taker,* gardien, ne, concierge, *m,f*. ~*worn,* rongé par les soucis. ¶ *v.i,* ~ *about,* se soucier de, s'intéresser à. *I don't* ~, ça m'est égal. *I couldn't* ~ *less,* je m'en fiche pas mal. ~ *for,* (*the sick*) soigner; (*garden*) entretenir. (*like*) *I don't* ~ *for that,* cela ne me plaît pas, cela ne me dit rien.
career, *n,* carrière, *f*. *in full* ~, en pleine course. ~*s guidance,* orientation professionnelle, *f*. ¶ *v.i,* ~ *along,* aller à toute vitesse.
careful†, *a,* soigneux (de), attentif (à); prudent. ~**ness,** *n,* soin, *m,* attention, *f*. **careless,** *a,* insouciant; négligent. ~**ly,** *ad,* négligemment. ~**ness,** *n,* négligence, *f,* manque d'attention, *m*.
caress, *n,* caresse, *f*. ¶ *v.t,* caresser.
caret, *n,* (*Typ.*) lambda, signe d'omission, *m*.
cargo, *n,* cargaison, *f,* chargement, *m*. ~ *boat,* cargo, *m*.
Caribbean Sea (the), la mer des Antilles.
caricature, *n,* caricature, *f*. ¶ *v.t,* caricaturer.
caries, *n,* carie, *f*.
Carmelite, *n,* (*friar*) carme, *m;* (*nun*) carmélite, *f*.
carmine, *n,* carmin, *m*.
carnage, *n,* carnage, *m*.
carnal†, *a,* charnel; sensuel. (*Law*) ~ *knowledge,* relations sexuelles, *f.pl*.
carnation (*Bot.*) *n,* œillet, *m*.
carnival, *n,* carnaval, *m*.
carnivore, *n,* & **carnivorous,** *a,* carnassier, carnivore, *m*.
carol, *n,* chant joyeux, *m*. [*Christmas*] ~, [chant de] Noël, *m*. ¶ *v.i,* chanter.
carousal, *n,* beuverie, bombe *P, f*. **carouse,** *v.i,* faire la bombe *P*.
carp[1], *n,* (*fish*) carpe, *f*.
carp[2], *v.i,* (& ~ *at*) critiquer.
Carpathians (the), les Carpathes, *m.pl*.
carpenter, *n,* charpentier, menuisier, *m*. ¶ *v.i,* faire de la charpenterie *ou* de la menuiserie. **carpentry,** *n,* charpenterie, menuiserie, *f*.
carpet, *n,* tapis, *m*. *fitted* ~, moquette, *f*. ~ *slippers,* pantoufles, *f.pl*. ~ *sweeper,* balai mécanique, *m*. ¶ *v.t,* recouvrir d'un tapis *ou* d'une moquette; (*fig.*) tapisser.
carping, *a,* chicanier.
carriage, *n,* (*horse*) voiture, *f,* équipage, *m;* (*Rly*) voiture, wagon; (*bearing*) port, maintien; transport, *m*. ~ *forward,* [en] port dû. ~ *free,* franco de port. ~ *paid,* [en] port payé.
carrier, *n,* (*bearer, Med.*) porteur, euse; entrepreneur de transports; transporteur, camionneur, *m;* (*firm*) entreprise de transports, *f*. *luggage* ~ (*cycle*) porte-baggages, *m*. ~ *bag,* sac en plastique, *m*. ~ *pigeon,* pigeon voyageur, *m*. (*Tel.*) ~ *wave,* onde porteuse.
carrion, *n,* charogne, *f*. ~ *crow,* corneille, *f,* corbeau, *m*.
carrot, *n,* carotte, *f*. ~**y,** *a,* (*hair*) carotte *inv,* roux; (*pers.*) poil-de-carotte *inv*.
carry, *v.t,* porter; (*goods*) transporter; (*money &c*) avoir sur soi; (*motion &c*) voter, adopter; (*Arith.*) retenir; (*pipe: water*) amener. ~ *the day,* l'emporter. ~ *the can,* payer les pots cassés. ~ *coals to Newcastle,* porter de l'eau à la rivière. ~ *away* (*off*), emporter, enlever; (*thrill*) emballer *P*. ~ *forward* (*Bkkpg*) reporter. ~ *on,* continuer, poursuivre; (*busi-*

ness) exercer, diriger; (*with s.o*) avoir une liaison avec qn. *what a ~-on!* quelle histoire! *~ out,* accomplir, exécuter, effectuer. ¶ *v.i,* (*sound*) porter.

cart, *n,* charrette; (*hand*) voiture, *f. tip~,* tombereau, *m. put the ~ before the horse,* mettre la charrue devant les bœufs. *~-horse,* cheval de trait, *m. turn a ~-wheel* (*Gym.*) faire la roue. ¶ *v.t,* transporter; charrier, charroyer; (*in truck*) camionner. *~ around P,* trimballer *P.* **~age,** *n,* charroi, camionnage; transport, *m.* **~er,** *n,* charretier, camionneur, *m.*

Carthusian [monk], *n,* chartreux, *m. ~ monastery,* chartreuse, *f.*

cartilage, *n,* cartilage, *m.*

cartoon, *n,* (*Press*) dessin [humoristique]; (*Cine.*) dessin animé; (*sketch*) carton, *m.* **~ist,** *n,* dessinateur, trice; caricaturiste, *m,f.*

cartridge, *n,* cartouche; (*cannon*) gargousse; (*pick-up*) cellule, *f;* (*Phot.*) chargeur, *m. ~ belt,* cartouchière, *f.*

carve, *v.t,* sculpter; tailler; (*meat*) découper. **carver** (*pers.*) *n,* sculpteur, *m.* **carving,** *n,* sculpture, *f;* découpage, *m. ~ knife* or *carver,* couteau à découper, *m.*

cascade, *n,* cascade, *f.* ¶ *v.i,* tomber en cascade.

case¹, *n,* cas, *m. in ~ of,* en cas de. *in any ~,* en tout cas, de toute façon. *just in ~,* à tout hasard. (*Med.*) *a serious ~,* un cas grave. (*instance*) exemple, *m;* (*Law*) cause, affaire, *f,* procès, *m. to have a good ~,* avoir de bons arguments. *a hard ~,* un dur *P.*

case², *n,* (*packing ~, crate*) caisse; (*suit~*) valise, *f;* (*necklace &c*) écrin; (*camera &c*) étui; (*jewelry*) coffret, *m. note~,* portefeuille, *m. show~,* vitrine, *f.* ¶ *v.t,* mettre dans une caisse &c.

caseharden, *v.t,* cémenter.

casement window, *n,* fenêtre à battants, croisée, *f.*

cash, *n,* espèces, *f.pl,* argent, *m. pay in ~* (*not cheque*) payer en espèces. *ready ~,* [argent] liquide. *~ down,* argent comptant. *pay ~ down,* payer comptant. *~ on delivery,* livraison contre remboursement *ou* paiement à la livraison. (*money*) *short of ~,* à court d'argent. *out of ~,* sans argent liquide, à sec *P. ~ book,* livre de caisse, *m. ~ box, ~ desk,* caisse, *f. ~ in hand,* espèces en caisse. *~ price,* prix au comptant, *m. ~ register,* caisse enregistreuse. ¶ *v.t,* (*cheque*) encaisser, toucher. **~ier,** *n,* caissier, ère.

cashier, *v.t,* (*Mil.*) casser.

cashmere, *n,* cachemire, *m.*

casing, *n,* enveloppe, *f.*

cask, *n,* tonneau, baril, fût, *m;* (*large*) pièce, barrique, *f.*

casket, *n,* cassette, *f,* coffret, *m.*

Caspian Sea (the), la mer Caspienne.

casserole, *n,* cocotte, *f;* (*dish*) ragoût en cocotte, *m.*

cassock, *n,* soutane, *f.*

cast, *n,* (*dice, net*) coup; (*Fish.*) lancer; (*gut*) bas de ligne, *m;* (*mould*) moule, *f,* moulage, *m. plaster ~,* moulage en plâtre. (*Theat.*) acteurs, *m.pl,* (*list*) distribution, *f. have a ~ in one eye,* avoir un œil qui louche. *~ of mind,* tournure d'esprit. *~ iron,* fonte, *f.* ¶ *v.t.ir,* jeter, lancer; (*light, shadow*) projeter; (*Tech., Art*) couler, fondre; (*statue*) mouler; (*play*) distribuer les rôles. *~ anchor,* jeter l'ancre, mouiller. *~ an eye* (*or glance*) *over,* promener son regard sur, jeter un coup d'œil sur. *~ lots,* tirer au sort. (*snake*) *~ its skin,* muer. *~ a vote,* voter. *~ down,* (*eyes*) baisser. (*Naut.*) *~ off,* larguer l'amarre.

castanet, *n,* castagnette, *f.*

castaway, *n,* naufragé, e; (*fig.*) réprouvé, e.

caste, *n,* caste, *f.*

castellated, *a,* crénelé.

castigate, *v.t,* châtier, corriger; critiquer sévèrement. **castigation,** *n,* châtiment, *m,* correction; critique sévère, *f.*

casting, *n,* (*Tech.*) (*process*) coulage, *m,* coulée, fonte, *f;* (*object*) pièce coulée *ou* fondue, *f;* (*Theat.*) distribution des rôles. *~ vote,* voix prépondérante.

castle, *n,* château, *m;* (*Chess*) tour, *f. ~s in the air,* châteaux en Espagne. ¶ (*Chess*) *v.i,* roquer.

castor *or* **caster,** *n,* (*sprinkler*) saupoudreuse, *f. ~ sugar,* sucre en poudre, *m;* (*wheel*) roulette, *f.*

castor oil, *n,* huile de ricin, *f.*

castrate, *v.t,* châtrer. **castration,** *n,* castration, *f.*

casual†, *a,* accidentel, fortuit; (*remark*) en passant; (*pers., off-hand*) sans-gêne *inv,* désinvolte; (*clothes*) sport *inv;* (*worker*) temporaire. *in ~ dress,* en décontracté. *~* (*farm*) *labourer,* journalier, ère. **~ty,** *n,* (*in accident*) accidenté, e, victime, *f;* (*Mil.*) *pl.* morts & blessés; pertes, *f.pl.*

casuistry, *n,* casuistique, *f.*

cat, *n,* chat, te. *tom ~,* matou, *m. ~ species,* race féline, *f. let the ~ out of the bag,* vendre la mèche. *to be like a ~ on hot bricks,* être sur des charbons ardents, être sur le gril *P. ~ burglar,* monte-en-l'air, *m inv. ~call,* sifflet, *m. ~gut,* boyau [de chat], *m. to be s.o's ~'s paw,* tirer les marrons du feu pour qn.

cataclysm, *n,* cataclysme, *m.*

catacomb, *n,* catacombe, *f.*

catafalque, *n,* catafalque, *m.*

catalyst, *n,* catalyseur, *m.*

catalogue, *n,* catalogue, *m.* ¶ *v.t,* cataloguer.

catamaran, *n,* catamaran, *m.*

catapult, *n,* (*Hist., Aero.*) catapulte; (*boy's*) fronde, *f,* lance-pierres, *m.* ¶ *v.t,* catapulter.

cataract (*falls & Med.*) *n,* cataracte, *f.*

catarrh, *n,* catarrhe, *m.*
catastrophe, *n,* catastrophe, *f.*
catch, *n,* prise; (*fish*) prise, pêche, *f;* (*trick*) attrape, *f;* (*Mach., pawl*) cliquet; (*door, window*) loqueteau. *safety ~,* cran de sécurité, *m. ~-as-~-can,* catch, *m. ~-phrase,* rengaine, scie, *f. ~word,* slogan, *m.* ¶ *v.t.ir,* attraper; saisir; (*fish*) prendre, attraper; (*train*) prendre, ne pas manquer; (*hear*) saisir; (*clothing in sth*) accrocher. *~ cold,* attraper (*ou* prendre) froid, s'enrhumer. *~ s.o. doing,* surprendre qn à faire. *~ s.o's eye,* attirer l'attention de qn. *~ fire,* prendre feu, s'enflammer. *~ sight of,* apercevoir. *~ on,* (*v.i*) prendre, avoir du succès. *~ up,* (*v.t*) rattraper. (*v.i*) (*with sth*) se rattraper. **~ing,** *a,* contagieux.
catechism, *n,* catéchisme, *m.* **catechize,** *v.t,* catéchiser.
categorical†, *a,* catégorique. **category,** *n,* catégorie, *f.*
cater, *v.i,* fournir de la nourriture. (*fig.*) *~ for,* pourvoir à; (*journal*) s'adresser à. **~er,** fournisseur, traiteur, *m.*
caterpillar, *n,* chenille, *f. ~ tractor,* autochenille, *f.*
caterwaul, *v.i,* miauler. **~ing,** *n,* miaulement, *m;* (*pers.*) braillements, *m.pl.*
cathedral, *n,* cathédrale, *f.*
catherine wheel, *n,* soleil, *m.*
catheter, *n,* cathéter, *m,* sonde creuse, *f.*
cathode, *n,* cathode, *f. ~ ray tube,* tube cathodique, *m.*
Catholic, *a,* (*Eccl.*) catholique. *the C~ Church,* l'Eglise catholique. *~ tastes,* goûts éclectiques, *m.pl.* ¶ *n,* Catholique, *m,f.* **~ism,** *n,* catholicisme, *m.*
catkin, *n,* chaton, *m.*
cattle, *n,* bétail, *m,* bestiaux, *m.pl. ~ market,* marché aux bestiaux, *m. ~ show,* concours agricole, *m. ~ truck,* wagon (*ou* fourgon) à bestiaux *m.*
Caucasian, *a,* caucasien. ¶ *n,* Caucasien, ne. **the Caucasus,** le Caucase.
caucus, *n,* clique politique, *f;* (*Am.*) comité électoral, *m.*
cauldron, *n,* chaudron, *m.*
cauliflower, *n,* chou-fleur, *m.*
caulk, *v.t,* calfater.
causal, *a,* causal; (*Gram.*) causatif.
cause, *n,* cause, raison, *f,* motif, *m. with good ~,* à juste titre. *~ for complaint,* sujet de plainte, *m. to have ~ for c.,* avoir lieu de se plaindre. *to make common ~ with,* faire cause commune avec. ¶ *v.t,* causer, occasionner, provoquer, entraîner; faire, *e.g, to ~ to vary,* faire varier.
causeway, *n,* chaussée, *f.*
caustic, *a. & n,* caustique, *m.* **cauterize,** *v.t,* cautériser. **cautery,** *n,* cautère, *m.*
caution, *n,* prudence, précaution, *f;* (*warning*) avertissement, *m. ~!* attention! ¶ *v.t,* avertir. **cautious,** *a,* prudent, circonspect. **~ly,** *ad,* avec circonspection.
cavalcade, *n,* cavalcade, *f.*
cavalier†, *a,* (*off-hand*) cavalier, désinvolte. ¶ *n,* cavalier, *m.* **cavalry,** *n,* cavalerie, *f.*
cave, *n,* caverne, grotte, *f. ~ dweller,* troglodyte, *m,f. ~* **in,** *v.i,* s'effondrer; (*pers.*) se dégonfler *P.*
cavern, *n,* caverne, *f.* **~ous,** *a,* caverneux.
caviar[e], *n,* caviar, *m.*
cavil, *v.i,* chicaner, ergoter.
cavity, *n,* cavité, *f,* creux, *m. ~ wall,* mur creux.
caw, *v.i,* croasser.
cayenne pepper, *n,* poivre de cayenne, *m.*
cease, *v.i. & t,* cesser (*doing,* de faire). *without ~,* sans cesse. **~less,** *a,* incessant. **~lessly,** sans cesse, sans arrêt.
cedar, *n,* cèdre, *m. ~ of Lebanon,* cèdre du Liban.
cede, *v.t,* céder.
ceiling, *n,* (*lit., fig.*) plafond, *m.*
celebrate, *v.t. & i,* célébrer; fêter; (*event with drink*) arroser *P.* **~d,** *a,* célèbre. **celebrity,** *n,* célébrité, *f.*
celery, *n,* céleri, *m. head of ~,* pied de c., *m.*
celestial, *a,* céleste.
celibacy, *n,* célibat, *m.* **celibate,** *n,* célibataire, *m, f.*
cell, *n,* cellule, *f;* (*Elec.*) élément [de pile], *m.*
cellar, *n,* cave, *f.*
cellist, *n,* violoncelliste, *m.* **cello,** *n,* violoncelle, *m.*
cellular, *a,* cellulaire. **celluloid,** *n,* celluloïd, *m.* **cellulose,** *n,* cellulose, *f.*
Celsius, *a,* Celsius *inv.*
Celt, *n,* Celte, *m,f.* **Celtic,** *a. &* (*language*) *n,* celtique, *m.*
cement, *n,* ciment, *m.* ¶ *v.t,* cimenter.
cemetery, *n,* cimetière, *m.*
cenotaph, *n,* cénotaphe, *m.*
cense, *v.t,* encenser. **censer,** *n,* encensoir, *m.*
censor, *n,* censeur, *m.* ¶ *v.t,* censurer. **~ship,** *n,* censure, *f.* **~ious,** *a,* critique, sévère.
censure, *n,* blâme, *m,* critique, *f. ~ motion,* motion de censure, *f.* ¶ *v.t,* critiquer, censurer.
census, *n,* recensement, *m.*
centaur, *n,* centaure, *m.*
centenarian, *n,* centenaire, *m,f.* **centenary,** *n,* centenaire, *m.*
centigrade, *a,* centigrade; Celsius *inv.*
centimetre, *n,* centimètre, *m.*
centipede, *n,* mille-pattes, *m inv.*
central, *a,* central. *C~ America,* l'Amérique Centrale, *f. ~ heating,* chauffage central, *m.* **~ize,** *v.t,* centraliser.
centre, *n,* centre; milieu, *m;* (*lathe*) pointe, *f. ~ bit,* mèche, *f. ~-board,* (*Naut.*) dérive, *f. ~-*

forward, -half, (*Sport*) avant-, demi-centre, *m.* ~ *parties,* partis du centre, *m.pl.* ¶ *v.t,* centrer; (*fig.*) concentrer. ~ *on,* (*talk*) tourner autour de.

centrifugal, *a,* centrifuge. **centripetal,** *a,* centripète.

century, *n,* siècle, *m. in the 10th* ~, au dixième s.

ceramic, *a,* céramique. ¶ *n,* ~*s,* la céramique.

cereal, *n,* céréale, *f.*

ceremonial, *n,* cérémonial, *m.* ¶ *a,* de cérémonie. **ceremonious**†, *a,* cérémonieux.

ceremony, *n,* cérémonie, façons, *f* (*pl*). *stand on* ~, faire des façons *ou* des cérémonies.

certain, *a,* certain, sûr; convaincu; (*cure*) infaillible. *for* ~, à coup sûr. ~**ly,** *ad,* assurément, bien sûr, sans aucun doute; (*readily*) volontiers. ~ *not,* certainement pas. ~**ty,** *n,* certitude, *f.*

certificate, *n,* certificat; diplôme; (*Sch.*) brevet, *m. birth* ~, acte (*ou* extrait) de naissance, *m.* ~**d,** *a,* diplômé. **certify,** *v.t,* certifier; attester. *certified true copy,* copie certifiée conforme.

cesspool, *n,* fosse d'aisances, *f.*

Ceylon, *n,* Ceylan, *m.* ~**ese,** *a,* cingalais, ceylanais.

chafe, *v.t,* frictionner; frotter. ¶ *v.i,* (*fig.*) s'irriter (*at,* de).

chaff[1], *n,* badinage, taquinerie, *f.* ¶ *v.t,* taquiner.

chaff[2], *n,* balle; menue paille, *f.*

chaffinch, *n,* pinson, *m.*

chafing dish, *n,* chauffe-plats, *m.*

chain, *n,* chaîne; chaînette, *f;* (*events*) suite, *f;* (*ideas*) enchaînement, *m.* ~*s,* (*fetters*) chaînes, fers, *m.pl.* ~ *reaction,* réaction en chaîne. ~ *saw,* tronçonneuse, *f.* ~ *stitch,* point de chaînette, *m.* ~ *store,* grand magasin, m. à succursales multiples, *m.* ¶ ~ & ~ *up, v.t,* enchaîner.

chair, *n,* chaise, *f. arm*~, fauteuil, *m. wheel*~, fauteuil roulant. (*Univ.*) chaire, *f. take the* ~, prendre la présidence, présider. ~*lift,* télésiège, *m.* ¶ *v.t,* (*meeting*) présider; (*pers.*) porter en triomphe.

chairman, *n,* président, e. ~**ship,** *n,* présidence, *f.*

chalice, *n,* calice, *m,* coupe, *f.*

chalk, *n,* craie, *f;* (*Bil.*) blanc, *m.* ~ *pit,* carrière de craie, *f.* ¶ *v.t,* marquer à la craie. ~**y,** *a,* crayeux.

challenge, *n,* défi, *m,* provocation; (*job*) gageure, *f;* (*sentry*) sommation; (*of juror*) récusation. *to issue a* ~, lancer un défi. (*Sport*) ~ *contest,* challenge, *f.* ¶ *v.t,* défier (qn de faire); (*decision*) contester; (*Mil.*) faire une sommation à; (*juror*) récuser.

chamber, *n,* pièce, salle; (*bed*~) chambre, *f.* ~*s,* (*judge &c*) cabinet, *m,* (*solicitor*) étude, *f. hear a case in* ~*s,* juger un cas en référé. (*Pol.*) *Upper, Lower C*~, Chambre haute, basse. ~*maid,* femme de chambre, *f.* ~ *music,* musique de chambre, *f.* ~ [*pot*], vase de nuit, *m.*

chameleon, *n,* caméléon, *m.*

chamfer, *n,* chanfrein, *m.*

chamois, *n,* chamois, *m.* ~ [*leather*], peau de chamois, *f,* chamois, *m.*

champ, *v.t,* ronger, mâcher.

champagne, *n,* champagne, vin de Champagne, *m.* ~ *glass,* coupe à c., *f.*

champion, *a,* sans rival, maître; (*P fine*) formidable *P,* du tonnerre *P.* ¶ *n,* champion, *m. world* ~, champion du monde. ¶ *v.t,* se faire le champion de, défendre. ~**ship,** *n,* championnat, *m.*

chance, *a,* de hasard; fortuit. ¶ *n,* hasard, *m;* (*lucky*) chance, *f. by* ~, par hasard. *on the off* ~, a tout hasard. possibilité, chance(s), *f.*(*pl*): *the* ~*s are that,* il y a de grandes chances que (+*subj.*). (*opportunity*) occasion, chance, *f.* ¶ *v.t,* risquer, se risquer (*doing,* à faire). *let's* ~ *it,* risquons le coup.

chancel, *n,* chœur, *m.*

chancellery, *n,* chancellerie, *f.* **chancellor,** *n,* chancelier, *m. C*~ *of the Exchequer,* Chancelier de l'Echiquier (*UK*), Ministre des Finances (*Fr.*), *m.*

chancre, *n,* chancre, *m.*

chandelier, *n,* lustre, *m.*

change, *n,* changement, *m.* ~ *of mind, opinion,* revirement, *m.* ~ *of front,* volte-face, *f.* ~ *of clothes,* vêtements de rechange, *m.pl.* (*money*) monnaie, *f. small* ~, petite monnaie. *to give* ~ *for 10 francs,* faire la monnaie de 10 francs. ¶ *v.t. & i,* changer de: ~ *one's mind,* changer d'avis; ~ *one's address,* changer d'adresse. ~ [*one's clothes*], se changer. (*money*) changer; faire la monnaie de; (*currency*) changer, convertir (*into,* en); (*alter*) modifier; transformer (*into,* en). ~**able,** *a,* changeant; variable, inconstant.

channel, *n,* (*Naut.*) chenal, *m,* passe, *f;* (*river*) lit; (*irrigation*) canal, *m,* rigole; (*TV*) chaîne, *f. through official* ~*s,* par la voie hiérarchique. *the* [*English*] *C*~, la Manche. *the C*~ *Islands,* les îles Anglo-Normandes, *f.pl. the C*~ *tunnel,* le tunnel sous la Manche. ¶ *v.t,* (*efforts &c*) canaliser, diriger.

chant, *n,* chant, *m.* ¶ *v.i. & t,* chanter, psalmodier; entonner.

chaos, *n,* chaos, *m.* **chaotic,** *a,* chaotique.

chap[1], *n,* (*skin*) crevasse, gerçure, *f.* ¶ *v.t,* crevasser, gercer. ¶ *v.i,* se crevasser, se gercer.

chap[2], *n,* = **chop**[2].

chap[3] *P, n,* type, bonhomme. *young* ~, jeune homme. *old* ~, mon vieux.

chapel, *n,* chapelle, *f;* (*non-conformist*) temple, *m.* ~ *of ease,* [église] succursale, *f.*

chaperon, *n,* chaperon, *m.* ¶ *v.t,* chaperonner.

chaplain, *n,* aumônier; chapelain, *m.*

chaplet, *n,* guirlande, *f;* (*beads*) chapelet, *m.*

chapter, *n,* chapitre, *m;* (*fig.*) page; série, *f.*
char[1], *v.t,* carboniser. ¶ *v.i,* charbonner.
char[2] *P, n,* (~*lady,* ~*woman*) femme de ménage, *f.* ¶ *v.i,* faire des ménages.
char[3] *P, n,* thé, *m.* **charabanc,** *n,* [auto]car, *m.*
character, *n,* caractère, *m,* nature, *f.* (*pers.*) *of good, bad* ~, de bonne, mauvaise réputation. *strong* ~, caractère, volonté, *f. he has* ~, il a du caractère. *he's quite a* ~, c'est un numéro *P.* (*Liter., Theat.*) personnage, *m;* (*testimonial*) références, *f.pl.* ~ *actor,* acteur de genre. ~**istic,** *a. & n,* caractéristique, *f.* ~**ize,** *v.t,* caractériser.
charade, *n,* charade, *f.*
charcoal, *n,* charbon de bois, *m.* ~ *burner* (*pers.*), charbonnier, *m.* ~ *drawing,* [dessin au] fusain, charbon, *m.* ~ [*pencil*], fusain, charbon [à dessin], *m.*
charge, *n,* (*Mil., Elec.*) charge, *f;* (*Law*) plainte, accusation, *f. bring a* ~ *against,* porter plainte contre. (*cost*) prix, *m,* frais, *m.pl. free of* ~, gratuit. *at a* ~ *of...,* moyennant... responsabilité, charge, *f. take* ~ *of,* se charger de. *be in* ~ *of s.o,* avoir la charge de qn. *the man in* ~, le responsable. ~*hand,* chef d'équipe, *m.* ¶ *v.t,* (*Mil., Elec.*) charger; (*Law*) accuser *ou* inculper (qn de qch); (*price*) demander, prendre, faire payer. ~ *up to s.o,* mettre sur le compte de qn. ¶ *v.i,* se précipiter. ~ *down on,* foncer sur.
charger (*horse*) *n,* cheval de bataille, *m.*
charily, *ad,* prudemment; avec circonspection.
chariot, *n,* char, *m.*
charisma, *n,* charisme, *m.* ~**tic,** *a,* charismatique.
charitable†, *a,* charitable, généreux. ~ *organization,* oeuvre *ou* association de bienfaisance, *f.* **charity,** *n,* charité; bienfaisance, aumône, *f.*
charlatan, *n,* charlatan, *m.*
Charlie, *n,* Charlot, *m.*
charm, *n,* charme, attrait, *m;* (*spell*) enchantement, sortilège, *m;* amulette, *f,* fétiche, *m;* (*trinket*) breloque, *f.* ¶ *v.t,* charmer, enchanter. ~**er,** *n,* charmeur, euse.
charnel house, *n,* charnier, ossuaire, *m.*
chart, *n,* carte [marine], *f;* (*graph &c*) graphique, diagramme, *m. temperature* ~, feuille de température, *f.* ¶ *v.t,* porter sur la carte, le graphique, &c.
charter, *n,* charte, *f;* (*plane &c*) affrètement, *m.* ~ *flight &* ~ *plane,* charter, *m.* ¶ *v.t,* accorder une charte à; (*plane &c*) affréter.
charwoman, *n,* femme de ménage, *f.*
chary, *a,* prudent; avare, peu prodigue (*of,* de).
chase, *n,* chasse, poursuite, *f.* ¶ *v.t,* chasser, poursuivre; donner la chasse à. ~ *away,* ~ *off,* chasser.
chasm, *n,* abîme, gouffre, *m.*
chassis, *n,* châssis, *m.*
chaste†, *a,* chaste, pudique.
chasten & chastise, *v.t,* châtier, punir, corriger. **chastisement,** *n,* châtiment, *m,* punition, correction, *f.*
chastity, *n,* chastete, pudeur, *f.*
chasuble, *n,* chasuble, *f.*
chat, *n,* causette, *f.* ¶ *v.i,* causer, bavarder (avec qn). ¶ *v.t,* ~ *up P,* (*girl*) baratiner *P.*
chattels, *n.pl,* biens, *m.pl,* possessions, *f.pl.*
chatter, *n,* bavardage; (*monkeys &c*) jacassement, *m.* ¶ *v.i,* bavarder, causer, jaser; jacasser; (*tool*) brouter. *my teeth were* ~*ing,* je claquais des dents. ~*box,* moulin à paroles, *m,* bavard, e. *to be a* ~*box,* avoir la langue bien pendue.
chauffeur, *n,* chauffeur, *m.*
chauvinism, *n,* chauvinisme *m.* **chauvinist,** *n,* chauvin, e.
cheap, *a,* bon marché; (*ticket, &c*) à prix réduit; (*price*) bas; (*joke*) facile. *on the* ~, au rabais. *feel* ~, n'être pas bien fier de soi, avoir honte. ~**er,** *a,* meilleur marché, moins cher. ~**[ly],** *ad,* à bon marché, à peu de frais. *get off* ~*ly,* s'en tenir à bon compte.
cheat (*pers.*) *n,* fourbe, *m,f;* tricheur, euse. ¶ *v.t,* tromper; duper; (*defraud*) frauder. ¶ *v.i* (*games*) tricher. ~**[ing],** *n,* tromperie; tricherie; fraude, *f.*
check[1], *n,* échec, arrêt [momentané]; (*Mil.*) échec, revers, *m. put a* ~ *on,* mettre un frein à. *keep in* ~, tenir en échec. (*tickets &c*) contrôle; (*goods*) pointage; (*medical*) examen médical, *m;* (*Chess*) échec. ~*mate,* échec & mat, *m.* ¶ *v.t,* arrêter, brider, enrayer; contrôler; pointer; (*accounts*) vérifier; (*Chess*) faire échec à. ¶ *v.i,* ~ *up,* se renseigner.
check[2], *n,* carreaux, *m.pl;* (*stuff*) étoffe à carreaux *ou* en damier.
cheek, *n,* joue, *f.* ~ *bone,* pommette, *f.* (*impudence*) toupet *P,* culot *P, m. what* ~*!* quel culot! ~**y,** *a,* effronté; culotté *P.*
cheep, *v.i,* (*bird*) piauler.
cheer, *n,* (*cry*) hourra, bravo, *m,* applaudissements, *m.pl;* consolation, *f,* encouragement, *m.* ~ *up!* [du] courage! (*food*) *good* ~, bonne chère. (*drinks*) ~*s!* à la vôtre! ¶ *v.t,* applaudir; consoler, réjouir. ~ *on* (*team*) encourager. ~ *up,* égayer, dérider, ragaillardir; *v.i,* s'égayer, se dérider. ~**ful**†, *a,* (*pers.*) gai, joyeux; (*news*) réjouissant. ~**fulness,** *n,* gaieté, allégresse, *f.* ~**less,** *a,* triste, morne.
cheese, *n,* fromage, *m.* ~ *board,* plateau à f., *m.* ~ *dairy,* fromagerie, *f.* ~ *industry,* industrie fromagère, *f.* ~ *maker,* fromager, ère. ~*paring,* économie de bouts de chandelle, *f.*
cheetah, *n,* guépard, *m.*
chemical†, *a,* chimique. ~ *engineer,* ingénieur chimiste, *m.* ¶ *n,* produit chimique, *m.*
chemist, *n,* (*scientist*) chimiste, *m,f;* (*druggist*) pharmacien, ne. ~*'s shop* pharmacie, *f.*

~**ry,** *n,* chimie, *f.*
cheque, *n,* chèque, *m.* ~ *book,* carnet de chèques, *m.* ~ *card,* identité bancaire, *f.*
chequered, *a,* à carreaux, en damier; (*career*) avec des hauts et des bas.
cherish, *v.t,* (*pers.*) chérir; (*hope &c*) nourrir, caresser.
cherry, *n,* cerise, *f.* ~ *orchard,* cerisaie, *f.* ~-*pie,* tarte aux cerises, *f.* ~-*red,* cerise *inv.* ~ *stone,* noyau de cerise, *m.* ~ [*tree*], cerisier; (*wild*) merisier, *m.*
cherub, *n,* chérubin, *m.*
chervil, *n,* cerfeuil, *m.*
chess, *n,* échecs, *m.pl.* ~*board,* échiquier, *m.* ~*men,* pièces, *f.pl,* échecs, *m.pl.*
chest[1], *n,* (*Anat.*) poitrine, *f.* ~ *measurement,* tour de poitrine, *m.*
chest[2], *n,* coffre, *m,* caisse, *f.* ~ *of drawers,* commode, *f.*
chesterfield, *n,* canapé, sofa, *m.*
chestnut, *n,* châtaigne, *f,* marron, *m.* *horse* ~, marron d'Inde. ~ [*tree*], châtaignier, marronnier, *m.*
cheval glass, *n,* psyché, *f.*
chew, *v.t. & i,* mâcher; (*tobacco*) chiquer. (*fig.*) ~ *over,* remâcher, ruminer. ~ *the cud,* ruminer. ~**ing,** *n,* mastication, *f.* ~ *gum,* chewing gum, *m.*
chiaroscuro, *n,* clair-obscur, *m.*
chicanery, *n,* chicane, chicanerie, *f.*
chick, *n,* (*chicken*) poussin; (*nestling*) oisillon, *m;* (*P girl*) nana *P,* pépée *P, f.*
chicken, *n,* poulet, te. ~ *P &* ~-*hearted,* froussard *P,* trouillard *P.* ~ *farmer,* volailleur, *m.* ~ *farming,* élevage de volaille, *m.* ~*pox,* varicelle, *f.* ¶ *v.i, to* ~ *out P,* se dégonfler *P.*
chicory, *n,* (*salad*) endive; (*coffee*) chicorée, *f.*
chide, *v.t.ir,* gronder.
chief, *a,* premier, principal; en chef. ~ *engineer,* ingénieur en chef, *m.* ~ *rabbi,* grand rabbin, *m.* ~ *town,* chef-lieu, *m.* ¶ *n,* chef, patron, *m.* ~**ly,** *ad,* principalement, surtout, ~**tain,** *n,* chef, *m.*
chiffon, *n,* mousseline de soie, *f.*
chilblain, *n,* engelure, *f.*
child, *n,* enfant, *m, f. from a* ~, dès l'enfance. *with* ~, enceinte. ~*birth,* accouchement, *m.* *in* ~*birth,* en couches. ~ *care,* ~ *welfare,* protection infantile, p. de l'enfance, *f.* ~ *guidance clinic,* centre psycho-pédagogique, *m.* *it's* ~*'s play,* c'est un jeu d'enfant. ~ *prodigy,* enfant prodige, *m,f.* ~**hood,** *n,* enfance, *f.* *in his* ~ *he . . ,* tout enfant il . . . ~**ish,** *a,* enfantin; puéril. ~**ishly,** *ad,* puérilement. ~**ishness,** *n,* enfantillage, *m,* puérilité, *f.* ~**less,** *a,* sans enfant. ~**like,** *a,* d'enfant, innocent. **children,** *n.pl of* **child.**
Chile, *n,* le Chili. **Chilean,** *a,* chilien. ¶ *n,* Chilien, ne.
chill, *a,* froid, frais; (*fig.*) glacé. ¶ *n,* froid, *m,* fraîcheur, *f;* (*Med.*) coup de froid, refroidissement, *m;* (*fig.*) froideur, *f;* (*of fear &c*) frisson, *m.* *to catch a* ~, prendre froid. *to take the* ~ *off,* (*water*) dégourdir; (*wine*) chambrer. ¶ *v.t,* (*pers.*) faire frissonner; (*fig.*) glacer; (*wine*) rafraîchir. ~*ed to the marrow,* transi jusqu'à la moelle. **chilly,** *a,* (*pers.*) frileux; (*wind*) froid, frais; (*look*) glacé. *it's* ~, il fait frisquet.
chime[s], *n.*[*pl.*], carillon, *m.* ¶ *v.i,* carillonner. *chiming clock,* horloge à carillon, *f.*
chim[a]era, *n,* chimère, *f.* **chimerical,** *a,* chimérique.
chimney, *n. &* ~ *piece,* cheminée, *f.* ~ *corner,* coin du feu, *m.* ~ *pot,* cheminée, *f.* ~ *sweep,* ramoneur, *m.*
chimpanzee, *n,* chimpanzé, *m.*
chin, *n,* menton, *m.* ~ *strap,* jugulaire, *f.*
china, *n,* porcelaine, *f.* *a piece of* ~, une porcelaine. ~ *cabinet,* vitrine, *f.* ~ *clay,* kaolin, *m.* ~ *shop,* magasin de porcelaines, *m.*
China, *n,* la Chine. ~*man,* Chinois, *m.* ~ *tea,* thé de Chine, *m.* ~*town,* le quartier chinois.
Chinese, *a,* chinois. ~ *curio &c,* chinoiserie, *f.* ~ *lantern,* lanterne vénitienne, *f.* ~ *puzzle,* casse-tête chinois, *m.* ¶ *n,* (*language*) chinois, *m;* (*pers.*) Chinois, e.
Chink *P* (*pej.*) *n,* Chinetoque *P* (*pej.*) *m,f.*
chink[1], *n,* (*slit*) fente, fissure, *f.*
chink[2], *n,* (*sound*) tintement, *m.* ¶ *v.i,* tinter.
chintz, *n,* chintz, *m.*
chip, *n,* (*wood*) copeau; (*stone, glass*) éclat, *m;* (*cup &c*) ébréchure, *f;* (*gaming*) jeton, *m;* (*Tech: micro*~) microplaquette, puce *P, f.* (*Cook.*) ~*s,* [pommes] frites, *f.pl.* *he's a* ~ *off the old block,* c'est bien le fils de son père. *he's had his* ~*s,* il est fichu *P.* ¶ *v.t,* (*cup*) ébrécher; (*furniture*) écorner; (*paint*) écailler.
chiropodist, *n,* pédicure, *m,f.* **chiropody,** *n,* soin des pieds, *m.*
chirp, *n,* pépiement, gazouillis; (*insect*) cricri, *m.* ¶ *v.i,* pépier; crier.
chisel, *n,* ciseau; (*engraving*) burin, *m.* ¶ *v.t,* ciseler, buriner.
chit & chitty, *n,* petit billet, *m,* note, *f.*
chit-chat, *n,* papotage, bavardage, *m.*
chivalrous, *a,* chevaleresque. **chivalry,** *n,* chevalerie, *f.*
chive, *n,* ciboulette, civette, *f.*
chiv[v]y, *v.t,* chasser; harceler.
chlorate, *n,* chlorate, *m.* **chloride,** *n,* chlorure, *m.* ~ *of lime,* c. de chaux. **chlorinate,** *v.t,* (*water*) javelliser. **chlorine,** *n,* chlore, *m.* **chloroform,** *n,* chloroforme, *m.* ¶ *v.t,* chloroformer.
choc-ice, *n,* esquimau, *m.*
chock, *n,* (*wedge*) cale, *f.* ¶ *v.t,* caler.
chock-a-block & chock-full, *a,* plein à craquer, plein comme un oeuf.

chocolate, *n,* chocolat, *m. a* ~, un bonbon au c., *m. bar of* ~, tablette de c., *f.* ~ *éclair,* éclair au chocolat, *m.* ~ *manufacturer* or *seller,* chocolatier, ère.
choice, *a,* de choix. ¶ *n,* choix, *m. for* ~, de préférence. *to make a* ~, faire un choix. *I had no* ~, je n'avais pas le choix.
choir, *n,* chœur, *m,* chorale, *f.* ~*boy,* enfant de chœur, petit chanteur. ~*master,* maître de chapelle, chef des chœurs, *m.*
choke, *v.t,* étrangler, étouffer; (*smoke*) suffoquer; (*pipe &c*) boucher. ¶ *v.i,* étouffer (*with anger, laughter,* de colère, de rire).
cholera, *n,* choléra, *m.*
choose, *v.t,* choisir; (*elect*) élire. ~ *to do,* décider, juger bon de faire. ¶ *v.i,* choisir. ~ *between,* opter, faire un choix entre. [*I'll go*] *when I choose,* quand il me plaira.
chop[1], *n,* coup, *m;* (*Cook.*) côtelette, côte, *f. pork* ~, côte de porc. ¶ *v.t,* couper; (*wood*) fendre; (*Cook.*) hacher. ¶ *v.i,* ~ *& change,* changer d'avis sans cesse. ~**ping block,** billot, *m.* ~**ping board,** planche à hacher. ~**sticks,** baguettes, *f.pl.* **choppy,** (*water*) *a,* agité.
chop[2], *n,* ~*s,* bajoues, babines, *f.pl. lick one's* ~*s,* se lécher les babines.
chopper, *n,* couperet, hachoir, *m;* (*Aero P*) hélicoptère, *m,* banane *P, f.*
choral, *a,* choral. ~ *society,* chorale, *f.*
chord, *n,* corde, *f;* (*Mus.*) accord, *m.*
choreography, *n,* chorégraphie, *f.*
chorister, *n,* choriste, *m,f;* enfant de chœur, *m.*
chorus, *n,* chœur; refrain. ~ *of praise,* concert de louanges, *m.* ~ *girl,* girl, *f.* ~ *singer,* (*opera*) choriste, *m,f.*
Christ, *n,* le Christ, Jésus-Christ. **christen,** *v.t,* baptiser. **Christendom,** *n,* chrétienté, *f.* **christening,** *n,* baptême, *m.* **Christian,** *a,* chrétien. ~ *name,* nom de baptême, prénom, *m.* ~ *science,* scientisme chrétien, *m.* ¶ *n,* chrétien, ne. **Christianity,** *n,* christianisme, *m.* **christianize,** *v.t,* christianiser.
Christmas *&* ~**tide** (*abb.* Xmas) *n,* Noël, *m. at* ~, à la [fête de] Noël, à Noël. ~ *box,* étrennes, *f.pl.* (*in Fr. given at New Year*). ~ *carol,* chant de Noël, noël, *m. Happy* ~*!* joyeux Noël! ~ *tree,* arbre de Noël, *m.*
chromatic, *a,* chromatique.
chrome, *n,* chrome, *m.* ¶ *a,* (*steel, leather*) chromé; (*yellow*) de chrome. **chromium,** *n,* chrome, *m.* ~*-plated,* chromé.
chronic, *a,* chronique.
chronicle, *n,* chronique, *f.* ¶ *v.t,* enregistrer, faire la chronique de. **chronicler,** *n,* chroniqueur, *m.*
chronological†, *a,* chronologique. **chronology,** *n,* chronologie, *f.*
chronometer, *n,* chronomètre, *m.*
chrysalis, *n,* chrysalide, *f.*
chrysanthemum, *n,* chrysanthème, *m.*
chub (*fish*) *n,* chevesne, *m.*
chubby, *a,* potelé. ~*-faced,* joufflu.
chuck[1] (*throw*) *v.t,* jeter, flanquer *P;* (*P friend*) plaquer *P.* ~ *on the ground,* flanquer par terre. ~ *s.o under the chin,* prendre le menton à qn. ~ *out,* (*clothes &c*) balancer *P;* (*pers.*) flanquer à la porte, vider *P.* ~ *up,* laisser tomber. *chucker-out P,* videur *P, m.*
chuck[2] (*lathe*) *n,* mandrin, *m.*
chuckle, *v.i,* glousser, rire sous cape.
chum, *n,* copain, *m,* copine, *f.*
chump *P, n,* (*fool*) idiot, e, ballot *P, m. off his* ~, timbré *P,* toqué *P.*
chunk, *n,* gros morceau; (*bread*) quignon, *m.*
church, *n,* église, *f;* (*Fr. protestant*) temple, *m. go to* ~, aller à l'église, aller à la messe. *the C*~ *of England,* l'Église anglicane. *the C*~ *of Rome,* l'Église catholique. *go into the* ~, entrer dans les ordres. ~*goer,* pratiquant, e. ~ *service,* office divin; (*protestant*) culte, *m.* ~*warden,* bedeau, *m.* ~*yard,* cimetière, *m.*
churl, *n,* rustre, malotru, *m.* ~**ish,** *a,* grossier; hargneux.
churn, *n,* baratte, *f. milk* ~, bidon, *m.* ¶ *v.t,* baratter, battre. ~ *out,* débiter. ~ *up,* (*sea &c*) faire bouillonner. (*pers.*) *to be all* ~*ed up,* être dans tous ses états.
cicada, *n,* cigale, *f.*
cider, *n,* cidre, *m.*
cigar, *n,* cigare, *m.* ~ *case,* étui à cigares, *m.* ~ *cutter,* coupe-cigares, *m.* ~ *holder,* fume-cigare, *m.*
cigarette, *n,* cigarette, *f.* ~ *case,* étui à c—s, *m.* ~ *end,* mégot, *m.* ~ *holder,* fume-cigarette, *m.* ~ *lighter,* briquet, *m.*
cinder, *n,* cendre, *f.* ~*s,* cendres; (*furnace*) scories, *f.pl. burn to a* ~, (*food*) calciner. ~ *track,* piste cendrée, *f.*
Cinderella, *n,* Cendrillon, *f.*
cine-camera, *n,* caméra, *f.*
cinema, *n,* cinéma. ~ *star,* vedette de cinéma, *f.* **cine-projector,** *n,* projecteur de cinéma, *m.*
cineraria (*Bot.*) *n,* cinéraire, *f.*
Cingalese, *a,* cingalais. ¶ *n,* Cingalais, e.
cinnamon, *n,* cannelle, *f.*
cipher, *n,* chiffre; zéro, *m;* (*fig.*) zéro, nullité, *f. in* ~, en chiffre. ¶ *v.t,* chiffrer.
circle, *n,* cercle; milieu, *m. the family* ~, le milieu familial. *financial, well informed* ~*s,* les milieux financiers, bien informés. (*Theat.*) balcon, *m.* ¶ *v.t,* entourer; (*go round*) faire le tour de. ¶ *v.i,* (*birds &c*) tournoyer, tourner en rond. **circuit,** *n,* circuit, tour, *m;* (*judge*) tournée, *f;* (*Elec.*) circuit. ~**ous,** *a,* détourné, indirect. **circular†,** *a. & n,* circulaire, *f.* **circulate,** *v.t,* faire circuler, répandre. ¶ *v.i,* circuler, rouler. *circulating library,* bibliothèque à prêt, *f.* **circulation,** *n,* circulation, *f;* (*Press*) tirage, *m.*
circumcise, *v.t,* circoncire.

circumference, *n,* circonférence, *f.*
circumflex, *a. & n,* circonflexe, *m.*
circumlocution, *n,* circonlocution, *f.*
circumscribe, *v.t,* circonscrire.
circumspect, *a,* circonspect. ~**ly,** *ad,* avec circonspection.
circumstance, *n,* circonstance, *f;* état de choses; cas, *m. in no ~s,* en aucun cas. *in similar ~s,* en pareil cas. *in easy ~s,* dans l'aisance, à l'aise, *f. in straitened ~s,* dans la gêne. *~s permitting,* sauf imprévu. **circumstantial,** *a:* *~ account,* relation circonstanciée, *f. ~ evidence,* preuve par présomption, *f.*
circumvent, *v.t,* circonvenir.
circus, *n,* cirque; (*in city*) rondpoint, *m.*
cirrhosis, *n,* cirrhose, *f.*
cirrus (*Met.*) *n,* cirrus, *m.*
cistern, *n,* citerne; (*W.C.*) chasse d'eau; (*barometer*) cuvette, *f.*
citadel, *n,* citadelle, *f.*
cite, *v.t,* citer. *~ as an example,* citer en exemple.
citizen, *n,* (*state*) citoyen, ne; (*town*) habitant, e. ~**ship,** *n,* citoyenneté, *f.*
citric, *a,* citrique.
city, *n,* cité, [grande] ville, *f. ~ centre,* centre [de la] ville, *m. ~ dweller,* citadin, e.
civet [cat], *n,* civette, *f.*
civic, *a,* civique, municipal.
civil†, *a,* civil; (*polite*) civil, poli. *~ commotion,* émeute, *f. ~ engineer,* ingénieur des travaux publics, *m. ~ servant,* fonctionnaire, *m,f. ~ service,* administration publique, *f.* ~**ian,** *n,* civil, e. ~**ity,** *n,* civilité, politesse, *f.* **civilization,** *n,* civilisation, *f.* **civilize,** *v.t,* civiliser. **civilizing,** *a,* civilisateur, trice.
clack, *n,* claquement; (*talk*) caquet, *m.*
claim, *n,* réclamation, revendication, *f. insurance ~,* demande d'indemnité, déclaration de sinistre, *f. pay ~,* demande d'augmentation. *lay ~ to,* prétendre à. ¶ *v.t,* réclamer, revendiquer, demander; prétendre. *~ damages,* réclamer des dommages et intérêts. *he ~s he can swim,* il prétend savoir nager. ~**ant,** *n,* (*benefits*) demandeur, eresse.
clairvoyance, *n,* seconde vue, *f.* **clairvoyant,** *n,* voyant, e.
clamber, *v.i,* grimper, se hisser. *~ up,* escalader.
clamminess, *n,* moiteur, *f.* **clammy,** *a,* moite [et froid].
clamorous, *a,* bruyant, vociférant. ~**ly,** *ad,* à cor & à cri. **clamour,** *n,* clameur, *f.* ¶ *v.i,* crier, vociférer. *~ for,* réclamer à grands cris.
clamp, *n,* crampon, *m;* pince, *f;* (*Carp.*) valet, *m.* ¶ *v.t,* cramponner, serrer. *~ down on,* (*pers.*) visser *P;* (*activity*) freiner.
clan, *n,* clan, *m.*
clandestine†, *a,* clandestin.
clang, *n,* son métallique. ¶ *v.i,* retentir.
clank, *n,* cliquetis, *m.* ¶ *v.i,* cliqueter.
clap, *n,* (*sound*) claquement; (*thunder*) coup; (*hands*) battement; applaudissement, *m. ~trap,* boniment, baratin *P, m.* ¶ *v.t. & i,* battre, frapper; (*into prison*) fourrer *P;* applaudir. *~ped out P,* crevé *P.* **clapper,** *n,* (*bell*) battant, *m.* **clapping,** *n,* applaudissements, *m.pl.*
claret, *n,* bordeaux [rouge], vin de Bordeaux, *m.*
clarify, *v.t,* clarifier.
clarinet, *n,* clarinette, *f.* **clarion,** *n,* clairon, *m.*
clash, *n,* (*noise*) choc, fracas; (*swords*) cliquetis, *m;* (*troops, police*) échauffourée, *f,* accrochage, *m;* (*interests*) conflit; (*colours & fig.*) heurt, *m,* discordance, *f.* ¶ *v.i,* s'entrechoquer; se heurter; être en conflit.
clasp, *n,* (*necklace*) fermoir, *m;* (*hand &c*) étreinte, *f. ~knife,* couteau pliant, *m.* ¶ *v.t,* étreindre, serrer. *to ~ s.o's hand,* serrer la main à qn.
class, *n,* classe; catégorie, *f;* (*lesson*) cours, *m,* classe. *the middle ~,* la classe moyenne, la bourgeoisie. *the working ~,* la classe ouvrière. *evening ~,* classe du soir. *take a ~,* faire un cours. *attend ~es,* suivre des cours. *~ consciousness,* conscience de classe. *~ mate,* camarade de classe, *m,f. ~room,* [salle de] classe, *f. ~ struggle, ~ war,* lutte des classes, *f.* ¶ *v.t,* classer; classifier. **classic & classical**†, *a,* classique. **classic,** *n,* classique, *m. the ~s,* les humanités, *f.pl.* **classification,** *n,* classification, *f.* **classify,** *v.t,* classer, classifier.
clatter, *n,* cliquetis, fracas, *m.* ¶ *v.i,* cliqueter, résonner.
clause, *n,* clause, *f;* (*Gram.*) proposition, *f.*
claustrophobia, *n,* claustrophobie, *f.*
claw, *n,* griffe; (*bird of prey*) serre; (*crab &c*) pince, *f;* (*hammer*) pied-de-biche, *m.* ¶ *v.t,* griffer, égratigner.
clay, *n,* argile; [terre] glaise, *f. ~ pigeon,* pigeon d'argile, *m. ~ pipe,* pipe en terre, *f. ~ pit,* glaisière, *f.* **clayey,** *a,* argileux.
clean, *a,* propre; net. *~ sheet of paper,* feuille blanche. *a ~ life,* une vie honnête. *have a ~ conscience,* avoir la conscience nette. *make a ~ sweep,* faire table rase. *~-out,* nettoyage à fond, *m. ~-shaven,* glabre, rasé de près. ¶ *v.t,* nettoyer; (*shoes*) cirer; (*blackboard*) essuyer; (*teeth*) se brosser (les dents); (*nails*) se curer (les ongles). ~**er,** *n,* femme de ménage, *f.* [*dry-*]~, teinturier, ière. ~**ing,** *n,* nettoyage, *m.* **cleanliness,** *n,* propreté, *f.* **cleanse,** *v.t,* nettoyer, purifier; (*street*) balayer; (*drain*) curer; (*blood*) dépurer. *cleansing cream,* démaquillant, *m.*
clear, *a,* (*glass, water*) transparent, limpide; (*distinct*) net, distinct; (*obvious*) clair, évident; (*sign*) manifeste, certain; (*road*) dégagé, libre. *in ~ weather,* par temps clair. *in a ~ voice,* d'une voix claire. *~ mind, ~ thinker,*

esprit clair, lucide, *m. make o.s.* ~, se faire comprendre. *all* ~*!* fin d'alerte!, la voie est libre. (*Tel.*) *in* ~, en clair. ~*-cut features,* traits bien dessinés. ~*-headed,* perspicace. ~*-sighted,* (*fig.*) clairvoyant. ¶ *v.t,* (*road &c*) dégager, déblayer; (*land*) défricher; (*pipe*) déboucher; (*suspect*) disculper; (*table*) débarrasser. ~ *the table,* desservir. (*Customs: goods*) dédouaner; (*fence*) sauter, franchir; (*cheque*) compenser. ~ *one's throat,* s'éclaircir la voix. ~ *away,* enlever, emporter. ~ **off** *P,* filer *P.* ~ *off!* fiche-moi le camp! ~ **out,** (*room*) nettoyer. ~ **up,** (*books, toys*) ranger. ¶ *v.i,* (*weather*) s'éclaircir; (*sky*) se dégager. ~**ance,** *n,* (*space*) espace libre; (*Customs*) dédouanement, *m.* ~ *sale,* soldes, *m.pl.* ~**ing,** (*glade*) *n,* clairière, *f.* ~ *house* (*Banking*), chambre de compensation, *f.* ~**ly,** *ad,* clair[ement], nettement, distinctement, évidemment. *to see* ~, voir clair. ~**ness,** *n,* clarté, netteté; transparence, *f.*

cleat, *n,* (*Naut.*) taquet, *m.*

cleavage, *n,* (*Geol.*) clivage, *m;* (*fig.*) division, *f.*

cleave, *v.t.ir,* fendre; cliver, diviser. ¶ *v.i.ir,* ~ *to,* coller à; (*fig.*) s'attacher à. **cleaver,** *n,* fendoir, couperet, *m.*

clef, *n,* clef, clé, *f.*

cleft, *n,* fente, fissure, *f.* ~ *stick,* piquet fourchu, *m;* (*fig.*) impasse, *f.*

clematis, *n,* clématite, *f.*

clemency, *n,* clémence, *f.* **clement,** *a,* clément.

clench, *v.t,* crisper; serrer.

clergy, *n,* clergé, *m,* membres du c., *m.pl.* ~**man,** *n,* ecclésiastique; (*Catholic*) prêtre, curé; (*Protestant*) pasteur, *m.* **cleric,** *n,* ecclésiastique, *m.* ~**al,** *a,* d'employé, de commis; (*of clergy*) ecclésiastique, clérical. ~ *error,* erreur d'écriture.

clerk, *n,* employé, e, commis [de bureau], *m;* (*Law*) clerc; (*court*) greffier, *m.* ~ *of works,* conducteur de travaux, *m.*

clever, *a,* intelligent; (*skilful*) habile, adroit; ingénieux, astucieux; (*crafty*) malin. ~**ness,** *n,* intelligence; habileté, adresse; ingéniosité, astuce, *f.*

click, *n,* déclic; (*tongue*) claquement; (*Mech.*) cliquet, *m.* ¶ *v.t,* (*tongue*) claquer. ¶ *v.i,* cliquer.

client, *n,* client, e. **clientele,** *n,* clientèle, *f.*

cliff, *n,* (*coast*) falaise, *f;* (*inland*) escarpement, *m.*

climate, *n,* climat, *m.* **climatic,** *a,* climatérique, climatique.

climax, *n,* point culminant, *m;* (*Rhetoric*) gradation, *f.*

climb, *n,* ascension, montée, *f.* ¶ *v.t,* monter; (*mountain*) gravir, faire l'ascension de, grimper, escalader; (*wall*) escalader. ~ *trees,* grimper aux arbres. ~ *a tree,* grimper dans *ou* sur un a. ¶ *v.i,* monter, grimper. ~**er,** *n,* alpiniste, ascensionniste, *m,f;* plante grimpante, *f.* ~**ing,** *n,* alpinisme, *m;* (*rock*) escalade, *f.* ~*ing boots,* chaussures de montagne, *f.pl.*

clinch, *n,* (*Box.*) accrochage, *m.* ¶ *v.t,* (*Tech.*) river; (*deal*) conclure. ¶ *v.i,* (*Box.*) s'accrocher.

cling, *v.i.ir,* se cramponner, s'accrocher; (*clothes*) coller. ~**ing,** *a,* (*garment*) collant.

clinic, *n,* clinique, *f;* (*health centre*) centre médico-social, *m.* ~**al,** *a,* clinique; (*thermometer*) médical. ~**ian,** *n,* clinicien, *m.*

clink[1], *n,* (*glasses*) tintement, *m.* ¶ *v.t,* faire tinter. ~ *glasses* (*toast*) trinquer. ¶ *v.i,* tinter.

clink[2], (*P prison*) *n,* violon *P, m,* taule *P, f.*

clinker, *n,* mâchefer, *m.* (*Naut*) ~*-built,* bordé à clin[s].

clip, *n,* (*paper*) attache, *f,* trombone, *m;* (*brooch*) clip, *m;* (*P blow*) taloche *P, f.* ¶ *v.t,* couper; (*dog*) tondre; (*hedge*) tailler; (*wings*) rogner; (*ticket*) poinçonner; (*P hit*) flanquer une taloche à. **clippers,** *n.pl,* tondeuse, *f.*

clique, *n,* clique, coterie, *f.*

cloak, *n,* grande cape, *f;* (*fig.*) manteau. ~*room,* vestiaire, *m;* (*Rly*) consigne, *f.* ¶ *v.t,* voiler, masquer.

clock, *n,* (*big*) horloge; (*small*) pendule, *f;* (*taximeter*) compteur, taximètre, *m;* (*car: milometer*) compteur. ~ *& watch maker,* horloger, *m.* ~**work,** *a,* (*toy*) mécanique. *go like* ~, marcher comme sur des roulettes.

clod, *n,* motte [de terre], *f.*

clog, *n,* sabot, socque, *m,* galoche, *f.* ¶ *v.t,* boucher, bloquer; encrasser; (*fig.*) entraver.

cloister, *n,* cloître, *m.* ¶ *v.t,* cloîtrer.

close[1] (kləus) *a,* (*near*) proche (*to,* de); voisin (*to,* de). ~ *to,* près de. (*friend*) intime; (*ages*) rapproché; (*ranks*) serré; (*control*) étroit. ~ *connection,* rapport étroit. (*study*) attentif; (*scrutiny &c*) détaillé, minutieux; (*attention*) soutenu; (*translation*) fidèle; (*weather*) lourd: *it's* ~, il fait lourd; (*room*) mal aéré. (*Sport*) ~ *season,* chasse *ou* pêche fermée. ~ *finish,* arrivée serrée. (*pers.*) (*secretive*) renfermé; (*mean*) avare. *keep a* ~ *watch on,* surveiller de près. *to have a* ~ *shave,* l'échapper belle. ¶ *ad,* de près, étroitement, attentivement. ~ *by,* ~ *at hand,* tout près. ~*-shaven,* rasé de près. ~**ness,** *n,* proximité; intimité; fidélité; (*weather*) lourdeur, *f;* (*room*) manque d'air, *m.* ¶ *n,* clos, *m;* (*cathedral*) enceinte, *f.*

close[2] (kləuz) *n,* fin, conclusion, *f. come, draw to a* ~, arriver, tirer à sa fin, se terminer. *the* ~ *of day,* la chute du jour. ¶ *v.t,* fermer, clore; (*road*) barrer; (*meeting &c*) terminer, mettre fin à; (*ranks*) serrer. ¶ *v.i,* (*shop &c*) fermer; (*end*) finir, se terminer, prendre fin.

closet, *n,* armoire, *f,* placard, *m;* (*study*) cabinet, *m. water* ~, toilettes, *f.pl,* cabinets, waters, *m.pl.*

closing, *n,* (*shop*) fermeture, *f.* ~ *time,* heure de fermeture, *f.* **closure,** *n,* (*factory &c*) fermeture; (*Pol.*) clôture; *f;* (*Theat.*) relâche, *f.*
clot, *n,* (*blood*) caillot, *m;* (*P idiot*) ballot *P, m,* gourde *P, f.* ¶ *v.t,* (*blood*) coaguler. ¶ *v.i,* se coaguler.
cloth, *n,* étoffe, *f,* tissu; (*wool*) drap, *m;* (*cotton, Bookb., Naut.*) toile, *f;* (*drying, duster*) torchon, *m. table* ~, nappe, *f.*
clothe, *v.t.ir,* habiller, vêtir; revêtir.
clothes, *n.pl,* habits, vêtements, *m.pl,* tenue, *f. in casual* ~, en tenue négligée, en décontracté. ~ *basket,* panier à linge, *m.* ~ *brush,* brosse à habits, *f.* ~ *hanger,* cintre, *m.* ~ *horse,* séchoir à linge, *m.* ~ *line,* corde à linge, *f.* ~ *peg,* pince à linge, *f.* ~ *shop,* magasin d'habillement *ou* de confection, *m.* **clothier,** *n,* marchand de confection; drapier, *m.* **clothing,** *n,* habillement, vêtements, *m.pl.*
cloud, *n,* nuage, *m;* (*fig.*) nuée, *f. to have one's head in the* ~*s,* être dans les nuages. ~*burst,* trombe d'eau, *f.* ¶ *v.t,* obscurcir, voiler, obnubiler; (*face*) assombrir; (*liquid*) troubler, rendre trouble. ¶ *v.i,* (*sky*) ~ *over,* se couvrir de nuages. ~**less,** *a,* sans nuage. ~**y,** *a,* nuageux, couvert; (*liquid*) trouble.
clout, *n,* torchon; chiffon, *m;* (*blow*) gifle, *f,* coup de poing, *m.*
clove, *n,* [clou de] girofle, *m.* ~ *of garlic,* gousse d'ail, *f.* ~ *tree,* giroflier, *m.*
cloven hoof, *n,* pied fourchu, *m.*
clover, *n,* trèfle, *m. to be in* ~, vivre comme un coq en pâte.
clown, *n,* clown, bouffon; (*fig.*) pitre, *m.* ¶ *v.i,* faire le clown &c. ~**ing,** *n,* bouffonneries, singeries, *f.pl.*
cloy, *v.t,* rassasier (*with,* de).
club, *n,* massue, matraque, *f,* gourdin, *m;* (*Golf*) club, *m;* (*people*) club, cercle, *m;* (*Cards, s. & pl.*) trèfle, *m.* ~ *foot,* pied bot, *m;* ¶ *v.t,* matraquer, assommer. ¶ *v.i,* ~ *together,* se cotiser.
cluck, *n,* gloussement, *m.* ¶ *v.i,* glousser.
clue, *n,* indice, *m,* indication; clef, *f. have a* ~, être sur une piste. *I haven't a* ~*! P,* aucune idée!
clump, *n,* (*trees*) bouquet; (*shrubs*) massif, *m;* (*flowers*) touffe, *f.*
clumsiness, *n,* gaucherie, maladresse, *f.* **clumsy†,** *a,* gauche, maladroit.
cluster, *n,* (*fruit &c*) grappe, *f;* (*trees*) bouquet; (*bananas*) régime; (*people*) groupe, *m.* ¶ *v.i,* se grouper.
clutch, *n,* étreinte; (*eggs*) couvée, *f;* (*car*) embrayage, *m. fall into s.o's* ~*es,* tomber sous les griffes de qn. ¶ *v.t. & i,* empoigner, agripper; saisir. ~ *at,* ~ *on to,* se raccrocher à, se cramponner à.
coach, *n,* (*horse*) carrosse, *f;* (*stage* ~) coche, *m;* (*Rly*) voiture, *f,* wagon, *m;* (*motor*) [auto]car, *m;* (*tutor*) répétiteur; (*Sport*) entraîneur, *m.* ~ *builder,* carrossier, *m.* ~ *work,* carrosserie, *f.* ~*man,* cocher, *m.* ¶ *v.t,* (*for exam*) préparer; (*Sport*) entraîner.
coagulate, *v.t,* coaguler. ¶ *v.i,* se coaguler.
coal, *n,* charbon *m,* houille, *f.* ~ *cellar,* cave à charbon, *f.* ~ *cutter,* haveur, *m.* ~ *face,* front de taille, *m.* ~*field,* bassin houiller. ~ *industry,* industrie houillère. ~*man,* ~ *merchant,* charbonnier, marchand de c., *m.* ~*mine,* mine de c., houillère, *f.* ~*miner,* mineur, *m.* ~ *scuttle,* seau à c., *m.* ¶ *v.t. & i,* (*ship*) charbonner.
coalesce, *v.i,* s'unir, se fondre. **coalition,** *n,* coalition, *f.*
coarse†, *a,* (*salt, sand*) gros; (*cloth*) grossier, rude; (*pers.*) grossier, vulgaire. ~**ness,** *n,* grossièreté, rudesse, vulgarité, *f.*
coast, *n,* côte, *f,* littoral, *m.* ¶ *v.i,* (*Naut.*) caboter. ~**er,** *n,* caboteur. ~**guard** & ~*guard vessel,* gardecôte, *m.* ~**ing,** *n,* cabotage, *m.*
coat, *n,* manteau; (*man*) pardessus, *m;* (*animal*) poil, pelage, *m;* (*horse*) robe, *f;* (*layer*) couche, *f,* enduit, *m.* ~ *of arms,* armoiries, *f.pl,* blason, *m.* ~ *of mail,* cotte de mailles, *f.* ¶ *v.t,* enduire, revêtir.
coax, *v.t,* enjôler, amadouer, cajoler.
cob, *n,* (*horse*) cob, *m;* (*corn*) épi, *m.* ~[*nut*], grosse noisette, *f.*
cobalt, *n,* cobalt, *m.*
cobble¹, *v.t,* rapetasser, rafistoler *P.* ~**er,** cordonnier, *m.*
cobble², *n,* ~*s* & ~*stones,* pavés, *m.pl.* ~*d street,* rue pavée.
cobra, *n,* cobra, *m.*
cobweb, *n,* toile d'araignée, *f.*
cocaine, *n,* cocaïne, *f.*
Cochin-China, *n,* (*now Vietnam*) la Cochinchine.
cochineal, *n,* cochenille, *f.*
cock, *n,* coq; (*tap*) robinet; (*hay*) meulon; (*of gun*) chien, *m;* (*P* penis*) bitte *P*, f.* ~*-a-doodle-doo,* cocorico, *m.* ~*-&-bull story,* histoire à dormir debout, *f.* ~ *bird,* oiseau mâle, *m.* ~*crow*[*ing*], chant du coq, *m.* ~ *of the walk,* coq du village, *m.* ~*-eyed P,* (*askew*) de traviole *P;* (*crazy*) ridicule, tordu, maboul *P. a* ~*-up P,* un vrai foutoire *P.* ¶ *v.t,* (*gun*) armer. ~ *one's ears,* dresser les oreilles. ~ *a snook,* faire un pied de nez. ~*ed hat,* chapeau à cornes, *m.*
cockade, *n,* cocarde, *f.*
cockatoo, *n,* cacatoès, *m.*
cockchafer, *n,* hanneton, *m.*
cockerel, *n,* jeune coq, *m.*
cockle, *n,* (*Zool.*) coque, *f.* ~ *shell* (*boat*), coquille de noix, *f.*
cockpit, *n,* arène, *f;* (*Aero.*) poste de pilotage, *m.*
cockroach, *n,* cafard, cancrelat, *m,* blatte, *f.*

cockscomb, *n,* (*lit., Bot.*) crête de coq, *f.*
cocktail & ~ party, *n,* cocktail, *m.*
cocky, *a,* suffisant, trop sûr de soi.
cocoa, *n,* (*bean*) cacao; (*drink*) chocolat, *m.*
coconut, *n,* noix de coco, *f.* ~ *oil,* huile de coco, *f.* ~ *palm,* cocotier. ~ *shy,* jeu de massacre, *m.*
cocoon, *n,* cocon, *m.*
cod[fish], *n,* morue, *f,* cabillaud, *m;* (*dried*) merluche, *f.* ~ *fisher,* morutier, *m.* ~ *liver oil,* huile de foie de morue, *f.*
coddle, *v.t,* dorloter, choyer.
code, *n,* (*Law*) code, *m. highway* ~, code de la route. *penal* ~, code pénal. (*cipher*) code, chiffre, *m. in* ~, en code, chiffré. ¶ *v.t,* coder, chiffrer. **codicil,** *n,* codicille, *m.* **codify,** *v.t,* codifier.
coeducation, *n,* éducation mixte, *f.* **~al,** *a,* mixte.
coefficient, *n,* coefficient, *m.*
coerce, *v.t,* contraindre.
coexist, *v.i,* coexister. **~ence,** *n,* coexistence, *f.*
coffee, *n,* café, *m. black* ~, café noir. *white* ~, c. au lait, c. crème. *instant* ~, c. soluble *ou* instantané. ~ *bean,* grain de c. ~*-coloured,* café au lait, *inv.* ~ *cup,* tasse à café, *f.* ~ *pot,* cafetière, *f.*
coffer, *n,* coffre, *m,* caisse, *f.*
coffin, *n,* cercueil, *m,* bière, *f.*
cog, *n,* dent, *f.* ~*wheel,* roue dentée, *f.*
cogency, *n,* force, *f.* **cogent,** *a,* convaincant, probant.
cogitate, *v.i,* méditer, réfléchir.
cognate, *a,* de même origine; apparenté.
cognizance, *n,* connaissance, *f. cognizant of,* instruit de.
cohabit, *v.i,* cohabiter.
coherence, *n,* cohérence; suite, *f.* **coherent,** *a,* cohérent; suivi. **~ly,** *ad,* avec cohérence. **cohesion,** *n,* cohésion, *f.*
cohort, *n,* cohorte, *f.*
coil, *n,* (*rope, hair*) rouleau, *m;* (*Naut.*) glène, *f;* (*snake*) anneau, *m;* (*Elec.*) bobine, *f;* (*Med.*) stérilet, *m.* ¶ *v.t,* enrouler; (*Elec.*) bobiner. ¶ *v.i,* s'enrouler; (*snake*) se lover. ~ *up,* se replier.
coin, *n,* pièce de monnaie, *f.* ~ *of the realm,* espèces sonnantes et trébuchantes. ~ *operated,* automatique. ¶ *v.t,* frapper; (*phrase*) inventer. **~age,** *n,* système monétaire, *m.*
coincide, *v.i,* coïncider. **coincidence,** *n,* coïncidence, *f.*
coiner, *n,* (*forger*) faux-monnayeur, *m.*
coir, *n,* fibre de coco, *f.*
coitus, *n,* coit, *m.*
coke, *n,* coke, *m.*
colander, *n,* passoire, *f.*
cold†, *a,* froid; (*pers.*) froid, distant, indifférent. *it is* ~, il fait froid. *it's freezing* ~, il fait un froid de canard. (*pers.*) *to be, feel* ~, avoir froid. *my feet are* ~, j'ai froid aux pieds. (*fig.*) *to get* ~ *feet,* avoir le trac *P ou* la frousse *P. grow* ~, (*food*) refroidir; (*weather*) se refroidir. ~*-blooded,* (*Zool*) à sang froid; (*pers.*) insensible, sans pitié. ~ *chisel,* ciseau à froid, *m.* ~ *cream,* crème de beauté, *f,* cold-cream, *m.* (*Met.*) *cold front,* front froid. *to* ~*-shoulder s.o,* battre froid à qn. ~ *snap,* coup de froid, *m.* ~ *storage,* conservation par le froid, *f.* ~ *store,* entrepôt frigorifique, *m.* ¶ *n,* froid; rhume, *m. head, chest* ~, rhume de cerveau, de poitrine. *heavy* ~, gros rhume. *to feel the* ~, craindre le froid, être frileux. *catch* ~, attraper *ou* prendre froid, s'enrhumer. **~ness,** *n,* froideur, *f.*
colic, *n,* colique, *f,* tranchées, *f.pl.*
collaborate, *v.i,* collaborer. **collaborator,** *n,* collaborateur, trice; (*pej.*) collabo *P, m,f.*
collapse, *n,* effondrement, écroulement, *m;* (*Govt.*) chute; (*army*) débâcle, *f;* (*lung*) collapsus, *m.* ¶ *v.i,* (*Build., fig.*) s'effondrer, crouler, s'écrouler, s'affaisser. ~ *with laughter,* se tordre de rire. ~ *into an armchair,* se laisser crouler dans un fauteuil. **collapsible,** *a,* (*chair &c*) pliant.
collar, *n,* col; (*detached*) faux col; (*dog*) collier, *m;* (*Tech.*) bague, *f.* ~*bone,* clavicule, *f.* ~ *stud,* bouton de col, *m.* ¶ *v.t,* (*lit.*) saisir au collet; (*fig.*) accrocher.
collate, *v.t,* collationner.
collateral, *a,* (*artery*) collatéral. ~ *security,* nantissement, *m.*
collation, *n,* collation, *f.*
colleague, *n,* collègue, *m,f,* confrère, *m.*
collect[1], *n,* (*Eccl.*) collecte, *f.*
collect[2], *v.t,* (*wealth &c*) amasser, accumuler; (*facts &c*) rassembler, recueillir; (*pers.*) aller chercher; (*people: together*) réunir, rassembler; (*objects*) (*pick up*) ramasser, (*call for*) passer prendre; (*stamps &c*) collectionner; (*taxes*) percevoir; (*rent*) encaisser. ~ *one's thoughts,* se recueillir. ¶ *v.i,* (*people*) se réunir, se rassembler; (*water, objects*) s'accumuler, s'amasser; (*for charity*) quêter. **~ed,** *a,* recueilli, calme. **~ion,** *n,* accumulation, *f;* rassemblement, *m;* réunion; collection; perception, *f;* encaissement, *m;* (*Eccl.*) quête, collecte, *f.* **~ive†,** *a,* collectif. **~or,** *n,* (*stamps &c*) collectionneur, euse; (*tax*) percepteur; (*rent*) encaisseur; (*charity*) quêteur, euse. *ticket* ~, contrôleur, euse.
college, *n,* collège, *m. agricultural* ~, institut agronomique, *m.* ~ *of art,* école des beaux arts, *f.* ~ *of music,* conservatoire [de musique], *f. technical* ~, ~ *of further education* &c, établissement d'éducation supérieur.
collide, *v.i,* se heurter, se tamponner, entrer en

collision; (*Naut.*) aborder.
collie (*dog*) *n,* colley, *m.*
collier, *n,* (*pers.*) mineur; (*ship*) charbonnier, *m.* **~y,** *n,* houillère, mine [de charbon], *f.*
collision, *n,* collision, *f,* heurt, tamponnement; (*Naut.*) abordage, *m. come into ~ with,* entrer en collision avec.
colloquial†, *a,* de la conversation; (*words, phrases*) familier. **~ism,** *n,* expression familière, *f.* **colloquy,** *n,* colloque, *m.*
collusion, *n,* collusion, *f.*
colon[1], *n,* (*Anat.*) colon, *m.*
colon[2], *n,* deux-points, *m.*
colonel, *n,* colonel, *m. C~ Lebrun,* le colonel Lebrun.
colonial, *a,* colonial. *C~ Office,* Ministère des Colonies, *m.* **colonist,** *n,* colon, *m.* **colonize,** *v.t,* coloniser.
colonnade, *n,* colonnade, *f.*
colony, *n,* colonie, *f.*
colossal†, *a,* colossal. **colossus,** *n,* colosse, *m.*
colour, *n,* couleur, teinte, *f.* (*fig.*) *full of ~* (*poem &c*) plein de couleur. *under ~ of,* sous couleur de. (*complexion*) teint, *m;* (*racial*) couleur. (*pers.*) *to change ~,* changer de couleur. (*Art*) coloris, *m. water ~[s],* aquarelle, *f.* (*Mil., Naut., club &c*) *~s,* couleurs, (*Mil.*) drapeau, (*Naut.*) pavillon, *m.* *~ bar,* discrimination raciale. *~-blind,* daltonien. *~ blindness,* daltonisme, *m. ~ film,* (*camera*) pellicule en couleur, *f;* (*movie*) film en c., *m. ~ photography,* photographie en c., *f. ~ problem,* problème racial. *~ television set,* téléviseur couleur, *m.* ¶ *v.t,* colorer. *~ in,* colorier. **~ed,** *a,* coloré, colorié; (*photo, slide &c*) en couleur; (*pers.*) de couleur. *cyclamen-, straw-~,* couleur cyclamen, c. paille. **~ful,** *a,* vif, éclatant; (*style &c*) coloré. **~ ing,** *n,* coloris, *m,* coloration, *f;* (*pers.*) teint, *m.* **~less,** *a,* sans couleur, incolore, pâle; (*fig.*) fade.
colt, *n,* poulain, *m.*
Columbia, *n,* la Colombie.
columbine (*Bot.*) *n,* ancolie, *f.*
column, *n,* colonne, *f;* (*gossip, sports &c*) rubrique, *f.*
coma, *n,* (*Med.*) coma, *m. in a ~,* dans le coma. **comatose,** *a,* comateux.
comb, *n,* peigne; coup de peigne, *m;* (*crest*) crête, *f;* (*honey*) rayon de miel, *m.* ¶ *v.t,* peigner; (*town &c*) fouiller. *~ one's hair,* se peigner, se donner un coup de peigne. *~ out* (*fig.*), éliminer.
combat, *n,* combat, *m.* ¶ *v.t,* combattre; lutter contre. **~ant,** *n,* combattant, *m.* **~ive,** *a,* combatif.
combination, *n,* combinaison, *f.*
combine, *n,* association, *f,* cartel, *m. ~ harvester,* moissonneuse-batteuse, *f.* ¶ *v.t,* combiner, réunir; joindre. ¶ *v.i,* s'associer, s'unir.
combustible, *a,* combustible. **combustion,** *n,* combustion, *f.* (*Mot.*) *~ chamber,* chambre de combustion, *f.*
come, *v.i.ir,* venir; arriver. *to ~ & go,* aller et venir. *~ running,* arriver en courant. [*I'm*] *coming!* j'arrive! *to ~,* (*life*) futur, (*years*) à venir. *in time to ~,* à l'avenir. *~, ~! ~ now!* allons! voyons! *~ along! ~ on!* allons! venez! dépêchez-vous! *what's ~ over you?* qu'est-ce qui vous prend? *come what may,* quoi qu'il arrive, advienne que pourra. *~* **about,** *~ to pass,* arriver, se produire. *how does it ~ about that..?* comment se fait-il que..? *~* **across,** *~* **upon,** trouver, rencontrer, tomber sur. *~* **after,** (*time*) suivre. *~* **along,** *~* **on,** (*work, studies*) avancer, faire des progrès. *~* **back,** revenir. *~* **forward,** (*candidate*) se présenter. *~* **from,** (*country, language*) provenir de; (*be a native of*) être originaire de. *~* **home,** rentrer [à la maison]. *~* **in,** entrer. *~* **into,** (*inherit*) hériter de. *~* **near to doing,** faillir faire. *~* **off,** se détacher; (*plan*) réussir; (*well*) s'en tirer (bien). *~* **off on,** (*dye*) déteindre sur. *~* **out,** sortir; (*book &c*) paraître; (*qualities*) se révéler; (*into society*) faire ses débuts dans le monde. *~* **round,** *~* **to,** revenir à soi, reprendre connaissance. *~* **to,** (*amount*) se monter à, revenir à; (*decision*) prendre. *~ to an agreement,* tomber d'accord. *~ to blows,* en venir aux mains. *~ to light,* se découvrir. *~ to terms,* s'arranger. *~* **undone,** se défaire, se découdre. *~* **up,** (*plant*) pointer, germer, sortir. **~back,** *n,* retour, *m,* rentrée, *f. stage a ~,* faire une rentrée. **~down,** *n,* abaissement, *m,* déchéance, *f.* **coming,** *a,* à venir, futur; (*promising*) d'avenir. ¶ *n,* arrivée, venue, *f;* (*of Christ*) avènement, *m. ~ & going,* va-et-vient, *m. ~s & goings,* allées & venues, *f.pl.*
comer, *n,* arrivant, e. *the first ~,* le premier venu, le premier arrivant.
comedian & comedienne, *n,* (*plays*) comédien, ne; (*variety*) comique, *m,* actrice comique. **comedy,** *n,* comédie, *f. ~ writer,* auteur de comédies, *m.*
comeliness, *n,* beauté, grâce, *f.* **comely,** *a,* beau, gracieux, charmant.
comet, *n,* comète, *f.*
comfort, *n,* (*material*) confort, bien-être, *m. ~s,* aises, commodités [de la vie], *f.pl. live in ~,* **vivre dans l'aisance** *ou* **à l'aise. (*mind*) consolation, *f,* réconfort, soulagement, *m.*** ¶ *v.t,* consoler, réconforter, soulager. **~able†,** *a,* (*bed &c*) confortable; (*pers.*) à l'aise. *I am very ~ here,* je suis très bien ici. *comfortably off,* à l'aise. **~er,** *n,* consolateur, trice; (*scarf*) cache-nez, *m.*
comic, *a,* comique, amusant. *~ opera,* opéra bouffe, o. comique. *~ strip,* bande dessinée. *~ verse,* poésie humoristique. ¶ *n,* (*Theat.*)

comique, *m*, actrice comique, *f;* (*magazine*) comic, *m.* ~**al,** *a*, drôle, amusant.
comma, *n*, virgule, *f.*
command, *n*, ordre, commandement, *m.* (*Mil.*) *under ~ of,* sous le commandement (les ordres) de. *his ~ of French,* sa maîtrise du français. *have at one's ~,* avoir à sa disposition. ¶ *v.t,* ordonner, commander (à qn de faire); (*a view of*) donner sur. ~**ing,** *a*, impérieux, imposant. *~ officer,* commandant, *m.* ~**ant,** *n*, commandant, chef, *m.*
commandeer, *v.t,* réquisitionner.
commander, *n*, commandant, chef; (*Nav.*) capitaine de frégate, *m.* *~-in-chief,* généralissime, commandant en chef, *m.*
commandment, *n*, commandement, *m.*
commemorate, *v.t,* commémorer.
commence, *v.t. & i,* commencer (à faire). ~**ment,** *n*, commencement, début, *m.*
commend, *v.t,* recommander; (*entrust*) confier (à qn), remettre (aux soins de qn); (*praise*) louer. ~**able,** *a*, recommandable, louable. ~**ation,** *n*, éloge, *m*, louange; recommandation, *f.*
commensurate, *a*, proportionné.
comment, *n*, commentaire, *m*, observation, remarque, *f.* ¶ *v.i,* remarquer. *~ on,* faire des observations sur; (*text*) commenter. ~**ary,** *n*, (*Radio, TV, text*) commentaire, *m. running ~*, c. suivi; (*Sport*) reportage, *m.* ~**ator,** *n*, (*Radio, TV*) reporter, *m;* (*text*) commentateur, trice.
commerce, *n*, commerce, *m;* affaires, *f.pl.* **commercial,** *a*, commercial, de commerce; (*district*) commerçant; (*value*) marchand. *~ traveller,* voyageur de commerce, commis voyageur, *m;* représentant, e. ~**ism,** *n*, mercantilisme, esprit commerçant, *m.* ~**ize,** *v.t,* commercialiser. ~**ly,** *ad*, commercialement.
commiserate with, *v.i,* s'apitoyer sur le sort de; témoigner de la sympathie à.
commissar, *n*, (*USSR*) commissaire du peuple, *m.*
commissariat, *n*, intendance militaire, *f.*
commission, *n*, ordre, *m*, commission, *f;* (*body*) commission, comité, *m. ~ of enquiry,* commission d'enquête. (*artist &c*) commande, *f;* (*Com.*) commission, courtage; (*officer*) brevet, *m.* ¶ *v.t,* donner mission à; charger (de faire); (*book &c*) commander; (*officer*) nommer; (*ship*) armer. ~**aire,** *n*, commissionnaire, chasseur, *m.* ~**er,** *n*, commissaire; (*Police*) préfet, *m.*
commit, *v.t,* commettre, faire. *~ perjury,* se parjurer. *~ suicide,* se suicider. (*entrust*) confier (à qn), remettre (aux soins de qn); (*Pol: bill*) renvoyer à une commission. *~ for trial,* mettre en accusation. *~ to writing,* coucher par écrit. *~ o.s,* s'engager (à faire); se compromettre. ~**ment,** *n*, responsabilité, *f;* (*Com.*) engagement, *m. without ~,* sans obligation. *committal order,* mandat de dépôt, *m.*
committee, *n*, comité, *m;* commission, *f.*
commode, *n*, chaise percée, *f.*
commodious, *a*, spacieux.
commodity, *n*, produit, article, *m;* marchandise; (*food*) denrée, *f.*
common, *a*, (*shared*) commun. *in ~,* en commun. *~ ground,* terrain d'entente, *m.* (*usual*) ordinaire, commun, courant; (*pers.*) vulgaire. *out of the ~,* hors du commun. *in ~ parlance,* dans le langage courant. *the ~ people,* le peuple, le commun. (*Mus.*) *~ time,* mesure à quatre temps, *f. ~ knowledge,* de notoriété publique, *f. ~ land,* terrain communal, *m. ~ law,* droit coutumier, *m. ~ sense,* sens commun, bon sens, *m.* *~place, a,* banal, commun; *n*, lieu commun, *m*, banalité, *f. ~ weal,* le bien public. ~**ly,** *ad*, communément, couramment, généralement, ordinairement. ~**ness,** *n*, fréquence, *f.*
commoner, *n*, roturier, ère.
commons, *n.pl,* le peuple, le tiers état. *the House of C~,* la Chambre des Communes, les Communes, *f.pl. to be on short ~,* faire maigre chère.
commonwealth, *n*, république, *f*, état, *m. the British C~,* le Commonwealth.
commotion, *n*, commotion, agitation, *f.*
communal, *a*, commun, communautaire. **commune,** *n*, communauté; (*Adm.*) commune, *f.* ¶ *v.i,* converser. **communicant,** *n*, communiant, e. **communicate,** *v.t. & i,* communiquer, transmettre; correspondre; (*Eccl.*) communier. **communication,** *n*, communication, *f. to be in ~ with,* être en rapport *ou* en contact avec. *~ cord,* sonnette d'alarme, *f.* **communicative,** *a*, communicatif. **communion,** *n*, (*gen. & Holy C~*) communion, *f. ~ service* (*protestant*) office de communion, *m. ~ table,* sainte table, *f.*
communism, *n*, communisme, *m.* **communist,** *n*, communiste, *m,f.*
community, *n*, communauté, *f. ~ centre,* maison de la culture, *f;* foyer socio-éducatif, *m. ~ singing,* chansons en chœur, *f.pl. ~ spirit,* esprit communautaire, *m.*
commutator, *n*, commutateur, *m.*
commute, *v.t,* (*Law, Elec.*) commuer. ¶ *v.i,* (*travel*) faire la navette. ~**r,** *n*, banlieusard, e.
compact, *a*, compact, serré. ¶ *n*, convention, entente, *f;* (*powder*) poudrier, *m.* ~**ness,** *n*, compacité, *f.*
companion, *n*, compagnon, *m*, compagne, *f.* [*lady*] ~, dame de compagnie. ~**able,** *a*, sociable. ~**ship,** *n*, compagnie, société; camaraderie, *f.*
company, *n*, (*gen., Com.*) compagnie, société, *f;* (*visitors*) invités, *m.pl,* du monde; (*Theat.*)

compagnie, troupe, *f;* (*ship's*) équipage, *m;* (*Mil.*) compagnie. *to keep s.o* ~, tenir compagnie à qn. *keep bad* ~, avoir de mauvaises fréquentations.

comparable, *a,* comparable. **comparative†,** *a,* comparatif; (*studies*) comparé. ¶ (*Gram.*) *n,* comparatif, *m.* **compare,** *v.t,* comparer, assimiler. **comparison,** *n,* comparaison, *f. in, by* ~ *with,* en comparaison de, par c. avec.

compartment, *n,* compartiment, *m;* case, *f.*

compass, *n,* boussole, *f;* (*Naut.*) compas, *m;* (*extent*) étendue, portée, *f;* (*Mus.*) diapason, *m.* ~*es,* (*Math.*) compas. (*Naut.*) ~ *card,* rose des vents, *f.* ¶ *v.t,* entourer; (*ends*) atteindre.

compassion, *n,* compassion, *f.* ~**ate,** *a,* compatissant.

compatible, *a,* compatible.

compatriot, *n,* compatriote, *m,f.*

compel, *v.t,* contraindre, obliger, forcer (qn à faire). *to be* ~*ed,* être forcé &c (de faire).

compendious, *a,* concis. **compendium,** *n,* compendium, abrégé, *m.*

compensate, *v.t,* compenser, indemniser, dédommager. **compensation,** *n,* compensation, indemnité, *f,* dédommagement, *m.*

compère, *n,* animateur, trice. ¶ *v.t,* animer, présenter.

compete, *v.i,* concourir. (*Com.*) ~ *for, with,* faire concurrence pour, à.

competence, -cy, *n,* compétence (*for,* pour; *in,* en); aptitude, *f.* **competent,** *a,* compétent, capable. ~**ly,** *ad,* avec compétence.

competition, *n,* concurrence; compétition, *f;* concours, *m.* **competitor,** *n,* concurrent, e.

compile, *v.t,* compiler.

complacence, -cy, *n,* contentement de soi, *m,* suffisance, *f.* **complacent,** *a,* content de soi, suffisant. ~**ly,** *ad,* d'un air suffisant, avec suffisance.

complain, *v.i,* se plaindre (de qch; que); faire une réclamation; porter plainte (contre qn). **complaint,** *n,* plainte, réclamation, *f. cause for* ~, sujet de plainte, grief, *m;* (*Med.*) affection, maladie, *f.*

complaisance, *n,* complaisance, obligeance, *f.*

complement, *n,* complément, *m. full* ~, effectif complet. ~**ary,** *a,* complémentaire.

complete†, *a,* complet; entier, total. ¶ *v.t,* compléter, achever, terminer. *to* ~ *his misfortune,* pour comble de malheur. **completion,** *n,* achèvement, *m;* (*of contract*) signature, *f.*

complex, *a,* complexe. ¶ *n,* complexe, ensemble, *m.*

complexion, *n,* (*face*) teint; (*fig.*) caractère, aspect, *m.*

complexity, *n,* complexité, *f.*

compliance, *n,* (*consent*) acquiescement (*with,* à), *m;* conformité (*with,* avec), *f. in* ~ *with,* conformément à. **compliant,** *a,* accommodant.

complicate, *v.t,* compliquer. **complication,** *n,* complication, *f.*

complicity, *n,* complicité, *f.*

compliment, *n,* compliment, *m.* ~*s,* compliments, respects, hommages, *m.pl. give him my* ~*s,* faites-lui mes compliments. ¶ *v.t,* complimenter, féliciter (*on,* de). ~**ary,** *a,* flatteur; (*ticket*) de faveur; (*copy*) en hommage.

complin[e] (*Eccl.*) *n,* complies, *f.pl.*

comply, *v.i,* ~ *with,* se soumettre à, se conformer à; (*order*) obéir à; (*request*) accéder à; (*rule*) observer.

component, *a,* constituant; composant. ~ *parts,* parties constituantes, *f.pl.* ¶ *n,* (*Chem.*) composant, *m;* (*Tech.*) pièce [détachée], *f.*

compose, *v.t,* composer. *to be* ~*d of,* se c. de. ~ *oneself,* se calmer. ~**d,** *a,* composé, calme. **composer** (*Mus.*) *n,* compositeur, trice. **composite,** *a,* composite, composé. **composition,** *n,* (*gen., Mus., Typ.*) composition; (*Chem., Tech.*) constitution; (*Sch.*) rédaction, *f,* (*foreign lang.*) thème, *m.* **compositor** (*Typ.*) *n,* compositeur, trice.

compost, *n,* compost, *m.* ~ *heap,* tas de c., *m.* ¶ *v.t,* composter.

composure, *n,* calme, sang-froid, *m.*

compound, *a,* (*Chem., interest, word*) composé; (*fracture*) compliqué; (*number*) complexe. ¶ *n,* (*Chem.*) composé; (*enclosure*) enclos, *m,* enceinte, *f.* ¶ *v.t,* (*Chem. &c*) composer, mélanger; (*debt &c*) arranger, régler à l'amiable. ¶ *v.i,* s'arranger (*with,* avec).

comprehend, *v.t,* comprendre. **comprehension,** *n,* compréhension, *f.* **comprehensive,** *a,* compréhensif, détaillé. ~ *school,* collège d'enseignement général, *m.*

compress, *n,* compresse, *f.* ¶ *v.t,* comprimer; (*report*) condenser. ~**ion,** *n,* compression, *f.* ~**or,** *n,* compresseur, *m.*

comprise, *v.t,* comprendre, contenir.

compromise, *n,* compromis, *m,* transaction, *f.* ¶ *v.t,* compromettre. ¶ *v.i,* transiger. ~ *o.s,* se compromettre.

compulsion, *n,* contrainte, *f.* **compulsorily,** *ad,* obligatoirement. **compulsory,** *a,* obligatoire, forcé.

compunction, *n,* remords, *m,* componction, *f. without* ~, sans scrupule.

computation, *n,* calcul, *m.* **compute,** *v.t,* calculer, supputer.

computer, *n,* ordinateur, *m.* ~ *programmer,* programmeur, euse. ~ *science,* informatique, *f,* ~**ize,** *v.t,* informatiser.

comrade, *n,* camarade, *m,f.* ~**ship,** *n,* camaraderie, *f.*

con[1], *v.t,* (*lesson*) étudier; (*ship*) gouverner. ~*ning tower* (*submarine*), kiosque, *m.*

con² *P, a,* ~ *man,* escroc, *m.* ¶ *v.t,* escroquer.
concave, *a,* concave. **concavity,** *n,* concavité, *f.*
conceal, *v.t,* cacher (qch à qn); (*feelings*) dissimuler; (*plan*) tenir secret. ~**ment,** *n,* dissimulation, *f.*
concede, *v.t,* accorder, concéder. ~ *that,* admettre que.
conceit, *n,* vanité, suffisance, *f.* ~**ed,** *a,* vaniteux, suffisant.
conceivable, *a,* concevable. **conceive,** *v.t,* concevoir. ¶ *v.i,* ~ *of,* concevoir.
concentrate, *v.t,* concentrer, rassembler. ¶ *v.i,* (*troops &c*) se concentrer, converger; (*mentally*) se concentrer, fixer son attention (sur qch). **concentration,** *n,* concentration, *f.* ~ *camp,* camp de c., *m.*
concentric, *a,* concentrique.
conception, *n,* conception, *f.*
concern, *n,* affaire, *f;* souci, *m,* inquiétude, *f;* (*Com.*) entreprise, maison de commerce, firme, *f. it's no* ~ *of mine,* ce n'est pas mon affaire, cela ne me regarde pas. ¶ *v.t,* concerner, intéresser, regarder. *as far as we are* ~*ed,* en ce qui nous concerne. *the lady* ~*ed,* la dame en question. *to be* ~*ed about,* s'inquiéter de. ~**ing,** *pr,* au sujet de, à propos de, à l'égard de, concernant, en ce qui concerne.
concert, *n,* concert, *m. in* ~ *with,* de concert avec. ~ *hall,* salle de concert, *f.* ~*goer,* amateur de concerts, *m.* ¶ *v.t,* concerter.
concerto, *n,* concerto, *m.*
concession, *n,* concession, *f.* **concessionaire,** *n,* concessionnaire, *m,f.*
conch, *n,* conque, *f.*
conciliate, *v.t,* concilier. **conciliation,** *n,* conciliation, *f.* ~ *board,* conseil d'arbitrage, *m.*
concise, *a,* concis. ~**ness,** *n,* concision, *f.*
conclave, *n,* conclave, *m;* assemblée, *f.*
conclude, *v.t,* conclure; terminer, achever. ¶ *v.i,* (*event*) se terminer (*with,* par). **conclusion,** *n,* conclusion; décision, *f. in* ~, en conclusion, pour conclure. *to try* ~*s with,* se mesurer contre. **conclusive,** *a,* concluant; décisif.
concoct, *v.t,* confectionner; (*fig.*) combiner, fabriquer. ~**ion,** *n,* mixture; (*action*) confection; (*fig.*) élaboration, *f.*
concomitant, *a,* concomitant.
concord, *n,* concorde, harmonie, *f;* (*Mus., Gram.*) accord, *m.* ~**ance,** *n,* accord, *m;* (*Bible*) concordance, *f.*
concourse, *n,* concours, *m,* affluence, *f.*
concrete, *a,* concret. ¶ *n,* béton, *m.* (*Philos.*) *the* ~, le concret. ¶ *v.t,* bétonner.
concubine, *n,* concubine, *f.*
concupiscence, *n,* concupiscence, *f.*
concur, *v.t,* (*agree*) être d'accord; coïncider; concourir (*to,* à). ~**rent†,** *a,* simultané.
concuss, *v.t,* (*Med.*) commotionner. ~**ion,** *n,* ébranlement, *m;* (*Med.*) commotion [cérébrale], *f.*
condemn, *v.t,* condamner. ~ *to death,* c. à mort. *the* ~*ed,* le (la) condamné(e). ~**ation,** *n,* condamnation, *f.*
condensation, *n,* condensation, *f.* **condense,** *v.t,* condenser. ~*d milk,* lait condensé, *m.* **condenser,** *n,* (*Elec., Opt.*) condensateur; (*gas*) condenseur, *m.*
condescend, *v.i,* condescendre (à faire); daigner (faire). **condescension,** *n,* condescendance, *f.*
condiment, *n,* condiment, *m.*
condition, *n,* condition, *f;* état, *m. on* ~ *that,* à condition de (faire); à c. qu'(on fasse). *in good* ~, en bon état. ~*s,* conditions, circonstances, *f.pl.* ¶ *v.t,* conditionner. ~**al†,** *a,* conditionnel.
condole with, exprimer ses condoléances à. **condolence,** *n,* condoléance, *f.*
condom, *n,* préservatif, *m.*
condone, *v.t,* passer sur, fermer les yeux sur.
conduce to, *v.i,* conduire à, contribuer à. **conducive to,** *a,* qui contribue à, favorable à.
conduct, *n,* conduite; (*affairs*) direction, gestion, *f.* ¶ *v.t,* conduire, guider, mener; (*manage*) diriger, gérer. ~*ed tour,* excursion accompagnée; (*house &c*) visite guidée, *f.*
conductor, *n,* (*Mus.*) chef d'orchestre, *m;* (*bus*) receveur, (*-tress,* -euse); (*Elec.*) conducteur. *lightning* ~, paratonnerre, *m.*
conduit, *n,* conduit; canalisation, *f.*
cone, *n,* cône, *m;* (*fir, pine*) pomme, *f.*
confectioner, *n,* confiseur, euse; pâtissier, ère, ~*'s shop,* confiserie, pâtisserie, *f.* ~**y,** *n,* confiserie, *f.*
confederacy, *n,* confédération, *f.* **confederate,** *n,* confédéré, e; complice, *m,f.* ¶ *v.i,* se confédérer. **confederation,** *n,* confédération, *f.*
confer, *v.t,* conférer, accorder (*on,* à). ¶ *v.i,* conférer, s'entretenir. ~**ence,** *n,* conférence, réunion, *f,* congrès, *m.*
confess, *v.t,* confesser, avouer. ¶ *v.i,* se confesser. ~**edly,** *ad,* de son propre aveu. **confession,** *n,* confession, *f,* aveu, *m.* (*Eccl.*) *make one's* ~, se confesser. *hear s.o's* ~, confesser qn. ~**al,** *n,* confessionnal, *m.* **confessor,** *n,* confesseur, *m.*
confidant, e, *n,* confident, e. **confide,** *v.t,* confier, avouer en confidence. ¶ *v.i,* ~ *in,* se confier à. **confidence,** *n,* confiance, *f. to have every* ~ *in s.o,* faire toute confiance à qn. (*self-*~) assurance; (*secret*) confidence, *f.* ~ *trick,* escroquerie, *f.* **confident,** *a,* confiant, assuré. **confidential,** *a,* (*matter*) confidentiel; (*clerk &c*) de confiance. ~ *secretary,* secrétaire particulier, ère. ~**ly,** *ad,* confidentiellement. **confiding,** *a,* confiant.
confine, *v.t,* enfermer, confiner, emprisonner; (*to barracks*) consigner; (*remarks*) borner, limiter. ~ *o.s to,* se borner à. (*Med.*) *to be* ~*d,* accoucher, être en couches. ~*d to bed,*

alité. ~**ment,** *n,* détention, *f;* (*woman*) couches, *f.pl,* accouchement, *m.* ~ *to barracks,* consigne, *f.* ~ *to bed,* alitement, *m.* **confines,** *n.pl,* confins, *m.pl,* limites, *f.pl.*
confirm, *v.t,* (*news*) confirmer, corroborer; (*treaty*) ratifier; (*s.o in an opinion*) fortifier. ~**ation,** *n,* confirmation; ratification, *f;* raffermissement, *m;* (*Rel.*) confirmation. ~**ed,** *a,* invétéré, incorrigible.
confiscate, *v.t,* confisquer (*from,* à). **confiscation,** *n,* confiscation, *f.*
conflagration, *n,* conflagration, *f,* incendie, *m.*
conflict, *n,* conflit, *m,* lutte, *f.* ¶ *v.i,* être en conflit (avec); se heurter; se contredire. ~**ing,** *a,* contradictoire.
confluence, *n,* (*river*) confluent, *m.*
conform, *v.t,* conformer. ¶ *v.i,* se conformer (*with,* à). ~**able,** *a,* conforme. ~**ation,** *n,* conformation, *f.* ~**ity,** *n,* conformité, *f. in* ~ *with,* conformément à.
confound, *v.t,* confondre. ~**ed** *P, a,* maudit, sacré *P.*
confront, *v.t,* confronter (*with,* avec); (*danger &c*) affronter, faire face à. ~**ation,** *n,* confrontation, *f.*
confuse, *v.t,* confondre, mêler; embrouiller. **confused,** *a,* confus, embrouillé. ~**ly,** *ad,* confusément. **confusion,** *n,* confusion, *f,* désordre, *m.*
confute, *v.t,* réfuter.
congeal, *v.i,* (*blood*) [se] coaguler; (*oil*) [se] figer.
congenial, *a,* sympathique; agréable.
congenital, *a,* congénital.
conger [eel], *n,* congre, *m.*
congest (*Med.*) *v.t,* congestionner. ~**ed,** *a,* (*road &c*) encombré, embouteillé. ~**ion,** *n,* (*Med.*) congestion, *f:* ~ *of the lungs,* c. pulmonaire; encombrement, embouteillage, *m.*
conglomerate, *v.t,* (*& i*), (s')agglomérer. ¶ *n,* conglomérat, *m.* **conglomeration,** *n,* agglomération, *f.*
congratulate, *v.t,* féliciter, complimenter (de qch, d'avoir fait). **congratulations,** *n.pl,* félicitations, *f.pl,* compliments, *m.pl.* ~*!* [toutes mes] félicitations!
congregate, *v.t.* (*& i*), (se) rassembler, (s')assembler, (se) réunir. **congregation,** *n,* rassemblement, *m;* (*Eccl.*) assemblée des fidèles, assistance, *f.*
congress, *n,* congrès, *m.* (*Am. Pol.*) *C*~, Congrès. ~*man,* ~*woman,* membre du C. *m,f.*
congruous, *a,* convenable, approprié (*with,* à).
conic(al) *a,* conique.
conifer, *n,* conifère, *m.* ~**ous,** *a,* conifère.
conjectural†, *a,* conjectural. **conjecture,** *n,* conjecture, *f.* ¶ *v.t,* conjecturer.
conjugal†, *a,* conjugal.
conjugate, *v.t,* conjuguer. **conjugation,** *n,* conjugaison, *f.*
conjunction, *n,* conjonction, *f.* **conjuncture,** *n,* conjoncture, *f.*
conjure, *v.t,* (*adjure*) conjurer (qn de faire). ¶ *v.i,* faire des tours de passe-passe. ~ *away,* escamoter. ~ *up,* faire apparaître; (*memories*) évoquer. **conjurer, -or,** *n,* prestidigitateur, illusionniste, *m.* **conjuring,** *n,* prestidigitation, *f.* ~ *trick,* tour de passe-passe, *m.*
connect, *v.t,* relier, joindre, réunir; (*Elec.*) connecter. ~ *up,* relier, brancher (*to,* sur). ~ *to earth,* remettre à la masse. (*Tel.*) mettre en communication avec; (*fig.*) associer. *to be* ~*ed with,* (*related*) être parent de; (*associated*) avoir des contacts *ou* des relations avec; (*subject*) avoir rapport à. (*Tech.*) ~*ing rod,* bielle, *f.* ¶ *v.i,* (*Rly*) ~ *with,* assurer la correspondance avec.
connexion, -nection, *n,* (*logical &c*) rapport, *m,* liaison, association; (*family*) parenté, *f;* (*relative*) parent, e; (*Rly*) correspondance; (*Com.*) clientèle, *f.*
conning tower, *n,* (*submarine*) kiosque, *m.*
connivance, *n,* connivence, *f. be in* ~ *with s.o,* être de connivence avec qn. **connive at,** fermer les yeux sur.
connoisseur, *n,* connaisseur, euse.
connubial, *a,* conjugal.
conquer, *v.t,* vaincre, conquérir. **conqueror,** *n,* vainqueur, conquérant, *m. William the C*~, Guillaume le Conquérant. **conquest,** *n,* conquête, *f.*
consanguinity, *n,* consanguinité, *f.*
conscience, *n,* conscience, *f. to have a clear* ~, avoir bonne c., avoir la c. tranquille. *have a guilty* ~, avoir mauvaise c. ~*-stricken,* pris de remords. **conscientious†,** *a,* consciencieux. ~ *objector,* objecteur de conscience, *m.* ~**ness,** *n,* conscience, *f.*
conscious, *a: to be* ~, avoir sa connaissance. *to be* ~ *of,* avoir conscience de, être conscient de, sentir. *become* ~ *of,* s'apercevoir de. ~**ly,** *ad,* sciemment. ~**ness,** *n,* (*Med.*) connaissance, *f. lose, regain* ~, perdre, reprendre c. (*awareness*) conscience, *f.*
conscript, *n,* conscrit, *m.* ~**ion,** *n,* conscription, *f.*
consecrate, *v.t,* consacrer; sacrer. **consecration,** *n,* consécration, *f;* sacre, *m.*
consecutive†, *a,* consécutif.
consensus, *n,* consensus, *m.*
consent, *n,* consentement, accord, *m. by common* ~, de l'aveu de tous. ¶ *v.i,* consentir (à qch, à faire), accéder (à qch).
consequence, *n,* conséquence, *f,* suites, *f.pl. in* ~, par conséquent. importance, *f. of no* ~, sans importance. **consequent,** *a,* résultant (*on,* de). ~**ly,** *ad,* par conséquent, en conséquence.
conservation, *n,* préservation, *f;* (*nature*) défense de l'environnement, *f.*

conservative, *a,* conservateur, traditionaliste. *the C~ Party,* le parti conservateur. ¶ *n,* (*Pol.*) conservateur, trice.
conservatory, *n,* (*Hort.*) serre, *f;* (*Mus.*) conservatoire, *m.*
consider, *v.t,* considérer, examiner; réfléchir à; (*possibility*) envisager; prendre en considération. *I ~ him* [*to be*] *innocent,* je le tiens pour innocent, je le considère comme i. *all things ~ed,* toute réflexion faite. **~able†,** *a,* considérable. **~ate,** *a,* prévenant. **~ation,** *n,* considération, *f;* égard, *m. out of ~ for,* par égard pour. *show ~ to, for,* ménager. *take into ~,* prendre en considération, tenir compte de. *after due ~,* après mûre réflexion. *without proper ~,* à la légère. (*factor*) considération; (*payment*) rémunération, *f. for a ~,* moyennant finance. *on no ~,* à aucun prix. **~ing,** *pr,* vu, étant donné.
consign, *v.t,* (*entrust*) confier, remettre; (*goods*) expédier. **~ee,** *n,* consignataire, *m.* **~ment,** *n,* expédition, *f;* envoi, chargement, *m. ~ note,* bulletin de chargement, *m.* **~or,** *n,* consignateur, trice; expéditeur, trice.
consist, *v.i,* consister (en qch; dans qch, à faire); se composer de. **~ence, -cy,** *n,* (*liquid*) consistance; (*actions*) uniformité, *f.* **~ent,** *a,* conséquent; logique; suivi. *~ with,* compatible avec.
consolation, *n,* consolation, *f. ~ prize,* prix de c., *m.* **console**[1], *v.t,* consoler (qn de qch).
console[2], *n,* (*organ & ~ table*) console, *f.*
consolidate, *v.t,* consolider; réunir. **consolidation,** *n,* consolidation; unification, *f.*
consoling, *a,* consolant, consolateur, trice.
consonant, *a, ~ with,* en accord avec. ¶ *n,* consonne, *f.*
consort, *n,* époux, ouse. *prince ~,* prince consort, *m.* (*Naut.*) conserve, *f.* ¶ *v.i, ~ with,* fréquenter.
conspicuous, *a,* voyant, en évidence; (*courage &c*) insigne, remarquable. *to make o.s ~,* se faire remarquer, se singulariser.
conspiracy, *n,* conspiration, conjuration, *f;* complot, *m.* **conspirator,** *n,* conspirateur, trice, conjuré, e. **conspire,** *v.i. & t,* conspirer, se conjurer (contre qn); comploter (de faire).
constable, *n,* (*town*) agent de police; (*country*) gendarme, *m.* **constabulary,** *n,* police; gendarmerie, *f.*
constancy, *n,* constance, *f.* **constant,** *a,* constant; continuel, incessant. ¶ (*Math.*) *n,* constante, *f.* **~ly,** *ad,* constamment; sans cesse.
constellation, *n,* constellation, *f.*
consternation, *n,* consternation, *f.*
constipate, *v.t,* constiper. **constipation,** *n,* constipation, *f.*
constituency, *n,* circonscription électorale, *f,* électeurs, *m.pl.* **constituent,** *a,* constituant, composant. ¶ *n,* (*part*) élément [constitutif], *m;* (*Pol.*) électeur, trice. **constitute,** *v.t,* constituer. **constitution,** *n,* (*Pol.*) constitution; (*health*) constitution, *f,* tempérament, *m.* **~al†,** *a,* constitutionnel.
constrain, *v.t,* contraindre, forcer (qn à faire). **constraint,** *n,* contrainte, gêne, sujétion, *f.*
construct, *v.t,* construire, bâtir. **~ion,** *n,* construction, *f;* bâtiment, *m;* (*on words*) interpretation, *f. under ~,* en construction. **~ional,** *a,* de construction. **~or,** *n,* constructeur, *m.*
construe, *v.t,* (*Gram.*) analyser; (*fig.*) interpréter.
consul, *n,* consul, *m.* **~ar,** *a,* consulaire. **~ate,** *n,* consulat, *m.*
consult, *v.t,* consulter. **~ant,** *n,* consultant, expert-conseil; (*Med.*) médecin consultant, spécialiste, *m.* **~ation,** *n,* consultation, *f.* **consulting,** *a: ~ engineer,* ingénieur-conseil, *m. ~ room,* cabinet de consultation, *m.*
consume, *v.t,* consommer; (*fire & fig.*) consumer, dévorer. *be ~d with desire, jealousy,* brûler de désir, être rongé par la jalousie. **consumer,** *n,* consommateur, trice.
consummate, *a,* consommé, achevé. ¶ *v.t,* consommer. **consummation,** *n,* consommation, *f.*
consumption, *n,* (*food &c*) consommation, *f;* (*Med.*) consomption, phtisie, *f.* **consumptive,** *a. & n,* tuberculeux, euse, poitrinaire, phtisique, *m,f.*
contact, *n,* contact, *m. be in ~ with s.o,* être en contact *ou* en rapport avec qn. (*Elec.*) *make, break ~,* établir, rompre le c. (*pers.*) relation, *f;* (*Med.*) contact. ¶ *v.t,* (*pers.*) se mettre en c. avec; contacter. *~ breaker,* interrupteur, *m. ~ lenses,* verres de contact, *m.pl.*
contagion, *n,* contagion, *f.* **contagious,** *a,* contagieux. **~ness,** *n,* contagion, *f.*
contain, *v.t,* contenir, renfermer; (*anger &c*) contenir, maîtriser; (*Mil., enemy*) contenir. **~er,** *n,* récipient, *m;* (*freight*) conteneur, *m.* ¶ *a,* (*ship*) porte-conteneurs, *inv.*
contaminate, *v.t,* contaminer, souiller. **contamination,** *n,* contamination, souillure, *f.*
contemplate, *v.t,* contempler; songer à. *~ doing,* envisager, méditer de faire, songer à faire. **contemplation,** *n,* contemplation, méditation, *f.* **contemplative,** *a,* contemplatif.
contemporaneous, *a,* contemporain (*with,* de). **contemporary,** *a, ~ with,* contemporain de, de la même époque que; moderne. ¶ *n,* contemporain, e.
contempt, *n,* mépris, dédain, *m. ~ of court,* outrage à la Cour, *m.* **~ible,** *a,* méprisable. **contemptuous,** *a,* dédaigneux, méprisant.
contend, *v.t. & i: ~ that,* prétendre que. *~ with,* combattre; lutter contre. *~ with s.o. for sth,* disputer qch à qn.
content[1], *a,* content, satisfait. ¶ *n,* contentement, *m.* ¶ *v.t,* contenter. *~ed with,* satisfait

de. ~**edly,** *ad,* content.
content², *n,* (*capacity*) contenance, *f;* (*book, play*) contenu, *m;* (*letter, metal*) teneur, *f.* ~*s,* contenu; (*book*) table des matières, *f.*
contention, *n,* démêlé, *m;* dispute, *f. my ~ is that...,* ce que je prétends, c'est que... **contentious,** *a,* (*pers.*) querelleur; (*issue*) litigieux.
contentment, *n,* contentement, *m.*
contest, *n,* lutte, *f,* combat; concours, *m. beauty ~,* concours de beauté. ¶ *v.t,* (*result*) contester; (*election, seat*) disputer.
context, *n,* contexte, *m.*
contiguous, *a,* contigu (*to,* à).
continence, *n,* continence, chasteté, *f.* **continent¹,** *a,* chaste.
continent², *n,* (*Geog.*) continent, *m. the C~,* l'Europe [continentale]. ~**al,** *a,* continental.
contingency, *n,* éventualité, *f,* événement imprévu, *m. should a ~ arise,* en cas d'imprévu. *~ fund,* caisse de prévoyance, *f.* **contingent,** *a,* contingent. *be ~ upon,* dépendre de. ¶ *n,* (*Mil.*) contingent, *m.*
continual†, *a,* continuel. **continuance,** *n,* continuation, *f.* **continuation,** *n,* continuation; (*serial*) suite; (*after a break*) reprise, *f.* **continue,** *v.t. & i,* continuer (à, de faire); (*task*) poursuivre; (*tradition &c*) maintenir. *~on one's way,* poursuivre sa marche; (*after halt*) reprendre son chemin. **continuity,** *n,* continuité, *f.* (*Cine*) *~ girl,* script-girl, *f.* **continuous,** *a,* continu. (*Cine*) *~ performance,* spectacle permanent, *m.* ~**ly,** *ad,* sans interruption; sans arrêt.
contort, *v.t,* (*face*) crisper, tordre. **contortion,** *n,* contorsion, crispation, *f.* ~**ist,** *n,* contorsionniste, *m,f.*
contour, *n,* contour; profil, *m. ~ line,* courbe de niveau, *f.*
contraband, *n,* contrebande, *f.* ¶ *a,* de c.
contraception, *n,* contraception, *f.* **contraceptive,** *a. & n,* contraceptif, *m.*
contract¹, *n,* contrat, *m. by ~,* par contrat. *enter into a ~ with s.o,* passer un c. avec qn. *~ work,* travail à l'entreprise *ou* à forfait. *~ bridge,* bridge contrat, *m.* ¶ *v.t,* (*disease*) contracter; (*habits*) prendre. *~ to do,* s'engager par contract à faire. *~ing party,* contractant, e.
contract², *v.t,* contracter; (*face*) crisper; (*pupils*) rétrécir. ¶ *v.i,* se contracter; se crisper; se rétrécir. ~**ion,** *n,* contraction, *f,* rétrécissement, *m;* (*Gram.*) forme contractée, *f.*
contractor, *n,* entrepreneur, fournisseur, *m.*
contradict, *v.t,* contredire, démentir. ~**ion,** *n,* contredit, démenti, *m.* ~**ory,** *a,* contradictoire.
contralto, *n,* contralto, *m.*
contraption, *n,* machin *P,* truc *P,* bidule *P, m.*
contrarily, *ad,* contrairement.
contrariness, *n,* esprit de contradiction, *m.*
contrary, *a,* contraire; opposé, *in the ~ direction,* en sens inverse. ¶ *ad, ~ to,* contrairement à, à l'encontre de. ¶ *n,* contraire, *m. on the ~,* au contraire. *unless you hear to the ~,* sauf avis contraire.
contrast, *n,* contraste, *m. in ~ to,* par contraste avec, par opposition à. ¶ *v.t,* mettre en contraste; contraster. ¶ *v.i,* contraster, faire contraste. *~ sharply with,* trancher sur. ~**ing,** *a,* contrasté.
contravene, *v.t,* violer, contrevenir à, enfreindre. **contravention,** *n,* infraction, violation, *f.*
contribute, *v.t,* (*money*) offrir, donner, contribuer [pour]. ¶ *v.i,* contribuer (*to,* à). *~ to* (*journal*), collaborer à. **contribution,** *n,* contribution, cotisation, *f;* (*to journal*) article, *m.* **contributor** (*to journal*) *n,* collaborateur, trice.
contrite, *a,* contrit, pénitent. **contrition,** *n,* contrition, pénitence, *f.*
contrivance, *n,* dispositif, mécanisme, *m;* (*scheme*) combinaison, *f,* artifice, *m.* **contrive,** *v.t,* combiner; ménager. *~ to,* s'arranger pour, s'ingénier à.
control, *n,* contrôle, *m;* maîtrise; (*over child*) autorité; (*rent, price, traffic*) réglementation, *f.* ~*s,* (*vehicle*) commandes, *f.pl.* (*experiment*) cas témoin, *m. self-~,* maîtrise de soi, contrôle de soi-même. *lose ~ of,* perdre c. de. *have well under ~,* (*child, situation*) avoir bien en main. ¶ *v.t,* contrôler, maîtriser; (*feelings*) dominer; (*business*) diriger; (*traffic, expenditure*) régler; (*child, class*) tenir [bien]; (*vehicle*) être maître de. *~ o.s,* se maîtriser. *~ group,* groupe témoin, *m. ~ panel* (*plane &c*) tableau de bord, *m. ~ tower,* tour de contrôle, *f.* **controller,** *n,* contrôleur, *m.*
controversial, *a,* de controverse; discutable. **controversy,** *n,* controverse, *f.*
contumacious, *a,* rebelle, récalcitrant.
contusion, *n,* contusion, *f.*
conundrum, *n,* devinette, énigme, *f.*
convalesce, *v.i,* entrer en convalescence. **convalescence,** *n,* convalescence, *f.* **convalescent,** *a. & n,* convalescent, e.
convene, *v.t,* convoquer.
convenience, *n,* commodité, *f. all modern ~s,* tout le confort moderne. (*public*) *~s,* toilettes, *f.pl.* **convenient,** *a,* commode, convenable. *if that's ~,* si cela vous arrange. ~**ly,** *ad,* d'une façon commode, sans inconvénient.
convent (*& ~ school*) *n,* couvent, *m.*
convention, *n,* (*meeting*) convention, *f;* (*custom*) usage, *m,* convenances, *f.pl.* ~**al,** *a,* conventionnel, de convention; conformiste. *~ weapons,* armes classiques, *f.pl.*
converge, *v.i,* converger. **convergent,** *a,* convergent.

conversant, *a, be* ~ *with,* être au courant de; s'y connaître en.
conversation, *n,* conversation, *f;* entretien, *m.* ~**al,** *a,* de la conversation. *in a* ~ *tone,* sur le ton de la c. ~**alist,** *n,* causeur, euse.
converse[1], *a. & n,* contraire, *m;* inverse, *m.*
converse[2], *v.i,* converser, causer, s'entretenir.
conversion, *n,* conversion, *f; (Build.)* aménagement, *m; (Rugby)* transformation, *f.*
convert, *n,* converti, e. ¶ *v.t,* convertir, changer (*into,* en); (*Relig.*) convertir; (*Build.*) aménager; (*Rugby*) transformer. ~**er,** *n,* (*Elec.*) convertisseur, *m.* ~**ible,** *a,* convertible; (*car*) décapotable.
convex, *a,* convexe. ~**ity,** *n,* convexité, *f.*
convey, *v.t,* transporter; (*pers.*) conduire; (*message*) transmettre, communiquer; (*Law: property*) transférer, transmettre. ~**ance,** *n,* transport; (*vehicle*) véhicule, *m,* voiture, *f;* (*property*) translation, transmission, *f;* (*deed*) acte translatif [de propriété], *m.*
convict, *n,* forçat, *m,* bagnard, *m.* ¶ *v.t,* déclarer coupable. ~**ion,** *n,* conviction; (*crime*) condamnation, *f. carry* ~, être convaincant.
convince, *v.t,* convaincre, persuader (qn de qch). **convincing,** *a,* convaincant; (*win*) décisif.
convivial, *a,* qui aime la compagnie; joyeux.
convocation, *n,* convocation; assemblée, *f.* **convoke,** *v.t,* convoquer.
convolvulus, *n,* volubilis, liseron, *m,* belle de jour, *f.*
convoy, *n,* convoi, *m;* escorte, *f.* ¶ *v.t,* convoyer, escorter.
convulse, *v.t,* bouleverser. *to be* ~*d with laughter,* se tordre de rire. **convulsion,** *n,* convulsion, *f,* bouleversement, *m.* **convulsive†,** *a,* convulsif.
cony, -ney, *n,* lapin, *m.*
coo, *n,* roucoulement, *m.* ¶ *v.i,* roucouler.
cook, *n,* cuisinier, ère. *to be a good* ~, faire bien la cuisine. ¶ *v.t,* [faire] cuire; (*books*) falsifier, truquer. (*fig.*) ~ *s.o's goose,* faire son affaire à qn. ~ *up P,* fabriquer. ¶ *v.i,* cuisiner, faire la cuisine. **cooker,** *n,* (*stove*) cuisinière, *f,* fourneau, *m.* **cookery,** *n,* cuisine, *f.* ~ *book,* livre de cuisine, *m.* **cooking,** *n,* cuisine; cuisson, *f.* ~ *time,* temps de cuisson, *m.* ~ *apples,* pommes à cuire, *f.pl.* ~ *salt,* sel gris, sel de cuisine, *m.*
cool†, *a,* (*water &c*) frais; (*pers.*) calme. *to keep* ~, garder son sang-froid. (*unfriendly*) froid; (*cheeky*) effronté, sans-gêne, *inv. he's a* ~ *customer,* il a du culot *P.* ~*-headed,* imperturbable. ¶ *n,* frais, *m,* fraîcheur, *f. in the* ~, au frais. ¶ *v.t,* rafraîchir; refroidir. ~ *one's heels,* faire le pied de grue. ~ *it! P,* ne t'énerve pas! (*v.i.*) se refroidir. ~ *down,* (*pers.*) se calmer. ~**er** *P, n,* (*jail*) taule *P, f.* ~**ness,** *n,* fraîcheur, *f;* calme, sang-froid, flegme, *m;* froideur, *f.*
coomb, *n,* combe, *f.*
coop, *n,* cage à poules, *f,* poulailler, *m.* ¶ *v.t,* enfermer. (*pers.*) ~ *up,* claquemurer.
cooper, *n,* tonnelier, *m.* ~**age,** *n,* tonnellerie, *f.*
cooperate, *v.i,* coopérer. **cooperation,** *n,* coopération, *f;* concours, *m.* **cooperative,** *a,* coopératif. ~ *society,* [société] coopérative, *f.* ¶ *n,* coopérative, *f.*
coordinate, *n,* ~*s* (*map*) coordonnées, *f.pl;* (*dress*) coordonnés, *m.pl.* ¶ *v.t,* coordonner.
coot, *n,* foulque, *f.*
cop *P, n,* (*policeman*) flic *P, m.* ¶ *v.t,* pincer *P. get* ~*ped,* se faire pincer. *to* ~ *it P,* écoper *P.*
cope[1], *n,* (*Eccl.*) chape, *f.*
cope[2], *v.i,* se débrouiller. ~ *with,* s'occuper de, se charger de; (*situation*) faire face à.
Copenhagen, *n,* Copenhague, *f.*
coping, *n,* (*Build.*) chaperon, couronnement, *m.*
copious†, *a,* copieux, abondant.
copper, *n,* cuivre *m;* (*wash*) lessiveuse, *f;* (*P policeman*) flic *P, m.* ~*s,* petite monnaie, *f.* ~ *beech,* hêtre pourpre, *m.* ~*-coloured,* cuivré. ~*-plate* [*engraving*], gravure sur cuivre, taille douce, *f;* (*handwriting*) écriture moulée. ~*smith,* chaudronnier, *m.* ¶ *v.t,* cuivrer.
coppice, copse, *n,* taillis, *m.*
copulation, *n,* copulation, *f.*
copy, *n,* copie; reproduction, *f;* (*book*) exemplaire; (*journal*) numéro, *m;* (*material*) copie, matière à reportage, *f.* ~*writer,* rédacteur, trice, publicitaire. ¶ *v.t,* copier. ~*ing ink,* encre à copier, *f.* **copyist,** *n,* copiste, *m,f.*
copyright, *n,* droit d'auteur, copyright, *m.* ~ *reserved,* tous droits de réproduction &c réservés.
coquetry, *n,* coquetterie, *f.* **coquette,** *n,* coquette, *f.* **coquettish,** *a,* coquet; provocant.
coral, *n,* corail, *m.* ~ *reef,* récif de c., *m.*
corbel, *n,* corbeau, *m.*
cord, *n,* corde, *f;* cordon, *m.* ¶ *v.t,* corder. ~**age,** *n,* cordages, *m.pl.*
cordial†, *a,* cordial, chaleureux. ¶ *n,* cordial, *m.* ~**ity,** *n,* cordialité, *f.*
cordon, *n,* cordon, *m.* ¶ *v.t,* ~ *off,* (*area*) interdire l'accès à.
corduroy, *n,* velours côtelé, *m.*
core, *n,* (*fruit*) trognon, coeur; (*magnet*) noyau, *m;* (*cable*) âme, *f.* ¶ *v.t,* (*fruit*) vider, enlever le coeur de.
co-respondent, *n,* co-défendeur, deresse.
cork, *n,* liège; (*bottle*) bouchon, *m.* ~*screw,* tire-bouchon, *m.* ~*-tipped* (*cigarettes*), à bouts de liège. ~ *tree,* chêne-liège, *m.* ¶ *v.t,* boucher. ~*ed,* (*wine*) qui sent le bouchon.
cormorant, *n,* cormoran, *m.*
corn[1], *n,* grain, blé; (*Indian*) maïs, *m;* céréales, *f.pl.* ~ *cob,* épi de maïs, *m.* ~ *field,* champ de

blé, *m.* ~*flakes,* céréales, *f.pl,* pétales de maïs *m.pl.* ~*flour,* farine de maïs, *f.* ~*flower,* bleuet, *m.*
corn², *n,* (*Med.*) cor, *m. tread on s.o's* ~*s,* toucher qn à l'endroit sensible.
corned beef, corned-beef, *m.*
cornelian, *n,* cornaline, *f.*
corner, *n,* coin, angle, *m;* encoignure, *f;* (*Mot.*) virage, tournant, *m: take a* ~, prendre un tournant. (*Foot.*) corner, *m.* (*att., house, shop*) du coin. ~ *cupboard,* encoignure, *f.* ~ *stone,* pierre angulaire, *f.* ¶ *v.t,* acculer; (*fig., pers.*) coincer *P;* (*market*) accaparer. ¶ *v.i,* (*car*) ~ *well,* prendre bien les virages.
cornet, *n,* (*Mus.*) cornet à pistons; (*ice cream*) cornet, *m.*
cornice, *n,* corniche, *f.*
Cornish, *a,* de Cornouailles.
cornucopia, *n,* corne d'abondance, *f.*
Cornwall, *n,* la Cornouailles.
corolla, *n,* corolle, *f.*
corollary, *n,* corollaire, *m.*
corona, *n,* (*Astr., Arch.*) couronne, *f.*
coronary, *a,* (*Anat.*) coronaire. ~ [*thrombosis*], *n,* infarctus [du myocarde], *m.*
coronation, *n,* couronnement, sacre, *m.* **coronet,** *n,* couronne, *f.*
corporal†, *a,* corporel. **corporal,** *n,* caporal-chef; (*cavalry*) brigadier-chef, *m.*
corporation, *n,* conseil municipal, *m,* municipalité; (*Com.*) société commerciale; (*P belly*) bedaine *P, f.*
corps, *n,* corps, *m. army* ~, corps d'armée.
corpse, *n,* cadavre, corps, *m.*
corpulence, *n,* corpulence, *f,* embonpoint, *m.* **corpulent,** *a,* corpulent.
Corpus Christi, la Fête-Dieu.
corpuscle, *n,* corpuscule, *m.* [*blood*] ~, globule sanguin, *m.*
correct†, *a,* correct; exact, juste. ¶ *v.t,* corriger; rectifier; (*pers.*) reprendre. ~*ed copy,* corrigé, *m.* ~**ion,** *n,* correction; rectification, *f.* ~**ive,** *n,* correctif, *m.* ~**ness,** *n,* correction, exactitude, justesse, *f.* ~**or,** *n,* correcteur, trice.
correlate, *v.t,* mettre en corrélation (*with,* avec). ¶ *v.i,* correspondre (à); être en corrélation (avec). **correlation,** *n,* corrélation, *f.*
correspond, *v.i,* (*write*) correspondre (*with,* avec); (*be equivalent*) correspondre (*to,* à); (*agree*) s'accorder (avec). ~**ence,** *n,* correspondance, *f.* ~ *course,* cours par correspondance, *m.* ~**ent,** *n,* correspondant, e. ~**ing,** *a,* correspondant; conforme (à); semblable.
corridor, *n,* couloir, corridor, *m.*
corroborate, *v.t,* corroborer.
corrode, *v.t,* corroder; ronger. **corrosion,** *n,* corrosion, *f.* **corrosive,** *a. & n,* corrosif, *m.*
corrugated, *a,* ondulé, ridé. ~ *iron,* tôle ondulée, *f.*
corrupt, *a,* corrompu; dépravé; vénal; (*text*) altéré. ¶ *v.t,* corrompre, dépraver; (*witness*) suborner. ~**ion,** *n,* corruption, *f.*
corsair, *n,* corsaire, *m.*
corset, *n,* (& ~*s*) corset, *m.* ¶ *v.t,* corseter.
Corsica, *n,* la Corse. **Corsican,** *a,* corse. ¶ *n,* Corse, *m,f.*
coruscate, *v.i,* scintiller.
cos, *n,* or **Cos lettuce,** [laitue] romaine, *f.*
cosily, *ad,* à son aise, confortablement.
cosmetic, *a. & n,* cosmétique, *m.*
cosmic *a,* (*gen., dust, rays*) cosmique.
cosmonaut, *n,* cosmonaute, *m,f.*
cosmopolitan, *a. & n,* cosmopolite, *m,f.*
cost, *n,* coût, prix, *m;* frais, *m.pl.* (*Law*) ~*s,* dépens, *m.pl. to be ordered to pay* ~*s,* être condamné aux dépens. *at all* ~*s,* coûte que coûte, à tout prix. *at a great* ~, à grands frais. ~ *of living bonus,* indemnité de vie chère, *f.* ~ *of living* [*index*], [index du] coût de la vie, *m.* ~ *price,* prix de revient, *m.* ¶ *v.t.ir,* (*job*) évaluer le coût de. ¶ *v.i,* coûter. *what does it* ~? combien ça coûte? ~ *a lot,* coûter cher. ~ *the earth,* c. les yeux de la tête.
coster[monger], *n,* marchand des quatre saisons, *m.*
costliness, *n,* cherté; somptuosité, *f.* **costly,** *a,* coûteux; dispendieux; somptueux.
costume, *n,* costume; (*lady's*) tailleur, *m.* ~ *play,* pièce historique, *f.* **costumier,** *n,* costumier, ière.
cosy, *a,* confortable, douillet. ~ *corner,* coin intime, *m.*
cot, *n,* lit d'enfant; petit lit, *m.*
coterie, *n,* coterie, *f,* cénacle, *m.*
cottage, *n,* petite maison à la campagne, cottage, *m;* (*thatched*) chaumière, *f.* **cottager,** *n,* paysan, anne.
cotton, *n,* (*Bot., cloth*) coton, *m;* (*thread*) fil de coton, *m.* ~ *goods,* cotonnades, *f.pl.* ~ *industry,* industrie cotonnière, *f.* ~ *mill,* filature de coton, *f.* ~ *plant,* cotonnier, *m.* ~ *waste,* déchets de c., *m.pl.* ~ *wool,* ouate *f,* coton *m.*
couch, *n,* canapé, divan, sofa, *m.* ¶ *v.t,* exprimer, formuler. ~*ed in these terms,* ainsi conçu. ~ **grass,** *n,* chiendent, *m.*
cough, *n,* toux, *f.* ~ *mixture,* sirop pour la toux, *m.* ~ *lozenge,* pastille pour la t., *f.* ¶ *v.i,* tousser. ¶ *v.t,* ~ *up,* expectorer; (*money P*) cracher *P.*
council, *n,* conseil; (*Eccl.*) concile, *m.* **councillor,** *n,* conseiller, ère.
counsel, *n,* conseil, *m;* délibération; consultation, *f;* (*pers.*) avocat, e, conseil, *m.* ¶ *v.t,* conseiller (à qn de faire). **counsellor,** *n,* conseiller, ère; (*guidance*) orienteur, *m.*
count¹, *n,* compte, calcul; (*votes*) dépouillement, *m. keep* ~ *of,* tenir compte de. (*Law*) chef

d'accusation, *m.* ~*down,* compte à rebours. ¶ *v.t,* compter; (*people*) dénombrer; (*votes*) dépouiller; (*consider*) tenir pour. ¶ *v.i,* ~ *on,* compter sur. ~ *on doing,* compter faire.

count[2], *n,* (*title*) comte, *m.*

countenance, *n,* figure, mine, expression, *f. out of* ~, décontenancé. ¶ *v.t,* approuver; encourager.

counter[1], *n,* (*shop*) comptoir; (*bank*) guichet; (*disc*) jeton, *m,* fiche, *f;* (*meter*) compteur, *m. Geiger* ~, compteur Geiger.

counter[2], *a,* contraire, opposé (*to,* à). ¶ *n,* riposte, *f;* (*Box.*) coup d'arrêt, *m.* ¶ *ad,* ~ *to,* à l'encontre de. *run* ~ *to,* aller à l'encontre de. ¶ *v.t,* riposter; s'opposer à; (*blow*) parer.

counter-, *pref,* contre-, *e.g:* ~*-attack,* contre-attaque, *f.* ~*-espionnage,* c.-espionnage, *m.* ~*-measure,* c.-mesure, *f.* ~*-revolution,* c.-révolution, *f.*

counteract, *v.t,* neutraliser.

counterbalance, *n,* contrepoids, *m.* ¶ *v.t,* contrebalancer, faire contrepoids à.

counterfeit, *a,* faux. ¶ *n,* contrefaçon, *f.* ¶ *v.t,* contrefaire. ~**er,** *n,* contrefacteur, *m;* (*money*) faux monnayeur, *m.*

counterfoil, *n,* souche, *f,* talon, *m.*

counter instructions, *n.pl,* contrordre, *m.*

countermand, *v.t,* annuler, révoquer; (*Com.*) décommander.

counterpane, *n,* couvre-lit, *m.*

counterpart, *n,* contrepartie, *f;* double, *m;* (*pers.*) homologue, *m,f.*

counterpoint, *n,* contrepoint, *m.*

counterpoise, *n,* contrepoids, *m.* ¶ *v.t,* contrebalancer, faire contrepoids à.

countersign, *v.t,* contresigner.

countersink, *v.t.ir,* fraiser.

counterweight, *n,* contrepoids, *m.*

countess, *n,* comtesse, *f.*

countless, *a,* innombrable.

country, *n,* pays, *m;* (*native*) patrie; (*opp. town*) campagne: *in the* ~, à la campagne; *surrounding* ~, région, *f.* ~ *cousin,* cousin(e) de province. ~ *dance,* danse folklorique, *f.* ~ *house,* (*weekend*) maison de campagne, *f;* (*large*) manoir, château, *m.* ~*man, -woman,* campagnard, e. [*fellow*] ~*man, -woman,* compatriote, *m,f.* ~*side,* campagne, *f.* ~ *town,* ville de province, *f.*

county, *n,* comté (*UK*), département (*Fr.*), *m.* ~ *town,* chef-lieu, *m.*

couple, *n,* couple, *m. young* ~, jeune couple, jeune ménage, *m.* ¶ *v.t,* [ac]coupler, atteler. **couplet,** *n,* distique, *m.* **coupling,** *n,* accouplement; (*Rly*) attelage; (*Elec.*) couplage, *m.*

coupon, *n,* coupon; bon; (*ration*) ticket, *m.*

courage, *n,* courage, *m.* ~**ous†,** *a,* courageux.

courier, *n,* courrier, *m.*

course, *n,* cours; courant, *m. in* ~ *of construction,* en cours de construction. (*river*) cours, lit, *m;* (*Naut.*) route, *f: set* ~ *for,* mettre le cap sur; (*Naut., fig.*) *go off* ~, faire fausse route. ~ *of action,* ligne de conduite, *f.* (*Sch., Univ.*) *attend a* ~, suivre des cours. (*meal*) plat, *m;* (*Med.*) traitement, *m;* (*bricks*) assise, *f.* (*sport*) terrain, parcours, *m,* piste, *f. in due* ~, en temps & lieu. *of* ~, naturellement, bien entendu. ¶ *v.t. & i,* chasser, courir. **coursing,** *n,* chasse au lièvre, *f.*

court, *n,* (*Law*) cour, *f,* tribunal, *m.* ~ *of enquiry,* commission d'enquête, *f.* (*royal, yard*) cour; (*tennis*) court, terrain, *m.* ~ *card,* figure, *f.* ~*-martial, n,* conseil de guerre, *m; v.t,* faire passer en c. de g. ~*s of justice,* palais de justice, *m.* ~*yard,* cour, *f.* ¶ *v.t,* (*woman*) faire la cour à, courtiser; (*favour*) solliciter, briguer; (*disaster &c*) inviter, aller au devant de. ¶ *v.i, be* ~*ing,* sortir ensemble. ~*ing couple,* couple d'amoureux, *m.*

courteous†, *a,* courtois, poli (*to,* envers). **courtesan,** *n,* courtisane, *f.* **courtesy,** *n,* courtoisie, politesse, *f.* **courtier,** *n,* courtisan, *m;* dame de la cour, *f.* **courtly,** *a,* élégant; (*love*) courtois. **courtship,** *n,* cour, *f.*

cousin, *n,* cousin, e.

cove[1] (*bay*) *n,* anse, crique, *f.*

cove[2] *P, n,* type, mec *P.*

covenant, *n,* convention, *f,* contrat, *m.* ¶ *v.i,* s'engager.

Coventry (to send to) (*fig.*), mettre en quarantaine.

cover, *n,* (*bowl &c*) couvercle, *m;* (*book*) couverture; (*chair &c, loose*) housse, *f. bed*~, dessus de lit, *m.* (*Com.*) *under separate* ~, sous pli séparé. (*shelter*) abri, *m: take* ~, se mettre à l'abri, s'abriter. (*Hunt.*) fourré, *m;* (*Insce*) couverture; (*at table*) couvert, *m;* (*Mil.* ~*ing fire*) feu de couverture, *m.* ¶ *v.t,* couvrir, recouvrir, revêtir (*with,* de); (*distance*) parcourir, couvrir; (*topics*) traiter, comprendre; (*sport*) marquer; (*animal*) couvrir. ~ *s.o. with a revolver,* braquer un revolver sur qn. ~ *up,* cacher, dissimuler. ~**age,** *n,* (*Press &c*) reportage, *m.* ~**ing,** *n,* couverture; (*layer*) couche, *f.* ~**let,** *n,* dessus de lit, couvre-lit, *m.*

covert, *a,* voilé, caché, secret. ¶ *n,* (*Hunt.*) fourré, *m.* ~**ly,** *ad,* en cachette.

covet, *v.t,* convoiter. ~**ous,** *a,* avide (*of,* de). ~**ously,** *ad,* avec convoitise. ~**ousness,** *n,* convoitise, *f.*

covey, *n,* compagnie, *f.*

cow, *n,* vache, *f;* (*att., of elephants &c*) femelle. ~*bell,* sonnaille, *f.* ~*boy,* cow-boy, *m.* ~ *catcher,* (*Rly*) chasse-pierres, *m inv.* ~*herd,* vacher, ère. ~ *hide,* peau de vache, *f.* ~ *shed,* étable, *f.* ¶ *v.t,* intimider.

coward, *n,* lâche, *m,* poltron, ne. ~**ice,** *n,* lâcheté, *f.* ~**ly,** *a,* lâche, poltron.

cower, *v.i,* se blottir, se tapir. (*fig.*) ~ *before s.o,* trembler devant qn.

cowl, *n,* (*monk, chimney*) capuchon, *m.*
cowrie, *n,* porcelaine, *f.*
cowslip, *n,* coucou, *m,* primevère, *f.*
coxcomb, *n,* fat, vaniteux, *m.*
coxswain (*abb.* cox) *n,* barreur; (*Naut.*) patron, *m.*
coy, *a,* qui simule la timidité. ~**ness,** *n,* timidité feinte; coquetterie, *f.*
crab[1], crabe, *m.* ~ [*louse*], morpion *P, m.*
crab[2], *n,* ~ [*apple*], pomme sauvage, *f;* (*tree*) pommier sauvage, *m.*
crabbed & crabby, *a,* revêche, grincheux.
crack, *a,* d'élite, de première classe. *a ~ skier,* un as *ou* un crack du ski. *~pot P,* cinglé *P,* loufoque *P,* tordu *P.* ¶ *n,* fente, fissure, crevasse; (*glass &c*) fêlure; (*paint*) craquelure; (*wall*) lézarde, *f;* (*of door ajar*) entrebaillement, *m;* (*noise*) craquement, claquement; (*rifle*) coup [sec]. *dirty ~ P,* vacherie *P,f. have a ~ at it P,* tenter le coup. ¶ *v.t,* fendre; (*glass &c*) fêler; (*ground*) crevasser; (*skin*) gercer; (*nuts*) casser; (*bottle*) déboucher; (*code*) déchiffrer; (*whip*) faire claquer. *~ a joke,* raconter une blague. *~ up P,* vanter, louer. ¶ *v.i,* se fendre, se fêler &c; (*whip*) claquer; (*voice*) se casser. *get ~ing P,* se mettre au boulot *P.* ~**ed** (*daft*) *a,* timbré, toqué. **cracker,** *n,* (*firework*) pétard, *m;* (*Christmas*) diablotin, *m.*
crackle, *v.i,* crépiter, pétiller. **crackling,** *n,* crépitement, *m;* (*Radio*) friture; (*pork*) couenne croquante, *f.* **cracknel,** *n,* craquelin, *m.*
cracksman, *n,* cambrioleur, *m.*
cradle, *n,* berceau; (*Surg.*) arceau, *m.* ¶ *v.t,* bercer.
craft, *n,* (*skill*) métier, art, *m;* (*cunning*) astuce, ruse; (*Naut.*) embarcation, *f,* petit bateau, *m.* **craftily,** *ad,* astucieusement. **craftsman,** *n,* homme de métier, artisan, *m.* ~**ship,** *n,* adresse, dextérité, connaissance du métier, *f.* **crafty,** *a,* astucieux, malin, rusé.
crag, *n,* rocher à pic, *m.* **craggy,** *a,* escarpé, à pic.
cram, *v.t,* bourrer (*with,* de). *~ into,* fourrer dans. (*with food*) gaver; (*pupil*) chauffer *P.* ¶ *v.i,* (*for exam*) bachoter. *~-full,* (*hall, bus*) bondé. *crammer's* (*school*) boîte à bachot, *f.*
cramp[1], *n,* (*Med.*) crampe, *f.* ¶ *v.t,* entraver, gêner. *~ s.o's style,* priver qn de ses moyens.
cramp[2], *n,* (*Build.*) agrafe, happe, *f,* crampon, *m.* ¶ *v.t,* cramponner.
cranberry, *n,* canneberge, *f.*
crane, *n,* (*bird & hoist*) grue, *f. ~ driver,* grutier, *m. ~ fly,* tipule, *f.* ¶ *v.t,* (*neck*) tendre.
cranium, *n,* crâne, *m.*
crank[1], *n,* (*Mach.*) manivelle, *f. ~ shaft,* vilebrequin, *m.* ¶ *v.t,* faire partir à la manivelle.
crank[2] **& cranky,** *n. & a,* eccentrique, loufoque *P, m,f.*
cranny, *n,* fente, crevasse, *f.*
crap *P**, *n,* merde *P**, *f;* (*nonsense*) conneries *P**, *f.pl.*
crape, *n,* crêpe, *m.*
crash, *n,* (*noise*) fracas; (*car, plane*) accident, *m;* (*car*) collision; (*Fin.*) faillite, *f;* (*Stk Ex.*) krach, *m.* ¶ *i,* patatras! ¶ *v.i,* retentir, éclater; (*car, plane*) s'écraser (*into,* contre); (*cars*) se rentrer dedans *P. ~ to the ground,* tomber, s'abattre avec fracas.
crass, *a,* crasse (*a.f.*), grossier.
crate, *n,* caisse à claire-voie, *f.*
crater, *n,* cratère; (*bomb &c*) entonnoir, *m.*
crave, *v.t,* implorer. *~ for,* avoir soif de.
craven, *a,* poltron, lâche.
craving, *n,* désir obsédant, grand besoin, *m,* soif, *f* (*for,* de).
crawl, *n,* (*Swim.*) crawl, *m.* ¶ *v.i,* ramper, se traîner; (*car*) avancer au pas, faire la poussette *P. to ~ with* (*lice &c*) grouiller de.
crayfish, crawfish, *n,* (*river*) écrevisse; (*sea*) langouste, langoustine, *f.*
crayon, *n,* [crayon] pastel, *m.*
craze, *n,* manie, marotte (*for,* de); toquade, *f* (*for,* pour). *it's all the ~,* cela fait fureur. ¶ *v.t,* rendre fou. **crazy,** *a,* fou, toqué *P,* dingue *P* (*about,* de). *~ paving,* dallage irrégulier, *m.*
creak, *v.i,* grincer, crier, craquer.
cream, *n,* crème, *f. ~ cheese,* fromage blanc, *m. the ~ of society,* la c. de la société. *~-coloured,* crème, *inv. ~ jug,* pot à c., *m. ~ puff,* chou à la crème, *m.* ¶ *v.t,* (*milk*) écrémer. ~**ery,** *n,* crémerie, *f.* ~**y,** *a,* crémeux.
crease, *n,* pli; (*unwanted*) faux pli, *m.* ¶ *v.t.*(*& i*), (se) plisser; (*crush*) (se) froisser, (se) chiffonner.
create, *v.t,* créer; faire, produire; provoquer. **creation,** *n,* création, *f.* **creative,** *a,* créateur. **creator, tress,** *n,* créateur, trice. **creature,** *n,* créature, *f,* être; animal, *m,* bête, *f. ~ comforts,* aises, *f.pl.*
crèche, *n,* crèche, garderie, pouponnière, *f.*
credence, *n,* croyance, *f. give ~ to,* ajouter foi à. **credentials,** *n.pl,* papiers d'identité, *m.pl;* lettres de créance, *f.pl.* **credibility,** *n,* crédibilité, *f.* **credible,** *a,* croyable; digne de foi. **credibly,** *ad, be ~ informed,* tenir de bonne source.
credit, *n,* (*belief*) foi, *f,* crédit, *m. give ~ to,* ajouter foi à. *gain ~* (*rumour*) s'accréditer, prendre crédit. (*Com., Fin.*) crédit; (*Bkkpg*) avoir, *m. give s.o ~,* faire crédit à qn. *buy on ~,* acheter à crédit. réputation, influence, *f,* crédit (*with s.o,* auprès de qn). *to his ~,* à son honneur. *reflect ~ on, bring ~ to,* faire honneur à. *~ balance,* solde créditeur, *m. ~ card,* carte de crédit, *f.* ¶ *v.t,* croire, ajouter foi à; (*qualities*) attribuer. *~ s.o with,* (*sum*) créditer qn de, porter au crédit de qn. ~**able,** *a,* honorable, estimable. ~**or,** *n,* créancier, ère.

credulity, *n,* crédulité, *f.* **credulous,** *a,* crédule.
creed, *n,* (*Rel.*) Credo, symbole [des Apôtres] *m;* (*gen.*) credo, principes, *m.pl.*
creek, *n,* crique, anse, *f. up the ~ P,* dans le pétrin.
creel, *n,* panier de pêche, *m.*
creep, *v.i.ir,* ramper. *~ into,* (*room*) entrer tout doucement *ou* à pas de loup; (*bed*) se glisser dans. *it makes my flesh ~,* cela me donne la chair de poule. *~ing paralysis,* paralysie progressive, *f.*¶ *n,* (*pers. P**) salaud *P*;* lécheur *P, m.* **~er,** *n,* plante grimpante, *f.* **~y,** *a,* qui fait frissonner.
cremate, *v.t,* incinérer. **cremation,** *n,* crémation, incinération, *f.* **crematorium,** *n,* four crématoire, *m.*
crenel[l]ate, *v.t,* créneler.
creole, *n. & a,* créole, *m,f.*
creosote, *n,* créosote, *f.* ¶ *v.t,* créosoter.
crêpe, *n,* (*cloth*) crêpe, *f. ~* [*rubber*] *soles,* semelles de crêpe, *f.pl.*
crept, *p.p. of* **creep.**
crescendo, *n,* crescendo, *m.*
crescent, *n,* croissant, *m. ~ moon,* croissant de la lune.
cress, *n,* cresson, *m. ~ bed,* cressonnière, *f.*
crest, *n,* (*bird, wave, mountain*) crête, *f;* (*helmet*) cimier, *m;* (*family*) armoiries, *f.pl.* ¶ *v.t,* franchir la crête de. *~ed,* (*bird*) huppé. *~fallen,* abattu, découragé.
Crete, *n,* la Crète.
cretin, *n,* & **~ous,** *a,* crétin, e.
cretonne, *n,* cretonne, *f.*
crevasse, *n,* crevasse, *f.* **crevice,** *n,* fente, lézarde, fissure, *f.*
crew, *n,* (*ship*) équipage, *m;* (*gun, rowing &c*) équipe, *f;* (*set, gang*) bande, *f.*
crib, *n,* mangeoire; (*Eccl.*) crèche, *f;* lit d'enfant, *m;* (*plagiary*) plagiat, *m;* (*Sch. P*) traduc *P, f.* ¶ *v.t,* (*Sch.*) *~ s.o's work,* copier sur qn.
crick (*in neck*) *n,* torticolis, *m.*
cricket[1], *n,* grillon, *m,* cri-cri, *m inv.*
cricket[2], *n,* (*game*) cricket, *m. ~ pitch,* terrain de c., *m.*
crier, *n,* crieur, *m.*
crime, *n,* crime, délit, *m.*
Crimea (the), la Crimée.
criminal†, *a,* criminel. *the C~ Investigation Department* (*C.I.D*), la police judiciaire (la P.J.). ¶ *n,* criminel, le.
crimp, *v.t,* friser, crêper.
crimson, *a. & n,* cramoisi, *m.*
cringe, *v.i,* reculer (*from,* devant); s'humilier. **cringing,** *a,* craintif; servile.
crinkle, *n,* plissement, *m,* fronce, *f.* ¶ *v.t.* (*& i*), (se) froisser.
cripple, *n,* estropié, e, boiteux, euse. ¶ *v.t,* estropier; (*fig.*) paralyser. *~d with rheumatism,* perclus de rhumatismes.
crisis, *n,* crise, *f.*
crisp, *a,* croquant, croustillant; (*air, style*) vif. *potato ~s,* [pommes] chips, *f.pl.* ¶ *v.t,* rendre croustillant.
criss-cross, *n,* entrecroisement, *m.* ¶ *v.i,* s'entrecroiser.
criterion, *n,* critère, *m.*
critic, *n,* critique; censeur, *m.* **critical,** *a,* (*pers., moment, condition*) critique. **criticism,** *n,* critique, *f.* **criticize,** *v.t,* critiquer; censurer.
croak, *v.i,* (*raven*) croasser; (*frog*) coasser.
crochet, *n. & ~ hook,* crochet, *m.*
crockery, *n,* faïence; (*dishes &c*) vaisselle, *f.*
crocodile, *n,* crocodile, *m. ~ tears,* larmes de crocodile, *f.pl. walk in ~,* aller deux par deux.
crocus, *n,* crocus, *m.*
crone, *n,* vieille femme ratatinée. **crony,** *n,* copain, *m,* copine, *f.*
crook, *n,* (*shepherd*) houlette; (*bishop*) crosse, *f;* (*river &c*) angle, *m;* (*pers. P*) escroc, gangster, *m.* ¶ *v.t,* [re]courber. **~ed,** *a,* crochu, tordu; de travers; (*pers.*) malhonnête. **~edly,** *ad,* de travers.
crop, *n,* produit agricole, *m;* (*harvest*) récolte, moisson; (*fruit*) cueillette, *f;* (*fig.*) tas, *m,* série, *f;* (*bird*) jabot, *m. hunting ~,* cravache, *f. ~ spraying,* pulverisation, *f.* ¶ *v.t,* (*hair*) tondre. *close ~ped,* coupé ras. (*animals: grass*) brouter, paître. ¶ *v.i, ~ up,* surgir, se présenter.
cropper, *come a ~ P,* ramasser une veste *P.*
croquet, *n,* croquet, *m.* ¶ *v.t,* croquer.
crosier, crozier, *n,* crosse, *f.*
cross, *a,* de mauvaise humeur, en colère. *get ~,* se fâcher, se mettre en colère (*with,* contre), ¶ *n.* croix; (*fig.*) croix; (*on letter t*) barre, *f;* (*Biol.*) hybride, croisement, *m;* (*fig.*) mélange, *m.* (*Need.*) *on the ~,* en biais. *~ bar* (*Foot.*) barre transversale, *f. ~-bred,* métis. *~-breed,* (*animal*) métis, se, hybride, *m. ~breeding,* croisement, métissage, *m. ~-country running, race,* cross[-country], *m. ~-examine s.o,* faire subir un interrogatoire à qn. *~-eyed,* qui louche. *~-patch,* grognon, *m. to be at ~-purposes,* se comprendre de travers. *~ reference,* renvoi, *m. ~roads,* carrefour, croisement, *m. ~ section,* coupe transversale, *f;* (*sample*) échantillon, *m. ~-stitch,* point de croix, *m. ~-word* [*puzzle*], mots croisés, *m.pl.* ¶ *v.t,* traverser, passer, franchir; (*arms, plants &c*) croiser; (*thwart*) contrarier, contrecarrer; (*cheque, a t*) barrer. (*Eccl.*) *~ o.s,* se signer. *~ out,* rayer, biffer, barrer. ¶ *v.i,* (*people, paths*) se croiser.
crossing, *n,* (*sea &c*) traversée, *f;* (*roads, plants*) croisement. [*pedestrian*] *~,* passage clouté, *m.*
crotch, *n,* (*tree, body*) fourche, *f.*
crotchet, *n,* (*Mus.*) noire, *f. ~ rest* (*Mus.*), soupir, *m.* **~y,** *a,* grincheux.

crouch, *v.i,* se tapir, s'accroupir.
croup[1] (*Med.*) *n,* croup, *m.*
croup[2] (*rump*) *n,* croupe, *f.*
crow, *n,* corbeau, *m,* corneille, *f;* (*cock's*) chant, *m.* ~[*bar*], pince [à levier], *f.* ~*foot* (*Bot.*), renoncule, *f.* ~*'s-foot* (*wrinkle*), patte d'oie, *f.* ~*'s-nest* (*Naut.*), nid de pie, *m. as the* ~ *flies,* à vol d'oiseau. ¶ *v.i.ir,* chanter. ~ *over,* chanter victoire sur.
crowd, *n,* foule, masse, *f;* beaucoup de monde; (*crush*) cohue; (*group*) bande, *f;* (*Theat.*) les figurants, *m.pl.* ¶ *v.i,* se presser, s'assembler. ~ *round,* assiéger. ~**ed,** *a,* (*room &c*) bondé, plein, comble.
crown, *n,* couronne, *f;* (*head, hill*) sommet; (*hat*) fond, *m.* (*Law*) *the C*~, la Couronne, *f.* ¶ *v.t,* couronner; (*Draughts*) damer. ~**ing,** *n,* couronnement, *m.* ¶ *a,* suprême.
crucial, *a,* décisif, critique.
crucible, *n,* creuset, *m.*
crucifix, *n,* crucifix, christ; (*wayside*) calvaire, *m.* ~**ion,** *n,* crucifiement, *m.* (*Eccl.*) *the C*~, la crucifixion, *f.* **crucify,** *v.t,* crucifier.
crude, *a,* (*oil &c*) brut; (*colour*) cru; (*pers.*) grossier; rudimentaire. ~**ly,** *ad,* crûment, grossièrement. ~**ness,** *n,* crudité, grossièreté, *f.*
cruel†, *a,* cruel (*to,* envers). ~**ty,** *n,* cruauté, *f.*
cruet, *n,* (*gen. & Eccl.*) burette, *f.* ~ *stand,* huilier, *m.*
cruise, *n,* croisière, *f.* ¶ *v.i,* croiser; (*car*) rouler. *cruising* (*taxi*), en maraude. **cruiser,** *n,* croiseur, *m.*
crumb, *n,* miette; (*opp. crust*) mie; (*fig.*) miette, *f,* brin, *m.* ~**y, crummy** *P, a,* minable *P.*
crumble, *v.t,* émietter. ¶ *v.i,* s'émietter; (*house*) crouler, tomber en ruines; (*hopes*) s'effondrer. **crumbly,** *a,* friable.
crumple, *v.t.* (*& i*) (se) froisser, (se) chiffonner.
crunch, *v.t,* croquer, faire craquer. ¶ *v.i,* craquer. ¶ *n,* (*gravel, snow*) craquement, crissement, *m. the* ~ *P,* le moment critique.
crupper, *n,* croupe; (*harness*) croupière, *f.*
crusade, *n,* croisade, *f.* **crusader,** *n,* croisé, *m.*
crush (*crowd*) *n,* cohue, foule, bousculade, *f.* *have a* ~ *on s.o P,* avoir un béguin pour qn. ~ *barrier,* rampe de sécurité, *f.* ¶ *v.t,* écraser, broyer; (*crumple*) froisser; (*fig.*) écraser. ¶ *v.i,* (*people*) se presser, se serrer.
crust, *n,* (*bread, earth's*) croûte, *f.*
crustacean, *a. & n,* crustacé, *m.*
crusty, *a,* (*bread*) croustillant; (*pers.*) bourru, hargneux. ~ *end* (*bread*), croûton, *m.*
crutch, *n,* béquille, *f.*
crux, *n,* nœud, point capital, *m.*
cry, *n,* cri, *m. let out a* ~, pousser un cri. *have a good* ~, pleurer un bon coup. ¶ *v.i,* crier. ~ *for help,* appeler, crier au secours. ~ *out,* s'écrier. (*weep*) pleurer. ~ *one's eyes out,* pleurer à chaudes larmes, verser toutes les larmes de son corps. ~ *off,* (*appointment*) se décommander. ~**ing,** *a,* (*fig.*) flagrant, criant. ¶ *n,* cris; pleurs, *m.pl,* larmes, *f.pl.*
crypt, *n,* crypte, *f.*
cryptic, *a,* énigmatique.
crystal, *n,* cristal, *m.* ¶ *a,* de cristal. ~ *ball,* boule de c. ~ *gazer,* voyant, e. **crystalline,** *a,* cristallin. ~ *lens* (*eye*), cristallin, *m.* **crystallize,** *v.t.* (*& i.*) (se) cristalliser. ~*d fruits,* fruits confits.
cub, *n,* (*animal*) petit, e. ~ *scout,* louveteau, *m.*
Cuba, *n,* Cuba, *m. in* ~, à C. **Cuban,** *a,* cubain. ¶ *n,* Cubain, e.
cube, *n,* cube, *m.* ~ *root,* racine cubique. ¶ *v.t,* cuber. **cubic,** *a,* (*shape*) cubique; (*measure*) cube. ~ *capacity,* volume, *m.* ~ *metre,* mètre cube, *m.*
cubicle, *n,* alcôve de dortoir; cabine, *f.*
cubism, *n,* cubisme, *m.* **cubist,** *n,* cubiste, *m,f.*
cuckoo, *n,* coucou, *m.* ~ *clock,* pendule à coucou, *f,* coucou, *m.*
cucumber, *n,* concombre, *m.*
cud, *chew the* ~, ruminer.
cuddle, *v.t,* serrer dans ses bras, caresser; (*child*) câliner. ¶ *v.i,* se serrer. ~ *up,* se pelotonner, se blottir (*to,* contre).
cudgel, *n,* gourdin, *m,* trique, *f.* ¶ *v.t,* battre à coups de trique. ~ *one's brains,* se creuser la cervelle.
cue, *n,* (*Theat.*) réplique, *f;* signal, *m;* (*Bil.*) queue, *f.*
cuff, *n,* (*shirt*) manchette, *f;* poignet; (*coat*) parement, *m.* ~ *links,* boutons de manchettes, *m.pl. off the* ~, impromptu. (*blow*) calotte *P,* taloche *P, f.* ¶ *v.t,* calotter *P.*
cul-de-sac, *n,* impasse, *f,* cul-de-sac, *m.*
culinary, *a,* culinaire.
cull, *v.t,* cueillir; (*fig.*) choisir, recueillir.
culminate, *v.i,* culminer; se terminer (*in,* par). **culminating,** *a,* culminant.
culpability, *n,* culpabilité, *f.* **culpable,** *a,* coupable. **culprit,** *n,* coupable, *m,f.*
cultivate, *v.t,* cultiver. **cultivation,** *n,* culture, *f.* **cultivator,** *n,* cultivateur, trice; (*machine*) cultivateur; motoculteur, *m.* **cultural,** *a,* culturel. **culture,** *n,* culture, *f.* ~**d,** *a,* (*pers.*) cultivé; (*pearl*) de culture.
cumber, *v.t,* encombrer. ~**some, cumbrous,** *a,* embarrassant, encombrant.
cumulative, *a,* cumulatif.
cumulus, *n,* cumulus, *m.*
cunning, *a,* astucieux, malin, rusé. ¶ *n,* finesse, astuce, ruse, *f.*
cunt *P**, *n,* con *P**, *m;* (*pers. P**) salaud *P**, *m,* salope *P**, *f.*
cup, *n,* tasse; (*metal*) timbale; (*goblet, sport*) coupe; (*Eccl.*) calice, *f.* ~ *bearer,* échanson, *m.* ~ *final,* finale de la coupe, *f.* ~*ful,* tasse, *f.* (*Med.*) ~*ping glass,* ventouse, *f.* ¶ *v.t,* (*Med.*) poser des ventouses à.

cupboard, *n,* armoire, *f;* (*wall*) placard, *m.* ~ *love,* amour intéressé, *m.*
Cupid, *n,* Cupidon, *m;* (*Art*) amour, *m.*
cupidity, *n,* cupidité, *f.*
cupola, *n,* coupole, *f.* ~ [*furnace*], cubilot, *m.*
cur, *n,* cabot, *m.*
curable, *a,* curable, guérissable.
curacy, *n,* vicariat, *m.* **curate,** *n,* vicaire, *m.*
curative, *a,* curatif.
curator, *n,* conservateur, *m.*
curb, *n,* (*harness*) gourmette; (*street*) bordure de pavés; (*fig.*) bride, *f,* frein, *m.* ¶ *v.t,* (*horse & fig.*) brider, tenir en bride.
curd[s], *n.*[*pl.*], caillé, *m.* **curdle,** *v.t,* cailler; (*fig., blood*) glacer, figer.
cure, *n,* guérison; cure, *f;* remède, *m;* (*souls*) charge, *f.* *water* ~, cure d'eau. *take a* ~, faire une cure. ¶ *v.t,* guérir; (*fig.*) remédier à, éliminer; (*salt*) saler; (*smoke*) fumer.
curfew, *n,* couvre-feu, *m.*
curiosity & curio, *n,* curiosité, rareté, *f,* bibelot, *m.* **curious†,** *a,* curieux; (*odd*) curieux, étrange, bizarre.
curl, *n,* (*hair*) boucle, *f;* (*ringlet*) frison, *m;* (*gen.*) courbe; (*smoke*) spirale, *f.* ~ *paper,* papillote, *f.* ~*ing tongs,* fer à friser, *m.* ¶ *v.t,* friser, boucler. ¶ *v.i,* (*lip*) se retrousser. ~ *up,* se mettre en boule, se pelotonner. **curler** (*hair*) *n,* rouleau, bigoudi, *m.*
curlew, *n,* courlis, *m.*
curling (*Sport*) *n,* curling, *m.*
curly, *a,* (*hair*) (*tightly*) frisé; (*loosely*) bouclé.
curmudgeon, *n,* bourru; hargneux, *m.*
currant, *n,* (*red, white*) groseille *f;* (*black*) cassis; (*dried*) raisin de Corinthe, *m.* ~ *bush,* groseillier; cassis, *m.*
currency, *n,* monnaie, *f,* argent, *m.* *in* ~, en circulation. *foreign* ~, devise *ou* monnaie étrangère, *f.* **current,** *a,* courant, actuel, en cours; (*rumour*) qui court. *to be* ~, avoir cours. *in* ~ *use,* d'usage courant. ~ *affairs,* actualités, *f.pl.* ¶ *n,* courant, *m.* ~**ly,** *ad,* actuellement.
curriculum, *n,* programme d'études, *m.*
curry[1] (*Cook.*) *n,* curry, cari, *m.* ~ *powder,* poudre de c., *f.*
curry[2], *v.t,* (*leather*) corroyer; (*horse*) étriller. ~ *favour with,* se faufiler dans les bonnes grâces de. ~*comb,* étrille, *f.*
curse, *n,* malédiction; (*oath*) imprécation, *f,* juron; (*bane*) fléau, *m.* (*woman*) *have the* ~ *P,* avoir ses règles. ¶ *v.t,* maudire. ¶ *v.i,* jurer. **cursed,** *a,* maudit, sacré *P,* (*both before n*). ~ *with,* affligé de.
cursory, *a,* hâtif, rapide, superficiel.
curt, *a,* sec, cassant, brusque.
curtail, *v.t,* raccourcir, écourter; (*fig.*) restreindre, réduire. ~**ment,** *n,* raccourcissement, *m;* réduction, *f.*
curtain, *n,* rideau; (*fig.*) rideau, voile, *f.* *draw the* ~*s,* tirer les rideaux. (*Theat.*) ~ *call,* rappel, *m.* ~ *raiser,* lever de rideau, *m.* ~ *rod,* tringle à rideaux.
curtly, *ad,* brusquement, d'un ton cassant.
curts[e]y, *n,* révérence, *f.* ¶ *v.i,* faire une r.
curvaceous *P, a,* (*woman*) bien balancée *P.*
curvature, *n,* courbure, *f.* ~ *of the spine,* déviation de la colonne vertébrale, *f.*
curve, *n,* courbe, *f;* (*road*) virage, tournant, *m.* ¶ *v.t.* (*& i*) (se) courber; (*Arch.*) cintrer. **curvet,** *n,* courbette, *f.* ¶ *v.i,* faire des courbettes. **curvilinear,** *a,* curviligne.
cushion, *n,* coussin, *m;* (*Bil.*) bande, *f.* ~ *cover,* taie de coussin, *f.*
cushy *P, a,* tranquille. ~ *job,* planque *P,f.*
cussed, *a,* têtu, entêté. *out of sheer* ~*ness,* pour embêter le monde.
custard, *n,* crème anglaise; (*set*) c. renversée, *f.* ~ *pie,* (*att. comedy*) tarte à la crème.
custodian, *n,* gardien, ne. **custody,** *n,* garde; arrestation, captivité, *f.*
custom, *n,* usage, *m,* coutume; pratique, *f;* (*Com.*) clientèle, *f,* clients, *m.pl.* ~**ary,** *a,* habituel, ordinaire, coutumier. ~**er,** *n,* client, e; (*at café*) consommateur, *m; P,* type, individu, *m.* *queer* ~, drôle de type *P.*
customs, *n.pl,* douane, *f.* ~ *duty,* droits de douane, *m.pl.* ~ *inspection,* visite de douane, *f.* ~ *officer,* douanier, *m.*
cut, *n,* (*hair, clothes*) coupe; (*wound; book, film; power*) coupure, *f;* (*stroke*) coup, *m;* (*Med.*) incision; (*pay &c*) réduction, diminution, *f;* (*meat*) morceau; (*saw*) trait, *m.* ~*back,* (*staff &c*) réduction, *f.* ~*-price,* au rabais, à prix réduit. ~*-throat,* assassin, *m;* (*att. competition*) acharné; (*rasor*) de coiffeur. ¶ *v.t,* couper; trancher; (*shape, trim*) tailler; (*lawn*) tondre; (*corn*) faucher. ~ *one's finger,* se couper au doigt. ~ *one's teeth,* faire ses dents. *get one's hair* ~, se faire couper les cheveux. (*pay &c*) réduire, diminuer; (*article &c*) couper. ~ *short* (*visit*) écourter; (*pers.*) couper la parole à. ~ *the ground from under s.o's feet,* couper l'herbe sous les pieds de qn. ~ *it very fine,* compter très juste. ~ *& dried,* tout fait. ~ **across,** (*fields*) couper à travers; (*plans*) aller à l'encontre de. ~ **back,** (*shrubs &c*) tailler, élaguer; (*production*) réduire. ~ **down,** (*tree*) abattre; (*costs*) réduire. ~ *down on,* économiser sur. ~ **in,** (*car, runner*) se rabattre. ~ **into,** (*flesh, metal, loaf*) entamer; (*conversation*) se mêler à. ~ **off,** (*phone, power*) couper; (*limb*) amputer. ~ **out,** (*picture*) découper; (*detail*) enlever, élaguer, supprimer; (*smoking*) arrêter de. ~ **up,** (*wood*) couper; (*meat*) (*carve*) découper, (*chop*) hacher. (*fig.*) *be* ~ *up about,* être affecté par.
cute, *a,* fin, rusé, astucieux; mignon.
cuticle, *n,* épiderme, *m;* (*nails*) petites peaux,

f.pl.
cutlass, *n,* coutelas, sabre d'abordage, *m.*
cutler, *n,* coutelier, ère. **cutlery,** *n,* & ~ *trade,* coutellerie, *f;* (*on table*) couverts, *m.pl.*
cutlet, *n,* côtelette; (*veal*) escalope, *f.*
cutter, *n,* (*clothes*) coupeur, euse; (*gems, stone*) tailleur; (*film*) monteur euse; (*tool*) couteau, coupoir, *m;* (*boat*) cotre; canot, *m.* **cutting,** *a,* coupant, tranchant; (*wind*) cinglant; (*remark*) mordant, acéré, caustique. ~ *edge,* tranchant, *m.* ~*-out scissors,* ciseaux à couture, *m.pl.* ¶ *n,* (*trees*) coupe, *f,* abattage; (*film*) montage, *m;* (*gem*) taille; (*newspaper*) coupure; (*Rly*) tranchée; (*plant*) bouture, *f.*
cuttle fish, *n,* seiche, *f.*
cyanide, *n,* cyanure, *m.*
cyclamen, *n,* cyclamen, *m.*
cycle, *n,* (*Astr., seasons, song &c*) cycle, *m;* (*bicycle*) bicyclette, *f,* vélo, *m.* ~ *track* (*path*), piste cyclable, *f.* ¶ *v.i,* aller à bicyclette, en vélo. *go cycling,* faire de la bicyclette, du vélo. **cycling,** *n,* cyclisme, *m.* ~ *track* (*races*), vélodrome, *m.* **cyclist,** *n,* cycliste, *m,f.* **cyclometer,** *n,* compteur de bicyclette, *m.*
cyclone, *n,* cyclone, *m.*
cygnet, *n,* jeune cygne, *m.*
cylinder, *n,* cylinder; (*typewriter*) rouleau, *m.* ~ *head,* culasse, *f.* **cylindrical,** *a,* cylindrique.
cymbal, *n,* cymbale, *f.*
cynic, *n,* cynique, *m,f.* **cynical†,** *a,* cynique. **cynicism,** *n,* cynisme, *m.*
cynosure (*fig.*) *n,* point de mire, *m.*
cypress, *n,* cyprès, *m.*
Cyprus, *n,* Chypre, *f.* *in* ~, à Chypre.
cyst (*Med.*) *n,* kyste, *m.*
Czech, *a.* & (*language*) *n,* tchèque, *m.* ¶ (*pers.*) *n,* Tchèque, *m,f.* **Czechoslovak,** *n,* Tchécoslovaque, *m,f.* **Czechoslovakia,** *n,* la Tchécoslovaquie.

D

D (*Mus.*) *letter,* ré, *m.* *D-day,* le jour J.
dab[1], *n,* petit coup, petit morceau; coup de tampon, *m.* ¶ *v.t,* tamponner.
dab[2], *n,* (*fish*) limande, *f.*
dabble, *v.i,* barboter. ~ *in,* s'occuper un peu de. ~ *on the stock exchange,* boursicoter.
dace, *n,* vandoise, *f.*
dachshund, *n,* teckel, *m.*
dad[dy], *n,* papa, *m.*
daddy-longlegs, *n,* tipule, *f.*
dado, *n,* lambris d'appui, *m.*
daffodil, *n,* jonquille, *f.*
daft, *a,* idiot, stupide, timbré *P.*
dagger, *n,* poignard, *m;* (*Typ.*) croix, *f.* *at* ~*s drawn,* à couteaux tirés.
dahlia, *n,* dahlia, *m.*
daily, *a,* quotidien, journalier. ~ *help,* femme de ménage, *f.* ~ [*paper*], [journal] quotidien, *m.* ¶ *ad,* journellement, quotidiennement, tous les jours.
daintily, *ad,* délicatement. **daintiness,** *n,* délicatesse. **dainty,** *a,* (*food*) délicat. ~ *morsel,* morceau de choix. (*girl*) mignon. ¶ *n,* friandise, *f,* mets délicat, *m.*
dairy, *n,* laiterie; (*shop*) crémerie, *f;* (*att. farm, cow*) laitier. ~*maid,* fille de laiterie. ~*man,* (*farm*) employé de laiterie, (*shop*) crémier. ~ *products,* produits laitiers.
dais, *n,* estrade, *f.*
daisy, *n,* marguerite, pâquerette, *f.*
dale, *n,* vallée, *f,* vallon, *m.*
dally, *v.i,* tarder; lambiner *P.* ~ *with* (*idea*) caresser.
Dalmatian, *n,* (*dog*) dalmatien, *m.*
dam, *n,* barrage, *m,* digue, *f.* ¶ *v.t,* endiguer.
damage, *n,* dommage, dégât, *m,* avarie, *f;* (*pl., Law*) dommages-intérêts, *m.pl.* ¶ *v.t,* (*goods*) endommager, abîmer; (*health*) abîmer; (*reputation*) nuire à.
Damascus, *n,* Damas, *m.* **damask,** *n,* damas, *m.*
dame, *n,* dame; (*Am P*) fille, nana *P, f.*
damn, *v.t,* damner; (*book &c*) éreinter. ¶ *i,* ~*!* ~ *it!* merde! *P.* ¶ *a, P* (& ~*ed*), sacré *P,* fichu *P* (*before n.*) ¶ *ad, P* (& ~*ed*), rudement *P,* bougrement *P,* vachement *P.* *I don't give a* ~, je m'en fiche pas mal. ~**able,** *a,* détestable. ~**ation,** *n,* damnation, *f.* ~**ing,** *a,* accablant.
damp, *a,* humide; moite. ~*-course,* couche isolante, *f.* ~*-proof,* imperméable. ¶ *n,* humidité, *f.* ¶ *v.t,* humecter, (*fig.*) refroidir; (*shock*) amortir. ~**er,** *n,* (*piano*) étouffoir; (*furnace*) registre, *m.* ~**ness,** *n,* humidité, *f.*
damsel, *n,* demoiselle, jeune fille, *f.*
damson, *n,* prune de Damas, *f.* ~ [*tree*], prunier de Damas, *m.*
dance, *n,* danse, *f;* (*event*) bal, *m,* soirée dansante, *f.* ~ *floor,* piste, *f.* ~ *hall,* dancing, *m.* *D*~ *of Death,* Danse macabre. ¶ *v.i.* & *t,* danser. ~ *attendance* (*on*), s'empresser (auprès de). **dancer,** *n,* danseur, euse. **dancing,** *n,* la danse. ~ *partner,* cavalier, *m,*

partenaire, *m,f.*
dandelion, *n,* pissenlit, *m.*
dandle, *v.t,* (*child*) faire sauter sur ses genoux; bercer.
dandruff, *n,* pellicules, *f.pl.*
dandy, *n,* dandy, élégant, *m.*
Dane, *n,* Danois, e.
danger, *n,* danger, péril, *m. out of* ~, hors de danger. *be in* ~ *of* (*doing*), risquer de (faire). ~**ous†,** *a,* dangereux.
dangle, *v.t,* balancer; laisser pendre. ¶ *v.i,* (*legs &c*) pendre, se balancer. *with arms dangling,* les bras ballants.
Danish, *a,* danois. ¶ (*language*) *n,* le danois.
dank, *a,* humide et froid.
dapper, *a,* pimpant; tiré à quatre épingles.
dappled, *a,* tacheté; (*sky*) pommelé.
dare, *v.i.ir,* oser (faire). *I* ~ *say,* sans doute. ~-*devil,* casse-cou, *m.* ¶ *v.t.ir,* ~ *s.o to do,* défier qn de faire. **daring†,** *a,* audacieux, osé, hardi. ¶ *n,* audace, hardiesse, *f.*
dark, *a,* obscur; sombre; noir; ténébreux; (*complexion*) brun, basané; (*colours*) foncé: ~ *blue,* bleu foncé, *inv. it is* ~, il fait noir, il fait nuit. *it is pitch* ~, il fait nuit noire. *look on the* ~ *side of things,* voir tout en noir. *keep sth* ~, tenir qch secret. *to be a* ~ *horse,* cacher son jeu. *the D*~ *Ages,* l'âge de l'ignorance. ~ *room* (*Phot.*), chambre noire, *f.* ¶ *n,* obscurité, nuit, *f,* ténèbres, *f.pl. after* ~, la nuit venue. *to be in the* ~ (*fig.*), être dans le noir; être tout à fait ignorant (*about,* de). ~**en,** *v.t.* (*& i*) (s')assombrir, (s')obscurcir; (*face*) se rembrunir. ~**ly,** *ad,* obscurément; (*hint*) mystérieusement. ~**ness,** *n,* obscurité, *f,* ténèbres, *f.pl;* teinte foncée, *f.* **dark[e]y,** *n, pej,* moricaud, e, *pej.*
darling, *a,* chéri, bien-aimé. ¶ *n,* chéri, e, bien-aimé, e; (*child*) petit chou, petit amour. *mother's* ~, chouchou, te. (*of the people*) idole, *f.*
darn[1], *n,* reprise, *f.* ¶ *v.t,* (*socks*) repriser; (*clothes*) raccommoder. ~**ing,** reprise, *f;* raccommodage, *m.* ~ *needle,* aiguille à repriser, *f.*
darn[2] *&* **darned,** *mild form of* **damn** *&* **damned.**
dart, *n,* (*weapon*) trait, javelot, *m;* (*game*) fléchette, *f.* ~*s,* jeu de fléchettes, *m.* ¶ *v.t,* (*look*) darder, lancer. ¶ *v.i,* s'élancer, se précipiter.
dash, *n,* (*rush*) élan, *m,* ruée, *f;* (*spirit*) fougue, *f,* entrain, *m;* (*drink*) goutte, *f;* (*Typ.*) tiret; (*morse*) trait, *m. make a* ~ *for it,* prendre ses jambes à son cou. *cut a* ~, faire de l'effet. ~*board,* tableau de bord, *m.* ¶ *i,* ~! ~ *it!* P, zut alors! *P,* flûte! *P.* ¶ *v.t,* jeter violemment; (*fig.*) abattre; (*hopes*) anéantir. ¶ *v.i,* (*rush*) se précipiter. ~**ed** *P, a, ad,* mild form of **damned.** ~**ing,** *a,* fougueux; fringant.
dastardly, *a,* lâche; ignoble.
data, *n.pl,* données, *f.pl.* ~ *processing,* informatique, *m.*
date[1], *n,* date, *f. what is the* ~*?* quelle est la date?, nous sommes le combien? *fix a* ~, prendre date. *up to* ~, (*pers.*) à la page; (*work*) à jour. *out of* ~, démodé. (*pers.*) *be out of* ~, retarder. (*P with s.o*) rendez-vous, *m.* ~ *stamp,* dateur, *m.* ¶ *v.t,* (*letter*) dater; (*pers.*) prendre rendez-vous avec.
date[2], *n,* datte, *f.* ~ *palm,* dattier, *m.*
dative [case], *n,* datif, *m.*
datum, *n,* donnée, *f.*
daub, *n,* (*painting*) barbouillage, *m,* croûte *P, f;* (*walls*) enduit, *m.* ¶ *v.t,* barbouiller, peinturlurer.
daughter, *n,* fille, *f.* ~-*in-law,* belle-fille, *f.*
daunt, *v.t,* intimider, décourager. ~**less†,** *a,* intrépide.
davit, *n,* bossoir, *m.*
dawdle, *v.i,* flâner, lambiner *P.* ~ *on the way,* trainer *ou* s'amuser en chemin.
dawn, *n,* aube, *f,* point du jour, *m,* aurore, *f;* (*fig.*) naissance, *f.* ¶ *v.i,* poindre; se lever; (*fig.*) naître. ~**ing,** *a,* naissant.
day, *n,* jour, *m;* journée, *f. the* ~ *before, after* (*sth*), la veille, le lendemain (de qch). *2* ~*s before, after* (*sth*), l'avant-veille, le surlendemain (de qch). *on that* ~, ce jour-là. *every* ~, tous les jours. *every other* ~, tous les deux jours. *from that* ~ *on,* à partir de ce jour. *this* ~ *week,* d'aujourd'hui en huit. *any* ~ *now,* d'un jour à l'autre. *one of these* ~*s,* un de ces jours. *live from* ~ *to* ~, vivre au jour le jour. *in those* ~*s,* à cette époque-là. *in the* ~*s of*.., au temps de.. *these* ~*s,* de nos jours. *the good old* ~*s,* le vieux bons temps. (*Sch*) ~ *boy, girl,* externe, *m,f.* ~ *boarder,* demi-pensionnaire, *m,f.* ~*break,* point du jour, *m,* ~ *dream,* rêverie, *f; v.i,* rêvasser. ~ *labourer,* journalier, *m.* ~ *nursery,* crèche, pouponnière, *f.* ~ *shift,* équipe de jour, *f. in the* ~ *time,* le jour, pendant la journée.
daylight, *n,* lumière du jour, *f. in broad* ~, en plein jour. *it is still* ~, il fait encore jour. ~ *saving time,* l'heure d'été, *f.*
daze, *v.t,* stupéfier, hébéter; étourdir; (*news*) abasourdir. ¶ *n, in a* ~, stupéfait, étourdi, ahuri; *P.* dans la lune.
dazzle, *n,* éblouissement, *m.* ¶ *v.t,* éblouir, aveugler. **dazzling,** *a,* éblouissant; aveuglant.
deacon, *n,* diacre, *m.* ~**ess,** *n,* diaconesse, *f.*
dead, *a,* mort; (*pers. only*) décédé. *to drop* [*stone*] ~, tomber [raide] mort. (*limbs*) engourdi; (*colour*) terne; (*secret*) profond. ~ *silence,* silence de mort, *m.* ¶ *ad,* absolument, complètement. ~ *in the middle,* au beau milieu. *stop* ~, s'arrêter net. ~ *broke P,* fauché [comme les blés] *P.* ¶ *n, the* ~, les morts, *m.pl.* ~-*ball line* (*Rugby*), ligne de ballon mort, *f.* ~-*beat,* ~ *tired,* éreinté,

crevé *P,* claqué *P.* ~ *calm,* calme plat, *m.* ~ *centre,* point mort, *m.* ~ *drunk,* ivre mort. ~ *end,* impasse, *f.* ~ *letter,* (*Post*) rebut, *m;* (*fig.*) lettre morte, *f.* ~ *line,* date *ou* heure limite, *f.* ~ *lock,* impasse, *f.* ~ *loss,* (*Com.*) perte sèche; (*pers.*) bon à rien, *m.* ~ *march,* marche funèbre, *f.* ~ *reckoning* (*Naut.*), estime, *f. D*~ *Sea,* mer Morte, *f.* ~ *season,* morte-saison, *f.* ~ *wire,* fil sans courant, *m.* ~**en,** *v.t,* (*blow*) amortir; (*sound*) assourdir; (*feeling*) émousser. ~**ly,** *a,* mortel, (*weapon*) meurtrier; (*P boring*) mortel, rasoir *P.* ~ *nightshade,* belladone, *f.* ~ *sins,* péchés capitaux, *m.pl.*

deaf, *a,* sourd. ~ *as a post,* s. comme un pot. *turn a* ~ *ear to,* faire la sourde oreille à. ~ *& dumb,* ~*-mute,* sourd(e)-muet(te), *m,f.* ~ *& dumb alphabet,* alphabet des sourds-muets. ~**en,** *v.t,* assourdir. ~**ness,** *n,* surdité, *f.*

deal[1], *n, a good* ~ *of, a great* ~ *of,* beaucoup de, pas mal de, une grande quantité de. (*ad.*) *a good* ~ *better,* bien meilleur, beaucoup mieux. (*Com.*) marché, *m,* affaire, *f. a raw* ~ *P,* un sale coup *P.* (*cards*) donne, main, *f.* ¶ *v.t,* (*cards*) donner; (*blow*) porter, asséner. ~ *out,* distribuer, répartir. ¶ *v.i,* ~ *with,* (*pers.*) avoir affaire à qn; (*Com.*) traiter, négocier (avec qn); (*shop*) se fournir chez; (*task*) s'occuper de. ~**er,** *n,* marchand, e, fournisseur, *m;* (*Cards*) donneur, euse. ~**ing,** *n,* (*&* ~ *out*) distribution, *f.* ~*s* (*with people*) rapports, *m.pl,* relations; (*Stk Ex.*) opérations, *f.pl.*

deal[2], *n,* [bois de] sapin, bois blanc, *m.*

dean, *n,* (*Eccl., Univ.*) doyen, ne. ~**ery,** *n,* doyenné, *m;* demeure du doyen, *f.*

dear, *a,* (*pers.*) cher; (*object*) précieux; (*costly*) cher, coûteux. (*letters*) ~ *Jean,* cher Jean. ~ *Sir,* Monsieur. ~ *Mme Dupont,* chère Madame. ¶ *n, my* ~, mon cher ami, ma chère amie. *my* ~*est.* mon chéri, ma chérie. *... there's a* ~, ... tu seras bien gentil. ¶ *i,* ~, ~*! oh* ~*!* ~ *me!* oh là! là! mon Dieu! ~**ly,** *ad,* tendrement. (*lit., & fig.*) *pay* ~ *for,* payer cher.

dearth, *n,* manque, *m.* (*food*) disette, *f.*

death, *n,* mort, *f;* décès, *m.* ~ *bed,* lit de mort, *m.* ~ *blow,* coup mortel, *m.* ~ *certificate,* acte de décès, *m.* ~ *duties,* droits de succession, *m.pl.* ~ *knell,* glas *m.* ~ *penalty,* peine de mort, *f.* ~ *rate,* mortalité, *f,* taux de m., *m.* ~ *warrant,* ordre d'execution; (*fig.*) arrêt de mort, *m.* ~*-watch* [*beetle*], horloge de la mort, vrillette, *f.* ~**less,** *a,* immortel.

debar, *v.t,* exclure, priver (*from,* de).

debase, *v.t,* avilir; ravaler; (*metal*) altérer.

debatable, *a,* discutable, contestable. **debate,** *n,* débat, *m,* discussion, *f.* ¶ *v.t,* débattre, discuter.

debauch, *v.t,* débaucher; corrompre. ¶ *n* (*&* ~**ery**) débauche, *f.* ~**ee,** *n,* débauché, e.

debilitate, *v.t,* débiliter. **debility,** *n,* débilité, *f.*

debit, *n,* débit, *m.* ¶ *v.t,* débiter. ~ *balance,* solde débiteur, *m.* ¶ *v.t,* ~ *s.o with a sum,* débiter qn d'une somme, porter une s. au débit de qn.

debris, *n,* débris, *m.pl.*

debt, *n,* dette, créance, *f. in* ~, endetté. *run into* ~, faire des dettes, s'endetter. *be in s.o's* ~ (*for sth*), être redevable à qn (de qch). ~ *collector,* agent de recouvrements, *m.* ~**or,** *n,* débiteur, trice.

decade, *n,* décennie, décade, *f.*

decadence, *n,* décadence, *f.* **decadent,** *a,* décadent, en décadence.

decamp, *v.i,* décamper, ficher le camp *P.*

decant, *v.t,* décanter, transvaser. ~**er,** *n,* carafe, *f;* (*small*) carafon, *m.*

decapitate, *v.t,* décapiter.

decarbonize, *v.t,* (*Mot.*) décalaminer.

decay, *n,* pourriture; (*teeth*) carie; (*fig.*) ruine, décadence, *f.* ¶ *v.i,* pourrir, se gâter; (*teeth*) se carier; (*house*) tomber en ruines.

decease, *n,* décès, *m.* ¶ *v.i,* décéder. ~**d,** *n,* défunt, e, décédé, e.

deceit, *n,* tromperie, fausseté, duplicité, *f.* ~**ful,** *a,* trompeur, mensonger. **deceive,** *v.t,* tromper, abuser, duper. **deceiver,** *n,* trompeur, euse.

December, *n,* décembre, *m.*

decency, *n,* décence; pudeur, *f;* convenances, *f.pl.*

decent, *a,* (*dress*) décent; (*pers.*) convenable, honnête. (*nice*) *a* ~ *sort P,* un chic type *P.* *that's* ~ *of him,* c'est chic de sa part. ~**ly,** *ad,* décemment; convenablement.

decentralize, *v.t,* décentraliser.

deception, *n,* tromperie, *f.* **deceptive,** *a,* trompeur, illusoire; mensonger.

decibel (*Phys.*) *n,* décibel, *m.*

decide, *v.i. & t,* (*to do*) décider (de faire); se décider (à faire); (*question*) décider, trancher. **decided,** *a,* (*pers.*) décidé, résolu; (*distinct*) marqué, net, incontestable. ~**ly,** *ad,* décidément.

deciduous, *a,* caduc; (*tree*) à feuilles caduques.

decimal, *a,* décimal. ~ *point,* virgule [décimale], *f. Note:*–The decimal point is indicated in French by a comma. ¶ *n,* décimale, *f.*

decimate, *v.t,* décimer.

decipher, *v.t,* déchiffrer.

decision, *n,* décision, *f;* (*Law*) jugement, arrêt, *m. reach a* ~, prendre une décision, prendre un parti. (*quality*) résolution, fermeté, *f.* **decisive,** *a,* décisif; (*manner*) décidé.

deck, *n,* (*Naut.*) pont, *m.* (*bus*) *top* ~, impériale, *f.* ~ *chair,* transatlantique, transat *P, m.* ¶ *v.t,* parer, orner (*with,* de). ~ *with flags,* pavoiser.

declaim, *v.i,* déclamer. **declamatory,** *a,*

déclamatoire.

declaration, *n,* déclaration, *f.* **declare,** *v.t,* déclarer, proclamer. ~ *o.s for, against,* se déclarer pour, contre. *well, I* ~*!* [ça] par exemple!

declension (*Gram.*) *n,* déclinaison, *f.*

decline, *n,* déclin, *m;* décadence, *f;* (*prices*) baisse, *f. on the* ~, moins fréquent. (*Med.*) *go into a* ~, dépérir. ¶ *v.t,* refuser, décliner. ¶ *v.i,* baisser; (*ground*) s'incliner. *in his declining years,* au déclin de sa vie.

declivity, *n,* déclivité, pente, *f.*

declutch, *v.i,* débrayer.

decode, *v.t,* déchiffrer.

decompose, *v.t.* (*& i*) (se) décomposer.

decorate, *v.t,* décorer; orner (*with,* de); (*room*) peindre, tapisser; (*Mil.*) décorer. **decoration,** *n,* décoration, *f;* décor, *m.* **decorative,** *a,* décoratif. **decorator,** *n,* décorateur, *m.*

decorous†, *a,* convenable, bienséant. **decorum,** *n,* décorum, *m;* bienséance, *f.*

decoy, *n,* (*bird*) appeau, *m,* chanterelle, *f;* (*imitation*) leurre, *m;* (*pers.*) compère, *m.* ¶ *v.t,* leurrer; attirer dans un piège.

decrease, *m,* diminution, décroissance, *f.* ¶ *v.i,* diminuer, décroître.

decree, *n,* décret, arrêt; jugement, *m.* ~ *absolute,* jugement définitif. ~ *nisi,* j. provisoire. ¶ *v.t,* décréter, ordonner.

decrepit, *a,* (*pers.*) décrépit; (*thing*) vermoulu. **decrepitude,** *n,* décrépitude, *f,* délabrement, *m.*

decry, *v.t,* décrier.

dedicate, *v.t,* dédier, consacrer. ~ *o.s to,* se dévouer à. **dedication,** *n,* consécration; (*book*) dédicace, *f;* (*quality*) dévouement, *m.*

deduce, *v.t,* déduire.

deduct, *v.t,* déduire, retrancher, défalquer, rabattre. ~**ion,** *n,* déduction, défalcation; (*from pay*) retenue, *f;* (*logical*) déduction.

deed, *n,* action, *f;* acte; fait; exploit; (*Law*) acte, contrat; (*title* ~) titre, *m.*

deem, *v.t,* juger, estimer, considérer.

deep, *a,* profond. *the water is 2 metres* ~, l'eau a 2 mètres de profondeur. (*snow*) épais; (*sound*) grave; (*colour*) foncé, intense; (*interest*) vif; (*pers.*) rusé, malin. ~ *in* (*thought, book*) plongé, absorbé dans. ~ *in debt,* criblé de dettes. ¶ *n,* océan, *m.* ~*-freeze,* congélateur, *m.* ~*-sea diver,* plongeur sous-marin. ~*-sea fisherman,* pêcheur de haute mer. ~*-sea fishing,* grande pêche. ~*-seated,* profond, enraciné. ~**en,** *v.t.* (*& i*) (s')approfondir; rendre (devenir) plus profond &c. ~**[ly],** *ad,* profondément, ~ *into,* (*forest*) très avant dans. (*grateful*) extrêmement, infiniment. *go* ~ *into sth,* approfondir qch.

deer, *n,* cerf, *m,* biche, *f;* (*fallow*) daim, *m;* (*roe*) chevreuil, *m.* ~*-stalking,* chasse au cerf à pied.

deface, *v.t,* dégrader; mutiler; barbouiller.

defamation, *n,* diffamation, *f.* **defamatory,** *a,* diffamatoire, diffamant, infamant. **defame,** *v.t,* diffamer.

default, *n,* défaut, *m.* (*Law*) *judgment by* ~, jugement par défaut *ou* par contumace. *in* ~ *of,* à défaut de, faute de. ¶ *v.i,* manquer à ses engagements; (*Law*) faire défaut. ~**er,** *n,* (*Mil.*) consigné, e.

defeat, *n,* défaite, *f.* ¶ *v.t,* vaincre, battre, défaire; (*hopes*) frustrer; (*plan*) faire échouer. ~**ist,** *a. & n,* défaitiste, *m,f.*

defecate, *v.t. & i,* déféquer.

defect, *n,* défaut, *m,* vice, *m;* imperfection, tare, *f.* ~**ion,** *n,* défection; apostasie, *f.* ~**ive†,** *a,* défectueux; (*Gram.*) défectif; (*Med.*) déficient.

defence, *n,* défense, *f.* ~**less,** *a,* sans défense. **defend,** *v.t,* défendre. ~**ant,** *n,* défendeur, eresse. ~**er,** *n,* défenseur, *m.* **defensible,** *a,* défendable, justifiable. **defensive,** *a,* défensif. ¶ *n,* défensive, *f.*

defer, *v.t. & i,* différer, remettre, renvoyer, retarder; (*submit*) déférer (à qn). ~**ence,** *n,* déférence, *f,* respect, *m* (pour qn). **deferential,** *a,* déférent, respectueux; (*tone*) de déférence.

defiance, *n,* défi, *m. in* ~ *of,* (*law*) au mépris de. **defiant,** *a,* de défi.

deficiency, *n,* insuffisance, *f;* manque, défaut; (*Fin.*) déficit, *m;* (*Med.*) carence, *f.* **deficient,** *a,* défectueux; insuffisant. *to be* ~ *in,* manquer de. **deficit,** *n,* déficit, *m.*

defile[1], *n,* (*gorge, march*) défilé, *m.*

defile[2], *v.t,* souiller, profaner. ~**ment,** *n,* souillure, profanation, *f.*

definable, *a,* définissable. **define,** *v.t,* définir. **definite,** *a,* défini; déterminé; précis. ~**ly,** *ad,* décidément, sans aucun doute. **definition,** *n,* définition, *f.* **definitive†,** *a,* définitif.

deflate, *v.t,* (*tyre*) dégonfler; (*pers.*) démonter. **deflation,** *n,* dégonflement, *m;* (*Fin.*) déflation, *f.*

deflect, *v.t,* détourner, faire dévier. ~**ion,** *n,* déviation, déflexion, *f.*

deflower, *v.t,* (*girl*) déflorer; (*Bot.*) défleurir.

defoliation, *n,* défoliation, *f.*

deforest, *v.t,* déboiser.

deform, *v.t,* déformer, défigurer. ~**ed,** *a,* difforme, contrefait. ~**ity,** *n,* difformité, *f.*

defraud, *v.t,* (*state*) frauder; (*pers.*) frustrer (qn de qch), escroquer (qch à qn).

defray, *v.t,* ~ *s.o's expenses,* défrayer qn, rembourser ses frais; (*cost*) couvrir.

deft†, *a,* adroit. ~**ness,** *n,* adresse, *f.*

defunct, *a,* défunt. ¶ *n,* défunt, e.

defy, *v.t,* défier, braver. ~ *s.o to do,* défier qn de faire.

degeneracy *&* **degeneration,** *n,* dégénérescence,

f. **degenerate,** *a.* & *n,* dégénéré, e. ¶ *v.i,* dégénérer, s'abâtardir.
degradation, *n,* dégradation, *f;* avilissement, *m.* **degrade,** *v.t,* dégrader; abaisser, avilir. **degrading,** *a,* dégradant, avilissant.
degree, *n,* (*Math., Geog., heat*) degré, *m. by* ~*s,* par degrés. *to some* ~, dans une certaine mesure. (*Univ.*) grade, *m,* licence, *f.*
dehydrate, *v.t,* déshydrater.
deify, *v.t,* déifier, diviniser.
deign, *v.i,* (*to do*) daigner (faire), condescendre (à faire).
deity, *n,* dieu, *m,* déesse, divinité, *f.*
dejected, *a,* déprimé, découragé, abattu. **dejection,** *n,* abattement, accablement, *m.*
delay, *n,* retard, délai, *m.* ¶ *v.t,* différer, retarder. ~ *doing,* tarder à faire.
delectation, *n,* délices, *f.pl.*
delegate, *n,* délégué, e. ¶ *v.t,* déléguer. **delegation,** *n,* délégation, *f.*
delete, *v.t,* rayer, barrer, biffer.
deleterious, *a,* délétère.
deliberate, *a,* (*action*) délibéré, voulu; réfléchi; (*manner*) posé. ¶ *v.i,* délibérer; réfléchir (*upon,* sur). ~**ly,** *ad,* exprès, délibérément; posément. **deliberation,** *n,* délibération, *f.*
delicacy, *n,* délicatesse, finesse, sensibilité, *f;* (*food*) friandise, *f.* **delicate†,** *a,* délicat; fin; (*health*) fragile.
delicious†, *a,* délicieux. **delight,** *n,* délectation, joie, *f,* grand plaisir. *be a* ~ *to,* faire la joie de. ~*s,* délices, *f.pl,* charmes, *m.pl.* ¶ *v.t,* enchanter, réjouir, faire la joie de *ou* les délices de. ~**ed,** *a,* enchanté, ravi. ~ *to meet you!* enchanté! ~**ful,** *a,* délicieux, ravissant, charmant. ~**fully,** *ad,* délicieusement.
delimit, *v.t,* délimiter.
delineate, *v.t,* tracer; dépeindre, décrire.
delinquency, *n,* délinquance, *f. juvenile* ~, d. juvénile. **delinquent,** *a.* & *n,* délinquant, e.
delirious, *a,* delirant. *to be* ~, délirer. ~*ly happy,* fou de joie. **delirium,** *n* délire, *m.* ~ *tremens,* delirium tremens, *m.*
deliver, *v.t,* (*goods*) remettre, livrer; (*post*) distribuer; (*speech*) prononcer; (*blow*) porter, asséner; (*save*) délivrer, sauver; (*Med.*) accoucher. *to be* ~*ed of,* accoucher de. ~**ance,** *n,* délivrance, *f.* ~**er,** *n,* libérateur, trice. ~**y,** *n,* remise, livraison; distribution, *f;* (*speech*) débit; (*Med.*) accouchement, *m.* ~ *man,* ~ *girl,* livreur, euse. ~ *note, van,* bulletin (*m*), voiture de livraison, *f.*
dell, *n,* vallon, *m.*
delphinium, *n,* pied-d'alouette, delphinium, *m.*
delta, *n,* delta, *m.*
delude, *v.t,* tromper, abuser, duper. ~ *o.s,* se faire des illusions.
deluge, *n,* déluge, *m,* inondation *f.* ¶ *v.t,* inonder (*with,* de).
delusion, *n,* illusion, *f.* **delusive†,** *a,* illusoire.
delve, *v.i,* creuser; fouiller.
demagogue, *n,* démagogue, *m.*
demand, *n,* demande; exigence; (*workers*) revendication, *f. on* ~, sur demande, sur présentation. ¶ *v.t,* exiger (qch de qn), réclamer (qch à qn); revendiquer.
demarcation, *n,* démarcation, *f.* ~ *dispute,* conflit d'attributions, *m.*
demean, *v.t,* ~ *o.s,* s'abaisser (à faire). **demeanour,** *n,* allure, *f,* maintien, comportement, *m.*
demented, *a,* dément. **dementia,** *n,* démence, *f.*
demerit, *n,* démérite, *m.*
demesne, *n,* domaine, *m.*
demigod, *n,* demi-dieu, *m.*
demijohn, *n,* dame-jeanne, *f.*
demise, *n,* décès, *m,* mort, *f.*
demisemiquaver, *n,* triple croche, *f.*
demobilize, *v.t,* démobiliser.
democracy, *n,* démocratie, *f.* **democrat,** *n,* démocrate, *m.* ~**ic,** *a,* démocratique.
demolish, *v.t,* démolir. **demolition,** *n,* démolition, *f.*
demon, *n,* démon, *m.*
demoniac[al], *a,* démoniaque, diabolique.
demonstrate, *v.t,* démontrer; (*system*) expliquer. ¶ *v.i,* (*Pol.*) manifester. **demonstration,** *n,* démonstration; (*Pol.* &c) manifestation, *f.* **demonstrative,** *a,* démonstratif. **demonstrator,** *n,* (*Pol.*) manifestant, e; (*Com.*) démonstrateur, trice.
demoralize, *v.t,* démoraliser.
demur, *n,* objection, *f.* ¶ *v.i,* faire des objections; (*Law*) opposer une exception. *without* ~, sans faire de difficultés.
demure, *a,* modeste, sage; aux airs de sainte nitouche (*pej*).
den, *n,* (*lion* &c) tanière, *f,* antre; (*thieves*) repaire, *m;* (*study*) antre, turne *P, f.*
denature, *v.t,* dénaturer.
denial, *n,* dénégation, *f,* démenti; reniement, *m.* *self-*~, abnégation, *f.*
denigrate, *v.t,* dénigrer.
denim, *n,* coton, *m,* toile de jean, *f.* (*Mil.*) ~*s,* treillis, *m.pl.*
denizen, *n,* habitant, hôte, *m.*
Denmark, *n,* le Danemark.
denominate, *v.t,* dénommer. **denomination,** *n,* dénomination; catégorie; (*Eccl.*) secte, confession, *f.* ~**al,** *a,* confessionnel. **denominator,** *n,* dénominateur, *m.*
denote, *v.t,* dénoter, indiquer.
denounce, *v.t,* dénoncer.
dense†, *a,* dense, compact, épais; (*P pers.*) bête, obtus. **density,** *n,* densité, épaisseur, *f.*
dent, *n,* bosselure, *f.* ¶ *v.t,* bosseler, cabosser.
dental, *a,* (*Anat.*) dentaire. ~ *surgeon,* chirurgien dentiste, *m.* **dentist,** *n,* dentiste, *m,f.* ~**ry,** *n,* l'art dentaire, *m.* **dentition,** *n,* dentition, *f.* **denture,** *n,* denture, *f;* ratelier *P, m.*

denude, *v.t,* dénuder, dépouiller.
denunciation, *n,* dénonciation, *f.*
deny, *v.t,* nier; (*news*) démentir. *there's no* ~*ing it,* c'est indéniable. ~ *s.o sth,* refuser qch à qn. ~ *o.s sth,* se priver de qch.
deodorant, *a. & n,* déodorant, désodorisant, *m.*
depart, *v.i,* partir; s'en aller. ~ *this life,* quitter ce monde. ~**ed,** *n,* défunt, e.
department, *n,* département, service; (*government*) ministère, *m;* (*shop*) rayon, comptoir, *m.* ~ *store,* grand magasin. ~**al,** *a,* du département &c; (*Fr.*) départemental.
departure, *n,* départ; (*from law*) manquement (à), *m;* (*new*) innovation, *f.* ~ *platform,* quai de départ, *m.*
depend, *v.i,* dépendre (*on,* de). *that* ~*s,* ça dépend, c'est selon. ~ (*rely*) *on,* compter sur, se fier à. ~**able,** *a,* digne de confiance. ~**ant,** *n,* personne à charge, *f.* ~**ence,** *n,* dépendance. *place* ~ *on s.o,* faire confiance à qn. ~**ency,** *n,* (*country*) dépendance, *f.* ~**ent,** *a,* dépendant. *to be* ~ *on,* dépendre de; être tributaire de.
depict, *v.t,* dépeindre, peindre.
deplete, *v.t,* réduire; épuiser.
deplorable†, *a,* déplorable, lamentable. **deplore,** *v.t,* déplorer, regretter vivement.
deploy, *v.t,* déployer. ~**ment,** *n,* déploiement, *m.*
depopulate, *v.t,* dépeupler. **depopulation,** *n,* (*action*) dépeuplement, *m;* (*state*) dépopulation, *f.*
deport, *v.t,* expulser. ~**ation,** *n,* expulsion, *f.*
deportment, *n,* maintien, *m,* tenue, *f.*
depose, *v.t,* déposer.
deposit, *n,* (*bank*) dépôt, *m;* (*on purchase*) arrhes, *f.pl,* acompte, *m;* (*bottle &c*) consigne, *f;* (*Geol.*) dépôt, gisement, *m.* ~ *account,* compte de dépôt, *m.* ¶ *v.t,* déposer, poser; (*money &c*) mettre en dépôt, consigner; (*Geol.*) déposer. ~**or,** *n,* déposant, e. ~**ory,** *n,* dépôt; entrepôt, *m.*
depot, *n,* (*Mil.*) dépôt; (*Com.*) dépôt, entrepôt; (*bus*) garage, *m.*
depravity, *n,* dépravation, perversité, *f.* **deprave,** *v.t,* dépraver, corrompre.
deprecate, *v.t,* désapprouver. **deprecating,** *a,* désapprobateur.
depreciate, *v.t,* (*Fin., fig.*) déprécier; (*fig.*) dénigrer. ¶ *v.i,* se déprécier. **depreciation,** *n,* dépréciation; (*Com.*) moins-value, *f;* (*annual*) amortissement, *m.* **depreciatory,** *a,* péjoratif.
depredation, *n,* déprédation, *f.*
depress, *v.t,* déprimer, attrister; (*price*) faire baisser; (*lever*) appuyer sur. *feel* ~*ed,* avoir le cafard. ~**ing,** *a,* déprimant, décourageant. ~**ion,** *n,* (*Med., Econ., Met.*) dépression, *f;* (*pers.*) découragement; (*ground*) creux; (*lever*) abaissement, *m.*
deprivation, *n,* privation, *f.* **deprive,** *v.t,* priver, déposséder (*of,* de).
depth, *n,* profondeur; hauteur; (*snow*) épaisseur; (*colour*) intensité; (*sound*) gravité, *f;* (*despair*) fond, *m. in the* ~ *of winter,* au plus fort de l'hiver. *to get out of one's* ~, perdre pied. ~ *charge,* grenade sous-marine, *f.*
deputation, *n,* députation, délégation, *f.* **depute,** *v.t,* députer, déléguer. **deputize for,** faire l'intérim de, remplacer. **deputy,** *n,* remplaçant, e; (*Fr. Pol.*) député, *m.* ~ *chairman,* vice-président, e. ~ *director,* sous-directeur, *m.* ~ *mayor,* maire adjoint.
derail, *v.i,* dérailler. ~**ment,** *n,* déraillement, *m.*
derange, *v.t,* déranger. ~**d,** *a,* (*pers.*) dérangé, détraqué; (*Med.*) aliéné.
derelict, *a,* abandonné. ¶ *n,* navire abandonné, *m;* (*pers.*) épave, *f.* ~**ion,** *n,* ~ *of duty,* manquement au devoir, *m.*
deride, *v.t,* se moquer de; tourner en dérision. **derision,** *n,* dérision, *f.* **derisive,** *a,* de dérision. **derisory,** *a,* dérisoire.
derivation, *n,* dérivation, *f.* **derivative,** *n,* dérivé, *m.* **derive,** *v.t,* (*pleasure &c*) tirer (de), trouver (dans); (*ideas*) puiser (dans). *to be* ~*d from,* dériver de, [pro]venir de.
derogatory, *a,* dénigrant; (*sense*) péjoratif.
derrick, *n,* (*ship*) mât de charge, *m;* (*oil well*) derrick, *m.*
derv, *n,* gas-oil, *m.*
descend, *v.i. & t,* descendre. ~*ed from,* issu de. ¶ *v.i,* (*rain &c*) tomber. ~ *to doing,* s'abaisser à faire. ~**ant,** *n,* descendant, e. **descent,** *n,* descente; (*lineage*) descendance, *f.*
describe, *v.t,* décrire, dépeindre. **description,** *n,* description, *f;* (*Police*) signalement, *m;* sorte, espèce, *f. of every* ~, de toutes sortes. **descriptive,** *a,* descriptif.
descry, *v.t,* apercevoir.
desecrate, *v.t,* profaner.
desert[1], *n,* ~*s,* mérites, *m.pl;* ce que l'on mérite.
desert[2], *n,* désert, *m;* (*att. region*) désertique; désert. ~ *island,* île déserte. ¶ *v.t,* déserter; abandonner, délaisser. ~**ed,** *a,* abandonné, désert. ~**er,** *n,* déserteur; transfuge, *m.* ~**ion,** *n,* désertion, *f;* abandon, délaissement, *m.*
deserve, *v.t,* mériter. **deservedly,** *ad,* à juste titre. **deserving,** *a,* (*pers.*) méritant; (*action*) méritoire, louable.
desiccate, *v.t,* dessécher. **desiccation,** *n,* dessiccation, *f.*
design, *n,* (*pattern*) dessin, motif, *m;* (~*ing*) création, conception; *f;* (*Mach.*) étude, *f;* (*product*) modèle, *m. our latest* ~*s,* nos derniers modèles. (*intention*) dessein, projet, *m,* intention, *f. by* ~, à dessein. *have* ~*s on s.o, sth,* avoir des visées sur qn, qch. ¶ *v.t,* dessiner, créer; concevoir. *well, badly* ~*ed,* bien, mal conçu. (*intend*) projeter (de faire).
designate, *v.t,* désigner. **designation,** *n,* dési-

gnation, *f.*
designedly, *ad,* à dessein. **designer,** *n,* dessinateur, trice; créateur, trice. **designing,** *a,* (*pers.*) intrigant.
desirable, *a,* désirable, à désirer, souhaitable. **desire,** *n,* désir, *m;* envie, *f.* ¶ *v.t,* désirer (qch, faire), avoir envie (de qch, de faire). **desirous,** *a,* désireux.
desist, *v.i,* cesser, s'arrêter (*from doing,* de faire).
desk, *n,* (*Sch.*) pupitre; bureau, *m;* (*shop*) caisse, *f.*
desolate, *a,* (*place*) désert, désolé; (*pers.*) affligé. ¶ *v.t,* désoler. **desolation,** *n,* désolation, *f.*
despair, *n,* désespoir, *m. to drive to* ~ *&* ~, *v.i,* désespérer. ~**ing,** *a,* désespéré.
despatch, *n. & v.t.* Same as *dispatch.*
desperate, *a,* (*pers.*) désespéré; (*fight*) acharné. ~**ly** *ad,* désespérément; (*in love*) éperdument. **desperation,** *n,* désespoir; acharnement, *m.*
despicable, *a,* méprisable. **despise,** *v.t,* mépriser, dédaigner.
despite, *pr,* malgré, en dépit de.
despoil, *v,t,* (*pers.*) dépouiller (*of,* de); (*country*) piller.
despondency, *n,* abattement, découragement, *m.* **despondent,** *a,* abattu, découragé.
despot, *n,* despote, tyran, *m.* ~**ic†,** *a,* despotique. ~**ism,** *n,* despotisme, *m.*
dessert, *n,* dessert, *m.* ~ *spoon,* cuiller à dessert.
destination, *n,* destination, *f.* **destine,** *v.t,* destiner (*for,* à). **destiny,** *n,* destin, *m,* destinée, *f.*
destitute, *a,* indigent, sans ressources; dépourvu, dénué (*of,* de). *the* ~, les pauvres. **destitution,** *n,* dénuement, *m,* misère, indigence, *f.*
destroy, *v.t,* détruire. ~**er,** *n,* destructeur, trice; (*Naut.*) contre-torpilleur, destroyer, *m.* **destruction,** *n,* destruction, *f;* ravages, *m.pl.* **destructive,** *a,* destructif, destructeur. ~ *person,* brise-tout, *m.*
desultory, *a,* décousu, sans suite; (*conversation*) à bâtons rompus.
detach, *v.t,* détacher; séparer. ~**able,** *a,* amovible, détachable. ~*ed house,* villa, *f.* ~**ment,** *n,* séparation; (*pers.*) indifférence, *f;* (*pers., Mil*) détachement, *m.*
detail, *n,* détail, *m. go into* ~*s,* entrer dans les détails. ¶ *v.t,* détailler; raconter en détail; (*Mil.*) affecter (*to do,* pour faire). ~*ed,* détaillé, circonstancié.
detain, *v.t,* retenir, empêcher de partir; (*in prison*) détenir; (*Sch.*) consigner.
detect, *v.t,* découvrir; surprendre; apercevoir. ~**ion,** *n,* découverte, *f.* ~**ive,** *n,* agent de la sureté, détective, *m.* ~ *story,* roman policier, *m.* ~**or** (*Radio &c*) *n,* détecteur, *m.*
detention, *n,* détention, *f;* arrêt, *m;* (*Sch.*) retenue, colle *P, f.*
deter, *v.t,* détourner (qn de qch, de faire); empêcher, décourager (qn de faire).
deteriorate, *v.i,* se détériorer.
determination, *n,* détermination; résolution, *f.* **determine,** *v.t,* déterminer, fixer; établir; (*s.o's career*) décider de. ~ *to do,* décider (de faire), se résoudre (à faire). ~**d,** *a,* déterminé, résolu.
detest, *v.t,* détester, avoir horreur de. ~**able,** *a,* détestable.
dethrone, *v.t,* détrôner.
detonate, *v.i,* détoner. ¶ *v.t,* faire détoner. **detonation,** *n,* détonation, *f.* **detonator,** *n,* détonateur; (*Rly*) pétard, *m.*
detour, *n,* détour, *m;* (*traffic*) déviation, *f.*
detract from, rabaisser, diminuer. **detractor,** *n,* détracteur, trice.
detriment, *n,* détriment, préjudice, *m. to the* ~ *of,* au préjudice de. ~**al,** *a,* préjudiciable, nuisible. *be* ~ *to,* nuire à.
detritus, *n,* détritus, *m.*
deuce[1], *n,* (*Cards, Dice*) deux, *m;* (*Ten.*) égalité, *f.*
deuce[2], *n,* diantre, diable, *m.* (*V also* **devil**).
devaluation, *n,* (*Fin.*) dévaluation, *f.* **devalue,** *v.t,* dévaluer.
devastate, *v.t,* dévaster, ravager. **devastating,** *a,* accablant, écrasant.
develop, *v.t,* développer; (*region*) exploiter, mettre en valeur; (*illness &c*) contracter. ¶ *v.i,* se développer, se manifester. ~*ing country,* pays en voie de développement. ~**er** (*Phot.*) *n,* révélateur, *m.* ~*ing bath,* bain révélateur, *m.* ~**ment,** *n,* développement, *m;* (*ideas*) évolution; (*region*) exploitation, *f;* (*story, events*) déroulement, *m. new* ~, fait nouveau. *await further* ~*s,* attendre la suite des événements.
deviate, *v.i,* dévier; s'écarter. **deviation,** *n,* déviation, *f;* écart, *m.*
device, *n,* moyen, expédient; (*mechanism*) dispositif, appareil; (*explosive*) engin; truc *P, m;* (*Her.*) devise, *f,* emblème, *m.*
devil, *n,* diable, démon, *m. what, how the* ~? que, comment diable? *the* ~ *of a noise,* un chahut de tous les diables. ~**ish†,** *a,* diabolique, infernal; satané, sacré (*before n*). ~**ment,** *n,* diablerie, espièglerie; (*spite*) malice, *f.*
devious, *a,* (*means*) détourné; (*pers.*) sournois.
devise, *v.t,* combiner, inventer, imaginer; (*Law*) léguer.
devoid, *a,* dépourvu, dénué (*of,* de).
devolution, *n,* (*Pol.*) décentralisation administrative.
devolve on, *v.i,* incomber à; retomber sur.
devote, *v.t,* (*life &c*) consacrer; (*funds*) affecter. ~ *o.s to,* se vouer à; (*study*) s'adonner à; (*pleasure*) se livrer à. ~**d,** *a,* fervent, dévoué. **devotee,** *n,* partisan, e; (*sport, music &c*) fervent, e; passionné, e. **devotion,** *n,* (*Rel.*)

dévotion; piété, *f;* (*zeal*) dévouement, attachement, *m.*
devour, *v.t,* dévorer, engloutir.
devout†, *a,* dévot, pieux; (*wish*) sincère. **~ness,** *n,* dévotion, *f.*
dew, *n,* rosée, *f.* ~*drop,* goutte de r., *f.*
dewlap, *n,* fanon, *m.*
dewy, *a,* couvert de rosée.
dexterity, *n,* dextérité, adresse, habileté, *f.* **dext[e]rous†,** *a,* adroit, habile.
dextrin, *n,* dextrine, *f.*
diabetes, *n,* diabète, *m.*
diabolic(al)†, *a,* diabolique.
diadem, *n,* diadème, *m.*
diaeresis, *n,* tréma, *m.*
diagnose, *v.t,* diagnostiquer. **diagnosis,** *n,* diagnostic, *m.*
diagonal†, *a,* diagonal. ¶ *n,* diagonale, *f.*
diagram, *n,* diagramme; schéma, *m.*
dial, *n,* cadran, *m.* ¶ *v.t,* (*Tel.*) (*number*) faire, composer. ~ *direct,* appeler par l'automatique. ~ *999,* appeler Police Secours. ~*ling code,* indicatif, *m.* ~*ling tone,* tonalité, *f.*
dialect, *n,* dialecte, parler; (*local*) patois, *m.*
dialectic[s], *n,* dialectique, *f.*
dialogue, *n,* dialogue, *m.*
diameter, *n,* diamètre, *m.* **diametric†,** *a,* diamétral.
diamond, *n,* diamant; (*Geom.*) losange; (*Cards*) carreau, *m.* ~ *wedding,* noces de diamant, *f.pl.*
diaper, *n, Am,* couche [de bébé], *f.*
diaphanous, *a,* diaphane.
diaphragm, *n,* diaphragme, *m.*
diarrhoea, *n,* diarrhée, *f.*
diary, *n,* agenda; (*of one's life*) journal, *m.*
diatonic, *a,* diatonique.
diatribe, *n,* diatribe, *f.*
dibble, *n,* plantoir, *m.*
dice, *n.pl,* dés, *m.pl. play* ~, jouer aux dés. ¶ *v.t,* (*Cook.*) couper en cubes.
dickens (the) *n,* diable, diantre, *m.*
dictaphone, *n,* dictaphone, *m.*
dictate, *v.t. & i,* dicter. ~ *to,* régenter. ¶ *n.pl,* ~*s,* ordres, *m.pl;* (*conscience*) voix, *f.* **dictation,** *n,* dictée, *f.* **dictator,** *n,* dictateur, *m.* **~ial,** *a,* dictatorial. **~ship,** *n,* dictature, *f.*
diction, *n,* diction, *f.* **~ary,** *n,* dictionnaire, *m.*
dictum, *n,* dicton, *m.*
didactic, *a,* didactique.
die[1], *n,* dé [à jouer], *m. the* ~ *is cast,* le sort en est jeté. (*Tech.*) matrice, *f.* ~*-sinker,* graveur de matrices, *m.*
die[2], *v.i.ir,* mourir, décéder; (*animal*) crever; (*love, memory*) s'éteindre. ~ *laughing, of fright,* mourir de rire, de peur. ~ *of boredom,* périr d'ennui. *I'm dying of hunger, of thirst,* je crève de faim, de soif *P. to be dying to do,* mourir d'envie de faire. *to be dying for sth,* avoir une envie folle de qch. ~ *away,* (*sound*) s'affaiblir, s'éteindre. ~ *down,* (*storm, anger*) se calmer, s'apaiser. ~ *out,* s'éteindre, disparaître. ~*hard, n,* réactionnaire; intransigeant, e.
diet, *n,* diète, *f,* régime [alimentaire], *m.* ¶ *v.t,* mettre au régime. ¶ *v.i,* suivre un régime. **~etics,** *n,* diététique, *f.* **~ician,** *n,* diététicien, ne.
differ, *v.t,* différer, être différent, se distinguer; (*about sth*) ne pas être d'accord.
difference, *n,* différence, *f,* écart, *m;* (*quarrel*) différend, *m. it makes no* ~, ça ne fait rien. *that makes all the* ~, voilà qui change tout. **different,** *a,* différent (*from,* de), autre (*from,* que); (*various*) divers. *that's quite a* ~ *matter,* c'est tout autre chose. *I feel a* ~ *person,* je me sens tout autre. **differential,** *a,* différentiel. ~ [*gear*], [engrenage] différentiel, *m.* **differentiate,** *v.t,* différencier. **differently,** *ad,* différemment, autrement.
difficult, *a,* difficile, malaisé; (*pers.*) difficile, peu commode. ~ *to get on with,* difficile à vivre. *I find it* ~ *to believe,* j'ai de la peine à croire. **~y,** *n,* difficulté; peine, *f. with* ~, avec difficulté, avec peine. *he has* ~ *in seeing,* il voit difficilement, il a du mal à voir. obstacle, *m,* difficulté, *f,* embarras, *m,* ennuis, *m.pl. to have money difficulties,* avoir des ennuis d'argent, être dans l'embarras. *to get out of a* ~, se tirer d'affaire. *I see no* ~ *about that,* je n'y vois pas d'inconvénient.
diffidence, *n,* défiance de soi; timidité, *f.* **diffident†,** *a,* qui manque de confiance en soi; timide.
diffuse, *v.t.* (*& i*) (se) diffuser, (se) répandre. ¶ *a,* diffus. ~*d lighting,* éclairage diffus *ou* indirect. **diffusion,** *n,* diffusion, *f.*
dig, *n,* coup. ~ *in the ribs,* coup de coude dans les côtes. (*sly* ~) coup de patte, *f;* (*Archaeol.*) fouille, *f.* ¶ *v.t.ir,* (*ground*) bêcher, retourner; (*hole &c*) creuser; (*thrust*) enfoncer. ¶ *v.i,* (*Archaeol.*) faire des fouilles. ~ *with P,* loger chez. *I* ~ *that music P,* cette musique m'emballe *P.* ~ *into,* fouiller dans. ~ *up,* déterrer; arracher.
digest, *v.t. & i,* digérer. **~ible,** *a,* digestible. **~ion,** *n,* digestion, *f.* **~ive,** *a. & n,* digestif, *m.*
digger, *n,* (*Mach.*) excavateur, *m,* pelleteuse, *f.* **digging,** *n,* bêchage, creusement, *m,* excavation, *f,* fouilles, *f.pl.*
digit, *n,* doigt; (*Math.*) chiffre, *m.* **~al,** *a,* (*computer, watch*) numérique.
dignified, *a,* digne, grave. **dignify,** *v.t,* donner de la dignité à. **dignitary,** *n,* dignitaire, *m.* **dignity,** *n,* dignité, *f;* haut rang, *m.*
digress, *v.i,* s'écarter; faire une digression.
digs *P, n.pl,* logement, *m,* piaule *P, f.*
dike, *n,* (*bank*) digue, *f;* (*ditch*) fossé, *m.*
dilapidated, *a,* (*house*) délabré. **delapidation,** *n,* délabrement, *m.* ~*s* (*by tenant*) détério-

ration, *f.*
dilate, *v.t.* (*& i*) (se) dilater. ~ *upon* (*subject*) s'étendre sur.
dilatory, *a,* (*pers.*) lent; (*policy*) dilatoire, d'attente.
dilemma, *n,* dilemme, *m.*
dilettante, *n,* dilettante, *m.*
diligence, *n,* assiduité *f,* zèle, *m.* **diligent†,** *a,* assidu.
dilly-dally, *v.i,* lanterner, lambiner *P.*
dilute, *v.t,* étendre, diluer.
dim, *a,* (*light*) faible, pâle; (*memory*) vague; (*sight*) trouble; (*P stupid*) bête, bouché *P.* ~*wit P,* imbécile, *m,f.* ¶ *v.t,* (*light*) baisser; (*memory*) effacer; (*sight*) troubler. ¶ *v.i,* (*& grow* ~) baisser; s'effacer; (*sight*) se troubler, s'obscurcir.
dimension, *n,* dimension, *f.*
diminish, *v.t.* & *i,* diminuer. **diminution,** *n,* diminution, *f.* **diminutive,** *a,* exigu; tout petit, minuscule; (*Gram.*) diminutif. ¶ (*Gram.*) *n,* diminutif, *m.*
dimple, *n,* fossette, *f.* ~**d,** *a,* à fossettes.
din, *n,* vacarme, tapage, *m.*
dine, *v.i,* dîner. ~ *out,* dîner en ville. **diner,** *n,* dîneur, euse.
dinghy, *n,* canot, youyou; (*Sailing*) dériveur, *m.*
dingy, *a,* terne; miteux.
dining: ~ *car,* wagon-restaurant, *m.* ~ *room,* salle à manger, *f.* **dinner,** *n,* dîner, *m. at* ~, à table. ~ *jacket,* smoking, *m. give a* ~ *party,* inviter du monde à dîner. ~ *service,* service de table, *m.* ~ *time,* heure du dîner, *f.* ~ *trolley,* ~ *wagon,* table roulante.
dint, *n, by* ~ *of* (*sth, doing*), à force de (qch, faire).
diocesan, *a,* diocésain. **diocese,** *n,* diocèse, *m.*
dip, *n,* (*in sea*) bain, *m,* baignade, *f;* (*sheep*) bain parasiticide; (*ground*) creux, *m,* dépression; (*slope*) déclivité, *f. to take a* ~ (*sea*), aller se baigner. (*car*) ~*stick,* jauge [de niveau d'huile], *f.* ¶ *v.t,* (*in liquid*) plonger, tremper; (*sheep*) baigner; (*car: headlights*) se mettre en code. ¶ *v.i,* (*ground*) descendre, s'incliner, plonger; (*price, sun*) baisser. ~ *into,* (*savings*) puiser dans; (*book*) feuilleter.
diphtheria, *n,* diphtérie, *f.*
diphthong, *n,* diphtongue, *f.*
diploma, *n,* diplôme, *m.*
diplomacy, *n,* diplomatie, *f;* (*fig.*) tact, doigté, *m.* **diplomatic,** *a,* (*lit., fig.*) diplomatique. ~ *bag,* valise d. ~ *service,* diplomatie, *f.* **diplomat[ist],** *n,* diplomate, *m,* femme d., *f.*
dipper, *n,* (*bird*) merle d'eau, *m;* (*at fair*) montagnes russes, *f.pl.*
dipsomania, *n,* dipsomanie, *f.* ~**c, dipso** *P, n,* dipsomane, alcoolique, *m,f.*
dire, *a,* (*distress*) extrême; (*poverty*) noir. ~ *necessity,* dure nécessité.
direct, *a,* direct; immédiat; (*pers*) franc. ~ *current* (*Elec.*), courant continu, *m.* (*Gram.*) ~ *speech,* style direct. ¶ *ad,* directement. ¶ *v.t,* (*business*) diriger, administrer, gérer; (*efforts*) orienter; (*remark*) adresser. ~ *s.o's attention to,* attirer l'attention de qn sur. (*order*) ordonner (à qn de faire). *to* ~ *me to the station,* m'indiquer le chemin de la gare. (*Theat.*) mettre en scène; (*Cine, TV*) réaliser. ~**ion,** *n,* direction, *f,* sens, *m. in the right, wrong* ~, dans la bonne, mauvaise direction. *in all* ~*s,* en tous sens. (*control*) direction, administration, *f;* ordre, *m,* instruction, *f.* ~*s for use,* mode d'emploi, *m.* (*Theat.*) mise en scène; (*Cine, TV*) réalisation, *f.* **directly,** *ad,* directement; immédiatement, tout de suite; exactement.
director, *n,* (*company &c*) directeur, trice, administrateur, trice; (*Theat.*) metteur en scène, *m;* (*Cine, TV*) réalisateur, trice.
directory, *n,* (*phone*) annuaire [des téléphones]; (*addresses*) répertoire, *m.*
dirge, *n,* chant funèbre, *m.*
dirk, *n,* dague, *f,* poignard, *m.*
dirt, *n,* saleté, crasse; (*mud*) boue; (*muck*) crotte, ordure, *f.* ~*-cheap,* à vil prix. *treat like* ~, traiter comme un chien; t. comme de la merde *P.* **dirtily,** *ad,* salement. **dirty,** *a,* sale, malpropre, crasseux; crotté; (*coarse*) grossier, cochon *P.* ~ *story,* histoire graveleuse *ou* cochonne *P. play a* ~ *trick on s.o,* jouer un sale tour à qn. ¶ *v.t,* salir.
disable, *v.t,* (*pers.*) rendre infirme, mutiler; (*tank &c*) mettre hors de combat; (*ship*) désemparer. ~**d,** *a,* infirme, handicappé. ~ *ex-servicemen,* mutilés de guerre, *m.pl.* ~**ment** & **disability,** *n,* incapacité, invalidité, infirmité, *f.*
disabuse, *v.t,* désabuser, détromper (*of,* de).
disadvantage, *n,* désavantage, inconvénient, *m. place at a* ~, désavantager. ~**ous†,** *a,* désavantageux.
disaffection, *n,* désaffection, *f.*
disagree, *v.i,* n'être pas d'accord, être en désaccord. ~ *with s.o,* (*climate*) ne pas convenir à qn. ~**able†,** *a,* désagréable. ~**ment,** *n,* désaccord, différend, *m.*
disallow, *v.t,* rejeter.
disappear, *v.i,* disparaître. ~**ance,** *n,* disparition, *f.*
disappoint, *v.t,* décevoir, tromper, désappointer. *don't* ~ *me,* ne manquez pas à votre parole. ~**ment,** *n,* déception, *f,* désappointement, *m.* ~*s,* déboires, *f.pl.* ~*s in love,* chagrins d'amour, *m.pl.*
disapproval, *n,* désapprobation, *f.* **disapprove,** *v.t.* & ~ *of,* désapprouver. **disapprovingly,** *ad,* d'un air *ou* d'un ton désapprobateur.
disarm, *v.t,* désarmer. **disarmament,** *n,* désarmement, *m.*
disarrange, *v.t,* déranger, mettre en désordre. ~

s.o's hair, décoiffer.
disarray, *n,* désarroi, désordre, *m.*
disaster, *n,* désastre, *m,* catastrophe, *f;* (*flood, fire &c*) sinistre, *m.* **disastrous,** *a,* désastreux, funeste.
disavow, *v.t,* désavouer. **~al,** *n,* désaveu, *m.*
disband, *v.t,* licencier; disperser.
disbelief, *n,* incrédulité, *f.* **disbelieve,** *v.t,* ne pas croire (*in,* à). **~r,** *n,* incrédule, *m,f.*
disbud, *v.t,* ébourgeonner.
disburse, *v.t,* débourser.
disc, *n,* (*gen., Med., Mus.*) disque, *m.* ~ *brakes,* freins à disque, *m.pl.* ~ *jockey,* disc-jockey, *m.*
discard, *v.t,* jeter; se débarrasser de, mettre de côté; (*Bridge*) se fausser de.
discern, *v.t,* discerner, distinguer. **~ible,** *a,* perceptible. **~ing,** *a,* judicieux. **~ment,** *n,* discernement, jugement, *m.*
discharge, *n,* (*gun, Elec.*) décharge, *f;* (*cargo*) déchargement, *m;* (*prisoner*) libération, mise en liberté, *f;* (*employee, patient*) renvoi, *m;* (*Mil: on med. grounds*) réforme; (*accused*) relaxe; (*duty*) exécution, *f;* (*debt*) acquittement; (*Med.*) écoulement, *m.* ¶ *v.t,* (*ship, gun, Elec.*) décharger; (*employee*) renvoyer, congédier; (*prisoner*) libérer, mettre en liberté; (*accused*) relaxer; (*bankrupt*) réhabiliter; (*debt*) acquitter; (*duty*) remplir, s'acquitter de. ~ *a patient,* renvoyer un malade [guéri]. ¶ *v.i,* (*Med.*) suppurer, suinter.
disciple, *n,* disciple, *m.* **disciplinary,** *a,* disciplinaire. **discipline,** *n,* discipline, *f. keep* ~, maintenir la d. ¶ *v.t,* discipliner.
disclaim, *v.t,* désavouer; dénier. **~er,** *n,* dénégation, *f;* désaveu; démenti, *m.*
disclose, *v.t,* révéler, divulguer, dévoiler. **disclosure,** *n,* révélation, divulgation, *f.*
discoloration, *n,* décoloration, *f.* **discolour,** *v.t,* décolorer.
disco *P, n,* discothèque, *f.*
discomfit, *v.t,* confondre. **~ure,** *n,* déconvenue, *f.*
discomfort, *n,* malaise, *m,* gêne; incommodité, *f.*
disconcert, *v.t,* déconcerter, décontenancer. **~ing,** *a,* troublant, déroutant.
disconnect, *v.t,* séparer, détacher; (*gas &c, phone, phone call*) couper; (*Elec. fitting*) débrancher. **~ed,** *a,* (*speech*) décousu.
disconsolate, *a,* abattu, inconsolable.
discontented, *a,* mécontent (*with,* de). **discontent[ment],** *n,* mécontentement, *m.*
discontinue, *v.t,* cesser, interrompre.
discord, *n,* discorde, *f;* désaccord, *m;* (*Mus.*) dissonance, *f.* **~ant,** *a,* discordant; (*Mus.*) dissonant.
discotheque, *n,* discothèque, *f.*
discount, *n,* escompte, *m;* remise, *f;* rabais, *m.* (*Fin.*) *at a* ~, en perte. ¶ *v.t,* escompter; (*fig.*) ne pas tenir compte de.
discourage, *v.t,* décourager (qn de qch, de faire). **~ment,** *n,* découragement, *m.*
discourse, *n,* discours, *m.* ¶ *v.i,* ~ *on,* discourir sur, traiter de.
discourteous, *a,* impoli, peu courtois. **discourtesy,** *n,* impolitesse, *f,* manque de courtoisie, *m.*
discover, *v.t,* découvrir; (*error &c*) s'apercevoir de. **~er,** *n,* découvreur, euse. **~y,** *n,* découverte; (*lucky find*) trouvaille, *f.*
discredit, *n,* discrédit, *m.* ¶ *v.t,* discréditer, déconsidérer; ne pas croire. **~able,** *a,* déshonorant, peu honorable.
discreet†, *a,* discret.
discrepancy, *n,* contradiction, divergence, *f;* décalage, *m.*
discrete, *a,* discret.
discretion, *n,* discrétion, retenue; prudence, *f. use your* ~, faites comme bon vous semblera. *years of* ~, l'âge mûr. **~ary,** *a,* discrétionnaire.
discriminate, *v.i,* distinguer, établir une distinction (*between,* entre); (*unfairly*) établir une discrimination (contre, en faveur de). **discrimination,** *n,* distinction, *f;* jugement, discernement, *m. racial* ~, discrimination raciale.
discursive, *a,* discursif.
discus, *n,* disque, *m.*
discuss, *v.t,* discuter (qch; de, sur qch), débattre (qch; de qch); (*question*) agiter. **~ion,** *n,* discussion, *f,* débat, *m. under* ~, en discussion.
disdain, *n,* dédain, *m.* ¶ *v.t,* dédaigner. **~ful†,** *a,* dédaigneux.
disease, *n,* maladie, *f;* mal, *m.* **~d,** *a,* malade.
disembark, *v.t. & i,* débarquer. **~ation,** *n,* débarquement, *m.*
disembowel, *v.t,* éventrer.
disenchant, *v.t,* désenchanter, désillusionner, **~ment,** désenchantement, *m,* désillusion, *f.*
disengage, *v.t,* dégager. **~d,** *a,* libre.
disentangle, *v.t,* démêler, débrouiller.
disestablishment [of the Church] *n,* séparation de l'Église & de l'État, *f.*
disfavour, *n,* défaveur, *f. incur s.o's* ~, s'attirer la d. de qn.
disfigure, *v.t,* défigurer. **~ment,** *n,* défiguration, *f,* enlaidissement, *m.*
disfranchise, *v.t,* priver du droit électoral.
disgorge, *v.t,* dégorger.
disgrace, *n,* disgrâce; honte, *f;* déshonneur, *m. there's no* ~ *in being*... il n'y a aucune honte à être... *it's a* ~*!* c'est une honte! ¶ *v.t,* déshonorer, faire honte à; (*dismiss*) disgracier. **~ful†,** *a,* honteux, scandaleux, déshonorant.
disgruntled, *a,* maussade, mécontent.
disguise, *n,* déguisement, *m. in* ~, en déguisé. ¶ *v.t,* déguiser (*as a boy,* en garçon); camoufler

(*as,* en); (*feelings*) dissimuler.
disgust, *n,* dégoût, *m,* répugnance, *f* (*at, for,* pour). ¶ *v.t,* dégoûter, écœurer. **~ing,** *a,* dégoûtant, écœurant.
dish, *n,* plat, *m;* (*Phot.*) cuvette, *f;* (*food*) plat, mets, *m. wash the ~es,* faire la vaisselle. *~washer,* (*Mach.*) lave-vaisselle, *m, inv;* (*pers.*) laveur, euse, de vaisselle; plongeur, *m. ~water,* eau de vaisselle, *f;* (*of soup &c*) lavasse *P, f.* ¶ *v.t,* (*P chances*) foutre en l'air *P. ~ out,* distribuer; (*food*) servir. *~ up,* (*meal*) servir.
dishearten, *v.t,* décourager, abattre.
dishevelled, *a,* échevelé, ébouriffé.
dishonest†, *a,* malhonnête, de mauvaise foi, déloyal. **~y,** *n,* malhonnêteté, *f.*
dishonour, *n,* déshonneur, *m.* ¶ *v.t,* déshonorer. *~ one's word,* manquer à sa parole. **~able,** *a,* déshonorant, honteux. *~ed cheque,* chèque impayé *ou* refusé.
disillusion, *n,* désillusion, *f.* ¶ *v.t,* désillusionner, désenchanter, désabuser.
disinclination, *n,* répugnance (à faire). **disinclined,** *a,* peu disposé (à qch, à faire).
disinfect, *v.t,* désinfecter. **~ant,** *a. & n,* désinfectant, *m.* **~ion,** *n,* désinfection, *f.*
disingenuous, *a,* peu sincère. **~ness,** *n,* manque de franchise, *m.*
disinherit, *v.t,* déshériter.
disintegrate, *v.t.* (*& i*) (se) désagréger, (s')effriter.
disinter, *v.t,* déterrer, exhumer.
disinterested, *a,* désintéressé. **~ness,** *n,* désintéressement, *m.*
disinterment, *n,* exhumation, *f.*
disjointed, *a,* décousu, sans suite.
disk = disc.
dislike, *n,* aversion, antipathie, *f* (*of,* pour). *to take a ~ to s.o, sth,* prendre qn, qch en grippe. ¶ *v.t,* ne pas aimer, avoir en aversion, avoir de l'aversion pour. *I ~ him, that,* il, cela me déplaît.
dislocate, *v.t,* disloquer, luxer, démettre, déboîter; (*fig.*) désorganiser. **dislocation,** *n,* dislocation, luxation; (*fig.*) désorganisation, *f.*
dislodge, *v.t,* déplacer, détacher, faire bouger.
disloyal†, *a,* déloyal, infidèle. **~ty,** *n,* déloyauté, infidélité, *f.*
dismal†, *a,* lugubre, morne, sombre.
dismantle, *v.t,* démonter.
dismast, *v.t,* démâter.
dismay, *n,* consternation, *f.* ¶ *v.t,* consterner.
dismember, *v.t,* démembrer.
dismiss, *v.t,* (*employee*) renvoyer, congédier; (*official*) destituer; (*idea, request*) rejeter, écarter, abandonner; (*Law: accused*) relaxer. (*Mil.*) *~!* rompez! **~al,** *n,* renvoi, congédiement, *m;* destitution, *f;* rejet, abandon, *m;* (*Law*) relaxe, *f.*
dismount, *v.i,* descendre, mettre pied à terre. ¶ *v.t,* (*rider*) démonter, désarçonner.
disobedience, *n,* désobéissance, *f.* **disobedient,** *a,* désobéissant. **disobey,** *v.t,* désobéir (à qn, à un ordre); (*law*) violer.
disobliging, *a,* désobligeant, désagréable.
disorder, *n,* désordre, *m,* confusion, *f;* (*Med.*) troubles, *m.pl,* maladie, *f;* (*Pol.*) désordres, *m.pl.* ¶ *v.t,* mettre en désordre, déranger. **~ly,** *a,* désordonné, en désordre.
disorganize, *v.t,* désorganiser.
disown, *v.t,* désavouer, renier.
disparage, *v.t,* dénigrer, rabaisser, déprécier, décrier. **~ment,** *n,* dénigrement, *m.* **disparaging,** *a,* peu flatteur.
disparity, *n,* disparité, inégalité, *f.*
dispassionate, *a,* calme, impartial. **~ly,** *ad,* avec calme, sans parti pris.
dispatch, *n,* expédition, *f,* envoi, *m;* (*report*) dépêche; (*speed*) promptitude, *f. ~ case,* serviette, *f. ~ rider,* estafette, *f.* ¶ *v.t,* envoyer; (*goods, business*) expédier; (*messenger*) dépêcher.
dispel, *v.t,* dissiper, chasser.
dispensary, *n,* officine, pharmacie, *f;* (*clinic*) dispensaire, *m.* **dispense,** *v.t,* distribuer; (*Phar.*) préparer; (*exempt*) dispenser (*from,* de). *~ with,* se passer de. **dispenser,** *n,* (*pers.*) pharmacien, ne; (*Mach.*) distributeur, *m.*
dispersal & dispersion, *n,* dispersion, *f.*
disperse, *v.t.* (*& i*) (se) disperser, (se) dissiper.
dispirit, *v.t,* décourager, déprimer.
displace, *v.t,* déplacer; (*from office*) destituer. *~d person,* personne déplacée. **~ment,** *n,* (*gen., Naut.*) déplacement, *m.*
display, *n,* (*goods*) exposition, *f,* étalage, *m;* (*feelings*) manifestation; (*ostentatious*) parade, *f,* étalage. *make a ~ of,* faire parade de. *~ cabinet,* vitrine, *f.* ¶ *v.t,* (*goods*) exposer, étaler; (*qualities*) montrer, faire preuve de; faire parade de.
displease, *v.t,* déplaire à; mécontenter. **displeasure,** *n,* déplaisir, mécontentement, *m.*
disposable, *a,* (*cups &c*) à jeter; (*available*) disponible. **disposal,** *n,* vente, *f;* (*matter in hand*) expédition, *f. at his ~,* à sa disposition. *waste ~ unit,* broyeur d'ordures, *m.* **dispose,** *v.t,* disposer. *~ of,* se débarrasser de, se défaire de; (*problem &c*) régler. **~d,** *a,* disposé (à faire). *well, ill ~,* bien, mal disposé (envers qn). **disposition,** *n,* disposition, *f;* (*pers.*) naturel, tempérament, *m.*
dispossess, *v.t,* déposséder (*of,* de).
disproportion, *n,* disproportion, *f.* **~ate,** *a,* disproportionné.
disprove, *v.t,* réfuter.
dispute, *n,* (*argument*) contestation, discussion, *f. in ~,* en discussion; (*Law*) en litige. (*quarrel*) dispute, *f. wages ~,* conflit salarial, *m.* ¶ *v.t,* disputer, contester.

disqualification, *n,* (*Sport*) disqualification; (*Law*) incapacité, *f.* **disqualify,** *v.t,* rendre incapable (de faire); (*Sport*) disqualifier. ~ *s.o from driving,* retirer le permis de conduire à qn.
disquiet, *v.t,* inquiéter, troubler. ~**[ude],** *n,* inquiétude, *f,* trouble, *m.*
disregard, *n,* (*feelings &c*) indifférence (*for,* à); (*danger &c*) mépris, dédain, *m;* (*law*) désobéissance (*for,* à). ¶ *v.t,* ne tenir aucun compte de; mépriser; désobéir à, méconnaître.
disrepair, *n,* délabrement, *m.*
disreputable, *a,* de mauvaise réputation, louche; (*action*) honteux; (*clothes*) minable *P.* **disrepute,** *n,* discrédit, *m.*
disrespect, *n,* manque de respect, *m,* irrévérence, *f.* ~**ful†,** *a,* irrespectueux, irrévérencieux.
disrupt, *v.t,* perturber, désorganiser, déranger.
dissatisfaction, *n,* mécontentement, *m.* **dissatisfied,** *a,* mécontent (*with,* de).
dissect, *v.t,* disséquer. ~**ion,** *n,* dissection, *f.*
dissemble, *v.t.* & *i,* dissimuler.
disseminate, *v.t,* disséminer.
dissension, *n,* dissension, *f.* **dissent,** *n,* dissentiment, *m;* (*Eccl.*) dissidence, *f.* ¶ *v.i,* différer d'opinion; (*Eccl.*) être dissident. ~**er,** *n,* (*Eccl.*) dissident, e.
dissertation, *n,* (*oral*) exposé; (*written*) mémoire, *m;* thèse, *f.*
disservice, *n,* mauvais service, *m.*
dissidence, *n,* dissidence, *f,* désaccord, *m.* **dissident,** *n.* & *a,* dissident, e.
dissimilar, *a,* dissemblable (à), différent (de). ~**ity,** *n,* dissemblance, différence, *f.*
dissimulate, *v.t,* & *i,* dissimuler.
dissipate, *v.t,* dissiper; (*efforts*) gaspiller. ~**d,** *a,* (*pers.*) débauché; (*life*) déréglé. **dissipation,** *n,* dissipation, *f;* gaspillage, *m;* débauche, *f.*
dissociate, *v.t,* dissocier.
dissolute, *a,* dissolu, débauché; (*life*) déréglé.
dissolution, *n,* dissolution, *f.* **dissolve,** *v.t,* dissoudre, faire fondre. ¶ *v.i,* se dissoudre, fondre; (*fig.*) s'évanouir. ~ *into tears,* fondre en larmes.
dissonance, *n,* dissonance, *f.* **dissonant,** *a,* dissonant, discordant.
dissuade, *v.t,* dissuader (qn de faire); détourner (qn de qch, de faire). **dissuasion,** *n,* dissuasion, *f.*
distaff, *n,* quenouille, *f.*
distance, *n,* distance, *f* (*between,* entre). *the ~ between the posts,* l'écartement des poteaux, *m. in the ~,* dans le lointain, au loin. *what ~ are we from . . ?* on est à quelle distance de . . ? *it's no ~ from here,* c'est à deux pas d'ici. *within shouting ~,* à portée de voix. *keep s.o at a ~,* tenir qn à distance. (*in time*) intervalle, *m.* [*long-*]~ *race,* course de fond, *f. long-~* [*phone*] *call,* appel interurbain, *m.* **distant,** *a,* éloigné, lointain; (*in time*) reculé, éloigné; (*relation*) éloigné.
distaste, *n,* dégoût, *m,* répugnance, *f* (*for,* pour). ~**ful,** *a,* désagréable, déplaisant.
distemper[1], *n,* (*paint*) détrempe, *f,* badigeon, *m.* ¶ *v.t,* peindre à la détrempe, badigeonner.
distemper[2], *n,* maladie des chiens, *f.*
distend, *v.t.* (& *i*) (se) distendre; (se) ballonner. **distension,** *n,* distension, dilatation, *f,* ballonnement, *m.*
distil, *v.t,* distiller. **distillate** & **distillation,** *n,* distillation, *f.* **distiller,** *n,* distillateur, *m.* ~**y,** *n,* distillerie, *f.*
distinct†, *a,* distinct, net, marqué; (*colours*) tranché. ~**ion,** *n,* distinction, *f.* (*author &c*) *of ~,* réputé. *win ~,* se distinguer. (*Univ.*) mention très bien, *f.* ~**ive,** *a,* distinctif. **distinctness,** *n,* netteté, *f.* **distinguish,** *v.t,* distinguer (*from,* de). ~ *o.s,* se distinguer. *to be ~able from,* se distinguer de. ¶ *v.i, ~ between,* distinguer *ou* faire la distinction entre. ~**ed,** *a,* distingué, de marque.
distort, *v.t,* (*shape*) déformer; (*words, truth*) déformer, dénaturer; (*face*) convulser. ~**ion,** *n,* (*gen., Radio, Opt.*) distorsion; déformation, *f.*
distract, *v.t,* distraire, détourner. ~**ed†,** *a,* éperdu, affolé. ~**ion,** *n,* distraction, *f;* divertissement, *m. drive to ~,* rendre fou.
distress, *n,* douleur, angoisse; (*poverty, danger*) détresse, *f.* ~ *signal,* signal de détresse, *m.* ¶ *v.t,* affliger, désoler, angoisser. ~**ing,** *a,* affligeant, pénible.
distribute, *v.t,* distribuer, répartir. **distribution,** *n,* distribution, répartition, *f.* **distributor,** *n,* (*Com.*) concessionnaire, *m,f;* (*car*) distributeur, Delco, *m.*
district, *n,* région, *f;* (*town*) quartier; (*Adm.*) district, arrondissement, *m.* ~ *manager,* directeur régional, *m.* ~ *nurse,* infirmière visiteuse, *f.*
distrust, *n,* méfiance, défiance, *f.* ¶ *v.t,* se méfier de, se défier de. ~**ful,** *a,* méfiant.
disturb, *v.t,* déranger; (*upset pers.*) inquiéter, troubler; (*water*) remuer. ~**ance,** *n,* dérangement; trouble, *m,* perturbation, *f;* (*Pol.*) troubles, *m.pl,* émeute, *f;* (*noise*) tapage, *m;* (*Met.*) perturbation, *f.*
disunion, *n,* désunion, *f.* **disunite,** *v.t,* désunir.
disuse, *n,* désuétude, *f. fall into ~,* tomber en d. ~**d,** *a,* (*building*) désaffecté, abandonné.
ditch, *n,* fossé, *m.* ¶ *P v.t,* (*pers.*) laisser tomber, plaquer *P;* (*car &c*) abandonner.
dither, *n, to be in a ~,* être indécis. ¶ *v.i,* hésiter.
ditto, *n.* & *ad,* idem.
ditty, *n,* chansonnette, *f.*
divan, *n,* divan, *m.*
dive, *n,* plongeon, *m;* (*deep-sea*) plongée, *f;* (*Aero.*) piqué, *m;* (*P bar &c*) bouge, *f.* ¶ *v.i,*

plonger. ~ *headfirst,* piquer une tête; (*Aero.*) piquer du nez. ~*-bomb,* bombarder en piqué. **diver,** *n,* (*Swim.*) plongeur, euse; (*in suit*) scaphandrier, *m;* (*bird*) plongeon, *m.*

diverge, *v.i,* diverger. **divergence,** *n,* divergence, *f.* **divergent,** *a,* divergent.

diverse†, *a,* divers, varié. **diversify,** *v.t,* diversifier, varier. **diversion,** *n,* diversion, *f;* divertissement, *m;* (*traffic*) déviation, *f. create a* ~, faire diversion. **diversity,** *n,* diversité, variété, *f.* **divert,** *v.t,* détourner, dériver, écarter; (*amuse*) divertir; (*traffic*) dévier.

divest, *v.t,* dépouiller (*of,* de).

divide, *v.t,* (*into parts*) diviser (en parties), partager, répartir; (*Math.*) diviser; (*from sth*) séparer. ¶ *v.i,* se diviser; (*road*) bifurquer. ~**d,** *a,* (*family &c*) désuni; (*opinion*) partagé. ~ *skirt,* jupe-culotte, *f.* **dividend,** *n,* dividende, *m.* **dividers,** *n.pl,* compas à pointes sèches, *m.*

divine†, *a,* divin. ¶ *n,* théologien, *m.* ¶ *v.t,* deviner. **diviner,** *n,* devin, *m,* devineresse, *f.*

diving: ~ *bell,* cloche à plongeur, *f.* ~ *board,* plongeoir; (*springboard*) tremplin, *m.* ~ *suit,* scaphandre, *m.*

divining rod, *n,* baguette divinatoire, *f.*

divinity, *n,* divinité; (*subject*) théologie, *f.*

divisible, *a,* divisible. **division,** *n,* division, séparation (*into,* en); répartition, *f,* partage, *m* (*among,* entre); (*Mil., Math.*) division; (*strife*) désaccord; (*Pol.*) vote, *m.* **divisor,** *n,* diviseur, *m.*

divorce, *n,* divorce, *m. get a* ~, obtenir le d. (d'avec). ¶ *v.t,* divorcer d'avec. *to get* ~*d,* divorcer. **divorcee,** *n,* divorcé, e.

divulge, *v.t,* divulguer.

dizziness, *n,* vertige, *m.* **dizzy,** *a,* (*pers.*) pris de vertige; (*height &c*) vertigineux. *it makes me* ~, ça me donne le vertige.

do, *v.t.ir,* faire. ~ *one's best,* faire de son mieux; f. tout son possible. *what did he* ~ *with the paper?* qu'est-ce qu'il a fait du journal? *to* ~ *2 years* [*in jail*], faire 2 ans de prison. (*speed*) *to* ~ *50* [*m.p.h.*], faire du 80 à l'heure, rouler à 80 à l'heure. (*cover a distance*) faire, parcourir. (*clean &c*) *to* ~ *one's teeth,* se brosser les dents. *to* ~ *the dishes,* faire la vaisselle. (*room:* & ~ *out*) faire, nettoyer; (*shoes*) cirer. ¶ *v.i.ir,* faire, agir; aller, marcher. *he did well to come,* il a bien fait de venir. *how* ~ *you* ~? comment allez-vous? comment ça va? (*patient*) *she's* ~*ing better,* elle va mieux. *business is* ~*ing well,* les affaires vont *ou* marchent bien. *that will* ~ *for a hat,* cela servira de chapeau. *that will* ~, ça suffit. *that has nothing to* ~ *with,* (*pers.*) cela ne regarde pas (mon frère); (*thing*) cela n'a rien à voir avec (la question). *to make* ~ *with,* se débrouiller avec. ~ *again,* refaire. ~ **away with,** abolir, supprimer. ~ **in,** (*kill*) supprimer, liquider *P.* ~ **over,** (*P pers.*) passer à tabac, tabasser *P.* ~ **up,** boutonner; (*dress &c*) attacher; (*repair*) refaire, mettre à neuf. ~ **without,** se passer de. **done,** *p.p, well* ~! bravo! (*steak*) *well* ~, bien cuit. ~ *to a turn,* à point. ~ *in,* éreinté, crevé *P,* claqué *P.* ~ *for,* fichu *P,* foutu *P**. *I have* ~, j'ai fini. *that's often* ~, ça se fait souvent.

docile†, *a,* docile. **docility,** *n,* docilité, *f.*

dock[1] *n,* (*Naut.*) bassin, dock, *m. the* ~*s,* les docks. ¶ *v*(*t*) & *i,* (faire) entrer au bassin.

dock[2], *n,* (*Law*) banc des accusés, *m.*

dock[3], *n,* (*Bot.*) patience, *f.*

dock[4], *v.t,* (*tail*) écourter; (*wages*) rogner.

docker, *n,* docker, débardeur, *m.* **dockyard,** *n,* chantier naval, *m.*

doctor, *n,* médecin, docteur, *m. D*~ *Duval,* le docteur Duval. *a woman* ~, une femme médecin. *she's a* ~, elle est docteur *ou* médecin. (*Univ.*) docteur (en droit, ès sciences &c). ¶ *v.t,* (*pers.*) soigner; (*cat*) châtrer; (*wine*) frelater; (*accounts*) tripatouiller *P.* ~**ate,** *n,* doctorat, *m.*

doctrinaire, *n.* & *a,* doctrinaire, *m,f.*

doctrine, *n,* doctrine, *f.*

document, *n,* document, *m.* ~ *case,* porte-documents, *m inv.* ¶ *v.t,* documenter. ~**ary,** *a,* documentaire. ¶ *n,* (*film*) documentaire, *m.*

dodderer, *n,* gâteux, euse; croulant, e *P.*

dodge, *n,* (*Box.* &c) esquive, *f;* truc *P, m,* combine *P, f.* ¶ *v.t,* esquiver, éviter. ¶ *v.i,* s'esquiver. *artful dodger,* roublard, e. **dodgy,** *a,* (*situation*) délicat, épineux.

doe, *n,* (*deer*) biche; (*hare*) hase; (*rabbit*) lapine, *f.* ~**skin,** *n,* peau de daim, *f.*

doff, *v.t,* ôter, enlever.

dog, *n,* chien, ne; (*fox, wolf*) mâle, *m. the* ~*s P,* les courses de lévriers, *f.pl. to lead a* ~*'s life,* mener une vie de chien. *go to the* ~*s,* mal tourner. *lucky* ~ *P,* veinard, e [*P*]. *dirty* ~ *P,* sale type *P. fire-*~, chenet, *m.* ~ *biscuit,* biscuit pour chien, *m.* ~*-cart,* charrette anglaise, *f.* ~*-eared,* écorné. *to be in the* ~ *house P,* ne plus être dans les petits papiers de qn. ~ *paddle,* nage en chien, *f.* ~ *rose,* églantine, *f;* (*bush*) églantier, *m.* ~*show,* exposition canine. ~*-tired,* crevé *P,* claqué *P.* ¶ *v.t, to* ~ *s.o's footsteps,* marcher sur les talons de qn. **dogged,** *a,* tenace. ~**ness,** *n,* obstination, *f.*

doggerel, *n,* méchants vers, *m.pl.*

doggy *or* **doggie,** *n,* toutou, *P, m.*

dogma, *n,* dogme, *m.* **dogmatic†,** *a,* dogmatique. **dogmatize,** *v.i,* dogmatiser.

doings, *n.pl,* faits & gestes, *m.pl.* ¶ *n.s,* (*P thing*) truc *P,* machin *P, m.*

do-it-yourself, *n,* bricolage, *m.* ¶ *a,* (*shop*) de bricolage.

doldrums (*Naut.*) *n.pl,* zone des calmes, *f. to be*

in the ~ (*fig.*), broyer du noir.
dole, *n,* allocation de chômage, *f.* ¶ *v.t,* ~ *out,* distribuer parcimonieusement.
doleful†, *a,* plaintif, dolent, lugubre.
doll, *n,* poupée, *f;* (*P girl*) nana *P,* môme *P, f;* pépée *P, f.* ~*'s house,* maison de poupée, *f.*
dollar, *n,* dollar, *m.*
dolphin, *n,* dauphin, *m.*
dolt, *n,* lourdaud, e; gourde, *f.*
domain, *n,* domaine, *m.*
dome, *n,* dôme, *m,* coupole, *f.*
domestic, *a,* domestique; familial; (*coal &c*) de ménage; (*affairs, trade*) intérieur; (*animal*) domestique. ~ *science,* arts ménagers. ~ *science college,* école ménagère. ¶ *n,* domestique, *m,f.* ~**ate,** *v.t,* (*animal*) apprivoiser. ~*d,* (*woman*) femme d'intérieur, (*man*) homme d'i. ~**ity,** *n,* vie de famille, *f.*
domicile, *n,* domicile, *m.* ¶ *v.t,* domicilier. *domiciliary visit,* visite domiciliaire.
dominant, *a,* dominant. ¶ *n,* (*Mus.*) dominante, *f.* **dominate,** *v.t,* dominer. **domination,** *n,* domination, *f.* **domineer,** *v.i,* se montrer autoritaire. ~**ing,** *a,* dominateur.
Dominican, *n,* dominicain, e.
dominion, *n,* domination, *f,* empire, *m;* territoire, dominion, *m.*
domino, *n,* domino, *m. play* ~*es,* jouer aux dominos.
don[1], *v.t,* mettre, endosser, revêtir.
don[2], *n,* professeur d'université, *m.*
donate, *v.t,* faire don de; (*blood*) donner.
donation, *n,* don, *m,* donation, *f.*
done, *p.p. of* **do.**
donkey, *n,* âne(sse) *m*(*f*), baudet, *m,* bourrique, *f;* (*P fool*) âne, imbécile, *m,f.* ~ *engine,* petit cheval, *m.* ~ *work,* le gros du travail. ~*'s years,* une éternité.
donor, *n,* donateur, trice; (*blood, heart*) donneur, euse.
doodle *P, v.i,* griffonner; gribouiller.
doom, *n,* destin, sort, *m;* ruine, *f.* ¶ *v.t,* condamner. ~*ed to failure,* voué à l'échec. **doomsday,** *n,* jour du jugement dernier, *m.* (*fig.*) *till* ~, jusqu'à la fin des temps.
door, *n,* porte; (*car*) portière, *f.* ~*bell,* sonnette, *f.* ~*frame,* chambranle, *m.* ~ *handle,* bouton (*m*) *ou* poignée de porte, *f.* ~*keeper,* (*flats*) concierge, *m,f;* (*hotel*) portier, *m.* ~*mat,* paillasson, *m.* ~*step,* pas de la porte, seuil, *m.* ~*-to-*~ *selling,* porte à porte, *m.*
dope, *n,* drogue, *f,* stupéfiant; (*athlete*) dopant, *m. take* ~, se droguer. (*P information*) tuyaux, *m.pl. get the* ~ *on,* se tuyauter sur. (*P pers.*) nouille *P,* gourde *P, f.* ¶ *v.t,* (*pers., horse*) doper; (*drink*) verser une drogue dans. ~**y,** *a,* abruti.
dormant, *a,* (*fig.*) endormi, en sommeil; (*volcano*) en repos. **dormer [window],** *n,* lucarne, *f.* **dormitory,** *n,* dortoir. *m.* ~ *suburb,* banlieue dortoir, *f.* **dormouse,** *n,* loir, *m.*
dosage, *n,* (*Phar.*) posologie, *f.* **dose,** *n,* dose; (*of illness*) attaque, *f.* ¶ *v.t,* administrer un médicament à.
dot, *n,* point, *m. on the* ~, à l'heure pile. ¶ *v.t,* marquer d'un point, pointiller; (*an i*) mettre un point sur. **dotted:** ~ *with,* parsemé de. ~ *line,* ligne pointillé.
dotage, *n,* seconde enfance, *f. in one's* ~, gâteux. **dote on,** *v.i,* être fou (folle) de, raffoler de.
dotty *P, a,* piqué *P,* toqué *P.*
double, *a,* double. (*letters*) ~ *'n',* deux 'n'. ~ *the size of,* deux fois plus grand que. ¶ *ad, see* ~, voir double. *bent, folded* ~*;* courbé, plié en deux. ¶ *n,* double, *m;* (*pers.*) double, sosie, *m.* ~ *or quits,* quitte ou double. *at the* ~, au pas de course; (*Mil.*) au pas de gymnastique. ~*-barrelled,* (*gun*) à deux coups. ~ *bass,* contrebasse, *f.* ~ *bed,* lit de deux personnes, *m.* ~*-breasted,* croisé. ~*-cross P,* tromper, trahir. ~*-dealing,* duplicité, *f.* ~ *entendre,* ~ *meaning,* double entente, *f.* ~*-decker,* (*bus*) autobus à impériale, *m.* (*Bkkpg.*) ~ *entry,* comptabilité en partie double, *f.* ~ *glazing,* doubles fenêtres, *f.pl.* ~ *room,* chambre pour deux personnes, *f.* ~ *saucepan,* [casserole *f*] bain-marie, *m.* ¶ *v.t,* doubler; plier en deux. *to be* ~*d up with laughter,* être plié en deux de rire. ¶ *v.i,* (*in room*) partager une chambre. **doubly,** *ad,* doublement.
doubt, *n,* doute, *m. to be in* ~ *about,* avoir des doutes sur. ¶ *v.t,* douter de (qn, qch). *I* ~ *it,* j'en doute. *I* ~ *whether he will come,* je doute qu'il vienne. ~**ful,** *a,* (*pers.*) incertain, indécis; (*thing*) douteux. ~**less,** *a,* sans doute.
douche, *n,* douche, *f;* (*Med.*) lavage, *m.*
dough, *n,* pâte, *f;* (*P money*) fric *P, m.* ~*nut,* beignet, *m.*
dour, *a,* sévère; peu démonstratif.
dove, *n,* colombe, *f.* ~*cot*[*e*], colombier, pigeonnier, *m.* ~*tail,* queue d'aronde, *f.*
dowdy, *a,* mal fagoté *P.*
dowel, *n,* cheville, *f,* goujon, *m.* ¶ *v.t,* goujonner.
down[1], *ad,* en bas, vers le bas; (*to the ground*) à terre, par terre. *go, come* ~, descendre. ~ *with fascism!* à bas le fascisme! (*to dog*) ~*!* couché! ~ *below,* en bas. ~ *there,* là-bas. (*sun, moon*) couché; (*blinds*) baissé. (*walk*) *with one's head* ~, la tête baissée. (*tyres*) dégonflé, à plat. *feel* ~, être déprimé, avoir le cafard. ~ *in the mouth,* abattu, découragé. ¶ *pr, walk* ~ *the street, go* ~ *the hill,* descendre la rue, la colline. *fall* ~ *the stairs,* tomber en bas de l'escalier. ¶ *n, have a* ~ *on s.o,* avoir une dent contre qn. ¶ *v.t,* (*opponent*) abattre, terrasser. ~ *tools,* cesser le travail. *comps:* ~*-and-out,* sur le pavé. *a* ~*-and-out,* un clochard. ~*-at-heel,* miteux. ~*fall, n,* chute, *f,* effondrement, *m,* ruine, *f.* ~*hearted, a,*

découragé, abattu. *~hill, a,* en pente; *ad* en descendant. *~pour,* forte averse; déluge, *m.* *~right,* (*pers.*) franc, direct; *ad,* franchement, carrément. *~stairs, ad,* en bas, au rez-de-chaussée; *a,* (*flat*) d'en bas. *~stream, ad,* en aval (*from,* de). *~-to-earth,* terre à terre, *inv.* *~trodden,* opprimé. *~wards, a,* descendant; de baisse, à la baisse. *~ward*[*s*], *ad,* en bas, vers le bas, en contre-bas.

down[2], *n,* (*bird, fruit, pers.*) duvet, *m.* **~y,** *a,* duveteux.

dowry, *n,* dot, *f. provide a ~ for,* doter.

dowser, *n,* sourcier, *m.* **dowsing,** *n,* hydroscopie, *f.* *~ rod,* baguette de sourcier, *f.*

doze, *v.i,* sommeiller. *to have a ~*, faire un petit somme. *~ off,* s'assoupir.

dozen, *n,* douzaine, *f. half a ~*, une demi-douzaine. *~s of times,* des douzaines de fois. *by the ~*, à la douzaine.

drab, *a,* terne; gris, morne.

draft, *n,* (*Mil.*) détachement, *m;* (*Am*) conscription, *f;* (*letter*) brouillon, *m;* (*plan*) ébauche; (*Com.*) traite, *f.* ¶ *v.t,* (*Mil.*) détacher; (*Am*) appeler sous les drapeaux; faire le brouillon de; (*plan*) esquisser, dresser; (*Pol: bill*) rédiger. **draftsman = draughtsman.**

drag, *n,* (*dredging & ~net*) drague, *f;* (*Aero.*) traînée, *f;* (*hindrance*) entrave, *f;* (*P pers.*) raseur, euse, casse-pieds, *m,f. inv.* (*thing*) *what a ~!* quelle barbe! *P.* (*P female attire*) travesti, *m. in ~*, en travesti. ¶ *v.t,* traîner, tirer; (*pers.*) entraîner; (*pond*) draguer. *~ the truth out of s.o,* arracher la vérité à qn. (*Naut.*) *~ anchor,* chasser ses ancres. *~ about,* (*bags*) trimbaler *P.* ¶ *v.i, ~ on,* traîner [en longueur].

dragon, *n,* dragon, *m.* *~fly,* libellule, *f.*

dragoon, *n,* dragon, *m.* *~ into,* forcer à.

drain, *n,* égout, canal de décharge; (*pipe*) tuyau d'écoulement, *m;* (*Agr.*) drain; (*fig.*) épuisement, *m,* perte, *f.* ¶ *v.t,* (*land*) drainer, assécher; (*boiler, pool*) vider; (*fig.*) épuiser, saigner. ¶ *v.i, ~ away,* (*liquid*) s'écouler. *~ing board, ~ing rack,* égouttoir, *m.* **~age,** *n,* drainage, assèchement, *m.* *~ system,* (*town*) système d'égouts, *m.*

drake, *n,* canard, *m.*

dram, *n,* (*drink*) goutte, *f,* petit verre, *m.*

drama, *n,* drame, *m,* pièce de théâtre, *f. the ~*, le théâtre, l'art dramatique, *m.* (*fig.*) drame. **~tic,** *a,* dramatique; (*effect*) théâtral. *dramatis personae,* personnages, *m.pl.* **~tist,** *n,* auteur dramatique, *m,* dramaturge, *m,f.* **~tize,** *v.t,* (*event*) dramatiser; (*book*) adapter pour la scène.

drape, *v.t,* draper; tendre. **draper,** *n,* marchand de nouveautés, *m.* **~y,** *n,* draperie, *f;* (*shop*) magasin de nouveautés, *m.*

drastic, *a,* (*measures*) extrême, énergique.

draught, *n,* courant d'air; (*chimney*) tirage; (*Naut.*) tirant d'eau; (*drink*) coup, breuvage, *m. in long ~s,* à longs traits. (*fish*) pêche, prise, *f.* (*game*) *~s,* dames, *f.pl.* *~ animal,* animal de trait, *m.* *~ beer,* bière [à la] pression, *f.* *~ board,* damier, *m.* **~y,** *a,* plein de courants d'air.

draughtsman, *n,* dessinateur, trice; (*game*) pion, *m.*

draw, *n,* loterie, *f;* tirage au sort, *m;* attraction, *f;* (*game*) partie nulle, *f,* match nul, *m.*

draw, *v.t.ir,* (*pull*) tirer, traîner; (*curtains - open & close*) tirer; (*caravan*) remorquer; (*crowd*) attirer; (*teeth*) arracher, extraire; (*pay*) toucher; (*cheque*) tirer; (*water*) puiser (*from,* dans); (*picture*) dessiner; (*plan*) tracer. (*boat*) *to ~ 3 metres,* caler 3 mètres. *~ lots* (*for sth*), tirer (qch) au sort. *~ blank,* revenir bredouille, faire chou blanc *P.* ¶ *v.i,* (*game*) faire match nul. (*train*) *~ into the station,* entrer en gare. *~ near,* s'approcher (*to,* de). *~ round* (*table*), s'assembler autour de. *~ to a close,* toucher à sa fin. *~* **aside,** *v.t,* tirer à l'écart; *v.i,* s'écarter. *~* **back,** *v.t,* retirer; *v.i,* reculer. *~* **down,** baisser, [faire] descendre. *~* **in,** (*days*), raccourcir. *~* **on,** (*source*) puiser dans. *~* **out,** (*days*), rallonger. *~* **up,** (*list &c*) dresser, rédiger; (*plan*) formuler; *v.i,* (*car*) s'arrêter.

drawback, *n,* désavantage, inconvénient, *m.*

drawbridge, *n,* pont à bascule; (*Hist.*) pont-levis, *m.*

drawer, *n,* (*receptacle*) tiroir, *m;* (*of cheque*) tireur, *m.* *~s,* (*men*) caleçon, *m;* (*women*) culotte, *f.*

drawing, *n,* dessin; (*lottery*) tirage, *m.* *~ board,* planche à dessin, *f.* *~ pen,* tire-ligne, *m.* *~ pin,* punaise, *f.* *~ room,* salon, *m.*

drawl, *v.i,* parler d'une voix traînante.

drawn, *p.p. of* **draw:** *~ battle,* bataille indécise, *f.* *~ face,* visage tiré, v. crispé. *~ game,* partie nulle, *f.*

dread, *a,* (*liter.*) redoutable. ¶ *n,* terreur, crainte, épouvante, *f.* ¶ *v.t,* redouter, craindre. **~ful†,** *a,* épouvantable, affreux, atroce. **~fully,** *ad,* affreusement, terriblement. *I'm ~ sorry,* je regrette infiniment.

dream, *n,* rêve; (*liter.*) songe, *m. to have a ~*, faire un rêve. *day-~*, rêverie. *in a ~*, dans la lune, dans les nuages. *my ~ house,* la maison de mes rêves. ¶ *v.i. & t.ir,* rêver (*of,* de; que); (*day-~*) rêvasser. **~er,** *n,* rêveur, euse. **~y,** *a,* rêveur, songeur.

dreary, *a,* morne, lugubre, monotone. **dreariness,** *n,* aspect morne &c, *m.*

dredge, *n,* drague, *f.* ¶ *v.t,* draguer. **dredger,** *n,* dragueur, *m.* **dredging,** *n,* dragage, *m.*

dregs, *n.pl,* lie, *f.*

drench, *v.t,* tremper, mouiller. *~ed to the skin,* trempé jusqu'aux os. *to get ~ed,* se faire saucer *P.* *~ing rain,* pluie battante, *f.*

Dresden, *n,* Dresde, *f.* ~ *china,* porcelaine de Saxe, *f,* saxe, *m.*

dress, *n,* habillement, *m,* tenue, *f,* vêtements, *m.pl;* (*frock*) robe, toilette, *f. evening* ~, tenue de soirée. *in full* ~, en grande tenue. *national* ~, costume national, *m. wedding* ~, toilette de mariée, *f.* ~ *circle,* premier balcon, *m.* ~ *designer,* couturier, *m,* modéliste, *m,f.* ~*maker,* couturière, *f.* ~*making,* couture, confection de robes, *f.* ~ *rehearsal,* répétition générale, *f.* ~ *suit,* habit de soirée, *m.* ¶ *v.t,* habiller, vêtir. ~*ed in a suit, in black,* habillé d'un complet, de noir. ~*ed for town,* en tenue de ville. (*play*) costumer; (*shop window*) faire l'étalage; (*ship with flags*) pavoiser; (*wound*) panser; (*food*) apprêter; (*salad*) assaisonner, garnir (*with,* de); (*stone*) tailler, dresser; (*Mil.*) aligner. ¶ *v.i,* s'habiller, se vêtir. ~ *for dinner,* se mettre en tenue de soirée. (*Mil.*) s'aligner. ~ *down P,* passer un savon à *P.* ~ *up,* se déguiser (*as,* en); (*in one's Sunday best*) s'endimancher. *get* ~*ed up to the nines,* se mettre sur son trente et un. ~**er**[1], *n,* (*Theat.*) habilleur, euse; (*window* ~) étalagiste, *m,f.* ~**er**[2], *n,* (*kitchen*) buffet, vaisselier, *m.* ~**ing,** *n,* (*Med.*) pansement, *m. French* ~, (*salad*) vinaigrette, *f.* ~ *gown,* robe de chambre, *f,* peignoir, *m.* ~ *room,* (*Theat.*) loge d'acteur, *f.* ~ *table,* [table de] toilette, coiffeuse, *f.*

dribble, *n,* bave; (*water*) petite goutte, *f.* ¶ *v.i,* baver; (*water*) tomber goutte à goutte; (*v.t, Foot.*) dribbler.

driblet, *n, in* ~*s,* (*fig.*) petit à petit; au compte-gouttes.

dried, *p.p. of* **dry,** *a,* séché; (*raisins, figs* &c) sec; (*milk*) en poudre.

drift, *n,* (*current*) direction; (*Naut.*) dérive; (*Artil.*) déviation; (*snow*) congère, *f,* amoncellement, *m;* (*meaning*) but, *m,* portée, *f;* (*Min.*) galerie, *f;* (*Geol.*) apports *m.pl.* ~ [*net*], traîne, *f.* ~*wood,* bois flotté, *m.* ¶ *v.i,* (*Naut.*) dériver, aller à la dérive; (*snow*) s'amonceler. (*fig.*) *let o.s* ~, se laisser aller. *let things* ~, laisser les choses aller à la dérive. ~**er,** *n,* (*boat*) chalutier, *m.*

drill[1], *n,* (*bit*) mèche, *f,* foret; porte-foret, *m,* perceuse, *f;* (*Min.,* &c) perforatrice, foreuse, sonde, *f;* (*dentist*) fraise. *electric* (*hand*) ~, perceuse électrique. ¶ *v.t,* percer, forer; (*tooth*) fraiser; (*oil well*) forer. ~**ing,** *n,* perçage, forage; fraisage, *m.*

drill[2], *n,* (*furrow*) sillon; (*Mach.*) semoir, *m.* ¶ *v.t,* (*seed*) semer; (*field*) ensemencer.

drill[3], *n,* (*Mil.*) exercice(s), *m(pl),* manoeuvre(s), *f(pl).* ¶ *v.t,* faire faire l'exercice à. ¶ *v.i,* faire l'exercice.

drill[4], *n,* (*cloth*) coutil, *m.*

drily, *ad,* (*coldly*) sèchement, d'un ton sec; (*with dry humour*) d'un air pince-sans-rire.

drink, *n,* boisson; (*in café*) consommation, *f. strong* ~, liqueurs fortes; spiritueux, *m.pl. give, stand s.o a* ~, donner, offrir à boire à qn. *have a* ~, prendre un verre, boire un coup *P. to take to* ~, s'adonner à la boisson. *celebrate with a* ~, (*event*) arroser. *that calls for a* ~, ça s'arrose. ¶ *v.t.* & *i.ir,* boire, prendre; (*soup*) manger. *to* ~ *like a fish,* boire comme un trou *P.* ~**able,** *a,* (*wine*) buvable; (*water*) potable. ~**er,** *n,* buveur, euse. ~**ing,** *att:* ~ *bout,* beuverie, *f.* ~ *fountain,* fontaine publique, *f.* ~ *song,* chanson à boire, *f.* ~ *trough,* abreuvoir, *m.* ~ *water,* eau potable, *f.*

drip, *n,* goutte, *f;* (*Med.*) perfusion, *f;* (*apparatus*) goutte-à-goutte, *m inv;* (*P weak pers.*) lavette, *f.* ¶ *v.i,* (*water*) tomber goutte à goutte, dégoutter; (*washing*) [s']égoutter; (*tap*) goutter; (*walls*) suinter. ~ *with sweat,* ruisseler de sueur. *to* ~*-dry,* laisser égoutter. ~*-dry, a,* à ne pas repasser. **dripping,** *n,* graisse de rôti, *f.* ~ *pan,* lèchefrite, *f.* ~ *wet,* tout trempé, saucé *P.*

drive, *n,* (*car*) promenade en voiture; (*house*) avenue, allée, *f;* (*quality*) énergie, *f,* dynamisme, *m;* (*export* &c) campagne, *f,* effort, *m;* (*Hunt.*) battue; (*Mach.*) commande, transmission; (*Golf, Ten.*) drive, *m. front-wheel* ~, traction avant, *f. left-hand* ~, conduite à gauche, *f.* ¶ *v.t.ir,* chasser, pousser; (*vehicle, passenger*) conduire; (*cattle*) mener, conduire; (*game*) rabattre; (*Mach.*) actionner, commander. ~ *s.o to do,* forcer qn à faire. ~ *s.o hard,* surmener qn. ~ *mad,* rendre fou. ¶ *v.i.ir,* conduire [une voiture], aller en voiture. *to* ~ *on the right,* rouler *ou* circuler à droite. ~ **along,** rouler, circuler. ~ **away,** *v.t,* chasser. ¶ *v.i,* (*car*) démarrer; (*pers.*) partir en voiture. ~ **back,** repousser, refouler; (*pers.*) ramener en voiture. ~ **in,** *v.t,* (*nail, post*) enfoncer; (*screw*) visser. ~ **out,** (*pers., thoughts*) chasser.

drivel, *n,* radotage, *m.* ¶ *v.i,* radoter.

driver, *n,* (*car, taxi* &c) conducteur, trice, chauffeur, *m;* (*Rly*) mécanicien, *m;* (*Golf*) driver, *m.* **driving,** *n,* (*car* &c) conduite, *f.* ¶ *a,* ~ *rain,* pluie battante. ~ *force,* force agissante. ~ *belt,* courroie de transmission, *f.* ~ *instructor,* moniteur, trice de conduite. ~ *licence,* permis de conduire, *m.* ~ *mirror,* rétroviseur, *m.* ~ *school,* auto-école, *f.* ~ *test,* examen du permis de conduire, *m.* ~ *shaft,* arbre moteur, *m.*

drizzle, *n,* bruine, *f,* crachin, *m.* ¶ *v.i,* bruiner.

droll, *a,* drôle, comique; bizarre.

dromedary, *n,* dromadaire, *m.*

drone, *n,* abeille mâle, *f,* faux-bourdon, *m;* (*fig.*) fainéant, e; (*sound*) (*bees*) bourdonnement, (*engine*) ronronnement, vrombissement; (*Mus.*) bourdon, *m.* ¶ *v.i,* bourdonner; ronronner, vrombir.

droop, *v.i,* (*head*) pencher; (*eyelids*) s'abaisser; (*body*) s'affaisser; (*plant*) languir, s'étioler. **~ing,** *a,* (*spirits*) défaillant.

drop, *n,* (*water &c*) goutte, *f.* *~ by ~*, goutte à goutte. *just a ~*, une larme, une petite goutte. *a ~ too much,* un verre de trop. (*fall*) baisse, chute, *f;* (*in altitude*) descente, dénivellation, *f;* (*parachute*) saut, *m.* *~ earrings,* pendant d'oreille, *m.* *~-forge,* marteau-pilon, *m.* (*Rugby*) *~ kick,* drop, *m.* (*Ten.*) *~-shot,* amorti, *m.* ¶ *v.t,* laisser tomber; (*let go*) lâcher; (*bomb*) lancer; (*pers. from car*) déposer; (*give up*) (*idea &c*) abandonner, renoncer à; (*friend*) laisser tomber. (*Naut.*) *~ anchor,* mouiller, jeter l'ancre. *~ a stitch,* sauter une maille. *~ a brick,* faire une gaffe. ¶ *v.i,* tomber; (*pers.*) se laisser tomber; (*price &c*) baisser; (*wind*) se calmer. *~ into an armchair,* s'écrouler dans un fauteuil. *I'm ready to ~*, je tombe de fatigue. ~ **in,** (*at the grocer's*) passer (chez l'épicier); (*on s.o*) passer voir (qn). ~ **out of,** se retirer de; (*society*) s'évader de, être un (une) drop-out *P;* (*Univ.*) abandonner. ~ **round,** (*to s.o's house*) faire un saut (chez qn.). **dropper,** *n,* (*Med.*) compte-gouttes, *m inv.* **droppings,** *n.pl.* (*animals*) crotte, *f;* (*birds*) fiente, *f.*

drought, *n,* sécheresse, *f.*

drove, *n,* troupeau, *m.* *come in ~s,* arriver en foule.

drown, *v.t,* noyer; (*sounds*) couvrir, étouffer. *~ one's sorrows,* noyer ses chagrins. ¶ *v.i,* se noyer. *~ed man,* un noyé. [*death by*] *~ing,* noyade, *f.*

drowse, *v.i,* somnoler. **drowsiness,** *n,* assoupissement, *m.* **drowsy,** *a,* somnolent, assoupi. *grow ~*, s'assoupir. *feel ~*, avoir sommeil.

drubbing, *n,* volée de coups, *f.* *give s.o a ~*, donner une bonne râclée à qn *P.*

drudge, *n,* homme *ou* femme de peine. ¶ *v.i,* trimer *P.* **~ry,** *n,* corvée, *f,* travail pénible *ou* fastidieux, *m.*

drug, *n,* drogue, *f;* stupéfiant, narcotique, *m.* *to be on ~s,* se droguer; (*Med.*) être sous médication. *to be a ~ on the market,* être invendable. *~ addict,* toxicomane, *m,f,* drogué, e. *~ addiction,* toxicomanie, *f.* *~ pusher,* revendeur, euse de drogue. *~ traffic,* trafic des stupéfiants, *m.* ¶ *v.t,* (*gen., Med.*) droguer.

Druid, *n,* druide, *m.*

drum, *n,* tambour, *m.* *big ~*, grosse caisse. *~s,* (*band, group*) batterie, *f.* *ear~*, tympan, *m.* *~-head,* peau de tambour, *f.* *~ major,* tambour-major, *m.* *~stick,* baguette de tambour, *f;* (*chicken*) pilon, *m.* ¶ *v.i,* battre du (*ou* le) tambour; (*with fingers*) tambouriner, pianoter. *~ sth into s.o,* seriner qch à qn, fourrer qch dans le crâne de qn *P.* **drummer,** *n,* tambour; (*band, group*) batteur, *m.*

drunk, *a,* ivre, soûl; (*fig.*) enivré, grisé (*with,* par, de). *to get ~*, s'enivrer, se soûler *P.* *~ as a lord,* soûl comme un Polonais *P.* **~ard,** *n,* ivrogne, esse, soûlard, e *P.* **~en,** *a,* (*orgy &c*) d'ivrogne; (*driving*) en état d'ivresse. **~enness,** *n,* ébriété, ivresse; (*habitual*) ivrognerie, *f.*

dry, *a,* sec; (*well &c*) à sec, tari; (*country*) aride; (*wine*) sec, brut; (*wit*) mordant. *~-clean,* nettoyer à sec. *~ cleaner,* teinturier, *m.* *~ dock,* cale sèche, bassin de radoub, *m.* *~ fly fishing,* pêche à la mouche sèche, *f.* *on ~ land,* sur la terre ferme. *man of ~ humour,* pince-sans-rire, *m.* *~ rot,* pourriture sèche. *~-shod,* à pied sec. ¶ *v.t. & i,* sécher; *v.t,* (*clothes*) faire sécher; (*dishes*) essuyer. *~ up, v.i,* (*stream &c*) se dessécher, [se] tarir. *~ up! P,* ferme-la! *P.* **~er, drier,** *n,* séchoir, *m.* *hair ~*, s. à cheveux. (*paint*) siccatif, *m.* **~ing,** *n,* séchage; essuyage, *m.* *~ room, ~ cupboard,* séchoir, *m.* **~ly = drily.** **~ness,** *n,* sécheresse, aridité, *f.*

dual, *a,* double. *~ carriageway,* route à chaussées séparées, *f.*

dub, *v.t,* (*nickname*) surnommer; (*Cine.*) doubler.

dubious†, *a,* douteux, incertain; suspect; (*shady*) équivoque, louche.

duchess, *n,* duchesse, *f.* **duchy,** *n,* duché, *m.*

duck, *n,* canard, *m;* (*female*) cane, *f.* *wild ~*, canard sauvage. *play ~s & drakes,* faire des ricochets. *~-board,* caillebotis, *m.* *~ pond,* mare aux canards, *f.* *~weed,* lentille d'eau, *f.* ¶ *v.i,* se baisser subitement. ¶ *v.t,* (*blow & fig.*) esquiver. **~ling,** *n,* caneton, *m,* canette, *f.* **~s, ~ie** *P, n,* mon chou *P.*

duct, *n,* (*Anat.*) canal, conduit, *m;* (*gas &c*) conduite, *f.*

ductile, *a,* (*metals*) ductile; (*pers.*) docile.

due, *a,* (*sum*) dû. *fall ~*, échoir, venir à échéance. (*suitable*) qui convient. *in ~ course,* en temps & lieu, en temps voulu; à la longue, finalement. *after ~ consideration,* après mûre réflexion. *I am ~ to leave at . .*, je dois partir à . . . *~ to,* dû à, provoqué par, attribuable à; (*P pr*) à cause de. ¶ *ad,* *~ east,* droit vers l'est. ¶ *n,* *give s.o his ~*, rendre justice à qn. *~s,* (*port &c*) droits, *m.pl.*

duel, *n,* duel, *m,* rencontre, *f.* ¶ *v.i,* se battre en duel.

duet, *n,* duo, *m.*

duffel, *a,* *~ bag,* sac marin, *m.* *~ coat,* duffel-coat, *m.*

duffer *P, n,* cruche *P, f;* (*Sch.*) cancre *P;* (*Sport*) nul, bon à rien, *m.*

dug, *p.p of* **dig.** *~-out, n,* tranchée-abri, *f.*

duke, *n,* duc, *m.* **~dom,** *n,* duché, *m.*

dull, *a,* (*pers.*) obtus, borné. *~ witted,* à l'esprit lourd. (*sight*) faible; (*boring*) ennuyeux. *dead-*

ly ~, mortel *P*, assommant *P*. (*ache, sound*) sourd; (*colour*) terne; (*weather*) couvert, sombre, gris. ¶ *v.t*, (*senses, edge*) émousser; (*colour*) ternir; (*sound*) assourdir. ~**ard,** *n*, lourdaud, e. ~**ness,** *n*, (*pers.*) lourdeur d'esprit, *f;* (*book*) manque d'intérêt; (*colour*) manque d'éclat, *m*.
duly, *ad*, dûment; en temps voulu.
dumb†, *a*, muet. ~ *animals*, animaux, *m.pl. to be struck* ~, rester muet. (*P pers.*) bête, gourde *P*. ~*-bell*, haltère, *m*. ~ *show*, pantomime, *f*.
dumbfound, *v.t*, abasourdir, ahurir, sidérer *P*.
dumbness, *n*, mutisme, *m*.
dummy, *a*, faux, factice. ¶ *n*, (*display*) mannequin; (*Com.*) [objet] factice, *m;* (*book*) maquette, *f;* (*ventriloquist*) pantin, *m;* (*Bridge*) mort, *m;* (*baby's*) tétine, *f*.
dump, *n*, (*tip*) décharge publique, *f;* (*Mil.*) dépôt, *m. to be down in the* ~*s*, broyer du noir. *P pej.* (*place*) trou *P*, *m;* (*hotel &c*) boîte *P*, *f*. ¶ *v.t*, (*rubbish*) déposer; (*thing*) se débarrasser de, bazarder *P*. ~**ing,** *n*, (*Com.*) dumping, *m*. ~**y,** *a*, boulot, courtaud.
dun[1], *n*, agent de recouvrements, *m*. ¶ *v.t*, (*s.o for money*) harceler, relancer.
dun[2], *a*, (*colour*) fauve gris.
dunce, *n*, ignorant, e, cancre, âne, *m*.
dune, *n*, dune, *f*.
dung, *n*, excrément, *m*, crotte, *f;* (*horse*) crottin, *m;* (*cattle*) bouse; (*bird*) fiente, *f;* (*manure*) fumier, *m*. ~*hill*, [tas de] fumier, *m*.
dungarees, *n.pl*, bleus [de travail], *m.pl*, salopette, *f*.
dungeon, *n*, cachot, *m*.
Dunkirk, *n*, Dunkerque, *m*.
duodenal, *a*, duodénal. ~ *ulcer*, ulcère du duodénum, *m*.
dupe, *n*, dupe, *f*. ¶ *v.t*, duper, tromper.
duplicate, *a*, double. ¶ *n*, double, duplicata, *m. in* ~, en deux exemplaires. ¶ *v.t*, (*document*) faire un double de, polycopier. ~*ing machine*, machine à polycopier, *f*, duplicateur, *m*. **duplication,** *n*, polycopie; (*work &c*) répétition, *f*. **duplicity,** *n*, duplicité, *f*.
durable, *a*, durable. **duration,** *n*, durée, *f*.
duress, *n*, contrainte, *f. under* ~, sous la c.
during, *pr*, pendant, durant, au cours de.
dusk, *n*, crépuscule, *m. at* ~, au c., entre chien & loup. ~**y,** *a*, (*pers.*) au teint foncé, noiraud.
dust, *n*, poussière, poudre, *f*. (*fig.*) *throw* ~ *in s.o's eyes*, jeter de la poudre aux yeux de qn. ~*bin*, poubelle, boîte à ordures, *f*. ~ *cover*, couvre-livre, *m*. ~*man*, boueux, éboueur, *m*. ~ *pan*, pelle à poussière, *f*. ~ *sheet*, housse, *f*. ~*-up P*, bagarre *P*, *f*. ¶ *v.t*, épousseter; (*sprinkle*) saupoudrer. ~**er,** *n*, torchon, chiffon, *m*. ~**y,** *a*, poussiéreux.
Dutch, *a*, hollandais, de Hollande, néerlandais. ~ *auction*, enchère au rabais, *f*. ~ *courage*, courage puisé dans la bouteille. ~ *East Indies*, Indes néerlandaises, *f.pl*. ~*man*, *-woman*, Hollandais, e, Néerlandais, e. *to go* ~, partager les frais. ¶ (*language*) *n*, le hollandais.
dutiable, *a*, soumis à des droits de douane.
dutiful†, *a*, obéissant, soumis, respectueux.
duty, *n*, devoir, *m. to do one's* ~, faire son d. (*duties*) fonction(s) *f.*(*pl*). *on* ~, (*Mil., Police*) de service; (*Med.*) de garde; (*Adm.*) de permanence. *off* ~, libre. *to do* ~ *for s.o*, remplacer qn. (*Fin.*) droit, impôt, *m*, taxe, *f*. ~*-free*, exempté de douane. ~*-free shop*, magasin hors-taxe, *m*.
duvet, *n*, couette, *f*.
dwarf, *n. & a*, nain, e. ¶ *v.t*, rapetisser.
dwell, *v.i.ir*, (*liter.*) habiter, demeurer. ~ *on*, arrêter sa pensée sur; (*point*) insister sur, appuyer sur. ~**er,** *n*, habitant, e. ~**ing,** *n*, habitation, *f*. ~ *house*, maison d'habitation, *f*.
dwindle, *v.i*, diminuer. ~ *away*, (*pers., strength*) dépérir.
dye, *n*, teinture, *f*. (*fig.*) *dyed-in-the-wool*, bon teint. ~*stuffs*, matières colorantes, *f.pl*. ~ *works*, teinturerie, *f. of the deepest* ~ (*fig.*), de la plus belle eau *ou* espèce. ¶ *v.t*, teindre. *to* ~ *blue*, t. en bleu. *to* ~ *one's hair*, se t. les cheveux. ~**ing,** *n*, teinture, *f*. **dyer [& cleaner],** *n*, teinturier, *m*.
dying, *a*, mourant; agonisant; moribond. *the* ~, les mourants, les agonisants, *m.pl*. ~ *words*, dernières paroles, *f.pl*.
dyke = dike.
dynamic, *a*, dynamique. **dynamics,** *n*, dynamique, *f*.
dynamite, *n*, dynamite, *f*. ¶ *v.t*. faire sauter à la d., dynamiter.
dynamo, *n*, dynamo, *f*.
dynasty, *n*, dynastie, *f*.
dysentery, *n*, dysenterie, *f*.
dyspepsia, *n*, dyspepsie, *f*.

E

E (*Mus.*) *letter,* mi, *m.*
each, *a,* chaque. ~ *day,* chaque jour, tous les jours. ¶ *pn,* chacun, e. ~ *of the women,* chacune des femmes. ~ *of us,* chacun d'entre *ou* de nous. (*fruit &c*) *one franc* ~, un franc [la] pièce. ~ *other,* l'un(e) l'autre, les un(e)s les autres. *they hate* ~ *other,* ils se détestent [l'un l'autre]. *they write to* ~ *other,* ils s'écrivent. *separated from* ~ *other,* séparés l'un de l'autre.
eager, *a,* ardent, passionné; avide, désireux, assoiffé (*for,* de). *to be* ~ *for,* désirer ardemment, ambitionner. ~**ly,** *ad,* ardemment, avidement. ~**ness,** *n,* ardeur, avidité, *f,* empressement, *m.*
eagle, *n,* (*bird*) aigle, *m,f;* (*standard*) aigle, *f.* **eaglet,** *n,* aiglon, ne.
ear[1], *n,* oreille, *f. to close one's* ~*s to sth,* faire la sourde oreille à qch. *I'm up to my* ~*s in work,* j'ai du travail par-dessus la tête. (*Mus.*) *to have a good* ~, avoir de l'oreille. *play by* ~, jouer à l'o. *to have* ~*ache,* avoir mal à l'oreille. ~*drum,* tympan, *m.* ~*mark,* (*funds &c*) affecter, assigner. ~*-phones,* casque, *m.* ~*piece,* (*Tel.*), écouteur, *m.* ~*ring,* boucle d'oreille, *f. within* ~*shot,* à portée de voix.
ear[2], *n,* (*corn*) épi, *m.*
earl, *n,* comte, *m.* ~**dom,** *n,* comté, *m.*
early, *a,* (*fruit*) précoce, hâtif; (*death*) prématuré. ~ *vegetables, fruit,* primeurs, *m.pl. to be* ~, arriver tôt *ou* de bonne heure. *to be an* ~ *riser,* être matinal. *in the* ~ *morning,* de bon matin. *from an* ~ *age,* dès l'enfance. (*Com.*) *at your earliest convenience,* dans les meilleurs délais. ¶ *ad,* de bonne heure, tôt. ~ *in the afternoon,* au début de l'après-midi. *as* ~ *as possible,* le plus tôt possible. *earlier,* plus tôt; auparavant.
earn, *v.t,* gagner; (*salary*) toucher; (*praise*) mériter; (*Fin.*) (*interest*) rapporter. *to* ~ *one's living,* gagner sa vie.
earnest, *a,* sérieux; ardent, fervent. ¶ *n, in* ~, sérieusement. *to be in* ~, ne pas plaisanter. (*pledge*) gage, *m.* ~ *money,* arrhes, *f.pl.* ~**ly,** *ad,* avec sérieux; (*beseech*) instamment. ~**ness,** *n,* sérieux, *m,* gravité; ardeur, instance, *f.*
earnings, *n.pl,* salaire, *m;* (*Com.*) bénéfices, profits, *m.pl.*
earth, *n,* (*world*) terre, *f,* monde, *m. on* ~, sur terre. *here on* ~, ici bas. *nothing on* ~, rien au monde. (*ground*) terre, sol, *m;* (*of fox*) terrier, *m,* tanière, *f.* ~*quake,* tremblement de t., *m.* ~*work,* terrassement, *m.* ~*worm,* ver de terre, *m.* ¶ *v.t,* (*Elec.*) mettre à la terre; m. à la masse. (*Hort.*) ~ *up,* butter. ~**en,** *a,* de terre. ~**enware,** *n,* poterie, faïence, *f.* ~**ly,** *a,* terrestre. *no* ~ *reason,* pas la moindre raison. ~**y,** *a,* terreux.
ease, *n,* aisance; facilité; (*mind*) tranquillité, *f;* (*body*) bien-être, *m. with* ~, facilement. *at one's* ~, à l'aise. *my mind is at* ~, j'ai l'esprit tranquille. (*Mil.*) *stand at* ~*!* repos! ¶ *v.t,* (*pain*) soulager; (*mind*) calmer, tranquilliser; (*cord &c*) desserrer, détendre. ¶ *v.i,* (& ~ *off*) diminuer.
easel, *n,* chevalet, *m.*
easily, *ad,* facilement, sans difficulté. (*by far*) de loin.
east, *n,* est; orient, *m. the E*~, l'Orient. *to the* ~ *of,* à l'est de. ¶ *a,* est *inv,* de l'est, oriental. ~ *wind,* vent d'est, *m. on the* ~ *side,* du côté est. *E*~ *Germany,* Allemagne de l'Est. *E*~ *Africa,* l'Afrique orientale. ¶ *ad,* à l'est, vers l'est.
Easter, *n,* Pâques, *m.s.* ~ *egg,* œuf de P., *m.*
easterly, *a,* (*wind*) d'est. **eastern,** *a,* est *inv,* de l'est, oriental.
easy, *a,* facile; (*in one's mind*) tranquille. ~ *as pie P, dead* ~, simple comme bonjour, bête comme chou. (*Com.*) *on* ~ *terms,* avec facilités de paiement. *I'm* ~ *P,* ça m'est égal. ¶ *ad,* doucement, tranquillement. *to take things* ~, en prendre à son aise. *take it* ~*!* ne vous emballez pas! ~ *chair,* fauteuil, *m.* ~*-going,* accommodant, insouciant. *by* ~ *stages,* par petites étapes, par degrés. ~ *to get on with,* (*pers.*) facile à vivre.
eat, *v.t. & i.ir,* manger; bouffer *P.* ~ *a meal,* prendre un repas. ~ *like a horse,* manger comme quatre. ~ *one's words,* se rétracter. ~ *one's heart out,* se ronger [de chagrin]. ~ *away,* ~ *into,* ronger. ~ *out,* dîner en ville. ~ *up,* finir; (*fig.*) dévorer. ~**able,** *a,* mangeable. ~**ables,** *n.pl,* comestibles, *m.pl.* ~**er,** *n,* mangeur, euse. ~**ing:** ~ *apples,* pommes à couteau, *f.pl.* **eats** *P, n,* bouffe *P, f.*
eaves, *n.pl,* avant-toit, *m.* **eavesdrop,** *v.i,* écouter aux portes. **eavesdropper,** *n,* écouteur (euse) aux portes.
ebb, *n,* jusant, reflux, *m.* ~ *tide,* marée descendante. ¶ *v.i,* refluer, descendre.
ebonite, *n,* ébonite, *f.*
ebony, *n,* ébène, *f;* (*tree*) ébénier, *m.*
ebullient, *a,* exubérant, plein de vie.
eccentric, *a.* & (*Mech.*) *n,* excentrique, *m.* ~**ity,** *n,* excentricité, *f.*
ecclesiastic, *n,* ecclésiastique, *m.* ~**al,** *a,* ecclésiastique.
echo, *n,* écho, *m.* ¶ *v.i,* faire écho, retentir,

résonner. ¶ *v.t,* (*fig.*) se faire l'écho de.
éclair, *n,* (*Cook.*) éclair, *m.*
eclectic, *a,* éclectique. **eclecticism,** *n,* éclectisme, *m.*
eclipse, *n,* éclipse, *f. to be in ~,* être éclipsé. ¶ *v.t,* (*lit. & fig.*) éclipser.
economic, *a,* (*situation &c*) économique; (*profitable*) rentable, qui rapporte. **~al,** *a,* (*pers.*) économe; (*speed &c*) économique. *to be ~ with,* économiser, ménager. **~s,** *n.pl,* science économique, économie politique, *f;* aspect financier, côté économique, *m.* **economist,** *n,* économiste, *m,f.* **economize,** *v.i,* économiser (*on,* sur), faire des économies. ¶ *v.t,* économiser. **economy,** *n,* économie, *f. make economies in,* faire des économies de.
ecstasy, *n,* extase, *f. to go into ecstasies,* s'extasier (*over,* sur). **ecstatic,** *a,* ecstasié.
Ecuador, *n,* l'Équateur, l'Ecuador, *m.*
ecumenical, *a,* œcuménique.
eczema, *n,* eczéma, *m.*
eddy, *n,* remous, tourbillon, *m.* ¶ *v.i,* tourbillonner.
Eden (*fig.*) *n,* éden, *m.* [*the Garden of*] *~,* l'Éden, le paradis terrestre.
edge, *n,* (*table*) bord; (*plate, cliff*) bord, rebord, *m;* (*river, lake*) bord, rive, *f;* (*wood*) lisière, *f;* (*knife &c*) tranchant, fil, *m. put an ~ on,* aiguiser, affiler. *take the ~ off,* (*lit., fig.*) émousser. *to be on ~,* avoir les nerfs à vif. *on ~,* (*object*) de chant, sur chant. ¶ *v.t,* border (*with,* de). ¶ *v.i,* se glisser. *~ways, ~wise,* de côté. **edging,** *n,* bordure, *f.*
edible, *a,* comestible, bon à manger.
edict, *n,* (*Hist.*) édit; (*Pol.*) décret, *m.*
edifice, *n,* édifice, *m.* **edify,** *v.t,* édifier.
Edinburgh, *n,* Édimbourg, *m.*
edit, *v.t,* (*newspaper*) diriger; (*text*) éditer; (*article*) mettre au point; (*film*) monter. **~ion,** *n,* édition, *f.* **editor,** *n,* (*newspaper*) rédacteur (trice) en chef; (*magazine*) directeur, trice; (*film*) monteur. **~ial,** *a,* de la rédaction; *~ staff;* rédaction; *f.* ¶ *n,* éditorial, *m.*
educate, *v.t,* instruire, donner de l'instruction à; (*bring up*) élever, éduquer. *he was ~d in Paris,* il a fait ses études à Paris. **~d,** *a,* instruit, cultivé. **education,** *n,* éducation, *f;* enseignement, *m;* instruction, *f;* (*training*) formation, *f.* **~al,** *a,* (*system*) d'éducation, d'enseignement; (*methods*) pédagogique; (*game*) éducatif. **educator,** *n,* éducateur, trice.
eel, *n,* anguille, *f. ~ pot,* nasse, *f.*
eerie, -y, *a,* sinistre, inquiétant.
efface, *v.t,* effacer; (*liter.*) oblitérer.
effect, *n,* effet, *m;* conséquence, suite; action, *f;* (*pl*) effets, *m.pl. to have an ~ on,* produire un effet sur. *to take ~,* (*drug*) agir; (*law*) entrer en vigueur. ¶ *v.t,* effectuer, faire, opérer. **~ive†,** *a,* efficace; (*actual*) effectif; (*striking*) qui fait de l'effet. ¶ *n,* (*Mil.*) *~s,* effectifs, *m.pl.*
effectual†, *a,* efficace.
effeminacy, *n,* caractère efféminé, *m.* **effeminate,** *a,* efféminé.
effervesce, *v.i,* être en effervescence; mousser, pétiller. **effervescence,** *n,* effervescence, *f.* **effervescent,** *a,* effervescent; (*drink*) gazeux.
effete, *a,* (*pers.*) mou; (*society*) décadent.
efficacious†, *a,* efficace.
efficiency, *n,* efficacité; (*pers.*) capacité, compétence, *f;* (*Mach.*) bon rendement, *m.* **efficient†,** *a,* efficace; (*pers.*) capable, compétent; (*Mach.*) qui fonctionne bien.
effigy, *n,* effigie, *f.*
effluent, *a. & n,* effluent, *m.*
effort, *n,* effort, *m. to make an ~ to do,* faire un effort pour faire, s'efforcer de faire. *to make every ~,* faire tout son possible (pour faire).
effrontery, *n,* effronterie, *f.*
effusion, *n,* effusion, *f;* (*fig.*) épanchement, *m.*
effusive, *a,* expansif, démonstratif.
egg, *n,* œuf, *m. ~s & bacon,* œufs au bacon. *~cup,* coquetier, *m. ~head P,* intellectuel, le. *~-shaped,* ovoïde. *~ shell,* coquille d'œuf, *f.* *~* **on,** *v.t,* pousser, inciter (à faire).
ego, *n,* (*Psych.*) *the ~,* le moi, l'ego, *m.* **egoism,** *n,* égoïsme, *m.* **egoist,** *n,* égoïste, *m,f.* **egoistic(al),** *a,* égoïste. **egotism,** *n,* égotisme, *m.* **egotist,** *n,* égotiste, *m, f.* **egotistic(al),** *a,* égotiste.
egregious, *a,* insigne, fameux.
egress, *n,* sortie, issue, *f.*
egret, *n,* aigrette, *f.*
Egypt, *n,* l'Égypte, *f.* **Egyptian,** *a,* égyptien. ¶ *n,* Égyptien, ne. **Egyptologist,** *n,* égyptologue, *m,f.* **Egyptology,** *n,* égyptologie, *f.*
eh, *i,* (*what?*) comment? hein? (*isn't it?*) n'est-ce pas? hein?
eider [duck], *n,* eider, *m. ~down,* édredon, *m.*
eight, *a. & n,* huit, *m. for phrases V* **four. eighteen,** *a. & n,* dix-huit, *m.* **eighteenth,** *a. & n,* dix-huitième, *m,f.* **eighth,** *a. & n,* huitième, *m,f;* (*fraction*) huitième, *m. for phrases V* **fourth. eightieth,** *a. & n,* quatre-vingtième, *m,f.* **eighty,** *a. & n,* quatre-vingts, *m. 81, &c,* quatre-vingt-un, &c. *for phrases V* **forty.**
either, *pn. & a,* l'un (l'une) ou l'autre; n'importe lequel (laquelle) des deux. *I didn't see ~,* je n'ai vu ni l'un ni l'autre. *on ~ side,* de chaque côté, des deux côtés. ¶ *c, ~... or,* ou [bien]... ou [bien], soit... soit; (*after neg.*) ni... ni. ¶ *ad,* (*after neg.*) non plus. *nor I* (*me*) *~,* ni moi non plus.
ejaculate, *v.t & i,* s'exclamer, s'écrier; (*semen*) éjaculer. **ejaculation,** *n,* exclamation; éjaculation, *f.*
eject, *v.t,* (*pers.*) expulser; (*Tech.*) éjecter. **~ion,** *n,* expulsion; éjection, *f.* **~or,** *n,* (*Tech.*) éjecteur. (*Aero.*) *~ seat,* siège éjectable, *m.*

eke out, *v.t,* faire durer; augmenter.
elaborate, *a,* compliqué; minutieux; (*style*) travaillé, recherché. ¶ *v.t,* élaborer. ¶ *v.i,* ~ *on,* développer, entrer dans les détails de.
elapse, *v.i,* s'écouler, [se] passer.
elastic, *a.* & *n,* élastique, *m.* ~ *band,* élastique, caoutchouc, *m.* ~**ity,** *n,* élasticité, *f.*
elated, *a,* transporté de joie; (*by news*) exalté, emballé *P.*
elbow, *n,* (*pers., pipe &c*) coude, *m. to rest one's* ~*s on,* s'accouder à *ou* sur. ~ *grease,* (*fig.*) huile de coude, *f. to have* ~ *room,* (*fig.*) avoir les coudées franches. ¶ *v.t, to* ~ *s.o aside,* écarter qn du coude. *to* ~ *one's way forward,* avancer en jouant des coudes.
elder[1], *a,* aîné [des deux]. ¶ *n,* aîné, e. *our* ~*s,* nos aînés. (*Eccl., village*) ancien, *m.* ~**ly,** *a,* d'un certain âge. **eldest,** *n,* & *a,* aîné, e.
elder[2], *n,* (*tree*) sureau, *m.* ~*berry,* baie de s., *f.*
elect, *v.t,* élire, nommer. *the* ~ (*Rel.*), les élus, *m.pl.* ~*ed member,* élu, e. **election,** *n,* élection, *f;* (*att. agent, campaign*) électoral. **electioneering,** *n,* propagande électorale. **elector,** *n,* électeur, trice. ~**al,** *a,* électoral. ~ *roll,* liste électorale. ~**ate,** *n,* corps électoral, électorat, *m.*
electric, *a,* électrique. ~ *blanket,* couverture chauffante. ~ *fire,* radiateur électrique, *m.* ~ *sign,* enseigne lumineuse, *f.* ~ *storm,* orage magnétique, *m.* ~**al,** *a,* électrique. ~ *engineer,* ingénieur électricien, *m.* ~ *failure,* panne d'électricité, *f.* ~ *fitter,* monteur électricien, *m.* ~**ally,** *ad,* par l'électricité. ~**ian,** *n,* électricien, *m.* ~**ity,** *n,* électricité, *f.* **electrify,** *v.t,* électriser; (*Rly &c*) électrifier. **electroconvulsive therapy,** *n,* électrochocs, *m.pl.* **electrocute,** *v.t,* électrocuter. **electrode,** *n,* électrode, *f.* **electrolysis,** *n,* électrolyse, *f.* **electromagnet,** *n,* électro-aimant, *m.* **electron,** *n,* électron, *m.* ~**ic,** *a,* électronique. ~**ics,** *n,* électronique, *f.* **electroplate,** *n,* vaisselle plaquée. ¶ *v.t,* argenter.
elegance, *n,* élégance, *f,* chic, *m.* **elegant,** *a,* élégant. ~**ly,** *ad,* élégamment.
elegy, *n,* élégie, *f.*
element, *n,* (*Chem., Met., fig.*) élément; facteur, *m;* (*heater &c*) résistance, *f. to be in one's* ~, être dans son élément. ~**ary,** *a,* élémentaire; (*Sch.*) primaire.
elephant, *n,* éléphant, *m. cow* ~, é. femelle. *baby* ~, éléphanteau, *m.* ~**ine,** *a,* (*huge*) éléphantesque.
elevate, *v.t,* élever; hausser. **elevation,** *n,* élévation; altitude, hauteur, *f.* **elevator,** *n,* élévateur, monte-charge; (*Am lift*) ascenseur; (*Aero.*) gouvernail de profondeur, *m.*
eleven, *a.* & *n,* onze, *inv* & *m.* **eleventh**†, *a.* & *n,* onzième, *m,f. the* ~ *of May,* le onze mai.
elf, *n,* elfe, lutin, *m.* **elfin,** *a,* d'elfe, de lutin, féerique.
elicit, *v.t,* (*reply*) tirer, obtenir; (*facts*) tirer au clair.
elide, *v.t,* élider.
eligible, *a,* (*for office*) éligible; (*for job*) admissible (*for,* à). (*pension*) *to be* ~ *for,* avoir droit à.
eliminate, *v.t,* éliminer. *eliminating heat,* [épreuve] éliminatoire, *f.*
elision, *n,* élision, *f.*
élite, *n,* élite, *f.* **élitism,** *n,* élitisme, *m.*
elixir, *n,* élixir, *m.*
elk, *n,* élan, *m.*
ellipse & **ellipsis,** *n,* ellipse, *f.* **elliptic(al)**†, *a,* elliptique.
elm [tree], *n,* orme, (*young*) ormeau, *m.*
elocution, *n,* élocution; diction, *f.*
elongate, *v.t,* allonger.
elope, *v.i,* se faire enlever (*with,* par); s'enfuir. ~**ment,** *n,* fugue amoureuse, *f.*
eloquence, *n,* éloquence, *f.* **eloquent,** *a,* éloquent. ~**ly,** *ad,* éloquemment.
else, *ad,* autre, d'autre, encore. *s.o, sth, no one* ~, qn, qch, personne d'autre. *nothing* ~, rien d'autre, plus rien. *anything* ~ *to say?* encore qch à dire? plus rien à dire? *any one* ~ *would accept,* n'importe qui d'autre *ou* tout autre accepterait. *somewhere* ~, ailleurs, autre part. *or* ~, sinon, ou bien, autrement. *sign or* ~! signez sinon! ~**where,** ailleurs, autre part.
elucidate, *v.t,* élucider, éclaircir.
elude, *v.t,* échapper à; se soustraire à, se dérober à. **elusive**†, *a,* insaisissable.
emaciated, *a,* émacié; (*limb*) décharné.
emanate, *v.i,* émaner.
emancipate, *v.t,* émanciper, affranchir.
emasculate, *v.t,* émasculer.
embalm, *v.t,* embaumer.
embankment, *n,* remblai, talus; (*river*) quai, *m,* levée, *f.*
embargo, *n,* embargo, *m.*
embark, *v.t.* (& *i*) (s')embarquer. ~**ation,** *n,* embarquement, *m.*
embarrass, *v.t,* embarrasser, gêner. ~**ment,** *n,* embarras, *m,* gêne, *f.*
embassy, *n,* ambassade, *f.*
embed, *v.t,* encastrer.
embellish, *v.t,* embellir, orner; (*tale*) enjoliver.
embers, *n.pl,* braise, *f,* charbons ardents, *m.pl.*
embezzle, *v.t,* détourner. ~**ment,** *n,* détournement de fonds, *m.*
embitter, *v.t,* (*pers.*) aigrir; (*relations*) envenimer.
emblem, *n,* emblème, *m.*
embodiment, *n,* incarnation, personnification, *f.* **embody,** *v.t,* (*pers.*) incarner, personnifier; (*work*) exprimer, renfermer.
embolden, *v.t,* enhardir.
emboss, *v.t,* graver en relief; estamper; (*leather, paper*) gaufrer.

embrace, *n,* étreinte, *f.* ¶ *v.t,* embrasser, enlacer; (*fig.*) embrasser, renfermer.
embrasure, *n,* embrasure, *f.*
embrocation, *n,* embrocation, *f.*
embroider, *v.t,* broder; (*tale*) broder, enjoliver. **~y,** *n,* broderie, *f.*
embroil, *v.t,* entraîner (*in,* dans).
embryo, *n,* embryon, *m. in ~,* (*fig.*) à l'état embryonnaire, en germe. **embryonic,** *a,* embryonnaire.
emend, *v.t,* corriger. **~ation,** *n,* correction, *f.*
emerald, *n,* émeraude, *f. ~ green,* vert é., *m.*
emerge, *v.i,* apparaître; émerger, surgir; déboucher. **emergence,** *n,* apparition, *f.*
emergency, *n,* cas urgent, imprévu, *m. in case of ~,* en cas d'urgence. (*att. brake, repairs*) d'urgence. *~ exit,* sortie de secours, *f. ~ landing,* atterrissage forcé.
emery, *n,* émeri, *m. ~ cloth,* toile d'é., *f.*
emetic, *a. & n,* émétique, *m.*
emigrant, *n,* émigrant, e. **emigrate,** *v.i,* émigrer. **emigration,** *n,* émigration, *f.*
eminence, *n,* distinction, *f. His E~* (*cardinal*), son Éminence. (*hill*) éminence, élévation, *f.* **eminent,** *a,* éminent, distingué. **~ly,** *ad,* éminemment.
emir, *n,* émir, *m.*
emissary, *n,* émissaire, *m.* **emission,** *n,* émission, *f,* dégagement, *m.*
emit, *v.t,* émettre, dégager; (*cry*) laisser échapper; (*sound*) rendre.
emollient, *a. & n,* émolient, *m.*
emoluments, *n.pl,* émoluments, *m.pl.*
emotion, *n,* émotion, *f;* sentiment, *m. to appeal to the ~s,* faire appel aux sentiments. **~al,** *a,* (*reaction, shock*) émotionnel; (*pers.*) émotif; (*voice*) ému.
empathy, *n,* communion d'idées, *f.*
emperor, *n,* empereur, *m.*
emphasis, *n,* (*stress*) accentuation, *f,* accent; (*fig.*) accent, *m. to lay ~ on* or **emphasize,** *v.t,* appuyer sur, insister sur; souligner, accentuer. **emphatic†,** *a,* énergique. *to be ~ about,* insister sur.
empire, *n,* empire, *m.*
empiric(al)†, *a,* empirique.
employ, *v.t,* (*pers., time*) employer; (*method*) employer, utiliser. **~ee,** *n,* employé, e. **~er,** *n,* patron, ne, employeur, euse, *the ~s,* le patronat, *m. ~s' federation,* syndicat patronal, *m.* **~ment,** *n,* emploi, travail, *m;* place, situation, *f. ~ agency,* bureau de placement, *m.*
empower, *v.t,* autoriser (qn à faire).
empress, *n,* impératrice, *f.*
emptiness, *n,* vide, *m.* **empty,** *a,* vide (*of,* de); (*stomach*) creux; (*house*) inoccupé. *~ words,* paroles creuses. *~-handed,* les mains vides. *to be ~-headed,* n'avoir rien dans la tête. *on an ~ stomach,* à jeun. ¶ *n.pl, empties,* bouteilles &c vides. ¶ *v.t,* vider; (*tank &c*) vidanger; (*vehicle*) décharger.
emulate, *v.t,* rivaliser avec, imiter. **emulation,** *n,* émulation, *f.* **emulator,** *n,* émule, *m.*
emulsion, *n,* émulsion, *f.*
enable, *v.t, ~ s.o to do,* permettre à qn de faire, mettre qn à même de faire; (*Law*) habiliter qn à faire.
enact, *v.t,* décréter, ordonner.
enamel, *n. & ~ ware,* émail, *m.* ¶ *v.t,* émailler. **enamelling,** *n,* émaillage, *m.*
enamoured, *a,* épris, amoureux (*of,* de).
encamp, *v.i. & t,* camper. **~ment,** *n,* campement, *m.*
encase, *v.t,* enfermer (*in,* dans); recouvrir (*in,* de).
enchant, *v.t,* (*lit.*) enchanter, ensorceler; (*fig.*) enchanter, ravir. **~er, ~ress,** *n,* enchanteur, eresse. **~ing,** *a,* enchanteur, ravissant. **~ment,** *n,* enchantement, ravissement, *m.*
encircle, *v.t,* encercler, ceindre, cerner.
enclave, *n,* enclave, *f.*
enclose, *v.t,* (*ground*) enclore, clôturer; enfermer; (*in letter*) inclure, joindre. **~d,** *a,* ci-inclus, ci-joint. **enclosure,** *n,* (*ground*) enceinte, clôture, *f;* (*in letter*) pièce jointe, document ci-inclus; (*Turf*) pesage, *m.*
encomium, *n,* panégyrique, éloge, *m.*
encompass, *v.t,* entourer, ceindre (*with,* de).
encore, *i. & n,* bis, *m.* ¶ *v.t,* bisser.
encounter, *n,* rencontre, *f.* ¶ *v.t,* rencontrer; (*difficulties*) éprouver.
encourage, *v.t,* encourager, inciter (qn à faire); (*arts &c*) favoriser. **~ment,** *n,* encouragement, *m.*
encroach on (to), empiéter sur. **~ment,** *n,* empiètement, *m.*
encumber, *v.t,* embarrasser, encombrer. **encumbrance,** *n,* embarras, *m;* charge, *f.*
encyclic(al), *a. & n,* encyclique, *f.*
encyclop[a]edia, *n,* encyclopédie, *f.*
end, *n,* (*finger, table &c*) bout, *m;* extrémité, limite, *f. on ~,* debout. *from ~ to ~,* d'un bout à l'autre. *to stand on ~,* (*hair*) se dresser. *to make both ~s meet,* joindre les deux bouts. *to keep up one's ~,* se défendre. (*completion*) (*week, story &c*) fin, *f,* bout. *in the ~,* finalement, à la fin. *at the ~ of July,* (*Com.*) fin juillet. *at the ~ of 3 days,* au bout de trois jours. *for 3 hours on ~,* trois heures de suite *ou* d'affilée. *no ~ of,* énormément de. *at the ~ of one's strength,* à bout de force. *to make an ~ of, put an ~ to,* mettre fin à. *to come to an ~,* prendre fin. *to come to a bad ~,* mal finir. (*purpose*) but, dessein, *m,* fin. *with this ~ in view,* dans ce but *ou* dessein. *~ paper,* [feuille de] garde, *f.* ¶ *v.t,* finir, achever, terminer, mettre fin à. ¶ *v.i,* finir, se terminer, s'achever; prendre fin. *~ up,* (*road*) aboutir (*in, at,* à); (*by doing*) finir (par faire).

endanger, *v.t,* mettre en danger.
endear, *v.t,* faire aimer. ~**ments,** *n.pl,* paroles tendres, *f.pl.*
endeavour, *n,* effort, *m,* tentative, *f.* ¶ *v.i,* s'efforcer, tâcher, essayer (de faire).
ending, *n,* fin, *f;* dénouement, *m;* (*Gram.*) terminaison, désinence, *f.*
endive, *n,* (*curly*) chicorée, *f.*
endless, *a,* sans fin, interminable. ~**ly,** *ad,* sans fin, interminablement.
endorse, *v.t,* endosser; (*fig.*) souscrire à. ~**ment,** *n,* (*cheque*) endossement, *m.*
endow, *v.t,* (*church*) doter; (*prize*) fonder. ~*ed with* (*pers.*), doué de. ~**ment,** *n,* dotation, *f.*
endue, *v.t,* revêtir; douer (*with,* de).
endurable, *a,* supportable. **endurance,** *n,* endurance; résistance, *f.* ~ *test,* épreuve d'endurance, *f.* **endure,** *v.t,* endurer, supporter; souffrir. ¶ *v.i,* durer.
enema, *n,* lavement, *m;* poire à l., *f.*
enemy, *n.* & *a,* ennemi, e.
energetic†, *a,* énergique. **energize,** *v.t,* donner de l'énergie à; (*dynamo*) amorcer. **energy,** *n,* énergie, vigueur, *f.*
enervate, *v.t,* affaiblir, amollir.
enfeeble, *v.t,* affaiblir.
enfilade, *n,* enfilade, *f.* ¶ *v.t,* prendre en e.
enfold, *v.t,* envelopper (*in,* de); étreindre.
enforce, *v.t,* imposer; (*law, decision*) mettre en vigueur, appliquer; (*rights*) faire valoir. ~**ment,** *n,* mise en vigueur, *f.*
enfranchise, *v.t,* accorder le droit de vote à; (*slave*) affranchir.
engage, *v.t,* (*room*) retenir, réserver; (*worker*) embaucher, engager; (*Mech.*) engrener, mettre en prise; (*Mil.*) engager le combat avec. ~ *in conversation,* lier conversation avec. ¶ *v.i,* (*Mech.*) s'engrener, se mettre en prise. ~ *to do,* s'engager à faire. *to* ~ *in,* s'engager dans. ~**d,** *a,* (*pers., seat*) occupé, pris; fiancé (*to,* a, avec). ~ *in doing,* occupé à faire. ~ *tone* (*Tel.*), tonalité pas libre, *f.* ~**ment,** *n,* (*appointment*) rendez-vous, *m;* fiançailles, *f.pl.* ~ *ring,* bague de fiançailles, *f.* **engaging,** *a,* engageant, attachant.
engender, *v.t,* engendrer.
engine, *n,* machine, *f,* moteur, *m;* (*Rly*) locomotive, *f;* (*car, plane*) moteur. ~ *driver,* mécanicien, *m.* ~ *room* (*ship*), salle des machines, *f.* **engineer,** *n,* ingénieur; (*tradesman*) technicien; (*ship*) mécanicien, *m.* (*Mil.*) *the E*~*s,* le génie. ¶ *v.t,* (*fig.*) machiner, manigancer. **engineering,** *n,* l'art (*m.*) (*ou* la science) de l'ingénieur; construction, *f;* génie, *m.* **engineless,** *a,* sans moteur.
England, *n,* l'Angleterre, *f.* **English,** *a,* anglais. *the* ~ *Channel,* la Manche. ~*man,* ~ *woman,* Anglais, e. ¶ (*language*) *n,* l'anglais, *m.*
engrave, *v.t,* graver. **engraver,** *n,* graveur, *m.*
engraving, *n,* gravure, estampe, *f.*
engross, *v.t,* absorber; (*Law*) grossoyer.
engulf, *v.t,* engouffrer, engloutir.
enhance, *v.t,* rehausser; augmenter.
enigma, *n,* énigme, *f.* **enigmatic(al)**†, *a,* énigmatique.
enjoy, *v.t,* aimer, prendre plaisir à; trouver bon, agréable. *I* ~*ed the film,* le film m'a plu. ~ *doing,* trouver du plaisir à faire. *to* ~ *o.s,* s'amuser. (*possess*) jouir de. ~**able,** *a,* agréable; (*meal*) excellent. ~**ment,** *n,* plaisir, *m;* (*rights &c*) jouissance, *f.*
enlarge, *v.t,* agrandir, augmenter, élargir. ~ *upon,* s'étendre sur. ~**ment,** *n,* agrandissement, *m.* **enlarger** (*Phot.*) *n,* agrandisseur, *m.*
enlighten, *v.t,* éclairer (qn sur qch). ~**d,** *a,* (*pers., views*) éclairé. ~**ing,** *a,* révélateur.
enlist, *v.t*(& *i*) (*Mil.*) (s')engager, (s')enrôler; (*v.t*) (*support &c*) s'assurer. ~**ment,** *n,* engagement, enrôlement, *m.*
enliven, *v.t,* animer, égayer.
enmity, *n,* inimitié, hostilité, *f.*
ennoble, *v.t,* anoblir; (*fig.*) ennoblir.
enormity, *n,* énormité, *f.* **enormous,** *a,* énorme. ~**ly,** *ad,* énormément.
enough, *a.* & *n,* assez de; assez. ~ *money* (*to buy*), assez d'argent (pour acheter). *I've had* ~ *of it,* j'en ai assez. ~ *to eat,* assez à manger. ~ *to live on,* de quoi vivre. *that's* ~*!* ça suffit! ¶ *ad,* assez, suffisamment. *good* ~, assez bon. *I've eaten* ~, j'ai assez mangé.
enquire, *&c.* = **inquire,** &c.
enrage, *v.t,* rendre furieux, mettre en rage.
enrapture, *v.t,* enchanter, ravir.
enrich, *v.t,* enrichir; (*soil*) amender.
enrol, -ll, *v.t,* (*Mil.*) enrôler; (*workers*) embaucher; (*students*) inscrire, immatriculer. **enrolment,** *n,* enrôlement; embauchage, *m;* inscription, immatriculation, *f.*
ensconced, *a,* installé.
ensemble, *n,* (*Mus., dress*) ensemble, *m.*
ensign, *n,* (*Naut.*) pavillon; (*Am Navy*) enseigne de vaisseau, *m.*
enslave, *v.t,* (*lit., fig.*) asservir.
ensnare, *v.t,* (*lit., fig.*) prendre au piège.
ensue, *v.i,* s'ensuivre, résulter. **ensuing,** *a,* (*days*) suivant; (*event*) qui s'ensuit.
ensure, *v.t,* assurer.
entail, *v.t,* entraîner, occasionner, nécessiter; (*Law*) substituer.
entangle, *v.t,* (*catch up*) empêtrer; (*wool*) emmêler; (*pers.*) mêler, entraîner. *to get* ~*d in,* (*lit., fig.*) s'empêtrer dans.
enter, *v.t,* entrer dans, pénétrer dans; (*vehicle*) monter dans; (*path &c*) s'engager dans; (*college*) se faire inscrire à; (*on form, list*) inscrire; (*item in ledger*) porter; (*pupil for exam*) présenter; (*horse for race*) inscrire (à). ¶ *v.i,* entrer; (*for exam*) se présenter; (*for race*) s'inscrire. ~ *into,* (*contract*) passer; (*negoti-*

ations) entamer. *his age doesn't ~ into it,* son âge n'y est pour rien.
enterprise, *n,* entreprise, *f;* esprit entreprenant, *m.* **enterprising,** *a,* entreprenant.
entertain, *v.t,* amuser, divertir; (*guest*) recevoir; (*thoughts*) méditer; (*doubt, hope*) nourrir; (*proposal*) accueillir favorablement. **~er,** *n,* artiste, *m,f.* **~ment,** *n,* amusement, divertissement; (*show*) spectacle, *m.*
enthral[l], *v.t,* captiver, passionner.
enthrone, *v.t,* introniser.
enthusiasm, *n,* enthousiasme, *m.* **enthusiast,** *n,* enthousiaste, *m,f,* fervent, e. *he's a ski ~,* c'est un passionné (un enragé *P*) de ski, il se passionne pour le ski. **~ic,** *a,* enthousiaste, fervent, passionné, enragé *P.* **~ically,** *ad,* avec enthousiasme.
entice, *v.t,* attirer, allécher; séduire. **~ment,** *n,* attrait, *m;* (*act*) séduction, *f.* **enticing,** *a,* séduisant, attrayant.
entire†, *a,* entier, intégral. **~ty,** *n,* intégralité, *f.* *in its ~,* en entier.
entitle, *v.t,* intituler; donner droit à.
entity, *n,* entité, *f.*
entomb, *v.t,* ensevelir.
entomologist, *n,* entomologiste, *m.* **entomology,** *n,* entomologie, *f.*
entr'acte (*Theat.*) *n,* entracte, *m.*
entrails, *n.pl,* entrailles, *f.pl.*
entrance¹, *n,* entrée; (*to school &c*) admission, *f.* *~ fee* (*club*), droit d'inscription, *m.*
entrance², *v.t,* ravir, transporter. *~d,* extasié.
entrap, *v.t,* prendre au piège.
entreat, *v.t,* supplier, prier instamment (qn de faire). **~y,** *n,* supplication, prière, *f.*
entrench, *v.t,* retrancher.
entrust, *v.t,* confier (qn, qch à qn). *to ~ s.o with a task,* charger qn d'une tâche.
entry, *n,* entrée, *f. to make an ~,* faire son e. *no ~,* (*one-way st.*) sens interdit; (*room &c*) entrée interdite. (*on list &c*) inscription; (*ledger*) écriture, *f.* (*Bkkpg*) *double-~,* comptabilité en partie double, *f. ~ form,* feuille d'inscription, *f. ~ permit,* visa d'entrée, *m.*
entwine, *v.t,* enlacer, entrelacer, entortiller.
enumerate, *v.t,* énumérer, dénombrer.
enunciate, *v.t,* (*word*) articuler; (*theory*) énoncer.
envelop, *v.t,* envelopper. **~e,** *n,* enveloppe, *f. to put into an ~,* mettre sous e. *in a sealed ~,* sous pli cacheté.
envenom, *v.t,* envenimer.
enviable, *a,* enviable. **envious,** *a,* envieux.
environment, *n,* environnement, milieu; (*moral &c*) climat, *m,* ambiance, *f.* **environs,** *n.pl,* environs, alentours, *m.pl.*
envisage, *v.t,* envisager; (*foresee*) prévoir.
envoy, *n,* envoyé, *m.*
envy, *n,* envie, *f.* ¶ *v.t,* envier (qch à qn).
epaulette, *n,* épaulette, *f.*
ephemeral, *a,* éphémère.
epic, *a,* épique. ¶ *n,* épopée, *f.*
epicure, *n,* gourmet, *m,* gastronome, *m,f.* **epicurean,** *a.* & *n,* épicurien, *m.*
epidemic, *n,* épidémie, *f.* ¶ *a,* épidémique.
epidermis, *n,* épiderme, *m.*
epiglottis, *n,* épiglotte, *f.*
epigram, *n,* épigramme, *f.*
epigraph, *n,* épigraphe, *f.*
epilepsy, *n,* épilepsie, *f.* **epileptic,** *a.* & *n,* épileptique, *m,f. ~ fit,* crise d'épilepsie.
epilogue, *n,* épilogue, *m.*
Epiphany, *n,* Épiphanie, fête des Rois, *f.*
episcopal, *a,* épiscopal. *the E~ Church* (*Sc., Am.*), l'église épiscopale.
episode, *n,* épisode, *m.*
epistle, *n,* épître, *f.* **epistolary,** *a,* épistolaire.
epitaph, *n,* épitaphe, *f.*
epithet, *n,* épithète, *f.*
epitome, *n,* abrégé; modèle, *m.* **epitomize,** *v.t,* abréger; personnifier.
epoch, *n,* époque, ère, *f.*
equable†, *a,* égal. **equal†,** *a,* égal. *~ to* (*task*), à la hauteur de. *on an ~ footing with s.o,* sur un pied d'égalité avec qn. *I don't feel ~ to going,* je n'ai pas le courage d'y aller. ¶ *n,* égal, e, pareil, le, pair, *m. our ~s,* nos égaux. *without ~,* hors pair. *to treat s.o as an ~,* traiter qn d'égal à égal. ¶ *v.t,* égaler. **~ity,** *n,* égalité, *f.* **~ize,** *v.t,* égaliser. **~izer,** *n,* (*Sport*) but égalisateur, *m.*
equanimity, *n,* sérénité, égalité d'âme, *f.*
equation, *n,* équation, *f.*
equator, *n,* équateur, *m. at the ~,* sous l'équateur. **~ial,** *a,* équatorial.
equestrian, *a,* équestre. ¶ *n,* cavalier, ère; écuyer, ère [de cirque].
equilibrium, *n,* équilibre, *m.*
equine, *a,* chevalin.
equinoctial, *a,* équinoxial; (*gale*) d'équinoxe. **equinox,** *n,* équinoxe, *m.*
equip, *v.t,* équiper, outiller; (*home*) monter; (*pers.*) munir, pourvoir (*with,* de); (*ship*) armer. **~ment,** *n,* équipement; (*factory*) outillage; (*office, camping*) matériel, *m.*
equitable†, *a,* équitable. **equity,** *n,* équité, *f.*
equivalent, *a.* & *n,* équivalent, *m. to be ~ to,* être équivalent à.
equivocal, *a,* équivoque, ambigu; (*conduct*) douteux, louche. **equivocate,** *v.i,* user de faux-fuyants. **equivocation,** *n,* faux-fuyants, *m.pl.*
era, *n,* ère, époque, *f.*
eradicate, *v.t,* extirper, supprimer, déraciner.
erase, *v.t,* effacer, gratter; gommer. **eraser,** *n,* (*rubber*) gomme, *f;* (*typing*) liquide correcteur, *m.* **erasure,** *n,* rature, *f.*
ere (*liter.*), *pr,* avant. *~ long,* sous peu. ¶ *c,* avant que.
erect, *a,* droit; debout; (*tail*) levé. *with head ~,* la tête haute. ¶ *v.t,* (*building*) construire,

bâtir; (*tent, mast, ladder*) dresser. **~ion,** *n,* érection; construction, *f;* dressage, *m.*
ermine, *n,* hermine, *f.*
erode, *v.t,* éroder. **erosion,** *n,* érosion, *f.*
erotic, *a,* érotique.
err, *v.i,* errer, se tromper; (*sin*) pécher.
errand, *n,* commission, course, *f. to run ~s,* faire des courses *ou* des commissions. *~ boy,* garçon de courses, *m.*
erratic, *a,* irrégulier; (*pers.*) capricieux; (*Geol., Med.*) erratique.
erratum, *n,* erratum, *m.* **erroneous,** *a,* erroné, faux. **~ly,** *ad,* à tort. **error,** *n,* erreur, faute, *f. in ~,* par erreur, par méprise.
erudite, *a,* érudit. **erudition,** *n,* érudition, *f.*
erupt, *v.i,* (*volcano*) entrer en éruption; (*violence*) éclater. **~ion,** *n,* éruption, *f.*
escalate, *v.i,* s'intensifier; (*costs*) monter en flèche. **escalation,** *n,* escalade, *f.*
escalator, *n,* escalier roulant, *m.*
escapade, *n,* équipée, frasque, fredaine, *f.*
escape, *n,* fuite; evasion, *f;* (*gas &c*) fuite, échappement, *m. to have a narrow ~,* l'échapper belle. *~ clause,* échappatoire, *f. ~ route,* route d'évasion, *f. ~ valve,* soupape d'échappement, *f.* ¶ *v.i,* (*pers., gas*) s'échapper (*from,* de); échapper (*from s.o,* à qn); (*prisoner*) s'évader (*from,* de). *an ~d prisoner,* un évadé. *to ~ unhurt,* sortir sain & sauf. ¶ *v.t,* échapper à, éviter. *his name ~s me,* son nom m'échappe. **~ment** (*clock*), *n,* échappement, *m.* **escapism,** *n,* évasion, *f.*
escarpment, *n,* escarpement, *m.*
eschew, *v.t,* éviter, fuir.
escort, *n,* escorte, *f;* (*at dance &c*) cavalier, *m.* ¶ *v.t,* escorter; accompagner. *~ back,* reconduire.
Eskimo, *a,* esquimau, de. ¶ *n,* Esquimau, de.
esoteric, *a,* ésotérique.
espalier, *n,* espalier, *m;* (*tree*) en espalier.
esparto [grass], *n,* alfa, *m.*
especial, *a,* particulier, spécial, exceptionnel. **~ly,** *ad,* surtout; notamment; particulièrement. *~ as,* d'autant plus que.
espionage, *n,* espionnage, *m.*
esplanade, *n,* esplanade, *f.*
espousal, *n,* (*cause*) adhésion (à), *f.* **espouse,** *v.t,* (*fig.*) épouser, embrasser.
espresso, *n,* [café] express, *m.*
esquire, *n,* (*formal: on envelope &c*) *John Jones Esq.,* Monsieur John Jones.
essay, *n,* (*Liter.*) essai, *m;* (*Sch.*) composition, rédaction; (*Univ.*) dissertation, *f* (*on,* sur). ¶ *v.t,* essayer.
essence, *n,* essence, *f,* essentiel, fond, *m. in ~,* essentiellement. **essential†,** *a,* essentiel; indispensable. ¶ *n.pl the ~s,* l'essentiel.
establish, *v.t,* établir; (*business*) fonder, créer; (*reputation*) se faire. *the ~d Church,* l'Eglise établie, *f.* **~ment,** *n,* établissement, *m;* fondation, création, *f;* (*Mil., Naut.*) effectif, *m. the E~,* les pouvoirs établis.
estate, *n,* (*land*) propriété, domaine, terre(s), *f* (*pl*); (*possessions*) biens, *m.pl;* (*of deceased*) succession, *f;* (*rank*) rang, *m,* condition, *f. ~ agency,* agence immobilière, *f. ~ agent,* agent immobilier. *~ car,* break, *m. ~ duty,* droits de succession, *m.pl.*
esteem, *n,* estime, *f.* ¶ *v.t,* estimer, avoir de l'estime pour; considérer, estimer comme.
Esthonia, *n,* l'Estonie, *f.*
estimate, *n,* estimation, évaluation, *f;* (*Com.*) état estimatif; (*Build.*) devis, *m.* (*Pol.*) *the ~s,* le budget. ¶ *v.t,* estimer, apprécier, évaluer. **~d,** *a,* estimatif. **estimation,** *n,* jugement, *m. in my ~,* à mon avis. (*esteem*) estime, considération, *f.*
estrange, *v.t,* éloigner. *~d couple,* époux séparés.
estuary, *n,* estuaire, *m.*
et cetera, *ad. & n,* et caetera, *m.*
etch, *v.t,* graver à l'eau-forte. **~ing,** *n,* gravure à l'eau-forte, *f.*
eternal†, *a,* éternel. **eternity,** *n,* éternité, *f.*
ether, *n,* éther, *m.* **ethereal,** *a,* éthéré.
ethical, *a,* éthique, moral. **ethics,** *n.pl,* éthique, morale, *f.*
Ethiopia, *n,* l'Éthiopie, *f.* **Ethiopian,** *a,* éthiopien. ¶ *n,* Éthiopien, ne.
ethnic, *a,* ethnique. **ethnography,** *n,* ethnographie, *f.* **ethnologist,** *n,* ethnologue, *m.*
ethyl, *n,* éthyle, *m.*
etiquette, *n,* étiquette, *f,* protocole, *m.*
Eton crop, *n,* coiffure en garçon, *f.*
etymologic(al), *a,* étymologique. **etymology,** *n,* étymologie, *f.*
eucalyptus, *n,* eucalyptus, *m.*
Eucharist, *n,* Eucharistie, *f.*
eugenics, *n.pl,* eugénie, *f,* eugénisme, *m.*
eulogize, *v.t,* faire l'éloge de. **eulogy,** *n,* éloge, panégyrique, *m.*
eunuch, *n,* eunuque, *m.*
euphemism, *n,* euphémisme, *m.* **euphemistic,** *a,* euphémique.
euphonic & euphonious, *a,* euphonique.
euphonium, *n,* saxhorn baryton, *m;* basse à pistons, *f.*
euphoria, *n,* euphorie, *f.*
Euphrates (the), l'Euphrate, *m.*
eurocrat, *n,* eurocrate, *m,f.*
Europe, *n,* l'Europe, *f.* **European,** *a,* européen. ¶ *n,* Européen, ne.
Eustachian tube, *n,* trompe d'Eustache, *f.*
euthanasia, *n,* euthanasie, *f.*
evacuate, *v.t,* évacuer.
evade, *v.t,* éviter, esquiver; (*duty*) se soustraire à. *to ~ tax,* frauder le fisc.
evaluate, *v.t,* évaluer, peser.
evanescent, *a,* évanescent.
evangelic(al)†, *a,* évangélique. **evangelist,** *n,*

évangéliste, *m.*

evaporate, *v.t,* faire évaporer. ¶ *v.i,* s'évaporer. **evaporation,** *n,* évaporation, *f.*

evasion, *n,* fuite, *f* (*of,* devant); (*of issue*) échappatoire, *f,* faux-fuyant, *m.* ~ *of tax,* fraude fiscale, *f.* **evasive†,** *a,* évasif. ~ *answer,* réponse de Normand, *f.*

eve[1], *n,* veille, *f. Christmas E~,* la v. de Noël.

eve[2] **& even** (*Poet.*) *n,* soir, *m.*

even, *a,* (*surface*) uni, plan, plat; (*temper, match*) égal; (*step, pulse*) régulier; (*number*) pair. (*Sport*) *to be* ~, être à égalité. *to get* ~ *with s.o,* se venger de qn. ¶ *ad,* même, jusqu'à. *they killed* ~ *the children,* on a tué même les enfants *ou* jusqu'aux enfants. (+ *compar.*) encore. ~ *faster,* encore plus vite. (+ *neg.*) même, seulement. *she didn't* ~ *reply,* elle n'a même pas répondu. *without* ~ *seeing me,* sans seulement me voir. ~ *so,* quand même, cependant. ~ *if,* même si.

evening, *n,* soir, *m;* (*period of time*) soirée, *f. in the* ~, le soir. *tomorrow* ~, demain soir. *the following* ~, le lendemain soir. *8 o'clock in the* ~, 8 heures du soir. *to spend the* ~ *dancing,* passer la soirée à danser. (*att. meal, paper, class*) du soir. ~ *dress,* (*man*) tenue de soirée; (*woman*) toilette de s., *f.* ~ *gown,* robe du soir, *f.*

evenly, *ad,* uniment; de façon égale.

evensong, *n,* (*Eccl.*) vêpres, *f.pl,* office du soir, *m.*

event, *n,* événement; cas, *m. in the* ~ *of death,* au cas de décès. (*Sport*) épreuve, *f.* ~**ful,** *a,* chargé en événements; mouvementé; mémorable.

eventual†, *a,* éventuel; qui s'ensuit. ~**ly,** finalement. ~**ity,** *n,* éventualité, *f.*

ever, *ad,* jamais. *nothing* ~ *happens,* il n'arrive jamais rien. *I hardly* ~ *read,* je ne lis presque jamais. *did you* ~ *see him?* l'avez-vous jamais vu? (*always*) toujours. *for* ~, (*gone*) pour toujours; (*talking*) sans cesse. *if* ~, si jamais. ~ *so slightly,* tant soit peu.

evergreen, *a,* (*tree, shrub*) à feuillage persistent.

everlasting†, *a,* éternel; immortel.

every, *a,* chaque; tout, e; tous (toutes) les. ~ *day,* chaque jour, tous les jours. ~ *other day,* tous les 2 jours. ~ *100 metres,* tous les cent mètres. *at* ~ *moment,* à chaque instant, à tout moment. ~ *bit as cold as,* tout aussi froid que. ~**body,** ~**one,** *pn,* tout le monde, chacun. ~*one knows that,* tout le m. (*ou* n'importe qui) sait cela. ~**day,** *a,* (*clothes*) de tous les jours; (*event*) commun, banal. ~**thing,** *pn,* tout. ~ *he has,* tout ce qu'il a. ~**where,** *ad,* partout.

evict, *v.t,* expulser. ~**ion,** *n,* expulsion, *f.*

evidence, *n,* évidence, *f;* témoignage, *m,* déposition, *f. to give* ~, témoigner, déposer. marque, *f,* signe, *m. to bear* ~ *of,* porter les marques de. *much in* ~, bien en vue. **evident,** *a,* évident. ~**ly,** *ad,* évidemment.

evil, *a,* mauvais; (*influence*) néfaste; (*spirit*) malfaisant. ~*-minded,* malveillant, malintentionné. *the E~ One,* le Malin. ¶ *n,* mal, *m. to speak* ~ *of s.o,* dire du mal de qn. *social* ~*s,* plaies sociales. ~*doer,* scélérat, *m.*

evince, *v.t,* manifester, témoigner.

evocation, *n,* évocation, *f.* **evoke,** *v.t,* évoquer.

evolution, *n,* (*Biol., gen.*) évolution, *f.* **evolve,** *v.t,* élaborer, développer. ¶ *v.i,* évoluer, se développer.

ewe, *n,* brebis, *f.* ~ *lamb,* agnelle, *f.*

ex-, *pref:* ~*-professor,* ex-professeur, ancien professeur, *m.* ~*-serviceman,* ancien combattant, *m.* **ex,** *pr,* (*out of*) *price* ~ *works,* prix départ usine, *m.*

exacerbate, *v.t.* exacerber.

exact, *a,* exact, précis, juste. ¶ *v.t,* exiger. ~**ing,** *a,* exigeant; (*work*) astreignant. ~**ion,** *n,* exaction, *f.* ~**ly,** *ad,* exactement, précisément, tout juste, justement. *at 4 o'clock* ~, à 4 heures précises. ~**ness,** ~**itude,** *n,* exactitude, *f.*

exaggerate, *v.t. & i,* exagérer.

exalt, *v.t,* (*in rank*) élever; (*praise*) exalter.

examination, *n,* examen, *m;* (~ *paper*) épreuve; (*Mach.*) inspection, *f;* (*suspect*) interrogatoire, *m;* (*witness*) audition; (*expert's*) expertise, *f. medical* ~, visite médicale. **examine,** *v.t,* examiner; (*Mach.*) inspecter; (*witness*) interroger; (*question*) étudier; (*accounts*) vérifier; (*documents*) compulser. **examinee,** *n,* candidat, e. **examiner,** *n,* examinateur, trice. [*board of*] ~*s,* jury, *m.*

example, *n,* exemple, *m. for* ~, par e. *to set a good* ~, donner l'e.

exasperate, *v.t,* exaspérer, pousser à bout.

excavate, *v.t,* excaver, creuser; (*Archaeol.*) fouiller. **excavation,** *n,* excavation, *f,* creusement, *m;* fouille, *f.* **excavator,** *n,* (*Mach.*) excavateur, *m,* excavatrice, *f.*

exceed, *v.t,* dépasser, excéder (*by,* de). *to* ~ *the speed limit,* dépasser la vitesse permise. ~**ingly,** *ad,* excessivement, extrêmement.

excel, *v.i,* exceller (à faire), briller (en). ¶ *v.t,* surpasser. ~**lence,** *n,* excellence, *f. His Excellency,* Son Excellence, *f.* ~**lent,** *a,* excellent. ~**ly,** *ad,* admirablement, parfaitement, à merveille.

except & ~**ing,** *pr,* sauf, excepté, à l'exception de, hormis. ~ *for,* à part. ~ *if,* sauf si. ~ *when,* sauf quand. sinon, si ce n'est: *what can one do* ~ *pay?* qu'est-ce qu'on peut faire sinon *ou* si ce n'est payer? ¶ *v.t,* excepter, exclure. ~**ion,** *n,* exception, *f. with the* ~ *of,* à l'e. de. *to take* ~ *to,* s'offenser de. ~**ional†,** *a,* exceptionnel, hors ligne.

excerpt, *n,* extrait, passage, *m.*

excess, *n,* excès; excédent, *m. to drink to* ~, boire à l'excès. ~ *fare,* supplément, *m.* ~

luggage, excédent de bagages. **~ive†,** *a,* excessif, immodéré, outré.
exchange, *n,* échange, *m. in ~,* en échange. (*Fin.*) change, *m. rate of ~,* taux de change, *m.* [*stock*] ~, la Bourse. (*telephone ~*) central, *m.* ¶ *v.t,* échanger; faire un échange de.
exchequer, *n,* ministre des Finances; (*UK*) Échiquier, *m;* (*of pers.*) finances, *f.pl.*
excise, *n,* contributions indirectes, *f.pl. E~ office,* la Régie.
excite, *v.t,* exciter; (*curiosity &c*) provoquer, susciter. **~d,** *a,* excité, agité. *to get ~,* s'exciter, s'énerver. *don't get ~!* ne t'énerve pas! du calme! **~ment,** *n,* excitation; exaltation; vive émotion, *f.*
exclaim, *v.i,* s'écrier, s'exclamer. **exclamation,** *n,* exclamation, *f.*
exclude, *v.t,* exclure. **exclusion,** *n,* exclusion, *f.* **exclusive†,** *a,* (*rights, story &c*) exclusif; (*group*) sélect. (*price*) *~ of tax,* taxe non compris.
excommunicate, *v.t,* excommunier.
excrement, *n,* excrément, *m.*
excrescence, *n,* excroissance, *f.*
excruciating†, *a,* (*pain*) atroce; (*grief*) déchirant. *~ly funny P,* à mourir de rire.
exculpate, *v.t,* disculper.
excursion, *n,* excursion; randonnée, balade, *f.* *~ ticket,* billet d'excursion, *m.*
excuse, *n,* excuse, *f,* prétexte, *m. there's no ~ for it,* cela est inexcusable. ¶ *v.t,* excuser, pardonner. *~ me!* excusez-moi! pardon! *to ask to be ~d,* se faire excuser. *~ s.o from,* exempter, dispenser (qn de qch, de faire).
execrable†, *a,* exécrable. **execrate,** *v.t,* exécrer.
execute, *v.t,* (*order, plan; Mus., dance; kill*) exécuter; (*movement*) effectuer; (*duties, task*) accomplir, s'acquitter de. **execution,** *n,* exécution, *f;* accomplissement, *m.* **~er,** *n,* bourreau, *m.* **executive,** *a,* (*powers*) exécutif; (*post*) administratif. ¶ *n,* (*pers.*) cadre, administrateur; (*group*) bureau, *m.* (*Pol.*) *the ~,* l'exécutif, *m.* **executor, trix,** *n,* exécuteur (trice) testamentaire.
exemplary, *a,* exemplaire; (*pupil*) modèle. **exemplify,** *v.t,* servir d'exemple de, illustrer.
exempt, *a,* exempt. ¶ *v.t,* exempter, dispenser (de qch, de faire). **~ion,** *n,* exemption, *f.*
exercise, *n,* (*gen., physical, Gram. &c*) exercice, *m. to take ~,* prendre de l'e. (*Sch.*) devoir, *m;* (*Mil.*) manœuvre, *f,* exercice. *~ book,* cahier, *m.* ¶ *v.t,* exercer; (*right*) user de, faire valoir; (*tact &c*) faire preuve de. ¶ *v.i,* prendre de l'exercice.
exert, *v.t,* exercer; (*force*) employer. *to ~ o.s,* s'appliquer, s'efforcer (de faire). **~ion,** *n,* effort, *m.*
exhale, *v.t & i,* (*pers.*) expirer. ¶ *v.t,* (*odour &c*) exhaler.
exhaust, *n,* échappement, *m. ~ pipe,* tuyau d'é. *~ fumes,* gaz d'é., *m.* ¶ *v.t,* (*supplies, pers.*) épuiser; (*pers.*) exténuer. *to be ~ed,* tomber de fatigue. **~ion,** *n,* épuisement, *m.* **~ive,** *a,* approfondi, minutieux. **~ively,** *ad,* à fond.
exhibit, *n,* objet exposé, *m;* (*Law*) pièce à conviction, *f.* ¶ *v.t,* exposer; (*goods*) étaler. **~ion,** *n,* exposition, *f;* (*goods*) étalage, *m;* (*Univ.*) bourse, *f. to make an ~ of o.s,* se donner en spectacle. **exhibitor,** *n,* exposant, e.
exhilarate, *v.t,* stimuler; vivifier; mettre la joie au cœur à.
exhort, *v.t,* exhorter, inciter (qn à faire).
exhume, *v.t,* exhumer, déterrer.
exigence, -cy, *n,* exigence, *f.*
exile, *n,* exil, *m;* (*pers.*) exilé, e. *in ~,* en exil. *to go into ~,* partir en e. ¶ *v.t,* exiler.
exist, *v.i,* exister. *which still ~s,* qui subsiste. (*live*) vivre, subsister. **~ence,** *n,* existence, *f.* *to come into ~,* naître, être créé.
exit, *n,* sortie, issue, *f;* (*Theat.*) sortie. *make one's ~,* quitter la scène. *~ X,* X sort.
exodus, *n,* exode, *m. E~* (*Bible*), l'Exode.
ex officio, *a,* (*member*) nommé d'office, ex officio.
exonerate, *v.t,* dispenser; (*from blame*) disculper.
exorbitant, *a,* exorbitant, extravagant, excessif.
exorcise, *v.t,* exorciser.
exotic, *a,* exotique. ¶ *n,* plante exotique, *f.*
expand, *v.t* (*& i*) (*gas &c*) (se) dilater; (*trade*) (se) développer; (*empire*) (s')étendre. **expanse,** *n,* étendue, *f.* **expansion,** *n,* expansion; dilatation, *f;* développement, *m.* **expansive,** *a,* expansif.
expatiate, *v.i,* s'étendre, discourir (*on,* sur).
expatriate, *v.t,* expatrier. ¶ *a. & n,* expatrié, e.
expect, *v.t,* attendre (qn), s'attendre à (qch). *to ~ to do,* compter *ou* penser faire. *to ~ the worst,* s'attendre au pire. *I ~ed as much,* je m'y attendais. *to ~ that,* s'attendre à ce que *+subj. to ~ s.o to do,* exiger, demander qu'on fasse. supposer, imaginer, croire. *I ~ he is ill,* je suppose qu'il est malade. *I ~ so,* je [le] crois. **~ancy,** *n,* attente, *f.* **~ant,** *a,* qui attend. *~ mother,* femme enceinte, *f.* **~ation,** *n,* attente, espérance, prévision, *f.*
expedience, -cy, *n,* convenance, *f;* opportunisme, *m.* **expedient,** *a,* convenable, opportun. ¶ *n,* expédient, *m.* **expedite,** *v.t,* expédier; hâter. **expedition,** *n,* expédition, *f.* **expeditious,** *a,* expéditif. **expel,** *v.t,* expulser, chasser; (*Sch.*) renvoyer.
expenditure, *n,* (*time &c*) dépense, *f;* (*Fin.*) dépense(s). **expense,** *n,* frais, *m.pl,* dépense, *f.* *at my ~,* à mes frais. *at little ~,* à peu de frais. *to have a laugh at s.o's ~,* rire au dépens de qn. *to live at s.o's ~,* vivre à la charge *ou* aux crochets de qn. *~ account,* frais de représentation. **expensive†,** *a,* cher, coûteux; (*tastes*) dispendieux.

experience, *n,* expérience; (*practical*) pratique, *f;* (*incident*) épreuve, aventure, *f. painful* ~, rude épreuve. ¶ *v.t,* essuyer, subir, rencontrer; (*feel*) éprouver. ~**d,** *a,* expérimenté, qui a de l'expérience. **experiment,** *n,* expérience, *f. as an* ~, à titre d'essai. ¶ *v.i,* expérimenter. ~ *on,* faire des expériences sur. ~**al†,** *a,* expérimental.

expert, *a. & n,* expert, *m* (en, à faire). ~**ise,** *n,* compétence, *f.*

expiate, *v.t,* expier.

expiration & expiry, *n,* expiration, *f.* **expire,** *v.t & i,* (*breathe out, die*) expirer; (*end*) expirer, arriver à terme.

explain, *v.t,* expliquer, éclaircir; (*ideas*) exposer. *that's easily* ~*ed,* cela s'explique facilement. ~**able,** *a,* explicable. **explanation,** *n,* explication, *f.* **explanatory,** *a,* explicatif. ~ *note* (*on map*), légende, *f.*

expletive, *n,* exclamation, *f;* (*oath*) juron; (*Gram.*) explétif, *m.*

explicit†, *a,* explicite; catégorique.

explode, *v.i,* exploser, éclater, sauter, faire explosion. ~ *with laughter,* éclater de rire. ¶ *v.t,* faire exploser, f. éclater, f. sauter; (*theory*) discréditer.

exploit, *n,* exploit, *m.* ¶ *v.t,* (*all senses*) exploiter. ~**ation,** *n,* exploitation, *f.*

exploration, *n,* exploration, découverte, *f.* **exploratory,** *a,* d'exploration, de découverte; (*talks &c*) préparatoire. (*Med.*) ~ *operation,* sondage, *m.* **explore,** *v.t,* explorer. **explorer,** *n,* explorateur, trice.

explosion, *n,* explosion; (*noise*) détonation, *f.* **explosive,** *a,* explosif; (*matter*) explosible. ¶ *n,* explosif, *m.*

exponent, *n,* interprète, *m,f.*

export, *v.t,* exporter. ¶ *n,* exportation, sortie, *f.* ~*s,* articles d'exportation, *m.pl,* exportations. ~ *trade,* commerce d'exportation, *m.* ~**er,** *n,* exportateur, trice.

expose, *v.t,* exposer, découvrir; (*wire*) mettre à nu; (*plot*) révéler, dévoiler; (*Phot.*) exposer. (*Mil.*) ~*d position,* lieu découvert, *m.* **exposition,** *n,* exposition, *f.*

expostulate, *v.i,* faire des remontrances.

exposure, *n,* découverte; mise à nu; révélation; (*Phot.*) pose, *f,* temps de p., *m.* ~ *meter,* posemètre, *m.*

expound, *v.t,* exposer.

express, *a,* exprès, formel; (*letter &c*) exprès *inv. by* ~ *post,* en exprès. ¶ *n,* (*train*) rapide, *m.* ~*way Am,* autoroute, *f.* ¶ *v.t,* exprimer; (*truth*) énoncer; (*wish*) formuler. *to* ~ *o.s,* s'exprimer. ~**ion,** *n,* (*all senses*) expression, *f.* ~**ive,** *a,* expressif. **expressly,** *ad,* expressément.

expropriate, *v.t,* exproprier.

expulsion, *n,* expulsion, *f;* (*Sch.*) renvoi, *m.*

expunge, *v.t,* effacer.

expurgate, *v.t,* expurger.

exquisite, *a,* exquis; (*pleasure*) vif. ~**ly,** *ad,* exquisément, de façon exquise.

extant (to be), exister.

extempore, *a,* improvisé, impromptu. ¶ *ad,* impromptu. *to speak* ~, parler d'abondance. **extemporize,** *v.t. & i,* improviser.

extend, *v.t,* étendre; prolonger; (*hand*) tendre; (*knowledge*) élargir. ¶ *v.i,* s'étendre, se prolonger. **extension,** *n,* extension, prolongation, *f;* (*road*) prolongement, *m;* (*table, flex*) rallonge, *f.* (*Tel.*) ~ *24,* poste 24. appareil supplémentaire, *m.* ~ *ladder,* échelle coulissante. **extensive,** *a,* étendu, vaste. ~**ly,** *ad,* largement. **extent,** *n,* étendue; importance, *f;* degré, point, *m,* mesure, *f. to a certain* ~, dans une certaine mesure, jusqu'à un certain point.

extenuate, *v.t,* atténuer.

exterior†, *a,* extérieur. ¶ *n,* extérieur; dehors, *m. on the* ~, à l'extérieur.

exterminate, *v.t,* exterminer.

external, *a,* externe, extérieur. ~**ly,** *ad,* extérieurement.

extinct, *a,* éteint. ~**ion,** *n,* extinction, *f.* **extinguish,** *v.t,* éteindre. ~**er,** *n,* (*fire*) extincteur [d'incendie], *m.*

extirpate, *v.t,* extirper.

extol, *v.t,* (*pers.*) louer; (*act*) exalter, prôner.

extort, *v.t,* (*money*) extorquer; (*secret*) arracher (*from,* à). ~**ion,** *n,* extorsion, *f.* ~**ionate,** *a,* exorbitant.

extra, *a,* supplémentaire, en supplément, de plus. (*Foot.*) ~ *time,* prolongation, *f.* ¶ *ad,* plus que d'ordinaire; extra-: ~ *fine,* extra-fin; ~ *smart,* ultra-chic. ¶ *n,* (*menu*) supplément, *m;* (*Cine*) figurant, e.

extract, *n,* extrait, *m.* ¶ *v.t,* extraire; (*tooth, promise*) arracher (*from,* à); (*money*) tirer. ~ *or fan,* ventilateur, *m.* ~**ion,** *n,* extraction; origine, *f.*

extradite, *v.t,* extrader. **extradition,** *n,* extradition, *f.*

extraneous, *a,* étranger (*to,* à).

extraordinary†, *a,* extraordinaire; remarquable; (*surprising*) étonnant, inouï.

extravagance, *n,* (*money*) prodigalité; (*act of* ~) dépense inutile *ou* excessive, folie; (*eccentricity*) extravagance, *f.* **extravagant,** *a,* (*pers.*) dépensier; (*tastes*) dispendieux; (*price*) exorbitant; (*ideas &c*) extravagant; (*praise*) outré. ~**ly,** *ad,* avec prodigalité; d'une façon extravagante; à outrance.

extreme†, *a,* extrême. ~ *case,* cas exceptionnel. ¶ *n,* extrême, *m. in the* ~, à l'extrême, au dernier degré. *to go to* ~*s,* pousser les choses à l'e. **extremist,** *a. & n,* extrémiste, *m,f.* **extremity,** *n,* extrémité, *f,* bout, *m.*

extricate, *v.t,* dégager. *to* ~ *o.s,* se dépêtrer; (*fig.*) se tirer.

exuberance, *n,* exubérance, *f.* **exuberant,** *a,* exubérant.
exude, *v.t. & i,* exsuder. *to ~ water,* suinter.
exult, *v.i,* exulter, triompher.
eye, *n,* œil, *m* (*pl.* yeux); (*needle*) chas, trou; (*hurricane*) œil, centre, *m. with blue ~s,* aux yeux bleus. *to have blue ~s,* avoir les y. bleus. *with tears in her ~s,* les larmes aux y. *with my own ~s,* de mes propres y. *as far as the ~ can see,* à perte de vue. *to keep an ~ on,* (*s.o, sth*) surveiller, avoir l'œil à. *to keep a close ~ on s.o,* surveiller qn de près. *I have my ~ on a house,* j'ai une maison en vue. *to catch s.o's ~,* attirer le regard de qn. *to keep one's ~s skinned,* avoir l'œil, ouvrir l'œil. *to cast an ~ over,* jeter un coup d'œil sur, parcourir du regard. *to make ~s at,* faire de l'œil à. *I'm up to my ~s in work,* j'ai du travail jusqu'au cou. (*Mil.*) *~s right!* tête [à] droite! *~s front!* fixe! *~ball,* globe oculaire, *m. ~ bath,* œillère, *f. ~brow,* sourcil, *m. ~brow tweezers,* pince à épiler, *f. ~-catching,* qui attire l'œil; voyant. *~glass,* monocle, *m. ~lash,* cil, *m. ~lid,* paupière, *f. ~ opener,* révélation, *f. ~shade,* visière, *f. ~sight,* vue, *f. my ~sight is failing,* ma vue baisse. *~sore,* objet qui choque la vue, *m. ~witness,* témoin oculaire, *m.* ¶ *v.t,* regarder, observer; (*girls*) lorgner, reluquer *P.* **eyelet,** *n,* œillet, *m.*
eyrie, *n,* aire (d'aigle), *f.*

F

F (*Mus.*) *letter,* fa, *m. ~ clef,* clef de fa, *f.*
fable, *n,* fable, légende, *f.* **~d,** *a,* légendaire, fabuleux.
fabric, *n,* tissu, *m,* étoffe; (*Build.*) structure, *f. ~ of society,* édifice social, *m.* **~ate,** *v.t,* fabriquer. **~ation,** *n,* fabrication; invention, *f.*
fabulous†, *a,* fabuleux, légendaire; extraordinaire; (*P wonderful, abb* fab) terrible *P,* sensationnel, sensass *P.*
facade, *n,* façade, *f.*
face, *n,* visage, *m,* figure; (*expression*) mine, *f;* (*clock*) cadran; (*Build.*) devant, *m,* facade, *f;* (*cards*) face, *f,* dessous; (*type*) œil; (*impudence*) toupet, *m. ~ to ~ with s.o,* face à face avec qn. *in the ~ of,* (*problems, danger &c*) face à, devant, en présence de. *on the ~ of it,* à première vue. *to fall* [*flat*] *on one's ~,* tomber à plat ventre. *he laughed in my ~,* il m'a ri au nez. *to keep a straight ~,* garder son sérieux. *to put a good ~ on it,* faire contre mauvaise fortune bon cœur. *to save* [*one's*], *lose ~,* sauver, perdre la face. *to make ~s,* faire des grimaces. *to take s.o at ~ value,* juger qn sur les apparences. *~ lift,* lifting, déridage, *m. ~ powder,* poudre de riz, *f. ~ value* (*Fin.*), valeur nominale, *f.* ¶ *v.t,* (*pers., danger &c*) faire face à, affronter, braver; (*window*) donner sur; (*wall*) revêtir. *to ~ the facts,* regarder les choses en face. *~d with* (*silk*), à revers de. ¶ *v.i,* (*pers.*) se tourner; (*house*) être exposé *ou* orienté (au sud).
facet, *n,* facette, *f.*
facetious, *a,* facétieux, plaisant.
facial, *a,* facial. ¶ *n,* soin du visage, *m.*
facile, *a,* facile. **facilitate,** *v.t,* faciliter. **facility,** *n,* facilité, *f.* **facilities,** facilités, installations, *f.pl;* (*sports*) équipement, *m.*
facing, *n,* (*Need.*) revers; (*Build.*) revêtement, *m.* ¶ *pr,* en face de, vis-à-vis de. (*Rly*) *~ the engine,* dans le sens de la marche.
facsimile, *n,* fac-similé, *m.*
fact, *n,* fait, *m,* réalité, *f. in ~, as a matter of ~* en fait, à vrai dire, en réalité. *to stick to the ~s,* s'en tenir aux faits.
faction, *n,* faction, *f.* **factious,** *a,* factieux.
factor, *n,* facteur; élément; (*pers.*) agent, *m. safety ~,* f. de sécurité. *human ~,* é. humain.
factory, *n,* usine, fabrique, *f. ~ hand,* ouvrier, ère [d'usine]. *~ inspector,* inspecteur du travail, *m.*
faculty, *n,* (*gen., Univ.*) faculté; aptitude, facilité, *f* (*for doing,* à faire).
fad, *n,* marotte, manie, *f.*
fade, *v.i,* se faner, se flétrir; (*colour, cloth*) déteindre; (*& ~ away*) (*sound*) s'affaiblir; (*sight, memory*) baisser; (*hope*) s'éteindre. *~ out,* (*Cine*) disparaître en fondu. *~-in, ~-out,* (*Cine*) ouverture, fermeture en fondu, *f.* **~d,** *a,* fané, défraîchi; (*cloth*) décoloré.
fag, *P, n,* corvée, *f. what a ~!* quelle barbe! (*P cigarette*) sèche *P, f. ~ end,* restes, *m.pl;* (*P cigarette*) mégot *P, m.* ¶ *& ~ out, v.t,* éreinter, épuiser. *~ged out,* éreinté, claqué *P.*
fag[g]ot, *n,* fagot, *m.*
Fahrenheit, *a,* Fahrenheit.
fail, *v.i,* échouer, ne pas réussir; (*in exam*) échouer, être recalé *P* (à un examen; en anglais); (*sight, health, light*) baisser, faiblir; (*Com.*) faire faillite; (*engine*) tomber en panne; (*supplies*) faire défaut. *his courage ~ed him,* son courage lui a fait défaut. *words ~ me,* les mots me manquent. *to ~ in one's*

duty, manquer à son devoir. ~ *to do*, manquer, négliger de faire. ¶ *v.t*, (*candidate*) refuser, recaler *P*. ¶ *n, without* ~, sans faute, à coup sûr. ~**ing**, *n*, défaut, *m*. ¶ *pr*, à défaut de, faute de. ~**ure**, *n*, (*exam, play, plan*) échec, *m;* (*Com.*) faillite; (*engine*) panne; (*crops*) perte, *f;* (*play*) fiasco, four, *m;* (*pers.*) raté, e.

faint, *a*, faible; léger; (*idea, smile*) vague; (*Med.*) défaillant. *to feel* ~, se trouver mal. ~*hearted*, craintif. ¶ *n*, évanouissement, *m*, syncope, *f*. ¶ *v.i*, s'évanouir, défaillir.

fair[1], *n*, foire, *f*. ~*ground*, champ de f., *m*.

fair[2], *a*, (*pers., hair*) blond; (*skin*) clair; (*weather*) beau; (*wind*) favorable; (*just*) juste, équitable, honnête; (*work*) assez bon, passable; (*size*) considérable. ~ *enough!* d'accord! ça va! ¶ *ad, to play* ~, jouer franc jeu. ~ *& square in the face* (*hit*), en plein visage. ~ *copy*, copie au net, *f;* (*Sch.*) corrigé, *m*. ~*-haired*, aux cheveux blonds, blond. *by* ~ *means or foul*, de gré ou de force, d'une manière ou d'une autre. ~ *play*, fair-play, *m*. *the* ~ *sex*, le beau sexe. ~*-sized*, assez grand. ~*way*, (*Naut.*) chenal, *m*, passe, *f;* (*Golf*) fairway, *m*. ~**ly**, *ad*, équitablement, honnêtement; assez. ~ *well*, passablement; absolument. ~**ness**, *n*, couleur blonde; (*skin*) fraîcheur; justice, équité, impartialité, *f*. *in all* ~, en toute justice.

fairy, *n*, fée, *f;* (*P homosexual*) tante *P*, *f*. ~ *godmother*, bonne fée; (*fig.*) marraine gâteau, *f*. ~*land*, royaume des fées, *m;* (*fig.*) féerie, *f*. ~ *lights*, guirlande lumineuse. ~*like*, féerique. ~ *tale*, conte de fées, *m*.

faith, *n*, foi (*in God*, en Dieu); confiance (*in s.o*, en qn); (*religion*) foi, religion, *f*. *in all good* ~, en toute bonne foi. *to act in bad* ~, agir de mauvaise foi. ~**ful**†, *a*, fidèle. *the* ~, les fidèles, les croyants, *m.pl*. ~**fully**, *ad*, *yours* ~, veuillez agréer, Monsieur, mes salutations distinguées. ~**fulness**, *n*, fidélité, *f*. ~**less**, *a*, perfide, déloyal.

fake, *n*, objet truqué; faux, *m*. ¶ *v.t*, truquer.

falcon, *n*, faucon, *m*. ~**ry**, fauconnerie, *f*.

fall, *n*, chute; (*Mil.*) chute, prise, *f*. *to have a* ~, faire une chute. (*temperature, Fin.*) baisse, *f;* (*Am.*) automne, *m*. *water* ~, ~*s*, cascade, chute d'eau, *f*. ¶ *v.i.ir*, tomber; (*ground*) descendre; (*temperature, Fin.*) baisser. *to* ~ *into bed*, se jeter au lit. *to let* ~, laisser tomber. *to* ~ *asleep*, s'endormir. *to* ~ *ill*, tomber malade. *to* ~ *due*, venir à échéance. *to* ~ *in love with, to* ~ *for P*, tomber amoureux de. *his face fell*, son visage s'allongea. ~*ing-off*, réduction, diminution, *f* (*in*, de). *fallout*, retombées [radioactives], *f.pl*. ~ **away**, (*ground*) descendre en pente. ~ **back**, (*Mil.*) reculer. ~ **down**, tomber [par terre]. ~ **in**, (*house*) s'écrouler, s'effondrer; (*Mil.*) former les rangs. ~ *in!* à vos rangs! ~ *in with*, (*view, decision*) se ranger à. ~ **off**, diminuer, baisser. ~ **out**, (*Mil.*) rompre les rangs. ~ *out!* rompez! ~ *out with*, ~ *foul of*, se brouiller avec. ~ **through** (*fail*), échouer.

fallacious, *a*, fallacieux. **fallacy**, *n*, erreur, *f;* faux raisonnement, sophisme, *m*.

fallen, *a*, tombé; (*angel, woman*) déchu; (*leaf*) mort. (*Mil.*) *the* ~, les morts.

fallibility, *n*, faillibilité, *f*. **fallible**, *a*, faillible.

fallow[1], *a*, (*Agr., fig.*) *to lie* ~, être en jachère, en friche.

fallow[2], *a*, ~ *deer*, daim, *m*.

false, *a*, faux; (*pers.*) perfide; (*report*) mensonger; (*hair &c*) artificiel, postiche. ~ *teeth*, dentier, *m*, fausses dents. (*Law*) ~ *pretences*, moyens frauduleux, *m.pl*. ~**hood**, *n*, (*lie*) mensonge, *m*. ~**ly**, *ad*, faussement, à faux. ~**ness**, *n*, fausseté, *f*. **falsetto**, *n*, fausset, *m*. **falsify**, *v.t*, (*accounts &c*) falsifier.

falter, *v.i*, hésiter; vaciller, chanceler.

fame, *n*, renommée, *f*, renom, *m*. *at the height of his* ~, en pleine gloire.

familiar†, *a*, familier, bien connu. *to be* ~ *with sth*, bien connaître qch. (*with pers.*) familier, intime. *to be on* ~ *terms with*, être intime avec. ~ [*spirit*], démon familier. ~**ity**, *n*, familiarité, *f;* (*pl. pej.*) familiarités, privautés, *f.pl*. ~**ize**, *v.t*, familiariser (qn avec qch).

family, *n*, famille, *f*. *att* (*name, doctor &c*) de famille; (*life*) de f., familial. ~ *man*, bon père de famille. ~ *planning*, planning familial, *m*. ~ *tree*, arbre généalogique, *m*. *to be in the* ~ *way P*, attendre de la famille.

famine, *n*, famine, disette, *f*.

famished, famishing, *a*, affamé. *I'm* ~, j'ai une faim de loup, je meurs (crève *P*) de faim.

famous†, *a*, célèbre, renommé; (*P splendid & ironic*) fameux.

fan[1], *n*, éventail; (*Mech.*) ventilateur, *m*. ~ *belt* (*car*), courroie de ventilateur, *f*. ~ *heater*, radiateur soufflant. ~*light*, imposte, *f*, vasistas, *m*. ~*tail*, pigeon paon, *m*. ¶ *v.t*, éventer; (*fire & fig.*) souffler, attiser.

fan[2], *n*, enthousiaste, *m,f;* (*of star*) fan, *m,f*, admirateur, trice. *football, jazz* ~ (*or fanatic*), fana *P*, mordu *P*, enragé *P* de f., de j. *he's a jazz* ~, il se passionne pour le j.

fanatic, *n*, fanatique, *m,f*. ~**(al)**, *a*, fanatique. **fanaticism**, *n*, fanatisme, *m*.

fancied, *a*, imaginaire. **fancier**, *n*, grand amateur (de . . .), *m*. **fanciful**, *a*, (*account*) fantaisiste; (*idea, plan*) chimérique; (*tale*) imaginaire. **fancy**, *n*, fantaisie, *f*, caprice, *m;* imagination, *f*. *as the* ~ *takes him*, comme cela lui chante. (*liking*) goût, *m*, envie, *f*. *to take a* ~ *to sth*, prendre goût à qch. *to take a* ~ *to s.o*, prendre qn en affection. ¶ *a*, de fantaisie. ~ *cakes*, pâtisseries, *f.pl*. ~ *dress*, déguisement, travesti, *m.* ~ *dress ball,* bal costumé, b. travesti, *m.* ~ *goods,* nouveautés, *f.pl.* *a* ~ *price,* un prix exorbitant. ¶ *v.t,* s'imaginer; se figurer. ~ *that!* tiens! (*think*) penser, croire; (*want*) avoir envie de; aimer. *I don't* ~ *that,* cela ne me dit rien. *I* ~ *her,* elle me plaît bien; elle me botte *P.*

fang, *n,* (*wolf*) croc; (*snake*) crochet, *m.*

fantasia, *n,* fantaisie, *f.* **fantastic,** *a,* fantastique; bizarre, incroyable; (*P superb*) fantastique, sensationnel. **fantasy,** *n,* fantaisie, *f.*

far, *ad,* loin. ~ *away,* au loin. ~ *& wide,* de tous côtés, partout. *how* ~ *is it to...?* combien y a-t-il jusqu'à...? *is it* ~ *to Lyon?* c'est loin pour aller à Lyon? *as* ~ *as the eye can see,* à perte de vue. (*fig.*) ~ *from it,* loin de là, tant s'en faut. *to go* ~ *towards sth,* contribuer beaucoup à qch. *how* ~ *have you got with...?* où en êtes-vous de...? *to carry too* ~, pousser trop loin. *that's going too* ~, cela dépasse la mesure. *so* ~ *as that goes,* pour ce qui est de cela. *as* ~ *as I am concerned,* en ce qui me concerne. *as* ~ *as I know,* autant que je sache. (*degree*) *by* ~, de loin. ~ *better,* beaucoup *ou* bien mieux. ~ *& away the best,* de très loin ce qui est de mieux. (*time*) *so* ~, jusqu'à présent. ~ *into the night,* fort avant dans la nuit. ¶ *a, on the* ~ *side of,* de l'autre côté de. *at the* ~ *end of,* à l'autre bout de. ~*away,* ~*-distant,* ~*-off,* lointain, éloigné. *the F*~ *East,* l'Extrême-Orient, *m.* ~*-fetched,* tiré par les cheveux, forcé. ~*-reaching,* de grande portée. ~*-sighted,* prévoyant.

farce, *n,* farce, *f.* **farcical,** *a,* grotesque, ridicule.

fare, *n,* prix du billet, p. du ticket, *m.* ~*s please!* les places s'il vous plaît! (*pers.*) voyageur, euse; (*taxi*) client, e; (*food*) chère, *f.* ~ *stage* (*bus &c*), section, *f.* ¶ *v.i,* aller. ~ *well,* réussir. ~**well,** *i. & n,* adieu, *m.* *to bid s.o* ~, dire adieu, faire ses adieux à qn.

farinaceous, *a,* farineux, farinacé.

farm, *n,* ferme, *f.* ~ *hand,* valet de ferme, *m.* ~*house,* ferme, *f.* ~ *labourer,* ~ *worker,* ouvrier agricole. ~*yard,* cour de f., basse-cour, *f.* ¶ *v.t,* cultiver. ¶ *v.i,* être fermier *ou* cultivateur. ~**er,** *n,* fermier, ère, cultivateur, trice, agriculteur, *m.* ~*'s wife,* fermière, *f.* ~**ing,** *n,* agriculture, exploitation agricole, *f.*

farrier, *n,* maréchal-ferrant, *m.*

farrow, *n,* portée de cochons, *f.* ¶ *v.t,* mettre bas.

fart *P**, *n,* pet, *m.* ¶ *v.i,* péter *P**.

farther, *a,* plus éloigné *ou* lointain. ¶ *ad,* plus loin. ~ *on, back,* plus en avant, en arrière. **farthest,** *a,* le plus é. *ou* l. ¶ *ad,* le plus loin.

farthing, *n,* le quart d'un ancien penny.

fascinate, *v.t,* fasciner. **fascinating,** *a,* fascinant. **fascination,** *n,* fascination, *f.*

fascism, *n,* fascisme, *m.* **fascist,** *n,* fasciste, *m,f.*

fashion, *n,* façon, manière, *f.* *in a stupid* ~, d'une façon *ou* manière stupide. *after a* ~, tant bien que mal. (*dress*) mode, vogue, *f.* *in* ~, à la mode. *out of* ~, démodé. *the latest* ~, la dernière mode, le dernier cri. ~ *designer,* couturier, *m.* ~ *house,* maison de couture, *f.* ~ *plate,* gravure de mode, *f.* ~ *show,* présentation de mode, *f.* ¶ *v.t,* façonner. ~**able,** *a,* à la mode, chic. ~ *society,* le beau monde. ~**ably,** *ad,* à la mode.

fast[1], *a,* rapide. *he's a* ~ *worker,* il travaille vite. *to pull a* ~ *one on s.o P,* rouler qn. (*watch &c*) *to be 5 minutes* ~, avancer de 5 minutes. (*pers.*) de mœurs légères. ~ *woman,* femme légère. (*colour*) bon teint; (*friend*) sûr. *to make* ~, (*boat, rope*) amarrer. ¶ *ad,* vite, rapidement. ~ *asleep,* profondément endormi. *to stand* ~, tenir bon.

fast[2], *n,* jeûne, *m.* ~ *day,* jour de jeûne, j. maigre, *m.* ¶ *v.i,* jeûner, rester à jeun.

fasten, *v.t,* attacher, fixer; (*dress*) fermer, agrafer, boutonner. *to* ~ *one's gaze on,* fixer son regard sur. ~**er,** ~**ing,** *n,* attache; (*box &c*) fermeture; (*hook*) agrafe; (*press stud*) pression; (*zip*) fermeture éclair, *f.*

fastidious, *a,* (*pers.*) difficile, pointilleux; (*care*) méticuleux.

fat, *a,* (*pers., meat*) gras; (*limb*) gros. *to grow* ~, engraisser, grossir. ~*head P,* imbécile, *m,f.* ¶ *n,* (*pers.*) graisse, *f;* (*on meat*) gras, *m;* (*Cook.*) graisse, matière grasse. *deep* ~, grande friture. *to live on the* ~ *of the land,* vivre grassement. *the* ~*'s in the fire,* le feu est aux poudres. ¶ *v.t,* ~*ted calf,* veau gras.

fatal†, *a,* (*blow &c*) mortel, fatal; (*fig.*) fatal. ~**ist,** *n,* fataliste, *m,f.* ~**ity,** *n,* accident mortel, *m;* tué, e.

fate, *n,* destin, sort, *m.* ~*d,* destiné (à faire). ~**ful,** *a,* fatal, décisif.

father, *n,* père, *m.* (*Rel.*) *F*~ *Paul,* le [révérent] père Paul, l'abbé P. *yes F*~, oui, mon père. *F*~ *Christmas,* le père Noël. ~*-in-law,* beau-père, *m.* ~*land,* patrie, *f.* ¶ *v.t,* engendrer. ~**hood,** *n,* paternité, *f.* ~**less,** *a,* sans père, orphelin de père. ~**ly,** *a,* paternel.

fathom, *n,* (*Naut.*) brasse, *f.* ¶ *v.t,* sonder, pénétrer. ~**less,** *a,* insondable.

fatigue, *n,* fatigue; (*Mil.*) corvée, *f.* ~ *dress* (*Mil.*), treillis, *m.* ¶ *v.t,* fatiguer.

fatness, *n,* embonpoint, *m,* corpulence, *f.* **fatten,** *v.t. & i,* engraisser. **fatty,** *a,* gras, graisseux; (*tissue*) adipeux.

fatuity, *n,* imbécillité, *f.* **fatuous,** *a,* imbécile.

fault, *n,* faute, *f.* *it's my* ~, c'est ma f. (*defect: pers., Tech.*) défaut, *m;* (*Ten.*) faute; (*Geol.*) faille, *f.* *to find* ~ *with,* (*sth*) trouver à redire à, (*s.o*) critiquer. ~**less,** *a,* sans faute; sans défaut; irréprochable. ~**y,** *a,* défectueux; (*reasoning*) erroné.

faun, *n,* faune, *m.* **fauna,** *n,* faune, *f.*

favour, *n,* faveur, grâce, *f;* service, *m.* (*Com.*)

your ~, votre honorée. *to ask s.o a* ~, demander un service à qn. *to do s.o a* ~, rendre service à qn. *do me a* ~ *and..*, sois gentil et... (*pers.*) *to be in, out of* ~, être bien, mal en cour. *to win s.o's* ~, gagner les bonnes grâces de qn. (*Law*) *to decide in s.o's* ~, donner gain de cause à qn. ¶ *v.t*, favoriser; appuyer; être partisan de; (*pers.*) préférer, avantager. **favourable†**, *a*, favorable; (*weather*) propice. **favourite**, *a. & n*, favori, ite, préféré, e. **favouritism**, *n*, favoritisme, *m*.

fawn[1], *n*, faon; (*colour*) *n. & a*, fauve, *m*.

fawn[2], *v.i*, ~ [*up*]*on*, flagorner, ramper devant. ~**ing**, *a*, servile, flagorneur.

fear, *n*, crainte, peur, *f*. *to tremble with* ~, trembler de peur. *numbed with* ~, transi de p. *for* ~ *of falling*, de peur de tomber. *for* ~ [*that*], de peur que + ne + *subj*. (*risk*) risque, danger, *m*. *no* ~! pas de danger! ¶ *v.t. & i*, craindre, avoir peur, redouter (*to do, doing*, de faire). *I* ~ *he will* (*not*) *do it*, je crains *ou* j'ai peur qu'il ne le fasse (pas). *I* ~ *so, not*, je crains que oui, que non. ~**ful†**, *a*, affreux, épouvantable; (*timid*) craintif. ~**less**, *a*, sans peur, intrépide.

feasibility, *n*, possibilité [de réalisation], *f*. **feasible**, *a*, faisable, praticable, possible.

feast, *n*, festin, banquet, *m*; (*Rel.*) fête, *f*. ¶ *v.i*, festoyer. ¶ *v.t*, (*pers.*) fêter, régaler. *to* ~ *one's eyes on*, repaître ses yeux de.

feat, *n*, exploit, *m*, prouesse, *f*. ~ *of arms*, fait d'armes. ~ *of skill*, tour d'adresse, *m*.

feather, *n*, plume; (*wing, tail*) penne, *f*. *birds of a* ~ *flock together*, qui se ressemble s'assemble. ~ *bed*, lit de plume, *m*. ~*-brain*, tête de linotte, *f*, écervelé, e. ~ *duster*, plumeau, *m*. ~*weight* (*Box.*), poids plume, *m*. ¶ *v.t*, (*oar*) plumer. *to* ~ *one's nest*, faire sa pelote.

feature, *n*, trait, *m*; caractéristique; (*Com.*) spécialité, *f*; (*Cine.*) grand film.

February, *n*, février, *m*.

fecund, *a*, fécond. ~**ity**, *n*, fécondité, *f*.

fed, *p.p. of* **feed**. *to be* ~ *up*, en avoir assez, en avoir marre *P* (*doing*, de faire).

federal, *a*, fédéral. **federate**, *v.t.* & (*i*) (se) fédérer. **federation**, *n*, fédération, *f*.

fee, *n*, (*doctor &c*) honoraires, *m.pl*; (*artist &c*) cachet; (*director*) jeton [de présence], *m*; (*exam*) droits, *m.pl*.

feeble†, *a*, faible, débile. ~**ness**, faiblesse, *f*.

feed, *n*, nourriture; alimentation, *f*; (*fodder*) fourrage, *m*; (*baby*) (*breast*) tétée, *f*; (*bottle*) biberon, *m*. *to have a good* ~, bien bouffer *P*. ~*back*, (*Tech.*) rétroaction; (*gen.*) réaction, *f*, feed-back, *m*. ¶ *v.t*, donner à manger à; (*baby*) allaiter; (*army*) ravitailler. ¶ *v.i*, manger; (*cattle*) paître, brouter. *to* ~ *on*, se nourrir de.

feel, *n*, toucher, *m*. *to recognize by* ~, reconnaître au toucher. sensation, *f*; (*fig.*) impression générale. ¶ *v.t*, (*blow &c*) sentir; (*pain, grief*) ressentir, éprouver. *to* ~ *the cold*, être sensible au froid, être frileux. (*touch*) tâter, palper. *to* ~ *one's way*, avancer à tâtons. *to* ~ *s.o's pulse*, tâter le pouls à qn. (*think*) estimer, juger, avoir l'impression. ¶ *v.i*, *to* ~ *ill*, se sentir malade. *to* ~ *hungry, sleepy &c*, avoir faim, sommeil &c. *to* ~ *sure*, être sûr. *to* ~ *like doing*, avoir envie de faire. (*thing*) *to* ~ *hard*, être dur au toucher. *to* ~ *around in*, (*pocket*) fouiller dans. ~**er**, *n*, antenne, *f*, tentacule, *m*. *to put out* ~*s*, tâter le terrain, lancer un ballon d'essai. **feeling**, *n*, sensation, *f*; (*impression*) sentiment, *m*; (*sensitivity*) sensibilité, émotion, *f*. ~*s*, sentiments, *m.pl*. ~**ly**, *ad*, avec émotion.

feign, *v.t*, feindre, simuler. **feint**, *n*, (*Box. &c*) feinte, *f*. ¶ *v.i*, feinter.

felicitous, *a*, heureux, à propos. **felicity**, *n*, félicité, *f*; bonheur, *m*.

feline, *a. & n*, félin, *m*.

fell[1], *v.t*, (*tree*) abattre. **fell**[2], *past of* **fall**.

fell[3], *n N*, coteau, *m*; montagne, *f*.

fellow, *n*, garçon, individu, type *P*, *m*. *a nice* ~, un brave garçon *ou* type. *an old* ~, un vieux bonhomme. *old* ~, mon vieux. *poor little* ~, pauvre petit. camarade, compagnon, *m*. ~ *citizen*, concitoyen, ne. ~ *countryman, -woman*, compatriote, *m,f*. ~ *men*, semblables, *m.pl*. ~ *feeling*, sympathie, *f*. ~ *traveller*, compagnon de voyage, *m*, compagne de v., *f*; (*Pol.*) communisant, e. ~ *worker*, (*factory*) camarade de travail; (*office*) collègue, *m,f*. ~**ship**, *n*, société; camaraderie, *f*.

felon, *n*, criminel, le. ~**y**, *n*, crime, *m*.

felt, *n*, feutre, *m*. ~ *hat*, [chapeau de] feutre, *m*. ~ *pen*, [crayon] feutre, *m*.

female, *a*, (*animal*) femelle; (*sex*) féminin. ¶ *n*, (*pers.*) femme; (*animal*) femelle, *f*. **feminine**, *a. & n*, féminin, *m*. **feminist**, *a. & n*, féministe, *m,f*.

femur, *n*, fémur, *m*.

fen, *n*, marais, marécage, *m*.

fence, *n*, clôture, barrière, palissade, *f*. *to sit on the* ~, ménager la chèvre et le chou. (*P pers.*) receleur, euse. ¶ *v.t*, ~ [*in*], (*land*) clôturer. ¶ *v.i*, (*sport*) faire de l'escrime. **fencer**, *n*, escrimeur, euse. **fencing**, *n*, clôture; (*sport*) escrime, *f*. ~ *master*, maître d'armes, *m*. ~ *school*, salle d'armes, *f*.

fend, *v.i*, ~ *for o.s*, se débrouiller. ¶ *v.t*, ~ *off*, parer, détourner. ~**er**, *n*, garde-feu, *m.inv*; (*Naut.*) pare-battage, *m*, défense, *f*.

fennel, *n*, fenouil, *m*.

ferment, *n*, ferment, *m*; (*fig.*) fermentation, effervescence, *f*. ¶ *v.i*, fermenter; (*v.t.*) faire f. ~**ation**, *n*, fermentation, *f*.

fern, *n*, fougère, *f*.

ferocious, *a,* féroce. **ferocity,** *n,* férocité, *f.*
ferret, *n,* furet, *m.* ¶ *v.i. & t,* fureter. ~ *about,* fureter. ~ *out,* dénicher.
ferrous, *a,* ferreux.
ferrule, *n,* virole, *f.*
ferry, *n,* (*place*) passage, *m.* ~ [*boat*], bac; (*car, train*) ferry[-boat], *m.* ~*man,* passeur, *m.* ¶ *v.t,* ~ [*over, across*], faire passer.
fertile, *a,* fertile, fécond. **fertility,** *n,* fertilité, fécondité, *f.* **fertilize,** *v.t,* fertiliser. **fertilizer,** *n,* engrais, *m. artificial* ~, e. chimique.
fervent, *a,* fervent, ardent. **fervour,** *n,* ferveur, ardeur, *f.*
fester, *v.i,* suppurer.
festival, *n,* (*Rel.*) fête, *f;* (*Mus. &c*) festival, *m.* **festive,** *a,* de fête. **festivity,** *n,* fête, réjouissance, *f.*
festoon, *n,* feston, *m.* ¶ *v.t,* festonner.
fetch, *v.t,* aller chercher; (*s.o*) amener; (*sth*) apporter; (*blow*) flanquer *P. to* ~ *a good price,* rapporter une jolie somme.
fête, *n,* fête; kermesse, *f.* ¶ *v.t,* fêter.
fetid, *a,* fétide, puant.
fetish, *n,* fétiche, *m.*
fetter, *n,* ~*s,* fers, *m.pl,* chaînes; (*horse, fig.*) entraves, *f.pl.* ¶ *v.t,* enchaîner; entraver.
fettle, *n, in fine* ~, en pleine forme.
feud, *n,* querelle vendetta, *f.* ¶ *v.i,* se quereller.
feudal, *a,* féodal. ~**ism,** *n,* féodalité, *f.*
fever, *n,* fièvre, *f. a bout of* ~, un accès de f. ~**ish**†, *a,* (*pers.*) fiévreux; (*state, fig.*) fébrile.
few, *a. & pn,* peu, peu de. ~ *dogs,* peu de chiens. *a* ~, quelques: *a* ~ *dogs,* quelques chiens; (*pn*) quelques-uns, -unes. *a* ~ *of us,* quelques-un(s) d'entre nous. *a good* ~, pas mal de, bon nombre de. ~ *& far between,* rare. ~**er,** *a,* moins; moins de.
fiasco, *n,* fiasco, four, *m.*
fiat, *n,* décret, *m.*
fib *P, n,* bobard *P, m.* ¶ *v.i,* raconter des b.
fibre, *n,* fibre, *f. moral* ~, force morale. ~*board,* bois aggloméré. ~*glass,* fibre de verre. **fibrous,** *a,* fibreux.
fibula, *n,* péroné, *m.*
fickle, *a,* volage, inconstant. ~**ness,** *n,* inconstance, *f.*
fiction, *n,* fiction, *f. the realms of* ~, le domaine de la f. *work of* ~, livre de f., roman, *m. science* ~, science-f., *f.* **fictitious**†, *a,* fictif.
fiddle, *n,* violon, crincrin *P, m;* (*cheat*) combine, *f,* tripotage, *m.* ~*sticks!* fadaises! ¶ *v.i,* jouer du violon. ¶ *v.t,* (*accounts &c*) truquer, maquiller *P. to* ~ *with,* (*pen &c*) tripoter. ~**r,** *n,* joueur, euse de violon; combinard *P, m.* **fiddling,** *a,* insignifiant.
fidelity, *n,* fidélité, *f.*
fidget, *v.i,* remuer, se trémousser. *to have the* ~*s,* avoir la bougeotte *P. stop* ~*ing!* arrête de bouger! ~**y,** *a,* remuant, agité.
field, *n,* (*Agric., Phys., Her.*) champ, *m;* (*Mil.*) champ de bataille. (*Mil.*) *to take the* ~, entrer en campagne. (*Sport*) terrain, *m;* (*Turf*) concurrents, partants, *m.pl;* (*fig. arts &c*) domaine, *m.* ~ *artillery,* artillerie de campagne, *f.* ~*fare,* litorne, *f.* ~ *glasses,* jumelles, *f.pl.* ~ *gun,* canon de campagne, *m.* (*Mil.*) ~ *marshal,* maréchal, *m.* ~ *mouse,* mulot, *m.* ~ *sports,* la chasse & la pêche. ~ *trials,* (*Mach.*) essais sur le terrain, *m.pl.*
fiend, *n,* démon; monstre, *m;* (*fanatic*) enragé, e. ~**ish,** *a,* diabolique.
fierce, *a,* féroce, violent; (*battle*) acharné; (*resistance*) farouche. ~**ly,** *ad,* férocement, violemment, avec acharnement. ~**ness,** *n,* férocité, *f.*
fiery, *a,* ardent, brûlant; (*pers.*) fugueux.
fife (*&* ~ *player*) *n,* fifre, *m.*
fifteen, *a. & n,* quinze, *m.* ~**th**†, *a. & n,* quinzième, *m,f.* **fifth**†, *a,* cinquième. (*Pol.*) ~ *column,* c. colonne, *f.* ~*-rate,* de dernier ordre. ¶ *n,* cinquième, *m,f;* (*fraction*) cinquième, *m;* (*Mus.*) quinte, *f. for phrases V* **fourth. fiftieth,** *a. & n,* cinquantième, *m,f.* ~ *anniversary,* cinquantenaire, *m.* **fifty,** *a. & n,* cinquante, *m.* ~ [*or so*], une cinquantaine.
fig, *n,* figue, *f.* ~ *leaf,* feuille de figuier; (*Art*) f. de vigne, *f.* ~ *tree,* figuier, *m.*
fight, *n,* (*Mil.*) combat, *m,* bataille; (*fig.*) lutte, *f;* (*Box.*) combat; (*brawl*) bagarre *P,* rixe, *f. to have a* ~ *with s.o,* se battre, se bagarrer *P* avec qn. ¶ *v.i.ir,* se battre, combattre; (*fig.*) lutter; (*quarrel*) se disputer. *to* ~ *against disease,* combattre la maladie. ¶ *v.t.ir,* (*pers., army*) se battre avec *ou* contre; (*disease &c*) lutter contre, combattre. *to* ~ *a battle,* livrer bataille. (*Law*) *to* ~ *a case,* défendre une cause. *to* ~ *one's way through,* se frayer un passage. ~**er,** *n,* combattant; boxeur, *m.* ~ [*plane*], chasseur, avion de chasse, *m.*
figment, *n,* (*of the imagination*) invention, *f.*
figurative, *a,* (*Art*) figuratif; (*sense*) figuré. *in the* ~ *sense,* au [sens] figuré.
figure, *n,* (*human*) forme, silhouette, *f. to keep one's* ~, garder la ligne. *she has a good* ~, elle est bien faite. (*pers.*) figure, *f,* personnage; (*Arith.*) chiffre, *m. in round* ~*s,* en chiffres ronds. *good at* ~*s,* doué pour le calcul. (*Geom.*) figure. ~*head,* (*ship*) figure de proue, *f;* (*pers.*) homme de paille, *m.* ~ *of speech,* figure de rhétorique; façon de parler, *f.* ~ *skating,* patinage artistique, *m.* ¶ *v.i,* (*appear*) figurer.
filament, *n,* filament, *m.*
filbert, *n,* aveline, *f.* ~ [*tree*], avelinier, *m.*
filch, *v.t,* voler, chiper *P,* barboter *P.*
file[1], *n,* (*tool*) lime, *f.* ¶ *v.t,* limer.
file[2], *n,* file, *f. in single* ~, en file, à la f, à la queue leu leu. ¶ *v.i,* ~ *in, out,* entrer, sortir en f. *to* ~ *past,* défiler.
file[3], *n,* dossier, classeur, *m.* ¶ *v.t,* classer.

filial†, *a,* filial. **filiation,** *n,* filiation, *f.*
filibuster, *n,* (*Am Pol.*) obstructionnisme, *m.*
filigree, *n,* filigrane, *m.* ¶ *a,* en filigrane.
filing, *n,* classement, *m.* ~ *cabinet,* classeur, *m.*
filings, *n.pl,* limaille, *f. iron* ~, l. de fer.
fill, *n, to have one's* ~ *of sth,* avoir [tout] son content de qch. *eat, drink one's* ~, manger, boire tout son soûl, manger à sa faim. ¶ *v.t,* remplir (*with,* de); (*hole*) boucher (*with,* avec); (*tooth*) plomber; (*pipe*) bourrer; (*post, job*) remplir. *to* ~ *a gap,* combler un vide. ¶ *v.i,* se remplir; se boucher; (*sail*) s'enfler, gonfler. ~ *in,* (*form*) remplir. ~ *up, v.i,* (*car*) faire le plein d'essence.
fillet, *n,* (*beef, fish*) filet, *m.* ¶ *v.t,* (*meat*) désosser; (*fish*) couper en filets. ~*ed sole,* filets de sole, *m.pl.*
filling, *a,* (*food*) bourratif *P.* ¶ *n,* (*tooth*) plombage, *m.* ~ *station,* poste d'essence, *m,* station-service, *f.*
fillip, *n,* chiquenaude, *f;* (*fig.*) coup de fouet, *m.*
filly, *n,* pouliche, *f.*
film, *n,* (*layer*) couche, pellicule, *f;* (*Phot.*) pellicule, film, *m;* (*movie*) film. *to make a* ~, tourner un f. *to go to the* ~*s,* aller au cinéma. ~ *fan,* cinéphile, *m,f.* ~ *maker,* cinéaste, *m,f.* ~ *script,* scénario, *m.* ~ *star,* vedette [de cinéma], *f.* ~ *strip,* film fixe. ¶ *v.t,* filmer, tourner. ~**y,** *a,* vaporeux.
filter, *n,* filtre; (*Phot.*) écran, *m.* ~ *tip,* bout filtre, *m.* ¶ *v.t. & i,* filtrer.
filth, *n,* saleté, crasse; ordure, *f;* (*fig.*) saleté. **filthy†,** *a,* sale, crasseux; dégoûtant; (*talk &c*) ordurier, obscène; (*weather*) affreux, sale.
fin, *n,* nageoire, *f;* (*shark*) aileron, *m.*
final, *a,* dernier; (*decision*) définitif, sans appel. *to put the* ~ *touches to,* mettre la dernière main à. ¶ *n,* (*Sport*) finale, *f.* (*Univ.*) ~*s,* examens de dernière année, *m.pl.* **finale,** *n,* (*Mus., fig.*) finale, *m.*
finance, *n,* finance, *f. F*~ *Minister,* ministre des Finances, *m.* ~*s,* finances, *f.pl,* situation financière. ¶ *v.t,* (*project*) financer, commanditer. **financial†,** *a,* financier. ~ *year,* année budgétaire, *f.* **financier,** *n,* financier, *m.*
find, *n,* trouvaille, découverte, *f.* ¶ *v.t.ir,* trouver; (*s.o, sth lost*) retrouver. *to go &* ~, aller chercher. *that is* [*to be*] *found everywhere,* cela se trouve partout. *to* ~ *that,* trouver, découvrir, s'apercevoir que. (*provide*) fournir. *how did you* ~ *the film?* comment avez-vous trouvé le film? *I* ~ *her very kind,* je la trouve très gentille. *to* ~ *some difficulty in doing,* éprouver quelque difficulté à faire. (*Law*) *to* ~ *s.o guilty,* prononcer qn coupable. ~ **out,** *v.t,* découvrir, apprendre. ¶ *v.i,* (*about sth*) se renseigner (sur qch). ~**ings,** *n.pl,* conclusions, *f.pl.*
fine[1], *n,* amende, contravention, *f.* ¶ *v.t,* condamner à une amende; donner une contravention à.
fine[2], *a,* (*dust, cloth &c*) fin; (*metal*) pur; (*feelings, adjustment*) délicat; (*weather*) beau. *it was* ~ *yesterday,* il a fait beau hier. *one* ~ *day,* (*lit.*) par une belle journée; (*fig.*) un beau jour. excellent, magnifique, beau. *of finest quality,* de premier choix. *that's all very* ~ *but...* tout cela c'est bien joli mais... ¶ *ad,* très bien. *to feel* ~, se sentir très bien. (*Cook.*) *to chop up* ~, hacher menu *ou* fin. *to cut it rather* ~, arriver un peu juste. ~**ly,** *ad,* (*worked*) finement, délicatement; magnifiquement; (*chopped*) menu, fin; (*adjusted*) délicatement. ~**ness,** *n,* finesse, *f;* (*gold &c*) titre, *m.* **finery,** *n,* parure, *f.*
finger, *n,* doigt, *m. first* ~, index. *little* ~, auriculaire. *ring* ~, annulaire, *m. he has a* ~ *in every pie,* il se mêle de tout. (*Mus.*) ~ *board,* touche, *f.* ~*nail,* ongle [de la main] *f.* ~ *mark,* trace de doigt, *f.* ~*print,* empreinte digitale, *f.* ~ *stall,* doigtier, *m.* ~ *tip,* bout du doigt, *m. to have sth at one's* ~ *tips,* connaître qch sur le b. du d. ¶ *v.t,* toucher, palper; (*Mus.*) doigter. ~**ing,** (*Mus.*) *n,* doigté, *m.*
finicky, *a,* (*job*) minutieux; (*pers.*) tatillon; (*over food*) difficile.
finish, *n,* (*end*) fin; (*Sport*) arrivée; (*car &c*) finition, *f. to fight to the* ~, se battre jusqu'au bout. ¶ *v.t,* finir, terminer, achever. ¶ *v.i,* finir, se terminer, prendre fin. *to* ~ *doing,* finir de faire. *to* ~ *with sth,* en finir avec qch. *I've* ~*ed with it,* je n'en ai plus besoin. *to put the* ~*ing touches to,* mettre la dernière main à. (*Sport*) ~*ing line,* ligne d'arrivée, *f.*
finite, *a,* (*gen., Gram.*) fini.
Finland, *n,* la Finlande. **Finn,** *n,* Finnois, e. Finlandais, e. **Finnish,** *a,* finnois, finlandais. ¶ (*language*) *n,* le finnois.
fir [tree], *n,* sapin, *m.* ~ *cone,* pomme de pin, *f.*
fire, *n,* feu; (*house &c*) incendie, *m. to catch* ~, prendre feu. *on* ~, en feu, en flammes. ~*!* au feu! (*Mil.*) feu. *to open* ~, ouvrir le f., faire f. *to come under* ~, essuyer le f. ~*!* feu! (*passion*) ardeur, fougue, *f,* feu. ~ *alarm,* avertisseur d'incendie, *m.* ~*arms,* armes à feu, *f.pl.* ~*brand,* tison, brandon; (*pers.*) fauteur de troubles, *m.* ~ *brick,* brique réfractaire, *f.* ~ *brigade,* [sapeurs-]pompiers, *m.pl.* ~ *engine,* pompe à incendie, voiture de pompiers, *f.* ~ *escape,* échelle d'incendie, *f.* ~ *extinguisher,* extincteur d'incendie, *m.* ~*fly,* luciole, *f.* ~*guard,* garde-feu, pare-étincelles, *m.* ~ *hydrant,* bouche d'incendie, *f.* ~ *insurance,* assurance-incendie, *f.* ~ *lighter,* allume-feu, *m.* ~*man,* [sapeur-] pompier; (*stoker*) chauffeur, *m.* ~*place,* cheminée, *f.* ~*proof, a,* ignifuge; (*v.t.*) ignifuger. ~*proof dish,* plat qui va au feu. ~ *raiser,* incendiaire, pyromane, *m,f.* ~*side,* coin du feu, foyer, *m.* ~ *station,* caserne des pom-

piers, *f.* ~*wood,* bois à brûler, b. de chauffage, *m.* ~*work,* feu d'artifice, *m.* ¶ *v.t,* (*set on* ~) mettre le feu à, incendier; (*fig.*) enflammer, échauffer; (*gun*) tirer, décharger; (*shot*) tirer; (*pot*) cuire; (*P sack*) renvoyer, flanquer à la porte *P.* ¶ *v.i,* faire feu, tirer (*at, on,* sur). **firing,** *n,* (*Mil.*) feu, tir, *m;* (*pottery*) cuisson, cuite, *f.* ~ *squad,* peloton d'exécution, *m.*

firkin, *n,* barillet, *m.*

firm[1], *n,* maison [de commerce], firme, compagnie, *f.*

firm[2], *a,* ferme, solide; (*faith &c*) constant; (*intention*) résolu. *to stand* ~, tenir bon, t. ferme.

firmness, *n,* fermeté, solidité; consistance; résolution, *f.*

first, *a,* premier; (*after 20, 30 &c*) unième. *the* ~ *of May,* le premier mai. *Henry the F*~, Henri Premier. *in the* ~ *place,* en premier lieu, d'abord. *at* ~ *sight,* à première vue. ~ *thing tomorrow,* dès demain matin. ¶ *ad,* d'abord, premièrement. ~ *of all,* tout d'abord. *I* ~ *saw him,* je l'ai vu pour la première fois. ¶ *n,* premier, ère. *to be the* ~ *to arrive,* arriver le premier. *at* ~, d'abord, au début. ~ *aid,* premiers soins *ou* secours, *m.pl.* ~ *attempt,* coup d'essai, *m.* ~*-born,* premier-né, première-née. *the* ~ *comer,* le premier venu, la première venue. ~ *cousin,* cousin(e) germain(e). ~ *finger,* index, *m. on the* ~ *floor,* au premier [étage]. ~*-hand,* de première main. *F*~ *Lord of the Admiralty,* ministre de la Marine, *m.* (*Naut.*) ~ *mate,* second, *m.* ~ *name,* prénom, *m.* ~ *night,* ~ *performance,* première, *f.* ~**-class,** *a,* (*ticket*) de première classe; (*hotel*) de première catégorie. *to travel* ~, voyager en p. [classe]. *also* = ~*-rate.* ~**ly,** *ad,* premièrement, primo. ~**-rate,** *a,* de premier ordre, excellent, fameux.

firth, *n,* estuaire, *m.*

fiscal, *a,* fiscal. ~ *year,* année budgétaire, *f.*

fish, *n,* (*pl.* ~ or ~*es*) poisson, *m. I've other* ~ *to fry,* j'ai d'autres chats à fouetter. *like a* ~ *out of water,* dépaysé. *a queer* ~ *P,* un drôle de numéro *P.* ~*bone,* arête, *f.* ~*bowl,* bocal, *m.* ~ *farm,* centre de pisciculture, *m.* ~ *fingers,* bâtonnets de p., *m.pl.* ~*hook,* hameçon, *m.* ~ *kettle,* poissonnière, *f.* ~ *knife,* couteau à p., *m.* ~ *market,* marché au p., *m.* ~*monger,* marchand de p., poissonnier, ère. ~ *pond,* étang à poissons, vivier, *m.* ~ *shop,* poissonnerie, *f.* ~ *slice,* pelle à p., *f.* ~*wife* (*pej.*) poissarde, harengère, *f.* ¶ *v.i,* pêcher. *to go* ~*ing,* aller à la pêche. *to* ~ *for salmon,* pêcher le saumon. ¶ *v.t,* (*river &c*) pêcher dans. ~ *out,* ~ *up,* [re]pêcher, sortir. ~**erman,** *n,* pecheur, euse. ~**ery,** *n,* pêche; (*ground*) pêcherie, *f.* ~**ing,** *n,* pêche, *f. att* (*boat, line, net*) de pêche. ~ *ground,* lieu de p., *m,* pêcherie, *f.* ~ *rod,* canne à p., *f.* ~ *tackle,* attirail de p., *m.* ~**y,** *a,* suspect, louche.

fissure, *n,* fissure, fente, *f.*

fist, *n,* poing, *m.* **fisticuffs,** *n.pl,* coups de poing, *m.pl.*

fistula, *n,* fistule, *f.*

fit[1], *n,* (*Med.*) accès, *m,* attaque, crise, *f. to throw a* ~, piquer une crise. ~ *of coughing,* quinte de toux, *f.* (*anger*) accès, mouvement, *m.* ~ *of the giggles,* crise de fou-rire. *by* ~*s & starts,* par à-coups.

fit[2], *a,* bon, propre (*for,* à); (*pers.*) capable (de qch, de faire). ~ *for a king,* digne d'un roi. ~ *to eat, wear, live in,* mangeable, mettable, habitable. (*proper*) correct, convenable. *do as you think* ~, faites comme bon vous semblera. (*physically*) en bonne santé. (*Mil.*) ~ *for service,* apte au service. ~ *to travel,* en état de voyager. *to keep* ~, se maintenir en forme. ¶ *n, it's a tight* ~, c'est un peu juste. ¶ *v.t,* ajuster, adapter. *this dress* ~*s you like a glove,* cette robe te va comme un gant. (*put in*) (*cupboard &c*) aménager, installer. ~*ted carpet,* moquette, *f.* ¶ *v.i,* (*clothes*) être bien ajusté, aller. ~ *in with,* (*story, ideas*) s'accorder avec, correspondre à. ~ *out, v.t,* (*boat, flat*) aménager; (*pers.*) équiper; (*workshop*) outiller. ~ *with, v.t,* (*Mach. &c*) équiper de, munir de. **fitful,** *a,* changeant; intermittent. **fitness,** *n,* (*pers.*) aptitude; santé physique; (*remark*) justesse, *f.* **fitter,** *n,* (*Tech.*) monteur, *m;* (*clothes*) essayeur, euse. **fitting**†, *a,* (*comment*) approprié, juste. ¶ *n,* (*lock &c*) pose, *f;* (*clothes*) essayage, *m.* ~*s,* (*house*) installations, *f.pl.* équipement, *m.* ~**ly,** *ad,* convenablement.

five, *a. & n,* cinq, *m. for phrases V* **four.** ~*-year plan,* plan quinquennal, *m. fiver P,* billet de cinq livres, *m.*

fix, *n,* difficulté, *f,* ennui, *m. to be in a* ~, être dans le pétrin, être coincé *P.* (*P drugs*) piqûre, injection, *f.* ¶ *v.t,* fixer, attacher. *to* ~ *one's eyes on,* fixer son regard sur. (*date &c*) décider, arrêter; (*Phot.*) fixer; (*mend*) réparer; (*match, trial*) truquer. *to* ~ *up with s.o,* s'arranger avec qn (pour faire). ~**ed**†, *a,* fixe; (*smile*) figé. ~**er,** *n,* (*Phot.*) fixateur, *m.* ~**ing,** *n,* (*Phot.*) fixage, *m,* fixation, *f.* ~**ture,** *n,* (*house*) installation, *f;* (*Sport*) match [prévu] *m.*

fizz[le], *v.i,* pétiller. *fizzle out,* n'aboutir à rien; (*firework*) rater.

flabbergast, *v.t,* ahurir, époustoufler *P.*

flabby & flaccid, *a,* flasque, mou.

flag[1], *n,* drapeau; (*Naut.*) pavillon, *m.* ~ *of convenience,* pavillon de complaisance. ~*ship,* vaisseau amiral, *m.* ~*staff,* mât [de pavillon] *m.*

flag², *v.i,* (*pers.*) s'alanguir; (*conversation*) languir, traîner; (*interest*) faiblir.
flag³, *n,* (*Bot.*) iris [des marais] *m.*
flag[stone]⁴, *n,* dalle, *f.*
flagellate, *v.t,* flageller.
flagon, *n,* grande bouteille, cruche, *f.*
flagrant, *a,* flagrant.
flail, *n,* fléau, *m.*
flair, *n,* flair, *m,* aptitude (*for,* à), *f.*
flake, *n,* (*snow*) flocon, *m;* (*metal &c*) écaille, paillette, *f.* ¶ *v.i,* ~ [*off*], s'écailler, s'effriter. **flaky**, *a,* floconneux; (*pastry*) feuilleté.
flame, *n,* flamme; (*fig.*) ardeur, flamme, *f,* feu, *m. in ~s,* en flammes, en feu. *to go up in ~s,* s'enflammer. *P an old ~ of mine,* un de mes anciens flirts. *~thrower,* lance-flammes, *m inv.* ¶ *v.i,* flamber. **flaming**, *a,* (*sun*) ardent; (*P blasted*) fichu *P,* sacré *P.*
flamingo, *n,* flamant, *m.*
flammable, *a,* inflammable.
Flanders, *n,* la Flandre.
flange, *n,* bride, collerette, *f.*
flank, *n,* flanc, *m.* ¶ *v.t,* flanquer.
flannel, *n,* flanelle, *f. face ~,* gant de toilette, *m.* **~ette**, *n,* pilou, *m.*
flap, *n,* (*counter, table*) abattant; (*pocket*) rabat; (*wings*) battement; (*flag*) claquement; (*Aero.*) volet, *m;* (*P*) panique, *f. in a ~ P,* dans tous ses états. *to get in a ~,* s'affoler. ¶ *v.t,* (*wings*) battre (des ailes). ¶ *v.i,* battre, claquer; *P* s'affoler. *don't ~!* pas de panique!
flare, *n,* flamme, *f,* flamboiement, *m;* (*Mil.*) fusée éclairante; (*skirt*) évasement, *m. ~ path,* rampe de balisage, *f. ~-up,* flambée de colère, *f.* ¶ *v.t* (*& i*) (*skirt*) (s')évaser. *~ up,* (*fire*) s'enflammer brusquement; (*pers.*) s'emporter, s'enflammer de colère; (*fighting &c*) éclater.
flash, *n,* éclat, *m. ~ of lightning,* éclair, *m. ~ of wit,* saillie, *f. in a ~,* en moins de deux, en cinq sec *P.* (*fig.*) *a ~ in the pan,* un feu de paille. (*Phot. & news ~*) flash, *m.* ¶ *v.i,* étinceler, briller; (*on & off*) clignoter. *~ past,* passer comme un éclair. ¶ *v.t, ~ about,* (*jewels &c*) étaler. *~back* (*Cine.*), retour en arrière, *m. ~light,* (*Phot.*) flash; (*torch*) lampe électrique, l. de poche, *f.* (*fig.*) *at ~ point,* sur le point d'exploser. **~er**, *n,* (*P indecent*) exhibitionniste, *m.* **~y**, *a,* tapageur, voyant.
flask, *n,* bouteille, *f;* (*hip ~*) flacon [plat], *m;* (*Chem.*) ballon, *m,* fiole, *f.*
flat¹, *n,* appartement, *m. ~let,* studio, *m.*
flat², *a,* plat; (*nose*) épaté; (*tyre, battery*) à plat; (*tyre*) dégonflé; (*denial*) net, catégorique; (*style*) plat, fade; (*beer*) éventé; (*Mus.*) bémol, *inv. ~ rate,* taux fixe, *m. feel ~,* se sentir à plat. *lay sth ~,* poser qch à plat. *fall ~ on one's face,* tomber à plat ventre. *fall ~* (*joke*), tomber à plat. *in a ~ spin,* dans tous ses états. ¶ *ad, he told me ~,* il m'a dit carrément. *~ out,* à toute vitesse; (*horse*) ventre à terre; (*rider*) à bride abattue. *work ~ out,* travailler d'arrache-pied. (*Mus.*) *sing ~,* chanter en dessous de la note. ¶ *n,* (*hand*) plat; (*Mus.*) bémol, *m. ~iron,* fer à repasser, *m. ~ race,* course de plat, *f. ~ racing,* plat, *m.* **~ly**, *a,* [tout] net, carrément, catégoriquement. **~ness**, *n,* (*surface*) égalité; (*style*) platitude, *f.* **flatten**, *v.t,* aplatir; (*road*) aplanir; (*crops*) écraser.
flatter, *v.t,* flatter. **~er**, *n,* flatteur, euse. **~ing**, *a,* flatteur. **~y**, *n,* flatterie, *f.*
flatulence, *n,* flatulence, *f.*
flaunt, *v.t,* étaler; (*knowledge*) faire parade *ou* étalage de.
flautist, *n,* flûtiste, *m,f.*
flavour, *n,* saveur, *f,* goût, *m.* ¶ *v.t,* assaisonner. **~ing**, *n,* assaisonnement, *m.*
flaw, *n,* (*gem, character*) défaut, *m,* imperfection, *f;* (*Law*) vice de forme, *m.* **~less**, *a,* sans défaut, parfait; impeccable.
flax, *n,* lin, *m.* **~en**, *a,* (*hair*) blond, de lin.
flay, *v.t,* écorcher; (*thrash*) rosser, fouetter.
flea, *n,* puce, *f. ~bite,* piqûre de puce, *f;* (*fig.*) vétille, *f. ~-pit P,* ciné miteux.
fledg[e]ling, *n,* oisillon, *m.*
flee, *v.i. & t. ir,* fuir, s'enfuir, se sauver.
fleece, *n,* toison, *f.* ¶ *v.t,* tondre *P,* plumer *P;* (*swindle*) escroquer. **fleecy**, *a,* floconneux; (*clouds, sky*) moutonné.
fleet, *n,* flotte, *f. F~ Air Arm,* aéronavale, *f.*
fleeting, *a,* fugace, fugitif, passager.
Fleming, *n,* Flamand, e. **Flemish**, *a. &* (*language*) *n,* flamand, *m.*
flesh, *n,* chair, *f. in the ~,* en c. et en os. *to put on ~,* prendre de l'embonpoint, grossir; (*animal*) engraisser. *to make s.o's ~ creep,* donner la chair de poule à qn. *~ colour,* couleur de chair, *f.* **~y**, *a,* charnu.
flex, *n,* fil [souple] *m.* ¶ *v.t,* fléchir; tendre.
flexible, *a,* flexible, souple.
flick, *n,* (*whip, tail*) petit coup, *m;* (*of finger*) chiquenaude, *f. P ~s,* ciné *P, m.* ¶ *v.t* donner un petit coup à.
flicker, *v.i,* (*light &c*) vaciller, trembloter.
flight¹, *n,* fuite, *f. to take to ~,* prendre la f., s'enfuir.
flight², *n,* (*bird, Aero.*) vol, *m;* (*group*) (*birds*) vol, volée, *f;* (*planes*) escadrille, *f;* (*of fancy*) élan, *m,* envolée, *f. ~ of stairs,* escalier, *m,* volée d'e., *f. ~ deck,* (*Naut.*) pont d'envoi, *m. ~ lieutenant,* capitaine, *m. ~ recorder,* enregistreur de vol, *m.* **~y**, *a,* volage, étourdi, frivole.
flimsy, *a,* peu solide; (*dress*) trop léger.
flinch, *v.i,* broncher. *without ~ing,* sans broncher.
fling, *n,* (*throw*) lancer, *m. to have one's ~,* se payer du bon temps. ¶ *v.t,* lancer, jeter. *to ~*

open (*door*), ouvrir à la volée. ~ *away*, jeter.
flint, *n,* silex, *m;* (*for lighter*) pierre [à briquet] *f.*
flippant, *a,* désinvolte, irrévérencieux, frivole.
flipper, *n,* nageoire, *f.* (*Swim.*) ~*s*, palmes, *f.pl.*
flirt, *n,* (*pers.*) flirteur, euse. ¶ *v.i,* flirter (avec qn). ~ *with* (*idea*), caresser. ~**ation,** *n,* flirt, *m.* ~**atious,** *a,* flirteur.
flit, *v.i,* voleter, voltiger; (*P*) déménager.
float, *n,* (*Fish., Tech., seaplane*) flotteur; (*cork*) bouchon; (*carnival*) char, *m.* ¶ *v.i,* flotter; (*ship*) être à flot; (*Swim.*) faire la planche. ¶ *v.t,* faire flotter, mettre à flot; (*Fin: loan*) lancer. ~**ing,** *a,* flottant. ~ *voter*, électeur, trice indécis, e.
flock[1], *n,* (*animals*) troupeau; (*birds*) vol, *m,* volée; (*people*) foule, *f;* (*Rel.*) ouailles, *f.pl.* ¶ *v.i,* aller, venir en foule, affluer. ~ *together*, s'assembler.
flock[2], *n,* bourre (de laine, de coton) *f.*
floe, *n,* (*ice* ~) banquise, *f,* glaces flottantes.
flog, *v.t,* flageller, fustiger.
flood, *n,* inondation, *f;* (*fig.*) déluge, flot, torrent, *m.* *the F*~, le déluge. *in* ~ (*river*). en crue. ~ [*tide*], flux, *m,* marée montante. ¶ *v.t,* inonder, submerger; (*carburettor*) noyer. ¶ *v.i,* (*river*) déborder; (*people*) aller, venir en foule; affluer. ~*gate*, vanne, porte d'écluse. ~*light*, projecteur, *m.* *v.t,* éclairer aux projecteurs. ~*lighting*, *n,* illumination, *f,* éclairage [aux projecteurs] *m.*
floor, *n,* sol; (*boarded*) plancher, parquet, *m.* *dance* ~, piste, *f.* (*storey*) étage, palier, *m.* *on the third* ~, au troisième [étage] ¶ *v.t,* planchéier; parqueter; faire le sol de; (*pers.*) terrasser. ~*board*, planche, *f.* ~*cloth*, serpillière, *f.* ~ *polisher*, cireuse, *f.* ~ *show*, spectacle de cabaret, *m.*
flop, *n,* *P,* (*gen.*) fiasco; (*play*) four, *m.* ¶ *v.i,* (*pers.*) s'affaler; (*scheme, play*) faire fiasco; (*play*) faire un four. **floppy,** *a,* (*hat*) à bords flottants. (*Tech.*) ~ *disc*, disque souple, *m,* disquette, *f.*
flora, *n,* flore, *f.* **floral,** *a,* floral. **florid,** *a,* (*style*) fleuri; (*complexion*) rubicond. **Florida,** *n,* la Floride. **florist,** *n,* fleuriste, *m,f.*
flotilla, *n,* flottille, *f.*
flotsam, *n,* épaves [flottantes] *f.pl.*
flounce[1], *n,* (*Dress*) volant, *m.*
flounce[2], *v.i,* ~ *in, out*, entrer, sortir dans un mouvement d'humeur.
flounder, *v.i,* patauger. ~ *about*, se débattre.
flour, *n,* farine, *f.* ~ *mill*, minoterie, *f.*
flourish, *n,* floriture, *f;* parafe, *m;* (*with stick*) moulinet, *m;* (*trumpets*) fanfare, *f.* ¶ *v.t,* brandir. ¶ *v.i,* prospérer, avoir du succès. ~**ing,** *a,* florissant.
floury, *a,* farineux; (*hands*) enfariné.
flout, *v.t,* narguer, se moquer de, faire fi de.
flow, *n,* (*blood, liquid*) écoulement; (*river*) courant, cours; (*tide*) flux; (*words*) flot, *m;* (*Elec: current*) passage, *m.* ¶ *v.i,* couler; (*Elec.*) circuler. ~ *in*, (*crowd*) affluer. ~*out*, s'écouler.
flower, *n,* fleur, *f.* ~ *bed*, plate-bande, *f,* parterre, *m.* ~ *garden*, jardin d'agrément, *m.* ~ *girl*, bouquetière, *f.* ~ *market*, marché aux fleurs, *m.* ~ *pot*, pot à fleurs, *m.* *at the* ~ *shop*, chez le fleuriste. ~ *show*, floralies, *f.pl.* ¶ *v.i,* (*lit., fig.*) fleurir. ~**ing,** *a,* (*shrub*) à fleurs. ¶ *n,* floraison, *f.* ~**y,** *a,* fleuri.
flowing, *a,* (*robes, hair*) flottant; (*style*) coulant.
flu, *n,* (*abb of influenza*) grippe, *f.*
fluctuate, *v.i,* fluctuer, varier. **fluctuation,** *n,* fluctuation, variation, *f.*
flue, *n,* conduit de fumée, *m;* (*stove*) tuyau, *m.*
fluency, *n,* facilité, *f.* **fluent,** *a,* (*style*) coulant. *to be a* ~ *speaker*, avoir la parole facile. ~**ly,** *ad,* couramment.
fluff, *n,* (*birds*) duvet, *m;* (*material*) peluche, *f;* (*on floor*) moutons, *m.pl.* ¶ *v.t,* ~ *up*, (*feathers*) ébouriffer; (*pillows*) faire bouffer. ~**y,** *a,* duveteux; pelucheux; (*toy*) en peluche.
fluid, *a,* fluide. ¶ *n,* fluide; liquide, *m.* ~**ity,** *n,* fluidité, *f.*
fluke[1], *n,* (*anchor*) patte, *f.*
fluke[2], *n,* coup de hasard, c. de veine *P,* *m.* *by a* ~, par raccroc.
flunk *P,* *v.t,* (*exam*) être recalé à *ou* collé à *P.*
flunkey, *n,* laquais, larbin, *m.*
fluorescent, *a,* fluorescent.
fluorine & fluoride, *n,* fluor, *m.*
flurry, *n,* (*snow &c*) rafale, *f;* (*fig.*) agitation, *f.* ¶ *v.t,* agiter. *to get flurried*, s'affoler.
flush[1], *n,* (*face*) rougeur, *f;* (*sky*) rougoiement, *m;* (*fig.*) éclat, élan, *m.* *in the first* ~ *of victory*, dans l'ivresse de la victoire. (*W.C.*) chasse d'eau; (*Cards*) flush, *m.* ¶ *v.t,* (& ~ *out*) nettoyer à grande eau; (*game*) lever. ¶ *v.i,* (*pers.*) rougir. ~*ed with success*, ivre de succès.
flush[2], *a,* (*door*) plan; (*cupboard*) encastré (*with*, dans). ~ *with*, au *ou* à ras de, au même niveau que. (*P rich*) en fonds, plein de fric *P.*
fluster, *v.t,* agiter, troubler.
flute, *n,* flûte, *f.* ~**d,** *a,* (*column*) canelé.
flutter, *n,* (*wings &c*) battement; (*emotion*) émoi, *m.* *all in a* ~, tout troublé. ¶ *v.i,* (*bird, flag*) voleter; (*heart*) palpiter. ~ *about*, (*bird*) voltiger. ¶ *v.t,* (*wings*) battre (des ailes).
fluvial, *a,* fluvial.
flux, *n,* *in a state of* ~, changeant sans arrêt.
fly[1], *n,* mouche, *f.* ~*-blown*, couvert de chiures de mouche. ~*catcher* (*bird*), gobe-mouches, *m.* ~ *fishing*, pêche à la mouche, *f.* ~ *paper*, papier tue-mouches, *m.* ~*swat*[*ter*], tapette, *f.* ~*weight* (*Box.*), poids mouche, *m.* ~ *whisk*, chasse-mouches, *m.*
fly[2], *a,* (*astute*) malin, rusé.
fly[3], *v.i.ir,* voler; (*travel*) voyager en avion;

(*flag*) flotter. *to* ~ *off, away,* s'envoler. *to* ~ *over the Alps,* survoler les Alpes. (*fig: time*) passer vite. *I must* ~*!* il faut que je file *P*! *to* ~ *into a rage,* ~ *off the handle,* s'emporter. *to* ~ *at s.o,* sauter sur qn. *to* ~ *into pieces,* voler en éclats. *to* ~ *open* (*door*), s'ouvrir en coup de vent. (*flee*) fuir (devant), s'enfuir (de); se réfugier (*to s.o,* auprès de qn). ¶ *v.t,* (*plane*) piloter; (*goods*) transporter par avion; (*flag*) battre. *to* ~ *a kite,* jouer au cerf-volant; (*fig.*) lancer un ballon d'essai. ¶ *n,* (*tent*) auvent, *m;* (*trousers & pl.*) braguette, *f;* (*Theat.*) *pl,* cintres, dessus, *m.pl.* ~ *leaf,* page de garde, *f.* ~*over,* autopont, *m.* ~ *past,* défilé aérien. ~*wheel,* volant, *m.* ~**ing,** *a,* volant. ¶ *n,* vol, *m;* aviation, *f.* ~ *boat,* hydravion, *m.* ~ *buttress,* arc-boutant, *m.* (*Police*) ~ *squad,* brigade volante. (*Sport*) ~ *start,* départ lancé. ~ *visit,* visite éclair, *f.*

foal, *n,* poulain, *m;* (*ass's*) ânon, *m.* ¶ *v.i,* pouliner, mettre bas.

foam, *n,* (*sea, horse*) écume; (*beer*) mousse, *f.* ¶ *v.i,* écumer, mousser; (*sea*) moutonner. ~**y,** *a,* écumeux; mousseux.

fob off, *v.t,* refiler *P* (*sth on s.o,* qch à qn).

focal, *a,* focal. ~ *length,* distance focale. ~*-plane shutter,* obturateur focal. **focus,** *n,* foyer; (*fig.*) centre, siège, *m.* (*Phot.*) *in* ~, au point. ¶ *v.t,* (*Phot.*) mettre au point; (*fig.*) concentrer. ¶ *v.i,* ~ *on,* fixer son regard sur.

fodder, *n,* fourrage, *m.*

foe, *n,* ennemi, e, adversaire, *m.*

foetus, *n,* fœtus, *m.*

fog, *n,* brouillard, *m,* (*sea*) brume, *f;* (*Phot.*) voile, *m.* (*fig.*) *to be in a* ~, être dans le brouillard, être embrouillé. ~*horn,* corne de brume, *f.* ~*lamp,* phare anti-brouillard, *m.* ¶ *v.t* (*& i*) (*glasses*) (s')embuer; (*Phot.*) (se) voiler. **foggy,** *a,* brumeux. *it is* ~, il fait du brouillard.

fog[e]y, *n, old* ~, vieille baderne *P, f.*

foible, *n,* marotte, manie, *f.*

foil¹, *n,* (*metal*) feuille, lame, *f;* (*Cook.*) [papier] alu, *m. to act as a* ~ *to,* servir de repoussoir à.

foil², *n,* (*Fenc.*) fleuret, *m.*

foil³, *v.t,* (*thwart*) déjouer, contrecarrer.

foist, *v.t,* refiler *P* (*sth on s.o,* qch à qn). ~ *o.s on s.o,* s'imposer à qn.

fold¹, *n,* pli, repli; (*Geol.*) plissement, *m.* ¶ *v.t,* plier; (*arms*) [se] croiser; (*hands*) joindre; (*s.o in one's arms*) serrer, étreindre. ~ [*up*], *v.t* (*& i*) (se) replier. (*P fail*) échouer, (*business*) fermer [ses portes]. ~**er,** *n,* (*file*) chemise, *f,* dossier; (*loose-leaf*) classeur; (*leaflet*) dépliant, *m.* ~**ing,** *a,* (*table, chair*) pliant. ~ *door,* porte en accordéon, *f.* ~ *seat,* (*taxi, Theat.*) strapontin, *m.* ~ *stool,* pliant, *m.*

fold², *n,* parc à moutons, *m.* (*Rel., fig.*) *to return to the* ~, rentrer au bercail.

foliage, *n,* feuillage, *m.* **foliation,** *n,* foliation, feuillaison, *f.*

folio, *n,* folio, *m;* (*book*) *n. & a,* in-folio, *m.*

folk, *n,* (*&* ~*s*) gens, *m.pl.* (*f.pl. with preceding adj.*) *good* ~*s,* de bonnes gens. *country* ~, campagnards, *m.pl. my* ~*s,* ma famille, les miens. ¶ *a,* (*dance, music, song*) folklorique; (*Mus., modern*) folk, *inv.* ~*lore,* folklore, *m.*

follow, *v.t,* suivre; (*suspect*) filer. (*understand*) *do you* ~ *me?* vous me suivez? *to* ~ *suit,* (*Cards*) fournir (*in hearts,* à cœur); (*fig.*) faire de même. ~*ed by,* suivi de. ~ *out,* (*plan*) poursuivre. ~ *up,* (*advantage*) exploiter; (*offer*) donner suite à. ¶ *v.i,* suivre; (*result*) s'ensuivre, résulter. *to* ~ *in s.o's footsteps,* marcher sur les traces de qn. ~*-through,* (*Bil.*) coulé; (*Golf. Ten.*) accompagnement, *m.* ~*-up,* suite, *f.* ~**er,** *n,* disciple, *m,* partisan, e. ~**ing,** *a,* suivant. *the* ~ *day,* le jour s., le lendemain. *the* ~ *dates,* les dates suivantes, les d. que voici.

folly, *n,* folie; sottise, *f.*

foment, *v.t,* (*lit., fig.*) fomenter. ~**ation,** *n,* fomentation, *f.*

fond†, *a,* tendre, affectueux. *to be* ~ *of,* (*gen.*) aimer; (*pers*) avoir de l'affection pour; (*music &c*) être amateur de; (*sweets*) être friand de.

fondle, *v.t,* caresser, câliner.

fondness, *n,* (*for people*) affection, tendresse; (*for things*) prédilection, *f,* penchant, *m.*

font, *n,* (*Eccl.*) fonts, *m.pl;* (*Typ.*) fonte, *f.*

food, *n,* nourriture, *f,* vivres, *m.pl.* ~*stuffs,* aliments, comestibles, *m.pl,* denrées alimentaires, *f.pl.* ~ *& drink,* le boire & le manger. *to give s.o* ~, donner à manger à qn. *to give s.o* ~ *for thought,* donner à penser à qn. ~ *poisoning,* intoxication alimentaire, *f.* ~ *value,* valeur nutritive.

fool, *n,* sot, te; imbécile, *m,f,* idiot, e; (*jester*) bouffon, *m. silly* ~*!* espèce d'idiot! *don't be a* ~, ne fais pas l'idiot. *to make a* ~ *of o.s,* se rendre ridicule. *to make a* ~ *of s.o,* se payer la tête de qn. *to play the* ~, faire l'imbécile. ~*hardiness,* témérité, *f.* ~*hardy,* téméraire. ~*-proof,* à toute épreuve. ¶ *v.t,* duper; avoir *P.* ¶ *v.i,* ~ *about,* faire l'imbécile *ou* l'idiot. *no* ~*ing?* sans blague? *P.* ~**ery,** *n,* sottises, bêtises, *f.pl;* bouffonnerie, *f.* ~**ish†,** *a,* idiot, bête, sot. ~**ishness,** *n,* bêtise, sottise, *f.*

foot, *n,* (*pl. feet*) (*pers., horse, cow*) pied, *m;* (*dog, cat, bird*) patte, *f. on one's feet,* debout. *to go on* ~, aller à pied. *to put s.o on his feet again,* remettre qn sur pied. *to put one's* ~ *in it,* mettre les pieds dans le plat. *to put one's* ~ *down,* faire acte d'autorité; (*P car*) appuyer sur le champignon *P. to set* ~ *in,* mettre les pieds dans, à. (*Meas.*) pied (= 0.3048 m); (*hill, bed*) pied; (*page, stairs*) bas, *m;* (*Mil.*) infanterie, *f.* ¶ *v.t,* (*bill*) payer. *to* ~ *it,* aller à pied. ~ *& mouth disease,* fièvre aphteuse, *f.* ~*brake,* frein à pied, *m.* ~*bridge,* passerelle, *f.* ~*fall,* [bruit de] pas, *m.* ~*hills,* contreforts, *m.pl.* ~*hold,* prise de pied, *f. to gain a* ~*hold,* prendre pied. ~*lights,* rampe, *f.* ~*man,* valet de pied, *m.* ~*note,* note en bas de la page, *f.* ~*pad,* détrousseur, *m.* ~*path,* sentier, (*street*) trottoir, *m.* ~*print,* empreinte de pied, *f.* ~ *soldier,* fantassin, *m. to be* ~*sore,* avoir mal aux pieds. ~*step,* pas, *m.* ~*-wear,* chaussures, *f.pl.* ~*work,* jeu de jambes, *m.*

football, *n,* (*Sport*) football; (*ball*) ballon [de f.], *m. att* (*match, team &c*) de f. ~**er,** *n,* joueur de f., footballeur, *m.*

footing, *n,* prise [de pied] *f. to lose one's* ~, perdre pied. *on an equal* ~, sur un pied d'égalité.

footling, *a,* insignifiant, dérisoire.

fop, *n,* dandy, *m.* **foppish,** *a,* de dandy.

for, *pr,* pour. *a present* ~ *you,* un cadeau pour toi. *what* ~*?* pourquoi? ~ *example,* par exemple. ~ *sale,* à vendre. *what's that* ~*?* c'est pour quoi faire? *it's not* ~ *me to decide,* ce n'est pas à moi de décider. *to leap* ~ *joy,* sauter de joie. ~ *all that,* malgré tout. ~ *all his strength,* malgré toute sa force. *as* ~ *him,* quant à lui. *but* ~ *them,* sans eux. (*time*) (*future*) pour, pendant: *I'm going away* ~ *10 days,* je pars pour 10 jours. *he'll be away* ~ *2 years,* il sera absent [pendant] 2 ans. (*past*) pendant: *he played* ~ *2 hours,* il a joué pendant 2 heures. (*continuing action*) depuis: *he has been waiting* ~ *20 minutes,* il attend depuis 20 minutes. *I haven't seen her* ~ *a month,* il y a un mois que je ne l'ai vue. (*distance*) *bends* ~ *3 km,* virages sur 3 km. *he's* ~ *it! P* qu'est-ce qu'il va prendre! *P* ¶ *c,* car.

forage, *n,* fourrage, *m.* ~ *cap,* calot, *m.* ¶ *v.i,* fourrager, fouiller.

foray, *n,* incursion, razzia, *f,* raid, *m.*

forbear, *v.i.ir,* s'abstenir, s'empêcher (*from doing,* de faire). ~**ance,** *n,* patience, *f.*

forbid, *v.t.ir,* défendre, interdire (à qn de faire). *passengers are* ~*den to...* il est défendu aux voyageurs de... *smoking* ~*den,* défense de fumer. ~**ding,** *a,* (*look*) rébarbatif; (*sky*) menaçant.

force, *n,* force, violence, *f. by sheer* ~, de vive force. *by* ~ *of habit,* par la force de l'habitude. (*Law*) *in* ~, en vigueur. (*Mil.*) *the* ~*s,* les forces armées. *the police* ~, la police, *f.* ¶ *v.t,* forcer, obliger (qn à faire). *to be* ~*d to do,* être forcé *ou* obligé de faire. *to* ~ *o.s to do,* se forcer à faire. *to* ~ *one's way through,* se frayer un passage à travers. *to* ~ *open a door,* forcer une porte. *to* ~ *back,* (*tears*) refouler. **forced,** *a,* (*smile, landing*) forcé. **forceful†,** *a,* (*pers.*) énergique; (*argument*) vigoureux, puissant.

forceps, *n.s. & pl,* (*Surg.*) pince, *f;* (*dental*) davier; (*obstetrical*) forceps, *m.*

forcible, *a,* (*entry*) de force, par f.

ford, *n,* gué, *m.* ¶ *v.t,* passer à gué.

fore, *a,* (*-foot, -leg, -paw*) antérieur, de devant. ¶ *ad,* (*Naut.*) à l'avant. ~ *& aft,* de l'avant à l'arrière. ¶ *n,* (*Naut.*) avant, *m.* (*fig.*) *to the* ~, très en évidence. *to come to the* ~, se faire remarquer. ¶ *i,* (*Golf*) attention! gare!

forearm, *n,* avant-bras, *m.*

forebode, *v.t,* présager. **foreboding,** *n,* pressentiment, *m,* prémonition, *f.*

forecast, *n,* prévision, *f.* ¶ *v.t.ir,* prévoir.

forecastle *or* **foc's'le,** *n,* gaillard d'avant; poste de l'équipage, *m.*

forecourt, *n,* cour de devant; avant-cour, *f.*

forefathers, *n.pl,* aïeux, ancêtres, *m.pl.*

forefinger, *n,* index, *m.*

forego, *v.t,* s'abstenir de, renoncer à. ~**ing,** *a,* précédent, susdit. *a* ~*ne conclusion,* à prévoir, réglé d'avance.

foreground, *n, in the* ~, au premier plan.

forehand [stroke], (*Ten.*) *n,* coup droit, *m.*

forehead, *n,* front, *m.*

foreign, *a,* (*gen., fig.*) étranger; (*trade &c*) extérieur. ~ *exchange market,* marché des changes, *m. F*~ *Legion,* Légion [étrangère]. *F*~ *Office,* Ministère des Affaires étrangères, *m. F*~ *Service,* le corps diplomatique. (*Mil.*) ~ *service,* service à l'étranger, *m.* ~ *policy,* politique étrangère *ou* extérieure. ~**er,** *n,* étranger, ère.

foreland, *n,* cap, *m,* pointe [de terre], *f.*

forelock (*hair*) *n,* mèche, *f,* toupet, *m.*

foreman, *n,* contremaître, chef d'équipe; (*jury*) président, *m.*

foremast, *n,* mât de misaine, *m.*

foremost, *a,* premier, principal. *first &* ~, tout d'abord.

forensic, *a,* du barreau; (*medicine*) légal. ~ *expert,* médecin légiste, *m.*

forerunner, *n,* avant-coureur, précurseur, *m.*

foresee, *v.t.ir,* prévoir.

foreshadow, *v.t,* annoncer, présager.

foreshore, *n,* laisse de mer; plage, *f.*

foreshortening, *n,* raccourci, *m.*

foresight, *n,* prévoyance, *f;* (*gun*) guidon, *m.*

forest, *n,* forêt, *f;* (*att.*) forestier. ~**er,** *n,* [garde] forestier, *m.* ~**ry,** *n,* sylviculture, *f.*

forestall, *v.t,* anticiper; prévenir; devancer.

foretaste, *n,* avant-goût, *m.*

foretell, *v.t.ir,* prédire, annoncer.

forethought, *n,* prévoyance, *f.*

forever, *ad,* toujours, sans cesse.

forewarn, *v.t,* prévenir, avertir.

forewoman, *n,* contremaîtresse, *f.*

foreword, *n,* avant-propos, *m,* préface, *f.*

forfeit, *n,* peine, *f.* ~*s* (*game*), gages, *m.pl.* ¶ *v.t,* perdre; (*one's life*) payer de. ~**ure,** *n,* perte, *f.*

forgather, *v.i,* se réunir.

forge, *n,* forge, *f.* ¶ *v.t,* (*metal, fig.*) forger;

(*money, picture*) contrefaire; (*accounts*) falsifier. ~*d*, faux. ~**r,** *n,* faussaire, *m,f.* ~**ry,** *n,* contrefaçon; falsification, *f;* (*object*) faux, *m.*

forget, *v.t.ir,* oublier. ~ *to do,* oublier, omettre de faire. *to* ~ *o.s,* (*misbehave*) s'oublier. ~ *about it,* n'y pensez plus. *let's* ~ *all about it,* passons l'éponge. ~*-me-not,* myosotis, *m.* ~**ful,** *a,* distrait, étourdi. ~ *of,* oublieux de. ~**fulness,** *n,* manque de mémoire, *m.*

forgive, *v.t.ir,* (*pers., sin*) pardonner. ~ *s.o for sth, for doing,* pardonner qch à qn, à qn de faire *ou* d'avoir fait. *to* ~ *s.o a debt,* faire grâce d'une dette à qn. ~**ness,** *n,* pardon, *m.*

forgo, *v.t.ir,* s'abstenir de; renoncer à.

fork, *n,* (*Agr., tree*) fourche; (*table*) fourchette; (*road &c*) bifurcation, *f.* ~*-lift truck,* chariot élévateur. ¶ *v.t,* ~ [*over*], (*ground*) retourner à la fourche. ~ *out,* (*money*) *P,* allonger *P.* ¶ *v.i,* bifurquer. ~ *right,* prenez à droite. ~ *out P,* casquer *P.* ~**ed,** *a,* fourchu. ~ *lightning,* éclair en zigzag, *m.*

forlorn, *a,* triste; abandonné, délaissé; (*cry*) désespéré.

form, *n,* (*shape, figure, Art, Mus.*) forme, *f. in the* ~ *of,* sous f. de. (*kind*) forme, espèce, *f;* (*paper*) formulaire, *m,* formule, fiche, *f;* (*Sch.*) classe, *f;* (*seat*) banc, *m. in fine* ~, en pleine forme. ¶ *v.t,* former, façonner, construire; (*plan*) arrêter; (*habit*) prendre; (*society*) organiser; (*Com: company*) fonder, créer. *to* ~ *a circle,* se mettre en cercle. (*Mil.*) *to* ~ *fours,* se mettre par quatre. ¶ *v.i,* se former, prendre forme. ~ *up,* se ranger. ~**al†,** *a,* (*function*) officiel; (*welcome*) cérémonieux; (*pers.*) guindé, compassé. ~ *dress,* tenue de cérémonie, *f.* ~ *agreement,* accord en bonne & due forme, *m.* ~**ality,** *n,* formalité, *f.* ~**ation,** *n,* formation; constitution, création, *f.* ~**ative,** *a,* formateur, trice.

former, *a,* ancien; précédent. ~ *pupil,* ancien élève. ¶ *pn, the* ~, celui-là. ~**ly,** *ad,* autrefois, jadis, anciennement.

formidable†, *a,* redoutable.

Formosa, *n,* Formose, Tai-wan, *f.*

formula, *n,* formule, *f.* **formulate,** *v.t,* formuler.

fornication, *n,* fornication, *f.*

forsake, *v.t.ir,* délaisser, abandonner.

forswear, *v.t.ir,* abjurer. ~ *oneself,* se parjurer.

fort, *n,* fort, (*small*) fortin, *m.* **forte** (*Mus.*) *ad,* forte. ¶ (*strong point*) *n,* fort, *m.*

forth, *ad,* en avant. *to go back &* ~, aller & venir. *and so* ~, et ainsi de suite. ~**coming,** *a,* qui va paraître; à venir; prochain; (*pers.*) ouvert, communicatif. ~**right,** *a,* franc, direct. ~**with,** *ad,* sur-le-champ, tout de suite.

fortieth, *a. & n,* quarantième, *m,f;* (*fraction*) quarantième, *m.*

fortification, *n,* fortification, *f.* **fortify,** *v.t,* fortifier. *fortified place,* place forte.

fortitude, *n,* force d'âme, *f,* courage, *m.*

fortnight, *n,* quinze jours, *m.pl,* quinzaine, *f.* ~**ly,** *a,* bimensuel. ¶ *ad,* tous les 15 jours.

fortress, *n,* forteresse, *f.*

fortuitous†, *a,* fortuit.

fortunate, *a,* (*pers.*) heureux, chanceux; (*time &c*) favorable, propice. ~**ly,** *ad,* heureusement, par bonheur. **fortune,** *n,* fortune, *f,* hasard, *m. by good* ~, par bonheur. (*wealth*) *to make a* ~, faire fortune. *to tell* ~*s,* dire la bonne aventure. ~ *teller,* diseur (euse) de bonne aventure.

forty, *a.* quarante. *inv. about* ~ *words.* une quarantaine de mots. *he is about* ~, il a dans les quarante ans. *to have* ~ *winks,* faire un petit somme. ¶ *n,* quarante, *m inv. she is getting on for* ~, elle va sur ses quarante ans. (*1940s &c*) *in the forties,* dans les années quarante. ~*-odd,* quarante et quelques *P.* ~*-one,* quarante et un. ~*-two,* quarante-deux. ~*-first,* quarante et unième. ~*-second,* quarante-deuxième.

forum, *n,* forum, *m.*

forward, *a,* (*movement*) en avant; (*with work*) en avance; (*child*) précoce; (*pers.*) hardi, effronté. (*Mil.*) ~ *post,* avant-poste, *m.* (*Rugby*) ~ *pass,* [passe *f*] en-avant, *m.* (*Com: prices &c*) à terme. ~[**s**], *ad,* en avant. *to go* ~, avancer. *to go straight* ~, aller droit devant soi. *from that day* ~, à partir de ce jour-là. ¶ *n,* (*Sport*) avant, *m.* ¶ *v.t,* expédier, envoyer; (*mail*) faire suivre. *please* ~, faire suivre S.V.P. ~*ing agent,* transitaire, *m,f.* ~*-looking,* tourné vers l'avenir. ~**ness,** *n,* précocité; hardiesse, *f.*

fossil, *a. & n,* fossile, *m. an old* ~ *P,* un vieux fossile *P,* une vieille croûte *P.*

foster, *v.t,* (*child*) élever; (*fig.*) encourager, favoriser; (*idea*) nourrir, entretenir. *comps:* (*child, family, parents*) adoptif, (*brother, sister*) adoptif, de lait.

foul, *a,* (*gen.*) infecte; (*place*) crasseux, immonde; (*weather*) moche, sale; (*air*) vicié; (*breath*) fétide; (*behaviour*) infâme; (*language*) ordurier. ~ *play,* acte criminel; (*Sport*) jeu déloyal. ¶ *n,* (*Sport*) coup défendu, c. irrégulier; (*Foot.*) faute, *f.* ~*-mouthed,* mal embouché. ~*-smelling,* puant. ¶ *v.t,* salir; (*air, river*) polluer; (*pipe, gun*) obstruer, encrasser; (*Naut.*) (*anchor &c*) engager; (*ship*) aborder, entrer en collision avec.

found[1], *v.t,* (*metal*) fondre.

found[2], *v.t,* fonder, créer; établir; (*opinion &c*) baser (*on,* sur). ~**ation,** *n,* fondation, *f,* établissement, *m.* (*Build.*) ~*s,* fondations, *f.pl.* (*fig.*) (*statement, belief*) fondement, *m,* bases, *f.pl. without* ~, sans fondement. ~ *garment,* gaine, *f.* ~ *stone,* première pierre.

founder[1], *n,* fondateur, trice; (*family, race*) souche, *f.*
founder[2], *v.i,* (*ship*) sombrer, couler; (*fig.*) (*plans &c*) s'effondrer, s'écrouler.
foundling, *n,* enfant trouvé, e.
foundry, *n,* fonderie, *f.*
fount, *n,* (*Typ.*) fonte; (*liter.*) source, *f.*
fountain, *n,* fontaine, source, *f;* jet d'eau, *m. drinking ~,* jet d'eau potable. *~head,* source, *f. ~ pen,* stylo, *m.*
four, *a,* quatre, *inv. he is ~* [*years old*], il a q. ans. *he lives at number ~,* il habite au [numéro] q. *the ~ corners of the world,* les q. coins du monde. ¶ *n,* quatre, *m inv. ~ of the men,* q. des hommes. *there are ~ of us,* nous sommes *ou* on est q. *all ~ of them* (*us, you*), tous les q. *it is ~ o'clock,* il est q. heures. *they are sold in ~s,* cela se vend par q. *on all ~s,* à q. pattes. *~-engined plane,* quadrimoteur, *m. ~fold, a,* quadruple, *ad,* au quadruple. *~-footed,* quadrupède; à q, pattes. (*Mus.*) *~-part,* à q. voix. *~-poster,* lit à colonnes, *m. ~score, a. & n,* quatre-vingts, *m. ~some* (*game*), partie à q., *f.* (*Mot.*) *with ~-wheel drive,* à q. roues motrices. **fourteen,** *a. & n,* quatorze, *m.* **~th,** *a. & n,* quatorzième, *m,f.* **fourth†,** *a,* quatrième. *on the ~ of May,* le quatre mai. *Henry the F~,* Henri Quatre. *he lives on the ~ floor,* il habite au quatrième. *she was the ~ to arrive,* elle est arrivée la quatrième. ¶ *n,* quatrième, *m,f;* (*fraction*) quart, *m;* (*Mus.*) quarte, *f.*
fowl, *n,* poule, volaille, *f;* (*liter.*) oiseau, *m. wild ~,* gibier d'eau, *m. ~ pest,* peste aviaire, *f.*
fox, *n,* renard, *m.* (*fig.*) *sly ~,* rusé, malin, *m.* ¶ *v.t, P,* mystifier; tromper. *~ cub,* renardeau, *m. ~ earth,* renardière, *f. ~glove,* digitale, *f. ~hound,* foxhound, *m. ~hunting,* chasse au renard, *f. ~ terrier,* fox-terrier, *m.*
foyer, *n,* foyer [du public], *m.*
fraction, *n,* fraction, *f.* **~al,** *a,* fractionnaire.
fractious, *a,* grincheux, hargneux.
fracture, *n,* fracture, *f.* ¶ *v.t* (*& i*) (se) fracturer, (se) casser.
fragile, *a,* fragile. **fragility** *n,* fragilité, *f.*
fragment, *n,* fragment, morceau; (*shell*) éclat, *m.* **~ary,** *a,* fragmentaire.
fragrance, *n,* bonne odeur, *f,* parfum, *m.* **fragrant,** *a,* odorant, parfumé.
frail, *a,* frêle; fragile. **~ty,** *n,* fragilité; (*moral*) faiblesse, *f.*
frame, *n,* (*human, Build.*) charpente, *f;* (*picture, cycle*) cadre; (*door, window*) chambranle; (*car, window, garden*) châssis, *m;* (*ship*) carcasse; (*spectacles*) monture, *f. ~ of mind,* disposition d'esprit, humeur, *f. ~-up P,* coup monté. *~work,* (*house*) charpente, *f;* (*society, play*) cadre, *m,* structure, *f.* ¶ *v.t,* (*picture, face*) encadrer; (*sentence*) construire; (*P pers.*) monter un coup contre.
framing, (*act*) *n,* encadrement, *m.*
franc, *n,* franc, *m.*
France, *n,* la France. *in ~,* en France.
franchise, *n,* droit de vote, *m.*
Franciscan, *n,* franciscain, *m.*
francophil[e], *a. & n,* francophile, *m,f.* **francophobe,** *a. & n,* francophobe, *m,f.*
frank†, *a,* franc, ouvert, sincère. **~ly,** franchement, en toute franchise.
frantic†, *a,* frénétique; effréné, fou.
fraternal†, *a,* fraternel. **fraternity,** *n,* fraternité, *f.* **fraternize,** *v.i,* fraterniser. **fratricide,** *n.* & **fratricidal,** *a,* fratricide, *m.*
fraud, *n,* fraude; supercherie, *f;* (*pers.*) imposteur, *m.* **fraudulent†,** *a,* frauduleux.
fraught with, plein de, gros de, chargé de.
fray[1], *n,* rixe, bagarre; bataille, *f,* combat, *m.* (*fig.*) *to enter the ~,* entrer en lice.
fray[2], *v.t.* (*& i*) (*cloth*) (s')effilocher, (s')effiler.
freak, *n,* monstre, phénomène, *m;* (*eccentric*) phénomène; (*of fortune*) caprice, *m. she looks a ~ P,* elle a l'air d'un épouvantail. *att* (*storm, result*) anormal, inouï. **~ish,** *a,* bizarre, grotesque; (*idea*) saugrenu.
freckle, *n,* tache de rousseur, t. de son, *f. ~d,* couvert de taches de r.
free, *a,* (*pers., choice, seat, room*) libre. *~ to do,* libre de faire. *to set ~,* mettre en liberté, libérer. (*from care &c*) dégagé. *~ & easy,* décontracté, désinvolte. (*at no cost*) gratuit. (*Com.*) *delivery ~,* livraison gratuite, franco de port. *~ on board,* franco à bord. *~ of tax, duty,* exempt de taxe, hors-taxe. *to be ~ with one's money,* dépenser son argent sans compter. *~board,* franc-bord, *m. ~ fight, ~-for-all,* mêlée générale. *a ~ hand* (*fig.*), carte blanche. *~hand* (*drawing*), à main levée. *~ kick* (*Sport*) coup franc, *m. ~lance,* (*journalist &c*) indépendant. *~mason,* franc-maçon, *m. ~-range* (*hens*), de ferme. *to give ~ rein to,* donner libre cours à. *~style,* nage libre, *f. ~thinker,* libre-penseur, euse. *~ trade,* libre-échange, *m. ~ verse,* vers libre, *m. ~way* (*Am.*), autoroute (sans péage) *f. ~wheel* (*cycle*), roue libre, *f. ~ will* (*Philos.*), libre arbitre, *m. of his own ~ will,* de son propre gré. ¶ *ad,* gratis. ¶ *v.t,* (*gen.*) libérer; (*slave, people*) affranchir; (*prisoner*) libérer, élargir; (*extricate*) dégager; (*of tax*) exempter; (*pipe*) débloquer. **freedom,** *n,* liberté, *f. ~ of speech,* l. de parole. *~ of the seas,* franchise des mers, *f.* **freely,** *ad,* (*act*) librement; (*speak*) franchement; (*give*) libéralement.
freeze, *v.i.ir,* geler, *it is freezing,* il gèle. *the pond has frozen,* l'étang est pris *ou* gelé. (*fig.*) (*smile*) se figer. *to ~ in one's tracks,* rester figé sur place. *~ over,* (*windscreen*) givrer. ¶ *v.t.ir,* (*food*) congeler; (*Ind.*) surgeler; (*Econ.*) (*prices, wages*) bloquer. (*fig.*) *frozen with*

terror, glacé d'horreur. ¶ *n,* gel, *m,* gelée, *f;* (*Econ.*) blocage, *m.* **freezer,** *n,* (*home*) congélateur; (*Ind.*) surgélateur, *m.* **freezing,** *a,* (*weather*) glacial; (*feet &c*) gelé, glacé. ~ *point,* point de congélation, *m.*

freight, *n,* (*load*) fret, *m,* cargaison, *f;* (*transport*) transport, *m.* ~ *plane,* avion-cargo, *m.* ~**er,** *n,* (*ship*) cargo, *m.*

French, *a,* français. ~ *embassy, team,* ambassade, équipe de France, *f.* ~ *Canadian, a,* canadien français; *n,* (*language*) français canadien, *m.* ~ *beans,* haricots verts, *m.pl.* ~ *dressing,* vinaigrette, *f.* ~ *fries,* [pommes de terre] frites, *f.pl.* ~ *horn,* cor d'harmonie, *m.* *to take* ~ *leave,* filer à l'anglaise. ~ *lesson, teacher,* leçon, *f,* professeur, *m,* de français. ~ *letter P,* capote anglaise *P.* ~ *loaf,* baguette, *f.* ~*man,* ~*woman,* Français, e. ~ *polish,* vernis [à alcool], *m.* ~ *seam,* couture anglaise. ~*-speaking* (*nation*), francophone. ~*-speaking Switzerland,* la Suisse romande. ~ *window,* porte fenêtre, *f.* ¶ (*language*) *n,* le français. **the** ~, *pl,* les Français, *m.pl.* **Frenchify,** *v.t,* franciser.

frenzied, *a,* (*pers.*) effréné; (*joy &c*) frénétique, délirant. **frenzy,** *n,* frénésie, *f.*

frequency, *n,* fréquence, *f.* **frequent,** *a,* fréquent. *it's quite* ~, cela arrive souvent. ¶ *v.t,* fréquenter, hanter, courir. ~**er,** *n,* habitué, e. ~**ly,** *ad,* fréquemment.

fresco, *n,* fresque, *f.*

fresh, *a,* (*food, breeze, colour*) frais; (*further, new*) nouveau. *to make a* ~ *start,* faire un nouveau départ. ~ *water,* eau douce. *in the* ~ *air,* en plein air, au grand air. *to go out for a breath of* ~ *air.* sortir prendre le frais. (*P cheeky*) culotté *P.* ~ *from school,* frais émoulu de l'école. ~*man* (*Univ.*), bizut[h], *m.* ~**en,** *v.i,* (*wind*) fraîchir. ~ *up,* faire une petite toilette. ~**ly &** ~, *ad,* récemment, nouvellement. ~[*ly*] *cut roses,* des roses fraîches cueillies. ~**ness,** *n,* fraîcheur, *f.*

fret[1], *n,* (*guitar*) touchette, *f.*

fret[2], *v.i,* se tourmenter, se ronger les sangs. ~**ful,** *a,* agité, énervé; (*child*) grognon.

fretsaw, *n,* scie à découper, *f.* **fretwork,** *n,* découpage, *m.*

friar, *n,* moine, frère, religieux, *m.*

friction, *n,* friction, *f,* frottement, *m.*

Friday, *n,* vendredi, *m.*

friend, *n,* ami, e; camarade, *m,f;* copain *P, m,* copine *P, f.* *a* ~ *of mine,* un de mes amis. *to make* ~*s with,* se lier d'amitié avec, se faire un ami de. ~**less,** *a,* sans amis. ~**liness,** *n,* bienveillance, *f.* ~**ly,** *a,* amical, gentil; bienveillant. ~ *society,* [société] mutuelle, *f.* ~**ship,** *n,* amitié, *f.*

frieze, *n,* frise, *f.*

frigate, *n,* frégate, *f.*

fright, *n,* peur, *f,* effroi, *m.* *to take* ~, prendre peur, s'effrayer. (*P pers.*) épouvantail, *m,* horreur *P, f.* ~**en,** *v.t,* effrayer, faire peur à. *to be* ~*ed to death, out of one's wits,* mourir de peur, avoir une peur bleue. ~**ening,** *a,* effrayant. ~**ful**†, *a,* effrayant, épouvantable, affreux.

frigid†, *a,* glacial, froid. ~**ity,** *n,* frigidité, froideur, *f.*

frill, *n,* ruche, *f;* jabot, *m;* (*Cook.*) papillote, *f.* (*fig.*) *without* ~*s,* simple, sans façons.

fringe, *n,* frange, *f,* bord, *m,* bordure, *f.* (*fig.*) *on the* ~ *of,* en marge de. ¶ *v.t,* franger; border.

frippery, *n,* colifichets, *m.pl.*

frisk, *v.i,* gambader. ¶ *v.t,* (*P search*) fouiller. ~**y,** *a,* fringant, vif.

fritter[1], *n,* (*Cook.*) beignet, *m.* *apple* ~, b. aux pommes.

fritter[2] **[away],** *v.t,* gaspiller, dissiper.

frivolity, *n,* frivolité, *f.* **frivolous,** *a,* frivole, léger.

frizz, *v.t,* (*hair*) faire friser. ~**[l]y,** *a,* crépu.

frizzle, *v.i,* (*bacon*) grésiller.

frock, *n,* robe, *f;* (*monk's*) froc, *m.* ~ *coat,* redingote, *f.*

frog, *n,* grenouille, *f.* *a* ~ *in one's throat,* un chat dans la gorge. (*P pej.*) *F*~, Français, e. ~*man,* homme-grenouille, *m.*

frolic, *n,* gambades, *f.pl,* ébats, *m.pl.* ¶ *v.i,* folâtrer, batifoler. ~**some,** *a,* folâtre.

from, *pr,* (*place*) de, depuis. ~ *Paris,* de Paris. *the train* ~ *Lyon,* le train [en provenance] de Lyon. *where are you* ~*?* d'où venez-vous? (*house &c*) *2 km* ~ *the station,* à 2 km de la gare. (*time*) de, dès, à partir de, à dater de. ~ *tomorrow,* à partir de demain. *right* ~ *the start,* dès le début. (*pers.*) de, de la part de. *a letter* ~.., une lettre de [la part de]... *tell him* ~ *me,* dites-lui de ma part. (*out of*) (*drink*) ~ *a glass,* dans un verre; ~ *a stream,* à un ruisseau; (*take*) ~ *a drawer,* dans un tiroir. (*away* ~) (*after* enlever, prendre, cacher, voler *&c*) ~ *s.o,* à qn. (*cause*) ~ [*sheer*] *habit,* par habitude. ~ *what he said,* d'après ce qu'il a dit. ~ *what I see,* à ce que je vois.

frond, *n,* fronde, *f.*

front, *a,* (*garden &c*) de devant; (*wheel*) avant; (*runner*) de tête. ~ *door,* porte d'entrée, *f.* (*Mil.*) ~ *line,* front, *m.* *on the* ~ *page,* en première page, à la une *P.* ~ *room,* pièce de devant, p. donnant sur la rue. *in the* ~ *row,* au premier rang. ~ *view,* vue de face, *f.* ~*-wheel drive,* traction avant, *f.* ¶ *n,* devant, avant; (*Build.*) front, *m,* façade; (*shop*) devanture, *f;* (*sea* ~) front de mer, *m.* *in* ~, *in* ~ *of,* devant. *at the* ~ *of,* (*train &c*) en tête de. (*fig.*) *to put on a bold* ~, faire bonne contenance. *on the sea* ~, (*prom*) sur le front de mer, sur la mer. ¶ *v.i,* ~ *on,* faire face à,

donner sur. ~**al,** *a,* (*attack*) de front; (*Anat.*) frontal.
frontier, *n. & att,* frontière, *f.*
frontispiece, *n,* (*book*) frontispice, *m.*
frost, *n,* gelée, *f,* gel; (*hoar* ~) givre, *m. 5 degrees of* ~, 5 degrés au-dessous de zéro. ¶ *v.t,* (*fruit &c*) geler. ~*ed over* (*window*), givré. ~*ed glass,* verre dépoli, *m.* ~*bite,* gelure, *f.* ~*bitten,* gelé. ~**y,** *a,* glacial, de gelée.
froth, *n,* écume; mousse, *f;* (*talk*) paroles creuses, *f.pl.* ¶ *v.i,* écumer; mousser. ~**y,** *a,* écumeux, mousseux.
frown, *n,* froncement de sourcils, *m.* ¶ *v.i,* froncer les sourcils, se renfronger. ~ [*up*]*on,* désapprouver.
frowzy, *a,* sale, peu soigné; (*room*) & **frowsty,** qui sent le renfermé.
frozen, *p.p of* **freeze.** *a,* (*toes &c*) gelé, glacé; (*credit*) gelé; (*food*) *V* **freeze.**
frugal†, *a,* frugal. ~**ity,** *n,* frugalité, *f.*
fruit, *n,* (*lit., fig.*) fruit, *m. here's some* ~, voilà des fruits. *take some* ~, prenez un fruit. *att* (*basket, knife*) à fruits. ~ *dish,* compotier, *m.* ~ *farm,* exploitation fruitière. ~ *fly,* mouche du vinaigre, *f.* ~ *machine,* machine à sous, *f.* ~ *salad,* salade de f-s, *f.* ~ *tree,* arbre fruitier. ~**erer,** *n,* marchand, e, de f-s, fruitier, ère. ~**ful**†, *a,* fertile, fécond; (*fig.*) fructueux. ~**fulness,** *n,* fertilité, fécondité, *f.* ~**ion,** *n,* réalisation, *f.* ~**less,** *a,* (*fig.*) vain, stérile.
frump, *n,* femme mal fagotée.
frustrate, *v.t,* (*pers., hopes*) frustrer; (*plot*) déjouer. **frustration,** *n,* frustration, *f.*
fry[1], *n,* (*fish*) fretin, *m.* (*fig.*) *small* ~, menu f.
fry[2], *n,* friture, *f.* ¶ *v.t,* [faire] frire. *fried eggs,* œufs sur le plat, *m.pl.* ~ *potatoes,* pommes [de terre] sautées; (*chips*) [pommes] frites, *f.pl.* ¶ *v.i,* frire. ~**ing,** *n,* & ~ *oil* or *fat,* friture, *f.* ~ *pan,* poêle [à frire], *f.*
fuchsia, *n,* fuchsia, *m.*
fuck *P*, v.t. & i,* baiser *P*.* ~ *off! P*,* va te faire foutre *P*.* ~**ing** *P*, a,* putain de *P*,* bordel de *P*.*
fuddled, *a,* [em]brouillé, confus; (*tipsy*) gris.
fudge, *n,* (*Cook.*) caramel mou. ¶ *v.t,* (*fake*) truquer.
fuel, *n,* combustible; (*Mot.*) carburant, *m. to add* ~ *to the flames,* jeter de l'huile sur le feu. ¶ *v.t,* (*stove*) charger, alimenter [en combustible]; (*ship*) ravitailler en c. ~ *oil,* mazout, *m.* ~ *tank,* réservoir à carburant, *m;* (*ship*) soute à mazout, *f.*
fug *P, n, what a* ~*!* ça pue le renfermé!
fugitive, *a,* fugitif. ¶ *n,* fugitif, ive, fuyard, e.
fugue, *n,* fugue, *f.*
fulcrum, *n,* [point d']appui, *m.*
fulfil, *v.t,* accomplir, réaliser; (*condition*) remplir; (*order*) exécuter; (*desire*) satisfaire à. ~**ment,** *n,* accomplissement, *m,* exécution, *f.*
full, *a,* plein, rempli (*of,* de); (*hall &c*) comble; (*bus, hotel* &c) complet; (*text*) intégral. *2* ~ *hours,* 2 heures entières, 2 bonnes h. *a* ~ *day* (*busy*), une journée chargée. ~ *of o.s,* plein de soi. (*food*) *I'm* ~ [*up*], je n'en peux plus. *in* ~ *bloom,* en pleine fleur. (*Mil.*) ~ *dress,* grande tenue. (*fall*) ~ *length,* de tout son long. (*Naut.*) ~ *steam ahead!* en avant toute! ~ *stop,* point, *m. at* ~ *strength,* au grand complet. *to be in* ~ *swing,* battre son plein. ¶ *ad,* ~ *well,* parfaitement, fort bien. ~ *in the face,* en plein visage. ¶ *n, in* ~, complètement, en détail; (*write*) en toutes lettres. (*Sport*) ~*back,* arrière, *m.* ~*-blooded,* vigoureux. ~*-blown,* (*flower*) épanoui; (*doctor &c*) diplômé. ~*-bodied* (*wine*), qui a du corps. ~*-length* (*portrait*), en pied. ~*-scale,* (*model*) grandeur nature, *inv;* (*enquiry*) approfondi. ~*-time,* (*job*) à plein temps. **ful[l]ness,** *n,* (*voice, dress*) ampleur; (*figure*) rondeur; (*detail*) abondance, *f.* **fully,** *ad,* complètement; entièrement; (*satisfied*) pleinement.
fulminate, *v.i. & t,* fulminer.
fulsome, *a,* excessif, exagéré.
fumble, *v.i,* fouiller, tâtonner. ¶ *v.t,* manier maladroitement.
fume, *n,* ~*s,* vapeurs, fumées, *f.pl.* ¶ *v.i,* fumer, émettre des vapeurs; (*rage*) rager, être furibond.
fumigate, *v.t,* désinfecter par des fumigations.
fun, *n,* amusement, *m. to have* ~, s'amuser. *it's good* ~, c'est très amusant. *in* ~, *for* ~, pour rire, par plaisanterie, *to make* ~ *of,* se moquer de, rire de. ~ *fair,* fête foraine.
function, *n,* fonction, *f;* (*pers.*) fonction, charge, *f;* (*social*) réunion; cérémonie publique, *f.* ¶ *v.i,* fonctionner, marcher. ~**al,** *a,* fonctionnel.
fund, *n,* fonds, *m,* caisse, *f. in* ~*s,* en fonds. *to start a* ~, lancer une souscription. ¶ *v.t,* (*debt*) consolider.
fundamental†, *a,* fondamental. ¶ *n,* ~*s,* principes de base, *m.pl,* essentiel, *m.*
funeral, *n,* enterrement, *m,* (*elaborate*) funérailles, *f.pl;* convoi, *m,* pompe funèbre, *f.* ¶ *a,* funéraire; funèbre. ~ *oration,* oraison funèbre, *f.* **funereal,** *a,* funèbre; lugubre.
fungus, *n,* champignon; (*Med.*) fongus, *m.*
funicular, *a. & n,* funiculaire, *m.*
funk *P n,* (*pers.*) froussard, e *P. to be in a blue* ~, avoir la frousse *P.* ¶ *v.t, to* ~ *it,* se dégonfler *P.*
funnel, *n,* entonnoir, *m;* (*ship &c*) cheminée, *f.*
funny, *a,* amusant, drôle, comique, rigolo *P,* marrant P. *screamingly* ~, tordant *P,* à mourir de rire, désopilant *P.* (*strange*) drôle, étrange, bizarre, curieux. *a* ~ *smell,* une drôle d'odeur. *to feel* ~, se sentir tout drôle. ~ *bone,* petit juif, *m.*

fur, *n,* fourrure, *f,* poil, pelage, *m.* ~ *coat,* manteau de fourrure, *m.* (*kettle*) tartre, *m.* ¶ *v.i,* ~ *up,* (*pipes &c*) s'entartrer, s'incruster. ~*red,* entartré; (*tongue*) chargé.
furbish, *v.t,* fourbir. ~ *up,* remettre à neuf.
furious†, *a,* furieux (*with,* contre); (*wind*) déchaîné; (*battle*) acharné; (*speed*) fou.
furl, *v.t,* serrer, ferler.
furlong, *n,* furlong, *m.* = $\frac{1}{8}$ mile, 201.17 m.
furlough, *n,* congé, *m;* (*Mil.*) permission, *f.*
furnace, *n,* four; fourneau, *m;* (*fig., room*) fournaise, *f.*
furnish, *v.t,* (*supply*) fournir, donner. *to* ~ *s.o with sth,* pourvoir qn de qch. (*house*) meubler. ~*ed flat,* appartement meublé. *in* ~*ed rooms,* en meublé. ~**ing,** *n,* ~*s,* ameublement, mobilier, *m.* ~ *fabrics,* tissus d'ameublement, *m.pl.* **furniture,** *n,* meubles, *m.pl;* ameublement, mobilier, *m. a piece of* ~, un meuble. ~ *polish,* encaustique, *f.* ~ *remover,* déménageur, *m.* ~ *van,* camion de déménagement, *m.* ~ *warehouse,* garde-meuble, *m.*
furore, *n,* débordement d'enthousiasme, *m;* (*uproar*) tempête de protestations, *f.*
furrier, *n,* fourreur, pelletier, *m.*
furrow, *n,* (*Agr.*) sillon, *m.* ¶ *v.t,* sillonner; (*brow*) rider.
furry, *a,* (*animal*) à poil; (*toy*) en peluche.
further, *a,* supplémentaire, nouveau. *2*~*points,* encore 2 points. *without* ~ *ado,* sans plus de cérémonie. *also* = **farther.** ¶ *ad,* davantage, plus. *without searching* ~, sans chercher davantage, sans plus chercher. *also* = **farther** & ~**more.** ¶ *v.t,* avancer, favoriser. ~**ance,** *n,* avancement, *m.* ~**more,** *ad,* de plus, en outre, par ailleurs. **furthest** = **farthest.**
furtive†, *a,* (*look*) furtif; (*pers.*) sournois.
fury, *n,* (*pers.*) furie, fureur; (*storm*) fureur, violence, *f;* (*battle*) acharnement, *m.* (*Myth.*) *the Furies,* les Furies, *f.pl. to work like* ~, travailler comme un fou.
furze, *n,* ajoncs, *m.pl.*
fuse, *n,* (*bomb, shell*) fusée, amorce, *f;* (*Min.*) cordeau; (*Elec.*) plomb, fusible, *m. to blow a* ~, faire sauter un p., un f. ¶ *v.t. & i,* (*metals*) fondre; (*Elec: lights &c*) faire sauter les plombs.
fuselage, *n,* fuselage, *m.*
fusillade, *n,* fusillade, *f.*
fusion, *n,* fusion, *f.*
fuss, *n,* bruit, tapage, *m;* histoires, *f.pl. what a* ~*!* que d'histoires! *to make a* ~, faire un tas d'histoires (*about,* pour). *without* ~, sans façons. *to make a* ~ *of s.o,* être aux petits soins pour qn. ¶ *v.t,* tracasser. ¶ *v.i,* s'agiter; (*fret*) se tracasser. ~ *around,* faire l'affairé. ~**y,** *a,* (*pers.*) tatillon; (*over food*) difficile; (*ornate*) tarabiscoté. *I'm not* ~ *P,* ça m'est égal.
fusty, *a,* qui sent le renfermé; moisi.
futile, *a,* futile, vain. **futility,** *n,* futilité, *f.*
future, *a,* futur; à venir; (*Com: delivery*) à terme. ¶ *n,* avenir, *m. in* [*the*] ~, à l'avenir. *in the near* ~, dans un proche avenir. *there's no* ~ *in it,* cela n'a aucun avenir. (*Gram.*) futur, *m. in the* ~, au f. ~ *perfect,* f. antérieur. **futuristic,** *a,* futuriste.
fuzz *P, n, the* ~, les flics *P.*
fuzzy, *a,* (*hair*) crépu; (*image*) flou.

G

G (*Mus.*) *letter,* sol, *m.* ~ *clef,* clef de sol, *f.* ~ *string,* corde de sol, *f;* (*Dress*) cache-sexe, *m.*
gabardine, *n,* gabardine, *f.*
gabble, *v.i,* bredouiller, bafouiller. ¶ *v.t,* (*speech*) baragouiner *P,* débiter à toute vitesse.
gable, *n,* pignon, *m.*
gad about, *v.i,* courir (la ville &c), vadrouiller *P.*
gad-fly, *n,* taon, *m.*
gadget, *n,* gadget; (*thingummy*) truc *P,* machin *P, m.*
gaff, *n,* (*spear*) gaffe; (*spar*) corne, *f.*
gaffer *P, n,* vieux bonhomme; (*Ind.*) patron; contremaître, *m.*
gag, *n,* bâillon, *m;* (*joke*) plaisanterie, blague, *f.* ¶ *v.t,* (*lit., fig.*) bâillonner.
gaga *P, a,* (*senile*) gaga *P,* gâteux.
gage = **gauge.**
gaiety, *n,* gaieté, *f.* **gaily,** *ad,* gaiement. ~ *coloured,* aux couleurs vives.
gain, *n,* (*Fin.*) gain, bénéfice, *m;* (*increase*) augmentation, *f;* (*fig.*) avantage, *m.* ¶ *v.t,* gagner, acquérir; (*reach*) atteindre; (*weight, speed*) prendre. (*watch*) *to* ~ *3 minutes,* prendre 3 m. d'avance. ¶ *v.i,* gagner (*in,* en; *by doing,* à faire) ~ *on,* (*runner ahead*) rattraper; (*r. behind*) prendre de l'avance sur.
gainsay, *v.t,* contredire, démentir, nier.
gait, *n,* démarche, *f,* pas, *m.*
gaiter, *n,* guêtre, *f.*
gala, *n,* gala, *m,* fête, *f.* (*att day, dress*) de gala.
galaxy, *n,* galaxie, *f.*

gale, *n,* grand vent, coup de vent, *m. it's blowing a ~,* le vent souffle très fort. *~ warning,* avis de coup de vent, *m.*
gall[1], *n,* (*Med.*) bile, *f;* (*fig.*) fiel, *m;* (*P cheek*) culot *P. ~bladder,* vésicule biliaire, *f. ~stone,* calcul biliaire, *m.*
gall[2], *v.t,* (*pers.*) contrarier, humilier. **~ing,** *a,* humiliant.
gallant ['gælənt], *a,* vaillant, brave; [gə'lænt] (*attentive to women*) galant. **~ly,** *ad,* vaillamment; galamment. **~ry,** *n,* courage, *m,* vaillance; galanterie, *f.*
galleon (*Hist.*) *n,* galion, *m.*
gallery, *n,* galerie; (*public, press*) tribune, *f;* (*Theat.*) troisièmes galeries, poulailler *P,* paradis *P, m;* (*art*) galerie, musée, *m.*
galley, *n,* (*boat*) galère; (*cook's*) cuisine. *~ slave,* galérien, *m.* (*Typ.*) galée, *f. ~ [proof],* épreuve en placard, *f,* placard, *m.*
Gallic, *a,* gaulois; français; (*charm*) latin. **gallicism,** *n,* gallicisme, *m.*
gallivant, *v.i, ~ [around],* courir, courir la prétentaine.
gallon, *n,* gallon, *m.* (*UK*=4.546 litres; *Am* = 3.785 l.).
gallop, *n,* galop, *m. at full ~,* au grand galop. ¶ *v.i,* galoper. *to ~ away, back &c,* partir, revenir &c au galop. *~ing consumption,* phtisie galopante, *f.*
gallows, *n,* potence, *f,* gibet, *m. ~-bird,* gibier de potence, *m.*
galore, *ad,* en abondance, à gogo *P.*
galoshes, *n.pl,* caoutchoucs, *m.pl.*
galvanize, *v.t,* (*Elec., fig.*) galvaniser. *~d iron,* tôle galvanisée. **galvanometer,** *n,* galvanomètre, *m.*
Gambia, *n,* la Gambie.
gambit, *n,* (*Chess*) gambit, *m;* (*fig.*) manœuvre, *f.*
gamble, *n,* jeu de hasard, *m,* entreprise risquée. ¶ *v.i,* jouer. *~ away,* perdre au jeu. (*fig.*) *~ on,* miser sur. **gambler,** *n,* joueur, euse. **gambling,** *n,* jeu[x], *m.[pl.]. ~ den,* tripot, *m.*
gambol, *n,* gambade, *f.* ¶ *v.i,* gambader.
game, *n,* (*gen.*) jeu, *m. card ~,* jeu de cartes. *~ of skill,* jeu d'adresse. (*of Ten., cards, chess*) partie, *f;* (*Foot. &c*) match, *m. to have, play a ~ of,* faire une partie de, jouer un match de. (*score*) (*Ten.*) jeu; (*Bridge*) manche, *f. one ~ all,* un jeu (une manche) partout. (*Sch.*) *~s,* sport, plein air, *m. good at ~s,* sportif. *he's off his ~,* il n'est pas en forme. (*scheme*) plan, petit jeu, *m,* combinaison, *f. to spoil s.o's ~,* déjouer les plans de qn. *the ~ is not worth the candle,* le jeu ne vaut pas la chandelle. (*Hunt.*) gibier, *m. big ~,* gros gibier. ¶ *a,* courageux. *~ for,* de taille à. *~ for anything,* prêt à tout. *~ birds,* gibier à plume. *~keeper,* garde-chasse, *m. ~ licence,* permis de chasse, *m. ~s master, mistress,* professeur d'éducation physique, *m,f.* **gaming,** *n,* jeu, *m. ~ house,* maison de j., *f. ~ table,* table de j., *f.*
gammon, *n,* jambon fumé, *m.*
gamut, *n,* gamme, *f.*
gamy, *a,* (*Cook.*) faisandé.
gander, *n,* jars, *m.*
gang, *n,* (*workmen*) équipe; (*crooks*) bande, *f,* gang, *m;* (*boys*) bande; (*convicts*) convoi, *m. ~ saw,* scie multiple, *f.* ¶ *v.i, ~ up, ~ together,* se mettre à plusieurs.
Ganges (the), le Gange.
gangling, *a,* dégingandé.
ganglion, *n,* ganglion, *m.*
gangrene, *n,* gangrène, *f.* **gangrenous,** *a,* gangreneux. *to go ~,* se gangrener.
gangster, *n,* gangster, bandit, *m.*
gangway, *n,* passage; (*bus*) couloir, *m;* (*Theat.*) allée; (*Naut.*) & **gangplank,** passerelle, *f.*
gannet, *n,* fou [de Bassan] *m.*
gantry, *n,* portique; (*for cask*) chantier, *m;* (*Space*) tour de lancement, *f.*
gaol, gaoler, = **jail, jailer.**
gap, *n,* (*in hedge, wall*) trou, *m,* ouverture, *f;* (*between curtains, planks*) interstice; (*spark plug*) écartement, *m;* (*Geog.*) trouée, *f;* (*fig.*) vide; (*in time*) intervalle, *m;* (*in knowledge*) lacune, *f.* (*Com.*) *trade ~,* déficit commercial, d. extérieur, *m. a ~ in one's memory,* un trou de mémoire. *to fill a ~,* combler un vide, boucher un trou.
gape, *v.i,* bâiller. *to stand gaping,* rester bouche bée (*at,* devant); bayer aux corneilles. *to ~ at sth, s.o,* regarder qch, qn bouche bée. **gaping,** *a,* (*hole &c*) béant; (*seam*) qui bâille.
garage, *n,* garage, *m. ~ mechanic,* mécanicien, *m. ~ proprietor,* garagiste, *m.* ¶ *v.t,* mettre au garage.
garb, *n,* costume, *m.*
garbage, *n,* ordures, *f.pl;* (*kitchen*) déchets, *m.pl. ~ can,* poubelle, *f. ~-collector,* éboueur, *m.*
garbled, *a,* (*muddled*) embrouillé; (*distorted*) dénaturé.
garden, *n,* jardin; (*small*) jardinet, *m. ~s,* parc, jardin public, *m. to lead s.o up the ~ path,* mener qn en bateau. *~ centre,* pépinière, *f. ~ city,* cité-jardin, *f. ~ hose,* tuyau d'arrosage, *m. the G~ of Eden,* le jardin d'Eden. *~ party,* garden-party, *f. ~ produce,* produits maraîchers. *~ tools,* outils de jardinage, *m.pl.* ¶ *v.i,* jardiner. **~er,** *n,* jardinier, ère. **~ing,** *n,* jardinage, *m.*
gardenia, *n,* gardénia, *m.*
gargle, *n,* gargarisme, *m.* ¶ *v.i,* se gargariser.
gargoyle, *n,* gargouille, *f.*
garish, *a,* voyant, tapageur, criard.
garland, *n,* guirlande, *f.*
garlic, *n,* ail, *m.*
garment, *n,* vêtement, *m.*
garnet, *n,* grenat, *m.*

garnish, *n,* garniture, *f.* ¶ *v.t,* garnir (*with,* de).
garret, *n,* mansarde, *f,* grenier, *m.*
garrison, *n,* garnison, *f.* ¶ *v.t,* (*town*) mettre une garnison dans. *to be ~ed at,* être en g. à.
garrulous, *a,* bavard, loquace.
garter, *n,* jarretière, *f.*
gas, *n,* gaz, *m;* (*Med.*) [gaz] anesthésique, *m. tear ~,* g. lacrymogène. *by ~,* (*cook, heat &c*) au gaz. (*Am gasoline*) essence, *f. to step on the ~ P,* mettre les gaz *P.* *~bag P,* moulin à paroles, *m.* *~ bracket,* applique à g., *f.* *~ burner, jet,* brûleur à g., *m.* *~ cooker, stove,* cuisinière à g., *f.* *~ fire,* radiateur à g., *m.* *~-fired,* chauffé au g. *~ fitter,* ajusteur-gazier, *m.* *~light,* lumière du g., *f.* *~ lighter,* (*cooker*) allume-gaz, *m;* (*cigarettes*) briquet à g. *~ main,* canalisation de g., *f.* *~ man,* employé du gaz, *m.* *~ mask,* masque à g., *m.* *~ meter,* compteur à gaz, *m.* *~ pipe,* tuyau à g., *m.* *~ ring,* réchaud à gaz, *m.* *~ worker,* gazier, *m.* *~ works,* usine à gaz, *f.* ¶ *v.t,* asphyxier; (*War*) gazer. **~eous & ~sy,** *a,* gazeux.
gash, *n,* balafre, estafilade, *f.* ¶ *v.t,* balafrer.
gasket, *n,* (*Mot.*) *cylinder head ~,* joint de culasse, *m.*
gasp, *n,* halètement, *m. to be at one's last ~,* être à l'agonie. ¶ *v.i,* (*for breath*) haleter. (*news &c*) *it made him ~,* il en a eu le souffle coupé.
gastric, *a,* gastrique; (*flu*) gastro-intestinal. *~ ulcer,* ulcère de l'estomac, *m.* **gastritis,** *n,* gastrite, *f.* **gastronome,** *n,* gastronome, *m,f.* **gastronomic,** *a,* gastronomique. **gastronomy,** *n,* gastronomie, *f.*
gate, *n,* (*town*) porte; (*field*) barrière; (*garden*) porte, (*iron*) grille; (*sluice*) vanne, *f;* (*Sport*) les spectateurs, *m.pl.* *~crash P,* s'introduire sans invitation *ou* sans payer. *~crasher P,* (*uninvited*) intrus, e; (*non-paying*) resquilleur, euse *P.* *~ keeper,* portier, ère; (*level crossing*) garde-barrière, *m,f.* *~ money,* recette, *f.* *~ way,* porte, *f.*
gather, *n,* (*Need.*) fronce, *f.* ¶ *v.t,* (*& ~ together*) (*people, things*) rassembler, (*people*) réunir; (*collect, pick*) (*& ~ up*) (*flowers*) cueillir, (*wood, dust, papers*) ramasser. *to ~ speed,* prendre de la vitesse. *to ~ one's strength,* rassembler ses forces. (*Need.*) froncer; (*infer*) déduire, comprendre, croire comprendre (*from,* d'après). ¶ *v.i,* (*people*) se rassembler, se réunir; (*crowd, clouds*) se former; (*dust &c*) s'amonceler, s'amasser; (*storm*) se préparer. **~ing,** *n,* rassemblement, *m;* réunion; accumulation, *f.*
gauche, *a,* gauche, maladroit.
gaudy, *a,* voyant, criard; tapageur.
gauge, *n,* (*Meas: wire &c*) calibre; (*Rly*) écartement, *m;* (*instrument*) jauge, *f;* (*Mot: temperature &c*) indicateur, *m. petrol, oil ~,* jauge d'essence, du niveau d'huile. *pressure ~,* manomètre. *rain ~,* pluviomètre, *m.*
gaunt, *a,* décharné, émacié.
gauntlet, *n,* gant [à crispin] *m.*
gauze, *n,* gaze, *f.* **gauzy,** *a,* vaporeux.
gavel, *n,* marteau, *m.*
gavotte, *n,* gavotte, *f.*
gawky, *a,* maladroit, godiche *P.*
gay, *a,* gai, joyeux; (*colours*) gai, vif. *~ dog,* gai luron, *m. to lead a ~ life,* mener une vie de plaisirs. (*P*) homosexuel.
gaze, *n,* regard [fixe], *m.* ¶ *v.i,* regarder. *~ at,* regarder [fixement], contempler.
gazelle, *n,* gazelle, *f.*
gazette, *n,* gazette, *f;* [journal] officiel, *m.*
gazetteer, *n,* dictionnaire géographique, *m.*
gear, *n,* (*camping, Phot. &c*) matériel, équipement, *m. my ~,* mes affaires, *f.pl,* mes bagages, *m.pl.* (*clothes*) vêtements, *m.pl,* tenue, *f;* fringues *P, f.pl;* (*Tech. & ~ing*) engrenage, *m;* (*Mot.*) vitesse, *f. in ~,* en prise. *top ~,* quatrième (cinquième) vitesse. *to change into second ~,* passer en deuxième. *~box,* boîte de vitesses, *f.* *~ lever,* levier de vitesse, *m.* *~ ratio,* multiplication, *f.* *~ wheel,* roue d'engrenage, *f;* (*cycle*) pignon, *m.* ¶ *v.t,* (*fig., to a need*) adapter.
gee-gee, *n,* dada, *m.* **gee up,** *i,* hue!
Geiger counter, *n,* compteur Geiger, *m.*
gelatin[e], *n,* gélatine, *f.* **gelatinous,** *a,* gélatineux.
geld, *v.t,* (*pig*) châtrer; (*horse*) hongrer. **~ing,** *n,* castration, *f;* [cheval] hongre, *m.*
gem, *n,* pierre précieuse, gemme, *f;* (*fig.*) bijou, trésor, *m,* merveille, *f.*
gen *P, n,* coordonnées *P, f.pl,* tuyaux *P, m.pl.* ¶ *v.t, ~ s.o up P,* mettre qn au parfum *P.*
gender, *n,* genre, *m.*
genealogical, *a,* généalogique. **genealogy,** *n,* généalogie, *f.*
general, *a,* général; (*overall: view, impression*) d'ensemble; (*widespread: opinion, criticism*) commun, répandu. *as a ~ rule,* en règle générale. *in ~ use,* d'usage commun. *~ education,* culture g-e. *~ election.* élections législatives. *~ knowledge,* connaissances g-es. *~ manager,* directeur g. (*Med.*) *~ practice,* médecine g-e. *~ practitioner,* [médecin] généraliste, *m. the ~ public,* le grand public. *the ~ reader,* le lecteur moyen. *~ servant,* bonne à tout faire, *f.* *~ staff,* état-major, *m.* *~ store,* grand magasin. ¶ *n,* (*Mil.*) général, *m. in ~,* en général. **~ity,** *n,* généralité, *f.* **~ize,** *v.t. & i,* généraliser. **~ly,** *ad,* généralement; en général. **~-purpose,** *a,* (*tool &c*) universel.
generate, *v.t,* engendrer; (*heat &c*) produire. *generating station,* centrale électrique, *f.* **generation,** *n,* génération, *f. the younger ~,* la jeune g. *the ~ gap,* le conflit des g-s. **gen-**

erator, *n,* (*Elec.*) génératrice, *f;* (*steam*) générateur; (*lighting*) dynamo, *m.*
generic, *a,* générique.
generosity, *n,* générosité, *f.* **generous†,** *a,* généreux; (*supply, helping*) abondant, copieux.
genesis, *n,* genèse, *f.* **G~** (*Bible*), la Genèse.
genetic, *a,* génétique. ¶ *n,* *~s,* génétique, *f.*
Geneva, *n,* Genève, *f. Lake of G~,* le lac Léman.
genial, *a,* (*pers.*) cordial; (*smile &c*) chaleureux. **~ity,** *n,* cordialité, *f.*
genitals, *n.pl,* organes génitaux, *m.pl.*
genitive [case], *n,* génitif, *m.*
genius, *n,* génie, *m. invention of ~,* invention géniale, *f. to have a ~ for,* avoir le génie de.
Genoa, *n,* Gênes, *f.* **Genoese,** *a,* génois.
genocide, *n,* génocide, *m.*
gent, *n,* (*abb of gentleman*) monsieur, *m;* (*Com.*) homme. *P the ~s,* toilettes [pour hommes], *f.pl.*
genteel, *a,* maniéré; qui affecte la distinction.
gentian, *n,* gentiane, *f.*
Gentile, *n,* Gentil, e. ¶ *a,* des Gentils.
gentle, *a,* (*pers., slope, voice*) doux; (*rebuke*) léger, peu sévère; (*heat*) modéré; (*breeze, touch*) léger. *~woman* (*court*), dame d'honneur, *f.* **~ness,** *n,* douceur, *f.* **gently,** *ad,* doucement, bellement; (*remind &c*) gentiment. *deal ~ with s.o,* ménager qn. **gentry,** *n,* petite noblesse, *f.*
gentleman, *n,* (*man*) monsieur; (*courteous*) homme bien élevé, gentleman, *m. a perfect ~,* un vrai gentleman. (*at court*) gentilhomme. *~'s ~,* valet de chambre, *m.* **~ly,** *a,* courtois, bien élevé.
genuflexion, *n,* génuflexion, *f.*
genuine, *a,* authentique, véritable, vrai. *that's the ~ article,* ça c'est du vrai. (*pers., belief*) sincère. **~ly,** *ad,* authentiquement; sincèrement.
genus, *n,* genre, *m.*
geographer, *n,* géographe, *m,f.* **geographic(al)†,** *a,* géographique. **geography,** *n,* géographie, *f.* **geological,** *a,* géologique. **geologist,** *n,* géologue, *m,f.* **geology,** *n,* géologie, *f.* **geometric(al)†,** *a,* géométrique. **geometry,** *n,* géométrie, *f.*
Georgia, *n,* (*USA, USSR*) la Géorgie.
geranium, *n,* géranium, *m.*
germ, *n,* (*Biol., fig.*) germe; (*Med.*) microbe, *m. ~ warfare,* guerre bactériologique, *f.*
German, *a,* allemand. *East-, West-~,* est-, ouest-allemand. *~ measles,* rubéole, *f. ~ shepherd* (*dog*), berger allemand. ¶ *n,* (*pers.*) Allemand, e; (*language*) l'allemand, *m.* **Germanic,** *a,* germanique. **Germany,** *n,* l'Allemagne, *f. East, West ~,* l'A. de l'Est, de l'Ouest.
germane to, se rapportant à.
germinate, *v.i,* germer. **germination,** *n,* germination, *f.*
gerund, *n,* gérondif, *m.*
gestation, *n,* gestation, *f.*
gesticulate, *v.i,* gesticuler.
gesture, *n,* geste, *m. with a ~,* d'un geste. ¶ *v.i,* faire des gestes; faire signe (à qn).
get, *v.t,* (*book, coat &c*) obtenir, trouver, acheter; (*Sch: mark*) avoir, obtenir; (*letter, shock*) recevoir; (*wages, salary*) gagner, toucher; (*disease, prison sentence*) attraper. (*have*) *what have you got?* qu'est-ce que tu as? (*fetch*) (*s.o*) faire venir, (*s.o, sth*) aller chercher. (*cause*) *to ~ the car mended,* faire réparer la voiture. *to ~ going,* (*car, clock*) mettre en marche. (*take, send*) (*s.o home*) ramener, (*s.o to hospital*) transporter, (*goods*) faire parvenir, transporter. *to ~ sth through the customs,* passer qch à la douane. (*understand*) comprendre, saisir. *do you ~ me? P,* tu y es? tu saisis? *I don't ~ it P,* je n'y suis pas du tout. ¶ *v.i,* (*grow, become*) devenir. *~ fat, thin,* grossir, maigrir. *to ~ dressed,* s'habiller. *to ~ caught,* se faire attraper. *it's ~ting late,* il se fait tard. *~ lost! P**, fous-moi le camp! *P**. (*reach, arrive*) aller, arriver, parvenir. *you can ~ there by bus,* on peut y aller en autobus. *when do we ~ to Rome?* à quelle heure arrivons-nous à R.? (*fig.*) *we're ~ting nowhere,* nous n'arrivons à rien. (*obligation*) *you've got to do it,* il faut absolument que tu le fasses. *you haven't got to answer,* vous n'êtes pas obligé de répondre. (*start*) *~ going,* commencer; s'y mettre; se mettre en marche, se m. en route. *to ~ cracking P,* se mettre au boulot *P.* ~ **about,** (*pers.*) se déplacer. ~ **across,** (*sth to s.o*) faire comprendre qch à qn; (*offend*) se faire mal voir de qn. ~ **at,** (*reach*) atteindre, parvenir à. (*fig.*) *what are you ~ting at?* où voulez-vous en venir? (*nag*) *she's always ~ting at him,* elle est toujours après lui. ~ **away,** partir; (*thief*) s'échapper. ~ **back,** *v.i,* revenir, rentrer. ¶ *v.t,* retrouver, recouvrer; (*sth lent*) se faire rendre. *to ~ one's own back,* prendre sa revanche. *to ~ one's money back,* se faire rembourser. ~ **by,** se débrouiller. ~ **down,** *v.i. & t,* descendre; *v.t,* décrocher; (*depress*) déprimer. ~ **in,** *v.i,* entrer, (*car &c*) monter, (*~ home*) rentrer. ¶ *v.t,* (*harvest, washing*) rentrer; (*coal &c*) acheter; (*police*) faire venir. *to ~ in supplies,* faire des provisions. ~ **into,** entrer dans, (*car &c*) monter dans; (*habit*) prendre. ~ **off,** *v.i,* (*bus &c*) descendre; (*leave*) partir, (*plane*) décoller. *tell s.o where to ~ off,* envoyer promener qn. *~ off to a good start,* prendre un bon départ. *~ off lightly* (*with a fine*), s'en tirer à bon compte (avec une amende). ~ **on,** (*bus &c*) monter; (*studies*) faire des progrès, avancer. *did you ~ on well?* ça s'est bien passé? ça a bien

marché? ~ **on with,** (*work*) continuer; (*s.o*) s'entendre avec. ~ **out,** *v.t,* (*sth from drawer*) prendre qch dans le tiroir, sortir qch du t.; (*stain*) enlever. ¶ *v.i,* (*bus &c*) descendre. ~ **out of,** (*habit*) perdre; (*trouble*) se tirer (d'affaire); (*duty*) se soustraire à. ~ **over,** (*river &c*) traverser, franchir; (*wall*) escalader; (*difficulties*) surmonter; (*illness, loss*) se remettre de; (*ideas &c to s.o*) faire comprendre à qn. *to ~ sth over,* en finir avec qch. ~ **round,** (*difficulty, rule*) contourner; (*pers.*) entortiller. ~ **through,** *v.t. & i,* (*hedge*) passer à travers; (*window*) passer par; (*Mil: lines*) percer; (*work*) terminer; (*food &c*) consommer; (*in exam*) être reçu. *to ~ through to s.o,* (*Tel.*) avoir qn, obtenir une communication avec qn; (*fig.*) se faire comprendre de qn. ~ **together,** *v.t.* (*& i*) (se) rassembler, (se) réunir. ~ **up,** *v.i,* se lever. ¶ *v.t,* (*fête*) organiser. **getaway,** *n,* (*thief*) fuite, *f. to make a ~,* filer. **getup,** *n,* mise, tenue, *f.*

geyser, *n,* (*spring*) geyser; chauffe-bain, *m.*

ghastly, *a,* horrible, affreux; (*pale*) blême, livide.

Ghent, *n,* Gand, *m.*

gherkin, *n,* cornichon, *m.*

ghetto, *n,* ghetto, *m.*

ghost, *n,* fantôme, spectre, revenant, *m.* (*fig.*) *the ~ of a smile,* une ombre de sourire. *not the ~ of a chance,* pas la moindre chance. ~ *story,* histoire de revenants, *f.* ~ *town,* ville morte. ~ *writer,* nègre, *m.* ~**ly,** *a,* spectral, fantomatique.

ghoul, *n,* goule, *f.* ~**ish,** *a,* macabre.

giant, *a,* géant; (*stride*) de géant; (*helping*) gigantesque. ¶ *n,* géant, *m.*

gibber, *v.i,* baragouiner; (*with rage*) bafouiller. ~**ish,** *n,* baragouin, charabia *P, m.*

gibbet, *n,* gibet, *m,* potence, *f.*

gibe, *n,* raillerie, *f.* ¶ *v.i,* ~ *at s.o,* railler qn.

giblets, *n.pl,* abattis [de volaille], *m.pl.*

giddiness, *n,* vertige, *m. a bout of ~,* un v. **giddy,** *a,* (*pers.*) pris de vertige; (*flighty*) écervelé; (*height*) vertigineux. *to make s.o ~,* donner le vertige à qn.

gift, *n,* cadeau, *m;* (*Com.*) prime; (*Law*) donation, *f,* don, *m. to make a ~ of sth,* faire cadeau *ou* don de qch. (*shop*) *is it for a ~?* c'est pour offrir? *it's a ~ P* (*easy*), c'est du gâteau *P.* (*talent*) don. *to have a ~ for sth,* avoir le don de qch. *to have the ~ of the gab,* avoir du bagou *P.* ~**ed,** *a,* doué.

gig *P, n,* (*Mus.*) gig, *f.*

gigantic, *a,* gigantesque, géant.

giggle, *v.i,* rire bêtement. *to have the ~s,* avoir le fou rire.

gild, *v.t.ir,* dorer. ~**ing,** *n,* dorure, *f.*

gill, *n,* (*Meas.*) = $\frac{1}{4}$ pint or 0.142 litre.

gills, *n.pl,* (*fish*) ouïes, branchies, *f.pl.*

gilt, *n,* dorure, *f.* ¶ *a,* doré. ~*-edged,* (*book*) doré sur tranche; (*security*) de premier ordre.

gimbals, *n.pl,* (*Naut.*) cardan, *m.*

gimcrack, *a,* de camelote, de pacotille.

gimlet, *n,* vrille, *f.*

gin, *n,* gin, *m.*

ginger, *n,* gingembre, *m. G~* (*nickname*), Poil de Carotte. ¶ *a,* (*hair*) roux, ronquin *P.* ~*bread,* pain d'épice, *m.*

gingham (*fabric*) *n,* vichy, *m.*

gipsy, *n,* bohémien, ne, gitane, *f,* tzigane, *m,f.*

giraffe, *n,* girafe, *f. baby ~,* girafeau, *m.*

gird, *v.t.ir,* ceindre. ~**er,** *n,* poutre, *f.* ~**le,** *n,* ceinture; (*corset*) gaine, *f.* ¶ *v.t,* ceindre.

girl, *n,* jeune fille, *f. little ~,* petite f., fillette, *f. English ~,* jeune Anglaise. *~s' school,* école (*f*), lycée de filles, *m.* ~*friend,* (*boy*) petite amie; (*girl*) amie, copine, *f.* ~ *guide,* éclaireuse, guide, *f.* ~**hood,** *n,* enfance, jeunesse, *f.* ~**ish,** *a,* de jeune fille.

giro, *n, National G~,* ≏ Comptes Chèques Postaux, *m.pl.*

girth, *n,* (*saddle*) sangle; (*waist*) tour de taille, *m;* (*tree*) circonférence, *f.*

gist, *n,* essentiel, fond, *m.*

give, *v.t,* donner; (*gift*) faire cadeau de, offrir; (*meal*) offrir; (*help, support*) prêter; (*permission*) accorder; (*details*) fournir; (*answer*) faire, donner; (*one's time, life*) consacrer; (*a cold*) passer, donner; (*cry, sigh*) pousser. (*pay*) *what did he ~ for it?* combien l'a-t-il payé? ~ *s.o sth to eat, drink,* donner à manger, à boire à qn. ~ *s.o a piece of one's mind,* dire son fait à qn. *they gave him 5 years,* on l'a condamné à 5 ans de prison. *to ~ as good as one gets,* rendre coup pour coup. (*Tel.*) ~ *me Eye 604,* passez-moi le 604 à Eye. ~ *her my love,* faites-lui mes amitiés. *he doesn't ~ a damn P,* il s'en fiche pas mal *P. to ~ way,* (*pers.*) céder (à qn, à qch); (*legs*) se dérober, fléchir; (*ice, floor*) céder, s'affaisser. (*Mot.*) *'~ way',* 'cédez la priorité'. ¶ *v.i,* (*legs, ice &c*) = ~ *way.* ~ **away,** faire cadeau de; (*prizes*) distribuer; (*secret*) révéler; (*pers., o.s*) trahir. *to ~ the game away,* vendre la mèche. ~ **back,** rendre. ~ **in,** (*to s.o*) céder; (*yield*) se rendre; renoncer. ~ **off,** (*smell &c*) émettre, dégager. ~ **out,** *v.i,* (*supplies*) s'épuiser, manquer. ¶ *v.t,* (*food*) distribuer; (*news*) annoncer. ~ **up,** *v.i,* abandonner, renoncer. ¶ *v.t,* (*friend*) abandonner; (*habit &c*) renoncer (à qch, à faire), laisser tomber; (*seat*) céder; (*time &c*) consacrer. *to ~ o.s up to sth,* se livrer à qch. *I ~ up!* je renonce! ~**-&-take,** *n,* concessions mutuelles, *f.pl.* **given to,** adonné à; enclin à. **giver,** *n,* donneur, euse. ~**-away,** *n,* révélation involontaire, *f.*

gizzard, *n,* gésier, *m.*

glacial, *a,* (*wind &c*) glacial; (*Geol.*) glaciaire. **glacier,** *n,* glacier, *m.*

glad, *a,* content; heureux (*about,* de; *to do,* de faire). *I'm ~ about it,* cela me fait plaisir.

~**den,** *v.t,* réjouir, rendre heureux. ~**ly,** *ad,* volontiers, avec plaisir. ~**ness,** *n,* joie, *f.*
glade, *n,* clairière, *f.*
gladiolus, *n,* glaïeul, *m.*
glamorous, *a,* (*pers.*) séduisant; (*job*) prestigieux; (*life*) brillant. **glamour,** *n,* (*pers.*) séduction(s), *f* (*pl*); (*job*) prestige, *m. to lend ~ to sth,* prêter éclat à qch. ~ *girl P,* pin-up *P,f.*
glance, *n,* coup d'œil, regard, *m.* ¶ *v.i,* ~ *at,* jeter un coup d'œil sur. ~ *through,* (*letter, book*) parcourir. ~ *off,* ricocher; dévier (sur qch). **glancing,** *a,* (*blow*) oblique.
gland, *n,* glande, *f.* ~**ular,** *a,* glandulaire.
glare, *n,* éclat; éblouissement; regard furieux, *m.* ¶ *v.i,* éblouir. ~ *at* (*pers.*), lancer un regard furieux à. **glaring,** *a,* éclatant, eblouissant; (*colour*) criard; (*mistake*) grossier; (*lie &c*) flagrant; (*eyes*) furibond.
glass, *n,* verre, *m. cut ~,* cristal taillé. *plate ~,* verre double. *pane of ~,* carreau, *m,* vitre, *f. wine ~,* verre à vin. ~ *of wine,* v. de vin. *beer ~,* bock, *m.* (*mirror*) miroir, *m,* glace, *f. magnifying ~,* loupe, *f. grown under ~,* cultivé sous verre. (*Met.*) *the ~ is falling,* le baromètre baisse. ~*es,* lunettes, (*field ~es*) jumelles, *f.pl.* ¶ *a,* en verre, (*eye, fibre*) de v., (*door*) vitré. ~ *case,* vitrine, *f.* ~ *cloth,* essuie-verres, *m.* ~ *cutter,* diamant, coupe-verre, *m.* ~ *house,* serre, *f.* (*Mil. P*) *in the ~house,* au trou *P.* ~ *maker,* verrier, *m.* ~ *making,* ~*ware,* ~*works,* verrerie, *f.* ~**y,** *a,* vitreux.
glaucous, *a,* glauque.
glaze, *n,* (*pottery*) vernis, *m.* ¶ *v.t,* (*pottery*) vernisser; (*window*) vitrer; (*picture*) mettre sous verre. ~**d,** *a,* (*look*) vitreux. **glazing,** *n,* vitrage, *m. double ~,* double-fenêtres, *f.pl.* **glazier,** *n,* vitrier, *m.*
gleam, *n,* lueur, *f,* rayon, *m;* (*metal*) reflet, *m.* ~ *of hope,* lueur d'espoir. ¶ *v.i,* (*star*) luire; (*shoes*) reluire; (*water*) miroiter. ~**ing,** *a,* brillant.
glean, *v.t,* (*lit., fig.*) glaner. ~**er,** *n,* glaneur, euse.
glee, *n,* joie, gaieté; (*Mus.*) chanson à plusieurs voix, *f.* ~**ful,** *a,* joyeux.
glen, *n,* vallon, *m.*
glib, *a,* (*answer*) spécieux, désinvolte; (*tongue*) délié. (*pers.*) *to be ~,* avoir la parole facile.
glide, *n,* glissement; (*Danc.*) glissé, *m.* ¶ *v.i,* glisser; couler. **glider** (*Aero.*) *n,* planeur, *m.* **gliding** (*Aero.*) *n,* vol plané, *m.*
glimmer, *n,* faible lueur, *f.* ¶ *v.i,* jeter une faible lueur.
glimpse, *n,* vision momentanée, *f.* ¶ *v.t,* (*& catch a ~ of*) entrevoir.
glint, *n,* reflet, *m;* (*in eye*) étincelle, *f.* ¶ *v.i,* étinceler, briller; (*water*) miroiter.
glisten, *v.i,* luire; (*water*) miroiter; (*eyes*) briller.
glitter, *n,* scintillement; (*fig.*) éclat, *m.* ¶ *v.i,* scintiller; (*eyes*) briller.
gloaming, *n,* crépuscule, *m.*
gloat, *v.i,* se réjouir avec malveillance (*over,* de).
global, *a,* global; (*world-wide*) mondial. **globe,** *n,* globe, *m,* sphère, *f;* (*fish bowl*) bocal, *m.* **globular,** *a,* globulaire, sphérique. **globule,** *n,* globule, *m;* (*water*) gouttelette, *f.*
gloom, *n,* (*darkness*) obscurité, *f,* ténèbres, *f.pl;* (~*iness*) mélancolie, tristesse, *f.* ~**y,** *a,* mélancolique, sombre, morne, lugubre.
glorify, *v.t,* glorifier. **glorious†,** *a,* (*saint*) glorieux; (*view, weather*) magnifique, superbe. **glory,** *n,* gloire, splendeur, *f. to give ~ to God,* rendre gloire à Dieu. ¶ *v.i,* ~ *in,* se glorifier de, se faire gloire de.
gloss[1], *n,* vernis, éclat, *m.* ¶ *a,* (*paint*) laqué. ~ *finish,* brillant; (*Phot.*) glaçage, *m.* ~**y,** *a,* luisant; (*Phot: paper*) glacé, brillant; (*magazine*) de luxe. ¶ *v.t,* ~ *over,* glisser sur; camoufler.
gloss[2], *n,* (*on text*) glose, *f;* commentaire, *m.* ~**ary,** *n,* glossaire, *m.*
glove, *n,* gant, *m.* ~ *compartment* (*car*), boîte à gants, *f.* ~ *maker,* gantier, ière. ~ *shop,* ganterie, *f.* ¶ *v.t,* ganter. *to put on one's ~s,* se ganter.
glow, *n,* (*gen.*) lueur, *f;* (*red: fire, sky*) rougeoiement, *m;* (*metal*) incandescence, *f;* (*skin*) éclat, *m.* ~*worm,* ver luisant, *m.* ¶ *v.i,* luire; rougeoyer; (*face: with pleasure &c*) rayonner; (*cheeks*) être en feu. ~**ing,** *a,* (*account*) enthousiaste; (*health*) florissant.
glower at, regarder d'un air hostile.
glucose, *n,* glucose, *f.*
glue, *n,* colle; (*marine*) glu, *f.* ¶ *v.t,* coller. *to stand ~d to the spot,* rester figé sur place. ~**y,** *a,* gluant.
glum, *a,* triste, maussade, lugubre.
glut, *n,* surplus, *m,* surabondance, *f.* ¶ *v.t,* gorger, rassasier (*with,* de).
glutinous, *a,* glutineux.
glutton, *n,* glouton, ne, gourmand, e. ~**ous†,** *a,* glouton, gourmand. ~**y,** *n,* gloutonnerie, gourmandise, *f.*
glycerin[e], *n,* glycérine, *f.*
gnarled, *a,* noueux.
gnash one's teeth, grincer des dents.
gnat, *n,* moucheron, *m.*
gnaw, *v.t. & i,* ronger. ~*ed by hunger,* tenaillé par la faim.
gnome, *n,* gnome, *m.*
go, *n,* (*energy*) entrain, dynamisme, *m;* (*attempt*) coup, essai, *m. at one ~,* d'un seul coup. *to have a ~ P,* tenter le coup *P. to make a ~ of sth,* réussir qch. *it's your ~,* à vous de jouer. ¶ *v.i.ir,* aller, se rendre; (*vehicle*) rouler. ~ *up, down the street,* monter, descendre la rue. *to ~ 5 km,* faire 5 km. *to ~ to the doctor,* aller voir le médecin. (*Mil.*) *who ~es there?*

qui va là? qui vive? (*future*) *I'm ~ing to come*, je vais venir. *he's just ~ing to leave*, il est sur le point de partir. (*activity*) *to ~ & do sth*, aller faire qch. *~ fishing*, aller à la pêche. *~ swimming*, aller nager. *~ sailing*, faire de la voile. *~ for a walk*, se promener, se balader *P*. *~ on a journey*, partir en voyage. (*depart*) s'en aller, partir; disparaître; (*time*) passer; (*fail: sight, health*) baisser, faiblir. *his mind is ~ing*, il n'a plus toute sa tête. *to let ~*, lâcher prise. *to let ~ of*, lâcher. *to let o.s ~*, se laisser aller. *to ~ cheap*, se vendre à bas prix. (*progress, succeed*) *how's it ~ing?* comment ça va? (*event*) *did it ~ well?* ça s'est bien passé? *to ~ well*, (*business, studies*) marcher [bien]. (*Mach.*) (*start*) démarrer; (*work*) marcher, fonctionner. *my watch isn't ~ing*, ma montre ne marche pas. *to set, get ~ing*, mettre en marche. (*become*) *~ pale, red*, pâlir, rougir; *~ mad*, devenir fou. (*sound*) *the bell has gone*, la cloche a sonné. *the story ~es that*, le bruit court que. *that ~es without saying*, cela va sans dire. **~-ahead,** *a*, entreprenant. (*n*) *to give s.o the ~*, donner le feu vert à qn. **~-between,** intermédiaire, *m,f*. **~-cart,** kart; (*child's*) chariot, *m*. **~-getter,** arriviste, *m,f*. **~-slow,** (*Ind.*) grève perlée. *comps:* ~ **about,** circuler; (*rumour*) courir; (*Naut.*) virer [vent devant]; (*work*) se mettre à. *how to ~ about it*, comment s'y prendre. ~ **across,** traverser. ~ **against,** (*decision, wishes*) aller à l'encontre de. ~ **ahead with,** (*scheme*) mettre à exécution. *~ ahead!* allez y! ~ **along with** *s.o, sth*, être d'accord avec qn, sur qch. ~ **away,** partir, s'en aller. ~ **back,** retourner; revenir; (*on promise*) revenir sur. ~ **by,** (*pers., time*) passer; (*appearances*) juger d'après. ~ **down,** descendre; (*sun*) se coucher; (*ship*) couler; (*swelling*) désenfler. *~ down well, badly*, être bien, mal reçu. ~ **for,** attaquer; (*verbally*) s'en prendre à. ~ **forward,** avancer. ~ **in,** entrer; (*sun*) se cacher. *~ in for*, (*exam*) se présenter à. ~ **into,** entrer dans; (*question*) étudier, examiner. ~ **off,** s'en aller, partir; (*gun*) partir; (*food*) se gâter. (*event*) *it went off well*, ça s'est bien passé. ~ **on,** continuer (*doing*, de, à faire); (*happen*) se passer. *~ on!* allons donc! *~ on at s.o*, s'en prendre à qn. ~ **out,** sortir; (*fire*) s'éteindre. *~ out for a meal*, manger en ville. ~ **over,** (*to enemy*) passer à; (*in one's mind*) repasser, retracer. ~ **through,** passer par, traverser; (*suffer*) subir; (*one's pockets*) fouiller dans. *to ~ through with it*, aller jusqu'au bout. ~ **up,** (*price &c*) monter; (*to bed*) monter se coucher; (*curtain*) se lever. ~ **without,** se passer de.

goad, *n*, aiguillon, *m*. ¶ *v.t*, aiguillonner, piquer.

goal, *n*, (*Sport, fig.*) but, *m*. *~ keeper, kick, post*, gardien, coup de pied, poteau de b., *m*. *~ie P*, goal *P*, *m*.

goat, *n*, chèvre, *f*; (*he-~*) bouc, *m*. *to get s.o's ~*, mettre qn en boule *P*. **~ee,** *n*, barbiche, *f*.

gobble, *v.t*, (*& ~ up*) manger goulûment, engloutir; (*v.i, of turkey*) glouglouter.

goblet, *n*, coupe, *f*; verre à pied, *m*.

goblin, *n*, lutin, farfadet, *m*.

God, *n*, Dieu, *m*. *my ~! P* mon Dieu! bon Dieu! *~ forbid!* Dieu m'en garde! **god,** *n*, dieu. *the ~s* (*Theat*), poulailler, paradis, *m*. *~-child*, filleul, e. *~-daughter*, filleule, *f*. *~-father*, parrain, *m*. *~head*, divinité, *f*. *~mother*, marraine, *f*. *~send*, aubaine, *f*. *~son*, filleul, *m*. **goddess,** *n*, déesse, *f*. **godless,** *a*, impie. **godlike,** *a*, divin. **godliness,** *n*, piété, *f*. **godly,** *a*, pieux.

goggles, *n.pl*, lunettes [protectrices], *f.pl*.

going, *a*, (*concern*) qui marche. *~, ~, gone!* une fois, deux fois, adjugé! ¶ *n*, état du terrain, *m*. *that was good ~*, ça a été rapide. *~s-on*, (*pej.*) conduite, *f*, agissements, *m.pl*.

gold, *n*, or, *m*. (*fig.*) *heart of ~*, cœur d'or, *m*. ¶ *a*, (*coin, mine*) d'or; (*watch &c*) en or. *~ braid*, galon d'or, *m*. *~-digger*, (*pej.*) aventurière, *f*. *~ dust*, poudre d'or, *f*. *~finch*, chardonneret, *m*. *~fish*, poisson rouge, *m*. *~fish bowl*, bocal, *m*. *~ plate*, vaisselle d'or, *f*. *~-plated*, plaqué or. *~ rush*, ruée vers l'or, *f*. *~smith*, orfèvre, *m*. *~smith's work*, orfèvrerie, *f*. *~ standard*, étalon d'or, *m*. **~en,** *a*, (*hair, corn*) doré; (*jewelry*) d'or, en or. *~ age*, âge d'or, *m*. *~ eagle*, aigle royal, *m*. *~ mean*, juste milieu, *m*. *~ rod*, gerbe d'or, *f*. *~ syrup*, mélasse raffinée, *f*. *~ wedding*, noces d'or, *f.pl*.

golf, *n*, golf, *m*. *~ club*, (*place, stick*) club de g, *m*. *~ course, ~ links*, [terrain de] golf, *m*. **~er,** *n*, joueur (euse) de golf.

gondola, *n*, gondole; (*Aero.*) nacelle, *f*. **gondolier,** *n*, gondolier, *m*.

goner *P*, *n*, *to be a ~*, être fichu *P ou* foutu *P*.

gong, *n*, gong, *m*.

gonorrhoea, *n*, blennorragie, *f*.

good, *a*, bon; (*child*) sage. *as ~ as gold*, sage comme une image. *a ~ man*, un brave homme, un h. bien. *my ~ man*, mon brave. *~ sort P*, brave type *P*, *m*, *ou* fille, *f*. (*kind*) bon, gentil. *be ~ to her*, soyez gentil avec elle. *would you be ~ enough to..* auriez-vous la bonté de..., seriez-vous assez aimable pour... (*weather*) beau; (*holiday*) agréable. *to have a ~ time*, bien s'amuser. (*beneficial*) *it's ~ for me*, ça me fait du bien. (*terms, offer*) favorable, avantageux. (*appearance*) *~ looks*, beauté, *f*. *you look ~ in that*, ça vous va bien. *you look ~*, tu es très bien. (*greetings*) *~ morning, ~ afternoon*, bonjour. *~ evening*, bonsoir. *~ night*, bonsoir, bonne nuit. *~bye*, au revoir. (*quantity*) *a ~ deal, a ~ many*, beaucoup de. *a ~ few*, pas mal de. *a*

~ *way*, un bon bout de chemin. *a ~ 2 hours*, 2 bonnes *ou* grandes heures. *to make ~, v.i,* (*pers.*) faire son chemin; *v.t,* (*damage*) réparer; (*promise*) remplir; (*losses*) compenser. ¶ *i,* bon!, bien! ¶ *n,* bien, *m. that will do you ~*, ça vous fera du bien. *for ~*, pour de bon, à jamais. *for ~ & all,* une fois pour toutes. *gone for ~*, parti pour toujours. (*advantage*) avantage, profit, *m. the common ~*, l'intérêt commun. *it's no ~ saying,* inutile de dire. *what's the ~ (of doing)?* à quoi bon (faire)? *~-for-nothing,* propre à rien; (*n*) vaurien, ne. *G~ Friday,* Vendredi saint. *~-humoured,* de bonne humeur; d'une heureuse nature. *~-looking,* beau, bien, joli. *~-natured,* (*pers.*) au bon naturel; (*smile*) bon enfant, *inv. ~-tempered,* qui a bon caractère. *~ will,* bonne volonté, bienveillance, *f.* **goodies,** *n.pl,* friandises, *f.pl.* **goody** *P, i,* chouette! *P* chic! *P.* **goodness,** *n,* bonté, *f. for ~ sake,* [par] pitié! *~ only knows,* Dieu seul le sait.

goods, *n.pl,* marchandises, *f.pl;* articles, *m.pl. ~ train,* train de marchandises, *m.*

goose, *n,* oie, *f. ~ flesh* (*fig.*), chair de poule, *f. ~ step,* pas de l'oie, *m.*

gooseberry, *n,* groseille à maquereau, *f. ~ bush,* groseillier [à maquereau] *m.*

gore[1], *n,* sang, *m.*

gore[2], *v.t,* blesser d'un coup de corne.

gorge, *n,* gorge, *f.* ¶ *v.t, ~ o.s,* se gorger (*on,* de).

gorgeous†, *a,* magnifique, splendide.

gorilla, *n,* gorille, *m.*

gormless *P, a,* mollasse *P;* bête.

gorse, *n,* ajoncs, *m.pl.*

gory, *a,* (*wound*) sanglant; (*pers.*) ensanglanté.

gosh *P, i,* ça alors! *P.*

goshawk, *n,* autour, *m.*

gosling, *n,* oison, *m.*

gospel, *n,* évangile, *m. ~* [*truth*], parole d'évangile, *f.*

gossamer, *n,* fils de la Vierge, *m.pl.*

gossip, *n,* commérages, potins, *m.pl;* (*pers.*) commère, *f. piece of ~*, ragot, *m. ~ column,* échos, *m.pl. ~ writer,* échotier, ière. ¶ *v.i,* bavarder, faire des commérages.

Gothic, *a,* gothique.

gouache (*Art*) *n,* gouache, *f.*

gouge, *n,* gouge, *f.* ¶ *v.t,* (*& ~ out*) gouger.

gourd, *n,* (*fruit*) courge; (*flask*) gourde, *f.*

gourmand, *a. & n,* gourmand, e.

gourmet, *n,* gourmet, *m.*

gout, *n,* goutte, *f.* **~y,** *a,* goutteux.

govern, *v.t. & i,* (*gen., Gram.*) gouverner; (*events*) déterminer. *~ing body,* conseil d'administration, *m.* **~ess,** *n,* gouvernante, *f.* **~ment,** *n,* gouvernement, *m. ~ in power,* gouvernants, *m.pl. ~ organ,* journal ministériel, *m. att,* (*policy &c*) du g., gouvernemental. *~ reshuffle,* remaniement ministériel. **~or,** *n,* gouverneur; (*Sch. &c*) administrateur, trice; (*Mach.*) régulateur, *m.*

gown, *n,* robe; (*Univ.*) toge, *f.*

grab, *v.t,* empoigner, agripper, saisir. ¶ *n,* (*Mach.*) benne preneuse.

grace, *n,* (*gen., Rel.*) grâce, *f. to be in s.o's good ~s,* être dans les bonnes grâces de qn. (*before meal*) le bénédicité; (*after*) les grâces. (*Mus.*) *~ note,* note d'agrément, *f. his G~,* (*archbishop*) Monseigneur. ¶ *v.t,* orner; honorer **~ful†,** *a,* gracieux.

gracious†, *a,* gracieux, bienveillant. **~ness,** *n,* bienveillance, *f.*

gradation, *n,* gradation, *f.* **grade,** *n,* (*Adm.*) catégorie, *f;* (*on scale*) grade, échelon; (*rank*) rang, *m;* (*goods*) qualité, *f. high ~*, de qualité supérieure. (*fruit, eggs*) calibre, *m.* ¶ *v.t,* classer; (*fruit &c*) calibrer. **gradient,** *n,* (*up*) rampe; (*down*) pente; (*gen.*) inclinaison, *f. ~ of 1 in 10,* inclinaison de dix pour cent. **gradual†,** *a,* graduel. **graduate,** *v.t,* graduer. ¶ *v.i,* obtenir sa licence. ¶ *n,* licencié, e.

graffiti, *n.pl,* graffiti, *m.pl.*

graft, *n,* (*Hort., Surg.*) greffe; (*bribery*) corruption, *f.* ¶ *v.t,* greffer.

grain, *n,* (*cereals, Phot.*) grain, *m;* (*of sand, rice &c*) grain; (*fig: truth &c*) grain, brin; (*wood*) fil, *m. against the ~*, à contre-fil. (*fig.*) *it goes against the ~*, c'est à contrecœur que je le fais.

grammar, *n,* grammaire, *f. that's bad ~*, cela n'est pas grammatical. *~ school,* lycée, *m.* **~ian,** *n,* grammairien, ne. **grammatical†,** *a,* grammatical.

gramophone, *n,* phonographe, *m. ~ record,* disque, *m.*

granary, *n,* grenier, *m.*

grand†, *a,* grand; magnifique, splendide; (*house &c*) grandiose; excellent, formidable *P. I don't feel too ~*, je ne suis pas dans mon assiette. *~child, ~son, ~daughter,* petit-fils, *m,* petite-fille, *f. ~children,* petits-enfants, *m.pl. grand*[*d*]*ad,* grand-papa, *m. ~father,* grand-père, *m. ~father clock,* horloge de parquet, *f. ~ma,* grand-maman, *f. ~-mother,* grand-mère, *f. ~parents,* grands-parents, *m.pl. ~piano,* piano à queue, *m. ~staircase,* escalier d'honneur, *m. ~stand,* tribune, *f. ~total,* somme globale, *f.* **grandeur,** *n,* grandeur, splendeur, *f.*

grandiloquence, *n,* grandiloquence, *f.* **grandiloquent,** *a,* grandiloquent.

grandiose, *a,* grandiose.

granite, *n,* granit, *m.*

granny, *n,* grand-maman, bonne maman, *f.*

grant, *n,* (*money*) allocation, subvention; (*student*) bourse, *f.* ¶ *v.t,* accorder; (*request*) concéder à; (*admit*) admettre, reconnaître. *take for ~ed,* présumer (*that,* que); considérer comme allant de soi; (*success*) escompter. *~ed!* d'accord!

granular, *a,* granuleux. **granulated sugar,** *n,* sucre cristallisé, *m.* **granule,** *n,* granule, *m.*
grape, *n,* [grain de] raisin, *m.* *~s,* du raisin, des r-s. *to gather ~s,* vendanger. *~ harvest,* vendange, *f.* *~ picker,* vendangeur, euse. *~fruit,* pamplemousse, *m.*
graph, *n,* graphique, *m.* *~ paper,* papier millimétré. **~ic†,** *a,* graphique; (*description*) vivant. **~ics,** *n,* art graphique, *m.*
graphite, *n,* graphite, *m,* plombagine, *f.*
grapnel, *n,* grappin, *m.* **grapple,** *v.t,* accrocher avec un grappin. ¶ *v.i, ~ with,* (*pers.*) lutter contre, se battre avec; (*problem*) s'attaquer à.
grasp, *n,* étreinte, *f.* *a strong ~,* une forte poigne. (*subject*) *to have a sound ~ of,* avoir une solide connaissance de. *within s.o's ~,* à la portée de qn. ¶ *v.t,* saisir, empoigner; (*understand*) saisir, comprendre. **~ing†,** *a,* avide, cupide.
grass, *n,* herbe, *f;* (*lawn*) gazon; (*pasture*) herbage, *m;* (*P marijuana*) herbe *P.* (*Bot.*) *~es,* graminées, *f.pl.* (*horse*) *put out to ~,* mettre au vert. (*land*) *under ~,* en pré. (*Ten.*) *on ~,* sur gazon. *~hopper,* sauterelle, *f.* *~land,* prairie, *f.* *~-roots, a,* (*Pol: movement &c*) populaire, du peuple. *~ snake,* couleuvre, *f.* *~ widow,* veuve à titre temporaire, *f.* ¶ *v.i,* (*P inform*) moucharder *P.* **~y,** *a,* herbeux, herbu.
grate[1], *n,* grille de foyer, *f;* (*fireplace*) foyer, *m,* cheminée, *f.*
grate[2], *v.t,* (*Cook.*) râper. *to ~ one's teeth,* grincer des dents. ¶ *v.i,* grincer. *~ on the ears,* écorcher les oreilles. *~ on the nerves,* taper sur les nerfs. *grating,* (*sound*) grinçant. **~r,** *n,* (*Cook.*) râpe, *f.*
grateful, *a,* reconnaissant (*to,* à; *for,* de).
gratification, *n,* satisfaction, *f,* plaisir, *m.* **gratify,** *v.t,* satisfaire, faire plaisir à.
grating, *n,* grille, *f;* grillage, *m.*
gratis, *ad,* gratis, gratuitement.
gratitude, *n,* reconnaissance, gratitude, *f* (*towards,* envers; *for,* de).
gratuitous†, *a,* gratuit, sans motif. **gratuity,** *n,* (*tip*) pourboire, *m,* gratification; (*Mil.*) prime de démobilisation, *f.*
grave†[1], *a,* grave, sérieux.
grave[2], *n,* tombe, *f,* tombeau, *m.* *~digger,* fossoyeur, *m.* *~stone,* pierre tombale, *f.* *~yard,* cimetière, *m.* *~yard cough,* toux qui sent le sapin, *f.*
gravel, *n,* gravier; (*fine*) gravillon, *m.* *~ path,* allée de gravier, *f.* *~ pit,* carrière de cailloux, *f.*
gravitate, *v.i,* (*lit., fig.*) graviter. **gravitation,** *n,* gravitation, *f.* **gravity,** *n,* (*Phys.*) pesanteur, *f.* *law of ~,* loi de la p., *f.* (*fig.*) gravité, *f;* sérieux, *m.*
gravy, *n,* jus de viande, *m,* sauce, *f.* *~ boat,* saucière, *f.*
gray, *V* **grey. grayling,** *n,* ombre, *m.*
graze[1], *n,* écorchure, *f.* ¶ *v.t,* (*skin*) écorcher, érafler; (*brush against*) frôler, effleurer; (*sea bottom*) labourer.
graze[2], *v.t. & i,* (*cattle*) paître, brouter; (*farmer*) faire paître. **grazing,** *n,* pâturage, *m.*
grease, *n,* graisse, *f.* *to remove ~ from,* dégraisser. *~ gun,* [pistolet] graisseur, *m.* *~paint,* fard, *m.* *~-proof paper,* papier sulfurisé, *m.* ¶ *v.t,* graisser. *to ~ s.o's palm,* graisser la patte à qn. **greasiness,** *n,* graisse, *f.* **greasing,** *n,* (*Mach.*) graissage, *m,* lubrification, *f.* **greasy,** *a,* graisseux; (*hair*) gras. *~ pole,* mât de cocagne, *m.*
great, *a,* (*size*) grand, gros; (*intensity: pain &c*) fort; (*man, lady, painter &c*) grand; (*P excellent*) magnifique, formidable *P,* terrible *P,* sensationnel *P,* au poil *P.* *~-aunt,* grand-tante, *f.* *G~ Britain,* la Grande-Bretagne. *~coat,* pardessus, *m;* (*Mil.*) capote, *f.* *~ Dane,* [grand] danois, *m.* *a ~ deal* [*of*], *a ~ many,* beaucoup [de]. *G~er London,* le grand Londres. *~-grandchildren,* arrière-petits-enfants, *m.pl.* *~-granddaughter, -son,* arrière-petite-fille, *f,* a.-petit-fils, *m.* *~-grandfather -mother,* arrière-grand-père, *m,* a.-grand-mère, *f,* bisaïeul, e. *~-~-grandfather, -mother,* trisaïeul, e. *~-uncle,* grand-oncle, *m.* *the G~ War,* la Grande Guerre. **~ly,** *ad,* grandement; fort. **~ness,** *n,* grandeur, *f.*
grebe, *n,* grèbe, *m.*
Greece, *n,* la Grèce. **Greek,** *a,* grec. ¶ *n,* Grec, Grecque; (*language*) le grec. *it's* [*all*] *~ to me,* tout ça c'est de l'hébreux pour moi.
greed[iness], *n,* avidité; (*for food*) gourmandise, *f.* **greedy†,** *a,* avide (*for,* de); gourmand, glouton, goulu.
green, *a,* vert; (*corn*) en herbe; (*inexperienced*) novice, inexpérimenté; naïf. *to turn ~,* verdir. *~ belt,* zone de verdure, *f.* *~finch,* verdier, *m.* *~fly,* puceron, *m.* *~gage,* reine-claude, *f.* *~grocer,* marchand de légumes, *m,* fruitier, ère. *~horn,* novice, blanc bec, *m.* *~house,* serre, *f.* *~ light,* (*Mot., fig.*) feu vert. *~ peas,* petits pois, *m.pl.* *~room,* foyer des artistes, *m.* *~ stuff* or **greens,** *n.pl,* légumes verts, *m.pl,* verdure, *f.* ¶ *n,* vert, *m;* (*Golf*) green, *m.* [*village*] *~,* place [du village] *f.* **~ery,** *n,* verdure, *f.* **~ish,** *a,* verdâtre.
Greenland, *n,* le Groenland.
greenness, *n,* verdure; verdeur; naïveté, *f.*
greet, *v.t,* saluer; accueillir. **~ing,** *n,* salutation, *f,* salut, *m.* *~s,* compliments, *m.pl,* salutations, *f.pl.* *~ card,* carte de vœux, *f.*
gregarious, *a,* grégaire; (*pers.*) sociable.
Gregorian, *a,* grégorien.
grenade, *n,* grenade, *f.*
grenadine, *n,* (*cordial*) grenadine, *f.*
grey, gray, *a. & n,* gris, *m.* (*hair*) *turning ~,* grisonnant. *~ matter P,* matière grise *P.* *~*

friar, franciscain, *m.* ~*-haired,* aux cheveux gris. ~*hound,* lévrier, *m;* levrette, *f.* ~*hound track,* cynodrome, *m.* ¶ *v.i,* (*hair*) grisonner. ~**ish,** *a,* grisâtre.

grid, *n,* (*gen., map*) grille, *f;* (*Elec.*) réseau, *m.* ~*iron,* gril, *m.*

grief, *n,* chagrin, *m,* douleur, peine, affliction, *f. to come to* ~, (*plan &c*) échouer, tourner mal.

grievance, *n,* grief, *m* (*against,* contre). *to have a* ~ *against s.o,* en vouloir à qn. **grieve,** *v.t,* chagriner, peiner; (*stronger*) désoler. ¶ *v.i,* avoir du chagrin de la peine; se désoler (*at, over,* de). **grievous**†, *a,* (*wrong*) grave; (*pain, loss*) cruel. (*Law*) ~ *bodily harm,* coups & blessures.

grill, *n,* gril, *m;* (*meat*) grillade, *f;* (~*room*) rôtisserie, *f.* ¶ *v.t,* [faire] griller; (*P question*) cuisiner *P.*

grill[e], *n,* grille, *f;* (*in door*) judas, *m.*

grim, *a,* sinistre; (*joke*) macabre: (*face*) sévère; (*truth*) brutal. ~ *determination,* volonté inflexible, *f.*

grimace, *n,* grimace, *f.* ¶ *v.i,* grimacer, faire la grimace, f. la moue; (*for fun*) f. des g-s.

grime, *n,* crasse, *f.* **grimy,** *a,* crasseux, sale.

grin, *n,* [grand] sourire, *m.* ¶ *v.i,* sourire.

grind, *n,* (*work*) corvée, *f,* boulot pénible, *m.* ¶ *v.t,* moudre, broyer; (*knife &c*) aiguiser [à la meule]. ~ *one's teeth,* grincer des dents. (*fig.*) ~ *down,* opprimer, écraser. ~*stone,* meule à aiguiser. ¶ *v.i,* (*grate*) grincer. (*work*) ~ [*away*], bûcher *P.* boulonner *P.* ~**er,** *n, coffee* ~, moulin à café, *m.* ~**ing,** *a,* (*poverty*) écrasant. ¶ *n,* (*sound*) grincement, *m.*

grip, *n,* prise, étreinte; *f. he has a strong* ~, il a la poigne forte. *to loosen one's* ~, lâcher prise. *to get a* ~ *on,* (*problem*) s'attaquer à. ¶ *v.t,* saisir, empoigner; (*hold*) serrer; (*fig.*) (*terror*) saisir; (*film*) empoigner. (*tyres*) *to* ~ *the road,* adhérer à la route. ~**ping,** *a,* (*film &c*) passionnant.

gripe, *n,* & ~*s,* coliques, *f.pl.* ¶ *v.i, P,* rouspéter *P.*

grisly, *a,* effrayant, horrible, affreux.

gristle, *n,* cartilage, *m.* **gristly,** *a,* cartilagineux, croquant.

grit, *n,* sable; gravillon, *m;* (*P courage*) cran *P, m.* ¶ *v.t,* (*road*) sabler. ~ *one's teeth,* serrer les dents.

grizzle, *v.i,* pleurnicher. **grizzled,** *a,* grisonnant. **grizzly,** *a,* ~ *bear,* ours gris, grizzly, *m.*

groan, *n,* gémissement, *m.* ¶ *v.i,* gémir.

grocer, *n,* épicier, ère. ~*'s shop* & **grocery,** *n,* épicerie, *f.*

grog, *n,* grog, *m.* **groggy** *P, a,* faible, chancelant; (*after blow*) groggy *P.*

groin, *n,* aine; (*Arch.*) arête, *f.*

groom, *n,* valet d'écurie, *m.* ¶ *v.t,* panser. (*pers.*) *well* ~*ed,* très soigné.

groove, *n,* rainure; cannelure, *f;* (*record*) sillon, *m.* (*fig: rut*) *in a* ~, encroûté. ¶ *v.t,* rainurer.

grope, *v.i,* tâtonner. ~ *for,* chercher à tâtons. ~ *one's way,* avancer à tâtons.

gross†, *a,* (*coarse*) grossier; (*fat*) obèse; (*error*) gros; (*injustice*) flagrant; (*Com: weight*) brut. ¶ *n,* (144) grosse, *f.*

grotto, *n,* grotte, *f.*

grotty *P, a,* minable *P,* moche *P.*

ground[1], *n,* terre, *f,* sol, *m. to fall to the* ~, tomber à *ou* par terre. *on the* ~, par terre, sur le sol. (*fig.*) *to get off the* ~, (*scheme*) démarrer *P. that suits me down to the* ~, ça me va à merveille. (*position*) terrain, *m.* (*Mil.*) *to give, lose* ~, céder, perdre du t. *to gain* ~, (*Mil.*) gagner du t.; (*idea*) faire son chemin. *to be sure of one's* ~, être sur son t. *to stand one's* ~, tenir bon *ou* ferme. (*football &c*) terrain. ~*s,* (*of house*) parc, *m;* (*coffee*) marc, *m.* (*reason*) & ~*s,* ~ *for complaint,* sujet de plainte, grief, *m.* ~*s for divorce,* motifs de divorce, *m.pl. on medical* ~*s,* pour des raisons médicales. *on what* ~*s?* à quel titre? ¶ *v.t,* (*Aero.*) empêcher de voler; (*fig: hopes &c*) fonder. (*Aero.*) ~ *crew,* équipe au sol, *f.* ~ *floor,* rez-de-chaussée, *m.* (*Mil.*) ~ *forces,* armée de terre, *f.* ~ *frost,* gelée blanche. *at* ~ *level,* au ras du sol. ~*nut,* arachide, *f.* ~*sheet,* tapis de sol, *m.* ~*sman,* gardien de stade, *m.* ~*swell,* lame de fond, *f.* ~*work,* base, *f,* travail préparatoire, *m.* ~**ing,** *n, good* ~ (*in subject*), base solide, *f.* ~**less,** *a,* sans fondement.

ground[2], *p.p of* **grind.** *a,* (*coffee*) moulu. ~ *rice,* farine de riz.

group, *n,* groupe, *m. in* ~*s,* par groupes. (*RAF*) *G*~ *Captain,* colonel, *m.* (*Med.*) ~ *practice,* cabinet collectif. ¶ *v.t.* (*& i*) (se) grouper.

grouse[1], *n,* (*bird*) grouse, *f.*

grouse[2], *n,* grief, *m.* ¶ *v.i,* rouspéter *P,* râler *P.*

grove, *n,* bocage, bosquet, *m.*

grovel, *v.i,* ramper (devant qn).

grow, *v.i. ir,* (*plant, hair; child P*) pousser; (*pers.*) grandir; (*amount*) augmenter; (*become*) devenir. ~ *old,* vieillir. ~ *pale, red,* pâlir, rougir. ~ *cold,* [se] refroidir. ~ *rare,* se faire rare. *to* ~ *up,* grandir. ¶ *v.t.ir,* (*crops*) cultiver; (*beard &c*) laisser pousser. ~**er,** *n,* cultivateur, trice. ~**ing,** *a* qui pousse; qui grandit; (*amount*) croissant, grandissant; (*fear &c*) croissant. ~ *crops,* récoltes sur pied, *f.pl.* ~ *pains,* douleurs de croissance, *f.pl.* **grown-up,** *a,* grand, adulte. ¶ *n,* grande personne, *f,* adulte, *m,f.* **growth,** *n,* croissance; augmentation, *f;* développement, *m;* (*hair*) poussée; (*Med.*) grosseur, tumeur, *f.*

growl, *n,* grognement, *m.* ¶ *v.i,* grogner.

groyne, *n,* brise-lames, *m inv.*

grub, *n,* larve, *f;* (*P food*) bouffe *P, f.* ¶ *v.t,* ~ *up,* (*tree*) déraciner, déterrer. **grubby,** *a,* sale, crasseux.

grudge, *n,* rancune, *f. bear a ~ against s.o,* en vouloir à qn, garder rancune à qn. ¶ *v.t,* donner à contrecœur; (*resent*) voir d'un mauvais œil. **grudgingly,** *ad,* à contrecœur.

gruelling, *a,* épuisant, éreintant.

gruesome, *a,* macabre, affreux, épouvantable.

gruff, *a,* brusque, bourru.

grumble, *v.i,* grogner, ronchonner (*about,* contre); rouspéter *P* (*at,* après). **grumpy,** *a,* grincheux, grognon.

grunt, *n,* grognement, *m.* ¶ *v.i,* grogner.

guarantee, *n,* garantie, *f. there's no ~ that,* il n'est pas garanti que. ¶ *v.t,* garantir. **guarantor,** *n,* garant, e, caution, *f. to stand ~ for s.o,* se porter garant *ou* caution de qn.

guard, *n,* (*gen., Mil., Box.*) garde, *f. on ~,* (*Mil.*) de garde, de faction; (*Fenc.*) en garde! *to be on one's ~,* être sur ses gardes. *to take s.o off his ~,* prendre qn au dépourvu. (*Mil: squad*) garde, *f;* (*man*) garde, *m. ~ of honour,* g. d'honneur. (*Rly*) chef de train, *m;* (*Mach.*) dispositif de sûreté, *m. fire-~,* garde-feu, *m. ~ dog,* chien de g., *m. ~house, ~room,* corps de garde, *m. ~'s van,* fourgon, *m.* ¶ *v.t,* protéger (*against,* contre); (*prisoner, frontier*) garder. ¶ *v.i, ~ against doing,* se garder de faire. **~ed,** *a,* réservé, prudent. **~ian,** *n,* gardien, ne; (*child*) tuteur, trice. *~ angel,* ange gardien.

guava, *n,* goyave, *f;* (*tree*) goyavier, *m.*

gudgeon, *n,* (*fish*) goujon, *m.* (*Mot.*) *~ pin,* goupille, *f.*

guer[r]illa, *n,* guérillero, *m. ~ band, ~ warfare,* guérilla, *f.*

Guernsey, *n,* Guernesey, *f.*

guess, *n,* conjecture, *f. to make a ~,* essayer de deviner. ¶ *v.t. & i,* deviner; (*size, number &c*) estimer; (*Am: believe*) croire, penser. *to ~ right,* deviner juste. *I ~ed as much,* je m'en doutais.

guest, *n,* invité, e, hôte; (*at meal*) convive, *m,f;* (*hotel*) client, e. *~ of honour,* invité(e) d'honneur. ¶ *a,* (*artist, speaker*) invité. *~-house,* pension de famille, *f. ~ room,* chambre d'amis, *f.*

guffaw, *n,* gros rire. ¶ *v.i,* rire bruyamment.

guidance, *n,* conseils, *m.pl. for your ~,* pour votre gouverne. *vocational ~,* orientation professionnelle. **guide,** *n,* guide, *m. rough ~,* indication, *f. ~* [*book*], guide. (*girl ~*) éclaireuse, guide, *f. ~ dog,* chien d'aveugle, *m. ~ line,* (*fig.*) ligne directrice. *~post,* poteau indicateur. ¶ *v.t,* guider, conduire. *~ed missile,* engin téléguidé. *~ing principle,* principe directeur.

guild, *n,* association; (*Hist.*) guilde, *f. ~hall,* hôtel de ville, *m.*

guile, *n,* ruse, astuce, *f,* artifice, *m.* **~less,** *a,* candide, sans astuce, franc.

guillotine, *n,* guillotine, *f;* (*for paper cutting*) massicot, *m.* ¶ *v.t,* guillotiner.

guilt, *n,* culpabilité, *f.* **~less,** *a,* innocent. **~y,** *a,* coupable. *to have a ~ conscience,* avoir mauvaise conscience.

guinea, *n,* (*21 shillings*) guinée, *f. G~* (*Geog.*), la Guinée. *~-pig,* cochon d'Inde, cobaye, *m.* (*pers.*) *act as ~-pig,* servir de cobaye.

guise, *n,* apparence, *f.*

guitar, *n,* guitare, *f.* **~ist,** *n,* guitariste, *m,f.*

gulf, *n,* (*lit., fig.*) gouffre, abîme; (*sea*) golfe, *m. Persian G~,* golfe Persique. *G~ Stream,* Gulf-Stream, *m.*

gull, *n,* (*sea*) mouette, *f,* goéland, *m;* (*pers.*) dupe, *f.* ¶ *v.t,* duper.

gullet, *n,* gosier, *m,* gorge, *f.*

gullible, *a,* crédule.

gully, *n,* ravine, *f;* (*gutter*) caniveau, *m.*

gulp, *n,* gorgée, *f.* (*drink*) *at one ~,* d'un trait. ¶ *v.t, ~ down,* (*drink*) boire à grandes lampées; (*food*) avaler à grosses bouchées. ¶ *v.i, he ~ed,* sa gorge s'est serrée.

gum[1], *n,* (*Anat.*) gencive, *f. ~boil,* fluxion dentaire, *f.*

gum[2], *n,* (*glue*) gomme, colle, *f. chewing ~,* chewing-gum, *m. ~boots,* bottes de caoutchouc, *f.pl. ~ tree,* gommier, *m. up a ~ tree P,* dans le pétrin. ¶ *v.t,* gommer, coller. *~ up the works P,* tout bousiller *P.*

gumption, *n,* initiative, *f,* allant, *m;* jugeote *P,f.*

gun, *n,* (*Artil.*) canon; (*rifle*) fusil; (*hand*) revolver, pistolet, *m. to be going great ~s P,* être en plein boum *P. ~boat,* canonnière, *f. ~ carriage,* affût, *m. ~ detachment,* peloton de pièce, *m. ~fire,* tir d'artillerie, *m;* (*rifle*) coups de feu, *m.pl. ~man,* bandit armé. *~powder,* poudre à canon, *f. ~shot wound,* blessure de balle, *f. ~smith,* armurier, *m.* ¶ *v.t, ~ down,* abattre. *~ for s.o,* chercher qn. **gunner,** *n,* artilleur, *m.* **~y,** *n,* tir au canon, *m.*

gunwale, gunnel, *n,* plat-bord, *m.*

gurgle, *n,* glouglou, *m.* ¶ *v.i,* glouglouter, gargouiller.

guru, *n,* gourou, *m.*

gush, *n,* jaillissement, *m.* ¶ *v.i,* jaillir. *~ing,* (*pers.*) trop démonstratif.

gust, *n,* coup [de vent], *m,* bourrasque, rafale, bouffée, *f.*

gusto, *n, with ~,* avec entrain, *m.*

gut, *n,* boyau; intestin, *m;* (*Mus.*) corde de boyau, *f.* (*fig.*) *he has ~s,* il a du cran. *to sweat one's ~s out,* se casser le cul *P.* ¶ *v.t,* vider, étriper.

gutter, *n,* (*roof*) gouttière, *f;* (*street*) ruisseau, caniveau, *m.* (*fig.*) *brought up in the ~,* élevé dans le ruisseau. *~ press,* presse à scandale, *f. ~-snipe,* gamin(e) des rues. ¶ *v.i,* (*candle*) couler.

guttural, *a,* guttural. ¶ *n,* gutturale, *f.*

guy[1], *n*, type *P*, mec *P*, *m*. *nice* ~, type bien. *tough* ~, dur *P*, *m*. ¶ *v.t*, tourner en ridicule.
guy[2], *n*, (~ *rope*) corde de tente, *f*.
guzzle, *v.i.* & *t*, bâfrer, se goinfrer (de).
gymnasium, *n*, gymnase, *m*. **gymnast**, *n*, gymnaste, *m,f*. ~**ic**, *a*, gymnastique. ~**ics**, *n.pl*, gymnastique, *f*.
gynaecology, *n*, gynécologie, *f*. **gynaecologist**, gynécologue, *m,f*.
gypsum, *n*, gypse, *m*.
gyrate, *v.i*, tourner. **gyration**, *n*, giration, *f*. **gyrocompass**, *n*, gyrocompas, *m*. **gyroscope**, *n*, gyroscope, *m*.

H

H, h, *n*, H, h, *m,f*. *aspirate, mute h*, h aspiré, muet. *H-bomb*, bombe-H, *f*.
haberdasher, *n*, mercier, ère. ~**y**, *n*, mercerie, *f*.
habit, *n*, habitude, coutume, *f*. *to be in the* ~ *of doing*, avoir l'habitude de faire. *get into bad* ~*s*, prendre de mauvaises habitudes. *get out of the* ~ *of doing*, perdre l'habitude de faire. (*dress*) habit, *m*. ~*-forming*, qui crée une accoutumance. ~**able**, *a*, habitable. **habitat**, *n*, habitat, *m*. **habitation**, *n*, habitation, *f*. **habitual**†, *a*, habituel; (*drinker &c*) invétéré. **habituate**, *v.t*, habituer.
hack[1], *n*, (*cut*) entaille, *f*. ~*saw*, scie à métaux, *f*. ¶ *v.t*, hacher. ~ *to pieces*, tailler en morceaux. (*Sport*) donner un coup de pied à. ~*ing cough*, toux sèche & bruyante.
hack[2], *n*, (*horse*) cheval de selle; (*hired*) c. de louage, *m*; (*nag*) haridelle, *f*. ~*-writing*, littérature alimentaire, *f*. ¶ *v.i*, *to go* ~*ing*, se promener à cheval.
hackney carriage, *n*, voiture de louage, *f*. **hackneyed**, *a*, (*subject*) usé, banal. ~ *phrase*, cliché, *m*, rengaine, *f*.
haddock, *n*, aiglefin, églefin, *m*.
haematology, *n*, hématologie, *f*. **haemoglobin**, *n*, hémoglobine, *f*. **haemophilia**, *n*, hémophilie, *f*. **haemorrhage**, *n*, hémorragie, *f*. **haemorrhoids**, *n.pl*, hémorroïdes, *f.pl*.
hag, *n*, [vieille] sorcière, *f*.
haggard, *a*, (*face*) hâve; (*look*) hagard.
haggle, *v.i*, marchander. ~ *over*, chicaner sur.
Hague (the), la Haye.
ha-ha (*sunk fence*) *n*, saut de loup, *m*.
hail[1], *n*, (*lit., fig.*) grêle, *f*. *to damage by* ~, grêler. ~*stone*, grêlon, *m*. ~ *storm*, orage [accompagné] de grêle, *m*. ¶ *v.i.imp*, grêler. *it's* ~*ing*, il grêle.
hail[2], *v.t*, saluer, acclamer; (*ship, taxi*) héler. ~ *from*, venir de. *within* ~, à portée de voix. ~*-fellow-well-met*, *a*, à tu & à toi avec tout le monde. *the H*~ *Mary*, le Je vous Salue Marie, *m*.
hair, *n*, cheveu, *m*; (*col*) les cheveux; (*head of* ~) chevelure, *f*. *to have red* ~, avoir les c. roux. *with grey* ~, aux c. gris. *to do one's* ~, se coiffer. *to wash one's* ~, se laver les c. *ou* la tête. *to get one's* ~ *cut*, se faire couper les c. (*on body*) poil, *m*. ~ *on one's chest*, du p. *ou* des p-s sur la poitrine. (*animal*) poil; (*coat*) pelage, *m*, (*horse*) robe, *f*. *by a* ~*'s breadth*, d'un poil, d'un cheveu, tout juste. ~*brush*, brosse à cheveux, *f*. ~ *curler*, bigoudi, *m*. ~*cut*, coupe de c., *f*. ~*do P*, ~ *style*, coiffure, *f*. ~*dresser*, coiffeur, euse. ~*-drier*, séchoir à c., *m*. ~*net*, filet à c, *m*, résille, *f*. ~*piece*, postiche, *m*. ~*pin*, épingle à c., *f*. ~*pin bend*, virage en é. à c., *m*. ~*-raising*, à vous faire dresser les c. ~ *remover*, crème épilatoire, *f*. ~*-splitting*, ergotage, *m*. ~ *spray*, laque, *f*. ~*-spring*, [ressort] spiral, *m*. ~**less**, *a*, sans poils; (*face*) glabre. ~**y**, *a*, velu, poilu.
hake, *n*, colin, merlu, *m*.
halcyon days, *n.pl*, jours sereins, *m.pl*.
hale, *a*, ~ *& hearty*, vigoureux, en pleine santé.
half, *n*, moitié, *f*, demi(e), *m(f)*. *2 & a* ~, deux et demi. *2 & a* ~ *hours*, 2 heures et demie. *to cut, break in* ~, couper, se casser en deux. *to do things by halves*, faire les choses à moitié. *to go halves with s.o*, se mettre de moitié avec qn. *too clever by* ~, un peu trop malin. (*Sport*) demi, *m*; (~ *of match*) mi-temps, *f*. ¶ *a*, demi. *a* ~ *cup*, ~ *a cup*, une demi-tasse. *a* ~ *hour*, ~ *an hour*, une demi-heure. ¶ *ad*, [à] moitié, à demi. ~ *full*, à moitié plein. ~ *dressed*, à demi vêtu. ~ *French* ~ *English*, moitié français moitié anglais. ~ *as big as*, moitié moins grand que. ~ *as big again*, moitié plus g. *not* ~*! P* tu parles! P. ~*-&-*~, moitié-moitié. ~*-back* (*Sport*) demi, *m*. ~*-baked*, (*idea*) à la manque. ~*-brother*, demi-frère, *m*. ~*-caste*, métis, se. ~ *fare*, ~ *price* (*Theat. &c*), demi-place, *f*, demi-tarif, *m*. ~*-hearted*, tiède, sans enthousiasme. ~*-holiday*, après-midi libre, *m*. ~*-length* (*portrait*), en buste. ~ *light*, demi-jour, *m*. *at* ~*-mast* (*flag*), en berne. ~*-open*, *a*, entrouvert, entrebâillé; (*v.t.*) entrouvrir. ~ *past twelve*,

midi, minuit & demi. ~ *past two*, deux heures & demie. *at ~ price*, à moitié prix. ~-*sister*, demi-sœur, *f.* (*Sch.*) ~-*term*, congé de demi-trimestre, *m.* ~-*time*, (*Sport*) mi-temps, *f;* (*Ind.*) *ad*, à mi-temps. ~*way*, à mi-chemin. ~*way up* [*the hill*], à mi-côte. ~*way line*, (*Sport*) ligne médiane. ~-*wit*[*ted*], idiot, e. ~-*year*, semestre, *m.* ~-*yearly*, *a*, semestriel.

halibut, *n*, flétan, *m.*

hall, *n*, (*entrance*) vestibule, hall, *m*, entrée, *f;* (*large room*) salle, *f. village* ~, salle paroissiale. *dining* ~, réfectoire, *m.* (*Univ.*) ~, ~*s of residence*, pavillon (*m*), cité universitaire, *f.* ~-*mark*, *n*, poinçon; (*fig.*) sceau, *m.* ~ *porter*, concierge, *m,f.* ~ *stand*, vestiaire, *m.*

hallo, *i*, bonjour! salut! (*Tel.*) allô! (*shout*) hé! (*surprise*) tiens!

hallow, *v.t*, sanctifier, consacrer. ~*ed ground*, terre sainte. **Halloween,** *n*, veille de la Toussaint, *f.*

hallucination, *n*, hallucination, *f.*

halo, *n*, (*saint*) auréole, *f;* (*Astr.*) halo, *m.*

halt, *n*, halte, *f*, arrêt, *m.* (*fig.*) *call a ~ to*, mettre le holà à, m. fin à. ¶ *v.i*, faire halte; s'arrêter. (*Mil.*) ~! halte[-là]! ~**ing,** *a*, hésitant.

halter, *n*, (*horse*) licou, *m;* (*noose*) corde, *f.*

halve, *v.t*, partager en deux; réduire de moitié. ~*d hole* (*Golf*), trou partagé, *m.*

halyard, *n*, drisse, *f.*

ham, *n*, jambon, *m.* ~ *& eggs*, œufs au jambon, *m.pl.* (*P actor*) cabotin, e; (*Radio*) radio-amateur, *m.* ~-*fisted*, maladroit. ~-*string*, *v.t*, couper les jarrets à; (*fig.*) couper les moyens à.

hamlet, *n*, hameau, *m.*

hammer, *n*, marteau; (*gun*) chien, *m.* ¶ *v.t*, marteler, battre; (*play &c*) éreinter. ~ *in*, (*nail*) enfoncer [à coups de marteau].

hamper[1], *n*, [gros] panier en osier, *m.*

hamper[2], *v.t*, gêner, entraver.

hand, *n*, main, *f. hold in one's* ~, tenir à la main. *take by the* ~, prendre par la m. *clever with his* ~*s*, adroit de ses m. *made, written &c by* ~, fait, écrit &c à la m. *at* ~, à portée de la m., sous la m. ~ *in* ~, la m. dans la m. *fall into the* ~*s of*, tomber entre les m. de. *take s.o, sth in* ~, prendre qn, qch en m. *have sth well in* ~, avoir qch bien en m. *keep one's* ~ *in*, garder la m. *give s.o a* [*helping*] ~, donner un coup de m. à qn. ~ *in glove with s.o*, de mèche avec qn. *live from* ~ *to mouth*, vivre au jour le jour. *on every* ~, de tous côtés. *on the one* ~. *on the other* ~, d'une part.. d'autre part. (*worker*) ouvrier, ère. ~*s*, (*Ind.*) main d'œuvre, *f;* (*Naut.*) hommes, *m.pl. lost with all* ~*s*, perdu corps & biens. (*clock*) aiguille, *f;* (*Cards*) main; (*game*) partie, *f.* ¶ *a*, (*brake, grenade, luggage, saw*) à main; (*cream &c*) pour les m. ~*bag*, sac à main, *m.* ~*book*, manuel, livret, *m.* ~*cuff*, *v.t*, mettre les menottes à; (*n.pl.*) menottes, *f.pl.* ~*ful*, poignée, *f. in* ~*fuls*, par poignées. ~*grip*, (*cycle*) poignée. ~*icraft*, [travail d']artisanat, *m.* ~*iwork*, ouvrage, *m*, œuvre, *f.* ~*kerchief*, mouchoir, *m.* ~*s off!* bas les mains! ~*out*, documentation, *f*, prospectus; (*press*) communiqué, *m.* ~-*picked*, (*fig.*) trié sur le volet. ~*rail*, (*stairs*) rampe, *f;* (*bridge*) garde-fou, *m.* ~*shake*, poignée de main, *f.* ~ *to* ~ (*fight*), corps à corps. ~*s up!* haut les mains! ~*writing*, écriture, *f.* ¶ *v.t*, passer. ~ *down* (*fig.*), transmettre. ~ *in*, remettre. ~ *out*, distribuer. ~ *over*, remettre; (*to justice*) livrer; (*surrender*) céder.

handicap, *n*, (*Sport*) handicap; (*fig.*) désavantage, *m.* ¶ *v.t*, (*Sport, gen.*) handicaper. ~*ped*, (*mentally, physically*) mentalement, physiquement handicapé.

handle, *n*, (*broom, knife*) manche; (*door, suitcase, umbrella*) poignée; (*basket, bucket*) anse; (*saucepan*) queue, *f;* (*pump, stretcher*) bras, *m;* (*crank* ~) manivelle, *f.* ~*bars*, (*cycle*) guidon, *m.* ¶ *v.t*, (*tool*) manier; (*goods*) manipuler; (*ship, car*) manœuvrer; (*pers., animal*) manier, s'y prendre avec; (*problem*) s'occuper de. ~ *roughly*, malmener. ~**r,** *n*, (*dog*) dresseur, euse [de chiens]. **handling,** *n*, maniement, *m*, manipulation; (*goods*) manutention; (*ship*) manœuvre, *f.*

handsome, *a*, beau; (*gift*) généreux. ~**ly,** *ad*, (*reward*) grassement, généreusement.

handy, *a*, (*at hand*) sous la main; (*useful*) commode, pratique; (*pers.*) adroit. *to be* ~ *with*, savoir se servir de. ~*man*, factotum, *m;* (*at home*) bricoleur, *m.*

hang, *v.t.ir*, (*&* ~ *up*) suspendre; accrocher (*on*, à); (*criminal*) pendre; (*wallpaper*) poser. (*fig.*) *to* ~ *fire*, traîner en longueur. ¶ *v.i*, pendre, être suspendu *ou* accroché; (*hair*) tomber. ~ **about,** (*dawdle*) traîner; *v.t*, (*streets*) traîner dans; (*place*) hanter. ~ **back,** hésiter. ~ **down,** pendre. ~ **on,** (*wait*) attendre; (*hold out*) tenir bon. ~ *on!* (*phone*) ne quittez pas! ~ *on to*, (*branch*) s'accrocher à. ~ **out,** (*washing*) étendre. *v.i*, (*P live*) percher *P.* ~-*dog look*, air de chien battu, *m.* ~-*glider*, aile volante, *f.* ~*man*, bourreau, *m.* ~*nail*, envie, *f. to have a* ~*over*, avoir la gueule de bois *P*, avoir mal aux cheveux *P.* ~-*up*, complexe, *m.* ~**er,** *n*, (*coat* ~) cintre, *m.* ~-*on*, (*pers.*) parasite, *m.* ~**ing,** *a*, suspendu; (*light*) pendant. ~ *cupboard*, penderie, *f. a* ~ *matter*, un cas pendable. ¶ *n*, (*execution*) pendaison, *f.* ~*s*, tentures, *f.pl.*

hangar, *n*, (*Aero.*) hangar, *m.*

hank, *n*, écheveau, *m.*

hanker after, aspirer à, avoir envie de.

hankie, *n, abb. of* **handkerchief.**
Hanover, *n,* Hanovre, *m.*
haphazard, *ad,* au hasard, au petit bonheur. ¶ *a,* ~ *arrangement,* disposition fortuite.
happen, *v.i,* arriver, se passer, se produire. *what* ~*ed?* qu'est-ce qui s'est passé? *whatever* ~*s,* quoiqu'il arrive. *sth ghastly* ~*ed to me,* il m'est arrivé qch d'affreux. *as if nothing had* ~*ed,* comme si de rien n'était. *how does it* ~ *that..?* comment se fait-il que..? (+*subj.*) (*chance*) *if I* ~ *to find it,* s'il m'arrive de le trouver. *I.* ~ *to know..,* il se trouve que je sais.. ~**ing,** *n,* événement, *m.*
happily, *ad,* (*play &c*) tranquillement; (*luckily*) heureusement. *live* ~, vivre heureux. **happiness,** *n,* bonheur, *m;* félicité, *f.*
happy, *a,* heureux, content (*with, about,* de; *to do,* de faire). *I'll be* ~ *to come,* je viendrai volontiers. (*phrase, result*) heureux. ~ *medium,* juste milieu, *m.* ~ *Christmas!* joyeux Noel! ~ *New Year!* bonne année! ~*-go-lucky,* insouciant.
harangue, *n,* harangue, *f.* ¶ *v.t,* haranguer.
harass, *v.t,* harceler; (*worry*) tracasser, tourmenter.
harbour, *n,* port, *m.* ~ *master,* capitaine de port, *m.* ¶ *v.t,* héberger, abriter; (*criminal*) receler; (*feelings*) nourrir, entretenir.
hard, *a,* dur; (*difficult*) difficile; (*work, life*) dur, pénible; (*study*) assidu; (*pers.*) dur, sévère, impitoyable; (*master*) exigeant; (*winter*) rude; (*water*) dur. ~ *cash,* espèces, *f.pl.* ~ *court* (*Ten.*), terre battue. ~ *currency,* devise forte. ~ *drinker,* gros buveur. ~ *drug,* drogue dure. ~ *facts,* réalité brutale. *no* ~ *feelings!* sans rancune! ~ *of hearing,* dur d'oreille. ~ *labour,* travaux forcés. ~ *luck!* ~ *lines! P* pas de chance! manque de pot! *P.* ~ *sell,* battage, *m.* ¶ *ad, hit* ~, frapper fort, sec, cogner dur. (*work*) dur, d'arrache-pied; (*look*) fixement; (*drink*) sec. *think* ~, penser bien; réfléchir profondément. (*rain*) à verse; (*snow*) dru; (*freeze*) fort, à pierre fendre. ~ *by,* tout près. (*Naut.*) ~ *a-starboard!* à tribord toute! ~*-&-fast,* (*rule*) absolu. ~*back,* (*book*) cartonné. ~*-board,* Isorel, *m.* ~*-boiled,* (*egg*) dur; (*pers.*) dur à cuire *P.* ~*core* (*Build.*), blocaille, *f.* ~*-fought,* âprement disputé. ~*-headed,* réaliste. ~*-hearted,* au cœur dur. ~*-up,* à court d'argent. ~*ware,* quincaillerie, *f;* (*computers*) matériel, hardware, *m.* ~*ware dealer,* quincailler, *m.* ~*-wearing,* résistant, durable. ~*-working,* travailleur. ~**en,** *v.t. & i,* durcir. ~ *one's heart,* s'endurcir. ~*ed,* (*criminal*) endurci. ~**ly,** *ad,* (*treat*) durement, sévèrement; (*scarcely*) à peine; ne... guère. ~ *anyone, ever,* presque personne, jamais. *I* ~ *know her,* c'est à peine si je la connais. ~**ness,** *n,* dureté; difficulté; rigueur, sévérité, *f.* ~**ship,** *n,* souffrance, *f;* privations, épreuves, *f.pl.*
hardy, *a,* fort, robuste; (*plant*) résistant [au gel]. **hardihood,** *n,* hardiesse, *f.*
hare, *n,* lièvre, *m.* ~*bell,* campanule, *f.* ~*-brained,* (*pers.*) écervelé; (*scheme*) insensé. ~*lip,* bec-de-lièvre, *m.* ¶ *v.i,* ~ *in &c,* entrer &c en trombe.
harem, *n,* harem, *m.*
haricot beans, *n.pl,* haricots blancs, *m.pl.*
hark, *i,* écoutez! ¶ *v.i,* ~ *back to,* revenir sur.
harlequin, *n,* arlequin, *m.*
harm, *n,* mal; tort, *m.* ¶ *v.t,* faire du mal à; nuire à. *you'll come to no* ~, il ne t'arrivera rien. *I see no* ~ *in that,* je n'y vois aucun mal. ~**ful,** *a,* nuisible (*to,* à). ~**less,** *a,* (*animal*) inoffensif; (*pers.*) pas méchant; (*action*) innocent.
harmonic†, *a. & n,* harmonique, *m.* **harmonica,** *n,* harmonica, *m.* **harmonious†,** *a,* harmonieux. **harmonium,** *n,* harmonium, *m.* **harmonize,** *v.t,* harmoniser. ¶ *v.i,* (*colours &c*) s'harmoniser (*with,* avec). **harmony,** *n,* harmonie, *f;* accord, *m. in* ~ *with,* en accord avec.
harness, *n,* harnais, *m. die in* ~, mourir debout. *get back into* ~, reprendre le collier. ~ *room,* sellerie, *f.* ¶ *v.t,* harnacher; (*to cart*) atteler; (*fig: resources*) exploiter.
harp, *n,* harpe, *f.* ¶ *v.i,* ~ *on,* rabâcher.
harpoon, *n,* harpon, *m.* ¶ *v.t,* harponner.
harpsichord, *n,* clavecin, *m.*
harrow, *n,* herse, *f.* ¶ *v.t,* herser; (*fig.*) déchirer le cœur de. ~**ing,** *a,* déchirant, angoissant.
harry, *v.t,* harceler; (*country*) dévaster.
harsh†, *a,* dur; (*climate*) rude; (*words*) âpre; (*voice*) aigre. ~**ness,** *n,* dureté; rudesse; âpreté; aigreur, *f.*
hart, *n,* cerf, *m.*
harum-scarum, *a. & n,* tête de linotte, *f.*
harvest, *n,* moisson; récolte; (*grapes*) vendange, *f.* ~ *festival,* fête de la moisson, *f.* ¶ *v.t,* (*grain, fig.*) moissonner; (*fruit*) récolter. ~**er,** *n,* moissonneur, euse; (*Mach.*) moissonneuse, *f.*
hash, *n,* (*Cook.*) hachis; (*fig.*) gâchis, *m. make a* ~ *of,* (*job*) bousiller *P,* faire un gâchis de, louper *P.*
hashish, *n,* (*abb.* **hash**) haschisch (*abb.* hasch) *m.*
hassle *P, n,* (*fuss, bother*) empoisonnements *P, m.pl,* histoire, *f;* (*chaos*) pagaïe, *f.*
hassock, *n,* agenouilloir; coussin, *m.*
haste, *n,* hâte, *f. in* ~, à la hâte. *in great* ~, en toute h. *to make* ~ **& hasten,** *v.i,* se dépêcher, se hâter, s'empresser (*to do,* de faire). **hasten,** *v.t,* hâter, précipiter. **hasty†,** *a,* (*glance*) rapide; (*departure*) précipité; (*words*) irréfléchi; (*pers.*) emporté.
hat, *n,* chapeau, *m.* ~ *in hand,* chapeau bas. *take off one's* ~, se découvrir (*to s.o,* pour saluer qn). *keep it under your* ~*!* gardez ça

pour vous! motus! ~ *stand,* porte-chapeaux, *m.*

hatch[1], *n,* (*Naut.*) écoutille, *f. under ~es,* dans la cale. *serving ~,* passe-plat, *m. ~back* (*car*), avec hayon arrière, *m.*

hatch[2], *v.i,* (*eggs*) éclore; (*v.t.*) faire éclore; (*fig: plot*) ourdir, tramer. **~ing,** *n,* éclosion, *f.*

hatchet, *n,* hachette, *f.* ~ *faced,* au figure en lame de couteau, *f.*

hate, *n,* haine, *f.* ¶ *v.t,* haïr; détester. ~ *to do, doing,* avoir horreur de faire. **~ful†,** *a,* haïssable; odieux. **hatred,** *n,* haine, *f. full of ~,* haineux.

hatter, *n,* chapelier, *m.*

haughtily, *ad,* avec hauteur, d'une manière hautaine. **haughtiness,** *n,* hauteur, morgue, *f.* **haughty,** *a,* hautain, altier, rogue.

haul, *n,* (*fish*) coup de filet; (*thieves*) butin; (*journey*) trajet, voyage, *m.* ¶ *v.t,* traîner, tirer; (*Naut. & ~ in*) haler. ~ *down,* (*sail*) amener. **~age,** *n,* transport routier, *m.* ~ *contractor,* entrepreneur de transports, *m.*

haunch, *n,* hanche, *f;* (*meat*) cuissot, *m. on its ~es,* (*dog*) assis sur son derrière.

haunt, *n,* (*pers., animal*) lieu fréquenté; (*thieves*) repaire. *favourite ~,* (*café &c*) lieu de prédilection, *m.* ¶ *v.t,* (*lit., fig.*) hanter.

Havana, *n,* la Havane. ~ [*cigar*], havane, *m.*

have, *v.t. ir,* (*& ~ got*) avoir, posséder; (*meals, food*) prendre. *I'll ~ coffee,* je prendrai du café. *to ~ a bath,* prendre un bain. (*news, letter &c*) recevoir. *to ~ good holidays,* passer de bonnes vacances. *to ~ a good time,* s'amuser bien. ¶ *v. aux,* avoir, être. *I ~ lost,* j'ai perdu. *I ~ come,* je suis venu. *I ~ got up,* je me suis levé. ¶ *v. modal, I ~* [*got*] *to leave,* je dois partir, il faut que je parte. *he doesn't ~ to come,* il n'est pas obligé de venir, il n'a pas besoin de v. (*causative*) *to ~ sth done,* faire faire qch. ~ *the car mended,* faire réparer la voiture. ~ *one's hair cut,* se faire couper les cheveux. ~ *a tooth out,* se faire arracher une dent. ~ *an operation,* se faire opérer. (*wish*) *what would you ~ me do?* que voulez-vous que je fasse? *I won't ~ her disturbed,* je ne veux absolument pas qu'on la dérange. *I had* (*I'd*) *rather speak to him,* j'aimerais mieux lui parler. *you had* (*you'd*) *better keep quiet,* vous feriez mieux de vous taire. *he was had P,* il s'est fait avoir *ou* rouler *P.* ~ *in,* faire entrer; (*doctor*) faire venir. ~ *it in for s.o,* avoir une dent contre qn. ~ *it off with s.o P*,* s'envoyer qn *P*.* ~ *on,* (*clothes*) porter; (*pers.*) faire marcher. ~ *it out with,* s'expliquer avec.

haven, *n,* (*fig.*) havre, refuge, abri, *m.*

haversack, *n,* musette, *f,* sac, *m.*

havoc, *n,* ravages, dégâts, *m.pl. play ~ with,* désorganiser complètement.

haw (*Bot.*) *n,* cenelle, *f. ~thorn,* aubépine, *f.*

hawk, *n,* (*& Pol. fig.*) faucon, *m. have eyes like a ~,* avoir des yeux de lynx.

hawker, *n,* colporteur; (*house to house*) démarcheur, *m.*

hawser, *n,* haussière, *f.*

hay, *n,* foin, *m. make ~,* faire les foins. ~ *fever,* rhume des foins, *m. ~loft,* fenil, *m. ~maker,* faneur, euse. ~ *wire P,* (*pers., Mach.*) détraqué. *~making,* fenaison, *f. ~rick, ~stack,* meule de foin, *f.*

hazard, *n,* hasard, *m;* (*risk*) risque, danger, *m.* ¶ *v.t,* (*life*) hasarder, risquer; (*opinion*) hasarder. **~ous,** *a,* hasardeux.

haze, *n,* brume, *f.* (*fig.*) *to be in a ~,* être dans le brouillard. **hazy,** *a,* brumeux; (*outline*) flou; (*idea*) vague. *to be ~ about,* avoir une idée très vague de.

hazel, *n,* noisetier, coudrier, *m;* (*att., colour, eyes*) noisette, *inv.* ~ *nut,* noisette, *f.*

he, *pn,* (*unstressed*) il. *~'s alive,* il vit. *there ~ is,* le voilà. *~'s an actor,* il est acteur, c'est un acteur. (*stressed*) lui. ~ *& I,* lui & moi. *taller than ~,* plus grand que lui. *HE didn't say so,* ce n'est pas lui qui l'a dit. ~ *who, ~ that,* celui qui. ¶ *n. & att,* mâle, *m. ~-goat,* bouc, *m.*

head, *n,* tête, *f.* ~ *of hair,* chevelure, *f.* ~ *down,* la tête baissée. ~ *downwards,* la t. en bas. ~ *first,* la t. la première. *my ~ aches,* j'ai mal à la t. *to be a ~ taller than s.o,* dépasser qn d'une t. *win by a short ~,* gagner d'une courte t. (*fig.*) *keep one's ~ above water,* se maintenir à flot. *give s.o his ~,* lâcher la bride à qn. (*mind*) tête. *to get it into one's ~ that,* se mettre dans la t. que. *it's gone out of my ~,* ça m'est sorti de la t. *he's got his ~ screwed on,* il a la t. sur les épaules. *it's above my ~,* ça me dépasse. *the wine went to his ~,* le vin lui est monté à la t. *go off one's ~,* perdre la tête, perdre le nord *P.* (*flower, hammer, nail*) tête; (*arrow*) pointe, *f;* (*bed*) chevet, *m;* (*on beer*) mousse, *f;* (*celery*) pied; (*page, stairs*) haut, *m;* (*river*) source, *f;* (*ship*) avant, cap, nez, *m;* (*tape recorder*) tête magnétique; (*coin*) face, *f. ~s or tails?* pile ou face? (*heading*) *under this ~,* sous ce titre *ou* cette rubrique. (*leader*) (*firm, family*) chef, *m;* (*Sch.*) directeur, trice. ~ *of state,* chef d'Etat. *at the ~ of,* (*list*) en tête de; (*firm*) à la t. de. ¶ *a,* principal; (*gardener*) en chef. *~ache,* mal de tête, *m. ~band,* bandeau, *m.* ~ *clerk,* chef de bureau, *m.* ~ *cold,* rhume de cerveau, *m.* ~ *cook,* chef [de cuisine] *m. ~dress,* coiffure; (*lace*) coiffe, *f. ~gear,* couvre-chef, *m. ~land,* cap, promontoire, *m. ~light,* (*Mot.*) phare; (*train*) fanal, *m. ~line,* (*news*) manchette, *f;* gros *ou* grands titres. *~long, a,* (*flight*) précipité; *ad,* (*fall*) la tête la première; (*run*) à toute allure. *~master,* directeur; (*lycée*) proviseur. *~mistress,* directrice, *f.* ~ *office,* bureau *ou* siège central. *~-on,* (*collision*) de front. ~*-phones*, casque, *m*. ~*quarters*, (*Mil.*) quartier général. ~*scarf*, foulard, *m*. ~*stone*, pierre tombale, *f*. ~*strong*, entêté, volontaire. ~ *waiter*, maître d'hôtel, *m*. ~*way*, progrès, *m*. *make* ~*way*, faire des progrès. ~*wind*, vent debout, *m*. ¶ *v.t*, (*list, poll*) venir en tête de; (*body of people*) être à la t. de. ~ *a procession*, ouvrir la marche. (*chapter*) intituler. (*Foot.*) ~ *the ball*, faire une tête. ¶ *v.i*, (*Naut.*) mettre le cap (*for*, sur; *out to sea*, au large). ~ *for*, se diriger vers. ~ *off*, *v.t*, détourner. *v.i*, partir. ~**ed**, *a*, (*paper*) à en-tête. ~**er**, *n*, plongeon, *m*. *take a* ~, piquer une tête. ~**ing**, *n*, titre, *m*, rubrique, *f*; (*letter*) en-tête, *m*. ~**y**, *a*, (*wine*) capiteux; (*success*) enivrant.

heal, *v.t*, guérir. ¶ *v.i*, ~ *up*, (*wound*) se cicatriser. ~**er**, *n*, guérisseur, euse. ~**ing**, *n*, guérison, *f*.

health, *n*, santé, *f*. *in good, bad* ~, en bonne, mauvaise santé. *Department of H*~, Ministère de la Santé publique, *m*. *to drink s.o's* ~, boire à la s. de qn. ~ *centre*, centre médico-social, *m*. ~ *insurance*, assurance maladie, *f*. ~ *resort*, station climatique, *f*. *National H*~ *Service* ≃ la Sécurité Sociale. ~ *visitor* ≃ infirmière visiteuse. ~**y†**, *a*, sain; bien portant; (*climate*) salubre.

heap, *n*, tas, amas, monceau, *m*. ~*s of things*, des tas de choses. *I've* ~*s of time*, j'ai largement le temps. ¶ *v.t*, entasser, amonceler.

hear, *v.t. & i. ir*, entendre. *I* ~*d him come in*, je l'ai entendu entrer. *I can't* ~ *you*, je ne vous entends pas. *make o.s* ~*d*, se faire entendre. (*news*) apprendre. ~ *from*, recevoir des nouvelles de. ~ *of s.o, sth*, entendre parler de qn, qch. ~**er**, *n*, auditeur, trice. ~**ing**, *n*, (*sense*) ouïe, *f*. *to be hard of* ~, avoir l'oreille dure. *in my* ~, en ma présence. *within* ~, à portée de voix. (*Law: case*) audience; (*witness*) audition, *f*. ~ *aid*, appareil acoustique, *m*. ~*say*, *n*, ouï-dire, *m*.

hearse, *n*, corbillard, *m*.

heart, *n*, cœur, *m*. *have a weak* ~, être cardiaque. *at* ~, au fond. *with all my* ~, de tout mon cœur. *in his* ~ *of* ~*s*, au fond de son c. *with a heavy* ~, le c. gros *ou* serré. *take sth to* ~, prendre qch à c. *to set one's* ~ *on* (*sth, doing*), vouloir à tout prix (qch, faire). *to one's* ~*'s content*, à cœur joie; (*eat, drink, sleep*) tout son soûl, t. son content. *to take, lose* ~, prendre, perdre courage. *learn by* ~, apprendre par cœur. ~*ache*, chagrin, *m*. ~ *attack*, crise cardiaque, *f*. ~*beat*, battement de c., *m*. ~*breaking*, à vous fendre le c. ~*broken*, au c. brisé. ~ *complaint*, ~ *disease*, maladie de c., *f*. ~ *failure*, arrêt du c., *m*. ~*felt*, sincère. ~*less*, (*pers.*) sans c.; (*action*) cruel. ~*rending*, déchirant. ~ *surgeon*, chirurgien cardiologue, *m*. ~*-to-*~, *a. & ad*, à c. ouvert. ~ *transplant*, greffe du c., *f*. ~**en**, *v.t*, encourager.

hearth, *n*, foyer, *m*, cheminée, *f*. ~ *rug*, tapis de foyer, *m*.

heartily, *ad*, cordialement; (*laugh*) de tout son cœur; (*eat*) de bon appétit. **hearty**, *a*, cordial; (*laugh*) gros; (*meal*) copieux; (*pers.*) vigoureux; jovial.

heat, *n*, chaleur, *f*. (*Cook.*) *at low* ~, à feu doux. (*passion*) feu, *m*, passion, *f*. *in the* ~ *of the moment*, dans le feu de l'action. (*Sport*) [épreuve] éliminatoire, *f*. (*animals*) *on* ~, en rut, *m*, en chaleur. ~ *stroke*, coup de chaleur, *m*. ~*wave*, vague de c., *f*. ¶ *v.t*, (& ~ *up*) chauffer; (*reheat*) réchauffer. ¶ *v.i*, (*room*) se réchauffer. ~**ed**, *a*, (*pers.*) échauffé; (*debate*) passionné. ~**er**, *n*, appareil de chauffage, *m*. ~**ing**, *n*, chauffage, *m*. *central* ~, c. central.

heath, *n*, (*land*) lande; (*shrub*) bruyère, *f*.

heathen, *a. & n*, païen, enne.

heather, *n*, bruyère, brande, *f*.

heave, *v.t.ir*, (*lift*) soulever; (*pull*) tirer, traîner; (*throw*) lancer; (*sigh*) pousser. ¶ *v.i*, (*sea, bosom*) se soulever; (*retch*) avoir des haut-le-cœur. ~ *to* (*Naut.*) *v.t.* (& *i*), (se) mettre en panne.

heaven, *n*, ciel, paradis, *m*. ~ *knows when &c.*, Dieu sait quand &c. ~ *only knows!* Dieu seul le sait! *good* ~*s!* mon Dieu! *thank* ~*!* Dieu merci! (*sky*) *the* ~*s*, ciel. ~**ly**, *a*, céleste; (*fig.*) divin, merveilleux.

heavily, *ad*, lourdement, pesamment; (*sleep*) profondément. ~*-built*, solidement bâti. **heaviness**, *n*, pesanteur, *f*, poids, *m*; lourdeur, *f*. **heavy**, *a*, lourd; pesant; (*rain, swell*) fort; (*sea, shower, loss, drinker*) gros; (*work*) pénible; (*blow*) violent. ~ *cold*, gros rhume. ~ *luggage*, gros bagages. ~ *goods vehicle*, poids lourd. *to be* ~*-handed*, avoir la main lourde. ~*weight*, (*Box.*) poids lourd, *m*.

Hebrew, *a*, hébraïque. ¶ (*language*) *n*, l'hébreu, *m*.

heckle, *v.t*, interpeller. **heckling**, *n*, interpellation, *f*, interruptions, *f.pl*.

hectic, *a*, (*life &c*) agité, bousculé, trépidant.

hector, *v.t*, rudoyer. ~**ing**, *a*, autoritaire.

hedge, *n*, haie, *f*. ~*hog*, hérisson, *m*. ~*row*, haie, *f*. ~ *sparrow*, fauvette des haies, *f*. ¶ *v.t*, (& ~ *in*) entourer d'une h.; (*fig.*) entourer. ~ *one's bets*, se couvrir. ¶ *v.i*, répondre évasivement.

heed, *n*, attention, *f*. ¶ *v.t*, faire attention à. ~**less**, *a*, insoucieux.

heel[1], *n*, talon, *m*. [*hot*] *on the* ~*s of*, aux trousses de, sur les talons de. *take to one's* ~*s*, prendre ses jambes à son cou. (*dog*) ~*!* au pied! (*fig.*) *bring to* ~, rappeler à l'ordre. (*P man*) salaud *P*, *m*. ¶ *v.t*, (*Rugby*) talonner.

heel[2], *v.i*, (& ~ *over*) (*boat*) gîter; (*truck*)

pencher.
hefty, *a,* solide, costaud.
heifer, *n,* génisse, *f.*
height, *n,* hauteur; (*mountain*) altitude; (*pers.*) taille, *f. what ~ are you?* combien mesurez-vous? (*folly &c*) comble, *m. at, in the ~ of,* (*summer, battle*) au plus fort de; (*season*) en pleine saison; (*fashion*) à la toute dernière mode. **~en,** *v.t,* rehausser, surélever; (*fig.*) augmenter, intensifier.
heinous†, *a,* odieux; atroce.
heir, ess, *n,* héritier, ère. *~loom,* meuble &c de famille, *m.*
helicopter, *n,* hélicoptère, *m.*
heliotrope, *n,* héliotrope, *m.*
helium, *n,* hélium, *m.*
hell, *n,* enfer, *m. a ~ of a din P,* un tapage du diable *P. go ~ for leather,* aller à un train d'enfer. *where the ~ can he be?* où est-ce qu'il peut bien être? *oh ~!* zut alors! *go to ~! P,* va te faire voir *P.* **~ish,** *a,* infernal, diabolique.
hello = hallo.
helm, *n,* barre, *f,* gouvernail, *m. be at the ~,* (*lit., fig.*) tenir la barre. [*take the*] *~,* (*Naut.*) barrer. *~sman, n,* homme de barre; barreur, *m.*
helmet, *n,* casque, *m.*
help, *n,* aide, assistance, *f,* secours, *m. ~!* au secours! à l'aide! *with the ~ of,* (*pers.*) avec l'aide de; (*tool*) à l'aide de. *to be of ~ to,* rendre service à. [*daily*] *~,* femme de ménage, *f. mother's ~,* aide familiale. ¶ *v.t, & i,* aider (qn à faire); secourir, venir à l'aide de. *~ one another,* s'entraider. (*food*) *~ s.o to soup,* servir du potage à qn. (*avoid*) *I can't ~ seeing,* je ne peux pas m'empêcher de voir. *I can't ~ it,* ce n'est pas ma faute; je n'y peux rien; c'est plus fort que moi. **~er,** *n,* aide, *m,f.* **~ful,** *a,* (*pers.*) serviable, obligeant; (*tool &c*) utile. **~ing,** *n,* (*food*) portion, *f.* ¶ *a, give a ~ hand,* donner un coup de main. **~less,** *a,* impuissant; impotent; (*powerless*) sans ressource.
helter-skelter, *ad,* à la débandade. ¶ *n,* débandade, *f.*
hem, *n,* ourlet; bord, *m. ~stitch,* ourlet à jour. ¶ *v.t,* ourler. *~ in,* cerner. **~ming,** *n,* point d'ourlet, *m.*
hemisphere, *n,* hémisphère, *m.*
hemorrhage = haemorrhage.
hemp, *n,* chanvre, *m.*
hen, *n,* poule; femelle, *f. ~ bird,* oiseau femelle, *m. ~ coop,* cage à poulets, mue, *f. ~ house,* poulailler, *m. ~-pecked,* mené par le bout du nez par sa femme.
hence, *ad,* (*therefore*) de là, d'où. (*time*) *2 months ~,* dans 2 mois, d'ici 2 m. **~forth,** *ad,* désormais, dorénavant, dès maintenant.
henchman, *n,* partisan; (*pej.*) acolyte, *m.*
henna, *n,* henné, *m.*
hepatitis, *n,* hépatite, *f.*
her, *pn object,* (*direct*) la, l'; (*emphatic*) elle. *it's ~,* c'est elle. *I know HER well,* elle, je la connais bien. (*indirect*) lui; (*after pr.*) elle: *for ~,* pour elle. *think of ~,* pensez à elle. ¶ *a,* son, sa, ses.
herald, *n,* héraut, *m.* ¶ *v.t,* annoncer. **~ic,** *a,* héraldique. **~ry,** *n,* héraldique, *f.*
herb, *n,* herbe, *f.* (*Cook.*) *~s,* fines herbes. **~aceous,** *a,* herbacé. *~ border,* bordure de fleurs vivaces, *f.* **~al,** *a,* d'herbes. **~alist,** *n,* herboriste, *m,f.* **~ivorous,** *a,* herbivore.
Herculean, *a,* herculéen. *a Hercules,* un hercule.
herd, *n,* troupeau, *m;* (*deer*) harde, *f. the ~ instinct,* l'instinct grégaire. ¶ *v.t,* mener. ¶ *v.i, ~ together,* s'attrouper. **~sman,** *n,* gardien de troupeau, bouvier, *m.*
here, *ad,* ici. *far from ~,* loin d'ici. *up, down to ~,* jusqu'ici. *from ~ to Paris,* d'ici à P. *Jean isn't ~,* J. n'est pas là. voici. *~ I am,* me voici. *~ are my friends,* voici mes amis. *~ comes Paul,* voici P. qui arrive. *my sister ~ says,* ma sœur que voici dit. *this boy ~,* ce garçon-ci. (*roll call*) *~!* présent! *~ you are!* (*take this*), tiens, voilà! (prends!) *~ & there,* ça & là, par-ci par-là. *~, there & everywhere,* un peu partout. *~ lies* (*grave*), ci-gît. *~ below,* ici-bas.
hereabouts, *ad,* près d'ici, dans les environs. **hereafter,** *ad,* après. *the ~,* l'au-delà, *m.* **hereby,** *ad,* par la présente. **herewith,** *ad,* sous ce pli, ci-joint.
hereditary†, *a,* héréditaire. **heredity,** *n,* hérédité, *f.*
heresy, *n,* hérésie, *f.* **heretic,** *n,* hérétique, *m,f.* **~al,** *a,* hérétique.
heritage, *n,* héritage, patrimoine, *m.*
hermaphrodite, *n,* hermaphrodite, *m.*
hermetic†, *a,* hermétique.
hermit, *n,* ermite, *m. ~ crab,* bernard-l'ermite, *m.* **~age,** *n,* ermitage, *m.*
hernia, *n,* hernie, *f.*
hero, *n,* héros, *m. ~ worship,* culte des héros, *m.* **~ic†,** *a,* héroïque. **~ine,** *n,* héroïne, *f.* **~ism,** *n,* héroïsme, *m.*
heroin, *n,* (*drug*) héroïne, *f.*
heron, *n,* héron, *m.* **~ry,** *n,* héronnière, *f.*
herpes, *n,* herpès, *m.*
herring, *n,* hareng, *m. ~ boat,* harenguier, *m. ~bone,* (*design*) chevrons, *m.pl.*
hers, *pn,* le sien, la sienne, les siens, les siennes. *my bed & ~,* mon lit & le sien. *a friend of ~,* un de ses amis [à elle]. *this ring is ~,* cette bague est à elle. **herself,** *pn,* (*reflexive*) se. *she hurt ~,* elle s'est blessée. *she said to ~,* elle s'est dit. (*emphatic*) elle-même. *she did it ~,* elle l'a fait elle-même. [*all*] *by ~,* toute seule.
hesitant, *a,* hésitant, irrésolu.
hesitate, *v.i,* hésiter (sur, devant qch; à faire;). **hesitation,** *n,* hésitation, *f.*

hessian, *n,* toile de jute, *f.*
het up *P, a,* agité (*about,* par). *to get ~,* s'énerver.
heterogeneous, *a,* hétérogène.
heterosexual, *a,* hétérosexuel.
hew, *v.t.ir,* couper; (*stone*) tailler.
hexagon, *n,* hexagone, *m.* **~al,** *a,* hexagonal.
heyday, *n, in his ~,* à l'apogée de sa gloire.
hi, *i,* hé! (*greeting*) salut!
hiatus, *n,* lacune, *f;* (*Gram.*) hiatus, *m.*
hibernate (*Zool.*) *v.i,* hiberner.
hiccup, hiccough, *n,* hoquet. *m, to have ~s,* avoir le h. ¶ *v.i,* hoqueter.
hidden, *p.p of* **hide.**
hide[1], *v.t.ir,* cacher (*from s.o,* à qn); (*feelings*) dissimuler. *hidden from sight,* dérobé aux regards. ¶ *v.i,* (*& go into hiding*) se cacher (*from,* de). *~ & seek,* cache-cache, *m. ~away, ~out, hiding place,* cachette, *f.*
hide[2], *n,* peau, *f,* cuir, *m. ~-bound,* (*fig.*) borné, rigide. *hiding,* (*P thrashing*) raclée, *f.*
hideous†, *a,* (*sight*) hideux; (*crime*) atroce.
hierarchy, *n,* hiérarchie, *f.*
hieroglyph & ~ic, *n,* hiéroglyphe, *m.*
hi-fi, *a. & n,* haute fidélité, hi-fi, *P, inv & f.*
higgledy-piggledy, *ad,* pêle-mêle.
high, *a,* haut. *how ~ is that tree?* quelle est la hauteur de cet arbre? *it is 9 metres ~,* il est haut de 9 m. *ou* il a 9 m. de haut. (*esteem, official, pressure, tension*) haut; (*price, salary, rent*) élevé; (*speed, value*) grand; (*fever, wind*) fort; (*character, ideal*) noble; (*Mus: note, voice*) aigu; (*meat*) avancé; (*game*) faisandé. *~ on drugs P,* défoncé par la drogue *P. ~ altar,* maître-autel, *m. in the ~est degree,* au plus haut degré. *~ & dry,* (*Naut.*) échoué. *leave s.o ~ & dry,* laisser qn en plan. *get up on one's ~ horse,* monter sur ses grands chevaux. *~ jump,* saut en hauteur, *m. he's for the ~ j. P,* qu'est-ce qu'il va prendre! *P. H~ Mass,* grand-messe, *f. to be ~ & mighty,* se donner de grands airs. (*Mus.*) *the ~ notes,* les aigus, *m.pl. pay a ~ price for,* payer cher. *to run a ~ temperature,* avoir de la température *ou* une forte t. *on the ~ seas,* en haute mer. *~ society,* le grand monde. *hit the ~ spots P,* faire la noce *P. ~ street,* (*town*) rue principale; (*village*) grand-rue, *f. in ~ summer,* en plein été. ¶ *ad,* haut; (*fly*) à haute altitude. *~ up,* en haut. *~ & low,* (*hunt*) partout. (*fig.*) *fly ~,* viser haut. *comps: ~-brow,* intellectuel. *~-class,* de premier ordre. *~-fidelity,* haute fidélité. *~-flown,* ampoulé. *~-flying,* (*pers.*) ambitieux. *~-handed,* tyrannique. *~light,* (*Art*) rehaut, *m;* (*of evening*) clou, *m. v.t,* souligner. *~-minded,* noble. *~-pitched,* (*sound*) aigu. *~-pressure,* (*salesman*) de choc *P. ~-rise block,* tour [d'habitation], *f. ~road,* grand-route, *f. ~-speed,* ultra-rapide. *~-spirited,* plein d'entrain. *~way,* grand-route, voie publique, *f. ~way code,* code de la route, *m. ~wayman,* voleur de grand chemin, *m.* (*Adm.*) *H~ways Department,* les Ponts & Chaussées. **~er,** *a,* supérieur (*than,* à). *~ bid,* surenchère, *f. ~ education,* enseignement supérieur. ¶ *ad,* plus haut. **~ly,** *ad,* très, extrêmement; (*paid*) très bien. *~ strung,* nerveux. **~ness,** *n,* hauteur; (*title*) Altesse, *f.*
hijack, *v.t,* détourner. ¶ *n,* (*& ~ing*) détournement, *m.* **~er,** *n,* pirate de l'air.
hike, *n,* excursion à pied, *f.* ¶ *v.i, go ~ing,* faire des excursions à p. **~r,** *n,* excursionniste [à p.], *m,f.*
hilarious, *a,* hilare; (*funny*) désopilant, marrant *P,* bidonnant *P.* **hilarity,** *n,* hilarité, *f.*
hill, *n,* colline, *f,* coteau, *m,* côte, pente, *f. up ~ & down dale,* par monts & par vaux. **~ock,** *n,* petite colline, tertre, butte, *f.* **~side,** *n,* flanc de coteau, *m.* **~y,** *a,* accidenté.
hilt, *n,* poignée; garde, *f.* (*fig.*) *up to the ~,* jusqu'à la garde, jusqu'au cou.
him, *pn object,* (*direct*) le, l'; (*emphatic*) lui. *it's ~,* c'est lui. *HE doesn't know,* il ne sait pas, lui. (*indirect*) lui; (*after pr.*) lui. *for ~,* pour lui. *think of ~,* pensez à lui. **himself,** *pn,* (*reflexive*) se. *he hurt ~,* il s'est blessé. *he said to ~,* il s'est dit. (*emphatic*) lui-même. *he did it ~,* il l'a fait lui-même. [*all*] *by ~,* tout seul.
hind[1], *n,* (*deer*) biche, *f.*
hind[2], *a, ~ legs, ~ feet,* pattes de derrière, *f.pl. ~most,* dernier. *~quarters,* arrière-train, *m. with ~sight,* rétrospectivement.
hinder, *v.t,* gêner, entraver; (*prevent*) empêcher (*s.o from doing,* qn de faire). **hindrance,** *n,* obstacle, *m.*
Hindu, *a,* hindou. ¶ *n,* Hindou, e. **Hinduism,** *n,* hindouisme, *m.*
hinge, *n,* (*door*) gond, *m;* (*box, stamp*) charnière, *f.* ¶ *v.i, ~ on,* (*lit.*) pivoter sur; (*fig.*) dépendre de. **~d,** *a,* à charnières.
hint, *n,* allusion; insinuation, *f. gentle ~,* allusion discrète. *drop a ~,* faire une allusion, faire comprendre. *know how to take a ~,* comprendre à demi-mot. (*trace*) soupçon; (*tip*) conseil, tuyau, *m.* ¶ *v.i, ~ at,* faire allusion à.
hip, *n,* hanche, *f. ~ bath,* bain de siège, *m. ~ flask,* flacon plat, *m. ~ pocket,* poche revolver, *f. ~ measurement,* tour de hanches, *m.*
hippie *P, n,* hippie, *m,f.*
hippopotamus, *n,* hippopotame, *m.*
hire, *n,* location, *f. for ~,* à louer. *~ purchase,* achat à crédit, *m.* ¶ *v.t,* louer; (*pers.*) engager.
his, *a,* son, sa, ses. *~ son,* son fils. *~ wife,* sa femme. *~ friend,* son ami(e). *~ books,* ses livres. ¶ *pn,* le sien, la sienne, les siens, les siennes. *my bed & ~,* mon lit & le sien. *a friend of ~,* un de ses amis [à lui]. *this pipe is ~,* cette pipe est à lui.

hiss, *v.t. & i,* siffler. ~**[ing],** *n,* sifflement; (*Theat. &c*) sifflet, *m.*
historian, *n,* historien, ne. **historic[al]**†, *a,* historique. **history,** *n,* histoire, *f.*
histrionic, *a,* théâtral. ~**s,** *n.pl,* de la comédie.
hit, *n,* coup, *m;* (*not miss*) coup réussi; (*shot*) tir réussi; (*Fenc.*) touche, *f;* chanson, pièce &c à succès, *f;* (*song*) tube *P, m. to be, make a big* ~, avoir un grand succès. ~ *or miss,* au petit bonheur. ¶ *v.t.ir,* frapper; (*knock against*) heurter, cogner; (*car, bus*) heurter, entrer en collision avec; (*target*) atteindre; (*fig.*) toucher, affecter. ~ *one's head against,* se cogner la tête contre. ~ *the nail on the head,* mettre le doigt dessus. ~ *back,* (*fig.*) riposter. ~ *it off with,* s'entendre bien avec. ~ *out at,* (*fig.*) attaquer. ~ *[up]on,* tomber sur.
hitch, *n,* anicroche, *f,* contretemps, *m.* ¶ *v.t,* accrocher (*to,* à). ~ *up,* (*trousers*) remonter. ~ *a lift &* ~ (*v.i*) = ~*-hike.* ~**-hike,** *v.i,* faire de l'auto-stop, f. du stop *P.* ~**-hiker,** *n,* autostoppeur, euse. ~**-hiking,** *n,* auto-stop, *m.*
hither & thither, *ad,* ça & là. **hitherto,** *ad,* jusqu'à présent, jusqu'ici.
hive, *n,* ruche, *f.* ¶ *v.t,* ~ *off,* séparer.
hoard, *n,* réserve, provision [secrète] *f;* (*of money*) trésor, magot, *m.* ¶ *v.t,* amasser, accumuler.
hoarding, *n,* palissade, *f;* (*for posters*) panneau-réclame, *m.*
hoarfrost, *n,* gelée blanche, *f,* givre, *m.*
hoarse, *a,* enroué. ~**ly,** *ad,* d'une voix enrouée. ~**ness,** *n,* enrouement, *m.*
hoary, *a,* (*hair*) blanc, blanchi; (*joke*) éculé.
hoax, *n,* mystification, *f;* canular, *m.* ¶ *v.t,* mystifier; faire un canular à. ~**er,** *n,* mystificateur, trice.
hobble, *v.i,* clopiner, boitiller. ~ *along,* aller clopin-clopant. ¶ *v.t,* (*horse*) entraver.
hobby, *n,* passe-temps favori, hobby, *m.* ~**horse,** *n,* dada, *m.*
hobnail, *n,* caboche, *f.* ~**ed,** *a,* clouté, ferré.
hobnob, *v.i,* ~ *with,* frayer avec.
hock[1], *n,* vin du Rhin, *m.*
hock[2], *n,* (*animal*) jarret, *m.*
hockey, *n,* hockey, *m.* ~ *stick,* crosse de h., *f.*
hocus-pocus, *n,* tour de passe-passe, *m;* mystification, *f.*
hod, *n,* oiseau [de maçon], *m.*
hoe, *n,* houe; binette, *f;* sarcloir, *m.* ¶ *v.t,* (*ground*) biner; (*weeds*) sarcler.
hog, *n,* cochon, porc [châtré], *m;* (*greedy* ~) goinfre, *m. go the whole* ~, aller jusqu'au bout.
Hogmanay, *n, Sc,* la Saint-Sylvestre.
hoist, *n,* appareil de levage; (*goods*) monte-charge, *m inv.* ¶ *v.t,* (*sail &c*) hisser.
hold, *n,* prise; (*over s.o*) influence, *f,* empire, *m* (sur qn). *get* ~ *of,* saisir, se procurer, s'emparer de; obtenir, trouver; (*pers.*) contacter, joindre. *keep* ~ *of,* ne pas lâcher. (*ship*) cale, *f;* (*rock climb*) prise. ¶ *v.t,* tenir. ~ *tight,* bien tenir, serrer. ~ *one's ground,* tenir bon, t. ferme. ~ *hands,* se tenir par la main. ~ *o.s ready,* se tenir prêt. (*interest, breath*) retenir; (*Sport: record; Fin: shares*) détenir; (*post*) occuper; (*weight*) supporter; (*contain*) contenir; (*possess*) posséder, avoir; (*opinion*) avoir; (*consider*) maintenir, considérer. ~ *s.o responsible,* considérer qn responsable, tenir qn pour r. (*retain; money, prisoner*) garder. (*Tel.*) ~ *the line!* ~ *on!* ne quittez pas! ~ *one's tongue,* tenir sa langue, se taire. ~ *water,* (*argument*) tenir debout. ¶ *v.i,* (*rope*) tenir [bon]; (*weather*) se maintenir; (*argument &* ~ *good*) être valable. ~ **back,** *v.t,* retenir; (*facts*) cacher. ¶ *v.i,* hésiter. ~ **down,** maintenir en place; (*job*) occuper. ~ **forth,** pérorer. ~ **off,** (*enemy*) tenir à distance. ~ **on,** tenir bon; attendre. ~ *on to,* se cramponner à; (*idea*) se raccrocher à; (*money*) garder. ~ **out,** *v.t,* tendre; (*hope*) offrir. ¶ *v.i,* tenir bon. ~ *out against,* résister à. ~ **up,** *v.t,* soutenir; (*delay*) retarder; (*pers.*) attaquer. ~ **with,** *I don't* ~ *with that,* je suis contre cela. ~**-all,** *n,* fourre-tout, *m.* ~**-up,** *n,* (*bank*) hold-up, *m,* attaque à main armée *f;* (*delay*) retard; (*traffic*) embouteillage, *m.* ~**er,** *n,* support, *m;* porte- (*always m.*): *menu* ~, porte-menu, *m.* (*pers: ticket, shares*) détenteur, trice; (*post &c*) titulaire, *m,f.* ~**ing,** *n,* (*land*) propriété, ferme, *f;* (*shares*) avoir, *m,* possession, *f.* ~*s,* intérêts, *m.pl.*
hole, *n,* (*gen., Golf*) trou; (*rabbit &c*) terrier, *m. make a* ~ *in,* trouer, faire un t. dans. (*fig.*) *to be in a* ~, être dans le pétrin. *get s.o out of a* ~, tirer qn d'embarras, dépanner qn *P.* (*place pej.*) trou, bled *P, m.* ¶ *v.t,* trouer. (*Golf*) ~ *out in one,* faire un trou en un.
holiday, *n,* (*official, Bank*) jour férié, [jour de] fête, *f;* (*annual &c*) vacances, *f.pl;* (*day off*) [jour de] congé, *m. the* ~*s,* (*Christmas, Easter &c*) les fêtes; (*Sch.*) les vacances [scolaires]. ¶ *a,* (*clothes, spirit*) de vacances. ~ *camp,* camp de v., *m;* (*children*) colonie de v., *f.* ~*maker,* vacancier, ère; (*summer*) estivant, e. ~ *resort,* villégiature, *f.* ¶ *v.i,* passer les vacances.
holiness, *n,* sainteté, *f. His H*~, Sa Sainteté.
Holland *n,* la Holland.
hollow, *a,* creux; (*eyes*) cave; (*voice*) caverneux; (*sound*) creux, (*from cave*) caverneux. ¶ *ad, sound* ~, sonner creux. *beat s.o* ~, battre qn à plate couture. ¶ *n,* creux, *m.* ¶ *v.t,* (*&* ~ *out*) creuser, évider.
holly, *n,* houx, *m.*
hollyhock, *n,* rose trémière, *f.*
holocaust, *n,* holocauste, *m.*
holster, *n,* étui de revolver, *m.*
holy, *a,* (*pers.*) saint; (*ground*) sacré; (*bread,*

water) bénit. *H~ Bible,* Sainte Bible. *H~ Ghost, Holy Spirit,* Saint-Esprit, *m. H~ Land,* Terre Sainte. *~ orders,* ordres, *m.pl. H~ See,* Saint-Siège, *m. ~-water stoup,* bénitier, *m.*

homage, *n,* hommage, *m. pay ~ to,* rendre hommage à.

home, *n,* foyer, chez-soi, *m;* maison, *f. he's at ~,* il est à la maison *ou* chez lui. *to leave ~,* quitter la maison. *near my ~,* près de chez moi. *to have a ~ of one's own,* avoir un foyer, un chez-soi. *a lovely ~,* un joli intérieur. *come from a good ~,* avoir une famille comme il faut. *broken ~,* foyer désuni. *make yourself at ~!* faites comme chez vous! *feel at ~ with s.o,* se sentir à l'aise avec qn. (*country*) pays [natal], *m,* patrie, *f. at ~ & abroad,* chez nous & à l'étranger. (*institution*) maison, foyer. *old people's ~,* maison de retraite. *children's ~,* m. pour enfants. ¶ *ad,* à la maison, chez soi. *return ~,* rentrer [à la maison]; (*from abroad*) r. au pays. *journey ~,* chemin du retour, *m. see s.o ~,* raccompagner qn chez lui, chez elle. *drive ~,* (*nail*) enfoncer. *bring sth ~ to s.o,* faire comprendre qch à qn. ¶ *a,* (*life, cooking, problems*) familial; (*life*) de famille; (*visit*) à domicile; (*policy, trade*) intérieur; (*news*) de l'intérieur. *~ help,* aide familiale. *~ match,* match [joué] à domicile. *H~ Office, H~ Secretary,* ministère, ministre de l'Intérieur, *m. ~ town,* ville natale. [*a few*] *~ truths,* ses quatre vérités, *f.pl.* ¶ *v.i,* (*pigeon*) revenir au colombier. *comps: ~-grown,* du jardin; du pays. *~land,* patrie, *f. ~-loving,* casanier. *~-made,* fait à la maison. *~less,* sans foyer. *to be ~sick,* avoir le mal du pays. *~sickness,* mal du pays, *m;* nostalgie (*for,* de), *f. ~ward, a,* du retour; *ad,* (*& ~wards*) vers chez soi, v. la maison. *~ward bound,* sur le chemin du retour. *~work,* devoirs [à la maison], *m.pl. homing pigeon,* pigeon voyageur.

homeopath, *&c.* = **homoeopath** *&c.*

homicidal, *a,* homicide. **homicide,** *n,* (*pers.*) homicide, *m,f;* (*act*) homicide, *m.*

homily, *n,* homélie, *f.*

homoeopath, *n,* homéopathe, *m,f.* **~ic,** *a,* homéopathique. **~y,** *n,* homéopathie, *f.*

homogeneous, *a,* homogène.

homonym, *n,* homonyme, *m.*

homosexual, *a. & n,* homosexuel, elle.

hone, *n,* pierre à aiguiser, *f.*

honest†, *a,* honnête; (*opinion*) sincère; (*face*) franc; (*profit*) honnêtement gagné. *the ~ truth,* la pure vérité. *to be ~ with you,* à vous dire la vérité. **~y,** *n,* honnêteté, *f. in all ~,* en toute sincérité. (*Bot.*) monnaie du pape, *f.*

honey, *n,* miel, *m.* (*P pers.*) *yes, ~,* oui, chéri(e). *she's a ~,* c'est un chou *P. ~-bee,* abeille, *f. ~comb,* rayon de miel, *m; v.t,* cribler (*with,* de). *~moon,* lune de miel, *f;* voyage de noces, *m. ~suckle,* chèvrefeuille, *m.* **~ed,** *a,* (*words*) mielleux, doucereux.

honorary, *a,* (*pers.*) honoraire; (*post*) à titre honorifique; (*degree*) honoris causa.

honour, *n,* honneur, *f. in ~ of,* en l'honneur de. *promise on one's ~,* promettre sur l'h. *I am in ~ bound to do,* l'h. m'oblige à faire. *on my ~!* parole d'h.! (*Univ.*) *~s degree in English* ≃ licence d'anglais, *f.* ¶ *v.t,* honorer. **~able†,** *a,* honorable.

hooch *P, n,* gnôle *P, f.*

hood, *n,* capuchon, *m,* cagoule, *f;* (*car*) capote, *f,* (*Am. car*) capot, *m. ~wink,* tromper.

hoof, *n,* sabot, *m.* **~ed,** *a,* à sabots.

hook, *n,* (*gen., Box.*) crochet; (*Fish.*) hameçon, *m;* (*coat ~*) patère; (*dress*) agrafe, *f;* (*Golf*) coup hooké, *m.* (*fig.*) *take the ~,* gober l'hameçon. *get s.o off the ~,* tirer qn d'affaire. *by ~ or by crook,* de façon ou d'autre. ¶ *v.t,* (*Fish.*) prendre; (*Rugby*) talonner. **~ed,** *a,* (*nose*) crochu, en bec d'aigle. *he's ~ on drugs, on jazz,* c'est un drogué, un mordu du jazz. **~er,** *n,* (*Rugby*) talonneur, *m;* (*P*) putain, *f.*

hookah, *n,* narguilé, *m.*

hooligan, *n,* voyou, *m.*

hoop, *n,* (*barrel*) cercle; (*toy*) cerceau; (*croquet*) arceau, *m.*

hoopoe, *n,* huppe, *f.*

hoot, *n,* (*owl*) hululement; (*Mot.*) coup de klaxon, *m;* (*jeer*) huée, *f.* ¶ *v.i,* hululer; klaxonner; (*& v.t*) huer; (*with laughter*) s'esclaffer. **~er,** *n,* (*factory*) sirène, *f;* (*Mot.*) klaxon, *m.*

hoover, *n,* aspirateur, *m.* ¶ *v.t,* passer l'a. sur *ou* dans.

hop¹, *n,* (*Bot. & ~s*) houblon, *m. ~ field,* houblonnière, *f. ~ pole,* perche à h., *f.*

hop², *n,* saut; (*bird*) sautillement, *m;* (*Aero.*) étape, *f.* ¶ *v.i,* sauter à cloche-pied; sautiller. *~ it! P,* allez! ouste! *P. ~scotch,* marelle, *f.*

hope, *n,* espoir, *m,* espérance, *f. past ~,* sans espoir. *some ~! P,* tu parles! *P.* ¶ *v.i,* espérer (*to do,* faire). *~ for sth,* espérer avoir qch. *I ~ so, not,* j'espère que oui, que non. *hoping to hear from you,* dans l'espoir d'avoir de vos nouvelles, (*Com.*) de vous lire. **~ful,** *a,* (*pers.*) plein d'espoir; (*sign &c*) encourageant. **~less,** *a,* (*pers.*) sans espoir, désespéré; (*state*) irrémédiable

hopper, *n,* (*Tech.*) trémie, *f.*

horde, *n,* horde, *f.*

horizon, *n,* horizon, *m. on the ~,* à l'horizon. **~tal†,** *a,* horizontal.

horn, *n,* corne, *f;* (*pl, deer*) bois, *m.pl;* (*insect*) antenne, *f;* (*Mus.*) cor; (*Mot.*) klaxon, *m. draw in one's ~s,* restreindre son train de vie. *~beam,* charme, *m. ~-rimmed spectacles,*

lunettes à monture d'écaille, *f.pl.* **~ed,** *a,* à cornes. **~y,** *a,* (*hands*) calleux.
hornet, *n,* frelon, *m.*
horoscope, *n,* horoscope, *m.*
horrible† *&* **horrid,** *a,* horrible, affreux; (*pers.*) méchant, détestable.
horror, *n,* horreur, *f. to have a ~ of,* (*sth, doing*) avoir horreur de (qch, faire). ¶ *a,* (*film*) d'épouvante. *~-stricken,* saisi d'horreur.
horse, *n,* cheval, *m;* (*Mil.*) cavalerie, *f;* (*gym*) cheval d'arçons. *clothes ~,* séchoir. *saw ~,* chevalet, *m.* (*fig.*) *straight from the ~'s mouth,* de source sûre. *on ~back,* à cheval. *~-box,* fourgon à chevaux, *m. ~-chestnut,* marron d'Inde; (*tree*) marronnier d'I., *m. ~ dealer,* maquignon, *m. ~fly,* taon, *m. ~hair,* crin, *m. ~man,* cavalier, *m. ~manship,* équitation, *f;* (*skill*) talent de cavalier, *m. ~ meat,* viande de cheval, *f. ~meat butcher's* (*Fr.*), boucherie chevaline. *~play,* jeux brutaux. *~power,* puissance [en chevaux], *f;* (*unit*) cheval-vapeur, *m. a 10 ~power car,* une dix-chevaux. *~ race,* course de chevaux, *f. ~ racing,* les courses, *f.pl. ~-radish,* raifort, *m. ~shoe,* fer à cheval, *m. ~ show,* concours hippique, *m. ~-trading,* (*lit., fig.*) maquignonnage, *m. ~whip, n,* cravache, *f;* (*v.t.*) cravacher. *~woman,* cavalière, *f*
hors[e]y, *a,* (*pers.*) féru de cheval; (*face*) chevalin.
horticultural, *a,* horticole. **horticulture,** *n,* horticulture, *f.* **horticulturist,** *n,* horticulteur, *m.*
hose, *n,* (*& ~pipe*) tuyau, *m;* (*Com: stockings*) bas, *m.pl.* ¶ *v.t,* (*garden*) arroser au jet; (*fire*) a. à la lance. *~ down,* laver au jet. **hosier,** *n,* bonnetier, *m.* **~y,** *n,* bonneterie, *f.*
hospitable, *a,* hospitalier.
hospital, *n,* hôpital, *m. in ~,* à l'hôpital. ¶ *a,* (*bed &c*) d'hôpital; (*staff, service &c*) hospitalier. *~ nurse,* infirmier, ère. *~ patients,* les hospitalisés. **hospitality,** *n,* hospitalité, *f.* **hospitalize,** *v.t,* hospitaliser.
host[1], *n,* hôte; (*hotel*) hôtelier, aubergiste, *m.* **~ess,** *n,* hôtesse; (*bar*) entraîneuse, *f. air ~,* hôtesse de l'air.
host[2], *n,* foule; (*liter.*) armée, *f;* (*of reasons*) tas *P, m.*
host[3], *n,* (*Rel.*) hostie, *f.*
hostage, *n,* otage, *m. take s.o ~,* prendre qn comme ôtage.
hostel, *n,* (*students &c*) foyer, *m. youth ~,* auberge de jeunesse, *f.*
hostile†, *a,* hostile. **hostility,** *n,* hostilité, *f.*
hot, *a,* chaud; (*sun*) brûlant. *to be ~,* (*pers.*) avoir [très, trop] chaud; (*sth*) être [très] c., (*Met.*) *it's very ~,* il fait très c. *to get ~,* (*pers.*) s'échauffer; (*sth*) chauffer, devenir c. *it's too ~ in here,* on a trop c. ici. *have a ~ meal, drink,* manger, boire c. (*Cook.*) piquant, fort; (*news*) tout frais. *~ chase,* poursuite acharnée. *~ favourite,* grand favori. *~ at maths,* calé en maths. *not so ~ P,* pas fameux *P. to have a ~ temper,* s'emporter facilement, être soupe au lait. *to get ~ under the collar,* s'échauffer, se mettre dans tous ses états. ¶ *ad, ~ on his trail,* sur ses talons. *give it to s.o ~ & strong,* passer un bon savon à qn. *~ up P, v.t,* (*food*) [faire] réchauffer; (*engine*) gonfler *P; v.i,* (*situation*) chauffer *P. ~-blooded,* ardent, passionné. *~foot,* à toute vitesse. *~head,* tête chaude. *~headed,* impétueux. *~house,* serre [chaude], *f. ~-water bottle,* bouillotte, *f.* **~ly,** *ad,* (*deny*) vivement; (*pursue*) de près.
hotchpotch, *n,* (*Cook., fig.*) salmigondis, *m.*
hotel, *n,* hôtel, *m. ~ keeper,* hôtelier, ère.
hound, *n,* chien courant, *m. the ~s,* la meute. *ride to ~s,* chasser à courre. ¶ *v.t,* (*pers.*) poursuivre. *~ down,* traquer. *~ out of,* chasser hors de.
hour, *n,* heure, *f. at all ~s,* à toute heure. *~ by ~,* d'heure en h. *from one ~ to the next,* d'une h. à l'autre. *pay by the ~,* payer à l'h. *it's 2 ~s by road, by train,* c'est à 2 h-s de route, de train. *I spent ~s doing it,* j'ai mis des h-s à le faire. *~glass,* sablier, *m. ~ hand,* petite aiguille, *f.* **~ly,** *a,* (*visit*) toutes les h-s; (*rate*) horaire. ¶ *ad,* toutes les h-s; (*expect*) à tout moment.
house, *n,* maison; (*detached*) villa, *f;* (*small*) pavillon *m. at our ~,* chez nous. *set up ~,* s'installer. *move ~,* déménager. *keep ~ for s.o,* tenir la maison de qn. *~ of cards,* (*lit., fig.*) château de cartes, *m. on the ~,* aux frais de la maison. *H~ of Commons, Lords,* Chambre des Communes, des Lords. *the H~ of Hanover,* la maison des Hanovre. (*Theat.*) salle, *f;* spectateurs, *m.pl. full ~,* salle pleine. *'~ full',* 'complet'. (*Com.*) maison [de commerce]. *publishing ~,* m. d'édition. *banking ~,* établissement bancaire, *m. ~ agent,* agent immobilier. *~breaker,* cambrioleur; (*Build.*) démolisseur, *m. ~coat,* peignoir, *m. ~ dog,* chien de garde, *m. ~ fly,* mouche commune, *f. ~hold,* ménage, *m;* (*staff*) maison, gens de la maison, *m.pl; a,* (*expenses &c*) de ménage, du m. *~hold linen,* linge de maison, *m. ~holder,* chef de famille, *m. ~keeper,* femme de charge; gouvernante, *f. a good ~keeper,* bonne ménagère. *~keeping,* ménage, *m;* économie domestique, *f. ~keeping money,* argent du ménage, *m. ~maid,* bonne, femme de chambre, *f. ~ martin,* hirondelle de fenêtre, *f. ~ painter,* peintre en bâtiments, *m. ~ physician, surgeon,* interne en médecine, en chirurgie, *m,f. ~proud,* méticuleux. *proclaim from the ~tops,* crier sur les toits. *to give a ~ warming,* pendre la crémaillère. *~wife,* ménagère; (*no career*) femme au

foyer, *f.* ~*work*, ménage, *m. to do the* ~*work*, faire le m. ¶ *v.t*, loger, héberger; (*building*) abriter. **housing,** *n*, logement, *m.* ~ *shortage*, crise du logement, *f.*
hovel, *n*, taudis, bouge, *m.*
hover, *v.i*, planer; (*pers:* ~ *around*) roder. ~**craft,** *n*, aéroglisseur, *m.*
how, *ad*, comment. ~ *are you?* comment allez-vous? ~ *do you do?* (*on introduction*) enchanté Monsieur &c. ~ *is it that?* comment se fait-il que? + *subj.* ~ *come? P*, comment ça se fait? *P.* ~ *was the film?* comment as-tu trouvé le film? ~ *much,* ~ *many*, combien [de]. ~ *long?* combien de temps? ~ *long is..?* quelle est la longueur de..? ~ *old is he?* quel âge a-t-il? comme, que. ~ *stupid you are!* comme *ou* que tu es bête! ce que tu es b.! *P.* ~ *about going to see?* si on allait voir?
however, *ad*, ~ *one does it*, de quelque manière qu'on le fasse. ~ *rich he may be*, quelque *ou* si riche qu'il soit. ~ *did you do that?* comment as-tu bien pu faire ça? ¶ *c*, pourtant, cependant, toutefois.
howl, *n*, hurlement, *m;* (*wind*) mugissement, *m.* ¶ *v.i*, hurler; mugir; (*cry*) pleurer, brailler. ~**er,** *n*, gaffe; (*Sch.*) bourde, perle [d'écolier], *f.*
hoyden, *n*, garçon manqué, *m.*
hub, *n*, moyeu; (*fig.*) centre, *m.* (*Mot.*) ~*-cap*, enjoliveur, *m.*
hubbub, *n*, brouhaha, *m.*
huddle, *v.i*, se blottir (*together*, les uns contre les autres). *go into a* ~, se réunir en petit groupe. ~*d over*, penché sur.
hue, *n*, teinte; nuance, *f.*
hue & cry, *with* ~, à cor & à cri. *raise a* ~, crier haro (sur qn).
huff, *n*, *in a* ~, froissé. *get into a* ~, prendre la mouche. ¶ *v.t*, (*Draughts*) souffler.
hug, *n*, étreinte, *f.* ¶ *v.t*, serrer dans les bras, étreindre. (*Naut.*) ~ *the shore*, serrer la côte.
huge, *a*, énorme, vaste. ~**ly,** *ad*, énormément, extrêmement.
hulk, *n*, vaisseau rasé; ponton, *m.* ~**ing,** *a*, gros, lourd.
hull, *n*, (*ship*) coque, *f.*
hullabaloo *P*, *n*, chambard *P*, raffut *P*, *m.*
hullo = **hallo.**
hum, *v.i. & t*, (*bee &c*) bourdonner; (*top*) ronfler; (*tune*) fredonner, chantonner; (*engine*) vrombir.
human†, *a*, humain. ~ *being*, être humain. **humane**†, *a*, humain. **humanist,** *n*, humaniste, *m,f.* **humanitarian,** *a. & n*, humanitaire, *m,f.* **humanity,** *n*, humanité, *f.* **humanize,** *v.t*, humaniser.
humble†, *a*, humble. *of* ~ *origin*, d'origine modeste. ¶ *v.t*, humilier. ~ *o.s*, s'abaisser.
humbug, *n*, (*pers.*) charlatan, *m*, fumiste *P*, *m,f;* (*talk &c*) fumisterie *P*, *f.*
humdrum, *a*, monotone; banal.
humerus, *n*, humérus, *m.*
humid, *a*, humide. ~**ity,** *n*, humidité, *f.*
humiliate, *v.t*, humilier. **humility,** *n*, humilité, *f.*
humming bird, *n*, oiseau-mouche, colibri, *m.*
hummock, *n*, mamelon, *m*, bosse, *f.*
humorist, *n*, humoriste, *m,f.* **humorous,** *a*, (*story, writer*) humoristique; (*pers., talk*) plein d'humour, amusant. ~**ly,** *ad*, avec humour. **humour,** *n*, (*mood*) humeur, *f. in a good, bad* ~, de bonne, mauvaise h. (*comic*) humour, *m. a sense of* ~, le sens de l'humour. ¶ *v.t*, ménager, faire plaisir à.
hump, *n*, bosse, *f.* ¶ *P v.t*, porter. ~ *around*, trimballer *P.* ~*backed*, (*pers.*) bossu; (*bridge*) en dos d'âne.
humus, *n*, humus, *m.*
hunch, *n*, (*hump*) bosse, *f;* (*idea*) intuition, petite idée, *f.* ¶ *v.t*, (*shoulders*) voûter. ~**back(ed),** *n.* (*& a.*), bossu, e.
hundred, *a. & n*, cent, *m. a* ~ *words*, cent mots. *2* ~ *words*, deux cents mots. *about a* ~ *words*, une centaine de mots. *101*, cent un. *200*, deux cents. *201*, deux cent un. (*year*) *in 1900*, en dix-neuf cents; *in 1910*, en dix-neuf cent dix. ~*s of*, des centaines de. *a* ~ *percent, ad*, à cent pour cent. ~**th,** *a. & n*, centième, *m,f;* (*fraction*) centième, *m.* ~**weight,** *n*, poids de 112 livres, *m.* (= 50.7 kg).
Hungarian, *a*, hongrois. ¶ *n*, Hongrois, e; (*language*) le hongrois. **Hungary,** *n*, la Hongrie.
hunger, *n*, faim, *f.* ~ *strike*, grève de la faim, *f.* ¶ *v.i*, ~ *for, after*, avoir faim de. **hungrily,** *ad*, avidement. **hungry,** *a*, *to be* ~, avoir faim. *to be very* ~, avoir très f., être affamé. *to be ravenously* ~, avoir une f. de loup. (*fig.*) ~ *for*, avide de.
hunk, *n*, gros morceau; (*bread*) quignon, *m.*
hunt, *n*, chasse, *f;* (*people*) chasse, chasseurs, *m.pl. tiger* ~, chasse au tigre. (*fig., search*) recherche, *f.* ¶ *v.t*, chasser; (*thief*) poursuivre. ¶ *v.i*, chasser, aller à la chasse. ~ [*around*] *in*, fouiller dans. ~ *down*, (*pers.*) traquer. ~ *up*, rechercher. ~**er,** *n*, chasseur; cheval de chasse. **hunting,** *n*, chasse à courre; (*fox* ~) c. au renard. ~ *lodge*, pavillon de c., *m.* **huntsman,** *n*, chasseur, *m.*
hurdle, *n*, claie; (*Sport*) haie, *f;* (*fig.*) obstacle, *m.* ~ *race*, course de haies, *f.*
hurl, *v.t*, lancer, jeter. ~ *o.s*, se jeter.
hurly-burly, *n*, tohu-bohu, *m.*
hurrah, -ray, *n. & i*, hourra, *m.*
hurricane, *n*, ouragan, *m.* ~ *lamp*, lampe-tempête, *f.*
hurry, *n*, précipitation, hâte, *f. to be in a* ~, être pressé. ¶ *v.t*, (*pers.*) faire presser, faire se dépêcher; bousculer; (*work*) presser. ¶ *v.i*, se dépêcher, se presser, se hâter (*to do*, de faire). ~ *in, out*, entrer, sortir à la hâte. ~*up!*

dépêchez-vous!
hurt, *n,* mal, *m;* blessure, *f.* ¶ *a,* blessé; (*offended*) blessé, froissé. ¶ *v.t.ir,* faire mal à; blesser. ~ *o.s,* se faire mal, se blesser. ~ *one's foot,* se blesser au pied. (*distress*) faire de la peine à. ~ *s.o's feelings,* froisser, blesser qn.
husband, *n,* mari, époux, *m.* ¶ *v.t,* ménager.
hush, *n,* silence, *m.* ~ *money,* prix du silence, *m.* ¶ *i,* silence!; chut! ¶ *v.t,* faire taire. ~ *up,* étouffer. ~-~ *P,* [ultra-]secret.
husk, *n,* (*grain*) balle; (*nut*) écale, *f.*
husky, *a,* (*hoarse: pers.*) enroué; (*voice*) rauque.
hussy, *n,* coquine, *f.*
hustle, *v.t,* bousculer.
hut, *n,* hutte, cabane, *f;* (*mountain*) refuge, *m.*
hutch, *n,* clapier, *m.*
hyacinth, *n,* jacinthe, *f.*
hybrid, *a. & n,* hybride, *m.*
hydrangea, *n,* hortensia, *m.*
hydrant, *n,* prise d'eau, *f. fire* ~, bouche d'incendie, *f.*
hydraulic, *a. &* **~s,** *n,* hydraulique, *f.*
hydrocarbon, *n,* hydrocarbure, *m.* **hydrochloric,** *a,* chlorhydrique. **hydroelectric,** *a,* hydroélectrique. **hydrofoil,** *n,* hydrofoil, *m.* **hydrogen,** *n,* hydrogène, *m.* ~ *bomb,* bombe à hydrogène, *f.* **hydrometer,** *n,* hydromètre, *m.* **hydrophobia,** *n,* hydrophobie, *f.* **hydroplane,** *n,* hydroglisseur, *m.*
hyena, *n,* hyène, *f.*
hygiene, *n,* hygiène, *f.* **hygienic†,** *a,* hygiénique.
hymn, *n,* hymne, *m;* (*Eccl.*) hymne, *f,* cantique, *m.* ~ *book,* livre de cantiques, *m.*
hypercritical, *a,* hypercritique. **hypermarket,** *n,* hypermarché, *m.* **hypertension,** *n,* hypertension, *f.*
hyphen, *n,* trait d'union, *m.*
hypnosis, *n,* hypnose, *f.* **hypnotic,** *a,* hypnotique. **hypnotism,** *n,* hypnotisme, *m.* **hypnotist,** *n,* hypnotiseur, euse. **hypnotize,** *v.t,* hypnotiser.
hypochondriac, *a. & n,* hypochondriaque, *m,f.* **hypocrisy,** *n,* hypocrisie, *f.* **hypocrite,** *n,* hypocrite, *m,f.* **hypocritical†,** *a,* hypocrite. **hypodermic,** *a,* hypodermique. ~ *syringe,* seringue hypodermique, *f.* **hypothermia,** *n,* hypothermie, *f.* **hypothesis,** *n,* hypothèse, *f.* **hypothetic(al)†,** *a,* hypothétique.
hysterectomy, *n,* hystérectomie, *f.*
hysteria, *n,* hystérie, *f.* **hysteric(al),** *a,* (*Med.*) hystérique; (*gen.*) surexcité; (*sobs &c*) convulsif. *become* ~, avoir une crise de nerfs. **hysterics,** *n,* crise de nerfs, *f;* (*laughter*) fou rire.

I

I, *pn,* je; (*stressed*) moi. *he &* ~ *are going,* lui & moi nous partons. *it's* ~, c'est moi.
ibex, *n,* bouquetin, *m.*
ibis, *n,* ibis, *m.*
ice, *n,* glace, *f;* (*black* ~) verglas, *m. my feet are like* ~, j'ai les pieds glacés. ~ [*cream*], glace. *strawberry* ~, g. à la fraise. ~ *age,* période glaciaire, *f.* ~ *axe,* piolet, *m.* ~*berg,* iceberg, *m.* ~*breaker* (*ship*), brise-glace, *m. inv.* ~ *cube,* glaçon, *m.* ~ *hockey,* hockey sur glace, *m.* ~*house,* glacière, *f.* ~ *rink,* patinoire, *f.* ~ *show,* spectacle sur glace, *m.* ~*-skating,* patinage [sur g.], *m.* ¶ *v.t,* (*cake*) glacer; (*wine*) frapper. ~*d coffee,* café glacé. ¶ *v.i,* ~ *over,* (*windscreen*) givrer.
Iceland, *n,* l'Islande, *f.* **~er,** *n,* Islandais, e. **~ic,** *a. &* (*language*) *n,* islandais, *m.*
icicle, *n,* glaçon, *m.* **icing,** *n,* (*Cook.*) glace, *f,* glaçage, *m.* ~ *sugar,* sucre glace, *m.*
icon, *n,* icône, *f.* **~oclast,** *n,* iconoclaste, *m,f.*
icy, *a,* (*wind, stare*) glacial; (*hands*) glacé; (*road*) verglacé.
idea, *n,* idée, *f. good* ~*!* bonne idée! *I haven't the faintest* ~, je n'ai pas la moindre idée. *to get some* ~ *of the problem,* se faire une idée du problème. *don't get* ~*s into your head,* ne te fais pas des idées. *I have an* ~ *that,* j'ai l'impression que. *I had no* ~ *that,* j'ignorais complètement que. **ideal†,** *a. & n,* idéal, *m.* **~ist,** *n,* idéaliste, *m,f.*
identical†, *a,* identique. **identification,** *n,* identification, *f;* (*papers*) pièce d'identité, *f.* **identify,** *v.t,* identifier. ¶ *v.i,* s'identifier (*with,* avec). **identity,** *n,* identité, *f.* ~ *card,* carte d'identité, *f.*
idiocy, *n,* idiotie, *f.*
idiom, *n,* (*dialect*) idiome; (*phrase*) idiotisme, *m,* expression idiomatique, *f.*
idiosyncrasy, *n,* particularité, petite manie, *f.*
idiot, *n. &* **~ic,** *a,* idiot, e; imbécile, *m,f.*
idle, *a,* (*without work: pers., life*) oisif; (*pers.*) désœuvré; (*unemployed*) en chômage; (*moments*) de loisir; (*machine*) au repos; (*lazy*) paresseux, fainéant; (*pointless*) oiseux, vain; (*promises*) en l'air. **~ness,** *n,* oisiveté, *f,* désœuvrement; chômage, *m;* paresse, *f.* **idler,** *n,* oisif, ive; paresseux, euse, fainéant, e. **idly,** *ad,* sans travailler; paresseusement.

idol, *n,* idole, *f.* **~atrous,** *a,* idolâtre. **~atry,** *n,* idolatrie, *f,* **~ize,** *v.t,* idolatrer.
idyl[l], *n,* idylle, *f.* **idyllic,** *a,* idyllique.
if, *c,* (*condition*) si. *~ it's fine I shall go out,* s'il fait beau je sortirai. *~ it were fine I would go out,* s'il faisait beau je sortirais. *~ I had known I would have invited him,* si j'avais su je l'aurais invité. *~ not,* sinon. *~ so,* si c'est le cas. *as ~,* comme si. (*although*) *even ~,* même si, bien que. *a fine rug ~ rather worn,* un beau tapis bien qu'un peu usé. (*whether*) si. *do you know ~ she is there?* savez-vous si elle est là?
igloo, *n,* igloo, *m.*
ignite, *v.t,* mettre le feu à. ¶ *v.i,* prendre feu. **ignition,** *n,* ignition, *f;* (*Mot.*) allumage, *m.* *~ key,* clef de contact, *f.*
ignoble†, *a,* ignoble.
ignominious†, *a,* ignominieux. **ignominy,** *n,* ignominie, *f.*
ignoramus, *n,* ignorant, e, ignare, *m,f.* **ignorance,** *n,* ignorance, *f.* **ignorant,** *a,* ignorant. *to be ~ of,* ignorer.
ignore, *v.t,* ne pas faire attention à, ne tenir aucun compte de; (*facts*) méconnaître.
ill, *n,* mal, *m. speak ~ of,* médire de, dire du mal de. ¶ *a,* (*sick*) malade, souffrant. *fall ~,* tomber malade. (*bad: health, omen, temper*) mauvais. *~ effects,* conséquences désastreuses. *house of ~ fame, ~ repute,* maison mal famée. *~ feeling,* ressentiment, *m,* rancune, *f.* *~ luck,* malchance, *f.* *~ will,* malveillance, *f. I bear him no ~ will,* je ne lui en veux pas. ¶ *ad,* mal. *~-advised,* malavisé, peu judicieux. *~-bred,* mal élevé. *~-considered,* irréfléchi. *~-fated, ~-starred,* (*day*) néfaste; (*pers.*) infortuné. *~-favoured,* laid. *~-gotten gains,* biens mal acquis, *m.pl.* *~-natured,* désagréable. *~-omened,* de mauvais augure. *to be ~-tempered,* avoir mauvais caractère. *~-timed,* intempestif, inopportun. *~-treat, ~-use,* maltraiter.
illegal†, *a,* illégal. **~ity,** *n,* illégalité.
illegible†, *a,* illisible.
illegitimacy, *n,* illégitimité, *f.* **illegitimate†,** *a,* illégitime.
illicit†, *a,* illicite.
illiterate, *a,* illettré, analphabète. **illiteracy,** *n,* analphabétisme, *m.*
illness, *n,* maladie, *f.*
illogical, *a,* illogique. **~ity,** *n,* illogisme, *m.*
illuminate, *v.t,* éclairer; (*festively*) illuminer; (*sky*) embraser; (*MS.*) enluminer. *~d sign,* enseigne lumineuse. **illumination,** *n,* éclairage, *m;* illumination, *f;* enluminure, *f.* **illumine,** *v.t,* éclairer.
illusion, *n,* illusion, *f. to have no ~s,* ne se faire aucune illusion (*about,* sur). **illusive, illusory,** *a,* illusoire.
illustrate, *v.t,* (*lit., fig.*) illustrer. **illustration,** *n,* illustration, *f.* (*fig.*) *by way of ~,* à titre d'exemple. **illustrator,** *n,* illustrateur, trice. **illustrious,** *a,* illustre. *to make ~,* (*liter.*) illustrer.
image, *n,* image, *f;* (*in water &c*) réflexion, *f;* (*public ~*) image de marque. *he's the ~ of his father,* c'est tout le portrait de son père. **~ry,** *n,* images, *f.pl.* **imaginable,** *a,* imaginable. *the best... ~,* le meilleur... qu'on puisse imaginer. **imaginary,** *a,* imaginaire. **imagination,** *n,* imagination, *f.* **imagine,** *v.t,* [s']imaginer, se figurer; (*suppose*) [s']imaginer, supposer, croire.
imbecile, *a. & n,* imbécile, *m,f;* idiot, e.
imbibe, *v.t,* (*lit.*) boire; (*fig.*) absorber.
imbue, *v.t,* (*fig.*) imprégner (*with,* de).
imitate, *v.t,* imiter. **imitation,** *n,* imitation, *f.* ¶ *a,* (*jewelry*) faux, en simili. *~ leather,* similicuir, imitation c., *m.* **imitative,** *a,* imitatif. **imitator,** *n,* imitateur, trice.
immaculate, *a,* (*gen.*) impeccable. *the I~ Conception,* l'Immaculée Conception, *f.*
immaterial, *a,* sans importance. *it's ~ to me,* cela m'est indifférent.
immature, *a,* qui n'est pas mûr; (*pers.*) qui manque de maturité.
immeasurable, *a,* infini.
immediate†, *a,* immédiat. *my ~ aim,* mon premier but.
immense, *a,* immense. **~ly,** *ad,* immensément. **immensity,** *n,* immensité, *f.*
immerse, *v.t,* immerger, plonger. **immersion,** *n,* immersion, *f.* *~ heater,* chauffe-eau électrique, *m. inv.*
immigrant, *a. & n,* immigrant, e; (*established*) immigré, e.
immigrate, *v.t,* immigrer. **immigration,** *n,* immigration, *f.* *~ authorities,* service de l'i., *m.*
imminence, *n,* imminence, *f.* **imminent,** *a,* imminent.
immoderate†, *a,* immodéré.
immodest†, *a,* immodeste.
immoral, *a,* immoral. **~ity,** *n,* immoralité, *f.*
immortal†, *a. & n,* immortel, le. **~ity,** *n,* immortalité, *f.* **~ize,** *v.t,* immortaliser.
immovable†, *a,* fixe; (*fig.*) inébranlable.
immune, *a,* immunisé (*to,* contre). **immunity,** *n,* immunité, *f.* **immunize,** *v.t,* immuniser.
immutable†, *a,* immuable.
imp, *n,* diablotin, *m;* (*child*) petit diable.
impact, *n,* choc, impact, *m;* (*fig.*) impression, *f.*
impair, *v.t,* (*health*) abîmer; (*relations*) détériorer; (*sight &c*) affaiblir.
impart, *v.t,* (*news*) communiquer.
impartial†, *a,* impartial. **~ity,** *n,* impartialité, *f.*
impassable, *a,* (*barrier*) infranchissable; (*road*) impraticable.
impassioned, *a,* passionné.
impassive, *a,* impassible.
impatience, *n,* impatience, *f.* **impatient,** *a,* impa-

I-N

tient. *to grow* ~, s'impatienter. ~**ly,** *ad,* impatiemment.
impeach, *v.t,* accuser; (*character*) attaquer.
impeccable, *a,* impeccable.
impecunious, *a,* besogneux, nécessiteux.
impede, *v.t,* entraver, gêner. **impediment,** *n,* obstacle, *m. speech* ~, défaut d'élocution, *m.*
impel, *v.t,* pousser; forcer, obliger (à faire).
impending, *a,* imminent.
impenetrable, *a,* impénétrable.
impenitent, *a,* impénitent. ~**ly,** *ad,* sans le moindre repentir.
imperative†, *a. & n.* (*Gram.*), impératif, *m. rest is* ~, le repos s'impose. *it is* ~ *that,* il faut absolument que (+ *subj.*).
imperceptible†, *a,* imperceptible.
imperfect†, *a.* & ~ **[tense],** *n,* imparfait, *m.* ~**ion,** *n,* imperfection, *f.*
imperial, *a,* impérial; (*weights & measures*) britannique. ¶ (*beard*) *n,* [barbiche à l']impériale, *f.* ~**ist,** *n. & a,* impérialiste, *m,f.*
imperil, *v.t,* mettre en danger.
imperious†, *a,* impérieux.
imperishable, *a,* impérissable.
impermeable, *a,* imperméable.
impersonal†, *a,* impersonnel.
impersonate, *v.t,* se faire passer pour. **impersonation,** *n,* (*Theat.*) imitation; (*Law*) supposition de personne, *f.*
impertinence, *n,* impertinence, *f.* **impertinent,** *a,* impertinent (*to s.o,* envers qn). ~**ly,** *ad,* avec impertinence.
imperturbable†, *a,* imperturbable.
impervious, *a,* imperméable; (*fig.*) fermé (*to,* à).
impetuosity, *n,* impétuosité, *f.* **impetuous**†, *a,* impétueux.
impetus, *n,* (*lit., fig.*) impulsion, *f,* élan, *m.*
impiety, *n,* impiété, *f.*
impinge, *v.i:* ~ *on,* venir en contact avec; (*fig.*) affecter, toucher.
impious, *a,* impie.
implacable†, *a,* implacable (*towards,* envers).
implant, *v.t,* implanter.
implement, *n,* outil, instrument, *m.* ¶ *v.t,* exécuter, mettre à effet; (*promise*) accomplir.
implicate, *v.t,* impliquer. **implication,** *n,* implication, *f* (*in,* dans); (*sth implied*) implication, insinuation, *f;* sous-entendu, *m. by* ~, implicitement. **implicit**†, *a,* implicite.
implore, *v.t,* implorer, supplier (qn de faire).
imply, *v.t,* (*fact*) impliquer, suggérer; (*pers.*) laisser entendre. *implied,* implicite, sous-entendu.
impolite†, *a,* impoli. ~**ness,** *n,* impolitesse, *f.*
impolitic, *a,* impolitique.
imponderable, *a. & n,* impondérable, *m.*
import, *n,* (*meaning*) portée, signification, *f,* sens, *m;* (*Com.*) importation, *f.* ~ *duty,* droit d'importation, *m.* ¶ *v.t,* importer. ~**ation,** *n,* importation, *f.* ~**er,** *n,* importateur, trice.
importance, *n,* importance, *f. of no* ~, sans importance. **important,** *a,* important.
importunate, *a,* importun. **importune,** *v.t,* importuner. **importunity,** *n,* importunité, *f.*
impose, *v.t,* imposer; (*fine &c*) infliger (*on,* à); (*tax*) mettre (*on,* sur). ¶ *v.i,* ~ *on s.o,* abuser de la gentillesse de qn. **imposing,** *a,* imposant. **imposition,** *n,* imposition; (*Sch.*) punition, *f.*
impossibility, *n,* impossibilité, *f* (de qch, de faire). **impossible,** *a,* impossible.
impostor, *n,* imposteur, *m.* **imposture,** *n,* imposture, *f.*
impotence, *n,* (*gen., sexual*) impuissance, *f.* **impotent,** *a,* impuissant.
impound, *v.t,* confisquer.
impoverish, *v.t,* appauvrir.
impracticable, *a,* impraticable.
impregnable, *a,* imprenable, inexpugnable.
impregnate, *v.t,* (*lit., fig.*) imprégner (*with,* de); (*fertilize*) féconder.
impresario, *n,* impresario, *m.*
impress, *n,* empreinte, *f.* ¶ *v.t,* (*pers., remark*) impressionner. ~ *favourably,* faire une bonne impression à. (*stamp*) imprimer; (*on memory*) graver. ~ *on s.o,* chercher à bien faire comprendre à qn. ~**ion,** *n,* impression, *f. make a good, bad* ~ *on s.o,* faire une bonne, mauvaise i. à qn. *I'm under the* ~ *that,* j'ai l'i. que. (*imprint*) empreinte, *f;* (*book*) tirage, *m.* ~**ionism,** *n,* impressionnisme, *m.* ~**ionist,** *a. & n,* impressionniste, *m,f.* ~**ive,** *a,* impressionnant.
imprint, *n,* empreinte, *f.* ¶ *v.t,* imprimer.
imprison, *v.t,* emprisonner. ~**ment,** *n,* emprisonnement, *m. 2 years'* ~, 2 ans de prison.
improbability, *n,* improbabilité, invraisemblance, *f.* **improbable,** *a,* improbable; (*story*) invraisemblable.
impromptu, *ad. a. & n,* impromptu, *m.*
improper, *a,* (*behaviour*) inconvenant; (*language*) indécent, incorrect; (*word usage*) abusif. ~**ly,** *ad,* pas convenablement; indécemment; abusivement. **impropriety,** *n,* inconvenance, *f.*
improve, *v.t,* améliorer; prefectionner; (*in appearance*) embellir; (*soil*) amender. ¶ *v.i,* s'améliorer; (*in subject, sport*) faire des progrès. ~ *on,* (*offer*) [r]enchérir sur. ~ *on acquaintance,* gagner à être connu. ~**ment,** *n,* amélioration, *f;* perfectionnement; embellissement; amendement, *m.*
improvidence, *n,* imprévoyance, *f.* **improvident,** *a,* imprévoyant.
improvise, *v.t,* improviser.
imprudence, *n,* imprudence, *f.* **imprudent,** *a,* imprudent. ~**ly,** *ad,* imprudemment.
impudence, *n,* impudence, *f.* **impudent,** *a,* impudent. ~**ly,** *ad,* impudemment.
impugn, *v.t,* attaquer.
impulse, *n,* impulsion, *f. sudden* ~, coup de tête,

m. to act on ~, agir par impulsion. **impulsive,** *a,* impulsif; primesautier.
impunity, *n,* impunité, *f. with* ~, impunément.
impure†, *a,* impur. **impurity,** *n,* impureté, *f.*
imputation, *n,* imputation, *f.* **impute,** *v.t,* imputer.
in, *pr,* (*place*) dans, en, à. ~ *the street,* dans la rue. ~ *town,* en ville. ~ *the country,* à la campagne. ~ *the garden,* au jardin, dans le j. ~ *here,* ici. ~ *there,* là-dedans. (*towns*) à: à Paris. (*countries*) *f:* en; *m:* au(x). en Grèce, au Pérou, aux États-Unis. (*time*) ~ *the morning,* le matin, dans la matinée. ~ *the evening,* le soir, pendant la soirée. ~ *the night,* pendant la nuit. ~ *May,* en mai, au mois de m. ~ *spring,* au printemps. ~ *summer, autumn, winter,* en été, automne, hiver. ~ *1984,* en 1984. *at 10 o'clock* ~ *the morning,* ~ *the evening,* à 10 heures du matin, du soir. *I did it* ~ *2 days,* je l'ai fait en 2 jours. *he's coming* ~ *3 days,* il viendra dans 3 jours. (*superlative*) *the best..* ~ *the world,* le meilleur .. du monde. (*manner*) ~ *Greek,* en grec. ~ *fashion,* à la mode. *dressed* ~ *black,* habillé en noir, vêtu de noir. ~ *a strange way,* d'une manière, d'une façon étrange. (*out of*) *one man* ~ *ten,* un homme sur dix. ¶ *n, the* ~*s & outs of a question,* les tenants & les aboutissants d'une affaire. ¶ *ad, to be* ~, (*home, office &c*) être là; (*train*) être en gare, être arrivé. *to have it* ~ *for s.o P,* avoir une dent contre qn *P. to be well* ~ *with s.o,* être bien avec qn. ~ *between,* entre les deux.
inability, *n,* incapacité (de faire); impuissance, *f* (à faire).
inaccessible, *a,* inaccessible.
inaccuracy, *n,* inexactitude, *f.* **inaccurate†,** *a,* inexact.
inaction, *n,* inaction, *f.* **inactive,** *a,* inactif.
inadequate, *a,* insuffisant. ~**ly,** *ad,* insuffisamment.
inadmissible, *a,* inadmissible.
inadvertently, *ad,* par inadvertance, par mégarde.
inadvisable, *a,* à déconseiller.
inane, *a,* inepte. **inanity,** *n,* ineptie, *f.*
inanimate, *a,* inanimé.
inapplicable, *a,* inapplicable.
inappropriate†, *a,* qui ne convient pas (*to,* à); (*word*) impropre.
inarticulate, *a,* (*pers.*) qui s'emprime avec difficulté; (*sound*) inarticulé. ~ *with rage,* bégayant de colère.
inasmuch, *ad,* ~ *as,* étant donné que, vu que.
inattentive, *a,* inattentif.
inaudible†, *a,* imperceptible, inaudible.
inaugurate, *v.t,* inaugurer.
inauspicious, *a,* peu propice.
inborn *&* **inbred,** *a,* inné.
incalculable, *a,* incalculable.
incandescence, *n,* incandescence, *f.* **incandescent,** *a,* incandescent.
incapable, *a,* incapable (de qch, de faire). **incapability & incapacity,** *n,* incapacité, *f* (de faire). **incapacitate,** *v.t,* rendre incapable.
incarcerate, *v.t,* incarcérer.
incarnate, *a,* incarné. **incarnation,** *n,* incarnation, *f.*
incautious, *a,* imprudent.
incendiary, *a. & n,* (*pers.*) incendiaire, *m,f;* (*bomb*) engin incendiaire, *m.*
incense[1], *n,* encens, *m.*
incense[2], *v.t,* mettre en colère. ~*d,* outré (*at, by,* de, par).
incentive, *n,* motif, stimulant, *m. he has no* ~ *to work,* rien ne le pousse à travailler. ~ *bonus,* prime d'encouragement, *f.*
inception, *n,* commencement, *m.*
incessant, *a,* incessant. ~**ly,** *ad,* sans cesse.
incest, *n,* inceste, *m.* **incestuous,** *a,* incestueux.
inch, *n,* pouce, *m.* (= 2.54 cm). (*fig.*) *to give an* ~, céder d'un pouce. (*fig.*) *within an* ~ *of,* à deux doigts de. ¶ *v.i,* ~ *forward,* avancer petit à petit.
incidence, *n,* fréquence, *f.* **incident,** *n,* incident; (*in book &c*) épisode, *m.* ~**al,** *a,* accessoire, d'importance secondaire; (*chance*) fortuit. ~ *expenses,* faux frais, *m.pl.* ~**ally,** *ad,* (*by the way*) à propos, en passant.
incinerate, *v.t,* incinérer. **incinerator,** *n,* incinérateur, *m.*
incipient, *a,* naissant.
incise, *v.t,* inciser. **incision,** *n,* incision, *f.* **incisive,** *a,* incisif, tranchant. **incisor,** *n,* [dent] incisive, *f.*
incite, *v.t,* inciter, pousser (qn à qch; qn à faire). ~**ment,** *n,* incitation, *f.*
incivility, *n,* incivilité, *f.*
inclement, *a,* inclément.
inclination, *n,* (*all senses*) inclination, *f;* (*liking*) penchant, *m. I have no* ~ *to,* je n'ai aucune envie de. **incline,** *n,* inclinaison, pente, *f.* ¶ *v.t,* (*tilt*) incliner, pencher. ~*d plane,* plan incliné. *I'm* ~*d to accept,* j'incline à accepter. ~*d to laziness,* enclin à la paresse. ~*d to believe,* porté à croire. *he's* ~*d to lie,* il a tendance à mentir. ¶ *v.i,* (*slope*) s'incliner. ~ *towards,* (*opinions*) tendre vers.
include, *v.t,* comprendre, englober, inclure. ~*d on the list,* inclus dans la liste. *service is* ~*d,* le service est compris. *Sundays* ~*d,* y compris le dimanche. **including,** *pr,* y compris. **inclusive,** *a,* compris; (*sum*) global. *from 3 - 9 May* ~, du 3 au 9 mai inclus. *to be* ~ *of,* comprendre, inclure. ~**ly,** *ad,* inclusivement.
incognito, *ad. & n,* incognito, *m.*
incoherence, *n,* incohérence, *f.* **incoherent,** *a,* incohérent.
incombustible, *a,* incombustible.
income, *n,* revenu, *m. oft. pl. private* ~, rentes,

f.pl. ~ *tax,* impôt sur le revenu, *m.* ~ *tax return,* déclaration d'impôts, *f. lowest* ~ *group,* les économiquement faibles.
incoming, *a,* qui arrive; (*tide*) montant; (*tenant &c*) nouveau.
incommensurate, *a,* disproportionné (*with,* à).
incomparable†, *a,* incomparable.
incompatibility, *n,* incompatibilité, *f;* (*in divorce*) i. d'humeur. **incompatible,** *a,* incompatible.
incompetence, -cy, *n,* incompétence, *f.* **incompetent,** *a,* incompétent, incapable.
incomplete†, *a,* incomplet.
incomprehensible, *a,* incompréhensible.
inconceivable, *a,* inconcevable.
inconclusive, *a,* peu concluant.
incongruous, *a,* en désaccord, incompatible; (*remark*) incongru, déplacé.
inconsequent[ial], *a,* inconséquent.
inconsiderable, *a,* insignifiant.
inconsiderate†, *a,* (*pers.*) qui manque d'égards.
inconsistency, *n,* inconséquence, *f.* **inconsistent,** *a,* inconséquent. ~ *with,* incompatible avec.
inconsolable†, *a,* inconsolable.
inconspicuous, *a,* peu (*ou* pas) en évidence.
inconstancy, *n,* inconstance, *f.* **inconstant,** *a,* inconstant, volage.
incontestable, *a,* incontestable.
incontinent, *a,* incontinent.
incontrovertible, *a,* incontestable, irréfutable.
inconvenience, *n,* inconvénient; dérangement, *m. put s.o to great* ~, causer beaucoup de dérangement à qn. ¶ *v.t,* déranger, incommoder; gêner. **inconvenient,** *a,* (*date &c*) qui ne convient pas, mal choisi; (*room, tool*) incommode, peu pratique; (*event*) gênant.
incorporate, *v.t,* incorporer (*in, into,* à, avec); (*Com: company*) se constituer en societé avec.
incorrect†, *a,* incorrect; inexact.
incorrigible†, *a,* incorrigible.
incorruptible, *a,* incorruptible.
increase, *n,* augmentation, *f,* accroissement, *m.* ¶ *v.t.* (*& i*), augmenter, (s')accroître; (*joy, noise*) (s')intensifier; (*pain*) (s')aggraver. **increasing,** *a,* croissant.
incredible†, *a,* incroyable. **incredulity,** *n,* incrédulité, *f.* **incredulous,** *a,* incrédule.
increment, *n,* augmentation, *f.*
incriminate, *v.t,* incriminer.
incrust, *v.t,* incruster.
incubate, *v.t. & i,* couver. **incubation,** *n,* incubation, *f.* **incubator,** *n,* couveuse, *f;* (*cultures*) incubateur, *m.*
inculcate, *v.t,* inculquer (qch à qn).
incumbent, *n,* titulaire, *m. to be* ~ *on s.o to do,* incomber à qn de faire.
incur, *v.t,* (*blame*) s'attirer; (*risk*) courir; (*expenses*) encourir; (*loss*) subir; (*debts*) contracter.
incurable†, *a. & n,* incurable, *m,f.*
incursion, *n,* incursion, *f.*
indebted, *a,* redevable (à qn de qch).
indecency, *n,* indécence, inconvenance, *f;* (*Law*) outrage public à la pudeur, *m.* **indecent,** *a,* indécent, inconvenant. (*Law*) ~ *assault,* attentat à la pudeur. ~**ly,** *ad,* indécemment.
indecision, *n,* indécision, *f.* **indecisive,** *a,* indécis.
indecorous, *a,* inconvenant, peu convenable.
indeed, *ad,* vraiment, en effet. *yes* ~, mais certainement, bien sûr. *very ill* ~, extrêmement malade. ¶ *i,* vraiment!, tiens!
indefatigable†, *a,* infatigable.
indefensible, *a,* indéfendable.
indefinable, *a,* indéfinissable. **indefinite†,** *a,* indéfini, incertain, vague; (*leave*) illimité.
indelible, *a,* indélébile, ineffaçable.
indelicacy, *n,* indélicatesse, *f.* **indelicate†,** *a,* indélicat; (*tactless*) indiscret.
indemnify, *v.t,* indemniser, dédommager. **indemnity,** *n,* indemnité; (*Insce*) assurance, *f.*
indent, *n,* (*Com.*) commande, *f.* ¶ *v.t,* (*edge*) denteler; (*coast*) échancrer; (*Typ.*) renfoncer. (*Com.*) ~ *for,* commander (qch à qn). ~**ation,** *n,* dentelure; échancrure, *f;* renfoncement, *m.* ~**ures,** *n.pl,* contrat d'apprentissage, *m.*
independence, *n,* indépendance, *f.* **independent,** *a,* indépendant. *an* ~ *opinion,* l'avis d'un tiers, *m. person of* ~ *means,* rentier, ère. ~**ly,** *ad,* indépendamment (*of,* de).
indescribable, *a,* indescriptible.
indestructible, *a,* indestructible.
indeterminate, *a,* indéterminé.
index, *n,* (*book*) index; (*card* ~) catalogue; (*Eccl.*) Index; (*indicator*) indice, *m. cost of living* ~, indice du coût de la vie. ~ *card,* fiche, *f.* ~ *finger,* index, *m.* ~*-linked,* indexé. ¶ *v.t,* classer, cataloguer; (*book*) faire l'index de.
India, *n,* l'Inde, *f.* ~ *paper,* papier bible, *m.* **Indian,** *a,* indien, de l'Inde. ~ *clubs,* massues de gymnastique, *f.pl.* ~ *elephant,* éléphant d'Asie, *m.* ~ *Empire,* empire des Indes, *m.* ~ *ink,* encre de Chine, *f.* ~ *Ocean,* océan Indien, *m.* ¶ *n,* Indien, ne. **indiarubber,** *n,* gomme [à effacer], *f;* (*material*) caoutchouc, *m.*
indicate, *v.t,* indiquer; signaler; faire comprendre. **indication,** *n,* indication, *f;* indice, *m. there is no* ~ *that,* rien ne porte à croire que. **indicative,** *a. & n.* (*Gram*), indicatif, *m. in the* ~, à l'i. **indicator,** *n,* indicateur, *m;* (*Mot.*) clignotant, *m.*
indict, *v.t,* accuser. ~**able,** *a,* ~ *offence,* délit [pénal], *m.* ~**ment,** *n,* acte d'accusation, *m.*
Indies (the) *n.pl,* les Indes, *f.pl. East* ~, les Indes orientales. *West* ~, les Antilles, *f.*
indifference, *n,* indifférence; médiocrité, *f.* **indifferent,** *a,* indifférent (*to,* à); (*talent*) médiocre.

~**ly,** *ad,* indifféremment; médiocrement.
indigenous, *a,* indigène.
indigestible, *a,* indigeste. **indigestion,** *n,* (*chronic*) une mauvaise digestion; (*attack*) une indigestion.
indignant, *a,* indigne. *get* ~, s'indigner (*at,* de, devant). *make s.o* ~, indigner qn. ~**ly,** *ad,* avec indignation. **indignation,** *n,* indignation, *f.* **indignity,** *n,* indignité, *f.*
indigo, *a. & n,* indigo, *inv. & m.*
indirect†, *a,* indirect; (*means*) détourné.
indiscreet†, *a,* indiscret. **indiscretion,** *n,* indiscrétion, *f.*
indiscriminate, *a,* sans aucun discernement; (*fines &c*) distribué au hasard. ~**ly,** *ad,* sans distinction, au hasard.
indispensable†, *a,* indispensable.
indisposed, *a,* indisposé, souffrant; (*reluctant*) peu disposé (à faire). **indisposition,** *n,* indisposition, *f,* malaise, *m.*
indisputable†, *a,* incontestable, indiscutable.
indissoluble†, *a,* indissoluble.
indistinct†, *a,* indistinct; (*memory*) vague.
individual†, *a,* individuel; (*style*) particulier. ¶ *n,* individu; particulier, *m.* ~**ist,** *n,* individualiste, *m,f.* ~**ity,** *n,* individualité, *f.*
indivisible†, *a,* indivisible.
Indo-China, *n,* l'Indochine, *f.*
indolence, *n,* indolence, *f.* **indolent,** *a,* indolent, mou. ~**ly,** *ad,* indolemment.
indomitable, *a,* indomptable.
indoor, *a,* (*shoes, work, Phot.*) d'intérieur; (*aerial*) intérieur; (*plants*) d'appartement; (*swimming pool*) couvert. ~**s,** *ad,* à la maison; à l'abri.
indubitable†, *a,* indubitable.
induce, *v.t,* persuader (qn de faire); (*sleep &c*) provoquer; (*Med: labour*) déclencher. ~**ment,** *n,* stimulant, encouragement; (*bribe*) pot de vin, *m.*
induct, *v.t,* (*Eccl. &c*) installer. ~**ion,** *n,* installation; (*Elec.*) induction, *f.* ~ *course,* stage préparatoire, *m.*
indulge, *v.t,* (*pers.*) gâter; (*feelings*) céder à. ~ *in,* se permettre; s'adonner à. **indulgence,** *n,* indulgence, *f.* ~*s,* petites faiblesses. **indulgent,** *a,* indulgent (*to,* envers).
industrial, *a,* industriel; (*disease*) professionnel; (*worker*) de l'industrie; (*dispute*) ouvrier; (*injury*) du travail. ~ *action,* action revendicative. ~ *estate,* zone industrielle. ~**ism,** *n,* industrialisme, *m.* ~**ist,** *n,* industriel, *m.* ~**ize,** *v.t,* industrialiser. **industrious†,** *a,* industrieux, travailleur. ~**ly,** *ad,* industrieusement. **industry,** *n,* industrie, *f. heavy, light* ~, industrie lourde, légère. *tourist, motor* ~, i. touristique, automobile. *Department of I*~, ministère de l'I., *m.* (*diligence*) application, assiduité, *f.*
inebriate, *a,* ivre. ¶ *n,* ivrogne, *m,f.* ¶ *v.t,* enivrer.
inedible, *a,* (*not for eating*) non-comestible; (*unfit to eat*) immangeable.
ineffective† & **ineffectual†,** *a,* inefficace, sans résultat; (*pers.*) incapable.
inefficient, *a,* inefficace; (*pers.*) incapable, incompétent. **inefficiency,** *n,* inefficacité; incapacité, incompétence, *f.*
inelegant, *a,* inélégant. ~**ly,** *ad,* sans élégance.
ineligible, *a,* inéligible. ~ *for,* n'ayant pas le droit de; (*Mil. service*) inapte à.
inept, *a,* inepte. **ineptitude,** *n,* ineptie, *f.*
inequality, *n,* inégalité, *f.*
inequitable†, *a,* injuste, inéquitable.
ineradicable, *a,* indéracinable.
inert, *a,* inerte. **inertia,** *n,* inertie, *f.*
inescapable, *a,* inéluctable.
inestimable, *a,* inestimable.
inevitable†, *a,* inévitable. **inevitably,** *ad,* forcément, fatalement, inévitablement.
inexact†, *a,* inexact. **inexactitude,** *n,* inexactitude, *f.*
inexcusable, *a,* inexcusable.
inexhaustible†, *a,* inépuisable, intarissable.
inexorable†, *a,* inexorable.
inexpedient, *a,* malavisé; inopportun.
inexpensive, *a,* peu coûteux, bon marché, *inv.*
inexperience, *n,* inexpérience, *f.* ~**d,** *a,* inexpérimenté; novice (*in,* dans.).
inexplicable, *a,* inexplicable.
inexpressible, *a,* inexprimable.
inextricable, *a,* inextricable.
infallible†, *a,* infaillible. **infallibility,** *n,* infaillibilité, *f.*
infamous, *a,* infâme; (*Law*) infamant. **infamy,** *n,* infamie, *f.*
infancy, *n,* petite enfance, *f;* bas âge, *m;* (*Law*) minorité, *f.* **infant,** *n,* bébé, *m;* tout(e) petit(e) enfant, *m,f;* (*Law*) mineur, e; (*Sch.*) petit, e. ~ *mortality,* mortalité infantile, *f.* ~ *school,* classes préparatoires (de 5 à 7 ans). **infanticide,** *n,* infanticide (*act*) *m;* (*pers.*) *m,f.* **infantile,** *a,* enfantin; (*Med.*) infantile.
infantry, *n,* infanterie, *f.* ~*man,* fantassin, *m.*
infatuated, *a, to become* ~ *with,* (*s.o, sth*) s'enticher de, s'engouer de *ou* pour. **infatuation,** *n,* entichement, engouement, *m.*
infect, *v.t,* infecter. ~**ion,** *n,* infection, *f.* ~**ious,** *a,* (*Med.*) infectieux; (*pers., fig.*) contagieux.
infer, *v.t,* inférer, déduire. ~**ence,** *n,* inférence, déduction, *f. by* ~, par déduction.
inferior†, *a,* inférieur (*to,* à); (*work &c*) de qualité inférieure. ¶ *n,* inférieur, e. ~**ity,** *n,* infériorité, *f.* ~ *complex,* complexe d'i., *m.*
infernal, *a,* infernal. ~**ly,** *ad,* abominablement. **inferno,** *n,* enfer, *m.*
infertile, *a,* infertile.
infest, *v.t,* infester (*with,* de).
infidelity, *n,* infidélité, *f.*
infiltrate, *v.i,* s'infiltrer (*into,* dans). ¶ *v.t,*

s'infiltrer dans. **infiltration,** *n,* infiltration, *f;* (*Pol.*) noyautage, *m.*

infinite†, *a,* infini. **the ~,** l'infini, *m.* **infinitesimal,** *a,* infinitésimal. **infinitive,** *n,* infinitif, *m. in the ~,* à l'i. **infinitude & infinity,** *n,* infinité; immensité, *f.* **infinity** (*Math., Phot.*) *n,* l'infini, *m.*

infirm, *a,* infirme. **~ary,** *n,* hôpital, *m.* **~ity,** *n,* infirmité, *f.*

inflame, *v.t,* (*Med.*) enflammer; (*fig.*) attiser. **inflammable,** *a,* inflammable. **inflammatory,** *a,* (*speech*) incendiaire. **inflammation,** *n,* inflammation, *f.*

inflate, *v.t,* (*tyre*) gonfler; (*price*) faire monter; (*bill*) grossir. **inflatable,** *a,* pneumatique. **~d,** *a,* (*prices*) exagéré; (*style*) enflé. **inflation,** *n,* gonflement, *m;* (*Econ.*) inflation, *f.* **~ary,** *a,* inflationniste.

inflect, *v.t,* (*voice*) moduler. **inflexible†,** *a,* inflexible. **inflexibility,** *n,* inflexibilité, *f.* **inflexion, -ction,** *n,* inflexion, *f.*

inflict, *v.t,* (*fine &c*) infliger (*on,* à). **~ion,** *n,* infliction, *f.*

influence, *n,* influence, *f. under the ~ of,* (*drugs, drink*) sous l'effet de; (*pers.*) sous l'influence de. ¶ *v.t,* influencer; influer sur. **influential,** *a,* influent. *to be ~,* avoir de l'influence.

influenza, *n,* grippe, *f.*

influx, *n,* afflux, flot, *m.*

inform, *v.t, ~ s.o of sth,* informer, avertir qn de qch; faire part de qch à qn. *~ s.o about sth,* renseigner qn sur qch. *keep s.o ~ed,* tenir qn au courant (*about,* de). **~ant,** *n,* informateur, trice. **~ation,** *n,* renseignements, *m.pl. a piece of ~,* un renseignement, une information. *to get ~ about,* se renseigner sur. **~technology,** télématique, *f.* **~ative,** *a,* instructif. **~er,** *n,* délateur, trice; (*police*) indicateur, trice.

informal, *a,* simple; sans cérémonie; (*unofficial*) officieux. **~ity,** *n,* simplicité, absence de cérémonie, *f.* **~ly,** *ad,* sans cérémonie; officieusement.

infra-red, *a,* infrarouge.

infrastructure, *n,* infrastructure, *f.*

infrequent, *a,* peu fréquent, rare.

infringe, *v.t,* contrevenir à. *~ on,* empiéter sur. **~ment,** *n,* infraction, *f. ~ of patent,* contrefaçon, *f.*

infuriate, *v.t,* rendre furieux.

infuse, *v.t,* infuser; (*tea &c*) faire infuser. **infusion,** *n,* infusion; (*herbal*) tisane, *f.*

ingenious†, *a,* ingénieux. **ingenuity,** *n,* ingéniosité, *f.*

ingenuous†, *a,* ingénu. **~ness,** *n,* ingénuité, *f.*

ingle nook, *n,* coin du feu, *m.*

inglorious†, *a,* honteux, déshonorant.

ingot, *n,* lingot, *m.*

ingrained, *a,* (*fig.*) enraciné, invétéré.

ingratiate oneself with, s'insinuer dans les bonnes grâces de.

ingratitude, *n,* ingratitude, *f.*

ingredient, *n,* ingrédient, *m.*

ingrowing (*nail*) *a,* incarné.

inhabit, *v.t,* habiter. **~able,** *a,* habitable. **~ant,** *n,* habitant, e.

inhale, *v.t,* inhaler, respirer; (*smoker*) avaler.

inherent, *a,* inhérent; propre (*in,* à).

inherit, *v.t,* hériter [de]; (*title*) succéder à. **~ance,** *n,* héritage, patrimoine, *m;* (*Law*) succession, *f.*

inhibit, *v.t,* (*Psych.*) inhiber; (*gen.*) gêner, entraver. **~ion,** *n,* inhibition, *f.*

inhospitable, *a,* inhospitalier.

inhuman†, *a,* inhumain. **~ity,** *n,* inhumanité, *f.*

inimical, *a,* ennemi, hostile.

inimitable, *a,* inimitable.

iniquitous†, *a,* inique. **iniquity,** *n,* iniquité, *f.*

initial, *a,* initial, premier. ¶ *n,* initiale, *f.* **~s,** initiales, *f.pl.* (*signing*) parafe, *m.* ¶ *v.t,* parafer.

initiate, *a. & n,* initié, e. ¶ *v.t,* (*talks &c*) amorcer, entamer; (*scheme*) inaugurer; (*s.o into secret*) initier. **initiation,** *n,* initiation, *f.* **initiative,** *n,* initiative, *f. take the ~,* prendre l'i.

inject, *v.t,* injecter; (*pers*) faire une piqûre à. **~ion,** *n,* injection; piqûre, *f.*

injudicious, *a,* peu judicieux.

injunction, *n,* ordre, *m;* (*court*) ordonnance, *f.*

injure, *v.t,* (*Med.*) blesser. *~ one's foot,* se blesser au pied. (*harm: pers., health*) nuire à; (*offend*) offenser. (*Law*) *the ~d party,* la partie lésée. **injurious†,** *a,* nuisible, préjudiciable (*to,* à). **injury,** *n,* blessure, *f;* (*wrong*) tort, *m.*

injustice, *n,* injustice, *f. to do s.o an ~,* être injuste envers qn.

ink, *n,* encre, *f. in ~,* à l'encre. *~ eraser,* gomme à l'e. *~pad,* tampon, *m. ~pot, ~stand, ~well,* encrier, *m.* ¶ *v.t,* encrer. *~ in,* repasser à l'e.

inkling, *n,* soupçon, *m,* idée, *f.*

inlaid, *a,* incrusté (*with,* de); (*table*) marqueté. *~ work,* incrustation, marqueterie, *f.*

inland, *a,* intérieur. *~ waterways,* canaux (*m.pl*) & rivières, *f.pl. I~ Revenue,* le fisc. ¶ *ad,* à l'intérieur.

inlet, *n,* (*sea*) crique, *f,* bras de mer, *m;* (*Tech.*) arrivée, *f. ~ valve,* soupape d'admission, *f.*

inmate, *n,* occupant, e; (*prison*) détenu, e; (*hospital*) malade, *m,f.*

inmost, *a,* le plus intime *ou* profond.

inn, *n,* auberge, *f. ~keeper,* aubergiste, *m,f.*

innate, *a,* inné, naturel.

inner, *a,* intérieur, interne. *~ harbour,* arrière-port, *m. ~ tube,* chambre à air, *f.*

innings, *n,* (*Cricket*) tour de batte, *m.*

innocence, *n,* innocence, *f.* **innocent,** *a. & n,* innocent, e. **~ly,** *ad,* innocemment.

innocuous, *a,* inoffensif.

innovate, *v.t. & i,* innover. **innovation,** *n,* innovation, *f.* **innovator,** *n,* novateur, trice.
innuendo, *n,* insinuation, allusion, *f.*
innumerable, *a,* innombrable.
inoculate, *v.t,* inoculer. **inoculation,** *n,* inoculation, *f.*
inoffensive, *a,* inoffensif.
inoperable, *a,* inopérable.
inoperative, *a,* inopérant.
inopportune, *a,* inopportun. **~ly,** *ad,* mal à propos, inopportunément.
inordinate†, *a,* démesuré; (*price*) exorbitant.
inorganic, *a,* inorganique.
input, *n,* (*Elec.*) énergie, puissance, *f;* (*data*) données, *f.pl.*
inquest, *n,* enquête, *f.*
inquire, *v.t,* demander (*from s.o,* à qn). ¶ *v.i,* s'informer (*about, after,* de); se renseigner (*about,* sur). '*~ at the office*', 's'adresser au bureau'. **inquiring,** *a,* (*look*) interrogateur. *~ mind,* esprit curieux. **inquiry,** *n,* (*from s.o*) demande de renseignements, *f.* (*sign*) '*Inquiries*', 'Renseignements'. *~ office, ~ desk,* bureau de renseignements, *m.* (*Law, Adm.*) enquête, *f. board of ~,* commission d'e.
inquisition, *n,* investigation, *f.* (*Eccl.*) *the I~* l'Inquisition, *f.* **inquisitive,** *a,* curieux.
inroad, *n,* (*Mil.*) incursion (*into,* en, dans), *f.* (*fig.*) *make ~s into,* (*funds &c*) entamer.
insane, *a,* (*pers.*) fou, (*Med.*) aliéné; (*act*) insensé. **insanity,** *n,* folie, démence, *f;* (*Med.*) aliénation mentale.
insanitary, *a,* insalubre, malsain.
insatiable†, *a,* insatiable.
inscribe, *v.t,* inscrire; (*carve*) graver; (*book*) dédier. **inscription,** *n,* inscription; dédicace, *f.*
inscrutable, *a,* impénétrable.
insect, *n,* insecte, *m. ~ powder,* poudre insecticide, *f. ~ repellent,* crème anti-insecte, *f.*
insecure, *a,* (*fixture*) peu solide; (*place*) peu sûr; (*future*) incertain. **insecurity,** *n,* insécurité, *f.*
insemination, *n,* insémination, *f.*
insensible†, *a,* insensible; sans connaissance.
inseparable†, *a,* inséparable.
insert, *n,* insertion, *f;* (*page*) encart, *m.* ¶ *v.t,* insérer. **~ion,** *n,* insertion, *f.*
inshore, *a,* (*fishing*) côtier; (*wind*) de mer.
inside, *n,* (*gen., Foot.*) intérieur, *m. on the ~,* à l'i., au dedans. *P ~[s],* ventre, *m,* (*animal*) entrailles, *f.pl. ~ out,* (*garment*) à l'envers. *know sth ~ out,* connaître qch à fond, comme sa poche. ¶ *a,* intérieur; d'i. ¶ *ad,* [au] dedans, à l'intérieur. ¶ *pr,* dans, à l'intérieur de.
insidious†, *a,* insidieux.
insight, *n,* pénétration, *f,* perspicacité, *f.*
insignia, *n.pl,* insignes, *m.pl.*
insignificant, *a,* insignifiant. **insignificance,** *n,* insignifiance, *f.*
insincere, *a,* peu sincère. **insincerity,** *n,* manque de sincérité, *m.*
insinuate, *v.t,* insinuer (*into,* dans; *that,* que).
insipid, *a,* insipide, fade.
insist, *v.t. & i, ~ that,* affirmer, soutenir que. *~ on,* exiger (*sth,* qch; *doing, my doing,* de faire, que je fasse); insister (pour faire, pour que je fasse). **~ence,** *n,* insistance, *f.*
insolence, *n,* insolence, *f.* **insolent,** *a,* insolent. **~ly,** *ad,* insolemment.
insoluble, *a,* insoluble.
insolvency, *n,* insolvabilité, *f.* **insolvent,** *a,* insolvable. *to become ~,* faire faillite.
insomnia, *n,* insomnie, *f.*
inspect, *v.t,* inspecter, examiner [de près]; (*Customs*) visiter; (*ticket, accounts*) contrôler. **~ion,** *n,* inspection, *f,* examen, *m;* visite, *f;* contrôle, *m;* (*Mil.*) revue, *f,* (*kit &c*) inspection. *~ pit,* fosse à réparations, *f.* **~or,** *n,* inspecteur, trice; (*ticket*) contrôleur, euse. **~orate,** *n,* inspection, *f.*
inspiration, *n,* inspiration, *f.* **inspire,** *v.t,* inspirer (*s.o with sth,* qch à qn). **inspiring,** *a,* (*force*) & **inspirer,** *n,* inspirateur, trice.
instability, *n,* instabilité, *f.*
install, *v.t,* installer. **~ation,** *n,* installation, *f.*
instalment, *n,* acompte, versement partiel; (*story &c*) épisode, *m. pay by ~s,* payer par acomptes. *~ plan,* vente à tempérament, *f.*
instance, *n,* cas, exemple, *m. for ~,* par exemple. *in the first ~,* en premier lieu. ¶ *v.t,* citer en exemple. **instant,** *a,* immédiat, instantané; (*coffee*) instantané; (*month*) courant. ¶ *n,* instant, moment, *m. go this ~,* vas-y tout de suite! **~ly,** *ad,* tout de suite. **instantaneous†,** *a,* instantané.
instead, *ad,* plutôt, au lieu de cela. *~ of,* au lieu de (*sth,* qch; *doing,* faire). *~ of him,* à sa place.
instep, *n,* cou-de-pied, *m;* cambrure, *f.*
instigate, *v.t,* inciter (qn à faire); (*revolt*) provoquer. **instigation,** *n,* instigation, *f.*
instil, *v.t,* (*courage*) insuffler; (*manners*) inculquer (*into s.o,* à qn).
instinct, *n,* instinct, *m. by ~,* d'instinct. **~ive†,** *a,* instinctif.
institute, *n,* institut, *m.* ¶ *v.t,* instituer, établir; fonder. *~ proceedings,* intenter un procès (contre, à qn). **institution,** *n,* institution, *f;* établissement, *m.*
instruct, *v.t,* (*teach*) instruire (qn en qch); enseigner (qch à qn); (*order*) ordonner (à qn de faire), donner des instructions à; (*counsel*) constituer. **~ion,** *n,* (*teaching*) instruction, *f.* *driving ~,* leçons de conduite, *f.pl.* (*pl.*) instructions, indications, *f.pl;* (*Mil.*) consigne, *f.* '*~ions for use*', 'mode d'emploi', *m.* *~ion book,* manuel, guide-âne, *m. ~ional film,* film éducatif. **~ive,** *a,* instructif. **~or,** *n,* professeur; (*Mil.*) instructeur; (*Ski*)

moniteur, *m.* ~**ress,** *n,* professeur, *m;* (*Ski*) monitrice, *f.*
instrument, *n,* instrument; (*Law*) instrument, acte, *m.* ~**al,** *a,* (*Mus.*) instrumental. *to be* ~ *in doing,* contribuer à faire. ~**alist,** *n,* instrumentiste, *m,f.*
insubordinate, *a,* insubordonné.
insufferable†, *a,* insupportable.
insufficiency, *n,* insuffisance, *f.* **insufficient,** *a,* insuffisant. ~**ly,** *ad,* insuffisamment.
insular, *a,* insulaire. ~**ity,** *n,* insularité, *f.*
insulate, *v.t,* (*Elec.*) isoler; (*sound*) insonoriser; (*heat*) calorifuger. **insulating,** *a,* ~ *material,* isolant, *m.* ~ *tape,* chatterton, *m.* **insulation,** *n,* isolation; insonorisation, *f;* calorifugeage, *m.* **insulator,** *n,* isolateur; (*material*) isolant, *m.*
insult, *n,* insulte, injure, *f.* ¶ *v.t,* insulter. ~**ing†,** *a,* injurieux, offensant.
insuperable, *a,* insurmontable.
insurance, *n,* assurance, *f. life* ~, assurance-vie, *f. National I*~, assurances sociales. ¶ *a,* (*policy, premium*) d'assurance; (*agent, company*) d'assurances. **insure,** *v.t,* [faire] assurer. ~ *one's life,* s'assurer sur la vie. (*ensure*) assurer. ¶ *v.i,* ~ *against,* s'assurer *ou* se faire a. contre. ~**d** (*pers.*) *n,* assuré, e. **insurer,** *n,* assureur, *m.*
insurgent, *n. & a,* insurgé, e, révolté, e.
insurmountable, *a,* insurmontable.
insurrection, *n,* insurrection, *f.*
intact, *a,* intact.
intake, *n,* (*air*) prise; (*gas &c*) admission, *f.* (*Univ.*) admissions, *f.pl;* (*Mil.*) contingent, *m;* (*food &c*) consommation, *f.*
intangible, *a,* intangible.
integral†, *a, to be an* ~ *part of,* faire partie intégrante de. (*whole & Math.*) intégral. **integrate,** *v.t.* (*& i*), (s')intégrer (*in, into,* dans). ~*d* (*personality*) bien intégré. **integration,** *n,* intégration, *f. racial* ~, déségrégation raciale. **integrity,** *n,* intégrité, *f.*
intellect, *n,* intellect, *m,* intelligence, *f.*
intellectual†, *a. & n,* intellectuel, le.
intelligence, *n,* intelligence, *f.* ~ *quotient* (*I.Q.*), quotient intellectuel. ~ *test,* test d'aptitude intellectuelle, *m.* (*information*) informations, *f.pl. I*~ *Service,* service de renseignements; (*Mil.*) deuxième bureau, *m.* **intelligent,** *a,* intelligent. ~**ly,** *ad,* intelligemment. **intelligible†,** *a,* intelligible.
intemperate, *a,* (*pers.*) intempérant, immodéré; (*climate*) sévère.
intend, *v.t,* avoir l'intention, se proposer (de faire); compter (faire). ~ *sth for s.o,* destiner qch à qn. ~**ed,** *a,* (*deliberate*) fait exprès, intentionnel; (*effect*) voulu.
intense, *a,* (*heat*) intense; (*interest*) vif; (*pers.*) trop sérieux. ~**ly,** *ad,* extrêmement. **intensify,** *v.t,* intensifier; (*Phot., colour*) renforcer.
intensity, *n,* intensité, *f.* **intensive,** *a,* intensif. *in* ~ *care,* en réanimation.
intent, *a,* (*look*) préoccupé. ~ *on sth,* tout entier à, absorbé par qch. ~ *on doing,* résolu, décidé à faire. ¶ *n,* intention, *f,* but, *m. to all* ~*s & purposes,* pratiquement. **intention,** *n,* intention, *f. with the* ~ *of doing,* dans l'intention de faire. ~**al†,** *a,* intentionnel, voulu. ~**ally,** *ad,* exprès. **-intentioned,** *a,* (*well, ill,* bien, mal) intentionné.
inter, *v.t,* enterrer, ensevelir.
inter-, *pref,* inter. ~*-city,* interurbain. ~*-school,* interscolaire.
interact, *v.i,* réagir réciproquement. ~**ion,** *n,* interaction, *f.*
intercede, *v.i,* intercéder (*with,* auprès de).
intercept, *v.t,* intercepter; (*pers.*) arrêter au passage.
intercession, *n,* intercession, *f.*
interchange, *n,* échange, *m;* (*motorway*) échangeur, *m.* ~**able,** *a,* interchangeable.
intercom, *n,* interphone, *m.*
intercourse, *n,* relations, *f.pl,* rapports, *m.pl.* [*sexual*] ~, rapports [sexuels].
interest, *n,* intérêt, *m. take an* ~ *in,* (*s.o, sth*) s'intéresser à. (*advantage*) intérêt, avantage, *m. it's in your* ~ *to do,* vous avez i. à faire. (*Com: stake; Fin.*) intérêts. *simple, compound* ~, intérêts simples, composés. *bear* ~ *at 9%,* porter intérêt à 9%. ~ *rate,* taux d'intérêt, *m.* ¶ *v.t,* intéresser. *to be, grow* ~*ed in,* s'intéresser à. *would you be* ~*ed in coming?* ça vous intéresserait de venir? ~*ed party,* intéressé, e. ~**ing,** *a,* intéressant.
interfere, *v.i,* s'ingérer, intervenir (*in,* dans); se mêler des affaires des autres. *he's always interfering,* il fourre son nez partout *P.* ~ *with* (*hinder*), contrarier, gêner, déranger. **interference,** *n,* ingérence; intervention, *f;* (*Radio*) parasites, *m.pl.*
interim, *n,* intérim, *m.* ¶ *a,* provisoire; (*dividend*) intérimaire.
interior†, *a. & n,* intérieur, *m.*
interject, *v.t,* placer. ~**ion,** *n,* interjection, *f.*
interlace, *v.t,* entrelacer.
interloper, *n,* intrus, e.
interlude, *n,* intervalle; (*Mus. &c*) interlude; (*Theat.*) intermède, *m.*
intermediary, *n. & a,* intermédiaire, *m,f.* **intermediate,** *a,* intermédiaire. ~ *classes,* (*Sch.*) cours moyen, *m.*
interminable, *a,* interminable.
intermingle, *v.t.* (*& i*), (s')entremêler (*with,* de).
intermission, *n,* interruption, *f;* (*Cine*) entracte, *m;* (*Med.*) intermission, *f.* **intermittent,** *a,* intermittent. ~**ly,** *ad,* par intermittence.
intern, *v.t,* interner. ¶ *n,* (*Am Med.*) interne, *m,f.* ~**ee,** *n,* interné, e. ~**ment,** *n,* internement, *m.*
internal, *a,* (*Geom., Med., Tech.*) interne; (*Ind.,*

Pol: dispute &c) intérieur, interne. ~ *combustion engine,* moteur à combustion interne, *m.* **~ly,** *ad,* intérieurement.
international, *a. & n,* (*player, match*), international, *m.* **I~e** (*hymn*) *n,* Internationale, *f.*
interplay, *n,* effet réciproque, *m.*
interpolate, *v.t,* interpoler.
interpose, *v.t.* (*& i*), (s')interposer.
interpret, *v.t,* interpréter. **~ation,** *n,* interprétation, *f.* **~er,** *n,* interprète, *m,f.*
interregnum, *n,* interrègne, *m.*
interrogate, *v.t,* interroger. **interrogation,** *n,* interrogation, *f;* (*Police*) interrogatoire, *m.* **interrogative,** *a,* (*tone*) interrogateur; (*Gram.*) interrogatif. *in the* ~, à l'i. **interrogator,** *n,* interrogateur, trice.
interrupt, *v.t,* interrompre. **~er,** *n,* (*pers.*) interrupteur, trice; (*switch*) interrupteur, *m.* **interruption,** *n,* interruption, *f.*
intersect, *v.t,* couper. ¶ *v.i,* s'entrecouper. **~ion,** *n,* intersection, *f.*
interspersed, *a,* ~ *with,* parsemé de.
interstice, *n,* interstice, *m.*
intertwine, *v.t.* (*& i*), (s')entrelacer.
interval, *n,* (*gen., Mus.*) intervalle; (*Theat.*) entracte, *m. at ~s,* par intervalles.
intervene, *v.i,* (*pers., event*) intervenir; (*time*) s'écouler. **intervention,** *n,* intervention, *f.*
interview, *n,* entrevue, *f. call for* ~, convoquer. (*Press &c*) interview, *m.* ¶ *v.t,* (*for job*) avoir une entrevue avec; (*Press*) interviewer. **~er,** *n,* interviewer, *m;* (*poll*) enquêteur, euse.
intestate, *a,* intestat (*inv.*).
intestine, *n,* intestin, *m.*
intimacy, *n,* intimité, *f;* (*sexual*) rapports intimes, *m.pl.* (*pl.*) familiarités, *f.pl.* **intimate†,** *a* intime. *be on ~ terms with,* être ami intime de. (*knowledge*) approfondi. ¶ *n,* intime, *m,f.* ¶ *v.t,* annoncer, faire savoir. **intimation,** *n,* annonce, indication, *f.*
intimidate, *v.t,* intimider.
into, *pr,* dans; en. *go* ~, (*room*) entrer dans; (*question*) étudier. *get* ~, (*train, plane*) monter dans; (*car*) monter en voiture, dans une v. ~ *town,* en ville. *change sth* ~, changer qch en. *fall ~ s.o's hands,* tomber entre les mains de qn. ~ *the bargain,* par-dessus le marché.
intolerable†, *a,* intolérable. **intolerance,** *n,* intolérance, *f.* **intolerant,** *a,* intolérant.
intonation, *n,* (*gen., Mus.*) intonation, *f.* **intone,** *v.t,* entonner.
intoxicate, *v.t,* enivrer. **~d,** *a,* (*lit.*) ivre. (*fig.*) ~ *with,* ivre de, grisé par. **intoxicating,** *a,* (*drink*) alcoolique. **intoxication,** *n,* ivresse, *f.*
intractable, *a,* intraitable; (*problem*) difficile à résoudre.
intransitive†, *a,* intransitif. (See Note under *se, s'* in French-English section).
intrepid†, *a,* intrépide.
intricacy, *n,* complication, complexité, *f.* **intricate,** *a,* compliqué, complexe.
intrigue, *n,* intrigue, *f.* ¶ *v.i,* (*plot*) intriguer. ¶ *v.t,* intriguer, éveiller la curiosité de. **~r,** *n,* intrigant, e. **intriguing,** *a,* fascinant.
intrinsic†, *a,* intrinsèque.
introduce, *v.t,* introduire; (*subject, show &c*) présenter; (*pers. to s.o*) présenter; (*Parliament: bill*) déposer. **introduction,** *n,* introduction; présentation, *f.*
introspection, *n,* introspection, *f.* **introspective,** *a,* introspectif.
introvert, *a. & n,* introverti, e.
intrude, *v.i,* être importun. ~ *on,* (*pers.*) s'imposer à; (*s.o's time*) empiéter sur. **intruder,** *n,* intrus, e. **intrusion,** *n,* intrusion, *f.*
intuition, *n,* intuition, *f.* **intuitive,** *a,* intuitif. **~ly,** *ad,* par intuition.
inundate, *v.t,* (*lit., fig.*) inonder (*with,* de).
inure, *v.t,* aguerrir (*to,* contre); habituer (*to,* à).
invade, *v.t,* (*lit., fig.*) envahir. **invader,** *n,* envahisseur, *m.*
invalid[1], *a. & n,* (*ill*) malade; (*disabled*) infirme, invalide, *m,f.* ¶ *v.t,* (*Mil.*) ~ *out,* réformer.
invalid[2], *a,* non valable, non valide. **~ate,** *v.t,* invalider; (*will &c*) rendre nul, vicier.
invaluable, *a,* inestimable, inappréciable.
invariable†, *a,* invariable.
invasion, *n,* invasion, *f,* envahissement, *m.*
invective, *n,* invective, *f.* **inveigh,** *v.i,* ~ *against,* invectiver; tonner contre.
inveigle, *v.t,* ~ *s.o into doing,* amadouer qn pour qu'il fasse.
invent, *v.t,* inventer. **~ion,** *n,* invention, *f.* **~ive,** *a,* inventif. **~iveness,** *n,* esprit inventif. **~or,** *n,* inventeur, trice.
inventory, *n,* inventaire, *m.*
inverse†, *a,* inverse. *in ~ proportion,* en raison inverse (*to,* de). **inversion,** *n,* inversion, *f;* (*Mus.*) renversement, *m.* **invert,** *v.t,* renverser. *~ed commas,* guillemets, *m.pl.*
invertebrate, *a. & n,* invertébré, *m.*
invest, *v.t,* (*pers., occasion*) revêtir, investir (*with,* de); (*Fin.*) (*capital*) investir, (*money*) placer; (*Mil: town*) investir. **~iture,** *n,* investiture, *f.* **~ment,** *n,* (*Fin.*) investissement, placement, *m;* (*Mil.*) investissement, *m.* **~or,** *n,* actionnaire, *m,f. the small* ~, la petite épargne.
investigate, *v.t,* (*question*) examiner, étudier; (*crime*) enquêter sur. **investigation,** *n,* investigation, enquête, *f.* **investigator,** investigateur, trice; (*Police*) enquêteur, *m.*
inveterate, *a,* invétéré.
invidious, *a,* qui suscite la rancune *ou* la jalousie; (*task*) ingrat; (*comparison*) blessant.
invigorate, *v.t,* fortifier; (*air, climate*) vivifier, tonifier.
invincible†, *a,* invincible.
inviolable†, *a,* inviolable.
invisible†, *a,* invisible; (*ink*) sympathique, *f.* ~

mending, stoppage, *m*.
invitation, *n*, invitation, *f*. *at s.o's* ~, à *ou* sur l'i. de qn. **invite,** *v.t*, inviter (qn à faire). ~ *to dinner*, inviter à dîner. (*ridicule*) appeler; (*trouble*) chercher. **inviting,** *a*, engageant, attrayant; (*dish*) appétissant.
invoice, *n*, facture, *f*. ¶ *v.t*, facturer.
invoke, *v.t*, invoquer.
involuntary†, *a*, involontaire.
involve, *v.t*, (*pers. in sth*) entraîner, engager, impliquer (dans qch); mêler (à qch). *get* ~*d in*, (*business &c*) s'engager dans. (*entail: expense &c*) entraîner, nécessiter. ~**d,** *a*, compliqué.
invulnerable, *a*, invulnérable.
inward, *a*, (*peace*) intérieur; (*thoughts*) intime; (*thrust*) vers l'intérieur. ¶ *ad*, ~[*s*], vers l'intérieur. ~**ly,** *ad*, (*laugh*) intérieurement.
iodine, *n*, iode, *m*.
ion, *n*, ion, *m*.
Ionian, Ionic, *a*, ionien, ionique.
iota, *n*, iota, *m*.
Iran, *n*, l'Iran, *m*, ~**ian,** *a*, iranien.
Iraq, *n*, l'Irak, *m*. ~**i,** *a*, irakien.
irascible, *a*, irascible. **irate,** *a*, furieux.
Ireland, *n*, l'Irlande, *f*. *Northern* ~, l'I. du Nord.
iridescence, *n*, irisation, *f*. **iridescent,** *a*, irisé; (*plumage*) chatoyant.
iris, *n*, (*Anat., Bot.*) iris, *m*.
Irish, *a*, irlandais. ~*man*, ~*woman*, Irlandais, e. ~ *Sea*, mer d'Irlande, *f*. ¶ (*language*) *n*, l'irlandais, *m*.
irksome, *a*, ennuyeux, fastidieux.
iron, *n*, (*metal, wrought, for linen, Golf &c*) fer, *m*; (*cast, pig*) fonte; (*sheet*) tôle; (*scrap*) ferraille, *f*. *man of* ~, homme de fer. *he has lots of* ~*s in the fire*, il a beaucoup d'affaires en train. ~*s*, (*fetters*) fers, *m.pl*. ¶ *a*, en fer, de fer; (*will, constitution*) de fer. *the I*~ *Age*, l'âge de fer, *m*. ~ *& steel industry*, industrie sidérurgique, *f*. ~ *foundry*, fonderie de fonte, *f*. ~ *lung*, poumon d'acier, *m*. ~ *ore*, minérai de fer, *m*. ~*monger*, quincaillier, *m*. ~*monger's &* ~*mongery*, quincaillerie, *f*. [*wrought*] ~*work*, ferronnerie, serrurerie [d'art], *f*. ~*works*, usine sidérurgique, *f*. ¶ *v.t*, (*linen*) repasser. ~ *out*, (*difficulties*) aplanir. ~**ing,** *n*, repassage, *m*. ~ *board*, planche à repasser, *f*.
ironic(al)†, *a*, ironique. **irony,** *n*, ironie, *f*.
irrational, *a*, déraisonable, irrationnel.
irreconcilable, *a*, (*pers.*) irréconciliable; (*belief*) inconciliable.
irreducible, *a*, irréductible.
irrefutable†, *a*, irréfutable.
irregular†, *a*, irrégulier; (*surface*) inégal. ~**ity,** *n*, irrégularité, *f*.
irrelevant, *a*, hors de propos, non pertinent. *that's* ~, cela n'a rien à voir avec la question.
irreligious†, *a*, irréligieux.
irremediable†, *a*, irrémédiable, sans remède.
irreparable†, *a*, irréparable.
irrepressible, *a*, irrépressible.
irreproachable†, *a*, irréprochable.
irresistible†, *a*, irrésistible.
irresolute, *a*, irrésolu.
irrespective of, sans égard pour; sans tenir compte de.
irresponsible, *a*, pas sérieux, irresponsable.
irretrievable†, *a*, irréparable.
irreverent, *a*, irrévérencieux.
irrevocable†, *a*, irrévocable.
irrigate, *v.t*, irriguer. **irrigation,** *n*, irrigation, *f*.
irritable, *a*, irritable. **irritate,** *v.t*, irriter; agacer.
irritant, *a. & n*, irritant, *m*. **irritation,** *n*, irritation, *f*.
irruption, *n*, irruption, *f*.
Islam, *n*, Islam, *m*.
island, *n*, île, *f*; (*traffic* ~) refuge, *m*. ~**er,** *n*, insulaire, *m,f*. **isle,** *n*, île, *f*. **islet,** *n*, îlot, *m*.
isolate, *v.t*, isoler. **isolation,** *n*, isolement, *m*. ~ *hospital*, hôpital de contagieux, *m*.
Israel, *n*, l'Israël, *m*. **Israeli,** *a*, israélien. ¶ *n*, Israélien, ne.
issue, *n*, (*matter*) question, *f*, sujet, *m*. *the point at* ~, la question dont il s'agit. *to be at* ~, être en cause. *evade the* ~, prendre la tangente. (*outcome*) résultat, *m*. *happy* ~, heureuse issue. (*stores &c*) distribution; (*shares, stamps*) émission; (*passport, receipt*) délivrance; (*offspring*) descendance, *f*. ¶ *v.t*, distribuer; émettre; délivrer. ~ *a statement*, faire une déclaration.
isthmus, *n*, isthme, *m*.
it, *pn*, (*m or f subject*) il, elle; (*m or f object*) le, la. *of, from* ~ *&c* (*de qch*) en. *I'm sure of* ~, j'en suis sûr. *he spoke of* ~, il en a parlé. *to, at, in* ~ *&c* (*à qch*) y. *we're going to* ~, nous y allons. *think about* ~, pensez-y. *in* ~, dedans. *on, above* ~, [au-]dessus. *under, below* ~, [au-]dessous. (*impersonal*) il, ce, cela, ça. ~ *'s your mother*, c'est ta mère. ~ *'s impossible*, c'est impossible. ~ *'s impossible to see*, il est impossible de voir. ~ *depends*, ça dépend. ~ *is raining*, il pleut. ~ *is said that*, on dit que.
Italian, *a*, italien. ¶ *n*, (*pers.*) Italien, ne; (*language*) l'italien, *m*.
italic, *a. &* ~**s,** *n.pl*, italique, *m*.
Italy, *n*, l'Italie, *f*.
itch, *v.i*, (*pers.*) éprouver des démangeaisons. *my arm* ~*es*, le bras me démange. (*fig.*) *I'm* ~*ing to do*, ça me démange de faire. ¶ ~**[ing],** *n*, démangeaison, *f*. (*Med.*) *the* ~, la gale. ~**y,** *a*, qui démange.
item, *n*, article; (*in programme*) numéro, *m*; (*on agenda*) question, *f*, point, *m*; (*Bkkpg*) poste, *m*. ~**ize,** *v.t*, détailler.
itinerant, *a*, itinérant; (*musician*) ambulant.

itinerary, *n,* itinéraire, *m.*
its, *a,* son, sa, ses; en.
itself, *pn,* (*emphatic*) lui-même, elle-même; (*reflexive*) se. *kindness* ~, la bonté même. *by* ~, tout[e] seul[e].
ivory, *n,* ivoire, *m.* ¶ *a,* d'ivoire, en ivoire. *the I~ Coast,* la Côte d'Ivoire.
ivy, *n,* lierre, *m.*

J

jab, *n,* coup, *m;* (*Med. P*) piqûre, *f.* ¶ *v.t,* enfoncer (*into,* dans); piquer (*with,* avec).
jabber, *v.i. & t,* jacasser; baragouiner *P. what's he ~ing about?* qu'est-ce qu'il baragouine?
jack, *n,* (*Mot.*) cric; (*Cards*) valet; (*Bowls*) cochonnet, *m.* ~*ass,* âne, baudet, *m.* ~*boots,* bottes à l'écuyère, *f.pl.* ~*daw,* choucas, *m.* ~*-in-the-box,* diable [à ressort], *m.* ~*knife,* canif, couteau de poche, *m;* (*dive*) saut carpé. ~*-of-all-trades,* homme à tout faire, *m.* ~*pot,* le gros lot.
jackal, *n,* chacal, *m.*
jacket, *n,* (*man*) veston, *m,* veste; (*woman*) veste, jaquette, *f;* (*lumber* ~) blouson, *m;* (*book*) jaquette; (*boiler &c*) chemise, *f.* ~ *potatoes,* pommes de terre en robe de chambre, *f.pl.*
jade, *n,* jade, *m.* ~ *green,* vert [de] jade, *inv.*
jaded, *a,* (*pers.*) las; (*palate*) blasé.
jagged, *a,* dentelé, déchiqueté.
jaguar, *n,* jaguar, *m.*
jail, *n,* prison, *f.* ¶ *v.t,* mettre en prison. ~ *for life,* condamner à perpétuité. ~*bird,* [vieux] cheval de retour, *m.* ~**er,** *n,* geôlier, ère.
jam[1], *n,* (*people*) cohue, *f;* (*traffic*) embouteillage, *m.* (*fig.*) *to be in a* ~, être dans le pétrin. ~*-full,* ~*-packed,* plein à craquer. ¶ *v.t,* (*into sth*) serrer, enfoncer; (*wedge*) coincer. ~ *one's finger,* (*in door &c*) se coincer le doigt. (*obstruct: Tel. line; street*) encombrer; (*gun, Mach.*) enrayer; (*Radio*) brouiller. ~ *on the brakes,* freiner à bloc.
jam[2], *n,* confiture, *f. plum* ~, c. de prunes. ~ *jar,* ~ *pot,* pot à confitures, *m.*
Jamaica, *n,* la Jamaïque. ~**n,** *a,* jamaïquain. ¶ *n,* Jamaïquain, e.
jamb, *n,* jambage, montant, *m.*
jangle, *v.i.* (*& t*) (*chains &c*) (faire) cliqueter.
janitor, *n,* concierge, *m.*
January, *n,* janvier, *m.*
Japan, *n,* le Japon. **Japanese,** *a,* japonais. ¶ *n,* (*pers.*) Japonais, e; (*language*) le japonais.
jar[1], *n,* pot, *m,* jarre, *f;* (*glass*) bocal, *m.*
jar[2], *n,* secousse, *f,* choc, *m.* ¶ *v.i,* rendre un son discordant; (*colours*) jurer. ~ *on,* agacer. *that ~s on my nerves,* ça me tape sur les nerfs. ~**ring,** *a,* (*sound*) discordant.
jargon, *n,* jargon, *m.*
jasmin[e], *n,* jasmin, *m.*
jaundice, *n,* jaunisse, *f. have a ~d view of life,* voir les choses en noir.
jaunt, *n,* excursion, balade *P, f. go for a* ~, aller se balader *P.* ~**y,** *a,* insouciant, désinvolte; (*gait*) vif.
Java, *n,* Java, *m.* **Javanese,** *a,* javanais. ¶ *n,* Javanais, e.
javelin, *n,* javelot, *m.*
jaw, *n,* mâchoire, *f.* ~ *bone,* maxillaire, *m.*
jay, *n,* geai, *m.* ~*walker,* piéton étourdi, *m.*
jazz, *n,* (*Mus.*) jazz, *m. & all that* ~ *P,* et tout le bataclan *P.* ¶ *v.t,* ~ *up,* animer; (*dress*) égayer.
jealous†, *a,* jaloux (*of,* de). ~**y,** *n,* jalousie, *f.*
jeans, *n.pl,* blue-jean, *m.*
jeep, *n,* jeep, *m.*
jeer, *n,* raillerie; (*crowd*) huée, *f.* ¶ *v.i,* railler; huer. ~ *at s.o,* railler qn. ¶ *v.t,* huer. ~**ing,** *a,* railleur.
jelly, *n,* gelée, *f. like* ~ (*legs*), en compote. ~*fish,* méduse, *f.*
jemmy, *n,* pince-monseigneur, *f.*
jeopardize, *v.t,* mettre en danger. **jeopardy,** *n,* danger, *m.*
jerboa, *n,* gerboise, *f.*
jerk, *n,* à-coup, *m,* saccade, secousse, *f. in ~s,* (*move*) par à-coups, par saccades. ¶ *v.t,* donner une secousse à. ~**y,** *a,* saccadé.
jerry-building, *n,* construction de camelote, *f.* ~**-built,** *a,* en carton-pâte.
jersey, *n,* tricot; (*football*) maillot; (*cloth*) jersey, *m.* **J~,** *n,* Jersey, *f. J~ cow,* vache jersiaise, *f.*
jest, *n,* plaisanterie, *f. in* ~, pour rire. ¶ *v.i,* plaisanter. ~**er,** *n,* bouffon, *m.*
Jesuit, *n,* Jésuite, *m.* ~**ical,** *a,* jésuitique.
Jesus, *n,* Jésus, *m.* ~ *Christ,* Jésus-Christ, *m.*
jet[1], *n,* jais, *m.* ~*-black,* noir de j.
jet[2], *n,* (*spurt*) jet; (*Mot.*) gicleur; (*gas*) brûleur, *m;* (~ *plane*) avion à réaction, jet, *m.* ¶ *a,* (*engine &c*) à réaction.
jettison, *v.t,* (*Naut.*) jeter à la mer; (*bombs*) larguer; (*fig.*) abandonner.
jetty, *n,* jetée, embarcadère, *f.*
Jew, *n,* Juif, *m.* ~*'s harp,* guimbarde, *f.* **Jewess,** *n,* Juive, *f.* **Jewish,** *a,* juif.

jewel, *n,* bijou, joyau; (*watch*) rubis, *m.* ~ *case,* coffret à bijoux, *m.* ~**ler,** *n,* bijoutier, ère, joaillier, ère. ~**[le]ry,** *n,* bijouterie, joaillerie, *f.*

jib, *n,* (*sail*) foc, *m;* (*crane*) flèche, *f.* ¶ *v.i,* regimber (*at,* devant); se refuser (*at doing,* à faire).

jibe, *n.* & *v.i,* = **gibe.**

jiffy, *n,* instant, *m. in a* ~, en moins de rien.

jig, *n,* (*dance*) gigue, *f;* (*Mach.*) calibre, *m.* ~*-saw,* scie à chantourner, *f.* ~*-saw puzzle,* puzzle, *m.* ¶ *v.i,* ~ *about,* se trémousser.

jilt, *v.t,* laisser tomber *P.*

jingle, *n,* tintement; cliquetis; (*TV, Radio*) couplet publicitaire, *m.* ¶ *v.i.* (& *t*), (faire) tinter.

jingoism, *n,* chauvinisme, *m.*

jinx *P, n,* porte-malheur, porte-poisse *P, m.*

jiu-jitsu, *n,* jiu-jitsu, *m.*

job, *n,* (*task*) tâche, besogne, *f,* travail, boulot *P, m;* (*post*) travail, poste, emploi, *m,* situation, *f,* boulot *P. out of a* ~, en chômage. *cushy* ~ *P,* planque *P,f.* ~*s for the boys,* des planques pour les copains. *he knows his* ~, il connaît son métier. *I had a* ~ *finding him,* j'ai eu du mal à le trouver. *it's a good* ~ *that,* heureusement que. ~ *analysis,* analyse des tâches, *f.* ~ *centre,* agence pour l'emploi, *f.* ~ *lot,* lot d'articles divers, *m.* ~**bing,** *a,* (*gardener*) à la journée; (*workman*) à la tâche.

jockey, *n,* jockey, *m.* ¶ *v.i.* & *t,* manœuvrer.

jockstrap, *n,* suspensoir, *m.*

jocular, *a,* jovial, badin. ~**ly,** *ad,* d'un ton badin.

jog, *n,* secousse, *f;* (~*-trot*) petit trot. ¶ *v.t,* (*arm*) pousser; (*memory*) rafraîchir. ¶ *v.i,* (*Sport*) faire du jogging. ~ *along,* (*pers., things*) aller son petit train; (*pers.*) aller cahin-caha. ~**ging,** *n,* (*Sport*) jogging, *m.*

join, *v.t,* (~ *together*) joindre, [ré]unir; (*link*) relier; (*wires, pipes*) raccorder; (*club, party*) devenir membre de, s'inscrire à; (*army*) s'engager dans; (*firm*) entrer dans; (*meet*) rejoindre, retrouver. *Alice* ~*s me in wishing you...* A. se joint à moi pour vous souhaiter... ~ *in,* participer à. ~**er,** *n,* menuisier, *m.* ~**ery,** *n,* menuiserie, *f.* **joint,** *n,* (*Anat.*) articulation, *f. put one's shoulder out of* ~, se démettre, se disloquer l'épaule. (*Tech.*) joint; (*Carp.*) assemblage, *m,* jointure, *f;* (*Cook.*), rôti, *m;* (*P place*) boîte, *f.* ¶ *v.t,* (*Cook.*) découper. ~*ed,* articulé. ¶ *a,* (*account, decision*) commun; (*committee*) mixte. ~ *author,* coauteur, *m.* ~ *manager,* codirecteur, *m.* ~ *owner,* copropriétaire, *m,f.* ~*-stock company,* société par actions, *f.*

joist, *n,* solive, *f.*

joke, *n,* plaisanterie, blague *P, f. for a* ~, pour rire. *it's no* ~, ce n'est pas drôle. *play a [practical]* ~ *on s.o,* faire une farce à qn. ¶ *v.i,* plaisanter, blaguer *P. you're joking!* sans blague! *P.* **joker,** *n,* blagueur, euse *P;* farceur, euse; (*Cards*) joker, *m.*

jollity, *n,* gaieté, *f;* réjouissances, *f.pl.* **jolly,** *a,* jovial, gai. ¶ *ad,* (*very*) drôlement *P,* rudement *P.*

jolt, *n,* cahot, *m,* secousse, *f.* ¶ *v.i.* & *t,* cahoter.

Jonah (*fig.*) *n,* porte-malheur, *m.*

Jordan, *n,* (*country*) Jordanie, *f;* (*river*) Jourdain, *m.*

jostle, *v.t,* bousculer.

jot, *n,* iota, brin, *m.* ¶ *v.t,* ~ *down,* noter. ~**ter,** *n,* bloc-notes, *m.* ~**tings,** *n.pl,* notes, *f.pl.*

journal, *n,* (*daily* & *diary*) journal, *m;* (*periodical*) revue, *f;* (*Com.*) livre journal. ~**ism,** *n,* journalisme, *m.* ~**ist,** *n,* journaliste, *m,f.*

journey, *n,* voyage; (*distance*) trajet, *m. go on a* ~, partir en voyage. *a 20 km* ~, un trajet de 20 km. ~ *there & back,* voyage aller & retour.

jovial†, *a,* jovial. ~**ity,** *n,* jovialité, *f.*

joy, *n,* joie, *f.* ~*s,* plaisirs, *m.pl. it's a* ~ *to see her,* c'est un vrai plaisir de la voir. ~*ride,* balade en voiture *P,f.* ~*stick,* (*Aero.*) manche à balai, *m.* ~**ful†,** *a,* joyeux. ~**fulness,** *n,* allégresse, *f.*

jubilant, *a, to be* ~, jubiler. **jubilation,** *n,* jubilation, *f.* **jubilee,** *n,* jubilé, *m.*

judge, *n,* juge, *m;* (*fig.*) connaisseur, euse. ¶ *v.t,* juger; estimer. ¶ *v.i,* ~ *for oneself,* juger par soi-même. *judging by,* à en juger par. **judg[e]ment,** *n,* (*Law*) jugement; (*opinion*) avis, *m,* opinion, *f. pass* ~ *on,* porter un jugement sur. (*sound* ~) discernement, jugement, *m.* (*Rel.*) *Last J*~, Jugement dernier.

judicial†, *a,* judiciaire. **judiciary,** *n,* magistrature, *f.* **judicious†,** *a,* judicieux.

judo, *n,* judo, *m.*

jug, *n,* (*milk &c*) pot, *m;* (*pottery*) cruche, *f;* (*P prison*) taule *P, f.* ~*ged hare,* civet de lièvre, *m.*

juggernaut, *n,* (*lorry*) mastodonte, *m.*

juggle, *v.i,* jongler. ~**ry & juggling,** *n,* jonglerie, *f;* (*fig.*) tours de passe-passe, *m.pl.* **juggler,** *n,* jongleur, euse.

jugular [vein], *n,* [veine] jugulaire, *f.*

juice, *n,* jus; suc, *m.* **juicy,** *a,* juteux; (*story*) sauvoureux.

jukebox, *n,* juke-box, *m.*

July, *n,* juillet, *m.*

jumble, *n,* fouillis, fatras, *m;* (*in* ~ *sale*) bric-à-brac, *m. in a* ~, pêle-mêle. ~ *sale,* vente de charité, *f.* ¶ *v.t,* brouiller.

jump, *n,* saut; (*startled*) sursaut, *m. at one* ~, d'un bond. (*show* ~*ing*) saut; (*fence*) obstacle, *m.* ¶ *v.i,* sauter, bondir; (*start*) sursauter. ~ *out of,* sauter (*bed*) à bas du lit, (*car*) d'une voiture, (*window*) par la fenêtre. ~ *over,* sauter par-dessus, franchir [d'un bond]. ~ *to a conclusion,* conclure à la légère.

¶ *v.t,* sauter, franchir. (*fig.*) ~ *the gun,* agir prématurément. ~ *the queue,* resquiller. (*Rly*) ~ *the rails,* dérailler. ~**ed up** *P, a,* parvenu. ~**er,** *n,* tricot, pull[over], *m.* ~**y,** *a,* nerveux.

junction, *n,* jonction; (*road*) bifurcation, *f;* (*Rly*) embranchement, *m;* (*station*) gare de jonction, *f.* **juncture,** *n, at this* ~, à ce moment-là; à présent.

June, *n,* juin, *m.*

jungle, *n,* jungle, *f.*

junior, *a,* (*younger*) cadet, plus jeune. *J.Brown* ~, J.Brown fils. (*in rank*) subalterne; (*Sport*) ≏ cadet. ~ *school,* école primaire, *f.* ¶ *n,* cadet, te. *my* ~ *by 2 years,* mon c. de 2 ans.

juniper, *n,* genévrier. ~ *berries,* [grains de] genièvre, *m*[*pl*].

junk[1], *n,* (*boat*) jonque, *f.*

junk[2], *n,* bric-à-brac, *m;* (*shoddy goods*) pacotille, camelote, *f.* ~ *heap, n,* dépotoir, *m.* ~ *shop,* boutique de brocanteur, *f.* ~**ie** *P, n,* drogué, e.

junket, *n,* lait caillé. ¶ *v.i,* (*revel*) faire la fête. ~**ing,** *n,* bombance, *f.*

junta, *n,* junte, *f.*

jurisdiction, *n,* juridiction, *f. within our* ~, de notre compétence.

juror, *n,* juré, *m. woman* ~, femme juré. **jury,** *n,* jury, *m.* ~ *box,* banc des jurés, *m.* ~*man,* juré. ¶ *a,* (*mast &c*) de fortune.

just, *a,* juste, équitable (*to,* envers). ¶ *ad,* (*exactly*) juste, au juste, exactement. ~ *opposite,* juste en face. ~ *what's needed,* juste *ou* exactement ce qu'il faut. ~ *as he was leaving,* juste au moment où il partait. ~ *what does he want?* qu'est-ce qu'il veut au juste? *everything was* ~ *so,* tout était bien en ordre. (*this moment*) *I'm* ~ *coming,* j'arrive. *I'm* ~ *leaving,* je suis sur le point de partir. *I have* ~ *seen,* je viens de voir. (*by a little*) ~ *enough,* [tout] juste assez. ~ *in time,* juste à temps. ~ *before, after,* juste avant, après. ~ *about,* à peu près. ~ *as big as,* tout aussi grand que. (*merely*) seulement, [tout] simplement. *I* ~ *told him...* je lui ai tout simplement dit... ~ *look at that!* regarde-moi ça! *P.* ~**ice,** *n,* justice, *f. do s.o* ~, rendre justice à qn. *do o.s* ~, se montrer à sa juste valeur. *do* ~ *to* (*meal*), faire honneur à. (*judge*) juge, *m. J*~ *of the Peace,* juge de paix. ~**ifiable,** *a,* justifiable. ~**ifiably,** *ad,* avec raison. ~**ification,** *n,* justification, *f.* ~**ly,** *ad,* (*treat*) avec justice. ~**ness,** *n,* justice, *f.*

jut [out], *v.i,* faire saillie, [s']avancer.

jute, *n,* jute, *m.*

juvenile, *a,* juvénile; (*books, court*) pour enfants. ¶ *n,* jeune, *m,f.*

juxtapose, *v.t,* juxtaposer.

K

kale, *n,* chou frisé, *m.*

kaleidoscope, *n,* kaléidoscope, *m.*

kangaroo, *n,* kangourou, *m.*

kaolin, *n,* kaolin, *m.*

karate, *n,* karaté, *m.*

kayak, *n,* kayak, *m.*

kedge [anchor], *n,* ancre à jet, *f.*

keel, *n,* quille, *f.* ¶ *v.i,* ~ *over,* chavirer.

keen, *a,* (*blade*) aiguisé, tranchant; (*air, wind; interest, intelligence*) vif; (*desire, pleasure*) intense; (*ear*) fin; (*sight*) perçant; (*competition*) serré; (*pers.*) ardent, enthousiaste, passionné. *to be* ~ *on,* (*sport, jazz*) se passionner pour, avoir la passion pour. *to be* ~ *to do, for s.o to do,* tenir à faire, à ce qu'on fasse. ~**ly,** *ad,* vivement; avec enthousiasme. ~**ness,** *n,* (*blade*) finesse; intensité, *f;* enthousiasme, *m.*

keep, *n,* frais de subsistance, *m.pl. earn one's* ~, gagner sa vie. (*castle*) donjon, *m.* ¶ *v.t.ir,* (*object*) garder, conserver; (*promise, accounts, diary*) tenir; (*order*) maintenir; (*rule*) observer; (*pigs &c*) élever. (*maintain*) ~ *clean,* garder *ou* tenir propre. *well kept,* (*garden &c*) bien [entre]tenu. (*hotel, shop*) tenir; (*detain*) retenir. *what kept you?* qu'est-ce qui vous a retenu? ~ *s.o waiting,* faire attendre qn. (*support: family*) faire vivre, nourrir. ~ *o.s to o.s,* se tenir à l'écart. ~ *s.o from doing,* empêcher qn de faire. ¶ *v.i.ir,* continuer de *ou* à faire. ~ *straight on,* continuer tout droit. ~ *still, calm,* rester tranquille, calme. ~ *silent, smiling,* garder le silence, le sourire. ~ *fit,* se maintenir en forme. (*food*) se garder, se conserver. ~ **away,** tenir éloigné. ~ **back,** (*money, crowd*) retenir; (*facts*) cacher. ¶ *v.i,* rester en arrière. ~ **down,** (*prices*) empêcher de monter. ~ **in,** (*Sch: pupil*) garder en retenue; (*stomach*) rentrer. ~ **off,** ~ *off!* n'approchez pas! ~ *off the grass',* 'défense de marcher sur les pelouses'. ~ **on,** continuer (*de, à faire*). ~ *on at s.o,* harceler qn. ~ **out,** (*pers.*) empêcher d'entrer; (*cold*) protéger de. ¶ *v.i,* rester en dehors. ~ *out'*, 'entrée interdite'. ~ *out of this!* ne vous en mêlez pas! ~ *out of sight*, ne pas se montrer. ~ **to**, ~ *to the left*, tenir la gauche. ~ *to one's bed*, garder le lit. ~ **up**, continuer; (*house &c*) entretenir, maintenir en bon état; (*appearances*) garder. ~ *up with*, (*friend*) rester en relations avec; (*s.o in race*) aller aussi vite que. ~**er**, *n*, gardien, ne; (*museum*) conservateur, trice; (*game* ~) garde-chasse, *m*. ~**ing**, *n*, *put in s.o's* ~, confier à qn. *in* ~ *with*, en accord avec. ~**sake**, *n*, souvenir, *m*.

keg, *n*, (*beer*) tonnelet, *m*; (*fish*) caque, *f*.

ken, *n*, connaissance, *f*.

kennel, *n*, niche, *f*; (*hounds*) chenil, *m*.

Kenya, *n*, Kenya, *m*.

kerb, *n*, bord du trottoir, *m*.

kernel, *n*, (*of nut, fruitstone*) amande, *f*.

kerosene, *n*, kérosène, *m*. ¶ *a*, (*lamp*) à pétrole.

kestrel, *n*, crécerelle, *f*.

ketch, *n*, ketch, *m*.

kettle, *n*, bouilloire, *f*. ~*drum*, timbale, *f*.

key, *n*, (*lit., fig.*) clef, clé, *f*; (*winder*) remontoir, *m*; (*piano, typewriter*) touche; (*flute &c*) clef, *f*; (*Mus.*) ton; (*Sch. book*) corrigé, *m*. ¶ *a*, clef, *inv*. ~ *industry, position*, industrie, position clef. ~ *man*, pivot, *m*. ~*board*, clavier, *m*. ~*hole*, trou de serrure, *m*. ~*note*, tonique, *f*; (*fig.*) note dominante. ~*ring*, porte-clefs, *m*. ~ *signature* (*Mus.*), armature, *f*. ~*stone*, clef de voûte, *f*. ¶ *v.t*, ~*ed up*, excité, tendu.

khaki, *a*. & *n*, kaki, *inv* & *m*.

kibbutz, *n*, kibboutz, *m*.

kick, *n*, coup de pied, *m*. *give s.o a* ~ *in the pants*, botter les fesses à *ou* de qn. (*fig.*) *a* ~ *in the teeth*, une gifle en pleine figure. (*P thrill*) *I get a* ~ *out of that*, ça me fait quelque chose. *for* ~*s*, pour le plaisir. (*horse*) ruade, *f*; (*gun*) recul, *m*. ~*-off* (*Foot.*), coup d'envoi, *m*. ¶ *v.t*, donner un coup (des coups) de pied à; (*horse*) lancer une ruade à. ~ *a goal*, marquer un but. ~ *over the traces*, ruer dans les brancards. ~ *one's heels*, faire le pied de grue. ~ *the bucket P*, casser sa pipe *P*. ~ *in*, (*door*) enfoncer à coups de p. ~ *out*, (*pers.*) mettre à la porte; *v.i*, (*horse*) ruer. ~ *up a fuss*, faire toute une histoire.

kid[1], *n*, (*goat, leather*) chevreau, *m*; (*P child & kiddy*) gosse *P*, mioche *P*, *m,f*. ¶ *a*, (*gloves*) de chevreau; (*brother*) petit.

kid[2] *P*, *v.t*, faire marcher. ~ *o.s*, se faire des illusions. ¶ *v.i*, raconter des blagues. *no* ~*ding!* sans blague! *P*.

kidnap, *v.t*, enlever, kidnapper.

kidney, *n*, (*Anat.*) rein; (*meat*) rognon, *m*. ¶ *a*, rénal, des reins. ~*-bean*, haricot rouge, *m*. ~ *machine*, rein artificiel. ~ *transplant*, greffe du rein, *f*.

kill, *n*, mise à mort, *f*. ¶ *v.t*, tuer; assassiner; (*shoot down*) abattre. ~ *time*, tuer le temps. ~ *two birds with one stone*, faire d'une pierre deux coups. ~*-joy*, rabat-joie, *m*. ~**er**, *n*, tueur, euse. ~**ing**, *a*, (*work*) tuant, crevant *P*; (*funny*) tordant *P*, crevant *P*.

kiln, *n*, four, *m*. ~*-dry*, sécher au four.

kilo, *n*, kilo, *m*. **kilogram[me]**, *n*, kilogramme, *m*. **kilometre**, *n*, kilomètre, *m*. **kilowatt**, *n*, kilowatt, *m*.

kilt, *n*, kilt, *m*.

kimono, *n*, kimono, *m*.

kin, *n*, parents, *m.pl*.

kind[1], *n*, genre, *m*, espèce, sorte, *f*. *what* ~ *is it?* c'est de quelle sorte? *pay in* ~, payer en nature.

kind[2], *a*, gentil, bon, aimable. *to be* ~ *enough to do*, avoir la gentillesse de faire. *that's very* ~ *of you*, c'est très gentil de votre part. *give her my* ~ *regards*, faites-lui mes amitiés.

kindergarten, *n*, jardin d'enfants, *m*.

kindle, *v.t*, allumer. **kindling**, *n*, petit bois, *m*.

kindliness, *n*, bienveillance, bonté, *f*. **kindly**, *a*, bienveillant. ¶ *ad*, avec bonté. *would you* ~ *tell him*, voulez-vous bien lui dire. **kindness**, *n*, bonté, gentillesse (*towards*, pour). *do s.o a* ~, rendre service à qn.

kindred, *n*, parents, *m.pl*. ¶ *a*, de la même famille. ~ *spirits*, âmes sœurs, *f.pl*.

king, *n*, roi, *m*; (*Draughts*) dame, *f*. *oil, steel* ~, roi du pétrole, de l'acier. ~*cup*, bouton d'or, *m*. ~*fisher*, martin-pêcheur, *m*. ~*pin*, (*Tech., fig.*) cheville ouvrière, *f*. ~**dom**, *n*, royaume; (*Nat. Hist.*) règne, *m*. ~**ly**, *a*, royal.

kink, *n*, (*in rope*) entortillement, *m*; (*fig.*) bizarrerie, *f*. ~**y**, *a*, bizarre; (*idea*) biscornu *P*.

kinship, *n*, parenté, *f*. **kinsman, -woman**, *n*, parent, e.

kiosk, *n*, kiosque, *m*.

kipper, *n*, hareng salé & fumé, kipper, *m*.

kiss, *n*, baiser, *m*. ¶ *v.t*, embrasser, donner un baiser à. ~ *s.o's hand*, baiser la main de qn. ¶ *v.i*, s'embrasser.

kit, *n*, équipement, matériel; (*model*) kit, *m*; (*clothes*) affaires, *f.pl*; (*Mil.*) fourniment, barda *P*, *m*; (*tool, first aid*) trousse, *f*. ~*bag*, sac [de marin &c]. ¶ *v.t*, ~ *out*, équiper (*with*, de).

kitchen, *n*, cuisine, *f*. ¶ *a*, (*table &c*) de cuisine. ~ *garden*, [jardin] potager, *m*. ~ *maid*, fille de cuisine, *f*. ~ *unit*, élément de c., *m*. ~ *utensils*, batterie de c., *f*.

kite, *n*, (*bird*) milan; (*toy*) cerf-volant, *m*.

kith & kin, amis & parents, *m.pl*.

kitten, *n*, chaton, petit chat, *m*, petite chatte, *f*.

kleptomania, *n*, cleptomanie, *f*. **kleptomaniac**, *n*, cleptomane, *m,f*.

knack, *n*, tour de main, truc *P*, *m*.

knacker, *n*, équarrisseur, *m*. ~**ed** *P*, *a*, crevé *P*.

knapsack, *n*, sac [à dos], havresac, *m*.

knave, *n,* fripon, coquin; (*Cards*) valet, *m.*
knead, *v.t,* pétrir. ~*ing trough,* pétrin, *m.*
knee, *n,* genou, *m. on one's* ~*s,* à genoux. ~*cap,* (*Anat.*) rotule. ~*pad,* genouillère, *f.*
kneel [down], *v.i.ir,* s'agenouiller, se mettre à genoux. ~*ing,* à genoux.
knell, *n,* glas, *m. toll the* ~, sonner le glas.
knickers, *n.pl,* slip [de femme], *m.*
knick-knack, *n,* bibelot, *m.*
knife, *n,* couteau, *m;* (*pocket* ~) canif, *m.* ~, *fork & spoon,* couvert, *m. have one's* ~ *into s.o,* s'acharner contre qn. *before you could say* ~, en moins de rien. ~ *grinder,* rémouleur, *m.* ~ *rest,* porte-couteau, *m.* ¶ *v.t,* poignarder.
knight, *n,* chevalier; (*Chess*) cavalier, *m.* ¶ *v.t,* faire chevalier. ~**hood,** *n,* titre de chevalier, *m.*
knit, *v.t.ir,* tricoter; (*fig.*) lier. ~ *one's brows,* froncer les sourcils. ¶ *v.i.ir,* tricoter; (*bones*) se souder. ~**ted,** *a,* en tricot. ~**ter,** *n,* tricoteur, euse. **knitting,** *n,* tricot; tricotage, *m.* ¶ *a,* (*wool &c*) à tricoter. ~ *needle,* ~ *pin,* aiguille à tricoter, *f.* **knitwear,** *n,* tricots, *m.pl.*
knob, *n,* (*door*) bouton; (*cane*) pommeau, *m;* (*butter*) noix, *f.* ~**bly,** *a,* noueux.
knock, *n,* coup, *m. there was a* ~ *at the door,* on a frappé [à la porte]. *I heard a* ~, j'ai entendu frapper. ¶ *v.t. & i,* frapper; cogner. ~ *one's head against sth,* se cogner la tête contre qch. (*engine*) cogner. ~ **about,** (*pers.*) brutaliser. ¶ *v.i,* (*travel*) vagabonder, vadrouiller *P.* ~ **back** *P,* (*drink*) s'envoyer *P.* ~ **down,** (*pedestrian*) renverser; (*Build.*) démolir; (*door*) enfoncer; (*price*) baisser; (*auction*) adjuger. ~ **in,** (*nail*) enfoncer. ~ **off,** (*from shelf &c*) faire tomber. ¶ *v.i,* (*from work*) s'arrêter [de travailler]. ~ **over,** renverser. ~ **out,** (*stun*) assommer; (*Box.*) mettre knock-out; (*Sport*) éliminer. ~ **together,** *v.i,* s'entrechoquer. ~ **up,** (*at night*) réveiller; (*meal*) préparer en vitesse. ¶ *v.i,* (*Ten.*) faire des balles. ~*ed up,* éreinté. ~**er,** (*door*), *n,* marteau, *m.* ~**-kneed,** *a,* cagneux. ~**out,** *n,* (*Box.*) knock-out, *m.*
knoll, *n,* terte, *m,* butte, *f.*
knot, *n,* nœud, *m. tie a* ~, faire un nœud. (*Naut.*) *make 10* ~*s,* filer 10 nœuds. ¶ *v.t,* nouer. **knotty,** *a,* noueux; (*problem*) épineux.
know, *v.t. & i.ir,* (*facts; why, where, when &c*) savoir. *he* ~*s Greek,* il sait le grec. ~ *by heart,* savoir par cœur. ~ *how to do sth,* savoir faire qch. *he* ~*s how to please,* il sait plaire. *I know nothing about it,* je n'en sais rien. ~ *more about,* en savoir plus long sur. *he* ~*s all about cars,* il s'y connaît en voitures. *as far as I* ~, autant que je sache. *not that I* ~ *of,* pas que je sache. *let s.o* ~, faire savoir à qn. *not to* ~ *sth, that,* ignorer qch, que. (*be acquainted with: pers., place, book &c*) connaître. *do you* ~ *Rome?* connaissez-vous Rome? (*recognize*) reconnaître. *I knew him by his voice,* je l'ai reconnu à sa voix. ¶ *n, to be in the* ~, être au courant. ~**-all,** *n,* je-sais-tout, *m,f.* ~**-how,** *n,* technique, *f.* ~**ing,** *a,* (*pers.*) malin; (*smile*) entendu. ~**ingly,** *ad,* (*consciously*) sciemment; d'un air entendu. **knowledge,** *n,* connaissance, *f. to* [*the best of*] *my* ~, à ma connaissance. *without my* ~, à mon insu. *have no* ~ *of,* ignorer. (*learning*) connaissances, *f.pl,* savoir, *m.* ~**able,** *a,* bien informé. **known,** *a,* (*thief*) connu. *well-*~, bien connu.
knuckle, *n,* articulation du doigt, *f;* (*veal*) jarret, *m.* ~*-duster,* coup de poing américain. ¶ *v.i,* ~ *down* [*to it*], s'y mettre. ~ *under,* se soumettre.
Koran, *n,* Coran, *m.*
Korea, *n,* la Corée. ~**n,** *a,* coréen.
kosher, *a,* kascher.
kowtow, *v.i,* se prosterner (*to,* devant).
kudos, *n,* gloire, *f.*

L

label, *n,* étiquette, *f.* ¶ *v.t,* étiqueter.
labial, *a,* labial. ¶ *n,* labiale, *f.*
laboratory, *n,* laboratoire, *m.* ~ **assistant,** laborantin, e.
laborious†, *a,* laborieux.
labour, *n,* (*gen., Med.*), travail, *m;* (*col; workers*) main-d'œuvre, *f,* ouvriers, *m.pl.* ~ *camp,* camp de travaux forcés, *m.* ~ *exchange,* Agence Nationale pour l'emploi, *f,* (A.N.P.E.). ~ *market,* marché du travail, *m.* ~ *pains,* douleurs [de l'accouchement], *f.pl. L*~ *party,* parti travailliste, *m.* ~*-saving,* qui allège le travail. ~*-saving device,* appareil ménager, *m.* ~ *troubles,* agitation ouvrière, *f.* ¶ *v.i.* (*with effort*) travailler dur à; (*with difficulty & engine*) peiner, (*at,* sur); (*ship*), fatiguer. ¶ *v.t,* insister sur, s'étendre sur. ~**ed,** *a,* (*fig.*), laborieux. ~**er,** *n,* ouvrier, *m,* travailleur, *m;* (*farm*) ouvrier agricole; (*Build. &c*) manœuvre, *m.*

laburnum. *n,* cytise, *m.*
labyrinth, *n,* labyrinthe, dédale, *m.*
lace, *n,* dentelle, *f;* (*boot &c*) lacet, cordon, *m.* *~maker,* dentellière, *f.* *~making,* fabrication de la dentelle, *f.* *~-up shoes,* chaussures à lacets, *f.pl.* ¶ *v.t,* lacer; (*drink*) arroser (*with,* de), corser. ¶ *v.i,* se lacer.
lacerate, *v.t,* déchirer, lacérer.
lack, *n,* manque, *m.* *for ~ of,* faute de, par manque de. ¶ *v.t,* manquer de. *to be ~ing,* faire défaut, manquer (à qn). *~ing in meaning,* dénué de sens. *~lustre, a,* terne.
lackadaisical, *a,* indolent, nonchalant.
lackey, *n,* laquais; (*pej.*) larbin *P, m.*
laconic†, *a,* laconique.
lacquer, *n. & ~ work,* laque, *m.* ¶ *v.t,* laquer.
lactate, *v.i,* produire du lait. **lactation,** *n,* lactation, *f.*
lacuna, *n,* lacune, *f.*
lad, *n,* garçon; gars, *m.* *come on ~s!* allez les gars! *he's a bit of a ~,* c'est un rude gaillard.
ladder, *n,* échelle; (*stocking &c*) échelle, maille filée, *f.* *~proof,* indémaillable. ¶ *v.t,* filer, faire une échelle à. ¶ *v.i,* filer, se démailler.
laden, *a,* chargé (*with* de).
ladle, *n,* louche, *f.* ¶ *v.t, ~ out,* servir [à la louche].
lady, *n,* dame, *f.* *Ladies & Gentlemen!* Mesdames, Messieurs! *ladies first!* place aux dames! *she's a real ~,* c'est une vraie dame. *she's no ~,* elle est fort commune. *young ~,* (*married*) jeune femme, (*single*) jeune fille, *f.* *his young ~,* sa bonne amie. *~bird,* coccinelle, bête à bon Dieu, *f.* *L~ chapel,* chapelle de la Vierge, *f.* *L~ Day,* fête de l'Annonciation, *f;* le 25 mars. *~-killer,* bourreau des cœurs, *m.* *his* (*my*) *~-love,* la dame de ses (de mes) pensées. *~ of the manor,* châtelaine, *f.* *~'s maid,* femme de chambre, *f.* *ladies' man,* homme galant. *~like,* comme il faut, distingué.
lag[1], *n,* (*delay*) retard, *m;* (*between two events*) décalage, *m.* ¶ *v.i,* traîner. *~ behind,* rester en arrière.
lag[2], *v.t,* (*pipes*) calorifuger. **~ging,** *n,* calorifuge, *m;* (*act*) calorifugeage, *m.*
lag[3], *n, old ~ P,* [vieux] cheval de retour, *m.*
lager, *n,* bière [blonde], *f.*
lagoon, *n,* lagune, *f.*
laid up, *a,* (*in bed*) alité; (*car*) remisé; (*ship*) désarmé.
lair, *n,* tanière, *f,* repaire, *m.*
laity, *n,* laïcs *ou* laïques, *m.pl.*
lake, *n,* lac, *m;* (*paint*) laque, *f.* *~ dwelling,* habitation lacustre, *f.*
lama, *n,* lama, *m.*
lamb, *n,* agneau; (*pers.*) agneau, *m.* *like a ~ to the slaughter,* comme un agneau qu'on mène à l'abbatoir. ¶ *v.i,* agneler. **~kin,** *n,* agnelet, *m.*
lambast *P, v.t,* (*beat*) rosser *P;* (*scold*) sonner les cloches à *P;* (*criticize*) éreinter, démolir.
lambent, *a,* [doucement] radieux, lumineux.
lame, *a,* boiteux, éclopé, estropié; (*fig.*) qui cloche. ¶ *v.t,* estropier.
lamé, *a. & n,* lamé, *m.*
lameness, *n,* claudication; boiterie, *f.*
lament, *n,* lamentation, *f;* chant funèbre, *m.* ¶ *v.i,* se lamenter (*over,* sur). **~able†,** *a,* lamentable. **~ation,** *n,* lamentation, *f.* **the [late] ~ed...,** le (la) regretté, e...
laminate, *v.t,* laminer. **~d,** *a,* (*metal*) laminé; (*windscreen*) en verre feuilleté.
lamp, *n,* lampe, *f;* (*train*) fanal; (*street*) réverbère, *m.* *~post,* réverbère. *~shade,* abat-jour, *m.inv.* *~stand,* pied de lampe, *m.* *~ standard,* lampadaire, *m.*
lampoon, *n,* satire, *f;* (*written*) pamphlet, libelle, *m.* ¶ *v.t,* railler, tourner en dérision. **~ist,** *n,* satiriste, pamphlétaire; (*in song*) chansonnier, *m.*
lamprey, *n,* lamproie, *f.*
lance, *n,* lance, *f.* *~ corporal,* (*infantry*) caporal; (*cavalry*) brigadier, *m.* ¶ (*Surg.*) *v.t,* inciser, percer, ouvrir.
land, *n,* terre, *f;* (*property*) terre(s), *f.*(*pl*); (*plot*) terrain; (*country, nation*) pays, *m.* *dry ~* terre ferme. *on ~* à terre. *over ~ & sea,* sur terre & sur mer. *live off the ~,* vivre de la terre. *throughout the ~,* dans tout le pays. *~locked,* enfermé dans les terres. *~lord, ~lady,* propriétaire, *m,f;* logeur, euse; (*pub &c*) patron, ne. *~lubber,* terrien, ne. *~mark,* point de repère, *m.* *~ of milk & honey, ~ of plenty,* pays de cocagne. *~owner,* propriétaire foncier, *m,f,* terrien, ne. *~scape & ~scape painting,* paysage, *m.* *~scape gardener,* architecte (*ou* jardinier) paysagiste, *m.* *~scape painter,* [peintre] paysagiste, *m.* *~slide, ~slip,* éboulement de terre, *m.* *~slide victory,* (*Pol.*) victoire écrasante. ¶ *v.t,* (*cargo*) décharger; (*passengers*) débarquer; (*aircraft*) poser; (*fish*) amener à terre. *~ a blow,* infliger un coup. (*job &c*) décrocher *P.* ¶ *v.i,* (*from ship*) débarquer; (*plane*) se poser, atterrir; (*pers. thing*) [re]tomber, arriver. *~ up,* atterrir *P,* échouer, [finir par] se retrouver.
landau, *n,* landau, *m.* **~let,** *n,* landaulet, *m.*
landed, *a,* (*property*) foncier. *~ gentry,* aristocratie terrienne. **landing,** *n,* (*from ship*) débarquement; (*aircraft*) atterrissage; (*stairs*) palier, *m.* *~ card,* carte de débarquement, *f.* *~ gear* (*Aero.*), train d'atterrissage, *m.* *~ net,* épuisette, *f.* *~ place, ~ stage,* débarcadère, *m.*
lane, *n,* (*country*) chemin, sentier, *m;* (*town*) ruelle; (*part of road*) voie; (*traffic*) file, *f.* *keep in ~!* ne changez pas de file! (*Aero.*) couloir aérien; (*Sport*) couloir, *m.* *shipping ~,* route

maritime, *f.*
language, *n,* (*means of expression*) langage, *m;* (*national &c*) langue, *f. they do not speak the same* ~, (*fig.*) ils ne parlent pas le même langage. *bad* ~, gros mots. *modern* ~*s,* les langues vivantes.
languid, *a,* mou; languissant; traînant. **languish,** *v.i,* languir. ~**ing,** *a,* languissant, mourant.
languor, *n,* langueur, *f.* ~**ous,** *a,* langoureux, alangui.
lank, *a,* (*hair*) plat, raide & terne; (*plant*) long & grêle. ~**y,** *a,* grand & maigre.
lanolin, *n,* lanoline, *f.*
lantern, *n,* lanterne, *f;* (*paper*) lanterne vénitienne, lampion, *m.* ~*-jawed,* aux joues creuses. ~ *slide,* plaque le lanterne magique, *f.*
lanyard, *n,* (*Naut.*) ride, *f;* (*Mil.*) cordon, *m.*
lap[1], *n,* genoux, *m.pl,* giron, *m. in the* ~ *of the gods,* entre les mains des dieux. *in the* ~ *of luxury,* dans le plus grand luxe. ~*dog,* chien d'appartement, *m.*
lap[2], *n,* (*Build.*) recouvrement, *m;* (*Sport*) tour de piste, *m.* ¶ *v.t,* (*Sport*) prendre un tour d'avance sur.
lap[3], *v.t,* (*milk*) laper. ¶ *v.i,* (*waves*) clapoter (*against,* contre).
lapel, *n,* revers, *m.*
lapis lazuli, *n,* lapis[-lazuli], *m.*
Lapland, *n,* la Laponie. **Lapp,** *a,* lapon. **Lapp, Laplander,** *n,* Lapon, one.
lapse, *n,* (*fault*) défaillance, *f;* (*in behaviour*) écart de conduite, *m;* (*of time*) intervalle, *m;* (*custom*) oubli, *m;* (*law*) déchéance, *f.* ~ *of memory,* trou de mémoire, *m.* ~ *of time,* laps de temps, *m.* ¶ *v.i,* tomber (*into,* dans); (*fig.*) déchoir, démeriter. ~ *into bad habits,* prendre de mauvaises habitudes. (*Law*) tomber en désuétude, être caduc; (*contract*) expirer; (*ticket &c*) se périmer. ~**d,** *a,* caduc; périmé. ~ *Catholic,* catholique non pratiquant.
lapwing, *n,* vanneau, *m.*
larceny, *n,* (*Law*) vol simple, *m.*
larch, *n,* mélèze, *m.*
lard, *n,* saindoux, *m.* ¶ *v.t,* (*Cook.*) larder, piquer; ~*ing needle,* lardoire, *f.* (*fig.*) larder. ~**er,** *n,* garde-manger, *m.*
large, *a,* (*town, house &c*) grand; (*pers., animal*) gros; (*sum, loss*) fort; (*amount*) important; (*family*) nombreux; (*meal*) copieux; (*Anat.*) ~ *intestine,* gros intestin. *to get* ~*r,* grossir, grandir. *to make* ~*r,* agrandir. *at* ~, en liberté; (*as a whole*) en général. ~*-scale,* (*plan &c*) à grande échelle. ~**ly,** *ad,* en grande partie. ~**ness,** *n,* grandeur, grosseur, *f.*
largess[e], *n,* largesse, *f.*
lark[1], *n,* alouette, *f.* ~*spur,* pied d'alouette, *m. rise with the* ~, se lever au chant du coq.
lark[2], *n,* blague, rigolade *P, f.* ¶ *v.i,* ~ *about,* faire le petit fou *P.*
larva, *n,* larve, *f.*
laryngitis, *n,* laryngite, *f.* **larynx,** *n,* larynx, *m.*
lascivious†, *a,* lascif.
laser, *n,* laser, *m.* ~ *beam,* rayon laser, *m.*
lash, *n,* (*of whip*) lanière, *f;* (*cut with a whip*) coup de fouet; (*eye*) cil, *m.* ¶ *v.t,* (*horse*) cingler; (*pers.*) fouetter; (*Naut.*) amarrer. ¶ *v.i,* (*rain*) cingler, fouetter. ~ *out,* (*horse*) ruer; (*pers. with hand, foot*) lancer un coup de poing, de pied; (*words*) invectiver; (*money*) les lâcher *P.*
lass[ie], *n,* [jeune] fille, *f.*
lassitude, *n,* lassitude, *f.*
lasso, *n,* lasso, *m.* ¶ *v.t,* prendre au lasso.
last[1], *a,* dernier. ~ *but one,* avant-dernier. *at the* ~ *minute,* à la dernière minute. ~ *night,* cette nuit, hier [au] soir. *in the* ~ *resort,* en dernier ressort. ~ *straw,* comble, *m.* ~ *week,* la semaine dernière *ou* passée. *the* ~ *word,* le dernier mot. *the* ~ *word in,* le dernier cri en. ¶ *ad,* (*time*) la dernière fois. *arrive* ~, arriver le (la) dernier (ère), en dernier. ¶ *n,* dernier, ère. *the* ~ *but one,* l'avant dernier, ère *ou* le (la) pénultième. *at* ~, enfin, à la fin. ~**ly,** *ad,* en dernier lieu, enfin.
last[2], *n,* (*shoe*) forme, *f.*
last[3], *v.i,* (*continue*) durer; (*hold out*) tenir. ~ *out,* (*pers.*) tenir [le coup]; (*money*) suffire. ~**ing,** *a,* durable.
latch, *n,* loquet, *m. the door is on the* ~, la porte n'est pas fermée à clef. ~ *key,* clef de maison, *f.* ¶ *v.t,* fermer au loquet. ~ *on to,* s'accrocher à; (*understand*) piger *P,* saisir.
late, *a,* en retard. *to be* ~ être en retard, avoir du retard. *to be* ~ *with payments,* avoir des arrières. (*edition, quartets*) dernier. *keep* ~ *hours,* se coucher tard. *in the* ~ *afternoon,* vers la fin de l'après-midi. *at a* ~*r date,* à une date ultérieure. *at the* ~*st,* au plus tard. (*former*) ancien, ex-: *the* ~*minister,* l'ancien ministre, l'ex-ministre. (*recent*) récent, de ces derniers temps. *the* ~*st,* (*news &c*) dernier. *of* ~, récemment, dernièrement, ces derniers temps. (*dead*) feu. *his* ~ *mother,* feu sa mère. défunt (*before n.*); (*of fruit*) tardif. ~*comer,* retardataire, *m, f.* ¶ *ad,* en retard; tard. ~*r on,* plus tard. *see you* ~*r!* à tout à l'heure! ~**ly,** *ad,* dernièrement, récemment. ~**ness,** *n,* retard, *m. the* ~*ness of the hour,* l'heure tardive *ou* avancée.
latent, *a,* latent; caché.
lateral†, *a,* latéral.
latex, *n,* latex, *m.*
lath, *n,* latte; (*blind*) lame, *f.*
lathe, *n,* tour, *m.*
lather, *n,* (*soap*) mousse; (*horse*) écume, *f.* ¶ *v.i,* mousser. ¶ *v.t,* savonner; (*thrash*) rosser *P.*
Latin, *a. & n,* latin, *m.*
latitude, *n,* latitude, *f.*
latrine, *n,* latrines, *f.pl.*

latter (the), ce dernier, cette dernière; celui-ci, celle-ci, ceux-ci, celles-ci. *the ~ half,* la deuxième moitié. **~ly,** *ad,* dernièrement.
lattice, *n,* treillis; (*fence*) treillage, *m.* ¶ *v.t,* treilliser.
Latvia, *n,* la Lettonie. **Latvian,** *a,* letton. ¶ *n,* Letton, one.
laud, *v.t,* louer. ~ [*to the skies*], louanger. **~able,** *a,* louable. **laudatory,** *a,* élogieux.
laugh, *n,* rire; (*brief*) éclat de rire, *m. what a ~!* quelle rigolade! *P.* ¶ *v.i,* rire, rigoler *P,* se marrer *P.* ~ *at,* rire de, se moquer de. ~ *like a drain P,* rire comme un fou, se gondoler *P. to burst out ~ing,* éclater de rire. *to split one's sides ~ing,* se tordre de rire. *it's no ~ing matter,* il n'y a pas de quoi rire. *to make o.s a ~ing stock,* se couvrir de ridicule. **~able†,** *a,* risible; dérisoire. **laughter,** *n,* rire[s], *m.* [*pl.*].
launch, *n,* (*patrol &c*) vedette, *f,* canot, *m;* (*carried by ship*) chaloupe, *f.* ¶ *v.t,* lancer; (*lifeboat*) faire sortir; (*ship's boat*) mettre à la mer. **~[ing],** *n,* lancement, *m.*
launder, *v.t,* blanchir. **launderette,** *n,* laverie automatique, *f.* **laundry,** *n,* blanchisserie, *f.*
laureate, *a. & n,* lauréat, e.
laurel, *n,* laurier, *m;* (*pl, fig.*) lauriers, *m.pl.*
lava, *n,* lave, *f.*
lavatory, *n,* toilettes, *f.pl,* W.-C., cabinets, *m.pl.* ~ *pan,* cuvette des W-C. *ou* cabinets, *f.* ~ *paper,* papier hygiénique, *m.* ~ *seat,* siège des W-C., *m.*
lavender, *n,* lavande, *f.*
lavish, *a,* prodigue. ¶ *v.t,* prodiguer (*sth on s.o,* qch à qn). **~ly,** *ad,* à profusion. **~ness,** *n,* prodigalité; extravagance, *f.*
law, *n,* loi, *f;* (*profession, study &c*) droit, *m;* (*in operation*) justice; (*sport*) règle, *f. take the ~ into one's own hands,* se faire justice soi-même. *~-abiding,* respectueux des lois. ~ *& order,* ordre public, *m.* ~ *courts,* cours de justice, *f.pl.,* tribunaux, *m.pl;* Palais de Justice, *m.* ~ *Faculty,* (*Univ.*) faculté de droit, *f. ~suit,* procès, *m. to go to ~,* recourir à la justice. **~ful†,** *a,* (*action*) légal, licite; (*marriage, child*) légitime; (*contract*) valide. **~less,** *a,* sans loi; déreglé. **~lessness,** *n,* anarchie, *f.*
lawn[1], *n,* pelouse, *f,* gazon, *m.* ~ *mower,* tondeuse [à gazon], *f.* ~ *tennis,* tennis, *m.*
lawn[2], *n,* (*Cloth*) batiste, *f;* (*fine*) linon, *m.*
lawyer, *n,* homme de loi; juriste; (*solicitor*) avoué; (*conveyancing*) notaire; (*barrister*) avocat, *m.*
lax, *a,* relâche. **~ative,** *a. & n,* laxatif, *m.* **~ity,** *n,* relâchement, *m.*
lay[1], *a,* laïque. ~ *brother,* frère lai *ou* convers. *~man,* (*Rel.*) laïc; (*fig.*) profane, *m.* ~ *reader,* prédicateur laïque.
lay[2], *n,* (*of land*) configuration, *f. she's an easy ~P,* elle couche avec n'importe qui *P. ~-about P,* fainéant, e. *~-by,* aire de stationnement, *f. ~out,* plan, *m,* disposition, *f.* ¶ *v.t,* mettre, poser; (*fire*) préparer; (*eggs*) pondre; (*trap*) tendre, dresser (*for,* a); (*P woman*) baiser, *P**. ~ *a bet* (*on sth*), parier (sur qch). ~ *the table,* mettre le couvert. ~ *bare,* mettre à nu, dévoiler. ~ **down,** [dé]poser; (*cards*) étaler; (*wine*) mettre en cave. ~ **in,** (*stock*) amasser, s'approvisionner de. ~ **into,** (*by word or blow*) prendre à partie. ~ **off,** (*Ind.*) licencier. ~ **on,** (*gas &c*) installer; (*provide*) fournir; (*paint*) étaler. ~ **out,** (*plan &c*) dessiner, faire le plan de. ~ **up,** amasser; (*car*) remiser; (*ship*) désarmer.
lay[3], *n,* (*Mus., Poet.*) lai, *m.*
layer, *n,* couche, *f,* lit, *m;* (*Hort.*) marcotte, *f;* (*of pipes &c*) poseur, *m.* ¶ *v.t,* (*hair*) couper en dégradé; (*Hort.*) marcotter.
lay figure, *n,* mannequin, *m.*
laying, *n,* mise; pose; (*eggs*) ponte, *f.*
laze, *v.i,* paresser, traînasser. **lazily,** *ad,* paresseusement; indolemment. **laziness,** *n,* paresse, *f.* **lazy,** *a,* paresseux. *~bones,* fainéant, e.
lea (*Poet.*) *n,* pré, *m.*
leach, *v.i,* (*liquid*) filtrer.
lead (lɛd) *n,* plomb, *m;* (*for pencils*) mine [de plomb]; (*Typ.*) interligne, *f;* (*Naut.*) plomb [de sonde], *m,* sonde, *f.* ~ *poisoning,* saturnisme, *m.* ~ *works,* fonderie de plomb, *f.* **~en,** *a,* de plomb.
lead (li:d) *n,* (*Sport*) tête; (*distance ahead*) avance, *f;* initiative, *f;* exemple, *m;* (*clue*) piste, *f;* (*Theat.*) rôle principal; (*leash*) laisse, *f;* (*Elec.*) fil, *m.* ¶ *v.t. & i.ir,* mener, conduire (*to,* à). ~ *s.o in, out, across,* faire entrer, sortir, traverser qn. (*induce*) amener, porter (à faire); (*be ahead, ~er of*) être en tête de; (*cards*) jouer; (*fig.*) aboutir (*to,* à); (*life*) mener. ~ *a dog's life,* mener une vie de chien. ~ *s.o astray,* détourner qn du droit chemin. ~ *back,* ramener, reconduire. ~ *up to* (*fig.*), amener à.
leader, *n,* chef, *m;* (*strike &c*) meneur, euse; (*political*) dirigeant, e, leader, chef [de file], *m;* (*orchestra*) premier violon; (*Sport*) coureur, cheval de tête, *m;* (*Press & ~ing article*) éditorial, *m.* **~ship,** *n,* direction, tête, *f.* **leading,** *a,* principal; premier; marquant. ~ *lady, man,* (*Cine.*) vedette féminine, masculine, (*Theat.*) premier rôle, rôle principal. ~ *rein,* (*horse*) longe, *f;* (*baby*) guides, *m.pl.* ~ *question,* question tendancieuse, *f.*
leaf, *n,* (*Bot.*) feuille, *f;* (*book*) feuillet, *m,* page, *f;* (*table*) rallonge, *f,* (*on hinges*) rabat, *m.* (*fig.*) *shake like a ~,* trembler comme une feuille. *take a ~ out of s.o's book,* prendre exemple sur qn. *turn over a new ~,* changer de conduite. ~ *bud,* bourgeon à feuilles, *m.* ~ *mould,* terreau [de feuilles], *m.* ¶ *v.t,* ~

through, feuilleter. ~**let,** *n,* prospectus; (*instruction*) mode d'emploi, *m.* ~**y,** *a,* feuillu.
league, *n,* ligue; (*of Nations*) société; (*Meas.*) lieue, *f;* (*Sport*) championnat, *m.*
leak & ~ **age,** *n,* fuite, voie d'eau, *f.* ¶ *v.i,* fuir; (*ship*) faire eau; (*shoes*) prendre l'eau.'¶ *v.t,* (*liquid*) répandre; (*fig.*) (*information*) divulguer. ~**y,** *a,* qui fuit; qui fait eau; qui prend l'eau.
lean[1], *a,* maigre. ¶ *n,* (*meat*) maigre, *m.* ~**ness,** *n,* maigreur, *f.*
lean[2], *v.t.ir,* appuyer (*up against,* contre); adosser (à). ¶ *v.i.ir,* (*rest*) s'appuyer, s'adosser; (*slope*) pencher; (*put pressure*) faire pression (*on,* sur). ~ *back, out,* se pencher en arrière, au dehors. ~ *on one's elbow,* s'accouder. ~**ing,** (*fig.*) *n,* tendance, *f,* penchant, *m* (*towards,* pour). ~ *tower* (*Pisa*), tour penchée, *f.* ~**-to,** *n,* appentis, *m.*
leap, *n,* saut, bond, *m.* (*fig.*) *by* ~*s & bounds,* à pas de géant. ~ *in the dark,* saut dans l'inconnu. ¶ *v.t. & i.ir,* sauter, bondir; (*flames*) jaillir. ~*-frog,* saute-mouton, *m.* ~ *year,* année bissextile, *f.*
learn, *v.t. & i.ir,* apprendre. ~**ed,** *a,* savant, érudit; (*profession*) libéral. ~**edly,** *ad,* savamment, avec érudition. ~**er,** *n,* débutant, e. ~**ing,** *n,* savoir, *m,* science, érudition, *f.*
lease, *n,* bail, *m. give s.o a new* ~ *of life,* (*fig.*) donner à qn un regain de vie. ¶ *v.t,* (*grant & take*) louer à bail. ~*hold property,* propriété louée à bail. ~ *holder,* locataire, *m,f.*
leash, *n,* laisse, *f. keep on a* ~, tenir en laisse.
least (the), *a,* le moindre; le plus petit. ¶ *ad. & n,* le moins. *at* ~, au moins; du moins. *not in the* ~, pas le moins du monde.
leather, *n,* cuir, *m,* peau, *f.* ~ *goods,* maroquinerie, *f.* ~ *jacket,* larve de la tipule, *f.* ~**ette,** *n,* similicuir, *m.* ~**y,** *a,* coriace.
leave, *n,* (*consent, Mil.*) permission, *f;* (*holiday*) congé, *m. on* ~, en permission, en congé. *take* ~ *of s.o,* prendre congé de qn. ¶ *v.t.ir,* laisser; (*place*) quitter; partir de; sortir de; (*pers.*) quitter. *his wife has left him,* sa femme l'a quitté. (*in will*) léguer. ¶ *v.i.ir,* partir, s'en aller. ~ *off,* (s')arrêter, cesser (*doing,* de faire). ~ *off!* arrête! ~ *out,* omettre.
leaven, *n,* levain. ¶ *v.t,* faire lever; (*fig.*) assaisonner.
leavings, *n.pl,* restes, *m.pl.*
lecher, *n,* débauché, *m.* ~**ous,** *a,* lubrique, luxurieux; (*look*) lascif. ~**y,** *n,* luxure, lubricité, *f.*
lectern, *n,* lutrin, *m.*
lecture, *n,* (*single*) conférence, *f;* (*in series*) cours (*on,* de), *m;* (*scolding*) sermon, *m.* ~ *course,* cours. ~ *hall,* salle de conférences, *f,* amphithéâtre, *m.* ~ *notes,* notes de cours, *f.pl.* ¶ *v.t,* réprimander, sermonner. ¶ *v.i,* faire *ou* donner une conférence, un cours.
lecturer, *n,* conférencier, ère, maître de conférences, *m.*
ledge, *n,* (*wall*) rebord, *m,* saillie, *f;* (*window*) rebord [de la fenêtre]; (*mountain*) corniche, *f.*
ledger, *n,* grand livre, *m.*
lee [side], *n,* côté sous le vent, *m.*
leech, *n,* sangsue, *f.*
leek, *n,* poireau, *m.*
leer, *n,* regard polisson, *m. to* ~ *at,* lorgner.
leeward, *a,* sous le vent. *L~ Islands,* îles sous le Vent, *f.pl.* **leeway,** *n,* dérive, *f.*
left, *a. & n,* gauche, *f. the* ~ (*Box.*), le [poing] gauche. ¶ *ad,* à gauche. ~*-hand,* (*page*) de gauche. ~*-hand drive,* conduite à g., *f.* ~*-handed, a.* & ~*-hander, n,* gaucher, ère.
left (to be), rester. *left luggage office,* consigne [des bagages], *f. left-overs,* restes, *n.pl.*
leg, *n,* (*pers., horse*) jambe; (*animals*) patte; (*fowl*) cuisse, *f;* (*mutton*) gigot; (*table &c*) pied, *m;* (*stage*) étape, *f.* ~ *of beef,* gîte, *m. on one* ~, sur un pied. (*fig.*) *he hasn't got a* ~ *to stand on,* il ne peut s'appuyer sur rien.
legacy, *n,* legs, *m.*
legal†, *a,* légal; légitime; (*in law*) judiciaire. ~ *aid,* assistance judiciaire, *f.* ~ *costs,* frais de justice, *m.pl.* ~ *tender,* monnaie légale, *f.* ~**ize,** *v.t,* légaliser.
legate, *n,* légat, *m.* **legatee,** *n,* légataire, *m,f.* **legation,** *n,* légation, *f.*
legend, *n,* légende, *f.* ~**ary,** *a,* légendaire.
legerdemain, *n,* prestidigitation, *f.*
leggings, *n.pl,* jambières, *f.pl;* (*for baby*) culotte [longue], *f.*
legible†, *a,* lisible.
legion, *n,* (*lit., fig.*) légion, *f.*
legislate, *v.i,* faire les lois. **legislation,** *n,* législation, *f.* **legislative,** *a,* législatif. **legislator,** *n,* législateur, *m.* **legislature,** *n,* législature, *f.*
legitimacy, *n,* légitimité, *f.* **legitimate†,** *a,* légitime. **legitim[at]ize,** *v.t,* légitimer.
leguminous, *a,* légumineux.
leisure, *n,* loisir, temps libre, *m. at* ~, à loisir, à tête reposée. *to be a lady of* ~, (*fig.*) faire la rentière. ~**ly,** *a,* (*pace*) lent, mesuré. ¶ *ad,* sans se presser.
lemon, *n,* citron, *m.* ~ *juice,* jus de citron; (*drink*) citron-pressé, *m.* ~ *squash,* sirop de citron, *m.* ~ *squeezer,* presse-citron, *m.* ~ *tree,* citronnier, *m.* ~**ade,** *n,* citronnade, *f.*
lemon sole, *n,* sole limande, *f.*
lend, *v.t.ir,* prêter. ~**er,** *n,* prêteur, euse. ~**ing,** *n,* prêt, *m.* ~ *library,* bibliothèque de prêt, *f.*
length, *n,* (*space*) longueur; (*time*) durée; (*of service*) ancienneté, *f;* (*section*) morceau, bout; (*material*) métrage [de tissu], *m;* (*skirt &c*) hauteur, *f. at* ~, enfin, à la fin; (*speak*) longuement. *fall one's* ~, tomber de tout son long. *to go to great* ~*s,* faire tout son possible. (*Sport*) *win by a* ~, gagner d'une

longueur. **~en,** *v.t.* (*& i*) (*object*) (s')allonger, (se) rallonger; (*visit, life*) (se) prolonger. **~ways, ~wise,** *ad,* en long. **~y,** *a,* long.
lenience, *n,* (*gen.*) indulgence; (*Pol.*) clémence, *f.* **lenient,** *a,* indulgent, clément (*to,* envers). **~ly,** *ad,* avec indulgence, clémence.
lens, *n,* lentille, *f;* (*camera*) objectif; (*spectacles*) verre, *m. contact ~,* verre de contact.
lent, *n,* carême, *m.* **~en,** *a,* de carême.
lentil, *n,* lentille, *f.*
leopard, *n,* léopard, *m.* **~ess,** *n,* l. femelle, *m.*
leotard, *n,* collant, *m.*
leper, *n,* lépreux, euse. *~ hospital,* léproserie, *f.* **leprosy,** *n,* lèpre, *f.* **leprous,** *a,* lépreux.
lesbian, *n,* lesbienne, *f.* ¶ *a,* lesbien. **~ism,** *n,* lesbianisme, *m.*
lesion, *n,* lésion, *f.*
less, *a. & pn,* moins (de). *I have ~ than you,* j'en ai moins que vous. *~ & ~,* de moins en moins. *even ~,* encore moins. ¶ *suffix,* sans. ¶ *ad,* moins. *~ often,* moins souvent. ¶ *pr,* moins. *~ 10%,* moins 10%.
lessee, *n,* preneur, euse [à bail].
lessen, *v.t. & i,* diminuer; (*Pol. tension*) (se) relâcher. **~ing,** *n,* diminution, *f.* (*Pol.*) *~ of tension,* détente, *f.*
lesser, *a,* moindre. *to a ~ degree,* à un moindre degré. *the ~ of two evils,* le moindre de deux maux.
lesson, *n,* leçon, classe, *f,* cours, *m. let that be a ~ to you!* que cela vous serve de leçon!
lessor, *n,* bailleur, eresse.
lest, *c,* de peur *ou* de crainte de (+*inf*); de peur *ou* de crainte que [ne] (+*subj*).
let[1], *v.t,* laisser; (*allow*) permettre (à qn de faire); (*cause*) faire; (*house*) louer. *~'s go,* allons-y. *just ~ him try!* qu'il essaie un peu! *~* **down,** (*lower*) baisser; (*hem*) descendre; (*tyre*) dégonfler; (*fail*) décevoir. *~* **off,** (*release*) dégager, lâcher; (*gun*) tirer. *to ~ off steam P* (*fig.*), se défouler. *~* **out,** laisser sortir; (*release*) relâcher; (*fire*) laisser s'éteindre; (*secret, cry &c*) laisser échapper; (*clothes*) élargir. *~* **up,** *v.i,* (*rain*) diminuer; (*cold weather*) s'adoucir.
let[2], *n,* (*Ten.*) balle let, *f.* (*Law*) *without ~ or hindrance,* librement.
lethal, *n,* fatal, mortel; (*weapon*) meurtrier.
lethargic, *a,* léthargique. **lethargy,** *n,* léthargie, *f.*
letter, *n,* lettre, *f. ~ bomb,* lettre piégée. *~ box,* boîte à *ou* aux lettres, *f. ~head,* entête, *m. ~ writer,* correspondant, e. ¶ *v.t, ~ sth,* marquer, inscrire des lettres sur qch; (*engrave*) graver. **~ed,** *a,* lettré. **~ing,** *n,* gravure, *f;* caractère, *m.*
letting, *n,* location, *f.*
lettuce, *n,* salade, laitue, *f;* (*Bot.*) laitue.
leukaemia, *n,* leucémie, *f.*
level, *n,* niveau; (*Pol. &c*) échelon, *m. at departmental ~,* à l'échelon départmental. *top ~ talks,* conférence au sommet, *f.* (*Rly, road*) palier, *m.* ¶ *a,* (*flat*) uni, plat; (*equal*) à égalité; (*voice*) calme; (*judgement*) sain. *do one's ~ best,* faire tout son possible. *~ crossing,* passage à niveau, *m. ~-headed,* équilibré. ¶ *v.t,* (*ground*) niveler, égaliser, aplanir; (*quantity*) répartir également; (*gun*) braquer (*at,* sur); (*accusation*) lancer (*at,* contre). ¶ *v.i, ~ off,* se stabiliser. **levelling,** *n,* nivellement, *m.*
lever, *n,* levier, *m. ~* **[up]** *v.t,* soulever au moyen d'un levier. **~age,** *n,* force de levier, *f;* (*fig.*) influence, prise (sur), *f.*
leveret, *n,* levraut, *m.*
levity, *n,* légèreté, *f;* manque de sérieux, *m.*
levy, *n,* (*act, amount*) taxation; (*tax*) taxe, *f,* impôt, *m.* ¶ *v.t,* prélever; imposer.
lewd, *a,* obscène, lubrique. **~ness,** obscenité, lubricité, *f.*
lexical, *a,* lexical. **lexicographer,** *n,* lexicographe, *m.* **lexicon,** *n,* lexique, *m.*
liability, *n,* responsabilité (*for,* de), *f;* (*handicap*) handicap; (*person*) poids mort. *m;* (*pl, Fin.*) engagements, *m.pl,* passif, *m.* **liable,** *a,* (*subject*) sujet; passible; (*law*) civilement responsable (*for,* de). (*likely*) *to be ~ to do,* risquer de faire.
liaison, *n,* liaison, *f. ~ officer,* officier de l., *m.*
liar, *n,* menteur, euse.
libel, *n,* diffamation, *f. ~ action,* action en diffamation, *f.* ¶ *v.t,* (*Law*) diffamer; (*gen.*) calomnier, médire de. **libellous,** *a,* diffamatoire.
liberal†, *a,* libéral. ¶ *n,* libéral, *m.* **~ism,** *n,* libéralisme, *m.* **~ity,** *n,* libéralité, *f.*
liberate, *v.t,* libérer. **liberation,** *n,* libération, *f.* **liberator,** *n,* liberateur, trice.
libertine, *a. & n,* libertin, e.
liberty, *n,* liberté, *f. at ~,* libre. *to take the ~ to do,* se permettre de faire.
libido, *n,* libido, *f.*
librarian, *n,* bibliothécaire, *m,f.* **library,** *n,* bibliothèque, *f.*
librettist, *n,* librettiste, *m,f.* **libretto,** *n,* livret, *m.*
licence, *n,* (*permit*) autorisation, *f,* permis, *m;* (*Com.*) licence, *f;* (*car*) vignette; (*TV*) redevance, *f. driving ~,* permis de conduire. *pilot's ~,* brevet de pilote, *m.* (*freedom*) liberté, *f.* **license,** *v.t,* (*allow*) autoriser; donner une licence à; (*car*) acheter une vignette de, pour. *~d,* (*hotel*) ayant une licence de débit de boissons. **licensee,** *n,* (*pub*) patron, ne. **licentiate,** *n,* diplômé, e. **licentious†,** *a,* licencieux.
lichen. *n,* lichen, *m.*
lick, *n,* coup de langue, *m. ~ & a promise,* petit brin de toilette. *~ of paint,* petit coup de peinture. ¶ *v.t,* lécher. *~ one's lips,* se lécher les lèvres; (*fig.*) se frotter les mains. (*defeat*)

battre; (*thrash*) rosser. ~ *up,* (*cat*) laper.
lid, *n,* couvercle, *m;* (*eye*~) paupière, *f.*
lie[1], *n,* mensonge, *m. give the* ~ *to,* démentir. ¶ *v.i,* mentir.
lie[2], *n,* (*of ground*) configuration; (*Golf &c*) position, *f;* (*Naut.*) gisement, *m.* ¶ *v.i.ir,* (~ *down*) s'allonger, s'étendre, se coucher; (*dead body*) reposer; (*in grave*) être enterré; (*object*) être; (*place*) se trouver; (*remain*) rester. ~ *still,* rester tranquille. (*on tombstone*) *here* ~*s...,* ci-gît... *to* ~ *dead,* être étendu mort. *see how the land* ~*s,* tâter le terrain. ~ *about,* (*object*) traîner; (*pers.*) traînasser. ~ *back,* se renverser [en arrière]. ~ *in,* faire la grasse matinée. ~ *low,* ~ *up,* se cacher. ~ *in wait,* se tenir à l'affût (*for,* de).
lien, *n,* (*Law*) droit de rétention, *m.*
lieu of (in), au lieu de.
lieutenant, *n,* lieutenant; (*naval*) l. de vaisseau, *m.* ~ *colonel,* lieutenant-colonel, *m.* ~ *commander,* capitaine de corvette, *m.* ~ *general,* général de corps d'armée, *m.*
life, *n,* vie; (*car, Govt. &c*) durée, *f. animal & plant* ~, vie animale & végétale. *a matter of* ~ *& death,* une question de vie & de mort. *have the time of one's* ~, s'amuser follement. *for* ~, (*prison*) à vie, à perpétuité. (*Art*) *from* ~, d'après nature. *how's* ~? *P,* comment ça va? *P. not on your* ~! *P,* jamais de la vie! ~ *& soul of the party,* boute-en-train, *m. take one's* ~ *in one's hands,* jouer sa vie. ~ *& death struggle,* combat à mort, *m.* ~ *annuity,* rente viagère. ~ *assurance,* assurance-vie, *f.* ~ *belt,* bouée de sauvetage, *f.* ~*blood,* élément vital. ~*boat,* canot de sauvetage, *m.* ~*guard,* ~*saver,* surveillant, e de baignade. ~*-saving,* sauvetage; (*first aid*) secourisme, *m.* ~*-size,* grandeur nature *inv.* ~ *span,* durée *ou* espérance de vie, *f.* ~*time,* vie. *during my* ~*time,* de mon vivant. ~**less,** *a,* sans vie; inanimé. ~**like,** *a,* vivant. ~**long,** *a,* de toute la vie.
lift, *n,* ascenseur; (*goods*) monte-charge, *m;* (*Aero.*) portance, *f. can I give you a* ~? est-ce que je peux vous déposer quelque part? *thumb a* ~ *P,* faire du stop *P.* (*fig.*) *it gave me a* ~, cela m'a remonté le moral. ¶ *v.t,* lever, soulever; (*Agr: potatoes*) arracher; (*restrictions*) supprimer; (*P steal*) chiper *P;* (*idea &c*) voler (*from,* à). ~ *down,* descendre. ~ *off,* (*lid*) enlever. ~ *up,* (se) soulever. ~ *up one's head,* lever *ou* redresser la tête.
ligament, *n,* ligament, *m.* **ligature,** *n,* ligature, *f.*
light[1], *a.* léger; (*rain*) fin. *as* ~ *as a feather,* léger comme une plume. *to make* ~ *of,* prendre à la légère. *to make* ~ *work of,* faire sans difficulté. ~*-fingered,* chapardeur. ~*-headed,* étourdi. ~*-hearted,* gai. ~*weight,* (*Box.*) poids léger, *m.* ~**en,** *v.t,* alléger. ~**ly,** *ad.* légèrement. ~**ness,** *n.* légèreté, *f.*
light[2], *n.* (*gen.*) lumière, *f;* (*electric, lamp*) éclairage, *m,* lumière; (*day*~) jour, *m;* (*Mot.*) (*gen.*) feu; (*headlamp*) phare, *m;* (*cycle, traffic*) feu. *against the* ~, à contre-jour. *at first* ~, au point du jour. *to be in s.o's* ~, faire l'ombre à qn. *put on the* ~, allumer. *put out the* ~, éteindre. *the* ~*s are red,* le feu est [au] rouge. *have you a* ~? avez-vous du feu? *throw* ~ *on sth,* éclaircir qch. ¶ *a,* clair; (*hair*) blonde. ~ *brown,* châtain clair. *it's* ~, il fait jour. ~ *bulb,* ampoule, lampe, *f.* ~*house,* phare, *m.* ~ *meter,* (*Phot.*) photomètre, *m.* ~ *wave,* onde lumineuse. ¶ *v.i,* allumer; (*match*) frotter; (*room*) éclairer. ¶ *v.i,* (*match*) s'allumer; (*coal &c*) prendre feu. ~ *up,* (*eyes &c*) s'éclairer. ~**en,** *v.t,* (*darkness*) éclairer; (*hair*) éclaircir. ~**ing,** *n,* ~*-up time,* heure de l'éclairage des véhicules, *f.*
lighter, *n,* (*cigarette* ~) briquet, *m.* ~ *fuel,* gaz à briquet, *m.* (*Naut.*) péniche, allège, *f.*
lightning, *n,* éclair, *m. oft. pl,* foudre, *f.* ~ *conductor,* paratonnerre, *m.* ~ *strike,* grève surprise, *f.*
lights (*animal lungs*) *n.pl,* mou, *m.*
like[1], *a,* semblable, pareil, du même genre, tel. ~ *father* ~ *son,* tel père tel fils. *to be as* ~ *as two peas,* se ressembler comme deux gouttes d'eau. *rather* ~, un peu dans le genre de. *very much* ~, tout à fait dans le genre de. ~*-minded,* de même opinion. ¶ *pr,* comme, en. *act* ~ *a fool,* se conduire comme un imbécile, en imbécile. *sth* ~ *that,* qch comme ça *P. that's more* ~ *it!* voilà qui est mieux! *there's nothing* ~, il n'y a rien de tel que. *what's he* ~? comment est-il? (*such as*) comme, tel que, par exemple. ¶ *ad, as* ~ *as not,* probablement. ¶ *n,* semblable, *m,f,* pareil, le. *his* ~, son pareil. *the* ~*s of me,* les gens comme moi. ~**en,** *v.t,* comparer (à). ~**ness,** *n,* ressemblance (*to,* avec; *between,* entre); forme, *f. in the* ~ *of,* sous la forme de. *a family* ~, un air de famille marqué. ~**wise,** *ad,* (*similarly*) de même; (*also*) aussi; (*moreover*) de plus.
like[2], *v.t,* aimer [bien]. *I* ~ *him,* je l'aime bien. (*less familiar*) il me plaît. (*want*) aimer, vouloir (*to do,* faire, *s.o to do,* que qn fasse). *if you* ~, si vous voulez. ¶ *n,* ~*s,* goûts, *m.pl,* préférences, *f.pl.* ~**able,** *a,* sympathique, agréable. ~**ing,** *n,* (*for pers.*) sympathie, *f;* (*for thing*) goût, *m. to take a* ~ *to s.o,* se prendre d'amitié pour qn.
likelihood, *n,* probabilité; chance, *f. there is little* ~ *of that,* cela ne risque pas d'arriver.
likely, *a,* probable; (*explanation*) plausible, vraisemblable. *a* ~ *story!* elle est bien bonne! *it is not* ~ *that,* il est peu probable que + *subj.* ¶ *ad,* probablement. *as* ~ *as not,* pour autant que je sache. *most* ~, très probablement. *not* ~! pas de danger! *P.*
lily, *n,* lis, *m.* ~ *of the valley,* muguet, *m.*

limb, *n,* membre, *m;* (*tree*) grosse branche. *tear ~ from ~,* démembrer, mettre en pièces. (*fig.*) *out on a ~,* isolé; (*vulnerable*) dans une situation délicate. **-limbed,** *a, long-, strong-~,* aux membres longs, forts.
limber, *a,* souple. *~ up, v.i,* (*Sport*) se dégourdir; (*fig.*) se préparer.
limbo[1], *n,* (*Rel.*) limbes, *m.pl;* (*fig.*) oubli, *m. to be in ~,* être tombé dans l'oubli.
limbo[2], *n, ~ dancer,* danseur, euse de limbo.
lime[1], *n,* chaux, *f. ~ kiln,* four à chaux, *m. ~ stone,* pierre à chaux, *f. to be in the ~light,* (*Theat.*) être sous les feux de la rampe; (*fig.*) en vedette. ¶ *v.t,* (*Agr.*) chauler; (*twig*) engluer.
lime[2], *n,* citron vert, *m.*
lime[3], *n,* (*tree*) tilleul, *m.*
limit, *n,* limite; limitation; (*fig.*) borne, *f. speed ~,* limitation de vitesse, *f. that's the ~!* c'est le comble! *there are ~s,* il y a une limite à tout. *within ~s,* dans une certaine limite, mesure. *without ~,* sans limitation, limite. ¶ *v.t,* limiter, borner, restreindre (à). *to ~ o.s to (doing) sth,* se borner à (faire) qch. *~***ation,** *n,* limitation, *f.* **limited,** *a,* limité; (*intelligence*) borné; restreint; (*edition*) à tirage restreint. (*Com.*) *X L~ (Ltd), X Public L~ Company (PLC),* X Société anonyme (S.A.). *~ [liability] company,* société à responsabilité limitée, *f.*
limousine, *n,* limousine, *f.*
limp[1], *a,* mou; (*flesh*) flasque; (*clothing*) avachi; (*binding*) souple. *~***ness,** *n,* mollesse, *f.*
limp[2], *n,* claudication, *f,* boitement, *m. to have a ~,* boiter. ¶ *v.i,* boiter, clocher.
limpet, *n,* patelle, *f.*
limpid, *a,* limpide. *~***ity,** *n,* limpidité, *f.*
linchpin, *n,* esse, *f;* (*fig.*) pivot, *m.*
line[1], *n,* (*gen.*) ligne; (*wrinkle*) ride; (*boundary*) frontière, *f;* (*pen mark*) trait, *m;* (*rope, washing &c*) corde, *f;* (*Com.*) article(s) *m.(pl.);* (*row: gen.*) rangée, (*traffic*) file; (*hills*) chaîne, *f;* (*descent*) ligne, lignée, *f;* (*Poet.*) vers, *m;* (*Rly*) voie, *f,* ligne; (*Ship.*) compagnie, *f;* (*route*) ligne; (*Tel.*) ligne; (*work*) genre d'affaires, métier, *m. that's not my ~,* ce n'est pas mon rayon. *~ of argument,* raisonnement, *m. ~ of fire,* ligne de tir. *to be on the right ~s,* être sur la bonne voie. *I draw the ~ at that,* je ne vais pas jusqu'à ce point-là. *to drop s.o a ~,* envoyer un [petit] mot à qn. *fall into ~,* se conformer (*with,* à). *hard ~s!* c'est dur! (*Am*) *to stand in ~,* faire la queue. *~ up, v.i,* s'aligner, faire la queue; *v.t,* aligner. *~***age,** *n,* lignée *f;* lignage, *m. ~***al,** *a,* en ligne directe. *~***ar,** *a,* linéaire, *inv. ~***d,** *a,* (*paper*) réglé; (*face*) ridé.
line[2], *v.t,* (*clothes*) doubler; (*nest, brakes*) garnir; (*streets: people*) faire la haie, (*trees*) border. *to ~ one's pockets,* s'emplir les poches.
linen, *n,* [toile de] lin, [*f.*]*m;* (*col.*) linge, *m. ~ sheets,* draps de fil. (*fig.*) *wash one's dirty ~ in public,* laver son linge sale en public. *~ basket,* panier à linge, *m. ~ cupboard,* armoire à linge, *f.*
liner, *n,* paquebot, *m.*
linesman, *n,* (*Ten.*) juge de ligne; (*Foot.*) juge de touche, *m.*
ling, *n,* (*fish*) lingue, morue longue, *f;* (*Bot.*) bruyère, brande, *f.*
linger, *v.i,* s'attarder; (*smell &c*) persister; (*doubt*) subsister; traîner. *~***ing,** *a,* (*look*) long; (*death*) lent.
lingerie, *n,* lingerie, *f.*
lingo, *n,* jargon, baragouin, *m.* **lingual,** *a,* lingual. ¶ *n,* linguale, *f.* **linguist,** *n,* linguiste, *m. ~***ics,** *n,* linguistique, *f.*
liniment, *n,* liniment, *m.*
lining, *n,* doublure; garniture, *f;* (*Tech.*) revêtement, *m.*
link, *n,* chaînon, maillon, anneau; (*fig.*) lien, *m;* (*connection*) liaison, *f. ~s of friendship,* liens d'amitié. (*fig.*) *the weak ~,* le point faible. *~-up,* (*gen.*) lien, rapport, *m;* (*Radio, TV*) liaison. ¶ *v.t,* relier; (*fig.*) lier. ¶ *v.i, ~ up,* se rejoindre; (*Com.*) s'associer.
links, *n.pl,* [terrain de] golf, *m.*
linnet, *n,* linotte, *f.*
linoleum, *n., also* **lino,** *abb,* linoléum, *m.*
linotype, *n. & a,* linotype, *f.*
linseed, *n,* graine de lin, *f. ~ oil,* huile de lin, *f.*
lint, *n,* tissu ouaté, *m.*
lintel, *n,* linteau, *m.*
lion, ess, *n,* lion, ne. *~ cub, ~ whelp,* lionceau, *m. ~'s share,* part du lion, *f.*
lip, *n,* lèvre; (*animal & P*) babine, *f;* (*jug*) bec; (*cup*) rebord; (*P insolence*) culot *P, m.* insolence, *f. he never opened his ~s,* il n'a jamais desserré les dents. *~-read,* lire sur les lèvres. *~-reading,* lecture sur les lèvres. *~stick,* [baton de] rouge à lèvres, *m.*
liquefaction, *n,* liquéfaction, *f.* **liquefy,** *v.t,* liquéfier.
liqueur, *n,* liqueur [de dessert], *f. ~ brandy,* fine champagne, *f.*
liquid, *a,* liquide; (*Com., Fin.*) liquide, disponible; (*fig.*) (*eyes &c*) limpide. *~ ammonia,* ammoniaque, *f. ~ assets,* disponibilités, *f.pl. ~ paraffin* (*Phar.*), huile de paraffine, *f.* ¶ *n,* liquide, *m;* (*Gram.*) liquide, *f.*
liquidate, *v.t,* liquider. **liquidation,** *n,* liquidation, *f. to go into ~,* déposer son bilan. **liquidator,** *n,* liquidateur, *m.* **liquidize,** *v.t,* liquéfier; (*Cook.*) passer au mixer. **liquidizer,** *n,* mixer, *m.*
liquor, *n,* spiritueux, alcool; (*Cook.*) liquide, *m.*
liquorice, *n,* réglisse, *f.*
lisle, *n,* fil d'Écosse, *m.*
lisp, *v.i,* zézayer. ¶ *n.* zézaiement, *m.*
lissom[e], *a,* souple.

list[1], *n,* liste, *f.* ~ *price* (*Com.*), prix de catalogue, *m.* ¶ *v.t,* faire la liste de; (*write down*) inscrire; énumerer, cataloguer. ~*ed building,* monument classé.
list[2], *n,* inclinaison, *f.* ¶ *v.i,* (*Naut.*) donner de la bande, gîter.
listen, *v.i.* écouter. *to* ~ *for sth,* prêter l'oreille à qch. ~ *in,* (*Radio &c*) être à l'écoute, écouter. ~**er,** *n,* auditeur, *m. the* ~*s,* l'auditoire, *m.*
listless†, *a,* apathique; sans énergie; mou. ~**ness,** *n,* apathie; mollesse, *f;* manque d'énergie, *m.*
litany, *n,* litanies, *f.pl.*
literacy, *n,* degré d'alphabétisation. ~ *campaign,* campagne d'a, *f.*
literal†, *a,* littéral. ~ *sense,* (*passage*) sens littéral; (*word*) [sens] propre, *m.*
literary, *a,* littéraire. ~ *man,* homme de lettres, *m.* **literate,** *a,* qui sait lire & écrire; (*educated*) instruit. **literature,** *n,* littérature, *f;* (*brochures*) documentation, *f,* brochure(s), *f.*(*pl.*).
lithe, *a,* souple, agile.
lithograph & ~**y,** *n,* lithographie, *f.* ¶ *v.t,* lithographier. ~**er,** *n,* lithographe, *m.* ~**ic,** *a,* lithographique.
Lithuania, *n,* la Lit[h]uanie.
litigant, *n,* plaideur, euse. **litigation,** *n,* litige, *m.* **litigious,** *a,* litigieux.
litmus, *n,* tournesol, *m.*
litre, *n,* litre, *m.*
litter, *n,* détritus, *m.pl;* ordures, *f.pl;* (*papers*) vieux papiers, *m.pl;* (*untidiness*) désordre, fouillis, *m;* (*bedding*) litière; (*Zool.*) portée; (*stretcher*) civière, *f.* ~ *bin,* boîte à ordures, poubelle, *f.* ¶ *v.t,* mettre en désordre. ~*ed with,* jonché de, couvert de, encombré de.
little, *a,* petit. ~ *finger,* petit doigt, auriculaire, *m.* ~ *hand,* (*clock*) petite aiguille. ~ *one*(*s*), le(s), la petit(s), e(s). *poor* ~ *thing!* pauvre petit(e)! ~ *toe,* petit orteil. *L*~ *Red Riding Hood,* le Petit Chaperon Rouge. *a tiny* ~ *piece of bread,* un tout petit bout de pain. ¶ *a.* & *n,* (*amount*) peu [de], *m.* ~ *money,* peu d'argent. *a* ~ *money,* un peu d'argent. ~ *by* ~, petit à petit *ou* peu à peu. ~ *or nothing,* rien ou presque rien. *for a* ~ *while,* un petit moment. *he knows very* ~, il ne sait pas grand-chose. ¶ *ad,* peu; ne . . . . guère. ~**ness,** *n,* petitesse, *f.*
live, (liv) *v.i.* & *t,* vivre; (*reside*) vivre, habiter. ~ *in Paris,* habiter [à] Paris. *they* ~ *together,* (*as man & wife*) ils vivent ensemble. *as long as I* ~, tant que je vivrai. *long* ~ *the King!* vive le roi! *you* ~ & *learn,* on apprend à tout âge. *to* ~ *on bread,* se nourrir de pain. *to* ~ *off the land,* vivre des produits de la terre. ~ *a happy life,* mener une vie heureuse. ~ *a life of crime,* vivre dans le crime. *to* ~ *up to,* (*reputation*) se montrer digne de.
live, (laiv) *a,* vivant, en vie; (*Elec.*) chargé, sous tension; (*ammunition*) actif, amorcé; (*broadcast*) en direct; (*coal*) ardent. ~ *bait,* vif, *m. a real* ~ . . ., . . . en chair et en os. (*fig.*) *to be a real* ~ *wire,* avoir un dynamisme fou. ~ *rail,* rail conducteur, *m.* ~*stock,* bétail, *m.* ¶ *ad,* (*Radio, TV*) en direct.
liveliness, *n,* vivacité, animation, *f.* **lively,** *a,* (*pers.*) vif; (*account*) vivant; (*discussion &c*) animé. **liven,** *v.t,* ~ *up,* animer.
livelihood, *n,* gagne-pain, *m.*
liver (*Anat.*) *n,* foie, *m.*
livery, *n,* livrée, *f.* ~ *stables,* écuries de chevaux de louage, *f.pl.*
livid, *a,* livide; (*furious*) furieux, furibond.
living, *a,* vivant; en vie. ~ *being,* vivant, *m. within* ~ *memory,* de mémoire d'homme. *there wasn't a* ~ *soul,* il n'y avait pas âme qui vive. ¶ *n,* vie, *f;* (*Eccl.*) bénéfice, *m. to earn a* ~, gagner sa vie. ~ *conditions,* conditions de vie, *f.pl.* ~ *standards,* niveau de vie, *m.* ~-*room,* salle de séjour, *f,* living, *m.* **the** ~, les vivants, *m.pl.*
lizard, *n,* lézard, *m.*
llama, *n,* lama, *m.*
load, *n,* charge; (*ship*) cargaison, *f;* (*lorry*) chargement, *m;* (*pressure, weight*) poids, *m;* (*fig.*) (*burden*) fardeau, *m;* (*strain*) poids. *that's a* ~ *off my mind!* quel soulagement! (*fig.*) ~*s of P,* des tas de *P. we've* ~*s of time,* nous avons largement le temps. ¶ *v.t,* charger (*with,* de); (*dice*) piper; (*cane*) plomber. ~**ed,** *a,* (*P rich*) bourré de fric *P;* (*P drunk*) plein *P;* (*P drugged*) défoncé *P.* ~ *question,* question insidieuse. ~**er,** *n,* chargeur, *m.* ~**ing,** *n* chargement, *m.*
loaf[1], *n.* & ~ *of bread,* pain, *m;* (*round loaf*) miche, *f. use your* ~! *P* fais marcher tes méninges! *P.* ~ *sugar,* sucre en morceaux, *m.*
loaf[2], *v.i.* fainéanter, traîner. ~**er,** *n,* fainéant, e; flâneur, euse.
loam, *n,* terreau, *m.*
loan, *n,* (*lent*) prêt; (*borrowed*) emprunt, *m.* ¶ *v.t.* prêter (qch à qn).
loath (to be), ne pas vouloir, répugner (à faire). **loathe,** *v.t,* détester; (*pers.*) haïr; (*thing*) avoir horreur de; abhorrer. **loathing,** *n,* dégout, *m,* repugnance, *f.* **loathsome,** *a,* répugnant.
lob, *n,* (*Ten.*) lob, *m.* ¶ *v.t,* lober.
lobby, *n,* vestibule; (*larger*) hall, *m;* (*Pol.*) groupe de pression, lobby, *m.* ¶ *v.i.* (& *t,*) faire pression (sur). ~**ing,** *n,* pressions, *f.pl.*
lobe, *n,* lobe, *m.*
lobelia, *n,* lobélie, *f.*
lobster, *n,* homard, *m.* ~ *pot,* casier à h., *m.*
local, *a,* local; (*shop &c*) du quartier; (*wine*) du pays; (*pain*) localisé; (*pers.*) du pays *ou* du coin *P. the* ~*s P,* les gens du pays, du coin *P.* (*Tel.*) ~ *call,* communication urbaine. ~ *education authority,* office régional de

l'enseignement. ~ *government elections,* élections municipales. ¶ *n,* (*P pub*) café du coin, *m.* ~**[e],** *n,* scène, *f.* ~**ity,** *n,* environs, *m.pl;* région, *f.* ~**ize,** *v.t,* localiser. ~**ly,** *ad,* localement.

locate, *v.t,* repérer; (*cause &c*) localiser; (*situate*) situer. *to be* ~*d,* être situé, se trouver. **location,** *n,* emplacement, *m. on* ~ (*Cine*), en extérieur.

lock, *n,* serrure, *f;* (*on steering wheel*) antivol, *m;* (*canal*) écluse; (*hair*) boucle, mèche; (*pl.*) chevelure, *f;* (*gun*) percuteur, *m;* (*Mot.*) rayon de braquage, *m.* ~ *stock & barrel,* en bloc. *under* ~ *& key,* sous clef; (*prisoner*) sous verrous. ~*jaw,* tétanos, *m.* ~ *keeper,* éclusier, ère. ~*-out,* lock-out, *m.* ~*smith,* serrurier, *m.* ~*-up,* (*garage*) box, *m;* (*prison*) cellule provisoire, *f;* (*a.*) fermant à clef. ¶ *v.t,* fermer à clef; (*pers., also* ~ *in*) enfermer; (*Mot: wheels*) bloquer. ~ *away,* mettre sous clef. ~ *out,* mettre à la porte; (*Ind.*) lock-outer. ~ *up,* fermer à clef; (*prisoner*) mettre sous les verrous; (*mental patient*) enfermer; (*Fin.*) immobiliser, bloquer.

locker, *n,* casier, *m.*

locket, *n,* médaillon, *m.*

locomotion, *n,* locomotion, *f.* **locomotive,** *n,* locomotive, *f.*

locum tenens, *n,* remplaçant, e.

locust, *n,* sauterelle, locuste, *f.*

locution, *n,* locution, *f.*

lode, *n,* filon, *m.* ~ *star,* étoile polaire, *f.* ~*stone,* aimant naturel, magnétite, *f.*

lodge, *n,* loge, *f;* (*house*) pavillon, *m.* ¶ *v.t,* loger; (*money*) déposer; (*report*) présenter (*with,* à). ¶ *v.i,* (*pers.*) être logé (chez); (*bullet*) se loger. **lodger,** *n,* locataire, *m,f.* **lodging,** *n,* logement, *m,* chambre, *f;* (*pl.*) meublé, *m.* ~ *house,* pension, *f.*

loft, *n,* grenier, *m;* (*church &c*) galerie, *f.* ¶ *v.t,* (*ball*) lancer en chandelle. ~**iness,** *n,* hauteur, *f.* ~**y,** *a,* (*high*) élevé, haut; (*fig: ideals, style &c*) noble, élevé; (*haughty*) hautain.

log, *n,* bûche, *f;* (*trunk*) rondin; (*Naut.*) loch, *m.* ~ [*book*], livre de bord, *m.* ~ *book,* (*car*) carte grise. ~ *cabin,* cabane de rondins, *f.* ~ *fire,* feu de bois, *m.* ¶ *v.t,* noter; (*Naut., Aero.*) inscrire.

loganberry, *n,* ronce-framboise, *f.*

logarithm, *n,* logarithme, *m.*

loggerheads (at), à couteaux tirés (avec).

logic, *n,* logique, *f.* ~**al†,** *a,* logique. ~**ian,** *n,* logicien, *m.*

loin, *n,* (*pl: Anat.*) reins, lombes, *m.pl;* (*Cook.*) filet; (*beef*) aloyau, *m;* (*veal*) longe, *f.* ~ *chop,* côte première. ~ *cloth,* pagne, *m.*

loiter, *v.i,* s'attarder, traîner. ~**er,** *n,* flâneur, euse; rôdeur, euse.

loll, *v.i,* se prélasser; (*tongue*) pendre.

lollipop, *n,* sucette, *f.* **lolly** = **lollipop;** (*P money*) fric *P, m.*

London, *n,* Londres, *m;* (*att.*) londonien. ~**er,** *n,* Londonien, ne.

loneliness, *n,* (*pers.*) solitude, *f;* (*place*) isolement, *m.* **lonely** *&* **lone[some],** *a,* solitaire, isolé. *to feel* ~, se sentir seul. *a loner, lone wolf,* solitaire, *m,f.*

long[1], *a,* long. *3m. long,* long de 3m. *a* ~ *time,* longtemps. *have a* ~ *memory,* avoir de la mémoire. ~*-distance,a,* (*race*) de fond; (*Tel.*) interurbain. ~*-drawn-out,* interminable. ~ *forgotten,* oublié depuis longtemps. ~*-haired,* (*pers.*) aux cheveux longs; (*animal*) à longs poils. ~*hand,* en écriture normale. ~*-jump,* saut en longueur, *m.* ~*-legged,* aux jambes longues. ~*-lived,* d'une grande longévité. ~*-lost,* perdu depuis longtemps. ~*-playing record,* 33 tours, *m.inv.* ~*-range,* (*gun*) à grande portée; (*forecast*) à long terme. ~*-shoreman,* débardeur, *m.* ~*-sighted,* hypermétrope; (*in old age*) presbyte. ~*-term,* à long terme. ~*-winded,* prolixe. ¶ *ad,* longtemps. *I have been here for a* ~ *time,* je suis ici depuis longtemps. ~ *ago,* il y a longtemps. ~ *before,* longtemps avant. *don't be* ~, dépêche-toi! *how* ~*?* combien de temps? *not* ~ *since,* il n'y a pas longtemps. *all day* ~, toute la journée. *so, as* ~ *as,* pourvu que + *subj.* ~*-suffering, a,* très patient. ¶ *n, the* ~ *& the short of it,* le fin mot de l'histoire. ~**ish,** *a,* assez long; longuet *P.*

long[2], *v.i, I* ~ *to do,* je meurs d'envie de faire. *I am* ~*ing to,* il me tarde de. *to* ~ *for s.o,* se languir de qn. ~**ing,** *n,* envie, *f,* désir, *m.*

longevity, *n,* longévité, *f.*

longitude, *n,* longitude, *f.* **longitudinal†,** *a,* longitudinal.

loo *P, n,* cabinets, waters, *m.pl,* petit coin *P.*

look, *n,* regard; coup d'œil, *m. to have, take a* ~ *at,* regarder, jeter un coup d'œil à. *to take a good* ~ *at s.o,* bien observer qn. *take a good* ~ *at it!* regarde-le bien! (*appearance*) air, aspect, *m. by the* ~ *of it,* selon toute apparence. ~*-out,* surveillance, *f;* guet, *m;* (*pers.*) guetteur, *m;* (*Naut.*) vigie, *f;* (*outlook*) perspective, *f. that's your* ~*-out,* c'est votre affaire. ¶ *v.i,* regarder; (*seem*) avoir l'air, sembler, paraître. ~ **after,** s'occuper de, soigner; (*possessions*) faire attention à, prendre soin de. ~ **at,** regarder; (*consider*) considérer, voir; (*check*) vérifier; s'occuper de. ~ **down on,** mépriser. ~ **for,** chercher; (*expect*) s'attendre à. ~ **forward to,** attendre avec impatience. ~ **in,** (*visit*) passer [voir]. ~ **into,** examiner; se renseigner sur. ~ **like,** ressembler à, avoir l'air de. *it* ~*s like, it* ~*s as though,* on dirait [que]. ~ **on,** regarder; (*front*) donner sur. ~ **out!** attention! gare! ~ *out for,* chercher; s'attendre à. ~ *out of the*

window, regarder par la fenêtre. ~ **over,** (*book &c*) parcourir; (*building*) visiter. ~ **to,** (*rely on*) compter sur. ~ **up,** (*word &c*) chercher. ~**ing-glass,** *n.* glace, *f,* miroir, *m.*
loom[1], *n,* métier [à tisser], *m.*
loom[2], *v.i,* se dessiner, surgir; (*fig.*) menacer.
loony *P, a,* timbré *P,* cinglé *P.* ¶ *n,* idiot, e; fou, folle. ~ *bin,* maison de fous, *f.*
loop, *n,* boucle, *f;* (*Elec.*) circuit fermé; (*Rly* ~ *line*) voie d'évitement, *f;* (*motorway*) bretelle, *f.* ~*hole,* meurtrière; (*fig.*) lacune, *f.* ¶ *v.t,* boucler. ~ *the* ~, boucler la boucle.
loose, *a,* (*knot, screw*) desserré; (*brick, tooth*) qui branle; (*page*) détaché; (*animal*) en liberté; (*hair*) dénoué. *to get* ~, échapper. *to work* ~, se desserrer. *let* ~, lâcher. (*clothes*) ample; (*not tight enough*) large; (*collar*) lâche; (*in bulk*) en vrac; (*discipline, morals &c*) relâché; (*pej. woman*) facile. ~ *living,* vie dissolue. (*translation*) libre. ~ *box,* fourgon à chevaux, *m.* ~ *chippings,* gravillons, *m.pl.* ~ *cover,* housse, *f. to be at a* ~ *end,* ne pas trop savoir quoi faire. *tie up the* ~ *ends,* régler les détails qui restent. ~*-fitting,* ample. ~*-leaf,* à feuilles volantes. ~*-limbed,* agile. ¶ *v.t,* (*undo*) défaire; (*untie*) délier; (*screw &c*) desserrer; (*free*) (*prisoner*) relâcher. ~**n,** *v.t,* desserrer; (*grip, bowels*) relâcher; (*tongue*) délier; (*soil*) rendre meuble.
loot, *n,* butin, *m;* (*P money*) fric *P, m.* ¶ *v.t. & i,* piller.
lop, *v.t,* (*tree*) élaguer, tailler; (*branch*) couper. ~*-eared,* aux oreilles pendantes. ~ *off,* (*head*) trancher. ~*-sided,* de guingois.
lope, *v.i, to* ~ *along,* courir à petits bonds.
loquacious, *a,* loquace. **loquacity,** *n,* loquacité, *f.*
lord, *n,* seigneur; (*UK*) lord, *m.* the [*House of*] *L*~*s,* la Chambre des Lords. ~ *of the manor,* châtelain, *m. the L*~ (*God*), le Seigneur. *L*~*'s prayer,* Notre-Père, *m. L*~*'s Supper,* la Cène. *In the year of our L*~ ..., en l'an de grâce... *Good L*~*!* mon Dieu! ¶ *v.t,* ~ *it over,* traiter avec arrogance. ~**ly,** *a,* hautain, arrogant. ~**ship,** *n,* seigneurie, *f. Your L*~, Monsieur le comte (*&c*); (*judge*) M. le juge; (*bishop*) Monseigneur.
lore, *n,* coutumes, *f.pl.*
lorry, *n,* camion, *m.* ~ *driver,* camionneur; (*long-distance*) routier, *m.*
lose, *v.t. & i.ir,* perdre; (*mislay*) égarer; (*clock*) retarder. *to* ~ *one's balance,* perdre l'équilibre. ~ *one's bearings,* être désorienté. ~ *face,* perdre la face. ~ *heart,* se décourager. ~ *one's temper,* se fâcher. ~ *one's way,* se perdre, s'égarer. ~ *weight,* maigrir. **loser,** *n,* perdant, e; (*good, bad*) joueur, euse. *he's a born* ~, il est né perdant. **loss,** *n,* perte, *f.* ~ *of voice,* extinction de voix, *f.* (*Mil.*) *heavy* ~*es,* pertes sévères. *it's no great* ~ *P,* ce n'est pas une grande perte. *sell at a* ~, vendre à perte. *to be at a* ~, être perplexe *ou* embarrassé. **lost,** *a,* perdu; égaré; (*in thought*) absorbé. ~ *property office.* bureau des objets trouvés, *m.*
lot, *n,* sort; (*random selection*) tirage au sort; (*auction &c*) lot, *m. throw in one's* ~ *with,* se ranger du côté de. *he's a bad* ~ *P,* il ne vaut pas cher *P. draw* ~*s,* tirer au sort. *the* ~, [le] tout; (*people*) tous, toutes. *a* ~ *of,* ~*s of,* beaucoup de. *a* ~ *of people,* beaucoup de monde. *quite a* ~ *of...,* pas mal de... *a hell of a* ~ *of people P,* un monde fou *P. parking* ~ *Am,* parking, *m.*
loth (to be), *V* **loath.**
lotion, *n,* lotion, *f.*
lottery, *n,* loterie, *f.*
lotus, *n,* lotus, *m.*
loud, *a,* (*voice*) fort, sonore; (*laugh, music*) bruyant; (*noise*) grand, sonore; (*applause*) vif; (*gaudy*) voyant. ~*-mouth* (*pej.*), grande gueule *P.* ~ *pedal,* pédale forte, *f.* ~ *speaker,* hautparleur, *m. out* ~, tout haut. ~**ly,** *ad,* fort, haut.
lounge, *n,* salon, *m.* ~ *suit,* complet[-veston], *m.* ¶ *v.i,* (*&* ~ *about*) flâner, paresser; (*in chair*) être vautré. ~**r,** *n,* (*pers.*) fainéant, *m;* (*sun* ~) lit de plage, *m.*
louse, *n,* pou, *m;* (*pej. pers.*) salaud *P, m.* **lousy,** *a,* (*lit.*) pouilleux; (*P bad*) moche *P.*
lout, *n.* & ~**ish,** *a,* rustre, *m.*
lovable, *a,* aimable, sympathique.
love, *n,* amour; (*Ten.*) zéro, rien, *m. in* ~, amoureux. *fall in* ~, tomber amoureux. *make* ~, faire l'amour. ~ *at first sight,* le coup de foudre. *for* ~ *or money,* pour rien au monde. *there's no* ~ *lost between them,* ils ne peuvent pas se sentir. [*with*] ~ [*from*], affectueusement, bons baisers. *everyone sends their* ~, tout le monde t'embrasse. ~ *affair,* liaison, *f.* ~*-in-a-mist,* cheveux de Vénus, *m.pl.* ~ *letter,* billet doux, *m.* ~ *match,* mariage d'amour, *m.* ~ *story,* histoire d'amour, *f.* ¶ *v.t,* aimer; (*activity &c*) aimer [beaucoup], adorer.
loveliness, *n,* beauté, *f.* **lovely,** *a,* (*pretty*) [très] joli, ravissant; (*pleasant*) charmant; (*day &c*) beau; (*food &c*) bon. *have a* ~ *time!* amusez-vous bien! *it's* ~ *to see you,* je suis vraiment content de vous voir. (*baby*) *isn't she* ~*!* qu'elle est mignonne!
lover, *n,* amant; (*in love*) amoureux; (*wine, music &c*) amateur, *m.* **loving,** *a,* affectueux; (*tender*) tendre; (*dutiful*) aimant.
low[1], *a,* (*gen.*) bas; (*speed*) petit, faible; (*density, standard, intelligence*) faible; (*depressed*) déprimé. *at a* ~ *heat,* à feu doux. *to be in* ~ *spirits,* ne pas avoir le moral *P. to be* ~ *on,* être à court de. *in a* ~ *voice,* à voix basse. *the* ~*est of the* ~, le dernier des derniers. *L*~ *Countries,* Pays-Bas, *m.pl.* ~*-cut,* (*dress*)

décolleté. ~*-key,* modéré. ~ *tide,* marée basse. ~ *trick,* sale tour *P, m.* ¶ *ad,* bas; (*bow*) profondément. ~**er,** *a,* inférieur. ~ *case,* (*Typ.*) bas de casse, *m.* ~ *income groups,* économiquement faibles, *m.pl.* ¶ *v.t,* amener, baisser; (*flag*) [a]baisser; (*boat*) mettre à la mer. ~ *o.s* (*fig.*), s'abaisser. ~**ness,** *n,* manque de hauteur, *m;* (*price &c*) modicité.

low², *v.i,* mugir, beugler.

lowlands, *n.pl,* plaine, *f. the L*~ [*of Scotland*], la Basse Écosse.

lowliness, *n,* humilité, *f.* **lowly,** *a,* humble.

loyal†, *a,* loyal, fidèle. ~**ist,** *n. & att,* loyaliste, *m,f.* ~**ty,** *n,* loyauté, *f;* (*to sovereign*) loyalisme, *m.*

lozenge, *n,* pastille, *f;* (*Geom.*) losange, *m.*

lubricate, *v.t,* lubrifier; (*car*) graisser. *lubricating oil,* lubrifiant, *m,* huile [de graissage], *f.* ~*d P,* (*drunk*) rond *P,* bourré *P.* **lubrication,** *n,* lubrification, *f,* graissage, *m.* **lubricator,** *n,* graisseur, *m.*

lucern[e], *n,* luzerne, *f.*

lucid, *a,* lucide. ~**ity,** *n,* lucidité, *f.*

luck, *n,* chance, *f,* hasard, *m. bad* ~, malchance, *f,* malheur, *m. good* ~, [bonne] chance, bonheur, *m,* veine *P, f. as* ~ *would have it,* comme par hasard. *better* ~ *next time!* ça ira mieux la prochaine fois. *good* ~*!* bonne chance! *hard* ~*!* pas de chance! manque de pot! *P. with any* ~, avec un peu de chance. *worse* ~, malheureusement. ~**ily,** *ad,* heureusement. ~**less,** malchanceux. ~**y,** *a,* heureux; (*pers.*) qui a de la chance, veinard *P;* (*charm*) porte-bonheur, *inv. how* ~*!* quelle chance! *you* ~ *devil! P,* veinard! *P.* ~ *break,* coup de veine *P, m.* ~ *star,* bonne étoile.

lucrative, *a,* lucratif. **lucre,** *n,* lucre, *m.*

ludicrous†, *a,* ridicule, absurde, risible.

lug, *n,* oreille, *f.* ~*hole P,* esgourde *P, f.* ¶ *v.t,* traîner.

luggage, *n,* bagage[s] *m.*[*pl.*]. ~ *label,* étiquette à b-s, *f.* ~ *rack,* porte-b-s, filet, *m.* ~ *van,* fourgon à b-s, *m.*

lugubrious†, *a,* lugubre.

lukewarm, *a,* tiède.

lull, *n,* (*storm*) accalmie; (*conversation*) pause, *f;* (*shooting*) arrêt, *m.* ¶ *v.i,* apaiser, calmer. **lullaby,** *n,* berceuse, *f.*

lumbago, *n,* lumbago, *m.* **lumbar,** *a,* lombaire.

lumber, *n,* (*wood*) bois de charpente; (*junk*) bric-a-brac, *m.* ~ *jack,* bûcheron, *m.* ~ *room,* [cabinet de] débarras, *m.* ¶ *v.t,* (*room*) encombrer. *get* ~*ed with P,* (*s.o, sth*) avoir sur les bras.

luminary, *n,* astre, *m;* (*pers.*) lumière, *f.*

luminous†, *a,* lumineux. ~ *dial* (*watch*), cadran lumineux, *m.*

lump, *n,* [gros] morceau, *m,* masse, *f;* (*soil*) motte, *f;* (*in sauce*) grumeau, *m;* (*Med.*) grosseur, *f. a* ~ *in one's throat,* la gorge serrée. ~ *sugar,* sucre en morceaux, *m.* ~ *sum,* somme globale, *f. in a* ~ *sum,* (*pay*) en une fois. ¶ *v.t,* (~ *together*) réunir. ~**y,** *a,* (*sauce*) grumeleux; (*bed*) défoncé.

lunacy, *n,* aliénation mentale, démence, *f.* **lunatic,** *n,* fou, folle; aliéné, e. ~ *asylum,* asile d'aliénés, *m. the* ~ *fringe,* les enragés *P.*

lunar, *a,* lunaire.

lunch, *n,* déjeuner, *m.* ~ *basket,* panier-repas, *m.* ~ *break,* heure du déjeuner, *f.* ¶ *v.t,* déjeuner. ~**eon,** *V* **lunch.** ~ *meat,* mortadelle, *f.* ~ *voucher,* ticket-restaurant, *m.*

lung, *n,* poumon, *m.*

lunge, *m.* (*Fenc.*) botte, *f.* ¶ *v.i,* se fendre. ~ *at,* porter une botte à; (*gen.*) envoyer un coup à.

lupin[e] (*Bot.*) *n,* lupin, *m.*

lurch, *n,* (*vehicle*) embardée, *f. leave in the* ~, planter là. ¶ *v.i,* (*pers.*) tituber; (*vehicle*) faire une embardée.

lure, *n,* (*attraction*) charme, attrait; (*false & decoy*) leurre, *m.* ¶ *v.t,* attirer par la ruse. ~ *s.o into a trap,* attirer qn dans un piège.

lurid, *a,* (*details*) atroce; (*tale*) effrayant; (*crime*) horrible; (*sensational*) à sensation; (*colour*) sanglant.

lurk, *v.i,* se cacher; (*doubt*) persister; (*danger*) menacer.

luscious, *a,* succulent.

lush, *a,* luxuriant; (*P house &c*) luxueux.

lust, *n,* (*sexual*) luxure; (*for fame &c*) soif (*for,* de), *f.* ¶ *v.i.* ~ *after,* convoiter; avoir soif de. ~**ful,** *a,* luxurieux.

lustre, *n,* lustre, *m.* ~**less,** *a,* terne.

lusty†, *a,* vigoureux, robuste.

lute, *n,* (*Mus.*) luth, *m.*

Luxemburg, *n,* Luxembourg, *m.*

luxuriance, *n,* exubérance, *f.* **luxuriant,** *a,* luxuriant, exubérant. **luxurious,** *a,* luxueux. **luxury,** *n,* luxe, *m.*

lying, *a,* (*story*) mensonger; (*pers.*) menteur. ¶ *n,* mensonge, *m.*

lymph, *n,* lymphe, *f.* ~ *gland,* ganglion lymphatique, *m.*

lynch, *v.t,* lyncher. ~**ing,** *n,* lynchage, *m.*

lynx, *n,* lynx, *m.*

Lyons, *n,* Lyon, *m.*

lyre, *n,* lyre, *f.* ~*-bird,* oiseau-lyre, *m.*

lyric & ~**al,** *a,* lyrique. ¶ *n,* ~*s* (*song*) paroles, *f.pl.* **lyricism,** *n,* lyrisme, *m.* **lyricist,** *n,* parolier, ière.

M

macabre, *a,* macabre.
macadam, *n,* macadam, *m.* **~ize,** *v.t,* macadamiser.
macaroni, *n,* macaroni, *m.*
macaroon, *n,* macaron, *m.*
macaw, *n,* ara, *m.*
mace, *n,* masse, *f;* (*spice*) macis, *m.* ~ *bearer,* massier, *m.*
macerate, *v.t,* macérer.
Machiavellian, *a,* machiavélique.
machination, *n,* machination, *f.*
machine, *n,* machine, *f;* (*fig.*) machine, appareil, *m;* (*pej. pers.*) automate, *m.* ~ *age,* le siècle de la machine. ~ *gun,* mitrailleuse, *f.* ~ *gunner,* mitrailleur, *m.* ~*-made,* fait à la machine. ~ *shop,* atelier d'usinage, *m.* ~*-stitch,* piquer à la machine. ~*-tool,* machine-outil, *f.* ¶ *v.t,* (*Tech.*) usiner; (*sew*) piquer [à la machine]. **~ry,** *n,* machinerie, *f,* machines, *f.pl;* (*part*) mécanisme, *m;* (*fig.*) rouages, *m.pl. the* ~ *of government,* les rouages de l'État. **machinist,** *n,* machiniste, *m,f;* (*sewing*) mécanicienne, *f.*
mackerel, *n,* maquereau, *m.* ~ *sky,* ciel pommelé, *m.*
mackintosh, *n,* imperméable, *m.*
mad, *a,* (*pers.*) fou; dingue *P;* (*dog*) enragé; (*bull*) furieux; (*rash: pers., plan*) incensé; (*race*) effréné; (*angry*) furieux. *drive* ~, rendre fou; (*exasperate*) exaspérer; (*anger*) faire enrager. *go* ~, devenir fou. *hopping* ~, fou furieux. *like* ~ *P,* comme un fou. *stark raving* ~, fou à lier. ~ [*keen*] *about,* fou de; mordu de *P.* ~*cap,* écervelé, e. ~*house,* maison de fous, *f.* ~*man, -woman,* fou, folle, aliéné, e. **~den,** *v.t,* rendre fou; exaspérer. **~dening,** *a,* exaspérant. **~ly,** *ad,* follement, comme un fou; (*hurriedly*) désespérément. **~ness,** *n,* folie; démence; (*dog*) rage, *f.*
madam, *n,* madame, *f.*
Madeira, *n,* Madère, *f.*
madonna, *n,* madone, *f.*
madrigal, *n,* madrigal, *m.*
magazine, *n,* revue, *f,* magazine, *m;* (*Mil.*) magasin du corps; (*of gun*) magasin, *m.*
maggot, *n,* ver; asticot, *m.* **~y,** *a,* véreux.
Magi, *n.pl,* mages, *m.pl.*
magic, *a,* magique. ~ *lantern,* lanterne magique, *f.* ¶ *n,* magie, *f,* enchantement, *m.* **~al,** *a,* magique. **~ally,** *ad,* comme par enchantement, d'une façon magique. **~ian,** *n,* magicien, ne; (*Theat.*) illusionniste, *m,f.*
magisterial, *a,* de magistrat; (*fig.*) magistral. **~ly,** *ad,* en magistrat; magistralement. **magistracy,** *n,* magistrature, *f.* **magistrate,** *n,* magistrat; juge, *m.*
magnanimity, *n,* magnanimité, *f.* **magnanimous†** *a,* magnanime.
magnate, *n,* magnat, *m.*
magnesia, *n,* magnésie, *f.* **magnesium,** *n,* magnésium, *m.* ~ *light,* lumière magnésique, *f.*
magnet, *n,* aimant, *m.* **~ic,** *a,* magnétique; (*bar, needle*) aimanté, e; (*fig.*) attirant. **~ics,** *n.* & **~ism,** *n,* magnétisme, *m.* **~ize,** *v.t,* aimanter; (*fig.*) magnétiser. **magneto,** *n,* magnéto, *f.*
magnificence, *n,* magnificence, *f.* **magnificent†,** *a,* magnifique.
magnify, *v.t,* (*image*) grossir; (*sound*) amplifier; (*incident &c*) exagérer; (*the Lord*) magnifier. ~*ing glass,* verre grossissant, *m,* loupe, *f.*
magnitude, *n,* ampleur; (*Astr.*) magnitude, *f.*
magnolia, *n,* magnolia, *m.*
magpie, *n,* pie, *f.*
mahogany, *n,* acajou, *m.*
maid, *n,* (*servant*) bonne, *f.* (*pej.*) *old* ~, vieille fille, *f.* ~*-of-all-work,* bonne à tout faire. *the M*~ *of Orléans,* la Pucelle. **maiden,** *n,* (*liter.*) jeune fille, *f.* ¶ *a,* (*voyage, speech &c*) premier. ~ *aunt,* tante célibataire, *f.* ~*hair* [*fern*], capillaire, *m.* ~ *lady,* demoiselle, *f.* ~ *name,* nom de jeune fille, *m.* **~hood,** *n,* virginité, *f.* **~ly,** *a,* de jeune fille, virginal.
mail[1], *n,* poste, *f;* (*letters*) courrier, *m.* ~ *bag,* sac postal. ~*boat,* paquebot-poste, *m.* ~*ing list,* liste d'adresses, *f.* (*Am*) ~*man,* facteur, *m.* ~*-order,* vente *f,* achat par correspondance *m,f.* ~*-order firm,* maison de vente par c., *f.* ~ *train,* train-poste, *m.* ~ *van,* voiture des postes, *f;* (*Rly*) wagon-poste, *m.*
mail[2], *n,* (*armour*) mailles, *f.pl.*
maim, *v.t,* estropier, mutiler.
main, *a,* principal; (*pipe, beam*) maître, esse. ~ *bearing,* (*Mot.*) palier, *m.* ~ *body* (*of the army &c*), gros (de l'armée &c), *m.* ~ *course,* (*Cook.*) plat de résistance, *m.* ~ *crop,* (*Agr.*) culture principale. ~ *idea* (*of book*), idée mère. ~*land,* continent, *m.* ~ *line,* (*Rly*) grande ligne. ~*mast,* grand mât. *the* ~ *point, thing,* l'essentiel, *m.* ~ *road,* grand-route, *f.* ~*sail,* grand-voile, *f.* ~*spring,* ressort principal; (*fig.*) mobile principal. ~*stay,* soutien, pilier, *m.* ~ *street,* grand-rue, *f.* ¶ *n,* (*pipe*) canalisation *ou* conduite maîtresse; (*Elec.*) conducteur principal; (*gas*) conduite principale; (*drainage*) égout collecteur; (*water*) conduite d'eau de la ville. *the* ~*s,* (*Elec.*) le secteur. *connected to the* ~*s,* branché sur [le] secteur. *turn off at the* ~*s,* couper au compteur. (*Poet.*) océan, *m. in the* ~, en général. **~ly,** *ad,* principalement.

maintain, *v.t,* maintenir; (*silence*) garder; (*contact*) entretenir; (*advantage*) conserver; (*strength, rights &c*) soutenir; (*support*) entretenir; (*road &c*) entretenir; (*assert*) maintenir, soutenir (*that,* que). **maintenance,** *n,* maintien, entretien, *m;* (*payments*) pension alimentaire, *f.* ¶ *a,* (*costs &c*) d'entretien. ~ *allowance, grant,* (*student*) bourse [d'études]; (*worker*) indemnité de déplacement. ~ *order* (*Law*), obligation alimentaire, *f.*

maisonette, *n,* duplex, *m.*

maize, *n,* maïs, *m.*

majestic†, *a,* majestueux. **majesty,** *n,* majesté, *f. His, Her, M~,* Sa Majesté.

major, *a,* majeur. *for the ~ part,* en grande partie. ~ *road,* route de priorité, *f.* (*Cards*) ~ *suit,* majeure, *f.* ¶ *n,* (*Mil.*) commandant, *m.* ~*-general,* général de division, *m.* (*Am. Univ.*) matière principale, *f.* ¶ *v.i,* (*Am. Univ.*) se spécialiser (en).

Majorca, *n,* Majorque, *f.*

majority, *n,* majorité, *f. to be in the ~,* être en majorité. *the ~ [of people],* la plupart [des gens]. ¶ *a,* (*decision &c*) majoritaire.

make, *n,* (*brand*) marque; (*manufacture*) fabrication, *f. be on the ~,* chercher à faire fortune à tout prix. ~*-believe,* semblant, *m. land of ~-believe,* pays de chimères, *m.* ~*shift, n,* expédient, *m; a,* de fortune. ~*-up,* (*nature*) constitution, *f;* (*cosmetics*) maquillage, *m.* ~*-up remover,* démaquillant, *m.* ~ *weight,* complément de poids, *m.* ¶ *v.t.ir,* (*gen.*) faire; (*Ind.*) fabriquer; (*Build.*) construire; (*score*) marquer; (*cause*) faire; forcer (à). ~ *o.s known,* se faire connaître. ~ *s.o happy,* rendre qn heureux. ~ *s.o* (*do sth*), faire qn *ou* obliger, forcer qn à (*faire qch*). (*earn*) gagner; (*business &c*) rapporter; (*profits*) faire. (*equal*) *2 & 2 ~ 4,* 2 & 2 font *ou* égalent 4. *how much does that ~?* combien ça fait? (*reach*) arriver à; (*catch train &c*) attraper; (*cards*) battre; (*trick*) faire. ~ *do with,* (*be satisfied*) se contenter de; (*manage*) se débrouiller avec. ~ *do & mend,* se débrouiller avec ce qu'on a. ~ *it,* (*succeed*) y arriver, (*arrive*) parvenir (à). ~ *[it with] a girl P*,* s'envoyer une fille *P*.* ~ *or mar,* faire la fortune ou la ruine de. *show what one is made of,* donner toute sa mesure. *what time do you ~ it?* quelle heure avez-vous? ~ **for,** se diriger vers. ~ **off,** se sauver, filer. ~ **out,** *v.t,* (*list, cheque etc.*) faire; déchiffrer; distinguer; comprendre; (*claim*) prétendre (*that,* que). ¶ *v.i,* (*P*) se débrouiller. ~ **over,** (*money &c*) céder. ~ **up,** (*friendship*) (se) réconcilier; (*face*) (se) maquiller; (*Theat.*) (se) grimer; (*put together*) faire; (*Typ.*) mettre en pages; (*story*) inventer; (*loss*) combler; (*lost time*) rattraper; (*lost ground*) regagner. ~ *up one's mind,* se décider. ~ *up for,* compenser.

maker, *n,* (*Com.*) fabricant, *m. Our M~* (*Rel.*), le Créateur. **making,** *n,* fabrication; (*dress, food*) confection, *f.* ~*s,* éléments essentiels.

maladjusted, *a,* inadapté.

maladministration, *n,* mauvaise gestion, *f.*

maladroit†, *a,* maladroit.

malady, *n,* maladie, *f.*

Malagasy, *a,* malgache. ¶ *n,* Malgache, *m,f.*

malaprop[ism], *n,* pataquès, *m.*

malaria, *n,* paludisme, *m,* malaria, *f.* **malarial,** *a,* paludéen.

Malay[an], *a,* malais. ¶ *n,* (*pers.*) Malais, e; (*language*) le malais. **Malaysia,** *n,* Malaysia, *f.*

malcontent, *a. & n,* mécontent, *m.*

male, *n,* mâle, *m.* ¶ *a,* mâle; (*sex*) masculin; (*clothes*) d'homme. ~ *chauvinist pig P,* [sale] phallocrate *P*, m.*

malediction, *n,* malédiction, *f.*

malefactor, *n,* malfaiteur, *m.*

malevolence, *n,* malveillance (*towards,* envers), *f.* **malevolent,** *a,* malveillant.

malformation, *n,* malformation, *f.*

malice, *n,* malice, méchanceté, *f.* ~ *aforethought,* préméditation, intention criminelle, *f.* **malicious,** *a,* méchant; (*Law*) criminel.

malign, *v.t,* calomnier, diffamer. ¶ *a,* pernicieux. **malignancy,** *n,* malfaisance; (*Med.*) malignité, *f.* **malignant,** *a,* malfaisant; (*Med.*) malin.

malinger, *v.i,* faire le malade, simuler la maladie.

mallard, *n,* col-vert, *m.*

malleable, *a,* malléable.

mallet, *n,* maillet, *m.*

mallow, *n,* (*Bot.*) mauve, *f.*

malt, *n,* malt, *m.* ¶ *a,* (*vinegar, extract*) de malt. ~ *whisky,* whisky pur malt, *m.* ~**ing,** *n,* malterie, *f.* ~**ster,** *n,* malteur, *m.*

Malta, *n,* Malte, *f.* **Maltese,** *a,* maltais. ~ *cross,* croix de Malte, *f.* ¶ *n,* (*pers.*) Maltais, e; (*language*) le maltais.

maltreat, *v.t,* maltraiter. ~**ment,** *n,* mauvais traitements, *m.pl.*

mam[m]a, *n,* maman, *f.*

mammal, *n,* mammifère, *m.*

mammoth, *n,* mammouth, *m.* ¶ *a,* géant.

man, *n,* homme; (*servant*) valet; (*in factory &c*) ouvrier; (*white collar*) employé; (*Mil.*) soldat; (*Naut.*) matelot; (*sport*) joueur; (*draughts*) pion, *m;* (*chess*) pièce, *f.* ~ *& wife,* mari & femme. *as one ~,* comme un seul homme. ~ *about town,* mondain, *m. my old ~ P,* (*father*) mon paternel *P;* (*husband*) mon homme *P. old ~,* vieillard, *m. yes, old ~,* oui, mon vieux. *the ~ in the moon,* l'homme dans la lune. *the ~ in the street,* l'homme de la rue. *to a ~,* sans exception. *to the last ~,* jusqu'au dernier. ~*-eater,* mangeur d'hommes, *m.* ~ *Friday,* (*Liter.*) Vendredi; (*fig.*) fidèle serviteur, *m.* ~*handle,* maltraiter; (*goods &c*) manutentionner. ~*hole,* regard, *m.* ~*hole cover,* plaque d'égout, *f.* ~*-hour,* (*Ind.*) heure de main-d'œuvre, *f.* ~*hunt,* chasse à l'homme, *f.* ~*-made,* (*fibre*) synthétique; (*lake &c*) artificiel. *M*~, (*human race*) l'homme. ~*-of-war,* bâtiment de guerre, *m.* ~*power,* main-d'œuvre, *f.* ~*slaughter,* homicide involontaire, *m.* ~**hood,** ~**kind,** ~**ly, &c** See below.

manacle, *v.t,* mettre des menottes à; (*fig.*) enchaîner. ~**s,** *n.pl,* menottes, *f.pl,* fers, *m.pl.*

manage, *v.t,* (*gen.*) gérer; (*organisation*) diriger, administrer; (*farm*) exploiter; (*vehicle*) manœuvrer; (*tool*) manier; (*pers., animal*) savoir s'y prendre avec. ¶ *v.i,* s'arranger; se débrouiller. ~ *to,* parvenir à. *can you* ~*?* tu y arrives? ~ *without sth, s.o,* se passer de qch, qn. ~**able,** *a,* (*vehicle &c*) facile à manœuvrer; (*pers., animal*) docile; (*size*) maniable. ~**ment,** *n,* gestion; direction, administration; exploitation, *f;* (*people*) cadres, *m.pl,* direction, *f.* ~ *consultant,* conseiller de gestion, *m.* **manager, ess,** *n,* (*gen.*) directeur, trice; (*hotel*) gérant, e; (*singer &c*) manager, *m.* **managing,** *a,* ~ *director,* directeur général. (*bossy*) autoritaire.

Manchuria, *n,* la Mandchourie. **Manchu[rian],** *a,* mandchou. ¶ *n,* Mandchou, e.

mandarin, *n,* mandarin, *m.*

mandarin[e] [orange], *n,* mandarine, *f.*

mandate, *n,* mandat; (*country*) pays sous mandat, *m.* **mandatory,** *a,* obligatoire; (*Pol. powers*) mandataire.

mandolin[e], *n,* mandoline, *f.*

mandrake, *n,* mandragore, *f.*

mandrill (*baboon*) *n,* mandrill, *m.*

mane, *n,* crinière, *f.*

manfully, *ad,* vaillamment.

manganese, *n,* manganèse, *m.*

mange, *n,* gale, *f.*

mangel[-wurzel] *or* **mangold[-wurzel],** *n,* betterave fourragère, *f.*

manger, *n,* mangeoire; (*Rel.*) crèche, *f.*

mangle, *n,* essoreuse [à rouleaux], *f.* ¶ *v.t,* (*wring*) essorer; (*body*) déchirer; (*text &c*) mutiler.

mango, *n,* mangue, *f.* ~ [*tree*], manguier, *m.*

mangy, *a,* galeux; (*P object*) miteux.

manhood, *n,* âge mûr, *m;* (*manliness*) virilité, *f.*

mania, *n,* manie, *f. have a* ~ *for,* avoir la manie de. **maniac,** *n,* (*Psych.*) maniaque, *m,f;* (*fig.*) fou, folle [à lier]. ¶ *a,* maniaque; fou. **manic,** *a,* maniaque. ~ *depression,* cyclothymie, *f.* ~*-depressive,* cyclothymique, *m,f.*

manicure, *n,* soin des mains, *m.* ~ *set, scissors,* trousse, ciseaux à ongles, *f, m.pl.* ¶ *v.t,* (*nails*) faire. **manicurist,** *n,* manucure, *f,m.*

manifest†, *a,* manifeste. ¶ (*Ship.*) *n,* manifeste, *m.* ¶ *v.t,* manifester. ~**ation,** *n,* manifestation, *f.*

manifesto, *n,* manifeste, *m.*

manifold, *a,* (*collection*) divers; (*duties*) multiple.

manipulate, *v.t,* manœuvrer; (*facts &c*) tripoter *P.* **manipulation,** *n,* manipulation, manœuvre, *f;* tripotage, *m.*

manliness, *n,* virilité, *f.* **manly,** *a,* mâle, viril.

manna, *n,* manne, *f.*

mannequin (*pers.*) *n,* mannequin, *m.*

manner, *n,* manière, façon; (*attitude*) attitude, *f,* comportement, *m;* (*type*) sorte, *f,* genre, *m.* ~*s,* manières; (*customs*) mœurs, *f.pl. all* ~ *of people,* toutes sortes de gens. *good, bad* ~*s,* bonnes, mauvaises manières. *comedy of* ~*s,* comédie de mœurs, *f.* ~**ed** (*style &c*) *a,* maniéré. ~**ism,** *n,* (*Art &c*) maniérisme; (*habit*) trait particulier; (*pej.*) tic, *m.* ~**ly,** *a,* poli.

mannish, *a,* masculin; (*pej.*) hommasse.

manœuvre, *n,* manœuvre, *f.* ¶ *v.i. & t,* manœuvrer.

manor, *n,* (*&* ~ *house*) manoir, *m.*

mansion, *n,* château; (*town*) hôtel particulier, *m.*

mantelpiece, mantel shelf, *n,* [tablette de] cheminée, *f.*

mantle, *n,* (*coat*) cape, *f;* (*gas, lamp*) manchon, *m.*

manual†, *a,* manuel. ¶ *n,* manuel; (*organ*) clavier, *m.*

manufacture, *n,* fabrication; (*clothes*) confection, *f.* ¶ *v.t,* fabriquer; confectionner. **manufacturer,** *n,* fabricant, *m.*

manure, *n,* fumier; (*artificial*) engrais, *m. liquid* ~, purin, *m.* ~ *heap,* tas de fumier, *m.* ¶ *v.t,* fumer, répandre des engrais sur.

manuscript, *n. & a,* manuscrit, *m.*

Manx, *a,* de l'île de Man; (*language*) mannois, *m.*

many, *a,* beaucoup (de), un grand nombre (de), bien des. ~ *a,* plus d'un. ~ *a time,* maintes fois. ~*-coloured,* multicolore. ~*-sided,* complexe. *a great, good* ~, un grand nombre (de). *as* ~ [*as*], autant [que]. *how* ~*?* combien (de)? *so* ~, tant. *the* ~, la multitude. *too* ~, trop (de).

map, *n,* carte, *f;* (*town, Rly*) plan, *m.* (*fig.*) *put a town on the* ~, faire connaître une ville. *wipe off the* ~, raser. *off the* ~, à l'autre bout du monde. ~ *maker,* cartographe, *m.* ¶ *v.t,* faire la carte, le plan de. ~ *out,* tracer; (*time*) organiser.

maple, *n,* érable, *m.*

mar, *v.t,* gâter.

maraschino, *n,* marasquin, *m.*

marathon, *n,* marathon, *m.* ¶ *a,* marathon; (*sport*) du marathon.

maraud, *v.t,* marauder. ~**er,** *n,* maraudeur, euse. ~**ing,** *n,* maraude, *f.* ¶ *a,* maraudeur.

marble, *n,* marbre, *m;* (*games*) bille, *f.* ¶ *a,* en marbre, de m.; (*industry*) marbrier. ~ *quarry,* marbrière, *f.* ¶ *v.t,* marbrer. **marbling,** *n,* marbrure, *f.*
marcasite, *n,* marcassite, *f.*
March, *n,* mars, *m.*
march, *n,* marche, *f.* ~ *past,* défilé, *m. on the* ~, en marche. ¶ *v.i,* marcher. ~ *in,* entrer. ~ *off,* se mettre en marche. ~ *out,* sortir. ~ *past,* défiler. ~ *up & down,* faire les cent pas. ¶ *v.t,* faire marcher [au pas]. ~*ing orders,* feuille de route, *f.* ~*ing song,* chanson de route, *f. give s.o his* ~*ing orders,* (*fig.*) envoyer promener qn.
marchioness, *n,* marquise, *f.*
mare, *n,* jument, *f.*
margarine, *n,* margarine, *f.*
margin, (*gen.*) marge; (*wood*) lisière, *f.* (*fig.*) *win by a wide, narrow* ~, gagner de loin, de peu. *a* ~ *of error,* une marge d'erre. ~**al,** *a,* marginal. *a* ~ *case,* un cas limite. (*Pol.*) ~ *seat,* siège disputé.
marguerite, *n,* marguerite, *f.*
marigold, *n,* souci, *m.*
marijuana, *n,* marijuana, *f.*
marine, *a,* (*life*) marin; (*products*) de mer; (*insurance*) maritime. ¶ *n,* (*Naut.*) marine, *f;* (*Mil.*) fusilier marin. *tell it to the* ~*s!* à d'autres! **mariner,** *n,* marin, *m.* ~*'s compass,* boussole marine.
marionette, *n,* marionnette, *f.*
marital, *a,* matrimonial; (*bliss*) conjugal. (*Adm.*) ~ *status,* situation de famille, *f.*
maritime, *a,* maritime.
marjoram, *n,* marjolaine, *f.*
mark, *n,* (*gen.*) marque; (*stain*) tache; (*Sch.*) note, *f,* point; (*target*) but, *m;* (*Sport*) ligne de départ, *f.* (*Tech.*) *M*~, série, *f.* (*fig.*) *make one's* ~, se faire un nom. *good, bad* ~*s,* bonnes, mauvaises notes. *on your* ~*s! get set! go!* à vos marques! prêts! partez! *get off the* ~, démarrer. *be wide of the* ~, être loin de la vérité. ¶ *v.t,* marquer; tacher; (*Stk Ex.*) coter; (*Sch.*) corriger; (*note*) noter; (*Sport*) marquer. ~ *my words,* écoutez-moi bien. ~ **down,** inscrire, noter. ~ **off,** (*on list*) cocher. ~ **out,** (*zone &c*) délimiter; (*field*) borner; (*single out*) désigner (pour). ~ **time,** (*Mil.*) marquer le pas; (*fig.*) piétiner. ~ **up,** (*price*) augmenter; (*goods*) majorer le prix de. ~**ed,** *a,* marqué; (*increase &c*) sensible. *a* ~ *man,* un homme marqué. ~**er,** *n,* (*pers.*) marqueur, euse; (*book*) signet; (*flag &c*) jalon; (*pen*) marker, *m.*
market, *n,* (*gen. & Stk Ex.*) marché, *m;* (*covered*) halles, *f.pl. find a* ~ *for,* trouver un débouché pour. *there's a good* ~ *for,* il y a une grosse demande pour. ¶ *a,* (*day &c*) de marché; (*square &c*) du marché; (*price, value*) marchand. ~ *garden,* jardin maraîcher, *m.* ~ *gardener,* maraîcher, ère. ~ *gardening,* culture maraîchère, *f.* (*Stk Ex.*) ~ *prices,* cours du marché, *m.* ¶ *v.t,* vendre; lancer sur le marché. ~**able,** *a,* vendable. ~**ing,** *n,* marketing, *m.*
marking, *n,* marquage, *m;* (*Sch.*) correction [de copies], *f;* (*on road*) signalisation horizontale. ~ *ink,* encre à marquer.
marksman, *n,* bon tireur, *m.* ~**ship,** *n,* adresse au tir, *f.*
marmalade, *n,* confiture d'orange, de citron &c, *f.*
marmoset, *n,* ouistiti, *m.*
maroon[1], *a,* (*colour*) bordeaux, *inv.*
maroon[2], *v.t,* (*on island &c*) abandonner; (*fig.*) bloquer.
marquee, *n,* grande tente, *f.*
marquet[e]ry, *n,* marqueterie, *f.*
marquis, -quess, *n,* marquis, *m.*
marriage, *n,* mariage, *m. by* ~, par alliance. *take in* ~, épouser. ~ *ceremony,* bénédiction nuptiale. ~ *certificate,* extrait d'acte de mariage, *m.* ~ *guidance counsellor,* conseiller, ère conjugal(e). ~ *licence,* dispense de bans, *f.* ~**able,** *a,* mariable, nubile. *of* ~ *age,* en âge de se marier. **married,** *a,* (*pers.*) marié; (*life*) conjugal. ~ *couple,* couple, *m.* [*newly*] ~ *couple,* nouveaux mariés, *m.pl.* ~ *name,* nom de femme mariée, *m.* ~ *quarters* (*Mil.*), appartements pour familles, *m.pl. get* ~, se marier.
marrow, *n,* moelle; (*vegetable*) courge, *f. frozen to the* ~, gelé jusqu'à la moelle des os. ~*bone,* os à moelle, *m.*
marry, *v.t,* épouser, se marier avec; (*priest, parents*) marier. ¶ *v.i,* se marier. ~ *again,* se remarier. ~ *beneath o.s,* se mésallier. ~ *into a family,* s'allier à une famille par le mariage.
Marseilles, *n,* Marseille, *f.*
marsh, *n,* marais, marécage, *m.* ~*mallow,* guimauve, *f.* ~ *marigold,* souci d'eau, *m.*
marshal, *n,* (*Mil.*) maréchal; (*Sport &c*) membre de service d'ordre, *m.* ¶ *v.t,* (*troops &c*) rassembler; (*Rly*) trier. ~*ling yard,* gare de triage, *f.*
marshy, *a,* marécageux.
marsupial, *n,* marsupial, *m.*
marten, *n,* martre, *f.*
martial, *a,* martial. ~ *law,* loi martiale.
martin, *n,* (*& house* ~) hirondelle de fenêtre, *f.*
martyr, *n,* martyr, e. ~**dom,** *n,* martyre, *m.* ~**[ize],** *v.t,* martyriser.
marvel, *n,* merveille, *f,* prodige, *m.* ¶ *v.i.* s'émerveiller, s'étonner (*at,* de; *that,* de ce que). **marvellous†,** *a,* merveilleux.
Marxism, *n,* marxisme, *m.* **Marxist,** *a. & n,* marxiste, *m,f.*
marzipan, *n,* pâte d'amandes, *f.*
mascara, *n,* mascara, *m.*
mascot, *n,* mascotte, *f,* porte-bonheur, *m.*

masculine, *a,* masculin; (*pej: woman*) hommasse. ~ [*gender*], [genre] masculin, *m.* **masculinity,** *n,* masculinité, *f.*
mash, *n,* (*Cook.*) purée; (*poultry*) pâtée, *f.* ¶ *v.t,* faire une purée de; (*gen.*) écraser. ~*d potatoes,* purée de pommes de terres, pommes mousseline.
mask, *n,* masque, *m.* ¶ *v.t,* masquer. ~*ing tape,* papier-cache adhésif.
masochism, *n,* masochisme, *m.* **masochist,** *n,* masochiste, *m,f.* **masochistic,** *a,* masochiste.
mason, *n,* maçon; (*free* ~) franc-maçon, *m.* ~**ic,** *a,* francmaçonnique. ~**ry,** *n,* maçonnerie; franc-maçonnerie, *f.*
masquerade, *n,* (*lit., fig.*) mascarade, *f.* ¶ *v.i,* ~ *as,* se faire passer pour, se déguiser en.
mass[1], *n,* masse, *f.* ~*es of P,* des masses de, des tas de. *the* ~*es,* (*people*) les masses populaires. ¶ *a,* (*culture*) de masse; (*education &c*) des masses; (*resignation*) en masse; (*hysteria &c*) collectif. ~ *grave,* fosse commune. ~ *media,* mass-media, *m.pl.* ~ *meeting,* réunion générale. ~ *murders,* tueries, *f.pl.* ~*-produce,* fabriquer en série. ~ *production,* fabrication en série. ¶ *v.t.* (*& i.*), (se) masser; (*clouds*) s'amonceler.
mass[2], *n,* (*Rel.*) messe, *f.*
massacre, *n,* massacre, *m.* ¶ *v.t,* massacrer.
massage, *n,* massage, *m.* ¶ *v.t,* masser; (*P figures*) maquiller. **masseur, euse,** *n,* masseur, euse.
massive†, *a,* massif.
mast, *n,* mât, *m;* (*pl.*) mâture, *f;* (*Radio*) pylône, *m.* ~ *head,* tête de mât, *f.*
master, *n,* (*gen.*) maître; (*Sch.*) (*secondary*) professeur; (*primary*) instituteur, maître; (*Naut.*) capitaine; (*fishing boat*) patron, *m. be one's own* ~, être son [propre] maître. (*Univ.*) *M*~ *of Arts, Science,* titulaire d'une maîtrise ès lettres, sciences. ~*'s degree,* maîtrise, *f.* ~ *of ceremonies,* maître des cérémonies. ¶ *a,* (*beam, card*) maître, esse; (*bedroom &c*) principal. ~ *builder,* entrepreneur, *m.* ~ *class,* cours de grand maître, *m.* ~ *key,* passe-partout, *m.inv.* ~ *mariner,* capitaine de la marine marchande; (*foreign going*) c. au long cours, *m.* ~*piece,* chef-d'œuvre, *m.* ~ *plan,* stratégie d'ensemble, *f.* ~ *stroke,* coup de maître, *m.* ¶ *v.t,* (*pers.; emotion*) maîtriser; (*learn*) apprendre; (*understand*) saisir. ~**ful,** *a,* dominateur, autoritaire. ~**ly,** *n,* magistral. *in a* ~ *way,* magistralement. ~**mind,** *n,* cerveau, *m.* ¶ *v.t,* diriger. ~**y,** *n,* (*skill, power*) maîtrise; (*opponent*) supériorité (sur), *f;* (*subject &c*) connaissance approfondie (de).
masticate, *v.t,* mâcher, mastiquer.
mastiff, *n,* mastiff, *m.*
mastoid, *a,* mastoïde.
masturbate, *v.i,* se masturber. **masturbation,** *n,* masturbation, *f.*
mat, *n,* (*floor*) tapis; (*door*) paillasson, *m;* (*of straw*) natte, *f;* (*table*) dessous-de-plat; (*in linen*) napperon, *m.* **matted,** *a,* (*hair*) emmêlé; (*wool*) feutré.
matador *n,* matador, *m.*
match[1], *n,* allumette, *f. put a* ~ *to,* mettre le feu à. ~*box,* boîte à allumettes, *f.*
match[2], *n,* (*Sport*) match, *m;* (*Ten. &c*) partie, *f;* (*equal*) égal, e; (*marriage*) mariage, *m.* (*colours &c*) *be a good* ~, aller bien ensemble. ~*maker,* marieur, euse. ~ *play* (*Golf*), partie par trous. ~ *point* (*Ten.*), balle de match, *f.* ¶ *v.t,* égaler; aller bien avec. ~ *against,* opposer à. *well* ~*ed,* (*opponents*) de force égale; (*couple*) bien assorti. ~ *up,* assortir. ~**less,** *a,* sans pareil.
mate, *n,* (*work &c*) camarade, *m,f;* (*P friend*) copain, ine; (*assistant*) aide, *m,f;* (*bird*) mâle, *m,* femelle, *f;* (*Naut.*) second, *m;* (*Chess*) mat, *m.* ¶ *v.t.* (*& i*), (s')accoupler (*with,* à); (*Chess*) mater.
material, *a,* (*Phys.*) matériel; (*important*) essentiel; (*relevant*) qui importe (à); (*Law*) pertinent; (*witness*) direct. ¶ *n,* (*substance*) matière, *f;* (*cloth &c*) tissu, *m,* étoffe, *f.* (*fig.*) [*officer*] ~, l'étoffe [d'un officier]. (*pl.*) fournitures, *f.pl,* articles, *m.pl. building* ~*s,* matériaux de construction, *m.pl.* (*for book &c*) matériaux, documentation, *f.* ~**ism,** *n,* matérialisme, *m.* ~**ist,** *n.* & ~**istic,** *a,* matérialiste, *m,f.* ~**ize,** *v.t.* (*& i,*) (*plan, wish*) (se) matérialiser; (*offer, loan*) (se) concrétiser. ~**ly,** *ad,* réellement; (*Philos.*) matériellement.
maternal†, *a,* maternel. **maternity,** *n.* & ~ *hospital,* maternité, *f.* ¶ *a,* (*clothes*) de grossesse.
mathematical†, *a,* mathématique; (*instruments*) de mathématiques. **mathematician,** *n,* mathématicien, ne. **mathematics,** *n.pl,* mathématiques, *f.pl.*
matinée, *n,* matinée, *f.* **matins,** = **mattins.**
matriarchy, *n,* matriarcat, *m.*
matriculate, *v.i,* s'inscrire. **matriculation,** *n,* inscription, *f.*
matrimonial†, *a,* conjugal; (*Law, agent &c*) matrimonial. ~ *triangle,* ménage à trois, *m.* **matrimony,** *n,* mariage, *m,* vie conjugale, *f.*
matrix, *n,* matrice, *f.*
matron, *n,* matrone; (*hospital &c*) infirmière en chef, *f.* ~**ly,** *a,* de matrone.
matt, *a,* mat.
matter, *n,* (*gen., Phys.*) matière, *f;* (*Med.*) pus, *m;* (*content*) fond, *m;* (*affair, concern*) affaire, question, *f. as a* ~ *of course,* automatiquement. *as a* ~ *of fact,* à vrai dire. *for that* ~, d'ailleurs. *it's no laughing* ~, il n'y a pas de quoi rire. *make* ~*s worse,* aggraver la situation. *no* ~*!* n'importe! *no* ~ *what, where,*

who, quoi, où, qui que ce soit. *no ~ what he says,* quoi qu'il dise. *there's nothing the ~,* il n'y a rien. *what's the ~?* qu'est-ce qu'il y a? *what's the ~ with him?* qu'est-ce qu'il a? *~-of-fact,* (*tone, assessment*) neutre; (*style*) prosaïque; (*pers.*) terre-à-terre. ¶ *v.i,* importer (à). *it doesn't ~,* ça ne fait rien.
Matterhorn (the), le [mont] Cervin.
matting, *n,* natte[s], *f.*[*pl.*].
mattins, *n.pl,* matines, *f.pl.*
mattress, *n,* matelas, *m.*
mature†, *a,* mûr. ¶ *v.i. & t,* mûrir; (*wine, cheese*) se faire; (*Com.*) échoir. **maturity,** *n,* maturité; échéance, *f.*
maudlin, *a,* larmoyant.
maul, *v.t,* malmener; (*tiger &c*) lacérer.
Mauritius, *n,* l'île Maurice, *f.*
mausoleum, *n,* mausolée, *m.*
mauve, *n. & a,* mauve, *m.*
maverick, *n,* (*fig: pers.*) dissident, e, franc-tireur, *m.*
mawkish, *a,* d'une sentimentalité excessive.
maxim, *n,* maxime, *f.*
maximum, *n,* maximum; plafond, *m.* ¶ *a,* maximum. *~ load,* charge limite. *~ temperature,* température maximale.
may[1], *n,* (*Bot.*) aubépine, *f.* (*month*) *M~,* mai, *m. M~ day,* le premier mai. *~fly,* éphémère, *m.*
may[2], *v. modal ir,* pouvoir, permettre. (*permission*) *you ~ go now,* vous pouvez partir. *~ I help you?* puis-je vous aider? (*in shop*) vous désirez? *~ I . . . ?* vous permettez (que je + *subj.*)? (*possibility*) *he ~ come,* il peut venir, il viendra peut-être. *it ~ be that,* il se peut que (+ *subj.*) *that's as ~ be,* c'est bien possible. *be that as it ~,* quoi qu'il en soit. *as soon as ~ be,* aussitôt que possible. *you might have told me,* vous auriez pu me le dire. *you might as well . . .* vous feriez aussi bien . . . **~be,** *ad,* peut-être.
mayonnaise, *n. & att,* mayonnaise, *f.*
mayor, *n,* maire, *m. Mr, Madam M~,* Monsieur, Madame le maire. **~ess,** *n,* femme du maire, *f.*
maze, *n,* labyrinthe, dédale, *m.*
me, *pn.* (*direct & indirect object*) me; (*emphatic & after pr.*) moi. *he can see ~,* il me voit. *he gave it to ~,* il me l'a donné. *give it to ~!* donnez-le-moi! *it's ~,* c'est moi. *he wants to see ME,* c'est moi qu'il veut voir.
meadow & (*Poet.*) **mead,** *n,* pré, *m,* prairie, *f. meadow-sweet,* reine des prés, *f.*
meagre†, *a,* maigre.
meal[1], *n,* repas, *m. ~ time,* l'heure du repas, *f. at ~ times,* aux heures de repas.
meal[2], *n,* farine [d'avoine &c], *f.* **~y,** *a,* farineux. *~-mouthed,* mielleux, doucereux.
mean[1], *a,* (*stingy*) avare (*with,* de), radin *P;* (*unkind*) mesquin, méchant; (*poor, inferior*) misérable, minable. *a ~ trick,* un sale tour.
mean[2], *n,* milieu, moyen terme, *m;* (*Math.*) moyenne, *f. ~s,* (*method, wealth*) moyens, *m.pl. by all ~s!* mais certainement! *by all manner of ~s,* par tous les moyens. *by any ~s,* n'importe comment. *by no ~s,* pas du tout. *by this ~s,* de cette façon. *live within, beyond one's ~s,* vivre selon, au-dessus de ses moyens. *~s test,* enquête sur les ressources, *f.* ¶ *a,* (*temperature &c*) moyen. [*in the*] *~ time, ~while,* en attendant.
mean[3], *v.t,* vouloir dire, signifier. *~ to do,* avoir l'intention de faire; compter, vouloir faire. (*gift &c*) destiner (*for,* à); (*remark*) adresser (*for,* à). *he ~s well,* il a de bonnes intentions. *I didn't ~* [*to do*] *it,* je ne l'ai pas fait exprès. *I ~ it!* c'est sérieux! *what do you ~ by that?* qu'entendez-vous par là?
meander, *n,* méandre, *m.* ¶ *v.i,* (*river*) serpenter; (*pers.*) errer.
meaning, *n,* (*word*) sens, *m;* (*phrase*) signification; intention, *f.* **~ful,** *a,* significatif, éloquent. **~less,** *a,* dénué de sens, sans signification; (*waste &c*) insensé.
meanness, *n,* avarice, mesquinerie, méchanceté; pauvreté, *f.*
measles, *n.pl,* rougeole, *f.*
measurable, *a,* mesurable.
measure, *n,* (*gen.*) mesure, *f;* (*tape*) mètre, *m;* (*step*) démarche, mesure, *f;* (*bill*) projet de loi, *m. I've got his ~,* je sais ce qu'il vaut. *made to ~* (*suit*), fait sur mesure. ¶ *v.t,* (*lit., fig.*) mesurer. *to be ~d for sth,* faire prendre ses mesures pour qch. *what does it ~?* quelles sont ses dimensions? *~ off, out, up,* mesurer. *~ up to, v.i,* être à la hauteur de. **~less,** *a,* incommensurable. **~ment,** *n,* mesurage, *m.* *~s,* mesures, dimensions, *f.pl.* **measuring,** *a, ~ jug,* pot gradué, *m. ~ rod,* règle, *f. ~ tape,* mètre à ruban, *m.*
meat, *n,* viande; (*fig.*) substance, *f. one man's ~ is another man's poison,* ce qui guérit l'un tue l'autre. *~ball.* boulette de viande. *f, ~-eating,* carnivore. *~ extract,* concentré de viande, *m. ~ pie,* pâté en croûte, *m. ~ safe,* garde-manger, *m.inv.* **~y,** *a,* de viande; (*fig.*) étoffé.
mechanic, *n,* mécanicien, *m.* **~al†,** *a,* mécanique; (*fig.*) machinal. *~ engineer,* ingénieur mécanicien, *m. ~ engineering,* construction mécanique; (*science*) mécanique, *f.* **mechanics,** *n.pl,* mécanique, *f.* **mechanism,** *n,* mécanisme, *m.* **mechanization,** *n,* mécanisation, *f.* **mechanize,** *v.t,* mécaniser.
medal, *n,* médaille, *f.* **medallion,** *n,* médaillon, *m.* **medallist,** *n,* médaillé, e.
meddle, *v.i,* se mêler (*in,* de), s'ingérer (dans); (*tamper*) toucher (*with,* à). **meddler,** *n,* touche-à-tout, *m.* **meddlesome,** *a,* qui touche à tout; qui fourre son nez partout.
media, *n.pl.* media, *m.pl. ~ man,* reporter, *m.*

mediaeval, *a,* médiéval, du moyen âge; (*also pej.*) moyenâgeux.
mediate, *v.i,* s'interposer (dans). ~ *between,* servir d'intermédiaire entre. ¶ *v.t,* (*peace &c*) obtenir par médiation. **mediation,** *n,* médiation, *f.* **mediator,** *n,* médiateur, trice.
medical, *a,* médical; (*school &c*) de médecine; (*student*) en médecine. ~ *officer,* médecin, *m.* ¶ *n,* (~ *examination*) visite médicale, *f.* **medicated,** *a,* traitant; médical. **medicinal,** *a,* médicinal. **medicine,** *n,* (*science*) médecine, *f;* (*drug*) médicament, *m.* ~ *cabinet,* armoire à pharmacie, *f.* ~ *man,* [sorcier] guérisseur, *m.*
medieval, = **mediaeval.**
mediocre, *a,* médiocre. **mediocrity,** *n,* médiocrité, *f.*
meditate ([up]on), *v.t. & i,* méditer (sur), contempler. **meditation,** *n,* méditation, *f.* **meditative,** *a,* méditatif.
Mediterranean, *a,* méditerranéen. **the M~ [Sea],** la [mer] Méditerranée.
medium, *a,* moyen. ~*-dry,* demi-sec. ¶ *n,* (*gen.*) milieu; (*Phys. &c*) véhicule; (*agency*) moyen, intermédiaire; (*Spiritualism*) médium, *m. the happy* ~, le juste milieu.
medlar, *n,* nèfle, *f.* ~ [*tree*], néflier, *m.*
medley, *n,* mélange; (*Mus.*) pot pourri, *m.*
meek, *a,* doux. ~ *& mild,* doux comme un agneau. ~**ly,** *ad,* avec douceur. ~**ness,** *n,* douceur, *f.*
meet (*Hunt.*) *n,* rendez-vous [de chasse], *m.* ¶ *v.t.ir,* (*gen.*) rencontrer; (*on purpose*) retrouver, rejoindre; (*danger &c*) affronter, faire face à; (*need &c*) satisfaire à; répondre à. *arrange to* ~ *s.o,* donner un rendez-vous à qn. ~ *Mr. X,* je vous présente Mr X. *pleased to* ~ *you,* enchanté [de faire votre connaissance]. ¶ *v.i.ir,* se rencontrer; se retrouver; se rejoindre; (*committee &c*) se réunir. *until we* ~ *again,* à la prochaine fois! ~ *with,* rencontrer; (*rebuff &c*) essuyer. ~**ing,** *n,* rencontre, *f;* rendez-vous, *m;* (*club &c*) réunion, *f;* (*Pol., Sport*) meeting, *m. call a* ~, convoquer une réunion. ~ *place,* lieu de réunion, *m.*
mega..., *pref,* méga... ~*cycle,* mégacycle, *m.* ~*lith,* mégalithe, *m.* ~*lithic,* mégalithique. ~*ton,* mégatonne, *f.*
megalomania, *n,* mégalomanie, *f.* ~**c,** *n. & a,* mégalomane, *m,f.*
megaphone, *n,* porte-voix, *m.*
melancholia & melancholy, *n,* mélancolie, *f.* **melancholic & melancholy,** *a,* mélancolique.
mellow, *a,* (*fruit*) mûr; (*wine, voice*) moelleux; (*colour*) doux, velouté; (*pers.*) mûri. ¶ *v.i,* mûrir; devenir moelleux; (*pers.*) s'adoucir.
melodious†, *a,* mélodieux. **melody,** *n,* mélodie, *f.*
melon, *n,* melon, *m.*
melt, *v.t.ir,* fondre; (*pers.*) attendrir. ¶ *v.i.ir,* fondre; (*sugar &c*) se dissoudre; (*fig.*) se fondre; s'attendrir. ~ *in the mouth,* fondre dans la bouche. ~ *away, v.i,* (*worry, fog*) se dissiper; (*crowd*) se disperser. ~ *down,* fondre. ~**ing,** *n,* fonte, *f.* ¶ *a,* fondant; (*fig.*) attendri. ~ *point,* point de fusion, *m.* ~ *pot,* creuset, *m.*
member, *n,* (*gen.*) membre, *m;* (*party, club*) adhérent, e. ~ *of Parliament,* député, *m.* ~ *of the public,* simple particulier, ère. ~ *of staff,* employé, e; (*Sch., Univ.*) professeur, *m.* ~**ship,** *n,* adhésion, *f;* (*numbers*) nombre de membres, *m.* ~ *fee,* cotisation, *f.*
membrane, *n,* membrane, *f.*
memento, *n,* souvenir, *m.*
memo, *n,* note, *f.* ~ *pad,* bloc-notes, *m.*
memoir, *n,* mémoire, *m;* notice biographique, *f.* ~*s,* mémoires.
memorable, *a,* mémorable. **memorandum,** *n,* mémorandum, *m,* note, *f.* **memorial,** *n,* monument, *m.* ¶ *a,* commémoratif. **memorize,** *v.t,* (*facts*) retenir; (*poem*) apprendre par cœur. **memory,** *n,* mémoire, *f;* (*recollection*) souvenir, *m. from* ~, de mémoire.
menace, *n,* menace, *f. a* ~ *to the public,* un danger public. ¶ *v.t,* menacer.
menagerie, *n,* ménagerie, *f.*
mend, *v.t,* réparer; (*clothes*) raccommoder. *to* ~ *one's ways,* s'amender. ¶ *n, to be on the* ~, s'améliorer; (*patient*) aller mieux. ~**ing,** *n,* raccommodage, *m.*
menial, *a,* servile; (*task*) inférieur; (*position*) subalterne.
meningitis, *n,* méningite, *f.*
menopausal, *a,* (*symptoms*) dû à la ménopause; (*woman*) à la ménopause. **menopause,** *n,* ménopause, *f.*
menstrual, *a,* menstruel. *pre-~ tension,* syndrome prémenstruel. **menstruate,** *v.i,* avoir ses règles. **menstruation,** *n,* menstruation, *f.*
mental, *a,* mental; (*ability*) intellectuel; (*treatment*) psychiatrique; (*P mad*) timbré *P. make a* ~ *note,* noter mentalement. ~ *arithmetic,* calcul mental. ~ *illness,* maladie mentale. ~ *institution,* hôpital psychiatrique. ~ *patient,* malade mental, e. ~ *reservations,* doutes (*about,* sur), *m.pl.* ~ *strain,* tension nerveuse. ~**ity,** *n,* mentalité, *f.* ~**ly,** *ad,* mentalement. ~ *defective,* mentalement déficient. ~ *handicapped person,* **handicapé(e) mental(e).**
menthol, *n,* menthol, *m;* (*cigarettes*) mentholé.
mention, *n,* mention, *f. make* ~ *of,* faire m. de ¶ *v.t,* mentionner, parler de, signaler; (*quote*) citer. *don't* ~ *it!* il n'y a pas de quoi! de rien! je vous en prie! *just* ~ *my name,* dites que c'est de ma part. *not to* ~...., sans compter... *without* ~*ing names,* sans citer personne.
menu, *n,* menu, *m;* carte [du jour], *f.*
mercantile, *a,* (*Naut.*) marchand; (*affairs*) commercial; (*nation*) commerçant. ~ *law,* droit commercial. ~ *marine,* marine marchande.
mercenary, *a. & n,* (*gen., Mil.*) mercenaire, *m.*

merchandise, *n*, marchandises, *f.pl.* **merchant,** *n*, négociant, e; (*shopkeeper*) commercant, e. ~ *bank,* banque de commerce, *f.* ~ *navy,* marine marchande. *wine* ~, marchand de vin; (*bigger*) négociant, *m.*
merciful†, *a,* miséricordieux, clément. **merciless†,** *a,* impitoyable.
mercurial, *a,* (*Chem.*) mercuriel; (*fig.*) vif. **mercury,** *n,* (*metal*) mercure, *m.*
mercy, *n,* pitié, indulgence; (*Rel.*) miséricorde, *f.* *at the* ~ *of,* à la merci de. *beg for* ~, demander grâce. *to have* ~ *on,* avoir pitié de. *show* ~, montrer de l'indulgence (pour, envers). *without* ~, sans pitié. ~ *killing,* euthanasie, *f.*
mere†, *a,* simple, pur, seul. *a* ~ *nothing,* une vétille. *he's a* ~ *child,* ce n'est qu'un enfant.
merge, *v.i,* (*colours &c*) se mêler (*into, with,* à); (*roads*) se rejoindre (avec); (*river*) confluer (avec); (*states*) s'unir (à); (*Com., Fin.*) & *v.t,* fusionner. **merger,** *n.* (*Com., Fin.*) fusion, *f.*
meridian, *n.* & *a,* méridien, *m.* **meridional,** *a.* & *n,* méridional, e.
meringue, *n,* meringue, *f.*
merit, *n,* mérite, *m.* ¶ *v.t,* mériter. **meritocracy,** *n,* méritocratie, *f.* **meritorious,** *a,* méritoire; (*pers.*) méritant.
mermaid, *n,* sirène, *f.* **merman,** *n,* triton, *m.*
merrily, *ad,* gaiement, joyeusement. **merriment,** *n,* gaieté, joie, hilarité, *f.* **merry,** *a,* gai, joyeux; (*P tipsy*) éméché *P. get* ~, se griser. ~ *Christmas!* joyeux Noël! *make* ~, s'amuser, se divertir. ~*-go-round,* manège, *m.* ~*-making,* réjouissances, *f.pl.*
mesh, *n.* maille, *f;* (*fabric*) tissu à mailles; (*fig.*) réseau; (*Mech.*) engrenage, *m. in* ~, en prise. ~ *tights,* collant indémaillable, *m.* ¶ *v.i,* s'engrener.
mesmerism, *n,* mesmérisme, *m.* **mesmerize,** *v.t,* hypnotiser; (*snake*) fasciner.
mess, *n,* (*object*) désordre, *m,* pagaïe *P;* (*dirt*) saleté, *f;* (*muddle*) gâchis; (*Mil.*) mess; (*Naut.*) carré, *m. be* [*in*] *a* ~, être en désordre, en pagaïe *P. get into a* ~, (*pers.*) se mettre dans de beaux draps. *make a* ~ *of,* gâcher, bousiller *P.* ~*-tin,* gamelle, *f.* ¶ *v.t,* salir, souiller. ¶ *v.i,* manger (avec). ~ *about,* perdre son temps; (*dawdle*) lambiner. ~ *up,* salir; mettre en désordre; (*hair*) ébouriffer; (*life &c*) gâcher.
message, *n,* message, *m. leave a* ~, laisser un mot. *will you give him a* ~*?* voulez-vous lui faire une commission? *to get the* ~ *P,* piger *P.* **messenger,** *n,* messager, ère; (*in office, hotel*) coursier, *m.* ~ *boy,* garçon de courses, *m.*
Messiah, *n,* Messie, *m.*
messy, *a,* sale; en désordre; (*job*) salissant; (*situation*) compliqué.
metal, *n,* métal; (*for roads*) empierrement, *m.* ¶ *v.t,* (*road*) empierrer. **metallic,** *a,* métallique. **metallurgist,** *n,* métallurgiste, *m.* **metallurgy,** *n,* métallurgie, *f.*
metamorphose, *v.t,* métamorphoser. **metamorphosis,** *n,* métamorphose, *f.*
metaphor, *n,* métaphore, *f.* ~**ical†,** *a,* métaphorique.
metaphysical, *a.* & **metaphysics,** *n.pl,* métaphysique, *f.*
mete [out], *v.t,* (*punishment*) infliger; (*reward*) décerner; (*justice*) rendre.
meteor, *n,* météore, *m.* ~**ic,** *a,* météorique; (*fig.*) fulgurant. ~**ite,** *n,* météorite, *m,f.* ~**ologic(al),** *a,* météorologique. ~**ologist,** *n,* météorologue, *m,f.* ~**ology,** *n,* météorologie, *f.*
meter, *n,* compteur, *m.*
methane, *n,* méthane, *m.*
method, *n,* (*gen.*) méthode; (*manner*) méthode, façon, *f.* ~**ical†,** *a,* méthodique. ~**ism,** *n,* méthodisme, *m.* ~**ist,** *n,* méthodiste, *m,f.* ~**ology,** *n,* méthodologie, *f.*
methyl (*Chem.*) *n,* méthyle, *m.* ~*ated spirit,* alcool à brûler, *m.*
meticulous†, *a,* méticuleux.
metre, *n,* (*all senses*) mètre, *m.* **metric & metrical,** *a,* métrique.
metronome, *n,* métronome, *m.*
metropolis, *n,* métropole, *f.* **metropolitan,** *a,* métropolitain.
mettle, *n,* fougue, *f. show one's* ~, faire ses preuves. ~**some,** *a,* fougueux.
mew, *v.i,* miauler. ~**[ing],** *n,* miaulement, *m.* **mews,** *n,* ruelle, *f.*
Mexican, *a,* mexicain. ¶ *n,* Mexicain, e. **Mexico** (*country*) *n,* le Mexique. ~ **City,** Mexico, *m.*
mezzanine, *n,* mezzanine, *f.*
mezzo-soprano, *n,* mezzo-soprano, *m.*
miaow, *n,* miaulement, *m.* ¶ *v.i,* miauler.
miasma, *n,* miasme, *m.*
mica, *n,* mica, *m.*
Michaelmas, *n,* la Saint-Michel. ~ *daisy,* aster d'automne, *m.*
mickey *P, n: take the* ~ *out of s.o,* se payer la tête de qn *P.*
micro.., *pref,* micro-. ~*chip,* microplaquette, puce, *P, f.* ~*dot,* micropoint-image, *m.* ~*film,* microfilm, *m.* ~*mesh, a,* super-fin. ~*processor,* microprocesseur, *m.* ~*wave,* micro-onde, *f.*
microbe, *n,* microbe, *m.*
microbiologist, *n,* microbiologiste, *m,f.* **microbiology,** *n,* microbiologie, *f.*
microcosm, *n,* microcosme, *m.*
microphone, *n,* microphone, *m.*
microscope, *n,* microscope, *m.* **microscopic(al),** *a,* microscopique.
mid, *a: in* ~ *air,* en plein ciel; (*fig.*) en suspens. *in* ~ *Channel,* au milieu de la Manche. *in* ~ *June,* à la mi-juin. ~*day,* midi, *m.* ~ *lent,* la

mi-carême. ~*night*, minuit, *m*. ~*riff*, diaphragme, *m*; (*dress*) taille, *f*. ~*shipman*, aspirant, midship *P*, *m*. ~*summer*, milieu de l'été, *m*. *M~summer day*, la Saint-Jean. ~*way*, à mi-chemin. *in* ~*winter*, en plein hiver.

middle, *a*, du milieu; (*size, quality*) moyen. ~-*aged*, d'un certain âge. *M~ Ages*, Moyen Age, *m*. ~-*class*, bourgeois. *the* ~ *class*[*es*], les classes moyennes, la bourgeoisie. ~ *course*, moyen terme, *m*. ~ *distance*, mi-distance; (*Art &c*) second plan, *m*. *M~ East*, Moyen-Orient, *m*. ~ *finger*, majeur, *m*. ~*man*, intermédiaire, *m*. ~*weight* (*Box*.), poids moyen, *m*. ¶ *n*, milieu, *m*; (*waist*) taille, *f*. *in the* ~ *of nowhere P*, en plein bled *P*. *right in the* ~, au beau milieu. ~-*of-the-road*, *a*, modéré.

middling†, *a*, moyen. ¶ *ad*, assez bien, comme ci comme ça.

midge, *n*, moucheron, cousin, *m*.

midget, *n*, nain, e. ¶ *a*, minuscule.

midst, *n*, *in the* ~ *of*, au milieu de, parmi.

midwife, *n*, sage-femme, *f*. **midwifery,** *n*, obstétrique, *f*.

mien, *n*, mine, *f*, air, *m*.

might¹, *v. modal*, *V* **may.** *a* ~-*have-been*, (*pers*.) un(e) raté, e.

might², *n*, puissance; force, *f*. *with* ~ *& main*, de toutes ses forces. **mightiness,** *n*, puissance; grandeur, *f*. **mighty†,** *a*, puissant; (*feat*) formidable; (*ocean*) vaste.

mignonette, *n*, (*Bot*.) réséda, *m*.

migrant, *a*, (*bird*) migrateur; (*worker*) migrant. **migrate,** *v.i*, émigrer. **migration,** *n*, migration, *f*. **migratory,** *a*, migrateur; (*journey*) migratoire.

mild†, *a*, (*gen*.) doux; (*beer, reproach &c*) léger; (*illness*) bénin; (*sauce*) peu épicé.

mildew, *n*, moisissure; (*on plants*) rouille, *f*; (*on vines*) mildiou, *m*. ~**ed,** *a*, moisi; piqué de rouille; mildiousé.

mildness, *n*, douceur; légèreté, *f*.

mile, *n*, mille [anglais], *m*. = 1·6093 km. (*50 miles = 80 km* approx.). (*long way*) lieue, *f*. *from a* ~ *off*, d'une lieue. ~ *stone*, pierre milliaire; (*Fr*.) borne kilométrique, *f*.

militant, *a*. *& n*, militant, e. **militarize,** *v.t*, militariser. **military†,** *a*. *&* ~ *man*, militaire, *m*. *the* ~, les militaires, *m.pl*. **militate,** *v.i*, militer. **militia,** *n*, milice, *f*. ~*man*, milicien, *m*.

milk, *n*, lait, *m*. ~*can*, ~*churn*, bidon à lait, *m*. ~ *chocolate*, chocolat au lait, *m*. ~ *diet*, régime lacté, *m*. ~*man*, ~*woman*, laitier, ère. ~*sop* (*pers*.), chiffe molle, *f*. ~ *tooth*, dent de lait, *f*. ¶ *v.t*, traire. ~**ing,** *n*, traite, *f*. **milky,** *a*, laiteux. *M~ Way*, voie lactée, *f*.

mill, *n*, moulin, *m*; (*Ind*.) minoterie; (*factory*) usine, fabrique, *f*; (*cotton*) filature, *f*. ~*hand*, ouvrier, ère de filatures. ~ *owner*, industriel du textile, *m*. *sea like a* ~*pond*, mer d'huile, *f*. ~*stone*, meule, *f*. (*fig*.) *a* ~*stone round one's neck*, un boulet qu'on traîne avec soi. ~*stream*, courant du bief, *m*. ¶ *v.t*, moudre; (*Tech*.) moleter; (*coin*) créneler. ~*ed edge*, crénelage, *m*. ¶ *v.i*, ~ *about*, (*fig*.) grouiller.

millennium, *n*, millénaire; (*fig*.) millénium, *m*.

millepede, *n*, mille-pattes, *m*.

miller, *n*, meunier, ère, minotier, *m*.

millet, *n*, millet, *m*.

milli.., *pref*, milli.. ~*bar*, millibar, *m*. ~*gramme*, milligramme, *m*. ~*litre*, millilitre, *m*. ~*metre*, millimètre, *m*.

milliner, *n*, modiste, *f*. ~**y,** *n*, modes, *f.pl*.

milling, *n*, moulure, *f*; moletage, *m*. ¶ *a*, (*crowd*) grouillant.

million, *n*, million, *m*. *a* ~ *men*, un million d'hommes. ~*s of P*, des milliers de *P*. **millionaire,** *n*, millionnaire, *m,f*. **millionth,** *a*. *& n*, millionième, *m*.

mime, *n*, mime, *m*. ¶ *v.i*, mimer. **mimic,** *n*, imitateur, trice. ¶ *v.t*, imiter. **mimicry,** *n*, imitation, *f*; (*Zool*.) mimétisme, *m*.

mimosa, *n*, mimosa, *m*.

mince, *n*, (*Cook*.) viande hachée, *f*. ¶ *v.t*, (*meat*) hacher. ¶ *v.i*, (*steps*) minauder. *not to* ~ *matters, one's words*, ne pas mâcher ses mots. ~*meat*, hachis de fruits secs, *m*. (*fig*.) *make* ~*meat of*, pulvériser. **mincer,** *n*, hachoir, *m*. **mincing** (*fig*.) *a*, minaudier, affété.

mind, *n*, (*gen*.) esprit, *m*; (*sanity*) raison; (*memory*) mémoire, *f*; (*opinion*) avis, *m*; (*intention*) intention, *f*. ~ *over matter*, la victoire de l'esprit sur la matière. *bear in* ~, tenir compte de. *bear it in* ~, songez-y bien. *change one's* ~, changer d'avis. *give s.o a piece of one's* ~, dire ses quatre vérités à qn. *have an open* ~, rester sans parti pris. *have in* ~, avoir l'idée. *have sth on one's* ~, être préoccupé de qch. *in the* ~*'s eye*, en imagination. *I've a good* ~ *to*, j'ai bien envie de. *let one's* ~ *wander*, laisser flotter ses pensées. *make up one's* ~, prendre une décision, se décider (*to do*, à faire). *of sound* ~, sain d'esprit. *set s.o's* ~ *at rest*, rassurer qn. *take s.o's* ~ *off sth*, changer les idées de qn. ~-*bending P*, renversant. ¶ *v.t*, (*pay attention to*) faire attention à; (*beware of*) prendre garde à; (*take charge*) garder. ~ *one's P's & Q's*, surveiller son langage; se tenir à carreau. ~*out!* attention! ~ *you... P*, remarquez... ~ *your own business*, mêlez-vous de ce qui vous regarde. *do you* ~ *if I smoke?* la fumée ne vous gêne pas? *I don't* ~, ça m'est égal. *if you don't* ~, si cela ne vous fait rien. *never* ~*!* (*don't be upset*) ne t'en fais pas!; (*no matter*) ça ne fait rien! *would you* ~ ...*?* cela vous ennuierait de...? ~**ed,** *a*, disposé (à faire). -~**ed,** *a*: *feeble-*, *healthy-*~, à l'esprit faible,

sain. ~**er,** *n,* (*child*) gardien(ne), *m,f.* ~**ful,** *a,* attentif. ~**less,** *a,* stupide, idiot.
mine[1], *pn,* le mien, la mienne, les miens, les miennes; à moi. *a friend of* ~, un de mes amis, un ami à moi.
mine[2], *n,* (*all senses*) mine, *f.* (*fig.*) *a real* ~ *of information,* une véritable mine de renseignements. *lay a* ~, poser une mine. ~*field,* champ de mines, *m.* ~ *sweeper,* dragueur de mines, *m.* ¶ *v.t,* (*Min.*) extraire; (*Mil., Naut.*) miner. **miner,** *n,* mineur, *m.* **mineral,** *a. & n,* minéral, *m.* ~ *water,* eau minérale *f;* (*soft drink*) boisson gazeuse. **mineralogist,** *n,* minéralogiste, *m,f.* **mineralogy,** *n,* minéralogie, *f.*
mingle, *v.t.* (*& i*), (se) mêler (*with,* à).
mini.., *pref,* mini... ~*bus,* minibus, *m.* ~*cab,* minitaxi, *m.* ~*skirt,* mini-jupe, *f.*
miniature, *n,* miniature, *f;* (*drink*) mini-bouteille, *f. in* ~, en miniature. ¶ *a,* [en] miniature; (*tiny*) minuscule. ~ *camera,* appareil de petit format, *m.* ~*-golf,* golf-miniature, *m.* ~ *poodle,* caniche nain. **miniaturist,** *n,* miniaturiste, *m,f.*
minim, *n,* (*Mus.*) blanche, *f.*
minimize, *v.t,* minimiser. **minimum,** *n. & a,* minimum, *m.* ~ *wage,* salaire minimum garanti, (S.M.I.G.), *m.*
mining, *n,* exploitation [de mines], *f;* (*att.*) minier. ~ *engineer,* ingénieur des mines, *m.*
minion, *n,* subordonné, e.
minister, *n,* ministre; (*Eccl.*) pasteur, *m.* ~ **to,** pourvoir à; (*pers.*) donner ses soins à; (*Eccl.*) desservir. ~**ial,** *a,* ministériel; (*benches*) de ministres. **ministration,** *n,* (*Eccl.*) ministère, *m.* ~*s,* soins, *m.pl.* **ministry,** *n,* ministère, *m. M*~ *of Health,* Ministère de Santé publique. *go into the* ~, devenir pasteur.
mink (*Zool. & fur*), *n,* vison, *m.*
minnow, *n,* vairon, *m.*
minor, *a,* (*gen., Mus., Law*) mineur; (*details, repairs, expenses*) menu; (*interest, importance*) secondaire. ~ *operation* opération bénigne. *a* ~ *role,* (*Theat., fig.*) un petit rôle. ¶ *n,* (*Law*) mineur, e; (*Am. Univ.*) matière secondaire, *f.*
Minorca, *n,* Minorque, *f.*
minority, *n,* minorité, *f. in the* ~, en minorité. ¶ *a,* minoritaire.
minstrel, *n,* (*Hist.*) ménestrel, *m.*
mint[1], *n,* [hôtel de la] Monnaie, [*m*]; (*fig.*) une *ou* des somme(s) folle(s). *in* ~ *condition,* à l'état neuf. ¶ *v.t,* (*coins*) battre; (*gold*) monnayer; (*fig.*) forger.
mint[2], *n,* (*Bot.*) menthe, *f;* (*sweet &c*) à la menthe.
minuet, *n,* menuet, *m.*
minus, *pr,* moins; (*without*) sans, avec... de moins. ~ *quantity,* (*Math.*) quantité négative. ~ *sign, n,* moins.
minute, (minit) *n,* (*time, Geog., Math.*) minute, *f;* (*fig.*) instant, *m,* minute; (*memorandum*) note, *f;* (*record*) procès-verbal, *m. any* ~ *now,* d'une minute à l'autre. *do it this* ~*!* fais-le tout de suite! *I won't be a* ~, j'en ai pour deux secondes. *up to the* ~, (*equipment*) dernier modèle; (*fashion*) d. cri, *inv;* (*news*) de dernière heure. *wait a* ~, attendez un instant. ~ *book,* registre des délibérations, *m.* ~ *hand,* grande aiguille. ~ *steak,* entrecôte minute, *f.* ¶ *v.t,* prendre note de.
minute, (mainjut) *a,* minuscule; (*change, differences*) minime, infime; (*examination, description*) minutieux. *in* ~ *detail,* dans les moindres détails. ~**ly,** *ad,* minutieusement. **minutiae,** *n.pl,* menus détails.
miracle, *n,* miracle, *m.* ~ [*play*], miracle, *m.* **miraculous†,** *a,* miraculeux.
mirage, *n,* mirage, *m.*
mire, *n,* fange, boue, *f.*
mirror, *n,* miroir, *m,* glace, *f;* (*Mot.*) rétroviseur, *m.* ~ *image,* image invertie. ¶ *v.t,* refléter.
mirth, *n,* gaieté, hilarité, *f.* ~**ful†,** *a,* joyeux, gai. ~**less,** *a,* sans gaieté.
misadventure, *n,* mésaventure, *f.*
misalliance, *n,* mésalliance, *f.*
misanthrope, -pist, *n,* misanthrope, *m,f.* **misanthropic(al),** *a,* misanthropique, misanthrope.
misapply, *v.t,* mal employer; (*money*) détourner.
misapprehend, *v.t,* mal comprendre. **misapprehension,** *n,* malentendu, *m.*
misappropriate, *v.t,* détourner.
misbehave [oneself], se comporter mal. **misbehaviour,** *n,* mauvaise conduite, inconduite, *f.*
miscalculate, *v.i,* se tromper. **miscalculation,** *n,* erreur de calcul, *f.*
miscarriage, *n,* (*letter &c*) égarement, *m;* (*Med.*) fausse couche, *f;* (*failure*) avortement, insuccès, *m.* ~ *of justice,* erreur judiciaire, *f.* **miscarry,** *v.i,* s'égarer; (*Med.*) faire une fausse couche; (*fail*) avorter, échouer, rater.
miscellaneous, *a,* divers. **miscellany,** *n,* (*objects*) collection, *f;* (*Liter.*) recueil, *m;* (*Radio, TV*) sélection, *f.*
mischance, *n,* malchance, *f. by* [*a*] ~, par malheur.
mischief, *n,* (*naughtiness*) sottises, *f.pl;* (*playful*) espièglerie; (*maliciousness*) méchanceté, *f;* (*P child*) polisson, ne. *do o.s a* ~, se faire mal. *get into* ~, faire des sottises. *make* ~, créer des ennuis (à qn). ~*-maker,* (*gossip*) mauvaise langue. **mischievous†,** *a,* méchant; espiègle.
misconceive, *v.t,* mal comprendre. ¶ *v.i,* se tromper. **misconception,** *n,* malentendu, *m.*
misconduct, *n,* inconduite, *f;* (*sexual*) adultère, *m.*
misconstruction, *n,* fausse interprétation. **mis-**

construe, *v.t,* mal interpréter.
miscount, *n,* mécompte, *m;* (*in election*) erreur dans le compte, *f.* ¶ *v.t. & i,* mal compter.
misdeal (*Cards*) *n,* maldonne, *f.*
misdeed, *n,* méfait, *m.*
misdemeanour, *n,* incartade; (*Law*) infraction, *f.*
misdirect, *v.t,* (*letter &c*) mal adresser; (*pers.*) mal renseigner; (*effort*) mal diriger; (*operation*) mener mal; (*jury*) mal instruire.
miser, *n. &* ~**ly,** *a,* avare, *m,f.*
miserable†, *a,* (*unhappy*) malheureux, triste; (*deplorable*) lamentable; (*wretched*) misérable; (*weather*) sale *P;* (*contemptible*) dérisoire. **misery,** *n,* (*unhappiness*) tristesse, *f;* (*suffering*) souffrances, *f.pl,* (*wretchedness*) misère, *f;* (*pers: child*) pleurnicheur, euse *P;* (*adult*) grincheux, euse.
misfire, *v.i,* rater; (*joke*) tomber à plat; (*Mot.*) avoir des ratés.
misfit, *n,* (*dress*) vêtement manqué; (*fig: pers.*) inadapté, e.
misfortune, *n,* malheur, *m,* infortune, *f.*
misgiving[s], *n.[pl],* crainte[s], *f.[pl],* doute[s], *m.[pl],* appréhension, *f.*
misgovern, *v.t,* mal gouverner. ~**ment,** *n,* mauvais gouvernement, *m.*
misguided, *a,* (*pers.*) abusé; (*attempt*) malencontreux; (*action*) peu judicieux.
mishandle, *v.t,* (*pers.*) maltraiter; (*object*) manier sans précaution; (*problem*) mal traiter.
mishap, *n,* contretemps, *m,* mésaventure, *f.*
mishear, *v.t,* mal entendre.
misinform, *v.t,* mal renseigner.
misinterpret, *v.t,* mal interpréter. ~**ation,** *n,* contresens, *m.*
misjudge, *v.t,* (*amount, time*) mal évaluer; (*underestimate*) sous-estimer; (*pers.*) méjuger.
mislay, *v.t,* égarer.
mislead, *v.t,* tromper. ~**ing,** *a,* trompeur.
mismanage, *v.t,* mal gérer. ~**ment,** *n,* mauvaise gestion, *f.*
misnamed, *a,* mal nommé.
misnomer, *n,* erreur de nom, *f.*
misogynist, *n,* misogyne, *m.*
misplace, *v.t,* mal placer.
misprint, *n,* faute d'impression, erreur typographique, coquille, *f.*
mispronounce, *v.t,* mal prononcer. **mispronunciation,** *n,* mauvaise prononciation.
misquotation, *n,* citation inexacte, *f.* **misquote,** *v.t,* citer à faux.
misrepresent, *v.t,* dénaturer. ~**ation,** *n,* déformation, *f.*
misrule, *n,* mauvaise administration, *f.*
miss[1], *n,* (*shot*) coup manqué *ou* raté; (*Bil.*) manque à toucher, *m. that was a near* ~, il s'en est fallu d'un cheveu. *have a near* ~, échapper belle. *give* (*s.o, sth*) *a* ~, passer le tour de (qn, qch); (*lecture &c*) ne pas assister à. (*sight*) négliger de voir. ¶ *v.t. & i,* manquer, rater; (*omit: page &c*) sauter; (*avoid*) échapper (à); (*long for*) regretter. ~ *the boat P,* manquer le coche *P. I do* ~ *her,* elle me manque beaucoup. *to* ~ *one's footing,* glisser. *you're* ~*ing the point,* vous n'y êtes pas. ~ *out on,* laisser passer; louper *P.*
miss[2], *n,* mademoiselle, *f.* (*on letter*) *M*~ *X,* Mademoiselle *ou* Mlle X. *Dear M*~ *X,* chère Mademoiselle. *modern* ~, jeune fille moderne.
missal, *n,* missel, *m.*
misshapen, *a,* contrefait, difforme.
missile, *n,* projectile; (*Mil.*) missile, *m.* ~ *launcher,* lance-missiles, *m. inv.*
missing, *a,* (*pers.*) absent; (*object*) manquant; (*lost*) perdu; (*Mil.*) disparu. (*Police*) ~ *person,* personne absente. *to be* ~, manquer.
mission, *n,* mission, *f.* ~**ary,** *n,* missionnaire, *m,f.* **missive,** *n,* missive, *f.*
misspell, *v.t,* mal orthographier. ~**ing,** *n,* faute d'orthographe, *f.*
misspend, *v.t,* gaspiller. *misspent youth,* folle jeunesse.
misstatement, *n,* rapport inexact, *m.*
mist, *n,* brume; (*on glass*) buée, *f;* (*before eyes*) brouillard; (*tears, ignorance*) voile; (*perfume &c*) nuage, *m. in the* ~*s of time,* dans la nuit des temps. ¶ *v.t.* (*& i*), (*eyes, mirror*) (s')embuer; (*landscape*) se couvrir de brume.
mistake, *n,* erreur, faute; (*misunderstanding*) méprise, *f. by* ~, par erreur. *make a* ~, se tromper. ¶ *v.t,* (*meaning*) mal comprendre; (*intentions*) se méprendre sur; (*time &c*) se tromper de; (*voice*) ne pas reconnaître; (*2 people*) confondre. **mistaken,** *a,* erroné; (*generosity*) mal placé. ~ *identity,* erreur d'identité. *in the* ~ *belief that,* croyant à tort que.
mister, *n,* monsieur, *m.*
mistletoe, *n,* gui, *m.*
mistranslation, *n,* contresens, *m.*
mistreat, *v.t,* maltraiter. ~**ment,** *n,* mauvais traitement.
mistress, *n,* (*gen.*) maîtresse; (*Sch: primary*) maîtresse, institutrice, *f;* (*secondary*) professeur, *m.*
mistrust, *n,* méfiance, *f.* ¶ *v.t,* se méfier de. ~**ful,** *a,* méfiant.
misty, *a,* brumeux; (*windscreen, eyes &c*) embué; (*fig: idea &c*) nébuleux.
misunderstand, *v.t.ir,* mal comprendre. ~**ing,** *n,* erreur, *f;* (*disagreement*) malentendu, *m.* **misunderstood** (*pers.*) *a,* incompris.
misuse, *n,* abus, *m.* ¶ *v.t,* abuser de; (*word, tool*) employer incorrectement; (*time, resources &c*) mal employer; (*funds*) détourner.
mite, *n,* (*small amount*) grain, atome, *m;* (*child*) petit, e; (*Zool.*) mite, *f. the widow's* ~, le

denier de la veuve.
mitigate, *v.t,* atténuer. *mitigating circumstances,* circonstances atténuantes. **mitigation,** atténuation, *f.*
mitre, *n,* (*bishop's*) mitre, *f;* (*Carp.*) onglet, *m.* ~**d,** *a,* mitré; (*Carp.*) à onglet.
mitt[en], *n,* (*no separate fingers*) moufle; (*cut-off fingers*) mitaine, *f.*
mix, *n,* mélange, *f.* ~*-up,* confusion, *f.* ¶ *v.t.* (& *i*), (se) mêler, mélanger; (*metals*) (s')allier; (*cement*) malaxer; (*Cook., drink*) préparer; (*salad*) retourner. ~ *in,* incorporer (*with,* à). ~ *up,* (*prepare*) mélanger, préparer; (*in disorder*) mêler; (*confuse*) confondre (avec); (*muddle*) embrouiller. ~*ing bowl,* terrine, *f,* grand bol, saladier, *m.* ~**ed,** *a,* (*gen.*) mixte; (*nuts &c*) assorti; (*feelings*) contradictoires; (*motives*) complexe; (*weather*) variable. ~ *doubles* (*Ten.*), double mixte, *m.* ~ *farming,* polyculture, *f.* ~**er,** *n,* (*Cook.*) batteur [électrique], *m;* (*Ind: liquid*) agitateur, *m. cement* ~, bétonnière, *f.* ~ *tap,* robinet mélangeur. **mixture,** *n,* mélange; (*Med.*) préparation, mixture, *f.*
mnemonic, *a,* mnémonique.
moan, *n,* gémissement, *m;* (*complaint*) plainte, *f.* ¶ *v.i,* gémir; se plaindre.
moat, *n,* fossé, *m.*
mob, *n,* foule; (*disorderly*) cohue, *f;* (*rioting*) émeutiers, *m.pl;* (*pej.*) populace; (*P group*) bande, *f;* (*criminal*) gang, *m.* ~ *rule,* la loi de la populace. ¶ *v.t,* (*pers.*) assaillir; (*place*) assiéger.
mobile, *a,* mobile. **mobility,** *n,* mobilité, *f.* **mobilization,** *n,* mobilisation, *f.* **mobilize,** *v.t.* & *i,* mobiliser.
mocha, *n,* moka, *m.*
mock, *a,* (*leather &c*) imitation, *inv. before n,* faux, *before n;* (*anger &c*) feint. ~ *battle,* simulacre de bataille, *m.* ~ *exam,* examen blanc. ¶ *v.t,* (*ridicule*) ridiculiser; (*laugh at*) se moquer de; (*mimic*) singer. ~*-up,* maquette, *f.* ~**er,** *n,* moqueur, euse. ~**ery,** *n,* moquerie, *f. make a* ~ *of,* tourner en dérision. ~*ing bird,* moqueur, *m.*
mode, *n,* (*way, fashion*) mode, *f;* (*form, method*) mode, *m.*
model, *n,* (*gen.*) modèle, *m;* (*Tech., Arch. &c*) maquette, *f;* (*fashion*) mannequin, *m;* (*att.*) modèle. ¶ *v.t,* modeler (*in,* en, *on,* sur). ¶ *v.i,* (*Art &c*) poser (pour); (*fashion*) être mannequin (*for,* chez). **modeller,** *n,* modeleur, *m.* **modelling,** *n,* modelage, *m.*
moderate, *a,* (*gen.*) modéré; (*climate*) tempéré; (*language, terms*) mesuré. ~*-sized,* de grandeur (grosseur, taille) moyenne. ¶ *v.t.* (& *i*), (se) modérer. ~**ly,** *ad,* modérément. **moderation,** *n,* modération, *f.*
modern, *a.* & *n,* moderne, *m. all* ~ *conveniences,* tout confort. ~ *language,* langue vivante, *f.* ~**ization,** *n,* modernisation, *f.* ~**ize,** *v.t,* moderniser.
modest†, *a,* modeste. ~**y,** *n,* modestie; (*demand &c*) modération; (*price &c*) modicité, *f.*
modicum, *n,* petite quantité; légère dose, *f,* grain, *m.*
modification, *n,* modification, *f.* **modify,** *v.t,* modifier.
modish, *a,* à la mode, de mode. ~**ly,** *ad,* à la mode.
modular, *a,* modulaire.
modulate, *v.t,* moduler. **modulation,** *n,* modulation, *f.* **module** & **modulus,** *n,* module, *m.*
mogul, *n,* manitou, *m.*
mohair, *n,* mohair, *m.*
Mohammedan, *n.* & *a,* mahométan, e. ~**ism,** *n,* mahométisme, *m.*
moist, *a,* humide; (*atmosphere*) moite; (*cake*) moelleux. ~**en,** *v.t,* humecter; mouiller. ~**ness** & ~**ure,** *n,* humidité; moiteur; (*on glass &c*) buée, *f.*
molar, *a.* & *n,* molaire, *f.*
molasses, *n,* mélasse, *f.*
mole, *n,* grain de beauté; (*jetty*) môle, *m;* (*Zool.*) taupe, *f.* ~ *hill,* taupinière, *f.*
molecular, *a,* moléculaire. **molecule,** *n,* molécule, *f.*
molest, *v.t,* (*torment*) importuner, tracasser; (*harm*) molester, brutaliser; (*Law: sexually*) attenter à la pudeur de. ~**ation,** *n,* tracasseries; brutalités, *f.pl;* attentat à la pudeur, *m.*
mollify, *v.t,* apaiser, calmer.
mollusc, *n,* mollusque, *m.*
mollycoddle, *v.t,* chouchouter.
molten, *a,* fondu, en fusion.
moment, *n,* moment; instant, *m;* (*importance*) importance, *f. a* ~ *ago,* il y a un instant. *at this* ~ *in time,* à l'heure qu'il est. *for a* ~, un instant. *not for a* ~, jamais de la vie. ~**ary†,** *a,* momentané, passager. ~**ous,** *a,* de la dernière importance. **momentum,** *n,* (*Mech.*) moment; (*impetus*) élan, *m.*
monarch, *n,* monarque, *m.* ~**ic(al),** *a,* monarchique. ~**ist,** *n,* monarchiste, *m,f.* ~**y,** *n,* monarchie, *f.*
monastery, *n,* monastère, *m.* **monastic,** *a,* monastique, monacal.
Monday, *n,* lundi, *m.*
monetary, *a,* monétaire.
money, *n,* argent, *m;* (*familiar*) sous, *m.pl,* fric *P, m;* (*Fin.*) monnaie, *f.* (*Law*) ~*s,* sommes d'argent, *f.pl. public* ~*s,* deniers publics. ~ *doesn't grow on trees,* l'argent ne se trouve pas sous le pas d'un cheval. ~ *talks,* l'argent est roi. *get one's* ~ *back,* être remboursé. *make good* ~, gagner gros. *to be rolling in* ~ *P,* rouler sur l'or *P.* ~*box,* tirelire, *f.* ~ *changer,* changeur, *m.* ~*grubber,* ~*grubbing,* grippe-sou, *a.* & *m.* ~*-lender,* prêteur, euse sur gages. ~*making, a,* lucratif. ~

market, marché monétaire, *m.* ~ *order,* mandat, *m.* ~ *spider,* araignée porte-bonheur, *f.* ~ *spinner,* mine d'or, *f.* ~**ed,** *a,* riche, cossu, argenté *P.*

monger, *n,* marchand, *m* de...

Mongolia, *n,* la Mongolie. **Mongol[ian],** *a,* mongol. (*Med.*) *m*~, mongolien. ¶ *n,* Mongol, e; (*Med.*) mongolien, ne. **mongolism,** *n,* (*Med.*) mongolisme, *m.*

mongoose, *n,* mangouste, *f.*

mongrel, *a.* & *n,* (*dog*) bâtard, *m.*

monitor, *n,* moniteur, *m;* (*Radio: pers.*) rédacteur, trice. ¶ *v.t,* contrôler.

monk, *n,* moine, religieux, *m.* ~*'s-hood* (*Bot.*), aconit, *m.*

monkey, *n,* singe, *m,* (*she*) guenon, *f;* (*fig: child*) polisson, ne. ~ *business,* fricotage, *m;* qch de louche. ~ *house,* singerie, *f.* ~ *nut,* arachide, cacahouète, *f.* ~ *puzzle,* araucaria, *m.* ~ *wrench,* clef anglaise. ¶ *v.i,* ~ *about,* faire l'idiot.

mono... *pref,* mono... ~**chrome,** *a,* monochrome. **monocle,** *n,* monocle, *m.* ~**gamous,** *a,* monogame. ~**gamy,** *n,* monogamie, *f.* ~**gram,** *n,* monogramme, *m.* ~**graph,** *n,* monographie, *f.* ~**lingual,** *a,* monolingue. ~**lith,** *n,* & ~**ic,** *a,* monolithe, *m.* ~**logue,** *n,* monologue, *m.* ~**mania,** *n,* monomanie, *f.* ~**phonic,** *a,* monophonique, monaural. ~**plane,** *n,* monoplan, *m.* ~**polist,** *n,* accapareur, euse. ~**polize,** *v.t,* monopoliser. ~**poly,** *n,* monopole; (*game*) Monopoly, *m.* ~**rail,** *n,* monorail, *m.* ~**syllabic,** *a,* monosyllabique, monosyllabe. ~**syllable,** *n,* monosyllabe, *m.* ~**tonous,** *a,* monotone. ~**tony,** *n,* monotonie, *f.*

monsoon, *n,* mousson, *f.*

monster, *n.* & *a,* monstre, *m.*

monstrosity, *n,* monstruosité, *f.* **monstrous†,** *a,* monstrueux; (*huge*) gigantesque.

month, *n,* mois, *m.* ~*'s pay, rent &c,* mois, *m. to be paid by the* ~, être payé au mois *ou* mensualisé. **monthly,** *a,* mensuel; au mois. ~ *payment, drawing, salary &c,* mensualité, *f.* ~ *period,* règles, *f.pl.* ~ *statement* (*Com.*), relevé de fin de mois, *m.* ¶ *ad,* mensuellement, par mois. ¶ *n,* revue mensuelle, *f.*

monument, *n,* monument, *m.* ~**al,** *a,* monumental. ~ *mason,* marbrier, *m.*

moo, *v.i,* beugler. ¶ *n,* beuglement, *m.*

mooch about *P, v.i,* traînasser.

mood, *n,* humeur, disposition, *f;* (*Gram.*) mode, *m. in no* ~ *for, to,* pas d'humeur à. *the* ~ *of the meeting,* l'état d'esprit de l'assemblée. ~**y,** *a,* (*variable*) d'humeur changeante; (*sulky*) maussade.

moon, *n,* lune, *f.* ~*beam,* rayon de l., *m.* ~ *landing,* alunissage, *m.* ~*light,* clair de l., *m.* ~*light flit,* déménagement à la cloche de bois, *m.* ~*lighting P,* travail noir. ~*lit,* éclairé par la l. ~*shine,* balivernes, *f.pl;* (*Am. spirits*) alcool de contrebande, *m.* ~*stone,* pierre de lune, *f.* ~*struck,* dans la lune. ~ **[about],** muser.

moor[1], *n,* lande, *f.* ~*hen,* poule d'eau, *f.* ~*land,* bruyère, *f.*

moor[2], *v.t,* (*ship*) amarrer. ¶ *v.i,* mouiller. ~**ing,** *n,* (*place*) mouillage, *m;* (*ropes &c*) amarres, *f.pl.* ~ *buoy,* bouée de corps-mort, *f.*

moose, *n,* élan, *m.*

moot, *a,* discutable. ¶ *v.t,* soulever.

mop, *n,* (*floor*) vadrouille, *f;* balai-éponge, *m;* (*dishes*) lavette, *f;* (*of hair*) tignasse, *f.* ¶ *v.t,* éponger. ~ *up,* essuyer, éponger; (*Mil.*) nettoyer.

mope, *v.i,* avoir le cafard, *P.* ~ *around,* traîner son ennui.

moral†, *a,* moral. ¶ *n,* (*of story*) morale; (*pl, standards*) moralité, *f;* (*pl, ethics*) morale, *f.* ~**[e],** *n,* moral, *m.* ~**ist,** *n,* moraliste, *m.* ~**ity,** *n,* moralité, *f.* ~**ize,** *v.i.* & *t,* moraliser.

morass, *n,* marais, marécage, *m.*

moratorium, *n,* moratorium, moratoire, *m.*

morbid, *a,* morbide; (*fear, dislike*) maladif.

more, *a.* & *pn,* plus [de], davantage [de]; (*additional*) encore du, de la &c; (*other*) d'autres. *let's say no* ~ *about it,* n'en parlons plus. *the* ~ *the merrier,* plus on est de fous plus on rit. ¶ *ad,* plus, davantage. ~ *important,* plus important. *he sleeps* ~ *than you,* il dort plus *ou* davantage que vous. ~ *or less,* plus ou moins. *once* ~, encore une fois. *he doesn't live here any* ~, il n'habite plus ici. ~**over,** *ad,* d'ailleurs, aussi bien, en outre, du reste, encore.

morgue, *n,* morgue, *f.*

moribund, *a,* moribond.

morning & (*Poet.*) **morn,** *n,* matin, *m;* matinée, *f. during the* ~, pendant la matinée. *in the* ~, (*tomorrow*) demain matin. *the next* ~, le lendemain matin. *the* ~ *before,* la veille au matin. ~ *coat,* jaquette, *f.* ~*-glory,* belle-de-jour, *f.* ~ *sickness,* nausée du matin, *f.* ~ *star,* étoile du matin, *f.*

Moroccan, *a,* marocain. ¶ *n,* Marocain, e. **Morocco,** *n,* le Maroc. *morocco* [*leather*], maroquin, *m.*

morose, *a,* morose.

morphia, -phine, *n,* morphine, *f.*

morphology, *n,* morphologie, *f.*

morsel, *n,* morceau, *m.*

mortal†, *a,* mortel; (*strife*) à mort. ¶ *n,* mortel, le. ~**ity,** *n,* mortalité, *f.*

mortar (*plaster, vessel, Mil.*) *n,* mortier, *m.*

mortgage, *n,* hypothèque, *f.* ¶ *v.t,* hypothéquer. **mortgagee,** *n,* créancier hypothécaire, *m.* **mortgagor,** *n,* débiteur h., *m.*

mortification, *n,* mortification, *f.* **mortify,** *v.t,* mortifier.

mortise, -ice, *n,* mortaise, *f.* ~ *lock,* serrure

encastrée.
mortuary, *a,* mortuaire. ¶ *n,* institut médico-légal, *m,* morgue, *f.*
mosaic, *n,* mosaïque, *f.*
Moslem, *n. & a,* musulman, e.
mosque, *n,* mosquée, *f.*
mosquito, *n,* moustique, *m.* ~ *net,* moustiquaire, *f.*
moss, *n,* mousse, *f.* ~ *rose,* rose moussue, *f.* ~ *stitch,* point de riz, *m.* ~**y,** *a,* moussu.
most, *a. & pn,* le plus [de], la plus grande quantité [de]; (*greater part*) la plus grande partie [de]; (*majority*) la plupart [des]; la majorité [des]. *at the* [*very*] ~, au maximum. *for the* ~ *part,* pour la plupart. *in* ~ *cases,* dans la majorité des cas. *make the* ~ *of,* (*time*) bien employer; (*opportunity &c*) bien profiter de; (*talents &c*) tirer le meilleur parti de; (*resources*) utiliser au mieux. ¶ *ad,* le plus; (*very*) bien, très. ~ *likely,* très probablement. ~**ly,** *ad,* pour la plupart; (*chiefly*) surtout.
motel, *n,* motel, *m.*
moth, *n,* papillon [de nuit], *m;* (*clothes*) mite, *f.* ~*-eaten,* mangé aux mites, mité.
mother, *n,* mère, *f.* ~*-in-law,* belle-mère, *f.* ~ *of pearl,* nacre, *f.* ~ *'s side* (*family*), côté maternel, *m.* ~ *superior,* mère supérieure, *f. M* ~*'s Day,* la fête des Mères. ~*-to-be,* future maman. ~ *tongue,* langue maternelle. ¶ *v.t,* servir de mère à; (*cosset*) dorloter. ~**less,** *a,* sans mère. ~**ly,** *a,* maternel, de mère.
motif, *n,* (*Art, Need.*) motif, *m.* **motion,** *n,* mouvement, *m,* marche, *f;* (*proposal*) motion; proposition; (*Med.*) selle, *f.* ¶ *v.i,* faire signe. ~**less,** *a,* sans mouvement, immobile. **motivate,** *v.t,* (*act*) motiver; (*pers.*) pousser (à faire). **motivation,** *n,* motivation, *f.* **motive,** *a,* moteur. ~ *power,* force motrice, *f.* ¶ *n,* raison, *f;* motif; (*Law*) mobile, *m.* ~**less,** *a,* immotivé.
motley, *a,* bariolé, bigarré; (*collection*) hétéroclite.
motor, *n,* moteur, *m.* ~*-assisted,* à moteur. ~*bike,* moto, *f.* ~*boat,* canot automobile, *f.* ~ *car,* auto, voiture, *f.* ~ *coach,* car, *m.* ~*cycle,* motocyclette; (*smaller*) mobylette, *f.* ~*cycling,* motocyclisme, *m.* ~*cyclist,* motocycliste, *m,f.* ~ *insurance,* assurance-automobile, *f.* ~ *mechanic,* mécanicien garagiste, *m.* ~ *mower,* tondeuse à moteur, *f.* ~ *racing,* course automobile, *f.* ~ *scooter,* scooter, *m.* ~ *show,* exposition d'autos, *f. the M* ~ *Show,* le Salon de l'Automobile. ~ *vehicle,* véhicule automobile, *m.* ~ *vessel,* navire à moteur, motorship, *m.* ~*way,* autoroute, *f.* ¶ *a,* (*accident*) de voiture; (*nerve*) moteur. ¶ *v.t,* conduire &c en auto. ¶ *v.i,* aller &c en auto. ~**ing,** *n,* tourisme automobile, *m;* (*att. holiday*) en voiture. ~**ist,** *n,* automobiliste, *m,f.* ~**ize,** *v.t,* motoriser.
mottled, *a,* tacheté; (*horse, sky*) pommelé; (*complexion*) brouillé.
motto, *n,* devise, *f.*
mould[1], *n,* moule, *m.* ¶ *v.t,* (*clay*) mouler; (*figure*) modeler (*in, out of,* en); (*fig; character &c*) former.
mould[2], *n,* moisissure, *f;* (*soil*) terreau, *m.* ~**er,** *v.t,* moisir, tomber en poussière.
moulding, *n,* moulure, *m.*
mouldy, *a,* moisi; (*P fig.*) moche *P.*
moult, *v.i,* muer, se déplumer. ~[**ing**], *n,* mue, *f.*
mound, *n,* tertre, *m;* (*Archeol.*) t. artificiel.
mount, *n,* mont, *m;* montagne, *f;* (*for photo &c*) carton de montage, *m;* (*horse &c*) monture, *f. M* ~ *Etna,* le mont E. ¶ *v.t. & i,* monter. ~ *up,* (*increase*) monter; s'accumuler.
mountain, *n,* montagne, *f.* ¶ *a,* (*people*) montagnard; (*gen.*) de montagne. ~ *ash,* sorbier, *m.* ~ *range,* chaîne de montagnes, *f.* ~**eer,** *n,* alpiniste, *m,f.* ~**eering,** *n,* alpinisme, *m.* ~**ous,** *a,* montagneux; (*fig.*) énorme.
mounted, *a,* à cheval; monté.
mourn, *v.t. & i,* pleurer. **the** ~**ers,** le cortège funèbre. ~**ful**†, *a,* lugubre; (*pers.*) mélancolique. ~**ing,** *n,* deuil, *m.* ~ *band,* crêpe, *m.* ~ [*clothes*], vêtements de deuil, *m.pl.*
mouse, *n,* souris, *f.* ~ *trap,* souricière, *f.*
mousse, *n,* mousse, *f.*
moustache, *n,* moustache(s), *f.*(*pl*). ~**d,** *a,* moustachu.
mouth, *n,* bouche; (*animal*) gueule; (*river*) embouchure; (*sack*) ouverture; (*cave &c*) entrée, *f;* (*bottle*) goulot, *m. a big* ~ *P,* une grande gueule *P. with one's* ~ *wide open,* bouche bée. ~ *organ,* harmonica, *m.* ~*piece,* (*Mus.*) embouchure, *f,* bec, *m;* (*Tel.*) microphone, *m;* (*pers.*) porte-parole, *m. inv.* ~*wash,* eau dentifrice, *f.* ~*-watering,* qui met l'eau à la bouche. ~**ful,** *n,* bouchée; (*liquid*) gorgée *f.*
movable, *a,* mobile; (*Law*) meuble, mobilier. **move,** *n,* mouvement; (*change of house*) déménagement; (*change of job*) changement d'emploi, *m;* (*within an organization*) mutation, *f;* (*Chess &c*) coup, *m. whose* ~ *is it?* à qui à jouer? ¶ *v.t,* (*object*) changer de place, déplacer; (*limbs*) remuer; (*troops &c*) transporter; (*Chess &c*) jouer; (*employee*) muter; (*fig.*) pousser, inciter (qn à faire); (*emotionally*) émouvoir; (*Adm. &c*) proposer. *to* ~ *house,* déménager. *to* ~ *to pity,* attendrir. ¶ *v.i,* bouger; (*go*) aller, se déplacer; (*clouds*) passer; (*act*) agir; (*progress*) avancer. *don't* ~*!* ne bougez pas! ~ **about,** (*fidget*) remuer; (*travel*) voyager; *v.t,* (*object*) déplacer. ~ **along,** (faire) avancer. ~ **away,** (s')éloigner; (*house*) déménager. ~ **back,** reculer; (*return*) retourner, revenir; faire reculer. ~ **down,** descendre. ~ **forward,** avancer; faire avancer. ~ **in,** emménager; faire entrer; (*goods*

&c) rentrer. ~ **off,** (*pers.*) s'éloigner; (*car*) démarrer; (*train &c*) s'ébranler ~ **on!** circulez! ~ **out,** déménager. ~ **over!** pousse-toi! ~**ment,** *n,* mouvement, *m.* **moving,** *a,* (*touching*) émouvant. ~ *part,* (*Mech.*) pièce mobile, *f.* ~ *staircase,* escalier roulant.

mow, *v.t.ir,* faucher; (*turf*) tondre. ~ *down,* faucher. ~**er,** *n,* (*pers.*) faucheur, *m;* (*Mach.*) faucheuse; (*lawn*) tondeuse, *f.*

Mr, Monsieur, M.; (*courtesy title of lawyers*) maître, *m.* **Mrs,** Madame, Mme; (*Law*) la dame.

much, *a, pn,* beaucoup (de); (*with neg.*) grand-chose. *as* ~, autant (de). *as* ~ *as,* autant que. *how* ~*?* combien (de)? *it's not up to* ~, ça ne vaut pas grand-chose. *make* ~ *of,* faire grand cas de. *so* ~ tant (de). *they're* ~ *of a muchness,* c'est blanc bonnet & bonnet blanc. *too* ~, trop (de). ¶ *ad,* (*& very* ~) beaucoup, bien, très. ~ *the same,* presque le même. *it doesn't matter* ~, cela ne fait pas grand-chose. *so* ~ *so that,* à tel point que. *too* ~, trop.

muck, *n,* (*manure*) fumier, *m;* (*dog*) crotte; (*mud*) boue, *f;* (*dirt*) saletés; (*fig.*) ordures, cochonneries, *f.pl. make a* ~ *of P,* saloper *P.* (*fig.*) ~ *raking,* remuage de boue, *m.* ~*-up,* gâchis, *m.* ¶ *v.i.* ~ *about,* faire l'idiot. ~ *in P,* (*help*) mettre la main à la pâte *P.* ¶ *v.t,* ~ *out,* nettoyer. ~ *up P,* (*spoil*) gâcher; (*dirty*) salir. ~**y,** *a,* boueux; crotté.

mucous, *a,* muqueux. ~ *membrane,* [membrane] muqueuse, *f.* **mucus,** *n,* mucus, *m.*

mud, *n,* boue, *f. sling* ~ *at,* (*fig.*) couvrir de boue. *stuck in the* ~, embourbé. ~*bank,* banc de vase, *m.* ~*bath,* bain de boue, *m.* ~ *flap,* pare-boue, *m.* ~*flat*[*s*], laisse de vase, *f.* ~*guard,* garde-boue, *m.inv.* ~ *hut,* hutte de terre, *f.* ~*pack,* masque de beauté, *m.* ~ *pie,* pâté, *m.*

muddle, *n,* (*mix-up*) confusion, *f,* embrouillamini *P;* (*disorder*) désordre, fouillis, *m.* ¶ *v.t,* embrouiller. ~ *through,* se débrouiller tant bien que mal. ~ *up,* confondre. **muddler,** *n,* esprit brouillon.

muddy, *a,* boueux; (*clothes, hands &c*) crotté; (*complexion*) terreux. ¶ *v.t,* rendre boueux; crotter; (*river &c*) troubler.

muff, *n,* manchon, *m.* ¶ *v.t,* rater. *to* ~ *it P,* rater son coup *P.* **muffle** *v.t,* assourdir. ~ *up,* emmitoufler. ~**d,** *a,* sourd. **muffler,** *n,* cache-nez, *m.*

mufti (in), en civil.

mug, *n,* chope, *f;* (*metal*) gobelet, *m;* (*P fool*) œuf *P, m;* (*P face*) gueule *P, f.* ¶ *v.t,* agresser. ~ *up P,* bûcher *P.* **mugger,** *n,* agresseur, *m.* **mugging,** *n,* agression, *f.*

muggy, *a,* mou. *it's* ~, il fait lourd.

mulatto, *n,* mulâtre, sse.

mulberry, *n,* mûre, *f.* ~ [*tree*], mûrier, *m.*

mulch, *n,* paillis, *m.* ¶ *v.t,* pailler.

mule, *n,* (*he & pers.*) mulet, *m,* (*she*) mule, *f;* (*pl, slippers*) mules, *f.pl.* **muleteer,** *n,* muletier, *m.* **mulish,** *a,* têtu.

mull, *v.t,* ~ *over,* ruminer. ~*ed wine,* vin chaud.

mullet, *n,* (*grey*) mulet; (*red*) rouget, *m.*

mullion, *n,* meneau, *m.*

multi... *pref,* multi.... ~*coloured,* multicolore. ~*millionaire,* multimilliardaire, *m,f.* ~*national, a,* multinational; *n,* multinationale, *f.* ~*purpose,* multi-usages, *inv.* ~*racial,* multiracial. ~*storey,* à étages.

multiple, *n. & a,* multiple, *m.* ~ *sclerosis,* sclérose en plaques, *f.* ~ *store,* ~ *shop,* magasin à succursales multiples, *m.* **multiplication,** *n,* multiplication, *f.* **multiplicity,** *n,* multiplicité, *f.* **multiply,** *v.t.* (*& i*), (se) multiplier (par).

multitude, *n,* multitude, *f.*

mum['s the word], motus!, bouche close!

mumble, *v.t. & i,* marmotter.

mummify, *v.t,* momifier. **mummy,** *n,* momie; (*mother*) maman, *f.*

mumps, *n,* (*Med.*) oreillons, *m.pl.*

munch, *v.t. & i,* mastiquer, croquer.

mundane, *a,* de ce monde; (*humdrum*) banal.

municipal, *a,* municipal. ~**ity,** *n,* municipalité, *f.*

munificence, *n,* munificence, *f.* **munificent,** *a,* munificent.

munitions, *n.pl,* munitions, *f.pl.*

mural, *a,* mural. ¶ *n,* peinture murale.

murder, *n,* meurtre; (*premeditated*) assassinat, *m.* ¶ *v.i,* assassiner; (*fig.*) massacrer. ~**er,** ~**ess,** *n,* meurtrier, ère, assassin, e. ~**ous,** *a,* meurtrier.

murky, *a,* sombre, obscur, ténébreux.

murmur, *n,* murmure, *m.* ¶ *v.i. & t,* murmurer.

muscle, *n,* muscle, *m.* **muscular,** *a,* (*gen.*) musculaire; (*pers.*) musclé.

muse, *v.i,* méditer; songer, réflechir (à).

museum, *n,* musée, *m.*

mush, *n,* bouillie, *f.*

mushroom, *n,* champignon [comestible], *m.* ¶ *a,* (*soup &c*) aux champignons; (*flavour*) de champignon; (*colour*) beige rose, *inv.* ¶ *v.i.* pousser comme un c.

music, *n,* musique, *f.* ~ *case,* porte-musique, *m.* ~ *centre,* chaîne compacte stéréo. ~ *hall,* music-hall, *m.* ~ *lover,* mélomane, *m,f.* ~ *master,* professeur de musique, *m.* ~ *stand,* pupitre à m., *m.* **musical,** *a,* musical; (*pers.*) musicien. ~ *box,* boîte à musique, *f.* ~ *chairs,* chaises musicales, *f.pl.* ~ *comedy,* opérette, *f.* ~ *evening,* soirée musicale, *f.* ~ *instrument,* instrument de musique, *m.* ~ *interlude,* entracte de musique, *m.* **musician,** *n,* musicien, ne.

musing, *n,* rêverie, *f.*

musk, *n,* musc, *m.* ~ *rat,* rat musqué, *m.* ~

rose, rose muscade, *f.*
musket, *n,* mousquet, *m.* ~**eer** (*Hist.*) *n,* mousquetaire, *m.* ~**ry** (*Mil.*) *n,* tir, *m,* exercices de tir, *m.pl.*
Muslim, *V* **Moslem.**
muslin, *n,* mousseline, *f.*
musquash, *n,* rat musqué; (*fur*) ondatra, *m.*
mussel, *n,* moule, *f.*
must, *v. modal,* (*obligation*) devoir, falloir. *he ~ do it,* il doit le faire, il faut qu'il le fasse. *if you ~,* si vous y tenez. (*certainty*) devoir. *he ~ be mad!* il doit être fou! *you ~ be joking!* vous plaisantez! *he ~ have seen me,* il a dû me voir.
mustard, *n,* moutarde, *f.* ~ *gas,* gaz moutarde, *m,* ypérite, *f.* ~ *plaster,* sinapisme, *m.* ~ *pot,* moutardier, *m.* ~ *seed,* graine de m., *f.*
muster, *v.t,* rassembler; (*money &c*) réunir. *to ~ up the courage,* prendre son courage à deux mains (pour).
musty, *a,* moisi; (*smell*) de renfermé.
mutation, *n,* mutation, *f.*
mute, *a,* muet. ¶ *n,* muet, te; (*Mus.*) sourdine, *f.* ¶ *v.t,* (*sound*) assourdir; (*colour*) adoucir; (*Mus.*) mettre la sourdine à. ~**d,** *a,* sourd; (*Mus.*) en sourdine; (*protest*) voilé.
mutilate, *v.t,* mutiler. **mutilation,** *n,* mutilation, *f.*
mutineer, *n,* mutin, *m.* **mutinous,** *a,* (*Mil., Naut.*) mutiné; (*fig.*) rebelle. **mutiny,** *n,* mutinerie; (*fig.*) révolte, *f.* ¶ *v.i,* [se] mutiner, se révolter.
mutter, *v.i,* murmurer [entre ses dents], marmotter; (*of thunder*) gronder.
mutton, *n,* mouton, *m. leg of ~,* gigot, *m. ~ chop,* côtelette de mouton, *f.*
mutual†, *a,* (*reciprocal*) mutuel, réciproque; (*Com.*) mutuel; (*shared: friend &c*) commun. *by ~ consent,* par consentement mutuel. *the feeling's ~,* c'est réciproque.
muzzle, *n,* (*animal*) museau, *m;* (*gun*) bouche, gueule; (*for dog*) muselière, *f.* ¶ *v.t,* museler.
muzzy, *a,* dans les vapes *P;* (*tipsy*) éméché; (*ideas*) confus; (*outline*) flou.
my, *a,* mon, ma, mes. *I've broken ~ arm,* je me suis cassé le bras. *that's MY idea,* c'est mon idée à moi.
myopia, *n,* myopie, *f.* **myopic,** *a,* myope.
myriad, *n,* myriade, *f.*
myrrh, *n,* myrrhe, *f.*
myrtle, *n,* myrte, *m.*
myself, *pn,* (*reflexive*) me; (*emphatic*) moi-même; (*after pr.*) moi. *all by ~,* tout seul. *I've hurt ~,* je me suis blessé. *I drive the car ~,* je tiens le volant moi-même. *I speak of ~,* je parle de moi. *I'm not ~ today,* je ne suis pas dans mon assiette aujourd'hui.
mysterious†, *a,* mystérieux. **mystery,** *n,* mystère, *m.* **mystic** (*pers.*) *n,* mystique, *m,f.* ~**(al)†,** *a,* mystique. **mysticism,** *n,* mysticisme, *m.* **mystification,** *n,* (*act*) mystification, *f;* (*state*) perplexité, *f.* **mystify,** *v.t,* mystifier; rendre perplexe. **mystique,** *n,* mystique, *f.*
myth, *n,* mythe, *m.* ~**ical,** *a,* mythique. ~**ologic(al),** *a,* mythologique. ~**ology,** *n,* mythologie, *f.*
myxomatosis, *n,* myxomatose, *f.*

N

nab *P, v.t,* (*catch in act*) pincer *P;* (*to speak to*) coincer *P.*
nabob, *n,* nabab, *m.*
nadir, *n,* nadir, *m.*
nag[1], *n,* (*horse*) bidet, *m.*
nag[2], *v.t,* (*doubts &c*) harceler; (*pers.*) être toujours sur le dos de. ¶ *v.i,* gronder sans cesse. **nagging,** *a,* harcelant; (*pers.*) criard.
nail, *n,* (*finger, toe*) ongle; (*metal*) clou, *m. pay on the ~,* payer rubis sur l'ongle. ~ *brush,* brosse à ongles, *f.* ~ *clippers,* pince à ongles, *f.* ~ *file,* lime à ongles, *f.* ~ *scissors,* ciseaux à ongles, *m.pl.* ~ *varnish,* vernis à ongles, *m.* ~ *varnish remover,* dissolvant, *m.* ¶ *v.t,* (*also ~ down, ~ up*) clouer; (*P catch*) pincer *P;* (*put ~s in*) clouter. ~ *down,* (*pers.*) coincer *P.* ~ *up,* (*picture &c*) fixer par des clous; (*door &c*) condamner.
naive†, *a,* naïf. **naivety,** *n,* naïveté, *f.*
naked, *a,* nu. *with the ~ eye,* à l'œil nu. ~**ness,** *n,* nudité, *f.*
namby-pamby, *a. & n,* gnangnan, *m,f.*
name, *n,* nom, *m;* réputation, *f. my ~ is Adam,* je m'appelle Adam. *get a bad ~,* se faire une mauvaise réputation. *in ~ only, ad,* de nom seulement; (*marriage*) nominal. (*Sport &c*) *have one's ~ taken,* recevoir un avertissement. *make one's ~,* se faire un nom. *mention s.o by ~,* désigner qn par son nom. ~ *plate,* plaque, *f.* ~ *sake,* homonyme, *m.* ¶ *v.t,* (*child &c*) appeler; (*ship*) baptiser; (*object*) donner un nom à; (*designate*) nommer; (*date &c*) fixer. ~**less,** *a,* sans nom; (*anonymous*) anonyme. ~**ly,** *ad,* à savoir, c'est à dire.
nancy, ~ **boy** *P, n,* (*pej.*) tante *P*, f.*
nanny, *n,* nurse, nounou, *f.* ~ [*goat*], chèvre,

bique, *f.*
nap, *n,* (*sleep*) somme, *m,* sieste, *f.* ¶ *v.i,* sommeiller. *to catch ~ping,* prendre au dépourvu.
napalm, *n,* napalm, *m.*
nape [of the neck], *n,* nuque, *f.*
napkin *n,* serviette [de table]; (*baby's*) couche, *f.* ~ *ring,* rond de serviette, *m.*
narcissus, *n,* narcisse, *m.* **narcissistic,** *a,* narcissique.
narcotic, *a,* narcotique. ¶ *n,* narcotique, stupéfiant, *m.*
narrate, *v.t,* raconter. **narration & narrative,** *n,* narration, *f,* récit, *m,* relation, *f.* **narrative,** *a,* narratif. **narrator,** *n,* narrateur, trice.
narrow, *a,* étroit; (*mind*) étroit, borné; (*majority*) petit. *to have a ~ escape,* l'échapper belle. *~-gauge railway,* chemin de fer à voie étroite, *m.* *~-minded,* à esprit étroit. ¶ *n,* (*Naut.*) passage étroit; (*harbour*) goulet; (*river*) étranglement, *m.* ¶ *v.t.* (*& i*), (se) rétrécir. *to ~ one's eyes,* plisser les yeux. ~ *down the field,* restreindre le champ. **~ly,** *ad,* (*by a small margin*) de justesse; (*strictly*) étroitement; (*closely*) minutieusement. **~ness,** *n,* étroitesse, *f.*
nasal, *a,* nasal. ¶ (*Gram.*) *n,* nasale, *f.*
nastiness, *n,* (*gen.*) caractère désagréable, *m;* (*spitefulness*) méchanceté; (*dirtiness*) saleté, *f.*
nasturtium, *n,* capucine, *f.*
nasty†, *a,* désagréable, mauvais; méchant; (*weather, accident &c*) vilain, sale (*before n.*); (*wound, experience*) dangereux. *a ~ moment,* un moment pénible. *have a ~ temper,* avoir très mauvais caractère.
nation, *n,* nation, *f,* peuple, *m.* *~-wide,* à travers tout le pays. **~al,** *a,* national. ~ *anthem,* hymne national. ~ *debt,* dette publique, *f.* *N~ Health Service, N~ Insurance,* Sécurité Sociale. ~ *holiday,* fête nationale. ~ *monument,* monument historique, *m.* *N~ Savings,* épargne nationale. ~ *service,* service militaire, *m.* **nationalism,** *n,* nationalisme, *m.* **nationalist,** *n. & att,* nationaliste, *m,f.* **nationality,** *n,* nationalité, *f.* **nationalization,** *n,* nationalisation, *f.* **nationalize,** *v.t,* nationaliser.
native, *a,* (*country &c*) natal; (*language*) maternel; (*innate*) inné; (*plant, animal*) indigène; (*resources &c*) natural, du pays. ~ *wit,* bon sens inné. ¶ *n,* (*pers.*) autochtone, *m,f;* (*Bot., Zool., pers.*) indigène, *m,f.* *he's a ~ of,* il est originaire de. **nativity,** *n,* nativité, *f.*
natter, *v.i,* bavarder; (*grumble*) grommeler. **~er,** *n,* moulin à paroles, *m.*
natty, *a,* (*pers., dress*) chic; (*gadget*) astucieux.
natural†, *a,* naturel. ¶ *n,* (*Mus.*) [note] naturelle, *f;* (*sign*) bécarre, *m.* **~ist,** *n,* naturaliste, *m.* **~ization,** *n,* naturalisation, *f.* ~ *papers,* déclaration de n., *f.* **~ize,** *v.t,* naturaliser. **~ness,** *n,* naturel, *m.* **nature,** *n,* nature, *f;* (*type*) genre, *m.* ~ *conservancy,* protection de la nature, *f.* ~ *lover,* amoureux, euse de la n. ~ *study,* (*Sch.*) sciences naturelles. ~ *trail,* circuit forestier éducatif. **-natured,** *a,* (*good-, ill-~*) d'un (bon, mauvais) naturel. **naturism,** *n,* naturisme, *m.* **naturist,** *n,* naturiste, *m,f.*
naughtiness, *n,* (*child &c*) désobéissance, mauvaise conduite, *f.* **naughty,** *a,* (*child &c*) méchant, vilain, pas sage; (*joke &c*) grivois, risqué; (*word*) vilain.
nausea, *n,* nausée, *f.* **nauseate,** *v.t,* écœurer. **nauseating,** *a,* écœurant.
nautical, *a,* (*science, almanac*) nautique; (*mile*) marin.
naval, *a,* (*battle &c*) naval; (*affairs*) de la marine. ~ *architecture,* construction navale. ~ *base,* base navale, port de guerre, *m.* ~ *cadet,* élève de l'école navale, *m.* ~ *dockyard,* arsenal maritime, *m.* ~ *officer,* officier de marine, *m.* ~ *warfare,* combat naval.
nave, *n,* (*church*) nef, *f.*
navel, *n,* nombril, *m.* ~ *orange,* [orange] navel, *f.*
navigable, *a,* navigable; (*missile &c*) dirigeable. **navigate,** *v.i,* naviguer; (*v.t.*) naviguer; diriger; (*aircraft*) piloter; (*seas*) naviguer sur. **navigation,** *n,* navigation, *f.* **navigator,** *n,* navigateur, *m.*
navvy, *n,* terrassier, *m.*
navy, *n,* marine [militaire], m. de guerre, *f.* ~ *blue,* bleu marine, *inv.*
nay, *neg. particle,* & qui plus est, voire. ¶ *n,* non, *m.*
Nazi, *a. & n,* nazi, e. **Nazism,** *n,* nazisme, *m.*
neap tide, *n,* morte-eau, *f.*
near, *a,* proche; (*result &c*) serré; (*guess*) à peu près juste; (*likeness*) assez exact; (*friend*) intime. *it was a ~ thing,* il s'en est fallu de peu. *my ~est & dearest,* mes proches. *the ~est equivalent,* ce qui s'en rapproche le plus. *the ~est way,* la route la plus directe. *to the ~est kilo,* à un kilo près. *the N~ East,* le proche Orient. ~ *relations,* proches [parents], *m.pl.* ~ *side* (*UK*) côté gauche, (*Fr.*) côté droit. *~-sighted,* (*person*), myope, *a.* (*& m,f*). ¶ *ad,* près. ~ *at hand,* tout près; (*event*) tout proche. *~by,* tout près. *come ~,* s'approcher (de). ~ *to tears,* au bord des larmes. ¶ *pr,* près de; auprès de. ~ *here,* près d'ici. ~ *the end,* vers la fin. ¶ *v.i,* s'approcher de. **~ly,** *ad,* presque. *he ~ fell,* il a manqué de tomber. *I ~ missed the train,* j'ai failli manquer le train. **~ness,** *n,* proximité, *f.*
neat, *a,* (*gen.*) net; (*clothes &c*) soigné; (*room*) bien tenu; (*hair*) bien coiffé; (*phrase &c*) élégant; (*plan*) habile; (*spirits*) pur, sec; (*legs &c*) fin. **~ly,** *ad,* (*tidily*) avec soin; (*write*)

proprement; (*skilfully*) habilement. **~ness,** *n,* netteté; habileté, *f.*
nebulous, *a,* nébuleux.
necessarily, *ad,* nécessairement, forcément. **necessary,** *a,* nécessaire. *if ~,* s'il est n., au besoin. ¶ *n.* & **necessaries,** *n.pl,* le nécessaire. **necessitate,** *v.t,* nécessiter. **necessitous,** *a,* nécessiteux. **necessity,** *n,* nécessité, *f.*
neck, *n,* cou, *m;* (*horse, garment*) encolure, *f;* (*bottle*) col; (*violin*) manche; (*P cheek*) culot *P, m.* ~ & ~, à égalité. (*Cook.*) *best end of ~,* côtelettes premières. *save one's ~,* sauver sa peau. *stick one's ~ out,* se mouiller *P,* prendre des risques. *to be in it up to one's ~,* être dans le bain *P. to be up to one's ~ in work,* avoir du travail par dessus la tête. *win by a ~,* gagner d'une encolure. *~band,* tour du cou, *m. ~lace,* collier, *m. ~line,* encolure. *~tie,* cravate, *f.* ¶ *v.i, P,* se peloter *P.* **~ing** *P, n,* pelotage *P, m.*
necromancer, *n,* nécromancien, ne. **necromancy,** *n,* nécromancie, *f.* **necrophilia,** *n,* nécrophilie, *f.*
nectar, *n,* nectar, *m.* **~ine,** *n,* brugnon, *m.*
need, *n,* besoin, *m. if ~ be,* si besoin est, s'il le faut. *in ~,* dans le besoin. *there's no ~ for you to go,* vous n'êtes pas obligé d'y aller. ¶ *v.i.* & *t,* avoir b. de. *~ I do it?* est-ce que je suis obligé de le faire? faut-il que je le fasse? *you only ~ to ask,* tu n'as qu'à demander. **~ful,** *a,* nécessaire.
needle, *n,* aiguille, *f;* (*record-player*) saphir, *m. look for a ~ in a haystack,* chercher une aiguille dans une botte de foin. *~ case,* porte-aiguilles, *m.inv. ~cord,* velours mille-raies, *m. ~work,* travail d'aiguille, *m;* (*Sch.*) couture, *f.* ¶ *v.t, P,* agacer.
needless†, *a,* inutile. **needs,** *ad,* absolument. **needy,** *a,* nécessiteux, besogneux.
ne'er (*Poet.*) *ad,* ne . . . jamais. *~-do-well, a.* & *n,* propre à rien, *m,f.*
nefarious†, *a,* abominable.
negate, *v.t,* annuler. **negation,** *n,* négation, *f.* **negative†,** *a,* négatif. ¶ *n,* (la) négative; (*Gram.*) négation, *f;* (*Phot.*) cliché, négatif, *m;* (*Elec.*) négatif. *in the ~,* (*reply*) négativement, par la négative. ¶ *v.t,* rejeter.
neglect, *n,* (*gen.*) manque de soins (*of,* envers); (*duty*) manquement, *m. in a state of ~,* mal tenu. ¶ *v.t,* (*gen.*) négliger; (*house, car &c*) ne pas s'occuper de; (*duty*) manquer à. **neglectful†** & **negligent†,** *a,* négligent. **negligence,** *n,* négligence, *f.* **negligible,** *a,* négligeable.
negotiable, *a,* négociable; (*road*) praticable; (*obstacle*) franchissable; (*river*) navigable. **negotiate,** *v.t.* & *i,* négocier; franchir; naviguer. **negotiation,** *n,* négociation, *f;* (*pl.*) pourparlers, *m.pl.* **negotiator,** *n,* négociateur, trice.
negress, *n,* négresse (*oft. pej*); Noire, *f.* **negro,** *n,* nègre (*oft. pej*); Noir, *m.* ¶ *a,* noir. **negroid,** *a,* négroïde.
neigh, *v.i,* hennir. **~[ing],** *n,* hennissement, *m.*
neighbour, *n,* voisin, e; (*Bible*) prochain, *m. in a ~ly way,* en bon voisin. **~hood,** *n,* voisinage; (*district*) quartier, *m;* (*area*) environs, *m.pl.* **~ing,** *a,* voisin, avoisinant.
neither, *pn.* & *a,* ni l'un (l'une) ni l'autre (+ ne *before v.*) ¶ *c,* ni; ne . . . pas non plus. *if you don't go ~ shall I,* si tu n'y vas pas, je n'irai pas non plus. *~ do I,* ni moi [non plus]. ¶ *ad, ~ . . . nor,* ni . . . ni (+ ne *before v.*).
nelson (*Wrestling*) *n, full ~,* nelson, *m. half ~,* clef du cou, *f.*
Nemesis, *n,* Némésis, *f.*
neo..., *pref,* néo-. *~classical,* néo-classique. *~fascist,* néofasciste. *~nazi,* néo-nazi. **~lithic,** *a,* néolithique. **~logism,** *n,* néologisme, *m.*
neon, *n,* néon, *m. ~ light,* lumière néon, *f.*
nephew, *n,* neveu, *m.*
nepotism, *n,* népotisme, *m.*
nerve, *n,* nerf, *m;* (*Bot.*) nervure, *f;* (*courage*) courage, sang-froid, *m;* (*P cheek*) culot *P, m. ~ centre* (*fig.*), centre d'opérations, *m. ~ gas,* gaz neuroplégique. *~-racking,* éprouvant. *~ specialist,* neurologue, *m,f.* **nervous†,** *a,* nerveux; (*apprehensive*) inquiet. *~ breakdown,* dépression nerveuse. **~ness,** *n,* nervosité, *f.*
nest, *n,* nid, *m. ~ of tables,* table gigogne, *f. ~ egg,* bas de laine, *m. ~ing box,* nichoir, *m.* ¶ *v.i,* nicher. **~[ful],** *n,* nichée, *f.* **nestle,** *v.i,* se blottir. **nestling,** *n,* oisillon, *m.*
net¹, *n,* filet; (*fabric*) voile, *m. hair ~,* résille, *f. ~ball,* netball, *m. ~ curtains,* voilage, *m. ~work,* (*gen.*) réseau; (*fig: streets &c*) lacis, *m.* ¶ *v.t,* prendre au filet.
net² & **nett,** *a,* net.
nether, *a,* inférieur, bas. *~ regions,* enfers, *m.pl.* **the Netherlands,** les Pays-Bas, *m.pl.* **nethermost,** *a,* (le) plus bas.
netting, *n,* (*nets*) filets, *m.pl;* (*mesh*) mailles, *f.pl;* (*fabric*) voile; (*wire*) treillis, *m.*
nettle, *n,* ortie, *f. ~ rash,* urticaire, *f.* ¶ *v.t,* agacer; piquer au vif.
neuralgia, *n,* névralgie, *f.* **neurasthenia,** *n,* neurasthénie, *f.* **neuritis,** *n,* névrite, *f.* **neurologist,** *n,* neurologiste, -logue, *m,f.* **neurosis,** *n,* névrose, *f.* **neurotic,** *a,* névrosé.
neuter, *a.* & *n,* neutre, *m.* ¶ *v.t,* (*Vet.*) châtrer. **neutral,** *a.* & *n,* neutre, *m;* (*Mot.*) point mort. **~ity,** *n,* neutralité, *f.* **~ize,** *v.t,* neutraliser.
neutron, *n,* neutron, *m. ~ bomb,* bombe à neutrons, *f.*
never, *ad,* ne . . . . jamais. *I've ~ tasted it,* je ne l'ai jamais goûté. *~ again,* plus jamais. *I ~ said a word,* je n'ai pas dit le moindre mot. *~ mind!* ça ne fait rien. *well I ~ did!* pas possible! *~-ending,* interminable. *~-~ land,*

pays de cocagne, *m.* *~more,* ne... plus jamais. **nevertheless,** *ad,* néanmoins; cependant; toutefois; pourtant, quand même.

new, *a,* nouveau (*before n.*); (*brand ~*) neuf; (*different*) nouveau, autre; (*fresh: bread &c*) frais; (*wine*) nouveau. *a ~ boy,* un nouveau. *a ~ girl,* une nouvelle. *good as ~,* comme neuf. *the ~ woman,* la femme moderne. *what's ~?* quoi de neuf? *~born,* nouveau-né, e. *~comer,* nouveau venu, nouvelle venue. *~-fangled,* nouveau genre. *~-found,* tout neuf. *N~ Guinea,* Nouvelle-Guinée. *N~ Hebrides,* Nouvelles-Hébrides. *~-laid,* tout frais [pondu]. *N~ South Wales,* la Nouvelle-Galles du Sud. *N~ Testament,* Nouveau Testament. *~ year,* nouvel an, nouvelle année. *~ year's day,* le jour de l'an. *~ year's eve,* la Saint-Sylvestre. *Happy N~ Year!* bonne année! *N~ York, n,* New York; *a,* new-yorkais. *N~ Zealand, n,* Nouvelle-Zélande; *a,* néo-zélandais. *N~ Zealander,* Néo-Zélandais, e.

newel, *n,* noyau, *m.*

Newfoundland, *n,* Terre-Neuve, *f.* ¶ *a,* terre-neuvien.

newly, *ad,* nouvellement, fraîchement. *~-weds,* jeunes mariés, *m.pl.* **newness,** *n,* nouveauté, *f.*

news, *n,* nouvelle[s], *f.* [*pl*]; (*Press, Radio &c*) informations; (*Cine., TV*) actualités, *f.pl.* *good, bad ~,* bonnes, tristes nouvelles. *make ~,* faire parler de soi. *is there any ~?* y a-t-il du nouveau? *what's your ~?* quoi de neuf? *~ agency,* agence de presse, *f.* *~agent,* marchand, e de journaux. *~ bulletin,* (*Radio*) informations; (*TV*) actualités. *~ flash,* flash, *m.* *~ item,* information, *f.* *~letter,* bulletin, *m.* *~paper,* journal, *m;* (*minor*) feuille, *f.* *~print,* papier de journal, *m.* *~reader,* speaker, ine. *~reel,* actualités. *~room,* salles de rédaction, *f.pl;* (*Radio, TV*) studio, *m.* *~ stand,* kiosque, *m.*

newt, *n,* triton, *m.*

next, *a,* (*place*) voisin, d'à côté, plus proche; (*time: future*) prochain; (*past*) suivant. *the ~ day,* le lendemain. *the ~ day but one,* le surlendemain. *~ door to,* à côté de. *~ morning,* le lendemain matin. *~ please!* au suivant! *the ~ size,* la taille au-dessus. *this time ~ week,* d'ici huit jours. *who's ~?* à qui le tour? ¶ *ad,* ensuite, après, puis. *~ to,* auprès de, à côté de; (*almost*) presque. *~ to last,* avant-dernier. *~ to nothing,* presque rien. *~ of kin,* plus proche parent, e, proches [parents], *m.pl.*

nib, *n,* plume, *f,* bec, *m.*

nibble (*Fish.*) *n,* touche, *f.* ¶ *v.t. & i,* grignoter, mordiller; (*grass*) brouter; (*fish*) mordre.

nice, *a,* (*gen.*) agréable; (*pers.*) sympathique, gentil; (*meal, smell &c*) bon; (*in looks*) joli, charmant, bien; (*subtle*) délicat. (*decent*) *~ people,* des gens bien. (*ironic*) *in a ~ mess,* dans de beaux draps. *have a ~ time,* s'amuser bien. *~***ly,** *ad,* agréablement, bien; (*kindly*) gentiment. *~***ness,** *n,* gentillesse; délicatesse, *f.* **nicety,** *n,* précision, *f;* (*pl.*) finesses, *f.pl.* *to a ~,* avec grande précision.

niche, *n,* niche, *f.*

nick, *n,* (*in skin, wood*) entaille; (*in blade*) ébréchure; (*P prison*) taule *P, f.* *in good ~ P,* impec *P.* *in the ~ of time,* juste à temps. ¶ *v.t,* entailler; ébrécher; (*P arrest*) pincer *P;* (*P steal*) piquer *P.*

nickel, *n,* nickel, *m.* ¶ *v.t,* nickeler.

nickname, *n,* sobriquet, surnom, *m.* ¶ *v.t,* surnommer.

nicotine, *n,* nicotine, *f.*

niece, *n,* nièce, *f.*

niggardly, *a,* (*pers.*) pingre, chiche.

nigger, *n.* (*pej.*), nègre, négresse (*pej*). *~-brown,* tête-de-nègre, *inv.*

niggle, *v.i,* tatillonner, pinailler *P.* ¶ *v.t.* (*conscience*) travailler. **niggling,** *a,* tatillon; (*doubt*) persistant; (*details*) insignifiant.

night, *n,* nuit, *f;* soir, *m.* *at ~,* la nuit, le soir; (*hour*) du soir. *by ~,* de nuit. *the ~ before,* la veille au soir. *the ~ before last,* avant-hier soir. *~cap,* bonnet de nuit, *m.* *~ club,* boîte de n., *f.* *~dress,* *~gown,* chemise de nuit, *f.* *~fall,* la tombée de la nuit. *at ~fall,* à la nuit tombante. *~ light,* veilleuse, *f.* *~mare,* cauchemar, *m.* *~'s lodging,* un gîte pour la nuit. *~-time,* nuit. *~ watchman,* gardien de n., *m.* *~ work,* travail de n., *m.*

nightingale, *n,* rossignol, *m.*

nightly, *ad,* (& *a.*) (de) toutes les nuits; (de) tous les soirs.

nihilist, *n,* nihiliste, *m.*

nil, *n,* néant; (*Sport*) zéro, *m.*

nimble†, *a,* agile; (*mind*) vif. *~***ness,** *n,* agilité; vivacité, *f.*

nincompoop, *n,* idiot, e.

nine, *a. & n,* neuf, *inv. & m.* *~ times out of ten,* neuf fois sur dix. *have ~ lives,* avoir l'âme chevillé au corps. *~ days' wonder,* la merveille d'un jour. *dressed up to the ~s,* sur son trente et un. *~pins,* quilles, *f.pl.* *for other phrases V* **four. nineteen,** *a. & n,* dix-neuf, *inv. & m.* *talk ~ to the dozen,* être un vrai moulin à paroles. **nineteenth,** *a. & n,* dix-neuvième, *m,f.* **ninetieth,** *a. & n,* quatre-vingt-dixième, *m,f.* **ninety,** *a. & n,* quatre-vingt-dix, *inv. & m.* *91, 92 &c,* quatre-vingt-onze, -douze &c. *to be in one's nineties,* être nonagénaire. *for other phrases V* **forty.**

ninny, *n,* cornichon *P, m.*

ninth, *a. & n,* neuvième, *m,f.* *for phrases* V **fourth.**

nip, *n,* (*pinch*) pinçon, *m;* (*bite*) morsure; (*liquor*) goutte, *f.* *there's a ~ in the air,* l'air est piquant. ¶ *v.t,* pincer; (*bite*) donner un coup de dent; (*cold &c*) brûler. ~ *in the bud* (*fig.*), écraser dans l'œuf. **nipper,** *n,* (*P child*) gosse *P, m,f.*

nipple, *n,* mamelon, bout du sein, *m;* (*nursing bottle*) tétine, *f.*

nit, *n,* lente, *f;* (*P fool*) niquedouille *P, m,f.* ~-*pick,* couper les cheveux en quatre. ~*wit,* nigaud, e *P.*

nitrate, *n,* nitrate, azotate, *m.* **nitre,** *n,* nitre, salpêtre, *m.* **nitric,** *a,* azotique, nitrique. **nitrogen,** *n,* azote, *m.* **nitroglycerin[e],** *n,* nitroglycérine, *f.* **nitrous,** *a,* azoteux.

no, *ad. & n,* non, *m.inv.* ¶ *a,* aucun, nul, pas de (+ ne *before v.*) *I've* ~ *idea,* je n'ai aucune idée. ~ *other person,* nul autre, personne d'autre. *he's* ~ *friend of mine,* il n'est pas de mes amis. ~ *longer,* ~ *more,* ne... plus. ~ *admittance* [*except on business*], entrée interdite, défense d'entrer [sans autorisation]. ~-*claims bonus,* bonification pour non-sinistre, *f.* ~ *doubt,* sans doute. ~ *entry* [*one way street*], sens interdit. ~ *flowers by request,* ni fleurs, ni couronnes. ~ *matter!* n'importe! ~ *nonsense!* pas d'histoires! ~ *one,* = **nobody.** ~ *parking,* stationnement interdit. ~ *smoking,* défense de fumer. ~ *thoroughfare,* passage interdit [au public].

Noah's ark, *n,* l'arche de Noé, *f.*

nobility, *n,* noblesse, *f.* **noble†,** *a,* noble; (*unselfish*) magnanime. ~[*man*], noble, *m.* ~-*woman,* noble, *f.* ~**ness,** *n,* noblesse, *f.*

nobody, *pn,* personne, nul (+ ne *before v.*). *I saw* ~, je n'ai vu personne. ~ *saw me,* personne ne m'a vu. ¶ *n, a* ~, un rien du tout; (*unknown*) inconnu, e.

nocturnal, *a.* & **nocturne,** *n,* nocturne, *m.*

nod, *n,* signe [de tête], *m,* inclination de t., *f.* ¶ *v.i,* incliner la tête; (*signify assent*) hocher la t., faire signe que oui; (*flowers &c*) se balancer. ~ *off,* (*doze*) s'endormir.

node, *n,* nœud, *m.*

noise, *n,* (*gen.*) bruit; (*loud*) tapage, vacarme, *m;* (*Tel.*) friture, *f;* (*Radio, TV*) parasites, *m.pl.* ~*s in the ears,* bourdonnements d'oreilles, *m.pl. a big* ~ *P,* une grosse légume *P.* ~ *abatement,* lutte anti-bruit, *f.* ~ *abroad, v.t,* ébruiter. ~**less†,** *a,* silencieux.

noisy†, *a,* bruyant. *to be* ~, faire du bruit *ou* du tapage.

nomad, *n.* & ~**(ic),** *a,* nomade, *m,f.*

nominal†, *a,* nominal; (*rent*) insignifiant. **nominate,** *v.t,* nommer, désigner; (*candidate &c*) proposer. **nomination,** *n,* nomination, désignation; proposition, *f.* **nominative [case],** *n,* nominatif, *m.* **nominee,** *n,* personne nommée.

non, *pref:* ~-*aggression,* non-agression, *f.* ~-*alcoholic,* sans alcool. ~-*aligned* (*Pol.*), neutraliste, non-aligné. ~-*believer,* incroyant, e. ~-*combatant, n. & a,* non-combattant, *m.* ~-*commissioned officer,* gradé, *m.* ~-*essential,* accessoire. ~-*existant,* inexistant. ~-*interference,* ~-*intervention,* non-intervention, *f,* laissez-faire, *m.* ~-*profitmaking,* sans but lucratif. ~-*resident,* non-résident. ~-*run,* indémaillable. ~-*skid,* antidérapant. ~-*smoker,* non-fumeur. ~-*starter,* non-partant. ~-*stop,* sans arrêt; (*train &c*) direct.

nonchalance, *n,* nonchalance, *f.* **nonchalant,** *a,* nonchalant. ~**ly,** *ad,* nonchalamment.

noncommittal, *a,* (*answer*) qui n'engage à rien; (*pers.*) réservé.

nonconformist, *n. & a,* non-conformiste, *m,f.*

nondescript, *a,* indéfinissable; (*pers.*) quelconque.

none, *pn,* aucun, e; (*pers.*) personne, aucun, e (+ ne *before v.*); (*form-filling*) néant, *m. there's* ~ *left,* il n'en reste plus. ~ *of us,* aucun d'entre nous. ~ *at all,* rien du tout; pas un(e) seul(e). ~ *of this,* rien de ceci. *it's* ~ *too soon,* ce n'est pas trop tôt.

nonentity, *n,* (*pers.*) nullité, *f.*

nonplus, *v.t,* dérouter.

nonsense, *n,* absurdités, sottises, inepties, *f.pl,* non-sens, *m. that's* ~ *!* c'est absurde! *a piece of* ~, une absurdité &c, un non-sens. *talk* ~, dire des absurdités &c. **nonsensical,** *a,* absurde.

noodle, *n,* (*Cook.*) ~*s,* nouilles, *f.pl.*

nook, *n,* recoin, *m.* ~*s & crannies,* coins & recoins.

noon & noonday & noontide, *n,* midi, *m.*

noose, *n,* nœud coulant; (*cowboy*) lasso, *m;* (*hangman*) corde, *f.*

nor, *c,* ni; (= *& not*) ne..... pas non plus. *neither you* ~ *I know,* ni vous ni moi ne [le] savons. *he doesn't know,* ~ *do I,* il ne le sait pas – ni moi non plus.

Nordic, *a,* nordique.

norm, *n,* norme, *f.* **normal†,** *a,* normal.

Norman, *a,* normand; (*Arch.*) roman. ¶ *n,* Normand, e. **Normandy,** *n,* la Normandie.

Norse, *n,* (*language*) norrois, *m.* ~**man,** *n,* Scandinave, *m.*

north, *n,* nord, *m. in the* ~ [*of*], dans le nord [de]. [*to the*] ~ [*of*], au nord [de]. ¶ *ad,* au nord, vers le nord. ¶ *a,* [du] nord; (*wind*) du n. *N*~ *Atlantic,* l'Atlantique Nord, *m. N*~ *Africa,* l'Afrique du Nord, *f. N*~ *African,* nord-africain. *N*~ *America,* l'Amérique du Nord, *f. N*~ *American,* nord-américain. ~*bound,* en direction du nord; (*carriageway*) nord. ~-*east,* nord-est (*m*). ~-*facing,* exposé au nord. *N*~ *Pole,* pôle Nord, *m. N*~ *Sea,* mer du Nord, *f.* ~-*west,* nord-ouest (*m*). **northerly,** *a,* du nord; (*direction*) vers le nord. **northern,** *a,* [du] nord. ~ *lights,* aurore boréale, *f.* **northerner,** *n,* homme, femme du nord, *m,f. the* ~*s,* le gens du nord. **northward[s],** *ad,* vers le nord.

Norway, *n,* la Norvège. **Norwegian,** *a,* norvégien. ¶ *n,* (*pers.*) Norvégien, ne; (*language*) le norvégien.
nose, *n,* nez; (*tool*) bec; (*sense of smell*) odorat; (*fig.*) flair, *m.* (*Mot.*) ~ *to tail,* pare-choc contre pare-choc. *blow one's* ~, se moucher. *poke one's* ~ *into,* fourrer son nez dans. ~ *bag,* musette, *f.* ~*bleed,* saignement de nez, *m.* ~*-dive, v.i,* descendre en piqué. ~ *drops,* gouttes nasales. ~*gay,* bouquet, *m.* ~ *about,* fouiner. ~ [*out*], *v.t,* flairer.
nostalgia, *n,* nostalgie, *f.* **nostalgic,** *a,* nostalgique.
nostril, *n,* narine, *f;* (*horse*) naseau, *m.*
nosy, *a,* fouinard *P,* curieux. *don't be* ~! mêlez-vous de vos affaires! *N*~ *Parker,* fouinard, e *P.*
not, n't, *ad,* ne... pas, ne... point (*usually liter.*). ~ *at all,* pas du tout; (*after thanks*) de rien, je vous en prie. ~ *a few,* pas mal de. ~ *guilty,* non-coupable. ~ *half! P* tu parles! *P.* ~ *negotiable,* non-négotiable. ~ *without reason,* et pour cause. ~ *yet,* pas encore. *he is* ~ *here,* il n'est pas ici. *he hasn't come,* il n'est pas venu. *I hope* ~, j'espère que non. *why* ~? pourquoi pas? (*tag questions*) *isn't it? hasn't he? &c,* non? n'est-ce pas?
notable, *a,* notable. **notably,** *ad,* (*in particular*) notamment; (*outstandingly*) notablement.
notary, *n,* notaire, *m.*
notation, *n,* notation, *f.*
notch, *n,* (*in wood*) encoche; (*in blade*) ébréchure, *f;* (*in belt*) cran, *m.* ¶ *v.t,* encocher; ébrécher; (*Need.*) cranter.
note, *n,* (*gen., Mus., Diplomacy*) note, *f;* (*informal letter*) mot; (*Com., Bank.*) billet, *m.* *make a* ~ *of,* prendre note de. *make* ~*s,* prendre des notes. *take* ~ *of,* remarquer. *play, sing a false* ~, faire une fausse note. *write s.o a* ~, mettre un petit mot à qn. ~*book,* carnet; (*Sch.*) cahier, *m.* ~*-case,* portefeuille, *m.* ~*pad,* bloc-notes, *m.* ~*paper,* papier à lettres, *m.* ~*worthiness,* importance, *f.* ~*worthy,* remarquable. ¶ *v.t,* noter (que), prendre note de; (*notice*) remarquer, constater. ~ *down,* noter, inscrire. **noted,** *a,* célèbre.
nothing, *n,* rien (+ ne *before v.*); (*Math.*) zéro, *m;* (*before a.*) rien de. ~ *but,* rien que. ~ *could be simpler,* rien de plus simple. ~ *else,* rien d'autre. ~ *on earth,* rien au monde. ~ *like as big,* loin d'être aussi grand. ~ *much,* pas grand-chose. ~ *new,* rien de nouveau. *it's* ~ *to do with you,* cela ne vous regard pas. *to say* ~ *of,* sans parler de. ~**ness,** *n,* néant, *m.*
notice, *n,* (*warning*) avis, *m,* notification, *f;* (*period*) délai; (*advance* ~) préavis; (*announcement*) avis, *m;* (*in paper*) annonce; (*poster*) affiche; (*sign*) pancarte, *f;* (*review*) compte rendu, *m,* critique, *f.* ~ *to quit,* congé, *m. at short* ~, à bref délai. *at a moment's* ~, sur-le-champ. *give* ~, (*to tenant*) donner congé; (*to landlord*) donner un préavis de départ. *give s.o* ~, (*employer*) licencier qn. *give one's* ~, (*employee*) donner sa démission. *public* ~, avis au public. *take no* ~! ne faites pas attention! *until further* ~, jusqu'à nouvel ordre. ~*board,* panneau d'affichage, *m.* ¶ *v.t,* (*perceive*) remarquer; (*heed*) faire attention à. ~**able†,** *a,* (*perceivable*) perceptible; (*obvious*) évident, net. **notification,** *n,* annonce, *f.* **notify,** *v.t,* aviser (qch à qn), notifier (qn de qch).
notion, *n,* idée, *f.*
notoriety, *n,* notoriété, *f.* **notorious,** *a,* notoire; (*place*) mal famé. ~**ly,** *ad,* notoirement.
notwithstanding, *pr,* malgré. ¶ *ad,* néanmoins, quand même.
nought, *n,* (*Math.*) zéro; (*liter.*) rien, *m. come to* ~, n'aboutir à rien.
noun, *n,* nom, substantif, *m.*
nourish, *v.t,* nourrir. ~**ing,** *a,* nourrissant. ~**ment,** *n,* nourriture, *f.*
Nova Scotia, *n,* la Nouvelle-Écosse.
novel, *a,* nouveau (*after n.*), original. ¶ *n,* roman, *m.* ~**ette,** *n,* nouvelle, *f.* ~**ist,** *n,* romancier, ère. ~**ty,** *n,* nouveauté; (*idea*) innovation, *f.*
November, *n,* novembre, *m.*
novice, *n,* novice, *m,f,* apprenti, e.
now, *ad,* (*gen.*) maintenant; (*these days*) actuellement; (*at that time*) alors; (*alternation*) tantôt. ~ *here,* ~ *there,* tantôt par ici, tantôt par là. [*every*] ~ *& then,* de temps en temps. ~ *or never,* c'est le moment ou jamais. *from* ~ *on,* à partir de maintenant. *just* ~, à l'instant. *right* ~, en ce moment. ¶ *c,* (~ *that*) maintenant que; (*introductory*) or. ~, *he loved his wife,* or, il aimait sa femme. ¶ *i,* ~ [*then*]! bon, alors; (*remonstrating*) allons! *well* ~! eh bien! **nowadays,** *ad,* de nos jours; aujourd'hui; actuellement.
nowhere, *ad,* nulle part (+ ne *before v.*). ~ *else,* nulle part ailleurs. ~ *to be found,* introuvable. ~ *near,* loin de. **nowise,** *ad,* nullement, aucunement.
noxious, *a,* nocif.
nozzle, *n,* (*hose &c*) ajutage; (*bellows*) bec; (*vacuum cleaner*) suceur, *m;* (*icing bag*) douille, *f.*
nubile, *a,* nubile.
nuclear, *a,* nucléaire. ~ *physicist,* physicien, ne atomiste. ~ *physics,* physique nucléaire *ou* atomique, *f.* ~ *power station* centrale nucléaire, *f.* ~ *scientist,* atomiste, *m.*
nucleus, *n,* noyau, *m.*
nude, *a. & n,* (*Art.*) nu, *m.*
nudge, *n,* coup de coude, *m.* ¶ *v.t,* donner up coup de coude à, pousser du coude.

nudism, *n,* nudisme, *m.* **nudist,** *n,* nudiste, *m,f.* **nudity,** *n,* nudité, *f.*
nugget, *n,* pépite, *f.*
nuisance, *n,* ennui, embêtement; (*pers.*) fléau, *m,* peste, *f;* (*Law*) dommage simple, *m. it's a ~,* c'est embêtant. *make a ~ of o.s,* embêter le monde. *what a ~!* quelle barbe! *P. you're being a ~,* tu me casses les pieds *P.*
null, *a,* nul. *~ & void,* nul & non avenu. **nullify,** *v.t,* annuler. **nullity,** *n,* nullité, caducité, *f.*
numb, *a,* engourdi; (*cold, fear*) transi. ¶ *v.t,* engourdir, transir.
number, *n,* (*gen., Gram. &c*) nombre; (*Math.*) chiffre, nombre; (*house, page, Paper, Tel.*) numéro, *m. N~s,* (*Bible*) les Nombres. *a large, small ~,* un grand, petit nombre. *in equal ~s,* en nombre égal. (*car*) *~* [*plate*], [plaque d']immatriculation, *f.* ¶ *v.t,* compter; (*give ~ to*) numéroter. **~ing,** *n,* numérotage, *m.* **~less,** *a,* innombrable.
numbness, *n,* engourdissement, *m.*
numeral, *a,* numéral. ¶ *n,* chiffre, *m.* **numerator** (*Arith.*) *n,* numérateur, *m.* **numerical,** *a,* numérique. **numerous,** *a,* nombreux.
numskull, *n,* imbécile, *m,f.*
nun, *n,* religieuse, *f.*
nuncio, *n,* nonce, *m.*
nunnery, *n,* couvent, *m.*
nuptial, *a,* nuptial. **~s,** *n.pl,* noces, *f.pl.*
nurse, *n,* infirmier, ère; (*children's*) nurse, *f. ~-maid,* bonne d'enfants, *f.* ¶ *v.t,* (*Med.*) soigner; (*suckle*) allaiter; (*in arms*) bercer [dans ses bras]; (*fig: hope &c*) nourrir. **nursery,** *n,* nursery, chambre d'enfants; (*day ~*) crèche; (*residential*) pouponnière; (*Hort. & fig.*) pépinière, *f. ~man,* pépiniériste, *m. ~ rhyme,* comptine, *f. ~ school,* école maternelle. (*Ski*) *~ slopes,* pentes pour débutants, *f.pl.* **nursing,** *n,* allaitement, *m;* (*care*) soins, *m.pl. ~ home,* clinique, *f. ~ mother,* mère qui allaite.
nurture, *n,* nourriture, *f.* ¶ *v.t,* (*rear*) élever; (*feed*) nourrir (*on,* de).
nut, *n,* (*Bot.*) *no generic term V* **walnut** *&c;* (*Tech.*) écrou, *m;* (*P mad pers. also ~case, nutter*) tout a fait toqué. *~ crackers,* casse-noisettes, casse-noix, *m.inv. ~ hatch,* sittelle, *f. ~house P,* maison de fous, *f. ~meg,* [noix] muscade, *m. ~shell,* coquille de noix, noisette &c, *f.* (*fig.*) *in a ~shell,* en un mot.
nutrition, *n,* nutrition, *f.* **~al,** *a,* alimentaire. **nutritious & nutritive,** *a,* nourrissant, nutritif.
nuzzle, *v.i, ~ up,* fourrer son nez.
nylon, *n,* nylon, *m.*
nymph, *n,* nymphe, *f.*
nymphomania, *n,* nymphomanie, *f.* **~c,** *a. & n,* nymphomane, *f.*

O

O, *i,* ô! ¶ *n,* (*Tel: number*) zéro, *m.*
oaf, *n,* (*awkward*) balourd, e; (*bad-mannered*) mufle, *m.* **~ish,** *a,* (*pers.*) mufle; (*behaviour*) de m.
oak [tree], *n,* chêne, *m. ~* [*wood*], [bois de] chêne. *~ apple,* galle [de chêne], *f.* ¶ *att.* & **~en,** *a,* de chêne.
oakum, *n,* étoupe, *f.*
oar, *n,* rame, *f. shove one's ~ in,* mettre son grain de sel. **oarsman,** *n,* rameur; (*Naut., Sport*) nageur. **oarswoman,** *n,* rameuse, *f.*
oasis (*lit. & fig.*) *n,* oasis, *f.*
oat, *n,* (*pl.*) avoine, *f. ~meal,* flocons d'avoine, *m.pl.*
oath, *n,* serment; (*profane*) juron, *m.*
obdurate, *a,* obstiné; inflexible; (*unrepentant*) impénitent.
obedience, *n,* obéissance, soumission; (*Eccl.*) obédience, *f.* **obedient,** *a,* obéissant; (*submissive*) soumis. **~ly,** *ad,* avec soumission; docilement.
obelisk, *n,* obélisque, *m.*
obese, *a,* obèse. **obesity,** *n,* obésité, *f.*
obey, *v.t,* obéir à; (*instructions*) se conformer à. ¶ *v.i,* obéir.
obituary, *n,* nécrologie, *f.*
object, *n,* (*gen.*) objet; (*Gram.*) complément [d'objet]; (*aim*) but, *m. ~ lesson,* (*fig.*) démonstration (*in,* de), *f.* ¶ *v.t,* objecter. ¶ *v.i,* élever une objection (*to,* contre); trouver à rédire. *I ~!* je proteste. *if you don't ~,* si vous ne voyez pas d'objection. **objection,** *n,* objection, *f;* (*drawback*) inconvénient, *m.* **~able,** *a,* (*pers., behaviour &c*) insupportable; (*language*) choquant. **objective†,** *a,* objectif. ¶ (*aim, Opt.*) *n,* objectif, *m. ~* [*case*], accusatif, *m.*
obligation, *n,* obligation, *f. be under an ~ to s.o,* devoir de la reconnaissance à qn. *meet one's ~s,* satisfaire à ses obligations. *under an ~ to do,* dans l'obligation de faire. *"without ~,"* "sans engagement". **obligatory,** *a,* obligatoire. **oblige,** *v.t,* obliger (qn; qn à faire). **obliging,** *a,* obligeant; aimable. **~ly,** *ad,*

obligeamment; aimablement.
oblique†, *a,* oblique; (*fig.*) indirect.
obliterate, *v.t,* effacer; (*cross out*) rayer; (*Post*) oblitérer. **obliteration,** *n,* effacement, *m;* rature, oblitération, *f.*
oblivion, *n,* oubli, *m.* **oblivious,** *a,* oublieux; (*unaware*) inconscient (de).
oblong, *a,* oblong. ¶ *n,* rectangle, *m.*
obnoxious, *a,* odieux; (*child*) insupportable.
oboe, *n,* hautbois, *m.* **oboist,** *n,* hautboïste, *m,f.*
obscene, *a,* obscène. **obscenity,** *n,* obscénité, *f.*
obscure, *a,* obscur. ¶ *v.t,* (*lit, fig.*) obscurcir; (*hide*) cacher. **~ly,** *ad,* obscurément. **obscurity,** *n,* obscurité, *f.*
obsequious†, *a,* obséquieux. **~ness,** *n,* obséquiosité, *f.*
observance, *n,* observation; (*Theol.*) observance, *f.* **observant,** *a,* observateur. **observation,** *n,* observation; (*Police, Mil.*) surveillance; (*remark*) observation, remarque, *f.* ~ *post* (*Mil.*) & **observatory,** *n,* observatoire, *m.* **observe,** *v.t,* (*gen.*) observer; (*say*) faire remarquer. ~ *closely,* scruter. **observer,** *n,* observateur, trice.
obsess, *v.t,* obséder. *to be ~ed by, with,* être obsédé par. **~ion,** *n,* obsession; (*sth. unpleasant*) hantise, *f.* **obsessive,** *a,* obsédant; (*Psych.*) obsessionnel.
obsolescence, *n,* (*goods, words*) vieillissement, *m;* (*Mach.*) obsolescence, *f. built-in* ~, obsolescence calculée. **obsolescent,** *a,* (*word*) désuet; (*goods*) vieux; (*Mach.*) obsolescent. **obsolete,** *a,* dépassé; désuet; (*word*) vieilli; (*goods, Mach.*) vieux; (*law*) caduc; (*Bio.*) atrophié. *become* ~, tomber en désuétude.
obstacle, *n,* obstacle, *m.* ~ *race,* course d'obstacles, *f.*
obstetric(al), *a,* obstétrical; (*clinic*) obstétrique. **obstetrician,** *n,* obstétricien, ne. **obstetrics,** *n.pl,* obstétrique, *f.*
obstinacy, *n,* obstination, *f,* entêtement, *m.* **obstinate,** *a,* obstiné, opiniâtre, entêté; acharné; (*fight &c*) acharné; (*pain &c*) persistant. **~ly,** *ad,* obstinément, opiniâtrement.
obstreperous, *a,* turbulent; (*rebellious*) rouspéteur.
obstruct, *v.t,* (*block*) bloquer (avec, par); (*artery*) obstruer; (*hinder*) entraver; (*Sport*) faire obstruction à. **~ion,** *n,* obstacle; (*to pipe*) bouchon, *m;* (*to artery*) embolie, *f. cause an* ~, (*on road*) encombrer la voie publique; (*Mot.*) bloquer la circulation. **~ive,** *a,* obstructionniste.
obtain, *v.t,* obtenir, procurer; (*v.i.*) régner.
obtrude, *v.t.* (*&i.*) (s') imposer.
obtuse, *a,* obtus.
obverse (*coin*) *n,* face, *f.*
obviate, *v.t,* obvier à.
obvious†, *a,* évident, manifeste.
occasion, *n,* occasion; circonstance, *f;* (*event*) événement.¶ *v.t,* occasionner, causer. **~al,** *a,* (*event*) qui a lieu de temps en temps; (*visits*) espacés; (*showers*) intermittent; (*Mus.*) de circonstance. ~ *table,* table volante, *f.* **~ally,** *ad,* de temps en temps, parfois.
occult, *a,* occulte. ¶ *n, the* ~, le surnaturel.
occupant, *n,* occupant, e; (*job*) titulaire, *m,f.* **occupation,** *n,* (*gen., Mil. &c*) occupation; profession, *f;* (*trade*) métier; (*work*) emploi, travail, *m.* *~al therapist,* ergothérapeute, *m,f.* *~al therapy,* ergothérapie, *f.* **occupier,** *n,* habitant, e, locataire, *m,f.* **occupy,** *v.t,* occuper.
occur, *v.i,* (*event*) avoir lieu, arriver; se rencontrer, se trouver; (*opportunity*) se présenter; (*change*) s'opérer. *it ~s to me that,* il me vient à l'esprit que. **occurrence,** *n,* événement, *m,* circonstance, *f. an everyday* ~, un fait journalier. *it's a common* ~, ceci arrive souvent.
ocean, *n,* océan, *m.* ~ *bed,* fond sous-marin. *~-going,* de haute mer. *~-going ship,* long-courrier, *m.* ~ *liner,* paquebot, *m.* **~ic,** *a,* océanique. **~ography,** *n,* océanographie, *f.*
ochre, *n,* ocre, *f.*
o'clock, *ad: at 3* ~, à 3 heures.
octagon, *n,* octogone, *m.* **~al,** *a,* octagonal. **octane,** *n,* octane, *m.* **octave,** *n,* octave, *f.* **octavo,** *a. & n,* inoctavo, *m.* **October,** *n,* octobre, *m.* **octogenarian,** *a. & n,* octogénaire, *m,f.* **octopus,** *n,* poulpe, *m,* pieuvre, *f.*
ocular, *a. & n,* oculaire, *m.* **oculist,** *n,* oculiste, *m.*
odd, *a,* (*strange*) bizarre, singulier, étrange, curieux; (*number*) impair; (*& a few more*) & quelques; (*left over*) qui reste; (*from pair*) déparié; (*from set*) dépareillé. ~ *moments,* moments perdus. *at* ~ *times,* par-ci par-là. ~ *jobs,* menus travaux. *~-job man,* factotum, *m.* **~ity,** *n,* (*pers.*) excentrique, *m.f;* drôle d'oiseau *P, m;* (*thing*) curiosité; (*trait*) singularité, *f.* **~ly,** *ad,* bizarrement, curieusement. ~ *enough,* chose curieuse. **~ments,** *n.pl,* fins de série, *f.pl.* **~ness,** *n,* singularité, *f.* **odds,** *n.pl,* (*Turf*) cote, *f;* (*fig.*) chances, *f.pl,* avantage, *m. it makes no* ~ *to me,* ça m'est complètement égal. *lay* ~ *of 3 to 1,* parier 3 contre 1. *the* ~ *are that,* il y a à parier que. ~ *& ends,* petits bouts.
ode, *n,* ode, *f.*
odious†, *a,* odieux.
odour, *n,* odeur, *f.* **~less,** *a,* inodore.
oesophagus, *n,* œsophage, *m.*
oestrogen, *n,* œstrogène, *m.*
of, *pr,* (*gen.*) de. *a friend* ~ *mine,* un de mes amis. *there are 4* ~ *us,* nous sommes quatre. *2* ~ *them,* deux d'entre eux.
off, *pr,* de; sur; dans; (*distance*) éloigné de; écarté de; (*Naut.*) au large de. *be* ~ *one's food,* avoir perdu l'appétit. *eat sth* ~ *a plate,* manger qch dans une assiette. *fall* ~ *the wall,*

O-S

tomber du mur. *take sth ~ the table,* prendre qch sur la table. *~beat,* original. *~-centre,* désaxé. *on the ~-chance,* au hasard. *~-colour,* mal fichu *P*. *~hand,* sans-gêne, *inv;* (*curt*) brusque. *~handedness,* sans-gêne, *m;* brusquerie, *f*. *~-key,* (*Mus.*) faux. *~-load,* débarquer; (*fig: task*) passer. *~-peak,* aux heures creuses; (*tariff*) réduit; (*heating*) par accumulation. *~-putting,* (*job*) rebutant; (*food*) peu ragoûtant; (*pers.*) peu engageant. *~-season,* morte saison, *f*. *~shoot,* (*Bot.*) rejeton, *m;* (*business*) ramification; (*action &c*) conséquence, *f*. *~shore,* (*breeze*) de terre; (*waters, fishing*) côtier. *~side,* (*Mot.*) (*UK*) côté droit; (*Fr.*) côté gauche; (*Sport*) hors-jeu. *~spring,* rejeton, *m,* progéniture, *f*. *~stage,* dans les coulisses. *~-the-cuff,* impromptu. *~-the-peg,* prêt à porter. *~-white,* blanc cassé, *inv*. ¶ *ad,* de distance, d'ici. *be ~,* partir, s'en aller; (*in restaurant*) n'y avoir plus de; (*cancelled*) être annulé; (*stale*) être mauvais. *~ & on,* de temps en temps.

offal, *n,* abats, *m.pl.*

offence, *n,* (*Law*) délit (contre), *m,* infraction (*against,* à); (*Rel.*) offense, *f*. *first ~,* premier délit. *give ~ to,* blesser, froisser. *take ~ [at],* se vexer (de); se froisser (de). **offend,** *v.t,* (*pers.*) blesser, froisser; (*ears, eyes &c*) choquer. ¶ *v.i,* commettre une infraction. *~ against,* (*law*) violer; (*taste*) offenser. *~***er,** *n,* (*Law*) délinquant, e; (*regulations &c*) contrevenant, e. *~***ing,** *a,* incrimé. **offensive,** *a,* (*shocking*) offensant, choquant; (*disgusting*) repoussant; (*insulting*) grossier; (*Mil. &c*) offensif. ¶ *n,* (*Mil.*) offensive, *f*.

offer, *n,* offre, proposition; (*of marriage*) demande, *f*. (*Com.*) *on ~,* en promotion. ¶ *v.t,* offrir (à); (*help, money &c*) proposer (à); (*opinion*) émettre. *~ up,* offrir. *~***ing,** *n,* offre; (*Rel.*) offrande, *f*. *~***tory,** *n,* offertoire, *m;* (*collection*) quête, *f*.

office, *n,* (*place*) bureau, *m;* (*lawyer*) étude; (*function*) fonction, *f;* (*duty*) fonctions; devoir, *m*. *be in, hold ~,* (*minister*) avoir un portefeuille; (*party*) être au pouvoir; (*mayor, chairman*) être en fonction. *through the good ~s of,* par les bons offices de. *~ automation,* bureautique, *f*. *~ block,* immeuble de bureaux, *m*. *~ boy,* garçon de bureau. **officer,** *n,* (*Mil. &c*) officier; (*Govt.*) fonctionnaire; (*police*) agent, *m*. **official†,** *a,* (*gen.*) officiel: (*language*) administratif; (*uniform*) réglementaire. ¶ *n,* (*gen. Sport &c*) officiel, *m;* (*Adm.*) fonctionnaire, *m,f;* (*Rly &c*) employé, e. *~***dom,** *n,* administration, *f*. **officiate,** *v.i,* (*Eccl.*) officier; exercer les fonctions (*as,* de). **officious,** *a,* empressé.

offing, *n, in the ~,* (*Naut.*) au large; (*fig.*) en vue.

offset, *n,* (*Typ.*) offset. ¶ *v.t,* compenser.

often & (*Poet.*) **oft,** *ad,* souvent. *as often as,* toutes les fois que. *every so often,* de temps en temps. *how often?* combien de fois? *more often than not,* le plus souvent.

ogle, *v.t,* lorgner, reluquer.

ogre, ogress, *n,* ogre, *m,* ogresse, *f*.

oh, *i,* oh!; ô!; ah!

oil, *n,* (*Com., Geol., Ind. &c*) pétrole, *m;* (*Art, Cook., Mot. &c*) huile, *f;* (*heating fuel*) mazout, *m*. *~ of cloves,* essence de girofle, *f*. ¶ *a,* (*industry*) pétrolier; (*millionaire &c*) du pétrole. *~-burning,* (*lamp*) à pétrole; (*stove*) à mazout. *~cake,* tourteau, *m*. *~can,* (*storage*) bidon à huile, *m;* (*nozzled*) burette à h., *f*. *~cloth, ~skin,* toile cirée. *~ colour, ~ paint[ing],* peinture à l'huile, *f*. *~field,* gisement pétrolifère, *m*. *~ filter,* filtre à huile, *m*. *~-fired,* (*heating*) au mazout; (*boiler*) à mazout. *~ lamp,* lampe à pétrole, *f*. *~ pressure,* pression d'huile, *f*. *~ refinery,* raffinerie de pétrole, *f*. *~ rig,* (*land*) derrick, *m;* (*sea*) plate-forme pétrolière. *~ slick,* nappe de pétrole, *f*. *~ stove,* poêle à mazout *ou* (*paraffin*) à pétrole. *~ tanker,* (*ship*) tanker, *m;* (*truck*) camion-citerne, *m*. *~ well,* puits de pétrole, *m*. ¶ *v.t,* graisser, lubrifier. (*fig.*) *to be well ~ed P,* être beurré *P*. *~***y,** *a,* (*consistency*) huileux; (*clothes, hands*) graisseux; (*food*) gras; (*fig.*) onctueux.

ointment, *n,* onguent, *m;* pommade, *f*.

O.K., *P i,* d'accord! O.K! ¶ *a,* (*not bad*) pas mal; (*very good*) très bien. *everything's ~,* tout va bien. ¶ *v.t,* approuver.

okapi, *n,* okapi, *m*.

old, *a,* (*gen.*) vieux; (*former*) ancien, *before n. any ~ thing P,* n'importe quoi. *how ~ is he? he is 10 years ~,* quel âge a-t-il? il a 10 ans. *in the ~ days,* autrefois. *~-age,* la vieillesse. *~-age pension,* pension vieillesse, *f*. *~-age pensioner,* retraité, e. *~-established,* ancien. *~-fashioned,* démodé; (*pers.*) vieux jeu, *inv*. *~ maid,* vieille fille. *~ man,* vieux, *m*. *~ master* (*Art*), tableau de maître, *m*. *~ people,* personnes âgées, vieux, *m.pl*. *~ people's home,* maison de retraite, *f*. *~-style,* à l'ancien mode. *O~ Testament,* Ancien Testament, *m*. *the good ~ days,* le bon vieux temps. *~ wives' tale,* conte de bonne femme, *m*. *~ woman,* vieille, *f*. *~-world,* (*charm &c*) d'autrefois. **in the ~en times,** [au temps] jadis.

oleander, *n,* laurier-rose, *m*.

oligarchy, *n,* oligarchie, *f*.

olive, *n,* olive, *f*. *~ [tree, wood],* olivier, *m*. ¶ *a,* (*complexion &c*) olivâtre. *~[-green],* vert olive, couleur [d']olive. *~ grove,* olivaie, *f*. *~ oil,* huile d'olive, *f*.

Olympic, *a,* olympique. *~ Games,* Jeux olympiques, *m.pl*.

ombudsman, *n,* médiateur, ombudsman, *m*.

omelet[te], *n,* omelette, *f*.

omen, *n,* augure, présage, *m.* **ominous,** *a,* de mauvais augure; (*look, voice &c*) menaçant; (*sign &c*) alarmant.

omission, *n,* omission, *f.* **omit,** *v.t,* omettre (*to do,* de faire).

omnibus, *n,* (*O: bus*) omnibus *O;* (*book*) recueil, *m.*

omnipotence, *n,* omnipotence, toute-puissance, *f.* **omnipotent,** *a,* omnipotent, toutpuissant. **omniscience,** *n,* omniscience, *f.* **omniscient,** *a,* omniscient.

omnivorous, *a,* omnivore.

on, *pr,* sur; à; (*train &c*) dans. ~ *& after,* à partir de. *& so* ~, & ainsi de suite. ~ *the blackboard,* au tableau. ~ *the left, right,* à gauche, droite. ~ *the radio, TV,* à la radio, télé. ~ *France-Inter,* sur France-Inter. ~ *the table,* sur la table. ~ *time,* à temps. ~*coming,* qui approche. ~*going,* en cours. ~*lookers,* spectateurs, *m.pl.* ¶ *ad,* en avant. ~ & ~, sans arrêt. ~ *there,* là-dessus. *be* ~, (*light, Radio &c*) être allumé; (*tap*) être ouvert; (*brake*) être serré; (*taking place*) être en cours. *be* ~ *the pill,* prendre la pilule. *be* ~ *drugs,* se droguer. *put* ~, mettre.

once, *ad,* une fois; (~ *only*) une seule fois. ~ *again,* ~ *more,* encore une fois. *at* ~, tout de suite. ~ *before,* déjà une fois. ~ *for all,* une fois pour toutes. ~ *or twice,* une fois ou deux. ~ *upon a time there was,* il y avait (*ou* il était) une fois.

one, *a,* un; (*sole*) seul; (*same*) même. ~ *& only,* seul & unique. ~ *day,* un jour. ~ *hundred,* cent. *for* ~ *thing,* d'abord. *in the* ~ *car,* dans la même voiture. ~*-armed* (*pers.*), manchot, e. ~*-armed bandit P,* machine à sous, *f.* ~*-eyed,* borgne. ~*-horse town P,* bled *P, m.* ~*-legged,* unijambiste. ~*-man band,* homme-orchestre, *m.* ~*-night stand* (*Theat.*), représentation unique. ~*-sided,* unilatéral; (*fig: contest*) inégal; (*account*) partial. ~*-way,* (*street*) à sens unique; (*traffic*) en s.u; (*ticket*) simple. ¶ *n,* un, e. *I for* ~, pour ma part. ~ *by* ~, un, e à un, e. *he's* ~ *of us,* il est des nôtres. ¶ *pn,* (*indefinite*) un, e; (*specific*) celui, celle; (*impers.*) (*subject*) on; (*object*) vous. *that* ~, celui-là, celle-là. *this* ~, celui-ci, celle-ci. *which* ~? lequel?, laquelle? *the little* ~, le petit. ~**ness,** *n,* unité, *f.*

onerous, *a,* (*task*) pénible; (*responsibility*) lourd.

one's, *pn,* son, sa, ses. **oneself,** *pn,* se; soi-même; (*after pr.*) soi[-même]. [*all*] *by* ~, tout seul. *hurt* ~, se blesser. *speak to* ~, parler à soi-même. *sure of* ~, sûr de soi.

onion, *n,* oignon, *m.* ~ *sauce,* sauce à l'oignon, *f.* ~ *skin,* ~ *peel,* pelure d'oignon, *f.*

only, *a,* seul, unique. ~ *child,* enfant unique, *m,f. it's the* ~ *one left,* c'est le seul qui reste. ¶ *ad,* seulement, ne... [plus] que. ~ *yesterday,* pas plus tard qu'hier. *not* ~ ... *but also,* non seulement ... mais aussi. *she's* ~ *6,* elle n'a que 6 ans. ¶ *c,* mais, seulement.

onomatopoeia, *n,* onomatopée, *f.*

onset, *n,* (& **onslaught**) attaque, *f,* assaut, *m;* (*illness*) début; (*winter, old age*) approche, *f.*

onus, *n,* responsabilité, charge, *f.*

onward, *a,* en avant. ~**[s],** *ad,* en avant; plus loin.

onyx, *n,* onyx, *m.*

ooze, *n,* vase, *f.* ¶ *v.i,* suinter; (*resin*) exuder. ~ *away,* (*courage &c*) disparaître. ~ *out,* sortir, suinter.

opacity, *n,* opacité, *f.*

opal, *n,* opale, *f.*

opaque, *a,* opaque; (*fig.*) obscur.

open, *v.t,* (*gen.*) ouvrir; (*bowels*) relâcher; (*legs*) écarter; (*conversation*) engager. ~ *slightly,* entrouvrir. ~ *again,* rouvrir. ¶ *v.i,* s'ouvrir; (*shop &c*) ouvrir; (*flower*) s'épanouir. ~*out,* (*street &c*) s'élargir. ~ *out on to,* déboucher sur. ¶ *a,* (*gen.*) ouvert; (*road*) dégagé; (*car*) décapoté; (*sewer*) à ciel ouvert; (*prison*) à régime libéral; (*pores*) dilaté; (*frank: pers.*) ouvert, franc; (*enemy*) déclaré; (*admiration &c*) manifeste; (*meeting*) public. ~*-air,* (*activities*) de plein air; (*swimming pool &c*) en p. a; (*Theat.*) de verdure. ~*-&-shut case,* cas incontestable, *m.* ~ *day,* jour de visite, *m;* (*Sch.*) porte[s] ouverte[s], *f.*(*pl.*). ~*-handed,* généreux. ~*-hearted,* franc, sincère. ~*-heart surgery,* chirurgie à cœur ouvert. ~*-minded,* sans parti pris. ~*-mouthed,* bouche bée. ~*-plan,* sans cloisons. ¶ *n, out in the* ~, en plein air; (*countryside*) au grand air. *come out in the* ~ (*fig.*) se faire jour. ~**er,** *n. tin, bottle* ~, ouvre-boîtes, -bouteilles, *m.inv.* ~**ing,** *n,* (*gen.*) ouverture; (*in trees &c*) trouée; (*in wall*) brèche; (*in roof*) percée; (*opportunity*) occasion, *f;* (*trade outlet*) débouché, *m.* ¶ *a,* (*time, price*) d'ouverture; (*remark*) préliminaire. ~ *night,* (*Theat.*) première, *f.* ~**ly,** *ad,* (*frankly*) ouvertement; publiquement. ~**ness,** *n,* franchise, candeur, *f.*

opera, *n.* & ~ *house,* opéra, *m.* ~ *glass*[*es*], jumelle[s] de théâtre, *f.*(*pl*). ~ *singer,* chanteur, euse d'opéra.

operable, *a,* opérable. **operate,** *v.i,* (*gen.*) opérer; (*Med.*) opérer (*on s.o for sth,* qn de qch); (*Mach.*) marcher; (*system, mind*) fonctionner; (*factors*) jouer. *be* ~*d on for,* être opéré de. ¶ *v.t,* faire marcher; faire fonctionner; (*business*) diriger; (*mine &c*) exploiter.

operatic, *a,* d'opéra.

operating theatre, salle d'opération, *f.* **operation,** *n,* (*gen.*) opération; (*Med.*) opération, intervention; exploitation, *f;* fonctionnement, *m;* (*business*) gestion, *f.* **operative,** *a,* en vigueur. ¶ *n,* ouvrier, ère. **operator,** *n,* opérateur, trice; (*Tel.*) standardiste, *m,f.*

operetta, *n,* opérette, *f.*

ophthalmia, *n,* ophtalmie, *f.* **ophthalmic,** *a,* ophtalmique; (*surgeon*) ophtalmologique.
opiate, *n,* opiat, *m.*
opinion, *n,* (*point of view*) opinion, *f,* avis, *m;* (*professional*) avis; (*belief*) opinion. *in my ~,* à mon avis. *in the ~ of,* d'après, selon. (*Med.*) *take a second ~,* prendre l'avis d'un autre médecin. *~ poll,* sondage, *m.* **~ated,** *a,* dogmatique.
opium, *n,* opium, *m. ~ addict,* opiomane, *m,f. ~ den,* fumerie, *f.*
opossum, *n,* opossum, *m.*
opponent, *n,* (*Mil., Sport, of ideas &c*) adversaire, *m,f;* (*in debate*) antagoniste, *m,f.*
opportune, *a,* opportun. **~ly,** *ad,* opportunément, à propos. **~ness,** *n,* opportunité, *f.* **opportunism,** *n,* opportunisme, *m.* **opportunist,** *n,* opportuniste, *m,f.* **opportunity,** *n,* occasion, *f. equality of ~,* chances égales. *when the ~ arises,* à l'occasion.
oppose, *v.t,* s'opposer à; (*Pol.*) faire opposition à; (*debate*) parler contre. **~d,** *a,* opposé (à). **opposing,** *a,* (*army*) opposé; (*minority*) opposant; (*Law*) adverse. *~ team,* adversaire[s], *m.[pl].* **opposite,** *n,* opposé, contraire, *m.* **~ (to),** *a,* opposé. ¶ *pr,* en face de. *~ one another,* en vis-à-vis. ¶ *ad,* en face. *the house ~,* la maison d'en face. **opposition,** *n,* opposition, *f;* adversaire, *m.*
oppress, *v.t,* opprimer; (*Med., fig.*) oppresser. **~ion,** *n,* oppression, *f.* **~ive,** *a,* (*Mil., Pol.*) tyrannique; (*tax &c*) oppressif; (*heat, anxiety &c*) accablant; (*weather*) lourd. **~or,** *n,* oppresseur, *m.*
opt, *v.i, ~ for,* opter pour. *~ to do,* choisir de faire. *~ out,* se récuser. *~ out of doing,* choisir de ne pas faire.
optic, *a,* optique. **~al,** *a,* optique; (*glass, instruments, illusion*), d'optique. **optician,** *n,* opticien, ne. **optics,** *n,* optique, *f.*
optimal, *a,* optimal.
optimism, *n,* optimisme, *m.* **optimist,** *n. &* **~(ic),** *a,* optimiste, *m,f.*
optimum, *a,* optimum.
option, *n,* choix, *m;* (*Com., Fin.*) option, *f.* **~al†,** *a,* facultatif.
opulence, *n,* opulence, *f.* **opulent,** *a,* opulent.
or, *c,* ou; (*neg.*) ni. *~ else,* ou bien, autrement. *2 ~ 3 times a day,* de 2 à 3 fois par jour.
oracle, *n,* oracle, *m.*
oral†, *a,* oral. *~ exam,* [examen] oral, *m.*
orange, *n,* orange, *f;* (*colour*) orange, *m,* orangé, *m.* ¶ *a,* orange, orangé; (*drink, flavour*) d'orange; (*liqueur*) à l'o. *~ [tree],* oranger, *m. ~ blossom,* fleurs d'oranger, *f.pl. O~man,* orangiste, *m. ~ peel,* écorce d'orange, *f.* **~ade,** *n,* orangeade, *f.* **~ry,** *n,* orangerie, *f.*
orang-outang, *n,* orang-outang, *m.*
oration, *n,* discours, *m;* (*funeral*) oraison, *f.* **orator,** *n,* orateur, *m.* **oratorio,** *n,* oratorio, *m.* **oratory,** *n,* l'art oratoire, *m,* éloquence, *f;* (*chapel*) oratoire, *m.*
orbit, *n,* orbite, *f.* ¶ *v.t. & i,* orbiter.
orchard, *n,* verger, *m.*
orchestra, *n,* orchestre, *m. ~ stall,* fauteuil d'orchestre, *m.* **orchestral,** *a,* orchestral. **orchestrate,** *v.t,* orchestrer.
orchid, *n,* orchidée, *f.* **orchis,** *n,* orchis, *m.*
ordain, *v.t,* décréter (que); (*Rel.*) ordonner.
ordeal, *n,* épreuve; (*Hist.*) ordalie, *f.*
order, *n,* (*gen., Mil., Rel.*) ordre; (*Adm.*) arrêté, *m;* (*social*) classe; (*Com.*) commande, *f;* (*Fin.*) mandat; (*permit*) permis, *m. holy ~s,* les ordres, *m.pl.* (*Law*) *judge's ~,* ordonnance, *f. court ~,* injonction de la cour, *f. ~!* à l'ordre! *in ~,* (*room &c*) en ordre; (*documents*) en règle. *in ~ that,* afin que, pour que. *in ~ to,* afin de. *keep ~,* (*police*) maintenir l'ordre; (*teacher*) maintenir la discipline. *out of ~,* en panne; (*Tel: line*) en dérangement. *~ book,* livre (*ou* carnet) de commandes, *m. ~ form,* bon (*ou* bulletin) de commande, *m. ~ paper* (*Parliament*), ordre du jour. ¶ *v.t,* ordonner (*s.o to do,* à qn de faire); (*goods*) commander; (*taxi*) retenir. ¶ *v.i,* (*in restaurant*) passer la commande. *~ about,* commander. **~ly,** *a,* ordonné; (*life*) rangé; (*crowd*) discipliné. ¶ *n,* (*Mil.*) ordonnance, *f,* planton, *m;* (*hospital*) garçon de salle, *m. ~ officer,* officier de service, *m. ~ room,* salle du rapport, *f.*
ordinal [number], *n,* nombre ordinal, *m.*
ordinance, *n,* ordonnance, *f.*
ordinary†, *a,* (*usual*) ordinaire, normal, habituel; (*average*) moyen; (*pej.*) quelconque. ¶ *n,* ordinaire, *m. out of the ~,* hors du commun.
ordination, *n,* ordination, *f.*
ordnance, *n,* artillerie, *f. ~ [survey] map,* carte d'État-major, *f.*
ore, *n,* minerai, *m.*
organ, *n,* organe; (*Mus.*) orgue, *m. ~ grinder,* joueur d'orgue de Barbarie, *m. ~ loft,* tribune d'orgue, *f. ~ pipe,* tuyau d'orgue, *m.*
organdie, *n,* organdi, *m.*
organic, *a,* organique. **organization,** *n,* organisation, *f.* **organize,** *v.t,* organiser. **organizer,** *n,* organisateur, trice.
orient, *n,* orient, *m. the O~* (*Geog.*), l'O. **~al,** *a,* oriental. **O~,** *n,* Oriental, e. **~[ate],** *v.t,* orienter.
orifice, *n,* orifice, *m.*
origin, *n,* origine, *f.* **~al†,** *a,* (*not copied*) original; (*primitive*) originaire, originel. ¶ *n,* original, *m.* **~ality,** *n,* originalité, *f.* **~ate,** *v.t,* être l'auteur de; (*effect*) produire. ¶ *v.i, ~ from,* (*pers.*) être originaire de; (*goods*) provenir de. *~ from s.o,* émaner de qn. **originator,** *n,* auteur, *m.*
oriole (*bird*) *n,* loriot, *m.*

Orkneys (the), les Orcades, *f.pl.*
orlon, *n,* orlon, *m.*
ormolu, *n.* (*& a*), (en) similor, *m.*
ornament, *n,* (*gen.*) ornement; (*object*) bibelot, *m.* ¶ *v.t,* (*Build.*) ornementer; (*dress, style*) orner. **~al,** *a,* ornemental; (*design*) décoratif; (*garden, lake*) d'agrément. **ornamentation,** *n,* ornementation, *f.* **ornate,** *a,* orné.
ornithologist, *n,* ornithologiste, ornithologue, *m.f.* **ornithology,** *n,* ornithologie, *f.*
orphan, *n. & a,* orphelin, e. **~age,** *n,* orphelinat, *m.*
orthodox, *a,* orthodoxe. **~y,** *n,* orthodoxie, *f.*
orthography, *n,* orthographe; (*Arch.*) orthographie, *f.* **orthopaedic,** *a,* orthopédique. **orthopaedics,** *n,* orthopédie, *f.*
oscillate, *v.i,* osciller; (*v.t.*) faire osciller. **oscillation,** *n,* oscillation, *f.*
osier, *n,* osier, *m.* ~ *bed,* oseraie, *f.*
osmosis, *n,* (*Phys., fig.*) osmose, *f.*
osprey, *n,* orfraie, *f.*
ostensible, *a,* prétendu. **ostensibly,** *ad,* en apparence, sous prétexte. **ostentation,** *n,* ostentation, parade, *f.* **ostentatious,** *a,* prétentieux; (*liter.*) ostentatoire.
osteopath, *n,* ostéopathe, *m.f.* **~y,** *n,* ostéopathie, *f.*
ostracism, *n,* ostracisme, *m.* **ostracize,** *v.t,* frapper d'ostracisme.
ostrich, *n,* autruche, *f.*
other, *a. & pn,* autre. *every ~ day,* tous les deux jours. *on the ~ side* or *hand,* de l'autre côté. *~s, ~ people,* d'autres, les autres; (*liter.*) autrui. **~wise,** *ad,* autrement. ¶ *c,* autrement, sinon, sans quoi, sans cela.
otter, *n,* loutre, *f.*
ottoman, *n,* ottomane, *f.*
ought, *v.modal,* devoir, falloir. *he ~ to do it,* il devrait le faire, il faudrait qu'il le fasse.
ounce, *n,* once, *f.* (*= 28.35 grammes*).
our, *a,* notre, nos, *pl.* **~s,** *pn,* le nôtre, la nôtre, les nôtres. *a friend of ~,* un de nos amis. *this table is ~,* cette table est à nous. **ourselves,** *pn,* (*reflexive & after pr.*) nous; (*emphatic*) nous-mêmes. *we said to ~,* nous nous sommes dit.
oust, *v.t,* évincer (*from,* de); supplanter.
out, *ad,* dehors; (*Elec., gas &c*) éteint; (*not at home, Sport: ball*) sorti; (*in flower*) en fleur. *~ & ~,* (*fool, liar &c*) fieffé; (*believer &c*) à tous crins; (*success*) éclatant; (*defeat*) écrasant. ~ [*for the count*] (*Box.*), K.-O. ~ *loud,* tout haut. ~ *there,* là-bas, là-dehors. *be ~,* (*games*) être éliminé; (*wrong*) se tromper. *it's just ~,* (*book &c*) il vient de paraître. *the tide is ~,* la marée est basse. **out of,** *pr,* (*outside*) en dehors de, hors de; (*motive*) par; (*source*) de, dans; (*from among*) sur; (*without*) sans. *drink ~ a glass,* boire dans un verre. *9 ~ 10,* neuf sur dix. ¶ *comps: ~ action,* hors de combat. ~ *bounds,* hors des limites. ~ *date,* démodé; (*ticket &c*) périmé. *be ~ date,* (*pers.*) retarder. ~ *doors,* dehors, au grand air. ~ *fashion,* démodé. ~ *hand,* sur-le-champ; échappé à tout contrôle. ~ *one's element,* hors de son élément, dépaysé. ~ *place* (*fig.*), déplacé, hors de propos. ~ *pocket,* en perte. ~ *pocket expenses,* débours, *m.pl.* ~ *practice,* rouillé. ~ *print,* épuisé. ~ *shape,* avachi. ~ *sight,* hors de vue. ~ *sorts,* pas dans son assiette. *to be ~ stock of,* être à court de, manquer de. *out-of-the-way, a,* écarté, retiré, isolé. ~ *true,* (*upright*) pas d'aplomb; (*beam*) gauchi; (*wheel*) faussé. ~ *tune,* faux. ~ *work,* en chômage; sans emploi. **out,** *i,* dehors! hors d'ici! *~ with him!* à la porte! *~ with it!* dis-le donc! accouche! *P.* *~ you go!* filez *P,* sortez!
outbid, *v.t.ir,* [r]enchérir sur, surenchérir sur.
outboard, *a,* hors-bord, *inv.*
outbreak, *n,* (*war, disease &c*) début; (*emotion, fever*) accès, *m;* (*violence, spots*) éruption; (*demonstrations*) vague, *f.* ~ *of fire,* incendie, *m. at the ~ of war,* quand la guerre éclata.
outbuilding, *n,* dépendance, *f.*
outburst, *n,* explosion, *f;* (*anger*) accès, *m.*
outcast, *n,* exilé, e, proscrit, e; (*social ~*) paria, *m,* réprouvé, e.
outclass, *v.t,* surclasser.
outcome, *n,* conséquence, issue, *f,* résultat, *m.*
outcrop (*Geol.*) *n,* affleurement, *m.*
outcry, *n,* cri, *m,* clameur, *f. general ~,* tollé [général]. *raise an ~,* crier haro (*about,* sur).
outdated, *a,* (*custom*) suranné; (*clothes, theory &c*) démodé; (*word*) vieilli.
outdistance, *v.t,* distancer.
outdo, *v.t.ir,* surpasser; l'emporter sur.
outdoor, *a,* (*activities*) de plein air; (*swimming pool*) en plein air.
outer, *a,* extérieur; (*garments*) de dessus. ~ *space,* cosmos, *m.* ~ *suburbs,* grande banlieue.
outfit, *n,* équipement, *m;* (*set of clothes*) tenue; (*P organization*) équipe *P, f.* **outfitter,** *n,* (*gents'*) maison d'habillement pour hommes; (*sports ~*) maison de sports, *f.*
outflank, *v.t,* déborder.
outflow, *n,* écoulement, *m.*
outgoing, *a,* (*president &c*) sortant; (*train, mail &c*) en partance; (*tide*) descendant; (*pers.*) ouvert. **~s,** *n.pl,* débours, déboursés, *m.pl.*
outgrow, *v.t.ir,* devenir trop grand pour.
outhouse, *n,* appentis, *m. the ~s,* les communs, *m.pl.*
outing, *n,* sortie, excursion, *f.*
outlandish, *a,* bizarre.
outlast, *v.t,* durer plus longtemps que.
outlaw, *n,* hors-la-loi, *m.inv.* ¶ *v.t,* proscrire, mettre hors la loi.
outlay, *n,* débours, frais, dépenses, *m.pl.*

outlet, *n,* issue, sortie, *f;* (*Com. & fig.*) débouché, *m.*
outline, *n,* (*object*) contour; (*face, building &c*) profil, *m;* (*Art*) ébauche; (*fig: summary*) esquisse, *f;* (*pl.*) grandes lignes. ~ *drawing,* dessin au trait, *m.* ¶ *v.t,* tracer le contour de; exposer les grandes lignes de.
outlive, *v.t,* survivre à.
outlook, *n,* vue (sur), perspective (de); (*fig: point of view*) attitude, *f.*
outlying, *a,* (*peripheral*) périphérique; (*remote*) isolé.
outmanœuvre, *v.t,* déjouer.
outnumber, *v.t,* surpasser en nombre.
out-patient, *n,* malade en consultation externe, *m,f.*
outpost, *n,* avant-poste, *m.*
outpouring, *n,* épanchement, *m,* effusion, *f.*
output, *n,* rendement, *m,* production; (*computer*) sortie, *f.*
outrage, *n,* atrocité, *f;* (*scandal*) scandale, *m.* ¶ *v.t,* outrager, faire outrage à; violer. ~**ous†,** *a,* atroce; (*action, price &c*) scandaleux; (*fashion*) impossible.
outrigger, *n,* (*boat*) outrigger, *m.*
outright, *a,* complet; (*rejection &c*) catégorique; (*winner*) incontesté. ¶ *ad,* complètement; catégoriquement; (*kill*) net; (*tell*) carrément; (*at once*) sur-le-champ.
outset, *n,* début, *m.*
outshine, *v.t.ir,* éclipser.
outside, *a,* extérieur. (*Mot.*) ~ *lane,* (*UK*) voie de droite; (*Fr.*) v. d. gauche, *f.* (*Foot.*) ~ *right, left,* ailier droit, gauche. ¶ *ad,* à l'extérieur, [au] dehors. ¶ *n,* extérieur, dehors, *m;* (*café*) terrasse, *f. at the* ~, tout au plus. ¶ *pr,* (*lit.*) à l'extérieur de, hors de; (*fig.*) en dehors de. **outsider,** *n,* (*pers.*) étranger, ère; (*horse*) outsider, *m.*
outsize, *a,* (*gen.*) énorme; (*clothes*) grande taille, *inv.*
outskirts, *n.pl,* environs, *m.pl;* banlieue, *f.*
outsmart *P, v.t,* se montrer plus malin que.
outspoken, *a,* franc. ~**ness,** *n,* franchise, *f.*
outspread, *a,* étendu.
outstanding, *a,* exceptionnel; (*feature*) dominant; (*business*) en suspens; (*account*) arriéré; (*debt*) impayé.
outstretched, *a,* étendu.
outstrip, *v.t,* devancer.
outward, *a,* vers l'extérieur; (*journey*) aller; (*fig: appearance &c*) extérieur. ¶ *ad,* vers l'extérieur. ~ *bound,* en partance.
outwit, *v.t,* (*gen.*) se montrer plus malin que; (*pursuer*) dépister.
oval, *a. & n,* ovale, *m.*
ovary, *n,* ovaire, *m.*
ovation, *n,* ovation, *f.*
oven, *n,* four, *m;* (*fig.*) étuve, *f.* ~ *glove,* gant isolant, *m.* ~*proof,* allant au four. ~*-ready,* prêt à cuire. ~*ware,* plats allant au four, *m.pl.*
over, *ad,* (*above*) [par-]dessus; (*finished*) fini; (*remaining*) en plus; (*too*) trop. *children of 7 &* ~, enfants au-dessus de 7 ans. ~ *again,* encore une fois. (*look*) *all* ~ (*for*), (chercher) partout. ~ *& above,* en sus de. ~ *there,* là-bas. ¶ *pr,* (*on top of*) sur, par-dessus; (*above*) au-dessus de; (*more than*) plus de, au-dessus de; (*across*) par-dessus, de l'autre côté de. ~ *all* (*Meas.*), de bout en bout. **over...** *pref,* sur...
overact, *v.t,* charger. ~**ive,** *a,* trop actif.
overall, *a,* (*view*) global; (*Meas.*) hors tout; (*total*) total. ~ *measurements* (*Mot.*), encombrement, *m.* ¶ *n,* blouse, *f.* ~*s* (*Ind. &c*), salopette, *f,* bleus [de travail], *m.pl.*
overarm, *ad,* (*throw &c*) par en-dessus.
overawe, *v.t.* intimider.
overbalance, *v.i,* perdre l'équilibre; (*object*) se renverser.
overbearing, *a,* insolent, arrogant, excédant.
overboard (*Naut.*) *ad,* par-dessus bord. [*a*] *man* ~*!* un homme à la mer!
overburden, *v.t,* surcharger.
overcast, *a,* couvert. *grow* ~, se couvrir.
overcautious, *a,* prudent à l'excès.
overcharge, *v.t,* ~ *s.o for sth,* faire payer qch trop cher à qn. *be* ~*d,* payer un prix excessif. (*Elec.*) surcharger. ¶ *v.i,* demander un prix excessif.
overcoat, *n,* pardessus, *m;* (*Mil.*) capote, *f.*
overcome, *v.t.ir,* (*enemy, opposition*) triompher de; (*obstacle*) surmonter; (*emotions*) maîtriser. *be* ~ *by grief &c,* succomber à la douleur &c. *we shall* ~*!* nous vaincrons!
overconfidence, *n,* (*assurance*) suffisance, présomption; (*trust*) confiance aveugle, *f.* **overconfident,** *a,* suffisant, présomptueux; trop confiant (en).
overcrowded, *a,* (*bus, room*) bondé; (*town, house*) surpeuplé; (*class*) surchargé. **overcrowding,** *n,* surpeuplement, *m;* effectifs surchargés; (*in bus &c*) encombrement, *m.*
overdo, *v.t.ir,* exagérer; outrer; trop cuire. **overdone,** *a,* exagéré, outré; (*Cook.*) trop cuit.
overdose, *n,* trop forte dose, *f.*
overdraft, *n,* découvert, *m.* **overdraw,** *v.t.ir,* (*an a/c*) mettre à découvert.
overdrive (*Mot.*), *n,* [vitesse] surmultipliée, *f.*
overdue, *a,* (*train &c*) en retard; (*reform*) qui tarde [à être réalisé]; (*reply*) tardif; (*account*) arriéré.
overelaborate, *a,* contourné; (*design*) trop compliqué.
overestimate, *v.t,* surestimer.
overexcite, *v.t,* surexciter.
overexpose, *v.t,* surexposer. **overexposure** (*Phot., fig.*), *n,* surexposition, *f.*
overfeed, *v.t.* (*& i.*)*ir,* (se) suralimenter.

overflow, *n,* (*outlet*) trop-plein; (*reservoir &c*) déversoir; (*excess: people, objects*) excédent, *m.* ¶ *v.i,* déborder. *full to ~ing,* plein à déborder.
overgrown, *a,* envahi (*with,* par); (*child*) trop grandi.
overhang, *n,* surplomb, *m.* ¶ *v.i. & t. ir,* surplomber. **~ing,** *a,* en saillie, en surplomb.
overhaul, *n,* (*Mach.*) révision, *f;* (*ship*) radoub, *m.* ¶ *v.t,* réviser; radouber.
overhead, *a,* aérien. *~s, ~ charges,* frais généraux, *m.pl.* ¶ *ad,* au-dessus de la tête; en haut, en l'air, au ciel.
overhear, *v.t.ir,* entendre [par hasard].
overheat, *v.t,* surchauffer. ¶ *v.i.* (*engine*) chauffer.
overindulgence, *n,* excès d'indulgence, *m.*
overjoyed, *a,* comblé de joie, ravi.
overladen, *a,* surchargé.
overland, *ad. & a,* par voie de terre.
overlap, *n,* chevauchement, *m.* ¶ *v.t,* (*tiles*) enchevaucher; (*edges*) dépasser; (*fig.*) empiéter sur. ¶ *v.i,* se chevaucher.
overleaf, *ad,* au verso.
overload, *v.t,* surcharger.
overlook, *v.t,* (*have view over*) donner sur; (*castle &c*) dominer; (*miss*) oublier; (*ignore*) fermer les yeux sur.
overlord, *n,* (*gen.*) chef suprême; (*Hist.*) suzerain, *m.*
overmuch, *ad,* [par] trop, à l'excès.
overnight, *a,* (*stay*) d'une nuit; (*journey*) de nuit; (*fig: sudden*) soudain. ¶ *ad,* pendant la nuit; (*fig.*) du jour au lendemain.
overpay, *v.t.ir,* surpayer, trop payer.
overpopulated, *a,* surpeuplé.
overpower, *v.t,* (*physically*) maîtriser; (*fig.*) accabler. **~ing,** *a,* (*strength, passion*) irrésistible; (*heat*) accablant, suffocant.
overproduction, *n,* surproduction, *f.*
overrate, *v.t.* surestimer. **~d,** *a,* surfait.
overreach, *v.t,* dépasser. *~ o.s,* trop entreprendre.
override, *v.t.ir,* (*decision*) annuler; (*law*) fouler aux pieds; (*order, wishes*) passer outre à. **overriding,** *a,* (*importance*) primordial; (*factor*) prépondérant.
overripe, *a,* trop mûr, blet.
overrule, *v.t,* (*decision*) annuler; (*claim &c*) rejeter.
overrun, *v.t.ir,* (*pests &c*) envahir, infester; (*army*) occuper. ¶ *v.i,* (*time*) dépasser l'heure prévue (*by,* de).
oversea[s], *a,* d'outre-mer. ¶ *ad,* outre-mer; à l'étranger.
oversee, *v.t,* surveiller. **overseer,** *n,* contremaître, *m.*
overshadow, *v.t,* ombrager; obscurcir; (*fig.*) éclipser.
overshoot, *v.t.ir,* dépasser.
oversight, *n,* omission, *f,* oubli, *m.*
oversleep, *v.i.ir,* dormir trop longtemps.
overspill, *n,* excédent de population, *m.*
overstate, *v.t,* exagérer.
overstep, *v.t,* outrepasser.
overstrain, *v.t,* surmener.
oversubscribed, (*Stk. Ex.*) *a,* sursouscrit.
overt, *a,* déclaré; non déguisé. **~ly,** *ad,* ouvertement.
overtake, *v.t.ir,* rattraper; (*storm &c*) surprendre; (*fate*) frapper; (*Mot.*) doubler.
overtax, *v.t,* (*Fin.*) surimposer; (*fig: strength &c*) abuser de; (*pers.*) surmener.
overthrow, *n,* (*Govt. &c*) chute; (*enemy*) défaite, *f.* ¶ *v.t,* (*Govt., dictator &c*) renverser; (*enemy, country &c*) vaincre [définitivement].
overtime, *n,* heures supplémentaires, *f.pl.*
overtone, *n,* (*Mus.*) harmonique, *m. or f;* (*fig.*) accent, *m.*
overture, *n,* ouverture, *f.*
overturn, *v.t,* (*lit. & fig.*) renverser; (*boat*) faire chavirer.
overvalue, *v.t,* surestimer.
overweening, *a,* outrecuidant; (*pride &c*) démesuré.
overweight (to be), peser trop, avoir des kilos de trop.
overwhelm, *v.t,* (*enemy*) écraser; (*emotions*) accabler; (*beauty*) bouleverser; (*flood*) engloutir. **~ing,** *a,* (*defeat*) écrasant; (*desire*) irrésistible; (*heat*) accablant.
overwork, *n,* surmenage, *m.* ¶ *v.t,* surmener; (*horse*) forcer.
ovulation, *n,* ovulation, *f.*
owe, *v.t,* devoir (à). **owing,** *a,* dû. ¶ *pr, ~ to,* à cause de, en raison de.
owl, *n,* hibou, *m,* chouette, *f.*
own, *a,* propre. *all my ~ work,* c'est moi qui ai tout fait moi-même. *not my ~,* pas à moi. *one's ~,* son [propre], à soi. *with my ~ eyes,* de mes propres yeux. ¶ *pr, on one's ~,* tout seul. *get one's ~ back,* prendre sa revanche (sur qn de qch). ¶ *v.t,* posséder; (*acknowledge*) avouer, reconnaître. *~ up,* confesser, avouer. **owner,** *n,* propriétaire, *m,f. at ~'s risk,* aux risques & périls du propriétaire. **~ship,** *n,* possession, *f. 'under new ~'* (*Com.*), 'changement de propriétaire'.
ox, *n,* bœuf, *m. ~-eye daisy,* grande marguerite, *f. ~tail,* queue de bœuf, *f.*
oxide, *n,* oxyde, *m.* **oxidize,** *v.t,* oxyder. **oxyacetylene,** *a,* oxyacétylénique. **oxygen,** *n,* oxygène, *m.* **oxygenate,** *v.t,* oxygéner.
oyster, *n,* huître, *f. ~ bed,* banc d'h-s, *m.*
ozone, *n,* ozone, *m.*

P

pace, *n,* pas, *m;* (*speed*) allure, *f. keep ~ with,* aller à la même allure que; (*fig.*) marcher de pair avec. *set the ~,* (*Sport*) mener le train; (*fig.*) donner le ton. *~maker,* (*Sport*) meneur de train; (*Med.*) stimulateur cardiaque, *m.* ¶ *v.t,* (*street &c*) arpenter; (*Sport*) régler l'allure de.

pacific, *a,* pacifique. **P~ [Ocean],** [océan] Pacifique, *m.* **pacifist,** *n. & a,* pacifiste, *m,f.* **pacify,** *v.t,* (*pers.*) apaiser; (*country*) pacifier.

pack, *n,* (*goods*) balle, *f;* (*pedlar*) ballot; (*~ animal*) bât; (*Mil.*) sac [d'ordonnance]; (*Com.*) paquet; (*cards*) jeu; (*Rugby*) pack, *m;* (*hounds*) meute; (*wolves, thieves*) bande, *f. ~ of lies,* tissu de mensonges, *m.* ¶ *v.t,* (*put in box &c*) emballer; (*fill: container*) remplir (*with,* de); (*room, car, memory*) bourrer (de); (*crush*) (*people*) entasser; (*objects*) tasser (*into,* dans). *~ one's bags,* faire ses bagages *ou* ses valises; (*fig.*) plier bagage. *~ed like sardines* (*people*), serrés comme des sardines. *~* **away,** ranger. *~***in** *P,* (*pers., job*) plaquer *P. ~* **off** *P,* envoyer promener; (*~ s.o. off*) expédier (qn à) *P. ~* **up,** faire sa valise; (*Mach.*) tomber en panne; (*P give up*) laisser tomber *P.* **~age,** *n,* colis, paquet, *m.* ¶ *a,* (*tour, holiday*) organisé. *~ deal,* marché global. ¶ *v.t,* emballer. **~aging,** *n,* emballage, *m.* **~et,** *n,* paquet; (*needles, sweets*) sachet, *m;* (*paper bag*) pochette, *f. cost a ~ P,* coûter les yeux de la tête *P.* **~ing,** *n,* emballage, *m. ~ case,* caisse d'emballage, *f.*

pact, *n,* pacte, traité, *m.*

pad, *n,* (*flute &c*) coussinet; tampon, *m;* (*Foot.*) protège-cheville, *m.inv;* (*Hockey*) jambière, *f;* (*writing ~*), bloc [de papier à lettres]; (*note ~*) bloc-notes; (*inking ~*) tampon encreur, *m;* (*dog*) coussin charnu; (*launching ~*) rampe [de lancement]; (*P room*) piaule *P, f.* ¶ *v.t,* (*clothing &c*) rembourrer; (*furniture*) capitonner; (*fig: ~ out*) délayer. ¶ *v.i,* aller à pas feutrés. *~ded cell,* cabanon, *m.* **~ding,** *n,* bourre, ouate, *f;* (*fig.*) délayage, *m.*

paddle, *n,* (*canoe*) pagaie; (*water wheel*) aube, *f. ~ boat,* bateau à roues, *m.* ¶ *v.t,* pagayer. ¶ *v.i,* (*in water, mud*) barboter; patauger. *paddling pool,* bassin pour enfants, *m;* [petite] piscine.

paddock, *n,* enclos; (*Turf*) paddock, *m.*

paddy *P, n,* (*rage*) rogne *P, f.*

paddy field, *n,* rizière, *f.*

padlock, *n,* cadenas; (*for cycle*) antivol, *m.* ¶ *v.t,* cadenasser; mettre un antivol à.

paediatric, *a,* (*department*) de pédiatrie; (*illness &c*) infantile. **~ian,** *n,* pédiatre, *m,f.* **~s,** *n,* pédiatrie, *f.*

pagan, *a. & n,* païen, ne. **~ism,** *n,* paganisme, *m.*

page[1], *n,* (*book*) page, *f.*

page[2], *n,* (*hotel*) groom, chasseur; (*court*) page, *m.* ¶ *v.t,* (*pers.*) faire appeler.

pageant, *n,* spectacle historique, *m.* **~ry,** *n,* pompe, *f,* apparat, *m.*

paid, *a,* (*gunman &c*) à gages. *~ up,* (*shares*) libéré; (*member*) qui a payé sa cotisation.

pail, *n,* seau, *m.* **~[ful],** *n,* seau, *m.*

pain, *n,* douleur, *f,* mal, *m;* (*mental*) peine, *f;* douleur. *be in ~,* souffrir. *cause ~ to,* faire mal à; faire de la peine à. *~ in the neck P* (*pers.*), casse-pieds *P. give s.o a ~ in the neck P,* enquiquiner qn *P. ~killer,* calmant, *m. on ~ of death,* sous peine de mort. ¶ *v.t,* faire souffrir; peiner. **~ful†,** *a,* douloureux; pénible. **~less,** *a,* sans douleur; (*operation*) indolore. **pains,** *n.pl,* peine, *f. take ~ over,* se donner beaucoup de mal pour. **~taking,** *a,* soigneux.

paint, *n,* peinture, *f; pl,* couleurs, *f.pl. ~box,* boîte de couleurs, *f. ~ brush,* pinceau, *m. ~pot,* pot de peinture, *m. ~ spray,* pulvérisateur, *m. ~-stripper,* (*chemical*) décapant; (*tool*) racloir, *m.* ¶ *v.t,* peindre; (*fig.*) dépeindre. *~ one's nails,* se vernir les ongles. *~ the town red* (*fig.*), faire la bombe *P.* **~er,** *n,* peintre, *m.* **~ing,** *n,* peinture, *f;* (*picture*) tableau, *m.*

pair, *n,* paire, *f;* (*man & wife*) couple, *m. ~ of scissors,* ciseaux, *m.pl. ~ of steps,* escabeau, *m. ~ of trousers,* pantalon, *m. in ~s,* à deux. ¶ *v.t,* (*~ off*) (*objects*) ranger par paires. ¶ *v.i,* (*people*) s'arranger deux par deux.

Pakistan, *n,* Pakistan, *m.* **Pakistani,** *a,* pakistanais. ¶ *n,* Pakistanais, e.

pal *P, n,* copain, *m,* copine, *f. P.*

palace, *n,* palais, *m.*

palatable, *a,* agréable [au goût]; (*fig.*) acceptable. **palate,** *n,* palais, *m.*

palatial, *a,* vaste & somptueux.

palaver, *n,* palabre, *f;* (*fuss*) histoire, affaire, *f.*

pale, *a,* pâle; (*sickly*) blême. *~face,* Visage pâle, *f. ~-faced,* au teint pâle; blême. ¶ *v.i,* pâlir; devenir blême. **~ness,** *n,* pâleur, *f.*

paleontology, *n,* paléontologie, *f.*

Palestine, *n,* la Palestine. **Palestinian,** *a,* palestinien. ¶ *n,* Palestinien, ne.

palette, *n,* palette, *f. ~ knife,* couteau à palette, *m;* (*Cook.*) spatule, *f.*

paling, *n,* (*fence*) palissade, *f.*

pall[1], *v.i,* perdre de son charme (*on,* pour).

pall[2], *n,* drap mortuaire, *m. be a ~ bearer,* tenir les cordons du poêle.

palliate, *v.t,* pallier. **palliative,** *a. & n,* palliatif, *m.*
pallid, *a,* blafard, blême. **pallor,** *n,* pâleur, *f.*
palm[1], *n,* (*tree*) palmier, *m;* (*branch*) palme, *f;* (*Rel.*) rameau, *m.* ~ *oil,* huile de palme, *f.* *P~ Sunday,* dimanche des Rameaux, *m.*
palm[2], *n,* (*hand*) paume, *f. grease s.o's* ~, graisser la patte à qn. ~ **off,** *v.t.* faire passer; refiler *P.* ~**ist,** *n,* chiromancien, ne. ~**istry,** *n,* chiromancie, *f.*
palpable, *a,* palpable; (*fig.*) manifeste. **palpitate,** *v.i,* palpiter. **palpitation,** *n,* palpitation, *f.*
paltry, *a,* dérisoire; (*excuse*) piètre.
pampas, *n.pl,* pampas, *f.pl.*
pamper, *v.t,* gâter; dorloter.
pamphlet, *n,* brochure, *f.*
pan[1], *n,* (*Cook.*) casserole; (*frying* ~) poêle, *f;* (*scales*) plateau, *m;* (*W.C.*) cuvette, *f.* ~ *scrubber,* tampon à récurer, *m.* ¶ *v.t,* (*P criticize*) esquinter *P.* ¶ *v.i,* (*Cine*) panoramiquer.
pan... *pref,* pan...
panacea, *n,* panacée, *f.*
panama, *n,* ~ [*hat*], panama, *m.*
pancake, *n,* crêpe, *f. as flat as a* ~, plat comme une galette. *P~ Day,* mardi gras.
pancreas, *n,* pancréas, *m.*
panda, *n,* panda, *m.*
pandemonium, *n,* tohu-bohu, *m.*
pander to, (*wishes*) se plier à; (*pers.*) encourager bassement.
pane, *n,* (*glass*) carreau, *m,* vitre, *f.*
panegyric, *n,* panégyrique, *m.*
panel, *n,* panneau; (*ceiling*) caisson; (*dress*) pan; (*Mot., Aero: instrument*~) tableau de bord; (*Law, Adm. &c*) jury, *m;* (*doctor's*) régistre, *m.* ¶ *v.t,* lambrisser.
pang, *n,* serrement de cœur, *m;* (*of death*) angoisse, *f;* (*pl.*) affres, *f.pl.*
panic, *n,* terreur, panique, *f.* ¶ *a,* de panique. ¶ *v.t.* (*& i*), (s')affoler.
pannier, *n,* panier, *m;* (*on cycle &c*) sacoche, *f.*
panoply, *n,* panoplie, *f.*
panorama, *n,* panorama, *m.* **panoramic,** *a,* panoramique.
pansy, *n,* pensée, *f;* (*P* pej.*) tante *P*, f.*
pant, *v.i,* haleter. ~ *for breath,* chercher à reprendre haleine.
pantechnicon, *n,* grand camion de déménagement.
panther, *n,* panthère, *f.*
pantomime, *n,* (*Theat.*) spectacle de Noël, *m;* (*mime*) pantomime, *f.*
pantry, *n,* garde-manger, *m.*
pants, *n.pl,* (*men, women*) slip; (*men*) caleçon; (*Am. trousers*) pantalon, *m.*
papa, *n,* papa, *m.*
papacy, *n,* papauté, *f.* **papal,** *a,* papal. ~ *nuncio,* nonce du Pape, *m.*
paper, *n,* papier; (*news*) journal, *m;* (*documents: pl.*) papiers, *m.pl;* (*Sch: exam questions*) épreuve [écrite]; (*answers*) copie, *f;* (*learned*) article, exposé, *m. old* ~*s,* paperasses, *f.pl. piece of* ~, (*sheet*) feuille de papier, *f;* (*smaller*) bout d. p., *m.* ~ *bag,* sac en papier, *m;* (*small*) pochette, *f.* ~ *boy,* livreur de journaux, *m.* ~ *chase,* rallye-papier, *m.* ~ *clip,* trombone, *m.* ~ *cup,* verre en carton, gobelet, *m.* ~ *knife,* coupe-papier, *m.* ~ *mill,* papeterie, *f.* ~ *money,* papier-monnaie, *m.* ~ *weight,* presse papiers, *m.* ~ *work,* paperasserie, *f.* ¶ *v.t,* tapisser.
papier mâché, *n,* carton-pâte, *m.*
papist, *n,* papiste, *m,f.*
paprika, *n,* paprika, *m.*
papyrus, *n,* papyrus, *m.*
par, *n,* pair; (*Golf*) par, *m. be on a* ~ *with,* être au niveau de, aller de pair avec.
para..., *pref,* para...
parable, *n,* parabole, *f.*
parachute, *n,* parachute, *m.* ¶ *a,* (*jump*) en parachute; (*regiment*) de parachutistes. ~ *drop, landing,* parachutage, *m.* ¶ *v.i,* descendre en parachute. **parachutist,** *n,* parachutiste, *m,f.*
parade, *n,* (*Mil.*) rassemblement, *m;* (*ceremonial*) parade, revue, *f;* (*procession*) défilé; (*fig: display*) étalage, *m.* ~ *ground,* terrain de manœuvres, *m. fashion* ~, présentation de collections, *f.* ¶ *v.t.* (*fig.*) faire étalage de. ¶ *v.i,* (*Mil.*) se rassembler; (*march*) défiler.
paradise, *n,* paradis, *m.*
paradox, *n,* paradoxe, *m.* ~**ical,** *a,* paradoxal.
paraffin, *n,* (*Chem.*) paraffine, *f;* (*fuel*) pétrole [lampant], *m. liquid* ~, huile de paraffine, *m.* ~ *lamp,* lampe à pétrole, *f.* ~ *wax,* paraffine.
paragon, *n,* parangon, modèle, *m.*
paragraph (*abb.* par[a]) *n,* paragraphe; alinéa; (*newspaper item*) entrefilet, *m.*
parakeet, *n,* perruche, *f.*
parallel†, *a,* parallèle (*with, to,* à). ~ *bars,* barres parallèles, *f.pl.* ¶ *n,* (*Geom., Geog., fig.*) parallèle, *f.* ~**ogram,** *n,* parallélogramme, *m.*
paralyse, *v.t,* paralyser. **paralysis,** *n,* paralysie, *f.* **paralytic,** *a. & n,* paralytique, *m,f;* (*P drunk*) ivre mort.
paramilitary, *a,* paramilitaire.
paramount, *a,* suprême; souverain.
paramour, *n,* amant, *m,* maîtresse, *f.*
paranoia, *n,* paranoïa, *f.* ~**c,** *a. & n,* paranoïaque, *m,f.* **paranoid,** *a,* paranoïde.
parapet, *n,* parapet, *m.*
paraphernalia, *n.pl,* attirail, *m.*
paraphrase, *n,* paraphrase, *f.* ¶ *v.t. & i,* paraphraser.
paraplegia, *n,* paraplégie, *f.* **paraplegic,** *a. & n,* paraplégique, *m,f.*
parasite, *n,* parasite, *m.* **parasitic(al),** *a,* parasite; parasitaire.

parasol, *n,* ombrelle, *f;* (*for table*) parasol, *m.*
paratrooper, *n,* parachutiste, para *P m.*
parboil, *v.t,* faire bouillir à demi.
parcel, *n,* colis, paquet, *m;* (*land*) parcelle, *f;* (*shares*) paquet. ~ *bomb,* paquet piégé. *by* ~ *post,* par colis postal. ~ *office,* bureau de messageries, *m.* ~ **[out],** *v.t,* distribuer; (*land*) lotir.
parched, *a,* (*land*) brûlé, desséché. *be* ~ (*pers.*), mourir de soif.
parchment, *n,* parchemin, *m.*
pardon, *n,* pardon, *m;* (*Rel.*) indulgence; (*Law: free* ~) grâce, *f. general* ~, amnistie, *f.* ¶ *v.t,* pardonner, pardonner à; gracier. ¶ *i,* pardon! excusez-moi!; (*not hearing*) comment? plaît-il? ~**able,** *a,* pardonnable, excusable.
pare, *v.t,* (*fruit*) peler, éplucher; (*nails*) rogner. ~ *down,* réduire.
parent, *n,* père, *m,* mère; (*fig.*) mère, *f;* (*pl.*) parents, *m.pl;* (*att.*) mère. ~**age,** *n,* origine, naissance, *f.* ~**al,** *a,* de père, de mère, des parents.
parenthesis, *n,* parenthèse, *f.* **parenthetic(al),** *a,* entre parenthèses. **parenthetically,** *ad,* par parenthèse.
parish, *n,* (*civil*) commune; (*Eccl.*) paroisse, *f;* (*att.*) communal; paroissial. ~ *church,* église paroissiale, *f.* **parishioner,** *n,* paroissien, ne.
Parisian, *a,* parisien. ¶ *n,* Parisien, ne.
parity, *n,* parité, *f.*
park, *n,* parc; (*public*) jardin public, parc, *m.* ~ *keeper,* gardien de parc, *m.* ¶ *v.t,* garer, parquer. ¶ *v.i,* se garer, stationner.
parka, *n,* parka, *m.*
parking, *n,* stationnement, *m.* ~ *attendant,* gardien de parking, *m.* ~ *lights,* feux de position, *m.pl.* ~ *metre,* parcmètre, *m.* ~ *ticket,* papillon *P, m.*
parlance, *n,* langage, *m.*
parley, *n,* pourparlers, *m.pl.* ¶ *v.i,* parlementer.
parliament, *n,* parlement, *m.* ~**ary,** *a,* (*government, &c*) parlementaire; (*election*) législatif; (*candidate*) à la députation.
parlour, *n,* [petit] salon; (*convent, school*) parloir, *m.* ~ *games,* jeux de société, *m.pl.* ~ *maid,* femme de chambre (*servant à table*) *f.*
parmesan, *n,* parmesan, *m.*
parochial, *a,* (*civil*) communal; (*Eccl.*) paroissial; (*fig.*) de clocher.
parody, *n,* parodie, *f.* ¶ *v.t,* parodier.
parole, *n,* (*Mil.*) parole d'honneur; (*Law*) liberté conditionelle, *f. on* ~, sur parole; en liberté conditionnelle.
paroxysm, *n,* paroxysme, *m.*
parquet, *n,* parquet, *m.* ¶ *v.t,* parqueter.
parrot, *n,* perroquet, *m;* (*hen*) perruche, *f.*
parry, *v.t,* parer; (*question*) éluder. ~**[ing],** *n,* parade, *f.*
parsimonious†, *a,* parcimonieux. **parsimony,** *n,* parcimonie, *f.*
parsing, *n,* analyse grammaticale, *f.*
parsley, *n,* persil, *m.*
parsnip, *n,* panais, *m.*
parson, *n,* pasteur; curé; ecclésiastique, *m.* ~*'s nose,* croupion, *m.* ~**age,** *n,* presbytère, *m.*
part, *n,* (*gen.*) partie; (*Tech.*) pièce; (*Cook.*) mesure, *f;* (*serial*) épisode, *m;* (*Mus: song*) voix, *f;* (*Theat., fig.*) rôle; (*side*) parti, *m;* (*behalf*) part; (*region*) région, *f;* ~*s of speech,* catégories grammaticales. *be* ~ *& parcel of,* faire partie intégrante de. *for my* ~, quant à moi; pour ma part. *for the most* ~, dans l'ensemble. *in these* ~*s,* dans ces parages, *m.pl. in foreign* ~*s,* à l'étranger. *take* ~ *in,* participer à. *take in good* ~, prendre du bon côté. *take s.o's* ~. prendre parti pour qn. (*fig.*) *play a large* ~ *in,* jouer un grand rôle dans. ~ *exchange,* reprise en compte, *f.* ~ *payment,* règlement partiel, *m.* ~*-time,* à temps partiel; (*half-time*) à mi-temps. ¶ *ad,* en partie. ¶ *v.t,* (*people*) séparer. ~ *company with,* quitter; (*fig.*) ne plus être d'accord avec. ~ *one's hair,* se faire une raie. ¶ *v.i,* se séparer; se quitter. ~ *with,* (*money*) débourser; (*belongings*) se défaire de.
partake, *v.i.ir,* participer (*in,* à). ~ *of,* (*food &c*) prendre.
partial†, *a,* (*biased*) partial; (*not entire*) partiel. *to be* ~ *to,* avoir un faible pour. ~**ity,** *n,* partialité; (*liking*) prédilection, *f,* faible, *m.*
participate, *v.i,* participer (*in,* à).
participle, *n,* participe, *m.*
particle, *n,* particule, parcelle; (*Gram.*) particule, *f.*
particular†, *a,* particulier; spécial; (*own*) personnel; (*fussy &c*) méticuleux, difficile. *for no* ~ *reason,* sans raison précise. ¶ *n,* détail, point, *m;* (*pl.*) détails, *m.pl;* description, *f;* (*pers.*) signalement, *m. in* ~, en particulier. ~**ity,** *n,* particularité, *f.* ~**ize,** *v.t,* préciser; spécifier.
parting, *n,* séparation, *f;* (*hair*) raie, *f.* ¶ *a,* (*words*) d'adieu. ~ *shot,* flèche du Parthe, *f.*
partisan, *n,* partisan, *m.*
partition, *n,* cloison; (*country*) partition, *f.* ¶ *v.t,* diviser; partager; (*room*) cloisonner. **partitive** (*Gram.*) *a,* partitif.
partly, *ad,* en partie; moitié; partiellement.
partner, *n,* (*Com.*) associé, e; (*Sports*) partenaire, *m,f;* (*in marriage*) époux, épouse; (*Danc.*) cavalier, ère. ¶ *v.t,* (*Danc.*) danser avec. ~**ship,** *n,* association, *f. to enter into* ~ *with,* s'associer avec.
partridge, *n,* perdrix, *f;* (*young*) perdreau, *m.*
party, *n,* (*Pol.*) parti, *m;* (*group: travellers*) groupe, *m;* (*workmen*) équipe, *f;* (*Mil.*) détachement, *m;* (*Law &c*) partie, *f.* ~ *to,* complice de. (*gathering*) réunion, réception; surprise-partie; (*birthday*) fête; (*evening*) soirée, *f.* ~ *dress,* robe habillée. ~ *line,* (*Pol.*)

ligne du parti, *f;* (*Tel.*) ligne commune à 2 abonnés. ~ *wall,* mur mitoyen.
pass, *n,* (*Geog.*) col, défilé, *m;* (*permit*) laissez-passer, *m.inv;* (*Mil.*) sauf-conduit, *m;* (*Foot.*) passe; (*Fenc.*) botte, *f.* ~ *degree,* licence, *f.* ~*key,* passe-partout, *m.inv.* ~*mark,* moyenne, *f.* ~*word,* mot de passe, *m.* ¶ *v.i,* (*come, go*) passer; (*time*) passer, s'écouler; (*occur*) se passer; (*in exam*) être reçu; (*Mot.*) doubler; (*Foot.*) faire une passe. ¶ *v.t,* (*food, object*) passer, faire p.; (*time*) passer (*doing,* à faire); (*frontier, customs*) passer; (*house*) passer devant, dépasser; (*overtake*) dépasser; (*Mot.*) doubler; (*exam*) être reçu à; rèussir; (*candidate*) recevoir; (*Pol. bill*) voter; (*judgement*) rendre, prononcer; (*remark*) faire. *to* ~ *water,* uriner. ~ **away,** (*die,* also ~ *on*) mourir, s'éteindre; (*memory*) disparaître. ~ **down,** transmettre. ~ **on,** (*clothes &c*) repasser; (*news*) faire circuler; (*message*) transmettre. ~ **off,** (*pain*) passer, ~ *o.s. off as,* se faire passer pour. ~ **out,** (*faint*) s'évanouir; (*from drink*) tomber ivre mort; (*distribute*) distribuer. ~ **over,** passer sur, omettre. ~**able**†, *a,* passable; (*road &c*) praticable. ~**age,** *n,* passage, *m;* (*Naut.*) traversée, *f,* (*corridor*) couloir, *m.*
passenger, *n,* (*train*) voyageur, euse; (*sea, air, car*) passager, ère; (*fig: pej.*) poids-mort, *m.* ~ *seat* (*Mot.*), siège de passagers, *m.*
passer-by, *n,* passant, e. **passing,** *a,* (*lit.*) qui passe; (*fig: brief*) passager; (*desire*) fugitif; (*remark*) en passant. ¶ *n,* passage, (*time*) écoulement, *m. in* ~, en passant, passagèrement. ~ *fancy,* caprice, *m;* (*liaison*) passade, *f.*
passion, *n,* passion, *f;* (*anger*) emportement, *m.* ~ *flower,* passiflore, *f.* ~ *fruit,* fruit de la Passion, *m.* ~ *play,* mystère de la Passion, *m.* ~**ate,** *a,* emporté; (*speech*) véhément; passionné. ~**ately,** *ad,* passionnément.
passive†, *a,* passif. ~ **[voice],** *n,* passif, *m.* **passivity,** *n,* passivité, *f.*
passover, *n,* pâque, *f.*
passport, *n,* passeport, *m.*
past, *n,* passé, *m.* ¶ *a,* passé. *be a* ~ *master at,* avoir l'art de. *the* ~ *few days,* ces derniers jours. ~ [*tense*], [temps] passé, *m.* ¶ *pr,* (*beyond*) plus loin que; au delà de; (*in time*) plus de. *half* ~ *4,* 4 heures & demie. *10* ~ *4,* 4 heures 10. ¶ *ad,* auprès, devant. *to go* ~, (*house*) passer devant.
pasta, *n,* pâtes, *f.pl.*
paste, *n,* (*gen., Cook.*) pâte, *f;* (*meat*) pâté, *m;* (*glue*) colle, *f;* (*jewellery*) strass, *m.* ~*board,* carton, *m.* ¶ *v.t,* coller; (*wallpaper*) enduire de colle.
pastel, *n,* pastel, *m.*
pasteurize, *v.t,* pasteuriser.
pastil[le], *n,* pastille, *f.*
pastime, *n,* passe-temps, *m.*
pastor, *n,* pasteur, *m.* ~**al,** *a,* pastoral. ~**al &** ~**ale,** *n,* pastorale, *f.*
pastry, *n,* pâte; (*cake*) pâtisserie, *f.* ~ *board,* planche à pâtisserie, *f.* ~ *brush,* pinceau à patisserie, *m.* ~ *case,* croûte, *f.* ~*cook,* pâtissier, ère.
pàsture, (*&* ~*land*) *n,* pâturage, *m.*
pasty, (pεisti) *a,* pâteux; (*face*) terreux. ¶ (pæsti) *n,* petit pâté, feuilleté, *m.*
pat[1], *a. & ad,* à propos, à point; (*answer*) tout prêt.
pat[2], *n,* petite tape; (*butter*) noix, *f. give o.s a* ~ *on the back,* se féliciter. ¶ *v.t,* taper, tapoter; (*animal*) caresser, flatter.
patch, *n,* (*for clothes*) pièce; (*for rubber*) rustine, *f;* (*for eye*) bandeau, *m;* (*face*) mouche; (*ground*) lopin, *m,* parcelle, *f;* (*vegetables*) carré; (*sky*) morceau, *m;* (*colour*) tache; (*ice*) plaque, *f.* ~ *pocket,* poche rapportée. ~*work,* patchwork, *m.* ¶ *v.t,* rapiécer; (*tyre*) réparer. ~ *up a quarrel,* se raccommoder. ~**y,** *a,* inégal.
patent, *a,* breveté; (*obvious*) patent. ~ *leather,* cuir verni, *m.* ~ *medicine,* spécialité pharmaceutique, *f.* ¶ *n,* brevet [d'invention], *m.* ¶ *v.t,* [faire] breveter.
paternal†, *a,* paternel. **paternity,** *n,* paternité, *f.*
path, *n,* sentier, chemin, *m;* (*in garden*) allée; (*storm &c*) trajectoire; (*sun*) route, *f.*
pathetic†, *a,* (*gen. & fig: pej.*) pitoyable; (*attempt*) désespéré.
pathological, *a,* pathologique. **pathologist,** *n,* pathologiste, *m,f.* **pathology,** *n,* pathologie, *f.*
pathos, *n,* pathétique, *m.*
patience, *n,* patience; (*Cards*) réussite, *f. lose* ~, s'impatienter. **patient**†, *a,* patient, endurant. ¶ *n,* malade, *m,f;* (*Med.*) patient, e; (*doctor's list*) client, e.
patriarch, *n,* patriarche, *m.* ~**al,** *a,* patriarcal.
patrician, *a. & n,* patricien, ne.
patrimony, *n,* patrimoine, *m.*
patriot, *n,* patriote, *m,f.* ~**ic,** *a,* patriotique; patriote. ~**ism,** *n,* patriotisme, *m.*
patrol, *n,* patrouille, *f.* ~ *car,* voiture de police, *f.* ¶ *v.i,* patrouiller; (*v.t.*) patrouiller dans.
patron, *n,* (*charity*) patron, ne; (*arts*) protecteur, trice; (*shop &c*) client, e; (*theatre*) habitué, e. ~ *saint,* saint, e patron, ne. ~**age,** *n,* patronage, *m,* protection, *f.* **patronize,** *v.t,* (*Com.*) donner sa clientèle à; (*pej.*) traiter avec condescendance. **patronizing,** *a,* condescendant.
patter[1], *n,* (*sales talk*) boniment; baratin, *m.*
patter[2], *n,* (*rain &c*) crépitement; (*footsteps*) petit bruit, *m.* ¶ *v.i,* (*rain*) battre; (*hail*) crépiter; (*footsteps*) trottiner.
pattern, *n,* (*on material &c*) dessin[s], *m*[*pl*]; motif; (*Need.*) patron; (*sample*) échantillon;

(*fig.*) modèle, *m.* ~ *book,* album d'échantillons, *m;* (*Need.*) catalogue de modes, *m.* ¶ *v.t,* modeler (sur).
patty, *n,* bouchée, *f.*
paunch, *n,* panse, *f.*
pauper, *n,* indigent, e, pauvre, *m.*
pause, *n,* pause, *f,* arrêt; (*Mus.*) point d'orgue, *m;* (*in conversation*) silence, *m.* ¶ *v.i,* faire une pause; hésiter. ~ *for breath,* s'arrêter pour reprendre haleine.
pave, *v.t,* paver. ~ *the way for* (*fig.*), frayer la voie à. ~**ment,** *n,* trottoir, *m.*
pavilion, *n,* pavillon, *m.*
paving, *n,* (*stones*) pavés; (*tiles*) carreaux, *m.pl;* (*flagstones*) dalles, *f.pl;* (*ground*) pavage, *m.* ~ *stone,* pavé, *m.*
paw, *n,* patte, *f.* ¶ *v.t,* (*P pers.*) tripoter *P.* ~ *the ground,* piaffer.
pawn[1], *n,* gage, *m.* ~*broker,* prêteur, euse sur gages. ~*shop,* mont de piété, *m. in* ~, en gage, au clou *P.* ¶ *v.t,* mettre en gage *ou* au clou *P.*
pawn[2], *n,* (*Chess*) pion, *m. a* ~ *in the game* (*fig.*), un pion sur l'échiquier.
pay, *n,* (*gen.*) salaire, *m;* (*manual worker*) paie *ou* paye, *f;* (*civil servant*) traitement, *m;* (*Mil., Naut.*) solde, *f,* paie; (*servant*) gages, *m.pl. in the* ~ *of,* à la solde de. *holidays with* ~, congés payés. ~ *day,* jour de paie, *m.* ~ *desk,* caisse, *f.* ~ *rise,* augmentation de salaire, *f.* ~ *slip,* bulletin de paie, *m.* ¶ *v.t,* (*pers., money*) payer; (*bill &c*) régler, payer; (*deposit*) verser; (*debt*) régler; (*be profitable*) rapporter à; (*compliment*) faire; (*visit*) rendre. ¶ *v.i,* payer. ~ *for sth* (*lit. & fig.*), payer qch. ~ **back,** (*pers., loan*) rembourser; rendre. ~ **in,** verser. ~ **off,** *v.t,* (*debts*) régler; (*pers.*) rembourser; (*discharge*) licencier; (*v.i,*) rapporter. ~ **out,** (*spend*) dépenser; (*cashier &c*) payer; (*rope*) laisser filer. ~ **up,** (*amount*) payer; (*arrears &c*) régler, s'aquitter de. ~**able,** *a,* payable; (*cheque*) à l'ordre (de). ~**ee,** *n,* bénéficiaire, *m,f.* ~**er,** *n,* celui qui paie; (*cheque*) tireur, euse; (*good, bad*) payeur, euse. ~**ing,** *a,* payant; (*profitable*) rémunérateur. ~ *guest,* pensionnaire, *m,f.* ~*-in slip,* bordereau de versement, *m.* ~**ment,** *n,* paiement; versement; règlement; acquittement; remboursement, *m.*
pea, *n,* [petit] pois, *m. they're as like as 2* ~*s,* ils se ressemblent comme 2 gouttes d'eau. ~*cock,* paon, *m.* ~*hen,* paonne, *f.* ~*nut,* (*plant*) arachide; (*nut*) cacahouète, *f.* ~*shooter,* sarbacane, *f.* ~ *soup,* soupe aux pois, *f.*
peace, *n,* paix; (*calm*) tranquillité, *f;* (*Law*) ordre public. *keep the* ~, (*police*) veiller à l'o. p.; (*fig.*) maintenir la paix. ~*maker,* pacificateur, trice. ~ *offering,* cadeau de reconciliation, *m.* ¶ *a,* (*talks, treaty*) de paix. ~**able,** *a,* pacifique. ~**ful†,** *a,* paisible; tranquille; (*meeting*) calme; (*demonstration*) non-violent; (*co-existence &c*) pacifique.
peach, *n,* pêche, *f.* ~ [*tree*], pêcher, *m.*
peak, *n,* cime, *f,* sommet; pic, *m;* (*roof &c*) arête; (*cap*) visière, *f;* (*graph*) sommet; (*fig: career &c*) apogée, *m.* ~ *times,* heures de pointe, *f.pl.*
peal, *n,* (*bells*) carillon; (*thunder*) coup; (*laughter*) éclat, *m.* ¶ *v.i,* carillonner; gronder; éclater.
pear, *n,* poire, *f.* ~ *tree &* ~ *wood,* poirier, *m.*
pearl, *n,* perle, *f.* [*mother of*] ~, nacre, *f.* ~ *button,* bouton de nacre, *m.* ~ *barley,* orge perlé, *m.* ~ *oyster,* huître perlière, *f.* ~**y,** *a,* (*made of pearl*) de *ou* en nacre; (*colour*) nacré.
peasant, *n. & a,* paysan, ne.
peat, *n,* tourbe, *f.* ~ *bog,* tourbière, *f.* ~**y,** *a,* tourbeux.
pebble, *n,* caillou; (*on beach*) galet, *m.* ~ *dash,* mouchetis, *m.*
pecan, *n,* pacane, *f.* ~ [*tree*], pacanier, *m.*
peck, *n,* coup de bec, *m;* (*kiss*) bise *P, f.* ¶ *v.t,* becqueter, picoter; (*food*) picorer. ~*ing order* (*fig.*), hiérarchie, *f. be* ~*ish,* avoir la dent *P.*
pectin, *m,* pectine, *f.*
peculiar†, *a,* (*odd*) bizarre, curieux, étrange; (*particular*) particulier. ~**ity,** *n,* bizarrerie; particularité, *f.*
pecuniary†, *a,* pécuniaire.
pedagogical, *a,* pédagogique. **pedagogue,** *n,* pédagogue, *m.*
pedal, *n,* pédale, *f.* ~*bin,* poubelle à pédale, *f.* ~*boat,* pédalo, *m.* ~*car,* voiture à pédales, *f.* ¶ *v.i,* pédaler.
pedant, *n,* pédant, e. ~**ic,** *a,* pédant. ~**ry,** *n,* pédantisme, *m.*
peddle, *v.t,* colporter; (*drugs*) faire le trafic de.
pedestal, *n,* piédestal, *m.* ~ *desk,* bureau-ministre, *m.* ~ *table,* guéridon, *m.*
pedestrian, *n,* piéton, *m.* ~ *crossing,* passage pour piétons, passage clouté, *m.* ~ *precinct,* zone piétonnière, *f.* ¶ *a,* à pied; pédestre.
pedigree, *n,* (*animal*) pédigree, *m;* (*pers.*) ascendance, *f.* ¶ *a,* de [pure] race.
pedlar, *n,* colporteur, *m;* (*drugs*) revendeur, euse.
peel, *n,* (*on fruit*) peau; (*from apples &c*) pelure; (*potato*) épluchure; (*citrus*) écorce, *f;* (*Cook.*) zeste, *m. candied* ~, écorce confite. ¶ *v.t,* (*fruit, potatoes*) éplucher; (*shrimps*) décortiquer. ~ [*off*], *v.i,* se peler; (*paint*) s'écailler. ~**er,** *n,* éplucheur, *m.* ~**ings,** *n.pl,* épluchures, *f.pl.*
peep, *n,* regard furtif, coup d'œil, *m.* ~*-bo!* coucou! ~*hole,* trou pour épier, *m.* ~*ing Tom,* voyeur, *m.* ¶ *v.i,* jeter un coup d'œil, regarder furtivement.
peer[1], *v.i,* ~ *at,* regarder; scruter.

peer², *n,* pair, *m.* ~**age,** *n,* pairie, *f. be given a* ~, être anobli. ~**ess,** *n,* pairesse, *f.* ~**less,** *a,* sans pareil.
peeved, *P, a,* fâché, en rogne *P.* **peevish,** *a,* maussade.
peewit, *n,* vanneau, *m.*
peg, *n,* (*wooden*) cheville; (*metal*) fiche; (*coat &c*) patère; (*clothes* ~) pince à linge, *f;* (*tent* ~) piquet, *m. bring s.o down a* ~ *or 2,* rabaisser le caquet de qn. ¶ *v.t,* (*Tech.*) cheviller; (*prices*) stabiliser.
pejorative, *a,* péjoratif.
Pekinese *or* **peke** (*dog*) *n,* pékinois, *m.* **Pekin[g],** (*Geog.*) *n,* Pékin, *m.*
pelican, *n,* pélican, *m.*
pellet, *n,* (*paper*) boulotte, *f;* (*for gun*) plomb, *m.*
pell-mell, *ad,* pêle-mêle.
pelt¹, *n,* peau, *f.*
pelt², *v.t,* bombarder, cribler (*with,* de). *it's* ~*ing down P,* il tombe des cordes *P.* ~*ing rain,* pluie battante.
pelvis, *n,* bassin, pelvis, *m.*
pen¹, *n,* plume, *f;* (*fountain* ~) stylo; (*ball-point*) stylo [à bille]; (*felt-tip*) feutre, *m.* ~ *& ink drawing,* dessin à la plume, *m.* ~*knife,* canif, *m.* ~ *name,* pseudonyme, *m.* ~ *nib,* bec de plume, *m.* ¶ *v.t,* écrire.
pen², *n,* parc, enclos, *m;* (*play* ~) parc [d'enfant]. ¶ *v.t,* (*animal*) parquer; (*pers.*) enfermer.
penal, *a,* pénal; (*colony*) pénitentiaire. ~ *servitude,* travaux forcés. ~**ize,** *v.t,* pénaliser. ~**ty,** *n,* pénalité, peine; (*Sport*) pénalisation, *f;* (*Foot.*) penalty, *m.* ~ *area,* (*Foot.*), surface de réparation, *f.* ~ *clause,* clause pénale, *f.* ~ *kick,* penalty. ~ *spot,* point de réparation, *m.* ~ *stroke* (*Golf*), coup d'amende, *m.* **penance,** *n,* pénitence, *f.*
pencil, *n,* crayon, *m. in* ~, au crayon. ~ *case,* trousse, *f.* ~ *sharpener,* taille-crayon, *m.* ¶ *v.t,* crayonner.
pendant, *n,* pendentif, *m.* **pending,** *a,* pendant. ¶ *pr,* en attendant. **pendulum,** *n,* pendule; (*clock*) balancier, *m.*
penetrate, *v.t. & i,* pénétrer (dans); (*business, Pol. Party*) s'infiltrer dans. **penetrable,** *a,* pénétrable. **penetrating,** *a,* pénétrant. **penetration,** *n,* pénétration, *f.*
penguin, *n,* pingouin; (*Antarctic*) manchot, *m.*
penicillin, *n,* pénicilline, *f.*
peninsula, *n,* péninsule, *f.* **peninsular,** *a,* péninsulaire.
penis, *n,* pénis, *m.*
penitence, *n,* pénitence, *f.* **penitent,** *a. & n,* pénitent, e. **penitentiary,** *a,* pénitentiaire. ¶ *n,* pénitencier, *m.*
pennant, *n,* flamme, *f.*
penniless, *a,* sans le sou.
penny, *n,* penny; (*very little money*) sou, *m. the* ~ *has dropped!* il a (j'ai &c) pigé! *P.* ~ *dreadful,* roman à deux sous, *m.* ~*royal,* pouliot, *m.* ~ *whistle,* flûteau, *m.*
pension, *n,* pension; retraite, *f.* ~ *fund,* fonds vieillesse, *m.pl.* ~ *scheme,* caisse de retraite, *f.* ¶ *v.t,* pensionner. ~ *off,* mettre à la retraite. ~**er,** *n,* retraité, e.
pensive, *a,* pensif, songeur.
pentagon, *n,* pentagone, *m,* ~ **al,** *a,* pentagonal.
pentathlon, *n,* pentathlon, *m.*
penthouse, *n,* (~ *flat*) appartement construit sur le toit d'un immeuble.
pent-up, *a,* (*emotions &c*) refoulé; (*pers.*) tendu.
penultimate, *a,* pénultième.
penury, *n,* misère, indigent, *f.*
peony, *n,* pivoine, *f.*
people, *n,* (*pl; persons*) gens, *m.pl, f.pl a. before n;* personnes, *f.pl;* (*crowd*) monde, *m;* (*pl. in general*) on, les gens; (*inhabitants*) habitants, *m.pl;* (*citizens*) peuple, *m;* (*general public*) public, *m;* (*family*) famille, *f;* (*nation, race*) peuple, race, nation, *f.* ~ *say,* on dit. *what a lot of* ~*!* que de monde! ¶ *v.t,* peupler (*with,* de).
pep, *n,* entrain, dynanisme, *m.* ~ *pill,* excitant, *m.* ~ *talk,* discours d'encouragement, *m.* ~ **up,** *v.t,* (*pers.*) remonter le moral à; (*party*) animer.
pepper, *n,* poivre; (*vegetable*) poivron, *m.* ~*corn,* grain de poivre, *m.* ~ *mill,* moulin à poivre. ~*mint,* (*sweet*) pastille de menthe, *f.* ¶ *v.t,* (*Cook.*) poivrer; (*shot*) cribler; (*questions*) assaillir. ~**y,** *a,* poivré; (*pers.*) irascible.
per, *pr,* par; pour. ~ *annum,* par an, l'an. ~ *cent,* pour cent.
perceive, *v.t,* (*sense*) percevoir; (*notice*) apercevoir, s'apercevoir de.
percentage, *n,* pourcentage, *m.*
perceptible, *a,* perceptible. **perception,** *n,* perception, *f.* **perceptive,** *a,* (*pers., analysis*) perspicace; pénétrant.
perch¹, *n,* (*fish*) perche, *f.*
perch², *n,* (*bird's*) perchoir, *m;* (*Meas.*) perche, *f.* ¶ *v.t,* (*& i*), (se) percher; (se) jucher.
percolate, *v.t. & i,* (*coffee*) passer; (*fig.*) filtrer.
percussion, *n,* percussion, *f.* ~ *instruments,* instruments de percussion, *m.pl,* batterie, *f.*
peregrine [falcon], *n,* faucon pèlerin, *m.*
peremptory†, *a,* péremptoire.
perennial, *a,* perpétuel; (*plant*) vivace. ¶ *n,* plante vivace, *f.*
perfect†, *a,* parfait; (*emphatic: pest &c*) véritable. ~ *pitch,* (*Mus.*), l'oreille absolue. ~ *tense* (*Gram.*), parfait, *m.* ¶ *v.t,* parachever; parfaire; (*skill*) mettre au point. ~**ion,** *n,* perfection, *f.*
perfidious†, *a,* perfide. **perfidy,** *n,* perfidie, *f.*
perforate, *v.t,* perforer.
perforce, *ad,* forcément.

perform, *v.t,* (*task*) exécuter, accomplir; (*function*) remplir; (*rite*) célébrer; (*Theat.*) donner; (*Mus.*) jouer; exécuter. ¶ *v.i,* donner une représentation; jouer; chanter; danser; (*Mach.* &c) marcher, fonctionner. **~ance,** *n,* (*Theat.*) représentation; (*Cine.* &c) séance; (*actor* &c) interprétation, *f;* (*Sport, vehicle*) performance, *f;* (*Mach.*) fonctionnement, *m;* (*duty*) exécution; (*P fuss*) histoire, *f.* *~ing dog,* chien savant, *m.* **~er,** *n,* (*gen.*) artiste, *m,f.*

perfume, *n,* parfum, *m.* ¶ *v.t,* parfumer. **~ry,** *n,* parfumerie, *f.*

perfunctory, *a,* pour la forme.

perhaps, *ad,* peut-être. *~ so, not,* peut-être que oui, non.

peril, *n,* péril, *m.* **~ous†,** *a,* périlleux.

perimeter, *n,* périmètre, *m.*

period, *n,* période; époque, *f;* (*Sch.*) cours; (*stop*) point, *m;* (*menstruation*) règles, *f.pl.* *~ costume,* costume de l'époque, *m.* *~ piece,* curiosité, *f.* **~ic** & **~ical†,** *a,* périodique. **~ical,** *n,* périodique, *m.*

peripatetic, *a,* ambulant; (*teacher*) qui enseigne dans plusieurs écoles.

peripheral, *a,* périphérique. **periphery,** *n,* périphérie, *f.*

periscope, *n,* périscope, *m.*

perish, *v.i,* (*die*) périr, mourir; (*rubber* &c) se détériorer, s'abîmer. *be ~ed* (*cold*), crever de froid *P.* **~able,** *a,* périssable. **~ing,** *a,* très froid; (*P*) foutu *P.*

peritonitis, *n,* péritonite, *f.*

periwinkle, *n,* (*Zool.*) bigorneau, *m;* (*Bot.*) pervenche, *f.*

perjure oneself, se parjurer; (*Law*) faire un faux serment. **perjurer,** *n,* parjure, *m,f.* **perjury,** *n,* faux serment; parjure, *m.*

perk, *n,* à-côté, *m;* (*pl.*) gratte *P, f.*

perk up, *v.i,* se ragaillardir; (*after illness*) se remonter. **perky,** *a,* éveillé; guilleret.

perm, *n,* permanente, *f.* *to have a ~,* se faire faire une p.

permanence, *n,* permanence, *f.* **permanent,** *a,* permanent. **~ly,** *ad,* de façon permanente.

permeate, *v.t,* pénétrer, filtrer à travers; (*ideas*) se répandre dans *ou* parmi. *~ed with,* saturé de. ¶ *v.i,* s'infiltrer; se répandre.

permissible, *a,* permis. **permission,** *n,* permission, *f.* *give ~,* autoriser. **permit,** *n,* autorisation écrite; (*specific*) permis, *m.* ¶ *v.t,* permettre (à qn de faire); autoriser (qn à faire).

pernicious†, *a,* nuisible; (*Med.*) pernicieux.

pernickety, *a,* difficile; pointilleux.

peroxide, *n,* peroxyde, *m.*

perpendicular†, *a.* & *n,* perpendiculaire, *f.*

perpetrate, *v.t,* perpétrer, commettre; faire. **perpetrator** (*crime*) *n,* auteur, *m.*

perpetual†, *a,* perpétuel. **perpetuate,** *v.t,* perpétuer. **perpetuity,** *n,* perpétuité, *f.*

perplex, *v.t,* rendre perplexe. **~ed,** *a,* perplexe. **~ing,** *a,* embarrassant. **~ity,** *n,* perplexité, *f,* embarras, *m.*

perquisite, *n,* à-côté, *m.*

perry, *n,* poiré, *m.*

persecute, *v.t,* persécuter. **persecution,** *n,* persécution, *f.* **persecutor,** *n,* persécuteur, trice.

perseverance, *n,* persévérance, *f.* **persevere,** *v.i,* persévérer (dans qch).

Persia, *n,* la Perse. **Persian** (*modern*) *a,* persan. *~ blind,* persienne, *f.* *~ carpet,* tapis de Perse, *m.* *~ Gulf,* golfe Persique, *m.* ¶ *n,* (*pers.*) Persan, e; (*language*) le persan. **Persian** (*ancient*) *a,* perse. ¶ *n,* Perse, *m,f.*

persist, *v.i,* persister, s'obstiner (dans qch, à faire). **~ence, ~ency,** *n,* persistance, *f.* **~ent,** *a,* persévérant; obstiné; (*smell*) persistant; (*warning, noise* &c) continuel. *~ offender* (*Law*), récidiviste invétéré(e).

person, *n,* personne, *f.* *in ~,* en personne, *~-to-~ call* (*Tel.*), communication avec préavis, *f.* **~age,** *n,* personnage, *m.* **~al†,** *a,* personnel; individuel; (*hygiene*) corporel; (*appearance*) en personne; (*Tel: call*) privé. **~ality,** *n,* personnalité, *f.* **~ification,** *n,* personnification, *f.* **personify,** *v.t,* personnifier.

perspective, *n,* perspective, *f.* *get sth into ~,* voir qch sous son vrai jour.

perspex, *n,* plexiglas, *m.*

perspicacious, *a,* perspicace. **perspicacity,** *n,* perspicacité, *f.*

perspiration, *n,* transpiration, sueur, *f.* *bathed in ~,* en nage. **perspire,** *v.i,* transpirer.

persuade, *v.t,* persuader (*s.o of sth,* qn de qch, *s.o that,* qn que); convaincre (qn de qch). **persuasion,** *n,* persuasion; (*Rel.*) religion, *f.* **persuasive,** *a,* persuasif; (*argument* &c) convaincant.

pert†, *a,* impertinent.

pertain, *v.i,* avoir rapport.

pertinent, *a,* pertinent, à propos. **~ly,** *ad,* à propos.

pertness, *n,* impertinence, *f.*

perturb, *v.t,* troubler, agiter. **~ation,** *n,* perturbation, agitation, *f.*

Peru, *n,* le Pérou.

perusal, *n,* lecture, *f.* **peruse,** *v.t,* lire attentivement.

Peruvian, *a,* péruvien. ¶ *n,* Péruvien, ne.

pervade, *v.t,* se répandre dans; s'étendre dans. **pervasive,** *a,* pénétrant; envahissant.

perverse, *a,* pervers; (*stubborn*) entêté. **perversion,** *n,* (*Psych.*) perversion, *f;* (*fact, justice* &c) travestissement, *m.* **perversity,** *n,* perversité, *f.* **pervert,** *n,* (*Psych: sexual ~*) perverti, e. ¶ *v.t,* pervertir.

pessimism, *n,* pessimisme, *m.* **pessimist,** *n.* & **~ic,** *a,* pessimiste, *m,f.*

pest, *n,* insecte, animal nuisible, *m;* (*pers.*) peste,

f. ~ *control,* (*insects*) désinsectisation, *f;* (*rats*) dératisation, *f.*
pester, *v.t,* tourmenter, importuner.
pesticide, *n,* pesticide, *m.*
pestilence, *n,* peste, *f.* **pestilential,** *a,* pestilentiel.
pestle, *n,* pilon, *m.* ¶ *v.t,* piler.
pet, *n,* animal familier; (*favourite*) chouchou, te *P,* câlin, e. *he's a* ~, c'est un chou *P.* ~ *aversion,* bête noire, *f.* ~ *dog,* chien favori, *m.* ~ *hare, snake &c,* lièvre, serpent &c apprivoisé. ~ *name,* petit nom d'amitié, *m.* ~ *scheme,* plan favori, *m.* ~ *subject,* dada, *m,* marotte, *f.* ~ *vice,* péché mignon, *m.* ¶ *v.t,* (*fondle*) câliner; (*indulge*) chouchouter *P;* (*sexually*) peloter *P.*
petal, *n,* pétale, *m.*
petite, *a,* menue.
petition, *n,* pétition; (*request*) requête, *f.* ¶ *v.t,* adresser une requête à; (*v.i.*) pétitionner. ~**er,** *n,* pétitionnaire, *m,f;* requérant, e; (*divorce*) demandeur, eresse.
petrel, *n,* pétrel, *m.*
petrifaction, *n,* pétrification, *f.* **petrify,** *v.t,* pétrifier.
petrol, *n,* essence, *f. high-octane* ~, supercarburant, super *P, m. run out of* ~, être en panne d'essence. ~ *can,* bidon [à essence], *m.* ~ *cap,* bouchon de réservoir d'e., *m.* ~ *gauge,* jauge d'e., *f.* ~ *pump,* pompe d'e., *f.* ~ *station,* station-service, *f.* ~ *tank,* réservoir, *m.* **petroleum,** *n,* pétrole, *m.*
petticoat, *n,* (*skirt*) jupon, *m;* (*slip*) combinaison, *f.*
pettiness, *n,* petitesse, *f.*
petting, *n,* pelotage *P, m.*
pettish, *a,* maussade.
petty, *a,* petit, menu; (*&* ~*-minded*) mesquin. ~ *officer,* second maître, *m.*
petulance, *n,* irritabilité, irascibilité, *f.* **petulant,** *a,* irritable, irascible.
petunia, *n,* pétunia, *m.*
pew, *n,* banc [d'église], *m.*
pewter, *n,* étain, *m.*
phallic, *a,* phallique. **phallus,** *n,* phallus, *m.*
phantom, *n,* fantôme, *m.*
pharmaceutical, *a,* pharmaceutique. **pharmacist,** *n,* pharmacien, ne. **pharmacy,** *n,* pharmacie, *f.*
pharyngitis, *n,* pharyngite, *f.* **pharynx,** *n,* pharynx, *m.*
phase, *n,* phase, *f. go through a difficult* ~, passer par une période difficile. ¶ *v.t,* ~ *in,* introduire progressivement. ~ *out,* retirer p.
pheasant, *n,* faisan, e; (*young*) faisandeau, *m.*
phenomenal, *a,* phénoménal. **phenomenon,** *n,* phénomène, *m.*
phial, *n,* fiole, *f.*
philander, *v.i,* courir après les femmes. ~**er,** *n,* coureur [de jupons], *m.*
philanthropic, *a,* philanthropique. **philanthropist,** *n,* philanthrope, *m,f.* **philanthropy,** *n,* philanthropie, *f.*
philatelist, *n,* philatéliste, *m,f.* **philately,** *n,* . philatélie, *f.*
philharmonic, *a,* philharmonique.
Philistine, *n,* philistin, *m.*
philologist, *n,* philologue, *m.* **philology,** *n,* philologie, *f.*
philosopher, *n,* philosophe, *m.* ~*s' stone,* pierre philosophale, *f.* **philosophic(al)**†, *a,* philosophique; (*calm*) philosophe. **philosophize,** *v.i,* philosopher. **philosophy,** *n,* philosophie, *f.*
phlebitis, *n,* phlébite, *f.*
phlegm, *n,* flegme, *m.* ~**atic,** *a,* flegmatique.
phlox, *n,* phlox, *m.*
phobia, *n,* phobie, *f.*
ph[o]enix, *n,* phénix, *m.*
phone, *n,* téléphone, *m.* ~ *book,* annuaire, *m.* ~*-in* [*programme*], programme à ligne ouverte, *m.* ¶ *v.i.* (*& t,*) téléphoner (à).
phonetic, *a,* phonétique. ~**s,** *n.pl,* phonétique, *f.*
phoney *P, a,* faux; du toc *P;* (*emotion*) factice; (*company*) bidon *P, inv.* ¶ *n,* fumiste *P, m,f.*
phosphate, *n,* phosphate, *m.* **phosphorescence,** *n,* phosphorescence, *f.* **phosphorescent,** *a,* phosphorescent. **phosphorus,** *n,* phosphore, *m.*
photo, *n,* photo, *f.* ~*copier,* photocopieur, *m.* ~*copy,* photocopie, *f; v.t,* photocopier. ~*-finish,* photo-finish, *f.* ~**genic,** *a,* photogénique. **photograph,** *n,* photographie, *f. take a* ~ *of s.o,* prendre une photo de qn; prendre qn en photo. ¶ *v.t,* photographier. ~**er,** *n,* photographe, *m,f.* ~**ic,** *a,* photographique. ~**y,** *n,* photographie, *f.* **photogravure,** *n,* photogravure, *f.* **photosynthesis,** *n,* photosynthèse, *f.*
phrase, *n,* expression; (*Gram.*) locution; (*Mus.*) phrase, *f;* (*linguistics*) syntagme, *m.* ~ *book,* recueil d'expressions, *m.* ¶ *v.t,* (*idea*) exprimer; (*Mus.*) phraser. **phraseology,** *n,* phraséologie, *f.*
physical†, *a,* physique; (*object &c*) matériel. ~ *examination,* examen médical. ~ *training,* gymnastique, *f.* **physician,** *n,* médecin, *m.* **physicist,** *n,* physicien, ne. **physics,** *n.pl,* physique, *f.*
physiognomy, *n,* physionomie. *f.*
physiological, *a,* physiologique. **physiologist,** *n,* physiologiste, *m,f.* **physiology,** *n,* physiologie, *f.*
physiotherapist, *n,* kinésithérapeute, *m,f.* **physiotherapy,** *n,* kinésithérapie, *f.*
physique, *n,* physique, *m;* constitution, *f.*
pianist, *n,* pianiste, *m,f.* **piano,** *n,* piano, *m.* ~ *duet,* morceau pour 4 mains, *m.* ~ *stool,* tabouret, *m.* ~ *tuner,* accordeur [de piano], *m.*
piccolo, *n,* piccolo, *m.*
pick, *n,* (*also* ~ *axe*) pioche, *f,* pic; (*choice*) choix, *m;* (*best*) meilleur, e. ~*lock,* crochet,

rossignol, *m.* ~*-me-up,* remontant, *m. the* ~ *of the bunch,* la fleur des pois. ~*pocket,* voleur à la tire, pickpocket, *m.* ~*up,* (*records, truck*) pick-up, *m.inv;* (*casual lover*) partenaire de rencontre, *m,f.* ¶ *v.t,* (*flowers*) cueillir; (*choose*) choisir; (*Sport: team*) sélectionner; (*lock*) crocheter; (*teeth*) curer; (*quarrel*) chercher; (*peck*) becqueter. ~ *at one's food,* manger du bout des dents. ~ *& choose,* faire le difficile. ~ *holes in,* relever les défauts de. ~ *one's nose,* se mettre les doigts dans le nez. ~ *s.o's brains,* faire appel aux lumières de qn. ~ **on,** (*blame*) s'en prendre à. ~ **out,** (*object*) distinguer; (*pers.*) identifier; reconnaître. ~ **over,** trier. ~ **up,** (*object*) ramasser; (*pers.*) relever; (*phone*) décrocher; (*survivors*) recueillir; (*from sea*) repêcher; (*habit, passenger*) prendre; (*information*) apprendre.

pickaback, *ad,* sur le dos.

picked, *a,* (*& hand* ~) sélectionné; (*men*) trié sur le volet. **picker,** *n,* cueilleur, euse.

picket, *n,* piquet; (*Ind: strike* ~) piquet de grève, *m.* ~ *line,* [cordon de] piquet de grève. ¶ *v.t,* mettre un piquet de grève à.

picking, *n,* cueillette, *f;* triage, *m;* (*pl. pilferings*) gratte, *f;* (*left-overs*) restes, *m.pl.*

pickle, *n,* (*brine*) saumure, *f;* (*plight*) le pétrin; (*child*) lutin, *m;* (*pl.*) pickles, *m.pl.* ¶ *v.t,* saler; conserver [au vinaigre]. ~**d,** *a,* (*vegetables*) au vinaigre; (*meat*) salé.

picnic, *n,* pique-nique, *m;* (*fig.*) partie de plaisir, *f.* ~ *basket,* panier pique-nique, *m.* ¶ *v.i,* faire un pique-nique, pique-niquer.

pictorial, *a,* (*record*) en images; (*magazine*) illustré. ¶ *n,* illustré, *m.* **picture,** *n,* (*gen.*) image, *f;* (*painting*) tableau; (*portrait*) portrait; (*drawing*) dessin; (*Cine.*) film, *m;* (*fig.*) image. *the general* ~, le tableau général de la situation. *put s.o in the* ~, mettre qn au courant. *look a* ~, être ravissant. ~ *book,* livre d'images, *m.* ~ *frame,* cadre, *m.* ~ *gallery,* (*public*) musée [de peinture], *m;* (*private*) galerie [de p.], *f.* ~ *postcard,* carte postale [illustrée]. ~ *rail,* cimaise, *f.* ~ *window,* fenêtre panoramique, *f.* ¶ *v.t,* (*imagine*) se figurer, s'imaginer; (*describe, draw &c*) représenter. **picturesque†,** *a,* pittoresque.

piddling *P, a,* insignifiant; de rien.

pie, *n,* (*fruit, meat in sauce &c*) tourte, *f;* (*meat*) pâté en croûte, *m.* ~ *in the sky,* des châteaux en Espagne. ~*crust,* croûte de pâté, *f.* ~ *dish,* terrine, *f.* ~*-eyed P,* rond *P.* ~ *plate,* tourtière, *f.*

piebald, *a,* pie.

piece, *n,* (*gen.*) morceau; (*smaller & string &c*) bout, *m;* (*coin, item, Chess*) pièce, *f;* (*Draughts*) pion, *m;* (*Mus.*) morceau. *in* ~*s,* en morceaux. ~ *of advice,* conseil, *m.* ~ *of furniture,* meuble, *m.* ~ *of information,* renseignement, *m.* ~ *of land,* (*Agr.*) parcelle de terre, *f;* (*Build.*) lotissement, *m.* ~ *of luck,* coup de chance, *m.* ~ *of news,* nouvelle, *f.* ~ *of work,* travail, *m. fall to* ~*s,* tomber en morceaux. *go to* ~*s,* (*pers.*) (*collapse*) s'effrondrer: (*lose grip*) lâcher pied. *in one* ~, (*pers.*) sain & sauf; (*object*) intact. *10 franc* ~, pièce de 10 francs, *f.* ~*work,* travail à la pièce, *m.* ¶ *v.t,* ~ *together,* (*facts, object*) rassembler; (*story*) reconstituer. **piecemeal,** *ad,* (*tell*) par bribes; (*construct*) petit à petit.

pied, *a,* bigarré, bariolé.

pier, *n,* (*with amusements*) jetée [promenade], *f;* (*landing stage*) embarcadère, *m.* ~*head,* musoir, *m.*

pierce, *v.t,* percer; (*cold*) transpercer. **piercing,** *a,* perçant; (*cold*) pénétrant.

piety, *n,* piété, *f.*

pig, *n,* cochon, porc, *m;* (*pers. pej.*) cochon. *buy a* ~ *in a poke,* acheter chat en poche. ~*s might fly!* c'est la semaine des quatre jeudis! ~ *breeding,* élevage porcin. ~*-headed,* têtu. ~ *iron,* gueuse de fonte, *f.* ~ *skin,* peau de porc, *f.* ~*sty,* (*lit. & fig.*) porcherie, *f.* ~*tail,* (*hair*) natte, *f.*

pigeon, *n,* pigeon; (*wood* ~) ramier, *m.* (*pidgin*) *that's not my* ~, ce n'est pas mes oignons *P.* ~*hole, n,* casier, *m; v.t,* classer. ~ *loft,* pigeonnier, *m.*

piglet, *n,* porcelet, *m.*

pigment, *n,* pigment, *m.*

pigmy, *n,* pygmée, *m.*

pike, *n,* (*fish*) brochet, *m.*

pilchard, *n,* pilchard, *m.*

pile[1], *n,* (*Build.*) pieu de fondation, pilot, *m.* ~ *driver,* sonnette, *f.*

pile[2], *n,* pile, *f;* tas, *m;* (*Phys.*) pile. *in a* ~, en pile, en tas. *P make one's* ~, faire fortune. *P* ~*s of,* un tas de *P;* des masses de *P.* ~ *of money,* un argent fou. ~*up,* (*Mot.*) carambolage, *m.* ¶ *v.t.* (*& i.*) (s')entasser; (*stack*) (s')empiler. ~ *up, v.i,* s'amonceler; (*work &c*) s'accumuler; *v.t,* accumuler; (*crash*) bousiller *P.*

pile[3], *n,* (*cloth, carpet*) poils, *m.pl.*

piles (*Med.*) *n.pl,* hémorroïdes, *f.pl.*

pilfer, *v.t,* chaparder *P.* ~**er,** *n,* chapardeur, euse. ~**ing,** *n,* chapardage, *m.*

pilgrim, *n,* pèlerin, e. ~**age,** *n. & place of pilgrimage,* pèlerinage, *m.*

pill, *n,* pilule, *f. to be on the* ~, prendre la p. ~*box,* (*Med.*) boîte à pilules, *f;* (*Mil.*) blockhaus, *m.inv;* (*hat*) toque, *f.*

pillage, *n,* pillage, *m.* ¶ *v.t,* piller.

pillar, *n,* pilier, *m;* (*fire, smoke*) colonne, *f.* ~ *of the Church,* pilier de l'Église. ~ *box,* boîte aux lettres, *f.* ~*-box red,* rouge sang.

pillion (*Motor.*) *n,* siège arrière, tan-sad, *m.* ~ *passenger,* passager de derrière, *m.*

pillory, *n,* pilori, *m.* ¶ *v.t,* mettre au pilori.

pillow, *n,* oreiller, *m.* ~*case,* ~ *slip,* taie d'oreiller, *f.*
pilot, *n,* pilote, *m.* ~ *boat,* bateau-pilote, *m.* ~ *film,* film-pilote, *m.* ~ *light,* veilleuse, *f.* ~-*scheme,* projet-pilote, *m.* ¶ *v.t,* (*Aero., Naut.*) piloter; (*guide*) guider, diriger.
pimento, *n,* piment, *m.*
pimp, *n,* souteneur, maquereau *P, m.*
pimpernel, *n,* mouron, *m.*
pimple, *n,* bouton, *m.* **pimply,** *a,* boutonneux.
pin, *n,* épingle; (*drawing* ~) punaise, *f;* (*safety* ~) épingle de sûreté; (*Elec.*) fiche; (*Mach. &c*) goupille; (*Med.*) broche; (*Bowling*) quille, *f. for 2* ~*s...,* pour un peu... *neat as a new* ~, propre comme un sou neuf. *you could hear a* ~ *drop,* on entendrait voler une mouche. ~*s & needles,* fourmis, *f.pl.* ~*ball,* flipper, *m.* ~ *cushion,* pelote à épingles, *f.* ~ *money,* argent de poche, *m.* ~*prick,* (*lit.*) piqûre d'épingle, *f;* (*fig.*) coup d'é., *m.* ~*up,* pin-up, *f.inv.* ¶ *v.t,* (*dress &c, also* ~ *up*) épingler; (*papers*) attacher avec une épingle, une punaise; (*Tech.*) goupiller. ~ *s.o against a wall,* clouer qn à un mur. ~ *back,* retenir. ~ *down,* (*trap*) coincer.
pinafore, *n,* tablier, *m.* ~ *dress,* robe-chasuble, *f.*
pincer, *n,* (*crab*) pince, *f;* (*pl. tool*) tenailles, *f.pl.*
pinch, *n,* (*salt*) pincée; (*snuff*) prise, *f;* (*action*) pincement, *m. at a* ~, au besoin. *feel the* ~, être serré. *take sth with a* ~ *of salt* (*fig.*), ne pas prendre qch pour argent comptant. *when it comes to the* ~, au moment critique. ¶ *v.t,* pincer; (*shoes*) serrer; (*P steal*) piquer *P,* chiper *P;* (*P arrest*) pincer *P.* ~**ed,** *a,* (*face &c*) tiré.
pine[1], *n,* (*&* ~ *tree*) pin, *m.* ~*cone,* pomme de pin, *f.* ~ *kernel,* ~ *nut,* pignon, *m.* ~ *marten,* martre, *f.*
pine[2], *v.i,* languir, dépérir; (*long*) désirer ardemment.
pineapple, *n,* ananas, *m.*
ping-pong, *n,* ping-pong, *m.*
pinion, *n,* (*Mech.*) pignon, *m.*
pink[1], *a,* rose; (*Pol.*) gauchisant. *turn* ~, (*thing*) rosir; (*pers.*) rougir. ¶ *n,* rose, *m;* (*Bot.*) mignardise, *f. be in the* ~, se porter comme un charme.
pink[2], *v.t,* (*Need.*) denteler les bords de. ~*ing shears,* ciseaux à denteler, *m.pl.*
pinnacle, *n,* pinacle, *m.*
pint, *n,* pinte, *f.* (= *0.57 litre*).
pioneer, *n,* pionnier, *m.*
pious†, *a,* pieux.
pip, *n,* (*seed*) pépin; (*cards, dominoes*) point; (*Tel.*) top, *m;* (*pl. Radio*) bip-bip, *m. he gives me the* ~ *P,* il me court sur le haricot *P.*
pipe, *n,* tuyau, conduit, *m,* conduite, *f;* (*tobacco*) pipe, *f;* (*flute*) pipeau, chalumeau; (*boatswain's*) sifflet, *m;* (*organ*) tuyau; (*tube*) tube; (*pl. bag*~*s*) cornemuse, *f.* ~ *of peace,* calumet de la paix, *m.* ~ *cleaner,* cure-pipe, *m.* ~ *dream,* château en Espagne, *m.* ~*line,* (*gen.*) pipe-line; (*oil*) oléoduc; (*gas*) gazoduc, *m.* ¶ *v.t,* transporter par tuyau; jouer (sur un pipeau &c); (*Naut.*) siffler; (*Need.*) passepoiler. ~ *down P,* mettre la sourdine *P.* ~ *up,* se faire entendre. **piping** (*braid*) *n,* passepoil, *m.*
pipit, *n,* pipi[t], *m.*
piquancy, *n,* goût piquant; (*fig.*) piquant, sel, *m.* **piquant,** *a,* piquant. **pique,** *n,* dépit, *m.* ¶ *v.t,* dépiter.
piracy, *n,* piraterie, *f.* **pirate,** *n,* pirate; (*Com: gen.*) contrefacteur; (*publishing*) démarqueur, *m.* ~ *radio,* radio pirate, *f.* ¶ *v.t,* (*idea*) s'approprier; (*book*) démarquer; (*product*) contrefaire.
pirouette, *n,* pirouette, *f.* ¶ *v.i,* pirouetter.
piss *P**, *v.t,* pisser *P**. ~ *off**, foutre le camp *P**. ~**ed** *P**, *a,* (*drink*) bourré *P. be* ~ *off,* en avoir marre *P.*
pistachio, *n,* (*nut*) pistache, *f.*
pistil, *n,* pistil, *m.*
pistol, *n,* pistolet, *m. to hold a* ~ *at s.o's head* (*fig.*), mettre le couteau sur la gorge à qn.
piston, *n,* piston, *m.* ~ *rod,* tige de piston, *f.*
pit, *n,* trou, *m;* (*coal*) mine; (*quarry*) carrière; (*garage*) trappe, *f;* (*motor racing*) stand; (*stomach*) creux, *m;* (*Theat.*) [fauteuils (*m.pl.*) d']orchestre, *m.* ~*fall,* piège, *f.* ¶ *v.t,* (*fruit*) dénoyauter; opposer (qn à qn). ~ *one's wits against,* se mesurer avec. ~**ted,** *a,* (*metal*) piqueté; (*face*) grêlé.
pit-a-pat (to go), (*rain*) crépiter; (*heart*) palpiter; (*feet*) trottiner.
pitch[1], *n,* (*degree*) degré, point, *m;* (*voice*) hauteur, *f;* (*Mus.*) diapason, ton; (*Sport*) terrain, *m;* (*trader*) place habituelle; (*roof*) degré de pente. ~*fork, n,* fourche, *f.* ¶ *v.t,* (*throw*) lancer; (*Mus: note*) donner; (*tent*) dresser; (*camp*) établir. ¶ *v.i,* (*fall*) tomber; (*Naut.*) tanguer. ~ *in P,* s'attaquer au boulot *P.* ~ *into P,* (*attack*) tomber sur; (*set about*) s'attaquer à. ~*ed battle* (*Mil.*), bataille rangée.
pitch[2], *n,* (*tar*) poix, *f.* ~-*black,* noir comme poix. *it's* ~ *dark,* il fait nuit noire. ~*pine,* pitchpin, *m.*
pitcher, *n,* cruche, *f,* broc, *m.*
piteous†, *a,* pitoyable.
pith, *n,* (*plant, bone*) moelle; (*orange*) peau blanche; (*fig.*) force, *f.* ~**y,** *a,* vigoureux; concis.
pitiable†, *&* **pitiful**†, *a,* piteux, à faire pitié, pitoyable, lamentable. **pitiless**†, *a,* impitoyable, sans pitié.
pittance, *n,* maigre revenu, revenu dérisoire; (*wage*) salaire de misère, *m.*
pity, *n,* pitié, *f;* (*regret*) dommage, *m. take* ~

on, feel ~ *for,* avoir pitié de. *what a* ~ *!* quel dommage! ¶ *v.t,* plaindre, avoir pitié de.
pivot, *n,* pivot, *m.* ¶ *v.i,* pivoter.
pixy, -xie, *n,* fée, *f.* ~ *hood,* bonnet pointu.
placard, *n,* placard, *m,* affiche, *f.* ¶ *v.t,* placarder, afficher.
place, *n,* (*gen.*) endroit; lieu, *m;* (*seat, position, vacancy &c*) place, *f.* ~ *of birth, work &c,* lieu de naissance, travail &c. *all over the* ~, partout. *at my* ~ *P,* chez moi. *from* ~ *to* ~, d'un endroit à l'autre. *know one's* ~, savoir se tenir à sa place. *lose one's* ~, (*book*) perdre sa page. *out of* ~, déplacé. *people in high* ~*s,* les gens en haut lieu. *put s.o in his* ~, remettre qn à sa place. *take* ~, avoir lieu. ~ *kick* (*Rugby*), coup placé, *m.* ~ *name,* nom de lieu, *m.* ~ *setting,* couvert, *m.* ¶ *v.t,* (*gen.*) placer; (*put*) mettre, poser; (*situate*) situer; (*Com: order*) passer (*with,* à); (*contract*) passer (avec); (*remember*) se rappeler, reconnaître. ~**ment,** *n,* placement, *m.*
placid†, *a,* placide.
plagiarism, *n,* plagiat, *m.* **plagiarist,** *n,* plagiaire, *m,f.* **plagiarize,** *v.t,* plagier.
plague, *n,* (*Med.*) peste, *f;* (*fig.*) fléau, *m;* (*pers.*) plaie, *f. avoid like the* ~, fuir comme la peste. ¶ *v.t,* tourmenter, harceler.
plaice, *n,* plie, *f,* carrelet, *m.*
plain, *a,* (*clear*) clair, évident; (*speech*) franc; (*simple*) simple; (*one colour*) uni; (*not pretty*) quelconque, sans beauté. ~ *as a pikestaff,* clair comme le jour. *make o.s* ~, se faire comprendre. *the* ~ *truth is...* à parler franc... ~ *chocolate,* chocolat à croquer, *m.* *in* ~ *clothes,* en civil. ~ *knitting,* tricot à l'endroit, *m. to be* ~ *sailing,* aller comme sur des roulettes. ~*-song,* plain-chant, *m.* ¶ *n,* plaine, *f.* ~**ly,** *ad,* clairement; (*unambiguously*) carrément; simplement. *speak* ~, parler sans détours. ~**ness,** clarté; simplicité, *f;* manque de beauté, *m.*
plaintif, *n,* demandeur, eresse, plaignant, e.
plaintive†, *a,* plaintif.
plait, *n,* natte, tresse, *f.* ¶ *v.t,* natter, tresser. *to* ~ *one's hair,* se natter.
plan, *n,* (*drawing &c*) plan; (*project*) projet, *m;* plan. ~ *of campaign,* plan de campagne. *go according to* ~, se passer comme prévu. ¶ *v.t,* dresser des plans de; (*holiday, campaign &c*) organiser; (*Econ.*) planifier; (*family*) contrôler; (*intend*) projeter (de); avoir l'intention (de). ¶ *v.i,* faire des projets.
plane[1], *n,* avion, *m. by* ~, par avion. ¶ *v.i,* planer.
plane[2] (*Carp.*), *n,* rabot, *n.* ¶ *v.t,* raboter.
plane[3] (*tree*), *n,* platane, *m.*
plane[4] (*Math, Arch. &c*) *a. & n,* plan, *m.*
planet, *n,* planète, *f.* **planetarium,** *n,* planétaire, *m.* **planetary,** *a,* planétaire.
plank, *n,* planche, *f.*
plankton, *n,* plancton, *m.*
planning, *n,* planification, *f;* (*Com., Ind.*) planning, *m.* ~ *permission,* permis de construire, *m.*
plant, *n,* (*Bot.*) plante, *f;* (*Ind., Tech.*) matériel, *m;* installation; (*factory*) usine, fabrique, *f.* ~ *life,* flore, *f.* ~ *pot,* pot [de fleurs], *m.* ¶ *v.t,* planter. ~ *out,* repiquer.
plantain, *n,* plantain, *m.*
plantation, *n,* plantation, *f.* **planter,** *n,* planteur, euse.
plaque, *n,* plaque, *f.*
plaster, *n,* plâtre, *m;* (*for cuts &c*) pansement adhésif, sparadrap, *m.* ~ *cast,* plâtre, *m.* ~ *of Paris,* plâtre de moulage, *m.* ¶ *v.t,* plâtrer; (*fig; cover*) couvrir. ~ *over, up* (*crack &c*), boucher. ~**ed,** *P* (*drunk*), *a,* bourré *P.* ~**er,** *n,* plâtrier, *m.*
plastic, *a. & n,* plastique, *m;* (*pl.*) matières plastiques. ~ *explosive,* plastic, *m.* ~ *surgery,* chirurgie esthétique, *f.* **plasticine,** *n,* pâte à modeler, *f.*
plate, *n,* assiette, *f;* (*platter*) plat; (*church*) plateau [de quête], *m;* (*metal: on wall, Phot. &c*) plaque; (*in book*) gravure, *f;* (*Turf*) prix; (*dental*) dentier, *m. have a lot on one's* ~ (*fig.*), avoir du pain sur la planche. ~ *glass window,* baie vitrée. ~ *layer* (*Rly*), poseur de rails, *m.* ~ *rack,* égouttoir, *m.* ~ *warmer,* chauffe-assiettes, *m.inv.* ¶ *v.t,* (*with metal*) plaquer; (*with gold*) dorer; (*with silver*) argenter; (*with nickel*) nickeler. ~**[ful],** *n,* assiettée, assiette, *f.*
plateau, *n,* plateau, *m.*
platform, *n,* (*on bus &c*) plate-forme; (*in hall*) estrade; (*at meeting*) tribune, *f;* (*Rly*) quai, *m;* (*Pol.*) plate-forme [électorale]. ~ *ticket,* billet de quai, *m.*
platinum, *n,* platine, *m.* ~ *blonde* (*colour*), blond platiné, *m.*
platitude, *n,* platitude, *f.*
Platonic, *a,* platonique.
platoon, *n,* (*Mil.*) section, *f.*
plausible†, *a,* plausible; (*pers.*) convaincant.
play, *n,* (*games &c*) jeu, *m;* (*Theat.*) pièce [de théâtre], *f;* (*performance*) spectacle; (*pl.*) théâtre; (*Mech.*) jeu, *m. make great* ~ *with,* faire grand cas de. ~*-back,* réécoute, *f.* ~*bill,* affiche [de théâtre], *f.* ~*-goer,* amateur de théâtre, *m.* ~*ground,* cour de récréation, *f.* ~*mate,* [petit, e] camarade; [petit] copain, [petite] copine. ~*-off* (*Sport*), belle, *f.* ~*pen,* parc d'enfant, *m.* ~*room,* salle de jeux, *f.* ~*thing,* jouet, *m.* ~*time,* récréation, *f.* ~*wright,* dramaturge, *m.* ¶ *v.t,* (*game &c*) jouer à; (*card &c*) jouer; (*team*) jouer contre; (*match*) disputer (*against,* avec); (*Mus: instrument*) jouer de; (*tune &c*) jouer; (*record*) passer; (*hose &c*) diriger; (*fish*) fatiguer. ~ *ball P,* coopérer (avec). ~ *it cool,* garder son

sang-froid. ~ *one's cards right,* bien jouer son jeu. ¶ *v.i,* jouer; (*lambs*) folâtrer; (*light &c*) jouer (sur). ~ *for time,* essayer de gagner du temps. ~ *about with,* tripoter. ~ **down,** minimiser. ~ **up,** *v.i,* (*motor, child*) faire des siennes. ¶ *v.t,* tracasser. ~**er,** *n,* (*gen.*) joueur, euse; (*Theat.*) acteur, trice; (*Mus.*) musicien, ne. ~**ful,** *a,* enjoué. ~**fulness,** *n,* enjouement, *m.*

plea, *n,* (*appeal*) appel, *m;* (*excuse*) excuse; (*claim*) allégation, *f;* (*Law*) défense, *f. make, enter a ~ of,* plaider. **plead,** *v.t,* (*Law*) plaider; (*ignorance &c*) alléguer. ¶ *v.i,* (*beg*) implorer (*with s.o to do,* qn de faire); (*Law*) plaider. ~ [*not*] *guilty,* plaider [non] coupable. ~ *for mercy,* implorer la clémence. ~**ing,** *a,* suppliant, implorant. ¶ *n,* prières (en faveur de qn), *f.pl.*

pleasant†, *a,* agréable. ~**ness,** *n,* (*pers.*) amabilité, *f;* (*place*) agrément, *m.* ~**ry,** *n,* plaisanterie, *f;* **please,** *v.t,* plaire à, faire plaisir à; (*satisfy*) satisfaire, contenter; (*v.i,*) plaire. ¶ *imperative,* s'il vous, te plaît; (*formal*) veuillez; (*notices*) prière de... ~**d,** *a,* content, heureux. *as ~ as Punch,* heureux comme un roi. ~ *to meet you!* enchanté! **pleasing** *a,* (*personality*) sympathique; (*aspect*) plaisant. ~**ly,** *ad,* agréablement. **pleasurable†,** *a,* agréable. **pleasure,** *n,* plaisir, *m. it's a ~,* je vous en prie. *with ~,* avec plaisir, volontiers. ~ *boat,* bateau de plaisance, *m.* ~ *cruise,* voyage d'agrément, *m.* ~*-seeking,* hédoniste. ~ *trip,* excursion, *f.*

pleat, *n,* pli, *m,* pince, *f.* ¶ *v.t,* plisser.

pledge, *n,* (*pawn, token*) gage, *m;* (*promise*) promesse, *f,* engagement, *m.* ¶ *v.t,* engager, mettre en gage; promettre.

plentiful†, *a,* abondant; (*meal, amount*) copieux. ~ *supply of,* abondance de, *f.* **plenty,** *n,* abondance, *f.* ~ *of,* [bien] assez de. *that's ~,* ça suffit. ~ *big enough,* bien assez grand.

pleurisy, *n,* pleurésie, *f.*

pliable, pliant, *a,* (*substance*) flexible; (*pers.*) souple.

pliers, *n.pl,* pince, *f,* pinces, *f.pl.*

plight, *n,* état critique, *m.*

plimsoll, *n,* [chaussure de] tennis, *f. P~ line* (*Naut.*), marque de Plimsoll, *f.*

plinth, *n,* plinthe, *f.*

plod, *v.i,* (~ *along*) avancer d'un pas lent *ou* lourd; (*work*) bosser *P,* bûcher *P.* ~ *on,* continuer son chemin; (*fig.*) persévérer. **plodder,** *n,* bûcheur, euse.

plonk, *n,* (*sound*) plouf, *m;* (*P wine*) pinard *P, m.* ¶ *v.t,* (~ *down*) poser [bruyamment]. ~ *o.s down,* se laisser tomber.

plop, *n,* plouf, *m.* ¶ *v.i,* (*stone*) faire plouf; (*rain*) faire flic flac.

plot, *n,* (*land*) terrain, carré; (*plan*) complot; (*novel, play*) intrigue, *f.* ¶ *v.t,* (*Naut. &c; course*) déterminer; (*graph &c*) tracer; (*plan*) comploter. ¶ *v.i,* comploter, conspirer. **plotter,** *n,* conspirateur, trice.

plough, *n,* (*Agr.*) charrue, *f. the P~* (*Astr.*), la Grande Ourse. ~*man,* laboureur, *m.* ~*share,* soc, *m.* ¶ *v.t,* (*&* ~ *up: field*) labourer; (*furrow*) creuser. ~ *through* (*mud &c*), avancer péniblement dans. ~ *back* (*profits*), réinvestir. ~**ing,** *n,* labourage, labour, *m.*

plover, *n,* pluvier, *m.*

ploy *P, n,* stratagème, *m.*

pluck, *n,* courage, cran *P, m.* ¶ *v.t,* (*flowers*) cueillir; (*Cook.*) plumer; (*Mus: strings*) pincer; (*guitar*) pincer les cordes de. ~ *one's eyebrows,* s'épiler les sourcils. ~ *at s.o's sleeve,* tirer doucement par la manche. ~ *off, out,* (*gen.*) enlever; (*feathers*) arracher. ~ *up courage,* prendre son courage à 2 mains. ~**y†,** *a,* courageux.

plug, *n,* (*bath &c*) bonde, *f;* (*to stop leak*) tampon; (*stopper*) bouchon, *m;* (*Elec.*) prise; (*switchboard*) fiche; (*Mot: sparking ~*) bougie, *f. give sth, s.o a ~ P,* donner un coup de pouce à qch, qn. ~*hole,* vidange, *f.* ¶ *v.t,* (*&* ~ *up*) (*hole*) boucher; (*leak*) colmater; (*publicize*) faire de la publicité pour. ~ *away at P,* bûcher *P.* ~ *in* (*Elec.*), (se) brancher.

plum, *n,* prune, *f.* ~ *job P,* boulot en or *P.* ~ *pudding,* plum-pudding, *m.* ~ [*tree*], prunier, *m.*

plumage, *n,* plumage, *m.*

plumb, *a,* vertical, d'aplomb. ¶ *ad,* en plein. ~ *crazy,* complètement fou. ¶ *n,* plomb, *m.* ~ *line,* fil à plomb, *m;* (*Naut.*) sonde, *f.* ¶ *v.t,* sonder. ~ *in,* (*washing machine &c*) faire le raccordement de. **plumber,** *n,* plombier, *m.* **plumbing,** *n,* plomberie, *f.*

plume, *n,* plumet; (*larger & smoke*) panache, *m.*

plummet, *v.i,* (*bird, plane*) descendre à pic; (*temperature, prices &c*) baisser brusquement; (*spirits*) tomber à zéro.

plump, *a,* (*pers.*) rondelet; (*chicken*) dodu. ¶ *v.t,* (~ *up: pillow*) tapoter. ~**ness,** *n,* rondeur, *f.*

plunder, *n,* (*act*) pillage; (*loot*) butin, *m.* ¶ *v.t,* piller. ~**er,** *n,* pillard, e.

plunge, *n,* plongeon, *m;* (*fall*) chute, *f. take the ~* (*fig.*), se jeter à l'eau, sauter le fossé. ¶ *v.t,* plonger (dans). ¶ *v.i,* (*dive*) plonger; (*fig.*) se lancer. **plunger** (*for blocked pipe*), *n,* ventouse, *f.*

pluperfect, *n,* plus-que-parfait, *m.*

plural, *a,* (*Gram.*) pluriel. ¶ *n,* pluriel, *m. in the ~,* au pluriel.

plus, *pr,* plus. ~ [*sign*], [signe] plus, *m.*

plush, *n,* peluche, *f.* ¶ *P a,* somptueux.

Pluto, *n,* (*Astr.*) Pluton, *f;* (*Myth.*) Pluton, *m.* **plutocracy,** *n,* ploutocratie, *f.* **plutocrat,** *n,* ploutocrate, *m.* **plutonium,** *n,* plutonium, *m.*

ply[1], *n*, *3-~ wool*, laine à 3 fils, *f.* *~wood*, contre-plaqué, *m*.
ply[2], *v.t*, (*oar, tool &c*) manier; (*river*) naviguer sur; (*trade*) exercer; (*with questions*) presser (*with*, de). ¶ *v.i*, faire le service.
pneumatic, *a*, pneumatique. *~ drill*, marteau-piqueur, *m*.
pneumonia, *n*, pneumonie, *f*.
poach[1], (*Cook*.), *v.t*, pocher. **~er**[1], *n*, pocheuse, *f*.
poach[2], *v.t. & i*, braconner. **~er**[2], *n*, braconnier, *m*.
pocket, *n*, (*gen. & fig.*) poche; (*Bil.*) blouse, *f;* (*Aero: air ~*) trou d'air, *m. be in ~*, s'y retrouver. *be out of ~*, en être de sa poche. *in one's ~* (*fig.*), dans sa poche. ¶ *a*, (*flask &c*) de poche. *~book*, (*wallet*) portefeuille; (*notebook*) carnet, *m. ~ money*, argent de poche, *m*. ¶ *v.t*, empocher. **~ful,** *n*, pleine poche, *f*.
pock-marked, *a*, grêlé; (*surface*) criblé de petits trous.
pod, *n*, cosse, gousse, *f*.
podgy, *a*, rondelet.
poem, *n*, poème, *m*. **poet,** *n*, poète, *m*. **~ess,** *n*, poétesse, *f*. **~ic,** *a*, poétique. **~ally,** *ad*, poétiquement. **~ry,** *n*, poésie, *f*.
poignant, *a*, poignant.
point, *n*, (*gen.*) point, *m;* (*knife &c*) pointe, *f;* (*Geog.*) pointe, cap, *m;* (*main idea: argument*) essentiel; (*joke &c*) piquant; (*meaning*) intérêt, sens, *m;* (*decimal ~*) virgule; (*Elec: power ~*) prise de courant, *f;* (*pl: Rly*) aiguilles, *f.pl. good ~s*, qualités, *f.pl. bad ~s*, défauts, *m.pl. his strong ~*, son fort. *beside the ~*, à côté de la question. *come to the ~*, en venir au fait. *4 ~ 5*, 4 virgule 5. *there's no ~ in it*, cela ne sert à rien. *~ of view*, point de vue. *off the ~*, hors de propos. *make a ~ of*, ne pas manquer de. *make the ~ that*, faire remarquer que. *up to a ~*, jusqu'à un certain point. *~-blank*, (*refuse, refusal*) catégorique(ment); (*request*) de but en blanc. *at ~-blank range*, à bout portant. ¶ *v.t*, (*direct*) pointer, diriger (sur); (*gun*) braquer (sur); (*Build.*) jointoyer. *~ [a finger] at*, montrer du doigt. *~* **out,** indiquer; (*mention*) faire remarquer. *~ sth. out to s.o*, signaler qch à qn. **~ed,** *a*, pointu; (*beard*) en pointe; (*arch*) en ogive; (*remark*) mordant. **~er,** *n*, (*needle*) aiguille, *f;* (*indicator*) index; (*clue*) indice (*to*, de); (*dog*) chien d'arrêt, *m*. **~ing,** (*Build.*), *n*, jointoiement, *m*. **~less†,** *a*, inutile, vain; (*cruelty*) gratuit. **~lessness,** *n*, inutilité, gratuité, *f*.
poise, *n*, équilibre, *m;* (*confidence*) assurance; (*grace*) grâce, *f*. ¶ *v.t*, mettre, tenir en équilibre.
poison, *n*, (*lit., fig.*) poison; (*snake*) vénin, *m*. ¶ *v.t*, empoisonner. *~ s.o's mind*, corrompre qn. *~ s.o's system*, intoxiquer qn. **~er,** *n*, empoisonneur, euse. **~ing,** *n*, empoisonnement, *m*, intoxication, *f*. **~ous,** *a*, (*gas &c*) toxique; (*snake*) vénimeux; (*plant*) vénéneux; (*fig.*) pernicieux.
poke, *n*, petit coup, *m;* (*push*) poussée, *f*. ¶ *v.t*, (*with a stick*) donner un coup (de canne) à; (*thrust; finger &c*) enfoncer (*into*, dans, *through*, à travers); (*fire*) tisonner. *~ one's nose into sth* (*fig.*), fourrer le nez dans qch. *~ about, in*, fourrager dans.
poker[1], *n*, tisonnier, *m*.
poker[2], (*Cards*), *n*, poker, *m*.
poky, *a*, exigu, misérable.
Poland, *n*, la Pologne.
polar, *a*, polaire. *~ bear*, ours blanc, *m*. **polarity,** *n*, polarité, *f*. **polarization,** *n*, polarisation, *f*. **polarize,** *v.t*, (*lit. & fig.*) polariser.
pole[1], *n*, (*gen.*) perche, *f;* (*telegraph, fencing*) poteau; (*flag, tent*) mât, *m. ~axe*, terrasser. *~ vault*, saut à la perche, *m*.
pole[2], *n*, pôle, *m. be ~s apart*, être aux antipodes [l'un de l'autre]. *~ star*, étoile polaire, *f*.
Pole, *n*, Polonais, e.
polemic, *n*, polémique, *f*.
police, *n*, police, *f. ~ car*, voiture de police, *f. ~ court*, tribunal de simple police, *m. ~ dog*, chien policier. *~ force*, la police. *~man*, agent de police, gardien de la paix. *m. ~ record*, casier judiciaire, *m. ~ state*, état policier. *~ station*, poste de police; (*divisional*) commissariat de p., *m. ~woman*, femme-agent, *f*. ¶ *v.t*, faire la police; (*Mil: frontier &c*) contrôler.
policy[1], *n*, politique, *f. a matter of ~*, une question de principe. *~ decision*, décision de principe, *f*.
policy[2], (*Insce*), *n*, police [d'assurance], *f. ~ holder*, assuré, e.
polio, *n*, polio, *f. ~ victim*, polio, *m,f*. **~myelitis,** *n*, poliomyélite, *f*.
Polish, *a*, polonais. ¶ *n*, le polonais.
polish, *n*, (*for shoes*) cirage, *m;* (*for floors &c*) cire, *f;* (*for nails*) vernis [à ongles]; (*metal ~*) produit d'entretien pour les métaux; (*fig: pers.*) raffinement, *m*. ¶ *v.t*, (*also ~ up*) (*shoes, floors &c*) cirer; (*glass, stones*) polir; (*car, metal*) astiquer; (*languages &c*) perfectionner. *~ off*, (*food*) finir; (*work*) expédier; (*P kill*) liquider, *P*.
polite, *a*, poli. *~ society*, bonne société. **politely,** *ad*, poliment. **~ness,** *n*, politesse, *f*.
politic *&* **~al†,** *a*, politique. **~ian,** *n*, homme, femme politique; (*pej.*) politicien, ne. **~s,** *n.pl*, politique, *f*.
polka, *n*, polka, *f. ~ dot*, pois, *m*.
poll, *n*, (*gen*) vote; (*ballot*) scrutin, *m;* (*survey*) sondage, *m. at the ~s*, aux élections. *~ing booth*, isoloir, *m. ~ing station*, bureau de vote, *m. ~ tax*, capitation, *f*. ¶ *v.t*, (*votes*)

obtenir; (*people*) sonder l'opinion de.
pollard, *n,* têtard, *m.* ¶ *v.t,* étêter.
pollen, *n,* pollen, *m.* **pollinate,** *v.t,* féconder.
pollute, *v.t,* polluer; (*fig.*) contaminer. **pollution,** *n,* pollution, contamination, *f.*
polo, *n,* polo, *m.* ~*necked,* à col roulé.
poltergeist, *n,* esprit frappeur, *m.*
polyanthus, *n,* primevère des jardins, *f.* **polyester,** *n,* polyester, *m.* **polygamist,** *n.* & **polygamous,** *a,* polygame, *m,f.* **polygamy,** *n,* polygamie, *f.* **polyglot,** *a.* & *n,* polyglotte, *m,f.* **polygon,** *n,* polygone, *m.* **Polynesia,** *n,* la Polynésie. **polyp,** *n,* polype, *m.* **polyphonic,** *a,* polyphonique. **polyphony,** *n,* polyphonie, *f.* **polystyrene,** *n,* polystyrène, *m.* **polysyllabic,** *a.* & **polysyllable,** *n,* polysyllabe, *m.* **polytechnic,** *n,* Institut Universitaire de Technologie (I.U.T.), *m.* **polythene,** *n,* polyéthylène, *m.* ~ *bag,* sac en plastique. **polyurethane,** *n,* polyuréthane, *m.*
pomegranate, *n,* grenade, *f.* ~ [*tree*], grenadier, *m.*
pomp, *n,* pompe, *f,* faste, *m.* ~ *& circumstance,* grand apparat.
pomposity, *n,* manières pompeuses, *f.pl.* **pompous†,** *a,* pompeux.
poncho, *n,* poncho, *m.*
pond, *n,* étang, *m;* mare, *f;* (*garden*) bassin, *m.*
ponder, *v.i,* réfléchir, méditer (sur). ¶ *v.t,* peser, ruminer. ~**able,** *a,* pondérable. ~**ous†,** *a,* pesant.
pong *P, n,* puanteur, *f.* ¶ *v.i,* puer.
pontiff, *n,* pontife, *m.* **pontifical†,** *a,* pontifical. **pontificate,** *n,* pontificat, *m.* ¶ *v.i,* pontifier (sur).
pontoon, *n,* ponton, *m;* (*Cards*) vingt-et-un, *m.* ~ *bridge,* pont flottant.
pony, *n,* poney, *m.* ~*tail,* queue de cheval, *f.* ~ *trekking,* randonnée à cheval, *f.*
poodle, *n,* caniche, *m,f.*
poof *P*,* (*pej.*) *n,* tante *P*,* tapette *P*, f.*
pooh-pooh, *v.t,* faire fi de.
pool, *n,* flaque; (*larger*) mare, *f;* (*pond*) étang; (*artificial*) bassin, *m;* (*swimming* ~) piscine, *f;* (*money*) cagnotte, *f;* (*fig.*) fonds commun; (*ideas &c*) réservoir, *m;* (*Bil.*) billard américain. ~ *table,* billard, *m.* ¶ *v.t,* mettre en commun; (*ideas &c*) unir.
poor, *a,* pauvre; médiocre; (*light*) faible; (*health*) mauvais; (*effort*) insuffisant. *as ~ as a church mouse,* pauvre comme Job. ~ *thing!* le, la pauvre! *be ~ at sth,* ne pas être doué pour qch. ¶ *n, the* ~, les pauvres, *m.pl.* ~**ly,** *a,* souffrant. ¶ *ad,* pauvrement; mal. ~**ness,** *n,* pauvreté, médiocrité, *f.*
pop¹, *n,* (*sound*) pan, *m;* (*drink*) boisson gazeuse. ~*corn,* popcorn, *m.* ~ *eyed,* aux yeux exorbités. ~*gun,* pistolet à bouchon, *m.* ~*per,* [bouton] pression, *f.* ¶ *v.t,* (*balloon*) crever; (*cork*) faire sauter; (*put*) mettre. ~ *the question,* faire sa demande. ¶ *v.i,* crever; sauter; (*ears*) se déboucher. ~ *in,* entrer en passant. ~ *over &c,* faire un saut. ~ *off,* (*leave*) partir; (*P die*) claquer *P.* ~ *up,* (*pers.*) surgir.
pop², (*Mus. &c*), *a.* & *n,* pop, *inv.* & *m.*
pope, *n,* pape, *m.*
poplar, *n,* peuplier, *m.*
poplin, *n,* popeline, *f.*
poppy, *n,* (*Bot.*) pavot; (*wild*) coquelicot, *m.*
populace, *n,* peuple, *m.* **popular†,** *a,* populaire; (*fashionable*) à la mode; (*journal*) de vulgarisation. *by ~ request,* à la demande générale. ~**ity,** *n,* popularité, *f.* ~**ize,** *v.t,* (*fashion &c*) rendre populaire; (*ideas &c*) vulgariser. **populate,** *v.t,* peupler. **population,** *n,* population, *f.*
porcelain, *n,* porcelaine, *f.*
porch, *n,* porche, *m.*
porcupine, *n,* porc-épic, *m.*
pore¹, *n,* pore, *m.*
pore², *v.i,* ~ *over,* (*book*) être absorbé dans; (*map*) étudier de près; (*problem*) méditer sur.
pork, *n,* porc, *m.* ~ *butcher,* charcutier, *m.* ~ *products,* charcuterie, *f.*
porn *P, n,* porno *P, m or f.* ~ *shop,* boutique pornographique, *f.* **pornographic,** *a,* pornographique. **pornography,** *n,* pornographie, *f.*
porous, *a,* poreux.
porpoise, *n,* marsouin, *m.*
porridge, *n,* porridge, *m.* ~ *oats,* flocons d'avoine, *m.pl.*
port¹, *n,* port; (*side*) bâbord, *m.* ~*hole,* hublot, *m.* ~ *of call,* escale, *f.*
port², (*wine*) *n,* porto, *m.*
portable, *a,* portatif. ¶ *n,* modèle portatif.
portend, *v.t,* présager. **portent,** *n,* présage, *m.* **portentous,** *a,* de mauvais présage.
porter, *n,* (*Rly &c*) porteur, *m;* (*door-keeper*) concierge, *m,f;* (*public building*) gardien, ne.
portfolio, *n,* portefeuille, *m.*
portion, *n,* (*gen.*) portion; (*train &c*) partie, *f.*
portly, *a,* corpulent.
portmanteau, *n,* grosse valise, *f.*
portrait, *n,* portrait, *m.* ~ *gallery,* galerie de portraits, *f.* ~ *painter,* portraitiste, *m,f.* **portray,** *v.t,* (*painter*) peindre; (*painting*) représenter. **portrayal,** *n,* représentation, *f.*
Portugal, *n,* le Portugal. **Portuguese,** *a,* portugais. ¶ *n,* (*pers.*) Portugais, e; (*language*) le portugais.
pose, *n,* pose, *f. strike a* ~, poser [pour la galerie]. ¶ *v.i.* & *t,* poser. **poser,** *n,* question difficile, *f.* **poseur,** *n,* poseur, euse.
posh *P, a,* (*gen.*) chic; (*pers.*) snob; (*accent*) distingué. *talk* ~, parler comme les gens bien. *get ~ed up P,* se pomponner.
position, *n,* (*gen.*) position; (*circumstances, job*) situation; (*Sport*) place, *f;* (*house &c, gun*) emplacement, *m. in a ~ to do,* en position *ou* en mesure de faire. *in a good* ~, bien placé.

in[to] ~, en place. ¶ *v.t,* placer; mettre en position.

positive, *a,* (*gen.*) positif; indéniable; (*proof*) formel; (*change*) réel; (*contribution*) effectif; (*pers.*) certain, sûr (de); (*tone*) assuré. *a* ~ *miracle P,* un vrai miracle. ~**ly,** *ad,* indéniablement; de façon certaine.

possess, *v.t,* posséder. ~**ion,** *n,* possession; (*Law: occupancy*) jouissance, *f. get* ~ *of,* aquérir; (*improperly*) s'emparer (de). *take* ~ *of,* prendre possession de; (*improperly*) s'approprier. ~**ive,** *a,* possessif. ~**iveness,** *n,* possessivité, *f.* ~**or,** *n,* possesseur, *m;* (*owner*) propriétaire, *m,f.*

possibility, *n,* possibilité, *f.* **possible,** *a,* possible. *it is* ~ *that,* il se peut que + *subj. as far as* ~, dans la mesure du possible. **possibly,** *ad,* peut-être. *he cannot* ~ ..., il est impossible qu'il ... + *subj.*

post[1], *n,* (*upright: gen.*) poteau; (*door &c*) montant, *m.* ¶ *v.t,* (~ *up*) afficher; (*announce*) annoncer. ~ *s.o missing* (*Mil.*), porter qn disparu.

post[2], *n,* (*gen., Mil.*) poste, *m.* (*Mil.*) *last* ~, sonnerie aux morts, *f.* ¶ *v.t,* (*sentry &c*) poster; (*send, assign*) affecter (à).

post[3], *n,* poste, *f;* (*letters*) courrier, *m. by return of* ~, par retour du courrier. *catch, miss the* ~, avoir, manquer la levée. *first, second class* ~, tarif normal, réduit. ~ *& packing,* frais de port & d'emballage. ~*-bag,* sac-postal. ~*box,* boîte aux lettres, *f.* ~*card,* carte postale. ~*-free,* franco de port. ~*haste,* à toute allure. ~*man,* facteur, *m.* ~*mark, n,* cachet de la poste; *v.t,* timbrer. ~*master, mistress,* receveur, euse des postes. *P*~ *General,* ministre des Postes & Télécommunications, *m.* ~ *office,* [bureau de] poste; (*organisation*) service des postes, *m. P*~ *Office Box* (*P.O. Box*), boîte postale (*B.P.*). *P*~ *Office Savings Bank,* Caisse [Nationale] d'Épargne. ~*-paid,* port payé. ¶ *v.t,* (*send*) envoyer par la poste; (*in box*) mettre à la poste, poster; (*Bkkpg.*) inscrire. ~ *sth on,* faire suivre qch. *keep s.o* ~*ed,* (*fig.*), tenir qn au courant. ~**age,** *n,* tarifs postaux; (*in account*) frais de port, *m.pl.* ~ *stamp,* timbre-poste, *m.* ~**al,** *a,* (*rates, code &c*) postal; (*application*) par la poste. ~ *order,* mandat[-poste], *m.* ~ *vote,* vote par correspondence, *m.*

post..., *pref,* post... ~*-1968,* postérieur à 1968, après 1968. ~*graduate,* de troisième cycle [universitaire]. ~*-impressionism,* post-impressionnisme, *m.* ~*-natal,* post-natal.

postdate, *v.t,* postdater.

poster, *n,* affiche, *f;* (*decorative*) poster, *m.*

posterior, *a. & n,* postérieur, *m.*

posterity, *n,* postérité, *f.*

posthumous, *a,* posthume.

posting, *n,* affectation, *f.*

post mortem, *n,* autopsie, *f.*

postpone, *v.t,* remettre, renvoyer, ajourner.

postscript (*abb.* P.S.) *n,* post-scriptum, P.-S., *m.*

postulate, *v.t,* poser comme principe; (*Philos.*) postuler.

posture, *n,* posture, *f.* ¶ *v.i,* poser.

post-war, *a,* d'après-guerre. ~ *period,* l'après-guerre, *m.*

posy, *n,* petit bouquet, *m.*

pot, *n,* (*flowers, jam &c*) pot, *m;* (*piece of pottery*) poterie, *f;* (*Cook.*) marmite; (*pan*) casserole; (*tea* ~) théière; (*coffee* ~) cafetière, *f;* (*chamber* ~) pot [de chambre]; (*P marijuana*) marie-jeanne *P, f.* ~*s & pans,* quincaillerie, *f,* casseroles. *go to* ~ *P,* (*pers.*) se laisser complètement aller; (*business*) aller à la dérive; (*plans*) aller à vau-l'eau. ~*bellied,* bedonnant *P.* ~ *boiler* (*fig.*), œuvre alimentaire, *f.* ~*hole,* (*in road*) nid-de-poule, *m;* (*cave*) caverne, *f,* gouffre, *m.* ~*holer,* spéléologue, *m,f.* ~*holing,* spéléologie, *f. take* ~ *luck,* (*food*) manger à la fortune du pot; (*gen.*) courir le risque. ~ *roast,* rôti braisé, *m. take a* ~ *shot,* tirer à vue de nez. ¶ *v.t,* (*plant &c*) mettre en pot; (*P shoot: bird*) descendre *P;* (*Bil.*) blouser.

potash, *n,* potasse, *f.* **potassium,** *n,* potassium, *m.*

potato, *n,* pomme de terre, *f. sweet* ~, patate douce, *f.* ~ *crisps,* [pommes] chips, *f.pl.* ~*-masher,* presse-purée, *m.inv.* ~*-peeler,* épluche-légumes, *m.inv.*

potency, *n,* puissance; (*drink*) teneur (en alcool), *f.* **potent,** *a,* puissant; fort. **potentate,** *n,* potentat, *m.* **potential,** *n,* potentiel; (*sales, uses*) possible. ¶ *n,* potentiel, *m;* (*fig.*) potentialités, *f.pl. have* ~, être prometteur.

potion, *n,* potion, *f;* (*magic* ~) philtre, *m.*

potpourri, *n,* (*flowers*) mélange de fleurs séchées; (*Mus.*) pot-pourri, *m.*

potted, *a,* en pot. ~ *meat,* rillettes [de viande], *f.pl.* ~ *version* (*fig.*), abrégé, *m.*

potter, *n,* potier. ~ *'s wheel,* tour de potier, *m.* ¶ *v.i,* mener sa petite vie tranquille. ~ *about,* bricoler *P.* ~**y,** *n,* (*craft*) poterie, *f;* (*objects*) poteries, *f.pl;* (*glazed*) faïencerie, *f.*

potty[1], *n,* pot [de bébé], *m.* ~*-trained,* propre.

potty[2] *P, a,* (*pers.*) dingue, toqué *P* (*about,* de); (*idea*) idiot.

pouch, *n,* petit sac; (*tobacco*) blague; (*Zool.*) poche, *f.*

poultice, *n,* cataplasme, *m.*

poultry, *n,* volaille[s], *f.*[*pl*]. ~ *dealer,* marchand de volailles, *m.* ~ *farm*[*ing*], élevage de volailles, *m.* ~ *farmer,* éleveur, euse de v.

pounce, *n,* bond, *m;* attaque subite, *f.* ¶ *v.i,* bondir, sauter (sur). ~ *on sth* (*fig.*), (*object*) se précipiter sur; (*idea*) sauter sur.

pound[1], *n,* (£) livre; (*weight*) livre, *f* = 453,6

grammes.
pound², *v.t,* (*drugs, spices &c*) piler; (*rocks*) concasser. ~ *to a pulp,* réduire en bouillie. ¶ *v.i,* (*heart*) battre fort; (*sea*) battre (contre). *take a* ~*ing,* (*team*) se faire battre à plate couture.
pour, *v.t,* verser. ¶ *v.i,* ruisseler. *come* ~*ing in,* (*sun, water*) entrer à flots; (*people, cars*) arriver en masse; (*letters*) arriver en avalanche. *it is* ~*ing* [*with rain*], il pleut à verse. ~ *out,* verser; (*empty*) vider; (*fig: emotions*) donner libre cours à; (*troubles*) épancher.
pout, *v.i,* faire la moue.
poverty, *n,* pauvreté, *f. live in* ~, vivre dans le besoin. ~*-stricken,* (*pers.*) dans la misère.
powder, *n,* poudre, *f.* ~ *compact,* poudrier, *m.* ~ *magazine,* poudrière, *f.* ~ *puff,* houppe, *f.* ¶ *v.t,* (*rocks, chalk*) pulvériser; (*body*) poudrer. ~ *one's nose,* se mettre de la poudre. ~*ed milk,* lait en poudre, *m.* ~**ing,** *n,* (*snow*) mince pellicule, *f;* (*sugar*) saupoudrage, *m.* ~**y,** *a,* poudreux.
power, *n,* (*ability*) pouvoir, *m,* capacité; (*strength*) puissance, force; (*energy*) énergie, *f;* (*authority; gen. & Pol.*) pouvoir. *mental* ~*s,* facultés mentales. ~ *of attorney* (*Law*), procuration, *f.* ~ *of veto,* droit de veto, *m. the* ~*s that be,* les autorités constituées. ¶ *a,* (*saw &c*) mécanique; (*Elec: cable*) électrique; (*line*) à haute tension. ~ *cut,* coupure de courant, *f.* ~*house* (*fig.*), personne très dynamique. ~ *point,* prise de courant, *f.* ~*-sharing,* partage du pouvoir, *m.* ~ *station,* centrale [électrique *ou* nucléaire], *f.* ~ *structure,* répartition des pouvoirs, *f.* ¶ *v.t,* faire fonctionner; (*propel*) propulser. ~**ful†,** *a,* puissant; fort. ~**less,** *a,* impuissant.
practicable, *a,* praticable. **practical†,** *a,* pratique. ~ *joke,* farce, *f.* **practice,** *n,* (*custom*) pratique, *f,* usage; (*Sport*) entraînement, *m;* (*rehearsal*) répétition, *f;* (*opp. theory*) pratique; (*doctor, lawyer*) exercice, *m. in* ~, en pratique. *be in* ~ (*doctor &c*), exercer. ¶ *a,* d'entraînement. **practise,** *v.t,* (*gen.*) pratiquer; (*method*) employer; (*Sport*) s'entraîner à; (*Mus: piano, song*) travailler. ~ *one's French,* s'exercer à parler français. ¶ *v.i* (*Mus.*) s'exercer; (*Sport*) s'entraîner; (*pro fessional*) exercer. **practising,** *a,* (*Rel.*) pratiquant; actif. **practitioner,** *n.* praticien, ne; (*Med.*) médecin, *m.*
pragmatic, *a,* pragmatique.
prairie, *n,* plaine [herbeuse]. *the* ~[*s*], la Grande Prairie.
praise, *n,* éloge, *m. in* ~ *of,* à la louange de. ¶ *v.t,* louer. ~ *s.o to the skies,* porter qn aux nues. ~**worthy,** *a,* digne d'éloges.
pram, *n,* voiture d'enfant, *f.*
prance, *v.i,* caracoler.
prank, *n,* frasque; (*joke*) farce, *f. childish* ~, gaminerie, *f.*
prattle, *v.i,* (*child*) babiller; (*people*) jacasser.
prawn, *n,* crevette rose, *f,* bouquet, *m.*
pray, *v.t. & i,* prier. **prayer,** *n,* prière, *f;* (*pl.*) office, *m. say one's* ~*s,* faire sa prière. ~ *book,* livre de messe, *m. The P*~ *Book,* le rituel d l'Église anglicane. ~ *mat,* tapis de prière, *m.* ~ *wheel,* moulin à prières, *m.*
pre..., *pref,* pré... ~*-1968, a,* antérieur à 1968, *ad,* avant 1968. ~*-arrange,* fixer à l'avance. ~*cast concrete,* béton précoulé. ~*date,* (*cheque &c*) antidater; (*come before*) précéder.
preach, *v.t. & i,* prêcher. ~**er,** *n,* prédicateur; (*protestant*) prédicant, *m.* ~**ing,** *n,* prédication, *f.*
preamble, *n,* préambule, *m.*
precarious†, *a,* précaire.
precaution, *n,* précaution, *f.* ~**ary,** *a,* de précaution.
precede, *v.t,* précéder; (*in rank*) avoir préséance sur. **precedence,** *n,* priorité; préséance, *f.* **precedent,** *n.* & **preceding,** *a,* précédent, *m.*
precept, *n,* précepte, *m.*
precinct, *n,* enceinte, *f;* (*pl.*) alentours, *m.pl.*
precious†, *a,* précieux. ~ *little,* très peu. *your* ~ *child* (*ironic*), ton enfant chéri.
precipice, *n,* précipice, *m.* **precipitancy** & **precipitation,** *n,* précipitation, *f.* **precipitate,** *v.t.* (*& i*), (se) précipiter; (*event &c*) hâter. ¶ *a,* irréflechi, hâtif. ~**ly,** *ad,* précipitamment. **precipitous,** *a,* escarpé, à pic; (*action*) hâtif.
précis, *n,* résumé, *m.*
precise, *a,* précis; (*pers.*) minutieux; (*pej: over* ~) pointilleux. ~**ly,** *ad,* precisément. *to state* ~, préciser. **precision,** *n,* précision, *f.*
preclude, *v.t,* empêcher; (*doubt*) écarter; (*possibility*) exclure.
precocious, *a,* précoce. ~**ness,** *n,* précocité, *f.*
preconceived, *a,* préconçu.
precursor, *n,* précurseur; (*event*) signe avant-coureur, *m.*
predator, *n,* prédateur, *m.* ~**y,** *a,* (*animal*) prédateur; (*pers.*) rapace.
predecessor, *n,* prédécesseur, *m.*
predestination, *n,* prédestination, *f.*
predicament, *n,* situation difficile, *f.*
predicate (*Logic & Gram.*) *n,* attribut, prédicat, *m.* ¶ *v.t,* affirmer.
predict, *v.t,* prédire. ~**able,** *a,* prévisible. ~**ion,** *n,* prédiction, *f.*
predilection, *n,* prédilection, *f.*
predispose, *v.t,* prédisposer.
predominance, *n,* prédominance, *f.* **predominate,** *v.i,* prédominer.
pre-eminent, *a,* prééminent. ~**ly,** *ad,* par excellence.
preen, *v.t,* (*feathers*) (se) lisser. ~ *o.s,* se pomponner.
prefabricate, *v.t,* préfabriquer.

preface, *n,* préface, *f,* avant-propos, *m.* ¶ *v.t,* faire précéder.
prefect, *n,* préfet, *m.* ~**ure,** *n,* préfecture, *f.*
prefer, *v.t,* préférer, aimer mieux. ~**able†,** *a,* préférable. ~**ably,** *ad,* de préférence. ~**ence,** *n,* préférence, *f.* ~ *shares* or ~**red stock,** actions de priorité, *f.pl.* ~**ential,** *a,* préférentiel.
prefix, *n,* préfixe, *m.* ¶ *v.t,* préfixer.
pregnancy, *n,* grossesse, *f.* **pregnant,** *a,* enceinte, grosse; (*animal*) pleine; (*fig.*) gros, plein.
prehensile, *a,* préhensile.
prehistoric, *a,* préhistorique.
prejudge, *v.t,* (*question*) préjuger de; (*pers.*) juger d'avance. **prejudice,** *n,* préjugé[s], *m.*[*pl*]; (*law*) préjudice, *m. without* ~ *to,* sans préjudice de. ¶ *v.t,* (*pers.*) prévenir (contre); (*Law &c*) porter préjudice à. ~**d,** *a,* (*pers.*) plein de préjugés; (*idea*) préconçu. **prejudicial,** *a,* préjudiciable.
prelate, *n,* prélat, *m.*
preliminary, *a,* préliminaire.
prelude, *n,* prélude, *m.* ¶ *v.i,* préluder.
premarital, *a,* avant le mariage.
premature†, *a,* prématuré; (*childbirth*) avant terme.
premeditate, *v.t,* préméditer. **premeditation,** *n,* préméditation, *f.*
premier, *a,* premier. ¶ *n,* premier ministre, *m.* **première,** *n,* première, *f.*
premise, *n,* prémisse, *f.* ~**s,** *n.pl,* locaux, lieux, *m.pl.*
premium, *n,* prime, *f. be at a* ~, faire p.
premonition, *n,* pressentiment, *m.*
preoccupation, *n,* préoccupation, *f.* **preoccupy,** *v.t,* préoccuper.
prepack[age], *v.t,* préemballer.
prepaid, *a,* payé d'avance; (*reply*) payé.
preparation, *n,* préparation; (*Sch.*) étude, *f;* devoirs, *m.pl;* (*pl.*) préparatifs, *m.pl.* **preparatory,** *a,* préparatoire; (*step*) préliminaire. ~ *school,* école primaire privée. **prepare,** *v.t,* préparer (*for,* pour, à).¶ *v.i,* faire des préparatifs (*for,* pour); se préparer (*for,* pour; *to do* à faire). ~**d,** *a,* (*pers. &c*) prêt; (*answer &c*) préparé à l'avance; (*Cook.*) tout prêt.
preponderance, *n,* prépondérance, *f.*
preposition, *n,* préposition, *f.*
prepossessing, *a,* (*appearance*) avenant.
preposterous†, *a,* absurde.
prerecord, *v.t,* enregistrer à l'avance. ~*ed broadcast,* émission en différé, *f.*
prerequisite, *n,* condition préalable, *f.*
prerogative, *n,* prérogative, *f,* privilège, *m.*
Presbyterian, *n. & a,* presbytérien, ne.
preschool, *a,* préscolaire; (*child*) d'âge préscolaire.
prescribe, *v.t,* prescrire. **prescription,** *n,* prescription; (*Med.*) ordonnance, prescription, *f. on* ~, sur ordonnance.
presence, *n,* présence, *f.* ~ *of mind,* présence d'esprit. *make one's* ~ *felt,* ne pas passer inaperçu. **present,** *a,* (*gen., Gram.*) présent; (*current*) actuel. *at the* ~ *time,* actuellement. *be* ~ *at something,* assister à qch. ~*-day,* actuel. ~ *perfect,* passé composé, *m.* ¶ *n,* (*time, Gram.*) présent; (*gift*) cadeau, *m. at* ~, actuellement, en ce moment, à présent. ¶ *v.t,* (*gen.*) présenter; (*evidence &c*) fournir; (*Law: case*) exposer; (*gift*) offrir, faire cadeau de; (*prize &c*) remettre; (*play, film, TV &c*) donner; (*act as presenter*) présenter. ~ *arms,* présenter les armes. ~**able,** *a,* présentable. **presentation,** *n,* présentation, *f.*
presentiment, *n,* pressentiment, *m.*
presently, *ad,* tout à l'heure.
preservation, *n,* conservation; (*from harm*) préservation, *f.* **preservative,** *n,* agent de conservation, *m.* **preserve,** *n,* (*jam, oft.pl.*) confiture, *f;* (*bottled*) conserve, *f;* (*Hunting*) réserve, *f.* ¶ *v.t,* (*maintain: gen.*) conserver; (*materials*) entretenir; (*memory, silence &c*) garder; (*peace*) maintenir; (*from harm*) préserver (de); (*Cook.*) mettre en conserve. ~**d,** *a,* en conserve. *well* ~, en bon état de conservation; (*pers.*) bien conservé [pour son âge].
preshrunk, *a,* irrétrécissable.
preside, *v.i,* présider. ~ *at, over,* présider [à]. **presidency,** *n,* présidence, *f.* **president,** *n,* président, e. *P*~ *of the Board of Trade,* ministre du Commerce, *m.* **presidential,** *a,* présidentiel.
press, *n,* (*wine &c*) pressoir, *m;* (*apparatus: gen.*) presse, *f.* (*newspapers*) *the* ~, la presse. *in the* ~, (*being printed*) sous presse; (*in the papers*) dans la presse. ~ *agency,* agence de presse, *f.* ~ *agent,* agent de publicité, *m.* ~ *box, gallery,* tribune de la presse, *f.* ~ *conference,* conférence de presse, *f.* ~ *cutting,* coupure de journal, *f.* ~ *fastener,* ~ *stud,* pression, *f.* ~ *release,* communiqué de presse, *m.* ¶ *v.t,* (*button &c*) appuyer sur; (*hand &c*) serrer; (*fruit, flowers*) presser; (*clothes*) repasser, donner un coup de fer à; (*fig: advantage, attack &c*) pousser; (*claim*) renouveler; (*opponent*) presser; (*creditor*) poursuivre. ~ *charges,* engager des poursuites (*against,* contre). ¶ *v.i,* appuyer, presser (sur); (*weight*) peser (sur); (*debts*) peser (*on,* à). ~ *down,* appuyer (sur). ~ *on,* continuer. ~ *out,* (*liquid*) exprimer; (*crease*) aplatir. ~**ing,** *a,* (*business &c*) urgent; (*danger*) pressant; (*invitation*) instant. **pressure,** *n,* pression, *f.* ~ *cooker,* cocotte-minute, *f.* ~ *group,* groupe de pression, *m.* ~ *gauge,* manomètre, *m.* **pressurize,** *v.t,* (*cabin &c*) pressuriser; (*pers.*) faire pression sur; forcer.
prestige, *n,* prestige, *m.* **prestigious,** *a,* prestigieux.
prestressed, *a,* ~ *concrete,* [béton armé] précon-

traint, *m*.
presume, *v.t*, (*suppose*) présumer; (*venture*) se permettre. ~ [*up*]*on*, abuser de. **presumption,** *n*, présomption; audace, *f*. **presumptuous,** *a*, présomptueux. ~**ness,** *n*, audace, *f*.
presuppose, *v.t*, présupposer. **presupposition,** *n*, présupposition, *f*.
pretence, *n*, semblant, *m*, feinte, *f;* (*pretext*) prétexte, *m;* (*affectation*) prétention, *f*. **pretend,** *v.t. & i*, faire semblant (de faire); feindre; (*claim*) prétendre. ~**er,** *n*, prétendant, e. **pretension,** *n*, prétention, *f*. **pretentious,** *a*, prétentieux.
preterite, *n*, prétérit, passé simple, *m*.
pretext, *n*, prétexte, *m*.
pretty†, *a*, joli. ~-~, un peu trop joli. ¶ *ad*, assez. ~ *good*, pas mal. ~ *much*, à peu près.
pretzel, *n*, bretzel, *m*.
prevail, *v.i*, prévaloir, l'emporter (*over*, sur); (*conditions &c*) prédominer. ~ [*up*]*on*, décider (à), persuader (de). **prevailing,** *a*, (*wind*) dominant; (*conditions*) actuel; (*opinion &c*) courant. **prevalence,** *n*, fréquence, prédominance, *f*. **prevalent,** *a*, courant; actuel; (*illness*) répandu.
prevaricate, *v.i*, tergiverser, équivoquer. **prevarication,** *n*, faux fuyant[s], *m*,[*pl*].
prevent, *v.t*, empêcher (*s.o from doing*, qn de faire); (*illness*) prévenir. ~**able,** *a*, évitable. ~**ative,** & ~**ive,** *a*, préventif. ~**ion,** *n*, prévention, *f*. *society for the ~ of cruelty to animals*, société protectrice des animaux, *f*.
preview, *n*, (*film &c*) avant-première, *f;* (*fig.*) aperçu, *m*.
previous, *a*, précédent, antérieur. *have a ~ engagement*, être déjà pris. ~**ly,** *ad*, (*before*) précédemment, auparavant, avant; (*in past*) dans le temps, jadis; (*already*) déjà.
pre-war, *a*, d'avant-guerre.
prey, *n*, proie, *f*. ~ [*up*]*on*, faire sa proie de; (*the mind*) miner, ronger.
price, *n*, (*gen, fig.*) prix; (*Stk.Ex.*) cours, *m;* (*Turf*) cote, *f*. *all at the same ~*, au choix. (*fig.*) *set a high ~ on*, faire grand cas de. ¶ *a*, (*index, rise*) des prix. ~ *cut*, réduction, *f*, rabais, *m*. ~ *freeze*, blocage des prix, *m*. ~ *list*, tarif, *m*, prix courant. ~ *tag*, étiquette, *f*. ¶ *v.t*, fixer *ou* marquer le prix de; (*value*) évaluer. ~**less,** *a*, sans prix, inestimable; (*amusing*) impayable. **pricey** *P*, *a*, couteux, cher.
prick, *n*, piqûre, *f;* (*P* penis*) bitte *P**, *f*. ¶ *v.t*, piquer. *my conscience ~s me*, j'ai mauvaise conscience. ~ *out*, repiquer. ~ *up* (*ears*), dresser. **prickle,** *n*, piquant, *m*. **prickly,** *a*, épineux, hérissé; (*pers.*) irritable. ~ *pear*, figue de Barbarie, *f*.
pride, *n*, (*self-respect*) amour-propre; (*arrogance*) orgueil, *m;* (*in s.o, sth*) fierté; (*of lions*) troupe, *f*. *to take ~ in*, être fier de. ¶ *v.t*, ~ *o.s on*, être fier de; s'enorgueillir de.
priest, *n*, prêtre, *m*. ~**ess,** *n*, prêtresse, *f*. ~**hood,** *n*, prêtrise, *f*, sacerdoce; clergé, *m*. ~**ly,** *a*, sacerdotal.
prig, *n*, pharisien, ne. **priggish,** *a*, suffisant.
prim, *a*, guindé, collet monté.
primacy, *n*, (*Rel.*) primatie; primauté, *f*.
prima facie, *ad*, à première vue, de prime abord.
primary†, *a*, (*gen.*) primaire; principal; (*colour*) fondamental; (*importance*) primordial. ~ *school*, école primaire. ~ *school teacher*, instituteur, trice. ¶ *n*, (*Am. Pol.*) primaire, *f*.
primate, *n*, (*Eccl.*) primat; (*Zool.*) primate, *m*.
prime, *a*, (*chief*) principal, primordial, fondamental; (*meat*) de premier choix; (*Math.*) premier. ~ *cost*, prix coutant. *m*. ~ *minister*, premier ministre, *m*. ~ *mover*, (*Tech.*) force motrice; (*fig.*) instigateur, trice. ~ *of life*, fleur de l'âge, *f*. *past one's ~*, sur le retour. ¶ *v.t*, (*pump, gen.*) amorcer; (*paint*) apprêter; (*fig: pers.*) mettre au courant. **primer,** *n*, (*book*) livre élémentaire; (*paint*) apprêt, *m*.
primeval, *a*, primordial; (*forest*) vierge. **primitive†,** *a*, primitif. **primordial,** *a*, primordial. **primrose,** *n*, primevère, *f*.
prince, *n*, prince, *m*. ~**ly,** *a*, princier. **princess,** *n*, princesse, *f*.
principal†, *a*, principal. ~ *parts* (*verb*), temps primitifs. ¶ *n*, (*gen, Sch.*) directeur, trice; (*lycée, college*) proviseur; (*Fin.*) principal, capital, *m*. ~**ity,** *n*, principauté, *f*.
principle, *n*, principe, *m*. *in ~*, en principe. *on ~*, par principe.
print, *n*, (*foot &c*) empreinte; (*Phot.*) épreuve; (*Art*) gravure, *f;* (*fabric*) imprimé, *m;* (*Typ: letters*) caractères, *m.pl;* (*material*) texte imprimé. *finger ~*, empreinte digitale. *out of ~*, épuisé. *in ~*, disponible. *~-out* (*computer*) listing, *m*, édition, *f*. ¶ *v.t*, (*Typ., fabric*) imprimer; (*Phot.*) tirer; (*by hand*) écrire en caractères d'imprimerie. *~ed matter*, imprimé, *m*. ¶ *v.i*, imprimer. ~ *out*, imprimer. ~**er,** *n*, imprimeur, *m*. *~'s error*, faute d'impression, coquille, *f*. ~**ing,** *n*, impression, *f;* tirage, *m*. ~ *ink*, encre d'imprimerie, *f*. ~ *office*, ~ *works*, imprimerie, *f*. ~ *press*, presse typographique, *f*.
prior, *a*, antérieur. ¶ *pr*, ~ *to*, antérieurement à, avant. ¶ *n*, prieur, *m*. ~**ess,** *n*, prieure, *f*. ~**ity,** *n*, priorité, *f*. **priory,** *n*, prieuré, *m*.
prise, *v.t*, forcer. ~ *off*, *up*, enlever, soulever en faisant levier.
prism, *n*, prisme, *m*. ~**atic,** *a*, prismatique.
prison, *n*, prison, *f*. ¶ *a*, pénitentiaire. ~ *camp*, camp de prisonniers, *m*. ~ *governor*, directeur de prison, *m*. ~ *officer*, gardien, ne de p. ~**er,** *n*, prisonnier, ère, détenu, e. ~ *at the bar*, accusé, e. ~ *of war*, prisonnier de guerre.
pristine, *a*, (*former*) d'antan; (*unspoilt*) virginal.
privacy, *n*, intimité, solitude, *f*. **private,** *a*, (*opp.*

public, official) privé; (*confidential*) confidentiel, personnel; (*on door*) privé, interdit au public; (*car, house &c*) particulier; personnel. ~ *hearing*, (*Law, Adm.*) audience à huis clos, *f.* ~ *parts*, parties [génitales], *f.*[*pl*]. ~ *secretary*, secrétaire privé, e *ou* personnel, elle. ¶ *n*, (*Mil.*) [simple] soldat, *m.* **privateer,** *n*, corsaire, *m.* **privately,** *ad*, (*secretly, personally*) dans son for intérieur; (*opp. publicly*) en privé; (*unofficially*) à titre personnel.
privation, *n*, privation, *f.*
privet, *n*, troène, *m.*
privilege, *n*, privilège, *m*; (*parliament &c*) prérogative, *f.* ~**d,** *a*, privilégié. *be* ~ *to*, avoir le privilège de.
privy, *a*, privé. ~ *council*, conseil privé, *m.* ¶ *n*, cabinets, W.-C., *m.pl.*
prize, *n*, prix, *m*; (*Nav.*) prise, *f*; (*lottery*) lot, *m.* ~ *bull*, taureau primé, *m.* ~ *court*, conseil des prises, *m.* ~ *fight*[*ing*], combat [de boxe] professionnel, *m.* ~ *fighter*, boxeur professionnel, *m.* ~ *giving*, distribution des prix, *f.* ~ *list*, palmarès, *m.* ~*money*, argent du prix, *m.* ~ *winner*, lauréat, e; (*lottery*) gagnant, e. ¶ *v.t*, (*value*) priser; faire grand cas de.
pro, *pref*, pro-. ¶ *n*, *the* ~*s & cons*, le pour & le contre. ~ *forma*, pour la forme. ~ *rata*, au pro rata.
probability, *n*, probabilité, *f.* *in all* ~, selon toute probabilité. **probable†,** *a*, (*likely*) probable; (*credible*) vraisemblable.
probate, *n*, homologation [d'un testament], *f.*
probation, *n*, (*Law*) mise à l'épreuve; (*minors*) mise en liberté surveillée; (*Rel.*) probation, *f.* *on* ~, (*job*) engagé à l'essai. ~**ary,** *a*, d'essai. ~**er,** *n*, employé(e), engagé(e) à l'essai; (*Rel.*) novice, *m,f*; (*Med.*) élève infirmière.
probe, *n*, (*gen., Med., Space*) sonde; (*fig.*) enquête (*into*, sur), *f.* ¶ *v.t*, (*gen., Med.*) sonder; explorer; (*mystery*) chercher à éclaircir.
probity, *n*, probité, *f.*
problem, *n*, problème, *m.* *no* ~*!* *P* pas de problème! *P* ¶ *a*, (*child*) caractériel; (*family*) inadapté; (*play &c*) à thèse. ~ *page* (*Press*), courrier du cœur, *m.* ~**atic(al),** *a*, problematique.
procedure, *n*, procédure, *f.* **proceed,** *v.i*, (*go*) aller, se rendre; avancer; continuer; (*act*) procéder; (*originate*) provenir (*from*, de). (*Law*) ~ *against*, poursuivre. ~**ing,** *n*, procédé, *m*; (*pl.*) (*ceremony*) cérémonie; (*meeting*) séance, *f*; débats; (*records*) actes, *m.pl*; (*Law*) procès, *m.* *take* ~*s*, (*gen.*) prendre des mesures; (*Law*) intenter un procès. **proceeds,** *n.pl*, produit, *m.*
process, *n*, processus; (*method*) procédé; (*Law: action*) procès, *m.* *in* ~, en cours. *in the* ~ *of doing*, en train de faire. ¶ *v.t*, (*Ind.*) traiter; (*Phot.*) développer; (*Adm. &c*) s'occuper de. ~*ed chesse*, fromage fondu, *m.* ~**ing,** *n*, traitement, *m.*
procession, *n*, (*Rel.*) procession, *f*; (*gen.*) défilé, cortège, *m.*
proclaim, *v.t*, (*gen.*) proclamer; déclarer; (*news*) annoncer; (*show*) révéler. **proclamation,** *n*, proclamation; déclaration, *f.*
procrastinate, *v.i*, faire traîner les choses; atermoyer. **procrastination,** *n*, procrastination, *f.*
procreate, *v.t*, procréer. **procreation,** *n*, procréation, *f.*
procure, *v.t*, obtenir; (*Law: prostitute*) procurer. ¶ *v.i*, (*Law*) faire du proxénétisme. **procurer,** *n*, proxénète, *m,f.* **procuring,** *n*, proxénétisme, *m.*
prod, *n*, (*push & fig.*) poussée, *f*; (*jab*) [petit] coup (de canne &c), *m.* ¶ *v.t*, pousser [doucement] (du doigt &c).
prodigal, *a. & n*, prodigue, *m,f.*
prodigious†, *a*, prodigieux. **prodigy,** *n*, prodige, *m.*
produce, *n*, produit[s], *m.*[*pl*]. ¶ *v.t*, produire; (*Fin.*) rapporter; (*child*) donner naissance à; (*cause*) causer; (*impression*) faire; (*interest &c*) susciter; (*Elec: current*) engendrer; (*Theat., TV*) mettre en scène; (*Cine.*) produire; (*TV, Radio*) réaliser. **producer,** *n*, (*Ind., Agr., Cine.*) producteur, trice; metteur en scène; réalisateur, *m.* **-producing,** *suffix*, producteur, trice. **product,** *n*, produit; (*fig.*) résultat, fruit, produit, *m.* ~**ion,** *n*, production; (*gen., Cine.*) mise en scène; réalisation, *f.* ~**ive,** *a*, (*gen.*) fécond; (*Econ.*) productif.
profane, *a*, profane. ¶ *v.t*, profaner. **profanity,** *n*, blasphème, *m.*
profess, *v.t*, professer. ~**ed,** *a*, déclaré; (*Rel.*) profès. ~**ion,** *n*, profession, *f.* *by* ~, de son métier. ~**ional,** *a. & n*, professionnel, le; (*diplomat, soldier*) de carrière; (*fig: job*) de haute qualité. ~ *army*, armée de métier, *f.* ~ *classes*, professions libérales, *f.pl.* ~**ionalism,** *n*, professionnalisme, *m*; haute qualité. ~**or,** *n*, professeur, *m.*
proffer, *v.t*, (*thanks, apology*) présenter; (*object*) offrir; (*remark*) faire.
proficiency, *n*, compétence, *f.* **proficient,** *a*, compétent.
profile, *n*, profil, *m*; (*fig: of pers.*) portrait, *m.* ¶ *v.t*, profiler; faire un portrait de.
profit, *n*, (*gen., Com., fig.*) profit; (*Com., Insce*) bénéfice, *m.* ~*-making*, à but lucratif. ~ *margin*, marge bénéficiaire, *f.* *non-*~*-making*, à but non lucratif. ~ *sharing*, participation aux bénéfices, *f.* ¶ *v.t*, profiter, tirer un profit. ~**able,** *a*, (*Com.*) rentable; (*fig.*) avantageux; (*discussion &c*) profitable. ~**ability,** *n*, rentabilité, *f.* ~**ably,** *ad*, (*sell*) à profit; (*deal & fig.*) avec profit. ~**eer,** *n*, profiteur, *m.* ¶ *v.i*, faire des bénéfices excessives.
profligacy, *n*, débauche, *f.* **profligate,** *a. & n*,

débauché, e.
profound†, *a*, profond. **profundity,** *n*, profondeur, *f*.
profuse, *a*, abondant; (*thanks &c*) profus. **~ly,** *ad*, (*grow*) à profusion; (*bleed &c*) abondamment; (*thank*) avec effusion. **profusion,** *n*, profusion, *f*.
progenitor, *n*, auteur, *m*. **progeny,** *n*, descendants, *m.pl;* progéniture, *f*.
prognosis, *n*, pronostic, *m*. **prognosticate,** *v.t*, pronostiquer.
programme, *n*, (*gen.*) programme, *m;* (*broadcast*) émission, *f*. ¶ *v.t*, (*gen., computer*) programmer. **programmer,** *n*, (*pers.*) programmeur, euse; (*device*) programmateur, *m*. **programming,** *n*, programmation, *f*.
progress, *n*, progrès, *m. oft. pl. in ~*, en cours. ¶ *v.i*, avancer, progresser, faire des progrès. **~ion,** *n*, progression, *f*. **~ive**†, *a*, progressif; (*pers., Pol.*) progressiste.
prohibit, *v.t*, défendre, interdire; (*Adm., Law*) prohiber; (*prevent*) empêcher (qn de faire). **~ion,** *n*, défense, interdiction, prohibition, *f*. **~ionist,** *n*, prohibitionniste, *m*. **~ive** *&* **~ory,** *a*, prohibitif.
project, *n*, (*scheme*) projet, plan (pour faire), *m;* (*undertaking*) entreprise; (*study*) étude (*on*, de), *f;* (*Sch.*) dossier (sur), *m*. ¶ *v.t*, projeter. ¶ *v.i.* se p., faire saillie, saillir, avancer. *~ beyond*, dépasser. **~ile,** *n*, projectile, *m*. **~ing,** *a*, en saillie, saillant; (*tooth*) en avant. **~ion,** *n*, projection; (*protruding*) saillie, *f;* ressaut, *m*. *~ room* (*Cine.*), cabine de projection, *f*. **~ionist,** *n*, projectionniste, *m,f*. **~or,** *n*, projecteur, *m*.
prolapse, *n*, prolapsus, *m*.
proletarian, *a*, prolétarien. ¶ *n*, prolétaire, *m*. **proletariat[e],** *n*, prolétariat, *m*.
proliferate, *v.i*, proliférer. **proliferation,** *n*, prolifération, *f*. **prolific,** *a*, prolifique.
prologue, *n*, prologue, *m*.
prolong, *v.t*, prolonger. **~ation,** *n*, (*in time*) prolongation, *f;* (*in space*) prolongement, *m*.
promenade, *n*, promenade, *f;* (*Theat. &c*) promenoir, *m*. *~ deck*, pont-promenade, *m*.
prominence, *n*, proéminence, *f*. **prominent,** *a*, proéminent; saillant; (*tooth*) qui avance; (*pers.*) important, bien en vue. **~ly,** *ad*, (*display &c*) bien en vue.
promiscuity, *n*, promiscuité, *f*. **promiscuous,** *a*, (*pers.*) de mœurs faciles; (*conduct*) léger. **~ly,** *ad*, immoralement; au hasard.
promise, *n*, promesse, *f;* (*hope*) espérances, *f.pl*. ¶ *v.t. & i*, promettre (qch à qn; à qn de faire). *~ ?* c'est promis? *land of ~*, terre promise, *f*. **promising,** *a*, prometteur. *promissory note*, billet à ordre, *m*.
promontory, *n*, promontoire, *m*.
promote, *v.t*, promouvoir (*to*, à); (*Com.*) lancer; (*Govt. bill*) présenter. *be ~d*, être promu, monter en grade; (*Foot.*) monter. **promoter,** *n*, (*Com.*) promoteur de vente, *m;* (*Sport*) organisateur, trice; (*company*) fondateur, trice. **promotion,** *n*, promotion, *f;* lancement, *m;* présentation, *f*.
prompt†, *a*, rapide, prompt; ponctuel. ¶ *v.t*, pousser, inciter (qn à faire); (*Theat.*) souffler. **~er,** *n*, souffleur, euse.
promulgate, *v.t*, promulguer.
prone, *a*, (*face down*) [couché] sur le ventre; (*liable*) enclin (à qch, à faire).
prong, *n*, (*fork*) dent; (*antler*) pointe, *f*.
pronominal, *a*, pronominal. **pronoun,** *n*, pronom, *m*.
pronounce, *v.t. & i*, prononcer. **pronunciation,** *n*, prononciation, *f*.
pronto *P*, *ad*, illico *P*.
proof, *n*, (*gen., Math.*) preuve; (*Typ.*) épreuve, *f*. *~ of identity*, pièce[s] d'identité, *f.*[*pl*]. *~ against*, à l'épreuve de; (*pity*) insensible à. *~read*, corriger les épreuves de. *~reader*, correcteur, trice d'é. *~ spirit*, alcool à 57° ¶ *v.t*, imperméabiliser.
prop, *n*, support; (*for wall, mine &c*) étai, *m;* (*for clothes line*) perche, *f;* (*fig.*) soutien, *m*. ¶ *v.t*, *~* [*up*], (*lean: bike &c*) appuyer; (*Build., régime*) étayer; (*business*) soutenir; (*Fin.*) venir au secours de.
propaganda, *n*, propagande, *f*.
propagate, *v.t*, propager.
propel, *v.t*, propulser. **propeller,** *n*, hélice, *f*. *~ shaft* (*Mot.*), arbre de transmission, *m*.
propensity, *n*, propension (à qch, à faire), *f*.
proper, *a*, (*correct*) bon, correct, qui convient; (*behaviour*) convenable; (*pers.*) comme il faut. *~ noun*, nom propre, *m*. **~ly,** *ad*, convenablement, correctement, comme il faut. *~ speaking*, à proprement parler. **~ty,** *n*, propriété, *f;* (*possessions*) biens, *m.pl;* (*pl. Theat.*) accessoires, *m.pl*. *~ market*, marché immobilier, *m*. *~ tax*, impôt foncier, *m*.
prophecy, *n*, prophétie, *f*. **prophesy,** *v.t*, prédire. ¶ *v.i*, prophétiser. **prophet,** *n*, prophète, *m*. **~ess,** *n*, prophétesse, *f*. **~ic(al)**†, *a*, prophétique.
propitiate, *v.t*, se concilier. **propitious,** *a*, propice.
proportion, *n*, proportion *f;* (*pl. size*) proportions; (*part*) partie, part, *f*. *in ~ to*, en proportion de. ¶ *v.t*, proportionner (à). **~al**†, **~ate**†, *a*, proportionnel, proportionné (*to*, à).
proposal, *n*, proposition; (*of marriage*) demande, *f;* (*plan*) projet (pour), *m*. **propose,** *v.t*, proposer (*sth to s.o*, qch à qn; *doing*, de faire; *that*, que + *subj*); (*toast*) porter; (*marriage*) demander. **proposition,** *n*, (*gen.*) proposition; (*fig.*) affaire, *f*. ¶ *v.t*, faire des propositions [indécentes] à.
propound, *v.t*, proposer.

proprietary, *a,* (*rights*) de propriété. ~ *brand,* marque déposée. *f.* ~ *medicine,* spécialité pharmaceutique, *f.* **proprietor, tress,** *n,* propriétaire, *m,f.* **propriety,** *n,* bienséance, convenance, *f.*

propulsion, *n,* propulsion, *f.*

prosaic†, *a,* prosaïque.

proscribe, *v.t,* proscrire.

prose, *n,* prose, *f.* ~ *writer,* prosateur, *m.*

prosecute, *v.t,* poursuivre. **prosecution,** *n,* (*Law: case*) accusation, *f;* (*act*) poursuites judiciaires, *f.pl. witness for the* ~, témoin à charge, *m.* **prosecutor,** *n,* plaignant, *m;* (*public* ~) procureur [de la République]; ministère public, *m.*

prosody, *n,* prosodie, *f.*

prospect, *n,* (*view*) vue; (*fig: outlook*) perspective, *f;* (*future*) avenir; (*hope*) espoir (de), *m.* ¶ *v.t. & i,* prospecter. ~**ing,** *n,* prospection, *f.* ~**ive,** *a,* (*home*) futur (*before n.*); (*client*) possible; (*journey*) en perspective. ~**or,** *n,* prospecteur, *m.*

prospectus, *n,* prospectus, *m.*

prosper, *v.i,* prospérer, réussir. ~**ity,** *n,* prospérité, *f.* ~**ous,** *a,* prospère.

prostate [gland], *n,* prostate, *f.*

prostitute, *n,* prostituée, *f. male* ~, prostitué, *m.* ¶ *v.t,* prostituer. **prostitution,** *n,* prostitution, *f.*

prostrate, *a,* à plat ventre; (*Med.*) prostré; (*in respect*) posterné; (*fig.*) accablé, effondré. ¶ *v.t,* (*fig.*) accabler. ~ *o.s,* se prosterner. **prostration,** *n,* (*Med.*) prostration, *f.*

protagonist, *n,* protagoniste, *m.*

protect, *v.t,* protéger; (*interests*) sauvegarder. ~**ion,** *n,* protection (contre); sauvegarde, *f.* ~**ionist,** *n. & a,* protectionniste, *m,f.* ~**ive,** *a,* de protection; (*Econ.*) protecteur. ~ *colouring* (*Zool.*), camouflage, *m.* ~ *custody* (*Law*), détention préventive. ~**ively,** *ad,* d'un geste protecteur. ~**or, tress,** *n,* protecteur, trice. ~**ate,** *n,* protectorat, *m.*

protein, *n,* protéine, *f.*

protest, *n,* protestation, *f.* ¶ *a,* de protestation. ~ *march,* manifestation, *f.* ¶ *v.t. & i,* protester (que); (*innocence*) protester de. ~**ant,** *n. & a,* protestant, e. ~**ation,** *n,* protestation, *f.* ~**er,** *n,* protestataire, *m,f;* (*demonstrator*) manifestant, e.

protocol, *n,* protocole, *m.*

prototype, *n,* prototype, *m.*

protract, *v.t,* prolonger. ~**or,** *n,* rapporteur, *m.*

protrude, *v.i,* faire saillie; (*teeth*) avancer.

protuberance, *n,* protubérance, *f.*

proud†, *a,* fier; (*arrogant*) orgueilleux, hautain; (*imposing*) majestueux. *as* ~ *as a peacock,* fier comme Artaban.

prove, *v.t,* prouver; (*test*) mettre à l'épreuve; (*will*) homologuer. ¶ *v.i,* se révéler, s'avérer; (*dough*) se lever.

proverb, *n,* proverbe, *m.* ~**ial†,** *a,* proverbial.

provide, *v.t,* fournir (qch à qn); (*equip*) munir, pourvoir (qn de qch); (*law*) stipuler, prévoir (que). ~ *for s.o,* pourvoir aux besoins de qn. ~ *for sth,* prévoir qch. ~*d* [*that*], *providing,* pourvu que + *subj.* ~*d with,* pourvu de. **providence,** *n,* providence; (*God*) Providence, *f.* **provident,** *a,* prévoyant. ~ *fund,* caisse de prévoyance, *f.* ~**ial†,** *a,* providentiel. **provider,** *n,* pourvoyeur, *m.*

province, *n,* province; (*pl.*) province; (*sphere*) compétence, *f,* domaine, *m.* **provincial,** *a,* provincial; de province.

provision, *n,* provision, *f;* (*pl. food &c*) provisions, *f.pl;* (*supplying*) fourniture, *f,* approvisionnement, *m;* (*Adm., Law*) disposition, *f.* ¶ *v.t,* approvisionner. ~**al,** *a,* provisoire. ~**ally,** *ad,* provisoirement, à titre provisoire.

proviso, *n,* condition; (*Law*) clause restrictive, *f.*

provocation, *n,* provocation, *f.* **provocative,** *a,* provocant. **provoke,** *v.t,* provoquer. **provoking,** *a,* agaçant.

provost, *n,* (*Univ.*) principal; (*Sc: mayor*) maire; (*Eccl.*) doyen, *m.*

prow, *n,* proue, *f.*

prowess, *n,* prouesse, *f.*

prowl, *v.i,* rôder. ~**er,** *n,* rôdeur, euse.

proximity, *n,* proximité, *f.*

proxy, *n,* (*power*) procuration, *f;* (*pers.*) mandataire, *m,f. by* ~, par procuration. ~ *vote,* vote par p., *m.*

prude, *n,* prude, bégueule, *f.*

prudence, *n,* prudence, *f.* **prudent†,** *a,* prudent. ~**ial,** *a,* de prudence.

prudery, *n,* pruderie, *f.* **prudish,** *a,* prude, pudibond, bégueule.

prune[1], *n,* pruneau, *m.*

prune[2], *v.t,* tailler, élaguer, émonder; (*fig.*) élaguer. **pruning,** *n,* taille, *f,* émondage, élagage, *m.* ~ *hook,* émondoir, *m.* ~ *knife,* serpette, *f.* ~ *shears,* sécateur, *m,* cisailles, *f.pl.*

pruriency, *n,* lascivité, *f.* **prurient,** *a,* lascif.

Prussia, *n,* la Prusse. **Prussian,** *a,* prussien. ¶ *n,* Prussien, ne. **prussic,** *a,* prussique.

pry, *v.i,* fureter, fouiller. ~**ing,** *a,* indiscret, curieux.

psalm, *n,* psaume, *m.* ~**ist,** *n,* psalmiste, *m.* **psalter,** *n,* psautier, *m.*

pseudo, *pref,* pseudo-. ¶ *a, P* insincère, faux.

pseudonym, *n,* pseudonyme, *m.*

psyche, *n,* psychisme, *m,* psyché, *f.*

psychedelic, *a,* psychédélique.

psychiatric, *a,* (*hospital &c*) psychiatrique; (*disease*) mental. **psychiatrist,** *n,* psychiatre, *m.* **psychic(al),** *a,* psychique. **psychoanalysis,** *n,* psychanalyse, *f.* **psychoanalyze,** *v.t,* psychoanalyser. **psychological,** *a,* psychologique. **psychologist,** *n,* psychologue, *m,f.* **psychology,** *n,* psychologie, *f,* **psychopath,** *n,*

psychopath, *m,f.* ~**ic,** *a,* (*pers.*) psychopath; (*condition*) psychopathique. **psychosis,** *n,* psychose, *f.* **psychosomatic,** *a,* psychosomatique. **psychotherapy,** *n,* psychothérapie, *f.* **psychotic,** *a,* psychotique.
ptomaine, *n,* ptomaïne, *f.* ~ *poisoning,* intoxication alimentaire, *f.*
puberty, *n,* puberté, *f.* **pubic,** *a,* pubien. ~ *hair,* poils du pubis, *m.pl.* **pubis,** *n,* pubis, *m.*
public†, *a,* public. *in the* ~ *eye,* très en vue. *make* ~, rendre public, publier. ~ *address system,* [installation de] sonorisation, *f.* ~ *convenience,* ~ *lavatory,* toilettes, *f.pl,* W.-C, *m.pl.* ~ *figure,* homme public. ~ *holiday,* jour férié, *m.* ~ *house,* pub, *m.* ~ *limited company* (*P.L.C.*), ≏ société anonyme (S.A.), *f.* ~ *library,* bibliothèque municipale. ~ *opinion,* opinion publique. ~ *opinion poll,* sondage d'o. p., *m.* ~ *ownership,* étatisation, *f.* ~ *relations,* relations publiques, public-relations *P, f.pl.* ~ *servant,* fonctionnaire, *m,f.* ~ *speaking,* l'art oratoire, *m.* ~ *spirit,* civisme, *m.* ~ *transport,* transports en commun, *m.pl.* ¶ *n,* public, *m.* ~**an,** *n,* patron, ne de bistrot, *m.* ~**ation,** *n,* publication, *f.* ~**ity,** *n,* publicité, *f.* **publicize,** *v.t,* (*make public*) rendre public; (*advertise*) faire la publicité pour. **publish,** *v.t,* publier; (*book*) éditer; faire paraître. *to be* ~*ed* (*book*), paraître. ~**er,** *n,* éditeur, *m,f.* ~**ing,** *n,* publication, *f.* ~ *house,* maison d'édition, *f.*
puce, *a,* puce.
pucker, *v.t,* (*Need.*) faire goder. ¶ *v.i,* (~ *up*) goder; (*face*) se plisser.
pudding, *n,* (*steamed &c*) pudding, pouding; (*dessert*) dessert, *m.* ~ *basin,* jatte, *f. black, white* ~, boudin [noir], blanc.
puddle, *n,* flaque, *f.*
puerile, *a,* puéril.
puff, *n,* (*smoke, wind*) bouffée, *f;* (*breath*) souffle, *m;* (*powder*) houppe, houppette, *f. jam* ~, feuilleté à la confiture, *m. take a* ~ *at a cigarette,* tirer des bouffées d'une cigarette. ~*ball,* vesse-de-loup, *f.* ~ *pastry,* pâte feuilletée, *f.* ~ *sleeves,* manches bouffantes, *f.pl.* ¶ *v.i,* (*blow*) souffler; (*pant*) haleter. ~ *out,* (*cheeks, sails*) gonfler. *be* ~*ed out P,* être à bout de souffle.
puffin, *n,* macareux, *m.*
puffiness, *n,* gonflement, *m,* bouffissure, *f.* **puffy,** *a,* gonflé, bouffi.
pug, *n,* carlin, *m.* ~ *nosed,* camus.
pugilism, *n,* pugilat, *m.* boxe, *f.* **pugilist,** *n,* pugiliste, *m.* **pugnacious,** *a,* pugnace, batailleur.
puke *P**, *v.i,* dégobiller *P**.
pull, *n,* (*act*) traction; (*magnet &c*) attraction; (*loyalties*) force; (*drink*) lampée, *f;* (*bell*) cordon, *m.* ¶ *v.t,* (*gen.*) tirer; (*trigger*) presser; (*oars*) tirer sur; (*teeth, weeds*) arracher; (*cork*) retirer; (*gun &c*) sortir; (*beer, thread*) tirer; (*muscle*) se déchirer. ~ *s.o's leg,* faire marcher qn. ~ *one's weight,* faire sa part du travail. ~ *strings,* se faire pistonner. ~ *to pieces,* démolir; (*pers., play*) éreinter, esquinter. ~ **away,** (*car &c*) démarrer. ~ **down,** (*blind*) baisser; (*skirt, hat*) tirer; (*building*) démolir. ~ **in,** (*car*) s'arrêter; (*train*) entrer en gare; (*rope &c*) ramener; (*P earn: pers.*) gagner; (*business*) rapporter. ~ **off,** (*clothes &c*) enlever; (*plan*) réaliser; (*deal*) mener à bien; (*attack*) réussir. ~ **out,** (*leave: car &c*) démarrer; (*withdraw*) (se) retirer (de); (*Mot.*) déboîter; (*extract*) arracher. ~ **over,** (*Mot.*) se ranger sur le côté. ~**over,** pull, pull-over, *m.* ~ **through,** (*illness*) se rétablir. ~ **o.s together,** se ressaisir. ~**up,** (*stop*) (s')arrêter; (*plant*) arracher. ~ *up one's roots,* se déraciner.
pullet, *n,* jeune poule, *f.*
pulley, *n,* poulie, *f.*
Pullman [car], *n,* pullman, *m.*
pulmonary, *a,* pulmonaire.
pulp, *n,* pulpe; chair; (*Paper making*) pâte à papier, *f.* ¶ *v.t,* réduire en pulpe, en pâte; (*book*) mettre au pilon.
pulpit, *n,* chaire, *f.*
pulsate, *v.i,* émettre des pulsations; (*heart*) palpiter; (*blood*) battre; (*music*) vibrer. **pulsation,** *n,* pulsation, *f,* battement, *m.* **pulse**[1], *n,* (*Anat.*) pouls, *m;* (*Elec. Phys.*) vibration; (*radar*) impulsion, *f.* ~ *rate,* fréquence des pulsations, *f.*
pulse[2], *n,* légume à gousse, *m;* (*plant*) légumineuse, *f.*
pulverize, *v.t,* pulvériser.
puma, *n,* puma, *m.*
pumice [stone], *n,* [pierre] ponce, *f.*
pummel, *v.t,* bourrer de coups.
pump, *n,* pompe, *f.* ~ *attendant,* pompiste, *m,f.* ~*ing station,* station de pompage, *f.* ~ *room* (*at spa*), buvette, *f.* ¶ *v.t. & i,* pomper; (*P fig.*) cuisiner. ~ *up,* gonfler.
pumpkin, *n,* citrouille, courge, *f,* potiron, *m.*
pun, *n,* calembour, jeu de mots, *m.*
punch, *n,* coup de poing; (*Box.*) punch, *m;* (*fig: speech*) force, *f;* (*tickets*) poinçonneuse, *f;* (*paper*) perforateur; (*drink*) punch, *m.* ~ *bowl,* bol à punch, *m.* ~ *card,* carte perforée. ~*-drunk,* abruti. ~*-line,* (*joke*) astuce; (*speech*) phrase-clé, *f.* ~*-up P,* bagarre *P, f.* *P*~, Polichinelle, *m.* ~ *& Judy show,* guignol, *m.* ¶ *v.t,* (*pers.*) donner un coup de poing à; (*object*) frapper d'un coup de p.; (*with tool*) poinçonner; perforer. ~ *s.o's face in P,* casser la gueule à qn *P.* ¶ *v.i,* frapper, cogner.
punctilious, *a,* pointilleux.
punctual†, *a,* ponctuel; (*on time*) à l'heure. ~**ity,** *n,* ponctualité, exactitude, *f.* **punctuate,**

v.t. & abs, ponctuer. **punctuation,** *n,* ponctuation, *f.* **puncture,** *n,* piqûre; (*Surg.*) ponction; (*tyre*) crevaison, *f.* ¶ *v.t. & i,* piquer; ponctionner; crever.

pundit, *n,* expert, pontife, *m.*

pungency, *n,* (*sauce*) goût piquant, *m;* (*smell, taste*) acreté, *f;* (*remark*) mordant, *m.* **pungent,** *a,* piquant; âcre; mordant.

punish, *v.t,* punir (*for sth,* de qch; *for doing,* pour avoir fait); (*fig: Sport*) malmener. **~able,** *a,* punissable. **~ment,** *n,* punition, *f.* **punitive,** *a,* (*measure*) de punition; (*expedition*) punitif.

punk, *n,*(*pers. pej.*) plouc *P;* (*rubbish*) foutaises *P, f.pl;* (*music, pers.*) punk, *m.* ~ *rock,* le punk rock.

punnet, *n,* carton, petit panier, *m.*

punt[1], *n,* bachot à fond plat, *m.* ¶ *v.t,* faire avancer à la perche. ¶ *v.i,* faire un tour de rivière.

punt[2], *v.i,* (*bet*) parier. **~er,** *n,* parieur, euse.

puny, *a,* chétif, malingre.

pup, *n,* petit(e) chien, ne. *sell s.o a ~* (*fig.*), rouler qn *P.*

pupa, *n,* chrysalide, *f.*

pupil[1], *n,* (*eye*) pupille, prunelle, *f.*

pupil[2], *n,* élève, *m,f.*

puppet, *n,* marionnette, *f.* ¶ *a,* (*show &c*) de marionnettes; (*fig: state &c*) fantoche. **~eer,** *n,* marionnettiste, *m,f.*

puppy, *n, V* **pup.** ~ *fat,* rondeur d'adolescent, e, *f.* ~ *love,* premier amour.

purchase, *n,* achat, *m;* (*hold*) prise, *f.* ¶ *v.t,* acheter. **purchaser,** *n,* acheteur, euse. **purchasing power,** *n,* pouvoir d'achat.

pure†, *a,* pur. **~ness,** *n.* pureté, *f.*

purgative, *a. & n,* purgatif, *m.* **purgatory,** *n,* purgatoire, *m.* **purge,** *n,* purge, *f.* ¶ *v.t,* purger.

purification, *n,* (*water &c*) épuration; (*pers.*) purification, *f.* **purifier,** *n,* (*air ~*) purificateur, *m.* **purify,** *v.t,* purifier; épurer. **purist,** *n,* puriste, *m,f.* **Puritan,** *n. & a.* & **puritanic(al),** *a,* puritain, e. **purity,** *n,* pureté, *f.*

purl, *n,* maille à l'envers. ¶ *v.t,* tricoter à l'envers.

purloin, *v.t,* dérober.

purple, *n. & a,* violet, pourpre, *m. go ~ in the face,* devenir cramoisi. ~ *heart* (*Drug*), pilule de bonheur *P, f. the ~* (*Eccl.*), la pourpre romaine. **purplish,** *a,* violacé.

purport, *n,* signification, portée, *f.* ¶ *v.t,* prétendre.

purpose, *n,* (*aim*) but, objet; (*use*) usage, *m;* utilité, *f. on ~,* exprès, à dessein. *to no ~,* en pure perte. *to some ~,* utilement. *~-built,* fonctionnalisé. **~ful,** *a,* résolu. **~fully,** *ad,* délibérément. **~ly,** *ad,* exprès, délibérément.

purr, *n,* ronronnement, *m.* ¶ *v.i,* ronronner.

purse, *n,* porte-monnaie, *m,* bourse, *f. hold the ~ strings,* tenir les cordons de la bourse. ¶ (*lips*) *v.t,* pincer. **purser,** *n,* commissaire du bord, *m.*

purslane, *n,* pourpier, *m.*

pursue, *v.t,* (*gen.*) poursuivre; (*pleasure, fame*) rechercher; (*course*) suivre. **pursuer,** *n,* poursuivant, e. **pursuit,** *n,* poursuite, recherche; occupation, *f;* passe-temps, *m.inv.*

purveyor, *n,* fournisseur, euse (*of sth,* en qch; *to s.o,* de qn).

pus, *n,* pus, *m.*

push, *n,* poussée; (*drive*) initiative, *f;* (*effort*) gros effort, *m;* (*Mil*) poussée, *f. at a ~ P,* au besoin. *give s.o, sth a ~,* pousser qn, qch. *give s.o the ~,* (*employer*) flanquer qn à la porte *P;* (*girlfriend &c*) plaquer qn *P*.* *~-bike,* vélo, *m.* *~-button* (*control &c*), presse-bouton. *~chair,* poussette, *f.* *~-up* (*Gym.*), traction, *f.* ¶ *v.t,* pousser; (*button &c*) appuyer sur; (*thrust: finger &c*) enfoncer; (*views*) mettre en avant; (*product*) pousser la vente de; (*candidate*) soutenir; (*force*) pousser, forcer (qn à faire); (*drugs*) revendre. ~ *one's way through* (*crowd &c*), se frayer un chemin (dans la foule &c). ¶ *v.i,* pousser; appuyer. ~ **around,** (*lit.*) pousser de-ci de-là; (*fig.*) marcher sur les pieds à *P.* ~ **aside,** écarter. ~ **back,** repousser; (*fig.*) réprimer ~ **off,** (*Naut.*) pousser au large; (*P leave*) filer *P.* ~ *off! P,* fiche-moi le camp! *P.* **~er,** *n,* (*drugs*) revendeur, euse [de drogue]. **~ing,** *a,* (*pers.*) entreprenant; (*manner*) arrogant. **~y,** *a,* (*pers.*) arriviste.

pusillanimous, *a,* pusillanime.

puss[y], *n,* minet, te, minou, *m. Puss in Boots,* le Chat botté. ~ *willow,* saule [blanc], *m.*

put, *v.t, ir,* (*gen.*) mettre; placer; (*lay down*) poser; (*time &c*) consacrer (*into,* à); (*money*) placer (dans); (*advertisement*) passer (dans); (*signature*) apposer (à); (*express*) dire, exprimer; (*case &c*) exposer; (*proposal, argument*) présenter; (*question*) poser; (*estimate*) estimer; évaluer (*at,* à). ~ *into port* (*Naut.*), entrer au port. ~ *to sea,* lever l'ancre. ~ *the shot,* lancer le poids. ~ **away,** ranger; (*car*) rentrer; (*in prison*) mettre en prison; (*drink*) siffler *P.* ~ **back,** (*replace*) remettre [à sa place]; (*retard*) retarder; (*postpone*) remettre (à). ~ **down,** (*aircraft*) (se) poser; (*Mot: passenger*) déposer; (*money*) verser (*on,* pour); (*wine*) mettre en cave; (*revolt*) réprimer; (*attribute*) attribuer; (*humiliate*) rabaisser; (*record*) noter; inscrire; (*kill: cat, dog*) faire piquer; (*horse*) abattre. ~ **forward,** avancer; (*plan*) proposer; (*opinion*) exprimer. ~ **in,** (*Naut.*) faire escale (*at,* à); (*insert*) insérer; (*remark*) ajouter; (*seeds*) semer. ~ **off,** remettre; (*hinder*) dérouter; (*light, gas &c*) éteindre; (*radio, TV*) fermer. ~ **on,** (*clothes*) mettre; (*record*) passer; (*pressure &c*) augmenter; (*weight*) prendre; (*assume:*

accent) se donner; (*light*) allumer; (*radio, TV*) ouvrir. ~ *on the brakes,* freiner. ~ **out,** mettre dehors, sortir; (*stretch*) étendre; (*tongue*) tirer; (*lay out: cards*) étaler; (*chessmen &c*) disposer; (*clothes, dishes &c*) sortir; (*light &c*) éteindre; (*heater*) fermer; (*annoy*) contrarier; (*inconvenience*) gêner, déranger; (*shoulder &c*) démettre. ~ **through,** (*Tel: call*) passer: (*caller*) mettre en communication. ~ **up,** *v.i,* (*at hotel, with friends*) descendre (dans, chez). ¶ *v.t,* (*erect*) ériger; (*tent*) dresser; (*friend*) loger; (*money*) fournir. *a ~-up job,* un coup monté. ~ *up with,* supporter. *be ~ upon,* se faire marcher sur les pieds. **~-you-up,** *n,* canapé-lit, *m.*

putative, *a,* putatif.

putrefaction, *n,* putréfaction, *f.* **putrefy,** *v.t,* (& *i.*) (se) putréfier. **putrid,** *a* putride.

putt, *n,* (*Golf*) putt, coup roulé, *m.* ¶ *v.t. & i,* putter. **putter** (*club*), *n,* putter, *m.* **putting green,** green, *m.*

putty, *n,* mastic, *m.* ¶ *v.t,* mastiquer.

puzzle, *n,* (*mystery*) mystère, *m,* énigme; (*bewilderment*) perplexité, *f;* (*game*) casse-tête, *m.inv;* (*word-game*) rébus, *m;* (*crossword*) mots-croisés; (*jigsaw*) puzzle, *m;* (*riddle*) devinette, *f.* ~*book,* livre de jeux, *m.* ¶ *v.t,* rendre perplexe. *to be ~d by,* ne pas arriver à comprendre. ~ *over,* essayer de résoudre *ou* comprendre. **~d,** *a,* perplexe. **~ment,** *n,* perplexité, *f.* **puzzler,** *n,* casse-tête, *m. inv.* **puzzling,** *a,* incompréhensible.

pygmy, *n,* pygmée, *m.*

pyjamas, *n.pl,* pyjama, *m.*

pylon, *n,* pylône, *m.*

pyorrhoea, *n,* pyorrhée, *f.*

pyramid, *n,* pyramide, *f.*

pyre, *n,* bûcher funéraire, *m.*

Pyrenees (the), les Pyrénées, *f.pl.*

Pyrex, *n,* pyrex, *m.*

pyromaniac, *n,* pyromane, *m,f.* **pyrotechnic,** *n,* pyrotechnique.

python, *n,* python, *m.*

Q

quack[1], (*duck*) *n,* coin-coin, *m.* ¶ *v.i,* faire coin-coin.

quack[2], *n,* charlatan *m;* (*P doctor*) toubib *P.* **~ery,** *n,* charlatanisme, *m.*

quadrangle, *n,* (*college*) cour, *f;* (*Math.*) quadrilatère, *m.*

quadrant, *n,* quadrant; quart de cercle, *m.*

quadraphonic, *a,* quadriphonique.

quadratic (*Math.*), *a,* de second degré.

quadrilateral (*Math.*), *n. & a,* quadrilatère, *m.*

quadruped, *n. & a,* quadrupède, *m.*

quadruple, *a. & n,* quadruple, *m.* **quadruplets, quads,** *n.pl,* quadruplé, es.

quagmire, *n,* bourbier, *m.*

quail[1], *n,* caille, *f.*

quail[2], *v.i,* faiblir (*before,* devant).

quaint, *a,* bizarre; pittoresque; (*old-world*) vieillot. **~ness,** bizarrerie, *f;* pittoresque; caractère vieillot, *m.*

quake, *v.i,* trembler.

qualification, *n,* qualité; aptitude (*for,* à), capacité (*to do,* pour faire); compétence (*for,* en; *to do,* pour faire), *f;* (*pl.*) titres, dîplomes, *m.pl;* (*limitation*) réserve, *f.* **qualified,** *a,* qualifié (pour, en matière de); (*doctor, teacher &c*) diplômé; (*modified: praise &c*) mitigé; (*support &c*) conditionnel. **qualify,** *v.t,* (*gen., Gram.*) qualifier; (*modify*) mitiger; (*support &c*) mettre des réserves à. ¶ *v.i,* obtenir son diplôme. **~ing,** (*Sport &c*) *a,* éliminatoire. **quality,** *n,* qualité, *f.*

qualms, *n.pl,* doutes, scrupules, *m.pl.*

quandary, *n,* embarras, *m.*

quantity, *n,* quantité, *f.* ~ *surveying,* métrage, *m.* ~ *surveyor,* métreur, *m.*

quantum, *n,* quantum, *m.*

quarantine, *n,* quarantaine, *f.* ¶ *v.t,* mettre en quarantaine.

quarrel, *n,* querelle, dispute; (*breach*) brouille, *f.* *pick a ~ with,* chercher querelle à. ¶ *v.i,* se quereller, se disputer (*with,* avec); se brouiller (avec). **~some,** *a,* querelleur.

quarry[1], *n,* carrière, *f.* ¶ *v.t,* (*stone*) extraire; (*hillside*) exploiter. ~*man,* carrier, *m.* ~ *tile,* carreau, *m.* ~*-tiled,* carrelé.

quarry[2], *n,* proie, *f.*

quart, *n,* *Imperial Meas.* = 1·136 litres.

quarter, *n,* (*gen.*) quart; (*beef, apple, moon &c*) quartier; (*3 months*) trimestre; (*Am. money*) quart de dollar; (*direction*) côté; (*part of town*) quartier, *m;* (*pl.*) résidence, *f;* (*Mil.*) quartiers, *m.pl;* (*temporary*) cantonnement, *m.* *a ~ of an hour,* un quart d'heure. *a ~ to 2, a ~ past 2,* 2 heures moins le quart, 2 h. et q. *ou* un q. ~ *day,* [jour du] terme, *m.* ~ *deck,* plage arrière, *f.* ~ *final,* quart de finale. ~*master,* (*Mil.*) intendant militaire de troisième classe; (*Naut.*) maître de manœuvre, *m.*

¶ *v.t,* diviser en quatre [parts égales]; (*Mil.*) caserner; cantonner. ~**ly,** *a,* trimestriel; (*ad.*) par trimestre.
quartet[te], *n,* quatuor; (*jazz*) quartette, *m.*
quartz, *n,* quartz, *m.*
quash, *v.t,* casser, annuler, infirmer.
quasi, *c.* & **quasi-,** *pref,* quasi (*ad.*), quasi-.
quaver (*Mus.*) *n,* croche, *f.* ¶ *v.i,* chevroter, trembler.
quay, *n,* quai, *m.*
queasiness, *n,* mal au cœur, *m.* **queasy,** *a,* (*stomach*) délicat. *feel* ~, avoir mal au cœur.
queen, *n,* reine; (*Cards, Chess*) dame, reine, *f.* ~ *bee,* reine des abeilles, *f.* ¶ (*Chess*) *v.t,* damer. ~**ly,** *a,* de reine.
queer†, *a,* (*odd*) étrange, bizarre, singulier; (*suspicious*) louche; (*P unwell*) mal fichu *P;* (*P* homosexual*) homosexuel. *a* ~ *fellow,* un drôle de corps *P. in Q*~ *Street,* en mauvaise posture. ¶ *n,* (*homosexual*) pédé *P*, m.* ¶ *v.t,* gâter. ~ *s.o's pitch,* couper l'herbe sous les pieds à qn.
quell, *v.t,* réprimer, étouffer.
quench, *v.t,* (*flames &c*) éteindre. ~ *one's thirst,* se désaltérer.
querulous, *a,* plaintif. ~**ly,** *ad,* d'un ton plaintif.
query, *n,* question, *f;* (*doubt*) doute, *m.* ¶ *v.t,* mettre en question, en doute. ~ *whether,* demander si. **quest,** *n,* quête, recherche, *f.*
question, *n,* (*gen.*) question, *f;* doute, *m;* (*Gram.*) interrogation, *f. that's out of the* ~, il n'en est pas question. *there's no* ~ *about it,* il n'y a pas de question. *without* ~, sans aucun doute. ~ *mark,* point d'interrogation, *m.* ~*master,* meneur de jeu; (*Radio, TV*) animateur, *m.* ¶ *v.t,* interroger, questionner (*on,* sur; *about,* au sujet de, à propos de); (*motive &c*) douter de; (*claim*) contester. ~**able,** *a,* discutable; (*pej.*) douteux. ~**er,** *n,* personne qui pose des questions, *f.* ~**ing,** *a,* interrogateur. ~**naire,** *n,* questionnaire, *m.*
queue, *n,* queue; (*cars*) file, *f.* ¶ *v.i,* ~ *up,* faire la queue.
quibble, *n,* chicane, *f.* ¶ *v.i,* chicaner (*over,* sur).
quick, *a,* (*gen.*) rapide; (*answer*) prompt; (*lively*) vif, éveillé. ~*lime,* chaux vive. ~*sands,* sables mouvants. ~*silver,* vif-argent, mercure, *m.* ~*-tempered,* soupe au lait *P,* prompt à s'emporter. ~*-witted,* à l'esprit vif. ¶ *ad,* vite. *be* ~*!* vite! dépêche-toi! fais vite! ¶ *n,* vif, *m. cut to the* ~, blesser au vif. ~**en,** *v.t,* accélérer, presser; (*fig.*) stimuler. ~**ly,** *ad,* vite, rapidement; promptement, sans tarder. ~**ness,** *n,* vitesse, rapidité; (*mind &c*) vivacité, *f.*
quid pro quo, *n,* compensation, *f.*
quiescence, *n,* calme, *m.* **quiescent,** *a,* calme, passif. **quiet,** *a,* (*gen.*) tranquille, calme; (*music*) doux; (*voice*) bas; (*sound*) léger; (*cough, laugh*) petit; (*subdued: pers.*) doux; (*animal*) docile; (*dress &c*) discret. *be* ~*!* taisez-vous! ¶ *n,* (*silence*) silence; (*peace*) calme, *m,* tranquillité, *f. on the* ~, en cachette; en sourdine; en douce *P.* ~**en,** *v.t,* calmer, apaiser. ~ *down,* (s')apaiser, (se) calmer. ~**ly,** *ad,* silencieusement; (*softly*) doucement; (*secretly*) en cachette, en catimini. ~**ness,** *n,* *V* **quiet,** *n.*
quill, *n,* (*porcupine*) piquant, *m.* ~ [*feather*], penne, *f.* ~ [*pen*], plume d'oie, *f.*
quilt, *n,* édredon [piqué], *m. continental* ~, couette, *f.* ¶ *v.t,* ouater & piquer; (*furniture*) capitonner.
quince, *n,* coing, *m.* ~ [*tree*], cognassier, *m.*
quinine, *n,* quinine, *f.*
quintessence, *n,* quintessence, *f.*
quintet[te], *n,* quintette, *m.*
quintuple, *a.* & *n,* quintuple, *m.* ¶ *v.t.* & *i,* quintupler. **quintuplet, quin,** *n,* quintuplé, e.
quip, *n,* mot piquant, *m.*
quire, *n,* main, *f.*
quirk, *n,* bizarrerie, *f. a* ~ *of fate,* un caprice du destin. **quirky,** *a,* capricieux.
quit, *a,* débarrassé (de). ¶ *v.t,* quitter; (*stop*) arrêter (*doing,* de faire). ¶ *v.i,* (*resign*) démissionner; (*give up*) se rendre.
quite, *ad,* (*entirely*) tout à fait, complètement; (*fairly*) assez. ~ [*so*]*!* exactement! *you are* ~ *right,* tu as bien raison. *it's* ~ *good,* c'est pas mal du tout. *I* ~ *like him,* je l'aime assez.
quits, *a,* quitte. *let's call it* ~, restons-en là.
quiver[1], *v.i,* trembler, frémir; frissonner. ~**[ing],** *n,* tremblement, frisson[nement], *m.*
quiver[2] (*for arrows*) *n,* carquois, *m.*
quixotic, *a,* donquichottesque. ~**ally,** *ad,* à la Don Quichotte.
quiz, *n,* (*Radio, TV*) quiz, jeu-concours, *m.* ¶ *v.t,* presser de questions. **quizzical,** *a,* narquois.
quoit, *n.* & ~**s,** *n.pl,* palet, *m.*
quorum, *n,* quorum, *m.*
quota, *n,* (*share*) quote-part, *f;* (*Adm.*) quota, *m.*
quotation, *n,* citation; (*Stk Ex.*) cote, *f;* cours; (*Com: estimate*) devis, *m.* ~ *marks,* guillemets, *m.pl.* **quote,** *v.t,* citer; (*Com: price*) indiquer; (*Stk Ex.*) coter.
quotient, *n,* quotient, *m.*

R

rabbi, *n,* rabbin, *m.*

rabbit, *n,* lapin, e; (*young*) lapereau, *m.* ~ *burrow,* ~ *hole,* terrier de lapin, *m.* ~ *hutch,* cabane à lapins, *f,* clapier, *m.* ~ *warren,* garenne, *f.*

rabble, *n,* (*crowd*) cohue, foule [confuse]; (*pej.*) canaille, populace, *f.* ~*-rouser,* agitateur, trice.

rabid, *a,* enragé; (*fig.*) furieux; farouche; fanatique. **rabies,** *n,* la rage, hydrophobie, *f.*

rac[c]oon, *n,* raton laveur, *m.*

race[1], *n,* race, *f.* ~ *relations,* rapports entre races, *m.pl.* ~ *riot,* bagarre raciale.

race[2], *n,* (*Sport*) course, *f;* (*in sea*) raz, *m. the* ~*s,* les courses de chevaux. ~ *card,* programme [des courses], *m.* ~*course,* champs de course, hippodrome, *m.* ~*goer,* turfiste, *m,f.* ~*horse,* cheval de course, *m.* ~*track,* piste, *f;* (*for horses*) champs de courses. ¶ *v.t,* faire une course avec; (*Sport*) faire courir. ¶ *v.i,* aller *ou* courir à toute allure; (*engine*) s'emballer; (*pulse*) battre très vite. **racer,** *n,* (*cycle*) vélo (*m*) *ou* bicyclette de course, *f;* (*car, yacht*) racer, *m.*

racial, *a,* racial. ~**ism** *&* **racism,** *n,* racism, *m.* ~**ist** *&* **racist,** *n. & a,* raciste, *m,f.*

racing, *n,* courses, *f.pl.* ~ *bike,* vélo de course, *m.* ~ *car,* voiture de c., *f.* ~ *cyclist,* coureur cycliste, *m.* ~ *driver,* pilote de course, *m.*

rack[1], *n,* (*fodder*) râtelier; (*bottles &c*) casier; (*in shops*) rayon; (*luggage*) filet; (*coats &c*) portemanteau, *m.*

rack[2], *n,* chevalet, *m.* ¶ *v.t,* (*pain*) torturer. ~ *one's brains,* se creuser la cervelle.

rack & ruin (to), (*economy*) à vau-l'eau; (*pers.*) à la ruine.

racket[1] *or* **racquet,** *n,* raquette, *f.* ~ *press,* presse à raquette, *f.*

racket[2], (*noise*) vacarme; (*crime*) racket, *m;* (*swindle*) escroquerie, *f.* ~**eer,** *n,* racketteur, *m.* ~**eering,** *n,* racket, *m.*

racy, *a,* plein de verve.

radar, *n. & a,* radar, *m. & inv.* ~ *trap,* piège radar, *m.*

radial, *a,* radial. ~ *tyre,* pneu à carcasse radiale, *m.* **radiance,** *n,* rayonnement, *m.* **radiant,** *a,* radieux. **radiate,** *v.i,* (*Phys.*) irradier; (*fig.*) rayonner. ¶ *v.t,* émettre. **radiation,** *n,* radiation, *f.* **radiator,** *n,* radiateur, *m.* ~ *cap,* bouchon de r., *m.* ~ *grill,* calandre, *f.*

radical†, *a. & n,* radical, *m.*

radio, *n,* poste de radio, *m,* radio, *f;* (*Tel.*) radio, radiotélégraphie, *f. on the* ~, à la radio. ¶ *a,* de radio, radiophonique. ~ *announcer,* speaker, ine. ~ *link,* liaison radio, *f.* ~ *operator,* radio, *m.* ~ *programme,* émission, *f.* ~ *station,* station de radio, *f.* ~ *taxi,* radio-taxi, *m.* ~ *telephone,* radiotéléphone, *m.* ~ *wave,* onde hertzienne.

radioactive, *a,* radioactif. **radiogram,** *n,* (*message*) radiogramme; (*apparatus*) combiné, *m.* **radiographer,** *n,* radiologue, *m,f.* **radiography,** *n,* radiographie, *f.* **radiologist,** *n,* radiologue, *m,f.* **radiotherapy,** *n,* radiothérapie, *f.*

radish, *n,* radis, *m.*

radium, *n,* radium, *m.*

radius, *n,* rayon, *m;* (*Anat.*) radius, *m.*

raffia, *n,* raphia, *m.*

raffle, *n,* loterie, tombola, *f.* ¶ *v.t,* mettre en loterie.

raft, *n,* radeau, *m.*

rafter, *n,* chevron, *m.*

rag[1], *n,* lambeau; (*for wiping*) chiffon, *m;* (*pl. waste*) chiffons; (*old clothes*) haillons, *m.pl;* (*P newspaper*) torchon *P, m.* ~*-&-bone man,* ~*picker,* chiffonnier, *m.* ~ *doll,* poupée de chiffon, *f.* ~, *tag & bobtail,* racaille, *f.* ~*time,* rag-time, *m.* ~ *trade,* confection, *f.* ~*wort,* jacobée, *f.*

rag[2], *n,* farce, blague, *f.* ¶ *v.t,* (*teacher*) chahuter.

ragamuffin, *n,* va-nu-pieds, *m.*

rage, *n,* rage, fureur, *f.* ¶ *v.i,* faire rage.

ragged, *a,* (*clothes*) en lambeaux; (*pers.*) en haillons; (*cuff*) effiloché. ~ *robin,* fleur de coucou, *f.*

raging, *a,* (*pers.*) furieux; (*thirst, fever*) ardent; (*pain &c*) atroce, violent; (*storm*) déchaîné. ~ *toothache,* rage de dents, *f.*

raglan, *a. & n,* raglan, *inv. & m.*

ragout, *n,* ragoût, *m.*

raid, *n,* (*Mil.*) incursion, *f,* raid, *m;* (*police*) descente, rafle; (*bandits*) razzia, *f;* (*thieves*) hold-up, *m.inv.* ¶ *v.t,* faire une incursion &c dans, à; (*Aero.*) bombarder; (*fig.*) marauder dans.

rail[1], *v.t,* ~ *at, against,* invecter contre.

rail[2], *n,* (*boat, bridge*) rambarde; (*balcony*) balustrade; (*bannister*) rampe; (*curtains &c*) tringle, *f;* (*Rly*) rail, *m. go off the* ~*s,* (*train*) dérailler; (*fig: pers.*) s'écarter du droit chemin; (*be mad*) être détraqué *P.* ~ *traffic,* trafic ferroviaire, *m.* ~**ing,** *n,* rambarde; balustrade; rampe, *f;* (*pl.*) grille, *f.*

railway & railroad, *n,* (*system*) chemin de fer, *m;* (*track*) voie ferrée, *f.* ~ *line,* ligne de c. de f., *f;* voie ferrée. ~*man,* cheminot, *m.*

rain, *n,* pluie, *f. in the* ~, sous la pluie. ~*bow,*

arc-en-ciel, *m.* ~*coat,* imperméable, imper *P, m.* ~ *cloud,* nuage de pluie, *m.* ~*drop,* goutte de pluie, *f.* ~*fall,* hauteur des précipitations, *f.* ~ *gauge,* pluviomètre, *m.* ~*water,* eau de pluie, *f.* ¶ *v.i,* pleuvoir. *it's* ~*ing cats & dogs,* il pleut à torrents; il tombe des cordes *P.* ¶ *v.t,* faire pleuvoir. ~**y,** *a,* pluvieux; (*season*) des pluies. *put sth away for a* ~ *day,* garder une poire pour la soif.

raise, *v.t,* (*gen.*) lever; (*dust*) soulever; (*voice*) hausser; (*salary &c*) augmenter; (*level*) élever; (*temperature*) faire monter; (*question*) soulever; (*objection*) élever; (*family, pigs*) élever; (*corn*) cultiver; (*money*) se procurer; (*the dead*) ressusciter. ~ *Cain,* ~ *hell P,* faire du boucan *P,* faire une scène de tous les diables *P.* ~ *one's hat to s.o* (*fig.*), tirer son chapeau à qn.

raisin, *n,* raisin sec, *m.*

rake[1], *n,* râteau, *m.* ~*-off P,* profit; (*illegal*) dessous de table, *m.* ¶ *v.t,* (*garden*) ratisser; (*leaves &c*) râteler; (*fire*) tisonner. ~ *in P,* amasser. ~ *up* (*fig.*), rappeler.

rake[2], *n,* débauché; (*O*) roué, *m.* **rakish,** *a,* (*pers.*) débauché; (*appearance*) cavalier.

rally, *n,* (*gen*) rassemblement; (*troops*) ralliement; (*Pol.*) meeting; (*Mot.*) rallye; (*Ten.*) échange, *m.* ¶ *v.t,* rassembler, rallier. ¶ *v.i,* (*people*) se rallier; (*sick pers.*) aller mieux; (*Stk Ex.*) reprendre.

ram, *n,* bélier; (*pile driving*) mouton, *m.* ¶ *v.t,* enfoncer, pilonner; (*Tech.*) damer; (*pack*) tasser (*into,* dans). ~ *sth down s.o's throat,* rebattre les oreilles à qn de qch.

ramble, *n,* randonnée, excursion [à pied], *f.* ¶ *v.i,* faire une randonnée &c à pied; (*wander*) se promener au hasard; (*rave*) radoter. **rambler,** *n,* (*pers.*) promeneur, euse; (*rose*) rosier grimpant, *m.* **rambling,** *a,* (*speech*) décousu; (*pers.*) qui radote.

ramification, *n,* ramification, *f.* **ramify,** *v.i,* se ramifier.

rampage, *n, go on the* ~, se déchaîner.

rampant *a,* (*Her.*) rampant; (*plants*) exubérant. *to be* ~, sévir, courir.

rampart, *n,* rempart, *m.*

ramrod, *n,* baguette, *f.*

ramshackle, *a,* délabré.

ranch, *n,* ranch, *m.*

rancid, *a,* rance.

rancour, *n,* rancune, rancœur, *f.*

random, *a.* & *at* ~, au hasard, à l'aventure.

range, *n,* (*gun &c*) portée, *f;* (*ship, plane*) rayon d'action, *m;* (*temperature*) variations, *f.pl;* (*prices, salaries*) échelle; (*Mus.*) étendue; (*colours &c*) gamme, *f;* (*patterns*) choix, *m;* (*row*) rangée; (*hills*) chaîne, *f;* (*shooting: Mil.*) champ de tir; (*at fair*) stand [de tir]; (*domain*) champ, *m;* sphère; (*Am. grazing*) prairie; (*stove*) cuisinière, *f.* ~*finder,* télémètre, *m.* ¶ *v.t,* (*objects*) ranger; (*troops*) aligner. ¶ *v.i,* (*talk*) s'étendre (*over,* sur); (*vary*) varier. **ranger,** *n,* garde forestier, *m.*

rank[1], *n,* (*row, position, Mil.*) rang; (*Mil: grade*) grade, *m;* (*cab*) station, *f. the* ~ *& file,* le commun. *rise from the* ~*s,* sortir du rang. ¶ *v.t. & i,* compter. ~ *high,* occuper un rang élevé.

rank[2], *a,* (*growth*) exubérant; (*smell*) fétide, rance; (*utter*) absolu, véritable; (*lie*) flagrant; (*liar*) fieffé.

rankle, *v.i,* rester sur le cœur (*with,* à).

ransack, *v.t,* (*town*) mettre à sac; (*house &c*) saccager, piller; (*in search: room*) fouiller [à fond].

ransom, *n,* rançon, *f.* ¶ *v.t,* (*hold to* ~) rançonner; racheter.

rant, *v.i,* déclamer. ~ *& rave,* tempêter (*at s.o.,* contre qn).

rap, *n,* petit coup sec; (*blow*) tape, *f. take the* ~ *P,* (*fig.*) payer les pots cassés. ¶ *v.t. & i,* frapper, taper. ~ *s.o's knuckles,* donner sur les doigts de qn.

rapacious, *a,* rapace.

rape[1], *n,* viol, *m.* ¶ *v.t,* violer.

rape[2], (*Bot.*) *n,* colza, *m.*

rapid†, *a,* rapide. ¶ *n,* rapide, *m.* ~**ity,** *n,* rapidité, *f.*

rapier, *n,* rapière, *f.*

rapist, *n,* violeur, auteur d'un viol, *m.*

rapt, *a,* (*attention*) profond; (*look*) ravi. **rapture,** *n,* ravissement, enthousiasme, *m;* (*ecstasy*) extase, *f. go into* ~*s over,* s'extasier sur. **rapturous,** *a,* extatique; (*applause*) frénétique.

rare†, *a,* rare; (*meat*) saignant; (*P excellent*) fameux *P.* **rarefy,** *v.t,* raréfier. **rareness** & **rarity,** *n,* rareté, *f.*

rascal, *n,* coquin, e, fripon, ne.

rash[1], *n,* éruption, *f.*

rash[2], *a,* imprudent. ~**ness,** *n,* témérité, *f.*

rasher, *n,* tranche, *f.*

rasp, *n,* râpe, *f.* ¶ *v.t,* râper. ¶ *v.i,* grincer.

raspberry, *n,* framboise, *f.* ~ *bush, cane,* framboisier, *m.*

rat, *n,* rat, *m;* (*pej: pers.*) salaud *P*, m;* vache *P, f.* ~ *catcher,* chasseur de rats, *m.* ~ *catching,* dératisation, *f.* ~ *poison,* mort-aux-rats, *f.* ~ *race,* foire d'empoigne, course au biftek *P, f.* ~ *trap,* ratière, *f.* ¶ *v.i, P,* ~ *on s.o.* abandonner, lâcher qn *P;* (*grass on*) moucharder qn *P.*

ratchet, *n,* cliquet, rochet, *m.*

rate, *n,* (*proportion*) taux, *m;* (*speed*) vitesse, allure, *f,* train, *m;* (*Com., Fin.*) taux, cours, tarif, *m;* (*pl. tax*) impôts locaux. *at a* ~ *of,* à une vitesse de. *at a* ~ *of knots P,* à toute allure. *at any* ~, (*fig.*) en tout cas, de toute façon. ~ *of pay,* taux de rémunération. ~*payer,* contribuable, *m,f.* ~*s office,* recette municipale. ¶ *v.t,* (*appraise*) évaluer; (*con-*

sider) considerer (*as*, comme); (*deserve*) mériter. ¶ *v.i*, être classé, se classer (comme). **~able,** *a*, (*property*) imposable. ~ *value*, valeur locative imposable.
rather, *ad*, plutôt; un peu; assez. *it's ~ expensive*, c'est un peu cher. ~ *pretty*, assez joli. ~ *plain*, plutôt laid. ~ *than*, plûtot que. ~*! P*, et comment! *I ~ think that*... je crois bien que... *I would ~*, j'aimerais mieux, je préférerais.
ratification, *n*, ratification, *f*. **ratify,** *v.t*, ratifier.
rating, *n*, classement, *m*; (*Nav.*) matelot, *m*.
ratio, *n*, rapport, *m*, raison, proportion, *f*.
ration, *n*, ration, *f*; (*pl*) vivres, *m.pl*. ~ *book*, carte de rationnement, *f*. ¶ *v.t*, rationner. **~al†,** *a*, (*pers, action*) raisonnable; (*explanation*) logique; (*faculty*) rationnel; (*Med.*) lucide. **~ale,** *n*, raisonnement, *m*. **rationalism,** *n*, rationalisme, *m*. **rationalist,** *n*, & **~ic,** *a*, rationaliste, *m,f*. **rationalization,** *n*, rationalisation, *f*. **rationalize,** *v.t*, (*Ind.*) rationaliser; (*event, conduct &c*) justifier après coup.
rattle, *n*, crécelle, *f*; (*baby's*) hochet; (*noise: vehicle*) bruit de ferraille; (*chains &c*) cliquetis; (*gunfire*) crépitement, *m*. *death ~*, râle, *m*. *~snake*, serpent à sonnettes, *m*. ¶ *v.i*, faire un bruit de ferraille; cliqueter, crépiter; (*objects*) s'entrechoquer. ¶ *v.t*, (*dice, box*) agiter; faire s'entrechocher; faire cliqueter. *get ~d*, se mettre dans tous ses états. ~ *off*, (*poem &c*) débiter à toute allure.
ratty *P a*, en rogne *P*.
raucous, *a*, rauque.
ravage, *v.t*, ravager. **~s,** *n.pl*, ravages, *m.pl*; (*of time*) injure[s], *f*.[*pl*.], outrage, *m*.
rave, *v.i*, (*with enthusiasm*) s'extasier (*about, over*, sur); (*delirious*) délirer; (*wildly*) divaguer; (*with fury*) tempêter.
raven, *n*, grand corbeau, *m*, corneille, *f*. *~-haired*, aux cheveux de jais.
ravenous, *a*, vorace; (*pers.*) affamé; (*hunger*) dévorant. *to be ~*, avoir une faim de loup. **~ly,** *ad*, voracement.
ravine, *n*, ravin, *m*.
raving, *n*, délire, *m*. ¶ *a*, délirant. ~ *mad*, fou à lier.
ravish, *v.t*, ravir. **ravishing,** *a*, ravissant. **ravishingly,** *ad*, à ravir.
raw, *a*, (*food*) cru; (*cloth, hide*) écru; (*sugar*) brut; (*silk*) grège; (*spirit*) pur; (*untrained*) novice; (*troops*) non aguerri; (*sore*) sensible, à vif; (*weather*) âpre; (*air*) vif. *a ~ deal P*, un sale coup *P*. ~ *materials*, matières premières. *to touch s.o on the ~*, piquer qn au vif.
rawlplug, *n*, cheville, *f*.
ray¹, *n*, rayon, *m*; (*fig.*) lueur, *f*.
ray² (*fish*), *n*, raie, *f*.
rayon, *n*, rayonne, soie artificielle, *f*.
raze, *v.t*, raser. **razor,** *n*, rasoir, *m*. ~ *blade*, lame de razoir, *f*.
re¹, (*Mus.*) *n*, ré, *m*.
re², *pr*, au sujet de.
re³, *pref*, re..., ré...; r... *~do*, refaire. *~heat*, réchauffer. *~open*, rouvrir. *~absorb*, réabsorber.
reach, *n*, portée, atteinte; (*river*) étendue, *f*; (*canal*) bief, *m*; (*Box.*) allonge, *f*. *within ~*, à portée. *out of ~*, hors d'atteinte. ¶ *v.t*, (*gen.*) atteindre; arriver à, gagner; (*agreement*) aboutir à. ~ *down*, descendre. ~ *out*, étendre. **~able,** *a*, accessible, à portée.
react, *v.i*, réagir. **~ion,** *n*, réaction, *f*; contrecoup, *m*. **~ionary,** *a. & n*, réactionnaire, *m,f*. **~or,** *n*, réacteur, *m*.
read, *v.t. & i. ir*, lire; (*Univ. &c*) étudier, faire des études de; (*instruments*) marquer, indiquer; (*meter*) relever; (*proofs*) corriger; (*Tel.*) recevoir. ~ *back*, ~ *over*, relire. ~ *for*, (*exam*) préparer. ~ *off*, (*without pause*) lire d'un trait; (*from sight*) lire à livre ouvert; (*instruments*) relever. ~ *out*, lire à haute voix. ~ *through*, parcourir. ~ *up* [*on*], étudier, potasser *P*. **~able†,** *a*, lisible.
readdress, *v.t*, faire suivre.
reader, *n*, lecteur, trice; livre de lecture, *m*.
readiness, *n*, (*willingness*) empressement, *m*. *be in ~*, être prêt (*for*, à, pour).
reading, *n*, lecture; (*proofs*) correction; (*recital*) séance de lecture, *f*. ~ *desk*, pupitre; (*Eccl.*) lutrin, *m*. ~ *glass*, loupe, *f*. ~ *glasses*, lunettes pour lire, *f.pl*. ~ *lamp*, lampe de travail, *f*. ~ *matter*, de quoi lire. ~ *room*, salle de lecture *ou* de travail, *f*.
readjust, *v.t*, rajuster; (*instrument*) régler [de nouveau]. **~ment,** *n*, réadaptation, *f*.
ready, *a*, prêt; (*inclined*) enclin; (*prompt: wit &c*) prompt; (*about to*) sur le point (*de faire*). *get ~*, se préparer. *~, steady, go!* prêts? 1-2-3, partez! ~ *cash*, liquide, *m*. *~-made*, tout fait. ~ *reckoner*, barème, *m*. *~-to-serve*, prêt à servir. *~-to-wear*, prêt à porter.
real†, *a*, véritable, vrai, réel; (*flowers, silk*) naturel. *in ~ life*, dans la réalité. *the ~ thing P*, du vrai de vrai *P*. ~ *estate*, biens fonciers. *for ~ P*, pour de vrai *P*. **~ist,** *n. & a*. réaliste, *m,f*. **~ity,** *n*, réalité, *f*. **~ization,** *n*, réalisation; (*awareness*) prise de conscience, *f*. **~ize,** *v.t*, se rendre compte de; (*be aware of*) [bien] savoir; (*understand*) comprendre; (*assets, plan*) réaliser; (*price*) atteindre.
realm, *n*, royaume; (*fig.*) domaine.
ream, *n*, rame, *f*.
reap, *v.t*, moissonner, faucher; (*fig.*) récolter. **reaper,** *n*, moissonneur, euse. **reaping,** *n*, moisson, *f*. ~ *machine* or **reaper,** *n*, moissonneuse, *f*.
reappear, *v.i*, reparaître, réapparaître. **~ance,** *n*, réapparition, *f*.
reappoint, *v.t*, renommer.

rear[1], *n*, arrière, derrière, *m*; (*P buttocks*) derrière; (*Mil.*) arrière-garde, *f*; (*column*) queue, *f*. *bring up the* ~, fermer la marche. ~ *admiral*, contre-amiral, *m*. ~ *door*, (*house*) porte de derrière; (*car*) portière arrière, *f*. ~-*view mirror*, rétroviseur, *m*. ~ *window*, glace arrière, *f*.

rear[2], *v.t*, (*children &c*) élever; (*head &c*) dresser. ¶ *v.i*, (*&* ~ *up*) se cabrer.

reason, *n*, raison, cause, *f*; motif, *m*; (*faculty*) raison. *for no* ~, sans motif, sans raison. *have* ~ *to believe that*, avoir lieu de croire que. *with* ~, avec raison. *it stands to* ~, il va sans dire. ¶ *v.i*, raisonner. ~ *with*, raisonner. ~**able**†, *a*, raisonnable; (*results*) passable. ~ *doubt* (*Law*), doute bien fondé. ~**ing,** *n*, raisonnement, *m*.

reassure, *v.t*, rassurer.

rebate, *n*, rabais; remboursement, *m*.

rebel, *n*, rebelle, *m,f*, révolté, e. ¶ *v.i*, se rebeller, se révolter. **rebellion,** *n*, rébellion, révolte, *f*. **rebellious,** *a*, rebelle.

rebirth, *n*, renaissance, *f*.

rebound, *n*, (*ball*) rebond; (*bullet*) ricochet, *m*. ¶ *v.i*, rebondir; (*fig.*) retomber (*on*, sur).

rebuff, *n*, rebuffade, *f*. ¶ *v.t*, repousser.

rebuild, *v.t.ir*, rebâtir, reconstruire.

rebuke, *n*, réprimande, *f*. ¶ *v.t*, réprimander.

rebut, *v.t*, réfuter.

recalcitrant, *a. & n*, récalcitrant, e.

recall, *n*, rappel, *m*. *beyond* ~, irrévocablement. ¶ *v.t*, rappeler; (*Parliament*) convoquer d'urgence; (*recollect*) se rappeler, se souvenir de.

recant, *v.t.* (*& i*), (se) rétracter; (*Rel.*) abjurer.

recapitulate, *v.t*, récapituler.

recapture, *n*, (*town &c*) reprise; (*prisoner*) arrestation, *f*. ¶ *v.t*, reprendre; (*emotion*) retrouver; (*evoke*) recréer.

recast, *v.t.ir*, refondre; (*script*) remanier.

recede, *v.i*, s'éloigner; (*tide*) descendre; (*hair*) se dégarnir. **receding,** (*forehead, chin*) *a*, fuyant. ~ *hairline*, front dégarni.

receipt, *n*, (*for payment*) reçu, *m*, quittance, *f*; (*for letter, parcel*) accusé de réception, *m*; (*Com.*) réception, *f*; (*pl.*) recette[s], *f*.[*pl.*]. *acknowledge* ~ *of*, accuser réception de. *be in* ~ *of* ... avoir reçu... *on* ~ *of*, dès la réception de. ~ *book*, livre de quittances, *m*. ¶ *v.t*, aquitter. **receive,** *v.t*, (*gen.*) recevoir; (*welcome*) accueillir; (*money*) toucher; (*stolen goods*) receler. (*Com.*) ~*d with thanks*, pour acquit. **receiver,** *n*, receveur, euse; (*letter*) destinataire, *m,f*; receleur, euse; (*Fin., Law*) liquidateur, trice; (*Tel., Radio*) récepteur, *m*. *lift the* ~, décrocher. *replace the* ~, raccrocher. **receiving,** *n*, recel, *m*.

recent†, *a*, récent; nouveau; de fraîche date. *in* ~ *years*, ces dernières années.

receptacle, *n*, récipient, *m*. **reception,** *n*, réception, *f*. ~ *centre*, centre d'accueil, *m*. ~ [*desk*], [bureau (*m*) de] réception. ~**ist,** *n*, réceptionniste, *m,f*. **receptive,** *a*, réceptif.

recess, *n*, renfoncement, *m*; (*bed*) alcôve; (*window &c*) embrasure; (*statue*) niche, *f*; (*pl. fig: mind &c*) recoin, repli, *m*; (*Parliament &c*) vacances, *f.pl.* ~**ion,** *n*, (*Econ.*) récession, *f*.

recipient, *n*, (*letter*) destinataire; (*cheque*) bénéficiaire, *m,f*; (*diploma*) récipiendaire, *m*; (*Law*) donataire, *m,f*.

reciprocal†, *a*, réciproque. **reciprocate,** *v.t*, (*kindness*) rendre. ~ *s.o.'s feelings*, payer qn de retour. ¶ *v.i*, en faire autant. **reciprocity,** *n*, réciprocité, *f*.

recital, *n*, récit, *m*; énumération, *f*; (*Mus.*) récital, *m*. **recitation,** *n*, récitation, *f*. **recitative,** *n*, récitatif, *m*. **recite,** *v.t*, réciter, déclamer, énumérer.

reckless, *a*, téméraire, imprudent; (*heedless*) insouciant. ~ *driving*, conduite imprudente. ~**ly,** *ad*, imprudemment; avec insouciance.

reckon, *v.t. & i*, compter, calculer; (*judge*) estimer, considérer; penser, croire. ~ *without*, ne pas tenir compte de. ~**ing,** *n*, compte, calcul, *m*; estimation, *f*. *to the best of my* ~, autant que je puisse en juger.

reclaim, *v.t*, réclamer (*from s.o*, à qn); (*land*) défricher; (*from sea*) assécher; (*Ind.*) récupérer.

recline, *v.i*, être couché, se reposer. *reclining seat*, siège à dossier réglable, *m*.

recluse, *n*, reclus, e.

recognition, *n*, reconnaissance, *f*. **recognizable,** *a*, reconnaissable. **recognize,** *v.t*, reconnaître.

recoil, *n*, recul, *m*. ¶ *v.i*, reculer (*from*, devant). ~ *in disgust*, r. de dégoût.

recollect, *v.t*, se rappeler, se souvenir de. ¶ *v.i*, se souvenir. ~**ion,** *n*, souvenir, *m*.

recommence, *v.t. & i*, recommencer.

recommend, *v.t*, recommander; conseiller (*s.o to do*, à qn de faire). *to be, not to be* ~*ed*, à conseiller, à déconseiller. ~**ation,** *n*, recommandation, *f*.

recompense, *n*, récompense, *f*; (*Law*) dédommagement, *m*. ¶ *v.t*, récompenser; dédommager.

reconcile, *v.t*, (*pers.*) réconcilier (*to*, avec); *facts &c*) concilier. ~ *o.s to*, se résigner à. **reconciliation,** *n*, [ré]conciliation, *f*.

recondition, *v.t*, remettre à neuf; (*Mot.*) réviser.

reconnaissance, *n*, reconnaissance, *f*. **reconnoitre,** *v.t*, reconnaître. ¶ *v.i*, faire une reconnaissance.

reconsider, *v.t*, reconsidérer. ~**ation,** *n*, remise en cause, *f*.

reconstruct, *v.t*, (*building*) reconstruire; (*fig.*) reconstituer. ~**ion,** *n*, reconstruction; (*fig.*) reconstitution, *f*.

record, *n*, (*of attendance*) registre; (*of evidence*, *meeting*) procès-verbal, *m;* (*of decision*) minute, *f;* (*Law*) enregistrement; (*historical*) document, *m;* (*pl: public* ~*s*) archives, *f.pl;* (*of society*) actes, *f.pl;* (*card*) fiche, *f;* (*police*) casier judiciaire; (*Sport &c*) record; (*disc*) disque, *m. break the* ~, battre le record. *make a* ~, graver un disque. ~*-breaking,* qui bat tous les records. ~ *dealer,* disquaire, *m,f.* ~ *holder,* détenteur, trice du record. ~ *library,* discothèque, *f.* ~ *player,* tourne-disque, électrophone, *m. in* ~ *time,* en un temps record. ~ *token,* chèque-disque, *m.* ¶ *v.t,* (*gen., facts, music*) enregistrer; (*in log &c*) noter; décrire; (*instrument*) enregistrer, marquer. ~*ed delivery,* avec avis de réception. ~**er,** *n,* (*tape* ~) magnétophone; (*Law*) juge suppléant, *m;* (*Mus.*) flûte à bec, *f.* ~**ing,** *n,* enregistrement, *m.* ¶ *a,* (*artist*) qui enregistre; (*equipment*) enregistreur; (*studio, session*) d'enregistrement. ~ *van,* car de reportage, *m.*

re-count, *v.t,* recompter.

recount, *v.t,* raconter.

recoup, *v.t,* récupérer.

recourse, *n,* recours, *m.*

re-cover, *v.t,* recouvrir.

recover, *v.t,* (*gen.*) retrouver; (*sth lent*) reprendre (*from s.o,* à qn); (*territory*) reconquérir; (*expenses &c*) récupérer; (*debt, health, sight*) recouvrer; (*breath, consciousness, strength*) reprendre. ~ *lost ground* or *time,* se rattraper. ~ *o.s, one's composure,* se ressaisir. ¶ *v.i,* (*from illness &c*) guérir, se rétablir (de); (*come to*) revenir à soi; (*economy*) se redresser. ~**y,** *n,* récupération, *f;* recouvrement; (*health*) rétablissement *m,* guérison, *f.*

recreation, *n,* récréation, *f.*

recrimination, *n,* récrimination, *f.*

recruit, *n,* récrue, *f.* ¶ *v.t,* recruter. ~ *s.o to help,* embaucher *P* qn pour aider. ~**ment,** *n,* recrutement, *m.*

rectangle, *n,* rectangle, *m.* **rectangular,** *a,* rectangulaire.

rectify, *v.t,* rectifier; (*omission*) réparer; (*Elec.*) redresser.

rectitude, *n,* rectitude, *f.*

rector, *n,* pasteur; (*Univ.*) président élu, *m.* ~**y,** *n,* presbytère, *m.*

rectum, *n,* rectum, *m.*

recumbent, *a,* couché. ~ *figure* (*statue*), gisant, e.

recuperate, *v.i,* se rétablir. ¶ *v.t,* récupérer. **recuperation,** *n,* récupération, *f;* (*Med.*) rétablissement, *m.* **recuperative,** *a,* (*powers*) de récupération.

recur, *v.i,* se reproduire, se répéter; (*theme*) réapparaître. *recurring decimal,* fraction périodique, *f.* ~**rence,** *n,* répétition: réapparition, *f.* ~**rent,** *a,* (*fever*) périodique.

red, *a. & n,* rouge, *m;* (*hair &c*) roux, *a. the* ~*s,* (*Pol.*), les rouges, *m.pl. be in the* ~ *P,* être à découvert. *go* ~, rougir. *see* ~, se fâcher tout rouge. *go through a* ~ *light* (*Mot.*), passer au rouge. ~ *admiral* (*butterfly*), vulcain, *m.* ~ *breast,* rouge-gorge, *m. the R*~ *Cross,* la Croix Rouge. ~*currant,* groseille, *f.* ~ *deer,* cerf commun. ~*-faced* (*person*), rougeaud, e; (*fig.*) rouge de confusion. ~*-haired,* (*person*), roux, rousse, rouquin, e. ~*-handed,* en flagrant délit. ~ *herring,* hareng saur, *m;* (*fig.*) diversion, *f.* ~*-hot,* chauffié au rouge. ~ *Indian* or ~ *skin,* Peau-Rouge, *m,* ~ *lead,* minium, *m.* ~*-letter day,* jour mémorable, *m.* ~ *light district,* quartier réservé. ~ *mullet,* rouget, *m.* ~ *pepper,* (*capsicum*) poivron rouge, *m. R*~ *Sea,* mer Rouge, *f.* ~ *spot* (*skin*), rougeur, *f.* ~*start,* rouge-queue, *m.* ~ *tape,* paperasserie, *f.* ~*wing,* mauvis, *m.* **redden,** *v.t. & i,* rougir; roussir. **reddish,** *a,* rougeâtre.

redeem, *v.t,* (*Rel., gen.*) racheter; (*from pawn*) dégager; (*debt*) amortir; (*mortgage*) purger; (*obligation*) s'aquitter de. **Redeemer,** *n,* Rédempteur, *m.* **redemption,** *n,* rachat; remboursement; amortissement; dégagement, *m;* (*mortgage*) purge, *f;* (*Rel.*) rédemption, *f.*

redirect, *v.t,* faire suivre.

redness, *n,* rougeur; rousseur, *f.*

redouble, *v.t,* redoubler; (*Cards*) surcontrer.

redoubtable, *a,* redoutable.

redound, *v.i,* retomber (sur).

redress, *n,* redressement, *m,* réparation, *f.* ¶ *v.t,* redresser, réparer.

reduce, *v.t,* (*gen.*) réduire; diminuer; (*price*) baisser; (*voltage*) diminuer; (*Med: swelling*) résorber; (*Cook: sauce*) faire réduire. ~ *speed* (*Mot.*), ralentir. ~ *to the ranks* (*Mil.*), casser. *in* ~*d circumstances,* dans la gêne. ¶ *v.i,* (*slim*) maigrir. **reduction,** *n,* réduction; diminution; (*temperature*) baisse, *f;* (*tax*) dégrèvement, *m. make a* ~ *on* (*Com.*), faire un rabais sur.

redundancy, *n,* excès, *m,* superfluité, *f;* (*Ind.*) licenciement, *m,* mise en chômage, *f.* ~ *payment,* prime de licenciement, *f.* **redundant,** *a,* superflu; redondant; au chômage. *be made* ~, être licencié *ou* mis en chomage.

reed, *n,* roseau; (*pipe*) chalumeau, *m;* (*Mus.*) anche, *f.*

reef[1], *n,* récif, écueil; (*fig.*) écueil, *m.*

reef[2], *n,* (*in sail*) ris, *m.* ~ *knot,* nœud plat, *m.* ¶ *v.t,* prendre un ris dans. ~**er,** *n,* (*jacket*) caban; (*P*) joint *P, m.*

reek, *v.i,* puer, empester (*of sth,* qch).

reel, *n,* bobine, *f;* (*Fish.*) moulinet, *m;* (*Cine.*) bande, *f;* (*Danc.*) reel, *m.* ¶ *v.i,* chanceler, vaciller; (*drink*) tituber. *my head is* ~*ing,* la tête me tourne. ~ *in,* (*Naut., Fish.*) ramener. ~ *off* (*list &c*), débiter.

re-enact, *v.t,* (*scene &c*) reconstituer.

re-enter, *v.i,* rentrer. ¶ *v.t,* rentrer dans. **re-entry,** *n,* rentrée, *f.*
re-establish, *v.t,* rétablir, restaurer.
re-examine, *v.t,* examiner de nouveau; (*Law*) interroger de nouveau.
refectory, *n,* réfectoire, *m.*
refer, *v.t,* (*problem*) soumettre; (*pers. to s.o, sth*) renvoyer. ~ *to drawer* (*cheque*), refuser d'honorer. ¶ *v.i,* ~ *to,* parler de, faire mention de; faire allusion à; (*words*) se rapporter à; (*consult*) se reporter à, consulter. ~**ee,** *n,* (*Sport & fig.*) arbitre, *m. be a* ~ *for s.o,* fournir des références à qn. ¶ *v.t,* arbitrer. ¶ *v.i,* être arbitre. **reference,** *n,* mention (de); allusion (à), *f;* (*connection*) rapport (*to,* avec), *m;* (*book, letter*) référence, *f;* (*map*) coordonnées; (*testimonial, oft. pl.*) références, *f.pl. with* ~ *to,* en ce qui concerne; (*Com.*) comme suite à. ~ *library,* bibliothèque d'ouvrages à consulter, *f.* **referendum,** *n,* referendum, *m.*
refill, *n,* (*gen.*) recharge; (*pen*) cartouche, *f.* ¶ *v.t,* remplir à nouveau; recharger.
refine, *v.t,* affiner; (*sugar, oil*) raffiner. ¶ *v.i,* s'affiner. ~**d,** *a,* (*fig: pers.*) raffiné; (*metal*) affiné. ~**ment,** *n,* (*fig.*) raffinement; (*Mach. &c*) perfectionnement, *m.* **refiner,** *n,* affineur; raffineur, *m.* **refinery,** *n,* (*oil*) raffinerie, *f.*
refit (*Naut.*), *n,* remise en état, *f.* ¶ *v.t,* remettre en état.
reflate (*Econ.*), *v.t,* relancer. **reflation,** *n,* relance, *f.* ~**ary,** *a,* de relance.
reflect, *v.t,* refléter; (*mirror*) réfléchir; (*sound, heat*) renvoyer; (*fig: show*) refléter; (*credit &c*) faire rejaillir (sur). ¶ *v.i,* (*ponder*) réfléchir, méditer (sur); penser (à). ~ *upon,* (*discredit*) faire tort à; nuire à. ~**ion,** *n,* réflexion; image, *f,* reflet, *m;* (*on s.o's honour*) atteinte, *f;* (*pl: thoughts*) réflexions, pensées, *f.pl. on* ~, réflexion faite. ~**or,** *n,* réflecteur, *m.* **reflex,** *a. & n,* réflexe, *m.* ~ *angle,* angle rentrant. ~ *camera,* [appareil] reflex, *m.* **reflexive** (*Gram.*) *a,* réfléchi.
refloat (*ship*) *v.t,* renflouer.
reform, *n,* réforme, *f.* ¶ *v.t,* réformer. ¶ *v.i,* (*pers.*) s'amender. ~**ation,** *n,* réforme, *f.* ~**er,** *n,* réformateur, trice.
refrain[1], *n,* refrain, *m.*
refrain[2], *v.i,* s'abstenir (*from sth,* de qch; *from doing,* de faire).
refresh, *v.t,* (*gen., memory*) rafraîchir; (*sleep &c*) délasser, reposer. ~*er course,* cours de recyclage, *m.* ~**ing,** *a,* rafraîchissant; (*sleep*) reposant. **refreshment,** *n,* rafraîchissement, *m.* ~ *room,* ~ *bar,* buvette, *f,* buffet, *m.*
refrigerate, *v.t,* réfrigérer. **refrigeration,** *n,* réfrigération, *f.* **refrigerator,** *n,* réfrigérateur, frigidaire, frigo *P, m.*
refuel, *v.t.* (*& i,*) (se) ravitailler [en carburant]. ~**ling,** *n,* ravitaillement en carburant, *m.* ~ *stop* (*Aero.*), escale technique, *f.*
refuge, *n,* refuge, *m. to take* ~, se réfugier. **refugee,** *n,* réfugié, e.
refund, *n,* remboursement, *m.* ¶ *v.t,* rembourser.
refurbish, *v.t,* remettre à neuf.
refusal, *n,* refus, *m.* **refuse[1],** (riˈfju:z) *v.t,* refuser (de faire; *s.o sth,* qch à qn); se refuser (à faire); (*request*) rejeter. ¶ *v.i,* refuser.
refuse[2], (ˈrefju:s) *n,* détritus, *m.pl;* ordures, *f.pl;* (*industrial waste*) déchets, *m.pl.* ~ *collection,* ramassage d'ordures, *m.* ~ *collector,* éboueur, *m.* ~ *disposal,* traitement d'ordures, *m.* ~ *disposal service,* service de voirie, *m.* ~ *dump,* décharge, *f.*
refute, *v.t,* réfuter.
regain, *v.t,* regagner; (*health &c*) recouvrer; (*territory*) reconquérir; (*consciousness*) reprendre. ~ *possession,* rentrer en possession (de).
regal, *a,* royal; (*fig.*) majestueux.
regale, *v.t,* régaler.
regard, *n,* considération; estime, *f,* respect, *m;* (*pl: in messages*) amitiés, *f.pl. out of* ~ *for,* par égard pour. *without* ~ *to, for,* sans égard pour. *with* ~ *to,* ~*ing,* quant à, en ce qui concerne. ¶ *v.t,* considérer, regarder. ~**less,** *a,* ~ *of,* (*danger*) insouciant de; (*result*) sans se soucier de. ¶ *ad,* quand même.
regatta, *n,* régate, *f. oft. pl.*
regency, *n,* régence, *f.*
regenerate, *v.t.* (*& i,*) (se) régénérer. **regeneration,** *n,* régénération, *f.*
regent, *n. & a,* régent, e.
régime, *n,* régime, *m.* **regiment,** *n,* régiment, *m.* **regimental,** *a,* régimentaire; du régiment. **regimentation,** *n,* discipline excessive.
region, *n,* région, *f.* ~**al,** *a,* régional.
register, *n,* (*gen.*) régistre, *m;* (*electoral*) liste, *f.* ¶ *v.t,* enregistrer; (*birth &c*) déclarer; (*car*) [faire] immatriculer; (*trademark*) déposer; (*Post*) recommander; (*dial &c*) indiquer, marquer; (*face*) exprimer. ¶ *v.i,* s'inscrire. ~**ed,** *a,* (*voter &c*) inscrit; (*vehicle*) immatriculé; (*letter*) recommandé; (*Rly: luggage*) enregistré; (*shares*) nominatif. ~ *office,* siège social, *m.* ~ *trademark,* marque déposée. **registrar,** *n,* greffier; (*births &c*) officier de l'état civil; (*Univ.*) secrétaire [général]; (*Med.*) interne, *m,f.* **registration,** *n,* enregistrement, *m;* inscription, *f.* ~ *document* (*Mot.*), carte grise. ~ *fee* (*Univ.*), droits d'inscription, *m.pl* ~ *number,* numéro d'immatriculation, *m.* **registry office,** *n,* bureau de l'état civil; (*mariage*) mairie, *f.*
regress, *v.i,* régresser. ~**ion,** *n,* régression, *f.*
regret, *n,* regret (*for,* de), *m. have no* ~*s,* ne rien regretter. ¶ *v.t,* regretter (de faire; que + *subj*); être désolé. ~**ful,** *a,* désolé, navré; (*look &c*) de regret. ~**table,** *a,* regrettable,

fâcheux.
regroup, *v.t.* (*& i,*) (se) regrouper.
regular, *a,* régulier; (*in order*) régulier, en règle; habituel; normal; (*reader*) fidèle; (*staff*) permanent; (*Mil: soldier*) de métier; (*officer*) de carrière. ¶ *n,* soldat de métier, *m;* (*customer &c*) habitué, e. **~ity,** *n,* régularité, *f.* **~ize,** *v.t,* régulariser. **~ly,** *ad,* régulièrement. **regulate,** *v.t,* régler. **regulation,** *n,* règlement, *m;* (*att.*) réglementaire. **regulator,** *n,* régulateur, *m.*
rehabilitate, *v.t,* (*Med. &c*) réadapter, rééduquer; (*ex-prisoner*) réhabiliter. **rehabilitation,** *n,* rééducation; réadaptation; réhabilitation, *f.*
rehash, *n,* rechauffé, *m.* ¶ *v.t,* (*book &c*) remanier.
rehearsal, *n,* répétition, *f.* **rehearse,** *v.t,* (*Theat.*) répéter; (*relate*) énumérer.
rehouse, *v.t,* reloger.
reign, *n,* règne, *m.* ~ *of terror,* régime de terreur, *m.* ¶ *v.t,* régner. **~ing,** *a,* régnant.
reimburse, *v.t,* rembourser.
rein, *n,* (*lit., fig.*) rêne; (*coach horse*) guide, *f* *give free ~ to,* lâcher la bride à.
reindeer, *n,* renne, *m.*
reinforce, *v.t,* renforcer; (*concrete*) armer; (*claim &c*) appuyer. **~ment,** *n,* renforcement, *m;* armature, *f;* (*pl: men*) renforts, *m.pl.*
reinstate, *v.t,* réintégrer, rétablir, réhabiliter.
reissue, *v.t,* (*book*) rééditer; (*film*) ressortir.
reiterate, *v.t,* réitérer.
reject, *a.* (*& n,*) (article) de rebut, *m.* ¶ *v.t,* (*gen.*) rejeter; (*manuscript*) refuser; (*Ind.*) mettre au rebut. **~ion,** *n,* rejet; refus, *m.*
rejoice, *v.i,* se réjouir, être enchanté (de). **rejoicing,** *n,* réjouissance, *f.*
re-join, *v.t,* rejoindre. ~ *ship,* rallier le bord.
rejoin, *v.t,* répliquer. **rejoinder,** *n,* réplique, *f.*
rejuvenate, *v.t,* rajeunir.
rekindle, *v.t,* rallumer; (*fig.*) raviver.
relapse, *n,* (*Med. &c*) rechute, *f.* ¶ *v.i,* rechuter. ~ *into crime,* retomber dans le crime.
relate, *v.t,* (*tell*) raconter; (*associate*) rapporter; établir un rapport entre. ¶ *v.i,* se rapporter, toucher (*to,* à). *~d to,* parent avec, apparenté à. **relation,** *n,* (*connection*) relation, *f;* rapport, *m;* (*family*) parent, e; (*kinship*) parenté, *f;* (*pl: diplomatic &c*) relations, *f.pl;* (*sexual*) rapports, *m.pl.* **~ship,** *n,* liens de parenté, *m.pl;* rapport[s], *m.*[*pl*]; relation[s], *f.*[*pl*]. **relative†,** *a,* relatif; (*respective*) respectif. ~ *to,* relatif à, qui se rapporte à. ¶ *n,* parent, e. **relativity,** *n,* relativité, *f.*
relax, *v.t,* relâcher; (*pers.*) détendre; (*muscles*) décontracter. ¶ *v.i,* se relâcher; se détendre. ~! du calme! **~ation,** *n,* détente, *f.* **~ed,** *a,* (*pers.*) détendu, décontracté. **~ing,** *a,* qui détend; (*holiday*) reposant.
relay, *n,* relais, *m.* ~ *race,* course de relais, *f.* ¶ *v.t,* relayer.
release, *n,* libération, *f;* (*news*) autorisation de publier; (*book &c*) sortie, *f;* (*from Customs*) congé, *m.* ¶ *v.t,* libérer; (*Law*) remettre en liberté; (*extricate*) dégager; (*let go*) lâcher; (*gas*) dégager; (*spring &c*) déclencher, faire jouer; (*handbrake*) desserrer. ~ *the clutch* (*Mot.*), débrayer.
relegate, *v.t,* reléguer. **relegation,** *n,* relégation, *f.*
relent, *v.i,* s'adoucir, se laisser fléchir. **~less†,** *a,* impitoyable.
relevance, *n,* pertinence, *f.* **relevant,** *a,* (*gen.*) pertinent (à); (*chapter*) approprié. *be ~ to,* avoir rapport à.
reliability, *n,* (*method, memory*) sûreté, *f;* (*pers.*) sérieux, *m.* **reliable†,** *a,* sérieux; sûr; (*Mach.*) solide. **reliance,** *n,* confiance, *f.*
relic, *n,* relique, *f.*
relief, *n,* soulagement; (*aid*) secours, *m,* assistance, *f;* (*tax*) dégrèvement; (*Art*) relief, *m;* (*Mil.*) relève, *f.* ~ *organization,* société de secours, *f.* ~ *road,* route de délestage, *f.* ~ *supplies,* secours, *m.pl.* ~ *train,* train supplémentaire, *m.* ~ *work,* œuvres de secours, *f.pl.* **relieve,** *v.t,* soulager; secourir, assister; dégrever; relever; débarrasser.
religion, *n,* religion, *f.* **religious†,** *a,* (*lit. & fig.*) religieux; (*book*) de piété; (*wars*) de religion.
relinquish, *v.t,* (*gen.*) abandonner; (*right*) renoncer à.
reliquary, *n,* reliquaire, *m.*
relish, *n,* goût (*for,* pour), *m.* *with ~,* avec délectation; (*eat*) de bon appétit. ¶ *v.t,* savourer.
reluctance, *n,* répugnance, *f.* **reluctant,** *a,* peu disposé (à). **reluctantly,** *ad,* à contrecœur, à regret.
rely, *v.i,* compter (*on,* sur); avoir confiance (en).
remain, *v.i,* rester; demeurer. **remainder,** *n,* reste, *m;* (*people*) autres, *m,f.pl;* (*pl. Com.*) fin[s] de série, *f.*[*pl*]. **remains,** *n.pl,* restes; (*building*) vestiges, *m.pl.*
remake, *v.t.ir,* refaire. ¶ *n,* (*Cine.*) remake, *m.*
remand, *v.t,* renvoyer (*to,* à). ~ *in custody,* renvoyer en détention provisoire. *on ~,* en détention préventive. ~ *home,* maison d'arrêt, *f.*
remark, *n,* remarque, observation, *f.* *worthy of ~,* digne d'attention. ¶ *v.t,* (faire) remarquer. **~able†,** *a,* remarquable.
remedy, *n,* remède; (*Law*) recours, *m.* ¶ *v.t,* remédier à.
remember, *v.t,* se souvenir de; se rappeler. ¶ *v.i,* se souvenir. **remembrance,** *n,* souvenir, *m;* mémoire, *f.*
remind, *v.t,* rappeler (*s.o of sth,* qch à qn; *s.o that,* à qn que). *you ~ me of someone,* vous me rappelez quelqu'un. **~er,** *n,* mémento; rappel, *m.*

reminiscence, *n,* réminiscence, *f.*
remiss, *a,* négligent. **~ion,** *n,* rémission; (*Law*) remise, *f.* **remit,** *v.t,* remettre; (*send*) envoyer; (*Law*) renvoyer. **remittance,** *n,* remise, *f;* envoi; (*money*) versement, *m.*
remnant, *n,* reste, restant; (*cloth*) coupon; (*food, fortune*) débris; (*splendour*) vestige, *m.*
remonstrance, *n,* remontrance, *f.* **remonstrate,** *v.i,* faire des remontrances (*with,* à); protester (*against,* contre).
remorse, *n,* remords, *m.* **~less,** *a.* & **~lessly,** *ad,* sans remords.
remote, *a,* éloigne; écarté; lointain; (*pers.*) distant; (*antiquity*) reculée, haute; (*slight*) vague. ~ *control,* télécommande, *f.* **~ness,** *n,* éloignement, *m.*
remould (*tyre*), *n,* pneu rechapé, *m.*
removable, *a,* amovible. **removal,** *n,* enlèvement; (*house*) déménagement, *m;* (*abuse, evil*) suppression, *f;* (*Med.*) ablation, *f.* ~ *man, remover,* déménageur, *m.* ~ *van,* camion de déménagement, *m.* **remove,** *v.t,* (*gen.* & *Med.*) enlever; déménager; supprimer; (*doubt, obstacle*) écarter; (*fear* &c) dissiper; (*official*) déplacer; (*child from school*) retirer. **~r,** *n,* (*stain*) détachant; (*varnish*) dissolvant; (*make-up* ~) démaquillant, *m.*
remunerate, *v.t,* rémunérer. **remuneration,** *n,* rémunération, *f.* **remunerative,** *a,* rémunérateur.
renaissance, *n,* renaissance, *f.*
renal, *a,* rénal.
render, *v.t,* (*gen.*) rendre; (*account*) présenter; (*Mus.*) interpréter; (*assistance*) prêter; (*Cook: fat* &c) faire fondre; (*Build.*) plâtrer. **~ing,** *n,* interprétation, traduction, *f.*
renegade, *n,* renégat, e.
renew, *v.t,* renouveler. **~al,** *n,* renouvellement, *m;* reprise, *f;* (*strength*) regain, *m.*
rennet, *n,* présure; (*apple*) reinette, *f.*
renounce, *v.t,* renoncer à; (*religion*) abjurer; (*friend, cause* &c) renier; (*principles*) répudier.
renovate, *v.t,* remettre à neuf; (*building* &c) restaurer.
renown, *n,* renommée, *f,* renom, *m.* **~ed,** *a,* renommé.
rent[1], *n,* loyer, *m.* ~*-free, a,* exempt de loyer; *ad,* sans payer loyer. ~ *rebate,* dégrèvement de l., *m.* ¶ *v.t,* louer. **~al,** *n,* prix de location, *m.*
rent[2], *n,* déchirure, *f,* accroc, *m.*
renunciation, *n,* renonciation, abjuration; dénonciation; (*Law*) répudiation, *f;* reniement, *m.*
reorganize, *v.t,* réorganiser.
repair, *n,* réparation; (*Build.*) réfection, *f;* (*condition: good, bad*) état, *m.* ¶ *v.t,* réparer. **~able** & **reparable,** *a,* réparable. **reparation,** *n,* réparation, *f.*
repartee, *n,* repartie, réplique, *f.*
repatriate, *v.t,* rapatrier. **repatriation,** *n,* rapatriation, *f.*
repay, *v.t.ir,* (*money*) rembourser, rendre; (*obligation*) s'aquitter de; (*pers.*) récompenser.
repeal, *n,* (*law*) abrogation; (*sentence*) annulation, *f.* ¶ *v.t,* abroger; annuler.
repeat, *n,* répétition; (*Mus., TV* &c) reprise, *f.* ¶ *v.t,* répéter; (*demand* &c) réitérer; (*Mus.*) reprendre; (*Com.*) renouveler. **~edly,** *ad,* fréquemment, à plusieurs reprises. **~ing** (*rifle, watch*) *a,* à répétition.
repel, *v.t,* repousser. **repellent,** *a,* repoussant, répugnant.
repent, *v.i,* se repentir. ¶ *v.t.* se repentir de. **~ance,** *n,* repentir, *m.*
repercussion, *n,* répercussion, *f.*
repertory, *n,* répertoire, *m.*
repetition, *n,* répétition; (*needless*) redite, *f.*
replace, *v.t,* (*put back*) replacer; remplacer (*by, with,* par). **~ment,** *n,* replacement; remplacement, *m;* (*pers.*) remplaçant, e. ~ *part* (*Tech.*), pièce de rechange, *f.*
replenish, *v.t,* remplir de nouveau (*with,* de). **replete,** *a,* rempli; (*fed*) rassasié. **repletion,** *n,* satiété, *f.*
replica, *n,* réplique, *f;* (*document*) fac-similé, *m.*
reply, *n,* réponse, *f.* ~ *paid,* avec réponse payée. ¶ *v.t.* & *i,* répondre.
report, *n,* rapport; (*speech* &c) compte-rendu; (*Press, TV* &c) reportage; (*weather*) bulletin; (*Sch.*) bulletin scolaire, *m;* (*noise*) détonation, *f;* coup de fusil, *m.* ¶ *v.t,* rapporter, rendre compte de; faire un reportage sur; déclarer; (*notify*) signaler; (*pers.*) dénoncer. ¶ *v.i,* se présenter. **~er,** *n,* reporter, *m;* (*Press*) journaliste, *m,f.* **~ing,** *n,* reportage, *m.*
repose, *n,* repos; (*sleep*) sommeil, *m. in* ~, en repos. ¶ *v.i,* se reposer; (*dead*) reposer.
repository, *n,* dépôt; (*fig.*) répertoire, *m.*
reprehend, *v.t,* (*pers.*) réprimander; (*conduct*) blâmer. **reprehensible,** *a,* répréhensible.
represent, *v.t,* représenter. ~ *s.o,* venir de la part de qn. **~ation,** *n,* représentation; (*pl.*) démarche, *f.* **~ative,** *a,* représentatif. ¶ *n,* représentant, e.
repress, *v.t,* réprimer; (*Psych.*) refouler. **~ion,** *n,* répression, *f;* refoulement, *m.* **~ive,** *a,* répressif.
reprieve, *n,* sursis, *m;* (*Law*) commutation de la peine capitale, *f.* ¶ *v.t,* surseoir à l'exécution de; accorder une commutation &c à.
reprimand, *n,* réprimande, *f.* ¶ *v.t,* réprimander.
reprint, *n,* réimpression, *f.* ¶ *v.t,* réimprimer.
reprisal, *n,* représaille, *f.*
reproach, *n,* reproche, *m. be a* ~ *to,* être la honte de. *beyond* ~, irréprochable. ¶ *v.t,* faire des reproches à; reprocher (*s.o for sth,* qch à qn). **~ful,** *a,* (*word*) de reproche; (*look* &c) réprobateur. **~fully,** *ad,* d'un ton de reproche.

reproduce, *v.t.* (*& i,*) (se) reproduire. **reproduction,** *n,* reproduction, *f.* ~ *furniture,* imitation de meuble ancien, *f.*
reproof, *n,* réprimande, *f.* **reprove,** *v.t,* reprendre, réprimander, blâmer (*for,* de).
reptile, *n,* reptile, *m.*
republic, *n,* république, *f.* ~**an,** *a. & n,* républicain, e.
republish, *v.t,* publier de nouveau; (*book*) rééditer.
repudiate, *v.t,* répudier; renier.
repugnance, *n,* répugnance, *f.* **repugnant,** *a,* répugnant. *be ~ to,* répugner à.
repulse, *v.t,* repousser. **repulsion,** *n,* répulsion, *f.* **repulsive,** *a,* repoussant; (*Phys.*) répulsif.
reputable, *a,* de bonne réputation. **reputation & repute,** *n,* réputation, *f. of repute,* réputé. **reputed,** *a,* réputé.
request, *n,* demande, requête, *f. by ~, on ~,* sur demande. ¶ *v.t,* demander; (*formal*) prier. ~ *programme,* programme des auditeurs, *m.* ~ *stop,* arrêt facultatif.
requiem, *n,* requiem, *m.*
require, *v.t,* (*need: pers.*) avoir besoin de; (*action, thing*) demander, exiger, nécessiter. *if ~d,* s'il faut, au besoin. ~**ment,** *n,* exigence, *f;* besoin, *m;* (*condition*) condition requise. **requisite,** *a,* requis, voulu. ¶ *n,* chose nécessaire, *f. toilet ~s,* accessoires de toilette, *m.pl.* **requisition,** *n,* réquisition, *f.* ¶ *v.t,* réquisitionner.
rescind, *v.t,* (*decision*) annuler; (*law*) abroger; (*judgement*) rescinder.
rescue, *n,* délivrance, *f;* secours, *m.pl;* sauvetage, *m. to the ~,* à la rescousse. ~ *party,* équipe de secours, *f.* ¶ *v.t,* délivrer; secourir; sauver.
research, *n,* recherche, *f.* ~ *worker,* chercheur, euse. ¶ *v.i.* (*& t,*) faire des recherches (pour) (*into, on,* sur).
resemblance, *n,* ressemblance, *f.* **resemble,** *v.t,* ressembler à.
resent, *v.t,* être indigné de. ~**ful,** *a,* rancunier. ~**ment,** *n,* ressentiment, *m.*
reservation, *n,* réserve, réservation; (*mental*) restriction, arrière-pensée; (*seats*) location, *f.* **reserve,** *n,* réserve, *f;* (*Sport*) remplaçant, e. ~ *price,* prix minimum, *m.* ~ *tank,* reservoir de secours, *m.* ~ *team,* équipe B, *f.* ¶ *v.t,* réserver. ~**d,** *a,* (*pers.*) renfermé. **reservist,** *n,* réserviste, *m.* **reservoir,** *n,* réservoir, *m.*
resettle, *v.t,* (*land*) repeupler; (*pers.*) établir.
reshuffle, *n,* (*Pol.*) remaniement, *m.* ¶ *v.t,* (*Cards*) rebattre; (*fig.*) remanier.
reside, *v.i,* (*lit., fig.*) résider (*in,* en, dans). **residence,** *n,* résidence, *f;* (*hostel*) foyer, *m. in ~,* en résidence; (*doctor*) résident. ~ *permit,* permis de séjour, *m,* carte de s., *f.* **resident,** *n,* habitant, e; (*foreigner*) résident, e; (*in street*) riverain, e; (*hotel*) pensionnaire, *m,f.* ¶ *a,* résident; (*tutor &c*) à demeure. ~**ial,** *a,* résidentiel.
residual, *a,* restant; (*Chem.*) résiduel. **residuary,** *a,* restant; (*Chem.*) résiduaire. ~ *legate* (*Law*), légataire universel, le. **residue,** *n,* reste[s], *m.*[*pl*]; (*Chem.*) résidu; (*Law*) reliquat, *m.*
resign, *v.t,* (*job*) se démettre de; (*rights*) renoncer à. ~ *o.s to,* se résigner à. ¶ *v.i,* démissionner. **resignation,** *n,* démission; (*mental*) résignation, *f. tender one's ~,* donner sa démission.
resilience, *n,* résistance, *f;* ressort, *m.* **resilient,** *a,* (*material*) élastique; (*pers.*) qui a du ressort.
resin, *n,* résine, *f.* ~**ous,** *a,* résineux.
resist, *v.t,* (*gen.*) résister à; s'opposer à; (*order*) refuser d'obéir à. ¶ *v.i,* résister. ~**ance,** *n,* résistance, *f.*
resit, *v.t,* (*exam*) se représenter à.
resolute†, *a,* résolu, déterminé. **resolution,** *n,* résolution, *f.* **resolve,** *n,* détermination, *f.* ¶ *v.t,* résoudre. ¶ *v.i,* résoudre, décider (de faire); se résoudre (à faire).
resonance, *n,* résonance, *f.* **resonant,** *a,* résonnant.
resort, *n,* recours, *m. as a last ~,* en dernier ressort. *seaside &c ~,* station balnéaire &c. *coastal ~,* plage, *f.* ~ **to,** avoir recours à, recourir à.
resound, *v.i,* résonner, retentir. ~**ing,** *a,* sonore; (*success &c*) retentissant.
resource, *n,* ressource, *f;* (*pl.*) ressources, *f.pl.* ~**ful,** *a,* de ressources; (*plan*) ingénieux.
respect, *n,* respect, *m;* considération, *f;* (*aspect*) égard, rapport, *m;* (*pl.*) respects, hommages, *m.pl. in many ~s,* à bien des égards. *with ~ to,* quant à, en ce qui concerne. ¶ *v.t.* respecter. ~**able,** *a,* (*gen.*) respectable; (*clothes, behaviour*) convenable. ~**ably,** *ad,* convenablement, comme il faut *P;* (*fairly well*) passablement, pas mal *P.* ~**ful†,** *a,* respectueux. ~**ing,** *pr,* concernant. ~**ive†,** *a,* respectif.
respiration, *n,* respiration, *f.* **respirator,** *n,* masque à gaz; (*Med.*) respirateur, *m.* **respire,** *v.t. & i,* respirer.
respite, *n,* répit, *m.*
resplendent, *a,* resplendissant.
respond, *v.i,* répondre (*to,* à; *with,* par); (*nerves &c*) réagir. **response,** *n,* réponse; réaction, *f;* (*Rel.*) répons, *m. in ~ to,* en réponse à. **responsibility,** *n,* responsabilité, *f.* **responsible,** *a,* responsable (*for,* de); (*pers.*) digne de confiance; (*job*) comportant des responsabilités. **responsive,** *a,* qui réagit bien.
rest, *n,* repos; (*Mus.*) silence; (*support*) support, appui; (*remainder*) reste, *m. & all the ~ of it,* & tout ça *P.* ¶ *v.i,* se reposer; (*be buried*) reposer; (*remain*) rester; (*lean &c*) [s']appuyer (*on,* sur; *against,* contre); (*fig: case &c*)

reposer; (*eyes*) se poser. ¶ *v.t*, poser, appuyer; (*fig.*) fonder.
restaurant, *n*, restaurant, *m*. ~ *keeper*, restaurateur, trice.
restful, *a*, reposant.
restitution, *n*, restitution, *f*. *make* ~ *of*, restituer.
restive, *a*, (*horse*) rétif; (*pers.*) agité, énervé.
restless, *a*, agité. *get* ~, s'impatienter. *have a* ~ *night*, mal dormir.
restoration, *n*, restauration, *f*; rétablissement, *m*. **restorative,** *a*. & *n*, reconstituant, *m*. **restore,** *v.t*, (*give back*) rendre; (*order &c, health, rights*) rétablir; (*confidence*) redonner; (*repair*) restaurer. **restorer,** *n*, restaurateur, trice.
restrain, *v.t*, retenir; (*emotions*) contenir. ~ *o.s*, se retenir. ~**ed,** *a*, (*manner &c*) mesuré; (*style*) sobre. **restraint,** *n*, contrainte; mesure; sobriété, *f*. (*Med.*) *place under* ~, interner.
restrict, *v.t*, restreindre; limiter. ~**ion,** *n*, restriction; (*speed*) limitation, *f*; (*price*) contrôle, *m*. ~**ive,** *a*, restrictif.
result, *n*, résultat, *m*. *as a* ~, en conséquence. *as a* ~ *of*, par suite de. ¶ *v.i*, résulter. ~ *in*, aboutir à.
resume, *v.t*, (*gen.*) reprendre; (*relations*) renouer; (*sum up*) résumer. ¶ *v.i*, reprendre. **resumption,** *n*, reprise, *f*.
resurrect, *v.t*, ressusciter; (*fig: custom &c*) faire revivre; (*memory*) réveiller. ~**ion,** *n*, résurrection, *f*.
resuscitate, *v.t*, (*Med.*) réanimer. **resuscitation,** *n*, réanimation, *f*.
retail, *n*, [vente *f* au] détail, *m*. ¶ *a*, (*business &c*) de détail. ¶ *v.t*, vendre au détail, détailler. ~**er,** *n*, détaillant, e.
retain, *v.t*, (*keep*) conserver, garder; (*hold, engage*) retenir. ~**er,** *n*, (*Hist.*) serviteur, *m*; (*to barrister*) provision, *f*.
retaliate, *v.i*, user de représailles (envers). **retaliation,** *n*, représailles, *f.pl*. **retaliatory,** *a*, de représailles.
retarded, *a*, (*Med.*) retardé, arriéré.
retch, *v.i*, avoir des haut-le-cœur.
retention, *n*, maintien, *m*, conservation; (*memory*) mémoire; (*Med.*) rétention, *f*. **retentive,** *a*, qui retient; (*memory*) fidèle.
reticence, *n*, réticence, *f*. **reticent,** *a*, réticent, réservé. *to be* ~, se montrer réticent.
retina, *n*, rétine, *f*.
retinue, *n*, suite, *f*, cortège, *m*.
retire, *v.t*, mettre à la retraite. ¶ *v.i*, se retirer; (*Mil.*) reculer; (*from work*) prendre sa retraite; (*to bed*) se coucher; (*Sport*) abandonner. ~**d,** *a*, retraité; (*secluded*) retiré. ~ *person*, retraité, e. ~**ment,** *n*, retraite, *f*. ~ *age*, âge de [la] retraite, *m*. ~ *benefit*, prime de r. **retiring,** *a*, réservé.
retort, *n*, réplique, riposte; (*Chem.*) cornue, *f*. ¶ *v.t*. & *i*, rétorquer, répliquer, riposter.
retrace, *v.t*, (*relate*) retracer. ~ *one's steps*, revenir sur ses pas, rebrousser chemin.
retract, *v.t*. (& *i*), (se) rétracter; (*Aero.*) rentrer.
retread (*tyre*) *n*, pneu rechapé.
retreat, *n*, (*Mil., Rel.*) retraite, *f*; (*place*) asile, refuge, *m*. ¶ *v.i*, se retirer (de); (*Mil.*) battre en retraite; (*glacier &c*) reculer.
retrench, *v.t*, réduire. ¶ *v.i*, faire des économies.
retribution, *n*, récompense, *f*, châtiment, *m*.
retrieval, *n*, (*Computer*) extraction, *f*, rapatriement, *m*. **retrieve,** *v.t*, (*recover: object*) récupérer (*from*, de); (*dog*) rapporter; (*information*) extraire; (*reputation*) rétablir; (*situation*) redresser. **retriever** (*dog*) *n*, retriever, *m*.
retrograde, *a*, rétrograde.
retrospect, *n*, *in* ~, rétrospectivement. ~**ive**†, *a*, rétrospectif; (*effect*) rétroactif.
return, *n*, (*gen., Ten.*) retour, *m*; (*to Sch., work*) rentrée, *f*; (*sending back*) renvoi, *m*; (*sth lost &c*) restitution, *f*; (*money*) remboursement, *m*; (*Com.*) rapport (*on*, de); (*pl: profits*) bénéfice, *m*; (*tax*) déclaration; (*election* ~*s*) résultats, *m.pl*. *in* ~, en revanche. *in* ~ *for*, en échange de. *many happy* ~*s!* bon anniversaire! ~ *flight*, vol de retour, *m*. ~ *half* (*ticket*), coupon de retour, *m*. ~*ing officer* (*Pol.*), scrutateur, *m*. ~ *match*, revanche, *f*, match retour, *m*. *by* ~ *of post*, par retour du courrier. ~ *ticket*, aller & retour, *m*. ¶ *v.t*, (*give back*) rendre; (*money*) rembourser; (*put back*) remettre; (*send back; Ten.*) renvoyer; (*bring back*) rapporter; (*compliment, verdict*) rendre; (*s.o's love*) répondre à; (*reply*) répliquer; (*candidate*) élire. '~ *to sender*', 'retour à l'envoyeur'. ¶ *v.i*, (*come back*) revenir; (*go back*) retourner; (*doubts &c*) réapparaître. ~ *home, to school*, rentrer. ~ *to*, (*work*) reprendre; (*subject*) revenir à. ~**able,** *a*, (*bottle*) consigné.
reunion, *n*, réunion, *f*. **reunite,** *v.t*, réunir.
rev *P*, *n*, (*Mot.*) tour, *m*. ~ *counter*, comptetours, *m.inv*. ~ *up*, emballer le moteur.
reveal, *v.t*, révéler (que); (*object*) découvrir. ~**ing,** *a*, révélateur.
reveille, *n*, réveil, *m*.
revel, *n*, (*pl.*) festivities, *f.pl*. ¶ *v.i*, se délecter (*in sth*, de qch; *in doing*, à faire).
revelation, *n*, révélation, *f*. *R*~ (*Bible*), Apocalypse, *f*.
reveller, *n*, noceur, euse. **revelry,** *n*, festivités, *f.pl*.
revenge, *n*, vengeance; (*Sport*) revanche, *f*. ~ **oneself,** se venger. ~**ful,** *a*, vindicatif.
revenue, *n*, revenu, *m*.
reverberate, *v.i*, se répercuter. **reverberation,** *n*, répercussion, *f*.
revere, *v.t*, révérer, vénérer. **reverence,** *n*, vénération, *f*. ¶ *v.t*, révérer. **reverend,** *a*, révérend.

reverent†, *a*, respectueux. **reverential,** *a*, révérenciel.
reverie, *n*, rêverie, *f*.
reversal, *n*, (*rôles*) interversion, *f;* (*opinion &c*) revirement; (*policy*) renversement, *m;* (*Law*) réforme, *f*. **reverse,** *a*, contraire; (*order*) inverse; (*gear*) arrière. ¶ *n*, contraire, opposé; (*coin*) revers; (*cloth*) envers; (*page*) verso; (*setback*) revers, *m*. *in* ~ (*Mot*.), en marche arrière. ¶ *v.t*, (*object &c*) retourner; (*order, current*) renverser, inverser; (*Law: judgment*) réformer. ~ *the charges* (*Tel*.), téléphoner en P.V.C. ¶ *v.i*, (*Mot*.) faire marche arrière. *reversing lights*, feux de marche arrière, *m.pl*. **reversible,** *a*, réversible; (*decision*) révocable. **reversion,** *n*, retour, *m;* (*Biol., Law*) réversion, *f*. **revert,** *v.i*, retourner (à); (*subject*) revenir (à). ~ *to type*, retrouver son caractère original.
review, *n*, revue, *f;* examen, *m;* (*Mil*.) revue; (*book &c*) critique, *f;* (*magazine*) revue. ¶ *v.t*, (*Mil., the past &c*) passer en revue; (*situation*) réexaminer; (*book &c*) faire la critique de. ~**er,** *n*, critique, *m*.
revile, *v.t*, insulter.
revise, *v.t*, réviser, modifier; (*text, subject*) réviser, revoir ¶ *v.i*, réviser (*for*, pour). **revision,** *n*, revision, *f*.
revival, *n*, reprise; renaissance, *f;* (*Rel*.) réveil, *m*. **revive,** *v.t*, (*pers., feelings, fire*) ranimer; (*joy, doubt*) faire renaître; (*memories*) réveiller; (*custom &c*) ressusciter; (*play*) reprendre. ¶ *v.i*, (*pers*.) reprendre connaissance; (*hope &c*) renaître; (*trade*) reprendre.
revoke, *v.t*, (*order*) révoquer; (*decision*) revenir sur; (*law*) abroger; (*licence*) retirer. ¶ *v.i*, (*Cards*) faire une fausse renonce.
revolt, *n*, révolte, *f*. ¶ *v.i*, se révolter, se soulever. ~**ing,** *a*, révoltant, dégoûtant; dégueulasse *P*.
revolution, *n*, révolution, *f*. ~**ary,** *a. & n*, révolutionnaire, *m,f*. ~**ize,** *v.t*, révolutionner. **revolve,** *v.i*. (*& t*,) (faire) tourner.
revolver, *n*, revolver, *m*.
revolving, *a*, tournant; (*chair &c*) pivotant; (*Tech*.) rotatif. ~ *door*, tambour, *m*.
revue, *n*, revue, *f*.
revulsion, *n*, dégoût, *m*.
reward, *n*, récompense, *f*. ¶ *v.t*, récompenser (*for*, de). ~**ing,** *a*, (*financially*) rémunérateur; (*fig*.) qui en vaut la peine.
rewire (*house*) *v.t*, refaire l'installation électrique de.
rhapsody, *n*, rhapsodie, *f*.
rhesus, *n*, rhésus, *m*.
rhetoric, *n*, rhétorique, *f*. ~**al,** *a*, (*style*) ampoulé. ~ *question*, question pour la forme, *f*.
rheumatic, *a*, rhumatismal. ~ *fever*, rhumatisme articulaire aigu. **rheumatism,** *n*, rhumatisme, *m*.
rhinoceros, *n*, rhinocéros, *m*.
rhododendron, *n*, rhododendron, *m*.
rhubarb, *n*, rhubarbe, *f*.
rhyme, *n*, rime, *f*. ¶ *v.t*, rimer. **rhythm,** *n*, rythme, *m*. ~ *method* (*Med*.), méthode ogino, *f*. ~**ic(al),** *a*, rythmique; rythmé, cadencé.
rib, *n*, (*Anat., Cook., Knit*.) côte; (*vault*) nervure; (*umbrella*) baleine, *f*. ¶ *v.t*, (*P tease*) mettre en boîte *P*.
ribald, *a*, paillard. ~**ry,** *n*, paillardises, *f.pl*.
ribbed, *a*, à côtes; à nervure(s).
ribbon, *n*, ruban, *m*. *in* ~*s*, en lambeaux.
rice, *n*, riz, *m*. ~ *field*, rizière, *f*. ~*-growing*, riziculture, *f*. ~ *paper*, papier de riz, *m*. ~ *pudding*, riz au lait.
rich, *a*, riche; (*furnishing &c*) de luxe; (*voice*) ample; (*food*) gras. *get* ~, s'enrichir. **riches,** *n.pl*, richesse, *f. oft. pl*. **richly,** *ad*, richement, somptueusement; (*deserve*) largement. **richness,** *n*, richesse, somptuosité, ampleur, *f;* (*colour*) éclat, *m*.
rickets, *n*, rachitisme, *m*. **rickety,** *a*, rachitique; (*furniture &c*) branlant.
rickshaw, *n*, pousse-pousse, *m*.
ricochet, *n*, ricochet, *m*. ¶ *v.i*, ricocher.
rid, *v.t*, débarrasser, délivrer (qn de qch). ~ *o.s of, get* ~ *of*, se débarrasser de; (*fears &c*) perdre. **riddance,** *n*, débarras, *m*.
riddle[1], *n*, énigme, devinette, *f*.
riddle[2], *n*, crible, *m*. ¶ *v.t*, passer au crible; (*stove*) agiter la grille de; (*fig*.) cribler (de).
ride, *n*, promenade (à cheval &c), *f;* tour; (*distance covered*) trajet, *m*. *take s.o for a* ~, (*in car &c*) emmener qn en promenade; (*P fool*) faire marcher qn *P;* (*swindle*) rouler qn *P*. ¶ *v.t.ir*, ~ *a horse, a bicycle, a donkey*, monter à cheval, à bicyclette, à dos d'âne. ¶ *v.i.ir*, monter à cheval &c; (*go*) aller à cheval &c; (*Sport*) faire du cheval. ~ *side-saddle*, monter en amazone. ~ *at anchor* (*Naut*.), être à l'ancre. ~ *out*, (*Naut: storm*) étaler; (*crisis*) surmonter. ~ *up* (*skirt*), remonter. **rider,** *n*, cavalier, ère; (*Turf*) jockey, *m;* (*circus*) écuyer, ère; (*clause*) annexe, *f*.
ridge, *n*, (*roof, nose, hills*) arête; (*mountain*) crête; (*on cliff*) strie, *f;* (*Met*.) ligne, *f*.
ridicule, *n*, ridicule, *m*. ¶ *v.t*, ridiculiser. **ridiculous†,** *a*, ridicule. ~**ness,** *n*, ridicule, *m*.
riding, *n*, équitation, *f;* (*Turf*) monte, *f*. ~ *boots*, bottes, *f.pl*. ~ *breeches*, culotte de cheval, *f*. ~ *habit*, amazone, *f*. ~ *school*, école d'équitation, *f*, manège, *m*. ~ *whip*, cravache, *f*.
rife (to be), régner, sévir, courir [les rues].
riff-raff, *n*, canaille, racaille, *f*.
rifle[1], *n*, fusil [rayé], *m;* (*Hunt*.) carabine de chasse, *f*. ~ *range*, (*outdoor*) champ de tir; (*indoor*) stand de t., *m*.

rifle², *v.t,* (*house, drawer*) vider, dévaliser; (*pockets*) puiser dans.

rift, *n,* fissure; (*clouds*) trouée; (*Pol: in party*) division, *f.*

rig, *n,* (*oil: land*) derrick, *m;* (*sea*) plate-forme petrolière, *f;* (*Naut.* & *~ging*) gréement, *m.* ¶ *v.t,* (*Naut.*) gréer; (*election*) truquer. *~ out,* habiller, fringuer *P.* *~-out,* tenue, *f.* *~ up,* (*ship*) gréer; (*with mast*) mâter; (*equipment*) monter; installer; bricoler *P.*

right, *a,* (*correct*) juste, exact; (*just*) juste, équitable; (*morally*) bien, *inv;* (*opp. left*) droit, de droite; (*Math.*) droit; (*road*) bon. *at the ~ time,* au bon moment. *be ~* (*pers.*), avoir raison; (*clock*) être à l'heure; (*answer*) être juste. *be in one's ~ mind,* avoir toute sa raison. *~-oh! P,* d'accord! *put ~,* corriger; (*pers.*) détromper; (*situation*) redresser; (*clock*) remettre à l'heure. *that's ~!* c'est ça! *~-angled,* rectangle; (*bend*) à angle droit. *~-hand,* droit. *~-handed person,* droitier, ère. *~ side,* (*fabric*) endroit, *m.* *~ thinking, ~ minded,* sensé. *~-wing,* (*Sport*) ailier droit, *m;* (*Pol.*) *a,* de droite. ¶ *ad,* (*straight*) tout droit; (*completely*) tout, tout à fait; (*remember*) bien; (*guess &c*) juste; (*answer*) correctement; (*opp. left*) à droite. *~ away,* tout de suite. *~ now,* en ce moment. *~ here,* ici même. *~ in the middle,* au beau milieu. *~ & left,* à droite & à gauche. *~ left & centre,* de tous les côtés. ¶ *n,* droit, *m;* raison; (*side & Pol.*) droite, *f.* *~ & wrong,* le bien & le mal. *be in the ~,* avoir raison. *within one's ~s,* dans son droit. *in one's own ~* (*Law*), de son propre chef. *by ~s,* en toute justice. *~-of way,* droit de passage; (*Mot.*) priorité, *f.* ¶ *v.t,* redresser.

righteous, *a,* (*pers.*) vertueux; (*indignation &c*) justifié. *~***ly,** *ad,* vertueusement. *~***ness,** *n,* droiture, *f.*

rightful†, *a,* légitime. **rightly,** *ad,* (*correctly*) bien; (*justifiably*) à juste titre.

rigid, *a,* rigide; strict; (*system*) qui manque de flexibilité. *~***ity,** *n,* rigidité, *f;* caractère strict; manque de flexibilité, *m.* *~***ly,** *ad,* rigidement; (*fig.*) rigoureusement.

rigmarole, *n,* (*speech*) galimatias, *m;* (*procedure*) comédie, *f.*

rigor mortis, *n,* rigidité cadavérique, *f.*

rigorous†, *a,* rigoureux. **rigour,** *n,* rigueur, *f.*

rim, *n,* (*cup &c*) bord, *m;* (*wheel*) jante; (*glasses*) monture, *f.* *~***less,** (*glasses*) *a,* sans monture.

rind, *n,* écorce, peau; (*cheese*) croûte; (*bacon*) couenne, *f.*

ring¹, *n,* (*gen.*) anneau, *m;* (*with stone, for bird*) bague; (*swimmer*) bouée de natation, *f;* (*napkin*) rond; (*piston*) segment; (*people*) cercle; (*smoke, water &c*) rond, *m;* (*group: gen.*) coterie, *f;* (*spies*) réseau; (*dealers*) cartel, *m;* (*circus*) piste; (*exhibition*) arène, *f;* (*Box.*) ring, *m.* *~s round the eyes,* des cernes sous les yeux. *wedding ~,* alliance, *f.* *~ binder,* classeur à anneaux, *m.* *~ finger,* annulaire, *m.* *~ leader,* meneur, *m.* *~ road,* route de ceinture, *f;* (*motorway*) périphérique, *m.* *~ worm,* teigne, *f.* ¶ *v.t,* (*bird, tree*) baguer; (*encircle*) entourer, encercler.

ring², *n,* (*bell*) sonnerie, *f;* (*fainter*) tintement, *m.* *give s.o a ~,* passer un coup de fil à qn. *have a ~ of truth,* sonner juste. ¶ *v.t,* (*bell*) faire sonner; (*Tel:* & *~ up*) téléphoner à. *~ the doorbell,* sonner. *~ a peal,* carillonner. *~ the changes in* (*fig.*), varier. ¶ *v.i,* sonner; retentir; résonner; tinter; téléphoner. *~ true, false* (*fig.*), sonner juste, faux. *~ back* (*Tel.*), rappeler. *~ off* (*Tel.*), raccrocher. *~ out,* (*bell*) sonner; (*voice*) résonner; (*shot*) retentir. *~***ing,** *n,* (*in ears*) bourdonnement, *m.* *~ tone* (*Tel.*), tonalité, *f.*

ringlet, *n,* frisette, *f.*

rink, *n,* (*ice*) patinoire, *f;* (*roller*) skating, *m.*

rinse, *n,* rinçage, *m.* ¶ *v.t,* (*& ~ out*) rincer. *~ one's hair* (*colour*), se faire un rinçage. *~ out one's mouth,* se rincer la bouche.

riot, *n,* émeute, bagarre; (*colour*) profusion, *f.* *~ police,* forces d'intervention, *f.pl.* ¶ *v.i,* faire une émeute. *~***er,** *n,* émeutier, ère. *~***ous†,** *a,* tapageur; (*P funny*) marrant *P.*

rip, *n,* déchirure, *f.* ¶ *v.t,* fendre, déchirer. *~ cord,* poignée d'ouverture, *f.* *a ~-off P,* coup de fusil *P, m.* *~-roaring,* bruyant. *~ saw,* scie à refendre, *f.*

ripe, *a,* mûr; (*cheese*) fait. **ripen,** *v.t. & i,* mûrir; se faire. **ripeness,** *n,* maturité, *f.* **ripening,** *n,* maturation, *f.*

ripple, *n,* ride, ondulation, *f.* ¶ *v.i,* se rider, onduler.

riposte, *n,* riposte, *f.* ¶ *v.t,* riposter.

rise, *n,* (*sun, curtain*) lever, *m;* (*prices, shares*) hausse; (*wages*) augmentation; (*ground*) élévation; (*slope*) côte, pente, *f.* *give ~ to,* donner lieu à. ¶ *v.i.ir,* se lever; (*from fall*) se relever; (*from dead*) ressusciter; (*go higher*) monter, s'élever; (*wind, sun*) se lever; (*dough*) lever; (*hair; fig: hills etc*) se dresser; (*barometer*) remonter; (*fish*) mordre; (*hopes &c*) croître; (*increase*) augmenter; (*meeting*) lever la séance; (*river*) prendre sa source (dans). *~ from the ranks,* sortir du rang. *~ to the bait,* (*fig.*) mordre à l'hameçon. *~ to the occasion,* se montrer à la hauteur de la situation. *~ up,* se lever; (*rebel*) se soulever (contre). **rising,** *n,* soulèvement, *m.* ¶ *a,* levant; en hausse; croissant; (*tide*) montant; (*ground*) qui monte en pente; (*generation*) nouveau.

risk, *n,* risque, *m.* *take, run ~s,* courir des risques. *at ~,* (*child*) en danger; (*job*) menacé. *at your own ~,* à vos risques & périls. ¶ *v.t,* risquer; (*defeat &c*) courir le risque de;

(*accident*) risquer d'avoir. *I'll ~ it,* je vais tenter le coup. **~y,** *a,* risqué, hasardeux.
risotto, *n,* risotto, *m.*
rissole, *n,* croquette, *f.*
rite, *n,* rite, *m.* **ritual,** *a. & n,* rituel, *m.*
rival, *a,* rival; (*claim*) opposé. ¶ *n,* rival, e. ¶ *v.t,* rivaliser avec (*in,* de). **~ry,** *n,* rivalité, *f.*
river, *n,* rivière, *f;* (*large*) fleuve, *m.* ¶ *a,* de rivière; fluvial. *~ bank,* rive, *f. ~ bed,* lit de rivière *ou* de fleuve. *~side,* bord de l'eau, *m.*
rivet, *n,* rivet, *m.* ¶ *v.t,* river. **~ing,** (*fig.*) *a,* fascinant.
Riveria (the), (*French*) la Côte d'Azur; (*Italian*) la Riviera [italienne].
roach (*fish*) *n,* gardon, *m.*
road, *n,* (*gen.*) route, *f;* (*minor*) chemin, *m;* (*urban*) rue, *f;* (*fig.*) chemin, voie, *f. the ~ to Paris,* la route de Paris. *on the right ~,* (*lit.*) sur la bonne route; (*fig.*) sur la bonne voie. *on the ~ to ruin,* sur le chemin de la ruine. *take to the ~,* se mettre en route. ¶ *a,* routier; (*accident*) de la route. *~block,* barrage routier. *~ book,* guide routier. *~ haulage, transport,* transports routiers. *~hog,* chauffard, *m. ~house,* relais, *m. ~man,* or *~ mender,* cantonnier, *m. ~ sense,* sens de la conduite [sur route], *m. ~ show* (*Theat*), spectacle de tournée, *m. ~side,* bord de la route, *m; a,* au b. de la r. *~ sign,* panneau indicateur, *m. ~stead* (*Naut.*), rade, *f. ~ sweeper,* (*pers.*) balayeur, euse; (*vehicle*) balayeuse, *f. ~-test,* essai sur route, *m. ~way,* chaussée, *f. ~works,* travaux, *m.pl;* chantier, *m. ~worthy,* en état de marche.
roam, *v.i,* errer, rôder; (*thoughts*) vagabonder. *~ [about] the streets,* traîner dans les rues.
roan, *a. & n,* rouan, *m.*
roar, *v.i. & t,* (*lion*) rugir; (*bull, wind, sea*) mugir; (*thunder, gun &c*) gronder; (*crowd*) hurler; vrombir; (*fire*) ronfler. *~ with laughter,* rire aux éclats. ¶ *n,* rugissement, mugissement &c, *m. ~ of the crowd,* clameur de la foule.
roast, *n. & a,* rôti, *m. ~ beef,* rôti de bœuf, rosbif, *m.* ¶ *v.t. & i,* rôtir; (*coffee beans*) torréfier; (*fig: with heat*) se faire rôtir, crever [de chaleur] *P.*
rob, *v.t,* (*pers.*) voler; (*shop &c*) dévaliser. *~ s.o of sth,* voler qch à qn; (*rights &c*) priver qn de qch. **robber,** *n,* voleur, euse. **~y,** *n,* vol, *m. ~ with violence,* vol à main armée.
robe, *n,* robe, *f.* ¶ *v.i,* revêtir sa robe.
robin [redbreast], *n,* rouge-gorge, *m.*
robot, *n,* robot, *m.* ¶ *a,* robotique, automatique. **~ics,** *n,* robotique, *f.*
robust, *a,* robuste, vigoureux; (*appetite*) solide.
rock[1], *v.t,* (*child*) bercer; (*chair, boat*) balancer; (*lit., fig: shake*) secouer. ¶ *v.i,* se balancer; être ébranlé. ¶ *n,* (*music*) rock, *m. ~-&-roll,* rock [and roll], *m. off one's ~er,* cinglé *P. ~ing chair, horse,* fauteuil, cheval à bascule, *m.*
rock[2], *n,* (*gen.*) roche, *f;* (*large & ~ face*) rocher, *m. ~-bottom,* fond rocheux; (*fig.*) le plus bas possible. *~ bun, ~ cake,* rocher. *~ climbing,* escalade, varappe, *f. ~ crystal,* cristal de roche, *m. ~face,* parois rocheuse. *~ garden,* rocaille, *f. ~ plant,* plante alpestre, *f. ~ salmon,* roussette, *f. ~ salt,* sel gemme, *m.* **~ery,** *n,* [jardin *m* de] rocaille, *f.*
rocket, *n,* fusée, *f. fire a ~,* lancer une fusée. *give s.o. a ~ P,* passer un savon à qn *P.* ¶ *v.i,* (*prices*) monter en flèche. *~ base, range,* base de lancement de missiles, *f. ~ launcher,* lance-fusées, *m.inv.* **~ry,** *n,* fusées, *f.pl.*
rocky[1], *a,* branlant; chancelant.
rocky[2], *a,* rocheux; rocailleux. *R~ Mountains,* montagnes Rocheuses, *f.pl.*
rococo, *n. & a,* rococo, *m.*
rod, *n,* (*wooden*) baguette; (*curtain, stair*) tringle; (*Mach.*) tige; (*fishing*) canne à pêche; (*usher's*) verge, *f. rule with a ~ of iron,* (*state*) gouverner d'une main de fer; (*pers.*) mener à la baguette.
roe, *n,* (*soft ~*) laitance, *f. hard ~,* œufs [de poisson], *m.pl.*
roe[-deer], *n,* chevreuil, *m.*
rogue, *n,* coquin, e. *~ elephant,* éléphant solitaire, *m.* **roguish,** *a,* espiègle, coquin.
roll, *n,* (*gen.*) rouleau, *m;* (*notes*) liasse, *f;* (*fat &c*) bourrelet; (*bread*) petit pain; (*ship*) roulis; (*Aero.*) vol en tonneau; (*thunder, drum*) roulement; (*organ*) ronflement; (*list*) tableau, *m,* liste, *f;* (*court, crew &c*) rôle, *m. ~ call,* appel, *m. ~ of honour,* liste de ceux qui sont morts pour le patrie. ¶ *v.t,* (*gen.*) rouler; (*pastry*) étendre au rouleau; (*road*) cylindrer; (*metal*) laminer. ¶ *v.i,* rouler; (*horse, dog*) se rouler. *be ~ing [in money],* rouler sur l'or. *be ~ing in the aisles P,* rire à se rouler par terre. *~ in,* (*letters &c*) affluer; (*pers.*) s'amener. *~-neck(ed),* (à) col roulé. *~-on,* gaine, *f. ~ on,* (*time*) s'écouler. *~ on the holidays!* vivement les vacances! *~ over,* (se) retourner; se rouler. *~-top desk,* bureau à cylindre, *m. ~ up,* (se) rouler; (*sleeves*) retrousser. **~ed gold,** *n,* plaqué or, *m.* **roller,** *n,* (*gen., wave*) rouleau, *m;* (*wheel*) roulette, *f. ~ blind,* store, *m. ~ coaster,* montagnes russes, *f.pl. ~ skate,* patin à roulettes, *m. ~ skating,* patinage à r., *m. ~ towel,* essuie-main à rouleau, *m.*
rollicking, *a,* bruyant & joyeux.
rolling, *a,* (*country*) onduleux; (*sea*) houleux; (*ship*) qui roule. *a ~ stone gathers no moss,* pierre qui roule n'amasse pas mousse. *~ pin,* rouleau à pâtisserie, *m. ~ stock,* matériel roulant, *m.*
Roman, *a,* romain; (*nose*) aquilin. *~ candle,* chandelle romaine, *f. ~ Catholic, a. & n,*

catholique, *m,f.* ~ *Catholicism,* catholicisme, *m.* ¶ *n,* (*pers.*) Romain, e.

romance, *n,* (*Liter.*) roman; (*love story*) roman d'amour, *m;* (*Mus.*) romance; (*love affair*) idylle, *f.* ¶ *v.i,* inventer à plaisir. **R~**, *a.* & *n,* roman, *m.*

Romanesque, *a,* roman.

romantic, *a,* (*gen.*) romantique; (*adventure*) romanesque. ¶ *n,* romantique, *m,f.* **~ism,** *n,* romantisme, *m.* **~ize,** *v.t.* & *i,* romancer.

romp, *n,* jeu bruyant, *m.* ¶ *v.i,* folâtrer. ~ *home* (*horse*), arriver dans un fauteuil *P.* **~ers,** (*child's*) *n.pl,* barboteuse, *f.*

roof, *n,* (*house, car*) toit; (*cave, tunnel*) plafond, *m;* (*fig.*) voûte, *f.* ~ *of the mouth,* voûte du palais. *hit the* ~ *P,* sortir de ses gonds. ~ *light,* plafonnier, *m.* ~ *rack* (*Mot.*), galerie, *f.* ¶ *v.t,* couvrir d'un toit.

rook, *n,* freux, *m,* corneille; (*Chess*) tour, *f.* **~ery,** *n,* colonie de freux, *f.*

room, *n,* (*in house* &c) pièce; (*large*) salle; (*bed~*) chambre; (*space*) place, *f, there's no* ~, il n'y a pas de place. ~ *divider,* meuble de séparation, *m.* ~*mate,* camarade de chambre, *m,f.* ~ *service,* service des chambres, *m. at* ~ *temperature* (*wine*), chambré. **~ful,** *n,* pleine salle. **~y,** *a,* spacieux; (*garment*) ample.

roost, *n,* juchoir, perchoir, *m.* ¶ *v.i,* [se] jucher, percher. **~er,** *n,* coq, *m.*

root, *n,* racine; (*fig: trouble* &c) cause, *f. pull up by the* ~*s,* déraciner. ~ *cause,* cause première. ~ *crops,* racines alimentaires. ~ *word* (*Gram.*), mot racine, *m.* ¶ *v.t,* enraciner. ¶ *v.i,* (*plants* &c) s'enraciner; (*pigs*) fouiller. ~ *out* (*fig.*), extirper.

rope, *n,* corde, *f;* (*Naut.*) cordage; (*bell*) cordon, *m. give s.o more* ~, lâcher la bride à qn. *know the* ~*s,* connaître les ficelles du métier. ~ *ladder,* échelle de corde, *f.* ¶ *v.t,* corder, (*climbers*) encorder. ~ *in,* (*fig.*) enrôler, embringuer *P.* ~ *off,* réserver par une corde. **ropey** *P, a,* pas fameux *P.*

rosary, *n,* rosaire, *m;* (*rose garden*) roseraie, *f.*

rose, *n,* rose, *f;* (~*bush*) rosier; (*colour*) rose, *m;* (*ceiling*) rosace; (*can*) pomme, *f. wild* ~, églantine, *f.* ~*bed,* massif de rosiers, *m.* ~ *bud,* bouton de rose, *m. see life through* ~-*coloured spectacles,* voir la vie en rose. ~ *grower,* rosiériste, *m.* ~-*hip,* gratte-cul, *m.* ~ *tree,* rosier, *m.* ~ *water,* eau de rose, *f.* ~ *window,* rose, rosace, *f.* ~*wood,* bois de rose, *m.* **rosé,** *n,* rosé, *m.* **rosemary,** *n,* romarin, *m.* **rosette,** *n,* rosette; (*Sport* &c) cocarde; (*Arch.*) rosace, *f.*

rosin, *n,* (*for violin*) colophane, *f.*

rostrum, *n,* tribune, *f.*

rosy, *a,* [de] rose, rosé.

rot, *n,* pourriture; (*Med., Bot.*) carie, *f;* (*P rubbish*) foutaises, *f.pl. stop the* ~, redresser la situation. ¶ *v.i.* (& *t*), (faire) pourrir. ~ *away,* tomber en pourriture.

rota, *n,* tableau, *m.* **rotary,** *a,* rotatif. **rotate,** *v.t,* (*turn round*) faire tourner; (*crops*) alterner. ¶ *v.i,* tourner, être alterné. **rotating,** *a,* tournant. **rotation,** *n,* rotation, *f;* (*crops*) assolement, *m. in* ~, à tour de rôle. **rotor,** *n,* rotor, *m.*

rotten, *a,* pourri; (*tooth*) gâté; (*fig: corrupt*) véreux; (*P bad*) moche *P. a* ~ *trick,* un sale tour *P. feel* ~, se sentir mal fichu *P.*

rotund, *a,* rond, arrondi; (*pers.*) rondelet.

rouge, *n,* rouge [à joues], *m.*

rough, *a,* (*to touch, manners, voice*) rude; (*cloth, ground, skin*) rugueux; (*ground*) accidenté, raboteux; (*skin, wine*) rêche; (*taste*) âpre; (*pers. play*) brutal; (*weather* &c) mauvais; (*sea*) agité; (*calculation*) approximatif; (*justice*) sommaire. *give s.o a* ~ *time,* malmener qn. *have a* ~ *time of it,* en baver *P.* ~-&-*ready,* rudimentaire; (*work*) grossier. ~ & *tumble,* mêlée, *f.* ~ *estimate,* approximation, *f.* ~*neck P,* dur à cuire *P, m. ride* ~*shod over,* fouler aux pieds. ~ *sketch,* croquis, *m,* ébauche, *f.* ~ *work, copy, draft,* brouillon, *m.* ¶ *ad,* (*live, sleep*) à la dure; (*play*) brutalement. ¶ *n,* (*Golf*) rough, *m;* (*P pers.*) dur *P, m.* ¶ *v.t,* ~ *it P,* vivre à la dure. ~-*hew,* ~ *out,* ébaucher, dégrossir. **~ly,** *ad,* rudement; brutalement; (*answer, order*) brusquement; (*make, sew*) grossièrement; approximativement, en gros, à peu près. **~ness,** *n,* rugosité; rudesse, brusquerie; brutalité; (*sea*) agitation, *f;* (*road*) inégalités, *f.pl.*

Roumania, *n,* la Roumanie. **Roumanian,** *a,* roumain. ¶ *n,* (*pers.*) Roumain, e; (*language*) le roumain.

round, *a,* rond. ~ *robin,* pétition, *f.* ~ *shoulders,* le dos vouté. ~ *trip,* voyage aller & retour, *m.* ¶ *n,* rond, cercle, *m;* (*slice*) tranche, *f;* (*tour: oft.pl. watchman* &c) ronde; (*postman* &c) tournée, *f;* (*doctor*) visites, *f.pl;* (*applause*) salve; (*Pol., Sport*) manche; (*Cards, Golf*) partie, *f;* (*Box.*) round; (*showring*) parcours, *m;* (*talks*) série, *f;* (*Mus.*) canon, *m.* ~ *of ammunition,* cartouche, *f.* ~ *of drinks,* tournée, *f.* ¶ *ad,* autour. ~ *about,* environ. *a long way* ~, un grand détour. ¶ *pr,* autour de. ¶ *v.t,* arrondir; (*corner*) tourner; (*bend*) prendre; (*cape*) doubler. ~ *off,* terminer; mettre fin à. ~ *up,* rassembler; (*criminals*) effectuer une rafle de. **roundabout,** *a,* (*route*) détourné; (*means*) contourné. ¶ *n,* (*fairground*) manège; (*Mot.*) rond-point [à sens giratoire], *m.* **roundly,** *ad,* rondement. **roundness,** *n,* rondeur, *f.* **roundsman,** *n,* livreur, *m.* **round-up,** *n,* rassemblement, *m;* rafle, *f.*

rouse, *v.t,* éveiller; (*feelings*) exciter, soulever; (*interest* &c) susciter. ~ *s.o* [*to anger*], mettre

qn en colère.
rout, *n,* déroute, *f.* ¶ *v.t,* mettre en déroute.
route, *n,* itinéraire, *m;* (*pl. shipping, air*) routes, *f.pl;* (*bus*) ligne, *f. on* ~, en route (*for,* pour). ~ *march* (*Mil.*), marche d'entraînement, *f.* ¶ *v.t,* faire passer (par).
routine, *n,* routine, *f;* (*office*) travail courant; (*Theat.*) numéro, *m. daily* ~, train-train journalier, *m.* ¶ *a,* d'usage; ordinaire.
rove, *v.i,* errer. **rover,** *n,* vagabond, e. **roving,** *a,* vagabond; (*ambassador*) itinérant; (*reporter*) volant. *have a* ~ *eye,* aimer reluquer les filles *P.*
row[1] (rou), *n,* (*gen., Knit.*) rang, *m;* (*trees &c*) rangée; (*file*) file, ligne; (*cars*) file, *f. in a* ~, (*events*) de suite.
row[2], *v.i,* ramer; (*Sport*) faire de l'aviron. ¶ *v.t,* faire aller à la rame. ~[*ing*] *boat,* canot [à rames], *m.*
row (rau), *n,* (*noise*) vacarme, tapage, *m;* (*quarrel*) querelle, dispute; (*scold*) engueulade *P, f. have a* ~, se disputer, s'engueuler *P* (avec). ¶ *v.i,* se disputer (avec).
rowan, *n,* sorbier, *m.* ~ *berry,* sorbe, *f.*
rowdy, *a,* (*noisy*) chahuteur; (*rough*) bagarreur *P.* ¶ *n,* voyou, *m.* **rowdiness,** *n,* tapage, *m;* bagarre *P, f.*
rower, *n,* rameur, euse; (*Nav.*) nageur, *m.* **rowing,** *n,* canotage; (*Sport*) aviron, *m;* nage, *f.* ~ *club,* cercle *ou* club d'aviron, *m.* **rowlock,** *n,* dame de nage, *f.*
royal†, *a,* royal. ~ *blue,* bleu roi, *inv. His, Your, R*~ *Highness,* son, votre, altesse royale. ~**ist,** *n. & a,* royaliste, *m,f.* ~**ty,** *n,* royauté, *f;* (*author's*) droit d'auteur, *m.*
rub, *n,* (*with cloth*) coup de chiffon, *m. give sth a* ~, frotter qch. *there's the* ~, c'est là le hic *P.* ¶ *v.t,* frotter. ~ *one's hands together,* se frotter les mains. ~ *shoulders with,* coudoyer. ~ **along,** s'accorder tant bien que mal. ~ **away,** effacer. ~ **down,** (*horse*) bouchonner; (*pers.*) frictionner. ~ **in,** faire pénétrer [en frottant]. (*fig.*) *don't* ~ *it in!* n'insistez pas davantage. ~ **off,** (*writing*) effacer; (*dirt*) enlever en frottant. ~ **out,** effacer. ~ **up,** frotter, astiquer. ~ *s.o up the wrong way,* prendre qn à rebrousse-poil. **rubber**[1], *n,* (*material*) caoutchouc, *m;* (*eraser*) gomme, *f.* ¶ *a,* de *ou* en caoutchouc. ~ *band,* élastique, *m.* ~ *ring,* bouée de natation, *f.* ~ *solution,* dissolution, *f.* ~ *stamp,* tampon, *m.* ~ *tree,* hévéa, *m.*
rubber[2] (*Cards*), *n,* robre, *m.*
rubberized, *a,* caoutchouté. **rubbery,** *a,* caoutchouteux. **rubbing,** *n,* frottement; (*Art*) frottis, *m.*
rubbish, *n,* (*gen., garden*) détritus, *m;* (*household*) ordures, *f.pl;* (*trash*) camelote *P, f;* (*nonsense*) bêtises, foutaises *P, f.pl. what* ~! quelle blague! ~ *bin,* poubelle, boîte à ordures, *f.* ~ *dump,* (*public*) dépotoir, *m.*
rubble, *n,* (*Build.*) blocaille, *f;* (*débris*) décombres, *m.pl.*
rubicund, *a,* rougeaud.
ruby, *n,* rubis, *m.* ¶ (*lips*) *a,* vermeille.
ruck, *n,* faux pli, godet, *m.*
rucksack, *n,* sac à dos, *m.*
rudder, *n,* gouvernail, *m.*
ruddy, *a,* (*complexion*) coloré; (*sky*) rougeoyant; (*P*) fichu *P,* sacré *P* (*before n.*).
rude†, *a,* grossier, mal élevé, impoli; (*improper*) indécent; (*shock &c*) brusque, rude; (*primitive*) primitif; (*health*) robuste. ~ *word,* gros mot. ~**ness,** *n,* impolitesse; insolence; grossièreté; brusquerie, *f.*
rudiment, *n,* rudiment, *m;* (*pl.*) bas éléments, *m.pl.* ~**ary,** *a,* rudimentaire.
rue[1], (*Bot.*) *n,* rue, *f.*
rue[2], *v.t,* se repentir de. ~**ful†,** *a,* triste.
ruffian, *n,* voyou, *m,* brute, *f.*
ruffle, *v.t,* (*hair &c*) ébouriffer; (*water*) rider; (*clothes, fig.*) froisser; (*disturb*) troubler.
rug, *n,* petit tapis; carpette; (*bedside*) descente de lit; (*travelling*) couverture, *f;* (*tartan*) plaid, *m.*
rugby [football], *n,* rugby, *m.* ~ *league,* rugby à treize. ~ *player,* rugbyman, *m.* ~ *union,* rugby à quinze.
rugged, *a,* (*features*) irrégulier; (*ground*) rugueux, accidenté; (*style*) raboteux; (*life*) rude.
ruin, *n,* ruine, *f. in* ~*s,* en ruine. ¶ *v.t,* ruiner; (*clothes*) abîmer; (*health &c*) gâter. ~**ous,** *a,* ruineux.
rule, *n,* (*gen., Gram.*) règle, *f;* (*regulation*) règlement, *m;* (*pl.*) règle; (*Pol.*) autorité, *f,* gouvernement, *m. as a* ~, en règle générale, normalement. *by* ~ *of thumb,* à vue de nez. ~ *of the road,* règle générale de la circulation. *work to* ~, grève du zèle, *f.* ¶ *v.t,* (*country*) gouverner; (*umpire &c*) décider; déclarer (que); (*paper*) régler; (*line*) tirer à la règle. ¶ *v.i,* (*monarch*) régner (*over,* sur); (*Law*) statuer (*on,* sur). ~ *out,* exclure. **ruler,** *n,* chef [d'État], *m;* souverain, e; (*for lines*) règle, *f.* **ruling,** *a,* (*passion*) dominant; (*principle*) souverain; (*price*) actuel; (*class*) dirigeant; (*Pol: party*) au pouvoir. ¶ *n,* decision, *f.*
rum, *n,* rhum, *m.*
Rumania, *&c.* Same as *Roumania,* &c.
rumble, *v.i,* gronder; (*bowels*) gargouiller. ¶ *n.* & ~**ing,** grondement; gargouillement, *m.*
ruminate, *v.i. & t,* ruminer.
rummage, *v.i,* fouiller (*in, among,* dans). ~ *sale,* vente de charité, *f.*
rumour, *n,* rumeur, *f,* bruit, *m. it is* ~*ed that,* le bruit court que.
rump, *n,* (*animal*) croupe; (*beef*) culotte, *f;* (*pers.*) derrière, *m.* ~ *steak,* rumsteck, *m.*
rumple, *v.t,* chiffonner; (*hair*) ébouriffer.

run, *n,* (*action*) course; (*outing*) promenade *f,* tour; (*bus &c: route*) parcours; (*distance*) trajet, *m;* (*Com: demand*) ruée (*on,* sur); (*ski*) piste, *f;* (*animal pen*) enclos, *m;* (*series*) série, suite; (*Cards*) séquence, *f;* (*Typ.*) tirage, *m. at a ~,* au pas de course. *go for a ~,* faire un peu de course à pied. *have a long ~,* durer longtemps. *in the long ~,* à la longue. *make a ~ for it,* se sauver, filer. *on the ~,* en fuite, en cavale *P.* **~-up,** période préparatoire (à), *f.* **~way,** piste. ¶ *v.i,* courir; (*flee*) fuir, se sauver; (*rope*) filer; (*drawer &c*) glisser; (*river, tears*) couler; (*pen*) fuir; (*sore &c*) suppurer; (*ink, colour*) baver; (*in wash*) détendre; (*play*) tenir l'affiche, se jouer; (*road, film*) passer; (*hills*) s'étendre; (*stocking*) filer; (*Knit.*) démailler; (*Mach. &c*) marcher; (*wheel*) tourner. *~ in, out &c,* entrer, partir &c en courant. ¶ *v.t,* (*gen., risks*) courir; (*business &c*) diriger; (*course &c*) organiser; (*fingers, comb &c*) passer (*over,* sur; *through,* dans); (*article*) publier; (*film*) présenter. *~ aground,* s'échouer. ~ **away,** partir en courant; (*flee: pers.*) s'enfuir; (*horse*) s'emballer; (*water*) s'écouler. ~ **down,** (*battery*) se décharger; (*watch &c*) s'arrêter; (*v.t.*) (*knock over*) renverser; (*~ over*) écraser; (*production*) restreindre de plus en plus; (*disparage*) dénigrer. *be ~ down,* (*Med.*) être fatigué. ~ **dry,** (*river*) se tarir; (*resources &c*) s'épuiser. ~ **errands,** faire des commissions. ~ **in,** (*car*) roder; (*arrest*) emmener au poste. *~ning in,* en rodage. ~ **into,** ~ **up against,** (*pers.*) tomber sur; (*problems*) se heurter à. ~ **off** (*Typ.*), tirer. ~ **out,** (*supplies*) s'épuiser; (*time*) s'écouler. ~ **out of,** manquer de. ~ **over,** (*Mot.*) écraser; (*reread*) revoir; (*details &c*) reprendre. ~ **riot,** (*pers., imagination*) être déchaîné. ~ **through,** (*notes &c*) jeter un coup d'œil sur, parcourir. ~ **to earth,** finir par trouver. ~ **up,** (*flag*) hisser; (*bill*) laisser accumuler; (*sew*) fabriquer. ~ **wild,** être déchaîné; (*animals*) courir en liberté. **runabout,** *n,* (*car*) petite voiture; (*boat*) runabout, *m.* **runaway,** *a,* (*pers.*) fugitif; (*horse*) emballé; (*car*) fou; (*inflation*) galopant. ¶ *n,* fugitif, ive.

rung, *n,* barreau; (*on scale*) échelon, *m.*

runner, *n,* (*pers.*) coureur; (*horse*) partant; (*messenger*) messager; (*sledge*) patin; (*drawer*) coulisseau; (*carpet & table ~*) chemin [de table]; (*Bot., Hort.*) stolon, *m. ~ bean,* haricot à rames, *m. ~-up,* (*Sport &c*) second, e. **running,** *n,* course; marche, direction, *f. be in the ~,* avoir des chances de réussir. ¶ *a,* courant; coulant; de suite. *~ board,* marchepied, *m. ~ commentary,* (*Radio, TV*) commentaire suivi; (*fig.*) c. détaillé (sur). *~ costs,* frais d'exploitation, *m.pl. ~ jump,* saut avec élan, *m. ~ stitch,* point de devant, *m. ~ water,* eau courante.

runt, *n,* avorton, *m.*

rupee, *n,* roupie, *f.*

rupture, *n,* rupture; (*Med.*) hernie, *f.* ¶ *v.t,* rompre. *to be ~d,* avoir une hernie.

rural, *a,* rural; (*scene &c*) de la campagne.

ruse, *n,* ruse, *f.*

rush[1], *n,* ruée (*for,* vers); bousculade; (*hurry*) hâte, *f. be in a ~,* être extrêmement pressé. *~ hours,* heures de pointe, *f.pl. ~ job,* travail d'urgence. ¶ *v.i,* (*pers.*) se précipiter; (*car*) foncer. *~ at,* se ruer sur. ¶ *v.t,* (*job*) dépêcher; (*order & through*) executer d'urgence. *~ s.o to hospital,* transporter qn d'urgence à l'hôpital. *~ed off one's feet,* débordé. *~ about, around,* courir ça & là.

rush[2] (*Bot.*), *n,* jonc, *m. ~ matting,* tapis tressé, *m.*

rusk, *n,* biscotte, *f.*

russet, *a,* feuille-morte, *inv.* ¶ *n,* (*apple*) reinette grise, *f.*

Russia, *n,* la Russie. **Russian,** *a,* russe. ¶ *n,* (*pers.*) Russe, *m,f;* (*language*) le russe.

rust, *n,* rouille, *f.* ¶ *v.t,* rouiller; (*v.i.*) se r. *~-coloured,* rouille, *inv. ~proof, ~ resistant,* inoxydable.

rustic, *a,* rustique.

rustle, *n,* bruissement, *m.* ¶ *v.i,* bruire; (*dress*) faire froufrou. ¶ *v.t,* faire bruire; (*cattle &c*) voler. *~ up,* (*make*) préparer en vitesse; (*find*) dénicher. **~r,** *n,* voleur de bétail, *m.*

rusty, *a,* rouillé.

rut, *n,* ornière, *f;* (*of animals*) rut, *m.*

ruthless†, *a,* impitoyable.

rye, *n,* seigle, *m. ~ grass,* ray-grass, *m.*

S

sabbath, *n,* sabbat; dimanche, *m.*

sable, *n,* (*Zool.*) zibeline, martre; (*fur*) zibeline, *f;* (*Her.*) sable, *m.*

sabotage, *n,* (*& act of ~*) sabotage, *m.* ¶ *v.t,* saboter. **saboteur,** *n,* saboteur, euse.

sabre, *n,* sabre, *m.*

saccharin[e], *n,* saccharine, *f.*
sachet, *n,* sachet, *m.*
sack[1], *n,* sac, *m. give s.o the* ~ (*fig.*), renvoyer qn, flanquer qn à la porte *P.* ~*cloth, sacking,* toile à sacs, *f.* ~*cloth & ashes,* le sac & la cendre. ~ *race,* course en sacs, *f.* ¶ *v.t,* renvoyer &c. ~**ful,** *n,* plein sac.
sack[2] (*plunder &c*) *v.t,* mettre à sac. ¶ *n,* & ~**ing,** sac, *m.*
sacrament, *n,* sacrement, *m,* communion, *f.* ~**al,** *a. & n,* sacramental, *m.* **sacred,** *a,* sacré; saint; inviolable; (*song &c*) religieux, spirituel; (*to the memory of*) consacré. **sacrifice,** *n,* sacrifice, *m.* ¶ *v.t. & i,* sacrifier. **sacrificial,** *a,* sacrificiel. **sacrilege,** *n.* & **sacrilegious,** *a,* sacrilège, *m.* **sacristy,** *n,* sacristie, *f.* **sacrosanct,** *a,* sacro-saint.
sad, *a,* triste; (*loss*) douloureux; (*mistake*) fâcheux. **sadden,** *v.t,* attrister.
saddle, *n,* selle, *f;* (*mountain*) col, *m.* ~*-backed,* ensellé. ~ *bag,* sacoche, *f.* ¶ *v.t,* seller; (*pack* ~) bâter; (*fig.*) coller *P* (*s.o with sth,* qch à qn.). **saddler,** *n,* sellier, *m.* **saddlery,** *n,* sellerie, *f.*
sadism, *n,* sadisme, *m.* **sadist,** *n,* & ~**ic,** *a,* sadique, *m,f.*
sadly, *ad,* (*unhappily*) tristement; (*regrettably*) fâcheusement. **sadness,** *n,* tristesse, *f.*
safari, *n,* safari, *m.* ~ *park,* réserve, *f.*
safe, *a,* hors de danger, en sécurité; (*not dangerous*) sans danger; (*method*) sûr; (*ice, ladder*) solide; (*choice*) prudent. ~ *journey!* bon voyage! ~ *& sound,* sain & sauf. *better* ~ *than sorry!* mieux vaux être prudent! ~ *conduct,* sauf-conduit, *m. feel* ~, se sentir en sécurité. ~ *from,* à l'abri de. ~ *keeping,* sécurité, *f. the* ~ *period* (*Med.*), la période sans danger. *to be on the* ~ *side,* par précaution. ¶ *n,* coffre-fort, *m.* ~ *breaker,* ~ *cracker,* perceur de coffre-fort, *m.* ~ *deposit,* dépôt de coffre-forts, *m.* ~ *guard,* sauvegarde, garantie, *f; v.t,* sauvegarder. ~**ly,** *ad,* en sûreté; sûrement; sans danger; sans accident; (*arrive*) bien. ~**ty,** *n,* sûreté; sécurité, *f;* salut, *m.* ~ *belt,* ceinture de sécurité, *f.* ~ *catch,* cran de sûreté, *m.* ~ *curtain,* rideau de fer, *m.* ~ *first,* sécurité d'abord. ~ *match,* allumette de sûreté, *f.* ~ *measure,* mesure de sécurité, *f.* ~ *pin,* épingle de sûreté, é. de nourrice, *f.* ~ *razor,* rasoir de sûreté, *m.* ~ *valve* (*lit., fig.*), soupape de sûreté, *f.*
saffron, *n,* safran, *m.*
sag, *v.i,* (*roof, chair*) s'affaisser; (*board, beam*) fléchir; (*breasts*) pendre; (*rope*) être détendu.
sagacious, *a,* sagace. **sagacity,** *n,* sagacité, *f.*
sage[1], *n,* (*herb*) sauge, *f.*
sage[2], *a. & n,* sage, *m.*
sago, *n,* sagou, *m.*
Sahara, *n,* Sahara, *m.*
said (the) (*Law*) *a,* ledit, ladite &c.
sail, *n,* (*boat*) voile; (*windmill*) aile, *f. go for a* ~, faire une promenade en bateau. *set* ~, prendre la mer. *set* ~ *for,* partir (*pers.*) pour; (*boat*) à destination de. *under* ~, à la voile. *under full* ~, toutes voiles dehors. ~*board,* planche à voile, *f.* ~*cloth,* toile à voile, *f.* ~ *maker,* voilier, *m.* ¶ *v.i,* faire voile (*towards,* vers); naviguer. *go* ~*ing,* faire de la v.; (*fig.*) glisser; (*boat*) partir. ~ *away, back &c,* partir, revenir en bateau. ~ *into harbour,* entrer au port. ~ *close to the wind* (*fig.*), jouer un jeu dangereux. ¶ *v.t,* (*seas*) parcourir; (*boat*) piloter. ~ *through,* réussir haut la main. ~**ing,** *n,* navigation [à voile], *f;* (*departure*) départ, *m.* ~ *boat,* ~ *ship,* voilier, *m.* ~ *dinghy,* dériveur, *m.* ~**or,** *n,* marin, matelot, *m. be a good, bad* ~, avoir, ne pas avoir le pied marin. ~ *suit,* costume marin.
saint, *n,* saint, e. ~*'s day,* fête, *f. All S*~*s' Day,* la Toussaint. *St Bernard* [*dog*], saint-bernard, *m.inv. Saint Helena,* Sainte-Hélène, *f. St-John's-wort,* mille-pertuis, *m. Saint Lawrence,* Saint-Laurent, *m. St. Vitus's dance,* danse de Saint-Guy, *f.* **saintliness,** *n,* sainteté, *f.* **saintly,** *a,* [de] saint.
sake, *n, for the* ~ *of s.o,* pour l'amour de qn. *for my, his &c* ~, pour moi, lui &c. *for old times'* ~, en souvenir du passé. *for your own* ~, pour ton bien. *for argument's* ~, à titre d'exemple.
salad, *n,* salade, *f.* ~ *bowl,* saladier, *m.* ~ *dressing,* vinaigrette, *f.* ~ *oil,* huile de table, *f.* ~ *servers,* couvert à salade, *m.*
salary, *n,* appointements, *m.pl,* traitement, *m.* ~ *bracket, scale,* fourchette, échelle des traitements, *f. salaried staff,* employés qui touchent un traitement.
sale, *n,* vente, *f;* (*Com: oft. pl.*) soldes, *m.pl.* ~ *by auction,* vente aux enchères. *'for* ~*',* 'à vendre'. *in a* ~, en solde. *on* ~, en vente. *put in the* ~, solder. *put up for* ~, mettre en vente. ~ *of work,* vente de charité. ~ *price,* prix de solde. ~*room,* salle des ventes, *f.* ~*s talk,* boniment, *m.* ~**able,** *a,* vendable. **salesman,** *n,* vendeur; représentant de commerce, *m.* ~*ship,* art de la vente, *m.* **saleswoman,** *n,* vendeuse, *f.*
salient, *a. & n,* saillant, *m.*
saliva, *n,* salive, *f.* **salivate,** *v.i,* saliver.
sallow, *a,* jaunâtre.
sally, *n,* (*Mil.*) sortie; (*wit*) saillie, boutade, *f.* ~ *forth,* sortir; se mettre en route.
salmon, *n,* saumon, *m.* ~ *pink,* rose saumon, *m.* ~ *trout,* truite saumonée, *f.*
salon, *n,* salon, *m.*
saloon, *n,* salle, *f,* salon, *m;* (*Naut.*) salon; (*Am: bar*) bar, *m;* (*car*) conduite intérieure, *f.*
salsify, *n,* salsifis, *m.*
salt, *n,* sel, *m. rub* ~ *in the wound* (*fig.*),

retourner le couteau dans la plaie. *take sth with a pinch of* ~ (*fig.*), ne pas prendre qch au pied de la lettre. *the* ~ *of the earth* (*fig.*), le sel de la terre. ~ *cellar*, salière, *f.* ~ *lake*, lac salé. ~ *marsh*, salin, *m.* ~ *spoon*, cuiller à sel, *f.* ~*water* (*fish &c*), de mer. ¶ *v.t*, saler. ~**iness,** *n*, (*water*) salinité, *f;* (*food*) goût salé. ~**ing,** *n*, salaison, *f.* **saltpetre,** *n*, salpêtre, *m.* **salty,** *a*, salé.

salubrious, *a*, salubre.

salutary†, *a*, salutaire. **salutation,** *n*, salutation, *f*, salut, *m.* **salute,** *n*, salut; (*guns*) salut, *m*, salve, *f.* ¶ *v.t*, saluer.

salvage, *n*, (*ship &c*) sauvetage, *m;* (*payment*) prime de s., *f;* (*for re-use*) récupération, *f;* (*things saved*) objets *ou* biens sauvés. ¶ *a*, (*operation &c*) de sauvetage. ¶ *v.t*, sauver (de); récupérer. **salvation,** *n*, salut, *m.* *S*~ *Army*, Armée du Salut, *f.* ~**ist,** *n*, salutiste, *m,f.* **salve,** *n*, baume, *m.* ¶ (*fig.*) *v.t*, calmer.

salver, *n*, plateau, *m.*

salvo, *n*, salve, *f.*

Samaritan, *n*, Samaritain, e. *the Good* ~, le bon Samaritain. *the* ~*s*, ≏ S.O.S. Amitié.

same, *a*, *& pn*, même, *m,f;* (*Law*) susdit, e. *all, just the* ~, tout de même, quand m. *at the* ~ *time*, en m. temps. ~ *here! P* moi aussi! *in the* ~ *way* .... de même .... *it's all the* ~ *to me*, ça m'est égal. ~**ness,** *n*, monotonie, *f.*

sample, *n*, (*gen. & Med: urine*) échantillon; (*blood, tissue*) prélèvement; (*poetry &c*) exemple, *m.*

sanatorium, *n*, sanatorium, *m;* (*Sch.*) infirmerie, *f.*

sanctify, *v.t*, sanctifier. **sanctimonious,** *a*, moralisateur. **sanction,** *n*, (*both senses*) sanction, *f.* ¶ *v.t*, sanctionner, approuver. **sanctity,** *n*, (*pers.*) sainteté; (*marriage*) inviolabilité, *f;* (*oath, place*) caractère sacré. **sanctuary,** *n*, sanctuaire; (*refuge*) asile, *m;* (*wild life*) réserve, *f.* **sanctum,** *n*, le saint des saints; sanctuaire, *m.*

sand, *n*, sable, *m;* (*pl.*) plage, *f.* ~ *bag*, sac à terre, *m.* ~ *bank*, banc de sable, *m.* ~ *blast*, jet de sable, *m.* ~ *box &* ~ *pit* (*children*), tas de sable, *m.* ~ *castle*, château de sable, *m.* ~ *dune*, dune [de sable], *f.* ~ *martin*, hirondelle de rivage, *f.* ~ *paper*, *n*, papier de verre, *m; v.t*, poncer. ~*piper*, bécasseau, *m.* ~ *pit*, sablonnière, *f.* ~*stone*, grès, *m.* ~ *storm*, tempête de sable, *f.* ¶ *v.t*, sabler. ~ [*up*], ensabler.

sandal, *n*, sandale, *f.*

sandwich, *n*, sandwich, *m. ham* ~, sandwich au jambon. *open* ~, canapé, *m.* ~ *loaf*, pain de mie, *m.* ~ *man*, homme-sandwich, *m.* ~ [*in*], (*visit*) intercaler. ~*ed* [*between*], pris en sandwich [entre].

sandy, *a*, (*soil*) sablonneux; (*water*) sableux; (*beach*) de sable; (*colour*) sable, *inv;* (*hair*) blond roux, *inv.*

sane, *a*, (*pers.*) sain d'esprit; (*views*) sain.

sanguinary, *a*, sanglant. **sanguine,** *a*, optimiste; plein d'espérance; (*complexion*) sanguin.

sanitary, *a*, sanitaire; hygiénique. ~ *engineer*, ingénieur sanitaire, *m.* ~ *inspector*, inspecteur, trice de la Santé publique. ~ *towel*, serviette hygiénique, *f.* **sanitation,** *n*, système sanitaire, *m;* installations sanitaires, *f.pl.*

sanity, *n*, (*pers.*) santé mentale; bon sens.

Santa Claus, *n*, le père Noël.

sap[1] *n*, (*Bot.*) sève, *f.*

sap[2] *v.t*, (*strength &c*) saper.

sapling, *n*, jeune arbre, *m.*

sapper, *n*, sapeur, *m. the S*~*s* (*Mil.*), le génie.

sapphire, *n*, saphir, *m.*

sarcasm, *n*, sarcasme, *m.* **sarcastic,** *a*, sarcastique.

sarcophagus, *n*, sarcophage, *m.*

sardine, *n*, sardine, *f.*

Sardinia, *n*, la Sardaigne. **Sardinian,** *a*, sarde. ¶ *n*, Sarde, *m,f.*

sardonic, *a*, sardonique.

Sark, *n*, Sercq, *m.*

sartorial, *a*, vestimentaire; (*art*) du tailleur.

sash[1], *n*, écharpe; ceinture à nœud, *f.*

sash[2], *n*, châssis à guillotine, *m.* ~ *cord*, corde, *f.* ~ *window*, fenêtre à guillotine, *f.*

Satan, *n*, Satan, *m.* ~**ic,** *a*, satanique.

satchel, *n*, cartable, *m.*

satellite, *n. & a*, satellite, *m.*

satiate, *v.t*, rassasier (*with*, de). **satiation,** *n*, rassasiement, *m. to* ~ [*point*], à satiété. **satiety,** *n*, satiété, *f.*

satin, *n*, satin, *m.* ~ *stitch* (*Emb.*), plumetis, *m.* ~ *wood*, bois satiné de l'Inde. ¶ *a*, (*dress*) de *ou* en satin; (*paper*) satiné.

satire, *n*, satire, *f.* **satiric** & ~**al,** *a*, satirique. **satirist,** *n*, écrivain satirique, *m.* **satirize,** *v.t*, satiriser, faire la satire de.

satisfaction, *n*, satisfaction, *f.* **satisfactorily,** *ad*, d'une manière satisfaisante. **satisfactory,** *a*, satisfaisant. **satisfy,** *v.t*, (*pers.*) satisfaire, contenter; (*need, hunger &c*) satisfaire; (*condition*) satisfaire à; convaincre, assurer (de qch, que). ~**ing,** *a*, satisfaisant.

saturate, *v.t*, saturer (*with*, de). **saturation,** *n*, saturation, *f. reach* ~ *point*, arriver à saturation.

Saturday, *n*, samedi, *m. on* ~, samedi. *on* ~*s*, le samedi. *next, last* ~, samedi prochain, dernier. *every* ~, tous les samedis, chaque s.

Saturn, *n*, (*Myth.*) Saturne, *m;* (*Astr.*) Saturne, *f.*

saturnine, *a*, sombre, mélancolique.

sauce, *n*, sauce; (*cheek*) impertinence, *f;* toupet *P*, *m.* ~ *boat*, saucière, *f.* ~*pan*, casserole, *f.* **saucer,** *n*, soucoupe, *f.* **saucy,** *a*, impertinent; culotté *P.*

Saudi Arabia, *n*, Arabie Séoudite, *f.*

sauerkraut, *n,* choucroute, *f.*
sauna *&* ~ **bath,** *n,* sauna, *m, or f.*
saunter, *v.i,* flâner.
sausage, *n,* (*fresh*) saucisse, *f;* (*smoked &c*) saucisson, *m.* ~ *meat,* chair à saucisse, *f.*
sauté potatoes, *n.pl,* pommes [de terre] sautées, *f.pl.*
savage†, *a,* sauvage; féroce; (*pers.*) brutal. ¶ *n,* sauvage, *m,f.* ¶ *v.t,* (*dog &c*) attaquer férocement. ~**ry,** *n,* férocité; brutalité, *f.*
save¹, *v.t,* sauver; (*money &c*) économiser, épargner; (~ *up*) mettre de côté; (*food, paper*) garder; (*time*) gagner. ~ *a goal* (*Sport*), sauver un but. ~ *face,* sauver la face. *God* ~ *the Queen!* vive la reine! ~ *one's bacon, one's skin.* sauver sa peau. ~ *one's strength.* ~ *o.s,* ménager ses forces. ¶ *v.i,* économiser (*on,* sur). ~ [*up*], faire des économies.
save², *pr,* sauf. **saving,** *n,* (*time, money &c*) économie; (*Econ.*) épargne, *f.* ~*s bank,* caisse d'épargne, *f.* ~*s stamp,* timbre-épargne, *m.*
saviour, *n,* sauveur, *m.* (*Rel.*) *the S*~, le Sauveur.
savory (*Bot.*) *n,* sarriette, *f.* **savour,** *n,* saveur, *f.* ¶ *v.t,* savourer. ~ *of sth,* sentir qch. **savoury,** *a,* savoureux; (*opp. sweet*) salé. *not very* ~, (*subject*) peu appétissant; (*area*) peu recommandable. ¶ *n,* mets non sucré, *m;* (*on toast*) canapé chaud.
Savoy, *n,* la Savoie. *s*~ *cabbage,* chou de Milan, *m.*
saw, *n,* scie, *f.* ~*dust,* sciure, *f.* ~*-edged knife,* couteau-scie, *m.* ~*mill,* scierie, *f.* ¶ *v.t.ir,* scier. ~ *off,* enlever à la scie. ~ *up,* débiter à la scie.
saxifrage, *n,* saxifrage, *f.*
Saxon, *a,* saxon. ¶ *n,* Saxon, ne. **Saxony,** *n,* la Saxe.
saxophone, *n,* saxophone, *m.*
say, *n,* mot, *m;* voix, *f. have a* ~ *in the matter,* avoir voix au chapitre. *have one's* ~, dire son mot. ¶ *v.t. & i,* (*gen.*) dire; (*poem &c*) réciter; (*dial &c*) marquer. ~, (*so much*), disons. ~ *after me,* répéter après moi. *I* ~*!* dites donc! *to* ~ *nothing of,* sans parler de. *you don't* ~*!* pas possible! ~ *again,* répéter. ~**ing,** *n,* dicton, *m.*
scab, *n,* croûte, *f;* (*Ind. pej.*) jaune, *m.*
scabious (*Bot.*) *n,* scabieuse, *f.*
scaffold, *n,* échafaud, *m.* ~**ing,** *n,* échafaudage, *m.*
scald, *n,* brûlure, *f.* ¶ *v.t,* ébouillanter; (*sterilize*) stériliser. ~**ing [hot],** *a,* brûlant.
scale¹, *n,* échelle; (*Mus.*) gamme, *f;* (*wages*) barème, *m. on a large, small* ~, en grand, petit. [*drawn*] *to* ~, à l'échelle. ~ *model,* modèle réduit. ¶ *v.t,* (*wall &c*) escalader; (*drawing*) dessiner à l'échelle. ~ *down,* (*production*) réduire; (*drawing*) r. à l'échelle.
scale², *n,* (*fish, rust*) écaille; (*skin*) squame, *f;* (*kettle &c, teeth*) tartre, *m.* ¶ *v.t,* écailler; détartrer.
scale³, *n,* (*pan*) plateau, *m.* ~*s* (*& pair of* ~*s*) balance, *f;* (*bathroom*) pèse-personne, *m.inv;* (*luggage &c*) bascule, *f. tip the* ~*s* (*fig.*), faire pencher la balance.
scallop, *n,* coquille Saint-Jacques, *f.* ~ *shell,* coquille.
scalp, *n,* cuir chevelu; (*trophy*) scalp, *m.* ¶ *v.t,* scalper.
scalpel, *n,* scalpel, *m.*
scaly, *a,* écailleux.
scamp, *n,* polisson, ne.
scamper away, s'enfuir en courant, détaler.
scampi, *n.pl,* langoustines, *f.pl.*
scan, *v.t,* (*horizon*) scruter; (*crowd*) fouiller du regard; (*newspaper*) parcourir [des yeux]; (*Radar, TV*) balayer; (*Computer*) scruter. ¶ *v.i,* (*verse*) se scander. ¶ (*Med.*) *n,* échographie, *f.*
scandal, *n,* scandale, *m;* (*gossip*) médisance, *f,* cancans, ragots *P, m.pl. it's a* ~, c'est une honte. ~*monger,* mauvaise langue. ~**ize,** *v.t,* scandaliser. ~**ous†,** *a,* scandaleux.
Scandinavia, *n,* la Scandinavie. **Scandinavian,** *a,* scandinave. ¶ *n,* Scandinave, *m,f.*
scanner (*Med.*), *n,* scanner, *m.* **scansion,** *n,* scansion, *f.*
scant[y], *a,* peu abondant, insuffisant; (*resources*) maigre, exigu; (*respect*) peu de; (*bikini*) minuscule. ~ *attire,* tenue sommaire, *f.*
scapegoat, *n,* bouc émissaire, *m.*
scar, *n,* (*gen.*) cicatrice; (*on face*) balafre, *f.* ¶ *v.t,* marquer d'une cicatrice; balafrer; (*fig.*) marquer.
scarce, *a,* (*food, money*) peu abondant; (*edition*) rare. *make o.s* ~ *P,* se sauver *P.* ~**ly,** *ad,* à peine. **scarcity,** *n,* rareté; disette, *f.*
scare, *n,* peur, *f. give s.o a* ~, faire peur à qn. *raise a* ~, semer la panique. *bomb* ~, alerte à la bombe, *f.* ~*monger,* alarmiste, *m,f.* ¶ *v.t,* effrayer, faire peur à. *be* ~*d stiff,* avoir une peur bleue *ou* la frousse *P.* ~*crow, n,* épouvantail, *m.* **scary,** *a,* qui fait peur.
scarf, *n,* écharpe, *f;* (*square*) foulard, *m.*
scarlatina, *n.* or **scarlet fever,** scarlatine, *f.* **scarlet,** *n. & a,* écarlate, *f.*
scathing, *a,* cinglant.
scatter, *v.t,* (*gen.*) éparpiller, répandre; (*clouds, crowd*) disperser; (*cushions*) jeter ça & là; (*enemy*) mettre en déroute. ¶ *v.i,* se disperser. ~*brain*(*ed*), étourdi, e, écervelé, e.
scavenge, *v.i,* fouiller [dans les rues &c]. **scavenger,** *n,* animal, insecte nécrophage, *m;* (*pers.*) chiffonnier, ère.
scenario, *n,* scénario, *m.* **scene,** *n,* scène, *f;* (*place: crime &c*) lieu, endroit; (*sight*) spectacle, *m. behind the* ~*s* (*Theat., fig.*), dans les coulisses. *outdoor* ~ (*Cine.*), extérieur, *m. set*

the ~ for, préparer le terrain pour. *~ change,* changement de décors, *m. ~ painter,* peintre de décors, *m. ~ shifter,* machiniste, *m.* ~**ry,** *n,* paysage, *m;* (*Theat.*) décors, *m.pl. a change of ~* (*fig.*), un changement de cadre. **scenic,** *a,* scénique. *~ railway,* montagnes russes, *f.pl.*

scent, *n,* parfum; (*animal track*) fumet, *m;* (*fig.*) piste, *f. lose the ~*, perdre la piste. *throw off the ~*, dépister. *~ bottle,* flacon à parfum, *m. ~ spray,* vaporisateur [à parfum]; (*aerosol*) atomisateur [à p.], *m.* ¶ *v.t,* (*perfume*) parfumer; (*game & fig*) flairer.

sceptic, *n.* & ~**al,** *a,* sceptique, *m,f.* **scepticism,** *n,* scepticisme, *m.*

sceptre, *n,* sceptre, *m.*

schedule, *n,* (*work &c*) programme; (*trains &c*) horaire; (*events*) calendrier, *m;* liste, *f,* inventaire; (*prices*) barème, *m. go according to ~*, se passer comme prévu. *be behind ~*, avoir du retard. *on, up to ~*, (*train*) à l'heure; (*job*) à jour. ~**d,** *a,* prévu; régulier.

scheme, *n,* projet, plan, *m;* (*pej.*) manigance, combine, *f.* ¶ *v.i,* comploter. **schemer,** *n,* intrigant, e; comploteur, euse. **scheming,** *a,* intrigant, rusé. ¶ *n,* machinations, *f.pl.*

schism, *n,* schisme, *m.*

schizoid, *a.* & *n,* schizoïde, *m,f.* **schizophrenia,** *n,* schizophrénie, *f.* **schizophrenic,** *a.* & *n,* schizophrène, *m,f.*

scholar, *n,* lettré, e, erudit, e. ~**ly,** *a,* savant, érudit. ~**ship,** *n,* savoir, *m,* érudition; (*award*) bourse, *f.* **scholastic,** *a,* scolaire.

school[1], *n,* (*gen., primary*) école, *f;* (*secondary*) collège; (*grammar ~*) lycée, *m;* (*Univ.*) faculté, *f.* ¶ *a,* scolaire. *~-age,* d'âge scolaire. *~ attendance,* scolarisation, *f. ~boy, ~girl, ~child,* élève, *m,f,* écolier, ère; collégien, ne; lycéen, ne. *~ bus,* car de ramassage scolaire, *m. ~days,* années d'école, *f.pl. ~ fees,* frais de scolarité, *m.pl. ~ leaving age,* âge de fin de scolarité, *m. ~master, ~mistress, ~ teacher,* (*primary*) instituteur, trice; (*secondary*) professeur, *m. ~mate,* camarade de classe, *m,f. ~room,* salle de classe, *f.* **schooling,** *n,* études, *f.pl.*

school[2] (*fish*), *n,* banc, *m.*

schooner, *n,* schooner, *m,* goélette, *f.*

sciatic, *a.* & **sciatica,** *n,* sciatique, *f.*

science, *n,* science, *f;* (*study*) sciences, *f.pl.* ¶ *a,* (*equipment &c*) scientifique; (*exam*) de sciences. *~ fiction,* science-fiction, *f.* **scientific**†, *a,* scientifique; (*instruments*) de précision. **scientist,** *n,* scientifique, *m,f;* savant, e.

Scilly Isles (the), les Sorlingues, *f.pl.*

scintillate, *v.i,* scintiller; (*fig: pers.*) pétiller d'esprit. **scintillating,** *a,* scintillant; pétillant.

scissors, *n.pl,* ciseaux, *m.pl.*

sclerosis, *n,* sclérose, *f.*

scoff *v.i,* se moquer (*at,* de). **scoffer,** *n,* moqueur, euse.

scold, *v.t,* réprimander; (*child*) gronder, attraper (pour avoir fait). ¶ *v.i,* grogner, rouspéter *P.* ~**ing,** *n,* réprimande, *f. get a ~*, se faire gronder &c.

scoop, *n,* (*food*) pelle; (*water*) écope, *f;* (*Press*) scoop, *m.* ¶ *v.t,* (*Press*) publier en exclusivité. *~ out,* (*water*) vider; (*hole*) creuser. *~ up,* ramasser.

scooter, *n,* trottinette, *f;* (*motor ~*) scooter, *m.*

scope, *n,* (*book*) limites; (*for sth*) possibilités, *f.pl;* (*range*) étendue, portée; (*enterprise*) envergure; (*capacity*) compétence, *f. ~ of one's activities,* champ de ses activités.

scorch, *v.t,* brûler; (*cloth*) roussir; (*sun*) déssecher. *~ mark,* brûlure légère. ~**er** *P, n,* journée torride, *f.* ~**ing,** *a,* torride; brûlant.

score, *n,* (*Sport*) score, *m;* (*Cards*) marque; (*mark*) rayure; incision; (*Mus.*) partition; (*film*) musique, *f. a ~* (20), vingt, une vingtaine. *on that ~*, à ce titre. *an old ~ to settle,* un compte à régler. *what's the ~?* (*Sport*) où en est le jeu *ou* le match? *~board,* tableau, *m.* ¶ *v.t,* (*goal &c*) marquer; (*mark*) rayer, érafler; (*Mus.*) écrire, orchestrer. ¶ *v.i,* marquer un point *ou* un but; (*fig.*) avoir l'avantage. **scorer,** *n,* marqueur, euse; (*goal*) marqueur [de but], *m.*

scorn, *n,* mépris, dédain, *m.* ¶ *v.t,* mépriser, dédaigner; (*advice*) négliger. ~**ful**†, *a,* dédaigneux.

scorpion, *n,* scorpion, *m.*

Scot, *n,* Écossais, e. **Scots,** *a.* & *dialect,* écossais, *m. ~sman, ~swoman,* Écossais, e. **Scottish,** *a,* écossais. **Scotland,** *n,* l'Écosse, *f. ~ yard* (*London*), ≏ le Quai des Orfèvres (*Paris*).

scotch, *v.t,* faire échouer; (*rumour*) étouffer.

Scotch, *a,* (*not in Sc.*), écossais. *~ mist,* bruine, *f,* crachin, *m. ~ tape,* scotch, *m.* ¶ *n,* whisky, scotch, *m.*

scot-free, *a,* indemne; impuni.

scoundrel, *n,* canaille, *f,* vaurien, *m.*

scour, *v.t,* (*pan*) récurer; (*metal*) décaper; (*country*) battre, parcourir. ~**er,** *n,* tampon à récurer, *m.*

scourge, *n,* fléau, *m.*

scout, *n,* (*Mil.*) éclaireur; (*boy ~*) scout, éclaireur, *m. ~ camp,* camp scout, *m.* ¶ *v.t, ~ out* (*Mil.*), (*route &c*) éclairer, reconnaître.

scowl, *n,* air maussade, *m.* ¶ *v.i,* se renfrogner.

scrag & ~ **end,** *n,* collet [de mouton], *m.* **scraggy,** *a,* (*body*) décharné; (*pers., beast*) efflanqué.

scram *P, v.i,* ficher le camp *P.*

scramble, *n,* bousculade, ruée, *f;* (*motorcycle ~*) [réunion *f* de] moto-cross, *m.* ¶ *v.t,* (*Cook., Tel.*) brouiller. *~d eggs,* œufs brouillés. ¶ *v.i,* (*Aero.*) décoller en cas d'alerte. *~ for* (*seats &c*), se bousculer pour [avoir]. ~ *up,* grimper tant bien que mal. **scrambler** (*Tel.*), *n,* brouilleur, *m.*

scrap[1], *n,* (*gen.*) bout; fragment, *m;* (*learning*) bribe, *f;* (*metal*) déchets, *m.pl;* (*pl. pieces*) débris; (*food*) restes, *m,pl. sell for* ~, vendre à la casse. ~*book,* album, *m.* ~ *iron,* ~ *metal,* ferraille, *f.* ~ *paper,* papier de brouillon, *m. throw on the* ~ *heap,* mettre au rebut. ~ *yard,* chantier de ferraille, *m.* ¶ *v.t,* jeter; (*car &c*) envoyer à la ferraille; (*project*) abandonner.

scrap[2], *n,* bagarre, *f.* ¶ *v.i,* se bagarrer (avec).

scrape, *n,* coup de racloir, *m;* (*mark*) éraflure, *f;* (*trouble*) embarras, *m.* ¶ *v.t,* (*clean*) racler; (*Cook.*) gratter; (*graze*) érafler. ~ *off,* enlever en raclant. ~ *mud off,* (*boots*) décrotter. ~ *the bottom* (*Naut.*), talonner. ~ *together,* ~ *up,* rassembler. ~ *every penny together,* racler les fonds de tiroir. ¶ *v.i,* racler, gratter; (*rub*) frotter. ~ *through,* réussir de justesse. **scraper,** *n,* racloir, grattoir; (*boot*) décrottoir, *m.*

scratch, *n,* égratignure; éraflure; rayure, *f;* (*claw, nail*) coup de griffe, d'ongle; (*Sport*) scratch, *m. start from* ~ (*fig.*), partir de zéro. *come up to* ~, se montrer à la hauteur. ¶ *a,* (*team &c*) de fortune; (*golfer &c*) scratch, *inv.* ¶ *v.t,* gratter; griffer; érafler; (*record*) rayer; (*Sport*) scratcher; (*game &c*) annuler. ~ *out,* rayer. ¶ *v.i,* [se] gratter.

scrawl, *n,* griffonnage, gribouillage, *m.* ¶ *v.t. & i,* griffonner, gribouiller.

scream, *n,* cri perçant, hurlement; (*laughter*) éclat, *m. it's a* ~ *P,* c'est vraiment marrant *P.* ¶ *v.i,* crier (*at,* après); hurler (*with,* de; *at,* à). ~*ingly funny,* tordant, désopilant.

screech, *n,* cri strident; hurlement; (*tyres*) crissement, *m.* ~ *owl,* effraie, *f.* ¶ *v.i,* crier; hurler; crisser.

screen, *n,* (*Cine &c*) écran; (*in room*) paravent; (*fire*) écran de cheminée; (*fig.*) rideau, *m.* ~*play,* scénario, *m.* ~ *test,* essai à l'écran, *m.* ~ *writer,* scénariste, *m,f.* ¶ *v.t,* (*hide*) masquer (à), cacher; (*protect*) abriter, protéger (de); (*film*) passer; (*sieve*) cribler. ~**ing,** *n,* projection, *f;* (*Med.*) test de dépistage, *m.*

screw, *n,* vis; (*Aero., Naut.*) hélice, *f;* (*action*) tour de vis; (*P prison warder*) garde-chiourme, *m.* ~*driver,* tournevis, *m.* ~ *top,* couvercle à pas de vis, *m.* ¶ *v.t,* visser (sur; à); (*extort: money*) soutirer (*out of,* à); (*information*) arracher (à); (*P* woman*) baiser *P*.* ~ *down,* ~ *on,* [se] visser. ~ *off,* [se] dévisser. *have one's head* ~*ed on all right,* avoir la tête sur les épaules. ~ *up one's courage* prendre son courage à deux mains. ~**y** *P, a,* cinglé *P.*

scribble, *n,* gribouillage, *m.* ¶ *v.t. & i,* gribouiller; (*a note*) griffonner; (*author pej.*) écrivailler. **scribbler,** *n,* écrivailleur, euse. *scribbling pad,* bloc-notes, *m.* **scribe,** *n,* scribe, *m.*

scrimmage, *n,* mêlée; bousculade, *f.*

script, *n,* (*Cine*) scénario; (*TV &c*) texte; (*writing*) script, *m;* (*Typ.*) scriptes, *f.pl.* ~ *writer,* scénariste, dialoguiste, *m,f.*

Scripture, *n. oft. pl,* l'Écriture, *f. oft. pl.*

scroll, *n,* (*parchment*) rouleau, *m;* (*Arch.*) volute, *f.*

scrounge *P, v.t,* se faire payer (par qn). ~ *money from s.o,* taper qn *P.* ~ *on s.o,* vivre aux crochets de qn. **scrounger** *P, n,* parasite, *m;* (*of meals*) pique-assiettes, *m,f. inv.*

scrub[1] (*bush*) *n,* broussailles, *f.pl.*

scrub[2], *n,* nettoyage à la brosse, *m.* ¶ *v.t,* (*washing*) frotter; (*floor*) nettoyer à la brosse; (*pan*) récurer. *scrubbing brush,* brosse dure. ~**ber** *P, n,* sauteuse *P*,* putain *P*, f.*

scruff of the neck, *n,* peau du cou, *f.*

scruffy, *a,* (*pers.*) débraillé; (*clothes*) miteux.

scrum[mage], *n,* (*Rugby*) mêlée; (*in crowd*) bousculade, *f. scrum half,* demi de mêlée, *m.*

scruple, *n,* scrupule, *m.* ~ **to,** se faire scrupule de. **scrupulous**†, *a,* scrupuleux.

scrutineer, *n,* scrutateur, trice. **scrutinize,** *v.t,* scruter; (*votes*) pointer. **scrutiny,** *n,* examen rigoureux; pointage, *m.*

scuff *v.t.* (*shoes &c*) érafler.

scuffle, *n,* rixe, bagarre, *f.*

scull, *n,* aviron de couple, *m;* (*stern oar*) godille, *f.* ¶ *v.t,* godiller. ¶ *v.i,* ramer en couple.

scullery, *n,* arrière-cuisine, *f.*

sculpt, *v.t. & i,* sculpter (*out of,* dans). **sculptor,** *n,* sculpteur, *m.* **sculptress,** *n,* femme sculpteur, *f.* **sculpture,** *n,* sculpture, *f.* ¶ *v.t,* sculpter.

scum, *n,* écume; (*fig.*) lie, *f.* ~ *of the earth,* rebut du genre humain, *m.*

scurf, *n,* pellicules [du cuir chevelu], *f.pl.*

scurrilous, *a,* calomnieux; grossier, vulgaire.

scurry, *v.i,* se précipiter. ~ *away,* détaler.

scuttle[1], *n,* (*coal*) seau, *m.*

scuttle[2], *v.i,* courir précipitamment.

scuttle[3], *v.t,* (*Naut.*) saborder; (*fig.*) faire échouer.

scythe, *n,* faux, *f.* ¶ *v.t,* faucher.

sea, *n,* mer, *f. by the* ~, au bord de la mer. *out to* ~, au large. *go to* ~, (*boat*) prendre la mer; (*pers.*) se faire marin. *over, beyond the* ~, outre-mer. *be all at* ~ (*fig.*), nager *P.* ~ *air,* air marin *ou* de la mer. ~ *anemone,* anémone de mer, *f.* ~ *bathing,* bains de mer, *m.pl.* ~ *bed,* fond de la mer, *m.* ~*board,* littoral, *m.* ~ *bream,* daurade, *f.* ~ *breeze,* brise de mer, *f.* ~ *captain,* capitaine [de la marine marchande], *m.* ~*coast,* côte, *f.* ~*farer,* marin, *m.* ~*food,* fruits de mer, *m.pl.* ~*front,* front de mer, *m.* ~*-going ship,* [navire] long-courrier, *m.* ~*-green,* vert glauque, *inv.* ~*gull,* mouette, *f.* ~ *kale,* crambe, chou marin, *m. have got one's ~ legs,* avoir le pied marin. ~ *level,* niveau de la mer. ~*-lion,* otarie, *f.* ~*man,* marin. ~*manship,* qualités de marin, *f.pl.* ~*plane,* hydravion, *m.* ~*port,* port de mer, *m.* ~*scape* (*Art*), marine, *f.* ~ *scout,* scout marin. ~ *shanty,* chanson de marins, *f.* ~ *shell,* coquillage, *m.* ~*shore,* rivage, *m;* plage, *f. by the ~shore,* au bord de la mer. ~*sickness,* mal de mer, *m. be ~sick,* avoir le m. de m. ~*side resort,* station balnéaire, *f.* ~ *urchin,* oursin, *m.* ~ *wall,* digue, *f.* ~*wards,* vers le large. ~ *water,* eau de mer, *f.* ~*way,* route maritime, *f.* ~*weed,* algue, *f.* ~*worthy,* en [bon] état de navigabilité.

seal[1], *n,* (*Zool.*) phoque, *m.* ~*skin,* peau de phoque, *f.*

seal[2], *n,* seau; (*on letter*) cachet; (*on package*) plomb, *m. set one's ~ of approval to,* donner son approbation à. ¶ *v.t,* sceller; (*envelope*) coller; (*fate*) régler. *my lips are ~ed,* mes lèvres sont scellées. ~ *off* (*door &c*), condamner; (*area*) mettre un cordon autour de. ~*ing wax,* cire à cacheter, *f.*

seam, *n,* couture; (*Geol.*) couche; (*Min.*) veine, *f.* ~**less,** *a,* sans couture. **seamstress,** *n,* couturière, *f. seamy side* (*lit. & fig.*), envers, *m.*

seance, *n,* séance de spiritisme, *f.*

search, *n,* recherches, *f.pl;* (*Law*) perquisition; (*of pers. &c*) fouille, *f. in ~ of,* à la recherche de. ~ *light,* projecteur, *m.* ~*-party,* équipe de secours, *f.* ~ *warrant,* mandat de perquisition, *m.* ¶ *v.t,* (*pers., room, memory*) fouiller; (*documents &c*) examiner en détail. ¶ *v.i,* chercher. ~ *through,* fouiller. ~**er,** *n,* chercheur, euse. ~**ing,** *a,* pénétrant; scrutateur.

season, *n,* saison, *f. be in ~* (*food*), être de saison. *the Christmas ~,* la période des fêtes. *the off-~,* la morte saison. ~ *ticket,* carte d'abonnement, *f.* ¶ *v.t,* assaisonner; (*spice*) relever, épicer; (*wood*) faire sécher; (*troops*) aguerrir. ~**able,** *a,* de saison; (*advice*) opportun. ~**al,** *a,* saisonnier. ~**ing** *n,* (*Cook.*) assaisonnement, *m.*

seat, *n,* (*gen*) siège; (*Theat.*) fauteuil, *m;* (*bus &c*) banquette; (*place*) place; (*on horse*) assiette, tenue, *f;* (*trousers, chair*) fond; (*buttocks*) postérieur *P, m;* (*parliament; of Govt., learning*) siège; (*infection*) foyer, *m. country ~,* château. *take a ~,* s'asseoir. *takes one's ~,* prendre place. ~ *belt,* ceinture de sécurité, *f.* ¶ *v.t,* (*child*) faire asseoir; (*guests*) placer. *2-~er car,* [voiture à] 2 places, *f.* ~**ing,** *n,* sièges; places assises, *f.pl.*

secateurs, *n,* sécateur, *m.*

secede, *v.i,* faire sécession. **secession,** *n,* sécession, *f.*

secluded, *a,* (*gen.*) isolé, à l'écart; (*life, spot*) retiré. **seclusion,** *n,* solitude, *f.*

second[1], *n,* (*time, Math.*) seconde, *f;* (*fig.*) seconde, instant, *m.* ~ *hand,* trotteuse, *f.*

second[2]†, *a,* second; deuxième; (*date*) deux; (*cousin*) issu(e) de germain. *Charles the S~,* Charles Deux. ~ *best,* pis-aller, *m. come off ~ best,* perdre. *be in one's ~ childhood,* retomber en enfance. ~*-class,* (*Rly &c*) seconde [classe]; (*mail*) [à] tarif réduit. *the ~ coming,* le second avènement. *in ~* [*gear*], en seconde. ~*hand,* d'occasion; (*fig.*) de seconde main. ~*hand bookseller,* bouquiniste, *m.* ~*hand dealer,* marchand, e d'occasion. ~ *-in-command,* (*Mil.*) commandant en second, *m.* ~ *lieutenant,* sous-lieutenant, *m.* ~ *to none,* sans pareil. *play ~ fiddle,* jouer un rôle secondaire. ~ *self,* autre soi-même. ~*-rate,* de qualité inférieure. ~ *sight,* le don de seconde vue. *have ~ thoughts,* changer d'avis. *on ~ thoughts,* reflexion faite. *get one's ~ wind,* (*lit., fig.*) trouver son second souffle. *for other phrases V* **fourth.** ¶ *ad,* en seconde place. *come ~,* (*in race &c*) se classer deuxième *ou* second; (*arrive*) arriver le deuxième. *the ~ largest &c,* le plus grand &c sauf un. ¶ *n,* deuxième, *m,f;* second, e; (*Box.*) soigneur; (*duel*) témoin, *m;* (*pl: Com.*) articles de second choix, *m.pl.* ¶ *v.t,* appuyer [la motion de]. ~**ary,** *a,* secondaire. ~ *school,* collège [d'enseignment secondaire]; lycée, *m.* ~**ment,** *n,* détachement, *m.*

secrecy, *n,* secret, *m;* discrétion, *f.* **secret,** *a,* secret; caché. *keep ~,* ne pas révéler. ¶ *n,* secret, *m. keep a ~,* garder un secret. *in the ~,* au courant. ~**arial,** *a,* de secrétariat, de secrétaire. ~**ariat,** *n,* secrétariat, *m.* **secretary,** *n,* secrétaire, *m,f. S~ of State,* ministre, *m.* **secrete,** *v.t,* cacher; (*Med.*) sécréter. **secretion,** *n,* sécrétion, *f.* **secretive,** *a,* secret; (*pej.*) dissimulé, cachottier. **secretly,** *ad,* en secret, secrètement, en cachette.

sect, *n,* secte, *f.* ~**arian,** *n. & a,* sectaire, *m.*

section, *n,* section, partie, *f;* (*country*) partie; (*town*) quartier; (*machine &c*) élément; (*Mil.*) groupe [de combat]; (*Adm.*) article, *m;* (*Press*) page[s], *f.*[*pl*]; (*cut*) coupe, *f;* (*department*) section; (*Com.*) rayon, *m.* ¶ *v.t,* sectionner. ~ *off,* séparer. ~**al,** *a,* démontable; (*interests*) d'un groupe; (*view*) en coupe. **sector,** *n,* secteur, *m.*

secular, *a,* (*authority*) séculier; (*school*) laïque; (*music &c*) profane.

secure†, *a,* (*safe*) en sûreté; (*place*) sûr; (*lock &c*) solide; (*rope*) bien attaché; (*door*) bien fermé; (*future*) assuré. ~ *from,* à l'abri de. ¶ *v.t,* attacher; bien fermer; (*tile*) fixer; assurer; (*get*) obtenir: (*pers.*) engager. **security,** *n,* (*gen., Pol. &c*) sécurité; (*Fin: for loan*) caution, garantie, *f;* (*pl. Stk. Ex.*) valeurs, *f.pl,* titres, *m.pl. S~ Council,* Conseil de sécurité, *m.* ~ *forces,* forces de sécurite, *f.pl.* ~ *guard,*

garde chargé de la sécurité, *m*.
sedate†, *a*, posé, calme. ¶ *v.t*, mettre sous sédation. **sedation,** *n*, sédation, *f*. **sedative,** *n*. & *a*, sédatif, *m*. **sedentary,** *a*, sédentaire.
sedge, *n*, laîche, *f*. ~ *warbler*, phragmite des joncs, *m*.
sediment, *n*, sédiment; (*in wine &c*) dépôt, *m*.
sedition, *n*, sédition, *f*. **seditious,** *a*, séditieux.
seduce, *v.t*, séduire. **seducer,** *n*, séducteur, trice. **seduction,** *n*, séduction, *f*. **seductive,** *a*, séduisant.
see[1], *n*, siège [épiscopal], *m*.
see[2], *v.t*. & *i*, *ir*, (*gen*.) voir; comprendre; (*escort &c*) [re]conduire, [r]accompagner; (*ensure*) s'assurer, veiller. *as far as I can* ~, à ce que je vois. *I* ~*!* ah bon! *let's* ~, voyons [un peu]. *you* ~, [vous] voyez, tu vois. ~ *you P!* salut! *P* ~ *you later!* à toute à l'heure! ~ *you on Saturday, next week*, à samedi, à la semaine prochaine. ~ *you soon!* à bientôt! ~ *about sth*, s'occuper de qch. ~ *in the New Year*, faire le réveillon du Nouvel An. ~ *through*, (*pers. &c*) ne pas se laisser duper par; (*finish*) mener à bonne fin. ~*-through*, transparent. ~ *to*, s'occuper de; réparer. ~ *to it that*, veiller à ce que (+ *subj*).
seed, *n*, graine; (*col*.) semence, *f*; (*grape &c*) pépin; (*fig*.) germe, *m*. *go to* ~, (*plant*) monter en graine; (*pers*.) se laisser aller. ~ *bed*, couche, *f*. ~ *box*, germoir, *m*. ~ *corn &c*, blé *m* &c de semence. ~ *merchant*, grainetier, *m*. ~ *pearls*, semence de perles. ¶ *v.t*, (*lawn*) ensemencer; (*grape &c*) épépiner. ~[*ed player*], (*Ten*.) tête de série, *f*. ~**less,** *a*, sans pépins. ~**ling,** *n*, semis, *m*. **seedy,** *a*, miteux; (*sick*) mal fichu *P*.
seeing, *n*, vision, *f*. ~ *is believing*, voir c'est croire. ~ *that*, vu que.
seek, *v.t*. & *i*. *ir*, chercher, rechercher. ~ *help, advice from s.o*, demander de l'aide, conseil à qn. ~**er,** *n*, chercheur, euse.
seem, *v.i*, sembler, paraître, avoir l'air. ¶ *v. imp*, sembler, paraître. *she* ~*s very young*, elle semble *ou* paraît *ou* a l'air très jeune. *I* ~ *to know you*, il me semble vous connaître. *it* ~*s like a dream*, on dirait un rêve. *it* ~*s to me*, il me semble. *it* ~*s the shop's closed* (*they say*), le magasin est fermé, paraît-il. *so it* ~*s*, à ce qu'il paraît. *it* ~*s not*, il paraît que non. **seeming**†, *a*, apparent, soi-disant. **seemly,** *a*, (*behaviour*) bienséant; (*dress*) décent.
seep, *v.i*, suinter, filtrer. ~ *away*, s'écouler. ~ *in*, s'infiltrer. ~ *out*, suinter. ~**age,** *n*, suintement, *m*; (*from tank*) fuite, *f*.
seersucker, *n*, crépon de coton, *m*.
seesaw, *n*, bascule, balançoire, *f*. ¶ *v.i*, se balancer; (*fig*.) osciller.
seethe, *v.i*, (*liquid*) bouillonner; (*with rage*) bouillir; (*with people*) grouiller, fourmiller. *seething*, furibond.
segment, *n*, segment, *m*.
segregate, *v.t*, séparer. **segregation,** *n*, (*Pol*.) ségrégation; (*gen*.) séparation, *f*.
seismic, *a*, sismique. **seismograph,** *n*, sismographe, *m*. **seismology,** *n*, sismologie, *f*.
seize, *v.t*, saisir; (*take by force*) s'emparer de; (*Law: pers*) arrêter; (*goods*) saisir. ¶ *v.i*, (*Mach*.) se gripper. **seizure,** *n*, saisie; prise; capture; (*Med*.) crise, attaque, *f*.
seldom, *ad*, rarement.
select, *a*, (*club*) fermé; (*group &c*) choisi. ~ *committee*, commission d'enquête, *f*. ¶ *v.t*, (*team &c*) selectionner; (*gift &c*) choisir. ~*ed works*, œuvres choisies. ~**ion,** *n*, choix, *m*; sélection, *f*; (*pl, from writings*) morceaux choisis, *m.pl*; (*Betting*) pronostic, *m*. ~ *committee*, comité de sélection, *m*. ~**ive,** *a*, sélectif.
self, *n*, moi, *m.inv*; moi-même &c. *pay* ~ (*on cheque*), payez à l'ordre de moi-même. ~*-acting*, automatique. ~*-adhesive*, autoadhésif. ~*-adjusting*, à réglage automatique. ~*-assurance*, ~*-confidence*, assurance, *f*. ~*-assured*, ~*-confident*, sûr de soi. ~*-centred*, égocentrique. ~*-confessed*, de son propre aveu. ~*-conscious*, gêné, embarassé. ~*-contained*, indépendant. ~*-control*, maîtrise de soi, *f*. ~*-defence*, légitime défense, *f*. ~*-denial*, abnégation, *f*. ~*-discipline*, discipline [personelle]. ~*-drive*, sans chauffeur. ~*-effacing*, effacé. ~*-employed*, qui travaille à son compte. ~*-esteem*, amour-propre, *m*. ~*-evident*, évident. ~*-government*, autonomie, *f*. ~*-importance*, suffisance, *f*. ~*-indulgent*, sybarite. ~*-inflicted*, volontaire. ~*-interest*, intérêt [personnel]. ~*-made man*, fils de ses œuvres; self-made man, *m*. ~*-opinionated*, opiniâtre. ~*-portrait*, autoportrait, *m*. ~*-possession*, sang-froid, aplomb, *m*. ~*-raising flour*, farine à levure, *f*. ~*-reliance*, confiance en soi, *f*. ~*-respect*, amour-propre, *m*. ~*-righteous*, pharisaïque. ~*-sacrifice*, abnégation, *f*. ~*-satisfied*, suffisant. ~*-seeking*, égoïste. ~*-service*, libre-service, *m.inv*. ~*-styled*, soi-disant, *inv*. ~*-sufficient*, indépendant. ~*-taught*, autodidacte. ~*-willed*, volontaire.
selfish†, *a*, égoïste, intéressé. ~**ness,** *n*, égoïsme, *m*. **selfless,** *a*, désintéressé, altruiste.
sell, *v.t*. (& *i*), (se) vendre; (*fig: idea &c*) faire accepter; (*betray &c*) tromper, avoir *P*. ~ *s.o a pup P*, rouler qn *P*. ~ *o.s*, (*fig*.), se faire valoir. ~ *off*, (*stock &c*) liquider; (*goods*) solder. *sold out*, (*item*) épuisé. ~*out*, *n*, trahison, capitulation, *f*. (*Theat*.) *it's a* ~*out*, on joue à guichets fermés. ~ *up*, liquider, vendre. **seller,** *n*, vendeur, euse.
sellotape, *n*, scotch, *m*. ¶ *v.t*, scotcher.
selvage, -edge, *n*, lisière, *f*.
semantic, *a*. & ~**s,** *n*, sémantique, *f*.

semaphore, *n*, sémaphore, *m*.
semblance, *n*, semblant, *m*, apparence, *f*.
semen, *n*, sperme, *m*.
semi, *pref:* ~*breve*, ronde, *f*. ~*circle*, demi-cercle, *m*. ~*colon*, point-virgule, *m*. ~*conscious*, à demi conscient. ~*darkness*, pénombre, *f*. ~*-detached house*, maison jumelle. ~*-final*, demi-finale, *f*. ~*-official*, semi-officiel; officieux. ~*quaver*, double croche, *f*. ~*-skilled*, (*worker*) spécialisé. ~*tone*, demi-ton, *m*.
seminar *&* **seminary,** *n*, séminaire, *m*.
Semitic, *a*, sémitique; (*people*) sémite.
semolina, *n*, semoule, *f*.
senate, *n*, sénat; (*Univ.*) conseil de l'université, *m*. **senator,** *n*, sénateur, *m*.
send, *v.t. & i. ir*, (*gen.*) envoyer; (*by post &* ~ *off*) envoyer, expédier. ~ *s.o mad*, rendre qn fou. ~ *s.o flying*, envoyer qn rouler à terre. ~ *s.o home*, renvoyer qn chez lui; (*from abroad*) rapatrier qn. ~ *s.o packing P*, envoyer promener qn *P*. ~ *to Coventry*, mettre en quarantaine. ~ **away,** faire partir; (*dismiss*) renvoyer. ~ **back,** renvoyer. ~ **for,** envoyer chercher. ~**off,** (*Foot. &c*) expulser. ~ *off for*, commander par correspondance. ~ **out,** envoyer; (*emit*) répandre. ~ **up** faire monter; (*P*) parodier; (*pers.*) mettre en boîte, *P*. ~*-up*, *n*, mise en boîte *P*; parodie, *f*. ~**er,** *n*, envoyeur, euse, expéditeur, trice.
Senegal, *n*, le Sénégal. ~**ese,** *a. & n*, sénégalais, e.
senile, *a*, sénile. **senility,** *n*, sénilité, *f*.
senior, *a*, (*older*) aîné, plus âgé; (*in rank*) supérieur. ~ *school*, (*top classes*) grandes classes; (*secondary school*) collège, *m*. *Jones S*~, Jones père. ~ *partner*, associé principal. ¶ *n*, aîné, e; (*Sch.*) grand, e. ~**ity,** *n*, priorité d'âge; supériorité; (*years of service*) ancienneté, *f*.
sensation, *n*, sensation (*of doing*, de faire), *f*. *cause a* ~, faire sensation. ~**al,** *a*, (*event*) qui fait sensation; (*film, book &c*) à sensation; (*account*) dramatique; (*P marvellous*) sensationnel *P*, sensass *P*, *inv*. **sense,** *n*, (*faculty*) sens, *m*; (*impression: physical*) sensation, *f*; (*mental*) sentiment, *m*; (*common* ~) bon-sens, intelligence, *f*; (*meaning*) sens; (*pl: sanity*) raison, *f*. *come to one's* ~*s*, revenir à la raison. ~ *of hearing, taste &c*, ouïe, *f*, goût, *m &c*. ~ *of humour, direction &c*, sens de l'humour, de l'orientation &c. *make* ~, avoir du sens. ¶ *v.t*, (*gen.*) sentir [intuitivement]; (*danger*) pressentir. ~**less,** *a*, insensé; sans connaissance. **sensibility,** *n*, sensibilité, *f*. **sensible**†, *a*, (*pers.*) raisonnable, sensé; (*act*) raisonnable, judicieux; (*clothes*) pratique; (*noticeable*) sensible, appréciable. **sensitive,** *a*, (*pers., tooth &c*) sensible (à); (*question, skin*) délicat; (*touchy*) susceptible. **sensitivity,** *n*, sensibilité; délicatesse; susceptibilité, *f*.
sensitize, *v.t*, sensibiliser.
sensual†, *a*, sensuel. ~**ity** *n*, sensualité, *f*.
sensuous†, *a*, voluptueux. ~**ness,** *n*, volupté, *f*.
sentence, *n*, sentence, condamnation; (*punishment*) peine; (*Gram.*) phrase, *f*. ¶ *v.t*, condamner. **sententious**†, *a*, sentencieux.
sentiment, *n*, (*feeling*) sentiment, *m*; opinion; sentimentalité, *f*. ~**al**†, *a*, sentimental. ~**ality,** *n*, sentimentalité, sensiblerie, *f*.
sentinel, *n*, sentinelle, *f*. **sentry,** *n*, sentinelle, *f*. ~ *box*, guérite, *f*. ~ *duty*, faction, *f*.
separate†, *a*, (*gen.*) séparé, distinct; indépendant; (*question &c*) différent, autre; (*entrance*) particulier. *sleep in* ~ *beds*, faire lit à part. ¶ *n.pl*, coordonnés, *m.pl*. ¶ *v.t*, séparer; (*divide*) diviser; (*strands*) dédoubler; (*milk*) écrémer. ¶ *v.i*, se séparer. **separation,** *n*, séparation, *f*.
sepia, *n*, sépia, *f*.
September, *n*, septembre, *m*. *in* ~, au mois de septembre.
septet[te], *n*, septuor, *m*.
septic, *a*, septique; (*wound*) infecté. *go* ~, s'infecter. ~ *tank*, fosse s., *f*.
sepulchral, *a*, sépulcral. **sepulchre,** *n*, sépulcre, *m*.
sequel, *n*, suite; conséquence, *f*. **sequence,** *n*, suite, succession; (*Cards*) séquence, *f*.
sequin, *n*, paillette, *f*.
serenade, *n*, sérénade, *f*. ¶ *v.t*, donner une sérénade à.
serene, *a*, serein. **serenity,** *n*, sérénité, *f*.
serge, *n*, serge, *f*.
sergeant, *n*, sergent; (*Artil., Cavalry*) maréchal des logis; (*Police*) brigadier, *m*. ~ *major*, adjudant; maréchal des logis chef, *m*.
serial, *n*, (*story &c*) feuilleton, *m*. ~ *number*, numéro de série, *m*. ~ *rights*, droits de reproduction en feuilleton, *m.pl*. **series,** *n*, série, suite, *f*.
serious†, *a*, (*gen.*) sérieux; (*look, loss, injury*) grave; (*damage*) important. *his condition is* ~ (*Med.*), il est dans un état grave. ~**ness,** *n*, sérieux, *m*; gravité; importance, *f*.
sermon, *n*, sermon, *m*. ~**ize,** *v.t*, sermonner.
serpent, *n*, serpent, *m*.
serrated, *a*, dentelé, en dents de scie.
serum, *n*, sérum, *m*.
servant, *n*, domestique, *m,f*; (*maid*) bonne, *f*; (*fig.*) serviteur, *m*, servante, *f*. **serve,** *v.t. & i*, (*gen, Mil., Rel., Ten.*) servir; (*food &* ~ *out*, ~ *up*) servir (*sth to s.o, s.o with sth*, qch à qn); (*bus: area*) desservir; (*Law; summons*) remettre (*on*, à); (*warrant*) délivrer (à). ~ *one's time*, (*apprentice*) faire son apprentissage; (*Mil.*) faire son [temps de] service; (*prison*) purger sa peine. ~ *time*, faire de la prison. ~ *a writ on*, assigner. ~ *no purpose*, ne servir à rien. ¶ *v.i.*, (*be of use*) servir (*as sth*, de qch; *to*

do, à faire). ¶ (*Ten.*) *n,* service, *m.* **server** *n,* (*Rel.*) servant, *m;* (*Ten.*) serveur, euse. **service,** *n,* service, *m;* (*bus*) ligne; (*on car &c*) révision, *f. the S~s,* les forces armées. ~ *area* (*motorway*), aire de services, *f.* ~ *charge,* service. ~ *families* (*Mil.*), familles de militaires, *f.pl.* ~ *hatch,* passe-plats, *m.* ~ *line* (*Ten.*), ligne de service, *f.* ~ *road,* voie de service, *f.* ~ *station,* station-service, *f.* ¶ *v.t,* (*car &c*) réviser. ~**able,** *a,* (*practical*) commode; (*usable*) utilisable; (*durable*) solide. ~**man,** *n,* militaire, *m.*

serviette, *n,* serviette, *f.* ~ *ring,* rond de serviette, *m.*

servile†, *a,* servile. **servility,** *n,* servilité, *f.* **servitude,** *n,* servitude, *f.*

sesame, *n,* sésame, *m.*

session, *n,* (*gen., Adm., Law*) séance, *f. be in* ~, siéger.

set, *n,* (*gen.*) jeu, *m,* série, *f;* (*golf clubs, knives &c*) jeu; (*pans, stamps &c*) série; (*kit*) trousse; (*dishes*) service; (*tyres*) train; (*Ten.*) set; (*Math.*) ensemble; (*Radio, TV*) poste, *m;* (*group*) bande, *f;* (*Cine*) plateau, *m;* (*Theat.*) scène, *f;* décor, *m;* (*hair*) mise en plis, *f.* ¶ *a,* fixe; déterminé, décidé d'avance; (*smile &c*) figé; (*meal*) à prix fixe; (*Sch: book &c*) au programme. *all* ~, prêt (*to do,* pour faire). *be* ~ *on doing,* vouloir à tout prix faire. ¶ *v.t,* (*gen.*) mettre; (*place*) placer, poser; (*signature*) apposer; (*clock &c*) régler; (*alarm*) mettre; (*type &c*) composer; (*Med: in plaster*) plâtrer; (*fracture*) réduire; (*hair*) faire une mise en plis à; (*date, time*) fixer; (*record*) établir; (*task &c*) donner; (*problem*) poser; (*gem*) monter; (*ring*) orner (*with,* de). ~ *fire to,* mettre le feu à. ¶ *v.i,* (*sun &c*) se coucher; (*limb &c*) se ressouder; (*jelly &c*) prendre; (*glue, concrete*) durcir; (*character*) se former. ~ *to work,* se mettre au travail. ~ **about,** se mettre à; attaquer. ~ **apart,** mettre à part. ~ **aside,** mettre de côté; (*will*) annuler; (*judgement*) casser. ~ **back,** remettre; (*work*) retarder. ~*back,* contretemps, revers, *m;* (*in health*) rechute, *f.* ~ **down,** déposer; (*note*) noter, inscrire. ~ *down in writing,* coucher par écrit. ~ **in,** *v.i,* commencer, se produire; *v.t,* (*Need.*) rapporter. ~ **off,** *v.i,* se mettre en route, partir (en voyage &c); *v.t,* (*firework*) faire partir; (*bomb*) faire exploser; (*mechanism*) déclencher; (*enhance*) mettre en valeur. ~ **out,** *v.i,* partir (*for,* pour); chercher (*to do,* à faire); se proposer (de faire); *v.t,* (*goods, ideas*) exposer. ~ **to,** s'y mettre *P.* ~*-to P,* bagarre; prise de bec *P, f.* ~ **up,** (*tent &c*) dresser; (*camp*) établir; (*institution*) fonder, créer; constituer. ~ *up house,* s'installer. ~ *up shop,* s'établir. ~*up P,* situation; affaire, *f.* ~ **upon,** attaquer.

settee, *n,* canapé, *m.*

setter, *n,* chien d'arrêt, setter, *m.* **setting,** *n,* (*gem.*) monture, *f;* (*fig: background &c*) cadre, *m;* (*Mus.*) arrangement, *m.* ~ *lotion,* lotion pour mise en plis, *f.* ¶ *a,* (*sun*) couchant.

settle[1], *n,* banc à haut dossier.

settle[2], *v.t,* (*question, account*) régler; (*date*) fixer; (*problem*) résoudre; (*debt*) rembourser; (*decide*) décider; (*pers.*) installer; (*calm*) calmer; (*doubts*) dissiper; (*colonize*) coloniser. (*Law*) ~ *out of court,* régler une affaire à l'amiable. *that* ~*s it,* ça me décide. ¶ *v.i,* décider (*to do,* de faire); (*dust &c*) retomber; (*sediment &c*) se déposer; (*bird &c*) se poser; (*in a place*) s'installer, se fixer ~ **down,** (*in chair &c*) s'installer (dans); se calmer; (*situation*) s'arranger. ~ **in,** s'installer. ~ **into,** (*job*) se faire à; (*routine*) adopter; (*habit*) prendre. ~ **on,** fixer son choix sur. ~ **up,** régler [la note]. ~ *up with s.o,* r. qn; (*fig.*) r. son compte à qn. ~**d,** *a,* décidé; (*weather*) au beau fixe. ~**ment,** *n,* règlement; accord, *m;* (*dowry*) dot; (*colony*) colonie, *f.* **settler,** *n,* colon, *m.*

seven, *a. & n,* sept, *m. for phrases V* **four. seventeen,** *a. & n,* dix-sept, *m.* **seventeenth,** *a. & n,* dix-septième, *m,f.* **seventh,** *a. & n,* septième, *m,f;* (*fraction*) septième, *m. in* ~ *heaven,* au septième ciel. *for other phrases V* **fourth. seventieth,** *a. & n,* soixante-dixième, *m,f.* **seventy,** *a. & n,* soixante-dix, *m. 71, 72,* soixante et onze, soixante-douze. *he's in his seventies,* il est septuagénaire. *for other phrases V* **forty.**

sever, *v.t,* couper; rompre; interrompre. ~**al,** *a. & pn,* plusieurs, *m,f.pl;* (*separate*) divers. ~**ally,** *ad,* séparément, individuellement. ~**ance,** *n,* séparation, *f.* ~ *pay,* indemnité de licenciement, *f.*

severe†, *a,* (*gen.*) sévère; (*pain*) violent; (*illness &c*) grave; (*winter, climate*) rigoureux; (*cold*) intense. **severity,** *n,* sévérité; violence; gravité; rigueur; intensité; difficulté, *f.*

sew, *v.t. & i.ir,* coudre. ~ *up,* (*tear &c*) recoudre; (*seam*) faire. *have sth all* ~*n up P,* avoir qch dans la poche *P.*

sewer, *n,* égout, *m.* **sewage,** *n,* vidange[s], *f.*[*pl*]. ~ *works,* ~ *farm,* champ d'épandage, *m.*

sewing, *n,* couture, *f.* ~ *machine,* machine à coudre, *f.*

sex, *n,* sexe, *m.* ¶ *a,* (*education &c*) sexuel. ~ *appeal,* sex-appeal, *m.* ~ *maniac,* obsédé(e) sexuel(le). ~ *offender,* délinquant(e) sexuel(le). ~ *pot P,* allumeuse *P, f.* ~ *shop,* sexshop, *m.*

sextet[te], *n,* sextuor, *m.*

sexton, *n,* sacristain, *m.*

sexual†, *a,* sexuel. ~ *intercourse,* rapports sexuels. ~**ity,** *n,* sexualité, *f.* **sexy** *P, a,* sexy *P, inv.*

shabby, *a,* (*clothes*) usé; râpé; (*pers.*) pauvrement vêtu; (*district, house*) miteux; (*behaviour*) mesquin.
shack, *n,* cabane, hutte, *f.*
shackle, *n,* fer, *m;* (*fig.*) entrave, *f.* ¶ *v.t,* entraver.
shade, *n,* ombre; (*colour, meaning &c*) nuance, *f;* (*lamp* ~) abat-jour, *m.inv;* (*ghost*) fantôme, *m.* ¶ *v.t,* ombrager, abriter du soleil; (*light*) voiler. ~ [*in*], (*Art*) ombrer; hachurer. ~ *off,* dégrader. **shading,** *n,* ombres, *f.pl;* hachure[s], *f.*[*pl*]. **shadow,** *n,* ombre, *f.* ~ *boxing,* boxe à vide, *f.* ~ *cabinet,* cabinet fantôme, *m.* ¶ *v.t,* filer. **shady,** *a,* ombragé; (*Poet.*) ombreux; (*disreputable*) louche, véreux.
shaft, *n,* (*arrow, spear*) hampe, *f;* (*hoe, golf club*) manche; (*cart*) brancard; (*column*) fût; (*Mech.*) arbre; (*Min.*) puits, *m;* (*lift*) cage; (*ventilation*) cheminée, *f;* (*light*) rayon; (*wit*) trait, *m.*
shaggy, *a,* (*beard*) hirsute; (*mane*) broussailleux; (*animal*) à longs poils rudes.
shake, *n,* secousse, *f;* (*head*) hochement, *m;* (*hand*) poignée; (*pl.*) tremblote *P, f. it's no great* ~*s P,* ça ne casse rien *P. in 2* ~*s,* en un clin d'œil. ¶ *v.t.ir,* (*gen.*) secouer; (*dice, bottle*) agiter; (*house, window*) ébranler; (*stick &c*) brandir; (*health, belief*) ébranler; (*disturb*) secouer, bouleverser. ~ *hands with,* serrer la main de. ~ *one's fist at,* menacer du poing. ¶ *v.i.ir,* trembler. *let's* ~ *on it,* topez là! ~ *off,* (*water*) secouer; (*cold &c*) se débarrasser de; (*habit*) se défaire de; (*pursuer*) semer. ~ *up,* secouer; (*bottle*) agiter. ~*-up,* grande réorganisation, *f.* **shaky,** *a,* tremblant; (*table*) peu solide; (*writing*) tremblé; (*memory &c*) assez mauvais.
shall, *v. modal ir,* (*lst pers. future tense*) *I* ~ *wait for you,* je vous attendrai. *we* ~ *be late,* nous serons en retard. (*in questions*) ~ *I wait for you?* voulez-vous que je vous attende? (*subj.*). ~ *we go?* on y va? (*command &c*) *you* ~ *do it!* vous le ferez, je le veux! *you* ~ *have it,* vous l'aurez.
shallot, *n,* échalote, *f.*
shallow, *a,* peu profond; (*fig: pers. &c*) superficiel. ~**s,** *n.pl,* hauts-fonds, *m.pl.*
sham, *a,* (*fake*) faux, en toc *P;* (*feigned*) feint, simulé, faux. ¶ *n, it's all* ~, c'est de la frime. ¶ *v.t,* feindre, simuler, faire semblant.
shambles, *n,* scène de carnage; (*P disorder*) pagaïe *P, f.*
shambling, *a,* traînant.
shame, *n,* honte, *f. the* ~ *of it!* quelle honte! *what a* ~*!* [quel] dommage! ¶ *v.t,* faire honte à. ~**faced,** *a,* honteux, penaud. ~**ful†,** *a,* honteux; scandaleux. ~**less,** *a,* éhonté; (*immodest*) impudique. ~**lessly,** *ad,* sans vergogne; de façon impudique.
shammy [leather], *n,* peau de chamois, *f.*
shampoo, *n,* (*wet*) schampooing, *m;* (*dry*) friction, *f.* ¶ *v.t,* faire un schampooing à; faire une friction à.
shamrock, *n,* trèfle, *m.*
shanty[1], *n,* baraque, *f.* ~ *town,* bidonville, *m.*
shanty[2], *n,* chanson de marins, *f.*
shape, *n,* forme, *f. be in good* ~, (*pers.*) être en forme; (*business*) marcher bien. *lick into* ~, (*pers.*) dresser; (*plan*) mettre au point. *in poor* ~, mal en point. *take* ~, prendre tournure. ¶ *v.t,* (*stone &c*) façonner (*into,* en); (*character*) pétrir; (*events*) influencer. ~ *up well,* faire des progrès; marcher bien. ~**less,** *a,* informe. ~**ly,** *a,* (*legs &c*) bien fait.
share, *n,* part (*of, in,* de); (*Fin.*) action, *f;* (*plough*) soc, *m. do one's* ~, fournir sa part d'effort. *take a* ~ *in,* participer à. ~*cropper,* métayer, ère. ~*holder,* actionnaire, *m,f.* ~ *index* (*Stk Ex.*), indice de la Bourse, *m.* ~ *prices,* prix des actions, *m.pl.* ¶ *v.t. & i,* partager (avec); (*have* ~ *of*) avoir part à. ~ [*out*], partager, répartir (*among,* entre). ~ *&* ~ *alike,* à chacun sa part.
shark, *n,* (*fish*) requin; (*pers.*) escroc, *m.*
sharp, *a,* (*point, angle*) aigu; (*pencil, nose*) pointu; (*blade*) tranchant, bien aiguisé; (*features*) anguleux; (*bend*) brusque; (*fall of price, change*) soudain; (*photo*) net; (*Mus.*) dièse; (*pain*) vif; (*wind, cold*) pénétrant; (*frost*) fort; (*taste*) piquant; (*reply*) brusque; (*rebuke*) sévère; (*pers.*) éveillé, dégourdi. ~ *practice,* procédés malhonnêtes. ~*shooter,* tireur d'élite, *m.* ¶ *ad,* (*sing*) trop haut. *at 2 o'clock* ~, à 2 heures pile. *look* ~*!* dépêche-toi! ¶ (*Mus.*) *n,* dièse, *m.* ~**en,** *v.t,* (*blade, appetite*) aiguiser; (*point*) tailler; rendre plus net; aviver. ~ *one's wits,* se dégourdir. ~**ener,** *n,* (*blades*) aiguisoir, *m;* (*pencil* ~) taille-crayons, *m.inv.* ~**ly,** *ad,* sévèrement; (*retort*) sèchement; (*abruptly*) brusquement; (*distinctly*) nettement. ~**ness,** *n,* netteté; (*pain*) violence; sévérité; brusquerie, *f;* piquant, *m.*
shatter, *v.t,* (*object*) fracasser; (*lit., fig.*) briser; (*fig.*) ruiner; détruire. ¶ *v.i,* voler en éclats; se fracasser. ~**ed,** *a,* (*with grief*) anéanti; bouleversé; (*P exhausted*) éreinté. ~**ing,** *a,* (*defeat*) écrasant; (*news &c*) bouleversant.
shave, *v.t.* (*& i*), (se) raser. ~ *off one's beard,* se raser la barbe. **shaving,** *n,* (*wood*) copeau, *m.* ~ *brush,* blaireau, *m.* ~ *cream,* crème à raser, *f.* ~ *stick,* bâton de savon à barbe, *m.*
shawl, *n,* châle, *m.*
she, *pn,* (*stressed & unstressed*) elle; (+ *relative pn.*) celle. *there* ~ *is,* la voilà. ¶ *n,* (*animal*) femelle, *f.* ~*-bear,* ourse, *f.* ~*-wolf,* louve, *f.*
sheaf, *n,* (*corn*) gerbe; (*papers*) liasse, *f.*
shear, *v.t.ir,* tondre. ~ *off, v.t,* arracher; emporter. ~**er,** *n,* tondeur, euse. ~**ing,** *n,* tonte,

f. **shears,** *n.pl,* (*Hort.*) cisaille[s], *f.*[*pl*]; (*Need.*) grands ciseaux.

sheath, *n,* (*sword*) fourreau, *m;* (*dagger, cable*) gaine; (*Biol.*) enveloppe, *f;* (*condom*) préservatif, *m.* ~*-knife,* couteau à gaine, *m.* **sheathe,** *v.t.* (*sword &c*) rengainer.

shed¹, *n,* (*garden &c*) remise; (*smaller*) hutte; (*cow* ~) étable, *f;* (*Agr., Rly &c*) hangar, *m.*

shed², *v.t,* (*petals, fur &c*) perdre; (*tears, blood*) verser; (*clothes*) enlever; (*light, warmth &c*) répandre. ~ *light on* (*fig.*), jeter de la lumière sur; (*problem*) éclaircir.

sheen, *n,* lustre, luisant; (*hair*) brillant, *m.*

sheep, *n,* mouton, *m;* (*ewe*) brebis, *f.* ~*-dip,* bain parasiticide, *m.* ~*dog,* chien de berger, *m.* ~*fold,* parc à moutons, *m,* bergerie, *f.* ~*shank* (*Naut.*), jambe de chien, *f.* ~*skin,* peau de mouton, *f.* ~*skin jacket,* canadienne, *f.* ~**ish,** *a,* penaud.

sheer¹, *a,* pur; absolu; vrai, veritable; (*material &c*) extrafin; (*rock &c*) à pic. *a* ~ *drop,* un à-pic.

sheer², *v.i,* ~ *off,* (*Naut.*) faire une embardée; (*fig.*) prendre le large *P.*

sheet, *n,* (*bed*) drap, *m;* (*dust* ~) housse; (*tarpaulin*) bâche; (*paper*) feuille, *f;* (*metal*) tôle; (*ice, glass &c*) plaque; (*water, flame*) nappe; (*Naut.*) écoute, *f.* ~ *lightning,* éclair en nappes, *m.* ~ *metal,* tôle, *f.* ~ *music,* partitions, *f.pl.*

sheik[h], *n,* cheik, *m.*

shelf, *n,* étagère; (*oven*) plaque, *f;* (*shop*) rayon; (*rock*) rebord; (*Naut.*) écueil, *m.* [*set of*] *shelves,* rayonnage, *m. on the* ~ (*unmarried*), laissé pour compte.

shell, *n,* (*nut, egg &c*) coquille; (*tortoise, lobster*) carapace, *f;* (*sea* ~) coquillage, *m;* (*peas*) cosse; (*building*) carcasse, *f;* (*Mil.*) obus, *m. come out of one's* ~, sortir de sa coquille. ~*fish,* coquillage; (*lobster, crab*) crustacé, *m;* (*Cook.*) fruits de mer, *m.pl.* ~ *hole,* entonnoir, *m.* ~ *shock,* psychose traumatique, *f.* ¶ *v.t,* (*peas*) écosser; (*nut, shrimp*) décortiquer; (*Mil.*) bombarder. ~**ing** (*Mil.*) *n,* bombardement, *m.*

shelter, *n,* abri; (*mountain*) refuge; (*Bus* ~) abribus; (*air-raid* ~) abri, *m. take* ~, se mettre à l'abri *ou* à couvert. ¶ *v.t,* abriter; protéger. ¶ *v.i,* s'abriter.

shelve, *v.t,* (*lit.*) garnir de rayons; (*fig.*) laisser en suspens. ¶ *v.i,* (*slope*) descendre en pente douce.

shepherd, *n,* berger; (*Rel.*) pasteur, *m.* ~*'s crook,* houlette, *f.* ~*'s purse,* bourse-à-pasteur, *f.* ¶ *v.t,* (*flock*) garder; (*fig.*) conduire. ~**ess,** *n,* bergère, *f.*

sheriff, *n,* shérif, *m.*

sherry, *n,* xérès, sherry, *m.*

shield, *n,* (*gen, fig.*) bouclier; (*Mach.*) écran [de protection]; (*Her.*) écu, écusson, *m.* ¶ *v.t,* protéger.

shift, *n,* changement (*in,* de); déplacement, *m;* (*of wind*) saute, *f;* (*linguistic*) mutation, *f;* (*Ind: work period*) poste; (*expedient*) expédient, truc *P, m. work* ~*s,* travailler par roulement *ou* en équipes. ¶ *v.t,* (*object*) déplacer, changer de place; (*limb &c*) bouger, remuer; (*scenery*) changer; (*fig: blame &c*) rejeter (sur). ¶ *v.i,* bouger; (*wind*) tourner; (*load*) se déplacer; (*opinion*) changer. ~ *for o.s,* se débrouiller tout seul *P.* ~**ily,** *ad,* sournoisement. ~**iness,** *n,* sournoiserie, *f.* ~**less,** *a,* peu débrouillard *P.* ~**y,** *a,* sournois.

shilly-shally, *v.i,* hésiter, vaciller.

shimmer, *v.i,* chatoyer; (*water &c*) miroiter.

shin, *n,* tibia; (*beef*) jarret, *m.* ~ *bone,* tibia, *m.* ~ *up a tree,* grimper à un arbre.

shindy, *n,* chahut; boucan *P, m. kick up a* ~, faire du boucan.

shine, *n,* brillant; éclat, *m. take the* ~ *off,* ternir; (*fig.*) diminuer l'effet de. ¶ *v.i.ir,* briller; (*face*) rayonner (de, *with*). ~ *on sth,* éclairer qch. ¶ *v.t,* faire briller.

shingle, *n,* galets, *m.pl;* (*Build.*) bardeau, *m.*

shingles (*Med.*), *n,* zona, *m.*

shining & shiny, *a,* brillant; reluisant; (*example*) resplendissant.

ship, *n,* (*gen.*) bateau; (*large*) navire; vaisseau, bâtiment, *m.* ~*'s boat,* chaloupe, *f.* ~ *building,* construction navale, *f.* ~ *canal,* canal maritime, *m.* ~*'s company,* équipage, *m.* ~*mate,* camarade de bord, *m.* ~*owner,* armateur, *m.* ~*shape,* à sa place. ~*wreck,* naufrage, *m. to be* ~ *wrecked,* faire naufrage. ~*wright,* constructeur de navires; charpentier de vaisseau, *m.* ~*yard,* chantier naval, *m.* ¶ *v.t,* transporter, expédier; (*take on*) embarquer, charger; (*oars*) rentrer. **shipment,** *n,* cargaison, *f.* **shipper,** *n,* expéditeur, *m.* **shipping,** *n,* navigation, *f;* (*col: ships*) navires, *m.pl.* ~ *agent,* agent maritime, *m.* ~ *charges,* frais d'expédition, *m.pl.* ~ *lane,* voie de navigation, *f.* ~ *line,* compagnie de navigation, *f.*

shire, *n,* comté, *m.* ~ *horse,* cheval de gros trait, *m.*

shirk, *v.t,* (*work, duty*) esquiver, se dérober à. ¶ *v.i,* tirer au flanc *P.* ~**er,** *n,* tire-au-flanc *P, m.inv.*

shirt, *n,* (*man's*) chemise, *f;* (*woman's*) chemisier, *m. in one's* ~ *sleeves,* en bras de chemise. *put one's* ~ *on* (*horse*), jouer sa fortune sur. **shirty** *P, a,* en rogne *P.*

shit *P*, n,* merde *P*, f.* ¶ *i,* merde! ¶ *v.i.ir,* chier, *P*.*

shiver, *v.i,* frissonner. ¶ *n,* frisson, *m.*

shoal, *n,* (*sand, fish*) banc; (*shallow*) haut-fond, *m.*

shock, *n,* (*gen.*) choc, *m;* (*explosion &c*)

secousse; (*Elec.*) décharge; (*of hair*) tignasse, *f. you gave me a* ~ , vous m'avez fait peur. ~ *absorber* (*Mot.*), amortisseur, *m.* ~*proof,* anti-choc, *inv.* ~ *resistant,* résistant aux chocs. ~ *therapy.* électrochoc, *m.* ¶ *a,* (*Mil: tactics*) de choc. ¶ *v.t,* choquer, scandaliser; secouer; bouleverser. ~**ing,** *a,* choquant; affreux; bouleversant.

shoddy, *a,* de mauvaise qualité.

shoe, *n,* soulier, *m,* chaussure, *f;* (*horse*) fer; (*brake* ~) sabot [de frein], *m. in your* ~*s,* à votre place. *shake in one's* ~*s,* trembler dans sa culotte, *P.* ~ *brush,* brosse à souliers, *f.* ~ *horn,* chausse-pied, *m.* ~*lace,* lacet de soulier, *m.* ~*maker,* ~ *repairer,* cordonnier, *m.* ~ *polish,* cirage, *m.* ~*shop,* magasin de chaussures, *m. on a* ~*string,* à peu de frais. ¶ *v.t.ir,* chausser; ferrer.

shoo away, ~ **off,** *v.t,* chasser.

shoot, *n,* (*game*) chasse; (*plant*) pousse; (*chute*) glissière, *f.* ¶ *v.t.ir,* (*game*) chasser; (*kill*) abattre; (*pers: hit*) atteindre; (*wound*) blesser d'un coup de fusil; (*execute*) fusiller; (*fire: gun*) tirer *ou* lâcher un coup de fusil (*at,* sur); (*arrow, missile &c*) lancer (sur); (*goal*) marquer; (*look*) lancer (à); (*Cine: film &c*) tourner; (*rapids*) descendre. (*fig.*) ~ *one's bolt,* jouer sa dernière carte. ~ *a line P,* en conter. ¶ *v.i,* tirer (sur); (*Foot. &c*) shooter, tirer; (*Bot.*) pousser, bourgeonner. *go* ~*ing,* chasser. ~ *on sight,* tirer à vue. ~ *down,* abattre. ~*-out,* fusillade, *f.* ~ *up,* (*grow*) pousser vite; (*water, flame*) jaillir; (*rocket, prices &c*) monter en flèche. **shooting,** *n,* chasse, *f;* (*shots*) coups de feu, *m.pl;* fusillade, *f;* meurtre *m;* exécution, *f.* ~ *brake,* break, *m.* ~ *gallery,* stand de tir, *m. the whole* ~ *match P* (*fig.*), tout le tremblement *P.* ~ *pains,* douleur lancinante, *f.* ~ *star,* étoile filante, *f.* ~ *stick,* canne-siège, *f.*

shop, *n,* magasin, *m;* (*small*) boutique, *f;* (*work*) atelier, *m. talk* ~ , parler boutique. ~ *assistant,* vendeur, euse. ~*-floor* [*workers*], ouvriers, *m.pl.* ~*keeper,* commerçant, e. ~*-lifting,* vol à l'étalage, *m.* ~*-soiled,* défraîchi. ~ *steward,* délégué, e syndical, e. ~ *window,* vitrine, *f.* ¶ *v.i,* faire ses courses *ou* achats (*at,* chez). *go* ~*ping,* faire des courses. ¶ *v.t,* (*P betray*) vendre, donner *P.* **shopping,** *n,* (*goods*) achats, *m.pl.* ~ *bag, basket,* sac, panier à provisions, *m.* ~ *centre,* centre commercial, *m.* ~ *precinct,* zone commerciale [piétonnière], *f.*

shore, *n,* (*sea*) rivage, bord, *m;* (*lake*) rive; (*coast*) côte, *f. on* ~, à terre. *go on* ~, débarquer. ~ *leave,* permission à terre, *f.*

shore up, *v.t,* étayer; (*fig.*) consolider.

short, *a.* (*gen.*) court; (*pers., step, walk*) petit; (*vowel, visit*) bref; (*manner*) brusque, sec; (*pastry*) brisé. ~ *of doing it,* à moins de le faire. *a* ~ *distance away,* à peu de distance. *a* ~ *time,* peu de temps. *be* ~ *of,* être à court de; manquer. *be taken* ~ *P,* être pris d'un besoin pressant. *be* ~ *for,* être l'abréviation de. *give* ~ *measure,* tricher sur le poids. ~*bread,* sablé, *m.* ~[*-circuit*], *a,* court-circuit; *v.t,* court-circuiter. ~*coming,* défaut, *m.* ~ *cut,* raccourci, *m.* ~*fall,* manque, *m.* ~*hand,* sténo[graphie], *f.* ~*hand-typist,* sténodactylo, *m,f.* ~*hand-writer,* sténo[graphe], *m,f.* ~*-lived,* (*fig.*) de courte durée. ~*-range,* ~*-term,* à court terme. ~*-sighted,* myope; (*fig.*) peu perspicace. ~*-sightedness,* myopie, *f;* manque de vision, *m.* ~ *story,* nouvelle, *f.* ~*-story writer,* nouvelliste, *m,f.* ~*-tempered,* coléreux; d'humeur irritable. ~*-wave,* ondes courtes. ~**age,** *n,* manque, *m,* pénurie, *f;* (*housing*) crise, *f. food* ~ , disette, *f.* ~**en,** *v.t. & i,* raccourcir. ~**ening,** (*Cook.*) *n,* matière grasse, *f.* ~**ly,** *ad,* bientôt; sous peu; (*curtly*) brusquement. ~ *before,* peu avant. ~**ness,** *n,* peu de longueur, *m,* brièveté; petite taille, *f.*

shot, *n,* (*act*) coup; (*sound*) coup de feu, de fusil &c, *m;* (*bullet*) balle, *f;* (*pellets*) plomb; (*pers.*) tireur; (*Foot., Ten., Golf*) coup; (*throw*) lancer; (*for putting*) poids, *m;* (*Phot.*) photo; (*Cine*) prise de vues; (*injection*) piqûre, *f;* (*alcohol*) coup; (*at goal, moon*) tir; (*attempt*) essai, coup, *m. have a* ~ *at it,* tenter le coup. *a* ~ *in the arm* (*fig.*), un coup de fouet. *get* ~ *of P,* se débarrasser de. *like a* ~ , (*move*) comme une flèche; (*accept*) sans hésiter. ~*gun,* fusil de chasse, *m.* ~*gun wedding,* mariage forcé. ~ *silk,* soie gorge-de-pigeon, *f.* ~ *with* (*fabric*), strié de.

should, *v.modal, is expressed in Fr. by conditional mood & by* devoir, falloir, *to express obligation, advisability & probability. I* ~ *like,* j'aimerais bien. *he* ~ *have arrived by this time,* il devrait être arrivé à l'heure qu'il est. *you* ~ *do it at once,* vous devriez le faire (il faudrait que tu le fasses) tout de suite.

shoulder, *n,* épaule, *f;* (*road*) accotement, bas-côté; (*hill*) contrefort, *m. put one's* ~ *to the wheel* (*fig.*), s'atteler à la tâche. ~ *bag,* sac à bandoulière, *m.* ~ *blade.* omoplate, *f.* ~ *strap,* (*dress &c*) bretelle, *f.* ¶ *v.t,* charger sur son épaule; (*fig.*) se charger de; (*responsibility*) endosser. ~ *arms* (*Mil.*), porter l'arme.

shout, *n,* cri; (*laughter*) éclat, *m.* ¶ *v.t,* crier. ¶ *v.i,* crier (*for help,* au secours); pousser des cris (de joie &c). ~ *with laughter,* éclater de rire. ~ *down,* huer. ~**ing,** *n,* cris; éclats de voix, *m.pl.*

shove, *n,* poussée, *f.* ¶ *v.t,* pousser [avec peine]; (*thrust*) enfoncer; (*jostle*) bousculer. ~ *sth in one's pocket,* fourrer qch dans sa poche. ¶ *v.i,* pousser. ~ *off P,* ficher le camp *P.* ~ *over P,* se pousser.

shovel, *n,* pelle; (*Mach.*) pelleteuse, *f.* ¶ *v.t,* pelleter. ~ *away,* (*snow*) enlever à la p. ~**ful,** *n,* pelletée, *f.*

show, *n,* (*emotion*) démonstration; (*of wealth*) parade, *f;* (*of power*) étalage, *m;* (*Art &c*) exposition; (*Com.*) foire; (*Agr.*) concours; (*Theat.*) spectacle; (*variety*) show, *m.* ~ *of hands,* vote à main levée, *m. just for* ~, pour l'effet. *make a poor* ~ *P,* faire piètre figure. *put up a good* ~ *P,* bien se défendre *P.* ~ *business,* le monde du spectacle. ~*case,* vitrine, *f.* ~*down,* épreuve de force, *f.* ~*girl,* girl, *f.* ~*ground,* champ de foire, *m.* ~*-house &c,* maison &c témoin. ~*jumping,* concours hippique, *m.* ~*man,* forain, *m.* ~*manship* (*fig.*), sens de mise en scène, *m.* ~*-off,* m'as-tu-vu, e. ~*room,* salle d'exposition, *f.* ¶ *v.t,* (*gen.*) montrer; (*film*) passer; (*Art &c*) exposer; (*feelings*) manifester, témoigner; (*clock &c*) indiquer, marquer. ~ *itself,* se révéler, devenir visible. ~ *one's age,* faire son âge. ~ *s.o the way,* indiquer le chemin à qn. ¶ *v.i,* être visible; se voir. ~ **in,** faire entrer. ~ **out,** ~ *to the door,* reconduire jusqu'à la porte. ~ **off,** *v.i,* crâner *P,* faire l'important; *v.t,* faire étalage de; (*to advantage*) mettre en valeur. ~ **round,** faire visiter. ~ **through,** se voir au travers. ~ **up,** *v.i,* ressortir; se voir; *v.t,* révéler; (*imposter*) démasquer.

shower, *n,* (*rain*) averse; (*stones, blows*) pluie, grêle, *f.* ~ [*bath*], douche, *f.* ~ *cap,* bonnet de douche, *m.* ~*proof,* imperméable. ¶ *v.t,* (*fig.*) combler (*on s.o,* qn de); (*blows*) faire pleuvoir (sur qn); (*abuse &c*) couvrir (qn de). ~**y,** *a,* pluvieux.

showing, *n,* (*film*) projection; (*Cine*) séance, *f.*

showy, *a,* éclatant; (*pej.*) voyant.

shrapnel, *n,* éclat d'obus, *m.pl.*

shred, *n,* lambeau; (*fig: truth*) grain, *m. not a* ~ *of evidence,* pas la plus petite preuve. *tear to* ~*s,* déchiqueter; (*fig.*) démolir. ¶ *v.t,* mettre en lambeaux, déchiqueter; (*Cook.*) couper en lanières. **shredder,** *n,* (*paper*) destructeur *m.*

shrew, *n,* (*Zool.*) musaraigne; (*woman*) mégère, *f.*

shrewd, *a,* perspicace; (*plan*) astucieux. ~**ness,** *n,* perspicacité; astuce, *f.*

shriek, *n,* hurlement, *m.* ¶ *v.i. & t,* hurler, crier (*with,* de). ~ *with laughter,* rire aux éclats.

shrill, *a,* aigu, perçant, strident. ~**ness,** *n,* ton perçant.

shrimp, *n,* crevette, *f.* ~**ing,** *n,* pêche à la crevette, *f.*

shrine, *n,* (*place*) lieu saint; (*reliquary*) châsse, *f;* (*fig.*) haut lieu.

shrink, *v.i.ir,* (*cloth*) [se] rétrécir, [se] rapetisser; (*wood*) se contracter; (*sum*) diminuer. ~ [*away*], ~ *back,* reculer. ¶ *v.t.ir,* [faire] rétrécir; contracter. ¶ *n, P,* psychiatre, psy *P,* *m,f.* ~**age,** *n,* rétrécissement, *m;* contraction; diminution, *f.*

shrivel [up], *v.t.* (*& i,*) (*face, apple*) (se) ratatiner; (*skin*) (se) rider; (*meat*) (se) racornir.

shroud, *n,* linceul; (*Naut.*) hauban, *m.* ¶ *v.t,* envelopper; ensevelir (*in,* de).

Shrove Tuesday, *n,* mardi gras, *m.*

shrub, *n,* arbrisseau; (*small*) arbuste, *m.* **shrubbery,** *n,* [massif *m* d']arbustes, *m.pl.*

shrug, *n,* haussement d'épaules, *m.* ¶ *v.i,* hausser les épaules.

shudder, *n,* frisson, *m;* (*engine &c*) vibration, *f.* ¶ *v.i,* frissonner; vibrer.

shuffle, *v.t,* (*Cards*) battre; (*dominoes*) mêler; (*papers*) remuer. ¶ *v.i,* traîner les pieds.

shun, *v.t,* éviter, fuir.

shunt, *v.t,* (*Rly*) aiguiller; manœuvrer; (*Elec.*) dériver. ~**ing,** *n,* manœuvres d'aiguillage, *f.pl.* ~ *yard,* gare de triage, *f.*

shut, *v.t.ir,* fermer. ¶ *v.i.* [se] f. ~ *away,* (*pers. &c*) enfermer; (*valuables*) mettre sous clef. ~ *down,* fermeture, *f.* ~ *in,* enfermer. ~ *out,* fermer la porte à; exclure. ~ *up,* fermer; enfermer; clouer la bec à *P; v.i,* se taire. ~ *up!* tais-toi! ferme-la! *P.* **shutter,** *n,* volet; (*Phot.*) obturateur, *m.*

shuttle, *n,* navette, *f.* ~*cock,* volant, *m.* ~ *service,* [service *m* de] navette. ¶ *v.i,* faire la navette.

shy[1], *v.t,* lancer, jeter.

shy[2]†, *a,* timide; (*unsociable*) sauvage. ¶ *v.i,* (*horse*) se cabrer (*at,* devant). ~ *away from doing* (*fig.*), répugner à faire. ~**ness,** *n,* timidité, sauvagerie, *f.*

Siamese, *a. & n,* siamois, e. ~ *cat,* [chat] siamois. ~ *twins,* [frères] siamois, [sœurs] siamoises.

Siberia, *n,* la Sibérie. **Siberian,** *a,* sibérien. ¶ *n,* Sibérien, ne.

sibilant, *a,* sifflant. ¶ *n,* sifflante, *f.*

siblings, *n.pl,* enfants de même parents, *m,f.*

Sicilian, *a,* sicilien. ¶ *n,* Sicilien, ne. **Sicily,** *n,* la Sicile.

sick, *a,* (*ill*) malade; (*fig: mind &c*) malsain. *be* ~, vomir, être malade. *feel* ~, avoir mal au cœur. *be* ~ *& tired,* ~ *to death of,* en avoir par-dessus la tête de. *you make me* ~*!* tu me dégoûtes! ~*bay,* infirmerie, *f.* ~ *leave, pay,* congé, *m,* indemnité de maladie, *f.* ~ *room,* chambre de malade, *f.* ~**en,** *v.t,* rendre malade; donner mal au cœur à; dégoûter. ¶ *v.i,* tomber malade. ~ *for sth,* couver qch. ~**ening,** *a,* écœurant; dégoûtant; agaçant.

sickle, *n,* faucille, *f.*

sickly, *a,* (*pers.*) maladif; (*complexion*) blafard; (*smile*) faible; (*plant*) étiolé; (*smell &c*) écœurant. **sickness,** *n,* maladie, *f. bouts of* ~, vomissements, *m.pl.* ~ *benefit,* assurance maladie, *f.*

side, (*gen.*) côté; flanc; (*river, road &c*) bord;

(*fig: problem &c*) aspect, *m;* (*character*) facette, *f;* (*group*) camp, côté, *m;* (*Sport*) équipe, *f;* (*Pol.*) parti, *m.* ~ *by* ~, côte à côte. *from* ~ *to* ~, d'un côté à l'autre. *pick* ~*s,* former des camps. *take* ~*s,* prendre parti (*with s.o,* pour qn). *whose* ~ *are you on?* qui soutenez -vous? ¶ *a,* (*chapel &c*) latéral; (*fig: effect*) secondaire. ~*board,* buffet, *m.* ~*boards,* ~*burns,* rouflaquettes, *f.pl.* ~*car,* side-car, *m.* ~ *door,* petite porte. ~*kick P,* sous-fifre *P, m.* ~*light,* (*Mot.*) feu de position, *m.* (*fig.*) *a* ~*light on,* un aperçu de. ~*line* (*Sport*), [ligne de] touche, *f;* (*job*) activité secondaire, *f. on the* ~*lines,* (*Sport*) sur la touche; (*fig.*) dans les coulisses. ~ *plate,* petite assiette. ~ *long,* de côté, oblique; (*glance*) en coulisse. ~ *road, street,* petite route, p. rue. ~*saddle,* en amazone. ~ *shows,* attractions, *f. pl.* ~*-step,* éviter, esquiver. ~*track,* (*train*) dériver; (*fig.*) faire dévier de son sujet. *get* ~ *tracked,* s'écarter de son s. ~ *walk Am,* trottoir, *m.* ~*ways,* de côté. ~ *whiskers,* favoris, *m.pl.* ~ **with,** se ranger du côté de. **siding,** *n,* voie de garage, *f.*

sidle, *v.i,* ~ *in &c,* entrer &c furtivement. ~ *up to s.o,* glisser vers qn.

siege, *n,* siège, *m.*

sienna, *n,* terre de sienne, *f.*

siesta, *n,* sieste, *f.*

sieve, *n,* tamis; (*riddle*) crible, *m.* ¶ *v.t,* = *sift.* **sift,** *v.t,* tamiser: passer au crible. ~ [*out*], (*facts &c*) dégager. ~ *through,* examiner. ~**er,** *n,* saupoudreuse, *f.*

sigh, *n,* soupir, *m.* ¶ *v.i,* soupirer.

sight, *n,* (*gen., faculty*) vue, *f;* spectacle, *m;* (*gun*) mire, *f. at* ~, *on* ~, à vue. *I can't stand the* ~ *of him,* je ne peux pas le sentir *P. catch* ~ *of,* apercevoir. *know by* ~, connaître de vue. *look a* ~, avoir l'air de Dieu sait quoi *P. lose* ~ *of,* perdre de vue. *out of* ~, hors de vue. *out of* ~ *out of mind,* loin des yeux loin du cœur. ~*-read,* déchiffrer. ~*seeing,* tourisme, *m.* ~*seer,* touriste, *m,f.* ¶ *v.t,* (*land &c*) apercevoir; (*gun*) viser.

sign, *n,* signe; (*notice: gen., traffic*) panneau, *m;* (*inn, shop*) enseigne, *f. as a* ~ *of,* en signe de. *in* ~ *language,* par signes. ~*post,* poteau indicateur, *m.* ~ *writer,* peintre d'enseignes, *m.* ¶ *v.t. & i,* (*letter &c*) signer; (*Foot. &c: player*) engager. ~ *one's name,* signer. ~ **in,** (*at work*) pointer; (*in hotel*) signer le registre. ~ **off,** (*Radio, TV*) terminer l'émission. ~ **on,** ~ **up,** (*Mil.*) (s')engager; (*employee*) (se faire) embaucher; (*enrol*) s'inscrire.

signal, *n,* signal, *m.* ~ *box,* cabine d'aiguillage, *f.* ~*man* (*Rly*) aiguilleur; (*Naut.*) signaleur, *m.* ¶ *a,* (*success*) insigne; (*importance*) capital. ¶ *v.t,* communiquer par signaux. ¶ *v.i,* faire des signaux. **signatory,** *n,* signataire, *m,f.* **signature,** *n,* signature; (*Mus. key* ~) armature, *f.* ~ *tune,* indicatif musical. **signet,** *n,* cachet, *m.* ~ *ring,* chevalière, *f.*

significance, *n,* signification; importance, portée, *f. look of deep* ~, regard très significatif, *m. it's of no* ~, ça importe peu. **significant,** *a,* (*look*) significatif; (*event*) important, de grande portée; (*increase*) considérable. **signify,** *v.t,* signifier. ¶ *v.i,* avoir de l'importance.

silence, *n,* silence, *m.* ¶ *v.t,* faire taire. **silencer,** *n,* silencieux, *m.* **silent**†, *a,* silencieux, taciturne; (*Gram. &c*) muet. *to be* ~. se taire.

silhouette, *n,* silhouette, *f.*

silicon, *n,* silicium, *m.* ~ *chip,* plaquette de s., microplaquette, *f.* **silicone,** *n,* silicone, *f.* **silicosis,** *n,* silicose, *f.*

silk, *n,* soie, *f.* ~ *dress &c,* robe &c de *ou* en soie. ~ *goods* or ~*s,* ~ *factory,* soierie, *f.* ~*screen printing,* sérigraphie, *f.* ~*worm,* ver à soie, *m.* **silky,** *a,* [à l'aspect] soyeux; (*voice*) doucereux.

sill, *n,* rebord; (*Mot.*) bas de marche, *m.*

silliness, *n,* bêtise, niaiserie, stupidité, *f.* **silly,** *a,* idiot, bête, sot; (*clothes &c*) ridicule. *feel* ~, se sentir ridicule. ¶ *n,* idiot, e, imbécile, *m,f.*

silo, *n,* silo, *m.*

silt, *n,* vase, *f,* limon, *m.* ~ **up,** s'envaser.

silver, *n,* argent, *m;* argenterie, *f,* ¶ *a,* d'argent, en argent. ~ *birch,* bouleau argenté. ~ *foil,* ~ *paper,* papier d'argent. ~ *fox,* renard argenté, *m.* ~*-gilt,* vermeil, argent doré. ~*-plate, n,* argenterie, *f; v.t,* argenter. ~*side,* gîte à la noix, *m.* ~*smith,* orfèvre, *m.* ~ *ware,* argenterie, *f.* ~ *wedding,* noces d'argent, *f.pl.* ¶ *v.t,* argenter; (*mirror*) étamer. ~**y,** *a,* (*colour, light*) argenté; (*sound*) argentin.

similar, *a,* semblable, pareil, similaire. ~**ity,** *n,* ressemblance (*to,* avec; *between,* entre); similitude (entre), *f.* ~**ly,** *ad,* de la même façon. **simile,** *n,* comparaison, *f.*

simmer, *v.i.* (*& t*), (*water*) (laisser) frémir; (*soup, stew*) (laisser) mijoter, (faire) cuire à feu doux. ~ *down P,* se calmer.

simper, *n,* sourire affecté, *m.* ¶ *v.i,* minauder.

simple†, *a,* simple; (*pers.*) niais; (*equation*) du premier degré. ~ *as ABC,* simple comme bonjour. ~ *interest,* intérêts simples, *m.pl.* ~*-minded,* simple d'esprit. **simpleton,** *n,* niais, e, nigaud, e. **simplicity,** *n,* simplicité, *f.* **simplify,** *v.t,* simplifier.

simulate, *v.t,* simuler, feindre. **simulation,** *n,* simulation, feinte, *f.* **simulator,** *n,* simulateur, *m.*

simultaneity, *n,* simultanéité, *f.* **simultaneous**†, *a,* simultané. ~ *equations,* équations équivalentes.

sin, *n,* péché, *m. live in* ~, vivre en concubinage (avec). ¶ *v.i,* pécher.

since, *ad. & pr,* depuis. ¶ *c,* depuis que; (*because*) puisque, comme.

sincere†, *a,* sincère. **sincerity,** *n,* sincérité, *f.*

sine, *n,* sinus, *m.*
sinecure, *n,* sinécure, *f.*
sinew, *n,* tendon, *m.* ~*s,* muscles, *m. pl.*
sinful, *a,* coupable; (*waste &c*) scandaleux.
sing, *v.t. & i. ir,* chanter; (*ears*) bourdonner, tinter. ~ *like a lark,* chanter comme un rossignol.
Singapore, *n,* Singapour, *m.*
singe, *v.t,* brûler légèrement; (*cloth*) roussir; (*hair*) flamber.
singer, *n,* chanteur, euse; cantatrice, *f.* **singing,** *n,* chant; (*ears*) tintement, *m.*
single, *a,* seul, unique; (*opp. double*) simple; (*unmarried*) célibataire. ~ *bed,* lit d'une personne, *m.* ~ *breasted,* droit. ~*-celled,* unicellulaire. ~ *combat,* combat singulier. ~*-decker,* sans impériale. ~*-engined,* monomoteur. *in* ~ *file,* en file indienne. ~*-handed,* tout seul, sans aide. *a* ~ *life,* le célibat. ~ *man, woman,* célibataire, *m,f.* ~*-minded,* résolu. ~ *room,* chambre à un lit, *f.* ~ *spacing,* simple interligne, *m.* ~*-track* (*Rly*), à voie unique. ¶ *n,* (*pl. Sport*) simple; (*ticket*) aller [simple], billet simple; (*record*) 45 tours, *m.* ~ **out,** distinguer. **singly,** *ad,* séparément; un(e) à un(e).
singsong, *a,* chantant. ¶ *n,* psalmodie, *f. have a* ~, chanter en chœur.
singular†, *a. & n,* singulier, *m. in the* ~, au s.
sinister, *a,* sinistre; (*Her.*) sénestre.
sink[1], *n,* évier, *m.* ~ *tidy,* coin d'évier, *m.* ~ *unit,* bloc-évier, *m.*
sink[2], *v.i.ir,* (*ship*) couler; (*ground, building &c*) s'affaisser; (*prices, temperature, level*) baisser; (*into a chair*) se laisser tomber, s'effondrer; (*fig: into sleep &c*) sombrer (dans). *be* ~*ing* (*dying*), décliner. *my heart sank,* j'ai été pris de découragement. ¶ *v.t,* couler; (*mine &c*) creuser; (*pipe &c*) noyer; (*money*) investir. ~ *one's teeth into,* mordre [à belles dents] dans. ~ **back,** retomber. ~ **down,** s'enfoncer. ~ **in,** (*pers. &c*) s'enfoncer; (*water &c*) pénétrer; (*fig.*) rentrer; faire son effet. *with* ~*ing heart,* le cœur serré.
sinless, *a,* innocent. **sinner,** *n,* pécheur, *m,* pécheresse, *f.*
sinuous, *a,* sinueux.
sinus, *n,* sinus, *m.*
sip, *n,* petite gorgée; goutte, *f.* ¶ *v.t. & i,* boire à petites gorgées; (*savour*) siroter *P.*
siphon, *n,* siphon, *m.* ~ [*off*], siphonner.
sir, *n,* monsieur, *m;* (*title*) sir. *no,* ~, (*Army*) non, mon colonel, &c; (*Navy*) non, amiral, *&c;* (*ship's captain*) non, commandant. *Dear S*~, (*letter*) Monsieur. **sire,** *n,* père; (*to kings*) sire, *m.* ¶ *v.t,* engendrer.
siren (*Myth. & hooter*) *n,* sirène, *f.*
sirloin, *n,* aloyau, *m. a roast* ~, un rosbif.
sisal, *n,* sisal, *m.*
sister, *n,* sœur; (*Med.*) infirmière en chef; (*Rel.*) [bonne] sœur, *f.* ~*-in-law,* belle-sœur, *f.* ~ *ship,* sister-ship, *m.* ~**ly,** *a,* de sœur.
sit, *v.i.ir,* s'asseoir; (*portrait*) poser; (*court &c*) siéger; (*hen*) couver. ~ *down,* s'asseoir. ~ [*for*] (*exam*), passer, se présenter à. *be* ~*ting down,* être assis. *be* ~*ting pretty,* tenir le bon bout *P,* ~ **down,** s'asseoir; ~ *down again,* se rasseoir. ~ [*down*], *v.t,* [faire] asseoir. ~*-down strike,* grève sur le tas, *f.* ~ **for,** (*portrait*) poser pour; (*Pol.*) représenter. ~**-in,** sit-in, *m.inv.* ~ *in for s.o,* remplacer qn. ~ *still,* rester *ou se* tenir tranquille. ~ *tight* (*lit., fig.*), ne pas bouger. ~ **up,** se redresser; (*stay up*) rester debout, veiller.
site, *n,* (*of building &c*) emplacement; (*Archeology*) site; (*Build.*) chantier [de construction, de démolition &c], *m.* ¶ *v.t,* placer.
sitting, *n,* (*assembly*) séance; (*portrait*) séance de pose, *f;* (*meals*) service, *m.* ~ *duck P,* cible facile, *f.* ~ *room,* salon, *m.* ~ *tenant,* locataire en place, *m,f.*
situated, *a,* situé; placé. **situation,** *n,* situation, *f.* ~ *vacant,* offre d'emploi, *f.* ~ *wanted,* demande d'emploi, *f.*
six, *a. & n,* six, *m. be at* ~*es & sevens,* (*place &c*) être en pagaïe *P;* (*pers.*) être tout retourné *P. it's* ~ *of one & half a dozen of the other,* c'est bonnet blanc & blanc bonnet. *for other phrases V* **four. sixteen,** *a. & n,* seize, *m.* **sixteenth,** *a. & n.* seizième, *m,f;* (*fraction*) seizième, *m.* **sixth**†, *a. & n,* sixième, *m,f;* (*fraction*) sixième, *m;* (*Mus.*) sixte, *f.* ~ *form,* classes de première & terminale, *f.pl. for phrases V* **fourth. sixtieth,** *a. & n,* soixantième, *m,f.* **sixty,** *a. & n,* soixante, *m. for phrases V* **forty.**
size[1], *n,* (*for paper &c*) colle, *f.* ¶ *v.t,* encoller.
size[2], *n,* (*room, car &c*) dimensions, *f.pl;* (*egg, fruit*) grosseur; (*pers., clothes, photo*) taille; (*shoes, gloves*) pointure; (*shirt*) encolure, *f;* (*sum*) montant, *m;* (*land, problem*) étendue; (*operation &c*) envergure, *f. what* ~ *do you take?* quelle taille *ou* pointure faites-vous? ~ **up,** (*pers.*) juger; (*situation*) mesurer. ~**able,** *a,* assez grand; assez gros; assez important; assez considérable.
sizzle, *n,* grésillement, *m.* ¶ *v.i,* grésiller.
skate[1], (*fish*), *n,* raie, *f.*
skate[2], *n,* patin, *m.* ~*board,* planche à roulettes, *f.* ¶ *v.i,* patiner. *go skating,* faire du patinage; (*roller*) faire du patin à roulettes. ~ *round,* glisser sur. **skater,** *n,* patineur, euse. *skating rink,* patinoire, *f;* (*roller*) skating, *m.*
skein, *n,* écheveau, *m.*
skeleton, *n,* squelette; (*plan &c*) schéma, *m. the* ~ *in the cupboard,* le honteux secret de la famille. ~ *key,* crochet, *m.*
sketch, *n,* esquisse, *f,* croquis; (*fig: ideas &c*) résumé, aperçu; (*Theat.*) sketch, *m,* saynète, *f.* ~ *book,* carnet à croquis, *m.* ~ *pad,* bloc à

dessins, *m.* ¶ *v.t,* esquisser. ~ *in,* ajouter. ~ *out,* ébaucher. ¶ *v.i,* faire des croquis *ou* des esquisses.

skew, *a,* biais, oblique. ¶ *n,* biais, *m.* ~*-whiff P,* de guingois *P.*

skewer, *n,* brochette, *f.*

ski, *n,* ski, *m.* ~ *binding,* fixation, *f.* ~ *boot,* chaussure de ski, *f.* ~*ing instructor,* moniteur, trice de ski. ~*jump,* tremplin de ski, *m.* ~*jumping,* saut à ski, *m.* ~ *lift,* remonte-pente, *m.inv.* ~ *pants,* fuseau [de ski], *m.* ~ *resort,* station de ski, *f.* ~ *stick,* bâton de ski, *m.* ¶ *v.i,* faire du ski. **skiing,** *n,* le ski. *go on a* ~ *holiday,* partir aux sports d'hiver.

skid, *n,* dérapage, *m. go into a* ~, déraper. *correct a* ~ , redresser un d. ~*lid P,* casque [de moto], *m.* ~ *mark,* trace de dérapage, *f.* ~*pan,* piste savonnée. ¶ *v.i,* déraper.

skiff, *n,* skiff, *m,* yole, *f.*

skilful†, *a,* habile, adroit. **skill,** *n,* habileté, adresse; (*manual*) dextérité, *f;* (*talent*) savoir faire, talent, *m;* (*in craft &c*) technique, *f.* ~**ed,** *a,* (*pers.*) habile, adroit; (*worker &c*) qualifié; (*work*) de spécialiste.

skillet, *n,* poêlon, *m.*

skim, *v.t,* (*milk*) écrémer; (*scum*) écumer; (*grease*) dégraisser; (*ground, water*) raser, effleurer. ~ *off,* enlever, ~ *through* (*fig.*), parcourir. ~ *milk,* lait écrémé, *m.*

skimp, *v.t,* (*food*) lésiner sur; (*praise &c*) être chiche de; (*work*) bâcler *P.* ~**y,** *a,* (*dress*) étriqué; (*meal*) insuffisant, maigre, chiche.

skin, *n,* (*gen.*) peau; (*for wine*) outre, *f. by the* ~ *of one's teeth,* d'un poil, de justesse. *escape by the* ~ *of one's teeth,* l'échapper belle. *get under s.o's* ~ , taper sur les nerfs à qn. ~*-deep,* superficiel. ~ *diver,* plongeur, euse sous-marin(e). ~*flint,* grippe-sou, *m,* radin, e. ~ *graft,* greffe de la peau, *f.* ~ *test,* cuti[-réaction], *f.* ~*tight,* collant. ¶ *v.t,* (*animal*) écorcher. **skinny,** *a,* décharné; maigrelet.

skip[1] (*for rubbish*), *n,* benne, *f.*

skip[2], *n,* petit bond, petit saut. ¶ *v.i,* sautiller; (*with rope*) sauter à la corde. ~ [*off*], (*run away*) filer. ¶ *v.t,* (*omit*) sauter. ~ *it! P* laisse tomber! *P.* ~ *school,* sécher les cours. **skipper,** *n,* (*Naut.*) capitaine, patron; (*Sport*) capitaine, *m. skipping rope,* corde à sauter, *f.*

skirmish, *n,* escarmouche, *f.*

skirt, *n,* jupe; (*beef*) bavette, *f.* ¶ *v.t,* (*coast, wall*) cotoyer, longer. ~ *round,* contourner; (*difficulty*) esquiver. ~**ing [board],** *n,* plinthe *f.*

skit, *n,* parodie, *f;* (*Theat.*) sketch satirique, *m.*

skittle, *n,* quille, *f.* ~ *alley,* piste de jeu de quilles, *f,* bowling, *m.*

skive *P, v.i,* tirer au flanc. **skiver,** *n,* tire-au-flanc *P, m.inv.*

skivvy *P, n,* boniche, *f.*

skulk, *v.i,* rôder furtivement.

skull, *n,* crâne, *m.* ~ *cap,* calotte, *f.*

skunk, *n,* mouffette, *f;* (*fur*) sconse, *m.*

sky, *n,* ciel, *m;* (*pl: fig.*) cieux, *m.pl. praise to the skies,* porter aux nues. ~*-blue,* bleu ciel, *inv.* ~ *diving,* parachutisme, *m.* ~*-high,* (*prices*) extrêmement haut. ~*lark,* alouette [des champs], *f; v.i.* (*fig.*), chahuter. ~*light,* lucarne, *f.* ~*line,* ligne d'horizon, *f.* ~*scraper,* gratte-ciel, *m.inv.*

slab, *n,* (*stone &c*) bloc, *m;* (*paving*) dalle; (*flat*) plaque, *f;* (*chocolate*) plaque, tablette; (*steak, cake*) pavé, *m.*

slack†, *a,* (*rope*) lâche; (*grip, market &c*) faible; (*lax*) négligent. ¶ (*coal*), *n,* poussier, *m.* ¶ ~ *&* ~**en [off],** *v.t,* (*rope, reins*) relâcher; (*nut*) desserrer; (*pressure &c*) diminuer. ~ *one's pace,* ralentir l'allure. ¶ *v.i,* se relâcher; se desserrer; diminuer; (*trade*) ralentir. ~**er,** *n,* flemmard, e. ~**s,** *n.pl,* pantalon, *m.*

slag, *n,* (*metal*) scories; (*Min.*) crasses, *f.pl.* ~ *heap,* crassier; terril, *m.*

slake, *v.t,* (*thirst*) étancher.

slam (*Cards*), *n,* chelem, *m.* ¶ (*bang*) *v.i. & t,* claquer.

slander, *n,* calomnie; (*Law*) diffamation, *f.* ¶ *v.t,* calomnier; diffamer.

slang, *n,* argot, *m.* ~ *word,* mot d'argot, argotisme, *m.* ~*ing match P,* prise de bec *P, f.*

slant, *n,* inclinaison, *f;* (*fig.*) angle, *m.* ¶ *v.i,* pencher. ¶ *v.t,* faire pencher. ~*ed,* (*report*) tendancieux. ~*-eyed,* aux yeux bridés. ~*wise,* obliquement.

slap, *n,* claque; (*on face*) gifle, *f;* (*on back*) grande tape, grande claque. *a* ~ *on the bottom,* une fessée. ~*dash,* (*work*) bâclé *P;* (*pers.*) négligent. ~*stick, a,* tarte a la crème. ¶ *ad,* en plein (*into,* dans). ¶ *v.t,* donner une tape *ou* claque à. ~ *s.o's face,* gifler qn. ~ *on,* appliquer à la va-vite.

slash, *n,* entaille, *f;* (*Need.*) crevé, *m.* ¶ *v.t,* entailler; taillader; (*face*) balafrer; (*prices*) casser *P.*

slat, *n,* lame; (*blind*) lamelle, *f.*

slate, *n,* ardoise, *f.* ~*-blue,* bleu ardoise, *m.inv.* ~*-coloured,* ardoise, *inv.* ~ *quarry,* ardoisière, *f.* ¶ *a,* (*roof*) en ardoise. ¶ *v.t,* couvrir d'ardoises; (*fig.*) éreinter.

slaughter, *n,* tuerie, *f,* massacre, carnage; (*cattle*) abattage, *m.* ~ *house,* abattoir, *m.* ¶ *v.t,* massacrer, égorger; (*cattle*) abattre.

Slav, *a,* slave. ¶ *n,* Slave, *m,f.*

slave, *n,* esclave, *m,f.* ~ *driver* (*fig.*), négrier, ère. ~ *labour* (*fig.*), travail de galérien, *m.* ~ *trade,* commerce des esclaves, *m.* ~ *trader,* négrier, *m.* ~ [*away*], *v.i,* travailler comme un nègre, trimer.

slaver, *n,* bave, *f.* ¶ *v.i,* baver.

slavery, *n,* esclavage, *m.* **slavish†,** *a,* servile.

slay, *v.t,* tuer. ~**er,** *n,* tueur, *m.*

sledge, *n,* luge, *f;* (*sleigh*) traîneau, *m. go sledging,* faire de la luge. ~ *hammer,* masse, *f.*
sleek, *a,* (*hair &c*) lisse; (*pers.*) soigné; doucereux. ~ *down one's hair,* se lisser les cheveux.
sleep, *n,* sommeil, *m. have a little* ~, faire un somme. *go to* ~, s'endormir. *my foot's gone to* ~, j'ai le pied engourdi. *put to* ~, (*kill: animal*) faire piquer. ~ *walker,* somnambule, *m,f.* ¶ *v.i,* dormir; (*spend night*) coucher. ~ *like a log,* dormir comme une souche. ~ *with s.o,* coucher avec qn *P. we can* ~ *6,* nous pouvons coucher 6 personnes. ~ *in,* faire la grasse matinée. ~**er,** *n,* dormeur, euse; (*Rly*) traverse; (*bed*) couchette, *f;* (*train*) wagon-lit, train-couchettes; (*earring*) clou, *m.* **sleepiness,** *n,* envie de dormir; (*place*) somnolence, *f.* **sleeping,** *a,* endormi. *let* ~ *dogs lie,* il ne faut pas réveiller le chat qui dort. ~ *bag,* sac de couchage, *m. the S*~ *Beauty,* la Belle au bois dormant. ~ *car,* wagon-lit, *m.* ~ *partner,* commanditaire, *m.* ~ *pill,* somnifère, *m.* ~ *sickness,* maladie du sommeil, *f.* **sleepless,** *a,* éveillé. *have a* ~ *night,* passer une nuit blanche. ~**ly,** *ad,* sans dormir. ~**ness,** *n,* insomnie, *f.* **sleepy,** *a,* (*pers.*) somnolent; (*place*) endormi. *feel* ~, avoir sommeil. ~*head,* endormi, e.
sleet, *n,* de la neige fondue, pluie mêlée de neige, *f.* ¶ *v.i,* tomber de la neige fondue.
sleeve, *n,* manche; (*cylinder &c*) chemise; (*record*) pochette, *f;* (*Mach.*) manchon, *m. laugh up one's* ~, rire sous cape. ~*board,* jeannette, *f.* ~**less,** *a,* sans manches.
sleigh, *n,* traîneau, *m.*
sleight-of-hand, *n,* tour de passe-passe, *m.*
slender, *a,* (*pers.*) mince; (*stem, waist &c*) fin; (*glass*) élancé; (*hope*) faible; (*income, knowledge &c*) maigre. ~**ness,** *n,* minceur; finesse, *f.*
sleuth, *n,* limier, *m.*
slice, *n,* (*gen.*) tranche; (*lemon, sausage*) rondelle; (*fish* ~) truelle, *f.* ~ *of bread & butter,* tartine [beurrée], *f.* ¶ *v.t,* couper [en tranches]; (*ball*) couper; (*rope*) trancher. ~*d loaf,* pain en tranches, *m.* **slicer,** *n,* coupe-jambon, *m.inv.*
slick, *a,* habile, adroit; (*answer*) trop facile. ¶ *n,* (*oil* ~) nappe de pétrole, *f.*
slide, *n,* (*action*) glissade, *f;* (*of land*) glissement, *m;* (*of prices &c*) chute; (*on ice*) glissoire, *f;* (*in playground*) toboggan; (*microscope*) porte-objet, *m;* (*Phot.*) diapositive; (*hair* ~) barrette, *f.* ~ *rule,* règle à calcul, *f.* ¶ *v.t. & i. ir,* glisser. *let things* ~, laisser les choses aller à la dérive. **sliding,** *a,* glissant; (*part*) mobile; (*door &c*) coulissant; (*roof*) ouvrant. ~ *scale,* échelle mobile, *f.*
slight†, *a,* léger, petit; faible; (*pers.*) menu, frêle. ¶ *n,* affront, *m.* ¶ *v.t,* offenser. *the* ~*est,* le (la) moindre.
slim, *a,* (*pers., book*) mince; (*hope, excuse*) faible. ¶ *v.i,* maigrir; (*by diet*) être au régime.
slime, *n,* (*mud*) vase; (*snail*) bave, *f;* dépôt visqueux.
slimming, *a,* (*dress*) amincissant; (*pills &c*) amaigrissant. **slimness,** *n,* minceur, *f.*
slimy, *a,* visqueux; (*muddy*) couvert de vase; (*fig: pers. &c*) obséquieux, servile.
sling, *n,* (*Med.*) écharpe; (*rifle*) bretelle; (*catapult*) fronde, *f.* ¶ *v.t.ir,* lancer; (*hammock &c*) suspendre; (*load &c*) hisser. ~ *away,* ~ *out,* balancer *P.* ~ *out* (*pers.*), flanquer à la porte. *slung over the shoulder,* en bandoulière.
slink away, *v.i.ir,* s'esquiver. **slinky,** *a,* (*walk, body*) ondoyant; (*dress*) moulant.
slip, *n,* (*slide*) dérapage, *m;* (*trip*) faux pas; (*mistake*) erreur, gaffe *P, f;* (*moral*) écart; (*oversight*) oubli, *m;* (*underskirt*) combinaison; (*pillow*) taie; (*paper*) fiche, *f;* (*pottery*) engobe, *m;* (*pl. Theat.*) coulisses, *f.pl;* (*Hort.*) bouture; (*Naut.*) cale, *f.* ~ *of the tongue,* ~ *of the pen,* lapsus, *m. give s.o the* ~, fausser compagnie à qn. ~ *knot,* nœud coulant. ~ *road,* bretelle d'accès, *f.* ~*shod,* négligé. ~ *stitch,* maille glissée. ~*-up,* bévue, *f.* ~*way,* cale, *f.* ¶ *v.i. & t,* glisser; (*Mot: clutch*) patiner; (*escape*) échapper à; (*Naut.*) filer; (*pers., vehicle*) se faufiler. *let* ~, laisser échapper. ~ *away,* s'esquiver. ~ *on,* (*garment*) passer, enfiler. **slipper,** *n,* pantoufle, *f;* chausson, *m;* mule, *f.* **slippery,** *a,* glissant; (*pers.*) fuyant.
slit, *n,* fente; (*cut*) incision; (*tear*) déchirure, *f.* ¶ *v.t.ir,* fendre; inciser; déchirer. ~ *s.o's throat,* trancher la gorge à qn.
slither, *v.i,* glisser; déraper.
sliver, *n,* (*glass, wood*) éclat, *m;* (*cheese &c*) lamelle, *f.*
slobber, *n,* bave, *f.* ¶ *v.i,* baver.
sloe, *n,* prunelle, *f.* ~ *gin,* [liqueur de] prunelle, *f.*
slog, *n,* corvée, *f;* boulot pénible *P, m.* ¶ *v.i,* (*Box.*) cogner dur. (*work*) ~ *away,* boulonner [dur] *P;* trimer (*at,* sur). ~ *along,* avancer d'un pas lourd. ~**ger,** *n,* cogneur, *m;* bosseur, euse *P.*
slogan, n, slogan, *m.*
slop [over], ¶ *v.i,* déborder. ¶ *v.t,* répandre; renverser.
slope, *n,* inclinaison; (*hill*) côté, pente, *f;* (*mountain*) versant, *m.* ~ *down,* descente, *f.* ~ *up,* montée, *f.* ¶ *v.t,* pencher, incliner. ¶ *v.i,* être en pente; pencher. ~ *away,* descendre en pente. ~ *off P,* filer *P,* ficher le camp *P.*
sloppy, *a,* (*work*) peu soigné; bâclé *P;* (*dress*) négligé; (*novel*) à l'eau de rose, fadement sentimental. **slops,** *n,* (*water*) eaux sales, *f.pl;* fond de tasse; (*food*) bouillon, *m.*

slosh, *v.t,* (*hit*) flanquer un gnon à *P;* (*paint*) flanquer. ~**ed** *P, a,* bourré *P. get* ~, se soûler la gueule *P.*
slot, *n,* (*slit*) fente; (*groove*) rainure; (*Radio, TV*) créneau, *m.* ~ *machine,* distributeur [automatique], *m.* ¶ *v.t.* (*& i*), (s')emboîter (*into,* dans).
sloth, *n,* paresse, indolence, *f;* (*Zool.*) paresseux, *m.* ~**ful,** *a,* paresseux, indolent.
slouch, *v.i,* ne pas se tenir droit.
slovenly, *a,* (*pers.*) débraillé; (*work*) négligé.
slow†, *a,* (*gen.*) lent; (*train*) omnibus; (*clock*) qui retarde; (*child*) retardé. *at a* ~ *speed,* à petite vitesse. ~ *but sure,* lent mais sûr. ~ *to act &c,* long à agir &c. *business is* ~, les affaires stagnent. ~*-burning,* à combustion lente. ~*coach,* lambin, e. ~*down,* ralentissement, *m.* ¶ *ad,* lentement. *go* ~ (*Ind.*), faire la grève perlée. ~ **down,** ralentir. **slowness,** *n,* lenteur, *f.*
slow-worm, *n,* orvet, *m.*
sludge, *n,* (*mud*) bourbe, *f;* (*sewage*) vidanges, *f.pl.*
slug, *n,* (*Zool.*) limace; (*bullet*) balle, *f;* (*blow*) coup, *m.* ¶ *v.t,* frapper de toutes ses forces.
sluggish†, *a,* (*gen.*) lent; (*pers.*) sans allant; (*liver*) paresseux; (*engine*) peu nerveux.
sluice, *n,* écluse, *f;* (*channel*) canal, *m.* ~ *gate,* vanne, *f.*
slum, *n,* taudis, *m. the* ~*s,* les quartiers pauvres, les bas q., *m.pl.*
slumber, *n,* sommeil, *m.* ¶ *v.i,* sommeiller.
slump, *n,* (*in prices*) effondrement, *m;* (*in trade*) crise, *f;* baisse soudaine. ¶ *v.i,* (*pers., prices*) s'effronder; (*pers.*) s'affaisser. ~*ed in a chair,* affalé dans un fauteuil.
slur, *n,* atteinte (*on,* à); (*Mus.*) liaison, *f.* ¶ *v.t,* (*Mus.*) lier; (*speech &c*) mal articuler. ~ *over,* glisser sur.
slush, *n,* neige fondante; (*mud*) gadoue, *f.*
slut, *n,* souillon; salope, *f.*
sly†, *a,* sournois; (*wily*) rusé. *on the* ~, en cachette; sournoisement.
smack¹, *n,* claque; (*on face*) gifle, *f;* (*kiss*) gros baiser. *a* ~ *in the eye,* (*fig: snub*) une gifle; (*setback*) un revers. ¶ *ad,* en plein. ¶ *v.t,* donner une claque à, gifler. ~ *s.o's bottom,* donner la fessée à qn. ~ *one's lips,* se lécher les babines. (*fig.*) *smack of sth,* sentir qch.
small, *a,* (*gen.*) petit; (*meal*) léger; (*waist*) mince; (*population &c*) peu nombreux. *feel* ~, se sentir humilié. *grow* ~*er,* diminuer; (*town &c*) décroître. *in* ~ *letters,* en minuscules. *make* ~*er,* diminuer; réduire; rapetisser. ~ *ads,* petites annonces. (*Mil.*) ~ *arms,* armes portatives. ~ *change,* petite monnaie. ~ *fry,* menu frétin. ~ *intestine,* intestin grêle. ~*-minded,* mesquin. ~*pox,* variole, petite vérole. ~*-scale,* peu important. ~ *talk,* menus propos, *m. pl.* ~*-town,* provincial. ¶ *n,* ~ *of the back,* creux des reins, *m.* (*Dress*) ~*s P,* dessous, *m.pl.*
smarmy *P, a,* flagorneur.
smart†, *a,* chic, *inv,* élégant; à la mode; (*clever*) dégourdi *P,* malin, astucieux; (*pace*) rapide. *look* ~! remue-toi! *the* ~ *set,* le grand monde. ¶ *v.i,* (*cut &c*) brûler; (*fig.*) être piqué au vif. ~**en,** *v.t,* embellir. ~ *up, v.i,* se faire beau. ~**ness,** *n,* chic, *m,* élégance; astuce; rapidité, *f.*
smash, *n,* accident, *m;* (*Mot., Rly*) collision, *f;* (*Fin.*) effondrement; (*Stk. Ex.*) krach; (*Ten.*) smash, *m.* ¶ *v.t,* casser, briser; (*shatter*) fracasser; (*Ten.*) smasher; (*fig: enemy*) écraser; (*hopes*) ruiner; briser. ¶ *v.i,* se briser; se fracasser; (*Fin.*) faire faillite. ~ *in,* enfoncer. ~ *s.o's face in,* casser la gueule à qn *P.* ~ *up* (*car*), bousiller *P.* ~**ing** *P, a,* formidable *P,* terrible *P.*
smattering, *n,* connaissances vagues, *f.pl.*
smear, *n,* trace; traînée; (*lit., fig.*) tache; (*insult*) calomnie, *f;* (*Med.*) frottis, *m.* ¶ *v.t,* enduire, barbouiller; (*print &c*) maculer; (*reputation &c*) salir; calomnier.
smell, *n,* odeur, *f;* (*sense of* ~) odorat; (*animal*) flair, *m. what a* ~! ça pue! *smelling salts,* sels, *m.pl.* ¶ *v.t.ir,* sentir; flairer; (*sniff at*) renifler; (*fig.*) pressentir. ~ *a rat* (*fig.*), soupçonner qch. ¶ *v.i.ir,* sentir (*good, bad,* bon, mauvais); (*stink*) puer. ~ *out,* découvrir.
smelt¹, *n,* éperlan, *m.*
smelt², *v.t,* fondre. ~*ing works,* fonderie, *f.*
smile, *n,* sourire, *m.* ¶ *v.i,* sourire. **smiling,** *a,* souriant.
smirk, *n,* petit sourire satisfait, affecté &c.
smith, *n,* forgeron, *m.* ~**y,** *n,* forge, *f.*
smitten, *a,* ~ *with,* (*remorse*) pris de; (*fear*) frappé de; (*in love*) épris de.
smock, *n,* blouse, *f.* **smocking,** *n,* smocks, *m.pl.*
smoke, *n,* fumée, *f. go up in* ~, (*house &c*) brûler; (*hopes &c*) tomber à l'eau. ~ *bomb,* bombe fumigène, *f.* ~*screen,* (*Mil.*) écran de fumée; (*fig.*) paravent, *m.* ¶ *v.t. & i,* fumer. ~ *like a chimney,* fumer comme un sapeur. ~ *out,* (*wasps &c*) enfumer; (*fig: criminal*) dénicher. ~**less,** *a,* sans fumée. ~ *fuel,* combustible non polluant, *m.* **smoker,** *n,* fumeur, euse; (*Rly*) wagon fumeurs, *m.* **smoking,** *n,* l'habitude de fumer, *f.* '*no* ~', 'défense de fumer'. **smoky,** *a,* (*fire*) qui fume; (*room*) enfumé; (*flame*) fumeux; (*glass*) fumé.
smooth, *a,* (*gen.*) lisse; (*surface*) uni, égal; (*skin*) doux; (*wine &c*) moelleux; (*running: Mach., pulse &c*) régulier; (*crossing*) par mer calme; (*pers., manners*) doucereux, mielleux. *a* ~ *talker,* un beau parleur. ~*-running,* qui marche bien. ~*-tongued,* doucereux. ¶ *v.t,* (*gen.*) lisser; rendre lisse. ~ *out,* (*material*) défroisser; (*creases & fig.*) faire disparaître. ~

things over, arranger les choses. **~ly,** *ad,* facilement; doucement; (*take off*) en douceur. *go ~,* marcher comme sur des roulettes. **~ness,** *n,* aspect lisse *ou* égal, *m;* régularité; douceur, *f.*
smother, *v.t,* étouffer; (*with kisses &c*) couvrir (de).
smoulder, *v.i,* couver.
smudge, *n,* macule, tache, *f.* ¶ *v.t,* (*print, writing*) maculer, brouiller.
smug†, *a,* béat; satisfait.
smuggle, *v.t,* passer en contrebande. ¶ *v.i.* faire la contrebande. *~ in, v.t,* entrer en fraude. **smuggler,** *n,* contrebandier, ère.
smut, *n,* (*soot*) flocon de suie, *m;* tache de s., *f;* (*obscenity*) cochonneries, *f.pl.* **smutty,** *a,* noirci; taché, sale; (*fig.*) cochon.
snack, *n,* casse-croûte, *m.inv. have a ~,* casser la croûte. *~ bar,* snack[-bar], *m.*
snag, *n,* (*Hort.*) chicot; (*tear & fig.*) accroc; inconvénient, *m. hit a ~,* tomber sur un os *P. that's the ~!* voilà le hic *ou* l'os *P.*
snail, *n,* escargot, *m. at a ~'s pace,* à pas de tortue.
snake, *n,* serpent, *m. a ~ in the grass,* traître, esse.
snap, *n,* bruit sec; (*Cards*) jeu de bataille, *m. a cold ~,* un coup de froid. *make a ~ decision,* décider tout d'un coup. *~dragon,* gueule-de-loup, *f. ~ fastener,* pression, *f. ~[shot],* photo, *f.* ¶ *v.t,* casser net. *~ one's fingers,* faire claquer les doigts. ¶ *v.i,* se casser net; claquer. *~ at,* (*dog*) essayer de mordre; (*pers.*) rembarrer. *~ out of it!* secoue-toi! **snappy,** *a,* (*& snappish*) hargneux; (*slogan*) accrocheur. *make it ~! P* grouille-toi! *P*.*
snare, *n,* piège, *m.* ¶ *v.t,* attraper.
snarl¹, *n,* grondement féroce, *m.* ¶ *v.i,* gronder; (*dog*) g. en montrant les dents.
snarl², *n,* (*wool &c*) nœud, *m. ~-up* (*traffic*) embouteillage, *m.* ¶ *v.i, get ~ed up,* s'enchevêtrer; (*traffic*) se bloquer.
snatch, *n* (*scrap*) fragment; (*action*) geste vif; (*fig: robbery*) vol, *m.* ¶ *v.t,* saisir; (*kiss*) voler; (*food, drink*) avaler à la hâte; (*steal*) voler (à qn).
sneak, *n,* (*Sch.*) mouchard, e *P. ~ thief,* chapardeur, euse. ¶ *v.t. & i,* glisser furtivement; (*steal*) chiper *P. ~ away,* s'esquiver, s'éclipser *P.* **~ers,** *n,* tennis, *f.pl.* **~ing,** *a,* caché, secret.
sneer, *v.t,* ricaner. *~ at,* parler avec mépris de.
sneeze, *n,* éternuement, *m.* ¶ *v.i,* éternuer.
sniff, *n,* reniflement, *m.* ¶ *v.t,* renifler; (*dog*) flairer; (*air &c*) humer; (*salts, glue*) respirer. ¶ *v.i,* renifler; (*with scorn*) faire la moue (*at,* à). **sniffle,** *n,* (*cold*) petit rhume de cerveau.
snigger, *n,* petit rire moqueur; ricanement, *m.* ¶ *v.i,* pouffer de rire; ricaner.
snip, *n,* coup de ciseaux; (*of cloth &c*) petit bout, *m;* (*bargain*) bonne affaire. ¶ *v.t,* couper.
snipe, *n,* bécassine, *f.* ¶ *v.t,* canarder. **sniper,** *n,* tireur isolé, franc-tireur, *m.*
snippet, *n,* petit bout; fragment, *m.*
snivel, *v.i,* pleurnicher.
snob, *n.* & **snobbish,** *a,* snob, *m.f. & inv.* **snobbery** & **snobbishness,** *n,* snobisme, *m.*
snoop, *v.i,* se mêler des affaires des autres. *~ [around],* fourrer son nez.
snooze, *n,* petit somme. ¶ *v.i,* sommeiller.
snore, *n,* ronflement, *m.* ¶ *v.i,* ronfler.
snorkel, *n,* (*swimmer*) tuba, *m.*
snort, *v.i,* (*pers.*) grogner; (*horse*) s'ébrouer.
snotty *P, a,* morveux; (*nose*) qui coule.
snout, *n,* museau; (*pig*) groin, *m.*
snow, *n,* neige, *f;* (*drug*) neige *P,* cocaine, *f. ~ball,* boule de neige, *f; v.i.* (*fig.*), faire b. de n. *~ blindness,* cécité des neiges, *f. ~-capped,* couronné de n. *~-covered,* enneigé. *~drift,* congère, *f. ~drop,* perce-neige, *f. ~fall,* chute de n., *f. ~flake,* flocon de n., *m. ~ line,* limite des neiges éternelles, *f. ~man,* bonhomme de neige, *m. ~ plough,* chasse-neige, *m. ~ shoes,* raquettes, *f.pl. ~ storm,* tempête de n., *f. ~-white,* blanc comme neige. *S~ White,* Blanche-Neige. ¶ *v.i,* neiger. *~ed in, up,* bloqué par la neige. *~ed under,* submergé. **~y,** *a,* neigeux.
snub¹, *n,* rebuffade, *f.* ¶ *v.t,* snober.
snub², *a,* (*nose*) retroussé.
snuff¹, *n,* tabac à priser, *m. to take ~* priser. *~ box,* tabatière, *f.*
snuff², *v.t,* moucher. *~ it P,* casser sa pipe *P.*
snuffle, *v.i,* renifler, nasiller.
snug†, *a,* (*house &c*) confortable; (*bed, garment*) douillet; (*fit*) bien ajusté.
snuggle, *v.i,* se pelotonner, se blottir (*up to s.o,* contre qn).
so, *ad. & c,* (*degree*) si, aussi, tellement; (*thus*) ainsi, comme ceci *ou* cela; (*therefore*) donc, par conséquent. *~ as to do,* pour faire, afin de f. *~ do I, ~ have I, ~ am I &c,* moi aussi. *I told you ~!* je vous l'avais bien dit! *just ~!* exactement! *~ long!* à bientôt! *30 or ~,* à peu près 30, une trentaine, environ 30. *~ what?* et alors? & apres? *~-&-~,* un tel, une telle. *~-called,* soi-disant; *a.inv,* prétendu. *~ ~,* comme ci, comme ça; couci-couça. *~ that,* pour que, afin que; de sorte que. *~ to speak,* pour ainsi dire.
soak, *v.t,* faire tremper (dans); (*bread*) imbiber; (*P for money*) faire casquer *P. ~ed to the skin,* trempé jusqu'aux os. ¶ *v.i,* tremper. ¶ (*P drunkard*) *n,* soulard *P, m.*
soap, *n,* savon, *m. ~ dish,* porte-savon, *m. ~flakes,* paillettes de s., *f.pl. ~-opera,* feuilleton à l'eau de rose, *m. ~-powder,* lessive, *f. ~suds,* mousse de savon, *f* ¶ *v.t,* savonner. **~y,** *a,* savonneux.
soar, *v.i,* (*rise*) monter en flèche; (*glide*) planer;

(*ball &c*) voler; (*spire*) s'élancer vers le ciel.
sob, *n*, sanglot, *m*. ~*-stuff*, sensiblerie, *f*. ¶ *v.i*, sangloter.
sober†, *a*, (*pers*.) sérieux; (*clothes &c*) sobre; (*occasion*) solennel; (*not drunk*) qui n'a pas trop bu. *never* ~, toujours ivre. ¶ *v.t*, (& ~ *up*) désenivrer, dessoûler. ~**ness** & **sobriety,** *n*, sérieux, *m*, sobriété; modération, *f*.
sociable†, *a*, sociable. **social,** *a*, social; (*in society*) mondain. ~ *climber*, arriviste, *m.f*. ~ *science*, sciences humaines. ~ *security*, sécurité sociale. ~ *studies*, sciences sociales. ~ *worker*, assistant(e) social(e). ~**ism,** *n*, socialisme, *m*. ~**ist,** *n*. & *a*, socialiste, *m,f*. **society,** *n*, société, association; (*fashionable* ~) haute société, *f*, le grand monde. ¶ *a*, mondain. **socio..** *pref*., socio... ~**logical,** *a*, sociologique. ~**logist,** *n*, sociologue, *m,f*. ~**logy,** *n*, sociologie, *f*.
sock[1], *n*, chaussette; (*short*) soquette, *f*. *pull up one's* ~*s* (*fig*.), se secouer.
sock[2] *P*, *n*, coup, gnon *P*, *m*. ¶ *v.t*, flanquer un gnon à *P*.
socket, *n*, (*gen*.) cavité; (*Elec: in wall*) prise de courant; (*for bulb*) douille; (*eye*) orbite, *f*; (*tooth &c*) alvéole, *m*.
sod[1], *n*, gazon, *m*; motte, *f*.
sod[2] *P**, *n*, con *P**, (*pej*.) salaud *P**, *m*. ¶ *v.t*, ~ *it!* merde! *P**. ~ *off P**, foutre le camp *P**.
soda, *n*, soude, *f*; (*washing*) cristaux de soude, *m.pl*. ~ [*water*], soda, *m*, eau de Seltz, *f*. ~ *siphon*, siphon [d'eau gazeuse], *m*.
sodden, *a*, détrempé.
sodium, *n*, sodium, *m*.
sofa, *n*, canapé, sofa, *m*. ~ *bed*, canapé-lit, *m*.
soft†, *a*, (*not hard*) mou. (*light, sound, colour, skin, rain &c*) doux; (*stone, wood, pencil*) tendre; (*leather*) souple; (*hair*) soyeux; (*toy*) de peluche; (*flabby: pers. &c*) avachi; (*life, job*) facile; (*stupid*) bête, imbécile. ~*-boiled egg*, œuf à la coque, *m*. ~ *drinks*, boissons non alcoolisées. ~ *drugs*, drogues douces. ~ *focus* (*Phot*.), flou artistique, *m*. ~ *fruit*, baies comestibles, *f.pl*. ~ *furnishing*, tissus d'ameublement, *m.pl*. ~*-hearted*, au cœur tendre. ~ *palate*, voile du palais, *m*. ~ *pedal*, pédale douce; *v.i*, (*fig*.) ne pas trop insister sur. ~ *soap*, flagornerie, *f*; *v.t*, passer de la pommade à *P*. ~ *spoken*, à la voix douce. *have a* ~ *spot for*, avoir un faible pour. *be a* ~ *touch*, se faire avoir [facilement]. ~ *verges*, accotements non stabilisés. ~ *water*, eau qui n'est pas calcaire. ~**en [up],** *v.t*, (& *i*,) (s')adoucir; (se) ramollir; (s')assouplir; (*outline*) (s')estomper; (*resistance*) amoindrir; (*pers*.) (s')attendrir. ~ *the blow*, amortir le choc. ~**ener,** *n*, (*water* ~) adoucisseur; (*fabric* ~) adoucissant, *m*. ~**ie** *P*, *n*, (*kind*) tendre, *m,f*; (*coward*) poule mouillée, *f*. ~**ness,** *n*, douceur; mollesse; souplesse, *f*; (*indulgence*) manque de sévérité, *m*. ~**ware,** *n*, (*Computers*) logiciel, software, *m*.
soggy, *a*, (*ground*) détrempé; (*bread*) mal cuit.
soil, *n*, sol, *m*, terre, *f*. ¶ *v.t*, salir, souiller. ~**ed,** *a*, (*linen*) sale; (*shop goods*) défraîchi.
solace, *n*, consolation, *f*. ¶ *v.t*, consoler.
solar, *a*, solaire; (*heating*) à énergie s. ~ *plexus*, plexus s., *m*.
solder & ~**ing,** *n*, soudure, *f*. ¶ *v.t*, souder. ~*ing, iron*, fer à souder, *m*.
soldier, *n*, soldat, militaire, troufion *P*, *m*. ¶ *v.i*, servir dans l'armée. ~ *on*, persévérer.
sole[1], (*fish*), *n*, sole, *f*.
sole[2], *n*, (*shoe*) semelle; (*foot*) plante, *f*. ¶ *v.t*, ressemeler.
sole[3], *a*, seul, unique; (*exclusive*) exclusif.
solecism, *n*, solécisme, *m*.
solemn†, *a*, solennel; (*warning*) formel; (*pers., face*) grave, sérieux. ~**ity,** *n*, solennité; gravité, *f*. ~**ize,** *v.t*, célébrer.
solicit, *v.t*, solliciter (*from*, de). ¶ *v.i*. (*prostitute*), racoler. ~**ing,** *n*, racolage, *m*. ~**or,** *n*, *in Fr*. ≏ avocat, *m*. ~**ous,** *a*, (*eager*) désireux; (*anxious*) inquiet. ~**ude,** *n*, sollicitude, *f*.
solid†, *a*, (*gen*.) solide; (*tyre, wall &c*) plein; (*silver, oak &c*) massif; (*vote*) unanime. *on* ~ *ground*, (*lit*) sur la terre ferme; (*fig*.) en terrain sûr. ~ *fuel*, combustible solide, *m*. ¶ *n*, solide, *m*; (*pl: food*) aliments solides, *m.pl*. ~**arity,** *n*, solidarité, *f*. ~**ify,** *v.t*. (& *i*), (*liquid, gas*) (se) solidifier; (*oil*) (se) congeler. ~**ity,** *n*, solidité, *f*.
soliloquy, *n*, soliloque, *m*.
solitaire (*gem, game*) *n*, solitaire, *m*. **solitary,** *a*, solitaire; seul; unique. ~ *confinement*, régime cellulaire, *m*. **solitude,** *n*, solitude, *f*.
solo, *n*, solo, *m*. ~ *violin*, violon solo, *m*. ~ *whist*, whist-solo, *m*. ¶ *ad*, (*fly, play*) en solo. ~**ist,** *n*, soliste, *m,f*.
solstice, *n*, solstice, *m*.
soluble, *a*, soluble. **solution,** *n*, solution, *f*. **solve,** *v.t*, résoudre; (*mystery*) éclaircir. **solvency,** *n*, solvabilité, *f*. **solvent,** *a*, dissolvant; (*Com*.) solvable. ¶ *n*, dissolvant, *m*.
sombre, *a*, sombre.
some, *a*, du, de la, des; quelque, quelques; certain; (*a lot*) pas mal de *P*. *would you like* ~ *cheese?* voulez-vous du fromage? ~ *day*, un de ces jours. ~ *people say*, il y en a qui disent. *after* ~ *time*, après un certain temps. *it takes* ~ *time*, ça prend pas mal de temps. *at* ~ *length*, assez longuement. ¶ *pn*, quelques-uns, -unes; certains, certaines; en. ~ *of my friends*, quelques uns *ou* certains de mes amis. *give me* ~! donnez-m'en! **somebody** & **someone,** *pn*, quelqu'un; on. ~ *else*, quelqu'un d'autre. *to be somebody*, être un personnage. **somehow [or other],** *ad*, d'une manière ou d'une autre; tant bien que mal.
somersault, *n*, culbute, *f*; (*Gym*.) saut périlleux;

(*car*) tonneau, *m.*
something, *n,* quelque chose (*good,* de bon; *to read,* à lire), *m. it's ~ like,* c'est un peu comme. *~ to live for,* une raison de vivre. **sometime,** *a,* (*former*) ancien. ¶ *ad, ~ or other,* tôt ou tard. *~ soon,* bientôt. **sometimes,** *ad,* quelquefois; parfois; de temps en temps. *~ the one ~ the other,* tantôt l'un tantôt l'autre. **somewhat,** *ad,* quelque peu, un peu. **somewhere,** *ad,* quelque part. *~ else,* ailleurs, autre part.
somnambulism, *n,* somnambulisme, *m.* **somnambulist,** *n,* somnambule, *m,f.* **somnolent,** *a,* somnolent.
son, *n,* fils, *m. ~-in-law,* gendre, beau-fils, *m.*
sonata, *n,* sonate, *f.*
song, *n,* chanson, *f;* (*formal & birds*) chant, *m.* (*fig.*) *for a ~,* pour une bouchée de pain, *f. ~bird,* oiseau chanteur, *m. ~book,* recueil de chansons, *m. ~thrush,* grive musicienne, *f. ~ without words,* romance sans paroles, *f. ~ writer,* auteur, *m, ou* compositeur, trice de chansons. **~ster, ~stress,** *n,* chanteur, euse.
sonic, *a,* sonique. *~ boom,* bang supersonique, *m. ~ depth finder,* sonde à ultra-sons, *f.*
sonnet, *n,* sonnet, *m.*
sonorous, *a,* sonore.
soon, *ad,* bientôt; tôt. *as ~ as,* aussitôt que; dès que. *as ~ as possible,* aussitôt que possible, dès que p., le plus tôt p. *how ~?* dans combien de temps? **~er,** *ad,* plus tôt; (*rather*) plutôt. *~ or later,* tôt ou tard. *no ~ said than done,* aussitôt dit, aussitôt fait.
soot, *n,* suie, *f.* **~y,** *a,* noir de suie.
soothe, *v.t,* (*pers., nerves*) calmer; (*anger &c*) apaiser. **soothing,** *a,* (*words &c*) apaisant; (*medicine*) lénitif; (*presence*) réconfortant.
sop, *n,* (*pl.*) aliments semi-liquides, *m.pl. as a ~ to,* (*pers.*) pour amadouer; (*pride*) pour flatter.
sophisticated, *a,* (*pers., Mach.*) sophistiqué; (*pers., taste*) raffiné; (*book &c*) subtil.
soporific, *a,* soporifique.
sopping [wet], *a,* trempé. **soppy** *P, a,* sentimental; (*silly*) bête, idiot.
soprano (*voice & pers.*) *n,* soprano, *m.*
sorbet, *n,* sorbet, *m.*
sorcerer, ess, *n,* sorcier, ère. **sorcery,** *n,* sorcellerie, *f.*
sordid, *a,* sordide; (*act*) ignoble.
sore, *a,* douloureux; irrité, enflammé; (*offended*) vexé. *I have a ~ finger,* j'ai mal au doigt. *~ eyes,* mal aux (*ou* d')yeux. *~ point,* point délicat, *m. ~ throat,* mal à la gorge; angine, *f.* ¶ *n,* plaie, *f.* **~ly,** *ad,* (*missed &c*) amèrement; (*tempted*) fortement.
sorrel, *n,* oseille, *f.* ¶ *a,* (*horse*) alezan clair, *inv.*
sorrow, *n,* chagrin, *m,* douleur, peine, *f.* ¶ *v.i,* s'affliger. **~ful†,** *a,* triste. **sorry,** *a,* désolé; (*state &c*) triste, lamentable. *~!* pardon! excusez-moi! je suis désolé! *be ~ for* (*pity*), plaindre. *I'm ~ to disturb you,* excusez-moi de vous déranger. *you'll be ~ for this!* vous le regretterez!
sort, *n,* sorte, *f,* genre, *m,* espèce; (*make: car &c*) marque, *f. ~ of,* en quelque sorte, plutôt. *out of ~s,* pas dans son assiette. ¶ *v.t, ~* [*out*], trier; (*classify*) classer. *~ out,* (*tidy: objects*) ranger; (*ideas*) mettre de l'ordre dans. *~ s.o out,* (*punish*) régler son compte à qn *P.* **~er,** *n,* trieur, euse.
sortie, *n,* sortie, *f.*
soul, *n,* âme, *f;* (*pers.*) âme, personne, *f. I didn't see a ~,* je n'ai pas vu âme qui vive. *the ~ of discretion,* la discrétion même. *~-destroying,* abrutissant. *~mate,* âme sœur, *f. ~-searching,* introspection, *f.* **~ful,** *a,* (*look*) éloquent. **~less,** *a,* sans âme; (*task*) abrutissant.
sound[1], *n,* (*gen.*) son; bruit, *m. I don't like the ~ of it,* ça m'inquiète. *~ barrier,* mur du son, *m. ~ effects,* bruitage, *m. ~proof,* insonoriser. *~ track,* bande sonore, *f. ~ wave,* onde sonore, *f.* ¶ *v.t,* [faire] sonner. *~ the horn* (*Mot.*), klaxonner. ¶ *v.i,* (*bell &c*) sonner; (*siren, order*) retentir; (*fig: seem*) sembler [être]; avoir l'air de. *how does that ~ to you?* qu'en penses-tu? *~ off at s.o,* engueuler qn *P.*
sound†[2], *a,* (*gen.*) sain; en bon état; (*heart, bank*) solide; (*investment*) sûr, sans danger; (*sleep*) profond; (*advice, policy &c*) sensé, valable, juste; (*pers.*) compétent. *be ~ in wind & limb,* avoir bon pied bon œil. *be ~ asleep,* dormir à poings fermés.
sound[3], (*Med.*) *n,* sonde, *f.* ¶ *v.t.* sonder. *~* [*out*] (*fig.*), sonder. **~ing,** *n,* (*Naut. &c*) sondage, *m. take ~s,* (*fig.*) faire un sondage, sonder l'opinion.
soundless, *a,* silencieux. **~ly,** *ad,* en silence, sans bruit.
soundness, *n,* santé; solidité; justesse; profondeur, *f.*
soup, *n,* soupe, *f;* potage; (*smooth*) velouté, *m. ~ ladle,* louche, *f. ~ plate,* assiette creuse, *f. ~spoon,* cuiller à soupe, *f. ~ tureen,* soupière, *f. ~ed-up P,* au moteur gonflé *P.*
sour, *a,* (*gen.*) aigre; (*fruit*) acide; (*milk*) tourné; (*pers. &c*) acerbe, revêche. *turn ~,* tourner; (*fig.*) tourner au vinaigre. *~[ed] cream,* crème aigre, *f. ~-puss P,* grincheux, euse. ¶ *v.t.* (*& i*), (s')aigrir. **~ish,** *a,* aigrelet. **~ly,** *ad,* aigrement. **~ness,** *n,* aigreur, acidité, *f.*
source, *n,* source, *f;* (*Med: infection*) foyer, *m.*
souse, *v.t,* tremper; (*Cook.*) mariner.
south, *n,* sud, *m. the S~ of France,* le Midi. ¶ *ad,* au sud. ¶ *a,* du sud; méridional. *S~ Africa,* l'Afrique du Sud, *f. S~ African,* sud-africain. *S~ America,* l'Amérique du Sud, *f. S~ American,* sud-américain. *~bound* (*carriageway*), sud. *~-east,* sud-est, *m. S~-East*

Asia, le Sud-Est asiatique. ~*-facing,* exposé au sud. *S~ Pole,* pôle sud, *m. S~ Sea Islands,* l'Océanie, *f. S~ Seas,* Mers du Sud, *f.pl.* ~*-west,* sud ouest, *m.* **southern,** *a,* [du] sud; méridional; austral. ~**er,** *n,* habitant, e du sud; (*in Fr.*) méridional, e. **southward[s],** *ad,* vers le sud.

souvenir, *n,* souvenir, *m.*

sou'wester (*wind, hat*) *n,* suroît, *m.*

sovereign, *a.* & (*pers.*) *n,* souverain, e. ~**ty,** *n,* souveraineté, *f.*

soviet, *n,* soviet, *m;* (*att.*) soviétique. *the S~ Union,* l'Union soviétique, *f.*

sow (sau), *n,* truie, *f.*

sow (sou), *v.t. & i. ir,* (*seeds & fig.*) semer; (*field*) ensemencer. ~**er,** *n,* semeur, euse. **sowing,** *n,* semailles, *f.pl.* ~ *machine,* semoir, *m.*

soy[a], *n,* ~ *bean,* grain de soja, *f.* ~ *flour,* farine de soja, *f.* ~ *sauce,* sauce de soja, *f.*

spa, *n,* station thermale, *f.*

space, *n,* (*gen., Phys. &c*) espace, *m;* (*for car &c*) place, *f;* (*Mus.*) interligne; (*Typ.*) espace; (*time*) laps de temps, *m,* période, *f. stare into* ~, regarder dans le vide. ¶ *a,* spatial. *S~ Age,* ère spatiale. ~ *bar,* barre d'espacement, *f.* ~ *capsule,* capsule spatiale. ~*craft,* engin spatial. ~ *heater,* radiateur, *m.* ~*-saving,* qui fait gagner de la place. ~ *travel,* voyages spatiaux *ou* interplanétaires. ¶ *v.t,* ~ [*out*], espacer; (*payments*) échelonner (*over,* sur). **spacing,** (*Typ.*) *n,* espacement; (*between lines*) interligne, *m.* **spacious,** *a,* spacieux; grand.

spade, *n,* bêche; (*child's*) pelle, *f;* (*Cards*) pique, *m. call a* ~ *a* ~, appeler un chat un chat. ~*work* (*fig.*), gros du travail, *m.* ~**ful,** *n,* pelletée, *f.*

spaghetti, *n,* spaghetti, *m.pl.*

Spain, *n,* l'Espagne, *f.*

span, *n,* (*hand, wing &c*) envergure; (*Build.*) portée; (*bridge*) travée; (*in time*) durée, *f.* ¶ *v.t,* franchir; (*time*) embrasser.

spangle, *n,* paillette, *f.* ~**d,** *a,* pailleté.

Spaniard, *n,* Espagnol, e. **spaniel,** *n,* épagneul, e. **Spanish,** *a,* espagnol; (*embassy, king*) d'Espagne; (*Cook.*) à l'espagnole. ~ *Main,* mer des Antilles, *f.* ~ *onion,* oignon d'Espagne, *m.* ¶ *n,* l'espagnol. *m.*

spank, *v.t,* donner une fessée à. ~**ing,** *n,* fessée, *f.*

spanner, *n,* clef, clé, *f.*

spar[1], *n,* (*Naut.*) espar, *m.*

spar[2], *v.i,* (*Box.*) s'entraîner [à la boxe]; (*fig.*) se disputer (avec). ~*ring partner,* sparring-partner, *m.*

spare, *a,* (*surplus*) de *ou* en trop, disponible; (*reserve*) de réserve, de rechange; (*pers.*) maigre. ~ [*bed*]*room,* chambre d'ami, *f.* ~ *capital,* fonds disponibles, *m.pl.* ~ *part,* pièce de rechange, *f.* ~*-rib,* travers de porc, *m.* ~ *time,* moments de loisir, *m.pl.* ~*-time activities,* loisirs, *m.pl.* ~ *tyre,* pneu de rechange, *m.* ~ *wheel,* roue de secours, *f.* ¶ *v.t,* (*do without*) se passer de; (*show mercy to*) épargner; (*use sparingly*) ménager. *can you* ~ *me a few moments?* pouvez-vous m'accorder quelques moments? ~ *s.o's feelings,* ménager les sentiments de qn. ~ *no expense,* dépenser sans compter. ~ *no pains,* ne pas ménager sa peine. **sparing,** *a,* modéré. ~ *of praise,* avare de compliments. *be* ~ *with,* économiser, ménager. ~**ly,** *ad,* (*live*) frugalement; (*spend*) avec modération.

spark, *n,* étincelle; (*interest, sense*) lueur, *f.* ~*ing plug,* bougie, *f.* **sparkle,** *v.i,* (*gen.*) étinceler; (*water, diamond &c*) scintiller; (*wine, conversation*) pétiller; (*pers.*) briller. **sparkling,** *a,* étincelant (de); scintillant; pétillant (de); (*wine*) mousseux.

sparrow, *n,* moineau, *m.* ~ *hawk,* épervier, *m.*

sparse, *a,* peu dense, clairsemé, rare.

Spartan, *a.* & *n,* spartiate, *m,f.*

spasm, *n,* spasme, *m.* **spasmodic,** *a,* intermittent; (*Med.*) spasmodique. ~**ally,** *ad,* par à-coups.

spastic, *a.* & *n,* handicapé, e moteur; (*movements*) spasmodique.

spate, *n,* (*words, abuse*) torrent, *m;* (*orders, letters &c*) avalanche, *f. in* ~, en crue.

spatter, *v.t,* éclabousser.

spatula, *n,* spatule, *f.*

spawn, *n,* (*fish*) frai; (*mushroom*) blanc, *m.* ¶ *v.i,* frayer. ¶ *v.t,* (*fig.*) engendrer.

speak, *v.t. & i. ir,* parler; (*truth &c*) dire. *so to* ~, pour ainsi dire. ~*ing personally,* personellement. *medically* ~*ing,* médicalement parlant. (*Tel.*) *Pat* ~*ing,* ici Pat, c'est P. à l'appareil. *'French spoken',* 'ici on parle français'. *it* ~*s for itself,* c'est évident. *I'll never* ~ *to him again,* je ne lui adresserai plus jamais la parole. ~ *one's mind,* dire ce que l'on pense. ~ *out,* ~ *up,* parler franchement. ~ *up!* [parle] plus fort! ~**er,** *n,* celui, celle qui parle; (*dialogue*) interlocuteur, trice; orateur, *m;* conférencier, ère; (*loud*~) haut-parleur, *m.* **speaking,** *a,* parlant. *we are not on* ~ *terms,* nous ne nous parlons pas. ~ *tube,* tuyau acoustique, *m.*

spear, *n,* lance; (*asparagus &c*) pointe, *f.* ~ *head,* fer de lance, *m; v.t,* mener. ~*mint,* menthe verte, *f.* ¶ *v.t,* transpercer d'un coup de lance.

spec (on) *P,* à tout hasard.

special†, *a,* (*gen.*) spécial; [tout] particulier, exceptionnel; (*Pol. &c*) extraordinaire. ~ *feature* (*Press*), article spécial. ~ *offer,* réclame, *f. nothing* ~, rien de spécial ~ *agent,* agent secret. ~ *correspondent,* envoyé, e special, e. *by* ~ *delivery,* en exprès. ~ *licence,* dispense spéciale. ~**ist,** *n,* spécialiste, *m,f.* ~**ity,** *n,* spécialité, *f.* ~**ize in,** se spécialiser dans.

species, *n,* espèce, *f.*

specific, *a,* précis; (*Phys., Chem. &c*) spécifique. ~ *gravity,* densité, *f.* ¶ *n,* remède spécifique, *m.* ~**ally,** *ad,* expressément. ~**ation,** *n,* spécification; (*in contract*) stipulation, *f.* **specify,** *v.t,* spécifier; préciser. **specimen,** *n,* (*rock, style, species*) spécimen; (*blood*) prélèvement; (*urine*) échantillon; (*fig.*) exemple, *m.* ~ *copy,* spécimen. ~ *signature,* spécimen de signature. **specious†,** *a,* spécieux.

speck, *n,* (*dust, truth &c*) grain, *m;* (*dirt*) petite tache. *a* ~ *on the horizon,* un point noir à l'horizon. ~**led,** *a,* tacheté.

spectacle, *n,* spectacle, *m;* (*pl.*) lunettes, *f.pl.* **spectacular,** *a,* spectaculaire. ¶ *n,* film &c à grand spectacle, *m.* **spectator,** *n,* spectateur, trice.

spectre, *n,* spectre; fantôme, *m.* **spectrum,** *n,* spectre, *m;* (*fig.*) gamme, *f.*

speculate, *v.i,* (*Philos., Fin.*) spéculer; (*ponder*) s'interroger; (*Stk Ex.*) jouer à la Bourse. **speculation,** *n,* spéculation, *f;* conjecture[s], *f*[*pl*]. **speculative,** *a,* spéculatif. **speculator,** *n,* spéculateur, trice.

speech, *n,* (*faculty, opp. writing*) parole; articulation; façon de parler, *f;* (*group language*) parler; (*Gram., address*) discours, *m.* ~ *day,* distribution des prix, *f.* ~ *defect,* défaut d'élocution, *m.* ~ *therapist,* orthophoniste, *m,f.* ~ *training,* leçons d'élocution, *f.pl.* ~**ify,** *v.i,* pérorer. ~**less,** *a,* sans voix, muet.

speed, *n,* vitesse; rapidité; promptitude, *f;* (*Tech. Mot: gear*) vitesse; (*Phot: film*) rapidité; (*exposure*) durée d'exposition, *f.* *3-~ gear,* boîte à 3 vitesses, *f.* ~*boat,* vedette, *f.* ~ *limit,* ~ *restriction,* limitation de vitesse, *f.* ~ *trap,* piège de police, *m.* ¶ *v.i.ir,* (*Mot.*) conduire trop vite. ~ *along,* aller à toute allure. ~ *up,* aller plus vite; (*Mot.*) accélérer; (*Mach.*) tourner plus vite. ~**ing,** *n,* excès de vitesse, *m.* ~**ometer,** *n,* compteur [de vitesse], *m.* ~**well** (*Bot.*) *n,* véronique, *f.* ~**y,** *a,* rapide.

spell[1], *n,* (*power & fig.*) charme, *m;* (*words*) incantation, *f.* *under a* ~, ensorcelé. ~*binding,* ensorcelant. ~*bound,* sous le charme.

spell[2], *n,* (*turn*) tour, *m;* (*period*) [courte] période, *f.* *for a* ~, pendant un certain temps.

spell[3], *v.t.ir,* (*writing*) écrire; (*aloud*) épeler; (*letters*) former; (*fig: mean*) signifier; (*entail*) mener à. *how do you* ~ *it?* comment écrit-on cela? *can you* ~ *that?* pouvez-vous l'épeler. ¶ *v.i,* épeler. ~ *out,* épeler; (*fig.*) expliquer bien clairement. **spelling,** *n,* orthographe, *f.* ~ *mistake,* faute d'o., *f.*

spend, *v.t. & i. ir,* (*money*) dépenser; (*time &c*) passer; (*devote: time &c*) consacrer. ~ *one's time reading,* passer son temps à lire. ~*thrift,* dépensier, ère. ~**ing,** *n,* dépenses, *f.pl.* ~ *money,* argent de poche, *m.* ~ *power,* pouvoir d'achat, *m.* **spent,** *a,* (*match &c*) utilisé. *be* ~, être épuisé.

sperm, *n,* sperme, *m.* ~ *whale,* cachalot, *m.*

sphere, *n,* sphère, *f;* (*fig.*) domaine, *f.* **spherical,** *a,* sphérique.

sphinx, *n,* sphinx, *m.*

spice, *n,* épice, *f;* (*fig.*) piquant, *m.* ¶ *v.t,* épicer; (*lit., fig.*) relever (*with,* de).

spick & span, (*pers.*) tiré à quatre épingles; (*room &c*) propre comme un sou neuf.

spicy, *a,* épicé, relevé; (*fig.*) piquant.

spider, *n,* araignée, *f.* ~*'s web,* toile d'a., *f.*

spiel *P,* *n,* baratin *P,* *m.*

spike, *n,* (*gen.*) pointe, *f;* (*Bot.*) épi, *m;* (*pl: shoes*) chaussures à pointes, *f.pl.* ¶ *v.t,* ~ *s.o's guns* (*fig.*), mettre des bâtons dans les roues à qn.

spill, *v.t,* (*liquid, salt &c*) renverser, répandre; (*blood*) verser, faire couler. ~ *the beans* (*fig.*), vendre la mèche. ¶ *v.i,* (& ~ *out*) se répandre. ~ *over, v.i,* déborder.

spin, *n,* tournoiement, *m;* (*Aero.*) vrille, *f;* (*on ball*) effet; (*washing machine*) essorage, *m.* *go into a* ~ (*Aero.*), tomber en vrille. *go for a* ~, faire une balade en voiture &c. *be in a flat* ~, être dans tous ses états. ¶ *v.t,* (*gen.*) filer; (*spider*) tisser; (*wheel*) faire tourner; (~*-dry*) essorer; (*Sport: ball*) donner de l'effet à. ~ *a coin,* jouer à pile ou face. ¶ *v.i,* filer; tisser sa toile; (*Fish*) pêcher à la cuiller. ~ [*round*], tourner; (*pers.*) se retourner vivement; (*Mot: wheel*) patiner; (*ball*) tournoyer. ~*drift,* embruns, *m.pl.* ~*-dryer,* essoreuse, *f.* ~*-off,* avantage inattendu, *m.* ~ *out,* faire durer.

spinach, *n,* (*Cook.*) épinards, *m.pl.*

spinal, *a,* spinal; (*column*) vertébrale. ~ *cord,* moelle épinière, *f.*

spindle, *n,* (*hand*) fuseau, *m;* (*Mach.*) broche, *f.* **spindly,** *a,* grêle; (*plant*) étiolé.

spine, *n,* (*Bot.*) épine; (*Anat.*) é. dorsale, *f;* (*of book*) dos, *m.* ~*-chilling,* à vous glacer la moelle des os. ~**less** (*fig.*), *a,* mou, sans caractère.

spinney, *n,* bosquet, *m.*

spinning, *n,* filature; (*Fish.*) pêche à la cuiller, *f.* ~ *jenny,* jenny, *f.* ~ *mill,* filature, *f.* ~ *wheel,* rouet, *m.*

spinster, *n,* célibataire; (*pej.*) vieille fille, *f.*

spiny, *a,* épineux. ~ *lobster,* langouste, *f.*

spiral, *a,* spiral; en spirale; (*staircase*) en colimaçon; (*Aero.*) en vrille. ¶ *n,* spirale, *f.* *inflationary* ~, la spirale inflationniste. ¶ *v.i,* (*smoke*) monter en spirale; (*prices*) monter en flèche.

spire, *n,* flèche, *f.*

spirit, *a,* (*soul, ghost, attitude &c*) esprit; (*courage*) courage, cran *P;* (*drive*) entrain, *m;* énergie, *f;* (*Chem.*) alcool, *m;* (*pl: drink*) spiritueux, *m.pl;* alcool. *in good* ~*s,* de bonne humeur. *in low* ~*s,* qui n'a pas le moral. *the right* ~, l'attitude qu'il faut. ¶ *a,* (*lamp &c*) à alcool. ~*-level,* niveau à bulle, *m.* ~ **away,** faire disparaître comme par enchantement, escamoter. ~**ed,** *a,* (*horse, speech*) fougueux; (*discussion*) animé; (*defence*) courageux. *give a* ~ *performance* (*Mus.*), jouer avec brio. **spiritual†,** *a,* spirituel. **spiritualism,** *n,* (*psychic*) spiritisme; (*Philos.*) spiritualisme, *m.* **spiritualist,** *n,* spirite; spiritualiste, *m,f.*

spit[1], *n,* (*Cook.*) broche; (*Geog.*) pointe de terre, *f.* ~ *roast,* faire rôtir à la broche. ¶ *v.t,* embrocher.

spit[2], *n,* (*spittle*) crachat, *m;* (*saliva*) salive, *f.* ~ *& polish,* astiquage, *m. the dead* ~ *of P,* le portrait craché de *P.* ¶ *v.t. & i. ir,* cracher; (*v.i*) (*fire, fat*) crépiter.

spite, *n,* dépit, *m,* malveillance, rancune, pique, *f. in* ~ *of,* en dépit de, malgré. *in* ~ *of the fact that,* bien que + *subj.* ¶ *v.t,* vexer. ~**ful,** *a,* malveillant; (*tongue*) venimeux. ~**fully,** *ad,* par dépit.

spittle, *n,* crachat, *m;* salive; (*animal*) bave, *f.* **spittoon,** *n,* crachoir, *m.*

splash, *n,* éclaboussement; (*sound*) plouf, *m;* (*spot*) éclaboussure; (*fig: colour*) tache, *f. make a* ~ (*fig.*), faire sensation. ~*down* (*Space*), amerrissage, *m.* ¶ *v.t,* éclabousser. ¶ *v.i,* faire des éclaboussures. ~ [*about*], barboter, patauger. ~ *down,* amerrir. ~ *out P* (*spend*), faire une folie. ~ *up,* gicler.

splay, *v.t.* (*& i*), (se) tourner en dehors.

spleen, *n,* (*Anat.*) rate, *f. vent one's* ~ *on,* décharger sa bile sur.

splendid†, *a,* splendide, magnifique; superbe. **splendour,** *n,* splendeur, magnificence, *f.*

splice, *n,* épissure, *f.* ¶ *v.t,* épisser.

splint, *n,* éclisse, attelle, *f.*

splinter, *n,* éclat, *m,* écharde; (*bone*) esquille, *f.* ~ *group,* groupe dissident, *m.* ¶ *v.t.* (*& i*), (*bone, glass*) (se) briser en éclats; (*wood*) (se) fendre en éclats.

split, *n,* déchirure; (*at seam*) fente; (*in wood, ground*) crevasse; (*quarrel*) rupture; (*Pol.*) scission, *f. do the* ~*s,* faire le grand écart. ¶ *v.t.* (*& i.*)*ir,* (*gen.*) (se) fendre; (*tear*) (se) déchirer; (*party &c*) (se) diviser; (*share*) (se) partager. ~ *the difference,* partager la différence. ~ *hairs,* couper les cheveux en 4. ~ *off, v.i,* se détacher; se séparer. ~ *on s.o,* dénoncer qn. ~ *one's sides* [*laughing*], se fendre la pipe *P.* ~ *peas,* pois cassés, *m.pl.* ~ *personality,* double personnalité, *f. in a* ~ *second,* en un rien de temps. ~ *sth in 2,* couper qch en deux. ~ *up,* (*married couple*) se séparer; (*friends*) rompre. *splitting headache,* affreux mal de tête, *m.*

splutter, *v.i,* (*pers., engine*) bafouiller; (*fire*) crépiter.

spoil, *v.t,* (*damage*) abîmer; (*child, food*) gâter; (*holiday &c*) gâcher. ~ *s.o's fun,* gâcher l'amusement de qn. ~ *one's appetite,* se couper l'appétit. ¶ *v.i,* (*goods*) s'abîmer; (*in storage*) s'avarier. *to be* ~*ing for a fight,* chercher la bagarre *P.* ~*sport,* trouble-fête, *m.* ~[**s**], *n,* butin, *m.*

spoke, *n,* rayon, *m. put a* ~ *in s.o's wheel,* mettre les bâtons dans les roues à qn.

spokesman, *n,* porte-parole, *m.inv.*

sponge, *n,* éponge, *f.* ~ *bag,* sac à éponge, *m.* ~ *cake,* biscuit de Savoie, *m.* ~ *finger,* boudoir, *m.* ¶ *v.t,* éponger. ~ *on s.o,* vivre aux crochets de qn. ~ *down,* laver à l'éponge. **sponger,** *n,* pique-assiette, parasite, *m.* **spongy,** *a,* spongieux.

sponsor, *n,* (*Fin.*) répondant, e; (*godparent, for club membership*) parrain, *m,* marraine, *f.* ¶ *v.t,* (*Fin.*) se porter caution pour; (*programme &c*) patronner, offrir; (*concert*) subventionner.

spontaneity, *n,* spontanéité, *f.* **spontaneous†,** *a,* spontané.

spook, *n,* revenant, *m.* ~**y,** *a,* qui donne le frisson.

spool, *n,* bobine, *f;* (*Fish.*) tambour; (*wire*) rouleau, *m;* (*sewing machine*) canette, *f.*

spoon, *n,* cuiller, cuillère, *f.* ~*bill,* spatule, *f.* ~*feed,* nourrir à la cuiller; (*fig.*) mâcher le travail à. ~*ful,* cuillerée, *f.*

Spoonerism, *n,* contrepetterie, *f.*

spoor, *n,* foulées, *f.pl,* trace, *f.*

sporadic†, *a,* sporadique.

spore, *n,* spore, *f.*

sport, *n,* sport; (*fun*) divertissement, *m.* ~*s,* réunion sportive; (*P pers.*) chic type *P, m,* chic fille *P, f. be a* ~*!* sois chic! ~*s car,* voiture de sport, *f.* ~*s club, editor &c,* club, rédacteur &c sportif. ~*s ground,* terrain de sport, *m.* ~*s jacket,* veste *f* sport, *inv.* ~*swear,* vêtements de sport, *m.pl.* ¶ *v.t,* exhiber. ~**ing,** *a,* sportif. **sportsman, -woman,** *n,* sportif, ive. ~**ship,** *n,* sportivité, *f.*

spot, *n,* tache, *f;* (*on dice &c*) point; (*polka dot*) pois; (*pimple*) bouton; (*place*) endroit, coin; (*in show*) numéro; (*advert.*) spot, *m;* (*Bil.*) mouche, *f. a* ~ *of,* un peu de; (*liquid*) une goutte de. *on the* ~, sur place; (*at once*) sur le champ. *in a tight* ~, dans le pétrin. ~ *cash,* argent comptant, *m.* ~ *light,* (*Theat.*) rayon de projecteur; (*lamp*) projecteur, spot. *in the* ~ *light* (*fig.*), en vedette. ¶ *v.t,* tacher (*with,* de); (*notice*) apercevoir, repérer; (*mistake*) relever. ~**less,** *a,* sans tache. **spotted,** *a,* tacheté; à pois. **spotty,** *a,* boutonneux.

spouse, *n,* époux, *m,* épouse, *f;* (*Law*) conjoint, e.

spout, *n,* (*gen.*) bec; (*of liquid*) jet, *m. up the* ~ *P,* fichu *P.* ¶ *v.t,* faire jaillir; vomir; (*P fig.*) débiter.

sprain, *n,* entorse, foulure, *f. to* ~ *one's...,* se

fouler le, la . . . se donner une entorse au, à la.
sprawl, *v.i,* s'étaler, se vautrer.
spray[1]**,** *n,* nuage de gouttelettes, *m; (sea)* embruns, *m.pl; (from hose)* pluie, *f; (Hort.)* vaporisateur, pulvérisateur, *m.* ~ *can,* bombe, *f,* aérosol, atomisateur, *m.* ~ *gun,* pistolet, *m.* ~ *nozzle,* pomme, *f.* ~ *paint,* peinture au pistolet, *f.* ¶ *v.t, (liquid)* vaporiser, pulvériser; *(crops)* faire des pulvérisations sur; *(room)* passer la bombe dans. ~ *with bullets,* arroser de balles.
spray[2]**,** *n, (flowers)* gerbe; *(greenery)* branche; *(Need.)* chute; *(jewels)* aigrette, *f.*
spread, *n, (wings)* envergure; *(ages &c)* échelle; *(fire &c)* propagation; *(knowledge)* diffusion, *f; (P meal)* festin, *m.* ¶ *v.t,* étendre; étaler; répandre *(over,* sur); *(bread)* tartiner *(with,* de); *(disease)* propager; *(germs, news)* disséminer; *(rumours)* faire courir. ¶ *v.i,* s'étendre; *(payments)* s'étaler; se répandre. ~ [*out*], *v.t, (things)* étaler; *(people)* disposer.
spree, *n,* fête, *f. go on a* ~ , faire la noce.
sprig, *n,* brin, rameau, *m.*
sprightly, *a,* actif, alerte.
spring, *n, (leap)* saut, bond; *(Tech.)* ressort, *m; (resilience)* élasticité; *(water)* source, *f; (season)* printemps, *m, (att.)* printanier. ~*board,* tremplin, *m.* ~ *chicken,* poussin, *m.* ~ *cleaning,* grand nettoyage. ~ *tide,* marée de vive eau, *f.* ¶ *v.i.ir,* bondir, sauter; *(originate)* provenir (de). ~ *to mind,* venir à l'esprit. ¶ *v.t, (catch &c)* faire jouer; *(news)* annoncer de but en blanc. ~ *a surprise on,* surprendre. ~ *up, (pers.)* se lever d'un bond; *(plants &c)* surgir; *(storm)* se lever; *(friendship)* naître. ~**y,** *a,* souple; flexible.
sprinkle, *v.t, (liquid)* asperger (de); *(sugar)* saupoudrer (de). **sprinkler,** *n, (for lawn)* arroseur; *(for sugar)* saupoudroir, *m.*
sprint, *n,* sprint, *m.* ¶ *v.i, (Sport)* sprinter; *(gen.)* foncer. ~**er,** *n,* sprinteur, euse.
sprout, *n, (on plant)* pousse, *f; (from seeds)* germe, *m.* [*Brussels*]~*s,* choux de Bruxelles, *m.pl.* ¶ *v.i,* pousser, germer. ~ [*up*], pousser.
spruce[1]**,** *n,* épicéa, *m.* **spruce**[2]**,** *a,* pimpant.
sprung *(provided with springs) a,* à ressorts.
spud *P, n,* patate *P, f.*
spur, *n,* éperon; *(fig.)* aiguillon, *m. on the* ~ *of the moment,* sous l'impulsion du moment. ¶ *v.t,* éperonner; aiguillonner.
spurious, *a,* faux; *(claim)* fallacieux.
spurn, *v.t,* repousser.
spurt, *n, (water, flame)* jet; *(anger, energy &c)* sursaut, *m. put on a* ~ , *(Sport)* démarrer; *(gen.)* foncer; *(fig.)* donner un coup de collier. ¶ *v.i.* ~ [*up*], ~ [*out*], jaillir.
spy, *n,* espion, ne; *(police)* indicateur, trice de police. ¶ *a, (story &c)* d'espionnage. ~*glass,* longue-vue, *f.* ~*hole, (in door)* judas, *m.* ¶ *v.i,* espionner; faire de l'espionnage. ¶ *v.t,* apercevoir. ~ *on,* épier. ~ *out,* reconnaître.
squabble, *n,* chamaillerie *P, f.* ¶ *v.i,* se chamailler. **squabbling,** *n,* chamailleries, *f.pl.*
squad, *n, (gen.)* escouade, *f; (Mil.)* groupe; *(Foot. &c)* contingent, *m.* ~ *car,* voiture de police, *f.* **squadron,** *n, (Mil.)* escadron, *m; (Nav., Aero.)* escadre, *f.* ~ *leader,* commandant, *m.*
squalid, *a,* sordide; *(motive)* vil, ignoble.
squall, *n, (at sea)* grain, *m; (Met.)* rafale *ou* bourrasque de pluie, *f.* ¶ *v.i,* brailler, hurler. ~**y,** *a,* à grains, à rafales.
squalor, *n,* conditions sordides, *f.pl;* misère noire.
squander, *v.t, (time, money)* gaspiller; *(fortune)* dissiper; *(chances)* perdre.
square, *a,* carré; *(accounts &c)* en ordre; *(honest)* honnête, régulier *P; (P opp. trendy)* vieux jeu, rétro *P.* ~ *metre,* mètre carré. *be all* ~ , être quitte; *(Sport)* être à égalité. *look s.o* ~ *in the face,* regarder qn bien en face. *get* ~ *with s.o,* régler son compte à qn. ~ *bracket (Typ.),* crochet, *m.* ~*-cut,* coupé à angle droit. ~ *dance,* ~ *dancing,* quadrille, *m.* ~ *meal,* repas convenable, *m.* ~ *root,* racine carrée. ¶ *n, (gen.)* carré; *(in pattern)* carreau, *m; (chessboard &c)* case; *(town)* place, *f; (with gardens)* square, *m; (Mil.)* cour, *f.* ¶ *v.t,* carrer; couper à angle droit; mettre en ordre. ~ *one's account with,* régler ses comptes avec. ¶ *v.t,* ~ *with,* cadrer, s'accorder avec. ~**ly,** *ad,* carrément.
squash, *n, (crush &c)* cohue, *f; (orange, lemon* ~) orangeade, citronnade *f; (Sport)* squash, *m.* ~ *court,* terrain de s., *m.* ¶ *v.t,* écraser; *(snub)* remettre à sa place. ~ *flat (box &c),* aplatir. ¶ *v.i,* ~ [*up*], se serrer, s'entasser.
squat, *a, (pers.)* ramassé; *(object)* petit & épais. ¶ *v.i,* ~ [*down*], s'accroupir; *(animals)* se tapir. ~ *in a house,* squatteriser une maison. ~**ter,** *n,* squatter, *m.*
squawk, *n,* couac; cri rauque; *(baby)* braillement, *m.* ¶ *v.i,* pousser un cri rauque; brailler.
squeak, *v.i, (hinge)* grincer; *(mouse)* vagir; *(shoe)* craquer; *(pers.)* glapir. ¶ *n,* grincement &c, *m.*
squeal, *n,* cri aigu; *(brakes)* hurlement; *(tyres)* crissement, *m.* ¶ *v.i,* pousser un cri aigu; hurler; crisser; *(P inform)* vendre la mèche.
squeamish, *a,* facilement dégouté; *(queasy)* qui a mal au cœur. ~**ness,** *n,* délicatesse exagérée.
squeeze, *n,* pression, compression; *(in crowd)* cohue, *f. it's a tight* ~ , on tient tout juste. *put the* ~ *on s.o P,* harceler qn. *credit* ~ , restrictions de credit, *f.pl.* ¶ *v.t,* presser; *(arm)* serrer. ~ [*out*], exprimer. ¶ *v.i,* se glisser *(under, into,* sous, dans). **squeezer,** *n,* presse-fruits, *m.inv.*
squelch, *v.i,* patauger.
squib, *n,* pétard, *m.*
squid, *n,* calmar, *m.*

squiggle, *n,* gribouillis, *m.*
squint, *n,* strabisme, *m.* ¶ *v.i,* loucher.
squire, *n,* châtelain; (*Hist.*) écuyer, *m.*
squirm, *v.i,* (*worm*) se tortiller; (*fig: pers*) ne pas savoir ou se mettre.
squirrel, *n,* écureuil, *m.*
squirt, *n,* (*liquid*) jet, *m,* giclée, *f.* ¶ *v.t,* faire gicler, f. jaillir. ¶ *v.i,* gicler.
stab, *n,* coup (de poignard, &c), *m. a ~ in the back* (*fig.*), un coup bas. *~ of pain,* élancement, *m. have a ~ at it,* tenter le coup. ¶ *v.t,* poignarder.
stability, *n,* stabilité; solidité; fermeté, *f;* équilibre, *m.* **stabilize,** *v.t,* stabiliser. **~r,** *n,* (*Mot., Naut.*) stabilisateur, *m.* **stable[1],** *a,* stable; (*marriage*) solide; (*pers.*) équilibré.
stable[2], *n,* écurie, *f;* (*pl: riding*) manège, *m. ~boy, ~ lad,* lad, *m.* ¶ *v.t,* mettre à l'écurie.
stack, *n,* (*Agr.*) meule; (*heap*) pile, *f,* tas; (*arms*) faisceau, *m;* (*chimney*) souche, *f. have ~s of time P,* avoir plein de temps *P.* ¶ *v.t,* empiler; mettre en meule.
stadium, *n,* stade, *m.*
staff, *n,* (*pole &c*) bâton; (*flag ~*) mât, *m;* (*Mus.*) portée, *f;* personnel, *m;* (*Sch., Univ.*) professeurs, *m.pl;* (*Mil.*) état-major, *m. ~room,* salle des professeurs, *f. ~ training,* formation du personnel, *f.* ¶ *v.t,* pourvoir en personnel.
stag, *n,* cerf, *m. ~ beetle,* cerf-volant, *m.*
stage, *n,* (*Theat.*) scène; (*in hall*) estrade; (*of journey*) étape, *f;* (*rocket*) étage; (*process, disease*) stade; (*career*) échelon, *m. in ~s,* par étapes. *in the early ~s,* au début. *on ~,* sur scène. *the ~,* le théâtre. *come on ~,* entrer en scène. *go on the ~* (*career*), monter sur les planches. *~coach,* diligence, *f. ~ designer,* décorateur, trice de théâtre. *~ director,* metteur en scène, *m. ~ door,* entrée des artistes, *m. ~ fright,* trac *P, m. ~hand,* machiniste, *m. ~ manager,* régisseur, *m. ~ name,* nom de théâtre, *m. in a ~ whisper,* en aparté. ¶ *v.t,* mettre en scène, monter; (*fig.*) organiser, monter.
stagger, *v.i,* chanceler, tituber. ¶ *v.t,* renverser, stupéfier; bouleverser; (*payments*) échelonner; (*holidays*) étaler. *~ing blow,* (*lit., fig.*) coup de massue, *m.*
stagnant, *a,* stagnant. **stagnate,** *v.i,* être stagnant; (*fig.*) stagner. **stagnation,** *n,* stagnation, *f.*
staid, *a,* posé, sérieux.
stain, *n,* (*mark*) tache, *f;* (*colour*) colorant, *m. without a ~ on one's character,* sans une tache à sa réputation. *~ remover,* détachant, *m. ~ed glass,* verre coloré; (*windows*) vitraux, *m.pl. ~ed-glass window,* vitrail, *m.* **~less,** *a,* (*steel*) inoxydable.
stair, *n,* marche, *f. ~ carpet,* tapis d'escalier, *m. ~case* & *~[s],* escalier, *m. ~ rod,* tringle d'e., *f.*
stake, *n,* (*gen.*) pieu, poteau; (*for plant*) tuteur; (*Hist.*) bûcher; (*bet*) enjeu; (*share*) intérêt; (*pl: Turf*) prix, *m. be at ~,* être en jeu. *have a ~ in sth,* avoir des intérêts dans qch. ¶ *v.t,* jouer (sur). *~ one's claim to,* établir son droit à. *~ [out],* marquer avec des piquets.
stalactite, *n,* stalactite, *f.*
stalagmite, *n,* stalagmite, *f.*
stale, *a,* (*meat &c*) qui n'est plus frais; (*bread*) rassis; dur; (*air*) confiné; (*beer*) éventé; (*joke*) rebattu. **~mate,** *n,* (*Chess*) pat, *m;* (*fig.*) impasse, *f.* **~ness,** *n,* manque de fraîcheur, *m.*
stalk[1], *n,* (*plant*) tige; (*fruit*) queue, *f;* (*cabbage*) trognon, *m.*
stalk[2], *v.t,* (*prey &c*) traquer; (*suspect*) filer.
stall, *n,* (*stable*) stalle, *f;* (*market*) éventaire; (*exhibition*) stand; (*Theat.*) fauteuil d'orchestre, *m. coffee ~,* buvette, *f. newspaper ~,* kiosque à journaux, *m. ~ holder,* marchand, e. ¶ *v.i,* (*Mot.*) caler; (*Aero.*) être en perte de vitesse; (*pers.*) temporiser. ¶ *v.t,* caler.
stallion, *n,* étalon, *m.*
stalwart, *a,* robuste, vigoureux; résolu ¶ *n,* fidèle, *m,f.*
stamen, *n,* étamine, *f.*
stamina, *n,* résistance, endurance, *f.*
stammer, *v.i. & t,* bégayer. **~er,** *n,* bègue, *m,f.* **~[ing],** *n,* bégaiement, *m.*
stamp, *n,* timbre, *m. postage ~* timbre-poste. (*mark*) cachet; (*on. metal*) poinçon, *m. rubber ~,* timbre. *date ~,* t. dateur. *~ collecting,* philatélie, *f. ~ collector,* philatéliste, *m,f. ~ duty,* droit de timbre, *m.* ¶ *v.t,* timbrer; (*passport*) viser; (*date*) apposer (*on,* sur); (*metal*) poinçonner. ¶ *v.i,* taper du pied; (*horse*) piaffer; (*rage &c*) trépigner; (*when cold*) battre la semelle. *~ed addressed envelope,* enveloppe timbrée pour la réponse. *~ on sth,* piétiner qch. *~ out,* (*custom*) supprimer; (*rebellion*) écraser.
stampede, *n,* sauve-qui-peut, *m.inv;* débandade; (*rush*) ruée, *f.* ¶ *v.i,* s'enfuir à la débandade; se ruer (*for,* vers). ¶ *v.t,* jeter la panique parmi.
stance, *n,* position, *f.*
stand, *n,* position; (*Mil.*) résistance, *f;* (*for plant &c*) guéridon; (*lamp*) support, pied; (*Mus.*) pupitre; (*Com.*) étalage; (*exhibition*) stand, *m;* (*fair*) baraque, *f. band ~,* kiosque à musique, *m. make a ~,* résister (*against,* à); prendre position (contre). *~point,* point de vue, *m. come to a ~-still,* s'arrêter. ¶ *v.t.ir,* (*put*) mettre, poser; (*tolerate*) supporter; (*pay for*) offrir, payer. *I can't ~ him,* je ne peux pas l'encaisser *P. ~ a chance* avoir une bonne chance. *~ one's ground,* tenir bon *ou* ferme. *~ the strain,* supporter la tension; (*pers.*) tenir le coup. *~ trial,* passer en

jugement. ¶ *v.i.ir,* être *ou* se tenir debout; se trouver; (*be left: liquid*) reposer; (*tea, coffee*) infuser. ~ *guard over,* veiller sur. ~ *on ceremony,* faire des manières. ~ *for election,* se présenter aux élections. ~ *in s.o's way,* barrer le passage à qn. ~ *on s.o's foot,* marcher sur le pied à. ~ *to lose,* risquer de perdre. *it* ~*s to reason,* il va sans dire. ~ **aside,** s'écarter. ~ **back,** reculer, s'écarter. ~ **by,** *v.i,* (*troops*) être en état d'alerte; (*pers.*) se tenir prêt; *v.t,* (*promise*) tenir; (*decision*) s'en tenir à; (*pers.*) ne pas abandonner. ~ **clear,** s'écarter. ~ **down,** (*Mil.*) être déconsigné; (*candidate*) se désister. ~ **fast,** ~ **firm,** tenir bon. ~ **for,** représenter; (*tolerate*) supporter, tolérer. ~**-in,** remplaçant, e; (*Cine*) doublure, *f.* ~ **in for,** remplacer. ~ **out,** (*project: ledge &c*) avancer; (*vein &c*) ressortir; (*be obvious*) ressortir, se détacher (*against,* sur). *it* ~*s out a mile!* cela crève les yeux! ~ **out against,** (*attack*) résister à; (*demands*) s'opposer fermement à. ~ **over s.o,** être sur le dos de qn. ~ **[up],** se lever, se mettre debout. ~ **up for,** défendre. ~ **up to,** (*opponent*) affronter; (*in argument*) tenir tête à; (*cold &c*) résister à.

standard, *n,* (*flag*) étendard; (*Naut.*) pavillon, *m;* (*norm*) norme, *f,* critère; (*Meas.*) étalon; (*education*) niveau; (*lamp &c*) pied, *m. gold* ~, étalon d'or. *up to* ~, (*pers.*) à la hauteur; (*thing*) de la qualité voulue. *apply double* ~*s,* appliquer deux mesures. ~ *of living,* niveau de vie. ~*-bearer,* porte-étendard, *m.inv.* ~*-lamp,* lampadaire, *m.* ¶ *a,* ordinaire, normal; étalon, *inv;* (*Com.*) standard, *inv;* (*pronunciation &c*) correct. *it's* ~ *practice,* c'est courant. ~ *model* (*car*), voiture de série, *f.* ~ *time,* l'heure légale. ~**ization,** *n,* standardisation, normalisation, *f.* ~**ize,** *v.t,* standardiser, normaliser.

standing, *n,* importance; réputation, *f;* standing, *m;* (*social*) position, *f;* standing; (*professional*) rang, *m. of long* ~, de longue date. ¶ *a,* debout; (*crops*) sur pied; (*Naut.*) dormant; (*water*) stagnant; (*orders, army &c*) permanent. ~ *expenses,* frais généraux. ~ *order* (*Bank*), virement automatique, *m.* ~ *orders,* règlement, *m.* ~ *room only!* places debout seulement.

stand-offish, *a,* distant, réservé. ~**ness,** *n,* réserve, froideur, *f.*

stanza, *n,* strophe, *f;* (*song*) couplet, *m.*

staple[1], *n,* (*wall*) crampon; (*wire*) cavalier, *m;* (*for papers*) agrafe, *f.* ¶ *v.t,* agrafer; cramponner. **stapler,** *n,* agrafeuse, *f.*

staple[2], *a,* (*crop, industry*) principal; (*food, product*) de base.

star, *n,* étoile, *f;* (*Typ. &c*) astérisque, *m;* (*Theat. &c*) vedette; (*actress*) star, *f;* (*pl: horoscope*) horoscope, *m. see* ~*s P,* voir 36 chandelles. *the S*~*s & Stripes,* la Bannière étoilée. ~*fish,* étoile de mer, *f. be* ~*gazing,* (*fig.*) être dans la lune. ~*lit.* (*night &c*) étoilé; (*scene*) illuminé par les étoiles. ~ *part,* premier rôle. *the* ~ *turn,* la vedette. ¶ *v.t,* étoiler; marquer d'un astérisque; avoir pour vedette. ¶ *v.i,* être la vedette.

starboard, *n,* tribord, *m.*

starch, *n,* amidon, *m;* fécule, *f.* ¶ *v.t,* empeser, amidonner. ~**y** *a,* (*food*) féculent.

stare, *n,* regard appuyé, *m.* ¶ *v.i,* écarquiller les yeux. ~ *at,* regarder fixement, dévisager.

stark, *a,* raide; (*country &c*) désolé, morne; (*décor*) austère. ~ *raving mad,* complètement dingue *P.* ~ *naked,* tout nu, nu comme un ver; à poil *P.*

starling (*bird*) *n,* sansonnet, étourneau, *m.*

starry, *a,* étoilé. ~*-eyed,* idéaliste; innocent.

start, *n,* (*jump*) tressaillement, sursaut; (*beginning*) commencement, début; (*race &c*) départ, *m;* (*negotiations*) ouverture; (*advantage: Sport*) avance, *f;* (*fig.*) avantage, *m. for a* ~, d'abord. *from* ~ *to finish,* de bout en bout. *give s.o a* ~, faire sursauter *ou* tressailler qn. ¶ *v.t,* (*gen.*) commencer (*to do, doing,* à faire, de faire); (*task*) entreprendre; (*bottle &c*) entamer. ~ *again, afresh,* recommencer. ~ *life as,* débuter dans la vie comme. ~ [*off*], ~ [*up*], (*discussions*) commencer, ouvrir, engager; (*rumour, quarrel*) faire naître; (*war, crisis*) déclencher; (*fashion, policy*) lancer. ~ [*off*], (*race*) donner le signal du départ. ~ [*up*], (*car &c*) mettre en marche. *let's get* ~*ed,* allons-y. ¶ *v.i,* (*jump*) sursauter, tressaillir; (*gen.*) commencer (*with,* par; *by doing,* par faire); (*road*) partir; (*car*) démarrer; (*clock*) se mettre en marche. ~ *on,* commencer; (*bottle*) entamer. ~ [*off*], ~ [*out*], partir. ~**er,** *n,* (*Sport*) starter; (*horse*) partant; (*Mot.*) démarreur; (*Cook.*) hors-d'œuvre, *m.* ~*ing price,* (*Turf*) cote de départ, *f.*

startle, *v.t,* (*sound &c*) faire sursauter *ou* tressaillir; (*news &c*) alarmer. *you* ~*d me!* vous m'avez fait peur! ~**d,** *a,* (*animal*) effarouché; (*pers.*) très surpris. **startling,** *a,* surprenant, alarmant.

starvation, *n,* inanition, *f.* ¶ *a,* (*wage, rations*) de famine. **starve,** *v.t,* priver de nourriture, affamer. ¶ *v.i* mourir de faim. **starving,** *a,* affamé.

state, *n,* état, *m. the S*~*s,* les États-Unis, *m.pl. get into a terrible* ~, se mettre dans tous ses états. ~ *banquet,* banquet de gala, *m.* ~*-controlled,* ~*-owned,* étatisé. ~ *education,* enseignement public. ~ *enrolled nurse,* infirmier, ère diplômé, e d'État. ~*room,* grande salle de réception; (*ship*) cabine de luxe, *f.* ¶ *v.t,* déclarer (*that,* que); (*problem &c*) exposer; (*time, place*) fixer, spécifier. ~ *one's case,* présenter ses arguments. ~**d,** *a,* (*limit*) prescrit; (*date, sum &c*) fixe. **~less,** *a,* & ~ *person,* apatride, *m,f.* **~liness,** *n,* majesté, *f.* **~ly,** *a,* majestueux. **statement,** *n,* déclaration, *f;* (*views*) exposition; (*conditions*) formulation; (*bill*) facture, *f. bank* ~ , relevé de compte, *m. make a* ~ , faire une déclaration. *official* ~ , communiqué officiel. **statesman,** *n,* homme d'État, *m.* ~*like,* diplomatique.

static, *a.* & **statics,** *n,* statique, *f.*

station, *n,* (*place*) station, *f,* poste, *m;* (*Mil.*) poste; (*Rly*) gare, *f;* (*metro*) station. ~*s of the Cross,* Chemin de la Croix, *m. one's* ~ *in life,* sa situation sociale. ~*master,* chef de gare, *m.* ~ *wagon,* break, *m.* ¶ *v.t,* (*gen.*) placer; (*Mil. &c*) poster. ~*ed at,* (*Mil.*) en garnison à; (*Naut.*) en station à. **~ary,** *a,* stationnaire.

stationer, *n,* papetier, ère. ~ *'s* [*shop*], papeterie, *f.* **~y,** *n,* papeterie, *f;* (*writing paper*) papier à lettres, *m.*

statistic(al), *a,* statistique; (*error*) de statistiques; (*expert*) en s. **statistician,** *n,* statisticien, ne. **statistics,** *n,* statistiques, *f.pl;* (*subject*) statistique, *f.*

statue, *n,* statue, *f.* **statuesque,** *a,* sculptural. **statuette,** *n,* statuette, *f.*

stature, *n,* stature, taille; (*fig.*) envergure, *f.*

status, *n,* position, situation, *f;* (*Law*) statut; (*social*) standing; prestige, *m.* ~ *symbol,* signe extérieur de standing. ~ *quo,* statu quo, *m.*

statute, *n,* loi, *f.* ~ *book,* code, *m.* **statutory,** *a,* (*right &c*) statuaire; (*holiday*) légal.

staunch[1], *v.t,* (*flow*) arrêter; (*blood*) étancher.

staunch†[2], *a,* (*support*) loyal; (*friend &c*) à toute épreuve.

stave, *n,* douve; (*Mus.*) portée, *f.* ~ *in, v.t.ir,* enfoncer, défoncer. ~ *off,* (*attack*) parer; (*defeat*) écarter, éviter; (*hunger*) tromper.

stay, *n,* séjour; (*Law*) sursis, *m.* ¶ *v.t,* arrêter; (*disease*) enrayer; (*delay*) retarder; (*Law: judgement*) surseoir à; (*proceedings*) suspendre; (*decision*) remettre. ~ *the course,* (*Sport*) aller jusqu'au bout; (*fig.*) tenir bon. ¶ *v.i,* rester; (*at hotel*) descendre à; (*in a place*) séjourner. ~ *with s.o.,* passer quelques jours chez qn. ~*-at-home,* casanier, ère, ~ **away,** s'absenter. ~ **in,** rester à la maison, ne pas sortir; (*Sch.*) être en retenue; (*screw &c*) tenir. ~ **out,** ne pas rentrer; rester dehors; (*on strike*) rester en grève. ~ *out late,* rentrer tard. ~ *out of trouble,* se tenir tranquille. ~ **up,** (*pers.*) veiller; ne pas se coucher; (*garment*) tenir. ~ *up late,* se coucher tard. *staying power,* endurance, *f.*

stead, *n,* place, *f. stand in good* ~ , être très utile à.

steadfast, *a,* constant, ferme. **~ly,** *ad,* fermement. **~ness,** *n,* fermeté, *f.*

steadily, *ad,* d'un pas *ou* d'une main ferme; (*look*) longuement; (*improve*) progressivement; (*rain*) sans arrêt. **steady,** *a,* (*firm: table &c*) stable; (*hand*) sûr; (*nerves*) solide; (*gaze*) franc; (*pers.*) sérieux, posé; (*regular*) constant, régulier; (*prices, job &c*) stable. **go** ~ *with s.o,* sortir avec qn. ¶ *v.t,* (*ladder*) assurer; (*voice*) [r]affermir; (*nerves*) calmer. ~ *o.s,* reprendre son aplomb. ¶ *i,* ~ *on!* doucement!.

steak, *n,* tranche, *f;* (*beef*) bifteck, steak, *m.*

steal, *v.t.ir,* voler (*from s.o,* à qn). ~ *a march on s.o,* gagner qn de vitesse. ~ *away,* s'en aller à pas de loup. ~ *into,* se glisser dans. **~ing,** *n,* vol, *m.* **by stealth,** furtivement. **stealthy**†, *a,* furtif.

steam, *n,* vapeur, *f. full* ~ *ahead!* en avant toute! *get up* ~ , (*engine*) chauffer. *let off* ~ (*fig.*), se défouler. ¶ *a,* à vapeur. ~ *roller,* rouleau compresseur, *m.* ~*ship,* paquebot, *m.* ¶ *v.t,* (*Cook.*) cuire à la vapeur. ~ *open a letter,* décacheter une lettre à la vapeur. ¶ *v.i,* (*liquid &c*) fumer; (*ship*) avancer, naviguer, ~ *up, v.t,* embuer; *v.i,* se couvrir de buée. *get* ~*ed up* (*fig.*), se mettre dans tous ses états. **~er,** *n,* vapeur; (*liner*) paquebot; (*Cook.*) couscoussier, *m.* **~y,** *a,* (*heat &c*) humide; (*room &c*) embué.

steel, *n,* acier; (*sharpener*) aiguisoir, *m.* ¶ *a,* (*tool &c*) d'acier; (*engraving*) sur a.; (*industry*) sidérurgique. ~ *band,* steel band, *m.* ~*-plated,* revêtu d'acier. ~ *wool,* paille de fer, *f.* ~*worker,* sidérurgiste, *m.* ~*works,* aciérie, *f.* ~ *o.s against,* se cuirasser contre.

steep[1], *v.t,* (*in liquid*) tremper (dans); (*Cook.*) macérer. ~*ed in* (*fig.*), imbu de; imprégné de; (*vice*) plongé dans.

steep[2], *a,* (*gen.*) raide; (*hill, path*) escarpé; (*cliff*) à pic; (*price*) élevé. **steeple,** *n,* clocher, *m.* ~*chase,* steeple-chase, *m.* **steeply,** *ad,* (*rise: road*) en pente raide; (*prices*) en flèche. **steepness,** *n,* raideur, *f.*

steer[1], *n,* bouvillon, *m.*

steer[2], *v.t,* (*car*) conduire; (*ship*) gouverner; (*boat*) barrer; (*fig: pers.*) guider. ¶ *v.i,* gouverner. ~ *clear of,* éviter. **~age,** *n,* (*Naut.*) entrepont, *m.* **~ing,** *n,* (*action*) conduite; (~ *gear*) direction, *f.* ~ *wheel,* volant, *m.*

stem[1], *n,* (*plant*) tige; (*fruit, leaf*) queue, *f;* (*glass*) pied; (*Gram.*) radical, thème, *m. from* ~ *to stern,* de bout en bout. ¶ *v.i,* ~ *from,* provenir de.

stem[2], *v.t,* (*flow*) contenir; (*attack &c*) refouler. ~ *the flow of* (*fig.*), endiguer.

stench, *n,* puanteur, *f.*

stencil, *n,* pochoir; (*of paper*) poncif; (*Typing*) stencil, *m* ¶ *v.t,* marquer au pochoir.

stenographer, *n,* sténographe, *m,f.* **stenography,** *n,* sténographie, *f.*

step, *n,* (*gen.*) pas, *m;* (*stair*) marche, *f;* (*door*) seuil; (*bus &c*) marchepied; (*pl: outdoor*) perron, *m. keep in* ~, marcher au pas. *get out of* ~, rompre le pas. *take* ~*s*, prendre des dispositions *ou* des mesures (pour faire). ~*brother*, demi-frère, *m.* ~*daughter*, belle-fille, *f.* ~*father*, beau-père, *m.* ~*ladder* or [*pair of*] ~*s*, escabeau, *m.* ~*mother*, belle-mère, *f.* ~*sister*, demi-sœur, *f.* ~*son*, beau-fils, *m.* ¶ *v.i*, faire un pas, aller; venir; monter. ~ *on it! P* dépêche-toi! ~ *on the brakes*, donner un coup de frein. ~ *on the gas P*, appuyer sur le champignon *P.* ~ *out of line*, s'écarter du droit chemin. ~ **aside,** s'écarter. ~ **down,** descendre; (*fig.*) se désister (en faveur de qn.). ~ **in,** entrer; (*fig.*) intervenir. *stepping stone*, pierre de gué, *f;* (*fig.*) tremplin (*to*, pour obtenir), *m.* ~ **up,** augmenter; intensifier; multiplier.

stereo, *n. & a,* stéréo, *f. & inv. in* ~, en stéréo. ~**phonic,** *a,* stéréophonique. ~**scope,** *n,* stéréoscope, *m.* ~**scopic,** *a,* stéréoscopique. ~**type,** *n,* stéréotype; (*Typ.*) cliché, *m.* ¶ *v.t*, stéréotyper.

sterile, *a,* stérile. **sterility,** *n,* stérilité, *f.* **sterilization,** *n,* stérilisation, *f.* **sterilize,** *v.t*, stériliser.

sterling, *a,* (*Eng. money*) sterling, *inv.;* (*silver &c*) fin; (*fig.*) à toute épreuve; solide.¶ *n,* livre sterling, *f.*

stern[1], *n,* arrière, *m,* poupe, *f.*

stern†[2], *a,* sévère; (*discipline*) strict. *be made of* ~*er stuff*, être d'une autre trempe. ~**ness,** *n,* sévérité, *f.*

stet (*Typ.*), à maintenir.

stethoscope, *n,* stéthoscope, *m.*

stevedore, *n,* docker, *m.*

stew, *n,* (*meat*) ragoût; (*game*) civet, *m.* ~*pot*, cocotte, *f.* ¶ *v.t*, cuire en ragoût *ou* en civet; (*fruit*) faire cuire. ¶ *v.i*, cuire. ~ *in one's own juice*, mijoter dans son jus. ~**ed,** *a,* en ragoût; (*fruit*) en compote.

steward, *n,* (*ship, plane*) steward; (*in club, estate*) intendant, *m.* ~**ess,** *n,* femme de chambre; (*air*) hôtesse, *f.* ~**ship,** *n,* intendance, *f.*

stick, *n,* (*gen.*) bâton, *m;* (*walking*) canne; (*twig*) brindille; (*Mus.*) baguette, *f;* (*for plants*) tuteur, *m;* (*Hockey*) crosse, *f;* (*pl.*) du petit bois; (*celery*) branche, *f;* (*bombs*) chapelet, *m. get hold of the wrong end of the* ~, mal comprendre. *give s.o* ~, engueuler qn *P. in the* ~*s P*, dans le bled *P.* ~ *insect*, phasme, *m.* ¶ *v.t*, (*thrust*) planter, enfoncer; (*pig*) égorger; (*put*) mettre, poser, placer; (*with glue*) coller; (*put up with*) supporter; (*pers.*) souffrir, sentir *P.* '~ *no bills*', 'défense d'afficher'. *I'm stuck P*, je sèche *P. stuck at home* cloué à la maison. ¶ *v.i*, se planter, s'enfoncer; (*glue*) tenir (*to*, à); (*stamp &c*) être collé (à); (*sauce &c*) attacher (à). ~ or *be stuck*, (*gen.*) être coincé; (*wheels*) être enlisé. ~ *to one's guns*, ne pas en démordre. ~*ing plaster*, sparadrap, *m.* ~ **at,** (*job*) persévérer dans. ~ **by,** (*pers.*) rester fidèle à. ~ **down,** coller. ~ **in,** enfoncer, planter; piquer; coller. ~*-in-the-mud* encroûté, e. ~ **on,** coller. ~*-on*, adhésif. ~ **out,** (*gen.*) sortir; (*teeth*) avancer; faire saillie; dépasser. ~*ing out* (*ears*), décollé. ~ **up,** (*notice &c*) afficher; (*rob*) dévaliser. ~ *'em up!* haut les mains! ~**er,** *n,* auto-collant, *m.*

stickleback, *n,* épinoche, *f.*

stickler, *n, be a* ~ *for*, insister sur.

sticky, *a,* (*label*) adhésif; (*hands, paste &c*) poisseux; (*surface, toffee*) gluant; (*sweaty*) moite. *come to a* ~ *end*, finir mal. ~ *tape*, scotch, *m.*

stiff, *a,* raide, rigide; (*brush*) dur; (*dough*) ferme; (*starched*) empesé; (*joint*) ankylosé; (*fig: pers.*) guindé; (*exam*) difficile; (*breeze, drink*) fort; (*resistance*) tenace. ~ *neck*, torticolis, *m.* ¶ *n,* (*P* corpse*) macchabée *P*, m.* ~**en,** *v.t*, raidir; ankyloser; (*fig.*) affermir. ¶ *v.i*, devenir raide, rigide &c; s'ankyloser; s'affermir. ~**ness,** *n,* raideur, rigidité &c; ankylose, *f.*

stifle, *v.t*, étouffer; (*fig.*) réprimer. ¶ *v.i*, étouffer.

stifling, *a,* (*heat*) étouffant; (*fumes*) suffocant.

stigma, *n,* stigmate, *m.* **stigmatize,** *v.t*, stigmatiser.

stile, *n,* échalier, *m.*

stiletto, *n,* stylet, *m.* ~ *heel*, talon aiguille, *m.*

still[1], *a,* calme; tranquille; (*quiet*) silencieux; immobile; (*drink &c*) non gazeux. *keep* ~*!* ne bouge pas! ~*born*, mort-né, e. ~ *life*, nature morte, *f.*

still[2], *ad,* encore, toujours; (*even*) encore; (*nevertheless*) quand même, tout de même; néanmoins. *he's* ~ *here*, il est toujours ici. ~ *more*, encore plus.

still[3], *n,* alambic, *m.*

stillness, *n,* calme, *m,* tranquillité, *f;* silence, *m;* immobilité, *f.*

stilt, *n,* échasse, *f.* ~**ed,** *a,* guindé.

stimulant, *n,* stimulant, *m.* **stimulate,** *v.t*, stimuler. **stimulation,** *n,* stimulation, *f.* **stimulus,** *n,* (*Phys.*) stimulus; (*fig.*) stimulant, *m.*

sting, *n,* (*bee &c*) dard, *m;* (*wound*) piqûre, *f;* douleur cuisante; (*fig.*) mordant, *m.* ¶ *v.t*, piquer; brûler; (*whip*) cingler; (*taunt*) piquer au vif. ¶ *v.i*, piquer; brûler. **stinging,** *a,* cuisant. ~ *nettle*, ortie, *f.*

stingy, *a,* avare, mesquin; chiche (*with*, de); (*meal*) mesquin. *to be* ~. lésiner (*with*, sur). **stinginess,** *n,* avarice, *f.*

stink, *n,* puanteur, *f. kick up a* ~ *P*, faire toute une scène. ¶ *v.i*, (*lit. & fig.*) puer; empester (*of sth*, qch). (*P fig.*) *it* ~*s!* c'est infect! ~ *to high heaven*, sentir à plein nez. ~ [*out*], empester. ~**er,** *n,* (*pers.*) salaud *P, m,* salope *P, f.*

stint, *n,* période de travail; besogne assignée, *f. without* ~, sans bornes. ¶ *v.t*, ~ [*on*], (*food*)

lésiner sur. ~ *o.s,* se priver (de).
stipend, *n,* traitement, *m.*
stipulate, *v.t,* stipuler. **stipulation,** *n,* stipulation, *f.*
stir, *n,* (*fig.*) agitation, sensation, *f. give sth a* ~, remuer qch. *make a* ~, faire du bruit. ¶ *v.t,* remuer, tourner; (*leaves*) agiter; (*pers.*) émouvoir. ~ *o.s,* se secouer. ¶ *v.i,* (*pers.*) bouger; (*trees*) remuer. ~ *up,* exciter; susciter; (*mob*) ameuter; (*trouble*) provoquer. **stirring,** *a,* excitant, émouvant.
stirrup, *n,* étrier, *m.*
stitch, *n,* point *m;* (*Knit., Crochet &c*) maille, *f;* (*Surg.*) point de suture. ~ *in the side* (*Med.*), point de côté. *be in* ~*es,* se tordre de rire. ¶ *v.t,* coudre; (*Mach.*) piquer; suturer.
stoat, *n,* hermine, *f.*
stock, *n,* (*descent*) lignée; (*tree &c*) souche; (*flower*) giroflée; (*goods, money*) réserve, *f;* (*Com.*) stock; (*learning*) fonds; (*Agr.*) cheptel [vif & mort]; (*Hort.*) porte-greffe; (*Cook.*) bouillon, *m;* (*Fin.*) valeurs, *f.pl;* titres, *m.pl;* (*Govt.* ~) fonds d'État, *m.pl;* (*pl: Hist.*) pilori, *m. on the* ~*s,* (*book &c*) en chantier. *in* ~, en stock. *out of* ~, épuisé. *take* ~, (*Com.*) faire l'inventaire; (*fig.*) faire le point. ¶ *a,* (*Com.*) courant; (*excuse*) classique. ~ *breeder,* éleveur, euse. ~*broker,* agent de change, *m.* ~*car,* stock-car, *m.* ~ *cube,* bouillon-cube, *m. on the* ~ *exchange,* à la Bourse. ~ *holder,* actionnaire, *m,f.* ~*-in-trade,* (*lit., fig.*) outils du métier, *m.pl.* ~ *market,* Bourse, *f;* marché financier. ~ *phrase,* cliché, *m. to* ~*pile,* stocker. ~*piling,* stockage, *m.* ~*pot,* marmite de bouillon, *f.* ~ *still,* complètement immobile. ~ *taking,* inventaire, *m.* ¶ *v.t,* (*shop*) approvisionner (*with,* en); (*Com: hold*) avoir, vendre. ~ *up,* *v.i,* s'approvisionner.
stockade, *n,* palissade, palanque, *f.*
stockinet, *n,* jersey, *m.* **stocking,** *n,* bas, *m.* ~ *stitch,* point de jersey, *m.*
stockist, *n,* stockiste, *m,f.* **stocky,** *a,* trapu.
stodge *P, n,* aliment bourratif, *m.* **stodgy,** *a,* (*food*) bourratif; (*cake*) lourd; (*book*) indigeste.
stoical†, *a,* stoïque. **stoicism,** *n,* stoïcisme, *m.*
stoke, *v.t,* (*engine, boiler*) chauffer; (*fire &c*) garnir; alimenter. **stoker,** *n,* chauffeur, *m.*
stole, *n,* étole, *f.*
stolid, *a,* impassible. ~**ly,** *ad,* avec impassibilité.
stomach, *n,* ventre; (*Anat.*) estomac, *m.* ~ *ache,* mal de ventre, *m.* ~ *pump,* pompe stomacale, *f.* ~ *trouble,* ennuis gastriques, *m.pl.* ¶ *v.t,* (*fig.*) tolérer, encaisser *P.*
stone, *n,* (*gen.*) pierre, *f;* (*fruit*) noyau; (*Med.*) calcul, *m;* (*Meas.*) = 6.35 kilos. *leave no* ~ *unturned,* remuer ciel & terre (pour faire). *within a* ~*'s throw of,* à 2 pas de. ¶ *a,* de pierre, en p. *S*~ *Age,* âge de la pierre, *m.* ~*-cold,* complètement froid. ~*-dead,* raide mort. ~*-deaf,* sourd comme un pot *P.* ~*mason,* tailleur de pierre[s], *m.* ~*ware,* poterie de grès, *f.* ~*work,* maçonnerie, *f.* ¶ *v.t,* lancer des pierres sur; (*to death*) lapider; (*fruit*) dénoyauter. **stoned** *P, a,* (*drink*) soûl; (*drugs*) défoncé *P.* **stony,** *a,* pierreux; (*heart*) de pierre; (*look*) froid. ~*-broke P,* fauché comme les blés *P.*
stooge, *n,* (*Theat.*) faire-valoir, *m.inv;* sous-fifre; (*pej.*) laquais, *m.*
stool, *n,* tabouret; (*folding*) pliant, *m;* (*Med.*) selle, *f.* ~ *pigeon,* mouchard, e.
stoop, *v.i,* se courber; (*fig.*) s'abaisser (*to sth,* jusqu'à qch); (*have a* ~) avoir le dos voûté.
stop, *n,* (*short*) halte, *f;* (*bus, train*) arrêt, *m;* (*ship, plane*) escale, *f;* (*organ*) jeu; (*Typ.*) point; (*Phot.*) diaphragme, *m. put a* ~ *to,* mettre fin à. ~*cock,* robinet d'arrêt, *m.* ~*gap, n,* bouche-trou, *m; a,* intérimaire. ~*over,* halte, *f.* ~ *press,* nouvelles de dernière heure, *f.pl.* ~*watch,* chronomètre, *m.* ¶ *v.t,* arrêter; (*activity*) cesser, interrompre; (*Box., fight*) suspendre; (*leave &c*) supprimer; (*wages*) retenir; (*hole, ears &* ~ *up*) boucher; (*tooth*) plomber; (*cheque*) faire opposition à; (*prevent*) empêcher. ~ *it!* ça suffit! ¶ *v.i,* s'arrêter; cesser; se terminer; (*remain*) rester; loger (*with s.o,* chez qn). ~ *off,* ~ *over,* s'arrêter, faire une halte. ~ *thief!* au voleur!
stoppage, *n,* arrêt, *m;* interruption; (*Ind.*) grève; suspension; retenue, *f.* **stopper,** *n,* bouchon, *m.* ¶ *v.t,* boucher.
storage, *n,* entreposage, *m;* (*energy*) accumulation; (*computers*) mise en réserve, *f.* ~ *heater,* radiateur électrique par accumulation, *m.* **store,** *n,* provision, réserve, *f;* (*knowledge &c*) fonds, *m;* (*pl.*) provisions; (*depot*) entrepôt; (*furniture*) garde-meuble; (*shop*) [grand] magasin, *m;* boutique, *f. set great* ~ *by* (*fig.*), faire grand cas de. ~*house,* entrepôt, *m.* ~ *keeper,* magasinier, *m.* ~*room,* réserve, *f.* ¶ *v.t, &* ~ *away,* (*gen., computer*) mettre en réserve; conserver; (*energy*) accumuler; (*crops*) engranger.
storey, *n,* étage, *m. 3-storied,* à 3 étages.
stork, *n,* cigogne, *f.*
storm, *n,* orage, *m;* (*gen., fig.*) tempête, *f. a* ~ *in a teacup,* une tempête dans un verre d'eau. *take by* ~, (*Mil.*) prendre d'assaut. ~ *cloud,* nuage orageux, *m;* (*fig.*) n. noir. ¶ *v.t,* (*Mil., fig.*) prendre d'assaut. ¶ *v.i,* (*pers.*) fulminer ~ *out,* sortir comme un ouragan. **stormy,** *a,* (*lit., fig.*) orageux; (*sea*) démonté. ~ *petrel,* pétrel, *m.*
story, *n,* (*gen.*) histoire; (*film, play*) action; (*short*) nouvelle, *f;* (*Press*) article, *m. it's the same old* ~, c'est toujours la même histoire.

~book, livre de contes *ou* d'histoires, *m.* *~ teller,* conteur, euse.

stout†, *a,* (*strong*) fort, solide; robuste; vigoureux; (*fat*) gros, corpulent. *~-hearted,* vaillant. ¶ (*beer*) *n,* stout, *m.* **~ness** (*of body*) *n,* embonpoint, *m.*

stove, *n,* (*heater*) poêle; (*cooker: solid fuel*) fourneau, *m;* (*gas, Elec.*) cuisinière, *f;* (*small*) réchaud; (*Ind.*) four, *m.*

stow (*Naut.*) *v.t,* arrimer. *~ away, v.t,* ranger; (*hide*) cacher; *v.i,* s'embarquer clandestinement. **~away,** *n,* passager (ère) clandestin(e).

straddle, *v.t,* être à cheval sur.

straggle, *v.i, ~ along,* traîner [en désordre]. **straggler,** *n,* traînard, e. **straggling & straggly,** *a,* (*hair*) ébouriffé; (*village*) tout en longueur.

straight, *a,* (*gen.*) droit; (*hair*) raide; (*route*) direct; (*house*) en ordre; (*pers.*) honnête; (*opp. homosexual*) hétéro *P;* (*answer*) franc; (*denial*) catégorique; (*whisky*) sans eau; (*Theat.*) sérieux. (*Box.*) *~ left,* direct du gauche, *m. keep a ~ face,* garder son sérieux. ¶ *ad,* (*walk &c*) droit; (*shoot*) juste; (*directly*) tout droit, directement. *go ~,* (*criminal*) rester dans le droit chemin. *~ ahead,* (*go*) tout droit; (*look*) droit devant soi. *~ away,* tout de suite, sur-le-champ. *~ out,* sans hésiter. ¶ *n,* (*Turf*) ligne droite, *f. cut on the ~,* couper droit fil. **~en,** *v.t,* redresser; (*hair*) défriser. *~ out,* (*problem*) résoudre; (*fig.*) débrouiller, mettre de l'ordre dans. *~ [up], v.t,* mettre de l'ordre dans; (*tie &c*) ajuster; (*picture*) remettre d'aplomb; *v.i,* (*pers.*) se redresser. **straightforward,** *a,* franc; simple.

strain[1], *n,* (*breed*) race; (*virus*) souche, *f.*

strain[2], *n,* (*Tech*) tension, pression, *f;* (*pers*) effort [physique], *m;* tension nerveuse; fatigue, *f;* (*overwork*) surmenage, *m;* (*Med.*) entorse, foulure, *f;* (*pl: Mus.*) accents, *m.pl.* ¶ *v.t,* tendre excessivement; (*Med: muscle*) froisser; (*ankle &c*) fouler; (*eyes*) abîmer; (*heart*) fatiguer; (*resources &c*) grever; (*meaning*) forcer; (*liquid*) passer; (*vegetables*) égoutter. *~ one's back,* se donner un tour de reins. *~ one's ears* (*to hear*), tendre l'oreille. ¶ *v.i,* faire un grand effort. **~ed,** *a,* (*smile*) forcé; (*look*) contraint; (*relations*) tendu. **~er,** *n,* passoire, *f.*

strait, *n,* (*s. & pl.*) détroit, *m;* (*pl.*) gêne, *f,* embarras, *m. S ~s of Dover,* Pas de Calais, *m.* **~-jacket,** *n,* camisole de force, *f.* **~-laced,** *a,* collet monté. **in straitened circumstances,** dans la gêne.

strand[1], *n,* (*thread*) brin; (*pearls*) rang, *m.*

strand[2], *n,* (*liter & Irish*) rive, plage, *f.*

stranded, *a,* (*ship*) échoué; (*pers.*) en rade *P.*

strange, *a,* (*odd*) étrange, bizarre; (*town &c*) inconnu; (*work &c*) inaccoutumé. **~ly,** *ad,* étrangement, curieusement. *~ enough,* chose curieuse. **~ness,** *n,* étrangeté, bizarrerie, *f.*

stranger, *n,* inconnu, e; étranger, ère.

strangle, *v.t,* étrangler. *have in a ~hold,* tenir à la gorge. **strangulation,** *n,* strangulation, *f.*

strap, *n,* courroie, sangle; (*shoe*) lanière; (*dress*) bretelle; (*shoulder ~*) bandoulière, *f;* (*watch*) bracelet, *m;* (*in tube &c*) poignée de cuir, *f.* ¶ *v.t,* attacher. **~less,** *a,* sans bretelles. **strapping,** *a,* costaud, *inv.*

stratagem, *n,* stratagème, *m,* ruse, *f.* **strategic(al)†,** *a,* stratégique. **strategist,** *n,* stratège, *m.* **strategy,** *n,* stratégie, *f.*

stratosphere, *n,* stratosphère, *f.*

stratum, *n,* couche, *f.*

straw, *n,* paille, *f. that's the last ~!* c'est le comble! *~-colour[ed],* paille, *inv. ~ hat,* chapeau de paille, *m.*

strawberry, *n,* fraise, *f. ~ ice,* glace à la fraise, *f. ~ plant,* fraisier, *m.*

stray, *a,* (*child, bullet*) perdu; (*sheep*) égaré; (*occasional*) isolé. ¶ *n,* enfant &c perdu, e. ¶ *v.i,* (*lit.*) s'égarer; (*thoughts*) errer. *~ from,* s'écarter de.

streak, *n,* raie, bande, *f;* (*blood*) filet, *m;* (*pl: in hair*) mèches, *f.pl. ~ of lightning,* éclair, *m. a jealous ~,* des tendances à la jalousie, *f.pl.* ¶ *v.t,* zébrer; strier; maculer (*with,* de). ¶ *v.i, ~ in &c,* entrer &c comme un éclair. **~y,** *a, ~ bacon* ≃ lard maigre, *m.*

stream, *n,* ruisseau; (*flow*) flot, courant; (*Sch.*) groupe, *m. ~lined,* (*Aero.*) fuselé; (*Mot.*) aérodynamique; (*fig.*) rationalisé. ¶ *v.i,* ruisseler (*with,* de). *~ in &c,* entrer &c à flots. ¶ *v.t,* (*Sch.*) répartir par niveau. *a streaming cold,* un gros rhume. **~er,** *n,* serpentin, *m.*

street, *n,* rue, *f. be on the ~s,* faire le trottoir *P. the man in the ~,* l'homme de la rue. *its right up my ~* (*fig.*), c'est tout à fait mon rayon. ¶ *a,* (*lighting, plan &c*) des rues. *~car* (*Am.*), tramway, *m. ~ door,* porte sur la rue, *f. ~ lamp,* réverbère, *m. ~ sweeper,* balayeur, *m;* (*Mach.*) balayeuse, *f. ~ urchin,* gamin des rues, *m.*

strength, *n,* (*gen.*) force[s]; (*materials*) solidité, *f;* (*Mil. &c*) effectif, *m. on the ~ of,* en vertu de. *~ of purpose,* résolution, *f. ~ of will,* volonté, *f. in ~,* en grand nombre. **~en,** *v.t,* renforcer; fortifier; (*Fin., table*) consolider. ¶ *v.i,* (*muscle &c*) se fortifier; (*wind &c*) augmenter.

strenuous, *a,* ardu, fatigant; (*life*) très actif; (*resistance &c*) acharné, vigoureux, énergique. **~ly,** *ad,* vigoureusement, énergiquement; avec acharnement.

stress, *n,* (*Tech.*) charge, *f;* travail, *m;* (*mental*) tension nerveuse, *f;* stress; (*Mus. &c*) accent, *m;* (*emphasis*) insistance, *f. under ~* sous tension. ¶ *v.t,* insister sur; accentuer. **~ful,** *a,* stressant, difficile.

stretch, *n,* (*sand*) étendue; (*span*) envergure, *f;* (*imagination*) effort, *m;* (*time*) période; élasticité, *f. for hours at a* ~, des heures d'affilée. *do a* ~, faire de la prison. ¶ *a,* (*fabric &c*) extensible; élastique. ¶ *v.t,* tendre; allonger; (*elastic*) étirer; (*shoes &c*) élargir; (*muscle*) distendre; (*rules, law*) tourner; (*student*) pousser. ~ *a point,* faire une concession. ~ *one's legs,* se dégourdir les jambes. ¶ *v.i,* (*pers.*) s'étirer; s'allonger; s'élargir; (*fabric &c*) prêter; (*in time*) se prolonger. ~ *out, v.i,* s'étendre; *v.t,* tendre; allonger, étendre. **stretcher,** *n,* brancard, *m;* civière, *f.* ~ *bearer,* brancardier, *m.*

strew, *v.t.ir,* répandre, éparpiller; (*floor*) joncher (*with,* de).

strict, *a,* (*gen.*) strict; (*pers.*) strict, sévère; (*order*) formel; (*limits*) précis. ~**ness,** *n,* sévérité, *f.* ~**ure,** *n,* critique, *f.*

stride, *n,* grand pas, *m;* enjambée; (*runner*) foulée, *f. get into one's* ~, prendre le rythme. *make great* ~*s* (*fig.*), faire de grands progrès. ¶ *v.i.ir,* ~ **along,** marcher à grands pas.

strident, *a,* strident.

strife, *n,* conflits, *m.pl;* dissensions, *f.pl.*

strike, *n,* (*Ind.*) grève; (*Min.*) découverte, *f;* (*Mil.*) raid [aérien], *m. go on* ~, se mettre en grève. ~ *breaker,* briseur de g., *m.* ¶ *v.t.ir,* frapper; heurter; (*clock*) sonner; (*match*) frotter; (*roots*) prendre; (*camp*) lever; (*tent*) démonter, plier; (*sail*) amener; (*coins*) frapper; (*gold, oil*) trouver; (*bargain*) conclure. ~ *dumb,* rendre muet. ~ *fear into s.o,* remplir qn d'effroi. *it* ~*s me,* il me semble. ~ *the first blow,* donner le premier coup. ¶ *v.i,* frapper; (*Mil.*) attaquer; (*snake*) mordre; sonner; (*Ind.*) faire grève. ~ **at,** (*pers.*) porter un coup à. ~ **back,** rendre les coups. ~ **down,** terrasser. ~ **out,** *v.t,* rayer; *v.i,* se débattre. ~ **up,** (*band*) se mettre à jouer. ~ *up a friendship &c with,* lier amitié &c avec. ~**r,** *n,* (*Ind.*) gréviste, *m,f;* (*Foot.*) buteur, *m.* **striking,** *a,* frappant, saisissant. *within* ~ *distance of,* à portée de.

string, *n,* (*gen.*) ficelle; (*Mus., racket*) corde, *f;* (*apron*) cordon; (*pearls*) rang; (*onions, excuses*) chapelet, *m;* (*people &c*) file, *f. the* ~*s* (*Mus.*), les cordes. *with no* ~*s attached,* sans conditions. *a second* ~, une deuxième ressource. ~ *bag,* filet à provisions, *m.* ~ *orchestra,* orchestre à cordes, *m.* ¶ *v.t.ir,* (*racket*) corder; (*violin*) monter; (*pearls*) enfiler. ~ *along P,* suivre. ~ *s.o. along,* faire marcher qn. ~ *up,* suspendre; (*P hang*) pendre. *strung up* (*pers.*), très tendu. ~**ed,** *a,* à cordes.

stringency, *n,* rigueur, *f.* **stringent†,** *a,* rigoureux.

stringy, *a,* (*food*) filandreux; (*plant*) tout en longueur.

strip, *n,* (*gen.*) bande, *f;* (*water*) bras, *m. tear s.o off a* ~ *P,* passer un savon a qn *P.* ~ *cartoon,* bande dessinée. ~ *lighting,* éclairage au néon, *m.* ~ *tease,* strip-tease, *m.* ¶ *v.t,* (*pers.*) déshabiller; (*room &c*) vider; (*wallpaper, thread*) enlever, arracher; (*tree, fig.*) dépouiller; (*engine*) démonter; (*bed*) défaire. ¶ *v.i,* ~ [*off*], se déshabiller.

stripe, *n,* raie, rayure, *f;* (*Mil. &c*) galon, *m.* ~**d,** *a,* rayé.

stripling, *n,* tout jeune homme, *m.*

stripper, *n,* (*paint*) décapant, *m;* stripteaseuse, *f.*

strive, *v.i.ir,* s'efforcer (*to do,* de faire).

stroke, *n,* (*gen.*) coup, *m;* (*Swim.*) nage, *f;* (*Med.*) coup de sang; (*pen &c*) trait, *m;* (*brush*) touche; (*Typ.*) barre, *f;* (*clock &c*) coup; (*Rowing*) chef de nage, *m;* (*piston*) course, *f. at a* ~, d'un seul coup. ~ *of luck,* coup de chance. *put s.o off his* ~, faire perdre son rythme à qn. *2-*~ *engine,* moteur à 2 temps, *m.* ¶ *v.t,* caresser.

stroll, *n,* tour, *m,* promenade, *f.* ¶ *v.i,* se promener; flâner. **strolling,** *a,* ambulant.

strong, *a,* (*gen.*) fort; (*magnet*) puissant; (*table, nerves, the dollar*) solide; (*eyesight*) très bon; (*contender &c*) sérieux; (*interest &c*) vif; (*protest &c*) vigoureux, énergique; (*well up in*) calé, fort; (*characteristic*) marqué; (*solution*) concentré; (*Elec: current*) intense. *as* ~ *as an ox,* fort comme un bœuf; (*in health*) avoir une santé de fer. *50* ~, au nombre de 50. ~*-arm,* brutal. ~*box,* coffre-fort, *m.* ~ *drink,* liqueurs fortes. ~*hold,* forteresse, *f;* (*fig.*) bastion, *m.* ~ *language,* grossièretés, *f.pl.* ~ *man,* hercule, *m.* ~*-minded,* ~*-willed,* résolu. ~*room,* chambre forte. ¶ *ad, be going* ~, (*car*) marcher toujours bien; (*pers.*) être toujours solide. ~**ly,** *ad,* (*feel*) profondément; (*believe*) fermement; (*protest*) énergiquement; (*desire*) vivement; (*indicate*) fortement; (*made*) solidement. *smell* ~ *of,* avoir une forte odeur de.

structural, *a,* (*gen.*) structural; (*fault*) de construction. ~*ly sound,* d'une construction solide. **structure,** *n,* (*gen.*) structure; (*Build*) armature, *f;* édifice, *m.*

struggle, *n,* (*gen.*) lutte, *f.* ¶ *v.i,* lutter, se battre; (*thrash about*) se débattre; (*resist*) résister (à); (*fig.*) se démener (pour faire). ~ *in, along &c,* entrer, avancer &c avec peine.

strum, *v.t,* (*piano*) tapoter; (*guitar*) racler.

strut[1], *v.i,* se pavaner.

strut[2], *n,* étai, support, *m.*

strychnin[e], *n,* strychnine, *f.*

stub, *n,* (*plant*) souche, *f;* (*pencil*) bout; (*cheque*) talon; (*cigarette*) mégot *P, m.* ¶ *v.t,* ~ *one's toe* se cogner le doigt de pied. ~ *out,* écraser.

stubble, *n,* (*Agr.*) chaume, *m;* (*on chin*) barbe de plusieurs jours, *f.*

stubborn, *a,* (*gen.*) opiniâtre; (*pers.*) têtu, obstiné, entêté; (*animal*) rétif. ~**ly,** *ad,* obstinément. ~**ness,** *n,* obstination, opiniâtre-

té; ténacité, *f.*
stucco, *n,* stuc, *m.*
stuck-up, *a,* prétentieux, bêcheur *P.*
stud[1], *n,* (*gen.*) clou. [*collar*] ~, bouton de col, *m.* (*Foot. boots*) crampon, *m.* ¶ *v.t,* clouter. ~*ded with,* parsemé de.
stud[2], *n,* (*horses*) écurie, *f;* (~ *farm*) haras, *m. be at* ~, étalonner. ~ *horse,* étalon, *m.* ~ *mare,* poulinière, *f.*
student, *n,* étudiant, e. *law* ~, étudiant, e en droit. ¶ *a,* (*life &c*) étudiant; (*residence &c*) universitaire. ~ *teacher,* élève professeur, *m,f.* **studied,** *a,* étudié; délibéré. **studio,** *n,* studio, *m.* ~ *couch,* divan, *m.* **studious,** *a,* (*pers.*) studieux, appliqué. **study,** *n,* étude, *f;* (*room*) bureau, cabinet de travail, *m.* ¶ *v.t. & i,* étudier.
stuff, *n,* étoffe, matière, substance, *f. it's good* ~, c'est bien *ou* bon. *what's this* ~*?* qu'est-ce que c'est que ça? *do your* ~*!* vas-y! *put your* ~ *away,* range tes affaires. ~ *& nonsense,* quelle bêtise! ¶ *v.t,* (*animal*) empailler; (*cushion*) bourrer (de); (*Cook.*) farcir (avec); (*hole*) boucher (avec); (*cram*) fourrer (*in, into,* dans). ~ *o.s,* se gaver. ~*ed-up* (*nose*), bouché. ~**iness,** *n,* manque d'air; (*pers.*) esprit vieux jeu, *m.* ~**ing,** *n,* rembourrage, *m;* (*Cook.*) farce, *f. knock the* ~ *out of s.o,* battre qn à plates coutures. ~**y,** *a,* mal aéré; (*pers.*) collet monté, *m.*
stumble, *v.i,* (*horse*) broncher; (*pers.*) trébucher (sur). ~ *upon,* tomber sur. *stumbling block,* pierre d'achoppement, *f.*
stump, *n,* (*tree*) souche, *f;* (*tooth*) chicot; (*limb*) moignon; (*pencil &c*) bout; (*Cricket*) piquet, *m.* ¶ *v.t,* (*baffle*) faire sécher. ~ *up, v.t,* cracher *P; v.i,* casquer *P.* ~**y,** *a,* trapu, boulot.
stun, *v.t,* étourdir; (*fig.*) stupéfier. **stunning,** *a,* étourdissant; stupéfiant; (*P lovely*) sensationnel.
stunt[1], *n,* (*Aero.*) acrobatie, *f;* (*feat*) tour de force, *m;* (*publicity*) truc publicitaire, *m.* ~*man,* cascadeur, *m.*
stunt[2], *v.t,* (*growth*) retarder; (*plant, pers.*) retarder la croissance de. ~**ed,** *a,* rabougri.
stupefy, *v.t,* étourdir; stupéfier; (*drink, drugs*) abrutir. **stupefaction,** *n,* stupéfaction, *f.*
stupendous†, *a,* prodigieux.
stupid†, *a,* stupide; bête. ~**ity,** *n,* stupidité; bêtise, *f.* **stupor,** *n,* stupeur, *f.*
sturdy†, *a,* robuste; (*fig.*) vigoureux, énergique.
sturgeon, *n,* esturgeon, *m.*
stutter, *v.i. & t,* bégayer. ~ *&* ~**ing,** *n,* bégaiement, *m.* ~**er,** *n,* bègue, *m,f.*
sty, *n,* porcherie, *f.*
sty[e] (*on the eye*) *n,* orgelet, *m.*
style, *n,* (*gen.*) style; (*type*) genre; (*dress &c*) modèle, *m;* (*hair* ~) coiffure; (*distinction: pers.*) allure, *f,* chic, *m. in the latest* ~, *a,* du dernier cri; *ad,* à la dernière mode. *it's not my* ~ (*fig.*), ce n'est pas mon genre. *do things in* ~, faire bien les choses. *live in* ~, vivre sur un grand pied. ¶ *v.t,* (*call*) appeler. **styling,** *n,* (*hair*) coupe, *f.* **stylish,** *a,* chic, *inv;* (*pers.*) qui a du chic. ~**ly,** *ad,* élégamment. ~**ness,** *n,* élégance, *f;* chic, *m.* **stylist,** *n,* coiffeur, euse; (*Liter.*) styliste, *m,f.* **stylistic,** *a. &* ~**s,** *n,* stylistique, *f.* **stylize,** *v.t,* styliser.
stylus, *n,* (*tool*) style, *m;* (*pickup*) pointe de lecture, *f.*
suave†, *a,* doucereux, mielleux. **suavity,** *n,* manières doucereuses.
sub . . . *pref:* sub . . ., sous-. ~*committee,* sous-comité, *m;* (*local govt.*) sous-commission, *f.* ~*continent,* sous-continent, *m.* ~*machine gun,* mitraillette, *f.* ~*normal,* au dessous de la normale; (*pers.*) arriéré. ~*standard, a,* (*goods*) de qualité inférieure; médiocre. ~*total,* total partiel.
subaltern, *n,* (*Mil.*) lieutenant, *m.*
subconscious, *a. & n,* subconscient, *m.*
subcontract, *n,* sous-traité, *m.* ~**or,** *n,* soustraitant, *m.*
subdivide, *v.t,* subdiviser.
subdue, *v.t,* subjuguer, soumettre, assujettir; (*passions &c*) contenir, maîtriser; (*light*) adoucir, tamiser. ~**d,** *a,* contenu; tamisé; (*voice*) bas; (*response &c*) faible. *be* ~, avoir perdu sa vivacité.
sub-editor, *n,* secrétaire de la rédaction, *m.*
subject, *n,* (*gen.*) sujet; (*Sch. &c*) matière, *f;* (*pers.*) sujet, te; ressortissant, e. ~ *heading,* rubrique, *f.* ~ *index,* index par matières, *m.* ~ *matter,* (*content*) contenu; (*theme*) sujet, *m.* ¶ *v.t,* soumettre; (*to heat &c*) exposer (à). ¶ *a,* ~ *to,* (*illness &c*) sujet à; (*tax &c*) soumis à; (*flooding &c*) exposé à; à condition de. ~**ion,** *n,* sujétion, soumission, *f.* ~**ive**†, *a. & n,* subjectif, *m.*
subjugate, *v.t,* subjuguer.
subjunctive [mood], *n,* subjonctif, *m.*
sublieutenant, *n,* enseigne de vaisseau, *m.*
sublimate, *v.t,* sublimer. **sublimation,** *n,* sublimation, *f.* **sublime**†, *a,* (*gen.*) sublime; (*P excellent*) fantastique; (*contempt &c*) suprême *before n.* **subliminal,** *a,* subliminal. **sublimity,** *n.* sublimité, *f.*
submarine, *a. & n,* sous-marin, *m.*
submerge, *v.t,* submerger. ¶ *v.i.* plonger.
submission, *n,* soumission, *f.* **submissive,** *a,* soumis. ~**ness,** *n,* soumission, *f.* **submit,** *v.t,* soumettre. ~ *to,* se soumettre à, obéir à, subir.
subordinate, *a,* (*gen.*) subalterne; (*Gram.*) subordonné. ¶ *n,* subordonné, e. ¶ *v.t,* subordonner (*to,* à).
subpoena, *n,* citation, assignation, *f.* ¶ *v.t,* citer, assigner.
subscribe, *v.t,* (*money*) donner. ¶ *v.i,* ~ *to,*

(*opinion, fund, book &c*) souscrire à; (*newspaper*) s'abonner à. **subscriber,** *n,* souscripteur, *m;* abonné, e. ~ *trunk dialling* (*STD*), automatique, *m.* **subscription,** *n,* souscription; (*club*) cotisation, *f,* abonnement, *m.*
subsequent, *a,* ultérieur, suivant. ~**ly,** *ad,* plus tard, à la suite.
subservience, *n,* servilité, *f.* **subservient,** *a,* (*role*) subalterne; (*pers.*) obséquieux, servile.
subside, *v.i,* (*building, land, pers.*) s'affaisser; (*flood*) baisser; (*wind, emotion*) tomber. **subsidence,** *n,* affaissement, *m.*
subsidiary†, *a,* subsidiaire; auxiliaire. ~ [*company*], [société] filiale, *f.*
subsidize, *v.t,* subventionner. **subsidy,** *n,* subvention, *f.*
subsist, *v.i,* subsister; vivre. ~**ence,** *n,* subsistance, existence, *f;* (*money*) frais de subsistance, *m.pl.* ~ *wage,* salaire à peine suffisant pour vivre.
subsoil, *n,* sous-sol, *m.*
substance, *n,* substance, *f. a man of* ~, un homme riche. *lack* ~, (*book &c*) manquer d'étoffe. **substantial,** *a,* considérable, important; (*meal*) substantiel. ~**ly,** *ad,* considérablement; en grande partie; (*built*) solidement. **substantiate,** *v.t,* justifier.
substantive, *a. & n,* substantif, *m.*
substitute, *n,* (*pers.*) remplaçant, e; (*object*) produit de remplacement; succédané, *m.* ¶ *v.t,* substituer (*for,* à). ¶ *v.i,* ~ *for s.o,* remplacer qn. **substitution,** *n,* substitution, *f.*
substratum, *n,* substrat, *m.*
subterfuge, *n,* subterfuge, *m.*
subterranean, *a,* souterrain.
subtitle, *n,* sous-titre, *m.* ¶ *v.t,* sous-titrer.
subtle†, *a,* subtil. ~**ty,** *n,* subtilité, *f.*
subtract, *v.t,* soustraire, retrancher. ~**ion,** *n,* soustraction, *f.*
suburb, *n,* faubourg, *m;* (*pl.*) banlieue, *f.* ~**an,** *a,* suburbain; de banlieue; (*pej: pers &c*) banlieusard *P.* **suburbia,** *n,* la banlieue.
subvention, *n,* subvention, *f.*
subversion, *n,* subversion, *f.* **subversive,** *a,* subversif. **subvert,** *v.t,* (*law &c*) saper, bouleverser; (*pers.*) corrompre.
subway, *n,* passage souterrain; (*Am. Rly*) métro, *m.*
succeed, *v.t,* succéder à; suivre. ¶ *v.i,* succéder; (*prosper*) réussir (dans qch, à faire); arriver, parvenir (à faire). ~**ing,** *a,* suivant; à venir, futur. **success,** *n,* succès, *m,* réussite, *f. make a* ~ *of,* (*project*) mener à bien; (*job, meal*) réussir. ~ *story,* réussite. ~**ful,** *a,* heureux; réussi; couronné de succès; (*in exam*) reçu; (*in election*) élu. ~**fully,** *ad,* avec succès. **succession,** *n,* succession; suite, *f. in* ~, successivement. **successive†,** *a,* successif; (*days &c*) consecutif. **successor,** *n,* successeur, *m;* (*to throne*) héritier, ère.
succinct†, *a,* succinct.
succour, *n,* secours, *m.* ¶ *v.t,* secourir.
succulent, *a,* succulent. ¶ *n.pl,* plantes grasses, *f.pl.* **succulence,** *n,* succulence, *f.*
succumb, *v.i,* succomber.
such, *a,* tel *before n,* pareil; semblable; (*so much*) tant de. ~ *as,* tel que, comme. ~ *a noise,* un tel bruit, tant de b. *in* ~ *cases,* en pareil cas. *there's no* ~ *thing!* ça n'existe pas! *in* ~ *a way that,* de telle sorte que. ¶ *ad,* si, tellement; (*in comparisons*) aussi. ~ *pretty flowers,* de si jolies fleurs. ~ *an ugly house as hers,* une maison aussi laide que la sienne.
suck, *v.t. & i,* (*gen.*) sucer; (*baby*) téter; (*with straw; pump &c*) aspirer. ~ *at,* sucer. ~ *down,* engloutir. ~ *in,* absorber; (*Mach.*) aspirer. ~ *up,* aspirer. ~ *up to s.o,* faire de la lèche à qn *P.* ~**er,** *n,* (*of insect*) suçoir, *m;* (*of leech*) ventouse, *f;* (*Hort.*) drageon, surgeon, *m;* (*P pers.*) poire *P, f.* ~**le,** *v.t,* allaiter, donner à téter à. **suction,** *n,* succion; aspiration, *f.* ~ *pump,* pompe aspirante, *f.*
sudden, *a,* (*gen.*) soudain, brusque; subit; (*unexpected*) imprévu. *all of a* ~, soudain, tout à coup. ~**ly,** *ad,* soudain, brusquement, subitement. ~**ness,** *n,* soudaineté, *f.*
suds, *n.pl,* (*lather*) mousse de savon; (*water*) eau savonneuse, *f.*
sue, *v.t,* poursuivre [en justice] (*for damages,* en dommages-intérêts.). ~ *s.o. for libel,* intenter un procès en diffamation à qn.
suede, *n,* daim, *m.* ¶ *a,* de daim; (*gloves*) de suède.
suet, *n,* graisse de rognon, *f.*
suffer, *v.t,* subir; supporter; (*pain*) éprouver; (*allow*) tolérer. ¶ *v.i,* souffrir. ~ *from,* souffrir de; (*deafness*) être atteint de. ~**ance,** *n,* tolérance, *f. on* ~, par t. ~**er,** *n,* victime, *f;* (*illness*) malade, *m,f.* ~**ing,** *n,* souffrance, *f.* ¶ *a,* souffrant.
suffice, *v.i,* suffire. ~ *it to say that,* suffit que. **sufficiency,** *n,* quantité suffisante. **sufficient†,** *a,* assez de; (*quantity*) suffisant.
suffix, *n,* suffixe, *m.* ~**ed,** *a,* suffixe.
suffocate, *v.t. & i,* suffoquer, étouffer; (*fig.*) suffoquer (*with,* de). **suffocation,** *n,* suffocation, *f,* étouffement, *m;* (*Med.*) asphyxie, *f.*
suffrage, *n,* suffrage, *m.* **suffragette,** *n,* suffragette, *f.*
suffuse, *v.t,* se répandre sur; baigner (*with,* de).
sugar, *n,* sucre, *m.* ~ *almond,* dragée, *f.* ~ *basin,* sucrier, *m.* ~ *beet,* betterave à s., *f.* ~ *cane,* canne à s., *f.* ~*-coated,* dragéifié. ~ *daddy P,* vieux protecteur. ~ *industry,* industrie sucrière. ~ *loaf,* pain de sucre, *m.* ~ *pea,* mange-tout, *m.inv.* ~ *refinery,* raffinerie de sucre, *f.* ~ *sifter,* saupoudreuse, *f.* ~ *tongs,* pinces à s., *f.pl.* ¶ *v.t,* sucrer. ~**y,** *a,* sucré; (*pej. voice*) mielleux.
suggest, *v.t,* suggérer, proposer; insinuer.

~**ible,** *a,* influençable. ~**ion,** *n,* suggestion; insinuation, *f.* *a* ~ *of,* un soupçon de. ~**ive,** *a,* suggestif.
suicidal, *a,* suicidaire. **suicide,** *n,* suicide, *m;* (*pers.*) suicidé, *m.* *to commit* ~, se suicider.
suit, *n,* (*man's*) complet, costume; (*woman's*) tailleur, ensemble, *m;* (*boiler* ~ *&c*) combinaison, *f;* (*Law*) procès, *m;* (*Cards*) couleur, *f.* *bring a* ~ *against,* intenter un procès à. ~*case,* valise, *f.* ~ *of armour,* armure complète, *f.* ¶ *v.t,* (*gen.*) convenir à; (*clothes &c*) aller à. ~*s me! P* ça me va! ~ *yourself! P* faites commes vous voulez! ~**ability,** *n,* (*remark &c*) à-propos, *m;* (*for job*) aptitude, *f.* ~**able,** *a,* (*gen.*) approprié (*to,* à); qui convient; qui va; (*time, place*) propice; (*socially*) convenable; (*for job*) apte. ~**ably,** *ad,* (*behave*) convenablement, comme il convient; (*reply*) à propos.
suite, *n,* suite, *f.* ~ [*of furniture*], mobilier, *m.*
suitor, *n,* soupirant, *m.*
sulk, *v.i,* bouder. ~**y,** *a,* boudeur.
sullen, *a,* renfrogné, maussade. ~**ness,** *n,* maussaderie, *f.*
sulphate, *n,* sulfate, *m.* **sulphide,** *n,* sulfure, *m.* **sulphite,** *n,* sulfite, *m.* **sulphur,** *n,* soufre, *m.* ~ *bath,* bain sulfureux. **sulphuric,** *a,* sulfurique. **sulphurous,** *a,* sulfureux.
sultan, *n,* sultan, *m.* **sultana,** *n,* sultane, *f;* (*fruit*) raisin sec de Smyrne, *m.*
sultry, *a,* étouffant, lourd; (*fig: look*) sensuel.
sum, *n,* somme, *f;* (*Math.*) calcul, *m;* (*pl: Sch.*) le calcul. ~ *total,* somme totale; (*money*) montant global; (*fig.*) résultat. ~ *up,* récapituler, faire un *ou* le résumé; (*Law*) résumer. **summarize,** *v.t,* résumer; (*facts &c*) récapituler. **summary†,** *a,* sommaire. ¶ *n,* sommaire, résumé, *m.*
summer, *n,* été, *m.* ~ *camp,* colonie de vacances, *f.* ~ *holidays,* grandes vacances, *f.pl.* ~ *house,* pavillon [de jardin], *m.* ~ *lightning,* éclair[s] de chaleur, *m.*[*pl.*]. ~ *resort,* station estivale, *f.* ~ *school,* cours de vacances, *m.pl.* ~*time,* été. ~ *time,* heure d'été, *f.* ~ *visitor,* estivant, e. ~**y,** *a,* d'été.
summing up, *n,* récapitualtion, *f,* résumé, *m.*
summit, *n,* sommet, *m,* cime, *f,* faîte; (*ambition*) summum, *m.* ~ *conference,* conférence au sommet, *f.*
summon, *v.t,* (*gen.*) appeler, faire venir; (*to meeting*) convoquer; (*Law*) citer, assigner (*as,* comme); (*help &c*) requérir. ~ *up,* (*courage*) faire appel à, rassembler. **summons,** *n,* (*gen., Mil.*) sommation; (*Law*) assignation, *f.* ¶ *v.t,* assigner; appeler en justice.
sump, *n,* (*Tech.*) puisard; (*Mot.*) carter, *m.*
sumptuous†, *a,* somptueux. ~**ness,** *n,* somptuosité, *f.*
sun, *n,* soleil, *m.* *in the* ~, au soleil. *the* ~ *is shining,* le soleil brille, il fait du s. ~*bathe,* prendre des bains de soleil. ~*bathing,* bains de s., *m.pl.* ~*beam,* rayon de s., *m.* ~ *bed,* ~ *lounger,* fauteuil bain de s., *m.* ~ *blind,* store, *m.* ~*burn,* bronzage, hâle; (*painful*) coup de soleil, *m.* ~*burnt,* bronzé, hâlé; brûlé par le s. ~*-dial,* cadran solaire, *m.* ~*flower,* tournesol, soleil, *m.* ~*glasses,* lunettes de s., *f.pl.* ~ *lamp,* lampe à rayons ultraviolets, *f.* ~*light,* lumière du s., *f.* ~*lit,* ensoleillé. ~*rise,* lever du s., *m.* ~[*shine*] *roof,* toit ouvrant. ~*set,* coucher du s., *m.* ~*shade,* (*parasol*) ombrelle, *f;* (*for table*) parasol, *m.* ~ *shield* (*Mot.*), pare-soleil, *m.* ~*shine,* soleil. ~*spot,* tache solaire, *f.* ~*stroke,* coup de soleil, *m.* ~*tan,* bronzage, *m.* *get a* ~*tan,* [se faire] bronzer. ~*tan lotion, oil,* lait *m,* huile *f,* solaire. ¶ *v.t,* ~ *o.s,* (*pers.*) prendre un bain de soleil; (*animal*) se chauffer au s.
sundae, *n,* glace aux fruits, *f.*
Sunday, *n,* dimanche, *m.* *in one's* ~ *best,* tout endimanché. ~ *rest,* repos dominical. ~ *school,* école du dimanche, *f.* *for other phrases V* **Saturday.**
sundries, *n.pl,* [articles] divers, *m.pl.* **sundry,** *a,* divers; différent. *all &* ~, tout le monde.
sunken, *a,* (*eyes &c*) creux; (*ship*) submergé; (*garden*) en contrebas.
sunless, *a,* sans soleil. **sunny,** *a,* ensoleillé. *it is* ~, il fait du soleil. ~ *intervals,* éclaircies, *f.pl.*
super *P,* *a,* fantastique *P,* super *P.*
super... *pref:* super..., sur..., hyper... ~*abundant,* surabondant. ~*fine,* surfin. ~*market,* supermarché, *m.* ~*power,* superpuissance, *f.* ~*sonic,* supersonique. ~*store,* hypermarché, *m.* ~*structure,* superstructure, *f.* ~*-tanker,* pétrolier géant, *m.*
superannuated, *a,* (*retired*) retraité; (*out of date*) suranné. *superannuation fund,* caisse des retraites, *f.*
superb†, *a,* superbe.
supercilious†, *a,* dédaigneux. ~**ness,** *n,* hauteur, *f.*
superficial†, *a,* superficiel. ~**ity,** *a,* caractère superficiel, manque de profondeur, *m.*
superfluity, *n,* surabondance, *f.* **superfluous,** *a,* superflu.
superhuman, *a,* surhumain.
super[im]pose, *v.t,* superposer. ~**d,** (*Phot. &c*) *a,* en surimpression.
superintend, *v.t,* surveiller; diriger. ~**ence,** *n,* surveillance; direction, *f.* ~**ent,** *n,* directeur, trice; chef; (*police*) commissaire, *m.*
superior†, *a. & n,* supérieur, e; (*pej: pers.*) suffisant; (*goods*) de qualité supérieure. ~**ity,** *n,* supériorité, *f.*
superlative, *a,* suprême; sans pareil; (*Gram.*) superlatif. ¶ *n,* superlatif, *m.* ~**ly,** *ad,* extrêmement.
superman, *n,* surhomme, *m.*

supernatural†, *a. & n,* surnaturel, *m.*
supernumerary, *a. & n,* surnuméraire, *m,f.* ¶ (*Theat.*) *n,* figurant, e.
supersede, *v.t,* remplacer.
superstition, *n,* superstition, *f.* **superstitious†,** *a,* superstitieux.
supervise, *v.t,* surveiller; diriger. **supervision,** *n,* surveillance, *f,* contrôle, *m.* **supervisor,** *n,* surveillant, e, directeur, trice.
supine, *a,* étendu sur le dos.
supper, *n,* (*main meal*) dîner; (*later*) souper, *m. the Last S~*, la Cène. *have ~*, dîner, souper. *~ time,* l'heure du dîner, *f.*
supplant, *v.t,* supplanter.
supple, *a,* souple. *to make ~*, assouplir.
supplement, *n,* supplément, *m.* ¶ *v.t,* augmenter. **~ary,** *a,* supplémentaire. *~ benefit,* allocation supplémentaire, *f.*
suppleness, *n,* souplesse, *f.*
supplication, *n,* supplication, *f.*
supplier, *n,* fournisseur, *m.* **supply,** *n,* provision, réserve, *f;* (*Com.*) stock, *m;* (*Elec., Gas &c*) alimentation, *f;* (*pl.*) provisions, réserves; (*food*) vivres, *m.pl;* (*Mil.*) approvisionnements, *m.pl. ~ & demand,* l'offre & la demande. *~ teacher,* remplaçant, e. ¶ *v.t,* (*gen.*) fournir; (*Com.*) approvisionner; alimenter; (*s.o's needs*) subvenir à.
support, *n,* appui, soutien; (*Build., Tech.*) support, *m;* (*fig: moral*) soutien. *give one's ~ to,* prêter son appui à. ¶ *v.t,* (*pers: lit., fig.*) soutenir; (*beam &c*) supporter; (*bridge*) porter; (*fig.*) être en faveur de, être partisan de; (*team*) être supporter de; (*family &c*) subvenir aux besoins de; (*endure*) supporter, tolérer. **~able,** *a,* supportable, tolérable. **~er,** *n,* partisan; (*Sport*) supporter, *m.* **~ing,** *a,* (*wall*) de soutènement; (*Theat: role*) secondaire.
suppose, *v.t,* supposer (*que + indic. or subj.*); (*believe*) imaginer, penser, supposer. *supposing that,* à supposer que, supposé que (+ *subj.*). *supposing we go for a swim?* et si on allait se baigner? *he was ~d to return yesterday,* il devait rentrer hier. *you aren't ~d to know,* tu n'es pas censé le savoir. **~d,** *a,* présumé, supposé; (*so-called*) prétendu. **~dly,** *ad,* soi-disant. **supposition,** *n,* supposition, *f.*
suppress, *v.t,* (*revolt, feelings, yawn*) réprimer; (*documents*) supprimer; (*facts*) dissimuler; (*Psych.*) refouler; (*Elec., Radio &c*) éliminer. **~ion,** *n,* répression; suppression, *f, &c.* **~or,** *n,* dispositif antiparasite, *m.*
suppurate, *v.i,* suppurer.
supremacy, *n,* suprématie, *f.* **supreme†,** *a,* suprême. **supremo** *P, n,* grand patron, *m.*
surcharge, *n,* surcharge; (*on letter*) surtaxe, *f.* ¶ *v.t,* surcharger, surtaxer.
sure, *a,* sûr. *~ of o.s,* sûr de soi. *for ~*, à coup sûr. *make ~ of,* s'assurer de. *be ~ to come,* ne manquez pas de venir. ¶ *ad,* (*yes*) bien sûr; (*Am: really*) pour sûr. *~ enough...,* effectivement... *~-fire,* certain, infaillible. *~-footed,* au pied sûr. **~ly,** *ad,* sûrement, certainement; (*disbelief*) tout de même. *~ not!* pas possible! **~ness,** *n,* certitude; (*method &c*) sûreté, *f.* **~ty,** *n,* caution, *f.*
surf, *n,* (*foam*) écume; (*wave*) vague déferlante, *f. ~board,* planche de surf, *f. ~boarder, ~rider,* surfeur, euse. *~boarding, ~riding,* surf, *m.* ¶ *v.i,* surfer. **~ing,** *n,* surf, *m.*
surface, *n,* surface, *f;* (*Math.*) face; (*~ area*) superficie, *f. on the ~*, (*Min.*) au jour; (*Naut.*) en surface; (*fig.*) à première vue. *under the ~* (*water*) sous l'eau. *road ~*, chaussée, *f.* ¶ *a,* (*vessel*) de surface; (*tension*) superficiel. ¶ *v.t,* (*road*) revêtir (*with,* de). ¶ *v.i,* remonter à la surface.
surfeit, *n,* excès, *m. have a ~ of,* être rassasié de.
surge, *n,* (*fear &c*) vague, *f. the ~ of the sea,* la houle. ¶ *v.i,* (*waves*) s'enfler; (*anger*) monter; (*crowds, cars*) déferler. *~ forward,* se lancer en avant.
surgeon, *n,* chirurgien, *m.* **surgery,** *n,* chirurgie, *f;* (*place*) cabinet [de consultation], *m;* (*activity*) consultation, *f.* **surgical,** *a,* chirurgical. *~ spirit,* alcool à 90 [degrés], *m.*
surly, *a,* bourru, maussade.
surmise, *n,* conjecture, *f.* ¶ *v.t,* conjecturer.
surmount, *v.t,* surmonter.
surname, *n,* nom [de famille], *m.*
surpass, *v.t,* surpasser; (*hopes*) dépasser.
surplice, *n,* surplis, *m.*
surplus, *n,* surplus; excédent, *m.* ¶ *a,* en surplus; excédentaire.
surprise, *n,* surprise, *f;* étonnement, *m;* (*event*) surprise. *give s.o a ~*, faire une surprise à qn. *take by ~*, (*pers.*) surprendre; prendre au dépourvu; (*Mil.*) p. par surprise. ¶ *a,* inattendu. ¶ *v.t,* surprendre, étonner. **surprising,** *a,* surprenant, étonnant. **~ly,** *ad,* étonnamment. *~ enough,* chose étonnante.
surrealism, *n,* surréalisme, *m.* **surrealist,** *n. &* **~ic,** *a,* surréaliste, *m,f.*
surrender, *n,* reddition, *f;* (*Insce*) rachat, *m.* ¶ *v.t,* (*arms*) rendre; (*town*) livrer; (*documents*) remettre; (*rights &c*) abandonner, ceder; (*Insce policy*) racheter. ¶ *v.i,* se rendre.
surreptitious†, *a,* subreptice; furtif.
surrogate, *n,* substitut, *m. ~ mother,* mère porteuse.
surround, *v.t,* entourer, encercler (*by, with,* de). ¶ *n,* bordure, *f.* **~ing,** *a,* environnant. **~ings,** *n.pl,* alentours, *m.pl;* (*setting*) cadre, *m.*
surtax, *n,* impôt supplémentaire, *m.*
surveillance, *n,* surveillance, *f.*
survey, *n,* (*overall view*) vue d'ensemble (*of,* de); (*study*) enquête (sur), étude (de), *f;* (*Surv.*) levé, *m;* (*house*) visite d'expert; (*report*)

expertise, *f.* ~ *ship,* bateau hydrographique, *m.* ¶ *v.t,* (*gen.*) regarder; promener ses regards sur; (*situation*) passer en revue; (*Surv.*) faire le levé de; inspecter. ~**or,** *n,* expert; (*land*) géomètre, *m;* (*country*) topographe, *m,f;* (*seas*) hydrographe, *m.*
survival, *n,* (*relic*) survivance; (*act*) survie, *f.* ~ *of the fittest,* persistance du plus apte, *f.*
survive, *v.t,* survivre à; (*accident &c*) réchapper de. ¶ *v.i,* survivre. **survivor,** *n,* survivant, e.
susceptibility, *n,* vive sensibilité; susceptibilité; (*Med.*) prédisposition, *f.* **susceptible,** *a,* sensible (*to,* à); (*touchy*) susceptible; (*Med.*) prédisposé (à); (*influence*) ouvert (à).
suspect, *a,* suspect. ¶ *n,* suspect, e. ¶ *v.t,* (*gen.*) soupçonner (qn de qch, de faire); suspecter; se douter (que; de qch).
suspend, *v.t,* (*gen.*) suspendre; (*bus service*) interrompre provisoirement; (*Sch., Univ.*) exclure temporairement. (*Law*) ~*ed sentence,* peine avec sursis, *f.* ~**er,** *n,* (*stocking*) jarretelle, *f;* (*Am. pl.*) bretelles, *f.pl.* ~ *belt,* porte-jarretelles, *m.inv.* **suspense,** *n,* incertitude, *f;* (*in book &c*) suspense, *m. in* ~, en suspens. ~ *account,* compte d'attente, *m.* **suspension,** *n,* suspension, *f.* ~ *bridge,* pont suspendu, *m.*
suspicion, *n,* soupçon, *m;* (*Law*) présomption, *f. under* ~, considéré comme suspect. **suspicious,** *a,* (*feel*) soupçonneux, méfiant; (*appear: pers.*) suspect; (*action &c*) louche. *be* ~ *about,* avoir des soupçons à l'égard de (qn), sur (qch). ~**ly,** *ad,* avec méfiance; d'une manière suspecte *ou* louche.
sustain, *v.t,* (*effort, theory*) soutenir; (*life*) maintenir; (*Mus: note*) tenir; (*suffer*) subir, éprouver, essuyer. ~*ed,* prolongé. ~**ing,** *a,* (*food*) nourissant. **sustenance,** *n,* nourriture, *f;* moyens de subsistance, *m.pl.*
swab, *n,* (*cloth*) serpillière, *f;* (*Med.*) tampon; (*throat &c*) prélèvement *m.* ¶ *v.t,* ~ [*down*], passer à la serpillière.
swagger, *n,* air fanfaron, *m.* ¶ *v.i,* ~ *about,* faire le bravache. ~**ing,** *a,* (*pers.*) bravache, fanfaron, crâneur; (*gait*) assuré.
swallow[1], *n,* hirondelle, *f.* ~ *dive,* saut de l'ange, *m.* ~*tail butterfly,* machaon, *m.*
swallow[2], *n,* (*act*) avalement, *m;* (*amount*) gorgée, *f.* ¶ *v.t,* avaler; (*pride*) ravaler. ¶ *v.i,* avaler. ~ *up,* engloutir.
swamp, *n,* marais, marécage, *m.* ¶ *v.t,* (*flood*) inonder; (*boat*) emplir d'eau; (*fig.*) submerger (*with,* de). ~**y,** *a,* marécageux.
swan, *n,* cygne, *m.* ~ *'s-down,* duvet de cygne, *m.* ~ *song,* chant du cygne, *m.*
swank *P, n,* fanfaronnade, *f;* (*pers.*) crâneur, euse *P.* ¶ *v.i,* crâner *P.*
swap, *n,* échange, troc, *m.* ¶ *v.t,* échanger, troquer (*for,* contre). ¶ *v.i,* échanger.
swarm, *n,* (*bees, people*) essaim; (*ants &c*) fourmillement, *m.* ¶ *v.i,* essaimer; fourmiller; (*town, streets*) fourmiller, grouiller (*with,* de).
swarthy, *a,* basané.
swastika, *n,* svastika, *m;* (*Nazi*) croix gammée.
swat (*fly*) *v.t,* écraser. [*fly*] ~[*ter*], tapette, *f.*
swathe, *v.t,* emmailloter.
sway, *n,* (*motion*) oscillation, *f;* (*boat*) balancement, *m;* (*liter.*) emprise (*over,* sur), *f.* ¶ *v.t,* balancer, faire osciller; (*hips*) rouler; influencer. ¶ *v.i,* osciller, se balancer; (*train*) tanguer.
swear, *v.t. & i.ir,* jurer (*to do,* de faire). ~ *an oath,* (*Law*) prêter serment; (*curse*) lâcher un juron. ~ *like a trooper,* jurer comme un charretier. ~ *in,* (*jury &c*) faire prêter serment à. ~ *word,* juron, gros mot, *m.*
sweat, *n,* sueur, *f. be in a cold* ~, avoir des sueurs froides. *no* ~*! P* pas de problème! ¶ *v.i,* suer (*with, from,* de); (*walls*) suinter. ¶ *v.t,* (*workers*) exploiter. ~ *blood,* suer sang & eau. ~*ed labour,* main-d'œuvre exploitée. ~*band* (*Sport*), bandeau, *m.* ~*shirt,* sweatshirt, *m.* ~**er,** *n,* pullover, pull *P,* chandail, *m.* ~**y,** *a,* (*body*) en sueur; (*hands*) moite; (*feet*) qui suent.
swede, *n,* rutabaga, *m.*
Swede, *n,* Suédois, e. **Sweden,** *n,* la Suède. **Swedish,** *a,* suédois. ¶ *n,* le suédois.
sweep, *n,* coup de balai; (*pers.*) ramoneur; (*of arm*) grand geste; (*scythe*) movement circulaire, *m;* (*land &c*) étendue, *f.* ¶ *v.t. & i.ir,* (*lit., fig.*) balayer; (*chimney*) ramoner; (*Naut.*) draguer. ~ *sth under the carpet* (*fig.*), tirer le rideau sur qch. ~ *the board,* remporter un succès complet. ~ **along,** emporter. ~ **aside,** écarter; (*pers., suggestion*) repousser. ~ **away,** balayer; (*current &c*) entraîner. ~ **out,** ~ **up,** balayer. ~**er,** *n,* (*pers.*) balayeur, *m;* (*Mach.*) balayeuse, *f.* ~**ing,** *a,* (*gesture*) large; (*change*) radical. ~ *statement,* généralisation mal fondée, *f.* ~**stake,** *n,* sweepstake, *m.*
sweet, *a,* doux; sucré; (*water*) pur; (*scent*) agréable; (*pers.*) gentil, charmant; (*child, house &c*) mignon; (*smile, revenge*) doux. ~ *& sour,* aigre-doux. ~*bread,* ris de veau, *m.* ~*briar,* églantier odorant. ~*corn,* maïs, *m.* ~ *Fanny Adams, P,* rien de rien *P.* ~*heart,* petit(e) ami(e). ~*meat,* sucrerie, *f.* ~-*natured,* d'un naturel doux. ~*pea,* pois de senteur, *m.* ~ *potato,* patate [douce], *f.* ~-*scented,* parfumé. ~ *talk,* cajoleries, *f.pl.* ~-*talk,* enjôler. ~ *william,* œillet de poète, *m.* ¶ *n,* bonbon; (*course*) dessert, *m.* ~*shop,* confiserie, *f.* ~**en,** *v.t,* sucrer; (*air*) purifier; (*fig: temper &c*) adoucir; (*P bribe*) graisser la patte à *P.* ~**ener,** *n,* édulcorant; (*P bribe*) pot-de-vin, *m.* ~**ish,** *a,* douceâtre. ~**ly,** *ad,* (*smile*) gentiment; (*sing*) mélodieusement; (*run: en-*

gine) sans à-coups. ~**ness,** *n,* (*nature &c*) douceur, *f.*

swell, *n,* (*sea*) houle, *f;* (*Mus.*) crescendo, *m.inv.* ¶ *a,* (*P Am*) chic, *inv.* ¶ *v.i.ir,* (*numbers &c*) grossir; (*sound*) s'enfler; (*sail, tyre*) se gonfler; (~*up: leg &c*) enfler; (*wood*) gonfler. ~ *with pride,* se gonfler d'orgueil. ¶ *v.t.ir,* gonfler; enfler; (*number*) augmenter. **swelling,** *n,* (*Med.*) enflure; (*lump*) grosseur; gonflement, enflement, *m.*

swelter, *v.i,* étouffer de chaleur.

swerve, *n,* (*vehicle*) embardée, *f;* (*boxer*) écart, *m.* ¶ *v.i,* faire une embardée *ou* un écart; (*driver*) donner un coup de volant; (*ball, fig.*) dévier (*from,* de).

swift, *a,* rapide; (*response &c*) prompt; (*movement*) vif. ¶ *n,* martinet, *m.* ~**ly,** *ad,* rapidement, vite. ~**ness,** *n,* rapidité, vitesse, promptitude, *f.*

swig *P n,* lampée *P, f;* coup, *m.* ¶ *v.t,* lamper *P.*

swill, *n,* (*pig's*) pâtée, *f;* (*slops*) eaux grasses. ¶ *v.t,* (~ *down*) laver à grande eau; (*drink*) boire à grands traits.

swim, *n, go for a* ~, aller se baigner; a. nager. *in the* ~ (*fig.*), dans le bain. ¶ *v.i,* nager; (*Sport*) faire de la natation. ~ *away &c,* s'éloigner &c à la nage. *eyes* ~*ming with tears,* yeux baignés de larmes. *my head is* ~*ming,* la tête me tourne. ¶ *v.t,* (~ *across*) traverser à la nage. **swimmer,** *n,* nageur, euse. **swimming,** *n,* nage, natation, *f.* ~ *bath,* ~ *pool,* piscine, *f.* ~ *cap,* bonnet de bain, *m.* ~ *costume, swimsuit,* maillot [de bain], *m.* ~ *trunks,* caleçon de bain, *m.*

swindle, *n,* escroquerie, *f.* ¶ *v.t,* escroquer, rouler *P.* **swindler,** *n,* escroc, *m.*

swine, *n,* pourceau; (*P fig: pers.*) salaud *P**, *m.* ~*herd O,* porcher, ère.

swing, *n,* balancement, *m;* (*pendulum*) oscillations; (*child's*) balançoire, *f;* (*Golf, Box., Mus.*) swing; (*Pol.*) revirement, *m. be in full* ~, battre son plein. *go with a* ~, très bien marcher. *get into the* ~, se mettre dans le bain. *take a* ~ *at s.o,* décocher un coup de poing à qn. ~ *bridge,* pont tournant. ~ *door,* porte battante. ~*-wing* (*Aero.*), à géométrie variable. ¶ *v.t.ir,* balancer; (*axe*) brandir; influencer. ¶ *v.i.ir,* (*gen.*) se balancer; (*pendulum*) osciller; (*Pol.*) virer; (*P be hanged*) être pendu. *with a* ~*ing step,* d'un pas rythmé. ~ [*round*], pivoter, tourner; (*pers.*) se retourner, virevolter; (*car &c*) virer. ~ *to,* (*door*) se refermer.

swingeing, *a,* (*tax*) énorme; (*blow*) violent.

swipe *P, n,* (*at ball*) grand coup. *take a* ~ *at s.o,* flanquer une taloche à qn *P.* ¶ *v.t,* (*hit*) frapper à toute volée; (*pers.*) calotter à toute v.; (*steal*) faucher *P.*

swirl, *n,* tourbillon, *m;* (*cream &c*) volute, *f.* ¶ *v.i,* tourbillonner.

swish, *a,* (*P smart*) rupin *P.* ¶ *n,* sifflement; (*skirt*) froufrou, bruissement, *m.* ¶ *v.i,* (*whip &c*) siffler, cingler l'air; (*skirt &c*) bruire. ¶ *v.t,* faire siffler.

Swiss, *a,* suisse. ~ *roll,* gâteau roulé, *m.* ¶ *n,* Suisse, *m,* Suissesse, *f.*

switch, *n,* (*Elec.*) interrupteur, commutateur; (*Mot: ignition*) contact, *m;* (*Rly*) aiguille, *f;* changement, revirement; (*funds*) transfert; (*stick*) badine, *f.* ~*back,* montagnes russes, *f.pl.* ~*board,* (*Elec.*) tableau de distribution; (*Tel.*) standard, *m.* ~*board operator,* standardiste, *m,f.* ¶ *v.t,* (*swap*) échanger; (*support*) reporter (*to,* sur); (*conversation*) détourner; (*Rly*) aiguiller. ~ **off,** *v.t,* (*gen.*) éteindre; (*Radio, TV*) éteindre; (*engine*) arrêter. ¶ *v.i,* (*fig.*) décrocher. ~ **on,** *v.t,* allumer. ¶ *v.i,* (*Mot.*) mettre le contact; (*Radio, TV*) allumer le poste. ~**over,** (*TV*) changer de chaîne. ~ **round,** changer de place.

Switzerland, *n,* la Suisse.

swivel, *n,* pivot, *m.* ~ *chair,* fauteuil pivotant. ¶ *v.i.* (*& t*), ~ *round,* (faire) pivoter.

swollen, *a,* (*face, arm*) enflé; (*eyes, stomach*) gonflé; (*river*) en crue; (*population*) accru. ~ *glands,* une inflammation des ganglions. *to be* ~*-headed P,* se gober *P.*

swoon, *v.i,* se pâmer; (*fig.*) se p. d'admiration (*over,* devant).

swoop, *n,* (*police*) descente (*on,* dans), *f. in one fell* ~, d'un seul coup. ¶ *v.i,* ~ [*down*], (*bird*) fondre; (*plane*) descendre en piqué; (*police*) faire une descente.

sword, *n,* épée, *f.* ~*fish,* espadon, *m.* ~ *stick,* canne à épée, *f.* ~*-swallower,* avaleur de sabres, *m.* **swordsman,** *n,* lame, *f.*

swot *P, n,* bûcheur, euse *P.* ¶ *v.t. & i,* bûcher *P.* ~ *up on,* potasser *P.* **swotting** *P, n,* bachotage, *m.*

sycamore, *n,* sycomore, *m.*

sycophant, *n,* flagorneur, euse.

syllabic, *a,* syllabique. **syllable,** *n,* syllabe, *f.*

syllabus, *n,* programme; (*Eccl.*) syllabus, *m.*

syllogism, *n,* syllogisme, *m.*

sylph, *n,* sylphe, *m.* ~*like,* (*figure*) de sylphide; (*pers.*) gracile.

symbol, *n,* symbole, *m.* ~**ic(al)**†, *a,* symbolique. ~**ism,** *n,* symbolisme, *m.* ~**ize,** *v.t,* symboliser.

symmetric(al)†, *a,* symétrique. **symmetry,** *n,* symétrie, *f.*

sympathetic, *a,* compatissant (envers); bien disposé (envers). **sympathize,** *v.i,* compatir (*with,* à). *I* ~ *with you,* je vous plains. **sympathy,** *n,* (*pity*) compassion (pour); sympathie (à, pour); solidarité (avec), *f. be in* ~ *with,* être du côté de. ~ *strike,* grève de solidarité, *f.*

symphony, *n,* symphonie, *f.* ¶ *a,* & **symphonic,** symphonique.

symptom, *n,* symptôme, *m.* **~atic,** *a,* symptomatique.
synagogue, *n,* synagogue, *f.*
synchronize, *v.t,* synchroniser. ¶ *v.i,* se passer en même temps (*with,* que).
syncopate, *v.t,* syncoper. **syncopation & syncope,** *n,* syncope, *f.*
syndicalism, *n,* syndicalisme, *m.* **syndicalist,** *n,* syndicaliste, *m,f.* **syndicate,** *n,* syndicat, *m;* coopérative, *f.*
syndrome, *n,* syndrome, *m.*
synod, *n,* synode, *m.*
synonym, *n.* & **synonymous,** *a,* synonyme, *m.* **synonymy,** *n,* synonymie, *f.*
synopsis, *n,* résumé, *m;* (*Theat.*) synopsis, *m. or f.*
syntax, *n,* syntaxe, *f.*
synthesis, *n,* synthèse, *f.* **synthesize,** *v.t,* synthétiser; produire par une synthèse. **synthetic,** *a,* synthétique.
syphilis, *n,* syphilis, *f.*
Syria, *n,* la Syrie, *f.* **Syrian,** *a,* syrien. ¶ *n,* Syrien, ne.
syringe, *n,* seringue, *f.* ¶ *v.t,* seringuer.
syrup, *n,* sirop, *m.* **~y,** *a,* sirupeux.
system, *n,* (*gen.*) système; (*Anat.*) organisme; (*Rly*) réseau, *m. get sth out of one's ~,* se purger de qch. **~s analyst,** analyste-programmeur, *m,f.* **~atic†,** *a,* systématique. **~atize,** *v.t,* systématiser.

T

T, *n,* T, té, *m. ~-junction,* intersection en T, *f. ~-shirt,* T-shirt, *m. ~-square,* té, *m. to a ~,* tout craché.
tab, *n,* (*on garment*) patte; (*loop*) attache, *f;* (*on file*) onglet, *m. keep ~s on s.o,* tenir qn a l'œil.
tabby cat, *n,* chat moucheté, chat tigré, *m.*
tabernacle, *n,* tabernacle, *m.*
table, *n,* (*gen., statistics, Math.*) table, *f;* (*Sport: league*) classement, *m. at ~,* à table. *lay the ~,* mettre le couvert *ou* la table. *have good ~ manners,* savoir se tenir à table. *~cloth,* nappe, *f. ~-cover,* tapis de t., *m. ~ d'hôte, a,* à prix fixe; *n,* menu [à prix fixe], *m. ~land,* plateau, *m. ~ leg,* pied de t., *m. ~mat,* dessous-de-plat; (*cloth*) napperon, *m. ~ napkin,* serviette [de t.], *f. ~-runner,* chemin de t., *m. ~ salt,* sel fin. *~spoon,* cuiller de service; (*measure*) cuillerée à soupe, *f. ~-tennis,* ping-pong, *m. ~ top,* dessus de t., *m. ~ware,* vaisselle, *f.* ¶ *v.t,* (*motion &c*) présenter. **tableau,** *n,* tableau, *m.* **tablet,** *n,* (*Phar.*) comprimé, cachet, *m;* (*stone*) plaque commémorative; (*wax, chocolate*) tablette, *f. ~ of soap,* savonnette, *f.*
tabloid (*newspaper*), *n,* tabloïd, *m.*
taboo, *a. & n,* tabou, *m.* ¶ *v.t,* interdire.
tabular, *a,* tabulaire, **tabulate,** *v.t,* mettre sous forme de table; classifier; (*Typing*) mettre en colonnes. **tabulator,** *n,* tabulateur, *m.*
tacit†, *a,* tacite. **taciturn,** *a,* taciturne. **~ity,** *n,* taciturnité, *f.*
tack, *n,* (*carpet*) broquette; (*upholstery*) semence, *f;* (*Need.*) point de bâti; (*Naut.*) bord, *m. on the right, wrong ~,* sur la bonne, mauvaise voie. ¶ *v.t,* (*flooring &c*) clouer; (*Need.*) faufiler, bâtir. ¶ *v.i,* (*Naut.*) virer de bord. *~ on,* bâtir; (*fig.*) ajouter après coup. **~ing,** *n,* faufilage, faufil, *m,* faufilure, *f. take out the ~ from,* défaufiler.
tackle, *n,* (*gen.*) équipement; (*hoist*) palan; (*Fish.*) matériel de pêche; (*Rugby*) plaquage, *m.* ¶ *v.t,* s'attaquer à; (*Rugby*) plaquer; (*Foot.*) tacler; (*thief &c*) saisir [à bras le corps].
tacky, *a,* (*surface*) poisseux; (*paint*) presque sec; (*glue*) qui commence à prendre.
tact, *n,* tact, doigté, *m.* **~ful,** *a,* plein de tact; (*inquiry*) discret. *be ~,* agir avec tact. **~fully,** *ad,* avec tact. **~less,** *a,* qui manque de tact; indiscret.
tactic, *n.* & **~s,** *n.pl,* tactique, *f.* **tactical,** *a,* tactique; (*error*) de tactique. **tactician,** *n,* tacticien, *m.*
tactile, *a,* tactile.
tadpole, *n,* têtard, *m.*
taffeta, *n,* taffetas, *m.*
tag, *n,* (*lace &c*) ferret, *m;* (*on garment*) attache; (*label*) étiquette, *f;* (*stock phrase*) cliché; slogan, *m.* ¶ *v.t,* étiqueter. *~ along,* traîner (*behind s.o,* derrière qn).
Tahiti, *n,* Taïti, Tahiti, *m.*
tail, *n,* (*gen.*) queue, *f;* (*shirt*) pan, *m;* (*coin*) pile, *f. be right on s.o's ~,* serrer qn de près. *~board* (*Mot.*), hayon, *m. ~coat* or *tails,* habit, *m,* queue de pie, *f. ~ light,* feu arrière, *m. ~spin,* vrille, *f. ~wind,* vent arrière, *m.* ¶ *v.t,* (*follow*) suivre, filer. *~ off,* diminuer petit à petit. *~back,* bouchon, *m.*
tailor, *n,* tailleur, *m. ~'s dummy,* mannequin, *m. ~-made,* fait sur mesure; (*fig.*) préparé spécialement. ¶ *v.t,* façonner; (*fig.*) adapter.
taint, *v.t,* polluer; (*food*) gâter; (*fig.*) porter

tache à. ~**ed,** *a,* pollué; gâté; entaché; (*money*) mal acquis.

take, *n,* (*Phot &c*) prise de vues, *f;* (*recording*) enregistrement, *m.* ¶ *v.t.ir,* (*gen.*) prendre (*from sth,* dans qch; *from s.o,* à qn); (*carry*) porter, apporter, emporter; (*lead*) emmener, conduire; accompagner. ~ *s.o round a house,* faire visiter une maison à qn. (*exam*) passer; (*tolerate*) accepter; (*hill*) grimper; (*fence*) sauter. ~ *2 hours to do,* mettre 2 heures à faire. ~ *a trick* (*Cards*), faire une levée. ~ *it or leave it,* c'est à prendre ou à laisser. *I* ~ *it that,* je suppose que. *I can't* ~ *it any more,* je n'en peux plus. ~ *cover,* s'abriter. ~ **after,** ressembler à, tenir de. ~ **apart,** démonter; (*P fig.*) démolir *P.* ~ **aside,** prendre à part. ~ **away,** (*object*) emporter; (*pers.*) emmener; enlever (à qn; de qch), prendre; (*Math.*) soustraire, ôter (de). ~ **back,** reprendre; (*return*) rapporter; (*pers.*) raccompagner. ~ **down,** descendre; (*picture &c*) enlever; (*trousers*) baisser. ~ **in,** rentrer; (*pers.*) faire entrer; (*orphan &c*) recueillir; (*friend*) recevoir; (*dress &c*) reprendre; (*include*) couvrir, inclure; comprendre, saisir; (*P deceive*) rouler *P,* avoir *P.* ~ **off,** *v.t,* enlever, ôter; (*train &c*) supprimer; imiter. ¶ *v.i,* partir (*for,* pour); (*Aero.*) décoller; (*jump*) s'élancer. ~ **on,** accepter, se charger de; (*employee*) *prendre;* (*cargo*) embarquer; (*form*) revêtir. ~ **out,** [faire] sortir; (*remove*) enlever (de); (*Insce*) prendre; (*licence*) procurer. ~ **over,** *v.i,* (*Pol.*) prendre le pouvoir; prendre la relève; *v.t,* (*debts*) prendre à sa charge; (*Fin.*) absorber. ~ **to,** (*pers.*) se prendre d'amitié pour; (*action &c*) prendre goût à; (*drink &c*) se mettre à. ~ *to one's bed,* s'aliter. ~ *to pieces,* démonter, démolir. ~ *to task,* prendre à partie. ~ **up,** (*object*) monter; (*pers.*) faire m.; (*carpet*) enlever; (*road &c*) dépaver; (*hem*) raccourcir; (*subject*) commencer l'étude de; (*hobby &c*) se mettre à; (*career*) embrasser; (*shares*) souscrire à; (*method, pers.*) adopter; (*room, time*) prendre. ~ *up with s.o,* se lier avec qn. ~**away,** *a,* à emporter. ~**off,** *n,* (*Aero.*) décollage; (*fig.*) démarrage; (*imitation*) pastiche, *m.* ~**over,** (*Fin. &c*) *n,* absorption, *f.* ~ *bid,* offre publique d'achat, *f.* **taker,** *n,* preneur, euse. **taking,** *a,* engageant, attirant. ¶ *n,* prise; (*pl.*) recette, *f.*

talc, *n,* talc, *m.*

tale, *n,* histoire, *f,* conte; (*account*) récit, *m. tell* ~*s,* cafarder *P,* rapporter. ~*bearer,* rapporteur, euse.

talent, *n,* talent, *m.* ~ *scout,* dénicheur, euse de vedettes &c. ~**ed,** *a,* doué (*pour*). *be* ~*ed,* avoir du talent.

talisman, *n,* talisman, *m.*

talk, *n,* conversation; (*chat*) causerie, *f;* (*formal*) entretien; (*lecture*) exposé (sur), *m;* propos, bavardages, (*pej.*) recontars, *m.pl. give a* ~ *on...* parler de... *there's some* ~ *of...* on dit que..., ¶ *v.t,* parler; bavarder; (*converse*) s'entretenir. ~ *over,* discuter de. ~**ative,** *a,* bavard, volubile. ~**er,** *n,* causeur, euse, bavard, e. ~**ie** (*Cine*) *n,* film parlant. ~**ing,** *a,* parlant. ~ *book,* livre enregistré. ~ *point,* sujet de conversation, *m.* ¶ *n,* bavardage, *m.*

tall, *a,* (*pers.*) grand, de haute taille; (*building*) haut, élevé. ~**boy,** *n,* commode, *f.* ~**ness,** *n,* haute taille; hauteur, *f.*

tally, *n,* compte, *m.* ¶ *v.i,* correspondre (*with,* à). ~**-ho,** *i,* taïaut!

talon, *n,* serre, *f.*

tamarisk, *n,* tamaris, *m.*

tambourine, *n,* tambourin, tambour de basque, *m.*

tame, *a,* apprivoisé; (*fig.*) insipide. ¶ *v.t,* apprivoiser, dompter. **tamer,** *n,* dompteur, euse.

tamper with, (*gen.*) toucher à; (*text*) falsifier; (*lock*) essayer de crocheter.

tampon, *n,* tampon, *m.*

tan, *n,* bronzage, *m.* ¶ *a,* brun roux, *inv.* ¶ *v.t,* (*hides*) tanner; (*sun*) bronzer; (*sailor &c*) basaner. ~ *s.o's hide P,* rosser qn *P.* ¶ *v.i,* bronzer.

tandem, *n,* tandem, *m.* ¶ *a. & ad,* en tandem.

tang, *n,* saveur *ou* odeur forte & piquante.

tangent, *n,* tangente, *f.*

tangerine, *n,* mandarine, *f.*

tangible†, *a,* tangible; (*fig.*) réel, matériel.

tangle, *n,* enchevêtrement; (*fig.*) confusion, *f. get into a* ~, s'enchevêtrer; (*hair*) s'emmêler; (*fig.*) s'embrouiller. ¶ *v.t,* & ~ *up,* enchevêtrer, embrouiller.

tank, *n,* (*petrol &c*) réservoir, *m;* (*water &c*) citerne; (*Phot.*) cuve, *f;* (*fish*) aquarium, *m;* (*Mil.*) char, tank, *m.*

tankard, *n,* chope [à bière], *f.*

tanker, *n,* camion-citerne; (*ship*) pétrolier; (*Rly*) wagon-citerne, *m.*

tanner, *n,* tanneur, *m.* ~**y,** *n,* tannerie, *f.* **tannin,** *n,* tanin, tannin, *m.*

tantalize, *v.t,* mettre au supplice.

tantamount to, équivalent à.

tantrum, *n,* crise de colère, *f.*

tap[1], *n,* petit coup, *m.* ¶ *v.t. & i,* frapper doucement, tapoter; taper. ~*-dance, n,* claquettes, *f.pl.*

tap[2], *n,* robinet, *m. on* ~, (*beer*) en fût; (*funds &c*) disponible. ~ *water,* eau du robinet, *f.* ¶ *v.t,* (*cask &c*) mettre en perce; (*tree*) inciser; (*Elec.*) capter; (*Tel.*) mettre sur écoute; (*fig.*) exploiter.

tape, *n,* ruban; (*sticky*) scotch; (*Sport*) fil d'arrivée, *m;* (*recording*) bande magnétique, *f.* ~ *deck,* platine de magnétophone, *f.* ~

measure, mètre à ruban, *m.* ~*-recorder,* magnétophone, *m.* ~*worm,* ver solitaire, ténia, *m.* ¶ *v.t,* (*record*) enregistrer. ~ [*up*], attacher avec du ruban &c. *have* ~*d P,* avoir bien en main.
taper, *n,* bougie fine, *f;* (*church*) cierge, *m.* ¶ *v.t,* (*leg*) fuseler; (*hair*) effiler; (*shape*) terminer en pointe. ~**ing,** *a,* fuselé; en pointe.
tapestry, *n.* & ~ *work,* tapisserie, *f.*
tapioca, *n,* tapioca, *m.*
tapir, *n,* tapir, *m.*
tar, *n,* goudron, *m.* ~ *spraying,* goudronnage, *m.* ¶ *v.t,* goudronner.
tarantella, *n,* tarentelle, *f.* **tarantula,** *n,* tarentule, *f.*
tardy†, *a,* tardif.
tare, *n,* (*Com.*) tare, *f.*
target, *n,* cible, *f;* (*Mil.*) objectif, *m.* ~ *practice,* exercices de tir, *m.pl.* ¶ *a,* fixé, prévu.
tariff, *n,* tarif, *m.*
tarmac, *n,* macadam goudronné, *m;* (*runway*) piste; aire d'envol, *f.* ¶ *v.t,* goudronner.
tarnish, *v.t.* (& *i,*) (se) ternir.
tarpaulin, *n,* toile goudronnée; (*sheet*) bâche [g.], *f.*
tarragon, *n,* estragon, *m.*
tart†[1], *a,* âpre, acide; (*answer &c*) acerbe.
tart[2], *n,* tarte; (*small*) tartelette; (*P**) putain *P*,* *f.*
tartan, *n,* tartan, *m.* ¶ *a,* écossais. ~ *rug,* plaid, *m.*
tartar, *n,* tartre, *m.* ~**ic,** *a,* tartrique.
tartness, *n,* aigreur, âcreté, acidité, *f.*
task, *n,* tâche; besogne, *f. take to* ~, prendre à partie. ¶ *v.t,* mettre à l'épreuve. ~ *force,* détachement spécial, *m. hard* ~*master,* véritable tyran, *m.*
Tasmania, *n,* la Tasmanie.
tassel, *n,* gland, *m.*
taste, *n,* goût, *m. in good, bad* ~, de bon, mauvais g. *to* ~, à volonté. ¶ *v.t,* sentir [le goût de]; goûter à; g. de; (*wine*) déguster. ¶ *v.i,* avoir un goût. ~**ful,** *a,* de bon goût. ~**less,** *a,* fade; (*remark &c*) de mauvais goût. ~**lessly,** *ad,* sans goût. ~**lessness,** *n,* fadeur, *f;* mauvais goût. **taster,** *n,* dégustateur, trice.
tasting, *n,* dégustation, *f.* **tasty,** *a,* savoureux.
tata *P, i,* salut!
tatter, *n,* lambeau, *m.* ~**ed,** *a,* déguenillé; en lambeaux.
tattle, *n,* commérages, cancans, *m.pl.* ¶ *v.i,* cancaner. **tattler,** *n,* commère, *f.*
tattoo, *n,* tatouage, *m;* (*Mil.*) parade militaire, *f.* ¶ *v.t,* tatouer.
taunt, *n,* raillerie, *f.* ¶ *v.t,* railler.
taut, *a,* raide, tendu. ~**en,** *v.t,* raidir.
tautologic(al), *a,* tautologique. **tautology,** *n,* tautologie, *f.*
tavern, *n,* taverne, *f.*
tawdriness, *n,* qualité médiocre, *f.* **tawdry,** *a,* médiocre; (*clothes*) tapageur, criard.
tawny, *a,* fauve. *f.*
tax, *n,* impôt, *m,* taxe, *f.* ~ *collector,* percepteur, *m.* ~ *dodger,* fraudeur, euse fiscal, e. ~*-free,* exempt d'impôts. ~*payer,* contribuable, *m,f.* ¶ *a,* fiscal. ¶ *v.t,* imposer; taxer; (*fig.*) mettre à l'épreuve; taxer (qn de qch). ~**able,** *a,* imposable. ~**ation,** *n,* taxation, *f,* impôts, *m.pl.* ~**ing,** *a,* éprouvant.
taxi, *n.* & ~*cab,* taxi, *m.* ~*-driver,* chauffeur de t., *m.* ~*meter,* taximètre, *m.* ~*-rank,* station de taxis, *f.* ¶ *v.i,* (*Aero.*) rouler lentement.
taxidermist, *n,* empailleur, euse. **taxidermy,** *n,* empaillage, *m.*
tea, *n,* thé, *m;* (*herbal*) infusion, tisane, *f;* (*meal*) thé, goûter, *m.* ~*-bag,* sachet de thé, *m.* ~*-break,* pause-thé, *f.* ~ *caddy,* boîte à thé, *f.* ~*-chest,* caisse, *f.* ~*cloth,* torchon, *m.* ~ *cosy,* couvre-théière, *m.* ~*cup,* tasse à thé, *f.* ~ *party,* thé, *m.* ~*pot,* théière, *f.* ~*room*(*s*), ~*shop,* salon de thé, *m,* pâtisserie, *f.* ~*-set,* service à thé, *m.* ~*spoon,* petite cuiller. ~*spoonful,* cuillerée à café, *f.* ~ *time,* l'heure du thé, *f.*
teach, *v.t,* apprendre (qch à qn; à qn à faire); (*Sch., Univ.*) enseigner (qch à qn). ¶ *v.i,* enseigner. ~**er,** *n,* (*gen.*) professeur, *m;* (*primary*) instituteur, trice, maître, esse; (*pl: profession*) enseignants, *m.pl.* ~*er*[*s'*] *training college,* école normale. ~**ing,** *n,* enseignement, *m.* ¶ *a,* (*staff*) enseignant; (*material*) pédagogique; (*machine*) à enseigner.
teak, *n,* teck, *m.*
teal, *n,* sarcelle, *f.*
team, *n,* (*gen.*) équipe, *f;* (*horses &c*) attelage, *m.* ~*-mate,* coéquipier, ère. ~*-member,* équipier, ère. ~ *spirit,* esprit d'équipe, *m.* ¶ *v.t.* & ~ *up,* (*pers.*) mettre en collaboration (avec). ~ *up, v.i,* faire équipe (avec).
tear, (tɛə) *n,* déchirure, *f;* accroc, *m.* ¶ *v.t.ir,* déchirer; (*snatch*) arracher (à qn; de qch). ~ *one's hair,* s'arracher les cheveux. *be torn between* ... balancer entre ... *that's torn it!* (*P fig.*) ça fiche tout par terre! *P.* ~ *away,* ~ *down,* arracher. ~ *out,* détacher (*from,* de).
tear, (tiə) *n,* larme, *f, burst into* ~*s,* fondre en larmes. ~ *gas,* gaz lacrymogène, *m.* ~*-stained,* barbouillé de larmes. ~**ful,** *a,* larmoyant.
tease, *v.t,* taquiner; tourmenter. ¶ (*pers.*) *n,* taquin, e.
teasel, *n,* cardère, *f.*
teaser, *n,* (*pers.*) taquin, e; problème, cassetête, *m.* **teasing,** *n,* taquinerie, *f.*
teat, *n,* (*bottle, animal*) tétine, *f;* (*woman*) tétin, bout de sein, *m.*
technical†, *a,* technique. ~ *college,* collège technique, *m.* ~ *offence* (*Law*), contravention, *f.* ~**ity,** *n,* détail technique, *m.* **technician,** *n,* technicien, ne. **technique,** *n,* techni-

que, *f.* **technology,** *n,* technologie, *f.*
teddy bear, *n,* ours en peluche, nounours, *m.*
tedious†, *a,* ennuyeux, fatigant. ~**ness** & **tedium,** *n,* ennui, *m.*
tee, (*Golf*) *n,* tee, *m.*
teem, *v.i,* (*crowds, street &c*) grouiller (*with,* de). ~ *with rain,* pleuvoir à verse. ~**ing,** *a,* grouillant; (*rain*) battant.
teenage, *a,* adolescent; (*behaviour*) d'a., de jeune; (*fashions*) pour jeunes. **teenager,** *n,* jeune, *m,f.* adolescent, e. **teens,** *n.pl,* adolescence, jeunesse, *f. in one's* ~, adolescent.
teeter, *v.i,* (*pers.*) chanceler; (*pile*) vaciller.
teethe, *v.i,* faire ses dents. **teething,** *n,* poussée des dents, *f.* ~ *troubles* (*fig.*), difficultés de démarrage, *f.pl.*
teetotal, *a,* (*pers.*) qui ne boit jamais d'alcool. **teetotaller,** *n,* buveur d'eau, *m.*
telecommunications, *n.pl,* télécommunications, *f.pl.*
telegram, *n,* télégramme, *m,* dépêche, *f.* **telegraph,** *n,* télégraphe, *m.* ~ *pole,* poteau télégraphique, *m.* ¶ *v.t. & i,* télégraphier. ~**ic,** *a,* télégraphique. ~**y,** *n,* télégraphie, *f.*
telepathy, *n,* télépathie, *f.*
telephone, *n,* téléphone, *m.* ~ *call,* coup de t., coup de fil *P, m.* ~ *operator,* standardiste, *m,f.* ~ *subscriber,* abonné, e au t. ¶ *v.t. & i,* téléphoner. ¶ *a.* & **telephonic,** *a,* téléphonique. **telephonist,** *n,* téléphoniste, *m,f.*
telephoto lens, *n,* téléobjectif, *m.*
teleprinter, *n,* téléscripteur, *m.*
telescope, *n,* (*reflecting*) télescope, *m;* (*refracting*) lunette d'approche, *f.* ¶ *v.i,* se télescoper; (*umbrella*) se plier. **telescopic,** *a,* télescopique; pliant.
televise, *v.t,* téléviser. **television,** *n,* télévision, *f;* (*set*) téléviseur, *m. on* ~, à la télé[vision]. ¶ *a,* (*play &c*) télévisé; (*actor &c*) de télévision. ~ *viewer,* téléspectateur, trice.
telex, *n,* télex, *m.* ¶ *v.t,* envoyer par t.
tell, *v.t,* dire (*s.o sth,* qch à qn; *s.o to do,* à qn de faire); (*story &c*) raconter (à); (*lie &c*) dire; (*secret*) révéler; (*future*) prédire; (*time*) lire; (~ *apart*) distinguer; (*know*) savoir. ~ *me another! P* à d'autres! *P. you're* ~*ing me! P* tu parles! *P.* ¶ *v.i,* parler (*of, about,* de); savoir; (*have effect*) se faire sentir (*on,* sur). ~ *off,* gronder, attraper *P.* ~**er,** *n,* (*voting*) scrutateur; (*bank*) caissier, *m.* ~**ing,** *a,* révélateur; (*argument &c*) efficace. ~*-off,* attrapade *P, f.* ~**tale,** *n,* (*pers.*) rapporteur, euse; cafard *P;* (*Tech.*) contrôleur [de ronde], *m.*
telly *P, n,* télé *P, f.*
temerity, *n,* témérité, *f.*
temper, *n,* (*nature*) caractère, tempérament, *m;* (*mood*) humeur, *f;* [accès *m* de] colère, *f;* (*metal*) trempe, *f. have a quick* ~, être soupe au lait. *in a good, bad* ~, de bonne, mauvaise humeur. *to be bad-*~*ed,* avoir mauvais caractère. *lose one's* ~, se mettre en colère. ¶ *v.t,* (*metal*) tremper; (*fig.*) tempérer (*with,* par). **temperament,** *n,* tempérament, *m;* humeur, *f.* ~**al,** *a,* capricieux; fantasque. **temperance,** *n,* modération; (*in drinking*) tempérance, *f.* **temperate,** *a,* tempéré. **temperature,** *n,* température, *f.*
tempest, *n,* tempête, *f.* **tempestuous,** *a,* (*fig. pers.*) passionné; (*meeting*) orageux.
template, *n,* patron, *m.*
temple[1], *n,* (*Anat.*) tempe, *f.*
temple[2], (*Rel.*) *n,* temple, *m.*
tempo, *n,* tempo, *m.*
temporal†, *a,* temporel. **temporary†,** *a,* temporaire; (*teacher*) suppléant; (*secretary*) intérimaire. **temporize,** *v.i,* atermoyer, temporiser.
tempt, *v.t,* tenter; inviter. *to be* ~*ed,* être tenté (de faire). ~**ation,** *n,* tentation, *f.* **tempter, tress,** *n,* tentateur, trice. **tempting,** *a,* tentant; (*food*) appétissant.
ten, *a,* dix. ¶ *n,* dix, *m;* dizaine, *f. about* ~, une dizaine de. *for other phrases V* **four.** ~**fold,** *a.* & *ad,* décuple. *to increase* ~, décupler.
tenable, *a,* défendable. **tenacious,** *a,* tenace. ~**ly,** *ad,* avec ténacité.
tenancy, *n,* location, *f.* **tenant,** *n,* locataire, *m,f.*
tench, *n,* tanche, *f.*
tend[1], *v.t,* (*sheep*) garder; (*garden*) entretenir; (*invalid*) soigner; (*machine*) surveiller.
tend[2], *v.i,* avoir tendance (à faire); incliner (*towards,* à, vers). ~**ency,** *n,* tendance, *f.* **tendentious,** *a,* tendancieux. **tender**[1], *n,* (*Com.*) soumission; (*boat*) vedette, *f;* (*Rly*) tender, *m. put out to* ~, mettre en ajudication. ¶ *v.t,* (*apologies*) offrir; (*resignation*) donner. ~ *for,* faire une soumission pour.
tender[2]**†,** *a,* tendre; (*spot*) sensible; (*flower, subject*) délicat. ~*-hearted,* sensible. ~**ness,** *n,* tendresse; délicatesse; (*eatables*) tendreté, *f.*
tendon, *n,* tendon, *m.*
tendril, *n,* vrille, *f.*
tenement, *n,* immeuble, *m.*
tenet, *n,* principe, *m.*
tennis, *n,* tennis, *m.* ~ *court,* [court de] tennis, *m.* ~ *elbow* (*Med.*), synovite du coude, *f.*
tenon, *n,* tenon, *m.* ~ *saw,* scie à t., *f.*
tenor, *n,* (*speech &c*) sens, *m,* substance, *f;* (*life &c*) cours; (*Mus.*) ténor, *m.* ~ *clef,* clef d'ut, *f.*
tense[1], (*Gram.*) *n,* temps, *m.*
tense[2], *n,* (*pers., voice &c*) tendu; (*time*) de tension; (*smile*) crispé. ¶ *v.t,* tendre. ~**ness** & **tension,** *n,* tension, *f.*
tent, *n,* tente, *f.* ~ *peg,* piquet de t., *m.*
tentacle, *n,* tentacule, *m.*
tentative†, *a,* provisoire; hésitant, timide.
tenterhooks (on), sur des charbons ardents.
tenth†, *a,* dixième. ¶ *n,* dixième, *m,f;* (*fraction*)

dixième, *m. for phrases V* **fourth.**
tenuous, *a,* ténu.
tenure, *n,* (*land*) bail, *m;* (*Law*) [période de] jouissance, *f.*
tepid†, *a,* tiède. ~**ness,** *n,* tiédeur, *f.*
term, *n,* (*gen.*) terme, *m;* période, *f;* (*Sch., Univ.*) trimestre, *m;* (*Law*) session, *f;* (*pl: conditions*) conditions, *f.pl;* (*contract*) termes; (*Com.*) prix, *m.pl;* tarif, *m. on good ~s with s.o,* en bons termes (*ou* rapports) avec qn. *come to ~s with,* (*pers.*) arriver à un accord avec; (*situation*) accepter. ¶ *a,* (*exams &c*) trimestriel. ¶ *v.t,* appeler, nommer.
terminal, *a,* terminal; (*illness*) dans sa phase t. ¶ *n,* (*Rly &c*) terminus, *m;* (*Elec.*) borne, *f;* (*computer*) terminal, *m,* périphérique, *f. air ~,* aérogare, *f.* **terminate,** *v.t,* terminer; (*contract*) résilier.¶ *v.i,* se terminer. **termination,** *n,* fin, *f;* résiliation; (*pregnancy*) interruption, *f.*
terminology, *n,* terminologie, *f.*
terminus, *n,* terminus, *m.*
termite, *n,* termite, *m,* fourmi blanche, *f.*
tern, *n,* sterne, *m.*
terrace, *n,* terrasse; (*houses*) rangée de maisons, *f;* (*pl: Sport*) gradins, *m.pl.* ¶ *v.t,* arranger en terrasses.
terracotta, *n,* terre cuite, *f.*
terra firma, *n,* la terre ferme. **terrain,** *n,* terrain, *m.*
terrestrial, *a,* terrestre.
terrible†, *a,* terrible.
terrier, *n,* [chien] terrier, *m.*
terrific†, *a,* énorme, fantastique; (*crowd, speed*) fou; (*noise*) épouvantable; (*heat &c*) terrible; (*P excellent*) terrible *P,* formidable. *P.* **terrify,** *v.t,* terrifier. ~**ing†,** *a,* épouvantable, terrifiant.
territorial, *a. & n,* territorial, *m.* **territory,** *n,* territoire, *m.*
terror, *n,* terreur, *f. ~-stricken,* épouvanté. ~**ism,** *n,* terrorisme, *m.* ~**ist,** *a. & n,* terroriste, *m,f.* ~**ize,** *v.t,* terroriser.
terse†, *a,* laconique. ~**ness,** *n,* laconisme, *m.*
terylene, *n,* tergal, *m.*
test, *n,* (*gen., Sch.*) épreuve, *f;* (*trial*) essai, *m;* (*Chem., Pharm., blood &c*) analyse, *f;* (*driving*) examen; (*Psych.*) test, *m;* épreuve. *stand the ~,* (*pers.*) se montrer à la hauteur; (*Mach.*) résister aux épreuves. *~ card* (*TV*), mire, *f. ~ case,* affaire-test, *f. ~-drive,* essai de route, *m. ~ flight,* vol d'essai, *m. ~ tube,* éprouvette, *f. ~-tube baby,* bébé-éprouvette, *m.* ¶ *v.t,* essayer, mettre à l'essai *ou* à l'épreuve; (*goods*) vérifier; (*water &c*) analyser; (*Psych.*) tester; (*sight &c*) examiner; (*reactions*) mesurer. *a ~ing time,* une période éprouvante.
testament, *n,* testament, *m.* **testicle,** *n,* testicule, *m.* **testify,** *v.t,* témoigner. ¶ *v.i,* porter témoignage. *~ against s.o,* déposer contre qn. *~ to,* témoigner de; (*Law*) attester. **testimonial,** *n,* recommandation, *f.* **testimony,** *n,* témoignage, *m.*
testy, *a,* irritable, irascible.
tetanus, *n,* tétanos, *m.*
tetchy, *a,* irritable.
tether, *n,* longe, *f. at the end of one's ~,* au bout de son rouleau. ¶ *v.t,* attacher.
text, *n,* texte, *m. ~book,* manuel, *m.*
textile, *n,* textile, tissu, *m.* ¶ *a,* textile.
textual†, *a,* textuel; (*error*) de texte.
texture, *n,* texture; (*cloth*) contexture, *f;* (*skin*) grain, *m.*
Thames (the), la Tamise.
than, *c,* que; (*with numerals*) de. *more ~,* plus que. *more ~ 10,* plus de 10.
thank, *v.t,* remercier; dire merci (*for,* de). *~ God!* Dieu merci! *~ oneself,* s'en prendre à soi-même. *~ you! & no ~ you!* merci! ~**ful,** *a,* reconnaissant (de). *be ~ that,* être content *ou* heureux que (+ *subj.*). ~**fully,** *ad,* avec reconnaissance. ~**fulness,** *n,* reconnaissance, gratitude, *f.* ~**less,** *a,* ingrat. **thanks,** *n.pl,* remerciements, *m.pl.* ¶ *i,* merci! *~ to,* grâce à. **thanksgiving,** *n,* action[s] de grâce, *f.*[*pl.*].
that, *a,* (*demonstrative*) ce, cet, cette; (*stressed or opp. this*) ce... &c -là. ¶ *pn,* (*demonstrative*) cela, ça; (*before relative*) celui, celle. *~* [*one*], celui-là, celle-là. *~'s all,* c'est tout, voilà tout. *~'s enough!* ça suffit! *~ is to say,* c'est-à-dire. ¶ *pn,* (*relative*) (*subject*) qui; (*object*) que; (*with pr.*) lequel, laquelle; (*expressions of time*) où. ¶ *ad,* si, aussi. *not ~ stupid,* pas si bête que ça. ¶ *c,* que. *so ~,* pour que, afin que (+ *subj.*).
thatch, *n,* chaume, *m.* ¶ *v.t,* couvrir en c. *~ed cottage,* chaumière, *f.*
thaw, *n,* dégel, *m;* (*Pol. &c*) détente, *f.* ¶ *v.i. & t,* dégeler; (*ice, snow*) (faire) fondre.
the, *art,* le, l', *m,* la, l', *f,* les, *m,f.pl. from ~, of ~,* du, de l', de la, des. *to ~, at ~,* au, à l', à la, aux.
theatre, *n,* théâtre, *m. lecture ~,* amphithéatre, *m. operating ~,* salle d'opération, *f.* ¶ *a,* de théâtre, du t. *~goer,* habitué, e du t. **theatrical†,** *a,* théâtral. **theatricals,** *n.pl,* (*fig: pej.*) comédie, *f:* (*amateur*) théâtre. *m.*
thee *O, pn,* te, t'; (*stressed & after pr.*) toi.
theft, *n,* vol, *m.*
their, *a,* leur, leurs (*pl.*). **theirs,** *pn,* le leur, la leur, les leurs; à eux, à elles. *that dog is ~,* ce chien est à eux (*ou* à elles).
them, *pn,* (*direct*) les; (*stressed & after pr*) eux, elles; (*indirect*) leur. *as for ~,* quant à eux. *both of ~,* tous (*ou* toutes) les deux. *I don't like ~,* je ne les aime pas; (*emphatic*) eux (*ou* elles), je ne les aime pas. *I gave ~ my address,* je leur ai donné mon adresse. *it's ~,* ce sont eux! les voilà! *~selves,* (*reflexive*) se; (*em-*

phatic) eux-mêmes, elles-mêmes; (*after pr.*) eux, elles.
theme, *n,* thème; sujet; (*Mus.*) motif, *m.* ~ *tune,* indicatif; (*fig.*) refrain habituel, *m.*
then, *ad,* (*at that time*) alors, à cette époque; à ce moment-là; (*afterwards*) puis, ensuite, alors; (*in that case*) donc, alors; (*& also*) & puis, d'ailleurs. ~ *& there* sur-le-champ. *& ~ what?* et puis après? *before ~,* avant cela. *from ~ on,* dès lors. *until ~,* jusqu'alors. **thence,** *ad,* de là. **thenceforth, thenceforward,** *ad,* dès lors.
theodolite, *n,* théodolite, *m.*
theologian, *n,* théologien, ne. **theological†,** *a,* théologique. ~ *college,* séminaire, *m.* **theology,** *n,* théologie, *f.*
theorem, *n,* théorème, *m.* **theoretic(al†),** *a,* théorique. **theorist,** *n,* théoricien, ne. **theorize,** *v.i,* élaborer des théories (*about,* sur). **theory,** *n,* théorie, *f.*
therapeutic, *a.* & ~**s,** *n.pl,* thérapeutique, *f.* **therapist,** *n,* thérapeute, *m,f.* **therapy,** *n,* thérapie, *f.*
there, *ad,* là; y. ~ *are 5 left,* il en reste 5. [*over, down &c*] ~, là-bas. ~ *& back,* aller & retour. ~ *& then,* sur-le-champ. ~ *is,* ~ *are,* il y a; (*pointing out*) voilà. ~*about*[*s*], par là; environ. ~*by,* par là; de cette manière. ~*fore,* c'est pourquoi; donc, aussi, par conséquent. ~*on,* là-dessus. ~*upon,* sur ce, là-dessus.
thermal, *a,* thermal; (*Elec., Phys.*) thermique. ~ *baths,* thermes, *m.pl.* **thermo...** *pref:* therm[o]... **thermometer,** *n,* thermomètre, *m.* **Thermos [flask],** *n,* [bouteille] thermos, *f.*
these, *a. & pn,* ces; ces...-ci; ceux-ci; celles-ci. *V* **this.**
thesis, *n,* thèse, *f.*
they, *pn,* ils, elles; (*stressed*) eux, elles; (*people in general*) on. ~ *say that...* on dit que... *there ~ are!* les voilà!
thick, *a,* (*gen.*) épais; (*beard, hedge*) touffu; (*stupid*) bête, borné; (*with s.o*) lié. ~ *with dust,* couvert de poussière. *that's a bit ~!* ça c'est un peu fort! *be as ~ as thieves,* s'entendre comme larrons en foire. ~*-lipped,* aux lèvres charnues. ~*set,* râblé, trapu. ~*skinned,* (*pers.*) peu sensible. ~**[ly],** *ad,* (*spread &c*) en couche épaisse; (*cut*) en tranches épaisses; (*fall: snow*) dru; (*speak*) d'une voix pâteuse. *in the ~ of,* (*crowd*) au plus fort de; (*fight*) en plein cœur de. *through ~ & thin,* à travers toutes les épreuves. ~**en,** *v.t,* épaissir. ¶ *v.i,* s'épaissir; (*crowd*) grossir. ~**ening,** *n,* épaississement, *m;* (*for sauce*) liaison, *f.* ~**et,** *n,* fourré, *m.* ~**ness,** *n,* épaisseur; (*lips &c*) grosseur; (*fog, forest*) densité, *f.*
thief, *n,* voleur, euse. *set a ~ to catch a ~,* à voleur voleur & demi. **thieve,** *v.t,* voler. **thieving,** *a,* voleur. ¶ *n,* vol, *m.*
thigh, *n,* cuisse, *f.* ~*bone,* fémur, *m.* ~ *boots,* cuissardes, *f.pl.*
thimble, *n,* dé [à coudre], *m.* ~**ful,** *n,* doigt, *m.*
thin, *a,* (*gen.*) mince; (*glass*) fin; (*skinny: pers.*) maigre; (*string*) petit; (*soup &c*) peu épais; (*hair*) rare, clairsemé; (*fog*) léger; (*crowd*) épars; (*voice*) grêle. *as ~ as a rake,* maigre *ou* sec comme un coup de trique. *vanish into ~ air* (*fig.*), se volatiliser. ~*-lipped,* aux lèvres minces. ~*-skinned,* (*pers.*) susceptible. ¶ *v.t,* ~ [*down*], délayer. ~ [*out*], éclaircir. ¶ *v.i,* ~ [*out*] (*fog &c*), se disperser.
thine *O, pn,* le tien, la tienne, les tiens, les tiennes; à toi.
thing, *n,* (*gen.*) chose, *f;* (*pl: belongings*) affaires, *f.pl,* effets, *m.pl. do my own ~,* faire ce qu'il me plaît. *have a ~ about,* être obsédé par. *it's quite the ~,* ça se fait beaucoup. *what with one ~ & another...* ce qui fait qu'en fin de compte... *the funny ~ is that...* ce qui est drôle c'est que... *poor ~!* le (*ou* la) pauvre! *Mrs. ~ P,* Madame Machin *P.* ~**ummy,** *P,* machin, *P,* truc *P, m.*
think, *v.i,* penser (*about, of,* à); songer (à); (*carefully*) réfléchir (à). ¶ *v.t,* (*opinion*) penser, croire, trouver. *what do you ~ of this book?* que penses-tu de ce livre? comment trouves-tu ce l.? (*believe*) penser, croire; (*reflect*) penser; [s']imaginer. *who do you ~ you are?* pour qui te prends-tu? ~ **back,** essayer de se souvenir (*to,* de). ~ **of,** (*imagine*) imaginer, se rendre compte de; (*devise*) avoir l'idée de. ~ **out,** (*answer &c*) préparer; (*problem*) étudier. ~ **over,** bien réfléchir à. ~ **up,** avoir [l'idée de]; (*answer*) trouver; (*excuse*) inventer. ~**able,** *a,* pensable. ~**er,** *n,* penseur, euse. **thinking,** *a,* (*being*) rationnel; (*pers.*) qui réfléchit. ¶ *n,* pensée, réflection, *f;* (*thoughts*) opinions, *f.pl.*
thinly, *ad,* (*wooded &c*) peu; (*disguised*) à peine; (*spread*) en couche mince; (*cut*) en tranches minces. **thinness,** *n,* minceur, maigreur, *f.*
third†, *a,* troisième. ~*-class,* (*gen., Rly &c*) de troisième classe; (*hotel*) de t. catégoire; (*Univ: degree*) sans mention. ~ *finger,* majeur, *m.* ~ *party,* ~ *person,* tiers, *m;* (*Gram.*) troisième personne, *f.* ~*-rate,* de qualité très inférieure. *the T~ World,* le Tiers-Monde. ¶ *n,* troisième, *m,f;* (*fraction*) troisième, *m;* (*Mus.*) tierce; (*Mot.*) troisième [vitesse], *f. for other phrases V* **fourth.**
thirst, *n,* soif, *f.* ~ **for,** avoir soif de. **thirsty,** *a,* (*pers. &c*) qui a soif; (*stronger*) assoiffé; (*fig: land*) désséché. *be ~,* avoir soif.
thirteen, *a. & n,* treize. ~**th†,** *a. & n,* treizième, *m,f;* (*fraction*) treizième, *m.*
thirtieth, *a. & n,* trentieme, *m,f;* (*fraction*) trentième, *m.* **thirty,** *a. & n,* trente, *m. about ~,* une trentaine. *for phrases V* **forty.**

this, *a,* ce, cet, cette; (*stressed & opp. that*) ce. . ., -ci &c. ~ *way!* par ici! ~ *way & that,* ça & là. ~ *week,* cette semaine. ~ *time last week,* la semaine dernière à pareille heure. ¶ *pn,* ceci, ce. ~ [*one*], celui-ci, celle-ci. *after* ~, après ceci. *like* ~, comme ceci. *who's* ~*?* qui est-ce?

thistle, *n,* chardon, *m.* ~ *down,* duvet du chardon, *m.*

thong, *n,* lanière, *f.*

thorax, *n,* thorax, *m.*

thorn *&* ~ [*bush*] *n,* épine, *f.* ~**y,** *a,* épineux.

thorough, *a,* (*search &c*) minutieux; (*work &c*) consciencieux; (*knowledge*) approfondi; (*fig.*) véritable (*before n.*); (*rogue &c*) fieffé; (*clean*) à fond. ~**bred,** *a,* (*horse*) pur sang; (*other animal*) de race. ¶ *n,* pur-sang, *m.inv;* bête de race, *f.* ~**fare,** *n.* rue; voie publique, *f.* *'no* ~', 'passage interdit'. ~**ly,** *ad,* à fond; tout à fait; parfaitement. ~**ness,** *n,* minutie, *f.*

those, *a. & pn,* ces; ces. . .-là; ceux, celles; ceux-là; celles-là. *V* **that.**

thou, *O, pn,* tu; (*stressed*) toi.

though, *c,* bien que (+ *subj.*); quoique (+ *subj.*). *as* ~, comme si. *it looks as* ~, il semble que (+*subj.*). ¶ *ad,* pourtant, cependant.

thought, *n,* (*gen.*) pensée; (*idea*) idée, *f. give a* ~ *to,* penser à. *give* ~ *to,* bien réfléchir à. *without* ~, sans réfléchir. ~*-provoking,* qui pousse à la réflexion. ~**ful,** *a,* pensif; (*serious*) sérieux; (*considerate*) prévenant; (*act, remark*) gentil. ~**fully,** *ad,* pensivement; avec prévenance. ~**fulness,** *n,* air pensif, prévenance, *f.* ~**less†,** *a,* (*behaviour*) irréflechi; (*pers.*) étourdi. ~**lessness,** *n.* étourderie, *f;* manque de prévenance, *m. to be a* ~**-reader,** lire dans les pensées des gens.

thousand, *a. & n,* mille, *inv. & m. 1* ~, mille. *10* ~, 10 mille. *about a* ~, un millier. ~*s of,* des milliers de. ~**th,** *a. & n,* millieme, *m,f;* (*fraction*) millième, *m.*

thrash, *v.t,* rosser, rouer de coups; (*punish*) donner une bonne correction à; (*P Sport*) rosser, battre à plate couture. ~ *about,* se débattre. ~ *out,* (*problem &c*) débattre de. ~**ing,** *n,* correction, raclée *P, f.*

thread, *n,* fil; (*screw*) pas, filet[age], *m.* ¶ *v.t,* (*needle &c*) enfiler; (*cotton &c*) faire passer. ~ *one's way,* se faufiler. ~**bare,** *a,* usé, rapé; (*fig.*) rebattu.

threat, *n,* menance, *f.* ~**en,** *v.t,* menacer.

three, *a.& n,* trois, *inv. & m.* ~*-cornered,* triangulaire. ~*-dimensional,* à trois dimensions; (*film*) en relief. ~*-ply* (*wool*), trois fils, *inv.* ~*-quarter* (*Rugby*), trois-quarts, *m.inv.* ~*-quarters,* trois quarts, *m.pl.* ~*some,* groupe de trois, *m. in a* ~*some,* à trois. ~*-wheeler,* (*car*) voiture à 3 roues, *f. for other phrases V* **four.** ~**fold,** *a,* triple.

thresh, *v.t,* battre. ~**ing,** *n,* battage, *m.* ~ *machine,* batteuse, *f.*

threshold, *n,* seuil, *m.*

thrice, *ad,* trois fois.

thrift, *n,* économie, *f.* ~**less,** *a,* prodigue, dépensier. ~**y,** *a,* économe, ménager.

thrill, *n,* frisson, *m;* vive émotion; (*excitement*) sensation, *f.* ¶ *v.t,* (*pers. &c*) exciter, électriser; emballer *P.* ¶ *v.i,* frissonner [de joie]. ~**er,** *n,* roman *ou* film à suspense, *m.* ~**ing,** *a,* palpitant; (*news*) saisissant.

thrive, *v.i,* (*gen.*) prospérer; (*pers., animal*) être florissant de santé; (*plant*) pousser bien. **thriving,** *a,* prospère; florissant de santé; robuste.

throat, *n,* gorge, *f;* gosier, *m. sore* ~, angine, *f. ram sth down s.o's* ~, (*fig.*), rebattre les oreilles de qn avec qch. **throaty,** *a,* guttural.

throb, *v.i,* (*heart*) palpiter; vibrer; (*Med.*) élancer, lanciner. ¶ *n,* battement, *m;* vibration, *f;* élancement, *m.*

throes, *n.pl, in the* ~ *of,* (*war &c*) en proie à; (*writing*) aux prises avec; (*death*) dans les affres de.

thrombosis, *n,* thrombose, *f.*

throne, *n,* trône, *m;* (*bishop's*) chaire, *f.*

throng, *n,* foule, presse, *f.* ¶ *v.t,* se presser dans. ¶ *v.i,* se presser.

throttle, *n,* (*Mot. &c*) papillon des gaz, *m. at full* ~, à pleins gaz. *open the* ~, mettre les gaz. ¶ *v.t,* étrangler.

through, *pr,* à travers; (*time*) pendant, durant; (*by, from*) par; (*thanks to*) grâce à; (*because of*) à cause de. *go* ~, (*place*) traverser; (*door*) passer par, franchir; (*fig: pockets &c*) fouiller. ¶ *ad,* à travers; (*completely*) jusqu'au bout. *all night* ~, toute la nuit. *be* ~ [*with*], avoir fini [avec]. *get* ~ (*exam*), être reçu. *wet* ~, trempé. ¶ *a,* (*train*) direct. ~**out,** *pr,* partout dans; pendant tout. ¶ *ad,* partout; tout le temps.

throw, *n,* jet; (*dice: game*) tour, *m.* ~*-in* (*Foot.*), remise en jeu, *f.* ¶ *v.t,* jeter, lancer; (*hurl*) projeter; (*pottery*) tourner; (*fig.*) rejeter (sur); (*P party*) organiser; (*P upset*) déconcerter; (*kiss*) envoyer. ~ **about,** ~ **around,** éparpiller. ~ *one's weight around,* se faire important. ~ **away,** (*rubbish*) jeter; (*fig: life &c*) gâcher; (*money, chances*) perdre. ~ **back,** rejeter; (*ball &c, image*) renvoyer; (*head*) rejeter en arrière. ~ **down,** jeter [à terre, par t.]; (*weapons*) déposer. ~ **off,** se débarrasser de. ~ **on,** (*log*) ajouter; (*clothes*) enfiler à la hâte. ~ **open,** (*door &c*) ouvrir tout grand. ~ **out,** jeter dehors; (*rubbish*) jeter; (*pers.*) mettre à la porte; (*heat*) émettre; (*calculations*) fausser. ~ **over,** abandonner, laisser tomber. ~ **up,** (*vomit*) vomir; (*arms*) lever; (*object*) lancer en l'air; (*job*) abandonner. ~**er,** *n,* lanceur, euse.

thrush, *n,* grive, *f;* (*Med.*) muguet, *m.*
thrust, *n,* (*gen., Mil., Mech.*) poussée, *f;* (*stab*) coup, *m;* (*energy*) dynamisme, *m.* ¶ *v.t.ir,* pousser brusquement; (*stick &c*) enfoncer; (*shove*) fourrer *P* (dans). ~ *aside,* écarter brusquement; (*suggestion*) rejeter violemment. ~ *upon* (*job &c*), imposer à. ~ *o.s upon s.o,* imposer sa présence à qn.
thud, *n,* bruit sourd, *m.* ¶ *v.i,* faire un b. s; (*fall*) tomber avec un b. s.
thug, *n,* voyou, *m.*
thumb, *n,* pouce, *m. be all ~s,* avoir deux mains gauches. *be under s.o's ~,* être sous la coupe de qn. *have s.o under one's ~,* mener qn à la baguette. *~nail sketch,* croquis sur le vif, *m.* *~screw,* vis à papillon, *f;* (*Hist.*) poucettes, *f.pl.* ¶ *a,* de pouce. ¶ *v.t,* feuilleter. ~ *a lift,* faire du stop. ~ *one's nose,* faire un pied de nez.
thump, *n,* bruit lourd & sourd; (*with fist &c*) grand coup de poing &c. ¶ *v.t,* (*pers.*) asséner un coup à; taper sur; cogner à. ¶ *v.i,* taper, cogner; (*heart*) battre fort.
thunder, *n,* tonnerre; (*din*) fracas, *m.* *~bolt,* coup de foudre; (*fig.*) c. de tonnerre, *m.* ~ *clap,* coup de tonnerre, *m.* ~ *cloud,* nuage orageux, *m.* *~storm,* orage, *m.* *~struck,* abasourdi. ¶ *v.i,* (*Met. & guns*) tonner; (*hooves*) retentir. ~**ous,** *a,* ~ *applause,* tonnerre d'applaudissements, *m.* ~**y,** *a,* orageux.
Thursday, *n,* jeudi, *m.*
thus, *ad,* ainsi. ~ *far,* jusqu'ici.
thwart, *n,* (*Naut.*) banc [de nage], *m.* ¶ *v.t,* contrecarrer; (*pers.*) croiser. *be ~ed,* essuyer un échec.
thy *O, a,* ton, ta, tes.
thyme, *n,* thym; (*wild*) serpolet, *m.*
thyroid, *a,* thyroïde.
tiara, *n,* diadème, *m.*
tibia, *n,* tibia, *m.*
tic, *n,* tic, *m.*
tick[1] (*insect*) *n,* tique, *f.*
tick[2], *n,* (*clock*) tic-tac; (*P fig.*) instant, *m;* (*mark*) coche, *f. just a ~! P,* un instant! ¶ *v.t,* cocher; (*answer*) marquer juste. ¶ *v.i,* faire tic-tac. ~ *off,* cocher; (*tell off*) passer un savon à. ~ *over,* (*Mot.*) tourner au ralenti. ~**er** *P, n,* cœur, palpitant *P, m. ticking-off P,* attrapade *P, f.*
ticket, *n,* (*gen.*) billet; (*bus, métro*) ticket; (*left luggage*) bulletin, *m;* (*label*) étiquette; (*library*) carte, *f;* (*parking fine*) P.V., papillon, *m.* ~ *collector,* contrôleur, *m.* ~ *office,* guichet, *m.* ¶ *v.t,* étiqueter.
ticking, *n,* toile [à matelas], *f.*
tickle, *v.t. & i,* chatouiller; (*P amuse*) faire rire. *~d pink,* heureux comme tout. ¶ *n,* chatouillement, *m.* **ticklish,** *a,* (*pers.*) chatouilleux; (*position*) délicat.
tidal, *a,* qui a des marées. ~ *wave,* raz-de-marée, *m.inv;* (*fig.*) immense vague, *f.*
tiddler *P, n,* petit poisson, *m.* **tiddly** *P, a,* éméché. *~winks,* jeu de puce, *m.*
tide, *n,* marée, *f;* (*fig: events &c*) cours, courant, *m. go against the ~,* aller à contre-courant. *~way,* chenal de marée, *m.* ¶ *v.t, tide s.o over* [*a difficulty*], dépanner qn.
tidiness, *n,* proprete, *f,* bon ordre, *m.*
tidings, *n.pl,* nouvelles, *f.pl.*
tidy, *a,* (*room, papers &c*) bien rangé, en ordre; (*neat*) net; (*pers.*) soigné, ordonné; (*mind*) méthodique; (*P sum*) rondelet. ¶ *v.t. & i,* (*& ~ up*) ranger. ~ *o.s up,* s'arranger.
tie, *n,* (*link*) lien, *m;* (*on curtain &c*) attache; (*neck*) cravate; (*Mus.*) liaison; (*Voting*) égalité de voix; (*Sport*) égalité [de points], *f;* match nul, *m.* *~-break,* (*Ten.*) tie-break, *m.* *~pin,* épingle de cravate, *f.* ¶ *v.t.ir,* (*knot*) nouer; (*fasten*) attacher; (*shoes*) lacer; (*ribbon*) faire un nœud à; (*link & Mus.*) lier. ~ *o.s. in knots* (*fig.*), s'embrouiller. ¶ *v.i,* faire match nul; (*runners*) être ex aequo. ~ **back,** (*hair*) retenir [en arrière]. ~ **down,** ~ **on,** attacher. ~ **in with,** *v.t,* combiner avec; *v.i,* être lié à; correspondre à. ~ **up,** (*parcel*) ficeler; (*horse*) attacher. *be ~d up,* (*busy*) être très pris.
tier, *n,* (*gen., cake*) étage; (*stadium*) gradin, *m.*
Tierra del Fuego, *n,* la Terre de Feu.
tiff, *n,* prise de bec *P, f.*
tiger, *n,* tigre, *m.* ~ *lily,* lis tigré, *m.* ~ *moth,* écaille, *f.*
tight, *a,* (*Knit., knot, credit*) serré; (*rope &c*) raide, tendu; (*garment*) collant, ajusté; (*shoes, space*) juste, étroit; (*control*) rigoureux, strict; (*schedule*) très chargé; (*budget, money*) juste, serré; (*P drunk*) soûl *P. get ~ P,* se soûler *P.* ~ *corner,* situation difficile, *f.* ~[*-fisted*], dur à la détente *P.* *~-fitting,* ajusté; (*lid &c*) qui ferme bien. *~rope,* corde raide, *f.* *~rope walker,* funambule, *m, f.* ~**en,** *v.t,* tendre; ajuster; (*screw &c*) resserrer; (*restrictions*) renforcer. ~ *one's belt* (*lit., fig.*), se serrer la ceinture. ¶ *v.i, & ~ up,* se tendre; se reserrer; être renforcé. ~[**ly**], *ad,* (*close, grasp*) bien; (*squeeze*) très fort. ~**ness,** *n,* étroitesse; dureté; sévérité, *f.* **tights,** *n,* collant, *m.*
tigress, *n,* tigresse, *f.*
tile, *n,* (*roof*) tuile, *m;* (*floor*) carreau, *m. be out on the ~s P,* faire la bringue *P.* ~ *floor*[*ing*], carrelage, *m.* ¶ *v.t,* couvrir de tuiles; carreler.
till[1] *V* **until. till**[2], *n,* caisse, *f.*
till[3], *v.t,* labourer.
tiller, *n,* barre [du gouvernail], *f.*
tilt, *n,* inclinaison, *f. at full ~,* ventre à terre. ¶ *v.t,* incliner; (*hat*) rabattre (*over,* sur). ¶ *v.i,* pencher, être incliné.
timber, *n.* bois de construction, *m;* (*trees*)

arbres, *m.pl;* (*Naut.*) membrure, *f.* ~-*merchant,* négociant en bois, *m.* ~ *yard,* chantier de bois, *m.* ~**ed,** *a,* (*land*) boisé; (*house*) en bois.

time, *n,* (*gen.*) temps; (*point*) moment, *m;* (*by clock*) heure; (*occasion, Math.*) fois; (*era*) époque; (*Mus.*) mesure; (*P prison*) prison, *f.* ~ *after* ~, maintes & maintes fois. *a long* ~, longtemps. *as* ~ *goes by,* avec le temps. *at* ~*s,* parfois, par moments. *at one* ~, à un moment donné. *at that* (or *the*) ~, à ce moment-là. *at this* ~, en ce moment. *at the present* ~, actuellement. *behind the* ~*s,* vieux jeu. *between* ~*s,* entre temps. *each* ~, chaque fois. *for a* ~, pendant un certain temps. *for the* ~ *being,* pour le moment. *4* ~*s 2 is 8,* 4 fois 2 font 8. *from* ~ *to* ~, de temps en temps. *in former* ~*s,* dans le temps, jadis. *on* ~, à l'heure. *only* ~ *will tell,* qui vivra verra. *some* ~ *ago,* il y a quelque temps. *what* ~ *is it?* quelle heure est-il? ~ *& motion study,* étude des cadences, *f.* ~ *bomb,* bombe à retardement, *f.* ~-*consuming,* qui prend du temps. ~ *exposure* (*Phot.*), pose, *f.* ~-*honoured,* consacré par l'usage. ~*keeper* (*Sport*), chronométreur, *m.* ~-*lag,* décalage, *m.* ~ *limit,* limite de temps, *f,* délai, *m.* ~-*saving, a,* qui fait gagner du temps; *n,* gain de temps, *m.* ~*server,* opportuniste, *m,f.* ~ *sheet,* feuille de présence, *f.* ~ *signal,* signal horaire, *m.* ~ *switch,* minuteur, *m;* (*for lights*) minuterie, *f.* ~ *table,* (*Rly &c*) horaire; (*Sch.*) emploi du temps, *m.* ~ *zone,* fuseau horaire, *m.* ¶ *v.t,* (*work*) minuter; (*race*) chronométrer; (*visit &c*) fixer (*for,* à). **timeliness,** *n,* à-propos, *m.* **timely,** *a,* à propos. **timer,** *n,* (*Cook.*) compte-minutes, *m.inv;* (*with sand*) sablier, *m.*

timid†, *a,* timide, peureux. ~**ity,** *n,* timidité, *f.* **timorous,** *a,* timoré.

timing, *n,* (*of event*) date; heure, *f;* (*Mot.*) réglage de l'allumage; (*Sport &c*) chronométrage; (*musician*) sens de rythme; (*actor*) minutage, *m.* ~ *mechanism,* (*bomb*) mouvement d'horlogerie; (*Elec.*) minuteur, *m.*

tin, *n,* étain, *m;* (*can*) boîte *f. cake* ~ (*oven*), moule à gateaux, *m. roasting* ~, plat à rotir, *m.* ~*foil,* papier aluminium, *m.* ~ *hat,* casque, *m.* ~-*opener,* ouvre-boîtes, *m.* ~[*plate*], fer-blanc, *m.* ~ *soldier,* soldat de plomb, *m.* ~ *tack,* semence, *f.* ¶ *v.t,* (*food*) mettre en conserve. *tinned food,* conserves, *f.pl. tinned salmon,* saumon en boîte, *m.*

tinder, *n,* amadou, *m.*

tinge, *n,* teinte, *f.* ¶ *v.t,* teinter.

tingle, *v.i,* picoter; fourmiller; (*ears*) tinter; (*fig. thrill*) frissonner. ¶ *n.* & **tingling,** picotement, fourmillement; frisson, *m.*

tinker, *n,* rétameur, *m;* (*gipsy*) romanichel, le.

tinkle, *v.i,* tinter. ¶ *n.* & **tinkling,** tintement. *m*

tinny, *a,* (*sound*) métallique; (*pej: car &c*) de camelote *P.*

tinsel, *n,* lamelles brillantes *f.pl;* (*fig*) clinquant, *m.*

tint, *n,* teinte, *f.* ¶ *v.t,* teinter.

tiny, *a,* minuscule. ~ *bit,* tout petit peu, *m.*

tip¹, *n,* bout, *m;* (*pointed*) pointe, *f;* (*ferrule*) embout; (*Bil. cue*) procédé, *m.* ~**ped,** *a,* (*cigarette*) filtre, *inv.*

tip², *n,* (*gratuity*) pourboire; (*advice*) conseil; (*information*) tuyau *P, m.* ¶ *v.t,* donner un pourboire à; (*winner*) pronostiquer. ~ *off,* donner un tuyau à; prévenir.

tip³, *n,* (*rubbish*) décharge, *f.* ¶ *v.t,* incliner, renverser. ~ [*out*], (*liquid*) verser; (*rubbish*) déverser. ¶ *v.i,* pencher. ~ *up,* (*tilt*) pencher; (*overturn*) basculer; se renverser. *'no* ~*ping',* 'défense de déposer des ordures.' ~**lorry,** ~**per,** *n,* [camion (*m*) à] benne, *f.*

tipple, *v.i,* picoler *P.* **tippler,** *n,* picoleur, euse *P.*

tipster, *n,* pronostiqueur, *m.*

tipsy, *a,* éméché, pompette *P.*

tiptoe (on), sur la pointe des pieds.

tiptop, *a,* excellent, parfait.

tirade, *n,* diatribe, *f.*

tire, *v.t.* (& *i.*), (se) fatiguer, (se) lasser. ~ *out,* épuiser, crever *P. be* ~*d of sth,* en avoir assez de qch. ~**dness,** *n,* fatigue, lassitude, *f.* ~**less,** *a,* infatigable. ~**some,** *a,* ennuyeux, fâcheux. **tiring,** *a,* fatigant.

tissue, *n,* tissu, *m;* mouchoir en papier, *m.* ~ *paper,* papier de soie, *m.*

tit, *n,* (*bird*) mésange, *f;* (*P* breast*) nichon *P*,* téton *P*,* sein, *m.* ~ *for tat,* un prêté pour un rendu.

titbit, *n,* (*food*) friandise, *f.*

titillate, *v.t,* titiller, chatouiller.

titivate, *v.t.* (& *i*), (se) pomponner.

title, *n,* titre, *m;* (*Law*) titres, *m.pl.* (*Cine &c*) *credit* ~*s,* générique, *m.* ~ *deed,* titre de propriété. ~ *holder,* détenteur, trice du titre. ~ *page,* page de t., *f.* ~**d,** *a,* titré.

titmouse, *n,* mésange, *f.*

titter, *v.i,* rire bêtement.

tittle-tattle, *n,* cancans, *m.pl,* commérage, *m.*

titular, *a,* titulaire, en titre.

to, *pr,* (*gen.*) à; (*direction*) à, vers, en, chez; (*of the hour*) moins. ~ *be,* être. ~ *read,* lire. ~ *France,* en France. ~ *Canada,* au Canada. ~ *Paris,* à Paris. *the road* ~ *Rome,* la route de Rome. *10* ~ *1* (*bet*), 10 contre 1. *count* ~ *10,* compter jusqu'à 10. *from town* ~ *town,* de ville en ville. *go* ~ *& fro,* (*pers.*) aller & venir; (*pace*) faire les cent pas. ~ *& from movement,* va-et-vient, *m. push the door* ~, fermer la porte. *here's* ~ *you!* à la vôtre!

toad, *n,* crapaud, *m.* ~*stool,* champignon [vénéneux], *m.* **toady,** *n,* flagorneur, euse. ¶ *v.i,* ~ *to,* flagorner. ~**ing,** *n,* flagornerie, *f.*

toast, *n,* pain grillé, toast; (*health*) toast, *m. on*

~, sur canapé. *a slice of* ~, un toast; une tartine grillée. ~ *rack,* porte-toast, *m.inv.* ¶ *v.t,* (*bread*) faire griller; (*health*) porter un toast à; (*victory &c*) arroser. ~**er,** *n,* grille-pain, *m.*

tobacco, *n,* tabac, *m.* ~ *pouch,* blague à t., *f.* **tobacconist,** *n,* marchand, e de tabac. ~*'s shop,* [bureau de] tabac, *m.*

toboggan, *n,* toboggan, *m;* luge, *f.*

today, *ad.* & *n,* aujourd'hui, *m.* ~ *week, fortnight,* d'aujourd'hui en huit, en quinze.

toddle, *v.i,* (*child*) marcher à pas hésitants. (*P*) ~ *off,* filer *P.* **toddler,** *n,* tout(e) petit(e).

to-do, *n,* toute une histoire.

toe, *n,* doigt [de pied], orteil; (*shoe, sock*) bout, *m.* ~ *the line* (*fig.*), se plier aux règlements. ~*cap,* bout renforcé. ~*nail,* ongle du pied, *m.*

together, *ad,* ensemble; à la fois, en même temps; (*Mus.*) à l'unisson. ~ *with,* avec, en compagnie de, ainsi que.

toil, *n,* travail, labeur, *m.* ¶ *v.i,* peiner.

toilet, *n,* toilette, *f;* (*lavatory*) toilettes, *f.pl;* waters, *m.pl.* ¶ *a,* (*bag, soap, water*) de toilette. ~ *paper,* papier hygiénique, *m.* ~ *roll,* rouleau de p. h., *m.* ~**ries,** *n.pl,* articles de toilette, *m.pl.*

token, *n,* marque, témoignage; (*phone &c*) jeton; (*voucher*) bon, *m. book, record* ~, chèque-livre, -disque, *m. gift* ~, bon-cadeau, *m.* ¶ *a,* symbolique.

tolerable, *a,* tolérable; passable. **tolerably,** *ad,* passablement. **tolerance & toleration,** *n,* tolérance, *f.* **tolerant,** *a,* tolérant. **tolerate,** *v.t,* tolérer; (*heat, pain*) supporter.

toll[1], *n,* (*gen., Mot.*) péage; (*number*) nombre, *m.* ~ *road,* route à péage, *f.*

toll[2], *v.t.* & *i,* sonner.

tom: ~*boy,* garçon manqué, *m.* ~ [*cat*], matou, *m.* ~*foolery,* âneries, *f.pl.* ~*tit,* mésange charbonnière, *f.*

tomato, *n,* tomate, *f.* ~ *sauce,* sauce t., *f.*

tomb, *n,* tombe, *f,* tombeau, *m.* ~*stone,* pierre tombale, *f.*

tome, *n,* tome, volume, *m.*

tommy gun, *n,* mitraillette, *f.*

tomorrow, *ad.* & *n,* demain, *m.* ~ *morning,* demain matin. ~ *night,* ~ *evening,* demain soir.

tomtom, *n,* tam-tam, *m.*

ton, *n,* tonne, *f* (UK = 1016 kilos; metric = 1000 kilos); (*Naut.*) tonneau, *m,* tonne.

tone, *n,* (*gen: sound, colour, Mus.*) ton, *m;* (*Mus: instrument*) sonorité; (*Tel., Radio &c*) tonalité, *f;* (*muscles &c*) tonus, *m. be* ~*-deaf,* ne pas avoir d'oreille. ¶ *v.i,* s'harmoniser (*with,* avec). ~ *down,* (*colour*) adoucir; (*fig.*) atténuer. ~ *up,* tonifier.

tongs, *n,* pinces; (*coal*) pincettes, *f.pl;* (*sugar*) pince à sucre, *f;* (*curling*) fer [à friser], *m.*

tongue, *n,* (*gen., language*) langue; (*shoe*) languette, *f;* (*bell*) battant, *m.* ~ *in cheek,* ironiquement. ~*-tied,* muet.

tonic, *a,* tonique; remontant. ~ *water,* Schweppes, *m.* ¶ *n,* (*Med. & drink*) tonique, remontant, *m;* (*Mus.*) tonique, *f.*

tonight, *ad,* ce soir, cette nuit.

tonsil, *n,* amygdale, *f.* **tonsillitis,** *n,* amygdalite, *f.*

tonsure, *n,* tonsure, *f.* ¶ *v.t,* tonsurer.

too, *ad,* trop; (*also*) aussi; (*besides*) en plus, en outre. ~ *long,* (*length*) trop long; (*time*) trop [longtemps]. ~ *much,* ~ *many,* trop; trop de. *eat* ~ *much,* t. manger. ~ *much butter,* t. de beurre.

tool, *n,* outil; (*fig.*) instrument, *m. the* ~*s of one's trade,* les outils de son métier. ~*box,* boîte à outils, *f.* ~*kit,* trousse à o., *f.* ~*maker,* outilleur *m.* ~*shed,* cabane à outils, *f.* ~**ed,** *a,* (*leather*) repoussé; (*silver*) ciselé.

tooth, *n,* dent, *f.* ~ & *nail,* avec acharnement; bec et ongles dehors. ~*ache,* mal de dents, *m;* (*violent*) rage de dents, *f.* ~*brush,* brosse à dents, *f.* ~*paste,* pâte dentifrice, *f.* ~*pick,* cure-dents, *m.* ~*powder,* poudre dentifrice, *f.* ~**less,** *n,* édenté.

top[1], *n,* (*toy*) toupie, *f.*

top[2], *n,* (*pile, street, wall &c*) haut; (*hill, head, tree*) sommet; (*container*) dessus; (*lid*) couvercle; (*list &c*) tête, *f;* (*profession*) plus haut point; (*bottle*) bouchon, *m,* capsule, *f;* (*pen*) capuchon; (*bus*) étage supérieur; (*Sch.*) premier, *m. at the* ~ *of one's voice,* à tue-tête. *from* ~ *to bottom,* de fond en comble. *from* ~ *to toe,* de la tête aux pieds. *go over the* ~ *Mil.*), monter à l'assaut. ¶ *a,* (*shelf, drawer*) du haut; (*Mus.*) le plus haut; (*step, storey, paint: coat*) dernier; (*rank &c*) premier; (*score &c*) [le] meilleur. ~*coat,* pardessus, *m.* ~ *hat,* haut-de-forme, *m.* ~*-heavy,* trop lourd du haut; (*fig.*) mal équilibré. ~ *job,* poste prestigieux, *m.* ~ *marks* (*fig.*), vingt sur vingt. ~*most,* le plus haut. ~*-secret,* ultrasecret. ~*side,* gîte [à la noix], *m.* ~*soil,* couche arable, *f.* ¶ *v.t,* (*exceed*) dépasser; (*list &c*) être en tête de. ~ *up,* remettre; (*Mot.*) remettre de l'eau &c dans. ~**less,** *a,* (*costume*) sans haut; (*girl*) aux seins nus. ~ *swimsuit,* monokini *P, m.*

topaz, *n,* topaze, *f.*

topic, *n,* sujet, thème, *m.* ~**al,** *a,* d'actualité. ~**ality,** *n,* actualité, *f.*

topography, *n,* topographie, *f.*

topple (& ~ *over*) *v.i.* & *t,* culbuter.

topsyturvy, *ad,* sens dessus dessous.

torch, *n,* lampe de poche, torche électrique, *f,* (*flaming*) flambeau, *m.* ~*light tattoo,* retraite aux flambeaux, *f.*

torment, *n,* supplice, *m.* ¶ *v.t,* tourmenter. ~*ed*

by, torturé par. **tormentor,** *n,* persécuteur, trice.
tornado, *n,* tornade, *f.*
torpedo, *n,* torpille, *f.* ~ *boat,* [bateau] torpilleur, *m.* ¶ *v.t,* torpiller.
torpid, *a,* engourdi. **torpor,** *n,* torpeur, *f.*
torrent, *n,* torrent, *m. in ~s,* à torrents. **~ial,** *a,* torrentiel.
torrid, *a,* torride.
torso, *n,* torse; (*Art*) buste, *m.*
tortoise, *n,* tortue, *f.* ~*shell,* écaille [de t.], *f.*
tortuous†, *a,* tortueux. **torture,** *n,* torture, *f,* supplice, *m.* ¶ *v.t,* torturer; mettre au supplice. **torturer,** *n,* tortionnaire, bourreau, *m.*
toss, *n,* (*throw*) lancement, *m;* (*from horse*) chute, *f.* ¶ *v.t,* (*ball*) lancer; (*head &c*) rejeter en arrière; (*pancake*) faire sauter; (*horse*) désarçonner; (*bull*) projeter en l'air; (*waves*) ballotter. ¶ *v.i,* (*pers.*) s'agiter; (*boat*) tanguer; (*trees*) se balancer. ~ *off,* (*drink*) avaler d'un coup. ~ [*up*], (*coin*) jouer à pile ou face; (*Sport*) tirer au sort.
tot[1], *n,* tout(e) petit(e) enfant; (*drink*) petit verre, *m,* goutte, *f.*
tot[2], *v.t,* (*&* ~ *up*) faire le total de.
total†, *a,* (*gen.*) total; complet; (*sum*) global. ¶ *n,* total, *m. grand* ~, somme globale, *f.* ¶ *v.t,* faire le total de; (*sum*) s'élever à. **~itarian,** *a. & n,* totalitaire, *m,f.* **totalizer, totalizator,** *n,* totalisateur; (*Turf*) pari mutuel, *m.*
totter, *v.i,* chanceler; s'ébranler.
toucan, *n,* toucan, *m.*
touch, *n,* (*sense, pianist, typist*) toucher; (*act*) contact; (*light*) frôlement, *m;* (*artist*) touche, *f;* (*sun*) petit coup, *m;* (*small amount*) tout petit peu; (*Rugby, Foot.*) touche. *keep in* ~ *with s.o,* rester en contact avec qn. *be out of* ~, ne plus être au courant. ~*-down,* (*land*) atterrissage &c, *m.* ~*line,* ligne de touche, *f.* ~*-type,* taper au toucher. ¶ *v.t,* toucher (*with,* de); frôler; (*fig.*) toucher à; (*topic*) effleurer; (*equal*) égaler. ~ *s.o for a loan P,* taper qn *P.* ¶ *v.i,* se toucher. ~ **on,** (*subject*) effleurer. ~ **down,** atterrir; (*sea*) amerrir; (*moon*) alunir. ~ **up,** retoucher. **~ed,** *a,* (*moved*) touché (de); (*P mad*) toqué *P.* **~iness,** *n,* susceptibilité, *f.* **~ing,** *a. & pr,* touchant. **~y,** *a,* susceptible.
tough†, *a,* (*pers*) robuste, résistant; (*mentally*) solide; (*hard*) dur; (*substance*) solide, résistant; (*meat*) dur; (*task*) fatigant, pénible, rude; (*problem*) épineux; (*struggle*) acharné; (*regulation*) sévère. ~ *luck!* pas de veine! manque de pot! *P;* (*too bad*) tant pis pour vous! *a* ~ [*guy*] *P,* un dur *P. get* ~ *with,* se montrer dur envers. **~en,** *v.t,* (*pers.*) endurcir; (*substance*) renforcer. **~ness,** *n,* résistance; solidité; dureté, *f;* caractère fatigant &c; acharnement, *m;* sévérité *f.*
tour, *n,* (*journey*) voyage; (*of town &c*) tour, *m;* visite; (*by team &c*) tournée; (*walking, cycling*) randonnée, *f.* ~ *of duty* (*Mil. &c*), ronde, *f.* ~ *of inspection,* tournée d'inspection, *f.* ¶ *v.t,* visiter. *go* ~*ing,* faire du tourisme. **~ing** *&* **~ism,** *n,* tourisme, *m.* **~ist,** *n,* touriste, *m,f.* ¶ *a,* (*ticket &c*) touriste, *inv;* (*guidebook, attraction, season*) touristique; (*industry*) du tourisme. ~ *agency,* agence de tourisme, *f.* ~ *office,* syndicat d'initiative, *m.*
tournament, *n,* tournoi, *m.*
tourniquet, *n,* tourniquet, garrot, *m.*
tousle, *v.t,* ébouriffer.
tout, *n,* racoleur; (*Turf*) pronostiqueur; (*ticket*) revendeur [de billets], *m.* ¶ *v.t,* vendre [avec insistance]; revendre. ~ *for,* (*customers*) racoler.
tow[1], *v.t,* (*boat, car*) remorquer; (*caravan*) tirer; (*barge*) haler. ¶ *n, on* ~, en remorque. ~*boat,* remorqueur, *m.* ~*line,* ~*rope,* cable de remorque, *m.* ~*path,* chemin de halage, *m.*
tow[2], *n,* filasse, *f.* ~*-headed,* aux cheveux filasse.
toward[s], *pr,* (*gen.*) vers; (*in attitude*) envers, à l'égard de, vis-à-vis de.
towel, *n,* serviette [de toilette], *f;* (*for hands*) essuie-mains; (*for glasses*) essuie-verres, *m.inv;* (*tea-*~) torchon, *m.* ~ *rail,* porte-serviettes, *m.* **towelling,** *n,* tissu éponge, *m.*
tower, *n,* tour, *f;* (*church*) clocher, *m.* ~ *block,* tour [d'habitation]. ~ *of strength,* grand soutien. ¶ *v.i,* s'élever très haut. ~ *above,* dominer. **~ing,** *a,* imposant. ~ *rage,* colère noire, *f.*
town, *n,* ville, *f. in* ~, *into* ~, en ville. *in the* ~, dans la v. *go out on the* ~, faire la bombe *P.* ~ *clerk,* secrétaire de mairie, *m.* ~ *council,* conseil municipal, *m.* ~ *hall,* mairie, *f,* hôtel de ville, *m.* ~ *house,* maison en ville, *f.* ~*-planner,* urbaniste, *m,f.* ~*-planning,* urbanisme, *m.* **~ship,** bourgade, *f.* **townspeople,** *n.pl,* citadins, *m.pl.*
toxic, *a,* toxique. **toxin,** *n,* toxine, *f.*
toy, *n,* jouet, *m.* ¶ *a,* petit, miniature; (*trumpet*) d'enfant. ~ *with,* jouer avec; (*idea*) caresser. ~*shop,* magasin de jouets, *m.*
trace, *n,* trace, *f;* (*Harness*) trait, *m.* ¶ *v.t,* (*draw*) tracer; (*with paper*) décalquer; (*find*) retrouver. ~ *s.o,* suivre la trace de qn. ~ *back,* faire remonter. **~r,** *n,* (*Biochem.*) traceur, *m;* (*bullet*) balle traçante. **~ry,** *n,* (*on window*) réseau, *m;* (*frost*) dentelles, *f.pl.* **tracing,** *n,* calque; calquage, *m.* ~*-paper,* papier-calque, *m.*
track, *n,* (*trail: animal, pers.*) trace, piste; (*radar, bullet &c*) trajectoire, *f;* (*path*) chemin, *m;* (*Sport, tape*) piste; (*record*) plage; (*Rly*) voie, *f;* rails, *m.pl;* (*tractor*) chenille, *f. be on the right* ~, être sur la bonne route. *be on the wrong* ~, faire fausse route. *keep* ~ *of,*

(*pers.*) suivre la trace de; (*fig.*) rester en contact avec. *make ~s P*, filer *P*. *~suit*, survêtement, *m*. ¶ *v.t*, suivre la trace de; s. la trajectoire de; (*prey*) traquer. *~ down*, (*prey, cause*) dépister. **~er,** *n*, poursuivant, e; (*Hunt.*) traqueur, *m*. *~ dog*, chien policier, *m*.

tract[1] (*pamphlet*), *n*, tract, *m*.

tract[2], *n*, (*land*) étendue, *f*; (*digestive*) appareil, *m*. **~able,** *a*, (*pers.*) accommodant, docile; (*material*) malléable. **traction,** *n*, traction, *f*. *~ engine*, locomobile, *f*. **tractor,** *n*, tracteur, *m*.

trade, *n*, commerce; (*job*) métier, *m*. ¶ *a*, commercial. *~ deficit*, balance commerciale déficitaire. *f*. *~ discount*, remise au détaillant, *f*. *~ figures*, résultats financiers, *m.pl*. *~ mark*, marque de fabrique, *f*. *~ name*, marque déposée. *~ price*, prix de gros, *m*. *~[s] union*, syndicat, *m*. *~[s] unionist*, syndicaliste, *m.f*. *~ winds*, alizés, *m.pl*. ¶ *v.i*, faire le commerce (*in*, de). ¶ *v.t*, échanger (*sth for sth.* qch contre qch). *~ in*, faire reprendre. *~-in*, reprise, *f*. **trader,** *n*, commerçant, e; négociant, e (*in*, en); (*street ~*) vendeur, euse de rue. **tradesman,** *n*, commerçant, *m*. **trading,** *n*, commerce, *m*. *~ centre*, centre de commerce, *m*.

tradition, *n*, tradition, *f*. **~al†,** *a*, traditionnel.

traffic, *n*, (*Mot.*) circulation; (*Naut., Aero., Rly. Tel., drugs*) trafic; (*trade gen.*) commerce, *m*. *~ controller* (*Aero.*), aiguilleur du ciel, *m*. *~ island*; refuge, *m*. *~ jam*, embouteillage, *m*. *~ lights*, feu[x], *m.*(*pl*). *~ police*, police de la route, *f*. *~ sign*, poteau de signalisation, *m*. *~ warden*, contractuel, le. **trafficker,** *n*, trafiquant, e.

tragedy, *n*, (*gen., Theat.*) tragédie, *f*. **tragic,** *a*, tragique. *~ actor, tress*, tragédien, ne. **~ally,** *ad*, tragiquement.

trail, *n*, (*tracks*) trace; (*Hunt.*) piste; (*of smoke &c*) traînée, *f*; (*path*) chemin, sentier, *m*. *~ blazer*, pionnier, ère. ¶ *v.t*, (*follow*) suivre la piste de; (*object*) traîner; (*Mot: tow*) tirer. ¶ *v.i*, traîner; (*plant*) ramper; (*Sport*) être en retard (*by*, de). *~ along*, se traîner. **~er,** *n*, (*Mot.*) remorque, *f*; (*Cine.*) film publicitaire, *m*.

train, *n*, (*Rly*) train, *m*; (*métro*) rame; (*events, entourage*) suite; (*camels &c*) file; (*powder*) traînée; (*dress*) traîne, *f*; (*thoughts*) fil, *m*. *~ ferry*, ferry-boat, *m*. *~ set*, train électrique, *m*. ¶ *v.t*, (*in work*) former; (*Sport*) entraîner; (*mind, ear &c*) exercer; (*voice*) travailler; (*animal*) dresser; (*gun &c*) braquer (*on*, sur); (*plant*) faire grimper. *~ s.o in a craft*, apprendre un métier à qn. ¶ *v.i*, recevoir sa formation (*as*, de); (*Sport*) s'entraîner; se préparer (à). **~ed,** *a*, compétent; (*profession*) qualifié; diplômé. **~ ee,** *n*, stagiaire, *m,f*. **~er,** *n*, (*Sport*) entraîneur, *m*; (*circus*) dresseur, euse; (*shoe*) chaussure de sport, *f*. **training,** *n*, formation, *f*; entraînement; dressage, *m*. *~ college*, (*gen.*) école professionnelle; (*teaching*) école normale, *f*. *~ course*, cours professionels, *m.pl*. *~ ship*, navire-école, *m*.

traipse around *P*, *v.i*, se balader *P*.

trait, *n*, trait, *m*.

traitor, tress, *n*, traître, *m*, traîtresse, *f*. **~ous,** *a*, traître. **~ously,** *ad*, en traître.

trajectory, *n*, trajectoire, *f*.

tram [car], *n*, tramway, *m*.

tramp, *n*, (*pers.*) vagabond, e; clochard, e. (*footsteps*) martèlement de pas, *m*; (*hike*) randonnée [à pied], *f*. *~ [steamer]*, tramp, *m*. ¶ *v.i*, marcher d'un pas lourd; (*hike*) cheminer. *~ the streets*, battre le pavé.

trample [on], [down], *v.t*, fouler [aux pieds], piétiner.

trampoline, *n*, trampolino, *m*.

trance, *n*, extase; (*hypnotic*) transe, *f*.

tranquil†, *a*, tranquille. **tranquillity,** *n*, tranquillité, *f*. **tranquillize,** *v.t*, mettre sous tranquillisants. **tranquillizer,** *n*, tranquillisant, *m*.

trans... *pref*: trans...

transact, *v.t*, traiter. **~ion,** *n*, transaction; (*in bank, shop*) opération, *f*.

transatlantic, *a*, transatlantique.

transcend, *v.t*, transcender; (*hopes*) surpasser. **~ent,** *a*, transcendant. **~ental,** *a*, transcendantal.

transcribe, *v.t*, transcrire. **transcript & transcription,** *n*, transcription, *f*.

transept, *n*, transept, *m*.

transfer, *n*, (*gen.*) transfert; (*bank*) virement, *m*; (*Pol: power*) passation; (*design*) décalcomanie, *f*. ¶ *v.t*, transférer; faire passer; (*affections, design &c*) reporter (*to*, sur). *~ the charges* (*Tel.*), téléphoner en P.C.V. ¶ *v.i*, être transféré. **~able,** *a*, transmissible.

transfiguration, *n*, transfiguration, *f*.

transfix, *v.t*, transpercer. **~ed** (*fig.*) *a*, cloué sur place.

transform, *v.t*, transformer (*into*, en). **~ation,** *n*, transformation, *f*. **~er,** *n*, transformateur, *m*.

transfuse, *v.t*, transfuser. **transfusion,** *n*, transfusion, *f*.

transgress, *v.t*, transgresser. ¶ *v.i*, pécher. **~or,** *n*. pécheur, eresse.

tran[s]ship, *v.t*, transborder. **~ment,** *n*, transbordement, *m*.

transient†, *a*, transitoire, passager.

transistor, *n*, transistor, *m*. **~ize,** *v.t*, transistoriser.

transit, *n*, transit, *m*. *in ~*, en transit. ¶ *a*, (*Mil: camp*) volant; (*Aero: lounge*) de transit. **~ion,** *n*, transition, *f*. **~ive†,** *a*, transitif. **~ory†,** *a*, transitoire.

translate, *v.t*, traduire; (*bishop*) transférer.

translation, *n,* traduction; (*Sch.*) version; (*bishop*) translation, *f.* **translator,** *n,* traducteur, trice.
translucence, *n,* translucidité, *f.* **translucent,** *a,* translucide.
transmission, *n,* transmission, *f.* ~ *shaft* (*Mot.*), arbre de t., *m.* **transmit,** *v.t,* transmettre; (*Radio, TV, Tel.*) & *v.i,* émettre. **transmitter,** *n,* transmetteur; émetteur, *m.* **transmitting,** *a,* émetteur.
transmute, *v.t,* transmuer.
transom, *n,* traverse, *f.*
transparency, *n,* transparence; (*Phot.*) diapositive, *f.* **transparent,** *a,* transparent.
transpire, *v.i,* (*Bot., Phys.*) transpirer; (*happen*) se passer. *it ~d that . . .,* on a appris par la suite que . . .
transplant, *v.t,* (*gen.*) transplanter; (*seedlings*) repiquer; (*Med.*) greffer. ¶ *n,* (*Med.*) transplantation, greffe, *f.*
transport, *n,* transport, *m.* ~ *café,* restaurant de routiers, *m.* ¶ *v.t,* transporter. **~ation,** *n,* transport, *m;* (*convicts*) transportation, *f.* **~er,** *n,* transporteur; (*for cars*) camion (*Mot.*) *ou* wagon (*Rly*) pour transport d'automobiles, *m.*
transpose, *v.t,* transposer.
transubstantiation, *n,* transsubstantiation, *f.*
transverse†, *a,* transversal.
transvestite, *n,* travesti, e.
trap, *n,* (*gen.*) piège; (*snare*) collet, *m;* (*~door*) trappe; (*P* mouth*) gueule *P*, f;* (*drain*) siphon, *m;* (*carriage*) charrette anglaise, *f.* *~shooting,* ball-trap, *m.* ¶ *v.t,* prendre au piège; (*pers., ship*) bloquer; (*object, finger*) coincer.
trapeze, *n,* trapèze, *m.* ~ *artist,* **trapéziste,** *m,f.*
trapper, *n,* trappeur, *m.*
trappings, *n.pl,* signes extérieurs, *m.pl.*
trash, *n,* (*goods*) camelote *P, f;* (*refuse*) ordures; (*nonsense*) blagues *P,* bêtises, *f.pl.* (*Am*) ~ *can,* poubelle, boîte à ordures, *f.* **~y,** *a,* sans valeur; (*goods*) de camelote *P.*
trauma, *n,* traumatisme, *m.* **~tic,** *a,* traumatisant.
travel, *n,* voyages, *m.pl.* *~-sickness,* mal de la route, de l'air, de mer. ¶ *v.i,* voyager; aller; (*news*) circuler. ~ *round the world,* faire le tour du monde. ~ *through,* parcourir. ¶ *a,* (*agent, book, film*) de voyages; (*organisation*) de tourisme. ~ *brochure,* dépliant touristique, *m.* **~ator,** *n,* tapis-roulant, *m.* **~ler,** *n,* voyageur, euse; représentant [de commerce], *m.* *~'s cheque,* chèque de voyage, *m.* **travelling,** *a,* (*clock, rug*) de voyages; (*circus*) ambulant. ~ *crane,* pont roulant.
traverse, *v.t,* traverser.
travesty, *n,* (*of justice*) simulacre, *m.*
trawl [net], *n,* chalut, *m.* ¶ *v.i,* pêcher au chalut. **~er,** *n,* chalutier, *m.* **~ing,** *n,* pêche au chalut, *f.*
tray, *n,* plateau; (*storage*) tiroir, *m,* corbeille, boîte, *f.* *~cloth,* napperon, *m.*
treacherous†, *a,* (*pers., action, fig.*) traître; perfide. **treachery,** *n,* traîtrise, *f.*
treacle, *n,* mélasse, *f.*
tread, *n,* pas; (*of stair*) giron, *m;* (*tyre*) chape, *f.* ¶ *v.i.ir,* marcher. ~ *carefully,* avancer avec précaution. ¶ *v.t,* (*path &c*) parcourir; (*grapes &c*) fouler. ~ *water,* nager sur place. *~mill,* routine ennuyeuse, *f.* **~le,** *n,* pédale, *f.*
treason, *n,* trahison, *f.* **~able,** *a,* (*act*) de trahison.
treasure, *n.* & ~ *trove,* trésor; *m;* (*fig: servant &c*) perle, *f.* ~ *hunt,* chasse au trésor, *f.* ¶ *v.t,* garder précieusement; (*memory &c*) chérir. **treasurer,** *n,* trésorier, ère. **treasury,** *n,* trésorerie, *f.* *T~* (*UK*), Ministère des Finances (*Fr.*) *m.*
treat, *n,* plaisir; (*gift*) cadeau, *m;* (*trip*) sortie, *f.* *it's my ~,* c'est moi qui paie *P.* ¶ *v.t. & i,* traiter. ~ *sth with care,* faire attention à qch. ~ *o.s to sth,* se payer qch *P.* **treatise,** *n,* traité, *m.* **treatment,** *n,* traitement, *m.* *have ~ for sth* (*Med.*), suivre un t. pour qch. **treaty,** *n,* traité, *m.*
treble, *a,* triple; (*Mus.*) de soprano. ~ *clef,* clef de sol, *f.* ¶ *ad,* trois fois plus que. ¶ *v.t. & i,* tripler.
tree, *n,* arbre, *m.* *~-covered,* boisé. *~-lined,* bordé d'arbres. *~top,* cime d'un arbre, *f.* ~ *trunk,* tronc d'arbre, *m.* **~less,** *a,* dépourvu d'arbres.
trefoil, *n,* trèfle, *m.*
trek, *n,* trajet long & pénible, *m.* ¶ *v.i,* voyager à la dure.
trellis, *n,* treillis, treillage, *m.*
tremble, *v.i,* trembler; (*with emotion*) frémir; (*ship &c*) vibrer. ¶ *n.* & **trembling,** *n,* tremblement, *m.* ¶ *a,* tremblant; frémissant.
tremendous, *a,* énorme; (*blow*) épouvantable; (*speed*) fou; (*P excellent*) du tonnerre *P.* **~ly,** *ad,* énormément, terriblement.
tremor, *n,* tremblement, *m.* **tremulous,** *a,* tremblant; timide.
trench, *n,* tranchée, *f,* fossé, *m.* *~coat,* trench-coat, *m.* **~ant,** *a,* tranchant, incisif.
trend, *n,* tendance. *f;* (*events*) cours, *m;* (*fashion*) mode, *f.* **trendy** *P, a,* (*pers., ideas*) dans le vent; (*clothes*) dernier cri, *inv.*
trepidation, *n,* vive inquiétude, *f.*
trespass, *n,* entrée non autorisée; (*O Rel.*) offense, *f.* ¶ *v.i,* s'introduire sans permission. ~ *on* (*fig*), abuser de; (*rights*) empiéter sur. *'no ~ing',* 'propriété privée'. **~er,** *n,* intrus, e. '*~s will be prosecuted',* 'défense d'entrer sous peine d'amende'.
trestle, *n,* tréteau, *m.* ~ *table,* table à tréteaux, *f.*
trial, *n,* (*Law*) jugement; procès; (*test*) essai, *m;*

(*pl: Foot. &c*) match de sélection, *m; (Athletics)* épreuve de s., *f; (sheepdog)* concours, *m; (hardship)* épreuve, *f; (worry)* souci, *m.* ~ *& error,* tâtonnements, *m.pl.* ~*s & tribulations,* tribulations, *f.pl.* ~ *balance,* balance d'inventaire, *f.* ~ *marriage,* mariage à l'essai, *m.* ~ *of strength,* épreuve de force, *f.* ~ *period,* période d'essai, *f.* ~ *run,* essai, *m; (fig.)* période d'essai, *f.*
triangle (*Geom. & Mus.*) *n,* triangle, *m.* **triangular,** *a,* triangulaire.
tribal, *a,* tribal; (*war*) entre tribus. **tribe,** *n,* tribu, *f.*
tribulation, *n,* tribulation, *f.*
tribunal, *n,* tribunal, *m.* ~ *of inquiry,* commission d'enquête, *f.*
tributary, *n,* affluent, *m.* **tribute,** *n,* tribut; hommage, *m.*
trice, *n,* clin d'œil, *m.*
trick, *n,* (*joke, conjuror*) tour, *m;* (*ruse*) ruse, *f;* (*skill*) truc *P* (*for doing,* pour faire), *m;* (*habit*) manie, [fâcheuse] habitude; (*Cards*) levée, *f.* ~ *of the light,* illusion d'optique, *f.* ~ *of the trade,* ficelle du métier, *f. do the* ~ *P,* faire l'affaire. *play a* ~ *on,* jouer un tour à. *dirty* ~, sale tour, *m.* ¶ *v.t,* (*deceive*) duper, attraper; (*swindle*) escroquer. ~**ery,** *n,* ruse, *f.*
trickle, *n,* filet, *m.* ~ *charger* (*Elec.*), chargeur à régime lent, *m.* ¶ *v.i,* couler goutte à goutte.
trickster, *n,* filou, *m.* **tricky,** *a,* (*situation*) délicat; (*pej. pers.*) rusé.
tricycle, *n,* tricycle, *m.*
trifle, *n,* bagatelle, *f,* rien; (*Cook.*) diplomate, *m.* ¶ ~ *with,* badiner avec, traiter à la légère. **trifling,** *a,* insignifiant.
trigger, *n,* (*gun*) détente, gachette, *f;* (*tool*) déclic, *m.* ~ [*off*], déclencher; provoquer.
trigonometry, *n,* trigonométrie, *f.*
trill, *n,* trille, *m.*
trilogy, *n,* trilogie, *f.*
trim, *a,* (*gen.*) net; soigné; (*house &c*) coquet. ¶ *n,* état, *m;* (*Naut: boat*) assiette; (*sails*) orientation, *f. in* [*good*] ~, (*garden &c*) en bon état; (*pers.*) en forme. ¶ *v.t,* (*hair*) rafraîchir; couper; (*hedge, wick*) tailler; (*nails*) rogner; (*boat*) équilibrer; (*decorate*) garnir, orner (*with,* de). **trimming,** *n,* garniture; (*edging*) bordure, *f;* (*pl: cuttings*) chutes, *f.pl;* (*pl: Cook.*) garniture; (*pl. fig.*) accessoires, *m.pl.*
trimaran, *n,* trimaran, *m.*
Trinidad, *n,* [l'île de] la Trinité.
trinity, *n,* trinité, *f.* (*Rel.*) *the T*~ *& T*~ *Sunday,* la Trinité.
trinket, *n,* colifichet, bibelot, *m.*
trio, *n,* trio, *m.*
trip, *n,* voyage, *m;* excursion, *f;* (*stumble*) faux pas; (*P drugs*) trip, *m.* ~*wire,* fil de détente, *m.* ~ [**up**], *v.t,* faire trébucher; faire un croc-en-jambe à; (*argument*) prendre en défaut; (*anchor*) déraper. ¶ *v.i,* trébucher; faire un faux pas; (*mistake*) gaffer *P.*
tripe, *n,* tripes; (*P nonsense*) bêtises, *f.pl.*
triple†, *a. & n,* triple, *m.* ¶ *ad,* trois fois plus que. ¶ *v.t. & i,* tripler. **triplets,** *n.pl,* triplé(e)s. **triplicate (in),** en trois exemplaires.
tripod, *n,* trépied, *m.*
tripper, *n,* excursionniste; touriste, *m,f.*
triptych, *n,* triptyque, *m.*
trite†, *a,* banal. ~**ness,** *n,* banalité, *f.*
triumph, *n,* triomphe; sentiment de t., *m.* ¶ *v.i,* triompher (*over,* de). ~**al,** *a,* triomphal, de triomphe. ~**ant,** *a,* triomphant, victorieux. ~**antly,** *ad,* triomphalement.
trivia, *n.pl,* futilités, *f.pl.* **trivial,** *a,* insignifiant; (*book &c*) banal. ~**ity,** *n,* caractère insignifiant, *m;* banalité, *f;* (*pl.*) futilités, *f.pl.*
Trojan, *a,* troyen; (*war*) de Troie.
trolley, *n,* (*supermarket &c*) chariot; (*2-wheeled*) diable, *m;* (*tea*) table roulante. ~*bus,* trolleybus, *m.*
trombone, *n,* trombone, *m.*
troop, *n,* (*gen.*) groupe, *m;* (*scouts*) troupe, *f;* (*pl: Mil.*) troupes. ~ *carrier,* (*Mot.*) transport de troupes, *m.* ~ *ship,* transport, *m.* ¶ ~ *in &c,* entrer &c en groupe. ~**er,** *n,* soldat de cavalerie, *m.*
trophy, *n,* trophée, *m.*
tropic, *n,* tropique, *m.* ~ *of Cancer, of Capricorn,* tropique du Cancer, du Capricorne. ~**al,** *a,* tropical.
trot, *n,* trot, *m. on the* ~ *P* (*fig.*), de suite. ¶ *v.i,* trotter. ~ *in &c,* entrer &c au trot. ~ *out,* (*excuse &c*) débiter. **trotter,** *n,* (*pig's*) pied [de porc], *m.* **troubadour,** *n,* troubadour, *m.*
trouble, *n,* (*difficulties*) ennuis, *m.pl;* (*effort*) mal; (*problem*) ennui, problème; (*worry*) souci, *m;* (*Pol.*) troubles, *m.pl. be in* ~, avoir des ennuis, être en difficulté. *cause* ~ *between,* causer des désaccords entre. *get into* ~, s'attirer des ennuis. *it's no* ~, ça ne me dérange pas. *it's not worth the* ~, ça ne vaut pas la peine. *take* ~ *over,* so donner du mal pour. *that's the* ~*!* c'est ça l'ennui! *what's the* ~*?* qu'est-ce qu'il y a? ~*-free,* sans ennuis *ou* problèmes. ~*maker,* provocateur, trice. ~*shooter* (*Ind., Pol.*), conciliateur, *m.* ~*spot,* point chaud, *m.* ¶ *v.t,* (*bother*) déranger; gêner; (*worry*) inquiéter; (*upset*) troubler; (*part of body*) faire souffrir. *I'm sorry to* ~ *you,* je suis désolé de vous déranger. ¶ *v.i,* se déranger; se donner la peine (*to do,* de faire). ~**d,** *a,* (*gen.*) inquiet; (*sleep, life*) agité; (*water*) trouble. ~**some,** *a,* ennuyeux; gênant; (*child*) difficile.
trough, *n,* (*dip*) creux; (*fig.*) point bas; (*drinking*) abreuvoir, *m;* (*feeding*) auge, *f.* ~ *of low pressure,* zone dépressionnaire, *f.*
trounce, *v.t,* rosser; (*Sport*) écraser.
troupe, *n,* troupe, *f.*
trousers, *n.pl & pair of* ~, pantalon, *m. who*

wears the ~? (P fig.) qui porte la culotte? *trouser-suit,* tailleur-pantalon, *m.*
trousseau, *n,* trousseau, *m.*
trout, *n,* truite, *f.* ~ *fishing,* pêche à la t., *f.* ~ *stream,* rivière à truites, *f.*
trowel, *n,* truelle; (*Hort.*) houlette, *f,* déplantoir, *m.*
truancy, *n,* absence non autorisée, *f.* **truant,** *n,* élève absent, e sans autorisation. *play* ~, (*Sch.*) manquer *ou* sécher les cours; faire l'école buissonnière.
truce, *n,* trêve, *f. call a* ~, faire la t.
truck[1], *have no* ~ *with,* refuser d'avoir affaire à.
truck[2], *n,* (*lorry*) camion; (*Rly*) wagon; (*hand*) chariot à bagages; (*2-wheeled*) diable, *m.* ~*load,* plein camion; wagon. ¶ *v.t,* camionner. ~ *driver* (*Am* ~*er*), *n,* camionneur, *m.*
truculence, *n,* agressivité, *f.* **truculent†,** *a,* brutal, agressif.
trudge, *v.i,* marcher péniblement. ~ *round,* traîner.
true, *a,* vrai; (*account &c*) véridique, exact; (*copy*) conforme; (*genuine*) vrai, véritable *before n;* (*faithful*) fidèle; (*straight: upright*) d'aplomb; (*Mus: note*) juste. *a* ~ *likeness of,* une parfaite ressemblance avec. ~ *love,* (*emotion*) le grand amour; (*lover*) bien-aimé, e. ~ *to life,* réaliste. ~ *to type,* conforme au type. *out of* ~, pas d'aplomb; (*wheel*) voilé.
truffle, *n,* truffe, *f.*
truism, *n,* truisme, *m.* **truly,** *ad,* vraiment, véritablement; fidèlement; (*truthfully*) franchement.
trump, *n,* (*Cards*), atout, *m. play* ~*s,* jouer atout. *turn up* ~*s,* (*fig.*) faire des merveilles. *one's* ~ *card* (*fig.*), son atout. ¶ *v.t,* couper. ~ **up** *v.t,* (*charge &c*) inventer, forger.
trumpet, *n,* trompette, *f.* ~ *call,* sonnerie de t., *f.* ¶ *v.t. & i.* (*fig.*) trompeter; (*elephant*) barrir. ~**er,** *n,* trompette, *m.*
truncate, *v.t,* tronquer.
truncheon, *n,* matraque, *f;* (*traffic duty*) bâton, *m.*
trundle, *v.t,* rouler, pousser. ~ *around,* trimbaler *P.*
trunk, *n,* (*Anat., Bot.*) tronc, *m;* (*elephant*) trompe; (*luggage*) malle, *f;* (*Am. Mot.*) coffre; (*pl: Swim.*) maillot de bain; (*pants*) slip [d'homme], *m.* ~ *call* (*Tel.*), communication interurbaine, *f.* ~ *line* (*Rly*), grande ligne. ~ *road,* [route] nationale, *f.*
truss, *n,* (*Build.*) ferme; (*hay &c*) botte; (*flowers*) grappe, *f;* (*Med.*) bandage herniaire, *m.* ¶ *v.t,* (*fowl*) trousser. ~ *up* (*prisoner*), ligoter.
trust, *n,* (*faith*) confiance (*in,* en); (*responsibility*) charge, *f;* (*Law*) fidéicommis; (*Com., Fin.*) trust, *m. put one's* ~ *in,* faire confiance à. *take sth on* ~, croire qn sur parole. ~ *fund,* fonds en fidéicommis, *m.* ¶ *v.t. & i.,* se fier à; (*entrust*) confier (à); (*hope*) espérer (*that,* que). ~ *to luck,* s'en remettre à la chance. ~**ed,** *a,* (*friend &c*) en qui l'on a toute confiance; (*method*) éprouvé. ~**ee,** *n,* fidéicommissaire; (*institution*) administrateur, trice. *the* ~*s,* le conseil d'administration. ~**ful** *or* ~**ing,** *a,* confiant. ~**worthy,** *a,* digne de confiance; (*account &c*) exact. ~**y,** *a,* fidèle.
truth, *n,* vérité, *f. in* ~, en vérité. *to tell the* ~ ... à vrai dire ... ~**ful,** *a,* vrai, véridique; (*pers.*) qui dit la vérité. ~**fulness,** *n,* véracité, *f.*
try, *n,* essai, *m;* tentative, *f;* (*Rugby*) essai. *it's worth a* ~, ça vaut le coup d'essayer. ¶ *v.t,* essayer, tâcher, tenter (de faire); chercher (à faire); (*test*) mettre à l'épreuve; (*Mach.*) tester; (*Law*) juger. ¶ *v.i,* essayer. ~ *on,* essayer. *a* ~*-on,* du bluff. ~ *out,* essayer; (*pers.*) mettre à l'essai. ~**ing,** *a,* pénible. *have a* ~ *time,* passer des moments difficiles.
tsar, *n,* tsar, *m.* ~**ina,** *n,* tsarine, *f.*
tub, *n,* (*gen.*) cuve, *f;* (*wash* ~) baquet, bac; (*bath*) baignoire, *f;* (*cream*) petit pot, *m.* ~**by** *P, a,* rondelet.
tuba, *n,* tuba, *m.*
tube, *n,* tube, *m;* (*tyre*) chambre à air, *f;* (*Rly*) métro, *m.* ~ *station,* station de métro, *f.* ~*-less,* sans chambre à air.
tuber & tubercle, *n,* tubercule, *m.* **tubercular,** *a,* tuberculeux. **tuberculin,** *n,* tuberculine, *f.* ~*-tested,* certifié. **tuberculosis,** *n,* tuberculose, *f.*
tubing, *n,* tubes, *m.pl.* **tubular,** *a,* tubulaire.
tuck, *n,* (*Need.*) rempli, *m.* ¶ *v.t,* mettre, faire un rempli dans. ~ *in, v.t,* (*flap &c*) rentrer; *v.i,* (*eat*) [bien] bouffer *P.* ~ *in!* tapez dedans! ~ *up* (*in bed*), border.
Tuesday, *n,* mardi, *m.*
tuft, *n,* touffe, *f.* ~**ed,** *a,* huppé.
tug, *n,* [petite] saccade, *f;* (*boat*) remorqueur, *m.* ~*-of-war,* lutte à la corde, *f;* (*fig.*) lutte acharnée. ¶ *v.t,* tirer [sur]; remorquer.
tuition, *n,* cours, *m.pl.*
tulip, *n,* tulipe, *f.* ~ *tree,* tulipier, *m.*
tulle, *n,* tulle, *m.*
tumble, *n,* (*fall*) chute, dégringolade; culbute, *f.* ¶ *v.i,* (*fall*) tomber; dégringoler (*downstairs,* dans l'escalier); (*trip*) trébucher (*over,* sur); faire culbute. ~ *to sth,* réaliser qch. ¶ *v.t,* renverser. ~ *down,* tomber en ruine. ~*down,* délabré. ~ *dryer,* séchoir à linge [à air chaud], *m.* **tumbler,** *n,* (*pers.*) acrobate, *m,f;* (*glass*) verre [droit]; (*plastic &c*) gobelet, *m.*
tummy, *P, n,* ventre, *m.* ~*-ache,* mal de ventre, *m.*
tumour, *n,* tumeur, *f.*
tumult, *n,* tumulte, *m.* **tumultuous†,** *a,* tumultueux.
tumulus, *n,* tumulus, *m.*
tuna, *n,* thon, *m.*
tundra, *n,* toundra, *f.*

tune, *n,* air, *m. be in, out of* ~, être accordé, désaccordé; (*singer*) chanter juste, faux. *change one's* ~ (*fig.*), changer de ton. *in* ~ *with* (*fig.*), en accord avec. ¶ *v.t,* (*Mus.*) accorder; (*Radio, TV*) régler (*to,* sur); (*Mot.*) régler. ~ *in,* se mettre à l'écoute (*to,* de). **tuner,** *n,* accordeur, *m;* (*Radio*) bouton de réglage, *m.* ~*-amplifier,* radio-ampli, *m.* **tuneful†,** *a,* harmonieux, mélodieux.
tungsten, *n,* tungstène, *m.*
tunic, *n,* tunique, *f.*
tuning, *n,* accordage, *m.* ~ *fork,* diapason, *m.*
Tunisia, *n,* la Tunisie. **Tunisian,** *a,* tunisien. ¶ *n,* Tunisien, ne.
tunnel, *n,* tunnel, *m;* (*Min.*) galerie, *f.* ¶ *v.i,* percer un tunnel.
tunny, *n,* thon, *m.*
turban, *n,* turban, *m.*
turbid, *a,* trouble.
turbine, *n,* turbine, *f.*
turbo.., *pref.* turbo... ~*prop,* turbopropulseur, *m.*
turbot, *n,* turbot, *m.*
turbulence, *n,* turbulence, *f.* **turbulent,** *a,* turbulent.
tureen, *n,* soupière, *f.*
turf, *n,* gazon, *m;* (*piece*) motte de g.; (*peat*) tourbe, *f. the* ~ (*Racing*), le turf. ~ *accountant,* bookmaker, *m.* ¶ *v.t,* gazonner. ~ *out P,* flanquer à la porte *P.*
turgid, *a,* turgide; (*fig.*) boursouflé.
Turk, *n,* Turc, *m,* Turque, *f.* **Turkey,** *n,* la Turquie. **Turkish,** *a,* turc. ~ *bath,* bain turc, *m.* ~ *delight,* loukoum, *m.* ~ *towel,* serviette-éponge, *f.* ¶ (*language*) *n,* le turc.
turkey, *n,* dinde, *f;* dindon, *m;* (*Cook.*) dinde. ~*-cock,* dindon.
turmeric, *n,* safran des Indes, *m.*
turmoil, *n,* trouble, *m,* agitation, *f.*
turn, *n,* (*movement*) tour; (*bend*) tournant, *m;* (*Theat.*) numéro, *m;* (*Med.*) crise, *f;* (*in game &c*) tour. *at every* ~, à tout instant. *done to a* ~, à point. *do s.o a bad* ~, jouer un mauvais tour à qn. *do s.o a good* ~, rendre service à qn. *it gave me quite a* ~, ça m'a fait un coup. *it's your* ~, c'est à vous. ~ *of phrase,* tournure, *f. one good* ~ *deserves another,* un prêté pour un rendu. *speak out of* ~, commettre une indiscrétion. *take it in* ~*s!* chacun à son tour! *take it in* ~*s to do,* faire à tour de rôle. ¶ *v.t,* (*gen.*) tourner; (*Mach.*) faire t.; (*car, thoughts, eyes &c*) tourner; (*steps*) diriger; (*gun &c*) braquer (*on,* sur); (*conversation, blow*) détourner (*to,* sur); (~ *over*) retourner; (*shape: wood &c*) tourner; (*change*) transformer (qch en qch); changer (qn en qch); (*translate*) traduire (en). ~ *the corner,* tourner le coin de la rue; (*fig.*) passer le moment critique. *he's* ~*ed 50,* il a 50 ans passés. ¶ *v.i,* (*handle &c, wind, milk*) tourner; (*tide*) changer de direction; (*weather*) changer; (*leaves*) jaunir; (*about* ~) faire demi-tour; (*ship*) virer; (*pers.*) se tourner; (*right round*) se retourner; (*road, river*) faire un coude. ~ *to drink,* se mettre à boire. *I don't know which way to* ~ (*fig.*), je ne sais plus où donner de la tête. ~ **aside,** (se) détourner. ~ **away,** (*gen.*) renvoyer; (*business*) refuser. ~ **back,** *v.t,* (*bedclothes &c*) rabattre; (*pers., vehicle*) faire faire demi-tour; (*clock*) reculer (*to,* jusqu'à); *v.i,* (*to page*) revenir (à). ~ **down,** rabattre; (*heat &c*) baisser; (*offer*) rejeter. ~ **in,** (*go to bed*) aller se coucher; (*hand over: object*) rendre; (*pers.*) livrer [à la police]. ~ **off,** tourner; (*light*) éteindre; (*gas, tap, radio &c*) fermer; (*engine*) arrêter. ~ **on,** (*tap*) ouvrir; (*electricity &c*) allumer; (*engine*) mettre en marche. ~ **out,** *v.t,* (*light, gas*) éteindre; (*pockets*) vider; (*room &c*) nettoyer à fond; (*pers.*) mettre à la porte; *v.i,* (*prove to be*) s'avérer; (*pers.*) se révéler. ~ **over,** (se) retourner; (*engine*) tourner au ralenti; (*book*) tourner la page. ~ **round,** se retourner; faire demi-tour; tourner. ~ *round & round,* tournoyer sur soi-même. ~ **up,** *v.t,* (*sleeve &c*) remonter; (*sth buried*) déterrer; (*find*) dénicher; (*volume*) augmenter; *v.i,* remonter; arriver; (*be found*) être retrouvé. ~*ed-up nose,* nez retroussé, *m.* ~**coat,** *n,* renégat, e. ~**ing,** *n,* (*side road*) route *ou* rue latérale, *f;* (*junction*) embranchement, *m.* ~*ing circle,* rayon de braquage, *m.* ~*ing point,* moment décisif, *m.* ~**over,** *n,* (*Com.*) chiffre d'affaires; (*of stock*) roulement; (*Cook.*) chausson *m.* ~**pike,** *n,* barrière de péage, *f.* ~**stile,** *n,* tourniquet, *m.* ~**table,** *n,* (*records*) plateau, *m;* (*Rly &c*) plaque tournante. ~**-up,** *n,* revers, *m.*
turnip, *n,* navet, *m.* ~ *tops,* fanes de navets, *f.pl.*
turpentine, *n,* térébenthine, *f.*
turquoise, *n.* (*& a,*) (*stone*) (de) turquoise, *f;* (*colour*) turquoise, *m.*
turret, *n,* tourelle, *f.*
turtle, *n,* tortue marine, *f. turn* ~, chavirer. ~*dove,* tourterelle, *f.* ~*necked,* à col montant.
Tuscan, *a,* toscan. ~**y,** *n,* la Toscane.
tusk, *n,* défense, *f.*
tussle, *n,* lutte, mêlée, *f.* ¶ *v.i,* se battre.
tutor, *n,* précepteur, trice (*in,* de); (*Univ.*) directeur, trice d'études. ¶ *v.t,* donner des cours particuliers à.
twaddle, *n,* balivernes, *f.pl.*
twang, *n,* (*voice*) nasillement; son vibrant, *m.* ¶ *v.t,* (*guitar*) pincer les cordes de. ¶ *v.i,* vibrer.
tweak, *v.t,* (*hair*) tirer; (*ear*) pincer, tordre.
tweed, *n,* tweed, *m.*
tweezers, *n.pl,* pinces; (*eyebrow*) pince à épiler, *f.*
twelfth†, *a. & n,* douzième, *m,f;* (*fraction*)

douzième, *m. T~ Night,* la fête des Rois *for phrases V* **fourth. twelve,** *a. & n,* douze, *m. ~month,* année, *f. ~ o'clock,* [*in the day*] midi; [*at night*] minuit, *m. for other phrases V* four.
twentieth, *a. & n,* vingtième, *m,f;* (*fraction*) vingtième, *m.* **twenty,** *a. & n,* vingt, *m. for phrases V* **forty.**
twerp *P, n,* andouille *P, f.*
twice, *ad,* deux fois. *~ as much,* deux fois plus.
twiddle, *v.t, ~* [*with*], tripoter. *~ one's thumbs,* se tourner les pouces.
twig¹, *n,* brindille, *f.*
twig² *P, v.t. & i.* piger *P.*
twilight, *n,* (*night*) crépuscule, *m;* (*morning*) aube naissante. *in the ~,* dans la pénombre.
twill, *n,* croisé, *m.*
twin, *a,* jumeau; (*town*) jumelé. ¶ *n,* jumeau, elle. *~set,* twin-set, *m.*
twine, *n,* ficelle, *f.* ¶ *v.t.* (*& i,*) (s')enrouler (*round,* autour de).
twinge, *n,* élancement, *m. ~ of sadness,* pincement au cœur, *m. ~ of conscience,* petit remords, *m.*
twining (*Bot.*) *a,* volubile.
twinkle, *n,* (*stars*) scintillement; (*eyes*) pétillement, *m.* ¶ *v.i,* scintiller; pétiller. *in the twinkling of an eye,* en un clin d'œil.
twirl, *n,* (*writing*) fioriture, *f;* (*body*) tournoiement, *m.* ¶ *v.t, ~* [*round*], faire tournoyer; (*moustache*) tortiller. ¶ *v.i,* tournoyer.
twist, *n,* (*in wire &c, of paper*) tortillon, *m;* (*yarn*) torsade, *f;* (*tobacco*) rouleau, *m;* (*Med.*) foulure, *f. give a new ~ to sth* (*fig.*), donner un tour nouveau à qch. *~ of the wrist,* tour de poignet, *m. round the ~ P,* dingue *P.* ¶ *v.t,* (*gen.*) tordre; (*turn*) tourner; (*coil*) enrouler (*round,* autour de); (*meaning*) déformer; (*P cheat*) rouler *P. ~* [*together*], entortiller. *~ one's ankle,* se fouler la cheville. *~ s.o's arm* (*fig.*), forcer la main à qn. ¶ *v.i,* s'enrouler. *~ & turn,* zigzaguer. *~ round* (*pers.*), se retourner. **~ed,** *a,* tordu; entortillé; foulé; (*mind*) tordu; (*logic*) faux. **~er** *P, n,* escroc, *m.*
twit¹, *v.t,* taquiner (sur, à propos de).
twit² *P, n,* andouille *P, f;* crétin, e.
twitch, *n,* (*face*) tic, *m;* (*jerk*) saccade, *f.* ¶ *v.i,* (*nose &c*) remuer; (*pers.*) avoir des mouvements convulsifs. ¶ *v.t,* tirer brusquement. *~* [*grass*], *n,* chiendent, *m.*
twitter, *n,* gazouillis, *m.* ¶ *v.i,* gazouiller.
two, *a. & n,* deux, *inv. & m. in ~s,* par deux. *in ~s & threes,* deux ou trois à la fois; par petits groupes. *put ~ & ~ together,* faire le rapport. *for other phrases V* **four.** *~-edged,* à double tranchant. *~-faced,* hypocrite. *~-legged,* bipède. *~-party* (*Pol.*), bipartite. *in a ~some,* à deux. *~-stroke* (*Mot.*) *n,* deux-temps, *m.inv. ~-way,* (*switch*) à deux départs; (*street*) à double sens; (*traffic*) dans les deux sens. **~fold,** *a,* double.
tycoon, *n,* gros homme d'affaires, magnat, *m.*
type, *n,* (*gen.*) type; (*sort*) genre, *m,* espèce, sorte; (*Typ.*) caractère, *m;* (*col.*) caractères, type, *m. he's not my ~,* ce n'est pas mon genre. *~face,* œil de caractère, *m. ~script,* manuscrit dactylographié, *m. ~set,* composer. *~setter,* compositeur, trice. *~setting,* composition, *f. ~writer,* machine à écrire, *f. ~writing,* dactylographie, *f. ~written,* tapé à la machine, dactylographié. ¶ *v.t,* (*class*) classifier; (*letter &c*) taper [à la machine]. ¶ *v.i,* taper à la machine.
typhoid, *n,* typhoïde, *f.*
typhoon, *n,* typhon, *m.*
typhus, *n,* typhus, *m.*
typical†, *a,* typique. *that's ~ of him,* c'est bien de lui. **typify,** *v.t,* être caractéristique de.
typing, *n,* dactylo, *f. ~ error,* faute de frappe, *f. ~ pool,* dactylo, *f.* **typist,** *n,* dactylo, *m,f.*
typographic(al), *a,* typographique. **typography,** *n,* typographie, *f.*
tyrannic(al†), *a,* tyrannique. **tyrannize [over],** tyranniser. **tyranny,** *n,* tyrannie, *f.* **tyrant,** *n,* tyran, *m.*
tyre, *n,* pneu, *m. ~ gauge,* manomètre [pour pneus], *m. ~ pressure,* pression de gonflage, *f.*
tyro, *n,* novice, *m,f.*

U

U, *n,* U, u, *m. ~-turn,* (*Mot.*) demi-tour, *m;* (*Pol. &c*) volte-face, *f.inv.*
ubiquitous, *a,* qui se trouve partout. **ubiquity,** *n,* ubiquité, *f.*
udder, *n,* mamelle, *f,* pis, *m.*
ugh, *i,* pouah!
ugliness, *n,* laideur, *f.* **ugly,** *a,* (*gen.*) laid, vilain, moche *P;* (*fig.*) répugnant. *as ~ as sin,* laid comme un singe.
ukulele, *n,* guitare hawaïenne, *f.*
ulcer, *n,* ulcère, *m.* **~ate,** *v.i,* s'ulcérer. **~ated,** *a,* ulcéreux.

Ulster, *n,* Ulster, *m.*
ulterior, *a,* ultérieur. ~ *motive,* arrière-pensée, *f.*
ultimate, *a,* ultime; final, définitif; (*authority*) suprême. **~ly,** *ad,* finalement; en fin de compte. **ultimatum,** *n,* ultimatum, *m.* **ultimo,** *ad,* du mois dernier.
ultra... *pref.,* ultra..., hyper... ~ *high frequency,* très haute fréquence, *f.* ~*marine,* bleu outremer, *m.* ~*-sensitive,* hypersensible. ~*violet,* ultra-violet.
umber, *n,* terre d'ombre, *f.*
umbilical, *a,* ombilical. ~ *cord,* cordon o., *m.*
umbrage, *n,* ombrage, *m.*
umbrella, *n,* parapluie; (*garden, beach*) parasol, *m.* ~ *stand,* porte-parapluies, *m.*
umlaut, *n,* tréma, *m.*
umpire, *n,* arbitre, *m.* ¶ *v.t,* arbitrer.
umpteen, *a,* je ne sais combien de. **~th,** *a,* énième.
unabashed, *a,* nullement décontenancé.
unabated, *a,* non diminué.
unable, *a,* incapable. *be ~ to,* être incapable de, ne pas pouvoir; (*swim &c*) ne pas savoir.
unabridged, *a,* intégral.
unacceptable, *a,* inacceptable; inadmissible.
unaccompanied, *a,* non accompagné; (*sing*) sans accompagnement; (*cello &c*) seul.
unaccountable†, *a,* inexplicable.
unaccustomed, *a,* peu habitué; inaccoutumé.
unacquainted with (to be), être ignorant de; ne pas connaître.
unadorned, *a,* sans ornement; (*truth*) pur.
unadulterated, *a,* pur; (*wine*) non frelaté; (*fig.*) pur & simple.
unaffected, *a,* (*pers.*) naturel, simple; (*behaviour*) sans affectation; non affecté (par).
unafraid, *a,* sans peur.
unalloyed, *a,* sans alliage; (*fig.*) parfait.
unalterable, *a,* inaltérable; (*rule*) invariable.
unambiguous, *a,* non ambigu. **~ly,** *ad,* sans ambiguité.
unambitious, *a,* sans ambition; (*aim*) modeste.
unanimity, *n,* unanimité, *f.* **unanimous,** *a,* unanime. **~ly,** *ad,* à l'unanimité.
unannounced, *a,* sans se faire annoncer.
unanswerable, *a,* sans réplique; irréfutable.
unappetizing, *a,* peu appétissant.
unappreciated, *a,* (*pers.*) méconnu; (*offer*) non apprécié. **unappreciative,** *a,* indifférent (*of,* à).
unapproachable, *a,* inabordable.
unarmed, *a,* (*combat*) sans armes; (*pers.*) non armé.
unasked, *a,* sans être invité.
unassailable, *a,* inattaquable.
unassisted, *a,* sans aide.
unassuming, *a,* sans prétentions.
unattached, *a,* non attaché; (*unmarried*) sans attaches; (*Mil.*) en disponibilité.
unattainable, *a,* inaccessible.
unattended, *a,* sans surveillance.
unattractive, *a,* (*thing*) peu attrayant; (*pers.*) peu sympathique.
unauthorized, *a,* non autorisé.
unavailable, *a,* indisponible. **unavailing,** *a,* inutile, vain.
unavoidable†, *a,* inévitable.
unaware of (to be), ignorer. **unawares,** *a,* (*catch s.o*) au dépourvu; (*do sth*) inconsciemment.
unbalanced, *a,* déséquilibré.
unbandage, *v.t,* débander.
unbearable†, *a,* insupportable.
unbeatable, *a,* imbattable. **unbeaten,** *a,* (*army*) invaincu; (*record*) non battu.
unbecoming, *a,* (*dress*) peu séyant; (*behaviour*) inconvenant.
unbelievable†, *a,* incroyable. **unbeliever,** *n.* & **unbelieving,** *a,* incrédule, *m,f.*
unbend, *v.t.ir,* redresser. ¶ *v.i.ir,* se détendre. **~ing,** *a,* inflexible.
unbias[s]ed, *a,* impartial.
unbleached, *a,* écru.
unblemished, *a,* sans tache.
unblock, *v.t,* (*pipe &c*) déboucher; (*road*) dégager.
unblushing, *a,* éhonté. **~ly,** *ad,* sans rougir.
unbolt, *v.t,* déverrouiller.
unborn, *a,* (*child*) qui n'est pas encore né; (*generation*) à venir, futur.
unbound (*book*) *a,* non relié.
unbounded, *a,* sans bornes, illimité.
unbreakable, *a,* incassable.
unbridled, *a,* débridé.
unbroken, *a,* intact; (*sleep*) ininterrompu; (*line*) continu; (*record*) non battu; (*horse*) non dressé.
unburden oneself, s'épancher (*to s.o,* avec qn).
unbusinesslike, *a,* (*trader*) peu commerçant; (*fig: pers.*) qui manque de méthode.
unbutton, *v.t,* déboutonner.
uncalled for, *a,* (*remark*) déplacé; injustifié.
uncanny, *a,* étrange, mystérieux; inquiétant; (*resemblance, knack*) troublant.
uncared for, *a,* (*appearance*) négligé; (*child*) délaissé; (*garden*) à l'abandon.
unceasing, *a,* incessant. **~ly,** *ad,* sans cesse.
unceremoniously, *ad,* sans cérémonie.
uncertain, *a,* incertain. **~ly,** *ad,* d'une manière hésitante. **~ty,** *n,* incertitude, *f.*
unchallengeable, *a,* incontestable. **unchallenged,** *a,* incontesté.
unchangeable, unchanging, *a,* immuable, invariable. **unchanged,** *a,* inchangé.
uncharitable, *a,* peu charitable.
uncharted, *a,* inexploré.
unchecked, *a,* non vérifié; (*script*) non relu; (*advance*) sans opposition.
unchristian, *a,* peu chrétien.
uncivil†, *a,* incivil. **~ized,** *a,* barbare.

unclaimed, *a,* non réclamé.
unclassified, *a,* non classé.
uncle, *n,* oncle, *m.*
unclean, *a,* sale, malpropre; (*Rel.*) impur.
unclouded, *a,* sans nuages.
uncoil, *v.t.* (*& i,*) (se) dérouler.
uncomfortable, *a,* (*thing, position*) inconfortable; (*time*) désagréable; (*pers.*) qui n'est pas à l'aise; (*uneasy*) mal à l'aise (*about sth,* au sujet de qch). *have an ~ time,* passer un mauvais quart d'heure.
uncommitted, *a,* non engagé; (*attitude*) neutraliste.
uncommon†, *a,* rare, peu commun; singulier.
uncommunicative, *a,* peu communicatif.
uncomplaining, *a,* résigné. **~ly,** *ad,* sans se plaindre.
uncompleted, *a,* inachevé.
uncomplicated, *a,* peu compliqué, simple.
uncomplimentary, *a,* peu flatteur.
uncompromising, *a,* intransigeant.
unconcealed, *a,* non dissimulé.
unconcern, *n,* calme; sang-froid, *m;* indifférence, *f.* **~ed,** *a,* imperturbable (*by,* devant); indifférent (à).
unconditional, *a. &* **~ly,** *ad,* sans condition.
unconfirmed, *a,* non confirmé.
uncongenial, *a,* (*pers.*) peu sympathique; (*place &c*) peu agréable.
unconnected, *a,* (*ideas*) décousu; (*facts &c*) sans rapport.
unconscious†, *a,* inconscient; (*dead faint*) sans connaissance. **~ness,** *n,* inconscience; perte de connaissance, *f.*
unconstitutional†, *a,* inconstitutionnel.
uncontested, *a,* incontesté; (*seat*) non disputé.
uncontrollable, *a,* (*child &c*) indocile, indiscipliné; (*emotion*) irrésistible. **uncontrolled,** *a,* effréné.
unconventional, *a,* peu conventionnel.
unconvinced, *a,* non convaincu. **unconvincing,** *a,* peu convaincant.
uncooked, *a,* cru.
uncooperative, *a,* peu coopératif.
uncork, *v.t,* déboucher.
uncorrected, *a,* non corrigé.
uncouple, *v.t,* découpler; détacher.
uncouth, *a,* grossier, fruste.
uncover, *v.t,* découvrir.
uncrossed (*cheque*) *a,* non barré.
unction, *n,* onction, *f.*
uncultivated & uncultured, *a,* inculte.
uncurl, *v.t,* dérouler; (*legs*) déplier.
uncut, *a,* (*gen.*) non coupé; (*gem*) non taillé; (*diamond*) brut.
undamaged, *a,* non endommagé; intact.
undated, *a,* sans date, non daté.
undaunted, *a,* intrépide; non intimidé.
undecided, *a,* indécis; incertain.
undefeated, *a,* invaincu.
undefined, *a,* (*word*) non défini; (*feeling*) vague.
undelivered, *a,* non livré; non distribué.
undemonstrative, *a,* peu démonstratif.
undeniable†, *a,* indéniable, incontestable.
under, *pr,* sous; au-dessous de; (*less than*) moins de; (*fig.*) sous; (*according to*) selon; conformément à. *~ there,* là-dessous. *~ my orders,* sous mes ordres. *~ the circumstances,* dans les circonstances. ¶ *ad,* au-dessous. ¶ *comps:* (*inadequately*) sous-; (*junior*) sous-, aide-. **~cooked, ~ done,** *a,* pas assez cuit; saignant. **~-developed,** *a,* trop peu développé; (*Econ.*) sous-développé. **the ~dog,** *n,* l'opprimé, *m.* **~estimate,** *v.t,* sous-estimer. **~-exposure,** n, (*Phot.*) sous-exposition, *f.* **~-gardener,** *n,* aide-jardinier, *m.* **~nourish,** *v.t,* sous-alimenter. **~paid,** *a,* mal payé. **~populated,** *a,* sous-peuplé. **~ privileged,** *a,* défavorisé; (*Econ.*) économiquement faible. **~rate, ~value,** *v.t,* mésestimer, sous-estimer. **~secretary,** *n,* sous-secrétaire, *m,f.* **~sexed,** *a,* de faible libido. **~staffed,** *a,* à court de personnel.
underclothing, *n,* sous-vêtements, *m.pl.*
undercoat, *n,* couche de fond, *f.*
undercover, *a,* secret, clandestin.
undercurrent, *n,* courant [sous-marin]; (*fig.*) c. sous-jacent, vague de fond, *m.*
undercut, *v.t.ir,* vendre moins cher que.
underfelt, underlay, *n,* thibaude, *f.*
undergarment, *n,* sous-vêtement, *m.*
undergo, *v.t,* subir; (*treatment*) suivre.
undergraduate, *n,* étudiant, e.
underground, *a,* (*gen.*) souterrain; (*fig.*) secret; clandestin. ¶ *ad,* sous [la] terre. *go ~,* (*fig.*) prendre le maquis. ¶ *n,* (*Rly*) métro, *m;* (*Mil., Pol.*) résistance, *f.*
undergrowth, *n,* broussailles, *f.pl.*
underhand, *a,* sournois; en sous-main; (*Sport*) par en dessous.
underlie, *v.t,* être à la base de.
underline, *v.t,* souligner.
underling, *n,* subalterne, sous-fifre *P, m.*
underlying, *a,* sous-jacent; (*principle*) fondamental.
undermentioned, *a,* ci-dessous.
undermine, *v.t,* saper; (*health*) miner.
underneath, *ad,* dessous; au-dessous. ¶ *pr,* sous.
underpass, *n,* (*pedestrian*) passage souterrain; (*Mot.*) p. inférieur.
underpin, *v.t,* étayer.
underrate, *v.t,* mésestimer.
underside, *n,* dessous, *m.*
undersigned, *a. & n,* soussigné, e.
understand, *v.t. & i. ir,* comprendre. *it is understood that,* il est entendu que. **~able,** *a,* compréhensible. *that's ~,* ça se comprend. **~ing,** *a,* (*pers.*) compréhensif; (*look &c*) bienveillant. ¶ *n,* compréhension, *f;* (*agreement*) accord; arrangement, *m. come to an*

~ *with*, s'entendre *ou* s'arranger avec.
understudy, *n*, doublure, *f.* ¶ *v.t*, doubler.
undertake, *v.t.ir*, (*task*) entreprendre; (*duty*) se charger de; s'engager (*to do*, à faire). **undertaker,** *n*, entrepreneur de pompes funèbres, *m.* **undertaking,** *n*, entreprise, *f;* (*promise*) engagement, *m. give an* ~, promettre.
undertone (in an), à mi-voix.
underwater, *a*, soumarin.
underwear, *n*, sous-vêtements, *m.pl.*
underworld, *n*, (*hell*) enfers, *m.pl;* (*criminal*) milieu, *m.*
underwrite, *v.t.ir*, (*Insce*) souscrire, s. pour; (*Fin.*) garantir. **underwriter,** *n*, souscripteur, *m.*
undeserved, *a*, immérité. ~**ly,** *ad*, indûment; sans l'avoir mérité. **undeserving,** *a*, peu méritant; indigne (*of*, de).
undesirable, *a.* & *n*, indésirable, *m,f.*
undetected (to go), passer inaperçu.
undeveloped, *a*, non développé; (*land*) inexploité.
undignified, *a*, sans dignité.
undiluted, *a*, non dilué; pur.
undischarged, *a*, (*bankrupt*) non réhabilité; (*debt*) non acquitté.
undisciplined, *a*, indiscipliné.
undiscriminating, *a*, qui manque de discernement.
undismayed, *a*, sans être découragé.
undisputed, *a*, incontesté.
undisturbed, *a*, (*papers &c*) non dérangé; (*sleep*) paisible; (*unworried*) sans inquiétude.
undivided, *a*, entier. *his* ~ *attention*, toute son attention.
undo, *v.t.ir*, défaire; (*good*) annuler. *come undone*, se défaire. ~**ing,** *n*, ruine, *f.*
undoubted†, *a*, indubitable.
undreamed of, *a*, insoupçonné.
undress, *v.t.* (& *i*,) (se) déshabiller.
undrinkable, *a*, imbuvable; (*harmful*) non potable.
undue, *a*, excessif.
undulate, *v.i*, onduler. **undulating,** *a*, onduleux; (*country*) vallonné.
unduly, *ad*, trop, excessivement.
undying, *a*, (*fig.*), éternel.
unearned, *a*, immérité. ~ *income*, rentes, *f.pl.*
unearth, *v.t*, déterrer. ~**ly,** *a*, sinistre, surnaturel; (*fig.*) incroyable. ~ *hour*, heure indue.
uneasiness, *n*, inquiétude, *f.* **uneasy,** *a*, inquiet; mal à l'aise, gêné; (*conscience*) non tranquille; (*sleep*) agité.
uneatable, *a*, immangeable.
uneconomical, *a*, peu économique; peu rentable.
uneducated, *a*, sans instruction.
unemployable, *a*, incapable de travail. **unemployed,** *a*, sans travail, en chômage. *the* ~, les chômeurs, *m.pl.* **unemployment,** *n*, chômage, *m.* ~ *benefit*, allocation de chômage, *f.*
unending, *a*, sans fin.
unenterprising, *a*, sans initiative.
unenviable, *a*, peu enviable.
unequal†, *a*, inégal. ~ *to* (*task*), pas à la hauteur de. **unequalled,** *a*, sans égal, sans pareil.
unequivocal, *a.* & ~**ly,** *ad*, sans équivoque.
unerring†, *a*, infaillible; sûr.
unethical, *a*, immoral.
uneven†, *a*, inégal. ~**ness,** *n*, inégalité, *f.*
unexceptionable, *a*, irréprochable.
unexpected, *a*, inattendu; inespéré. ~**ly,** *ad*, subitement; (*arrive*) à l'improviste.
unexplained, *a*, inexpliqué.
unexplored, *a*, inexploré.
unexpurgated, *a*, intégral.
unfailing, *a*, (*supply*) inépuisable; (*cure*) infaillible.
unfair†, *a*, injuste; (*play &c*) déloyal. ~**ness,** *n*, injustice; déloyauté, *f.*
unfaithful†, *a*, infidèle. ~**ness,** *n*, infidélité, *f.*
unfamiliar, *a*, inconnu, peu familier. *be* ~ *with*, mal connaître.
unfasten, *v.t*, défaire; détacher; desserrer.
unfavourable†, *a*, défavorable; (*moment*) inopportun.
unfeeling, *a*, insensible. ~**ly,** *ad*, sans pitié.
unfinished, *a*, inachevé.
unfit, *a*, (*pers.*) inapte (à); (*unworthy*) indigne (de); impropre (*for*, à); (*road*) impraticable. ~ *to drive*, pas en état de conduire. ~ *for habitation*, inhabitable.
unflattering, *a*, peu flatteur.
unfold, *v.t*, (*gen.*) déplier; (*arms*) décroiser; (*wings*) déployer; (*fig: plans*) exposer. ¶ *v.i*, (*plot*) se dérouler.
unforeseeable, *a*, imprévisible. **unforeseen,** *a*, imprévu.
unforgettable, *a*, inoubliable.
unforgivable†, *a*, impardonnable. **unforgiving,** *a*, implacable.
unfortunate†, *a*, (*gen.*) malheureux; (*event*) fâcheux, regrettable, triste. *how* ~ *!* quel dommage! ¶ *n*, malheureux, euse.
unfounded, *a*, sans fondement.
unfriendly, *a*, (*pers.*) froid; (*behaviour*) inamical; hostile.
unfulfilled, *a*, (*condition*) non rempli; (*promise*) non tenu; (*ambition*) non réalisé.
unfurl, *v.t*, déployer.
unfurnished, *a*, non meublé.
ungainly, *a*, gauche, dégingandé.
ungodly, *a*, impie. ~ *hour* (*fig.*), heure indue, *f.*
ungovernable, *a*, ingouvernable; (*anger*) irrépressible.
ungracious, *a*, peu gracieux. ~**ly,** *ad*, avec mauvaise grâce.
ungrammatical, *a*, incorrect, non grammatical.
ungrateful, *a*, ingrat. ~**ness,** *n*, ingratitude, *f.*

ungrudgingly, *ad,* de bon cœur.
unguarded, *a,* (*Mil.*) sans défense; (*remark*) irréfléchi; (*moment*) d'inattention.
unhappiness, *n,* tristesse, *f.* **unhappy,** *a,* (*pers*) malheureux, triste; mécontent; (*worried*) inquiet; (*event*) malheureux; regrettable.
unharmed, *a,* (*pers.*) indemne; (*thing*) intact.
unhealthy, *a,* (*pers.*) maladif; (*place &c*) malsain.
unheard of, *a,* inouï.
unheeded, *a,* (*warning*) négligé.
unhesitatingly, *ad,* sans hésitation.
unhindered, *a,* sans encombre.
unholy, *a,* impie; (*P mess*) épouvantable.
unhook, *v.t,* décrocher.
unhoped for, *a,* inespéré.
unhurt, *a,* indemne, sauf.
unhygienic, *a,* non hygiénique.
unicorn, *n,* licorne, *f.*
unidentified, *a,* non identifié. ~ *flying object* (*U.F.O.*), objet volant non identifié (O.V.N.I), *m.*
uniform, *a,* uniforme; (*colour*) uni. ¶ *n,* uniforme, *m. in* ~, en uniforme. *out of* ~, en civil. ~**ity,** *n,* uniformité, *f.* ~**ly,** *ad,* uniformément. **unify,** *v.t,* unifier.
unilateral†, *a,* unilatéral.
unimaginable, *a,* inimaginable. **unimaginative,** *a,* qui manque d'imagination.
unimpeded, *a,* sans entraves.
unimportant, *a,* sans importance.
unimpressed, *a,* peu impressionné.
uninhabitable, *a,* inhabitable. **uninhabited,** *a,* inhabité.
uninhibited, *a,* (*pers.*) sans inhibitions; (*urge*) non refréné.
uninitiated (the), *n.pl,* les non-initiés, *m.pl.*
uninjured, *a,* indemne.
uninsured, *a,* non assuré.
unintelligent, *a,* inintelligent. **unintelligible†,** *a,* inintelligible.
unintentional†, *a,* involontaire.
uninterested, *a,* indifférent. **uninteresting,** *a,* sans intérêt.
uninterrupted, *a,* ininterrompu. ~**ly,** *ad,* sans interruption.
uninvited, *a,* sans invitation. **uninviting,** *a,* peu attrayant; peu appétissant.
union, *n,* (*gen.*) union, *f;* (*Ind.*) syndicat, *m. U~ of Soviet Socialist Republics* (*U.S.S.R.*), Union des Républiques socialistes soviétiques (U.R.S.S.). ¶ *a,* (*leader*) syndical; (*office*) du syndicat. ~**ism,** *n,* syndicalisme, *m.* ~**ist,** *n,* syndicaliste; (*Pol.*) unioniste, *m,f.*
unique†, *a,* unique.
unisex, *a,* unisexe.
unison, *n,* unisson, *m. in* ~, à l'unisson.
unit, *n,* (*gen., Elec., Mil., Math. &c*) unité, *f;* groupe; (*furniture*) élément, *m. sink* ~, bloc-évier, *m.* ~ *price,* prix unitaire, *m.* ~ *trust,* société d'investissements, *f.* **unite,** *v.t,* (*join*) unir (*with,* à); (*unify*) unifier. ¶ *v.i,* s'unir; (*Ind., Fin.*) fusionner. **united,** *a,* uni; unifié. *U~ Kingdom,* Royaume-Uni, *m. U~ Nations* [*Organisation*] (*U.N.*[*O.*]), Organisation des Nations unies (O.N.U.), *f. U~ States* [*of America*] (*U.S.*[*A.*]), États-Unis, *m.pl.* **unity,** *n,* unité, *f.*
universal†, *a,* universel. **universe,** *n,* univers, *m.* **university,** *n,* université, *f.* ¶ *a,* universitaire; (*student*) d'université.
unjust†, *a,* injuste. **unjustifiable,** *a,* injustifiable. **unjustified,** *a,* injustifié.
unkempt, *a,* débraillé; (*hair*) mal peigné.
unkind, *a,* peu aimable; méchant; (*fate*) cruel. ~**ness,** *n,* manque de gentillesse, *m;* méchanceté, *f.*
unknown, *a,* inconnu; ignoré. ~ *person,* inconnu, e. ~ [*quantity*], [quantité] inconnue, *f.* ~ *to,* à l'insu de. *the* ~, l'inconnu, *m. the U~ Warrior,* le Soldat inconnu. **unknowing†,** *a,* inconscient.
unladylike, *a,* mal élevée; peu distinguée.
unlawful†, *a,* illégal, illicite.
unleavened, *a,* sans levain; (*bread*) azyme.
unless, *c,* à moins que...[ne]; à moins de; si (+ *neg*); sauf. ~ *I see him,* à moins que je [ne] le voie; à moins de le voir. ~ *I am mistaken,* si je ne me trompe [pas]. ~ *otherwise stated,* sauf indication contraire.
unlicensed, *a,* illicite; (*vehicle*) sans vignette; (*hotel &c*) non patenté pour la vente des spiritueux.
unlike, *a,* dissemblable, différent. ¶ *pr,* à la différence de. **unlikelihood,** *n,* improbabilité, *f.* **unlikely,** *a,* peu probable; (*news*) invraisemblable.
unlimited, *a,* illimité.
unlined, *a,* (*dress*) sans doublure; (*face*) sans rides; (*paper*) non réglé.
unload, *v.t,* décharger; (*Fin.*) se défaire de.
unlock, *v.t,* ouvrir.
unlooked for, *a,* inattendu.
unluckily, *ad,* malheureusement. **unlucky,** *a,* (*choice*) malheureux; (*pers.*) malchanceux; malencontreux; (*number*) qui porte malheur. *he's* ~, il n'a pas de chance.
unmade, *a,* (*bed*) défait; (*road*) non goudronné.
unmanageable, *a,* (*object*) peu maniable; (*child*) indocile, intenable.
unmanned, *a,* (*spacecraft*) inhabité.
unmarried, *a,* non marié; célibataire. ~ *mother,* mère célibataire.
unmask, *v.t,* démasquer.
unmentionable, *a,* dont on ne parle pas.
unmerciful†, *a,* impitoyable.
unmethodical, *a,* peu méthodique.
unmistakable, *a,* évident; indubitable; (*sound &c*) impossible de ne pas reconnaître. **unmistakably,** *ad,* manifestement.

unmitigated, *a,* pur; absolu; (*rogue*) fieffé; (*disaster*) total.
unmixed, *a,* sans mélange, pur.
unmounted, *a,* non monté.
unmoved, *a,* indifférent.
unmusical, *a,* (*pers.*) peu musicien; (*sound*) peu mélodieux.
unnatural, *a,* anormal; (*tastes*) dénaturé, contre nature.
unnecessary†, *a,* inutile; superflu.
unnerve, *v.t,* déconcerter.
unnoticed, unobserved, *a,* inaperçu. **unobservant,** *a,* inattentif.
unobstructed, *a,* non obstrué; (*view*) dégagé.
unobtainable, *a,* impossible à obtenir.
unobtrusive†, *a,* discret.
unoccupied, *a,* inoccupé; (*seat, zone*) libre.
unofficial, *a,* (*source*) officieux; (*visit*) privé. **~ly,** *ad,* officieusement.
unopened, *a,* non ouvert.
unopposed, *a,* sans opposition.
unorganized, *a,* inorganisé; mal organisé; (*pers.*) qui ne sait pas s'organiser.
unorthodox, *a,* peu orthodoxe.
unostentatious, *a.* & **~ly,** *ad,* sans ostentation.
unpack, *v.t,* (*case*) défaire; (*contents*) déballer. **~ing,** *n,* déballage, *m.*
unpaid, *a,* (*bill, &c*) impayé; (*debt*) non acquitté; (*leave*) non payé. *to work ~,* travailler gratuitement.
unpalatable, *a,* (*fact &c*) désagréable; (*food*) d. au goût.
unparalleled, *a,* sans pareil.
unpardonable, *a,* impardonnable.
unpatriotic, *a,* antipatriotique.
unperceived, *a,* inaperçu.
unperturbed, *a,* non déconcerté.
unpick, *v.t,* défaire.
unpin, *v.t,* détacher.
unplaced, *a,* (*horse*) non placé; (*athlete*) non classé.
unpleasant†, *a,* désagréable; déplaisant. **~ness,** *n,* caractère désagréable *ou* déplaisant; désaccord, *m,* frottements, *m.pl.*
unplug (*Elec.*), *v.t,* débrancher.
unpolished, *a,* non poli; (*shoes*) non ciré; (*manners, style*) peu raffiné.
unpolluted, *a,* non pollué.
unpopular, *a,* impopulaire. **~ity,** *n,* impopularité, *f.*
unpractical, *a,* peu pratique.
unprecedented, *a,* sans précédent.
unpredictable, *a,* (*gen.*) imprévisible; (*weather*) incertain.
unprejudiced, *a,* sans préjugés, impartial.
unpremeditated, *a,* non prémédité.
unprepared, *a,* (*pers.*) sans être préparé, au dépourvu; (*speech &c*) improvisé.
unprepossessing, *a,* peu engageant.
unpretentious, *a,* sans prétentions.
unprincipled, *a,* sans scrupules.
unprintable, *a,* impubliable.
unproductive, *a,* improductif.
unprofessional, *a,* contraire au code professionnel.
unprofitable, *a,* peu rentable; (*job*) peu lucratif; inutile.
unpronounceable, *a,* imprononçable.
unprotected, *a,* sans défense; (*exposed*) découvert.
unprovided-for, *a,* sans ressources.
unprovoked, *a,* sans provocation.
unpublished, *a,* inédit. **unpublishable,** *a,* impubliable.
unpunctual, *a,* peu ponctuel.
unpunished, *a,* impuni.
unqualified, *a,* non qualifié; (*profession*) non diplômé; inconditionnel; (*praise*) sans réserve.
unquestionable†, *a,* indiscutable. **unquestioning,** *a,* inconditionnel; (*belief*) aveugle.
unravel, *v.t,* (*threads*) démêler; (*cloth*) effiler; (*fig.*) débrouiller; (*plot*) dénouer.
unread, *a,* sans être lu. **~able,** *a,* illisible.
unreal, *a,* irréel. **~istic,** *a,* peu réaliste. **~ity,** *n,* irréalité, *f.*
unreasonable†, *a,* déraisonnable; excessif; (*price*) exagéré. **~ness,** *n,* déraison, *f.* **unreasoning,** *a,* irraisonnable.
unrecognizable, *a,* méconnaissable.
unrefined, *a,* (*sugar &c*) non raffiné; (*pers.*) fruste.
unrehearsed, *a,* impromptu, improvisé.
unrelenting†, *a,* implacable.
unreliable, *a,* (*pers.*) sur qui on ne peut pas compter; (*Mach.*) peu fiable; (*memory*) peu fidèle.
unremitting†, *a,* incessant, inlassable.
unremunerative, *a,* peu rémunérateur; p. lucratif.
unrepentant, *a,* impénitent.
unrequited, *a,* non partagé.
unreservedly, *ad,* sans réserve.
unrest, *n,* agitation, *f;* troubles, *m.pl.*
unrestrained, *a,* immodéré; effréné.
unrestricted, *a,* (*access*) libre; (*power &c*) illimité.
unrewarded, *a,* sans récompense.
unripe, *a,* vert; (*corn*) en herbe.
unrivalled, *a,* sans égal.
unroll, *v.t,* dérouler.
unruffled, *a,* calme; (*hair*) lisse.
unruly, *a,* indiscipliné.
unsaddle, *v.t,* desseller.
unsafe, *a,* dangereux, hasardeux; (*method*) peu sûr.
unsalable, *a,* invendable.
unsatisfactorily, *ad,* d'une manière peu satisfaisante. **unsatisfactory,** *a,* peu satisfaisant.
unsavoury, *a,* (*dish*) peu savoureux; (*subject*) répugnant; (*reputation*) équivoque.

unscathed, *a,* indemne.
unscientific, *a,* peu scientifique.
unscrew, *v.t,* dévisser. *come ~ed,* se d.
unscripted (*TV &c*) *a,* improvisé.
unscrupulous, *a,* (*pers.*) sans scrupules; (*act*) malhonnête. **~ly,** *ad,* sans scrupule.
unseasonable, *a,* hors de saison; (*weather*) pas de saison. **unseasoned** (*wood*) *a,* vert.
unseat, *v.t,* (*rider*) désarçonner.
unseaworthy, *a,* pas en état de naviguer.
unsecured, *a,* (*Fin.*) à découvert.
unseemly, *a,* inconvenant.
unseen, *a,* inaperçu. ~ [*translation*], version, *f.*
unselfish, *a,* (*pers.*) sans égoïsme; (*act*) désintéressé. **~ly,** *ad,* sans penser à soi. **~ness,** *n,* générosité, *f.*
unserviceable, *a,* inutilisable.
unsettle, *v.t,* perturber. **~d,** *a,* (*weather*) incertain; (*question*) indécis.
unshakable†, *a,* inébranlable.
unshaven, *a,* non rasé.
unshrinkable, *a,* irrétrécissable.
unsightliness, *n,* laideur, *f.* **unsightly,** *a,* laid.
unsigned, *a,* non signé.
unsinkable, *a,* insubmersible.
unskilful, *a,* malhabile, maladroit. **~ly,** *ad,* avec maladresse. **unskilled,** *a,* inexpérimenté; (*work*) de manœuvre. ~ *worker,* manœuvre, *m.*
unsociable, *a,* insociable.
unsocial, *a,* (*hours*) incommode.
unsold, *a,* invendu.
unsolicited, *a,* non sollicité.
unsolved, *a,* non résolu.
unsophisticated, *a,* naturel, simple.
unsound, *a,* (*roof*) en mauvais état; (*business &c*) peu solide; (*judgment*) mal fondé; (*investment*) hasardeux; (*policy, advice*) peu judicieux. *of ~ mind,* qui ne jouit pas de toutes ses facultés mentales.
unsparing, *a,* prodigue (*of,* de); (*cruel*) impitoyable. **~ly,** *ad,* (*give*) généreusement; (*work*) inlassablement.
unspeakable, *a,* indicible, indescriptible.
unspoiled, *a,* (*country*) qui n'est pas déparé; (*pers.*) qui reste simple.
unsporting, *a,* déloyal.
unstable, *a,* instable.
unstamped, *a,* (*letter*) non affranchie.
unsteady, *a,* (*structure*) instable; (*gait, voice*) mal assuré; (*rhythm*) irrégulier. *be ~ on one's feet,* ne pas très bien tenir sur ses jambes; (*from drink*) tituber, chanceler.
unstick, *v.t,* décoller. *come unstuck,* se décoller; (*P plan*) tomber à l'eau *P;* (*pers.*) tomber sur un bec *P.*
unstressed, *a,* inaccentué.
unsuccessful, *a,* (*visit*) infructueux; (*candidate*) refusé; (*marriage*) malheureux; (*writer, book*) manqué. *be ~,* ne pas réussir; échouer. **~ly,** *ad,* sans succès.
unsuitable, *a,* (*gen.*) qui ne convient pas; (*size &c*) qui ne va pas; peu approprié; (*time*) inopportun. *be ~ for,* ne pas convenir à; (*film &c*) ne pas être pour. **unsuited,** *a,* (*pers.*) inapte (*to,* a); (*thing*) impropre (à).
unsupported, *a,* (*gen.*) non soutenu; (*evidence*) non corroboré.
unsuspected, *a,* insoupçonné. **unsuspecting,** *a,* qui ne se doute de rien.
unsweetened, *a,* non sucré.
unswerving, *a,* inébranlable.
unsympathetic, *a,* indifférent (à).
untangle, *v.t,* démêler.
untaxed, *a,* (*income*) non imposable; (*goods*) exempt de taxes.
untenable, *a,* (*position &c*) intenable; (*assertion &c*) insoutenable.
unthinkable, *a,* impensable. **unthinking,** *a,* irréfléchi.
untidiness, *n,* désordre; (*habits*) manque d'ordre; (*dress*) débraillé, *m.* **untidy,** *a,* en désordre; (*pers.*) désordonné; (*clothes*) débraillé; (*hair*) ébouriffé; (*page, pupil*) brouillon.
untie, *v.t,* (*knot*) défaire; (*pers., legs*) détacher.
until, *pr,* jusqu'à. ~ *now,* jusqu'ici, jusqu'à présent. ~ *then,* jusque-là. *not ~,* pas avant. ¶ *c,* jusqu'à ce que + *subj;* en attendant que + *subj. wait ~ he comes back,* attendez qu'il revienne. *not ~,* ne... pas avant de; ne... pas avant que + *subj.*
untimely, *a,* (*death*) prématuré; (*remark*) inopportun.
untiring†, *a,* infatigable.
untold, *a,* (*wealth*) incalculable.
untouchable, *a. & n,* intouchable. **untouched,** *a,* (*unharmed: thing*) intact; (*pers.*) indemne; (*unmoved*) insensible (*by,* à).
untoward, *a,* fâcheux.
untrained, *a,* inexercé; (*animal*) non dressé.
untranslatable, *a,* intraduisible.
untravelled, *a,* (*country*) non parcouru; (*pers.*) qui n'a jamais voyagé.
untroubled, *a,* calme.
untrue, *a,* faux; (*lover*) infidèle.
untrustworthy, *a,* indigne de confiance; (*report*) douteux.
untruth, *n,* contrevérité, *f,* mensonge, *m.* **~ful,** *a,* (*pers.*) menteur; (*report*) mensonger.
untwist, *v.t,* détordre, détortiller.
unusable, *a,* inutilisable. **unused,** *a,* inutilisé; (*new*) neuf. ~ *to,* peu habitué à. **unusual,** *a,* exceptionnel; insolite, étrange. *it is ~ to see him here,* il est rare qu'on le voie ici. **~ly,** *ad,* exceptionnellement.
unutterable, *a,* indicible, indescriptible.
unvarnished, *a,* non verni; (*truth*) pur & simple.
unvarying, *a,* invariable.
unveil, *v.t,* dévoiler. **~ing,** *n,* inauguration, *f.*

unventilated, *a,* sans ventilation.
unvoiced, *a,* inexprimé.
unwanted, *a,* (*child*) non désiré; (*clothes*) superflu.
unwarranted, *a,* injustifié.
unwary, *a,* imprudent.
unwavering, *a,* inébranlable.
unwelcome, *a,* (*visitor*) inopportun; fâcheux.
unwell, *a,* indisposé, souffrant.
unwholesome, *a,* malsain.
unwieldy, *a,* difficile à manier.
unwilling, *a,* peu disposé, mal disposé (*to do,* à faire). **~ly,** *ad,* à contre-cœur. **~ness,** *n,* mauvaise volonté; répugnance, *f.*
unwind, *v.t,ir,* dérouler. ¶ *v.i,* se dérouler; (*P pers.*) se détendre.
unwise†, *a,* imprudent.
unwitting†, *a,* involontaire.
unwonted, *a,* inaccoutumé.
unworkable, *a,* impraticable.
unworldly, *a,* détaché de ce monde.
unworthy, *a,* indigne.
unwrap, *v.t,* défaire, ouvrir.
unwritten, *a,* non écrit; (*agreement*) verbal. ~ *law,* droit coutumier.
unyielding, *a,* (*pers.*) inflexible; opiniâtre.
up, *ad,* en haut, en l'air; (*risen*) debout, *inv,* levé; (*curtains &c*) posé; (*picture*) accroché; (*building*) construit; (*tent*) planté; (*flag*) hissé; (*notice*) affiché; (*sun*) levé; (*tide*) haut; (*river*) monté. ~ *above,* au-dessus (*sth,* de qch). ~ *& about,* sur pied & à l'ouvrage. *~-&-coming,* plein d'avenir. ~ *& down,* en haut & en bas; (*walk*) de long en large. ~ *north,* dans le nord. ~ *there,* là-haut. ~ *to,* jusqu'à; (*job*) à la hauteur de, capable de faire. ~ *to date,* (*news*) très récent; (*pers.*) à la page; moderne. *~ to now, here,* jusqu'ici. ~ *to there,* jusque-là. *~-to-the minute,* de dernière heure. *be ~ ,* (*prices &c*) avoir augmenté; (*level, temperature*) avoir monté; (*standard*) être plus élevé. *be ~ to sth,* manigancer qch. *be 2 goals ~ ,* mener de 2 buts. *go ~ ,* monter; (*river*) remonter. *it's ~ to you,* c'est à vous (*to,* de). *'this side ~ ',* 'haut'. *well ~ in* (*subject*), fort en, calé en. *what's ~ ?* (*wrong*) qu'est-ce qui ne va pas? (*happening*) qu'est-ce qu'il y a? *where are you ~ to?* où en êtes-vous? *~-beat* (*Mus.*), levé, *m.* *~date,* mettre à jour. *~grade,* (*pers.*) promouvoir; (*job*) revaloriser. *~stairs,* en haut. *~stream,* en amont; (*sail*) vers l'amont. *be slow on the ~take,* avoir l'esprit lent. *~tight P,* très tendu. *ups & downs,* hauts & bas, *m.pl.*
upbraid, *v.t,* reprocher.
upbringing, *n,* éducation, *f.*
upheaval, *n,* (*Geol.*) soulèvement; (*fig.*) bouleversement, *m;* (*in home*) remue-ménage, *m.*
uphill, *a,* (*road*) qui monte; (*task*) pénible. *go ~ ,* monter.
uphold, *v.t,* (*Law: verdict*) confirmer; (*law*) faire respecter. **~er,** *n,* défenseur, *m.*
upholster, *v.t,* rembourrer; garnir (*in,* de). **~er,** *n,* tapissier, ère. **~y,** *n,* garniture, *f.*
upkeep, *n,* entretien, *m.*
upland, *n,* [haut] plateau, *m.*
uplift, *v.t,* (*soul*) élever; (*pers.*) grandir.
upon, *pr,* sur; dessus. *V* **on.**
upper, *a,* (*gen.*) supérieur; (*part, floor*) du dessus, supérieur; (*place name*) haut. ~ *case,* haut de casse, *m.* ~ *circle* (*Theat.*), deuxième balcon, *m.* *~-class,* aristocratique. ~ *crust* (*fig.*), gratin *P, m.* *the ~ hand* (*fig.*), l'avantage, le dessus. ~ *income bracket,* tranche des revenues élevés, *f.* ~ *middle class,* haute bourgeoisie, *f.* ~ *school,* grandes classes. ¶ *n,* (*shoe*) empeigne, *f.* *be on one's ~s P,* manger de la vache enragée. **~most,** *a,* le plus haut, le plus élevé; (*on top*) en dessus. ¶ *ad,* en dessus.
upright, *a. & ad,* droit. ¶ *n,* (*door &c*) montant; (*goal-post*) montant de but, *m.* ~ *piano,* piano droit. **~ness,** *n,* droiture, honnêteté, *f.*
uprising, *n,* soulèvement, *m.*
uproar, *n,* tumulte, vacarme, tapage, *m.* **~ious†,** *a,* bruyant, tapageur.
uproot, *v.t,* déraciner, arracher.
upset, *a,* (*pers*) vexé; peiné; fâché; (*ill*) indisposé; (*stomach*) dérangé. ¶ *n,* remue-ménage; (*in plans &c*) renversement; (*emotional*) chagrin, *m.* ¶ *v.t,* (*overturn*) renverser; (*boat*) faire chavirer; (*fig: plans*) déranger; (*pers.*) vexer; faire de la peine à; fâcher; rendre malade.
upshot, *n,* résultat, aboutissement, *m.*
upside down, *a. & ad,* à l'envers; sens dessus dessous. ~ *cake,* gâteau renversé.
upstart, *n,* parvenu, e.
upward, *a,* (*movement*) ascendant, ascensionnel; vers le haut; (*trend*) à la hausse. **~[s],** *ad,* en montant, vers le haut. *look ~ ,* regarder en haut. *~s of,* plus de.
uranium, *n,* uranium, *m.*
urban, *a,* urbain. **urbane,** *a,* courtois, urbain. **urbanity,** *n,* urbanité, *f.* **urbanization,** *n,* urbanisation, *f.*
urchin, *n,* polisson, ne.
urge, *n,* désir ardent, démangeaison *P, f.* ¶ *v.t,* (*pers.*) pousser, exhorter (à faire), presser (de faire); (*caution &c*) conseiller vivement. ~ *on,* (*pers.*) faire avancer; (*horse*) presser; (*team*) encourager. **urgency,** *n,* urgence; (*tone &c*) insistance, *f.* **urgent,** *a,* urgent; insistant. **~ly,** *ad,* d'urgence; (*plead*) instamment.
urinal, *n,* urinoir, *m,* vespasienne, *f;* (*vessel*) urinal, *m.* **urinate,** *v.i,* uriner. **urine,** *n,* urine, *f.*
urn, *n,* urne, *f.* *tea ~ ,* fontaine à thé, *f.*
us, *pn,* nous. *he's one of ~ ,* il est des nôtres. *let's go!* allons-y!
usage, *n,* (*custom; of word*) usage; (*pers.*) traitement, *m.* **use,** *n,* usage, emploi, *m;* utilisation,

f. *be of* ~, servir, être utile (à). *be* [*of*] *no* ~, ne servir à rien. *in* ~, en usage. *make* ~ *of*, se servir de. *not in* ~, hors d'usage. *what's the* ~ *of protesting?* à quoi bon protester? ¶ *v.t,* se servir de, utiliser, employer; (*s.o's name*) faire usage de; (*car*) prendre; (*opportunity*) profiter de; (*method*) employer; (*consume; petrol &c*) user, consommer; (*pers.*) agir envers, traiter. ~ [*up*], finir; utiliser; (*stores*) épuiser. ¶ *v.aux, translated in Fr. by imperfect tense: I* ~*d to go,* j'allais. ~**d,** *a,* (*car*) d'occasion. *be* ~ *to,* avoir l'habitude de, être habitué à. *get* ~ *to,* s'habituer à. ~**ful†,** *a,* utile; compétent. ~**fulness,** *n,* utilité, *f.* ~**less,** *a,* (*pointless*) inutile; inutilisable; qui ne vaut rien; (*remedy*) inefficace; (*pers.*) incompétent. ~**ly,** *ad,* inutilement. **user,** *n,* (*road &c*) usager, *m;* utilisateur, trice.

usher, *n,* (*court*) huissier; (*church*) placeur, *m.* ~ **in,** *v.t,* introduire, annoncer; (*fig.*) inaugurer. ~**ette,** *n,* ouvreuse, *f.*

usual, *a,* habituel; (*word*) usuel; (*conditions &c*) d'usage. *as* ~, comme d'habitude. ~**ly,** *a,* d'habitude, d'ordinaire.

usurp, *v.t,* usurper. ~**er,** *n,* usurpateur, trice.

usury, *n,* usure, *f.*

utensil, *n,* ustensile, *m.*

uterine, *a,* utérin. **uterus,** *n,* utérus, *m.*

utilitarian, *a,* utilitaire.

utility, *a,* utilitaire. ¶ *n,* utilité, *f;* service public, *m.* **utilize,** *v.t,* utiliser.

utmost, *a,* le plus grand; (*danger*) extrême. *do one's* ~, faire tout son possible. *to the* ~, au plus haut degré.

utopia, *n,* utopie, *f.* **utopian,** *a,* utopique.

utter[1], *v.t,* (*word*) prononcer; (*cry*) pousser; (*threat &c*) proférer; (*money*) passer.

utter[2], *a,* complet, total; (*madness*) pur; (*fool*) fini; (*rogue &c*) fieffé *before n.* ~**ly,** *ad,* complètement, tout à fait.

uvula, *n,* luette, uvule, *f.*

V, *n,* V, v, *m.* ~*-neck, n,* décolleté en V, *m.*

vacancy, *n,* poste vacant, chambre à louer, *f.* **vacant,** *a,* (*job*) vacant; (*room &c*) libre; (*stare*) vague. **vacate,** *v.t,* quitter; (*premises*) vider. **vacation,** *n,* vacances, *f.pl.*

vaccinate, *v.t,* vacciner. **vaccination,** *n,* vaccination, *f.* **vaccine,** *n,* vaccin, *m.*

vacillate, *v.i,* vaciller.

vacuity, *n,* vacuité, *f.* **vacuous,** *a,* (*stare*) vide; (*remark*) vide de sens, bête. **vacuum,** *n,* vide; (*Phys.*) vacuum, *m.* ~ *cleaner,* aspirateur, *m.* ~ *flask,* bouteille thermos, *f.* ~ *packed,* emballé sous vide. ~ *pump,* pompe à vide, *f.* ¶ *v.t,* passer à l'aspirateur.

vade-mecum, *n,* vade-mecum, *m.*

vagabond, *n,* vagabond, e.

vagary, *n,* caprice, *m.*

vagina, *n,* vagin, *m.* **vaginal,** *a,* vaginal.

vagrancy, *n,* vagabondage, *m.* **vagrant,** *a. & n,* vagabond, e.

vague, *a,* (*gen.*) vague, imprécis; (*outline, memory*) flou; (*pers.*) distrait. ~**ly,** *ad,* vaguement. ~**ness,** *n,* imprécision; (*pers.*) distraction, *f.*

vain, *a,* vaniteux; (*useless*) vain *before n;* (*promise*) vide. *in* ~, en vain, vainement. ~**ly,** *ad,* vaniteusement; en vain, vainement.

valedictory, *a,* d'adieu.

valentine [card], *n,* carte de la Saint-Valentin, *f.*

valet, *n,* valet [de chambre], *m.*

valiant†, *a,* vaillant, brave.

valid, *a,* valable. ~**ate,** *v.t,* valider. ~**ity,** *n,* validité; (*argument*) justesse, *f.*

valley, *n,* vallée, *f;* (*smaller*) vallon, *m.*

valorous†, *a,* valeureux. **valour,** *n,* valeur, vaillance, bravoure, *f.*

valuable, *a,* de valeur; (*time, help &c*) précieux. ~**s,** *n.pl,* objets de valeur, *m.pl.* **valuation,** *n,* (*house &c*) évaluation; (*Com., Law*) expertise; (*fig.*) appréciation, *f.* **value,** *n,* valeur, *f;* (*pl: moral standards*) valeurs, *f.pl. get* ~ *for one's money,* en avoir pour son argent. *put a* ~ *on,* évaluer. *V*~ *Added Tax* (*V.A.T.*), taxe sur la valeur ajoutée (T.V.A.), *f.* ¶ *v.t,* évaluer; expertiser (*at,* à); apprécier; (*liberty &c*) tenir à. ~**less,** *a,* sans valeur. **valuer,** *n,* expert, *m.*

valve, *n,* (*Anat.*) valvule; (*Bot., Zool., tyre &c*) valve; (*Mach.*) soupape; (*Radio*) lampe, *f;* (*Mus.*) piston, *m.*

vampire, *n,* vampire, *m.*

van, *n,* (*Mot.*) camion, fourgon, *m;* (*small*) camionnette, *f;* (*Rly*) fourgon. ~[*guard*], avant-garde, *f.*

vandal, *n,* vandale, *m.* ~**ism,** *n,* vandalisme, *m.* ~**ize,** *v.t,* saccager, saboter.

vane, *n,* (*weather* ~) girouette, *f.*

vanilla, *n,* vanille, *f.* ~ *ice,* glace à la v., *f.*

vanish, *v.i,* disparaître; se volatiliser. ~*ing point,* point de fuite, *m.*

vanity, *n,* vanité, *f.* ~ *case,* sac de toilette, *m.*
vanquish, *v.t,* vaincre.
vantage, *n,* (*Ten.*) avantage, *m.* ~ *point,* ~ *ground,* position avantageuse.
vapid, *a,* insipide, fade, plat.
vaporize, *v.t.* (& *i*), (se) vaporiser. **vaporizer,** (*Med.*) *n,* inhalateur, *m.* **vaporous,** *a,* vaporeux. **vapour,** *n,* vapeur; (*on glass*) buée, *f.* ~ *trail* (*Aero.*), traînée de condensation, *f.*
variable, *a,* variable; (*mood*) changeant. ¶ (*Math.* &*c*) *n,* variable, *f.* **at variance,** en désaccord. **variant,** *n,* variante, *f.* **variation,** *n,* variation, *f.*
varicose vein, *n,* varice, *f.*
varied, *a,* varié, divers. **variegated,** *a,* bigarré; (*Bot.*) panaché. **variety,** *n,* variété, *f;* (*Theat.*) variétés, *f.pl. a large* ~ *of,* un grand choix de. ~ *artist,* artiste de variétés, *m,f.* ~ *show,* (*Theat., TV*) spectacle de v.
various†, *a,* divers *before n. at* ~ *times,* en diverses occasions; à plusieurs reprises.
varnish, *n,* vernis, *m.* ¶ *v.t,* vernir. ~**ing,** *n,* vernissage, *m.*
vary, *v.i,* varier, se modifier, changer (*with,* selon). ¶ *v.t,* [faire] varier. ~**ing,** *a,* varié, variable. *with* ~ *degrees of success,* avec plus ou moins de succès.
vascular, *a,* vasculaire.
vase, *n,* vase, *m.*
vasectomy, *n,* vasectomie, *f.*
vaseline, *n,* vaseline, *f.*
vast, *a,* vaste. ~ *sums* [*of money*], des sommes folles. ~**ly,** *ad,* infiniment; immensément. ~**ness,** *n,* immensité, *f.*
vat, *n,* cuve, *f,* bac, *m.*
Vatican, *n,* Vatican, *m.* ~ *City,* la Cité du Vatican.
vaudeville, *n,* spectacle de music-hall, *m.*
vault[1], *n,* (*Arch.*) voûte; (*cellar*) cave, *f;* (*tomb*) caveau, *m;* (*bank, oft. pl.*) salle des coffres, *f.* ~**ing** (*Arch.*), *n,* voûtes, *f.pl.*
vault[2] **[over],** *v.t.* & *i,* sauter [d'un bond]. ~*ing horse,* cheval d'arçons, *m.*
vaunt, *v.t.* & *i,* se vanter (de).
veal, *n,* veau, *m.* ~ *cutlet,* côtelette de v., *f.*
veer, *v.i,* (*wind: opp. back*) tourner [du nord vers l'est &c]; (*car, ship, road*) virer; (*opinion*) changer.
vegetable, *n,* légume, *m.* ¶ *a,* végétal. ~ *dish,* légumier, *m.* ~ *garden,* potager, *m.* ~ *knife,* couteau à éplucher, *m.* ~ *marrow,* courge, *f.* ~ *soup,* soupe de légumes, *f.* **vegetarian,** *a.* & *n,* végétarien, ne. **vegetate,** *v.i,* végéter. **vegetation,** *n,* végétation, *f.*
vehemence, *n,* véhémence, *f.* **vehement,** *a,* véhément; (*actions*) violent. ~**ly,** *ad,* avec véhémence; avec violence.
vehicle, *n,* véhicule, *m. vehicular traffic,* circulation, *f.*
veil, *n,* (*gen., fig.*) voile, *m;* (*on hat*) voilette, *f. draw a* ~ *over,* mettre un voile sur. ¶ *v.t,* voiler.
vein, *n,* veine; (*leaf*) nervure, *f. in the same* ~, dans le même esprit. ~**ed,** *a,* veiné; nervuré.
vellum, *n,* vélin, *m.*
velocity, *n,* vitesse, vélocité, *f.*
velours, *n,* velours épais, *m.*
velvet, *n,* velours, *m.* **velveteen,** *n,* velvet, *m.* **velvet[y],** *a,* velouté.
venal†, *a,* vénal. ~**ity,** *n,* vénalité, *f.*
vendetta, *n,* vendetta, *f.*
vending, *n,* vente, *f.* ~ *machine,* distributeur automatique, *m.* **vendor,** *n,* vendeur, euse.
veneer, *n,* placage; (*fig.*) vernis, *m.* ¶ *v.t,* plaquer.
venerable, *a,* vénérable. **venerate,** *v.t,* vénérer. **veneration,** *n,* vénération, *f.*
venereal, *a:* ~ *disease,* maladie vénérienne.
Venetian, *a,* vénitien. ~ *blind,* store vénitien. ~ *glass,* cristal de Venise, *m.*
vengeance, *n,* vengeance, *f. take* ~ *on,* se venger de *ou* sur. *with a* ~, pour de bon *P;* (*work*) d'arrache-pied.
venial†, *a,* véniel.
venison, *n,* venaison, *f,* chevreuil, *m.*
venom, *n,* venin, *m.* ~**ous,** *a,* venimeux.
vent, *n,* (*hole*) orifice; (*pipe*) conduit; (*chimney*) tuyau; (*fig.*) libre cours, *m.* ¶ (*fig.*) *v.t,* décharger (*on,* sur). **ventilate,** *v.t,* (*room* &*c*) ventiler. **ventilation,** *n,* ventilation, *f.* ~ *shaft,* conduit d'aération, *m.* **ventilator,** *n,* ventilateur; (*Mot.*) déflecteur, *m.*
ventricle, *n,* ventricule, *m.*
ventriloquism, -quy, *n,* ventriloquie, *f.* **ventriloquist,** *n,* ventriloque, *m,f.*
venture, *n,* aventure; entreprise, *f. business* ~, tentatives commerciales, *f.pl.* ¶ *v.t,* (*life* &*c*) risquer; (*opinion* &*c*) hasarder. ~ *to,* oser, se permettre de. ¶ *v.i,* se risquer, s'aventurer.
venue, *n,* lieu [de rendez-vous], *m.*
veracious†, *a,* véridique. **veracity,** *n,* véracité, *f.*
veranda[h], *n,* véranda, *f.*
verb, *n,* verbe, *m.* **verbal†,** *a,* verbal. **verbalize,** *v.t,* exprimer. **verbatim,** *ad.* & *a,* mot à mot, m. pour m.
verbena, *n,* verveine, *f.*
verbiage, *n,* verbiage, *m.* **verbose,** *a,* verbeux. **verbosity,** *n,* verbosité, *f.*
verdict, *n,* verdict, *m. give one's* ~ *on,* se prononcer sur.
verdigris, *n,* vert-de-gris, *m.*
verge, *n,* (*road*) accotement, *m;* (*forest*) orée, *f. on the* ~ *of,* (*tears*) au bord de; (*ruin* &*c*) à deux doigts de; (*a discovery*) à la veille de; (*doing*) sur le point de. ¶ *v.i,* incliner, tendre. ~ *on,* (*ideas, actions*) approcher de; (*pers.*) frôler. **verger,** *n,* bedeau, *m.*
verification, *n,* vérification, *f.* **verify,** *v.t,* vérifier; (*documents*) contrôler. **véritable†,** *a,* véritable.

vermicelli, *n,* vermicelle, *m.*
vermilion, *a. & n,* vermillon, *inv. & m.*
vermin, *n,* (*insects, people*) vermine, *f;* (*animals*) animaux nuisibles, *m.pl.* ~**ous,** *a,* couvert de vermine.
verm[o]uth, *n,* vermouth, *m.*
vernacular, *n,* langue vulgaire, *f.*
veronica, *n,* véronique, *f.*
verruca, *n,* verrue, *f.*
versatile, *a,* (*mind*) souple; (*pers.*) aux talents variés. **versatility,** *n,* souplesse; variété de talents, *f.*
verse, *n,* (*poetry*) poésie, *f;* vers, *m:pl;* (*stanza: poem*) strophe, *f;* (*song*) couplet; (*Bible*) verset, *m.* **versed in,** *a,* versé dans. **versification,** *n,* versification, *f.* **versify,** *v.t,* mettre en vers. **version,** *n,* version, *f.*
versus, *pr,* contre.
vertebra, *n,* vertèbre, *f.* **vertebral,** *a,* vertébral. **vertebrate,** *a. & n,* vertébré, *m.*
vertex, *n,* sommet; (*Anat.*) vertex, *m.* **vertical,** *a,* vertical; (*cliff*) à pic. ¶ *n,* verticale, *f.* ~**ly,** *ad,* verticalement.
vertigo, *n,* vertige, *m.*
verve, *n,* verve, *f.*
very, *a,* (*precise*) même; (*extreme*) tout; (*mere*) seul. *that ~ day,* ce jour même. *at the ~ end,* (*road*) tout au bout; (*year*) tout à la fin. *the ~ idea!* quelle idée alors! *by the ~ fact that,* du seul fait que. *his ~ words,* ses propres paroles. ¶ *ad,* (*extremely*) très, bien; (*absolutely*) tout, de loin. *~ much,* beaucoup.
vespers, *n.pl,* vêpres, *f.pl.*
vessel, *n,* vaisseau, *m.*
vest[1], *n,* (*man's*) maillot, tricot de corps, *m;* (*woman's*) chemise américaine, *f;* (*Am.*) gilet, *m.*
vest[2], *v.t,* investir (qn de qch). *~ed interests,* (*Com., Fin.*) droits acquis, *m.pl. have a ~ed interest in* (*fig.*), être directement intéressé dans.
vestibule, *n,* vestibule, *m.*
vestige, *n,* vestige, *m,* trace, *f.*
vestment, *n,* vêtement sacerdotal, *m.*
vestry, *n,* sacristie, *f.*
vet, *n,* vétérinaire, *m,f.* ¶ *v.t,* (*scheme*) examiner de près; approuver.
vetch, *n,* vesce, *f.*
veteran, *n,* vétéran, *m.* [*war*] ~, ancien combattant. ¶ *a,* expérimenté; de longue date. *~ car,* voiture d'époque, *f.*
veterinary, *a,* vétérinaire. *~ surgeon,* vétérinaire, *m,f.*
veto, *n,* veto, *m.* ¶ *v.t,* mettre son v. à.
vex, *v.t,* contrarier, fâcher. ~**ation,** *n,* ennui, *m.* **vexatious, vexing,** *a,* contrariant. **vexed,** *a,* fâché; (*question*) controversé.
via, *pr,* par; via.
viability, *n,* viabilité, *f.* **viable,** *a,* viable.
viaduct, *n,* viaduc, *m.*
vibrant, *a,* vibrant. **vibrate,** *v.i,* vibrer (*with,* de). **vibration,** *n,* vibration, *f.*
vicar, *n,* pasteur, *m.* ~**age,** *n,* presbytère, *m.* **vicarious,** *a,* à la place d'un autre. ~**ly,** *ad,* indirectement.
vice[1], *n,* vice; (*weaker*) défaut, *m.* ~ *squad* (*Police*), brigade des mœurs, *f.*
vice[2] (*tool*), *n,* étau, *m.*
vice-, *pref,* vice-. *~-chairman, ~-president,* vice-président, e. *~-chancellor,* (*Univ.*) recteur, *m;* (*Law*) vice-chancelier, *m.* *~roy,* vice-roi, *m.*
vice versa, *ad,* vice versa.
vicinity, *n,* voisinage, *m,* environs, alentours, *m.pl;* (*closeness*) proximité, *f. in the ~ of,* aux alentours de.
vicious†, *a,* (*circle, habit, animal*) vicieux; (*remark &c*) méchant; (*attack*) brutal; (*tongue*) de vipère. ~**ness,** *n,* méchanceté; brutalité, *f.*
vicissitude, *n,* vicissitude, *f.*
victim, *n,* victime, *f.* ~**ization,** *n,* représailles, *f.pl.* ~**ize,** *v.t,* prendre pour victime; (*Ind.*) exercer des représailles contre.
victor, *n,* vainqueur, *m.* **victorious**†, *a,* victorieux. **victory,** *n,* victoire, *f.*
victuals, *n.pl,* victuailles, *f.pl.*
vide, *v. imperative,* voir.
video, *a,* vidéo, *inv. ~ cassette,* vidéocassette, *f.* *~ recorder,* magnétoscope, *m.* *~ recording,* enregistrement sur m., *m.*
vie, *v.i,* rivaliser (*with s.o,* avec qn).
view, *n,* (*gen.*) vue, *f;* avis, *m,* opinion, *f;* (*survey*) vue, aperçu, *m. overall ~,* vue d'ensemble. *come into ~,* apparaître. *come into ~ of,* arriver en vue de. *in ~ of,* étant donné, vue. *in full ~ of,* en plein devant. *on ~,* exposé. *have in ~,* envisager. *with a ~ to,* dans l'intention de. *~ finder,* viseur, *m.* *~point,* point de vue, *m.* ¶ *v.t,* (*house &c*) visiter; (*consider*) envisager. ¶ *v.i,* (*TV*) regarder la télévision. ~**er,** *n,* (*TV*) téléspectateur, trice; (*for slides*) visionneuse, *f.*
vigil, *n,* veille; (*by the dead*) veillée; (*Eccl.*) vigile, *f.* ~**ance,** *n,* vigilance, *f.* ~**ant,** *a,* vigilant. ~**antly,** *ad,* avec vigilance.
vigorous†, *a,* vigoureux. **vigour,** *n,* vigueur, *f.*
vile, *a,* vil, ignoble; (*very bad*) exécrable. ~**ness,** *n,* vilenie, bassesse, *f.* **vilification,** *n,* calomnie, *f.* **vilify,** *v.t,* calomnier.
villa, *n,* (*country*) maison de campagne, *f;* (*town*) pavillon, *m;* (*seaside*) villa, *f.* **village,** *n,* village, *m;* bourgade, *f.* *~ green,* pré communal, *m.* **villager,** *n,* villageois, e.
villain, *n,* scélérat, e; (*P crook*) bandit, *m;* (*Theat. &c*) traître, esse. ~**ous,** *a,* infâme. ~**y,** *n,* infamie, *f.*
vindicate, *v.t,* justifier. **vindication,** *n,* justification, *f.*
vindictive†, *a,* vindicatif.
vine, *n,* vigne, *f.* *~ grower,* vigneron, viti-

culteur, *m.* **vinegar,** *n,* vinaigre, *m.* **vineyard,** *n,* vignoble, *m.* **vintage,** *n,* (*season, harvest*) vendanges, *f.pl;* (*year*) année, *f.* ~ *wine,* vin de grand cru, *m.* ~ *car,* voiture d'époque, *f.*
vinyl, *n,* vinyle, *m.*
viola[1], *n,* (*Mus.*) alto, *m.*
viola[2], (*Bot.*), *n,* pensée, *f.*
violate, *v.t,* violer. **violation,** *n,* violation, *f.* **violence,** *n,* violence, *f. do* ~ *to,* faire violence à. *crime of* ~, voie de fait, *f. robbery with* ~, vol avec coups & blessures, *m.* **violent†,** *a,* violent; (*dislike*) vif.
violet, *n,* (*Bot.*) violette, *f;* (*colour*) violet, *m.* ¶ *a,* violet.
violin, *n,* violon, *m.* ~**ist,** *n,* violoniste, *m,f.*
viper, *n,* vipère, *f.*
virago, *n,* dragon, *m,* mégère, *f.*
virgin, *n,* vierge, *f;* garçon vierge, *m. the Blessed V*~, la Sainte Vierge. ¶ *a,* (*forest*) vierge; (*snow*) frais. **Virginia creeper,** *n,* vigne vierge, *f.* **virginity,** *n,* virginité, *f.*
virile, *a,* viril. **virility,** *n,* virilité, *f.*
virtual, *a,* de fait, en fait. *it was a* ~ *admission,* de fait c'était un aveu. ~**ly,** *ad,* pratiquement; en fait.
virtue, *n,* vertu, *f.* **virtuosity,** *n,* virtuosité, *f.* **virtuoso,** *n,* virtuose, *m,f.* **virtuous†,** *a,* vertueux.
virulence, *n,* virulence, *f.* **virulent,** *a,* virulent. **virus,** *n,* virus, *m.* ~ *infection,* maladie virale.
visa, *n,* visa, *m.*
vis-à-vis, *pr,* vis-à-vis de.
viscera, *n.pl,* viscères, *m.pl.*
viscous, *a,* visqueux. **viscose,** *n,* viscose, *f.* **viscosity,** *n,* viscosité, *f.*
viscount, *n,* vicomte, *m.* ~**ess,** *n,* vicomtesse, *f.*
visibility, *n,* visibilité, *f.* **visible†,** *a,* visible.
vision, *n,* vision; (*eyesight*) vue, *f.* ~**ary,** *a. & n,* visionnaire, *m,f.*
visit, *n,* (*call, tour*) visite, *f;* (*stay*) séjour, *m. be on a* ~ *to,* (*pers.*) être en visite chez; (*place*) faire un séjour à. ¶ *v.t,* (*pers.*) aller voir; rendre visite à; (*Med.*) visiter; (*place*) aller à; visiter; (*stay with*) faire un séjour chez ~**ation,** *n,* (*Eccl.*) visite pastorale. ~**ing,** *a,* (*card, hours*) de visite; (*professor*) associé. ~**or,** *n,* (*guest*) invité, e; (*hotel*) client, e; (*tourist; to zoo &c*) visiteur, euse. ~*s' book,* livre d'or; (*hotel*) registre, *m.*
visor, *n,* visière, *f.*
vista, *n,* panorama, *m;* (*fig.*) perspective, *f.*
visual†, *a,* visuel. ~ *display unit* (*VDU*), écran de visualisation, visu *P, m.* ~**ize,** *v.t,* se représenter.
vital, *a,* vital; indispensable; (*importance*) capital. ~**ity,** *n,* vitalité, *f.* ~**ize,** *v.t,* vivifier; (*fig.*) animer. ~**ly,** *ad,* absolument. **vitamin,** *n,* vitamine, *f.* ~ *deficiency,* carence en vitamines, *f.*
vitiate, *v.t,* vicier.
vitreous, *a,* vitreux; (*enamel*) vitrifié. **vitrify,** *v.t,* vitrifier. **vitriol,** *n,* vitriol, *m.* ~**ic,** (*fig.*) *a,* venimeux.
vituperation, *n,* vitupérations, injures, *f.pl.*
vivacious, *a,* enjoué. *to be* ~, avoir de la vivacité. ~**ly,** *ad,* avec vivacité. **vivacity,** *n,* vivacité, *f.* **viva,** *n,* oral, *m.* **viva voce,** *ad,* de vive voix. **vivid,** *a,* vif, éclatant; (*memory*) très net; (*imagination*) vif; (*description*) vivant. ~**ness,** *n,* éclat, *m;* (*style*) vigueur, *f.* **vivisection,** *n,* vivisection, *f.*
vixen, *n,* renarde; (*woman*) mégère, *f.*
viz, *ad, abb,* c'est-à-dire, [à] savoir.
vizi[e]r, *n,* vizir, *m.*
vocabulary, *n,* vocabulaire; (*in textbook*) lexique, *m.* **vocal†,** *a,* vocal. ~ *cords,* cordes vocales. ~**ic,** *a,* vocalique. ~**ist,** *n,* chanteur, euse. ~**ize,** *v.t,* vocaliser.
vocation, *n,* vocation, *f.* ~**al,** *a,* professionnel. ~ *guidance,* orientation professionnelle.
vocative [case], *n,* vocatif, *m.*
vociferate, *v.i,* vociférer. **vociferous,** *a,* bruyant. ~**ly,** *ad,* bruyammant.
vodka, *n,* vodka, *f.*
vogue, *n,* vogue, *f.*
voice, *n,* voix, *f. at the top of one's* ~, à tue-tête. *with one* ~, à l'unanimité. ¶ *v.t,* exprimer; (*consonant*) voiser. ~**less,** *a,* sans voix; (*consonant*) sourd.
void, *a,* vide; (*Law*) nul. ¶ *n,* vide, *m.*
voile (*textile*) *n,* voile, *m.*
volatile, *a,* (*Chem.*) volatil; (*situation*) explosif; (*behaviour*) capricieux.
volcanic, *a,* volcanique. **volcano,** *n,* volcan, *m.*
vole (*Zool.*) *n,* campagnol, *m.*
volition, *n,* volition, *f. of one's own* ~, de son propre gré.
volley, *n,* (*Mil., Sport*) volée; (*fig: insults*) bordée; (*applause*) salve, *f.* ~*ball,* volley [-ball], *m.* ¶ (*Ten.*) *v.t,* reprendre de volée.
volt, *n,* volt, *m.* ~**age,** *n,* voltage, *m,* tension, *f.*
volubility, *n,* volubilité, *f.* **voluble,** *a,* volubile.
volume, *n,* (*book, size &c*) volume; (*of smoke &c*) nuage, *m;* (*tank*) capacité, *f.* ~ *1, 2 &c* (*book*), tome premier, deux &c. **voluminous,** *a,* volumineux.
voluntary†, *a,* (*done freely*) volontaire; (*unpaid*) bénévole. ¶ (*organ*) *n,* morceau d'orgue, *m;* (*final*) sortie, *f.* **volunteer,** *n,* (*gen., Mil.*) volontaire, *m,f.* ¶ *v.t,* offrir de son plein gré. ¶ *v.i,* s'offrir; (*Mil.*) s'engager comme volontaire.
voluptuous†, *a,* voluptueux. ~**ness,** *n,* volupté, sensualité, *f.*
vomit, *n,* vomi, *m.* ¶ *v.t. & i,* vomir. ~**ing,** *n,* vomissements, *m.pl.*
voracious, *a,* vorace; (*reader*) avide. ~**ly,** *ad,* avec voracité. **voracity,** *n,* voracité, *f.*
vortex, *n,* vortex; (*fig.*) tourbillon, *m.*
votary, *n,* fervent, e. **vote,** *n,* (*gen.*) vote, *m;* (~

cast) voix, *f. give the ~ to,* donner le droit de vote à. *~s for women!* droit de vote pour les femmes! *~ of no confidence,* motion de censure, *f. ~ of thanks,* discours de remerciement, *m.* ¶ *v.t,* (*sum &c*) voter; (*~ in*) élire. ¶ *v.i,* voter. *~ on sth,* mettre qch au vote. **voter,** *n,* électeur, trice. **voting,** *n,* (*process*) scrutin; (*result*) vote, *m. ~ paper,* bulletin de vote, *m.* **votive,** *a,* votif.
vouch for, *v.i,* (*pers.*) répondre de; (*truth*) garantir. **voucher,** *n,* bon; (*receipt*) reçu, *m.*
vow, *n,* vœu, *m.* ¶ *v.t,* vouer. ¶ *v.i,* jurer.
vowel, *n,* voyelle, *f.* ¶ *a,* vocalique.
voyage, *n,* voyage par mer, *m;* traversée, *f.* ¶ *v.i,* voyager [par mer]. *~***er,** *n,* voyageur, euse.
vulcanite, *n,* ébonite, *f.* **vulcanize,** *v.t,* vulcaniser.
vulgar†, *a,* (*gen.*) vulgaire; (*pej.*) grossier; (*fraction*) ordinaire. *~***ity,** *n,* vulgarité, *f. ~***ize,** *v.t,* vulgariser. *the Vulgate,* la Vulgate.
vulnerable, *a,* vulnérable.
vulture, *n,* vautour, *m.*

W

wad, *n,* tampon, *m;* (*banknotes*) liasse, *f.* ¶ *v.t,* (*quilt*) rembourrer; (*garment*) ouater. **wadding,** *n,* bourre; ouate, *f.*
waddle, *n,* dandinement, *m.* ¶ *v.i,* se dandiner.
wade, *v.i,* marcher dans l'eau. *~ through,* (*water &c*) patauger dans; (*P book*) venir péniblement à bout de. ¶ *v.t,* traverser à gué. **wader,** *n,* (*bird*) échassier, *m;* (*pl. Fish.*) cuissardes, *f.pl.*
wafer, *n,* gaufrette; (*Rel.*) hostie, *f.*
waffle[1], *n,* gaufre, *f. ~ iron,* gaufrier, *m.*
waffle[2] *P, n,* verbiage, *m.* ¶ *v.i,* parler pour ne rien dire.
waft, *v.t,* (*smell, sound*) apporter. ¶ *v.i,* flotter.
wag, *v.t,* agiter, remuer. ¶ *v.i,* (*tail*) remuer. *~ its tail* (*dog*), frétiller [de la queue]. *set tongues ~ging,* faire jaser.
wage, *n. oft. pl,* salaire, *m;* paye, *f;* (*servant*) gages, *m.pl. ~ claim,* demande de révision de salaire, *f. ~ earner,* salarié, e. *~ freeze,* blocage des salaires, *m. ~ packet,* paye, *f. ~s slip,* fiche de paye, *f.* ¶ *v.t,* (*campaign*) mener. *~ war,* faire la guerre.
wager, *n,* pari, *m.* ¶ *v.t,* parier.
waggle, *v.t,* agiter; (*hips*) tortiller de. ¶ *v.i,* (*tooth*) branler, (*tail*) frétiller.
wag[g]on, *n,* (*horse*) chariot; (*Mot.*) camion; (*Rly*) wagon [de marchanises], *m;* (*tea-~*) table roulante, *f;* chariot. *go on the ~* (*fig.*), ne plus boire [d'alcool]. *~load,* (*Agr.*) charretée, *f;* (*Rly*) wagon. *~***er,** *n,* charretier, roulier, *m.*
wagtail, *n,* bergeronnette, *f,* hochequeue, *m.*
waif, *n,* enfant abandonné, e, *m,f.*
wail, *n,* (*pers., wind*) gémissement; (*baby*) vagissement; (*siren*) hurlement, *m.* ¶ *v.i,* gémir; vagir; hurler. *~***ing,** *a,* gémissant; plaintif. *the W~ Wall,* le mur des Lamentations.
wainscot, *n,* lambris, *m.*
waist, *n,* ceinture, taille, *f. ~ band,* ceinture, *f. ~coat,* gilet, *m. ~line,* taille. *watch your ~line!* attention à la ligne! *~ measurement,* tour de taille, *m.*
wait, *n,* attente, *f. lie in ~,* être à l'affût; (*for s.o.*) guetter. ¶ *v.i,* attendre (*for s.o,* qn; *for s.o to do, until s.o does,* que qn fasse). *~ & see,* attends voir. *~ a minute!* un instant! *keep s.o ~ing,* faire attendre qn. *~ at table,* servir à table. *~ on,* servir. *~ upon,* se présenter chez. **waiter,** *n,* garçon [de café], *m. ~!* garçon! monsieur! **waiting,** *n,* attente, *f. 'no ~'* (*Mot.*), 'stationnement strictement interdit'. *play a ~ game* (*fig.*), attendre son heure. *~ list,* liste d'attente, *f. ~ room,* salon d'attente, *m;* (*Rly*) salle d'a., *f.* **waitress,** *n,* serveuse, *f. ~!* mademoiselle!
waive, *v.t,* renoncer à; abandonner.
wake[1], *n,* (*ship*) sillage, *m. in the ~ of* (*fig.*), à la suite de.
wake[2], *v.t.ir,* & **waken,** réveiller; (*fig.*) éveiller. ¶ *v.i, ~* [*up*], se réveiller; (*fig.*) se secouer. *~ up to sth* (*fig.*), prendre conscience de qch. ¶ *n,* veillée mortuaire, *f. ~***ful,** *a,* éveillé; (*alert*) vigilant; (*time*) sans sommeil. *~***fulness,** *n,* insomnie, *f.*
Wales, *n,* le pays de Galles.
walk, *n,* promenade; (*path: garden*) allée, *f;* (*in country*) chemin, *m;* (*gait*) démarche, *f. go for a ~,* se promener, faire une promenade; (*short*) faire un tour; (*hike*) faire une randonnée. *5 minutes' ~ from here,* à 5 minutes à pied d'ici. *all ~s of life,* toutes conditions sociales. ¶ *v.i,* (*gen.*) marcher; (*opp. run*) aller au pas; (*opp. ride*) aller à pied; (*take a ~*) se promener. *~ into,* (*trap &c*) tomber sur; (*pers. &c*) se cogner à. ¶ *v.t,* (*distance*) faire à pied; (*road &c*) parcourir; (*pers.*) (*dog*) promener; (*horse*) conduire à pied. *~ the streets,* se promener dans les rues; (*prostitute*) faire le trottoir. *~ about,* aller & venir. *~about, n,*

bain de foule, *m.* ~*-in* (*cupboard*), de plain-pied. ~ *on,* (*Theat.*) être figurant, e. ~*-on part,* rôle de figurant, e. ~ *out,* sortir. ~*out,* (*Ind.*), grève surprise, *f.* ~*over,* (*Sport*) walk-over, *m;* (*fig.*) victoire facile, *f.* ~*way,* passage pour piétons, *m.* **walker,** *n,* (*Sport*) marcheur, euse; (*invalid*) déambulateur; (*baby*) trotte-bébé, *m.* **walkie-talkie,** *n,* talkie-walkie, *m.* **walking,** *n,* marche à pied, promenade, *f.* ¶ *a,* ambulant; (*shoes*) de marche. ~ *stick,* canne, *f.* ~ *tour,* excursion à pied, *f.*

wall, *n,* (*gen.*) mur, *m;* (*high*) muraille; (*inside*) paroi, *f;* (*tyre*) flanc, *m;* (*fig.*) muraille. *the Great W~ of China,* la grande muraille de Chine. (*fig.*) *have one's back to the* ~, être acculé. (*fig.*) *go to the* ~, perdre la partie; (*Fin.*) faire faillite. *drive s.o up the* ~ *P,* rendre qn dingue *P.* ¶ *a,* (*cupboard, clock &c*) mural. ~*flower,* giroflée, *f.* ~*paper,* papier-peint, *m.* ~*-to-*~ *carpeting,* moquette, *f.* ¶ *v.t,* ~ [*in*], entourer d'un mur. ~ *up,* murer. ~*ed garden,* jardin clos, *m.*

wallaby, *n,* wallaby, *m.*

wallet, *n,* portefeuille, *m.*

Walloon, *a,* wallon. ¶ *n,* Wallon, ne; (*language*) le wallon, *m.*

wallop, *n,* grand coup. ¶ *v.t,* rosser. ~**ing** *P, a,* énorme. ¶ *n,* raclée *P,* rossée *P, f.*

wallow, *v.i,* se vautrer (*in,* dans).

walnut, *n,* noix, *f;* (*tree, wood*) noyer, *m.*

walrus, *n,* morse, *m.*

waltz, *n,* valse, *f.* ¶ *v.i,* valser.

wan, *a,* blême, pâle; triste. ~**ly,** *ad,* tristement.

wand, *n,* baguette, *f.*

wander, *v.i,* errer; (*saunter*) flâner; (*stray*) s'égarer; (*in mind*) divaguer. ~ *around,* flâner. ~*lust,* bougeotte *P, f.* ~**er,** *n,* vagabond, e. *the Wandering Jew,* le Juif errant.

wane, *v.i,* (*moon*) décroître; (*fig.*) décliner, diminuer.

wangle *P, n,* combine, *f.* ¶ *v.t,* se débrouiller pour obtenir; (*not pay*) carotter *P.*

want, *n,* (*lack*) manque; (*poverty*) besoin, *m,* misère, *f. for* ~ *of,* faute de. ¶ *v.t,* vouloir; avoir envie de, désirer; (*need: pers.*) avoir besoin de; (*task &c*) exiger. *be* ~*ed by the police,* être recherché par la police. ~ *for sth,* manquer de qch. ~**ed** (*advt.*), on demande.

wanton, *a,* (*cruelty &c*) gratuit, injustifié; (*pers.*) dévergondé, lascif.

war, *n,* guerre, *f. at* ~, en guerre. *go to* ~, (*country*) entrer en g. *period between the* ~*s,* l'entre-deux-guerres, *m.inv.* ¶ *a,* de guerre. ~ *clouds,* nuages avant-coureurs de la guerre, *m.pl.* ~ *cry,* cri de guerre, *m.* ~ *dance,* danse guerrière. ~*fare,* guerre. ~*like,* guerrier. ~ *memorial,* monument aux morts, *m.* ~*-monger,* belliciste, *m,f.* ~*mongering, n,* bellicisme. *W~ Office,* ministère de la Guerre, *m.* ~*ship,* navire de guerre, *m.* ~ *time,* temps de g., *m.* ~*-weary,* las de la guerre. ¶ *v.i,* faire la guerre (*against,* à).

warble, *v.i,* gazouiller; (*singer pej.*) roucouler. **warbler** (*bird*) *n,* fauvette, *f.*

ward, *n,* (*pers.*) pupille, *m.f;* (*Local Govt.*) section électorale; (*hospital*) salle, *f.* ~ *of court,* pupille sous tutelle judiciaire. ~*room,* carré, *m.* ~ **off,** *v.t,* parer. ~**en,** *n,* directeur, trice; (*park &c*) gardien, ne. *traffic* ~, contractuel, le. **warder, dress,** *n,* gardien, ne [de prison]. **wardrobe,** *n,* armoire; garde-robe, *f;* (*Theat.*) costumes, *f.pl.* ~ *mistress* (*Theat.*), costumière, *f.*

warehouse, *n,* magasin, entrepôt, *m.* ~*man,* magasinier, *m.* ¶ *v.t,* emmagasiner; entreposer.

wares, *n.pl,* marchandises, *f.pl.*

warily, *ad,* avec circonspection. **wariness,** *n,* précaution, *f.*

warm†, *a,* (*gen.*) [assez] chaud; (*oven &c*) moyen; (*fig: gen.*) chaleureux; (*colour, discussion*) chaud; (*supporter*) ardent; (*thanks*) vif. *be* ~, avoir chaud. *it's* ~, il fait chaud. ~*-blooded,* à sang chaud. ~*-hearted,* chaleureux. ¶ *v.t,* (*pers., room*) réchauffer; (*water &c*) [ré]chauffer. ~ *one's hands,* se [ré]chauffer les mains. ¶ *v.i,* ~ [*up*], se réchauffer; chauffer. ~ *up, v.t,* (*engine*) faire chauffer; (*audience*) mettre en train; *v.i,* se réchauffer; (*athlete &c*) s'échauffer; (*discussion*) s'animer. ~**th,** *n,* chaleur, *f.*

warn, *v.t,* avertir, prévenir; (*police &c*) alerter. ~**ing,** *n,* avertissement; (*written*) avis, *m;* (*signal*) alerte, *f. without* ~, (*happen*) inopinément; (*arrive*) à l'improviste. ~ *device,* dispositif d'alarme, *m.* ~ *light,* voyant avertisseur, *m.*

warp, *n,* (*cloth*) chaîne; (*in wood*) voilure, *f.* ¶ *v.t,* voiler; (*character*) corrompre; (*judgment*) fausser. ¶ *v.i,* se voiler. ~**ed,** *a,* (*mind &c*) tordu, morbide.

warrant, *n,* (*voucher*) bon, *m;* garantie, *f;* (*Mil.*) brevet; (*Law, Police*) mandat, *m.* ~ *officer,* adjudant, *m.* ¶ *v.t,* justifier; garantir. ~**able,** *a,* justifiable. ~**y,** *n,* garantie, *f.*

warren, *n,* garenne; (*fig: house &c*) taupinière, *f.*

warrior, *n,* guerrier, ère.

Warsaw, *n,* Varsovie, *f.* ~ *Pact,* pacte de V., *m.*

wart, *n,* (*Med.*) verrue, *f.* ~*-hog,* phacochère, *m.*

wary, *a,* prudent; (*manner*) précautionneux. *be* ~ *about,* se méfier de. *keep a* ~ *eye on,* surveiller de près.

wash, *n,* (*linen*) lessive, *f;* (*Art*) lavis, *m;* (*mouth*) eau, *f;* (*ship*) sillage, *m. to have a* ~, se laver. ~*basin,* lavabo, *m.* ~*house,* lavoir, *m.* ~*leather,* peau de chamois, *f.* ~*-out P,* (*event &c*) fiasco, *m;* (*pers.*) nullité, *f.* ~*room,* toilettes, *f.pl.* ~*stand,* lavabo, *m.* ¶ *v.t,* (*gen.*) laver; (*coast &c*) baigner. ¶ *v.i,* (*pers.*) & ~

o.s, se laver, faire sa toilette; (*linen*) faire la lessive. ~ **away,** *v.t,* (*stain*) faire partir au lavage; (*mud &c*) enlever à l'eau; (*fig: sins*) laver; (*banks*) éroder. ~ **down,** *v.t,* (*car &c*) laver à grande eau; (*food*) arroser (de). ~ **off,** *v.i,* partir au lavage; p. à l'eau. ~ **over,** *v.t,* (*waves &c*) balayer. ~ **up,** *v.i,* faire la vaisselle; *v.t,* (*cups &c*) laver; (*sea &c*) rejeter [sur le rivage]. ~**able,** *a,* lavable. **washer,** *n,* (*ring*) rondelle, *f;* (*windscreen*) lave-glace, *m.inv.* **washing,** *n,* (*car*) lavage, *m;* (*linen*) lessive, *f;* (*walls*) lessivage; (*items to* ~) linge, *m;* lessive. ~ *day,* jour de lessive, *m.* ~ *line,* corde à linge, *f.* ~ *machine,* machine à laver, *f.* ~ *powder,* lessive [en poudre], *f.* ~ *soda,* cristaux de soude, *m.pl. do the* ~*-up,* faire la vaisselle. ~*-up bowl,* bassine, *f.* ~*-up liquid,* lave-vaisselle, *m.inv.* ~*-up water,* eau de vaisselle, *f.*

wasp, *n,* guêpe, *f.* ~*s' nest,* guêpier, *m.*

wastage, *n,* (*gen.*) gaspillage; (*of heat &c*) déperdition, *f.* **waste,** *a,* (*matter*) de rebut; (*gas, heat*) perdu; *lay* ~, dévaster. ¶ *n,* (*gen.*) gaspillage, *m;* (*time*) perte; (*rubbish*) ordures, *f.pl.* ¶ *comps:* ~*bin,* poubelle, *f.* ~*-disposal unit,* broyeur d'ordures, *m.* ~*land,* terres à l'abandon, *f.pl;* (*in town*) terrain vague, *m.* ~*-paper,* vieux papiers, *m.pl.* ~*-paper basket,* corbeille à papier, *f.* ~*-pipe,* [tuyau *m* de] vidange, *f.* ¶ *v.t,* gaspiller (*on,* pour); (*time &c*) perdre; (*opportunity*) laisser passer. ~ *one's breath,* dépenser sa salive pour rien. ¶ *v.i,* se perdre, être gaspillé. ~ *away,* dépérir. **waster, wastrel,** *n,* dépensier, ère; propre à rien, *m,f.* **wasteful,** *a,* (*pers.*) gaspilleur, prodigue. ~**ness,** *n,* manque d'économie, *m.* **wasting,** *a,* (*disease*) qui ronge.

watch, *n,* montre, *f;* (*Naut.*) quart, *m. keep* ~, faire le guet. *be on the* ~ *for,* guetter; être à l'affût de. *on* ~, de quart. ~ *dog,* chien de garde, *m;* (*fig.*) gardien, ne. ~*maker,* horloger, ère. ~*man,* gardien, *m.* ~*strap,* bracelet de montre, *m.* ~*tower,* tour de guet, *f.* ~*word,* mot d'ordre, *m.* ¶ *v.t,* (*gen.*) regarder, observer; (*birds &c*) observer; (*look after*) surveiller; (*be careful of*) faire attention à. ¶ *v.i,* regarder; faire attention; (*by sick pers.*) veiller. ~ *out,* faire attention, prendre garde. ~ *out!* attention! ~**er,** *n,* observateur, trice; guetteur, *m;* spectateur, trice. ~**ful,** *a,* vigilant.

water, *n,* eau; (*tide*) marée, *f;* (*pl: spa &c. & Med.*) eaux, *f.pl. it won't hold* ~, (*lit.*) cela n'est pas étanche; (*fig.*) ça ne tient pas debout. *make* ~ (*ship*), faire eau. *pass* ~, uriner. ¶ *a,* (*level, pipe, pressure, hen*) d'eau; (*pump, mill, pistol*) à eau; (*plant &c*) aquatique. ~ *bed,* matelas à eau, *m.* ~ *biscuit,* craquelin, *m.* ~ *bottle,* carafe, *f;* (*Mil.*) bidon, *m.* ~ *butt,* citerne [à eau de pluie], *f.* ~ *cannon,* grande lance à eau. ~ *closet,* cabinets, waters, W. C., *m.pl.* ~ *colour,* aquarelle, *f.* ~*course,* cours d'eau, *m.* ~*cress,* cresson [de fontaine], *m.* ~ *diviner,* sourcier, ère. ~*fall,* chute d'eau; cascade, *f.* ~ *fowl* (*pl.*), gibier d'eau, *m.* ~*front,* (*docks*) quais, *m.pl;* (*sea*) front de mer, *m.* ~ *heater,* chauffe-eau, *m.inv.* ~ *hole,* mare, *f.* ~ *ice,* sorbet, *m.* ~ *jacket,* chemise d'eau, *f.* ~ *jug,* pot à eau, *m.* ~ *jump* (*Turf*), brook, *m.* ~ *lily,* nénuphar, *m.* ~ *line,* ligne de flottaison, *f.* ~*logged,* imbibé d'eau; (*land*) détrempé. ~*man,* batelier, *m.* ~*mark,* (*tidal*) laisse, *f;* (*paper*) filigrane, *m.* ~ *meadow,* noue, *f.* ~ *melon,* pastèque, *f.* ~ *nymph,* naïade, *f.* ~ *on the brain,* hydrocéphalie, *f.* ~ *on the knee,* épanchement de synovie, *m.* ~*proof, a,* imperméable; (*watch*) étanche; *n,* imperméable, *m; v.t.* imperméabiliser. ~ *polo,* waterpolo, *m.* ~ *rat,* rat d'eau, *m.* ~ *rate,* taxe sur l'eau, *f.* ~*-repellent,* hydrofuge. ~*shed,* (*Geog.*) ligne de partage des eaux, *f;* (*fig.*) grand tournant. ~*side,* bord de l'eau, *m;* (*att.*) riverain. ~*-ski*[*ing*], ski nautique, *m.* ~ *softener,* adoucisseur d'eau, *m.* ~*spout,* (*rain*) tuyau de descente; (*Met.*) trombe, *f.* ~*-tight,* étanche; (*fig.*) inattaquable. ~ *tower,* château d'eau, *m.* ~*way,* voie navigable, *f.* ~ *wheel,* roue hydraulique, *f.* ~ *wings,* flotteurs de natation, *m.pl.* ~ *works,* station hydraulique, *f.* ¶ *v.t,* (*garden &c*) arroser; (*horse &c*) abreuver; (*drink*) couper, baptiser. ¶ *v.i.* (*eyes*) pleurer, larmoyer. *it makes one's mouth* ~, cela fait venir l'eau à la bouche. ~*ed silk,* soie moirée, *f.* ~ *down,* (*drink*) couper, baptiser; (*fig.*) édulcorer; (*effect*) atténuer. ~**ing,** *n,* arrosage, *m.* ~ *can,* arrosoir, *m.* ~ *place,* abreuvoir, *m;* (*spa*) station thermale. ~**y,** *a,* aqueux; humide; (*fluid*) ténu; (*soup*) trop liquide.

watt, *n,* watt, *m.* ~**age,** *n,* puissance en watts, *f.*

wave, *n,* (*gen., fig.*) vague, *f;* (*hair, surface*) ondulation; (*Radio, Tel. &c*) onde, *f;* (*of hand*) signe de main, *m.* ~*band,* bande de fréquences, *f.* ~*-length* (*lit., fig.*), longueur d'ondes, *f.* ¶ *v.t,* (*flag &c*) agiter; (*stick &c*) brandir; (*hair*) onduler. ¶ *v.i,* faire signe de la main; (*flag*) flotter au vent; (*tree &c*) être agité; (*hair, corn &c*) onduler. ~ *to s.o,* saluer qn de la main. **waver,** *v.i,* hésiter; (*flame, courage*) vaciller; (*voice*) trembler. **wavy,** *a,* (*hair &c*) ondulé; (*line*) onduleux.

wax[1], *v.i,* (*moon*) croître; (*lyrical &c*) devenir.

wax[2], *n,* cire, *f;* (*in ear*) bouchon de c.; (*for skis*) fart, *m.* ~ *candle,* bougie en cire, *f.* ~ *paper,* papier paraffiné, *m.* ~*works,* (*museum*) musée de cire, *m.* ¶ *v.t,* cirer; (*car*) lustrer. ~**en,** ~**y,** *a,* cireux.

way, *n,* (*road &c*) chemin, *m;* voie; (*route*) chemin (*to,* de); (*distance*) distance; (*method*) façon, *f*, moyen, *m;* (*direction*) direction, *f*, sens, *m;* (*custom*) coutume, façon; (*Naut.*) vitesse, *f*. *in some* ~*s*, à certains égards. *be in a bad* ~, (*pers.*) aller mal; (*car &c*) être en piteux état. *be in s.o's* ~, barrer le passage à qn; gêner qn. *be under* ~, (*ship*) faire route; (*meeting &c*) être en cours. *each* ~ (*bet*), gagnant ou placé. *get one's own* ~, obtenir ce qu'on désire. *get out of the* ~, s'écarter. *know one's* ~ *about* (*fig.*), savoir se débrouiller. *a long* ~ [*off*], loin. *make* ~ *for s.o*, s'écarter pour laisser passer qn; (*fig.*) laisser la voie libre à qn. *be on one's* ~, se mettre en route. *on the* ~, en route. *on the* ~ *to*, sur le chemin de. *over the* ~, en face, de l'autre côté [de la rue]. *the other* ~ *round*, dans l'autre sens. *this* ~, par ici. ~*farer*, voyageur, euse. ~*faring*, voyages, *m.pl.* ~ *in*, entrée, *f*. ~*lay*, (*attack*) attaquer; (*speak to*) accrocher *P*. ~ *of life*, manière de vivre, *f*. ~ *out*, sortie, *f*. ~*side*, *n*, bord de la route, *m;* *a*, au bord de la route. *fall by the* ~*side* (*fig.*), abandonner en route.

wayward, *a*, capricieux, rebelle; (*horse*) rétif.

we, *pn*, nous; (*P*) on. ~ *English*, nous autres Anglais.

weak, *a*, (*gen.*) faible; (*drink*) léger; (*Med.*) fragile; (*heart*) malade. *have* ~ *eyesight*, avoir la vue faible. *go* ~ *at the knees*, avoir les jambes de coton. ~*-kneed*, mou. ~*-minded*, faible d'esprit. ~*-willed*, faible ~**en,** *v.t*, affaiblir; rendre moins solide; (*heart*) fatiguer; (*drink &c*) diluer. ¶ *v.i*, faiblir; (*health*) s'affaiblir; (*power &c*) baisser. ~**ening,** *n*, affaiblissement, *m*. ~**ling,** *n*, mauviette, *f*. ~**ly,** *a*, faible, chétif. ¶ *ad*, faiblement. ~**ness,** *n*, faiblesse, *f;* (*for sth, s.o*) faible; manque de solidité, *m;* fragilité, *f*.

weal, *n*, trace d'un coup, *f*.

wealth, *n*, richesse, *f;* (*riches*) richesses, fortune, *f*. ~**y,** *a*, [très] riche.

wean, *v.t*, sevrer; (*fig.*) détourner.

weapon, *n*, arme, *f*.

wear, *n*, (*use*) usage, *m;* (~ *& tear*) usure, *f;* (*Com.*) vêtements, *m.pl.* *town &c* ~, tenue de ville &c. *the worse for* ~, fatigué. ¶ *v.t.ir*, (*gen.*) porter; (*rub &c*) user; (*hole, track*) faire peu à peu. ¶ *v.i*, s'user. ~ *away*, (s')user; (s')effacer. ~ *down* (*resistance*) miner. ~ *out*, (s')user; (*patience &c*) (s')épuiser. ~ *thin*, (*cloth*) être râpé; s'épuiser. ~ *well*, faire beaucoup d'usage; (*fig.*) résister au temps. ~**able,** *a*, mettable.

weariness, *n*, fatigue, lassitude, *f*.

wearing, *a*, épuisant.

wearisome, *a*, (*boring*) ennuyeux, lassant; (*tiring*) épuisant. **weary,** *a*, (*pers.*) las (de); (*work*) fatigant; (*sigh*) de lassitude. ¶ *v.t*, fatiguer, lasser (*with*, à force de).

weasel, *n*, belette, *f*.

weather, *n*, temps, *m*. *under the* ~ *P* (*fig.*), mal fichu *P*. ~ *permitting*, si le temps le permet. ¶ *a*, (*station &c*) météorologique; (*conditions &c*) atmosphérique; (*Naut: side &c*) du vent. ~*-beaten*, (*pers.*) tanné. ~*boarding*, planches de recouvrement, *f.pl.* ~ *chart*, carte du temps, *f*. ~*cock*, girouette, *f*. ~ *forecast*, bulletin météorologique, météo *P*, *m*. ~*proof*, (*house*) étanche; (*clothes*) imperméable. ¶ *v.t*, (*storm &c*) réchapper à.

weave, *n*, tissage, *m*. ¶ *v.t.ir*, tisser; (*basket*) tresser; (*strands*) entrelacer; (*fig: plot*) tramer. ¶ *v.i*, (*river &c*) serpenter. ~ [*one's way*] *through*, se faufiler à travers. **weaver,** *n*, tisserand, *m*.

web, *n*, (*spider*) toile, *f;* (*cloth, fig.*) tissu, *m*. **webbed,** *a*, palmé. **webbing,** *n*, sangles, *f.pl.*

wed, *v.t*, épouser; (*fig.*) allier. ¶ *v.i*, se marier. **wedded,** *a*, (*pers.*) marié; (*bliss &c*) conjugal. **wedding,** *n*, mariage, *m;* (*golden &c*) noces (d'or &c), *f.pl.* ~ *breakfast*, lunch de mariage, *m*. ~ *cake*, gâteau de noces, *m*. ~ *day*, jour de mariage, *m*. ~ *dress*, robe de mariée, *f*. ~ *march*, marche nuptiale, *f*. ~ *present*, cadeau de mariage, *m*. ~ *ring*, alliance, *f*.

wedge, *n*, (*splitting*) coin, *m;* (*for wheel*) cale, *f*. ¶ *v.t*, caler; (*push*) enfoncer. *be* ~*d*, être coincé.

Wednesday, *n*, mercredi, *m*. *for phrases V* **Saturday.**

wee, *a*, tout petit.

weed, *n*, mauvaise herbe; (*pers. pej.*) mauviette, *f*. ~*-killer*, désherbant, *m*. ¶ *v.t*, désherber. ~ *out* éliminer; trier. ~**ing,** *n*, désherbage, *m*.

week, *n*, semaine, *f;* huit jours, *m.pl.* *in a* ~, dans huit jours. *in 2* ~*s*, dans quinze jours. ~ *in* ~ *out*, semaine après s. ~ *day*, jour de semaine, *m*. ~ *days only*, la semaine seulement. ~*end*, week-end, *m*, fin de semaine, *f*. ~*end cottage*, maison de campagne, *f*. ~**ly,** *a. & n*, hebdomadaire, *m*. ¶ *ad*, une fois par semaine.

weep, *v.i. & t.ir*, pleurer (*for s.o*, qn; *for joy*, de joie); (*sore*) suinter. **weeping,** *n*, larmes, *f.pl.* ¶ *a*, qui pleure; (*tree*) pleureur. **weepy,** *a*, larmoyant.

weevil, *n*, charançon, *m*.

weewee *P*, *n*, pipi *P*, *m*. ¶ *v.i*, faire pipi *P*.

weft, *n*, trame, *f*.

weigh, *v.t*, peser; (*anchor*) lever. ¶ *v.i*, peser (*on*, sur). ~ *on s.o's mind*, tracasser qn. ~*bridge*, pontbascule, *m*. ~ *down*, faire plier. ~*ed down by* (*fig.*), accablé de. ~*-in*, pesage, *m*. ~*ing machine*, bascule, balance, *f*. **weight,** *n*, (*lit., fig.*) poids, *m*. *carry* ~, (*argument*) avoir du poids (*with*, pour); (*pers.*) avoir de l'influence. ~ *lifter*, haltérophile, *m*. ~**ing** (*on pay*) *n*, indemnité, *f*. ~**lessness,** *n*, apesanteur, *f*. ~**y,** *a*, (*load*) lourd; (*matter*) de poids, grave.

weir, *n*, barrage, *m*.

weird†, *a*, bizarre, étrange; mystérieux. ~**ness**, *n*, étrangeté, *f*. ~**o** *P*, *n*, drôle d'oiseau, *m*.
welcome, *a*, (*pers.*) bienvenu; (*event*) opportun; agréable. *you're ~ to..*, libre à vous de... ¶ *n*, accueil, *m*. *get a cold ~*, être reçu froidement. ¶ *v.t*, accueillir [chaleureusement]; souhaiter la bienvenue; (*news*) se réjouir de.
weld, *v.t*, souder. ~**er**, *n*, (*pers.*) soudeur, *m*; (*Mach.*) soudeuse, *f*. ~**ing** *&* **weld**, *n*, soudure, *f*.
welfare, *n*, (*gen.*) bien; (*comfort*) bien-être, *m*; (*physical &c*) santé, *f*. *child ~*, protection de l'enfance, *f*. *~ centre*, centre d'assistance sociale, *m*. *W~ State*, État-providence, *m*; Sécurité Sociale, *f*. *~ work*, travail social.
well[1], *n*, puits, *m*; (*stairs &c*) cage, *f*. ¶ *v.i*, ~ [*out*], sourdre. ~ [*up*], monter.
well[2], *a*, bien; (*healthy*) bien, en bonne santé. *feel ~*, se sentir bien. *get ~*, se remettre. *it's all very ~*, c'est bien beau. ¶ *ad*, bien. *as ~*, aussi, par-dessus le marché. *~ & truly*, bel & bien. *you may ~ ask!* belle question! *~-behaved*, sage. *~-being*, bien-être, *m*. *~-bred*, (*behaviour*) bien élevé; (*family*) de bonne famille; (*animal*) de bonne race. *~-built*, solide. *~-disposed*, *~-meaning*, bien intentionné. *~ done*, (*Cook*) bien cuit. *~ done!* bravo! *~-educated*, qui a reçu une bonne éducation. *~-fed*, bien nourri. *~-heeled P*, nanti. *~ known*, bien connu, célèbre. *~-mannered*, bien élevé. *~-nigh*, presque. *~-read*, cultivé, instruit. *~-spoken*, qui parle bien. *~-thought-of*, bien considéré. *~-thought-out*, bien conçu. *~-timed*, opportun. *~-worn*, (*path*) battu; (*clothes*) usagé; (*fig.*) rebattu. ¶ *i*, eh bien; (*hesitation*) c'est que..; (*question*) et alors? *~ I never!* ça alors! pas possible!
wellingtons, *n.pl*, bottes de caoutchouc, *f.pl*.
Welsh, *a*, gallois. *~ dresser*, vaisselier, *m*. *~ rabbit*, *~ rarebit*, toast au fromage, *m*. ¶ *n*, le gallois. *~man*, *~woman*, Gallois, e.
welsh *P*, *v.i*, (*Turf*) filer sans régler ses dettes.
welterweight (*Box.*) *n*, poids welter, *m*.
wend one's way, aller son chemin.
wer[e]wolf, *n*, loup-garou, *m*.
west, *n*, ouest, *m*. *in the ~*, dans l'o. [*to the*] *~ of*, à l'o. de. *the W~*, (*Pol.*) l'Occident, l'Ouest. ¶ *a*, ouest, *inv.*; (*wind*) d'ouest. *W~ Africa*, l'Afrique occidentale. *~ coast*, côte ouest, *f*. *W~ Indies*, Antilles, *f.pl*. ¶ *ad*, à l'ouest, vers l'o. **westerly**, *a*, (*wind*) de l'ouest. **western**, *a*, [de l']ouest, *inv*. *W~ Australia, Europe*, Australie, Europe occidentale. ¶ *n*, (*film*) western, *m*. ~**er**, *n*, homme *ou* femme de l'ouest; (*Pol.*) occidental, e. ~**ize**, *v.t*, occidentaliser.
wet, *a*, [tout] mouillé; (*damp, climate*) humide; (*soaking*) trempé; (*weather*) pluvieux; (*day*) de pluie; (*season*) des pluies; (*ink, paint*) frais. *~ blanket*, rabat-joie, *m*. *~suit*, combinaison de plongée, *f*. *~ through*, trempé jusqu'aux os. ¶ *n*, pluie; humidité; (*P pers.*) lavette *P*, *f*. ¶ *v.t*, mouiller. *~ o.s*, *~ one's pants*, mouiller sa culotte. ~**ness**, *n*, humidité, *f*.
whack, *n*, (*blow*) grand coup; (*sound*) claquement, *m*; (*P share*) part, *f*. ¶ *v.t*, donner un grand coup à; (*spank*) fesser. ~**ed** *P*, *a*, crevé *P*. ~**ing**, *n*, fessée; raclée *P*, *f*. *~ great*, énorme.
whale, *n*, baleine, *f*. *have a ~ of a time*, se payer une pinte de bon sang. *~bone*, fanon de baleine, *m*, baleine, *f*. *~ oil*, huile de b., *f*. ¶ *v.i*, pêcher la baleine. **whaler**, *n*, baleinier, *m*.
wharf, *n*, quai, *m*. ~**age**, *n*, droits de quai, *m.pl*.
what, *a*, (*question & exclamation*) quel, quelle. *~ a lovely dress!* quelle jolie robe! *~ an idiot!* quel idiot! *~ film did you see?* quel film as-tu vu? *~ little I had*, le peu que j'avais. ¶ *pn*, (*questions: subject*) qu'est-ce qui; (*object*) que, qu'est-ce que; (*after pr.*) quoi; (*that which*) ce qui; ce que. *~ about a drink?* si on prenait un verre? *~ about me?* et moi? *~ for*, pourquoi? *& ~ is more*, & qui plus est. *I don't know ~ to say*, je ne sais pas quoi dire. ¶ *i*, quoi! comment! *~'s-it*, *~'s-his-name*, machin *P*. **whatever**, *a*, quel que. *~ his courage*, quel que soit son courage. ¶ *ad*, *nothing ~*, absolument rien. ¶ *pn*, quoi que. *~ he may say*, quoi qu'il dise. (*all that*) tout ce qui, tout ce que.
wheat, *n*, froment, blé, *m*. ¶ *a*, (*flour, field*) de blé. *~germ*, germes de blé, *m.pl*.
wheedle, *v.t*, cajoler. **wheedling**, *a*, enjôleur. ¶ *n*, cajoleries, *f.pl*.
wheel, *n*, roue, *f*; (*Naut.*) [roue de] gouvernail; (*steering*) volant; (*spinning*) rouet; (*potter's*) tour, *m*; (*pl: fig.*) rouage, *m*. *~barrow*, brouette, *f*. *~-base*, empattement, *m*. *~chair*, fauteuil roulant, *m*. *~wright*, charron, *m*. ¶ *v.t*, pousser, rouler. ~ [*round*], (*birds*) tournoyer; (*pers.*) se retourner brusquement; (*Mil.*) effectuer une conversion. *~ing & dealing*, manigances, combines *P*, *f.pl*. **wheeled**, *a*, à... roues.
wheeze, *v.i*, respirer bruyamment. **wheezy**, *a*, poussif.
whelk, *n*, buccin, *m*.
when, *ad*, quand? à quelle époque? à quel moment? ¶ *c*, quand, lorsque; une fois que; (*whereas*) alors que. *one day ~ it was raining*, un jour qu'il pleuvait. *the day ~ he left*, le jour où il est parti. *at the time ~*, au moment où. **whence**, *c*, d'où. **whenever**, *c*, (*at whatever time*) quand; (*every time*) chaque fois que.
where, *ad*, où. *~ is he going?* où va-t-il? ¶ *c*, [là] où; là que. *tell me ~ he is*, dites-moi où il est. *this is ~ we left it*, c'est là que nous l'avons laissé. **whereabouts**, *ad*, où. *one's ~*, où on

est. **whereas,** *c,* tandis que, alors que; (*Law: since*) attendu que. **whereat,** *ad,* sur quoi. **whereby,** *c,* par quoi. **wherefore,** *ad,* pourquoi. **whereupon,** *c,* sur quoi, & sur ce. **wherever,** *c,* (*no matter where*) où que + *subj.;* (*anywhere*) [là] où; (*everywhere*) partout où. ~ *you are,* où que tu sois. *sit* ~ *you like,* asseyez-vous [là] où vous voulez. ~ *I go,* partout où je vais. ¶ *ad,* ~ *did you find it?* mais où donc l'as-tu trouvé? *the wherewithal,* les moyens (*to,* de), *m.pl.*

whet, *v.t,* aiguiser. ~*stone,* pierre à aiguiser, *f.*

whether, *c,* si; que + *subj.;* soit. *I don't know* ~ *he'll come,* je ne sais pas s'il viendra. ~ *or not he comes,* qu'il vienne ou non. ~ *now or later,* soit maintenant soit plus tard. *I doubt* ~ , je doute que + *subj.*

whey, *n,* petit-lait, *m.*

which, *a,* quel. ~ *one?* lequel? laquelle? *in* ~ *case,* auquel cas. ¶ *pn,* (*interrogative*) lequel, laquelle; (*relative: subject*) qui; (*object*) que; (*after pr.*) lequel &c; (*& that: subject*) ce qui; (*object*) ce que. *of* ~, dont. ~ *do you like?* lequel aimez-vous? *she was late* ~ *didn't please him,* elle était en retard, ce qui ne lui plaisait pas. *after* ~ , après quoi. *things* ~ *I need,* les choses dont j'ai besoin. ~ *way?* par où? **whichever,** *a,* le... qui, que; n'importe quel; *take* ~ *book you want,* prenez le livre que vous voudrez, prenez n'importe quel livre. ¶ *pn,* celui, celle &c qui *ou* que.

whiff, *n,* (*puff*) bouffée; (*smell*) odeur, *f.*

while, *n,* temps, *m. a* ~ , quelque temps. *between* ~*s,* entre-temps. *it is worth* ~ , cela vaut la peine. **while & whilst,** *c,* pendant que; (*as long as*) tant que; (*whereas*) tandis que; alors que; (*although*) bien que, quoique + *subj.* ¶ *v.t,* ~ *away,* [faire] passer.

whim, *n,* caprice, *m,* fantaisie, *f.*

whimper, *v.i,* (*pers.*) gémir faiblement; (*dog*) pousser des petits cris plaintifs.

whimsical, *a,* (*pers.*) fantasque, capricieux; (*idea*) bizarre, biscornu.

whine, *v.i,* (*pers., wind*) gemir; (*child*) pleurnicher; (*fig.*) se lamenter.

whinny, *n,* hennissement, *m.* ¶ *v.i,* hennir.

whip, *n,* fouet, *m;* (*riding*) cravache, *f;* (*Pol: pers.*) chef de file, *m.* ~*hand,* avantage, *m.* ~*lash,* coup de fouet, *m.* ¶ *v.t,* fouetter; (*Cook.*) battre au fouet. ~*ped cream,* crème fouettée, c. chantilly. ~ *sth away,* enlever qch brusquement. ~ *up,* battre au fouet; (*fig.*) stimuler; (*P*) préparer en vitesse. **whipper-in,** *n,* piqueur, *m.* **whipper-snapper,** *n,* freluquet, *m.* **whipping,** *n,* correction, *f.* ~ *cream,* crème fraîche [à fouetter]. ~*-boy,* bouc émissaire, *m.*

whippet, *n,* whippet, *m.*

whir[r], *v.i,* (*wings*) bruire; (*Mach.*) ronronner; vrombir.

whirl, *n,* tourbillon, *m. my head's in a* ~ , la tête me tourne. ¶ *v.i,* (*wheel &c*) tourner; (*leaves &c*) tourbillonner. ~*pool,* tourbillon, *m.* ~*wind,* tornade, trombe, *f.*

whisk, *n,* (*Cook.*) fouet; (*rotary*) batteur à œufs, *m.* ¶ *v.t,* battre au fouet; (*egg white*) b. en neige.

whiskers, *n.pl,* favoris, *m.pl;* (*cat*) moustache, *f.*

whisky, *n,* whisky, *m.*

whisper, *n,* chuchotement; (*wind &c*) murmure; (*fig.*) bruit, *m.* ¶ *v.i. & t,* chuchoter, dire à voix basse. ~**ing,** *n,* chuchotement, *m.* ~ *gallery,* galerie à écho, *f.*

whist (*Cards*) *n,* whist, *m.*

whistle, *n,* sifflet; (*sound*) sifflement; coup de sifflet, *m.* ¶ *v.t. & i,* siffler; (*casually*) siffloter. *you can* ~ *for it!* tu peux toujours courir *P.*

whit, *n,* iota, *m.*

white, *a,* blanc. *as* ~ *as a sheet,* pâle comme un linge. *go* or *turn* ~ , (*hair*) blanchir; (*with fear &c*) blêmir. ~*bait,* petite friture, *f.* ~*-collar worker,* employé(e) de bureau, col blanc. ~*-haired,* aux cheveux blancs. ~ *horses* (*sea*), moutons, *m.pl.* ~*-hot,* chauffé à blanc. *the W*~ *House,* la Maison Blanche. ~ *lie,* pieux mensonge. ~ *man,* ~ *woman,* Blanc, che. (*Pol.*) ~ *paper,* livre blanc, *m.* ~ *sale,* vente de blanc, *f.* ~ *sauce,* béchamel, *f.* ~*wash, n,* lait de chaux, *m; v.t,* blanchir à la chaux; (*fig.*) blanchir. ~ *wedding,* mariage en blanc, *m.* ¶ *n,* (*colour, egg, eye*) blanc, *m;* (*whiteness*) blancheur, *f;* (*pers.*) Blanc, che. **whiten,** *v.t,* blanchir. **whiteness,** *n,* blancheur, *f.*

whiting, *n,* (*fish*) merlan, *m.*

whitish, *a,* blanchâtre.

whitlow, *n,* panaris, *m.*

Whitsun[tide], *n,* la Pentecôte. *Whit Sunday,* dimanche de la Pentecôte, *m.*

whittle, *v.t,* tailler au couteau (*out of,* dans). ~ *down,* tailler; (*fig.*) réduire.

whiz[z], *n,* sifflement, *m.* ~ *kid P,* jeune prodige, *m.* ¶ *v.i,* ~ *past &c,* passer &c à toute vitesse.

who, *pn,* (*question & relative*) qui. ~*dunit,* roman policier, *m. W*~*'s W*~ , Bottin Mondain, *m.*

whoa, *i,* ho! hola!

whoever, *pn,* (*anyone that*) quiconque; (*no matter who, whom*) qui que ce soit qui, que + *subj.*

whole, *a,* entier; intact; (*set &c*) complet; (*unhurt*) sain & sauf. ~ *number* (*Math.*), nombre entier. *the* ~ *truth,* toute la vérité. *the* ~ *lot,* le tout. ~*hearted,* sans réserve. ~*heartedly,* de tout cœur. ~*meal bread,* pain complet, *m.* ¶ *n,* tout, *m. as a* ~ , dans son ensemble; (*sell*) en bloc. *on the* ~ , dans l'ensemble. *the* ~ *of,* tout. **wholesale,** *n,* [vente *f* en] gros, *m.* ¶ *a,* (*Com.*) de gros; (*fig.*) en masse; en bloc. ¶ *ad,* (*buy, sell*) en gros; (*get*) au prix de gros; (*fig.*) en masse; en bloc. ~**r,** *n,* grossiste, *m,f.*

wholesome, *a,* sain; (*air*) salubre. **wholly,** *ad,* entièrement, complètement.
whom, *pn* (*question*) qui; (*relative*) que; (*after pr.*) qui. *of* ~, dont.
whoop, *n,* cri, *m.* ¶ *v.i,* pousser des cris; (*Med.*) avoir des quintes de toux. ~**ing cough,** *n,* coqueluche, *f.*
whore, *n,* putain *P**, *f.*
whose, *pn,* (*question*) de qui; à qui; (*relative*) dont, de qui. **whosoever,** *pn,* quiconque.
why, *ad. & c,* pourquoi. ¶ *i,* eh bien! (*surprise*) tiens! *the* ~*s & wherefores,* les pourquoi et les comment.
wick, *n,* mèche, *f.*
wicked†, *a,* (*pers.*) méchant; (*act*) mauvais; (*smile*) malicieux. ~**ness,** *n,* méchanceté, malice, *f.*
wicker, *n,* osier, *m.* ~*work,* vannerie, *f.*
wicket, *n,* (*cricket*) guichet; (*gate*) portillon, *m.*
wide, *a,* (*gen.*) large; (*variety*) grand; (*knowledge*) vaste; (*powers*) étendu; (*interests*) divers. *how* ~ *is the carpet?* quelle largeur a le tapis? *it is 3 metres* ~, il a 3 mètres de large. ¶ *ad, go* ~, (*shot*) passer de côté. ~ *apart,* (*trees*) largement espacés; (*eyes*) très écartés. ~ *awake,* bien éveillé; (*smart*) dégourdi. ~ *of the mark,* loin de la vérité. ~ *open,* grand ouvert. ~*-ranging,* (*report*) de grand envergure. ~*-spread,* très répandu. ~**ly,** *ad,* (*spaced*) largement; (*believed*) généralement; (*differ &c*) radicalement. **widen,** *v.t,* élargir; (*knowledge*) étendre; (*margin*) augmenter.
widgeon, *n,* canard siffleur, *m.*
widow, *n,* veuve, *f. the* ~*'s mite,* le denier de la v. ¶ *v.t, to become* ~*ed,* devenir veuf, ve. ~**er,** *n,* veuf, *m.* ~**hood,** *n,* veuvage, *m.*
width, *n,* largeur; (*garment*) ampleur, *f.*
wield, *v.t,* manier; (*power*) exercer.
wife, *n,* femme; (*Law, Adm.*) épouse, *f.*
wig, *n,* perruque, *f;* (*hairpiece*) postiche, *m.*
wiggle, *v.t,* (*toes &c*) agiter; (*tooth, screw*) faire jouer; (*hips*) tortiller de. **wiggly,** *a,* ondulé.
wild, *a,* (*animal &c*) sauvage; (*rabbit*) de garenne; (*weather*) gros; (*wind &c*) furieux, déchaîné; (*appearance*) farouche; (*eyes*) égaré, hagard; (*idea, laughter*) fou; (*angry*) furieux. *I'm not* ~ *about it,* ça ne m'emballe pas. ~ *boar,* sanglier, *m.* ~*cat,* chat sauvage, *m.* ~*cat strike* (*fig.*), grève sauvage, *f. spread like* ~*fire,* se répandre comme une traînée de poudre. ~ *goose chase,* folle entreprise. *sow one's* ~ *oats,* jeter sa gourme. *the W*~ *West,* le Far West. **wild & wilderness,** *n,* région sauvage *ou* reculée, *f;* (*fig.*) desert, *m.* ~**ly,** *ad,* (*happy*) follement; (*blow &c*) furieusement; (*behave*) de façon extravagante; (*hit out, guess &c*) au hasard. ~**ness,** *n,* aspect sauvage, *m;* (*tribe*) sauvagerie; fureur, *f.*
wiles, *n.pl,* ruses, *f.pl;* (*charms*) artifices, *m.pl.*
wilful, *a,* (*pers.*) têtu, obstiné, volontaire; (*action*) délibéré; (*murder*) prémédité. ~**ly,** *ad,* obstinément; délibérément. ~**ness,** *n,* obstination, *f.*
will, *n,* volonté, *f;* (*Law*) testament, *m. have a* ~ *of one's own,* être très volontaire. *the last* ~ *& testament of,* les dernières volontés de. *where there's a* ~ *there's a way,* vouloir, c'est pouvoir. ~*power,* volonté, *f,* vouloir, *m.* ¶ *v. modal, is expressed in Fr. by future tense* or *by* vouloir. *he* ~ *see him on Sunday,* il le verra dimanche. ~ *you help me?* voulez-vous m'aider? ¶ *v.t, regular,* (*wish, intend*) vouloir (*that,* que + *subj.*); (*bequeath*) léguer. **willing,** *a,* (*help &c*) spontané; (*helper &c*) de bonne volonté. *be* ~, vouloir [bien]. ~**ly,** *ad,* volontiers; (*volontarily*) volontairement, spontanément. ~**ness,** *n,* bonne volonté.
will-o'-the-wisp, *n,* feu follet, *m.*
willow, *n,* saule, *m.* ~*herb,* épilobe, *m.* ~*-pattern, n,* motif chinois [bleu], *m.* ~**y,** *a,* élancé; mince.
willynilly, *ad,* bon gré, mal gré.
wilt, *v.t,* flétrir; (*v.i.*) se f., se faner, s'étioler; (*fig.*) faiblir.
wily, *a,* rusé, astucieux.
wimple, *n,* guimpe, *f.*
win, *n,* victoire, *f.* ~ *on points,* v. aux points. ¶ *v.t.ir,* (*gen.*) gagner; (*prize*) remporter; (*fame &c*) trouver; (*friends*) se faire. ~ *one's way to,* gagner, parvenir à. ~ *sth from s.o,* gagner qch à qn. ~ *the day,* l'emporter; (*Mil.*) remporter la victoire. ¶ *v.i.ir,* gagner, l'emporter. ~ *back,* regagner; (*land*) reconquérir; (*trophy*) reprendre. ~ *over,* ~ *round,* convaincre.
wince, *v.i,* tressaillir.
winch, *n,* treuil, *m.*
wind[1] (wind) *n,* vent; (*breath*) souffle, *m;* (*Med.*) vents, *m.pl.* (*Naut.*) *head* ~, vent debout. *following* ~, v. arrière. *break* ~, lâcher un v. *bring up* ~, avoir un renvoi. *get* ~ *of,* avoir vent de. *get a second* ~, trouver son second souffle. *have the* ~ *up,* avoir la frousse *P. put the* ~ *up s.o,* flanquer la frousse à qn *P. there's something in the* ~, il y a anguille sous roche. ~*bag,* hâbleur, euse. ~*break,* pare-vent, *m.inv.* ~*fall,* fruit abattu par le vent, *m;* (*fig.*) aubaine, *f.* ~ *gauge,* anémomètre, *m.* ~ *instrument,* instrument à vent, *m.* ~*mill,* moulin à vent, *m.* ~*pipe,* trachée, *f.* ~*screen,* pare-brise, *m.inv.* ~*screen washer,* lave-glace, *m.inv.* ~*screen wiper,* essuie-glace, *m.inv.* ~*sock,* manche à air, *f.* ~*surfer,* (*pers.*) véliplanchiste, *m,f;* (*board*) planche à voile, *f. go* ~*surfing,* faire de la p. à v. ~*swept,* battu des vents. ¶ *v.t,* essouffler; (*boxer &c*) couper le souffle à.
wind[2] (waind), *v.t.ir,* (*roll*) enrouler; (*clock &c*) remonter; (*handle*) donner des tours de. ¶ *v.i,* serpenter. ~ *down,* (*path &c*) descendre en

serpentant. ~ *up,* (*meeting &c*) terminer, clore; (*Com.*) liquider; (*account*) clore; (*watch &c*) remonter; monter en serpentant. ~**ing,** *a,* sinueux, tortueux, qui serpente. **windlass,** *n,* treuil, *m.*

window, *n,* fenêtre; (*car, train*) vitre, *f;* (*stained-glass*) vitrail, *m;* (*shop &c*) vitrine, *f;* (*ticket office &c*) guichet, *m.* ~*-box,* jardinière, *f.* ~*-cleaner,* laveur, euse de carreaux. ~*-dresser,* étalagiste, *m,f.* ~*-dressing,* présentation de l'étalage; (*fig.*) façade, *f.* ~*-ledge,* ~*sill,* (*inside*) appui de fenêtre; (*outside*) rebord de f., *m.* ~ *pane,* vitre, *f,* carreau, *m.* ~*-seat,* banquette, *f.* ~*-shopping,* lèche-vitrines, *m.*

windward, *n,* côte du vent, *m.* **windy,** *a,* (*day, weather*) de grand vent; (*place*) exposé au vent, battu par les vents. *it is* ~, il fait du vent. *get* ~ *P,* paniquer.

wine, *n,* vin, *m.* ~*glass,* verre à vin, *m.* ~ *grower,* vigneron, ne, viticulteur, *m.* ~*-growing, n,* viticulture, *f; a,* (*district &c*) viticole. ~ *list,* carte des vins, *f.* ~ *merchant,* marchand(e) de vin; négociant(e) en vins. ~*-tasting,* dégustation [de vins], *f.* ~ *waiter,* sommelier, *m.*

wing, *n,* (*gen.*) aile; (*chair*) oreillette, *f;* (*pl: Theat.*) coulisses, *f.pl.* ~ *mirror,* rétroviseur de côté, *m.* ~ *nut,* papillon, écrou à ailettes, *m.* ~*span,* envergure, *f.* ~ *tip,* bout de l'aile, *m.* **wing & winger** *n,* (*Sport*) ailier, *m.* ~**ed,** *a,* ailé.

wink, *n,* clin d'œil; (*blink*) clignement, *m.* ¶ *v.i,* faire un clin d'œil; cligner des yeux; (*star*) clignoter. *easy as* ~*ing,* simple comme bonjour.

winkle, *n,* bigorneau, *m.*

winner, *n,* (*game &c*) gagnant, e; (*fight*) vainqueur, *m. pick a* ~, (*Turf*) choisir un gagneur; (*gen.*) tirer le bon numéro. **winning,** *a,* (*pers. &c*) gagnant; (*goal*) décisif; (*smile*) charmeur. ~*-post,* poteau d'arrivée, *m.* ~**s,** *n,* gains, *m.pl.*

winter, *n,* hiver, *m.* ¶ ~, *a.* & **wintry,** *a,* d'hiver.

wipe, *n,* coup de torchon, de chiffon &c, *m.* ¶ *v.t,* essuyer; (*blackboard*) effacer. ~ *one's bottom,* s'essuyer. ~ *one's feet,* s'e. les pieds. ~ *one's nose,* se moucher. ~ *out,* (*memory &c*) effacer; (*army &c*) anéantir. ~ *up,* essuyer.

wire, *n,* fil de fer; (*Elec.*) fil [électrique]; (*fencing*) grillage; (*Tel.*) télégramme, *m.* ~ *brush,* brosse métallique, *f.* ~ *cutters,* cisaille, *f.* ~ *netting,* treillis métallique, *m.* ~ *wool,* paille de fer, *f.* ¶ *v.t,* (*circuit*) installer; (*house*) faire l'installation électrique de; télégraphier. ~ *sth to sth,* (*Elec.*) brancher qch sur qch. ~ *for sound,* sonoriser. ¶ *v.i,* télégraphier. ~**less,** *n,* T.S.F., radio, *f. by* ~, par sans-fils. ¶ *a,* (*programme*) radiophonique. ~ *message,* radio, sans-fils, *m,* ~ *operator,* radiotélégraphiste, *m,f.* ~ *set,* poste de T.S.F., *m,* radio, *f.* **wiring,** *n,* installation électrique, *f.* **wiry,** *a,* (*hair*) dru; (*pers.*) nerveux, vigoureux.

wisdom, *n,* sagesse; prudence, *f.* ~ *tooth,* dent de sagesse, *f.* **wise**[1]†, *a,* (*pers.*) sage; (*action*) judicieux; prudent. *grow* ~*r,* s'assagir. ~ *guy P,* gros malin *P, m. the* [3] *W*~ *Men,* les [3] Rois Mages.

wise[2], *n,* façon, *f.* ¶ *ad. suffix,* du point de vue de.

wish, *n,* désir; vœu, souhait, *m. best* ~*es,* meilleurs vœux; (*letter end*) bien amicalement. *give her my best* ~*es,* faites-lui mes amitiés. ¶ *v.t,* (*want*) souhaiter, désirer; (*s.o luck &c*) souhaiter (bonne chance &c à qn). ¶ *v.i.* faire un vœu. ~ *for sth,* souhaiter qch. ~**bone,** *n,* fourchette, *f.* ~**ful thinking,** pensée née du désir.

wishy-washy, *a,* fadasse *P;* (*colour*) délavé.

wisp, *n,* (*hair*) mèche, *f;* (*straw*) brin, *m.*

wistaria, *n,* glycine, *f.*

wistful, *a,* plein d'un vague regret. ~**ly,** *ad,* d'un air songeur & triste.

wit, *n,* esprit, *m;* (*pers.*) homme *ou* femme d'esprit; (*pl.*) intelligence, *f;* esprit. *be at one's* ~*s' end,* ne plus savoir que faire.

witch, *n,* sorcière, *f.* ~*craft,* sorcellerie, *f.* ~ *doctor,* sorcier, *m.* ~ *hazel,* hamamélis, *m.* ~*hunt* (*fig.*), chasse aux sorcières, *f.*

with, *pr,* avec; (*having*) à, qui a. *I'm staying* ~ *friends,* je suis chez des amis. ~ *all my heart,* de tout mon cœur. ~ *both hands,* à deux mains. ~ *pleasure,* avec plaisir. *the girl* ~ *blue eyes,* la fille aux yeux bleus. ~*-it P,* dans le vent *P.*

withdraw, *v.t.ir,* retirer (*from,* de); rappeler; (*statement &c*) rétracter; (*order*) annuler; (*claim*) renoncer à. ¶ *v.i,* se retirer; reculer; (*candidate*) se désister; se rétracter. ~**al,** *n,* retrait; (*Mil.*) repli, *m. have* ~ *symptoms* (*Med.*), être en état de manque. **withdrawn,** *a,* renfermé.

wither, *v.t,* flétrir. ¶ *v.i,* se flétrir; (*beauty*) se faner; (*hope &c*) s'évanouir. ~**ed,** *a,* flétri; (*limb*) atrophié; (*pers.*) ratatiné. ~**ing,** *a,* (*look*) foudroyant; (*remark*) cinglant.

withhold, *v.t.ir,* (*money*) retenir; (*news*) cacher (à qn); (*help &c*) refuser (à qn).

within, *pr,* (*inside*) à l'intérieur de. *live* ~ *one's income,* vivre selon ses moyens. ~ *a year of,* moins d'un an avant *ou* après. ~ *call,* ~ *earshot,* à portée de voix. ~ *sight,* en vue. *from* ~, de dedans.

without, *pr,* sans. *do* ~, se passer de.

withstand, *v.t.ir,* résister à.

witness, *n,* (*pers.*) témoin; (*evidence*) témoignage, *m.* ~ *box,* barre des témoins, *f.* ~ *for the defence, prosecution,* témoin à décharge, t. à charge. ¶ *v.t,* être témoin de;

(*document &c*) attester l'authenticité de; (*signature*) certifier. ¶ *v.i*, témoigner (*to sth*, de qch).
witticism, *n*, mot d'esprit, trait d'esprit, *m*. **witty†,** *a*, plein d'esprit, spirituel.
wizard, *n*, sorcier, magicien, *m*; (*fig.*) génie, *m*. **~ry,** *n*, magie, *f*; génie, *m*.
wizened, *a*, ratatiné.
wobble, *v.t*, trembler; (*table*) branler; (*wheel*) avoir du jeu; (*cyclist*) osciller.
woe, *n*, malheur, *m*. *~ betide*, malheur à. **~begone,** *a*, désolé. **~ful†,** *a*, triste, malheureux.
wolf, *n*, loup, *m*; (*she-~*) louve, *f*; (*fig: man*) courreur, *m*. *~ cub*, (*Zool., scouting*) louveteau, *m*. *~hound*, chien-loup, *m*. *give a ~ whistle*, siffler une fille. **~ish,** *a*, vorace.
woman, *n*, femme, *f*. *~ doctor*, femme médecin, doctoresse, *f*. *~ driver*, chauffeuse, *f*. *women drivers*, les femmes au volant. *~ hater*, misogyne, *m*. *Women's Libration Movement* (*Women's Lib P*), mouvement de libération de la femme (M.L.F.), *m*. *women's page* (*Press*), page des lectrices, *f*. *women's rights*, droits de la femme, *m.pl*. **~hood,** *n*, féminité, *f*. **~izer,** *n*, coureur [de femmes], *m*. **~ly,** *a*, féminin. *to be very ~*, être très femme.
womb, *n*, utérus; (*fig.*) sein, *m*.
wonder, *n*, étonnement, émerveillement; (*object &c*) miracle, *m*, merveille, *f*. *it's a ~ that*, c'est extraordinaire que. *no ~*, pas étonnant! ¶ *v.i. & t*, s'étonner (*at*, de; *that*, que + *subj.*); se demander (*why*, pourquoi); (*reflect*) penser, songer. **~ful†,** *a*, merveilleux. **~ment,** *n*, émerveillement, *m*.
wonky *P*, *a*, (*chair &c*) bancal; (*Mach.*) détraqué.
woo, *v.t*, faire la cour à; (*fig.*) chercher à plaire à.
wood, *n*, bois, *m*; (*Bowls*) boule, *f*. *you can't see the ~ for the trees*, les arbres vous cachent la forêt. *~ anemone*, anémone des bois, *f*. *~bine*, chèvrefeuille, *m*. *~ carver*, sculpteur sur bois, *m*. *~cock*, bécasse, *f*. *~cut*, gravure sur bois, *f*. *~ cutter*, bûcheron, *m*. *~land*, *n*, région boisée, *f*; *a*, des bois. *~louse*, cloporte, *m*. *~man*, forestier, *m*. *~pecker*, pic, *m*. *~ pigeon*, [pigeon] ramier, *m*. *~ pulp*, pâte à papier, *f*. *~ shavings*, copeaux [de bois], *m.pl*. *~shed*, bûcher, *m*. *the ~wind*, les bois, *m.pl*. *~work*, menuiserie, *f*. *~worm*, ver de bois, *m*. **~ed,** *a*, boisé. **~en,** *a*, de bois, en b; (*fig: movement*) raide. **~y,** *a*, ligneux.
woof, *n*, trame, *f*.
wool, *n*, laine, *f*. *pull the ~ over s.o's eyes*, en faire accroire à qn. *to be ~-gathering*, être dans la lune. ¶ *a*, de laine, en l.; (*shop*) de laines. **woollen,** *a*, (*cloth*) de laine; (*garment*) en *ou* de laine; (*industry*) lainier. **~s,** *n.pl*, lainages, *m.pl*. **woolly,** *a*, laineux; (*ideas*) confus. ¶ *n*, tricot, *m*; (*pl.*) lainages.
word, *n*, (*gen.*) mot, *m*; (*spoken*) mot, parole, *f*; (*pl: song*) paroles; (*promise*) parole; (*fig: message*) mot; (*news*) nouvelles (de), *f.pl*. *the W~* (*Rel.*), le Verbe. *keep one's ~*, tenir sa parole. *by ~ of mouth*, de vive voix. *~ for ~*, (*repeat*) mot pour mot, textuellement; (*translate*) m. à m. *have ~s with s.o* (*quarrel*), se disputer avec qn. *in other ~*, autrement dit. *in so many ~s*, explicitement. *put in a good ~ for*, glisser un mot en faveur de. *take s.o at his ~*, prendre qn au mot. *be ~-perfect in sth*, savoir qch sur le bout du doigt. ¶ *v.t*, formuler. **~-processor,** *n*, machine à traitement de texte, *f*. **wordiness,** *n*, verbosité, *f*. **wording** (*letter &c*) *n*, termes, *m.pl*. **wordy,** *a*, verbeux.
work, *n*, (*gen.*) travail, *m*; (*Art, Liter., Mus.*) œuvre, *f*; (*book &c*) ouvrage (sur qch), *m*; (*Need.*) ouvrage; (*social*) œuvres, *f.pl*; (*pl: gen, Adm., Mil.*) travaux, *m.pl*; (*clock &c*) mécanisme, *m*; (*factory*) usine, *f*. *out of ~*, en chômage. *~bag*, sac à ouvrage, *m*. *~basket*, corbeille à ouvrage, *f*. *~bench*, établi, *m*. *~box*, boîte à ouvrage, *f*. *~load*, part du travail, *f*. *~man*, ouvrier, *m*. *~manlike*, professionnel; bien fait. *~manship*, habileté professionnelle; travail. *~mate*, camarade de travail, *m,f*. *~out* (*Sport*), séance d'entraînement, *f*. *~room*, salle de travail, *f*. *~s manager*, chef d'exploitation, *m*. *~shop*, atelier, *m*. *~ shy*, fainéant. *~-study*, étude du travail, *f*. *~-to-rule*, grève du zèle, *f*. ¶ *v.t*, (*pers. &c*) faire travailler; (*Mach.*) faire marcher, actionner; (*miracle &c*) faire, accomplir; (*change*) apporter; (*mine &c*) exploiter; (*metal, dough &c*) travailler. *~ one's passage*, payer son passage en travaillant. *~ wonders*, (*pers.*) faire des merveilles; (*thing*) faire merveille. ¶ *v.i*, (*gen.*) travailler; (*Mach.*) marcher; (*medicine*) agir; (*brain*) fonctionner. *~ hard*, travailler dur. *~ like a Trojan*, t. comme un forçat. ~ **in with,** (*plans &c*) cadrer avec. ~ **off,** (*fat &c*) éliminer, se débarrasser de; (*anger*) passer (*on s.o.* sur qn). ~ **out,** *v.t*, (*sum, problem*) résoudre; (*plan*) élaborer; (*idea*) mettre au point; *v.i*, (*plan*) réussir; (*sum &c*) se résoudre exactement; (*total*) se monter (*at*, à). ~ **up,** (*business*) développer. *get ~ed up*, se mettre dans tous ses états. *~ up to*, préparer le terrain pour. **~able,** *a*, réalisable, possible. **~er,** *n*, travailleur, euse, ouvrier, ère; (*office*) employé, e. **~ing,** *a*, (*clothes, week &c*) de travail; (*wife*) qui travaille; (*model*) qui marche. *~ capital*, fonds de roulement, *m.pl*. *~ class*, classe ouvrière. *~-class*, (*background &c*) ouvrier. *~ day*, journée de travail, *f*. *~ drawing*, épure, *f*. **~ings,** *n*, (*Mach.*) mécanisme, *m*; (*Govt. &c*) rouages, *m.pl*: (*Min.*) chantier d'exploitation, *m*.
world, *n*, monde, *m*. *do s.o a ~ of good*, faire à

qn énormément de bien. *where in the ~ ...?* où donc...? ¶ *a,* (*gen.*) mondial; (*language*) universel; (*record, tour*) du monde. *the W~ Cup,* la Coupe du Monde. *W~ Fair,* Exposition Internationale. *~-famous,* de renommée mondiale. *W~ Health Organization* (*W.H.O.*), Organisation mondiale de la Santé (O.M.S.), *f.* **~-wide,** *a,* mondial, universel. **worldly,** *a,* (*pers.*) matérialiste; (*matters*) de ce monde; (*Rel.*) temporel. *all one's ~ goods,* tout ce qu'on possède.

worm, *n,* ver, *m.* *~-eaten,* (*fruit*) véreux; (*wood*) vermoulu. *~ oneself into,* s'insinuer dans. *~ sth out of s.o,* tirer les vers du nez à qn. **~wood,** *n,* armoise, *f.*

worn, *a,* (*object*) usé; (*pers.*) las. *~-out,* complètement usé; épuisé.

worry, *n,* souci, *m.* ¶ *v.t,* tracasser, inquiéter; (*sheep*) harceler. *~ o.s sick,* se rendre malade d'inquiétude. ¶ *v.i,* s'inquiéter, se faire du souci; s'en faire *P;* se faire du mauvais sang. **~ing,** *a,* inquiétant.

worse, *a,* pire, plus mauvais; (*feel*) plus mal; (*liter.*) pis. *get ~,* se détériorer; (*illness &c*) empirer. *all the ~ for him,* tant pis pour lui. ¶ *ad,* plus mal; (*more*) plus. ¶ *n,* pire, *m.* *for better or for ~,* pour le meilleur et pour le pire. **worsen,** *v.i,* se détériorer; empirer; (*chances*) diminuer.

worship, *n,* culte; (*Rel: service*) office, *m.* *Your, His W~,* Monsieur le Juge; (*mayor*) M. le Maire. ¶ *v.t,* (*Rel.*) adorer; (*pers.*) vénérer, adorer; (*money &c*) avoir le culte de. ¶ *v.i,* faire ses dévotions. **~per,** *n,* adorateur, trice; (*pl. in church*) fidèles, *m.pl.*

worst, *a,* le (la) plus mauvais(e); le (la) pire. ¶ *ad,* le plus mal. ¶ *n,* pire, *m.* *at* [*the very*] *~,* [en mettant les choses] au pire.

worsted, *n,* worsted, *m.*

worth, *n,* valeur, *f.* *£5 ~ of,* pour £5 de. ¶ *a,* qui mérite; digne de. *be ~,* valoir. *be ~ a great deal,* avoir beaucoup de valeur. *it's well ~ the effort, time &c,* ça vaut bien la peine. **~less,** *a,* sans valeur; qui ne vaut rien. **~while,** *a,* qui en vaut la peine; (*cause*) louable. **~y,** *a,* (*gen.*) digne (de); (*pers.*) digne *before n;* (*effort &c*) louable.

would, *v.modal, is expressed in Fr. by the conditional mood or by* vouloir. *she ~ come if you asked her,* elle viendrait si vous l'invitiez. *he ~n't wait,* il ne voulait pas attendre. *~ to God that...* plût au ciel que... *~ that,* si seulement. **~-be,** *a,* soi-disant, *inv,* prétendu.

wound, *n,* blessure, *f.* ¶ *v.t,* (*lit., fig.*) blesser (*in,* à). *the ~ed,* les blessés, *m.pl.*

wrangle, *n,* altercation, dispute, *f.* ¶ *v.t,* se disputer, se chamailler *P* (à propos de).

wrap, *n,* peignoir; châle, *m;* (*rug &c*) couverture, *f.* ¶ *v.t,* *~* [*up*], envelopper; (*parcel &c*) emballer. *~* [*o.s.*] *up,* s'habiller chaudement, se couvrir. *~ped up in one's work,* absorbé par son travail. *~over* (*skirt*), *a,* portefeuille, *inv.* **~per,** *n,* (*book*) jaquette; (*newspaper*) bande, *f;* (*sweets &c*) papier [d'emballage], *m.* **~ping,** *n,* emballage, *m.* *~ping paper,* papier d'e.; (*patterned*) p. cadeau, *m.*

wrath, *n,* courroux, *m.*

wreath, *n,* couronne, *f.* **wreathe,** *v.t,* envelopper (*in,* de). *~d in smiles,* rayonnant.

wreck, *n,* (*ship, plans &c*) naufrage, *m;* (*ship itself*) épave, *f;* (*car &c*) voiture &c accidentée. ¶ *v.t,* détruire; démolir; (*train*) faire dérailler; (*fig: marriage &c*) briser; (*health*) ruiner. *be ~ed,* (*ship*) faire naufrage. **~age,** *n,* débris; (*building*) décombres, *m.pl;* (*ship*) épave. **~er,** *n,* vandale; (*Build.*) démolisseur; (*cars*) marchand de ferraille, *m.*

wren, *n,* roitelet, *m.*

wrench, *n,* (*tool*) clef [à écrous]; (*Med.*) entorse, *f;* (*emotional*) déchirement, *m.* ¶ *v.t,* tirer violemment sur; (*Med.*) tordre. *~ open,* forcer.

wrestle, *v.i,* (*lit., fig.*) lutter (*with,* contre). *~ with,* (*problem &c*) se débattre avec. **wrestler,** *n,* lutteur, euse; (*all-in*) catcheur, euse. **wrestling,** *n,* lutte, *f;* (*all-in*) catch, *m.* *~ match,* rencontre de lutte *ou* de catch, *f.*

wretch, *n,* misérable, *m,f.* **~ed,** *a,* (*poor*) misérable; (*unhappy*) malheureux; (*small*) dérisoire; (*weather &c*) lamentable.

wrick, *n,* entorse, *f;* torticolis, *m.* ¶ *v.t,* *~ one's ankle,* se tordre la cheville. *~ one's neck,* attraper un torticolis.

wriggle, *v.i,* (*gen.*) se tortiller; (*fish, pers.*) frétiller. ¶ *v.t,* (*toes*) remuer. *~ out of,* (*difficulty &c*) esquiver.

wring, *v.t.ir,* (*clothes, hands, neck*) tordre; (*fig: heart*) fendre; (*s.o's hand*) serrer. *~* [*out*], (*linen*) essorer; (*water*) exprimer (*from,* de); (*confession*) arracher. **~er,** *n,* essoreuse, *f.* **~ing wet,** *a,* (*garment*) trempé; (*pers.*) t. jusqu'aux os.

wrinkle, *n,* (*skin*) ride, *f;* (*clothes &c*) pli, *m.* ¶ *v.t,* rider, plisser; (*nose*) froncer; (*carpet*) faire des plis dans. ¶ *v.i,* se plisser; se froncer; faire des plis.

wrist, *n,* poignet, *m.* *~band,* poignet, *m.* *~-watch,* montre-bracelet, *f.*

writ, *n,* acte judiciaire, *m.* *serve a ~ on s.o,* assigner qn.

write, *v.t. & i.ir,* (*gen.*) écrire; (*cheque, list*) faire; (*report &c*) rédiger. *~ back,* répondre. *~ down,* mettre par écrit; noter. *~ off,* (*Fin.*) passer aux profits & pertes; (*car*) détruire. *~-off,* (*Com.*) perte sèche, *f.* *~ out,* (*essay &c*) recopier. *~ up,* faire un compte rendu de; (*experiment*) rédiger; (*diary*) mettre à jour. *~-up,* compte-rendu, *m;* (*review*) critique, *f.* **writer,** *n,* auteur; (*career*) écrivain, *m.*

writhe, *v.i,* se tordre.

writing, *n,* écriture, *f;* quelque chose d'écrit. *in ~,* par écrit. *~ case,* necessaire de correspondance, *m. ~ desk,* secrétaire, *m. ~ pad,* bloc-notes, *m. ~-paper,* papier à lettres, *m. ~ table,* bureau, *m.* **written,** *a,* par écrit, écrit.
wrong, *a,* (*guess &c*) erroné; (*answer*) faux, inexact; (*number, horse*) mauvais; (*Mus: note*) faux; (*bad*) mal, *inv.*; (*unfair*) injuste; (*amiss*) qui ne vas pas. *be ~,* se tromper, avoir tort, faire erreur. *get a ~ number,* se tromper de numéro. *on the ~ side,* du mauvais côté. *what's ~?* qu'est qui ne va pas? qu'est-ce qu'il y a? *the ~ way round,* dans le mauvais sens. *the ~ way up,* sens dessus dessous. *rub s.o up the ~ way* (*fig.*) prendre qn à retrousse-poil. *~doer,* malfaiteur, trice. *~doing,* méfaits, *m.pl. ~-headed,* buté. ¶ *ad,* mal, incorrectement. *go ~,* (*gen.*) se tromper; (*on road*) se t. de route; (*plan*) mal tourner; (*clock &c*) se détraquer. ¶ *n,* (*evil*) mal, *m;* injustice, *f.* ¶ *v.t,* faire tort à. **~ful,** *a,* injustifié. **~fully,** *ad,* à tort. **~ly,** *ad,* incorrectement; injustement; (*dismiss, accuse*) à tort.
wrought iron, *n,* fer [forgé] *m.*
wry, *a,* désabusé; (*smile*) mi-figue, mi-raisin. *~ face,* grimace, *f.* **~ly,** *ad,* avec une ironie désabusée.
wych-elm, *n,* orme de montagne, *m.*

X

xenophobia, *n,* xénophobie, *f.*
xerox, *v.t,* photocopier.
Xmas, *abb.* See *Christmas.*
X-ray, *n,* (*ray*) rayon X, *m;* (*photo*) radiographie, radio *P, f. have an ~,* se faire radiographier. ¶ *v.t,* radiographier.
xylophone, *n,* xylophone, *m.*

Y

yacht, *n,* yacht, *m. ~ club,* cercle nautique, *m.* **~ing,** *n,* yachting, *m,* navigation de plaisance, *f.* **~sman,** *n,* yacht[s]man, plaisancier, *m.*
yam, *n,* igname, *f.*
yank, *v.t,* tirer à coup sec.
Yank *P* (*pej.*) *n,* Amerloque *P, m,f;* Amerlo[t] *P, m.* **~ee,** *n,* Yankee, *m,f.*
yap, *v.i,* (*dog*) japper; (*pers.*) jacasser.
yard[1], *n,* (*Meas.*) yard, *m;* (*Naut.*) vergue, *f. ~ stick,* mesure, *f.*
yard[2], *n,* (*gen.*) cour; (*builder's*) chantier; (*storage*) dépôt; (*Am.*) jardin, *m.*
yarn, *n,* (*thread*) fil, *m;* (*tale*) histoire, *f.*
yarrow, *n,* mille-feuille, achillée, *f.*
yawn, *n,* bâillement, *m.* ¶ *v.i,* (*pers.*) bâiller; (*chasm &c*) s'ouvrir. **~ing,** *a,* béant.
year, *n,* an, *m;* année, *f;* (*Sch., Univ., wine, coin &c*) année. *next ~,* l'an prochain, l'année prochaine. *this ~,* cette année. *~ in, ~ out,* d'année en année. *to be 5 ~s old,* avoir 5 ans. *to last 6 ~s,* durer 6 ans. *in the ~ 1000,* en l'an mille. *in the ~1984,* en 1984. *~s of discretion,* l'âge adulte. *~book,* annuaire, *m.* **~ling** (*Turf*) *n,* yearling, *m.* **~ly,** *a,* annuel. ¶ *ad,* annuellement. *twice ~,* 2 fois par an.
yearn, *v.i,* languir (après qn); aspirer (à qch; à faire). **~ing,** *n,* désir ardent (de).
yeast, *n,* levure, *f.*
yell, *n,* hurlement, *m.* ¶ *v.i,* hurler.
yellow, *a,* jaune; (*hair*) blond; (*P cowardly*) froussard *P. ~ fever,* fièvre jaune, *f. ~hammer* (*bird*), bruant jaune, *m.* ¶ *n,* jaune, *m.* ¶ *v.t. & i,* jaunir. **~ish,** *a,* jaunâtre.
yelp, *n,* (*fox*) glapissement; (*dog*) jappement, *m.* ¶ *v.i,* glapir, japper.
yes, *particle,* oui; (*contradicting neg.*) si. ¶ *n,* oui, *m. ~-man,* (*pej.*) béni-oui-oui *P, m.inv.*
yesterday, *n,* hier, *m. the day before ~,* avant-hier. *~ morning, evening,* hier matin, soir.
yet, *c,* pourtant, néanmoins, quand même. ¶ *ad,* (*still & as ~*) encore, toujours, jusqu'ici, jusqu'à présent; (*till then*) jusqu'alors.
yew [tree], *n,* if, *m.*
Yiddish, *a. & n,* yiddish, *inv. & m.*
yield, *n,* rendement; rapport, *m;* production, *f.*

¶ *v.t,* (*gen.*) rendre; (*business, tax: profit*) rapporter; produire. ¶ *v.i,* (*Mil, gen.*) céder (*to,* à).
yob[bo] *P, n,* voyou. *m.*
yodel, *v.i,* jodler.
yoga, *n,* yoga, *m.*
yog[ho]urt, *n,* yaourt, *m.*
yoke, *n,* (*lit.* & *fig.*) joug; (*dress*) empiècement, *m.* ¶ *v.t,* accoupler.
yokel, *n,* rustre, *m.*
yolk, *n,* jaune [d'œuf], *m.*
yonder, *ad,* là-bas.
you, *pn,* (*subject*) vous; tu; (*object*) vous; te; (*stressed* & *after pr.*) vous; toi; (*one: subject*) on; (*object*) vous; te.
young, *a,* jeune; (*wine*) vert. ~ *blood,* sang nouveau. ~ *lady,* (*unmarried*) jeune fille; (*married*) j. femme; (*address*) mademoiselle, *f.* ¶ *n,* (*animals*) petits, *m.pl. the* ~, ~ *people,* les jeunes, les j. gens, *m.pl.* **~er,** *a,* [plus] jeune, cadet; (*generation*) jeune. ~ *brother, sister,* frère, sœur cadet, te. *grow* ~, *make* (*s.o*) *look* ~, rajeunir (qn). **~ster,** *n,* jeune, *m,f.*
your, *a,* ton, ta, tes; votre, vos; (*emphatic*) votre &c... à vous; ton &c... à toi; (*one's*) son, sa, ses; ton &c; votre &c. **yours,** *pn.* & **your own,** le tien, la tienne, les tien(ne)s; le vôtre, la vôtre; les vôtres; à toi; à vous. ~ *faithfully,* ~ *truly,* veuillez agréer (*ou* recevez) mes salutations distinguées. ~ *sincerely* (*informal*), amicalement à vous. **yourself,** *pr,* (*reflexive*) te, vous; (*pl.*) vous; (*after pr.*) toi, vous; (*pl.*) vous; (*emphatic*) toi-même, vous-mêmes; (*pl.*) vous-mêmes.
youth, *n,* jeunesse, *f;* (*young man*) jeune homme, *m;* (*pl.*) jeunes gens, *m.pl;* (*coll.*) jeunesse, jeunes, *m.pl.* ~ *club,* foyer *ou* centre de jeunes, *m.* ~ *hostel,* auberge de jeunesse, *f.* ~ *leader,* animateur, trice de groupes de jeunes. **~ful,** *a,* jeune; (*mistake*) de jeunesse; (*quality*) juvénile.
yule[tide], *n,* Noël, *m,* la [fête de] Noël. *yule log,* bûche de Noël, *f.*

Z

Zaire, *n,* le Zaïre.
Zambia, *n,* la Zambie.
zany, *a,* dingue *P.*
zeal, *n,* zèle (pour), *m.* **zealot,** *n,* fanatique, *m,f.* **zealous,** *a,* zélé; dévoué. **~ly,** *ad,* avec zèle.
zebra, *n,* zèbre, *m.* ~ *crossing,* passage pour piétons, *m.*
zenith, *n,* zénith, *m.*
zephyr, *n,* zéphyr, *m.*
zero, *n,* zéro, *m.* ¶ *a,* zéro; nul. ~ *hour,* (*Mil.*) l'heure H; (*fig.*) le moment critique. ¶ *v.i,* ~ *in on,* piquer droit sur.
zest, *n,* entrain; (*fig.*) piquant; (*lemon &c*) zeste, *m.*
zigzag, *n,* zigzag, *m.* ¶ *v.i,* zigzaguer.
zinc, *n,* zinc, *m.* ¶ *a,* de zinc; (*roof*) zingué.
zip, *n,* & ~ **fastener, zipper,** fermeture éclair, *f.* (*Am.*) ~ *code,* code postal, *m.* ~ *pocket,* poche zippée, *f.* ¶ *v.t.* (& *i*), ~ [*up*], ~ *on,* (se) fermer, s'attacher avec une fermeture éclair.
zircon, *n,* zircon, *m.*
zither, *n,* cithare, *f.*
zodiac, *n,* zodiaque, *m.*
zombie *P n,* crétin, e; automate, *m.*
zone, *n,* zone, *f;* (*of city*) secteur, *m.* ¶ *v.t,* diviser en zones.
zoo, *n,* zoo, *m.* **zoological,** *a,* zoologique. **zoologist,** *n,* zoologiste, *m,f.* **zoology,** *n,* zoologie, *f.*
zoom, *v.i,* vrombir. ~ *in* (*Cine.*), faire un zoom (*on,* sur). ~ *lens,* zoom, *m.*

ENGLISH IRREGULAR VERBS

Except as otherwise stated, order of parts is

(1) Infinitive (*i.*) & Present (*pr.*);
(2) Past (*p.*);
(3) Past Participle (*p.p.*).

Prefixed verbs not included in the list, such as **arise, regild,** follow the second or last element (**rise, gild**).

abide; *p. & p.p.* abode.
awake; awoke; awoke, awaked.
i. **be;** *pr. indicative* am, art, is, *pl.* are; *p. ind.* was, wast *or* wert, was, *pl.* were; *pr. subj.* be; *p. subj.* were; *imperative* be; *p.pr.* being; *p.p.* been. *Contractions:* 'm = am, 's = is, 're = are.
bear; bore, borne. *When referring to birth* born & borne, *e.g.* born 19–; has borne a child; born of, borne by, woman.
beat; beat; beaten.
beget; begot; begotten.
begin; began; begun.
bend; bent; bent.
bereave; *p. & p.p.* bereaved *or* bereft.
beseech; besought; besought.
bespeak; bespoke; bespoke, -spoken.
bestride; bestrode; bestridden, bestrode.
bid; bade, bid; bidden, bid.
bind; bound; bound.
bite; bit; bitten *sometimes* bit.
bleed; bled; bled.
blow; blew; blown.
break; broke; broken.
breed; bred; bred.
bring; brought; brought.
build; built; built.
burn; *p. & p.p.* burnt *sometimes* burned.
burst; burst; burst.
buy; bought; bought.
can.–*pr.* I, he, &c, can, thou canst. *neg.* cannot, can't. *p. & conditional,* I, he, &c, could, thou could[e]st. *i., p.pr. & p.p. wanting; defective parts supplied from* be able to.
cast; cast; cast.
catch; caught; caught.
chide; chid; chidden *or* chid.
choose; chose; chosen.
cleave; clove *or* cleft; cloven *or* cleft.
cling; clung; clung.
clothe; *p. & p.p.* clothed *or* clad.
come; came; come.
cost; cost; cost.
could. See *can.*
creep; crept; crept.
crow; crew *or* crowed; crowed.
cut; cut; cut.
dare; dared & durst; dared.
deal; dealt; dealt.
die; died; *p.pr.* dying; *p.p.* died.
dig; dug; dug.
i. **do;** *pr. indicative* do, doest (*as auxiliary* dost), does, *pl.* do; *p.* did, didst, did, *pl.* did; *p.p.* done. *Contractions:* don't = do not. doesn't = does not. didn't = did not.
draw; drew; drawn.
dream; *p. & p.p.* dreamt *or* dreamed.
drink; drank; drunk.
drive; drove; driven.
dwell; dwelt; dwelt.
eat; ate *or* eat; eaten.
fall; fell; fallen.
feed; fed; fed.
feel; felt; felt.
fight; fought; fought.
find; found; found.
flee; fled; fled.
fling; flung; flung.
fly; flew; flown.
forbear; forbore; forborne.
forbid; forbad *or* -bade; forbidden.
forget; forgot; forgotten.
forsake; forsook; forsaken.
freeze; froze; frozen.
get; got; got, *also* -gotten *in combination as* ill-gotten.
gild; *p. & p.p.* gilded & gilt.
gird; *p. & p.p.* girt & *poet.* girded.
give; gave; given.
go; *pr.* I go, thou goest, he goes, we, &c, go; *p.* went; *p.p.* gone.
grave; graved; graven & graved.
grind; ground; ground.
grow; grew; grown.
hang; *p. & p.p.* hung & hanged.
i. **have;** *pr.* I have, *O* thou hast, he has, we, you, they, have; *p.* had, *O* thou hadst; *p.p.* had; *abb.* I've, we've, &c; I'd, we'd, &c; 's = has; *colloquially neg.* haven't, hasn't; hadn't.
hear; heard; heard.
heave; *p. & p.p.* heaved *or* hove.
hew; hewed; hewn *or* hewed.
hide; hid; hidden & hid.
hit; hit; hit.
hold; held; held.
hurt; hurt; hurt.
inset; *p. & p.p.* inset *or* insetted.
keep; kept; kept.
kneel; knelt; knelt.
knit; *p. & p.p.* knitted *or* knit.
know; knew; known.
lay; laid; laid.
lead; led; led.

lean; *p. & p.p.* leaned *or* leant.
leap; *p. & p.p.* leapt *or* leaped.
learn; *p. & p.p.* learnt, learned.
leave; left; left.
lend; lent; lent.
let; let; let.
lie; lay; *p.pr.* lying; *p.p.* lain.
light; *p. & p.p.* lit *or* lighted.
lose; lost; lost.
make; made; made.
pr. **I may,** he may; *p.* might.
mean; meant; meant.
meet; met; met.
melt; melted; melted, molten.
mow; mowed; mown.
pr. **I must,** he must; *p.* must.
pr. **ought;** *p.* ought.
overhang; overhung; overhung.
pay; paid; paid.
put; put; put.
read; read; read.
rid; ridded, rid; rid.
ride; rode; ridden.
ring; rang; rung.
rise; rose; risen.
run; ran; run.
saw; sawed; sawn.
say; said; said.
see; saw; seen.
seek; sought; sought.
sell; sold; sold.
send; sent; sent.
set; set; set.
sew; sewed; sewed *or* sewn.
shake; shook; shaken.
pr. **I shall,** he, &c, shall; *p. & conditional* I should, he, &c, should; *neg.* shall not *or* shan't; should not *or* shouldn't.
shear; sheared; shorn.
shed; shed; shed.
shine; shone; shone.
shit; shat; shat.
shoe; shod; shod.
shoot; shot; shot.
should. See *shall.*
show; showed; shown.
shrink; shrank; shrunk.
shut; shut; shut.
sing; sang; sung.
sink; sank; sunk.
sit; sat; sat.
slay; slew; slain.
sleep; slept; slept.
slide; slid; slid.
sling; slung; slung.
slink; slunk; slunk.
slit; slit; slit.
smell; smelt; smelt.
smite; smote; smitten.
sow; sowed; sown *or* sowed.
speak; spoke; spoken.
speed; sped; sped.
spell; *p. & p.p.* spelt *or* spelled.
spend; spent; spent.
spill; *p. & p.p.* spilt *or* spilled.
spin; spun *or* span; spun.
spit; spat; spat.
split; split; split.
spread; spread; spread.
spring; sprang; sprung.
stand; stood; stood.
steal; stole; stolen.
stick; stuck; stuck.
sting; stung; stung.
stink; stank *or* stunk; stunk.
strew; strewed; strewn, strewed.
stride; strode; (*rare*) stridden.
strike; struck; struck & stricken.
string; strung; strung.
strive; strove; striven.
swear; swore; sworn.
sweep; swept; swept.
swell; swelled; swollen.
swim; swam; swum.
swing; swung; swung.
take; took; taken.
teach; taught; taught.
tear; tore; torn.
tell; told; told.
think; thought; thought.
throw; threw; thrown.
thrust; thrust; thrust.
tie; tied; *p.pr.* tying; *p.p.* tied.
tread; trod; trodden.
wake; woke, waked; waked, woken.
wear; wore; worn.
weave; wove; woven & wove.
weep; wept; wept.
pr. I, he, &c, **will** *or* 'll; *p. & conditional* I, he, &c, would *or* 'd; *neg.* will not *or* won't; would not *or* wouldn't *or* 'd not.
win; won; won.
wind; wound; wound.
would. See *will.*
wring; wrung; wrung.
write; wrote; written.

APPENDICES/APPENDICES

ABBREVIATIONS MOST COMMONLY USED IN FRENCH

A.C.F.	Automobile-Club de France
A.P.	assistance publique *(public assistance)*
a/s	aux soins de *(care of; c/o)*
A.S.	assurances sociales
ap. J.-C.	après Jésus-Christ *(A.D.)*
av. J.-C.	avant Jésus-Christ *(B.C.)*
B.E.P.C.	Brevet d'études du premier cycle
B.I.T.	Bureau International du Travail *(I.L.O.)*
B.N.	Bibliothèque Nationale
B.N.C.I.	Banque Nationale pour le Commerce et l'Industrie
B.O.	Bulletin Officiel
B.p.F.	bon pour francs
B.U.S.	Bureau Universitaire de Statistique
Bx.A.	beaux-arts
C/, Cpte	compte
c.à.d.	c'est-à-dire *(that is; i.e.)*
C.A.P.	certificat d'aptitude pédagogique; certificat d'aptitude professionnelle
C.A.P.E.S.	certificat d'aptitude au professorat de l'enseignement secondaire
cc, Cie C^{t}	compte courant
C.C.	cours complémentaire
C.E.C.A.	Communauté Européenne du Charbon et de l'Acier
C.E.E.	Communauté Economique Européenne *(E.E.C.)*
C.E.P.	certificat d'études primaires
C.F.T.C.	Confédération Française des Travailleurs Chrétiens
C.G.A.	Confédération Générale de l'Agriculture
C.G.A.F.	Confédération Générale de l'Artisanat Français
C.G.C.	Confédération Générale des Cadres
C.G.T.	Confédération Générale du Travail; Compagnie Générale Transatlantique
C.G.T.—F.O.	Confédération Générale du Travail—Force Ouvrière
ch.-v., C.V.	cheval-vapeur *(horsepower; H.P.)*
Cie, C^{o}	compagnie
C.N.P.F.	Conseil National du Patronat Français
C.N.R.	Conseil National de la Résistance
C.N.R.S.	Centre National de la Recherche Scientifique
C.R.S.	compagnies républicaines de sécurité
C^{t}	courant
Cte, Ctesse	comte, comtesse
C.U.	charge utile
D.B.	division blindée
D.C.A.	défense contre avions
D.P.	défense passive
dz	douzaine

E	est
Ed.	édition
E.-M.	État-major
E.N.	École normale
E.N.S.	École Normale Supérieure
E.N.S.I.	École Nationale Supérieure d'Ingénieurs
E.O.R.	Élève-officier de réserve
E.P.S.	École Primaire Supérieure
Esc.	escompte
Etabl.	Établissement
E.-U.	États-Unis *(U.S.A.)*
E.V.	en ville *(local)*
F.F.I.	Forces Françaises de l'Intérieur
F.F.L.	Forces Françaises Libres
G.Q.G.	grand quartier général *(G.H.Q.—general headquarters)*
H.C.	hors concours
H.E.C.	Hautes Études Commerciales
H.L.M.	habitation à loyer modéré
I.D.H.E.C.	Institut des Hautes Études Cinématographiques
I.N.E.D.	Institut National des Études Démographiques
I.P.E.S.	Institut de préparation aux enseignements du second degré
I.P.N.	Institut Pédagogique National
J.A.C.	Jeunesse agricole chrétienne
J.-C.	Jésus-Christ
J.E.C.	Jeunesse étudiante chrétienne
J.M.F.	Jeunesses musicales de France
J.O.	Journal Officiel
J.O.C.	Jeunesse ouvrière chrétienne
L. en D.	Licencié en droit
L. ès L.	Licencié ès lettres
L. ès Sc.	Licencié ès sciences
M.	monsieur
Me	maître
Mgr	monseigneur
Mlle	mademoiselle
MM.	messieurs
Mme	madame
M^{on}	maison
M.P.C.	Cerificat de Mathématiques, Physique et Chimie
M.R.P.	Mouvement Républicain Populaire
N	Nord
N.-D.	Notre-Dame
N.F.	nouveau franc
N^{o}	numéro
O	ouest
O.A.S.	Organisation de l'Armée Secrète
O.C.D.E.	Organisation de coopération et de développement économiques *(O.E.C.D.)*
O.N.M.	Office Nationale Météorologique

O.N.U. Organisation des Nations Unies *(U.N.)*

O.T.A.N. Organisation du Traité de l'Atlantique Nord *(NATO)*

P.C. Parti Communiste; Poste de Commandement

P.C.B. Certificat de Physique, Chimie, Biologie

p.c.c. pour copie conforme

P.C.N. Certificat de Physique, Chimie, Sciences Naturelles

p.ex. par example *(e.g.)*

P.G. prisonnier de guerre *(P.O.W.)*

P.J. police judiciaire

P.M.U. pari mutuel urbain

p.p. profits et pertes; port payé

P.P.C. pour prendre congé

P.-S. post-scriptum *(P.S.)*

P.T.T. Postes, Télégraphes et Téléphones

P.V. procès-verbal

Q.G. quartier général *(H.Q.—headquarters)*

R.A.T.P. Régie autonome de transports parisiens

R.C. Registre du Commerce

r.d. rive droite

R.F. République Française

r.g. rive gauche

R.I. régiment d'infanterie

R.P. révérend père *(Fr.)*

R.P.F. Rassemblement du Peuple Français

R.S.V.P. réponse, s'il vous plaît

S Sud

s/ sur

S.A. société anonyme *(Inc.)*

S.A.R. son altesse royale *(H.R.H.)*

S.A.R.L. société anonyme à responsabilité limitée *(Ltd.)*

s.d. sans date

S.D.N. Société des Nations

S.Em. son éminence

S.E., S.Exc. son excellence

S.Gr. sa grandeur

S.M. sa majesté

S.N.C.F. Société Nationale des Chemins de Fer Français

S.P. sapeurs-pompiers; service de presse

S.P.A. société protectrice des animaux

S.S. sa seigneurie; sa sainteté; sécurité sociale

Sté société

S.V.P. s'il vous plaît

T.C.F. Touring Club de France

T.G.V. train à grande vitesse *(high-speed train)*

T.N.P. Théâtre National Populaire

U.R.S.S. Union des Républiques Socialistes Soviétiques *(U.S.S.R.)*

Vve veuve

W.C. water-closet

FALSE COGNATES AND "PART-TIME" COGNATES

Many French words appear to be cognates of English words, but they are not: e.g., *nuisance* in French does **not** mean *nuisance* in English. Other words sometimes suggest an English equivalent, but can also have a very different meaning: e.g., *actuel* in French can be interpreted at times to mean *real* in English but more often should be translated as *current*.

The following list contains many such false cognates. It is far from complete and is simplified, but it includes the most common difficulties that can be clarified in a short list. As a general rule, the English-speaking student of French is well advised to (1) become familiar with the meanings of a French word before using it; (2) be very suspicious of the meanings that English loan words such as *footing* and *cross* have assumed (for brevity, none of these are included, but with a very few exceptions they are *all* false friends); (3) remember that in French a change of gender can involve a drastic change of meaning: e.g., *la somme,* "sum," and *le somme,* "nap"; and (4) be aware of the diverse meanings of English words and realize that these meanings might each require a different French word: e.g., *habit* meaning "custom" and *habit* meaning "clothing."

In the French-to-English column, certain English words are in brackets to indicate that the French word *sometimes* has the meaning of the bracketed English word. If there is a sense in which the meanings of the French and English words overlap, the French-to-English column will be the one that catalogs it. In the English-to-French column the abbreviations *(a)* = "adjective," *(n)* = "noun," and *(v)* = "verb" are used in a few cases for clarity.

French-English

accommodation adaptation

actuel current, topical [actual]

adéquat appropriate, suitable

adresse [address], skill

agonie death agony, death throes

agréer accept, suit

allée driveway, path

alléger lighten, lessen

allure walk, gait, speed

altérer change for the worse, tamper with, spoil

amateur lover, [amateur]

angine sore throat

appointer pay a salary to

apprécier [appreciate], value, judge

argument argument in the sense of set of reasons for or against something

aspersion sprinkling

assistant bystander, [assistant]

attendre wait for

English-French

accommodations logement, chambre

actual véritable

adequate suffisant, passable

address addresse

agony douleur affreuse

agree être d'accord

alley ruelle, passage

allege alléguer

allure charme, attrait

alter changer

amateur amateur

angina angine de poitrine

appoint nommer

appreciate apprécier, estimer

argument dispute

aspersion calomnie

assistant assistant

attend s'occuper de, servir (qn), faire attention à

French-English

attractif magnetic
audience hearing, [audience *(royal)*]
auditoire audience
avertir warn
avertissement warning, notice

balance scales
ballot bundle, kit bag
banc bench, seat

biais angle, slant
blindé armored, hardened
blocage blocking, freezing *(prices)*
bomber bulge, stick out
bosser work hard
boulet cannonball
brasier fire, blaze, embers
brassière a baby's sleeved vest
bribes scraps, bits
bride bridle

caméra movie or TV camera
candeur innocence, naiveté
canoter go boating
casserole saucepan
caution surety, bail
cave cellar
cellier storeroom
chagrin grief
chair flesh
chandelier candlestick
clairvoyance clearsightedness, perspicacity
comédien, -ne actor, actress
commande order *(for goods)*
conducteur driver

confection making, especially of ready-made clothes
confidence secret
confortable comfortable, of things

English-French

attractive attrayant, séduisant
audience assistance, auditoire
auditorium salle
avert détourner, éviter
advertisement affiche, réclame

balance équilibre
ballot tour de scrutin
bank **1.** *(river)* rive. **2.** *(money)* banque.

bias parti pris, préjugé
blind aveugle. **˜ed**, aveuglé
blockage obstruction
bomb bombarder
boss *(v)* être affairé et autoritaire
bullet balle
brazier brasero
brassiere soutien-gorge
bribe pot-de-vin
bride (nouvelle) mariée

camera appareil (photographique)
candor franchise
canoe *(v)* faire du canoë
casserole ragoût en cocotte
caution précaution, prudence
cave caverne
cellar cave
chagrin dépit
chair chaise
chandelier lustre
clairvoyance voyance

comedian comique
command commandement, ordre
conductor **1.** *(streetcar)* receveur. **2.** *(orchestra)* chef d'orchestre.
confection confiserie

confidence confiance
comfortable à l'aise

French-English	English-French
conforter confirm, reinforce	**comfort** consoler
conjurer plot, scheme	**conjure** faire de la sorcellerie, évoquer
consistant well founded, substantial	**consistent** logique, conséquent, régulier
convenir be agreeable, agree	**convene** convoquer
corps de garde guardroom	**bodyguard** garde du corps, gorille
courtier broker	**courtier** courtisan
crayon pencil	**crayon** crayon de couleur
crier shout, cry (out)	**cry** *(weep)* pleurer
cynique Cynic *(philosopher),* shameless person	**cynic** railleur
décade ten days, [ten years]	**decade** décennie
décevoir disappoint	**deceive** tromper
défiant mistrustful	**defiant** réfractaire *(person)*, de défi *(action)*
défiler unstring, file past	**defile** souiller
déguster sample, taste, relish	**disgust** *(v)* dégoûter
demande request, [demand]	**demand** exigence
déportement swerve, skid. **~s,** misconduct	**deportment** conduite
déranger disturb, upset	**deranged** détraqué
dérober steal, hide	**disrobe** se dévêtir
déshonnêteté unseemliness	**dishonesty** malhonnêteté
destitution dismissal, firing	**destitution** dénuement
déterrer unearth	**deter** décourager
deviser converse, chat	**devise** trouver un moyen, inventer
disposer arrange, lay out, have at one's disposal	**dispose of** se débarrasser de
distraction diversion, absent-mindedness	**distraction** interruption
donjon keep *(of a castle)*	**dungeon** cachot
dresser erect, plan, train	**dress** s'habiller
éducation [education], training, breeding, manners	**education** enseignement, instruction, formation
effectivement [effectively], in fact	**effectively** efficacement
embarrassé hampered, in an awkward position	**embarrassed** gêné, confus
énergétique concerned with energy	**energetic** énergique
énerver upset, irritate	**enervate** affaiblir

French-English	English-French
engagé committed	**engaged** **1.** *(marriage)* fiancé. **2.** *(not free)* occupé.
errer wander	**err** se tromper
estimer [estimate], value, esteem, think	**estimate** apprécier, évaluer, estimer
exhibition showing *(of documents),* showing off	**exhibition** exposition
extra *(a)* extra special	**extra** en supplément, supplémentaire
extravagance wildness of behavior	**extravagance** folles dépenses
fade insipid, dull	**faded** décoloré, fané
fastidieux dull, tiresome	**fastidious** difficile, délicat
fatalité fate, bad luck	**fatality** mort
félonie treachery	**felony** crime
fixer place firmly in position, stare at	**fix** arranger
flair sense of smell	**flair** aptitude, penchant
formellement categorically	**formally** cérémonieusement
fournitures supplies, equipment	**furniture** meubles
futile trivial	**futile** **1.** vain. **2.** bête.
garde-corps handrail	**bodyguard** garde du corps, gorille
gendre son-in-law	**gender** genre
génial brilliant	**genial** bienveillant, jovial
gentilhomme nobleman, [gentleman]	**gentleman** homme poli, homme galant, monsieur
gentiment kindly	**gently** doucement
gratuité the fact of being given without charge	**gratuity** pourboire
grossesse pregnancy	**grossness** grossièreté
harassé tired	**harassed** tourmenté
hardi bold	**hardy** robuste
humeur mood, temper	**humor** humour
hurler yell, roar	**hurl** lancer
idiome local language	**idiom** idiotisme
impotence helplessness, disability	**impotence** impuissance
inconvenant unseemly, improper	**inconvenient** incommode
inconvénient disadvantage	**inconvenience** dérangement
s'infatuer conceited	**be infatuated** s'enticher
information **1.** (legal) inquiry. **2.** news.	**information** renseignements
inhabitable uninhabitable	**inhabitable** habitable
injurier insult	**injure** blesser

French-English

insolation sunstroke
instant insistent, pressing
interrogation set of questions
intoxicant poisonous
inusable hard-wearing, long-lasting
inusité unusual
job temporary job
journée day, whole day
justesse exactness, accuracy
labour plowing, tilling
lard bacon
lecture reading
libeller write out, draw up
librairie bookstore
licencier discharge *(workers)*
limonade carbonated soft drink
location renting
luxure lewdness
magasin large shop, department store
magnifier glorify, idealize
manucure manicurist
manufacture large factory
marmot urchin
médecin doctor
médecine study of medicine
menu set meal
monnaie change, [currency]
muter transfer *(employees)*
noise quarrel
nouvelliste short-story writer
nuisance harmful effect
oblitérer cancel, [obliterate]
offensif on the offensive
officieux informal
oppresser weigh down, suffocate
originalement in an original way
ostensible visible, conspicuous
outrage insult, offense

English-French

insulation isolement
instant **1.** immédiat. **2.** instantané.
interrogation interrogatoire
intoxicating alcoolique, enivrant
unusable inutilisable
unused inutilisé
job **1.** travail, boulot *P.* **2.** tâche.
journey voyage
justice justice
labor travail
lard saindoux
lecture **1.** conférence. **2.** sermon.
libel *(v)* diffamer
library bibliothèque
license *(v)* autoriser
lemonade citron pressé
location emplacement
luxury luxe
magazine magazine
magnify grossir, aggrandir
manicure soin des mains
manufacture fabrication
marmot marmotte
medicine médicament
menu carte
money argent
mute assourdir
noise bruit
novelist romancier
nuisance chose, personne embêtante
obliterate effacer
offensive offensant
officious trop zélé, importun
oppress opprimer
originally originellement, primitivement
ostensible prétendu
outrage scandale

French-English	English-French
parole words of a song, promise, way of speaking	**parole** liberté conditionelle
partialement unfairly	**partially** en partie
partie part	**party** **1.** réunion, fête. **2.** *(political)* parti.
passer [pass], take *(an exam),* overlook	**pass** **1.** dépasser. **2.** *(exam)* réussir à.
pathétique touching, moving	**pathetic** lamentable
pervers evil, depraved	**perverse** entêté, désobligeant
pétulance liveliness, verve	**petulance** irritabilité
photographe photographer	**photograph** photographie
physicien, -ne physicist	**physician** médecin
pièce play, a room in an apartment	**piece** morceau
piler crush	**pile** empiler, entasser
pilot pile *(engineering)*	**pilot** pilote
pistole an ancient gold coin	**pistol** pistolet
plaisant amusing, [pleasant]	**pleasant** agréable
pratiquer practice *(religion, medicine)*	**practice** s'exercer
préjudice detriment, harm, damages	**prejudice** parti pris, préjugé
prescription instructions	**prescription** ordonnance
prétendre claim, assert	**pretend** faire semblant de
prévenir avert, bias, forewarn	**prevent** empêcher
procès *(legal)* proceedings, trial	**process** processus, cours, progrès
propre clean, [proper]	**proper** correct, comme il faut
propriété property, [propriety *(of expression)*]	**propriety** bienséance
prune plum	**prune** pruneau
quitter leave	**quit** abandonner
raisin grape	**raisin** raisins secs
rater miss, fail	**rate** évaluer, considérer
réaliser fulfill, carry out	**realize** se rendre compte
réassurer reinsure	**reassure** rassurer
récipient receptacle	**recipient** destinataire
recouper cut again, cross-check	**recoup** récupérer
recouvrir cover again or cover over	**recover** recouvrer, retrouver, récupérer
récupérer retrieve, get back	**recuperate** se rétablir
regard look	**regard** estime, amitié
relief relief *(sculpture)*	**relief** soulagement
rentable profitable	**rentable** louable

French-English	**English-French**
rente annuity	**rent** *(n)* loyer
replacer put back	**replace** remplacer
réprouver condemn, reject	**reprove** réprimander
résignation submission, [resignation]	**resignation** **1.** *(quitting)* démission. **2.** soumission, résignation.
rester remain	**rest** *(v)* se reposer
résumer sum up	**resume** continuer, reprendre
retiré secluded	**retired** en retraite
rétribution reward, payment	**retribution** vengeance
revue [*(military)* review, review *(magazine)*], *(theatrical)* revue	**review** critique
rude harsh, gruff, hard	**rude** impoli, grossier
sensible sensitive, noticeable	**sensible** sensé
stage training period	**stage** *(theater)* scène
stationner park *(a car)*	**station** poster, aposter
succéder follow in succession	**succeed** réussir
supplier beg, beseech	**supply** fournir, approvisioner
supporter tolerate	**support** soutenir
surnom nickname	**surname** nom de famille
sympathique likeable	**sympathetic** compatissant
traiteur caterer	**traitor** traître
trouble murky, confused	**troubled** en peine, tracassé
typer classify	**type** taper (à la machine)
usé worn out	**used** **1.** employé. **2.** *(secondhand)* d'occasion.
versatile changeable, fickle	**versatile** ayant beaucoup de talents
vexation humiliation	**vexation** ennui
virtuel potential	**virtual** de fait, en réalité
zeste peel of orange, lemon, etc.	**zest** entrain

BUSINESS CORRESPONDENCE IN FRENCH

The following selected phrases are indicative of the style and tone of business letters in France.

Accusé de réception	**To acknowledge receipt**
We acknowledge receipt of your letter of the 10th of October...	Nous vous accusons réception de votre lettre du 10 octobre...
I have received your letter informing me ...	J'ai bien reçu votre lettre indiquant...
Pour commencer le texte d'une lettre	**To begin the body of a letter**
In reply to your ad..., I have the honor of ...	En réponse à votre annonce..., j'ai l'honneur de...
To follow up our telephone conversation, I confirm...	Comme suite à notre conversation téléphonique, je vous confirme...
I would be grateful to you for sending me ...	Je vous serais obligé(e) de m'envoyer...
I have the honor of asking you to issue me ...	J'ai l'honneur de vous demander de me délivrer...
We have the pleasure of informing you that...	Nous avons le plaisir de vous informer que ...
Pursuant to your request, we have the pleasure of mailing you the enclosed...	Suite à votre demande, nous avons le plaisir de vous adresser ci-inclus...
I have the honor of placing an order for ...	J'ai l'honneur de vous passer commande de...
We regret to inform you that...	Nous regrettons de vous informer que...
We are sorry for the error that crept into ...	Nous sommes désolés de l'erreur qui s'est glissé dans...
We have learned with regret about the fact of your missing ___...	Nous avons appris avec regret le cas de vos ___ manquant(e)s...
We have noticed, in balancing our accounts, that...	Nous avons remarqué, en balançant nos écritures, que...
Pour demander une réponse	**To request an answer**
Please acknowledge receipt of this letter and my enclosed check and send me by return mail...	Veuillez accuser réception de cette lettre, ainsi que de mon chèque ci-inclus, et m'envoyer par retour du courrier...
While waiting for your reply,...	Dans l'attente de votre réponse,...
Pour terminer une lettre commerciale	**To close a business letter**
Accept, sir, the expression of my cordial consideration.	Croyez, Monsieur, à l'expression de ma considération cordiale.
Please accept the expression of my respectful wishes.	Veuillez agréer, Madame, l'expression de mes respectueux hommages.

I beg you to receive the respectful expression of all my compliments.	Je vous prie de recevoir, Mademoiselle, l'expression respectueux de tous mes compliments.
Condescend to receive my respectful compliments.	Daignez recevoir mes compliments respectueux.

USEFUL EXPRESSIONS

à compter du starting from

à l'exception de except for

à la semaine weekly

à nouveau again

à partir de starting from

à réception upon receipt

à titre de by way of

à titre gratuit free of charge

à votre convenance according to your preference

ailleurs elsewhere

au mois monthly

au prix coûtant at cost

au reçu de upon receipt of

au verso on the back *(of the page)*

ci-après below

ci-avant above

ci-inclus enclosed

ci-joint attached

comptant cash

conforme à in accordance with

dans le courant de during

de toute urgence with utmost urgency

dès réception upon receipt

dispensé de exempt from

en bon, mauvais état in good, bad condition

en cas de retour in case of return

en cours de in the process of

en recommandé by registered mail

en temps utile in good time

indépendant de notre volonté beyond our control

la nuit per night

par ailleurs furthermore

par erreur by mistake

par l'intermédiaire de through the intermediary of

par le passé in the past

port dû postage due

port payé postage paid

sans réserve without (mental) reservations

soumis à subject to

sous peu in a short time

sur place on the spot

vers le 10 décembre around the 10th of December

y compris included

MONETARY UNITS OF FRENCH-SPEAKING COUNTRIES
UNITÉS MONÉTAIRES DES PAYS FRANCOPHONES

Country/Pays	Name/Nom	Symbol/Symbole
Algérie	1 dinar = 100 centimes	AD
Belgique	1 franc = 100 centimes	FB
Bénin	1 franc = 100 centimes	CAF Fr
Burkina Faso	1 franc = 100 centimes	CAF Fr
Burundi	1 franc = 100 centimes	BuFr
Cameroun	1 franc = 100 centimes	CAF Fr
Canada	1 dollar = 100 cents	$Can
Congo, République Populaire du	1 franc = 100 centimes	CAF Fr
Côte d'Ivoire	1 franc = 100 centimes	CAF Fr
France	1 franc = 100 centimes	FF
Guinée, République de	1 franc = 100 centimes	Fr
Haïti	1 gourde = 100 centimes	G
Luxembourg	1 franc = 100 centimes	FL
Mali, République de	1 franc = 100 centimes	Fr
Mauritanie, République Islamique de	1 franc = 100 centimes	CAF Fr
Niger, République de	1 franc = 100 centimes	CAF Fr
République Centrafricaine	1 franc = 100 centimes	CAF Fr
République Gabonaise	1 franc = 100 centimes	CAF Fr
République Rwandaise	1 franc = 100 centimes	RwFr
République Togolaise	1 franc = 100 centimes	CAF Fr
Sénégal, République de	1 franc = 100 centimes	CAF Fr
Suisse	1 franc = 100 centimes	FS
Tchad	1 franc = 100 centimes	CAF Fr
Zaïre, République de	1 zaïre = 100 makuta	Z

WEIGHTS AND MEASURES/POIDS ET MESURES

In the following chart, the figure under the column labeled *x* is the conversion factor. Multiply the standard measure by the appropriate factor to get the metric equivalent.

Longueurs	**Symbole**	**x**	**Length**	**Symbol**
1 millimètre	mm	.254	1 inch	in
1 centimètre = 100 mm	cm	2.54		
			1 foot = 12 in	ft
1 mètre	m	.9144	1 yard = 3 ft	yd
1 kilomètre	km	1.609	1 mi = 5280 ft	mi

Surfaces	**Symbole**	**x**	**Area**	**Symbol**
1 centimètre carré	cm^2	6.452	1 square inch	in^2
		929.03	1 square foot = 144 in^2	ft^2
1 mètre carré = 10,000 cm^2	m^2	.836	1 square yard = 9 ft^2	yd^2
1 are = 100 m^2	a	.025	1 acre = 4840 yd^2	
1 hectare = 100 a	ha	2.471		

Capacité	**Symbole**	**x**	**Capacity**	**Symbol**
1 centilitre	cl	2.957	1 ounce	oz
		.237	1 cup = 8 oz	c
		.473	1 pint = 2 c	pt
1 litre = 100 cl	1	.946	1 quart = 2 pt	qt
		3.785	1 gallon = 4 qt	gal
1 hectolitre = 1000 1	hl			

Poids	**Symbole**	**x**	**Weight and Mass**	**Symbol**
1 milligramme	mg			
1 gramme = 1000 mg	g	28.35	1 ounce	oz
1 livre = 500 g	*	.907	1 pound = 16 oz	lb
1 kilogramme = 1000 g	kg	.454	1 pound = 16 oz	
1 tonne = 1000 kg	t	.907	1 ton = 2000 lb	T

NUMBERS/NUMÉROS

Cardinal Numbers		Numéros cardinaux	Cardinal Numbers		Numéros cardinaux
zero	0	**zéro**	twenty	20	**vingt**
one	1	**un**	twenty-one	21	**vingt et un**
two	2	**deux**	twenty-two	22	**vingt-deux**
three	3	**trois**	twenty-three	23	**vingt-trois**
four	4	**quatre**	twenty-four	24	**vingt-quatre**
five	5	**cinq**	twenty-five	25	**vingt-cinq**
six	6	**six**	twenty-six	26	**vingt-six**
seven	7	**sept**	twenty-seven	27	**vingt-sept**
eight	8	**huit**	twenty-eight	28	**vingt-huit**
nine	9	**neuf**	twenty-nine	29	**vingt-neuf**
ten	10	**dix**	thirty	30	**trente**
eleven	11	**onze**	forty	40	**quarante**
twelve	12	**douze**	fifty	50	**cinquante**
thirteen	13	**treize**	sixty	60	**soixante**
fourteen	14	**quatorze**	seventy	70	**soixante-dix**
fifteen	15	**quinze**	seventy-one	71	**soixante-et-onze**
sixteen	16	**seize**	eighty	80	**quatre-vingt**
seventeen	17	**dix-sept**	ninety	90	**quatre-vingt-dix**
eighteen	18	**dix-huit**	one hundred	100	**cent**
nineteen	19	**dix-neuf**	one thousand	1000	**mille**

Ordinal Numbers		Numéros ordinaux	
1st	first	1er	-ère **premier, première**
2nd	second	2e	-ième **second, deuxième**
3rd	third	3e	**troisième**
4th	fourth	4e	**quatrième**
5th	fifth	5e	**cinquième**
6th	sixth	6e	**sixième**
7th	seventh	7e	**septième**
8th	eighth	8e	**huitième**
9th	ninth	9e	**neuvième**
10th	tenth	10e	**dixième**
11th	eleventh	11e	**onzième**

12th	twelfth	12e	**douzième**
13th	thirteenth	13e	**treizième**
14th	fourteenth	14e	**quatorzième**
15th	fifteenth	15e	**quinzième**
16th	sixteenth	16e	**seizième**
17th	seventeenth	17e	**dix-septième**
18th	eighteenth	18e	**dix-huitième**
19th	nineteenth	19e	**dix-neuvième**
20th	twentieth	20e	**vingtième**
21st	twenty-first	21e	**vingt et unième**
22nd	twnety-second	22e	**vingt-deuxième**
30th	thirtieth	30e	**trentième**
40th	fortieth	40e	**quarantième**
50th	fiftieth	50e	**cinquantième**
60th	sixtieth	60e	**soixantième**
70th	seventieth	70e	**soixante-dixième**
80th	eightieth	80e	**quatre-vingtième**
90th	ninetieth	90e	**quatre-vingt-dixième**
100th	hundredth	100e	**centième**

TEMPERATURE/TEMPÉRATURE

0° Celsius (C)	Water freezes	32° Fahrenheit (F)	Congélation de l'eau
37° C	Human body temp.	98.6° F	Temp. du corps humain
40° C	Fever	104° F	Fièvre
100° C	Water boils	212° F	Ébullition de l'eau

Formula/Formule: $C = 5/9\ (F - 32)$; **e.g.:** $C = 5/9\ (104° - 32) = 5/9\ (72) = 360 \div 9 = 40°\ C$

$F = 9/5C + 32$; **e.g.:** $F = 9/5 \text{x} 100° + 32 = 9 \times 20 + 32 = 180 + 32 = 212°\ F$

GEOGRAPHICAL NAMES: ENGLISH-FRENCH
NOMS GÉOGRAPHIQUES: ANGLAIS-FRANÇAIS

Abidjan, Ivory Coast: Abidjan
Addis Ababa, Ethiopia: Addis-Ababa
Adriatic Sea, Eastern Mediterranean: la mer Adriatique
Aegean Islands, Eastern Mediterranean: les îles Égées *[f.pl]*
Aegean Sea, Eastern Mediterranean: la mer Égée
Aleutian Islands, Northern Pacific Ocean: les îles Aléoutiennes *[f.pl]*
Alexandria, Egypt: Alexandrie
Algeria, North Africa: l'Algérie *[f]*
Algiers, Algeria: Algiers
Alps, Europe: les Alpes *[f.pl]*
Alsace, France: l'Alsace *[f]*
Amazon River, South America: l'Amazone *[m]*
Antarctica: l'Antarctique *[m]*
Antarctic Ocean: l'océan Antarctique *[m]*
Antilles, Central America: les Antilles *[f.pl]*
Antwerp, Belgium: Anvers
Apennines, Italy: les Apennins *[m]*
Arabian Sea, Western Indian Ocean: la mer d'Oman
Aral Sea, Western Asia: la mer d'Aral
Arctic: l'Arctique *[m]*
Arctic Ocean: l'océan Arctique *[m]*
Argentina, South America: l'Argentine *[f]*
Asia Minor: l'Asie mineure *[f]*
Athens, Greece: Athènes
Atlantic Ocean: l'océan Atlantique *[m]*
Atlas Mountains, North Africa: les monts de l'Atlas *[m]*
Australia: l'Australie *[f]*
Austria, Central Europe: l'Autriche *[f]*
Avignon, France: Avignon
Azores, Atlantic Ocean: les Açores *[f.pl]*

Balearic Islands, Western Mediterranean Sea: les Baléares *[f.pl]*
Balkan States or the Balkans, Europe: les Balkans *[m.pl]*
Baltic Sea, Eastern Atlantic Ocean: la mer Baltique
Bayonne, France: Bayonne
Belgium, Europe: la Belgique
Belgrade, Yugoslavia: Belgrade
Belize, Central America: Belize
Benin, West Africa: Bénin
Bering Sea, Pacific Ocean: la mer de Béring
Bern, Switzerland: Berne
Bethlehem, Near Eastern city: Bethléem
Black Sea, Western Asia: la mer Noire
Bordeaux, France: Bordeaux
Borneo, Indonesia: le Bornéo
Bosporus, Eastern Mediterranean Sea: le Bosphore
Brazil, South America: le Brésil
British Columbia, Canada: la Colombie britannique
British Isles, Western Europe: les îles Britanniques *[f.pl]*
British West Indies: les Indes occidentales britanniques
Brittany, France: la Bretagne
Bruges, Belgium: Bruges
Brussels, Belgium: Bruxelles
Bucharest, Romania: Bucarest
Budapest, Hungary: Budapest
Bulgaria, Central Europe: la Bulgarie
Burgundy, France: la Bourgogne
Burkina Faso, Western Africa: le Burkina Faso
Burma, Southeast Asia: la Birmanie

Calcutta, India: Calcutta
Cambodia or Kampuchea, Southeast Asia: le Cambodge *ou* le Kampuchéa
Cameroon, Western Africa: le Cameroun
Canada, North America: le Canada
Canary Islands, Atlantic Ocean: les îles Canaries *[f.pl]*
Cancer, Tropic of: le Tropique du Cancer
Cap Haitien, Haiti: Cap-Haïtien
Capricorn, Tropic of: le Tropique du Capricorne
Caribbean Sea, Central America: la mer des Antilles *ou* la mer des Caraïbes
Carpathian Mountains, Eastern Europe: les Carpates (Carpathes) *[f.pl]*

Caspian Sea, Western Asia: la mer Caspienne
Catalonia, Spain: la Catalogne
Caucasus Mountains, Southeastern Europe: le Caucase
Cayenne, French Guiana: Cayenne
Cayman Islands, West Indies: les îles Caïmans *[f.pl]*
Central African Republic, Central Africa: la République Centrafricaine
Central America: l'Amérique centrale
Central Asia: l'Asie centrale *[f]*
Central Europe: l'Europe centrale *[f]*
Ceylon, South Asia: Ceylan
Chad, Central Africa: le Tchad
Chad, Lake, Central Africa: le lac Tchad
Champagne, France: la Champagne
Channel Islands, English Channel: les îles Anglo-Normandes *[f.pl]*
China, East Asia: la Chine
Cologne, West Germany: Cologne
Congo (Zaïre) River, Africa: le Zaïre
Congo, People's Republic of the, West Africa: la République Populaire du Congo
Cophenhagen, Denmark: Copenhague
Corinth, Greece: Corinthe
Corsica, Mediterranean Sea: la Corse
Cracow, Poland: Cracovie
Crete, Eastern Mediterranean: la Crète
Cyprus, Eastern Mediterranean: la Chypre
Czechoslovakia, Central Europe: la Tchécoslovaquie

Dahomey: V. Benin.
Dalmatia, Yugoslavia: la Dalmatie
Damascus, Syria: Damas
Danube River, Europe: le Danube
Dardanelles, Eastern Mediterranean Sea: le détroit des Dardanelles *[f.pl]*
Dead Sea, Near East: la mer Morte
Denmark, Northern Europe: le Danemark
Dordogne River, France: la Dordogne
Dover, Strait of, English Channel: le Pas de Calais
Dresden, East Germany: Dresde
Dunkirk, France: Dunkerque

East China Sea, Western Pacific: la mer de Chine orientale
East Indies, Southeast Asia: les Indes *[f.pl]*
Edinburgh, Scotland: Édimbourg
Edirne, Turkey: Edirne
Egypt, Northeast Africa: l'Égypte *[f]*
Elbe River, Europe: l'Elbe *[m]*
England, Great Britain: l'Angleterre *[f]*
English Channel, North Sea: la Manche
Equator: l'équateur *[m]*
Ethiopia, East Africa: l'Éthiopie *[f]*
Euphrates, Near East: l'Euphrate *[m]*

Falkland Islands, South America: les Malouines *[f.pl] ou* les îles Falkland *[f.pl]*
Far East: l'Extrême-Orient *[m]*
Finland, Northern Europe: la Finlande
Florence, Italy: Florence
France, Western Europe: la France
French Guiana, South America: la Guyane française

Gabon, West Africa: le Gabon
Galapagos Islands, South America: les îles Galápagos *[f.pl]*
Garonne River, Western Europe: la Garonne
Gascony, France: la Gascogne
Geneva, Switzerland: Genève
Geneva, Lake, Switzerland: le lac Léman
Genoa, Italy: Gênes
Germany, Europe: l'Allemagne *[f]*
Ghana, West Africa: le Ghana
Ghent, Belgium: Gand
Gibraltar, Straits of, Mediterranean Sea: le détroit de Gibraltar *[m]*
Gobi Desert, Central Asia: le désert de Gobi
Good Hope, Cape of, South Africa: le cap de Bonne-Espérance
Great Britain, Western Europe: la Grande-Bretagne
Greater Antilles, Central America: les Grandes Antilles *[f.pl]*
Great Salt Lake, Western North America: le Grand Lac Salé
Greece, Southeastern Europe: la Grèce

Greenland, North America: le Groenland
Guinea, West Africa: la Guinée

Hague, The, Netherlands: La Haye
Haiti, West Indies: Haïti *[f]*
Havana, Cuba: La Havane
Hawaiian Islands, Pacific Ocean: les îles Hawaii *[f.pl]*
Hebrides, The, Scotland: les îles Hébrides *[f.pl]*
Himalayas, South Asia: l'Himalaya *[m]*
Hispaniola, West Indies: l'Haïti *[f]*
Holland (Netherlands), Western Europe: la Hollande
Horn, Cape, South America: le cap Horn
Hungary, Central Europe: l'Hongrie *[f]*

Iberian Peninsula, Western Europe: la péninsule ibérique
Iceland, Northern Europe: l'Islande *[f]*
India, South Asia: l'Inde *[f]*
Indian Ocean: l'océan Indien *[m]*
Indonesia, Southeast Asia: l'Indonésie *[f]*
Indus River, South Asia: l'Indus *[m]*
Ionian Sea, Eastern Mediterranean Sea: la mer Ionienne
Iran, Near East: l'Iran *[m]*
Iraq, Near East: l'Irak *[m]*
Ireland, Western Europe: l'Irlande *[f]*
Israel, Near East: Israël *[m]*
Istanbul, Turkey: Istanbul
Italy, Southern Europe: l'Italie *[f]*
Ivory Coast, West Africa: la Côte d'Ivoire

Jamaica, West Indies: la Jamaïque
Japan, East Asia: le Japon
Japan, Sea of, Western Pacific Ocean: la mer du Japon
Jerusalem, Near East: Jérusalem
Jordan, Near East: la Jordanie
Jutland Peninsula, Northern Europe: la presqu'île du Jutland

Kampuchea, Southeast Asia: le Cambodge *ou* le Kampuchéa
Kenya, East Africa: le Kenya
Kuwait, Near East: le Koweït
Kyoto, Japon: Kyōto

Lapland, Northern Europe: la Laponie
Lausanne, Switzerland: Lausanne
Lebanon, Near East: le Liban
Leeward Islands, West Indes: les îles sous le Vent *[f.pl]*
Leningrad, USSR: Leningrad
Lesser Antilles, Central America: les Petites Antilles *[f.pl]*
Libya, North Africa: la Libye
Liege, Belgium: Liège
Lille, France: Lille
Lisbon, Portugal: Lisbonne
Lithuania, Northern Europe: la Lituanie
Loire River, France: la Loire
London, England: Londres
Lorraine, France: la Lorraine
Louisiana, United States: la Louisiane
Louvain, Belgium: Louvain
Low Countries, Western Europe: les Pays-Bas *[m.pl]*
Lucerne, Switzerland: Lucerne
Luxembourg, Western Europe: le Luxembourg
Lyons, France: Lyon

Madagascar, Southeastern Africa: le Madagascar
Magellan, Strait of, South America: le détroit de Magellan
Mainz, West Germany: Mayence
Majorca, Spain: Majorque
Malay Peninsula, Southeast Asia: la péninsule Malaise
Malaysia, Southeast Asia: la Malaisie
Maldive Islands, Arabian Sea: les Maldives *[f.pl]*
Mali, Republic of, West Africa: la République du Mali
Malta, Mediterranean Sea: Malte
Marmara, Sea of, Aegean Sea: la mer de Marmara
Marseilles, France: Marseille
Martinique, West Indies: la Martinique
Massif Central, France: le Massif Central
Mauritania, Islamic Republic of, North Africa: la Mauritanie

Mauritius, Indian Ocean: la Maurice
Mediterranean Sea: la mer Méditerranée
Mekong River, Southeast Asia: le Mékong
Melanesia, Western Pacific Ocean: la Mélanésie
Meuse River, France: la Meuse
Mexico, North America: le Méxique
Mexico, Gulf of: le golfe du Méxique
Micronesia, Western Pacific Ocean: la Micronésie
Middle East: le Moyen-Orient
Minorca, Spain: Minorque
Mississippi River, United States: le Mississippi
Missouri River, United States: le Missouri
Mongolia, Central Asia: la Mongolie
Montreal, Quebec, Canada: Montréal
Morocco, North Africa: le Maroc
Moscow, USSR: Moscou
Moselle River, Western Europe: la Moselle

Nantes, France: Nantes
Naples, Italy: Naples
Near East: le Proche-Orient
Netherlands, Western Europe: la Hollande
Newfoundland, Canada: la Terre-Neuve
New Guinea, Western Pacific Ocean: La Nouvelle-Guinée
New Orleans, Louisiana, United States: La Nouvelle-Orléans
New York, United States: New York
New Zealand, South Pacific Ocean: La Nouvelle-Zélande
Nice, France: Nice
Niger, Republic of, West Africa: la République du Niger
Nigeria, West Africa: le *ou* la Nigeria
Niger River, West Africa: le Niger
Nile River, Africa: le Nil
Normandy, France: la Normandie
North Africa: l'Afrique du Nord *[f]*
North America: l'Amérique du Nord *[f]*
North Korea, East Asia: la Corée du Nord
North Sea, Eastern Atlantic Ocean: la mer du Nord
Norway, Northern Europe: la Norvège
Nova Scotia, Canada: la Nouvelle-Écosse

Odessa, Ukraine, USSR: Odessa
Ostend, Belgium: Ostende

Pacific Ocean: l'océan Pacifique *[m]*
Panama Canal, Central America: le canal de Panamá
Peru, South America: le Pérou
Perugia, Italy: Pérouse
Philippines, East Asia: les Philippines *[f.pl]*
Poland, Central Europe: la Pologne
Polynesia, Eastern Pacific Ocean: la Polynésie
Port Said, Egypt: Port-Saïd
Port-au-Prince, Haiti: Port-au-Prince
Port-of-Spain, Trinidad: Port of Spain
Prague, Czechoslovakia: Prague
Provence, France: la Provence
Pyrenees, Western Europe: les Pyrénées *[f.pl]*

Quebec, Canada: le Québec
Queen Charlotte Islands, Canada: les îles de la Reine-Charlotte

Rangoon, Burma: Rangoon
Red Sea, Northeast Africa: la mer Rouge
Rhine River, Western Europe: le Rhin
Rhodes, Aegean Sea: la Rhodes
Rhodesia, South Africa: la Rhodésie
Rhone River, France: le Rhône
Rio Grande, North America: le Rio Grande del Norte
Riviera, The, France and Italy: la Côte d'Azur
Rocky Mountains, North America: les montagnes Rocheuses
Rouen, France: Rouen
Rumania, Eastern Europe: la Roumanie
Russia, USSR: la Russie

Sahara, The, North Africa: le Sahara
St. Lawrence River, North America: le Saint-Laurent
Sardinia, Western Mediterranean: la Sardaigne

Saudi Arabia, Southwest Asia: l'Arabie saoudite *[f]*
Scandinavia, Northern Europe: la Scandinavie
Scotland, Great Britain: l'Écosse *[f]*
Seine River, France: la Seine
Senegal, Republic of, West Africa: la République du Sénégal
Siberia, Northeast Asia: la Sibérie
Sicily, Western Mediterranean Sea: la Sicile
Singapore, Southeast Asia: Singapour
Smyrna, Turkey: Smyrne
South Africa: l'Afrique du Sud *[f]*
South Africa, Union of: l'Union Sud-Africaine *[f]*
South America: l'Amérique du Sud *[f]*
South China Sea, Western Pacific Ocean: la mer de Chine Méridionale
South Korea, East Asia: la Corée du Sud
Spain, Western Europe: l'Espagne *[f]*
Sri Lanka, South Asia: Sri Lanka
Stockholm, Sweden: Stockholm
Strasbourg, France: Strasbourg
Sudan, The, North Africa: le Soudan
Suez Canal, Egypt: le canal de Suez
Surinam, Amérique du Sud: le Surinam
Sweden, Northern Europe: la Suède
Switzerland, Western Europe: la Suisse
Syria, Near East: la Syrie

Tangier *or* **Tangiers, Morocco:** Tanger
Taurus Mountains, Turkey: le Taurus
Tehran, Iran: Téhéran
Thailand, Southeast Asia: la Thaïlande
Thames River, England: la Tamise
Togo, Republic of, West Africa: le Togo
Tokyo, Japan: Tōkyō
Toulon, France: Toulon
Toulouse, France: Toulouse
Trinidad, West Indies: (l'île de) la Trinité
Tunisia, North Africa: la Tunisie
Turkey, Near East: la Turquie
Tyrrhenian Sea, Western Mediterranean Sea: la mer Tyrrhénienne

Ukraine, The, USSR: l'Ukraine *[f]*
Union of Soviet Socialist Republics (USSR): l'Union des républiques socialistes soviétiques (URSS) *[f]*
United Kingdom of Great Britain and Northern Ireland, Western Europe: le Royaume-Uni de Grande-Bretagne et d'Irlande du Nord
United States of America, North America: les États-Unis d'Amérique *[m.pl]*
Ural Mountains, Europe and Asia: l'Oural *[m]*

Van, Lake, Turkey: le lac de Van
Venice, Italy: Venise
Victoria, Lake, East Africa: le lac Victoria
Vienna, Austria: Vienne
Vienne, France: Vienne
Virgin Islands, West Indies: les îles Vierges *[f.pl]*

Wales, Great Britain: le pays de Galles
Warsaw, Poland: Varsovie
West Indies, Central America: les Antilles *[f.pl]*
Windward Islands, West Indies: les îles du Vent *[f.pl]*

Yangtze River, China: le Yang-tseu-kiang *ou* le fleuve Bleu
Yellow River, China: l'Houang-Ho *[m]* *ou* le fleuve Jaune
Yellow Sea, Western Pacific Ocean: la mer Jaune
Yugoslavia, Southeastern Europe: la Yougoslavie

Zaire, Republic of, Central Africa: la République de Zaïre
Zaire River, Africa: le Zaïre
Zambezi River, Africa: le Zambèze

NOMS GÉOGRAPHIQUES: FRANÇAIS-ANGLAIS
GEOGRAPHICAL NAMES: FRENCH-ENGLISH

Abidjan, Côte d'Ivoire: Abidjan
Açores, les *[f.pl]*, **océan Atlantique:** Azores
Addis-Ababa, Éthiopie: Addis Ababa
Adriatique, la mer, Méditerranée orientale: Adriatic Sea
Afrique du Nord, l': North Africa
Afrique du Sud, l': South Africa
Alexandrie, Égypte: Alexandria
Algérie, l' *[f]*, **Afrique du Nord:** Algeria
Algiers, Algérie: Algiers
Allemagne, l' *[f]*, **Europe:** Germany
Alpes, les *[f.pl]*, **Europe:** Alps
Alsace, l' *[f]*, **France:** Alsace
Amazone, l' *[m]*, **Amérique du Sud:** Amazon River
Amérique Centrale, l' *[f]*: Central America
Amérique du Nord, l' *[f]:* North America
Amérique du Sud, l' *[f]:* South America
Angleterre, l', Grande-Bretagne: England
Anglo-Normandes, les îles *[f.pl]*, **la Manche:** Channel Islands
Antarctique, l'*[m]:* Antarctic Ocean
Antarctique, l'océan *[m]:* Antarctica
Antilles, la mer des, *ou* **la mer des Caraïbes, Amérique centrale:** Caribbean Sea, Central America
Antilles, les *[f.pl]*, **Amérique centrale:** Antilles, West Indies
Antilles, les Grandes, Amérique du Nord: Greater Antilles
Anvers, Belgique: Antwerp
Apennins, les *[m]*, **Italie:** the Apennines
Arabie saoudite, Asie du Sud-Ouest: Saudi Arabia
Aral, la mer d', Asie occidentale: Aral Sea
Arctique, l' *[m]:* the Arctic
Arctique, l'océan *[m]:* Arctic Ocean
Argentine, l' *[f]*, **Amérique du Sud:** Argentina
Asie centrale, l' *[f]:* Central Asia
Asie mineure, l' *[f]:* Asia Minor
Athènes, Grèce: Athens
Atlantique, l'océan *[m]:* Atlantic Ocean
Atlas, l' *[m]*, **Afrique du Nord:** Atlas Mountains
Australie, l' *[f]:* Australia
Autriche, l' *[f]*, **Europe centrale:** Austria
Avignon, France: Avignon
Azur, la Côte d', France et Italie: The Riviera

Baléares, les *[f.pl]*, **mer Méditerranée:** Balearic Islands
Balkans, les *[m.pl]*, **Europe:** Balkan States *or* the Balkans
Baltique, la mer, océan Atlantique oriental: Baltic Sea
Bayonne, France: Bayonne
Belgique, la, Europe: Belgium
Belgrade, Yougoslavie: Belgrade
Belize, Amérique centrale: Belize
Bénin, Afrique occidental: Benin
Béring, la mer de, océan Pacifique septentrional: Bering Sea
Berne, Suisse: Bern
Bethléem, ville du Proche-Orient: Bethlehem
Birmanie, la, Asie du Sud-Est: Burma
Bleu, le fleuve (*ou* **le Yang-tseu-kiang), Chine:** Yangtze River
Bonne-Espérance, le cap de, Afrique méridionale: Cape of Good Hope
Bordeaux, France: Bordeaux
Bornéo, le, Indonésie: Borneo
Bosphore, le, mer Méditerranée orientale: The Bosporus
Bourgogne, la, France: Burgundy
Brésil, le, Amérique du Sud: Brazil
Bretagne, la, France: Brittany
Britanniques, les îles, Europe occidentale: British Isles
Bruges, Belgique: Bruges
Bruxelles, Belgique: Brussels
Bucarest, Roumanie: Bucharest
Budapest, Hongrie: Budapest
Bulgarie, la, Europe centrale: Bulgaria
Burkina Faso, le, Afrique occidentale: Burkina Faso

Caïmans, les îles *[f.pl]*, **Grandes Antilles:** Cayman Islands

Calais, le Pas de, la Manche: Strait of Dover
Calcutta, Inde: Calcutta
Cambodge, le, Asie du Sud-Est: Cambodia *or* Kampuchea
Cameroun, le, Afrique occidentale: Cameroon
Canada, le, Amérique du Nord: Canada
Canaries, les îles ***[f.pl]*****, océan Atlantique:** Canary Islands
Cancer, le Tropique du: The Tropic of Cancer
Capricorne, le Tropique du: The Tropic of Capricorn
Carpates (Carpathes), les ***[f.pl]*****, Europe orientale:** Carpathian Mountains
Caspienne, la mer, Asie occidentale: Caspian Sea
Catalogne, la, Espagne: Catalonia
Caucase, le, Europe du Sud-Est: Caucasus Mountains
Cayenne, Guyane française: Cayenne
Ceylan, Asie méridionale: Ceylon
Champagne, la, France: Champagne
Chine, la, Asie orientale: China
Chine méridionale, mer de, océan Pacifique occidental: South China Sea
Chine orientale, mer de, océan Pacifique occidental: East China Sea
Chypre, la, mer Méditerranée orientale: Cyprus
Cologne, Allemagne occidentale: Cologne
Colombie britannique, la, Canada: British Columbia
Congo (Zaïre), le, Afrique: Zaire River
Congo, la République Populaire du, Afrique occidentale: People's Republic of the Congo
Copenhague, Danemark: Copenhagen
Corée du Nord, la, Asie orientale: North Korea
Corée du Sud, la, Asie orientale: South Korea
Corinthe, Grèce: Corinth
Corse, la, mer Méditerranée: Corsica
Côte d'Ivoire, la, Afrique occidentale: Ivory Coast
Cracovie, Pologne: Cracow
Crète, la, mer Méditerranée orientale: Crete

Dalmatie, la, Yougoslavie: Dalmatia
Damas, Syrie: Damascus
Danemark, le, Europe septentrionale: Denmark
Danube, le, Europe: Danube River
Dardanelles ***[f.pl]*****, le détroit des, mer Méditerranée orientale:** The Dardanelles
Dordogne, la, France: Dordogne River
Dresde, Allemagne orientale: Dresden
Dunkerque, France: Dunkirk

Écosse, l', Grande-Bretagne: Scotland
Édimbourg, Écosse: Edinburgh
Edirne, Turquie: Edirne
Égée, la mer, mer Méditerranée orientale: Aegean Sea
Égypte, l' ***[f]*****, Afrique du Nord-Est:** Egypt
Elbe, l' ***[m]*****, Europe:** Elbe River
équateur, l' ***[m]*****:** The Equator
Espagne, l' ***[f]*****, Europe occidentale:** Spain
États-Unis d'Amérique, les, ***[m.pl]*****, Amérique du Nord:** The United States of America
Éthiopie, l' ***[f]*****, Afrique orientale:** Ethiopia
Euphrate, l' ***[m]*****, Proche-Orient:** Euphrates River
Europe centrale, l' ***[f]:*** Central Europe
Extrême-Orient, l' ***[m]:*** The Far East

Falkland, les îles ***[f.pl], ou*** **les Malouines** ***[f.pl]*****, Amérique du Sud:** Falkland Islands
Finlande, la, Europe septentrionale: Finland
Florence, Italie: Florence
France, la, Europe occidentale: France

Gabon, le, Afrique occidentale: Gabon
Galápagos, les îles ***[f.pl]*****, Amérique du Sud:** Galapagos Islands
Galles, le pays de, Grande-Bretagne: Wales
Gand, Belgique: Ghent
Garonne, la, Europe occidentale: Garonne River

Gascogne, la, France: Gascony
Gênes, Italie: Genoa
Genève, Suisse: Geneva
Ghana, le, Afrique occidentale: Ghana
Gibraltar, le détroit de, mer Méditerranée: Straits of Gibraltar
Gobi, le désert de, Asie centrale: Gobi Desert
Grand Lac Salé, le, Amérique du Nord occidentale: Great Salt Lake
Grande-Bretagne, Europe occidentale: Great Britain
Grandes Antilles, les, Amérique centrale: Greater Antilles
Grèce, la, Europe du Sud-Est: Greece
Groenland, le, Amérique du Nord: Greenland
Guinée, Afrique occidentale: Guinea
Guyane française, la, Amérique du Sud: French Guiana

Haïti, l'île d', Grandes Antilles: Hispaniola
Haïti, Grandes Antilles: Haiti
Havane, La, Cuba: Havana
Hawaii, les îles ***[f.pl]*****, océan Pacifique:** Hawaiian Islands
Haye, La, Hollande: The Hague
Hébrides, les îles, Écosse: The Hebrides
Himalaya, l' ***[m]*****, Asie septentrionale:** Himalayas
Hollande, la, Europe occidentale: The Netherlands *or* Holland
Hongrie, l' ***[f]*****, Europe centrale:** Hungary
Horn, le cap, Amérique du Sud: Cape Horn
Houang-Ho (*ou* le fleuve Jaune), l' ***[m]*****, Chine:** Yellow River

Ibérique, la péninsule, Europe occidentale: Iberian Peninsula
Îles Aléoutiennes, les ***[f.pl]*****, océan Pacifique septentrional:** Aleutian Islands
Îles du Vent, les ***[f.pl]*****, Petites Antilles:** Windward Islands
Îles Égées, les ***[f.pl]*****, mer Méditerranée orientale:** Aegean Islands
Îles sous le Vent, les ***[f.pl]*****, Petites Antilles:** Leeward Islands
Inde, l' ***[f]*****, Asie méridionale:** India
Indes, les ***[f.pl]*****, Asie du Sud-Est:** East Indies
Indes occidentales britanniques, les ***[f.pl]*****:** British West Indies
Indien, l'océan ***[m]*****:** Indian Ocean
Indonésie, l', Asie du Sud-Est: Indonesia
Indus, l' ***[m]*****, Asie septentrionale:** Indus River
Ionienne, la mer, mer Méditerranée orientale: Ionian Sea
Irak, Proche-Orient: Iraq
Iran, Proche-Orient: Iran
Irlande, l' ***[f]*****, Europe occidentale:** Ireland
Islande, l' ***[f]*****, Europe septentrionale:** Iceland
Israël ***[m]*****, Proche-Orient:** Israel
Istanbul, Turquie: Istanbul
Italie, l'***[f]*****, Europe septentrionale:** Italy

Jamaïque, la, Grandes Antilles: Jamaica
Japon, la mer du, océan Pacifique occidentale: Sea of Japan
Japon, le, Asie orientale: Japan
Jaune, la mer, océan Pacifique occidental: Yellow Sea
Jaune, le fleuve (*ou* Houang-Ho ***[m]*****,) Chine:** Yellow River
Jérusalem, Proche-Orient: Jerusalem
Jordanie, la, Proche-Orient: Jordan
Jutland, la presqu'île du, Europe septentrionale: Jutland Peninsula

Kampuchéa, le, Asie du Sud-Est: Cambodia *or* Kampuchea
Kenya, le, Afrique orientale: Kenya
Koweït, le, Proche-Orient: Kuwait
Kyōto, Japon: Kyoto

Laponie, la, Europe septentrionale: Lapland
Lausanne, Suisse: Lausanne
Léman, le lac, Suisse: Lake Geneva
Leningrad, URSS: Leningrad
Liban, le, Proche-Orient: Lebanon
Libye, la, Afrique du Nord: Libya
Liège, Belgique: Liege
Lille, France: Lille
Lisbonne, Portugal: Lisbon

Lituanie, la, Europe septentrionale: Lithuania
Loire, la, France: Loire River
Londres, Angleterre: London
Lorraine, la, France: Lorraine
Louisiane, la, États-Unis: Louisiana
Louvain, Belgique: Louvain
Lucerne, Suisse: Lucerne
Luxembourg, le, Europe occidentale: Luxembourg
Lyon, France: Lyons

Madagascar, le, Afrique du Sud-Est: Madagascar
Magellan, le détroit de, Amérique du Sud: Strait of Magellan
Mali, la République du, Afrique occidentale: Republic of Mali
Majorque, Espagne: Majorca
Malaise, la péninsule, Asie du Sud-Est: Malay Peninsula
Malaisie, la, Asie du Sud-Est: Malaysia
Maldives, les *[f.pl]*, mer d'Oman: Maldive Islands
Malouines, les *[f.pl], ou* Falkland, les îles *[f.pl]*, Amérique du Sud: Falkland Islands
Malte, mer Méditerranée: Malta
Manche, la, mer du Nord: English Channel
Marmara, la mer de, mer Égée: Sea of Marmara
Maroc, le, Afrique du Nord: Morocco
Marseille, France: Marseilles
Martinique, la, Petites Antilles: Martinique
Massif Central, le, France: Massif Central
Maurice, la, océan Indien: Mauritius
Mauritanie, la, Afrique du Nord: Islamic Republic of Mauritania
Mayence, Allemagne occidentale: Mainz
Méditerranée, la mer: Mediterranean Sea
Mékong, le, Asie du Sud-Est: Mekong River
Mélanésie, la, océan Pacifique occidental: Melanesia
Meuse, la, France: Meuse River
Méxique, le, Amérique du Nord: Mexico
Méxique, le golfe du: Gulf of Mexico
Micronésie, la, océan Pacifique occidental: Micronesia
Minorque, Espagne: Minorca
Mississippi, le, États-Unis: Mississippi River
Missouri, le, États-Unis: Missouri River
Mongolie, la, Asie centrale: Mongolia
Montréal, Québec, Canada: Montreal
Morte, la mer, Proche-Orient: Dead Sea
Moscou, URSS: Moscow
Moselle, la, Europe occidentale: Moselle River
Moyen-Orient, le: The Middle East

Nantes, France: Nantes
Naples, Italie: Naples
New York, États-Unis: New York
Nice, France: Nice
Niger, le, Afrique occidentale: Niger River
Niger, la République du, Afrique occidentale: Republic of Niger
Nigeria, le *ou* la, Afrique occidentale: Nigeria
Nil, le, Afrique: Nile River
Nord, la mer du, océan Atlantique oriental: The North Sea
Normandie, la, France: Normandy
Norvège, la, Europe septentrionale: Norway
Nouvelle-Écosse, la, Canada: Nova Scotia
Nouvelle-Guinée, la, océan Pacifique occidentale: New Guinea
Nouvelle-Orléans, la, Louisiane, États-Unis: New Orleans
Nouvelle-Zélande, la, océan Pacifique méridionale: New Zealand

Odessa, Ukraine, URSS: Odessa
Oman, la mer d', océan Indien occidental: Arabian Sea
Ostende, Belgique: Ostend
Oural, l' *[m]*, Europe et Asie: Ural Mountains

Pacifique, l'océan *[m]*: Pacific Ocean
Panamá, le canal de, Amérique centrale: Panama Canal

Pays-Bas, les, Europe occidentale: Low Countries
Pérou, le, Amérique du Sud: Peru
Pérouse, Italie: Perugia
Petites Antilles, les *[f.pl]*, **Amérique centrale:** Lesser Antilles
Philippines, les *[f.pl]*, **Asie orientale:** Philippines
Pologne, la, Europe centrale: Poland
Polynésie, océan Pacifique oriental: Polynesia
Port-au-Prince, Haïti: Port-au-Prince
Port of Spain, la Trinité: Port-of-Spain
Port-Saïd, Égypte: Port Said
Prague, Tchécoslovaquie: Prague
Proche-Orient, le: The Near East
Provence, la, France: Provence
Pyrénées, les *[f.pl]*, **Europe occidentale:** Pyrenees

Québec, Canada: Quebec

Rangoon, Birmanie: Rangoon
Reine-Charlotte, les îles de la, Canada: Queen Charlotte Islands
République Centrafricaine, la, Afrique centrale: Central African Republic
Rhin, le, Europe occidentale: Rhine River
Rhodes, mer Égée: Rhodes
Rhodésie, la, Afrique du Sud: Rhodesia
Rhône, le, France: Rhone River
Rio Grande del Norte, le, Amérique du Nord: Rio Grande
Rocheuses, les montagnes, Amérique du Nord: Rocky Mountains
Rouen, France: Rouen
Rouge, la mer, Afrique du Nord-Est: Red Sea
Roumanie, la, Europe orientale: Rumania
Royaume-Uni de Grande-Bretagne et d'Irlande du Nord, le, Europe occidentale: United Kingdom of Great Britain and Northern Ireland
Russie, la, URSS: Russia

Sahara, le, Afrique du Nord: The Sahara
Saint-Laurent, le, Amérique du Nord: Saint Lawrence River
Sardaigne, la, mer Méditerranée: Sardinia
Scandinavie, la, Europe septentrionale: Scandinavia
Seine, la, France: Seine River
Sénégal, la République du, Afrique occidentale: Republic of Senegal
Sibérie, la, Asie du nord-est: Siberia
Sicile, la, mer Méditerranée occidentale: Sicily
Singapour, Asie du Sud-Est: Singapore
Smyrne, Turquie: Smyrna
Soudan, le, Afrique du Nord: The Sudan
Sri Lanka, Asie du Sud: Sri Lanka
Stockholm, Suède: Stockholm
Strasbourg, France: Strasbourg
Suède, la, Europe septentrionale: Sweden
Suez, le canal de, Égypte: Suez Canal
Suisse, la, Europe occidentale: Switzerland
Surinam, le, Amérique du Sud: Surinam
Syrie, la, Proche-Orient: Syria

Tamise, la, Angleterre: Thames River
Tanger, Maroc: Tangier *or* Tangiers
Taurus, le, Turquie: Taurus Mountains
Tchad, le, Afrique centrale: Chad
Tchad, le lac, Afrique centrale: Lake Chad
Tchécoslovaquie, la, Europe centrale: Czechoslovakia
Téhéran, Iran: Tehran
Terre-Neuve, la, Canada: Newfoundland
Thaïlande, la, Asie du Sud-Est: Thailand
Togo, le, Afrique occidentale: Republic of Togo
Tōkyō, Japon: Tokyo
Toulon, France: Toulon
Toulouse, France: Toulouse
Trinité, la, Antilles: Trinidad
Tunisie, la, Afrique du Nord: Tunisia
Turquie, la, Proche-Orient: Turkey
Tyrrhénienne, la mer, mer Méditerranée occidentale: Tyrrhenian Sea

Ukraine, l' *[f]*, **URSS:** The Ukraine
Union Sud-Africaine, l' *[f.]:* Union of South Africa

Van, le lac de, Turquie: Lake Van
Varsovie, Pologne: Warsaw
Venise, Italie: Venice
Victoria, le lac, Afrique orientale: Lake Victoria
Vienne, Autriche: Vienna
Vienne, France: Vienne
Vierges, les, îles *[f.pl]*, **océan Atlantique occidental:** Virgin Islands

Yang-tseu-kiang (*ou* le fleuve Bleu), le, Chine: Yangtze River
Yougoslavie, la, Europe du Sud-Est: Yugoslavia

Zaïre, le, Afrique: Zaire River
Zaïre, la République de, Afrique centrale: Republic of Zaire
Zambèze, le, Afrique: Zambezi River

PAS DE CALAIS
LA MANCHE
Anvers
Gand
BRUXELLES
BELGIQUE
Liège
LUXEMBOURG
LUXEMBOURG
R.F.A.
Lille
Dieppe
Amiens
Cherbourg
Le Havre
Rouen
Saint-Quentin
Sedan
Meuse
Caen
Beauvais
Brest
Saint-Brieuc
Saint-Malo
Seine
PARIS
Reims
Verdun
Metz
Douarnenez
Quimper
Versailles
Marne
Nancy
Chartres
Melun
Rennes
Lorient
Fontainebleau
Troyes
Strasbourg
Le Mans
Orléans
Colmar
Nantes
Angers
Loire
Mulhouse
Saint-Nazaire
Tours
N
C
E
Belfort
F
R
A
Bourges
Dijon
Besançon
Poitiers
Châteauroux
Le Creusot
SUISSE
La Rochelle
Montluçon
Mâcon
OCÉAN
ATLANTIQUE
Royan
Limoges
Vichy
Roanne
Cognac
Angoulême
Clermont-
Ferrand
Rhône
Lyon
MASSIF
CENTRAL
Saint-Étienne
Chambéry
Périgueux
Brive
Grenoble
Bordeaux
Arcachon
Dordogne
Le Puy
Valence
ALPES
ITALIE
Cahors
Gap
Agen
Garonne
Montauban
Millau
Alès
Avignon
Nîmes
Bayonne
Biarritz
Pau
Montpellier
Aix-en-
Provence
Nice
Tarbes
Lourdes
Beziers
Cannes
Carcassonne
Narbonne
Marseille
Toulon
PYRÉNÉES
Perpignan
GOLFE DU LION

FRANCE

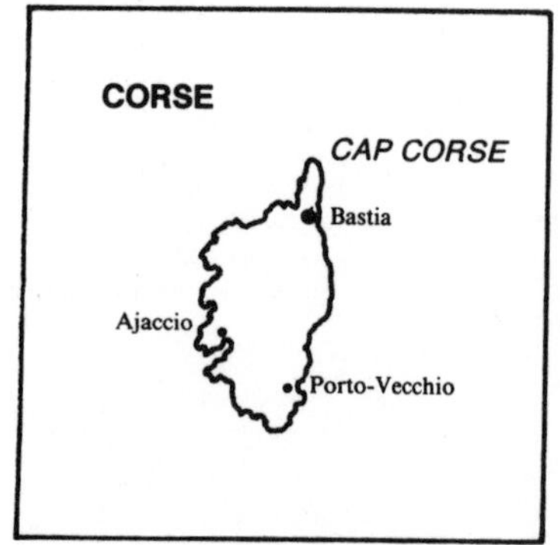
CORSE
CAP CORSE
Bastia
Ajaccio
Porto-Vecchio

DEPARTEMENTS
LIMITE DES DEPARTEMENTS
CHEF-LIEU
PAS-DE-CALAIS
NORD
SOMME
AISNE
ARDENNES
SEINE-MARITIME
OISE
MANCHE
CALVADOS
EURE
Paris
NEW DEPARTMENTS
SEINE- ET MARNE
MARNE
MEUSE
MOSELLE
BAS-RHIN
MEURTHE-ET-MOSELLE
FINISTÈRE
CÔTES - DU-NORD
ORNE
EURE-ET-LOIR
AUBE
HAUTE-MARNE
VOSGES
HAUT-RHIN
ILLE-ET-VILAINE
MAYENNE
SARTHE
LOIRET
YONNE
HAUTE-SAÔNE
MORBIHAN
LOIRE-ATLANTIQUE
MAINE-ET-LOIRE
INDRE-ET-LOIRE
LOIR-ET-CHER
CÔTE-D'OR
DOUBS
T. DE BELFORT
NIÈVRE
CHER
JURA
VENDÉE
DEUX-SÈVRES
VIENNE
INDRE
SAÔNE-ET-LOIRE
ALLIER
AIN
HAUTE-SAVOIE
RHÔNE
CHARENTE-MARITIME
CHARENTE
CREUSE
HAUTE-VIENNE
PUY-DE-DÔME
LOIRE
SAVOIE
ISÈRE
CORRÈZE
DORDOGNE
CANTAL
HAUTE-LOIRE
DRÔME
HAUTES-ALPES
GIRONDE
LOT
ARDÈCHE
LOZÈRE
LOT-ET-GARONNE
TARN-ET-GARONNE
AVEYRON
VAUCLUSE
BASSES-ALPES
ALPES-MARITIMES
LANDES
GERS
TARN
GARD
HÉRAULT
BOUCHES-DU-RHÔNE
VAR
BASSES-PYRÉNÉES
HAUTES-PYRÉNÉES
HAUTE-GARONNE
AUDE
ARIÈGE
PYRÉNÉES-ORIENTALES
NOUVEAUX DEPARTEMENTS DE LA REGION PARISIENNE DEPUIS JUILLET 1964
VAL D'OISE
SEINE-ST-DENIS
YVELINES
HAUTS-DE-SEINE
PARIS
VAL-DE-MARNE
ESSONNE
CORSE
HAUTE-CORSE
CORSE-DU-SUD

PLAN DES ARRONDISSEMENTS DE PARIS

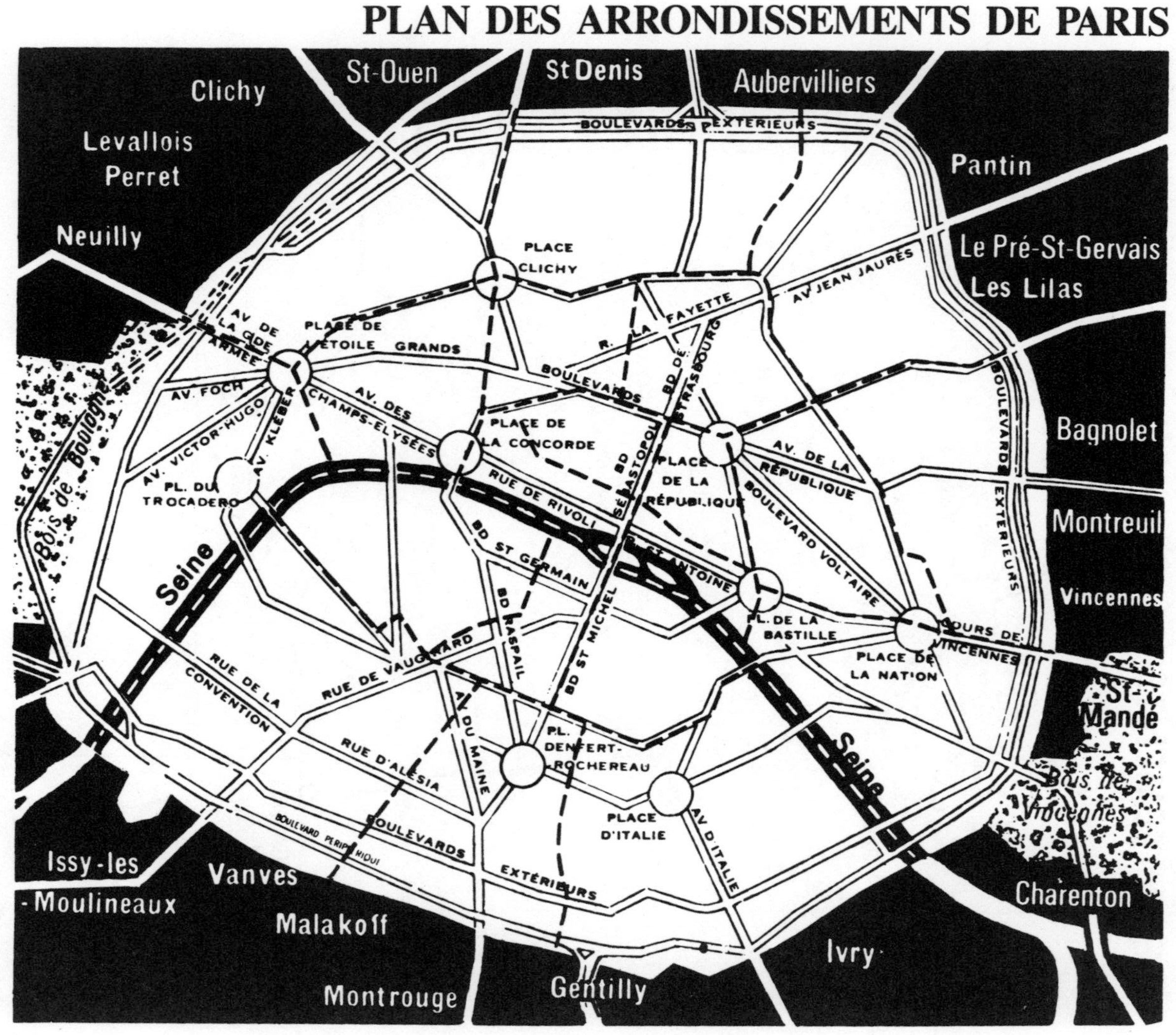

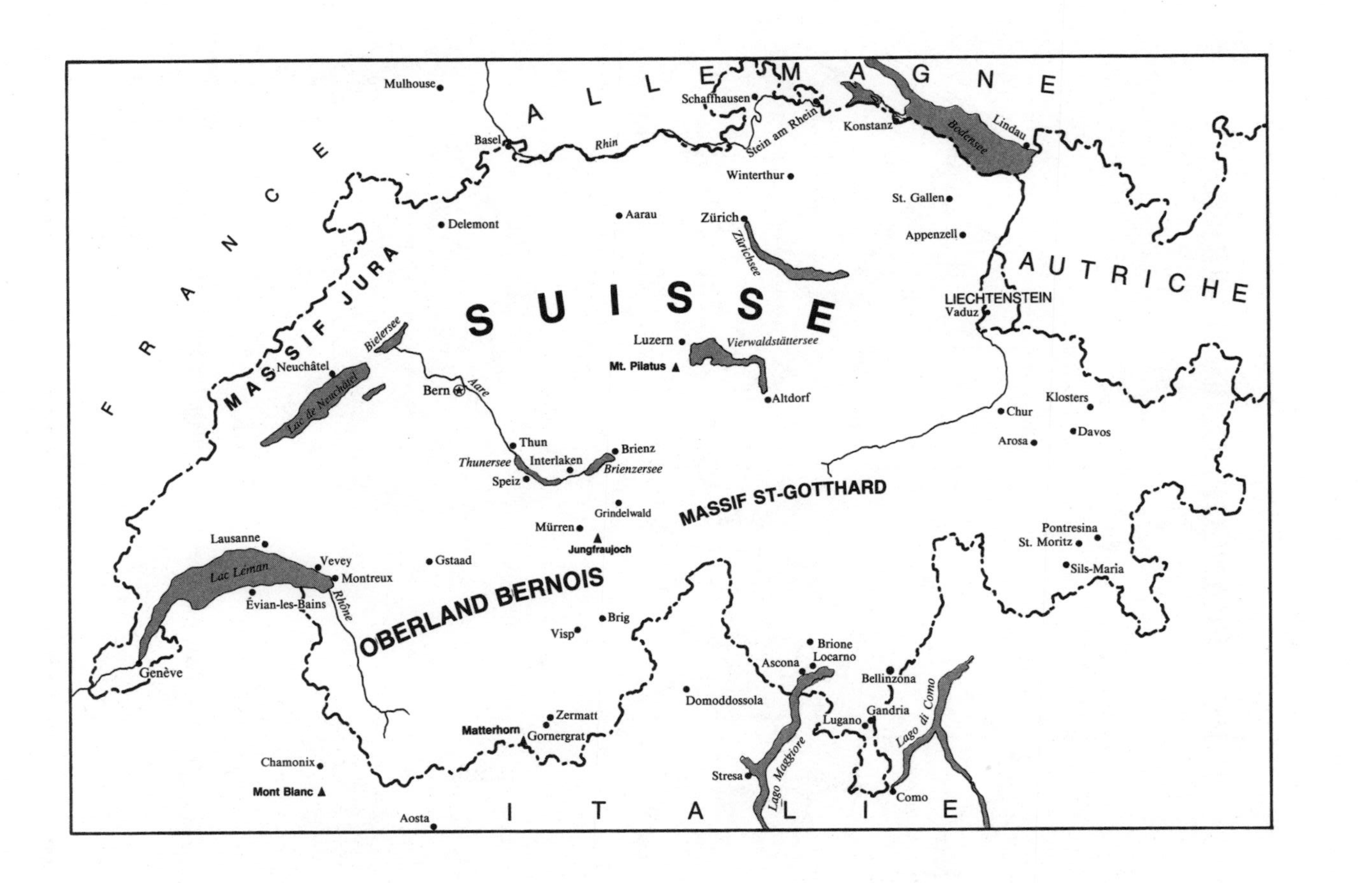

ALLEMAGNE
AUTRICHE
LIECHTENSTEIN
SUISSE
FRANCE
ITALIE
MASSIF JURA
MASSIF ST-GOTTHARD
OBERLAND BERNOIS
Mulhouse
Basel
Rhin
Schaffhausen
Stein am Rhein
Konstanz
Bodensee
Lindau
Winterthur
St. Gallen
Appenzell
Vaduz
Klosters
Davos
Chur
Arosa
Pontresina
St. Moritz
Sils-Maria
Delemont
Aarau
Zürich
Zürichsee
Luzern
Vierwaldstättersee
Altdorf
Mt. Pilatus
Bielersee
Lac de Neuchâtel
Neuchâtel
Bern
Aare
Thun
Thunersee
Interlaken
Speiz
Brienz
Brienzersee
Grindelwald
Mürren
Jungfraujoch
Gstaad
Brig
Visp
Zermatt
Gornergrat
Matterhorn
Domoddossola
Ascona
Brione
Locarno
Bellinzona
Lugano
Gandria
Como
Lago di Como
Lago Maggiore
Stresa
Aosta
Lausanne
Lac Léman
Vevey
Montreux
Rhône
Évian-les-Bains
Chamonix
Mont Blanc
Genève

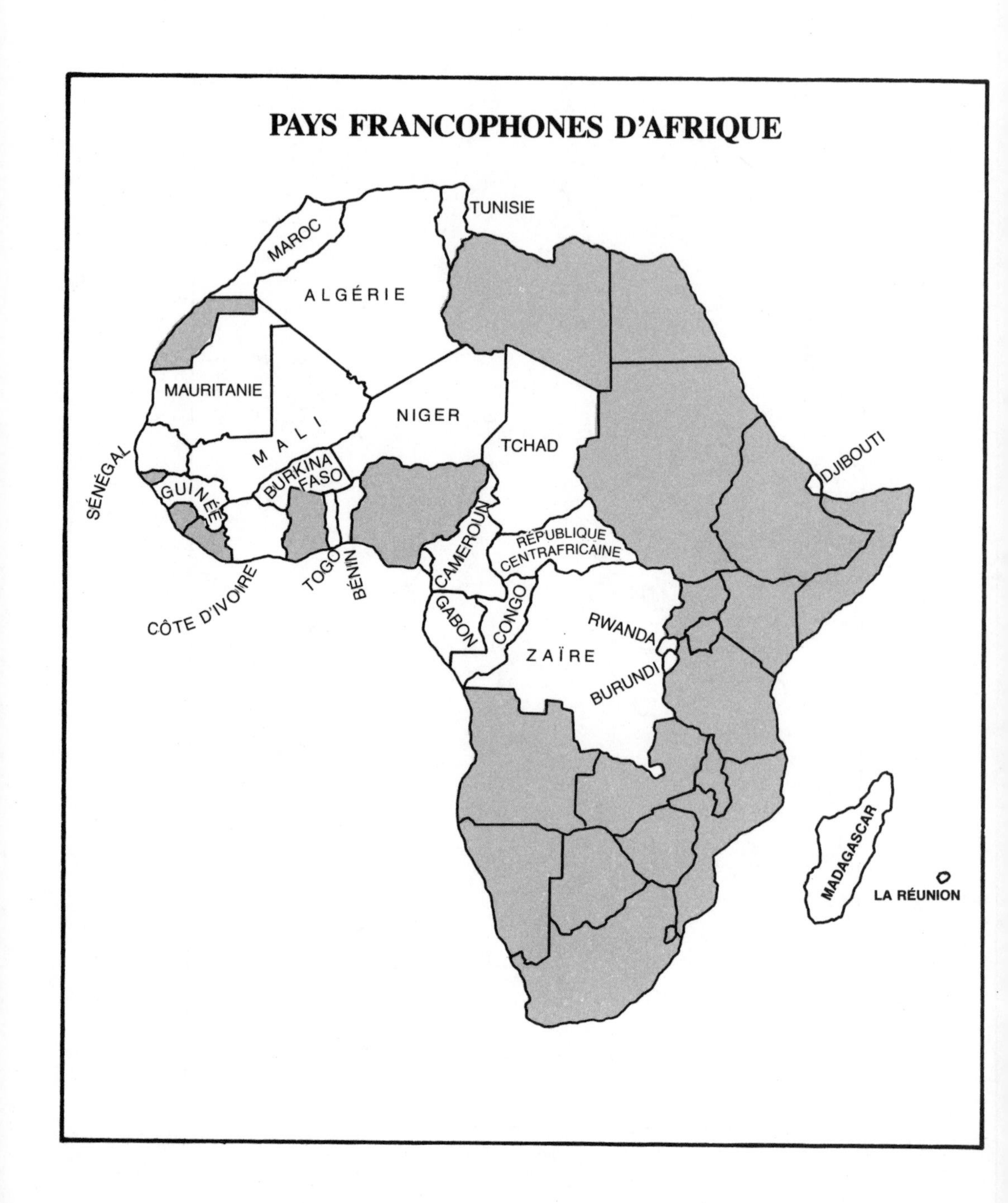
PAYS FRANCOPHONES D'AFRIQUE
TUNISIE
MAROC
ALGÉRIE
MAURITANIE
NIGER
MALI
TCHAD
DJIBOUTI
SÉNÉGAL
BURKINA FASO
GUINÉE
CAMEROUN
RÉPUBLIQUE CENTRAFRICAINE
CÔTE D'IVOIRE
TOGO
BÉNIN
GABON
CONGO
RWANDA
ZAÏRE
BURUNDI
MADAGASCAR
LA RÉUNION

RÉGIONS
FRANCOPHONES
DU CANADA
ÎLES DE LA REINE ÉLIZABETH
ELLESMERE
ÎLE DU
PRINCE PATRICK
ARCHIPEL DE PARRY
MELVILLE
DEVON
BANKS
VICTORIA
BAFFIN
YUKON
MONTAGNES ROCHEUSES
TERRITOIRES DU NORD-OUEST
Grand Lac de l'Ours
Yellowknife
Grand Lac des Esclaves
Whitehorse
Détroit d'Hudson
LABRADOR
Goose Bay
St. John's
Povungnituk
TERRE-
NEUVE
I.-P.-E.
Golfe du
Saint
Laurent
Baie d'Hudson
QUÉBEC
MTS LAURENTIENNES
Gaspé
Rimouski
Chicoutimi
N-E
Halifax
Fredericton
N-B
Québec
Trois-Rivières
Montréal
Ottawa
Toronto
ÎLE
REINE
CHARLOTTE
COLOMBIE-BRITANNIQUE
Lac Athabasca
ALBERTA
Lac Caribou
MANITOBA
Edmonton
SASKA-
TCHEWAN
Lac Winnipeg
ONTARIO
Saskatoon
VANCOUVER
Vancouver
Victoria
Calgary
Regina
Winnipeg
Thunder Bay
Entre 10%
et 100%
Entre 5%
et 10%

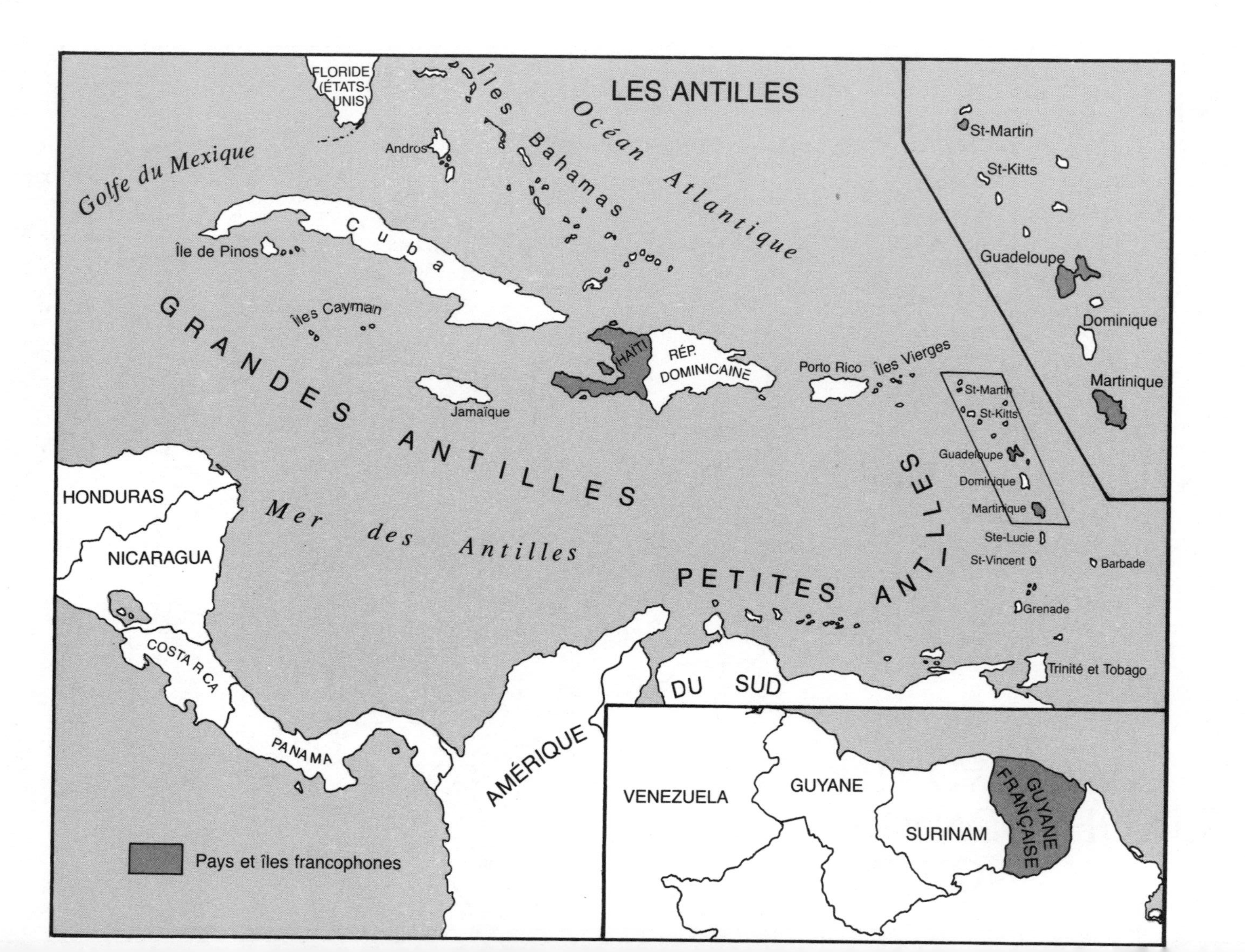
LES ANTILLES
Océan Atlantique
Îles Bahamas
Golfe du Mexique
FLORIDE (ÉTATS-UNIS)
Andros
Cuba
Île de Pinos
Îles Cayman
Jamaïque
HAÏTI
RÉP. DOMINICAINE
Porto Rico
Îles Vierges
GRANDES ANTILLES
PETITES ANTILLES
Mer des Antilles
St-Martin
St-Kitts
Guadeloupe
Dominique
Martinique
St-Martin
St-Kitts
Guadeloupe
Dominique
Martinique
Ste-Lucie
St-Vincent
Barbade
Grenade
Trinité et Tobago
HONDURAS
NICARAGUA
COSTA RICA
PANAMA
AMÉRIQUE DU SUD
VENEZUELA
GUYANE
SURINAM
GUYANE FRANÇAISE
Pays et îles francophones

OCÉANIE
FRANÇAISE
EIAO
NUKU HIVA
UA HUKA
UA POU
HIVA OA
TAHUATA
FATU HIVA
ÎLES MARQUISES
ARCHIPEL TOUAMOTOU
ÎLES DU DÉSAPPOINTEMENT
PUKAPUKA
MANIHI
MATAIVA
APATAKI
TAKUME
FANGATAU
FAKAHINA
ÎLES SOUS-LE-VENT
MANUAE
MAUPITI
BORA-BORA
HUAHINE
RAIATEA
TETIAROA
FAKARAVA
MAKEMO
TAHANEA
MOOREA
TAHITI
Papeete
TATAKOTO
ÎLES DU VENT
RAVA HERE
HAO
PUKA RUHA
REAO
ÎLES DE LA SOCIÉTÉ
MANUANGI
VAHITAHI
AHUNUI
HEREHERETUE
ÎLES DU
DUC DE GLOUCESTER
TUREIA
MARIA
POLYNÉSIE
FRANÇAISE
TEMATANGI
MARUTEA
RIMATARA
RURUTU
MURUROA
MARIA
FAGATAUFA
ÎLES TOUBOUAI
TUBUAI
MORANE
MANGAREVA
TEMOE
RAIVAVAE
ÎLES GAMBIER
OCÉAN
PACIFIQUE

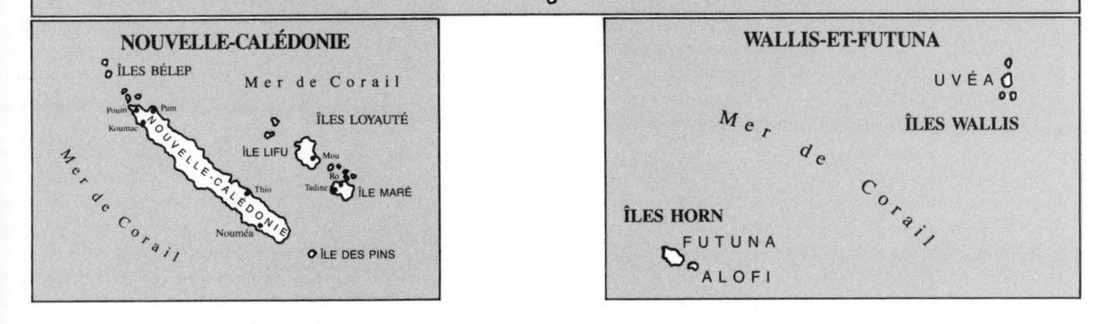
NOUVELLE-CALÉDONIE
ÎLES BÉLEP
Mer de Corail
Poum
Pam
Koumac
NOUVELLE-CALÉDONIE
ÎLES LOYAUTÉ
ÎLE LIFU
Mou
Ro
Tadine
ÎLE MARÉ
Thio
Nouméa
Mer de Corail
ÎLE DES PINS
WALLIS-ET-FUTUNA
UVÉA
ÎLES WALLIS
Mer de Corail
ÎLES HORN
FUTUNA
ALOFI